Child and family:
Concepts of
nursing practice

Child and family: Concepts of nursing practice

Marjorie J. Smith, R.N., M.S., C.N.M.
Rochester Community College
Rochester, Minnesota

Julie A. Goodman, R.N., M.S., C.N.M.
Rochester Community College
Rochester, Minnesota

Nancy Lockwood Ramsey, R.N., M.S.N.
Los Angeles City College
Los Angeles, California

Sarah B. Pasternack, R.N., M.A.
Boston University
Boston, Massachusetts

McGraw-Hill Book Company

NEW YORK ST. LOUIS SAN FRANCISCO AUCKLAND BOGOTÁ GUATEMALA HAMBURG
JOHANNESBURG LISBON LONDON MADRID MEXICO MONTREAL NEW DELHI PANAMA
PARIS SAN JUAN SÃO PAULO SINGAPORE SYDNEY TOKYO TORONTO

NOTICE

Medicine is an ever-changing science. As new research and clinical experience broaden our knowledge, changes in treatment and drug therapy are required. The editors and the publisher of this work have made every effort to ensure that the drug dosage schedules herein are accurate and in accord with the standards accepted at the time of publication. Readers are advised, however, to check the product information sheet included in the package of each drug they plan to administer to be certain that changes have not been made in the recommended dose or in the contraindications for administration. This recommendation is of particular importance in regard to new or infrequently used drugs.

Child and family: concepts of nursing practice

Copyright © 1982 by McGraw-Hill, Inc. All rights reserved.
Printed in the United States of America. Except as permitted under the
Copyright Act of 1976, no part of this publication may be reproduced or
distributed in any form or by any means, or stored in a data base or
retrieval system, without the prior written permission of the publisher.

1 2 3 4 5 6 7 8 9 0   RMRM   8 9 8 7 6 5 4 3 2

ISBN 0-07-048720-0

This book was set in Zapf Book by Monotype Composition Company, Inc.;
the editors were David P. Carroll, Stuart D. Boynton, and Mark W. Cowell;
the production supervisor was Jeanne Skahan. The cover was designed by
Charles A. Carson.

Rand McNally & Company was printer and binder.

Library of Congress Cataloging in Publication Data:
Main entry under title:

Child and family.

    Includes bibliographical references and index.
    1. Pediatric nursing.   2. Family—Health and
hygiene.   I. Smith, Majorie J., R.N. [DNLM:
1. Pediatric nursing.   2. Family—Nursing texts.
WY 159 C533]
RJ245.C465   610.73'62   81-17227
ISBN 0-07-048720-0   AACR2

To those who said it was possible,
  and to all those who made it possible.

Contents

part two
**impact of
illness on
the child,
the family,
and the
nurse**

Chapter 18   *Legal, ethical, and moral considerations in pediatric nursing*   409
Catherine M. Kneut

**part three
alterations
in child
health**

Chapter 37   *Perception and coordination*   1033
Susan Steiner Nash and Marjorie J. Smith

part four
appendix

List of Contributors

Frances Barber Drewry Austin, R.N., M.N.
Nursing Supervisor, Wadsworth Veterans Administration Medical Center, Los Angeles, California

Arlene V. Baia, R.N., B.S., N.Ed., M.S.
Health Division Chairperson, North Iowa Area Community College, Mason City, Iowa

Joan Brosnan, R.N., Ph.D.
Director of Nursing, Paramount General Hospital, Paramount, California

Dorothy J. DeMaio, Ed.D., R.N., F.A.A.N.
Associate Dean, Professor, College of Nursing, Rutgers–The State University, Newark, New Jersey

Phyllis Nie Esslinger, R.N., M.S.
Lecturer (Professor), California State University, Los Angeles, California

Sandra A. Faux, R.N., M.N.
Formerly Assistant Professor of Pediatric Nursing, University of Illinois, Champaign-Urbana, Illinois

Jacqueline Prokop Ficht, R.N., B.S., N.P.
Women's Health Care Nurse Practitioner, Division of Adolescent Medicine, Children's Hospital of Los Angeles, California

Vivian L. Fick, B.S.N.
Instructor, Nursing of Children, St. Luke's Hospital School of Nursing, Fargo, North Dakota

Mona Clare Lotz Finnila, R.N., P.H.N., P.N., M.S.
Formerly Family Health Coordinator, Family Development Project, Children's Hospital of Los Angeles, Los Angeles, California

Geanne M. Friedland, R.N., M.S.N.
Formerly Director of Nursing Education, Primary Children's Medical Center, Salt Lake City, Utah

Marlene Singer Garvis, R.N., M.S.N.
Research Associate, Research Center, University of Minnesota School of Nursing, Minneapolis, Minnesota

Jo Ann Dillingham Glasscock, R.N., B.S., M.N.
Instructor, Pediatric Nursing, California Hospital School of Nursing, Los Angeles, California

Julie A. Goodman, R.N., M.S.N., C.N.M.
Instructor, Maternal-Child Nursing, Rochester Community College, Rochester, Minnesota

Sandra Sonnessa Griffiths, M.N.
Instructor in Pediatric Nursing, Associate in Nursing—University Hospitals, Case Western Reserve University, Cleveland, Ohio

Deane Hatteberg, R.N., B.S.N.
Formerly Staff Nurse, Alcoholism and Drug Dependency Unit, Rochester Methodist Hospital, Rochester, Minnesota

Barbara Haugan, R.N., M.S.
Formerly Instructor, Los Angeles City College, Los Angeles, California

Carol J. Hill, R.N., M.S.N.
Associate Professor, Maternal-Child Health Nursing, College of Nursing, University of North Dakota, Grand Forks, North Dakota

Nancy B. Horvath, R.N., B.S.N.
Formerly Education Coordinator, Pediatrics, Saint Marys Hospital, Rochester, Minnesota

Elaine L. Ambrosini Hurley, R.N., M.S.
Assistant Professor, College of Nursing, Northeastern University, Boston, Massachusetts

Joanette Pete James, R.N., M.N.
Instructor, Department of Nursing, University of West Florida, Pensacola, Florida

Linda L. Jarvis, R.N., M.S.N.
Assistant Professor, Baccalaureate Program, School of Nursing, Boston University, Boston, Massachusetts

Catherine M. Kneut, R.N., M.S.
Instructor, School of Nursing, Boston University, Boston, Massachusetts

Carol Zinger Kotsubo, R.N., M.P.H., M.S.
Nurse Education Coordinator, Pediatric Pulmonary Center, Kapiolani Children's Medical Center, Honolulu, Hawaii

Sylvia L. Lee, R.N., P.H.N., M.P.H.
Assistant Clinical Professor, Pediatrics, University of Southern California, School of Medicine, Los Angeles, California

Nada Light, R.N., M.A.
Former Associate, Child Psychiatric Nursing Track, School of Nursing, Graduate Division, Columbia University, New York, New York

Lois L. Lux, R.N., B.S.N.
Formerly Urology Nurse Clinician, Children's Hospital of Philadelphia, Philadelphia, Pennsylvania

Barbara Macpherson, B.S.N.
Valley Children's Hospital, Fresno, California

Madeleine Martin, R.N., M.S.N.
Project Director, Burn and Trauma Nursing Program, University of Cincinnati, Cincinnati, Ohio

Ida M. Martinson, R.N., Ph.D.
Director of Nursing Research, University of Minnesota, Minneapolis, Minnesota

Margo McCaffrey, R.N., M.S., F.A.A.N.
Nursing Consultant, Santa Monica, California

Mary Jo McCracken, R.N., B.S.N.
Pediatric Pulmonary Nurse Specialist, University of Minnesota Hospitals and Clinics, Minneapolis, Minnesota

Patricia Maguire Meservey, R.N., B.S., M.S.
Instructor, School of Nursing, Boston University, Boston, Massachusetts

Jean R. Miller, R.N., Ph.D.
Associate Dean of Research and Development, College of Nursing, University of Utah, Salt Lake City, Utah

Robert T. Miller, P.A.
Department of Pediatrics, Hematology-Oncology, Los Angeles County, University of Southern California Medical Center, Los Angeles, California

D. Gay Moldow, R.N., M.S.W.
Research Associate, School of Nursing, University of Minnesota, Minneapolis, Minnesota

Susan Steiner Nash, R.N., M.S.
Formerly Assistant Professor, Augsburg College, Minneapolis, Minnesota

Carol R. Notaro, R.N., M.S., M.P.A.
Assistant Director of Nursing, Raritan Bay Health Services Corp., Perth Amboy General Hospital, Perth Amboy, New Jersey

Linda Waldrop Olivet, R.N., M.S.N.
Assistant Professor of Nursing, Capstone College of Nursing, University of Alabama, University, Alabama

Kathy Orth, R.N., B.S.
Clinical Nursing Instructor, College of St. Teresa, Winona, Minnesota

Sarah B. Pasternack, R.N., M.A.
Assistant Professor, School of Nursing, Boston University, Boston, Massachusetts

Andrea Piens, R.N., B.S.N., M.S.
Instructor, Maternal-Child Nursing, Rochester Community College, Rochester, Minnesota

Rosalyn Podratz, R.N., M.A.
Program Director, Continuing Education, University of Minnesota, Rochester Center, Rochester, Minnesota

Nancy Lockwood Ramsey, R.N., M.S.N.
Associate Professor, Los Angeles City College, Department of Nursing, Los Angeles, California

Linda Richelson, R.N., M.P.H.
Project Coordinator, Department of Medical Statistics and Epidemiology, Mayo Clinic, Rochester, Minnesota

Karen E. Roper, R.N., M.S.N.
Assistant Director of Nursing Education, The Children's Hospital of Philadelphia, Philadelphia, Pennsylvania

Sara Sacksteder, B.S.N.
Valley Childrens Hospital, Fresno, California

Patricia Salisbury, R.N., M.S.N., P.N.P.
Nurse Clinician, Pediatric Endocrine Clinic, Department of Pediatrics and Human Development, College of Human Medicine, Michigan State University, East Lansing, Michigan

Nancy L. Schamber, R.N., M.S., C.N.M.
Hennepin County Medical Center, Minneapolis, Minnesota

Gladys M. Scipien, R.N., M.S., F.A.A.N.
Associate Professor, School of Nursing, Boston University, Boston, Massachusetts

Ann R. Sloat, R.N., M.S.
Assistant Professor, School of Nursing, University of Hawaii, Honolulu, Hawaii

Marjorie J. Smith, R.N., M.S., C.N.M.
Coordinator, Continuing Education in Nursing, Rochester Community College, Rochester, Minnesota

Roberta W. Stroebel, B.A., B.S.N.
Rehabilitation Consultant, International Rehabilitation Associates, Inc., Minneapolis, Minnesota

Lyn Steele Ultsch, R.D., M.S.
Formerly Assistant Clinical Professor, Union County Community College, Cranford, New Jersey

William E. Walsh, M.D., F.A.C.A.
Clinical Assistant Professor, University of Minnesota, Minneapolis, Minnesota

Janet Louise Wilde, M.S.N.
School Nurse, Sulphur Springs Union School District, Canyon Country, California

Stephanie Wright, R.N., M.S.N.
Instructor, Nursing Program, Montgomery College, Takoma Park, Maryland

Christy Yapuncich, B.A., C.D.S.
Director, Program Development and Youth Specialist, Trinity Substance Abuse Treatment Corp., San Francisco, California

Preface

This book was written to answer the need for a pediatric text of manageable size that combined theory with detailed coverage of pediatric nursing procedures. It has been our intention to blend up-to-date theoretical content with enough applications to pediatric nursing practice to help overcome the nurse's inexperience with procedures when the nursing of children becomes a reality.

The nursing practices described are founded on the nursing process, which is carefully explained in Chapter 5. The description of the steps in the nursing diagnostic process should be helpful to students and instructors. Furthermore, individualized nursing care plans, incorporating nursing diagnoses, are presented in many chapters. They demonstrate how the nursing process is used to systematically gather and analyze data and to formulate priorities in nursing care.

The book has been organized around the health and illness care needs of the growing child within the developing family. Throughout there are frequent suggestions for anticipatory guidance. These should be useful in nursing care and for teaching parents to understand better their child's needs in health and in illness.

A special feature of this book is the concise approach to the nursing care of hospitalized children. Chapter 16 prepares the nurse to understand the child's and family's psychological reactions to hospitalization and offers age-appropriate interventions for easing their adjustment. Chapter 17 presents in a capsule the nursing procedures for meeting the basic needs of the child in the hospital. Thus in the span of just two chapters the nurse about to enter the hospital can learn the essentials of giving safe nursing care to children. Such succinct presentation of this important content is unique to our book and should be welcomed by the student and the instructor.

The ground plan we have adopted was designed to facilitate access to the great amount of information the book contains. Part One follows a growth and development framework. Part Two, on the other hand, focuses on selected problems such as the high-risk infant, acute illness, chronic illness, and terminal illness, treating each through all periods of childhood. Part Three also takes up alterations in health, but in this case they are arranged by body system or function. Chapters in Part Three begin, where appropriate, with a brief review of embryology, anatomy, and physiology. There follow discussions of diagnostic tests, common alterations, medical management, and nursing management, all with emphasis on changes specific to children and spanning all childhood ages. Special attention is paid to patient and family education and discharge planning. In addition, Part Three includes important chapters devoted to social problems such as substance abuse, child abuse and neglect, developmental disabilities, and behavioral problems.

We urge the user of this book to regard it as a companion through the nursing career. The book is generously furnished with information of reference value. Besides the nursing procedures and guidelines summarized in tables there are appendix sections devoted to metric conversion, growth charts, nutritional guidelines, poison treatment, and samples of personal information forms.

Finally, an instructor's manual has been prepared that will assist the instructor in making lesson plans, writing tests, designing learning experiences, and guiding students to further reading on the content of the chapters.

We gratefully thank our families for the support, sacrifice, patience, help, and encouragement we have received since the inception of this book. We could not have made it without you! The actual writing and preparation was greatly aided by the efforts and expertise of countless numbers of people. Our contributors, colleagues, and friends all made essential contributions. We thank you!

We also value the opportunity, direction, guidance, and patience provided by the McGraw-Hill editorial staff, in particular, Stuart Boynton, David Carroll, and the late Mary Ann Richter. For manuscript typing we are indebted to Gail Jimenez. For support, review, and direction we gratefully thank Jeanne Howe.

Marjorie J. Smith
Julie A. Goodman
Nancy Lockwood Ramsey
Sarah B. Pasternack

The cover
The drawing was prepared by a boy of 6½ years, who had not begun formal schooling, while at a day care center in Minneapolis. He and the other children were given an outline with eyes and mouth and 30 minutes in which to draw what they imagined was inside their bodies. When asked about his drawing the child explained that "bones helped you stand" but could not explain the function of the heart. He chose black and brown to distinguish layers of the skin and included a fly in the stomach. Arrows in the bones represent joints. (Courtesy of Andrea Piens, R.N., M.S.)

Part One Maintenance and promotion of child health

Chapter 1 **Conceptual framework**

Sarah B. Pasternack

Upon completion of this chapter, the student will be able to:

1. Identify "child," "family," and "health" as key concepts in pediatric nursing practice.
2. Discuss the central role of the family in the child's growth and development.

3. Explain the importance of health in the child's growth and development.
4. Analyze the role of the nurse as a health care provider for children and their families.

The child and family

Early life experiences are critical in preparing a child for a self-sufficient role in society. A child is highly dependent on his or her family for many years. Thus the family, or child-rearing unit,* assumes an important role in protecting the child's growth, development, health, and well-being. The family bears primary responsibility for meeting the child's basic physiological needs, such as food, shelter, and protection. Love and affection are as essential to the child's growth and development as food, water, and play. Emotional and psychological well-being are influenced by the quality of the child's relationships within the family. The love given a child by parents and family assures the child of "belonging" and nurtures feelings of self-worth.

The family serves as a unit of socialization for the child, providing the means through which the child gains self-knowledge, learns about other people, and becomes aware of the world in general. Optimally, experiences within the child-rearing unit afford the child opportunities to cultivate interpersonal relationships, to experience pleasure, and to give and receive affection. The family teaches the growing child how to assume responsibility and provides motivation for achieving personal goals.

---

* Since there are various forms of "family" in today's society, the terms *family* and *child-rearing unit* are used interchangeably in order to denote a broad meaning for the term *family*.

Health

Health is a desirable quality of life which enables an individual to experience physical, emotional, and psychological well-being. A dynamic quality which is difficult to define and impossible to measure, "health" is different for every individual. A person's health is not static; it changes from moment to moment. A multitude of both internal and external factors influence the individual's health at any given point in time. Health is a necessary prerequisite for optimum growth and development during the period of rapid change which occurs between conception and late adolescence.

During childhood, adequate nutrition, shelter, activity, affection, and intellectual stimulation are effective in promoting health. Measures which prevent communicable diseases and accidental injury are particularly important during childhood. Responsibility for child health promotion and maintenance is shared by the child-rearing unit, health care providers, and eventually by the individual child. Health may be altered when the child's basic needs are not fulfilled as a result of: (1) alterations in body structure, function, or growth and development; (2) traumatic injury; (3) neglect or abuse; and (4) lack of knowledge.

The nurse

The nurse has a unique role in relation to the health of children and their families. The nurse's role is different from the role of any other health provider because the nurse is concerned with the well-being of the child during health and illness. The nurse uses a holistic approach to provide care, comfort, counsel, and teaching for the child and family. Child health care is given by nurses in the home, school, hospital, clinic, and community. During an acute illness, direct nursing care is of utmost importance to the child's recovery. The nurse provides emotional support and guidance for the family during the child's illness.

A theoretical knowledge base is the foundation for nursing practice. The nurse's care is guided by scientific principles. Thorough knowledge of growth and development is indispensable for the nurse who provides care to children and their families. The nurse uses a problem-solving approach, the nursing process, to identify child health problems, including potential problems, and design a plan of care. The nursing process is used in child health promotion and in meeting the needs of the ill child and his or her family. Keen observation and good interpersonal skills are essential for the nurse who provides care to children and families. In order to be effective, the nurse must also use sound judgment, set priorities accurately, and collaborate with others.

The nurse has a responsibility to serve as a child and family advocate. In this role, the nurse promotes the health, growth, development, and independence of the child and the family. The nurse assists both child and family in becoming knowledgeable health care consumers who are able to assume responsibility for their own health.

Chapter 2 **The family: A dynamic, open system**

Carol Notaro

Upon completion of this chapter, the student will be able to:

1. Discuss the importance of families in relation to the development and socialization of children.

2. Differentiate among the following terms: *nuclear family, extended family, family of origin.*

3. Discuss at least three qualities demonstrated by families as open systems.

4. Discuss developmental changes that affect families.

5. Cite at least four factors that influence family interactions.

6. Identify at least five contemporary forces that influence family life.

7. Assess a given family with regard to structure, interactions as a system, roles, communication patterns, and significant contemporary forces.

When a nurse provides care to a child, whether within a health care institution or within the home, knowledge of the family and its operations is of prime importance. It is essential for nurses to view the child as part of a family system, noting particularly: the family composition, the interactions among the family members, the members' roles, and the family's functions. This *family-oriented approach* helps the nurse conduct an assessment of the family and develop an appropriate plan of care for the child. This chapter will identify elements of the family system that the nurse must understand and incorporate into pediatric nursing practice.

A *family* may be most simply defined as two or more adults living together and engaged in the care and rearing of their own or adopted children. A commonly held perception, then, is that a family comprises at least two generations living within the same household. As will be made clear later and in Chap. 3, many alternative arrangements also exist and, from the nurse's point of view, function as the patient's family.

Family structures

Structure (the membership and organization of a family group) sets the foundation for the roles and responsibilities the family, as a unit, carries out. The structure of the family provides the means for the achievement of family objectives (see Table 2-1). The family functions include giving an identity to its members, educating them for the roles of family life, and preparing

Table 2-1 Objectives common to all families

1. Satisfaction of the affectional needs of its members
2. Satisfaction of the spouses' sexual needs
3. Socialization and enculturation of children
4. Assisting members to relate effectively with social systems, organizations, and agencies
5. Providing an environment conducive to the growth and development of its members (such as food, shelter, health care, and economic support)

them for community interactions. With respect to children, specifically, the family provides training for their becoming social beings able to participate in society.

Historically, a multigenerational household fulfilled the family's objectives. That is, economic support, emotional support, child rearing, homemaking, and the like were shared by grandparents, parents, siblings, and possibly aunts and uncles, living under one roof. More recently, however, the nuclear family has become the most common form of family in Western culture. The *nuclear family* is one composed of a mother, a father, and dependent children.

In contemporary society, family structures vary considerably. These variations are not necessarily unhealthy. If a family's structure allows for the achievement of its goals, it is productive and appropriate. Even though the nuclear family is the most prevalent and perhaps most accepted family composition, different forms of family structure may also be viewed in a positive light. Other types of families that exist in today's society include the following: (1) the childless couple; (2) the couple whose children have separated from the family and now have their own families; (3) the single-parent family in which the adult is widowed, separated, divorced, or unmarried; (4) the commune family; (5) the extended family (nuclear family plus parents, siblings, and/or in-laws of the adults of that nuclear family).[1] At least one study of four different family life-styles (single-parent families, commune families, unmarried couples, and traditional nuclear families) found that each met the socialization and caretaking needs of children in a similar manner. In all these family types, parents used the parenting practices they were exposed to as children in bringing up their own children.[2] Each of the family structures mentioned has its as-

sociated strengths and weaknesses. The extended family, for example, may provide support but it may also interfere in the mobility of the family by limiting the family's ability to use new means to achieve its goals. The nuclear family, though relatively stable, may not have the resources available to the extended family. Reliance upon one wage earner in the nuclear family can lead to difficulties if that person is incapacitated.[3]

For many people, including some children, the "family" includes people who are not related to the patient either by blood or by marriage. Examples include individuals living together who provide emotional support for one another in institutional settings, foster homes, and, in some instances, neighborhood networks. The nurse's assessment must not focus on the structure or the stereotyped perception of "what ought to be," but rather on the achievement of the basic goals of the family. Variations in family structure are discussed further in Chap. 3.

The family as a child-rearing unit

The family is the environment that helps the child become a functioning adult. Parent-child interactions have an important bearing on the ability of the child to develop emotionally and intellectually (see Fig. 2-1). For example, a lack of positive parent-child interaction, characterized by minimal conversation between the two, may result in impairment of language development and scholastic ability.[4] Children learn about themselves and how to relate with others through their experiences within the family. Consistency, warmth, and dependability of interactions help a child become confident and, eventually, a productive member of society.

The family provides general health care and protection for its children. The well-functioning family ensures that children are immunized, that proper attention is given to food and clothing needs, and that health care is provided.

It is evident that the significance of the family in child rearing relates to the foundation it provides the child. The saying "What is past is prologue" is fitting to describe the relationship of the family to a child's development and later adulthood. What is learned in the family carries over into succeeding generations, perpetuating the system known as *family* for the individual.

Figure 2-1 The emotional and psychological well-being of a child is influenced by the quality of family relationships. (*Photo by Erika.*)

The family as an open system

A social *system* is made up of interrelated elements (people or groups of people) who interact with each other. An *open system* is one that is in continuous exchange with its environment, i.e., with people and institutions outside the system. At the same time, there is exchange among the system's own component parts (called *subsystems*). A *closed system* utilizes energy, but it is not in exchange with the environment. In communicating with its subsystems and relating to the larger social system, the family acts as an open system. Doing so helps the child learn about the outside world.

Qualities of open systems

Several processes characterize the functioning of open systems. Among them are *negentropy*, *equifinality*, and *feedback*. Families that are open systems demonstrate all these processes.

Negentropy *Negentropy* is increase in complexity, flexibility, and structure of a system as time passes. Negentropy is fostered by the constant energy transfer between the system and its environment. The open family system draws on resources from the environment around it, as well as providing input to that environment. The family with a child who attends school is an example of the exchange relationship between the open family system and the environment. There is a transfer of ideas, attitudes, and behaviors between the two institutions. The child brings to the school a manner of relating to others that was learned at home. In return, the school modifies the method used by the child in relating to others. A different way of handling a situation may result from the child's exposure to the school system. A child may resort to tantrums when denied something at home, but redirection and explanations offered at school may help the child accept disappointment in a more effective manner.

Equifinality An open system is marked not only by the exchange between the system and its environment but also by the process of equifinality. *Equifinality* is the ability of the system to tolerate the achievement of a goal through various means. For example, one young adult prefers part-time work and part-time college attendance, whereas her sibling attends college full-time. In this instance, the ability of the family to accept both methods in the attainment of higher education reflects an open system.

Feedback Feedback is another essential property associated with open systems. *Feedback* is the information that comes back into the system from its interchange with its environment. There are two types of feedback: positive and negative. *Positive feedback* leads to change within the system, while *negative feedback* maintains the status quo. Both types of feedback may have either desirable or undesirable effects on the family.

Positive feedback is desirable if it results in a growth-producing change in the family's behavior. On the other hand, positive feedback is undesirable when it causes a change that is detrimental to the family.

Consider the following examples:

EXAMPLE A: Trish, a 12-year-old, was teased by family members, who said she was "tall and clumsy." One day Trish came home and announced that she had just made the girls' varsity basketball team. Family members began to view her differently and within 2 weeks they no longer called her "clumsy." The change, positive feedback from the school, where Trish's height is valued, was growth-producing for this family.

EXAMPLE B: Susie J., 15 years old, demonstrated numerous behavior problems at school during the last 2 years. When the frequency of her acting-out episodes increased despite special counseling at school, her parents decided that Susie should transfer to a school offering more individualized attention. Shortly after the transfer, Susie's behavior problems became more frequent and she became argumentative and disruptive at home. One night, Susie was escorted home by a police officer who found her in possession of a controlled substance. In this case, the school transfer (positive feedback) increased the family's problems.

When negative feedback helps a family maintain its strengths, it is desirable. However, negative feedback is detrimental if it reinforces aspects of the family that are not in its best interests. Consider these examples:

EXAMPLE A: The Christopher family has six children. They are a close-knit family who are admired in the community. As the children became old enough, each sought after-school jobs to offset family expenses. In this instance, the family uses a variety of behaviors to maintain cohesiveness.

EXAMPLE B: Mr. and Mrs. Geraci have been married 2 years and have a 9-month-old daughter, Lily. Mrs. Geraci has always been fond of staying at home, but over the last year and a half she has been fearful of going out of the house to places like the supermarket, bank, or of just walking Lily in the carriage. The neighbors are concerned about Mrs. Geraci and Lily. However, Mr. Geraci has been brought up believing that a "woman's place is at home." He is not concerned that his wife never leaves the house and is completely dependent on him. He loves his wife and daughter and is pleased that his wife is such a good housekeeper and cook. In this instance, Mr. Geraci's beliefs help maintain behaviors indicative of poor mental health.

Wholeness *Wholeness* refers to the system's quality of being more than and different from the sum of its parts. In relation to families, wholeness is the interdependence of members on one another as a functioning unit. Individual members and combinations of members form subsystems of the larger family. The subsystems may consist of one person, such as the mother or father, or may be composed of two people, such as the parents or mother and child. Also, the subsystem can be gender-related, such as all females of the family, or it can consist of all of the siblings. Although each subsystem performs as a separate entity, the entire family functions in its own unique manner. Included in the idea of wholeness is the interrelatedness of the members who give the family its uniqueness. Although each member may function independently, the relationships among members give the family its own characteristic qualities that are greater than and distinct from the characteristics of individual family members or subgroups.

Wholeness also relates to the ability of the family members to carry out, to a certain extent, one another's functions, enabling the family to continue its existence as a family even if one member drops out. For example, if the breadwinner becomes unable to perform in this capacity, sharing of this responsibility among various members will maintain the family.

Unidirectionality of family system development

As time passes, open systems move along lines of increasing complexity, diversity, and structure. While doing so, families change. The family usually begins as a combination of two individuals forming a marital couple. Involved in the couple stage are negotiating, compromising, and exchanging activities that establish the couple as a distinct family, different from their families of origin (the families into which they were born).

As the couple becomes a family with children, there is further change in the family's interactions and focus. Nurturing of the young child adds a dimension that alters the time and attention that the couple can expend on each other. Energies are directed toward the caretaking aspects of child rearing at this stage of family development.

Each phase of family life has certain tasks for parents and children to accomplish, as will be further described in Chap. 3. For example, the family provides intensive support, satisfaction of needs, and supervision and direction during infancy, toddlerhood, and the preschool period. There is less intense parental intervention as the child enters school and learns to function outside the family system. Peer relationships develop and intersystem articulation between family and society increases. Parents must make allowances for increasing independence of offspring but at the same time must provide structure, direction, and the guidance necessary for their children's development. As children continue to get older, parents must continually modify their parenting. The period of adolescence requires pronounced adaptations in parent-child interaction and in roles of both child and parents. The adolescent is faced with the dilemma of maintaining family ties while also separating from the family. Parents must learn how to monitor behavior and set rules while at the same time supporting the independent actions of the child. (See Fig. 2-2.)

The developmental tasks of the family coincide with the development of its members and the family's own increasing maturity. As children become adults and separate from their family of origin, they make lives of their own and establish new families. Eventually the family encounters the aging and death of parents, the normal sequence of life.[5]

Assessment of family system interactions

By now it should be clear that the health care of a child must be provided in a way that is compatible with the child's family system. Hence the success of pediatric nursing depends on the nurse's accurate assessment of the family's established ways of interacting among themselves and with the other systems in the environment. The following section provides guidelines for assessing families by identifying their roles and communication patterns.

Family roles

Roles are responsibilities and actions that differentiate one family member from another. For example, the role of parents is to rear children by supporting and protecting them. Children occupy the dependent role in the family.

Male and female roles Traditionally, certain roles have been ascribed exclusively to either males or females in our society. Variations in these roles were thought pathological or at least inappropriate until recently. One of the expected roles for a man has been wage earner for the family. Associated with the provider role are other responsibilities, such as protector, community interactor, financial manager, disciplinarian, and, perhaps, one who does heavy house repairs. The wife was given the role of homemaker. The wife was expected to interact with the school system and care for the children. There has recently been an impetus toward shared responsibility for parenting between spouses. Family income has become more of a combined effort, and both parents may work. Gender-linked roles are no longer rigidly defined, allowing for more flexibility in assigning family responsibilities.

Roles and child development and socialization Roles play a part in the development of

Figure 2-2 The period of adolescence requires alterations of roles and responsibilities within the family as the young person develops independence. (*From D. Papalia and S. W. Olds, Human Development, McGraw-Hill, New York, 1978, p. 271.*)

children because patterns of behavior are learned by the child. The behavior patterns of children are eventually transmitted to their offspring. Roles, then, can be continued through multigenerational lines.

Roles are involved in the socialization of children. *Socialization* is the process by which a child learns to interact appropriately in society. It involves learning how to communicate with peers, adults, institutions, agencies, and the like in a manner that is acceptable and that gives the child satisfaction. Through this process, the child learns what it is like to be part of the larger system outside the family.

Changing roles within the family As the cycle of family life continues, each member adopts new roles to meet the requirements of the new aspect of the family's development. For example, addition of another child to a family that consists of mother, father, and one child alters the role of the firstborn. Until this time, the firstborn child has not been required to share parental love, affection, time, and interest with any other child. Consequently, there is change in the child's role, now that he or she is not the only child. The relationships this child has with the parents will be modified, and eventually the older child will acquire roles of protector, teacher, and model for the younger child. Similarly, all family members modify some of their roles as individual and family development proceed. The changes in parent roles in regard to protection and supervision have already been discussed. Moreover, parents may become the caretakers of their own elderly parents. As their parents age and become ill and in need of attention, roles are reversed. At one time the child was taken care of, but now the child provides care and support for the parents. Integration of grandparents into a family system almost inevitably alters the relationships and roles between family members. Children may be asked to offer support within the family by providing companionship and caretaking functions for their grandparents. Three-generation families are further discussed in Chap. 3.

Ordinal position in the family Another influence on the interactions of the family is birth order of the children. A person's position within the family system has implications for the individual's behavior throughout life. Firstborn children usually assume the same relationship with their peers as they do within their families. More often than not, this is a leadership role. On the other hand, the secondborn often takes on the follower role.

Sibling position has implications for the child's future family relationships. Complementarity of marriage partners is often related to their former positions within their families of origin. A smooth marital relationship is more likely if the positions of the spouses is similar to their sibling positions. For example, if a firstborn daughter, who has three younger brothers, marries a youngest son in the family of three older sisters, the arrangement is similar to the relationships experienced by each in the families of origin. The firstborn daughter may be comfortable with mothering and used to responsibility. As a wife, she complements the position of the youngest son, who, as a husband, may be content having someone take care of him. Conflict is sometimes generated when the marriage partners occupy the same ordinal positions, such as when two youngest children marry and expect each other to take the responsible role: The ordinal positions of the partners have not prepared either of them for this role.

Family communication patterns

As part of the assessment of family functioning, the nurse must examine communication patterns within the family system. *What* is communicated is often not as crucial as *how* it is communicated and to whom. The communication process, rather than merely the content of communication, should be observed. The nurse must remember that there are two kinds of communication, verbal and nonverbal. Each type of communication is transmitted from a sender to a receiver.

Verbal communication The nurse considers *who* speaks, *how* the message is said, and *for whom* the message is intended. For example, the nurse notes that Mr. Houston expresses himself to his children only through his wife. This can mean many things. The children may think they are not worthy of their father's attention, respect, or love. Or they may believe that this is how all families operate. The children are likely to adopt this pattern and use indirect communication when they have their own families.

Nonverbal communication Verbal communication that is inconsistent with the nonverbal message may cause confusion for the recipient. A child who is told that he or she is loved but who does not also have nonverbal communication to substantiate this claim will be perplexed. If a parent tells a child that he is loved but pushes the child away when the child demonstrates affection, the child is left wondering. If a family reprimands the children for fighting with others while the family is physically abusive within its own system, the children get a confusing message.

In assessing nonverbal communication, the nurse should note the frequency and kind of physical contact among family members. Support is often effectively conveyed from one person to another through touch. A hug, pat on the back, caress, all convey a positive message. Families differ in the degree to which physical contact is used. This often depends on cultural and familial heritage. However, a certain amount of touching is necessary for the growth and development of children. Taking care of the physical needs of the child without the warmth of touch ignores the total needs of the growing individual (see Fig. 2-3).

In addition to meeting the need for verbal and nonverbal human interactions among family members, communication in a family must have certain qualities. A characteristic of an open family system is the ability of its members to communicate clearly with each other. Communication among families considered "healthy" is spontaneous rather than contrived. Conversations in these families are sprinkled with frequent interruptions. Members may not often finish sentences, but they are understood by other members of the family.[6] Verbal and nonverbal communication between spouses is further discussed in Chap. 3.

Family values   *Values* are defined as principles or precepts of meaning, behavior, or thinking. Each family has its own values by which it holds its members accountable. In the early stages of the family's development, both spouses come to agreements about differences in their own values. Compromises over differing value systems are negotiated in order to maintain a smoothly functioning marriage (see Chap. 3). The agreed-upon values become the norm that the family transmits to offspring. Part of the child's socialization process is the development of a value system.

Figure 2-3 The parent's loving touch provides warmth and security for the growing child. (*From D. Papalia and S. W. Olds, Human Development, McGraw-Hill, New York, 1978, p. 31.*)

When a family is exposed to values different from its own, conflicts associated with the contrasting beliefs and behaviors need to be dealt with. Maintaining the family's value system may require support for members, discussions about values, and compromises. Further discussion of value systems is included in Chap. 18.

Family "boundaries" One of the most important aspects of the family's interactional system is its boundaries. Boundaries refer to the "territories" belonging to the family and each of its members. The family system's boundaries are not tangible. Rather, they are boundaries that exist within the family's communication patterns. For example, it is acceptable to use certain kinds of language or discuss certain topics with some family members but not with others. Boundaries are circumscribed "areas" surrounding each family member and the family as a unit and ensuring the family's functioning. In a sense, a boundary separates one person from another. It also helps to screen or control which interactions may enter the family's system, which may leave, and which are blocked from entering or exiting. Well-defined boundaries enable family members to carry out their roles and responsibilities as mother, father, and child.

When assessing family interaction with regard to boundaries, the nurse should remember that most healthy families have flexible boundaries. There may be times in the family's development when "loosening" boundaries is appropriate. There are also times when rigid boundaries are appropriate. For example, when the child is very young the boundary between mother and child may be loose and overlapping because of the closeness involved in the caretaking process. As the child matures, the boundary between mother and child becomes more distinct, allowing for the child's increased independence and maturity.

Familes that have flexible boundaries are usually very close. When stress is experienced by one member, the others feel the effects and quickly respond to alleviate it.[7] In families where the boundaries are always rigid, distance among family members is pronounced. Little interaction occurs and minimal support is given by family members.

Boundaries between the family and society are also important. Rigid boundaries decrease interaction between the family and the surrounding social system. If the boundaries are rigidly maintained, the family cannot accept input from society. Thus it must rely entirely upon its own internal support system. As previously stated, any system that does not allow for an exchange of input and output eventually becomes nonfunctioning and begins to decline. Some families with rigid boundaries between their own systems and the community also have diffuse boundaries within the family. These families often close ranks and shut out even beneficial external influences. Eventually these families become unable to function productively. As they become more and more like a closed system, energy dissipates. There may be little energy available to continue the existence of the family as an open system.

Contemporary influences on family systems

The nurse must be familiar with influences that affect present-day family life. Among the factors impinging on families are ideas about child rearing presented on television, in literature, and in courses and seminars. Some ideas offered to parents are sound; others may need careful examination.

Child-rearing practices

One of the most popular current practices is including the father as an equal participant in the parenting process. It has become acceptable for the father to participate in the childbirth process by supporting his wife during labor and delivery. Following this, the father may share responsibility for the actual care of the newborn (see Fig. 2-4). Today, many fathers are likely to bathe, feed, and dress their children. Child care has become a mutual endeavor for both parents.

Child day care

The loosening of traditional male and female roles and rapid increase in the number of single-parent families have favored the development of child day care. Many children spend all or part of their parents' working day in a setting designed to provide a substitute for home care. Child day care is not considered harmful, even for infants and toddlers, as long as the *quality* of the parent-child relationship is good.[8]

Figure 2-4 Fathers are often eager to be equal participants in the parenting process. (*From G. M. Scipien et al., Comprehensive Pediatric Nursing, 2d. ed., McGraw-Hill, New York, 1979, p. 406.*)

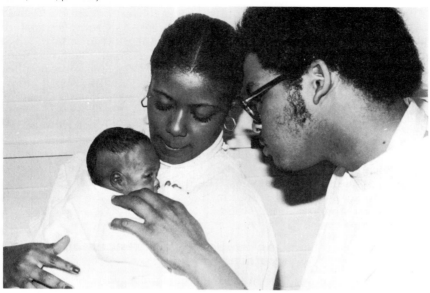

The extended family

The influence of the extended family varies depending on whether the extended family members live with the younger family, nearby, or at a distance. If the extended family is part of a household with several generations, its impact may be very strong. Elder family members' ideas about child rearing may be quite traditional. For example, acceptable behavior for family members may be more stringently defined by grandparents than by parents. Extended family members who live close to the young nuclear family are usually somewhat influential. If the family boundaries are flexible, there may be a continual exchange of services, communication, and information (see Fig. 2-5). Reliance on extended family members may be accepted as the norm, but if they live far away they are unlikely to influence the family's day-to-day activities.

Increasing dependency on parents

Another factor affecting families is the increasing length of time that a child is dependent on parents for financial support. The value placed on the attainment of higher education has pushed dependency upward into the young adulthood years. Previously, children finished high school or college, became employed, and embarked on lives of their own. Preparation for many careers and professions requires schooling well beyond the twenty-first birthday. Consequently, parents frequently provide economic support for their children until they are well into their twenties.

The "me" generation

Perhaps as an offshoot of increased dependency, many children hold the belief that "someone will always take care of me." A relatively affluent society may contribute to the feeling that the individual is "entitled" to satisfaction of his or her needs. The danger in this is that the individual may not assume responsibility for his or her own welfare. Some believe that this phenomenon signifies the family's failure to prepare children for adulthood.

Two-career families

There are many two-career families in today's society. When two parents are employed, arrangements for the care of children and sharing of household responsibilities must be made.

Support may be necessary from outside agencies, or, perhaps, from the extended family. Although both parents may exert a combined effort in family life, parent-child interaction can diminish if both parents are involved in careers.

Economic factors

The economic status of a family affects how the functions of the family are carried out. The health-promotion function is hard to carry out in the absence of adequate income, and individuals who live in poverty have poor health. It is no surprise that economic security is commonly conducive to a well-functioning family.

Death, separation, divorce, and remarriage

Other influences on the family's interactions include death, separation, divorce, and remarriage. Each of these has great impact on members in the family system. The effect of a death depends on: (1) whether it was anticipated or sudden; (2) when it occurs within the family's

development; (3) the ages of children involved. There may be need to reorder roles of family members as they take on the family functions of the individual who has died.

Separation and divorce may present similar problems. There may be guilt associated with a parent's leaving a family. Children often feel that they are the cause of the separation or divorce. Bitterness and recrimination between spouses may affect the children's relationships with the parents.

One of the newer developments affecting the family system in relation to divorce is the matter of joint custody. Rather than granting custody to one parent and allowing the other visitation rights, the court assigns children to both parents. Frequently, children live with each parent 6 months of the year. This allows both parents access to their children. Joint custody works only if both parents have a commitment to it and if consistency is maintained between the two households.[9]

Figure 2-5 The relationship between children and grandparents can be rich and rewarding for both. (*Photo by Erika.*)

The nurse and the family system

Until a child is old enough to assume management of his or her own health care, usually in late adolescence, health maintenance and therapy are family matters. Systems theory makes clear two pertinent points: The adequacy of the family's methods of operating directly affects a child's well-being, and the health status of each family member impacts on the family system as a unit as well as on the community, school, and other environmental systems with which the family interacts.

In both preventive maintenance of well children and interventive care for those who are ill, the nurse often has a critical role to play in helping the family system function effectively and in facilitating the family's interactions with the health care system. Assessment of the family, as outlined above, is an essential part of pediatric care and enables the nurse to adapt health services to the family system's established ways of operating and to help the family obtain and use supportive input from its environment.

References

1. Marvin B. Sussman, "The Family Today: Is It an Endangered Species?" *Children Today* 7:32–37 (March–April 1978).
2. Bernice Eiduson, "Child Development in Emergent Family Styles," *Children Today* 7:24–31 (March–April 1978).
3. Sussman, op. cit., p. 45.
4. *Task Panel Reports Submitted to the President's Commission on Mental Health*, vol. 2, 1978.
5. Ellen H. Janosik and Jean R. Miller, "Theories of Family Development," in Debra P. Hymovich and Martha Underwood Barnard, *Family Health Care*, McGraw-Hill, New York, 1979, pp. 3–16.
6. Jerry M. Lewis, *No Single Thread: Psychological Health in Family Systems*, Brunner/Mazel, New York, 1976.
7. Salvador Minuchin, *Families and Family Therapy*, Harvard, Cambridge, Mass., 1974.
8. Jerome Kagan, Richard B. Kearsley, and Philip R. Zelazo, "The Effects of Infant Day Care on Psychological Development," in Jerome Kagan, *The Growth of the Child*, Norton, New York, 1978, pp. 74–100.
9. Alice Abarbanel, "Shared Parenting After Separation and Divorce: A Study of Joint Custody," *American Journal of Orthopsychiatry* 49:320–329 (April 1979).

Chapter 3 **Family structure and development**

Jean R. Miller

Upon completion of this chapter, the student will be able to:

1. Describe various types of family structures.
2. Identify the developmental tasks of newly established families.

3. Identify the essentials of planning and preparation for parenthood.
4. Identify the major responsibilities of parenthood.

Families are described in broader terms today than previously. Families were traditionally defined as nuclear families consisting of husbands, wives, and offspring. Families, regardless of definition, still remain the basic unit of communities and the larger society.

Life within families is constantly evolving. Structure, which refers to the organization of the family, changes through additions and losses of family members. The roles or activities of family members are modified when the structure changes. Increased life span, economic influences, and changing values are other factors that affect how families are organized. The various types of family structure have similar as well as different tasks and problems, as will become evident through the following discussion of family structure.

Family structures

Traditional family structures

Nuclear family The structure of the nuclear family has the following three positions: husband-father, wife-mother, and offspring-sibling. Persons in these positions are expected to behave in certain ways and contribute to the emotional gratification of one another. Parents are expected to nurture and socialize their children, and children are expected to behave in ways that meet the norms established by the parents.

Contemporary marriages have at least three different types of husband-wife structures: husband as head of the household and wife as complement; husband as senior partner and wife as junior partner; and husband and wife as equal partners.[1] Until recently the husband-father was the head of the house with major decision-making powers in most households. The wife-mother maintained the household and took care of the children. Today wives and husbands frequently adjust their roles and responsibilities according to their interests and capabilities rather than assuming roles prescribed by society for women and men. The ability to perform a number of different tasks in the home has eased the chaos which often occurs when a family member becomes ill, dies, or leaves the home, since other members are able to assume the responsibilities of the missing member.

The nuclear family has been viewed as the ideal family type for many years, but the current rate of divorce suggests that the nuclear family is not without its problems. Just as in other types of families, clear and continuous communication among family members is a necessity. Healthy family relationships in all types of family structures require consistent effort in order that all members will be emotionally gratified and grow to be all they are capable of becoming.

In a growing number of nuclear families both the husband and wife have careers outside the home. The most logical family structure in two-career families is one in which the husband and wife share equally in household tasks and decision making. Many husbands, however, have not been socialized to know what needs to be done in the home or even how to do the tasks if they understand what needs to be done. More often than not, the wife assumes the responsibility of a full-time job outside the home in addition to responsibilities for maintaining the home. This type of role structure is the beginning of many family problems, since the resultant inequities are irritating and stressful. Healthy family relationships are strengthened when both husband and wife agree on the way everyday tasks can best be accomplished.

Single-parent family Single-parent families consist of one parent who may be either the mother or father of one or more children. Such arrangements are the result of separation, divorce, desertion, or death. Many single-parent families operate successfully, while others do not. Finances is one of the largest problems among female-headed households. Most single mothers must enter the labor force but often cannot

obtain the level of job they formerly held, since their former jobs may not exist or they are no longer prepared for comparable positions. Arrangements for children in either day-care centers or school place another burden on the working single parent. Single parents who play the dual role of mother and father to the children often feel frustrated and inadequate. Such arrangements are confusing to the child. Loneliness is a prevalent feeling for single parents regardless of their socioeconomic class, since American society is oriented toward couples rather than single persons.

Three-generation family Three-generation families usually consist of elderly parents, their adult children, and the adult children's children. When elderly parents live with their children, the structure and roles of the family often need clarification. It is relatively easy for elderly parents to inappropriately assume the parenting role with their adult children or, conversely, to seek parenting from their adult children. Neither type of relationship provides the autonomy and independence both generations need. Since elderly parents who live with their adult children are usually physically dependent, it is important that the elderly be able to maintain some autonomy through doing physical tasks within their capability and making decisions that are related to their own lives. The elderly also can increase their sense of self-worth through interaction with their grandchildren, who readily respond to love and nurturing (Fig. 3-1).

It is also important within three-generation structures that there is clarity about who assumes the parenting role and who assumes the grandparenting role. One approach is to have the grandparents assume the parenting role when the parents are out of the home but to have them relinquish the responsibility when the parents are home. It is most important that children understand who sets the limits, and at what times. Three-generation family living can be mutually beneficial, but it is one of the most difficult family structures because past relationships influence the enactment of present roles.

Social-support networks Social-support networks include the nuclear family, the kin of every family member, friends, neighbors, work associates, and sometimes helpers from such social agencies and institutions as churches and schools. This network serves as a source of support during easy and difficult times. Furthermore, the support is reciprocal in nature. Persons within the network share resources that can be used to solve problems experienced by members of the network.

The structure of the network changes according to the circumstances and the need for leadership. The intensity, durability, and frequency of interaction within the network also vary for numerous reasons. Crises may bring the whole network together, whereas subgroups may meet together as a matter of routine. The structure within the smaller subgroups of the network is less apt to change, since these tend to be more stable groups, as is the case with various friendship and work groups. The value of social-support networks is that families know there are others beyond the nuclear family to support them, especially in times of trouble.

Emerging family structures

Blended families Blended families, also called *reconstituted families*, consist of a husband and wife who have been married previously and who bring one or more children from a previous marriage into a new family relationship. The former marriage(s) may have been dissolved through either divorce or death of the partner. Decisions about the structure of blended families are no different from the decisions made about structure and roles in first-time marriages. Blended families, however, seem to have additional challenges.

As reported by stepparents and their partners, the major problem areas can be categorized as follows: (1) problems concerning the children, (2) financial difficulties, and (3) marital misunderstandings and alienation.[2] Problems between stepparents and children are often caused by negative expectations of how new family members will relate to one another and by the tendency to misinterpret various responses as representing rejection. The expectation that there will be instant love and affection between stepparents and children is unrealistic. In the initial stages of the blended family, previous parent-child relationships may be maintained without allowing the new family members to share in the relationship. Gradually, family members become more open and both parents share

Figure 3-1 A grandparent's loving interaction with grandchildren can be beneficial to both. (*Photo by Erika.*)

in the rearing of one another's children. Younger children seem to more easily develop a close and affectionate relationship with stepparents than do older children.

Family members often are hypersensitive to behaviors that might incorrectly be interpreted as rejection and lack of love. Stepparents may rightfully feel rejection when the stepchild expresses a preference for the biological parents, who may or may not be living in the same household. Time is needed for relationships to grow and mature.

Financial problems may seem less difficult than interpersonal problems, although inadequate finances can cause strains that hinder positive interpersonal relationships. Economic difficulties in blended families are the result of a number of factors, including alimony payments to former partners and a larger number of family members living on the salary of one parent. It is often necessary for both parents to work outside the home.

Marital misunderstandings are common at the beginning of a new relationship between divorced partners, as is also true for first-time married couples. The disadvantage remarried couples face is that habits formed with the previous partner may not be easily understood by the new partner. This is partly a function of the length of the previous marriage(s) and the age of the spouses.

Unmarried, single parent The number of unmarried, single parents is rising because of unwed mothers electing to keep their children and single persons adopting children. Unmarried, single-parent families can be very happy families, although the problems these families face are similar to those experienced by single-parent family heads. Finances, employment, loneliness, social relationships, role conflicts, child care, and child rearing are some of the problems faced by the unmarried, single parent. In addition, the predominant lack of social acceptability for these arrangements intensifies feelings of alienation.

Unmarried couples The number of unmarried couples is also increasing in American society. Unmarried couples live together for a number of reasons, which include gaining a knowledge about how to live with someone, preparing for marriage, testing a potential marriage relationship, and obtaining a convenient and economical living arrangement. Two general issues that affect the success of the relationship are the responses of the partners' families of origin (the families into which they were born) and the community surrounding the unmarried couple, and the degree to which the couple feels the relationship is permanent.[3] Some unique problems of cohabitation may be guilt due to religious beliefs, instability of the relationships, conflicts, inability to share lives with others, loss of other relationships, different expectations, children, legal problems, and housing difficulties.

Commune families Commune families are similar to social-support networks except that commune families are countercultural. The group lives together and consists of married couples, unmarried couples, single persons, and children. Many members seek the social support discussed in the section on social-support networks. Other reasons for living in a commune include wanting personal growth through small group processes, seeking spiritual rebirth, desiring to get back to nature, and desiring to rebel against the establishment. Communes tend to have little or no structure with very little authority given to any one person. Consequently, there is a certain amount of emotional and financial instability in most commune families. It is difficult in many communes to establish an intimate relationship with any one person, and the numerous relationships tend to be superficial and lack closeness, which is supposed to characterize commune families. Many communes lack privacy, have poor sanitation, provoke conflict with the outside community, and develop legal problems.

There are both advantages and disadvantages to commune child rearing. Children have the opportunity to learn cooperation as a part of everyday living. They are exposed to many adult role models who willingly care for the children. On the other hand, overly permissive discipline, high turnover with the accompanying instability that often diminishes children's sense of security, and poor education are some of the disadvantages of communal living. The long-range effects upon adults as well as children are not known at this time. As is true of all types of family structures, there is much variation within commune groups.

Family establishment
Communication
Communication is an essential part of the foundation upon which families are established. The verbal and nonverbal messages family members send to one another are vitally important to the well-being of each individual and to the family system as a whole. The way people communicate to one another reflects the nature of their relationship and affects future satisfaction or discord.

There are two main functions of communication: message sending and behavioral guidance for the receiver of the message. Dimensions of message sending include content, representational accuracy, information, and vocal properties.[4] Content refers to what is said, while representational accuracy is the degree to which the content is depicted accurately or inaccurately. When the content about events, people, or objects is misrepresented, it is usually done by lack of speech specificity, overgeneralization, or other representational inaccuracies. Information about a topic reduces uncertainty for the listener, but too much or too little information, or overly redundant or insufficient information, merely confuses the listener. The vocal properties of verbal behavior include volume of the message and feeling tones that convey pleasant or unpleasant messages. The person who receives the message affects the sender by his or her response. Sometimes family members inappropriately affect one another's message sending by excessive control, inappropriate control, and ineffective control. All of these aspects of communication need to be taken into consideration as couples develop their relationships with one another and later, as children or others enter the family system.

When couples are establishing communication patterns, understanding the several sources of difficulty in verbal behavior can be helpful. Verbal behavior is influenced by both the present and past responses to messages a person sends or has sent. A wife may talk incessantly to her new husband because she may have never learned to let others talk, or the husband may remain quiet and uncommunicative because this is the verbal behavior modeled by his father. During the establishment of a family, there are many conditions that stimulate misunderstandings in communication. There may be high stress due to money problems, conflicts with in-laws, or activities within the home.

Couples quickly learn that there are good and poor times for discussing issues. For instance, conversations about serious matters do not go well when the husband, wife, or both are hungry, tired, or angry. Regular times need to be established for talking to one another, although this is especially difficult when both partners work at different times of the day. When times are available for talking, it is important that partners reinforce appropriate verbal behaviors rather than precipitate or sustain such inappropriate verbal behaviors as pessimistic talk, excessive responses, or verbal tantrums.

Nonverbal behavior communicates as much if not more than verbal behavior. Touch, body positions, and facial expressions all convey messages. For example, shaking hands conveys such messages as acceptance and friendship; feelings of love often are expressed with physical contact. Differences in body position communicate information about how a person is feeling. The way one sits in a chair or where one looks reveal how interested the person is in the subject being discussed. It is of utmost importance that the nonverbal behavior be congruent with the verbal behavior so that there are not mixed messages.

Developmental tasks

Learning to communicate with one another is probably the most important developmental task of a new family, but there are other tasks that also must be accomplished. For the purposes of this chapter, the tasks of developing interdependence, deciding on roles, making decisions, and understanding sexual needs will be discussed.

Interdependence Couples vary in their desire to be dependent upon one another. At one extreme are couples who prefer to live relatively separate lives while living together and who obtain satisfaction in life from the activities they do as individuals rather than as couples. At the other extreme are couples who prefer to do everything together and who receive most of their satisfaction in life from their activities as couples. Partners who live relatively disengaged from each other tolerate a wide range of individual differences. It takes considerable stress in such relationships to activate support for each other, since the partners may be unaware of the stress being experienced by the other partner. Couples who are extremely close discourage autonomous exploration and mastery of problems.[5] A small amount of stress in one member of the couple activates a response from the other. Sometimes the support given is suffocating and hinders personal growth. The majority of couples are somewhere in the middle, where they strive for interdependence and where it is possible to grow and behave as an individual and as a couple.

Another way to understand interdependence is through the term *bond*, which refers to the ties that keep a couple together in a relationship. Each couple determines the desirable strength of their interpersonal bonds. Although most couples want to be close to each other for reasons just discussed, it should not be inferred that extremely strong bonds are an optimal goal. Many couples, however, need to strengthen their bonds in the early stages of marriage.

Turner[6] developed the principles about bonds

and Burr[7] amplified the ways that couples can increase the strength of their bonds. Burr's first principle is that the more couples share experiences with one another, the more likely they are to increase the strength of their bonds to one another. These experiences may be related to work around the home or to relaxing activities with one another. Second, couples who become involved in long-term activities tend to increase the strength of their bonds. Looking forward to the results of joint efforts creates a mutually shared anticipation that enhances feelings of togetherness. Third, open and unreserved interactions tend to increase the strength of the bonds. The nature of the communication needs to be constructive rather than divisive, even in stressful times. Fourth, interdependent roles influence the strength of the bonds. Fifth, the amount of support in a relationship influences the strength of the bonds. Finally, the more partners enhance each other's self-esteem, the greater will be the strength of their bonds to each other. These principles suggest ways that couples can encourage interdependence in the first stages of family development. The principles also, of course, pertain to later parent-child relationships, child-sibling bonds, and other subsystem relationships that may develop as the family expands.

Roles The successful establishment of the family requires considerable communication between partners about the roles and activities each will assume. Symbolic interaction theory provides guidelines on how roles affect relationships.[8] Each person comes to a relationship with expectations of how she or he will behave in the relationship and of how the partner should behave. These expectations are like rules about how people should or should not think, feel, and behave in a particular role. When the activities are important to the couple, the more congruence between what is expected and what actually occurs, the more satisfied the couple tends to be with the relationship. Similarly, couples tend to be more satisfied with their relationship when they agree about who makes what decisions and what should or should not be done in a designated role. It is not easy for individuals to give up beliefs about who should do certain tasks in a household, especially when these beliefs come from years of living in situations where the beliefs

successfully guided behavior. When possible, couples need to assume roles that are compatible with the other roles that each person assumes. Partners who understand each other's conflicts regarding the demands of the many different roles are more likely to have more satisfaction than partners who do not accurately understand each other and the role each plays in the relationship. Also, partners who are similar and who do not dominate one another are likely to ease the transition of establishing the family unit.

Decision making Clarification of roles in the family helps to delineate decision making, since the person who is responsible for a certain area of activities in the family is usually the person who is in charge of the decisions in that area. When leadership is not clearly defined, decisions often are not made. Decisions that have an important impact on both partners need to be discussed even though one member might be in charge of the issue being decided. The key to good decision making lies in open communication between members about the alternatives to the problem that needs to be solved and consensus about the best alternative. It is unusual to have complete consensus on all issues, although a family will sense greater satisfaction about decisions if they agree at least on the majority of issues, especially the important decisions.

Management of finances is an important area that demands decision making by the newly established family. Each person needs to clarify what he or she values, especially when there is not an overabundance of money. Furthermore, couples need to discuss what they value not only as individuals but as a couple and how they plan to achieve what they value. Open communication is essential in the decision-making process as it relates to money, since hidden feelings of hostility and rivalry are often revealed through discussions of finances.

Decisions also must be made about whether or not to have children, since a satisfactory method of conception control must be instituted if the couple wishes to postpone childbearing. Many factors influence the decision about whether a couple wants to become parents. If they choose to have a child, it is important that both persons desire a child and that both are willing to make the sacrifices that are a normal part of child rearing. Some couples find that one or both do not have the temperament, emotional stability, or ability to care for a child. Others find that children do not fit in with their desired lifestyle or life goals. It is most difficult when one partner wants a child and the other does not. If the couple goes ahead under such circumstances, the person wanting the child is usually the one who takes major responsibility for the child in the future.

Couples who want children must decide on when to have children and the number of children they desire. The number and timing of children is influenced by the age of the couple, health, financial status, and the emotional desire for children. Again, open communication is a key to the decision-making process as it relates to childbearing.

Sexual relations There are many speculations about the basis of good sexual relations. Perhaps the most important factor is that the couple be free of tension and worry at least while making love. Satisfaction in sexual relations is increased by active participation by both partners and a sense of security and love. When couples are fearful about conception, adequate measures should be taken to prevent conception at that time so that the couple can be free of this tension. Different techniques have been suggested to reach maximum pleasure, although techniques have little value in the long run unless there is a positive interpersonal relationship between the couple.

Preparation for parenthood

The childbearing family is faced with many transitions from the time the couple learns that the woman is pregnant through the birth of the child. This is both an exciting and stressful time for most couples.

Impact of pregnancy

The impact of pregnancy on couples is affected by the reasons for conception in the first place. It is less of a shock if the pregnancy is planned and desired by the couple. The impact is likely to be stressful, however, if it is unrealistic for the couple to handle the preparation and, later, the care of the child. Regardless of the reason for conception, most couples find that the transition into the parent role is a challenging time.

The first pregnancy affects couples in various ways, depending on the circumstances surrounding the pregnancy. If the couple is psychologically, mentally, physically, and financially prepared for the arrival of their first child, their reaction is likely to be joyous. A couple who has been wanting a child for years but without success is likely to be ecstatic unless, of course, they are no longer prepared to care for a child. There may be mixed reactions when a couple already has adopted a child with the thought there was no hope of bearing their own child. Again the circumstances affect the impact of the pregnancy on the couple. If the adopted child is old enough to understand the implications of a new child in the home, it is important that the adopted child feel that she or he is still loved and just as important to the parents as is the new baby.

When marriage is precipitated by pregnancy, the pregnancy may be viewed as a burden, but this is not true for all couples. Age of the parents also affects the impact of the pregnancy on the couple. A new baby could create serious complications in the lives of adolescent parents under 18 years of age or to first-time parents over 35 years of age. Older parents may have the financial resources to support a child, but they have the worry of physical risks involved in childbirth for babies born to older mothers. Although the news of pregnancy always has an impact on parents, news of the first pregnancy has special significance.

Subsequent pregnancies affect the couple, the children, and the family as a whole. For instance, the toddler who has been the center of attention as the only child may resent having a new addition to the family. The time before the birth of the second child may not be as easy for the mother, since she now must care for her growing child as well as herself. The family as a whole will feel the impact of pregnancy in many ways, financially, time-wise, and interpersonally.

Developmental tasks

Roles Couples planning for parenthood have several tasks they need to take care of as they prepare for parenthood. Roles, as well as sexual relations, again need to be adjusted. In addition, preparations need to be made for the baby, and parenting responsibilities need to be learned.

Special responsibilities come with the roles of

mother and father. As couples prepare for these new responsibilities, they need to make room for additional tasks that come with these roles. Couples who are already extremely busy need to determine how to handle increased responsibility so that the transition can be made with ease. This may mean changing expectations one has of oneself, eliminating roles that are not essential, and rearranging activities that might cause conflict.

Sexual preparations Sexual relations need not become an issue during pregnancy, but some adjustments are necessary. This is a time when women tend to feel unattractive. Understanding and loving support can help the woman during this time. Adjustments need to be made in the manner in which couples make love, since certain positions are no longer comfortable for the woman. Differing opinions about the safety of having sexual relations during the third trimester require that each couple seek the counsel of their physician during this period.

Financial preparations Financial preparations must be made so that there are adequate funds for normal expenditures and for unexpected events. Such baby equipment as car seats, clothing, and insurance are a few examples of items that need to be included in the budget. Health insurance usually covers most of the costs of medical and hospital care, but this should be assessed so that proper arrangements can be made if the insurance is not adequate. Family members' and friends' contributions to the new baby are usually most welcome.

Parent education The couple needs to prepare for the actual birth of the child. Childbirth classes for both partners are readily available in most localities, and, if not, literature and couple counseling can be substituted for the classes. It is most important that both the man and woman be involved in the process, since they can help each other.

Most new parents have some idea of parenting responsibilities from their past experiences; however, many new parents desire additional information. This can be obtained from published material, friends and relatives, and classes on parent education. The more new parents can learn about what will be expected of them in their role as parents, the less stressful the transition seems to be. Information about what is normal growth and development helps to ease the worries that so often accompany changes in the child. Such knowledge can also be used to detect abnormal behavior that can be taken care of if assessed early. Parents also need to learn about signs and symptoms indicative of physical illness. They need information on when to call for professional help and when to take action on their own. Since accidents are so prevalent among children, parents also need to know how to prevent such occurrences. The home setting must be assessed for areas where mishaps could easily occur. Falls, burns, ingestion of harmful substances, and cuts all can be prevented with the appropriate precautions.

Parenthood

Parenthood begins when the first child is born and, in a sense, continues throughout life (Fig. 3-2). The active period of parenting ends, however, when the last child leaves home. Early parenthood usually refers to the time when the children are young and in elementary school. Later parenthood occurs after the last child leaves home or finishes college. The parental couple continues to work through developmental tasks as the children grow and mature.

Developmental tasks

Duvall[9] listed a large number of specific developmental tasks through which developing families must progress. Only major tasks will be discussed here. These tasks revolve around the following: (1) responding to maturational and situational crises, (2) formulating child-rearing and discipline practices, (3) formulating health-seeking behaviors, and (4) maintaining growth and productivity in the family and community.

Maturational and situational crises All members of the family face individual crises as each matures, and these crises in turn affect the family as a whole. For example, the teething baby is experiencing a maturational crisis that affects the well-being of the baby, but the baby's cries also affect the total family. Adolescents go through maturational crises as they move through the stages of dependence, independence, and finally interdependence with their parents. Adult family members also experience maturational crises, such as realizing that they may not become what they had hoped to become in their careers. Reactions related to this realization permeate the feeling tones of the family, just as responses by other family members to their own maturational crises affect the family as a system. It is through these experiences that the family grows and matures as a supportive unit.

The ability of families to recover from maturational and situational crises is dependent upon a number of factors, including the family's adaptability, integration, and prior learning.[10] The family that is flexible and able to change its ways of doing things is likely to have an easier time when crises hit the family. Families that are interdependent and organized in a way that is conducive to getting things done seem to recover more easily from crises. Prior experiences with stressful events contribute to the skill with which families adjust to difficult circumstances. Families without prior experience with a stressful event can modify the effects of what they are dreading by anticipating what such an experience would be like and by planning what they would do under the circumstances. This is a particularly helpful exercise for dramatic happenings, such as death of a family member, but it is also helpful for maturational crises, such as working through feelings when the last child enters school.

Child-rearing and disciplining practices Child-rearing practices in American society tend to fluctuate from indulgent treatment to stern discipline of children. Just before the turn of the twentieth century, child-rearing advice tended to be rather indulgent, and the child regulated the activities surrounding its care. In the early 1900s, discipline changed from a reward system to a punishment-based system that emphasized obedience. Babies were allowed to cry at length and parents were discouraged from cuddling the baby too much, since this might spoil the child. In midcentury the pendulum returned to more permissive child rearing and disciplining. Today there tends to be more of a balance between permissiveness and sternness, although there is great variation among families. Parents often try to correct what they feel was undesirable in their

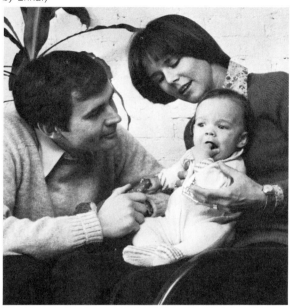

Figure 3-2 Active parenthood begins with the birth of a child and ends when he leaves home. However, in a sense parenthood extends through the life of the parents. (*Photo by Erika.*)

past, thus perpetuating the cycle of permissive and authoritarian child rearing.

Societal norms for child-rearing practices change over time, but parents must also adapt their child-rearing practices as their children move from infancy to adulthood, as was described in Chap. 2. Parenting during infancy centers around providing for the physical and emotional needs of the child. The early years of the child's life are filled with tension and gratification for both the child and parents, as the adults seek to meet the child's needs. As the child matures, the emphasis on restraining, controlling, and directing the child in the interest of the child's physical safety moves to more verbal and psychological directions. Clear and open communication between parent and child provides the foundation upon which the child's development depends.

Parenting styles are important in the child-rearing process because of the way that the style affects open and honest communication among family members (Fig. 3-3). It is not helpful to label parents as authoritarian, democratic, or laissez-faire, since the best approach a parent

Figure 3-3 Parenting styles affect the open and honest communication among family members. A democratic approach may best fit the goal of allaying children's fears. (*Photo by Erika.*)

can take depends on the particular situation. In some instances, a parent must be authoritarian in order to protect the child or get something done as soon as possible. If the goal of the parent is to allay fearful feelings, then the approach needs to be more democratic. Parenting style depends on what needs to be accomplished, and the successful accomplishment of the task usually depends on clear and open communication.

Berger and Benson[11] classified parenting styles according to a communication framework. The seven different parenting styles are neither "good" nor "bad"; rather they are "good" or "bad" depending on the effect that is desired in the child. Berger and Benson's seven styles are labeled as follows: The Commander General, Cross-Examiner, Family Psychologist, Disqualifier, Preacher, Cynic, and Facilitator. The Commander General bosses and gives orders to the children, who in turn tend to resent the parent. The Cross-Examiner continually asks why the child did such and such an act and blames the child for his or her actions, thus inhibiting further communication. The Family Psychologist evaluates messages, sometimes even diagnoses the

child's condition, but seldom allows the child a part in the process. The Disqualifier sends irrelevant or insensitive messages to the child, which makes the child feel as though he or she will never quite meet the expectations of the parents. The Preacher lectures or moralizes about an issue, which causes the child to think he has done something wrong. The Cynic uses sarcasm to belittle or make fun of the child, so that the child feels as though he or she can do nothing right. Finally, the Facilitator shows understanding of the child through verbal and nonverbal responses.

These styles of parenting are especially applicable to communication between adolescents and their parents. Adolescence is the time when conflicts frequently arise as the adolescent alternately moves between dependence and independence. During this period it is necessary that the adolescent realize that she or he is important in the decision-making process, since creative problem solving involves the assessment of alternative solutions, regardless of who offers the suggestion of how the issue might be solved. Trust and acceptance of the adolescent facilitate open communication between adolescents and their parents. Parent-child relations are influenced by the norms of society, but more specifically by the family's cultural background and socioeconomic class. In some cultures, adolescents are not expected to participate in the decision-making process as described earlier. Children are expected to comply with the parents' demands and to do so without question in many cultures. There are mixed findings on the effect of socioeconomic class on child-rearing practices, since the widespread viewing of television cuts across all classes and provides one norm for child rearing. It has been thought in the past, however, that middle-class parents stress reasoning, isolation, and guilt when disciplining children. Some studies indicate that lower-class families tend to discipline their children in terms of the consequences of the behavior and to physically punish them more often than middle-class parents punish their children. Again, there is much variation between families within any socioeconomic class.

Health-seeking behavior Another developmental task of parenthood is to teach and model health-seeking behavior, i.e., physical, emotional, and spiritual well-being. Children's food habits are established in the family through the selection, preparation, and consumption of food in the home. Sleep, relaxation, and exercise patterns also are established in the home. Health-seeking behaviors need to become a part of children's lives as parents aid their children through the various health crises that are normal in childhood.

Growth and productivity A final developmental task of parenthood to be discussed here is to ensure that individual family members grow to be all that they are capable of becoming as individuals and as a family and that they be provided opportunities to give to one another and to the community in which they live. The explorations and activities of each family member have the potential for enriching and complementing the lives of the other members of the family. Compromises that augment the growth of family members enrich family life as a whole and the community in which the family lives. Just as individuals are part of the family system, so is the family a part of the larger community system. This implies that there must be give-

and-take between the family and the larger system in order for both to survive in the long run.

Early parenthood

There are specific issues that must be addressed in early parenthood in addition to the more general developmental tasks just described. Duvall[12] listed the tasks of a family with a new infant as those of adapting housing arrangements to the child, meeting the financial costs of child bearing, assuming mutual responsibility for the child and household care, facilitating one another's role learning, communicating with one another, planning for future children, relating to relatives and others, maintaining motivation and morale, and establishing family rituals and routines. Although couples cognitively realize that all of the above activities must be performed, it often comes as a surprise to new parents that the complexity of their lives increases dramatically following the birth of a child. The more the couple can be mutually involved in the total process, the easier the adjustment to life with a new baby.

The addition of other children to the family increases the complexity of the tasks that must be accomplished. Conflicts arise for the other children when a new baby comes on the scene. Firstborn children who are toddlers at the time the second child is born are apt to experience frustration, since the only child is robbed of the attention and power to which he or she has become accustomed. As the children grow older and the number of children in the family increases, sibling rivalry is not uncommon. Children need assistance as they grow older with assuming responsibility for themselves as well as for other members of the family.

Later parenthood

Adult partner roles change again as children leave home to establish families of their own. Couples differ in their responses to this stage in their lives. Some couples adjust to the changing responsibilities with hopeful anticipation for a period when they can enjoy one another without the responsibilities of the children and careers. Other couples dread this stage because of feelings of uselessness and because the individuals in the couple unit are not comfortable with each other over long periods. The most ideal situation is when parents grow with and through their children, so that when the children leave home, the parents are prepared for the next stage in their lives.

Many couples look forward to the "empty nest" stage as a time of freedom, forgetting that their elderly parents may need assistance at this time. The assistance may only involve phone calls and letters but also could mean financial assistance, visits, errands, tasks around the parent's home, and even having him live with the adult children, if his physical condition necessitates such care. Family relationships remain important throughout life from the establishment of the family through the "empty nest" stage.

References

1. John Scanzoni, "Contemporary Marriage Types," *Journal of Family Issues* 1:125–140 (March 1980).
2. E. B. Visher and J. S. Visher, "Major Areas of Difficulty for Stepparent Couples," *International Journal of Family Counseling* 6:70–80 (1978).
3. Kathline Kuhn and Ellen H. Janosik, "Establishment of a Family System," *Family-Focused Care*, Jean R. Miller and Ellen H. Janosik (eds.), McGraw-Hill, New York, 1980, p. 155.
4. Edwin J. Thomas, *Marital Communication and Decision Making: Analysis, Assessment, and Change*, Free Press, New York, 1977, p. 11.
5. Salvador Minuchin, *Families and Family Therapy*, Harvard, Cambridge, Mass., 1974, p. 55.
6. Ralph H. Turner, *Family Interaction*, Wiley, New York, 1970, pp. 81–83.
7. Wesley R. Burr, *Successful Marriage: A Principles Approach*, Dorsey, Homewood, Ill., 1970, pp. 327–347.
8. Ibid., pp. 295–325.
9. Evelyn M. Duvall, *Marriage and Family Development*, 5th ed., Lippincott, Philadelphia, 1977, pp. 185–350.
10. Burr, op. cit., pp. 393–422.
11. Michael Berger and Loren Benson, *Family Communication Systems: Instructors Handbook*, Human Synergistics, Inc., Minneapolis, 1971, p. 10.
12. Duvall, op cit., pp. 231–247.

Chapter 4 **History of child health care**

Dorothy J. DeMaio

Upon completion of this chapter, the student will be able to:

1. Identify four societal factors that impeded progress in the delivery of child health care prior to the twentieth century.
2. Describe the historical roots of the nurse as a provider and promoter of sick- and well-child services.
3. List four major governmental activities or programs that significantly influenced the delivery of child health services in the United States.

4. List two documents on child health that reflect U.S. and worldwide concern for children to grow and develop in health.
5. Give examples of the variety of roles and settings in which maternal-child nurses function.
6. Discuss the standards of maternal-child nursing practice and their value to practicing nurses and the consumer.

Introduction

"Maintenance and promotion of health care are the nation's first line of defense in building a healthy society."[1] Finding someone to oppose this statement would be as difficult as finding someone to challenge the belief that health care is the right of every citizen. Yet endless reports from health planners, local and federal health agencies, and consumer health advocates conclude that broad-spectrum health care is lacking for children. A look at history may be helpful in explaining why children in the United States still have problems gaining access to health care.

Health care in primitive societies

Very little has been recorded about the health care of children in early primitive societies. However, from the evidence it seems clear that, although most children received the physical care essential for survival, some received very different treatment from others. Vitality and strength were often the key to survival. Weak or malformed infants were commonly allowed to die from neglect. In some primitive cultures males were valued and females, if born in excess numbers, were destroyed.

The advent of health care of the child

As civilization advanced and humans learned to grow their food, manufacture clothing and tools, and shelter themselves, children became important to the group.

Religious teachings strongly influenced attitudes toward children as individuals and as family members. In ancient Israel the health practices prescribed by Mosaic law improved the quality of life for children. Christianity placed stress on the love of one for another and the need to care for the weak as well as the strong.

Recognition that children had special needs did not become widespread until the sixteenth century, when certain religious orders took as their special mission the care and nursing of children. Vincent de Paul (later St. Vincent) championed the cause of abandoned children and established the Hospital for Foundlings. He was horrified by the way La Couche, the existing institution for abandoned children, indiscriminately gave the children to professional beggars, who sometimes mutilated them to make them more useful in begging. Vincent de Paul founded the Sisters of Charity, one of the earliest nursing orders. The Sisters made the bodily and material needs of children their cause.

In the seventeenth century, the educator John Amos Comenius sought in his writings to aid parents in understanding their children. He provided information of child-rearing practices that fostered emotional health. He believed that in this way the child would find it easier to undertake learning. He also wrote about the importance of age-appropriate sensory stimulation beginning in the home. His important writings included *The School of Infancy* (also known as *The School of the Maternal Bosom*),[2] which was published in 1633 and advocated a healthy relationship between the mother and the child. For Jean Piaget in our century, Comenius was a pioneer in developmental psychology.[3]

In the eighteenth century the problem of neglected and abandoned children grew worse. It became common for impoverished mothers to place infants on the doorsteps of the rich or to leave them in the street, where they often died from starvation or exposure.[4] In London between 1730 and 1750, 75 percent of all babies christened died before the age of 5. At times mothers rid themselves of their own newborn children so that they could help support their families by serving as wet nurses for the infants of wealthy women who considered breast-feeding unfashionable. Hospital records of this period show repeated entries noting "death from want of breast milk."[5] In 1761 the educator Jean Jacques Rousseau attempted in his book *Emile* to persuade mothers to breast-feed and nurture their own infants. Another drawback to the use of wet nurses was the spread of disease from these impoverished women to the children they nursed, further contributing to the high rate of infant mortality.

Child health care in the United States

The nineteenth century was a period of rapid industrialization in the United States. Little thought was given to the special needs of children. In fact, ordinary working people lacked even the basic health services. Children were considered the

Figure 4-1 Boys' ward, circa 1900. (*Boston City Hospital School of Nursing Alumnae, Boston, Massachusetts. Used with permission.*)

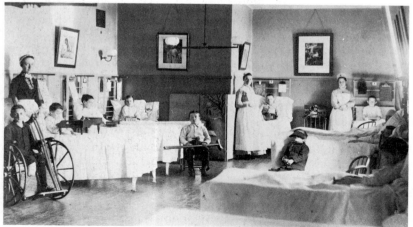

property of their parents and were often used by them to increase their income.

Children were an essential part of the work force. They were often given dangerous jobs in mines and mills. They also worked on farms and as servants in homes. Parents valued having many children as insurance against the inevitable loss of some family members to disease.

Specialization in the care of sick children

Although educators like Comenius and Rousseau were concerned with the emotional health and the education of children, specialists in their physical health did not emerge until the latter half of the nineteenth century. Of course, great physicians as far back as Hippocrates had reported on diseases peculiar to children, but little interest was shown in the management of childhood illness. It was common for hospitalized children to share a bed with six to eight others or even with seriously ill adults.[6]

In 1855 the first hospital for sick children, Children's Hospital of Philadelphia, was established. In 1860 Dr. Abraham Jacobi opened a clinic for children in New York City and lectured on childhood diseases. In time Harvard University's medical school and others developed children's clinics and educational programs primarily focused on the diseases of organ systems.[7]

Early role of nurses in care of sick children

Although nurses attended lectures on the care of sick children during this period, the first reference to formal education of nurses in midwifery and the care of sick children occurred in 1798. At New York Hospital, a physician presented 24 lectures on "Early Discovering when the Aid of a Physician is Necessary and Cautions for Nurses."[8] Were these lectures, by chance, the seed from which the concept of nursing diagnosis grew?

The need for "trained nurses" was first recognized in 1849 when a sanitary commission appointed by the Massachusetts Legislature to develop plans for promoting the health of the public recommended that nurses be educated to care for the sick.[9] The first U.S. nursing school began at the New England Hospital for Women and Children. Lectures were given on medical, surgical, and obstetrical conditions but none were specifically about child care. In 1903, almost 30 years after the first school was established, nurses were registered by the states. Early boards of nurse examiners refused to register nurses whose training school did not provide a special unit in the hospital for children and relevant education in the care of sick children (Figs. 4-1 and 4-2). This position strengthened the movement to improve hospital care of children.

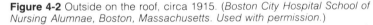

Figure 4-2 Outside on the roof, circa 1915. (*Boston City Hospital School of Nursing Alumnae, Boston, Massachusetts. Used with permission.*)

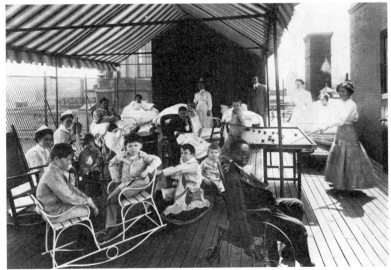

Early role of nurses in well-child care

Although Massachusetts recognized public health as a governmental responsibility, for a time there was little systematic or organized activity throughout the United States. Special committees and boards of health were set up to deal with specific crises, usually cholera epidemics, but had little to do otherwise.[10] Infant mortality rates were extraordinarily high. In Newark, New Jersey, the third oldest city in the nation, 2 of every 10 babies died within the first year of life. Deplorable living conditions, poor sanitation, bacteria-laden milk, ignorance of the essentials of prenatal and delivery care, and neglectful and ignorant infant feeding were the major causative factors.[11] See Fig. 4-3.

Recognizing the impact of unsanitary conditions on the raging infant mortality rate, citizens groups, physicians, and nurses established "milk stations." "Pure milk" was distributed by nurses who also visited and instructed in the homes of "improperly fed and sick infants only."[12]

In the early part of the twentieth century the concept of providing maternal and child health services developed in the urban areas. The first governmental unit of any kind devoted solely to maternal and child health services, the Bureau of Child Hygiene in the New York City Department of Health, was organized in 1908.[13] Soon after, other major cities created divisions of child hygiene within boards of health. Some segments of society had finally come to believe that the welfare of infants and children was the responsibility of the state. Physicians, in general, protested government involvement in the delivery of health services. Those physicians who practiced in the public health sector were very careful to assure physicians that they would not care for children who had private physicians.

Nurses were integral to the delivery of child health services from the inception of child hygiene bureaus. For example, in the city of Newark graduate nurses were employed to teach infant hygiene and carry out the health supervision of children in the home. Additional activities included case finding, treating ophthalmia neonatorum, managing all sickly infants delivered by midwives, caring for unmarried mothers, and resolving the problems of housing, sanitation, and poverty. Nurses also supervised hygienic practices of midwives and boarding homes for children.[14] See Fig. 4-4.

The role of nurses in school health was noted in the official records of the Board of Health of the City of Newark. In 1917 the record reported the dismissal of five physicians who provided medical inspection for the children in the 26 parochial schools in Newark. Six graduate nurses were employed to replace the physicians. These nurses were required to perform physical examinations on all the children. Physical examination was fully described in the records and was clearly distinguished from class inspection, which was an examination for cleanliness and open lesions.[15]

The historical literature reflects that child hygiene nurses, public health nurses, and school nurses were the main providers of child health services and, in many instances, the only child health care providers.[16] Physician focus was almost exclusively on the care of sick children. In fact as late as 1960, almost 30 years after the American Academy of Pediatrics was organized, there were constant pleas that physicians should "expand" their practices to provide child health services "whether they were completely enthusiastic about them or not."[17]

Figure 4-3 A nurse from the New York City Department of Health instructing tenement dwellers about health and sanitation in 1895. (*From Annie M. Brainard, The Evolution of Public Health Nursing, Saunders, 1922, p. 229. Used with permission.*)

Federal government concern for child health care

President Theodore Roosevelt initiated the first national effort to address the issues relevant to the needs of children. Known as the White House Conference of 1909, it was an assembly of representatives of consumer groups, federal, national, state, and voluntary human services organizations. Subsequently, White House conferences on the needs of children have been held every 10 years. A concern through all the conferences has been the developmental and physical health needs of children. Recommendations have included expressed concerns for changing existing services, providing new services, and reordering the nation's priorities.

Major governmental positions and programs have resulted from the White House conferences. A consequence of the 1909 conference was the creation, in 1912, of the Children's Bureau. By legislative command the Children's Bureau was ordered to study and report on all aspects of child life regardless of social class. Concern for increased and quality health care services for children emerged consistently in the study reports and recommendations. Improvements had been demonstrated in the areas of prenatal care, natal care, infant feeding, and sanitation, but little, if anything, was done for the child surviving beyond infancy. The first legislation introduced in Congress to establish a maternal and infant health program was hotly debated in 1920 and 1921. Known as the Maternity and Infancy Act, or the Sheppard-Towner Act, the bill was scored by key legislators as "radical, socialistic and bolshevistic" and a departure from "common sense."[18] Counterdebate by Representative Alben Barkley, who endorsed the act, stated that children should have "an equal chance with every child in the world, not only to be born in health and proper environment, but an equal chance to survive after they have been brought into the world." A strong lobbying effort against the bill was made by the American Medical Association.[19]

Although the opposition was intense, the Sheppard-Towner Act was signed into law in 1921. Matching funds were provided to the states, and by 1927 forty-five states and the territory of Hawaii were using the funds for a variety of related purposes. These included licensing midwives, sponsoring maternal health conferences,

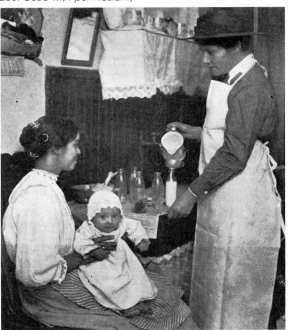

Figure 4-4 The baby welfare nurse. (*From Annie M. Brainard, The Evolution of Public Health Nursing, Saunders, 1922, p. 230. Used with permission.*)

improving the supply of public health nurses, fostering education of doctors and nurses, and creating child health centers. Although a significant number of states established child-hygiene clinics, there clearly was no standardized delivery pattern throughout the country.[20]

The Great Depression of the thirties stimulated research in the Children's Bureau on nutrition and child health. The 1930 White House conference had as its theme child health and protection. As a consequence of the disturbing findings, conference participants developed the *Children's Charter*, a document of great importance in the history of child health. The *Children's Charter* recommended that every child be given health protection from birth through adolescence, including periodic health examinations and, where needed, care from specialists and hospital treatment; regular dental examinations and care of the teeth; protective and preventive measures against communicable diseases; assurance of purity for food, milk, and water. The *Children's Charter* gave direction to the nation regarding the essentials of comprehensive child health care.

However, it was the Social Security Act of 1935 that made the most significant impact on the delivery of child health services. Through this legislation the government pledged support for state efforts to extend and improve health and welfare services for mothers and children.

Title V of the act created a structure to promote maternal and child health, to provide full medical services for handicapped children, to establish a governmental unit for crippled children's services, to develop projects to illustrate innovative and effective ways of providing maternal and child health services, and to expand child welfare services. Frequent amendments of Title V clearly reflect the nation's continuing concern for maternal and child health.[21]

The sweeping provisions of Title XIX (Medicaid) were incorporated in the 1965 amendments that were intended to influence primary care systems to provide comprehensive child health services to children from birth to age 21. Commonly known as *EPSDT* (*e*arly and *p*eriodic *s*creening, *d*iagnosis, and *t*reatment), it was mandated for all Medicaid-eligible children receiving aid to families with dependent children. Guidelines were developed defining the child health services as well as designating time intervals at which care was to be provided. Again the Medicaid-EPSDT program did not achieve the goal of comprehensive well-child care for all eligible children. Although the federal government reimbursed the states 55 percent for EPSDT services, the services were still not being provided because of some states' reluctance to put up matching funds.[22] The latest federal effort to remedy this dilemma is the Comprehensive Health Assurance Program, the CHAP bill. At this writing the bill has been amended several times and the sponsors have not been successful in getting it passed. One major argument against the bill is that it is too costly.

In 1969, when the Department of Health, Education, and Welfare (now Department of Health and Human Services) was restructured, the Children's Bureau became part of the Office of Child Development, and some of its functions were redistributed. Maternal-child health programs are now located in a number of divisions, such as the Bureau of Community Health Services,

Health Services Administration, the Office of Maternal and Child Health, the National Health Service Corps, the Indian Health Services, and others. Research activities take place in all programs but are the primary focus of the National Institute of Child Health and Human Development, located in the Public Health Service.

More than 70 years have passed since the first White House Conference on Children. The country still struggles with many of the old problems and new child health problems continue to emerge. Why do children, the nation's most valuable asset, continue to be deprived of needed health care? Why has this society neglected to create a reasonable, sensible health care delivery system?[23] Borgatta, an anthropologist, points out that "even a fleeting contact with the comparative study of cultures will indicate that accepted ways of doing things do not necessarily exist because of some rational basis or because they are effective."[24]

A worldwide perspective

The problems in delivering child health care are not unique to the United States. Established nations and developing countries the world over face many of the same child health care issues. In the case of developing countries, they are confronted with different cultural problems, both complex and serious, in providing for child health. Developing countries, even those rural in nature and not significantly affected by socioeconomic change, are attempting to improve the standard of living by extending public health programs. The welfare of children is now perceived as a global issue for civilized humankind. The World Health Organization (WHO), historically the first international organization for health, was organized within the structure of the United Nations in 1948. Along with the United Nations Children's Fund (formerly UNICEF) and other organizations, the World Health Organization has provided direction, education, and in some cases financial support to improve the health care services for children. The *Declaration of the Rights of the Child* is a substantive document, approved by the United Nations in 1959, that acknowledges the right of every child in this world to a happy childhood, and to grow and develop in health (Table 4-1).

Table 4-1 Declaration of the rights of the child*

WHEREAS the peoples of the United Nations have, in the Charter, reaffirmed their faith in fundamental human rights, and in the dignity and worth of the human person, and have determined to promote social progress and better standards of life in larger freedom,

WHEREAS the United Nations has, in the Universal Declaration of Human Rights, proclaimed that everyone is entitled to all the rights and freedoms set forth therein, without distinction of any kind, such as race, colour, sex, language, religion, political or other opinion, national or social origin, property, birth or other status,

WHEREAS the child, by reason of his physical and mental immaturity, needs special safeguards and care, including appropriate legal protection, before as well as after birth,

WHEREAS the need for such special safeguards has been stated in the Geneva Declaration of the Rights of the Child of 1924, and recognized in the Universal Declaration of Human Rights and in the statutes of specialized agencies and international organizations concerned with the welfare of children,

WHEREAS mankind owes to the child the best it has to give,

NOW THEREFORE

The General Assembly proclaims this Declaration of the Rights of the Child to the end that he may have a happy childhood and enjoy for his own good and for the good of society the rights and freedoms herein set forth, and calls upon parents, upon men and women as individuals and upon voluntary organizations, local authorities and national governments to recognize and strive for the observance of these rights by legislative and other measures progressively taken in accordance with the following principles:

I. The child shall enjoy all the rights set forth in this Declaration. All children, without any exception whatsoever, shall be entitled to these rights, without distinction or discrimination on account of race, colour, sex, language, religion, political or other opinion, national or social origin, property, birth or other status, whether of himself or of his family.

II. The child shall enjoy special protection, and shall be given opportunities and facilities, by law and by other means, to enable him to develop physically, mentally, morally, spiritually and socially in a healthy and normal manner and in conditions of freedom and dignity. In the enactment of laws for this purpose the best interests of the child shall be the paramount consideration.

III. The child shall be entitled from his birth to a name and a nationality.

IV. The child shall enjoy the benefits of social security. He shall be entitled to grow and develop in health; to this end special care and protection shall be provided both to him and to his mother, including adequate prenatal and postnatal care. The child shall have the right to adequate nutrition, housing, recreation and medical services.

V. The child who is physically, mentally, or socially handicapped shall be given the special treatment, education and care required by his particular condition.

VI. The child, for the full and harmonious development of his personality, needs love and understanding. He shall, wherever possible, grow up in the care and under the responsibility of his parents, and in any case in an atmosphere of affection and of moral and material security; a child of tender years shall not, save in exceptional circumstances, be separated from his mother. Society and the public authorities shall have the duty to extend particular care to children without a family and those without adequate means of support. Payment of state and other assistance towards the maintenance of children of large families is desirable.

VII. The child is entitled to receive education, which shall be free and compulsory at least in the elementary stages. He shall be given an education which will promote his general culture, and enable him on a basis of equal opportunity to develop his abilities, his individual judgment and his sense of moral and social responsibility, and to become a useful member of society.

The best interests of the child shall be the guiding principle of those responsible for his education and upbringing; that responsibility lies in the first place with his parents.

The child shall have full opportunity for play and recreation, which should be directed to the same purposes as education; society and the public authorities shall endeavour to promote the enjoyment of this right.

VIII. The child shall in all circumstances be among the first to receive protection and relief.

IX. The child shall be protected against all forms of neglect, cruelty and exploitation. He shall not be the subject of traffic in any form.

The child shall not be admitted to employment before an appropriate minimum age; he shall in no case be caused or permitted to engage in any occupation or employment which would prejudice his health or education or interfere with his physical, mental or moral development.

X. The child shall be protected from practices which may foster racial, religious and any other form of discrimination. He shall be brought up in a spirit of understanding, tolerance, friendship among peoples, peace and universal brotherhood and in full consciousness that his energy and talents should be devoted to the service of his fellowmen.

* As approved by the 14th General Assembly of the United Nations, November 20, 1959

Source: *Children,* vol. 7. United States Department of Health, Education and Welfare, Social Security Administration, Children's Bureau.

Nursing practice today—a perspective

The American Nurses' Association (ANA) has provided leadership toward assuring the public of quality nursing services by establishing *standards of practice*. These standards serve as a guide for all practicing nurses in that they assist them in assuring the public of quality nursing care. In addition, the standards establish a baseline for nursing practice for which the nurse must be responsible and accountable when providing nursing care. All nurses must be familiar with and guide their practice by the concepts included in the standards. Logically, with time and research, these standards will change. Presently in some states the standards are used as a guide for state boards of nursing in their interpretation of the Nursing Practice Acts.

Standards specific to the specialty of maternal-child health were published by the American Nurses' Association in 1973. The *Standards of Maternal-Child Health Nursing Practice* provide a rationale for each standard and the steps in the process essential to good nursing care. The standards are listed in Table 5-7.

Nursing expertise and services are essential on the total health-illness continuum. Whether the child is in a primary (health maintenance), secondary (acute care), tertiary (specialty hospitals), or long-term health care setting, the nurse needs to synthesize many different pieces of information about the child and family in order to provide maximum benefits to the clients. Nurses must have a substantial knowledge base in order to make the multitude of judgments and decisions required when attending to the unique and highly individualized emotional and physical needs of children.

Rapid technological advances have brought about many changes in nursing practice. Specialization in pediatric nursing is common at the master's level. Increased emphasis is placed on peer review programs and quality assurance (see Chap. 5), and nursing research. Current continuing education programs in pediatric nursing are broad in scope, focusing on child health maintenance and illness prevention as well as care of the ill child.

Pediatric nurses who wish to validate the quality of their practice may seek certification in nursing of the child or adolescent with acute or chronic illness or disabling condition. Certification in this area of practice is sponsored by the ANA Division on Maternal-Child Health Nursing Practice. Registered nurses who meet minimum clinical experience requirements and who are currently practicing in a pediatric clinical setting are eligible to apply.

Candidates for certification are required to pass a written examination. They must also submit written documentation and peer references "to provide evidence of the nature and quality of a candidate's clinical practice."[25] Written documentation includes a description of the nurse's practice setting, the individual's personal philosophy of nursing, and a case study which demonstrates use of the ANA standards of practice. Case studies are evaluated anonymously by at least two nurse reviewers who are knowledgeable in pediatric nursing and nursing process. Nurses who successfully demonstrate the established criteria are awarded certification.

Certification in ambulatory child care nursing practice is also available through the ANA. Only registered nurses who practice in ambulatory settings and who meet certain educational requirements are eligible, however. The process for certification in this area of practice is similar to the one described above.

Providing care to assist children in regaining health is a large part of the contemporary pediatric nurse's role. Nurses prepared at both the technical (A.D.) and professional (B.S.) levels provide care to ill children. As a care provider, the modern pediatric nurse's responsibility includes patient counseling and teaching as well as serving as a child and family advocate. Nurses prepared at the baccalaureate and master's levels assume the additional responsibilities of planning and coordinating care and maintaining and promoting child health. Healthy children are the first line of defense in building a healthy society.[26]

References

1. Martha Rogers, *An Introduction to the Theoretical Basis of Nursing*, Davis, Philadelphia, 1970, p. 122.
2. David Benham, "A Sketch of the Life of the Author," in John Amos Comenius, *The School of Infancy*, W. Mallalieu, London, 1858, p. 117.
3. Jean Piaget, "The Significance of John Amos Comenius at the Present Time," in *John Amos Comenius on Education*, Teachers College, New York, 1967, p. 2.

4. Josephine A. Dolan, *Nursing in Society*, Saunders, Philadelphia, 1978, p. 112.

5. Ibid., p. 112.

6. J. Stokes, *Pediatrics, Choice of a Medical Career*, Lippincott, Philadelphia, 1961, p. 2.

7. Ibid., p. 31.

8. Philip A. Kalisch and Beatrice J. Kalisch, *The Advance of American Nursing*, Little, Brown, Boston, 1978, p. 72.

9. Ibid., p. 77.

10. Stuart Galishoff, *Safeguarding the Public Health—Newark, 1895–1918*, Greenwood Press, Westport, Conn., 1975, p. 109.

11. Ibid., p. 110.

12. Yssabella Waters, *Visiting Nurses in the United States*, Wm. F. Ball, Philadelphia, 1909, p. 166.

13. Edward R. Schlesinger, "The Impact of Federal Legislation on Maternal-Child Health Services in The United States," *Health and Society*, Milbank Memorial Fund Quarterly, Winter 1974, p. 3.

14. New Jersey, City of Newark, Board of Health, *Annual Report*, 1915, p. 177.

15. New Jersey, City of Newark, Board of Health, *Annual Report*, 1917.

16. Dorothy DeMaio, "Comprehensive Well-Child Care: A Descriptive Analysis of a System in Which Services Were Provided by Physicians and Primary Health Care Nurses/ Pediatric Nurse Practitioners," Ed.D. dissertation, Rutgers, The State University of New Jersey, 1979, p. 46.

17. Committee on Child Health, *Health Supervision of Children*, American Public Health Association, New York, 1960, p. 18.

18. U.S. Department of Health, Education, and Welfare, *Child Health in America*, Public Health Service, Rockville, Md., 1976, p. 29.

19. Ibid., p. 30.

20. Ibid., p. 32.

21. Arthur J. Lesser, *Maternal and Child Health Service Programs*, U.S. Department of Health, Education, and Welfare, Maternal-Child Health Service, Washington, February 1973, Introduction.

22. *A Guide to Screening EPDST*, U.S. Department of Health, Education, and Welfare, Medicaid, Washington.

23. Dorothy DeMaio, op. cit., p. 30.

24. Edgar F. Borgatta, "Research Problems in Evaluation of Health Services," in John B. McKinlay (ed.), *Research Methods in Health Care*, Milbank Memorial Fund, New York, 1973, p. 20.

25. American Nurses' Association Division of Maternal-Child Health Nursing Practice: *Guidelines for Written Documentation, Certification in Nursing of the Child/Adolescent with Acute or Chronic Illness or Disabling Condition*, American Nurses' Association, Kansas City, 1980.

26. M. Rogers, op. cit., p. 122.

Chapter 5 The nursing process in child health care

Sarah B. Pasternack

Upon completion of this chapter, the student will be able to:

1. Discuss the use of the nursing process as a clinical practice tool for care of children and their families.

2. Describe each step of the nursing process.

3. Cite the importance of an accurate and thorough nursing assessment in providing care to a child and the child's family.

4. Identify the type of information which should be included in the nursing assessment of a child and family.

5. Differentiate between a nursing diagnosis and a medical diagnosis.

6. Formulate individualized nursing diagnoses for pediatric patients and their families.

7. Write care plan goals that describe the desired patient/family condition or behavioral outcome.

8. Cite the importance of priorities in planning and implementing nursing care.

9. Explain the purpose of evaluation and revision in the nursing process.

10. Write an accurate and concise nursing care plan for a given patient and family.

11. Discuss the purpose of quality assurance in pediatric nursing practice.

12. Discuss the implementation of the American Nurses' Association's *Standards of Maternal-Child Health Nursing Practice*.

The nursing process in pediatric nursing practice

Pediatric nursing is concerned with promoting, maintaining, and restoring the health of children and their families. The *nursing process* is a series of purposeful intellectual and technical activities used by the nurse in providing care to patients and their families. The nursing process is based on the problem-solving method and therefore its steps are arranged in a logical order. The *steps* of the nursing process are: (1) assessment; (2) nursing diagnosis; (3) planning; (4) implementation; and (5) evaluation and revision. Overall, the nurse applies the steps sequentially: assessment precedes diagnosis, diagnosis precedes making the treatment plan, and so forth. In the reality of daily practice, however, the steps of the nursing process often recur during the course of caring for any one client, and they sometimes overlap. The nursing process can be used effectively in providing care to ill children and in promoting and maintaining the health of well children.

Nursing is not a rote activity and it cannot be practiced in a simplistic "cookbook" fashion. The contemporary practice of nursing requires the practitioner to use a scientific knowledge base in order to prevent, minimize, or resolve children's health problems. The nursing process is an indispensable clinical practice tool which enables the nurse to identify patient health problems and make decisions in clinical practice.

Nursing care plans

It is essential that the nursing process be communicated, both orally and in writing, to others who participate in the patient's care. The *nursing care plan* is the written form of the nursing process. This chapter ends with a sample care plan. The exact design of the nursing care plan varies among health care agencies.

A nursing care plan documents nursing activities performed on the patient's and family's behalf. It also facilitates continuity of the patient's care among nursing staff members. The nursing care plan is often placed in the patient's record or in a location which is convenient for the nursing staff. In some states, the nursing care plan is part of the patient's legal medical record.

The nursing care plan should always be individualized in order to meet the needs of the child and family. The length and complexity of nursing care plans vary among patients. A patient and family with complex health problems might require an elaborate plan, whereas a child with minor health problems may need only a brief care plan.

Accountability through the nursing process

Today, consumers are knowledgeable and they demand quality from those who provide services and products. As health care providers, nurses are no exception. In pediatric nursing, the nurse is *accountable* to both the child and family for the care given. This means that the nurse is responsible for implementing a plan of care which will best resolve or minimize the child's health problems.

The nursing process is important because it explains the practice of nursing. It is more accurate, perhaps, than any other description of nursing. It tells the consumer and other health professionals what the nurse *does* in practice. The nursing process serves as the basis for the legal definition of nursing in some state nurse practice acts. Therefore, the nursing process can be used as the *legal standard* against which a nurse's practice may be judged. Many schools of nursing and health agencies evaluate nurses in relation to their ability to demonstrate use of the nursing process in clinical practice.

Steps of the nursing process

Assessment

The nurse cannot provide care to a child without knowledge of the child's health status. It is essential, therefore, that the nurse start the assessment before attempting to provide care.

Nursing assessment consists of (1) collecting information about the health status of the child and the family, (2) organizing this information, and (3) analyzing this information. Assessment is the first and most important step in the nursing process because it is the foundation for the steps that follow.

The nurse's assessment must be *thorough* and *accurate*. If the assessment is incomplete or inaccurate, the nursing diagnoses and care plan will be neither individualized nor effective. Invalid assumptions do not belong in the nurse's assessment. All interactions between the nurse and the patient and family provide opportunities for assessment. The nurse must continually be alert for new information about the patient. New data may suggest additional nursing diagnoses and changes in the care plan. Periodic reassessment is especially important in pediatric nursing because a child's condition can change rapidly. Thus, the nurse's assessment may serve as the basis for critical and, frequently, lifesaving decisions about the patient. The general categories of information which should be included in the pediatric nursing assessment are listed in Table 5-1.

Collecting information Two nursing skills are essential in assessment: observation and interviewing. The nurse should use as many senses as possible in performing the assessment. The nurse can learn much about the child and family by making astute observations. Initially, the nurse appraises the patient's *overall condition and appearance*. Is the child alert and active or lethargic? Does the child look uncomfortable or relaxed? As the nurse continues with the assessment, additional information about the patient's physical status is obtained. (Specific ob-

Table 5-1 Categories of information in the pediatric nursing assessment

1. Child's physical status
2. Child's behavior and response to illness and hospitalization
3. Child's level of growth and development
4. Behavior of parents and significant others
5. Patient's and parents' knowledge of child's condition and reason for hospitalization
6. Social/environmental factors influencing the child (siblings and others at home, religion and culture, school performance, financial resources, living conditions)

servations about the child's physical status that should be included in the assessment are listed in Table 6-4.) The extensiveness of the nurse's physical assessment varies according to the nurse's preparation, experience, and practice setting.

The nurse should observe the *verbal and nonverbal behavior* of the child and the child's family. These observations assist the nurse in assessing the child's developmental level and emotional status and the family's interaction patterns. Close observation of behavior is an important skill in pediatric nursing. Infants and very young children cannot adequately verbalize their discomfort. Children use symbolic language and play in order to communicate their feelings. Adolescents use various behaviors to (unconsciously) reveal feelings and fears which they are unable or unwilling to verbalize. It may be necessary to observe the child's and parents' behavior several times before the nurse can make an accurate assessment.

The nurse can elicit important assessment data during the *interview.* If the child is very young, the nurse interviews the parents, guardian, or primary caretaker. Children who are old enough to answer questions should also be given an opportunity to respond during the interview. The nurse uses the interview to obtain information about the child's past health history, growth and development, and family and home environment. When the patient is in need of immediate nursing care or if the patient or parents are very upset, it is best to defer the interview to a more suitable time. Information to be elicited during the interview and specific interview techniques are discussed in Chap. 6. Assessment of parental anxiety and of responses to a child's illness and hospitalization are presented in Chap. 17.

Consulting with other members of the health team and *reviewing the patient's medical records* are also part of the nursing assessment. The physician's orders for the patient should be carefully scrutinized. Results of diagnostic and laboratory tests, the physical examination, and the progress notes often yield valuable information about the child's health status.

A sample nursing assessment is provided in Table 5-2.

Organizing information The information which the nurse collects about the patient and family must be organized in a meaningful way. Many hospitals have a specific pediatric nursing assessment form on which the nurse can record this information. In some agencies, the assessment data are incorporated into the nurses' notes.

Analyzing information The nurse's ability to draw upon a scientific knowledge base is important at this point in the assessment. Theoretical information from the basic sciences, human behavior and development, and pathophysiology is used to determine whether the patient's condition deviates from the norm. This analysis prepares the nurse to begin the next step in the process, nursing diagnosis.

Nursing diagnosis

A *nursing diagnosis* is a brief statement describing an aspect of the child's health status at a given time. Although having perhaps only one *medical* diagnosis, a child is likely to have several *nursing* diagnoses. The nursing diagnoses are derived from the assessment data.

Nursing diagnosis has often been cited as the weakest step in the nursing process because nurses have a tendency to act before examining the problems that result in patients' needs.[1, 2] It is impossible to establish goals and implement care without first considering the patient's unique problems. Nursing diagnosis is therefore an essential step in the nursing process because it requires the nurse to identify the patient's actual and potential health problems *before* attempting to provide care.

Nursing diagnosis vs. medical diagnosis Since nursing practice differs from medical practice, a nursing diagnosis is not like a medical diagnosis. The term *diagnosis* has been used so frequently in relation to medical practice that the word *diagnosis* and the diagnostic process have often been regarded as the exclusive province of the physician.

A diagnosis is actually a conclusion formed by an individual after conducting an analysis of something. The same process is used by professionals and nonprofessionals alike. An automobile mechanic, for example, uses the diagnostic process in order to determine what is wrong with a car. But just as auto mechanics limit the diagnostic process to their area of expertise, automobiles, so nurses also limit the diagnostic process to judgments within the scope of nursing practice.

It is important to differentiate between medical diagnoses and nursing diagnoses. Medical diagnoses specify the actual pathophysiological or emotional *causes* of illnesses. On the other hand, nursing diagnoses describe *patients' responses* to actual or potential alterations in health.[3, 4] An

---

Table 5-2 Nursing assessment

Jimmy Markus, a 22-month-old male, was admitted to the pediatric unit at 1:30 A.M. with a diagnosis of bronchiolitis. The following information was related by the night nurse during the morning report. Jimmy was brought to the emergency room (ER) by his parents at 12:30 in the morning. Upon arrival at the ER, Jimmy's mother told the nurse that she and her husband were worried about Jimmy because "he is having so much difficulty breathing and he has a fever that will not stay down."

During the initial assessment and interview with Jimmy's parents, the ER nurse learned that Jimmy had had a "runny nose" and cough for the last 3 days. His mother also said Jimmy's temperature during the last few days had ranged from 37.7°C (99.8°F) to 38.1°C (100.6°F), rectally. Yesterday at 7:30 P.M., his temperature went up to 38.9°C (102°F). Jimmy's parents gave him both 120 mg of acetaminophen and a tepid sponge at that time. They also tried to give Jimmy fluids to drink, but he refused all but a few sips. At 9:30 P.M., his temperature was 38.7°C (101.6°F); by 11:30 P.M., it was back up to 38.9°C (102°F).

Jimmy's mother said that Jimmy's appetite had steadily decreased over the last 3 days. He had refused most solids and would only drink fluids. Mrs. Markus estimated that Jimmy had drunk about 16 oz of fluids during the last 24 h. Jimmy's parents said that his coughing had increased during the last 2 days and that his irritability also had increased sharply.

His parents said they brought him to the hospital because they were "afraid he's getting very sick." "He never got this way before," sobbed Mrs. Markus. Both parents repeatedly asked the ER nurses for assurances that Jimmy would be "OK."

Upon Jimmy's arrival on the pediatric unit, the night nurse made the following observations.

General appearance

Lethargic

Vital signs

Temperature: 38.6°C (101.4°F) (acetaminophen had been administered in the ER at 1:00 A.M.)
Apical heart rate: 160 beats per minute and regular
Respirations: 82 breaths per minute and shallow

Respirations

Breathing labored with moderate to severe intercostal and subcostal retractions; chest distended; nasal flaring; frequent hacking cough

Color

Skin pale; cyanosis of oral mucous membranes, circumoral region, and nail beds

Urine specific gravity

1.034

Behavior

Irritable; cries during examinations and treatment procedures

The night nurse reported that Mr. and Mrs. Markus seemed quite upset about Jimmy's illness and admission. Both parents insisted upon remaining at his side until Mr. Markus left for work at 6:00 A.M. His mother remained at Jimmy's side. Mrs. Markus did not sleep during the night, and she told the night nurse that she had slept only 3 hours during the previous night. The night nurse also reported that Mrs. Markus said, "This could have been avoided if I had called the doctor the other day—but it seemed like just a little cold at first—I was afraid that the doctor would think that I was foolish for calling him."

At 7:30 A.M. the day nurse made the following observations:

General appearance

Relaxed; dozing at intervals

Vital signs

Temperature: 38.1°C (100.6°F) (a dose of acetaminophen was given at 5:00 A.M. for a temperature of 38.6°C (101.4°F)

Respirations

Shallow; prolonged expiration with minimal chest movement, but respiratory movement equal bilaterally; bilateral expiratory rales and scattered wheezing, audible by auscultation; profuse white mucoid nasal secretions requiring frequent bulb suctioning

Color

Pale; cyanosis of circumoral region, oral mucous membrane, and nail beds

Behavior

Patient sleeping; mother present, anxiously watching child and nurse

Physician's orders

1. Mist tent with Fi_{O_2} at 34%
2. D_5 and 0.2 normal saline IV, to run at 65 ml/h
3. NPO if respiratory rate exceeds 40 breaths per minute; clear liquids if respiratory rate is below 40 breaths per minute
4. Acetaminophen 120 mg PO or PR q4h; PRN for rectal temperature over 38.3°C (101°F)
5. Vital signs q2h
6. Chest physical therapy and postural drainage q3h
7. Normal saline nose drops and bulb suction nasal
8. Secretions q3h and PRN

example of the difference between a medical diagnosis and the nursing diagnoses is given in Table 5-3.

Qualities of nursing diagnoses Certain qualities should be present in the nurse's diagnostic statements. The nursing diagnoses should be *individualized* so that they accurately reflect the patient's health status at a given time. In pediatric nursing, nursing diagnoses related to the parents' or family's behavior should also be written when indicated by the assessment data. When the patient's condition changes, new nursing diagnoses should be written to replace ones which no longer apply. Nursing diagnoses may focus on overt, covert, or potential health problems.[5] See Table 5-3 for examples. Some believe that the patient's and family's strengths should also be identified during the diagnostic process. Thus, the nurse can include measures in the care plan to enhance the patient's strengths.

The nursing diagnoses must be based on *valid*

assessment data. Nursing diagnoses cannot be pulled from thin air. A nursing diagnosis that lacks substantiating assessment data suggests either or both of the following: (1) the assessment was inadequate or (2) the diagnosis is invalid. The list of nursing diagnoses should be as *complete* as possible. The nurse cannot overlook significant assessment data when formulating nursing diagnoses. Nurses are advised to use diligence during the diagnostic process. Failure to use adequate care and accuracy in making nursing diagnoses can result in an incorrect or harmful care plan. This may place the nurse in danger of committing malpractice.[6]

Formulating nursing diagnoses Writing nursing diagnoses is a challenging intellectual process. The nurse must utilize both theoretical knowledge and judgment in order to identify the patient's health problems. At first, many nurses find it difficult to formulate diagnoses for their patients. Indeed, nursing diagnosis is not a simple process. Concentration and critical thinking are required in order to identify clear, individualized nursing diagnoses. Most students and practicing nurses, however, find that their ability to write comprehensive nursing diagnoses improves with persistence, practice, and experience.

Both students and practicing nurses often ask, "*How* do I go about making a nursing diagnosis?" At present, there is no universally accepted method of deriving nursing diagnoses from the assessment data. The most widely used method relates each nursing diagnosis to its underlying etiology, or cause, and the patient's signs and symptoms.[7,8] This method includes four basic steps which the nurse performs mentally. The nurse begins by scrutinizing the objective and subjective signs and symptoms manifested by the patient.* Next, the nurse reviews the pathophysiological processes underlying the patient's *medical* diagnosis. Following this, the nurse identifies symptoms related to these pathophysiological processes. Sometimes, only one or two symptoms may be evident; at other times, the

Table 5-3 Nursing diagnoses derived from nursing assessment

Patient
See Table 5-2

Medical diagnosis
Bronchiolitis

Nursing diagnoses, according to their priority*
1. Ineffective breathing patterns due to mucus obstruction in bronchioles (overt problem)†
2. Impaired gas exchange due to inefficient ventilation of alveoli (covert problem)†
3. Alteration in thermoregulation due to viral invasion (overt problem)†
4. Potential fluid volume deficit due to tachypnea and reduced oral fluid intake (potential problem)†
5. Potential impairment of skin integrity due to cool, damp environment (potential problem)†
6. Fatigue due to dyspnea (overt problem)
7. Fear due to dyspnea and exposure to strange environment (covert problem)†
8. Parental guilt due to illness and hospitalization of child (overt problem)
9. Parental fatigue due to care of ill child at home and vigilance in hospital (overt problem)

* These nursing diagnoses were formulated during the child's first 24 h of hospitalization.

† Denotes nursing diagnosis which has been accepted by the National Conference Group for Classification of Nursing Diagnosis and which is among those recommended for clinical testing in practice settings.

* *Objective* signs are detectable by the nurse or individuals other than the patient. Examples include vital signs, skin color, or diaphoresis. *Subjective* symptoms are those experienced by the patient but known to the health provider only if the patient communicates them. Examples include pain, numbness, thirst, fear.

nurse may be able to identify a "cluster" of symptoms. In doing this, the nurse relates the patient's symptoms to their etiology, or cause. In the fourth step, the nurse selects phrases that describe the patient's responses to alterations in health status. These are the nursing diagnoses. The terminology of the phrases should be as accurate and concise as possible. Only one health problem should be included in each nursing diagnosis. Symptoms should not be cited as nursing diagnoses. Table 5-4 shows how this method was used to formulate several nursing diagnoses for a patient.

It is important that the *words* which make up a nursing diagnosis describe the patient's health status as closely as possible. The profession's attention to the importance of nursing diagnosis and to the process by which nursing diagnoses are developed and expressed is rather recent. The First National Conference on Classification of Nursing Diagnoses was held in 1972. Its purpose was "to initiate the process of preparing an organized, logical, comprehensive system for classifying those health problems or health states diagnosed by nurses and treated by means of nursing interventions."[9] The National Conference Group on Nursing Diagnosis has convened three more times since 1972 in order to develop a diagnostic nomenclature that represents nursing practice. At present, over 100 nursing diagnoses, representing over 30 general problem categories, have been developed.[10, 11] The system of classifying nursing diagnoses is still evolving and the participation of many nurses is welcomed in this process. It is therefore not necessary for nurses to restrict diagnostic statements to those "accepted" by the National Conference Group. Table 5-3 includes selected examples of "accepted" nursing diagnoses and some original nursing diagnoses that apply to a patient. Nurses who are interested in obtaining more information about the development and classification of nursing diagnoses are encouraged to write the Clearinghouse for Nursing Diagnosis and the Northeastern Regional Depository for Nursing Diagnosis.*

---

* Clearinghouse for Nursing Diagnosis, St. Louis University School of Nursing, 3525 Caroline Street, St. Louis, MO 63104.

Northeastern Regional Depository for Nursing Diagnosis, Northeastern Regional Nursing Library, Boston College School of Nursing, Chestnut Hill, MA 02167.

Assigning priorities among nursing diagnoses The nurse should complete the list of nursing diagnoses before moving to the planning step of the nursing process. This enables the nurse to review the patient's problems and *rank them according to priority.* The most urgent problems are listed first and the other diagnoses are listed in decreasing order of importance. Physiological problems tend to be more acute than other types of patient problems. Therefore, physiological problems are usually given a higher priority than other problems. The nurse uses judgment and analysis of the patient's unique health status in order to assign a priority to the nursing diagnoses. The nursing diagnoses in Table 5-3 are listed according to priority.

Planning

The third step of the nursing process, *planning,* consists of two phases. In the first phase, the nurse writes patient goals. During the second phase, the nurse identifies nursing actions that will assist the patient and family in reaching the established goals.

Goal setting The nursing care plan goals should be written in terms of patient outcomes. *Patient outcomes* are conditions and behaviors that signify a positive improvement in the child's health status. Goals should describe, as clearly as possible, how the patient should look and act after health problems specified in the nursing diagnoses are resolved or minimized by nursing actions. If there are nursing diagnoses pertaining to the parents or family, the nurse also writes goals specifying parent or family outcomes. The nurse should include the patient and family in the goal-setting process as much as possible.

Goals should specify *desired* patient outcomes rather than "negative" outcomes. Negative outcomes are those the nurse intends to eliminate or avoid. For example, "no cyanosis of nail beds or oral mucous membranes" is a negative outcome because it cites a skin color the patient should *not* have. A positive outcome should specify what the patient's skin color *should* be. The goal could be improved by stating this desired outcome: "pink nail beds and oral mucous membranes." The goals cited in the nursing care plan (see page 49) are written in terms of the desired patient and parent outcomes.

The nurse uses the most *descriptive words*

Table 5-4 Steps in the nursing diagnostic process

Step 1: scrutinize assessment data	Step 2: consider pathophysiology and the patient's/family's behavior	Step 3: identify signs and symptoms of the patient's pathophysiological processes and the patient's/family's behavioral alterations	Step 4: formulate a nursing diagnosis describing the patient's/family's alteration in health status
Identify objective and subjective signs and symptoms manifested by the patient and the patient's family; see assessment example in Table 5-2 for specific information	Mucus obstruction in bronchioles	Respirations: 60–64 breaths per minute and shallow; bilateral expiratory rales and wheezing; labored breathing, with intercostal and subcostal retractions; chest distended; prolonged expiration with minimal chest movement; profuse, white mucoid nasal secretions; frequent nonproductive cough	Ineffective breathing patterns due to mucus obstruction in bronchioles
	Inefficient ventilation of alveoli	Pale skin color; oral mucous membrane, nail bed, and circumoral cyanosis; shallow respirations; prolonged expiration with minimal chest movement	Impaired gas exchange due to inefficient ventilation of alveoli
	Viral invasion	Elevated temperature for at least 48 h	Alteration in thermoregulation due to viral invasion
	Compensatory tachypnea interferring with ability to ingest food and fluids	Steadily decreasing appetite for last 2–3 days; oral fluid intake limited to 16 oz in the last 24 h; urine specific gravity: 1.034	Potential fluid volume deficit due to tachypnea and reduced oral fluid intake
	Constant cool, damp environment	Oxygen mist tent creates high humidity and cool environmental temperature; child's skin and bedding rapidly become moist and cold to touch	Potential impairment of skin integrity due to cool damp environment
	Dyspnea	Increasing irritability over last 48 h; "exhaustion" of patient cited by parents	Fatigue due to dyspnea
	Dyspnea; exposure to strange, frightening environment	Becomes irritable and cries during examinations and treatments	Fear due to dyspnea and exposure to strange environment
	Illness and hospitalization of child	Child not responsive to parents' care measures; mother stated: "This could have been avoided if I had called the doctor . . . but it seemed like just a little cold at first. . . ."	Parental guilt due to illness and hospitalization of child
	Care of ill child at home for at least 3 days before child's hospitalization	Mother slept only 3 h in the 24 h prior to the child's admission; neither parent slept from the time of admission, choosing instead to remain at child's bedside	Parental fatigue due to care of ill child at home and vigilance in hospital

possible in writing patient goals. Only words describing outcomes that can be *observed or measured* should be used. The nurse avoids words which are vague, unmeasurable, or which describe conditions that cannot be observed by someone other than the patient. Goals related to the patient's physiological condition are sometimes easier to write than those that describe feelings, behavior, or knowledge. Table 5-5 differentiates between suitable and unsuitable words for writing goals related to patient behavior.

A general *time framework* for goal achievement should be stated whenever possible. Short-term goals alone may be sufficient to alleviate some patient problems. (See care plan at end of this chapter.) Most patient problems, however, require the nurse to establish both short- and long-term goals. Long-term goals should be broken down into manageable short-term or intermediate-term goals. The feeling of success which accompanies short- and intermediate-term goal achievement helps the patient and nurse persist in working toward the long-term goal.

The *number* of patient goals varies according to the complexity of the child's health problems. Generally, if a patient has several nursing diagnoses, it is likely that there will also be several goals in the care plan. Some nursing diagnoses may have only one related goal, whereas others need several goals. In some instances, the same

goals can help resolve more than one health problem. (See goals related to the first and second nursing diagnoses in the care plan on page 49.)

Care plan goals must be *individualized, realistic,* and *appropriate* for the child's and family's unique situation. Goals that sound nice, but that are unattainable or inappropriate for the patient, are useless. Nurses and patients quickly lose interest in trying to reach irrelevant goals.

The nurse assigns a *priority* to the goals corresponding to the priority given the nursing diagnoses. (See care plan.) In daily practice, however, it is often possible to work toward achievement of several goals simultaneously.

Identifying nursing actions After the goals have been written, the nurse identifies measures likely to assist the patient and family in reaching the established goals. Nursing actions are individualized for the child and family and are based on sound theoretical rationales. The nurse's interventions should be appropriate for the child's level of growth and development.

The nurse uses *precise words* in entering the nursing actions on the care plan. Vague words and phrases only render the care plan useless to other nurses involved in the patient's care. For example, phrases such as "provide emotional support" (often found in pediatric care plans) are meaningless. "Emotional support" could represent different nursing actions, depending on the child's age and unique needs. It might mean rocking an infant to sleep instead of allowing the infant to cry herself or himself to sleep. Encouraging the parents of a toddler to be present as much as possible is another form of "emotional support." For an older child, emotional support could mean giving explanations before carrying out treatment procedures.

Specific *details* concerning the planned nursing actions must be written on the care plan. If, for example, the planned nursing action is "to assist the patient to walk to the end of the hall and return to room at least every two hours while awake," the care plan should say so. The mere statement "ambulate frequently" is open to misinterpretation by others. When planned nursing actions include patient or family teaching, both content and teaching methods are written in the care plan.

It should be possible for a nurse who is unfamiliar with the patient to implement care in

Table 5-5 Suitable and unsuitable words for writing goals describing behavior

Suitable	Unsuitable
Do use the following words, which are clear, measurable, and observable:	*Avoid* using these vague words:
Choose	Accept
Cite	Appreciate
Demonstrate	Feel
Describe	Know
Differentiate	Learn
Explain	Understand
Identify	
List	
Recall	
Verbalize	

the same manner intended by the writer of the care plan. The nurse must remember that inadequate care plans may hinder recovery of patients.

Implementation

The fourth step of the nursing process is *implementation*. At this point, the nursing actions specified in the care plan are carried out. The nurse's care should be organized according to the priorities assigned the nursing diagnoses and goals. Therefore, nursing actions designed to relieve severe or urgent problems are implemented first. The nurse attends to less pressing health problems later.

As previously indicated, the steps of the nursing process are recurrent and they often overlap. Since the nurse is in direct contact with the patient and family while implementing the care plan, the implementation phase is an opportune time to obtain new assessment data. It is important that the nurse *reassess* the patient and family periodically while providing care. Also, the nurse often begins the next step of the nursing process, evaluation, while implementing care.

Evaluation and revision

In *evaluation*, the nurse identifies the extent to which the patient and family have reached the established goals. Evaluation also requires the nurse to examine the effectiveness of the nursing actions in relation to the patient's goal achievement or lack of goal achievement.

The evaluation should be *recorded* on the care plan. The nurse indicates in writing the *specific criteria* which suggest either that the goal has been attained or that the patient is making progress toward the goal. The *date* of the nurse's evaluation of a goal is written on the care plan. When goal achievement suggests that the related nursing diagnosis has been resolved, the nurse indicates this in writing on the care plan along with the date. Once a nursing diagnosis has been resolved, the associated nursing actions are discontinued.

Revision occurs when the nurse determines that the nursing diagnoses, goals, or nursing actions should be changed. If the patient has not made sufficient progress in reaching a goal, the nurse must reevaluate the assessment, nursing diagnosis, goals, and nursing actions to deter-

Table 5-6 Reasons why goals may not be achieved

Any one or all of the following may interfere with a patient's or family's ability to achieve the care plan goals.

1. Inadequate assessment
2. Inaccurate assessment data
3. Invalid assessment data
4. Incorrect nursing diagnosis
5. Invalid nursing diagnosis
6. Omission of a nursing diagnosis
7. Unattainable goals
8. Vague goals
9. Failure to identify another goal which must be achieved before the patient can reach the goal in question
10. Ineffective nursing actions
11. Incorrect nursing actions

mine if they are appropriate. Table 5-6 lists the most common reasons why patients and families fail to achieve nursing care goals. The nurse uses information obtained during the evaluation to revise the care plan. The nurse may need to assess the patient more carefully. New or revised nursing diagnoses, goals, and nursing actions may be indicated. Thus, the nursing process begins again. A complete plan of care for a hospitalized toddler and his parents appears at the end of this chapter.

Quality assurance in pediatric nursing practice

As a profession, nursing must be concerned with the quality of care its members give to consumers. The term *quality assurance* denotes a system by which criteria representing excellence in nursing care may be developed and through which nursing care may continually be evaluated and improved. Students sometimes think that the nursing process and written care plans are merely academic exercises that do not have relevance in daily practice. Quite the contrary is true. Nursing process is the foundation for quality assurance measures in pediatric nursing.

The American Nurses' Association Standards of Maternal-Child Health Nursing Practice

The American Nurses' Association (ANA) has developed standards enumerating the characteristics of quality nursing practice. These standards are based on the nursing process. The ANA

Table 5-7 American Nurses' Association Standards of Maternal-Child Health Nursing Practice

Standard I

Maternal and child health nursing practice is characterized by the continual questioning of the assumptions upon which practice is based, retaining those which are valid and searching for and using new knowledge.

Standard II

Maternal and child health nursing practice is based upon knowledge of the biophysical and psychosocial development of individuals from conception through the childrearing phase of development and upon knowledge of the basic needs for optimum development.

Standard III

The collection of data about the health status of the client/patient is systematic and continuous. The data are accessible, communicated and recorded.

Standard IV

Nursing diagnoses are derived from data about the health status of the patient.

Standard V

Maternal and child health nursing practice recognizes deviations from expected patterns of physiologic activity and anatomic and psychosocial development.

Standard VI

The plan of nursing care includes goals derived from the nursing diagnoses.

Standard VII

The plan of nursing care includes priorities and the prescribed nursing approaches or measures to achieve the goals derived from the nursing diagnoses.

Standard VIII

Nursing actions provide for client/patient participation in health promotion, maintenance and restoration.

Standard IX

Maternal and child health nursing practice provides for the use and coordination of all services that assist individuals to prepare for responsible sex roles.

Standard X

Nursing actions assist the client/patient to maximize his health capabilities.

Standard XI

The client's/patient's progress or lack of progress toward goal achievement is determined by the client/patient and the nurse.

Standard XII

The client's/patient's progress or lack of progress toward goal achievement directs reassessment, reordering of priorities, new goal setting and revision of the plan of nursing care.

Standard XIII

Maternal and child health nursing practice evidences active participation with others in evaluating the availability, accessibility and acceptability of services for parents and children and cooperating and/or taking leadership in extending and developing needed services in the community.

Source: American Nurses' Association, *Standards of Maternal-Child Health Nursing Practice*, American Nurses' Association, Kansas City, 1973. Used by permission.

has published the general *Standards of Nursing Practice,*[12] which can be used in any practice setting, and standards for each of the clinical specialties. Included are a rationale to support each standard and specific factors that can be used to evaluate a nurse's ability to demonstrate the ANA standards in practice. Gaining wide acceptance since they were first introduced in 1973, they are frequently used in quality-assurance programs. Some individual standards of ANA *Standards of Maternal-Child Health Nursing Practice* are listed in Table 5-7. Copies of the complete ANA *Standards of Maternal-Child Health Nursing Practice* and the other standards of practice can be purchased from the ANA.*

Nursing audit

Nursing audit is a method for evaluating the outcomes of nursing care. Three basic steps are used in carrying out a nursing audit. First, the desired outcomes, or criteria, are established. The outcomes of nursing care for a group of patients are then compared with the established criteria. In the third step, differences between the actual care and the desired outcomes are analyzed and actions to improve care in the future are identified.

The nursing audit is usually conducted by a

* American Nurses' Association, 2420 Pershing Road, Kansas City, MO 64108.

committee composed of staff nurses who meet regularly. The audit committee develops the evaluation criteria and selects the audit methods. *Retrospective* audits evaluate nursing care of patients after they have been discharged. Patients' medical records, especially nurses' notes and care plans, are carefully examined in a retrospective audit. *Concurrent* audits evaluate nursing care while patients are still hospitalized. A concurrent audit often includes direct observations of nurses providing care to patients in addition to review of nursing care plans and nurses' notes.

Peer review

The performance of practicing nurses has traditionally been evaluated by head nurses or supervisors. Contemporary emphasis on nursing process, implementation of the ANA *Standards of Practice*, and the growth of primary nursing* have resulted in the need for different methods to evaluate staff nurses. In *peer review*, a staff nurse's performance is evaluated by a group of nurse colleagues rather than by a supervisor.

Nurses who practice on the same clinical unit as the nurse who is being evaluated are included on the panel of reviewers. Nurses who have expertise in practice but who do not personally know the nurse who is being evaluated are also appointed to peer review panels. The review may include any or all of the following: (1) direct observation of the nurse as care is being provided; (2) interview of patients cared for by the nurse; (3) interview of the nurse regarding his or her practice; (4) written self-evaluation (completed by the nurse who is being evaluated); and (5) review of written documentation by the nurse, i.e., care plans and nurses' notes. Although peer review is still quite new to nurses, it is likely to replace older methods of staff-nurse evaluation.

* *Primary nursing* is a system of care delivery in which one nurse assumes responsibility for the planning, implementing, and evaluating of a patient's care from the time of admission until the patient is discharged.

Nursing Care Plan

Patient: James (Jimmy) Markus   **Age:** 22 months   **Date of Admission:** 10/28, at 1:30 A.M.

Nursing diagnosis	Nursing goals	Nursing actions	Evaluation/revision
1. Ineffective breathing patterns due to mucus obstruction in bronchioles **2.** Impaired gas exchange due to inefficient ventilation of alveoli	☐ Effective oxygenation and breathing patterns as evidenced by: **a.** Pink mucous membranes, nail beds, and general skin color **b.** Respiratory rate: 32–38 breaths per minute **c.** Breath sounds clear upon auscultation **d.** Clear nasal passages	☐ Mist tent at 34% Fi_{O_2}, check O_2 concentration q2h ☐ Observe skin color q30min ☐ Record respiratory rate q2h ☐ Position in semi-Fowler's or on abdomen to aid in breathing ☐ Perform chest P.T. and postural drainage q3h ☐ Instill normal saline nose drops in both nostrils and bulb suction q3h and PRN	☐ 10/28, 10 A.M.: skin, oral mucous membranes, and nail beds pink; decreased respiratory efforts ☐ 10/28, 12 P.M. to 3:00 P.M.: no retractions noted; skin color pink; respirations 32–36 breaths per minute. Rales and wheezing still present but diminished after treatments; nasal secretions easily removed by bulb suction q3h ☐ *Continue plan*
3. Alteration in thermoregulation due to viral invasion	☐ Temperature regulation within a range of 37.2–38.2°C(R) [99–100.8°F(R)]	☐ Monitor temperature q1h if temperature exceeds 38.4°C(R) [101°F(R)] and q2h when temperature reaches desired range ☐ Administer acetaminophen, 120 mg PO or PR q4h, PRN for temperature over 38.3°C(R) [101°F(R)] ☐ Maintain IV infusion at 65 ml/h while NPO or drinking sips of fluids	☐ 10/28: Temperature: 38.1°C (100.6°F) at 9 A.M. and at 11:00 A.M.; Temperature: 37.9°C (100.2°F) at 1 P.M. and at 3 P.M. ☐ 10/28, 3:00 P.M.: IV site unremarkable; IV infusing well. Oral fluids started at 2 P.M. (see evaluation of nursing diagnosis 4 below) ☐ *Continue plan*
4. Potential fluid volume deficit due to tachypnea and reduced oral fluid intake	☐ Fluid balance as evidenced by: **a.** Oral fluid intake of at least 520 ml every 8 h **b.** Voiding qs (quantities sufficient) at least 4 times in 24 h **c.** Specific gravity of urine between 1.002 and 1.022 **d.** Moist oral mucous membranes **e.** Firm skin turgor	☐ Maintain IV at 65 ml/h while NPO or drinking sips ☐ Offer clear fluids q20–30 min while awake if respiratory rate is below 40 per minute ☐ Observe fluid intake at 2-h intervals and notify physician when oral intake averages 90 to 100 ml for 4 h ☐ Encourage mother to offer Jimmy fluids at intervals ☐ Use a bottle, as Jimmy prefers a bottle at bedtime and when ill ☐ Offer apple juice and ginger ale, Jimmy's favorites ☐ Record intake and output q2h ☐ Measure specific gravity after each voiding	☐ 10/28: 12 noon: sips of H_2O; 2:00 P.M.: 70 ml of apple juice ☐ Reevaluate oral fluid intake at 5:00 P.M. and 7:00 P.M.; maintain IV at 65 ml/h ☐ 10/28: specific gravity 1.030 at 8:00 A.M. and decreased to 1.024 by 3:00 P.M.; voiding q2h ☐ 3:00 P.M.: Mucous membranes moist and skin turgor firm ☐ *Continue plan*

49

Nursing diagnosis	Nursing goals	Nursing actions	Evaluation/revision
5. Potential impairment of skin integrity due to cool, damp environment	☐ Skin will remain pink, smooth, and unbroken	☐ Tepid sponge PRN to cleanse and refresh skin ☐ Avoid excessive use of soap ☐ Use lotion (nonalcoholic content) to protect skin and massage pressure areas q4h ☐ Change clothing and bed linen frequently ☐ Protect head and ears from direct line of cool mist ☐ Avoid direct contact between skin and plastic equipment ☐ Inspect skin condition q8h	☐ 10/28, 3:00 P.M.: Skin remains pink, smooth, and unbroken ☐ *Continue plan*
6. Fatigue due to dyspnea	☐ At least three 2-h nap periods within the next 8h	☐ Provide measures to improve oxygenation as outlined for nursing diagnoses 1 and 2 ☐ Structure day to allow 2-h intervals with minimal or no interruptions: 7–9 A.M.: rest 9–10 A.M.: treatment, nourishment, and other care as needed 10–12 noon: rest 12 A.M. to 1 P.M.: treatments, nourishment, and other care as needed 1–3 P.M.: rest 3–4 P.M.: treatments, etc. ☐ Parent or a familiar nurse should remain nearby	☐ 10/28: Slept quietly from 8–9:00 A.M.; 10:30 A.M. to 12:15 P.M.; and 1:30–3:00 P.M. ☐ Appeared less fatigued at 3:00 P.M., but could use more sleep ☐ *Continue plan* for next 24 h
7. Fear due to dyspnea and exposure to strange environment	☐ Appears "relaxed" as evidenced by: **a.** ease of respirations **b.** ability to tolerate routine care and treatment provided by familiar nurse or parent	☐ Provide measures to improve oxygenation as for nursing diagnoses 1 and 2 ☐ Spend time talking with parents within Jimmy's view, to show him that his parents "approve" of the nurse ☐ Use pleasant tones of voice while in Jimmy's room ☐ Encourage parents to participate in care when possible (see nursing diagnosis 8 below) ☐ Minimize number of persons providing care; assign a primary nurse ☐ Administer painful treatments in treatment room only, not at bedside	☐ 10/28, 3:00 P.M.: Jimmy's facial expression less apprehensive than at 7:30 A.M.; smiles and says "Hi" to familiar nurse; willing to allow nurse to do treatments ☐ *Continue plan*

Nursing diagnosis	Nursing goals	Nursing actions	Evaluation/revision
8. Parental guilt due to illness and hospitalization of child	☐ Mother will be able to verbalize her feelings about Jimmy's illness and hospitalization	☐ Encourage mother to take short "breaks" from beside (e.g., for coffee, a walk, etc.) ☐ Allow mother to talk about events leading to Jimmy's admission; praise parents' appropriate actions at home; assure parent that Jimmy's illness could not have been prevented ☐ Provide quiet area for mother to discuss feelings ☐ Suggest mother also take short "nap" periods (see nursing diagnosis 9 below) ☐ Allow parents to assist with care when ready; assure parents that they do not have to participate in care if they don't feel ready ☐ Explain all treatments and procedures to parents in advance; keep explanations simple and honest ☐ Praise parents' efforts to participate in care	☐ 10/28: 2:00 P.M.: Mother expressed relief that Jimmy is looking better; said she now realizes that his illness was not her "fault." Helping to provide care; seems less tense ☐ Parents may be ready to assist with chest physical therapy by 10/29 ☐ *Continue plan*
9. Parental fatigue due to care of ill child at home and vigilance in the hospital	☐ Parents able to obtain at least 8 h of sleep each day Jimmy is in the hospital	☐ Suggest that mother take short "nap" periods, especially while Jimmy is sleeping; assure her that a nurse will watch Jimmy while she rests ☐ Suggest that mother go home to sleep this evening, after Jimmy falls asleep ☐ Assure parents that a nurse will care for Jimmy in their absence	☐ 10/28, 3:00 P.M.: mother able to sleep for about 2 h during the day; stated she is "very tired"; seems willing to consider going home and returning around 6:30 A.M. ☐ *Continue plan*

* See Table 5-2 for assessment data for this patient; see Table 5-3 and Table 5-4 for information regarding the patient's nursing diagnoses.

References

1. Mary Jo Aspinall, "The Why and How of Nursing Diagnosis," *MCN: The American Journal of Maternal-Child Nursing* 2:354–357 (November–December 1977).
2. ———, "Nursing Diagnosis—The Weak Link," *Nursing Outlook* 24:433–437 (July 1976).
3. Ibid., p. 434.
4. Jacqueline D. Fortin and Jean Rabinow, "Legal Implications of Nursing Diagnosis," *Nursing Clinics of North America* 14:556 (September 1979).
5. Sandra J. Sundeen et al., *Nurse Client Interaction: Implementing the Nursing Process*, Mosby, St. Louis, 1976.
6. Fortin and Rabinow, op. cit., p. 558.
7. Marjory Gordon, "The Concept of Nursing Diagnosis," *Nursing Clinics of North America* 14:490 (September 1979).
8. ———, "Nursing Diagnosis and the Diagnostic Process," *American Journal of Nursing* 76:1298–1300 (August 1976).
9. Kristine M. Gebbie and Mary Ann Lavin, *Proceedings of the First National Conference on Classification of Nursing Diagnoses*, Mosby, St. Louis, 1975, p. 1.
10. Fourth National Conference for the Classification of Nursing Diagnoses, April 9–13, 1980, "Unofficial List of Accepted Nursing Diagnoses," Boston University School of Nursing, Boston, 1980. (Mimeographed.)
11. Gordon, op. cit., p. 443.
12. American Nurses' Association, *Standards of Nursing Practice*, American Nurses' Association, Kansas City, 1973.

Chapter 6 **Child health maintenance**

Joan Brosnan and Frances Drewry Barber Austin

Upon completion of this chapter, the student will be able to:

1. List the two goals of child health maintenance.
2. Describe the role of the nurse in child health maintenance.
3. List four contemporary influences on child health.
4. List the information needed for a health history.
5. Define the four techniques used in physical assessment.
6. Describe three common screening tests in terms of timing and purpose.

7. State the four major factors contributing to dental health.
8. Contrast deciduous and permanent teeth in terms of number, time of eruption, and shedding.
9. List four common causes of child death and injury and describe at least one preventive measure for each one.

Health is defined not only as the absence of disease but also in terms of the level of physical, psychological, and social well-being. Both the child and the adults responsible for the child must plan care to maintain his or her state of health. Child health maintenance is the management of routine preventive care and includes counseling about growth and development and common health problems.

The family as well as the child must be active participants in implementing child health maintenance. The family, as the child's main support system, is responsible for seeing that child health maintenance continues during the child's developmental years. Eventually, the child will become responsible for his or her own health maintenance. Active participation by the child increases the child's interest, understanding, and

sense of responsibility; it also encourages the child to develop his or her own health maintenance strategies.

The goals of child health maintenance programs are twofold:

1. To assist the child to reach adulthood in the best possible state of health.
2. To enable the child, the future adult, to become ultimately responsible for personal health maintenance.

The relationship of nursing to child health maintenance

State nursing laws commonly define professional nursing to include "diagnosing and treating human responses to actual or potential health problems through services such as casefinding, health teaching, health counseling, and the provision of care supportive to or restorative to life and well-being."[1] Thus nursing has a critical role and can make a significant impact on child health maintenance.

The nurse should be familiar with the signs of health as well as those of illness. Nursing includes assessing the total health status of the child, diagnosing human response to actual or potential health problems, and maintaining the child's normal health status through preventive and promotive health regimens.

The nurse can minimize the child's loss of health by early diagnosis and intervention. Anticipatory planning with the family can assist in developing patterns of living conducive to health. Nurses also promote child health by functioning as health teachers and counselors for children, families, and communities. Sometimes nurses must act as advocates for children to ensure that their health maintenance needs are met.

Contemporary influences on child health

Social conditions

Social conditions influence both the emotional and physical health of children. Today's changing society makes it more difficult for parents to raise healthy children as well as for children to grow up.

Child care Whether because of the increase in the number of single-parent families, the desire to fulfill career goals, or the need to supplement the family income in times of economic pressure, more and more mothers work outside the home than mothers of previous generations. This has resulted in the demand for more and improved child-care facilities.

School system Schools have had difficulty in meeting the needs of children. In fact, a quarter of all children who complete the fifth grade drop out of school prior to high school graduation. Schools also have problems in their ability to physically protect children who do attend school. Sixty-eight percent of the robberies and fifty percent of the assaults on children occur while children are in school.[2]

Community The mobility of families continues to increase. As a result youths have difficulty becoming attached to their community since they may move three or more times while growing up. Even if they remain in the community, they must constantly adjust to their friends' moving away. As a result, children may have less commitment both to their community and to their friends.

Social values Social values are not as clear-cut as they used to be. Rules and regulations for acceptable behavior are changing. As children grow older, their developing values are likely to differ from their parents' values. Sexual attitudes and practices have become more liberal. Sex is frequently exploited by the mass media, and teenagers find themselves under peer pressure to experience sexual intercourse. These influences frequently lead to unplanned pregnancy.

Socioeconomic status Socioeconomic conditions have a direct impact on physical problems. In fact, the socioeconomic status of the family is the most important single indicator of the child's nutritional health.[3] Children of lower socioeconomic status have a much higher incidence of illness. Their parents are more likely to lack the educational and financial resources that would enable them to want to secure adequate health maintenance care for their family.

Social stress The social stresses in growing up have contributed to a rise in emotional problems among teenagers. The current suicide rate among teenagers has almost tripled since 1950. Delinquent behavior among them has also risen. Currently, 77,000 children under the age of 18 are in prison.[4] Drug and alcohol abuse has become a major problem, even in schools. Reports of physical and sexual abuse are increasing.

Role of the nurse Nurses can help to improve social influences which may be detrimental to child health. They can encourage the development of day care facilities to assist working parents, can become politically active in resolving problems in the community, and can advocate the use of community resources that may minimize the stress for children new to a community. Mental health centers should be easily accessible to the child. Special effort should be made by the nurse to develop such health maintenance programs as free health screening programs and immunization outreach projects.

The parent-child relationship

The most important influence on a child is the family. The love and support of a family helps a child develop a strong sense of self-esteem. Helping parents build self-esteem in children should be a major nursing goal. The parent-child relationship has its most significant impact on the child during the first 18 years and as such has a great influence on the health maintenance care of the child.

Parent-child bond The parent-child relationship begins when pregnancy is first discovered and the couple begins adjusting to their new role of becoming parents. Parental reactions to pregnancy may influence the future parent-child relationship. Couples with an unplanned pregnancy, an unexpected change in their lives, may react to the child with apathy or hostility and may find it difficult to become attached to the child. The first few minutes after birth have significant impact on the future parent-child relationship.[5] Parent-infant bonding begins with a planned pregnancy and is strenghtened immediately after birth when parents and the infant maintain eye contact and touch and cling to each other. A lack of emotional attachment between the parents and the child could lead to psychological neglect, or even physical abuse, of the child.

Importance of the parent-child relationship Children need a continuous, warm relationship with an adult caretaker in order to thrive and grow normally. Usually children develop such a relationship with one or both of their parents. If children do not have this relationship, its absence can affect them for the rest of their lives. Infants deprived of such a relationship may lag behind in development and weight gain. These children may later be unable to develop anything but superficial relationships. Increased incidences of delinquent and antisocial behaviors are found among teenagers deprived of this initial parent-child relationship.

Breakdown of the family As society changes, the family changes. Parenting is a more difficult task now than in previous years because there are fewer extended family support systems. Previously, several generations of relatives usually lived in the same vicinity and were available to give advice on and provide assistance with raising children. Now, families usually consist of two generations. The "nuclear family," consisting of only parents and children, is the norm. Presently, the nuclear family is often further subdivided as a result of divorce.

Children in divorced families have special parent-child relationship problems. These children may feel responsible and assume that something they did caused the divorce. Parents need to reassure their children that they did not cause the divorce and that they are still loved by both parents. Remarriage by parents may put further stress on the parent-child relationship as the child must adjust to the new stepparent and siblings. Any loss of a parent, whether due to divorce or death, has a significant effect on the child and can result in feelings of guilt, rejection, shame, and anger. These children are at risk for developing behavioral and emotional problems.

Role of the nurse The parent-child relationship can help assure optimal health maintenance for the child. Concerned parents can be the child's strongest advocates. Nurses can help to promote this bond by encouraging immediate visual and physical contact between parents and child after birth, by encouraging parents to develop realistic expectations for a child's behavior, by politically supporting legislation which will lessen family stress, by promoting education for parenting, and by counseling or referring families for counseling if the family is having problems coping with its level of stress.

Emphasis on health promotion

Traditionally health care professionals have focused on an illness model in which a specific illness is diagnosed and treated. Today this focus is changing and there is a definite trend toward prevention of illness. Health promotion efforts include a consideration of the psychosocial and the physiological aspects of health and illness and how they affect each other. There is a growing awareness on the part of the public, the government, and health care professionals of the logic in utilizing nurses in such new settings and

Table 6-1 Techniques for successful interviews

Set the stage

Provide privacy and comfort.
Introduce yourself and explain your role.
Be interested and concerned about this family—focus on the child.
Young children may need a play activity while parent is being interviewed.

Open-ended questions

Begin interview with such statements as:
    "Before I ask any questions, do you have any?"
    "How have things been?"
    "Tell me why you came today."
    "Tell me about your daughter's or son's health."
    "Is there anything you want to remind me about?"

Less directive techniques

Listening:
    Let the parent or child tell you how it is.
    Observe the facial expression, posture, movement.
        (Adolescents usually do not tolerate silence as well as adults do.)
Facilitation:
    Show by your manner, words, or actions that you want to hear more but don't specify topic. "Mm-hmm," "Yes," "I understand."
Reflection:
    Repeat appropriate words, watch for cues.
Clarification:
    "Tell me what you mean by. . . ."

More directive techniques

Confrontation:
    Describe something striking about verbal or nonverbal behavior: "You seem to have difficulty talking about that." "You seem worried about ———."
    Ask directly about feelings, problems.
    Adolescents may ask questions about a "friend's" problem when it is really their own.

Direct questions

Use questions to encourage a chronological account, to fill in gaps, or to go from general information to specific.
Avoid *leading* questions.
Ask one question at a time.

Miscellaneous

Answer specific questions that parents have as you are able to during the interview.
Avoid asking: "Why did you ———?" Instead say, "Tell me your reasons for ———."
How, who, where, how much, how often are all good words to use to begin questions.

Terminating the interview

Before ending the interview ask:
    "Are there any other concerns that you have?"
    "Is there anything else bothering you that you'd like to talk about?"
    "Is there anything else you think I should know?"

roles as pediatric nurse practitioners or pediatric nurse associates. The demand for more accessible health care at a more reasonable cost is another force operating to create these new roles for nurses in the health care system.

Nurses skilled in physical assessment take patient histories and perform physical examinations. From the data collected, a judgment is made regarding whether growth, development, and behavior are progressing in a normal pattern and at at normal rate. Using the interpreted data, the nurse develops the nursing diagnoses and an evaluation of the health status of the child. In some settings, nurses assume responsibility for meeting nearly all of the health and illness needs of the child, referring to other health professionals only those children judged by the nurse to have complex problems. In other settings, nurses see only well children for assessment and may be obligated by agency policy to refer to other health professionals any child with symptoms of illness or abnormal laboratory and physical findings. In most agencies, nurses coordinate health services for patients and assist the family in setting health care goals.

Health assessment

The health history

A child's health history helps the nurse make an organized assessment of the child's current health. It includes information about the child's development, health practices, health problems, and environment. The history is obtained from the child, the family, or other knowledgeable persons. Personal interviews with the child and family are the most common way of obtaining a health history. A combination of personal interview and written questionnaire also works well. The nurse's attitude and interviewing skills are important factors in determining the success of an interview. A friendly, nonjudgmental, but direct approach will usually help the nurse obtain the necessary information without delay or embarrassment. The nurse should be tactful and courteous, and should provide a comfortable and private setting for the interview. The sequence of questioning and the language level used by the nurse are important.

The goals of the history-taking process are:

1. To establish a relationship with the child and family that will help them trust and confide in the nurse interviewer.

Table 6-2 Outline of a pediatric health history

Date of interview
Identifying data
Chief complaint
Historian (sources)
Sources of health care
Present problem or current health status
Past health

Birth history
    Maternal obstetrical history
    Patient's condition at birth
    Neonatal period
Early infancy
Childhood and adolescent health
    Common childhood illnesses
    Serious illnesses
    Obstetrical, menstrual, and contraceptive history
    Accidents and injuries
    Medications, drugs, alcohol
    Allergies
    Immunizations
    Screening procedures

Patient profile

Current life situation (social history)
    Household members
    Physical characteristics of home
    Primary care-givers at home
    Cultural beliefs, religious traditions
    School, educational data
    Economic situation
    Agencies involved in care
Development
    General description
    Affect, energy, and fears
    Child's relationship with family members

Habits
Child-school relationships
Play
Language and communication skills
Motor skills
Adaptive or problem-solving ability

Family health history

Family members—age, sex, health status (construct pedigree)
    Incidence of: heart disease, hypertension, diabetes, kidney disease, stroke, cancer, tuberculosis, arthritis, birth defects, genetic disease, headaches, mental illness

Review of symptoms (subjective data—gathered in response to questions)

General—fever, vomiting, weight change
Skin, hair, nails
Head—headaches
Eyes—vision, "cross-eyed"
Ears—earaches, decrease in hearing
Nose—incidence of colds, drainage
Mouth, teeth, gums, tongue—dental care, tooth eruption, bleeding
Throat and neck—infections, swallowing, stiffness
Respiratory—chest, difficult breathing, pneumonia, infections
Cardiovascular—any history of murmurs
Gastrointestinal—nausea, vomiting
Genitourinary—frequency, pain, menstruation
Musculoskeletal—joint pain, muscle soreness
Neurological—seizures, head injury
Endocrine—growth pattern
Mental health—get along with peers, family, fears

Source: Adapted from J. Deborah Ferholt, *Clinical Assessment of Children,* Lippincott, Philadelphia, 1980, pp. 21–22.

2. To establish a data base to use in formulating the nursing care plan.
3. To help the child and family, through education or counseling, to learn about development or solve problems.

Health history taking can be facilitated by deciding what information is needed and by using the specific interview technique expected to obtain the information. Collecting the data in an organized way helps the nurse gain parents' and children's confidence and obtain complete data quickly. Table 6-1 lists guidelines for interviewing a child and family.

The depth and form of the health history vary with its purpose. A complete history is obtained the first time the patient is seen. During subse-

quent visits the nurse obtains an interval history relating to the specific problem for which the child is now being seen.

The health history provides both subjective and objective data. The physical examination and laboratory tests furnish objective data used to confirm information obtained in the health history. Table 6-2 provides an outline of a pediatric health history. The following is a general discussion of the kind of information that should be obtained under each major heading of the health history.

Identifying data It is important to record not only age, sex, name, nickname, and address, but also the country of origin and primary language of the child. Any serious or chronic illness should also be noted. Names of the parents are usually included.

Chief complaint The primary reason for seeking health care for the present problem is a short, simple statement in the child's or parent's own words. In the case of an illness, the duration of symptoms should be noted.

Historian The reliability of the historian should be noted. Teachers or other care-givers can be helpful historians.

Sources of health care Names and addresses of other care-givers should be included.

Present problem If the child has come for a health-maintenance visit, the nurse should de-

Table 6-3 Assessment of cultural beliefs and practices

1. What does this condition or illness mean to the child and/or family?
2. What bodily responses are viewed by the cultural system as life threatening?
3. What foods, herbs, or objects are viewed as possessing qualities of healing?
4. Are there behaviors of the nurse (or care-giver) that could be threatening to the well-being of the child?
5. Are the family's (or child's) goals compatible with those of nurses or other care-givers?
6. Depending on the age of the child, it may be helpful to determine what beliefs the mother/father/grandparents have in regard to:
   a. The umbilical cord (a belly band is very important in some cultures until the cord falls off).
   b. Skin care—some cultures bathe the infant with oil.
   c. Feeding—some Mexican-American women believe colostrum is filthy. What foods are avoided and why? Some traditional Chinese foods are considered "hot" or "cold."
   d. Outings—a Chinese mother may miss a 2-week checkup because she will not take her baby out for 1 month after birth.
   e. Crying—it may be an indication that evil spirits are lurking around the baby.
   f. Naming—a child may be named after religious figures or family members.
   g. Interactions with others—Filipinos have a great concern for interpersonal relationships and will follow the health professional's advice exactly.
   h. Discipline—Indians quietly tell a child what is expected. Physical punishment and loud reprimands are not used.
   i. Religious practices and healing—Mexican-Americans may believe that "mal ojo" or "evil eye" can be caused when someone wishes to hold an infant but does not. Touching the child is thought to keep the "mal ojo" away.

scribe the child's current health status. If the child is ill, the nurse describes in chronological order such pertinent factors as onset, character, location, severity, duration, and frequency of symptoms, and aggravating or relieving circumstances. Exposure to contagious disease within the past 3 weeks should be noted.

Birth history Birth history is especially important during the early years and includes the mother's prenatal, intrapartum, and postpartum course. The weight, length, and condition of the neonate should also be described.

Early infancy Descriptions of the child's health and illness, behavior, routines, and family relationships are given.

Childhood and adolescent health This section of the health history includes an organized account of the child's past physical and emotional health. The past medical history allows the nurse to determine the adequacy of health maintenance, identify current immunization needs, assess frequency and types of illness or accidents, and be alert to patterns suggesting more serious problems.

Current life situation The social history describes the names, ages, and relationships of all household members as well as primary caretakers. Any significant deaths should be recorded. The nurse must also be aware of any beliefs and practices of health or illness care that are part of the child's culture. Nurses must become sensitive to beliefs and behaviors in order to anticipate what is culturally acceptable behavior for specific families. The nurse should ask appropriate questions to determine the meaning a symptom, illness, or health practice may have to the family. Table 6-3 suggests questions and topics the nurse can use to assess beliefs about health care practices. When nurses do not understand a family's cultural system, they can make inappropriate value judgments and cause the family to lose confidence in the health care system.

Development The nurse can obtain an impression of the child's past and current developmental status by combining a developmental history with structured and unstructured observations. Ask the parent to describe the child. "What is she like?" "How does she respond to other people? To separation?" When discussing relationships, ask questions about discipline and response to siblings. When a particular kind of behavior is described, ask how the parent feels about that. Observe the child's behavior during the interview.

Ask for a description of what the child eats, how and where the child sleeps, and how the child cares for himself or herself. In assessing play, determine what the child likes to do best, both with others and alone. Ask the parent of the younger child how the child communicates needs. The nurse can evaluate the communication skills of the older child according to intelligibility and age-appropriateness of the child's language.

In assessing motor skills look at fine and gross motor development. Determine how a child solves a problem such as drawing a circle, completing a puzzle, or naming a color. (See later discussion of developmental screening tools.)

Family health history Reviewing the family health history and constructing a pedigree chart (see Chap. 8) give the nurse the opportunity to look for hereditary or familial predisposing factors to illness. The child's and family's reaction to a family disability can also be evaluated. Serious infectious diseases should be noted.

Review of symptoms The review of symptoms helps establish the data base and helps the nurse assess the effectiveness and pattern of the child's functioning and coping behaviors. It may vary depending on the child's problems. It is essentially a checklist about recent symptoms.

Physical assessment of the child
The process of physical assessment begins during the interview as the nurse observes the child's appearance and behavior. Assessment utilizes all the senses of the nurse, but relies most frequently on sight, touch, and hearing. The technique of applying the hands to the body of the child to evaluate the size, shape, contour and consistency of organs or tissues is *palpation*. The technique of listening with a stethoscope is *auscultation*. Tapping upon the body to produce sounds is called *percussion*. *Inspection* is observation of the patient for physical signs. Inspection is the most difficult technique to master, but more diagnoses are made by inspection than by all other methods combined.[6]

The child's age and health problems influence the manner and sequence in which the physical examination is performed. Newborns must be examined quickly and protected from heat loss. (See Chap. 10 for details about neonatal examinations.) Infants and toddlers can be examined best if they are held or restrained by their parents. Both toddlers and preschoolers can be very frightened by an examination so they will need extensive reassurance and comfort. School-age children and adolescents are generally cooperative and interested in what is happening. The examination can be a useful educational tool for parents and older children.

Physical assessment must be done systematically so that no area is overlooked. Begin at either the head or feet and examine all nearby structures before moving upward or downward to include the whole body. Assessment usually begins at the head but may need to be altered with very young children. Allowing children to look at or hold the stethoscope or tongue blade may allay their fears and gain their cooperation. Complete physical assessment requires that the nurse learn new skills of auscultation and percussion; inspection and palpation have long been part of the nurse's responsibility. Nurses inspect and describe body wounds and drainage, and palpate to assess temperature changes and to locate and count various pulses. A large part of the body can be assessed by using only inspection and palpation; these skills do not require the nurse to use specialized and unfamiliar equipment. Since this book is directed to students of nursing and not to experienced nurses, the discussion of physical assessment concentrates on assessment by palpation and inspection. Table 6-4 outlines a guide for physical assessment of well children. More detailed information on assessment of each body system is found in the appropriate body system chapters.

Physical assessment requires the use of a systematic approach along with patience, tact, and sensitivity to the needs of the child and parent. Decisions, both large and small ones, are constantly being made by the nurse. Does this visit require a complete assessment or only an investigation of the particular symptoms presented? How should the child be positioned for the examination? Is the lighting in this room adequate for evaluating jaundice, cyanosis, and pallor? Is the child too tired to continue the

Table 6-4 Guide for physical assessment of well children

General appearance

Apparent state of health
Hygiene
Responsiveness

Measurements

Height
Weight
Head circumference
Vital signs
Blood pressure

Skin

Color
Rash
Bruise

Head

Size, shape, fontanels, hair
Face: features
Ears: position, hearing
Eyes: pupils, tears, sclerae, vision, movement
Nose: patency
Mouth: lips, tongue, mucous membrane, teeth
Throat: tonsils, swallowing

Chest

Respirations
Shape and symmetry of breasts
Retractions

Cardiovascular system

Apical and peripheral pulses
Presence of edema

Abdomen

Shape (contour)
Movement
Muscles (herniations, tenderness)

Genitalia

Hair pattern
Discharge
Female: labia, vagina
Male: penis, scrotum (testes)

Musculoskeletal system

Strength
Movement
Posture and gait
Pain

Neurological system

Developmental age, behavior
State of consciousness
Cerebral functioning
Cerebellar functioning
Cranial nerve functioning
Motor-sensory functioning

examination, and if so, when should the return visit be scheduled? Is this a normal variant or an abnormal finding? If it is an abnormal finding, what should be done about it? Should the parent be reassured by the nurse, or is a referral to a physician necessary? If a child is unable to perform a particular task, the nurse must decide whether the child understands the question or instructions, does not have the necessary maturity and motor skill to perform the task, or simply refuses. The ability to make sound decisions and judgments is developed with practice. Feedback from nursing colleagues, other health care workers, and from the patients and families will help the beginning nurse to perfect both decision-making and assessment skills.

Temperature Taking temperatures rectally is more reliable than taking temperatures orally in determining body temperature of pediatric patients up to 5 years of age. The average rectal temperature usually does not drop below 37.5°C (99°F) until the child reaches the age of 36 months; a variation of 1 to 2°F in 24 h is not unusual. Illness does not always accompany a temperature rise in children. Anxiety, physical activity, and a high environmental temperature may cause body temperature to increase. Infants may have normal or subnormal temperatures with severe infections, and also may have temperatures up to 40.6°C (105°F) with only minor illness.[7]

Pulse A child's heart rate is more readily affected by exercise, illness, and emotion than an adult's. An infant's pulse can be taken by palpation at the anterior fontanel or the femoral or carotid artery, or by auscultation over the heart. Auscultation is the preferred method if the rate is irregular or very rapid.

A single measurement of pulse, respiratory rate, temperature, and blood pressure is not nearly as useful as a series of measurements of each one taken over a period of time and under similar conditions. Each child has his or her own normal rate for each vital sign. For average normal pulse and respiratory rates see Table 17-20.

Respirations The nurse must assess the rate, quality, and depth of respirations. Respiratory rate is more variable in children than in adults and is easily influenced by illness, exercise, and anxiety. Because babies and young children use primarily the diaphragm in breathing, there is little chest movement; it is easier to count the respirations by observing abdominal movement. Respiration is predominantly costal by 7 years of age, so it is easier after that to count respirations by looking at chest movement. The nurse also observes for chest expansion and retractions.

Blood pressure Blood pressure measurement is considered part of routine screening for all children over 3 years of age. Emotion and activity affect the accuracy of blood pressure readings, as does cuff size. Blood pressure should be measured after other vital signs are taken and before the child becomes excited or upset.[8] Having a variety of cuff sizes enables the nurse to choose the correct size after measuring the limb. (See Table 17-22 for guidelines in selecting sphygmomanometer cuffs.) Percentiles for blood pressure measurements for girls and boys are shown in Fig. 6-1.

Weight and height Measurements of height and weight should be taken at least five times during the first year of life and then yearly throughout childhood and adolescence. The readings are plotted on a graph that shows the child's measurements in relation to percentile norms compiled from large groups of children in the same age group. The chart shows weight, length in lying position, height in standing position (stature), and head circumference as they relate to age. Different charts are available for boys and girls.

The National Center for Health Statistics (NCHS) growth charts of 1976 were prepared from data obtained from 1962 through 1974 in

Figure 6-1 Percentiles of blood pressure measurement (right arm, seated). (*A*) Girls. (*B*) Boys. (*From "Report of the Task Force on Blood Pressure Control in Children," Pediatrics* **59** *(suppl.):803, May 1977.*)

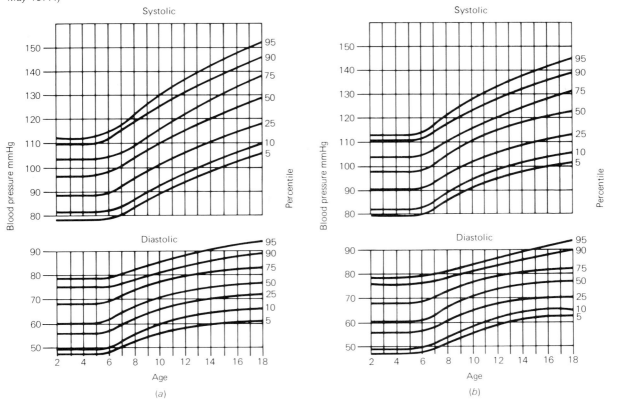

Figure 6-2 Physical growth of girls from birth to 36 months. [*Courtesy of Ross Laboratories. Adapted from National Center for Health Statistics, NCHS Growth Charts, 1976, Monthly Vital Statistics Report, vol. 25, no. 3, suppl. (HRA) 76-1120. Health Resources Administration, Rockville, Md., June 1976. Data from The Fels Research Institute, Yellow Springs, Ohio.*]

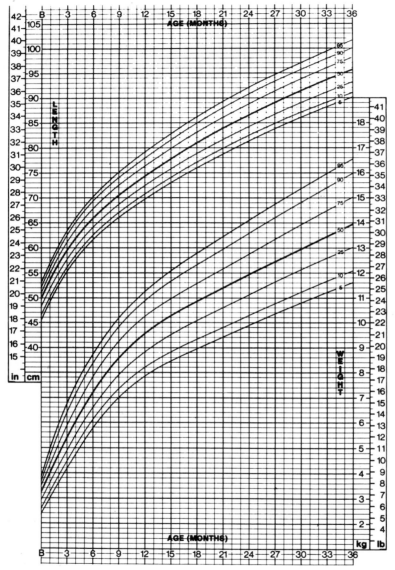

three separate surveys. Figure 6-2 shows a sample chart. The complete set of NCHS growth charts is included in Appendix B. Each chart shows curves at the 5th, 10th, 25th, 50th, 75th, 90th, and 95th percentiles.

A child below the 5th percentile is considered small or underweight. A child above the 95th percentile is considered large or overweight. Family patterns of growth and size must be considered in evaluating those children at the extremes of height or weight.

Newborns who are in the 50th percentile for

height and weight will usually remain in that percentile throughout their life span. Patterns of growth that need further investigation are (1) a wide disparity between height and weight, (2) a failure to show expected increases in height and weight, and (3) sudden increases or decreases in height, weight, or head circumference when previous growth was steady.

Infants should be weighed without clothing; older children are more comfortable when light clothing or a gown is worn. Balance scales are preferable to spring scales because of their greater accuracy. Figure 6-3 shows the measuring of an infant's weight. The average full-term infant weighs 3.4 kg at birth. This birth weight doubles by 4 to 5 months, triples by 1 year, and quadruples by 3 years.

Infant length can be assessed with a measuring board (see Fig. 17-3). One can measure an infant's length also by placing the baby on a long piece of paper, extending the legs, marking the points where the crown of the head and the bottom of the heel fall on the paper, and measuring between these marks.[9] Obtaining an accurate measurement of an infant's length with a measuring tape requires someone to hold the child still in a stretched-out position with the knees fully extended. Height measurement in children over 24 months of age can best be done with the child standing against a wall that has been measured and marked. The child should stand erect with the heels, buttocks, upper back, and back of the head touching the wall; the nurse then places atop the child's head a flat object that touches the wall at a 90° angle. The child should be told to stand as tall as possible. A balanced adult scale with an *accurate* built-in tape measure can also be used. The average length of the full-term infant is 50 cm at birth. Length increases by 50 percent by the first birthday, doubles by 4 years of age, and triples by age 12 for girls and age 13 for boys. From the preschool years to puberty, height increases approximately 6 cm each year.

Head circumference Periodic measurement of head circumference during the first year is important because skull growth must keep up with the rapid brain growth that is taking place. The nurse uses a nonstretchable tape measure at the largest circumference of the baby's head, as shown in Fig. 6-4. A child with a height and weight in the 50th percentile will usually have

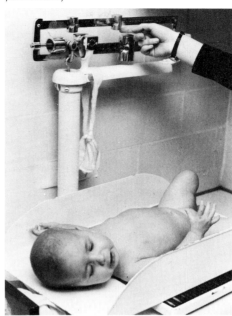

Figure 6-3 Weighing the infant. (*From M. Alexander and M. Brown, Pediatric History-Taking and Physical Diagnosis for Nurses, McGraw-Hill, New York, 1979. Used by permission.*)

a head circumference in the 50th percentile. At birth the average head circumference is 34 to 35 cm. It increases 6 cm by 3 months and another 6 cm by 1 year. Its growth rate then decreases so that there is only a 5-cm increase from 5 to 18 years of age.

Measurement accuracy It is essential that nurses obtain *accurate* measurements of height, weight, and head circumference. Generally children under 2 years of age are measured shorter than they really are, and children over 2 years of age are measured taller. Reliable equipment must be used and its accuracy checked. It is imperative that height or length be measured at right (90°) angles to the wall or table against which the child is standing or lying.

Developmental screening tools

The *Denver Developmental Screening Test (DDST)* is a tool designed to identify developmental delays in babies and children under 6 years of age.[10] The *DDST* provides a developmental profile of a child in the areas of gross motor, language,

Figure 6-4 Measuring head circumference. (*From M. Alexander and M. Brown, Pediatric History-Taking and Physical Diagnosis for Nurses, McGraw-Hill, New York, 1979. Used by permission.*)

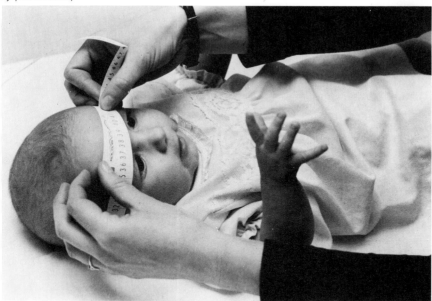

personal-social, and fine motor-adaptive abilities (see Figs. 6-5 and 6-6). If a child is scored as questionable or abnormal on any of the four areas of the *DDST*, the child should receive further evaluation.[11] Even though the *DDST* is fairly simple for both professionals and non-professionals to administer, score, and interpret, the test should not be used without adequate training. There is an instructional program that provides a manual, a workbook, a film, and a practice testing session with a proficiency evaluation. Periodic checks of the screening practices of all examiners using the *DDST* should be done in order to ensure the accuracy of test results.[12]

The *Denver Pre-screening Developmental Questionnaire (PDQ)* is a simplified adaptation of the DDST that can be used to decide whether or not a child needs to be tested with the *DDST*. The *PDQ* is a 10-item questionnaire that is answered by the parent. The questions vary according to the child's age. Like the *DDST*, the *PDQ* is suitable for children from infancy through the sixth birthday. The nurse interprets the questionnaire results and decides whether more thorough testing is necessary.[13]

Another questionnaire used by parents is the *Developmental Profile.* It relies heavily on verbal answers from a person who knows the child well. Included are five age scales that measure physical, self-help, social, academic, and communication development.[14]

Vision and hearing screening

Vision Vision screening is done to detect conditions that may cause blindness or visual impairment less severe but sufficient to delay development or interfere with education. Reduced visual acuity is a common problem in children. Amblyopia, or "lazy eye," is a major problem detectable by screening. Further loss of vision in the "unused" eye is preventable if amblyopia is detected and treated early (see Chap. 39). The recommended schedule for vision screening of all children is at birth, 3 years of age, before school, and then every 2 or 3 years.[15] (See Fig. 6-7.) Suspected problems should be verified with repeated screening before referring the child. When the estimated visual acuity is below 20/40, the child should be referred to a pediatrician or ophthalmologist.

Figure 13-4 Denver Developmental Screening Test Form.

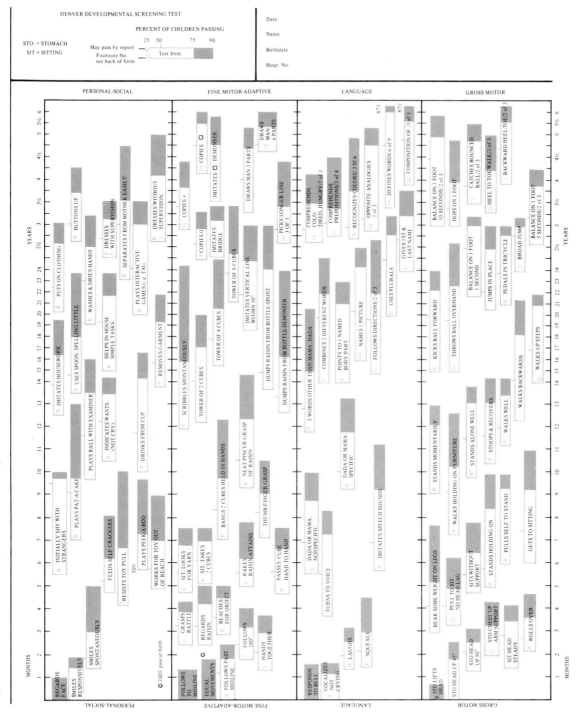

Figure 6-6 Instructions for administering some of the items in the *Denver Developmental Screening Test*.

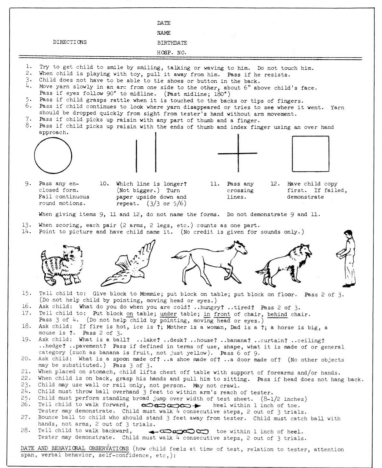

```
                              DATE
                              NAME
           DIRECTIONS         BIRTHDATE
                              HOSP. NO.
```

1. Try to get child to smile by smiling, talking or waving to him. Do not touch him.
2. When child is playing with toy, pull it away from him. Pass if he resists.
3. Child does not have to be able to tie shoes or button in the back.
4. Move yarn slowly in an arc from one side to the other, about 6" above child's face. Pass if eyes follow 90° to midline. (Past midline; 180°)
5. Pass if child grasps rattle when it is touched to the backs or tips of fingers.
6. Pass if child continues to look where yarn disappeared or tries to see where it went. Yarn should be dropped quickly from sight from tester's hand without arm movement.
7. Pass if child picks up raisin with any part of thumb and a finger.
8. Pass if child picks up raisin with the ends of thumb and index finger using an over hand approach.

9. Pass any enclosed form. Fail continuous round motions.
10. Which line is longer? (Not bigger.) Turn paper upside down and repeat. (3/3 or 5/6)
11. Pass any crossing lines.
12. Have child copy first. If failed, demonstrate

When giving items 9, 11 and 12, do not name the forms. Do not demonstrate 9 and 11.

13. When scoring, each pair (2 arms, 2 legs, etc.) counts as one part.
14. Point to picture and have child name it. (No credit is given for sounds only.)

15. Tell child to: Give block to Mommie; put block on table; put block on floor. Pass 2 of 3. (Do not help child by pointing, moving head or eyes.)
16. Ask child: What do you do when you are cold? ..hungry? ..tired? Pass 2 of 3.
17. Tell child to: Put block on table; under table; in front of chair, behind chair. Pass 3 of 4. (Do not help child by pointing, moving head or eyes.)
18. Ask child: If fire is hot, ice is ?; Mother is a woman, Dad is a ?; a horse is big, a mouse is ?. Pass 2 of 3.
19. Ask child: What is a ball? ..lake? ..desk? ..house? ..banana? ..curtain? ..ceiling? ..hedge? ..pavement? Pass if defined in terms of use, shape, what it is made of or general category (such as banana is fruit, not just yellow). Pass 6 of 9.
20. Ask child: What is a spoon made of? ..a shoe made of? ..a door made of? (No other objects may be substituted.) Pass 3 of 3.
21. When placed on stomach, child lifts chest off table with support of forearms and/or hands.
22. When child is on back, grasp his hands and pull him to sitting. Pass if head does not hang back.
23. Child may use wall or rail only, not person. May not crawl.
24. Child must throw ball overhand 3 feet to within arm's reach of tester.
25. Child must perform standing broad jump over width of test sheet. (8-1/2 inches)
26. Tell child to walk forward, ⊂⊃⊂⊃⊂⊃► heel within 1 inch of toe. Tester may demonstrate. Child must walk 4 consecutive steps, 2 out of 3 trials.
27. Bounce ball to child who should stand 3 feet away from tester. Child must catch ball with hands, not arms, 2 out of 3 trials.
28. Tell child to walk backward, ◄⊂⊃⊂⊃⊂⊃ toe within 1 inch of heel. Tester may demonstrate. Child must walk 4 consecutive steps, 2 out of 3 trials.

DATE AND BEHAVIORAL OBSERVATIONS (how child feels at time of test, relation to tester, attention span, verbal behavior, self-confidence, etc,):

Hearing Hearing screening is done to detect hearing loss and ear disease, since both are often treatable. Finding severe hearing loss is crucial in infants because the development of language skills is dependent upon the child's ability to hear. Severe hearing loss at birth is present in 1 in 2000 infants; by 2 years of age about 1 in 25 children has mild to moderate hearing loss.[16] The incidence of hearing loss is greater in disadvantaged children. Screening is recommended from birth through early childhood by gross hearing testing and assessment of language development. Pure-tone audiometry can be used at 3 to 4 years of age and then repeated every 2 to 3 years. Any child who has otitis media may develop temporary or permanent hearing loss and should be retested. Chapter 39 discusses vision and hearing screening in more detail.

Scoliosis screening

Scoliosis is a lateral curving of the spine. There are two types: functional and structural. Functional scoliosis is often the result of poor posture. Structural scoliosis occurs most frequently between the ages of 12 and 16 years, and affects girls more often than boys. The cause of structural scoliosis is not known. Its diagnosis is made by means of inspection and x-ray examination.

Exercise programs may improve functional scoliosis, but this is not generally true of the structural type. Prevention of progression of the spinal curve in the structural type can sometimes be accomplished by braces or surgery (see Chap. 36).

Screening for scoliosis is recommended throughout the school-age years. It has been learned that the heart grows normally in children with structural scoliosis. Because lung growth is abnormal (due to crowding of the organs in the chest cage), these children may develop pulmonary hypertension. Early recognition is important because early treatment often prevents an increase of the curvature. Early counseling can help the child cope with the altered body image.[17]

Other screening tests

Recently there has been a large increase in the number of conditions recommended (and legislated) for screening. Certain principles are used in making decisions regarding what, whom, when, and how to screen. It is important to screen for:

1. Conditions that can be diagnosed with certainty.
2. Conditions that will benefit from early diagnosis and treatment.
3. Conditions for which the screening procedures are highly accurate.

It is implied that positive results can be followed up by appropriate evaluation and treatment and that the benefits will be great in terms of the number of affected children identified or disabilities prevented.[18]

Galactosemia affects approximately 1 in 60,000 neonates.[19] Jaundice, poor eating, vomiting, weight loss, and an enlarged liver usually suggest the disease within the first weeks of life. Untreated infants usually die within 6 weeks, and the few who recover are severely handicapped.[20] Babies should be screened for the disease if symptoms are present or if the family is known to be at risk for the disease. Many physicians screen all newborns. A lactose-free diet using milk substitutes is the treatment, and infants so treated usually develop normal intelligence levels.

Figure 6-7 Child being tested with E Chart. (*From M. Alexander and M. Brown, Pediatric History-Taking and Physical Diagnosis for Nurses, McGraw-Hill, New York, 1979. Used by permission.*)

Phenylketonuria (PKU) occurs about once in every 10,000 births and is due to the child's inability to process phenylalanine, an essential amino acid found in natural protein food.[21] Signs and symptoms are not usually seen until 4 months of age, when some brain damage has already occurred. PKU is treated with dietary restriction of foods containing phenylalanine—breads, meats, fish, cheese, nuts, and eggs. Even with such treatment the outcome is sometimes poor, but some authorities believe that if the diet can be restricted until 4 to 6 years of age mental retardation can be prevented.[22]

PKU testing is required by law in some states. Some hospitals screen for PKU before babies are discharged from the nursery by using a Guthrie test on heel blood, ensuring that these babies will be tested at least once. Testing at 3 to 4 days of age, however, will obtain some false negative test results because the baby has not ingested enough milk to raise the phenylalanine in the blood to abnormal levels. For this reason, repeat screening may be done for PKU at 4 to 6 weeks of age.[23]

Congenital hypothyroidism (cretinism) results from too little secretion of thyroid hormone and is one of the most common endocrine diseases in children, occurring in 1 of every 6000 to 7000 births.[24] No signs or symptoms are present at birth, but may appear in the first weeks or months of life. Measurement of T_4 (thyroxine) in the neonatal period is a commonly used screening technique for hypothyroidism. Treatment is thyroid hormone replacement; even when treatment is successful and begun early, the child may have some degree of mental retardation.

Tuberculosis affects children of all ages; children under 3 years of age and during adolescence are especially susceptible. When children live for extended periods of time with persons who have tuberculosis, they often develop the disease. Routine screening for tuberculosis, using the Mantoux test, should be done at 12 months of age, before immunization with live viral vaccines, and again at 5 and 12 years of age. Children in high exposure groups should be tested every 1 to 2 years.

Anemia is a common childhood disorder that can impair health and development and may be indicative of numerous underlying health problems. Hemoglobin and hematocrit should be evaluated routinely at birth, at 1 and 5 years of age, and in early adolescence.

Urinary tract infections are also common and require treatment to prevent structural damage to the urinary tract as well as impairment of health and development. Because of their shorter urethras and greater risk of fecal contamination through the urinary meatus, girls have more urinary infections than boys. A urine culture should be done on all toilet-trained girls at 2 years of age. Urine protein should be evaluated in both sexes during the preschool period and at preadolescence.

Children who are at high risk for lead poisoning because of their environment or life circumstances should be screened at 9 to 12 months of age and at least yearly thereafter until the age of 5. High-risk children are: those who live in houses built before the mid-1940s, when lead paints were in use; those who practice pica (ingestion of nonfood substances, which may include paint chips containing lead); and those with previously elevated levels of lead.

Neonates of African, Mediterranean, or Arab ancestry are routinely screened for sickle cell hemoglobin in some hospitals. Certainly all newborns of parents who are known carriers of the sickle cell disorder should be screened by subjecting hemoglobin from cord blood to electrophoresis.

Components of routine health maintenance

Dental care

Dental health begins with a good prenatal diet since some of the primary teeth calcify in utero. At approximately 6 months of age the first of the primary (deciduous) teeth erupt. Formation of the permanent teeth begins soon after birth. Permanent teeth do not erupt until the primary teeth are lost, between 6 and 12 years of age (Fig. 6-8). Two important functions of primary teeth are to chew food and to maintain space in the mandible or maxilla for the permanent teeth. If a primary tooth is lost early, the child should see a dentist for evaluation of the need for a space-maintaining device.

The major factors in dental health are brushing teeth regularly, eating an adequate diet, applying fluoride or drinking flouridated water for the prevention of cavities, and preventing and correcting malocclusion. All the surfaces of the teeth should be brushed for 3 min within 10 min after eating (Fig. 6-9). The diet should be balanced,

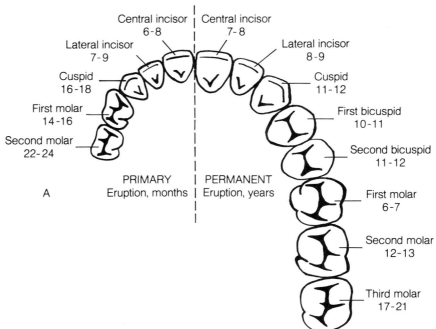

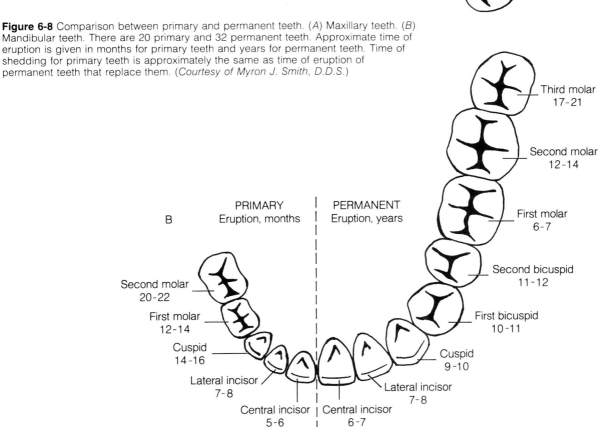

Figure 6-8 Comparison between primary and permanent teeth. (*A*) Maxillary teeth. (*B*) Mandibular teeth. There are 20 primary and 32 permanent teeth. Approximate time of eruption is given in months for primary teeth and years for permanent teeth. Time of shedding for primary teeth is approximately the same as time of eruption of permanent teeth that replace them. (*Courtesy of Myron J. Smith, D.D.S.*)

Figure 6-9 Brushing teeth after meals and before bed helps prevent tooth decay.

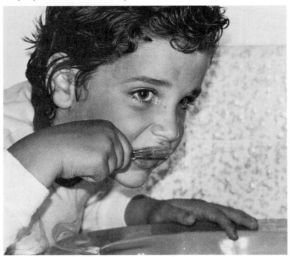

adequate in amount, and low in sugars and starches. Fluoridation of the water supply in communities with low-fluoride water is of tremendous value in reducing dental decay. Flossing between teeth is essential.

Malocclusion is faulty alignment of the teeth so that upper and lower teeth do not come together correctly when the mouth is closed. Common causes of malocclusion are teeth that are too large or small, one jaw that is too large or small, thumb-sucking, early loss of primary teeth, failure of a tooth to form where one should be, and a delayed or distorted pattern of tooth eruption. Malocclusion can interfere with chewing, cause facial deformity, interfere with speech, and cause body image problems. Parents should be encouraged to obtain regular dental care for children beginning at 3 years of age and to seek dental care immediately for children with injuries to the mouth, gums, or teeth. Family patterns of missing teeth, abnormal tooth eruption, or malocclusion are often significant factors to note in the health history.

Immunizations

Vaccines provide an inexpensive and effective method for preventing several of the common childhood diseases. Recent outbreaks of these illnesses provide evidence of the apathy toward immunizations that exists among some people today. Many states now require up-to-date immunizations for any child entering public school.

The nurse is often responsible for preparing the vaccine, administering it, and explaining the purpose, schedule, and reactions of it to parents. If a schedule is interrupted, final immunity can be achieved as long as the schedule is resumed and completed.

Table 6-5 recommends a schedule for active immunization of infants and children. It also contains the schedule for those not immunized in infancy.

Diphtheria, pertussis, tetanus (DPT) Children can receive protection against these three diseases using combined vaccines administered at 2, 4, and 6 months of age. Booster doses should be given at 18 months of age and again at 4 to 6 years of age. Pertussis is usually not necessary after the age of 6 since the disease is not as serious after early childhood. Tetanus boosters are given every 10 years or when a deep wound occurs more than 5 years after the last booster.

Poliomyelitis Initial protection should be given at 2, 4, 6, and 18 months of age with trivalent oral polio vaccine (TOPV). A booster should be given between 4 and 6 years of age.

Measles (rubeola) Until about 13 months of age infants are protected from rubeola with antibodies received from their mother. Passive immunity from the vaccine can be destroyed by these antibodies if the immunization is given before 13 months of age. During an outbreak of measles infants 6 months of age or older can be immunized. Reimmunization is necessary again at 15 months of age. Measles vaccine is usually administered in combination with mumps and rubella vaccines (MMR) at 15 months of age. Measles can be a severe disease with frequently serious complications.

German measles (rubella) Immunization is recommended for all children and is usually given at 15 months of age in combination with measles and mumps vaccine. Special emphasis should be placed on immunizing all preschool and elementary school children. Children of pregnant women can receive the vaccine, but pregnant women should not be vaccinated because of risk to the fetus.

Mumps Mumps vaccine can be given at 1 year of age, but it is usually given at 15 months of age in combination with measles and German measles. Twenty to thirty percent of males who get mumps after puberty develop mumps orchitis. Orchitis (testicular inflammation) can cause sterility in a small percentage of those affected. Other complications of mumps are meningitis, encephalitis, and deafness. Mumps vaccine is recommended for all older children and adolescents who are still susceptible to the disease.

Smallpox This vaccination is not recommended for children living in the United States because the risk of acquiring the disease is so slight. Because deaths have occurred from reactions to the vaccine, reactions are considered a greater risk than the chance of getting smallpox at this time.

Contraindications to immunizations Contraindications to immunizations include the following:

1. Acute febrile illness, chronic debilitating disease, or acute neurological disease.
2. Cancer, immunological disease, or anticancer therapy.
3. Pregnancy (except for polio vaccine).
4. Previous allergic reaction to vaccines.

Parents should be instructed to keep careful records of the type of protection their child received and the dates of administration. They should understand the recommended schedule of immunizations. Parents also need to know the common reactions their child might experience after an immunization. The nurse should explain the use of antipyretics (aspirin or acetaminophen) in appropriate doses for mild reactions. Table 6-6 describes the common side effects of immunizations.

Physical examination schedule

Well infants are usually examined at birth, 6 to 8 weeks, 4 months, 6 months, 9 months, and 1 year of age. Sick infants should be assessed at

Table 6-5 Recommended immunization schedules

a) Children immunized as infants		b) Children immunized at later ages			
		15 months through 5 years		**6 years and older**	
Age	**Substance**	**Timing**	**Substance**	**Timing**	**Substance**
2 months	DPT, TOPV	First visit	DPT, TOPV, tuberculin test	First visit	Td, TOPV, tuberculin test
		Interval after first visit		Interval after first visit	
4 months	DPT, TOPV	1 month	MMR		
6 months	DPT, TOPV			1 month	MMR
15 months	MMR	2 months	DPT, TOPV		
18 months	DPT, TOPV			2 months	Td, TOPV
4–6 years	DPT, TOPV	4 months	DPT, TOPV		
14–16 years	Td (repeat every 10 years)			8–14 months	Td, TOPV
		10–12 months	DPT, TOPV	Age 14–16 years	Td (repeat every 10 years)
		Age 14–16 years	Td (repeat every 10 years)		

Key: DPT, diphtheria and tetanus toxoids combined with pertussis vaccine.
TOPV, trivalent oral polio vaccine.
MMR, measles, mumps, and rubella combined vaccines.
Td, combined tetanus and diphtheria toxoids for children 6 years and older.
Source: *Parents Guide to Childhood Immunization*, DHEW Publication (OS) 77-50058, October 1977, pp. 20–23.

Table 6-6 Possible side effects of recommended immunizations

Immunizations	Reaction
Diphtheria	Fever within 24–48 hours; soreness, swelling, redness at site of vaccination
Tetanus	Same as diphtheria plus urticaria and malaise
Pertussis	Same as diphtheria. Rare reaction includes loss of consciousness, convulsions, thrombocytopenia
TOPV	Usually no side effects
Rubeola	Transient rash, anorexia, fever; malaise may occur 7–10 days later.
Rubella	Rash, lymphadenopathy, transient pain in peripheral joints
Mumps	Usually no side effects except brief, mild fever

each illness. If the child has had a recent well-child assessment, then a complete examination need not be done when an illness occurs; focus should be on the systems showing signs and symptoms. A yearly assessment of a child's physical and developmental status is generally recommended up to the age of 6 and at any time the parent feels the child is not progressing normally. After the age of 6, if the child appears well, has no symptoms, and is doing well socially and academically, routine assessment can be done every 2 years.

The nurse's role in child health maintenance

Anticipatory guidance

Anticipating potential child health problems and effectively intervening to avert them are nursing interventions used to promote child health. Many health problems are avoided by early detection and reduction of risk factors. By anticipating problems and assisting families to avoid or minimize them, the nurse promotes health maintenance.

Subsequent chapters in this book describe the normal growth and development for children from before birth to adolescence. For each age group the developmental steps, psychosocial tasks, and typical health problems are outlined. Using that information, the nurse can make an assessment of the child, the child's family (Chaps.

2 and 3), and developmental status to provide anticipatory guidance to the family.

A typical health maintenance guide for a 6-month-old infant is outlined in Table 6-7. Using this format, the reader can construct similar guides for the younger and older child.

In addition to health history, physical exam, screening tests, and immunizations, consideration is given to counseling and health education regarding nutrition, sleep, play and exercise, safety, physical-emotional-social development, sexuality, discipline, language skills, and school adjustment. Whether the child is seen on a health maintenance visit or hospitalized for an acute illness, the nurse has an obligation to anticipate educational needs of the child and family.

For example, since accidents are a leading cause of death and injury among children, parents need to be counseled regarding potential dangers for each age group (Fig. 6-10). Table 6-8 describes safety hazards for each age group and appropriate interventions.

The nurse must also be alert to common potential health problems in children. In 1978 the American Nurses' Association appointed a commission to investigate the unmet health needs of children and youth. In their 1979 report the commission listed the following unmet needs:[25]

1. Teenage pregnancy and venereal disease
   The rate of sexual activity among young people is increasing with more than 1 million becoming pregnant each year.
2. Drug abuse
   Children are using drugs at an earlier age and in greater numbers.
3. Child abuse
   Most cases go unreported. Possibly 1 million children are abused each year.
4. Sexual exploitation
   The incidence of sexual assault, incest, child pornography, and child prostitution is increasing.
5. Suicide
   Suicide is the second leading cause of death among young people of ages 12 to 24.
6. Physical fitness
   Accidents, nutritional problems, and dental problems greatly affect growth and development.
7. Developmental disabilities and chronic illness
   Estimates suggest 7 to 10 million children are handicapped.

8. Immunizations

It is estimated that in 1977, 20 million out of 52 million children had not been immunized against the most common preventable diseases.

These needs must be considered by all health professionals in all health maintenance settings.

Teaching and counseling

In teaching, an essential component of the nursing process, the nurse transmits knowledge to families and children to ensure continuity of care and long-term health maintenance. When teaching families, the nurse should attempt to elicit feedback from them in order to judge whether information was heard and understood. Even though the nurse may believe the information was clear and descriptive, if the family does not understand, or if they misinterpret instructions, the teaching has been ineffective. Family members may be embarrassed to admit they do not understand what the nurse or physician has told them. To confirm that they understand, the nurse may request that family members describe in their own words what the nurse has told them. The nurse should also ask questions that cannot be answered by a simple "yes" or "no." It is the nurse's responsibility to clarify any misconceptions or gaps in his or her teaching. The nurse should be supportive and

Table 6-7 Health maintenance guide for a 6-month-old child

Assessment	Counseling/health education
Age	
Height, weight, head circumference	Weight should double by 5 months; plot on growth chart
Physical exam	Complete exam performed
Hearing	Infant should localize sound by turning to it
Vision	Check ability to follow object, recognize mother
Hematocrit	Appropriate time to check for anemia since fetal iron stores depleted
Immunizations	DPT no. 3, TOPV no. 3
Dental screening	Time of first tooth eruption. Discuss use of fluoride. Relate use of sugar to caries. Discourage putting child to bed with bottle.
Nutrition	Begin solids—1 tbsp of rice cereal mixed with formula and fed from a spoon. Can be increased to 2–4 tbsp 1–2 times daily. Add one new food every 4–5 days. First cereal, then 2 weeks later start vegetables, then fruits. Next begin protein foods (chicken, meat, eggs). Review label reading and home preparation of baby food Add finger foods—soft cooked vegetables, crackers, fruits (counsel regarding choking) Continue use of multivitamin preparation
Sleep	Infant should be sleeping all night; total sleep 14–15 h.
Elimination	Behavior with wet and soiled diapers; number of voidings, stools per day.
Play	Self-playing with hands, feet. Rolls over into various positions; likes mobiles, swings.
Language	Babbling intensifies; imitates sounds, m-m-m when crying.
Physical development	Sits without support; grasp—hand to mouth.
Safety considerations	Electric outlets; discuss syrup of ipecac. Falls—accidents for age group.
Responses to people	Beginning of period of separation anxiety. Observe how baby acts with mother, strangers.
Parenting	How is primary care-giver getting time away from the baby? Does family agree on child-care procedures, discipline?
Sexuality	Baby has usually found genitals. Discussion of early sexuality is appropriate.

Figure 6-10 Learning to cross the street with stop and go lights.

encourage families' questions about points they do not understand. Effective teaching is planned and measured by the comprehension of learning.

Because of the nurse's expertise, families may request advice from the nurse about their life situations. In counseling, the nurse refrains from making a decision for the family. At the same time, the nurse can listen to the problem, help the family focus on the real issues, and assist the family in making their own decision.

Advocacy

Since children are not often in a position to advocate effectively for themselves, others must do so for them. Legal measures have been instituted to help ensure child health maintenance. Most states have laws that require nurses to report any suspected incidence of child abuse to official authorities. These rulings are based on the doctrine of *parens patrice*, which gives the state the authority to protect children.[26] Federal regulations requiring child-proof medication caps, flame-retardant night clothes, and safety standards for car seats are examples of legislation designed to protect the health of the child. (See Chap. 18 for additional information on advocacy.)

Protection of children's rights Previously, health professionals adopted a paternalistic attitude and included neither the family nor the child in the treatment plan. With increased emphasis on patients' rights, consumer pressure has forced professionals in recent years to include the patient in the decision-making process. More recently, children's rights, an outgrowth of the patients' rights movement, are being clarified.

In 1974 the *Pediatric Bill of Rights* was adopted by the National Association of Children's Hospitals as a proposed legislative model.[27] This bill of rights provides that every person, regardless of age, has the right to seek and consent to treatment involving contraception, venereal disease, pregnancy (including consent for abortion), and psychiatric problems. The bill protects the confidentiality of the patient and prevents the physician from disclosing any information to the child's parents without the child's consent.

Although court cases have not yet arisen, the

Table 6-8 Developmental safety: anticipatory guidance

Age	Developmental characteristics	Hazard	Preventive intervention
6 months–1 year	Creeping	Falls	Do not leave on high unprotected surface.
	Exploring	Putting foreign objects in mouth	Pick up buttons, pins, and small objects from the floor. Keep medicines and poisons locked up. Discard broken toys.
		Scalding	Keep hot liquids away from reach.
		Car accident	Use car safety seats (not parent's lap) fitted according to child's height and weight.
1–3 years	Walking, curious	Running in front of car	Supervise constantly. Enclose yard with fence. Don't let child cross street alone. Set up practice situations so child can learn to cross street.
		Overdosing on medication; poisoning	Keep safety cap on medication. Keep poisons out of reach.
		Car accident	Use car safety seat.
3–6 years	Investigator, wants to play in neighborhood	Car accident	Intensive safety instruction. Supervise activities. Use car seats up to 4 years of age, seat belts thereafter.
		Drowning	Do not allow to swim without responsible adult present. Wear life jacket while playing near lake, pool. Teach child appropriate behavior at lake or pool.
		Setting a fire	Keep matches locked up. Equip home with fire and smoke alarm.
6–12 years	Tries to be independent in play	Causing fires, using dangerous household equipment	Teach safe use of household tools and appliances. Practice fire drill at home.
		Hit by car on bicycle	Teach bicycle safety. Use lights. Put reflectors on bike and child.
		Car accidents	Use safety belts.
9–18 years	Competes in sports and tournaments Uses skateboards	Falls, knee injuries, head injuries	Use appropriate safety equipment (padding, helmets, etc.). Continue adult supervision.
12–18 years	Wants to drive a car or motorcycle	Mopeds, motorcycles, car accidents	Require completion of driver's education classes, use of helmets.
	Identifies with peer group. Is tempted to experiment with cigarettes, drugs, alcohol, and sex.	Long-term effects to lungs, liver, brain cells, teenage pregnancy	Counsel regarding harmful effects to body. Continue to monitor activities. Promote peer group support to say "no."

child may have the right to refuse treatment when the parents want the child to have treatment. Therefore, the nurse should see that consent is obtained from any minor of age 14 or older.

Rehabilitation

Through rehabilitation, the health maintenance of the handicapped child is emphasized. Rehabilitation involves retraining the handicapped child to the fullest physical, emotional, social, and vocational usefulness possible. Recent federal legislation (P.L. 94-142) mandates that handicapped children receive the same education in the same classrooms as normal children. This concept, called *mainstreaming*, is based on the philosophy that integration is necessary for optimal rehabilitation.

Referral

Nurses frequently refer children and families to other health care professionals or agencies. Community resources may include physicians, psychologists, social workers, dentists, physical therapists, and nurses. Handicapped children's services provide care to children with orthopedic problems; fees are based on the family's income. Local health departments are excellent sources for immunizations, well-child clinics, treatment for communicable diseases, screening programs, and developmental or psychological testing.

Preparing the child for self-care

The ultimate goal of child health maintenance is self-care. Effective transmission of knowledge and responsibility to the child and family enables them to be their own advocates. Both continuity of care and lifetime health maintenance are thus ensured.

To facilitate health care, both the child and the family should be actively included in the decision-making process for the health maintenance plan from the beginning. This involvement enables the child to develop problem-solving skills for health maintenance and increases the child's level of compliance. If children as well as adults are included in decision making, they will feel more involved and committed to the resulting plan.

With effective health maintenance programs, children and their families can eventually do much of the screening for disease and the preventing of potential health problems themselves. Health habits formed during childhood will continue throughout adulthood.

References

1. Rita Numerof, "Expanded Nursing Role from the Perspective of the New Medicine," *Health Care Management Review*, Aspen Publications, vol. 3, no. 3, Summer 1978, pp. 45–51.

2. National Commission on the International Year of the Child, *What are the Issues?*, 1979, pp. 1–4.

3. M. K. Duvak, "Highlights from the Ten State Nutrition Survey," *Nutrition Today* 7:4–11 (July–August 1972).

4. National Commission on the International Year of the Child, *What are the Issues?*, 1979, pp. 1–4.

5. Marshall Klaus, and John Kennel, *Maternal Infant Bonding*, Mosby, St. Louis, 1976, p. 90.

6. Elmer L. DeGowin, and Richard L. DeGowin, *Bedside Diagnostic Examination*, 2d ed., MacMillan, Collier Books, New York, 1969, p. 28.

7. Barbara Bates, *A Guide to Physical Examination*, Lippincott, Philadelphia, 1979, p. 376.

8. Ibid., p. 377.

9. Ibid., p. 379.

10. Dorothy R. Marlow, *Textbook of Pediatric Nursing*, Saunders, Philadelphia, 1977, p. 32.

11. Marcene L. Erickson, *Assessment and Management of Developmental Changes in Children*, Mosby, St. Louis, 1976, p. 174.

12. Ibid., p. 175.

13. Mary Alexander and Marie Brown, *Pediatric History-Taking and Physical Diagnosis for Nurses*, McGraw-Hill, New York, 1979, p. 412.

14. Erickson, op. cit., p. 194.

15. Robert A. Hoekelman, et al., *Principles of Pediatrics, Health Care of the Young*, McGraw-Hill, New York, 1978, p. 202.

16. Ibid., p. 197.

17. P. A. Zorab, *Scoliosis, Proceedings of a Fifth Symposium*, Sept. 21 and 22, 1976, Academic Press, New York, 1977.

18. Hoekelman, op cit., p. 182.

19. F. P. Hudson, "Screening for Inborn Errors of Metabolism in Infancy," *Nursing Mirror*, Aug. 28, 1975, p. 64.

20. Ibid., p. 63.

21. Marlow, op cit., p. 466.

22. Ibid., p. 467.

23. Ibid.

24. Ibid., p. 465.

25. "A Report on the Hearings of the Unmet Health Needs of Children and Youth," American Nurses' Association, Kansas City, 1979.

26. Angela Roddey Holder, *Legal Issues in Pediatrics and Adolescent Medicine*, Wiley, New York, 1977, p. 220.

27. G. Emmett Raitt, "The Minor's Right to Consent to Medical Treatment," *So. Cal. Law Rev.* 48: 1417 (1975).

Chapter 7 **Principles of growth and development**

Nancy Lockwood Ramsey

Upon completion of this chapter, the student will be able to:

1. State and identify examples of eight principles of growth and development.

2. Compare the definitions of the following terms: maturation vs. development, growth vs. development, developmental task vs. developmental milestone.

3. Define and compare critical periods and stage theory.

4. Describe the three components of consciousness according to Freudian theory.

5. Compare Freud's stages of development to Erikson's stages of psychosocial development.

6. Identify three major ways in which Erikson's theory differs from Freud's.

7. Define the following terms: cognitive development, assimilation, accommodation, schemata, organization.

8. Support or refute the following: "Children's cognitive development increases in complexity. A child learns by experience."

The nurse is in a strategic position to help the child and family obtain optimal health.[1] The first step in promoting and safeguarding health is, like the first step of the nursing process, assessment. Only after collecting data can the nurse make accurate nursing diagnoses and plan and prioritize appropriate, individualized interventions. Assessment of every child client includes growth and development.

The assessment of growth and development must be based on scientific knowledge and theory rather than on intuition, habit, or value judgment. The facts and theories nurses use in assessing growth and development come from various biological and psychosocial disciplines and include anthropometry (measurement of height, weight, body proportions, and the other aspects of physical growth), nutrition, physiol-ogy, psychology, sociology (especially as it applies to families and childhood peer groups), and others.

Perhaps the outstanding feature of growth and development during childhood is rapid change. (See Fig 7-1.) What is normal at one age is often abnormal a short time later. Only by thoroughly knowing growth and development can the nurse accurately assess the well-being of a child and, equally important, help parents and others in the child's environment anticipate what the child will need to ensure well-being in the next phases of continuing change.

The changes that occur with normal growth and development are both physical and behavioral. Many of the physical changes are obvious even to the unsophisticated observer: The child increases in size, and body proportions change.

Figure 7-1 Interests and activities that characterize one age are later replaced by other behavioral patterns that are better suited to the developmental tasks of that later period. (*Courtesy of David Carroll.*)

Other changes are less conspicuous. Internal structural changes take place as growth occurs, and physiological functions are modified as time passes. For example, the ability to digest milk is not well developed until around 3 months of age, when the infant begins to secrete lactase. Metabolic rates are higher in young children than in older ones; this fact accounts for differences in fluid and caloric requirements at different ages, influences temperature regulation, and affects medication dosage and physiological utilization of drugs. Maturation of the myelin sheath influences physiological activity; slow and erratic motor responses, for example, are typical of infants because the immature myelin sheath does not permit efficient muscular control. As the neuromuscular system matures, reflexes and other motor activities expected in young infants become abnormal during later months of infancy. A 2-month-old child does not have good control of the neck muscles that steady the head, but a 5-month-old baby should.

Behavioral changes that accompany growth and development result in part from physical changes. For example, varying maturation of different brain areas is believed to be partly responsible for the toddler's tantrums. Hormonal secretions contribute to the moodiness of adolescents. Increased heart and lung capacities, in addition to improved motor control, enable school-age children to engage in vigorous activities, such as tag and ball games, that are beyond the behavioral capacity of younger children. Behavioral changes that take place as children get older are not caused only by physical changes but are often due to increasing experience and the effect that has on interests and understanding.

Definitions

Growth refers to increase in the physical size of the body or body part. It is usually assessed in units of measurement, such as kilograms, centimeters, inches, or pounds. Growth occurs by two processes: an increase in the *number* of cells, called *hyperplasia*, and increase in the *size* of individual cells, termed *hypertrophy*. Most, if not all, organs and tissues grow by both processes. Obviously, cell multiplication (hyperplasia) is a very active part of prenatal growth, since new cells are necessary for the creation of all body structures of the unborn child. Hyperplasia depends on adequate nutritional intake, both before and after birth. Hypertrophy often depends on use of the body part. For example, the muscles of the back, buttocks, and legs become larger when the child learns to walk, and the myocardium hypertrophies to an abnormal extent in certain kinds of heart malformations that cause the heart to work hard in its effort to push the blood past a small valve or through a partially obstructed vessel.

Development refers to a gradual change in function, not size, that results in more complex skills and abilities. These new functions expand the child's capacity for achievement. For example, the school-age child who has progressed to abstract thinking is now able to anticipate and empathize with the feelings of other people and is perfecting fine and gross motor coordination. These developmental changes prepare the child for team play, as they enable the child to compromise for the welfare of the group, to analyze the effects of his or her own behavior upon winning, and to develop the neuromuscular coordination to play the game.

Maturation, a part of development, refers to the attainment of new competencies or characteristics that are transmitted genetically and hence are expected to "unfold" naturally in each member of the species. The word *maturation* is often incorrectly used to mean growth and development. Maturation is due to genetic endowment transmitted in the cell nuclei, not to practice or learning from the environment. For example, the maturation of the myelin sheath, the attainment of body height, and the secretion of lactase are governed by heredity and maturation, not practice or experience.

A *developmental task* is a global behavioral skill or ability that is best learned or accomplished during a specific time period of the child's life. Each particular developmental task occurs at approximately the same age in most children. Mastery of the task prepares the child to deal successfully with later developmental tasks. If the skill or ability is not learned at the appropriate time period, the child will probably have greater difficulty mastering it at a later time. Examples of developmental tasks include learning to manipulate symbols (such as letters and numbers used in reading and arithmetic) during the school-age period and becoming able to live independently from parents in late adolescence.

Learning is an increase in understanding or skill as a result of development or experience. Learning may or may not lead to an observable change in behavior. For example, children who have learned to cope with separation from their mothers no longer cry or cling when left at nursery school, but adolescents who have learned about the health hazards of smoking may or may not alter their smoking behavior. Learning is often dependent on maturation; a preschooler cannot learn cognitive skills such as algebra, for example, and toilet training cannot be learned until myelinization makes sphincter control possible. Learning is often made necessary by developmental changes as well as by situational requirements: Adolescents learn, for example, to deal with the physical changes of puberty, and they learn how to behave in new social situations, such as dating.

Readiness refers to the child's capability to begin learning a new skill or developmental task. Readiness requires neurological maturity and also involves motivation and prerequisite skills. For example, school readiness is said to be present at age 6, when children have the social and emotional maturity and self-help skills (toileting, eating, etc.) to adapt to being in school and, in addition, the cognitive maturity and motivation to receive teaching in the relatively structured instructional setting. Reading readiness consists of the perceptual maturation to distinguish letters and their associated sounds, the intellectual maturity to see the connection between written words and their meanings, and the motivation to learn to read.

A *developmental milestone* is a specific task, skill, or learned behavior that can be used to assess a child's development at a particular age. For example, children are expected to begin walking around 12 to 18 months, and failure to do so is a danger signal that calls for more thorough developmental assessment. Infants' developmental milestones are mainly neuromuscular responses to stimuli that reflect neurological maturation. Only gradually do the developmental milestones reflect increasing interactions with the environment.

Principles of growth and development

Researchers in child development have observed a number of common patterns of growth and behavior. These patterns are useful because they identify general principles, or laws, underlying children's growth and development. Most authorities agree on the following principles.

1. Each child has an individual rate and style of growth and development

As pertains to growth, for example, some children get bigger than others, some grow faster than others, and some reach puberty earlier than others. Although normative growth charts such as those in Appendix B are of great value in assessing a child's growth, it is important to remember that individual variations among children are entirely normal. Each child's own growth record is in many ways the best standard by which to evaluate his or her present growth data. A child who is relatively small or large in comparison with children of the same age may be experiencing a growth abnormality or may simply be following his or her own appropriate, individual growth pattern. A long-term growth record is invaluable in making the distinction between these two possibilities. That is, a child whose height is at the 25th percentile for children in that age group should not arouse concern if she has in the past consistently been near the same percentile on the height chart. A drop from earlier 50th percentile data would be an indication that she is deviating from the earlier pattern and is in need of further evaluation to rule out some health problem that is being manifested in growth retardation.

Individual differences in behavioral "style" are often evident even from birth. Observation of babies in a newborn nursery reveals some infants are slower than others to wake up and fall asleep, some are more insistent than others about feedings, some are easier than others to comfort, and so forth. Children naturally differ in their general style of interacting with the environment (alertness, assertiveness, consolability, etc.), as well as many other behavioral traits, with each child

Figure 7-2 One child's usual response to a new or difficult situation may be to sit back and size things up; another might jump right in; still another might seek adult intervention.

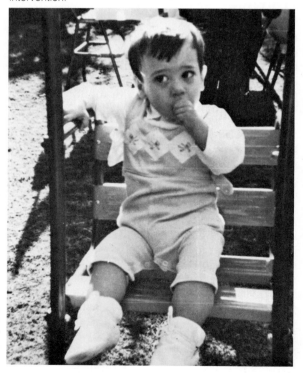

following his or her own pattern throughout the various developmental phases for the most part. (See Fig. 7-2.)

Child-to-child variations in growth and development result from both genetic inheritance and environmental influences. Inherited factors that influence growth and development include sex, race, and certain inherited diseases. For example, boys are somewhat larger than girls from birth through the preschool years, after which girls as a group are larger until the boys reach puberty. Boys generally reach the developmental milestones later than girls. Musculoskeletal differences among races are numerous and generally of little or no practical significance. Such inherited disorders as phenylketonuria, which affects intelligence, or cystic fibrosis, which affects growth as well as general health, obviously have great potential for influencing growth or development or both.

Environmental influences, such as the amount and consistency of stimulation, religion, ethnic background, education, and discipline techniques, affect the child's rate and style of development. For example, a child living with eight other children in a two-room apartment and locked in the apartment each day while parents work, may receive inadequate stimulation, education, and nutrition and as a consequence may demonstrate developmental delays or distortions.

2. Both growth and development are asynchronous

Different body parts and developmental areas (language, motor skills, etc.) develop at different rates. Each body part has its own time to grow. Brain growth, for example, predominates during early development, for it forms the foundation for later neuromuscular development. During each phase of development, the child focuses intensely on mastering the pertinent developmental tasks and skills. Other developmental areas recede into the background at that time. The toddler concentrates on learning to walk; only after walking is mastered does vocabulary greatly increase. Support for development includes providing toys and muscular activities to stimulate the predominant developmental activity. For example, when an infant is crawling, opportunities should be provided for the child to exercise that skill; perhaps the adult would place a soft blanket on the floor, sit on the floor, and encourage the child to crawl toward toys.

3. All areas of growth and development are interrelated

Growth and development are artificially divided into such subparts as physical, psychosocial, moral, language, and cognitive development to ease studying. In reality, each area of development is inseparably integrated with every other. For example, providing for the child's basic physiological needs forms a foundation for cognitive and psychosocial development. Language and social development go hand in hand. Physical maturation continually makes new experiences, hence new learning, possible. (See Fig. 7-3.)

4. Newly learned skills predominate

The child is preoccupied with practicing and perfecting the current new skill. A majority of the waking hours may be spent practicing the skill. The infant who has recently learned to throw an object for someone else to retrieve, the kindergartner who has just discovered how to whistle, and the school-age child who can make bubbles with bubble gum provide clear examples of the strong drive to repeat and practice newly acquired skills.

5. Growth and development occur in an orderly sequence

Both growth and development are predictable and orderly, not haphazard, develop in sequence, and are approximately the same among most children of the same age. That is why it has been possible to identify developmental milestones. Even children who pass their milestones unusually early or late can be expected to follow the usual childhood developmental *sequence*, and so milestones can be used not only to compare a child to others of a similar age but also to predict what developmental changes will occur next and to provide appropriate stimulation and parental guidance for the next stage. Structured developmental assessments such as can be obtained by use of the Denver Developmental Screening Test (DDST) (see Figs. 6-5 and 6-6) permit the nurse both to identify deviations from normal development and to give anticipatory guidance to parents. In other words, developmental assessments help the nurse to prevent

Figure 7-3 Physical, psychological, social, cognitive, and the other aspects of development occur simultaneously. This kind of play, for example, involves exercise and motor coordination; cognitive experience in how things work; perceptual learning about colors, textures, and judging distances; and practice in imitating adult roles.

or minimize developmental disability by early detection and to promote wellness.[2]

6. Growth and development progress from head to toe (cephalocaudally)

This principle is true both before and after birth. For example, the head and upper body portions are relatively large in the fetus and develop before the lower parts. The infant first learns head control, then trunk control, and then control of the legs.

7. Growth and development progress from the body midline toward the periphery (proximodistally)

Body parts near the infant's midline mature and develop before the areas farther away from the midline. Even in utero, the vital organs within the trunk develop before the limb buds form. Arm and hand control precede finger coordination, so that the infant uses sweeping and raking gestures to acquire a desired object, then a whole-hand grasp to pick it up, and finally a pincer grasp that involves thumb and forefinger.

8. Development progresses from simple to complex and from general to specific

The child's maturation and development become increasingly advanced and specialized as time passes. For example, development proceeds from simple to complex in utero when the heart, originally a simple, one-chambered tube, evolves into a more complex, four-chambered structure. The child's language also obviously develops from simple to complex. The child forms sounds, syllables, words, short sentences, and then several sentences. An example of the way development goes from general to specific is easily seen in the way an infant reacts at first to stimuli with a general response and later with a specific response. A young infant reacts to a noise with the entire body (the Moro reflex); only later does the baby turn the eyes and head toward the noise, a more specific response.

9. Children's behavior is directed toward competency

A child has an inherent drive toward normal, competent behavior. Competent behavior includes activities that ensure survival and those that promote independence and self-knowledge. Even a neonate demonstrates competence: The rooting reflex enables the newborn to locate food, and the pleasurable feelings that follow strengthen the quest for food. Recognizing the mother's face and odor promote attachment, and attachment enhances the child's access to further food and parenting.

Children have a strong drive to overcome genetic and environmental obstacles. Children raised under inadequate circumstances are remarkably resilient and strive toward competency when given even minimal opportunities. Nurses need to remember this. Nurses too often focus on the pathological, the weaknesses, instead of equally emphasizing the child's and family's strengths and competencies. Focusing on strengths builds trust, increases competence, promotes independence, and promotes the expectation of success.

Stages of development

The commonalities among children at specific ages have led developmentalists to classify growth and development into stages. The following stages, based strictly on age, are very commonly used by health professionals, educators, and others who work with children.

Stage	Age
Prenatal	Before birth
Neonatal	Birth to 28 days (1 month)
Infant	1 to 12 months
Toddler	1 to 3 years
Preschooler	3 to 6 years
School-age	6 to 12 years
Adolescent	12 to 18 years

Stage theories of development Other developmental stages that are not so rigidly based on age are also widely used. For example, Freud's, Piaget's, and Erikson's theories classify development into sequential stages that are linked roughly but not precisely to age. Each stage is typified by (and named for) some predominant developmental task or other developmental characteristic that makes it distinctive from earlier and later stages. Each stage builds on the foundations established in previous stages. The child who succeeds at accomplishing the tasks of a particular stage is prepared to succeed at the next stage. If he or she has failed to master the present stage, success in later stages will be more difficult. At each stage new areas of development become organized and consolidated into orderly patterns of behavior. During each stage, the child builds more complex activities on old foundations. The present stage is thus linked to the past and prepares or hinders the child for future development.[3]

Critical periods A *critical period*, also called *sensitive period*, is a specific time period when the child is most vulnerable or sensitive to a particular incoming stimulus. The same stimulus provided before or after the critical period will have less impact on the child.

Critical periods are clearly demonstrated in embryology. A critical period exists for cell specialization. For example, if a brain cell is transplanted to the kidney before the critical period for specialization begins, it will take on the characteristics of a kidney cell. If the brain cell is transplanted after the specialization period, it will not adopt the characteristics of the new location but will continue as a brain cell. The first trimester of pregnancy is the period of inital development (formation) of the organ systems. At this time the embryo and fetus are especially vulnerable to harmful stimuli such as the rubella virus. Unborn infants exposed in the first trimester to the rubella virus may develop cataracts, deafness, cardiac abnormalities, and mental retardation. Exposure to rubella after the critical period, when the body organs are less vulnerable, does not cause such severe defects. Critical periods also exist for visual development and color perception. The neonate must be stimulated with color during the first 2 weeks of life for optimal development of the cones and rods of the eye.

Critical periods also seem to exist for psychological development. Klaus and Kennell[4] believe a critical period exists for mother-child bonding (attachment). Knowledge of critical periods enables the nurse to prioritize nursing care by listing the critical phenomenon at the top of the nursing care plan. If the neonate is in the critical period for attachment, the nurse plans nursing interventions to promote attachment. These interventions include providing skin-to-skin contact in the delivery room; promoting early contact between mother, father, and child; assessing attachment behavior; and providing continuous contact through rooming in and maximum mother-child interaction (see Chaps. 10 and 11). The attachment period used to be designated as ages 3 to 6 months. More recent research indicates that it begins within minutes after birth.

Theories of behavioral development

A *theory* is an unproved speculation about probable cause-and-effect relationships among a series of events. When a theory is proven, it becomes fact. None of the theories discussed here has been conclusively proven. All are speculative outgrowths of the theorists' observational studies. Each observer is, in turn, an outgrowth of his own upbringing, culture, socioeconomic class, and era. Each theorist's conclusions reflect his own "universe" and contain personal biases. For this reason, theories should never be taken as ironclad, eternal rules for normal development. Small portions of theories should not be used to explain a child's total development. No theory explains all behavior, growth, and development.

Freudian theory

Sigmund Freud (1856–1939) was an Austrian physician whose revolutionary ideas about behavior gained popularity in the United States during the 1930s and have had worldwide impact. He founded the method of treatment known as psychoanalysis. Freud conceived the following psychiatric concepts. He related increased anxiety to threatened self-image; stated that *all* behavior has meaning; theorized that emotions, thoughts, and strivings originate in the unconscious; defined defense mechanisms; proposed that dreams are communicators of unconscious thought; and conceptualized the unconscious mind and stage theories of sexual development. Freud taught that adult behavior originates in childhood.

The acceptance of Freudian theory today is controversial. Some people consider Freud's theories to be outmoded, constricted by Freud's Victorian society, and nonscientific. Freud trained in neurology and treated adult nervous disorders; he did not study children directly. Other people believe that Freudian theory is a sound and fully developed approach to an understanding of behavior. Freud's beliefs are included here because of their familiarity in American life and because they are a basis upon which later theories have been built by others.

Freudian theory focuses upon studying and understanding the person's innermost, personal strivings, thoughts, and experiences. Because adult behavior and mental illness are believed to originate in childhood, parent-child interactions are thoroughly explored to discover the cause of the present behavior. Data are collected through remembering and *free association* (thoughts emerging spontaneously into awareness). Children are observed through nondirective play (see Chap. 16) because the child's innermost thoughts are expressed during play. Thus Freudian theory focuses upon the person's inner motivations rather than on interactions with society and culture.

Freud stressed that anxiety is the major motivation for behavior. Anxiety, which is increased when the person's self-esteem is threatened, has its origins in the unconscious. Freud delineated the *defense mechanisms*, or the unconscious methods used by the person to ward off threats to self-esteem. These mechanisms are used by children and adults to distort reality in order to decrease anxiety. (See psychology books for discussions of defense mechanisms.)

Freud sensed a polarity of opposing forces in human development: a drive toward pleasure opposing a "death wish," or unconscious drive to destroy oneself and others. Pleasurable feelings result in gratification and reduce anxiety.

Freud's theory can be divided into two main topics: *consciousness* and *personality*.

Consciousness The mind is comprised of conscious, unconscious, and preconscious portions. The *conscious* mind contains all the thoughts, feelings, actions, and strivings that can be easily remembered. The *preconscious* contains thoughts and experiences that are difficult, but possible, to remember. The *unconscious* portion contains thoughts, feelings, and memories still more difficult to bring into conscious awareness without special help, as from a psychoanalyst. Even if a person were presented with these unconscious experiences, they would usually not be recognized. Extremely threatening experiences and thoughts are *repressed*, or "buried," in the unconscious. These unconscious thoughts are believed by Freudians to be a major influence on behavior. Dreams, irrational fears, slips of the tongue ("Freudian slips"), selective forgetting, and tics are believed to reveal unconscious wishes when carefully analyzed. The belief that all behavior is meaningful is based upon the conviction that behavior reflects unconscious wishes.

Personality Freud found it useful to imagine the personality as embracing three parts: id, ego, and superego. The *id* is believed to be a seething vortex of life energy, primitive impulses, and passions. It strives for immediate achievement of its goals, no matter what the cost. The id drives take the form of urges to kill, to steal, to enjoy, and to destroy. Thoughts originating in the id motivate one to seek food, to satisfy greed, and to obtain sexual gratification. These feelings are believed to be present in the infant at birth and to be a source of the child's (and adult's) motives and energies.

The *ego* is the reality-based, executive manager of the personality. It mediates the opposing urges of the id and those of the superego, the ethical-moral unit. The ego is rational, assesses reality, and enables the individual to react in socially acceptable ways to make gratification possible without overwhelming guilt. It houses personality functions necessary to maintain contact with reality and the environment: memory, intelligence, thinking, analytical problem solving, learning, distinguishing reality from fantasy, and directing body movement. The ego is thought to begin developing during infancy.

The *superego* is essentially the conscience or moral-ethical portion of the personality. It is formed as a result of the child's socialization, as he internalizes the parents' values, customs, standards, and beliefs (see Chap. 13). The superego shows in the toddler and preschooler as they learn acceptable behavior. In the preschooler, the superego is rigid, tyrannical, and cruel, only later becoming flexible and tolerant. It is the "inner voice" that opposes the id's wishes: "Don't kick your father. He won't like it and will spank you." The superego exercises control by generating guilt.

Freud divided the life span into five stages, listed in Table 7-1. He believed sexual energy to be a main motivator of behavior. He originally called this sexual energy *libido*. It was a broad definition meant to include basic psychic energy, or *life force*, incorporating sexual drive, which directs the person's development through stages of development.[5] At each stage, the psychic energy is focused upon a body region (*erogenous zone*) that is the main source of pleasure and gratification; each stage is named for the dominant body region. (See Table 7-1.)

Freudian psychoanalysts believe the personality is essentially formed by the end of the phallic period. The personality develops through the child's response to physiological growth, frustrations, conflicts, and threats.[6] Freud believed that a person who mastered all stages of personality development would be emotionally mature.

Later psychoanalysts have added social and cultural aspects to Freud's basic tenets. These psychoanalysts include Alfred Adler, Karen Horney, Carl Jung, Harry Stack Sullivan, and Erik Erikson.

Eriksonian theory

Erik H. Erikson (b. 1902) is a psychoanalyst who has added a new dimension to the work of Freud: society. He considers Freud's work to be a rock upon which later theoretical advances are

Table 7-1 Psychoanalytical (Freudian) stages of development

Stage of development	Time frame	Characteristics	Examples of unsuccessful experience
Oral	Birth to 18 months	Learning to deal with anxiety-producing experiences by using the mouth and tongue	Defenses centered around oral experiences: smoking, alcoholism, obesity, nail-biting, drug addiction, difficulty with trust
Anal	18 months to 3 years	Learning muscle control, especially that involved with urination and defecation	Defenses centered around holding on and letting go: constipation, obsessive-compulsive personality, fastidiousness, perfection drive
Phallic	3 to 6 years	Learning sexual identity and developing awareness of the genital area	Difficulty with sexual identity: transsexuality, difficulty with authority, homosexuality, Oedipus complex (erotic attachment of male child to mother), Electra complex (erotic attachment of female child to father)
Latency	6 to 12 years	Quiet stage during which sexual development lies dormant	Defenses centered on inability to conceptualize: lack of self-motivation in school and job.
Genital	12 years to early adulthood	Developing sexual maturity and learning to develop satisfactory relationships with the opposite sex	Unsatisfactory relationships with the opposite sex: frigidity, impotence, premature ejaculation, serial marriages

From Pamela Ruffin, "Theoretical Models," in Judith Haber et al., *Comprehensive Psychiatric Nursing*, McGraw-Hill, New York, 1978, p. 35. Used with permission.

built. Unlike Freud, Erikson has extensively studied children.

Erikson sees development as a lifelong process under the influences of heredity, society, and culture. He believes that the child's hereditary blueprint and social and cultural influences are inseparably intertwined to form the personality.[7] According to Erikson, the child learns to balance inner wishes with outer reality through interactions with the environment.[8]

Erikson divided the life span into eight stages. (See Table 7-2.) Each stage contains a predominant "crisis" to be resolved in order to prepare a firm foundation for success in later stages. The developmental crisis of each stage consists of two opposing favorable and unfavorable potential outcomes. Erikson believes anxiety results from not mastering the crisis of a stage and that unless the favorable alternative is better developed than the unfavorable one, subsequent development will be difficult. Erikson thus retained Freud's stage format and the concept of polarity or opposing forces. Erikson further believes an inherent drive toward mastery coexists with a desire to regress to an earlier time of comfort and security.[9]

The theories of Erikson differ from Freud in three main ways:

1. Erikson believes the ego, not the id, is the main motivating force in human development. By focusing on the ego, he stresses realistic, healthy behavior; socialization (learning acceptable behavior sanctioned by society); and the ego's relationship with society, culture, and the environment. In contrast, Freud focused upon inner motivations and struggles.

2. Erikson focuses on the child's relationship with parents and family within their culture. He believes the child and family develop together; the action of one influences the other. He addresses social, political, and moral upheavals and the wide diversity of opinions in our society and discusses these pressures on the individual. His theory integrates insights from anthropology, social psychology, the arts, and child development. Freud, in contrast, focused on the drive of psychic energy and an inner, almost mystical, power struggle among id, ego, and superego.

3. Erikson focuses upon the healthy personality. In contrast, Freud dealt primarily with psychopathology. Erikson believes opportunities exist throughout the life span to master a developmental crisis. Each new life phase presents an older crisis in a subordinate position, disguised in new form. His theory is hopeful, for new opportunities are presented to rework older, unmastered crises. The

ultimate goal of development is thought to be a strong identity, healthy body, and a discerning, creative, and curious mind.[10]

Erikson's theory has been widely adopted by nursing and other health professions. His theory provides a useful pattern for observing behavior. However, Erikson is criticized for not describing the precise behaviors indicating whether or not mastery of the crisis has been accomplished. With no exact behaviors to assess, further testing and validation of his observations are difficult.

Piagetian theory

Jean Piaget (1896–1980) was a Swiss psychologist who pioneered the study of children's cognitive development. *Cognitive development* is the development of thinking, or the process of knowing. Early in his life, Piaget became very interested in psychoanalysis but preferred to study the normal development of thinking and intelligence. He extensively studied large groups of children throughout the world. The data collected worldwide coincide with the data he initially collected from his own children. Piaget thus extensively studied children in order to discover "how we know."[11]

Piaget believed each child has an inherent biological blueprint that outlines his or her intellectual potential. Whether or not the child reaches that potential depends upon stimulation from the environment. He believed that children's thoughts are derivatives of motor actions which began in utero. He stressed that experiences are the roots of all later, more complex thoughts. Children learn by *"experiencing their experiences."* Thus, experiences, not maturation, are the foundations of cognitive development.[12]

Children are active learners and seekers of new experiences. Piaget believed that each child knows best what he or she needs and is always ready to learn more.[13] Each child seems to have an inherent need to make sense out of the environment. As soon as one problem is solved,

Table 7-2 Erikson's psychosocial development

Stage of development	Approximate time frame	Development tasks	Examples
Sensory	Birth to 18 months	Trust vs. mistrust	Experiences with the nurturing person are the foundations of the level of trust a person will develop.
Muscular	1 to 3 years	Autonomy vs. shame and doubt	The toddler learns the extent to which the environment can be influenced by direct manipulation.
Locomotor	3 to 6 years	Initiative vs. guilt	The child learns the extent to which being assertive will influence environment. If important others disapprove of beginning assertiveness, the child will experience guilt.
Latency	6 to 12 years	Industry vs. inferiority	Either the child learns to utilize energies to create, develop, and manipulate, or the child learns to shy away from industry, feeling inadequate to the task.
Adolescent	12 to 20 years	Identity vs. role diffusion	The adolescent either integrates all life experiences into a coherent sense of self or is unable to integrate these experiences and feels lost and confused.
Young adulthood	18 to 25 years	Intimacy vs. isolation	The young adult is primarily concerned with developing an intimate relationship with another person.
Adulthood	21 to 45 years	Generativity vs. stagnation	The adult is primarily concerned with establishing a family and guiding the next generation.
Maturity	45 years to death	Integrity vs. despair	The life-style gives life meaning and the person must come to accept his or her life as fulfilling and meaningful. The lack of ego integration results in fear of death.

From Pamela Price, "Theoretical Models," in Judith Haber et al., *Comprehensive Psychiatric Nursing*, McGraw-Hill, New York, 1978, p. 37. Used with permission.

the child turns to new experiences.[14] As the child associates thoughts in an organized and increasingly complex manner, he or she learns to deal more effectively with the environment and distinguish reality from fantasy. The child's intellectual capacity depends mainly on the developing cognitive ability to organize the environment.

The following are basic concepts of Piaget.

1. Development is continually evolving and occurs in a predictable, sequential order.
2. New schemata (see below) are introduced within the existing structure, are consolidated, and equilibrium is reestablished. This process repeats continually.
3. Each new developmental phase builds upon previous learning in earlier stages. Piaget thus retains Freud's concept of stage theories.
4. Each new phase has a period of learning and forming, followed by a period of attainment.
5. New organizations of thoughts are increasingly complex and build a hierarchy.
6. Each person will achieve an individual level of development though all have the same potential.[15]
7. The goal of cognitive development is to attain emotional, biological, and intellectual balance.

There are two important ideas to grasp in understanding the basis of Piaget's theory.* These are what he terms *function* and *structure*. The *process* of interaction between child and environment is what Piaget calls *function*. There are two major functions or tendencies that govern how a child interacts with the environment: organization and adaptation.[16]

Organization refers to the biological way in which the infant is organized. It refers to the tendency to combine two schemata into a more complex schema (see below). Think of the baby's mind as a computer with the program representing the organizational function or the way in which information is processed by the infant. If the child reaches for a toy, the act of reaching (first schema) is coordinated with seeing the toy (a second schema) and the motivation to get the toy.

The second major function governing the child's interaction with the environment is *adaptation*. The adaptation process describes the way in which the child maintains a balanced orga-

nization and creates new structures to interact effectively with the environment. There are two parts to adaptation—assimilation and accommodation. According to Piaget, these processes are interrelated and operate simultaneously. *Assimilation* refers to the mental process of taking in new information and interpreting it in light of past experiences. In other words, the child uses old thoughts and actions to understand new events. *Accommodation* is changing earlier ideas or actions (schemata) to better meet or adapt to a new situation or to solve a more complex problem. An example from biological sciences that might help to illustrate would be the infant's taking in breast milk. The baby's digestive system is functional in that it breaks down the milk to elements that are then assimilated into the infant's body. When we introduce solid foods, however, the infant must accommodate by producing new gastric juices to digest the food. This is very close to what Piaget means when he uses the terms *assimilation* and *accommodation*. The two processes are always going on together. In our example above, as long as only breast milk is given, the infant may be assimilating more than accommodating. When solids are first given there may be a period where there is accommodating more than assimilating. The two processes may not always be in balance. The child at play is assimilating more than accommodating. He is acting on information that is already a part of him. When the child imitates, he is accommodating more than assimilating. The behavior is new and does not stem from an integration of his own experiences.

Those processes of function (accommodation and assimilation) are constant—are always going on in the same way. (See Fig. 7-4.) Structure, however, is continuously changing and that change is what accounts for development. Structure refers to a structural framework that information must fit into in order to be assimilated. Visualize structure as the structural framework of a building under construction. New information coming into the child must have the potential to relate to past experience or thoughts as the child has organized them, just as new additions to the building under construction must fit onto the basic framework. Think of your own learning and this may become clearer. Information you learned in a lecture may not be meaningful or "stick" until you are in the situation where you can see its usefulness. The

---

* The remainder of this discussion of Piaget is by Ann Sloat.

Figure 7-4 Interaction with the physical and social environment is a major source of learning; each child continually influences and is influenced by the surroundings.

1. Sensorimotor period, which lasts approximately the first 1½ to 2 years of life
2. Preoperational period, which lasts from 1½ or 2 years of age to 6 or 7 years
3. Concrete operations period, which encompasses middle childhood from age 6 or 7 to age 11 or 12 years
4. Formal operations period, which spans the ages of 11 or 12 years to about 15 years and brings the individual to the level of adult thought

Piagetian development is further discussed in Chaps. 10 through 15.

Cognitive development has prime importance for nurses and all adults working with children. Once the adult knows how a child associates thoughts, how he interprets adults' words and events in the environment, the adult can choose words and phrases to best communicate with the child. The adult can interpret what the child is really saying. An adult who has studied Piaget's work will never again communicate with children in the same way.

structure of your thoughts has been organized and reorganized to finally show where the information fits. The same thing is going on with infants' and children's thinking. This organization and reorganization of structure is always in the direction of seeking a balance, or equilibrium. As the structure approaches equilibrium, it becomes sharper and more delineated. As this happens, inconsistencies and gaps of information become apparent and the child's activities are directed toward filling in the gaps.

Cognitive development, then, consists of a series of changes. These changes are orderly, structural, and directional in that they move toward seeking equilibrium. Piaget uses the term *schema* (plural, *schemata*) to describe the units of thought in the structure. A *schema* is an organized pattern of behavior or action (a habit). It is a concept of experiences, the child's way of organizing or classifying earlier sensory events.[17] Each new schema or reorganization of structure incorporates the one before it.

The sequence of development is orderly and recognizable from one child to the next. Piaget describes this progression in terms of periods, subperiods, and stages. The basic periods are:

References

1. Debra P. Hymovich and Robert W. Chamberlin, *Child and Family Development, Implications for Primary Care*, McGraw-Hill, New York, 1980, p. 1.
2. Sharon R. Stangler et al., *Screening Growth and Development of Preschool Children: A Guide for Test Selection*, McGraw-Hill, New York, 1980, p. 1.
3. Mollie S. Smart and Russell C. Smart, *Children*, Macmillan, New York, 1972, p. 647.
4. Marshall H. Klaus and John H. Kennell, *Maternal-Infant Bonding*, Mosby, St. Louis, 1976, p. 14.
5. Henry W. Maier, *Three Theories of Child Development*, Harper & Row, New York, 1978, p. 81.
6. Hymovich et al., op. cit., p. 5.
7. Maier, op. cit., pp. 79, 81.
8. Ibid., pp. 75–76.
9. Ibid., p. 81.
10. Ibid., pp. 75–76.
11. Ibid., pp. 13, 16.
12. Ibid., p. 21.
13. Ibid., p. 20.
14. Ruth Ault, *Children's Cognitive Development, Piaget's Theory and the Process Approach*, Oxford, New York, 1977, pp. 12, 13.
15. Maier, op. cit., p. 29.
16. Ault, op. cit., p. 18.
17. Ibid., p. 87.

Chapter 8 **Human genetics**

Marjorie J. Smith

Upon completion of this chapter, the student will be able to:

1. Define terms used to describe genetic diseases.
2. Contrast the terms *DNA*, *gene*, and *chromosome*.
3. Compare mitosis and meiosis.
4. Describe the significance of nondisjunction and translocation in chromosomal abnormalities.
5. Diagram the inheritance pattern for (1) an autosomal dominant disorder, (2) an autosomal recessive disorder, and

(3) an X-linked recessive disorder in a carrier mother and affected male.
6. List three inborn errors of metabolism.
7. List three polygenic disorders.
8. List four environmental factors that influence genetic expression.
9. Describe the nurse's role in genetic evaluation.

Nurses who work with children and their families are asked many questions about the children's development, characteristics, and illness. In the case of hospitalized children, what is often behind these questions is the concern that heredity is involved in the illness and that in some way the parents are responsible. Nurses must understand the role of heredity in disease. Disease is part of a complex interplay between heredity and the environment. The hereditary (genetic) influence may be great and the environmental one slight, as in Down syndrome and in many of the conditions discussed in this chapter. The reverse may also be true, as in infections, some congenital defects, and multifactorial disorders (Table 8-1).

Inherited disease can be evident at birth or can appear later in development. Below are

examples of inherited characteristics that become evident at different stages of an individual's development:[1]

1. Polydactyly (extra fingers and toes): early embryonic stage
2. Eye pigmentation: a few days or weeks after birth
3. Tay-Sachs disease: about 1 year of age
4. X-linked muscular dystrophy: 10 to 15 years of age
5. Hereditary baldness: 25 to 50 years of age
6. Huntington's chorea (progressive mental and nervous deterioration): 30 to 50 years of age

Genetics and information transfer

Genetics concerns the flow of biological information from one generation to the next. Humans have always found this subject intriguing. Most

Table 8-1 Terms used in describing inherited disorders

Congenital defect

A condition present at birth that may be caused by genetic factors or by such environmental factors as irradiation, infection, trauma, or chemicals

Familial disorder

Any defect or disorder that appears more often in a family than would be predicted by chance

Genetic disorder

Any disorder due to:
1. A chromosome abnormality
2. A single mutant gene (e.g., Mendelian disorders)
3. Multiple *mutant genes* (polygenic)
4. Multifactorial causes (combination of genetic and environmental factors)

Inherited

Same as genetic. Also called heritable, hereditary. Transmitted by genes from parent to offspring

often our interest takes the form of deciding which parent contributed to a child's physical features, intelligence, or special skills. Little scientific knowledge was available about genetic information transfer before the development of the microscope in the 1600s. Afterward some curious theories were developed about which parent was responsible for the genetic endowment of the child. Near the end of the century a Swiss naturalist claimed to have seen a miniature human, which he termed a *homunculus*, in sperm cells. This "preformed" adult had merely to grow to become a full-sized human. Others thought that the homunculus existed in the ovum instead.

In the nineteenth century it became clear that fertilization produces a zygote that divides many times, leading to development of the embryo, fetus, and finally the infant. For a time it was widely believed that the blood carried hereditary factors that somehow entered the fertilized egg. From this notion comes such expressions as "It's in his blood," "blue blood," and "blood brothers."

In 1865 Gregor Mendel, an Augustinian monk, after carefully breeding peas over 8 years and analyzing the results mathematically, announced that inheritance of traits followed a predictable pattern; there are *laws* of heredity. His highly original contribution was neglected until 1900 but then, upon "rediscovery," accelerated the pace of genetic investigations. Since

then much has become clear about the physical basis of heredity.

Physical basis of heredity

Chromosomes—the carriers

The actual units of inheritance, the genes, reside on *chromosomes*, the coiled threadlike bodies in the cell nucleus. As genes are too small to be seen, for a long time their nature could only be deduced from experiments with chromosomes. Using fruit flies and certain plants, investigators, especially after 1900, built up a considerable knowledge of both genes and chromosomes from observable traits.

Information about human chromosomes, more difficult to isolate and to visualize, accumulated slowly. Only in 1956 was it determined that the normal human body cell contains 46 chromosomes. Human gametes, the sperm and ova, contain half that number, but in sexual union the male gamete's 23 chromosomes join the female's 23 in the fertilized cell, or *zygote*, which then has the normal complement of 46 chromosomes. The term *diploid* refers to the normal complement of chromosomes in body cells (46) and *haploid* to the normal number in mature gametes (23).

After staining, the 46 chromosomes can be grouped by shape into 22 pairs of autosomes and two sex chromosomes. The sex chromosomes look alike in the female but are unalike in the male. They are symbolized XX in the female, but XY in the male. It is the Y chromosome that determines maleness.

When a photograph of stained chromosomes is cut up and all the chromosomes from a single body cell are arranged by size and shape, the result is known as a *karyotype*. For a normal female it is expressed as 46,XX. Figure 8-1 shows a normal female karyotype and the original picture from which it was prepared. One member of each homologous (matching) pair is from the mother and one is from the father.

Genes—the units of heredity

Every chromosome carries hundreds of genes. A single gene is said to reside at a *point* or *locus* on a chromosome. As chromosomes come in pairs, there is a gene at the corresponding locus on the other member of the pair. Either member of a gene pair can be referred to as an *allele*.

If both alleles are alike, that is, produce an identical trait, the person is *homozygous* for the trait. If they are not alike, the individual is *heterozygous* for the trait.

In a heterozygous person, the allele that is expressed is *dominant;* the unexpressed, nonidentical allele is *recessive.* The latter exists in the *genotype,* the genetic makeup of the person, but not in the *phenotype,* the observable traits. A child's genotype may include a gene for black hair, for instance, and a corresponding allele for blond hair. As black is dominant, black hair will be part of the phenotype, but the genotype remains a mixture of genes for both black and blond hair. The child would be blond (phenotype) only if he or she were homozygous for the trait, that is, if all alleles were for blond hair. Some traits that display these simple Mendelian patterns are shown in Fig. 8-2. Current information suggests that several genes may determine hair or eye color.

DNA—chemical basis of the gene

Intensive research in the 1940s led to the conclusion that genetic information is stored in the DNA (deoxyribonucleic acid) of the chromosomes. In 1953 Francis Crick and James Watson announced their finding that DNA is actually a double strand resembling a twisted stepladder, a shape that chemists call a *double helix* (Fig. 8-3). The vertical sides are sugars and phosphates; the rungs are small molecules known as bases, linked at the middle by hydrogen bonds. Buried in this complex shape in coded form is the cell's genetic message, the information that dictates its nature and that serves to regulate and direct its functions.

A gene has been defined as a length of DNA that directs the manufacture of a polypeptide. Long polypeptide molecules are proteins. Protein synthesis is an important task directed by DNA.

Proteins are unique molecules of the body. They may be "structural" (such as keratin, collagen, and elastin) or "functional" (as in antibodies, hormones, and enzymes). Protein synthesis is directed by DNA but employs many other molecules, including amino acids, which serve as building blocks of polypeptides (Fig. 8-4).

A second vital function of DNA is the transfer of the genotype from one cell generation to the next. It does this shortly before each cell division. The double strand of chromosomal DNA comes

Figure 8-1 Normal female 46,XX. The X chromosomes are marked with arrows. A karyotype is prepared from lymphocytes or fibroblasts cultured from skin, gonad, or amniotic cells. The cells are grown in a nutrient medium and stimulated to undergo mitosis. Colchicine is applied to stop growth in metaphase, when the chromosomes are contracted and duplicated. Chemicals are added to cause swelling and enhance visibility. A photograph is taken of the magnified chromosomes (top half of figure). Then the chromosomes are cut from the picture, matched into homologous pairs, and numbered. The resultant arrangement of homologous chromosomes is known as a *karyotype.* (*Courtesy of Dr. Gordon DeWald, Rochester, Minnesota.*)

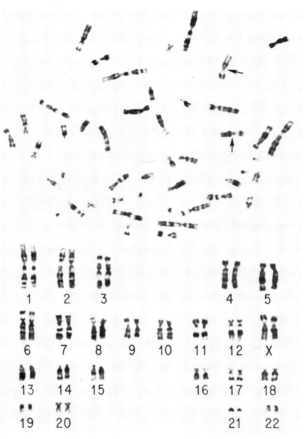

apart. Each strand acts as a template, or model, on which molecules from the cell are assembled to reproduce the missing strand. This self-reproduction is known as *replication.* As replication must precede each cell division, it is remarkable that a person's genotype can be carried faithfully through the many thousands of cell divisions that begin with the zygote. It is little wonder that

Figure 8-2 Some simple Mendelian traits found in humans. (*Source: Ana Pai, Foundations of Genetics, McGraw-Hill, New York, 1974. Used with permission.*)

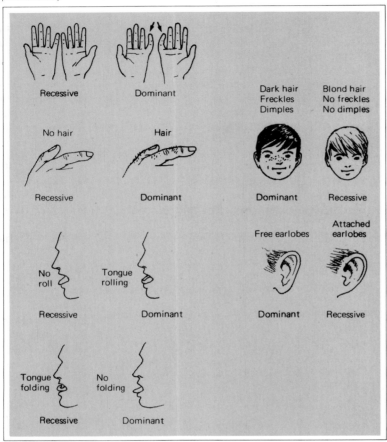

copying errors or other changes occasionally take place, as will be discussed under inborn errors of metabolism.

Cell division

While it is true that cell division is not the only time when genetic changes, or *mutations*, as they are known, occur, the cell engaged in reproducing itself is peculiarly vulnerable to chance occurrences and outside influences. There are two types of cell division, *mitosis* and *meiosis*. *Mitosis* is responsible for cellular growth. *Meiosis* is responsible for reproduction and genetic variation.

Mitosis

In all multicellular organisms, dividing cells undergo *mitosis*. Figure 8-5 shows mitosis in a cell that has a diploid number of four chromosomes. During the first step of mitosis, *prophase*, chromosomes in the cell nucleus form a two-stranded coil and take on a short, thick appearance. The constricted portion where the two strands join is called the *centromere*.

During the second phase, *metaphase*, chromosomes line up across the middle of the cell (equatorial plate). *Anaphase* begins when the strands separate at the centromere. Each strand, now itself a chromosome, moves away from its partner toward opposite poles of the cell. In

Figure 8-3 The DNA molecule is a double helix composed of sugars and phosphates along the sides. The following bases make up the cross bars: adenine (A), thymine (T), guanine (G), cytosine (C). (*Source: E. Dickason and M. Schult, Maternal and Infant Care, McGraw-Hill, New York, 1979. Used with permission.*)

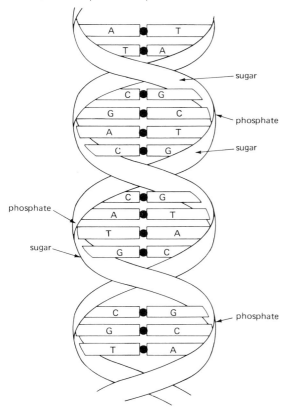

Meiosis with its reduction division serves an essential purpose. Mitosis without meiosis would leave gametes with 46 chromosomes and the fertilized egg would begin life with 92 chromosomes. Each cell of the new individual would contain 92 chromosomes. With sexual union the number would be doubled again. Clearly, cell function as we know it would be impossible.

In meiosis, prophase I brings paternal chromosomes opposite homologous maternal chromosomes in a tight pairing known as *synapsis.* The nuclear membrane dissolves and spindle fibers attach to the centromeres.

During metaphase I the homologous pairs arrange themselves across the middle of the cell. In anaphase I the pairs separate and move to opposite poles. Note that the chromosomes do not split lengthwise at the centromere; therefore, no doubling of the chromosome number occurs as in mitosis. Telophase I is very brief and the cell completes its first meiotic division, the reduction division, in which each daughter cell

Figure 8-4 Protein synthesis employs messenger ribonucleic acid (mRNA) as the intermediary. In *transcription* mRNA takes the genetic message from DNA in the cell nucleus. In *translation* the message is used to direct protein synthesis in the cytoplasm.

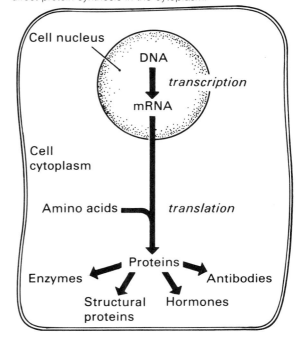

telophase, the cell nucleus is re-established and the cell prepares to divide. Cell division occurs next. Each resulting cell has a diploid number of four chromosomes that are identical to those of the parent cell.

Meiosis

Production of sperm and ova entails a unique additional step, a reduction division. The number of chromosomes provided by each parent cell is thereby reduced to one-half in the mature gamete. In human beings this means that, while the sex cell begins with 46 chromosomes, the gametes produced contain 23 chromosomes. The overall process is called *meiosis* (Fig. 8-5), of which reduction division is one step.

Figure 8-5 Comparison of *mitosis* in somatic cells with *meiosis* in reproductive cells in an organism (fruit fly) with a *diploid number of four*. (*Source: Ana Pai, Foundations of Genetics, McGraw-Hill, New York, 1974. Used with permission.*)

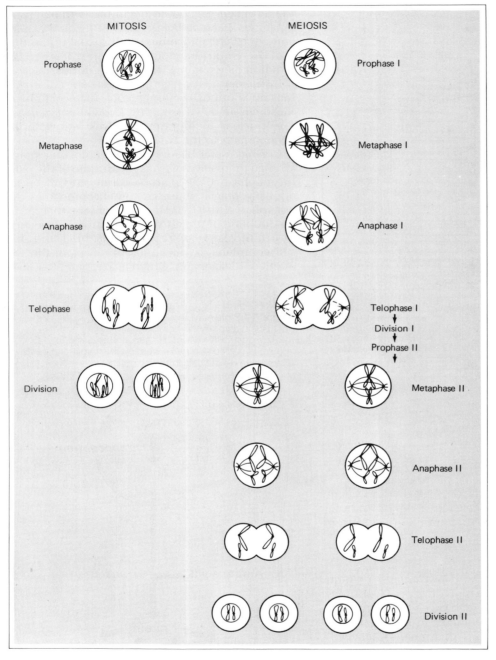

contains half the number of chromosomes of the parent cell.

The second meiotic division begins in the daughter cells immediately. In prophase II the pairs condense again and in metaphase II line up along the cell's equator. This time the centromere divides and daughter chromosomes move to opposite poles in anaphase II. In telophase II the nuclear membrane re-forms around the nuclear substance at each pole, and the second cell division follows. This division is not a reduction division; the haploid condition of the parent cell is preserved in the daughter cells. However, there are significant differences between sperm and ova in the details of maturation (Fig. 8-6).

Spermatogenesis begins in the testes at puberty. Sexually mature males continuously produce sperm; however, the lifetime supply of oocytes is present in the female at birth. They remain arrested at prophase I until puberty. Then, as each ovarian follicle matures, meiotic division resumes and is completed at the time of ovulation. The older a woman is, therefore,

Figure 8-6 Spermatogenesis and oogenesis. In preparation for fertilization sperm and ovum go through the process of meiosis, in which the number of chromosomes is reduced from 23 pairs (2n) to 23n. The four spermatozoa resulting from sperm maturation are all capable of reproducing. Of the four cells resulting from maturation of the ovum, however, three of the nuclei are not supplied with cytoplasm and become polar bodies, leaving only *one* capable of being fertilized. (*Source: Ana Pai, Foundations of Genetics, McGraw-Hill, New York, 1974. Used with permission.*)

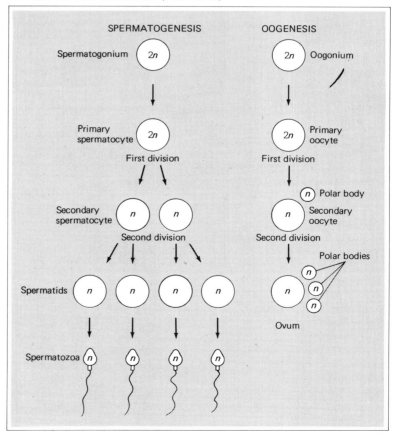

the older her ova are. There is evidence that, with increasing age, ova are more likely to carry abnormal chromosomes.

Chromosomal abnormalities

In a broad sense mutation refers to any change in genetic information, including addition or loss of chromosomes, alterations of chromosome structure, or changes within a gene.

Too much or too little chromosomal material in all or some of a person's cells leads to a clinical disorder. Chromosomal abnormalities have a significant impact on the individual, and therefore on the family of the individual and possibly even on society. Chromosomal alterations are:

1. Present in 6 to 7 of every 1000 live-born infants[2]
2. Responsible for 50 percent of all early spontaneous abortions[3]
3. Associated with 7 percent of perinatal mortalities[4]
4. Found in at least 10 percent of couples who give a history of *at least two* early abortions, stillbirths, or births with multiple congenital anomalies.[5]

Alterations in chromosomes usually involve either *number* or *structure*. The following types of chromosomal abnormalities are recognized:

1. Abnormal chromosome number—aneuploidy
   a. *Monosomy* The absence of *one* of a pair of chromosomes.
   b. *Trisomy* The presence of *three* chromosomes instead of the usual pair (Fig. 8-7).
   c. *Polyploidy* The presence of *extra sets* of chromosomes; a multiple of the haploid number. Polyploidy is common in plants but *lethal* in humans.
2. Abnormal morphology or structure
   a. *Deletions* The *absence* of part of a chromosome.
   b. *Reciprocal translocations* The *exchange* of chromosomal material between two nonhomologous chromosomes during cell division.
   c. *Inversion* During cell division a section of a chromosome breaks apart, turns end to end, and is reinserted, resulting in the reverse order of the genes.

Mechanisms of chromosome alteration

Nondisjunction Abnormal *numbers* of chromosomes usually result from an error during cell division. The most common cause of monosomy or trisomy is failure to separate, that is, *nondisjunction*, during the first or second division of meiosis (Fig. 8-8). If an ovum missing one chromosome is fertilized, the zygote, with 45 chromosomes, is said to be *monosomic*. Monosomy of the X chromosome is found both in spontaneously aborted fetuses and in live births. Monosomy of an autosome is lethal and so is found only in spontaneous abortions.

When an ovum with one extra chromosome is fertilized, the zygote, with 47 chromosomes, is said to be *trisomic*. It is also possible for a sperm to be responsible for the extra chromosome. Trisomy occurs in autosomes and sex chromosomes. Trisomy of autosomes 8, 13, 18, and 21 is seen in live infants. Trisomy of the larger chromosomes is usually lethal (see Table 8-2).

Nondisjunction may also occur during mitosis soon after the zygote has been created. This leads to the presence of at least two different cell lines, which is called *mosaicism* (Fig. 8-9). A person can be mosaic and have a normal phenotype, or can exhibit some abnormal traits. Most often, a mosaic person shows some signs that would be expected if the whole body were composed of cells bearing the abnormal chromosome number.

Translocation A *translocation* occurs when a part of a chromosome moves and attaches itself to another chromosome. Translocations change

Figure 8-7 Trisomy 21 karyotype from a male with Down syndrome. Note *three* No. 21 chromosomes. The shorthand description is 47,XY,+21. (*Courtesy of Dr. Gordon DeWald.*)

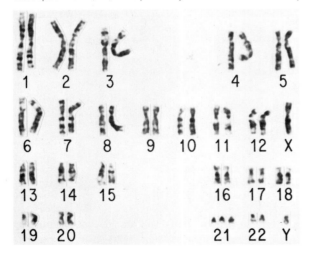

Figure 8-8 Nondisjunction at the first or second meiotic division. (*A*) The results of nondisjunction at the first meiotic division, which results in two cells having an extra chromosome (trisomy) and two having that chromosome missing (monosomy). (*B*) The results of nondisjunction at the second meiotic division. Here one cell is trisomic, one monosomic, and two normal. (*Adapted from Ana Pai, Foundations of Genetics, McGraw-Hill, New York, 1974. Used with permission.*)

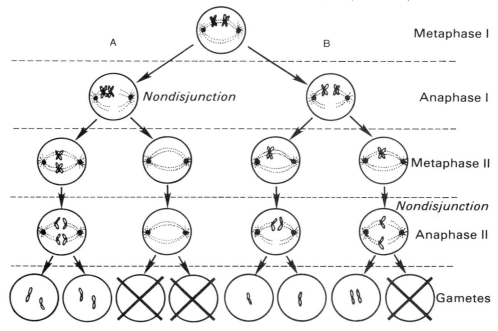

chromosome *structure*. They take place during cell division. Occasionally pieces of two nonhomologous chromosomes join to form a single chromosome. This is known as a *balanced translocation* (Fig. 8-10). As none of the genetic material is lost, the person whose cells carry such a translocation will appear normal, although the abnormal structure will be revealed in a karyotype. The significance of a balanced translocation appears in the next generation, when a person carrying this abnormal karyotype becomes a parent. If part of chromosome No. 21 becomes attached to 14 in the formation of gametes, both this 14-21 and a normal 21 may be passed to the child. If the other parent contributes a normal chromosome 21, the child will be trisomic for 21.

Deletion Structural defects of chromosomes are best understood as the consequence of breakage. Deletion occurs when one end of a chromosome breaks off and is lost. For example, deletion of the small arm of chromosome 5 results in the cri-du-chat syndrome (Table 8-2).

Trisomy 21

Trisomy 21 is one of the more common trisomies (Table 8-2). The clinical condition, which includes mental retardation and other defects, is known as *Down syndrome* (Fig. 8-11). An outmoded name for it is *mongolism*. The incidence of Down syndrome in relation to maternal age is described in Table 8-3. Recent data show a substantial decrease in the average age of mothers bearing Down syndrome babies. By the early 1970s only about 20 percent of such infants were born to mothers 35 years and older.[6] In the 1950s and 1960s 50 percent of Down syndrome babies were born to mothers in that age range.[7] This change may be due to fewer births after age 35, the declining birth rate in developed countries, liberalized abortion policies, and increased availability of prenatal diagnosis with amniocentesis. (In amniocentesis, cells shed by the growing fetus are withdrawn through the mother's abdomen from the amniotic sac by means of a large-bore needle and cultured. The cells and fluid can be analyzed for certain biochemical defects and chromosomal patterns.)

Table 8-2 Common chromosomal (autosomal) abnormalities*

Autosomal disorders	Abnormality	Incidence	Characteristic features	Genetic significance
Down syndrome	Trisomy 21	1:570 live births	Mental retardation; congenital anomalies; flat facial features; large protruding tongue; upward slanting eyes; prominent epicanthal folds; short, broad, stubby hands with simian crease; hypotonia; usually sterile but some females can reproduce with 50% risk of trisomic offspring	Related to advanced maternal age unless due to translocation (5–10%). Father has been shown to be source of extra chromosome in 24% of cases†
Edward syndrome	Trisomy 18	1:8000	Microcephaly; small eyes; deformed ears; small mouth; congenital heart disease; over-riding, clenched fingers; 85% die within 6 months; mental retardation	Related to advanced maternal age
Patau syndrome	Trisomy 13	1:6000	Microcephaly; microophthalmos; cleft lip and palate; low-set ears; congenital heart disease; polycystic kidneys; polydactyly; deafness; mental retardation	Death occurs in infancy without mosaicism. Related to advanced maternal age
Cri-du-chat syndrome	Deletion of short arm of No. 5	1:15,000	Severe mental retardation; microcephaly; weak, high-pitched cry due to hypoplasia of the larynx; low set ears; downward slanting eyes; retarded growth	10–15% due to inherited translocation
Warkany syndrome	Trisomy 8	Unknown	Growth and mental retardation; congenital skeletal defects and contractures; urinary tract anomaly; micrognathia	Due to mosaicism or to translocation

* Theoretically all are detectable in utero.

† L. B. Holmes, "Genetic Counseling for the Older Pregnant Woman: New Data and Questions," *New England Journal of Medicine* **298**(25): 1419 (June 1978).

Figure 8-9 Moisaicism due to nondisjunction during mitosis. In (*A*) one cell line is monosomic (45). If this involves an autosome, the cell line will not survive. However a mosaic with a cell line 45,X/47,XXY could survive. In (*B*) the cell line 45 will also not survive, but the individual would have two normal cell lines (46) and one with an extra chromosome (47). Survival is then possible if a small autosome or sex chromosome is involved.

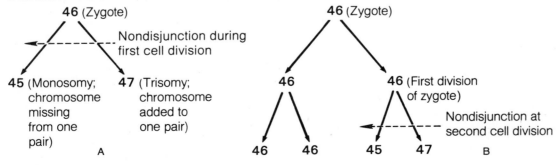

Holmes[8] reports that the father of the affected baby is the source of the extra chromosome in 24 percent of the cases studied. This information may cause revision of statistics of risk for the condition as a function only of maternal age. Honest genetic counseling of parents who have a baby with Down syndrome may free mothers from feeling solely responsible.

Nondisjunction causes 94 percent of trisomy 21 births. The risk in the general population for an offspring with trisomy 21 is 1 in 1000. If one parent's genotype contains a balanced translocation, however, the risk of a trisomic offspring increases greatly. When the father is the balanced translocation carrier, the chance of having a trisomic baby is 1 in 20, or 5 percent. For a carrier mother, the chance is 1 in 5, or 20 percent. Translocation is responsible for 5 percent of trisomy 21 births; mosaicism accounts for 1 percent.

Balanced translocations in close relatives of an affected child may also serve as a clue to increased risk of Down syndrome.

Figure 8-10 Trisomy 21 resulting from translocation of an extra chromosome 21 to chromosome 14. The father of this subject had one regular chromosome No. 21 and one No. 21 attached to chromosome No. 14. With only two No. 21 chromosomes the father had a *balanced* translocation and appeared normal. However, during spermatogenesis, the sperm received both the normal No. 21 chromosome and the No. 21 attached to the No. 14 chromosome. When this sperm fertilized an ovum containing one No. 21 chromosome, the resulting male child received *three* No. 21 chromosomes and is said to have an *unbalanced translocation*. This is written 46,XY, + 21. (*Courtesy of Dr. Gordon DeWald.*)

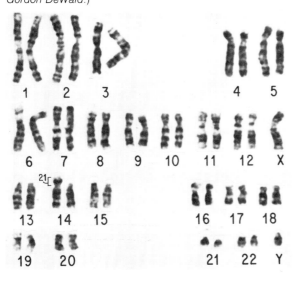

Figure 8-11 Child with trisomy 21. This smiling 18-month-old child shows some of the characteristics of Down syndrome. Note (A) epicanthal folds on eyes, (B) prominent tongue, (C) single transverse palmar crease (simian crease), (D) a short fifth finger, and (E) wide spacing between first and second toes.

A 24-year-old female, 6 weeks pregnant, came to her physician concerned about her sister's child with Down syndrome. She wondered if this could happen to her child. Her karyotype revealed a 14-21 translocation. When she learned of the 20 percent risk of having a Down syndrome baby, she decided to have an amniocentesis. When this was performed, at 16 weeks, a fetus with trisomy 21 was revealed. She elected to terminate the pregnancy.

Amniocentesis and karyotyping of fetal cells make it possible to determine whether the fetus is genetically normal, a balanced translocation carrier, or an affected individual with trisomy.

Alterations in sex chromosomes

Sex chromosomes can undergo the same abnormal changes as autosomes; nondisjunction during meiosis plays a major role. Twenty-five per-

Table 8-3 Risk of Down syndrome due to nondisjunction

| Mother's age in years | Risk for Down syndrome | |
	Incidence	Percentage
Less than 29	1:3000	
30–34	1:800	
35–39	1:290	0.3
40–44	1:100	1
45–49	1:50	2

Source: J. Miles and M. Kaback, "Prenatal Diagnosis of Hereditary Disorders," *Pediatric Clinics of North America*, August 1978, p. 598.

cent of all spontaneous abortions are due to abnormalities in sex chromosomes. Sex chromosome abnormalities are manifested anytime from birth to beyond puberty by ambiguous genitalia, delayed onset of puberty, hypogonadism, amenorrhea, infertility, variation in stature, or other congenital anomalies. Table 8-4 describes common sex chromosome abnormalities.

In *all* cells of a 46,XX female one X becomes inactivated in early embryonic development. If this did not happen, the female would have twice as many X chromosome genes as the male. This inactive X, visible at interphase as a dark spot in the cell, is called the *X-chromatin*, also known as the Barr body (Fig. 8-12*A*) An XX female has one X chromatin in all cells. An XY male and an X female have *none*. An XXX female will have two X-chromatin bodies. Regardless of genetic makeup, an individual will have only one active X chromosome per cell.

The presence of the Y chromosome can be detected at metaphase when the cell is stained with fluorescing dye, quinacrine mustard. The *Y-chromatin body* is shown in Fig. 8-12*B*. These two tests can usually determine the sex chromosome complement of the person from whom the cell was taken without necessitating a karyotype.

Single-gene disorders

Single-gene defects are due either to a single mutant gene (inherited from one parent) or to a mutant gene pair derived from both parents. Diseases due to mutant genes are classified as

Table 8-4 Common sex chromosome abnormalities*

Chromosomal disorders	Abnormality	Phenotype	Incidence†	Characteristics
Monosomy X, Turner syndrome (gonadal dysgenesis)	45,X (mosaicism possible)	Female	1:2500 female births	Amenorrhea; short stature; webbed neck; lack of sexual development at puberty; hypoplastic nails; sterility
Klinefelter syndrome	47,XXY (most common) 48,XXYY 49,XXXXY	Male	1:400 male births	Hypogonadism; infertility; low birth weight; delayed speech; poor gross motor coordination; variable mental retardation. The more X chromosomes, the more serious is the disease. Often are phenotypically abnormal at birth, have frequent school problems, gynecomastia, increased height, decreased libido, decreased testosterone secretion
Triple X	47,XXX 48,XXX 49,XXXXX	Female	1:000 female births	Often phenotypically normal at birth; ⅓ may be mentally retarded, have irregular menses, decreased fertility, increased speech and language problems, variety of major or minor congenital malformations. Incidence increased with increase in age of parents (offspring have normal karyotype)
Superman syndrome	47,XYY 48,XYYY	Male	1:900 male births	Normal birth weight; phenotypic male; behavior problems; increased height; delayed speech, language development; acne; increase in aggressive behavior (offspring have normal karyotype)

* Theoretically all are detectable in utero.

† General frequency of sex chromosomal abnormalities in males = 2.7:1000 and in females = 1.5:1000.

Figure 8-12 (*A*) Dark spot at edge of this cell nucleus is X-chromatin and represents inactivated X in cell with two XX chromosomes. (*B*) Light spot in this cell nucleus represents Y-chromatin and indicates presence of Y chromosome in cell. (*Courtesy of Dr. Gordon DeWald.*)

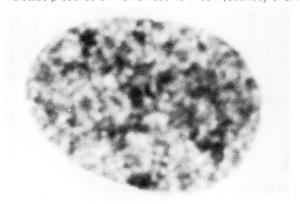 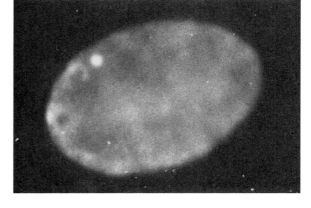

autosomal, X-linked, dominant, and recessive. Since the Y chromosome is known to carry only one or two traits, no single-gene disorders have been related to it. Single-gene diseases, though rare, produce significant effects on families and children.

Mendel's laws of inheritance

To understand single-gene disorders, it is helpful to review Mendel's laws of inheritance.

Law of dominance and recessiveness When two contrasting genes for a certain trait are paired, one is *dominant* over the other.

Law of segregation When gametes are formed, each gene is *separated from its allele* and passes into a different germ cell (sperm or egg).

Law of independent assortment Different genes segregate independently of one another (i.e., genes are transmitted *independently* of each other).

All genetic traits vary in their *expression* or the degree to which they are observable in the individual. *Penetrance* is a statistical term referring to the percentage of individuals with a given gene who express the trait produced by that gene. If only one-half with a mutant gene show its effects, penetrance is 50 percent.

Occasionally two alleles are expressed *equally*. This is true for the major blood groups, A, B, and O. A and B antigens are dominant over O (no antigens). A person with type A blood (phenotype) can be of the genotype AA or AO. When one parent contributes the gene for A antigen and the other parent the gene for B antigen, the offspring will be AB and have both antigens. This is known as *codominance*, i.e., neither gene is dominant over the other.

Autosomal dominant disorders

Autosomal dominant disorders are usually less severe than recessive disorders. They tend to involve defects in the embryo or have a late onset as in Huntington's chorea. The characteristic genetic pattern includes these points:

1. All affected children have one affected parent.
2. Affected individuals are found in successive generations.
3. Male and female are equally likely to transmit or have the trait.
4. In the long run, half the children of an affected parent will have the disorder.
5. The trait is not transmitted by an unaffected person.

Achondroplasia, or dwarfism, is often the result of a new mutation in the offspring, so the rule of affected parent may not apply. However, an offspring of an achondroplastic parent has a 50 percent chance of being affected. Some 80 percent of dominant disorders represent new mutations. Figure 8-13 represents the inheritance pattern of an autosomal dominant disorder. Table 8-5 describes selected autosomal dominant disorders.

Autosomal recessive disorders

Because both alleles are mutants in true homozygous conditions, autosomal recessive disorders are often severe. Sickle cell anemia (hemo-

Figure 8-13 Inheritance pattern for autosomal dominant disorder. D is dominant gene; r is recessive gene. Punnett square shows 50% of offspring will be affected, 50% will be unaffected. *Note:* With *each pregnancy* the chance of having an affected child will be 50% whether or not previous offspring were affected.

Parents: **Dr** × **rr**
(affected) (unaffected)

Gametes: **D** **r** **r** **r**

Affected

	D	**r**
r	**Dr**	**rr**
r	**Dr**	**rr**

Unaffected

50% Affected = **Dr**
50% Unaffected = **rr**

globin SS disease) is a well-known example. This disease stems from a genetically defective form of hemoglobin in red blood cells. The red cells are extremely fragile. Fever, anemia, and other symptoms are present (Table 8-6). The infant, whose blood until a few months of age contains fetal hemoglobin, is normal; the symptoms usually appear in the first year when fetal hemoglobin is replaced by the adult form. Hemoglobin SS disease is almost exclusively found among blacks.

Everyone carries three to five mutant genes capable of bringing about severe genetic disease. Because these usually are masked by dominant normal alleles, the mutant genes are not expressed. The risk that such mutant genes will be carried in someone heterozygous for the trait increases among parents who have ancestors in common. With such *consanguineous mating* recessive disorders appear more frequently than in the general population. Each person has half his or her genes in common with his or her parents, sibling, and children (first-degree relatives): one-fourth with his grandparents, grandchildren, aunts, uncles, nieces, and nephews (second-degree relatives); and one-eighth and one thirty-second, respectively, with his first and second cousins (third-degree relatives). The closer the genetic relationship of the parents, the greater the chance that a child will be born with a genetic defect.

Table 8-5 Autosomal dominant disorders

Disorder	Characteristics
Conradi disease	Asymmetric shortening of limbs; dry, scaly skin; scoliosis; alopecia; rounded face; flattening of nasal bridge and face; cataracts
Holt-Oram syndrome	Congenital heart disease; defects of thumbs
Polysyndactyly	Deformed fingers and toes—webbing, extra digits
Marfan syndrome	Appears in childhood or early adulthood; tall, thin body; scoliosis; pigeon breast; mitral or aortic valve insufficiency; retinal tears (connective-tissue defects)
Stickler syndrome	Myopia; retinal detachment; deafness; arthropathies; Pierre Robin syndrome may occur in same family
von Recklinghausen disease, neurofibromatosis	Defect in cells of neural crest; 50% of cases represent new mutations; neurofibromas of skin and central and peripheral nervous system; kyphoscoliosis; cutaneous pigmentation
Polycystic kidney disease	Adult onset (usually after child-bearing years); cystic disease of liver and kidneys; intracranial aneurysms; incidence is 1:500
Huntington's chorea	Adult onset usually after 30 (usually live 15 years after onset of symptoms); choreiform movements; decreasing intellectual function; mental deterioration
Bilateral retinoblastoma	Onset in infancy; x-ray therapy *before symptoms appear* has been successful in treating malignancy
Multiple endocrine adenomatosis I, II, III (medullary carcinoma of thyroid, parathyroid, pituitary)	Other signs include thickened nerve fibers in eyes and benign wartlike changes in tongue. Treat with thyroidectomy. May involve parathyroid, pituitary
Familial polyposis of colon	Adenomatous polyps can become cancerous. Begin screening at 10 years. Observe closely and do resection early
Cancer family syndrome	Familial excess of adenocarcinoma involving colon and endometrium (less frequent in stomach, breast, ovary), occurring at much earlier ages than in general population

The characteristic genetic pattern for autosomal recessive disease includes these points:

1. Affected individuals tend to group in the same generation.
2. Both parents are heterozygous for the disorder and are rarely affected.
3. Both sexes show the trait with equal frequency.
4. For each pregnancy, the chance of having an affected offspring is 25 percent, or 1 in 4.

Table 8-6 Autosomal recessive disorders

Disorder	Characteristics
Meckel syndrome	Microcephaly; encephalocele; cleft lip and palate; congenital heart defects; polycystic kidneys; polydactyly
Oculocutaneous albinism	Failure of normal melanin pigmentation (absence of tyrosine); visual impairment leading to blindness; susceptibility to ultraviolet light; no pigment in eyes, skin, hair
Infantile multicystic kidney disease	Renal failure
Cystic fibrosis	Onset at birth or up to adulthood; disorder of exocrine glands of: gastrointestinal tract, pancreas, respiratory tract; males are usually sterile
Usher syndrome	Sensory deafness; retinitis pigmentosa; sometimes mental illness and cataracts
Wilson disease	Degeneration of hepatolenticular system; defect in copper transport; anemia; greenish brown ring in iris of eyes; cirrhosis, jaundice; neurological defects
Sickle cell anemia (and other hemoglobinopathies)	Fever; anemia; sickle-shaped erythrocytes; infarction of small blood vessels
Adrenogenital syndrome	Excessive androgen production before birth causes masculinization of the female external genitalia. Can have enlargement of clitoris or fusion of labia. For girls: high physical energy level and low maternal caretaking behavior. Affected males show advanced somatic and genital growth and tend to have high physical energy levels

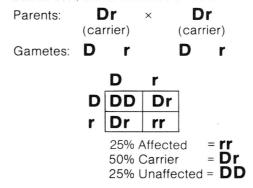

Figure 8-14 Inheritance pattern for an autosomal recessive disorder. Both parents are heterozygous for the recessive gene (r). They are unaffected although carriers. With *each pregnancy* the chance of bearing an affected child is 25%, a carrier 50%, and an unaffected child 25%.

Figure 8-14 shows the inheritance pattern for an autosomal recessive disorder. Table 8-6 describes selected autosomal recessive disorders.

X-linked dominant disorders

These conditions are extremely rare. Severity is usually much greater in the male because he does not have the normal allele on his Y chromosome to balance the effects of the abnormal gene on his X chromosome. An example of an X-linked dominant disorder is focal dermal hypoplasia. It is characterized by digital, oral, and ocular abnormalities, and when it occurs in males, it is lethal. Vitamin D–resistant rickets also fits in this category. The characteristic genetic pattern for X-linked dominant disorders includes these points:

1. Heterozygous affected females transmit to one-half their sons and one-half their daughters.
2. Homozygous affected females transmit to all offspring.
3. Affected males transmit to *all daughters* but to none of their sons.
4. Both sexes can be affected.

Figure 8-15 shows the inheritance pattern for an affected mother (*A*) and affected father (*B*).

X-linked recessive disorders

Over 150 X-linked recessive disorders have been identified. Males are frequently affected in X-linked recessive disorders because there is no

Figure 8-15 Inheritance pattern for X-linked dominant disorder. (*A*) Affected females transmit the disorder to one-half of their daughters and one-half of their sons. (*B*) Affected males transmit the disorder to *all* of their daughters and *none* of their sons. The risk of having an affected child is 50% for each pregnancy when either parent is affected with an X-linked dominant disorder.

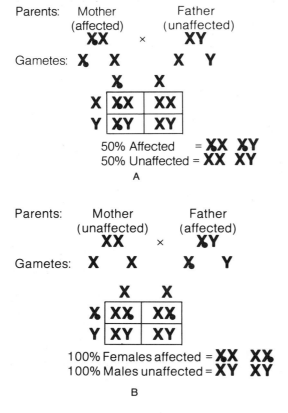

Figure 8-16 Inheritance pattern for X-linked recessive disorder. (*A*) Carrier females transmit the disorder to one-half of their sons. One-half of their daughters are carriers. (*B*) Affected fathers transmit their affected X chromosome to *all* of their daughters and none of their sons. The risk of having an affected child is 50% with each pregnancy. (See pedigree chart Fig. 8-8B)

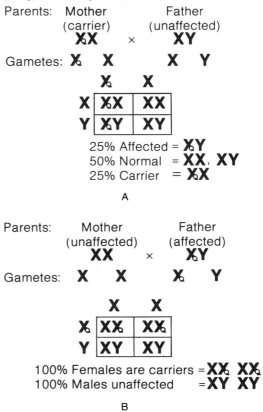

normal allele on the Y chromosome to balance the mutant recessive gene on the X. In rare cases the recessive allele may be partially expressed in females because of the inactivation of their second X chromosome. The characteristic genetic pattern for X-linked recessive disorders includes these points:

1. All sons of affected males are normal (males do not transmit the X chromosome to sons).
2. All daughters of affected males are carriers.
3. One-half the sons of carrier females are affected.
4. One-half the daughters of carrier females are carriers.
5. To be affected a female must (usually) have an affected mother and a carrier father.

Figure 8-16 shows the inheritance pattern for a carrier mother (*A*) and an affected father (*B*). Table 8-7 describes selected X-linked recessive disorders.

Polygenic disorders

Many normal traits such as eye color, intelligence, blood pressure, height, and pigmentation of skin are determined by the cumulative effect of several gene pairs. Disorders of such *polygenic* traits can be predicted like other genetic abnormalities. Very often parents of an affected child are normal. When their genes are combined, however, the proportion of abnormal genes is increased to the critical threshold and a defect is produced. Polygenic disorders are characterized by the following points:

1. Usually present in one sex more than the other.
2. A *single* organ system is involved.
3. Recurrence risk rises with the severity of the disorder.
4. Recurrence risk increases in proportion to the number of affected first- and/or second-degree relatives. Table 8-8 lists common disorders that can have a polygenic etiology.

Inborn errors of metabolism

Genes produce the enzymes that are the regulators of the many biochemical reactions of metabolism. Each such reaction is under the control of a different gene, and a change in the nature of a gene, that is, a mutation, may alter the ability of a cell to carry out some primary chemical reaction. An inborn error of metabolism is thus created. The immediate consequences may be (1) an accumulation, (2) a deficiency, or (3) an overproduction of a substance produced by the primary chemical reaction (Fig. 8-17).

At birth the child may appear normal. The nurse's first contact with the child may be for hospitalization due to failure to thrive, abnormal laboratory tests, or unexplained drug responses. Once the diagnosis of a biochemical disorder is made, it may not be long before the progressive, diffuse nature of the illness becomes evident. Many inborn errors of metabolism result in a typical pattern that includes liver or spleen enlargement, renal or cardiac involvement, changes in growth, anemia, and a progressive downhill course. Table 8-9 describes selected inborn errors of metabolism.

Fortunately, most genetic mutations have little if any effect on the phenotype. For one thing, each person carries two complete sets of chromosomes. Even if an allele on one chromosome is a mutant, its duplicate on the other chromosome is likely to be unaffected and to continue normal functioning.

Environmental influences

There is always interaction between genetic and environmental influences in utero. At various times one or the other will dominate. Traits or

Table 8-7 X-linked recessive disorders

Disorder	Characteristics
Anhydrotic ectodermal dysplasia	Absence of sweating; short, fragile hair; misshapen teeth; can be partially expressed in carrier females
Aqueductal stenosis	Hydrocephalus
Fabry's disease*	Fever; paresthesias (burning pains); skin lesions; heart and kidney failure; corneal opacities
Duchenne muscular dystrophy	Onset 3–5 years; progressive loss of muscle strength; contractures; pseudohypertrophy of calf muscles (usually death occurs in twenties and thirties)
Hemophilia A	Disorder of blood coagulation (factor VIII deficiency); bleeding from wounds and into tissues and joints
Hemophilia B	Disorder of blood coagulation (factor IX deficiency), not as serious as hemophilia A
Testicular feminization syndrome	Failure of embryonic end organs to respond to androgenic steroids despite presence of Y chromosome. 46,XY appears as female with blind-ending vagina, amenorrhea (tubes, uterus, upper vagina absent). Testes immature or found in groin or labia majora (1–2% of girls with inguinal hernias have this syndrome)

* Can be detected in utero.

Table 8-8 Common polygenic disorders*

Allergies (atopic)	Congenital scoliosis
Ceft lip and palate	Pyloric stenosis
Cleft palate	Hirschsprung's disease
Neural-tube defects	Mental retardation, nonspecific
Hydrocephalus (in isolation)	Urinary tract malformations
Congenital heart disease	Diabetes mellitus (adult onset)
Talipes equinovarus (clubfoot)	Schizophrenia
Congenital dislocation of the hip	

* Recurrence rates for first-degree relatives is 2–5%.
Source: Vincent Riccardi, *The Genetic Approach to Human Disease*, Oxford, New York, 1977, p. 90.

Figure 8-17 Types of metabolic abnormalities resulting from enzyme defects. (*A*) Normal. (*B*) Accumulation of excess substance at the block, as in tyrosinosis and alkaptonuria. (*C*) Lack of the product, as in albinism and cretinism. (*D*) Abnormal metabolites such as in phenylketonuria. (*Adapted from V. A. McKusick (ed.), Human Genetics, 2d ed., Prentice-Hall, Englewood Cliffs, N.J., 1969, p. 69. By permission of the publisher.*)

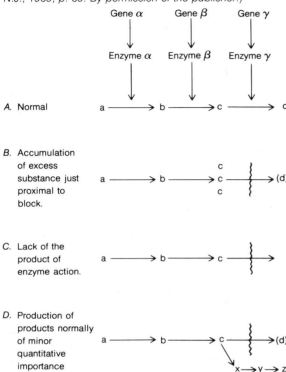

disorders determined by both the environment and by genes are known as *multifactorial*. A perfect environment will not overcome the effects of an extra chromosome as in trisomy 21. But a genetically normal infant, born to a mother with untreated phenylketonuria, will show the influence of the uterine environment. The child will have low birth weight, microcephaly, and eventual mental retardation.

Anything that causes change in genetic material is *mutagenic*. When an agent acts to change the structure or function within the fetus during pregnancy, it is known as a *teratogen* (*terato* = monster or anomaly; *gen* = causative agent). The resulting anomaly is said to be *congenital*.

There are four major environmental influences that can act as mutagens or teratogens: physical agents, infection, chemical agents (including drugs), and the maternal intrauterine environment.

Table 8-9 Inborn errors of metabolism

Disorder	Characteristics
Errors of amino acid metabolism	
Phenylketonuria*†	Absence of liver enzyme phenylalanine hydroxylase causes excess of phenylalanine in blood; irritability; vomiting; seizures; mental retardation
Maple syrup urine disease*†	Failure to thrive; seizures; sweet-smelling urine
Errors of lipid metabolism	
Tay-Sachs disease*†	Found in Ashkenazic Jews (frequency: 1:3600); failure to thrive; neurological deterioration; blindness; seizures; death; 1 in 36 Jews heterozygous for gene
Gaucher disease*†	Deficiency of β-glucoside; splenomegaly; thrombocytopenia; bone pain; leads to death
Errors in carbohydrate metabolism	
Galactosemia*†	Absence of enzymes galactose 1-phosphate uridyl transferase; intolerance to lactose; failure to thrive; weight loss; seizures; cataracts
Mucopolysaccharidosis* (Hurler, Hunter, etc.)	Results from accumulation of acid mucopolysaccharides in the liver, brain, heart. Coarsening features; cataracts; enlarged head and tongue; mental and growth retardation. Most inherited in autosomal recessive except Hunter's, which is X-linked recessive
Altered structural proteins	
Hemoglobinopathies	Disorders of clotting, bleeding—need fetal blood to test for in utero diagnosis; tests not conclusive at present time.

* Follows autosomal recessive pattern of inheritance.

† May be detected in utero.

Physical agents

Ultraviolet (sun) and ionizing (nuclear, x-ray) radiation and extremes of temperature can damage DNA directly by altering its structure. X-rays greatly increase the risk of mutation. Because the effects are cumulative, the risk is proportional to the amount of irradiation received. X-rays in the early weeks of pregnancy should be avoided unless absolutely necessary. Radioactive iodine (used for diagnostic tests) can become concentrated in the fetal thyroid gland and have a teratogenic effect. The effects of radiation may also become apparent in later life with an increased likelihood of cancer.

Infection

Viral illness during pregnancy can cause specific congenital syndromes as well as temporary chromosomal breakage. When a woman develops rubella (German measles) during the first trimester of pregnancy, she is likely to produce an infant with microcephaly, cataracts, deafness, and mental retardation. Other infections known to act as teratogens are toxoplasmosis, cytomegalovirus, *Treponema pallidum* (syphilis), and herpes simplex II virus. Infants infected in utero may have intrauterine growth retardation, microcephaly, anemia, jaundice, and poor motor development.

Chemical agents

Chemical teratogens are eaten or inhaled as drugs or pollutants in air, water, and food.

Organic mercurials, often found in fish, can cause neurological defects and blindness. Mustard gas, formaldehyde, and caffeine can produce mutations.

Drugs constitute a significant hazard to the pregnant woman. No drug should be taken unless its benefit *clearly overrides* any harmful effects it might have. Table 8-10 lists selected drugs and their known or suspected teratogenic effects.

Intrauterine environment

The physiological status of the mother has a definite effect on the fetus. Most drugs and metabolites cross the placental barrier and affect the fetus. Poor maternal nutrition is associated with a decrease in fertility and infant birth weight. At the present time maternal endocrine imbalance, diabetes mellitus, phenylketonuria, and alcoholism are known to be teratogenic to the fetus.[9] Factors putting the fetus at risk are discussed in more detail in Chap. 19.

It is helpful for the nurse to remember that mutations that occur in somatic cells (as in leukemia) will not be passed on to offspring, but will be passed on to all daughter cells. If the mutation occurs in a gamete, the mutant gene or chromosome will be transmitted to the offspring. Since not all gonadal cells may be involved, the risk of producing an affected offspring is calculated on the basis of population frequency of that trait or disorder.

Table 8-10 Drugs with known or suspected teratogenic effects

Drug	Known effects	Suspected effects
Thalidomide	Phocomelia (absence of parts or entire limbs)	
Amethopterin, aminopterin	Abortion; intrauterine growth retardation; cranial and facial abnormalities	
Progestins (birth control pill)	Masculinization of female fetus	Isolated limb defects; increase in abortion
Cigarette smoking		Low birth weight
Anticonvulsants (hydantoins)		Cleft palate; intrauterine growth retardation; congenital heart disease; hypoplasia of fingers and toes
Ethyl alcohol		Growth retardation; mental retardation; microcephaly; distinctive facies

Genetic counseling

Genetic counseling is an important part of health care. It is part of the process by which the affected individual or involved family is evaluated for risk and counseled so that rational decisions can be made about childbearing. In addition, there may be more immediate goals of psychological support, improved management of certain disorders, and referral for help in carrying out decisions the individual or family must make.

Genetic counseling involves nondirective counseling. The counselor presents information in a variety of ways so that the family has a clear understanding of the genetic basis of the disorder as well as the risks involved for future children. Riccardi has described guidelines for the counselor that include the following:[10]

1. Accurate diagnosis.
2. Communication—useful information regarding risks and alternatives.
3. Nondirective counseling—client chooses between alternatives.
4. Respect for and adjustment to the family's psychological and emotional turmoil.
5. The focus of health care is the *family unit*, not just the affected individual.
6. A team approach is optional but often helpful.

Components of a genetic evaluation

History and pedigree construction

Essential to genetic counseling is a detailed family history, pregnancy history, and postnatal history. Frequently the nurse can obtain the initial information needed.

Commonly used symbols and a sample pedigree chart are shown in Fig. 8-18. A complete pedigree includes second- and third-degree relatives. Family histories help the geneticist to diagnose a heritable disorder, define recurrence risks, and develop an understanding of the possible medical, social, and emotional burden the disorder has for affected and unaffected family members.

The maternal-fetal history should provide information on any infections, drugs, or environmental agents the mother was exposed to during pregnancy. A detailed description of the events at birth and postnatally is an important extension of the history. It is important to elicit the *parent's perception* of significant events, developmental steps, and possible causative factors. Frequently, parents describe events they believe may have caused the problem; they may talk about feelings of guilt. The counselor can correct misconceptions and misunderstandings.

Physical examination

A detailed and precise physical exam is required for a genetic evaluation. Special attention is given to the involved organs and to the reproductive and central nervous systems. The dermal creases and ridges on hands and feet reveal characteristic patterns in many syndromes. *Phenocopies*, developmental diseases that mimic genetic disorders, must be carefully distinguished from hereditary disease.

Laboratory data

Routine laboratory tests, specialized tests, and genetic diagnostic tests are the three types of laboratory procedures required for a genetic workup. Specialized lab exams are selected on the basis of presenting symptoms and can include x-rays and biopsies. Specialized genetic diagnostic tests include: chromosome analysis, karyotype, enzyme assays, and amniocentesis.

Chromosome analysis Analysis of chromosomes has become extremely important in genetics. Usually lymphocytes from a blood sample or fetal cells in amniotic fluid are grown in a special medium. During metaphase the cell nucleus is photographed after the chromosomes are stained. Special stains allow the identification of each chromosome and its specific parts. Buccal smears (scrapings of the inside of the cheek) are often used for sex chromatin studies.

Amniocentesis Prenatal diagnosis of genetic disorders is becoming a more common part of obstetric care. Amniocentesis, usually done 16 weeks from the last menstrual period, allows the physician to preview the genetic constitution of the fetus. It is usually done as an outpatient procedure after gestational age is carefully calculated. Maternal blood samples are drawn, ultrasound localizes the placenta, and the patient is carefully monitored (vital signs, fetal heart tones) both before and after this sterile procedure. Chromosomal analysis takes 3 to 5 weeks after the amniocentesis.[11]

The National Registry for Amniocentesis Study reported on 1040 subjects at nine institutions who had the procedure.[12] They concluded that: (1) no significant difference in fetal death was found between the amniocentesis group (3.5 percent) and the control group (3.2 percent); (2) there were no significant differences in complications of labor, delivery, or infant outcome; (3) the accuracy of diagnosis was 99.4 percent; (4) maternal and fetal risks are 1 in 200 when the procedure is performed by experienced physicians in large medical centers. Prenatal diagnosis using amniocentesis should be considered in the following situations:[13, 14]

1. Advanced maternal age (The most common reason for doing an amniocentesis is to detect chromosomal abnormality in fetuses carried by women over 35 years of age.)
2. Previous child with a chromosomal abnormality
3. Parent who is a balanced translocation carrier
4. Mother who is a habitual aborter
5. Occurrence of multiple congenital anomalies in a previous child
6. X-linked recessive disorders in the family (even if biochemical diagnosis cannot be made, sex can be determined)
7. Child is at risk for inborn errors of metabolism (It is now possible to identify many rare disorders such as Fabry's disease and Tay-Sachs disease.)
8. Previous child with a neural tube defect

Role of the nurse

Nurses can play a key role in the genetic counseling process by virtue of specialized training (nurse-geneticists or pediatric nurse associates) or by their close involvement with families in any nursing setting. They may participate in genetic evaluation by constructing pedigrees, visiting families at home, and helping in clinics. Often nurses are the first ones to be asked about the possible untoward effects of environmental agents during pregnancy. Nurses should be able to construct a simple pedigree chart, obtain a relevant history, understand genetic principles, make appropriate referrals, and appreciate the psychological aspects of counseling the affected family.

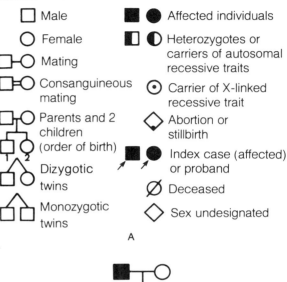

Figure 8-18 (A) Symbols used in constructing a pedigree. A pedigree should include all first-, second-, and third-degree relatives of the affected individual. (B) A characteristic X-linked recessive pedigree. Males are affected and they are related through unaffected (or carrier) females. All daughters of affected males are carriers.

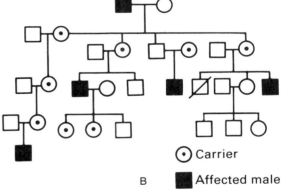

Referral

Usually referral is made to answer the question "Will it happen again?" It makes no difference whether the question is asked by the client, family, nurse, social worker, or physician. The question should be asked. The nurse should encourage families to verbalize their concerns and seek answers to their questions. Conditions that call for referral to a clinical geneticist are summarized in Table 8-11.

Table 8-11 Indications for referral to a clinical geneticist

1. Known or presumed congenital abnormalities
   a. Congenital malformations
   b. Ambiguous genitalia
   c. Mental retardation
   d. Fetal or parenteral exposure to environmental factors (drugs, irradiation, infections)
2. Acknowledged familial disorders
3. Known inherited disorders
4. Metabolic, biochemical disorders
5. Known or suspected chromosomal abnormalities
6. Multiple miscarriages, stillbirths
7. Infertility
8. Premarital counseling
9. Consanguinity, incest
10. Prenatal diagnosis
    a. Either parent is a known carrier
    b. Previous child with chromosomal abnormality
    c. Mother 35 or older
    d. Inordinate parental concern or anxiety
    e. Either parent has specific metabolic disorder
    f. Mother a known or presumed carrier for X-linked recessive

Adapted from Vincent Riccardi, *The Genetic Approach to Human Disease*, Oxford, New York, 1977, p. 6.

Once the data base is gathered (history, physical exam, and laboratory data), the geneticist counsels the client and family regarding the risks involved, the *probability* of recurrence, and the probable prognosis of an existing condition. Information is given about available health care, community agencies, and sources of financial support.

Nursing management

Families who experience the birth of a child who is less than perfect will experience loss and grief. They must mourn for the perfect child they expected before they can come to terms with the reality of the child they have. Nurses can expect reactions that include shock, denial, anger, and depression. The grief will resolve in time, but it will never disappear completely.

Parents experience profound disappointment and guilt. They may look on this child as punishment for something they did wrong. Grief and guilt can strain a marriage as well as interfere with other family relationships. There is potential for a decline in family self-esteem and a breakdown in communication. The nurse can antici-

pate and recognize these expected effects and explore them with the family as support is given to them.

Parents need to be involved in the care of their child as soon as possible. Seeing, touching, and fondling the infant promote attachment and development of parenting skills. With acceptance, parents can begin to focus their energy on problem solving. Parents need support as they gather information and make decisions regarding the care of their child. See Chap. 19 for further discussion of parenting the high-risk child.

Nurses, too, may experience feelings similar to those of parents. Parents are comforted when nurses participate in their grief. However, parents also look to the nurse's reactions as representative of how others may react to them and their child. They are sensitive to verbal or nonverbal cues that suggest shock, revulsion, or blame. A warm, caring, empathic nurse can provide support that will help parents cope with this crisis in their lives.

There are several ways that the nurse can help parents and the child who has genetic disease.

1. Accept family's feelings and reactions.
2. Help family explore their feelings and work through their grief.
3. Clarify misconceptions.
4. Help the family (and the child, when old enough) identify concerns and questions.
5. Fill in gaps in information.
6. Repeat information as often as necessary.
7. Provide opportunities for parents and family to care for child.
8. Teach family members (and child, when old enough,) to provide the care needed.
9. Get the family in touch with other parents or associations of parents who have similar children.
10. Make appropriate public health and social service referrals.
11. Provide written information to family.
12. Anticipate concerns and problems the family is likely to experience in the future.
13. Coordinate efforts of other health team members.
14. Continue care and follow-up.

Genetics is a rapidly growing specialty. New techniques and knowledge are added constantly. Nurses have a responsibility to become aware of developments in diagnosis, treatment, and prevention of hereditary disorders.

References

1. James F. Crow, *Genetics Notes*, Burgess, Minneapolis, 1976, p. 77.
2. J. Miles and M. Kaback, "Prenatal Diagnosis of Hereditary Disorders," *Pediatric Clinics of North America* **25**(3): 593–618 (August 1978).
3. Ann Clark and Dyanne Affonso, *Childbearing: A Nursing Perspective*, Davis, Philadelphia, 1979, p. 217.
4. Vincent M. Riccardi, *The Genetic Approach to Human Disease*, Oxford, New York, 1977, p. 4.
5. Clark et al., op. cit., p. 218.
6. L. B. Holmes, "Genetic Counseling for the Older Pregnant Woman: New Data and Questions," *New England Journal of Medicine* **298**(25): 1419–1421 (June 22, 1978).
7. Ibid., p. 1420.
8. Ibid., p. 1420.
9. Riccardi, op. cit., p. 148.
10. Ibid., p. 200.
11. M. Golbus, W. Loughman, C. Epstein, G. Halbasch, J. Stephens and B. Hall, "Prenatal Diagnosis in 3,000 Amniocenteses," *New England Journal of Medicine* **300**(4): 157–163 (Jan. 25, 1979).
12. NICHD National Registry for Amniocentesis Study Group, Midtrimester Amniocentesis for Prenatal Diagnosis: Safety and Accuracy," *Journal of the American Medical Association*, **236**: 1471–1477 (1976), p. 1471.
13. Miles et al., op. cit., pp. 597–600.
14. Golbus et al., op. cit., p. 158.

Chapter 9 **Prenatal development**

Marjorie J. Smith

Upon completion of this chapter, the student will be able to:

1. Define the three stages of human development that occur before birth.

2. Differentiate between menstrual and conceptual age.

3. Describe the timing of events leading to fertilization.

4. Trace the path of the egg from ovulation through implantation.

5. List three functions of amniotic fluid.

6. List three organ systems arising from each germ layer.

7. Identify the period of organ systems' greatest sensitivity to teratogens.

8. List four mechanisms used to transport products across the uteroplacental barrier.

9. Describe the functions of the placenta and its hormones.

Human development is the life process that begins at conception and concludes at death. In this chapter prenatal growth and development are briefly described to provide a basis for understanding later growth and development and arrests in development that lead to birth defects.

The human embryo progresses through stages of development similar to those of other creatures. Development occurs through cell division and growth. At first all cells seem to be alike, but soon they become *differentiated* according to coded information carried within them by genes. Some cells, known as *inducers*, influence other cells around them to develop in a certain way. Because the organism grows in a confined space, and because certain cells grow more rapidly than others, sheets of cells *fold* and *invaginate*. At the same time other cell groups *migrate* to different areas of the organism.

Development of function and size occurs in a cephalocaudal direction in the embryo and fetus, just as it does in the infant. Growth also occurs from the center, or medial aspect, of the body outward, or laterally.

Timetable of development

The first 14 days of human development are referred to as the *preembryonic stage* or the period of the *zygote* (fertilized egg). During this time implantation occurs; that is, the zygote embeds itself in the uterine lining. The *embryonic stage* begins the third week after conception and concludes at the end of the eighth week. This is the period of major organ system formation. The *fetal stage* encompasses the ninth through the thirty-eighth week, or to the end of pregnancy.

From birth to maturity weight increases 20 times, but from fertilization to birth, weight increases 6 billion times.[1] Relative proportions change markedly during fetal development. Figure 9-1 shows the relative proportions of head, trunk, and extremities at different ages.

The gestational age of the conceptus, as the product of conception is called, can be calculated from the first day of the last menstrual period, *menstrual age*, or from the time of conception, *conceptual age*. The normal length of pregnancy is 266 days (38 weeks) after conception or 280 days (40 weeks) after the last menstrual period. Figure 9-2 presents major milestones of the fetal life span.

The preembryonic stage

Fertilization

For pregnancy to occur healthy spermatozoa, deposited in the vagina at the cervical os, must find their way into a normal, patent fallopian tube at the time when a healthy ovum is present for fertilization.

The fertilization of the ovum usually occurs in the distal part of the fallopian tube approximately 24 h after ovulation. Once a single sperm penetrates the egg, changes occur in the outer membrane of the ovum that prevent others from entering.

Meanwhile the second meiotic division occurs (review Fig. 8-7) in the nucleus of the ovum and the male and female chromosomes come together. Thus the zygote is formed containing a full set of 44 autosomal chromosomes and two sex chromosomes, either XX or XY.

The fallopian tube propels the zygote toward the uterus by cilial and muscular movement. During this time the zygote is dividing mitotically by a process known as *cleavage*. In about 3 days it has become a tiny ball of 16 cells known as the *morula*.

Blastocyst

When the morula reaches the uterine cavity, it begins to absorb uterine fluid, creating a cystlike space within. The zygote is now known as a *blastocyst* (Fig. 9-3A) and is composed of three parts:

1. *Blastocoele* An inner, central cavity filled with nourishing fluid.
2. *Inner cell mass* The *embryoblast* that will eventually form the embryo.
3. *Trophoblast* (*tropho* = "nutrition") The protective outer-cell coating that invades and digests the endometrium. The trophoblast eventually forms the chorion (outer layer of fetal membranes) and fetal part of the placenta.

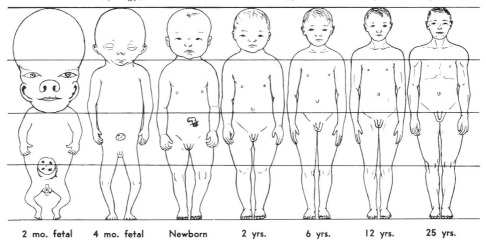

Figure 9-1 Fetal and postnatal stages drawn to same total height to show characteristic age changes in the proportion of various parts of the body. (*From B. M. Patten and B. Carlson, Foundations of Embryology, McGraw-Hill, New York, 1974, p. 13. Used with permission.*)

2 mo. fetal   4 mo. fetal   Newborn   2 yrs.   6 yrs.   12 yrs.   25 yrs.

Figure 9-2 The fetal life span in weeks. (*Adapted from Robert Hoekelman et al., Principles of Pediatrics, McGraw-Hill, New York, 1978, p. 374. Used with permission.*)

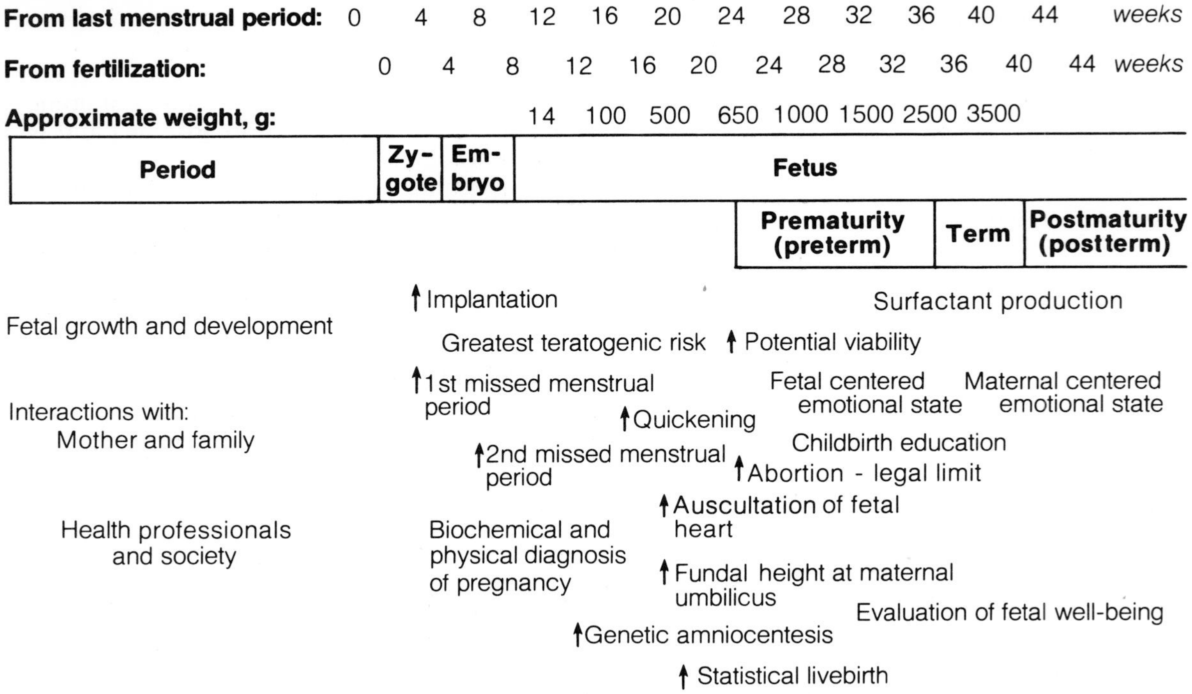

From last menstrual period:	0	4	8	12	16	20	24	28	32	36	40	44	*weeks*
From fertilization:		0	4	8	12	16	20	24	28	32	36	40	44 *weeks*
Approximate weight, g:				14	100	500	650	1000	1500	2500	3500		

Period	Zy-gote	Em-bryo	Fetus		
			Prematurity (preterm)	Term	Postmaturity (postterm)

Fetal growth and development
- ↑ Implantation
- Surfactant production
- Greatest teratogenic risk ↑ Potential viability

Interactions with:
  Mother and family
- ↑1st missed menstrual period
- ↑Quickening
- Fetal centered emotional state
- Maternal centered emotional state
- ↑2nd missed menstrual period
- Childbirth education
- ↑Abortion - legal limit

Health professionals and society
- ↑Auscultation of fetal heart
- Biochemical and physical diagnosis of pregnancy
- ↑Fundal height at maternal umbilicus
- Evaluation of fetal well-being
- ↑Genetic amniocentesis
- ↑ Statistical livebirth

Implantation

On about the fifth day after fertilization the zona pellucida (membrane surrounding the ovum) disappears and by the sixth day the blastocyst attaches itself to the endometrium (inner uterine lining). The usual site for implantation is the upper posterior uterine wall.

During the second week the trophoblast continues to penetrate the endometrium. At the same time two cavities, the amniotic cavity and the primitive yolk sac, appear within the trophoblast. The inner cell mass begins to differentiate into two layers, *endoderm* (inner layer) and *ectoderm* (outer layer). This *bilaminar embryonic disk* lies between the amniotic cavity and primitive yolk sac.

Under the influence of progesterone, the endometrium has greatly thickened. Its glands have become increasingly active and rich in glycogen. The invading trophoblast breaks down the endometrial cells, making nutrients available to the developing embryo until the placenta is formed.

Decidua, meaning "to shed," is the name given

the endometrium during pregnancy because it is extensively sloughed and rebuilt after delivery of the baby. The endometrium directly under the blastocyst is known as the *decidua basalis*, and that over the site of implantation is the *decidua capsularis*. The remaining endometrium is called the *decidua parietalis* (Fig. 9-4).

Early development of the placenta

The placenta is the specialized contact between the fetus and uterus. It develops partly from the invading trophoblast and partly from the endometrium.

By the end of the second week, the blastocyst is usually buried in the endometrium. The trophoblast enlarges and two layers are recognized.

The first, the outer layer, is known as the *syncytiotrophoblast*. This layer of cells expands rapidly into the endometrium. Spaces appear in the syncytiotrophoblast and are filled by blood from venules and capillaries of the endometrium.

The second, inner layer of the trophoblast, the *cytotrophoblast*, sends columns of cells into the decidua basalis. About then the trophoblast is renamed the *chorion* and these fingerlike extensions are *chorionic villi*. Eventually, fetal blood vessels grow into them and the villi become the major surfaces for fetal-maternal exchange. By then, intervillous spaces have formed around the villi and become pools for maternal blood, which reaches the site by spiral (later uteroplacental) arteries. The chorion is the outer layer of the fetal membranes.

Chorionic villi are originally present over the entire surface of the blastocyst. As it enlarges, however, the decidua capsularis becomes compressed. Circulation to the villi is cut off and all but those under the embryo atrophy by 4 months. This smooth portion of the chorion is known as the *chorion laeve*. Where the chorionic villi continue to enlarge and proliferate the surface is called the *chorion frondosum* (*frondosum* = "leafy").

Figure 9-5 shows the anatomic relationship of the fetus and the fetal membranes.

Amnion and amniotic fluid

The fetus develops within the amniotic cavity, which is lined by a layer of cells called the *amnion*. This smooth, shiny membrane secretes a fluid that bathes the fetus. Amniotic fluid is essential for fetal well-being because it provides:

1. A medium for fluid exchange
2. Protection from injury (by cushioning the embryo in fluid)
3. A constant body temperature (by absorbing heat)
4. Prevention of adhesion of body parts

Figure 9-3 Diagram showing early formation and implantation of the embryo. (*A*) 6–7 days: Beginning implantation; (*B*) Day 7½: Blastocyst embedded in uterine wall; (*C*) Day 12; and (*D*) Day 14. (*From M. Tudor, Child Development, McGraw-Hill, New York, 1981, after C. E. Corliss and K. L. Moore, p. 210. Used with permission.*)

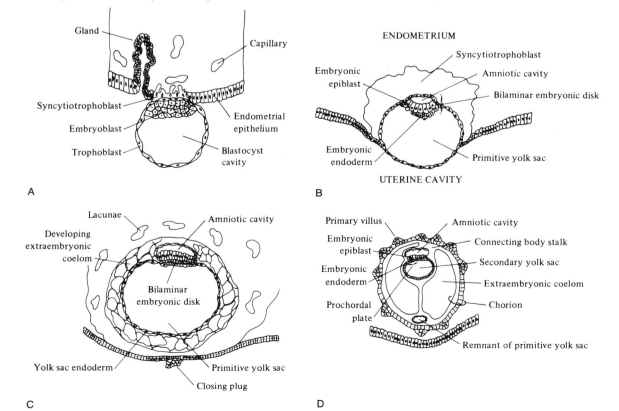

Figure 9-4 Diagram showing uterus, embryo, and membranes at 8 weeks after conception. (*From B. M. Patten and B. Carlson, Foundations of Embryology, McGraw-Hill, New York, 1974, p. 342. Used with permission.*)

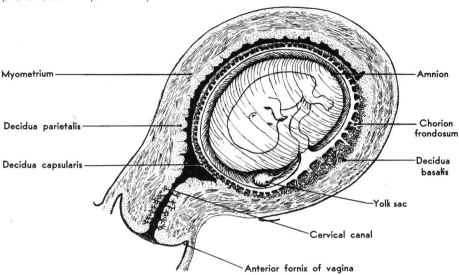

The amnion produces increasing amounts of amniotic fluid until near term, when 800 to 1000 ml are present. Upon examination amniotic fluid is found to contain hormones, enzymes, and fetal cells. The fluid can be withdrawn by amniocentesis and examined for genetic diagnosis at 16 weeks and for fetal well-being and maturity near the end of pregnancy.

Umbilical cord

As the placenta develops, the umbilical cord is being formed from a connecting structure known as the *body stalk*. Cells of this structure proliferate into the villi, acting as a core into which the fetal blood vessels penetrate. These vessels extend along the body stalk to form the two umbilical arteries and single umbilical vein that connect fetal circulation to the placenta. In some ways the fetal circulation resembles that of extrauterine circulation to the lungs. Oxygen-depleted blood circulates to the placenta through the two umbilical arteries and oxygen-enriched blood returns to the fetus through the umbilical vein.

The embryonic stage

The beginning of the embryonic stage, the third week after conception, is signaled by the devel-

opment of the third or middle cell layer, the *mesoderm*, between the ectoderm and endoderm. These three germ layers form the basis for differentiation and specialization of different body parts. Figure 9-6 shows the various parts of the body derived from each germ layer.

During the third week the primitive streak, formed from ectoderm, develops in the posterior midline of the embryo. The streak thickens, the embryonic disk elongates, and the neural plate forms. The neural plate then folds inward, creating the neural tube, forerunner of the central nervous system.

Thickened groups of mesodermal cells, called *somites*, begin to form in pairs alongside the neural folds. The somites eventually give rise to the skeleton and skeletal muscles.

Also by the third week the heart tubes and a simple vascular system have developed sufficiently to begin circulating the early blood cells that are formed in the yolk sac.

The body of the 4-week-old embryo is C-shaped. The embryo has folded longitudinally, pinching the yolk sac from the gut and thereby hastening the formation of the umbilical cord. Transverse folding causes incorporation of the embryonic coelom, leading to the formation of the peritoneal and pleural cavities.

Thickened areas of tissue, called *placodes*, appear in the cephalic end of the embryo where the eyes, ears, and nose will develop. Tiny arm and leg buds appear.

During the fifth week the greatest development continues at the head of the embryo. The brain grows rapidly and is composed of five vesicles. Facial features move closer together. All 44 pairs of somites are now present. Septa begin to develop within the heart while the primitive umbilical cord is developing from the body stalk.

By the middle of the sixth week the face is more identifiable and the arm and leg buds resemble paddles (Fig. 9-7). Cartilage centers develop and tooth buds form. The trachea enlarges and bifurcates (forks) to form lung buds.

During the seventh week the limbs continue to develop. Fingers are evident and limbs move laterally, causing palms and soles to face toward the middle of the body. Gonads are beginning to differentiate internally, to form ovaries or testes.

By the end of the eighth week all major organ systems have begun their development. The heart has four chambers and is beating 40 to 80 times per minute. The head is one-half the body length and is more rounded and less flexed than before. The embryo has grown 10 mm during this week and is now 30 mm long and weighs 1

Figure 9-5 Diagram showing relationships to the uterus of a 5-month-old fetus and its membranes. Amnion is drawn as a solid, black line; amniotic cavity is striped, and chorionic laeve is represented by a broken line. (*From B. M. Patten and B. Carlson, Foundations of Embryology, McGraw-Hill, New York, 1974, p. 348. Used with permission.*)

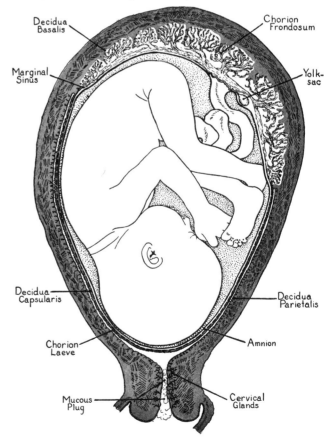

Figure 9-6 Chart showing the derivation of various body parts from the three primary germ layers.

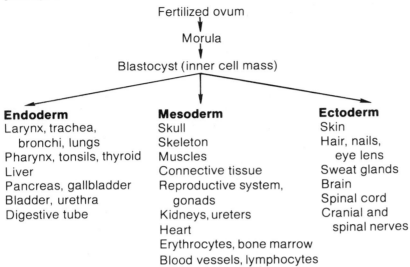

Fertilized ovum
↓
Morula
↓
Blastocyst (inner cell mass)

Endoderm
Larynx, trachea,
bronchi, lungs
Pharynx, tonsils, thyroid
Liver
Pancreas, gallbladder
Bladder, urethra
Digestive tube

Mesoderm
Skull
Skeleton
Muscles
Connective tissue
Reproductive system,
gonads
Kidneys, ureters
Heart
Erythrocytes, bone marrow
Blood vessels, lymphocytes

Ectoderm
Skin
Hair, nails,
eye lens
Sweat glands
Brain
Spinal cord
Cranial and
spinal nerves

to 2 g. The mother has missed two menstrual periods and probably suspects she is pregnant. It is during this crucial, embryonic period, while the organs are forming, that the unborn child is most vulnerable to insults that can cause congenital anomalies. Table 9-1 describes the time periods of greatest sensitivity to teratogenic influences (factors causing birth defects) for various organs.

Table 9-1 Sensitivity of fetal organs to teratogens (periods of development in weeks)

Organ	Most sensitive	Less sensitive
Central nervous system	2–5	5–38
Heart	3–6	6–12
Eyes	4–8	8–38
Ears	6–12	12–20
Arms	4–8	8–12
Legs	4–8	8–12
Palate	7–12	12–16
Teeth	7–12	12–20
External genitalia	7–16	16–38

Adapted from Seymour Romney et al., *Gynecology and Obstetrics: The Health Care of Women*, McGraw-Hill, New York, 1975, p. 71.

The fetal period

From 9 weeks until birth the fetus grows rapidly in length and weight. At 16 weeks there is hair on the head and body and the mother feels the fetus move (Fig. 9-8). By 24 weeks the fetus looks like a shriveled old man with red and wrinkled skin. By 30 weeks fat is beginning to accumulate. From then on the fetus continues to gain weight while the body systems mature to enable the baby to survive in extrauterine life.

Embryologic and fetal development is outlined in Table 9-2. Later chapters on alterations in child health describe the embryologic development of each body system in more detail.

Placentation

Structure

As the placenta becomes established, the anchoring villi enlarge and divide it into 15 to 30 segments, or lobes, known as *cotyledons*. Each lobe is composed mainly of a single large main stem villus and its surrounding branches. Each cotyledon is bathed by the blood from a single uteroplacental artery[2] (Fig. 9-9). By 6 weeks the placenta covers one-sixth of the uterus; by 20 weeks it covers one-half. At 8 to 10 weeks after conception the placenta has achieved its definitive form, and no new lobules are added after 12 weeks. Placental growth then occurs in depth rather than in size through the addition of new peripheral villi to the stem villi.

By the end of pregnancy the placenta weighs approximately 500 to 600 g (one-sixth as much as the fetus) and measures 15 to 20 cm by 2.5 to 3 cm. The fetal surface is shiny and slightly grayish. The umbilical vessels that enter the cord appear like a branching root system just beneath the amnion and chorion. The maternal surface is dark red, rough, and liverlike. The cotyledons can be seen, divided by shallow clefts.

The placenta as an organ of homeostasis

The placenta is the main organ of homeostasis for the fetus. It functions as an immunological barrier and as an organ of respiration, excretion, endocrine production, and alimentation.

Maternal and fetal blood do not normally intermix. The two circulations are separated by (1) fetal capillary endothelium, (2) connective tissue of the villous core, and (3) trophoblastic cells covering the villi.

Numerous substances cross the uteroplacental barrier by several mechanisms.[3]

Figure 9-7 Human embryo about the middle of the sixth week after conception. Small sketch, lower right, shows *actual size* of the embryo and its chorionic vesicle. (*From C. E. Corliss, Patten's Human Embryology, McGraw-Hill, New York, 1976, p. 57. Used with permission.*)

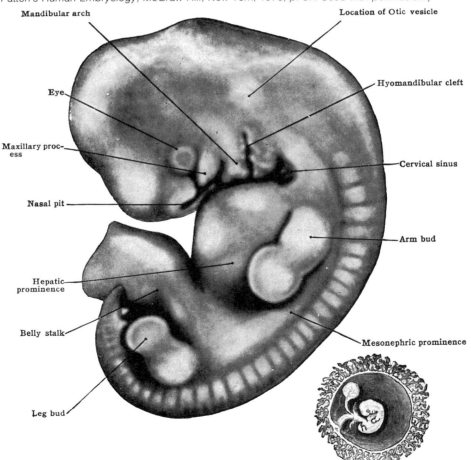

Mandibular arch

Location of Otic vesicle

Hyomandibular cleft

Eye

Maxillary process

Cervical sinus

Nasal pit

Arm bud

Hepatic prominence

Belly stalk

Mesonephric prominence

Leg bud

Figure 9-8 Photograph of a 4-month-old fetus with intact membranes and attached placenta. (*From E. Page, C. Villee, and D. Villee, Human Reproduction, Saunders, Philadelphia, 1972, p. 209. Used with permission.*)

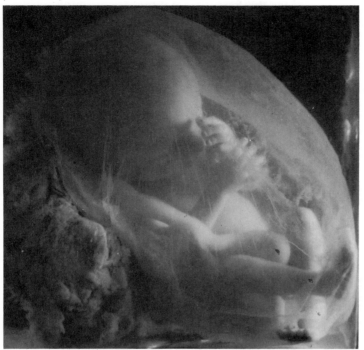

1. *Passive diffusion* Water, electrolytes, drugs, oxygen, and carbon dioxide move from an area of high concentration to one of low concentration.
2. *Facilitated diffusion* Glucose is transferred to an area of lower concentration by means of a carrier system.
3. *Active transport* Amino acids, water-soluble vitamins, and calcium and iron ions (Ca^{2+} and Fe^{2+}) are transferred by metabolic energy.
4. *Pinocytosis* Cells of the syncytiotrophoblast engulf serum proteins and antibodies, transferring them from maternal plasma to fetal circulation.
5. *Bulk flow* Rapid transfer of water and electrolytes occurs through submicroscopic channels in the placenta.
6. *Breaks* Accidental breaks in the fetal capillary wall and villous covering permit passage of maternal and fetal blood cells. Usually this occurs at the time of delivery and placental separation, but it can happen earlier. This process accounts for the production of maternal antibodies by an Rh negative mother against an Rh positive fetus.

Uteroplacental blood flow is of prime importance in the maintenance of maternal-fetal exchange. It increases 10 to 12 times over the course of a normal pregnancy reaching a flow of 500 to 600 ml/min near term.[4] Uteroplacental blood flow decreases under severe stress, during labor, and in chronic disease of the mother. As the placenta ages near term, it becomes less effective. This places the postterm fetus at risk.

Any chronic disease, fetal abnormality, or maternal infection is likely to affect placental functioning and result in growth retardation in the fetus. When vascular disease, such as maternal hypertension or preeclampsia, is present, the placenta is small and thin and often functions poorly. As a result fetal growth is impaired. Maternal diabetes produces a hypertrophied, edematous placenta.

If placental insufficiency develops rapidly, as it might in diabetes or in early separation of the placenta from the implantation site, the fetus can die quickly from hypoxemia and acidosis.

The placenta as an endocrine organ

Human chorionic gonadotropin (HCG) Besides functioning as an organ of homeostasis for the fetus, the placenta produces hormones essential to the continuation of the pregnancy. During the first 3 months of pregnancy, almost all necessary steroid hormones (estrogen and progesterone) are supplied by the corpus luteum of the ovary. Corpus luteum degeneration is prevented by a hormone produced by the trophoblastic cells that is known as *human chorionic gonadotropin*. HCG secretion increases rapidly during early pregnancy, reaching a peak 60 to 80 days after the last menstrual period. HCG forms the basis for pregnancy testing. The decrease in HCG is associated with an increase in placental production of estrogen and progesterone during the last 6 months of pregnancy (Fig. 9-10).

Human chorionic somatomammotropin (HCS)

Trophoblastic cells also produce human somatomammotropin, or human placental lactogen. HCS is similar to human pituitary growth hormone. It stimulates certain maternal metabolic adjustments that increase the availability of protein and glucose to the fetus and free fatty acids for the mother. Because it counteracts the action of insulin it is known as the diabetogenic factor in pregnancy.

Progesterone Progesterone is essential for the continuation of the pregnancy, especially during the early months. It reduces the contractility of

Figure 9-9 Schematic diagram to show interrelationships of fetal and maternal tissues in formation of placenta. Chorionic villi are represented as becoming progressively further developed from left to right across the illustration. (*From B. M. Patten and B. Carlson, Foundations of Embryology, McGraw-Hill, New York, 1974, p. 344. Used with permission.*)

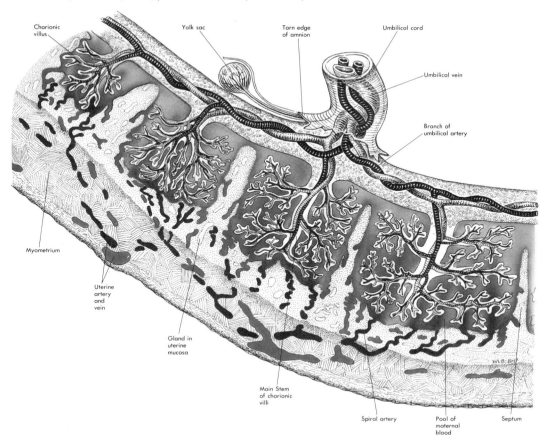

Table 9-2 Overview of embryonic and fetal development

Age, wk	Length, cm	Weight, g	Development/appearance
	Crown to rump:		
2			Three germ layers Primitive streak and notochord present
3	0.2		Neural tube forms from closure of neural groove Formation of oral cavity Digestive tract forming Liver function begins Blood begins circulating Primitive kidneys forming Somites develop in cephalocaudal direction
4	0.4	0.4	Heart tube fuses at 22 days and beats at 24 Anterior end of neural tube closes to form brain. Posterior end closes to form spinal cord Esophagotracheal septum begins division of tubular esophagus and trachea Limb buds present Stomach forms Intestine becomes tubular Auditory pit enclosed Head is 1/3 of total body length
5	0.8	1	Embryo is C-shaped Brain differentiated into five areas 10 pairs of cranial nerves present Division of cardiac atria occurs Permanent kidney begins to form Optic cups and lens vesicles of eyes form Somite formation complete
6	1.2	1.5	Tracheal bifurcating to begin lung formation Primitive skeletal shape forming Beginnings of muscle and cartilage formation Upper lip formed; upper and lower jaw recognizable. Tooth buds form Ear formation continues Liver forming red blood cells Tail still present but is beginning to regress
7–8	2–3	2	Eyes, ears, nose and mouth recognizable Inferior vena cava and valves form Heart basically developed and beating 40–80 times per minute Differentiation of sex glands into ovaries or testes Optic nerve formed; eyes converging, eyelids forming Diaphragm separates abdominal and thoracic cavities Muscle development continues and ossification begins Beginning fetal movements Bladder and urethra separate from rectum Stomach attains final form Digestive tract rotates in midgut All components of reflex arc present
10	6	10	Fusion of palate; development of face and mouth Nail growth begins Formation of tooth enamel begins Basic division of brain present Intestines enclosed in abdomen Bladder sac forms, urine forming Testes can form testosterone Responds to tactile stimulation Bone marrow forms and functions Eyelids fuse

Table 9-2 Overview of embryonic and fetal development (*Continued*)

Age, wk	Length, cm	Weight, g	Development/appearance
	Crown to heel:		
12	11.5	45	Palatal fusion complete Respiratory motion visible Swallows in response to thumb-sucking Distinctive external genitalia present Head is ½ size of fetus Human growth hormone produced in pituitary Movement more pronounced in lower trunk
16	15	200	Phase of rapid growth, looking more human Bladder assumes adult form Ossification of bone will show on x-ray Meconium present in intestines; anus open Lanugo growing on body; hair on head Differentiation of hard and soft palate Cerebral lobes delineated General sense organs differentiated Vagina open Nipples appear
16–20			Fetal heart tones heard by fetoscope Mother feels movement (quickening)
20	25	300–400	Sucking reflex present; swallows amniotic fluid First patterns (rhythms) of respiratory movement Vernix caseosa begins to form Eyelashes and eyebrows forming Myelinization of spinal cord begins Brown fat begins to be formed
24	30	650	Skin red and wrinkled Vernix present Alveolar ducts and sacs present Testes at inguinal ring Eyes structurally complete
28	35	1100	Lean body; less red Surfactant forming on alveolar surfaces Cerebral fissure and convolutions appear Pupils react to light Movements poorly sustained
32	40	1800	Lecithin/sphingomyelin ratio (L/S ratio) 1.2:1 Testes descending Lanugo beginning to be shed Subcutaneous fat beginning to collect Skin pink and smooth Movements sustained Moro reflex present Hunger cry Primordia of permanent teeth forming
36	45	2900+	Skin pink, body rounded L/S ratio 2:1 or greater Spinal cord ends at L3 Lanugo disappearing Good hunger cry
40	50	3350+	Skin smooth, covered with vernix Pulmonary branching ⅔ complete Myelinization of brain begins Testes descended into scrotum Lanugo on shoulders, upper body only Strong sucking reflex Lifts head in prone position Cartilage in nose and ears

Figure 9-10 Urinary excretion levels of estrogen, progesterone, and human chorionic gonadotropin during pregnancy. Urinary excretion rates reflect blood concentrations and actual production. (*From A. Vander, J. Sherman, and D. Luciano, Human Physiology, 3d ed., McGraw-Hill, New York, 1980, p. 508. Used with permission.*)

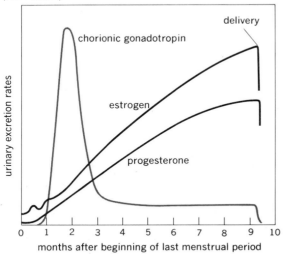

uterine smooth muscle and other smooth muscles, maintains the endometrium, and prepares the breasts for lactation.

Estrogens The placenta, using essential precursors from the fetal adrenals, synthesizes estriol. It also produces other estrogens—estradiol and estrone. Placental estrogens increase markedly during pregnancy, causing growth and enlargement of the uterus and breasts and increase of uterine blood flow. The level of maternal urinary estriol is indicative of fetal well-being and uteroplacental functioning. Estrogens continue to increase until just before delivery. They appear to promote mothering behavior at term.

References

1. Clark Edward Corliss, *Patten's Human Embryology*, Mc-Graw-Hill, New York, 1976, p. 112.
2. Chester B. Martin and Barbara Gingerich, "Uteroplacental Physiology," *Journal of Obstetrics-Gynecology Nursing*, suppl., September-October 1976, p. 17.
3. Ibid., pp. 19, 20.
4. Ibid., p. 21.

Chapter 10 **The Neonate**

Elaine L. Ambrosini Hurley

Upon completion of this chapter, the student will be able to:

1. Describe the physiological changes necessary in the transition from fetal to neonatal life.

2. Identify the special needs of the neonate immediately after birth and describe nursing actions to meet these needs.

3. Describe the characteristics of the normal neonate.

4. Identify the goals of nursing care for the neonate and correlate nursing interventions to meet these goals.

5. Teach parents about their newborn infant's characteristics and needs.

6. Describe parent-infant bonding and identify nursing actions to facilitate and assess this process.

7. Describe the ability of the neonate to interact with and affect the environment, and the subsequent impact of this ability on parent-child bonding.

8. Assess parental readiness to assume care of the neonate.

9. Identify the nutritional needs of the neonate and contrast the qualities of human breast milk and cow's milk formulas in meeting these needs.

10. Provide parents with anticipatory guidance to maximize the developmental potential of the infant during the first month of life.

The neonatal period is the first 28 days of life. It is a period of great change, during which the infant must recover from exhaustion of the birth process, undergo physiological changes for adaptation to independent functioning, and begin the lifelong process of psychological adaptations to life experiences.

The nurse must understand these physiological and psychological processes to be able to meet the newborn's nursing care goals. Clark and Affonso[1] have identified the goals of care for newborns as *assessment, protection, nurturance,* and *stimulation;* these four goals will be discussed throughout this chapter. The nurse has a primary role in parent teaching and should translate these nursing goals to parenting goals for neonatal care. Expert neonatal management

and parental guidance during this 28-day period lay the foundation for healthy parent-child development.

The infant at birth

Transition to extrauterine life

Perhaps the most important adjustment a human being must make during his lifetime is the transition from fetal-placental circulation to independent cardiopulmonary functioning. The first few minutes and hours of life are a critical time of dramatic adjustment.

Initiation of respiration The immediate change after birth is the onset of breathing. During passage through the birth canal, the neonate experiences pressure on the thoracic cage that can force out as much as 5 to 10 ml of tracheal fluid. This fluid is expelled from the nose and mouth when the face is exposed to atmospheric pressure. Following delivery, the chest walls recoil to the position they had prior to labor, drawing in air to fill the airways.[2] The alveolar surfaces of term infants are covered by a substance called *pulmonary surfactant*, which diminishes surface tension during expiration, thus allowing the alveolar sacs to remain partly open. The second breath requires much less effort than the first, because the sacs are already open, and successive breaths require even less effort.

In addition to these mechanical processes, there are sensory and chemical stimuli which aid in the initiation and maintenance of respiration. Birth is potentially an asphyxiating process because it stimulates chemical changes that lead to the following conditions in the blood: increased carbon dioxide, lowered oxygen, and lowered pH. These conditions stimulate the respiratory center in the medulla, either by acting upon it directly or by affecting chemoreceptors in the carotid artery or aorta, thus initiating respiration. However, if asphyxiation and these altered blood conditions are prolonged, respiration will be inhibited rather than stimulated.

Upon birth the neonate passes from an environment relatively deprived of sensory experiences to one in which the infant is bombarded with sensations of pressure, pain, noise, light, and cold. Chilling may act as a stimulus to sensory receptors in the skin. Nerve impulses are then transmitted to the respiratory center in the medulla, thus stimulating respiration. In animal studies on thermoregulation, it has been found that chilling stimulates breathing even when fetal-placental circulation is still intact and the level of blood gases is unchanged, and that respirations are inhibited by a heat stimulus.[3] However, excessive cooling interferes with respiration by increasing the need for oxygen and by producing acidosis. The practice of slapping the baby on the backside or feet to induce respiration is essentially a misuse of precious time if initiation of respiration is delayed.

Transition from fetal to neonatal circulation

Simultaneous with the beginning of respiration, critical changes from fetal to neonatal circulation must be made. Fetal circulation is discussed in detail in Chap. 26, being only briefly reviewed here (Fig. 10-1). Oxygenated blood leaves the placenta and enters the fetal circulation via the umbilical vein. This oxygenated blood mainly bypasses the fetal liver via the *ductus venosus*, then empties into the inferior vena cava. The majority of the blood entering the right atrium from the inferior vena cava crosses directly to the left atrium via the *foramen ovale* ("open window"), then follows the normal route through the left ventricle and out the ascending aorta to the head and upper extremities.

Most of the deoxygenated blood entering the right atrium from the superior vena cava passes through the right ventricle, then out via the pulmonary artery. There is no functional need for this blood to pass through the pulmonary system. Because of high fetal pulmonary vascular resistance, most of this blood bypasses the lungs via a third fetal shunt, the *ductus arteriosus*. The ductus arteriosus connects the pulmonary artery and the aorta. Blood passing through the ductus arteriosus enters the descending aorta, mixing with some oxygenated blood from the left ventricle. Some of this pool of blood supplies the lower extremities and visceral organs, but most of it returns to the placenta via the two umbilical arteries, for reoxygenation. Only about 12 percent of the blood in the fetal circulation actually reaches the pulmonary vascular beds.

Increases in systemic and decreases in pulmonary vascular resistance at birth serve to close these fetal blood shunts. It is important for the nurse to realize that closure of these structures at birth is not absolute. The ductus arteriosus closes gradually over the first 3 to 4 days of life. Functional heart murmurs are not uncommon during this period. Likewise, closure of the foramen ovale is not absolute during the first few days of life. Situations such as stress or crying increase pressure in the venae cavae and right atrium and may cause shunting of unoxygenated blood across the foramen ovale to the left side of the heart. This results in transient cyanosis in the newborn.

Nursing care of the neonate in the delivery room.

Nursing care of the neonate in the delivery room should be consistent with meeting the previously stated goals of assessment, protection, nurturance, and stimulation.

Initial assessment: the Apgar score Because of the extensive physiological changes undergone by the neonate during the first few minutes after birth, it is important that caretakers make astute and systematic observations of the neonate. The most uniform criterion used to evaluate the neonate in the delivery room is the Apgar scoring system, developed by Dr. Virginia Apgar in 1952. This method for assessing the cardiopulmonary status of the neonate is based on five evaluative criteria: heart rate, respiratory effort, muscle tone, reflex irritability, and color. Each criterion is given a score of 0, 1, or 2; then these individual values are totaled to yield the actual score. The Apgar score is usually obtained at 1 and at 5 min of age (Table 10-1).

Figure 10-1 Fetal circulation. (*Clinical Educational Aid No. 1, courtesy of Ross Laboratories, Columbus, Ohio.*)

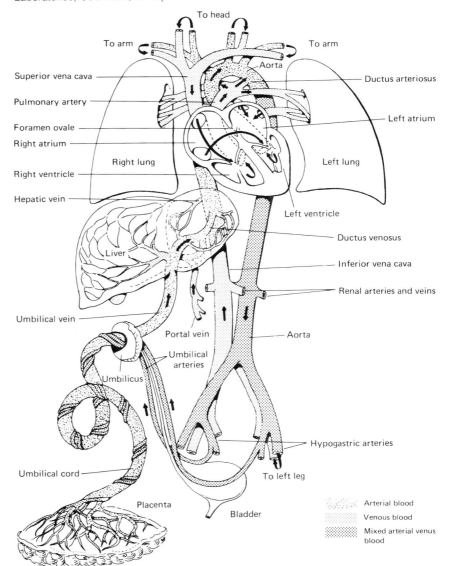

The *heart rate* is the most valuable indicator of the effects of asphyxia associated with the process of delivery. It is most reliably counted for at least 15 s, with a stethoscope. Palpation or visualization of pulsations in the umbilical cord, at the abdominal junction, are acceptable assessment techniques. A rate of less than 100 beats per minute indicates severe asphyxia. These infants usually require immediate resuscitative efforts.

Respiratory effort, an indicator of adequate ventilation, can be assessed while the heart rate is being checked.

Muscle tone refers to the degree of flexion and resistance offered by the infant when the examiner attempts to straighten the extremities. A score of 2 is given if the infant actively resists alteration of the normally flexed position, a score of 1 is given for less vigorous resistance, and a score of 0 is given if the infant is limp and therefore offers no resistance.

Reflex irritability may be evaluated by either (1) eliciting a grimace or gag reflex when suctioning the nostrils, or (2) slapping the soles of the feet with the examiner's hand. The normal healthy infant will respond to either of these stimuli with a loud cry, the moderately depressed by a facial grimace, and the severely depressed infant will exhibit no reaction to the stimulus.

Color is indicative of peripheral tissue oxygenation, and is the least significant of the five criteria. Few infants are completely pink at birth; most will manifest some blueness of the extremities, *acrocyanosis*. Generalized pallor and cyanosis indicate a severely asphyxiated baby. Reliable techniques for assessing color include inspection of the mucous membranes of the mouth and inspection of the lips, the palms of the hands, and the soles of the feet.

The Apgar score is of particular value for two reasons: First, it provides a uniform assessment scale for use in a variety of delivery settings. Second, and perhaps of greater significance, it allows anticipatory planning in the management of newborns. With a 1-min Apgar score, the clinical management of infants may be summarized as follows:

Apgar 0 to 2 These infants require immediate endotracheal intubation and positive-pressure ventilation with oxygen.

Apgar 3 to 6 These infants will frequently respond to gentle suctioning and receiving oxygen supplied by mask. If they do not promptly improve, or if signs of deterioration occur, immediate endotracheal intubation should be performed.

Apgar 7 to 10 These infants will rarely need any resuscitation, unless the Apgar score suddenly drops several minutes after birth. Appropriate management should be instituted if any danger occurs.[4]

The severely asphyxiated infant may be recognized and resuscitation begun *before* determination of the 1-min Apgar score. (See Chap. 19 for additional information regarding assessment and clinical management of the high-risk neonate in the delivery room.)

Protection: maintenance of a patent airway
The neonate is subject to airway occlusion for a variety of anatomic and situational reasons:

1. The newborn is a nose breather and has very narrow nasal passages, which are easily occluded.
2. The tongue is large and the trachea and glottis small.
3. The respiratory tract of the neonate is especially susceptible to edema.

Table 10-1 The Apgar scoring system

Sign	0	1	2
Heart rate	Absent	Slow (below 100)	Over 100
Respiratory effort	Absent	Slow, irregular	Good crying
Muscle tone	Flaccid, limp	Some flexion of extremities	Active motion
Reflex irritability	No response	Grimace	Cough, sneeze, or cry
Color	Blue, pale	Body pink, extremities pale	Completely pink

4. Pressure exerted on the thoracic cage during delivery expresses fluid via the mouth and nose.
5. Excessive amounts of mucus are produced during the first few hours of life.

For these reasons, it is of utmost importance that the nurse pay careful attention to maintenance of a patent airway. The oropharynx and nostrils are cleared with a bulb syringe as soon as the head is delivered to prevent aspiration of secretions into the bronchi. For most healthy newborns, a bulb syringe is both adequate and the preferred instrument for suctioning the oropharynx and nose. If there is need for additional suctioning, a DeLee or mechanical suction apparatus is used. The nurse must exercise care and careful judgment in selecting the appropriate size catheter and suctioning technique. It is important that only gentle suction, for periods no longer than a few seconds, be used; vigorous or prolonged suctioning can cause bradycardia and cardiac arrhythmias which are the result of vagus-nerve stimulation and laryngospasm. During and after suctioning the infant should be placed in a position which facilitates drainage of fluids from the airway. Usually this position is achieved by placing the infant on his or her side with the head slightly lower than the chest.

Protection: thermoregulation Heat loss by the neonate occurs through four distinct mechanisms: evaporation, conduction, radiation, and convection. *Evaporation* of amniotic fluid from the skin surface immediately after birth is a major cause of heat loss. Immediate drying of the skin and hair and placement of the baby in a warmed environment are essential nursing actions to minimize heat loss by evaporation. The warmed environment may be supplied by a warmed blanket, which is wrapped around the baby, or by a radiant heater, under which the infant is placed. Studies have shown that for most full-term infants, the relatively simple procedure of immediately drying and wrapping the infant in a warm blanket is nearly as effective as using a radiant heater.[5]

Heat loss also occurs by *conduction;* that is, when the neonate's skin is in direct contact with a cooler solid object, heat is conducted away from the body to the cooler object. Placing the baby on a padded, warm surface, as opposed to a cold examining table, and warming all examining devices that come in contact with the baby are some ways to avoid heat loss by conduction.

Infants also lose heat by *radiation;* that is, heat in the form of radiation is emitted by the body and absorbed by objects in the room. Heat loss by radiation increases as the cooler objects are brought nearer the baby, regardless of the temperature of the surrounding air. A critical point for the nurse to remember is that even though the ambient (surrounding) air may be at an optimal temperature for the infant, heat loss can still occur by radiation. A key factor in preventing heat loss by radiation is keeping the infant in the center of the room, preferably near the mother and as far away from cooler external walls as possible.

The last major mechanism for heat loss is *convection*—a mechanism in which body heat is lost to surrounding cooler air. This can be minimized by increasing the temperature in the delivery room, keeping the infant away from air currents (drafts, air conditioning), and placing the newborn in a recessed crib to shield him or her from cross-ventilation during examinations.

Protection from infection Newborns are routinely given treatment against *Neisseria gonorrhoeae*, which can cause blindness in babies born to mothers who harbor gonorrhea in their birth canal. The most commonly used prophylaxis is putting 1 drop of silver nitrate (1%) into each eye. The drops should be carefully placed on the inner aspect of the conjunctival sac, and allowed to flow laterally. The practice of irrigating the eye with normal saline following instillation of silver nitrate is no longer recommended as it dilutes the drug and decreases its potency. Local antibiotics, such as penicillin, tetracycline, or sulfonamides, are sometimes used for protection against gonorrheal ophthalmia neonatorum, but their use is not without some danger. One percent silver nitrate is considered to be the safest prophylactic agent available. Prophylaxis against ophthalmia neonatorum is required by law in 47 states; the nurse should be acquainted with local public health department regulations regarding this treatment.[6]

Protection against bleeding Newborn infants are susceptible to bleeding disorders because they lack adequate supplies of vitamin K during the first 3 to 4 days of life. This is because vitamin

K is normally produced by bacterial action in the large bowel, and infants have sterile bowels at birth. Vitamin K is mainly used in the production of prothrombin, necessary for the clotting process. Diminished amounts of vitamin K interfere with the coagulation process. A single dose of a water-soluble vitamin K preparation, 0.5 mg vitamin K_1, is given intramuscularly in the anterolateral aspect of the thigh.[7] The drug should be given shortly after birth, either in the delivery room or upon admission to the newborn nursery.

Protection by identification Every mother and baby must be properly identified before either of them leaves the delivery room. This is accomplished by the use of matched identification bands: one on the mother's wrist and one on the infant's wrist and ankle. The bands should include the mother's full name, hospital number, infant's sex, date and time of birth, and a code number. The nurse in charge of the delivery room is responsible for preparing and securely fastening the identification bands.[8] Care must be taken in attaching the bands to the infant; if they are too tightly placed, they might impede circulation; if too loose, they may fall off. The possible occurrence of the latter situation is the reason for placing *two* bands on the infant. Some hospitals also take a footprint of the baby and a fingerprint of the mother using a special form that remains a part of the baby's medical record. If taken carefully, a footprint provides a means for making positive identification of the infant, since arrangement of ridges on the infant's soles is unique. Nurses responsible for this procedure should carefully study instructions for the particular material used (Fig. 10-2).

Final delivery room assessment Before the infant leaves the delivery room, a cursory physical examination should be done. In addition to making a cardiopulmonary evaluation by using the Apgar score and inspecting the infant to determine the presence of birth trauma, the American Academy of Pediatrics recommends that the following screening tests be made before the infant leaves the delivery room to determine the presence of congenital anomalies:[9]

1. A brief appraisal of total body appearance and size relationships of various parts of the body.

2. Palpation of the abdomen for masses.
3. Observation of breathing to see if the infant can breathe with a closed mouth (rule out choanal atresia).
4. A soft tube may be passed through the mouth to the stomach (rule out esophageal atresia).
5. Gastric contents aspirated and measured (more than 15 to 20 ml of gastric content could suggest high intestinal obstruction).

These guidelines are modified by many hospitals to include other maneuvers, such as palpating the palate to rule out cleft palate and counting the number of vessels in the umbilical cord. There should be two arteries and one vein. A single umbilical artery, found in 1 percent of all single births, may indicate other congenital anomalies.[10]

Nurturance The decision to breast- or bottle-feed the newborn is central to every new mother's thinking; factors influencing this decision are discussed later in the chapter. If a woman has made the decision to breast-feed her infant, the nurse can enhance breast-feeding by helping the mother and baby begin a feeding as soon after birth as possible. This may begin in the delivery room, or, if more appropriate, in the recovery room. It is important for the nurse to realize that breast-feeding is not instinctive with humans, as it is with some lower animal species. Mothers require assistance in this process. Although this is especially true of mothers who are breast-feeding for the first time, the nurse must carefully assess the teaching and support needs of mothers who may have breast-fed other infants. Studies have suggested that for successful breast-feeding, mothers who choose to nurse should begin as soon as possible, preferably within the first hours following delivery.[11]

Stimulation Facilitating optimum stimulation for the infant is one of the most important and rewarding of the nursing goals. During the first 30 min to 1 h after birth, the infant is usually alert, with open eyes, and appears very interested in the environment. The nurse should capitalize on this state by allowing the parents uninterrupted time with their infant.

Klaus and Kennell, pioneers in the field of parental bonding, state, "Immediately after birth the parents enter into a unique period during

Figure 10-2 The identification process. (*A*) Footprint pad. (*B*) Inky foot. (*C*) Printing. (*D*) Mother's right index fingerprint. (*From Dickason and Schult, Maternal and Infant Care, 2d ed., McGraw-Hill, New York, 1979. Used with permission of McGraw-Hill Book Company.*)

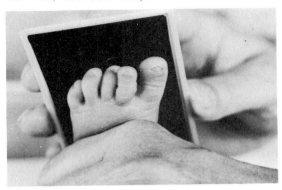

A

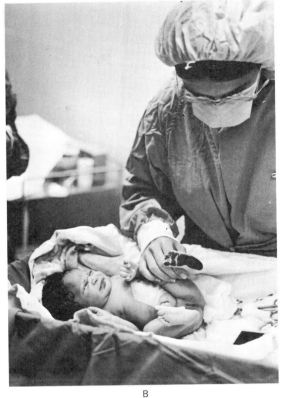

B

C

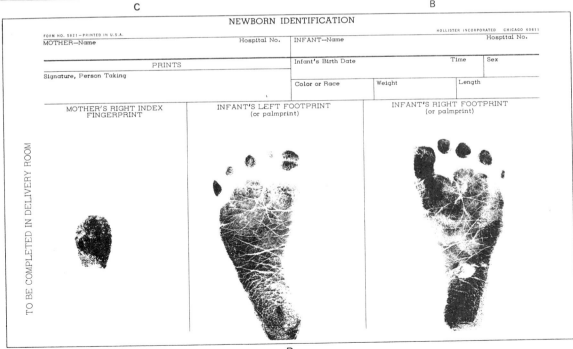

D

which events may have lasting effects on the family. This period, which lasts a short time, and during which the parents' attachment to their infant blossoms, we have named the *maternal sensitive period*."[12] Mothers who are left alone with their infants shortly after birth exhibit specific bonding behaviors. Perhaps the most notable is touch. In Klaus and Kennell's research, when nude infants were placed next to their mothers shortly after birth, most mothers touched them in a progressive pattern that began with placing the fingertips against the infant's extremities, from where they proceeded to use the palm to massage, stroke and encompass the trunk. Actual eye-to-eye contact, or at least an intense desire for it, was expressed by 70 percent of the mothers. Many assumed the *en face* position.[13] *En face* is defined as the position in which the mother's face is rotated so that her eyes and those of the infant meet fully in the same vertical plane of rotation.[14] Mothers speak to their infants in a higher-pitched voice than that used in normal conversation, which appears to alert and attract the infant.[15] Recent studies have also demonstrated that fathers exhibit specific behaviors during the first few minutes after birth. They hover over, point at, look into the eyes of, gaze at, and present their faces to their infants.[16]

The infant stimulates further parental response by the reciprocal behaviors of eye-to-eye contact, crying, and touch. Hence, the nurse must realize that the initial bonding process is one of mutuality, in which each party plays a unique role. Parents and infants who are allowed time for this acquaintance process ultimately demonstrate healthier parent-child relationships than those separated at birth.

Nursing actions that may facilitate parent-child bonding include:

1. Placing the infant on the mother's abdomen or chest immediately after birth.
2. Providing the parents privacy with their infant for 30 to 40 min shortly after birth.
3. Allowing the mother to have the baby in bed with her.
4. Encouraging the parents to unwrap and examine the infant (a radiant heater may be necessary to prevent chilling).
5. If the mother plans to breast-feed, encouraging the initiation of nursing.

6. Withholding the application of silver nitrate to the eyes for 1 h to allow maximum eye-to-eye contact.
7. Accurately recording these observed behaviors and responses.

Dr. Frederick Leboyer, a French physician, incorporates many of these guidelines into his conceptual approach to childbirth, commonly referred to as "birth without violence." This physician demonstates unusual sensitivity to the infant as a sensitive and unique human being. He utilizes some practices which are unconventional by U.S. standards. All unnecessary stimuli in the delivery room are minimized. The delivery is conducted either in silence or with soft music. Lighting is lowered, admitting only the amount of illumination necessary for initial assessment of the newborn. The delivery progresses naturally. The cord is tied when pulsations cease. The infant is then placed on the mother's abdomen for 3 to 6 min, and is given a gentle back massage. The infant is then transferred to a warm bath for another 3 to 6 min, with his or her head carefully supported out of water, and allowed to move freely. Dr. Leboyer feels that this bath simulates the amniotic-fluid environment to which the infant is accustomed, thereby reducing stress. Following the bath, the infant is dried, diapered, wrapped in a warm blanket, and given back to the mother for extended contact.[17]

The Leboyer method of childbirth, although controversial, obviously facilitates early bonding. There is a planned time for increased skin contact. The diminished lighting in the delivery room stimulates the infant's eyes to remain open for longer periods of time, thus allowing for maximum eye contact. In addition, the low-key, nonthreatening environment allows parents to "take in" all infant behaviors, and generally to respond to them without inhibition.

Signs of newborn transition

The infant undergoes intense physiological and psychological adjustment during the first 24 h of life. Extensive research on the newborn during this transition period resulted in findings of two distinct periods of activity. These are termed the *first* and *second periods of reactivity*. The *first period of reactivity*, which begins with birth, is normally characterized by "outbursts of diffuse, purposeless movements, alternating with brief periods of relative immobility." During this period, there may be transient flaring of the nares, retracting of the chest, and grunting upon expiration. The respiratory rate is rapid and can reach up to 80 breaths per minute during the first hour, before decreasing to 35 to 60 breaths per minute. Tachycardia is initially present, reaching a maximum of approximately 180 beats per minute at 3 min of age and falling gradually to 120 to 140 beats per minute at 30 min of age. Following this period of intense activity, the infant becomes quiet, relaxes, and usually falls asleep. The average age at which the infant falls asleep is 2 h, with sleep lasting from a few minutes to 2 to 4 h.

Upon awakening from this sleep, the infant enters the *second period of reactivity*. During this time, the infant may be hyperresponsive to all stimuli. The heart rate fluctuates appropriately with stimulation, and there are marked changes in color. The appearance of increased oral mucus is frequently a problem during this period, and may cause gagging, swallowing, vomiting, and, occasionally, choking. The second period of reactivity lasts for varying periods of time; when it is over the infant becomes relatively stable.[18]

Normal physical caracteristics of the newborn

General appearance

The neonate is differentiated from the older infant by specific structural and physiological characteristics. The head of the neonate is relatively large, accounting for approximately one-fourth of the total body length; the limbs are short; and the abdomen is prominent. The predominant posture of the neonate is one of flexion, or persistent fetal position. The neonate should demonstrate symmetry in size and movement.

Weight and length

The average weight, at sea level, for a Caucasian infant born at term is approximately 7 lb 8 oz (3400 g) for the male and 7 lb (3200 g) for the female. The average weight for non-Caucasian infants (black, Oriental, Indian) born at term is usually slightly lower; full-term black infants tend to weigh 8 oz (200 g) less than full-term Caucasian infants.[19] Approximately 95 percent of all full-term infants weigh between $5\frac{1}{2}$ lb (2500 g) and 10 lb (4600 g).[20]

The average length of a full-term infant is 20 in (51 cm), with approximately 95 percent of term infants having lengths between 18 and 22 in (45 to 55 cm).[21] Male infants tend to be slightly longer (0.8 in, or 2 cm) than female infants.

The head

The head circumference of the full-term infant is almost invariably between 13 and 15 in (33 to 37 cm). The skull is composed of six bony plates, joined loosely by membranous suture lines (Fig. 10-3). The junction of several sutures forms an irregular space. These spaces are enclosed by a membrane and are called *fontanels*, the two most important of which are designated as the *anterior fontanel* and the *posterior fontanel*. The *anterior fontanel*, located between the sagittal and coronal sutures, is diamond-shaped and varies in size up to approximately 5 cm. This fontanel closes by approximately 18 months of age. The *posterior fontanel*, located between the sagittal and lambdoid sutures, is triangular in shape and much smaller than the anterior fontanel. It may actually appear, upon palpation, to be nearly closed at birth, and at any rate usually closes by 2 to 3 months of age. A third fontanel, located between the anterior and posterior fontanels along the sagittal suture line, is found in some normal

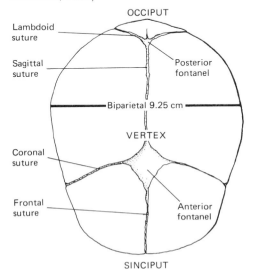

Figure 10-3 Anterior and posterior fontanel. (*Clinical Education Aid No. 13, courtesy of Ross Laboratories, Columbus, Ohio.*)

Figure 10-4 Diagram demonstrating molding of the bones of the head, with overlapping caused by the normal process of compression during passage of the head through the birth canal. By the third day of life the bones have returned to their normal position. (*Courtesy of Meade Johnson Company.*)

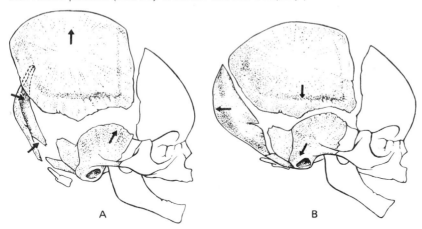

neonates. A much more important consideration than size is the tension exhibited by the fontanels. A bulging fontanel may indicate increased intracranial pressure, while a depressed or sunken fontanel is indicative of dehydration.

Molding The fact that the bones of the head are not fused, but rather held together by these membranous sutures, allows the cranium to change shape in response to the external pressure exerted on the head during labor and delivery (Fig. 10-4). This process is termed *molding*, and may result in an elongated head at birth. This distortion diminishes rapidly, and the head assumes its normal shape within 1 week.

Figure 10-5 Cephalhematoma. (*Courtesy of Meade Johnson Company.*)

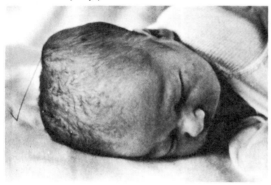

Caput succedaneum Profuse edema caused by pressure on the presenting part of the head during vertex deliveries is termed *caput succedaneum*. This edema, which crosses suture lines, usually subsides by 2 to 3 days of life.

Cephalhematoma Occasionally a neonate will develop a cephalhematoma, caused by bleeding from a ruptured blood vessel between the surface of a cranial bone and the periosteum covering that bone (Fig. 10-5). This will appear during the first few hours of life as a swelling confined to the area over the cranial bone involved; it will not cross suture lines. It is possible to have cephalhematoma over more than one cranial bone simultaneously. A cephalhematoma will disappear spontaneously, but may take up to 6 weeks to do so. Since the cephalhematoma is a collection of blood, significant amounts of serum bilirubin may result as the blood breaks down and is absorbed (Fig. 10-6).

The face

The nose and mouth. Proper anatomic and physiological function of the nose and mouth is of utmost importance in the neonate. Since neonates are primarily nose breathers, any obstruction of the nasal passages is of extreme significance.

The neonate normally exhibits a *sneeze* reflex in response to obstruction or irritation of the nasal passages. This should persist throughout life. In addition, the neonate has the ability to *differentiate odors*, although the precise developmental sequence of this is unknown. Neonates are able to distinguish their own mother's breast pads from those of other mothers and seem to respond to various other olfactory stimuli.[22]

When the *tongue* is touched, the neonate responds by forcing it outward. This *extrusion reflex* normally disappears by 4 months of age. The tongue is attached to the floor of the mouth by the frenulum, which is short and inelastic. This structure occasionally appears to limit the mobility of the tongue. This condition is termed *tongue-tie*, and is frequently accused falsely of causing feeding difficulties in the neonate. Since it is recognized that limited tongue protrusion is needed for the activities of the normal newborn, intervention is seldom indicated. The short frenulum will lenghten in the course of normal development, thus increasing tongue mobility.[23]

The neonate is known to have a discriminating sense of *taste*, demonstrating differing responses to sugar, salt, quinine water, and citric acid solutions. There is increased sucking in response to sweets, and a decrease in sucking when exposed to the others.[24] The tongue of the neonate is not controlled well enough to propel food from the lips to the pharynx; therefore, food must be delivered to the back of the tongue before swallowing is possible.[25]

The neonate is equipped with deposits of fatty tissue, called *sucking pads*, in each cheek. These assist the sucking/feeding process by preventing the pulling in of the cheeks during the sucking process. Even in the presence of malnutrition, these sucking pads remain intact until sucking ceases to constitute a major portion of the infant's ability to obtain nutrition.

Approximately 80 percent of neonates have small inclusion cysts visible at the junction of the hard and soft palates. These are called *Epstein's pearls*, and are of no significance. It is estimated that 1:5000 to 1:10,000 neonates are born with, or experience the eruption of, *teeth*. These are commonly termed "natal teeth," and, if their roots are inadequate, should be pulled to prevent their being aspirated or ingested.[26]

The eyes

The neonate's eyes appear slightly large when compared with the rest of the body. The eyeballs

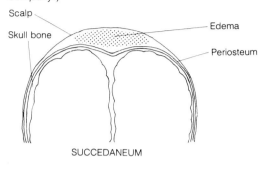

Figure 10-6 Comparison between caput succedaneum and cephalhematoma. (*From Dickason and Schult, Maternal and Infant Care, 2d ed., McGraw-Hill, New York, 1979. Used with the permission of the McGraw-Hill Book Company.*)

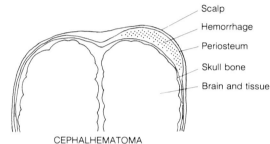

should be equal in size. The irises of all neonates are blue, slate blue–gray, or blue–brown. Pigmentation of the iris, which will determine permanent eye color, may begin to be evident at 3 months of age but is not complete until 6 to 12 months of age. The sclerae of the neonate appear to be slightly bluish gray because they are thin. Any yellow tinge found in the sclerae is indicative of jaundice and warrants further investigation.

Most neonates exhibit pseudostrabismus, commonly known as "cross-eyes," because they seldom make attempts at visual accommodation. A wide, flattened bridge of the nose in some newborns also enhances this appearance. This is a normal finding requiring no intervention.

Subconjunctival hemorrhage A bright red, crescent-shaped band located on the eyeball near the iris may be evident at birth. This is due to pressure on the neonate's face during delivery. This subconjunctival hemorrhage is of no long-term significance, and disappears during the first few weeks of life.

Ophthalmia neonatorum Many infants exhibit ophthalmia neonatorum, or an acute conjunctivitis of varied etiology. A *chemical conjunctivitis* secondary to prophylactic treatment with silver nitrate is frequently seen. This condition manifests itself by profuse edema and redness of the eyelids, frequently accompanied by copious amounts of purulent drainage. This inflammation may appear 2 to 4 h after the instillation of silver nitrate, and should subside without sequelae by the fifth or sixth day of life. Perhaps the most significant problems posed by chemical conjunctivitis center around its interference with parental-infant eye contact and thus bonding, and the inaccessibility of the eye itself to examination during this period.

In the past, the term *ophthalmia neonatorum* usually denoted an eye infection secondary to a gonorrheal infection. In spite of preventive measures, ophthalmia neonatorum caused by *Neisseria gonorrhoeae* continues to be seen. Gonorrheal conjunctivitis usually appears on the second or third day of life. Untreated, this condition progresses rapidly with symptoms similar to those of chemical conjunctivitis, with a constant discharge of *green* purulent material. Without proper treatment ocular involvement progresses to blindness.

Fortunately, since the advent of widespread prophylaxis against this organism, most neonatal conjunctivitis is caused by a variety of other organisms. Once identified, these may be treated appropriately.

Figure 10-7 Position of the ear. (*A*) Normal position. (*B*) True low-set ears. In the normal infant the insertion of the ear falls on the extension of a line drawn across the inner and outer canthus of the eye. (*Courtesy of Meade Johnson Company.*)

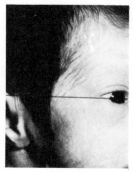
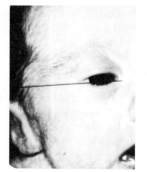

A   B

Eye reflexes Three reflexes are noted when examining the eye. The first is the *blinking*, or corneal, reflex, in which the infant blinks at the sudden appearance of a bright light or object. This is a protective reflex, and should continue throughout life. The second is the *pupillary response*, in which the pupil of the infant constricts when a bright light is shone toward it. This also persists throughout life. The *doll's eye reflex* is seen only early in life. It is demonstrated by moving the infant slowly to the right, left, or vertically. The neonate's eyes remain in a fixed position. This reflex disappears as fixation develops.

The ears

The ears of the full-term neonate should be of normal shape, with some palpable cartilage on examination. Preauricular skin tags are not uncommon. Placement of the ears is of utmost significance. Low-set and malformed ears are associated with kidney or chromosome abnormalities.[27] The pinna of the ear should arise from a point above the level of the inner canthus of the eye (Figs. 10-7A and B). Neonates have a well-developed sense of hearing, and are able to discriminate between high- and low-pitched voices.

The skin

Color The skin color of a neonate is an important indicator of overall status. The skin often looks slightly bluish red because of the visibility of the capillary bed through the thin epidermis. Central cyanosis, evidenced by blueness of the mucous membranes, and/or circumoral cyanosis, is indicative of inadequate general oxygenation. *Acrocyanosis*, or cyanosis localized in the hands and feet (and occasionally also in the nose), is a normal finding which usually disappears during the first few days of life. Pallor of the skin, mucous membranes, and nail beds is indicative of shock and necessitates further assessment and intervention. *Cutis marmorata*, or mottling, is seen most often in pre-term babies, but also in some full-term babies, as a response to chilling. It is due to immaturity of the neonate's vasoconstrictive ability, and disappears with increasing maturity.

Jaundice, or yellowness of the skin, is frequently seen during the first week of life. The normal finding, termed *physiological jaundice*, is due to two major factors: (1) There is an increased rate of red blood cell breakdown during the first week of life, resulting in increased amounts of bilirubin to metabolize, and (2) the immature neonate liver has a limited capacity to conjugate bilirubin. These two factors combine to result in serum bilirubin levels above the normal value (0.2 to 1.4 mg per 100 ml) in nearly all full-term infants. Only about 50 percent of all neonates demonstrate observable jaundice. It is interesting to note that bilirubin levels must exceed 5 mg per 100 ml of serum before jaundice is observable in the skin or sclera. In full-term neonates, physiological jaundice appears *after* the first 24 h of life, and usually peaks by the second or third day. At this time, it averages 6 mg per 100 ml, then rapidly declines to normal levels by the seventh to tenth days of life. See Chap. 19 for a discussion of pathological jaundice and phototherapy.

Common neonatal variations The skin of the neonate manifests several variations specific to this age. *Vernix caseosa*, a white cheesy substance formed on the fetus during the fifth lunar month, is present to some degree on the skin of most neonates. It is seen in abundance in premature infants, but may be noticeable primarily in skin creases in full-term infants. *Lanugo*, a fine downy hair which forms during the fourth lunar month of gestation and starts to disappear during the eighth month, may still be present to some degree in the full-term infant. *Milia* are tiny white epidermal inclusion cysts (plugged sebaceous glands) which appear mainly on the face, primarily on the nose and chin. They are a normal finding, require no treatment, and usually disappear within a few weeks.

Erythema toxicum, or the typical newborn rash, affects approximately 50 percent of all full-term neonates.[28] The rash usually develops during the first or second day of life and disappears spontaneously by the end of the first week of life. It appears on all parts of the body as small papules surrounded by areas of redness and resembling insect bites.

Desquamation, or the flaking off of skin, is normally seen in the neonate. This usually begins with the second or third day of life, and continues through the second or third week. During this period, the skin may appear to be dry, and there may be fissures in the skin folds of the ankles

and wrists. This is a normal, transient occurrence. Excessive desquamation may be indicative of postmaturity. *Harlequin color change*, not to be confused with a different disorder called *harlequin fetus*, is sometimes seen in neonates, especially during the first 4 days of life. It is characterized by blushing of one-half of the body, with simultaneous blanching of the other side. It is assumed to be related to the immaturity of the neurovascular control of the neonate, is of no physiological significance, and in most cases disappears by the third week of life.[29]

Skin trauma It is not uncommon for the newly born infant to have evidence of trauma secondary to labor and delivery. General *abrasions*, and those associated with the application of obstetrical forceps, usually heal without incident. *Ecchymoses*, appearing as black and blue areas, may be associated with trauma during the delivery process. *Petechiae*, or minute subcutaneous hemorrhages, are frequently noted after delivery, particularly in the head and trunk areas. They are due to rupture of capillaries too fragile to withstand the pressure exerted by the labor and delivery process. Ecchymoses and petechiae secondary to birth trauma usually disappear by the second day of life; persistence is worthy of investigation for pathological etiology.

Birth marks The neonate frequently has a variety of "birth marks." Perhaps the most common of these are telangiectatic nevi, more commonly known as *nevus flammeus*. These are typically flat, pale red, and found most often over the eyelids, between the eyes, or at the base of the skull. Because of the last location, these lesions have come to be commonly referred to as "stork-beak's marks" or "stork bites." These are a normal finding and tend to fade with age. However, nevi on other areas, such as the cheeks, do not fade, but develop a purplish coloration. This gives them the common name "port-wine stains."[30] These frequently cause cosmetic difficulties later in life.

Strawberry hemangiomas may be present at birth, or may develop during the neonatal period. These small red lesions grow outwardly and become raised, aquiring a strawberry-like texture—hence the common name. Most of these lesions disappear spontaneously during childhood. *Cavernous hemangiomas*, benign vascular tumors, can cause difficulty because they some-times impinge on specific structures; if this is the case, intervention is indicated. However, the vast majority of these also remit spontaneously.[31]

Mongolian spots are deep brown to greenish or blue-black pigmented areas of varying shape and size. They are located most often over the lumbosacral area and/or legs, and found most often in infants of Asian, African, or Mediterranean descent. These lesions are a normal finding, and bear absolutely no relationship to Down syndrome, formerly referred to as "mongolism." They fade or disappear by early childhood, although some remain as slate-gray discolorations.

The neurological system: major reflexes

The newborn is born with a repertoire of basic reflexes that are important to note as evidence of normal development. Their presence or absence, time of appearance and disappearance, and character yield valuable information regarding the general neurological status of the individual.

The Moro reflex The Moro reflex is an important indicator of neurological status, as it requires activity of both the central and peripheral nervous systems. It is best elicited, with the infant in the supine position, by either lifting the head approximately 2 in and releasing it abruptly, or by pulling the infant up slightly by both hands, then releasing them. The baby first stiffens, then throws both arms out and brings them forward as though he or she were embracing something. It is usually noted that the infant extends fingers three through five on each hand, and frequently will end the response with crying (Fig. 10-8). The Moro response should be present in all term infants and will gradually diminish and disappear by 3 to 4 months of age. Retention of this response after that age is an abnormal finding.

The tonic neck reflex In the tonic neck reflex (TNR), often referred to as the "fencer's position," the turning of the baby's head to one side will result in partial or complete extension of the arm and leg on the side to which the head is

Figure 10-8 The Moro reflex. (*A*) Infant at rest prior to testing for Moro reflex. (*B*) First stage in the Moro response. Note the abduction of the arms and fanning of the fingers. (*C*) Second stage in the Moro response. (*From Clausen et al., Maternity Nursing Today, 2d ed., McGraw-Hill, New York, 1977. Used with the permission of McGraw-Hill Book Company.*)

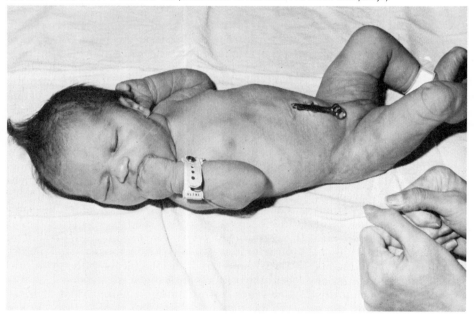

A

turned, and flexion of the opposite leg. The infant normally is able to break this posture after a few seconds; any infant who sustains this position for prolonged periods is demonstrating an abnormal response. This developmental reflex should disappear by 2 to 3 months of age.

The grasp reflex The neonate has grasp reflexes present in both hands and feet. In the palmar (hand) grasp reflex, the fingers will flex around anything placed in the palm of the hand. This should diminish by 3 months of age and be replaced later by voluntary action. The plantar

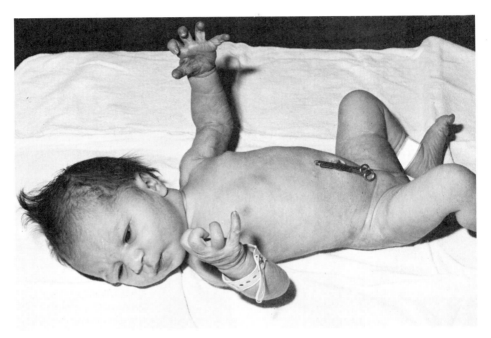

B

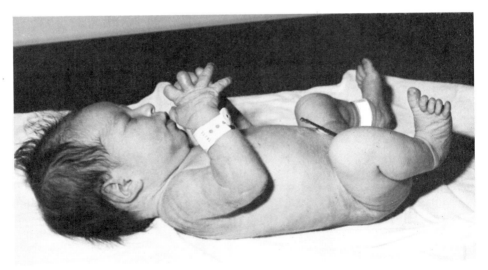

C

grasp is elicited by pressing something against the balls of the feet, which will cause the toes to curl around the object. The plantar grasp lessens by 8 to 10 months of age.

Reflexes used in feeding Basic reflexes aid the infant in the feeding process. The baby seeks food by use of the *rooting reflex*, which is elicited whenever the cheek is touched by the mother's breast, a hand, or any other object. The baby will respond to this stimulus by turning the face toward the stimulus, and opening the mouth in the anticipation of food. The *sucking, swallowing, cough,* and *sneeze* reflexes should be adequately developed to allow safe and effective feeding.

Placing, stepping, and crawling reflexes Responses present with the baby in the upright

Figure 10-9 The stepping reflex. (*From Dickason and Schult, Maternal and Infant Care, 2d ed., McGraw-Hill, New York, 1979. Used with the permission of McGraw-Hill Book Company.*)

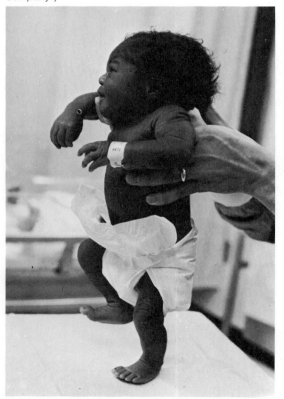

position include *placing* and *stepping*. When the infant is held so that the top of the foot lightly touches the edge of a surface, the foot will normally lift onto the surface. This is placing. Likewise, when the infant is lowered so that the soles of the feet lightly touch the surface of a table or bench, the infant's legs exhibit an alternating stepping motion (Fig. 10-9). These two reflexes normally disappear by 4 weeks of age. Full-term babies will make *crawling* movements when placed on their abdomen. This should disappear at 6 months of age.

The Babinski reflex This reflex should be present, and is demonstrated by lightly stroking the sole of the foot from the heel to toe. This should result in dorsiflexion or extension of the great toe with spreading of the smaller ones. Persistence of this reflex beyond 1 year of age indicates a pyramidal tract lesion.

The gastrointestinal tract

The mouth and its characteristics, senses, and reflexes have been discussed earlier in this chapter. General characteristics of the gastrointestinal tract of the neonate include the following:

1. The intestinal tract of the neonate is relatively longer than that of an older child or an adult.
2. The musculature of the intestinal tract, including sphincters, is underdeveloped.
3. There is a deficiency of elastic fibers.
4. The digestive and absorptive surfaces of the intestine are almost completely developed.

The stomach The stomach capacity of the full-term neonate is approximately 90 ml at birth, and reaches approximately 150 ml by the end of the first month of life. The infant normally swallows a considerable amount of air when eating and especially when crying. Peristaltic movements occur less frequently in the neonatal period than later in life, but reverse peristalsis is not uncommon. This, coupled with an immature and relaxed cardiac sphincter, frequently results in regurgitation. Regurgitation is the backflow of a small amount of milk from the stomach. It is spitting up, not vomiting.

Stomach emptying and intestinal transit times during the neonatal period differ from those found in the older child. The first part of the meal reaches the pylorus 1 to 2 min after ingestion (when the infant is lying on his or her right side). The stomach *empties* more slowly during the neonatal period than at any other time of life. Although the major portion of the meal leaves the stomach in 3 to 4 h, a considerable amount may remain for up to 8 h. Human milk passes through the stomach more rapidly than cow's milk. Stomach contractions due to hunger have been detected 2 to 4 h after eating, frequently before the stomach has emptied. These waves do not necessarily mean that the infant needs more food, and are not regularly a cause for crying or waking.

The intestines Food enters the cecum approximately 3 to 6 h after reaching the stomach, and the first part of the meal appears in the stool in a little over 8 h from the time ingested. The normal full-term neonate appears to possess the conditions and enzymes necessary for the digestion of nutrients commonly fed during this period. However, there is a deficiency in pancreatic amylase, impairing the utilization of complex carbohydrates, and of pancreatic lipase, which limits the absorption of fats.

The stools undergo major changes during the neonatal period. The first stools are *meconium.* Meconium begins to appear in the fetal intestine toward the end of the fourth month of gestation. Meconium is a black, odorless, sticky substance. It contains vernix caseosa and lanugo, which have been swallowed in the amniotic fluid, digestive secretions, desquamated epithelium, mucus, and bile pigments. Passage of the first meconium stool is frequently preceded by a meconium "plug," which is usually grayish white in color and 3 to 5 cm long with the consistency of rubber. Meconium may be passed in utero, in response to hypoxia, or as a result of a breech presentation. Some meconium should be passed during the first 24 h of neonatal life. If this does not occur, concern regarding the possibility of intestinal obstruction arises.

The character of the stools changes rapidly during the first week of life. During the first day of life, meconium stools will vary from black to blackish green in color. From the second through fourth days, stools contain some mucus and are greenish brown, brownish yellow, or greenish yellow. These are appropriately called *transitional* stools.

From about the fifth day on, the characteristics of the stools will depend largely on what the infant is fed. Infants who are breast-fed have soft, yellow stools which change to a pasty golden yellow, with a characteristic sour odor. The stools of infants fed cow's milk formula are somewhat drier and more formed, paler in color, and have a foul odor.

The liver The neonatal liver has a decreased or limited capacity to conjugate bilirubin. Unfortunately, this enzymatic deficiency occurs at a time when the increased red blood cell breakdown and resulting increased serum bilirubin levels place high demands on the system. This limited ability to conjugate bilirubin results in physiological jaundice.

The neonatal liver also has a decreased ability to form plasma proteins. The subsequent decreased plasma protein concentration may contribute to the generalized edema seen in the neonate. Another very important hepatic deficiency is that of adequate gluconeogenesis, frequently resulting in low blood sugars. For this reason, early feedings are advisable.

During this period the liver is unable to form adequate amounts of prothrombin and other factors necessary for adequate blood coagulation. As has been discussed earlier in this chapter, the newborn lacks vitamin K, necessary for the clotting process, and therefore is given a supplement of this vitamin shortly after birth.

The chest and abdomen
At birth the infant's chest circumference is 1 or 2 cm less than the head circumference. The normal chest is approximately cylindrical and symmetric. Breath sounds should be equal on both sides, as should the chest wall movements that occur with respiration. Neonates are "abdominal breathers"; that is, the abdomen rises and falls more noticeably than the chest expands and contracts with each breath.

As a result of the influence of maternal hormones, the breasts of babies of both sexes may be enlarged. A milky fluid called "witch's milk" may be secreted from the swollen breasts. Engorgement and secretion diminish rapidly after the first week of life and should disappear by 1 month of age.

The abdomen of the neonate is normally cylindrical in shape. Bowel sounds should be audible within a few hours after birth. If meconium is not passed during the first 24 h, the anus should be examined for patency.

An *umbilical hernia*, or skin-covered protrusion at the umbilicus, is not an unusual finding, especially in Negro children. This normally requires no intervention, and usually disappears early in childhood.

The *liver* is palpable 2 to 3 cm below the right costal margin. The tip of the *spleen* is normally felt in the lateral portion of the left upper quadrant. Deep palpation is necessary to locate the *kidneys*, which are felt as small oval structures between the examiner's thumb and index finger. The lower pole of each kidney should be 1 to 2 cm above the level of the umbilicus; if felt below this level, the kidneys may be enlarged, warranting further investigation.

The genitourinary system

The kidney The kidney of the full-term neonate is anatomically well developed, and capable of basic and essential excretory functions.[32] The neonatal kidney is functionally immature. It is limited in its ability to excrete some metabolites, in buffering capacity, and in controlling sodium excretion. The newborn's kidney is unable to concentrate water in response to dehydration.

The neonate has an average of 6 ml of urine in the bladder at birth. Studies have shown that as many as 17 percent first void in the delivery room. Approximately 90 percent void in the first 24 h of life.[33] Average urine output increases from 20 ml during the first days of life to 227 ml on day 7. The neonate voids two to six times per 24 h during the first few days of life; voidings then increase to 10 to 20 voidings per day.

The urine of the neonate has very little odor, and is normally clear. There is an increased excretion of uric acid, which may crystallize and be seen as red spots on the diaper. These spots are frequently mistaken for blood. Concentration of urine *may* be slightly elevated during the first 2 to 3 days of life—a condition secondary to low fluid intake. After the baby is about 3 days old, urine normally has a low specific gravity, rarely reaching 1.025. Infants who are breast-fed have urine with an unusually low specific gravity, averaging 1.008 after the third day of life. Protein is normally present in small amounts (under 10 mg per 100 ml). Excessive proteinuria may occur in pathological situations, such as neonatal asphyxia, and warrants further investigation.[34]

Male genitalia The *scrotum* of the full-term male infant frequently appears unusually large and may contain some fluid at birth. This fluid disappears during the first few days of life. The *testes* have descended into the scrotal sac in approximately 96 percent of full-term male infants. They are approximately 1 cm in diameter, and should be easily palpable. The testes of most neonates who have undescended testicles, or *cryptorchidism*, will descend spontaneously during the first year of life.

The urinary meatus is normally at the tip of the penis. The foreskin covers the glans penis completely, and is usually seen extending somewhat beyond the tip and narrowing to leave a small opening. During the neonatal period the foreskin is relatively inelastic and adherent to the glans. It cannot be retracted without trauma until about 3 years of age. In *phimosis*, the foreskin is so tightly fitted over the glans of the penis that it cannot be retracted. This is a normal finding in the neonate and becomes abnormal only if present after 3 years of age.

Circumcision of the male infant Circumcision, or the surgical removal of the foreskin, continues

Figure 10-10 Penis of infant after circumcision with Gomco clamp. (*From Scipien et al., Comprehensive Pediatric Nursing, 2d ed., McGraw-Hill, New York, 1979. Used with the permission of McGraw-Hill Book Company.*)

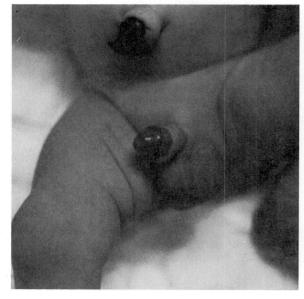

to be widely practiced in this culture. There are three basic methods for performing a circumcision. The first, and simplest, is the "dorsal-slit method," in which a small incision is made in the foreskin to allow complete retraction without the actual removal of the foreskin. The second is a clamp method (Fig. 10-10). In this method the glans and prepuce (foreskin) are separated, the glans covered, and the prepuce amputated by cutting. The third method is use of the *plastibell* (Fig. 10-11). In this method, a small plastic bell is placed over the glans and the prepuce draped over it. A suture is then tied tightly around the prepuce and bell. This is left in place, and the foreskin drops off in 1 to 2 weeks, thus requiring no cutting.[35]

Circumcision is performed on the eighth day of life, as a religious rite, by Orthodox Jews. On other babies it is usually done on the day before discharge from the newborn nursery; or if the procedure is contraindicated at that time, it may be done later on an outpatient basis.

Although few would argue the relevance of circumcision when performed as a religious ritual, the medical value of the procedure is very controversial. Proponents of circumcision argue that circumcision promotes the following: (1) the prevention of permanent phimosis; (2) greater cleanliness because it eliminates a blind pouch in which smegma, a cheeselike substance, can collect with ensuing infection; (3) avoidance of the potential trauma of pulling or tearing a nonretractable foreskin during sexual intercourse; and (4) a possible reduction in the risk of cancer of the penis in men and uterine cancer in their mates.

Opponents of circumcision as a routine procedure cite the following reasons for their disapproval: (1) hemorrhage secondary to the procedure; (2) infection at the circumcision site, which may escalate to generalized sepsis; (3) removal of the prepuce leaves the glans exposed and liable to injury or ulceration, frequently leading to meatal stenosis; (4) reports of complications, including gangrene, with use of the plastibell; (5) mild distortion of the penis secondary to scarring, which may lead to physical and psychological trauma; and (6) constant exposure of the glans to air may cause it to lose some tactile sensation, decreasing pleasure during intercourse.

Although the pros and cons regarding circumcision continue to be argued vehemently by those concerned, perhaps the most substantial considerations regarding circumcision lie in its relationship to cancer. Attempts have been made

Figure 10-11 Circumcision. (*A*) The Hollister plastibell. (*B*) Suture around the rim of plastic controls bleeding. (*C*) Plastic rim and suture drop off in 7 to 10 days. (*Courtesy of Hollister, Inc. From Dickason and Schult, Maternal and Infant Care, 2d ed., McGraw-Hill, New York, 1979. Used with the permission of McGraw-Hill Book Company.*)

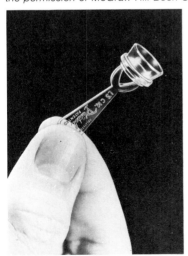

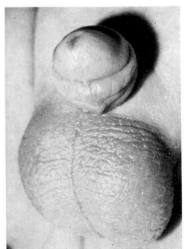

A   B   C

to demonstrate a decreased cancer rate both in circumcised males and in their sexual partners, but results of such studies continue to be controversial.

Female external genitalia The labia and clitoris of the female neonate are unusually edematous because of maternal hormonal influences. The labia minora are more fully developed than the labia majora, and because of this the latter seem to be somewhat separated when compared with those of the older child. Vernix caseosa is found between the labia of the newly born infant.

The urinary meatus is frequently difficult to see. The vaginal opening is seen without difficulty. From it there frequently is the protrusion of a hymenal tag. The female infant usually has a mucous discharge from the vagina, sometimes blood-tinged, during the first week of life. This is also due to the influence of maternal hormones and is called *pseudomenstruation.*

The Cardiovascular system

The transition from fetal to neonatal circulation has been discussed earlier in this chapter. Once this transition has been adequately accomplished, the circulatory pattern of the neonate is like that of the older child and adult.

The heart The neonatal heart is proportionately larger than that of the older child and therefore occupies proportionately more space within the thoracic cavity. Because the heart assumes a more lateral position at this age, the maximum impulse is heard at the third to fourth intercostal space, lateral to the midclavicular line.

The apical pulse rate changes markedly in the neonatal period. At birth, or shortly thereafter, it may reach as high as 180 beats per minute, typical of the first period of reactivity. As the neonate progresses through the period of transition, the rate will vary. By the second day of life the rate should have stabilized, and is most often heard in the range of 120 to 140 beats per minute. However, it may range from 100 to 160 beats per minute, depending upon activity. Soft systolic murmurs are often heard, caused by incomplete closure of the fetal shunts. These usually are of no significance, and disappear by the end of the first month of life.

Hematologic values The blood volume of full-term infants varies from an average of 99 ml/kg for those infants who have received a "placental transfusion" to 86 ml/kg for those who have not. *Placental transfusion* refers to the baby's receipt of 50 to 100 ml of blood from the placenta, which occurs if the umbilical cord is allowed to stop pulsating before it is clamped. Obstetrical practice in this regard varies. The corresponding hematocrit values are an average of 59 percent for the transfused group and 46 percent for the others.[36] The white blood cell count varies from a value of 9000 to 30,000 per cubic millimeter at birth, rising to 13,000 to 38,000 per cubic millimeter at 12 h of age, then declining to 5000 to 20,000 per cubic millimeter by 14 days of age.[37]

Respirations

Initiation of respirations was discussed earlier in the chapter. The normal respirations of the neonate are usually between 30 to 60 per minute, are irregular, and are more abdominal than thoracic. Neonates experience both apnea and periodic breathing.

A 1977 study revealed that apnea (cessation of breathing exceeding 6 s) was a normal phenomenon in the normal full-term infant. The study found that the incidence of apnea was highest in the newborn period, during which some periods of apnea exceeded 15 s. Periodic breathing, or the cessation of breathing for periods shorter than 6 s and occurring twice within a 24-s period, were common throughout the first 6 months of life.[38] More detailed information regarding evaluation of respiratory status will be found in Chap. 19.

The musculoskeletal system

The skeletal frame of the neonate is soft because it has relatively low amounts of mineral deposits and contains a large amount of cartilage. These facts, coupled with the increase in mobility of the joints during this period, make the body of the neonate extremely flexible. The neonate's trunk is disproportionately long, the extremities disproportionately short, and the head disproportionately large when compared with the same structures of older infants and children.

The legs normally appear so bowed that the soles of the feet may appear to meet. The spine is normally straight and without dimples or sinuses.

The normal neonate has good muscle tone, preferring to flex the extremities. This is demonstrated when an extremity is pulled to an extended position. It will attempt to return to the flexed position.

When being picked up, the baby should have head and back support. When prone, the neonate is able to lift his head momentarily and rotate it from side to side.

Body defenses

At the moment of birth, the neonate passes from an environment that is essentially sterile to one laden with pathogens. The nurse should understand what mechanisms are available to the baby to cope with this changing situation. The skin, traditionally considered the body's first line of defense, provides an effective barrier to pathogens. The reticuloendothelial system, the second line of defense, is capable of mobilizing phagocytes, such as neutrophils and monocytes. However, for reasons not fully understood, their phagocytic action does not reach full strength in the neonate. The inflammatory response, so important in dealing with pathogens that succeed in penetrating the skin, depends in large part on the activity of phagocytic cells. Therefore, the inflammatory response is less vigorous in the neonate than in older infants, in children, and in adults.

Immune responses, the third line of the body's defenses, are of mixed value to the neonate. There are two kinds of immune responses: cell-mediated and antibody-mediated. Cell-mediated responses depend on encounters between pathogens and certain prepared lymphocytes. These encounters can begin only at birth and for a time are unable to set off a fully effective counterattack against pathogens. Thus cell-mediated immune responses are deficient. Cell-mediated responses are ordinarily effective against fungi, cancer cells, parasites, and certain viral infections.

Antibody-mediated immune responses mainly provide protection against such bacteria as pneumococci, streptococci, and staphylococci. Antibodies may provide some initial protection against certain viruses. Antibodies are serum proteins that are better known as immunoglobulins (Ig). Immunoglobulins G (IgG) and M (IgM) are the most important in the neonate. IgG crosses the placenta, and throughout neonatal life the bulk of the infant's IgG is that received from the mother in the fetal period. IgG provides protection against such bacterial toxins as diphtheria and tetanus; viruses that cause such diseases as measles, rubella, and chickenpox;

and some gram-positive bacteria, notably staphylococci, streptococci, pneumococci, *Neisseria*, and *Haemophilus influenzae*. The nurse should recognize that no protection is available for the enteric gram-negative organism *Escherichia coli*, which frequently invades the newborn child.[39,40]

IgM does not cross the placenta but is made by the fetus beginning in the twentieth week of gestation. IgM is produced in response to such infections as syphilis, toxoplasmosis, rubella, cytomegalic inclusion disease (CID), and herpes simplex. These five diseases are commonly abbreviated as STORCH, and the last four as TORCH, infections. Because the fetus responds to the presence of these pathogens by producing IgM, a cord blood level of IgM greater than 20 mg per 100 ml is probably a sign of intrauterine infection. (The normal cord blood IgM is 8 mg per 100 ml.)[41]

Immunoglobulin A (IgA) does not cross the placenta. It is detectable in the serum by the end of the first month after birth, but normal adult levels are not reached until 10 years of age.[42] IgA can neutralize some viruses, especially influenza and polio. It is not active against bacteria.

Immunoglobulin E (IgE) does not cross the placenta. It is responsible for allergic skin reactions. Since the neonatal level of IgE is only about one-tenth that of the adult, one can safely assume that skin problems in the neonate are not allergic in nature.[43]

In summary, although the neonate is not without some ability to combat pathogens in its new environment, the nurse must take care to offer protection against known pathogens, to recognize the presence of infection immediately, and to take appropriate actions to combat the infection.

Hospital nursery care of the neonate

Admission to the newborn nursery

When the newborn is transferred to the nursery, effective communication between delivery room nurses and nursery nurses is critical. During this time, nursing actions generally revolve around meeting the goals of protection and assessment.

The neonatal nurse first acts to protect the newborn by verifying the infant's identification tags with the delivery room nurse and with the medical record. The record is checked to confirm that prophylactic treatment for *Neisseria gonorrhoeae* has been administered. If vitamin K has not been given in the delivery room, the nursery nurses will administer it as ordered.

The nursery nurse should carry out the assessment of the newborn by proceeding in an orderly and systematic manner.

Obtaining an accurate history

The nurse in attendance in the delivery room should report to the nursery nurse, who now assumes responsibility for care of the neonate. From direct knowledge or by notation on the medical records, the nurse provides the following information:

1. A history of hereditary conditions in the mother's or father's family.
2. The estimated date of confinement (EDC).
3. The mother's blood group and Rh type—evidence of sensitization and/or immunization (such as the administration of RhoGAM after previous deliveries—this subject is covered in more detail in the discussion of erythroblastosis fetalis in Chap. 19.
4. Results of testing for syphilis (including dates performed).
5. Number, duration, and outcome of previous pregnancies, with dates.
6. Any maternal disease (diabetes, hypertension, preeclampsia, infections, etc.).
7. Drugs taken during pregnancy, labor, and delivery (with time of administration if during labor and delivery).
8. Results of measurements of fetal maturity and well-being.
9. The duration of ruptured membranes and of labor.
10. The method of delivery, including indications for operative or instrumental intervention.
11. Any complications of labor and delivery.
12. A description of the placenta, including the number of umbilical vessels.
13. The estimated amount and description of amniotic fluid.
14. The Apgar scores at 1 and 5 min, the age at which respirations became spontaneous and sustained, and a description of any resuscitative measures employed.[44]
15. The results of any screening tests done, with a description of any observed anomalies.
16. A summary of parental involvement during the labor and delivery, with nursing observations about bonding behavior. Nursing observations of parental responses have long-range implications

for bonding and for the establishment of positive parenting patterns. This information allows the nurse to deliver comprehensive psychological care to the new family. Based on observations the nurse can give anticipatory guidance.

Initial physical assessment of the newborn

If the infant appears stable on admission to the nursery, assessment is begun by obtaining an accurate weight and vital signs.

The nurse then briefly examines the infant for congenital anomalies and assesses the general physical status of the infant. Take the infant's temperature, then wrap the infant in a warmed blanket, and place him or her in a side-lying position in clear view of the nursery nurse. If the temperature is below 35.5°C (96°F) on admission to the nursery, or fails to rise and stabilize with wrapping, warming lights or an incubator may be indicated. Many institutions routinely lower the head of the bassinet to facilitate drainage of mucus.

If the infant appears to be stable at this point, it is wise to provide a time for rest and recovery from the birth process before continuing to meet the goals of assessment, protection, nurturance, and stimulation.

Assessment

A basic understanding of the characteristics of the normal newborn, as discussed earlier in this chapter, is essential background knowledge which enables the nurse to systematically assess the neonate. Assessment began with interpretation of data regarding the history of the family, pregnancy, labor and delivery, fetal status, and status of the newborn in the delivery room. This information was obtained on admission of the infant to the nursery, and augmented by the brief physical inspection done by the nursery nurse. Comprehensive, ongoing assessment of the newborn is the responsibility of the neonatal nurse.

Physical assessment

A detailed and systematic physical examination of the newborn should be carried out by the nurse or physician. The purposes for doing a neonatal assessment are to:

1. Determine whether the infant has made a successful transition from intrauterine life to being an air-breather.

2. Determine the presence of congenital anomalies.
3. Collect baseline data against which future findings may be assessed.
4. Learn things about the baby's unique qualities that can be used in providing parents with appropriate anticipatory guidance in the care of their newborn.

There are some basic guidelines to consider when undertaking a physical assessment of the newborn. Chilling must be avoided. It is wise to take the infant's temperature prior to the examination, and to defer the procedure if the temperature is below 36.1°C (97°F). The examination should be done in an environment which will minimize heat loss.

The assessment should proceed in an orderly cephalocaudal (head-to-toe) progression. However, it is advisable to begin the examination by listening to the heart, lungs, and abdomen. Undressing and manipulating the infant may lead to crying, making these important observations impossible or inadequate. The nurse must use the techniques of inspection, palpation, percussion, and auscultation to obtain data. The guideline for physical assessment of the neonate (Table 10-2), used in conjunction with the previous section "Normal Physical Characteristics of the Newborn," will provide the nurse with direction in this phase of newborn assessment.

Vital signs Regular measurement of the neonate's vital signs will provide valuable information regarding physical status. Because these measurements may fluctuate markedly with activity, the nurse increases the accuracy of their interpretation if the activity, or behavioral state, of the infant is recorded at the time the measurement is made. Behavioral states (deep sleep, active sleep, and so forth) are explained below in the section on behavioral assessment.

Temperature Axillary temperatures are safest and hence preferable. The use of a rectal thermometer involves risk; inserting it more than 2 to 3 cm into the rectum can cause severe damage, not the least of which is perforation of the bowel. However, many institutions routinely take the *initial* temperature rectally to rule out imperforate anus. If the nurse does this, great care must be exercised. Since studies have indicated there is a high correlation between axillary and rectal temperatures, the taking of axillary temperatures

is recommended for this age group.[45] At delivery the newborn has an average rectal temperature of 37 to 37.8°C (98.6 to 100°F); and a decrease of 1 to 3°F is not unusual before the infant leaves the delivery room, despite the use of measures to minimize loss of body heat.[46,47] The infant's temperature should be monitored hourly for the first 2 h following transfer to the newborn nursery, then at least every 8 h. Once stabilized, the usual axillary temperature for the normal full-term infant ranges from 36 to 37°C (96.8 to 98.6°F), the corresponding rectal temperature being 0.4 to 0.5°C (1°F) higher than the axillary value.[48-50] It is important for the nurse to realize that thermoregulation in the neonate is a complex process, and that optimal body temperature may vary with each infant.

Heart rate The neonatal heart rate varies greatly with activity within a range of 100 to 140 beats per minute. Some authorities cite acceptable ranges as low as 70 during deep sleep and as high as 180 when active.[51] The usual range is between 120 and 140 beats per minute. When obtaining the apical pulse, it is important to use the appropriate stethoscope, and to count the rate for a full 60 s.

Respiratory rate The rate at which a neonate breathes, like the heart rate, varies with activity. The normal range is 30 to 60 breaths per minute. Because the newborn normally has an extremely irregular breathing pattern, it is especially important to monitor respiration for a full minute.

Blood pressure The blood pressure of the normal full-term newborn ranges from 60 to 80 mmHg systolic and 40 to 50 mmHg diastolic. The systolic rises to 95 to 100 mmHg by day 10, with a slight rise in the diastolic pressure.[52] For an accurate reading, the appropriate-sized cuff (2.5 to 4 cm) must be used. The pressure may be obtained by auscultation, palpation, or by the flush method. See Chap. 17 for discussion of methods of measuring blood pressure. It is the practice of many hospitals to omit routine blood pressure monitoring in the normal, healthy full-term newborn.

Laboratory tests for the newborn Biochemical and other laboratory screening tests are used to supplement data obtained through the history

Table 10-2 Newborn assessment guide

Manifestation/normal findings	Minor abnormalities/common variations	Major abnormalities/signs of potential problems
Measurements		
Length = 45–55 cm (18–22 in) Weight = 2500–4600 g (5½–10 lb) Head circumference = 33–37 cm (13–15 in) Chest circumference = 30–33 cm (12–13 in)	Neonate normally loses 10% of birth weight by 3–4 days, regains by 10 days	Head circumference more than 4 cm greater than chest (may indicate hydrocephaly) Head circumference less than chest may indicate microcephaly
Position/movement		
Assumes "fetal position"; head is flexed and extremities rest on chest and abdomen Size and movement of body parts should be symmetrical	Frank breech—abducted, externally rotated thighs, extended legs and neck	Hypotonia (limpness); extension of extremities
Skin		
Color—pink Epidermis is red, soft, smooth, delicate at birth; by 2d or 3d day becomes dry, flakes, or peels Vernix caseosa Lanugo Good skin turgor	Jaundice after first 24 h Acrocyanosis Milia Erythema toxicum (newborn rash) Harlequin color change Mongolian spots Cutis marmorata (mottling) Telangiectatic nevi ("stork bites") Petechiae or ecchymoses caused by birth trauma	Jaundice during first 24 h of life Generalized, central cyanosis Excessive vernix caseosa (may indicate preterm) Absence of vernix caseosa (may indicate post-term) Poor skin turgor Persistent and/or generalized petechiae
Cranium		
Anterior fontanel diamond-shaped (to 5 cm) (2 in) Posterior fontanel, triangular-shaped (0.5–1 cm) (0.2–0.4 in) Fontanels should be flat, soft, and firm	Third sagittal fontanel Caput succedaneum Cephalhematoma	Bulging or depressed fontanels Fused suture lines
Eyes		
Eyes usually closed—strong blink reflex Lids frequently edematous Color usually gray-blue or gray-brown Sclera usually has a bluish tint Fixes on bright object, has ability to follow to midline	Chemical conjunctivitis Subconjunctival hemorrhage Pseudostrabismus	Purulent discharge Congenital cataracts Mongoloid slant Inability to follow
Ears		
Top of ear should be at level of eye Some cartilage should be palpable	Lack of cartilage is indicative of preterm infant	Low-set ears (may indicate chromosome abnormality and/or renal disorder)
Nose		
Both nares patent Thin, white mucous discharge		Nonpatent nares Unusual nasal discharge Nasal flaring

Table 10-2 Newborn assessment guide (*Continued*)

Manifestation/normal findings	Minor abnormalities/common variations	Major abnormalities/signs of potential problems
Mouth and throat		
Intact palate Minimum salivation	Inclusion cysts (Epstein's pearls) Natal teeth Thrush	Cleft lip and/or palate Inability to pass nasogastric tube Large protruding tongue Excessive salivation
Neck		
Full lateral (side-to-side) and anterior-posterior range of motion Short and thick		Excessive skin folds Webbing Restricted movement Hyperextension
Chest		
Ribs should be flexible Xyphoid process observable	Supernumerary (extra) nipples Breast enlargement Secretion of "witch's milk" from nipples Funnel chest (pectus excavatum)	Marked retraction of chest and intercostal spaces with respirations Asymmetric chest expansion Redness around nipples Depressed sternum Widely spaced nipples
Lungs		
Bilateral breath sounds Respiratory rate 40–60 breaths per minute Abdominal breathing Irregular respirations	Apnea of 6–15 sec Periodic breathing Rales shortly after birth	Reduced or asymmetric breath sounds Apnea exceeding 15 s, dyspnea, tachypnea, grunting
Heart		
Rate: 120–140 beats per minute Regular rhythm Apex near fourth intercostal space on left, lateral to midclavicular line First and second sounds clearly discernible	Murmurs Rate: 100–120 beats per minute Rate: 140–180 beats per minute with activity	Apex abnormally placed Obvious enlarged heart Tachycardia Bradycardia
Abdomen		
Cylindrical with slight protrusion Umbilical stump: at birth, blue-white and shiny; by 24 h, yellow-brown, dull, dry; eventually black-brown; shrivels and falls off in 7–14 days Liver palpable 2–3 cm below right costal margin Spleen feels like slight mass in lateral aspect left upper quadrant Kidneys palpable 1–2 cm above umbilicus Femoral pulses should be palpable, equal	Umbilical hernia Visible peristalsis in thin infants Bladder distention—firm globular mass felt in suprapubic area	Distention Localized bulging at the flanks Red, oozing, and/or malodorous umbilical stump (or area) Any abnormal mass Persistent bladder distention after voiding Absent, diminished, or unequal femoral pulses
Male genitalia		
Both testes palpable in scrotum Urethral opening at tip of penis Smegma present Foreskin adherent to glans, difficult to retract	Testes palpable in inguinal canal Inability to retract foreskin Hydrocele Small scrotum Inguinal hernia Penile erection	Testes nonpalpable Hypospadias Epispadias

Table 10-2 Newborn assessment guide (*Continued*)

Manifestation/normal findings	Minor abnormalities/common variations	Major abnormalities/signs of potential problems
Female genitalia		
Labia minora larger than labia majora	Pseudomenses (blood-tinged mucous discharge from vagina)	Fused labia
Vernix caseosa between labia folds		No vaginal opening
Labia and clitoris edematous		
Urinary meatus difficult to visualize		
Hymenal tag		
Anus		
Patent anal opening		Imperforate anus
Anal opening normally placed		
Musculoskeletal system		
Spine intact with no prominent curves, masses, or openings	Pilonidal dimple in coccygeal area	Spina bifida
Full range of motion, including hips	Simian crease in palm	Pilonidal cyst or sinus
Sole usually flat	Occasional momentary tremors	Polydactaly (extra digits)
Symmetric extremities		Syndactaly (webbing or fusion of digits)
Head lag while sitting but momentarily able to hold head erect		Dislocated hip—symptoms:
Able to hold head in horizontal line with back when held prone		1. Limitation in abduction
		2. Audible "click" on abduction
Able to turn head from side to side when prone		3. Unequal leg length
		4. Unequal gluteal or thigh skin folds
Extremities maintain some degree of flexion		Hypotonia
		Paralysis
		Marked head lag
		Tremors, twitches, myoclonic jerks
Neurological system		
Reflexes: blinking, pupillary, sneeze, suck, gag, rooting, extrusion, yawn, cough, grasp, Babinski, Moro, tonic neck, crawling, stepping.	Response will vary depending on state	Absent or asymmetrical reflexes
	See text	Constant tongue protrusion
Doll's eye response		

* Head circumference should exceed chest circumference by 2–3 cm.

and physical examination. Which of these tests are routine and which will be done only when specifically indicated vary greatly from institution to institution.

Tests on cord blood In a sense, the newborn has one advantage not found in any other period of life: that of a ready-made blood sample. Blood obtained in the delivery room from the umbilical cord can be used to gather valuable diagnostic data. The baby's blood type and Rh factor are determined from this blood source. The Coombs' test is performed to detect sensitized red blood cells in hemolytic disease of the newborn. A weakly positive Coombs' test is indicative of mildly low levels of antibodies, therefore most likely causing only mild hemolysis; while a strongly positive (3^+ to 4^+) Coombs' test result indicates the presence of high concentrations of antibodies and, most likely, ensuing severe hemolysis. In many hospitals cord blood is tested for serology, to detect the presence of syphilis. Blood cultures are done if infection is suspected. Several other screening and diagnostic tests may be performed if indicated. It is wise for the laboratory to retain a sample of each infant's cord blood until the baby is discharged.

Blood and urine tests Depending on the nursery policy, a routine hematocrit, hemoglobin, and urinalysis may be done on all infants. Other services are of the opinion that these tests should only be carried out if the history and physical assessment of the infant yield abnormal or suspicious findings.

Cultures Most nurseries do not culture each infant routinely, although some institutions do culture the rectum, cord stump, and nasopharynx. The nurse should be aware of the severity and rapidity of progression of sepsis in newborns. If an infection is suspected, the appropriate culture should be taken.

Screening tests Screening tests for several congenital and inherited disorders may be done, either before the infant leaves the hospital or on an outpatient basis. For detailed information regarding testing, refer to material regarding specific diseases.

Behavioral assessment The behavioral evaluation is perhaps the most recent component of infant assessment. Little more than a decade ago, newly born infants were regarded by most professionals as passive beings, with no capacity to react to or affect their environment. We are becoming more and more aware that this is far from the truth. The *Brazleton Neonatal Assessment Scale* was developed by Dr. T. Berry Brazleton.[53] This tool evaluates a baby's behavior toward and responses to stimuli in the environment and the way in which this young individual attempts to control his or her environment.

The *Brazleton Behavioral Assessment Scale* scores babies on 27 behavioral and 20 neurological responses. The behavioral portion of the evaluation tests and documents the infant's behavioral states (deep sleep, active sleep, etc., described just below) and response to external cues administered by a caretaker. Behavioral state is plotted throughout the examination. The ability of an infant to vary his or her behavioral state directly relates to the infant's capacity for self-organization. The neurological items included in the examination act as a screening test for neurological adequacy. Dr. Brazleton advocates a complete neurological examination if there is any reason to question the neurological status of the infant.

The test has a relatively high degree of so-

phistication. To achieve an acceptable level of reliability, which is necessary before data collected from different samples of neonates can be compared, observers must undergo an intensive 2-day training period. Although this test was developed as a research tool, it is easily used as part of the nurse's clinical assessment. Infant responses elicited during this examination should be shared with parents to increase their awareness of the reciprocal effects of their own and their baby's behavior and responses. Nurses interested in utilizing all or portions of this scale in their newborn assessment should seek out and study Dr. Brazleton's original test.

The neonate demonstrates distinctly different behavioral states. The six states used by Brazleton and many others are described below. Some classification systems omit drowsiness and use only the other five states.

Deep sleep In this state, the infant has closed eyes and regular respirations. There is no spontaneous activity except for startles or jerky movements at regular intervals. External stimuli produce startles with some delay, but these are rapidly suppressed. There are no eye movements. State changes are less likely from deep sleep than from other states.

Active sleep Although the eyes are closed, rapid eye movement (REM) can be detected under the lids. For this reason this state is also known as *REM sleep*. There is little activity except random movements and startles. Movements are less jerky than in deep sleep. Respirations are irregular; sucking movements occur sporadically. The infant responds to stimuli with startles, often resulting in a change of state.

Drowsiness The eyes may be open or closed, with the eyelids fluttering. The activity level is less variable, with mild startles interspersed. Although the infant is responsive to sensory stimuli, the response is often delayed. Movements are usually smooth. There is frequently a state change after stimulation.

Alert inactivity The infant appears to focus on some source of stimulation (e.g., a visual or auditory stimulus). Impinging stimuli may break through, but with a delay in response. There is a minimum of motor activity in this state.

Alert activity The eyes are open. There is considerable motor activity with thrusting movements of the extremities. Spontaneous startles may be seen. The infant reacts to external stimuli with increased startles or motor activity. However, because of the high activity level, discrete reactions are difficult to discern.

Crying This state is characterized by intense crying which is difficult to break through with stimulation.

The cycle of these states of sleep is highly variable and heavily influenced by environmental stimuli. It is therefore extremely helpful for parents to understand the characteristics of the states and the methods for altering them. For instance, wrapping an infant will usually promote drowsiness, feeding will usually terminate crying if the cause of the crying is hunger. In addition, observation of the neonate in various states assists the parent in appreciating the individuality and potential of the infant. See Chap. 11 for further discussion of ways the nurse can apply knowledge about behavioral states to support infant development and foster parent-child relationships.

Protection from infection

Because newborns have diminished capacities to ward off infection in the neonatal period, careful attention must be paid to protecting them against pathogens in the environment. The nurse must act as infant-advocate in this regard.

Control of infections in the nursery includes measures directed toward personnel, physical environment of the nursery, and the infants, particularly identification and management of infants with a proven or potential transmissible infection.

Personnel The nursery techniques and health status of personnel caring for infants are the most important factors in infection control. The number of people coming in contact with the newborn should be limited to those directly involved in neonatal care. Nursery personnel and others who have contact with the newborn should be free of transmissible diseases. The American Academy of Pediatrics suggests that all personnel assigned to newborn infant services should have at least an annual health assess-

ment, including screening for tuberculosis. Nurses who have a respiratory, skin, mucocutaneous (especially herpes) lesions, intestinal, or other transmissible infection are a clear threat to newborn infants. Infected personnel should be excluded from working with infants, and not return to work until the infection has subsided. It is recommended that personnel health policies should be arranged so that staff feel free to report infections without fear of loss of income.[54] Unfortunately, this is not always the case. Neonatal nurses must exercise sound ethical judgment regarding their own health status and that of other hospital staff, parents, and visitors to ensure that none of these people, perhaps unknowingly, harbor infections which might affect the neonate.

After individuals have been screened and are considered safe to come in contact with the newborn, the foremost guard against the transmission of infection is thorough hand-washing. All persons caring for newborns should carry out a 2-min scrub at the beginning of each shift. This is most effectively done with an antiseptic agent, such as hexachlorophene or iodophor. Table 17-12 details hand-washing technique. Following the initial scrub, the hands should be thoroughly washed *immediately* before and after handling each infant. Even more specifically, the nurse should be conscientious about washing hands if she or he plans to examine or feed the infant. This should also be done following a diaper change. Following hand-washing, touching any part of one's own body (face, hair, nose, etc.) will contaminate the caretaker's hands, necessitating rewashing. Nurses must develop an unceasing awareness of this aspect of infection control, since touching of one's head is an unconscious habit of many people. In general, jewelry should not be worn while caring for the newborn, as it provides a harbor for pathogens. The one common exception to this is a flat wedding band.

Caps and masks are no longer considered necessary for routine nursery care. Long hair must be tied back so that it will not come in contact with the infant or equipment during examinations or treatments. To facilitate the scrubs and hand-washing procedure, nurses caring for neonates should wear short-sleeved garments. Hospital staff regularly assigned to the nursery should wear short-sleeved gowns to cover their clothing and to facilitate scrubbing to the elbow. Some nurseries also require this of regular staff, but many policies state *only* that it is necessary that a "barrier" be provided between the nurse's body and the infant during care. *Barrier* may be interpreted as a cover-gown, in the case of extended nurse-infant contact, or merely an infant blanket placed against the nurse while the infant is being held to the nurse's body. If gowning is done, the gown should be discarded after each use. Parents and others who might touch the infant should be instructed in hand-washing and gowning techniques before handling the infant.

The physical environment Another very important aspect of protecting the neonate from infection is maintaining a safe physical environment. Each infant's bassinet and equipment should be thought of as an "island." Nothing contaminated should come in contact with this island, and everything leaving it should be considered "dirty" and be disposable or cleaned appropriately. Each nursery should have a manual describing the policies for care of the physical environment and the nurse should be aware of these policies and procedures. This should include approved materials for cleaning, disinfecting, and sterilizing equipment, as well as for taking care of the bassinet itself.

Common scales and examining tables should not be used unless protected with a cloth or paper barrier, or properly disinfected after each use.

Parents should be taught the importance of hand-washing and infection control while they are in the hospital, and encouraged to continue these practices at home.

Infections transmitted from other infants The third major factor in infection control within the nursery situation is preventing the spread of infection from one infant to others. Obviously, good technique relative to the first two points, control of personnel and physical environment, will greatly reduce this danger. Despite conscientious care in these other two areas, once a neonate becomes infected, that infection may spread rapidly from infant to infant, with devastating results. For this reason, the nurse has a responsibility in the early identification of infected infants. Many of the symptoms of gen-

eralized infection in the neonate are subtle and subjective, such as hypothermia, lethargy, irritability, a general change in behavior, a change in feeding habits, and jaundice. Because the nurse is the one professional person most aware of the norms for any particular baby, the nurse is best equipped to detect possible infection. In addition to these generalized signs, the nurse should be alert for symptoms such as any pustules, obviously inflamed or infected skin lesion, and diarrhea. If a mother develops an infection of unknown origin during the postpartum period, the infant should also be suspected of harboring the infection.

Infants who have, or are suspected of having, any infection should be cultured and separated from the others. This may involve placing them in a separate nursery, to be closely observed, or maintaining the infant in the mother's room. The nurse should ensure that the parents have adequate instructions for the indicated precautions (putting on a gown, mask, gloves) so that contact with the baby will continue. The nurse must always be aware of the significance of uninterrupted contact in the bonding process.

Protection by physical care
The newborn is also protected by the nurse's appropriately meeting the infant's physical care needs.

Protection from heat loss Since the infant is frequently admitted to the nursery in a slightly hypothermic state, great care must be taken to arrest further heat loss. On admission to the nursery, the infant's temperature should be measured. Further procedures, such as bathing or making a formal and complete assessment, should be delayed for at least 2 to 6 h, or until the temperature has stabilized. The nurse should then utilize the concepts of care related to thermoregulation as they are discussed relative to nursing care of the newborn in the delivery room.

Bathing the newborn The initial bath should be given in the nursery, after the temperature has stabilized. The bath is frequently given with warm water, using a mild soap. However, the "dry technique" is preferred by many authorities for the following reasons: (1) it reduces heat loss by exposure, (2) it diminishes skin trauma, (3) it does not expose the infant to agents with known or unknown side effects, and (4) it requires less time.[54] In the dry technique, cotton balls or a washcloth are soaked with water (a mild soap may be used also) and used to remove blood from the face and head and meconium from the perineal area. The rest of the skin is not touched, unless grossly soiled. During the remainder of the hospital stay, only the diaper area is cleansed. Bathing the infant also provides opportunity for ongoing assessment. There are many other acceptable "wet" and "dry" techniques for bathing the newborn.

Diaper care The perineal and anal area should be thoroughly cleansed of any urine or fecal material. This may be done with plain warm water or with mild soap and water; cotton balls or a soft cloth should be used. The area should then be dried well, because a warm, moist environment promotes the growth of bacteria. Diapers are always applied and removed in a front-to-back motion, to avoid contamination of the urinary tract with fecal material. Diapers should be fastened with the back overlapping the front, so that hip flexion is not inhibited. Cloth diapers are folded in such a way as to provide extra thickness in the front for the male infant, and in either the front or back for the female infant, depending upon her lying position. The nurse should discuss with the parents the relative cost and convenience factors of using cloth diapers laundered at home, a diaper service, or disposable diapers. If cloth diapers are used, great care must be taken to prevent injury to the infant by contact with open pins. The safety pin should be placed in the diaper with the pin pointing to the rear of the infant; if the pin accidentally opens, there is less danger of damage to the abdomen, thighs, or genitalia. In addition, during diaper changes, all pins should be closed and kept well out of the active grasp reflex of the baby.

Diaper rash results from inadequate cleansing and may lead to excoriation of the area and a secondary bacterial or yeast infection. When redness or rash appears in the area, the buttocks or groin should be left exposed to the air. This simple treatment is most effective if done faithfully. A mild ointment may also be used to protect the skin. Plastic pants should not be used on infants with this condition; they promote the rash by increasing warmth and decreasing air circulation. Cloth diapers should be soaked in an agent designed to reduce ammonia, washed with soap, and rinsed well. Disposable diapers may cause a reaction similar to plastic pants in some infants. The ability to properly attend to the infant's diapering needs appears to play an important role in the achievement of tasks of parenting. Nurses should not underestimate the importance of parental guidance in this matter.

Care of the umbilical stump Careful attention must be paid to the care of the umbilical stump. It is essentially an open wound. After the baby is bathed and inspected for potential signs of infection, such as redness, induration, or oozing of foul-smelling drainage, alcohol or an antiseptic agent may be applied to the stump. The diaper should be kept below the cord to promote drying.

Care of circumcision Following a circumcision, the glans is covered with a gauze petroleum dressing, and the diaper applied loosely. The nurse should observe the infant carefully for bleeding from the site and check voiding to ensure that the procedure did not cause edema or trauma of the urethra. The initial gauze dressing may be left in place until it naturally falls off or removed by moistening with water or hydrogen peroxide. Any attempt to forcibly remove it may lead to bleeding. Once this dressing is off, the circumcision site appears as a raw, reddened, and sensitive area. Petroleum jelly should be applied after each voiding for a few days, or until the circumcision appears healed. Following a circumcision, the nurse should instruct the parents in proper care of the site, and also in wiping stool from front-to-back, when diapering, to avoid contamination. The penis should be examined regularly, and any sign of infection or bloody urine reported to the surgeon immediately.

Protection by identification

In the section of this chapter dealing with care of the neonate in the delivery room, an explanation of the technique and importance of adequate mother-infant identification was given. Caution should be continuously exercised. The neonatal nurse has the responsibility of ensuring that each infant has two coded identification tags on at all times. Before placing a baby with the mother, the nurse should ask the mother to read the code numbers on her bracelet. The nurse then verifies that the baby belongs to the woman questioned. The nurse also has the responsibility of monitoring other personnel to ensure that they also can verify the infant's identification.

Nurturance

The question, "Do you plan to breast-feed your baby?" is one that is frequently asked of pregnant women. Many factors will affect her decision— her cultural background, her own general attitude concerning nursing, the feelings of her husband or other people important to her, and her previous experiences with breast-feeding. The nurse should support the mother in *her* decision regarding breast- or bottle-feeding, and give her the guidance and support to make the venture pleasurable and successful.

It is imperative that the nurse maintain an awareness of the traditional role that feeding has played in development of positive maternal self-esteem. A mother who can successfully, comfortably, and satisfyingly manage her newborn infant's feeding needs has mastered one of her most basic mothering tasks. Positive reinforcement from the nurse will have a sustaining effect on the mother's ability to progress to other "tasks" of motherhood.

Breast-feeding Human breast milk is the most nearly perfect food for babies. In addition, breast-feeding offers certain advantages to both mother and infant. Perhaps the most striking of these is the promotion of a close mother-infant relationship. During the feeding the infant is nestled close to the mother's body, can sense her warmth, can hear her heart beat, and appears to develop a sense of security. This response by the infant frequently has a reciprocal effect on the mother, who has her nurturing role reinforced.

In addition to the psychosocial aspects of breast-feeding, there are physiological advantages. Colostrum, which is secreted from the breasts during the first 2 to 3 days, contains many antibodies in which the newborn is deficient, thus affording the infant passive immunity against some infections.

Colostrum and breast milk appear to have a laxative effect, helping the infant avoid the problem of constipation and speeding meconium passage.

Breast milk is always available, sterile, and at the appropriate temperature. It is the most economical form of infant feeding, although not actually free: the nursing mother must have a high-protein, high-calorie diet. There appears to be less overfeeding and subsequent obesity in breast-fed infants, because they are not encouraged to "finish their bottle."

Breast-feeding is inadvisable only in rare circumstances. Debilitating or infectious diseases in the mother, such as tuberculosis, severe heart of kidney disease, or advanced cancer may prevent the mother from nursing. Mothers who have inverted or cracked nipples may experience difficulty, but with proper support and guidance, the mother who truly wants to breast-feed her infant usually succeeds.

Perhaps the most common deterrent to breast-feeding for some mothers is the amount of time it takes. In our society today many mothers return to a career shortly after delivery, and therefore must be away from their infants for extended periods of time. It is important to communicate to these mothers that they can pump their breasts every 3 to 4 h while away from their infants to sustain lactation and that either this breast milk or formula may be given by bottle for one to two feedings each day. This method is not ideal and can cause frustrations, but is a viable option for the working mother who wishes to breast-feed her infant. Breast milk can be refrigerated in a clean bottle or other container and used within 24 h. If longer storage is desired, the milk can be frozen in a plastic container ("self-zipping" bags are ideal) for up to 6 months. All milk to be used within 24 h should be labeled with the time it was collected; frozen milk is labeled with the date.

There are known advantages to nursing the infant as soon after birth as possible. From that time on the mother and infant will develop a rhythm, a signaling system, and a unique pattern for feeding. Breast-fed infants tend to be hungry every 2 to 3 h and, since lactation depends only upon the stimulation of sucking, can and should be fed at these times. The nurse must remember that the breast-feeding mother needs a tremendous amount of teaching, guidance, and psychological support. However, the success a mother experiences in breast-feeding will be largely due to her desire to nurse her baby.

An analysis of the components of breast milk,

necessary supplements, and a comparison to cow's milk formula are covered in the section on nutrition at the end of this chapter.

Bottle-feeding Bottle-feeding is the most popular method of infant feeding used in the United States today. Many commercially prepared cow's milk formulas closely resemble human milk and provide adequate nutrition for the healthy neonate. A comparison between human milk and commercially prepared formulas, along with nutritional requirements of the neonate, appears later in this chapter.

If a mother chooses to bottle-feed the infant, she should of course be supported in her efforts. Support includes the teaching of both feeding techniques and formula preparation. The emphasis on teaching nursing mothers proper breast-feeding techniques is so great that the teaching of bottle-feeding mothers is sometimes overlooked (see later section on meeting the nutritional needs of the neonate).

The age at which the first bottle-feeding is given is largely dependent upon the neonate's condition. If the baby appears to be awake and alert and does not have excessive mucus, feeding may be instituted within 1 or 2 h after birth. In some infants, it appears to be wise to withhold feedings until after the second period of reactiv-

ity, during which time most infants have a lot of mucus and therefore may have difficulty tolerating fluid intake. For the first one or two feedings, a "test" meal of plain, sterile, or dextrose water may be given, following which the infant is started on the cow's milk formula prescribed. Bottle-fed babies should be allowed to adjust to a "demand" feeding schedule. Newborn infants usually require six to eight feedings in 24 h.

Stimulation

Little more than a decade has passed since the days when it was assumed that newborn infants were only passive individuals, unable to react to or affect their environment. It is now a recognized fact that this is not the case. The nurse has a tremendous opportunity and responsibility to ensure that the infant receives appropriate stimulation and that parents recognize the importance of their role in this regard.

The nursing goal of stimulation is met in two ways: (1) by promoting the bonding process, and (2) by providing an environment which is stimulating for the infant.

Facilitating the bonding process This process of parental attachment, or "the unique relationship between two people (infant and parent) that is specific and endures through time,"[55] begins in the prenatal period. We have discussed the importance of encouraging activities to promote the bonding/attachment process beginning with the moment of birth. The nurse may continue to facilitate this process by allowing the parents and infant as much uninterrupted contact as possible (Fig. 10–12). During this period, it is important that the nurse allow the parents control over the care and handling of the infant; the nurse should act as a "consultant" rather than "manager" in the relationship. The nurse may point out to the parents the unique capabilities of an infant by helping them identify the infant's various behavioral states, and by helping them to learn how to interact with these states. Parents who have an awareness of the behavioral and neurological capabilities of their own infant will cease to regard the infant as "a" baby and begin to know "their" child.

During the time spent with the parents, the nurse should capitalize on the positive aspects of the observed parenting role. Positive reinforcement will increase the parents' self-esteem and

Figure 10-12 Allowing the mother and infant time to become acquainted will facilitate the bonding process. Note *en face* position.

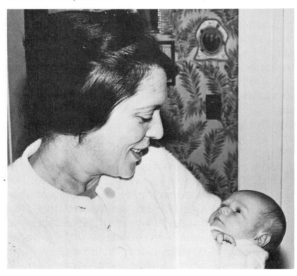

confidence and they will be open to learning new concepts. By gaining an awareness of the unique behaviors of each infant, and sharing these sensitivities with the parents, the nurse has a special opportunity to have a lasting impact on the eventual quality of the parent-child relationship.

As caretakers, nurses do not always allow the parents and their infants as much contact as they should; many institutional practices tend to separate adults from their infants. Dr. T. Berry Brazleton believes that this occurs for three reasons:

1. As physicians and nurses, we basically like to help people depend on us. If we allow them too much choice or autonomy, our rewards are minimized.
2. To do this most effectively, we must push a pathological model, one in which childbirth and neonatal care are based on treating pathology, rather than reinforcing for strengths that are present in most people and for the odds that are enormously in favor of a good outcome.
3. All adults who care about babies are competitive with all other adults. and each of us would like to be the primary caretaker of the attractive helpless infant. *Unconsciously*, we devalue the role of parents to fulfill our own role as *the* important caretaker of this new infant. No one would ever admit this drive, but it is universal.[56]

This is a strong and disturbing statement by Dr. Brazleton, one which all neonatal nurses should consider in light of their own feelings and activities. The role of the nurse is to unite and strengthen the family unit, not to come between its members.

In addition to facilitating and promoting attachment behavior, the nurse must assess and document the progression of this process. Criteria for assessing positive parent-infant bonding include the following:

1. The parents understand the infant's "states," and react appropriately.
2. The parents derive pleasure from interfacing with their infant, and in caretaking tasks.
3. The parents refer to the infant by name, and demonstrate an awareness of his or her unique personality and potential.
4. Discussion of future plans include the infant as a positive factor.

There are exhaustive lists of criteria and evaluating tools available regarding assessment of bonding; these are a sample of points to consider. Likewise, there are behaviors that are exhibited when parents are not bonding adequately. These center around general displeasure regarding the infant; disgust caused by such normal infant activities as drooling, defecation, urination, and regurgitation; abnormal or unfounded fears that the infant has an abnormality or serious illness; and inappropriate response to infant needs. These parents usually fail to demonstrate the behavior seen in the normal progression of the bonding process. They may lack eye contact with their infants, may not hold them close to their bodies, or refer to them as "it," rather than by name. Early assessment of this process is essential if crisis intervention is to be effective.

Provision of a stimulating environment In the process of developing behavioral assessment scales, much has been learned about infant stimulation techniques. Sharing this information with parents can serve to enhance their relationship with the child as well as enhance the infant's development. Parents must be aware that *touch* not only plays an important role in bonding but is a stimulating activity for the baby. *Visual interaction* and stimulation are also important parts of a healthy newborn's environment. The ability of an infant to follow a bright object, and to fixate on a face, should be demonstrated to parents. *Verbal interactions* play an essential role in infant development. The nurse should act as a role model, interacting verbally with the newborn, to alleviate any feelings of "foolishness" that the parents might feel in conversing with so young a being. The infant's varying responses to different noises and tones should be explored.

Discharge from the nursery

Many mothers and infants leave the hospital when the infant is 2- or 3-days-old, and the trend is toward even earlier discharge. This practice leaves little time for the nurse to meet the goals of neonatal care while the mother and infant are available. The nurse must use every opportunity to fulfill these goals during hospitalization, then appropriately plan for ongoing care at home.

Preparation for discharge from the hospital should begin with the newborn's admission to the nursery. The ongoing assessment of the infant and of the parental-infant interaction gives important clues as to the readiness of the family to function as an independent unit, outside the confines and security of the hospital setting. Mature infants are usually discharged on the third or fourth day of life, although some may leave earlier if stable.

The physical examination Within the 24 h preceding discharge, the neonate should have a complete physical examination by a physician, or, in some cases, a pediatric nurse practitioner. Significant maternal, fetal, and neonatal observations and treatments should be summarized in writing so they can be made available to health care workers who will provide follow-up services. The examination should include consideration of any laboratory tests done on the neonate.

Evaluation of maternal readiness By the day of planned discharge, the nurse should have completed the evaluation of the mother's readiness to assume independent care of her infant. This should include evaluation of bonding behavior, assessment of skill in infant care, and demonstration of appropriate judgment regarding needs of the infant. Any uncertainty the nurse feels regarding the mother's ability to cope in any of these areas should be sufficient reason for postponing discharge.

Home preparations The nurse should explore with the parents the home preparations for the baby, discussing the *physical environment*, such as the home temperature. If it is particularly cool, the nurse should emphasize the importance of keeping the baby warmly dressed and of placing the bassinet or crib away from outside walls.

The nurse should determine the answer to several questions and provide appropriate intervention when indicated. Do the parents *have* a bassinet? If the infant is bottle-feeding, do the parents have the formula or ingredients for the formula and directions and equipment for preparing it? Does a breast-feeding mother know how to prepare glucose water or formula in the event that she must use an alternative feeding method? Is there anyone in the household with a transmissible infection, such as a severe cold, skin infection, or diarrhea? If there are other children, have the parents considered their response to a new family member? Will the new mother have adequate support services for home and child care, so that she may fully recover from the labor and delivery experience? All these, and in some cases many more, issues should be addressed when the nurse is evaluating home preparation.

Birth registration The registration of the baby's birth is of utmost importance and should be done before the infant leaves the hospital. The law requires that the birth attendant submit notification of the birth to the local registrar, with specified information about the infant's name, date of birth, and parents. Each state has its own certificate standard, and these records are legal documents filed permanently with the state bureau of vital statistics. The parents should be aware that a copy of this certificate will be made available to them.

Preparations for follow-up care Plans for medical supervision of the newborn should be made. Appropriate referral should be made, if the infant will be transferring to a different care-giver. Contact should be made with the clinic or private physician to arrange for the first pediatric visit and to establish contact for emergency care or intermediate guidance. If the neonatal nurse feels it advisable, a referral to the visiting nurse should be completed, and the agency contacted by phone to ensure immediate follow-up care.

Home care of the neonate

Although the newborn has undergone the most dramatic changes during the first few days of life, the remainder of the first month continues to be a dynamic period during which the incorporation of the infant into the family system becomes more solidified. *Adaptation* may best describe the task of each participant.

Although it is hoped that the new parents have had adequate instruction regarding infant care while in the hospital, they need to be aware of modifications in this care after discharge from the hospital.

Bathing

The newborn should continue to have sponge or dry baths until the umbilical cord has fallen off and the site is completely healed, about 1 to 2 weeks, at which time tub baths may be started. The first bath may consist merely of placing the baby in a tub of warm water in order that he or she may adjust to the new experience. Parents need to learn to hold and support their baby in the tub, with one arm and hand, while leaving the other hand free. There is no reason for the baby to be bathed daily, unless it becomes a stimulating and enjoyable experience for both infant and parent(s). A mild soap should be used, and afterwards rinsed carefully to avoid excessive dryness of the skin.

The hair and scalp should be shampooed twice a week. Active sebaceous glands lead to sebum on the scalp, frequently causing a "cradle cap," or a crusting of these secretions. If cradle cap does occur, it is helpful to rub mineral oil into the skin of the scalp the night before the shampoo is to be given.

Cotton-tipped applicators should not be used to cleanse either the nose or ears, as they may cause damage to delicate tissues; it is adequate to gently wipe away obvious mucus with the twisted end of a washcloth or a cotton ball. Parents may feel that they want to moisturize the baby's skin, which frequently appears to be dry during the first few weeks. Lotion should be used rather than oil, as the latter clogs skin pores.

Bath time provides an excellent opportunity for parents to utilize their skills in assessment and stimulation. A pleasant bath experience can play a main role in the parent-infant bonding process.

Cord care

If the umbilical cord is still on, parents should be instructed to keep it clean and dry. It is important to apply the diaper in such a way that the stump is exposed. When the cord dries and falls off, a small amount of serous drainage, occasionally blood-tinged, is normal. At this time it is helpful to cleanse the area with alcohol three or four times a day. Parents should be advised that if there is a large amount of drainage or bleeding, a foul odor, or reddening or swelling of the skin around the umbilicus, the doctor should be notified immediately. The use of belly-binders is discouraged, as they hinder the healing process.

Clothing for the neonate

Clothing should be considered in relationship to family economics. This is an exciting time for most parents. Enthusiasm leading to the purchase of expensive wardrobes may need to be tempered with the reality that the baby will grow rapidly during the first few weeks and months of life and have a limited need for "special outfits."

The infant will need about two to three dozen cloth diapers. Since neonates are "droolers," parents should be advised that they will need an adequate supply of tops. A few nighties, receiving blankets, caps, and a bunting may be needed, depending upon the weather and climate. It is sometimes helpful for parents to know that they should dress their infants in approximately the same amount of clothing that is comfortable for other members of the family in the same environment. Any new clothing should be laundered before using, as much of it is often fuzzy and contains sizing, which is very irritating to the infant's delicate skin.

Sleeping and crying

Few parents leave the hospital prepared for how disturbing their own infant's *cry* is, nor do they realize that young infants spend much of their awake time in this activity. It may be helpful to point out that the infant's cry is an effort to communicate, and by trial and error, they will learn to differentiate what a specific cry means. Parents need to be told that if rocking, holding, walking, or talking to the neonate appears to be comforting, they should not be concerned about "spoiling" the infant. Infants derive a great deal of comfort from sucking; use of a pacifier is acceptable and may be gradually withdrawn as the infant gets older.

Colic is described as paroxysmal abdominal cramping accompanied by loud crying and drawing of the legs up to the abdomen, as if in pain. In spite of this, the infant appears to tolerate the feeding and gains weight. Many theories related to the type, amount, and technique of feeding have been investigated. The effect of emotional stress between parent and child has been explored as a causative factor. Generally, colic is thought to be caused by excessive fermentation and gas production in the intestines.[57] Regardless of the etiology of the problem, a crying, irritable baby with colic creates great stress and feelings of inadequacy in the parents. Occasionally, the reason for the problem is discerned and nursing intervention is successful. More often, the most helpful role the nurse can play is to provide support for the family during this difficult period, assuring them that in the normal growth and development process infants do outgrow these spells.

Parents also have questions regarding how much time they can expect their baby to *sleep* when at home. The neonate rarely sleeps more than 3 to 5 h without waking to be fed. Although parents should be encouraged to allow their healthy newborns to sleep as much as possible at night, the new mother should attempt to sleep several hours during the day. She will lose several hours of nighttime sleep during the first 4 weeks of her baby's life. It is helpful to know that as babies get older the amount of time they spend sleeping at night gradually increases.

Adjustment to the new infant

Just as the infant undergoes a series of adaptations during the neonatal period, so do other members of the family. They need to adjust to the newcomer. If the infant is a first-born, parents undergo phenomenal psychological maneuvers in adjusting to their new roles as a mother and father. If there are other children, they now must adapt their lifestyle to include someone they may see as a "stranger," perhaps even an unwanted stranger in their lives. Sibling rivalry needs to be recognized and dealt with openly. Assess adaptive behavior within the family structure and intervene if indicated. Provide guidance and support for family members in their changing roles. If indicated, refer the family that is experiencing difficulty to family counseling.

Socializing of the neonate

The neonate actively participates in a socialization process as she or he attempts to become acquainted with the environment and to develop a social relationship with others. The newborn is well equipped to begin this process. The newborn can see, hear, smell, and feel from the moment of birth. By processing external stimuli through these senses, the infant begins immediately to interact with the environment. Specific neonatal actions and reactions observed in behavioral assessments demonstrate that the infant's responses to stimuli vary greatly with her or his behavioral state. At a very early age the neonate is able to control the effect of the environment and stimuli by moving from one state to another, thereby "shutting out" unwanted stimuli.

Studies of maternal-infant bonding show that each infant, through behavior, modifies markedly how much interaction and stimulation he or she elicits.

During the first 4 weeks of life, the infant becomes increasingly active in the socialization process. This is a great joy to parents as they watch their baby develop into a unique personality.

Smiling and verbalization The ability of the neonate to smile plays a paramount role in socialization. The old belief that a young infant's smile could be nothing more than a response to "gas" has been discarded by child development experts. Neonates smile in response to stimuli as early as 2 weeks of age. By the fourth week the newborn is sophisticated enough to smile when eye-to-eye contact is made with a caretaker. The neonate also employs many different sounds in an attempt to interact with the environment. These range from miscellaneous noises at birth to a well-organized ability to respond with gurgles and "coos" by the end of the first month.[58] Both smiling and cooing are attempts by the infant to relate to others. In addition to these signals, the cry of the neonate becomes increasingly differentiated during this period. Parents learn to recognize these cries and respond to meet their baby's needs.

Appropriate toys

The selection of appropriate toys adds necessary stimulation to the neonate's life. It is important that all the senses through which the infant perceives stimuli be considered and that toys to stimulate as many of these senses as possible be provided. Rattles and mobiles are particularly good selections for the 1-month-old. If mobiles are used, they should be designed with the infant's age in mind. Dr. Burton White suggests the following guidelines for making a mobile for a 3- to 8-week-old infant:

1. A mobile should be placed where the infant tends to look. Since infants of this age prefer to look either

to the far right or far left, mobiles should be placed to the side, rather than midline, of the infant.

2. A mobile should be placed at a distance the infant prefers—at this age about 12 in from the head.

3. In designing a mobile, one should keep in mind what the baby sees while lying in the crib.[59]

Safety measures for the neonate

Parents need guidelines for providing a safe environment for their rapidly developing infant. At 1 month of age the infant retains much of the vulnerability of the first week of life but is gaining new motor skills that endanger his or her safety.

Parents should have a plan for medical emergencies in the home and an awareness of the nearest medical facility. Because the neonate, even at 4 weeks, is still immunodeficient, crowds and exposure to infectious diseases should be avoided. Parents need to be thoughtful of surfaces, such as countertops, beds, bath tables, from which the infant may roll. The parent should not leave the infant unattended on high surfaces or even in infant seats. Cribs and playpens should be checked to ensure that the bars are spaced so that the infant's head cannot get caught. Also, since automobile accidents are a leading cause of death during the first year of life, parents should be encouraged to restrain their infant in an approved infant seat while riding.[60] Infants should not be held in a passenger's (or the driver's) lap.

Anticipatory guidance is necessary on a frequent and regular basis in order to guide parents in accident prevention as the infant passes through the forthcoming developmental stages.

Meeting the nutritional needs of the neonate

During the first few months of life, the growth rate of the infant exceeds that of any other time during life. Therefore, careful attention should be given to providing the infant with nutrients necessary for healthy development. Unfortunately, health care professionals frequently overlook the role of nutrition in maintenance of a healthy neonate.

Nutritional requirements

The nutrients that a full-term infant needs for healthy development are based on body weight. Since the weight is constantly changing, so are nutritional requirements. Dietary allowances are expressed in daily requirements unless otherwise indicated.

Caloric needs The infant from birth through 6 months of age requires 117 kcal per kilogram of body weight, or about 54 kcal per pound. To calculate the daily caloric requirements, the nurse simply multiplies the infant's weight in kilograms by 117. For instance, an infant weighing 3.2 kg would require 3.2 × 117, or 374 kcal each day.

Fluid requirements The amount of fluid an infant needs is related to his or her caloric requirements and is approximately 1.5 ml for each kilocalorie required. Fluid requirement can also be calculated, as in caloric requirements, directly by the infant's weight. The infant should receive 165 ml per kilogram of body weight per day. Thus, our 3.2-kg infant should have 3.2 × 165, or 528 ml of fluid per day.

Vitamins and minerals Recommended dietary allowances vary somewhat; see Appendix C for a summary of average values.

Feeding methods and techniques

Following the establishment of feeding during the hospital stay, parents need continuing guidance and support to gain maximum satisfaction for both themselves and their infants.

Position during feeding *Nursing* mothers find a variety of positions comfortable for breastfeeding. Soon after delivery, many mothers find the side-lying position—placing the infant in a horizontal plane beside them—most comfortable. Others may sit upright in bed to nurse. By the time of discharge, most mothers find sitting the most satisfactory. Far more important than the general position of the mother and infant is the specific position of the child's mouth in relation to the areola. For successful nursing, the infant must have the nipple well back in the mouth. The gums then are able to press on the areolar surface, and the lips can close tightly around the breast tissue to permit suction (Fig. 10-13). In this position, the infant is able to apply pressure to the lactiferous sinuses and obtain milk by a process of compression and suction. The mother who, for one reason or another, experiences difficulty with breast feeding, becomes very frustrated. This frustration and tension then interfere with her "let-down" reflex and creates a cycle that may set both mother and infant up for failure in nursing. Prompt nursing assessment and intervention may alleviate this problem.

Bottle-feeding is the most common infant feeding method used in the United States. Yet mothers may not know how to bottle-feed their infants. Many mothers may need as much teaching and support as do those who are nursing. It is important to stress to mothers that thoughtful bottle-feeding allows a mother and infant a time for intimacy, much the same as breast-feeding does. Holding the infant closely and cuddling help to insure the realization of the emotional component of the feeding. Encourage parents to position the infant close to their bodies to allow eye contact. Emphasize to the parents that neonates tolerate formula-feeding best when the formula is at room temperature. The bottle should be kept tipped to keep the nipple filled with milk. This will decrease the amount of air consumed with the feeding. Propping the bottle should be very strongly discouraged, as it denies the infant parental contact and may result in choking and aspiration.

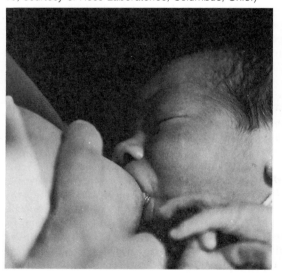

Figure 10-13 Proper position of the infant's mouth on the breast during breast-feeding. (*Clinical Education Aid No. 10, courtesy of Ross Laboratories, Columbus, Ohio.*)

Bubbling During the process of feeding, particularly bottle-feeding, infants ingest varying amounts of air. "Burping" them, or allowing them to expel this air, periodically, will reduce the possibility of vomiting. During burping all babies regurgitate small amounts of feeding. Mothers usually refer to this as "spitting up," and come to view it as a normal process.

Techniques for bubbling a baby vary. The traditional method is for the parent to place a diaper or cloth on the shoulder, then hold the infant against his or her chest and gently rub the baby's back. This is a position of comfort for both infant and parent. However, during the first few weeks of life there is some advantage in bubbling with the infant sitting on the parent's lap. If the infant is leaned slightly forward, and the head and face supported with one hand, the parent is free to gently rub the back with the other. (Fig. 17-16.) This position allows greater visibility of the infant and is especially preferred when caring for babies who tend to regurgitate particularly large amounts of formula with their feeding.

Position after feeding Following the feeding, the infant should be placed on his right side or stomach. Positioning on the right side will permit the feeding to flow toward the lower end of the stomach, and allow any excess air to rise above the feeding and escape via the esophagus, thus preventing vomiting and abdominal distention. A rolled blanket may be placed behind the back to keep the infant from changing position. Caution parents against placing the infant on his back after feeding, as regurgitation may lead to aspiration.

Feeding problems

The normal full-term infant encounters few feeding problems. However, it is important for the nurse to recognize them in order to intervene appropriately.

The problem of overfeeding In the case of breast-feeding mothers and infants, it is the *infant* who decides how much milk will be drunk; sucking continues until the baby's needs are met. The mother actually does not know how much fluid the infant has consumed. Therefore, overfeeding is rarely a problem for the breast-fed infant. Conversely, overfeeding is the greatest nutritional hazard of bottle-feeding. Parents frequently encourage their infants to "finish the bottle" and see the infant's compliance with this wish as a demonstration of love. There is much research currently being conducted to determine a relationship between early feeding in infancy and obesity in later life. The mother who is bottle-feeding her baby needs much guidance and encouragement to let her infant signal her when satisfied.

Problems related to prepared formula The infant who is breast-fed has the advantage of always receiving food that is suited to meet his or her physiological needs. Unfortunately, the use of home or commercially prepared formula leaves room for human error. It is not uncommon for mothers unknowingly to prepare formula incorrectly. In such cases, the infant may receive a feeding so rich that the baby cannot process it, or one so dilute that the infant receives inadequate nutrients per fluid ounce.

Drug companies are currently under scrutiny for promoting the use of commercially prepared formula in low-socioeconomic communities in this country as well as in underdeveloped countries throughout the world. When bottle-feeding replaces breast-feeding in these areas, it presents two basic problems. The first is one of contamination. Mothers from these environments may have difficulty understanding or applying principles of asepsis relative to preparation of the feeding and also frequently have inadequate refrigeration available for safe storage. Second, these mothers, many of whom do not understand written instructions and have limited resources to purchase formula, overdilute the mixtures to gain the volume their infants need. Obviously, the end result of such a continued practice is severe malnutrition. These infants would be far better served if resources spent on purchasing formula were spent to improve nutrition of breast-feeding mothers.

Formula allergies Approximately 1 to 2 percent of all infants become allergic to cow's milk. Sensitivity can be to different components of the milk. Clinical manifestations of milk allergy include vomiting, diarrhea, and colic. Diagnosis of milk allergy is made by the disappearance of these symptoms following the withdrawal of milk from the diet.

Once a diagnosis of sensitivity to cow's milk has been made, substitute formulas such as commercially available soy formulas, including Prosobee and Isomil, may be used. Infants also demonstrating a sensitivity to soybean milk may be placed on a meat-base formula such as Nutramigen.

Formula vs. breast milk

Human breast milk is uniquely suited to meet the needs of human infants. However, prepared cow's milk formulas are widely accepted as adequate to meet the needs of healthy infants.

Calories Cow's milk and human milk both provide 20 kcal/oz. Human milk appears to have an advantage in that it contains a higher amount of lactose, a component that is eventually converted to galactose, essential for the formation of galactolipids, necessary for the growth of the central nervous system.

Protein Adequate intake of protein is necessary to accommodate the rapid growth which takes place during the neonatal period. Human milk contains 1.1 grams of protein per 100 ml, while cow's milk has 3.5 grams per 100 ml. The type of protein in each kind of milk varies. Human milk contains 60 percent lactalbumin and 40 percent casein. Since lactalbumin is a more complete protein, containing a higher percentage of amino acids than does casein, human milk is easily digested, resulting in a soft stool. Cow's milk contains more casein than lactalbumin, resulting in the formation of large, hard curds in the stool. This difference also accounts for the more rapid stomach emptying time and subsequent necessity for more frequent feeding in breast-fed infants.

Fats The amount of fat in both human and cow's milk is approximately the same. However, human milk contains a higher percentage of unsaturated fats than does cow's milk.

Iron Iron is available in sufficient amounts in both human and cow's milk. The full-term infant is actually born with an iron reserve that should last for 5 to 6 months. However, iron deficiency anemia is not uncommon in the United States, and for that reason the Committee on Nutrition of the American Academy of Pediatrics recommends the addition of iron at the rate of 1 mg per kilogram of body weight per day for both breast- and bottle-fed infants. Because increased concentrations of protein appear to interfere with the utilization of iron, formula-fed babies appear to have a greater need for supplemental iron than do those who are breast-fed. Some physicians argue that breast-fed infants maintain adequate iron levels without being supplemented and oppose the use of iron-fortified formulas, because they believe that such feeding results in fussiness, spitting up, diarrhea, or constipation. The strongest argument against the administration of iron to breast-fed infants concerns the possibility that it might increase the risk of infection. Microorganisms added to human milk multiply more rapidly if iron is added.[61]

Other minerals and vitamins Both human and cow's milk are inadequate in fluoride content, even if the lactating woman drinks fluoridated water. Supplements of fluoride are usually recommended for both breast- and bottle-fed infants. That determination should be made regarding each specific infant.

Commercially prepared formulas are fortified with necessary vitamins and minerals, in an attempt to simulate breast milk. Infants receiving evaporated milk formula need to be supplemented with vitamin C. Both breast-fed neonates and those who receive cow's milk require vitamin D supplementation.

Similac, Enfamil, and SMA, the three major brands of commercially prepared formulas, all meet the nutritional needs during infancy. Similac and Enfamil are essentially the same. SMA is somewhat closer to human milk than the other two in protein and sodium chloride concentration.

Additional comparisons between breast milk and formulas are presented in Chap. 11.

Preparation of formula

The composition of unmodified cow's milk makes it unsuitable for young infants' nutrition. Therefore, infants who are not breast-fed must have their nutritional needs met by careful consideration of formula composition.

Evaporated milk formula Cow's milk formula may be easily prepared at home. Evaporated whole milk is usually modified to meet the specific needs of the infant. Care must be taken not to confuse evaporated milk with either canned condensed or skim milk. Condensed milk is a form of evaporated milk that has large amounts of sugar added to it; it is disproportionately high in sugar and low in fat and protein, making it inappropriate for infant feeding. Skim milk should not be given to infants because it has a low caloric concentration, would deprive the body of essential fatty acids, and places increased demands on the kidney.

One evaporated milk formula is prepared by mixing 13 oz of evaporated milk with 18 oz of water, and adding 2 tbsp of corn syrup. This formula yields approximately 20kcal/oz. Errors in the preparation of evaporated milk formula are usually of two kinds: (1) parents reverse the proportion of milk to water, and (2) there is confusion between tsp (teaspoon) and tbsp (tablespoon). The nurse should be aware of the potential problems and incorporate avoidance of these hazards into the teaching plan.

Infants receiving evaporated milk formula should receive supplements of vitamin C and iron. Fluoride may be recommended, depending upon supply available in the water. This should be discussed with the pediatrician at the first pediatric visit.

Commercially prepared formulas These prepared formulas, such as Similac, Enfamil, and SMA, have a cow's-milk base and have been modified to closely resemble human milk. They are available in three forms: (1) a powdered form, which must be diluted according to the manufacturer's directions; (2) a concentrated liquid form, which must be diluted with an equal amount of water; and (3) a ready-to-feed form, available in either cans or bottles. The manufacturers of these products supply explicit directions for their use, but the major problem encountered in their use is either underdilution or overdilution.

Each type of preparation varies, and needs to be understood by parents. These prepared formulas offer the busy parent much-appreciated convenience. They are considerably more expensive than preparation of an evaporated-milk formula. Most of these formulas are fortified with vitamins D and C and iron.

Calculation of caloric and fluid requirements

The information gathered thus far should enable the nurse to easily calculate the amount of formula an infant must consume each day to fulfill caloric and fluid requirements.

Caloric requirements To calculate the number of ounces of formula needed by an infant per day, the following formula should be used:

$$\frac{\text{Weight (kg)} \times 117 \text{ kcal/kg}}{20 \text{ kcal/oz}}$$

$$= \text{total number of ounces per day}$$

If this formula is used to calculate the number of ounces of formula a 3.2 kg-infant needs each day, results are as follows:

$$\frac{3.2 \text{ kg} \times 117 \text{ kcal/kg}}{20 \text{ kcal/oz}} = 19 \text{ oz}$$

Fluid requirements To calculate the daily fluid requirement for each infant, a simple calculation is used:

$$\text{Weight (kg)} \times 165 \text{ ml} = \text{total ml needed per day}$$

If this formula is used to calculate the number of ounces needed by the same infant per day, results are as follows:

$$3.2 \text{ kg} \times 165 \text{ ml} = 528 \text{ ml}$$

To convert 528 ml to ounces, divide by 30 (30 ml = 1 oz):

$$528 \text{ ml} \div 30 \text{ ml/oz} = 14 \text{ oz}$$

Therefore, by doing these two calculations, we find that 19 oz of formula will supply the caloric requirements, plus 5 oz of fluid more than the baby requires.

Prevention of contamination Great care must be taken in the preparation and storage of formula to prevent contamination. There are several different ways of accomplishing this.

Terminal heating method Bottles, nipples, caps, and utensils used for preparing the formula should be clean. The formula is prepared and poured into the bottles. The nipple, turned downward, is put into the mouth of the bottle. Caps are applied loosely to allow steam to escape.

The bottles are placed in a sterilizer, or deep kettle, and water is poured into the container until it covers the lower third of the bottles. A tight cover is applied to the sterilizer or kettle and the water is boiled for 20 to 25 min. After the boiling period, the sterilizer should be allowed to cool slowly. When the bottles are cool enough to handle, the caps are tightened and the bottles placed in the refrigerator for the daily supply of formula.

The aseptic or modified method All equipment is washed before starting the procedure, as in the terminal method. Then the bottles, nipples, and utensils (including measuring cups) needed for formula preparation should be boiled for 5 min. Next, water to be used in mixing the formula should be also boiled for 5 min (allowing a few extra ounces for evaporation). In actually mixing the formula, water should be remeasured to the exact amount needed and the other ingredients added. This is then poured into the presterilized bottles. Care should be taken not to touch the inner surfaces of caps and nipples when they are put on and tightened. Formula may then be refrigerated.

Note: Except for premature infants or others who for some reason need protection from bacteria normally tolerated by infants, families who use city water or tested well water can simplify the preparation of bottle feedings by using a dishwasher, if one is available. In this method the bottles, nipples, and caps are washed in the hot-water cycle of the dishwasher. The formula, which has been prepared with unboiled water, is then poured into the bottles. Bottles are capped and refrigerated until used. No terminal heating or other sterilization is used in this method. Still more simply, dry formula powder can be premeasured into clean bottles when they are taken from the dishwasher; the bottles are capped and stored at room temperature, and tap water is added at feeding time.

Disposable bottles Several companies market plastic bottles with disposable bag-liners into which the sterile formula is placed. Many families prefer that convenience. If this method is used, directions given by the manufacturer of the product used should be followed.

References

1. Ann L. Clark and Dyanne D. Affonso, with Thomas Harris, *Childbearing: A Nursing Perspective*, 2d ed., Davis, Philadelphia, 1979, pp. 564–565.
2. Victor Vaughn III, R. James McKay and Waldo E. Nelson, (eds.), *Nelson Textbook of Pediatrics*, 10th ed., Saunders, Philadelphia, 1965, p. 122.
3. Ibid., p. 127.
4. American Academy of Pediatrics, *Standards and Recommendations for Hospital Care of Newborn Infants*, 6th ed., Evanston, Ill., 1977, pp. 53–54.
5. Joann K. Williams and Jean Lancaster, "Thermoregulation in the Newborn," *Maternal-Child Nursing*, November–December 1976, p. 512.
6. Alexander J. Schaffer and Mary Ellen Avery, *Diseases of the Newborn*, 4th ed., Saunders, Philadelphia, 1977, pp. 992–993.
7. American Academy of Pediatrics, op. cit., p. 64.
8. Ibid., p. 59.
9. Ibid., pp. 57–58.
10. Schaffer and Avery, op. cit., p. 388.
11. Mary Winters Johnson, "Breast-feeding at One Hour of Age," *The American Journal of Maternal-Child Nursing*, January–February 1976, p. 15.
12. Marshall H. Klaus and John H. Kennell, *Maternal-Infant Bonding*, Mosby, St. Louis, 1976, pp. 50–51.
13. Ibid., pp. 68–70.
14. Ibid., p. 56.
15. Ibid., p. 73.
16. Darrel L. McDonald, "Paternal Behavior at First Contact with the Newborn in a Birth Environment without Intrusion," *Birth and the Family Journal* 5(3):126 (Fall 1978).
17. Frederick Leboyer, *Birth Without Violence*, Knopf, New York, 1975.
18. Helen W. Arnold et al., "Transition to Extrauterine Life," *The American Journal of Nursing* 65(10):78–79 (October 1965).
19. Schaffer and Avery, op. cit., p. 18.
20. Vaughn, McKay, and Nelson, op. cit., p. 19.
21. Ibid., p. 19.
22. Schaffer and Avery, op. cit., p. 44.
23. Ibid., pp. 318–319.
24. Ibid., p. 44.
25. Erna Zeigal and Mecca S. Cranley, *Obstetric Nursing*, 7th ed., Macmillan, New York, 1978, p. 444.
26. Schaffer and Avery, op. cit., p. 319.
27. Ibid., p. 7.
28. Ibid., p. 975.
29. Ibid., p. 973.
30. Ibid., pp. 957–959.
31. Ibid., pp. 960–961.
32. Clement A. Smith and Nicholas M. Nelson, *The Physiology of the Newborn Infant*, 4th ed., Thomas, Springfield, Ill., 1976, p. 421.
33. Schaffer and Avery, op. cit., p. 413.
34. Ibid., pp. 413–414.
35. Myron M. Faber, "Circumcision Revisited," *Birth and the Family Journal* 1(2):19–20 (Spring 1974).
36. Smith and Nelson, op. cit., p. 159.
37. Ibid., p. 287.
38. Toke Hoppenbrowers et al., "Polygraphic Studies of Normal Infants During the First Six Months of Life: III. Incidence of Apnea and Periodic Breathing," *Pediatrics* 60(4):422 (October 1977).
39. Schaffer and Avery, op. cit., p. 765.
40. Smith and Nelson, op. cit., p. 740.
41. Ibid., p. 739.
42. Schaffer and Avery, op. cit., p. 766.
43. Smith and Nelson, op. cit., p. 737.
44. American Academy of Pediatrics, op. cit., pp. 60–61.
45. Clark and Affonso, op. cit., p. 458.
46. American Academy of Pediatrics, op. cit., p. 510.
47. Williams and Lancaster, op. cit., p. 358.
48. American Academy of Pediatrics, op. cit., p. 106.
49. Schaffer and Avery, op. cit., p. 24.
50. Smith and Nelson, op. cit., p. 400.
51. Vaughn, McKay, and Nelson, op. cit., p. 332.
52. Lucille F. Whaley and Donna L. Wong, *Nursing Care of Infants and Children*, Mosby, St. Louis, 1979, p. 265.
53. T. Berry Brazleton, *Neonatal Behavioral Assessment Scale*, Clinics in Developmental Medicine, No. 50, Lippincott, Philadelphia, 1973.
54. American Academy of Pediatrics, op. cit., p. 110.
55. Klaus and Kennell, op. cit., p. 2.
56. Ibid., p. 97.
57. Whaley and Wong, op. cit., pp. 493–494.
58. P. Wolff, "Observations on the Early Development of Smiling" in B. M. Foss (ed.), *Determinants of Human Behavior*, vol. 2, Wiley, New York, 1963, pp. 117–130.
59. Burton L. White, *The First Three Years of Life*, Prentice-Hall, Inc., Englewood Cliffs, N.J., 1975, p. 27.
60. Gladys M. Scipien et al., *Comprehensive Pediatric Nursing*, 2d ed., McGraw-Hill, New York, 1979, p. 214.
61. Samuel J. Fomon et al., "Recommendations for Feeding Normal Infants," *Pediatrics* 63(1):53 (January 1979).
62. Peggy L. Pipes, *Nutrition in Infancy and Childhood*, Mosby, St. Louis, 1974, p. 104.

Chapter 11 **The infant**

Ann R. Sloat

Upon completion of this chapter, the student will be able to:

1. List at least four characteristics of infant growth and development.

2. Describe four or more factors that contribute to positive parenting.

3. Describe at least three methods the young infant uses to communicate with adults.

4. Select appropriate stimulation (e.g., toys) for the infant based upon the infant's age.

5. Describe a schedule for introducing solid foods to infants.

6. Describe the physical growth and function of the infant's body systems.

7. Describe Erikson's psychosocial stage of trust vs. mistrust.

8. Identify at least four caretaking measures that promote the development of a sense of trust in the infant.

9. Summarize each of the three stages of the infant's attachment behavior.

10. Identify the characteristics of each of the four stages of the infant's cognitive development.

11. Identify essential nursing interventions in infant care with regard to diapering, diaper rash, teething, weaning, feeding schedule, introducing solid foods, and taking safety precautions.

This chapter discusses the child between the ages of 1 month and 1 year. This is the period termed *infancy*. There is rapid growth and change this first year. The child starts as a tiny, relatively helpless and dependent individual and becomes an active, mobile, expressive person. This rate of growth and development will not be equaled, let alone surpassed, in the rest of the individual's lifetime.

Development—expectations and reality

Fortunately, the growth and change infants experience is patterned and predictable. Because of this predictability, it is possible to anticipate each new development. Knowing what to expect makes health care-givers and parents better able to provide for the needs of infants. Being able to predict the general pattern of development has other advantages as well. The infant's environment can be enriched to support whatever developmental adventure he or she is about to embark upon. The parents and other significant people are able to provide stimulation that will facilitate the infant's development. This knowledge helps parents be prepared and realistic about the demands and rewards of parenthood. And, very importantly, knowing what to expect of the infant increases the enjoyment parents and family experience in living with this new little person.

Characteristics of infant development

Babies are individuals. They have their own personalities from the very beginning. Each one expresses himself somewhat differently as he progresses in his own way through the first year. One of the differences among infants is the timing of the developmental sequence. While the pattern is predictable and each child goes through generally the same sequence of developmental milestones, the rate with which each progresses varies from child to child. One infant sits unsupported at 6 months, another not until 8 months. These differences do not predict the child's later abilities. If the infant is healthy, he is simply expressing his own timetable. He will remain consistent with himself. For example, if he's a late crawler, he will probably be a late walker as well.

Babies can progress best when the environment provides opportunities for them to practice whatever it is they are ready for. At the same time, it is important not to push the infant ahead of his schedule. Infants give us cues when they are ready to do something new. It takes a fairly observant infant watcher to tune in to their messages. Usually, parents are very good at this, but sometimes they need help. The 2-month-old may "tell" us he's ready to practice grasping objects by attending to and reaching toward a parent's earring or tie. If his playpen and crib lack attractive and reachable playthings or if he spends much of his day in an infant seat, then no one is hearing his message. The nurse can point out the baby's emerging capabilities and suggest ways the parents could cooperate with his endeavor.

All areas of the infant's growth and development are *interdependent*. A cognitive achievement such as removing a barrier to find a toy may be dependent on a motor skill such as the ability to crawl and grasp, which in turn is dependent on visual maturity, and so on. Not only is the whole process interdependent but *interrelated* as well. Language development, for example, is not only dependent on some degree of neurological maturity, but also is interrelated with cognitive and psychosocial development.

Another characteristic of development is that it does not always progress in a smooth, forward movement. There are spurts and stops and regressions. An infant may seem to concentrate on one certain skill while everything else waits in the wings for its time on stage. Infants may master a skill then seemingly lose it only to have it reappear later on. Regressions may occur, especially as a response to stress.

The pattern of infant development is from the *head downward.* The infant has head control before he can control his arms or legs. He can use his head to look about before he can crawl or walk. Development also progresses from the *main axis outward.* This means he will be able to move his arms about before he develops the ability to pick up objects with his fingers. In this way development follows the pattern of neurological maturation.

Infants are active participants in their growth and development. The process they are experiencing is not something that simply happens to them. They engage in activities that in many ways make it happen. They are *active stimulus seekers.* The amount of stimulation babies seek depends on their own temperament and other individual differences. Some infants have higher stimulus thresholds than others. This means that they can tolerate more intense or greater levels of stimuli. When stimulation becomes too intense, however, infants are able in some measure to block it out. Thus they are able to regulate the stimulation they need to foster their growth and maturation.

Individual differences

Infants differ in a number of ways. One important difference is in the *amount* and *intensity of stimulation* they can tolerate. Infants in general need a moderate level of stimulation in order to keep their attention. They lose interest or do not attend to stimulation that is low in intensity. They withdraw (by avoidance or crying) from overly intense stimuli. Type of stimulation, as well as intensity, must be varied to keep the infant interested. The complexity of stimulation needed differs among infants and among age levels as well.

Some infants respond to stimuli more slowly than others. These infants will not show the same degree of vigor in their response as a baby that reacts strongly and rapidly. They may also have less activity in general. Some infants seem to be always moving and on the go. Others are content to sit back, watch, and think it over.

Most babies have periods of fussiness, especially during the first few months. These periods generally follow a daily pattern and are often, much to parents' displeasure, at about dinner time in the evening. Some babies carry fussiness to extremes, however. These same infants are often the more active, responsive ones. They can be more difficult to console than their less fussy peers.

Cuddliness is another way in which infants differ significantly. Some infants mold to the adult's body when picked up and cuddled. They give the impression of relaxation and pleasure at being held. Other infants simply are not that fond of being held. They are stiffer in the adult's arms and may push away. They are not content, as others are, to snuggle in.

Influence of family on development

Parents come in all sizes and shapes and have all varying degrees of skills. They come in pairs, or as singles, with extended supports, or with no supports. Whatever their circumstances, temperaments, and experience with the parent role, they are a critical factor in the infant's development. Besides supplying basic physiological needs, which include nutrition, protection, nurturance, and stimulation, parents also carry out more complex tasks and responsibilities. The infant must learn about being human within a society of other humans. His beginning self-concept, his ability to learn to interact with others, his incorporation of the values of his culture will all depend a great deal on the parents' abilities in child rearing and the attitudes they hold about it.

Conditions of good parenting

Good parenting is not just a matter of instinct. Though the importance of good parenting is well established, we really don't know what conditions make it possible. The following list is tentative and will no doubt be expanded and refined as research increases our understanding.

1. *Manageable stress* There are limits to the individual parent's coping ability. Stress, which we all experience in some degree, should be within the individual's ability to effectively manage. We know that such highly stressful conditions as poverty and severe illness are detrimental to positive parenting.
2. *Healthy state of mind* Parents need the capacity to get out of themselves and sometimes put their children first. Depression or other psychiatric con-

ditions limit this ability. Acute grief may in some instances also have this effect, though its influence should be temporary.

3. *Positive childhood experience* Parents whose own childhood experience was enriching and nurturing have a better base to build upon than those who were less fortunate. Being loved as an infant and child builds in the capacity for love and makes possible the positive reciprocal relationship we call good parenting.
4. *Reasonable health* Good health allows the parent a full range of responsiveness. Chronic poor health can limit or influence the ability to be responsive and positive toward the child.
5. *Early bonding opportunity* There is evidence that early bonding has an influence on the parent-infant relationship. Many hospitals are adjusting their policies to allow for extended contact between the newborn and both parents to facilitate this parent-to-infant attachment. (Refer to Chap. 10 for discussion of bonding.)
6. *Adequate knowledge about children* Parents who have had experience with young children are more able to accurately interpret their infant's behavior. They are likely to be more skilled in such parenting activities as feeding, diapering, bathing, and generally communicating with their infants. Unfortunately, many parents of this generation may be lacking in this experience. The decrease of size and the increased mobility of nuclear families and subsequent loss of contact with extended families have reduced exposure to infants and small children.

The infant and his environment

Communication in infancy

By the time the infant is 1 month old, he is awake over a third of the day. Most of his time awake is during daylight hours, giving him a significant amount of time to interact with people in his environment. Additionally, he is perfecting the use of basic equipment he was born with and developing new skills that aid him in communicating.

Infant-to-parent communication One of the most potent communication tools the infant has is *gaze*. He has the ability at birth to follow and fixate on an object, but this is limited by a visual field of about 8 to 10 in (perfect distance for viewing a mother's face while nursing or being

Figure 11-1 An infant's gaze is a potent means of communication.

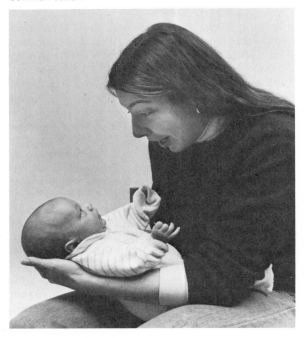

held). At 1 to 3 months he can fixate momentarily on his mother's face and follow an object almost as well as an adult. He can follow her visually as she moves about the room and let her know of his interest. Infants communicate with their gaze. They look into the care-giver's eyes and brighten

Figure 11-2 Complex facial expressions serve the infant as a means of communication.

with excitement. This kind of stimulation given by the infant elicits a good deal of social behavior from the parent. See Fig. 11-1.

The infant of 3 to 4 months has the ability to determine how much eye-to-eye communication he is willing to engage in. He can seek out eye contact or look away. His head movements are under his control and he can turn his head to facilitate seeking or disengaging. This puts him on equal footing with the adult. He has become a true partner in the interaction.

Facial expressions, of which babies have an impressive repertoire, are another means infants use to communicate with adults. The smile is present at birth, but is most often seen when the infant is in a drowsy state or REM sleep. At about 6 weeks infants smile in response to tickling, a happy voice, a human face, or a gaze. By about 3 to 4 months infants use the smile to elicit a response from someone else. They have enough control over facial expressions to mix the smile with other gestures, communicating such complex feelings as ambivalence by just 4 to 5 months. See Fig. 11-2.

Laughing, another means of communication, appears between the fourth and seventh months. Laughing is first a response to tactile stimulation, such as tickling, playing patty-cake, or the like. Soon the infant begins to laugh at visual or auditory stimulation. He then learns to utilize laughter to initiate an interaction or get a desired response from his care-giver. Crying and the cry face or pout are methods infants use to communicate displeasure. The infant learns to expand on all the behaviors leading up to a cry to express varying degrees of unhappiness. The face sobering and then the frown may be all he needs in some situations. The full-blown cry is a call for some action.

Sensitivity of infant to feeling tones Infants are very sensitive to the mood or tone of the environment around them. If the mother is relaxed, they are likely to be relaxed as well. If there is tension, the infant will probably show it in his behavior. The baby may respond with an increase in restlessness or fussiness. He may be difficult to comfort, especially by the tense or upset care-giver. There may be a decrease in his willingness to play or engage in playful interactions. Whatever behavior is displayed, the infant shows that he is a part of and sensitive to the activities of his family and immediate surroundings.

Infant behavioral states The concept of behavioral state is included here because of its importance in understanding the relationship of the infant to his environment. In the last few years there has been considerable research looking at aspects of this relationship. Most descriptions of infant states identify the following clusters of infant behaviors:

Deep sleep state The breathing is deep and regular, eyes are closed, and there are no movements except occasional startles.

Active sleep state The breathing is irregular, the eyes are closed and rapid eye movements are evident, and there are small muscle movements.

Drowsiness Eyes open and close but seem unfocused; there is little activity, and responses to stimuli are slowed.

Quiet alert state Eyes are open and there are no large movements.

Active alert state Eyes are open and there is diffuse movement and irregular breathing.

Crying state Eyes are usually closed or partly closed, and there are large movements and vigorous crying.

For the first 6 months and perhaps longer, the state the infant is in at any given time influences how he reacts to stimuli from his environment. A major part of the care-giver's task is to recognize the state and accordingly modify the stimulation the infant receives. A playful tickle when the infant is asleep may have little effect (unless of course it is quite vigorous; in which case it may bring the baby from deep sleep all the way to crying). The same tickle may be thoroughly enjoyed in an active alert state. It may aggravate the baby in a crying state and make him even more difficult to console. The mother's ability to approach the infant according to his state is very important in their developing relationship. How the mother perceives her infant's state will determine what she does and the kind of stimulation she provides. Conversely, what state the infant is in will determine his readiness for interaction and receptiveness to types and levels of stimulation.

Infant states can be modified by the care-giver and by the infants themselves. Some infants seem to have better inner resources and can keep themselves from reaching a crying state by self-consoling measures. Thumb-sucking, for instance, is a calming tactic employed by some infants. Picking an infant up is one method mothers use to bring an infant from crying to a quiet, alert state. Holding the infant upright, bouncing, swaying, or other vestibule-stimulating movements (such as rocking) are methods mothers seem to use naturally.

The quiet alert state is the time when the infant is ready to interact by gaze. We have already mentioned how significant this behavior is in terms of attracting and maintaining social interaction with the care-giver. If parents are not tuned into the readiness of their infant, their efforts to communicate may be frustrating and misleading. Insensitivity to state can lead to misinterpretation of the infant's behavior as dislike or rejection. For example, the infant's response to a friendly peek-a-boo game when he is in a drowsy state may be interpreted by the parent as boredom. Parents need to feel that the infant is responsive to the care and love they give. Parents need positive feedback from their infants to maintain the kind of mutual relationship that is so beneficial for growth and development.

The nurse has an important function here. It is important to assess the infant's state and the care-giver's sensitivity to it. Parents can be taught how to observe their infants, what to look for, and what approach might be best. They can also be taught how to bring the infant into an alert state from crying or sleep. No parent and infant pair will be perfectly in tune all the time. Neither will all the techniques they learn work every time. The quality of reading each other's cues and being sensitive to each other's signals is a vital characteristic of a healthy parent-infant interaction. Sometimes it takes a few months to establish this kind of harmony. The nurse who is involved with parents and infants throughout this first year should consider the quality of interaction a priority for assessment.

Parent-to-infant communication Parents hold, handle, stroke, cuddle, rock, sing, talk, play, and make faces when communicating with their infants. Adults, even those who are not parents, will automatically alter their interaction style to the infant. Mothers tend to be more gentle and comforting; fathers more playful. If one characteristic stands out, though, it is *touch*. Touch is an important component in almost all parent-to-infant communication.

The timing of parent-to-infant interaction is one of the most crucial variables. This along with the intensity and type of stimulation offered to the infant should be within the context of affection and interest in the child.

The function of play

Ask a mother why she plays with her infant. The answer may well sound something like: "Because I like to; it's fun!" Daniel Stern, in his book *The First Relationship: Infant and Mother*[1] expressed this by writing: "The immediate goal of a face-to-face play interaction is to have fun, to interest and delight and be with one another. During these stretches of purely social play, there are no tasks to be accomplished, no feeding or changing or bathing on the immediate agenda. ... We are dealing with a human happening, conducted solely with interpersonal 'moves' with no other end in mind than to be with and enjoy someone else."

This kind of experience is invaluable for the infant. Learning is not the goal of playful interaction of this type but of course learning is going on. The infant experiences how to be with another individual, how to share moments in his life. Appropriate toys and other stimulating objects for infant play are listed in Table 11-1.

Playful periods are framed within the optimal stimulus level for the infant. If the mother-infant pair are enjoying one another, then the stimulation being directed toward the baby is at the right level of intensity and is novel enough to

Table 11-1 Toys and stimulation for infants

1 month	7 months
Pacifiers	Floating bath toys
Lullabies	Kitchen objects
Tape recordings of heartbeat	String
Rocking chair	Soft rubber squeeze toys
Small, textured clutch toys	Small, soft, washable toys to clutch
Mobile	
Large, bright pictures	**8 months**
Your face close by	Nested cups
	Roly-poly toys
2 months	Space to creep
Music box	Toys to bang together
Mobiles, dangle toys for crib	Big soft blocks
Your smile	
	9 months
3 months	Toys tied to high chair
Rattles (ring or dumb-bell shaped)	Mirror (unbreakable)
Music	Jack-in-the-box
4 months	**10 months**
Crib or playpen gym	Pegboard
Bells tied to crib	Cardboard or cloth books
Plastic disk on chain	Push-and-pull toys without handle
5 months	**11–12 months**
Suction toy for surface	Stacking disks
Toy to kick	Large crayons
Interlocking plastic rings	Small items to place inside container
	Own drinking cup
6 months	Bright, medium-sized ball
Household objects to bang and throw	
Cups, spoons, pot lids, plastic containers	
Teething rings	
Squeaky, clutch toys	

maintain the infant's interest. At the same time, the infant is giving the mother positive signals, which is gratifying to her (Fig. 11-3).

Mothers and infants are not the only playful pairs in the family. Fathers and babies play, too. In fact, fathers often take on the play role—especially the more rough-and-tumble type—within the family. When dad comes into view, the baby may anticipate this play and be ready in an alert and aroused state.

Siblings also provide playful stimulation for the infant. Having a sister or brother is a very enriching factor in the infant's environment. Eye-to-eye playful interactions may be shorter in duration than with the adult or older child and infant. The enjoyment of being in each other's company and the acceptance small children demonstrate for each other can help create a very positive atmosphere. The function of this play among all members of the care-giving unit is to deepen the affectional relationship they share with each other. See Fig. 11-4.

Nutrition in infancy

Relationship of nutrition to growth and development

The healthy infant grows at a very fast rate. Parents will claim that their son or daughter seems to get bigger right before their eyes. This is not far from fact. Normally, the birth weight is doubled by 5 months and tripled by 1 year. During this time the infant is gaining an average of 30 g a day.

The process through which food becomes available to each cell is called *nutrition*. The American Medical Association defines nutrition as "the science of food, the nutrients and other substances therein, their action, interaction and balance in relation to health and disease, and the process by which the organism ingests, digests, transports, utilizes and excretes food substances." This is a very broad and complete definition. Studying it closely helps to focus our attention on the special needs of the infant's immature body rather than looking only at the nutrients contained in specific foods the infant may eat. This is necessary to understand what the infant's needs are for optimal growth and development and how important nutrition is to his well-being. Nutrition is one of the most important factors determining the child's growth

Figure 11-3 This infant is giving her mother positive signals.

and development. Conversely, the infant's growth is a sensitive measure of his nutritional status.

Think a moment of the body's composition. Our bodies are composed of fluids and cells. These are made of the same elements that are in food. Every cell has a job to do. Each one needs a constant supply of certain elements in order for it to accomplish its specific function. If a cell's job is to produce an enzyme, then it needs the raw materials to work with. The extracellular and intercellular fluids require their own specific proteins, minerals, lipids, or carbohydrates in order to carry nutrients to the cells that make up the organs or other tissues. The human body uses nutrients first to maintain itself and then to support growth. The infant normally is very active and has high energy needs for maintenance. Because the organs and tissues of the infant are growing rapidly, the

Figure 11-4 Siblings offer stimulation and opportunities for play. Note the interest this 10-month-old infant shows in his older brother.

need for a constant supply of raw materials or nutrients is of paramount importance.

Consequences of inadequate nutrition

The infant under 1 year of age is particularly vulnerable to inadequate nutrition. Inadequate nutrition may take several forms. First, the infant may not get enough of the calories or nutrients needed to support both maintenance requirements and growth. Consider the consequences if this happens at a time when an organ or body part is growing by increasing its number of cells. The optimal number of cells for that infant's organ or tissue will simply not be produced. The size in terms of cell number is then fixed when this stage is completed.

Secondly, the infant may have adequate calorie intake but lack specific necessary nutrients. An example of this might be inadequate iron ingestion or absorption with resultant anemia.

Thirdly, inadequate nutrition can occur when the infant ingests too much of certain nutrients as well as too little. Cow's milk, for instance, given undiluted to the young infant would be harmful because of the higher protein concentration. The young infant lacks the enzymes necessary to convert the type and amount of protein in cow's milk until about 1 year of age. The extra protein puts a burden on the immature kidneys. In addition, milk proteins cause injury to the intestinal mucosa of the infant, thereby causing small amounts of blood to be lost through the infant's stool. This compounds the possibility of anemia through loss of iron.

Next, overnutrition may be considered inadequate nutrition because it is not optimal for the infant's health and well-being. There has been much discussion of overfeeding producing chubby infants who may then grow to be obese adults. The relationship of overfeeding in infancy to adult obesity is not yet entirely clear from research. The possibility exists, however, that not only the physiological results of overnutrition, such as an increase number of fat cells, but also the behavioral results are significant. Food habits are formed early, and constant overeating may be detrimental in a number of ways.

Lastly, nutrition may be inadequate if the infant receives a food to which he has developed an allergy. Here, again, cow's milk and milk-based formulas are often the culprits. It has been estimated that between 0.3 to 7 percent of children are sensitive to cow's milk.[2]

The result of inadequate nutrition is, very broadly, the inability of the human body to function optimally. For the infant this may include growth retardation, problems in development, or both. It may also include a weaker body system unable to fight against pathogens and thus greater susceptibility to infection and disease. Severe forms of inadequate nutrition such as marasmus and kwashiorkor are rarely seen in the United States. These do exist in developing countries, during famine years particularly. Infants under 1 year are always the group most affected by lack of food or starvation. The morbidity and mortality rate worldwide is still high for nutrition-related causes.

Breast milk vs. infant formula

There is no doubt that breast milk is the optimum food for infants. Health professionals have sound reasons for encouraging mothers to nurse their babies. In recent years the trend is toward an increasing percentage of women choosing to breast-feed. This increase in numbers follows a general decline in breast-feeding in the industrialized countries that began about 50 years ago.

Most commercial formulas employ cow's milk and have been made to resemble human milk in nutritional composition. Generally speaking, infants do well on these formulas. For mothers who choose not to breast-feed, or for whom breast-feeding is contraindicated, these formulas offer very acceptable alternatives.

The advantages and disadvantages of breast- and bottle-feeding are compared in Chap. 10. Recent research on formulas is presented here as additional information.

Nutritional comparisons There are important differences between the amino acid content of the proteins of breast milk and of formula milk. Lactalbumin contains more cystine and less methionine than casein. Human infants cannot utilize the methionine efficiently until about 1 year of age, so they need lots of cystine. Taurine, a rare amino acid, is present in human milk but not in cow's milk. This amino acid is involved in the transmission of nerve impulses.[3] Since the infant's nervous system is quite immature, this may be of special benefit. Breast milk also contains more of an enzyme which helps to digest protein than does cow's milk. This enzyme, though present in cow's milk, is inactivated by pasteurization and sterilization.

Lactose is the major source of carbohydrate calories in milk. It not only provides energy but aids in the absorption of amino acids and minerals. Lactose is broken down into glucose and galactose, used in building the infant's nervous system. Human milk contains a higher amount of lactose. Cow's milk must be diluted because the protein concentration is too high to be tolerated by the infant. This dilution reduces the concentration of lactose as well. If milk-based formulas are not fortified by additional sugar, they will not meet the energy requirements of the infant. The fortification should be with lactose since sucrose (table sugar) or corn syrup contains no galactose. A galactose deficiency could be damaging to the growing and developing infant.

A high percentage of the infant's weight gain during the first 4 months is fat (75 percent). This percentage continues to be high (44 percent) for the first year then declines rapidly. In these first few months of life, the infant builds up a store of reserves. The infant with adequate fat reserves is better able to withstand infections and regulate

body temperature and draws upon these reserves for energy as well.

Human milk fat differs from that of cow's milk in several ways. It contains less total saturated fatty acids and three times as much polyunsaturated fatty acids as cow's milk. Infants digest and absorb fat from human milk better than from cow's milk. This in part is due to the fatty acid composition. Polyunsaturated fatty acids perform another important job for the infant. They are incorporated into cell membranes and help to make hormone-type substances. These substances help regulate the transmission of nerve impulses and help control blood pressure and digestion.

Vegetable oils have replaced butter fat in many of the infant formulas to improve fat absorption. Average breast milk is about 14 percent polyunsaturated fatty acid. Formulas with vegetable oil are higher by two or three times that amount. The effect of the higher levels of polyunsaturated fats on the infant is not yet known. There is a possible danger of vitamin E deficiency, however. This replacement of butter fat with vegetable oils has removed cholesterol from most formulas. Breast milk is a rich source of cholesterol. There is some thought that the cholesterol in early feeding may stimulate the body to produce enzymes that help in metabolizing cholesterol later in life. Cholesterol may also be important in the formation of nerve tissue.

Infants need the right amount of minerals in their diet. Salts are needed for bone growth, tissue growth, in conducting nerve impulses, and in muscle movement. Human milk contains the right amount for humans. Cow's milk contains three times as much calcium and six times as much phosphate. These higher concentrations of minerals overwork the infant's immature kidneys. The undesirable ratio of calcium to phosphate can result in convulsions in the infant. This is another reason why cow's milk must be diluted, modified, or both for use with young infants.

Zinc is an important element needed by the infant. Cow's milk contains more zinc than human milk. Human milk, however, contains a special zinc-binding protein that makes it possible for the infant to absorb zinc more readily. The infant therefore absorbs more zinc from human milk. Neither cow's milk nor human's milk is a rich source of iron.

All vitamins except vitamin D are present in the breast milk of a well-nourished mother. Vitamin D is supplied by exposure to sunlight. Infant formulas are fortified by vitamins A and D.

Body defense systems There are some advantages to breast milk that go beyond the nutrient value. Infants receive maternal antibodies in breast milk that protect against infection. In addition, breast milk contains white cells—macrophages and lymphocytes. Macrophages ingest and digest pathogenic bacteria. Lymphocytes, when suitably stimulated, can produce antibodies against bacteria.

Other disease fighters are friendly bacteria which discourage the growth of pathogens. Human milk encourages the growth of these friendly organisms in the infant's intestine. In addition, ingestion of human milk helps to prevent allergies by providing antibodies that coat the intestine and prevent allergens from being absorbed. Human milk is in itself nonallergenic.

Feeding patterns

No single feeding pattern or schedule will fit every mother-infant pair. Mothers and infants seem to adapt to each other's schedules to find the most satisfying and convenient times to feed. Most infants will establish a pattern of feeding that is predictable before the end of the first month.

A *demand feeding* schedule is the term used to indicate that the infant is fed whenever he is hungry. Most health care workers advocate feeding on demand. This is based on the belief that the infant creates his own schedule that is best for meeting his nutritional and psychological needs. For many years, however, scheduled feedings were advocated—usually on a basis of every 4 h. Strict scheduling of feeding times does not meet the individual needs of the child and is rarely suggested today.

Parents have many concerns centering around infant feeding. Many of these concerns and anxieties could be relieved if parents knew what to expect of their infants. Breast-fed infants, for example, may require feeding every 2 to 3 h during the first weeks. If mothers have not been prepared for this, they may think something is wrong with the infant or themselves. New mothers, especially, are sometimes apprehensive about their mothering skills and ability to provide for their infant. They may fear the infant is not getting enough milk and assume their milk supply is inadequate. This uncertainty leads to discouragement.

After this first few weeks, infants usually require between six and eight feedings a day. This gradually decreases until at 1 year they have adapted to the cultural feeding practices of the family. For most infants in western culture, that would be three meals a day, possibly supplemented with milk at naptime or before bed.

Infants differ greatly in their need for night feedings. Most infants are sleeping through the night by 2 months. Some lucky parents may get a relatively complete night's sleep by 3 weeks. It is not unusual for an infant to wake for night feedings until 10 or 11 months. Parents need to know that this is normal.

Breast-fed infants will regulate the amount of milk they take in to meet their needs. The bottle-fed baby must depend on the person feeding him to be sensitive to the cues he gives that he is done. There is a tendency to overfeed formula fed infants. The feeder may think the meal is over when the bottle is empty rather than when the infant signals he's full. A pattern of constant overfeeding may be detrimental to the infant in that it may form habits that persist into adult life.

Parents are sometimes tempted to use the bottle as a pacifier. This practice has some inherent dangers as does going to bed with a bottle. Young infants should *never* be left with a bottle propped. Most babies can begin to handle the bottle themselves by about 6 or 7 months. By this time they are mobile and adept enough to avoid the dangers of aspiration. However, these infants are erupting their first teeth. The infant who goes to sleep with the bottle in his mouth has milk or juice remaining in his mouth, too. This gives rise to a condition called *nursing bottle mouth*. Bacteria in the mouth convert the carbohydrate in the milk to acid products which cause the teeth to decay. If the fluid in the bottle has sugar or any freely fermentable carbohydrate, such as soda pop, kool aid, punch, juice, or honey water, the process of decay and damage to the teeth increases. Babies who are breast-fed to sleep do not develop this syndrome if held in an upright or semiupright position (the usual nursing position). It's very important for parents to know about this easily preventable problem.

Weaning Mothers sometimes ask when they should wean their babies. There is no magic time that this should be done. In general, the mother should be encouraged to breast-feed for as long as she and the infant gain satisfaction from the experience. Societal pressures in the past have seemed to discourage all but the most single-minded mothers. Now there is better acceptance of breast-feeding for longer periods.

Many infants gradually wean themselves. The pattern is generally from several feedings per day to one a day to several per week. The process may take a month or two to complete. The same pattern can be followed for weaning older infants from the bottle. It is a good idea to wean bottle-fed infants by 1 year in order to help prevent nursing bottle mouth.

Caution parents not to attempt to wean their infants during periods of disequilibrium for the family. A family vacation, move, or any other change in routine may increase the infant's dependency on the bottle or breast. Parents can be sensitive to this when it is pointed out and wait for better timing.

The eruption of teeth is not a reason in itself for weaning a child from the breast. The infant may try his new teeth out on the breast but he can be taught that this is not in his best interest. Simply stopping the feeding immediately when the infant bites will usually get the message across. Nutritionally, it is sound practice to continue breast feeding through the first year and longer.

Introduction of solid foods There is a term for foods other than milk or formula that are introduced into the baby's diet. The term is *beikost*. In the past, the suggested age at which beikost should be introduced has been based more on opinion than sound understanding of infant physiology. Recent information would suggest that there is no physiological advantage to introducing solid foods before 6 months. In fact, probably the liquid diet is best suited to the infant's physiological needs throughout the first year of life.

The practice in the United States until very recently has been toward early introduction of beikost, usually beginning with rice cereal as

early as 2 to 3 weeks. This may have been encouraged because infants seem to tolerate these feedings without obvious distress. There are dangers, however. Introducing solids before 4 or 5 months may cause food allergies. Furthermore, if solids such as cereal are given in place of a formula or breast-feeding, the infant may not get enough calories to maintain energy requirements and grow. If solids are given in addition to the formula, breast, or both, he runs the risk of being overfed with resultant overweight by 3 to 6 months of age. In addition, the high-solute load of beikost creates a problem of hyperosmolarity. This, among other things, compounds the problem of obesity in infants.

There are natural compounds in food which can be harmful to the infant. These include sucrose, gluten, salt, and nitrates. And of course food additives, which are most likely harmful to all of us, are particularly dangerous to the more vulnerable young infant. The ingestion of food additives and contaminants can be reduced by preparation of baby foods in the home and careful label-reading of commercially prepared infant foods.

The currently suggested age for introduction of beikost is between 4 and 6 months. It may be difficult to convince parents to wait this long. Parents are open to good information and advice, however. According to a Ross Laboratory survey, between 40 and 50 percent of mothers seek information about infant feeding from health professionals—the physician and nurse both being sought out for questions.[4]

When semisolid foods are introduced, the usual order is cereal, fruits, vegetables, and finally meats. Variations in this order are common and depend on the preference of the family and the advice they get from health professionals and friends. The order is not critical but there are some ground rules that should be carefully explained to parents and reinforced as the infant begins solid foods. First, new foods should be introduced one at a time in a small amount (1 tbsp), and not more often than every 1 or 2 weeks. The infant should then be carefully watched for intolerance of the food. This intolerance would most likely take the form of a food allergy. The symptoms indicating a food intolerance might be rash, colic, gas, diarrhea, or vomiting. Secondly, if there is a history of allergies in the family, foods of high allergic potential should be avoided. Egg white and orange juice are examples of foods likely to produce allergic responses in susceptible infants. Third, it is important to be sensitive to the infant for the right timing. Infants show a readiness to accept beikost as the neuromuscular physiology of their mouth develops. The *extrusion reflex* (pushing food out with the tongue) begins to disappear at about the third or fourth month of life. The infant can then accept food on his tongue and swallow without most of the food ending up on his chin. The infant begins to chew with lateral motion of his jaw at about 6 or 7 months. It is at this time that he can handle foods with more texture.

When the infant's erupting teeth urge him to bite, introduce junior (lumpy) foods. Instruct the parents to simply mash table foods for the baby. Use bite-size pieces of food, such as bananas or other soft-cooked fruits and vegetables. Give the child a few pieces of food and replenish them as necessary. Allow the child to put his hands in the food; infants accept food better when allowed to explore and play with it. Protect the floor with newspapers or towels. Then the child can hold a graham cracker, for instance, and enjoy practicing his skill, eating at his own pace.

At 9 months introduce the spoon. Allow the child to continue finger-feeding himself. Encourage him to practice drinking a small amount of liquid from a cup. Eliminate junior foods by 12 months and use finger foods from the family dinner.

Caution and common sense should go together when determining what foods are appropriate for the infant. Nuts, raisins, small candies, corn, or other small foods are difficult to manipulate in the mouth and impossible to chew with the infant's limited teeth. They can cause choking and are therefore dangerous. In addition, it's amazing how often peanuts, in particular, find their way into even the older child's nostrils and ears. Parents can be warned about these hazards. See Table 11-2 for guidelines for introducing new foods.

Preparation of infant foods There are a multitude of commercially prepared baby foods on the market. There are no nutritional advantages to these foods over those prepared at home. The primary advantage is one of convenience. See Table 11-3 for guidelines for buying prepared baby food.

Infant foods can easily and economically be prepared at home. A blender or food processor can be very helpful if parents are planning to prepare foods at home. Home preparation is very likely to reduce the amount of food additives, sugar, and salt the infant ingests. Instruct the parents to use only fresh foods; canned and frozen foods usually contain salt. Pureed foods are easily frozen in ice cube trays; a food cube is easily reheated. Stress scrupulously clean hands and utensils and prompt refrigeration of food.

Many babies are fed foods from the table that fit into the cultural eating patterns of the family. Pacific island infants are fed poi (made from taro root), while mashed potatoes or beans might be given to other infants, depending on the family's preference. In general, infants accept semisolid foods well and will express individual likes and dislikes just as any other member of the family.

Food supplements The breast-fed infant of a healthy woman receives all the vitamins necessary for his growth except vitamin D. Commercially prepared formulas are enriched with vitamins. Almost all strained commercial baby foods and junior foods are vitamin-supplemented as well. Many infants, either from prescriptions or over-the-counter preparations, are receiving daily supplemental vitamins. The effects, if any, of oversupplementation of vitamins are not known. However, because of the trend in our culture for all family members, including infants, to eat fast foods and snack foods, there is concern that vitamin intake may be inadequate. The need for supplemental vitamins should be based on an assessment of the family's and infant's eating habits and the nutritional soundness of their diet. See Appendix C for a listing of the recommended daily dietary allowances of essential nutrients for the infant.

Fluoride strengthens the enamel of the teeth and increases their resistence to decay. This is particularly important in infancy and early childhood, when teeth are being formed. Fluoride appears naturally in the water supply of some areas and in many vegetables grown where fluoride is in the soil or water used for irrigation. Some cities and counties routinely add fluoride to the water supply. Fluoride supplements are recommended for infants even if they live in areas where fluoride occurs naturally or is added.

Table 11-2 Introduction of new foods

Total daily food intake	How	What	Why
0–4 months 20–23 oz of formula or milk 5–7 feedings per day	No	Nothing	1. Formula, breast milk, or evaporated milk (with appropriate vitamins and minerals) are adequate 2. Solids replace formula with nutritionally inferior food 3. Solids, especially commercial, are more expensive 4. Easier to overfeed with solids and induce obesity 5. Infants are more vulnerable at earlier age to such additives as salt, sugar, nitrates, and modified food starches 6. No substantiation for theory that babies sleep through the night with solids at bedtime. 7. Increased renal solute load with some solids.
4–5 months* 32 oz of formula 2–4 tbsp of dry cereal 4–5 feedings/per day	Give 1–2 tbsp of dry cereal mixed with an equal amount of formula. Give once a day for several days. Increase to twice a day as infant learns to enjoy this experience	Dry cereals preferred. Begin with rice, save wheat and mixed until after 6 months	1. Iron stores becoming depleted; iron-fortified cereals are needed 2. Normal solid swallowing pattern appears 3. Age of increased acceptance 4. Drooling appears and pancreatic amylase increases to allow starch digestion
5–6 months* 32 oz of formula 4–6 tbsp of dry cereal 4–8 tbsp of fruit 4 tbsp of vegetable 4 feedings per day	Add one fruit or vegetable every 3–4 days. Start with 1–2 tbsp and increase to 4 tbsp per feeding	Fruits, vegetables, and egg yolks. Pureed table food (except beets, spinach, carrots) may be used before seasoning. Regular frozen or canned juice, standard dilution; wait until 6 months to introduce orange juice	1. Fortified juice is a source of vitamin C 2. "Baby" juices are high in sugar and more expensive 3. Dark green and deep yellow vegetables and fruits are a source of vitamin A 4. Beets, spinach, and carrots are potentially high in nitrate—should be postponed until infant is taking variety of foods at each meal or use commercial preparation

Table 11-2 Introduction of new foods (*Continued*)

Total daily food intake	How	What	Why
6–7 months 32 oz of formula 4–6 tbsp of dry cereal 4–8 tbsp of fruit 4 tbsp of vegetable 2–4 tbsp of meat 4 feedings per day	Give 1–2 tbsp of meat mixed with vegetable. Increase to a total of 4 tbsp per day	Meat. Pureed or milled meats and some casseroles from family table	1. Acceptable protein content 2. Some iron, expecially in liver 3. High-protein and high-meat dinners are an expensive source of protein. Whole-meat preparations should be used 4. Milk is the major source of protein for the infant's diet
6–8 months 28 oz of formula or milk 1.2 c. cereal 4–8 tbsp of vegetable 4–8 tbsp of meat 4 feedings per day	Encourage self-feeding. Provide toast, pieces of fruit, vegetables and cheese that the child can hold while being fed	Finger foods, whole pieces of soft fruits and vegetables, milled meats. Junior foods	1. Helps transition to table food 2. Feeding self encourages eating only to hunger satiation 3. Better food acceptance if allowed to feed self, mash and experiment
8–12 months 24 oz of milk ½ cup of cereal 2 slices of bread or crackers 8–12 tbsp of fruit 4–8 tbsp of vegetable 4–8 tbsp of meat	Switch to table food. Encourage child to try new textures	Table foods. Cut up meat finely. Encourage self-feeding. Provide spoon but allow hands. Still withhold seasonings. Drain syrup from canned fruit. Discontinue junior foods by 12 months. Decrease milk intake to 20–24 oz by 12 months	1. Encourage independence 2. Table food contains less sodium than commercial baby foods

* Some experts recommend starting solid foods at 6 months.

Source: Catherine DeAngelis et al., "Introduction of New Foods into the Newborn and Infant Diet," *Issues in Comprehensive Pediatric Nursing 1* (5): 30–33 (April 1977). Used with permission of the publisher. Adapted from E. Satter, R.D. and M. Morgan, R.D. University of Wisconsin Hospitals.

The reason for this is that most infants do not drink water in quantities large enough to supply their need.

Physical growth and maturation

Why study growth?

The infant's pattern of growth and the rate at which he progresses toward maturity give us a great deal of information about his health status. Comparing his progress to others of his same age, sex, and race, and to himself over time, provides the data we need to monitor his growth. The usefulness of this information is based on several known characteristics of growth itself. First, human growth proceeds in an overall pattern that is similar for all healthy individuals. Secondly, this overall pattern is consistent over time. There are wide variations in individuals when it comes to actual size and rate of growth. The pattern remains consistent, however, and the individual remains consistent with himself.

The measurement of growth

Growth is measured by length or height, weight, volume, and tissue thickness. The most common measurements made of the growing infant are length and weight. Newborn infants, tiny as they may seem, are almost one-third their adult height. If all is going well, they will increase in length to about half their adult height in the first 2 years. Along with this rapid early gain in height comes an equally impressive weight gain. Infants can be expected to triple their weight by the end of the first year of life.

Skeletal growth

Bone tissues provide a number of important functions for the infant and child. The first functions that usually come to mind are the mechanical support, the mobility, and the protection provided by bones. The bones also store minerals that the body can draw upon to maintain a proper balance. Also, the body manufactures blood cells in marrow tissues which help to maintain the blood supply. Infants have blood-producing marrow throughout most of their skeleton. During childhood some of this marrow is replaced by fatty tissue.

Skull growth The infant's head is larger in proportion to the rest of his body than that of

Table 11-3 Guidelines for buying commercial baby foods

1. Meats are vastly superior to meat combinations. High-meat dinners contain one-half the protein of whole-meat dinners
2. Fruit juices with added sugar should be avoided
3. Baby desserts are high in calories, low in nutrients, and usually contain additives
4. Labels from different brands of food should be compared for the best nutrition
5. Foods with water listed first or foods with added salt, sugar, or starches should be avoided
6. Lids should have an unbroken seal with no debris between the jar and lid
7. Food should be removed from the jar before being warmed and fed to infant. When the baby is fed from the jar, the enzymes from the saliva may spoil the remaining food

From Catherine DeAngelis et al., "Introduction of New Foods into the Newborn and Infant Diet," *Issues in Comprehensive Pediatric Nursing* April, 1977, pp. 23–33.

the adult. At birth the infant's head is one-quarter the length of his body while the adult's head is only one-eighth the length of the body. As can be seen, the head is one of the more rapidly growing body parts. The skull reaches adult size by about 6 years of age.

Skull growth closely parallels brain growth. Measurements of head circumference and assessment of fontanel status are the ways used by health professionals to monitor this growth. The posterior fontanel usually closes by 3 months. The anterior fontanel remains open throughout the first year.

Facial skeletal growth The facial skeleton does not grow as fast as the skull. While the skull will be about adult size by age 6, the facial skeleton grows into late adolescence. If you look closely at the infant, you can see that his eyes are about in the middle of his face, dividing the face equally from top to chin. As the facial skeleton grows, the facial proportions change. The largest amount of growth is in the lower portion of the face. The respiratory passages are increased and the jaw develops to accommodate permanent teeth.

Dentition

Teeth begin to form during the third fetal month. Usually the first teeth emerge through the gum when the infant is about 6 or 7 months of age. There is wide variation among infants, however, with some infants showing teeth as early as 3 months and others not before a year. These first teeth are called *primary* or *deciduous* teeth.

Teeth developed in the upper jaw, or maxilla, are called *maxillary teeth*. Lower teeth, those developed in the mandible, are called *mandibular teeth*. The infant's first two teeth are usually the lower central incisors. Next to emerge are usually the upper central incisors followed by the upper lateral incisors. These six teeth are what the infant of 1 year of age usually sports as basic equipment.

Each infant responds differently to *teething*, the process of erupting his first teeth. Some babies become fussy and irritable during this time and others have little discomfort. Most babies drool what seems like cupfuls. The salivary glands are active at this time and teething stimulates them to produce. The infant has not yet developed the habit of swallowing saliva, and so it simply comes out of the mouth. While they are teething, infants also gum or bite whatever is in reach.

Other infants have diarrhea, refuse food, have "cherry cheeks," or a teething rash around the mouth. Symptoms of an upper respiratory tract infection are often caused by the erupting teeth irritating the upper respiratory tract. The erupting tooth ruptures blood vessels and causes pain. This kind of behavior can go on for several weeks until the tooth emerges.

Teething can be stressful for parents. Instruct them to rub an analgesic ointment on the gums. Teething rings can be placed in the refrigerator. Teething biscuits quickly become messy and soft. Infants prefer to bite cold items. A spoon, piece of celery, or banana placed in the freezer effectively numbs the gums.

Neurological maturation

Neural tissue grows faster than other tissues or organs of the body during infancy. In many ways the neurological system provides both the foundation and structure upon which the child grows and develops. This system, unlike other body tissues, experiences only one growth cycle. This cycle begins in the embryonic stage and continues at a rapid rate through the first year of life.

Myelinization *Myelinization* is the process whereby a fatty substance called a *myelin sheath* surrounds or coats the axon portion of some nerves. This seems to serve the same kind of function as insulating an electrical wire. It helps the nerve impulse to travel more rapidly and with less expenditure of energy.

The process of myelinization begins before the infant is born. By the time of birth the pathways of sensation and equilibrium are already myelinated in the brain. Most of the afferent (sensory) nerves are myelinated as well. This is very important when we consider the capabilities of the newborn and young infant. Many of these capabilities, such as sense of smell, are used in establishing his initial attachment with his mother.

Myelinization continues at a rapid rate for the first 2 years. Just after birth, there is a lot of activity in the cerebral cortex. The descending motor fibers (efferent nerve fibers) are myelinated from the head downward and correspond to the infant's developing capabilities.

Brain growth Before birth the brain is developing by hyperplasia—an increase in cell numbers by cell division. From about the time of birth to 10 or 12 months of age, the brain is growing by both hyperplasia and hypertrophy—an increase in cell number and size. After 1 year and until maturity, the brain grows by hypertrophy only.

Most brain growth is accomplished while the infant is still in utero, but it is still developing rapidly until about age 2. At 2 years of age the brain is two-thirds the adult size. The importance of nutrition for the pregnant mother and the infant *cannot be over emphasized*. All of this rapid growth is compromised if the necessary nutrients are not present and available.

A continuous supply of adequate oxygen is also necessary for the infant's brain development. Hypoxia results in nerve cell death and thus compromises brain growth. Like malnutrition during this critical period, hypoxia may leave brain development permanently retarded.

Reflexes Reflexes begin diminishing as voluntary muscle control develops and the cortex matures. Rooting, sucking, and swallowing come under voluntary control fairly rapidly as the infant refines these reflexes into well-organized complex behaviors. Other reflexes, such as the survival reflexes, similarly disappear as voluntary behavior makes them unnecessary. Health professionals use the character and disappearance of reflexes to assess the neurological maturation of the infant. Refer to Chap. 10 for a listing of the infant's reflexes.

Muscle growth

Muscles are another rapidly growing tissue during infancy. Muscles are developed and innervated early in uterine life, making movement possible. The newborn infant's body is about 20 to 25 percent muscle tissue. As he grows, this percentage will increase until he reaches his adult proportion, which is about one-third muscle.

Probably the number of muscle fibers does not increase much after 1 month of age. In other words, the period of hyperplasia is over and from early infancy the predominant growth is from an increase in muscle fiber size. The muscle growth rate throughout the first year is about twice that of bones.

Muscle growth is influenced by a number of factors, including nutrition, exercise, general health, and hormones. The hormones most influential during this period are the pituitary growth hormone, thyroid hormones, and insulin.

Gross and fine motor development

Motor development refers to the process by which the infant or child gains control over his body. It requires the infant to practice in order to gain skill and strength. An alert, healthy infant is engaging in this process almost constantly.

Gross motor development refers to the development and maturation of the large muscles involved in the infant's sitting, crawling, standing, walking, and head control.

Motor development progresses from reflexive and generalized movement of the entire body to a more purposeful, differentiated movement in the infant. The head and neck muscles are the strongest and most developed at birth. The infant by 3 months is able to lift his head to look around when lying on his stomach and has some amount of head control when pulled to a sitting position or when held upright. Development progresses from the head downward and from the main axis outward. The trunk of the infant is then the next expected area of increased strength and differentiation. The infant demonstrates this by coordination of head, neck, and trunk to turn himself over. As gross motor behaviors become mastered and integrated into more complex behaviors and myelinization continues, the infant learns to sit, crawl, and then pull to standing. Table 11-4 presents gross motor developmental milestones of the first year of life.

Fine motor development requires use of hands, fingers, and the smaller muscles of the legs and feet. Fine motor follows gross motor development. The infant coordinates hand movements before finger movements. The infant is able to support his weight on his legs before he can develop the skill necessary to balance and step in order to walk. Table 11-5 includes fine motor developmental milestones of infancy.

Digestive system

It is amazing to think that the infant's digestive system is so well-developed that it can swing into action at the moment of birth. It is ready to digest and assimilate breast milk or a suitable substitute. Even the structure of the mouth is ready to assist the infant in supplying nutrients to his own body.

For the first 6 months of life the infant swallows differently from later in life. He has some built-in safeguards to prevent choking while he is sucking and swallowing. The posterior portion of the tongue is raised against the soft palate while the infant sucks. This separates the mouth from the throat and provides a place to hold the milk. In this way the infant can suck and breathe at the same time. When he swallows, respiration is inhibited briefly while the epiglottis closes and the milk goes into the stomach. This whole process is aided by the infant's anatomic structure. The infant has a longer posterior soft palate than the older child or adult to assist him in holding milk. Additionally, the passageway from the mouth to the pharynx is smaller.

The infant's taste buds are present at birth, but taste discrimination is not fully developed until about 3 months of age. Infants are fast learners and can tell the differences in tastes and textures of food quite well by the time beikost should be introduced into their diets.

Intestinal flora is introduced through the infant's mouth almost immediately after birth. By 2 days it is well-established. These bacteria are essential in the digestive process and also help to protect the infant from infections.

Parents are often distressed if their infant spits up often. Many infants do this on a regular basis.

Table 11-4 Developmental milestones: Gross motor development*

	1 month	2 months	3 months	4 months	5 months	6 months
Reflexes	Reflexes govern all movements Rooting, Moro, tonic neck, walking, grasp reflexes are strong	Tonic neck, Moro reflexes still strong	Movements becoming voluntarily controlled Tonic neck, Moro, walking, fading	Voluntary movements predominate Tonic neck, Moro, rooting, grasping disappeared		Swimming reflex disappears
Head	Head sags unless supported Turns head side to side when on stomach Lifts head momentarily	Head sags forward when held in sitting position Lifts head momentarily at 45° angle when on stomach	Head sags minimally May lift chest off surface for 10 s when on stomach	Head erect. Turns head in all directions. Briefly holds head erect Raises head and chest off surface when on stomach. Bears weight on arms	Head held erect when sitting or pulled up to sitting position. Helps to pull up body. Balances head well Lifts head and shoulders when on back	
Sitting			Sits supported, back rounded, knees flexed	Sits with minimal support, if propped for 10–15 min. Back less rounded. May flex legs to lift hips when on back	Sits for longer periods (30 min) when well supported	Sits with slight support, pulls self up to sitting position. Sits well-balanced in chair

Kicking, rolling

Straightens out arms and legs when playing

Rolls side to back part way

Kicks well when excited or playful

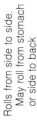

Rolls from side to side. May roll from stomach or side to back

Rolls from stomach to back

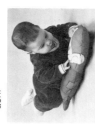

Rolls from back to stomach.

Turns, twists toward all directions

Pushes on hands and flexes knees when on stomach

Crawling

Makes crawling or swimming movements when on stomach

Moves arms and legs together on one side of body, then other

Crawls

Walking

Stands briefly with feet on surface when held in position

Stamps foot, supports most of weight in standing position

Stands with support

(continued)

Table 11-4 (Continued)

7 months	8 months	9 months	10 months	11 months	12 months
Reflexes					
	Parachute, plantar reflexes disappear				
Sitting					
Sits alone steadily and briefly. Pushes self into sitting position	Sits alone steadily, bounces	Sits alone for long time periods	Lowers self to sit		Lowers self to sit
Crawling					
Rocks in crawling position	Creeps	Crawls and creeps instead of hitching (often backwards at first)	Creeps forward Creeping and crawling well-coordinated		Prefers to crawl
	Pivots on stomach				

Walking

Hitches

Bounces, supports weight when held in standing position

Supports weight well when standing. Stands leaning on furniture. Pulls self up on furniture

Cruises

Pulls self to feet with help

Stands alone briefly
Stands holding onto furniture

Stands with little support

Walks holding two hands

Cruising continues
Pulls self to stand
Lifts one foot while standing
Walks with help

Stands by self

Walks around small objects

Table 11-5 Developmental milestones: Vision and fine motor development*

1 month	2 months	3 months	4 months	5 months	6 months
Hand					
Immediately drops object placed in hand	Holds object momentarily (voluntary movement replacing grasp reflex)	Holds objects placed in hands	Grasps, holds objects, better coordination	Picks up object at will, often misses	Picks up object well
			Puts objects in mouth	Holds one block, drops it to pick up another	Turns wrists to examine object
Fists usually clenched (grasp reflex)	Hands often open (grasp reflex fading)	Hands open (grasp reflex absent)	Hits at objects, still misses	Immediately puts object in mouth	Holds object well (bottle)
		Begins to hit at and often misses objects by large distance	Picks up object with entire hand, often misses it	Begins to use thumb when picking up object	Transfers toy from one hand to another
		Begins to reach for object with closed fist	Plays with small objects and hands	Reaches for object with two hands. Pulls paper off face. Plays with toes. Plays with rattle in hand	Holds block no. 1, reaches for block no. 2, looks at block no. 3
		Explores own hands and feet			Reaches with one arm
Vision					
Follows light with eyes up, down, sideways	Follows moving light from outer edge to past midline	Follows object 180°	Follows moving objects well	20/20 vision	Moves body to better view object
Stares at objects	Coordinates eye movements in circle	Looks toward sound	Binocular vision coordinated	Stares at small objects	Examines objects upside down to change perspective
Prefers pattern to color	Begins to focus on color	Looks from one object to another	Increased eye-hand coordination	Eye-hand coordination improving	Eye movements coordinated, mature
	Close object (8–10 in)	Focus on objects throughout room	Sees in color		
			Looks at and grabs object		
			Perceives depth and distance		

(continued)

Table 11-5 (Continued)

	7 months	8 months	9 months	10 months	11 months	12 months
Hand	Holds 2–3 blocks	Holds object 3 min	Plays with two objects held at same time. Hits them together	Holds two objects in one hand	Holds crayon to mark on paper	Reaches for object without looking
	Picks up small objects, bangs object on table	Begins to use pincer grasp to pick up objects	Hand preference obvious			
	Searches for dropped object	Reaches for toys	Pokes with index finger			
	Lifts cup by handle	Rakes at objects				
		Releases objects				
				Pincer grasp well-coordinated	Places several objects in container	Pincer grasp complete
				Finger-feeds self	Finger-feeding better coordinated	Places tiny objects in bottle
				May build two-block tower	Pushes toys	Removes covers of containers
						Turns book pages
					May pull off socks and untie shoes	Feeds self with spoon
						May undress self
Vision	Stares at tiny objects	Looks before reaching for object	Depth perception more acute	Reaches for unseen object		
	Depth and space perception begins					
	Searches for fallen objects					

* Compiled by Nancy L. Ramsey.

189

Unless the amount is substantial (in which case it is more like vomiting than spitting up), there are no ill effects. Infants will grow out of this by 6 or 7 months as their digestive system matures. Holding the infant in an upright position after feeding and burping may help.

Small and large intestines Milk is held in the stomach and released slowly into the small intestine. In the infant, the stomach is usually emptied within 3 hours after a meal. The rapidity with which the stomach is emptied can vary depending upon the type of food ingested. Breast milk leaves the stomach at a faster rate than formula.

Most of the actual digestion occurs in the small intestine. Bile and pancreatic secretions join with the food to break it down into usable nutrients. These nutrients are then absorbed into the bloodstream from the small intestine. What is not absorbed, plus the waste, continues on to the large intestine.

The composition of the infant's bile is not mature until he reaches about 6 months of age. Bile and pancreatic lipase, which is being secreted adequately by about 3 months of age, are necessary for the digestion of fats. The infant is not capable of digesting all fats until about 1 year of age.

The large intestine absorbs water into the bloodstream. Infants' stools are usually watery and frequent. This is partly due to food passing swiftly through the large intestine so that there is not enough time for water absorption. Another reason is that the infant is simply not absorbing water as well as an older child because his system is relatively immature. More residue remains in the intestine, which in turn keeps more water from being absorbed. By the time the infant is 1 year old, his system has become more efficient and his stools are firmer and less frequent.

Liver function related to digestion The liver performs a great many functions in our bodies, some of which are directly related to digestion. Besides producing bile, the liver helps to metabolize proteins, fats, and some vitamins. It acts as a storage center for iron, supplying the infant with this needed mineral for several months. The liver converts glucose into glycogen and stores it in order to keep a relatively stable blood sugar. Though the infant's liver is immature, it performs these functions well, increasing in efficiency as he grows.

Excretory system: kidneys and bladder

The newborn infant's kidneys are quite immature. They are equipped to handle breast milk. Increased fluids or foods with high solute load (i.e., cow's milk) endanger the infant by overtaxing the kidneys. The kidneys mature at a rapid rate during the first few weeks of life. Specifically, there are maturation changes in the tubules and in Bowman's capsules. The tubules become longer and wider and the epithelial membranes of Bowman's capsules become thinner and better able to filter. By 6 months, the kidneys have become better able to adapt and renal function is markedly improved. Because of the relative immaturity of the kidney function, infants are especially vulnerable to fluid and electrolyte imbalance.

During early infancy, the bladder empties automatically when it contains about half an ounce of urine. The amount of urine the bladder can hold increases by small amounts over the first year. The infant is not ready for voluntary bladder control. The child develops an awareness of a full bladder after 1 year of age.

Immune system

The infant begins life protected from infection by antibodies given him by his mother through placental transfer. Shortly after birth, he begins to develop his own antibodies through his own immune system. At first his system is sluggish and responds slowly or not at all. With more antigenic stimulation the infant begins to respond more quickly in making antibodies. By about 5 months of age the infant's immunoglobulin level is based almost completely on antibodies made by his own system. It takes the entire first year to approach levels similar to the older child's or adult's, however. Even then, not all types of immunoglobulins are being produced at the same level as by an adult. Immunoglobulin A (IgA), for instance, found in saliva and secretions of the respiratory tract, does not reach adult levels until adolescence.

The thymus is the most important of the infant's lymphoid structures. It has a particularly important function for the young infant and child. The thymus secretes a hormone called the *thymic factor.* It is believed to be essential for production by the thymus of T lymphocytes, which are important in cell-mediated immune reactions. Normal functioning of the infant's immune system is dependent on a healthy thymus.

Other lymphoid tissues include the tonsils, adenoids, spleen, and lymph nodes throughout the body. Certain lymphoid tissues are responsible for producing activated lymphocytes in the course of an immune response. The nodes and other lymphoid tissues also act as filters to trap pathogens before they enter the bloodstream so that phagocytic cells can attack them. Because the ability to make antibodies is not well-developed in infancy, this filtering system is especially important. The lymphoid tissues grow rapidly during infancy and reach peak volume at about 12 years.

Vision

Vision does not depend strictly on the maturity of the eye. The infant must learn to utilize his eye and all its properties plus interpret what he sees. Much of this process is cognitive in nature.

Vision is dependent on a number of capabilities that the infant must develop. *First* he must focus the image on the macula while adjusting to differences in distance. *Secondly*, both eyes must function together. This is accomplished by control of the extraocular muscles. Most infants coordinate their eye movements well by 3 months, and by 6 months this function is mature. *Third*, the infant must develop the capacity to perceive differences in color and brightness. The macula is mature at about 6 months of age. The rods are probably well-developed by birth. The cones, however, take longer and mature as the macula develops. Color vision then would follow brightness discrimination. Infants seem to begin to respond to specific colors by 1 or 2 months. Maturation of the macula also allows the infant to see smaller items in detail. *Fourth*, the infant must learn to perceive depth. This is dependent on being able to focus the image on the macula in both eyes simultaneously. The image seen with each eye is slightly different because of the different angle and distance of each eye to the object. These images must be fused in the brain to get depth perception. Crawling infants avoid steps or steep drops. Because of this, we can assume that depth perception is developed in the infant by crawling age—6 to 9 months. Table 11-5 includes visual development throughout the first year of life.

Hearing

Hearing is one of the better-developed senses in the infant. The fetus can hear in utero and responds to loud sounds. The newborn can distinguish sound frequencies and will turn his head toward a voice or other sound. He may even already be familiar with his mother's voice. By just a few months of age he can locate his mother by her voice even if in a crowded or noisy room. The progressive development of the infant's hearing is outlined in Table 11-6.

Psychosocial development
Building a sense of trust

Erik Erikson's work has had an enormous impact on the study of children. He offers the hypothesis that there are eight stages of social development, each with a task that must be mastered before a stage is achieved. The task of infancy is development of a sense of *trust.* The counterpart of trust is mistrust. Establishment of this basic sense of trust or mistrust will determine how the child approaches all the future stages of his growing identity. If he establishes a basic trust in people, himself, and the environment, he will have a healthy beginning. His future relationships will be characterized by this trust, allowing for deeper commitments and intimacy on his part. Need gratification is important to establishment of basic trust. So are the quality of his interpersonal relationships and the amount of stress encountered in new situations. The trusting infant feels secure, safe, and physically comfortable.

Factors influencing the establishment of trust
Predictability Part of developing trust is dependent on the infant's ability to predict what will happen in his environment. Some families have very well-established routines while the lifestyles of others are not, at least on the surface, so well-organized and patterned. Generally, babies are very adaptive and can pick out those consistencies and people they can count on. Difficulties arise, however, when there are events such as illness and hospitalization that have the

Table 11-6 Developmental milestones: Hearing and language*

1 month	2 months	3 months	4 months	5 months	6 months
Hearing					
Startled by sounds (Moro reflex) Quiets when hears voice	Turns head toward close, familiar sound Listens to bell	Turns head toward sound, searches for it in room Stops sucking to listen		Locates sounds below ear	
Crying					
Cries, makes throaty sounds	Crying predominates Crying becomes differentiated. Pattern, pitch, intensity vary	Cries less	Cry increasingly varies in volume, tone, duration		
Laughing					
		Chuckles, squeals with pleasure when talked to by parents or when happy	Laughs aloud Smiles, gurgles, grunts "Talks" with pleasure, 20 min	Still squeals	Belly laughs Laughs, squeals Babbles (one syllable) with pleasure Enjoys listening to own voice
Talking					
Responds to voice Begins to coo	Coos, still makes throaty sounds "Talks" to family members	Babbles and coos "Talks" when spoken to	Cooing changes pitch, volume Talks more to objects than face "Talkative" "Talking" varies with moods Begins consonant sounds: H, N, K, G, P, B	Makes vowel sounds (ee, ah, ooh) Consonant sounds increase Attempts to imitate sounds	Combines vowel, consonant sounds (ee, ka) Imitates sounds, varies pitch and rate "Talks" to toys and image in mirror Calls for help

(continued)

Table 11-6 *(Continued)*

	7 months	8 months	9 months	10 months	11 months	12 months
Hearing	Reacts to changes in music volume	Recognizes familiar words. Responds to familiar sounds	Listens to talking Understands and responds to one or two simple commands	Listens to common words	Begins to differentiate between words	
Talking	Makes four different vowel sounds Combines syllables (da-da, ma-ma) "Talks" with adultlike inflections when others are talking	Shouts for attention Talking shows emotion Responds to "no, no," "bye-bye" May label object with sound (kitty, meows)	Says "ma-ma, da-da" meaningfully "Talking" increasingly shows emotions Initiates coughing Intonation becomes patterned	Says one word (hi, no) Combines consonants Understands, responds to own name, and "bye-bye" Associates action with word (waves), says bye-bye Understands simple commands ("come here")	Says two or three words with meaning. Uses jargon Uses few definite speech sounds Continues to imitate intonation, expression Recognizes word as symbol for object	Says three words with meaning Enjoys jabbering expressively, in short sentences Vocalization decreases when walking Comprehends meaning of word before speaking Understands commands ("go get my shoes") Knows own name May have one word for a whole class of objects

* Compiled by Nancy L. Ramsey.

potential to remove the infant from any possibility of predicting what will happen. Such events should be viewed as grave threats to the infant's ability to establish trust. Every effort should be made to restore a sense of normalcy and predictability to the infant's life.

Needs gratification   The infant is dependent on those around him to meet his basic needs. He can let others know that he wants something but is dependent on their sensitivity and willingness to provide for him. When the infant's needs are met, he is in the best possible position to grow and develop and to establish a sense of trust.

Sucking can be considered a basic need in the infant. Sucking has a specific function, that of getting nutrients into his body. Apart from the

Figure 11-5 An infant tote is an excellent way of maintaining close contact with an infant.

need to obtain food, however, babies seem to need to exercise their ability to suck. Here again we see individual differences. Some babies seem to experience a great deal of need gratification from sucking both with feeding and with a pacifier or thumb. These babies use this mechanism to help establish a state of quiet and comfort, allowing them to devote more of their energies to the task at hand—developing basic trust.

Another need that must be gratified in the infant is relief from *hunger*. Hunger may be one of the most intense need states that the infant experiences. If the infant's need for food brings a quick response, he is likely to perceive the environment as trustworthy. He learns to rely on his primary caretaker, who is usually the mother. Infants who are deprived of food or who receive an inconsistent response are at risk for viewing the world with distrust.

The infant needs to be kept warm. Very young infants, because of their relatively low proportion of body fat, large amount of body surface area, and physiological immaturity, cannot adequately regulate their temperatures. In providing for *physical warmth*, we are helping the infant maintain some physiological equilibrium and thus helping him conserve energy. When the infant is comfortable, behavior is much better organized. His development of trust is assisted.

Psychological warmth is just as important to the infant as physical warmth. Psychological warmth is difficult to look at in isolation because it is related so closely to stimulation and affection. Infants need to be in close human contact. They need to be held, enveloped, and cuddled. They need to be *touched*—skin to skin with gentleness and warmth.

Infant carriers of the type pictured in Fig. 11-5 are excellent aids for providing this close human contact to young infants. They allow the mother or care-giver to spend more time with the infant while attending to daily tasks. The alternative is for the infant to spend this time in his crib, stroller, or infant seat, none of which provide the same mobility or person-to-person contact. The mother is in close contact and is better able to anticipate changes and respond to the baby's states or needs.

Infants need *stimulation* to maintain their growth both physically and psychosocially. Stimulation that is appropriate for the individual child in amount, intensity, and timing characterizes the loving and responsive relationship and helps to establish the infant's basic trust.

Interpersonal relations The quality of the *interpersonal relationships* that the infant is engaged in is of utmost importance in developing trust. There are several characteristics the nurse can look for when assessing these relationships. First, the response the infant gets should be related to his behavior. Something should happen as a result of what the baby does. It is confusing if he smiles at his mother in a face-to-face position and nothing happens. He must learn what his effect on the environment is. Much of this contingency is dependent on the care-giver's ability to respond to and interpret his cues (Fig. 11-6).

The relationship should be characterized by *affection* and *nurturance*. The care-giver is genuinely interested in the well-being of the child and emotionally involved in the interaction. The emotional involvement may include elements of protectiveness and possessiveness. There is identification with the infant as well. When the infant gets his immunization injection, the mother may shed tears right along with the child. As a whole, the relationship is loving and responsive.

It is a normal part of the infant's experience to encounter new situations. Because of his rapid development, his world expands almost continually. The parents' function is first to make sure the new encounter is not needlessly stressful, overwhelming, or dangerous, and second, to provide a base from which the infant can try out short periods of independent exploration. The child who faces these new happenings with the support of a loving adult establishes trust and maintains his curiosity and openness to the world and events around him. Table 11-7 summarizes psychosocial developmental milestones of the first year of life.

Attachment behavior indicative of trust Babies become attached to their primary care-givers. The quality of this attachment is important in the establishment of basic trust. It is also a major determinant of how an infant will face new situations or tolerate and enjoy independent exploration.

In order for an infant to show attachment behavior, several skills related to his cognitive

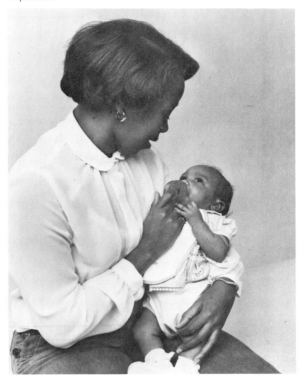

Figure 11-6 The care-giver's response to an infant is important.

development must be evident. First, he must be able to differentiate his mother or other primary care-giver from other individuals. To do this, he will first have to develop the ability to view himself as separate from the environment and to distinguish between objects and people and finally between his mother and other people. These abilities probably develop gradually over the first few months. The infant becomes aware of himself as separate but dependent on his environment (Fig. 11-7). As he experiences contingent relationships, he senses his own power to have control over what happens to him. If he cries when he is hungry, he brings Mom to the rescue. These interactions help him to become more differentiated from the environment and focused in his responses.

Next, the infant must develop a set of expectations for the mother or primary care-giver. This requires even more cognitive skill for he must anticipate the mother's behavior based on what he knows of her. He has then developed a

Table 11-7 Developmental milestones: Psychosocial development*

1 month	2 months	3 months	4 months	5 months	6 months
Interaction					
Watches parent's face. Establishes eye contact	Follows movement of caretaker around room Prefers people to objects Sucking need continues to be maximal	Watches environment; alert up to 45 min Recognizes mother Recognizes and distinguishes between family members	Increased interest in mother; shows trust—knows mother Discriminates among faces; adjusts responses to people	Distinguishes self from mother Begins to explore mother's body; playful Lifts arms to be picked up Clings when held Interested in other family. Distinguishes adults from children Shows emotions of fear, anger Protests when toy removed Delays gratification Begins to smile at self in mirror	Knows parents. Begins to stop indiscriminate socializing with adults. Begins to show stranger anxiety Imitates parents' behavior Smiles at self in mirror Plays peek-a-boo
Molds and cuddles when held. Interested in mother					
Intense need to obtain satisfaction and comfort through sucking, being held, rocked, touched	Shows satisfaction, delight in response to pleasurable stimuli Smiles and "talks" to family members	Social stimulation more important Moves entire body and facial expression changes when stimulated	Demands social attention. Fussy and bored if left alone Enjoys attention	Plays with rattle Pats mother's breast	Plays with feet
Becomes excited when sees parent or toy	Excitedly anticipates movement of objects	Smiles immediately	Chuckles, laughs, "talks." Talks more to face than object Entire body shows excitement		

(continued)

Table 11-7 (Continued)

7 months	8 months	9 months	10 months	11 months	12 months
Cries					
Cries for attention, help, or when distressed. Cries are result of inner needs, not reaction to environment Quiets when picked up or watching parent's face	Crying differentiated; volume, pitch, and strength vary with inner need Show distress Sucks to quiet self	Marked decrease in crying. Stops crying when parent enters room and holds him Awake longer periods without crying Squeals when frustrated Quiets quickly when concentrating on face	Has mood changes Responds to "No!" Wails when pleasurable activity interrupted Quiets self Music quiets		
Interaction					
Stranger anxiety increases. Cries when mother leaves Wants to be included in family's social interaction Distinguishes between angry and happy voices Mood swings increasing; shows humor. Bites, mouths objects aggressively Resists unwanted objects, food Pats image in mirror	Stranger anxiety at height Separation anxiety increasing. Fearing separation, follows mother around house Resists and avoids isolation or confinement Continues to reject unwanted objects Kisses image in mirror	Perceives mother as separate being Anticipates mother feeding Performs for family members if rewarded Plays out fears and problems Begins to evaluate moods	Tenderly cuddles toy Begins sexual identity. Jealous cries if other child receives attention Still shows emotions; happy, sad Increasingly aware of approval or disapproval	Increasingly dependent on mother Asserts self among family members Seeks approval, avoids disapproval Shows guilt	Separation anxiety increases Prefers certain people, especially women Fears strange people and places Expresses all emotions. Has sense of humor; affectionate Negative. Refuses toys, meal, etc.
Play					
Chews feet; explores body Excitedly anticipates play Plays with toys	Constantly reaches for toys Loves play	Imitates play Chooses specific toy Plays ball, pat-a-cake	Enjoys music	Parallel play Imitates other children's play	Plays games

* Compiled by Nancy L. Ramsey.

Figure 11-7 Hand regard is an indicator of the infant's growing awareness of himself as separate from the environment.

concept of mother that requires both memory and object permanence. These expectations reveal the quality of the trusting relationship.

Infants seem to progress through three very broad stages in developing attachments. In the first stage the very young infant is undifferentiated in his attachment behavior. He will respond to all adults who give him appropriate social stimulation. He smiles and brightens as a result of face-to-face attention and shows general arousal. He may show preference for his mother by visually pursuing her, looking at her when there is a choice, but he is happily responsive to all.

In the second stage, between about 4 and 8 months, the infant progresses to an exclusive or single attachment to his care-giver—usually the mother. At this time the infant shows a definite preference for the mother. He clearly would like to be in her presence and shows this in no uncertain terms. He brightens when she comes into view, reaches up to be held, follows both visually and literally to the extent of his mobility.

In this stage the infant does not respond happily to all. Social stimulation from a stranger is likely to elicit a sober face from the attached infant. In fact, sometime soon after this single attachment becomes evident, the infant shows some degree of fear of strangers. The term for this behavior is *stranger anxiety*. It is typically very strong at 8 months.

The third stage of attachment formation is an expansion to multiple attachments. Here the infant adds father, siblings, grandparents, and other significant and constant people in his environment to his little social group.

Babies differ not only in the age at which they develop the foregoing attachment behaviors, but also in the intensity and strength of the attachment. The quality of attachment depends upon the quality of the mother-infant relationship. Infant-mother pairs who are adept at reading each other's cues and responding to each other's needs could well be those whose interpersonal bonds are firmer and less ambivalent. These infants may show very strong attachments. The behavior of firmly attached infants is most indicative of trust. These babies expect the mother to be there and meet their needs. They can delay gratification because there is no doubt in their minds that whatever they need is forthcoming.

The assessment of the infant's attachment to his primary care-giver is an important function of the nurse. This relationship is critical for the child and represents his main source of security. Infants demonstrate their attachment with specific kinds of behaviors that the nurse can observe. These behaviors will vary among infants and according to the situation. Infants placed in a strange environment may show more disturbance and stronger dependency than in familiar surroundings. The amount of stranger anxiety displayed will also be different for each infant. The familiarity of the setting, whether or not the mother is present, the behavior of the stranger, and possibly the behavioral state of the infant will all have some effect. Stranger anxiety is sometimes used as an indication of attachment because it clearly shows the infant has preference for the mother, but a high degree of stranger anxiety may indicate some ambivalence in the attachment to the mother.

Infants will demonstrate individual differences in their response to brief and prolonged separations. The firmly attached, trusting infant is more able to tolerate periods when the mother is absent. When the parent returns, this infant shows delight in his greeting and an immediate rapport. The infant that is ambivalent tolerates the experience less well. He may show more *separation anxiety*, crying, general distress, or possibly a decrease in animation and ability to play. When the mother returns, there is not always the immediate rapport. He may respond by crying or by wanting to be held but without the obvious comfort and delight holding usually elicits.

Parents sometimes have concerns about separation anxiety. The nurse can help by assuring them that this phenomenon is normal and common among infants. It can be lessened by simple measures of keeping the surroundings as familiar as possible when separations are anticipated. Such suggestions as having the mother and infant spend some time together with a new baby-sitter before the mother leaves may be very helpful. Most importantly, parents and health care workers should realize that the mother's presence is very necessary to the infant who is hospitalized or undergoing unusual stress of any kind. Maintaining the integrity of this relationship should be a priority goal.

Sex role identification

There are differences in male and female infants besides the obvious one of anatomy. Male babies are on the average larger and have proportionately more muscle body mass at birth. Female infants are generally smaller in size but physiologically more mature at birth than males and less vulnerable to stress. Differences in activity level, cuddliness, and the like are not due to gender, however. Such differences are more likely to cluster around temperament than sex.

Sex differences are usually reinforced very early. Little girls are dressed in ruffles and lace and boys in overalls and baseball caps. Stereotypes in male or female behavior are encouraged as well. Because of this, it is difficult to know how much femaleness and maleness is due to true gender differences and how much to learning. What we know so far would suggest that behavioral and aptitude differences are not gender-based. Children do not identify themselves as male or female until after the infancy period. Their play and choice of toys does not take on gender identity until early childhood.

Cognitive development

The amazing newborn infant is something like a computer that has already been programmed to sort and process data. He is born with all sorts of abilities and a built-in method for interacting with his environment. Jean Piaget, a prominent theorist in the area of cognitive development, put forth a framework for explaining how children develop thinking or cognition.

The sequence of development is orderly and recognizable from one child to the next (see Chap. 7). Piaget described this progression in terms of periods, subperiods, and stages. The sensorimotor period is where we will focus for a better understanding of the infant and his cognitive development.

Sensorimotor period

There are six stages in the sensorimotor period. The important things to remember about the stages are that they are sequential and that each is built upon the one before. The first four generally occur during the first year of life; the last two are discussed in Chap. 12. Ages are assigned to the stages but are meant only as guidelines. Different children may progress through the sequence at different rates.

Stage 1 **Exercising sensorimotor reflexes (0–1 month)** The infant comes equipped with a group of behavioral activities called *reflexes*. (Refer to Chap. 10, "The Neonate," for a listing of these reflexes.) Piaget feels that the sucking and palmar grasp reflexes are particularly important. The infant practices these reflex patterns during the first month. The infant becomes better at finding the nipple and sucking after a few days' practice. He may soon find his thumb and suck that. He thus begins to experience these basic reflexive behaviors in a pattern. In order to suck his thumb, he must coordinate arm and hand movements with his mouth. This goes beyond reflex behavior.

Stage 2 **Primary circular reactions (1–4 months)** During this stage the infant assimilates more and more information into the sensorimotor schemata. What he sees becomes related to what he hears, grasps, mouths, and touches. He learns to stop crying as he sees his mother approach with the bottle. He begins to show preference for some things over others and develops more pattern to his behavior (similar to habits). His increased neuromuscular development is an important factor in this stage. He is capable of repeating behaviors he finds interesting and abandoning those that are no longer gratifying or helpful. There is no evidence that the child at this stage has any notion of time or space. For him there are only events and these events are related to his own functioning. There is also no relationship between the means and the end. The infant of this age does not seem to have an end in mind when he begins an activity (Fig. 11-8).

Stage 3 Secondary circular reactions (4–8 months)

In this stage the baby begins to identify the means to an end. For instance, if he has a mobile with a cord hanging down which he can grasp and pull to make the mobile move, he figures out this relationship and purposely pulls the cord. If you place another toy above his crib, he looks for the cord. At the beginning of this stage, he is very actively grasping everything he can get his hands on. He is building on the patterns of behavior he developed earlier (that's why this stage is termed secondary), and his behaviors are repeated over and over because he gets pleasure out of them (that's why the term *circular* is used.). He is interested in the results of his actions and prolonging them. Piaget describes infants in the early part of this stage as being on the threshold of intelligence. They are beginning to link vision with prehension (Fig. 11-9).

During this stage, too, infants begin to develop what is called *object permanence*. Before this

Figure 11-9 This 7-month-old child has toys that can be put together and pulled apart. Manipulating these objects will help him practice means-to-end relationships.

time, if an object were removed from the infant's vision or grasp, he would change his focus to something else. Now the child will look for the object (Fig. 11-10). This has implications for the onset of separation anxiety; the child can think about (remember) his parents even if he cannot see them.

Stage 4 Coordination of secondary schemata (8–12 months)

In this stage the infant refines those behaviors and mental associations that were begun in stage 3. There is now a clear difference between the means and the end goal. The infant may try several ways to get at his goal in spite of barriers. Object permanence continues to develop in this period and is related to the child's beginning knowledge of space. It is in this period that objects begin to take on symbolic meaning for the child (Fig. 11-11). He can begin to experience an event or object by watching it, without having to touch it.

In summary, Piaget describes how he believes the infant progresses from essentially reflex behavior to the ability to use symbols in his thinking. The infant develops from a very narrow conception of reality which is limited to the experience of his own actions to a beginning understanding of causality, space, time, and object permanence. The infant is very active in bringing about this process. He acts upon his environment and it in turn acts upon him as he assimilates new information and accommodates

Figure 11-8 At this age an infant does not yet seem to have an end in mind when he begins an activity.

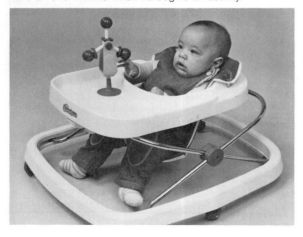

Figure 11-10 The 8-month-old infant begins to become mobile by creeping. Increased mobility aids development of object permanence. He can actively seek objects that he thinks about.

to new situations. Cognitive development during infancy is summarized in Table 11-8.

Language development

The infant makes almost incredible progress in developing language during the first year of life. He goes from crying as his only vocal sound to the beginnings of patterned speech in just 12 short months! We can observe what the child does and identify the general rules that seem to govern the language development. Deeper questions concerning the hows and whys of language development are more difficult. There are a number of theories but none very complete. Current thoughts suggest that the infant may come already programmed to develop language. He may already be tuned in to sorting and analyzing language in terms of specific rules. It may also be that language, as opposed to production of sounds, depends on cortical development. Development of the two seem to coincide in the second half of the first year of life. Table 11-6 includes milestones of language development throughout the first year.

Stages of prelanguage development

***Stage 1* Crying** The neonate's only vocal sound is crying. He may vary the intensity, pattern, and duration of his cry, but crying it still is. Even at this early stage the infant is positively responding to voice sounds. Listening skills and attentiveness are important in overall language development and can be encouraged even in this first month.

***Stage 2* Cooing** The infant begins to make cooing sounds by about 1 month of age. Cooing sounds are noncrying, voluntary sounds. Usually the infant makes these sounds when he seems contented and happy. Parents can be clued in to listening for these first sounds. When the infant is cooing, it is an opportune time for "conversation" between parent and child. Saying the sounds back to the baby and attending to his efforts can be stimulating and rewarding.

***Stage 3* Babbling** By about 6 months (the range is wide: 3 to 7 months) the baby is babbling.

Figure 11-11 This infant is able to transfer objects from hand to hand. Increasing motor skills are closely related to development of cognition.

Table 11-8 Developmental milestones: Cognition*

1 month	2 months	3 months	4 months	5 months	6 months
Memory					
Remembers existence of object for 2–3 s		Alert up to 45 min Memory obvious	Memory span: 5–7 min Recognition of strange places indicates memory	Remembers own actions in immediate past	Alert 1½–2 h
Causality: Repeated behavior causes same response					
Expects feedings at specific routine times Daily responses to activities disorganized	Anticipates movement of objects	Anticipates feedings (a reward)	Shows anticipation and excitement	Anticipates entire object when sees part Anticipates, searches for dropped or fast-moving objects	Reaches quickly for things seen and desired
Separation of self and others from environment					
Perceives self and parent as one Totally self-centered Does not recognize objects in environment	Discriminates between people, voices, objects	Begins to be aware of self Differentiates among family members Explores body parts with hand; begins to realize they are part of him	Becomes aware of self as separate from environment and external objects Begins to separate act from result Distinguishes between strange and familiar places	Recognizes objects external to self	Recognizes mother in other clothes, places
Reflexive or voluntary movement					
Movements are reflexive, not voluntary (initiated by infant) Repeated reflex movements establish a pattern of experiences Relates to world by touch and orally (not verbally)	Repeats reflex movements May associate action with people (bottle with mother)	Still repeats actions for pleasure, more than result. May associate action and result. Becomes bored with repeated sounds or images Begins to coordinate body movements and vision Begins to combine reflexes and voluntary actions	Combines behaviors to vary them or to reach goal Plays with favorite toy and games; shows discrimination	Voluntarily begins movements in pattern, or order Repeats actions to make environment interesting	Manipulates objects to change their position. Senses relationship between hands and objects being manipulated Interested in movement and action

(continued)

Table 11-8 (Continued)

7 months	8 months	9 months	10 months	11 months	12 months
Memory					
Concentrates more in detail Interested in detail Remembers series of events only if involved	Remembers series of events even if not involved Remembers time sequence Imitates behavior of people by memory	Remembers series of actions and ideas Remembers event of past day			Remembers events for increasing long times
Causality: Repeated behavior causes the same response					
Expects event to be repeated Searches for object he sees being hidden. Believes it remains in last place seen Remembers part of series of behaviors; knows it represents the entire series of behaviors Interested in results of own behavior Realizes goal only after attaining it Distinguishes near and far	Recognizes objects as separate from self Begins to learn; combines behaviors, problem solves to obtain toy Further separates action from result Begins to differentiate one from several objects Uses hands to learn concepts of in, out	Anticipates return of person or object Uncovers hidden toy Plays out solution to problems (shows use of symbols) Bored with repetition of same stimuli Explores toys: pokes finger in hole; mouths, sucks, chews Compares size, similarities, differences of objects Fears height	Searches for object hidden in several places Experiments and changes actions to attain goal; changes old actions by trial and error Sees objects as increasingly distinct; explores, manipulates toys Begins to match similar objects	Aware of result of some actions Associates sounds with object (barks for dog) Separates action from object Explores boxes. Inserts and removes objects in container Symbol recognition developing (enjoys books)	Perceives objects as separate, used for play Perceives self as unique from other objects Finds new solutions and removes barriers to problems Continues to associate symbol with event, object; classifying is based on own experience Experiments with object displacement: removes, turns, inserts objects in container Visualizes actions before acting them out in play

* Compiled by Nancy L. Ramsey.

Babbling sounds are often consonant sounds combined with a vowel repeated several times, i.e., "da da da da da da." The infant uses many sounds and seems to play and experiment with them. Babbling may take on similar rhythms and intonations. One predominant characteristic of babbling is that babies do it a lot.

There is not a clear understanding of the relationship between babbling and true language. Babbling does not seem to have the same intent as the infant's first words or language—that of communicating. It is interesting to note that all infants babble with the same sounds. When they begin to speak words, different sounds are used depending upon the language of their environment.

***Stage 4* Patterned speech** The infant's first words appear sometime between 9 and 14 months of age. These words are usually in the form of sounds used consistently to mean particular objects, people, or whatever. Often they are invented words created by the infant. Parents become adept at interpreting the meaning of the word used by the infant. The one word may convey variations of meaning depending on the context and tone in which it is used. For example, the infant may say "ball" meaning "there is my ball," expressing delight at discovery. Another time he may say "ball" meaning "play ball with me" or another time "I want my ball."

Babbling continues during this fourth stage but becomes less repetitive and more like the sound of regular speech. This later type of babbling is termed *jargon*.

One thing is certain, infants can understand language and follow simple instructions before patterned speech develops. "No-no" is generally responded to before the child is 9 months. The infant will also respond to his own name by this time. He is likely to be able to wave "bye-bye" when requested to do so or when he wants to go.

Factors influencing language development

Although it is not clear how and why children learn language, there are observations that can be made about the *way* they learn. Imitation of adult speech by the child cannot constitute a full explanation of language development. Children do not put words together the way adults do, as would be expected if they were learning by imitation alone, although imitation must have some role. Children do learn the language of their environment. We can assume that some aspects of language are at least in part learned by imitation of words they hear. Similarly, reinforcement for words spoken cannot account for the actual development of language. It may, however, play an important role in how much the infant vocalizes and the rate at which he progresses with language. The infant who is given attention and praise for attempts at language may vocalize more than the one who is ignored.

Parents play a significant role in language development. It is interesting to note that there are similarities across cultures in the way parents talk to infants and young children. Adults raise the pitch of their voice when speaking to infants. They also exaggerate speech with pitch, tone, intensity, and facial expression. The conversation of an adult to an infant is much richer and more varied with respect to these qualities than adult to adult. Vowel sounds are often elongated and the pace is slower with longer pauses between vocalizations. Mothers and fathers tailor their speech to the infant as he grows and progresses. They lead him, in a way, by slowly increasing the complexity of their sentences as he keeps pace with his own language development.

The amount the baby is talked to also makes a difference in his overall development. Infants from culturally deprived environments do not score as high on language or cognitive skills as those from rich environments. Talking to the infant probably does not speed up language acquisition. It does, however, broaden the repertoire of the young child and has a positive overall effect on his development.

Health maintenance

It is the nurse's role to assist the parents in promoting the health and well-being of their infant. In order to do this, the nurse must understand and appreciate what is involved in the daily care of an infant. Many times it is the "small" things that occur within the usual day that disturb and worry parents the most. It is also these same routine occurrences that can blow up into major threats to the well-being of the infant and family. Nurses must be sensitive to the cues parents give. Listening skills are of paramount importance here. Often parents feel uneasy about asking what they view as simple or trivial questions of the health professional.

The nurse should use her interviewing skills to open up areas of conversation concerning the infant's home routine. Specific information can be asked to help the nurse assess the care and environment of the infant. This also gives opportunity to encourage the mother or care-giver. Mothers need to know they are doing a good job.

Daily infant care

Safety Accidents are a tremendous threat to the child's health. As the infant becomes mobile, the hazards increase. The following list is not meant to include every hazard but rather some of the more common ones.

1. Never leave an infant unattended on a changing table, examining table, crib with side rail down, or other area where he might fall off. It is a good idea when working with the infant to place your hand on his body when you turn or look away.
2. Remove all small items—including safety pins (which, of course, are always closed) from the infant's reach. The infant puts virtually everything in his mouth. This is especially important for the infant that is creeping. A particularly hazardous item is a plugged-in extension cord on the floor. Parents should be warned to remove these.
3. Keep all soaps, cleansers, lotions, insecticides, and the like locked up or out of baby's reach. Kitchens, service porches, and bathrooms are particularly dangerous areas because of low cupboards and storage areas. Hospitals are full of dangerous solutions, as well, which sometimes find their way to the bedside table.
4. Never leave an infant unattended in a bathtub or other water, such as a wading pool.
5. Be especially careful of medicines. Childproof caps should be used but not depended upon to do any more than slow the child down. The aspirin in mother's purse or the vitamins on the table are sometimes overlooked in a routine safety check and remain accessible to the infant.
6. Strongly encourage parents to use infant car seats that have been tested and approved for safety. Automobile accidents are the number one cause of injury and death in childhood. Even a sharp curve or sudden stop can cause injury to an infant who is lying or sitting unrestrained on the seat. Parents

should be cautioned not to hold the infant on their lap—especially in the front passenger seat as an alternative to a safe car seat. Parents may feel they can protect the infant if an accident occurs, but this has not proven to be the case (Fig. 11-12).

7. Never leave small children alone in automobiles. Cars are filled with hazards. Remember that automobiles can become very hot when left parked in the sun. This can be very dangerous to the infant.

Feeding Mealtime for the infant should be unrushed and as free from distraction as possible. If the mother is nursing the infant, this is a good opportunity to get in a comfortable position and rest. Whether nursed or bottle-fed, the infant should have an enjoyable and satisfying experience. Beginning the infant on beikost may take some patience and skill. Mothers will find it easier to use an infant-sized spoon with a long handle. Having what is needed ready and in position helps. Placing the infant at eye level directly in front of and facing the person doing

Figure 11-12 An infant seat is the safe way for travel in a car.

the feeding will allow for the best visibility and control. If the bowl of the food is within reach, it will likely be explored by a tiny fist and end up on the floor.

Infants enjoy being with the family at mealtime. By the time the baby is 9 or 10 months old, he is capable of sitting in a high chair or feeding table and managing some finger foods.

Constipation Constipation (the passage of dry, hard stools) in infants is usually caused by inadequate water intake or by iron supplement added to the diet. Many mothers do not offer water to their children. Assess the infant's daily water intake. Instruct mothers to add 1 tsp of corn syrup, molasses, or honey to sweeten each bottle of water. The sugar pulls fluids from the gut into the stool. Instruct mothers to dilute prune juice in the bottle of water and add fruits to the diet. This increases bulk and stimulates defecation. Refer the child to a physician if the child's abdomen is distended or if constipation has lasted longer than 3 days.

Sleeping Infants need a lot of sleep, especially in the first few months. This is good because so do mothers. Encourage mothers to take rest periods when the baby naps instead of trying to "get everything done" in that period.

Infants differ in their ability to sleep with noise and other activity. Very young infants are able to block out some stimulation but as they grow older may require a quieter environment. Some infants drop off to sleep easily and seem to prefer the crib. Others have difficulty and may desire to be rocked or sung to sleep.

Infants have sleep cycles during the course of a nap or night. They may go from deep sleep to active sleep and back to deep sleep again several times. Be sure the infant is ready to wake up before disturbing him. A stretch and change of position may not be the signal for waking.

The infant should be kept warm when sleeping but not restricted by bed clothes. A blanket sleeper or sleeping sack may be appropriate for cool climates. Plastic pants on the young infant, especially for overnight, should be avoided. They hold in the moisture, which is not good for the baby's skin. A double diaper and cotton-backed waterproof sheet may be adequate for use overnight.

Diapering It's a good thing infants begin life small and relatively easy to diaper because parents need this time to practice. Diapering an 8-month-old can be a real challenge if you're not fairly skilled and swift. Diapering is discussed in Chaps. 10 and 17.

Diaper rash Diaper rash may exist until the infant is toilet-trained. Most infants, in spite of their mothers' best efforts, occasionally develop diaper rash. If the rash stubbornly persists, assess the following areas: (1) How often does the mother change the diapers? Is the child double-diapered? Urine continuously contacting the skin irritates it. The double thickness of the diaper absorbs the urine and draws it away from the skin. (2) Are the diapers rinsed twice? If the diapers are washed in a laundromat, second rinsing the diapers is more difficult and expensive. (3) Are irritating substances being added to the water? Harsh detergents, water softeners, and bleach irritate the skin. (4) Is the feces being completely washed off the skin before a non-water-soluble ointment is applied? Using water to rinse feces off the skin is not an adequate cleanser. A mild soap or cleansing lotion (without alcohol), followed by a rinse with a soft cloth, removes the irritating feces and bacteria. (5) Is the mother using adequate amounts of a non-water-soluble ointment to protect the skin? Petroleum jelly is one of the most economical products. (6) Can the mother remove the diaper for a period of time each day to allow air and sunlight to reach the rash? (7) Is the child wearing plastic pants? Instruct the mother to remove them. Plastic encourages a bacteria-supporting environment: airless, warm, and moist. (8) Is the child allergic to disposable diapers? (9) Do the diapers have an ammonia odor? Ammonia, which is formed by the bacteria on the diapers and by urea, irritates the skin. Instruct the mother to add 1 cup of vinegar to the rinse water or an antiseptic to the wash water. (10) Does the choice of diapers fit the parent's life-style and budget? Disposable diapers are most expensive but convenient for the family with no laundry facilities. Diaper service is approximately one-half the cost of disposable diapers. Cloth diapers are most economical. Always assess the mother's knowledge of diaper care. A persistent diaper rash can be detrimental to a mother's self-concept.

Bathing Babies are slippery when wet. It is very important to have the infant well-supported and everything that is needed within easy reach. Water should be warm and care taken not to chill the infant if the air temperature is cool. Bathing is discussed in Chap. 17.

Shampooing the hair helps to remove *cradle cap* from the infant's scalp. Cradle cap is common in young infants. It looks like yellowish, crusty, scaly patches on the infant's scalp. The patches are unappealing in appearance, may cause the baby discomfort, or may contribute to inflammation or infection. Applying petrolatum or mineral oil to the infant's scalp several hours before shampooing will help to soften the crusts so that they may be removed.

Cleaning the infant's head and scalp is often the last part of the infant's bath. Young infants can be wrapped in a towel and held securely under one arm with the hand supporting the head (like a football hold). This leaves the caretaker with one hand free to wash the scalp and the baby feeling secure. Most infants enjoy this procedure. A bath often relaxes the infant and provides an especially good time for interaction between the baby and care-giver. Instruct parents *never* to leave the infant alone in the bath.

Clothing The infant's clothing should be non-constrictive. Babies, don't forget, grow rapidly and could care less if all the shower gifts were size 0. Many mothers have friends or family that rotate infant clothing from family to family. Others discover thrift shops or simply buy larger-sized clothes that the infant can wear for a longer period. Avoid strings, ribbons, and reachable buttons on infant's clothing. All these things can present a hazard. Soft, comfortable garments that allow full range of motion for the infant are appropriate.

Well-baby health care The well-baby visit to the pediatrician or nurse practitioner provides the opportunity for effective health care maintenance. A physical and developmental exam is performed and an assessment of the infant's overall health status is made. This is also an excellent opportunity to assess and support the positive interaction between the infant and care-giver. Astute observations are critical at this time. A positive outcome for the infant may depend on the identification of problems or potential problems and initiation of early intervention.

The infant's growth and development are monitored. Nurses can use their knowledge to point out specific gains the infant is making. Suggestions for activities the parents can do to foster their child's progress can be made. The nurse can also encourage the parents by letting them know that the things they usually do with their infant—singing, rocking, and playing—are critical to his development. Parents are not always aware of the importance of their actions.

This is also the time to take preventive health care measures. Immunizations should be started (see Table 6-5). Health teaching, including preventive guidance about avoiding accidents, should be going on. Instructions for handling common illness at home are especially important. Make sure parents know how to use a thermometer safely, how to recognize illness in the child, and when to call in professionals to help.

A major part of the role of the nurse is anticipatory guidance. Parents should be informed about what to expect of their infant and, just as importantly, what to expect of themselves. Letting the parents know that they may feel anger and frustration at the infant can be very helpful. Parents can experience a sense of guilt because of feelings that come quite appropriately because of the demands accompanying the presence of an infant in the house.

In summary, the first year of life represents a critical period. The rapid development and far-reaching implications of environmental influences on the child's potential serve to underline the reason for concern. The nurse, physician, family, and even the child all have a role in ensuring the child's well-being.

References

1. Daniel Stern, *The First Relationship: Infant and Mother*, Harvard, Cambridge, Mass. 1977, p. 71.
2. Samuel Fomon, *Infant Nutrition*, 2d ed., Saunders, Philadelphia, 1974, p. 436.
3. Sherman Dickman, "Breast Feeding and Infant Nutrition," *Family and Community Health*, vol. 1, no. 4, 1979, p. 22.
4. Myron Winick, "The Physician's Role in Nutrition Counseling," *Year One: Nutrition Growth Health*, Ross Laboratories, 1975.

Chapter 12 **The toddler**

Nancy Lockwood Ramsey and **Barbara Haugan**

Upon completion of this chapter, the student will be able to:

1. Summarize the toddler's physical maturation within the following areas: changes in body size, vision, teeth, and musculoskeletal, nervous, and respiratory systems.

2. Identify the toddler's nutritional requirements and use interventions to cope with food jags, food refusal, and eating rituals.

3. Describe the development and characteristic behaviors of Erikson's developmental task autonomy vs. shame and doubt.

4. Relate the impact of parental methods of and attitudes toward toilet training on the toddler's attainment of autonomy or feelings of shame and doubt.

5. Cite key steps in toilet training a toddler.

6. List guidelines for disciplining a toddler and relate these guidelines to socializing the toddler.

7. Identify the cause of, and interventions to cope with, the following behaviors: temper tantrums, negativism, dawdling, and ritualism.

8. List five functions of the toddler's play and state an example for each function.

9. Describe the toddler's cognitive development in stages 5 and 6 of the sensorimotor period.

10. Cite several accidents a toddler may have and describe methods of preventing each.

The foundations for the toddler years are built in infancy. The infant learned to trust his parents and to perceive the world as safe to explore and able to fulfill his needs. He gradually began to separate from the mother and learned he had a predictable effect upon others.

The toddler years, which last from 1 to 3 years, are an age of discovery and exploration. The boundless energy and maturing neuromuscular system of toddlers support an insatiable need to explore and to master skills. With walking, toddlers enter a new world. They explore everything in sight and are in perpetual motion. They curiously investigate objects, using more senses than they did as infants: mouthing, shaking, poking, smearing. By exploring, toddlers learn new skills, feel new sensations, and learn about the environment.

A toddler gradually separates himself or herself from the mother and learns to tolerate her absence. Toddlers want to be in control, to do things alone, and to be independent. To be independent they must begin to learn self-control and self-care. They struggle with emotional control, caught between following their wishes and the parent's demands. Temper tantrums, negativism, and dawdling have helped label this period "the terrible twos." They learn to care for themselves, to dress, eat, toilet, and talk. Toddlers want and seek discipline to help them behave acceptably. Their autonomous behavior eventually results in accomplishment and mastery. They experiment, solve problems, and think using symbols. They imitate sex-role behavior. Their play includes fantasy and imitation.

The nurse who cares for the toddler and the

family unit must understand the growth and development of this exciting age. Understanding what is normal at this age enables the nurse to understand the toddler's behavior, anticipate problems, counsel parents, and design age-appropriate nursing care plans.

Physical maturation

Changes in body size

The toddler's height and weight increase, although the growth rate slows in comparison to that of the infant. The toddler gains more height in proportion to weight. Height increases from 3 to 5 in per year in comparison to the infant's growth of 4 in in the first 3 months. Boys tend to be taller than girls, although the difference is very small. Adult height can be estimated by multiplying the child's height at 2 years by 2. (Refer to Appendix B for growth charts.)

The toddler's rate of weight gain declines sharply because of decreased appetite, reduced metabolic rate, and resulting loss of subcutaneous fat. A newborn gains 7 oz per week; the toddler gains approximately 7 oz per month. A toddler gains 5 to 6 lb per year and begins the second year weighing 20 lb and the third year weighing 30 lb. Weight gain is steplike rather than smoothly continuous, and weight gains are made in spurts.[1]

Toddlers appear top-heavy when beginning to walk. Their legs are relatively short and stublike, and the trunk is long and "pot-bellied" (see Fig. 12-1). The chest, after the second year, is larger than the head in circumference. The abdomen protrudes because of an immature musculature and a relatively large liver. The arms and legs grow faster than the trunk because of the rapid ossification and growth of epiphyseal centers in the legs. Toddlers begin to lose their chubby appearance as walking improves their musculature, fat storage is altered, and increased muscle development replaces baby fat. The legs often appear bowed (tibial torsion) and the feet flat as a residual of the intrauterine position. This appearance gradually decreases as the muscles strengthen. The toddler's arch develops and becomes noticeable, and walking causes the fat pads on the soles of the feet to disappear.

Vision

The toddler's vision is well developed by 2 years and reflects neuromuscular maturation. (See Ta-

Figure 12-1 Toddlers have proportionally large heads and protruding abdomens. (*Photo courtesy of David Carroll.*)

ble 12-1.) During childhood the eyeball becomes increasingly rounded instead of remaining short, as in infancy. The rounded shape causes the farsightedness of infancy to decrease. Perception of light and dark, color, and detail is developed by 8 months. Visual acuity is approximately 20/40 at 2 years. The toddler needs large objects and pictures in order to make clear distinctions between objects. Binocular vision, the fusion of images, is developed at 1 year. Distance focusing remains poor; the toddler needs to be within a 6-ft range to see an object clearly.

Teeth

The development of teeth begins in utero and ends at approximately age 10. The eruption of *deciduous teeth*, or baby teeth, is completed by 2½ years. The lower lateral incisors appear at 12

Table 12-1 Visual development*

12–18 months

Identifies forms
Displays an intense interest in pictures
Scribbles on paper
Convergence becomes well established
Crude depth perception

18–24 months

Accommodation well developed
Vision acuity: 20/40
Discriminates between simple geometric shapes

2–3 years

Convergence smooth
Fixes on small objects or pictures for 50 s
Recalls visual images
Vision acuity: 20/30

* Adapted from Peggy L. Chinn, *Child Health Maintenance*, Mosby, St. Louis, 1979, p. 871.

to 18 months. Both cuspids appear at 18 to 24 months. Both first molars appear at 12 to 18 months. Second molars appear at 24 to 30 months. (See Fig. 6-8 for the tooth eruption schedule.) See the "Child Health Maintenance" section later in this chapter for prevention of caries.

Musculoskeletal system

The rate of skeletal growth decreases during the toddler years. Bone ossification continues. The height increase is primarily a result of growth of the legs. More than 25 new ossification centers appear during the second year.[2] Brain and skull growth rates also decrease. The anterior fontanel closes by 18 to 24 months, and the posterior fontanel closes by 2 to 3 months because brain growth slows and rapid skull growth is no longer necessary. Rickets or hypothyroidism may delay fontanel closure.[3] The infant's head circumference increases 4 to 5 in the first year. In contrast, the 2-year-old's head circumference increases less than 1 in per year and the 3-year-old's less than $\frac{1}{2}$ in per year. Appendix B shows head circumference norms.

Muscle size increases in response to hereditary predisposition and increased use. The child's strength increases as the muscle mass increases. Greater strength is needed to support the more complex muscular functions needed to explore the world, such as walking, climbing, and running.

Nervous system

The brain increases from an average of 350 g at birth to 1000 g at 2 years[4] and reaches two-thirds of adult size at 2 years. The nervous system's development and function become more refined during the second and third years because of increased *myelinization*. Growth of the myelin sheath continues for many years and is not completed until late adolescence. At 2 years the myelinization is complete enough to allow for most general movements. The myelinization proceeds cephalocaudally, as evidenced, for example, by children's ability to grasp a bottle with their arms before learning to walk. Completion of myelinization ensures that nerve impulses speedily reach their destination. When the myelin sheath is incomplete, the slower impulse may not reach the destination. For example, if a 14-month-old toddler spikes a fever of 40.3°C (104.5°F) and the fever is not reduced within 20 min of a tepid water bath and administration of an antipyretic drug, the incomplete myelinization may have caused the delayed response.

The limbic system controls temperament and emotional control of behavior and also sleep and wakefulness (arousal). Feelings are monitored by this system. While young children function by feelings, not logic, the immature limbic system cannot associate the feelings in a mature, rational pattern; this is thought to be a factor in toddlers' inability to control their emotions.[5]

The various areas of the cerebrum develop differently and correspond to the development of the child's intellect. The integration of these areas is intricately complex; the immature development of some areas is believed to limit the child's attention span. Because the nervous system cannot handle more than one incoming stimulus at a time, the introduction of another, second stimulus will intensify and prolong the action resulting from the first stimulus. For example, when a toddler is slapped for touching a forbidden object, the child's grasp (a result of the first stimulus) momentarily tightens or is prolonged instead of releasing the object. The child's inability to respond immediately to the parents' command is physiological, not a refusal to cooperate.

The brain also requires its largest supply of oxygen in early childhood: 5.21 ml/100 g.[6] The prevention of anoxia is therefore vitally important.

Stimulation of the nervous system is crucial for organ development. For example, untreated strabismus in toddlerhood causes the affected eye not to be stimulated, and the capacity for vision in that eye is lost as a result of inadequate stimulation. Physical maturation, changed body proportions, advanced neural development, and increased muscle strength are far more crucial than practice in determining the child's neuromotor progress.[7] For example, the overly zealous mother who toilet trains her child by repeatedly placing him on the potty chair before the child is walking is training herself, not the child. All the practice in the world will not toilet train the child if the myelin sheath has not matured far enough down the spinal cord to permit sphincter control. When the child can walk, the myelin sheath is sufficiently mature to transmit the messages to voluntarily empty bowel and bladder.

Gastrointestinal system

Food travels more swiftly through the toddler's gut than through the infant's. The acidity of the digestive juices increases, and their composition compares with those of the adult's. The salivary glands mature by age 3.[8]

Endocrine system

The functioning of the toddler's endocrine system is minimal and is not completely understood. However, it is known that insulin and glucagon production is limited and erratic.[9]

Respiratory system

The lungs grow and expand to hold a greater volume of air. The anatomic portions of the respiratory tract are farther apart, which decreases the incidence of infection. However, the adenoids and tonsils increase in size.[10] The middle ear and eustachian tube are short and horizontal, which provides easier access of nasal bacteria to the ear. These changes, coupled with entering nursery school, contribute to the numerous upper respiratory infections of the toddler.

Nutrition

The toddler's appetite decreases at approximately 2 years. If toddlers continued to eat and to grow at the same rate as during infancy, they would weigh over 200 lb by the time they reached the age of 10 years.[11] (The "finicky, birdlike appetite" of toddlers is a major parental concern.) To offer more calories than the toddler needs increases the risk of food refusal. The growth and metabolic rates of toddlers have slowed; they no longer require so much food. Short attention span and fascination with the environment distract children from eating.

Nutritional requirements Toddlers need a well-balanced diet that meets their nutritional requirements for maintenance and growth of body tissue and supports their large expenditures of energy. The diet should include essential nutrients from the four food groups to meet the minimum daily requirements. Toddlers need three regularly timed meals and several nutritious snacks each day. (Serving sizes and the recommended daily dietary allowances of proteins, fats, carbohydrates, minerals, and vitamins are given in Appendix C.)

The toddler's total amount of body water has decreased and the cell water has increased. Fluid intake needs are now 100 to 125 ml/kg per day, unless illness, increased temperature, or hot weather are present. Average calorie, protein, and water requirements of the 1- to 3-year-old are:

Calories	Protein	Water
100–120 kcal/kg per day or 45 kcal/lb per day	3.5 g/kg per day	100–125 ml/kg per day

The toddler's skeletal growth rate has slowed, but more minerals are deposited in the bones for weight-bearing support. Calcium and phosphorus are also needed for tooth development. Two to three cups of milk per day are adequate; allowing the child to drink larger amounts of milk decreases intake of other essential foods.

Psychological and cultural factors influence food intake. The old adage "Clean your plate, many children in the world are starving" is an unnecessary and meaningless anxiety to impose on any child. Adults must know that toddlers can choose adequate diets in the amount needed. In many subcultures, children who do not eat heartily and are not enjoying food are thought to be ill, unhappy, or manipulative of the care-givers. Some people equate health, beauty, and prosperity with hearty eating. Greeks, Italians, Germans, and Jews often associate food consumption with love and excellent parenting. Often, the family unit is knit around festive or large daily meals.

American parents have unknowingly encouraged poor food habits in their children by demanding that the children "clean the plate," giving children huge, adult-sized portions instead of tiny, toddler-sized portions, providing high sugar content snacks, and using desserts as bribes for desired behavior. Dietary trends today encourage high-protein, nutritious snacks, which prevent tooth decay and maintain the blood sugar at higher levels and for longer periods than refined-sugar snacks. Instruct parents to offer their children snacks of cheese, peanut butter and jelly sandwiches, fruit juice, and home-made juice popsicles instead of cookies, chips, or colas. Give toddlers small portions. When toddlers eat all their food, they feel proud, powerful, and in control and can request second helpings.

Figure 12-2 Toddlers enjoy mealtimes if permitted to feed themselves in their own way, which is messy because hand and arm control are not well developed. Pleasant social interaction is an important aspect of eating and of social learning. Excessive adult interference can easily lead to parent-child conflict and eating problems that may last for years.

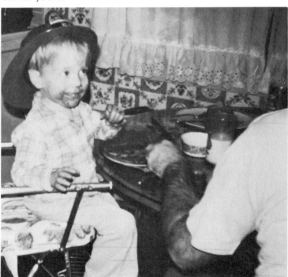

Food jags The toddler frequently goes on *food jags*, or "binges," on several foods for a few days, excluding other foods. If given a nutritious, well-balanced selection of food, toddlers will choose a balanced diet over several weeks. Many children change preferred foods on a 3- or 4-day cycle; knowing this calms the parents' fears. Parents who are worried that their toddler is not getting a complete diet may be advised to keep a food diary for a few weeks and to record what the child eats. This record generally shows that the quantity and variety of food intake are greater than the parent had supposed.

Food refusal Toddlers frequently refuse food and often imitate the food dislikes of parents or siblings. The child should *not* be forced to eat. Parents should ignore poor eating and praise healthy eating and should allow the child to avoid disliked foods. Food can be introduced in minute portions or disguised in other foods. Parents should allow the child to eat foods in his or her preferred sequence.

When a toddler says "No!" to eating, avoid reacting to the "no" and distract the child to another food. A child may test the parents and will feel more secure with specific food choices, such as "Do you want the potato or the beans?" Negative behavior at suppertime may be caused by fatigue from play or by being too hungry. A short rest period or nutritious snack 1 to $1\frac{1}{2}$ h before a meal may increase the toddler's cooperation. Most toddlers enjoy eating attractive, small portions of food served in a relaxed, pleasant atmosphere. (See Fig. 12-2.)

"Milk babies" are infants or young toddlers who primarily drink milk and refuse most solid food. These children are obese and pale and have low levels of hemoglobin. They are anemic because milk contains inadequate amounts of iron. Taking the bottle away (out of sight) until the child becomes hungry enough to accept solids works well. Milk in a glass is then offered after the meal. The child will cry for milk, and parents need reassurance of the need for solids and of the fact that retraining will take only a few days if they do not give in.

Eating rituals The toddler is object-oriented and attempts to control the environment by manipulating objects in a rigid pattern. The toddler cannot rationally relate actions and events and so establishes many ritualistic behavior patterns, some of which have to do with eating.

The child should be fed small portions on the same unbreakable plate and given child-sized utensils and a wide-bottomed cup. It is best that the child be fed at the same place and the same time. The child can be given favorite foods initially and gradually and inconspicuously new foods can be introduced.

The toddler's interest in objects, coupled with the short-attention span, makes the child easily lose interest in eating. Parents can encourage the child to eat in "one place" and not to run throughout the house eating. Having one place to eat teaches the child that sitting on his or her chair has one meaning: It's time to eat. The child should not be made to wait at the table until adults are finished. If the child loses interest in eating, apropriate play activities can stimulate eating. (See Fig. 12-3.) Feed the teddy bear saying, "Yum! I love this. It's good. I want more!" The child will often immediately begin eating. Serve colorful, attractive food: Design pancakes in the shape of a face, make a face on cottage cheese with raisins and peaches, or put a cheese "sail" in a potato "boat."

Toddlers should be allowed to feed themselves, although they are clumsy, and to choose the foods they prefer. Toddlers love *finger foods*, small, bite-sized pieces of food that do not require use of a spoon. They prefer raw vegetables to soft, cooked ones. Cereal or raisins will stimulate fine motor development. Spilled foods are to be expected. The floor can be covered with newspapers or large towels and the toddler should wear a bib. An absorbent cloth should be kept at the table. Young children develop creativity and learn about foods by touching, tasting, and playing in them (Fig. 12-4).

Motor development

The toddler's maturing neuromuscular system, including the myelinization of the spinal cord, readies the child for walking and exploring. The majority of the motor movements of toddlers have been learned by 2 years; the remaining toddler and preschool years are spent perfecting these skills. Toddlers have an insatiable, inherent need to perfect new skills. They spend long hours repeatedly practicing and refining these skills during play (see Fig. 12-5). Their repetitious

Figure 12-3 Pretending to feed a doll may increase a finicky eater's food intake and willingness to take time for eating.

practice is directed toward new skills and is selective, persistent, and satisfies an intrinsic need to deal with and learn about the environment. For example, a child may repeatedly climb upstairs until she drops from exhaustion. When the toddler becomes excessively frustrated learning a new skill, the child retreats to an old, favorite activity to increase his or her sense of competence and self-esteem.

The toddler's motor development is the most

Figure 12-4 Self-feeding skills are initially quite primitive, and toddlers eat with their hands before they learn to use utensils. (*Photo courtesy of David Carroll.*)

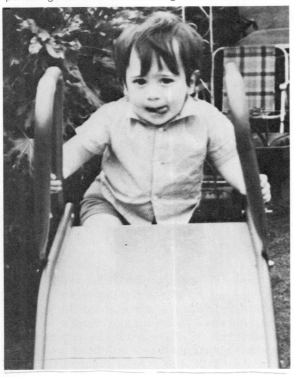

Figure 12-5 The toddler applies great determination in perfecting new skills and mastering the environment.

accurate criterion for assessing development level until verbal skills increase. If the child has not learned to walk by 20 to 22 months, he or she should be referred to a physician for a thorough pediatric and developmental assessment. Failure to walk may be a symptom of inadequate stimulation or mental retardation.

Gross motor development In order to walk, the toddler must first be able to hold head and shoulders erect, sit up, stand, and make stepping movements.[13] Cruising (walking while holding on to furniture) develops the infant's walking skills. Most toddlers walk alone by 15 months, walk backward and run by 18 months, and climb up stairs and kick a ball by 2 years. By 2½ years the child walks tip-toed and walks up and down stairs on alternating feet (see Table 12-2). The age at which the toddler masters these skills depends upon personality, stimulation in the environment, and heredity. For example, the trusting child eagerly forges ahead into the new environment and learns to walk faster than the more cautious child, who is hesitant to explore the environment. Children who have received inadequate sensory input will not reach out to interact with the environment and their developmental skills will be delayed (see Chap. 16).

Table 12-2 Gross motor development

Behavior	15 months	18 months	24 months	30 months
Walking	Walks alone (usually since 13–14 months) Loses balance with sudden stops	Walks sideways and backwards Walks pulling pull toy Pushes furniture around room	Walks steadily	Tiptoes a few steps
Standing	Stands up alone			Stands on one foot momentarily
Running		Runs awkwardly, falls often	Runs well with wide base of support, rarely falls	
Jumping	Jumps in place, falls forward often		Jumps with both feet in place	
Climbing	Creeps up stairs	Walks up stairs while holding on to rail Creeps downstairs	Goes up and down stairs, placing both feet on same step	Walks up and down stairs, one foot on a step
Sitting		Sits down on chair alone		
Throwing and kicking	Falls when throws ball	Throws ball overhand, doesn't fall	Kicks ball forward with good balance	Throws large ball 3–4 ft
Riding				Rides toy car

The toddler with athletic parents will probably walk earlier than the child of more sedentary parents.

The toddler beginning to walk has an unsteady gait, points the toes outward or inward, toddles with flat feet, and places the feet far apart to gain a wide base of support and improve balance (see Fig. 12-6). Practice steadies walking. Parents can promote the development of strong foot, ankle, and leg muscles by permitting the toddler to walk barefoot. Shoes should be soft and pliable and should not brace the foot or ankle (see the section "Shoes" in this chapter).

Toddlers' increased competence in walking, climbing, and opening doors gives them the confidence to explore the fascinating world. Because children have no earlier experience with new and occasionally dangerous objects, it is *absolutely imperative* that the parents constantly supervise children and provide a *safe indoor and outdoor* world to explore. (See the section "Accidents" in this chapter.)

Fine motor development The increasingly refined fine motor development of toddlers is illustrated by their ability to move a single muscular group instead of a larger, less differentiated group of muscles. For example, the infant could pick up a pencil with an entire-hand grasp whereas the toddler uses a perfectly refined pincer grasp. At 15 months toddlers can grasp a cup but cannot scoop up food. They turn a spoon upside down when bringing it close to the lips. The 18-month-old child fills the spoon but spills the food when turning it upside down. At 24 months the child eats with a spoon correctly. By 30 months the child can pour from a pitcher. The 15-month-old builds a two-block tower; the 24-month-old builds a five- to six-block tower (see Table 12-3).

Psychosocial development

Developmental task: autonomy vs. shame and doubt

The psychosocial developmental task of toddlers is to achieve a feeling of autonomy instead of shame and doubt. This stage lasts approximately from 18 months to 3 years. Toddlers must attain a sense of *autonomy*, or develop a sense of selfhood, i.e., a sense of being separate from others. Autonomous children feel competent, are able to assert their will and to do things independently. Toddlers who don't achieve autonomy feel *shame and doubt* and small, dependent, and worthless. Both of these opposing forces will be discussed in detail in this section.

Autonomy The toddler's burgeoning sense of autonomy originated during infancy and strengthens to dominate the toddler's behavior (see Table 12-4). The infant complied with the mother's wishes in order to develop trust but

Figure 12-6 The toddler walks and runs awkwardly at first, with feet apart and arms held out for balance.

probably protested being returned to bed by screaming and resisted being diapered by rolling away. Feelings of self-assertion began as the infant learned to influence the environment and make it respond to meet his or her needs. Trusting infants learned that the world and its caretakers were dependable and would meet their needs; the world became a safe place to explore. The toddler's readiness for becoming aware of selfhood, for being in control, and for influencing the world began in infancy.

The achievement of autonomy is based upon mastery of four concepts learned during infancy: (1) permanence of objects, (2) discrimination between inner and outer worlds, (3) recognition of the self as separate, and (4) gaining control over the body and the environment.[14] Each of these concepts will be discussed and related to the development of autonomy.

The infant learned that objects (people and toys) were permanent and existed when out of sight. This meant that the infant was developing a memory (could remember the lost toy), thought symbolically (mentally visualized the out-of-sight toy), and recognized the toy as separate from self. The child must discriminate between inner and outer worlds; without this distinction, there would be no outer world to control. The toddler's awareness of being separate from others increases the inner need to control the environment.

The toddler's need to autonomously control the environment and "to do things my way" permeates all aspects of development. *Negativism*, responding "No!" to most requests, is an automatic response of this age group. For example, a toddler will respond "No!" when asked if she wants a cookie. The "No!" has little meaning for the toddler, who then immediately grabs the cookie and gobbles it. This negative toddler is

Table 12-3 Fine motor development

Behavior	15 months	18 months	24 months	30 months
Building	Builds tower of two blocks	Builds tower of three blocks	Builds tower of five to six blocks Makes train of cubes	Builds tower of seven to eight blocks
Opening	Opens small boxes	Closes small boxes	Opens doors by turning knob Unscrews lid of jar	
Poking/turning	Pokes fingers in holes	Picks up small objects and places in box Puts blocks in hole Turns book pages		
Feeding	Grasps cup but frequently spills when tipping cup Grasps empty spoon. Cannot scoop up food. Turns spoon upside down when bringing to mouth	Drinks well from cup Fills spoon but spills often when bringing to mouth Turns spoon upside down in mouth	Drinks well, holds glass in one hand Puts filled spoon in mouth without turning it over	Pours from pitcher, spills often
Drawing	Scribbles	Scribbles. Tries to draw straight lines	Scribbling is more controlled. Copies vertical and circular strokes	Draws horizontal and vertical line. Makes two lines for cross Holds crayon with fingers rather than entire hand
Self-care	Pulls shoes and socks off. Sticks out arm or leg to help dressing	Removes own mittens. Helps pull off shirt. Helps unzip clothes	Removes most of own clothing. Puts on own shoes, socks, and pants (inside out and backwards)	

Table 12-4 Psychosocial development

Behavior	18 months	24 months	30 months
Ritualism		Ritualistic behavior begins; child is upset by changes in routine	Ritualistic behavior peaks
Imitation	Imitates parents' behavior, focuses on actions. Imitates actions during play		Imitates adult behavior, such as sex-role behavior. Imitation is increasingly symbolic
Exploration	Explores drawers, house, everything	Explores constantly. Resists restrictions on exploring.	
Autonomy	Autonomous behavior increasing but child is still dependent on mother. Temper tantrums begin	Increased independence away from mother. Temper tantrums continue. Negativism increases; focuses on own wishes. Dawdles	Independent behavior continues; reluctant to go to bed. Temper tantrums decrease. Negativism continues. Dawdles
Separation anxiety	Recognizes strangers but has less fear of them. Sucks thumb for comfort.	Separation anxiety at height. Fears parents' leaving. Thumb-sucking decreases.	Separation anxiety still at peak. Beginning to learn to cope with separation anxiety. Begins to use transitional object (security blanket or favorite toy) for comfort
Toileting	Increased readiness for toilet training. Will eliminate in potty. Fecal smearing common	Begins to cooperate at toilet training.	Has mastered daytime bladder control. Beginning nighttime bladder control. "Accidents" common
Play	Solitary play predominates. Possessiveness begins	Parallel play begins. Cannot share toys; still possessive	Parallel play continues
Attention span	Short attention span; shifts rapidly	Attention span longer	

simply asserting her will and testing her power to control other people. <u>Negativism is the observable aspect of the child's inner need to assert autonomy</u>.

The physical maturation of toddlers prepares them to assert their will and to control their actions and pushes them toward selfhood. The refining neuromuscular maturation of toddlers enables them to begin exploring the world. Fine and gross motor coordination mature. Toddlers can open the lids of jars to touch and taste the contents and turn doorknobs to explore the outside world. They can run and may chase a ball into the street. Increased physical and psychological energy is needed to support these explorations. The increased energy levels of toddlers coincide with the development of increased ego growth.[15] Myelinization of the central nervous system readies toddlers to control elimination.

A greatly expanding vocabulary allows toddlers to express their needs and wants.

Gaining control over elimination, feeding, and dressing increases the toddlers' feelings of self-control and autonomy (see Fig. 12-7). The toddler period corresponds to Freud's anal stage. The child must learn "to hold on and to let go." The child must let go of an inner wish to hold onto the stool and defecate when and where he or she wishes. Instead, the child must defecate when and where the parent decides. The toddler learns self-control and compromise. The toddler is also proud of the ability to feed and dress almost alone.

Self-control and compromise are two key components of *socialization*. Socialization is the learning of behavior needed to function successfully in a society: table manners, manners, modesty, and other social norms. Parents devote large amounts of time to the socialization of toddlers and preschoolers. The toddler must learn self-control and give-and-take. If children are allowed always to "have their way," and

Figure 12-7 This child has partially undressed and attempted to put on her mother's stocking and shoes. Toddlers learn early to remove their clothing, but they lack the perceptual and motor skills to get dressed without help.

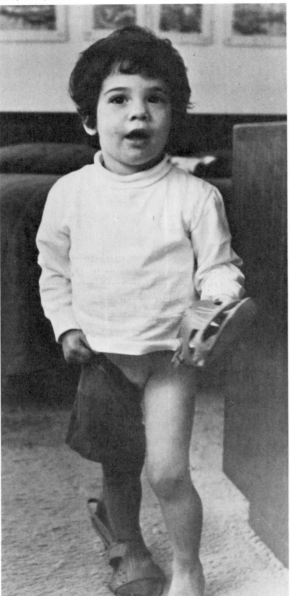

believe they can always dominate others, they will not learn to compromise. Awareness of the needs and wishes of others must begin in toddlerhood in order to assure future adaptation. Toddlers must learn to tolerate frustration of their own wishes to control others and to remain in emotional control.[16]

Shame and doubt Toddlers who do not achieve autonomy learn to feel shame and doubt. Shamed children feel small, self-conscious, dependent, worthless, and incompetent. While they feel increasingly in control, toddlers also recognize their inability to control everything and are aware of their dependency upon parents. These feelings plant the seeds of self-doubt. Toddlers recognize that their emotional outbursts may result in parental disapproval. When parents consistently restrict the child's attempts to manipulate objects, the toddler feels ineffectual, thwarted, and unable to learn about the environment. Overprotected children (see Chap. 21) are classic examples of children who feel shame and doubt. Overprotected children are kept dependent upon parents and have difficulty achieving their potential. It is important that children avoid learning shame and doubt, for feelings of viciousness and hostility seem to result from a sense of worthlessness.[17]

Sex-role distinction

The toddler learns the appropriate sex-role behavior by observing and imitating the behavior of same-sex models within the family. Sex roles are learned by age 3 (see Fig. 12-8). Toddlers imitate the same-sex parent's gestures, actions, tasks, posture, body movements, verbal expressions, and emotional control. For example, boys pretend to smoke pipes like daddy and girls apply make-up and jewelry like their mothers. The depth of the child's learning of a sex role is obvious in the older toddler's play. He or she frequently copies the parent's exact movements, posture, actions, word choice, and inflection of voice. Parents are often surprised to see and hear an exact child-sized replica of themselves punishing a doll during play!

Children imitate the parents' behaviors that produce social and material rewards. They appreciate the parents and want to be like the desired parent and gain the parents' approval. Children will not imitate behavior that is punished.[18] If a child sees a same-sex parent repeatedly demeaned or abused, the child may avoid learning the sex-role behavior to avoid punishment.

Despite the loosening of sex-role stereotypes that has taken place recently, most parents expect different behavior from boys than from girls. This molding of the child's sex-role behavior began during infancy and continues throughout childhood. Girls generally are allowed more emotional expression than boys. They are allowed to cry, pout, and whine longer than boys. Boys are traditionally expected to act stoically and are told, "Boys don't cry!" Girls are expected to be quieter and cleaner than boys. Boys are expected to show more aggression and physical exertion, as in rough-and-tumble play.

The parents' expectations of appropriate sex-role behavior differ with their cultural backgrounds. For example, boys in the United States are not encouraged to hug, kiss, or hold hands. In Middle Eastern cultures this behavior is acceptable. If the two parents have different expectations for behavior, the child will be confused about expected behavior and will have difficulty learning a sex role. The parents should discuss their different expectations, compromise, and give the child consistent expectations to learn.

Boys may have more difficulty than girls in learning their role. This occurs because a boy is physically close to a different sex-role model, the mother, for extended periods of time. He must thus copy the behavior of a frequently absent parent. In order to clarify sex-role differences and sexual identification, children of both sexes need role models of both sexes. Fathers should participate in child care, play with their children, and be physically present during the early years of childhood. Male teachers in nursery schools and male nurses in hospitals will strengthen the child's sex-role learning.

Young toddlers normally mix up sex-role behavior for they are only beginning to distinguish between the sexes. Boys experiment with smearing lipstick and wearing jewelry; girls with shaving. This normal behavior does not indicate future homosexuality but demonstrates the child's learning about the world.

Toddlers begin to develop a sense of body awareness and a sense of body image. Toddlers are determining the outer boundaries of their

Figure 12-8 Play and imitation promote sex-role learning. (*Photo courtesy of David Carroll.*)

body. The parents' sense of comfort or anxiety with their own bodies is easily transmitted to toddlers. Toddlers will imitate the parents and easily integrate feelings of shame about their bodily parts. The child learns shame if the parents exhibit shame, disapproval, or cover-up behavior when the child runs outside naked or touches the genitals. The child is *not* expressing precocious sexual urges but is simply learning about the body by touching it. Masturbation is normal and is universally practiced by both sexes. The child should not be shamed or slapped. Ways for helping parents deal with masturbation are discussed in Chap. 13.

Dolls that have genitals do not develop precocious sexual feelings in the child. The toddler's hormonal secretions are *not* mature enough to awaken these sexual feelings. The child identifies with the doll and is pleased by their similar bodies. One mother bought her toddler a boy doll with genitals after his toilet training had slowed after hospitalization. The boy undressed the doll and excitedly exclaimed, "Mom, he looks just like me!" He then immediately rushed to the bathroom and "toilet trained" the doll. From then on, the child's toilet training progressed smoothly.

The feminist movement has altered the traditional sex roles. Toddlers should be allowed to play with toys they prefer. Girls can use tools and garden, and boys can learn about work in the kitchen. Boys can learn parenting skills and express emotion by practicing on dolls. By having a variety of play experiences instead of being restricted to traditional boy or girl toys, children will learn more about the world and its people. (See Fig. 12-9.)

Toilet training

Toilet training is a main task that the toddler must master. Toilet training refers to the learned process of eliminating in a place and manner

Figure 12-9 Toddlers are not sex-role traditionalists, but seek and enjoy experimenting with adult roles of all kinds.

sanctioned by society. Attitudes toward toilet training vary among cultures. In many poorer socioeconomic classes of the world, infants and toddlers run through the house and yard eliminating at will. Parental attitudes toward toilet training are thus more lenient, and the children may essentially train themselves. In America children are trained earlier and the excreta is confined to bathrooms.

The parents' methods and attitudes toward toilet training will influence various aspects of the toddler's present and future life. They will affect the child's feelings and attitudes toward the body, sexuality, cleanliness, generosity versus miserliness (the ability to give and receive), self-esteem, and the achievement of autonomy or shame and doubt.

Toilet-trained toddlers are increasingly autonomous and able to care for themselves and take pride in their independence and ability to please parents. If children are shamed, perhaps for fecal smearing, they feel inadequate and incompetent, and their self-esteem will be lowered. Children learn to associate these negative feelings with the body. Toddlers perceive their body with indefinite boundaries, are establishing a separate identity, and may label their entire body as negative. In attempting to avoid parental displeasure, children may try to overcontrol toileting and may even avoid it.

Freud placed prime emphasis on toilet-training methods as indicators of later adult adjustment. He believed that the adult personality trends of generosity versus miserliness (to hold on versus let go) were outgrowths of toilet training during toddlerhood. Research suggests that emotional problems in older children are related to premature bowel training with the use of coercive methods. These children exhibited restlessness, tics, body manipulation, speech disturbances, psychosomatic ailments, or school failure despite adequate intelligence. Other symptoms included compulsiveness, aggression, negativism, fearfulness, timidity, overconformity, and inability to make decisions.[19]

Toilet training is an area in which an early mother-child contest of wills takes place. The mother requires the child to become socialized, to eliminate in a certain place and at a certain time. Following inner urges to defecate when and where the child wishes will risk parental disapproval. The toddler wants to retain the mother's approval and so bows to her wishes. This submission in order to obtain later gratification of wishes is one area wherein the toddler learns compromise, an essential ingredient of successful adult relationships.

Timing Children should not be rushed or forced into toilet training. Toddlers learn bowel control earlier than bladder control. They achieve daytime bowel control by 15 months to 2 years, daytime bladder control by 2 years, and nighttime bladder control by 3 to $4\frac{1}{2}$ years. There are several reasons why bowel control is mastered first. Bowel movements are more regular, easier for parents to predict, and fewer in number than urination. Bowel movements also cause a stronger sensation and urge; it is easier for the toddler to associate these feelings with defecation. Girls toilet train earlier than boys. This is believed to be due to boys' slower development in general.

Readiness Several criteria must be achieved before a toddler is ready to be toilet trained. There must be the neuromuscular maturity to walk to the bathroom, pull down clothing, recognize the urge to urinate or defecate, and have the sphincter control to hold in the urine or stool until on the potty. The child must be able to communicate his or her need to defecate by words, actions, or facial expression. The mother must be alert to the child's nonverbal behavior indicating a need to eliminate because the child has limited verbal ability (see Fig. 12-10). The toddler must recognize the sensation of the urge to defecate and associate it with the releasing of the stool on the potty.

In order for the child to learn bowel and bladder control, the central nervous system must be fully myelinated. Myelinization ensures that the brain's message will speedily reach the bladder or rectum. Only then can the child hold in and excrete voluntarily. Toilet training should begin after the child walks. (See Table 12-5 for readiness behaviors and training procedures.)

Fecal smearing Most toddlers smear feces, commonly between 15 and 18 months. The toddler has not learned that stool is dirty and should be avoided. To the toddler it is not shameful but is something warm and smearable that he produced. The toddler is proud of this product and smears it to learn about it. Parents should not shame the child. They should instead tell the child not to play with the stool and offer clay, paste, finger paints, or another, more ac-

Figure 12-10 The child indicates his toileting needs by gestures and facial expressions before he learns to use words for that purpose.

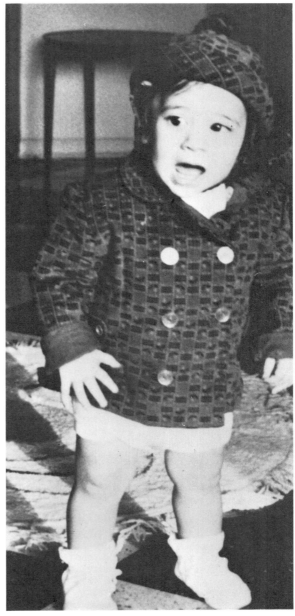

ceptable substance that allows smearing. (See Fig. 12-11.) The toddler thus learns a new method of handling this urge to smear.

Wetting accidents "Wetting" accidents occur among all children *throughout* the preschool years. Parents need not be overly concerned about wetting. Toddlers frequently are so absorbed in play that they do not feel or heed the urge to urinate until it is too late. If a child wets the bed several times each week, a casual wait-and-see attitude after a negative physical examination is best. The child should not be punished. Parents should preserve the child's self-esteem by saying, "It's okay. Next time I bet you'll come in earlier to pee." Excessive spanking reinforces the unwanted behavior; ignoring weakens it.

Table 12-5 Guidelines for toilet training

1. Indications that child is ready for training	Rationale
Walks	Indicates myelinization of spinal cord to bladder and anus
Dry for 2 h or awakens from nap dry	Bladder size will expand to hold urine
Neuromuscular maturity: Can walk to bathroom, pull down pants, and attempts to hold in urine or feces (may not succeed at first)	Child has sufficiently mature nervous and musculo-skeletal system and is ready for more self-care, toileting
Indicates wish to be trained. May pull down diapers, point to puddles on the floor, or bring dirty diapers to parent	Child feels uncomfortable in wet diapers, wants to control elimination
Has characteristic behaviors before defecation: grunting, glassy stare, or red face	Each child has individual behaviors which the mother can "read" to help predict defecation

2. Training procedure	Rationale
Parents can record time of child's elimination for several days	Child will train more easily on own schedule than on parent's schedule
Do not start training if child is under stress of illness, hospitalization, divorce, or has new baby sitter or new sibling	Child needs to deal with present stress. Learning new task during stress will take longer and be less successful.
Approach child with nurturant, nonthreatening, and expectant attitude	Parent is setting up expectancy to succeed, not fail
Tell child in simple words what to do: "This is your potty chair and where you sit down and go poop." Use the family term for excreta	Child needs to be told clearly what is expected in simple words.
Use potty chair or toilet seat. Set the child on it for 10-min periods at usual time for defecation or about 1 h after meals.	Chair feels more secure to child than adult's toilet. Extremely long time periods will cause child to reject potty

2. Training procedure (*Cont.*)	Rationale
Stay with child	Child left alone may feel abandoned
Place potty in bathroom, *one* place	Toddler must know there is *one* place to defecate. Moving potty may tell child it's okay to defecate in several places
No toys while on potty	Child needs to know there is *one* reason to sit on potty. Toddler's attention span is short and toys will distract him or her from defecation
When child defecates, reward her: "Susi, that's great! You went in the potty"	Rewarding the desired behavior strengthens it. This statement increases the child's self-esteem and emphasizes the achieved behavior
Toddlers frequently wet pants accidentally going to bathroom or while playing. Ignore the accident and don't punish the child.	Accidents usually occur. Toddler has not perfected sphincter control and does not heed elimination urge while playing until too late
Dress child in training pants or "fancy" pants	Training pants are associated with "big girls and boys," whereas diapers are associated with babies
Slacks should have elastic waistband	Elastic waists are easy to pull down and encourage self-care
Have both sexes sit to void at beginning. If boy stands to urinate, be certain toilet seat will not fall and hit penis	Toilet seat may injure penis. Pain associated with toilet may delay training
Have child with same-sex adult in bathroom each day	Child will imitate parent's behavior
Child is ready for night training when dry the entire day. Protect mattress with plastic	Bladder is storing urine for longer periods. Mattress protector decreases the mother's anxiety and work

Ill or anxious children regress, and toddlers usually regress by losing their newly acquired toilet training. They regain control when unstressed. Additional nursing interventions are listed in Chap. 13, and regression is discussed in Chap. 16.

Learning self-control

Toddlers must learn to control primitive, emotional outbursts and learn more constructive methods of emotional control. Learning emotional self-control and balance is not easy. Many people do not achieve emotional control until adulthood. In order to develop self-control, a toddler must recognize his own actions in a situation, want to copy the behavior of a role model, and imitate the role model's behavior while trying to control his behavior.[20]

Discipline *All* children need and want discipline. The goals of discipline are to help the child learn (1) self-control, (2) compliance with the behavior approved by the parents and society, and (3) how to get along with others. Each goal will be discussed in this section.

Punishment and discipline are not synonymous. Discipline includes both power-assertive (punishment) and love-oriented techniques. Punishing helps the punisher feel better, appeases the punisher's anger, and may prevent a recurrence through fear. Punishment makes the child feel powerless, forces submission, does not teach acceptable behavior, and lowers the child's self-esteem. Love-oriented techniques, discussed later under "Guidelines," correct behavior. They increase motivation to behave by building on the child's inherent wish to please the parents and increase self-esteem.

Children must learn respect for authority. Parents are the first teachers of authority, and the parent-child relationship is the model for all later relationships. If parents want to be respected during the teen years, they must be worthy of and establish respect during the preschool years.[21] For example, a parent can establish authority during a fight by bodily removing a biter or kicker from the victim and use spoken words to reinforce the physical command: "Stop biting Johnny now. It hurts." Respectful and responsible children result from the use of love and discipline.[22]

Discipline helps children learn self-control.

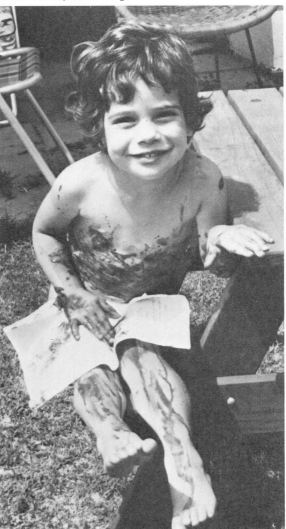

Figure 12-11 Toddlers like to play with mud and finger paints. Smearing is a natural way of enjoying and learning at this developmental stage.

Toddlers intensely feel the emotions of love, hate, and aggression. Only with the parents' limit setting will they learn to control these emotions, to channel them in constructive ways, and to learn new methods of coping.

Discipline is an essential component of accepting the self and successfully interacting with others. Many parents are afraid that discipline will squelch the child's development. This is one of the most widespread fallacies about discipline.

One child psychologist writes, "The greatest social disaster of this century is the belief that abundant love makes discipline unnecessary."[23] Discipline *is* necessary. Children do *not* know how to act and must be told how to behave. Each neighborhood has an "obnoxious kid" or a "holy terror" who causes parents to cringe when he or she arrives. This child, who has not learned the rules of society's "game plan" through discipline, begins life and school at a disadvantage. He or she must later learn the rules from strangers with a greater risk of rejection, disapproval, and even ostracism. Discipline helps children learn to live within the rules of their society and sociocultural group.

Limit setting may cause temporary anger but will make the child feel secure. The toddler's limit testing indicates a need for consistent limits and help in controlling primitive impulses. For example, 2-year-old John has broken the television and has been told not to "touch or kick the TV." John touches the TV, is told "No," and reaches toward the TV again while looking at his mother's face for disapproval. The mother again says, "John, don't touch it. No." John withdraws his hand, slaps it as if to reinforce the mother's command, and says, "John, no touch!" The mother was patient, repeated the instructions several times, and used action-oriented words (kick, touch) instead of abstract terms ("don't go near it" or "cool it!"). John illustrates the toddler's reaching out for consistent discipline.

Discipline is necessary to prevent accidents. Toddlers do not know the consequences of their actions and are often on the brink of an accident. (See Fig. 12-12.) Eventually children learn to trust parents' words, that the iron *is* hot, that injuries *do* result from unsafe play. They listen to parents' warnings and feel more comfortable, self-assured, and secure.

Figure 12-12 Toddlers develop the curiosity and motor skills to get into unsafe situations but lack the experience and judgment to avoid hazards. Discipline and safe, supervised play settings are essential to prevent accidents.

Guidelines While there are many theories and approaches to disciplining children, these are essential components which pervade all techniques.

1. Discipline must be *consistent.* When toddlers receive different responses to breaking rules, they become confused and unsure how they are expected to act and insecure, anxious, and doubtful of their self-control. Toddlers need consistency in order to predict responses to their actions.
2. Discipline must be *immediate.* Toddlers have a very short attention span and are easily distracted. If forced to wait for discipline, toddlers will forget what they did wrong and the discipline will have no meaning. Some mothers "wait until Daddy gets home" to discipline. Some theorists believe this practice allows the mother to project her anger onto her husband, forcing him to be the "bad guy." Discipline should be *jointly* practiced by all caretakers.
3. Discipline must be *related* to the incident. When a toddler is caught digging up a neighbor's flowers the child should be led firmly away from the neighbor's new garden and directed to her own sandbox or garden to dig. The parent should tell the child, "You cannot dig in Mrs. Clark's garden. You can dig here or in your sandbox." Preventing the toddler from watching television is not related to the incident, does not tell the child how to act, and would have less impact upon the child.

4. Instructions should be *repeated* many times. Toddlers should not be expected always to respond after being told one or two times. It takes several repetitions for many adults to learn a procedure, and it is unrealistic to expect a small child to learn so quickly.

5. Toddlers must be given time to respond to instructions; an immediate response cannot be expected. The toddler's nervous system is immature and cannot process two messages at the same time (see earlier discussion of the nervous system). The child may be physiologically unable to respond immediately. Toddlers should be given time to weigh their inner urges with minding parents. They must be given the *time* to learn self-control.

6. If the toddler does not mind, he or she probably did *not understand* the parent's directions. Parents often give instructions using colloquial or abstract terms. The toddler thinks concretely and does not understand the parent's slang words. If a parent says, "Bug off," "Simmer down," or "You're cruisin' for a bruisin'," the child thinks concretely and may visualize a bug or simply be confused. To the child these statements are not clearly related to the broken rule. Parents should use action-oriented words and focus on feelings. For example, "Suzi, don't touch the waffle iron. It's hot and will hurt!"

7. Adults should *not* expect each detail of the toddler's behavior to be correct. This expectation is incompatible with a toddler's development and imposes adult standards on a small child. Even most adults do not have perfect behavior. An adult expecting a toddler to act perfectly is setting the child up to fail.

8. Behaviors to be disciplined should be *prioritized.* The highest-priority behaviors needing discipline are usually potentially *unsafe* activities, such as running into the street, playing in a parked car, or exploring medicine cabinets or shelves under kitchen sinks. Both parents should jointly decide which behaviors to focus upon. When these are mastered, new behaviors can be addressed. The toddler will be overwhelmed and shamed by a burden of many behaviors to control simultaneously.

9. Children must be given *clear limits.* They must be told exactly what behaviors will not be tolerated. Their energies should be redirected to acceptable outlets. Clear instructions will tell a child exactly what is expected. For example, a 3-year-old started chasing a playmate, shouting, "I'll kill you! Go away," and was swinging wildly, attempting to hit her on the head with a large board. Her mother took the board away and said, "Alice, you *cannot* hit Suzi on the head with a board. It will hurt her." Then she redirected the child's energy to an acceptable outlet, a bean bag toss. The child was also told how to act: "Alice, when you get so angry next time, come and tell me and we'll toss the bean bag."

10. If the child is out of control, is unsafe, or is harming another child, *soft restraint* should be employed. For example, the mother can hold the child in her lap while calmly and quietly saying, "I will hold you to help you be calm and quiet. You cannot pull the cloth off the table." While continuing to hold the child, the mother speaks softly until the child regains control. The mother then tells the child what behavior is acceptable and chooses an activity to help the child express aggression.

11. Withdrawal of love should *not* be used as a punishment. The phrase "If you don't mind me, I won't love you anymore," establishes distrust and insecurity in the child. Loss of parental love is the toddler's greatest fear. If a toddler cannot trust the parent, it is difficult to achieve autonomy and may adversely affect later relationships. Instead, the *action* should be focused on, not the love. For example, "John, I love you but you *cannot* poke the dog's eye." This statement separates the love from the action. Children need to *know* they are loved in spite of wrong actions.

12. Extensive explanations and arguing should be *avoided.* The toddler cannot think logically and cannot understand the adult's point of view. Valuable time is wasted on explanations of "why" the adult is correct.

13. The child must have a *reason* for minding. "Do it because I said so," communicates only anger and power and does not provide a basis for learning. Toddlers believe there is a reason for everything and understand (although they may not like) such a simple reason as "because Grandmother would be sad if you broke her dish."

14. *Bribing* must be avoided. Bribing statements such as "If you stop screaming, I'll buy you a new toy" establish child-parent manipulation. The screaming behavior was rewarded with a new toy and the child will use it again. Instead, word statements to *expect* compliance: "Suzi, it's time for your bath now. After your bath, do you want to play paper dolls or something else?"

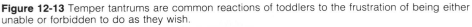

Figure 12-13 Temper tantrums are common reactions of toddlers to the frustration of being either unable or forbidden to do as they wish.

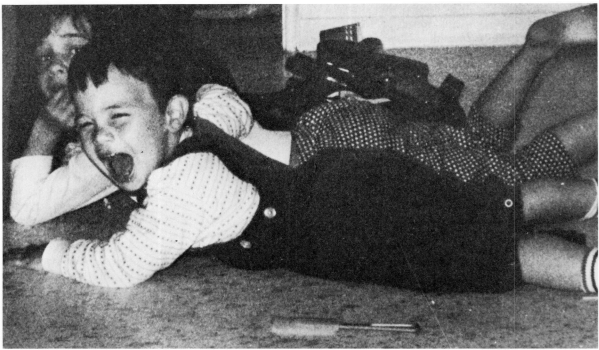

Techinques Ideal discipline techniques for the toddler are time out, reward, and diversion and are discussed in Chap. 13. Doll play is an ideal, pleasurable method of disciplining and communicating with children (see Chap. 16).

Temper tantrums A *temper tantrum* is a violent outburst of emotional and physical energy in response to anger (see Fig. 12-13). Toddlers express anger and frustration by falling to the floor, screaming, kicking, biting, and even holding their breath until they faint. Tantrums are a notorious cause of the label "the terrible twos" and parents frequently seek the nurse's counsel.

Toddlers have limited methods of expressing frustration when their wishes are thwarted. They have limited verbal ability and so have difficulty expressing their wishes and their increasing frustration. They have not learned emotional control. The toddler cannot solve problems, cannot delay gratification, cannot anticipate the consequences of the tantrum, and cannot see the parent's increasing anger. Instead, the tod-

dler is immersed in feelings of rage and frustration.

When toddlers have temper tantrums, it is very important *not* to give in and let them have their way. Rewarding the behavior (giving in to the toddler's wishes) strengthens the tantrum behavior. Toddlers then use tantrums increasingly to control their parents, even in markets or restaurants. Toddlers will stop using tantrums to control others when they do not achieve their goals. Wise parents give negative reinforcement by *ignoring* the behavior. Toddlers quickly stop screaming when the audience (the parent) leaves the room. Toddlers' breath holding should also be ignored. If the breath is held until fainting is induced, remember that breathing (driven by carbon dioxide build-up) resumes automatically.[24]

The disciplinary methods of bribing, screaming, or spanking are less effective than ignoring. Bribing the child sets up child-parent manipulation. Screaming at the child or comparing the child to the sibling's "bad" behavior or television tyrants is ineffective. Toddlers are self-centered and cannot compare their behavior with that of other children.

Ignoring tantrum behavior works well. After the toddler has calmed down enough to listen, do the following: (1) Label the child's feeling: "Jill, the way you feel now is called angry or mad." (2) Teach the child a more socially acceptable method of expressing anger: "Jill, instead of screaming say, 'Mom, I'm angry' and hit the punching bag as hard as you can!" (3) Offer the child alternative play materials designed to express anger: punching bags and gloves, hammer and peg sets, bean bags, stuffed animals or pillows, or pounding clay. Many toddlers are reluctant to express aggression and at first hit the toys gingerly. Approve of the child's expression of anger saying, "Jill, that's it! Hit it harder! Harder! It's OK. Hit the punching bag when you're mad!" (4) Reassure the child of your love. Toddlers' loss of self-control makes them feel insecure. The egocentric toddler thinks everyone thinks like him; he assumes the parent hates him as he hates the parent. The toddler is therefore afraid of the parent's hate and possible withdrawal of love. Verbal approval can be reinforced with touch, perhaps a hug or pat. (5) Offer a task which the toddler can do. This will encourage feelings of competence and decrease the shame and insecurity caused by the loss of emotional control and the parent's disapproval.

Negativism *Negativism* refers to the toddler's "No!" given in response to almost every request. Negativism is the observable behavior resulting from children's inner need to assert their will and their wish to dominate others. Parents frequently need assurance that the toddler's "No!" is an automatic response and is not a defiant testing of their authority. Toddlers are egocentric, believe everyone thinks as they do, and cannot imagine what adults are thinking.

Nurses can instruct parents to use several methods of handling negativism. Parents should be instructed not to overreact by spanking but instead offer the toddler safe, alternative choices. Choices give children an opportunity to assert their will within reasonable limits that are acceptable to parents. For example, a parent says, "It's time to eat dinner now. Do you want to eat the meat or the vegetables first?" This wording does not encourage a "No!" answer and gives a toddler an opportunity to make a choice and assert himself. Parents should be urged to not ask "yes" or "no" questions, because "Suzi, do you want to go to bed now?" will always elicit a "No!" response. Instead, the mother can use clear, action-oriented statements about her expectations and then allow a choice: "Suzi, you must go to bed now. Which doll do you want to take to bed?" Parents can easily divert the toddler's attention to another object and the toddler will quickly forget the "No!" Finally, the toddler should not be given a time-consuming choice when the parent is in a hurry. It increases the parent's frustration and promotes dawdling.

Destructiveness Parents should be instructed to avoid saying constant "No's!" to the toddler. Constant "No's!" will stifle the child's development, thwart exploration, promote shame and doubt by making the child feel powerless and incompetent, and decrease the child's creativity and independence. When the parent constantly says "No," the child stops hearing it. Instead, "No's!" should be saved for important safety hazards.

The toddler has limited self-control and cannot be expected to leave the parents' treasures alone indefinitely. Instead, breakable, treasured objects should be moved to high places and perhaps the toddler could be given "her own" drawer in the living room and "her kitchen drawer" filled with old plastic lids, cups, and pans. Toddlers must be given the opportunity to make choices and safely explore. Without these toddlers will not learn to assert their will and will have difficulty becoming separate, autonomous people.

Dawdling *Dawdling* occurs when toddlers resist parents' requests and do nothing. Dawdling reaches its height during toddlerhood. Children are caught in an ambivalent conflict, choosing between their own wishes and parents' requests. The toddler then does nothing while making a decision. The child can be affectionately helped to make a decision and act by being told, "I will help you put your jacket on this time. Next time perhaps you can do it alone." This guidance helps children to obey and establishes the expectation for cooperating in the future.

Ritualism Rituals give the toddler control over

the environment and nurture feelings of security. The toddler relies upon the sameness of all minute objects to maintain consistency and security in the environment. Field dependence, a characteristic of cognitive development, causes the toddler to believe that the entire environment is changed if one small object is altered. This accounts for the toddler's occasional hysterical, anxious overreactions when given a different cup, when two foods touch on a plate, or when the security blanket is missing.

The understanding parent encourages security in the toddler and avoids tantrums and frustration by catering to the child's need for rituals. Favorite times for rituals are meals and bedtimes. The toddler therefore needs the same cup, plate, and silverware, and the same bedtime sequence of a quieting-down time, a story, lullaby, prayers, and favorite doll.

Sleep Toddlers are reluctant to go to bed, have nightmares, and often disrupt their parents' sleep. Parents frequently seek the nurse's advice. The toddler's need for sleep decreases to 12 to

Figure 12-14 Toddlers are attracted to other people and, with experience, gradually learn the rules of social give-and-take.

14 h a night. Toddlers gradually relinquish the morning nap but most need an afternoon nap of 1 to 2 h. REM (rapid eye movement) sleep, during which dreams occur, comprises 25 percent of sleep at age 2 and 20 percent between 3 and 5 years. NREM (non-rapid eye movement) sleep increases from 75 percent at age 2 to 80 percent at 3 to 5 years.

Toddlers are extremely reluctant to go to bed and will try every excuse and delay tactic to stay up. They appear afraid of missing some excitement while sleeping. Nightmares peak at 2 to 4 years. Toddlers need parents' support and consistent limit setting to obtain adequate rest and sleep. They should be placed in bed for a nap

Table 12-6 Content of play*

Content of play	Examples
Social play. Toddlers receive pleasurable stimulation and learn social skills as toddlers relate to others. Learns slowly to play with others. (Fig. 12-14.)	Plays alongside others. Nuzzling, patty cake, smiling, teasing siblings
Sense pleasure play. Stimulation from both animate and inanimate objects brings pleasure. The toddler reaches out for stimulation.	Finger paint (smearing), pounding pegs, sand play, masturbation, bouncing to music, fondling a soft blanket, feeling the heat of the sun, smelling flowers.
Skill play. Reaches out for stimulation by an object. Involves more than one sense. Repetition of skills to master skill	Blocks, throwing ball, push-pull toy play, stair climbing, tricycle riding, dressing dolls, running
Dramatic play. Imitates or copies everyday events or scenes, usually within family. Introduces sex roles, socialization	Dress up with lipstick like Mommy; copy Daddy shaving or reading (copies both sexes)

* Adapted from L. J. Stone and J. Church, *Childhood and Adolescence*, Random House, New York, 1973, pp. 235–238.

or rest and kept there for a "rest time" even if they resist sleep. The child may take one favorite cuddly toy, but several toys divert the child to play, not sleep. Specific interventions for putting a child to bed and dealing with nightmares are discussed in Chaps. 13 and 16. Toddlers need adequate sleep to avoid frequent infections, irritability, and dulled intellectual functioning. The toddler with enough sleep has the following behaviors: ability to get up in the morning, relaxed and happy behavior, good appetite, bright eyes, erect posture, vibrant skin, curiosity, enthusiasm, and sufficient energy for active play.[25]

Play Toddlers would rather play than do anything else. They spend most of their time at play. (See Tables 12-6 and 12-7.) Play is not wasted time but is serious business, i.e., the child's *work*. The toddler works very hard to master tasks and seems to concentrate his entire being on gaining proficiency. When the toddler gains skill, he integrates it into other movements and play activities. For example, the child will run slowly, falteringly, then faster, more solidly, will soon run up stairs, backwards, in circles, in short spurts and fast stops, and eventually master running. The child then adapts the reciprocal leg motion to riding a kiddie car.

Play is a crucial part of physical, cognitive, and psychosocial development. The purposes of the toddler's play are to:

1. Refine fine and gross motor skills, eye-hand coordination, and spatial orientation (Fig. 12-15). Muscular strength and coordination are increased by banging drums, throwing balls, hammering nails, and feeding dolls.
2. Gain independence and differentiation of self. Play allows once-dependent toddlers to explore all objects in a search for new stimulation. Ambulation increases their exploration to new vistas. Exploration of each object brings new sensations and a realization of self as separate from the object.
3. Gain self-esteem. The toddler learns she can begin an action, has the power to affect movement, and

Table 12-7 Play activities*

Type of play	18 months	2–3 years
Gross motor play	Large hollow wooden blocks Low slide Low swing with arms and back Large riding toys (car, fire engine, etc.) Rocking chair Small table and chair	Sand box Large blocks, cardboard boxes Interlocking block trains
Creative play	Nesting blocks Hammer boards Toys with shaped openings to receive different shaped blocks Wrist bells	Large beads to string Braided strings with rigid tips to lace Wooden puzzles Finger paints Clay Colored construction paper Blunt scissors
Dramatic play	Wooden train Sand toys (pail, shovel, sieve) Stuffed toys	Strong vehicles (car, truck, etc.) Toy telephone Housekeeping toys (mixer, iron, broom) Carriage, doll bed, and high chair Washable doll to bathe Baby doll
Quiet play	Fingerpaints Clay	Wooden shoe to lace Paint Large crayons Cloth or cardboard books Cloth boards to lace with string Toys for water play (sponge, soap, rotary beater, sieve)

* Adapted from Ruth E. Hartley and Robert M. Goldonson, *The Complete Book of Children's Play*, Thomas Crowell, New York, 1957, pp. 39–67, 399–400.

Figure 12-15 Play activities develop balance, perception, learning, and control of large and small muscles.

5. Learn sex-role identification. Young toddlers begin to adopt a sex role and frequently are mixed up. Boys may parade around in mommy's jewelry, faces smeared with makeup, and girls may pretend to shave their faces and smoke daddy's pipe. With parental feedback toddlers quickly adopt traditional sex roles. Young toddlers spend long hours working and imitating household activities: washing dishes, bathing, mowing, and cooking.

Toddlers have progressed from the solitary play of infancy to *parallel play*. In parallel play two or more toddlers play side by side, even in the same sand pile. They are too egocentric to play together. Toddlers frequently grab each other's toys and are very possessive. They hit and fight to obtain the coveted toy, not to hurt the other child. They do not realize they're hurting the other child because they are self-centered and it doesn't hurt them. They feel no shame because no conscience is yet developed.

Figure 12-16 Toddlers take great delight in physical activity and in their abilities.

studies the results (Fig. 12-16). How powerful she must feel, being able to manipulate objects and cause results! When disciplined for misbehaving and her self-esteem is lowered, the toddler retreats to the small, safe harbor of toys. She manages these toys, practices solutions to the problem, and once again feels powerful and autonomous.

4. Learn to control inner urges within the limits set by parents and begin socialization. Toddlers cannot play with medicines, cross the street unescorted to retrieve a ball, or hit the dog with a hammer. They practice emotional control by projecting feelings onto toys, especially dolls, and playing out emotions. They practice controlling these emotions and expressing them during play.

Toddlers still function in a sensorimotor modality. They learn about objects by exploring and manipulating them. (Fig. 12-17.) For this reason, play that stimulates the senses is especially beneficial for the toddler: sandboxes with strainers, buckets, shovels, funnels, and spoons; water play with cups, boats, bubbles, colanders, plastic cups, and eggbeaters; mud pies and finger paints.

Play is a superb method of encouraging socialization and teaching the child. Many child care activities are made fun and educational by using play. Favorite dolls are bathed; bath toys encourage fun and new sensations; cutting out cookies teaches geometrical shapes. Doll play reflects the feelings of the child and is an excellent method of eliciting the child's thoughts. (See Chap. 16.)

Parents should be observers of play, guardians of safety, and arbitrators of fights. Toddlers need freedom to explore in a safe environment. The yard and house must be child-proofed *daily*. Toys must be safe, strong, and too large to swallow or insert in an ear. Parents must lock up medicines and tools and put away household breakables; they must use caution when they allow the child to explore the yard or neighborhood. Firmly forbid crossing the street without an adult for any reason, and provide close supervision to enforce this rule. In unsafe situations, instructions should be simple and authoritarian in tone, and no choices should be given.

Parents should allow the toddler to choose among his or her toys without adult interference. Child-development theorists believe a child will instinctively choose the most healing, beneficial toy. A toy selected by the parent meets the parent's needs. Further discussion on the nurse's role in play is found in Chap. 16.

Fear and anxieties

Separation anxiety The greatest fear of toddlers is losing their parents. Toddlers separated from their parents progress through a series of grief reactions called *separation anxiety*. Children attached themselves to the parents during infancy and learned that unseen objects still exist. Paradoxically, the urge of toddlers to separate from parents intensifies the fear of losing them. They want to do things alone but realize they are dependent upon the parents and want their attention and care. These ambivalent feelings

Figure 12-17 The toddler's learning depends on experience that involves the senses—touch, smell, taste, vision, and hearing.

increase feelings of insecurity and foster separation anxiety.

One of the main tasks of toddlerhood is to master separation from parents for short periods. Games such as peekaboo and hide-and-seek help toddlers master separation. Toddlers gradually learn that parents leave for work and then return home, and they associate the return with a meaningful activity, such as dinnertime. However, toddlers have no true concept of time. One hour may seem like an eternity, which increases a child's feelings of vulnerability.

Parents can decrease the toddler's separation

anxiety by having consistent baby-sitters. A new sitter should be introduced gradually to the child. If the sitter visits several times in the home, interacts with the parents and child, and the child sees the parents' approval of the sitter, the child will accept the sitter more easily. Parents should leave behind some object associated with them, such as keys, wallet, purse, or jewelry. The toddler is object-oriented and will feel reassured that the parents will return for the object. Toddlers also cling to a *transition object*, a security blanket or favorite toy that represents the home and is used for self-comfort. Finally, parents should relate their return to an activity, not time: "We'll be back after you eat lunch." (See Chap. 16 for a detailed discussion of separation anxiety.)

Reality vs. fantasy The distinction between reality and fantasy is totally unclear to toddlers. They engage in *magical thinking*, i.e., they believe that whatever they think is real and that whatever is in their minds will become true. Their tendency to focus on one feature of an object at a time and their self-centeredness distort reality. For example, a toddler fearfully focuses on the great size of a television monster while overlooking the monster's good deeds. Egocentricity

makes him believe the monster is after him. Cartoons with victims being killed and immediately recovering further distort reality.

Young toddlers will kick or slap a monster on television, expecting it to leap out of the television as a real person. Parents should help the child distinguish between reality and fantasy by saying, "Look, that is a TV picture of a monster. It is not real. It is a picture of a man dressed up in green paint." When children are afraid of pictures in books, parents can draw a picture saying, "This is drawn with crayons. It is not real, doesn't move, and will always be a picture." Parents can help the toddler in make-believe play distinguish reality from fantasy by saying, "That's a wonderful make-believe animal story. It's fun to pretend that animals really talk, but real animals don't talk."

Cognitive development

The toddler years encompass two phases of cognitive development. From 12 to 24 months the toddler is in Piaget's *sensorimotor phase*, classified as part of infancy; the toddler then proceeds through the *preconceptual phase* from 2 to 7 years (see Table 12-8; see also Chap. 13.)

Table 12-8 Cognitive development

Behavior	12–18 months	18–24 months
Experimentation/inferring	Uses trial-and-error experimentation to reach goal. Varies activities to observe result. Learns about object by experiencing it. Uses tools to reach goal	Invents new methods, through trial and error, to solve a problem. Infers cause from observing event and predicts result from observing cause
Causal relationships	Begins to sense causal relationship between objects being manipulated	
Object permanence	Increasingly aware of object permanence. Searches briefly for hidden object. Ventures further away from parent for longer time.	More aware of object permanence. Will search several places for longer time for hidden object
Spatial awareness	Spatial awareness begins. Recognizes different shapes	
Memory	Memory beginning	Memory increases
Time sense	Can enter into middle of series of actions without returning to beginning	Anticipates events, waits for brief period before anticipated event
	Beginning sense of time and anticipation of events	Beginning knowledge of past, present, and future
Symbolic thought	Concrete thought	Symbolic thought begins, can "pretend." Begins to think about own behavior. Imitates nonpresent behavior or objects
Characteristics of thought	Egocentric Ritualistic Global organization Magical thinking	

Sensorimotor period

Stage 5: Tertiary circular reactions (12 to 18 months)*
The same processes that are going on in stage 4 (see Chap. 11) continue in stage 5, but at a higher level. In stage 5 children actually experiment much as scientists do by varying their activities and changing the environment in order to see the different results. They thus learn to separate the means of achieving a goal from the goal itself. Space and time perception continue to develop in relation to object permanence. They begin to recognize different geometric shapes and investigate relationships among them. They learn to use tools to aid them in obtaining their goals. For instance, a toddler may use a stick to push a toy off the table so she can get at the toy. She has learned about and understood the event by experiencing it. Using a stick to get the toy indicates her understanding of causality is developing: she is aware of a causal relationship between her action and the resultant accessibility of the toy. Toddlers become very systematic in accommodating to new situations so that their actions become very deliberate and efficient. However, they cannot transfer information from one event to another and must repeatedly reinvestigate the situation. These children are curious and are seeking out new experiences.

Stage 6: Invention of new means through mental combinations (18 to 24 months)*
This is truly a transitional stage to the next period. Infants are capable of mentally putting together schemata (discussed in Chap. 11) through the process of assimilation to develop new ways or behaviors to reach their goals. In the first stages they applied familiar schemata to new situations and then modified these schemata. Now they invent new ways to do things, developing insight into the problems they are solving. Their muscles may involuntarily do the same things they're thinking about as the solution to the problem. For instance, a child's hand or mouth may open and close before he tries to open a box to reach a toy (adults do this, too). At this stage toddlers can also infer causes from observing events and can predict the results by observing causes.

---

*The authors are grateful to Ann Sloat for most of the discussion of stage 6.

The ability of children to imitate has changed considerably by stage 6. Earlier imitation was limited to mimicking certain actions, such as another's laughter. Imitation now shows deeper meanings as children begin to imitate sex-role behavior. They are now able to imitate models that are not physically present at the moment. They have a beginning sense of time. They think about out-of-sight objects, past events, and events in the immediate future. They think about what they are going to do before they do it. This ability is very important in the development of play. Children in stage 6 no longer play by simply manipulating objects, experimenting with them, and focusing on their actions. They are now able to visualize an event in their minds and can make believe. Their play is truly symbolic at this stage.

At this age children's thoughts are *egocentric*, or self-centered. The toddler views himself as the center of his world; he believes it is he who causes all outer events to happen and that the events happen for the purpose of bringing him pleasure or frustration. He believes that his opinion is the only one that exists. Egocentrism predominates all aspects of the toddler's behavior and is illustrated by the following quote:

> The magician is seated in his high chair and looks upon the world with favor. He is at the height of his powers. If he closes his eyes, he causes the world to disappear. If he opens his eyes, he causes the world to come back. If there is harmony within him, the world is harmonious. ... His wishes, his thoughts, his gestures, his noises command the universe.[26]

Magical thinking also predominates during these years. Toddlers believe their thoughts have the same far-reaching power as an action. Toddlers feel supremely powerful and responsible for events but are also vulnerable to feelings of guilt and remorse. A classic example: if a child wishes his mother dead, and the mother dies, the child believes he caused the death. Adults need to help children distinguish between reality and fantasy, but confusion will continue through the preschool years.

Language development
Language develops very markedly during the toddler period (see Table 12-9). Language varies greatly according to subcultures, experience in hearing others speak, involvement in sensori-

Table 12-9 Language development

Behavior	15 months	18 months	24 months	30 months
Word usage/ sentence length	Expresses self with jargon	Imitates adult words	Combines three to four words to form short sentence	Uses plurals
	Combines two to three words in a sentence	Uses short phrases with adjectives and nouns	Uses short sentences	Talks constantly
Communication	Points to desired objects. Responds with "No" to all requests. Understands simple commands	Uses few words to communicate need. Points to some objects when named. Uses gestures and few words to communicate needs	"Telegraphic" speech. Refers to self with pronoun (I, me) or own name. Names familiar objects	Speech is "telegraphic" and a monologue. Knows first and last name. Knows one color
Communication		Follows directions. Understands simple requests	Vocalizes needs for food, drink, or "potty." Understands and obeys simple commands	
Vocabulary size	20 words	25 words	275 words	900 words

motor skills, sense of self-esteem, and stimulation to acquire language. Some children are reluctant to speak when there are (1) problems in interrelationships with parents and siblings, (2) lack of stimulation, or (3) overstimulation. The sense of self-esteem is generally lowered with the above three occurrences and the child then withdraws. In an overstimulating home, the child "turns off" the stimuli.

The development of language is closely associated with the expansion of cognition (thinking). Delay in one area causes delay in the other. Verbal ability enhances thinking, problem solving, and autonomy.

There are differences in the speed of language acquisition. Girls develop language faster than boys, who catch up in midchildhood. Crowded ghettos or institutions produce slow acquisition of speech. Seemingly, this is due to sensory overload or understimulation or emotional and intellectual deprivation. Role models may not be available to imitate. Bilingual children acquire language more slowly. (See "Sensory Deprivation" in Chap. 16.)

The child imitates sounds and words and receives rewards for correct usage. The toddler may create sentences without ever hearing them before. The acquisition of grammar may be con-

trolled by special programmed neural structures in the brain that spew out correct grammar. Only a small number of errors occur in relation to the amount of words spoken by toddlers. There is no satisfactory explanation for the phenomenonally rapid acquisition of grammatical structure at this time.[27]

Toddlers understand more words than they express. The average vocabulary is about 20 words at 15 months, 25 words at 18 months, 120 words at 21 months, and 275 words at 24 months. By age 2 toddlers use sentences of two to three words and at 3 years use about 900 words.

Children of all races proceed through language development at the same rate. Stuttering and hesitation in speaking are common. Listening to people read stories exposes the child to language and speeds acquisition. At 1 year stories with simple pictures and one-word explanations of each picture and at age 3 paragraphs with pictures are appropriate. Children's readiness for various kinds of stories is indicated by their sentence structure. When two or more words are used in an expression, books with two or more word captions are appropriate for the toddler's short attention span. Toddlers learn nouns first, such as baby, milk, banana, cookie, and use subjects, objects, and verbs by 3 years, i.e., "Mom go store," "Suzie want cookie." They are also capable of learning numbers and colors.

Parents should talk often to their children, explaining reasons for objects and occurrences, and expanding the child's one to two word phrases of "See doggie?" to "See the big doggie? He has long hair and is brown. He says woof woof." This helps stimulate speech and cognitive development. If a child is not speaking by age 3, he or she should be referred to a physician or speech therapist for diagnosis and referral.

Child health maintenance

Accident prevention

Accidents are the leading cause of death among toddlers. Accident prevention is extremely important, and the nurse's role in prevention can be critical. The nurse can counsel parents, neighbors, friends, and clients to help the parents control the child's behavior to prevent accidents, understand the child's level of cognitive development, and predict potential safety hazards for this age group.[28] The accidental causes of death and measures for preventing them are discussed in Chap. 13.

Toddlers have an insatiable need to explore: the ability to climb, crawl, and walk greatly increases exposure to potential safety hazards. Toddlers cannot reason and cannot anticipate accidents that may result from exploration. They are egocentric. A toddler can be immersed in the joys of chasing a ball into the street and totally oblivious of the car racing toward him. For these reasons, toddlers need parents committed to keeping a safe environment. Safety locks must be secured on cabinet doors, all medicines must be locked away, and covers for electrical outlets should be installed. All caustic substances should be removed from under sinks to high, locked cupboards because toddlers can climb and sit on top of counters. It takes only one taste of a drain opener to injure a child's mouth and esophagus. Dishwasher soap is also caustic, and a toddler should not be allowed to play in it. Many poisonings occur from 4:30 to 6:30 P.M., when the mother is busy cooking dinner and unable to watch the child. The mother should consider placing the child in the playpen or providing a favorite television program to increase safety during these hours.

The garage, yard, and car must be child-proofed. Poisonous substances should never be stored in drink bottles or food containers. Caustic substances, sharp tools, and ladders should be safely stored. Ladders should not be left upright, ready for a toddler to climb. Toddlers should not be allowed to play in cars because of their urges to move the gears and "drive" the car. They should not be allowed to lie under the car's rear window or scramble around in the car. Toddlers should always wear seat belts. In a collision unrestrained toddlers become projectiles flying at several miles per hour. Additional safety precautions are discussed in Table 12-10 and in Chap. 13.

Vision

Vision should be tested at 3 years. Obvious eye problems such as nystagmus or strabismus ("cross-eyes") must be referred to the physician. Untreated strabismus results in amblyopia ("lazy eye") and vision suppression in the affected eye. Such subtle behavior changes as spatial discoordination seen in missing a step, reaching unsuccessfully for a toy, squinting excessively, or inability to fix the gaze on objects should be reported to the physician. See Table 12-1 for milestones in visual development. Since language and thought processes are very simplistic and self-oriented at this age, it is difficult but possible to test for visual impairments. Early diagnosis and treatment of eye problems will prevent future reading problems and alterations in the musculature of the eye.[29]

Dental care

Preventive dental care is an important health teaching concept to be emphasized to the toddler's caretaker. Tooth decay is the result of bacteria acting on carbohydrates on the surfaces of teeth. An acid environment is produced, resulting in destruction of the enamel. Frequent snacks, sticky foods, and bedtime bottles cause caries. Bottle caries result from the constant contact of the child's teeth with liquid containing sugar, such as milk, juice, or carbonated beverages. Fluoridated water at 0.7 to 1.2 parts per million or fluoridated vitamins are optimal for caries prevention. Health departments can recommend dosages of fluoride drops to the teeth if water levels are not optimal and will notify consumers of fluoride levels in different localities. Thumb-sucking beyond the age of 4 or 5 years can result in significant malocclusion, and referral to a dentist is appropriate. The parent can clean the infant's and toddler's teeth by gently wiping them with a washcloth. As toddlers' fine motor coordination becomes more refined, they can brush their teeth. Their teeth brushing should be closely supervised by the parents. Daily brushing and flossing, the latter performed by an adult, are recommended by dentists. Parents can encourage toddlers to practice brushing on doll's teeth and other household objects.

Table 12-10 Accident prevention*
*(Age: 1 to 3 years)**

Dangers at home

Gravity
    Falls from one level to another
    Falls on dangerous surfaces or objects
Water
    Tub, pool, puddle or toilet bowl
Heat
    Stoves, fireplaces, hot foods or liquids, matches, lighters
Poisons
    Medicines, caustics, cleaning compounds, paint thinner, bleaching fluid, etc.
Machines
    Electrical, the car, the lawn mower

What they do

They are in perpetual motion. They are curious about everything. They run almost as soon as they walk
They put things in their mouths whether these things are edible or not
They pull on everything they can reach
They crawl into boxes and cupboards and behind and under furniture
They climb. They can go up more easily than they can get back down.
They play alone and will wander away from a group
They are fascinated by fire
They may fear animals or chase dogs and cats, often provoking them
They have no fear of water
They are big operators who leap before they look

What they can do to protect themselves

At 1 year they haven't learned anything to protect themselves. Their locomotion makes them more susceptible than before
At 3 they may know that stoves and fire are hot, but they cannot be depended on to remember
They act largely without previous planning and cannot anticipate danger

What they need

They need protection; safety education and discipline must begin
They need good examples to imitate

They need a happy but orderly home in which to grow and learn how to behave safely

What the family can do to protect them

Anticipate their activities in the home environment. Remove potential hazards. Look around for "attractive nuisances." Demonstrate safe living. Integrate education for safety into daily living, showing "why."
Improve housekeeping—avoid keeping poisonous substances or bottled or packaged nonfoodstuffs anywhere they can reach them or climb for sampling
Provide a place for toys and a place to play on the floor. Remove destructible bric-a-brac and loose scatter rugs. Teach the meaning of "hot," "hurt," and "tastes bad," rather than "don't"
Unless they are in playpens or closed-off areas, keep crawling babies and toddlers out of the kitchen and traffic areas. Place playpens or high chairs as far away from stoves or other potential hazards as possible
Put a fence around pools and ponds, and *never* allow a potential crawler or toddler to be alone near water wherever it may be. Even the empty bathtub or sink, or 2 to 3 in of water in a plastic pool, are dangerous
Check bed and sleeping room for potential hazards, including inviting places to put the head
Assume that toddlers are in danger unless they can be seen. Danger may be most imminent when they are quiet; they have probably found something new to try
Be sure child can be seen before moving the family car or driving over empty packing cases

* Written by Hope Ecklund, R.N., R.H.N., M.P.H. Used with the permission of city and county of San Francisco, Calif., Department of Public Health.

Shoe selection

Regular monitoring of shoe size is important because during rapid growth children may need shoes every other month. The child's shoes should be $\frac{1}{2}$ to $\frac{3}{4}$ in longer than the feet when standing. Parents can press the thumb on the edge of the shoe to estimate the space felt between the longest toes and the end of the shoes. The main criteria for shoe selection are that they be soft and flexible, have a protective sole, and offer protection from the climate. Recommended shoes are no longer only high-topped, leather shoes. Tennis shoes have cloth uppers that provide maximal ventilation. They protect well, dry easily, and are flexible, which provides for maximal development of the muscles of the feet and legs. Primitive people who do not wear shoes have very strong muscles; for this reason orthopedists today recommend more flexible shoes and believe high-topped leather shoes are not necessary and may actually retard muscular development. If a child cries when standing or walking, or if he or she sits down when trying to walk, the shoes may be too small.

References

1. Isobel Thorp, "The Toddler, 1–3 years," in G. Scipien et al., *Comprehensive Pediatric Nursing*, 2d ed., McGraw-Hill, New York, 1979, p. 234.
2. Lucille F. Whaley and Donna L. Wong, *Nursing Care of Infants and Children*, Mosby, St. Louis, 1979, p. 511.
3. Eugenia Waechter and F. Blake, *Nursing Care of Children*, Lippincott, Philadelphia, 1979, p. 373.
4. P. Mussen, J. Konger, and J. Kagan, *Child Development and Personality*, Harper & Row, New York, 1969, p. 244.
5. Peggy L. Chinn, *Child Health Maintenance, Concepts in Family Centered Care*, Mosby, St. Louis, 1979, p. 319.
6. Ernest H. Watson and George H. Lowry, *Growth and Development of Children*, Year Book, Chicago, 1967, p. 219.
7. Mussen, loc. cit.
8. Chinn, op. cit., pp. 320–321.
9. Ibid., p. 321.
10. Ibid., p. 320.
11. William E. Homan, *Child Sense*, Basic Books, New York, 1969, p. 94.
12. R. W. White, "Motivation Reconsidered: The Concept of Competence," *Psychological Review*, 1966, pp. 318–319.
13. Mollie S. Smart and C. Russel, *Children, Development and Relationships*, Macmillan, New York, 1972.
14. Waechter, op. cit., p. 385.
15. Henry W. Maier, *Three Theories of Child Development*, Harper & Row, New York, 1978, p. 85.
16. Thorp, op. cit., p. 237.
17. Joseph L. Stone and J. Church, *Childhood and Adolescence*, Random House, New York, 1973, p. 243.
18. Ronald C. Johnson and Gene R. Medinuss, *Child Psychology, Behavior and Development*, Wiley, New York, 1969, p. 381.
19. Mussen, op. cit., p. 264.
20. Thorp, op. cit., p. 229.
21. James Dobson, *Dare to Discipline*, Tyndale House, Wheaton, Ill. and G/L, Regal Books, Glendale, Calif., 1974, p. 12.
22. Ibid., p. 7.
23. Ibid.
24. Whaley, op. cit., p. 522.
25. Smart, op. cit., p. 209.
26. Selma Fraiberg, *The Magic Years*, Scribner, New York, 1959, p. 107.
27. Mussen, op. cit., p. 254.
28. Thorp, op. cit., p. 238.
29. Watson, op. cit., p. 222.

Chapter 13 **The Preschooler**

Phyllis Nie Esslinger

Upon completion of this chapter, the student will be able to:

1. Describe the physiological development of the preschooler in the following areas: body proportions, weight gain, brain size, metabolic rate, vision, and neuromuscular development.
2. Summarize the preschooler's nutritional needs and problems: caloric, protein, mineral, and milk needs; food jags, food intake, and serving size.
3. Summarize the preschooler's characteristic behavior with respect to Erikson's initiative vs. guilt stage of psychological development.
4. Relate the following concepts to the preschooler's sex role development: identification, child-rearing practices, and sex role stereotypes.
5. List four guidelines for educating the preschooler about sex.

6. Compare the following types of play: cooperative, creative, dramatic, and quiet.
7. Define socialization and describe how the following types of learning socialize the preschooler: learning by insight and unfolding, conditioning, positive reinforcement, and negative reinforcement.
8. Identify, and illustrate each with an example, the characteristics of the preschooler's cognitive development in the preconceptual and intuitive phases.
9. Identify eight criteria for selection of a nursery school.
10. Describe methods of preventing the three most common accidents among preschoolers.

The preschool period, from age 3 through 5 years, is delightful—a period of enthusiasm, energy, activity, and creativity. The preschooler is an autonomous, discerning little individual who can run, jump, skip, ride a tricycle, and enjoy moving rapidly through space. Control over many bodily processes has been achieved; the child has much pride in these accomplishments.

The preschooler is highly social and independent. He or she is now beginning to know right from wrong, developing a conscience. Play often takes the form of imitation as the child assumes appropriate sex roles and dresses or acts like "Mama or Papa." This child constantly asks "Why"—evidence of the child's burgeoning vocabulary. The preschooler volunteers much information peppered with continual expressions of likes and dislikes.

This age period is one of rapid learning in which the preschooler is naturally curious and pushes out into the world (Fig. 13-1). This child needs to have freedom to explore, to test, and to control his or her individual actions as well as the actions of others. The child needs to know what makes things tick—what things look like inside and how they work and why. This insatiable curiosity often gets the little preschooler in trouble with Mama's watch, Daddy's tools, and the medicine cupboard. The child's curiosity explores his or her body, its functions, and the bodies of others. What the child lacks in knowledge is made up through fantasy or magical thinking. Observation is keen, with the pre-

Figure 13-1 Preschoolers are highly social and curious beings who love to play and explore.

schooler seeing, hearing, and feeling every detail of the environment.

This is a vital time in the development of the child since so much of the personality is being molded. Children need love, adequate role models, attention, and consistent guidance. They also need a safe, stimulating place where they can explore their own attributes, satisfy their curiosity, and master skills. To provide a more expansive world for preschoolers, their families often put them into nursery schools. Here they can expand their social and play world under the supervision and guidance of trained personnel. Nursery schools provide safe equipment to foster stimulation, curiosity, and activity in an environment that is tailored for preschoolers.

Health professionals must be aware of the preschooler's activity and curiosity and of the necessity of providing a *safe environment*. This need is reflected in the fact that accidents are the leading cause of death in this age group. Approximately one-third of all deaths in the preschool period are attributed to accidents, most of which are preventable. The next leading causes of death are congenital malformations, influenza and pneumonia, and malignant neoplasms.[1]

Physical development

The preschooler, unlike the chubby toddler with a protuberant abdomen, is a sturdy child standing straight and appearing tall and thin (Fig. 13-2). Physical development during this period is slow and follows an orderly sequence at a rate that is unique for each individual child.

Physical maturation

The child grows relatively more in height than weight during these years, gaining about 2 to 2½ in in height and approximately 5 lb. in weight per year.[2] Changes in body proportion occur because there are relatively large increments of growth in the trunk and legs. The head slows in growth rate as the brain approaches adult proportions. There is little difference in growth rate or size between boys and girls. (See Appendix B for growth charts.)

The preschooler's metabolic rate decreases from that of the toddler period. This decrease is reflected in the lowered vital signs. (See Tables 17-19 and 17-20 for normal ranges of the preschooler's vital signs.) Elevated vital signs in the preschooler often indicate stressful circumstances, such as extreme physical activity or

Figure 13-2 Preschoolers are thinner and stand taller than toddlers.

infections. Exposure to upper respiratory infections and childhood diseases increases during this period, when the child starts nursery school and has not yet developed immunity through frequent exposure. The eustachian tube is nearly horizontal at this stage, which causes more susceptibility to ear infections. A significant increase in respirations or pulse rate is the first evidence of an elevated temperature due to infection.

The preschooler's body systems undergo gradual development at varying rates. The most conspicuous development during the preschool period is related to the neuromuscular system.

Neuromuscular development Some of the most exciting behavioral changes or milestones noted in the physical development of the preschooler are related to the ability to control and coordinate the small and large voluntary muscles and to maintain visual attention.[3]

Development of the corticospinal tract is advanced enough to permit most movements, but full control does not occur until later adolescence. By 4 years of age, the child is clearly right- or left-handed.[4] Left-handed children may need encouragement and extra help in accomplishing such tasks as cutting with a scissors or tying a shoelace. Parents should allow children to utilize the dominant side since children not only do better in fine motor coordination but many emotional upsets can be avoided.

Visual development continues throughout the preschool period. The child of 4 has approximately 20/30 vision. The 4-year-old is usually ready to read, but since farsightedness (hyperopia) is normally present, print must be large to avoid eye strain. During this period referral to an ophthalmologist is indicated when strabismus is present or the eyes cross when the child is ill or fatigued. If strabismus is not corrected, amblyopia (dimming of vision and possibly loss of sight) can occur[5] (see Chap. 39).

Gross and fine motor development When vision and neuromuscular development are proceeding normally, gross and fine motor development can be assessed (see Tables 13-1 and 13-2). *Normative* (average for age) behaviors are helpful guidelines for determining a child's level of functioning. Decisions about individual needs of the child, play equipment, and health assessment can be made from these guidelines. Children who deviate significantly from average behaviors should be referred for workup and assistance. Chronological age by itself can be

Table 13-1 Gross motor development

Activity	3 years	4 years	5 years
Walking and running	Tandem walks a line without watching feet	Heel-toe walk	Backward heel-toe
	Walks backward		Skips
	Runs with smoothness, turns sharp corners, stops suddenly	Runs easily	Runs with skill, speed, and agility and plays games simultaneously
		Skips clumsily	
Stepping	Climbs upstairs alternating feet	Climbs downstairs alternating feet	
		Climbs without holding rail	
	Hops down three stairs on one foot	Hops on one leg	Hops well
		Hops down four to six stairs on one leg	
Throwing	Balances on one foot for 1 s	Balances on one foot for 5 s	Balances on one foot for 10 s
	Throws ball overhand		Throws and catches ball
	Catches ball with arms fully extended one out of three times	Catches ball thrown at 5 ft two to three times	Uses hands more than arms to catch ball
Jumping	Jumps from low step		Jumps three to four steps
	Jumps in place		Jumps rope
Other	Pedals tricycle	Climbs jungle gym	Roller-skates
	Swings		

Table 13-2 Fine motor development

Activity	3 years	4 years	5 years
Dressing	Undresses self, helps dress self	Dresses and undresses self except tying bows, closing zipper, putting on boots	Dresses self without assistance
	Undoes buttons on side or front of clothing	Buttons	Ties shoelaces
		Laces shoes but cannot tie bow	
		Distinguishes front	
Self-care	Washes hands, feeds self	Brushes teeth alone	Washes self without wetting clothes
	May brush own teeth		
Writing and drawing	Recognizes and draws a complete circle	Recognizes and draws crude square	Copies triangle for diamond
			Prints few letters or numbers crudely
	Draws crude cross	Combines two simple geometric forms	Can combine more than two geometric forms
	Tries to draw picture and name it	Draws crude three-part man	Draws six-part man
	Scribbles	Form and meaning in drawing apparent to adult	Draws clearly recognized lifelike representations, differentiates parts of drawing
			Prints some letters correctly
			Prints first name
			Knows there is a right and left side but cannot distinguish
			Definite hand preference
Play	Pours fluid from pitcher, with occasional spills	Likes water play	Likes water play
	Hits large pegs on board with hammer		Uses hammer to hit nail on head
	Begins to use scissors	Uses scissors without difficulty	Uses scissors and tools, like screwdriver, well
	Strings large beads	Enjoys fine manipulation of play materials	Folds paper diagonally
	Does puzzles by trial and error	Surveys puzzle before placing pieces	Does simple puzzles quickly and smoothly
		Matches simple geometric forms	
		Poor space perception	
	Builds tower of 9 to 10 blocks	Builds complicated structure extending vertically and laterally	Builds things out of large boxes
	Builds three-block gate	Builds five-block gate	Builds complex three-dimensional structure
		Notices missing parts—requests to fix	Disassembles and reassembles some objects

misleading as a basis for identifying deviations. To assess development, many aspects of gross and fine motor coordination are considered as well as the child's overall developmental pattern. Some children develop faster than others and some at a slower pace than the average. The pace depends on inherent factors and the extent to which these factors are stimulated by the environment.

Different types of movement emerge as a child develops. Much of a young child's movement is expressive; that is, these motor activities express emotions and needs. The young child expresses curiosity by direct involvement with objects; for example, a 3-year-old might be seen poking or pulling at the nose or eyes of a doll to see what it is all about. To relieve frustration a preschooler enjoys pounding on a peg board, molding play dough, swinging intensely, and doing other kinds of vigorous activity (Fig. 13-3).

Figure 13-3 Large-muscle activities express emotions and "let off steam" in the preschool period.

As hand-eye coordination becomes more precise and fine muscles are better controlled, the child becomes involved in *instrumental* movement, in which he or she learns to use instruments and tools. For example, a 3-year-old is usually unable to hammer a nail, while the 5-year-old can use a hammer to hit a nail on the head.

Physical health maintenance and promotion

Because of the high activity level of the preschooler, it is especially important to prevent accidents and promote good nutrition, exercise, and sleep to maintain adequate growth patterns and health. Signs of pathophysiology should be watched for since the child is often too busy to complain. Yearly visits should be made to the physician for preventive health examinations and immunization (see Table 6-5 for immunization schedule). Dental examinations should begin.

Accident prevention

Accidents are the leading cause of death of children between the ages of 2 and 5 years. One-third of preschool children suffer injuries requiring medical assistance, and many children develop permanent disabilities. Two-thirds of these serious accidents occur in the home. The leading types of accidents are injuries from motor vehicles, drowning, and burns. Other major causes include poisons; machinery, such as power tools and electrical equipment; projectile toys, such as darts, bows and arrows, and guns; and old refrigerators, freezers, and ditches.

Preschoolers under the age of 4 or preschoolers weighing less than 40 lb should be placed in car seats recommended by the National Safety Council. After the age of 4 lap safety belts should be used to avoid serious injury in case of accident. This should be emphasized to parents since these children resist restraint; this often causes the parents to become lax. Children in this age range are more frequently in pedestrian-vehicle accidents than within-vehicle accidents because of their spontaneity, well-developed gross motor abilities, and inability to recognize immediate dangers. The preschooler never seems to hesitate to chase a ball into the street, run the tricycle or big wheel down a driveway, or play between parked cars. Preschoolers climb fences, open gates, and unlock doors in order to gain access to the street.

The child, who is now old enough to understand simple explanations, should be taught to look both ways before entering a street, what red and green traffic lights mean, and to recognize pedestrian crossings. Explanations are not enough; good examples must be set by the parents. This is the age of imitation.

Prevention of household accidents should be approached from three aspects: removing dangers in the environment, providing adequate adult supervision, and teaching the child to understand potential dangers. Parents should be advised to make a complete inspection of the home and yard to identify and remove possible dangers before accidents occur. Caustic materials and medicines should be placed in locked and inaccessible cabinets; electrical equipment, machinery, and appliances should be put out of reach of children; dangerous toys should be removed or repaired; pools should have high fences and locked gates; and unused equipment such as refrigerators and freezers should have the doors removed or be removed from the premises (note Table 13-3).

Adequate adult supervision is still essential during the preschool period. Children this age do not have the ability to judge dangers. Because of their inquisitiveness, imagination, and physical activity, they can get into dangerous situations quickly. The preschooler must *never* be left alone and unsupervised, and it is certainly ill-advised to leave the preschooler in the care of older siblings unless the sibling is a responsible teenager who can make mature decisions and take aggressive action should danger occur. *At no time* is the preschooler to be left unattended around a swimming pool even when the child is able to swim. The child's swimming abilities are often overestimated, and the child may not recognize the potential danger.

Children cannot be protected against all dangers and must gradually learn to live in the world around them. Preschoolers are ready to learn to use simple equipment safely. Learning to saw, to use the stove, to carry scissors, to turn on the TV, or plug in a lamp can all be accomplished safely with simple explanations and praise. Encouraging these children to help around the home and introducing them to new experiences help them learn appropriate use of equipment and toys. Rules of safety for daily living must be learned: how to cross a street, how to behave in a swimming pool area, how and when to approach animals, and how to react to strangers. Nurses can help parents teach their children and can help them understand that their children need to be shown how to do things and given simple explanations. Often explanations must be repeated over and over again before they take on meaning and become part of a child's behavioral pattern. *Praise* should be given children when they do things safely and well. In addition, parents should not approach children with "don't" but should concentrate positively on *"how"* things are done safely and *"why"* things are done in certain ways to prevent accidents. Preschoolers are usually willing learners, enjoy assuming more responsibilities, and like receiving praise.

Table 13-3 Accident prevention for preschoolers*

Dangers at home	What they can do to protect themselves	What they need	What the family can do to protect them
Falls From windows, roofs, and trees **Burns** Food and caustics **Fire** Matches, lighters, inflammable clothing **Poisons** Liquid medicines, pills or colored particles, fluid in bottles, caustics, plant sprays, insect paste **Water** Bathtub, pools, ponds, and streams **Machinery** Wringers, lawn mowers, power tools, automobiles **Electricity** Probing outlets, tinkering with TV and light sockets **Toys** Projectile toys, guns, bow and arrow, darts, toys with points or sharp edges, cap guns	Have better muscles and coordination and are less likely to fall on stairs, etc. May have learned that stoves are hot, and that fire burns. Begin to get out of way of objects moving toward them. May have developed fear of water. Begin to reason and remember what has been taught. Begin to have a better concept of time and distance but have a long way to go.	They need kindness and affection. They need education integrated with protection and discipline for self-reliance and ability to perform safely. They need good examples of safe, orderly, and kind behavior from adults. They need exposure to new experiences and weaning from complete protection to be able to make decisions for themselves. They need to learn that limitations and rules are for their protection as well as for the rights of others. They need to share and to take turns. They need the basis for the kinds of attitudes and actions which will last them the rest of their lives.	Think ahead. Make plans and carry them out. Learn the common developmental sequences which all children reach sooner or later. Anticipate the subtle as well as obvious hazards which the children will be exposed to or will seek on their way to learning what life is all about. Survey the home and eliminate those danger spots. Do it *before*, not after. Educate—show and explain over and over again (sometimes 10 times a day) *how to do things safely*. Concentrate on "how" and "why" rather than "don't." Provide experience rather than limiting activity. Provide *planned* play equipment, including large packing boxes, large blocks or construction toys, colored books and art materials, dolls, simple toys that do things, and housekeeping toys.

Table 13-3 Accident prevention for preschoolers* (*Continued*)

Dangers at home	What they can do to protect themselves	What they need	What the family can do to protect them
Odds and ends			
Old refrigerators, old wells and ditches, sharp garden and household knives and tools			Expect them to do as you do—not as you say. Demonstrate respect for law and order, and the need to be considerate of the rights and feelings of others. Set limits and explain "why." Let them make choices but don't expect them to make decisions which are beyond them. Let them help with every task that is within their ability and help them use their mind and muscles. Give them "on the job" safety education. Teach them to do things and to use tools and toys. Teach them how to swim, how and when to cross the street, who they are and where they live, situations where they must ask permission, and manners. Plan with them and arrange for them to visit friends after school and to be away from the family for several hours or overnight. Teach them to be courteous, but not to accept favors or rides from strangers. Plan and do live safely and relax!

* Compiled by Hope Ecklund, R.N., P.H.N., M.P.H.
Source: *Accident Prevention Through Growth and Development Patterns*, San Francisco Department of Public Health.

Nutrition

The preschooler's appetite fluctuates continually. Periods of overeating or refusing certain foods occur but do not persist. Food fads and strong taste preferences, common in the toddler period, also occur among some young preschoolers. Around the age of 4 finicky eating is not unusual. The attention span of 3- and 4-year-olds often prohibits them from sitting quietly through a family meal. In contrast, 5-year-olds are more open to the introduction of new foods because of their maturity level, acquisition of new interest in taste, lengthened attention span, and sociability.

Parents should be aware of this fluctuation to prevent overconcern that can readily lead to conflict between the parents and child. Generally speaking, the child who is offered an adequate diet, in small portions, including the four major food groups, will over a period of time (1 month or longer) be eating an adequate diet. Parents' concern regarding food "jags" can be eased by having them keep a daily log for several weeks of the amount and type of food consumed by the child. It is comforting for the parents to see the actual quality and amount of food consumed over time and the gradually diminishing food jag. Parents should know that it is the quality of foods consumed, not the quantity, which is of primary importance, and that the appetite will improve as school age approaches and the growth rate increases.

Preschoolers need approximately 1400 to 1800 cal per day (90 cal/kg or 40 cal/lb.). Of the total caloric intake the child should receive about 1.0 g of protein per pound of body weight, half of which should be from animal origin to ensure adequate intake of amino acids, B complex vitamins, vitamin D, and such minerals as calcium and iron. During this period there is an increase in the deposit of minerals in the bones. Specifically, calcium and phosphorus are necessary for bone and tooth mineralization.

Preschoolers eat only a little more than toddlers. Servings for the preschooler are about half the size of an adult serving. An adequate daily diet for the preschooler includes approximately $1\frac{1}{2}$ pints of milk, four or more servings of vegetables and fruits, two servings of meat or meat substitutes, and four servings of bread and cereal. Three meals daily plus a midmorning, midafternoon, and evening snack should be provided because of the child's high activity level and inability to sit for long periods at a meal. Parents should choose snacks that augment the daily diet and avoid such "empty calorie" foods as potato chips, candy, and carbonated drinks. Snacks may include milk, juice, ice cream, raisins, cut-up fresh vegetables and fruits, cheese, and peanut butter with crackers. Such a diet not only begins to establish good eating habits and adequate nutrition but also prevents health problems associated with a poor diet, such as malnutrition, dental caries, and anemia.

Children should eat with their families. The family meal time is an important aspect of the socialization process and ideally provides a happy, warm, and accepting time in the daily routine. Children learn social customs, language skills, and the family's standards of behavior through interaction and identification with their parents and older siblings. Table manners should not be emphasized since this may lead to rebellion. Children learn adequately by example but do make mistakes and have accidents. Compliments on good behavior reinforce good table manners, but negative comments are to be avoided.

To encourage children to eat new foods or increase food consumption, no snacks should be allowed during the hour before meals. Other suggestions might include having the child assist in meal preparation, providing a quiet time before meals, providing a chair that is high enough and utensils that are small enough for the child, allowing the child sufficient time to eat, and allowing the child to leave the table when he or she appears restless. During meals avoid making food an issue through coaxing, bribing, or threatening since this is the root of many later eating problems.

Children's plates embossed with "Superman" or "Wonderwoman" do wonders for the appetite. Large servings tend to "turn off" the appetite. If the child desires he or she may ask for more; this promotes a feeling of achievement in the child. In preparation of foods, flavor, texture, form, and color should be considered. Foods should have a mild flavor, be served attractively, and where possible be served individually rather than in such mixtures as casseroles, stews, or salads. Preschoolers prefer meat, cut up in bite-sized pieces, and fruit. They are resistant to vegetables unless the vegetables are uncooked and cut into bite-sized pieces that can be picked up with the fingers. New foods should be introduced gradually. Parents should not insist that new foods be eaten. Children will eventually experiment with new foods if exposed to them often enough.

The exact amount of food intake must be determined before a conclusion is made that a child is eating insufficiently. If the child is eating poorly, the following causes should be explored: (1) poor eating habits, such as excessive snacking, unavailability of adequate varieties and quantities of foods, foods too highly seasoned; (2) poor meal-time socialization, such as irregular family meal schedule, unhappy or confusing mealtime atmosphere, excessive parental expectations, nagging; (3) physical problems, such as illness, overfatigue, tooth decay; and (4) emotional disturbances, such as phobias, fears, sibling rivalry. Specific causes must be identified and where necessary the child referred for further evaluation and intervention before physical or psychological damage occurs.

Exercise, rest, and sleep

Since this is a period of great activity and energy, there usually is little need to be concerned about exercise. If a child is "glued" to television or other passive activities, outside play should be encouraged and television limited. One or two hours of selected television programs are more than adequate each day. Family outings and nursery school are two modes for encouraging physical activity.

For the normally active child activity periods should be alternated with periods of rest or quiet (Fig. 13-4). Quiet times may include a rest or nap period after lunch, a reading time with mother or father, or perhaps watching "Sesame Street" on television. Without adequate rest periods during the day the child can readily become fatigued, which may lead to irritability, poor resistance to infections, and restless nighttime sleep. The 3-year-old may not sleep at naptime but will usually rest quietly for at least an hour. Four- and five-year-olds usually do not need naps if they get adequate sleep at night. Nevertheless, a quiet time is still important for reducing fatigue.

Nighttime sleep decreases for the preschooler

Figure 13-4 Care must be taken to alternate activity with rest periods.

to 10 to 12 h. However, children vary widely in the amount of sleep they need. Some function well with as little as 8 h of sleep while others require 14. Parents need to understand this variation and provide for a period of uninterrupted sleep in a conducive environment. Bedtime around 8 P.M. will achieve a long enough sleep period during the night.

Since it is a common practice for children to watch television in the early evening hours, parents should select television programs appropriate for a preschooler's viewing. High-action, bizarre, and violent programs should be avoided since they tend to overstimulate the child and promote nightmares or difficulty settling down to sleep. Ideally, early evening television is a family affair where parents and children together view carefully selected programs that parents discuss with their children. Not only are the children participating with adults in a mutually enjoyable experience, they also are being provided with an excellent learning experience. In addition, parents can monitor their children's reactions to the content of programs and prevent misunderstanding and overstimulation by providing simple and logical explanations.

If possible, the child should sleep in his own room and in his own bed. The room should be located away from noise and other distractions, such as television and the dishwasher. Frequently siblings do share rooms; it is helpful to place children with similar sleep patterns in the same room. Sleeping conditions should be carefully assessed. Poor sleeping patterns are related to physical illness and poor learning performance. Some children from large families in the lower socioeconomic level sleep on the floor or in the same bed with several siblings—a practice which is not conducive to good sleep.

Although they like to postpone bedtime, preschoolers are quite ritualistic about bedtime and respond well to routines and a specific hour for bed. There should be a quieting down period before bedtime that may include bathing, reading, listening to records, and saying prayers. This is a prime time for the preschooler to spend with parents in slowly unwinding from the activities of the day and gradually moving toward bedding down. Some preschoolers still feel more secure when taking a favorite toy or blanket to bed with them. Instruct parents to allow this. This *tran-*

sitional object, the favorite blanket or teddy bear, is something special. It represents security and familiarity which helps the child separate from "Mommy" and the active household to enter the quiet and seclusion of his own room.

Three and four-year-olds may wake up during the night to urinate, and most still have an occasional "accident." Often these accidents are associated with dreams and nightmares, a normal occurrence in this period. When awaking from dreams, a child is often extremely fearful and upset. It is difficult for the child to separate reality from the dream or fantasy world. The preschooler's active imagination can lead to terrifying experiences. The curtains become moving monsters in the dark, the unlit lamp a lurking vulture, the electric cord a snake! Parents should reassure a child upon awakening from such dreams by turning on the light and gently talking to him or her. The child should be reassured that there are no "monsters," and what is actually being seen should be explained. This helps the child distinguish reality from fantasy. Rocking in a chair, gently stroking the back, and singing lullabies often calm the child. If these measures are not sufficient to get the child back to sleep, it may be well to sleep with the child for a few hours. Allowing the child frequently to crawl in bed with the parents can lead to a habit most difficult to break. It is best to sleep with the child in his or her own room. Parents should be cautioned not to make a _habit_ of sleeping with the child since some children may use night fears as a way of gaining attention from the parents.

Psychological health and development

The development of a healthy personality is as important as physical development. Healthy psychological and emotional development is critically important throughout the preschool years. Hereditary, physical, environmental, and social factors play a significant role in the development of a healthy personality. The influence of methods of socialization on personality development are discussed in the following section.

Freud first identified the preschool period as the _Oedipal stage_ of development, emphasizing heredity (gender) as the prime factor for development. He recognized that sexual identification and development of the superego (conscience) occur between the ages of 3 and 5. Later Erik Erikson, who expanded Freud's stages and included the importance of socialization, posited that the child gains a sense of _initiative_ during this period as a result of adequate environmental stimulation and support from family members and other significant adults.

Initiative vs. guilt[6]

Initiative is the channeling of energy to plan and undertake activities or attack problems. That is, preschoolers learn to give direction and purpose to activities by _making things_ and by _making like_ or imitating other people in their play. For example, little boys love to build castles in the sand or wooden rockets to fly to Mars or play astronaut or fireman. Little girls love to make mud cakes, dress dolls, and dress up like admired adults. The preschooler's high energy level, motor development, cognitive development, curiosity, and imagination motivate the child to seek activities with assertion and aggression tempered with some judgment and self-confidence. To accomplish a sense of initiative the child must have a safe but stimulating environment where exploration can be _freely_ carried out under _adult supervision_. The child must have the opportunity to explore the wonderful world of people and the fascinating world of things (Fig. 13-5). The supervising adult should praise appropriate behavior and encourage imagination and creativity. Discipline should be restricted to acts which are morally wrong, socially unacceptable, destruc-

Figure 13-5 The child must be provided with a safe and stimulating environment under adult supervision.

tive, or harmful to the child or others. When discipline is necessary, the child needs to have a simple explanation of why the behavior was inappropriate and to be guided to more constructive activities. For example, the nurse might say, "You must stop hitting Johnnie because it hurts him like it hurts when someone hits you. You feel angry and want to hit. Maybe if you pound this clay you will feel better." In this way a true sense of initiative can be developed. As part of the process, too, the child is learning self-confidence, sex and social role identification, social behavior and self-control, and moral and ethical values.

If the child does not develop a positive sense of initiative, then a sense of *guilt* is developed. The child feels defeated, angry, afraid of attempting projects, accountable for things he or she really is not responsible for, and generally guilty. The child is often timid about people and new experiences and lacks interest in other children or adults. The sense of guilt develops from lack of positive recognition for achievement, stifled initiative because an adult does things for the child, lack of opportunity to try out new things, and limited play time to fantasize and interact with other children. Criticism, too, can cause feelings of guilt in children. Too often, one can hear adults saying to a preschooler, "That's nice, but you could do it better if . . .," or "Try it again, that's not good." Such comments cause the child to become anxious, frightened, and reluctant to attempt new tasks. The child should be approached more positively with comments such as, "You really worked hard."

The sense of guilt is frequently evident in the passive child, who will become an inhibited and dependent adult, avoiding new experiences and responsibilities. Some symptoms of serious disturbances in personality development during this period include: enuresis (see Chap. 42), nonspeaking, inappropriate play, withdrawal from peers, assaultiveness, destructiveness, night terrors, and persistent fears.

Sex and social role identification

The preschooler's insatiable curiosity, awareness of himself or herself as different from others, increased sense of balance and spatial orientation, development of cognitive and language skills, and increased neurological maturation lead to the development of *body image*, i.e., what the child believes his or her own body to be. One aspect of body image is gender. Children examine themselves, compare their own physical attributes with those of others, and soon become aware that there are sexual differences. The preschooler's play of "doctor" and attempts to hide in the bathroom with a friend to explore are both normal behaviors at this period. The child is simply learning about his or her body; this does not indicate later homosexuality. Parents should avoid shaming the children but distract them to another activity. By 3 and 4 years the child has developed an awareness of gender and is becoming increasingly aware of the physical attributes of the two sexes. Boys know they are boys; girls know they are girls.

Sex roles, those roles that society approves as characteristic of males and females, involve behavior as well as feelings, attitudes, motives, and beliefs. The actual behaviors, feelings, attitudes, motives, and beliefs a child takes on become part of the child's personality and determine that child's *sex-role identity*. The process by which the child develops sex-role identity is *identification*[7] (see Fig. 13-6).

Identification is the process whereby the child imitates and acquires some of the attributes of parents, siblings, or others. Freud, who first introduced identification, believed that girls identify with their mothers and boys with their fathers. Research has found that a child actually identifies with a person or persons who have certain qualities that the child *values*. Those qualities are (1) that there is a physical or psychological similarity between the child and the person, (2) that the person is nurturant to the child, and (3) that the person holds a position desired by the child such as a special power, love from others, or task competence.[8] A child may identify with people other than the same-sex parent. Identification is the strongest when all the three qualities are present. For example, Johnnie's father is a loving person, gives Johnnie much attention, and is a well-known football player. Johnnie feels his father's concern over him and is impressed with his father's fame and physical prowess. He wants to be like "Daddy." Johnnie, then, begins to walk like Daddy, talk like Daddy, and even has his own football uniform which he wears constantly—Johnnie is identifying with his father.

Our society traditionally defines masculine

attributes to include aggressiveness, independence, and emotional control; while feminine attributes are passiveness, nurturance, poise, and attractiveness.[9] A child who adopts the sex role behaviors that are approved in his or her social group is likely to be accepted by peers because he or she behaves the way a boy or girl is expected to behave. Conversely, a child who does not behave as expected by society may have difficulty being accepted by peers during later childhood.

Five-year-old Erica, whose family consists of a passive father, a mother who is aggressive and independent, and three older brothers, has identified with her mother and to some extent her oldest brother, who is the family favorite. Erica's nursery school teacher reports that Erica is frequently involved in fighting, uses foul language, and has little involvement in cooperative play. Erica is not playing the role that is expected by society. Erica, and other "tomboys," will probably be pressured to adopt traditional feminine roles at puberty.

To prevent serious personality disturbances, especially those associated with sex-role identity, children must be exposed to adequate female and male role models. This is not always easy to do because of the many different family structures in our society. One-parent families may not provide adequate adult role models for the child to imitate and identify with. A mother or father raising a child alone needs to provide a same-sex figure from whom the child can learn sex roles. Relatives or "Big Brother" organizations often provide positive, substitute relationships.

Although extremely important, identification is only one aspect of learning sex-role behavior. Child-rearing practices also play a significant part. The parents' method of rewarding the child for specific male or female behaviors and their attitudes and expectations of the child help to mold the child into the appropriate sex role. Parents' expectations are continually displayed.

Until World War I sex roles were strictly defined and were handed down from generation to generation. These sex roles, often described in "gothic novels," are traditional sex role stereotypes. Sex stereotypes are today less rigid but continue to exist. The blend of sex role stereotypes learned by the child depends upon the family's orientation and socioeconomic class. The lower socioeconomic classes tend to have

Figure 13-6 Preschoolers learn sex-role identity by identifying with and imitating their like-sexed parents.

more traditional sex stereotypes, wherein the mother cares for the home without the father's help and the father is the breadwinner. The expectations of middle-class parents are more flexible. Middle class parents allow their children to play with either traditional boy or girl toys until age 6 or 7 years. Lower economic class parents restrict their children's toys appropriate to the traditional sex role at an early age.

Sex role adoption begins with learning to act the appropriate sex role. The child learns which objects are appropriate for his or her role. Parents choose toys, books, and clothes they consider suitable. Though both sexes may today wear jeans, many parents would disapprove of their son's repeated experimentation and application of lipstick. They would probably substitute a traditionally appropriate razor or pipe. Since sex role learning is a gradual process, the child next adopts the attitudes of parents and society toward that role. Girls are often, even today, protected from injury, restricted from frequent fighting, and encouraged to cry and to express emotions. Boys are often expected to express aggression, fight more, be dirtier than girls, and not be a "crybaby." A parent may typically scold Bobby for kicking Jenny but instead tell Bobby, who was kicked and beaten by another boy, "Boy, go out and kick him harder, and don't cry!" Parents use these responses almost automatically and are not always aware of their influence on molding sex role behavior.

Even with the feminist movement, traditional sex role stereotypes remain. Because girls receive conflicting messages and male sex role behavior is more strictly defined, girls, such as Erica, often have more difficulty than boys in adopting the socially expected sex role attitudes and behavior.

All children seek approval, and approval is one of the most common and powerful motivators for behavior. When approval is given consistently and repeatedly for a specific sex role behavior, such as bravery or gentleness, children usually adopt the behavior to gain approval.

Sex education

Parents' attitudes and approach towards sex education also influence the child's attitudes and beliefs about sex roles. Because of their curiosity and developing sexual identity, preschoolers invariably are interested in "where did I come from" or "how are babies made." For such information they must rely almost exclusively on parents. If parents refuse answers, appear highly anxious in discussing sexual subjects, or imply to a child that the subject is "taboo" or "dirty," children often develop similar attitudes. When approached with questions about sex, parents tend either to close communication or to overwhelm the child with information. Four helpful guidelines to follow in answering preschoolers' questions are: (1) remain calm—do not show anxiety, confusion, or concern over the question; (2) find out from the child *why* he or she is asking the question; (3) find out *what* the child *knows* about the subject in question; and then (4) provide the child with a *simple, honest* answer.

Parents should be advised that these questions will come up during the preschool period. In this way the parents can be prepared with appropriate information and can provide their children with objective answers. This will also prevent the transference of anxiety or negative attitudes. Asking *why* a child asked a question will aid the parent in understanding what type of answer the child expects. For example, 4-year-old Sandy asks, "Mommie, where did I come from?" The mother replies, "Why do you ask?" The child responds, "Because Riza came from New York, did I too?" With this approach the mother discovers that the child's intent was not for sexual information at all, which is often the case.

Now assume that the mother's inquiry of why was met with the following question from Sandy: "Well—how did you make me?" In order to respond adequately the mother needs to be aware of what the child actually knows in order to provide a simple answer or to correct any misconceptions. Preschool children often have strange ideas about procreation as a result of misinformation, their inability to think logically, and their absorption in the world of fantasy. Mother may now ask, "Sandy, how do you think I made you?" Sandy will now tell mother what she needs to know: "Well, I thought I grew in your stomach but my food goes there!" Now the mother knows that the child needs to know the difference between the stomach, abdomen, and uterus. The child wants only one short explanation, a *simple* answer that she can comprehend. Honest, simple, and factual information is given with the use of anatomic terms which build a pathway for further knowledge. If the child does not comprehend at first, or forgets or misinterprets the explanation, factual material can be restated when the child is able to absorb the information. When the child is ready for further information and is able to handle more complexities, questions will follow about eggs, sperm, or how the baby "gets in" and "comes out." Questions should be answered one at a time and only as they are presented.

Often pictures aid in explanations to questions, and parents may need assistance in providing adequate explanations to children. There are many excellent sex education books to help parents meet the needs of the preschooler.[10] Books should be reviewed by the parents before presenting the material to the child, so that the parents will be comfortable and familiar with the material.

Conscience and moral development

Moral development, which Freud called super-ego or conscience development, has strong roots in the preschool years. *Moral development* is the adoption of cultural standards of social behavior. The child is learning what constitutes "right" and "wrong" and "good" and "bad" behavior. The preschooler begins to behave morally to avoid feelings of guilt and is beginning to use self-control to resist temptation.

Moral development is an outgrowth of identification and of child-rearing practices, especially those associated with reward and punishment. Through identification the child begins to imitate the parents by following social rules such as not eating with a knife but with a fork, not pushing or shoving others around, and answering honestly when asked a question. At the same time parents acknowledge the child for "obeying the rules" by approving and disapproving. For example, if a child lies, the parent may respond, "Don't tell lies, people won't like you if you do," or "Lies will get you in big trouble." If the child is truthful, a response from the parent may be, "I am glad you told the truth, that makes me feel really good." Through consistent rewards for good behavior and punishment for bad behavior, children develop a conscience. They begin to accept the rules and to feel guilty when they do not follow the rules, even when an adult is not present to reprimand them. Guilty feelings are highly uncomfortable, and so children try to avoid "breaking the rules" in order to prevent discomfort. Children avoid breaking the rules by self-control or the postponement of desires. For example, 5-year-old Traci just loves her friend's little doll lying on the table and wants it very badly. No one is in the room at the moment, so she picks it up and is tempted to put it in her pocket. Suddenly Traci feels very uncomfortable and can almost hear her mother say, "I don't want to be around anybody who steals." She puts the doll back on the table.

Conscience development is dependent on a *warm, consistent* relationship with adults, especially the parents. If the child perceives the parent as loving, wants to please the parent, and is fearful of losing parental love if he or she does not please the parent, the child will develop a healthy conscience. However, if the child feels greatly threatened by the parent, especially with regard to the loss of parental love, initiative and creativity can be inhibited. That is, the "overde-veloped" conscience can prevent the child from becoming involved in new activities or social situations simply because there is fear of not performing well enough to please the parent. This type of situation can be avoided if the parents do not demand more than that of which the child is capable and use punishment wisely. When the child is reprimanded for poor behavior, an explanation of *why* the behavior was unacceptable should be given. Focus is made on *the behavior itself* rather than on the relationship betweeen the parent and child. For example, the parent might say, "I don't like to hear the language you are using," not "I don't want you around me when you are talking that way," or "you're a bad boy for talking that way."

Lack of a consistent, warm relationship with a parent can result in the child's developing a weak conscience. This can occur in families where the parents are too busy to bother with their children. The child does not internalize the social rules and feels no guilt over not following the rules. These children appear unruly and mischievous and may later become delinquent. They are unable to follow the social and moral standards of society.

Socialization and the learning process

Socialization, the eventual transformation of a child into an adult participant in society, begins actively in the preschool years. At this time the child moves beyond the home environment out into a social world. Rules of behavior are learned and enforced and social roles defined, practiced, and learned.

A child is socialized by formal and informal means. Formal social learning (socialization) is the deliberate and controlled attempt to mold children into specific social roles by such social institutions as schools and churches. The young child is primarily socialized informally through exposure to parents and family. The preschool years are significant because very few demands can be imposed on the infant or toddler, while the preschooler is able and must learn to adapt to society. Informal types of social learning include insight and unfolding, imitation and identification, reinforcement and conditioning, and guidance and discipline.

Learning by insight and unfolding occurs as a result of the child's maturation. Natural unfolding refers to the child's spontaneously becoming able to carry out a behavior when the physiological capacity is present. For example, a child may suddenly learn to skip without ever having seen another person skip. *Insightful learning* refers to that moment when a child realizes a relationship or some significance during play, exploration, or experimentation. Reinforcement, conditioning, guidance, and discipline are modes of teaching. How these modes are utilized by parents is termed *child rearing practices*.

Reinforcement and conditioning

So much must be learned by the child in these preschool years, and so much must be taught by the parent: How to behave toward adults and peers; how to bathe, dress, and pick up the bedroom or playroom; how to behave at the table or in the living room; and so on. Much of this learning is determined in the preschool years through the use of reinforcement and conditioning. Parents value certain behaviors while others may not be accepted. Almost automatically or unconsciously parents reward or punish their children until the "right" behavior is finally carried out. This is called *conditioning*, a form of learning in which the frequency of a certain behavior is increased or decreased by a system of rewards or punishment to influence the behavior. *Reinforcement* has occurred when the behavior has increased because of the reward. For example, mother wants Janie to wash her hands before every meal. Each time Janie washes her hands before a meal without being asked, mother rewards Janie's behavior by a hug and the comment, "You make me so happy that you remembered to wash your hands." After a time Janie washes her hands before every meal (reinforcement has occurred).

Rewards, parental actions which give the child approval or pleasure, are most influential in leading the child to learn and adopt the rewarded behavior. Behaviors that gain disapproval, punishment, or no reaction from the parents tend to be abandoned. Therefore, how the parents or other significant adults react to the child's behavior determines which behaviors will be learned.[11]

Reinforcement not only helps explain the social development of the child but also is an important tool with which to improve child behavior. To teach a child a set of behaviors, the desired behaviors must be identified and only one small behavior change must be required at a time. Too much cannot be expected of the child. Once parents are aware of the behavior they wish to encourage, advise parents to show *consistent* approval of the behavior when it occurs. Reward must occur right after the behavior appears if the reward is to be effective and given each time the behavior appears over several weeks. This can be a most effective method of teaching a child how to behave appropriately in the social world.

Guidance and discipline

The preschooler must learn to understand and obey the rules and get along with others. *Discipline*, guidance in helping the child to understand and follow social rules and behavior, is essential to the attainment of this goal. The preschooler is struggling to gain control over inner impulses and needs, first of all, the establishment of limits of behavior.

Setting limits for the child provides a frame in which the child can function with freedom and safety. For example, the preschooler may be told to "play in the back yard and not on the street" or "not to hit or shove." If the child goes beyond these limits, disciplinary action is carried out. Children of all ages need to have established limits; limits are essential for the adventurous and ever-curious preschooler. The establishment and enforcement of limits provides the child with a clear definition of what he or she can and cannot do. This gives the child a feeling of security. When limits are set, they must be clearly explained to the child. Limit setting and disciplinary action must be consistent in order to be effective. If a rule is in effect one day, it should also be in effect the next; or if disciplinary action has been suggested to the child, it should be immediately carried out. Being consistent avoids confusion and anxiety in the child. However, limits must have some flexibility since extenuating circumstances do arise.

Disciplinary measures which are most effective with preschoolers include time-out, diversion, and offering restricted choices. *Time-out* consists of removing a child from a situation for a short period. For example, 4-year-old Scotty and Tony are suddenly pounding each other and pulling each other's hair. Mother requests they stop but the fight continues on! Mother picks up kicking

Scotty and removes him to his room, where he must remain for several minutes until he settles down. She then offers Scotty an explanation. A few minutes alone seems like an eternity to the preschooler and has an amazing calming effect.

Diversion is most effective when used with a child who repeats unacceptable behavior. With this technique the child is diverted to another activity and is given an explanation. For example, Karen persists in throwing sand at her playmates. She is asked to stop but refuses. The teacher then states, "You must stop throwing sand—it may get in someone's eye. Here, let's throw the big red ball instead." Karen takes the ball and throws it to her teacher. She has been diverted from an unacceptable behavior to one that is acceptable. The preschooler is quickly interested in and diverted to another activity because of his or her short attention span.

Offering restricted choices is a helpful technique when there is some danger involved in a child's activity. It offers an alternative to repeating "Stop it." In this technique, the child may continue the activity but in some way must modify it. For example, Jackie and his 4-year-old friends are furiously and continuously riding their big wheels down the driveway toward the street. Mother is worried they might enter the street and requests a change in the activity: "You may ride your wheels, but you will have to do it in the backyard. There is too much danger if you would accidentally go into the street." Here the children have the choice of continuing to ride if they go to the backyard or of ceasing the activity.

Play and socialization

Play, often referred to as the *child's work*, is one of the major modes of learning during the preschool years. Play enhances physical and cognitive development by providing opportunities for coordination of fine and gross motor development and development of depth perception, spatial relationships, and other sensory experiences. Play also stimulates curiosity and the development and use of vocabulary.

Play nurtures psychological and social development by providing situations where the child can imitate and practice adult roles to learn sex-role identification. Social behaviors and rules are developed and practiced in social play. Play also helps the child to overcome the feeling of powerlessness in the big world of adults as the child exercises control over the small world of manageable toys. Through the medium of play, the child is able to work out such negative feelings as anxiety, fear, and anger in a relatively non-threatening and socially acceptable manner. (See Chap. 16 for a discussion of play and the hospitalized child.) If the child is angry, a ball can be kicked, a hammer pounded, or a doll spanked without punishment.

The child can play alone, with peers, or with adults. Preschool children primarily enjoy play with peers and adults. They are very social. For this reason parents should be encouraged to seek opportunities for children to socialize with their own age group and to provide time in which to play with each of their children on a daily basis. Parental involvement in play activities is considered "prime time" for learning and establishing relationships. Games and activities are taught and learned that otherwise may not be and warm relationships are developed through mutual pleasure and enjoyment. Also, a mutual appreciation of one another as individuals is developed.

The preschooler's tremendous drive for social involvement sometimes leads to having an *imaginary playmate*. The adoption of an imaginary playmate is directly related to the child's ability to fantasize and is a normal behavior at this period. Imaginary playmates serve several purposes: They provide companionship in times of loneliness, are patient and understanding of accomplishments and failures, are sympathetic about problems that no adults seem to comprehend, and always play what the child wishes. Children soon give up the imaginary playmate as they become more involved with real friends and activities and as they approach entrance into school.

Solitary and parallel play, most frequently seen in the toddler period (see Chap. 12), persist in the preschool years, when the child feels a need to withdraw from the group or be alone. However, preschoolers are very social, and their predominant forms of play are *associative* and *cooperative* play. *Associative play* occurs when children engage in a common activity with only loosely established rules. (Fig. 13-7). No child takes leadership, there are no goals, and there is no division of functions. An example of associative play is seen when two children are playing in a sandbox

Figure 13-7 Associative play occurs when children engage in a common activity where rules are loosely established.

next to one another. They pass each other shovels, strainers, and other toys and carry on a conversation about their activities. They play in association with one another.

In *cooperative play* children cooperate in activities such as games, playing house, and building a spaceship. Children assume specific functions and roles, such as mother, father, or fire chief. Rules are established for play, and there is a feeling of belonging to the group. The group is structured so that there are definite leaders and followers with one or several children assuming the leadership and directing the activity.

Children, however, are not always involved in direct social interaction. A child who feels insecure about joining a group or is tired may become an *onlooker*. The onlooker may not actively be participating in an activity but is passively involved by observing and learning. This type of play is normal but if prolonged may also suggest that a child needs adult assistance in entering a group. Onlooker behavior must be differentiated from that of withdrawal, a symptom of psychological disturbance. The withdrawing child shows little interest in what is going on and manifests this behavior in much of the daily routine. When wthdrawal is a pattern of behavior, referral for assessment and treatment is necessary.

Children actively socializing with their peers need constant adult supervision. Parents must provide adequate opportunities for play, stimulating and safe play equipment and materials,

and a safe environment and safety rules before play begins. Allow children to develop their own play activities, try things out for themselves, and work out their own differences whenever possible. Structuring activities limits the child's interest and curiosity. Allow the child to play freely with little adult interference unless the child needs help or the play is unsafe. When children cannot work out their problems, divert the child or substitute an activity. An adult should join in the child's play only when requested by the child; these occasions provide wonderful opportunities for the adult to view the fascinating world of the child.

Play activities, equipment, and materials should provide for gross motor play, creative play, dramatic play, and quiet play. *Gross motor play* provides opportunity for the development and refinement of motor skills, such as running, jumping, climbing, and tricycle riding. *Creative play* promotes fine motor coordination, self-expression, and practice in manipulation and construction. Creative activities including painting, pasting, cutting, manipulation of carpentry tools, musical toys, and building with small blocks. *Dramatic play* enhances the process of identification and the learning of social roles by providing an opportunity to imitate and pretend. This type of play is most characteristic of the preschooler. Play houses, dress-up clothes, housekeeping toys, dollhouses, farm sets, trucks, little cars, planes, and dolls all provide materials with which to carry out dramatic play. *Quiet play* occurs primarily where activity is very limited or where the child is passively involved. Quiet play activities include looking at books, listening to stories, being read to, listening to records, or watching television. Some aspects of creative play may also be included under quiet play activities (see Fig. 13-8), such as the making of puzzles or doing simple handcrafts. All children need periods of quiet play to wind down from more strenuous activities before mealtimes and bedtime. Quiet play also plays a significant role when children feel tired or are ill.

Play activities and equipment should be selected in accordance with the developmental level of the child and the desired goals (note Table 13-4). Goals may include providing a specific learning experience, an opportunity for socializing, a chance to release energy, or a moment of relaxation. Toys must be durable since damage occurs from use and experimentation. Toys that will cause family disturbances if lost or damaged must not be purchased. The preschooler is not able to appreciate value and cannot be responsible for all his or her actions. A great many play materials are inexpensive (see Fig. 13-9). Children love cuddly handmade rag dolls, dollhouses built out of wooden boxes, old clothes from the parents' closet, homemade play dough, large cardboard boxes, and spare wood, nails, and hammers. Jungle gyms, play houses, and housekeeping furniture can be made from poles, ladders, pipes, large boxes, and wood. Sandboxes can easily be dug in the yard. Pieces of cloth, beans, macaroni, sticks, and leaves with paper and glue make great inexpensive creative materials. Puppets can be made from peanut shells, paper bags, or discarded toilet-paper rolls. Plastic jars, boxes, and discarded juice containers are perfect toys for sand and water play. For the preschooler some of the best things in life to play with are free and easily accessible.

Figure 13-8 A child may need time out from group activities to engage in quiet play.

Table 13-4 Suggested play activities for the preschooler

	3 years	4 years	5 years
Gross motor play	Swings Slides Tricycles Sandbox Wading pool Wagons	Rope ladders Jungle gym Swimming Trapeze	Roller skates Ball playing Bicycle with training wheels
Creative play	Sand play Water play Play dough and clay Finger painting Large blocks Musical toys	Crayons and chalk drawing Easel painting Rhythm band Simple puzzles	Cutting pictures Carpentry tools Simple sewing and handcraft Puzzles
Dramatic play	Block building Farm animal toys Dolls Dollhouses Trucks, cars, planes Toy phones	Dress-up clothes Group play Housekeeping toys Store play toys Nurse and doctor kits Wooden boxes	Paper puppets Handkerchief puppets Large wooden and cardboard boxes Pedal cars and trucks
Quiet play	Books—fairy tales Nursery rhymes and stories Children's records	Books—fairy tales and adventures	Books about real adventures of people and animals Selected television programs
Games	Where is Thumbkin? Mulberry bush Clapping games Eentsy-weentsy spider	Simon Says Dog and Bone Two little blackbirds	Bean bag throw Skip tag Ball play Hide and seek

Figure 13-9 A nursery school jungle gym built entirely of discarded materials found in the community.

Nursery school

As parents become more aware of their children's social needs and more mothers are working, increased numbers of children are attending nursery schools. There has recently been an upsurge of nursery schools called *day care centers*, which provide care over extended periods. The intent of day care centers is to provide complete child care for children whose parents work or attend school. In the past nursery schools have focused primarily on providing the child with supplemental social and learning experiences.

The more time the child spends in nursery school, the greater the influence the school will exert on the child's social and psychological development. Careful selection of nursery schools is very important. The following criteria are necessary to provide an optimum environment for the child:

1. The nursery school or day care center must be licensed by the state. This establishes minimum standards for safety and care.
2. The staff must include several members with 1 or more years of academic preparation in early childhood education or child development. One staff member to every four children is considered a safe ratio of supervision.
3. Facilities must include a safe environment for both indoor and outdoor play, including appropriate play equipment for gross motor, creative, dramatic, and quiet play.
4. Parents should know and agree with the philosophy of the staff regarding education, child rearing, and discipline.
5. Facilities must include adequate meal services, bathrooms, areas for rest, and individual places for the child's personal belongings.
6. Health services may not be provided but health histories and emergency information must be on file and adequate health policies established.
7. Food services must include a nutritious noon meal and healthy snacks.
8. Routines for play and rest periods must be established but flexibly administered.

In selecting a nursery school parents must consider price, closeness to the home, and obligations parents might have to the school. Many nursery schools require parents to participate in activities such as fund raising, administration, or actual child care. Before the final decision is made, it is imperative that parent and child visit the nursery school. There is no better way for the parents to evaluate the quality of child care than through direct observation, attending to the following questions. Is the staff competent? Are they warm and attentive toward the children? Do the children appear happy—and are they working and playing with one another? Does the program *actually* provide stimulation and freedom to explore? Is the food adequate, and the environment safe? The child's visit to the nursery school will introduce him or her to the new environment, the teachers, the children, and the program.

Once the selection of a nursery school has been made, the child needs adequate preparation. Parents can tell the child what to expect in a simple, direct fashion. If the child is willing and wants to attend the nursery school or has friends in attendance his or her adjustment will be facilitated.

Encourage parents to accompany the child on the first day and remain until the child feels secure enough to let the parent go. The process of separation may take several hours, days, or weeks; moving at the child's pace will prevent the trauma associated with separation anxiety. Parents also feel anxious about leaving their child for the first time. When they recognize the security of the nursery school, separation from the child becomes much easier. The parents need to inform the child exactly when and who will pick him or her up. When the parent and child feel secure and confident about the nursery school, a wonderful learning and socializing experience is their reward.

Intellectual and language development

Preoperational stage

The preschooler makes tremendous advances in his or her cognitive development. These strides lead to readiness for formal schooling. They result from maturation, experience, and social interaction.[12] (See Fig. 13-10.) Preschoolers between 2 and 7 years are in Piaget's preoperational stage of cognitive development. This stage is divided into two phases: the *preconceptual phase* (2 to 4 years) and the *intuitive phase* (4 to 7 years). The preschooler's greatly expanding language skills are an outgrowth of the child's cognitive development.

Preconceptual phase During the *preconceptual phase* the child begins to use symbolism. The child can now discriminate an object from an event. He or she recognizes that a high chair is not a part of the eating process but something to sit upon. Preconceptual thought is characterized by egocentrism, distortion of reality, lack of generality, and transductive reasoning.

The preschooler continues to have egocentric thought and views himself or herself as the center of the universe. From the perspective of preschoolers all events are either occurring to them or happening because of them. Such statements as "I got sick because I was bad," and "He fell down because I wanted him to get hurt," reflect such thought.

Symbolism, the ability to let one thing stand for or represent another that is not there, is developing throughout these years. These mental symbols allow the 3-year-old to remember the

past and act on it. The child knows about "grandmother's house" because he or she has learned the words and can associate them with past visits to grandmother's.

Symbols allow the child to "remember." With symbolic words the preschooler can describe something that happened in the past or ask for something that is not present. This child does not have a true concept of time so that explanations regarding time should be related to events *known* by the child. For example, a child should be told that "mother is coming to pick you up from the nursery school when you have finished lunch"—not, "at twelve o'clock"—since lunch, not twelve o'clock, has meaning for the child. Objects are used symbolically in "make believe" play. Play dough can be transformed into a tea party, a box on a cart can become a tank or a bulldozer, and a blanket over a table can become a house.

In *animistic thought*, objects are endowed with qualities adults reserve for animals and human beings, so that the teddy bear talks or protects from the dark or a doll becomes a "real" friend or crying baby. This type of symbolic play is vitally important for both cognitive and emotional development. If children are feeling overpowered by the adults around them, they may regain a sense of power and well-being by pretending to be Superman or a ferocious lion. After a traumatic experience, a child may work out his or her feelings through symbolic play, or

Figure 13-10 Much of the preschooler's learning comes from experience and from association with significant adults.

imagination. Four-year-old Susie left the doctor's office very angry after being given a "shot." Susie worked out her feelings at home by pulling out her doctor bag and "shooting" her doll many times.

Distortion of reality is in part caused by *transductive reasoning*. Adults reason from particular to general or vice versa, but the preconceptual child reasons from particular to particular or transductively. This kind of reasoning assumes relationships that do not exist and results in marvelous distortions of reality. A 3-year-old asked her father, "Why are you giving the dog a bath?" Father replied, "To wash the dirt and grease away." The child questioned "What is grease?" "A fatty substance," responded the father. After a pause the child answered, "Oh, then if Grandma took more showers she wouldn't be so fat!" This type of reasoning is accompanied by the inability to view the whole in relation to its parts or to reverse the thought process.

Preschoolers also have difficulty focusing on the important aspects of a situation. For a child everything is important and interrelated; this kind of thinking is called *field dependency*. For example, a preschooler might have difficulty going to sleep if one night the parent fails to read the usual bedtime story. This is to the child as important as closing his eyes in order to get to sleep. Objects, people, and routines are equally important. Because of this the preschooler has a great need for sameness and routine.

Preconceptual thought lacks generality and individuality; the child cannot form true and stable concepts or classes. If the child sees a dog and later sees another dog, the two dogs may be considered the same dog rather than members of the same class of animals called dogs. Because the preschooler's thought lacks generality and the child cannot yet form true concepts, classifying is inconsistent. For example, Janie is collecting shells at the beach when suddenly she adds a rock to her collection because "it was pretty, too."

The combination of elements of preconceptual thought (symbolism, egocentrism, transductive reasoning, and the associated distortion of reality) lead to the wonderful world of fantasy and magical beliefs of the preschool child whose Puff the Magic Dragon is under the piano and whose cape will transport her as Wonder Woman to Mars!

Intuitive phase The *intuitive phase* spans the ages from 4 through 7 and is still dominated by the child's perceptions rather than logic. Characteristics of this phase are centration, a static quality, and lack of reversibility. *Centration* names the child's tendency to *center* or focus on one part of a problem and ignore the other parts. The child therefore fails to consider the relationship between the parts or between parts and the whole. For example, a child may have difficulty in doing a relatively complex puzzle since she is determined to match colors when shapes of pieces and the picture are also important to the solution. However, unlike in the earlier phase, a child can form true classes and hierarchies. For example, blocks could be sorted into groups by shape or color.

The child's thought has a static quality whereby the child may focus on the *state* of an object rather than on the transformation of one object to another. For example, a ball of clay is made into a pie. Once the pie is made, the child is unable to recognize that the ball and pie had the same amount of clay. The child focuses only on the shape of the clay.

The child in the intuitive phase lacks *reversibility* in thought. A 4- or 5-year-old might correctly perceive that two identical glasses contained the same amount of water; if one glass is then poured into a third glass of a different shape, the child would believe that the different-shaped glass had a different amount of liquid. The child under 7 years does not realize that if the water were poured back in the original glass it would be the same amount he or she originally had. This demonstrates lack of reversibility. Another example might be seen in simple addition and subtraction since a 5-year-old might add $1 + 1 = 2$ but to reverse the problem $(2 - 1 = 1)$ would be too difficult.

When the child's thought becomes decentered, when the child is able to focus on transformations, and when reversibility occurs, the child then enters the stage of concrete operations—the age of reason—and is ready for academic work and school. Understanding a preschool child's way of thinking aids not only in assessing developmental level but also in communicating. By being aware of poor conceptual abilities, transductive reasoning, distortion of reality, centering, and lack of reversibility, the knowledgeable nurse understands that when children ask "Why?" they need simple, concise answers. Since the preschooler's thought has a magical and fantastic quality, it is all right to believe in Santa Claus and the Tooth Fairy at this age. Reality comes later as the child moves into the age of reasoning and understanding cause and effect relationships. But it is important that parents help preschoolers distinguish what is *pretend* from what is *reality*. A parent might say, "I see you are pretending you are Superman today," not "Here comes my little Superman." Adults should become concerned only when a child withdraws into the fantasy world, forsaking relationships with peers and the spontaneity and driving curiosity that are so much a part of the normal behavior of this period.

Language development

Language development parallels the rapid intellectual development of the preschool period. The child's vocabulary increases by approximately 600 words a year. The preschooler's constant activity is reflected through vocalization. Four- and five-year-olds constantly talk and tend to boast, exaggerate, and playfully use silly language. Speech is used as an aggressive behavior by the 4-year-old, who now uses full sentences. Little girls, especially, tend to be verbally aggressive toward each other at this age, and children of both sexes may use profanity for attention. Such behavior will usually disappear if ignored as will the tendency to mix fantasy with reality, which the adult may perceive as lying. It is most helpful if parents understand that this verbal behavior is normal at this age.

Language is used as a part of the learning and socialization process to get information, seek meaning about experiences, gain attention, and relieve anxiety. Language development involves the *expressive capacity*, or the actual vocalization of the child, and the *receptive capacity*, or the comprehension of the language. Reading and writing at this period as part of language development would identify an exceptionally bright child. The child's receptive capacity exceeds the expressive capacity; that is, the child understands words and phrases which are not yet part of his or her daily talking. The development of language depends upon the child's ability to learn the language, the quality and amount of language used in the home, the opportunity to express oneself, and the amount of exposure outside the home. Without exposure to the language, whether the child is partially deaf, deaf, or isolated, language development will be limited. Exposure of the child to talking is extremely important. It is during the preschool period that normal children acquire and master the basic syntactic structure of their language. The child learns to express himself or herself like the adults in the environment (although vocabulary and refinement of the structure will continue to grow throughout life). The child gradually learns to speak in full sentences.

The preschooler constantly asks "why, what, when, where, and how" in the determination to explore the world. Adults should readily respond with simple, short, and honest answers. Language is learned through direct communication with others, through reading, and through television. Encourage parents to discuss things with their children since verbal explorations are essential to learning. Adults must be attentive and show that they care about what the child is saying.

Some helpful modes of communicating with children include the following:

1. Be positive and provide no alternatives if the child must conform to a request. For example, "You must eat now," not "Would you like to eat?"
2. Use a positive phraseology since preschoolers tend to respond to them more readily instead of "Don't do this or that." Be instructive, telling the child what to do, what the choices are, and point out the consequences. For example, "You will need to hold your arm still so the doctor can get the bandage on evenly and fast," not "Don't move your arm."
3. Praise should be given for good behaviors. Praise is recognition of achievement. Avoid evaluative phrases and words such as *good*, *bad*, *nice*, and *naughty*. Acknowledge specific acts and efforts. For example, "You have learned how to do that very well, thank you for helping," not "What a big boy you are, that is nice." Immediate praise and reward foster the child's learning.
4. When a child appears upset, precede statements of advice or instructions with a statement of understanding of how the child feels. For example, "I understand that you are angry that mother left you, but she will be back at lunch time," or "I know that shot hurt you, but now wouldn't you like to go back to the playroom?" This also helps the child label his or her feelings and builds adult-child trust.

5. If a child has an anger outburst, the adult should stay with the child until calmness is regained. The child may need to be picked up and comforted, though not all children will respond to this or accept it. The parent might say, "That was a painful thing to happen to you. The way you feel is called angry. I think you'll be ready to play again."

6. If a child has an anger outburst following interference or physical restraint by an adult, the child usually benefits by bodily contact. You might say calmly, "I can help you hold still so you can stop and listen. You're angry now. Soon you can go back to play with Jane." Undue attention, however, should be avoided.

Table 13-5 Cognitive and language skills

3 years	4 years	5 years
Much egocentrism	**Less egocentrism**	**Little egocentrism**
Knows own sex	Sees self as individual in a group	Aware of cultural differences
Knows he or she is a separate person	Uses "I" frequently	Knows name and address
Uses "me" and "I" frequently		
Much distortion of reality	**Less distortion of reality**	**Little distortion of reality**
Imaginative	Highly imaginative	Less imaginative
Talks to self	Talks with imaginary playmate	Can tell story accurately
Does not care if another is listening	Tells family secrets	May use fantasy in stories but is aware
Some inappropriate answers	Exaggerates, boasts, and tattles	of the distortions made
	Tells stories mixing reality with fantasy	
Weak concept formation and symbolism	**Concepts weak but improving in accuracy**	**Symbolic thought and concepts improved**
Vocabulary of 900 words	Vocabulary of 1500 words	Vocabulary of 2100 words
Uses language experimentally	Concrete speech	Uses language correctly—full syntax
Talks in simple sentences (uses some adjectives and verbs), three to four words	More complex sentences (uses prepositions and plurals)	Meaningful sentences
	Defines simple words	Can follow plot of a story
Needs simple explanations	Knows one or more colors	Knows four or more colors
May repeat several numbers by rote	Concepts of 1, 2, and 3	
	Counts to 5	Counts to 10
Attention span: 10 min	Attention span: 20 min	Begins to understand money
		Attention span: 30 min
No generalization	**Some generalization**	**Generalizes**
Slight understanding of past and future	Conception of time of day	Knows days of week
	Knows days of week	Knows month and year
		Sense of time and duration
Transductive reasoning	**Some logic with crude comparison**	**Begins to reason logically**
Thinks illogically	Begins to organize experiences	Grasps some cause and effect relationships
Understands very simple reasoning	Asks "why" frequently	Likes to know how to use objects
		Frequently asks "how," "when," and "where"
		Knows meanings of words
Field dependency	**Centration**	**Centration**
Thrives on routine	Focus on one thing at a time	
Lack of reversibility	Lack of reversibility	Lack of reversibility
		May do simple addition
		Unable to subtract
Little awareness of feelings of others when talking	Some awareness of feelings of others when talking	Awareness of others' feelings and differences
Desires to please, is friendly	Bosses and criticizes others	Increasing independence
Needs directions	Uses profanity for attention	

7. Children need to be warned of impending changes in activities in order to prepare for them. For example, "In a few minutes, it'll be lunch time. Finish what you are doing." "Time in the playroom will be over in a few minutes and you need to get ready to go back to your room."
8. Do not make promises unless you can keep them. Children feel insecure with adults who do not fulfill promises.

Table 13-5 presents a summary of cognitive and language skills of the 3-, 4-, and 5-year-old.

Dealing with common problems

Maintaining and promoting optimum physical and mental health is the goal for all nurses. This goal is approached by providing education, counseling, and anticipatory guidance. Education is the communication of information to the parents with the goal of changing their behavior. Counseling assists parents to identify problems and find alternative approaches to child rearing. Anticipatory guidance assists parents in preparing for future developmental behaviors. Education and anticipatory guidance are preventive approaches toward health promotion and maintenance. Anticipatory guidance will help prevent undesirable habits and feelings, conflicts, and frustrations. Explain normal behaviors and milestones of development to parents, make an assessment of the family, and anticipate situations and behaviors for the parents and explain them before they occur. Through understanding, parents will be able to take a healthy attitude toward their children's behavior and use desirable methods of dealing with it. Parents need to be informed of the common normal behaviors of children of each age group which may cause parental concerns but which, in reality, are not problems and, if ignored, usually pass (are extinguished) when no mention (reinforcement) is made of them. Some normal behaviors in the preschool period which cause parental concern include masturbation, messiness, stuttering and stammering, temper tantrums, and short-lived unreasonable fears (note Table 13-6). It is only when behaviors become *persistent* and *interfere* with the normal daily routine of the child that they may be considered symptoms of physiological or psychological disturbances. To determine whether or not a child's behaviors are interferring with normal development, it is necessary to observe the child in his or her own environment. The nurse should observe the child's toileting, speech, play and peer relationships, sibling relationships, eating patterns, fears, and other general behaviors. Children with problems should be examined by a pediatrician; other referrals (e.g., to a speech pathologist or psychologist) may also be necessary.

Sibling rivalry

Sibling rivalry involves one child's negative feelings toward a sibling because of competition or jealousy. Rivalry occurs when the child's need to feel worthwhile is frustrated. It usually is directed toward an older sibling or occurs when a child tries to do better than a sibling. Jealousy occurs when the child's need to be loved and to love is frustrated and is commonly directed toward younger siblings. Behaviors characteristic of sibling rivalry may include acting out the negative feelings through fighting and verbal aggression or expressing the feelings in such regressive behaviors as bed-wetting, nail biting, or nightmares. Although a quiet period of sibling truce often occurs around the age of 4, sibling rivalry is of concern during the preschool period since this is a time when aggressive behaviors are common. Fighting with an older sibling or one close in age can readily disrupt a household, while fighting and aggression toward a younger sibling can lead to injury.

Although some sibling rivalry is normal, severe symptoms can be prevented by preparing the preschooler for the arrival of a new baby, and by recognizing each child for individual accomplishments. Instruct parents to provide the child with her *own time* of love and affection, include her in the infant's care, with the parent, and by treating her as an individual. Praise the child each time visitors praise the baby and give her an inexpensive present when the baby receives one. Encourage the child to voice any negative feelings without judgment, and to channel aggressive behavior in other directions.

If the regressive behaviors associated with sibling rivalry interfere with the child's daily routine and are persistent or if the aggressive verbal or physical behavior seems to be inflicting psychological or bodily harm to the other sibling, referral should be made for psychological counseling.

Table 13-6 Anticipated behaviors of the preschooler

Areas of observation	Normal behaviors	Behaviors which are not typically problems	Behaviors which are signs of disturbance
Toileting	Successful toilet training (2–2½ yr)	Occasional soiling and wetting	Persistent soiling past 5 years—enuresis, encopresis
Speech	Creative use of speech (3–4 yr)	Stuttering and stammering Aggressive speech—some swearing and lying Talks to self (2½ yr)	Nonspeaking beyond 2 yr Persistent lying
Play and peer relationships	Associative play (3 yr) Cooperative play (4 yr)	Aggressive and possessive play Messy play Won't put things away	Inappropriate play (death, torture) Withdrawal from peers Assaultive and distructive
Eating	Food preferences Sometimes finicky	Won't try new foods	Persistent eating problems
Sibling relationships	Some sibling rivalry (3 yr)	Some conflict between siblings	Persistent signs of jealousy or assaultiveness
Sleep	Bedtime ritual (including transitional object)	Some dreams	Persistent signs of disturbed sleep, night terrors, excessive body rocking
Fears		Short-lived and unreasonable fears	Persistent fear of dark, ghosts, burglars Shyness
General behaviors and daily routine	Sexual curiosity Aggressive, stubborn Accepts reasonable limits (2–2½ yr)	Masturbation Finger-sucking Temper tantrums Wants own way Regressive behavior with stress	Tics

Fighting, which is the most common symptom of sibling rivalry and one that few families avoid, is most effectively reduced by the use of "time-out." The children are placed in separate rooms, alone, or told to sit on a chair for a short duration.[13] This cooling down period may be as short as 2 min but must not be more than 10 to 15 min. The parent makes no attempt to determine who was to blame for the fight. Siblings are then discouraged from arguing with the parent or from baiting each other into starting another fight. To be effective, this approach must be used consistently and coupled with praise and attention when the siblings are playing cooperatively together.

Thumb-sucking

Thumb-sucking is reported in approximately 46 percent of children between birth and 16 years of age.[14] Although it may cause social embarrassment to both child and family, it has little significance before the age of 4. If continued when the permanent teeth appear, it contributes to malocclusion. It is desirable to extinguish the habit between the ages of 4 and 5, before school. Proposed causes for thumb-sucking include strong instinctual drives for sucking and regressive behavior and need for security when the child is under stress. If the behavior is ignored, in most children thumb-sucking usually disappears. For those in which this is not the case, action must be taken. Home management or interventions that have been used with varied success include wearing special mittens or restraints, applying bitter-tasting chemicals to the thumb, and reward for good behavior (positive reinforcement). Reward for good behavior is often successful with young children if managed consistently over a period of weeks. For example, a mother might suggest that every morning her 4-

year-old daughter wakes up with a dry thumb the child will receive a gold "big girl" star on a chart and that at the end of the week if each day has a gold star she can have a party or other reward. Success with this approach depends upon the mother's remembering to reward the child *every day* with the star. Each star and unsucked thumb *must* receive lavish praise, while the child's failure is ignored.

Thumb-sucking often is associated with an object such as a security blanket. The child picks up the blanket when watching TV, resting, or going to bed; this blanket usually has been a treasured object since infancy. Interestingly, if the blanket slowly is reduced to disappearance (mother washes it to nothing), the thumb-sucking may also disappear.

If the problem persists beyond the age of 4, referral is made to an orthodontist, who may intervene with the use of dental devices to prevent malocclusion. Such intervention has proved quite successful.

Sexual curiosity and masturbation

A child's sexual curiosity and masturbation rank among the top concerns of parents during this period, yet they are *normal* behaviors if not carried to excess. Both behaviors are triggered by the child's developing sexual identification and also result from the child's insatiable curiosity to learn about his or her own body and the world.

Preschoolers manifest sexual curiosity by asking many questions about sex (see the section on sex education), and in their play activities. Preschoolers are commonly found in the bathroom or playhouse engaging in mutual exploration while playing doctor, nurse, mother, or father. The preschooler frequently "peeps" around or under the bathroom door. Peeping behavior is usually quite limited in children who receive adequate answers to sexual questions at home and where the child is exposed to siblings and parents who comfortably accept their own sexuality. Sexual curiosity seems more intensified in children when parents are overly modest or where there are no siblings or close siblings with whom to compare.

When parents are confronted with these behaviors, the problem is more one for the parents than for the child. Parents need to know that most children exhibit this type of sexual curiosity in the preschool years and to be prepared to handle the situation. The most effective approach to the child's sexual explorations with others is to actually intrude on the activity, suggesting some diversional activity while avoiding embarrassment of the child in front of others. Later, when the child is alone, the parent can explain that undressing or touching each other's genitals is not acceptable behavior and suggest that the child ask any questions she or he has.[15] A calm and rational approach will limit sexual experimentation without damaging the child's interest in body or sex.

A calm, rational approach is also necessary in the management of the child who is masturbating. Masturbation is more common in boys than girls in the preschool period, probably because of the anatomic availability of the penis. Children frequently masturbate in bed; some do so openly in public. It is not unusual to see a 5-year-old walking about holding his penis in public. Such behavior, though harmless, can cause the parent embarrassment and anxiety. Parents should be reassured that the practice is normal in the preschool years and is absolutely harmless.

A small number of children use this form of self-gratification to retreat from relationships with parents and peers. Normally, children receive gratification primarily from interpersonal relationships. Excessive masturbation is usually indicative of some difficulty such as loneliness, boredom, or rejection.[16] Ignoring the behavior completely, therefore, is not beneficial to the child. Children must be told that it is not appropriate behavior in public. Effort to provide the child with more attention from the parents, more structured activity, and more involvement with peers is beneficial. Parents should set aside an hour or two a day to give personal attention to the child and, perhaps, enter the child in a nursery school to increase activities and widen peer associations. With such an approach, as the child passes through the preschool period normal masturbatory activity subsides.

Bed-wetting and soiling

Bed-wetting and soiling of underwear with urine or feces are common problems in the preschool years. It is estimated that 19 percent of normal 5- and 6-year-olds wet the bed at night (nocturnal enuresis) and that 1.5 percent soil their pants.[17] These problems occur more frequently in boys than girls. These behaviors tend to disappear by school age so that no treatment is usually initiated before the age of 5. Differentiation between occasional episodes and actual lack of control of bladder and/or bowel must be made. Total or partial lack of control often are symptoms of serious physical or psychological disturbances. Assessment of the problem is made over a period of several weeks by actually counting the number of accidents a child has had. One or two episodes a week is not considered significant. If bed-wetting or soiling occurs more frequently and persists past 5 years a physician's examination is necessary to rule out a pathological basis for the symptoms.

"Accidents" during both day and night occur occasionally to almost *all* preschoolers under the age of 5. During the day the child is often just too busy to be interrupted for going to the toilet. Overfatigue, illness, night dreams and disturbances may trigger nighttime accidents. Occasional accidents are to be expected and no significance should be attached to them. Soiling during the preschool period causes greater concern to parents than to children. The parents frequently feel they have failed at toilet training or are inconvenienced when they must change clothing or bed linens.

When accidents occur, clothing or beds are changed with recognition of the occurrence but *without* recrimination. Parents might say, "I know you are uncomfortable, let's quickly change your clothes." The less made of the accident, the better for the child for, indeed, *it is an accident*. Some measures that are helpful in limiting enuresis or encopresis are: (1) to encourage children to use the toilet following meals and before midmorning and midafternoon snacks so they will not have to interrupt play; (2) to encourage using the toilet before going to bed; (3) to restrict the intake of fluids an hour before naptime and 2 hours before going to bed; and (4) to avoid having meals too close to bedtime. If a child wets the bed frequently, it may be helpful to awaken the child once during the night for toileting. With patience and understanding, accidents will subside—they are but a part of development!

Temper tantrums

Temper tantrums are violent outbursts of anger characterized by complete loss of control, screaming, and kicking. Occasional temper tantrums, although most common around the age of 2, continue to be normal in the 3- and 4-year-old. Tantrums are the only way some children know for coping with an emotional crisis.[18] Children often have tantrums when they face a frustrating situation. Tantrums that occur frequently (e.g., daily) and tantrums in children over 4 years old are indicative of psychological disturbances. Referral for counseling is made since standard procedures for handling tantrums in younger children may have little effect or may even be damaging.

Temper tantrums are greatly distressing for parents since tantrums arouse feelings of helplessness, fear, and lack of control. How frustrating it is to see 3-year-old Laurie throw herself on the floor screaming, kicking, and holding her breath until "blue"! There is no reasoning, no action, no way to stop the tantrum immediately. As a result the parent gives in to the child's demands or desires, which reinforces the tantrum behavior. Laurie knows she gets what she wants.

The lesson the child must learn is that of *frustration tolerance*, the ability to put off desires and handle disappointment—a very important aspect of personality development. Frustration tolerance is learned and temper outbursts disappear when limits are enforced through methods such as time out.[19] When the child throws a tantrum, providing there is no danger, he or she is left alone and *no* attention whatsoever is paid to the child's actions until the tantrum has passed. The parent must stand firm and under no circumstances concede to the child's wishes. Coupled with this approach, the child is consistently rewarded (praised) for appropriate behavior. An example might be Laurie, who always interrupts adult conversations with her own wishes. If she is asked to wait she has a tantrum. Today she approaches mother, who is talking to a neighbor. She wiggles with impatience but does not interrupt. Mother acknowledges the child when her conversation is through with, "I'm so happy you waited until I was through talking—what do you wish, Honey?"

Inform parents of the necessity of carrying out this approach consistently and over a period of several weeks or months if it is to be successful. Acknowledge to the parents that the task of ignoring a child's behavior is most difficult but the reward is the child's own psychological growth and family peace.

Lying and stealing

Between the ages of 3 and 5 lying and stealing are common. Both behaviors are consequences of cognitive and moral development and should be approached as learning experiences for the child.

Lying occurs for two reasons: (1) it is an attempt to avoid punishment for an act which the child knows is wrong, or (2) it is an attempt to have something in fantasy which is lacking in reality. In either case, the preschooler is *not* deliberately being dishonest. Dishonesty, however, can be encouraged if the child consistently needs to tell a lie in order to avoid punishment. In this case, lying brings the reward of avoiding discipline. On the other hand, when the child does tell the truth about some wrongdoing, parents initiate punishment, not recognizing that it is painful enough to admit guilt and tell the truth. Advise parents to approach lying as an opportunity to encourage growth. If the parent knows that Johnnie broke the vase or Susie robbed the cookie jar, parents can assist the child in telling the truth by verbalizing the problem for him. "Johnnie, I see my new vase is broken. I am very unhappy about it. It really was my favorite one." After the child admits guilt, the parent may say, "I am so happy you told me the truth. I will not punish you." This statement not only aids the child in being truthful but affords a feeling of parental understanding. No further discipline is necessary since displeasure with the child's action has already been made clear.

Fantasizing something the child desires is part of the wonderful world of the preschooler. When a little girl says she is going to star on television next week or a little boy says he got a motorcycle for his birthday, the child is revealing wishful fantasies. This is an excellent opportunity for the adult to help the child distinguish between wishful thinking and reality. Avoid confronting the child with "That's not true" or labeling the child with "You are a liar!" Instead say, "You wish you could star on television; you wish you were all grown up. Maybe someday you will be a big star."

Stealing during the preschool period is also a form of fulfilling desires. At this period moral development is just beginning; the child is not always in control of his or her own actions. When a "theft" is discovered, approach it directly. The theft is verbalized by the adult and restitution demanded. If the child stole a little car from nursery school the parent says, "You took the car, but it is not yours. You must return it to the nursery school. It belongs there." The car must then be returned. If the child has difficulty giving up the object, it is important that parents either guide the child through the process of returning the object or secure the object from the child and return it themselves. The latter is done in the presence of the child and provides a role model for the child.

The act of returning an object is often enough punishment in itself. The use of a statement of disapproval may emphasize the seriousness of the situation to the child and foster learning. The mother says, "You took Janie's doll dress when I told you not to. I am really disappointed."

Whatever the cause for lying, distortion of the truth, or stealing, advise parents to be calm, understanding, factual, and realistic. These behaviors are an inherent part of the developmental process and provide experiences that are necessary for learning.

Fears and phobias

Although fantasy, magical thought, and transductive reasoning lead to many exciting adventures in the mind of the preschooler, they also lead to the production of fears. *Fears* are negative emotions caused by the anticipation of danger. No other period in the development of the child is so laden with fears. They are reflected in the child's daily behavior and in dreams. Common childhood fears include fear of the dark, solitude, heights, animals, monsters, bodily injury, and strange sights and sounds. Little girls tend to be more fearful of strange sights and sounds, of being alone, and of small crawling things like spiders and bugs. Little boys tend to be more fearful of body injury. These fears can be managed by the parent if approached realistically and tend to disappear by the age of 5. If the fear is irrational and becomes persistent, a *phobia*, and disrupts the child's daily patterns, professional assessment and treatment must be sought (see Chap. 40).

Informed parents will anticipate fear behaviors in their children and be prepared to recognize fear when it occurs. Instruct parents that fear is *very real* to the child. Never ridicule or tease a child when fear is expressed as it causes concealment of feelings. Encourage parents to talk with the child about the fears and to express them. Both communication techniques are important in reducing tension and anxiety. They also assist in exploring the fear with others who can point out the irrationality of fears and give explanations. An example of this would be the child who sees "spiders" moving on the dark shadowy wall of his room. He screams with fear. The parent identifies the fear and then reassures the child that nothing is there—that it is just the shadows from the moving trees outside the window. The child has an opportunity to explore the situation and to ask questions which in turn reduce the fear.

Once a fear is identified children must *not* be forced to directly confront fears. This may only intensify the fear. Four-year-old Felissa expressed fear of water and heights. Thinking that facing the problem directly would help, her father held her out over a river bridge. Felissa became terrified! In adulthood Felissa never learned to swim nor would she ever fly! Her fears became phobias.

Several approaches may help reduce a child's fear. One is providing the child with an opportunity to observe a non-fearful model in the fearful situation. Three-year-old Sara had great fear of dogs. Her little playmate Traci had a large friendly dog with whom she continually played in the yard. Arrangements were made to have Sara play at Traci's house several times a week, where playful interaction between Traci and her dog were observed. After a period of 6 months Sara was able to approach and pet Traci's dog with comfort. Subsequently she made friends with many dogs and was able to have one of her own.

Another approach is that of *desensitizing* the child through indirect exposure to the fearful situation. Johnnie, 4-years-old, is terrified of being examined by the doctor but must visit the doctor frequently to receive allergy treatments. A plan was developed to introduce stories and books about doctors, followed by providing Johnnie with a doctor's kit so that he could manipulate the play equipment and through play confront the doctor's visits without the actual threat of the doctor's office. The child was encouraged to tell stories about the doctor's office.

After exposure to this routine for several weeks, the fear was reduced significantly.

Assist parents to recognize that the process of reducing fear takes much time and patient understanding. Children do not readily comprehend the cause of their fears. They must learn to connect the object of their fear with safe and positive events. As children learn to handle themselves with safety and think more logically fears are slowly conquered.

References

1. *Vital Statistics of the U.S.—1969*, vol. 2; *Mortality*, U.S. Public Health Service, 1973, part B, sec. 2, tables 5–7.
2. Ruth Murray and Judith Zentner, *Nursing Assessment and Health Promotion Through the Life Span*, Prentice-Hall, Englewood Cliffs, N.J., 1975, p. 90.
3. Peggy Chinn, *Child Health Maintenance*, Mosby, St. Louis, 1974, p. 209.
4. J. H. Menkes, "The Neuromotor Mechanism," in R. H. Cooke, (ed.), *The Biological Basis of Pediatric Practice*, McGraw-Hill, New York, 1978, p. 257.
5. Marie Brown and Mary Murphy, *Ambulatory Pediatrics for Nurses*, McGraw-Hill, New York, 1975, pp. 209–210.
6. Erik Erikson, *Childhood and Society*, Norton, New York, 1963, pp. 255–257.
7. Jerome Kagan, "Acquisition and Significance of Sex Typing and Sex Role Identity," in A. Hoffman and L. Hoffman (eds.), *Review of Child Development Research*, vol. 2, Russell Sage Foundation, New York, 1964, pp. 144–146.
8. Jerome Kagan, "The Concept of Identification," *Psychol. Rev.* 65:296–305 (1958).
9. Kagan, "Acquisition and Significance of Sex Typing and Sex Role Identity," pp. 141–144.
10. Sara Stein, *Making Babies*, Walker, New York, 1974.
11. R. R. Sears, "Social Behavior and Personality Development," in T. Parsons, and E. A. Shils (eds.), *Toward A General Theory of Action*, Harvard, Cambridge, Mass., 1951, p. 465.
12. H. Ginsberg and S. Opper, *Piaget's Theory of Intellectual Development*, Prentice-Hall, Englewood Cliffs, N.J., 1969.
13. Charles Schaefer and Howard Millman, *Therapies for Children*, Jossey-Bass Publications, San Francisco, 1977, p. 419.
14. Schaefer et al., ibid., p. 253.
15. Haim Ginott, *Between Parent & Child*, Avon, New York, 1969, pp. 191–193.
16. Ginott, ibid., p. 191.
17. Schaefer et al., op. cit., p. 177.
18. Schaefer et al., op. cit., p. 267.
19. Schaefer et al., op. cit., p. 271

Chapter 14 **The school-age child**

Janet L. Wilde

Upon completion of this chapter, the student will be able to:

1. Identify the school-age child's growth and developmental changes within the following areas: height, weight, physique, and organ development.

2. Define Erikson's developmental task of industry vs. inferiority and compare the child's behavior in each task.

3. Identify four functions of the peer group.

4. Describe the attributes of the ideal school and teacher.

5. Describe the school-age child's characteristic behavior related to mealtimes, snacking, and school lunches.

6. Analyze the reasons for the school-age child's rigid behavior.

7. Define Piaget's stage of cognitive development (concrete operations) and compare it to cognitive development in the preschooler and adolescent.

8. Define and illustrate each of the following characteristics of cognitive development with an example: conservation, classification, ordering, and syncretic thinking.

9. Compare the characteristics and functions of the following types of play: cooperative, aggressive, and dramatic.

10. Identify the nursing interventions to prevent the two most common accidents in school-age children.

The keynote themes of the school-age years (ages 6 through 12) are freedom and *expansion*. At no other developmental stage does a person have such freedom and lack of responsibilities. The child's freedom and inexhaustible energy enable him or her to explore the boundless expanses beyond the home.

Several factors are responsible for the school-age child's readiness to explore the world. One factor is mastery of the earlier stages of psychosocial development. Having learned trust during infancy, the child expects the world to be safe and meet his needs. Having mastered autonomy as a toddler, he has learned to believe in himself. From mastering initiative as a preschooler, the child has enough self-confidence to be independent of his parents in much of what he does.

A child who has not mastered a previous stage will be psychologically handicapped. This child will lack one of the earlier psychological building blocks supporting the present stage. However, there is hope for this child, for each psychosocial stage is reworked in later stages.[1]

The child's maturing cognitive development also prepares him or her to explore the world. Learning to think logically, classify information, use symbols, remember a series of past events, and tell time, readies the school-age child for gathering new information. The child encounters new, differing opinions and value systems from schoolmates and teachers, during overnight visits to friends' homes and while camping, scouting, shopping, etc. The parents' role dimishes while the role of important adults besides the parents increases. The school-age child is learning acceptable behavior within different parts of society. Through significant adults the child learns the roles and technical skills necessary to function as a competent adult in society. This preparation for adulthood is called *socialization*. The school-age child becomes socialized within society, whereas the preschooler learned socialization within the family.

Physical maturation

Weight and skeletal development

The rapid height and weight gain of earlier years decreases significantly in the school-age period. Physical growth in this age group develops slowly and steadily (see Appendix B for growth charts). The average weight gain is 2 to 3.5 kg (5 to 7 lb) per year. This increase in weight is more noticeable in late summer and autumn.[2] The school-age child grows an average of 6 to 7 cm (2.5 to 3 in) per year. Boys are generally taller than girls until 10 years of age; then girls are taller until approximately age 14. A growth spurt will occur by age 11 to 13 in girls and 14 to 15 in boys. Head circumference increases much more slowly during the school-age years than earlier, increasing from about 51 cm (20 in) to 53–54 cm (21 in). The brain and skull grow slowly because 90 percent of brain growth has already occurred by 5 or 6 years of age. At the end of the early school-age years, the brain has achieved virtually adult size.[3] The child's facial appearance changes because the face grows faster than the skull.

The slower increase in height results from a skeletal system delayed in its general growth pattern. The bones are largely cartilaginous and soft in early childhood. These cartilage cells are ultimately replaced by bone as growth proceeds. (See Chap. 36 for a detailed discussion of skeletal development.) Physical activities for the school-age child must be planned accordingly with "close supervision to detect any complaint of injury to any bone or joint."[4]

During the last 10 years there has been an increased attempt to detect potential scoliosis cases. Scoliosis is a lateral curvature of the spine. Screening programs routinely performed in this age range will not only discover mild cases early enough to avoid surgery but will ensure greater success in cases requiring surgery.

The nurse's role in bringing this important information to local school communities and in assisting with the screenings is invaluable.[5]

The school-age child often complains of leg pains. It is common but erroneous to call these "growing pains" because growing itself is *not* painful. The cause of leg pains may be overexertion, bruising, or injury. Pains in the knees with no exertional signs are also common in school-age children. Such pains, especially if they occur late in the day or night and disappear in the morning, are usually not significant. This is true even if the pains are fairly severe.[6] Children with persistent leg pains should be referred to a physician.

The school-age child looks slimmer, more graceful, and better coordinated than the preschooler. Posture improves, the legs are longer, and the preschooler's pot belly and "baby fat" have disappeared. The child appears increasingly in control and has far fewer collisions and falls. Movements appear increasingly skilled and precise.

Fine and gross motor development

The reduced growth rate allows time for refinement and expansion of newly developed motor coordination. The child learns to refine skills by practicing specialized games. His muscular strength doubles; he can play games for longer periods of time. However, his strength is not comparable to an adult's. He is increasingly able to concentrate and play as a team member. School-age children need regular exercise and should spend time each day in games such as tag, jump rope, basketball, swimming, skating, soccer, or football. Regular exercise develops new muscle groups necessary to perform these games. (See Fig. 14-1.)

Fine motor coordination and creativity develop as the child refines printing and writing skills. The preschooler's gross motor skills of running and climbing give way to these finer motor skills. Children enjoy writing plays and stories and publishing neighborhood newspapers. Artistic talents blossom as children develop skills at drawing, ceramics, embroidery, or macrame. Refinement of fine motor skills is dramatically seen in the 9-year-old child who was unable to color within the lines when a preschooler but who can now paint a scenic landscape. Other children excel at music. School-age children commonly enjoy composing songs, playing in orchestras, singing in concerts, and studying ballet.

Organ growth and development

The school-age child's body is physiologically more mature than in earlier years. The myelinization of the school-age child's central nervous system is complete; hence physiological responses are more stable. The child's bladder capacity increases and the kidneys are better able to filter and concentrate urine. The gastrointestinal tract is also more stable. The school-age child can go without food for longer periods than a younger child and experiences diarrhea and vomiting less often. The eyes mature and achieve 20/20 vision during these years. The immunological system responds faster than before to antigen invasion. The antibody response is faster and higher antibody levels are achieved. The school-age child therefore catches fewer childhood diseases and is sick less often.

The heart grows at a slow rate in the school-age years. Only after the growth spurt of puberty will it grow rapidly and double its weight to reach adult size in the middle to late teens.[7] During the school years the heart is smaller in relation to body size but must continue to supply the needs of metabolism, rapid growth, and physical activity. For this reason, sustained physical activity is not desirable. No damage to the heart will result, but the young child is not yet capable of the same athletic performance as an older child. Evidence of this can be seen in the young school-age child who can seemingly play all day with friends only to collapse in a tired bundle at the dinner table,[8] or to say, "Mom, I'm tired. I need a nap." Knowing the physiological reasons for fatigue will enable parents to understand rather than criticize this behavior. The school-age child's vital signs approach adult levels. The blood pressure increases and the heart and respiratory rates decrease (see Tables 17-20 and 17-21).

Perceptual development

Perceptual development is crucial for the development of body image and coordination. Directional and positional skills (i.e., up vs. down; right vs. left; behind vs. in front of) are also learned at this time. All these aspects of development are precursors to the ability to read from left to right,

Figure 14-1 This school-age child is practicing swimming skills and refining gross motor coordination.

to follow directions, and to generally begin to conceive of one's self within one's surroundings.

Dental development

Dentition changes are readily apparent in the school-age child. The 6-year molars, which erupt at age 5 or 6, are the first secondary (permanent) teeth to appear. These teeth serve as the focal points in the dental arch. They determine to a large extent the spacing of the other secondary teeth and the ultimate shape of the jaw. For this reason, children who are evaluated for braces are often not fully evaluated until all four 6-year molars have come in (see Fig. 6-8 for tooth eruption schedule).

Nutrition

Nutritional needs change with the age of the child. During periods of rapid growth, caloric needs are particularly high. In the school-age years, caloric, protein, vitamin A, carbohydrate, and calcium needs particularly increase. (See Appendix C for daily requirements.) The later school-age years are a period of preparation for the rapid physiological changes of puberty; consequently caloric needs increase.

The caloric needs of the school-age child, though not as high as those for the infant, are still approximately *double* the average adult's requirements per kg of body weight. Maintenance of the basal metabolism for the 6- to 12-year-old uses 50 percent of the caloric intake. Physical activity uses 25 percent of the caloric intake. The other 25 percent is divided between growth (12 percent); specific dynamic action of food (5 percent); and loss by way of feces (8 percent).[9]

Mealtime and discipline Mealtime provides more than just a time for eating. It is an ideal time for family interaction and the child's learning of social skills. It may be the only time of the day when the whole family is together. Mealtime can be a time of great satisfaction for individual family members as they relate the day's achievements or have an opportunity to ask questions or voice opinions about items of interest to them. This is an ideal time to praise the accomplishments of individual children.

Often mealtime becomes a time of conflict instead of fellowship. Too often parental concern over table manners and the picky eating habits of this age group are so overemphasized that the dinner table loses its restful, pleasant atmosphere. A power struggle then results between parent and child. The child's eating habits will improve as the child grows older. The 6-year-old who stuffs her mouth, grabs for food, and is an active talker at mealtime will gradually become a 10- or 12-year-old who eats like the adults around her.

The dinner table is not the appropriate place for discipline. If discipline during meals is necessary, it should be kept to a minimum. When mealtime becomes a time of stress, digestion does not occur as readily. Poor eating habits or a temporary aversion to food can result from tense situations or from periods of great excitement.

As the school-age child's world expands, he or she may visit friends for meals and eat new foods or observe other people's eating habits. A favorite friend's food likes and dislikes may be copied. The child may refuse a new food or method of preparation at home by saying "so-and-so doesn't eat that." An understanding of why the child responds in this way, insisting that "one bite" be tried before a decision is made, and pointing out favorite foods containing the rejected item will help the family through the situation in a positive manner. It will also set the precedent for other family members.

School lunches As the child's desire to be liked by peers increases, the kind of lunch preferred often depends upon whether friends take lunch to school or eat in the cafeteria. Whether the food comes from home or is prepared at school, the school-age child often trades lunches or parts of lunches with members of the peer group. As a result, portions of well-planned meals may not be eaten.

If the school is located near a shopping center, the older school-age child will sometimes save the money for a cafeteria lunch until after school, when the peer group goes to the local store to buy "junk" foods (foods without nutritional value). If vending machines are located in the school a source of nonnutritional food becomes readily available. To combat this, some parent groups are working to eliminate vending machines or, at least, have nutritional snacks, such as oranges and food bars, replace the traditional candy bars and soft drinks.

School cafeteria lunches are regulated by federal and state standards when the school is part of the National School Lunch Program. Lunches must provide approximately one-third of the daily food requirements of the school-age child. However, because the food may be prepared in unfamiliar styles or served in portions too large for the child to eat, lunches that are paid for are often not eaten.

Nutritional status The types of situations just described are common in the life of today's school-age child. The parents need to be aware of these possibilities and make up for the deficiency at breakfast and dinner. The school-age child usually eats well and has fewer food fads than in earlier years. At home, eating problems are more apt to relate to a disrupted mealtime environment (distraction by friends or television) than to specific food dislikes.

After-school snacks can help make up for lack

of food at the noon meal and can satisfy the hunger usually experienced when the child returns home. Snacks eaten 1 h or longer before meals will not diminish food intake at mealtimes. Milk, cheese, fresh fruits and vegetables, peanut butter, unsugared nuts, yogurt, or fruit juices are desirable snacks both for general nutritional needs and for good dental health. Minimizing sugar content will protect against dental decay.

The school-age child's increased responsibility can be extended in the home to the area of nutrition. Children can be encouraged to "work as a team" and help at mealtime to prepare food. They can help plan menus, shop for the food, prepare some of the simpler foods, set the table, and wash the dishes. They thrive on mastering these tasks. However, the amount of participation should not be so great as to reduce time spent in the necessary outdoor play. Working parents should not leave cooking to school-age children. Children need specific foods set out in front of them to eat.

The school-age child usually learns about the basic four food groups in school. The child should be encouraged to share and use this information with other family members. This becomes a link between home and school as information learned in the classroom is demonstrated and discussed at home for every one's benefit.

Psychosocial maturation

Developmental task: Industry vs. inferiority

The basic psychosocial maturational process of the school-age child is to develop the sense of industry vs. inferiority. According to Erikson, it is during this stage that the child "must begin to be a worker and a potential provider."[10] The child now "becomes ready to apply himself to given skills and tasks"[11] and thus "learns to win recognition by producing things."[12] It is common to see children repeatedly practicing motor skills on the baseball diamond or math and spelling skills in the classroom.

Achievement vs. failure Children who are skilled on the playing field, in the classroom, or in the neighborhood will receive praise and recognition by peers and adults for a job well done. This praise makes them feel good about themselves and helps them see that others also consider them worthwhile, competent individ-

uals. (See Fig. 14-2.) These are the children who are frequently seen surrounded by peers in play and who are "everyone's" first choice "for the team." But the situation is different for children who fail or are not readily able to master skills such as reading or playing ball. These children will view themselves as a poor performers who cannot compete or who will not be sought after as valued persons. For example, a boy who is consistently rejected for the football team begins to see himself as a failure, unwanted, and inferior; his self-concept is tarnished. Such a child is in danger of establishing a "sense of inadequacy and inferiority."[13]

Children who feel inadequate may despair of their skills or status among peers. Self-esteem suffers, and they may be unable to identify with others who do succeed in the world of skills and

Figure 14-2 This girl's self-esteem is increased by receiving praise for perfecting her skill at baseball. Note her choice of baseball, a nontraditional sex-role activity.

tools.[14] Children often sit quietly and unnoticeably in the back of classrooms or stand at the back of a group, not participating unless coaxed over and over to do so. These children fear exposing themselves to laughter and criticism. They rarely ask questions or seek explanations. These children need the help of significant adults or peer partners to find meaningful roles in which they can achieve. Although they do have skills to develop and contribute, often these children drop out because no one takes the extra time necessary to start them on the way to experiencing recognition for skills they *can* master.

Hobbies are common among school-age children and can play an important role in the accomplishment of developmental tasks, including a sense of achievement. By learning everything he or she can about a subject, such as sewing, painting, soccer, electronics, the child acquires new skills. These skills help perfect gross and fine motor coordination while new information is gained for successful functioning as an adult. Organizations for children, such as Girl and Boy Scouts of America, Camp Fire, and

Figure 14-3 The school-age child with high self-esteem feels accepted by others, accepts criticism, states her beliefs, and feels competent.

4-H Clubs also provide opportunities to develop the skills of this age group. In addition, these groups provide opportunities to develop skills to help them function in their respective sex roles.

Self-esteem As new skills are learned and new thought processes develop, self-esteem becomes increasingly important. *Self-esteem* is self-respect or appreciation of one's own worth. The "primary antecedents for fostering self-esteem seem to be: (1) a high degree of acceptance by parents and others; (2) clear and consistent limits; and (3) flexibility within those limits to permit individual actions."[15]

The child with high self-esteem accepts criticism, states his or her beliefs even if they challenge authority, and feels competent. This child enters new situations confidently. Because nothing succeeds like success, this child usually succeeds. This repeated achievement increases self-esteem.[16] (See Fig. 14-3.)

Popularity results from many aspects of a child's personality. The school-age child who feels confident that others accept her shares freely with others and sets aside some of her own desires while contributing to the good of other people and the group as a whole. The intellectual growth at this age enables the child to cooperate with others and to understand and respect their thoughts and opinions. She is ready for team activities. She now feels empathy for others who experience happiness and sorrow.

The child with low self-esteem often withdraws from new situations; it's easier than failing again. This child may destroy other people's possessions, doesn't try hard, has psychosomatic pain, and worries whether her actions are correct. She may go to extremes to please adults and receive their approval.[17]

The school-age child receives messages about self-worth from many sources: parents, teachers, classmates, and team members. This child perceives her parents as all-powerful. She judges her performance by her parent's comments and by comparing it to an inner vision of her ideal self. Therefore, teachers and parents need to establish activities that promote success.

The child needs to experience success in the tasks she masters *and* receive recognition for those achievements. This recognition is as important to the child who is able to recognize all letters of the alphabet for the first time as it is to the 10-year-old who creates her own short story for the first time. It cannot be assumed that the child knows she has done well because how the child views herself is a reflection of how she perceives others feel about her.[18] Each new achievement should be praised, no matter how small.

School The school is the main socializing agent of our society. It indoctrinates children into the rules, values, and cultures of our society. It prepares them to function as adults in society.

The school should adapt learning experiences to the individual needs of the child. The school has a mutual and cooperative role with the parent to ensure that the school program meets each child's needs. Through this joint effort, the child will learn to develop positive attitudes towards his or her own and other ethnic, social, economic, and religious groups. The child will also learn the concepts necessary for success in daily living.

School readiness Children who have successfully completed prior stages of emotional maturation will be better prepared to begin school and to accomplish its many social and educational tasks. Those who have experienced encouragement and support of normal curiosity and exploration and manipulation (investigation of his or her own body, of toys, and of other objects), recognition of success in physical and mental endeavors (first steps or the first recitation and/or recognition of the alphabet), and maximum stimulation and life experiences in earlier years (trips to the zoo or beach and interactions with other children and adults) will be more ready and eager for the further development of intellectual skills in a more formal setting. These positive experiences of the past will decrease anxiety and allow children to concentrate more easily on the tasks of this period.

Reading is a primary focus of the school-age years. But reading does not just happen. Many skills and developmental tasks must be attained before reading can occur. Visual motor skills (drawing shapes), gross motor skills (jumping, hopping) and recitation, sequencing (ordering), and perceptual skills such as alphabet recognition all contribute to readiness for reading. Studies have even established crawling as a precursor to reading readiness. If crawling was not actually performed in the developmental sequence of events, the child may be taught to crawl. Usually, the development of this skill will result in an improvement in reading ability.

A variety of life experiences, verbal fluency, and exposure to books (including manipulation of them) also contribute to reading readiness. Adequate functioning of the auditory and visual systems is essential for the child to learn to read.

School-age children live largely in a visual mode. Many new tasks and concepts must be visually seen and manipulated in order to be understood and assimilated. Their cognitive system is now at a level which allows them to organize and control the environment in order to understand it. Children of this age are better able to understand something if they can concretely experience it through handling, seeing, or hearing it.

As children progress through the school years, it becomes less necessary for objects to be present for the children to understand and experience them. That is, conceptualization gradually replaces the earlier reliance on sensorimotor learning. Thus the ability to use symbols when thinking increases.

The teacher Next to parents, the teacher is the most powerful and influential adult in the school-age child's life. The teacher affects the child's attitudes towards adult authority, school, and society. Through the teacher, the child learns more about society and how to obtain the knowledge and skills necessary to live in it successfully.

Children want a teacher to resemble the ideal parent. In the early years the teacher takes on the role of parent by helping the child to go to the bathroom, conform to the group, and control aggressive impulses. The ideal teacher is warm, nurturant, kind, enthusiastic, a consistent, fair disciplinarian, sympathetic, attractive, and understanding. Children do not want a teacher who yells, has unbending expectations, and uses ridicule and sarcasm to control students.

Children strive to fulfill the teacher's expectations and avoid disapproval. Children want to be regarded as valuable human beings, capable of individual learning. The teacher is obviously extremely important in molding children's self-esteem.

Parents often seek the advice of their child's teacher to help them find solutions to the problems they have in understanding or dealing with their child. School-age children gain new ideas from adults such as teachers, television performers, parents of friends, and authors of textbooks. Often these ideas and attitudes conflict with those of the parents. The parents and teachers ideally should communicate well and have compatible ideas about both the child's strengths and areas needing improvement.

The peer group The school-age child spends more and more time with and relies increasingly on his or her *peer group*, a group of friends of similar age. Societies throughout history have described special subcultures of children. All subcultures require strict conformity to rules. This increases the group's security and isolates it from other groups, in this case, adults. School-age gangs have characteristics of a primitive society: oral communication of traditions, rituals, and magical incantations. School-age children have secret clubs and teach one another secret languages like pig latin, passwords, and jingles. Superstitious rituals represent children's attempts to increase power over the future: "If you step on a crack, you'll break your mother's back."

Figure 14-4 Friendship helps school-age children evaluate themselves, share information, and learn sex roles and acceptable behavior.

Prospective members of the peer group are closely examined and are admitted or rejected on a pass-fail basis. Potential members must conform to the group's standards of acceptable behavior. The rules become increasingly rigid as the child grows older. Children are admitted on the basis of physical development, strength, height, weight, athletic ability, dress, and skills benefiting the group. Conformity to the group is healthy: the accepted child feels satisfied, secure, and comfortable.

The peer group has several functions:

1. It provides a mirror into which the child looks to examine and evaluate himself or herself. By receiving group feedback, the child practices behavior to conform to the group's standards. This feedback increases the child's security and self-esteem.
2. It socializes the child. Members must conform to the group's rules. Children learn acceptable behavior and learn to compromise individual needs for the total group's benefit. Because groups usually consist of neighborhood friends and most neighborhoods are grouped by socioeconomic class, the group helps the child learn the standards of the economic class.
3. It encourages sharing of information. Members expose one another to differing value systems and opinions and evaluate their own thoughts. They learn that acceptable behaviors vary within different parts of society. This sharing, which is enhanced by television, decreases the child's self-centeredness.
4. It provides an environment for practicing sex role behavior. Friendship groups during the school-age period are sexually segregated. Within these same-sex clubs the child practices skills and actions needed to solidify his or her sex role. Best friends are inseparable, sharing secrets, jokes, clothes, and family secrets. They buoy up each other in times of stress. Occasionally they fight, learn to solve their conflicts, and reunite. These secret club friendships strengthen the child's sex role learning in preparation for boy-girl relationships during adolescence. (See Fig. 14-4).

Rigid behavior

Rigid behavior pervades many aspects of the school-age child's life, in rules followed, in thinking, in rituals, and in learning new roles. This rigidity is strong and results in a driving desire to complete such tasks as games, sewing projects, and building with an erector set. This rigidity is seen in the homework assignment of a 10-year-old who finds herself unable to try to write a sentence for the second word on the list until she has thought of one for the first word.

Though certain behavior expectations are necessary within the family setting, clear and consistent limits are more important than rigidity. Rigidity not only adds to the rigidity that is self-imposed by the child, but does not allow for flexibility and development of individuality. Too many rigid rules discourage the child from trying to solve problems by himself as he develops his sense of initiative.[19]

New roles Taking on new roles also entails rigid, concrete behavior. Any new role or situation is experienced in a very precise, rigid manner to successfully master feelings of inferiority and anxiety. Unless the child perfectionistically practices the actions of the role, she fears she may be unable to achieve the approval of peers and the important adults in her life. For example, the child may be seen making precise work out of cleaning her desk at school. She may actually appear to be moving in slow motion as she completes this task.

Bedtime rituals An extension of rigid behavior is the nighttime routine. In earlier stages, the fear of death was expressed in the child's fear of the dark and fear of going to sleep in the dark. Now the school-age child's thinking becomes more concrete. The child begins to conceive of death as happening to others but is unable to accept it as a part of his own life. When logical thinking occurs about 9 or 10 years of age, the child begins to view death as final and inevitable. While emotional capacity grows with experiences related to dying (seeing a dead bird, pet, or fish), an unconscious fear of death often continues to exist. The child often attempts to define death in terms of being good and thereby hopes to keep death away. He may project his fears onto others or onto inanimate objects, like a stuffed animal, skeletons, witches, or vampires. (See Fig. 14-5.) He believes that maintaining a routine makes things predictable. This allows less anxiety to surface. The rituals of the age are normal unless the child becomes so obsessed that he is no longer able to function without them.

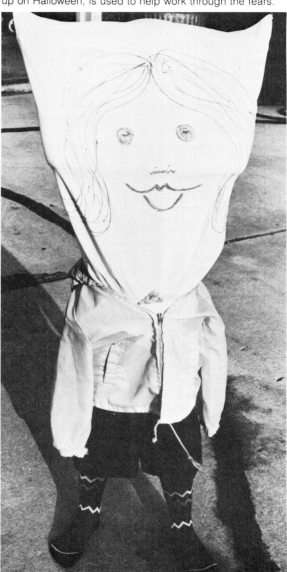

Figure 14-5 Children project their fears onto inanimate objects and fantasy characters. Play, in this case dressing up on Halloween, is used to help work through the fears.

Play

Play for the school-age child revolves around social interaction. The child seldom any longer plays alone, but in organized and unorganized groups. Group acceptance and the need for friends with whom to share experiences and thoughts takes on great urgency. Groups and their opportunities for socialization give the child the opportunity to feel secure while slowly becoming less dependent upon the family.

The 6-year-old at play displays endless energy and constant activity, often overdoing in the process. This age group is self-centered, and conflicts erupt because of the child's tendency to show off and be bossy while trying to dominate the situation. Boys and girls play together in a rough and tumble manner. Inhibitions are weak; aggressive thoughts are acted out in kicking, hitting, and even biting. Hand coordination allows for printing of large letters and gross motor hand skills like hammering nails. Six-year-olds are able to bounce and throw a ball, jump and run in games, and do elementary stunts on a bar. Athletic endeavors are still at a beginning performance level.

The 7-year-old has a more cautious approach to activity and is less demanding in desires and opinions. Thus the 7-year-old is easier to deal with. Gross motor skills are improving. Children can catch now, throw a ball, and may try to use a baseball bat. If not already riding a bicycle, most will want to learn. Pencils are now preferred over crayons and printing is not only smaller but easier to do. Fine motor development is improving.

Muscle movement is becoming smoother and more coordinated in the 8-year-old. Boys prefer

Table 14-1 Play activities

Purpose or function	Age 6	Age 7	Age 8
Gross motor development	Bicycle Skates Baseball bat, mitt Rough-and-tumble play Relay races, tag, hide-and-seek	Baseball Pogo stick Football equipment Flying planes Kite Bouncing balls Jump rope Skating	Badminton Basketball, hoop Bicycle Tennis racket Swimming Ping Pong
Fine motor development	Puppets Rhythm instruments, piano Bead jewelry-making sets Coloring books, crayons Clay Paint, drawing Paper dolls Hammer, pliers	Yo-yo Checkers Chinese checkers Dominoes Collages Clay Puzzles Magic tricks	Making and building objects Interlocking small plastic brick sets Dart set Leathercraft set Watercolor paints and brush Recorder
Sex-role establishment	Cooking sets Fishing tackle Large trucks, machinery toys Sewing machines Toys for playing store Dress-up play Household furniture	Costumes Household play Brownies, Cubs, Blue Birds	Performs dramatic shows Dolls
Collections and completion of task	Rake leaves Collect insects Collects minute objects ("odds and ends") Games (simple) Small play sets	Parcheesi Erector set Quiz and puzzle sets Simple games Magic tricks	Coin books Interlocking small plastic brick sets Group games
Quiet play	Card games Stories Darts (magnetic)	Reading Comics	Books Comics

Adapted from Ruth E. Hartley, and Robert M. Goldenson, *The Complete Book of Children's Play*, Thomas Y. Crowell, New York, 1957, pp. 402–405.

soccer, baseball, and may even try skate-boarding. Girls now play jump rope and roller skate. Printing is now slowly replaced by cursive writing.

Perfection of skills already learned at a younger age can be seen in the 9-year-old. Differences between the abilities of those who are increasing their skill levels and those who are not become more noticeable.

During the rest of the school-age years, children of both sexes develop increasing physical strength and endurance, but boys are stronger than girls. Many late school-age children come close to adult levels of proficiency as they perfect individual skills.

Table 14-1 lists common, appropriate play activities for school-age children and groups those activities according to some of the purposes or functions they serve, such as development of gross motor skills. The age categories are useful guidelines but are not intended as absolutes.

Cooperative play *Cooperative play* (playing together and sharing, as when two children build together with an erector set) now predominates, as did solitary and parallel play in earlier years. Cooperative play and the maturity level that allows sharing between more than two children at one time now offer the opportunities to ex-

Age 9	Age 10	Age 11–12
Rough and tumble activities	Bicycles	Bicycle (large)
Baseball	All gross motor activities	Archery sets (fine also)
Swimming	Out-of-door games	Swimming
Skating	Sliding	Horseback riding
Dancing: ballet, tap	Climbing	
Hiking	Running	
All competitive sports		
Wrestling		
Practical jokes, tricks	Tool set	Electric train set
Steam engine	Dart set	Chemistry set
Radio-controlled vehicles	Electrical model kits	Model cars with engines
Wood-burning set	Typewriter	Shell jewelry sets
		Wire cutters
		Papier-mâché
		Weaving
		Woodworking
		Knitting, sewing
Little-girl dolls		
Male role-model dolls		
Collections of objects	Card games	Various aids for collections of
Doll collections	All collections	objects and mementos
Card games	Erector set with motor	("movie stars")
	Stamp album	Perfume-making set
		Model cars with engines
Table games	Books	Electrical table games
Reading books	Games	

periment with life in group situations. The child now cognitively differentiates herself from her environment. This gives her the capacity to see and respect another's point of view. It makes her capable of true cooperative play and allows her to become a valued member of the group or team.

In cooperative play the child learns to relinquish her own needs for the overall good of a team. The group members learn to work together and to rely on each other. Each member has a specific role; the members learn to combine their efforts and win. Through group play the school-age child learns to compete successfully and to handle feelings of anger, disappointment, loss, and success.

A desire to play games with rules emerges about 7 years of age. The peer group members now have the ability to agree on rules, adhere to them, and compete with and control each other for the benefit of the entire team. Games with rules range all the way from table games to football and baseball; red light–green light and statues are familiar examples that illustrate the young school-age child's strict adherence to rules.

Rules for games give everyone playing specific guidelines. Rules also reduce the child's anxiety about a new situation. Conforming to rules promotes peer acceptance, while nonconforming,

Figure 14-6. These girls are playing *dramatically*, dressed up to imitate real-life situations. Dramatic play helps children feel in control and learn solutions to problems and reduces their anxiety.

"different" children are excluded. The rules also give the child an opportunity to measure herself against an external standard (the rules). After children have become familiar with the rules, they may modify them by group consent.

As a member of the team or play group, a child who successfully competes (by winning or by playing by the rules) experiences increased self-esteem. Her skills give her group status, confidence about her competency, and feelings of control. Successfully creating, following instructions, and completing the task, such as a painting or model car, also increase self-esteem. It takes some children longer to learn and follow the rules or instructions. They may choose to give up without giving much effort to complete the project. For these children, encouragement and support are necessary so that a decreased self-esteem does not result.

Dramatic play Children enjoy *dramatic play* in the early school-age years. (See Fig 14-6.) They create plays about real-life situations and enjoy presenting them to adults. The children jointly develop a set of rules (script), entertain, and gain approval from others. They express emotions, such as anger and sadness, and use their imaginations to play through problems to find solutions. The children learn to master their anxiety over a situation while expressing creativity within a group. They need to feel in control and powerful over their foes. The older children often wish to take a drama class.

Aggressive play *Aggressive play* is more common in boys than girls in this period. All children need room to run, jump, skip, and express pent-up hostility and tension. Aggressive play involves expressing hostility and boldness. (See Fig. 14-7.) It represents a symbolic way of conquering an enemy and may be accompanied by squeals of delight! Watching westerns, space programs, or competitive sports on television can be a vicarious means of mastering the enemy. Television, however, is *not* a substitute for active or creative dramatic play.

Parent approval Many children need parental approval before they can make their "own" choice of games and activities. The Oedipal conflict of the preschool years has been resolved. The child loves and respects both parents and

Figure 14-7 *Aggressive* play allows children to express hostility and boldness, releases tension, and provides an opportunity to overpower "the enemy." Note this boy's traditional sex-role identity.

imitates the parent of the same sex. He strengthens his sex-role identity by imitating that parent's actions and verbalizations. What the parent of the same sex likes or approves of thus has a great influence on the child's choices.

Sex-role identification

The preschooler began to assume behaviors characteristic of sex role identity and to turn his or her interest to the parent of the opposite sex. The school-age child becomes more interested in, and identifies with, the parent of the same sex. The school-age child associates with a same-sex group to reinforce sex identity and to practice the sex role which will be assumed later in life. By focusing on the same sex and its role, the child's earlier feelings of anxiety, anger, and conflict surrounding feelings about the opposite sex submerge for a few years. This liberates psychological energy to be used to learn, explore, and develop new skills free from sexual conflict.

Once the important skills of this period are mastered, the child will be better able to cope with heterosexual relationships in adolescence.

The school-age child also learns his or her sex role by participating in same-sex peer groups. These may be formally organized (Girl or Boy Scouts of America; Blue Birds or Blue Jays; etc.) or informal neighborhood groups and secret clubs. (See Fig. 14-8.) The peer group activities also enable children to explore sex roles through choice of toys and activities. Girls may still learn crafts, cook, use play dolls, and play house. Boys are more concerned with developing some physical prowess within the play group and/or on the athletic field. Because of the feminist movement, the traditional sex roles have become blurred. Today, children of both sexes explore areas and choose toys once reserved for one sex. Boys play with dolls (often exploring the male role in child rearing), cook, and clean the house. Girls compete on athletic teams and take carpentry and fix-it classes. By learning these roles, children will perhaps be increasingly self-reliant as adults and may also better understand people of the opposite sex.

The child learns the actions of new roles before the symbolic meanings. The girl learns the mother's sex role actions: cooking, giving first aid, housework, etc., before she understands the concept of mothering.

Figure 14-8 The school-age child learns her sex role by joining same-sex clubs, such as Girl Scouts.

Sexual curiosity Many school-age children are increasingly interested in sex within the peer group and are often involved in sex play. Curiosity about sexual differences intensifies. Many children explore their own bodies and those of peers. This is due to curiosity, not sexual urges. Secret conversations commonly involve sharing information (often incorrect) found in books, in magazines, or on television. The child may view a television program and report to a parent about the scene "where the man tore all her clothes off" rather than the story of the whole program.

Sex education Early in the preadolescent period, the child may be eager to learn biological facts with relative comfort since sexual feelings are not yet causing anxiety. But later, conflicts about sex become heightened so that information about sex is received with apprehension as well as interest. Preadolescents sometimes test adults' reactions to "touchy" subject matter. By such testing, the child learns whether a particular adult will discuss emotional or controversial subjects such as sex.

Sex education, although controversial, is included in many school curricula. The information may, however, be incompletely understood or quickly forgotten. Answers to questions should be honest and at the child's level of understanding, and information should be given when the child seeks the knowledge. Sex education may include the information that sex is necessary for survival of all species; drawings about anatomic differences; a discussion about body changes common to all children and their effects upon skin care, nutrition, and the need for rest and exercise; information for girls about personal care during the menses; general information about voice changes in boys; how twins are conceived; marriage and sex as an expression of love and sensitivity; communications; and other items of general interest to this age group. An objective approach provides emotional distance that encourages group participation.

Preadolescents are also becoming aware of many ambivalent and conflicting aspects of sex in our society. On the one hand, they learn about cultural prohibitions and disapprovals of sexual activity, while witnessing the mass media emphasis on sexuality. Parental reluctance to discuss sex may be confusing, blocks communication, and leads children to turn to peers for information. Misinformation and misconceptions acquired from peers may increase anxiety and prevent understanding of body functions. Misinformation can lead to difficulties later in life when attempting to handle the social and emotional aspects of sexuality as an adult.

Absent parent For the child who has lost the parent of the same sex through death, divorce, or other means, learning the sex role may be difficult. In the case of a boy, Big Brother programs, a grandfather, or a favorite uncle can provide a male role model. For girls, a grandmother, aunt, or concerned "Big Sister" may be appropriate. Relationships with adults of their own sex are crucial, since children need a sex-role model to copy and a same-sex adult to share and clarify new experiences.

For the older school-age child (10 to 13 years), the beginnings of interest in the opposite sex result in an increased effort to become more closely related to members of the same sex. If the parent of the same sex is absent from the home, the increased anxiety of this age group may further increase unless the child has developed a trusting relationship with a surrogate parent. As much as a single parent tries to be both parents to the child, the youngster needs close ties with adults of both sexes to learn to understand people and develop his or her own sex role.

Role unification Feminist life-styles of recent years have contributed another dimension to child rearing. Children raised in families subscribing to these life-styles are raised in nonsexist ways. These children experience and observe from very young ages that roles played by men and women need not be strictly linked to one of the sexes. Men cook, clean house, and participate in child rearing just as women go out to work to contribute to financial aspects of family life and to seek self-fulfillment.

It remains to be seen, but children raised in a nonsexist environment may grow up to be more self-reliant and share roles even more easily than their parents. Reduced sexual stereotyping may cause them to be more tolerant, loving, and understanding of other people of both sexes.

Hero worship For the preadolescent, an older friend of the same sex becomes a "worshipped" hero who provides support as parental ties are gradually loosened. This hero is usually an older teenager or young adult who is viewed as protective, warm, and someone the preadolescent wishes to be like.

Hero worship softens the child's previous dependency on parents and helps in the transition to the adolescent's developmental task of establishing greater self-reliance and interdependence with nonparent adults. The child who has a hero commonly is quite critical of the same-sex parent, who is perceived as not comparing favorably to the admired person. This can become a potential source of friction in the home, especially between girls and their mothers. However, if the parent maintains stability in the face of these expressions of contempt, it will serve to prevent the preadolescent from becoming overly anxious or rebellious about split loyalties. This child does not actually hate his parents but is moving toward appropriate independence from parents and home.

Boys usually experience less intense hero worship than girls, probably because society tends to frown upon strong attachments between males. Boys may master their fear of continuing dependence on parents by becoming heavily involved in a sport or by looking for a job outside the home.

The family

While the child's world expands beyond the home, the family stabilizes her total development. School-age children, whenever they feel vulnerable, need to retreat to their families. Here they can recharge their emotional energy, discuss topics, find solutions to problems, and experience companionship, affection, comfort, and stimulation for their emotional and moral growth.

The family also enhances the child's intellectual development and teaches the basic skills necessary to function as a valued, competent adult. Parents help children develop intellectually by having high expectations for them, being interested in their activities, praising their efforts, and encouraging their curiosity and explorations.

School-age children, at least until preadolescence, usually consider themselves closer to the same-sex parent. They also see the same-sex parent as more punitive. Even when the mother works, they tend to view the mother as the homemaker providing nurture and giving attention to their feelings and needs. Fathers are seen as the breadwinners, stronger, bigger, dirtier, and more menacing.

Social class affects the child's perceptions of her parents. Middle-class parents reason with their children, accept their behavior more, and give them attention. Lower-class fathers are more authoritarian and often punish physically; middle-class fathers are more often companions and are interested in their children's school activities and in promoting a positive self-concept.

Parents As the school-age child progresses developmentally, the parents often need support and knowledge of normal growth and development to help them adapt to their child's changes. For the new parent of a school-age child, this is particularly true. The ease with which the parents adapt to their child's travels away from them depends upon their ability to accept the child's new image and the child's new, more realistic view of them. Often parents say, "What a big girl she is now! She's in school and doesn't need me much anymore!"

The child of this age sees her parents more realistically than she did as a preschooler. She becomes independent of her parents in most daily activities and questions their expertise and their standards. This behavior threatens the parents. They may feel inadequate and disappointed. Both parents and child may feel hurt and angry and may reject each other. The nurse can ensure that this rejection remains temporary by educating the parents about the causes of these feelings, what to expect, and how to recognize the former strengths still existing in their "new" child. Parents need reassurance that even the most critical children will *not* tolerate any outside criticism of their parents.

Siblings Siblings generally experience the same basic child-rearing patterns, but parent and child personality characteristics modify the parenting styles. For example, a parent may be warmer toward one child than another even while being restrictive toward both in the same situation. This results in one child's appearing to be more socialized, self-confident, and friendly than the other child. Likewise, one parent may relate better to some children in the family and the other parent relate better to other children. Parents should share responsibilities to ensure that each child receives equal affection, attention, and discipline.

Discipline School-age children need realistic and consistent limits on their behavior, even while protesting and testing the rules. They need help in controlling their outbursts. These children respect and feel secure with the adult who establishes consistent rules and discusses the issues involved. Children who "run wild" without realistic parental controls feel insecure and are begging, by their misdeeds, for help in controlling their behavior.

Each child learns, as he grows older, which behaviors bring positive or negative results in which circumstances. Punishment (withdrawal of love, isolation, spanking) is not the only aspect of discipline that teaches the child consequences of misbehavior. It has been hypothesized that the parent who *talks* and *reasons* with the child about misbehavior is more likely than one who simply punishes to give the child a clear idea of what he did wrong. This allows the child's anxiety about misbehavior to be connected to the right cues. Explanations and reasons also give the child internal resources for evaluating his own behavior. This gives the child specific training in making moral judgments about his behavior. For the child whose parent does not talk about misbehaviors but only punishes him, anxiety may continue to exist but not be related to the specific consequences of misbehavior.

Development of the conscience

The conscience, which Freud called the *super-ego*, evolves as a part of cognitive development. As the child approaches the late preschool years, the conscience strengthens as the child incorporates the same-sex parent's moral values into her personality and behavior patterns. These values, which previously spoke to her from the parent as "thou shalt" and "thou shalt not," now speak to the child in her own voice as "I must" and "I must not." These statements, in turn, arouse feelings of guilt and the child now uses various mechanisms of defense (rationalization, regression, etc.) to reduce the guilt.

Initially, the school-age child's conscience is tyrannical and rigid. This is demonstrated in the moralistic school-age child who learns and applies rules of right and wrong in a rigid, strict, absolute manner that makes no allowances for extenuating circumstances. For example, a young school-age child might think losing one's shoes or stealing cookies is an offense as serious as a crime. This unyielding standard of right and wrong leads children to be highly condemning of others' behavior and even of the unfairness of uncontrollable events. Again as an example, a planned trip to the beach may be cancelled for one group of children and not for another. Despite explanations that appear clear and reasonable to an adult, the group unable to go continues to protest. It is not unusual to hear phrases like "It's not fair" in protest of being denied a desire. Having been told that she lives in a free country makes it difficult for the child to understand why she can't do what she wants when she wants to do it. This literal translation of right and wrong will gradually become more flexible. The child will become less harsh in judging herself and others and will learn to allow for extenuating circumstances.

Piaget pointed out two main characteristics of the child's moral judgments. The first of these is termed *moral realism* and involves the assumption that moral rules exist in their own right (similar to the idea of natural law). The second part is the idea that misdeeds have their own built-in punishments. An example of this is the situation where a child disobeys a class rule and cheats, unknown to her teacher, on a test. When she receives a failing grade, she is convinced that the low grade was a punishment for her misdeed.

School-age children actually judge themselves and one another more stringently than adults would and are likely to suggest punishment that sounds tantamount to an execution. It is possible, in terms of Freudian theory, that this behavior represents the child's attempts to maintain control over her impulses.

Because the school-age child is in such a rigid stage of morality, the adults around her must help the child to understand the reasons for punishment and to understand what distinguishes right from wrong. It is most important to help the child understand that punishment is for *deeds* she has done and not because she personally is not liked. The child's self-concept must be preserved and positively supported as she is being punished. For example, saying "I'm angry at what you did to your sister" instead of "I'm angry at you" separates the child's unacceptable action from the still accepted child herself and preserves her self-concept.

Any child's moral behavior depends upon the degree to which that child's family environment has taught her moral behaviors and judgments which conform to the moral codes of her socioeconomic class and culture. Fair rules and good role models will help the child internalize desirable societal values. As the child moves toward a more democratic morality and her own sense of right and wrong develops, she will begin to experience guilt after breaking a rule and will worry about the type and timing of punishment. If the child has learned that punishment is consistent, immediate, and appropriate to the nature of the infringement, she will experience less anxiety and feel more secure in relating to others. She will be less unsure about what constitutes acceptable and unacceptable behavior.

Cognitive development

Concrete operations

The cognitive development of the school-age child is in Piaget's phase of *concrete operations*. The school-age child is able to use symbols to organize his thoughts and manipulate the world around him. The preschooler had to experience an object physically before he could think about it (concrete thinking). The school-age child can experience an event *without* touching or seeing it. (See Fig. 14-9.) For example, this child can "taste" a chocolate cake by thinking about it (symbolic thinking). He can think about the past, present, and future and can use parts of past experiences to help understand the meaning of the present. He gradually becomes less self-centered and is able to see another person's point of view. The child is gradually moving towards the abstract thinking of the adolescent and adult.

Conservation A characteristic of the school-age child is the ability to *decenter* or focus on several aspects of a situation simultaneously. A child in this stage also is sensitive to *transformations* (for example, he knows that the amount of a fluid remains the same even when it is poured into different-sized containers with varying fluid levels) and can *reverse* his thinking (if half the

Figure 14-9 The school-age child thinks symbolically. She is tasting the raindrops (a concrete experience) and will later think symbolically by remembering the mental image of the raindrops.

contents of a 2-cup container is poured into a second cup, then the first cup will again contain 2 cups when the second cup is emptied back into the first cup). Piaget believes these three aspects of cognition (decentering, transformation, and reversibility) are interdependent and not able to exist individually. These three characteristics form the basis for the development of the characteristic of conservation. *Conservation* is the ability to be aware of the constancy of the properties of objects as they undergo transmutations (i.e., conservation of volume: the amount of fluid remains constant even as it is poured from a tall, thin glass into a short, squatty one).

Classification The school-age child gathers information, sorts it by defining properties, understands relations between classes and subclasses, and moves closer to the abstract thought of the next cognitive stage. The child may collect stamps or shells, separate them into groups, and classify them in any number of ways (for example, by size, color, or place of origin). In the process, new relationships between the objects may be discovered and new ideas created.

By gathering, sorting, and classifying information, the child determines the causes or reasons for events in his life. The child of this age delights in learning and collecting all the facts about things of interest to him, such as airplanes, or in learning about what will happen to him, such as in a medical procedure. He manipulates symbols and information to order, interpret, and understand his world. In this stage he collects all information on a subject. During abstract thought of adolescence he will judge its merits and form conclusions.

Syncretic thinking *Syncretic thinking* is characteristic of the school-age child. This means the child has a "tendency to connect a series of separate ideas into one confused whole."[20] He links coincidental but actually unrelated happenings and erroneously believes some cause-and-effect relationship exists. The child cannot focus simultaneously on differences among things and on their common relationships. The result is a conglomerated whole (syncretism) that lacks logical cause-and-effect relationships.

Ordering *Ordering* of information also demonstrates the child's inability to think simultaneously about several aspects of a situation. The child is able to determine, for example, that a city is part of a larger whole (Los Angeles is in California). But when he is questioned, he is unable to see that people living in Los Angeles are Californians. The child sees the part and whole separately, as if they were unrelated.

Symbol manipulation The cognitive system of the school-age child enables him to organize and manipulate the surrounding world. He does this by starting with what is immediately present or concrete. He can think of future events or possibilities only to a limited degree. This use of manipulation consists mainly of simple generalizations of the immediate present leading to new content. The child will take several math symbols and create new problems and relationships with them. In the process he may discover simple truths about higher levels of math but is not yet able to appreciate their scope.

Time recognition By age 7, the child is becoming more oriented in time and space. The ability to recognize time relationships, to place events in successive order, and to understand time intervals between events enables the child to begin to understand time in relation to a clock. Seasons and months are known, especially those involving something of special interest—birthdays, Halloween, etc.

Health maintenance

Safety

Motor vehicle accidents are the most common cause of accidental injury and death among children between the ages of 6 and 12 years. Injuries occur not only while children are riding in cars but also while they are walking between parked cars, crossing streets against the light, or riding bicycles or skate boards.

Statistics continue to support the use of auto seat belts as the best way to prevent severe injury or death when used appropriately for age and size. School-age children should be strapped into seat belts and not allowed to sit in the back of a station wagon or climb boisterously around the car.

Drowning is another major cause of death in this age group. Water safety and survival skills should be taught with basic swimming skills at an early age.

Many nurses include counseling regarding smoke detectors in their visits with parents. Smoke detectors are effective in preventing injury or death due to fires. A family-designed fire escape plan should be initiated and practiced one or two times a month. Burns among children also frequently result from curiosity and fascination with matches and fire.

Accidents frequently occur while children are playing, skating, or riding school buses. Children of this age are energetic and in almost constant motion. In their activities, they are not aware of potentially harmful situations. Thus burns, bumps, bruises, sprains, and even eye injuries may result. Accident prevention should be taught and enforced in schools and homes, and nurses need to promote safety by helping parents and children identify and avoid hazards. Skateboard and motorcycle enthusiasts should use helmets and knee and elbow pads to prevent serious injury and possible death. Parents should be encouraged to enforce strict safety rules before children are allowed to participate in these dangerous sports. When a child does become injured, treatment should include being helped to identify the reasons for the accident and planning clearcut methods for preventing subsequent accidents.

As children spend increasing amounts of time away from parental supervision, new aspects of safety become important for their well-being. At this age they must be taught to refuse to accept things from, speak to, or ride with strangers. This concept is often integrated into the classroom teaching of the preschooler and then reinforced in kindergarten and primary years. If safety measures designed to prevent accidents are emphasized early, children increasingly can avoid accidents common to school age.

Sleep disturbances

Nightmares and sleep disturbances are common in the early school years. One reason for this is that these children have reached a stage of mental development in which they have a concept of death. At home, the bedtime hour should be a quiet time of sharing and support between parent and child. It is an optimal time to exchange experiences, explore and answer questions, and have quiet talks. The consistent routines of prayers and preparing for bed can be a source of comfort and ritual for the child who is frightened of the dark or going to sleep.

Fears of death and mutilation are very real for children this age. Television movies (especially violent ones), discussions with friends, and pictures in books can provoke anxiety and cause reluctance to go to bed, fear of the dark, and bad dreams. This anxiety may seem unreasonable to an adult, but it is a reflection of a child's feelings of powerlessness and fear of death. An adult the child trusts can, through presence and support, strengthen the child's coping and alleviate at least some of the fears. Empathetic adults also understand that pretenses of independence and bravado are actually defenses to cover up the child's feelings of helplessness and fear.

Parents can reassure the fearful child by maintaining as much bedtime ritual as necessary to make the child feel secure. Nightlights, authoritative reassurances that the child's fears will not come true, and assurances that the parent is in the next room if needed at all during the night often reduce fears and improve sleep.

Self-care and hygiene The school-age child is eager to learn about his body and become self-reliant in caring for himself as he grows older. The school can assist the family in health education. As the child grows, he should assume responsibility for more aspects of self-care. This gradual process is reinforced by the three main influential groups: parents, teachers, and peers.

The health curriculum within the school setting reinforces the importance of good basic self-care habits, such as bathing, washing hair, using only one's own comb and brush, eating nutritious basic foods, and getting exercise and adequate rest each day. Each of these content areas should be included in the health curriculum and presented in interesting and creative ways. Class projects can be included. For the child approaching adolescence, a knowledge of basic hygiene will help eliminate peer group rejection that can result from body odor, unbrushed teeth, and dirty hair. The peer group influences the older child's conformity to hygiene standards.

Dental care Dental decay is the single most prevalent health problem during the school years. Ninety-five percent of school-age children are affected by dental caries. By age 16, the average person has had seven teeth and fourteen tooth surfaces attacked by decay. This is unfortunate; dental caries are completely preventable. Parents and children should be taught to exercise good oral hygiene habits (brushing and flossing) at least twice a day; to maintain good nutrition; to use fluoride toothpaste; to avoid sticky, sweet foods or at least to brush immediately after eating them; and to obtain regular 6-month dental visits.

Many children of school age wear dental braces. In some settings braces are well accepted or even considered to increase one's social status, but some children experience teasing by peers. Comments such as "railroad tracks" or "tin grin" are commonly heard. Group conformity is important during the school-age period. Any slight difference will increase group pressure to conform and increase the "different" child's anxiety level. A trusted adult can give support to alleviate the child's anxieties. Discuss feelings and attitudes with students. Others in the group may realize that it is all right to be different, especially when it leads to self-improvement.

Drug use Parents frequently feel uninformed and inadequate to approach children about drugs, and many believe in delaying the discussion of alcohol and other drug abuse for children above 12 years of age. Parent and child denial of substance abuse is widespread. Encourage parents to discuss topics as general as feelings about oneself in relation to others and peer pressures and how to deal with them. Adults as role models can serve to initiate some thinking and discussion with students before they reach upper grade levels, where all kinds of experimentation is common. See Chap. 42 for a discussion of substance abuse.

The handicapped child Current education laws are increasing the "mainstreaming" of physically and emotionally handicapped children into the regular classroom. This requires many school nurses to use increasing nursing skills in their daily work. They act as resources to school staffs and as liaisons between the school, the family, and the health care professions. See Chap. 21 for a discussion of the chronically ill child.

Mental health Mental health is of overriding importance to the child's well-being and healthful view of himself. Parents and other adults can support mental health by (1) taking time to share themselves and not just things with the child; (2) being good listeners to make the child feel worthwhile; and (3) directly telling the child the good things about himself. The adult who can be genuine and not afraid to say he's sorry and who lives a life worthy of respect sets a positive mental health example.

Developmental milestones*

The 6-year-old

The 6-year-old is self-centered, opinionated, a "know-it-all," bossy, and easily hurt by criticism. His boundless energy allows him to explore the world. He has an insatiable appetite for new experiences and is easily distracted by fascinating objects.

*This section was compiled by Nancy L. Ramsey.

Fine and gross motor development The 6-year-old is a whirlwind of constant motion: jumping, hopping, rolling on the floor, and wiggling while sitting on a chair. This child's gross movements are awkward at times. His skill increases while practicing skating, skipping, running, bicycling, and jumping rope. Fine motor coordination is less developed than gross muscle coordination. The 6-year-old cuts with scissors, hammers, ties shoelaces, and dresses himself. He prints unevenly and frequently reverses letters.

Family and social relationships The 6-year-old's relationship with his parents varies widely. One moment he seeks affectionate hugs and kisses; the next moment he defies a parent's request, blames the parent for everything, whines, argues, and dawdles when hurried. This child wants to accept complete responsibility for tasks or projects, but frequently lacks the experience and attention span to complete them.

The 6-year-old is in emotional upheaval. He is innocent, charming, affectionate, but is also tense and upset. He frequently returns briefly to earlier patterns of tension-reducing behaviors: chewing on fingers or sucking his thumb. As this child leaves home, separation anxiety briefly recurs. This child, when leaving for a new school, needs praise and consistent home routines. He frequently vacillates between acting like a baby and acting like a big child. The 6-year-old is fearful of strange noises, witches, skeletons, fantasized persons, and the elements of air, wind, fire, and rain.

This child seeks out a same-sex play group. He is too self-centered, expecting people to adapt immediately to his wishes, to be truly a team member. Six-year-olds play together, but their play is often independent. Group play frequently ends in brawls because this age child doesn't know when to withdraw to avoid getting hurt.

School The 6-year-old's day centers on the school. His language is well developed; it shows thought and gives him pleasure. He can read, count to 20, and define shapes. He begins to understand the abstract concepts of afternoon, morning, and tomorrow. He defines objects by their use and is interested in religion, including the concepts of heaven and God.

Self-care The 6-year-old plays in the tub but resists getting washed. This child must be reminded to wash before dinner but dresses and undresses alone. He drops toys on the floor and clothes wherever they were removed. He goes to the bathroom alone.

The 7-year-old

The 7-year-old is quiet, pensive, and reflective. He is consolidating past life experiences into an understandable whole. The 7-year-old is less satisfied with himself and the world. He demands perfection from himself and his family, is conscientious, and values the opinions of others. Mood swings range from exuberance to anger when family members do not fulfill his expectations.

Fine and gross motor development The 7-year-old is more cautious than the boisterous 6-year-old. His activity level is lower. This child practices skills to perfect them. He swims, bicycles, skates, and enjoys reading and quiet games.

Family and social relationships The 7-year-old's relationship with his parents is closer. He wants to be liked by family, peers, and teachers. This child is eager to cooperate and please these people and is sensitive to their opinion of him.

The child at this age enjoys teasing others but tolerates criticism and teasing poorly. He may feel "picked on" and may threaten to run away when feeling mistreated. The 7-year-old knows right from wrong and establishes very high standards for himself and the family. Even tiny failures to reach these high standards may make him feel inferior, withdraw, act shy, or be angry.

This child's fears of the dark, robbers, ghosts, and of feeling inadequate in a new situation continue.

School The 7-year-old enjoys school and seeks the teacher's approval. He can tell time and recognize the day, month, and season. He understands the basic concepts of addition and subtraction. He prints several sentences and reverses letters less frequently.

The 7-year-old is less egocentric, is able to see the other person's point of view, and can identify with and feel the other child's emotion (such as

hurt). He has a more realistic understanding of cause and effect.

Self-care This child needs less help from parents in caring for himself. He can dress, undress alone, brush his own teeth, scrub himself clean, brush his own hair, and go to bed alone. However, he still needs reminding to wash before meals. Like the 6-year-old, he dawdles during self-care activities and drops his clothes on the floor.

The 8-year-old

The 8-year-old is more self-confident, enthusiastic, and friendly. He curiously explores "the whys" of new experiences in the world. Eight is an age of creative intellectual expansion. This child enjoys learning about science and nature. He excitedly begins new activities but has difficulty completing them.

Fine and gross motor development The 8-year-old perfects his skills, whether playing jump rope or wrestling. His body movements appear more graceful and coordinated.

Family and social relationship The 8-year-old's relationship with both parents is closer and more sensitive. He wants their approval. He is interested in adult activities and closely scrutinizes the adults around him. He is less self-centered and listens to and tries to understand his parents' explanations.

This child increasingly merges into the same-sex peer group's activities. He wants to join their activities rather than play alone. He often has a love-hate relationship with friends of the opposite sex. Boys tend to be secretive about a girlfriend. This child may have a best friend of the same sex, and hero worship begins at this age. The 8-year-old is truthful and lies less. He more clearly distinguishes reality from fantasy and has fewer fears than younger children.

School Eight is a year of intellectual expansion, growing from the child's explorations of the world. His memory increases and his vocabulary soars. He is learning to write rather than print. He is able to categorize objects by both similarities and differences. This child enjoys studying rocket ships and science.

He is proud of his accomplishments, fears

poor grades, and wants to be praised by both teachers and parents. He is friendly and enjoys playing with friends at school.

Self-care The 8-year-old dresses himself completely. His social manners are better. He eats food more reasonably, rather than grabbing and cramming it into his mouth. He still enjoys being tucked into bed with a consistent routine. This child should have the responsibility for completing a stable list of chores and enjoys being paid in money for the work.

The 9-year-old

The 9-year-old plays hard and works hard. He is very interested in all group activities, both the team play of friends and the activities of his family. This child's behavior appears more mature, refined, and independent. He is less restless than the 8-year-old.

Fine and gross motor development The 9-year-old's eye-hand coordination is almost perfected. This age child enjoys activities to develop this coordination: writing, sewing, knitting, and model building. He spends long hours also perfecting gross muscle skills, such as baseball. His muscular control and timing show more expertise.

Family and social relationships The 9-year-old is more interested in his friends than in his parents. However, he enjoys taking part in family decisions. He enjoys helping his mother with housework and running errands. He is easier to discipline and begins to take responsibility for his actions. He has fewer fears and knows Santa Claus is not real.

If this child's peer group and parents' wishes collide, he will follow his friends. He is more empathetic, sympathetic, and loyal. These attributes enable him to become a valued team or group member. He still prefers same-sex friends. He is loyal to his peers and the group increasingly dominates his behavior. Hero worship intensifies; crushes on teachers are common. Nine-year-olds, however, do occasionally chase the opposite sex around the playground.

School The 9-year-old's attention span is longer. He is increasingly interested in the subject rather than the teacher. He understands explanations and strives to follow the teacher's directions. He now enthusiastically completes tasks. This child describes the characteristics of objects, not simply defining them in terms of usage. He multiplies, divides, and recites five numbers in reverse order. The 9-year-old loves historical sagas, reading, constructing projects, and winning at team sports. Good students are accepted by classmates while they reject superior students. At this age girls are usually intellectually superior to boys.

Self-care The 9-year-old can care for himself completely. He has good table manners but often needs reminding to brush his teeth. Boys are unaware of dirty clothes while girls are interested in cleanliness and clothes. The 9-year-old cleans up his room and toys. He is still reluctant to go to bed.

The 10-year-old

The 10-year-old is on a peaceful plateau. He is at peace with himself and the world. He is happy, confident, serene, and content. This child's behavior is more predictable and consistent, for he has more control over his emotions, behavior, and the environment. This child's social manners are courteous with adults outside the home.

Fine and gross motor development The 10-year-old has greater muscular strength, stamina, and coordination. This child thoroughly enjoys all physical activity: climbing, jumping, and skating. Fine motor development is perfected. This child spends hours practicing skills, such as playing the clarinet, for a child's talents are increasingly obvious at this age. Girls begin the pubertal growth spurt and tower over boys, whose height varies widely.

Family and social relationships The 10-year-old is closer to his family than at 9 years and has a better relationship with his mother. He enjoys attention from his dad and wants to join him in activities.

The 10-year-old is more relaxed and more easily expresses affection toward his parents. This child adapts more easily to rules, tolerates frustration better, and lives more harmoniously within the family. He explosively but briefly expresses emotions ranging from impulsive hugs and kisses to crying and depression. He gets angry but does not hold grudges.

Ten is the age of intense peer group memberships. This child desperately wants to join clubs and teams. He delights at competing and winning at competitive games. He often loves and praises a best friend. Hero worship intensifies. The 10-year-old is a successful group member.

School The 10-year-old reasons by cause and effect but has difficulty visualizing abstract relationships (combining facts and seeing the relationship). He ponders solutions to the world's social problems. This child believes in fairness and stern punishment for misdeeds. He focuses on the wrong more than the right.

This child enjoys learning in school. He writes clearly and fast. He relishes detective and adventure stories and magic tricks. The 10-year-old manipulates fractions and numbers over 100. He memorizes longer material. However, this child is impulsive and, although working hard, performs better when following a schedule. He would rather listen and play than work.

Self-care The 10-year-old neglects self-care. He hates and masterfully avoids self-care activities. His room is a mess and clothes are dropped on the floor throughout the house. This child hates to change to clean clothes and needs prodding to take a bath.

The 11-year-old

In contrast to the happy, serene 10-year-old, the 11-year-old gives his parents a glimpse of adolescent mood swings. He is resentful and critical of adults in authority. He rebels against instruction and rules. This child is often moody, unhappy, and in turmoil.

The 11-year-old wants to be independent. He thrives on exploration and adventure through which he learns about the world. The child at this age is highly moralistic, interested in religion, and attacks injustices in the world. He expects fairness and believes in unyielding punishment for misdeeds. However, this child wants friends to lie to protect him from punishment.

Eleven is a fearful age. The 11-year-old worries about everything—school, parents, money, and illness.

Fine and gross motor development The 11-year-old is active and energetic. This child enjoys outdoor activities and loves sports. He is agile at sports, but because of this child's rapid body changes, he may be clumsy at home. The body changes of puberty become more noticeable. Girls are more interested in their body changes than boys are.

Family and social relationships The 11-year-old is constantly with the family and enjoys family activities. He scrutinizes how adults (and parents) treat each other. His emotions are ambivalent: one moment sneaking affectionate hugs and the next moment criticizing and rebelling against parents. However, his behavior away from parents is courteous and considerate.

In contrast to his parents, the 11-year-old is gay and kind toward friends. He wants approval and acceptance by his friends. He confides innermost secrets to them, not parents. This child often works together with other young people in a group effort to improve the community. He wants to be financially independent and seeks small jobs after school.

School The 11-year-old is excited about learning and asks constantly "why and how" questions. He resists and complains about homework. This preadolescent begins to describe things abstractly, such as peace and justice. He wants the teacher, and his peer group, to challenge his learning.

Self-care The 11-year-old is capable of completely caring for himself. However, this child rebels against all rules and authority. Therefore, this young person needs urging to wash the back of his neck and behind his ears, and to shampoo his hair. The 11-year-old still resists going to bed and arising in the morning.

The 12-year-old

The 12-year-old is more cooperative, friendly, and even-tempered. He is more self-reliant and independent. This preadolescent is more satisfied with himself and the world. This young person is less tormented and is obviously growing up. He misbehaves less because he thinks abstractly and can analyze the consequences of his behavior. He will lie to protect a friend.

Fine and gross motor development The 12-year-old thrives on frantic, intense activity, at which he persists until collapsing. He enthusiastically enjoys all gross motor activity.

Both sexes' interest in sex increases. Girls height and weight gain is at a peak. Breasts develop and axillary hair appears. A girl at 12 may flaunt her developing body or be embarrassed and hide it. She comfortably discusses sexuality and masturbation with an older female friend. Boys are increasingly interested in their own sexual development. Discussions with friends often center on sex. Boys masturbate and have frequent erections.

Family and social relationships The 12-year-old relates to his parents better but is less affectionate. He expects parents to respect his privacy. Although he tests limits, the 12-year-old wants consistent limits.

The 12-year-old's peer group decreases in size. He often pairs off with a best friend. This child appears constantly accompanied by one or more friends. At school, interest in the opposite sex intensifies. Girls talk about boys, and both sexes play games involving close accidental contact with each other.

School The 12-year-old learns quickly. He enjoys collecting facts, doing math, playing sports, and reading on travel, science, home, and nature. Girls prefer romantic novels, while boys prefer adventure and mystery stories.

This child asks many questions. He wants to excel at school and be liked by teachers and classmates.

Self-care The 12-year-old is more concerned with his appearance. Boys bathe more frequently and change into clean clothes more frequently. Girls are intrigued by makeup and stylish clothes. Both sexes are still reluctant to go to bed at night, but arise more easily in the morning.

References

1. Erik H. Erikson, *Childhood and Society*, Norton, New York, 1950, pp. 219–234.
2. Alma Nemir and Warren E. Schaller, *The School Health Program*, Saunders, Philadelphia, 1975, p. 16.
3. V. C. Vaughn and R. I. McKay (eds.), *Nelson Textbook of Pediatrics*, Saunders, Philadelphia, 1975, p. 30.
4. Ibid., p. 21.
5. *Why Is Your Child Being Screened for Scoliosis?* Children's Hospital of Los Angeles, 1979, p. 77.
6. Vaughn et al., op. cit., p. 77.
7. Ibid., p. 21.
8. Ibid., p. 254.
9. Ibid., pp. 109–110.
10. Erikson, op. cit., p. 226.
11. Ibid., p. 227.
12. Ibid., p. 226.
13. Ibid., p. 227.
14. Ibid., p. 22.
15. Mari Sieman, "Mental Health in School-Aged Children," *The American Journal of Maternal Child Nursing* 3(4):215 (July-August 1978).
16. Diane E. Papalia and Sally W. Olds, *Human Development*, McGraw-Hill, New York, 1978, p. 236.
17. Ibid., p. 237.
18. Sieman, op. cit., p. 215.
19. Ibid., p. 215.
20. Herbert Ginsburg and Sylvia Opper, *Piaget's Theory of Intellectual Development, an Introduction*, Prentice-Hall, Englewood Cliffs, New Jersey, 1969, p. 110.

Chapter 15 **The adolescent**

Jacqueline Prokop Ficht

Upon completion of this chapter, the student will be able to:

1. Define the terms *adolescence* and *puberty*.
2. Describe the nutritional requirements of an adolescent.
3. Describe the psychosocial developmental task identity vs. role confusion.
4. Describe the adolescent's body-image changes.
5. Describe the functions of peer groups in adolescence.

6. Describe the adolescent's cognitive development.
7. Describe moral development during adolescence.
8. Describe accident prevention for adolescents.
9. Identify five guidelines to facilitate communication with teenagers.

Introduction—viewpoints on adolescence

Adolescents are the focus of a lot of public attention. It is unfortunately often true that the most conspicuous teenage activity is that which "causes problems" of one kind or another. Until there is trouble, people often do not notice what adolescents do, and a great deal of positive behavior goes unrecognized and unrewarded. Bandura[1] has suggested that a self-fulfilling prophecy may take place: Adults, having been brainwashed to expect trouble from adolescents, may unintentionally act in ways that foster problematical behavior.

No one exists in a vacuum, and this is perhaps most true of adolescents. They are subjected almost daily to a barrage of sexually stimulating books, magazines, and advertisements, yet the reason behind their early sexual activity is questioned. Violence is glorified by television and movies, yet when young people behave violently or commit crimes, people wonder why. Adolescents reflect the society in which they grow up; adults often lose sight of this fact.

Since World War II, teenagers have had to deal with threats unknown to previous generations: technological "advances" that make possible the destruction of the world or its inhabitants, pollution that makes the quality of life in some areas questionable, energy shortages, radical religious cults, and brainwashing and deprogramming. Little wonder, then, that an adolescent's attitude may be one of "live for today."

Our incredible technological advances also hold little for the teenager. A modern technological society cannot avoid alienating its young people from adult value systems.[2] Western technology and society have become so complex that it is increasingly difficult for adolescents to obtain the qualifications for entry into the adult world of work, economic independence, and social position. Advanced technology also fosters a relatively demanding, specialized, and impersonal approach to living that does not inspire much enthusiasm or commitment among young people. They often feel Western society has worshipped technological advances and has forgotten humanistic and spiritual aspects of human development.

A further difficulty for adolescents is that there are few if any clear-cut landmarks to signify to young people or others *when* a child has entered adolescence or when an adolescent has become an adult. In primitive societies, *rites of passage* mark these transitions and make each person's status as child, adolescent, or adult clear to everyone. In our own social practices, there are no universally recognized milestones into or out of adolescence, although Christian confirmation, the Jewish bar mitzvah and bat mitzvah, and marriage signify adolescent and adult status to some extent within some social subgroups. One important outcome of the uncertainty about when adolescence begins and ends is that many people, including adolescents themselves, have conflicting expectations about how "grown up" teenagers should be in various situations. One may be considered old enough to date but not old enough to drive a car on a date, for example, or old enough to choose an abortion but not old enough to sign a legal contract. Until a few years ago, young people could join the armed forces several years before they could vote. Adolescents often feel that they are expected to act like adults without receiving the privileges that accompany adulthood.

Stages of adolescence by age

Adolescence is a rather long developmental period, spanning several years. Adolescence is defined by a dictionary as "The state or process of growing up, the period of time from puberty to maturity."[3] *Puberty* is "the period of becoming first capable of reproducing sexually, marked by

maturing of the genital organs and development of the secondary sex characteristics."[4] It is useful to see adolescence as a process of adaptation to puberty.[5]

There is such a difference between children entering and young adults emerging from adolescence that it is helpful to subdivide the period into stages. It is important to remember that these age divisions are only guidelines for assessing and understanding adolescents, not absolute rules. Each adolescent has his or her own developmental pace and schedule; furthermore, we are all familiar with the teenager who is "13 going on 30" or "20 going on 15."

Early adolescence

Early adolescence, usually from about 11 to 13 years of age in girls and from about 12 to 14 in boys, is characterized by the rapid physical and phychosocial changes that terminate childhood. Physical changes are pronounced, as will be described later, and the young adolescent is preoccupied with them and worries whether the changes are progressing normally and will "turn out all right." Early adolescents form strong loyalties to friends who are in about the same stage of physical maturity; childhood friendships tend to dissolve if some members of the friendship group begin their pubertal changes earlier than the others. Family relationships become somewhat strained, especially between girls and their mothers, as the young person begins the necessary but awkward process of loosening ties to parents and strengthening alliances with peers and adults outside the family. Most early adolescents decrease their involvement in family activities and tend to "put down" parents and resent parental criticism. Although the early adolescents are not as strongly tied to the family as earlier, they also are not as firmly allied with the peer group as they will be in middle adolescence, and they move freely between the two.

Early adolescent males, because of their rapid growth, are often clumsy, lazy, and uninterested in their appearance. They may have to be reminded frequently of the need for good hygiene. Boys are acutely aware of the change in their genitals. They need to be reassured that masturbation is engaged in by virtually all teenage males and that it is normal—it will not cause hair to grow on their palms! Boys assess their masculinity primarily in relationship to other boys by comparing their chest, muscle, and genital size and their capacity to ejaculate. Involvement in an all-male peer group provides support and a needed sense of security. Masturbation and other sexual experimentation with friends of the same sex is common, especially among boys, and at this age is not predictive of a homosexual orientation in later life. Seminal emissions, or "wet dreams," should be explained to boys, and when they occur the vulnerable adolescent male should not be teased. Likewise, *gynecomastia*, the development of breast tissue in early adolescent males, should be explained as a normal consequence of temporary hormone imbalances so that the young man does not suffer needlessly from doubts about his masculinity. Both boys and girls at this age are extremely sensitive to the opinions of others, and even gentle teasing can be very distressing.

Early adolescent girls may become intensely preoccupied with their physical appearance very early in puberty and often feel that, in a society that places such a premium on beauty, they do not measure up. The new stresses of becoming an adolescent, combined with hormonal fluctuations and imbalances, often cause them to be moody and tense. Girls compare breast size and menstrual function with one another but use boys to assess their femininity.

The young girl is vulnerable to sexual exploitation. If she is to develop a healthy sense of her sexuality, it is important that there be men in her life who care about her and do not view her as a sexual object. Fathers are often uncomfortable with their daughters as they begin to develop sexually. As a result they may rebuff the girl's attentions and say, "You're too old to sit on my lap or hug or kiss me." The young adolescent is unable to perceive that her father is having difficulty dealing with the fact that she is growing up, and she often blames his changed behavior on herself. In extreme cases this misunderstanding may lead to embarrassment and dislike of her developing body and make her journey through adolescence more difficult.

Girls, like boys, need accurate information about physical changes to expect during puberty. The young girl who has her first menstrual period without having received information beforehand will imagine that she is going to bleed to death or that she is terribly ill or injured. Even girls who have been adequately prepared for menstruation routinely call it "the curse." Often well-meaning parents make menstruation even more difficult to accept by insisting that the young girl curtail her activities, thereby making her feel that growing up is hampering her life.

Early adolescent girls often form intense attachments with a best friend of the same sex. Usually the attraction is based on complementing each other—one is looking to the other for some trait she would like in herself and vice versa. By forming a close relationship with one who possesses this trait, it is almost as if she has it herself. These early adolescent best friends are often inseparable and tend to dress, talk, and think alike. The friendship usually does not stand the test of time well, however, for eventually one girl fails to live up to the standards the other has set, and the relationship crumbles. These intense relationships are replaced by the peer group in middle adolescence.

Girls are usually about 2 years ahead of the same-age boys, not only in physical maturity but also in their capacity for imagination and abstract thought, in their ability to perceive the feelings of others, and in their tolerance for frustration. Girls often are quite creative and record their deepest thoughts and feelings in diaries, a prelude to the journals kept by adults.

Toward the end of early adolescence, both boys and girls begin fuller participation in their peer groups. At this time, while complaining about parental restrictions, they eagerly take on the restrictions imposed by the peer group. As they move away from the family, they have a new sense of belonging within the peer group.

Middle adolescence

Middle adolescence is the period between about 13 and 16 years of age in girls and 14 to 17 in boys. The period of most rapid physical change is past, and the adolescent now focuses somewhat less on growth and other body changes and becomes absorbed in personal identity: Who am I? What will I do with my life?

As a necessary part of developing a strong, personalized sense of self, middle adolescents typically become rather harsh critics of parents and other authoritative adults and of their attitudes and values. As they "declare independence" from their families, they become intensely involved in their peer groups and the adolescent subculture. Adolescents mimic peers and other acquaintances and public figures they admire, borrowing portions of the behavior and opinions of these figures as part of the process of establishing who they are and what they want to be like. Some career planning takes place at this age. Dating is usual, and romantic and sexual interests or activities are a preoccupation for many middle adolescents (see Fig. 15-1).

Late adolescence

Late adolescence usually lasts from about 16 or 17 to 21. Physical changes are far less apparent than earlier as the growth process draws to a close. In late adolescence young people step up their preparations for living an adult life-style. They must now make career choices, an important step toward financial independence.

Intimacy and maintaining an intimate rela-

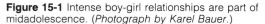

Figure 15-1 Intense boy-girl relationships are part of midadolescence. (*Photograph by Karel Bauer.*)

tionship with another person are developmental goals for late adolescence. The large peer group often is replaced by a smaller group of closer friends, and dating activities commonly become narrowed to one or a small number of dating partners; many adolescents marry or form other exclusive love relationships during this period. Before adolescents can engage in genuine psychological intimacy with others, they must have a fairly firm sense of personal identity. Intimacy requires sharing one's inner self, and they cannot share what they do not yet have; moreover, such self-exposure causes anxiety until identity is secure.

Relationships with parents are far less stormy as young people become increasingly confident about their independence and therefore find adult guidance and advice less threatening. Parents and adolescents begin to develop a new relationship in which they enjoy one another as adults.

Late adolescents also typically become involved in issues that have to do with their concern about the future of the society in which they are about to take their place as adults. They exert much energy toward peace, ecology, population control, and racial harmony.

In summary, late adolescents are involved in applying the psychosocial development that has built up during childhood and the earlier adolescent years. They are putting the final touches to their readiness to function as adults. Maturity in late adolescence is characterized by the capacity to be loving, to put the welfare of others before one's own pleasure, to wait for emotional gratification, to control aggression and impulsivity, and to plan for the future.

Physical development during adolescence

Adolescence causes pronounced changes in body size, structure, and shape. One-fourth of adult height is acquired during the adolescent growth spurt that begins at about age 10 in girls and about 13 in boys. Children of both sexes approximately double their weight between 10 and 18 years of age. The extremities grow first; this fact is responsible for the young adolescent's characteristic "leggy," gangly appearance and large hands and feet. The hips, chest, and shoulders widen next, and finally the trunk and spinal cord lengthen so that adult height is reached. Girls usually achieve their full height by 17, boys by 21. The longer growth period of males results in their usually having greater height, larger muscles, larger heart and lungs, bigger skeletal frame, and a larger oxygen-carrying capacity of the blood at maturity than most females.

If the nurse were to observe a group of 13-year-old boys and girls, marked differences in stage of physical maturity would be apparent. Some of the young adolescents would be *prepubertal* children (not yet beginning puberty), some would be just starting their pubertal changes, and others would be close to their adult height and weight.

The triggering mechanism by which puberty occurs is unknown, but it is clear that hormonal changes play a central role in producing the increased growth rate and sex differences that take place in early adolescence. An increase in production of gonadotropin releasing factor (GnRF) from the hypothalamus causes increased pituitary secretion of gonadotropins [follicle-stimulating hormone (FSH) and luteinizing hormone (LH)], and these hormones in turn cause the gonads to increase their production of estrogen and testosterone, as shown in Fig. 15-2. Estrogen and testosterone are responsible for the maturation of the genital organs and the development of the secondary sex characteristics (voice changes, breast development, and growth of pubic, facial, and axillary hair). Under the influence of the pubertal hormone changes, females acquire a characteristically rounded body. The hips widen to accommodate childbirth, the breasts enlarge, and adipose tissue is laid down in the breasts, hips, and thighs. Estrogen also stimulates uterine endometrial and vaginal growth and accelerates linear growth and skeletal maturation. In males, testosterone stimulates the growth of pubic, axillary, and facial hair; accelerates skeletal growth and maturation; produces the male characteristics of broad shoulders, large chest, and narrow hips; and increases the number and size of muscle cells. Sexual development of adolescents of both sexes is further described below.

Figure 15-2 Hormonal interactions of sexual maturity. (*Adapted from L. Whaley and D. Wong, "The Adolescent Years," in Nursing Care of Infants and Children, Mosby, St. Louis, 1979.*)

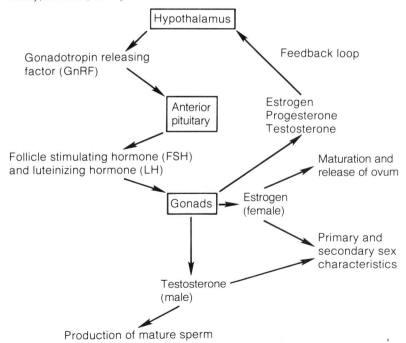

Female physical development

Pubertal changes in females are assessed according to breast development and pubic hair growth. In American girls the average age of *thelarche* (initial breast development) is 10.8 years. *Pubarche* (first appearance of pubic hair) follows soon after, at the average age of 11.0 years. *Menarche* (first menstruation), which is widely used as the indication that adolescence has begun, is actually a rather late event in puberty and does not occur until the average girl is within 3 or 4 in of her adult height. The average age at menarche among American girls is reported to range between 12.6 and 12.9 years, but it is not unusual for menarche to take place as early as 10 or as late as 16. Over the past century or so, the age at which girls first menstruate has declined. This earlier maturation may be due to better nutrition, better medical care of children with severe illness, and other environmental factors. A direct relationship may exist between height, weight, and onset of puberty, so that when a "critical" weight for a given height is attained, adolescent maturation begins. In the United States, menarche is achieved at an average

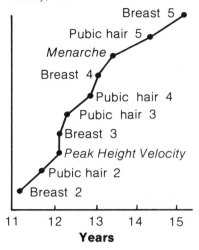

Figure 15-3 The sequence and mean ages of pubertal events in females. [*Adapted from the data of Marshall and Tanner. Numerals refer to the Tanner growth stages described in Table 15-1. From A. Root, "Endocrinology of Puberty," Journal of Pediatrics* **83**:1–19 (July 1978).]

height of 158.5 cm and a weight of 43 kg (ranging from 32 to 60 kg).

J. M. Tanner[6] has developed a standard method of assessing and classifying physical development in adolescence. The five Tanner stages of female maturation are reviewed in Table 15-1. Figure 15-3 shows the average ages at which the stages are achieved.

Other aspects of physical development can be expected to occur in conjunction with certain of the Tanner stages. For example, the adolescent height spurt begins in stage 2. Total body fat increases, hips widen, and, with breast enlargement, the adult female form begins to emerge.

In stage 3, the vagina enlarges and the vaginal epithelium, under estrogen stimulation from the ovaries, increases in thickness. *Döderlein's bacillus*, which is actually a group of microorganisms that produce lactic acid, appears in vaginal mucus, making the vaginal environment acidic and thereby protecting it against pathogenic bacteria. The height spurt reaches its peak late in stage 3.

If menarche did not occur late in stage 3, it occurs in stage 4. Axillary hair appears just before or just afterward. Ovulation during the first few menstrual cycles is rare; hence most early adolescent girls are infertile.

Table 15-1 Stages of female maturation

Stage	Breast	Pubic hair
1	Only the papilla shows elevation	None
2	Breast bud appears as a small mound formed by the elevation of the breast and papilla. Areola increases in diameter	Sparse, long, slightly pigmented, downy. It is straight or only slightly curled, primarily along the labia
3	Further enlargement of breast and areola with no separation of their contours	More widespread, darker, coarser, curlier
4	Areola and papilla may rise to form a secondary mound above the level of the breast	Adult in type but not as widespread
5	Areola has recessed to general breast contour. Breast is now mature	Adult in type, quantity, and distribution pattern

Source: J. M. Tanner, *Growth at Adolescence*, Blackwell, Oxford, 1962.

Table 15-2 Stages of male maturation

Stage	Genitalia	Pubic hair	Facial hair
1	Penis, testes, and scrotum are of childhood size	None	Like that in childhood
2	Scrotum and testes enlarge, but not penis. Scrotal skin reddens	Sparse, long, slightly pigmented, downy. It is straight or slightly curled, primarily at base of penis	Little change
3	Continued growth of scrotum and testes. Penis grows mainly in length	Darker, coarser, curlier, spreading sparsely over the junction of the pubes	About 50% of males show a small amount of short, lightly pigmented hair at corners of upper lip and on sides of face in front of ears
4	Continued growth. Penis grows mainly in width	Adult in type but not as widespread	Moderate amount of short, lightly pigmented, coarse down on upper lip; also long, fine, unpigmented hair on cheeks and occasionally along borders of the chin
5	Adult in size	Adult in type, quantity, and distribution pattern	Conspicuous growth on upper lip. Longer, more pigmented hair on sides of face

Source: J. M. Tanner, *Growth at Adolescence*, Blackwell, Oxford, 1962.

Male physical development

Pubertal progress in males is measured according to genital growth and pubic hair development. In the United States, pubic hair appears in males between 11.5 and 11.8 years of age on the average. The pubertal growth spurt is accompanied by an increase in number and size of muscle cells, which leads to the greater muscular strength of the male.

Tanner's classification of male maturation is reviewed in Table 15-2. Figure 15-4 shows the average ages at which the Tanner stages are reached. The rapid gain in weight and height begins in stage 1. There is also an increase in body fat. These trends continue in stage 2, and the male physique begins to appear. The height spurt continues through stage 3. Shoulders broaden, and muscle mass increases in proportion to fat. The cartilage of the larynx enlarges and the voice begins to deepen. In stage 4, axillary hair appears, the voice deepens, and the boy may experience ejaculation. There is a distinct enlargement of the breasts with a slight projection of the areola. The conspicuous breast enlargement (gynecomastia) ends in stage 5 as hormonal balance is established and the body reaches adult form.

Psychosocial development

Emotional characteristics of adolescents

The emotional status of adolescents is often unpredictable and labile (changeable). Teens live enthusiastically in the present, reaching emo-

Figure 15-4 The sequence and mean ages of pubertal events in males. [*Adapted from the data of Marshall and Tanner. Numerals refer to the Tanner growth stages described in Table 15-2. From A. Root, "Endocrinology of Puberty," Journal of Pediatrics* **83**:1–19 (July 1978).]

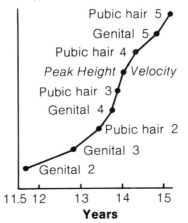

Pubic hair 5
Genital 5
Pubic hair 4
Peak Height Velocity
Pubic hair 3
Genital 4
Pubic hair 2
Genital 3
Genital 2

11.5 12   13   14   15
Years

tional heights (see Fig. 15-5). They may quickly then plunge to the depths of moodiness and depression. These emotional outbursts may be precipitated by what seem to be minor events to the parents but are interpreted as major crises by teenagers.

All teens occasionally lose control of themselves in an emotional outburst; this outburst releases accumulated anxiety. Teens then feel guilty, fear future loss of control, and retreat to reassess their behavior. They plan methods of maintaining self-control in the future, and later reassert themselves. Teenagers may daydream deeply, not hearing others talking to them. Do not ridicule the unstable emotions or behavior of adolescents. Allow teens time to be alone. Accept their feelings, saying, "It's okay to be

Figure 15-5 The teenager enjoys life to the fullest.

angry." Discuss other ways to express anger next time. "What else can you do when you're so angry?" Avoid immediately criticizing the outburst of behavior, for teens will usually quickly gain self-control; praise them for this.

Developmental task: Identity vs. role confusion

Before puberty school-age children have a well-developed self-identity. From infancy on they have developed their sex role identity, their moral standards, and their various roles as a member of their family, neighborhood, and school group. They know how other people feel about them (the Gonzales child, a C student, shy, good looking, athletic, etc.) and they are fully familiar with their own body and abilities. But adolescence brings many extensive changes that put the childhood sense of self out of date; one cannot be the same at 15 as one was at 10 or 12. By the end of adolescence one must be a worker or homemaker (or both), not a school child. One must be a person who makes provisions for day-to-day needs, not one who is taken care of by parents. Adolescents must make some satisfactory adaptation to their new sexual maturity. They must develop their own standards of behavior, which necessarily vary from their childhood beliefs.

Adolescence, then, is dominated by the process of becoming someone rather different from the person one was as a child. Accordingly, the main developmental task of adolescence is to build a new sense of personal identity, and adolescent psychosocial development is directly related to accomplishing this task. Erik Erikson[7] has described the sense of *identity* as the feeling that one's self (personality) has continuity (consistency and predictability) and that one's self-appraisal is essentially the same as the views other people have about oneself. According to Erikson, failure to accomplish the adolescent developmental task of achieving identity is *role confusion*, in which the adolescent lacks a firm sense of inner sameness; he feels he is not who people think he is and he has chameleon-like fluctuations in life goals, personal beliefs, or ways of relating to others. It must be understood that identity is not attained all at once and that a firm sense of identity is not to be expected before the end of the adolescent period.

During adolescence the earlier developmental

tasks are reworked so that adolescents can master them in an adult way rather than in the earlier ways that were appropriate to childhood. They now reestablish trust, not with the mother, but within peer friendships, relationships with nonparent adults, and, eventually, intimate heterosexual relationships. The struggle for autonomy now centers not upon resisting the control of the mother, but upon establishing themselves as individuals whose activities and beliefs are under their own control rather than dominated by the family. Initiative is tested anew as adolescents put themselves into dating situations and other unfamiliar experiences. Industriousness now focuses on entering or preparing to enter the competitive arenas of employment or post-high school education.

While establishing who they are, adolescents experience periods of self-doubt. Several factors contribute to this inner uncertainty. These young people no longer feel in control of their bodies or know just what to expect from them. The growth spurt produces a larger, unfamiliar, and sometimes awkward and displeasing body. New thoughts about oneself and changing attitudes toward parents are confusing and upsetting. Sexuality is something new and must be dealt with in some way. The peer group on which adolescents rely for a sounding board is itself quite changeable and uncertain. As social experience expands into new arenas, young people have to learn new roles and adapt to new expectations. They are frequently dissatisfied with their own performance and feel pessimistic about ever becoming the kind of persons they would like to be. Society, itself changing, offers little in the way of clear, universally approved standards for behavior or goals for the future.

Incorporating physical changes into identity

Adolescents experience changes in height, weight, body build, and secondary sex characteristics. Because so many changes occur at once, the early adolescent's body often does not feel like his or her own. A boy's body may also betray him by its awkwardness, sudden changes in voice, or an embarrassing sexual response. Breast development and onset of menses often occur before a young girl feels she is ready to cope with them.

Teenagers believe their bodies are the main criterion by which others will accept or reject them, and, therefore, become acutely aware of their bodies. They spend hours inspecting themselves for a blemish or imperfection. In a society that idealizes perfect beauty, one pimple can cause the adolescent to despair. The teen's body must meet peer group standards. The tall girl, the short boy, or the obese or handicapped teen of either sex will have a difficult time winning peer acceptance. Illnesses that impair the development of primary or secondary sexual characteristics may have serious psychological and social consequences. An 18-year-old male who looks age 12, the girl of 11 who has fully developed breasts, and the young woman of 18 who does not may suffer greatly from real or imagined unacceptance by peers.

An important aspect of identity is *body image*, the mental picture people have of their own body. When physical changes occur, the body image must be revised to incorporate the changes. Revising the body image takes time, as anyone can attest who has gotten a new hair style and is surprised for a few days to see himself in a mirror. The rapid physical changes of early adolescence take time to incorporate into the body image. This lag between body configuration and body image accounts in part for the young adolescent's awkwardness; for example, a teenage male may bump into objects because he has not become accustomed to his new size. The desire to update one's body image in order to feel familiar with one's body is one reason why adolescents, especially young ones, are so preoccupied with their appearance and with examining themselves in photographs and mirrors.

All people are critical of their own body image, but adolescents are especially so. Teenagers are renowned for thinking they are too fat, too tall, too thin, too short, or in some other way not built satisfactorily. Even sincere reassurances offered by others (especially adults) usually provide little comfort. Unfortunately, an unsatisfactory body image can undermine self-concept and self-confidence.

Development of independence: Relationship with parents

In order to become people who will, as adults, make their own decisions and provide for their own needs, teenagers have to reduce drastically their childhood reliance on parents. Both teenagers and parents usually experience considerable stress and strain in making the necessary role realignments. Parents feel uneasy about turning over their previous functions as supervisor, protector, advisor, and decision maker to teenagers, who are inexperienced and whose judgment is relatively untested. Adolescents are often awkward and ambivalent about making the transition toward independence. Early and middle adolescents may protest almost any parental interaction as "interference," but they may fluctuate between insisting that they are grown up and then at times behaving quite childishly or expecting parents to do things the adolescents could do for themselves.

Middle adolescents refight the battle of the preschool period: ambivalence toward the same-sex parent and a romantic attachment to the parent of the opposite sex. Working through these relationships helps the adolescent move on to love relationships outside the family. The teenager vacillates between emulating the same-sex parent and irritably trying to prove how different he or she is. The parent of the opposite sex is at times viewed through rose-colored glasses. Hence mother-son and father-daughter relationships are frequently smoother than those between parents and adolescents of the same sex, and the stage is set for family conflict unless the parents are in good agreement about how the two of them will respond to their child.

Adolescence is as difficult a time for parents as it is for their teens. Parents have historically raised their children the way they were raised. In today's advanced society, that is no longer easy. Teens today have access to a vast array of all our society has to offer. They are courted by the media to use their significant purchasing power to buy cosmetics, clothes, records, magazines, cars, etc. Parents want to provide their children with more than they had but are often hard pressed financially to do so.

Conflicts frequently occur over such issues as curfew, study hours, friends, dress, makeup, and allowance. Teenagers constantly test the limits set by parents, who interpret this to mean that teens want no limits placed on their behavior. The opposite is true. Teens want and need limits as an expression of their parents' love and concern. Adolescents who have no parental rules governing their behavior often are secretly envious of their peers who have curfews or other family rules to follow. Teens need to know that their parents have controls on which they can depend. The parent who sets no limits will make adolescence more difficult for all concerned. Consistent discipline strengthens their security.

A frequent struggle between adolescents and their parents turns on the issue of privileges. Parents usually view privileges as being earned by responsible behavior. Because the behavior of most adolescents vacillates between that of a mature adult and a toddler who throws tantrums, it is hard for parents to decide how much responsibility to give them.

Parents who have unresolved conflicts from their own adolescence will have a more difficult time raising a teenager. Those parents who were raised in a controlling family may be too lax with their own children, and those raised in an exceedingly permissive environment may be too controlling. Parental expectations are often greater than teens can be expected to meet, causing unhappiness and frustration for all. The son who is expected to be a better football player than his father and the daughter who is expected to follow in her mother's footsteps as a nurse are rarely seen by parents as having the right to make their own life choices. Parental attitudes have a significant effect on adolescent behavior, as Table 15-3 shows.

Adolescents and their parents live best in an atmosphere of mutual trust. Teens need to know they can depend on their parents' love and support. Parents need to be able to trust that their teens will use good judgment in making decisions. Perhaps the areas of greatest difficulty are sexuality and drugs. The age of first intercourse continues to be lower and the incidence of teenage pregnancy rises. Many parents are justifiably concerned that their teens will become involved in a sexual relationship before they are able to handle it (see Chap. 30). Likewise, with adolescent drug use rampant and many students attending classes "high," parents are frightened about the use of drugs and their effect. However, parents who have always attempted to keep the lines of communication with their children open will have a closer relationship than the parents who periodically search their teen's possessions for drugs and birth control devices.

By late adolescence parent-child relationships usually improve markedly; both teenager and parents have gained confidence in the young person's increasing ability to manage himself or

Table 15-3 Influence of parents on adolescent behavior

Parental attitude or behavior	Adolescent reaction or behavior
1. Overcoercive: rigid, demanding, very high, and controlled standards for children. Perfectionistic, compulsive, often belittling or punitive, or both (child can't possibly satisfy)	1. (a) Adoption of same behavior; hypercritical of self, drives self ("workaholic"); or (b) rebellion or resistance, or both (active or passive): to protect his or her individuality; or (c) withdrawal or regression or somatic symptoms, or all three: downgrades self, poor self-esteem, depression.
2. Overpermissive (indulgent): oversubmission, overindulgence, unable or unwilling to set limits, rarely punish or deny child privileges or gratification	2. Decreased capacity for self-control; increased need for immediate gratification. Bored and not easily impressed. Expects much reward without effort or responsibility. Needs and seeks new thrills and pleasures
3. Overprotective: shielding child from ordinary or imaginary hazards of living. Parent(s) often have phobias; may be narrow or generalized fear. Parent(s) may have guilt and fear of retribution and therefore overprotect	3. (a) Fearful person with lowered self-esteem, decreased curiosity, and fear of new experiences; or (b) anger at having been so restricted; rebellious toward parent(s) who have caused the adolescent's fears and bad feelings about self
4. Rejecting: feelings of not wanting or not loving the child openly or subtly conveyed by parent(s). Ambivalent feelings conveyed or actual neglect or belittling behavior. Child may be scapegoat or "black sheep" or actually unwanted. Distrustful: parent has little faith and tends to assume child has same weaknesses as parent	4. Child feels unwanted or unloved; may retaliate and evoke further rejection. Feeling of worthlessness; poor self-concept. Strangers are perceived as rejecting. Defenses used—aggression, self-aggrandizement, withdrawal, clowning (all these interfere with interpersonal relationships). Child yearns for friendships; has great need for acceptance and approval. May develop strong talents or skill or close relationships. Child tends to fulfill the parents' distrust
5. Symbiotic: abnormally close tie between one parent, usually the mother, and a child. Prevents normal contact with peers and outside world. "You and I against the world" attitude	5. Damaged self-concept: doesn't develop independent personality. Feels inadequate when separated. Social relationships and curiosity are damaged. As adolescent realizes handicap, anger and hostility develop to parent and others
6. Vicarious: the parent lives through the child. Pressure on child to achieve in areas important to parent	6. At first compliance, then anxiety, and finally rebellion or withdrawal. Self-concept suffers since never quite lives up to parent's expectations. Socialization may suffer because of narrowing of activities
7. Inconsistent: opposite of rigidity, rules constantly changing. Parents unpredictable in their response. Often marital disharmony, alcohol or drug abuse	7. Adolescent may show frustration, anxiety; may withdraw, or may rebel
8. Neglectful: parents who show lack of responsibility or actual emotional or physical abuse of their children	8. Self-esteem damaged, not able to trust or rely on others. Seeks out others (individuals or groups, e.g., "gangs") to substitute for parents. Often angry

From G. Comerci, E. Lightner, and R. Hansen, *Adolescent Medicine Case Studies*, Medical Examination Publishing, New York, 1979, pp. 510–511.

herself, and the fears and frustrations of both have lessened considerably. Until this time comes, parents need to maintain their own "center," a sense of keeping calm while living in the eye of the hurricane. When parents can maintain their control while adolescents are losing theirs, teenagers will feel more secure in their periods of instability, uncertainty, and regression.

There are four ways in which adolescents accomplish their emancipation from parents:*

*This section on the four ways of emancipation was written by Jean I. Clarke.

1. Teenagers may abruptly leave home and subsequently be viewed as adults.
2. Adolescents gradually move from being dependent children to becoming independent adults without ever having left home. As inflation soars and rents and the cost of living increase, many young people are continuing to live at home. This gradual role change while remaining in the parents' residence may complicate and extend the separation struggle.
3. Young people will leave home to be independent, then feel the need of the family unit, and move back home. This pattern will be repeated until they are finally able to manage independently away from home.

4. Adolescents who need a "kick" out of the family nest may be ready to leave but unable to do so. Through repetitions of unacceptable behavior, they force the family to provide the impetus to leave, often in the form of a parental order to pack their belongings and go.

Relationships with peers The peer group plays an essential role for adolescents. It provides security and support as teenagers separate from their families. Peer groups are usually made up of people of the same sex in early adolescence, in midadolescence are composed of one or both sexes, and in late adolescence incorporate couples. Within these groups, conversation revolves around school, clothes, and the opposite sex. The safety of the peer group allows adolescents to practice adult roles, social skills, and communication with the opposite sex. Peers provide a group conscience to determine appropriate behaviors and a review board to pass judgment on actions that have already taken place. There are teens who "march to their own drummer" and reject or are rejected by the peer group. The lives of most adolescents, however, are centered in the peer group. It dictates how they walk, talk, act, and dress. To behave differently is to risk exclusion from the group, a risk most adolescents are unwilling to take. Adolescents need others like themselves with whom to share the joys and sorrows experienced in the transition from childhood to adulthood.

The adolescent peer group is a subculture of society. A subculture has distinctly different values, sets of expectations, and approved behaviors that separate it from the mainstream of society. The members of a subculture may have insecure, fragile self-concepts and therefore isolate themselves from outside opinions. They live in protected, closed environments that insulate them from potentially threatening influences. This isolation reinforces their acceptance of only rigidly approved behaviors. Much of the adolescent's seemingly strange behavior can be explained by understanding the characteristics of a subgroup. Each subculture has the following characteristics:

1. There is a distinctive communication system, for example, slang, which reduces communication with outside groups, such as parents.
2. There are distinctive behaviors that isolate members of the subculture and help them identify with their chosen peer group. This isolation also reinforces their own rigid definitions of acceptable behavior. Earmarks of the adolescent subculture include distinctive dress, dance, hair styles, body posturing, and other nonverbal behavior.
3. Accepted behaviors change quickly, even every few days.

Identification with and participation in the adolescent subculture provides opportunities to try out (and eventually adopt, adapt, or discard) many attitudes and behaviors of other people who are not members of one's family. This experience provides a necessary bridge for emancipating oneself from the overinfluence of parents and finally developing one's own sense of identity that makes mimicking others unnecessary. In middle adolescence, teenagers readily adopt the peer group's style of dress, language, ideas, and values. Gang activity is seen in some lower economic groups. Gangs are usually made up of young people with a poor or negative sense of identity. By becoming part of a gang, they achieve a status and recognition they would not have otherwise. Unfortunately, the destructive activities the gang engages in may hamper the adolescent's chances of becoming a successful, contributing, member of society.

Peer activities and dating During early adolescence each sex remains socially separate. Boys practice and compete in active sports, practice muscle-strengthening activities, join clubs, and watch television. Girls' activities focus on endless phone conversations, parties, hobbies, nature study (Fig. 15-6), and volunteering. The trend seems to be toward earlier dating. Young adolescents begin group dating at school dances at least by the 8th and 9th grades.

In middle adolescence, an automobile or motorcycle brings optimal status. The car brings the opportunity for increased freedom and independence from parents. Males often experiment with adult roles by taking part-time jobs. Females spend hours experimenting with dress, hairstyles, and makeup. They converse endlessly on the phone. Part-time jobs increase their clothes allowance. By the 10th grade, couples pair up and group date.

Older adolescents continue to enjoy rock concerts, music on the stereo, reading, and phone conversations. Double-dating is common in the 11th grade and single dating in the 12th grade.

Throughout adolescence, dating is a means to help discover self-identity through interaction with others. "Going steady" means not having to worry about having a date and gives teenagers a sense of security and belonging. The young person who is sexually promiscuous is often searching for sexual identity but has not yet achieved that goal. A broad range of social and sex role–related skills as well as more specifically sexual attitudes and behaviors are gradually refined by dating, and each refinement brings the young person closer to a sense of identity. Young and middle adolescents use dating primarily as a medium for finding out who they are and how others feel about them. It is generally not until late adolescence that love in the sense of deep concern for the well-being of the other is possible.

Sexuality and sex-role identity The adolescent must achieve a mature sexual identity—an understanding and acceptance of self as a sexual male or a sexual female. Young adolescents often have difficulty accepting their maturing bodies, particularly when they appear to be changing almost daily. Girls, especially those who mature earlier than their friends, often slouch and wear baggy clothing to hide their breasts and hips. The pleasure of becoming an adult male is mixed with displeasure for the young man experiencing ill-timed erections.

As adolescents progress toward adulthood, they must integrate the biological and psychological aspects of sexuality into their lives. Sexuality is a major theme of adolescence. Sexual self-concept, sex roles, and sexual behavior are affected by each young person's past experiences as a male or female, and by his or her ideas about what it means to be a man or woman.

Society has an impact on adolescent sexuality. Social values and cultural patterns vary according to the adolescent's social subgroup and the times in which he or she lives. Economic and political conditions and laws regulating marriage, contraception, abortion, drinking, and equal rights influence sex roles and sexual behavior. The feminist movement has loosened sex role restrictions for both men and women, so that marriage, child rearing, and careers outside the home are truly options for all. In many

Figure 15-6 Adolescents enjoy activities with peers.

segments of society, greater permissiveness has developed in recent years, so that marriage is now not the only setting in which sexual intimacy and long-term love relationships are acceptable. While these social changes permit young people a wider range of options, they also can make choosing life-styles and life goals more confusing.

As has been pointed out earlier, adolescents actively involve other people in their search for identity. Sexual self-concept and sex role identity are largely developed in an interpersonal context. By middle adolescence teenagers want to feel that they are attractive to members of the opposite sex, and many are eager to try out their own sexual capacities. Preoccupation with one's own and others' physical attractiveness intensifies (Fig. 15-7). Crushes and going steady are common ways of experimenting with adult romantic and sexual behavior.

According to Feinstein, adolescents pass through four stages of sexual development:[8]

1. *Sexual awakening* Usually between ages 13 and 15 years, adolescents are confronted with their body image in comparison with their peers. They scrutinize and compare breast or penis size, height, weight, and pubic hair development. These comparisons can be devastating if the teen is "out of sync" with the peer group.
2. *Practicing stage* Generally extending from about 14 to 17, this involves experimentation and practice of the social skills necessary to form intimate relationships. Often the skills valued by the family and

Figure 15-7 The girl in midadolescence may spend hours on makeup, hair, and dress in striving for physical perfection. (*Photograph by Karel Bauer.*)

society are not those valued by the peer group, so that conflict results for the adolescent.

3. *Acceptance of sexual role* Between about 16 and 19, the adolescent develops a sense of comfort with the sexual role he or she has chosen. Couple dating replaces some of the activities that earlier involved the larger peer group.

4. *Permanent relationship choice* This stage may take place between ages 18 and 25 or so and is often delayed by prolonged post-high school education. In choosing a life partner, the adolescent must also decide between (1) a fairly traditional marriage, in

Figure 15-8 Some adolescents turn to religion to express their need to establish an identity, both personal and in relation to the universe. (*Photograph by Karel Bauer.*)

which the husband is responsible for family support and finances and the wife is responsible for the home and children and usually does not have a career, and (2) a companionship marriage, in which mutual love and support are considered most important and the responsibility for financial support and nurturing the family are shared.

Moral development A child's simplistic way of looking at right and wrong is inadequate for the needs of the adolescent, who must build a philosophy of life, a collection of moral values and truths to give meaning, direction, and purposes to life. In gradually establishing their own system of moral and ethical beliefs, adolescents become greatly interested in moral viewpoints that differ from those of their parents. Adolescents have a keen eye for noticing differences that may exist between parents' *standards* and parents' *practices*, that is, between what parents claim to believe in and what they actually do. Whether or not parents live up to their own standards, most adolescents go through a stage of questioning, condemning, and rebelling to some degree against the family's beliefs about morality. School teachers and other authoritative adults are also subjected to the critical evaluation of adolescents as they sort through various moral standards in search of those they will incorporate into their own identity.

Many adolescents turn to religion to strengthen their identity and to provide a set of clear-cut rules for belief and behavior. Until they have their own well-established, internalized code of behavior and philosophy of life, they find security and impulse control by adopting external rules of conduct. Religion may take the place of family authority and provide peer acceptance. Adolescents think deeply about religion (see Fig. 15-8). They may view themselves (when they are not despondent, embarrassed, or self-accusing) as pure spirit. Adolescents frequently feel a special link to the mysteries and austerities of religion, the beauties of nature, and poetry or music. These alliances are part of the process of loosening one's ties to one's family and childhood in order to search in broader fields for beliefs and standards that can be used in building one's identity not only as a member of one's family but also of the human family and the universe.

Career choice In order to achieve adult status and to acquire the part of identity that has to do with occupation, adolescents must work out an adequate career choice. This choice must be one that is compatible with their sense of who they are, and it must gain them self-sufficiency and recognition from family and friends.

Career choice usually begins to be an issue in middle adolescence, and many teenagers take part-time jobs at that time. Work gives them a sense of responsibility, reduces their financial dependence on parents, and allows them to experience the work role and a particular kind of work. Working also gives teenagers a glimpse of their own adulthood, which is rapidly approaching, without the extensive responsibilities of an adult's career commitment and management of a home.

Independence, which includes financial independence, is an important goal of adolescents. For many young people, the temptation to quit school and take a full-time job is strong. However, most people who go to work without graduating from high school, and often also those who do not acquire post-high school career training, put themselves at a disadvantage to compete in the job market. Hence, many who begin work early instead of going on to school may find that they cannot qualify for the kind of work that would give them the degree of financial independence they desire. Those who do choose post-high school education or other career training usually continue to depend on their families for economic support until their career preparation is completed. In this era of high technology and specialization, the length of training programs such as graduate and postgraduate study may prevent the young person from achieving financial independence until his or her middle or late twenties.

Cognitive development

According to Piaget, between approximately 13 and 15 years of age the final stage of cognitive development takes place. The adolescent enters the stage of *formal operations* and acquires adult cognitive capacities. Formal operations are characterized by abstract thinking. People at this stage now become capable of thinking *hypothetically*; that is, they are no longer limited to thinking only about things they have experienced

or observed but can conceptualize beyond the realm of reality to reason about things that are contrary to fact or beyond the range of possibility as we now understand it. The adolescent is able to understand and use the rules of logic for the first time and can think both deductively and inductively.

The person in the stage of formal operations grasps symbolic meanings and hence can appreciate and interpret jokes with double meanings, art forms such as symbolic poetry and abstract paintings, and sayings like "A rolling stone gathers no moss." This person's understanding goes beyond the surface meanings of things and picks up subtleties and deeper meanings.

The capacity to use abstract thought has a lot to do with the adolescent's general behavior. For example, the formulation of a personal code of ethics or a set of religious beliefs requires the ability to think about hypothetical possibilities beyond the scope of one's own past experience.

In early adolescence and to a lesser degree in middle adolescence, the young person's thinking is characterized by *egocentrism*. Young teenagers are heavily engaged in thinking about themselves in abstract ways they were not capable of as children: Am I normal? Why am I behaving this way? What do I mean to others? Who am I, really? As a consequence of this egocentrism, young people behave much of the time as if they were as central and important in the thoughts of others as they are in their own thoughts. They imagine that they are the center of everyone's attention and interest, that others are impressed by their good points (from character traits to facial features), and critical of their every flaw—whether those good points and flaws are real or only imagined by them. Adolescents frequently experience a "personal fable," in which they truly believe that they are unique among all of humanity, that no one has ever loved, enjoyed, or despaired as deeply as they. Adolescents may see themselves as "saviors" who will be able to solve problems that others have been unable to correct. Teenagers also tend to believe that they are not subject to the laws of probability that affect "ordinary" people, and that they can safely engage in drug use, sexual activity, and dangerous activities without suffering any serious consequences.

Health maintenance

Morbidity and mortality

Adolescents are often considered to be the healthiest segment of the population. It is true that mortality rates are highest for infants under 1 year of age, decline precipitously during childhood, and reach their lowest level during adolescence.

Accidental injuries are the leading cause of death among teenagers (60 deaths per 100,000 adolescents in the 15- to 24-year-old age group). Among adolescent males, motor vehicle accidents are responsible for approximately 40 percent of the deaths. The second most common cause of accidental deaths in adolescence is drowning. Fifteen- to twenty-four-year-olds have the highest number of fatalities due to drowning. Most spinal injuries and fatalities due to diving accidents involve teenage and young adult males.

Adolescents die from other forms of violence besides accidents. Homicide is the second leading cause of death in the 15- to 24-year-old group (approximately 14 deaths per 100,000 young people), and suicide is a close third (approximately 13 deaths per 100,000 population this age). The number of suicides in young people between ages 10 and 14 has increased by a third since 1968.

Neoplasms, both malignant and benign, and cardiovascular diseases are the fourth and fifth leading causes of death, with mortality rates approximating 7 and 5.4 deaths per 100,000 young people, respectively.

The low incidence of disease among adolescents presents an inaccurate impression of abundant health and reduced health care requirements for this age group. Nurses and teenagers need to be aware that adolescents, who have primary control of their day to day health-related behavior, adopt many practices that compromise their health in ways that typically do not show up for several years. Among the common health hazards for young people are poor nutrition, including obesity; cigarette smoking, which involves about one-fourth of adolescents; and use of beverage alcohol by about a third. Experimental use or frank abuse of other drugs can of course damage health, as can sexual practices that lead to infection.

Mental health problems are substantial during adolescence, although their exact incidence is unknown. Signs the nurse should be alert for are drug abuse (see Chap. 42), fatigue, lack of sleep, recurrent accidents or visits to health care professionals, poor school attendance or a decline in school performance, "acting out" behavior, and lack of friends or a peer group. These young people are psychologically in trouble and need intervention by mental health professionals.

Delivery of health care to adolescents

There has been much debate over who should provide health care to the adolescent (see Fig. 15-9). Traditionally parents took their children to a pediatrician until the teenager rebelled against being taken to the "baby doctor." At that point, the pediatrician was often replaced by an internist. Over the past few years a new physician specialty, adolescent medicine, has developed; physicians who complete a period of specialized training become skilled in dealing with the medical and psychosocial needs of adolescents. Nurses may obtain postgraduate degrees or certification as adolescent health care nurse practitioners. These physicians and nurses frequently work in adolescent clinics whose aim is to provide primary care. Many hospitals provide adolescent inpatient units that have special facilities and specially trained staff.

Teenagers may also obtain health care at free clinics in many communities. These clinics usu-

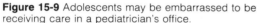
Figure 15-9 Adolescents may be embarrassed to be receiving care in a pediatrician's office.

ally provide a wide range of service—medical and dental care, counseling, and job placement. Free clinics usually are staffed by volunteers and provide service without charge, since cost is a severe problem for adolescents, who generally have limited funds.

Legal issues in adolescent health care

Until the mid-1960s, minors were legally totally under the control of their parents and had few rights of their own. While laws are changing very rapidly, the right of minors to give legally binding consent for health care varies from state to state. In many states a minor may give consent for routine or emergency medical care, marriage, treatment of venereal disease, contraceptive counseling and supplies, and abortion. Parental consent is not required in these settings; in fact, giving parents confidential medical information without the patient's consent subjects the health provider to prosecution.

In situations in which minors are allowed to give consent for certain health care procedures, the care-giver must first be sure that the adolescent is intelligent and mature enough to understand the treatment and its consequences. A full explanation must be given of the proposed treatment, its risks, and alternatives. *Informed consent* is a patient's agreeing to receive treatment that has been thoroughly explained. Recent supreme court decisions have struck down barriers that previously prevented adolescents from obtaining, without their parents' consent, health care related to sexual activity. As laws change, nurses have a responsibility to their adolescent patients to keep informed about the laws in their state. Sources of legal information include:

Regional planned parenthood offices
Regional bar associations
State and county medical associations
State and federal departments of health and social services
State attorneys general
Counsel for the health provider's malpractice insurance company

Safety

The role of accidents in adolescent mortality and morbidity mandates that accident prevention be a major component of health maintenance for teenagers. Because adolescents are so mobile and independent, it is too late now for the "don't touch" approaches and close adult supervision that were helpful in promoting safety for young children. The focus of accident prevention must be on teaching adolescents how to operate safely in their expanded environment, and on helping them to identify hazards and act responsibly to avoid injury to themselves and others.

School-sponsored driver's education courses, provided by law in some states, should be strongly encouraged. The same educational principles—instruction about the hazards involved and supervised teaching about how to proceed safely—need to be applied to other activities besides driving. Adolescents must be taught (and need attractive role models who demonstrate) that certain activities are never to be undertaken without a companion who knows the rules of safety and can provide help in case the need arises. Hunting, wilderness hiking, swimming, and activities involving such hazardous equipment as power saws are examples. Health educators should take advantage of the natural influence of attractive peers or older role models with whom adolescents identify and whom they believe and trust. Particularly in the area of alcohol and other drug use, which is heavily linked to accidents in adolescence, there is probably no other preventive or corrective educational approach to equal the effectiveness of peers who "have been there," who can tell what their experience was like, and who can convincingly testify that it wasn't worth it.

Sex education

Adolescents desperately need information about their sexuality. While an understanding of male and female anatomy and physiology is necessary, they need to understand more than just their "plumbing." Sex education must not focus only on reproduction. Adolescents need to recognize how sexuality can help or harm them and how sexual relationships can enhance or destroy their sense of worth. To learn this, it is imperative that they have adult role models from whom they may learn honest, responsible behavior.

A 1976 study found that 55 percent of young women were sexually active by age 19 and only 30 percent consistently used birth control methods (see Chap. 30). A number of factors are probably responsible for the low use of contraception among adolescents:

1. An inability to accept the fact that one is sexually active.
2. Ignorance about body function, types of contraceptives, and their availability.
3. Embarrassment—many teenagers find it difficult to purchase tampons or sanitary pads, much less contraceptive foam or condoms.
4. Adolescent magical thinking and denial: "It can't happen to me."

Table 15-4 Guide to nutritional assessment of adolescents

History

Family: Obesity, diabetes mellitus, or heart disease in close family members? Preventive diet may be indicated
Dietary: Appetite, total daily food intake, special diet, frequency of meals, snacking habits, food preferences and allergies, vitamin supplements
Medications: On oral contraceptive? If so, may need increased vitamin C, pyridoxine, and folic acid
Exercise: Daily exercise pattern. Participation in sports. Which sports? How often? May need increased calories, vitamins C and B complex, water, and salt
Past health problems: Significant weight gain or loss? Obesity, anemia, thyroid imbalance, or diabetes?
Special considerations: Pregnant? Consider needs for increased calories, protein, calcium, iron, B vitamins, and vitamins C and A. Intrauterine device in place? May need increased iron to replace losses during menstrual flow

Review of systems

If the following symptoms are present, consider corresponding mineral and vitamin deficiencies.
Dryness and cracking of skin or lips, itching of genital area—*riboflavin*
Nervousness, irritability, insomnia, muscle cramps—*calcium*
Indigestion, constipation, nervousness, irritability, fatigue, mental depression—*thiamine*
Night blindness, roughness of skin, dryness of hair—*vitamin A*
Bleeding of gums, slow wound healing, easy bruising—*vitamin C*
Fatigue, irritability, anorexia, headache, increased menstrual flow—*iron*

Physical assessment

Height and weight: Far below mean on growth chart for age? Consider protein and calorie deprivation. Far above mean? Consider obesity, overweight
Clinical signs: Lethargy; general depression; dry skin or hair; lesions on lips, skin, or genitalia; dental caries; swollen or bleeding gums; tachycardia; and enlarged thyroid may indicate nutritional inadequacies

Laboratory data

Consider iron deficiency anemia if hemoglobin and hematocrit levels are low

From C. Torre, "Nutritional Needs of Adolescents," *The American Journal of Maternal-Child Nursing* **2:**118–127 (March-April 1977).

5. Poor impulse control.
6. Belief that the use of contraception will inhibit spontaneity and pleasure.
7. Lack of male commitment to the prevention of pregnancy.
8. Fear of side effects.
9. A wish to become pregnant.

Teenagers need answers to their questions about sex. While nurses should have this information and be able to relay it to their teenage patients, it does not mean they must have all the answers. If you do not have the information, refer the teen to an appropriate person. Emphasize that you are not putting him off, merely referring him to another source such as a health educator or one with training in human sexuality.

Sex education for adolescents should include anatomy and physiology; clarification of value systems; and information about sexually transmitted diseases, pregnancy, contraception, abortion, parenting, communication in marriage, alternative life-styles, and sexual function and dysfunction.

Nutrition

Nutrition is a prime area for health maintenance in adolescence. Growth is greater during adolescence than at any other time except the fetal period and infancy. The nutritional needs of the adolescent are greatest during the growth spurt (Tanner stage 1 in girls and stage 2 in boys). Nutritional needs are summarized in Appendix C. While these recommended dietary allowances (RDA) are estimates for age groups and cannot be applied stringently to individuals, they are helpful in evaluating nutrition.

The efforts of teenagers to become independent of family and conform to peer group standards and cultural ideals have an effect on their nutritional practices. Young people make their own decisions about what to eat. Adolescents need to be taught that healthful foods have a direct, positive effect on health, appearance, physique, and physical function; this information often positively influences food selection habits.

A guide to assessing the nutritional status of the adolescent is listed in Table 15-4. A growth chart (see Appendix B) should also be used with every adolescent to plot height and weight to assess growth.

Table 15-5 Food sources of nutrients commonly deficient in adolescent diets

Common nutrient deficiencies	Foods high in these nutrients
Vitamin A	Direct sources: liver, fish liver oils, butter, cheese, eggs, and milk Sources of carotene (a substance the body converts to vitamin A): yellow vegetables, green leafy vegetables, tomatoes, yellow fruits
Vitamin C	Citrus fruits, strawberries, broccoli, bell peppers, tomato juice, rose hips
Calcium	Milk, cheese, yogurt, ice cream, soybeans, mustard and turnip greens
Iron	Red meats (especially liver), wheat germ, brewer's yeast, egg yolks, dark green leafy vegetables, apricots, whole-grain cereals, fish
Riboflavin	Milk, liver, brewer's yeast, whole grains, green leafy vegetables, fish, eggs
Thiamine	Brewer's yeast, wheat germ, rice polish, pork, milk, nuts, whole grains, liver, peas, lentils

From C. Torre, "Nutritional Needs of Adolescents," *The American Journal of Maternal-Child Nursing* **2:**118–127 (March-April 1977).

Nutritional research indicates no evidence of calorie or protein deficiency among American adolescents as a group today. Studies do, however, reveal deficiencies in both vitamins and minerals, particularly calcium, iron, vitamin A, and ascorbic acid (vitamin C). Table 15-5 shows the nutrients most lacking in the diets of adolescents, and lists the foods in which they are found.

Fast foods may not be a nutritional disaster (Fig. 15-10). A hamburger, french fries, and a milk shake provide close to one-third of daily nutritional needs. Most fast food meals are deficient in vitamin A and certain B vitamins (biotin, folacin, and pantothenic acid). To ensure proper nutritional intake the teenager should have daily servings of whole-grain breads, cereals, dark green leafy and yellow vegetables, beans, and fresh fruit.

Vegetarians An increasing number of young people are turning to vegetarianism for moral and health reasons. Strict vegetarians—those who eat no meat, fish, dairy products, or eggs— are most susceptible to nutritional deficiencies in amino acids, calcium, iron, zinc, and vitamin B_{12}. Lacto-ovo- and lacto-vegetarians are less likely than strict vegetarians to develop nutritional deficiencies. The lacto-ovo-vegetarian diet includes milk and eggs, the lacto-vegetarian diet only milk. The adolescent who adopts a vegetarian diet should be counseled by a nurse or nutritionist familiar with the particular needs of vegetarians. The Seventh Day Adventist Church, which advocates a meatless diet, is an excellent source of nutritional information and menu plans.

Snacks Adolescents are often ravenous snackers. Snacks are perfectly acceptable and if well planned can significantly contribute to the teenager's total daily nutritional intake. Teenagers tend to snack on whatever is available—too often this means relying on foods high in sugar and starches (with subsequent excess calories and dental caries) but low in calcium and iron. Snacks should consist of milk, cheese, fruits, nuts, veg-

Figure 15-10 Fast foods are a staple of the teenager's diet. (*Photograph by Karel Bauer.*)

etables, and other sources of protein and calcium. There is currently a trend in schools to replace soda and candy vending machines with those dispensing juices and fresh fruits. The substitution of nutritionally sound snacks should be promoted and supported by school nurses.

Breakfast Adolescents frequently skip breakfast because they fear gaining weight or have little time in the morning. Breakfast is probably the most important meal of the day because the needed amounts of ascorbic acid, calcium, and riboflavin may not be adequately provided by other meals. It has been shown that teenagers, particularly girls, who routinely eat breakfast rely less on "junk food" snacks for energy than do those who skip breakfast. Eating such "nontraditional" breakfasts as a grilled cheese sandwich is perfectly acceptable (Table 15-6).

Athletics and nutrition Adolescents who take part in athletics must meet nutritional needs for

Table 15-6 Snack foods common in the adolescent's diet

Food	Portion	Approx. cal
Devil's food cake with chocolate icing	1 (2 × 3 × 2 in)	203
Plain cake donut	1	125
Oreo creme cookie	1	50
Vanilla wafer	1	15
Plain Jello	1 cup	130
with whipped cream	1 tbsp	182
D-Zerta gelatin	1 cup	20
with whipped cream	1 tbsp	72
with Dream Whip topping	1 tbsp	34
Thin pretzel stick	1	1
Potato chip	5	54
Popcorn	1 cup	54
Chocolate milk shake	8 oz	421
Whole milk (white)	8 oz	161
Skim milk	8 oz	81
Coca-Cola	8 oz	104
Tea	8 oz	2
with sugar	1 tsp (level)	18
Ice cream (vanilla)	4 oz	145
Sherbet (orange)	4 oz	134
Ice milk (vanilla)	4 oz	102
Popsicle (twin)	1	95

Derived from H. V. Barnes, "Physical Growth During Puberty," *Medical Clinics of North America* **59**:(6):1305 (1975).

growth and energy expenditure (Table 15-7). Their diets should include sufficient protein, calories, carbohydrates, fat, water, vitamins, and minerals. Caloric intake should range from 2300 to 5000 cal per day for those involved in strenuous exercise. A greater percentage of the additional calories (up to 70 percent) should come from complex carbohydrates (bread, cereals) to provide a readily available source of energy before an event. Because athletic events may lead to sodium depletion and water loss, instruct the athlete to:

1. Avoid dehydration by maintaining an adequate fluid intake before and during the game.
2. Avoid sodium depletion by eating salted foods. Salt tablets are usually not indicated.

Athletes competing for a particular weight class should be counseled to avoid crash dieting to lose weight or binge eating to gain weight. Crash dieting, causing a rapid loss of water, is common among wrestlers. A rapid water loss, representing 5 percent of body weight, decreases the work capacity of muscles by 20 to 30 percent.

Contraceptives and nutrition Oral contraceptives have no serious effect upon nutritional status, although blood levels of some vitamins and minerals are reported to be altered. Folic acid deficiencies have been reported. The young woman taking birth control pills should perhaps be given supplemental folic acid. Those who have IUDs may have increased menstrual bleeding and their iron intake should by supplemented.

Underweight adolescents The adolescent who is underweight needs nutritional guidance. Teens who are too thin are often envied by their obese peers but are often no happier with their body image. A steady weight gain program should be encouraged with extra calories obtained from regular, nutritionally balanced meals and frequent, nourishing snacks.

Obesity Obesity among adolescents is a significant problem. Recent evidence suggests that "excessive weight gain during critical periods of development may result in laying down of excessive numbers of fat cells which will remain

Table 15-7 Energy expenditures of various activities

Activity	Cal/min	Activity	Cal/min
1. Personal necessities		Stone, masonry	6.3
		Truck and auto repair	4.2
Sitting, eating	1.5		
Sleeping	1.2	**6. Recreation**	
Washing and dressing	2.6	Baseball (not pitcher)	4.7
		Basketball	8.6
2. Sedentary		Canoeing, 2.5 mi/h	3.0
Classwork, lecture	1.7	4.0 mi/h	7.0
Sitting, reading	1.3	Dancing	
Sitting, playing cards	2.0	Waltz	5.2
Standing at ease	1.7	Rock	8.5
Lying at ease	1.4	Football	10.2
Typing at 40 wpm	1.3	Gardening, weeding	4.8
		Golfing	5.0
3. Locomotion		Gymnastics	
Cycling, 5.5 mi/h	4.5	Balancing	2.5
9.4 mi/h	7.0	Trunk bending	3.5
Driving a car	2.8	Horseback riding	
Walking, 2 mi/h	3.2	Walk	3.0
4 mi/h	5.8	Trot	8.0
downstairs	7.1	Mountain climbing	
upstairs	18.6	Light load w/slope	10.7
		Heavy load w/slope	13.2
4. Domestic work		Ping Pong	4.9
Bedmaking	3.5	Running, cross country	10.6
Dusting	2.5	Squash	10.2
Preparing a meal	2.5	Swimming	5.0–11.0
Scrubbing floors	4.0	Skiing, hard snow	
		Level, moderate speed	10.4
5. Light industry		Sprinting	23.3
Assembly work in factory	2.3	Tennis	7.1
House painting	3.5	Volleyball	3.5

Adapted from the following:

J. V. G. A. Durnin and R. Passmore, *Energy, Work & Leisure,* Heinemann Educational Books, London, 1967, pp. 49, 57, 72, 76.
R. Passmore and J. V. G. A. Durnin, "Human Energy Expenditure," *Physiological Reviews* **35:**(4):811–813 (1955).
C. F. Consolazio, R. E. Johnson, and L. J. Pecora, *Physiological Measurements of Metabolic Functions in Man,* McGraw-Hill, New York, 1963, pp. 330–332.

for the rest of that person's life."[9] Obese infants often become obese children and adults. The odds of an overweight adolescent's becoming an average-weight adult are 28 to 1. Studies have shown that obese youth experience less acceptance from their peers and from significant adults and have greater body image disturbances and poorer self-concepts than their normal-weight peers. Obese adolescents are also at risk for such physical illnesses as diabetes and cardiovasular problems.

A normal increase in fat deposition usually occurs in girls between 11 and 13 years and in boys between 12½ and 14½ years. By the end of adolescence, due to sex differences in hormone secretion and physical activity, males' body composition includes 7.9 percent fat and females' is 22.8 percent fat.

An adolescent is considered overweight if his or her weight falls more than two standard deviations from the mean on a growth chart. The diagnosis of obesity also depends upon what

Figure 15-11 Factors that contribute to obesity. (*From P. Pipes and J. Aus, Nutrition in Infancy and Childhood, Mosby, 1977. Diagram by B. Lucas, Nutritional Clinical Training Unit, Child Development and Mental Retardation Center, University of Washington, Seattle.*)

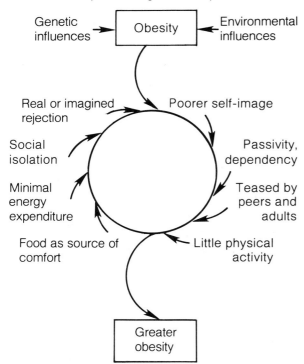

1. Duration and degree of obesity
2. Depression
3. Maturity and independence
4. Motivation
5. Self-esteem
6. Eating and activity patterns
7. Socialization

By reviewing these areas the nurse can set realistic treatment goals with the adolescent. The depressed, poorly motivated teenager will probably not respond well to a weight loss program, but would benefit from counseling.

Table 15-8 Nursing management of obese adolescents

1. Provide supportive counseling

See obese adolescents on a regular basis whether weekly, biweekly, or monthly

2. Encourage eating regular meals

Eating breakfast will improve performance and may lead to a lowered carbohydrate intake throughout the day

3. Set realistic goals with the teenager

Encourage a weight loss of no more than 1 to 2 lb per week. Focus on the amount of weight that can be lost in a week or a month, rather than on the total amount, which often sounds unmanageable to an obese teenager

4. Encourage exercise

Exercise will burn calories (Table 15-7) as well as helping teens to look and feel better

5. Provide nutrition counseling

Teenagers need nutritional education. Often they are not aware of the calorie content of their favorite foods (Table 15-5)

6. Provide psychosocial support

Often obese adolescents feel different from their peers. Encourage involvement in support groups. Refer the obese teen to Overeaters Anonymous, Weight Watchers, or a summer camp which offers exercise

7. Encourage family involvement

Family members responsible for doing the marketing and cooking should be involved and counseled on nutrition. Encourage them to eliminate high-calorie foods and to prepare nutritious, low-calorie meals

8. Have patience, show patience

Remind the teenager weight loss takes time just as weight gain did. Treatment of a teenager's obesity is one of long-term management

proportion of excess weight is fat, measured by use of a skin caliper.

Obese adolescents often find it difficult to lose weight. Often they are more sedentary than their normal-weight peers. Exercise has been shown to be extremely valuable in the treatment of obesity. Overweight teenagers, embarrassed by their weight and poor body image, usually restrict their activity. This further blocks their attempts at weight loss. They become more overweight and restrict their activity even more. This frustrating cycle of events is seen in Fig. 15-11.

The nurse can assist the teenager in treating obesity. First, however, the nurse should assess the following critical areas in the individual adolescent:

Guidelines to assist nurses concerned about management of obese adolescents are found in Table 15-8.

Communicating with adolescents

Communicating with teenagers can be easy to do if simple guidelines are followed:

1. *Don't preach* Teenagers often believe their parents and teachers preach to them; they do not want this also from health care providers.
2. *Listen* Let adolescents know you are interested in what they have to say, then let them say it. Use therapeutic interviewing techniques; do not "jockey" for the floor.
3. *Be aware of nonverbal cues* Often the manner of speaking and posture of people indicate their feelings. Does the adolescent make eye contact with you, sit comfortably in the chair, fidget, or turn away?
4. *Use as few words as possible when asking questions* This encourages a lengthy response.
5. *Ask open-ended questions and avoid "why" questions* Open-ended questions are those that allow for more than a yes or no answer. "Why" questions require a self-evaluation that promotes defensiveness. For example:

Closed-ended questions "Do you like school?" "Do you and your parents get along?"

Open-ended questions "What's school like for you this year?" "Tell me how you and your parents get along." "Go ahead." "What happened then?"

References

1. A. Bandura, The Stormy Decade: Fact or Fiction? *Psychology in the School* **1**(3):224–231 (1964).
2. Kenneth Kenniston, *The Uncommitted: Alienated Youth in American Society*, Harcourt, Brace & World, New York, 1965, p. 7.
3. *Webster's New Collegiate Dictionary*, Merriam, Springfield, Mass., 1973, p. 16.
4. Ibid, p. 932.
5. P. Blos, *On Adolescence*, Free Press, New York, 1967, p. 20.
6. J. M. Tanner, *Growth at Adolescence*, Blackwell, Oxford, 1962.
7. Erik Erikson, *Childhood and Society*, 2d ed., Norton, New York, 1963, p.261.
8. S. Feinstein, and M. Ardon, "Trends in Dating Patterns—Adolescence," *Journal of Youth and Adolescence* **2**:157 (June 1973).
9. P. Pipes, and J. Aus, "Special Concerns of Dietary Intake During Infancy-Adolescence," *Nutrition in Infancy and Childhood*, Mosby, St. Louis, 1977, p. 146

Part Two **Impact of illness on the child, the family, and the nurse**

Chapter 16 **Effects of hospitalization on the child and the family**

Nancy Lockwood Ramsey

Upon completion of this chapter, the student will be able to:

1. List at least two causes of stress in the hospitalized child for each age group.
2. Identify at least three factors influencing the child's ability to cope with hospitalization.
3. List at least four functions of play.
4. Describe situational (directive) and free (nondirective) play and ways the nurse can use each to communicate with the child.

5. Compare the procedures for preoperative preparation of an infant, toddler, preschooler, school-age child, and adolescent.
6. List at least five common feelings of parents of hospitalized children.
7. Describe reactions to hospitalization and appropriate nursing interventions for each age groups.

During the past 30 years there has been an increasing emphasis by medical and nursing personnel on meeting the child and family's psychological needs. In the early twentieth century it sometimes happened that children were given meticulous physical care but died of emotional starvation. Parents were allowed to visit their hospitalized children for only 2 to 3 h per week. Many nurses believed that parents upset their children and excluded the parents from the children's care.

Hospitals have gradually become more family-centered. Nurses have discovered the valuable part parents play in their children's recovery. The child's sense of security, reaction to the hospital, psychological health, and physical recovery are greatly influenced by the parents.

With knowledge of growth and development, the nurse can create a hospital environment designed to prevent psychological trauma and enhance the child's development. Through the nurse's interventions, hospitalization can be a positive, constructive experience for the child and the child's family.

Child-centered hospital

Ideally children's hospital units are homelike and geared to the child's developmental age and size. Small tables and chairs are there for use in family-style dinners (Fig. 16-1). Beds are close to the floor. Rockers and parents' cots are available on each unit. Nurses wear colored uniforms to prevent children from associating white with fear

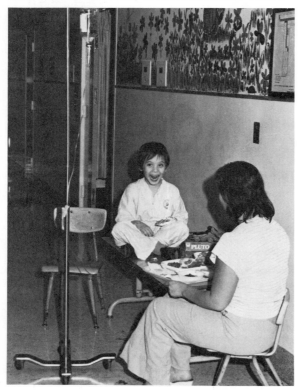

Figure 16-1 Child-sized furniture and unlimited visiting hours make the hospital more homelike. This child eats better at a small table with his mother present. (*Photo by Theresa Friedrich. Courtesy of LAC/USC Medical Center.*)

and discomfort. Colorful rooms, play areas, and lofts with toys invite healing play. Children are encouraged to bring favorite toys, "security blankets," and clothes from home whenever possible.

Children's units should welcome visits by parents and siblings. Rooming-in and open visiting hours enable parents to be available during stressful events, for feeding, and at bedtime. Many hospitals have short-admission surgery rooms, where the child is admitted and discharged in the same day. Other hospitals have outpatient areas where children can be observed or treated without formal admission. Ill children can be successfully cared for in parent-participation units. Preadmission tours and improved admission procedures reduce the child's anxiety.

Hospitalization and stress

Whenever a child is sick or hospitalized, stress is created within the entire family. A child or adult in stress or crisis is at a turning point. The child cannot solve the problem by previously developed coping mechanisms. Anxiety increases; the child may feel helpless, overwhelmed, and unable to find workable solutions to the problem.

Nursing interventions are crucial to help the child and family deal with the stresses of hospitalization. By helping the parents and child meet both psychological and physical needs, the nurse can help them experience success in coping with the hospitalization.

Hospitalization separates the child from a familiar and predictable environment and places him or her in an unfamiliar world dominated by strange people and unknown equipment (Fig. 16-2). The child must cope with situations for which he or she lacks preparation. The child fantasizes to find solutions for the missing information.[1] Intrusive procedures can threaten the child's body image. The child may feel dependent, insecure, and vulnerable. A child's ability to cope with hospitalization depends on numerous factors, among which are the following:

1. Age and cognitive development. The older child can more easily understand the reasons for hospitalization. The younger child's tendency to indulge in fantasy and distort reality increases.
2. Previous experience with illness or hospitals. The child's experience will establish expectations for the present hospitalization.
3. Relationship to parents. The stronger the parent-child relationship, the longer the child trusts parents to return and to protect him or her in the hospital.
4. Length and severity of the illness. Stores of psychic energy may be depleted by pain or illness, leaving the child less able to adapt to hospitalization.
5. Type and frequency of intrusive procedures. For a preschooler, several needle punctures within a short time may be overwhelming.
6. Anxiety level of parents. Anxiety in parents increases anxiety in a child.
7. Preparation. A child's anxiety will be less if he or she knows what to expect and how to act.
8. Prior stresses. If the child has been under stress

Figure 16-2 Strange, unfamiliar equipment may increase the young child's anxiety level. (*Photo by Theresa Friedrich. Courtesy of LAC/USC Medical Center.*)

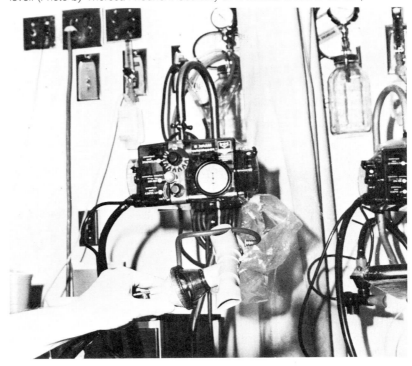

before hospitalization, the child will have less energy available to focus on recovery. On the other hand, if the child has learned to cope with stress, he or she is likely to deal with hospitalization well.

Communicating with children

Children respond not only to words but to the nurse's "feeling tone." Furthermore, they pick up unspoken attitudes. For this reason, the guidelines listed in Table 16-1 may be helpful in communicating with the young patient.

Television provides an innovative way of communicating with children of all ages. Children delight in seeing their friends' get-well messages flashed on the closed-circuit TV screen and hearing a puppet read the personal greeting. Sometimes a child's favorite stuffed animal is used to give a special message like "Drink lots of juice and water today, Amy" or "Take your medicine, Jason." Parents and nurses coach the TV director on appropriate messages. Before going to surgery one boy wanted to see the rocket he had drawn make a safe landing. After surgery he said seeing his rocket land safely made him feel "good." Children can also participate in these TV productions as they recuperate. Self-esteem is increased and the child is entertained and even educated.

Play and the hospitalized child

Play is the child's natural means of dealing with new experiences and stress. Play enables the child to express or project anger, aggression, insecurity, fear, fantasy, and conflict. If these emotions are suppressed instead, psychic energy is lost that could have been directed toward physical recovery. Much can be learned by watching a child at play (Table 16-2).

Table 16-1 Guidelines for communicating with children

1. Be gentle in manner and tone.
2. Talk soothingly in a low voice to a distressed or shy child.
3. Talk to preschoolers at their level of understanding:
   a. Use concrete terms: "You'll get well," or "I am busy now giving medicines. When I am finished in 5 minutes, I will play with you."
   b. Give them one direction at a time.
   c. Meet them at their eye level.
4. Praise school-age children for their accomplishments.
5. Be sensitive to teenagers' ambivalent need to approach and withdraw. Join them in their "dance" of moving toward and away from you.
6. Be honest and sincere; teenagers sense dishonesty immediately.
7. Children want to please. They want to know what is expected of them. Emphasize what they *can do.*
8. Give clear, brief directions. Reward them for correct actions. Praise *increases* in learning.
9. Place yourself in the child's position. How would you react and feel?

The value of toys

No child should be in bed without a toy. Even in isolation the child should have an age-appropriate toy. Toys that stimulate the imagination and permit manipulation can be made inexpensively in the hospital. The characteristics of safe toys are reviewed in Chap. 17.

By manipulating a small world of easily managed toys, the child gains feelings of control, power, and security. He or she can practice new methods of coping with problems. Furthermore, if play can be combined with procedures (Table 16-3), the child is helped to tolerate procedures.

Ideally every pediatric ward has a playroom. Playrooms provide a sanctuary from painful procedures. Here the child can control the environment, make decisions, and be active.

Play for communication

The nurse may use two types of play for communicating with the child: *situational,* or directive, play and *nondirective,* or free, play. In the former the play situation is structured around the procedure or other cause of the child's distress: injections, blood pressure cuff, diagnostic test, operation, or separation anxiety (Fig. 16-3). Materials and equipment used in the situation, such as syringes and alcohol sponges, should be gathered together. The nurse should take part in the play, for example, by shouting "ouch" when pretending to give or receive an injection. The child is allowed to handle the objects to make them less frightening.

The nurse may use a nurse-doll to teach a child the reasons for a procedure. After a procedure, the child and nurse play through it to assess the child's fantasies and distortions about the procedure. The nurse-doll can then be used to reteach or clarify the child's distortions. The nurse's sharing and approval of such play gives the child confidence and strength to master the problem.[2] By the proper use of play, a child can

Table 16-2 Guidelines for observing a child's play

Observation	Rationale
What toy did the child first select?	The preferred toy is usually the most healing one.
Did the child reject toys that were related to his or her treatment or diagnosis?	Refusal of toys is a method of denying the fear or of maintaining a distance from the fear. For example, a chronically ill child may refuse to play with a hospital model.
Is the child able to play?	Inability to play is a symptom of severe anxiety.
What emotions (affect) were expressed by the child as he or she played? Did the child's facial expression change? How did the child's body move during the play? Did the child express aggression in play? What toys did the child use to express it? What themes did the child communicate in his or her play?	The child expresses inner feelings through play. Observing the young child's body movements and actions is especially revealing if the child cannot talk fluently. Many children have been taught not to express aggression. They may gingerly begin to play aggressively and look at the nurse for approval to continue.
Did the child interact with others during play?	Children play alone and side by side (parallel play) until 4 years of age; then they learn to share (cooperative play)
Did the parents choose the child's toys or allow him or her to play freely?	Many parents need information about the benefits of free play.

Table 16-3 Playing to ease procedures

Procedure	Examples of play
Soaks	Play with small toys or objects (cups, syringes, soap dishes) in water. Wash dolls. Bubbles may be added to bath water.
Range of motion exercise	Throw bean bags at fixed or movable target. Touch or kick balloons held or hung in different positions.
Circulation check	Play "tickle toes"; wiggle them on request.
Deep breathing exercise	Blow bubbles with straw (no soap). Blow on pinwheel, feathers, whistle, harmonica. Draw face on rubber glove to expand when blown up.
Changing diapers	Nurse sings nursery rhymes or lullabies. Nurse smiles, laughs. Nurse moves child's legs and arms in rhythmical manner. Plays peek-a-boo.
Tuberculin testing	After injection, nurse or child draws face around site with washable pen.
Examination	Have child "blow out" little flashlight. Child can listen with stethoscope.
Observing or feeding (when there are many young children in a noninfectious ward)	Place children and toys on floor (covered with sheet) for play time.
Forcing of fluid	Make game of taking sip when turning page of book. Use small medicine cups. Color water with food coloring. Have tea party. Pour at small table.

Adapted from Lucille F. Whaley, and Donna L. Wong, *Nursing Care of Children*, Mosby, St. Louis, 1979, pp. 947–950.

be instructed and persuaded so that it is unnecessary to use force. For example, if a toddler refuses her medicine, a doll can be used as a subject, given medicine, made to tell its taste, and used to instruct the child to accept the medicine. The nurse should reflect the child's words back, especially the themes revealed in play. The preschooler spontaneously gives the doll her own name and diagnosis and projects her feelings onto it.

Nondirective, or free, play is based on the belief that children have the ability to solve their own problems and have a drive toward satisfying, normal behavior.[3] Children, therefore, instinctively choose comforting, self-healing toys.

Before the play session begins, the nurse establishes safety limits with the child. The child is then encouraged to choose toys. The child must learn that the nurse accepts him or her without evaluation or pressure to change. When trust is established, the child can play freely.

Parents and the hospitalized child

Reactions of parents

Parents experience a variety of feelings when their child is hospitalized. The majority of parents experience *anxiety*. If the child's progress is unknown or recovery questionable or the parents' sense of competency is threatened, their anxiety level will be high. In severe anxiety the parents' perceptual field narrows. Their attention focuses on one segment of the environment; what they hear is often distorted and they cannot learn or listen to others. These parents frequently

Figure 16-3 The nurse is using play to prepare this child for a procedure. Note the child's anxious facial expression. [*Courtesy of Nancy Conroy. From Gladys Scipien (ed.), Comprehensive Pediatric Nursing, McGraw-Hill, New York, 1979.*]

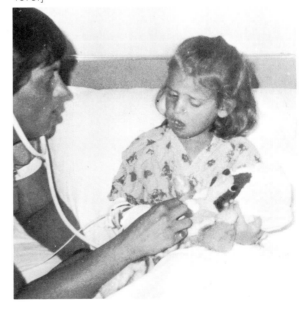

question nurses repeatedly and appear to test the nurses' competence. Characteristic behaviors of anxiety are rapid talking, a high-pitched voice, agitated hand movements, diaphoresis (sweating), and diarrhea. Anxiety must be recognized and reduced, for it is depleting and highly contagious.

Parents may also experience *fear*. Common causes of parents' fears are: inadequate information about test results, treatments, procedures, or prognosis; leaving the child alone; distrust of nursing and medical staff; strange equipment; and the costs of hospitalization. Parents may also worry about children at home, especially if the child care is inadequate. An ill or hospitalized child causes reverberations throughout the family constellation; children at home absorb their parents' anxiety. They may become jealous of their parents' time at the hospital and may become increasingly accident prone. (See Chap. 21.)

A *feeling of powerlessness* is a common parental reaction (Fig. 16-4). Before hospitalization the parents were the experts in control of their child's life. In the hospital medical and nursing personnel assume control of the child's care. Parents may feel helpless, dependent, uninformed, and powerless. Inadequacy is a common parental feeling. Parents may lack information about their role in the hospital. They do not know how they are expected to act. (One mother confided, "I haven't eaten in two days, but if I finish my daughter's tray, the head nurse will bawl me out!") The nurses had not assessed the mother's needs.

Parents frequently feel *guilt*, blaming themselves for their child's illness. Anger turned inward can result in guilt and depression. Parents express *anger* when they ask, "Why me? Why didn't the doctor diagnose it sooner? Why would God let this happen?" Anger is often directed at nurses or doctors because they are close, convenient targets. It is important for nurses to recognize the parents' anger, acknowledge it, help them express it, and realize it is not a personal attack. Parents may *deny* (or not consciously acknowledge) their child's illness. They take the child to various doctors and are unable to comprehend or believe the doctors' diagnoses or explanations. They may appear to disbelieve the doctor's diagnosis or search for errors. *Jealousy* of nurses occurs because parents feel inadequate, powerless, useless, and unimportant in the child's care. *Physical exhaustion* changes the parents' behavior. Inadequate sleep may reduce their ability to make rational decisions, cope with the stresses of the illness, and maintain a functioning routine at home. Parents who need sleep become irritable and unable to concentrate.

Parents in the hospital

Parents often have unclear expectations about their role in the hospital.[4] When people in any social encounter perceive their roles in the same way, they are in *role congruency*. If they do not, they may react unacceptably to each other. This is called *role incongruency* and often occurs between parents and nurses. Giving parents role cues or role information helps them learn how they are expected to act in a hospital.[5] Such aid is especially helpful when there is a cultural difference between nurse and parents. The four-step method shown in Table 16-4 may help the nurse increase the parents' sense of competence and ease any role incongruency that exists.

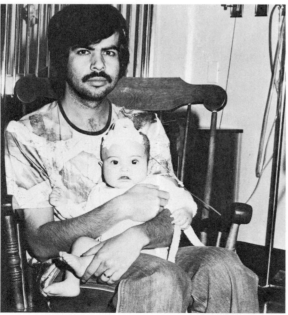

Figure 16-4 Hospitalization increases parents' feelings of anxiety, distrust, and powerlessness. Note this father's protective posture. (*Photo by Theresa Friedrich. Courtesy of LAC/USC Medical Center.*)

Table 16-4 Four-step teaching method*

1. *Paying attention* This first step validates your nursing diagnosis of the mother's source of anxiety. Directly address her, turn your body toward her, and say, for example: "Mrs. Smith, you look as if you're ready to cry. You seem really reluctant to pick up your child since she's had her IV." The mother then has the opportunity to agree (and validate) or reject your assessment. You then know if the observations and nursing diagnosis are correct. Focus your communication and teaching on the mother's main source of increased anxiety.
2. *Information-giving* In the second phase give the mother information about her role. Tell the mother that her feelings of fright are acceptable by saying, "Yes, Mrs. Smith, it must be frightening to pick up Jennifer with all of those tubes and wires attached to her body. Has anyone told you the reasons for them?" After giving an explanation for the IV, say: "Would you like me to teach you how to pick her up?" Demonstrate the procedure, telling her the essential points in *simple* words.
3. *Participation* Have the mother pick up Jennifer and stress the important points. Encourage the mother to ask questions.
4. *Evaluation* Evaluate your teaching: Did you consider the mother's main concern? Was your information given in small amounts and simple language during the demonstration? Document the mother's learning. What areas were her strengths and weaknesses? What teaching methods appeared most effective? How did the mother's behavior change after the teaching? What were her main concerns? Document these on the chart.

* Adapted from Roy.[4]

In most hospitals, teaching of role expectations begins before hospitalization. Usually there are booklets available that instruct parents on visiting hours, rooming-in, cafeteria hours, and other policies. Ideally, such guides also welcome them and encourage them to participate in their child's care.

The nurse can offer important help to the parents in search of an appropriate role. A few points of guidance can be given:

1. Allow a parent to be with the child during procedures, provided this makes the parent and child less anxious.
2. Encourage parents to participate in their child's care (Fig. 16-5). According to one study,[6] parents want to do more for their children than nurses realize. They gain a feeling of competence if they actively contribute to their child's recovery. The nurse who wishes to ensure that parents get to provide care can learn which jobs they prefer to do

and establish a contract, written on the Kardex, listing the parents' and nurse's tasks (Fig. 16-6). Parents should be assured that the nurse will teach them, answer questions, and check the child frequently.
3. Praise them for rearranging schedules in order to be with the child. Assure them that they are making an important contribution to the child's recovery. At the same time, assess their ability to cope with the illness. Can other family members support the parents by caring for children left at home? If appropriate, refer them to sources of financial aid.
4. Support and help parents when it is time for them to separate from the child. Explain that they should honestly tell the child they are going home and that this truthfulness will increase the child's trust. Educate them about separation anxiety and encourage them to leave a personal article (sweater, tie, keys) with the child and to telephone the child.

The nurse should make it a priority to win the parents' trust. They should be asked each day if they have questions, and these should be

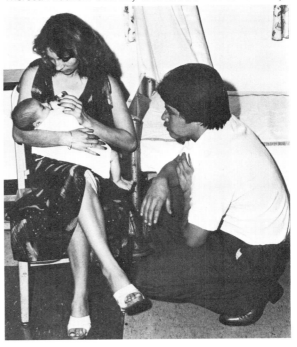

Figure 16-5 Children need their parents. Being fed by his parents increases this infant's sense of trust. (*Photo by Theresa Friedrich. Courtesy of LAC/USC Medical Center.*)

Figure 16-6 A completed nurse-parent contract is placed in the Kardex. [*From Annette Ayer, "Is Partnership with Parents Really Possible?" American Journal of Maternal Child Nursing 3(2):109 (March/April 1978).*]

Parent Participation in Hospital Care

What would you like to do for your child during his or her hospitalization as far as physical care is concerned?

Feed child _____
Bathe child _____
Take temperature _____
Give pills or liquid medications_____
Record amount child eats and drinks _____
Record amount of urination or bowel movement _____
Stay with child during doctor's examination _____
Stay with child during painful procedures_____
Take child to bathroom or change diaper _____
Go with child to x-ray department or bathroom _____
Change bed linen _____

Is there anything else you would like to do for your child during this hospitalization? _____

answered carefully; following through is important in establishing trust. After a doctor has finished an explanation, the parents should be asked what they understood the physician to mean. In this way the nurse can assess their understanding. Many parents see nurses as less threatening than physicians and as persons who have more time to talk. Finding out how parents interpret what the doctors said gives the nurse an opportunity to teach, clarify, and reinforce the physician's explanations. Simple, everyday words should be employed. If necessary a translator, perhaps another family member, should be used. Medical phrases can be written out on cards in two languages.

It will help communication if the nurse addresses the parents while turned toward them, using direct eye contact, after greeting them courteously by name. (The author once observed two nurses in an intermediate intensive care unit who failed to speak to or even acknowledge five of the six parents present over a 6-h period!)

Preparing the child for procedures

Nurses who understand how children think and know how to communicate and play with them are more successful in preparing them for procedures. The nurse may need guidelines on the needs of each age group, which naturally differ a great deal. Table 16-5 reviews the preteaching phase. Table 16-6 identifies the concerns and expectations of patients in the age groups from infancy to adolescence and offers suggestions for appropriate teaching and nursing care.

The infant's reactions to hospitalization

All infants have similar reactions to hospitalization. Because of their immature body systems, they frequently experience instability in temperature regulation, fluid and electrolyte balance, and absorption of medicine (see Chaps. 10 and

Table 16-5 Preparing the child for procedures: 1. Preteaching phase

Preparation for teaching	Rationale
Nurse who has established trust should teach child; relief person should be designated on Kardex and introduced to the child. Preoperative teaching should start 1 day before surgery at a time when child is rested.	If the child trusts the nurse-teacher, the child's anxiety will be less and he or she will be better able to grasp and believe what is said.
Review child's cognitive development	Teaching must be adapted to child's ability to think.
Confer with doctors or nurses in ICU or in surgery regarding special treatments, procedures, etc. Many hospitals use a "roller file" of doctor's special instructions about procedures. Notebooks of teaching plans are also used (e.g., Will anesthesia be given by mask; will child be on respirator?).	It is important for the nurse to maintain trust by giving the child correct information.
Assess if child wants parents present. Many preschoolers and school-age children do.	Presence of parents increases child's sense of security.
Gather together equipment for teaching: doll with tubes, IV tubing, etc. Assess if school-age child or adolescent is embarrassed by presence of doll.	Child needs to see equipment. Toddlers and preschoolers think concretely and respond best to dolls.

Table 16-6 Preparing the child for procedures: 2. Information-giving phase

Characteristics of cognitive development	Guidelines for teaching and nursing care
Infant (birth to 1 year)	
No understanding of procedure or effect Feels pain.	No preparation needed. Keep procedure brief. Comfort and hold the child securely. Talk in a soothing voice during procedure.
Familiar routines of care establish security and trust in mother/nurse.	Have familiar person hold infant during procedure. Give pacifier if appropriate. Encourage mother to comfort infant during procedure.
Relates to world through touch. Greatest comfort is in sucking.	After procedure, hold and cuddle infant. Give bottle or pacifier.
Toddler (1 to 3 years)	
Fear of separation from parents causes greatest anxiety. Parent provides greatest security, even while child is experiencing pain.	Urge parents to stay with and comfort child during procedure. Suggest that a parent hold the child afterward.
Has no vocabulary for explaining fears and anxieties. Toddler has less experience than an older child in dealing with stress. Understands only one concept at a time.	Use simple words. Explain one concept at a time (e.g., "Hold your leg still," not "Hold your leg still and don't cry.") Tell child how to act (e.g., first say, "Hold your leg still," then later, "You can cry.").
Relates to the world by touch, feel, taste. Uses play to learn about equipment and how to act in a new situation.	Let child use syringe (without needle), catheter, etc. and play at giving you or a doll an injection. Tell child how it will feel. If possible, leave equipment for child to play with.
Has no concept of passing time	Prepare child one-half h ahead or just before the procedure.
Preschooler (3 to 5 years)	
Still has no concept of passing time.	Prepare child one-half h ahead (if surgery is complicated, divide the information in sections). Tell child when procedure is completed.
Egocentric. Thinks he or she is the center and causes everything to happen. Cannot analyze own thinking. Only his or her opinion matters.	Tell child he or she did not cause the procedure. Use doll play to discover thoughts. (Doll will "say" what child thinks.) Don't argue about the procedure with the child.
Lives in the present. Interested only in "how it will feel." Still relates to the world primarily by touch.	Tell child what will happen now and how it will feel. (He or she has no interest in the cause or the disease.)
Sense of autonomy is well developed. Answers requests with "no."	Tell parent what you expect of the child. Allow child some control by giving him or her a choice (e.g., "which leg do you want the shot in?") If the child procrastinates, announce that you are going to give the injection, and proceed.
Child may be unable (though willing) to cooperate during a procedure; he or she may not have full control of emotions	Do not punish or get angry. Instead say, "I will help you hold your leg still this time. Maybe you can hold it still next time." Praise the child for something he or she did well (even crying loudly).
Child may become angry (without knowing the name for it) because he or she cannot escape the procedure.	Encourage expressions of anger through play (clay, hammer, bean bags). Tell child he or she is angry and it is all right.
As part of establishing boundaries of self, child fears body intrusion. Fantasies of body mutilation are very vivid.	Stress that only a limited part of the body will be involved. Describe how the body will feel, look, or "work" afterward.
Child may fear general anesthesia as being like dying.	Stress that "special sleep" keeps pain away and he or she will wake up.
Child thinks parent (or nurse) is omnipotent and can do anything for him.	Support the need for the procedure. Don't say, "I don't want to but I have to."
School-age child (6 to 12 years)	
Child needs to maintain emotional control.	Carry out procedure in a room away from child's peers to prevent embarrassment. Tell child what to do and say during the procedure. Explain the procedure beforehand.
With increase in vocabulary child wants to know cause of the disorder, how procedure affects body functioning, how procedure will feel.	Ask child to label a body outline or to draw a picture of the affected part. Reinforce his or her correct associations and correct any mistakes about anatomy and physiology. Explain cause of disorder. Draw a picture of the body and part, describing function, procedure, and aftermath. Tell child how procedure will feel.

Table 16-6 Preparing the child for procedures: 2. Information-giving phase (*Continued*)

Characteristics of cognitive development	Guidelines for teaching and nursing care
Despite larger vocabulary, child may not understand meaning of medical words he or she uses.	Ask the child word meanings. Teach the child scientific terms for body parts and procedures.
Child tends to blame himself or herself for illness.	Correct this misunderstanding.
Child needs to feel proud of accomplishments. May display more self-confidence than he or she actually has. Praise increases self-esteem.	After procedure, praise the child for what he or she did correctly (no matter how trivial). Encourage child to visit other well-adjusted children facing similar treatments.
Adolescent (12 to 21 years)	
The adolescent wants to be well informed on how procedure may affect body image.	Explain procedure and its effect on the body, what clothes or activities will be possible afterward. With a mutilating operation (e.g., colostomy or amputation) stress how the adolescent's normal activities can be adapted. Have a well-adapted teenager who has experienced the procedure visit.
Adolescent needs to have some control and feeling of independence.	Allow the adolescent to wear own clothes. Encourage the adolescent to make health care decisions and to execute them. Give adolescent privacy when requested. If he or she appears unduly dependent on parents, ask adolescent necessary questions when he or she is alone.
Adolescent fears loss of acceptance by peers.	Encourage visits by friends and other adolescent patients. Encourage adolescent to eat with friends in the cafeteria. Discuss school and friends with adolescent.

11). Furthermore, the parent-child relationship is likely to be disturbed. The trusting infant perceives the world as safe when experiencing consistency, continuity, and sameness in the daily routine. The inevitable disruptions brought on by hospitalization may promote distrust. The bonding process may be interrupted (see Chap. 10) and the older infant may experience separation anxiety, discussed later in the section "The Toddler's Reactions to Hospitalization."

To offset these reactions the nurse should attempt to adapt hospital routines to resemble those of the home. It has been found helpful to provide a "primary" nurse for each child and to encourage a family member to be with the child each day.

The remainder of this section will focus on the impact of disturbing a child's daily routines, such as feeding, sucking, sleeping, and crying. It will also examine how a changed sensory environment like the hospital affects a child.

Feeding

A reluctance to eat is very common in sick infants. This makes feeding a very time-consuming and frustrating experience for the nurse and parents. Feeding suggestions are listed in Table 16-7.

Infants need their mothers to hold and feed them whenever possible. Infants are acutely sensitive to the feeder; the environment; the texture, temperature, and taste of food; the type and size of nipple; the bottle; and the feeding schedule. All these must be considered when feeding the infant, and the experience should be made as homelike as possible. Painful procedures should be scheduled between feedings to avoid upsetting the baby just before or just after eating.

Sucking

Sucking is the infant's main source of emotional satisfaction and brings food and pleasurable feelings to the infant. Sick infants often have difficulty sucking. When the infant's sucking needs are not met through feeding, provide a pacifier. Position the infant to make the pacifier accessible.

Sleep

Changes in routine and environment result in disturbances of sleep patterns. Use information obtained in the admission history to simulate the home routine. Pay attention to bedtime, favorite position, nighttime bottle, bedtime rituals, and type and location of bed.

Crying

Infants communicate their needs by crying. Cries of pain are high-pitched and shrill; cries of hunger are lower-pitched and increase in loudness to reflect the intensity of hunger. Cries of anger are loud.

Learn to interpret infant cries. Ask the parents to interpret the cries and suggest successful remedies.

First check the baby's physical comfort: Are the diapers wet? Is a pin sticking the infant?

Table 16-7 Feeding problems of the hospitalized infant

Problem	Nursing intervention	Rationale
Excessive crying, gas, or pain from colic.	Burp infant before and frequently during feeding. Place infant on abdomen or use suppository, thermometer, or rectal tube to expel gas.	When crying, infant swallows air, which distends stomach, increasing pressure and discomfort. Release of air as burp brings food with it.
	Keep formula cool or at room temperature.	Excessively warm formula increases pressure in the enclosed stomach.
	Comfort child to decrease crying. Be sure diapers are not wet.	
	Offer pacifier if infant is unable to take enough formula to appease hunger.	
Anxious, anorexic infants.	A relaxed, secure nurse or preferably a parent should rock and comfort child before, during, and after feeding.	Relaxed tone of caretaker will be communicated to infant. Rocking simulates intrauterine movement and increases sense of security.
	Feed small amounts of food.	
Frequent regurgitation or vomiting of food.	Burp infant before and often during feeding.	Normal newborn children have weak cardiac sphincters, which allows food to ascend easily to mouth. This may be accentuated in sick infants.
	Thicken the formula slightly with rice cereal.	
	Take time in feeding. Allow child to rest in nurse's arms between feedings.	
	Keep child in upright position before, during, and after feeding. Do not feed in infant seat.	
	Perform any scheduled procedures before feeding.	
	Do not overfeed.	
Refuses solid foods or is hungry but is unable to take in adequate quantity.	Flavor cereal slightly with fruit (apricots, bananas).	Critically ill child (e.g., cardiac disease) may lack energy to suck or eat.
	Thin formula. Serve in small demitasse spoon.	In premature or brain-damaged infants, sucking reflex is weak.
	Offer small amounts of food using a gloved, clean finger.	Sucking requires considerable energy.
	Give child small frequent feedings, with rest periods between.	
	Reassess hospital routine. Is it homelike and consistent with data from admission interview.	

Note: Although some of these measures may help the nurse to feed the normal newborn, certain others will not. For instance, a pacifier is not to be used to appease a well infant instead of feeding. Furthermore, the nurse should not thicken the feeding of a normal infant to prevent regurgitation.

When was the infant last fed? How much was eaten? Does the infant need to be burped? Does the child have appropriate toys? When was the child last taken out of the crib to play? Is the child in pain? Make necessary corrections, then comfort the child by rocking or walking, singing and cooing, or offering toys.

Place babies in backpacks while working in noninfectious areas. Hold babies on laps while charting. Utilize others (foster grandparents) to consistently feed and care for infants when parents are unable to visit.

Sensory stimulation: Impact of the hospital

Infants and children need stimulation of their senses for normal psychological and neurological development. The newborn is especially alert immediately after birth. Infants move their eyes searching for human faces, which they prefer to other visual stimuli. They also prefer colorful, moving objects to unmoving, colorless forms.[7]

Auditory stimuli, like visual ones, can be highly significant. Hospitalized infants fall asleep almost immediately when recordings of intrauterine sounds are placed close by. It is probably no accident that a mother naturally cradles her child over her heart. The heart beat may simulate intrauterine sounds. Infants also move in synchronous rhythm with the sounds of the parent's speech.[8] All such auditory stimuli are believed to promote a feeling of security and the process of bonding.

Sensory stimulation of certain kinds also appears to foster physical development. Infants stimulated with rocking and tape recordings of a woman's voice and heartbeat have been shown to grow better than infants not receiving the stimulation.[9] In another study[10] infants exposed to auditory, visual, tactile, and motor stimulation matured faster than children not receiving it. Several studies have found that premature infants are especially vulnerable to developmental delays if the hospital environment provides inadequate stimulation and does not encourage the mother's presence.

For these reasons the modern-day maternity unit is a far different place from the one of years past, when infants were placed in white rooms, enclosed in bassinets with white-sheeted sides, and viewed by parents through a window. Infants were handled and rocked minimally. The practices of such institutions may have unintention-ally contributed to developmental delays and inadequate parent-child bonding.

Sensory deprivation The importance of sensory stimulation appears to derive from the need of the cerebrum for a certain level of input from the environment by way of the nervous system. The level is believed to be preset in each individual. A prolonged drop below this level brings about *sensory deprivation.* Premature infants, chronically ill children, and institutionalized children are at risk for sensory deprivation.

If a child's crying brings no response from an adult, the child cries less and learns not to expect adults to meet his or her needs. Infants who rarely see adults will not learn to imitate the facial expressions, body movements, or speech of adults. The faces of these infants bear stonelike or bland expressions. Speech development is delayed. Their speed of response is below normal, as is the number of words they learn to speak. Severely deprived infants fail to develop stranger anxiety (a behavior indicative of bonding) and to learn to mold to the caretaker's arms.

Older sensory-deprived children may exhibit self-stimulatory behavior such as body rocking, head banging, and repetitive rubbing or picking of the sheets. Such children are more likely than others to experience hallucinations.[11]

Sensory overload Excessive sensory stimulation may lead to *sensory overload.* Infants and children in critical care units are especially vulnerable, given the constant beeping of cardiac monitors, the sound of respirators, and the continuous, monotonous lighting. The behaviors of sensory overload are similar to those of sensory deprivation. The infant has difficulty perceiving new stimuli among the inflow of others. He or she needs a general reduction in stimuli and an individualized, age-appropriate plan for sensory stimulation.

Nursing management Using appropriate stimuli, the nurse is the critical person to design the plan for enrichment of the infant's environment. The nurse should assess the child for symptoms of sensory deprivation or overload and identify environmental sources if either condition exists.

Chosen stimuli should have maximal meaning for the child. A recording of the mother's heartbeat or voice may be right for an infant but less effective for an older child. The stimuli should relate to the child's greatest need. If the child screams for the mother, for example, the nurse should fetch her or provide a substitute. The intensity of the stimulus should be varied. Television should not be the source for an extended period. The visual and auditory stimuli, especially in the daytime with continuous game shows, may become monotonous and hence ineffective. Because of the infant's short attention span, stimuli for infants should be varied frequently.

Stimuli selected by the nurse for an infant should be age-appropriate and engage the infant's main ways of experiencing the world: touch, movement, vision, and hearing. Suggestions are given in Table 16-8.

The toddler's reactions to hospitalization

Toddlers usually react to hospitalization with three main behaviors: (1) separation anxiety (which begins in infancy but peaks in the toddler years); (2) regression; and (3) disturbances in

Table 16-8 Suggestions for sensory stimulation

Tactile

Fuzzy blankets
Toys of different colors and textures to touch and hold
Holding and cuddling during feedings and whenever possible
Diaper rolls to place behind infant's back (to simulate mother's backbone)
Pacifiers to bring pleasurable feelings and satisfaction

Movement

Rocking chairs to simulate intrauterine movement
Cradle gyms to pull self up
Toys to bounce, crunch, squeeze
Minimal restraint on child, with toy in reach

Visual

Mirrors in crib or incubator
Pictures of parents and pets
Brightly colored mobiles placed in child's line of vision, not at foot of bed

Auditory

Singing lullabies
Recordings of mother's heartbeat
Recording of parent's voice
Music boxes, records

Figure 16-7 This toddler is in the protest stage of separation anxiety. She angrily protests her mother's departure. *Photo by Theresa Friedrich. Courtesy of LAC/USC Medical Center.*

daily routines. Each of these behavioral disturbances will be discussed in this section.

Separation anxiety

This is essentially a grief reaction and is characterized by stages of (1) protest, (2) despair, and (3) denial or detachment. Children from 7 months to 3 years of age are most vulnerable to separation anxiety. The toddler's response to separation is strongly influenced by the existence of a strong parental bond, the illness itself, and previous experience of separation.

Stage 1: Protest After the mother has gone, the toddler angrily protests (Fig. 16-7). The toddler refuses to eat, tries frantically to climb over the siderail, keeps watching for her return, and cries loudly and angrily until dropping from exhaustion. The toddler depends on his mother. Her absence increases his feelings of vulnerability. The hospitalized child needs his mother as much as food. The environment is strange. The toddler may feel punished or abandoned by the mother. This lowers self-esteem and increases feelings of shame and doubt. Behavior is thus focused upon regaining the mother. During the protest stage, the toddler still trusts that his parents will return.

Nursing management The goal during protest is to preserve the child's trust in his parents. Do not feel rejected if the child stiffens when comforted; the child simply prefers his mother. Nurses instinctively say, "Shh, don't cry." Instead, encourage the child to cry and express anger by saying, "Go ahead, cry! I know you want your mommy." Expressing, instead of suppressing, anger is psychologically healthy for the child.

Figure 16-8 This toddler is in the despair stage of separation anxiety. Her depression deepens; she sits listlessly in the crib. *Photo by Theresa Friedrich. Courtesy of LAC/USC Medical Center.*

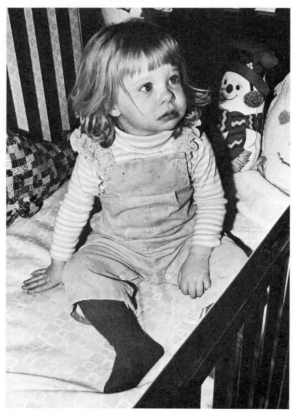

Encourage and accept expression of aggression in play: pounding boards or clay, throwing bean bags, or hitting balloons hung from the bed. Tell the child you will stay with him. Help the toddler remember his parents by talking about them and their activities together at home. The toddler thinks in the present: "My parents are gone and may not return." Because the toddler's security is associated with objects, he believes they will return for an object. The parent should leave with the child a personal object from home: a tie, keys, purse, or scarf.

Favorite toys, pajamas, dishes, or security blankets bridge the transition from home and bring hours of comfort. New toys and clothes brought by the parents are not the same. Tape pictures of family members and pets to the crib to connect the child to home. If the parent cannot come in, tape-record the mother telling a story or singing a bedtime lullaby. Foster grandparents can also help the child when parents can't be present. Allowing the parents to *room in* is ideal for promoting the toddler's security.

Stage 2: Despair In this stage the child's depression deepens (Fig. 16-8). The trust for parents wavers. The child begins to wonder if the parents will ever return. The child becomes sad, withdrawn, subdued, and less angry. He submits to intrusive procedures with little resistance, picks at food and sits quietly and forlornly in the crib. The child's cry is whining, listless, and pitiful. His behavior regresses. When the parents return the child may not go to them immediately but stands back as if to say, "You have caused me so much pain that I really don't know if I want to be closely involved with you again." When the child does approach them, he may cry, show anger, or frantically cling to them. The child occasionally runs away from the mother as if to punish and reject her, but soon clings tightly to her again.

Nursing management The nurse's goal with a child in despair is to increase the child's trust in the parents and to facilitate the expression of anger. If rooming-in is not possible, demand consistent staff to help the child develop trust in consistent care-givers. Encourage the child to talk about the parents. Use the interventions described in the section "Stage 1: Protest" to promote the child's trust in the parents. Encourage the parents or a familiar person to consistently visit and feed the child. When nurses do not actively intervene with a child in despair, the child's depression will deepen and progress to distrust of the parents.

Stage 3: Denial or detachment In past years nurses erroneously thought that settling-in, or an outward denial of parents, was a positive change in the child's behavior. Certainly a compliant child is easier to care for than a screaming protester. If the nurse does not strengthen a child's trust in the parents, and the child's hospitalization is traumatic and prolonged, the child may lose trust in the parents.

The child in the denial stage eats, plays with toys, begins to resist intrusive procedures again, and makes "overtures" to all nurses on the unit. He appears to have sad eyes, brimming with tears, and a permanent, plastic, or fake, smile. The child rejects the parents and their presents when they return and deliberately expresses affection for the nurses. He denies the need for the parents' love and suppresses longing and hostility toward them. Instead the child relates to others on a superficial level, no longer willing to risk intimate, trusting involvement with the parents. If the health team does not actively promote the child's trust, he may no longer be able to maintain in-depth, intimate relationships with adults.

Nursing management Encourage the child to express fears and perceptions (doll play is the ideal medium for the toddler's self-expression, "showing" the child that the parents will return and take him home). Promote the consistent presence of the mother or surrogate mother. Continue to use all nursing interventions described earlier.

Regression
While all children and adults regress to some degree when ill or faced with a stressful event, regression is an especially common coping mechanism during the toddler and preschool years. The child usually drops the most recently learned behavior and returns to an earlier, more firmly established satisfying behavior.[12]

Toddlers may revert to the bottle, refuse to drink from a cup, and wet their pants. Regression enables the child to withdraw, conserve energy,

and eventually develop new methods of problem-solving. This healthy, beneficial, "time-out" behavior is an attempt to regain control. The amount of regression is directly related to the degree of frustration and stress experienced by the child.

Nursing management Accept the child's behavior. Many nurses respond to regression in a cold, disapproving manner and label it as bad or obstructive.[13] This increases the child's stress. Therefore, let the child play baby or drink from a bottle. Hold, rock, and cuddle the child. Help parents understand the healthy psychological benefits of regression. Relate regression to their own need for hot chicken soup and tender, loving care when ill. Explain that regression reduces the child's anxiety level, helps him or her regain control, and facilitates the child's physical recovery. Assess the toddler's readiness to stop regressing by noting the child's willingness to share and play with the nurse.[14]

Disturbance of daily routines and behavior
Toilet training Make a Kardex note about stage of training, specific words, and usual time of elimination. Instead of automatically placing toddlers in diapers, establish a routine for placing the child on the potty-chair (see Chap. 12).

Sleeping Continue the child's bedtime ritual in the hospital with a story, lullaby, favorite animal or security blanket (see Chap. 12).

Eating behavior The toddler's eating patterns are erratic and ritualistic. The child is very sensitive to changes in the environment, type of food, and the person doing the feeding. Provide small portions of foods that can be easily handled and eaten by the child without help.

Negativism The toddler often repeats "No!" to every request whether it is a cookie or a nap. These constant no's are the toddler's method of proving his or her individuality with needs separate from the mother's.

Avoid questions inviting a "no" answer, such as "Suzy, do you want to take a nap now?" Help the child respond by holding her hand and leading her to the bed. Emphasize what to *do*, rather than what *not to do*. If the child is immersed in a forbidden activity, say no and divert her attention to another toy. Give the toddler a choice between two acceptable alternatives: "Suzy, do you want the red or green medicine first?"

Temper tantrums Temper tantrums provide a safety valve for releasing pent-up, explosive emotions. Toddlers have limited control over their feelings. Ignore, do not punish, tantrums. Some children respond well to being held firmly while regaining control. Hold the child and say, "I will help you hold still. The way you feel is called 'mad'." If a toddler is biting a child or behaving in some other unacceptable manner, move his head away from the other child, be on equal eye level, and say, "Stop biting him now. That hurts." Avoid saying, "You're a bad boy" for this may diminish the child's self-esteem.

Ritualistic behavior Toddlers depend upon their familiar routines and objects for security. They cannot reason, have a short attention span, and live in the present; toddlers have less ability to control and understand their environment. Provide homelike routines to meet basic needs and a safe environment appropriate for toddler's size.

Dawdling The toddler dawdles when caught in an ambivalent situation. Help him or her perform the activity needed.

Reactions at home after hospitalization

Help parents anticipate possible changes in their child's behavior when their toddler returns home. After a prolonged or traumatic hospitalization, the child may show any or all of the following behaviors: aggression, regression, nightmares, fear of falling asleep or of the dark, eating disturbances (food refusal, overeating, or rituals), overdependence, and unwillingness to let the mother out of sight.[15] The child is afraid that if the parent disappears, he or she will again be left alone. One mother said, about her daughter Sara,

> She follows me everywhere! I can't even go to the bathroom alone. She wakes up screaming five or six times at night, shaking and crying, "The nurses are giving me shots! I can't run away! They're tying me down." She's regressed, and when I approach her, she backs away and shakes like a hurt puppy!

Before her hospitalization, Sara had gone to nursery school, fed herself, and was toilet-trained. After hospitalization, which included 22 injections in 2 days, she regressed. The nurse reviewed the child's illness and history with the parents to analyze their effects on Sara's behavior. Together they planned methods of handling her fears that would neither punish nor reward the behavior. For example, the nurse advised the mother to use the interventions listed for dealing with protest behavior: stay with Sara, help her return to a meaningful activity, allow her to regress, and use needle play. She gleefully "shot" everything in the house—walls, pillows, couch, daddy—and within a few weeks her behavior had returned to normal.

The preschooler's reactions to hospitalization

Preschoolers have the following reactions to hospitalization: (1) fear of body mutilation, (2) misinterpretation of hospital events, (3) withdrawn behavior, (4) aggressive behavior, (5) sleep disturbances, (6) masturbation, and (7) separation anxiety. Each of these reactions will be discussed in this section.

Fears of mutilation

The main fear of preschoolers is loss of body integrity. They have violent fantasies about mutilation (Fig. 16-9). A preschooler is just defining his body's outer boundaries, is unsure of his completeness, and is acutely sensitive to physical sensations and threats of attack. When asked to open his mouth and say "Ah," one preschooler refused and clutched his penis as if to reassure himself of its intactness. Preschoolers are acutely interested in physical deviations among people. Preschoolers suppose that such deviations are the results of violence and egocentrically assume that body intrusions or mutilation may also happen to them.

Preschoolers have only general ideas about body functions. For example, they picture a whole hamburger or cola inside the body and are unable to visualize the digestion and elimination of food. Preschoolers may know they have a heart, but lack information about its function and location. They have minimal knowledge of other body organs and fantasize the information

Figure 16-9 An injection seen through a child's eyes. Preschoolers fear body invasion and mutilation. (*Photo by Theresa Friedrich. Courtesy of LAC/USC Medical Center.*)

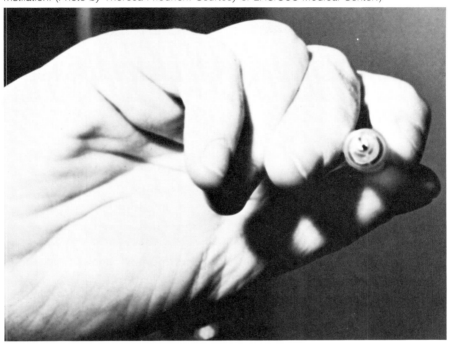

they lack. Selected nursing interventions to promote body integrity are described in Table 16-9.

Misinterpretation of events

Preschoolers commonly misinterpret hospital events. Thinking at this age is magical and concrete, and these children readily create fantasy explanations for events they don't understand. They don't clearly differentiate their fantasies, which are very real to them, from facts, which they poorly comprehend. They believe angry thoughts can make bad things happen. For example, if Mark is angry with his mother and she leaves, he will think he caused her to go away.

The thinking of children is egocentric; hence they are unable to understand or accept the points of view of others. They "know" what they "know," and arguing does not change their opinions.

Preschoolers focus on one aspect of an event while overlooking its other features. This characteristic causes them, for example, to attend only to the anticipated pain of an injection and

to be unconsoled by promises that it will hurt only for a moment.

They also are very present-oriented and cannot spontaneously anticipate that the current situation will improve (for example, that a procedure will soon be completed or that mother will return and eventually take the child home).

The thinking of young children is animistic; that is, they think everything that makes noise or has moving parts or blinking lights is alive. Consequently, preschoolers are commonly frightened of respirators, elevators, monitors, and other unfamiliar and noisy equipment.

Preschoolers also think adults are omnipotent and that adults' motivations for causing or allowing unpleasant things to happen to children must be malevolent, since they imagine that adults have the power to exercise control over such events.

A forthright, honest, sympathetic, firm approach does much to support young children through hospitalization even though they are still developmentally limited in their ability to understand what they are experiencing. Help

Table 16-9 Nursing interventions to reduce preschooler's fears about body mutilation

Source of fear	Intervention
Bleeding, even a tiny amount	Use adhesive bandages liberally, including after every injection and finger-stick and for small abrasions. Tell the child the bandage will plug the hole. Explain that when the blood comes out it gets "gluey" and "fixes" the hole and that the body makes new blood all the time.
Surgery	In preparation for surgery, explain that the doctor stops the bleeding and fixes the skin with needle and thread. Explain that surgery doesn't hurt because the child is in a special sleep. Have child sew doll's skin and apply bandage. Avoid words like *cut* and *knife;* use words like *take away, sew up,* and *fix.* Describe postoperative body function, e.g., "You will go to the bathroom just like before."
Casts and cast removal	Have child apply and remove cast from doll. Explain that body part is protected inside cast and remains attached to the body, that body parts do not "break off" from people as the child may have seen happen to toys and dolls or in cartoons. Demonstrate cast remover; use on own skin or parent's to show it doesn't cut.
Disfigurements observed in others, especially other patients	Explain how the observed person's condition differs from the child's and reassure child (realistically) that whatever happened to the other person (amputation, burn, birthmark, etc.) will not happen to the child. Emphasize restoration of body intactness, for example, "The doctors and nurses give her medicine and a new bandage every day, and her arm is getting better so that she will be able to play again."
Teasing, "jokes," and other threatening remarks about body damage	*Never* joke or threaten about accidental or intentional body injury. Young children interpret such remarks literally.
Equipment (sphygmomanometer, thermometer, traction, oxygen tents, respirators, etc.)	Emphasize therapeutic purpose for equipment, for example, "That machine helps the boy breathe until he gets better and can breathe by himself." Arrange doll play and manipulation of sphygmomanometer, thermometer, and other equipment used in the child's care. Demonstrate use and explain what the child will experience; for example, taking blood pressure on doll or parent, say, "It doesn't hurt. It feels tight like a belt. Now it's getting looser and I will take it off." Of rectal thermometer say, "See, it isn't sharp. It only goes in this far. It tells me how hot you are, and then I take it out again." Allow mother to insert thermometer.
Injections	See Chap. 17

children separate fact from fantasy: children have to take medicine because it helps them get well faster so they can go home, not because they are naughty; mothers leave the hospital because it is time for them to go to work, not because children are angry. Use play to discover children's perceptions and imaginings, and use play, story telling, and simple explanations to correct misperceptions and reduce fears. Prepare children in advance of procedures by demonstrating and explaining what is to be done and providing opportunities to examine and manipulate equipment. When a child is too upset about an injection or other treatment to tolerate explanations about it, it is usually best to provide external controls (restraints) and proceed as quickly and kindly as possible; preschoolers often are more amenable to teaching and reassurance afterward than before. Do not argue or

coax. Offer choices only if a choice truly exists; otherwise, explain what is to be done and do it. Tell the child when the procedure is over. Provide simple explanations about equipment that do not support fearful fantasies. Adults' motives can be explained without claims to powerlessness. For example, of a venipuncture say, "The doctor needs to see a little of your blood so we can tell how to make you well. We are sorry the needle hurts for a few minutes," rather than "We don't want to do this, but we have to."

Withdrawn behavior

Some preschoolers withdraw from threatening stimuli. They often appear passive, immobile, and apathetic when faced with threatening procedures or separation from parents. Accept such behavior. Help them to recognize and accept their emotions, to learn new methods of coping with stress, and to express themselves in play. Consistent nurses are vital in maintaining the child's trust.

Aggressive behavior

Aggressive behavior is common among preschoolers. Many children want to, but are unable to, control their impulsive behavior. Preschoolers are less socialized and have not yet learned to hide their true feelings. Label the child's emotion, saying, "Johnny, the way you feel is called anger. It is *okay* to be angry. I understand that you want your mommy, not me. Let's talk about what else you can do besides kicking me when you feel angry. You can . . ." Restrain the child to protect him from hurting others. Explain the reasons for holding him: "I am holding you until you stop biting. You cannot bite Andy again. He bleeds easily. Chew on this biscuit or bite the rubber duck. I will help you stop biting. It hurts." Accept his feelings of anger and structure an outlet for his aggression, such as hitting a punching bag or pounding clay.

Sleep disturbances

Fear of "monsters" at bedtime peaks at $2\frac{1}{2}$ to 4 years of age (Fig. 16-10). The boundary between dreams and reality is shadowy. Preschoolers cling to bedtime rituals to increase control over their lives. Repeat the home bedtime ritual. If a child is afraid of monsters, comfort her and emphatically tell her monsters are *not* real. Pretending to "search" for monsters is poor policy, since it may reinforce their possible existence.

Masturbation

Preschoolers are establishing sexual identity. They learn that masturbation is pleasurable and tension-releasing. Instead of shaming them, which communicates that sexual organs are bad, tell them to rub themselves in their room instead of in the hall, or divert their attention.

Separation anxiety

The separation anxiety of preschoolers is less intense than that of toddlers. Preschoolers have learned to handle their parents' absence, and they may previously have been away from home overnight. Their security is still closely bound to their parents, however, and at times of stress they need their parents nearby. The reactions to separation described in the section "The Tod-

Figure 16-10 Fear of nighttime "monsters" peaks during the preschool years.

dler's Reactions to Hospitalization" may also be seen in the preschooler, and the nursing interventions are the same.

The school-age child's reactions to hospitalization

School-age children frequently react to hospitalization with (1) fear of pain and body injury, (2) the perception of illness as punishment, (3) fear of loss of control, and (4) distress over separation from friends, school, and family. Each of these topics will be discussed in this section.

Fear of pain and bodily injury

These are important concerns of school-age children. Furthermore, they fear that body changes will make them different and result in rejection by their friends. They no longer focus on how the illness will feel, but are interested in learning about the *results* or outcomes of the disease or surgery.

School-age children's understanding of things is likely to be incomplete. They use words correctly but fantasize to complete their knowledge. A nursing student reported:

> My patient, a 10-year-old hemophiliac, seemed to know everything about his disease. When I asked

him what happened when he bled, he said, "Oh ... well, there's a hemophiliac bug eating his way in and out of my blood vessels, and that's what makes me bleed." And when asked what caused his disease, he answered, "Well, it's 'cause I ate too much candy after my mom told me not to."

Carefully question children to reveal and clarify their fantasies. Guidelines for teaching the school-age child are given in Table 16-6.

Use a projective technique for older school-age children reluctant to discuss their fears. Encourage them to draw a picture of the hospital and describe it, or make up a story about a child in the hospital and ask the child to describe what's happening in the drawing. Use one of the prepared and validated tests, such as *The Hospital Picture Test* (developed by Dr. Pauline Barton at the University of Florida[17]).

As children unconsciously project their feelings in the pictures or stories, the nurse learns about their level of growth and development, their perceptions of the hospital, and their relationships with others.[18] In one study children drew pictures of the hospital. After discussing the pictures with the nurse, they had a greater sense of confidence, a focus on reality, and a decrease in fear of the unknown.[19]

Perception of illness as punishment

Children have a very rigid, moralistic code of behavior. Because they are learning new roles, they scrutinize their own behavior and compare it to their parents' expectations. By acting "good," they can win approval and increase their self-esteem. Since they associate pain and hospitalization with unpleasant negative feelings, they assume they are being punished for breaking a rule. Assess their beliefs about their illness and reassure them about the cause of their condition and the motivations behind the therapy.

Fear of losing emotional control

All children want to be courageous and successfully cope with a frightening event; this bravery enhances their self-image. They mobilize their resources to control their emotions and want to receive praise for remaining in control. Help them discuss their feelings and methods of handling emotions. Plan play activities to allow expression of aggression. Encourage activities based on their interests.

Immobilized children feel powerless and vulnerable. School-age children have endless energy to explore and gain information about their environment. Being able to move quickly is associated with being in control and with being able to express aggression and protect themselves. Immobilized children have fewer opportunities to express aggression and feel less able to protect themselves from intrusive procedures.

Separation from friends, schools, and family

Younger school-age children may occasionally experience separation anxiety during traumatic procedures, but their reaction is shorter and less intense than that of preschoolers. Older children may miss their friends and activities more than they do their parents. They often have difficulty finding stimulating activities and become bored, frustrated, and lonely.

Nursing management of the school-age child

Promoting self-esteem The security of school-age children is directly related to living in an organized, predictable, and scheduled world. Children who know the rules of expected behavior will know how to react and gain approval. Tell them what to expect and how to act. Promote self-esteem by affirming their success in coping with hospitalization.

Increase the children's sense of power or control over their hospital environment by allowing them to make decisions about daily routines and giving them appropriate mobility (Fig. 16-11). School-age children help make beds, straighten rooms, pass out nourishments, use addressographs, answer lights, put charts together, or orient new children to the unit.

Dealing with rigid, moralistic behavior School-age children may have rigid, moralistic behavior because they are learning precisely how to act in a new role. They want to "play by the rules," and to them things are either right or wrong. They cannot yet think abstractly to learn the principle underlying social expectations. Therefore, they must still rely on "actions," and if they gain approval from their parents or other authority figures, their self-confidence will be bolstered.

Compulsive, ritualistic behavior pervades all aspects of the life of school-age children. They may increase their feelings of control over procedures by "ordering" nurses' actions in a certain way.

Johnny, aged 10, was crying and extremely upset during his dressing change. He said, "I want Judy to do it! She changes my bandage different!" Later during the dressing change, Johnny whined, "You're doing it all wrong! Why don't you put on the tape this way? No! It's not put on that way! Your tape is too long!" The nurse recognized his distrust, slowed her pace, and explained her upcoming actions. She knew this was one of his only ways left of maintaining control; therefore, she didn't scold him or tell him to be quiet. Instead, she let him tell her exactly how he wanted it done and followed his directions. To promote trust, she also wrote down his directions on the Kardex. Because she knew he was interested in the reasons for her actions, she explained them to him. Johnny's behavior the next day was vastly different; he greeted her with a smile. She suggested he help, play nurse, and wear sterile gloves. He glowed with satisfaction; during the procedure the nurse asked him questions to assess his views of the procedure.

Communicate acceptance of children's ritualistic behavior by discussing it in an honest, open manner. Explore the causes of their fear and discuss the "rules" of their behavior. Other team members can follow the same routine when it is reported verbally and recorded in the Kardex.

School, friends, and home If most of the school-age child's day is spent in school, it is logical that the hospital day include educational activities. Observe the child's attitude toward homework, help her when needed, assess areas of difficulty, and communicate observations to the teacher. Before discharge, contact the school nurse and plan for home teachers if they will be required.

Preserving communication with friends at home is difficult for a school-age child. She is dependent upon parents to form car pools and bring friends and siblings to the hospital. Call the school requesting her class to send letters. She loves to collect their cards and paste them on the wall. Help the child write letters or make a tape recording about hospital life to send to her friends. List the child's favorite toys and games on the Kardex. The toys should allow her

Figure 16-11 This school-age child's increased mobility enhances his feelings of self-control and power. (*Photo by Theresa Friedrich. Courtesy of LAC/USC Medical Center.*)

to complete a task successfully (crossword puzzles, erector sets, embroidery sets), promote her motor coordination (Ping Pong, jump rope, painting), and teach her to follow rules (card games, hide and seek).

Provide opportunities for school-age children to interact with other members of the same sex. Place children together in rooms with others of the same age and sex. Encourage volunteers to form clubs built around crafts, interests, or activities. For chronically ill children, arrange visits from local celebrities, rock stars, puppet groups, dramatic groups, or zoo programs.

The adolescent's reactions to hospitalization

Adolescents who become hospitalized are chiefly concerned about (1) the loss of their independence and identity, (2) the possibility of changes in body image, (3) peer rejection, and (4) loss of emotional control.

Loss of independence and identity

Major threats to the hospitalized adolescent are loss of independence and identity. The enforced dependency of illness and hospitalization occurs just when the adolescent is trying to establish independence and identity at home. Illness may prevent him or her from driving a car, from participating in peer group activities, or even

from going to the bathroom alone. These feelings of powerlessness, or lack of control over the environment, cause anger, frustration, and withdrawal (Fig. 16-12).

Nursing management Plan nursing care *with* teenagers. Too often, decisions are made about treatments, medicines, and daily routines without asking the patients. Joint planning will increase these feelings of power, independence, cooperativeness, and control. After all, "adolescents are ... best equipped to know which actions will fit most comfortably into their own life-styles. They know their home routines and school days better than anyone else and they need to help determine what actions are reasonable and workable for them in their own lives and settings."[20]

Adolescents thrive on demonstrating feelings of responsibility and independence. Encourage them to take care of a younger child, answer lights, or take snack orders to maintain their recently established identity in the hospital. Allow them to order preferred foods (within diet guidelines), order double portions, prepare food in a diet kitchen on the unit, wear their own clothes, and visit and eat in friends' rooms. Adolescents successfully orient new patients, help prepare each other for tests, and publish unit newsletters.

Families and friends remain an important base in their security system. Visiting hours should be liberal, allowing parents, friends, and siblings to visit freely. Place adolescents in their own section or ward. Imagine an adolescent's chagrin and embarrassment at being assigned to a room with a baby!

Continuation of school work in the hospital provides relief from boredom. Tutoring allows the adolescent to maintain academic progress on par with that of peers. Obtain a school referral. Assess the teenager's motivation for homework, favorite classes, and areas needing improvement. Communicating these needs to the teacher will ensure an individually designed school program.

Discuss with the teacher the teenager's physical limitations, upcoming stresses, and their effect on the child's ability to learn. After eye surgery, for example, the adolescent may be able to tolerate only 1 h of studying at a time. The seriously ill child may not be able to manage the entire school program.

Figure 16-12 This teenager has lost his independence and identity, and is bored. He stated, "There ain't no action here!" (*Photo by Theresa Friedrich. Courtesy of LAC/USC Medical Center.*)

Figure 16-13 Teenagers fear body image changes and rejection by peers. This girl is being visited by family and friends. (*Photo by Theresa Friedrich. Courtesy of LAC/USC Medical Center.*)

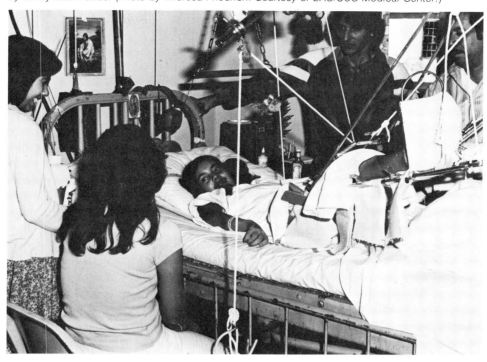

Body image changes

A second cause of the hospitalized teenager's anxiety is the fear of body image changes (Fig. 16-13). This anxiety increases in direct proportion to the severity of the threat to the body image. Body image is defined as a changing or evolving mental picture of one's own body. Teenagers believe their bodies are the main criteria by which others will accept or reject them. The normal adolescent experiences rapid physical growth and changes in body shape. When these normal changes are coupled with any threat to body image from surgery or illness, the adolescent's feelings of vulnerability increase. The threat of more body changes makes the adolescent feel more insecure, less in control, and incapable of succeeding.

Nursing management For a teenager with a body image change:

1. Assess the meaning and value of her body

2. If surgery has been done, assess her understanding of what went on during the operation
3. Assure her of being "resewn," that portions of her body are intact
4. Discuss and provide opportunities for her to see the body changes but do not force her to look at them
5. Assess talents which can be used to compensate for lost body functions
6. Help the young person value her positive attributes.

Help adolescents feel successful in using their bodies. This will promote a more positive self-image. Post-surgical patients can join a group meeting and discuss common adjustment problems, such as, "How do I go to a dance in a wheelchair?" "What can I wear around these body casts?" Groups are very tolerant of practicing social behavior on each other. One 14-year-old boy stated, "It's easier for me if I talk about what's happening to me, and it's better to talk to a group my own age—I feel less uncomfortable with teenagers than adults."[21]

Teen meetings were begun at the University of Minnesota Hospitals to encourage adolescents to share their feelings, to support each other during the stresses of hospitalization and the transition to home, and to convey the nurses' caring and concerned attitudes toward the patients. The teenagers who had become disfigured were able to be accepted within the group.[22] For teen meetings like these to succeed, a high level of commitment is necessary from the group leaders and nursing staff. Treatments and doctor's appointments must be scheduled around group meeting times.[23]

Provide privacy. The hospitalized teenager's need for privacy is often overlooked. Body changes make him or her especially sensitive to being displayed in front of medical personnel or strangers.

Fear of rejection

Normal adolescents are exquisitely aware of their body's defects. Physical perfection is idealized by our culture. Any physical imperfection may exclude them from the peer groups. The peer group's acceptance of behavior is rigidly controlled, is centered on physical perfection, and changes very quickly. Their fear of peer rejection is, therefore, very real!

Nursing management During the hospitalization assess teenagers' interactions with peers of both sexes. Do they initiate conversation (with what sex) or do they withdraw? Do they enter other teenagers' rooms? What are the behavioral reactions and common interests of their chosen friends? How are they treated by their roommates? Are they acknowledged as worthwhile people or are they ignored by other patients? Are they likely to go to the activity room? Certainly, young people who refuse to interact with other adolescents, keep the curtains drawn, door closed, and stay alone need nursing interventions designed to increase social interaction. Encourage peer interaction through parties, games, visits from friends, and flexible visiting hours. If they are consistently withdrawn, arrange a team meeting with a mental health nurse to assess behavior and plan an appropriate, consistent 24-h plan of care.

Fear of losing emotional control

Teenagers are famous for rapid mood changes. They are also afraid of losing control of their emotions and may be reluctant to express their frustration, anger, and aggression. Teenagers may lose control or overextend themselves. Their emotions may be released in temper tantrums, or tears. This leads to anxiety and fear. They then retreat to reassess their actions. Their withdrawal and regression make them feel guilty, for teenagers aren't supposed to act like "babies."

Nursing management Accept teenagers' regressed, dependent behavior. When they experience approval, their self-esteem soars. Regression allows them to recharge their psychological energy and then forge on ahead, independently.

Refrain from immediately reacting to their outbursts. Wait a few moments and their behavior will usually change to a more easily tolerated, more balanced and mature level.

Respect the teenagers' need to be alone. Observe "keep out" signs, and accept their behavior by saying, "You look really sad today," or "I will leave you alone. But call me if you need me. I will help you." Avoid saying, or implying, "Don't act like a baby!" Plan activities to encourage expression of aggression (Table 16-10).

Success in communicating with teenagers depends upon an understanding of their needs, growth, and development, and upon gaining genuine satisfaction from working with them. Help them to achieve self-esteem and to learn self-reliance. When the nurse shows flexibility, openness, acceptance, and tolerance, teenagers respond. Adolescents talk with a vengeance. As Eileen Tiedt has written:

Table 16-10 Activities that allow teenagers to express aggression

1. Boxing gloves or punching bags. (At one hospital the children demolished one every 3 to 4 months!)
2. "Graffiti boards" encourage anonymous expression of feelings (both washable walls and large wall-size sheets of paper work well).
3. Dart boards (with suction cups for safety)
4. Hammering and sawing
5. Pillow fights

Note: Always establish safety limits and rules before beginning these games, like "No throwing above the head. If a pillow hits someone's head or an IV, the game is over."

The nurse must consider it equally important to listen. As a listener she must allow the patient to tell about his plans, his successes, and failures. Those nurses who "cannot take the time," and those who have been "trained" to feel most useful when they're active, will find it hard to listen to them. The patient feels much more comfortable when a nurse is willing to sit and listen. And no other person is so insistent on attention as the adolescent. He is susceptible to the advances of anyone who shows genuine interest in him, but he is equally quick to reject anyone who tries to impose his will or ideas on him, whose interest is feigned, or who seems to have little regard for what the adolescent is, does, thinks, or says. The nurse, therefore, must pay as much attention to him as she does to his symptoms.[24]

References

1. Lucy Kunzmman, "Some Factors Influencing a Young Child's Mastery of Hospitalization," *Nursing Clinics of North America* 7:13–26 (March 1972).

2. Jacqueline Hott, "Play PRN in Pediatric Nursing," *Nursing Forum* 9(3):288–309 (1970).

3. Virginia Axline, *Play Therapy,* Random House (Ballantine Books), New York, 1947, p. 10.

4. Sister Mary Callista Roy, "Role Cues and Mothers of Hospitalized Children," *Nursing Research* 16:178–182 (Spring 1967).

5. Loc. cit.

6. Dorothy Merrow and Betty S. Johnson, "Perceptions of the Mother's Role with Her Hospitalized Child," *Nursing Research* 17:155–156 (March–April 1968).

7. L. P. Lipsitt, "The Study of Sensory and Learning Processes of the Newborn," *Clinics in Perinatology* 4: 163–186 (March 1977).

8. W. Condon and L. Sander, "Neonate Movement is Synchronized with Adult Speech: Interactional Participation and Language Acquisition." *Science* 183:99–101 (Jan. 11, 1974).

9. L. Kramer and M. Pierpont, "Rocking Waterbeds and Auditory Stimuli to Enhance Growth of Preterm Infants," *Journal of Pediatrics* 88:297–299 (February 1976).

10. V. Katz, "Auditory Stimulation and Developmental Behavior of the Premature Infant," *Nursing Research* 20:196–201 (May–June 1972).

11. Jerome Kagan, "Personality Development," in Nathan Talbot, Jerome Kagan, and Leon Eisenberg (eds.), *Behavioral Science in Pediatric Medicine,* Saunders, Philadelphia, 1971, pp. 282–349.

12. Marjorie S. Audette, "The Significance of Regressive Behavior in the Hospitalized Child," *The American Journal of Maternal Child Nursing* 3:4–48 (Spring 1974).

13. Ibid. p. 33.

14. Ibid. p. 34.

15. Anne L. Wilkinson, "Behavioral Disturbances Following Short-Term Hospitalization," *Issues in Comprehensive Pediatric Nursing* 3:12–18 (July 1978).

16. Elizabeth Gellert, "What Do I Have Inside Me? How Children View Their Bodies" in *Psychological Aspects of Pediatric Care,* Grune, New York, 1978, p. 22.

17. P. H. Barton, "The Relationship Between Fantasy and Overt Stress Reactions of Children to Hospitalization." Unpublished Ed. D. dissertation, University of Florida, 1964.

18. Jeanine M. Allen, "Influencing School-Age Children's Concept of Hospitalization," *Pediatric Nursing* 4:26–28 (November–December 1978).

19. Helen L. Gelhard, "Drawing and Development," *Pediatric Nursing* 4:23–25 (November–December 1978).

20. Mary Jean Denyes, and Anne Altschuler; "Illness: The Adolescent," in G. Scipien (ed.), *Comprehensive Pediatric Nursing,* McGraw-Hill, New York, 1979, p. 478.

21. Anne Altschuler, and Ann H. Seidl, "Teen Meetings: A Way to Help Adolescents Cope With Hospitalization," *The American Journal of Maternal-Child Nursing* 2:348–353 (November–December 1977).

22. Ibid.

23. Ibid., p. 349.

24. Eileen Tiedt, "The Adolescent in the Hospital: An Identity-Resolution Approach," *Nursing Forum* 11(2):120–140 (1972).

Chapter 17 **Basic needs of the hospitalized child**

Linda W. Olivet

Upon completion of this chapter, the student will be able to:

1. Describe the role of the nurse in preparing and admitting a child and the child's family for hospitalization.

2. Describe nursing approaches to the common procedures to be performed during admission.

3. Explain how to use various restraints.

4. Describe the Heimlich maneuver and how to use it with a child and infant.

5. Describe feeding techniques and methods for motivating children to eat.

6. Compare dehydration and volume overload.

7. Describe the role of the nurse in starting and maintaining intravenous therapy in children.

8. Describe methods for administering and monitoring moist oxygen.

9. Compare cardiopulmonary resuscitation of children with that of adults.

10. Explain how to measure temperature, pulse rate, respiratory rate, and blood pressure in children.

11. Name potential problems and appropriate nursing intervention in assessment of vital signs.

12. Describe hygiene for the hospitalized child.

13. List manifestations of pain in children.

14. Describe the nurse's role in the care of the child with fever, pain, and nausea and vomiting.

15. Determine the dosage for a common pediatric drug using body surface area (BSA).

16. Describe approaches to administering oral medications to children.

17. Compare the various sites for intramuscular injection in children.

18. Identify safety measures in administering any medications to children.

19. Discuss the role of the nurse in dismissal planning for the hospitalized child.

In recent years the number of children being hospitalized has decreased. This is due partially to improved health education, outpatient services, and emphasis on cost-effectiveness. Nevertheless, there are some occasions when a child must enter a hospital for health care.

When a child becomes a hospital patient, whatever the diagnosis, there are many areas of need that make the nursing care special. The fact that a hospitalized child is usually accompanied by a parent or concerned loved one makes pediatric nursing family-centered as well as patient-centered. Hospitalization has the potential for being an enriching experience for family and patient; it can also be difficult, emotionally draining, and even devastating. Appropriate intervention by caring, knowledgeable nurses can make the difference.

Admission to the hospital

Preparation for admission

A child must be prepared in advance for hospitalization. Preparation lessens anxiety and fear because the "unknown" becomes somewhat familiar. The child may work through uncomfortable feelings and determine some methods of coping with the anticipated experience. Even if a child has multiple hospitalizations, adequate preparation is essential to identify misconceptions and fears. Preparation also helps parents examine their own fears, expectations, and feelings and prepares them to cope in the hospital setting.

Role of the hospital Over the years hospital personnel have identified specific activities which prepare children for hospitalization. Some programs are offered in cooperation with the local schools. Children learn about hospital activities and the roles of health professionals. This approach increases their awareness of certain "helpers" in the community and may decrease their fears of hospitals. If a child who has attended the program later becomes a patient, the child may be able to apply the learning.

Another type of program is set up specifically for children who are soon to be admitted. A puppet show, preadmission party, tour, or similar activity is held at the hospital. Children can see the hospital setting, meet other children who may be with them as patients in the hospital, and prepare for a specific experience. These sessions may include time for the children to handle equipment and play "doctor" or "nurse" with dolls. They may also try on masks, gowns, and gloves like those worn by hospital personnel in surgery (Fig. 17-1). Some programs include films or slides that show many aspects of hospital life.

In addition to specific admission orientation programs, the hospital provides the environment which affects the child as a patient. An awareness of the needs of children and parents and a desire to provide for them is reflected in the facilities available. Brightly colored walls and curtains, playrooms and toys, sleeping provisions for parents, age-appropriate furniture, child-proof nurses' stations, personnel wearing colorful uniforms—these are a few of the ways a hospital says, "We want to make your time as a patient in our institution as easy and pleasant as possible."

Role of the parents Children reflect the attitudes of parents. If parents are anxious and worried, the child will react in a similar manner. A calm, informed parent encourages the child's confidence and trust in the care-givers.

Parents need to be encouraged to ask questions and express concerns to the doctor and nurse in the outpatient setting. This increases their understanding and allows them to be more effective as a resource and support to their child. Because each person faces a new experience in light of the past, an assessment of the parents' previous hospital experiences and present concerns provides the nurse with vital information in preparing both parents and child.

Specific preparation should begin a few days

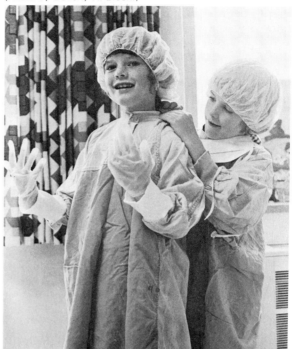

Figure 17-1 Children dressing up in masks and gowns during a "come-and-see" hospital orientation program. (*Photo by Beverly K. Bisek.*)

prior to admission. A variety of ways to prepare the child are available for parents to use at home. Reading appropriate books can answer many questions. (See Table 17-1.)

Children may also act out being in a hospital by role-playing various procedures. Informal discussions among the family members and simulated situation storytelling ("If this happened, what would you do?") are also helpful. Siblings should be included in the preparatory activities to decrease their unspoken fears.

Table 17-1 A selection of books about hospitalization

1. Bettina Clark and Lester Coleman, *Pop-Up Book: Going to the Hospital,* Random House, New York, 1971.
2. H. A. Rey, *Curious George Goes to the Hospital,* Houghton Mifflin, Boston, 1966.
3. Florence Whitman Rowland, *Let's Go to a Hospital,* Putnam, New York, 1968.
4. Sara Bonnet Stein, *A Hospital Story,* Walker, New York, 1974.
5. Arthur Shay, *What Happens When You Go to the Hospital,* Contemporary Books, Chicago, 1969.

Some children enjoy making scrapbooks about hospitals. This kind of activity increases the patient's involvement in preparation. The child may select toys, pajamas, and "security blanket," and can help with the packing. Special "homecoming" activities to be enjoyed when hospitalization ends may also be planned with the child.

Throughout this preparatory period, parents should be encouraged to answer the child's questions simply, directly, and honestly. If questions arise which they cannot answer, they may call the hospital for clarification.

Role of the outpatient clinic nurse Many of the ideas mentioned in the section "Role of the Parents" are alternatives that the outpatient nurse may offer to the parents. The parents will determine the methods that seem most appropriate for their circumstances, but the outpatient nurse has the responsibility of encouraging them to prepare the child.

The outpatient nurse also acts as a resource person and may be asked questions about hospitalization by both the patient and the patient's family. By visiting the hospital periodically, the nurse can be familiar with hospital staff routines. If the patient or the patient's family has special needs, the nurse should call before admission and share these with the hospital staff. Ideally, a written nursing care plan should be forwarded for the hospital nurse to use as a resource.

Teaching, explaining, preparing—all are functions of the outpatient nurse. An accurate assessment of the patient's and family's present knowledge can make the approaching hospitalization much easier for them.

The admission process

During admission to the hospital the child and parents develop their "first impressions." It is very important that they are greeted warmly and welcomed to the nursing unit as guests. Hospitality can be expressed in any hospital setting if the nursing staff value such an approach. Being welcomed, called by name, and accompanied to the appropriate room can help the child and family feel important and reassured.

Orientation to the environment Upon arriving in the room, the patient and family should receive an orientation to the surroundings. The extent of the orientation may vary according to the time available to the nurse at that moment and whether or not the child has been hospitalized there previously. Explain where the bathroom is and how to call the nurse, turn on the TV, and operate the "buttons" or "cranks" on the bed. Make the child and parents as comfortable as possible and tell them when the admission procedures will begin and what they can do in the meantime. Explain about visiting hours and facilities that are available for parents—cafeteria, sleeping facilities, and so forth.

As soon as possible, preferably before any procedures are done, take the patient and family on a brief tour of the nursing unit. This allows time for the child to see the surroundings and for the nurse to begin an informal assessment. Introductions of the child to the staff convey that the unit is friendly, pleasant, and nonthreatening. During the "tour" the child may walk or be carried in the parent's arms. Give the patient a chance to see the playroom or, if no playroom is available, other pleasant activities which are provided for young patients. Wait until later in the admission to undress the child or begin procedures.

A tour is not meant to mislead a child into thinking all is "fun and games," but it is one way to develop rapport. Children will respond in a variety of ways according to their level of growth and development, their previous experiences with hospitalization, and their illness.

If a patient is acutely ill or anticipating major surgery, decide whether or not a tour is appropriate. The anxiety level of the child, parents, or both may be so great that the admission procedure must begin another way. Sit down and talk with them to plan the admission together. Establish a climate of reassurance and understanding.

Whatever the initial activity, the nurse begins assessment of the patient's and family's needs at the time of the first encounter. The nurse may then determine well-chosen interventions based on that assessment.

In the immediate environment, items and equipment that are routine and normal to the nurse may be very strange and frightening to the patient. Determine the unspoken concerns through attention to nonverbal cues. Brief, honest explanations of equipment or of what another nurse is doing can alleviate fears.

Admission procedures Many hospitals provide admission packets containing helpful information about services available, routines, visiting hours, facilities for families, patient rights and responsibilities, and similar items. Encourage use of the material by mentioning it in conversation and using it when questions arise.

During initial conversations the patient and family may comprehend only part of the information. Give general information at first; prior to each activity give a more detailed explanation.

Table 17-2 provides an outline of admission activities and information to be given.

Admission history The Kardex nursing history card (Fig. 17-2) contains items of information that should be obtained during the admission interview. The use of assessment in nursing process and specific assessment components are discussed in Chaps. 5 and 6. If a patient is to be in the hospital for a very brief stay, the Kardex history may be adequate. It is the most practical approach if a child is admitted and whisked off for surgery or diagnostic tests.

The American Academy of Pediatrics has developed information guidelines for use with various age groups (Appendix D). These are useful for obtaining more detailed information about the child and are essential for longer stays.

Table 17-2 Admission activities

1. Tour of unit
2. Orientation to room, equipment
3. Identification
4. Admission history
5. Vital signs
6. Height and weight
7. Give information about:
   a. Clothing in the hospital
   b. Meal and snack time
   c. Rules about bringing food from home
   d. Daily activities—bath, naptime, bedtime
   e. Visiting hours
   f. Facilities for parents
   g. Physician's examination and visits
   h. Laboratory tests

It is important that parents are available for the admission interviews by the nurse and the physician. Advise them to remain until these are completed. Direct appropriate questions to the child so that he or she will feel included. If the parent or child is exhausted, delay a long interview.

The Kardex and American Academy of Pediatrics forms can be used as a guide for setting up personal information forms for pediatric patients of various ages and can be adjusted to fit the needs of particular hospital units.

Figure 17-2 An example of Kardex information to be obtained during admission of a young child to the hospital. (*Courtesy of Rochester Methodist Hospital, Rochester, Minn.*)

Name		Date .... By	
Nickname	Age	Religion	
DIET:	Food Allergies .... NURSING	Food Dislikes	
	Formula, Kind .... HISTORY	Amount	
	Bottle .... Breast	Cup .... Warm .... Cold	
	Types of foods: Strained	Junior .... Regular	
SLEEPING:	Usual Bedtime	Does he climb out of crib	
	What, if anything, does he take to bed with him		
	Any problem with sleeping .... If so, what helps		
ELIMINATION:	Any problems bowel .... Urine .... If so, what helps		
	Toilet trained .... Taken to B.R. at regular times .... at noc		
	Term used bowel movement .... Urination		
PLAYING:	Favorite toy with him		
Hospitalized before .... Why		Unpleasant experiences	
Exposed to any communicable diseases within the past 2 weeks			
Has he been on any drugs at home			
What is your understanding of your hospitalization			

FAMILY - INTERESTS - HOBBIES ....

ORIENTATION	Pt. Unit	Telemike	Visiting Hrs.	Pamphlet to Parents	Pre-Op Teaching	Chaplain
					Post-Op Teaching	

Identification and vital signs Identification (ID) of the patient during admission and throughout the hospital stay is a necessary safety precaution. The ID band contains information such as the patient's name, hospital number, room number, age, address, and date of admission. It is attached to the wrist with approximately a finger-breadth's space between the band and the arm to prevent constriction.[1] A preschooler or early school-age child will not usually object to the band if told that it is a bracelet that tells who he or she is. An infant or toddler may need to have the ID band placed on an ankle rather than a wrist if it is irritating or slips off easily. If the child's skin is sensitive to the plastic or tape, the band can be pinned to the child's clothing. The patient should wear an identification band at all times throughout the hospital stay.

Figure 17-3 Using a measuring board to determine the length of an infant. (*From G. Scipien, M. U. Barnard, M. A. Chard, J. Howe, and P. J. Phillips (eds.), Comprehensive Pediatric Nursing, McGraw-Hill, New York, 1979, p. 221. Used by permission.*)

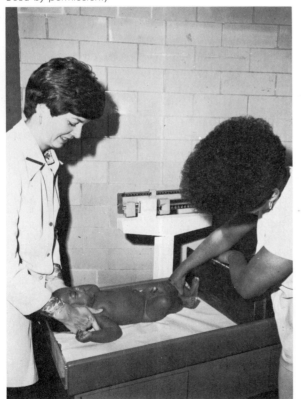

Vital signs include temperature, pulse rate, respiratory rate, and blood pressure. Procedures for obtaining vital signs are described later in this chapter. Taking a rectal temperature is an intrusive procedure to a young child and may cause crying. Perform this toward the end of the physical assessment. The assistance of parents in holding the thermometer in place or in remaining beside the child may help alleviate fears. Use dolls or puppets, if appropriate, to show how procedures are to be done.

Height and weight Height and weight determinations are very important and must be obtained soon after admission. The physician calculates fluid and drug amounts using this data. Upright scales for weight may be used by any patient who can stand alone. Young children may be frightened of the scales and refuse to cooperate. Stand on the scale first or ask a parent to do so, demonstrating that being weighed is painless. If this is ineffective, a parent can hold the child and both can be weighed. The parent is then weighed alone and his or her weight is subtracted from the total. Ideally the weight should be done when the child is wearing only underwear. This may be done without embarrassment in the room while the child is changing from street clothes to pajamas.

Height determinations are made pleasant through the use of decorative tape measures on the wall. A demonstration by the nurse or parent of standing against the wall may be adequate preparation for the child. Comments about how tall the child is can reward the child for cooperative behavior.

Height and weight for infants must be obtained in a different manner. Infant scales allow the child to be weighed lying down or sitting. Weigh with as little clothing as possible—preferably none. The younger the patient, the more significant a few ounces will be in weight determination. The patient's length may be obtained by placing him or her on a measuring board (Fig. 17-3). Measure from the crown of the head to the stretched-out heel. Documentation of height and weight on a growth chart is a good method of determining general health status. (See Appendix B.)

The use of a bed scale may be necessary in weighing an acutely ill child. More than one person will be required to gently move the patient from the bed to the scale and back again. A metal tape measure which remains straight will give a rough estimate of height, or the parents or child may know the child's height.

Personal belongings The patient will have various personal belongings with him or her upon arrival at the hospital. Store them in the area provided in the room. Write the patient's name and room number on toys, stuffed animals, security blankets, or other personal equipment which might be confused with hospital items or other children's toys.

Clothing Will the patient wear his or her own clothes, pajamas, or hospital clothing? Some children need and want the security of their own clothes. Honoring this desire as much as possible is another way to make hospitalization easier. A surgical patient must wear a hospital gown to the operating room. Gowns are easier then pajamas to change when intravenous lines and other equipment are in use, but the emotional needs of the patient should have priority in influencing what will be worn upon return to the hospital room.

Obtaining specimens Routine laboratory tests during admission include blood work and urinalysis. A stool specimen and x-ray may also be necessary. Each of these tests is brief and explanation can be most effective and least frightening if given just prior to the test.

Blood work A heel stick in the infant or finger stick in an older child or adolescent is used to obtain capillary blood. Certain tests require venipuncture with a needle and syringe.

Blood work can be painful and the patient may need restraining in order to lie still. Give a brief explanation just as the procedure begins, describing how it will feel.[2] Have the child squeeze your hand, count to 10, or hold the siderail of the bed when it hurts. Tell the child that you will help him or her hold still during the procedure so that it will be over faster.

The nurse can be a patient advocate in this situation by suggesting appropriate sites for venipuncture. If the child is right-handed, suggest that the left arm be used. Though the laboratory technician may not find adequate veins at the suggested site, such an effort reassures the patient that the nurse cares about what is happening to him or her.

Urine specimens Routine urinalysis is done on admission to identify the presence of infection in the urinary tract or changes in the end products of metabolism.[3] It is nonintrusive and less threatening than some tests.

Urinalysis is done on a clean specimen of urine. Assist the child to clean gently around the meatus with a warm, moist cloth. Explain how to hold the container without touching the inside. A child of either sex can obtain the urine by voiding directly into the container. If this is difficult for a girl, place a clean bedpan or collecting pan ("Sani-Pan") in the toilet, replace the seat, and have her void normally. Transfer the urine from the pan to the specimen bottle.

Though obtaining a urine specimen is one of the simpler diagnostic procedures, it can be embarrassing to children. The school-age child wants privacy and can usually collect the specimen alone. Preschoolers and toddlers will need adult assistance, preferably from a parent.

Obtaining specimens from infants and toddlers in diapers requires the use of plastic urine bags—unless one happens to catch a specimen during a diaper change (keep the specimen bottle nearby at this time). Figure 17-4 illustrates the use of the U-bag pediatric urine collector for boys and girls. The procedure requires three steps: (1) cleaning, (2) applying the collector, and (3) removing and folding the bag.

1. The child is placed on his or her back on a clean towel folded in quarters. The entire area between the legs is washed with a soapy washcloth.
   a. With a boy, first the testicles and then the penis are washed. The rectal area is washed last with a different corner of the washcloth. A cup of lukewarm water is used to rinse the area. The area is gently dried with a towel or dry washcloth.
   b. With a girl, each skin fold is washed with a different corner of the soapy washcloth. A top-to-bottom motion is used and care taken not to touch the rectum. The rectum is cleaned with a fourth corner of the washcloth. The area is rinsed with a cup of lukewarm water. Next, with the left thumb and index finger, the nurse separates the skin folds and repeats the entire cleaning procedure with a second soapy wash-

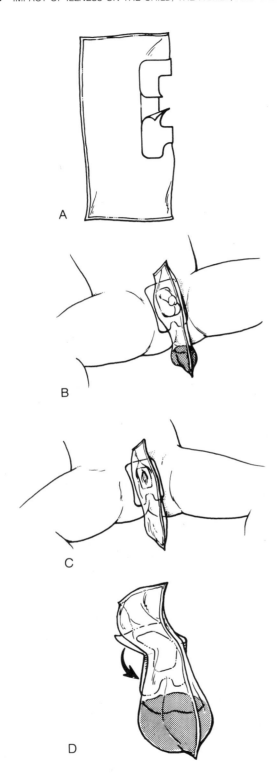

Figure 17-4 Collection of a urine specimen by means of a U-Bag. (*Courtesy of Hollister, Inc.*) The perineum is first carefully washed and dried.
(*A*) The collector is opened by removing the protective paper from the bottom section first.
(*B*) The bag is placed over the penis and testicles, flaps pressed firmly to the area between the anus and testicles. Remaining protective paper is removed and adhesive is pressed to skin.
(*C*) After skin folds are separated, the bag is placed over the vagina. Adhesive is pressed firmly against the bridge of skin separating the rectum from the vagina. Remaining protective paper is removed and the adhesive surface is pressed against the skin.
(*D*) When specimen is obtained, the bag is removed and closed by folding the sticky adhesive sides together. It may be placed into a cup for transportation.

cloth. After another rinse, the area is dried gently and thoroughly with a towel or dry washcloth.

2. The protective paper is removed from the bottom of the collector bag. The bag is fitted over the boy's penis and testicles; a girl's skin folds are separated to expose the urethra and the bag placed over it. Be sure the bag adheres securely, especially to the perineum (most leaks occur there). A diaper may be reapplied to help secure the bag in place.

3. When the specimen is obtained, the bag is removed and closed by folding the sticky adhesive sides together.

Stool specimens For infants and toddlers the stool specimen may be obtained from the diaper. It should be a fresh specimen and uncontaminated by urine. Older children may use a clean bedpan or potty chair for obtaining the stool. The nurse can explain to the child that the stool specimen must be obtained before he or she voids into it. The stool is transferred to a cardboard container with a tight-fitting lid and sent to the laboratory immediately.

This can be an embarrassing procedure and can best be handled matter-of-factly. Terminology used for explanation should include words for bodily functions which the child understands.

School-age children and adolescents may not have a daily bowel movement. A child who has been told that a stool specimen is needed may, out of embarrassment or lack of understanding, try to avoid having a stool or may go to the bathroom without telling the nurse. Use tact and good observation to intervene appropriately.

Other procedures Two common procedures with which the nurse assists are x-rays and enemas.

X-rays If a child needs a chest film on admission, explain that it is like having a picture made of the inside of the body and it is important to hold still "just like when Mommy or Daddy takes your picture at home." Practice taking a deep breath with the child. Encourage the parent to accompany the child to the x-ray department, but explain that he or she will remain in the waiting area during the procedure.

Enemas Discuss with the physician the purpose and type of solution to be used before proceeding with an enema. Pediatric disposable enemas are available and easy to use. Normal saline is also a safe solution for a cleansing enema. Do not use tap water on a child suspected of having megacolon.[4] Some of the enema solution might be retained, and if tap water is absorbed in large quantities, the child might suffer water intoxication. Only isotonic solutions should be used in these patients.[5]

Table 17-3 describes the steps in giving an enema to a child and the amounts of solution used for different age groups.

Preoperative preparation When a child is admitted for a surgical procedure, preoperative preparation is a vital part of the admission "routines." Good preoperative teaching lessens anxiety, postoperative pain, and other complications.

The admission assessment allows the nurse to determine what the child and parents already know. The nurse must also determine the child's level of development and select approaches which are most effective for the age of the child.

Children under 3 years of age may have difficulty conceptualizing and have no awareness of time. Use of pictures and explanations may be of no value to them but can be helpful to their parents. Use of equipment and dolls to show what will happen may be of some help to young children. Preoperative preparation is further discussed in Chap. 16.

The presence of parents is the most important thing to children in the hospital. Throughout the preparation, references to where the parents will be can provide continuing reassurance.

Table 17-3 Enema procedure for children

Recommended amounts of solution*

Infant: 150–250 ml
18 months to 10 years: 250–500 ml
10 years to 14 years: 250–750 ml

Position for infant or toddler

1. Place pillow under head and back.
2. Pad infant bedpan and place under buttocks.†

Position for older child

1. Turn to left side.
2. Pad bed well with towel and/or bath blanket.
3. Instruct child to hold enema solution after instillation. Use the bedpan or assist the child to the bathroom for expulsion.

Procedure

1. Use no. 10 or 12 French catheter inserted 2 to 4 in into the rectum.‡ Lubricate tip with small amount of water-soluble lubricant. (Commercially prepared enemas are prelubricated and may be inserted without additional lubrication.)
2. Use enema can or 50-ml syringe barrel for solution. Warm no greater than 40.6°C (105°F).
3. Instill by gravity with solution no higher than 18 in above the level of the hips.§
4. For the infant or toddler, the solution and the stool will be expelled simultaneously during the procedure. If retention enema is necessary, hold the buttocks together for a short time.¶
5. Be gentle and do not exhaust the child. If results are inadequate, allow a rest time and repeat procedure.
6. Clean buttocks, bed, and equipment after procedure.
7. Chart amount and type of solution, results of enema, and the condition of the child after the procedure.

* **Source:** Leifer [6].
† **Source:** Leifer [7].
‡ **Source:** Marlow [8].
§ **Source:** Marlow [9].
¶ **Source:** Whaley and Wong [10].

The following are content areas to be covered in preparing the child for surgery:

1. Nothing by mouth (NPO)—"so that your tummy will be empty and you won't throw up during your operation."
2. Surgical cart—"a bed on wheels to carry you to the operating room."
3. Preoperative medications—Explain to the patient receiving medicine that it will make him or her sleepy before leaving the room to go to surgery. If an injection is to be used, explain it just prior to administration rather than the evening before.

Nevertheless, if the patient asks, "Will I have a shot?" be honest but brief in discussing it. Tell the patient that it will "pinch" or "sting" but will be over very quickly.[11] Describe things to do to make it easier—count to 10, squeeze the bed rail or nurse's hand. (See later section for intramuscular injection procedure.)

4. Anesthesia—"a special sleep so that you don't feel the operation." Children may be very fearful of mask anesthesia. In order to decrease anxiety, some institutions allow a parent to hold the young child during induction by mask anesthesia. Intravenous medications are an alternative for older children. Communicate with the anesthesiologist preoperatively if the patient is extremely anxious.

5. Descriptions, visits to, and pictures of various areas of the hospital—preoperative area, surgical suite, recovery room—are helpful to the child and parents.

6. How the child may feel—"You may be dizzy and sleepy when you wake up. A nurse will be with you until you are brought back to your room with your parents." It is most helpful to the child to describe the sensations he or she will feel.

7. Location of parents during the procedure.

8. Postoperative nursing care—Vital signs will be done frequently. Describe intravenous fluid, mist, emesis basin, coughing and deep breathing, and other routines and equipment. Allow the patient to see and touch equipment. Use terms that are appropriate for the patient's level of understanding and describe activities according to how he or she will feel.

Support of the family

A great deal of emphasis is being placed on family-centered nursing care. *Family-centered* means that there is an awareness that the family is important, has the right to be involved in what happens to the child, and can be therapeutic in the child's recovery from illness. Giving the family support and encouragement may assist the patient as much, or more, than working directly with the child! When the family members have their emotional needs met, they are much more able to support the child.

Parental anxiety

It is very important to identify the causes of parents' anxiety in order to effectively intervene. Table 17-4 lists some possible causes of parental anxiety.

Anxiety is manifest in various behaviors. For instance, a mother who has never been in a hospital may avoid touching her child or helping with care. She may be fearful of doing the wrong thing and causing harm to her child. If the nurse takes time to determine reasons for her lack of involvement in care, teaching can be done to decrease the mother's insecurity. The nurse is a helper, not a substitute parent. The nurse's role is to aid parents to meet their child's needs, for they are the most significant people to the child.[12]

Rooming in

Some hospitals provide facilities for sleeping, personal hygiene, and cooking so that a parent may remain with a child overnight. The "rooming-in" concept allows continuous involvement of the family in the patient's care. This is especially helpful when (1) a child is too young to understand why he or she is hospitalized, (2) the child is seriously ill or, (3) the parents are very concerned and need to feel useful in caring for the child.

When a rooming-in policy is utilized, there may be a tendency for one parent to remain at the hospital constantly. This can be very tiring and can decrease that parent's effectiveness as a support person. It also divides the family and deprives those at home of parental attention. Encourage a system of taking turns so that some other familiar person is with the child at times. Show interest in what is happening at home: "How are your other children being cared for while Billy is in the hospital?" Provide times when the parent can take breaks and leave the room. By making observations that the child is

---

Table 17-4 Causes of parental anxiety during a child's hospitalization

1. Concern for the child's recovery.
2. Hospital environment—strange, frightening equipment with which they are unfamiliar.
3. Feelings of loss of control.
4. Feelings of being subordinate to the nurse.
5. Sense of guilt or self-condemnation because of the child's illness.
6. Concern about other family members at home.
7. Financial concerns.

Source: Compiled from G. Scipien et al. (eds.), *Comprehensive Pediatric Nursing*, McGraw-Hill, New York, 1979, pp. 417–418.

improving, the nurse assures the parent that it is all right to leave. Provide open visiting hours for siblings to encourage family solidarity and increase their understanding of what is happening in the hospital.

Parental rights

In order to decrease parental anxiety and increase effective support to the child, the nurse must be aware of parental rights. Following are the parental rights identified by Hilt[13] and nursing approaches designed to ensure them.

1. Right to be with their child.
   Nursing approaches
   a. Provide rooming-in facilities.
   b. Encourage their involvement in care.
   c. Talk with them while giving care.
2. Right to understand the diagnosis and treatment.
   Nursing approaches
   a. Accompany the physician when he or she visits.
   b. Spend time with the parents after rounds to clarify what they have been told.
   c. Explain each treatment and medication before administration.
   d. Use pamphlets and books to increase their understanding.
3. Right to question anything they do not understand or feel may be detrimental to their child.
   Nursing approaches
   a. Listen carefully to parents' concerns.
   b. Encourage questions by maintaining an open attitude.
   c. Intervene with the physician or other health team members and explain parental concerns.
4. Right to participate in decisions on their child's behalf.
   Nursing approaches
   a. Confer with parents about all planned activities. Keep phone number available and call them if they are away when a new treatment is to begin.
   b. Include them in setting goals for the patient.
   c. Ask their opinion about what is best for their child.

Cultural differences

Identify and record specific cultural needs and determine nursing interventions at admission. Patient and parental anxiety can be greatly decreased when cultural needs are recognized.

For example, an orthodox Jewish boy was admitted to a pediatric unit for 2 weeks of treatment for a skin problem. The admitting nurse learned that he always wore a skull cap, said prayers twice a day for 30 min, and needed kosher food to meet religious requirements. This information was recorded on the Kardex. His treatment schedule was arranged so that he could have his prayer times undisturbed. A sign was placed on his door to prevent interruptions. The nurse discussed the schedule with the physician so that rounds were planned accordingly. The nurse also conferred immediately with the dietitian so that the boy's first meal in the hospital met the requirements. This took extra time during admission but made the hospital experience very positive for the patient.

Language differences may indicate the need for an interpreter. Use word charts showing common hospital terms in the patient's language and the corresponding English word. Learn to pronounce the words in the foreign language. Use pictures to communicate with the child who cannot read. Label toys and equipment with the appropriate word in the patient's language.

Identify ethnic food preferences and obtain them through the diet kitchen if possible. Allow parents to bring food from home to encourage adequate nutrition.

According to Farris, culturally different people generally intend to retain their respective identities. "Becoming aware of cultural differences and similarities is the first priority in becoming an effective health care provider."[14] The nurse's role in cultural differences is to be sensitive to the differences; understand the reticence in accepting new and strange ideas; move slowly and patiently if changes are necessary for improved health.[15]

Behavior and discipline

Discipline can be described as guiding behavior. In past years it was equated with punishment. As efforts have been made to encourage effective parenting, the concept of discipline has been broadened to include a more positive approach.

Care of pediatric patients involves their activities both as individuals and in groups. Many pediatric units have written guidelines for patient activities. These should be explained to the child and parents during admission. Most children will follow the rules if they understand them. Use a kind but firm approach in setting limits.

Rewards

Rewards of various kinds may be used as positive reinforcement of acceptable behavior. School-age children respond favorably to "star charts" or "schedules." Star charts can include any activities the child resists that are a necessary part of his or her care. The child receives a star each time he or she successfully completes an activity.

Schedules provide time limits for unpleasant activities and encourage homework, rest, and play in the child's hospital day. The child will respond to the schedule more cooperatively if he or she helps to develop it. The schedule can be combined with a star chart and posted near the child's bed so that it can easily be seen (Fig. 17-5).

It may seem unrealistic to encourage the busy nurse to use these methods. They can, however, significantly increase patient cooperation, decrease inappropriate behavior, and ultimately save time.

Television

When children are hospitalized, they can easily spend many hours watching television. Ill children are more vulnerable to fears of separation, mutilation, and death—frequent themes of TV programs. These fears may be increased by long hours of watching TV. Small children vent feeling and fears through creative play. TV viewing does not encourage this kind of expression. In addition, parents and visitors may become absorbed in TV programs and ignore the needs of the sick child.[16] Encourage appropriate TV use in the following ways:

1. Assist the child and parents in choosing programs appropriate for the age of the child.
2. Encourage parental participation in viewing.
3. Plan treatments and care so that the child is free to watch a selected program.
4. Provide play activities, crafts, music, and games that are interesting, stimulating alternatives.
5. Help the child select times when TV is turned off.
6. Make the TV an ally in health teaching by developing closed-circuit TV systems and videotapes appropriate for children.

Providing for safety during hospitalization

Safety during activities and procedures

Identification of the child During the admission procedure the child receives an identification band and must wear it at all times. A card on the bed is used as a double check of the patient's identity. It should include the same information that is on the identification band and should be securely attached to the bed or the wall above the bed.

On occasion children will find it amusing to swap beds or try to exchange identity with another patient. Difficulties may occur also if siblings are hospitalized in the same room. Check the identification band and bed card carefully to ensure that the right patient receives the right care.

Figure 17-5 Schedule of Daily Activities. Use stars to indicate successful completion of tasks. (*Courtesy of Teresa Atkinson.*)

	Sun.	Mon.	Tue.	Wed.	Thur.	Fri.	Sat.
BATH (8:30-9:00 A.M.)	★	★					
SHAMPOO (9:15-9:30 A.M.)		★					
DRESSING CHANGE		★					
HOMEWORK (11:00 A.M. to noon, 2:00-3:00 P.M.)	★ ★	★					
MEDICINE (9:00 A.M., 1:00 P.M., 5:00 P.M.)	★★ ★	★★ ★					

Siderails Siderails are available on cribs, youth beds, and adult beds to prevent falls. Cribs are available in two lengths—one for infants, the other for toddlers. They are generally used for patients under 3 years. Youth beds may be used up to age 10. Practice raising and lowering siderails so that care may be given without disturbing a sleeping child.

In caring for an infant in a crib, lower the siderail only halfway. When alone, have only one side down at a time. When leaving an infant in bed—even in restraints—be sure that siderails are *up all the way.* Everyone on the nursing unit should be alert to checking siderails frequently. (When a child is in a mist tent, the plastic sides tucked under the mattress may give a false sense of protection. Make sure that siderails are not accidentally left down.)

A youth bed looks like a "high twin bed" with siderails. Because the bed is higher than the child's bed at home, the siderails act as a reminder to the child to seek assistance before getting out of bed. A step stool, or the supportive arms of an adult, are adequate to assist the child when the rails are down. These siderails can be raised 1 ft above the mattress. Although rails can prevent a young patient from falling out of bed when lying down, they cannot prevent the child from *climbing out.* The nurse must choose the appropriate bed according to the child's age and ability to call for assistance. Restraints other than siderails may be necessary.

Teach parents how to use the siderails. Stress the importance of raising them when leaving the child alone in bed.

Restraints The use of restraints as a safety measure may be a necessary, but unpleasant, part of caring for hospitalized children. The nurse must assess the need for restraints and select the appropriate kind. Restraints should be used sparingly. Dowd and others, in a study of 29 children, found that none of the children attempted to remove or disturb their tubes and suture lines when restraints were removed.[17] Restraints are not essential for every child with a tube or line attached. Simply covering the area with a cloth or dressing may adequately prevent disturbance.

If a child must remain in a certain position, or if he or she is tampering with equipment and interfering with necessary treatments, some method to decrease mobility must be employed. Restraints are necessary if no other means (e.g., parent present to hold the child) is available.

Give careful explanation about restraints to the child and parents to lessen fears and increase cooperation. Use a kind, gentle manner in application.

Various kinds of restraints are available or can be improvised. A few to be discussed are as follows:

1. Bubble top or crib net
2. Elbow restraints
3. Mittens
4. Clove-hitch restraint
5. Mummy restraint
6. Jacket

Bubble top or crib net Full siderails will usually prevent infants and small children from falling out of cribs. However, a toddler may be able to climb over the rail. If a child is too young to be moved to a youth bed, a bubble top (Fig. 17-6) or net can provide further protection.

A clear, heavy plastic bubble top can be secured on a track attached to the top of the endrails. When care is being given, the top will slide to the side by release of a catch at each end. A bubble top allows the child to stand in the crib and see out through the clear top.

An alternative to the bubble top is a crib net placed snugly over the top of the crib and attached securely to each corner of the bedsprings. It will stretch to allow the child to stand, but activity is more restricted than with the bubble top.

Elbow restraints (Fig. 17-7) These are most often used when children have had head or neck surgery or a scalp-vein infusion. Elbow restraints keep the arms extended. The child is unable to bend the elbow or touch his or her head. The restraint consists of a rectangular heavy-duty cloth divided into compartments. Tongue blades are placed into each compartment. If presewn restraints are not available, tape tongue blades close together across a washcloth. Wrap the restraint around the child's arm so that it extends about halfway up between the elbow and shoulder and down to the wrist. Secure with gauze ties or pins. To prevent slipping, extend the child's gown or pajama sleeve below the restraint,

Figure 17-6 The bubble top attached to a crib prevents the toddler from climbing out and provides visibility of surroundings. The ultrasonic nebulizer attached to the crib provides an environment of high humidity for the child with respiratory problems. (*Photo by Pearl Sheps.*)

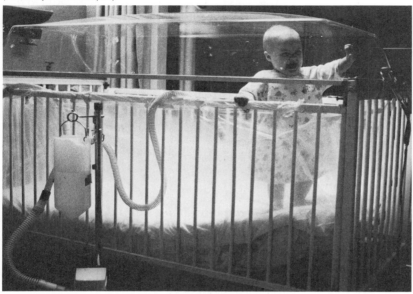

Figure 17-7 Elbow restraint. (*From G. Scipien, M. U. Barnard, M. A. Chard, J. Howe, and P. J. Phillips (eds.), Comprehensive Pediatric Nursing, McGraw-Hill, New York, 1979, p. 1033. Used by permission.*)

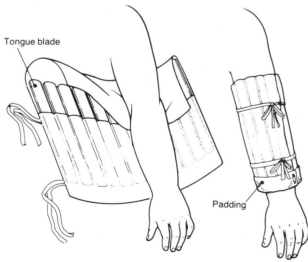

Tongue blade

Padding

turn it up, and pin it to the restraint. Apply the restraint loosely enough to allow insertion of a finger underneath it. Check the circulation of the arm frequently.

Mittens These can be used to prevent the child's fingers from manipulating tubes or to prevent scratching in dermatologic disorders. Use snug socks over the hands and pin the socks to the gown sleeves.

Clove-hitch restraint This type secures the extremities but cannot tighten to decrease circulation. Place a gauze pad over the wrist or ankle before the restraint is applied. Use a long piece of gauze or heavy-duty cloth and loop around the limb as illustrated in Fig. 17-8. Secure the restraint to the mattress spring, not to the side-rail.

Somewhat similar to the clove-hitch restraint is a commercially manufactured cuff restraint padded with sheepskin or foam. This may be

Figure 17-8 Clove-hitch Restraint. A figure eight is formed with gauze and then placed over padding on an extremity and tied by a slip knot to a stationary part of the crib. (*From G. Scipien, M. U. Barnard, M. A. Chard, J. Howe, and P. J. Phillips (eds.), Comprehensive Pediatric Nursing, McGraw-Hill, New York, 1979, p. 1033. Used by permission.*)

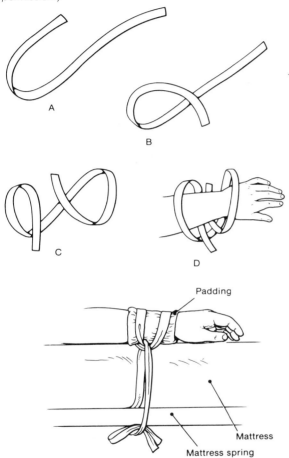

as a bed restraint to allow some mobility, but this proved unsafe because children frequently became entangled in the long tapes. It is best to use the jacket when positioning a child in a high chair, feeding table, wheelchair, or stroller. Secure the tapes snugly.

Nursing care of the restrained child Table 17-5 presents some nursing approaches to be used with any child who is restrained. Remember that the patient is a child and that the restraints may seem like punishment. Give the child attention frequently. Hold and cuddle him or her and provide distractions. Change the patient's position and check circulation frequently. Take special care not to restrain supine in spread-eagle

Figure 17-9 Mummy restraint. *A* and *B*. Material is first folded over right arm and then corner is tucked under left side. *C*. The opposite corner is then folded over the infant's left arm and tucked under the right side to secure. (*From G. Scipien, M. U. Barnard, M. A. Chard, J. Howe, and P. J. Phillips (eds.), Comprehensive Pediatric Nursing, McGraw-Hill, New York, 1979, p. 1033. Used by permission.*)

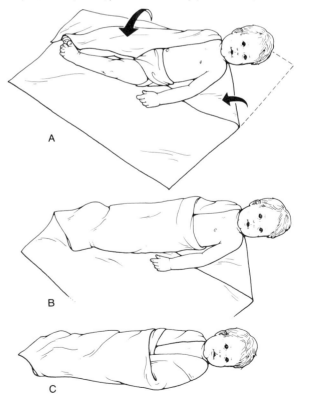

adequate for older children, but active toddlers and infants can slip their small fists out of them.

Mummy restraint This is useful when a small child must be positioned for a jugular venipuncture or a scalp-vein infusion. (See Fig. 17-9 for steps in applying the mummy restraint.)

Jacket Jacket restraints are available in various sizes and are applied with ties at the back. Long tapes extending from the sides of the jacket are tied to a chair. In the past the jacket was used fashion. Leave at least one extremity free. If a child is restrained on his or her back, elevate the head of the bed at least 15° to prevent aspiration in case of vomiting. Give the child stroller or wagon rides to increase mobility.

Positioning for procedures Proper positioning of a child is essential for the child's safety and successful completion of a procedure. Provide good explanation and a comfort measure (i.e., pacifier, stuffed animal, blanket, or parent). When holding the child use a minimum number of personnel. Imagine what it is like for a 4-year-old in a strange, new place to be approached by several strangers who restrain him for a painful procedure! With advance planning, two people can usually provide restraint while the third performs the procedure.

Find ways the child can help during the procedure, such as holding some of the equipment. Plan something pleasant to anticipate following the procedure. Praise the child fre-quently for helping. Encouraging the child's cooperation and allowing him to make some decisions will increase his sense of control over what is happening.

In positioning the child, be sure that adequate light is available and that those restraining the child do not obstruct the light source. Position the child as comfortably as possible while main-taining adequate restraint.

Positions for injections Common sites for in-tramuscular injections are the thigh and hip. When the thigh is used, position the child on her back in bed. Maintain her knees in an extended position, since the tendency is to flex the knees when the needle penetrates the skin. Restrain the child's hands by asking her to squeeze your hands or place her hands on her chest and restrain the hands and chest simul-taneously. The latter prevents the child from sitting up during the injection.

Vary the location of the procedure so that the

Table 17-5 Intervention regimen for children in restraints

Nursing action	Rationale
Explain to the child why his body part is restrained. This may be done through the use of a doll, puppet, or story for a toddler or preschooler.	It is important that the child understand why he is not allowed to use mobility at this time to meet his needs.
While remaining with the child, remove the restraints for 10 min every 2 h and allow random movement.	Removing the restraints will allow the child self-expression, to maintain contact with the environment, and to preserve his physiological integrity.
Change the child's position in relation to gravity as much as possible while he is unrestrained.	Position change is necessary to increase respiratory volume, to maintain autonomic control of the heart and peripheral circulation and to provide the proprioceptive stimulation which is necessary for neuromuscular function.
Talk soothingly to the child while he is unrestrained; use touch and body contact and provide play as appropriate.	Interaction with the child increases sensory input, encourages self-expression, and decreases boredom, feelings of lone-liness, and helplessness.
Before reapplying necessary restraints, change child's po-sition and talk soothingly. Restrain as little and as loosely as possible to maintain safety while allowing enough freedom so the child can touch some part of the body.	Position change helps prevent skin ischemia and breakdown, provides comfort, and allows for a variety of stimulation. The emotional attitude of the restraining person plays a role in the child's response.* The degree of restriction influences the effect of restraint on the child.† The infant and toddler develops a knowledge of his body and distin-guishes it from other objects through motor sensations.
Provide stimulation for the child while he is restrained.	Restricting the child's mobility has deprived him of his most important means of learning about and mastering his environment. Compensatory stimulation will facilitate the child's development.

* **Source:** Bernabeau [18].
† **Source:** O'Grady [19].

Source: From E. L. Dowd, J. Novak, and E. Ray, "Releasing the Hospitalized Child from Restraints," *American Journal of Maternal-Child Nursing*, November–December 1977, p. 372. Used by permission.

child does not associate the bed with "shots" and refuse to sleep. One alternative is for the nurse or parent to hold the young child on the lap; the adult can hold the child's hands with one hand and restrain the knees with the other. The child's lower legs can also be restrained between the thighs of the adult upon whose lap he or she is held.

When the site for the injection is the hip, position the child on her abdomen. Extend the child's hands over her head so that she can grip the head of the bed or the mattress. Have the child turn her toes inward to enhance relaxation of the hip muscles. Ask the child to concentrate on something (e.g., count to 10 or take slow, deep breaths). Maintain knees in an extended position and restrain the child's trunk to prevent flexion of the hip.

In giving an injection to an infant, turn toward the child's feet (Fig. 17-10) and secure the buttocks between your elbow and hip. Use the appropriate sites in the thigh. (See Fig. 17-37 for intramuscular sites.)

An experienced nurse can administer injections safely and also restrain the child. For example, the nurse can extend an arm across the patient's knees and still have a hand free to hold the syringe. Avoid becoming overconfident, however, because children's movements can be quick and unexpected. An inexperienced nurse must concentrate on the injection itself and have adequate assistance in positioning the patient so there is no worry about sudden movement.

Positions for venipuncture Careful selection of a potential site for venipuncture must be done before the child is held down. This lessens the restraint time and may also allow the child to participate in the procedure.

When the site is determined, ask for the child's cooperation so that the procedure can be completed quickly. Advise the child that you will assist him if necessary to stay in position. Restrain the child's hands or joints near the site. Remind him that after the needle is in place it will not hurt or "stick."

Use the mummy restraint (Fig. 17-9) for a venipuncture of the jugular vein. Turn the child's head to the side and extend it slightly over the edge of the bed (Fig. 17-11A). This hyperextends the neck so that the jugular vein is more accessible. (*Note:* After puncture of the jugular vein

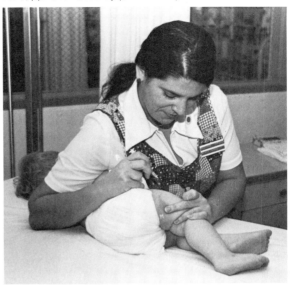

Figure 17-10 Small child being restrained for an intramuscular injection. (*From L. Whaley and D. Wong, Nursing Care of Infants and Children, Mosby, St. Louis, 1979, pp. 940. Used by permission.*)

apply pressure for at least 10 min to prevent hematoma formation.)

For a scalp-vein infusion, mummy the child and position him flat in bed. Hold the child's head firmly to one side. Avoid obstructing his nose and mouth.

Femoral sticks may be necessary for infants when no other veins are available or when arterial blood tests are needed. Place the infant's legs in frog-leg position with knees flexed and hips abducted (Fig. 17-11B). Place a diaper over the genitalia to prevent contamination of the site. (Infants commonly void during this kind of procedure.) Restrain the infant by holding the child's knees from above. The person performing the procedure works from below.

Positions for lumbar puncture Position the child on the side with knees and head flexed toward the abdomen (Fig. 17-11C). Place one arm behind the patient's knees and one behind the child's neck to maintain the flexion. This produces separation of the spinous processes and assists the physician in inserting the spinal needle properly. Keep the patient's back parallel to the edge of the bed or treatment table and maintain the flexion throughout the procedure.

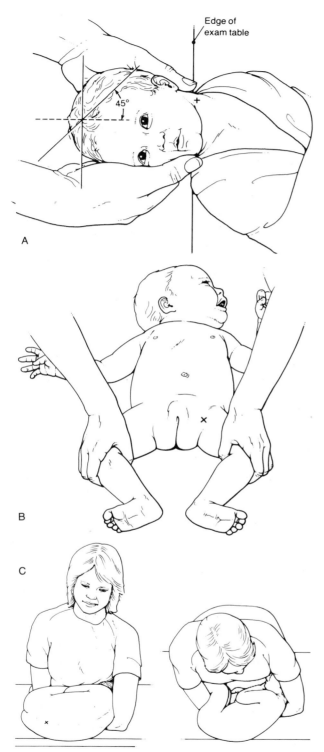

Figure 17-11 Positions for venipuncture. (*A*) Position for jugular venipuncture. The puncture site is indicated by X. The mummy restraint shown in Fig. 17-9*C* is being used. (*B*) Positioned for femoral venipuncture procedure. The X indicates the puncture site. (*C*)(Left) Position for lumbar puncture with back at or over table edge. The X indicates the puncture site. (Right) View of lumbar puncture restraint from above. (*From G. Scipien, M. U. Barnard, M. A. Chard, J. Howe, and P. J. Phillips (eds.), Comprehensive Pediatric Nursing, McGraw-Hill, New York, 1979, pp. 1034–1035. Used by permission.*)

Remember to talk to the child. Observe the child's appearance and check respirations as you hold him or her.

The sitting position for a lumbar puncture may be used in prematures who have a low spinal-fluid pressure.[20] Infants are supported sitting and leaning forward so that the spine is rounded.

Positions for physical examination of the head
To position a small child's head securely, place the child in a supine position, extend the arms up beside the head, restrain the elbows, and hold the head simultaneously. This facilitates eye, ear, nose, and throat examinations.

Reassurance following procedures During any procedure remember that you are holding a frightened child who is uncomfortable. He or she may also be very ill. Observe the child closely. Check vital signs and appearance during and after any stressful procedure. As soon as it is over, give comfort and reassurance. Though other nursing responsibilities are necessary (getting specimens to the lab, cleaning trays and equipment, etc.), the comfort and well-being of the patient have top priority. Encourage parents to hold the child. Provide a play activity or a treat as a pleasant change.

Role of parents in restraining for procedures
There are a variety of opinions about parents holding their child during painful procedures. Some authors feel that the child does not understand why parents will allow him or her to have pain. Their presence may cause the child to distrust them. Others believe that when parents assist, it lets the child know that the procedure, though painful, is necessary for getting well. This enhances the child's acceptance of the procedure and increases his or her feelings of

security. Each situation must be assessed individually. Remember that some parents cannot tolerate seeing their child in pain and prefer to leave the room. A child may become anxious if he or she senses the parents' anxiety. Maintain open communication among the parents, the child, physician, and nurses to determine what role the parents should play.

Toy safety Most of a child's waking hours are filled with play activities. Toys of all kinds are usually available on a pediatric unit and each child will find some object to play with—whether it is a "real" toy or not. Be aware of the safety hazards of all toys and equipment within the child's reach. A set of tiny building blocks appropriate for a 7-year-old can be lethal to a 14-month-old who puts everything in his mouth. Be aware of the developmental needs at various ages in order to determine what is appropriate and safe for each child.

In general, toys for children through age 5 should meet the following safety characteristics: no sharp edges, allergy-free, no small removable parts, unbreakable, washable, and lead-free.[21] With older children it is difficult to restrict toys to these requirements.

Explain to both children and parents that toys must be put away when no longer in use. Have each patient keep his or her own toys at the bedside or on a nearby shelf inaccessible to other children. Make sure that each patient has age-appropriate, safe, and varied toys so that he or she will be less likely to look for unsafe toys.

Choking Choking on food is the sixth leading cause of accidental death in the United States (1976 data). Twenty-five percent of these deaths are of children under 16.

The guidelines for prevention of choking and the signs of choking listed below are for general use but can be applied in the hospital setting.

For prevention of choking:[22]

1. Introduce solid foods to infants only when they have teeth for proper chewing.
2. Do not give children under 2½ years such foods as peanuts, popcorn, or whole-kernel corn, potato chips, or pieces of apple.
3. Do not let children eat while lying down or while overly active—running or playing. Both can cause a bolus of food to become lodged in the larynx.

4. Remove small objects from the reach of young children. When changing diapers, close safety pins and remove them from the infant's reach.
5. Teach by example—do not hold foreign objects in lips or mouth (tacks, pins, pencils).

The common signs of true choking[22] are for the child to:

1. Grab at his or her throat
2. Be unable to cry or speak
3. Turn bluish
4. Collapse

When true choking is identified, the rescuer must act *very quickly*. The Heimlich maneuver is a simple, effective method to use. It is described for a standing victim in Table 17-6 and shown in Fig. 17-12.

If the child is sitting, wrap your arms around the chair and the youngster from behind and proceed as if the child were standing (Fig. 17-13). The back of the chair provides support which may enhance the effectiveness of the quick upward thrust. Do not compress the ribs. Press the fist only.

If a child is lying on his back, face him. Kneel astride the child's hips, *not* beside him. Place the heel of one hand on the child's abdomen below the rib cage and above the navel and cover

---

Table 17-6 The Heimlich maneuver

Do this

1. Stand or kneel behind the victim. Place one fist, palm side in, against the victim's abdomen below the rib cage and slightly above the navel. Grasp this fist with your other hand.
2. Press the fist into the abdomen with a quick upward thrust.
3. Repeat the thrust if necessary.

Don't do this

1. Don't slap the victim's back.*
2. Don't squeeze the chest.
3. Don't give fluids.
4. Don't hold him upside down.
5. Don't turn victim's head to one side during the maneuver.

---

* The American Heart Association recommends that blows to the center of the back be used in combination with the Heimlich maneuver to relieve choking. This continues to be an area of controversy, for both methods have been used effectively.

Source: Adapted from C. R. Block and C. E. Block [22] and H. Heimlich [23].

Figure 17-12 Heimlich maneuver with child standing. (*Photo by Brian Kaihoi.*)

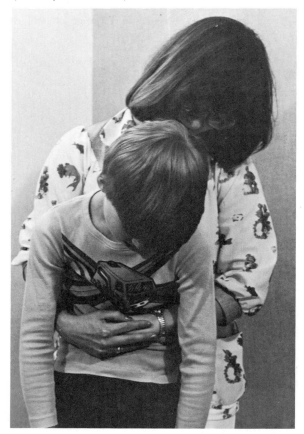

it with the other hand. Press with the quick upward thrust. Keep the child's head *up* during the thrust, not turned to one side.[23]

Dr. Henry Heimlich, who originated the maneuver, states that it has been performed on infants as young as 3 months. With an infant use two fingers of each hand to compress the abdomen. This may be acomplished with the infant lying on his back or sitting in your lap (Fig. 17-14).

Certain cautions should be followed. The Heimlich maneuver is not a punch, bear hug, or squeeze. It is a quick inward and upward pressing of the abdomen. Do not compress or squeeze your arms against the patient during the procedure or injury may result. Should vomiting occur, turn the victim to his side with face down and wipe out his mouth to prevent aspiration.[24]

Once breathing has been restored, the child should receive medical treatment to determine if complications have occurred.

The Heimlich maneuver is thought to mobilize the respiratory reserve volume in the lungs. Pressure on the abdomen forces the reserve air out of the lungs, carrying the bolus of food or other object along with it.[25] This is an effective rescue method which every nurse should be able to perform and share with others.

Carrying and holding infants Being held gently but firmly increases an infant's feelings of security and comfort. Safe methods for holding and carrying infants are as follows:

1. *Cradle* Hold the infant in your arm with her head above your elbow. Hold her thigh with your hand in order to keep the infant securely in place (Fig. 17-15).
2. *Football* Support the infant's head with your hand and her back on your forearm and press the infant's buttocks between your elbow and hip (Fig. 17-16).

Figure 17-13 Heimlich maneuver with child sitting. The fist is placed with the thumb next to the abdomen. The other hand is used to push on the fist and extend an inward and upward thrust. (*Photo by Brian Kaihoi.*)

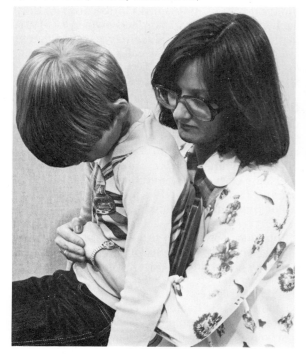

Figure 17-14 There are two ways to apply the Heimlich maneuver on an infant. (*A*) Hold the infant in your lap and place the index and middle fingers of both hands against the abdomen above the navel and below the rib cage. Press into the abdomen with a quick upward thrust. (*B*) Place the infant face upward on a firm surface and perform the maneuver while facing him. (*From H. J. Heimlich, "The Heimlich Maneuver: Where It Stands Today," Emergency Medicine, July 1978. Redrawn by permission.*)

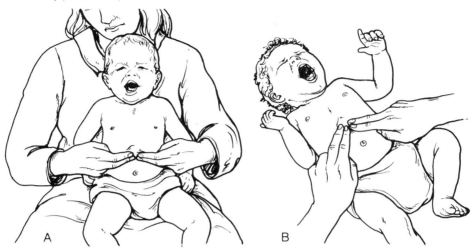

This allows one hand to be free for changing bed linen, shampooing the hair, or other activities.

3. *Upright* Support the infant's buttocks on one forearm and rest her head against your shoulder. Keep the other hand on her back to catch the unexpected backward movement which can easily occur. This hold is modified for the toddler, as shown in Fig. 17-17.

Movements of small children are unpredictable. While carrying a young child always remain alert to the possiblity of sudden movement and be able to compensate for it immediately.

Supervision of children's activities Maintaining safety in caring for children involves looking at the hospital unit with a critical eye and constantly identifying safety hazards.[26] Written guidelines developed by the nursing staff should be shared with children and parents. These must be supported and reinforced by all the staff—nurses, physicians, nursing assistants, housekeeping personnel, and other hospital workers. When parents are well informed about the guidelines, they can help their own child and other patients as well. See Table 17-7.

To provide a safe means of expanding the young child's environment and decreasing boredom, place the child in a playpen at the door of his or her room or at the nurse's station. Use strollers, wagons, or wheelchairs to give the

Figure 17-15 Infant cradled in caretaker's arms. Note eye contact between adult and child.

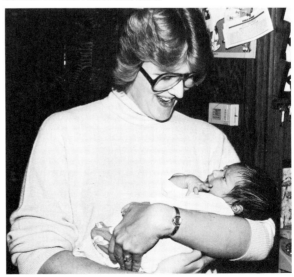

Figure 17-16 Football hold.

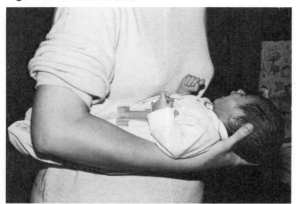

Table 17-7 A sample of nursing unit guidelines for children's activities

The following guidelines have been developed for the safety of all the children who are patients in the unit. Please try to follow them. If you have questions contact one of the nurses. Thank you!
1. No running on the nursing unit.
2. Please remain outside of the medication area at all times.
3. Return toys to the playroom shelves after use.
4. Feel free to use playroom toys in your room, unless you are in isolation. In that case, talk with a nurse before taking toys into the room.
5. Daily quiet time: 12:30–2:00 P.M.
6. Playroom hours: 7:30 A.M.–8:30 P.M.
7. Please be in your own room by 8:30 P.M.
8. Talk with the nurse before bringing in food from outside.
9. Small children must be accompanied by an adult when out of bed.

child rides around the unit or for transportation to other departments. Use restraints to ensure the child's safety and do not leave a child alone in the movable equipment unless he or she is old enough to safely get in and out and operate the vehicle (e.g., 12-year-old can easily move a wheelchair alone).

Figure 17-17 Holding a small child in an upright position. The caretaker holds the child's arm to prevent her from falling backwards. (*From G. Scipien, M. U. Barnard, M. A. Chard, J. Howe, and P. J. Phillips, Comprehensive Pediatric Nursing, McGraw-Hill, New York, 1979, p. 220.*)

Infection control

Medical asepsis The word *asepsis* means germ-free, and the purpose of medical asepsis is to eliminate all *disease-producing* organisms from the environment.[27] A clean, noninfectious item or area becomes contaminated if it comes in contact with anything infected.[28]

Handwashing Handwashing is the *single most important factor in infection control* on a nursing unit. Good, thorough, and frequent handwashing prevents the accumulation of bacteria. Soap mixes with and loosens dirt and oils on the hands while friction—good rubbing—actually removes the germs. Hands should be washed after each patient contact and after handling contaminated materials (e.g., elimination products). Table 17-8 describes proper handwashing technique.

Clean environment One aspect of the nurse's role in infection control is to help maintain a clean environment. Housekeeping personnel are responsible for *daily* cleaning of floors, furniture, and other equipment. Maintain close communication with the housekeeping department and notify them when an area needs additional cleaning.

If children eat together in the playroom, it is important that the floors be cleaned immediately afterward. Food is a potential source of bacterial growth. Periodically check the bedside or overbed tables for snacks or leftover food which may be a source of bacteria.

Provide a mat, sheet, or rug for play on the floor. This allows children to play without sitting directly on the floor; it can be cleaned between patients.

Playroom toys are used by many different patients and should be cleaned regularly—especially those used by young children who will put them in their mouths. Develop a plan for effectively accomplishing this task, perhaps by including it in the daily assignments for the nursing assistants.

Toys used by children in their rooms should be cleaned before being returned to the playroom. Send the equipment to a central cleaning department for terminal sterilization or wash it with an antibacterial solution. Consult the hospital's infection control policies for specific guidelines.

Preparing food Nurses commonly prepare snacks, food, and formula for infants on the nursing unit. A kitchenette with a sink and refrigerator for patients' food should be available. No medications or staff lunches should be kept in the same refrigerator. Careful handwashing before preparing any food is essential.

Presterilized formula and disposable bottles for juice or milk are often used for infants in the hospital. Parents may ask that a child's own bottle be used. The nurse must decide if facilities permit proper cleaning without cross-contami-

Table 17-8 Handwashing technique

With the newborn

1. Keep nails short and carefully trimmed.
2. Remove all jewelry, including watch.
3. Perform a 2-min scrub upon entering the nursery:
   a. Moisten hands, apply soap, and, using friction, wash palms, backs, and sides of hands, and between fingers. Use a brush for most effective scrubbing. Clean nails.
   b. Rinse hands.
   c. Moisten arms and apply soap, scrubbing to the elbows.
   d. Rinse hands and arms.
4. Dry carefully with disposable towels.
5. Wash hands for at least 30 s between infants.

With older children

1. Keep nails short and carefully trimmed.
2. Watch and plain ring may be worn.
3. Perform initial scrub of 1 min on the hands (as above).
4. Wash hands for 30 s between patients.

Table 17-9 Signs of possible infection

1. Nasal discharge	7. Stiff neck
2. Cough	8. Malaise
3. Skin rash	9. Enlarged lymph nodes
4. Fever	10. Vomiting
5. Draining wound	11. Diarrhea
6. Headache	

nation. On a busy nursing unit, the safest way is to use only hospital equipment.

Keep a good supply of prepared cereal and baby food on the unit. Infants do not conform to routine food service hours.

In preparing the food, use a clean cup and spoon for each child. Close dry cereal boxes securely after use so that the contents remain clean and dry. When a jar of baby food is opened, remove the amount needed, close the jar tightly, and label it with the date and time opened. Store it in the refrigerator no longer than 24 h. Do not feed an infant directly from a jar of food. The saliva which adheres to the spoon contaminates the food in the jar and provides a medium for bacterial growth. Discard a partially used bottle of milk or juice and *use a fresh bottle for each feeding.*

Room assignments The nurse has primary responsibility for selecting appropriate rooms and beds for patients. When possible, group patients by age and similarity of diagnosis. Be alert to signs that isolation may be necessary and report these to the physician. (See Table 17-9 for some signs of possible infection.) If in doubt about the need for isolation, place the patient in a private room until diagnostic tests are done to determine the presence of a communicable disease. If the patient has had recent exposure to a communicable disease, note this on the Kardex and be alert for symptoms during the child's hospitalization.

Equipment Various items such as stethoscopes and blood pressure cuffs are kept in the nurses' station for use in physical assessment. Wipe the bell, ear pieces, and tubing of the stethoscope with alcohol and allow it to dry before use. Blood pressure cuffs should be cleaned periodically by terminal sterilization. When feasible wipe all equipment with antiseptic solution before and after use. If a patient is isolated, frequently used equipment should remain in the room throughout the patient's stay and be sterilized after dismissal.

Isolation procedures Table 17-10 lists a variety of communicable diseases and the type of isolation precautions necessary.

Preparing the child and parents Explain carefully why isolation is needed. Sometimes a child does not fully understand the reason for isolation and believes it is punishment for wrongdoing. It may help to use play techniques—dolls with masks and gowns, drawing pictures—to explore the child's feelings. It always helps to spend time with the child "for fun," not only for specific physical care.

Instruct not only the child but also the parents in handwashing and gown procedures. The involvement of the parents in care should be encouraged by teaching them proper isolation techniques. However, the nurse should continue working with them rather than leaving them alone once they are trained. That maintains a high level of involvement.

Table 17-10 Infectious diseases grouped according to degree of recommended isolation*

Private room	Mask	Gown	Gloves	Excreta and excreta-soiled articles	Blood	Secreta and secreta-soiled articles	Diseases
Strict isolation							
R	R	R	R			R	Anthrax, inhalation; eczema vaccinatum; melioidosis, pulmonary, or extrapulmonary with draining sinus(es); plague, pulmonary or bubonic; smallpox; vaccinia, generalized and progressive.
R	C	C	C			R	Burns, extensive (when infected with *Staphylococcus aureus* or Group A streptococcus).
R	R	C	C			R	Staphylococcal enterocolitis; staphylococcal or streptococcal pneumonia.
R	R	C				R	Diphtheria.
R		C		R	R	R	Neonatal vesicular disease (herpes simplex); rubella, congenital syndrome.
R			C			R	Rabies.
Respiratory isolation							
R	R					R	Tuberculosis, pulmonary—sputum-positive (or suspect); Venezuelan equine encephalitis.
R	R						Meningitis, meningococcal; meningococcemia.
R	S					R	Chickenpox; herpes zoster; measles (rubeola); mumps; rubella (German measles); pertussis (whooping cough).
Enteric precautions							
D		C	C	R			Cholera; *Escherichia coli* gastroenteritis; salmonellosis, including typhoid fever; shigellosis.
D				R	R		Hepatitis, infectious or serum.

Table 17-10 Infectious diseases grouped according to degree of recommended isolation* (*Continued*)

Private room	Mask	Gown	Gloves	Excreta and excreta-soiled articles	Blood	Secreta and secreta-soiled articles	Diseases
Wound and skin precautions							
D						R	Gas gangrene.
D	C	C	C			R	Staphylococcal skin or wound disease.
D		C	C			R	Impetigo; streptococcal skin infection; wound infections, extensive—other than staphylococcal; burns, extensive—infected other than with *Staphylococcus aureus* or Group A streptococcus.

Discharge precautions

Special handling of excreta and excreta-soiled articles is recommended for the following diseases:

Herpangina
Leptospirosis
Meningitis, aseptic

Pleurodynia
Poliomyelitis
Taeniasis, pork

Viral diseases, enteric (if not covered elsewhere)

Special handling of secreta and secreta-soiled articles is recommended for the following diseases:

Actinomycosis with draining lesions
Anthrax, cutaneous
Brucellosis with draining lesions
Burns and wounds, minor (infected)
Clostridium perfringens food poisoning
Coccidioidomycosis with draining wounds
Conjunctivitis, acute bacterial (including gonococcal)
Cryptococcosis

Gonococcal ophthalmia neonatorum
Gonorrhea
Granuloma inguinale
Herpes simplex
Keratoconjunctivitis, infectious
Listeriosis
Lymphogranuloma venereum
Pneumonia, bacterial (if not covered elsewhere)
Psittacosis
Q fever

Scarlet fever
Staphylococcal food poisoning
Streptococcal pharyngitis
Syphilis, mucocutaneous
Trachoma, acute
Tuberculosis, extrapulmonary with open lesions
Tularemia, cutaneous
Viral diseases, respiratory (if not covered elsewhere)
Wound infections, not extensive (other than staphylococcal)

Blood precautions

Special handling of secreta and secreta-soiled articles is recommended for the following diseases:

Arthropod-borne viral fever (dengue and so forth)

Anthropod-borne viral hemorragic fever

Hepatitis, infectious or serum
Malaria

Key: R—recommended; C—with direct contact; S—for susceptibles; D—desirable but optional.

Source: Committee on Hospital Care, *Hospital Care of Children and Youth,* American Academy of Pediatrics, Evanston, Ill., 1978, p. 94–96. Used by permission.

Disposition of equipment Check daily for adequate supplies and reorder from central supply. Room facilities should include:[29]

1. A table or cart outside the door for gowns, masks, gloves, and plastic bags
2. Facilities for handwashing
3. Separately covered containers for soiled linen and diapers
4. Individual equipment for the child's care
5. Paper towels

Organize activities and gather necessary equipment and medications before entering the room.

If a piece of equipment is needed one time only (e.g., an otoscope) place it on a paper towel barrier on the bedside table. Wash it off with an antiseptic solution and return it to the unit.

Provide toys which can be easily sterilized after isolation is terminated.

Use disposable trays and dishes for mealtimes and snacks.

Personal hygiene Use good handwashing before and after each patient contact. Remove rings and watch before scrubbing and during care. Wear long hair pinned up off the shoulders. Wear a fresh disposable gown when entering the room. When a mask is necessary, cover both the nose and mouth. Wear a mask for only 30 min and replace.

Do not touch your hair, face, neck, uniform, or other "clean" item with contaminated hands. Wash hands before removing the gown (i.e., do not handle the neck of the gown with contaminated hands).

Do not assign a staff member who is pregnant, has skin lesions, or has an upper respiratory infection to care for a child with a communicable disease. A nurse who is caring for a child in isolation should not concurrently be assigned to another patient with a fresh surgical incision or lowered resistance to infection.

Disposal of contaminated items Dispose of diapers, contaminated dressings, and linen in covered containers kept in the room. Make certain that the child cannot get into these containers.

At the end of each shift, clean the room and remove all trash and linen. This requires two staff members dressed in isolation attire. One works inside the room while the other remains at the door and holds a clean bag. A soiled bag from the room is placed into the clean bag at the door. The outside person secures the bag and disposes of it properly. *No contaminated articles should be carried outside the room unless double-bagged.*

Reverse isolation This technique is used to protect children who have a reduced resistance to disease (e.g., a severely burned child or one with reduced white blood cell count). Mask, gown, and gloves for direct care are required. Staff members with any sign of infection must not care for these patients.

Surgical asepsis Surgical asepsis is an extension of medical asepsis. It includes good handwashing, maintenance of a clean environment, and use of sterile technique in the care of surgical wounds. It is more rigorous because open wounds are more vulnerable to infections than normal, intact tissues.[30]

Sterile dressings are applied to surgical wounds in the operating room. The initial dressing may be large and bulky in order to provide pressure to minimize bleeding. It is usually removed after the first day and replaced by either a smaller dressing or none at all.

Soiled, wet dressings act as a wick and allow bacteria to soak through to the site of the incision. In order to prevent this, the dressing can be changed or reinforced (added to) with additional sterile dressings. The physician must be notified if drainage is excessive; physician's instructions regarding dressing care should be followed.

The physician may prefer to do the first postoperative dressing change, but the nurse may be asked to perform subsequent ones. Steps in performing dressing changes are as follows:

1. Explain to the child and parents. Demonstrate dressing application and removal on a doll. Encourage the child to do the same.
2. Gather dressing supplies, masks, two pairs of sterile gloves, and a plastic bag.
3. Have the parent or another nurse assist in restraint or handling equipment.
4. Open all dressings and gloves on the table at the bedside.
5. If masks are necessary (determine according to the type of incision or wound, doctor's recommendation, and hospital policy), each attendant and the patient must wear one. A crying child may be unable to tolerate a mask, so omit and turn the child's head away when the wound is exposed.
6. Remove old tape gently by pulling skin and tape away from each other. This may be the most painful part of the procedure for the child. Encourage the child to help with the tape removal.
7. Put on gloves.
8. Remove all old dressings and discard in plastic bag.
9. Note the condition of the incision or wound, the type of drainage, and the surrounding skin.
10. Remove gloves and discard in bag. Put on a clean pair.
11. Replace dressings and secure well with gauze and tape. Prevent future discomfort of tape removal by using paper tape rather than adhesive, or wrap the area securely with gauze and apply tape to the gauze rather than the skin.
12. Remove gloves and discard in bag.
13. Discard bag in a closed container inaccessible to the child.

14. Comfort the child.
15. Chart the dressing change and the conditon of the incision.

Documentation to promote safety

Safety requires that complete charting be done *as soon as possible after care is given.* A young patient cannot and will not always tell the nurse, "Oh, I've already had that medicine." As a result, omissions in charting can cause errors in care.

Nursing care of children under 10 should be documented on a flow sheet at least every hour. Observe the patient's activities frequently when not giving direct care. With infants or seriously ill patients, charting may be more frequent. Write a thorough nurses' note at least once a day to document needs and progress. Observe for problems or needs related to the medical diagnosis, emotional status, growth and development, or parental concerns.

Keep accurate records of fluid intake and output throughout hospitalization. Record all intake in milliliters and the number of voidings. When a patient is receiving intravenous fluids or has a condition affecting renal function, the urinary output should be measured and recorded. The parents and the child may assist in documenting intake and output by keeping a record at the bedside.

Nutrition of hospitalized children

Requirements for different nutrients vary according to the growth rate of various body tissues, the patient's sex, stage of maturation, physical activity, and body build. The patient's general health and conformity to percentiles of growth in height and weight are the best indications of his or her nutritional state. Sample growth charts for males and females are presented in Appendix B, showing percentiles for particular age groups.

Caloric needs

The total caloric needs of children increase with age and with gains in height and weight. Appetite gives a good indication of a child's caloric needs. During the period of early infancy when growth occurs at a fast pace, the appetite is good and the caloric intake tends to increase accordingly. At the beginning of the second year there is a decrease in the rate of weight gain as the child becomes more mobile and growth slows.

Throughout childhood there are times when growth speeds up and the caloric needs increase, such as in adolescence.

Segar has developed a simple method of determining caloric needs according to body weight (Table 17-11).

Assessing nutritional patterns

On admission determine the child's weight and height and plot on a growth chart to show how the child compares with others his or her age. Discuss with parents and child the child's eating habits and food preferences and share this information with the dietitian. If a detailed nutritional history is needed, have the mother recall and write down a typical day's intake at home. Since a child's eating habits may be altered significantly by hospitalization and illness, the child's "normal" nutrition cannot be determined only by what he or she eats in the hospital.

Calorie counts

When a child is not eating properly in the hospital, it may be necessary to determine the child's daily caloric intake. Adequate caloric intake for the ill child is based on replacing the calories normally expended plus extra calories used in recuperating from the disease or in healing after surgery. To estimate the child's caloric intake, observe and record exactly how much he or she eats. The child and family can be taught to help keep this record so that nothing will be overlooked. The dietitian will know exactly what amount was served and can help calculate the calorie count. Be sure that everything the child eats during a period of "calorie count" is served from the diet kitchen. Obtain daily weights

Table 17-11 Caloric expenditures of children

Body weight in kilograms*	Caloric expenditure per day
Up to 10 kg	100 kcal/kg
11–20 kg	1000 kcal plus 50 kcal/kg for each kg over 10
Above 20 kg	1500 kcal plus 20 kcal/kg for each kg over 20

* 1 kg = 2.2 lb.

Source: V. C. Vaughan and J. R. McKay, *Nelson Textbook of Pediatrics*, 10th ed., Saunders, Philadelphia, 1975, p. 252. Used by permission.

on any child whose nutritional status is questionable.

Techniques of feeding

In order to encourage good nutritional intake in the hospitalized child, the nurse must use creativity, initiative, and intuition. A child who is away from home and family, feeling ill, in a strange environment, faced with a tray of food served in bed, with an intravenous line in one arm and a cast on the other, cannot be expected to eat enthusiastically!

Positioning Assist a bedridden child to assume a natural position at mealtime. If the child can sit with legs over the side of the bed and feet on the floor, he will eat more easily. Free a hand for the child to use at mealtime if at all possible. If the child must remain in bed, support him in an upright position to facilitate eating. Use an over-bed table for the older child or a bed tray in the youth bed or crib. (A bed tray allows siderails to be left up during mealtime.) Remove equipment like oxygen masks or mist tents during the meal.

Infant feeding Infant feedings of baby food and formula are usually prepared on the nursing unit rather than in the diet kitchen. (Review the section in infection control concerning cleanliness in preparing infant foods.) The food and formula may be served warm or cold according to the infant's routine at home. Dilute dry cereal with the formula to a liquid consistency. Prepared baby foods require no dilution. Have food

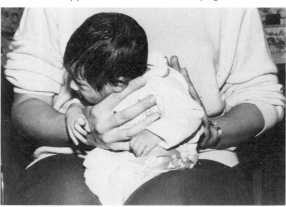

Figure 17-18 Method of holding the infant to burp. The mandible is supported to hold the head upright.

and formula available on the nursing unit before needed. Babies won't wait! Table 17-12 lists methods for feeding infants.

Although an infant usually requires only formula or breast milk until the age of 6 months, the physician may choose to start the child on solid foods earlier. Do not overfeed the infant. Stop feeding when the infant begins to spit food back or lose interest.

When an infant is able to sit alone, secure him or her in a high chair with a strap or jacket restraint. Never leave an infant alone in a chair. Falls from high chairs are a major cause of injury in young children.

An older infant can be encouraged to participate in the meal by holding a piece of dry toast and "gumming" it. Offer the infant a cup with a small amount of liquid at about 6 months to prepare the child for weaning later on. Toward the end of the first year, children can begin to feed themselves as the diet is progressed to soft, chopped table foods.

Even though an infant is old enough to have a meal in a high chair, hold the baby for the bottle-feeding. Some infants are accustomed to taking a bottle to bed for naps or bedtime. If the child demands a bottle in bed, remove it as soon as it is empty or the child falls asleep. It is unwise to try to break this habit in the hospital. It is far better to talk with the parents about how this can be done at home. Explain that going to sleep with a bottle of milk or sweet liquid increases the chance of dental caries and ear infections.

Exclude sweetened foods such as desserts,

Table 17-12 Feeding the infant

1. Put a bib on the infant and have a cloth handy.
2. Position the infant in your lap or in an infant seat or high chair for solid foods.
3. If the infant is very hungry and crying vigorously, offer a few sips from the bottle before feeding solids.
4. Using an infant spoon, put a small amount of the food on the end of the spoon and place it on the center of the infant's tongue, not on the tip.
5. Burp the newborn after every ounce. Set him or her upright and support the head and chest by placing the fingers over the mandible (the lower jaw) and upper chest.* (See Fig. 17-18.) The older infant can be burped after every 2 to 3 oz. Pat the infant's back gently to obtain a burp.
6. When solids are completed, cradle the infant in your arms for the bottle-feeding.

Source: Leifer [31].

Figure 17-19 The toddler likes to feed himself. (*From R. B. Howard and N. H. Herbold, Nutrition in Clinical Care, McGraw-Hill, New York, 1978, p. 233. Used by permission.*)

pastries, candy, and soft drinks from the infant's diet. If clear liquids are necessary, use plain water, sugar water, and clear juices, such as apple juice, rather than soft drinks or Kool-aid. When an infant is teething or needs a snack, use hard toast or a cracker served with fruit juice.

Toddler and preschooler Use a feeding table or high chair for the toddler. Allow the toddler to help feed himself or herself (Fig. 17-19). The preschooler can use the bed tray or sit at a small table in the hospital room or in the playroom. These children are at an age when the length of time between one meal and the next may be too long. Provide a carefully planned midmorning and midafternoon snack; this creates a pleasant change of pace and decreases irritability and crying due to hunger or thirst. A drink of water or juice after naptime also helps the child wake up and be in a more pleasant mood.

Gavage feeding When an infant or child is too ill to eat normally, or oral feedings are contrain-

dicated, gavage feeding may be the method of choice. A nasogastric tube is passed into the stomach for a single feeding and removed, or it may be left in place for one to three days before replacement is needed. The equipment required for gavage feeding is listed in Table 17-13. The steps in tube insertion and gavage feeding are described below. The technique outlined is for infant gavage, but the principles are the same for older children. Modification in the size of the tube and the type of feeding are necessary to accommodate the older child's nutritional needs.

Table 17-13 Equipment needed for gavage feeding

1. No. 5 to 8 French catheter 15 in long (nasogastric tube)
2. Nonallergenic tape
3. 3-ml syringe
4. Cup of sterile water
5. Stethoscope
6. Bulb suction
7. 30-ml syringe
8. Formula as ordered by physician (warm to room temperature)

Inserting the tube Using the nasogastric tube, measure from the tip of the infant's nose to the ear to a point midway between the xiphoid process and the umbilicus.[32] Using a small piece of tape, mark the tube to show how far it should be inserted.

Place the infant on his or her back. While restraining the head with one hand, quickly insert the tube through one nostril to the tape marker. (Use a mummy restraint to position the child if necessary.) Lubricate the tube with normal saline if mucous membranes are dry and the tube does not pass easily. If the infant begins to cough or choke or becomes cyanotic, remove the tube and reinsert.[33]

Check placement of the tube as follows:

1. Hold or tape the tube in place. Inject 1-ml air while listening with a stethoscope over the stomach. A "pop" indicates correct placement. Gently withdraw the injected air.
2. Aspirate gently for gastric contents.
3. Stimulate the infant to cry.
4. Invert the tube in a cup of sterile water while the child exhales. If bubbles appear, the tube may be in the lungs and should be removed immediately. Test only during exhalation to avoid the possibility that, if the tube is in the respiratory tract, the child might pull water from the cup into the lungs during inhalation.

Once correct placement is confirmed, secure the tube by wrapping one strip of tape around it and attach the free end above the upper lip. Place a second strip of tape over the tube. Secure the tube to the cheek by means of a third short strip of tape. Take care not to obstruct the nose.[34] Avoid taping the tube in any position that could cause pressure necrosis of the nasal cartilages. For example, this might happen if the tube were bent upward in order to tape it to the forehead.

The position of the tube should be checked every hour in infants and immediately prior to any feeding, using the preceding steps.

Feeding procedure Check the physician's order for the type, amount, and frequency of feeding. Draw up the formula in a 30-ml syringe. Position the infant on the right side, with the back supported by a blanket roll.[35] Elevate the head of the bed 15 to 30°.

Attach a syringe of formula to the tube and infuse contents by gravity at the rate of 3 ml/min. If the infant coughs, gags, or vomits, stop the feeding until this passes. (If respiratory distress occurs, stop the feeding, suction the infant, and recheck the tube's position.)[36]

To add formula, pinch the tube just before the syringe becomes empty. Refill the syringe and reattach it to the tube. Unclamp the tube so that flow resumes.

At the conclusion of the feeding, clear the tubing with 1 to 2 ml sterile water and either clamp the tube or leave it unclamped, according to physician's orders. If vomiting is a problem, it may be necessary to leave it unclamped so that aspiration does not occur. The infant should be left undisturbed on his or her right side 30 to 45 min with the bed elevated 15 to 30°.

To remove the tube, first remove the tape at the nose, clamp the tube so that formula does not drip into the pharynx, and remove the tube quickly.[37,38]

Prior to each feeding, gastric contents should be aspirated. If residual fluid measures more than 2 ml, refeed it, and subtract the amount from that ordered for the next feeding. Report to the physician any abdominal distention and excessive amounts of formula remaining in the stomach at the time of the next feeding. Amounts fed may need to be reduced temporarily until the infant's tolerance increases.

Chart time and location of gastric-tube insertion. Record the time, type, and amount of each feeding and the amount of the residual measured prior to the feeding.

Give oral care every 3 h while the tube is in place by wiping the infant's mouth with wet sterile gauze. Check for irritation of the nostril.

During the feeding, talk to the infant and stroke his or her back gently to increase relaxation and comfort. Provide a pacifier so that the infant can associate the feeling of fullness with sucking. If intermittent oral feedings are given, it is preferable to remove the nasogastric tube. This should be discussed with the physician. Hold and cuddle the infant for all oral feedings.

Snacks

Children need additional fluids and nutrients between meals. Confer with the physician (and dietitian) about the patient's specific needs so that snacks—as well as meals—may be planned wisely.[39] Plan a snack time in the midmorning, midafternoon, and evening. This may be an excellent time to increase the caloric intake for a child recuperating from surgery (by giving a milk shake or other high-calorie food), but it must be planned to avoid interference with the appetite at mealtime. Some hospitals use a "five-meal-a-day" plan so that the diet is divided into five small meals rather than three large ones. This may be a good alternative for a child who is not eating well and cannot tolerate a large meal all at once.

The problem eater

Motivation Hospitalization and illness may decrease appetite and increase dependence. This is especially noticeable in the young child who is accustomed to feeding herself and then refuses to do so in the hospital. During the acute phase of her illness, it is appropriate to feed the child. Each meal can be a time to encourage her involvement. As she improves, help her assume a normal position for eating at a table. Use small servings and remind her that she is improving and can now do more for herself.

A school-age child may be motivated by recording his own intake and output. Provide an easily accessible chart at his bedside so that he can write down what he eats and drinks. A star chart or similar poster can also be a good motivational tool.

Give praise liberally for all evidence of improvement in eating habits. Include the doctor in the efforts to encourage a child to eat. The doctor's praise may also be very significant to the patient.

Improving the appearance of food Institutional food prepared in large amounts may not look very appetizing to a young child. Work with the dietitian to make the food trays appear more pleasant. Request small servings for young children. Tray favors and placemats made by volunteers or by patients themselves can brighten up the serving trays.

Offer children the opportunity to request foods they wish to eat or which are special favorites. Hamburgers, pizza, peanut butter and jelly sandwiches, milk shakes, and foods specific to a particular ethnic group can be highly nutritious. If the diet kitchen cannot provide them, encourage parents to do so.

Socialization at mealtime An area with child-sized tables and chairs creates a pleasant eating environment. Sometimes children who are not eating well will be encouraged by seeing others eating. The distraction provided by the conversation of others may also help children forget about their discomforts and fears for a while and encourage them to eat.

When a child cannot leave his room to eat in the playroom, the parents may help by eating with him in the room. Provide guest trays or allow them to bring in their own meals.

Fluids for hospitalized children

Fluid requirements

A child's metabolic rate is much faster than that of an adult. As a consequence, a child needs more fluid in proportion to body weight than an adult. This is especially true of the younger child, whose fastest-growing tissues are the ones most active metabolically. It has been pointed out that, because the younger child weighs so much less than an adult, "there's a greater chance of overhydration through improper intravenous therapy."[40]

Determining fluid needs

The Segar table (Table 17-11) gives guidelines for determining caloric expenditures per kilogram of body weight. Since water needs (in milliliters) are approximately equal to caloric needs (in calories), the Segar guide can be used to determine fluid needs also.

EXAMPLE: How much fluid does a 30-lb child need per day?

Convert pounds to kilograms:

30 lb ÷ 2.2 lb/kg = 13.6 kg

Find weight excess over 10 kg:

13.6 − 10 = 3.6 kg

From Segar formula:

100 kcal/kg for first 10 kg = 100 × 10 = 1000 kcal

50 kcal/kg for each kilogram over 10 kg = 50 × 3.6 = 180 kcal

Total caloric requirement = total fluid requirement = 1000 + 180 = 1180 kcal, or ml per day

This child requires maintenance fluids of 1180 ml per day.

Dehydration results from inadequate fluid intake in relation to normal or excessive fluid losses. When the body is unable to eliminate fluids adequately, fluid retention occurs. Signs of dehydration and fluid retention are compared in Table 17-14.

A child may receive an excessive amount of fluid and tolerate it well as long as electrolyte balance and renal function are normal. Such a situation would be accompanied by passage of a large volume of dilute urine. Treatment involves decreasing the intravenous rate or oral intake.

The physician is responsible for calculating and ordering the fluids needed by the patient, but the nurse should double-check the orders for accuracy and appropriateness according to patient size. Fluids for maintaining adequate balance are made up of water plus electrolytes, and such nonelectrolytes as dextrose or proteins. (Chapter 24 describes fluid and electrolyte balance in children.) The amount and type of fluids required are influenced by diagnosis, general condition, blood chemistry, and intake and output.[41] Consideration must be given not only to maintenance fluid requirements, but also to existing fluid deficits and abnormal, ongoing fluid losses.

Intake and ouput

Measuring fluid intake The nurse must accurately measure fluid intake on every pediatric

Table 17-14 Signs of dehydration and fluid retention

Dehydration	Fluid retention
1. Dry skin and mucous membranes	1. Edema—puffy eyes, face, ankles
2. Depressed fontanel	2. Dyspnea
3. Poor skin turgor	3. Abdominal distention
4. Sunken eyeballs	4. Weight gain
5. Thirst	5. Scanty urine output
6. Elevated temperature or, in severe cases, lowered temperature	6. Elevated blood pressure
7. Increased pulse rate	7. Decreased hematocrit
8. Weight loss	8. Distended neck veins
9. Dark or concentrated urine	
10. Decreased urine output	
11. Exhaustion and collapse	
12. Increased hematocrit	

patient. The child and parents can help by keeping a daily record at the bedside. Transfer this information to the chart and make a cumulative total every 24 h. Fluid intake includes the following:

1. Oral fluids—including ice cream, popsicles, Jello, and so forth
2. Intravenous fluids
3. Oral medications in liquid form
4. Intravenous medications
5. Irrigating fluids

The child can also absorb fluids from a high-humidity environment (mist tent or oxygen hood) or may lose excessive fluid during phototherapy (e.g., for hyperbilirubinemia). Discuss these factors with the physician when fluid needs are being determined.

It is helpful to have a standard list of the amount of fluid contained in various size cups and containers, as shown in Fig. 17-20. Any nurse who removes a tray or soiled cup from a child's room is responsible for reporting or charting the amount taken.

Maintaining "nothing by mouth" It is challenging to care for the child whose fluid intake is restricted. Children may get water from the sink when thirsty. Roommates sometimes share their drinks. Carefully explain the rationale for fluid restriction to the child, the parents, and other patients and families in the same room. Place signs at the door, on the bed, and on the child as reminders (Figs. 17-21 and 17-22).

Fluid output Urine output in children is monitored in a general way by placing a checkmark on the chart each time a patient voids. Keeping accurate measurements of urine is essential when fluid balance is questionable. It is far better to measure urine when it is unnecessary than to overlook a measurement. When uncertain—measure! Have the child void in a bedpan, urinal, or a potty chair or place a collecting device in the toilet.

Measure and record each voiding and calculate 24-h cumulative totals on any child who is:

1. Receiving intravenous fluids
2. Receiving medication which requires urinary output for excretion (to be sure that the child will not

Figure 17-20 Chart of fluid volume of various containers appears on the flow sheet of each chart at Rochester Methodist Hospital to facilitate recording of fluid intake. (*Courtesy of Rochester Methodist Hospital, Rochester, Minn.*)

Coffee mug	240 ml	Creamer	15 ml
Fruit juice cup	120 ml	Isolation bowl	270 ml
Soup bowl	240 ml	All soft drinks	360 ml
Styrofoam cup	240 ml	(12-oz can)	
Disposable cup	120 ml	Milk shake (7 oz)	210 ml
Milk:		Sherbet-ice cream	
8 oz.	240 ml	(Dixie cup)	65 ml
4 oz.	120 ml	Gelatin	200 ml
Isolation cup	210 ml	Popsicle	120 ml

Figure 17-21 Nurse placing an NPO sign at the patient's door. (*Photo by Brian Kaihoi.*)

be overdosed by an accumulation of medication) or which affects renal function

3. Dehydrated, retaining fluids, or in acid-base disequilibrium
4. Has a known or suspected impairment of renal function
5. Within the first 24 h after surgery or longer as necessary

All types of fluid output must be measured to give an accurate picture of fluid needs. Measure fluid from drains, chest tubes, nasogastric tubes, liquid stools, and emesis.

Weighing diapers Diapers are weighed to determine infant output. Use a metric scale and weigh the diaper immediately; do not let it dry out. Subtract the weight of a dry diaper from the wet one. The difference (in grams) is approximately equal to the amount of urine (in milliliters) in the wet diaper. One milliliter weighs approximately one gram. Record the amount of urine on the chart and indicate that it was obtained by weighing the diaper.

Body weight Body weight is an indicator of fluid needs and should be measured daily before breakfast for any patient on accurate intake and output. Weight is always obtained on admission. A later weight is required, however, if a child receives intravenous fluids or begins retaining fluids.

Methods of encouraging fluid intake Pain or drug therapy which causes drowsiness or irritability may adversely affect the child's ability to

cooperate and willingness to drink. A thorough assessment of all the reasons why the child's intake is diminished must be done before appropriate intervention can be initiated.

Encourage the child to take oral fluids by offering choices. Popsicles, ice cream, milk shakes, slushes, and juices provide variety. Use small cups—even medicine glasses—rather than large containers. Give pain medication judiciously to increase comfort before encouraging intake. Star charts, "cup" posters (the child makes paper symbols and pastes one on the poster for each cup of liquid he or she drinks), and tea parties in the playroom are other possible activities. Effective approaches should be documented on the Kardex nursing care plan. It is well worth the time spent getting a child to drink if intravenous therapy can be avoided.

Figure 17-22 NPO sign to be placed on a child's bed or back as a reminder to prevent oral intake. (*Courtesy of Teresa Atkinson.*)

I can't eat or drink today. I'm going to surgery.

Intravenous fluid therapy

Intravenous (IV) fluid therapy is used to:

1. Provide adequate fluids to the child who cannot take them orally
2. Provide a means for safe and effective administration of parenteral medications
3. Correct electrolyte imbalance

Initiation of intravenous therapy Because children have smaller veins than adults, different sites for intravenous infusions may be used. Scalp veins are often used in infants. Superficial veins of the arms, hands, and lower legs may be used on a child of any age.

Of special concern to the nurse is prevention of circulatory overload and subsequent heart failure. To ensure the child's safety, the nurse

Figure 17-23 The nurse is preparing intravenous fluid. The clear plastic chamber (volume control chamber) and the pump are safety features to control rate and volume. (*Photo by Brian Kaihoi.*)

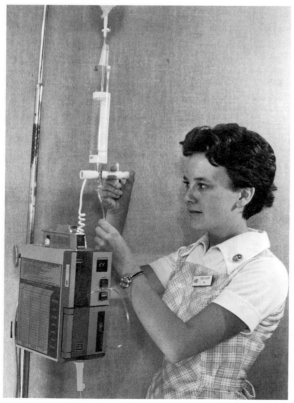

must provide the correct equipment, monitor the infusion closely, and maintain the patency of the infusion.

Intravenous fluids are usually available in plastic bags or glass bottles in sizes of 250 ml, 500 ml, and 1000 ml. A volume control chamber, attached to the intravenous fluid container, allows only small amounts (100 to 150 ml maximum) to be available for infusion at a given time (Fig. 17-23). A stopcock between the chamber and the IV bag allows the nurse to control the flow to the chamber and is a safety feature in preventing fluid overload. Intravenous infusion sets have either the standard drip chamber (15 gtt/ml) or the minidrip chamber (60 gtt/ml). Minidrip sets are preferable for use with children so that the flow may be regulated to a very slow rate.

Intravenous tubing is available in various lengths and with Y connections to allow IV medications to be attached and infused as needed. Needles used include scalp-vein needles, short plastic needles for standard infusions, and intravenous catheters for infusion into a cutdown site (Fig. 17-24).

An infusion pump is very helpful in delivering intravenous fluids at a controlled even rate (Fig. 17-23). The pump gives added safety to pediatric infusions by helping to prevent fluid overload. Some pumps can infuse at rates as low as one drop per minute. Audible and visible alarms alert the nurse to an empty bag, occlusion of the tubing, high resistance due to a positional change, or infiltration of the intravenous needle.

The nurse's role in starting intravenous therapy is described below. It is assumed that the physician or specially prepared nurse will perform the venipuncture.

1. Prepare the child and parents for the procedure. Describe how it will feel and the child's expected activity level during the infusion. Remind the child that the needle will not hurt after the initial venipuncture. Show the child the equipment. Begin the procedure soon after preparation is completed.
2. Wash hands well.
3. Gather and prepare equipment (Table 17-15).
4. Bring the child to a treatment room away from other patients.
5. Get adequate assistance: one nurse to help restrain the child, one to handle equipment, and the

Figure 17-24 Various needles used in intravenous therapy.

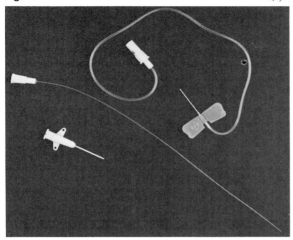

physician or intravenous nurse to perform the venipuncture. It is generally best to have the parents wait outside and comfort the child afterwards, unless they or the child insist on their presence.[43]

6. Prepare syringe of sterile saline in case needed to check site.

7. Connect the tubing and volume chamber to the IV fluid and hang on the pole. Fill volume chamber and clear tubing of air.

8. Mount pump on pole and check alarm and battery. Plug in but leave switch off until needed.

9. Help with site determination so that the dominant hand may be free for play, thumb-sucking, or eating. Millam advises that, "If infusion time is to be long-term and successive starts are anticipated over a number of days, beginning with the superficial vessels in the hand will permit progressively upward selection of later sites."[44]

10. Position the child and talk to the child gently during site selection. Do not restrain until absolutely necessary for needle insertion. Tell the child it's "okay to cry" but that he or she can help by being very still during the procedure.

11. If an extremity is used, assist physician to secure it to an arm board. Place gauze pads under tape to decrease discomfort and prevent skin abrasion. Check circulation to make sure that tape is not too tight. Scalp site must be shaved and head positioned securely for needle insertion.

12. Site will be cleansed and the needle inserted. Apply small strips of tape to secure the needle.

Figure 17-25 shows a method of taping the needle at the site.

13. Cover site with one half of a medicine cup and tape the cup in place or wrap site and board with gauze or stockinette (Fig. 17-26) to cover the site and prevent need for restraint. The site must be checked frequently for signs of infiltration or phlebitis, so it must be accessible as well as protected.

14. Tape connections throughout tubing.

15. Attach intravenous line to pump, set rate, and switch "ON."

16. Comfort the child and have the parents come in to be with him or her.

17. Check pump rate by counting the drops infused per minute.

18. Return child to room, and provide a pleasant activity.

19. Clean and replace equipment used.

Maintaining the IV site A major part of the nurse's role is that of maintaining the site after intravenous therapy is initiated. The younger and more active the child, the more difficult it is to maintain the site. Being aware of the possible problems is essential.

Infiltration is the accumulation of intravenous fluid in extravascular tissue. It is the most common complication of an infusion and occurs

Table 17-15 Equipment needed for intravenous therapy

IV fluid (check type, amount. Make sure it is clear and free of foreign material.)
Tubing with minidrip chamber, needles, and scalp vein sets (Have a variety of sizes available.)
3-ml syringe
Bottle of parenteral normal saline
Volume control chamber
Tourniquet or rubber band (used as a tourniquet for scalp-vein infusions)
Safety razor
Tape
Padded arm board
Gauze roll or stockinette
Betadine or alcohol (for cleansing site)
Antibiotic or iodine ointment for application to site after insertion*
One half of a med cup padded with tape for site protection (Fig. 17-26)
3 by 3-in gauze pads, cotton balls
Infusion pump
Intravenous pole
Light source

* **Source:** Millam [44].

Figure 17-25 A method of securing an intravenous needle for infusion. (*Courtesy of Vicra Division, Travenol Laboratories, Inc.*)

(*A*) The intravenous catheter is inserted into the vein.

(*B*) To secure the catheter properly, place a 5-in long, ½-in wide piece of tape under the wings of the catheter, adhesive side up.

(*C*) Fold each end forward in the direction of the catheter insertion forming a V configuration. A second piece of tape should be placed over the catheter hub. The tape is not placed over or near the skin puncture site.

(*D*) Topical ointment can be applied after the catheter is securely taped to the patient.

(*E*) The skin puncture site should be covered with a sterile dressing.

(*F*) The dressing can be removed easily for site inspection and maintenance without risk of disturbing or cutting the tape securing the catheter hub.

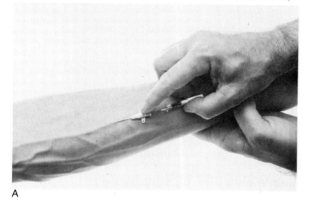
A

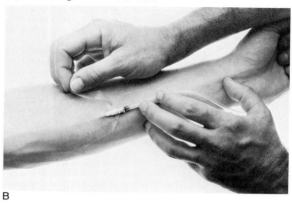
B

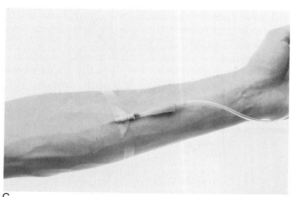
C

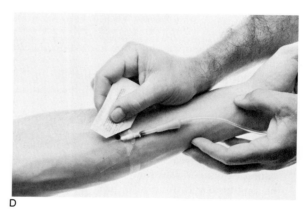
D

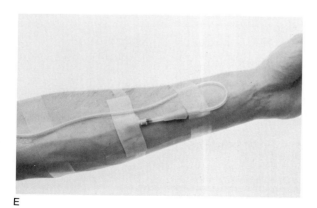
E

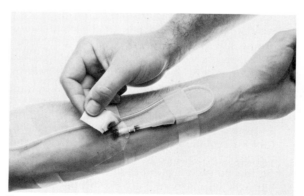
F

when the venipuncture device penetrates the vein and the wall beyond or becomes dislodged during normal insertion.[45]

Phlebitis is an inflammation of the vein. Some factors which contribute to the development of phlebitis include:

1. Chemical irritation by the intravenous solution
2. Mechanical irritation by the intravenous device
3. Allergic reaction to the intravenous device
4. Trauma during venipuncture
5. Infection via skin defect or contamination of intravenous apparatus[46]

Although the signs of phlebitis and infiltration are similar, there are a few differences which are important to note (Table 17-16).

In maintaining the intravenous site, the nurse must maintain the correct flow rate, prevent infection, and keep the needle in place. Specifically, the nurse must take the following steps:

1. Check and record the intravenous flow rate at least every hour.
2. Watch for kinks in the tubing and position the child so that he is not lying on the tubing. Assist the parent who wishes to hold the child and keep the tubing free of obstruction.
3. If flow rate is affected by normal movement:
   a. Use sandbags to prevent the infant's head from resting on the scalp-vein site.
   b. Use a short, padded and lightweight arm board. Secure it to the skin with adhesive padded with gauze.[47]
   c. Secure armboard to bed with pin or tape if necessary.
4. Observe the site at least every hour for signs of infiltration. Stop the intravenous flow and call the physician or venipuncture nurse if infiltration occurs. Since certain drugs and electrolytes are extremely irritating and can cause tissue damage, infiltration should be the signal to stop infusion.
5. Perform site care according to the hospital's infection control policies. This usually means changing the tape, cleansing with antiseptic, and applying an iodine or antibiotic ointment at the site every 24 to 48 h.
6. Secure the needle well at the site. If the flow seems to be obstructed, the bevel of the needle may be against the vein wall; a small piece of cotton placed under the hub of the needle may position it properly.

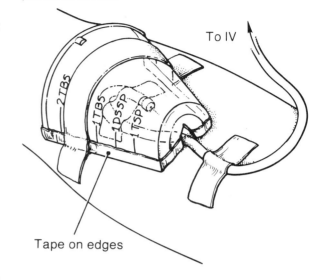

Figure 17-26 Half a medication cup to be used for protecting an intravenous site. the edges should be padded for comfort.

To IV

2 TBS

1 TBS

1 DSSP

1 TSP

Tape on edges

7. Restrain the child's other extremity (i.e., the opposite leg or arm) if it interferes with the intravenous infusion.

Cutdown At times it is impossible to find an appropriate venipuncture site on a small child and a cutdown (incision into a vein) becomes necessary. This is a sterile procedure which can be performed in the nursing unit. In addition to standard IV fluid equipment, a cutdown tray, sterile gloves, masks, and an intravenous catheter are needed. The physician incises the skin, dissects a vein free, inserts the sterile catheter, sutures it in place, and attaches the intravenous

Table 17-16 Signs of infiltration vs. phlebitis

Infiltration	Phlebitis
Blanching	Redness
Cold skin	Hot skin
Pain	Palpable, cordlike vein
Sensation of heaviness	Pain
Swelling	Sensation of heaviness
Tenderness	Swelling
	Tenderness

Adapted from "Fundamentals of IV Maintenance," programmed instruction, *American Journal of Nursing*, July 1979, p. 1275.

tubing. The ankle is a common site for a cutdown on an infant.[48] Check the specific hospital procedure for information about site care. Observe the site and the skin above it frequently for signs of phlebitis, since the catheter may extend several inches into the vein. The physician is responsible for discontinuing a cutdown.

Discontinuing an intravenous infusion Explain to the child what is going to be done and reassure him or her that taking the needle out does not "hurt" as it did during insertion. Allow the child to assist in tape removal.

To discontinue the infusion, clamp off the tubing and remove the tape. Hold an alcohol sponge (or sterile gauze—alcohol stings and has an anticoagulant property) over the site and withdraw the needle. Elevate the extremity and apply pressure with a gauze pad over the site of skin puncture and over the site of entry into the vein which may be 1 to 2 cm higher in the extremity. Maintain pressure for 1 to 2 min. Place an adhesive bandage over the site. If a large-gauge needle (no. 19 or larger) was used for the infusion, a pressure dressing (gauze pad secured tightly with gauze bandage) may be necessary for 10 to 15 min to stop the bleeding.[49]

Safety during intravenous therapy There are a number of areas of concern during intravenous therapy with children. The following are important to carry out:

1. Use a volume control chamber on all pediatric infusions except when a patient is receiving more fluid per hour than the chamber will hold.
2. Do not put more than a 2-h supply of fluid into the volume chamber at any time.
3. As a general rule, the following guidelines may be used for amounts of fluid to be hung: No more than 150 ml for a child under 2 years. No more than 250 ml for a child under 5 years. No more than 500 ml for a child under 10 years.[50]
4. Change fluid and tubing every 24 h and label with date, time changed, and nurse's initials.
5. The physician's order should include the type of fluid and a specific rate—not "KVO" (keep vein open).[51]
6. Frequently check restraints and tape for effectiveness and adequate circulation. Release restraints every 2 h and do range of motion exercises, unless contraindicated by the intravenous site.

7. Frequently check extremities and scalp for signs of pressure sores.
8. Tape connections and the rate control clamp to prevent tampering by a curious child.[52]
9. Supervise a child who has an intravenous infusion at all times when out of bed.
10. Do not develop a false sense of security when the intravenous pump is used. Double check the pumping rate by your watch. Use an *air eliminating filter with infusion tubing when a pump is to be used.* Some pumps will pump air as well as fluid.[53] Know the pump's limitations and check it frequently.
11. Throughout intravenous therapy remember that you are caring for a child and not an intravenous bag. Observe the child's general condition, vital signs, and emotional response to the infusion. Provide comfort and diversional activities; remember that a child can be up in a chair or wagon and have a change of scenery even with an intravenous infusion.
12. *Document* carefully: date, time, type and amount of fluid hung; rate and volume infused every hour; site care and condition of the site; accurate intake and output; daily weight.

Heparin lock The heparin lock is an ideal temporary measure for maintaining an infusion site for intermittent use. There is less chance of fluid overload and phlebitis, and the child is more mobile and comfortable.[54]

Heparin sodium is an anticoagulant now available in a Heparin Lock Flush Solution (Wyeth). A heparin lock infusion set (a needle and a short catheter with injection cap) is inserted into a vein, usually in the arm, and taped securely. Dilute heparin sodium is injected via the injection hub in a quantity sufficient to fill the set to the needle tip. The dilute heparin must be reinstilled after each use (e.g., after an intravenous medication is infused or blood is drawn).[57] For children a heparin solution of 10 units per milliliter may be adequate to keep the lock open.[56] If a drug to be administered is incompatible with heparin, the entire heparin lock set should be flushed with sterile water or normal saline before and after the medication is administered; following the second flush the dilute heparin may be reinstilled into the heparin lock set.[57]

Contraindications to a heparin lock include

an allergy to heparin or the presence of any type of bleeding disorder.

To maintain a heparin lock the nurse must check the site frequently, give site care, and protect the site by wrapping, using a medicine cup, or both.

Oxygenation

Methods of providing moist oxygen

When a respiratory problem is identified, one important treatment may be the provision of oxygen with moisture. Increased oxygen in the inspired air facilitates the transfer of oxygen to the blood in the lungs. Added moisture prevents drying of mucous membranes and may help in decreasing inflammatory processes in the airway.

Oxygen hood The hood is an effective device for administering high levels of oxygen to an infant. The cylindrical plastic hood fits over the infant's neck and surrounds the head. Vital signs and other care can be given without affecting the oxygen concentration. The hood allows administration of oxygen in concentrations up to 100%. Since it covers the head, nursing responsibilities include maintaining a warm environment and monitoring the infant's temperature so that oxygen requirements are not unduly increased by efforts to stay warm. The moist oxygen should be warmed [31 to 34°C (87.8 to 93.2°F)] to prevent cold stress. An oxygen hood, (Fig. 25-4) has an attached thermometer which constantly registers the temperature of the hood air.

Oxygen mask or face tent Moist oxygen can also be administered through masks or face tents. They are convenient for older children, but patient and family cooperation in their use is essential. Although the percentage of oxygen delivered is variable, masks are usually adequate for the administration of moist oxygen during the immediate postoperative period. A face tent (Fig. 17-27) is better tolerated by most children than the face mask because it fits loosely and does not resemble the anesthesia mask, which is frightening to some children. The face tent is held near the child's face while the child sits with his parent or is placed near him in bed. As the child moves in his sleep, the family member in attendance helps by moving the tent with

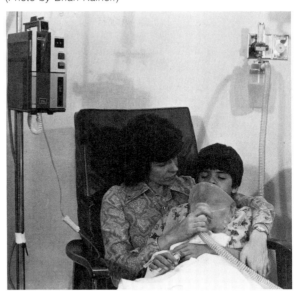

Figure 17-27 Oxygen face tent on the child. He can be held by his mother despite the presence of the equipment. (*Photo by Brian Kaihoi.*)

him. Although straps are available to secure the tent to the child's face, they usually are not tolerated well.

Mist tent A mist tent is a large plastic canopy which can be used for a child of any age. It provides oxygen in high humidity and allows the child freedom of movement. Its small counterpart, the croupette, can be used with infants and children under 3.

Mist tents are available with a nebulizer for the water, and may have an open-topped canopy or closed canopy with an air-conditioning unit (Fig. 17-28). In the first type, the top is open to allow circulation of the air and escape of the carbon dioxide. Since oxygen is heavier than room air, it settles to the lower part of the tent. Do not place a towel or blanket over the open top to keep the mist from escaping. Though such a covering does not totally prevent the escape of carbon dioxide, it creates a "stuffy" atmosphere. If a greater mist concentration is needed, an ultrasonic nebulizer may be attached through the zippered opening or the top of the canopy. Some tents have ice troughs which may be used to decrease the tent temperature and cool a feverish child.

Figure 17-28 Ohio Pediatric Aerosol Tent. (*Courtesy of Ohio Medical Products, Madison, Wis.*)

The mist tent with air conditioner cools and circulates the air for removal of carbon dioxide. This type of tent is essential in a nursing unit which is not air-conditioned. Any type of plastic tent becomes very warm in a warm environment.

Nursing care activities for a child in a mist tent are as follows:

1. Prepare the child and the parents by age-appropriate means:
   a. Set the tent up. Let the child feel the mist and hear the sound inside.
   b. Place a toy inside.
   c. Have a parent extend head inside.
   d. Explain how, why, and when mist tent is to be used.
2. Prior to placing the child inside, turn on the oxygen flow for 10 to 15 min so that it is mist-filled and cool.

3. Place the child inside with a "safe" toy. See later section on fire prevention.
4. Tuck the top and sides of the tent under the edge of the mattress. Secure the bottom edge by folding a blanket over the end and securing it under the mattress on each side.
5. Check the oxygen concentration periodically—every 4 to 24 h, according to the respiratory therapy policy of the hospital—and record on the chart.
6. Check the nebulizer or water reservoir and refill with sterile distilled water every 8 h or more often as needed.
7. Change the child's clothing and bed linen when it is damp. Use a bath blanket on top of the bottom sheet. (A blanket is more comfortable and warm in the tent because it absorbs some of the moisture.)
8. Organize nursing care to decrease the frequency with which the tent is opened.
9. Set times for the child to be out—i.e., during meals, every 2 h to be held—according to the patient's needs and tolerance for room air. Return the child to the tent if signs of respiratory distress develop. (See Chap. 25, for signs of respiratory distress.)
10. Keep the tent oxygen on if the child is out for a brief period. For longer periods, turn it off and then flush with oxygen 15 min before the child returns to it.
11. In transporting a child in bed with the tent, raise the sides of the tent to prevent hypoxia when the oxygen is turned off.
12. Monitor the child's physical response, color, rate and type of respirations, and other vital signs frequently.
13. Give the child attention and diversion. Play with the child even though he or she is in the tent.
14. Change the tent and equipment according to hospital policy. Mist tents readily become contaminated with bacteria.

Ultrasonic nebulizer The ultrasonic nebulizer provides high humidity in very fine droplets which are easily absorbed and helpful in resolving inflammation of the airway (Fig. 17-6). Because the ultrasonic nebulizer provides large amounts of easily absorbed moisture, some authors recommend that it not be used for small children because it may alter fluid balance. If an infant receives treatment with an ultrasonic nebulizer, monitor the infant's weight and vital signs frequently.

Safety factors in oxygen therapy

Maintaining oxygen saturation Room air contains approximately 20 percent oxygen. Forty percent oxygen is generally considered therapeutic, though physicians may order higher concentrations in certain situations. In order to maintain a saturation of approximately 40 percent, the following flow meter rates are recommended:

2 to 4 liters per minute—infant incubator
5 to 8 liters per minute—croupette
10 to 12 liters per minute—larger tents[58]

Monitoring oxygenation When a patient is receiving oxygen therapy, the oxygen concentration must be monitored with an oxygen analyzer at least every 8 h. Oxygen for the newborn must be monitored continuously. For older children periodic analysis is usually sufficient.

To accurately determine the oxygen content of the patient's environment, place the analyzer tube near the child's face—not just inside the top of a mist tent or isolette. The analysis should be done when the tent or isolette has been closed for at least 15 min.

Since various types of oxygen monitors are available, check the instructions for use printed on the side of the monitor. To ensure accuracy each monitor must be calibrated (i.e., checked for the accuracy of its reading) periodically according to the manufacturer's instructions.

Chart the results of oxygen analysis on the patient's medical record and indicate calibration of the monitor as necessary.

Oxygen toxicity Prolonged exposure to high oxygen tensions can be damaging to some body tissues and functions.[59] Use of oxygen for a long period, or high concentrations of oxygen (70% to 80%) for a short time, may result in pulmonary changes.[60] There is evidence to indicate damage to lung capillaries causing diffuse microhemorrhagic changes, diminished mucus flow, and inactivation of surfactant. Ventilation is gradually impaired as these changes occur.[61]

The premature infant treated with high concentrations of oxygen can develop *retrolental fibroplasia*. In this condition of the eyes vasoconstriction of the blood vessels of the retina progresses to endothelial damage, obliteration of the vessels, and eventual blindness.[62]

The nurse who cares for a child receiving long-term or high concentrations of oxygen must be alert to signs of oxygen toxicity: depressed respirations, somnolence, and coma. Check vital signs and oxygen concentration every 1 to 4 h (or continuously in the newborn and premature infant). Periodic blood gas determinations are made to monitor arterial oxygen levels.[63]

Infection control during oxygen therapy The high humidity environment used in oxygen administration provides a good medium for bacterial growth. The following steps are helpful in maintaining cleanliness of the equipment.

1. Change all equipment every 5 to 7 days.
2. When needed, add sterile distilled water to the water reservoir or nebulizer in the following manner:
   a. Discard any remaining water first.
   b. Rinse nebulizer and tubing before adding sterile distilled water.
   Distilled water is used in respiratory equipment because the minerals and salts in tap H_2O or saline are damaging.
3. Take periodic cultures of the equipment according to recommendations of the infection control committee.

Accumulation of moisture With the mask, hood, or ultrasonic nebulizer, there may be accumulation of moisture in the tubing connecting the oxygen source to the equipment. This interferes with oxygen flow, makes a disturbing "bubbling" noise, and can soak the patient thoroughly if the tubing is moved. Watch the tubing for moisture accumulation and drain the water into a basin rather than returning it to the nebulizer.

Fire prevention Because oxygen supports combustion, several safety principles must be adhered to during its use:

1. *Do not* use electrical equipment in an oxygen tent.
2. Use all-cotton clothing and bed linens to prevent production of static electricity.
3. Do not use alcohol or oil products on a child or infant during oxygen therapy.
4. Choose toys carefully so that they meet the above guidelines (i.e., no toys which produce sparks).
5. Check electrical cords in the room for frayed wires.

6. No smoking by visitors.
7. Place signs in the room, on the bed, and at the door of the room indicating that oxygen is in use and necessary safety precautions must be taken.

Techniques to improve oxygenation

Positioning Elevate the head of the bed to facilitate an open airway and chest expansion. This may be accomplished for an infant by elevating the mattress with a blanket or pillow or positioning the child in an infant seat. Do not use a pillow under the head of an infant or young child. A pillow may push the head forward and obstruct the trachea. Elevating the mattress provides a more physiological position. If an infant seat is used, secure it with a sandbag and strap the infant in place to prevent falling.

Suctioning Keep a bulb suction in the crib of an infant for aspiration of mucus and emesis from the child's mouth and nose. Turn the infant to the side to suction so that obstructing fluids are more accessible. Rinse the bulb with water after each use. Replace with a clean one daily.

If congestion is severe, use a mechanical suction machine with a catheter small enough to pass easily through the nose and into the child's throat. Table 17-17 lists specific steps in suctioning a child.

Chest physiotherapy Chest physiotherapy is used to prevent or treat conditions in which there is excessive mucus in the bronchi which is not being removed by normal coughing or ciliary action.[65] Techniques used include deep breathing, coughing, postural drainage, percussion, vibration, and suctioning when necessary.

Table 17-17 Suctioning the child

1. Use normal saline for lubrication.
2. Clamp the catheter during insertion. Pass the catheter through the nose to the back of the throat.
3. Unclamp and suction during catheter removal.
4. Suction quickly (5–10 s maximum in the airway) and allow the child to catch his breath before reinserting the catheter.[64]
5. Rinse the catheter in saline and reinsert.
6. Suction only in the back of the throat. Do not perform deep tracheal suction. There is danger of laryngospasm and apnea, especially in young infants.
7. Suction the mouth as needed.

Deep breathing Have the child take several deep breaths. Ask him or her to blow up a balloon or use "blow bottles" or incentive spirometer (Tri-Flow R) to stimulate deep breathing.[66] Make a game of blowing objects across the bedside table.

Coughing Encourage periodic coughing during deep breathing as well as during other components of chest physiotherapy. Have the child sit up. Encircle the child's chest with your hands and compress the rib cage as he or she tries to cough. Splint any abdominal or chest incisions with a folded bath blanket or towel to decrease discomfort during coughing.

Postural drainage Position the infant over a pillow or elevate the foot of the bed 15 to 25° to encourage removal of secretions by gravity. Position the older child over the elevated knee rest of the bed.

Postural drainage is especially helpful with the infant who cannot cough or deep breathe on command. The following nursing actions are needed:

1. Raise the end of the mattress by using a towel or blanket roll.
2. Position the infant on abdomen with head down for 10 to 15 min. Support the head with a pillow or blanket roll to prevent slipping.
3. Suction nose and mouth as drainage accumulates and at the end of the procedure.
4. Repeat every 4 h or as needed.
5. Chart: (a) Time, (b) length of procedure, (c) type and amount of mucus, (d) suctioning done, (e) child's response.

Percussion Percussion (or clapping) involves cupping the hands or using an object to trap air over portions of the chest wall to loosen secretions during postural drainage. See Fig. 17-29 for positions and areas to percuss to achieve drainage of specific portions of the lungs. The physician will determine which areas need percussion. Vibration may be done in conjunction with percussion.

Special precautions Chest physiotherapy requires the following precautions:

1. It should be performed an hour before meals to improve nutritional intake. If procedures must be done after meals, delay at least 1 h to avoid vomiting.

Figure 17-29 Positions for postural drainage and percussion. (*A*) Cupped hand position for percussion. Percussion is done in all positions for 1½ to 2 min. (*B*) Hand position for vibration. Vibration is done two to three times in positions 1 to 9. (*Demonstrator: Surina Geoffroy, R.P.T., California Medical Center, Los Angeles. Photographer: Theresa Friedrich.*)

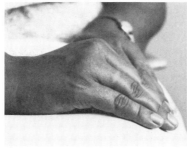 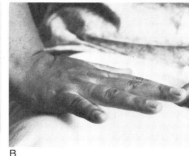

A   B

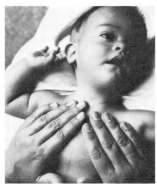 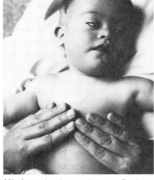 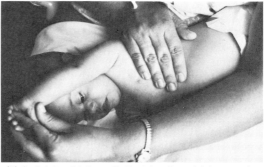

(*3*) Left lateral lobes. Patient is placed lying on the right side with left arm overhead. Head is lowered 45°.

(*1*) Anterior upper lobes. Patient is supine.

(*2*) Anterior lower lobes. Patient is supine with head lowered 45°.

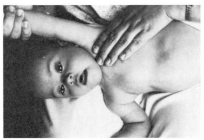 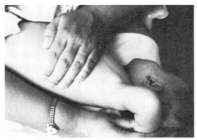 

(*4*) Left lingual lobe. Patient is placed with half side lying on right with left arm over head. Head is lowered 45°.

(*5*) Right lateral lobe. Patient is placed lying on right side with left arm over head. Head is lowered 45°.

(*6*) Right middle lobe. Patient is placed with half side lying on left with right arm over head. Head is lowered 15°.

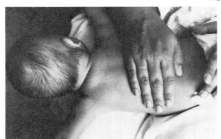  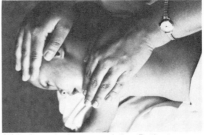

(*7*) Posterior lower lobes. Patient in prone position with head down 45°.

(*8*) Right posterior upper lobe. Patient prone with left shoulder elevated 30°.

(*9*) Left posterior upper lobe. Patient prone with left shoulder elevated 45°.

2. Modify length of treatment and positions for drainage according to the child's tolerance and physical limitations.
3. Do not percuss over the kidneys, lower back, or clavicle.[67]
4. Use cupped hands—do not slap—conforming to the contour of the chest and percuss over the rib cage. A rubber bottle stopper, small anesthesia mask, padded stethoscope head, or 2 to 3 fingers tented together should be used for the infant.[68]
5. If postoperative pain interferes with chest physiotherapy, give pain medication approximately 30 min before the procedure.

Cardiopulmonary resuscitation

Cardiopulmonary resuscitation for infants and children is patterned after that for adults with a few modifications to accommodate size differences.

If you are the rescuer In an emotionally charged situation like a respiratory or cardiac arrest, speed is essential but accuracy of diagnosis is equally important. The first step is to make sure resuscitation is needed.

1. Shake the child, shout, call his name. Slap the feet of an infant. To determine if there has been respiratory arrest, place the child in a horizontal position

and listen at the nose and mouth to hear or feel whether air is being exhaled. This allows you to focus on actual ventilation rather than chest movements, which may not be achieving ventilation.
2. Open the airway by extending the neck slightly. Shout for help simultaneously. Note the time. Avoid hyperextending the neck of infants and small children. The tissues of the trachea are very soft and pliable; if hyperextended they may obstruct the airway.
3. Carry out rescue breathing (mouth to mouth) and ventilate four times. Use:
   a. Puffs of air from cheeks for infants
   b. Small breaths for young children
   c. Normal breaths for children over 10 years old
   With a young child, cover the mouth and nose to ventilate; release to allow exhalation. Forward traction on the mandible keeps the root of the tongue from obstructing the airway in the hypopharyngeal area.
4. Palpate the carotid or femoral artery for pulse.
5. If there is no pulse, begin cardiac massage (see Table 17-18).
6. Continue cardiopulmonary resuscitation until the child begins breathing or until relieved by another rescuer.

If you are the helper Your job is to mobilize the resources of the hospital and to supplement the actions of the rescuer:

1. Get additional help by following hospital protocol.
2. Bring emergency equipment to the bedside—suction, oxygen, medications.
3. Connect manual resuscitation bag (e.g., Ambu) and mask and ventilate the child.
   a. Stand at the child's head.
   b. Pull forward on the angles of the lower jaw to keep the tongue from obstructing the airway.
   c. Hold the mask securely with the thumb over the mask at the bridge of the nose, the forefinger of the mask at the chin, and three fingers under the jaw to keep it forward.
   d. Gently deflate the bag and watch for the rise of the chest to check adequacy.
   e. Release the bag quickly.
   f. Use caution to prevent overinflation of the lungs. (Ventilation with bag and mask should be assumed by specially trained personnel as soon as possible.)
4. Check femoral or temporal pulse for adequate compression. Check pupils for reaction to light.

Table 17-18 Cardiac massage of children

1. Ventilate after every five compressions (watch the chest rise to determine adequacy of ventilation).
2. Compress the center of the sternum. In a child, the ventricles of the heart lie higher in the chest than in an adult. For this reason, the center of the sternum is recommended for safe, effective compression.[69] Depth of compression is based on the child's size (ages given are suggestions):
   a. Newborn or small infant: Compress $\frac{1}{2}$ to $\frac{3}{4}$ in at 80 to 100 per minute. Place thumbs on sternum with hands around chest (Fig. 17-30).
   b. Older infant: Compress $\frac{3}{4}$ to $1\frac{1}{2}$ in at 80 per minute. Use two fingers on child's chest with hand of solid flat object placed under the back.
   c. Child of 1 to 4 years: rate of 80 per minute. Use heel of one hand.[70]
   d. Child over 4 years: rate of 60 to 80 per minute. Use heel of one hand over heel of the other.
3. Remember that the purpose of compression is to produce blood flow to vital organs by compression of the heart between the sternum and the spinal cord. Adequate compression is indicated by the presence of femoral, carotid, or temporal pulse.

Figure 17-30 During cardiopulmonary resuscitation of a small infant, to compress the middle of the sternum the thumbs are used (*A*) side by side or (*B*) one on top of the other. Fingers encircling the chest provide back support. The pressure should be applied only with the thumbs. The rib cage should not be squeezed.

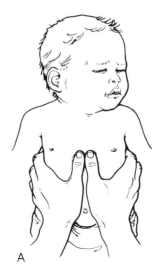
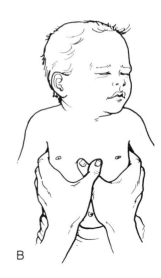

A   B

5. When relieved, set up intravenous infusion equipment and other items as needed.
6. Document all activities. Be very aware of time and length of resuscitation effort.

Throughout any resuscitation effort the child must be checked frequently to see if he or she is breathing or if the heart is beating on its own.

During cardiopulmonary resuscitation an infant's stomach can easily become distended with air. Compress the stomach periodically during the procedure, but not simultaneously with chest compression. If decompression is not effective, consider passing a nasogastric tube.

Locate all emergency equipment soon after arriving on any nursing unit and be familiar with steps in cardiopulmonary resuscitation. Be prepared to act quickly.

Vital signs

Temperature

Average normal temperatures for children are shown in Table 17-19. Variations of a degree or more can occur after activity, crying, or periods of excitement. There are also slight differences in temperature according to age. Since the body temperature reflects metabolic rate, heat production steadily declines as the child grows. During the first year, for example, the average normal temperature is 37.5°C (99.5°F). This de-

creases to 37.2°C (99.0°F) at 3 years. Females have a slightly higher temperature than males.

Taking the temperature Ideally a child should rest in bed 5 min or more before a temperature is taken. However, this is not always possible. The nurse should stay with the child throughout the procedure. Afterward, be sure the child's thermometer holder is labeled with his or her name, room, and bed number, as well as the type of temperature taken. Wash the thermometer with soap under cold running water after each use. Change the thermometer weekly or more often according to infection control procedures at the hospital. In charting temperatures, indicate *R* or *A* if rectal or axillary rather than oral is taken.

Rectal method Take a rectal temperature if a child is under 6 years of age. However, there are several exceptions. The rectal method should be

Table 17-19 Average normal temperatures for children

	Celsius	Fahrenheit
Rectal	37.6°C (37.2–37.8)	99.6°F (99–100)
Oral	37°C (36.7–37.2)	98.6°F (98–99)
Axillary	36.3°C (36.1–36.7)	97.4°F (97–98)

Source: S. M. Tucker et al. [71].

avoided if the patient faces rectal surgery, has diarrhea, or suffers from other rectal problems.

An oral or axillary temperature may be substituted if the child has grown accustomed to either method or finds the rectal method unduly frightening.

Finally, another exception is the newborn. The first temperature should be rectal so that the nurse can check for imperforate anus. Subsequent temperatures as a neonate should be axillary.

Every method starts with shaking the thermometer down below 35.6°C (96°F). After that, the rectal procedure is as follows:

1. Lubricate the thermometer, which has a rounded bulb, with a water-soluble lubricant.
2. Position the child on the abdomen or side. The infant may be laid on the back, side, or abdomen (Fig. 17-31).
3. Look at the anus and insert the thermometer the length of the bulb.
4. Hold the thermometer in place for 1 to 3 min until the mercury stops rising.
5. Keep a diaper over the infant's genitalia because the child may be stimulated to void.
6. Withdraw the thermometer, read the temperature, and wipe the child's rectal area with a tissue to remove the lubricant.

Figure 17-31 Taking an infant's rectal temperature. Thermometer is steadied by little finger and fingers holding it, while opposite hand restrains feet and legs.

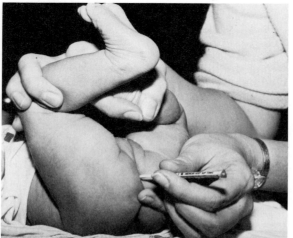

Oral method The oral thermometer is slightly pointed. It is to be used for children 6 years of age and older.

1. After shaking it down, insert the thermometer under the child's tongue. Tell the child to keep his lips closed during the procedure and not to bite the thermometer. (Be certain he has not just had a meal, snack, or cold drink!)
2. Do not let the child move around the room with a thermometer in his mouth. It is best to keep the child seated or lying down. *Stay with him.*
3. After about 3 min, remove the thermometer and record the reading.

Axillary method A clean oral or rectal thermometer should be used.

1. After shaking down the thermometer, insert it under the child's arm in the axilla and hold it in place with the child's arm at his side. Do not allow movement.
2. After 3 to 5 min, when the mercury has stopped rising, remove the thermometer and record the reading.

Electronic thermometers These are safe and effective for children. The probe is held in place (mouth or axilla) until a signal light comes on and the digital readout stops changing. Time required is 15 to 30 s.

Temperature variations If a child has a ½°C increase or decrease in temperature, a recheck is required. If it is confirmed, the variation should be reported to the physician (either at once or on the next medical rounds). A certain percentage of glass thermometers lose accuracy after some months of use.[73] It is wise for a nurse to question the accuracy of any temperature reading which does not fit the patient's signs and symptoms. A second thermometer should be used for the recheck.

Temperature variations are significant in children. In the newborn, hypothermia may indicate sepsis just as an elevated temperature (hyperthermia) indicates possible infection in an older child. A continuous low-grade fever [37.8 to 38.3°C (100 to 101°F) rectally] may indicate that tests need to be done to determine the source of the fever.

When the temperature exceeds 40°C (104°F)

rectally, a young child may have seizures. Efforts must be made to reduce a temperature approaching the high range. (See later section on comfort measures.)

Antipyretics—aspirin (acetylsalicylic acid) or acetaminophen (Tempra, Tylenol, Datril, and other trade names)—should be reserved for temperatures over 38.9°C (102°F) rectally. Otherwise they may mask the course of the fever and prevent accurate diagnosis by the physician.

Pulse

The heart rate is very rapid at birth and slows down with age, as shown in Table 17-20. Other factors that influence pulse rate are (1) age, (2) sex of the child, (3) fever, which increases the rate, (4) drugs (including anesthetics), which may increase or decrease pulse rate or cause arrhythmias, (5) emotions (excitement, anxiety), (6) activity, and (7) environmental temperature—pulse rate increases as metabolic rate increases to provide warmth.

If the child is under 10, the nurse should take an apical pulse while the child is sitting or lying quietly (Fig. 17-32). Warm the bell of the stethoscope by holding it in your hand for a short time or carry it in a pocket close to your body. Check the rate for a full minute. A radial pulse is accurate on the child over 10, but should also be checked for a full minute.

Respirations

Respirations are counted for a full minute by observation or with a stethoscope. The latter is more accurate under age 10, and can be done along with an apical pulse. This also provides an opportunity to assess respiratory sounds. Normal respiratory rates by age are given in Table 17-20.

Count respirations when the child is quiet. If the child cries, defer the count until a later time. Otherwise indicate *C* for *crying* when recording the respiratory rate.

Blood pressure

Blood pressure determination should be a routine part of taking vital signs in children 3 years and over because of the possibility of hypertension.[74] Detection is essential because:[75]

1. Hypertension in children and adolescents is usually secondary to a primary disease and may be cured by treating the underlying cause.

Table 17-20. Normal pulse and respiratory rates for specific ages

Age	Pulse	Respirations
Newborn	110–160	30–60
2 years	100–140	28–32
4 years	90–96	24–28
6 years	80–90	24–26
8 years	80–84	22–24
10 years	80–84	22–24
12 years	78–80	18–20

* These are averages only and vary with the sex of the child.

Source: G. Scipien et al. *Comprehensive Pediatric Nursing*, 2d ed., McGraw-Hill, New York, 1979, p. 28. Used by permission.

2. Unrecognized and uncontrolled high blood pressure may interfere with normal growth and development during critical childhood years.
3. Irreversible damage may occur in major organs.

Blood pressure measurement is also necessary to identify hypotension (e.g., postoperatively), though in infants the blood pressure may drop suddenly rather than decrease gradually as in adults.

Normal blood pressure values according to age are listed in Table 17-21. It is important to realize that one measurement is unreliable because the normal range is wide. The most useful blood pressure readings in children are serial readings, which show an upward or downward trend.

Figure 17-32 Apical pulse rate being determined while child sits with mother. (*Photo by Brian Kaihoi.*)

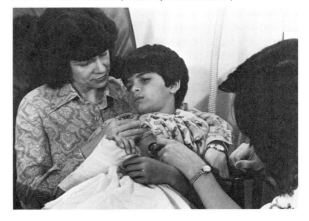

Table 17-21 Average normal blood pressure values by age

Age	Systolic Diastolic
Neonate (to 1 month)	80 ± 16* 46 ± 16
Infant (1–12 months)	96 ± 30 65 ± 25
Preschool (2–6 years)	60 to 110 40 to 75
School age (8–10 years)	105 ± 15 60 ± 10
Adolescent (11–16 years)	85 to 130 45 to 85
Adults	90 to 140 60 to 90

* The student should interpret a range presented in this way as follows: the average extends from 64 (80 − 16) to 96 (80 + 16).

Source: S. M. Tucker et al. [73].

Cuff size Appropriate cuff size is essential for accurate blood pressure measurement. A cuff too small causes an incorrectly high reading and a cuff too large causes an erroneously low reading. The cuff width should be no less than one-half nor more than two-thirds of the upper arm or be 20 percent wider than the limb on which it is used. A general guide to diameter of the cuff size by age is shown in Table 17-22.

Standard blood pressure Steps in standard blood pressure measurement on the arm are as follows.

1. Prepare the child by explaining how the blood pressure cuff will feel ("It will feel tight") and letting the child handle equipment.
2. Help the child assume a relaxed postion on the bed or in his or her mother's lap. (Place the infant supine in bed.) Measure the blood pressure after the child has been quiet for a few minutes to ensure greater accuracy.
3. Apply the cuff snugly. (Do not apply cuff over clothing. Remove or raise sleeve.)
4. Place aneroid gauge so that it can be seen directly, not at an angle. If a mercury manometer is used, make sure the meniscus of the mercury is at zero and can be viewed at eye level.

5. Palpate the radial pulse and inflate the bag 20 to 30 mmHg past the point at which the pulse disappears.
6. Place the stethoscope over the brachial artery. (The stethoscope must not be applied under the edge of the cuff. It can cause uneven pressure from the cuff's inflatable bag and distort the reading.)[76]
7. Release the cuff at a rate of 2 to 3 mmHg per second.
8. Repeat the reading once if in doubt. If still uncertain, have a coworker check it or delay another reading for 15 to 20 min.

Under normal circumstances two numbers are noted: (1) systolic, highest reading at which two consecutive sounds are heard, and (2) diastolic, where the sound becomes muffled. The two consecutive sounds are known as Korotkoff sounds. If they cannot be heard with the stethoscope, the brachial or radial artery should be palpated with two fingers. The cuff should be inflated and released. Where the pulse can be felt is the systolic reading. The diastolic cannot be determined by palpation.

If the child is suspected of hypertension[77] three numbers are recorded: (1) systolic, (2) diastolic, and (3) where the sound ceases.

Thigh blood pressure Blood pressure readings may also be obtained in the lower extremity. The cuff must be 20 percent wider than the diameter of the thigh. Place the patient on his or her abdomen or back. Apply the cuff over the mid-thigh with the compression bag (the part that

Table 17-22 Guideline for selection of standard blood pressure cuffs (*Dimensions of approximate size cuff**)

Cuff name	Range of dimensions of bladder	
	Width, cm	Length, cm
Newborn	2.5–4.0	5.0–10.0
Infant	6.0–8.0	12.0–13.5
Child	9.0–10.0	17.0–22.5
Adult	12.0–13.0	22.0–23.5
Large adult arm	15.5	30.0
Adult thigh	18.0	36.0

* Selection of proper size is dependent on the size of the extremity, not cuff name.

Source: "Report of the Task Force on Blood Pressure Control in Children," *Pediatrics* **59**(5):801 (May 1977). Used by permission.

fills with air) over the *back* of the thigh. Place the stethoscope over the popliteal space behind the knee. (If the patient is on his back, flex the knee slightly to place the stethoscope.) Note right or left thigh when recording blood pressure.

In the child under 1 year of age the thigh blood pressure is the same as the arm blood pressure. Over 1 year of age the thigh systolic pressure is 20 to 40 mmHg higher, but the diastolic remains the same.[78]

Flush blood pressure Flush blood pressure is an indirect method used in children under 1 year of age when a standard blood pressure reading is not obtainable (see Fig. 17-33). Steps in flush blood pressure technique are described below.

1. Select an appropriate infant cuff.
2. Place the cuff on the infant's wrist or ankle.
3. Elevate the extremity.
4. Compress the extremity distal to the cuff by wrapping it firmly with an elastic bandage.
5. Rapidly inflate the cuff to 120 to 140 mmHg.[79]
6. Remove the bandage. The extremity should appear blanched.
7. Gradually lower the manometer at a rate of 2 to 3 mmHg per second.
8. Take a reading at the moment the extremity appears flushed.

It is wise to have two people present for a flush blood pressure: one to watch the manometer and one to signify when the flush occurs. Be sure that the room is well lighted. If alone, place the manometer so that it can be seen simultaneously with the extremity.

The pressure determined by the flush method is the mean blood pressure—a point between the systolic and the diastolic. A range of 30 to 60 mmHg is considered normal for an infant over 2500 g (5.5 lb).[80]

Doppler method The use of oscillometry, or instrument measurement of pulsation, for determining blood pressure is popular in intensive care areas and may become more common because of its accuracy. An instrument using the Doppler effect is especially useful in neonates. It translates changes in sound frequency caused by blood motion to audible sound. It can also

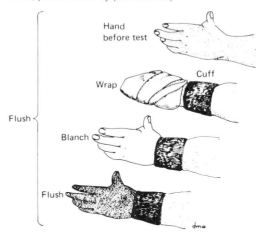

Figure 17-33 Flush blood pressure. (*From G. Scipien, M. U. Barnard, M. A. Chard, J. Howe, and P. J. Phillips (eds.) Comprehensive Pediatric Nursing, McGraw-Hill, New York, 1979, p. 29. Used by permission.*)

measure both systolic and diastolic pressures.[81] (See Fig. 17-34.)

A sphygmomanometer cuff is wrapped snugly around the child's limb. The transducer is applied with connecting gel over the brachial or popliteal artery. The cuff is then inflated 20 to 30 mmHg above the systolic sound and slowly deflated. The systolic reading is the first sound heard, and the diastolic pressure is the point at which the sound changes from loud and sharp to a soft, muffled sound.[82]

Comfort

Daily care

Bathing A daily bath can be pleasant and relaxing for a sick, anxious child. Allow flexibility in scheduling bath time so that it is as much like home as possible. For instance, if a parent is able to assist, a child who is embarrassed to have a "stranger" bathe him or her will feel more at ease. Furthermore, for the younger child, toys should be provided. Young children enjoy having toys at bath time—even for a bed bath from a small basin. Rubber water toys, cups, bubbles, and washcloth mittens may be welcome.

The infant should have an individual bath basin, infant tub, or regular tub. The older child can bathe in a tub or shower. (Check to make sure that the child bathes the genitalia and anal

Figure 17-34 Ultrasound stethoscope, an instrument for the detection of blood flow. Using the Doppler effect. (*Courtesy of MedaSonics, Inc., Mountain View, Calif.*)

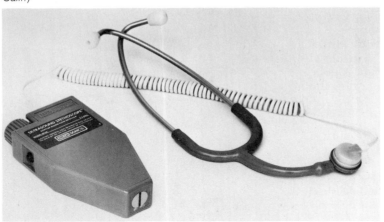

area. A tub bath allows better cleansing of these areas for the child who bathes reluctantly.)

The following safety precautions should be observed:

1. A water thermometer should be used to check temperature just before placing the child into the water. Water should be tepid or slightly warmer [31.1 to 34.4°C (88 to 94°F)]. Young children are especially sensitive to extremes in temperature; bath water that seems too cold to an adult may be just right to the child. Prepare the bath for the child. The water controls may be different from those in the child's home. Do not let the child play with the water controls during the bath.
2. Stay with an infant or young child at all times when he or she is in a tub or basin. Check up frequently on the older child or adolescent. Show the child the nurse's call light in the bathroom and advise him or her to call for assistance as needed.
3. When patients have been bedridden, accompany them to their first tub bath or shower. Remain there or outside the door.
4. While bathing an infant, support the infant behind the shoulders and hold the opposite arm firmly.

The bath routine will be carried out more efficiently if the nurse increases the temperature in the room 15 to 30 min prior to bath time and gathers equipment before the child is undressed or water is prepared. At the conclusion, the tub or basin should be cleaned with disinfectant solution.

Routine skin care Good skin care includes cleansing as well as prevention of dryness and itching. Skin dryness is a result of lack of moisture in the skin and can be remedied by appropriate use of bath oil, lubricant, bathing, and drying techniques.

Use a nonirritating, unscented, and inexpensive bath oil (for example, Robathol) in the basin or tub or on the skin for a shower. (Oil should not be used for newborns and teenagers with acne.) Unscented bath oil is soothing and prevents dryness; the use of soap is unnecessary unless desired for the groin or axillary area. After the bath, gently pat the skin dry. Do not rub vigorously. Use additional lubrication, such as a water-in-oil emulsion (Eucerin) to hold moisture in the skin.[83]

Shampoos A shampoo is very beneficial in helping a child, and especially a teenager, feel that he or she is returning to normalcy. The nurse must be familiar with hospital policy regarding the need for a doctor's order. When in doubt, discuss the plan for the shampoo with the physician. Suggestions for giving shampoos are listed in Table 17-23.

Nail care It is easy to overlook care of the child's nails because he or she will not remind you about it. Safety clippers or nail scissors should be available on every unit. Wipe them with alcohol before and after each use. A doctor's order is necessary for nail care in some hospitals.

In young children the nails should be clipped straight across with care that no sharp edges are left. Trim hang nails carefully. Nail care can sometimes be done for infants and toddlers when they are sleeping. When a young child is awake, he or she can hold a toy or be distracted by someone else while the nails are being clipped.

Oral hygiene As soon as a child has teeth and shows an interest in brushing (around 12 to 18 months) parents can begin brushing the child's teeth. Even prior to that, teeth should be wiped with a clean cloth or gauze sponge after meals. Regular toothbrushing habits should be established by age 3, but children should be *supervised* until age 8. Morning and evening routines in the hospital should include brushing teeth.

Toothbrushing techniques Most dentists recommend a brush with: (1) soft bristles, (2) straight handle, (3) flat brushing surface, and (4) head small enough to reach every tooth. When the bristles become bent and the brush does not clean well, obtain a new brush.[84]

The following brushing procedure was compiled from *Care of Children's Teeth* (American Dental Association, 1978):

1. Place the head of the toothbrush alongside the teeth.
2. Angle bristle tips against the gum line.
3. Gently "scrub" the brush back and forth with short, quick strokes.
4. Brush the inner, outer, and biting surfaces of each tooth both top and bottom.
5. Use the front toe of the brush to get the inside area of the front teeth.
6. Gently brush the tongue.
7. Rinse the mouth with water.

Teaching the technique requires spending time with the child and using the same procedure consistently. Older children who have already developed toothbrushing habits will probably prefer to continue as they have learned, though a tactful discussion of appropriate methods may be well received. Bedridden children will need to be taught to use a cup and basin for brushing.

When children are seriously ill and unable to brush their own teeth, the nurse or parent must assist them. Use a toothbrush or sponge stick with toothpaste, followed by a mouthwash. When oral surgery has been done or the gums are susceptible to bleeding, an oral irrigating device is helpful. Discuss this with the physician.

Nursing bottle mouth As soon as a child's teeth appear, they are susceptible to decay. If the child is allowed to go to bed with a bottle of sugary liquid, the teeth can be badly damaged. The liquid pools around the teeth and bacteria in the mouth change the sugar into decay-causing acids. Milk, fruit juices, formula, and other drinks can become harmful under these circumstances.[85]

To prevent "nursing bottle mouth":

1. Clean the infant's mouth after each feeding with a clean washcloth or gauze pad.
2. Don't give the child a bottle of sugary liquid at bedtime. Use water if he must take a bottle to bed.[86] Remove the bottle as soon as the child is asleep.

Table 17-23 Giving a child a shampoo

1. Shampoo preparations—Various shampoos are available and each hospital has its stock supply of recommended products. Do not use bar soap for shampooing because it is drying and difficult to apply and rinse off. A nonallergenic shampoo which can be used for all patients is desirable.
2. Moisten the hair, apply shampoo, lather, massage the scalp gently, and rinse well. Repeat the procedure. (A second shampoo is usually unnecessary in infants.)
3. Keep the temperature of the water warm, but not hot.
4. Young children:
   a. Give an infant a shampoo during the bath, but avoid getting soap and water in the infant's eyes.
   b. Use the football hold while holding the child's head over a basin or sink.
   c. Sing and/or talk pleasantly to the infant to make the procedure more tolerable.
   d. Ask the toddler to help by holding a cloth over the eyes or rubbing his or her scalp.
5. Older children:
   a. Allow capable older children to do their own shampoos in the tub or shower.
   b. Use bed shampoo equipment when necessary.
   c. An older child may be placed on a cart and moved to the sink. Extend the child's head over the end of the cart and support it during the procedure.
6. After the shampoo assist the child to towel dry his or her hair. Use a hair dryer for an older child if towel drying is inadequate.

Dressing Dressing young children can be made easier by allowing them to wear their own clothes if possible, encouraging their help, and learning their idiosyncrasies. When putting on a T-shirt gather the excess fabric up to the neck opening so that the child's face is covered only briefly. Gather up a sleeve or pant leg and pull the child's extremity through it. Use a loose-fitting gown or shirt which opens up the front or back for a seriously ill child.

Do not allow children to walk barefooted in the hospital. Provide slippers with nonskid soles in a variety of sizes, or ask the parents to bring slippers from home.

Diapers The nurse who is inexperienced in caring for infants may have difficulty in applying diapers snugly. The following suggestions may be helpful:

1. Use disposable diapers or cloth diapers if the child is sensitive to plastic. (See Fig. 17-35 for folding cloth diapers.)
2. Place the diaper underneath the child—extra thickness at the back for girls and at the front for boys.
3. Secure with self-adhesive tabs or pins. To pin the diaper, place the fingers of one hand between the diaper and child's skin to guide the pin through the cloth and prevent the infant from being stuck. Pin with back over front to fit body contours. Direct both pins horizontally and posteriorly in case the pin should accidentally open.
4. Change the diaper frequently. As an infant walks the diaper will stretch and loosen. Voiding will compound the problem.

5. For an older infant, apply two diapers at nap time or bedtime. Use plastic pants or a waterproof flannel pad on the bed.

Diaper rash is often caused by skin irritation from urine. At each diaper change cleanse the skin with a mild soap and warm water. If a beginning rash is noted, apply a protective, non-water-soluble ointment. If the rash persists, leave the diaper off when the infant is asleep to allow for "airing." Eliminate the use of plastic pants and use cloth rather than disposable diapers. The physician may want to culture the diaper area to determine if a medicated ointment is needed.

Sleep Adequate rest and sleep are essential for normal growth and development in children as well as for recovery from illness. When they are sick, children need more sleep than usual. Table 17-24 shows the average sleep needs of children at different ages.

Determine the child's sleep pattern at home. Some small children want or need both the morning and afternoon naps. Others take one long nap. Children use various comfort measures to help them go to sleep—a blanket, stuffed animal, thumb-sucking. Many parents will hold and rock children to sleep when they are in the hospital simply because the child needs the extra love and security during that time. As a child's condition improves, parents may prefer to break this habit and try to help the child regain his or her ability to go to sleep without being rocked.

Figure 17-35 Folding the diaper to provide extra thickness. (*A*) Place the diaper on a flat surface. (*B*) Fold it into thirds. (*C*) Place thickest part under the buttocks for a girl and over the penis for a boy. (*From G. Leifer, Principles and Techniques in Pediatric Nursing, Saunders, Philadelphia, 1977, p. 48. Used by permission.*)

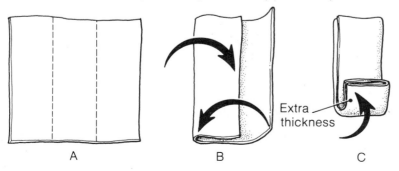

Extra thickness

A   B   C

Table 17-24 Sleep needs

Age	Hours per day	Naps
Infant	16–18	A.M. and P.M.
1 to 3	13	2 hr, P.M.
3 to 6	11–13	2 hr, P.M.
6 to 12	8–10	Rest time
Adolescent	8	

Source: From data in S. M. Tucker, et al. [73].

Provide a quiet rest time each day. Turn lights down, close doors of rooms, and turn off TVs to enhance the rest time. Even older children and adolescents may welcome a time to read, be alone, or take a nap as they recuperate. On an adolescent unit it is important to post rest and "lights out" times.

Parents may want to "sneak away" while a child is asleep so they do not have to go through the child's tears at separation. Discourage this because the child may resist sleep if she thinks her parents will leave each time she tries to rest. Honest, open communication with the child about when parents are leaving is the best approach. Refer to Chap. 16 for ways of dealing more effectively with separation anxiety.

Rest and nursing care Plan vital sign checks, dressing changes, medications, and other activities so that the child does not have to be awakened from a nap or night's rest. When it is necessary to awaken the child, maintain a quiet atmosphere and use a flashlight rather than the room light. When possible take vital sign measurements while the child is still sleeping. If the child *must* be awakened, rub his or her back or sing lullabies to encourage the child to fall asleep again.

Sometimes children are awakened by nursing care given to other patients in the same room. Plan room assignments to allow patients with similar care schedules to be in the same room.

Discomfort

Pain Pain is not usually a severe or long-lasting problem with children. In fact an infant can usually do well without any pain medication following major surgery, because of the immaturity of the neurological system.

When pain is present, however, it is difficult to assess. This is true especially in preschoolers and toddlers who may be unable to verbalize effectively. (See Chap. 21 for additional information on pain assessment.)

Identifying pain In a study of pain in children ages 2 to 7 years, Smith[87] identified some ways in which pain may be expressed:

1. Aggressive behavior
2. Dependency
3. Some verbalization
4. Physiological response (adrenal and sympathetic stimulation)
   a. Vasoconstriction of vessels to the internal organs (except the heart, lungs, and brain), causing hypomotility of the gastrointestinal tract
   b. Increase in circulating blood glucose with an increased amount of energy available
   c. Vasodilatation of peripheral vessels, increasing oxygen content and glucose in the muscles
5. Observable manifestations
   a. Flushing of the skin
   b. Vomiting
   c. Elevated pulse rate
   d. Restlessness (whole body movement)
   e. Dilatation of the pupils

If pain is identified and treated early, the child is more comfortable, more cooperative, and more tolerant of hospitalization. The nurse must observe the child carefully and be alert to behaviors indicative of pain.

Pain management Pain management does not necessarily mean use of medications. In fact, narcotics for pain relief are generally unnecessary for children because relief can be obtained with safer analgesics and nursing measures. Ways to help a child become more comfortable include: providing a change of position; loosening tight dressings; wrapping child comfortably in a blanket; rocking; singing; providing a favorite drink or play activity.

If comfort measures are inadequate, confer with the physician about medications. For some children the thought of a "shot" is worse than tolerating pain. The nurse must use all the signs of pain to determine if medication is needed—especially if the child is denying pain in fear of an injection. Explain that the pain of the medication is very brief and will make his or her body feel better. Consider the possibility of oral or rectal medications as alternatives to injections. Give medications as often as needed to control the discomfort.

Persistent pain not relieved by mild analgesics and comfort measures should be reported to the physician. There may be complications occurring which will require additional medical intervention.

Irritability and crying Irritability and aggressive behavior may be the result of conditions other than pain. Crying may occur simply because a child is hungry or tired. Try a cracker, some juice, or a nap as a means of helping the child.

Children also cry because of the presence of strangers, separation from parents, fear of the environment or procedures, uncertainty about what is happening, and boredom. Talk with the parents and spend time with the child to assess causes of irritability and to determine relief measures.

Some anesthetics cause irritability and irrational behavior. Reassure the parents and encourage comfort measures—rocking, singing, giving back rubs—so that the child can "sleep off" the side effects of the medications.

Fever Fever can cause irritability, crying, and lethargy. It is the most frequent cause of seizures in young children and may be a sign of infection. Report fever to the physician and discuss control measures needed.

Antipyretics may be ordered by the physician. The most common drugs for temperature control are aspirin (acetylsalicylic acid, ASA) and acetaminophen (Tylenol, etc.). For high fever it has been recommended that aspirin and acetaminophen be used together in half their individual dose. The combination works better than either used alone and the effect is prolonged.[88]

Additional nursing measures can be recommended:

1. Dress the child lightly. Remove the bed clothes to promote heat loss.
2. Encourage taking of fluids to replace those lost because of fever and to overcome any mild dehydration, which can raise the temperature.
3. Give a sponge bath (see Table 17-25).

Nausea and vomiting Nausea and vomiting occur as symptoms of gastrointestinal disease or as side effects of medications, pain, surgery, and anxiety.

If a patient is in the immediate postoperative period, the nurse must be familiar with side effects of the preoperative medications and anesthesia which the patient received. The side effects will be relieved when those drugs have been metabolized and eliminated. Blood and mucus swallowed during surgery may cause postoperative vomiting, which is relieved when the stomach empties itself.

Young children cannot verbalize the feeling of nausea. They may become restless, perspire, look flushed or pale, begin to cough, gag, or hold the stomach or throat. They may say that their throat hurts. Nursing measures for care of the child who is vomiting include the following measures:

1. Keep an emesis basin, tissues, and a washcloth at the bedside at all times. Include these in preparing *all* postoperative beds.
2. Tell the child and parents why the basin is available and to call the nurse if any vomiting occurs.
3. When the child is vomiting, have him or her sit up and lean over the basin. Support the head and wipe the child's mouth as needed. If sitting is contraindicated, turn the child to the side.
4. Position the child on abdomen, right side or with head of bed elevated at least 15° while resting.
5. Provide a cool cloth to the child's throat or head.
6. Provide a quiet environment and use a soft speaking voice.
7. Measure and record the amount of emesis, rinse the basin quickly, and return it to the bedside.
8. Remove soiled clothing and linen and use an air deodorizer to freshen the room.
9. Provide a mouthwash or water with which the

Table 17-25 Sponge bath technique for a child with fever

1. Fill a tub to 1- to 1½-in depth with lukewarm water.
2. Place the child in the tub and sponge him or her for 30 to 45 min.
3. Do not use alcohol to enhance the cooling effect. It may cause chills and shivering, which tend to raise body temperature. There is also danger of alcohol intoxication.
4. If the child cannot be moved from bed, use a basin of water at the bedside. Sponge the extremities, trunk, axilla, and groin with light, gentle strokes. Chilling can be prevented by keeping half the body covered while sponging the other part.
5. If the child feels chilled or begins to shiver, stop the sponging and resume later if necessary.
6. Check the child's temperature occasionally during bathing and at half-hour intervals afterward until it is down or at least has halted its rise.

child can rinse his or her mouth. Tell the child not to swallow it.

10. Confer with the physician about restricting the oral intake to avoid stimulating the gastrointestinal tract. Discuss the use of antiemetics. (Great care must be taken in the use of phenothiazines in children.)

11. Resume fluids and food by slow progression from ice chips or sips of carbonated beverages to full liquids and then to a regular diet.

Medications

Dosages

Pediatric dosages are calculated according to body weight (for instance, 10 mg/kg per 24 h) or body surface area. Body surface area (BSA) is considered to be the most accurate means of determining dosage.[89]

Determination of the body surface area with the West nomogram (Fig. 17-36) utilizes the

Figure 17-36 West nomogram (for estimation of surface areas). The surface area is indicated where a straight line connecting the height and weight intersects the surface area (SA) column or, if the patient is roughly of normal proportion, from the weight alone (enclosed area). (*Nomogram modified from data of E. Boyd by C. D. West; from H. C. Shirkey in V. C. Vaughan and R. J. McKay (eds.), Nelson, Textbook of Pediatrics, 10th ed., Saunders, Philadelphia, 1975, p. 1713. Used by permission.*)

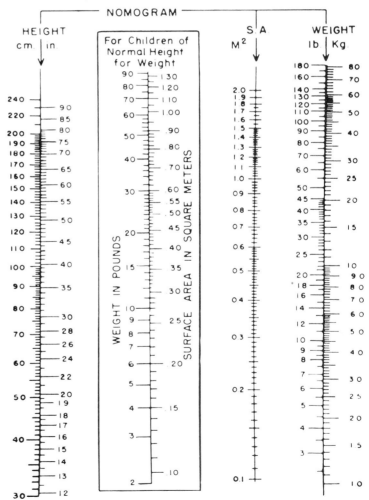

child's height and weight. The dose is then determined as follows:

Surface area in m² × recommended dose/m²
= approximate child's dose

For example, what is the appropriate dose of Benadryl for a child who weighs 30 lb and is 30-in tall? Recommended dosage is 150 mg/m² per 24 h. To find the answer using the nomogram, draw a straight line between 30 lb and 30 in; the surface area is 0.56 m². Therefore:

0.56 m² × 150 mg = 84 mg per day

This amount is then divided into four evenly spaced doses.

Table 17-26 Factors that affect drug dosage in neonates and older children

Factors related to drug absorption

Reduced intestinal motility typical of the neonate slows passing of drugs taken orally.

Delay in intestinal· enzyme development of the newborn impairs ability of intestine lining cells to process the drug for absorption.

Reduced acidity within the neonate's intestinal tract lowers drug uptake by lining cells.

Factors related to drug distribution

Continual change in relative tissue mass and fat content during growth and development make predictions as to drug delivery and tissue uptake unreliable.

Greater volume of body water in neonate relative to total weight requires adjustment of dosage calculations for certain drugs if desired serum concentration is to be achieved; adult water-vs.-tissue proportions are achieved in the teen years.

Factors related to drug metabolism

The normal slow maturing of hepatic enzymes during the first 2 to 3 weeks postnatally, if unrecognized, may lead to unmetabolized drugs accumulating to toxic levels.

From about the fourth week, the fully functioning liver can process larger quantities of drugs than BSA calculations would indicate because the liver is proportionately larger in the child than the adult

Factors related to drug excretion

The expected decreased glomerular filtration rate (GFR) during the first 3 weeks requires recognition to avoid drug accumulation to toxic levels. Full renal function at adult levels is reached by 5 to 7 months.

The neonate's decreased renal tubular function poses the same danger as decreased GFR.

Source: Adapted from G. Udkow, in R. Hoekelman et al. (eds.), *Principles of Pediatrics*, McGraw-Hill, New York, 1978, pp. 235–245.

BSA determinations may be used through the entire lifespan *except* with premature and full-term neonates. Because their excretory function is immature, neonates must receive special care in all drug administration; body surface area determinations are not appropriate.[90]

Factors affecting dosage are listed in Table 17-26.

Understanding medications

The nurse has the responsibility of knowing or learning about each drug to be given. Specific resources usually available are the *Hospital Formulary*, *Physician's Desk Reference*, a pediatric source such as Shirkey's *Handbook of Pediatric Dosages*, and the hospital pharmacist. Some hospital units have a drug dosage file with commonly used drugs and dosages on individual cards. A list of drugs used for emergencies is usually kept with the resuscitation equipment.

In checking physicians' orders, note any aspect of an order which may be inappropriate, and discuss it with the physician before the drug is administered. Dosages for drugs are based on the average amount of medication needed to achieve therapeutic effects without causing signs of overdose. The physician may have a specific reason for giving more or less than the average. However, the nurse must communicate *specific concerns* so that dosages can be determined with all aspects of correct therapy in mind.

Administration of medications

Prior to giving any medication explain to the child and parents what the medication is and why it is given. Use terms which the child understands—how it will feel, taste, look—but make the explanation brief, and then give the medication. It is best to have the medication prepared when the explanation is given so that a long period of time will not elapse between explanation and administration. (See Chap. 16 for more details about preparation for procedures and use of therapeutic play.) In some instances the parent may be more effective than the nurse in obtaining the child's cooperation.

When administering medications, the nurse must choose the appropriate route (enteric vs. parenteral) as well as the appropriate interval between doses to maintain the desired serum drug level. The child's response is influenced by fever (increased metabolic rate), the disease process itself, other drugs being taken, and the time of administration (with meals or between).

Oral medication This comes in tablets, capsules, liquids, and, occasionally, powders. Equipment for oral administration includes the medicine cup, spoon, plastic dropper, and plastic syringe.

Ormond and Caulfield have developed a helpful guide for administering oral medications to children ages 1 month through 6 years based on developmental tasks and behaviors (Table 17-27). The authors note that the charts are presented as "guides for normal behavior, but 'normal' is not an absolute and there is plenty of room for variation."[91]

Some additional suggestions are given below according to the form of oral medication to be used.

Table 17-27 Pediatric medication guidelines

Developmental tasks and behaviors	Nursing implications
1 to 3 months	
Motor	
Reaches randomly toward mouth; shows strong palmar grasp reflex.	Infant's hands should be monitored or controlled to prevent spilling of medications.
Head drops or exhibits bobbing control.	Head must be well supported.
Feeding	
Sucks reflexively in response to tactile stimulation.	Medication should be administered using this natural behavior: medication should be given via nipple.
Corners of the mouth may not seal effectively and the tongue may be reflexively forced against the palate.	Correct position of the nipple, if used, must be assured for adequate sucking.
Tongue movement may project food out of mouth.	A syringe or dropper, if used, should be placed in the center back portion of the mouth. If placed along the gums, it must be toward the back of the mouth.
Sucking strength increases (3 months)	Amount of medication presented must be controlled. Infants may choke or drool because they can take in more medication than they can control.
Stops taking fluids when full; sucking reflex begins to fade (3 months).	Medication more easily given in small volumes and when infant is hungry.
Interactive: Stage: Basic trust vs. mistrust	
Infant becomes socially responsive.	Medication administration requires feeding behavior which establishes an easy, comfortable situation. This is part of the child's learning to form a trust relationship.
3 to 12 months	
Motor	
Advances from sitting well with support (3–4 months) to crawling (10 months).	Safety precautions regarding where medications are placed and kept become extremely important.
Begins to develop fine motor hand control.	
Advances from lying as placed (3 months) to standing with support (12 months)	Child who does not want to cooperate has ability to resist with whole body.
Feeding	
Starting at 12-month-old level:	
Smacks and pouts lips in act of shifting food in mouth and in swallowing. Lower lip active in eating.	Children may spit out food and medicine they do not want.
Tongue may protrude during swallowing.	Eating is inefficient, so medications may need to be retrieved and refed.
Learns to drink from cup. Generally has poor approximation of corners of the mouth when drinking.	A small medicine cup may be more effective than a nipple or syringe because the cup can catch and refeed parts of the medicine the baby spits out.
Learns to finger-feed self.	
Feeding behaviors become individualized.	Feeding patterns and routines at home need to be considered.

Table 17-27 Pediatric medication guidelines (*Continued*)

Developmental tasks and behaviors	Nursing implications
3 to 12 months	
Interactive: Stages: Basic trust vs. mistrust and oral sensory	
Communication skills develop from random social responses (3 months) to making simple requests by gesturing (12 months).	One must be alert for children indicating their own needs (12 months).
Is sensitive and responsive to tactile stimulation. Begins developing responsiveness to other stimuli	Physical comforting will be most effective with child. Verbal comforting secondary.
Recognizes immediate family and, very importantly, may exhibit intense separation anxiety.	Exhibits early memory. May recall negative experiences, precipitating negative response in another similar situation.
12 to 18 months	
Motor	
Advances from standing with support to independent walking.	Have children choose a position for taking medication or hold them to provide control and comfort. Forcing children to take medicine when they are lying down takes away their sense of independence and will frequently result in very resistive behavior.
Feeding	
Begins independent self-feeding but is still messy.	Home feeding habits should be considered.
Develops voluntary tongue and lip control.	Spits out disagreeable taste effectively. Disguise crushed tablets and contents of capsules in a small amount of familiar solid. Be prepared to refeed.
Spits deliberately.	
Interactive: Stage: Autonomy vs. shame and doubt	
Indicates needs and wants by pointing.	Find out what words child uses for drinking, swallowing, and how oral medicines have been given at home.
Speaks four to six words. Uses individual jargon.	Let children explore an empty medication cup. They will likely be more cooperative if familiar terms are used.
Responds to familiar commands.	When possible, involve the parents. They are familiar and trusted persons, which is an important factor during an unfamiliar experience.
Responds to and participates in the routines of daily living.	Tell parents and staff the approach used for medication. Report its effectiveness.
	Allow children as much freedom as possible.
Exhibits notable independence, resistance, self-assertiveness, and ambivalence. Begins to have temper tantrums.	Allow children to assert themselves by choosing a drink to wash down the medicine.
	Use games to gain cooperation.
	Tell the child what you expect and then follow through. A consistent, firm approach is essential.
18 to 30 months	
Motor	
Walks, climbs into chair (18 months).	Child is able to run away and kick.
Advances to running without falling (24 months)	
Advances to obtaining and throwing small objects.	Children may throw materials placed within their reach. Never leave medications sitting on the bedside stand.
Feeding	
Generally feeds self. Advances to proficiency with minimal spilling.	Allow children opportunity to drink liquids from a medicine cup by themselves.
Second molars erupted (20–30 months).	Permits greater flexibility in choosing form of medication.
Exhibits increased rotary chewing; manages solid food particles.	
Controls mouth and jaw proficiently.	Child is effective in spitting out unwanted medications and in clamping mouth tightly closed in resistance.

Table 17-27 Pediatric medication guidelines (*Continued*)

Developmental tasks and behaviors	Nursing implications
18 to 30 months	
Interactive: Stage: Autonomy vs. shame and doubt	
Has some sense of time, but no words for time (18 months). Then responds to "just a minute" (21 months). Advances to understanding, "Play after you drink this" (24 months). Carries out two to three directions given one at a time.	Tell the child getting medicine that any bad taste will only last "a minute." Learn child's level of time awareness from nursing history. Give simplified directions: "Open your mouth, drink, and then swallow." Include child in establishing medicine-taking routine.
Shows ability to respond to and participate in routines of daily living. Helps put things away; carries breakable objects. Exhibits independence, resistance, self-assertiveness, and ambivalence. Throws temper tantrums frequently. Shows pride in accomplished skills. Does not know right from wrong. Shows conflict between holding on and letting go.	Use a firm, consistent approach. Resistive behaviors are at a peak. Give immediate, positive tactile and verbal response to cooperative taking of medicine. Ignore resistive behavior. Give choices when possible: "Do you want to sit in the chair or on my lap to take your medicine?"
2½ to 3½ years	
Motor	
Continues to develop proficiency. Basic skills have all been initiated.	Child may be quite adept in resistive behavior.
Feeding	
Becoming more proficient in skills. Eating likes and dislikes are definite but changeable. May be influenced by others' reactions in responding to new food experiences.	Medication taste can be disguised with variable effectiveness. A calm, positive approach is needed to gain a cooperative response from the child; quick, tense approach is likely to produce similar behavior in the child.
Interactive: Stage: Initiative vs. guilt	
Gives full name.	Begin asking for verbal identification of patient before giving medications.
Is ritualistic. Has little understanding of past, present, or future. Shows concrete thinking, egocentricity.	Communicate administration methods. Use concrete and immediate rewards. Tolerates frustration poorly. Child's initial response to reason appears positive, but without consistent effect. Prolonged bargaining is frustrating and frightening to the child because no one is in control of the situation.
Exhibits early aggressiveness; coercive, manipulative behavior. Has many fantasies.	Give a choice when possible. Do not give a choice if the child does not have one. Begin giving simple, honest explanations of why the medication is given (not because the child was bad).
May be frightened by his or her "power."	Child's sense of security is dependent upon the nurses' consistent expectations of his behavior.
3½ to 6 years	
Motor	
Develops proficiency of coordination. Can identify the parts of a complete movement or task.	Child can attempt and master pill taking.
Feeding	
Exhibits olfactory, gustatory, and kinesthetic refinement.	Disguising tastes is generally less effective than it is at younger ages. Child can distinguish medicine tastes and smells.
Begins to lose temporary teeth (5 years).	Loose teeth may need to be considered when selecting form of medication.

Table 17-27 Pediatric medication guidelines (*Continued*)

Developmental tasks and behaviors	Nursing implications
3½ to 6 years *Interactive: Stage: Initiative vs. guilt* Makes decisions.	Children should be active in making decisions which affect them.
Sense of time allows enjoyment of delayed gratification. Is able to tolerate frustration. Seeks companionship. Shows pride in accomplishments. Has ability to follow directions and remember several instructions for a period of minutes to hours. Exhibits developing conscience.	Rewards which are not immediately received and social interaction can be used as effective motivators. Child is able to understand the purpose of medications in simple terms. Teaching can have long-term benefits.
Needs limits set to help control frightening sense of "power." Exhibits genital interest, general mutilation fears.	Prolonged reasoning or arguing may frighten the child; a simple command by a trusted adult may be more effective. Explain the relationship between cause, illness, and treatment. Use simple terms.
Illness often seen as punishment. Shows changeable response to parents.	Give control when possible—child needs to make choices. Child may be more cooperative in medicine taking for the nurse than for the parent.

Source: E. A. R. Ormond and C. Caulfield, "A Practical Guide to Giving Oral Medications to Young Children," *Journal of Maternal Child Nursing,* September–October 1976, pp. 320–325. Used by permission.

Tablets Chewable tablets are generally taken easily by young children as long as a "chaser" such as water, soft drinks, or Kool-aid is available. If it is necessary to crush a tablet in order to give only part of it, ask the pharmacist to crush it for greater accuracy in dosage. If this must be done on the unit, crush the tablet between two spoons.

Crushed medications may be mixed with a *small* amount of syrup, jelly, or applesauce to facilitate administration. Do not mix the medication with essential foods (i.e., egg, milk, or formula) because the child may not eat the food later.[92] Mix the medication and the camouflage thoroughly on a small spoon and administer in one or two bites. Have a drink of the child's choice immediately available.

For the child on extremely limited fluid intake, offer the medications in baby food, thus saving the fluids for later.

Capsules Capsules should not be opened to facilitate administration without conferring with the pharmacist. If a child refuses a capsule, another form of the drug or another drug with similar actions may need to be substituted by the physician.

Liquids Because the stomach is not primarily an organ for absorption, oral medication must pass into the small intestine. Liquids pass more quickly and easily than tablets. Hence a liquid is the preferred form of oral drug for infants and small children. Measure the dose in a syringe to ensure accuracy. Do not depend on a medication cup for any amounts smaller than 5 ml. Use a tuberculin syringe if the amount is smaller than 1 ml.[93]

Giving liquid medicine to infants To prevent aspiration, always hold the infant in an upright position or with the head and shoulders elevated for oral medications. Use a soft plastic dropper or small plastic syringe for administration. Insert it into the side of the mouth between the cheek and gum. Slowly release the medicine so that it passes around the gums and into the esophagus. The sucking reflex may be used, as indicated in Table 17-27, by placing the dropper or syringe directly on the tongue.

Very young infants may take medications easily if they are given through a nipple. Dilute the medication in a little water or juice and administer when the infant is hungry. Use only a small amount of diluent so that the infant will be more likely to take the total amount.

When a child is crying vigorously, do not give the medication. Help the child to settle down and then try again. Never hold the child's nose to forcefully give medicine. The child will associate the medicine with the feeling of suffocation and will fight harder the next time. Forcing also creates a risk of aspiration.

Giving liquid medicine to toddlers Older toddlers should have a good explanation prior to receiving medications. If the child resists the medication, give choices between using the med cup, a paper cup, a straw, or a syringe. If this does not help, the child should be held firmly on the parent's or nurse's lap (see Fig. 17-37). Explain kindly, but firmly, that the medication must be taken now. Open the child's mouth by pressing on the chin and put the medication in. If the child spits it out, repeat the dose so that he or she understands that the medicine is essential. Remind the child that as soon as the medicine is taken he or she can play.

If a child regurgitates the medication immediately after receiving it, give the total amount again. If vomiting occurs within 30 min after medication, contact the physician so that new orders about repeating the drug can be given.

Rectal medications The advantages of rectal medication are: no chance of aspiration; it may be given without concern about excessive oral fluid intake; the child cannot spit it out; it can be used when oral intake is contraindicated, as in the presence of nausea and vomiting; insertion is brief and painless when compared to injections. Though medications given rectally may not be absorbed as readily as those given orally, there are times when it is the best alternative available.

Prior to administration, use a finger cot to check the child's rectum for the presence of stool. A suppository administered into a bolus of stool is *totally* ineffective. Lubricate the suppository *as directed.* Most are prelubricated, but moistening with a small amount of warm water may be helpful. Insert the suppository past the anal sphincter. Remain with a young child for a few minutes and hold the buttocks together in order to prevent expulsion of the medication. While waiting, talk, sing, and play with the child as a distraction. Fifteen to thirty minutes after the suppository is administered, check the child's diaper or underwear for expulsion.

Most suppositories cannot be divided because the manufacturer does not guarantee that the drug is evenly dispersed throughout the suppository.[94] Talk with the pharmacists before attempting to divide a suppository.

Time of administration The nurse should be aware of which drugs are to be given with or without food. Clarify orders for tid or qid medications. Every 6 h or every 8 h may be more appropriate for maintaining therapeutic blood levels.

Intramuscular medication Because an injection is a very brief procedure, it is best to prepare the child just prior to giving it. In this way the child does not have a long time to build up unnecessary anxieties.

Figure 17-37 Small child being restrained for oral medication from a syringe. (*From L. Whaley and D. Wong, Nursing Care of Infants and Children, Mosby, St. Louis, 1979, pp. 937. Used with permission.*)

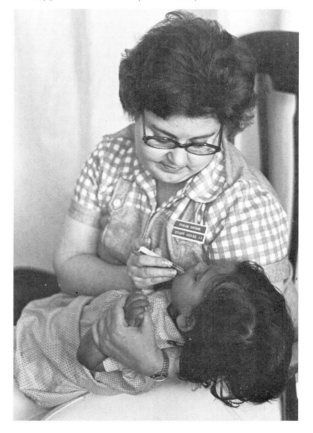

In children the appropriate sites for intramuscular injections are as follows:

1. Vastus lateralis (used in newborns) or anterolateral thigh (Figs. 17-38A and B). These sites are recommended in children under age 2 years in order to avoid the gluteal site. The gluteal muscle is not well developed until the child is walking.

2. Posterolateral gluteal (Fig. 17-38C). In children over 2, the upper outer quadrant of the gluteal may be used.

3. Ventrogluteal (Fig. 17-38D). This is an excellent site because there are no important nerves or blood vessels in the area.

4. Deltoid (Fig. 17-38E). The deltoid should not be used for intramuscular injections on small children

Figure 17-38 Sites for intramuscular injections in children. (*A*) Vastus lateralis. The vastus lateralis is the primary site for intramuscular injections in the thigh. The needle penetrates on a front-to-back course of the midlateral anterior thigh. Grasp thigh as shown to stabilize extremity and concentrate muscle mass. (*B*) Anterolateral thigh. An alternate site for intramuscular injections in the thigh is the anterolateral surface. The needle is directed distally into the rectus femoris muscle at a 45° angle to the horizontal and long axes of the leg. Compress thigh as suggested in *A*. (*C*) Posterolateral gluteal. Posterolateral aspect of the gluteal area is located by palpating the posterior superior iliac spine and the head of the greater trochanter. An imaginary line is drawn and the needle inserted on a straight back-to-front course as shown. (*D*) Ventrogluteal. Ventrogluteal area provides good muscle density and is free from major nerves and vessels. If injection is to be given on child's left side, use right hand in determining landmarks and vice versa. Place palm on greater trochanter, index finger on anterior iliac spine, and middle finger on posterior edge of iliac crest. The intramuscular injection is given in the center of the V or triangle formed by the hand with the needle directed upward toward iliac crest. (*E*) Deltoid. The injection site is determined by the acromion and the axilla as shown. Because muscle mass is limited in the middeltoid area, repeated injections and large quantities of medication are not recommended. Compress muscle mass prior to inserting needle. (*From G. Scipien, M. U. Barnard, M. A. Chard, J. Howe, and P. J. Phillips (eds.), Comprehensive Pediatric Nursing, McGraw-Hill, New York, 1979, pp. 1031–1032. Used by permission.*)

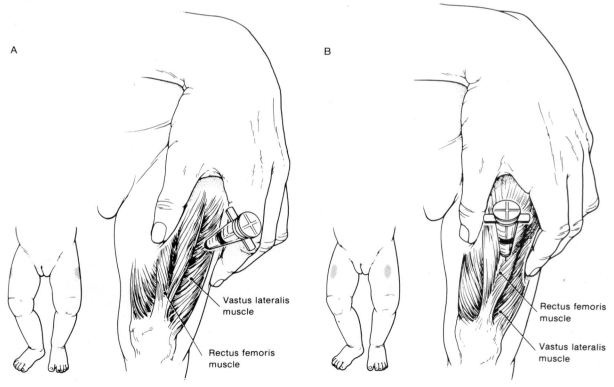

A

B

Vastus lateralis muscle

Rectus femoris muscle

Rectus femoris muscle

Vastus lateralis muscle

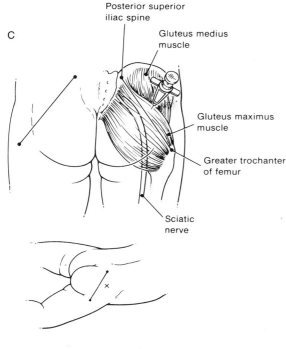

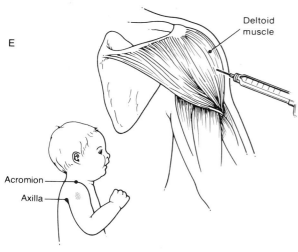

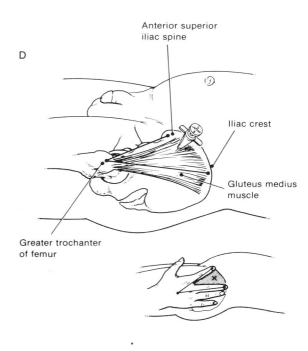

but can be used in school-aged and adolescents for small dosages (e.g., immunizations). Thick, long-acting antibiotics should always be administered in the large muscles of the leg or hip.

The deltoid has a faster absorption rate than the larger muscles, so it is appropriate when faster absorption is desired.

Needle size The needle chosen should be long enough to ensure that the medication is in the muscle without hitting the bone and large enough for the medication to pass through easily with minimal tissue trauma.

Suggested sizes are as follows:

Infants and toddlers $\frac{5}{8}$ in (very small infants) to 1 in (most infants)
Older children 1 to $1\frac{1}{2}$ in depending on size of child and injection site
Thin liquid medications 23–25 gauge
Thick antibiotics 21–22 gauge

Tubex syringes are available for many pediatric injections. Because these are sometimes frightening to children, the plastic disposable syringes and needles may be preferred. After an injection the child may have the used syringe without the needle as a souvenir. (Mutilate the end of the syringe to prevent re-use.)

Administration Table 17-28 lists steps in administering an intramuscular injection to a child.

Intravenous medication When administering an intravenous medication the nurse must be thoroughly familiar with the drug and its side

Table 17-28 Administering an intramuscular injection

1. Prepare the medication out of the child's sight. Bring it in inconspicuously on a tray.
2. Explain briefly that the medicine is needed to help the child get well or prepare him or her for surgery. It will stick or sting and be over quickly. (See earlier section on restraints.)
3. Position the child as needed for the appropriate site. Ask the child to help by turning toes in, squeezing the siderail, counting, and remaining as still as possible.
4. Cleanse the skin with an alcohol sponge and keep the sponge in hand to cleanse the site afterwards.
5. Pinch up the skin and muscle for a thigh injection on a small child, but release when injecting the medication.
6. Insert the needle with wrist positioned as if throwing a dart. If the injection must be given at a 45° angle, as in the anterior thigh, turn the bevel up to aid smooth insertion.
7. Aspirate the syringe and slowly inject the medication.
8. Maintain firm restraint of the child throughout the injection. The pain of the medication entering the tissue may be more uncomfortable than the needle and the child may try to move away.
9. Remove the needle and apply the alcohol sponge to the site. If bleeding occurs, apply pressure with a dry cotton ball for a few seconds.
10. Let the child help with the application of a Band-aid.
11. Explain that the injection is over and change the child's position to increase comfort. Distract with a pleasant activity. Apply ice to the site if the child continues to complain.

effects, the correct dosage, length of time necessary for administration, and the compatibility of the drug with the other intravenous medications and fluids being given. The effect of intravenous drugs is immediate and errors which may be well tolerated by an adult can be fatal in a small child.

Intravenous medications may be given:

1. Directly into the IV line through a medication inlet or the rubber flush ball (used in emergencies and generally under direct supervision by a physician).
2. Via the intravenous volume control chamber. (See Fig. 17-23 for a picture of the chamber.)
3. Via a separate intravenous medication bag or bottle.

When medication is given through the volume control chamber, it is added through the medication inlet on top of the chamber. The volume of intravenous fluid added to the chamber for medication administration is determined by the amount needed to prevent pain and irritation to the child's vein and the length of infusion time desired.

Use of a separate medication bag or bottle is the safest means of intravenous medication administration. The pharmacist prepares the medication and carefully determines the appropriate amount of diluent. The medication is administered through secondary intravenous tubing attached to the primary tubing through a Y inlet (Fig. 17-39).

Several important precautions in intravenous medication administration are listed in Table 17-29.

Ear drops Warm ear drops to body temperature prior to administration. An infant may be held on the mother's lap but an older child should be positioned on the bed so that he or she can

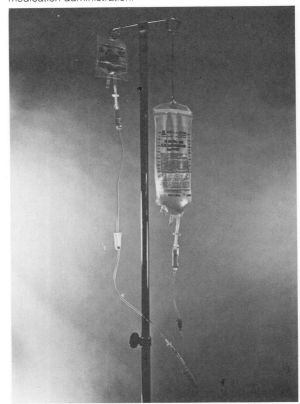

Figure 17-39 Intravenous medication being infused through a Y inlet in the main tubing. Note that medication bag must be raised above regular intravenous bag during medication administration.

Table 17-29 Precautions in administering intravenous medications

1. Check the intravenous site for patency before beginning the medication infusion.
2. Label the medication bag or volume control chamber with the drug name, date, time hung, time of expiration, and nurse's initials or name.
3. Administer the drug as soon as possible after it is prepared and complete the infusion before the expiration time to ensure drug potency.
4. Clear the secondary set tubing of all medication solution before discontinuing. All medication is not infused unless the line is cleared.
5. Use an intravenous pump to regulate the flow rate accurately.
6. Observe for signs of phlebitis or infiltration.
7. If there is local irritation of the vein only during infusion of the medication, the following alternatives may be helpful:
   a. Talk with the pharmacist about increasing the dilution of the medication. Confer with the physician about limits on fluid intake.
   b. Slow down the rate of infusion.
   c. Apply warm packs to the site (i.e., a warm washcloth changed frequently).
8. Flush the medication out of the tubing before another drug is infused. If a secondary set is used, as in Fig. 17-39, use different secondary tubing for each drug to prevent drug incompatibility.
9. Include the amount of fluid used for intravenous medications in the child's total daily fluid intake.

remain in bed for a few minutes after the drops are inserted. To accommodate for anatomic differences at different ages, use the following guidelines:[95]

Children under 3. Hold the pinna of the ear *down* and back.
Children over 3. Hold the pinna of the ear *up* and back.

Turn the child's head to the opposite side, insert ear drops, and keep the head turned for 2 to 3 min. It may be more comfortable to the child to have a cotton wick inserted loosely into the ear upon completion of the procedure to prevent the drops from rolling out during activities.

Eye drops Restrain the child as necessary. The hand which holds the dropper should rest on the head of the child.[96] Pull down the lower lid and insert the drops in the center of the pocket formed by the lid. The child should remain flat on his or her back for several minutes after the drops are inserted so that the medication may reach the entire cornea. Provide a tissue to absorb tears but restrain the child from rubbing the eyes.

Nose drops Nose drops should be given before meal time to open the nasal passages and make eating easier. This is especially necessary for infants who are still nursing because it is very difficult for them to suck when they cannot breathe through their nose.

Position the child's head by placing a towel roll under the neck or extending the head over the edge of the mattress. Keep his head back for 2 to 3 min after the drops are inserted.

After frequent use, certain kinds of nose drops create a chemical congestion in the nose and are no longer useful. It is best to use them only 2 to 3 days at a time.

Comfort measures after medications
The child may be very frightened or uncomfortable after a medication. Spend time with the child to provide comfort and distraction through a pleasant play activity. Help the child to realize that the medication was not given as punishment and that he or she is still "loved." This may be a good time for the child to try "giving medicine" to a doll or toy animal. Encourage the parents to provide comfort measures and distraction, because parents are the most significant "comforters."

Record specific approaches and comfort measures on the Kardex that are helpful to individual patients.

Safety factors in giving medications
The basic medication administration principles are vital in giving drugs safely to children:

1. Right medication
2. Right dosage
3. Right route
4. Right time
5. Right patient

The small amounts of medication involved mean that incorrect measurement or loss of medication is a proportionately greater error in children than in adults.

Be aware of side effects in children that may be different than in adults.

Be cautious and never leave medications at the patient's bedside. After injections remove the equipment from the room immediately. Even such seemingly harmless items as topical creams and lotions should never be left near a young patient. The patient may decide to apply the cream or eat it!

Document medication administration immediately. Chart the name, time, dosage, and route. Indicate effective approaches on the Kardex nursing care plan.

Dismissal planning

According to Scipien[97] the general objectives of dismissal planning are:

1. To ensure that there will be no interruption in the care required by the child and family.
2. To provide the family with adequate information and instruction to care for the child.
3. To involve other appropriate agencies as needed and provide them with the necessary information to ensure continuity of care.

Begin on admission

Dismissal planning begins during the initial nursing assessment of the patient and family. Assess the home situation and the level of understanding of the illness. Confer with the physician about the probable length of the patient's hospitalization and discuss the anticipated care to be done at home. Continue to assess learning needs throughout hospitalization.

Involve the child and family in setting goals and planning for the return home. They need to know what is to be accomplished before dismissal and anticipate home care needs in order to make arrangements in advance. Prepare a written plan on the Kardex containing goals for the child and family and specific instructions needed to carry out the plan. Provide the patient and family with a copy.

Teaching the child and family

Utilize principles of teaching and learning in preparation for dismissal:

1. Determine readiness to learn. Teach when the parent and child are receptive and motivated to learn.

2. Determine reading and comprehension level. Do not assume printed instructions can be understood.
3. Use repetition.
   When the parents and child are anxious, they may remember only portions of what they hear. Be prepared to repeat information patiently. Remind them, in the physician's presence, of those questions they "needed to ask the doctor but forgot."
4. Build on present knowledge.
   Be sure there is *real* understanding of simple information before moving to more complex.
5. Use teaching aids—pamphlets, books, films—as appropriate.
6. If medications are to be continued at home, be sure the parents (and child) have a clear understanding of the dosage, frequency and length of administration, and possible side effects of the drugs involved. Be aware of what equipment will be used at home and teach with that in mind.
7. Provide time for questions, discussion, demonstration, and practice in giving care.
8. Evaluate teaching effectiveness through quizzes and return demonstrations.[98]

Community resources

Community resources include public health nursing agencies, school nurses, support groups for patients with specific illnesses and their families, clergy, educational facilities, friends, relatives, and others. Determine those appropriate for the patient and family. Talk with a representative of any community agency needed and arrange a meeting in the hospital before dismissal.

A written referral may be necessary to assure adequate follow-up. Consult the child and family and obtain their permission. Complete a written nursing referral including:

Child's diagnosis
Treatments during hospitalization
Medications and treatments to be done at home
Reasons for the referral
Special needs of the child and family
Teaching done in the hospital
Goals for the patient
Planned follow-up activities
Hospital resource person who may be contacted.

Documentation

1. Chart all teaching on the Kardex nursing care plan and in the nurses' progress notes to ensure continuity of care from one shift to the next. Indicate

receptiveness of the patient and family and an evaluation of learning.

2. Record plans for a nursing referral in the Kardex nursing care plan.

3. Obtain parents' and child's permission for referral to a community agency and chart this in the nurses' notes.

4. Give written instructions to the child and family about medications and treatments.

5. Complete written referral at dismissal time.

6. Chart the dismissal procedure; include medications and equipment taken and the child's physical and emotional state.

Dismissal procedure

When dismissal is ordered, the nurse must confer with the physician about all medications and treatments to be done at home. Obtain medications and review the schedule of administration with the child and family. Review all previous teaching and written instructions. Assist the child to dress and gather belongings. Encourage the parents to go to the hospital business office to complete dismissal details before they take the child from the room. Give the child an opportunity to say "good-bye" to staff members and patients. Some pediatric units provide a dismissal gift (stuffed animal, coloring book) as a memento of hospitalization.

It is important to accompany the patient and family to the entrance of the hospital to assist in carrying belongings and to ensure that they are safely dismissed. Encourage them to call the nursing unit or physician if questions arise.

A follow-up telephone call by the child's primary nurse a few days later may be welcomed by the family. Any questions can be answered and the current conditions at home can be assessed.

References

1. G. Leifer, *Principles and Techniques in Pediatric Nursing*, Saunders, Philadelphia, 1977, p. 12.
2. J. Johnson, K. T. Kirchoff, and P. M. Endress, "Easing Children's Fright During Health Care Procedures," *American Journal of Maternal-Child* Nursing 1 (4):206 (July–August 1976).
3. G. Scipien, M. U. Barnard, M. A. Chard, J. Howe, and P. J. Phillips, *Comprehensive Pediatric Nursing*, McGraw-Hill, New York, 1975, p. 15.
4. Leifer, op. cit., pp. 75–77.
5. D. Marlow, *Textbook of Pediatric Nursing*, Saunders, Philadelphia, 1977, p. 456.
6. Leifer, op. cit., p. 76.
7. Ibid.
8. Marlow, op. cit., p. 457.
9. Ibid.
10. L. Whaley and D. Wong, *Nursing Care of Infants and Children*, Mosby, St. Louis, 1979. pp. 946–947.
11. Johnson, et al. loc. cit.
12. Scipien, et al. op. cit., p. 418.
13. N. Hilt, "Pride, Prejudice, and Parents," *Pediatric Nursing* 2(3):34 (May–June 1976).
14. L. S. Farris, "Approaches to Caring for the American-Indian Maternity Patient," *American Journal of Maternal-Child Nursing* 1(2):82 (March–April 1976).
15. Ibid., pp. 80–87.
16. D. McCown, "TV: Its Effects on Children," *Pediatric Nursing* 5(2):19 (March–April 1979).
17. E. L. Dowd, J. C. Novak, and E. J. Ray, "Releasing the Hospitalized Child from Restraints," *American Journal of Maternal-Child Nursing* 2(6):373 (November–December 1977).
18. E. P. Bernabeu, "The Effects of Severe Crippling on the Development of a Group of Children," *Psychiatry* 21:169–194 (May 1958).
19. R. S. O'Grady, "Restraint and the Hospitalized Child," *Current Concepts in Clinical Nursing*, vol. 2, ed. by B. S. Bergerson et al., Mosby, St. Louis, 1969, pp. 192–202.
20. Leifer, op. cit., p. 68.
21. Ibid., p. 33.
22. C. R. and C. E. Block, "Help, My Child is Choking," *Pediatric Nursing* 2(5):48 (September–October 1976).
23. H. Heimlich, "The Heimlich Maneuver: Where It Stands Today," *Emergency Medicine* 10(7):90 (July 1978).
24. Ibid., p. 99.
25. Ibid.
26. Scipien, et al., op cit., p. 241.
27. M. M. Seedor, *Introduction to Asepsis*, 2d rev. ed., Teacher's College, Columbia University, 1979.
28. P. M. Hamilton, *Basic Pediatric Nursing*, Mosby, St. Louis, 1974, p. 147.
29. Leifer, op. cit., p. 81.
30. Seedor, op. cit.
31. Leifer, op. cit., p. 90.
32. M. Zeimer and J. S. Carroll, "Infant Gavage Reconsidered," *American Journal of Nursing* 78(9):1543 (September 1978).
33. Leifer, op. cit., p. 99.
34. Zeimer and Carroll, op. cit., p. 1543.
35. Ibid.
36. Ibid.
37. Leifer, op. cit., p. 101.
38. Marlow, op. cit., p. 198.
39. Leifer, op. cit., p. 91.
40. L. J. Guhlow and J. Kolb, "Pediatric IVs: Special Measures You Must Take," *RN* 42(3):40 (March 1979).
41. Hamilton, op. cit., p. 216.
42. D. A. Millam, "How to Insert an IV," *American Journal of Nursing* 79(7):1268 (July 1979).
43. Guhlow and Kolb, op. cit., p. 47.
44. Millam, op, cit., p. 1270.

45. "Fundamentals of IV Maintenance," programmed instruction, *American Journal of Nursing* **79**(7):1275 (July 1979).
46. Ibid.
47. Millam, op. cit., p. 1269.
48. Hamilton, op. cit., p. 217.
49. Millam, op. cit., p. 1270.
50. C. H. Kempe, H. K. Silver, and D. O'Brien, *Current Pediatric Diagnosis and Treatment*, Lange Medical Publications, Los Altos, Calif., 1976, p. 933.
51. Guhlow and Kolb, op. cit., p. 50.
52. "Pediatric IVs: Nursing Implications at a Glance," tear-out guide, *RN* **42**(3) (March 1979).
53. Guhlow and Kolb, op. cit., p. 47.
54. Guhlow and Kolb, op. cit., p. 50.
55. "Wyeth R Heparin Lock Flush Solution, USP," Wyeth Laboratories, Philadelphia, 1978.
56. Guhlow and Kolb, op. cit., p. 50.
57. Wyeth, op. cit.
58. H. C. Shirkey (ed.), *Pediatric Therapy*, 5th ed., Mosby, St. Louis, 1975, p. 306.
59. Whaley and Wong, op. cit., p. 1200.
60. Scipien, op. cit., p. 590.
61. Ibid.
62. Whaley and Wong, op. cit., p. 1200.
63. Ibid.
64. Whaley and Wong, op. cit., p. 347.
65. Whaley and Wong, op. cit., p. 1201.
66. Jan S. Tecklin, "Positioning, Percussing, and Vibrating the Patient for Effective Bronchial Drainage," *Nursing 79* **9**(3):68 (March 1979).
67. Ibid., p. 69.
68. Ibid., p. 68.
69. A. Proctor, "Pediatric Arrest: Scaling Down CPR," *RN* **42**(9):58–64 (September 1979).
70. American Heart Association and National Research Council Report, "Standards for Cardiopulmonary Resuscitation and Emergency Cardiac Care," Supplement to *Journal of the American Medical Association* **227**(7):846 (Feb. 18, 1974).
71. S. M. Tucker et al., *Patient Care Standards*, Mosby, St. Louis, 1975, p. 407.
72. Whaley and Wong, op. cit., pp. 62–63.
73. J. Abbey et al., "How Long is That Thermometer Accurate?", *American Journal of Nursing* **78**(8):1375–1376 (August 1978).
74. E. D. Botwin, "Should Children Be Screened for Hypertension?", *Journal of Maternal-Child Nursing*, **1**(3):152 (May–June 1976).
75. D. Greenfield, R. Grant, and E. Lieberman, "Children Can Have High Blood Pressure Too," *American Journal of Nursing* **76**(5):771 (May 1976).
76. J. Lancour, "How to Avoid Pitfalls in Measuring Blood Pressure," *American Journal of Nursing* **76**(5):774 (May, 1976).
77. Ibid., p. 775.
78. Whaley and Wong, op. cit., p. 116.
79. Ibid.
80. Ibid.
81. Greenfield, et al., op. cit., p. 771.
82. A. Hernandez, D. A. Meyer, and D. Goldring, "Blood Pressure in Neonates," *Contemporary OB/GYN* **5** (March 1975).
83. J. Daniels, "Winter Skin Care: Change Your Skin's Personality," *Rochester Methodist Hospital News*, Rochester, Minn., Winter 1977, pp. 10–11.
84. American Dental Association, *Care of Children's Teeth*, 1976, p. 15.
85. American Dental Association, *Your Child's Teeth*, 1976, p. 4.
86. Ibid.
87. M. E. Smith, "The Preschooler and Pain," in P. A. Brandt, P. L. Chinn, and M. E. Smith, *Current Practice in Pediatric Nursing*, Mosby, St. Louis, 1976, p. 206.
88. S. K. Dube and S. H. Pierog, *Immediate Care of the Sick and Injured Child*, Mosby, St. Louis, 1978, p. 14.
89. Shirkey, op. cit., p. 21.
90. Ibid., p. 22.
91. E. Armond and C. Caulfield, "A Practical Guide to Giving Oral Medications to Young Children," *American Journal of Maternal-Child Nursing* **1**(5):325 (September–October 1976).
92. Whaley and Wong, op. cit., p. 935.
93. Ibid., p. 936.
94. Ibid., p. 940.
95. Ibid., p. 941,
96. Ibid.
97. Scipien, op. cit., p. 506.
98. Ibid., p. 508.

Chapter 18 **Legal, ethical, and moral considerations in pediatric nursing**

Catherine M. Kneut

Upon completion of this chapter, the student will be able to:

1. List and describe three ways in which the nurse functions as a child and family advocate.

2. Define the concept of *informed consent*.

3. Describe a clinical situation involving value system differences.

4. Identify the role of the courts in medical treatment for children.

5. Describe at least one situation that is likely to produce stress in pediatric nurses.

6. Describe three factors which inhibit the caring process.

7. Define the concept of *burnout*.

8. Differentiate between "quality of life" and "sanctity of life" philosophies.

9. List three factors which contribute to role conflict in the nurse.

10. Identify factors which may produce a situational crisis for the pediatric nurse.

The nurse as a child and family advocate

Patient advocacy as an integral component of the nurse's role

Within the scope of daily practice, the nurse performs many activities which are designed to promote the health and well-being of the child and the child's family. This role affords nurses the opportunity to establish and maintain therapeutic relationships with children and their families. These relationships are based on knowledge of the child and the family as a system. (See Chaps. 2 and 3.) A therapeutic nurse-client relationship is important in all areas of nursing, but it is paramount in the pediatric setting.

To be effective, the nurse-client relationship must be based on an awareness of and respect for the uniqueness of the individuals involved in the interaction. Nurses are human beings, as are clients, and this shared humanity forms the basis of the relationship between them.[1] This statement may appear simplistic, but all too frequently the focus is on the child as a "patient" only. The child's humanity may be neglected and his or her family excluded. Concern for children as individuals and awareness of their needs and rights enable the nurse to advocate on behalf of children and their families.

Advocacy means to intercede for another. One can fulfill this role by pleading a cause, providing support, or making recommendations. The nurse-client relationship provides the medium for the nurse's advocacy role. In order to intercede or put forth the rights of the child and family, the nurse must know what their needs are. The child and family are considered as people first. Therefore, both human needs and health needs are identified. Physical needs are not a priority except in life and death situations. The nurse cannot divide a child into isolated entities and deal with each separately. The child's needs and personal and developmental characteristics interact to form that child's uniqueness as an individual. The nurse must provide care that includes the whole being.

Advocacy in daily practice The nurse uses the nursing process to advocate for the child and family. As a care-provider in clinical settings, the nurse advocates directly for the child in order to meet the child's physiological, safety, and psychosocial needs. For example, in caring for an infant with gastroenteritis, maintenance of a patent intravenous site and the correct rate of infusion meets the child's physiological need for fluid and electrolyte balance. A toddler's psychosocial need for security is met by the nurse who encourages a mother to room in and par-

Figure 18-1 Nurses must be advocates for both the child and the parents.

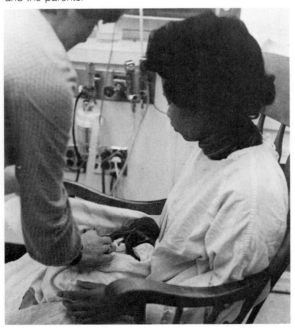

ticipate in the child's care. In this instance, the nurse helps the mother fulfill her parenting role. Safety needs of a child are met, for example, by giving the right dose of medication as well as by assessing and recording the child's response to it.

As an advocate, the nurse communicates with other members of the health care team to ensure that quality care is provided the child and family. Consultation with other disciplines is often necessary to ensure that needs of the child and family are met. For example, an unemployed father may be concerned about the cost of his child's hospitalization. A referral to social service can help this father work out a plan and, at the same time, reassure him that his child's care will not be jeopardized.

Teaching is both an important and a continuous aspect of nursing advocacy. Providing information to parents about immunizations for their child is one example of this nursing function. Reminding parents to keep hazardous household products out of a toddler's reach is another.

Advocacy in the management of care is accomplished by using nursing care plans. A written plan communicates the needs of a child and family to others responsible for the health care of the child. Consistency among those providing nursing care reassures the child and family that they are important and that their concerns are respected.

Advocacy is not confined to the legal definition of the term. All of these components of the nursing role are encountered in daily practice regardless of the health care setting. Each child and family unit is unique, and the nurse is professionally responsible to act as an intercessor for them in order to meet their particular needs. (See Fig. 18-1.)

Patients' rights

As human beings, children are entitled to certain rights just as adults are. They have a right to grow up healthy, to be educated, to be cared for, and to be protected from harm. Parents are legally responsible for the health and well-being of their children. In the majority of states, children below the age of 18 years are considered minors. This means they are considered legally incompetent to make decisions in regard to their own person. Parents are responsible for exercising and protecting the child's rights. However, this does not mean the rights of the parents supersede those of the child. The rights of children and the rights of parents are considered of equal value by the courts. Promotion of the child's best interest is part of parental responsibility.

Informed consent Since parents are legally accountable for the health of their children, only they can authorize medical treatment. For example, if a child has appendicitis and surgery is necessary, only the parent (or legal guardian) can legally consent to the operation and sign the permit. The surgeon must adequately explain the risks and benefits of the procedure before the parents can give their informed consent. Words which can be understood by the parents should be used in the explanation. After the parents have been given sufficient information, they can agree or disagree with the surgeon's decision. The signed operative permit is evidence that this exchange of information has occurred. Parents should not be forced to consent to any procedures because they fear reprisal for themselves or their child. Coercion, whether verbal or nonverbal, is a violation of parental rights.

Nurses also have a responsibility to inform parents of any treatments they intend to carry out. They have an obligation to explain or clarify the child's nursing care. Suppression of information by nurses or any other health care provider denies parents the legal right to knowledge that affects decisions made on the child's behalf.

Children are considered legally incapable of giving consent to medical treatment. Giving such consent is a parental right. Any touching of a minor by a physician, nurse, or other health worker, even with the child's consent, is technically battery.[2] Exceptions to this rule will be discussed further on in this chapter.

Special consent circumstances Under special circumstances, such as renal and bone marrow transplants, the informed consent of a child, as well as of the parents, may be required. In several instances, a minor child has donated a kidney to an ailing sibling. The courts have found, for the most part, that minor children are capable of understanding the risks and benefits involved and of consenting to them. (Risks to donors for renal transplant and bone marrow transplanta-

tion are minimal.) In these situations, both a consent from the donor and a court review of the parents' decision to permit the transplant may be required.[3] The risk involved in these procedures is significant for the child who receives the foreign tissue, because it can stimulate an immunological response directed against his or her own tissues (graft vs. host syndrome). However, since these treatment modalities are often the only option left for parents to choose for the ill sibling, the courts view the decision as one which promotes the best interests of the child.

Parents who must decide whether to give or withhold consent for one child to act as an organ donor for another sibling bear a heavy burden. They have equal responsibility for and accountability to both children. It is extremely difficult to jeopardize (however minimally) the life of one child for the benefit of the other. Conversely, it is just as painful for parents to deal with a child's illness and possible death without an attempt to forestall that conclusion. Nurses must be sensitive to the tremendous pressures parents experience in these circumstances. Parental support is a nursing responsibility regardless of the decision. Support can take many forms. It includes answering questions, listening to parental concerns about either child, and dealing with the parents' understandable anger or feelings of guilt.

It is important for the nurse to keep matters in perspective during this stressful period. Anger is a normal part of parents' response to such stress. The nurse should not take parental reactions personally. Rather, the nurse should regard them as coping mechanisms and handle the situation accordingly. Personalization of angry or hostile remarks will only make the situation more disruptive for the parents. Once the parents have reached a decision, the nurse's support must continue. They need reassurance from the nurse that their decision was the right one for them.

Even in the absence of such special circumstances as those just discussed, parents of course may experience great distress as they struggle toward a decision about whether or not to seek treatment for a child whose prognosis, even with the therapy, will be uncertain. The Nursing Care Plan at the end of the chapter demonstrates the application of the nursing process in the care of one child's parents.

Consent by minors Children are generally considered minors until the age of 18 years. However, a child under this age may be declared *emancipated.* Children achieve this status by marriage, judicial decree, consent of the parent(s), or failure of the parents to meet their legal responsibilities.[4] A minor who is financially independent of parents and lives apart from them is often considered emancipated. Emancipated children can, in most instances, consent to medical care without parental consent.

Another legal situation involves mature minors. The term *mature* is difficult to define. In most court cases where this has been an issue, the children involved were older adolescents. Mature minors are legally competent to consent to medical treatment. A child may give consent if he or she: (1) has been given the proper information, (2) is capable of reason, and (3) is intelligent enough to comprehend the risks involved in a procedure. Parental consent is waived in such instances. Some states, for example, allow treatment of children for venereal disease without parental knowledge or consent.

Consent during emergencies In an emergency, medical and nursing care can be given without the consent of a parent or guardian. However, an emergency must truly exist or those involved are liable to charges of battery. If the nature of the child's illness or injury is not serious and harm will not result if treatment is delayed, professionals are legally bound to wait for parental authorization. In situations that are not life-threatening, the courts will not overrule parents who decide against treatment.

Religious issues and consent for treatment The courts do not allow parents to make martyrs of their children even on religious grounds. Some religions hold beliefs that are inconsistent with medical treatment. The Jehovah's Witness sect does not believe in blood transfusions. If a child of this religion requires such treatment to save his or her life, and the parents refuse consent, the courts can intercede on the child's behalf and permit the transfusion. Parents cannot terminate treatments required to keep their child alive even when the parents believe discontinuation of therapy is in the child's best interest.[5] The child is of value to the state or society in which he or she lives. The state also has a responsibility to uphold the child's rights. The courts protect the interests of the state and the child when they intervene to override a parent's prerogative.

Legal and religious issues surrounding pediatric nursing practice are not rare occurrences. Nurses have an obligation to know the rights of parents and children and to respect them. However, parents can not place their child's health and well-being in jeopardy or the courts will intercede on the child's behalf.

Value system differences and the nurse
Values play an important role in our daily lives. A value is an affective disposition toward a person, object, or idea.[6] In essence, values are the importance or general worth we attach to persons, objects, or ideas. Values are the motivating force behind the way of life and patterns of conduct individuals choose. Values may differ to a greater or lesser degree from person to person. What one individual considers very important may be less so to another. An individual ranks values according to his or her ideas about their general worth. One value system is not necessarily better than another since these systems are individualized.

The family is the primary agent in the formation of value systems. As children grow and develop, they learn what their families consider important and desirable. Gradually children incorporate family values into their own lives and patterns of conduct. Their values may change over time as they become socialized and their sphere of nonfamily contacts increases. The priority of values, or the degree of worth attached to certain values, may also change over time. For example, a young girl may strive to achieve good grades in school because her parents place a high value on this goal. As she grows older, grades may become less important to her while learning itself becomes a motivating force. Similarly, as the child grows older, what the child's peers think of her becomes more important than family values.

Nurses have personal and professional ideas that they consider important. These ideals result from their own socialization and professional education. A nurse's manner and interactions with a child and family can convey acceptance or rejection of their value system. A nurse who makes value judgments is not able to perceive the unique needs of a child and family. A nurse who makes unfair judgments implies that the child and family, or their values, do not have worth. Whether verbal or nonverbal, value judgments can impede or completely obstruct meaningful communication between the nurse and the child and family.

Differences in value systems are common and are a part of daily nursing practice. The manner in which these conflicts are managed is crucial. The nurse must accept the child and family in order to provide the care necessary for their health and well-being. Acceptance of needs, value systems, and the individuality of family members enables the nurse to be an effective health care provider.

Sources of value system conflict Certain situations can be major sources of value system conflict between the nurse and the child and family. In child abuse, most nurses have a difficult time overcoming their negative feelings toward the battering parent. A child who has been deliberately harmed or neglected arouses strong emotions. Nurses will tend to give enormous attention to the child and neglect the parent. This only diminishes the parent's low self-esteem even further. Neglect of the parent does nothing to meet his or her needs. A nurse who thinks the parent inflicted harm because of lack of love for a child has made a value judgment. It may not be true. It is more beneficial to the child and family when the nurse shows concern for the parents and their problems. This attitude neither condones the abusive action nor condemns the parents. Support and counsel will be more readily accepted from the nurse who shows concern for *both* the child and parents.

Another situation full of conflict is caring for an adolescent who has repeatedly tried to commit suicide and is presently being cared for with life-support devices. Providing for his or her physical care is strenuous in itself. The nurse may feel this is a waste of valuable time and effort for someone who obviously does not want to live. But is this really so? Repeated drug abuse and suicidal attempts do not necessarily indicate a desire for death. These gestures can be cries for help. The adolescent may have sought an escape because of overwhelming peer and family expectations. The nurse must be sensitive to both the patient's needs and those of family members, who are probably experiencing guilt and turmoil over the situation.

Nurses give high priority to the protection and preservation of human life. Those who abuse life therefore present them with value system conflicts. In each situation, nurses need to analyze their feelings to avoid making harsh and inaccurate value judgments, which would render them incapable of providing needed support and counsel. Children and their families face many problems in the course of their development. Nurses need to be sensitive to these difficult and often overwhelming realities. If a nurse discovers that she or he is unable to refrain from making negative value judgments in certain situations, then the nurse has an obligation to the child, family, and the profession to withdraw from that situation.

The nurse who practices in a stressful setting

Stressful pediatric nursing settings

Nurses are normally subjected to many stresses in the course of practice. Stress is a personal reaction based on an individual's perception of an event. Certain practice settings, such as intensive care units, are more likely than others to create stress in that stressful events are more numerous, more frequent, and last longer.

Stress is defined as a physical and emotional experience which may result when a person is required to change from one condition to another condition.[7] For example, while in some settings care is provided usually through a routine and stress is an exception, in a pediatric intensive care unit, stress is the norm. The children's conditions are usually unstable. A child's needs change frequently and the nurse must be constantly alert to these changes in order to meet the child's needs. Intensive care units are challenging and demanding both physically and psychologically for nurses who work in them. In addition to providing care to critically ill children, nurses must provide support to parents and cope with physicians' demands and orders. The necessity for coordinating care and setting priorities in an everchanging environment compounds the stress in a pediatric intensive care unit.

Neonatal intensive care units Neonatal intensive care units produce the same climate as pediatric units, but they present additional unique stresses. The parents of a neonate who is premature or seriously ill, or who has a birth defect, experience two crises at once. The parents must cope simultaneously with grief reactions to the "loss of the perfect child" and the reality of an ill or defective newborn. Not only must the neonatal intensive care nurse provide support to the family, this nurse must also cope with her or his own emotions regarding the ill neonate. (See Fig. 18-2.) Nurses in this setting often unconciously feel responsible for failing to provide the parents with a perfect child. A broader discussion of the nurse's role in neonatal intensive care units can be found in Chap. 19.

Emergency rooms An emergency room is another area where stress is ever-present. Caring for children after such major trauma as burns, poisonings, and car accidents is difficult for the nurse. Parents are often in a crisis state and require the nurse's support. The emergency room nurse knows that "anything can happen at any moment." Therefore, the nurse must be prepared to change in order to act during the next crisis or emergency. This setting offers few if any opportunities for the nurse to relax or "settle down." She or he must continually cope with multiple stressors. (See Chap. 20 for further discussion of the emergency room nurse's role.)

Working with multiproblem families One does not need to work in an intensive care unit or an emergency room to experience stress. It can be difficult for the nurse to cope with families who have multiple problems. Just the *number* of problems in a given family can be overwhelming for the nurse. The nurse may be capable of meeting the child's or family's immediate needs, but long-term problems may be more than the nurse can handle. At such times, the nurse needs to recognize that one person cannot meet all needs for all people. There are other professionals who can manage some of the family's problems, and indeed they should do so.

Nurses who work in community settings are

Figure 18-2 Providing care to critically ill infants and children can evoke stress and crisis for the nurse.

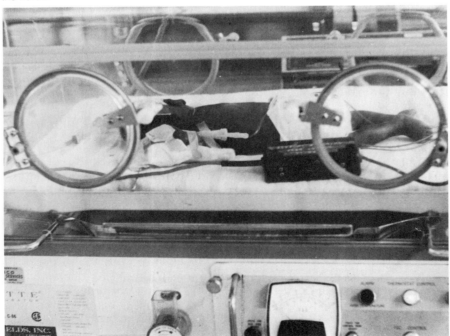

often faced with multiproblem families on a larger scale. The community health nurse often encounters inadequate health care, housing, and sanitation among clients. Although families may appear apathetic about these conditions, they are usually overwhelmed and unable to cope with their numerous problems without help. Frequently nurses become angry at political systems which allow such inadequacies to exist. Again, the nurse needs to recognize that there are some problems for which she or he is not responsible. Other professions and political systems are accountable for dealing with some of these family and community concerns.

Concerns of nurses who practice in stressful pediatric settings

Intensive care units, emergency rooms, and other stressful settings present the nurse with situations that continually demand fast, accurate assessments and actions. This pace and the intensity of providing care to seriously ill children can affect nursing practice. Nursing involves caring for and caring about another's pain, illness, or distress. It implies an interest in a child's needs and problems, whether physical or psychosocial. Caring is the humanistic element present in the therapeutic relationship between the nurse and the child and family. This humanistic caring is the essence of nursing practice.

Depersonalization Patient care in stressful settings can be burdensome for the nurse. In order to deal with stress, nurses frequently focus on the physical needs of the child. The "caring for" takes priority; the "caring about," or attachment process, is lost or never even considered. The uncertainty of the child's recovery makes the nurse reluctant to become involved and risk the chance of another loss.

Intensive care units demand special skills of the nurse. It is all too easy to concentrate one's attention on the perfection of these skills. Advances in technology have been beneficial to many children. In some instances, however, it has also made nurses and others overly concerned with mechanical equipment. Concern about technical skills, mechanical devices, and the rapid pace all lead the nurse to focus on the physiological problems of the children. It becomes easier to talk about them in terms of "system failure" or "functioning" rather than the children themselves.

Fragmentation of care Each person on the health care team has contact with physicians, nurses, respiratory therapists, physical therapists, occupational therapists, and numerous others. All these individuals have a valuable role in the child's care; however, their functions can contribute to fragmentation of the child's and family's care. One person needs to be responsible for the coordination of care. That person is the nurse. Interdisciplinary teams can produce positive outcomes in the child's health. However, quality of care is something quite separate from outcome of treatment.[8] Quality of care is concern and caring about *all* aspects of the child's growth and development in relation to health and illness.

Powerlessness in making life and death decisions Decision making is an ongoing process in any pediatric setting, but major decisions affecting life and death are continually made in intensive care units. Most if not all these decisions are made by the physicians, the child's family, or both. Nurses are rarely consulted even though they may have had intimate and prolonged contact with the child and family. Understandably, nurses feel powerless to alter the course of treatment. If a nurse has a caring relationship with a child and family and is aware of their needs and problems, then the nurse has a responsibility to voice these concerns to physicians if the family is unable to do so. Frustration results when the nurse must carry out physicians' orders with which the nurse disagrees. The nurse can refuse to follow orders which she or he believes will jeopardize a child's life, but a nurse cannot legally refuse to carry out an order on the basis of disagreement.

It is ironic that the nurse is expected to know all about a child's condition and manage the child's care but is given no power or role in decision making. Nurses are traditionally placed in the position of being "double agents." That is, nurses are expected to represent the interests of both the patient and the physician as the focus of authority.[9] Thus the nurse often experiences conflict. Individual autonomy and the nurse's role as a child advocate are threatened in this type of situation. Lack of power contributes to the stress nurses encounter.

Inadequate support systems Support systems for dealing with stress are sadly lacking in many practice settings. Nurses working together in stressful or difficult situations tend to reinforce each other in a manner that can increase rather than decrease stress. For example, two nurses may agree that a particular circumstance is stressful but be unable to find methods of coping with the stress. Agreement about stress does not necessarily alleviate it.

Nurses in administrative roles are often unaware of the problems faced by nurses at the bedside. This is usually due to their geographical distance from the setting. Nurse administrators must be made aware of these problems so the administrators can provide the leadership which will help nurses resolve the situation.

Status within the organizational hierarchy Another factor leading to stress among nurses is nursing's status within the organizational hierarchy. Both hospitals and community health agencies have some type of organizational structure. The effect of the organizational hierarchy is most evident in situations where nurses continually receive and implement physicians' orders, such as in intensive care units. The nature of the nurse-physician relationship can place the nurse in a role subordinate to that of the physician. For many nurses, the role strain which results is a source of stress.

Supportive resources for nurses experiencing stress Nursing leaders can lend considerable support, but only if they are aware of the difficulties. Nurses in stressful settings have a responsibility to make their own needs known to those who can help them.

Nursing clinical specialists and staff development educators also have an important role in supporting nurses. The clinical specialist can hold support group sessions for nurses who are experiencing stress. Difficult situations can be discussed and methods of coping explored. Alternative solutions to problems can also be a topic of discussion. Whether the specialist's expertise is in parent-child or psychiatric nursing, one of the clinical specialist's primary roles is allowing nurses to vent their feelings without fear of repercussion. Clinical specialists can often be more objective than staff nurses because they are usually less involved in the daily care of patients. Clinical specialists are, however, capable of understanding the stress experienced by staff nurses. Providing support for families is another way clinical specialists can temporarily relieve staff nurses of stress.

Staff development educators can help staff nurses by offering programs on decision making, ethical dilemmas, role conflict, and stress management, for example. They can also arrange "support group" sessions for staff nurses. Programs which involve nurses from other hospitals or agencies can aid nurses in identifying common sources of stress and methods of coping.

Members of other disciplines are also support resources in stressful situations. A psychiatrist or social worker can be an effective listener to problems of staff nurses. Such people have no vested interest and are therefore less likely to feel personally or professionally threatened. By virtue of their professions, they are capable of providing needed support and counsel to nurses in times of stress.

Burnout

When support systems are unavailable, nurses may withdraw from the situation psychologically. This method of coping is ineffective in changing stress or reducing it. Further depersonalization and fragmentation of care result. It may begin to seem that the nurses' role is of little value because no one confers with them except to give orders or make more demands. A psychological withdrawal or the denial of their needs or practice problems by others can lead to "burnout." *Burnout* may be defined as "a progressive loss of idealism, energy, and purpose experienced by people in the helping professions as a result of the conditions of their work."[10] Emotional exhaustion, cynicism, physical exhaustion, and, eventually, total disgust with one's self are symptoms of burnout.[11]

Factors leading to burnout Burnout is the result of any one or combination of the following: (1) working in stressful situations for too long; (2) inadequate support systems; (3) loss of professional perspectives; and (4) lack of professional challenges. The first two factors have already been discussed. Loss of professional perspective occurs when nurses become either too close to or too distant from children and families.[12] For example, intensive care unit nurses may become technically oriented in order to distance themselves from patients. Other nurses may be unable to provide care to a child or family because of their close emotional involvement with them.

Lack of professional challenges often results from the daily routine nurses allow themselves to fall into. Nurses can become complacent in their practice setting and fail to look for opportunities to learn or improve nursing care. In effect, these nurses fail to challenge themselves.

Remedies to prevent or counter burnout

Burnout is not an inevitable result of job or professional circumstances. Nurses can prevent burnout by effective stress management and by finding challenges or new experiences in either their personal or professional lives. Finding methods of relaxation or ways of easing the pressures of daily interactions with both clients and professionals does much to prevent burnout.

If burnout occurs, the nurse needs to reevaluate personal and professional goals. The remedy may involve a new job or a transfer to a new situation. However, before such a drastic move is made, the nurse must clearly identify the reasons for moving.[13] Sometimes all that is needed is time away from work to sort out problems and to put things in perspective.

Burnout is common among nurses because of the responsibilities their practice entails. Nurses need to recognize that they have needs, and they must be sensitive to them in order to prevent burnout. One cannot be effective in nursing practice if concern for self as a person is not present.

Ethical/moral decisions and the nurse

The decision to prolong life

Medical, surgical, and technological advancements now allow professionals to prolong life in situations where previously death would have occurred as a natural course of events. While beneficial to countless children and families, these developments have also generated ethical and moral controversies. One of the issues involves the "sanctity of life" versus the "quality of life" philosophies. In other words, just because we have the means to do so, are we obligated to attempt to save *all* lives or can we save only *some* lives?

"Quality of life" and "sanctity of life" issues

Quality of life means that certain criteria or characteristics need to be present in order for a child to be considered human. The child must be capable of or have the potential for human relationships.[14] Self-awareness is another factor considered essential for personhood.[15] Basically, quality of life involves more than the maintenance of heart rate and respirations. Both the child's physical and intellectual endowment and potential familial and societal contributions are used to determine the child's quality of life.[16] Believers of this philosophy think some lives are of more value than others and quality of life factors should be weighed when deciding whether to prolong life.

Proponents of the *sanctity of life* position believe that life is a value in and of itself. The ability to interact with others, intellectual capabilities, and potential contributions to family, for example, are not factors in the child's status as a person. Just the child's existence, regardless of abilities or potential, entitles a child to consideration as a person. Sanctity of life philosophers hold that medical criteria for care should remain physiological.[17] For example, they believe that life-prolonging measures should be used for a defective child because the child's illness warrants the use of such measures. They assert that the defect should not be a factor in the decision. However, they also believe that no treatment is indicated when none exists that can do any more than just prolong dying.[18]

The decision to implement life-prolonging measures is usually made by physicians, parents, or both. Some physicians feel the responsibility rests with them because parents are not emotionally capable of making a rational choice.[19,20] Others contend that parents need to participate in any decisions regarding treatment and be fully informed of the consequences of giving and witholding consent.[21] These authorities believe parents are fully capable of reaching a decision if they are provided with the proper information.[22] Regardless of whether their child is normal or defective, the decision about prolonging life is a major stress for parents. "Quality of life" criteria may or may not have an influence on their decision. Physicians, as decision-makers, do not necessarily have the best interests of the child in mind when they institute life-prolonging measures. Their actions may be based on a sense of duty to save life. The decision to prolong life is not necessarily made on a conscious level by either parents or physicians but is rather implemented as the next step in the child's treatment.

Legal implications of the decision The decision about prolonging life has many legal implications which affect the child, parents, physicians, and nurses. As cited previously, parents are legally responsible for the health and well-being of their child. Thus only they are legally capable of consenting to medical treatment. A person, in the legal or constitutional sense, is "anyone born."[23] Courts do not usually attempt to make quality of life decisions. Courts will, however, act to protect the best interests of the child by giving "proxy consent." In using proxy consent, a judge may override the parents' legal right to consent to or withhold consent for their child's treatment. The court can order life-prolonging treatment for someone incompetent to make such decisions if there is any potential for the life to be saved. For example, a court may order an open heart operation for a severely retarded child against the parents' wishes. The surgical procedure will prolong the child's life but will not affect mental capacity. In this situation, the sanctity of life rather than the quality of life is the major consideration. Furthermore, this decision means that no one life is more valuable than another—all are the same. Courts are expanding their role as the protectors of the best interests of the child.[24]

Physicians are legally accountable for their actions and decisions. The decision to prolong life or withhold treatment is not their choice to make alone. Decisions which bear on public attitudes regarding the value of human life should not be made in the relative secrecy of hospital wards. Neither should they be made by individuals who are not institutionally responsible to the public for making principled and impartial decisions.[25] Legally, then, one cannot decide the value of one life versus another. Parents and physicians are not necessarily impartial decision-makers for a child. Courts generally order the use of life-prolonging measures for children unless brain death is undeniably present.

Even though nurses are not often participants in the decision-making process, they are affected by the legal ramifications of the decision. The withholding of life-prolonging measures from an infant or child in the absence of clearly defined and documented brain death may result in legal action. In many states, such action is subject to criminal prosecution under child abuse and neglect statutes. To date no such legal procedure has been taken against physicians or nurses, but the possibility is always present. In the legal sense, a nurse could conceivably be subjected to prosecution for neglecting to report the withholding of treatment from an infant or child. This "passive euthanasia" is most often encountered in critical care or newborn intensive care units and involves defective infants and children. Nurses must be attentive to the legal as well as moral and ethical implications of such actions.

The nurse and life-prolonging measures

Physicians and parents are the primary decision-makers for a child. Parents have a role because they are legally and morally responsible for the child and they are expected to protect and promote the child's best interests. Physicians have expertise in medical treatment and therefore they are considered capable of prescribing the best course of treatment for a child. The nursing role with regard to the implementation of life-prolonging measures is seldom considered. However, it is necessary for nurses to participate in the outcomes of the decision. Again, the nurse is placed in the middle. The nurse has many responsibilities and is required to have many skills, and yet the nurse possesses few powers of decision.[26]

Conflicting values and loyalties This difficult position leads to role and rule confusion and conflict for the nurse because of the nurse's many loyalties. The nurse has responsibilities to the child, the parents, other nursing staff members, the employing agency, and the nursing profession. The nurse is also responsible for carrying out physicians' orders. In some circumstances involving life-prolonging measures, these loyalties can become contradictory.

Use of life-prolonging measures for infants and children who have pathophysiological problems with a good prognosis is seldom a conflict situation. Although it may be stressful for parents and professionals in terms of the child's care and condition, role and rule conflicts are rarely a problem. The use of life-prolonging measures for a defective infant or child, however, may lead to serious and sustained conflict for professionals. The quality of life versus the sanctity of life becomes the center of controversy. The matter of who is the most qualified decision-maker—parent or physician—can also surface.

Do parents have a right to refuse treatment for their defective infant or child if the treatment will only prolong life without changing the underlying defect? Do physicians have the right, despite parents' wishes, to prolong a life which will never be normal? These are only basic questions in the current moral and ethical debate. Nursing is not and cannot be a silent bystander because of the very nature of professional practice. Nurses may not be involved in the decision to implement life-prolonging measures, but they are frequently the ones who initiate such measures. In situations involving a defective infant or child, the issues become extremely confusing and complex.

The nurse may experience conflict in the role of child and family advocate. Because of their close proximity to the child's family, nurses may believe they know more than the physician about the impact of the situation on the family. Conflict may arise between physicians and nurses over what is best for a particular child or family unit. Also, strife may occur among nursing staff members with regard to the rightness or wrongness of prolonging the life of a defective infant or child.

What is the effect of such issues and concerns on nursing care? Physical care of the child may easily become the focus of the nurse's attention. Care of the machines may replace care for the child. The personalized dimension of care may also suffer. Furthermore, the nurses' emotional support for parents may be affected because the nurses disagree with the parents' decision to implement life-prolonging measures or because life-prolonging measures were implemented against the parents' desires. In either case it becomes difficult for nurses to provide crucial emotional support to parents. Nurses may feel they are doing more harm than good in such circumstances. Feelings and beliefs are based on a nurse's personal value system and moral code. How can one provide counseling to parents whose beliefs contradict the nurse's personal codes? It is extremely difficult and demanding and oftentimes is simply left undone.

The nurse in crisis Inner conflict and turmoil often result when a nurse is confronted with events that challenge or are directly opposed to the nurse's personal standards. The nurse becomes frustrated because of powerlessness to alter the situation even though the nurse is a participant in it. In order to cope with such circumstances, nurses may employ defense mechanisms which enable them to function. Some nurses use denial; others withdraw emotionally. Such nurses may find themselves in a crisis state.

The elements related to a crisis state are: (1) perception of the event; (2) available situational support; and (3) coping mechanisms. Weakness in any one of these factors can set the stage for disequilibrium and crisis.[27] For example, a defective infant requiring life-prolonging measures can upset the nurses's state of equilibrium. See Figure 18-3). The nurse is a nonparticipant in the decision-making process. Lack of situational support promotes the continuation of the crisis. Withdrawal and denial are inadequate coping mechanisms because they promote anxiety over the care of the infant and family. These coping mechanisms do not allow for resolution of the problem. Rather, they continue the process of disequilibrium, which leads to crisis.

Nurses in a crisis state need situational support that will enable them to realistically confront the situation and cope with it. Often nurses agree with one another that a particular situation is stressful, but they do not always follow through and attempt to understand why it is stress-producing and employ means to deal with it. Careful examination and analysis, coupled with professional support, can enable nurses to provide personalized care to an infant requiring life-prolonging measures. This is good situational support. Emotional support for parents can be provided either by the nurse involved in the care of the child or by an objective nurse consultant.

Legal, ethical, and moral issues in contemporary practice

This chapter has identified a few of the legal, ethical, and moral aspects of pediatric nursing practice. This area of nursing is quite complex. There are far more questions than there are answers, and more doubts than there are facts. As a result of increased technology and scientific knowledge, nurses will more frequently encounter the problems discussed here. Health care institutions are establishing ethics committees to deal with gray areas of life and death issues. Awareness of these dilemmas is not enough, however. Each nurse must realize that she or he will be confronted with difficult moral and ethical problems at some point in professional practice. At that point, each individual must appraise her or his own practice, value system, and moral code and must also be sensitive to those of the child, of the child's parents, and of other professionals.

Figure 18-3 Handling a stress situation: two possible outcomes. (*Adapted from Donna C. Aguilera and Janice M. Messick, Crisis Intervention: Theory and Methodology, 3d ed., Mosby, St. Louis, 1978. Used by permission.*)

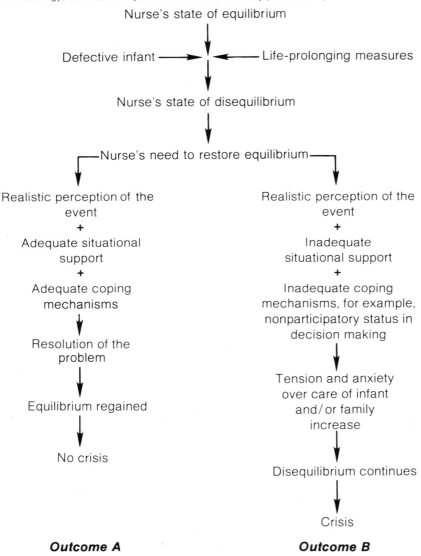

Nursing Care Plan–Infant with Multiple Defects

Assessment

Mr. and Mrs. James have just become parents of a son, born at 35 weeks gestation. During the course of the initial physical examination, a strong suggestion of Down syndrome is noted. Cardiac and gastrointestinal anomalies are evidenced by cyanosis, tachycardia, tachypnea, and his rapidly distending abdomen.

The parents are informed of their son's condition. They are visibly upset. Because of the labor and delivery process, both parents are physically and emotionally drained. Now they must deal with their infant's poor condition, mental retardation, and multiple anomalies. The parents must make a decision about surgery to repair the digestive defect. The danger of operating is compounded by the infant's prematurity and cardiac status.

The parents ask to see their son and are taken to the neonatal intensive care unit. The baby is attached to various monitors, has a nasogastric tube inserted, is receiving oxygen, and has an intravenous line. The Jameses appear extremely anxious and concerned. They ask several times about their child's mental retardation and what can be done to help it. They are also concerned about what the operation will do for their son.

The physical assessment suggests that the James infant requires comprehensive medical and nursing care. (See Chapter 19, "Care of the High-Risk Infant.") The care plan which follows focuses on the parents. Although the nurse is responsible for the physical care of the infant, it is also important that the nurse consider the needs of the parents in planning and providing care for this family unit.

Nursing diagnosis	Nursing goals	Nursing actions	Evaluation/revision
1. Parental grief secondary to birth of defective infant. **2.** Parental guilt feelings due to birth of defective infant.	☐ Parents will be able to verbalize feelings of anger and sadness (short-term goal).	☐ Provide privacy when talking with parents. ☐ Help parents explore their feelings and emotions. ☐ Tell parents that their reactions are normal; repeat this as much as necessary. ☐ Keep parents informed of baby's condition and care being provided. ☐ Do not wait for parents to ask questions; provide frequent opportunities for them to discuss their baby.	☐ Day after admission: Parents are confused and bewildered. They keep saying that their son is sick "because of us." Mrs. James can touch the baby with her fingertips, but Mr. James only looks at him. *Revision* (day after admission): ☐ Reinforce that the baby's condition did not occur because of something the parents did or didn't do.
	☐ Parents will be able to participate in their son's care (long-term goal).	☐ Encourage parents to visit the nursery at any time. ☐ Encourage parents to hold child. ☐ Allow parents privacy when visiting their son. ☐ Encourage parents to participate in son's care and increase their participation gradually. ☐ Expect that parents may direct some of their anger at nursing staff—do *not* react personally!	☐ Continue to explore parents' feelings. ☐ Spend time with each parent individually in order to assess personal and unique reactions. ☐ Accept father's reluctance to touch infant, but offer positive comments about his visits to the nursery. ☐ Continue nursing actions stated in plan.

Nursing diagnosis	Nursing goals	Nursing actions	Evaluation/revision
3. Impaired decision-making ability due to crisis state.	☐ With the aid of informed consent, parents will be able to make a decision regarding the proposed operative procedure (short-term goal).	☐ Reiterate the infant's physical problems as necessary to aid parents' understanding (parents' anxiety and overload of information may interfere with comprehension). ☐ Explain that the operation will repair only the gastrointestinal defect so that the baby can be fed by mouth. ☐ Answer questions patiently. ☐ Explain the purpose of equipment used in baby's care. ☐ Clarify what physician has already told parents about infant's condition and the planned surgery. ☐ Tell parents that nurses understand that the decision they face is a heavy burden.	☐ Day after admission: Mr. James says he knows that his son is mentally retarded, but he keeps asking how it can be treated. Mrs. James wants to know how retarded her son will be. ☐ Parents seem overwhelmed at the prospect of surgery for so small an infant. *Revision* (day after admission): ☐ Explain that mental retardation is permanent, but many children with Down syndrome can learn to be productive in some way. ☐ Explain that although surgery does pose a risk for the baby, it is the only way he can survive (parents need to know consequences if they withhold consent).
	☐ Parents will verbalize satisfaction with the decision they made.	☐ Continue to provide parents support measures described for Nursing Diagnoses 1, 2, and 3, regardless of their decision.	☐ Continue to update parents on baby's condition. ☐ Continue nursing actions stated in plan.
4. Impaired parent-infant interaction due to potential loss of infant and presence of physical defects and mental retardation.	☐ Parents will be able to verbalize feelings about the potential loss of their son (short-term goal). ☐ Parents will progress through stages of grief (long-term goal).	☐ Listen patiently to parents' fears. ☐ Encourage as much acquaintance with newborn as they are ready to accept (even with normal infants, this process takes time!). ☐ Encourage parents to engage in care-taking activities, but do *not* push them. ☐ Acknowledge that baby could die even after surgery. ☐ Continue nursing interventions for Nursing Diagnoses 1, 2, and 3. ☐ Talk to infant as a person, so parents will know the nurses care about them as a family unit.	☐ Day after admission: Mr. James says he knows that he should love his son but he finds it hard because the baby is not what he expected. Mrs. James said: "I am afraid to love him too much. . . ." *Revision* (day after admission) ☐ Acknowledge Mr. James' feelings of disappointment without being judgmental. ☐ Tell Mrs. James nurses understand that she is fearful of loving her child and then losing him.

References

1. Leah L. Curtin, "The Nurse as Advocate: A Philosophical Foundation for Nursing," *Advances in Nursing Science* 1:3 (April 1979).
2. George J. Annas, *The Rights of Hospital Patients: The Basic ACLU Guide to a Hospital Patient's Rights*, Avon, New York, 1975, p. 137.
3. George J. Annas, et al., *Informed Consent to Human Experimentation: The Subject's Dilemma*, Ballinger, Cambridge, 1977, p. 94.
4. Ibid., p. 70.
5. Ibid., p. 69.
6. Shirley M. Steele, *Values Clarification in Nursing*, Appleton-Century-Crofts, New York, 1979, p. 1.
7. David E. Hartl, "Stress Management and the Nurse," *Advances in Nursing Science* 1:91 (July 1979).
8. Barbara A. Carper, "The Ethics of Caring," *Advances in Nursing Science* 1:13 (April 1979).
9. Elsie Bandman and Bertrand Bandman, "The Nurse's Role in Protecting the Patient's Right to Live or Die," *Advances in Nursing Science* 1:22 (April 1979).
10. Jerry Edelwich and Archie Brodsky, *Burn-Out: Stages of Disillusionment in the Helping Professions*, Human Sciences Press, New York, 1980, p. 14.
11. Seymour Shubin, "Burnout: The Professional Hazard You Face in Nursing," *Nursing 78* 8:25 (July 1978).
12. Ibid., p. 24.
13. Ibid., p. 27.
14. Richard A. McCormick, "To Save or Let Die: The Dilemma of Modern Medicine," *Journal of the American Medical Association* 229:174, (July 8, 1974).
15. Michael Topley, "Abortion and Infanticide," *Philosophy and Public Affairs*, 2:37–65 (Fall 1970).
16. Anthony Shaw, "Defining the Quality of Life," *Hastings Center Report* 7:11 (October 1977).
17. Paul Ramsey, *Ethics at the Edges of Life*, Yale New Haven, 1978, p. 206.
18. Ibid., p. 192.
19. J. F. Inglefinger, "Bedside Ethics for the Hopeless Case," *New England Journal of Medicine* 289:914 (Oct. 25, 1973).
20. John M. Freeman, "To Treat or Not To Treat: Ethical Dilemmas of Treating the Infant with a Myelomeningocele," *Clinical Neurosurgery* 20:141 (1973).
21. Anthony Shaw, "Dilemmas of Informed Consent in Children," *New England Journal of Medicine* 289:890 (Oct. 25, 1973).
22. Raymond S. Duff and A. G. M. Campbell, "Moral and Ethical Dilemmas in the Special Care Nursery," *New England Journal of Medicine* 289:893 (Oct. 25, 1973).
23. Ramsey, op. cit., p. 199.
24. Annas, *Informed Consent to Human Experimentation*, p. 94.
25. Charles H. Baron, "Medical Paternalism and The Rule of Law: A Reply to Dr. Relman," *American Journal of Law and Medicine* 4:362, (Winter 1979).
26. Andrew Jameton, "The Nurse: When Roles and Rules Conflict," *Hastings Center Report*, 8:22, (August 1977).
27. Donna Aguilera and Janice Messick, *Crisis Intervention: Theory and Methodology*, Mosby, St. Louis, 1978, pp. 70–71.

Chapter 19 Nursing care of the high-risk infant

Julie A. Goodman

Upon completion of this chapter, the student will be able to:

1. Relate the state of preconceptional maternal health to fetal and newborn health.

2. Describe the use of prenatal assessment tools to predict fetal well-being.

3. Use the gestational age assessment tool to evaluate gestational age.

4. Identify the role of transport and the neonatal intensive care unit in the care of the high-risk infant.

5. Identify the immediate care needs of the depressed newborn.

6. Describe the problems specific to an infant who has inappropriate growth for gestational age.

7. Identify the problems common to the postmature infant.

8. Relate the physiological immaturity of the preterm infant to the physiological handicaps of that infant.

9. Contrast the methods of feeding the high-risk infant.

10. Describe the alterations caused by faulty oxygenation found in the high-risk newborn.

11. Contrast physiological and pathological jaundice.

12. Compare the disease process and supportive care for ABO and Rh hemolytic disease.

13. Describe the effects of maternal diabetes on the infant of a diabetic mother.

14. Identify the signs of fetal alcohol syndrome in the affected newborn.

15. Describe the signs of drug addiction in a newborn.

16. Discuss the commonalities underlying birth trauma.

17. Assess the steps in parenting affected by the birth of a high-risk infant.

High risk is a comprehensive term applied to a wide range of infants—from the minimally ill to the critically ill. High-risk babies are those born too early, too late, too large, or too small, and those who have a congenital anomaly or who were injured during birth. Whatever the cause or severity of the illness, a high-risk newborn needs special medical and nursing assistance to maintain the bodily functions that normal newborns are capable of supporting independently. Often the factors that place the newborn at risk are classified according to preconceptional, prenatal, intrapartum, and postpartum events. A special report by the Johnson Foundation states one out of every seven births has some element of high risk.[1]

Identification of the high-risk infant
Preconceptional factors

The fetus is almost totally dependent on its mother for a healthy environment; therefore, preparation for pregnancy should begin long before conception occurs. Ideally, this preparation takes place by maintaining a high level of wellness, especially between puberty and childbearing age. Often the initial opportunity to evaluate a woman's health arises when she comes for birth control or a premarital physical examination. History and physical examination will reveal physical problems, and the visit can be utilized for education to prevent future risks. Important subjects for preconceptional counseling are listed in Table 19-1.

Table 19-1 Topics for preconceptional counseling

1. Timing of pregnancy

Ages 20–35 are optimal ages for childbearing. Women 16 and under and over 35 are at higher risk. A 2-year interval between pregnancies is recommended.

2. Nutrition

Reinforce the need for a well-balanced diet. Discuss control of weight.

3. Prenatal care

Emphasize the need for a prepregnant physical examination to correct or control health impairments. Discuss the need for early prenatal care even when healthy.

4. Drugs

Avoid all drugs durings the first trimester and while trying to become pregnant. Consult a doctor about prescribed drugs before attempting to become pregnant. Street drugs and pot have unknown effect and should be avoided.

5. Alcohol use

Advise to stop drinking or not to drink more than 2 oz of alcohol (two mixed drinks or two cans of beer) a day. Fetal alcohol syndrome is discussed later in the chapter.

6. Genetic counseling

Premarital genetic counseling should be considered if a close relative has a disorder considered to be inherited. Indications for genetic counseling are listed in Table 8-11.

7. Smoking

Smoking retards fetal growth and should be decreased or stopped before beginning a pregnancy.

8. Effects of diseases (see also Chap. 34)

A. Rubella (measles)

All girls should be immunized. A rubella titer greater than 1:8 indicates immunity. If not immune, females should receive measles immunization at least 3 months before attempting a pregnancy. Avoid contact with sick children during pregnancy. Rubella causes cataracts, hearing defects, and heart defects in the fetus during the first 3 months of pregnancy.

B. Toxoplasmosis

The protozoon causing toxoplasmosis crosses the placenta. When planning a pregnancy, avoid eating undercooked red meat or contact with a cat. (Cats confined entirely to the home that eat commercial cat food present little risk). Mental retardation, hydrocephaly, microcephaly, and jaundice from liver damage can result in the fetus.

C. Gonorrhea

Treat early to prevent infertility from tubal adhesions. Treat mother before birth to prevent blindness in the newborn (ophthalmia neonatorum). The disease is acquired from the infected birth canal.

D. Syphilis

Treat with penicillin to prevent the disease in fetus. Syphilis crosses the placental barrier after about 20 weeks gestation.

E. Herpes Simplex, type II

Discuss herpes infections during prenatal care. Notify physician if any genital blisters appear. If active infection at term, there is danger of massive fetal infection (encephalitis). May need cesarean section if disease is active.

Prenatal factors

After conception, certain prenatal factors have proven to be important predictors of newborn health. These are (1) quality of prenatal care, (2) education, (3) socioeconomic status, (4) father's occupation, (5) nutrition, and (6) genetic factors and race.

All of these factors are interrelated. The pregnant woman living in a poverty situation is often poorly educated and has little access to good prenatal care or nutritious food. Low birth weight and high fetal morbidity (illness) are frequently correlated with race, being higher in blacks and Indians than in whites. Low birth-weight infants occur in 4 to 15 percent of whites and 12 to 15 percent of nonwhites.[2] However, this is actually related more to poverty, poor nutrition, and deficient prenatal care than to any inherent quality of a specific population. The greatest positive influence on the health of newborns remains the quality and number of prenatal visits.

Attempts to break the high-risk cycle prenatally are seen in the federal government's funding of neighborhood health clinics and providing supplemental food programs for pregnant women.

Prenatal fetal risk scoring sheet There are many assessment tools for evaluating the prenatal risks to the fetus. These tools provide convenient checklists and are used at prenatal visits to review risks present in the pregnancy.

The risk scoring system of Goodwin, Dunne, and Thomas, Table 19-2, is an example of such

Table 19-2 Scoring form for serial identification of the high-risk fetus

Check off all risk factors present (even if maximum score is reached) and tabulate the fetal risk score and gestation at each visit in the space provided below.

Part A — Score 0, 1, 2 or 3 to a maximum of 3   A
Part B — Score 0, 1, 2 or 3 to a maximum of 3   B
Part C — Score 0, 1, 2, 3 or 4 to a maximum of 4   +C
                         Fetal risk score:

A. BASELINE DATA

Age 35+ .... 1 ☐
    40+ .... 2 ☐
Para 0 .... 1 ☐
    6+ .... 2 ☐
Interval less than 2 yrs .... 1 ☐
Obesity 200 lbs+ .... 1 ☐
Diabetes mild-moderate .... 2 ☐
    severe .... 3 ☐
Chronic renal disease .... 1 ☐
    With diminished renal function .... 3 ☐
Preexisting hypertension
    140+ /90+ .... 1 ☐
    160+ /110+ .... 2 ☐

PREVIOUS OBSTETRICAL HISTORY:

Abortion .... ☐
Stillbirth .... ☐
Neonatal death .... ☐
Surviving premature infant .... ☐
Antepartum hemorrhage .... ☐
Toxemia .... ☐
Midforceps delivery .... ☐
Cesarean section .... ☐
Major congenital anomaly .... ☐
Baby 10 lbs+ .... ☐
    One instance of above .... 1 ☐
    Two or more instances
    of above .... 2 ☐
Rh isoimmunized mother .... 2 ☐
+ History of erythroblastosis .... 3 ☐

B. PRESENT PREGNANCY

Bleeding, before 20 weeks
    Alone .... 1 ☐
    With pain .... 2 ☐
Bleeding, after 20 weeks
    Ceased .... 1 ☐
    Continues .... 2 ☐
    With pain .... 3 ☐
    With hypotension .... 3 ☐
Spontaneous premature rupture
of membranes .... 1 ☐
    Latent period 24 h' .... 2 ☐
Anemia 8 to 10 g .... 1 ☐
    Less than 8 g .... 2 ☐
No prenatal care .... 2 ☐
    1 to 3 prenatal visits .... 1 ☐

Toxemia mild-moderate .... 1 ☐
    severe .... 3 ☐
Hydramnios (single-fetus) .... 3 ☐
Multiple pregnancy .... 2 ☐
Abnormal glucose tolerance .... 1 ☐
    Decreasing insulin requirement .... 3 ☐
    Maternal diabetic acidosis .... 3 ☐
Maternal pyrexia .... 1 ☐
Pyrexia + FHR greater than 160 .... 2 ☐
Rh negative
    With antibody titer .... 2 ☐
    With amniotic fluid Liley zone 111 .... 3 ☐

C. GESTATIONAL AGE (AT TIME OF SCORING)

28 wk or under .... 4 ☐
29–32 wk .... 3 ☐
33–35 wk .... 2 ☐
36–37 wk .... 1 ☐

38–41 wk .... 0 ☐
42 wk .... 1 ☐
43 wk or more .... 2 ☐

PRENATAL VISITS* (Goodwin, Dunne, and Thomas fetal risk scoring system)

1st visit (e.g.)	2d visit	3d visit	4th visit	5th visit	6th visit
Date: Jan. 2/79	Date:	Date:	Date:	Date:	Date:
Gestational age: 29/40	Gestational age: /40	Gestational age: /40	Gestational age: /40	Gestational age: /40	Gestational age: /40
Fetal risk score: 7/10	Fetal risk score: /10	Fetal risk score: /10	Fetal risk score: /10	Fetal risk score: /10	Fetal risk score: /10
7th visit	8th visit	9th visit	10th visit	11th visit	12th visit
Date:	Date:	Date:	Date:	Date:	Date:
Gestational age: /40	Gestational age: /40	Gestational age: /40	Gestational age: /40	Gestational age: /40	Gestational age: /40
Fetal risk score: /10	Fetal risk score: /10	Fetal risk score: /10	Fetal risk score: /10	Fetal risk score: /10	Fetal risk score: /10

Final Fetal Risk Score ——————/10
(= fetal risk score just prior to labor)

* The actual number of visits will of course vary.

Source: J. Goodwin, J. Dunne, and B. Thomas, "Antepartum Identification of the Fetus at Risk," *Canadian Medical Association Journal* 101(458):57–65 (Oct. 18, 1969).

a risk sheet. It consists of three parts. Part A is the baseline data usually obtained at the initial visit. Part B lists the factors relating to problems in the present pregnancy, as well as to the limitations of prenatal care. Part C consists of the gestational age in weeks. Gestational age is important in determining the maturity of the fetus and is directly related to the ability of the fetus to survive outside the uterus. Table 9-2 lists the appropriate weight and development for gestational age.

Gestational age, calculated by using the last menstrual period (LMP), is used to get the estimated date of confinement (EDC) or delivery. It is sometimes difficult to accurately assess gestational age because of variations in the menstrual-cycle length and the presence of implantation bleeding. Both *quickening* (first fetal movement, felt at about 18 to 20 weeks) and *fetal heart tones* (heard with a fetoscope by 20 weeks or a Doppler ultrasound instrument by 12 weeks) will help confirm the accuracy of dates. Most large medical centers also use ultrasound (B-Scan) to establish gestational age and monitor fetal growth.

Uterine size is monitored and the rate of enlargement compared to normal. An unusually rapid increase of uterine size may indicate twins, hydramnios (excessive amniotic fluid), or hydatidiform mole (degeneration of embryo into a group of grape-like vesicles). An abnormally slow rate of fetal growth and small uterine size often result from poor placental blood flow and may indicate intrauterine growth retardation or even fetal death.

Prenatal risks are assessed at each visit. The risk sheet accompanies the patient's chart to the hospital. Evaluation of the risks will help the obstetric staff determine special precautions and care needed for safety in labor and delivery. The back of the risk sheet (not shown) provides space for a discharge summary of labor, delivery, and newborn outcome.

Tools for assessment of fetal well-being Advances in fetal medicine have made it possible to study fetal status in utero. Biochemical samples can be obtained to give information about genetic disease, sex, fetal maturity, and certain congenital anomalies. Many of these tests are used to diagnose chronic fetal distress. Tools for assessing fetal status are discussed in greater detail in any current obstetrics book. Table 19-3 summarizes the significant features of some common procedures for fetal assessment.

Fetal monitoring is used to diagnose acute fetal distress in labor and to closely observe the status of the fetus who previously experienced stress. Monitoring helps to predict the infant's condition at birth. It consists of two tracings—the heart rate of the fetus and the uterine contraction pattern. *External monitors* are applied abdominally and are used in early labor and for both the nonstress and the stress (OCT) test. Using the *internal monitor* is a much more intrusive procedure than external monitoring. A thin spiral wire is introduced through the vagina and cervix and attached superficially to the fetal scalp to monitor the fetal heart. The normal fetal heart rate is 120 to 160 beats per minute, but a rate between 100 and 180 is usually considered a safe range. A Teflon catheter, placed inside the uterus, monitors the pressure of the contractions as reflected in the amniotic fluid. (The reader is referred to a current obstetrics book for a detailed discussion of fetal monitoring patterns.)

Intrapartum risk factors (labor and delivery)

Labor and delivery is a time of stress even for the healthy fetus. For the fetus who has previously experienced stress, this is a time when fetal well-being hangs in the balance. The outcome of labor and delivery is directly related to: (1) oxygenation of the fetus, (2) safe passageway through the birth canal, (3) fetal maturity and condition at birth. Table 19-4 summarizes the factors that affect each of these three areas.

Assessment of the high-risk infant at birth

The previous discussion of risk factors focused on the assessment of fetal condition. Assessment of the newborn's condition includes birth weight, gestational age, and an evaluation of any disease process or congenital anomaly present.

The *Apgar score* is the most commonly used tool for assessment of the newborn's condition. It provides a good evaluation of the newborn's condition right after birth. Most normal newborns have Apgar scores of 7 to 10. (Apgar scoring is discussed in detail in Chap. 10, and low Apgar scores will be discussed in a later section on respiratory distress.)

The Silverman scale (Fig. 19-1) is frequently used to assess respiratory status at birth. The

Table 19-3 Fetal assessment procedures

Test	Method	Purpose
1. Fundal height	Measure height of uterus in relationship to symphysis in early pregnancy, and umbilicus and xiphoid process as pregnancy advances	Shows progression of fetal growth. Normal findings are: 12 weeks—uterus above symphysis 20 weeks—uterus at umbilicus 39–40 weeks—uterus just below xiphoid process
2. Leopold's maneuvers	Manually palpate abdomen.	Gives an estimation of fetal size, fetal presentation (breech, vertex), and single or multiple fetuses.
3. Amniocentesis Analysis of fetal cells	Withdrawal of amniotic fluid from the amniotic cavity through a needle, often used with ultrasound to determine where placenta, cord, and fetus are located.	At about 16 weeks gestation, test can determine sex and many genetic defects (Down syndrome, Tay-Sachs, and others). See also Chap. 8.
Analysis of bilirubin in amniotic fluid		Bilirubin usually disappears from amniotic fluid by 36 weeks gestation. Increased levels after 30 weeks indicate destruction of red blood cells. Done for evaluation of Rh incompatibility.
Creatinine in amniotic fluid		Value of 2 mg per 100 ml at 36 weeks indicates maturity of kidneys.
Color of amniotic fluid		Normally straw colored. Meconium will color the fluid brown or green, indicating fetal hypoxia (lack of oxygen). Bilirubin will color fluid yellow.
Phospholipids level		L/S (lecithin-sphingomyelin ratio) 2:1 indicates fetal lung maturity. Sphingomyelin is present all during pregnancy and decreases at term. Lecithin increases with gestational age.
Alpha-fetoprotein		Possible neural-tube defect is indicated by presence of alpha-feto-protein from leakage of spinal fluid into the amniotic fluid.
4. Fetal scalp pH	Fetal scalp blood sample is obtained vaginally through a dilated cervix.	Fetal pH of 7.25–7.35 is normal. Fetal pH below 7.20 indicates beginning acidosis and is a danger signal. A pH of 7 usually indicates fetal death.
5. Amnioscopy	Vaginal inspection of the bag of waters (amniotic fluid seen behind the membranes with a lighted scope) for change in color of amniotic fluid.	Brown or green color indicates passage of meconium.
6. Serial estriols	Collection of 24-h urine specimen done several times to obtain a baseline. Can also be done using blood.	Measures the hormonal function of the placenta. The estriol content of urine and blood in pregnancy rises from 28 weeks to delivery. Values of 12 mg or above indicate adequate placental and fetal adrenal function; 4–12 mg usually indicate fetal death. A sudden drop of 25% is a warning that the fetus is in danger.

Table 19-3 Fetal assessment procedures (*Continued*)

Test	Method	Purpose
7. Shake test	Collect amniotic fluid (or in a newborn, gastric aspirant) and shake with alcohol.	A positive test shows the presence of lecithin and stability of surfactant and will indicate about 95% chance infant will not have respiratory distress syndrome (RDS). Enough bubbles form to make ring around the fluid in the test tube. A negative shake test shows lack of surfactant with few or no bubbles.
8. Ultrasound	Scan using ultrasound waves. Patient needs full bladder.	Used to establish fetal presentation, presence of twins. Detects some abnormalities of fetus (hydrocephalus, anencephaly, hydatidiform mole).
Measurement of biparietal diameter (BPD) of fetal head		Assess fetal gestational age and growth rates: 8.9–10.1 cm normal range of full term BPD. Average is about 9.4 cm.
Placental localization		Visualize implantation site, can see abnormal implantation (placenta previa).
9. Oxytocin challenge test (OCT) or stress test	Use external fetal monitor to check fetal heart tones and contractions. Then give Pitocin to produce 3 contractions in 10 minutes.	Baseline fetal heart rate is established. A delay in return of fetal heart tones (FHT) to normal after a contraction indicates uteroplacental insufficiency. Baby may tolerate stress of labor poorly. A C section must be considered. There are both false negatives and false positives with this test and it should be used as only one of many evaluation tools.
10. Non-stress test (NST) Sometimes called fetal acceleration determination (FAD)	Attach external fetal heart monitor. Use mild, normally present contractions (Braxton-Hicks) or fetal activity and mark each movement.	Fetal heart should accelerate with fetal movement or contractions. Lack of fluctuations (5–20 per minute), a straight baseline (poor variability), or decrease in heart rate predicts a poor reaction to the stress of labor. Called a nonreactive test. Usually done before the stress test.

Silverman scale is scored in the opposite direction from the Apgar, with 10 being the worst score. It evaluates chest movements, retractions, nasal dilatation, and grunting.

Statistics show that the highest number of neonatal deaths occur in the first hour after birth during the difficult transition to independent life. In reporting statistics the following terms are used to describe fetal death (mortality) and illness (morbidity).

Fetal death Death between 20 and 40 weeks gestation. 20 weeks is the legal age of viability. Most states require a birth certificate at 20 weeks.

Neonatal death Death of a newborn in the first 28 days of life. Expressed per 1000 live births.

Perinatal death Death from the period of viability (20 weeks) through the first 28 days of life, expressed per 1000 births.

The largest number of newborn deaths are related to low birth weight and immaturity. In the past, the term *premature* was used for any infant weighing 2500 g ($5\frac{1}{2}$ lb) or less. Both the

American Academy of Pediatrics Committee on the Fetus and Newborn and the Expert Committee of the World Health Organization recommend that the following distinctions be made on the basis of birth weight and gestational age.[3]

1. *Low birth weight:* Under 2500 g or 5½ lb
2. *Gestational age:*

Preterm or premature: Under 37 full weeks gestation regardless of weight
Full-term: 38 to 42 weeks gestation
Postterm: Over 42 weeks gestation

Lubchenco further subdivided each gestational age category. Figure 19-2 is the newborn classification and neonatal mortality risk chart

Table 19-4 Risk factors related to labor and delivery outcome for the fetus

	Risk factors	Causes or results of the risk
1. Oxygenation of the fetus in utero	Hemorrhage	Placenta previa Placenta abruptio Uterine atony Uterine rupture Tears of uterus, vagina or cervix
	Maternal disease	Hypertension, diabetes, heart disease, toxemia, anemia, Rh sensitization, renal disease
	Fetal hypoxia	Cord compression Congenital anomalies Placental insufficiency Anemia
	Maternal hypotension	Positional—often related to pressure on the vena cava Effects of anesthetic, analgesics
	Placental aging	Postmaturity Intrauterine fetal growth retardation or fetal death
2. Factors related to fetal movement through the pelvis	Prolonged labor	Faulty position or presentation
	Arrest of labor	Excessively large fetus Small pelvis Uterine inertia (lack of muscle tone or coordinated contractions) Excessive anesthesia
	Precipitous labor	Hypertonic contractions Excessive use of oxytocins to stimulate contractions Trauma to baby
	Trauma to the fetus	Difficult delivery related to large baby, twins, breech or faulty position Premature Forceps
3. Health and maturity of the fetus at birth	Gestational age	Prematurity is largest factor Postmaturity Small-for-dates
	Respiratory distress	Hypoxia in utero Drugs and analgesics Congenital anomalies Immaturity of the respiratory system Aspiration of meconium, blood, or mucus
	Sepsis	Prolonged rupture of membranes Maternal communicable disease
	Type of delivery	C section Difficult forceps delivery Faulty position (breech, face)
	Diseases	See no. 1 above and Table 19-1

Figure 19-1 Silverman-Anderson Index for evaluation of respiratory status. Five criteria are used to arrive at a retraction score. The values 0, 1, or 2 are assigned to each factor, and the total score indicates the degree of distress, from 0 (none) to 10 (severe). [*After W. A. Silverman and D. H. Anderson, Pediatrics* **17**:1(1956). *From G. Scipien et al. (eds.) Comprehensive Pediatric Nursing, 2d ed., McGraw-Hill, New York, 1979.*]

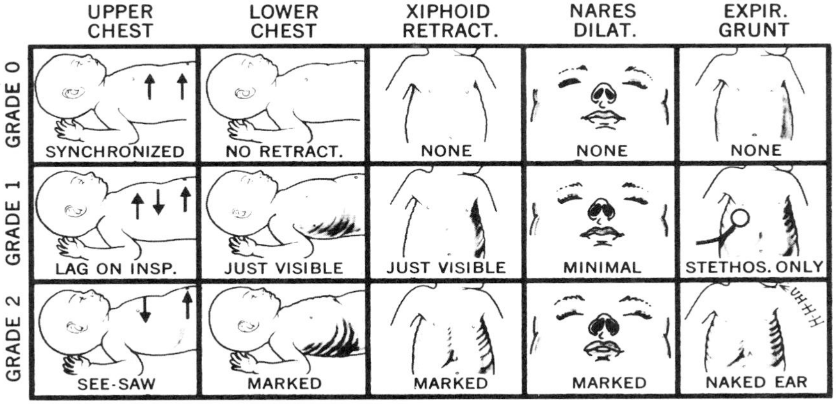

that can be used to estimate fetal mortality. On this chart, a fetus with growth that is *AGA* (appropriate for gestational age) will fall between the 10th and 90th percentile. A fetus below the 10th percentile is classified as *SGA* (small for gestational age) and above the 90th percentile is *LGA* (large for gestational age). Using this chart, the nurse can estimate that a 1500-g fetus at 28 weeks gestation will have a 60 percent survival rate, while the same fetus at 34 weeks will have an 81 percent survival rate.

Gestational age assessment It is important that nurses caring for newborns be able to make accurate gestational age assessments. Even when they are not responsible for the formal assessment, nurses who know gestational age characteristics will be alert for signs of prematurity or postmaturity and will be able to anticipate appropriate care needed for each infant.

The *Dubowitz gestational age assessment tool* consists of two parts—physical characteristics and neurological signs. This tool was tested by nurses during its development. Dubowitz found nurses could do this assessment accurately and quickly. With practice, the entire exam takes about 10 min.

Table 19-5 shows Dubowitz's 11 physical characteristics of the newborn used to detect maturity of body tissue development. These char-

acteristics can be easily seen at birth, and the assessment should be done within 12 h after birth. Table 19-6 is the score sheet.

Figure 19-3 describes 10 signs for evaluating muscle tone. This neurological examination is more difficult to do than the physical evaluation, especially with a sick or sleepy baby. It is quite accurate if done when the newborn is in an alert, quiet state. Table 19-7 gives instructions for estimating gestational age. Figure 19-4 compares characteristics of term and preterm infants.

Intensive care of the high-risk newborn

Since about 1960, there has been a rapid increase in the use of intensive care for newborns. This trend has greatly decreased the neonatal mortality rate. No guidelines for establishing a neonatal intensive care unit existed prior to 1971, however, and units proliferated without specified standards of care.

In 1971, the American Medical Association (AMA) formally recognized the need to centralize and organize newborn care facilities to ensure quality of care. The AMA issued a statement supporting the regionalization of care and levels of caregiving organized by geographic area. The National Foundation–March of Dimes financed a Committee on Perinatal Health that studied

Figure 19-2 Newborn classification and neonatal mortality risk by birth weight and gestational age. [From L. O. Lubchenco, D. T. Searls, J. N. Brazie, Journal of Pediatrics **81**:814–822(1972).]

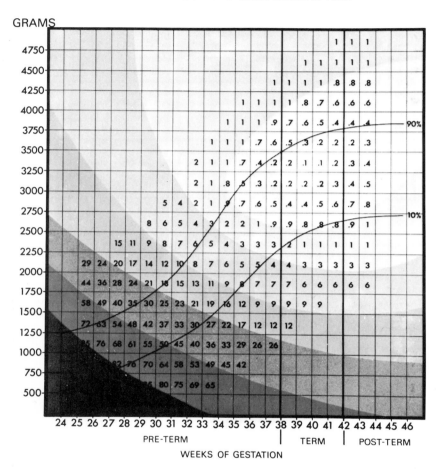

NEWBORN CLASSIFICATION AND NEONATAL MORTALITY RISK
BY BIRTH WEIGHT AND GESTATIONAL AGE

the issue and recommended three levels of care. The levels range from level 1, the least complex, to level 3, the most complex (Fig. 19-5).

Levels of care

Level 1—*primary care*—is provided in a small community hospital designed to give care to full-term, uncomplicated deliveries. Primary care also should detect risks and stabilize the unexpected sick newborn until transfer can be made to a higher level of care, usually a tertiary center.

Level 2—*secondary care*—handles compli-

cated obstetrics and is able to care for certain types of neonatal illnesses. These units have a minimum of 2000 births per year. Staff includes at least two obstetricians, pediatricians, and neonatal nurses. An organized system of transport for patients is set up.

Level 3—*tertiary care*, the most complex—is provided at a large medical center and includes all levels of complex obstetrics and care for high-risk newborns. Obstetricians, RNs with perinatal specialty training, a neonatologist, and specially trained pediatricians are available in a neonatal

Table 19-5 Score sheet for external physical characteristics of the newborn, for use in estimating gestational age*

External sign	Points					Score
	0	1	2	3	4	
Edema	Obvious edema of hands and feet; pitting over tibia	No obvious edema of hands and feet; pitting over tibia	No edema			
Skin texture	Very thin, gelatinous	Thin and smooth	Smooth; medium thickness; rash or superficial peeling	Slight thickening and peeling especially of hands and feet	Thick and parchment-like; superficial or deep cracking	
Skin color	Dark red	Uniformly pink	Pale pink; variable over body	Pale; only pink over ears, lips, palms, or soles		
Skin opacity (trunk)	Numerous veins and venules clearly seen, especially over abdomen	Veins and tributaries seen	A few large vessels clearly seen over abdomen	A few large vessels seen indistinctly over abdomen	No blood vessels seen	
Lanugo (over back)	No lanugo	Abundant; long and thick over whole back	Hair thinning especially over lower back	Small amount of lanugo and bald areas	At least one-half of back devoid of lanugo	
Plantar creases	No skin creases	Faint red marks over anterior half of sole	Definite red marks over > anterior one-half; indentations over < one-third	Indentations over > anterior one-third	Definite deep indentations over > anterior one-third	
Nipple formation	Nipple barely visible, no areola	Nipple well defined; areola smooth and flat, diameter < 0.75 cm	Areola stippled, edge not raised, diameter < 0.75 cm	Areola stippled, edge raised, diameter > 0.75 cm		
Breast size	No breast tissue palpable	Breast tissue on one or both sides, < 0.5 cm diameter	Breast tissue both sides; one or both 0.5–1.0 cm	Breast tissue both sides; one or both >1 cm		
Ear form	Pinna flat and shapeless, little or no incurving of edge	Incurving of part of edge of pinna	Partial incurving whole of upper pinna	Well-defined incurving whole of upper pinna		
Ear firmness	Pinna soft, easily folded, no recoil	Pinna soft, easily folded, slow recoil	Cartilage to edge of pinna, but soft in places; ready recoil	Pinna firm, cartilage to edge; instant recoil		
Genitals Male	Neither testis in scrotum	At least one testis high in scrotum	At least one testis down			
Female (with hips one-half abducted)	Labia majora widely separated, labia minora protruding	Labia majora almost cover labia minora	Labia majora completely cover labia minora			

	External Total:

*Score from this table is combined with score obtained from Table 19-6, and then Table 19-7 is consulted for gestational age determination.

Source: L. S. M. Dubowitz, Victor Dubowitz, and Cissie Goldberg, "Clinical Assessment of Gestational Age in the Newborn Infant," *Journal of Pediatrics* **77**:1–10 (1970).

Table 19-6 Instructions for scoring the neurological assessment of the newborn*

Posture

With the infant supine and quiet, score as follows:

Arms and legs extended	= 0
Slight or moderate flexion of hips and knees	= 1
Moderate-to-strong flexion of hips and knees	= 2
Legs flexed and abducted, arms slightly flexed	= 3
Full flexion of arms and legs	= 4

Square window

Flex the hand at the wrist. Exert pressure sufficient to get as much flexion as possible. The angle between the hypothenar eminence and the anterior aspect of the forearm is measured and scored according to Fig. 18-1. Do not rotate the wrist.

Ankle dorsiflection

Flex the foot at the ankle with sufficient pressure to get maximum change. The angle between the dorsum of the foot and the anterior aspect of the leg is measured and scored as in Fig. 18-1.

Arm recoil

With the infant supine, fully flex the forearms for 5 s, then fully extend by pulling the hands and release. Score the reaction according to:

Remain extended or make random movements	= 0
Incomplete or partial flexion	= 1
Brisk return to full flexion	= 2

Leg recoil

With the infant supine, fully flex the hips and knees for 5 s, then extend them by traction on the feet and release. Score the reaction according to:

No response or slight flexion	= 0
Partial flexion	= 1
Full flexion (less than 90° at knees and hips)	= 2

Popliteal angle

With the infant supine and the pelvis flat on the examining surface, flex the leg on the thigh, and fully flex the thigh with the use of one hand. With the other hand extend the leg, then score the angle attained as in Fig. 18-1.

Heel-to-ear maneuver

With the infant supine, hold the infant's foot with one hand and move it as near to the head as possible without forcing it. Keep the pelvis flat on the examining surface. Score as in Fig. 18-1.

Scarf Sign

With the infant supine, take the infant's hand and draw it across the neck and as far across the opposite shoulder as possible. Assistance to the elbow is permissible by lifting it across the body. Score according to the location of the elbow:

Elbow reaches the opposite anterior axillary line	= 0
Elbow between opposite anterior axillary line and midline of thorax	= 1
Elbow at midline of thorax	= 2
Elbow does not reach midline of thorax	= 3

Head lag

With the infant supine, grasp each forearm just proximal to the wrist and pull gently so as to bring the infant to a sitting position. Score according to the relationship of the head to the trunk during the maneuver:

No evidence of head support	= 0
Some evidence of head support	= 1
Maintains head in the same anteroposterior plane as the body	= 2
Tends to hold the head forward	= 3

Ventral suspension

With the infant prone and the chest resting on the examiner's palm, lift the infant off the examining surface and score according to the posture shown in Fig. 18-1.

*Score obtained by use of this table is added to the score from Table 19-5, and infant's estimated gestational age is found in Table 19-7. See also Fig. 19-B.

Source: L. M. S. Dubowitz, Victor Dubowitz, and Cissie Goldberg, "Clinical Assessment of Gestational Age in the Newborn Infant," *Journal of Pediatrics* **77**:1–10 (1970).

intensive care unit (Fig. 19-6). A well-organized team transports sick newborns and pregnant women at risk.

Transport of the high-risk patient

Referral involves moving pregnant women (maternal transport) or babies after birth (neonatal transport) from a smaller community hospital to a larger medical center hospital. *Transport* is accomplished through the use of a van or ambulance equipped with special life support systems for the newborn. Most neonatal intensive care units also have the capability for airplane or helicopter transport. A specially trained perinatal nurse and pediatrician are members of the transport team for a critically ill newborn.

Since the uterus is the ideal incubator, it is preferred that the high-risk woman be transported *before* delivery. This significantly decreases the severity of newborn illness, subsequent complications, and fetal mortality.[4] If transport occurs after delivery, the neonate must be stabilized before being moved to the neonatal unit.

Factors related to transport that increase the stress to the family and health care personnel involved are:

1. Separation of mother and infant from the family.
2. Separation of the infant from the mother when the baby is put in the neonatal intensive care unit.
3. Increased hospital costs for intensive care, transport, and lengthy hospitalization.
4. Problems with the actual transport (poorly supervised and disorganized transport).

5. Poor communication between referral centers (this may make the physician reluctant to refer patients).
6. Lack of education of personnel in referring communities. Failure to recognize the perinatal risks and the need for referring maternal and infant patients.[5]

Stabilizing the infant after birth

Stabilization of the sick newborn begins in the delivery room. To be ready, the nurse must recognize the signs indicating a high-risk birth.

Figure 19-3 Score sheet for neurological characteristics of the neonate. Instructions for use of this chart are presented in Table 19-6. resulting score is combined with score obtained by use of Table 19-5, and infant's gestational age is then found in Table 19-7. [*From L. M. S. Dubowitz, Victor Dubowitz, and Cissie Goldberg, "Clinical Assessment of Gestational Age in the Newborn Infant," Journal of Pediatrics, **77**:1–10(1970).*]

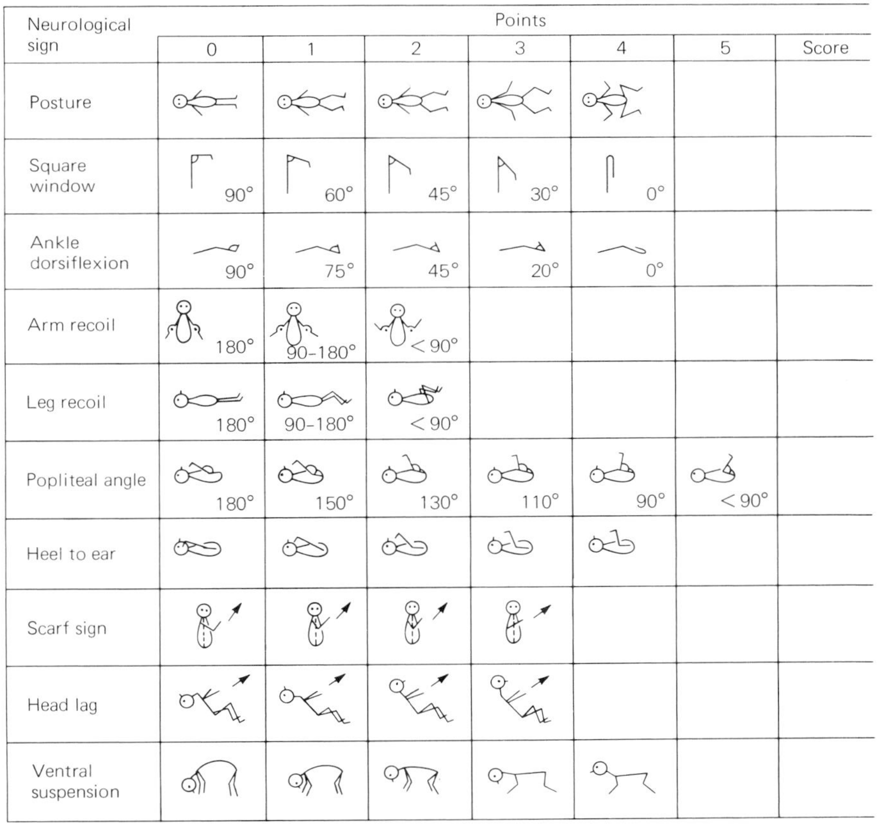

Neurological sign	Points						Score
	0	1	2	3	4	5	
Posture							
Square window	90°	60°	45°	30°	0°		
Ankle dorsiflexion	90°	75°	45°	20°	0°		
Arm recoil	180°	90–180°	<90°				
Leg recoil	180°	90–180°	<90°				
Popliteal angle	180°	150°	130°	110°	90°	<90°	
Heel to ear							
Scarf sign							
Head lag							
Ventral suspension							

Neurological Total: _____

External Total: _____

TOTAL SCORE: _____

Gestation Age: (in weeks) _____

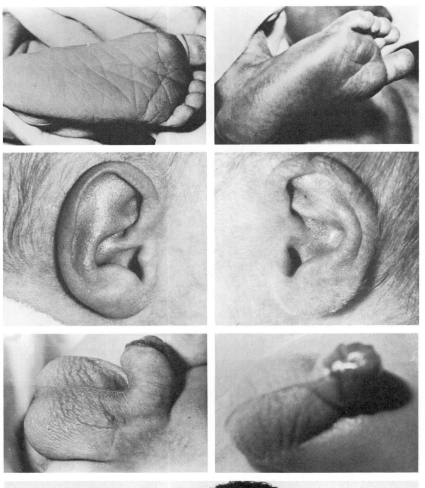

Figure 19-4*A* A comparison of the sole creases of a full-term and pre-term infant. Creases cover the entire sole of the full-term infant's foot. Preterm's sole is smooth and shiny.

Figure 19-4*B* A comparison of the ears shows a well-formed ear with much incurving and good cartilage tone in the full-term infant and an ear with less incurving, much lanugo, and softer cartilage in the preterm infant.

Figure 19-4*C* A comparison of the male genitals shows a full pendulous scrotum with the testes descended in the full-term infant and a small scrotum with few rugae and undescended testes in a preterm infant.

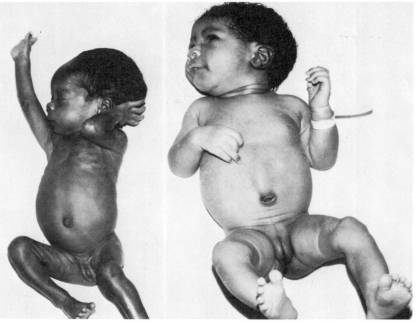

Figure 19-4*D* The same preterm infant pictured in Fig. 19-12 is shown with a 2-day-old black female born at 40 weeks gestation and weighing 3140 g (6 lb, 14 oz) at birth. This comparison demonstrates the full-term infant's characteristically greater muscle tone, darker genital pigmentation, curlier hair, and more abundant subcutaneous fat (including the genital region where the labia majora cover the clitoris). Open, mature eyes contrast with the birdlike lids of the preterm infant. [*From Scipien et al. (eds.), Comprehensive Pediatric Nursing, 2d ed., McGraw-Hill, New York, 1979. Used with permission.*]

Table 19-7 Maturity score sheet for estimating newborn gestational age*

Total score	Gestational age, weeks
5	26
10	27
15	29
20	30
25	31
30	33
35	34
40	35
45	36
50	38
55	39
60	40
65	42
70	43
75	44

*For estimating gestational age after scores have been obtained by neurological characteristics (see Fig. 19-2 and Table 19-6) and external physical characteristics (see Table 19-6)

Source: L. M. S. Dubowitz, Victor Dubowitz, and Cissie Goldberg, "Clinical Assessment of Gestational Age in the Newborn Infant," *Journal of Pediatrics* **77**:1–10 (1970).

Premature labor, maternal history of disease, and fetal distress alert the nurse to prepare for a compromised newborn. The nurse is often responsible for making sure a pediatrician or someone skilled in resuscitation is available when the infant is born. It is important to have one person in the delivery room whose sole responsibility is the well-being of the depressed baby. The nurse usually is responsible for calling the transport team.

The goals of care immediately after birth are to:

1. Establish ventilation
2. Maintain temperature
3. Provide fluids and electrolytes
4. Prevent infection
5. Maintain vital signs.

Establishing ventilation The life of the newborn depends on the early initiation of respirations. Most newborns breathe spontaneously in less than 30 s and need only gentle bulb or DeLee suctioning. If spontaneous respirations are not

Figure 19-5 Schematic representation of regionalized perinatal care. Note equal responsibility and reciprocal interaction between levels. [*From R. Hoekelman et al. (eds.), Principles of Pediatrics: Health Care of the Young, McGraw-Hill, New York, 1978. Used with permission.*]

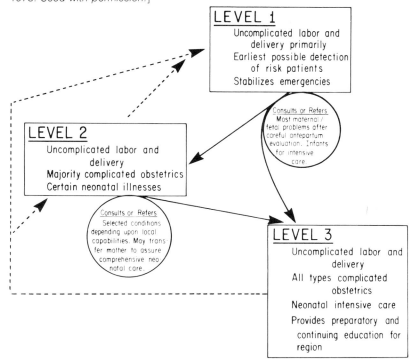

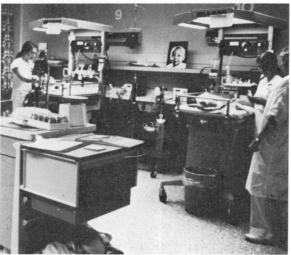

Figure 19-6 This scene shows a typical neonatal intensive care unit with a ratio of one nurse to one or two patients.

established within 1 min, resuscitation is required.

Asphyxia in the newborn may be due to many reasons (Table 19-4). If depression is due to narcotics given to the mother during labor, 0.01 to 0.02 mg/kg of naloxone (Narcan) is given intramuscularly. When signs of asphyxia are visible, the resuscitation begins. This is frequently long before the 1-min Apgar scoring is done. Occasionally the newborn's condition will deteriorate, resulting in a low 5-min Apgar score.

The moderately depressed infant, with an Apgar of 4 to 6, needs intervention to improve oxygenation. The baby appears cyanotic or pale, and limp. The cry is weak. Respirations are irregular and shallow, but the heart rate is above 100. Suctioning is done gently, with low suction, to avoid airway trauma. (Chapter 17 describes safety measures for suctioning.) Oxygen is administered by face mask or a ventilator bag. If not easily ventilated with a mask, the baby is treated like a severely depressed infant. A laryngoscope is inserted, and, under direct visualization, any foreign material, blood, mucus, or meconium is suctioned. Intubation may be necessary.

The severely depressed infant has an Apgar score of 0 to 3. The infant looks pale, blue, and limp and has few spontaneous respirations and no cry. The heart rate is below 100. It is easy to

see this infant needs immediate resuscitation. The laryngoscope is inserted and suctioning done under direct visualization; then the baby is intubated. Oxygen is given with a bag resuscitator or, if one is not available, by short puffs of air given by mouth. Often improvement is dramatic once oxygen is delivered to the lungs. If the heart rate has decreased to 60 or less, the baby is susceptible to cardiac arrest and may need cardiac massage. (See Chap. 17 for the technique for cardiopulmonary resuscitation.)

Acidosis is usually present in the depressed, hypoxic newborn. Oxygen alone will not always correct this state, and additional measures are needed. Initially 2 to 4 milliequivalents (meq) of $\frac{1}{2}$ strength sodium bicarbonate are given by direct infusion through one of the umbilical vessels. Continued doses of sodium bicarbonate are given until resuscitation is completed. An infusion of 10% glucose is started to replace the infant's stores lost by hypoxia and chilling and to prevent further acidosis.

Blood gas measurements to determine the oxygen and carbon dioxide levels in the blood are done every 5 to 15 min during resuscitation and then less frequently. P_{O_2}, the measurement of oxygen in solution in the blood, should be maintained above 50 mmHg, though cyanosis is not visible until it drops to about 40 mmHg.

Blood oxygen levels are done using arterial blood. An arterial catheter is inserted through the umbilical artery. Though complications of blood clots, infection, and reflex arterial spasms may occasionally occur, arterial catheterization is most frequently used to obtain a series of arterial blood samples. Without this source, repeated samples must be taken from punctures of the temporal, radial, or brachial artery. A new device, called a *transcutaneous oxygen monitor* (across the skin), gives continuous oxygen readings without the need to sample blood. It uses a skin contact plate. While it is too early to determine the exact benefits of this technique, early reports are encouraging.

Since capillary blood is of no value for arterial blood readings, a heel stick cannot be used. Heel sticks can be used for pH, P_{CO_2}, and hematocrit levels.

Blood drawn for blood gases should never be left at room temperature because the pH drops and the P_{CO_2} rises. The nurse should put the blood on ice or refrigerate it immediately. Normal

Table 19-8 Normal and abnormal blood gas values for the newborn

Blood component	Normal Range	Range in respiratory depression
P_{O_2}	80–100 mmHg	Below 50 mmHg (hypoxia)
P_{CO_2}	35–45 mmHg	Above 65 mmHg (hypercapnea)
pH	7.35–7.45	Below 7.20 (acidosis)

and abnormal levels of blood gases are given in Table 19-8.

Methods of administering oxygen The infant's oxygen needs after initial resuscitation are provided through a face mask, nasal prongs, or, more frequently, by a hood, incubator, or ventilator.

The incubator or isolette is often used and will allow concentrations of oxygen between 40 and 70 percent. It is difficult to raise the level above 70 percent because the lids may not fit perfectly and the portholes lose oxygen when opened for care (Fig. 19-7).

The oxygen hood gives a higher level of oxygen, 40 to 100 percent, and can be used inside an isolette or in a radiant warmer. A hood is a small plastic bubble that is placed over the infant's head and does not have to be removed for most care. It is essential to warm the oxygen to prevent chilling, because with a hood the oxygen blows directly on the head and face.

Positive-pressure ventilators provide intermittent positive pressure. One type delivers a preset volume of air and the other is controlled by the amount of pressure in the respiratory tract during delivery.

Continuous positive airway pressure (CPAP) provides constant distending pressure in the lungs to keep the alveoli slightly inflated. CPAP can be administered by a hood, face mask, nasal prongs, or by an endotracheal tube. Recent research indicates nasal prongs significantly increase the work of breathing and are therefore less desirable. The distending pressure in the lungs is maintained by adjusting the outflow setting to keep the lungs pressurized. The pressure gauge is usually kept between 2 and 12 mmHg and gradually decreased or increased as the lung condition requires.

Positive end expiratory pressure (PEEP) is another way of maintaining continuous airway pressure *with an endotracheal tube* (Fig. 19-8).

CPAP and PEEP are very similar and are frequently used for babies who have respiratory distress syndrome.

The *negative-pressure ventilator* provides a negative pressure outside the infant's body, allowing outside air to enter the lungs. The iron lung for polio is an example of a negative pressure ventilator.

Nursing management Whatever the method of administration, all oxygen is warmed to 31 to 34°C (89 to 93°F) and humidified between 40 and 60 percent. Oxygen level of the air the infant breathes is controlled through frequent analysis. A portable continuous analyzer can be used. The advantage of the continuous analyzer is the alarm that sounds if the oxygen rises above or falls below the desired concentration. If continuous analysis is not used, the oxygen is analyzed at least every hour and each time blood gases are drawn. (Chapter 17 discusses the technique of oxygen analysis.)

Blood gases are monitored as long as the infant is in oxygen. It is important to use blood oxygen (P_{O_2}) levels when adjusting oxygen concentration,

Figure 19-7 A sick infant is in an isolette with an oxygen hood.

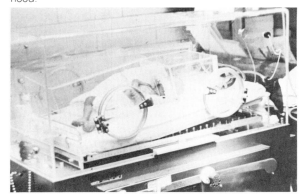

Figure 19-8 An intubated preterm infant attached to the ventilator. A heat sensor and cardiac monitors can also be seen.

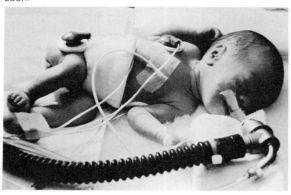

rather than flow rates. The infant's poor respiratory function may make it impossible to raise the blood P_{O_2} level above 50 mmHg even in 100 percent oxygen.

Pulmonary care includes suctioning, postural drainage, chest physiotherapy, and frequent position changes. Frequent observations of color, air flow into the lungs, and respiratory sounds are needed. Signs of respiratory distress are discussed in the section "Respiratory Distress Syndrome."

Removing the infant from oxygen Oxygen is adjusted by using blood oxygen level concentrations and by observing for cyanosis. The infant is gradually weaned off the oxygen. Oxygen concentration is lowered by no more than 10 percent at a time about every 3 to 4 h. If the infant becomes slightly cyanotic, the level may have to be increased. It is important to keep the oxygen adjusted to a therapeutic level and yet at the lowest possible level to prevent oxygen toxicity. Damage can be caused to the developing eyes (retrolental fibroplasia) and lungs by high concentrations of oxygen.

Temperature regulation One of the nurse's most important tasks in the care of the high-risk newborn is to keep the child warm. Because of immaturity, asphyxia, or hypoxia, the baby often cannot maintain its body temperature. A wet newborn in a cold environment can become chilled very quickly. The simple measures of drying and warming the newborn are essential for its survival.

An adult responds to cold by shivering and using muscle activity to produce heat. This is called *shivering thermogenesis.* An infant is unable to shiver and has little muscle activity or flexion to produce heat. The infant responds to cold stress by *nonshivering thermogenesis.* Its body heat is raised by metabolism. Norepinephrine is released by the body in response to chilling. This stimulates metabolism, using oxygen and glucose to raise body heat. To raise a low temperature, many times the normal number of calories are burned.

Chilling initiates a cycle leading to hypoxia. After available glucose and oxygen are used, glycogen is converted without oxygen. *Lactic acid* is a by-product of this conversion and builds up in the body leading to *metabolic acidosis.* The lungs respond to hypoxia and acidosis by vasoconstriction. Intralung vascular resistance increases, causing a return to the fetal circulation pattern. Decreased blood flow and gas exchange impair oxygenation of the lung tissue and eventually respiratory acidosis also occurs. (Chapter 24 discusses respiratory and metabolic acidosis.)

In the mature newborn, *brown fat* is a source of heat. It is found at the nape of the neck, between the scapulae, in the mediastinum, and around the kidneys. It is used especially for heat production in the first few weeks of life; after this time, it atrophies. While it has a very rich blood supply and produces much heat, the brown fat supply is limited in amount and is quickly depleted in the cold-stressed infant.

In addition to causing impaired pulmonary function, cold stress decreases the amount of glucose available to other organs. It depletes organ stores of glucose, particularly in the liver, and produces hypoglycemia. Because the brain requires a constant source of glucose, hypoglycemia can cause brain damage with subsequent mental retardation.

Equipment used for maintaining temperature Usually critically ill infants are left undressed, for easier observation, in an open radiant heater (Fig. 19-9) or an enclosed isolette. The baby is not removed from the heat source for nursing care; in the isolette, the portholes are kept closed as much as possible to prevent loss of heat and oxygen. Forty to sixty percent humidity is used because it contributes to maintaining body temperature by decreasing evaporation loss. Since bacteria grow well in water (humidity), a routine for cleaning isolettes and humidifiers every 8 to 24 h must be followed. Sterile distilled water is used in the humidifier and often a solution of silver nitrate is added as a disinfectant. Equipment is changed frequently. (Chapter 17 discusses maintenance of asepsis in the nursery.)

Nurses can keep an infant warm in a crib by wrapping him snugly in blankets and putting a cap on his head. The head accounts for 20 to 30 percent of the infant's body surface area and it must be covered in unstable infants to prevent heat loss.

Nursing management The best environment for the infant is neither cold nor hot since both of these conditions are damaging to the newborn. The nurse attempts to keep the baby in an environment that does not require the use of additional calories to maintain body temperature. In this *neutral thermal environment* the baby's skin temperature is maintained at 36.1 to 36.8°C (97 to 98.2°F). Most body heat is produced by body organs and muscle. The skin temperature is a reflection of organ (core) temperature. The amount of external heat needed to maintain the temperature depends on the weight, age, maturity, and physical condition of the infant, but is much higher than normal room temperature. If the high-risk infant does not have temperature support, calories are used for heat production instead of body growth. (Chapter 10 discusses the prevention of heat loss.)

Axillary temperatures are measured every hour until the temperature is stable, then every 2 to 4 h. Most high-risk nurseries have units with automatically controlled heat regulators, Infant Servo-Control (ISC). The ISC units respond to a skin temperature probe that is put on the abdomen over the area of the liver, the point of maximum body skin temperature. The probe should be shielded, with a foam-back aluminum shield, from the direct source of heat to prevent an inaccurate reading. Placing the infant on his or her stomach also makes the temperature reading inaccurate, unless the probe is moved to the flank.

Whenever the infant is under an artificial source of heat, the nurse must monitor both the baby's temperature and the temperature of the warmer. It is easy to overlook a drop in the infant's temperature when it is compensated for by an automatic rise in the warmer's temperature. Since a drop in temperature may signify a change, such as infection or hypoglycemia, this becomes an important observation.

Changing levels of heat Some sources suggest that infants who have been severely chilled should be warmed gradually with the heat source 1° above the body temperature. Too rapid warming, as well as chilling, can cause apnea.

Overheating the newborn may be as damaging as chilling. Remember the newborn does not have the adult response of sweating to cool his body. In addition to checking the temperature of the newborn and his environment, the nurse looks for the following signs of hyperthermia: flushed skin, labored respirations, tachycardia, and seizures.

Infants need to be weaned from added heat gradually; usually the temperature is reduced a degree or less at a time. The infant's temperature is taken to make sure it is stable.

Fluid and electrolytes The sick newborn needs an open route for administration of fluids and

Figure 19-9 Open radiant heater used in care of sick neonate. Warmth from the heating units at the top is radiated toward the bed surface below.

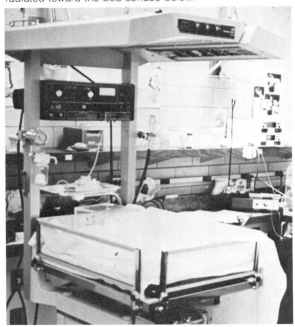

electrolytes. All small newborns under 1500 g or 32 weeks gestation will need intravenous fluids (IV) for at least the first 24 to 48 h and usually longer. A 10% glucose solution will be given intravenously at a rate of about 80 to 100 ml/kg/ per day for the first day and then increased to about 150 ml/kg/per day. When this is computed in an hourly requirement, it is only 4 to 6 ml/kg/ per hour. This is an extremely small flow rate, and it is important that the infusion be monitored carefully. The danger of error is very great. Volume overload with cardiac failure can result if the IV fluid infuses too fast. Usually an IV infusion pump is used to deliver these small amounts at a steady rate.

The IV site (right after birth) is usually the umbilical artery catheter. The scalp vein or cut-down into the saphenous vein of the leg are also frequent choices for infusion. The veins are fragile and small; the IV can easily infiltrate or become dislodged. The sites for IV infusion are limited and the nurse must protect the site with such devices as half a plastic medication cup taped over the site and small arm or leg boards. (See Chap. 17 for a discussion of IV therapy.)

Preventing infection The trauma and stress of resuscitation increase the danger of infection for the high-risk infant. Preterm babies have additional risks because their body defenses are immature.

The birth canal serves as a source of infection when organisms ascend from the vagina through a ruptured amniotic sac to the fetus. Other organisms cross the placenta from the mother's bloodstream. Nursery personnel, other infants, and contaminated equipment can also infect a neonate.

When infection is suspected, especially if the amniotic sac has been ruptured for more than 24 h, cultures should be done within 1 to 2 h of birth. In the delivery room cultures are taken from stomach aspirate, placenta, membranes, or amniotic fluid. The infant's external ear, nares, throat, axillae, inguinal folds, cord, and rectum are also cultured. When an infant shows signs of sepsis, blood, urine, and spinal fluid cultures will be done. Because infections that seem mild in the newborn can rapidly become massive and fatal, they are treated vigorously.

While many different organisms are responsible for newborn infections, a review of nursery infections shows some trends. In the 1960s *Staphylococcus aureus* caused epidemics of infections. Staph infections declined with the use of hexachlorophene soap and improved nursery asepsis. In 1972, the Federal Drug Administration (FDA) recommended that hexachlorophene bathing of infants be discontinued because of possible liver toxicity through skin absorption. The incidence of staph did rise after hexachlorophene was discontinued, but never again to the epidemic level.

Today *Pseudomonas*, which grows in water, and *Escherichia coli* cause about 75 percent of bacterial infections. *Streptococcus* is the major cause of the remaining 25 percent. *Group B hemolytic streptococci* has recently increased as a cause of infection in the nursery. Formerly it was regarded as a benign inhabitant of the body found frequently in the vagina. B strep causes acute infections in the newborn that are sometimes confused with respiratory distress syndrome. Meningitis and even death may result if the infection is not quickly recognized and treated. Survivors may be left with seizures and mental retardation. Suspected infants should be cultured and treated prophylactically with antibiotics.

Nursing management The nurse working with an infected newborn often finds only vague, nonspecific symptoms. The baby doesn't "act right." Lack of fever does not indicate absence of infection in the newborn. The following is a list of signs that may be seen in sepsis:

1. Lethargy or hyperirritability
2. Changes in color, activity, or muscle tone
3. Changes in temperature—hypothermia is more common in preterm infants than hyperthermia
4. Feeding difficulties—distended abdomen, poor suck, spitting up
5. Rapid respirations—apnea may also occur, especially in the preterm
6. Blood pressure may drop, resulting in shock
7. Jaundice

Broad spectrum antibiotics, often penicillin and gentamicin, are used to combat the infection. Supportive therapy includes oxygen, IV fluids and electrolytes, transfusions, and temperature control measures.

The best prevention for the spread of infection

is good handwashing techniques and clean protective clothing. All linen and nursery equipment should be clean or sterile and individual equipment used for each infant when possible. The machines in the nursery containing water (even soap dishes) are good sources for water-borne infection. Zephiran chloride (benzalkonium chloride) actually is used in a medium to grow *Pseudomonas* and should not be used for nursery disinfection. Nursing personnel must be healthy and not act as carriers of infection from one infant to another. Persons with herpes Type I or II are not allowed to work in the nursery. Posterior nares or throat cultures for streptococcus are routine. (Infection control is discussed further in Chap. 17.)

Specific problems of the high-risk newborn

Small-for-dates newborn (SGA)

The infant who is small for gestational age may be preterm, full-term, or postterm. The general characteristics seen in the baby will be similar to those of any baby of that gestational age.

The full-term small-for-dates newborn weighs less than 2500 g (5½ lb) even though it is gestationally mature. This small size is usually the result of placental insufficiency, maternal disease, poor maternal nutrition, smoking, excess alcohol intake, intrauterine infections, or a congenital anomaly.

When intrauterine growth is not progressing normally, the doctor will investigate by doing serial estriols, amniocentesis, and, near term, a nonstress and a stress test. When the intrauterine environment is poor, the baby's health may be better outside the uterus. If test results show sufficient maturity, poor response to stress, or falling estriols, the baby is delivered by C section or labor induction.

At birth, hypoxia, hypothermia, and hypoglycemia are frequent problems. Chronic low levels of oxygen before birth may trigger the fetus to pass meconium, leading to meconium aspiration. Resuscitation and thorough suctioning to remove meconium are needed.

This baby appears long, thin, and wasted with poor muscle growth—especially over the buttocks and cheeks. Loss of subcutaneous fat, used as an energy source before birth, gives the skin a loose, baggy appearance. Loss of body fat also

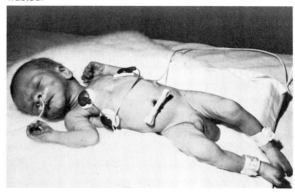

Figure 19-10 This infant shows intrauterine growth retardation. The infant appears typically long, thin, and wasted.

decreases body insulation and makes the baby vulnerable to chilling. The skin is dry and parchment-like and the hair is sparse. Nails, skin, and umbilical cord are often stained yellow from the meconium. The abdomen appears sunken and the skull sutures are wide. *Polycythemia*, an increase in red blood cells with a high hematocrit, may occur in response to prolonged lack of oxygen in utero (Fig. 19-10).

Nursing management This baby has depleted its stores of glucose prenatally and needs to be fed soon after birth. If oral feedings cannot be given, an IV of 10% glucose will be started. The baby is usually very active and has a strong suck. He often acts starved, sucks on his hands and clothes, and appears wide-eyed and birdlike. A pacifier helps satisfy the strong sucking urge and avoids overfeeding. These babies are often irritable and difficult to comfort.

Large-for-gestational-age (LGA) newborn

Ninety percent of LGA babies weigh 4000 g (9 lb) and 10 percent weigh 4500 g (10 lb) or over.

Large size at birth is associated most frequently with two factors: a diabetic mother and heredity. The large size makes it difficult for the head and shoulders to pass through the birth canal, contributing to the frequent problem of trauma during labor and delivery. Injuries to the infant from pulling and stretching are common.

The best choice of delivery for an excessively large baby is a C section. The diabetic infant and birth-related trauma will be discussed later in this chapter.

The postmature newborn

Twelve percent of all newborns are delivered after 42 weeks gestation. These postmature newborns have a two to three times higher mortality rate than do term infants. They appear about 1 to 2 weeks old at birth. Some may have little difficulty, while others have multiple complications.

Sometimes it is difficult to pinpoint gestational age to validate postmaturity. Ultrasonography, amniocentesis, and serial estriols are done. Before labor begins, nonstress and stress tests will be used to determine the infant's response to stress. As a rule, postterm babies do not respond well to the stress of labor. Seventy-five to eighty percent of the fetal deaths in postmature infants occur during labor. When a firm diagnosis of postmaturity is made, the baby is delivered by induction of labor or C section.

Intrauterine weight loss in the postmature fetus may result from decreased blood supply to the fetus due to placental aging. The fetus begins to use its own subcutaneous fat for an energy source. At birth, the lack of fat gives the skin a loose, baggy appearance and makes it difficult for the baby to maintain its body temperature.

The skin is dry, parchment-like and often stained yellow from meconium. Passing meconium is common, and meconium aspiration is a frequent problem. The skin will frequently *desquamate* (peel in sheets) after birth. No vernix is present to protect the skin and little lanugo is seen. The nails are long and ragged and cover the ends of the fingers. The hair is long. The baby appears wide-eyed, alert, and suffers from problems similar to the SGA baby: hypoxia, hypoglycemia, hypothermia, and polycythemia (Fig. 19-11).

Meconium aspiration

A wide variety of mild to severe respiratory problems result from meconium aspiration. Passage of meconium is usually related to an episode of fetal hypoxia. The underlying causes are many and are listed in Table 19-4. Meconium aspiration, although found in other babies, is most frequent in postterm infants.[6]

Etiology Fetal circulation responds to an episode of decreased oxygen by conserving blood for vital organs (brain or heart) and restricting blood flow to less vital areas (intestines). Diminished supply of oxygenated blood causes hyperperistalsis and rectal sphincter relaxation, allowing meconium to pass.

Meconium can be aspirated by the baby before,

Figure 19-11 Postmature black male born at 43 weeks gestation and weighing 2840 g (6 lb, 4 oz), 2 days old when photographed. Note the diminished subcutaneous fat, cracked skin, and long nails typical of a postmature infant. The chest tube is for treatment of pneumothorax following meconium aspiration. [*From G. Scipien et al. (eds.), Comprehensive Pediatric Nursing, 2d ed., McGraw-Hill, New York, 1979.*]

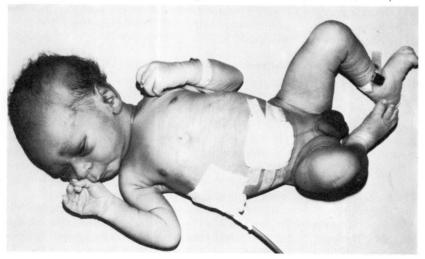

during, or after birth. Hypoxia actually causes an increase in strength of fetal breathing efforts, resulting in strong, reflex gasps. This can draw the meconium into the lungs. Meconium-filled amniotic fluid present in the respiratory tree at birth can also be aspirated by the baby as it begins breathing. The degree of newborn respiratory distress depends on the amount of meconium aspirated and how deeply it spreads into the lungs.

Medical management Complications of meconium aspiration are reduced from 25 percent in nonsuctioned to 1 percent in suctioned infants. To prevent the newborn from aspirating meconium with the first breath, oral and nasopharyngeal suctioning is done before the chest is born. After birth, the respiratory passages and stomach are suctioned. The vocal cords are inspected for meconium and, if it is present, intubation and suctioning are done. When resuscitation is needed, suctioning must be completed before beginning positive pressure ventilation since positive pressure ventilation will spread meconium throughout the lungs, causing severe meconium aspiration pneumonia.

Meconium aspiration can also cause complete blockage of portions of the lung, resulting in *atelectasis*, a condition in which an area of the lung is uninflated. A partial blockage of the lung with meconium allows air to enter, but not to leave, the lungs because airways expand on inspiration and are smaller in diameter on expiration. This can trap air in the alveoli, overdistending the lungs and leading to rupture of the alveoli. If air escapes from the lungs into the chest or mediastinum, it will cause a *pneumothorax* or *pneumomediastinum*. The infant then has severe respiratory distress. Pneumothorax causes mediastinal shift, and displaced heart sounds are heard on the affected side. To allow lung expansion the air will need to be released from the chest by needle aspiration and chest suction.

Most newborns recover from meconium aspiration rapidly with adequate suctioning and care. Mild symptoms usually subside in 1 to 2 days. Severe aspiration or aspiration with inadequate suctioning takes a week or longer for recovery. This newborn needs transfer to an intensive care unit and the same support as any other severely asphyxiated newborn. Chest x-

Table 19-9 Percent of survival of preterm infants related to weight*

Weight	Survival
2000–2500 g	90–95%
1500–2000 g	75–85%
1000–1500 g	40–50%
400–1000 g	10%

*Adapted from Lucille Whaley and Donna Wong, *Nursing Care of Children*, Mosby, St. Louis, 1979, p. 333.

rays are done to determine the extent of involvement and broad spectrum antibiotics are used for the pneumonia. Prognosis depends on the degree of respiratory impairment.

Nursing management Infants who have aspirated meconium should receive postural drainage and intermittent chest physiotherapy for the first 8 h. They should be closely observed for signs of respiratory distress: a respiratory rate of 60 or above, retractions, grunting, flaring, and cyanosis. A change in location of heart sounds may indicate a pneumomediastinum.

The preterm infant

The preterm infant has a mortality rate 20 to 30 times that of a full-term infant. Survival is in direct proportion to the maturity of body systems (gestational age), weight of the fetus, and the availability of intensive care. Table 19-9 lists the percentages of survival of preterm infants related to weight.

Preterm infants also have a higher incidence of serious congenital anomalies, developmental learning defects, anemia, and serious residual problems related to the trauma of resuscitation and asphyxia. These infants are the most likely group to suffer from cerebral palsy (due to lack of oxygen) and blindness (from too much oxygen).

Characteristics of the preterm infant A group of physical attributes are typical of the premature infant. Tables 19-5 and 19-7 contain the Dubowitz criteria for gestational age assessment and include descriptions of both physical and neurological characteristics of a premature infant. The baby in Figure 19-12 is of 32 weeks gestation; a description of its physical characteristics follows.

Figure 19-12 A 38-day-old preterm black female weighing 1415 g (3 lb, 1½ oz). Birth weight was 1300 g (2 lb, 14 oz) at estimated gestational age of 32 weeks. Note thinness of the skin. Absence of subcutaneous fat is especially noticeable in thigh folds, labia majora, and over the ribs. The open hands and scarflike "draped" position denote the diminished muscle tone of the preterm infant. [*From Scipien et al. (eds.), Comprehensive Pediatric Nursing, 2d ed., McGraw-Hill, New York, 1979. Used with permission.*]

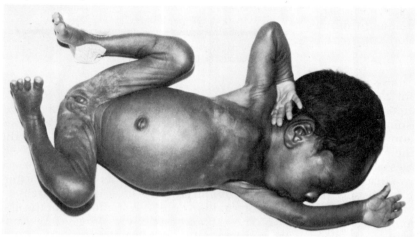

Weight 1300 g

Length Less than 47 cm (18 in)

Posture The baby often lies with the legs and arms extended or, after about 34 weeks of gestation, assumes the froglike position when prone. The muscles are hypotonic. There is little muscle resistance and the heel will nearly touch the ear. The elbow extends well past the midline of the body (positive scarf sign).

Head The head is large, 33 cm (13 in), about one-third the total body size. Skull bones are soft and spongy. The hair is fine, sticking out from the head in clumps. The eyes appear large.

Ears The cartilage is soft and the ears fold easily. They are shapeless with little incurving of the pinna.

Body The body is long with a protruding abdomen. *Lanugo* covers the forehead, shoulders, body, and thighs. At birth the body is covered with thick, white, cheesy *vernix*. *Breast masses* are not felt, but the nipples and areolae are visible.

Extremities The nails are soft and extend just to cover the nail beds of the fingers and toes. *Sole creases* are beginning to show with one to two anterior creases near the toes.

Skin The skin is thin and, especially in Caucasians, reddish pink in appearance. The lack of subcutaneous fat makes it appear loose or wrinkled. Blood vessels are abundantly visible over the abdomen.

The extremities may appear mottled or cyanotic, especially if the baby becomes cold.

Genitalia In the male, the scrotum is small with few rugae; the testicles can be palpated at the external inguinal ring after 30 weeks. They usually descend into the scrotal sac by 37 weeks. In the 32-week female, the labia majora are small and widely separated and the clitoris and labia minora are prominent. The labia majora increase in size as the baby nears term.

Physiological handicaps of the preterm infant

Temperature regulation Heat loss is greater for preterm infants than for other infants. The brainstem temperature regulatory center, though completely formed, does not efficiently control the constriction or dilation of blood vessels. The premature's muscles are often flaccid and inactive. The infant does not raise heat by body movement or muscle flexion. The body surface area is very large in proportion to body weight. A full-term infant's weight represents 5 percent of an adult's body weight but his body surface represents 15 percent of an adult's body surface area.[7] The proportion of body weight to surface area is significantly less for a preterm baby. Since most body fat is gained in the last trimester, these infants have little subcutaneous fat. Heat loss is rapid because the capillaries are not protected by the subcutaneous layer. Preterm babies have little insulation to conserve heat and few fat reserves to use for energy. The amount of brown fat available for use in heat production is not documented, but presumably it is less than in a full-term infant.

Circulation Congenital heart disease and a continuation of fetal circulation patterns are more common in the preterm. Patent ductus arteriosus (failure of closure of the opening between pulmonary and systemic circulation) is especially prevalent. (Congenital heart disease is discussed in Chap. 26.)

The capillaries in preterm infants are more fragile and hemorrhage from birth trauma often occurs. This increased incidence of hemorrhage results in higher levels of bilirubin as the red blood cells are broken down. Intracranial hemorrhage and elevated bilirubin levels are discussed later in the chapter.

Immunity The usual defenses against infection—the skin barrier, antibodies, and phagocytosis—are all less effective than those of a normal newborn. The skin is thin, frequently edematous, and breaks down easily. Antibodies against specific bacteria and diseases the mother has had cross the placenta to the fetus after the first 3 months of pregnancy, but not in large numbers until the last trimester. The infant born early never receives a full complement of antibodies. The full-term baby begins manufacturing antibodies by 3 months when the mother's antibodies are normally depleted. A preterm infant's immune response is delayed.

The decreased number of white blood cells reduces the ability to localize infections (phagocytosis). Even a mild infection in a premature can spread systemically causing sepsis, pneumonia, or meningitis.

Digestive function The preterm infant has a high metabolic rate, increasing caloric and fluid needs. Adequate nutrition is needed to continue the fast rate of intrauterine growth that was interrupted by early birth. The baby's small stomach size, poor sucking ability, and immature gastrointestinal tract limit his ability to take in food. Typically, the feeding reflexes—rooting, sucking, swallowing, gag, and cough—are weak and uncoordinated. This combination of immature reflexes makes it difficult to coordinate sucking and swallowing and increases the danger of aspiration. If milk is aspirated, the weak gag and cough reflex do not help the infant clear its air passages.

The acidity of the digestive juices of the stomach is low and though carbohydrate digestion is normal, fat utilization is very poor. The stomach's capacity is as little as 2 ml in a 1200-g baby and about 15 ml in a 2000-g baby.[8] Over a period of several weeks the capacity increases to 30 ml or more. The small gastric size makes it very easy to overfeed these babies. Since the stomach's cardiac sphincter is hypotonic, regurgitation of milk into the esophagus occurs easily. A full stomach and milk regurgitation predispose the infant to irritation of the diaphragm and aspiration of feedings with resulting respiratory distress.

Methods of feeding the high-risk infant Early feeding of high-risk infants is essential to prevent hypoglycemia and meet body growth needs. The method of feeding will vary with the infant's condition. A sick preterm infant will often receive IVs; an infant with a poor suck, who is otherwise well, may be fed by gavage. Most infants are bottle-fed when they can tolerate the effort required to suck and still continue to gain weight.

The amount and type of the feeding is based on calculations using gestational age, weight, and body requirements. "The caloric, water, electrolyte, mineral, and vitamin requirements of low-birth-weight infants are dependent on body stores, absorption, rate of utilization, expenditure, and excretion of the substances."[9] Table 19-10 gives general estimates of nutritional and vitamin requirements for low-birth-weight infants. Nevertheless, it is impossible to make

Table 19-10 Daily nutritional and vitamin requirements for low-birth-weight infants

Nutrients	Amount per kilogram of infant's weight	
Calories	110–150 (120 average)	
Water	130–200 ml	
Protein	3–4 g	(10–15% of diet)
Carbohydrate	12–15 g	(45–55% of diet)
Fat	5–8 g	(30–45% of diet)

one statement that fits all infants. Many have these deficiencies: sodium, potassium, chloride, phosphorus, magnesium, and vitamins A, B, C, D, and E. Iron and calcium are deficient in the preterm because they are stored in the last trimester. Fluid requirements are also high because the infant's body composition is 80 to 90 percent water and the immature kidneys lack the ability to conserve water or electrolytes. In addition, fluid losses through the skin increase by 10 percent when artificial heat and phototherapy lights are used.

Intravenous feedings *Intravenous feedings* are needed to ensure required fluid and caloric input for many infants. An IV will be used until the infant can take adequate nourishment by another route. It is then frequently continued as a route for medication.

Nutrition for maintaining body organs and growth cannot be supplied by regular IV's for prolonged periods of time. *Total parenteral nutrition* (TPN) is used in babies that continue to be too sick to take food via the GI tract. The TPN fluid is a highly concentrated solution of protein, glucose, and other nutrients put into a large blood vessel using a constant infusion pump. TPN requires meticulous nursing care to prevent infection and is discussed in Chap. 23.

Oral or gavage feedings Before beginning gavage or bottle feedings, the nurse must be sure the infant can tolerate them. Requirements for oral or gavage feedings are:

1. Establishment of normal respirations (less than 60).
2. No abdominal distention.
3. Bowel sounds are heard.
4. Color, tone, and cry are normal.
5. Before bottle feeding a strong suck and swallow are needed.

The first feeding is usually sterile water because it is less irritating then either 5% glucose or milk if aspirated into the lungs. Most infants are fed within 2 to 4 h after birth. The formula used is often diluted for the early feedings and gradually brought to full strength. Concentrated, high-caloric lipid solutions are also used to provide additional calories.

Recently there has been concern expressed by pediatricians about high solute concentration formula. This is of special concern in preterm babies because they have immature kidney function that is taxed by excreting additional solute loads. Breast milk has been favored in some centers because it has a composition that is more dilute and more compatible with the needs of the sick infant.

Gavage feedings are used when the infant cannot take bottle feedings but can receive food through the GI tract. A tube is inserted through the nose or mouth into the stomach. Remember that babies are nose breathers and anything blocking the nostrils (feeding tube, mucus, or blood) can cause respiratory distress. Bleeding and irritation of the nares can also lead to infection, a serious complication in a high-risk newborn. Passing the tube through the mouth also provides an opportunity to watch the baby's sucking response. For these reasons, the oral gastric insertion is preferred. The technique for correct placement and use of the feeding tube is described in Table 17-13.

Some centers prefer jejunal or duodenal (rather than gastric) placement of a feeding tube. This method is usually used in very small infants with long-term tube feedings. Proponents of this type of feeding say there is less fatigue, less gastric distention and irritation, no reflux from the stomach into the esophagus, and therefore, less danger of aspiration.

Feedings usually begin with a few milliliters and are increased 2 to 3 ml at a time every 1 to 2 h. Before each feeding the stomach is aspirated to see if digestion has taken place. When two or more milliliters of the previous feeding are present, the amount of feeding needs to be decreased. The stomach aspirate is put back in the stomach and the current feeding is reduced by that amount. Large amounts of residual formula are a sign of poor digestion.

It is important to protect the infant from overfeeding. A distended abdomen causes pressure on the diaphragm with apnea and respiratory distress in the infant. The baby may need to return to IV fluids if the feeding distress is severe. Vomiting or "spitting up" formula indicates the feeding volume is too large. It will need to be decreased until vomiting stops. The stomach can also be overdistended with air; so remember to burp the baby after every $\frac{1}{2}$ oz is given.

Handle the infant gently during and after

feeding to prevent regurgitation of milk through a weak cardiac sphincter. Position the baby on his right side with his head up or on his abdomen after feeding.[10]

Complications that accompany gavage feedings are intestinal perforation, changes in intestinal flora, necrotizing enterocolitis, vomiting, diarrhea, and infection of the nasal passages.

Bottle-feeding The nurse watches for signs that the infant is ready for *bottle-feeding*. The baby will begin to be awake before feedings and suck on the tube during feeding. Touching the cheek elicits a rooting response and the baby will begin sucking its fingers. Using a pacifier during gavage feeding and at periodic intervals helps the baby learn how to suck. Bottle feeding is usually begun with one feeding a day and then increased slowly until all the feedings are by bottle. The nurse watches the baby carefully so the amount of energy required to eat is not so great that weight gain is sacrificed. Many of the feeding precautions for gavage feedings also apply to bottle-feeding.

Most well infants over 32 weeks gestation can coordinate sucking and swallowing. A preterm infant sucks in short, rapid bursts and then rests. It is important to let the infant follow this natural feeding pattern. Many nurses become frustrated because the high-risk infant is lethargic and sucks poorly. It is helpful to use a soft nipple, set the baby upright, and burp the child frequently. Though patience is needed, the feeding time is usually limited to 20 to 30 min to prevent exhausting the baby. Inability to feed during that amount of time or respiratory distress usually indicates the need to return to gavage feeding. Bottle and gavage feedings are often alternated.

Breast-feeding Breast milk has more easily digestible protein and fat and more carbohydrate than cow's milk. (See Chap. 10 for a discussion of breast milk.) It also contains the mother's antibodies and macrophages, which help prevent infection. Breasts can be pumped and the milk fed by bottle or gavage.

Presently, there is much controversy among pediatricians regarding the benefits of feeding breast milk to sick babies. Donor breast milk is not used as frequently as in the past because some research suggests the mother's antibodies are beneficial only for her own baby.

Sick or preterm babies often do not have the energy it takes to suck from a breast at birth. The mother who wants to breast-feed should be encouraged to use a breast pump every 3 to 4 h until the baby can nurse.

Most experts agree that fresh breast milk is best to prevent antibody loss. However, it can be refrigerated and used within 2 days or kept frozen for 6 months.[11] For future use put enough milk for one feeding in a plastic bag and label it with the name, date, and time of freezing.

Nursing management The nurse monitors the reaction of the baby to feedings and is alert to signs that indicate the baby can be graduated from IV to gavage or oral feedings. The baby's strength is conserved by using gentle handling and by organizing care. Note how the feeding is tolerated and watch the infant for abdominal distress, vomiting, and respiratory distress. Dextrostix are used frequently to determine glucose levels. The baby is kept in a head-elevated position on its right side or on the abdomen after feedings. Intake and output are carefully monitored. Diapers are weighed; color, amount, and consistency of stools is noted. Body weights are done two or more times a day because weight is the most accurate indicator of hydration. A weight loss between 5 to 10 percent in the first week is acceptable. Weight gain after this should be about 10 to 30 g a day. All feedings, amounts, kind, and route, along with observations of how the feeding was tolerated, are charted.

Necrotizing enterocolitis (NEC)

Necrotizing enterocolitis, an ulceration and possible perforation of the bowel, is found most frequently in small (1250 g or less), sick, premature infants.[12] It occurs in 2 to 15 percent of premature infants and varies greatly among neonatal intensive care units.[13] An explanation of the cause is incomplete and the mortality rate is high. An ischemic insult to the bowel, tube feedings, sepsis, an exchange transfusion, or the use of umbilical catheters have all been related to the incidence of NEC.

Animal studies also indicate a relationship between NEC and feeding hypertonic formula.[14] Breast milk, with its human-specific composition, immune substances, and macrophages that combine to inhibit bacterial action in the bowel, is thought by some pediatricians to be helpful in preventing NEC.

Pathology The decreased blood supply to the bowel causes large numbers of mucus-producing cells to be damaged. These cells stop secreting the mucus barrier that protects the bowel wall. With this barrier removed, the normally present acids erode the bowel, allowing bacteria to invade the deteriorated area. As the bacteria infiltrate the bowel, submucosa and subserosa, gas is released. This results in the distinguishing sign of NEC, *pneumatosis intestinalis*, free gas in the intestinal wall or the peritoneum.

Clinical manifestations Signs of NEC may develop insidiously. The first signs may be those of sepsis, poorly controlled temperature, poor feeding, vomiting, lethargy, gastric distention, reduced or absent bowel sounds, blood in the stools, and jaundice. Eventually, apnea, shock, and circulatory collapse will occur.

Medical management The small infant receiving gastric tube feedings should have abdominal girth measured for abdominal distention. If signs of NEC are detected, IVs are started and no feedings are given. Nasogastric suction is begun and broad spectrum antibiotics are given systemically and by nasogastric tube. Diagnosis is usually confirmed by the presence of free abdominal air in x-rays. Surgery is indicated for perforation or severe disease. Often intestinal resection and a colostomy or ileostomy are done.

Hypoglycemia

Hypoglycemia in newborns is found most frequently in prematures, small-for-gestational-age infants, and infants of diabetic mothers. It also occurs in conjunction with sepsis, hypothermia, respiratory distress, and birth asphyxia.

Prenatally, the fetus receives transplacental supplies of glucose. At birth, the baby's glucose level normally reflects the mother's blood glucose level of about 50 to 60 mg per 100 ml. After birth, internal supplies (liver stores of glycogen) and any external glucose source (feedings or IV) will determine the baby's blood glucose level.

If a fetus is stressed it will have decreased glucose stores. When available maternal glucose is used up, the fetus's liver glucose stores and body fat are used. Birth stresses of cold and hypoxia raise the metabolic rate and very rapidly deplete the baby's glucose.

A blood glucose level of 30 mg per 100 ml is normal for a full-term infant and 20 mg per 100 ml is normal for a preterm infant. Glucose levels should be monitored in the first 1 to 2 h for all babies. Two consecutive low glucose levels are diagnostic of hypoglycemia. If blood levels are low, glucose is given and blood glucose levels are monitored for 1 to 2 days until they stabilize. An infant on normal feedings will have a gradual increase in blood glucose levels to at least 45 mg per 100 ml.

While blood sugars are more accurate for diagnosis, Dextrostix are often used for screening. A heel prick can be used to obtain blood. Warm the heel for at least 5 min to dilate the capillaries. Prick the heel, less than 2.4 mm deep, but never use the bony back of the heel.[13] Use of the lateral heel and good antiseptic technique prevent bone necrosis. Put a drop of blood on the filter end of the Dextrostix and wash it off with water exactly 60 s later. Compare the color with the chart provided. A level less than 45% on a Dextrostix is considered low.

Clinical manifestations Hypoglycemia usually occurs a few hours after birth, but may develop from 1 to 2 days to as long as a week later. Few signs of hypoglycemia are specific and it is easily confused with hypocalcemia and central nervous system trauma. All of the following signs are significant: refusal to feed, weak cry, lethargy, tachypnea, tremors, dyspnea, cyanosis, apnea, convulsions, and coma. To confirm the presence of hypoglycemia, glucose is given. If symptoms disappear after about 5 min, there is good evidence the problem was due to hypoglycemia.

Medical management In the infant who feeds well, oral glucose and continuation of normal oral feedings will prevent or treat hypoglycemia. If the infant is not able to feed orally, IV glucose is given. The following regimen is often used:

1. 25% glucose 2 to 4 ml/kg IV immediately to treat symptoms
2. 15% glucose 65 to 75 ml/kg IV for 24 h until stable
3. 10% glucose IV for a 12-h period reduced to 5% for the next 12 h.[15]

IV infusions of glucose are tapered off gradually to prevent a severe rebound hypoglycemic reaction.

Treatment of hypoglycemia is very important because lack of glucose can cause brain damage with subsequent mental retardation. Untreated, the problem can progress to cause an infant's death.

Idiopathic respiratory distress syndrome

Idiopathic respiratory distress syndrome (RDS), also called *hyaline membrane disease (HMD)*, is the largest cause of respiratory disease in the newborn. It is responsible for the deaths of thousands of infants annually.[16]

RDS is primarily a disease of the immature infant and is seen most often in infants under 32 weeks gestation weighing less than 1500 g. It also occurs more often in infants whose mothers have diabetes, placental bleeding, or C sections. Though these reasons are mentioned separately, in each case, it is the baby's immaturity that underlies the RDS. For example, the immature infant delivered by emergency C section has a high rate of RDS, and yet RDS is not common in mature infants born by C section. Another related cause of RDS, that often coexists with immaturity, is fetal asphyxia. However, decreased oxygen, prenatally or at birth, can precipitate respiratory distress syndrome, even in mature infants, by decreasing surfactant production.

Pathology In contrast to the salmon pink, spongy, air-filled lungs of the normal infant, on autopsy the lungs of the infant with RDS are a livery red, solid mass. A fibrous membrane is found in the terminal bronchioles and alveolar ducts. This membrane consists of products of cellular necrosis, bloody exudate, and fibrin and is sometimes called a *hyaline membrane*. Hyaline membrane is found only in the previously aereated portions of the lung and, therefore, is the result, not the cause, of RDS. X-rays show a typical *reticulogranular pattern*, a clouded appearance with the grainy look of ground glass. Small comma-like areas of density (dark spots) mark the areas of collapsed alveoli (atelectasis). At the hilar regions (larger bronchi opening into the lungs) there are dark streaks that are air-filled bronchi. These are called *air bronchograms*.

Laboratory findings Characteristic biochemical abnormalities of RDS are: *hypoxemia* (decreased blood oxygen levels), *hypercapnia* (increased levels of carbon dioxide), *acidosis*, and *rising potassium levels*, due to released potassium from injured alveolar cells.

Etiology Understanding fetal lung development and surfactant production is essential to the understanding of RDS. The alveoli of the fetal lungs multiply rapidly in the third trimester and continue growth after birth. Before 28 weeks thick-walled alveoli with scanty capillary blood supply are present. As the alveoli mature and increase in numbers, the alveolar walls become thin and become more closely approximated to the capillary membranes, facilitating gas exchange.

The fetal lung secretes a fluid that is found in the lung at birth. The composition is different than amniotic fluid. It contains the phospholipids *sphingomyelin* and *lecithin*. Sphingomyelin is present early and decreases at term, while lecithin increases as the fetus matures. The fetus breathes in and exhales amniotic fluid, contaminating that fluid with phospholipids from the lung. Therefore the amniotic fluid can be tested for phospholipid levels. A ratio of two parts lecithin to one part sphingomyelin (L/S = 2:1) in the amniotic fluid indicates mature fetal lungs. Lungs are usually mature at about 32 to 35 weeks gestation.

Immature lungs with insufficient surfactant production cause RDS. Surfactant is composed largely of lecithin, which is secreted by the alveoli in two cycles. The first, at about 24 weeks gestation, is small in amount and easily stopped by hypoxia, hypothermia, and other stress events commonly associated with premature birth. The second, and largest, surge of surfactant occurs at 32 to 35 weeks gestation. The amount secreted continues to rise until term and its production is stable.

Surfactant decreases the work of respiration by decreasing surface tension in the lung. It exerts the strongest influence on the relaxed lung. In this state, the surfactant is in a thick layer and can counteract surface tension most effectively. As the alveoli expand with inspiration, the layer of surfactant thins. Its effect decreases, reducing resistance to the recoil of the lung and allowing expiration to occur. The presence of surfactant keeps the alveoli partially distended after the first breath and makes subsequent breaths easier. Various sources estimate that the lungs remain 25 to 50 percent expanded. This remaining air in the lungs is known as the *functional residual capacity* (FRC).

A factor recently associated with increased fetal lung maturity is fetal stress. Fetal stress stimulates the fetal adrenals to produce gluco-corticoids (steroids) that speed production of surfactant and increase lung maturity. To repli-cate this stress effect, betamethasone, a steroid preparation, is given at least 24 h before delivery when premature delivery is imminent. Studies indicate increased lung maturity and decreased RDS when this treatment is used.

Clinical manifestations In the infant with de-creased surfactant, the first breath does not result in an adequate functional residual capac-ity. The alveoli collapse with each breath, greatly increasing the work of breathing. The lungs are inelastic and gradually become even more stiff. The infant soon becomes exhausted and has difficulty continuing the effort of breathing. The alveoli collapse, resulting in progressive atelec-tasis with increased intrapulmonary pressure. This decreases the pulmonary blood flow and eventually the circulatory flow pattern reverts to that found in fetal circulation, largely bypassing the lungs. Unless the lungs are expanded, aci-dosis and respiratory failure result. Correction of respiratory failure was discussed earlier.

The infant with RDS may immediately show signs, requiring resuscitation, or may seem stable and develop signs of distress 2 to 3 h after birth. The course of the disease ordinarily runs 3 to 5 days with death much less likely after the first 72 h. When prolonged ventilation support is needed, the prognosis is poor.

The symptoms usually begin with *tachypnea*. A respiratory rate above 60 is a sign of distress, but the rate often rises much higher to 80 or 100. Tachypnea is the infant's response as it tries to increase blood oxygen levels by breathing faster.

As the infant expends energy to increase res-pirations, signs of progressive respiratory distress occur. *Grunting*, the sound made when the infant closes its glottis to stop exhalation of the air by forcing air against the vocal cords, is heard. Grunting increases back pressure in the lungs,

maintaining some degree of alveolar expansion. The baby may improve respiratory status with grunting but soon becomes exhausted and is unable to continue. The baby will need artificial ventilation, often with intubation. Intubation eliminates grunting, because it does not permit closure of the glottis. An artificial means of maintaining end pressure, such as PEEP or CPAP, is needed with intubation.

Nasal flaring, a primitive reflex, is frequently seen in response to respiratory distress. The widening of the nostrils seems to be a way of reducing resistance of the narrow nasal passages to respirations.

The visible effect of inadequate lung expansion, combined with a flexible chest wall and use of accessory muscles, is *retraction*. There are sev-eral types of retractions: *intercostal* (the chest wall is pulled in between the ribs), *suprasternal* (above the sternum), and *substernal* (below the sternum). Retraction may actually decrease the volume of lung expansion.[17] If the inflation of the lungs is greatly decreased, the chest appears flattened and the abdomen bulges. This is called *see-saw* or *paradoxical respirations* and can be seen on the Silverman scale (Fig. 19-1). The only effective muscle of respiration left, in this case, is the diaphragm, which still ventilates the lower part of the lungs.

Cyanosis is a late major sign of respiratory distress. *Central cyanosis*, or blueness of the body and head, is a serious sign of oxygen deprivation. Cyanosis around the mouth, *circumoral cy-anosis*, often precedes central cyanosis. Periph-eral cyanosis of the extremities, *acrocyanosis*, is not a significant sign of respiratory distress and is often seen in newborns.

Cyanosis is a late sign of low blood oxygen. It is not apparent until a P_{O_2} of 40 mmHg is reached even though respiratory distress may occur at a P_{O_2} of 50 mmHg. Observations of the skin for cyanosis are not completely accurate. Factors such as lighting, color of the skin, and the nurse's vision are influential factors. Peripheral vasocon-striction may also give the skin a pale color.

Nursing management The nurse is responsible for monitoring all the vital functions: respirations, heart rate, blood pressure, temperature, and intake and output. Usually this includes oper-ating many machines that regulate intravenous fluid flow, oxygen, ventilation, apnea, heart rate, and blood pressure. Frequent laboratory tests and arterial blood gases may be the nurse's responsibility. Turning is needed every 1 to 2 h to prevent skin breakdown. Respiratory care includes suctioning, postural drainage, chest physiotherapy, and observation for signs of respiratory deterioration. The nursing care discussed earlier for stabilizing the sick infant after birth also applies to the infant with RDS.

Apnea and periodic breathing

Apnea is the lack of spontaneous respirations for periods of up to 15 to 30 s accompanied by functional changes such as: a decrease in heart rate, cyanosis, hypotonia, or acidosis. These episodes can cause brain damage and are related to an increased mortality rate. Apnea may be secondary to sepsis, hypoxia, hypothermia, hyperthermia, hypoglycemia, an immature respiratory center, airway obstruction, an overdistended abdomen (after feeding), or CNS injury.

Periodic breathing is common and should be differentiated from apnea. It is characterized by a cessation of breathing for less than 20 s with absence of bradycardia or cyanosis. It is found especially in preterm infants and is probably due to an immature central nervous system. Respirations resume spontaneously with no ill effects.

Nursing management When a baby has frequent episodes of apnea, a mechanical apnea monitor with an alarm is used to alert the nurses. If apnea is observed, the infant is stimulated by light rubbing of the body and face; this will usually initiate breathing. If not, suctioning of the airway to remove any obstruction and of the stomach to reduce overdistention may initiate breathing. If these measures are unsuccessful and apneic episodes increase, an Ambu-Bag and mask are used until a mechanical ventilator can be started. Apnea usually disappears with increased maturity and improved physical status.

Oxygen toxicity

Improved efficiency of oxygen administration has led to the ability to give high oxygen concentrations. While this is lifesaving for sick infants, it can also be destructive to body systems. The effects of oxygen toxicity are seen primarily on the eyes and the lungs of premature infants.

Retrolental fibroplasia (RFP) Blindness in immature infants (retrolental fibroplasia) was first reported in 1942. About 10 years later, oxygen was discovered to be the cause. High concentrations of oxygen cause constriction and spasm of the retinal blood vessels. Premature infants of 1500 to 2000 g are most susceptible because their retinal capillary development is incomplete and their blood vessels are fragile. RFP is related directly to high blood oxygen levels. Controlling oxygen flow rate will not guarantee safety for the premature's eyes. Damage is prevented by careful monitoring of blood gases and by keeping the blood level under 100 percent oxygen concentration. Though many sources say only 40 percent oxygen should be given, it is impossible to set an exact concentration as safe. The damage to the eye depends on the maturity of the infant, blood level of oxygen, and the length of oxygen exposure. Oxygen concentration is reduced as soon as the infant's condition permits and is maintained on the lowest possible therapeutic setting.

Retrolental fibroplasia progresses in two stages. The first stage involves *vasoconstriction* of the retinal arterioles. At this point the process may be reversible if exposure to oxygen is of short duration. An ophthalmologist should periodically check all prematures receiving oxygen for retinal vasoconstriction.

The second stage, or *proliferative stage*, usually begins 1 to 2 months after oxygen therapy is terminated. There is an overgrowth and dilation of capillaries and retinal edema. This leads to hemorrhage and eventual separation of the retina with scarring. Once RFP has reached the stage of retinal detachment, it is progressive and leads to blindness. Approximately 25 percent of infants who experience retinal vasospasms in early oxygen treatment will become blind.[18] (See Chap. 39 for additional discussion of RFP.)

Lung toxicity Oxygen administered in concentrations of 70 percent or above for periods of longer than 4 to 5 days can cause pulmonary disease in the infant.[19] The high oxygen concentration of inspired air, not the blood level, damages the linings of the alveolar walls. It causes thickening of the basement membranes and epithelial lining of the alveoli. In addition, ciliary action is impaired and mucus is not cleared from the lung. Surfactant is inhibited and atelectasis and hypoventilation occur. Several diseases are identified in the literature as being associated with oxygen toxicity.

Bronchopulmonary dysplasia (BPD) is associated with mechanical ventilation with an endotracheal tube. The signs of increasingly severe respiratory distress and the lung damage described above complicate the course of this infant's condition. The infant with BPD is very difficult to wean off the ventilator. It may take 6 months or longer for the lung disease to resolve.

Pulmonary dysmaturity, or Wilson-Mikity syndrome, has an insidious onset with mild respiratory symptoms. The disease usually begins after the first week of life in babies under 1500 g. Its chief manifestation is the appearance of multiple cystlike bubbles of the lungs on x-ray. Symptoms become severe in 4 to 8 weeks after onset and take 6 months to 2 years to completely disappear. The early cystic portion of the disease is often confused with bronchopulmonary dysplasia. Klaus states that "It is our impression that bronchopulmonary dysplasia and pulmonary dysmaturity (Wilson-Mikity disease) are separate entities, though their radiographic and clinical courses may at times be similar."[20] With skillful management, these infants seem to recover and survive with few permanent effects.

Hyperbilirubinemia in the newborn

Hyperbilirubinemia, an elevated blood bilirubin level, is seen in the newborn for a variety of reasons. The basic process of bilirubin production is the same, whatever the cause. Red blood cell breakdown with the release of hemoglobin is the main source (80 to 85 percent) of bilirubin.[21]

When the red blood cells become aged or damaged, the fragile cell membrane ruptures, releasing its contents. The hemoglobin portion divides into *globin*, a protein that is reused in the body, and *heme*, the iron-containing portion which is converted to bilirubin after much of the iron is salvaged.

Although the liver and spleen are chiefly responsible for red blood cell breakdown, *macrophages*, found in other parts of the reticuloendothelial system, can also reduce hemoglobin to bilirubin by phagocytosis. Through the action of enzymes these macrophages produce *unconjugated* (fat-soluble or indirect) bilirubin that will attach to other molecules in the body. In the blood, it attaches to the protein albumin and is carried to the liver. The liver separates bilirubin from the blood albumin through the action of the enzyme *glucuronyl transferase* and converts it to a *conjugated* water-soluble or direct bilirubin. Water-soluble bilirubin cannot diffuse through the cell membranes and is carried, as a part of bile, through the bile ducts to the duodenum. In the intestines, it interacts with bacteria to produce urobilinogen and stercobilin. The stercobilin is excreted in the stool, giving it a dark brown color. Urobilinogen is absorbed and excreted in the urine and will make it brown when the level is elevated.

Newborn jaundice Jaundice, the yellow color derived from bilirubin deposits, is seen when the albumin binding sites in the blood are filled and the unconjugated bilirubin attaches to molecules in other sites in the body. Bilirubin will commonly deposit in the subcutaneous fat, the eyes, under the nails, and eventually, if the level rises very high, in the brain cells.

The bilirubin level must exceed 5 mg/per 100 ml of blood before jaundice becomes visible. (Normal levels in newborns are 0.2 to 1.4 mg/per 100 ml of blood.) Levels of 12 mg/per 100 ml are usually treated. Jaundice progresses in a cephalocaudal direction, present first on the head and gradually moving down the body to the legs and the feet. Pathological levels that can cause harm in the body are not reached until the jaundice has spread to at least the trunk of the body.[22]

Physiological jaundice Physiological or developmental jaundice, is the most common process involving elevated levels of bilirubin seen in the newborn. A number of factors contribute to this process. High fetal hemoglobin, present in response to normal low intrauterine oxygen levels, is reduced by breakdown of red blood cells. The number of cells is decreased from 5 to 6 million to about 4 to 5 million as the newborn adjusts to higher environmental oxygen. The shorter life span of fetal RBCs (90 days) when compared to nonfetal RBCs (120 days) also leads to an increased rate of destruction. Additional factors include the immaturity of the liver function and relatively low levels of blood albumin. Bilirubin can also be reabsorbed from meconium through the intestines. In the fetal and neonatal intestines, the bacteria necessary for breaking down conjugated bilirubin for excretion are absent. An enzyme (β-glucuronidase) is present and converts the conjugated bilirubin back to unconjugated bilirubin, which can be reabsorbed into the bloodstream. In the fetus, the placenta efficiently clears this bilirubin. In the newborn, reabsorption raises the body levels of bilirubin and increases the work of the liver. Since meconium contains 1 mg of bilirubin per gram, an obstruction or delay in passing meconium can be significant. (See Chap. 10 for additional discussion of physiological jaundice.)

Pathological jaundice Pathological jaundice refers to an increased bilirubin level that poses a threat to the well-being of the baby. It begins early, rises very high, or may persist for a prolonged length of time. Hyperbilirubinemia may be the first clue to the presence of an undiagnosed disorder. Table 19-11 describes factors that relate to hyperbilirubinemia. A distinction between physiologic and pathologic jaundice can be made on the basis of time of onset, course of the jaundice, levels of bilirubin, and maturity of the infant. Table 19-12 compares physiological and pathological jaundice.

Table 19-11 Factors related to hyperbilirubinemia

Classification	Examples/further information
1. Hemolytic disorders	Rh and ABO incompatibilities
	Genetic red blood cell abnormalities
2. Extravascular blood	Hematomas, swallowed blood, hemorrhages
3. Polycythemia	Excessive numbers of red blood cells
4. Drug reactions	Maternal sulfonamides and aspirin
5. Infections	Prenatal or postnatal
6. Reabsorption of bilirubin from the intestines	Delayed meconium passage, bowel obstruction
7. Breast milk	Prolonged jaundice from hormone pregnanediol
8. Prematurity	Fragile blood vessels and immature body systems
9. Hypoxemia	Asphyxia, respiratory or cardiac disease
10. Hypoglycemia	Delayed oral intake or prematurity
11. Hypoalbuminuria	Infants of diabetic mothers
12. Impaired liver function or excretion	Biliary atresia
	Neonatal hepatic disease

Table 19-12 Comparison of physiological and pathological jaundice

Physiological jaundice	Pathological jaundice
Onset	
After 24 h—full-term After 48 h—preterm	Before 24 h
Course	
Full-term—disappears in 1 week	Full-term—lasts more than 1 week
Preterm—disappears 9–10 days	Preterm—lasts more than 2 weeks
Level	
Less than 12 mg per 100 ml	20 mg per 100 ml in full-term
	15 mg per 100 ml in preterm
Rate of elevation	
Less than 5 mg per 100 ml daily	More than 5 mg per 100 ml daily
General condition	
Infant is well	Sick infant

* Adapted from Sheldon B. Korones, *High-Risk Newborn Infants*, Mosby, St. Louis, 1972, p. 171.

Kernicterus When bilirubin enters the basal ganglia of the brain, causing a disruption in function or even cell death, the infant is said to have *kernicterus*. While this usually occurs at levels above 15 mg/per 100 ml for a premature, and above 20 mg/per 100 ml for a full-term infant, it is possible to have brain damage at lower bilirubin levels, especially in sick or preterm infants with low albumin binding levels. Bilirubin that is bound to albumin does not leave the bloodstream. However, if the amount of bilirubin exceeds the available blood albumin-binding sites, other sites, such as the brain cells, are used. Factors affecting albumin binding power include cold stress, acidosis, and drugs that compete for binding sites, especially sulfonamides and salicylates.[23]

Kernicterus can cause central nervous system depression or excitation (see Table 19-13). The infant affected by kernicterus may die or sustain permanent damage. Mental retardation, sensorineural hearing loss, and delayed or abnormal motor development are found in infants who survive.

Table 19-13 Central nervous system signs of kernicterus

CNS depression	CNS excitation
Lethargy	Tremors
Poor feeding, decreased suck and rooting	Twitching
	Seizures
Decreased reflexes, absent Moro reflex	High-pitched cry
Decreased muscle tone (hypotonia)	Opisthotonus (hyperextension of the back)

Nursing management The nurse checks all newborns for signs of jaundice by using a finger to press the skin over a bony area of the nose, forehead, sternum, or tibia. When the skin color leaves (blanches), observe for a yellow color. Check the conjunctival sac or oral mucosa of dark-skinned babies. Also note the pattern of jaundice, how much of the body it covers, and the time when it first appears. Be aware that various colored articles and lighting around the baby will distort color perception. Observations are more accurate in white light. Early feeding is important to prevent hypoglycemia and dehydration and to stimulate intestinal peristalsis. Early passage of meconium will prevent bilirubin reabsorption from the intestines. As the bilirubin level rises, the baby will become lethargic and very sleepy, and suck poorly. The nurse is responsible for notifying the doctor when the symptoms seem to indicate the need for bilirubin testing or other treatment.

Hemolytic disease in the newborn

Rh and ABO incompatibilities result from isoimmunization and are responsible for the majority of hemolytic diseases in the newborn. Antibodies are produced by the mother against Rh or AB antigens from her baby, endangering its healthy survival. Of these two diseases, two-thirds of the incompatibilities involve the ABO factor and the other one-third the Rh factor.[24]

When each parent has a different blood type (A, B, AB or O) the offspring can inherit a blood type that is incompatible with that of the mother. Red blood cells, except those from type O blood, carry an antigen. The serum, except that in type AB blood, contains antibody reactive to blood cells of other types (Table 19-14). Though the placenta usually acts as an effective barrier, some fetal red blood cells may still enter the maternal circulation. If a blood-type incompatibility exists, it will stimulate maternal antibody production; these antibodies can pass to the fetus and destroy fetal RBC's. This often occurs at the time of delivery, when the placenta tears or separates. It takes as little as 0.5 ml of blood to cause a significant antibody response in the mother. Sensitization before pregnancy is possible from blood transfusions or other unknown sources. The process takes about 72 h to be stimulated and from 6 weeks to 6 months for antibodies to be produced. After the first antibody response, the subsequent exposures to the same antigen will elicit a more rapid formation and higher level of antibodies. The plasma cells and the reticuloendothelial system have a "memory" response to this antigen.

ABO incompatibility ABO incompatibility is the most common cause of hemolytic disease; it usually results in fewer problems before birth and milder disease after birth than does Rh

Table 19-14 ABO system of antigens and antibodies for determining blood compatibility (includes genotype)

Blood group				Compatibility	
Genotype	Phenotype	Antigen	Antibody	Can be donor to type	Can receive transfusion from type
AA, AO	A	A	Anti-B	A or AB	A or O
BB, BO	B	B	Anti-A	B or AB	B or O
AB	AB	A and B	No antibodies	AB	A, B, AB, or O
OO	O	No antigen	Anti-A and anti-B	A, B, AB or O	O

Adapted from G. Scipien et al., *Comprehensive Pediatric Nursing*, McGraw-Hill Book Co., New York, 1979.

sensitization. The child inherits one allele for the ABO blood group from each parent. Since a type O allele is inactive when paired with an A or B allele, only a genotype of OO in the newborn will produce type O blood (see Table 19-14). Agglutination (clumping of RBC's) results from the contact between the antigen of one blood group and the antibodies of another group.

In ABO incompatibilities the mother is usually type O and the fetus type A; less commonly the fetus will have type B. It is rare to have an ABO incompatibility in other combinations.

The variable reaction in the fetus is thought to be due to a lower antigenicity of the fetal and neonatal red blood cell or because the maternal anti-A and anti-B antibodies are of the IgM type. Naturally produced IgM molecules are larger than the IgG molecules formed in an active immunity response and do not pass the placental barrier as easily. When type A or B red blood cells enter the mother's bloodstream, the anti-A and anti-B antibodies already present destroy them. Therefore the mother's body is not as likely to be stimulated to produce more "immune" antibodies and is less likely to have sensitization due to "memory response" for future pregnancies. For unexplained reasons, not all women produce IgG molecules in ABO incompatibilities. ABO incompatibility can occur in firstborn children and the numbers of pregnancies do not influence the severity of the disease.

At birth the newborn may show a rise in bilirubin, varying degrees of anemia, and later jaundice. Spherocytes, immature RBCs, increase and can be seen in blood cell counts. A direct Coombs test (measuring maternal antibodies attached to fetal blood cells) will be weakly positive. Treatment with phototherapy or exchange transfusions may be needed.

Rh sensitization The Rh factor was first recognized in 1940 in work with the Rhesus monkey. Though six factors are present in the Rh system— Cc, Dd, Ee— the capital D is present in 95 percent of the incompatibilities.[25] The term *Rh-positive* simply means the Rh antigen is contained on the outer membrane of the red blood cell; *Rh-negative* signifies its absence. The Caucasian population is 85 percent Rh-positive and 15 percent Rh-negative. Most other racial groups,

such as the blacks and American Indians, have fewer Rh-negative members.

Incompatibility can occur when an Rh-negative woman carries an Rh-positive fetus. The father of the baby may be a heterozygous or homozygous Rh-positive male. If he is homozygous, he carries only Rh-positive genes and all babies will be Rh-positive. If he is heterozygous, he carries both an Rh-positive and Rh-negative gene and has a 50 percent chance of passing the Rh-positive gene to his offspring.

The first pregnancy is usually unaffected unless the woman was previously sensitized. Sensitization can be the result of an Rh-positive blood transfusion, any pregnancy, or an abortion. A newer theory suggests the mother may sometimes be sensitized as a fetus by her own Rh-negative mother.[26]

Sensitization reaction in pregnancy is the result of fetal red blood cells entering the maternal circulation. These Rh-positive fetal cells act as an antigen in the mother's body and stimulate production of antibodies. These antibodies pass through the placenta into the fetus, where they destroy fetal red blood cells and cause continued hemolysis.

Each successive pregnancy of the Rh-sensitized mother will produce a greater antibody response. However, the degree and response of sensitization is variable, depending on the circumstances of birth, the woman's physiology, and many other factors.

An $Rh_o(D)$ immune human globulin, or RhoGAM, is given intramuscularly to the Rh-negative mother within 72 h after the birth of an Rh-positive baby. It is also given following each abortion or miscarriage when the blood type might be unknown. An immune globulin prevents Rh sensitization (Fig. 19-13).

$Rh_o(D)$ immune globulin gives the mother artificial antibodies that attach to and destroy the fetal red blood cells in her body. Since these antibodies give passive immunity, the mother's immune system is not stimulated to produce antibodies for active immunity. In about 4 to 6 weeks the immune serum's antibodies are destroyed. Since the mother's own immune system was never activated, it will have no memory for this antibody reaction. Without an immune globulin like RhoGAM the body produces active immunity with each succeeding pregnancy,

Figure 19-13 Maternal Rh sensitization and prevention by use of RhoGAM (Rho(D) gamma globulin). (*From S. H. Pierog and A. Ferrara, Medical Care of the Sick Newborn, 2d ed., Mosby, St. Louis, 1976, p. 188. Used with permission.*)

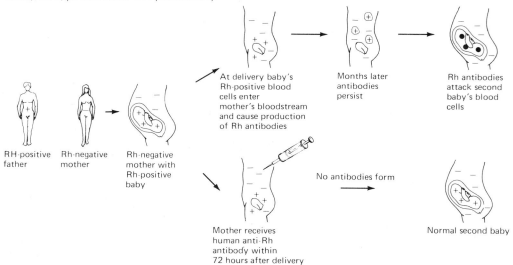

RH-positive father

Rh-negative mother

Rh-negative mother with Rh-positive baby

At delivery baby's Rh-positive blood cells enter mother's bloodstream and cause production of Rh antibodies

Months later antibodies persist

Rh antibodies attack second baby's blood cells

Mother receives human anti-Rh antibody within 72 hours after delivery

No antibodies form

Normal second baby

causing a more severe sensitization. The immune globulin is not used if the mother is already sensitized. Both maternal and fetal Coombs' tests and maternal antibody titers should be negative before an $Rh_o(D)$ immune globulin is given.

Clinical manifestations of hemolytic disease

Hemolytic disease of the newborn has largely replaced the older term *erythroblastosis fetalis.* The older term was derived from the immature red blood cells, *erythroblasts,* that are released in response to red blood cell hemolysis. Since this is only one diagnostic sign of the disease, hemolytic disease of the newborn, along with the designated cause, is preferable.

The severity of the hemolytic reaction in an Rh sensitization depends on the length of time the baby is exposed to antibodies and the degree of sensitization. Rh-negative women are usually monitored with indirect Coombs' tests, which measure anti-D antibody levels in maternal serum, initially at 16 to 20 weeks. If positive, a repeat Coombs' test is done at frequent intervals during the pregnancy.

Amniocentesis is indicated in pregnancy if the indirect Coombs' test shows rising antibody titers. The amniotic fluid is withdrawn and examined for levels of bilirubin. Though bilirubin is normally found in the amniotic fluid until 36 weeks, a rapidly increasing rate or high level indicate red blood cell destruction.

Anemia is the primary symptom in the fetus. It may cause the liver and spleen to enlarge and may lead to heart failure. Usually jaundice is not present. Excess bilirubin is excreted through the placenta and maternal circulation. There may be exceptions, however, in the severely ill fetus. Massive edema of the fetus, as a result of low blood protein, is referred to as *hydrops fetalis.* This subcutaneous edema sometimes becomes so severe it doubles fetal body weight. Fetuses this severely affected are often stillborn.

An *intrauterine transfusion* can be given to a severely anemic fetus if the infant is too immature to survive birth and is suffering from such severe disease that its life is endangered. This procedure is similar to an amniocentesis. Prior to the transfusion, a radiopaque dye is injected into the amniotic fluid. When the fetus swallows the dye, the GI tract is outlined and the tiny peritoneal cavity can be seen on the fluoroscope.

Type O Rh-negative blood is used for the transfusion because the fetal blood type is unknown. About 75 to 150 ml of packed red blood cells are injected into the peritoneum. They are absorbed into the fetal circulation, reducing the anemia. The transfusion may need to be repeated after several weeks to maintain life; as soon as the fetus is mature enough, he is delivered. A danger of injuring the fetus with the needle puncture exists, but, since most infants would die without the transfusion, the risk is worth taking. The nurse checks fetal heart tones and watches for leakage of amniotic fluid or maternal bleeding after the transfusion. Since the advent of $Rh_o(D)$ immune serums, Rh-sensitized women are rare and intrauterine transfusions are used very infrequently.

The clinical signs of the less severely affected newborn are those discussed under hyperbilirubinemia of the newborn. Whenever incompatibility is suspected, a direct Coombs' test is done at birth using the infant's cord blood. The test is positive if maternal antibodies are attached to the fetal red blood cells. The newborn is watched closely for jaundice and treated by phototherapy and exchange transfusion if needed.

Supportive care for newborn hemolytic disease The two usual therapies for hemolytic disease of the newborn are phototherapy and exchange transfusions. Of the two, phototherapy is used much more frequently.

Before initiating treatment for jaundice, the physician must attempt to determine the cause. Laboratory tests include serum bilirubin levels, blood type and Rh on both mother and infant, direct Coombs' test, hematocrit, hemoglobin, and peripheral blood smears. Often these tests do not reveal the reason for jaundice, and further investigation for less obvious causes, such as sepsis and biliary atresia, is needed. Even with careful examination, a reason for the jaundice is discovered in only about half of the cases.

Phototherapy Phototherapy had its beginnings when it was observed that light broke down the bilirubin in unshielded blood samples and that babies in sunny parts of the nursery were less jaundiced. Bilirubin lights (phototherapy) are artificial light sources used to reduce bilirubin levels of 12 mg per 100 ml or higher. The nude baby is placed under the lights with the eyes shielded. Some sources also suggest covering the gonads with a paper face mask (Fig. 19-14). Bilirubin in the skin decomposes when exposed to light and is reduced to a form that can be excreted in the stool and urine. Some controversy

exists over the long-range effects and appropriate use, but it is not used to prevent developmental jaundice from appearing.

While it is generally recognized that the blue-light spectrum is more effective in reducing bilirubin, there is disagreement regarding the use of blue or white light. Blue light, especially the super-blue type, produces headaches, dizziness, and nausea in some care-givers. Proponents of white light say that skin changes are more easily seen under white light and the undesirable effects of blue lights on personnel may indicate some unrecognized, but similar, effects on babies.

Whatever the type of light, a Plexiglas shield is used to prevent undesirable ultraviolet rays from reaching the baby. Usually a bank of 4 to 8 fluorescent bulbs are used. Though estimates of the correct length of time to use each bulb for maximum effectiveness vary, about 200 h is recommended. Keeping an accurate record will enable the nurse to set up a maintenance schedule and observe differences in clinical effectiveness. An accurate way to judge light effectiveness is by using a spectroradiometer (light meter) for

Figure 19-14 Infant receiving phototherapy.

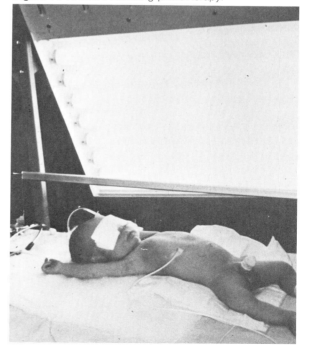

monitoring energy output. At the present time these are not often used because they are expensive and difficult to maintain.

While no ill effects from phototherapy have been documented, the nurse should watch for harmful effects to either the newborn or nursing personnel. When working with blue lights, sunglasses and a hair covering may reduce the nurses' nausea and dizziness. Protective measures for the newborn include shielding the gonads and covering the eyes. Since the head is a large part of the newborn's body surface area (one-third to one-fourth), the eye mask should be adequate to protect the eyes but leave most of the head unshielded. Before the mask is put on, make sure the baby's eyes are shut. The mask is secured in place so it does not slip down and obstruct the nose. It is removed for feedings and the eyes are cleansed. These measures will prevent corneal abrasions. The baby is turned every 1 to 2 h to increase exposure of all skin surfaces since unexposed areas will not have reduced bilirubin.

Infants under lights can have difficulty regulating temperature and experience an insensible water loss two to three times above normal. Heat is usually controlled by putting the baby in a radiant warmer or isolette. A skin temperature probe is the most accurate and safest way to control the temperature. Observe the skin turgor and fontanels for signs of dehydration and weigh every 8 to 12 h. Make sure the infant is receiving adequate fluids to compensate for the losses. Fluids are also lost through the stools. Loose green stools are often seen as the bilirubin is excreted. Special attention must be given to keeping the baby clean and dry.

A body rash is common and usually disappears spontaneously. A very severe skin change called *bronze baby syndrome* may develop as a result of obstructive jaundice. The skin becomes a dark, gray-brown color. Phototherapy is then usually discontinued or used with caution.[27]

Table 19-15 Indications for exchange transfusion

Cord blood bilirubin over 4 mg per 100 ml at birth
Bilirubin—rising more than 0.5 to 1 mg per 100 ml in 1 h
   15 mg per 100 ml in a preterm infant
   20 mg per 100 ml in a full-term infant
Hemoglobin—Under 12 g in a full-term infant
   Under 14 g in a preterm infant

Serum bilirubin levels will be tested every 6 to 8 h while the baby is under lights. After phototherapy is discontinued, bilirubin is checked in 8 to 12 h for the rebound level. The usual level of decrease in bilirubin is 3 to 4 mg per 100 ml in 8 to 12 h of therapy. The baby needs close observation because levels rebound during the first 12 h after removal from lights.

Parenting is easily disrupted at this early newborn stage. The nurse should assure parents that jaundice is not related to prenatal neglect (not keeping appointments, poor diet) or to any other factor under the parents' control. Remove the eye covers when they feed the baby and encourage them to hold and cuddle their infant. Between feedings parents and nurses can touch and stroke the baby. The sensory deprivation of an infant under lights can be severe, and relief from the isolated environment is an absolute necessity.

Exchange transfusions Newborn exchange transfusions are done to treat anemia caused by a hemolytic process and to prevent the rapid rise in bilirubin that can progress to kernicterus. An exchange transfusion will replace the infant's sensitized RBC's, remove circulating antibodies, and lower the bilirubin level. Table 19-15 lists the indications for an exchange transfusion.

The transfusion blood type for Rh incompatibility is the infant's blood type or type O Rh-negative blood. In ABO incompatibility, type O with the infant's Rh is used.[28] The blood is also cross-matched for compatibility with the mother's serum. Albumin, given intravenously in amounts of 1 g/kg before an exchange transfusion, will increase the binding sites available in the blood. This is called *priming*. It will increase the amount of bilirubin removed with an exchange transfusion.

A catheter is inserted into the umbilical vein and 5 to 20 ml of the newborn's blood is withdrawn and replaced with an equal transfusion volume. This is continued until double the volume of the newborn's blood is replaced. This is estimated as 85 ml/kg and removes about 85 percent of the sensitized cells. Serum bilirubin is lowered by about 50 percent, but this soon rises as bilirubin is drawn out of the tissues. The infant may need several repeat transfusions and may continue to show a progressive decrease in hemoglobin for as long as 6 weeks. Maternal antibodies can be found in the infant's blood for at least that long.

Fresh whole blood is the first choice for the transfusion. Blood more than 48 h old is not used because it is high in potassium and can cause acidosis. Heparinized blood is sometimes used, but protamine sulfate must be given at the completion of the exchange to prevent bleeding. Blood preserved with sodium citrate combines with the infant's serum calcium and depletes the calcium. Infusions of 0.5 to 1.0 ml of 10% calcium gluconate are given after each 100 ml of citrated blood exchanged to prevent tetany, convulsions, and possible death.

The nurse removes the blood from the refrigerator to warm, accurately identifies the blood type and Rh, and verifies the infant's name. It is important to keep the baby warm during the procedure and monitor the vital signs and blood pressure. Record the amounts of blood infused and watch for signs of calcium deficiency, cardiac arrythmias, or circulatory overload. During the infusion make sure the catheter is filled with normal saline prior to insertion to prevent air embolism and to maintain a closed system.

After the procedure is completed, a Dextrostix is used to measure blood glucose every 2 to 4 h. It is important to continue to monitor the vital signs frequently and observe the umbilical site for bleeding and infection.

The infant of a diabetic mother (IDM)

Prior to the discovery of insulin in 1921, a diabetic woman had little chance of becoming pregnant and producing a live, full-term baby. With the advent of insulin, effective control of diabetes, and improved techniques for maternal and fetal assessment, the maternal mortality rate for diabetics has continued to drop until it has nearly reached the level for other pregnant women. Despite treatment, the stillbirth and neonatal death rate for the offspring of diabetic mothers is several times higher than that for newborns of nondiabetic women.[29] Estimates of perinatal mortality range from 10 percent at high-risk centers to 20 or 30 percent in less advanced centers.[30]

The larger numbers of babies born to diabetic women today has led to more experience with their problems. An increased awareness exists of the need for close supervision of prenatal and newborn care as well as precise timing of the birth. The most complicated pregnancies and the poorest fetal outcomes are found in women with diabetes of early onset (before 10 years of age), of long standing (20 years), and with vascular changes such as retinopathy (vascular changes in the eyes).

It is important to control maternal diabetes, maintain the blood glucose near normal levels, and prevent ketosis to ensure fetal welfare. Careful medical care, close observation for vascular disease progression, periodic hospitalization for regulation of the diabetes, and a greater emphasis on self-care have improved fetal and maternal outcomes.

The timing of delivery is also critical to the survival of the baby. If delivery is too soon, prematurity is a great risk; if it is too late, stillbirths increase. Most physicians prefer to deliver the infant between 36 to 38 weeks, before placental degeneration has affected the fetus.

The decision to deliver the baby is made on the basis of tests to determine fetal size, maturity, intrauterine condition, and placental function. See Table 19-3. Serial estriols for the diabetic woman are done daily or at least two to three times a week beginning at 32 to 34 weeks. They establish a baseline of placental function and are used to watch for the normal estriol rise during the third trimester. A 25 percent drop in estriols indicates a serious placental dysfunction and danger to the fetus. Ultrasound determines fetal head size and assists in judging fetal growth and gestational age. Amniocentesis is always used before early delivery to determine fetal lung and kidney maturity. The nonstress test evaluates the fetal condition in the uterus by recording the reaction to the stress of movement or contractions. If the fetus shows signs of distress, the OCT (stress) test is used as a follow-up.

The decision to do a vaginal delivery or a cesarean section is based on information gained from these tests and observations of the pregnant woman. Since diabetic babies are often large, a vaginal delivery in a woman with an inadequate pelvis may cause severe trauma to both mother and baby; a C section is the safest choice. Toxemia and uteroplacental insufficiency also contribute to a high (70 percent) C section rate.

Clinical manifestations Usually infants of diabetic mothers are very large, weighing over 4500 g or 10 lb. They have fat cheeks, a tomato-like face, flushed appearance, and a large edematous body (Fig. 19-15*A* and *B*). Their muscles are often hypotonic, but the slightest stimulus will cause a tremulous and hyperirritable response. These

Figure 19-15 Infant of 36 weeks gestation, weighing 4500 g, of diabetic mother. Note round face and fat, almost edematous-appearing, body.

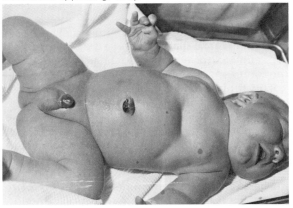

A

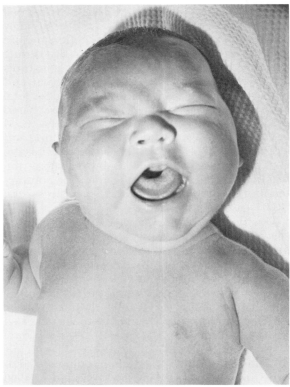

B

babies have a very poor suck and do not seem interested in eating. Their large, mature appearance is deceptive. They are usually premature and their physiological characteristics are those of their true gestational age. As with other prematures, respiratory distress syndrome is very common. Major congenital anomalies are present in about 5 percent of these infants.[31] The most common anomalies involve the spine and heart. Tracheoesophageal fistulas and malformations of the lower extremities are also more frequent. In contrast to this large baby, a small, intrauterine growth retarded infant may be born to a diabetic woman with severe vascular involvement.

Vaginal delivery of a large fetus can result in birth trauma. Common birth injuries are fractures of the clavicle, facial nerve paralysis, and damage to the brachial nerve plexus.

High levels of maternal glucose passing through the placenta stimulate fetal insulin production, thereby increasing both fetal growth and fat deposits. At birth, the newborn's glucose level will be close to that of his mother. Since the insulin-producing cells of the fetal pancreas are hypertrophied, they continue to produce excessive amounts of insulin the first few days after birth, causing depletion of body glucose supplies. A sharp drop in blood glucose level 1 to 4 h after birth is common.

The degree of hypoglycemia is affected by the severity of the maternal diabetes, prenatal control of the disease, and the level of maternal blood glucose. An extremely high maternal blood sugar or the administration of large amounts of glucose during labor and delivery will increase the insulin level in the newborn, and the resulting hypoglycemic reaction will be more severe. If the mother has relatively normal blood sugar levels, the infant will have lower insulin levels and less hypoglycemia.

It is important to remember that hypoglycemia is asymptomatic in about 30 percent of these infants. Early diagnosis is urgent. Fetal and maternal blood glucose levels should be measured at delivery. Blood glucose in the IDM is monitored every 1 to 2 h for the first 8 h and then about every 4 h for the next 24 h. (Refer to the earlier discussion of hypoglycemia for manifestations and treatment.)

Hypocalcemia, a calcium level below 7 mg per 100 ml, is another common problem in infants of diabetic women. Early signs of hypocalcemia may be similar to those of hypoglycemia and include apnea, cyanotic episodes, edema, high-pitched cry, or abdominal distention. Low calcium levels are often seen in stressed premature infants. Hypocalcemia is likely to occur either at 24 to 48 h or at 5 to 10 days after birth. (Hypocalcemia is further discussed in Chap. 24.)

Infants of diabetic mothers frequently develop hyperbilirubinemia due to excess red blood cell hemolysis. Polycythemia (excessively high number of red blood cells), extravascular bleeding related to traumatic deliveries, and prematurity all contribute to the high bilirubin levels in these infants. Polycythemia with increased blood viscosity, can also cause renal vein thrombosis, a rare, but serious condition seen in infants of diabetic mothers.

If infants born to diabetic women survive the perils of the neonatal period, the prognosis is good. However, according to White, 7 percent of them will develop diabetes by age 20.[32]

Nursing management Essential information in establishing a data base on which to build a nursing care plan includes: maternal diabetic classification; fetal gestational age; the course of pregnancy, labor, and delivery; Apgar score; fetal blood glucose; calcium levels; and respiratory status. Table 19-16 lists the common problems of the infant of the diabetic mother. The nursing management and other details of care for these problems are discussed earlier in this chapter or can be found in other parts of the book. It is obvious that an infant with such a multitude of problems needs close observation in an intensive care nursery.

Fetal alcohol syndrome (FAS)

Since 1973 studies have described the pattern of fetal alcohol syndrome in babies of chronically alcoholic women.[33] Research shows that maternal blood alcohol levels determine the effect on the fetus. "Binge drinkers," women who drink large amounts periodically, also risk FAS. Even social drinkers may be causing unidentifiable damage to their offspring.

Clinical manifestations Not all children of chronic alcoholics are affected. Smith estimates that "the risk of fetal alcohol syndrome in the offspring of alcoholic women is about 33% and

Table 19-16 Problems of the infant of the diabetic mother

Hypoglycemia
Respiratory distress syndrome
Hyperbilirubinemia
Hypocalcemia
Poor temperature control
Congenital anomalies
Birth trauma
Renal vein thrombosis

the risk of mental deficiency is about 50%."[34] The fetus seems to be affected during the first 11 weeks of gestation. The defects result from a decreased number of cells (hypoplasia), causing an uneven rate of body growth.

The affected children show growth deficiency in many specific areas. Microcephaly may be present. The face has a typical pattern with undersized eyes and a small midface. Cardiac and limb defects occur. Associated with the physical retardation are developmental delays and mental deficiency. These children tend to be hyperactive, poorly coordinated, and irritable and have many behavior problems.

Medical management Diagnosis is usually made on the basis of the mother's history and the appearance and symptoms of the child. Pregnant women should be told to abstain or reduce their alcohol intake to no more than 2 oz a day, the equivalent of one drink. Health professionals must actively educate pregnant women about the dangers of alcohol. Accurate histories and the use of effective birth control for known alcoholics are also essential.

Infant of a drug-addicted mother

Heroin, methadone, or barbiturates are the most common drugs abused by pregnant women. The typical characteristics of drug abusers affect the quality of their pregnancy and motherhood. The abuser is usually young, in her early twenties, and has an unplanned pregnancy. Poor prenatal care, malnutrition, and associated diseases such as hepatitis, septicemia, preeclampsia, and venereal diseases are common.

Clinical manifestations The addicted fetus may show signs of hyperactivity, such as kicking a lot, at the times the mother is due to take drugs. As many as 50 percent of these newborns are premature by weight and gestational age. Severe addiction in early pregnancy may lead to abortion and stillbirth. Two-thirds of the newborns of addicted mothers will be affected, showing visible signs of addiction.

Symptoms usually appear 24 to 96 h after birth with occasional delays up to a week or more. The newborn shows such signs of central nervous system stimulation as hyperactivity, hypertonicity, irritability, tremors, high-pitched cry, and, infrequently, convulsions. Gastrointestinal symptoms include vomiting, diarrhea, and poor feeding with a constant sucking need. The newborn may also sweat, sneeze, yawn, and have excessive mucus.

A complete maternal history for addicting drugs is essential. Observation of the newborn for the symptoms listed above will help detect addicted infants. A urinalysis done within 12 h after birth will show traces of morphine and quinine, a substance often used to dilute the drug's strength.

Medical and nursing management Control of withdrawal symptoms is achieved through administration of chlorpromazine or phenobarbital to relieve CNS symptoms and paregoric to control diarrhea. IV therapy prevents dehydration. These babies are extremely irritable, tense, and difficult to comfort. Their tension level and sucking needs can best be satisfied by a pacifier. These babies need a calm, quiet environment and soothing activities such as swaddling and very gentle rocking. One must anticipate that the mother may experience long-term difficulty caring for the infant. Referral to a community health nurse and follow-up by a counselor or social worker are essential.

Injuries related to birth trauma

The process of birth causes some degree of trauma to all babies. Soft tissue injuries such as petechiae, conjunctival hemorrhage, and subperiosteal hemorrhage (cephalhematoma) are common, and the recovery is usually spontaneous and complete. Injuries to the skeleton of the baby also occur frequently. Most injuries are related to large fetal size. Other factors involved are breech presentation, small maternal pelvic size, and a complicated delivery with excessive force.

Fractures most commonly involve the clavicle, but the femur, humerus, spine, and skull are also affected. Skull fractures are most often caused by pressure of the head against the promontory of the mother's sacrum. Forceps are also a factor, although they usually produce a linear rather than a depressed fracture. Linear fractures (cracks) are usually not treated, while depressed fractures are surgically corrected. Chapter 36 discusses treatment of fractures.

Neurological trauma is most often related to hemorrhage and excessive pulling on the neck or spine and manipulation during a difficult delivery. Brachial nerve plexus injuries affect the arm and shoulder. A partial disruption damaging the fifth or sixth cervical nerves causes a high injury called *Erb-Duchenne paralysis.* The newborn will have a flaccid arm with the elbow extended, the arm adducted and internally rotated. There is muscle weakness on the affected side and motion is limited. The Moro reflex on the affected side is absent. The grasp is intact. An injury at the seventh or eighth cervical and first thoracic nerve, called *Klumpke's paralysis,* affects the lower arm. The wrist and hand are flaccid and the grasp reflex is absent.

The affected arm and shoulder are protected from injury by gentle handling and support. In about 10 days passive range of motion exercises to the shoulder, elbow, wrist, and hand are begun. The "Statue of Liberty" position is no longer advised because it can enhance contractures and shoulder damage. Recovery is spontaneous with minimal residual in over three-fourths of the children.[35] If the nerve has been disrupted, the return of function will depend on the degree of regeneration. It takes about 6 months to determine what the degree of recovery will be. If reconstructive surgery is attempted, it will be done when the child is about 4 years of age.

Facial palsy results from damage of the seventh cranial nerve. When the baby cries, the eye on the affected side may remain open and the mouth will droop or be asymmetrical. The prognosis for recovery is good and permanent residual is rare. Pressure of the face against the sacrum during delivery or during pregnancy is the most frequent cause. A comparison of forceps deliveries and normal deliveries shows no increase of facial palsy with forceps.[36]

Intracranial bleeding in the newborn infant is *related* most often to asphyxia and mechanical trauma occuring during the birth process. Although it may not be the cause of death, intracranial bleeding is often seen in autopsy. Prematures, with their soft skulls and fragile capillary system, are predisposed to hemorrhage. Subarachnoid bleeding is most common in prematures. Clinical signs of intracranial bleeding range from almost no signs to severe neurological signs. Signs of intracranial pressure are discussed in Chap. 37.

Medical intervention is designed to relieve intracranial pressure. Prognosis is variable, depending on the amount of bleeding, the amount of pressure, and the success relieving it. IV fluids are begun and the baby is positioned with the head slightly elevated. Residual damage may include cerebral palsy, learning disabilities, seizure disorders, or mental retardation.

Alterations in parenting of high-risk infants

When caring for parents of high-risk infants, it is readily apparent that special parenting and attachment needs exist. These needs result from a disruption of the usual opportunities for attachment surrounding the birth process. They can also be affected by the parent's past experiences with pregnancy, their own parenting, the planning, course, and events of this pregnancy, relationships with their family and spouse, culture, socioeconomic background, and personal maturity.

Pregnancy

The usual tasks of midpregnancy include bonding to the fetus and preparing physically and emotionally for the baby (nesting). The final task of pregnancy, separation, establishes the baby with an identity apart from its mother's.

Separation is mastered in part by fantasy. The baby's characteristics are imagined: blue eyes "like me," black hair "like daddy's," a boy, a girl, and always "normal." The pregnant woman also works out her own mothering role through comparisons and mimicry of her own mother and other mothers she knows. At the end of pregnancy, although she may still fear labor, the increased discomforts of pregnancy make her welcome the birth of her baby.

Premature birth of an infant interrupts the normal psychological development of pregnancy. The birth of a sick infant destroys the fantasies of a perfect baby. It becomes a very disruptive and traumatic event for the entire family.

Labor

The woman in premature labor is acutely aware of a sense of sadness and fear. This is in sharp contrast to the usual aura of anticipation and joy. Frequently the time in labor is spent reviewing her pregnancy and searching for an explanation for this unexpected event. Feelings of guilt are often verbalized: "If only I hadn't scrubbed the floor," or "Maybe if I had rested more."

Birth

The time during the birth is especially anxiety-producing for the mother. Some physicians feel it is not appropriate for the father to be in the delivery room for an "abnormal" birth, and so the mother loses her best source of support. The delivery room is crowded with medical experts and the mother waits anxiously for some word of her baby. It is easy to ignore the mother when the baby needs resuscitation. Even with a very sick baby, someone should give the mother a quick summary of the baby's condition and provide a brief look at the baby.

Sick infants are usually taken to the neonatal intensive care unit or their condition is stabilized and they are moved to another hospital. In most hospitals the baby is taken to the mother's bedside in the transporter. The parents can see and touch the baby. The nurse can offer contact with the baby but should wait for the parents to be ready for this. Some parents will be too frightened to touch or afraid that touching the baby will harm it. Taking the mother's hand in yours and gently touching the baby sometimes helps. Seeing and touching the baby are important to help the parents accept the reality of the baby's birth. It also lets them see for themselves that the baby is alive. The father often follows the transporter team to the intensive care unit and sees what is happening to the baby.

Learning to cope with the reality of a high-risk infant

Caplan has identified four major tasks the mother needs to accomplish after the birth of a high-risk infant.[37]

1. She must realize that she may lose the baby and may do some anticipatory grieving; she still hopes for survival, but prepares for death.
2. She must acknowledge failure in her maternal function to deliver a full-term baby.
3. If the baby improves, she must respond with hope and anticipation. After the separation from the infant due to prolonged hospital stay, she must resume her interrupted relationship with it in preparation for the infant's homecoming.
4. She must prepare herself for the job of caring for the baby through understanding of its special needs and growth patterns while still recognizing that the baby will eventually develop normal growth patterns.

During the first few days, the mother spends her time in the maternity ward and the father is often the messenger between her and the inten-

Figure 19-16 This family is getting acquainted with the newborn in the intensive care area. Notice the brotherly attention to the pacifier.

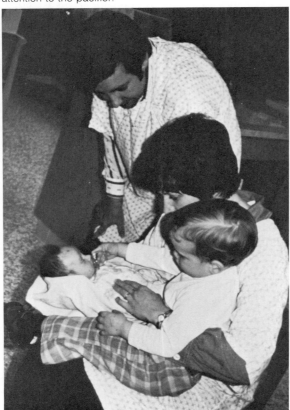

sive care unit. She feels isolated, alone, and a deep sense of loss. The father has similar feelings and, additionally, is torn between spending time with his wife, the baby, or the rest of their family.

Siblings often find it difficult to understand why the baby does not come home. They may also feel neglected because their parents spend most of their time in the hospital. Pictures of the baby and visits to the hospital will help the siblings to understand (Fig. 19-16).

Nurses and doctors can help parents by listening to them and facilitating visits to the ICU.

1. Allow the mother to retell her experiences—how labor began, what she saw in delivery, and how the baby appears to her.
2. Encourage the couple to talk together and help the father share information with his wife.
3. Talk with the parents about the baby. Give realistic, correct information. Klaus suggests stressing the positive and being optimistic since the outlook for high-risk infants is greatly improved. He suggests that once a mother believes the baby will die, she begins to mourn and is reluctant to attach to the baby.[38]
4. Assist the parents with early NICU visits. Prepare them for the tubes, monitors, and appearance of the baby, and discuss the policies of the unit. Arrange transportation and, if possible, go with them.
5. If the mother is not able to visit, maintain as much contact between her and her infant as possible. Pictures of the baby and phone calls to the unit, as well as visits from the pediatrician, are essential.
6. Allow parents to grieve and accept their crying and even their anger. At times a private room may help the mother to be able to express herself and work out her feelings. While anger may be directed toward the people around them, it is a response to deep fear and hurt. Remember that withdrawal can also be a protective mechanism, and when parents are overloaded with information, or have heard as much as they can bear, they may mentally shut off.

Once the mother has physically recovered from the birth, she is ready to begin the acquaintance process with the baby. It evolves through three steps: What are you really like? What do you think of me? What do I really think of you? The parents answer these questions through interaction with the baby. Parents can reach through the incubator portholes and touch their newborns. Progression of touch follows

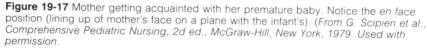

Figure 19-17 Mother getting acquainted with her premature baby. Notice the *en face* position (lining up of mother's face on a plane with the infant's). (*From G. Scipien et al., Comprehensive Pediatric Nursing, 2d ed., McGraw-Hill, New York, 1979. Used with permission.*

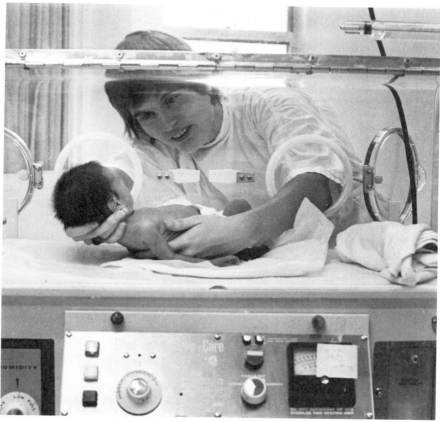

Rubin's progression from poking and handling the extremities to stroking, whole-hand touching, and holding close. This is the normal progression but is delayed because of separation. Establishing eye contact is very important to parents. You will often see them align their face with the baby's (the *en face* position) (Fig. 19-17).

The critical time period for attachment seems to be the first 10 to 14 days. If parents are not permitted contact during this time, their interest wanes and visiting decreases. In the early 1900s, Dr. Martin Cooney treated more than 5000 prematures in incubators. He prohibited parents from contact with their baby. After Dr. Cooney's babies were well, he had extreme difficulty persuading parents to take their infants home.[39]

Fortunately today, ICU policies usually permit early visiting, touching, and caretaking by par-ents. Visiting hours are unrestricted and many units provide areas for overnight stays. The staff orients the parents to the area and implements a systematic teaching and discharge plan.

The amount of caretaking progresses with the parents' readiness and the improvement of the baby's condition. The nurse is an ally, not a competitor who will replace the mother. It's important to give positive feedback to help the mother feel competent. Having the mother bring in special clothes or toys for the baby and leaving notes for her, like "Hi, Mom. I'm glad you came to feed me," will foster a healthy relationship.

Preparing for discharge

Criteria for discharge are no longer as rigid as they were in the past. Usually discharge depends on the following:

Table 19-17 Discharge planning tool

Infant's name _____ Birthdate _____ Discharge date _____
Parents' name _____ Address _____ Telephone _____
Physician _____ Primary nurse _____
Summary of birth events: Reason for admission _____
Gestational age _____ Weight _____ Height _____ Head circ. _____ Eye exam. _____

Parent demonstrates:	Yes	No	Comments
1. Bathing baby			
2. Feeding baby			
3. Diapering			
4. Cord care			
5. Rectal and/or axillary temperature			
6. Circumcision care on male			
7. Knowledge of formula preparation			
8. Comfortable with breast-feeding and milk supply is established, identifies a support source			
9. Any additional treatment: _____			
10. Giving medications, knows actions, side effects, and correct schedule			
11. Preparation for baby at home and a plan for integrating baby into family			
12. Correct expectations for development and knowledge of techniques for appropriate stimulation			
13. Bonding (calls, visits, cares for infant—include behaviors)			

Follow-up: Referral: Public health nurse _____
Social worker _____ Parent support group _____
Appointment: Dr. _____ Clinic _____
Date _____ Time _____

1. The baby's condition is stable.
2. Body temperature is maintained.
3. The baby is gaining weight and feeds easily.
4. The mother is willing and able to care for the infant.
5. The home environment is free of infection.

When the parents are having spontaneous interaction with the baby, and the baby's condition permits, the medical team can begin to focus on discharge. Though teaching is a continuous process, a formal tool is useful to make sure discharge planning is complete. See Table 19-17. Some tools include the number of times the parents visit or phone and the length of the visit, since these are reliable indicators of attachment. After parents have completed the cares and are proficient in comforting and caring for the infant, they are ready to take the baby home. A referral to a community health nurse should be made and parents should be clear about whom they can call for help.

The tension of taking the baby home is reduced by discharge planning. Rooming-in for a night at the hospital will also decrease anxiety. However, the parents will still be fearful. As the baby grows and remains healthy, their anxiety and fear will decrease. The parents anxiously compare their baby to others his age, however, and focus much attention on the baby's size, weight gain, and food intake. Using the expected birth date rather than the actual birth date for comparison helps parents be more realistic about expectations for their infant.

As these infants grow older, their parents have more frequent problems with certain areas than do parents of full-term, normal babies. They seem to have difficulty setting normal limits, tend to be more restrictive, and have undue concern over minor illnesses and body functions. The incidence of failure-to-thrive infants and battered children is higher among this group.[40] This may reflect a failure to complete attachment and an inability to complete Caplan's fourth task of seeing the baby as normal.

The following Nursing Care Plan is for a preterm infant with respiratory distress syndrome. Supports for parent-infant bonding and other aspects of the nursing care for parents would readily apply regardless of the neonate's particular medical problem.

Nursing Care Plan–Premature Infant*

Assessment

Name: Boy Peterson

Diagnosis: Respiratory distress syndrome. Prematurity—33 weeks gestation

Birth date: September 3

Sex: Male

Parents' marital status: Married

Siblings: None

Family's hospital experience: Mother presently hospitalized at local hospital. Neither parent hospitalized before.

Reason for child's hospitalization: "His lungs aren't mature enough."

Allergies: None known

Date: 9/03

Admission date: 9/03

Religion: Roman Catholic

General appearance

Infant arrived from referring hospital accompanied by a neonatal nurse and pediatric resident. He is 2 h old and presents with moderate subcostal retractions, prominent expiratory grunting, and nasal flaring. Air entry in lungs is decreased bilaterally. Coloring of mucous membranes is pink when in 68% oxygen, although acrocyanosis and half-nail bed cyanosis continue. Generalized hypotonia is present.

Physical assessment

Length: 44 cm

Weight: 2020 g

Occipitofrontal circumference: 32.5 cm

Dubowitz score: 32 points—33 weeks gestation.

Temperature: 37°C (98.6°F) axillary

Pulse: 158

Dextrostix: 45 mg%

Hematocrit: 56%

Respiratory rate: 68

Blood pressure: 50/20 (arterial) 34 mean 40 flush

Skin: Generalized pink coloring when in oxygen. Acrocyanosis present. Vernix covering half of skin surface. Skin smooth. Lanugo covering entire body, except face

Head: Anterior and posterior fontanels present. Hair fine

Eyes and ears: Normal positioning. Ears flat and shapeless with scant cartilage

Nose: Catheter passes easily through both nares

Mouth: Negative

Chest: Intercostal retractions. No palpable breast tissue. Areola and nipple visible

Abdomen: No masses palpable. Three cord vessels

Genitalia: Normal appearing male with undescended testes. Testes palpable in inguinal canal. Scrotum with few rugae

Extremities: Symmetrical movement. Two anterior sole creases

Hips: Negative

Spine: Negative

Reflexes: Moro and sucking reflex present

Heart: Soft systolic murmur

Elimination: Has voided 10 ml of urine and passed small amount of meconium. Anus patent

Psychosocial history

Parents have been married for three years. This is a first-born child and a planned pregnancy. Families of the parents live in close proximity. Parents carry insurance through the husband's business.

Maternal history

Mother is gravida I, para 0, 28-year-old white female with blood type A^+. Prenatal care sought after the third month of pregnancy. EDC: November 4. No medications were taken during pregnancy other than multiple vitamins and iron. Mother is a nonsmoker and is a light social drinker (2 to 3 glasses of wine per month). Weight gain during pregnancy has been 25 lb. Vital signs remained within normal limits during the course of the pregnancy. The pregnancy was uncomplicated until the event of premature labor and delivery. Spontaneous rupture of membranes occured 12 h prior to delivery. Amniotic fluid was clear and odorless. Betamethasone was given 16 h prior to delivery. Fetal heart tones remained stable during labor and delivery. Vaginal delivery.

Neonatal history

Infant's Apgar score was 6 at 1 min (points off for heart rate, color, respiratory effort, muscle tone) and 8 at 5 min (points off for color and respiratory effort). An umbilical arterial catheter was placed. Initial blood gases were $Pa_{O_2} = 52$, $Pa_{CO_2} = 62$, and pH = 7.20 on 68% oxygen. The infant was transported to the regional neonatal referral center in the same community after stabilization measures were accomplished. Upon arrival, the infant was intubated and placed on 68% oxygen and CPAP of 6 cm water pressure.

Nursing diagnosis	Nursing goals	Nursing actions	Evaluation/revision
1. Impaired gas exchange due to inefficient ventilation of the alveoli and immaturity of the lungs.	☐ The infant's mucous membranes and skin will be pink. ☐ The infant's respiratory rate will be 30 to 50 per minute and respirations will occur without retractions. ☐ The infant's circulatory flow will be maintained at the level needed for adequate oxygenation and perfusion.	☐ Administer warm, humidified oxygen as ordered according to blood gas determinations and assessment of respiratory status and color. ☐ Observe for signs of respiratory distress, degree and location of retractions, grunting, nasal flaring, tachypnea, character of breath sounds, rate of respirations. Record and report. ☐ Assess rate, rhythm, and quality of heart sounds. Record and report. ☐ Administer chest physiotherapy (percussion, vibration, and postural drainage) q1h to q2h, as indicated by quality of breath sounds and secretions. Maintain patent airway by suctioning. ☐ Change position frequently, at least q2h. Assess positioning in reference to color and respiratory status. ☐ Assess perfusion of extremities by observing quality of pulses, color of skin, capillary filling, and warmth. ☐ Record the arterial blood pressure noting the systolic and diastolic components, mean, and pulse pressure.	☐ 9/13: Placed in room air. Pa_{O_2} maintained above 70 mmHg; presently 88. ☐ 9/13: Respiratory rate is 38–50. Respirations easy, without retractions. Breath sounds clear. ☐ 9/11: Heart rate 120–146, regular. Soft systolic murmur. ☐ 9/14: No murmur present. ☐ 9/7: Minimal secretions. Chest PT now q2–3h. ☐ 9/14: Chest PT discontinued. Breath sounds clear. ☐ 9/6: Color improves when on abdomen or right side. ☐ 9/13: Color remains pink when on either side or abdomen. ☐ 9/6: Pulses equal. Extremities warm and pink. Skin, when blanched, quickly returns to normal. ☐ 9/7: Arterial BP, 62/36; mean remains 40–50. ☐ 9/9: Umbilical arterial catheter removed. Flush BP, 50.
2. Potential for hypoglycemia due to decreased intake and decreased energy stores of brown fat and glycogen.	☐ Infant's blood glucose will consistently remain above 45 mg per 100 ml.	☐ Administer constant infusion of intravenous glucose as ordered. Record accurately. ☐ Observe, record, and report signs and symptoms such as jitteriness, lethargy, seizures, change in color, heart rate, or respiratory effort. ☐ Monitor Dextrostix values. Report if below 45 mg per 100 ml or above 130–170 mg per 100 ml. ☐ Assess potential for hypoglycemia by determining gestational age, weight, and length and plotting these values on intrauterine	☐ 9/8: 10% glucose with 0.2% NaCl infusing, rate decreased from 8 ml/h to 3 ml/h. NG feedings started. ☐ 9/4: No symptoms noted. ☐ 9/8: No symptoms noted. ☐ 9/4: Dextrostix values are 45–90. ☐ 9.8: Values as stated above. ☐ 9/3: Weight, 50th percentile, is AGA. Length, 50th percentile.

Nursing diagnosis	Nursing goals	Nursing actions	Evaluation/revision
		growth curve. Determine if infant is appropriate size for gestational age. □ Feed as early as safety permits. Advance to naso-gastric feedings cautiously; gradually increase amounts. Advance to oral feedings as indicated by infant's clinical course.	□ 9/8: NG feedings of 5 ml/h of breast milk initiated. □ 9/12: NG feedings increased to 15 ml/h. □ 9/16: First oral feeding (15 ml).
3. Instability of body temperature due to prematurity, decreased layer of subcutaneous tissue and immature neuromuscular control.	□ Infant's temperature will remain between 36.5–37°C (97.7–98.6°F) (axillary) or 37–37.5°C (98.6°–99.5°F) (rectally).	□ Prevent heat loss due to evaporation, radiation, conduction, and convection. Keep baby dry and out of drafts. Avoid chilling. □ Assist maintenance of temperature with use of radiant warmer or incubator. Apply shielded servo-control probe to exposed skin area. Set control to maintain skin temperature at 36.5°C. □ Record axillary temperature every 1 h initially. When temperature has stabilized, every 2 h. □ Monitor temperature q1h when weaning from the incubator begins. □ Double wrap and put on cap when out of warmer or incubator.	□ 9/3: Environment adjusted to prevent heat loss. □ 9/9: Temperature remains 36.5–37°C (97.7–98.6°F) (axillary). □ 9/10: Infant moved from warmer to incubator. □ 9/4: Temperature remains within normal limits. □ 9/20: Weaned from incubator. Temperature is 36.7°C (98°F) (axillary) and above. □ 9/10: Double wrap in blankets when being held. Mother brought in baby cap.
4. Potential for fluid and electrolyte imbalances due to immature regulatory mechanisms and inadequate intake.	□ The major body electrolytes will remain within normal limits. □ Hydration will remain within normal limits.	□ Administer calcium and potassium as ordered. □ Observe for signs and symptoms of electrolyte imbalance. Record and report: **a.** *Hypocalcemia* — twitching, tremors, jitters **b.** *Potassium imbalance—*cardiac irregularities **c.** *Sodium imbalance—*neurological changes, feeding intolerance, edema □ Observe for any change in alertness, pattern of activity, or movement. □ Observe and report skin turgor. □ Accurately record output (nasogastric, blood loss, urine, stools). Weigh diapers. □ Measure specific gravity q8h.	□ 9/8: While on IV fluid, 200 mg/kg of calcium gluconate and 10 meq/l of KCl given per day. □ 9/8: No symptoms noted. Serum values: sodium, 136 meq/l; potassium; 4.0 meq/l; calcium; 8.8 mg per 100 ml. □ 9/10: No changes noted. □ 9/12: Elasticity of skin present. No "tent" sign. □ 9/8: Intake approximating output. Urine output adequate. □ 9/8: Specific gravity averages 1.010. Frequency of testing changed to one time per day.

Nursing diagnosis	Nursing goals	Nursing actions	Evaluation/revision
		☐ Weigh daily.	☐ 9/5: Weight 100 g below birth weight. ☐ 9/10: Regained birth weight. ☐ 9/20: Gaining an average of 10–15 g per day.
5. Impaired oral feeding related to gastrointestinal immaturity and immature sucking reflex.	☐ The infant will be feeding orally and gaining weight at time of dismissal.	☐ Encourage mother to breast-feed, if this was her initial intention. Discuss breast care, milk expression, and hints of how she can keep her supply of breast milk while the infant is not nursing. Identify a source of support for her. ☐ Gavage feedings may be indicated initially. Follow procedure for insertion of gastric tube. Allow feedings to flow in over time it would take for normal oral feeding. Check gastric residuals prior to each feeding. Measure abdominal girth prior to each feeding. Increase amount of feedings gradually. ☐ Pacifier practice every 3 h while on gavage feedings in order to develop sucking reflex. ☐ Use premature (soft) nipple when feeding orally. ☐ Allow infant to sleep or rest 1 h before feeding. Allow for cuddling and rocking before and after feeding.	☐ 9/3: Mother wishes to breast feed. Obstetrical nurses are assisting mother with information. A mother from LaLeche League will be contacting Mrs. P. ☐ 9/8: NG feedings started at 5 ml/h of breast milk. ☐ 9/12: NG feedings increased to 15 ml/h. ☐ 9/10: Gastric residuals are consistently less than 20% of total feeding. Abdominal girth is 28 cm. ☐ 9/12: Weak sucking movements. ☐ 9/14: Sucking improving, coordination with swallowing present. ☐ 9/16: Infant sucks strongly on soft nipple. ☐ 9/20: Infant does take feeding with increased vigor if allowed to rest.
6. Potential for hyperbilirubinemia due to liver immaturity.	☐ Infant's bilirubin will remain below 15 mg per 100 ml (indirect).	☐ Maintain fluid intake as specified according to protocol for age. Anticipate increased insensible fluid loss with phototherapy. ☐ Record intake and output accurately. Note stool pattern—frequency, type, and consistency of stools. ☐ Initiate phototherapy as ordered if indicated by bilirubin level. Place protective shields over eyes. Remove shields q4h to cleanse and note condition of eyes. ☐ Provide time for parental interaction during the period of phototherapy. Allow parents to hold and touch their	☐ 9/6: Infant appears well hydrated—skin elastic. ☐ 9/10: Urine output adequate. ☐ 9/6: Meconium stools, five times per day. ☐ 9/9: Transitional stools. ☐ 9/7: Indirect bilirubin reached level of 13 mg per 100 ml and then decreased. ☐ 9/9: Bilirubin lights are not indicated. ☐ 9/9: Not applicable.

Nursing diagnosis	Nursing goals	Nursing actions	Evaluation/revision
		infant. If parents do not visit frequently, nurses should provide for stimulation.	
7. Delayed parent-infant bonding due to the separation of parents and infant and parental anxiety.	☐ Parents will demonstrate appropriate bonding behaviors. ☐ Baby will give positive feedback (eye-to-eye contact, quieting) to parents when touched.	☐ Allow parents the opportunity to see and touch their infant prior to transport. ☐ Encourage the father to come to the referral hospital as soon as possible. Have him take pictures of infant back to mother. ☐ Encourage early initial contact. Provide for 24-h visiting and phoning. ☐ Provide knowledge about their infant's problems. Repeat concepts as necessary. Emphasize the normal as well as the abnormal. ☐ Encourage parents to touch, hold, caress, and talk to their baby. Comment on their baby's individuality and things he can do. ☐ Call mother frequently while she is hospitalized to update her on the infant's condition. Encourage her to call at any time. Arrange a schedule of the most convenient times for phone calls and visits. ☐ Provide continuity of care through primary nursing. ☐ Record on parent interaction sheet (allows easy evaluation of phone calls, visits, types of interaction, caretaking skills). ☐ Encourage grandparents to visit infant so they will begin to feel attached and provide parental support. ☐ Encourage the parents to visit frequently and give care to the infant. Have them spend time alone with the infant, if possible. Try to coincide visits with baby's alert state. Help parents interpret baby's behavior. ☐ Plan patient care conference every week with unit staff to evaluate progress of family and reassess attachment behavior and record.	☐ 9/3: Parents touched baby prior to transport. ☐ 9/3: Father followed ambulance to hospital. He brought pictures of infant to the mother. ☐ 9/4:Mother came to visit infant while on pass from hospital. ☐ 9/3: Basic information provided. Unit handbook given to parents. ☐ 9/4: Parents received a more in-depth explanation of infant's problems. ☐ 9/5: Parents verbalize what their baby's major problem is. ☐ 9/5: Parents held baby for first time. ☐ 9/5: Mother called five times yesterday. She was dismissed from the hospital. ☐ 9/6: Parents wish to call at their convenience. We will call with any significant changes. ☐ 9/4: Primary nurse—V. Fick; associate nurse—B. Rojas. ☐ 9/3: Interaction sheet started. ☐ 9/4: All grandparents visited. ☐ 9/13: Grandparents visit every other day with parents. ☐ 9/6: Parents change infant's diapers. Mother gave bath. ☐ 9/16: First time parents completely alone with baby. ☐ 9/4: Weekly conferences will be held on Monday mornings. See nurse's notes for comments.

Nursing diagnosis	Nursing goals	Nursing actions	Evaluation/revision
8. Parental anxiety and grieving due to the premature's illness and the loss of the anticipated perfect baby.	☐ The parents will be able to verbalize their feelings regarding their baby's illness and hospitalization.	☐ Assess and identify parental reactions in the following areas: **a.** Parental reaction to illness **b.** Parental perception of infant's condition **c.** Parental behaviors in relation to the baby **d.** Parental coping mechanisms (what support systems are available to them, how have they handled stress before, what are their religious ties) **e.** Parental relationships with each other **f.** Family support and reaction	☐ 9/6: Mother states, "We didn't expect any problems. It really overwhelmed us. We feel everything will turn out fine, but how does anyone ever know?" ☐ 9/7: Parents continue to touch and talk to their infant. ☐ 9/5: Parents have had their minister visit every day with them. Parents talk with and touch each other during visits. ☐ 9/7: Grandparents come with parents to visit.
		☐ Involve the social service representative. ☐ Be aware of the grieving process that the parents are going through (the loss of the normal child they anticipated during the pregnancy and the realization that the baby is less than perfect initiates a grief reaction). ☐ Encourage the parents to express feelings. Reflective statements may help.	☐ 9/5: Ms. Johnson met with parents. ☐ 9/8: Mother has cried quite often today. She stated, "This is not what I expected. We had been so happy with the thought of a baby. Everything was going so perfectly."
9. Environmental deprivation of baby due to need for hospitalization.	☐ Upon discharge, the baby will: **a.** Participate actively in his environment through visual perception **b.** Socialize with his caretakers **c.** Become alert and quiet with tactile stimulation ☐ Parents will verbalize expectations for infant's development and plans for appropriate stimulation.	☐ Encourage parents to participate in infant's care. Emphasize that this is one area that they can really be of assistance. ☐ Provide tactile and sensory stimulation in the following ways: **a.** Frequent changes of position (turning, infant seat, rocking, cuddling) **b.** Appropriate toys, such as bright colored rattle, bright colored mobile attached to crib or warmer, music boxes, soft cuddle toys, bells, and bright colored pictures placed within 9 in of infant's face ☐ Provide baby with bright colored blankets, dress, and crib materials, when his condition is stable. Encourage parents to bring these for the baby.	☐ 9/13: Parents usually do physical cares, such as bathing and diaper changes, when visiting. They stroke and hold him as much as possible. ☐ 9/10: Parents brought music box, mobile, and cuddle toy for baby. ☐ 9/20: Infant quiets when talked and sung to. His movements become calmer and slower. ☐ 9/20: Parents continue to bring appropriate toys. They verbalize the rationale behind the activities. ☐ 9/15: Mother brought in sleepers and knitted caps.

Nursing diagnosis	Nursing goals	Nursing actions	Evaluation/revision
		☐ Provide darkened atmosphere to establish infant's sleep pattern and maintain a day-night cycle.	☐ 9/15: Lights continue to be dimmed at night.
		☐ Provide parents with the information to continue the stimulation program at home.	☐ 9/20: Parents have been instructed about the infant stimulation program for their infant.
10. Parental teaching is needed due to the special care necessary for care of the premature infant.	☐ Parents will exhibit confidence in their ability to care for their infant at time of discharge. They will: **a.** Demonstrate ability to bathe the baby, take the baby's axillary/rectal temperature, use a bulb syringe for suctioning secretions, and feed the baby by breast or bottle. **b.** Demonstrate knowledge of actions and side effects of prescribed medications, administer meds, and verbalize the schedule **c.** Verbalize time and place for follow-up care of infant **d.** Verbalize situations for which the physician should be called for advice	☐ Assess parents' readiness to perform care activities. Observe parents for signs of stress. Initiate caregiving activities early and gradually increase the amount of care parents give. Reinforce parents' positive interactions with their infant. ☐ Demonstrate the bath, temperature taking, feeding, and use of the bulb syringe and have parents do a return demonstration. ☐ Discuss medications, side effects, and schedule for administration. Have parents administer the meds at least twice prior to dismissal.	☐ 9/13: Mother is consistently giving baby his bath each day. Father changes diapers. Parents stay at baby's bedside for long periods. ☐ 9/20: Mother is spending the entire afternoon with infant. ☐ 9/27: Demonstrations given to parents by primary nurse. ☐ 9/28: Return demonstration of care activities done by mother.
		☐ Inform parents about the premature's special needs: temperature regulation, development of suck reflex, need for touch and stimulation, and nutritional needs. ☐ Explain what types of signs and symptoms the parents should be alert for and concerned about regarding their baby's actions and behaviors and when they should call their physician. ☐ Provide for follow-up care when child is dismissed (public health nurse, social service, physician, follow-up clinic, and follow-up calls).	☐ 10/5: Parents instructed by nurse and pharmacist about the administration of vitamins. Parents verbalized reasons why their child was on the preparations and how to administer. ☐ 9/23: Parents attended scheduled class for the parents of prematures. ☐ 10/5: Parents verbalized to primary nurse the symptoms they should be alert for that may signify their baby is in need of medical care. ☐ 9/14: County public health nurse notified of baby's admission to high-risk nursery. ☐ 10/6: Parents informed of scheduled follow-up clinic visit on 10/24. ☐ 10/6: Primary nurse will call family on 10/9, 10/24, and 11/9.

*Prepared by Vivian Fick, B.S.N., Instructor, St. Lukes Hospital School of Nursing, Fargo, North Dakota.

References

1. The Robert Wood Johnson Foundation, *Special Report— Perinatal*, abstracted in *Perinatal Press*, vol. 3, no. 1, January 1979, p. 9.
2. Elizabeth Dickason, and Martha Schult, *Maternal and Infant Care*, 2nd ed., McGraw-Hill, New York, 1979, p. 691.
3. *Standards and Recommendations for Hospital Care of Newborn Infants*, American Academy of Pediatrics, Evanston, Ill., 1971, p. 11.
4. T. R. Harris et al., "Maternal Transport at Work," *Obstetrics and Gynecology* 52(3):294 (September 1978).
5. Ibid., p. 295.
6. Robert D. Bacsik, "Meconium Aspiration Syndrome," *Pediatric Clinics of North America* 24(3):463 (August 1979).
7. Sheldon B. Korones, *High Risk Newborn Infants*, Mosby, St. Louis, 1972, p. 60.
8. Ibid., p. 211.
9. Marshall Klaus and Avroy Fanaroff, *Care of the High-Risk Newborn*, 2d ed., Saunders, Philadelphia, 1973, p. 84.
10. Ibid., p. 79.
11. Diana Steward and Carol Gaiser, "Supporting Lactation When Mothers and Infants are Separated," *Nursing Clinics of North America* 13(1):59 (March 1978).
12. R. Hoekelman et al. (eds.), *Principles of Pediatrics: Health Care of the Young*, McGraw-Hill, New York, 1978, p. 844.
13. Klaus and Fanaroff, *op. cit.*, p. 136.
14. B. Barlow et al., "An Experimental Study of Acute Neonatal Enterocolitis," *Journal of Pediatric Surgery* 9:587–595 (1974).
15. Korones, *op. cit.*, Mosby, pp. 185–186.
16. Ibid., p. 126.
17. George Polgar, "Practical Pulmonary Physiology," *Pediatric Clinics of North America*, May 1973, p. 303.
18. Korones, op. cit., p. 139.
19. Klaus and Fanaroff, op. cit., p. 177.
20. Ibid., p. 194.
21. Ibid., p. 243.
22. Ann L. Clark and Dyanne D. Alfonso, *Childbearing: A Nursing Perspective*, 2d ed., Davis, Philadelphia, 1979, p. 882.
23. Korones, op. cit., p. 170.
24. Korones, op. cit., p. 156.
25. Korones, op. cit., p. 156.
26. Alexander Schaffer and Mary Ellen Avery, *Diseases of the Newborn*, 4th ed., Saunders, Philadelphia, 1977, p. 641.
27. Jeffry M. Maisel, "Neonatal Jaundice," *Pediatric Clinics of North America* 19(2):480 (May 1972).
28. Klaus and Fanaroff, op. cit., p. 255.
29. Ibid., p. 8.
30. Ibid., p. 9.
31. Schaffer and Avery, op. cit., p. 81.
32. Ibid., p. 83.
33. F. Jones and K. Smith, "The Fetal Alcohol Syndrome," *Teratology* 12:1–10 (1975).
34. F. Jones, K. Smith, C. Ulleland, and A. Strussgath, "Pattern of Malformation in Offspring of Chronic Alcoholic Women," *Lancet* 1:1262–1271 (1973).
35. Schaffer and Avery, op. cit., p. 701.
36. Ibid., p. 698.
37. Gerald Caplan, Edward Mason, and Daniel Kaplan, "Four Studies of Crisis in Parents of Prematures," *Community Mental Health Journal* 1(2):149–160 (Summer 1965).
38. Klaus and Fanaroff, op. cit., p. 159.
39. Ibid., p. 98.
40. L. Stern, "Prematurity as a Factor in Child Abuse," *Hospital Practice* 8:117–123 (May 1973).

Chapter 20 **Emergency room**

Carol Zinger Kotsubo

Upon completion of this chapter, the student will be able to:

1. List at least two functions of the nurse as manager/care-provider in an emergency room.

2. Describe two nursing approaches used to relieve the anxiety of children and parents in the emergency room.

3. List five variables used in Nelson's Severity Index for acute pediatric illness.

4. Describe three principles that are useful in teaching children and families cared for in the emergency room.

5. List the two leading types of accidents in the age groups of 0 to 1, 1 to 4, and 5 to 14 years.

6. Evaluate the child's life support system in terms of priority of need, nursing assessment, and intervention.

7. Describe the nurse's role in care of a child with a laceration.

8. List five specific observations indicating vascular occlusion distal to a fracture.

9. List three goals of emergency treatment of burns.

10. Identify at least five activities of the nurse in the care of a child with accidental ingestion of a poisonous substance.

11. Describe at least three preventive measures a nurse could suggest to parents in an effort to decrease the number of poisonings in children.

12. Compare the physiological effects of fresh water and sea water near-drownings.

13. Identify three nursing actions that assist parents of a SIDS infant to deal with the reality of death.

14. Discuss five nursing goals for the sexual assault victim.

15. Discuss the procedure for evidence collection from the sexual assault victim.

Role of the nurse

"Emergency room!" These words immediately conjure up a variety of images. To the lay person, the emergency room (ER) is often a frightening scene of traumatic injuries, upset families, and fast-moving, all-knowing nurses and doctors. To health professionals, the ER can mean a tense, stressful atmosphere, a challenge to skill and knowledge, and often, a fight for life over death. When one considers the ER after these intitial reactions, it is evident that the emergency room is much more. The nurse who cares for patients in this setting has a multifaceted role; it is more than just racing down the hall with resuscitation equipment. In the emergency setting, the nurse uses assessment skills, performs complicated procedures, and communicates with numerous people. Giving emotional support and teaching are important parts of the ER nurse's role. Often, the nurse must fulfill several of these responsibilities within a short span of time.

An acutely ill child in the emergency room, with or without family, adds unique dimensions to the functions and responsibilities of the nurse. Although nursing principles are the same, children are not little adults and the emergency care of pediatric patients offers special challenges. There are physiological as well as emotional and developmental differences among children of different ages which require a special approach and response. This chapter will discuss some common pediatric emergencies not dealt with in other chapters and the nurse's role in providing care for children and their families in specific emergency situations.

Emergency room contact with patients and their families is often brief and hurried. It is generally not conducive to a full range of nursing interventions. At the same time, the situation demands that nurses meet numerous patient needs by utilizing a variety of nursing interventions. The nurse in the ER is often the first health professional and hospital representative the child and family encounter during an acute illness. The manner in which the nurse greets and treats the child and family in the ER may influence their opinions of the entire hospital experience.

Providing care

Many types of patients seek care in the pediatric emergency room. The following are typical examples: a school-age girl with asthma who is audibly wheezing and in slight respiratory distress; a 2-month-old infant with a fever; a toddler with an upper respiratory infection; an unconscious teenager with multiple trauma suffered in a motorcycle accident; a 6-year-old boy who has fallen from a tree and is crying from pain in his arm. If these patients came to the ER at the same time, the nurse could not possibly attend to all of them at the same time. Therefore, as a manager of patient care, the nurse begins with triage. *Triage* is "a system of assigning priorities of medical treatment on the basis of urgency [or] chance for survival."[1] In order to set priorities

accurately, the nurse makes an initial assessment of each patient. The assessment needs to be quick and thorough and to serve as a tool for determining the immediate needs of the patient. The focus of the initial assessment is on airway, breathing, and circulation—the ABCs (see Table 20-3). With this type of assessment, the nurse will immediately recognize life-threatening situations and be able to deal with them by initiating appropriate action.

If the patient is not in immediate danger, the nurse then assesses in more detail other body systems and assigns priorities for medical attention and treatment. A quick review of body systems, beginning with the neurological, is an organized, efficient approach. Other valuable information is obtained by talking with the child and the family. This interviewing can be done while completing the systems assessment. The knowledge obtained from the brief medical history can be used as a partial basis for triage decisions. Questions such as "Why did you bring your child to the hospital?" "How long has your child been like this?" "How is your child acting differently from usual?" will give needed information about the duration and seriousness of the illness.

Nelson's index for rating the severity of acute nontraumatic illness (Table 20-1) in pediatric patients can be used as a screening device for triage in an emergency room.[2] Children with a score of 10 are judged "not sick," those with 8 or 9 are judged "moderately sick," and those

Table 20-1 An index of severity for acute pediatric illness

| Variable | Point value | | |
	0	1	2
Respiratory effort	Labored or absent	Some distress	No distress
Color	Cyanotic	Pale, flushed, mottled	Normal
Activity	Delirium, stupor, coma	Lethargy	Normal
Temperature	<36.4 or >40°C (<97.4 or >104°F)	38.4–40°C (101.1–104°F)	36.4–38.4°C (97.4–101°F)
Play	Refuses to play	Decreased play activity	Normal play activity

* **Source:** Kathleen G. Nelson, "An Index of Severity for Acute Pediatric Illness," *American Journal of Public Health* **70:**804–807 (1980). Used with permission.

with 7 or less "very sick." Table 20-1 can be used by the emergency room nurse as an aid in deciding which pediatric patient should be attended to first.

In addition to setting priorities for medical treatment, the nurse doing triage in the ER maintains close contact with the other health professionals. She or he alerts them to the number of children who are waiting, informs them of the findings of the brief assessments, and discusses with them the possible treatments which may be needed. The families and patients who are waiting are not left unattended. The nurse explains to them briefly the system of priorities and tries to estimate when they will be seen. The nurse returns to the child and family periodically to reassure them that they haven't been forgotten and that they will be taken care of as soon as possible.

The emergency room nurse strives to create an atmosphere of calm and reassurance. For the nurse is not only a manager but also a care-provider who realizes that the patients and their families are under stress. Families who have brought a sick or injured child to the ER are in a foreign environment and are fearful about their child's welfare. The nurse is usually the first health professional they encounter. If the nurse greets the patient and family in a hurried, insensitive manner, their anxiety is increased and their attitude toward the entire experience can be colored. Once a negative reaction is developed, it is difficult to overcome. One of the most important roles of the nurse in the emergency room is to provide the physical and emotional support required to assist a family through the anxieties and stress of such an experience.

One area in which the nurse attempts to provide physical support is the performance of therapeutic procedures. In the ER there are vital signs to be taken, medications to be given, IVs to be started, or dressings to be applied. The nurse carries out such procedures in a competent, calm manner. Despite the urgency of the situation, accuracy and safety are indispensable. It would be of no value to hurriedly draw up and administer an emergency medication only to have it seriously jeopardize the child's life because it is an incorrect dose. To prepare a medication for a child requires strict and careful mathematical calculation, even in the tense atmosphere of an emergency room.

Other nursing procedures, in addition to medication administration, require safety and caution. Preparing a struggling 2-year-old for a lumbar puncture is greatly different from instructing an alert 17-year-old how to bend for the same procedure. It is the nurse's responsibility to prepare the patient adequately for procedures in order to ensure the safety of the child and the accuracy of the treatment.

Communication and counseling

In the role of care-provider the nurse gives competent physical care and provides the family with a safe and reassuring environment, but it is in the role of communicator and counselor that emotional support becomes the primary focus. This role is often easily sidestepped in a busy emergency room. The rapid succession of injured and ill children and families makes it difficult to establish a significant nurse-patient relationship. The tension and excitement of a life-threatening situation seem to delegate a lesser priority to the feelings and emotions of the people involved. It is not only possible but essential for emergency room personnel to provide emotional support for the patient and family.

Any situation or event becomes stressful when it is perceived as a threat. The stress produces feelings of anxiety. An emergency room situation is stressful to almost everyone involved. A health emergency may threaten a life as well as physical well-being. It can threaten security, stability, and love. It places people in an environment where they have little control over what happens to their own bodies or those of their loved ones.

There are different levels of anxiety. At a low level, a person becomes more alert and more aware of the surroundings and is open to learning and understanding. As anxiety increases, perception decreases. Listening and comprehension become more difficult. At the panic level, the inner turmoil is so great as to make perception of external stimuli almost impossible. Knowledge of the levels of anxiety and the effects is essential for a nurse who communicates with patients and families in an emergency room. It will determine the type of explanation and the method of instruction used, as shown in the following examples.

EXAMPLE: An 8-year-old girl is driven to the emergency room by her mother. She has twisted her ankle while roller-skating. The ankle is swollen and painful but the child can walk with assistance. Both she and her mother are nervous but think that it is not a serious injury. After the x-rays have been taken and the foot is examined by the doctor, a diagnosis of sprain is made. The nurse begins to explain how the foot will be bandaged and how it should be cared for at home. Both mother and daughter listen attentively and ask pertinent questions about when she can go to school and how long it will hurt. They are functioning at a low level of anxiety: Their perceptions are sharpened and their responses are appropriate and interested. They may experience such bodily reactions as increased pulse and respirations or nervousness, but they are in control of their reactions.

EXAMPLE: Far greater anxiety is exhibited by the young parents of a 5-month-old boy who has died from sudden infant death syndrome. The mother is crying almost hysterically. The father sits with his head bowed and his face in his hands. The physician is explaining the causes. The parents are unable to respond. They are at a panic level of anxiety and have very little perception of what is going on around them. This couple requires brief, simple explanations and direct, basic instructions. Explanations will need to be repeated more than once because their grief prevents them from grasping what is said to them.

Aware of the varying degrees of comprehension due to anxiety, the nurse will need to verify a patient's and family's understanding of what they have been told. This is not done by simply asking, "Do you understand what I have just said?" An automatic response would be to say yes. But to determine if the patient really did comprehend, the nurse can ask the person to repeat the information that has just been given. This alerts the nurse to the anxiety level of that person and to the effectiveness of the communication that is taking place. When a person is in a stage of panic, it is often necessary to give instructions to another person who is not so immediately involved, such as a friend or another relative, to provide written instructions to be taken home, or to make a referral to another professional for future follow-up, or all of these.

In addition to tailoring communication to the anxiety level of the patient, the nurse who works with children realizes that such communication needs also to be age-specific. The developmental level of a child determines to a great extent what a child wants to hear and how it needs to be said. The 3-year-old wants an explanation of what is happening. It should, however, be brief and pertain to what is going on in the child's immediate surroundings. What is going to be done? What will it feel like? How will the child be positioned? A school-age child, ever-inquisitive, might like to be told the reasons for treatments and to be given basic explanations of anatomy. The teenager wants to be treated as the adult he or she is becoming and to be given choices. An adolescent is concerned about body image and future implications of an injury or illness. A knowledge of the developmental stages of childhood is as essential for any nurse working in the emergency room as it is for the nurse in pediatrics.

With an understanding of developmental stages and anxiety levels, the nurse in the emergency room also utilizes an awareness of family theory. Children are usually accompanied by family and friends who are concerned and closely involved. Everything that happens to the child affects the family also. Therefore, nurses need to realize that they are not caring for just one individual but for several, if not many. Nursing actions are more effective if the nurse is aware of the close bond that exists between child and primary care-giver (usually the mother or father) and if the nurse provides for close and prolonged contact between the child and the primary care-giver.

The parent should be allowed to accompany the child during procedures and needs to have a clear explanation of what to expect and how to help the child cope. Emotionally, parent and child are linked very closely. A child is sensitive to the feelings of parents. These feelings are often transmitted to the child without a word. The child may sense fear in the person who has always been strong and protective. The child may then be afraid simply because the parent is. A child who is afraid and anxious often becomes restless, squirms, and even thrashes about. This may complicate the injuries or the illness. Calming the child can be accomplished at least to an extent by calming the parent. A parent who is given complete explanations and honest information becomes less anxious and then is more able to focus on the child's fears and assist the nurse to support the young patient. Direct involvement of parents continues throughout the entire time that the child is being treated in the emergency room. Equipment is demonstrated, procedures explained, and plans discussed in an effort to keep the family included in the care.

It is reassuring to parents to be with their children during a stressful experience. They are able to actually observe what is happening. How many horrible things are imagined in a waiting room while the loved one is behind closed doors? Parents who are permitted to stay often remark, "Is that all there is to it? I thought it would be much worse." Somehow reality is far less frightening than the imagination. Several institutions have discovered that allowing families to remain, even during life-threatening situations, is beneficial to both parents and children. Allowing parents to remain also seems to relieve them of some of the guilt they experience because they could not prevent the illness or injury.

Every parent is an individual, and every family has a unique way of relating to one another. The nurse adapts care to the needs of each specific family and child. Not all parents want to stay with their children during treatment. Some prefer to wait outside the room. Their decision should be accepted and supported. Parents should inform the child where they will wait. The nurse then provides support for the child during the treatment.

There are also parents who are not emotionally able to remain in attendance during medical treatments. The nurse should be able to assess the coping abilities of the parent and to determine if it would be detrimental to the welfare of the child if the parent remains. If, after receiving reassurance and explanations, the parent is still unable to focus on what is being said or is still extremely agitated, the nurse should ask the parent to leave. Parents should be told where to wait and reassured that their decision is appropriate and good for both them and their child. Communication with parents who remain in the waiting room continues throughout the time the child is being treated. The nurse gives parents frequent information concerning the condition of their child and of what is being done. The child also needs to know where the parents are, that they are concerned, and that they will be waiting when the treatment is finished.

Occasionally a child is admitted to an emergency room without any family member present. Such a child may be brought from camp, from school, or by ambulance from the scene of an accident. Except in immediate life-threatening situations, emergency personnel may be legally unable to provide any type of treatment without the express permission of the parents or guardian. State law and hospital policy together fix what can be done. It is frequently the nurse who must contact the parents and inform them of what has happened to their child. It is important to be aware of the impact that this communication will have on parents. Simple, accurate information will be most clearly understood. The parents may also need to be told how to locate the emergency room and to be reminded to drive carefully. If it is true, the nurse reassures them that their child is in no danger and will be waiting for them when they arrive.

Patient education

In addition to the roles of manager/care-provider and communicator/counselor, the nurse in the emergency room is a patient educator. Though the time families spend in an emergency room is short, it is a period during which they become a captive audience, being sometimes both receptive and responsive. Recalling the theory of anxiety levels and responses, the nurse is aware that under stress a person often becomes more alert and perceptive. It is at the low anxiety stage that teaching is most effective. The majority of children who enter an emergency room have minor illnesses and injuries. They are usually eager to understand what has happened and what they can do to facilitate recovery. Parents often suffer guilt feelings, assuming that it was their neglect or their actions that caused the injury or illness of their child. They want to learn how to prevent further problems and how to care for their child. Yet not wishing to display what they assume is poor parenting or ignorance, many parents do not speak up; they do not ask questions. The nurse must recognize a parent's needs and intervene to meet them. Every encounter with a health care provider should be a learning experience for both child and parent.

Several categories of teaching are pertinent to the emergency room setting. They are: (1) instructions regarding follow-up care for the present problem, (2) general health care teaching, and (3) anticipatory guidance.

Instructions for follow-up care are important because much of the treatment initiated in the emergency room can be undone if care is not continued at home. Instructions given hurriedly or offhandedly can easily be misunderstood by the most well-meaning parent. Once at home, the parent may wonder, "Did the nurse say to use ice the first 24 hours and then warm compresses or heat the first day followed by ice?" Here are several principles that the nurse may employ to facilitate effective teaching:

1. Assess the educational background and intellectual level of the parents and teach them at an appropriate level.
2. Instructions should be clear and simple and phrased according to parent's and child's level of understanding.
3. Essential instructions should be written down and sent home with the family.
4. Parents should be asked to repeat in their own words what they have been told.
5. Measurements should be adapted to household equivalents like teaspoons or tablespoons.
6. Parents should be urged to call the emergency room to check on instructions or to have questions answered. Include a written telephone number.

Compliance with instructions is often very low. One reason usually cited is lack of understanding. Once the nurse has clearly taught a procedure that must be performed at home, it is usually beneficial to explain the purpose of it, including simple physiology and effects of the action. Most patients and family will respond better when they understand what they are doing and why. Patients and families are partners with health care personnel in their health care.

The nurse in the emergency room also has many opportunities to provide general health care teaching. For example, while taking a history from the mother of a 4-year-old, the nurse learns that the child has never been immunized. After attending to the problem which brought the mother in, the nurse talks with her about immunizations, explaining what they are, how they protect the child, and where to get them. The nurse discovers that the mother has no pediatrician and that evidently no one had ever really explained immunizations before. The immunizations were not the reason for the visit to the emergency room, but the patient's need was recognized and appropriate nursing intervention followed.

Along with general health care teaching, anticipatory guidance is often a function of the emergency room nurse. Anticipatory guidance is preparation for the future care of the child. It focuses on growth and development. In the emergency room a primary goal of anticipatory guidance is prevention of accidents. As the mother of a toddler with an upper respiratory tract infection is preparing to go home, the nurse may begin a discussion of accidental poisonings and ways to "child-proof" the home. Always included in any type of preventive teaching are concrete, simple suggestions for the parent to put into practice at home.

Finally the nurse in the emergency room must remember that no matter what condition brings the child to the hospital, careful and accurate documentation are required. Baseline data, procedures, medications, treatments, the child's response and reaction, all follow-up care and instruction, and the patient's and family's understanding of follow-up care should be written in the child's record.

Accidents and injuries

Accidents and traumatic injuries are the chief causes of children's emergency room visits. Accidents are the leading cause of death in children 1 to 14 years of age, and they also cause far larger numbers of nonfatal injuries that require treatment and hospitalization.

As children grow and develop new skills and abilities, the type of accident to which they are susceptible changes accordingly. A breakdown of specific accidents by age reveals the progression of developmental stages and physiological growth (Table 20-2).

The infant is most likely to be injured by falling or when improperly restrained in an automobile. As the child becomes mobile, he or she may suffer injury or death from motor vehicles as a passenger or pedestrian. Later the adolescent is involved as a driver.

No matter how accidents happen, they can lead to multiple injuries, fractures and sprains, lacerations, burns, poisonings, and drownings. They have a significant physical, emotional, social, and financial impact on the child and the entire family.

Multiple trauma

Automobile and motorcycle accidents frequently result in multiple trauma injuries. Several major organs of the body may sustain serious damage. The nurse in the emergency room quickly assesses the child with multiple traumatic injuries. Evaluation of the life-support systems—airway, breathing, and circulation—is a primary focus. Then a more detailed assessment of damage to other organs is performed. Head injuries, abdominal trauma with internal hemorrhage, and fractured bones are the most common sequelae of motor vehicle accidents. Table 20-3 illustrates a triage system of assessment and intervention for multiple trauma.

Of all accidents, 25 to 50 percent involve head injury. Many head injuries are minor, resulting in a brief loss of consciousness, and cause no serious effects. Others involve damage to brain tissue and can lead to sudden deterioration and death. The nurse in the emergency room must be able to evaluate the seriousness of a head injury and use appropriate interventions. The severity of a head injury depends on the involvement of the soft brain tissue. A skull fracture alone is of little consequence. The nurse performs a thorough neurological examination to determine the extent of injury and to document the child's condition for future reference. Evaluation of level of consciousness and detection of any signs that indicate location of brain damage are of primary importance. A neuro checklist is very helpful and ensures consistent examinations by different personnel over a period of time (Tables 37-3 and 37-19). Children with minor head injuries are usually discharged and are observed at home by their parents. The parents should be given clear instructions about the importance of evaluating the alertness of their child. They should be informed of changes that could indicate a problem and of what to do if the changes occur (Chap. 37).

A child with a head injury rarely goes into shock. So, if the emergency room nurse detects symptoms of shock (hypotension, rapid thready pulse, cold and clammy skin), other causes must be suspected. A frequent source of shock is internal bleeding from abdominal injuries. The mortality rate from abdominal trauma is relatively high in comparison to other types of injuries. The organs most frequently injured from abdominal trauma to a child are the spleen, the liver, the kidneys, and the intestine. The primary symptoms are abdominal pain and tenderness, distention, rigidity, and vomiting. Occasionally

Table 20-2 Types of accidents by specific age

0–1 years	1–4 years	5–14 years
Falls	Motor vehicles	Motor vehicles
Poisoning	Poisoning	Drowning
Burns	Burns	Burns
Aspiration of foreign objects	Drowning	Firearms
		Bicycle accidents

shock may be the only important sign. Children frequently vomit after trauma, and so vomiting is nonspecific and of value only in conjunction with other symptoms. At times bleeding from abdominal injuries is gradual and the development of an acute abdomen is insidious. Children with multiple trauma require close observation for several days to rule out the possibility of significant but covert injuries. Because of the small blood volume of a child, it is important for the nurse to correctly calculate actual blood loss. In a child, hemorrhage may seem insignificant until it is compared to total blood volume.

The nursing care plan for a child with possible abdominal injuries consists of frequent evaluation of vital signs, consistent measurements of abdominal girth, and accurate monitoring of urinary output with a retention catheter. Children often develop paralytic ileus after trauma, and so a nasogastric tube is inserted and connected to intermittent suction while the child is still in the emergency room. Then careful nursing observation for signs of physiological deterioration continues as the child is transferred to an inpatient unit. Throughout the entire time the nurse is aware that both child and parents are very frightened. The nurse explains procedures and provides emotional support.

Fractures, sprains, and strains

Falls frequently result in an emergency room visit. Although falls can lead to a multiplicity of injuries, fractures (broken bones), sprains (partial tearing of a ligament), and strains (overstretching of a muscle) are the most frequent consequences.

When a child comes to the emergency room with a history of an injury and with pain localized to a particular area of bone, a fracture should be suspected. The nurse's first responsibility is to assess the child for respiratory and circulatory

Table 20-3 Triage for victims of multiple trauma

Priority order of care	Assessment	Intervention
Airway	Air movement—look, listen, feel; check if tongue is back in throat over trachea Presence of mucus, blood, emesis, or foreign body in mouth	Hyperextend neck; lift chin with head and spinal injuries. Suction; remove foreign bodies. Nurse assists with: cricoid puncture, endotracheal intubation, tracheostomy.
Breathing	Auscultate breath sounds; feel for crepitus or deviation of trachea; check chest movement for asymmetry; and note skin color, difficulty in breathing, retractions. Open chest wound Arterial blood gases	Begin rescue breathing, oxygen therapy, or assist with chest tube insertion. Apply gauze soaked with petroleum jelly to seal hole; assist with chest tube insertion. Begin oxygen therapy.

Circulation	Carotid pulse
	Areas of bleeding
	
	Vital sings:
	    Pulse (<60/min or >130/min)
	    Respiration (<12/min or >50/min)
	    Blood pressure (<80/50 or >160/100)
	Skin temperature, color
	Urine output
		If absent, start closed chest cardiac massage.
		Control external bleeding with sterile compression dressing. Elevate extremity that is bleeding
		Nurse assists with: fluid replacement, blood replacement, insertion of IV lines, arterial blood gas analysis, and vasopressor administration.
		
		Insert Foley catheter—metered output.

Consciousness	Level of consciousness: alert, drowsy, stuporous, comatose Increased intracranial pressure Head or scalp injury: Assess bleeding, lacerations, and CSF drainage. Pupillary response: size, equality of size, reaction to light. Bilateral movement and sensation of extremities: Check hand grasp, elbow lift, hip and knee flexion, and toe wiggle.	If level of consciousness diminishes, nurse increases frequency of observation and becomes more watchful of patient safety. Hyperventilation—nurse also assists with medication such as steroids and diuretics. Sterile dressing to injury If abnormal, nurse increases concern for patient safety and assesses more frequently.
Digestive organs	Inspection for signs of abdominal trauma: contusions, abrasions, wounds. Auscultation for bowel sounds. Assess tenderness by gentle palpation. Observe: nausea, vomiting, distention, rigidity, and guarding.	Sterile dressing to site of injury; sterile saline dressing to protruding organs; NPO; flex knees; give tetanus prophylaxis. Nurse assists with: insertion of nasogastric tube, lab tests, x-rays, paracentesis, medications, IV insertion, and exam of pelvis and rectum.
Excretory organs	Observe for hematuria. Measure output; check specific gravity. Observe injury.	Insert Foley catheter—metered output. Nurse assists with: IV insertion and preparation for surgery.
Skeletal system	Observe extremities for pain, pulses, paresthesias, paralysis or movement, pallor; check pulses distal to injury; note movement and sensation; note swelling, deformity, and asymmetry.	Medicate as ordered; immobilize body part and elevate it. Nurse assists with: x-rays of affected joint plus one joint above and below: splint, tape, or cast.

status and then for the following local and systemic signs of fracture:

1. Deformity—shortening, angulation, or rotation
2. Local pain and tenderness
3. Grating or crepitation
4. Swelling
5. Bruising and discoloration
6. Loss of function or abnormal mobility
7. Appearance of fragments
8. Shock

A careful history should describe the kind and amount of trauma involved, when it occurred, the direction of force, other possible injuries, and any emergency treatment at the scene.

Several basic principles of care should be followed. With a suspected fracture, unnecessary handling must be avoided and the area immobilized. Splints are used to prevent further damage to skin, muscles, nerves, and blood vessels. Clean dressings should be applied to any wounds and hemorrhage controlled with direct pressure. The nurse should be familiar with the five P's of vascular occlusion distal to the injury and check for them. They include *pain*, *pulselessness*, *paresthesia*, *pallor*, and *paralysis*. It is often helpful to compare the injured extremity with the uninjured one.

Once the injured part has been initially evaluated and protected by splinting, x-rays are taken to provide a definitive diagnosis. In children the uninjured extremity may also be x-rayed if a comparison of epiphyseal growth plates is desired.

The child with an orthopedic injury experiences fear, anxiety, and pain. The nurse will need to establish rapport quickly to make an assessment possible. Gentle, firm handling is necessary while the child and family are prepared for what will happen next. If the possibility of surgery exists, the child is given nothing orally. The time the child last ate, allergies, and significant medical or surgical history should be determined.

Severe strains and sprains respond to immobilization of the joint with splinting, wrapping or taping, application of ice, and elevation. Sometimes splints are applied and the patient instructed to return in 2 to 5 days for application of a plaster cast. If crutches are necessary, the child will need instruction on correct use.

When a plaster cast is applied, the child and family should be given written instructions to take home regarding cast care and warning signs and symptoms. An example of appropriate instructions is given below.

1. Your cast will require 24 to 48 hours to dry. Walking casts are not ready for walking until they are dry.
2. Report any of the following to the emergency room: excessive swelling above or below the cast; continuous color change after elevation of the extremity for 30 minutes; an excessively loose cast; marked pain if someone moves your fingers or toes; irritation or rubbing sensation of skin around or under cast leading to redness or blisters; decreased ability to move fingers or toes; increasing pain not relieved by medication.
3. Do not cover your cast with paint as it must be able to "breathe."

The nurse, too, must remain alert for changes in color, warmth, sensation, and motion following cast application. (A more extensive discussion of orthopedic injuries and their treatment, including cast care, is found in Chap. 36.)

Lacerations

Lacerations occur commonly in children. They usually affect only the skin and fatty tissue beneath it. Sometimes muscles, tendons, blood vessels, ligaments, or nerves are cut. Minor lacerations are often treated at home. Usually cuts on the trunk or face should be examined by the physician in the emergency room. Parents may also bring their child in after a laceration has begun to show signs of infection.

The nurse will first determine when and how the laceration occurred. Other important historical data include the date of the last tetanus immunization, allergies, and significant medical conditions, such as bleeding or circulatory problems. The size and depth of the laceration should be described and the amount of bleeding and accompanying injuries noted. Vital signs are documented.

If there is profuse bleeding, pressure applied with a sterile compress, elevation, and ice are indicated. Minimal bleeding may be controlled with a sterile compress.

Next the wound should be cleansed. (It may be wise to check for allergies again.) A sterile 4- by 4-in pad and a Zephiran solution are often used for facial lacerations. Hands and feet may be soaked in a basin of cool water to which

Betadine soap solution has been added. Betadine soap solution and sterile 4- by 4-in pads are used to cleanse other areas.

After the wound is cleansed it can be protected with a sterile towel until treatment is begun. X-ray films may be taken to detect the presence of a foreign body such as fragments of glass, wood, or metal.

The wound is then dressed or stitched. The nurse has the responsibility to maintain a sterile field, provide necessary equipment, and assist in holding the child still during the procedure. Xylocaine (1%) is frequently used for anesthesia. Epinephrine may be added if control of bleeding is important. Epinephrine is never used on fingers, toes, ears, the nose, or the penis since vasoconstriction could cause circulatory impairment.

Any significant laceration threatens the child's sense of body integrity. It is always helpful to ask the child what he or she expects to happen. There is often time after the wound is cleansed, and before stitches are placed, to read a story to the child called "Becky Gets Stitches." If the parents read the story, or hear it, they, too, are prepared for this experience. The child should

Table 20-4 Instructions to parents—care of the child with an open wound

After initial emergency care of a wound, it is as important to care properly for the injury until healing is complete. Attend to the following:
1. Keep wounds clean and dry.
2. Notify the doctor if any of the following signs of infection appear:
    a. Redness, particularly if increasing and streaking from the area of the wound
    b. Pain, especially if increasing in severity
    c. Heat or warmth in the area of the wound.
    d. Swelling
    e. Drainage, especially if there is a bad odor or there is pus
    f. Chills, elevated temperature, or both

Keep your outpatient visit appointment.

Doctor _____

Phone _____

Source: City of Boston, Department of Health and Hospitals.

be encouraged to express his or her feelings about the entire experience.

Tetanus prophylaxis is necessary in most lacerations, puncture wounds, and open fractures and in any case of multiple injury. If the wound is "dirty" or made by a rusty object, a tetanus booster is given if the last immunization was given more than 2 to 3 years before the injury. If the wound is "clean," the last tetanus injection is usually considered adequate for 5 to 8 years. Antibiotic therapy may also be given if deemed appropriate. Table 20-4 gives an example of written instructions that can be given to parents and the child regarding care of a laceration upon discharge from the emergency room.

Burns

Burns, whether thermal, electrical, or chemical, are a major source of accidents among children. The consequences can be devastating, with treatment and hospitalization ranging from 6 weeks to 2 years. Electrical burns are particularly serious because passage of the electrical current through the body can cause cardiac arrhythmia, aneurysm, or late cataracts.

Burns are now one of the top five causes of death in children. There are approximately 200,000 burn cases in the United States yearly. About one-half of these affect children. Of the total, 80 percent are avoidable accidents, and of that number 50 percent are the result of the child's actions and 15 percent of carelessness or neglect on the part of the caretaker. Only 15 percent involve the child as an innocent bystander. Only about 10 percent of all burns have children as the intended victim.[3] These burns are classified as child abuse.

When a burned child arrives in the emergency room, the major goals of treatment are (1) to assess respiratory status, (2) to begin fluid replacement, (3) to evaluate extent and depth of wounds, and (4) to initiate cleansing measures.

Smoke inhalation accounts for 80 percent of the deaths associated with burns. The emergency room nurse immediately determines patency of the airway. Initially respiratory status may be unaffected, but edema of the respiratory tract due to burns or smoke inhalation can lead to airway obstruction any time from 4 to 24 h after the actual burn. Signs of smoke inhalation, such as burned or singed areas of the face and throat, smoky smelling breath, charcoal in the sputum, or any symptoms of respiratory distress, should alert the nurse to the possibility of future airway obstruction.

The extent and depth of burns forms a basis for type of treatment and calculation of fluid replacement (Fig. 32-2). It is generally agreed that any child with second- to third-degree burns of over 10 to 15 percent of the body requires hospitalization. Burns of the hands and feet are also usually treated on an inpatient basis to ensure correct splinting of the extremity and to prevent contractures. First-degree burns produce red skin that is extremely painful. Usually the application of cold wet towels is the most comfortable bandage. Greasy dressings are difficult to remove and may retain moisture and therefore encourage growth of bacteria.

Second-degree burns are best treated by removal of broken blisters, cleansing of the area with saline, and application of a Xerofoam gauze dressing with a layer of absorbing gauze over it.

More severe burns are initially cleansed with warmed saline and then dressed with an ointment application such as providone-iodine (Betadine) or Silvadene. Care must be taken to prevent hypothermia since heat loss occurs with severe burns. Vital signs, including temperature, are monitored frequently.

Fluid loss begins immediately after any burn. Therefore fluid replacement is a priority of treatment. Initially a solution of Ringer's lactate may be started while calculation of fluid replacement is determined. A cutdown in an unaffected part of the body is preferred because it provides stability for long-term IV therapy and a large lumen for colloid infusion if needed. A urinary retention catheter is necessary for accurate measurement of urine output as a determination of adequate fluid therapy. The burned child is weighed if at all possible, or a close estimation of weight is obtained from the family. Tetanus toxoid is also administered to the burn victim in the ER.

The immediate treatment for chemical burn is to flush the area with large amounts of warm water for approximately 20 min. If the eyes are burned, they too are flushed with water. A shower works well for burns covering large areas of the body. Then the child is transported to the ER, where the burns are washed again. Burned eyes should be flushed with physiological saline. If only one eye is involved, it is important to rinse the fluid away from the other, uninvolved eye. No attempt is made to neutralize the chemical because the neutralization produces heat which can cause further damage. Chemical burns may continue to cause damage for some time, and so multiple washings may be ordered. Most household containers stress the need to flush a contact area with water, but parents may need to be reminded to read labels for warnings and treatment as they are making purchases. Some items may be so dangerous that they are not advisable for use in homes with children. Further care and treatment of burns is discussed in Chap. 32.

Poisoning

Poisoning is the number one acute emergency in children. Seventy percent of the more than 2 million yearly ingestions in the United States occur in children under 5 years and are termed accidental.[4] When poisonings occur after the age of 5, the nurse must be alert to this "cry for help," or suicide attempt, which indicates a need for careful investigation and intervention.

Toddlers and preschoolers are prone to accidental poisoning because of their rapid motor maturation and new-found mobility. Compared to the infant, the 18- to 36-month-old seems to be "everywhere" and "into everything." The child touches and pokes, listens, sees, smells, and frequently tastes and swallows.

Children will taste and swallow almost anything that is within their reach. Availability and frequency of use determine the substances that are most commonly ingested. Soaps, detergents, and "cleaners" are the number one agents in poisonings. They are followed by plants, vitamins and minerals, and then aspirin.[5] Child-proof bottle caps have brought aspirin down from its former position as the number one child poisoner. Prescription medications belonging to anyone in the family are a potential risk. Children love to explore purses, a place in which visitors often store their medications. Small children may also take an overdose of their own medication, e.g., lanoxin. Because the parent gives the child a medication every day, the drug may seem as harmless as food to the child. Other commonly ingested poisons include bleach, paint thinners, insecticides, and petroleum distillates.

While in the past it was generally assumed that the child who ingested poisonous substances came from a home that was not an adequately safe environment, recent studies seem to conclude that stress in the family plays an important part.[6] Accidental poisonings in the young child may be seen as the child's efforts to cope with the family disorganization that surrounds him or her. Such crises as divorce, pregnancy, academic difficulties, illness, and death may precipitate accidental poisoning in the young child or deliberate self-poisoning in the older child. Once a child has had an ingestion episode, there is a 50 percent chance that he or she will repeat the episode within the year. The nurse must understand that a variety of factors, including stress and availability, interact to precipitate the incidence of accidental and deliberate self-poisoning.

Some ingested substances are considered "nontoxic." They include such things as antacids, chalk, deodorant, glue, ink, lipstick, laxatives, latex paint, perfume, shampoo, toothpaste, and vitamins. To designate an ingestion nontoxic, the single product must be absolutely identified, there must be no signal word on the container ("Danger," "Call physician immediately," or "Caution"), the amount ingested is known, and the victim is free of symptoms. For the average drug the toxicity is five times the average dose.

When the poison is unknown, the nurse or physician will have to investigate thoroughly to determine the culprit. Clues in the child that a poisoning has occurred include:[7]

1. An abrupt onset of signs and symptoms
2. "At risk" age group (1 to 4 years)
3. Previous ingestion history
4. Multiple organ system involvement

The nurse can ask specific questions in an attempt to determine the type of substance: "What was the child doing before symptoms developed?" "Where was the child playing? In the garage? In the kitchen? In the bathroom?" "What types of substances are stored there?" "What types of containers are they in?" "When did the child become symptomatic?" "How much of the product was available and in what form?" In any case of poisoning the nurse considers the possibility that other children may also have ingested the substance. Children are known to share their discoveries.

"The emergency management of poisoning is aimed at preventing absorption of the poison beyond that point which the body can safely detoxify or which can be effectively antagonized by antidotes."[8] When a child is known, or suspected, to have ingested a poisonous substance, the treatment begins immediately—at home, if possible. Induction of vomiting is generally the most immediate, effective method of removing the poison if the child's vital signs are stable. Mechanical methods, such as placing the finger at the back of the throat, are often ineffective and a waste of time. Syrup of ipecac is the recommended emetic and may be purchased by parents without a prescription. It is a drug which should be kept in all homes with small children. The dose is 10 ml for a child 6 months to 1 year of age, 15 ml for a child aged 1 to 5 years, and 30 ml for an older child, followed by at least 200 ml of any fluid. If there is no vomiting within 15 min, the same dose may be repeated. No further doses of ipecac should be given since the drug is cardiotoxic and may have dangerous side effects when administered in large doses. The "universal antidote" of burned toast, milk of magnesia, and charcoal is usually not effective, and valuable time is spent trying to persuade the child to swallow it.

Vomiting should never be induced if a child (1) has taken a corrosive alkali or acid, (2) has swallowed a petroleum product, (3) is unconscious or has lost gag or cough reflexes, or (4) is having seizures. An alkali or acid such as bleach, Draino, or the like, damages the mucous membrane of the esophagus as it is swallowed, and vomiting may cause further damage. If a child who has ingested a petroleum product such as paint thinner or furniture polish vomits, there is an increased danger of aspiration and of development of lipoid pneumonia, which is very difficult to treat. Any person who is unconscious or seizuring and vomits has an increased risk of aspiration and possible airway obstruction. If there is question about whether or not to induce vomiting, a parent should call a poison control center. Most large communities have such a resource and they are generally listed in the front of the phone book with other emergency numbers. Emergency room personnel will find it useful to have a poison treatment chart available for quick reference since many frightened parents will call a hospital when their child has swallowed a dangerous substance. (See Appendix E).

Once a child who has ingested poison is brought to the emergency room, treatment is basically supportive. Few of the harmful substances have specific antidotes, and unless information is readily available, medical care should be begun without it. Parents should be advised to bring the empty container to the hospital and should be asked if they have any estimation of how much was ingested. The volume of a swallow in a 1½- to 3-year-old is 4.5 ml and in an adult is 15 ml. Medical treatment is more precise if the type and amount of ingested substance is known.

If the substance is unknown, the nurse must observe the child carefully for signs and symptoms that will aid the physician in the differential diagnosis. These signs and symptoms are listed in Table 20-5. Substances that are known to have specific antidotes are listed in Table 20-6 along with their specific antidotes.

The goal of treatment in the emergency room is removal of the poison. Syrup of ipecac is given if indicated. When vomiting has been initiated in the home, the results are evaluated in the emergency room. Parents should be instructed to bring all emesis with them.

Although gastric lavage is not as effective in removing gastric contents as emesis, it can be used as long as the child is not convulsing or if the child has an endotracheal tube in place. A no. 22 to 26F Ewald or Jacques *orogastric tube* is used for a child and 34 to 36F is used for an adult. After the tube is passed, the stomach contents are aspirated and the initial material saved for toxicologic study. The lavage fluid is half-normal or normal saline used in quantities of 50- to 100-ml amounts for children. When returns are clear, the lavage is stopped. Oftentimes activated charcoal and later a cathartic are given by stomach tube and left in the stomach. The tube must be pinched off before it is withdrawn.

Activated charcoal is being used increasingly in the treatment of poisoning. It may be the most potent general antidote available. It is an *adsorbent* that inactivates many poisonous substances in the stomach. It decreases the amount of the poison available for absorption into the blood supply. The charcoal should not be given before syrup of ipecac because charcoal will absorb the ipecac and drastically reduce its effectiveness. It may be given after the child has vomited. Charcoal is given orally or by tube in doses of 2 g per kilogram of body weight mixed with 60 ml of water.

Throughout the treatment of the child with accidental poisoning, the nurse maintains close observation of vital signs and neurological status. A child may arrive in the emergency room crying loudly but within half an hour begin to exhibit

Table 20-5 Signs and symptoms as aids in differential diagnosis of poisoning

Signs and symptoms	Substance
Abdominal colic	Corrosives, heavy metals, insect bites
Ataxia	Alcohol, barbiturates, anticonvulsants
Breath odor	Acetone, petroleum distillates
Coma and drowsiness	Narcotic opiates, barbiturates, tranquilizers
Convulsions and muscle twitching	Amphetamines, camphor, organic phosphate insecticides
Mouth dryness	Anticholinergics, atropine, or excessive salivation as in the case of organic phosphate insecticides
Nystagmus	PCP, barbiturates, anticonvulsants
Oliguria or anuria	Heavy metals, ethylene glycol
Paralysis	Botulism, organic phosphate insecticides, heavy metals
Pulse rate	Slow: digitalis; fast: atropine
Pupil size	Miosis: narcotic opiates; mydriasis: antihistamines and anticholinergics
Respiratory alterations	Rapid: salicylates; Slow: narcotic opiates
Violent emesis, often with hematemesis	Aminophylline, iron, plants

Source: Joseph Greensher and Howard C. Mofenson, "Emergency Room Care of the Poisoned Child," *Issues in Comprehensive Pediatric Nursing* **4**(3):8 (June 1980).

Table 20-6 Poisonings and their specific antidotes

Poisoning	Specific antidote
Alcohol, methyl	Alcohol, ethyl
Amphetamines	Chlorpromazine
Anticholinergic poisonings	Physostigmine
Carbon monoxide	Oxygen
Coumarin anticoagulants	Vitamin K
Cyanide	Nitrites
	Thiosulfate
Ethylene glycol	Alcohol, ethyl
Heavy metals:	
Arsenic	Dimercaprol
	Penicillamine
Iron	Deferoxamine
Lead	Dimercaprol
	Calcium disodium edetate
	Penicillamine
Mercury	Dimercaprol
	Penicillamine
Narcotic opiate depressants:	Naloxone
Nitrates and nitrites	Methylene blue
Phenothiazines	Diphenhydramine (only idiosyncratic effect)
Phosphate ester insecticides	Atropine
	Pralidoxime

Source: Joseph Greensher and Howard C. Mofenson, "Emergency Room Care of the Poisoned Child," *Issues in Comprehensive Pediatric Nursing* **4**(3):12 (June 1980).

signs of serious respiratory depression. Sedation is rarely administered to a child after a poison ingestion because of the danger of central nervous system depression. If necessary, life support measures and monitors are used. The nurse is also responsible for assisting with the many laboratory and other tests used, including the following: (1) electrolytes, blood sugar, blood type, arterial blood gases; (2) urinalysis; (3) x-rays; and (4) electrocardiograms. See the nursing care plan at the end of this chapter.

Children who have ingested corrosive substances will probably have one or more of the following: visible burns of the mouth; increased salivation; retching, vomiting, or both; pain; cardiovascular collapse; or airway stenosis. Antibiotics, steroids, fluids, maintenance of the airway, and giving nothing orally form the basis of treatment. These children often require long periods of hospitalization with many dilatation procedures and even reconstruction surgery to replace the esophagus. The physical, emotional, and financial stress this places on the child and family is unimaginable and presents a tremendous nursing challenge.

The child who has ingested poison will be admitted to the hospital if symptoms are severe, the poison is highly toxic, the child shows signs of toxicity such as decreased level of consciousness or abnormal vital signs, or if there are signs of tissue destruction such as oral ulcerations, salivation, or dysphagia.

If the ingestion appears to be intentional self-poisoning, the child will need reassurance that something will be done and that he or she is safe from such self-destructive impulses. At some point a detailed history will be needed. The family will also need help and counseling. The nurse should take the child seriously and find out the details of the child's social setting, intent, method, stress, and support system. Psychiatric consultation is usually necessary. Follow-up care is essential.

Teaching is an important part of care of children who have been poisoned, especially since about half of such children repeat their ingestion accident. Parents should be reminded of the following safety measures:

1. Keep safety closures on medications and dangerous household products.
2. Keep all household products in their original containers.
3. Store all drugs and cleaners in locked cupboards or out of reach of children.
4. Get rid of all old drugs by flushing them down the toilet.
5. Keep purses away from children.
6. Use anticipatory guidance based on the child's age and behavior.

Drowning

Drowning or near-drowning is common in many localities of the country because of the availability not only of natural bodies of water but also of artifical lakes and swimming pools. Any age child may be a victim of drowning. Infants and toddlers fall in bathtubs and into pools and lakes. School-age children and teenagers may attempt to swim farther than they are able. Some drownings are the result of games or dares that children play with one another.

When a near-drowning victim is brought to the emergency room, it is important to determine whether the accident occurred in fresh water or salt water. This information is vital because the physiological effects of each are different and affect the type of treatment to be given.

A sample of the immersion fluid should be collected for chemical analysis and bacterial culture. Sometimes the water will contain pulmonary toxins such as chlorine or hydrocarbons that further complicate recovery.

The interval of anoxia and submersion should be determined. Any resuscitation efforts should be described. Other important aspects of the history include injuries, past medical and drug history, and tetanus immunization status.

In fresh-water near-drowning, the water aspirated into the lungs is absorbed into the pulmonary capillaries by osmosis because it is hypotonic in relation to the 0.9% salinity of capillary blood. In significant amounts the absorbed water causes intravascular overload, hemodilution of plasma, and hemolysis of red blood cells. The ruptured red blood cells release plasma-free hemoglobin that can lead to acute renal tubular necrosis.

When salt water enters the lungs, its hypertonicity draws fluid from the blood into the lungs, which then leads to increased intraalveolar fluid and fulminating pulmonary edema. Acidosis, hypoxemia, and hemoconcentration result.

The most common clinical symptoms are related to asphyxia and pulmonary edema and include cyanosis, frothy sputum, tachypnea, tachycardia, and rales. Hemoglobinuria may result from liberation of plasma-free hemoglobin by ruptured (fresh water) or dehydrated (sea water) red blood cells.

The treatment of serious submersion includes the establishment of an airway with a cuffed endotracheal tube, 100% oxygen, external cardiac massage, correction of acidosis, continuous monitoring, suctioning, treatment of arrhythmias, IV therapy, Foley catheterization, treatment of related injuries such as spinal cord compression, antibiotics, and evaluation of electrolytes and blood gases.

Frequently near-drowning victims arrive at the hospital alert, oriented, and feeling "fine." Most children are very frightened and only want to go home with their parents. Because of the secondary complications due to the aspiration of fairly large volumes of water, however, a thorough evaluation must be done. This evaluation includes blood gas analysis while breathing room air, chest x-rays, and a thorough auscultation of the lungs. Some physicians admit all near-drowning victims to the hospital for overnight observation. However, if there are no apparent problems, many children are discharged to be closely watched by their parents and to be re-evaluated the next day for any possible pulmonary complications.

Sudden infant death syndrome

Accidents are the leading cause of death in children between the ages of 1 and 14 years. Between the ages of 1 month and 1 year, however, the leading cause of death is *sudden infant death syndrome* (SIDS). The emergency room nurse has a significant role in the care of families whose child succumbs to SIDS. The true incidence of sudden infant death syndrome is not clearly apparent because of confusion in reporting. The cause of death may be listed as "pneumonia" or "found dead (cause unknown)" when it is actually SIDS. With recent recognition of SIDS as a distinct entity, more accurate reporting has become possible. At present the incidence is estimated to be as many as 12 to 20 deaths per 1000 live births.

Approximately 50 percent of all SIDS infants and families are seen in a hospital emergency room. This percentage is expected to increase as emergency medical services and communications improve. There is little that can be done for the actual victim since the child is already dead. The emergency room nurse must focus attention on the care of the survivors—the family. Understanding the nature and incidence of sudden infant death syndrome will enable the nurse to give more effective care.

While it is clearly accepted that SIDS is not caused by any lack of medical treatment or parental care, the exact etiology of sudden infant death is still not known. Many years ago it was believed that the baby had suffocated in its blankets. Then evidence seemed to suggest a respiratory infection because a number of the infants displayed symptoms of a cold the day or two before they died, and autopsy revealed occasional pulmonary infiltrates. But autopsies also demonstrated that the apparent respiratory infection was not severe enough to cause the death of the child. It has been recently postulated that the respiratory infection is a precipitating factor rather than a cause of SIDS. Although the specifics of sudden infant death syndrome remain unclear, there does seem to exist a group of common characteristics that indicate that SIDS does not strike randomly just any infant. (See Table 20-7.) These characteristics seem to describe a group of infants who may be at risk.

Over 70 theories have been postulated about the cause of SIDS. Much research is being conducted throughout the country in an attempt to discover the etiology of the infants' deaths. The prominent studies are related to airway narrowing, to sleep, to the immune system, and to virology. SIDS infants die in their sleep. The relationships between apnea and the developmental changes in sleep form the core of several research projects. The question "Why are some infants unable to recover from the brief periods of apnea that all infants experience during sleep?" is being investigated in one study. Other studies focus on the relationship of the thymus and the immune system in victims of SIDS. The epidemiology of the syndrome, along with the fact that 90 percent of the victims have an inflammation of the pharynx, seems to suggest that a virus plays a role. Many research projects are studying complex virology issues. It appears likely that one single cause of death will not emerge. Rather, several factors may be found to be the basis of sudden infant death syndrome.

The lack of knowledge about SIDS often subjects the parents and family to unnecessary accusation and hostility. No one is comfortable with the sudden unexplained death of an infant. Frequently a police officer is among the first responders to the scene. While ambulance attendants may be attempting to revive the child, the officer questions the parents. The questions may be repeated, reworded, and delivered with the attitude that the parents have caused the baby's death. There are even a few cases reported in which the parents were arrested for manslaughter or murder. Fortunately more information about SIDS is now available, and it is being disseminated among the general public and law enforcement officers. It is hoped that in the future the first response to parents will be one of understanding and support.

The emergency room nurse must be able to assess the problems of the family of a SIDS infant and to plan the care they require. Although specific for each family, problems generally center on two areas: confusion as to the reality of the death and its cause and the need to handle the multiplicity of emotions with which they are suddenly bombarded.

Table 20-7 Common factors in sudden infant death syndrome

Maternal	Child	Environmental
No prenatal care	2–6 months of age	Temperate zone areas
Young age	Low birth weight	Late fall or winter
	Siblings of SIDS baby	Low socioeconomic class

The ER nurse should provide a separate, quiet environment for the family. There they will be away from the stares of others in the waiting area and will be able to begin to sort out what has happened. Many times the parents are not actually aware that the baby is dead. If resuscitation measures were begun in the home, and continued until the baby was admitted to the ER, the parents may be hoping to hear that the baby has been revived. The nurse accompanies the physician when informing the family that the infant is dead. By being present, the nurse listens to what is said and watches reactions in order to ascertain that the parents have really heard that the baby died. If there is a language barrier, it is important to have an interpreter. It is no time for sign language and guessing. After being informed of the death, it is essential that the parents are told that sudden infant death syndrome is the apparent cause and that nothing could have been done to prevent it. They should also be assured that their baby did not suffer and that the death was quick and painless. While the parents may not be able to fully integrate and comprehend what they are told, they need information to begin their mourning and to form a basis for handling the many emotions they will experience. It is recommended that the parents be given written information about SIDS to take home with them. The National Sudden Infant Death Syndrome Foundation has published a pamphlet entitled "Facts about SIDS." It is available from the foundation at 310 S. Michigan Ave., Chicago, IL 60604.

The nurse may also act as a type of buffer as the parents are questioned by various professionals. The questions are occasionally lengthy but are necessary for records and reports. In their shock and grief the parents may have difficulty responding to the inquiries. The nurse can facilitate the process by keeping the questions simple and clear and by providing time for the parents to think before answering. It is essential that the atmosphere be one of understanding and empathy rather than blame and accusation.

To correctly determine that SIDS was the cause of death, an autopsy is necessary. The laws governing autopsies for SIDS cases vary in different states. In many areas autopsy is required because the death is sudden and unexplained. In those instances the coroner or medical examiner is authorized to conduct the autopsy. If a postmortem examination is not required, the nurse should attempt to facilitate arrangements for one in every case of SIDS. It further substantiates the cause of death as being unpreventable and not caused by the parents. The nurse and the physician should clearly explain to the parents the need for an autopsy and the benefits to them if one is performed.

After the questioning, the parents must leave their baby and go home. It is essential to the grieving process that the parents begin with a separation from their *dead* baby. This is facilitated by having the parents see the baby after the body has been cleaned. It reinforces their awareness that the child is dead and gives them a chance to say good-bye in their own way. It also reassures them that the infant is whole, and peaceful. If they desire, they should be given the opportunity to hold their baby. Some parents need to call other family members to be present at this time of grieving. If it is possible, it should be encouraged. Privacy is of great importance since this is a highly emotional time.

The nurse's knowledge of mourning and grief assists the family of SIDS. The nurse is prepared for a variety of parental responses. An overwhelming feeling experienced by SIDS parents is guilt. What could they have done to prevent the death? Unless this feeling is initially handled with information as discussed earlier, it can leave the parents open to self-blame and distrust of themselves and others. Because the death is sudden and unexplained, the parents often are stunned, reacting with disbelief and denial. Again the nurse reinforces the facts of the death.

The intensity of the grief that accompanies SIDS has been described as almost unbearable. There is no warning, no preparation, and parents have no explanation to offer to other family members and friends. Often these other people react with suspicion and blame at a time when their support is most needed.

The family of a SIDS baby has an overwhelming need for professional counseling and follow-up. The nursing care of the family does not end as they leave the emergency room. The nurse should make a referral to Social Services or to a community health nurse to make arrangements for a family follow-up or a home visit within 1 to 2 weeks. Often another SIDS parent can be the most helpful resource to this family.

It is during the early period of grief that the family may experience a total disruption of their family life. The parents may have difficulty continuing their daily functions. They may report that they hear the baby cry or go to check on the infant as if he or she is still there. They may fear that they are going crazy. Intervention at this time reassures the parents that what they are experiencing is normal. It may also mobilize other family members to provide specific types of support such as assisting with household duties. More information about SIDS can be given. Many states have chapters of the National SIDS Foundation. This organization is composed of health professionals, and parents who have experienced a SIDS in their family. These groups are particularly helpful to parents.

Often overlooked in the trauma and pain of the death are the siblings of the infant. They too will respond to the death of the baby. Their reactions will depend to a great extent on their stage of development. The toddler will suffer most from a disruption of parenting. He or she will be aware of the great changes in family but will not understand why. The grief and sadness of the parents will disturb the toddler, as will the sudden lack of attention and routine. The toddler may react with aggressive, attention-getting actions, or with regressive behavior. A surrogate parent who provides affection and daily routine will often be of assistance to the toddler.

The preschooler realizes the baby is gone but does not clearly understand where or why. He or she may ask many questions that parents are unable to answer. The preschooler often experiences feelings of guilt possibly having wished at some time that the baby was gone so he or she could have the parents exclusively. Now he or she may believe that the death was caused by this wish. Magical thinking and feelings of omnipotence are characteristic at this stage. The preschooler may also fear that he or she may be the next victim of whatever happened to the baby. This is reinforced by the fact that one day the baby was there, apparently healthy, and the next day the baby was gone. The preschooler also needs reassurance, affection, and stability in daily life.

The school-age child, while beginning to have an understanding of death, is not fully aware of its finality yet may be fascinated by the details of the preparations being made. The school-age child, who is greatly affected by the grief of the parents, needs reasonable explanations, as well as reassurance of love and signs of affection.

The professional who is making follow-up visits will assess the response of the total family and intervene appropriately. The immediate family may be too intimately involved to be aware of any disturbed relationships which might be developing. Thus it is essential in the emergency room care of the family whose infant is a SIDS victim that the nurse initiate the procedure for follow-up care.

Sexual assault

The first contact the nurse has with a child or adolescent who has been sexually assaulted often takes place in the emergency room. Because thousands of children are victims of this violent crime each year, the nurse must be cognizant of his or her role in providing initial care and follow-up treatment.

Over 50 percent of rape victims are between 10 and 19 years of age. In most states the suspected rape of a minor child *must* be reported to the police. An adolescent over the age of consent can decide whether or not to report the crime. States also define the age at which a minor can be treated for drug-related problems or gonorrhea or given contraceptives without parental consent. (Because laws and enforcement policies vary from state to state, the nurse must be familiar with those in the state where he or she is practicing.)

Criminal sexual conduct is legally defined as any sexual contact to which one party does not consent. Family sexual abuse, or *incest*, can be defined as the involvement of a minor child in sexual activity by his or her parent, close relative, guardian, or caretaker. Many more children are involved in an incestuous relationship (some estimate a million per year) than are ever reported to the authorities.

It is estimated that only 1 in 5 to 10 cases of sexual abuse or rape is reported. Of those cases reported, 1 in 4 results in an arrest and 1 in 60 leads to a conviction. According to the task force of the National Commission on Causes and Prevention of Violence, 52 percent of rapists are strangers to their victims and another 30 percent are slightly acquainted. However, when criminal sexual assault involves the younger adolescent or child, the rapist is known to the child or family in more than 75 percent of cases.

Rape is a crime of aggression and violence, not sex. The victim, usually female but sometimes male, feels violated and humiliated by this highly stressful, often life-threatening experience. It is *not* the role of the health professional to determine whether or not rape or incest has occurred. It *is* the responsibility of the health professional to accept the victim's story in a nonjudgmental and supportive manner and to provide treatment and follow-up care. The nurse must realize that the quality of the initial treatment of the victim in the emergency room is crucial to the victim's long-term resolution of this crisis. The nursing goals for the sexual assault victim are summarized below:

1. Provide a safe, secure, and supportive environment.
2. Provide information about: consent forms and rights, procedures to be done, reporting of crime to police, options available, community support services, follow-up care.
3. Involve the victim in the decision making in regard to treatment and examinations.
4. Listen to the victim in an accepting, nonjudgmental manner.
5. Maintain an accurate legal record. Document the victim's description of the attack accurately in the patient's own words, and record the observations made and the specimens collected.
6. Assist in evidence collection through a careful history, physical examination, and collection of specimens.
7. Assist in the care of physical injuries.
8. Maintain the chain of custody of evidence collected. [All people participating in evidence collection (nurse, doctor, laboratory personnel) must sign a slip that evidence placed in the collection kit came from the patient. The collection kit is kept refrigerated in a locked area and monitored until it is turned over to the police upon written consent of the victim.]
9. Arrange for a change of clothes to be brought for the victim and safe transportation home or to protective custody.

The child or adolescent who has been raped should be treated as a high-priority medical emergency. She should be quickly brought to a private examining room and not left alone. The very young child may need her mother present at all times. In cases of incest the child will also need to tell her story when parents aren't present. Older adolescents, too, will desire privacy during statements and examination.

The victim may initially exhibit verbal or physical signs of anger, fear, and anxiety. She may rub her arms or other sore spots and tend to hold her arms around her body for protection. She may be crying, shaking, and agitated. Some victims may appear calm and detached and even laugh. These are methods of denying their true feelings. They may also express statements of denial and self-blame. Because the victim has experienced the ultimate violation of self (other than murder), she feels fear, distrust, and loss of control.

During the whole ER examination and treatment process the nurse should use measures that enable the older victim to gain some control by involving her in decision making. Sometimes the very young child will not even realize what has happened, and then it is important not to make the situation any worse. Unless the victim is a minor, she has a right to refuse tests or treatment, reporting to the police, and, finally, prosecution of the assailant. Consent must be given by the adolescent and parents for examination and treatment, evidence collection, and reporting. If the victim is not sure about reporting the crime, the nurse will need to explain the value of collecting the evidence then so that it is not lost in the event she does decide to report the crime later.

History taking

The nurse will need to collect the regular identifying information in addition to medical history, allergies, and data regarding menses. The menstrual cycle, last menstrual period, and use of any birth control method should be noted. If intercourse has occurred within 72 h preceding the assault, that should be recorded. It is wise to determine if the girl has ever had a vaginal or rectal exam. Whether she showered, douched, or changed clothes should also be noted. If the victim is willing, other information needed regarding the attack includes: date, time, place, witnesses, body orifices involved, occurrence of ejaculation, and injuries. If incest information is needed, include when it started, other family members involved, and who knows about it.

When the victim is very young, every effort should be made not to upset the child any further. Dolls or illustrations can often aid the child in pointing out the affected areas or in describing what happened.

Children under 10 will frequently respond better to questions phrased in physical rather than sexual terms. Ask parents the common terms used by the family for body parts. When the child is interviewed, the nurse can assess the child's verbal ability as well as psychological and physical reactions. Burgess and others[9] suggest that early questions should be neutral in character. Examples include the following: "Do you know why you were brought to the hospital?" "Were you able to tell your mother or father what happened?" "I would like you to tell me what happened so I can help you." Have you ever been to a hospital before?" "Do you know what will happen here?" "How do you feel about being here?"

Children should be allowed to use their own language. The nurse must be extremely careful not to make any judgments or to put words into the child's mouth. Questions should be neutral and not leading. "Show me where he touched you," is much better than "Did he touch your breast?" This holds true no matter what the age of the patient.

During the interview the child should be given the opportunity to talk about her feelings as this will help her to express them later on during the recovery phase.

The parents may feel guilty also and be more upset than the child. If family abuse is not involved, help the parents to provide the strength and support that the child needs. Part of the nurse's role is to facilitate better communication between the child and the parents. Parents need to understand that it will be healing for the child to be able to talk about the assault later on.

When a family member is involved, the child must be protected from further injury. The child may feel betrayed by the parent who left the child unprotected as well as by the person committing the act. The family may be divided between loyalty to the child and to the family member.

Physical examination

After the history and vital signs are done, the physician or nurse practitioner will assess phys-ical and gynecological trauma. The victim is also examined for the presence of sperm and indications of forcible rape. The skin is examined for bruises, scratches, lacerations, tooth imprints, pressure imprints, or tenderness. The findings of the exam and tests are termed *clinical evidence* of rape. They do not become legal evidence until turned over to the police.

Parents are often particularly concerned about their child's welfare and anxiously await the examination report. The exam can be very upsetting to the child, especially the gynecological part. Sometimes a visual exam and swabbing of the vagina will be sufficient for the very young child. A nasal speculum may also be used instead of the small vaginal speculum. Whatever is done must be done very gently and with a great deal of sensitivity.

Table 20-8 describes equipment needed and the methods used for collecting specimens often needed from sexual assault victims.

The victim

The adolescent will need counseling about prevention of venereal disease and the possibility of pregnancy. Tests for syphilis and gonorrhea will need to be repeated 4 to 6 weeks after the attack. A written handout describing the symptoms of these venereal diseases may be given to the victim along with a return appointment.

The possibility of becoming pregnant exists for the adolescent who is not using any birth control method. The physician may offer the victim several choices, such as menstrual extraction, insertion of an IUD, diethylstilbestrol (the "morning after" pill), or abortion if pregnancy is determined to exist at a later date. Unfortunately it may be very difficult for the victim to make a choice when she is experiencing the shock and confusion precipitated by the assault.

For a short time after the rape, most victims experience mixed feelings of shock, dismay, denial, anxiety, and anger. Nightmares and insomnia are common. These feelings are coupled with somatic complaints of loss of appetite, headache, dizziness, abdominal pain, and loss of libido. The reaction is one of grief and loss. This acute phase of disorganization may cause regressive behavior, but it also makes the victim more amenable to crisis intervention. The reorganization phase that follows will last much longer

(Continued on page 500)

Table 20-8 Collection of specimens—ER examination of sexual assault victim*

Specimen	Equipment	Procedure	Comments
Clothing	*Paper* bags, labels	Have patient place each piece of clothing in separate paper bag. Handle as little as possible. Label.	Document in record who takes clothing. (Plastic bags may cause damp clothing to mold.)

Blood
    VDRL†
    Typing
	Collection tubes, tourniquet, alcohol sponge, syringe, needle	Routine. Label.	Check for syphilis and repeat in 4–6 weeks. Check patient's blood type to differentiate it from assailant's.

Saliva test	Sterile gauze, forceps, sterile container, label	Place gauze in patient's mouth with forceps. Have patient wet gauze. Place on 4- by 4-in pad to dry. Place in sterile container. Label.	Do not touch gauze! Specimen will be examined for blood group antigens.
Oral washing	Sterile water, test tube, top, label	4–5 ml sterile water—rinse around mouth. Collect in test tube.	Examined for blood group antigens.
Fingernail scrapings	Sterile fingernail file, sterile gauze, envelope, label	Scrape under patient's fingernails. Place debris in gauze and then put in envelope. Label.	Specimen will be examined for blood, skin, and clothing fibers belonging to assailant.

Hair
    Scalp
 	
    Pubic
	Forceps, envelopes, labels	Pull 10–12 hairs from different parts of head. Place in envelope. Label.
		Pull 6–8 pubic hairs. Place in envelope. Label.
			The hair follicle is needed to make an accurate comparison of patient's hair with that of assailant.

Pregnancy testing†	Urine container, label	Have patient collect urine specimen.	If patient is bleeding, obtain a midstream sample.
Vaginal smear	Sterile, dry swab, glass slide and holder, envelope	Swab vagina with dry swab. Make smear on slide. Dry slide and place in labeled envelope.	Do before introducing saline for sperm collection. May detect sperm. Useful for ABO typing.
Gonococcus (GC) culture†	3–4 Thayer-Martin plates, sterile swabs, labels	Collect specimens from: cervix, vagina, rectum, and throat if oral intercourse occurred. Label all specimens.	Repeat in 4–6 weeks.

Sperm
    Vaginal
 	
    Dried semen and blood on skin
	Speculum, gloves, test tube, top, saline, aspirator, labels
	
	Saline, thread, test tube, top, label
		Place saline in vagina and aspirate. Place aspirant in test tube. Label.
		Moisten spot with sterile saline and rub stain with thread. When dry, place in test tube. Label.
			Sperm may be tested to determine blood type of assailant.
			To be done on areas of body where dried semen or blood is noted. Be careful not to touch specimen.

* Prepared by Diane K. Olsen, R.N.

† The pregnancy test, GC culture, and VDRL are done in the hospital laboratory. They are repeated in 4–6 weeks. If results are postitive, then they may be used as evidence in court.

Note: It is suggested that the nurse wear clean gloves when handling any specimens to avoid contaminating them. The nurse should explain to the patient that it is important for the nurse to avoid contamination because of the importance of identification of blood type, not because he or she fears touching the patient. *All specimens collected should be carefully documented in the medical record.*

Nursing Care Plan–Accidental Poisoning*

Patient: Cindy S.　　　**Age:** 22 months　　　**Date of Admission:** July 7

Cindy, 22 months old, is rushed to the emergency room by her frightened, crying mother, Mrs. S. Cindy apparently swallowed some diazepam about one-half hour previously while in the care of a baby-sitter. The baby-sitter thought the pill container had been empty before Cindy began playing with it.

Mrs. S. had left the pill container on the coffee table while preparing to leave to visit her own mother, who is terminally ill with cancer. Mrs. S. estimates she has used 15 to 20 tablets of the original thirty 5-mg tablets prescribed.

Mother appears extremely upset, distraught, and frightened. She says, "I never should have gotten the Valium. Why did I leave it on the coffee table? Will Cindy be OK?" And later, "I'll never leave her alone again."

Assessment

Mother is holding Cindy. The child is too sleepy and too weak to stand or walk by herself. Cindy responds to her name by opening her eyes.

Temp.: 37.2°C
Apical pulse: 80
Respirations: 15
BP: 80/56 mmHg
Weight: 11.8 kg (26 lb)

No treatment given at home for poisoning.

Physician's orders

VS q 15 min
Neurological check q 30 min
Orogastric tube
Gastric lavage with 0.5 N saline
D5/0.2 NaCl IV at 40 ml/h
Activated charcoal 20 g per OG tube
3 g of NaSO$_4$
Endotracheal tube and oxygen available at bedside
Routine lab tests
Intake and output
Transfer to Peds ICU when stable

Nursing diagnosis	Nursing goals	Nursing actions	Evaluation/revision
1. Potential for central nervous system depression related to ingestion of diazepam	☐ To prevent further CNS depression as evidenced by maintaining: **a.** Respiratory rate >12/min **b.** Blood pressure >85/50 **c.** Response to verbal stimuli **d.** Absence of seizures	☐ Monitor vital signs with specific emphasis on respiratory status q 15 min ☐ Notify physician if respiratory rate less than 12/min ☐ Have endotracheal tube and oxygen available at bedside ☐ Monitor neuro status (orientation, alertness, response, movement) q 30 min ☐ Observe for seizure activity ☐ Assist with gastric lavage: **a.** Set up equipment. **b.** Observe level of consciousness, seizure activity, and gag reflex prior to insertion of orogastric tube; if unconscious or seizuring or if gag absent, child should be intubated prior to procedure	☐ Vital signs are stable: pulse: 90; resp.: 18; BP: 90/58; respirations are easy; child continues to be drowsy but responds to name

Nursing diagnosis	Nursing goals	Nursing actions	Evaluation/revision
		c. Position Cindy with head slightly down and to the side or flat **d.** Restrain as needed during insertion of oral/nasogastric tube **e.** Assist with insertion of oral/nasogastric tube **f.** Check placement of tube **g.** Collect specimen of initial gastric contents withdrawn **h.** Record amount of fluid instilled and withdrawn **i.** Record results of procedure including color and consistency of fluid withdrawn **j.** Prepare and administer dose of 30 g activated charcoal as ordered by physician after lavage. **k.** Prepare and administer $NaSO_4$ 60 min after charcoal is given **l.** Maintain IV of D5/0.2 NaCl at 40 ml/h (to maintain BP) **m.** Record strict intake and output **n.** Recognize that symptoms of Valium overdose may persist 24–48 h	
2. Potential for child anxiety and uncooperativeness related to intrusive procedures and separation from mother as primary support	□ Cindy will cooperate during gastric lavage and will not be separated from her mother unnecessarily	□ Briefly explain procedures to Cindy in language comprehensible to her level of development □ Inform Cindy of acceptable behavior during procedures, i.e., "It's OK to cry, but you must hold very still for a short time" □ Restrain child only as necessary. □ Allow Cindy's mother to be present during procedures (if she can cope with the situation) to provide support and comfort. Mother should *not* help to restrain child during procedures □ If mother not able to cope with situation, nurse should comfort child through touch and language □ Praise Cindy for appropriate behavior and cooperativeness during procedures	□ Cindy needed minimal amount of restraint during gastric lavage because of sleepiness □ Mother present during lavage, and she continually stroked Cindy's head, squeezed her hand, and talked to her saying, "You will be all right. You have just got to be all right. Mommy loves you."

Nursing diagnosis	Nursing goals	Nursing actions	Evaluation/revision
3. Parental guilt feelings and anxiety related to accidental poisoning and hospitalization.	☐ Mother will exhibit increased coping through altered behaviors such as less crying, appropriate responses to questions, and increased ability to comfort daughter	☐ Explain purpose of procedures, how procedures are to be performed, and expected outcomes of procedures to mother ☐ Allow mother to ventilate anger directed at: **a.** Baby-sitter for allowing Cindy to play with pillbox **b.** Self for having diazepam available to child and leaving Cindy with baby-sitter **c.** Her mother for having terminal illness ☐ Allow mother to remain with Cindy as support and comfort during procedures ☐ Notify husband of incident and wife's need for support person ☐ Prepare mother (parents) for transfer to Peds ICU	☐ Mother very upset at self for leaving Cindy with school-age baby-sitter and for leaving diazepam pillbox on coffee table by telephone ☐ Father will be arriving shortly
4. Lack of parental knowledge concerning prevention and emergency treatment of accidental poisoning	☐ Mother (parents) will be able to repeat information regarding prevention and treatment of poisoning	☐ Discuss with mother (parents) the implications of growth and development as pertains to poisonings ☐ Inform parents of services of local poison control center and telephone number ☐ Recommend purchase of syrup of ipecac for home medicine chest ☐ Explain use of syrup of ipecac ☐ Discuss preventive measures: i.e., lock all cabinets containing medicine, place all medicine, household cleaning substances, and plants out of child's reach, do not store harmful (caustic) substances in food containers, and do not refer to medicine as *candy*.	☐ Mother remains too upset for comprehension of this plan. Inform nurses in Peds ICU of need to discuss prevention and treatment of poisoning

* Prepared by Andrea Piens, R.N., M.S.

as the victim (and family) repairs the physical, emotional, and social disruption of her life. Depression is common in the reorganization phase.

The adolescent who has just begun to date may be concerned about the effect the rape will have on her relationship with young men. Parents must be cautioned against conveying the idea to her that she is somehow "altered" or "damaged" because of the rape. For the adolescent who is beginning to deal with her own sexuality the rape may have a real effect upon how she feels about herself and others. Emotional counseling and support should be made available to the victim and her family through referral to a sexual assault counseling service and by medical follow-up. During follow-up the victim will need to talk about the experience with those who cared for her during the immediate crisis.

References

1. *Webster's New World Dictionary of the American Language*, Second College Edition, Collins, Cleveland, 1980.
2. K. G. Nelson, "An Index for Severity of Acute Pediatric Illness," *American Journal of Public Health* 70:804–807 (1980).
3. J. R. Lloyd, Y. Silva, A. J. Walt, and R. F. Wilson, "Trauma in Infants and Children," in Alexander J. Walt and Robert F. Wilson (eds.), *Management of Trauma: Pitfalls and Practice*, Lea and Febiger, Philadelphia, 1975, p. 130.
4. Joseph Greensher and Howard C. Mofenson, "Emergency Room Care of the Poisoned Child," *Issues in Comprehensive Pediatric Nursing* 4(3):1–21 (June 1980).
5. Ibid.
6. Raymond Sobel, "Psychiatric Indications of Accidental Poisoning in Childhood," *Pediatric Clinics of North America*, August 1970, pp. 653–685.
7. Greensher and Mofenson, op. cit., p. 7.
8. Robert H. Dreisbach, *Handbook of Poisoning*, Lange, Los Altos, Calif., 1974, p. 12.
9. Ann W. Burgess, Lynda Holmshom, and Maureen Mc-Causland, "Counseling the Child Rape Victim," *Issues in Comprehensive Pediatric Nursing* 1(3):52–53 (November-December 1976).

Chapter 21 **The chronically ill child**

Jo Ann Dillingham Glasscock

Upon completion of this chapter, the student will be able to:

1. Differentiate between chronic illness, disability, and handicap.

2. State the incidence of chronic illness in children.

3. List at least three types of causes of chronic conditions.

4. Identify at least two factors that influence the consequence of chronic illness on children.

5. Describe the effects of chronic illness in each developmental level of the child.

6. List four nursing interventions used to assist the confined child.

7. Discuss three interventions used to provide healthful grieving in the child.

8. Describe the reactions of parents and siblings to a chronically ill child.

9. Compare the nursing care during shock and disbelief to that during overprotection.

10. Identify the effects of chronic illness on the family.

11. Describe the nurse's role as a child-family advocate.

12. Implement four nonpharmacologic pain relief measures.

Chronic illnesses are diseases or other alterations in body function that are long-term rather than acute. They may last for months, years, or even a lifetime. Chronic illnesses cause varying degrees of disability, handicap, or both.

The terms *disability* and *handicap* are used interchangeably by many nonprofessionals, but the nursing literature currently makes a distinction. A *disability* is simply a limitation of function, and inability to perform some normally expected physical or mental activity. For example, a child with cerebral palsy may have motor disabilities that make it impossible to run smoothly. *Handicap* is a more complicated concept and involves organic, functional, and social limitations.[1] The *organic* component is the unchanging impairment that underlies the disorder, such as blindness, deafness, or paralysis. The *functional* component is the same as *disability*, defined above; for example, a visually impaired child may have difficulty functioning in a regular classroom. The *social* component of handicap is the psychosocial limitations that may arise secondary to organic and functional problems and interfere with the person's social roles or relationships. For example, social stigma or poor self-concept can prevent a disabled person from participating in activities of which he or she actually is capable.

While the exact number of children who have a chronic illness is unknown, the incidence is high. If problems with vision, speech and hearing, mental retardation, and learning and behavioral problems are included, the incidence of chronic illness may be as high as 30 to 40 percent of American children. If these are excluded, the incidence of chronic illness is around 7 to 10 percent.[2] The most common chronic conditions are asthma, epilepsy, cardiac abnormalities, cerebral palsy, orthopedic conditions, and diabetes mellitus.

Mattson[3] classifies chronic conditions as:

1. Diseases due to chromosomal abnormalities, such as Down syndrome
2. Genetic diseases, such as sickle cell anemia, cystic fibrosis, hemophilia, and diabetes mellitus
3. Disorders resulting from harmful intrauterine factors, such as drugs, infections, radiation, or hypoxia
4. Disorders resulting from birth trauma or perinatal infections, such as cerebral palsy or sepsis
5. Disorders due to postnatal infections, physical injuries, or neoplasms, such as meningitis, rheumatic fever, leukemia, or chronic renal disease

In addition, chronic disorders can result from prematurity (for example, respiratory distress syndrome and bronchopulmonary dysplasia) and from medical therapy itself (for example, retrolental fibroplasia and disorders due to lack of sensory stimulation or interruption in maternal bonding).

Significance of chronic illness in childhood

The duration of chronic illness in children varies from a few months to several years. Many chronically ill children have had the condition for most of their lives. Their degree of disability varies from being able to participate in normal activities to being severely incapacitated and in need of frequent hospitalization.

Chronic illness causes disruption in family functioning, is very costly financially for the family and the government, and raises serious moral and ethical issues. The greatest impact, though, is on the child. Chronic illness interferes with socialization[4] and the development of skills by which the child learns to be like others and to function independently.

Influencing factors

Chronic illness has various effects on children's development. Some factors which influence the consequence of chronic illness are age, personality, and family attitudes.

Influence of age The child who has been ill since birth has always been treated as "different." Many such children have been overprotected (or overindulged) or rejected. Either overprotection or rejection causes the child to lose self-confidence because he sees himself as not capable or not deserving of love. Children who acquire a chronic illness at a later age have been brought up as "normal" and have acquired confidence in their ability to cope with their environment.

Children who are in a critical stage of development at the onset of chronic illness or when the illness is diagnosed are very vulnerable to the effects of the illness.[5] For example, the adolescent is vulnerable to conditions that affect peer acceptance, body image, or mobility, such as the loss of a limb. A school-age child is affected by illnesses that interfere with motor activity and peer interaction. A child who is deaf from birth does not learn to imitate sounds. The child who is blind before the age of 5 or 6 has little or no visual memory of color or letters and therefore has more difficulty learning braille than the child who is older when he becomes blind.

Influence of personality The influence of the individual's personality is difficult to specify. Children cope with illness in various ways. Some are passive, some are stoical and courageous, while others are extremely fearful. (This is further discussed in Chap. 16.)

The number and type of life experiences the child encounters and the emotional support provided by the parents in new situations help develop the child's coping capacity. As the child matures cognitively, past experiences and ways of coping can be recalled (see cognitive development discussions in Chaps. 14 and 15). Children who have developed coping skills that were successful in the past are likely to approach new situations confidently.[6]

Influence of family attitudes The feelings and attitudes the family gives the child about his or her competence and ability determine how the child responds to the illness. The family's approach is determined by family members' own experiences and their ways of coping with stress. Steinhauer[7] identifies some factors that influence the family's feelings about the illness:

1. The severity of the illness and prognosis. The more

severe the illness and the poorer the prognosis, the greater the stress on the family.

2. Whether the disease is congenital or acquired. Congenital illnesses cause more intense feelings of guilt.

3. The child's age at illness onset and diagnosis. If a diagnosis is made after the child's place in the family is established, a greater sense of loss is felt than when the child has never been thought of as "normal." The earlier the diagnosis is made, the more likely the parents are to see the child as handicapped and overprotect the child.

4. The presence of preexisting emotional problems in the family. The greatest psychological and social problems develop in a child whose family relationships are already disturbed.

5. The nature of the disease itself. Pain or malaise may cause the child to be irritable or demanding and may cause feelings of resentment and guilt in the parents.

Other influences Other factors that influence family responses are restrictions and demands of home management programs such as those required for children with cystic fibrosis or spina bifida, the presence or absence of other affected siblings, repeated hospitalizations, and the cost of the illness.

Impact of illness on the child

Developmental level

Nothing is more important in determining the effects of illness on the child than developmental level. For example, the very young child who is healthy relates to the environment through sensory and motor activity, but many children who are chronically ill are also physically disabled and are limited in the use of mobility as a way to handle emotions and to explore their environment.

Infant A physical defect may be visible at birth and interfere with the normal bonding between mother and child. (See Chaps. 10 and 16.) For example, a facial defect such as a cleft lip is a reminder of the parents' failure to produce a perfect child and their powerlessness to determine the future. Sick infants often must be hospitalized for days or even weeks. If the mother is unable to see or hold the child, sensory and maternal deprivation may occur.

The socialization process begins in the immediate postpartum period when the child begins to associate pleasant feelings with people who consistently respond to his feelings and satisfy his needs. If the child's cry, smile, or other responses to the mother are delayed, the mother may have difficulty relating to the child. This may delay or decrease bonding.[8] If the child is difficult to feed or cuddle, cries constantly, or is very restless or placid, the mother may feel frustrated and perceive herself as an inadequate mother at a time when the child needs to establish a trusting relationship.

Toddler The toddler is recognized as being the most vulnerable to separation from parent. (See Chaps. 12 and 16.) The chronically ill toddler may be repeatedly separated from parents, lacks the ability to understand "why," has no concept of time, and lacks confidence that the parents will return. The hospitalized toddler is in a strange place with strange people who may cause pain, give little comfort, and confine the child to bed or to the room. Repeated hospitalization leads to distrust of parents and a denial of the need for them. Nursing intervention is mandatory, because untreated separation anxiety influences later relationships (see Chap. 16, "Separation Anxiety").

Toddlers are trying to achieve the developmental task of autonomy (see Chap. 12). They demonstrate this need by actions and words. They want to explore, climb, jump, run, and say "No." The chronically ill child's parents may overprotect and caution, "Don't go out in the cold," "You aren't strong enough to do that," or "Don't get excited." So these children are forced to be dependent on the parents, fearful, or rebellious. They receive messages that they are incapable of venturing out on their own or of initiating actions by themselves.

Preschooler The feelings of initiative that began when the child was a toddler now become more prevalent and the child is expected to master certain tasks. One of these is the establishment of sexual identity, which the child learns by identification with the parents, especially the parent of the same sex. Sex-role attainment may be difficult for the disabled or chronically ill child. One adult may have withdrawn from the family or the parents may be divorced. The child, as a result, may feel frustrated or rejected. He or she may be unable to find a substitute role model because of physical limitations. The parent with whom the child is living may be too busy coping with everyday life to find social activities for the child that involve sex-role models.

The opportunity and ability to play with peers is especially important in the preschool years. Only the family is more important than the peer group in socialization. Other children help the child to learn roles, cooperative and competitive behavior, independence, and appropriate ways to express aggression. Peers help children to see themselves as competent, increase their self-esteem, and are reference points for sexuality.[9]

Body-integrity fears are at a peak in the preschool years. All children have these fears, but the chronically ill child is likely to experience more tests, treatments, and hospitalizations than the normal child. In addition, children of this age often think of illness and hospitalization as punishment for bad thoughts and actions. (See Chap. 16.)

School-age child The task of the school-age child is to master the skills required by society—expand beyond the family to the school, the peer group, and the outside world. The inability to achieve in academics or sports or to be like others of the group causes loss of self-esteem and feelings of inferiority or rejection. The chronically ill child may miss school because of illness or hospitalization or may be so incapacitated as to be unable to attend school at all. Repeated absences may cause the child to have to repeat a school grade and may further contribute to feelings of inferiority. Some chronically ill children find school a place where they can achieve intellectually, develop their talents, and thus compensate for impaired physical functioning.

The child's education is important in long-term hospitalization. Many hospitals that provide long-term care have a classroom teacher. Tutors are available in most public school systems. Education should not be left to the teachers alone. Changes in environment are important in the development of intelligence and nurses must find ways for children confined to bed or who are in body casts to move around and interact with other children.[10] (See Chaps. 14 and 16.) Children who cannot attend school should have a homebound teacher.

The school-age child who has experienced multiple hospitalizations becomes very knowledgeable about hospital routines and procedures. School-age children are becoming able to understand cause and effect and want to learn about body functions. However, repeated hospitalizations or surgeries do *not* make procedures less traumatic. More often anxiety increases with repeated hospitalization, even though the child may have learned to control expressions of fear. (Nursing interventions to reduce anxiety, teach school-age children, and communicate with them are described in Chap. 16.)

Adolescent Adolescence is one of the most difficult of all developmental stages for many normal teenagers because they are confronted with problems of establishing identity, deciding on a career, trying to achieve independence, establishing emotional control, and coping with physical changes and emerging sexual drives. These tasks may seem insurmountable for the chronically ill or handicapped adolescent. If a teenager has physical or intellectual disabilities or if family supports are limited, adolescence can become a nightmare. Our society values physical beauty, mobility, athletic prowess, and intelligence and has little tolerance for the disabled adolescent.

Body image, the way people appear to themselves or believe they appear to others, is especially important to adolescents (refer to Chaps. 15 and 16). Teenagers are constantly undergoing body changes. Many chronically ill adolescents are short and thin and have delayed sexual development, physical abnormalities, and limited mobility. Teenagers with chronic illnesses or disabilities commonly have a poor body image and low self-esteem, both because of their own responses to their health problems and because of the opinions of the peer group, which are accepted as accurate.[11]

Chronic illness also interferes with the adolescent's need to achieve independence from parents. It causes the teenager to have feelings of helplessness and lack of control and threatens the sense of personal identity. Chronic illness also limits the adolescent's social experience and skills. The ability to compete for dates is jeopardized since adolescents select dates who are most desirable according to the criteria of the peer group. Ill adolescents often feel insecure and inadequate in their sex roles.[12]

Adolescents can be helped to adjust to their disability by their family, peer group, and the health care team. Peers, especially those who have experienced similar problems, are often very helpful to the teenager.[13] Organized teen groups in the hospital or treatment center facilitate expression of feelings and adaptation.

Independence should be fostered in the hospital and at home by allowing the adolescent to take part in decision making and self-care. Vocational counseling is important for those who want to be independent but are limited physically or intellectually. The nurse may need to arrange for genetic counseling or family planning assistance for adolescents or young adults considering marriage or who are sexually active. Psychological or psychiatric counseling is often needed by chronically ill children and their families. Many low-cost services are available. Information about these services can be obtained from state or local medical or psychological associations.

Immobility and confinement

Mobility is very important in childhood. The ability to explore the environment is crucial in developing skills and achieving a sense of mastery and control. It is an important way of expressing emotions, controlling anxiety, and learning to relate to people. It is a way to find stimulation from friends and care-givers or to find solitude. It serves a protective function and makes it possible for the child to escape from threats.[14] Confinement differs from immobility. *Confinement* means restriction to a certain area; *immobility* is the inability to move. One definition of the word *confine* is "imprison," which is undoubtedly what hospitals mean to many children.

While immobility and confinement are not synonymous, they may have similar outcomes. They deprive the child of meaningful sensory stimulation and contact with peers, parents, and others. Confinement creates a barrier to exploration, thwarts attempts to master the environment, and isolates the child from other people. Nursing interventions suggested by McGuire et al.[15] are to:

1. Extend physical space by moving the child to hallways, playrooms, etc.
2. Facilitate meaningful social interaction by encouraging visits from staff, family, and peers and letter writing
3. Provide opportunities for recreation, such as games and puzzles, and provide outlets for aggression, such as wall games, clay, punching bags
4. Provide opportunities for education, encourage school work, and arrange for tutoring
5. Promote independence and allow child to help plan and provide care
6. Maintain sense of identity and orientation, encourage patient to wear his or her own clothes, and encourage the presence of pictures and belongings from home

Sensory impairment

Many chronically ill or handicapped children are sensorially impaired and consequently are unable to receive adequate stimulation from the environment. The most obvious conditions causing sensory impairment are blindness and deafness. Conditions in which there is limited tactile stimulation, such as burns or osteogenesis imperfecta, can also result in sensory restriction.

The importance of stimulation in the development of cognitive abilities is well known. Infant stimulation and developmental programs have been shown to be beneficial to children with such conditions as cerebral palsy and Down syndrome, and also to low birth weight infants.[16] Sensory impairment retards psychosocial growth and development but especially affects cognitive development because the child learns about the world by sensorimotor activity. Deprived of sight, the child must rely on hearing and touch to learn about the environment. Deprived of sound, the child does not learn to imitate speech and does not hear warnings of danger such as a car horn or train whistle. Sensory impairment also interferes with the ability of the parents as caretakers to communicate with the child and increases fear and anxiety of both.

Pain

All children with chronic illness will experience pain at some time from diagnostic procedures, treatments, or their disease condition. A child in pain can have problems sleeping, eating, concentrating, or completing activities at home or school. The child may become anxious, depressed or irritable.

Children may believe pain is a punishment for bad behavior. Some children have described pain as "abandonment," "being afraid," "when something hurts and no one comes," and "something you have no control over." [17]

Children have been thought to have a greater tolerance to pain, but this is *not* so. Haslam's study of children 5 to 18 years old showed that the younger the child, the more susceptible he was to pain.[18] Adults may also believe that children perceive less pain because children typically have difficulty describing their pain. The very young child may lack words; the older child may come to accept pain as being normal. Children may be reluctant to talk about their pain for fear of receiving medicine and injections or to avoid treatments.

To help a very young child describe pain the nurse might need to use other words, such as "sting" or "hurt," or to ask the child to point out the sore spot on her body or on a drawing. The nurse can ask a school-age child or adolescent to rate pain on a scale of 1 (mild discomfort) to 10 (severe or unbearable discomfort). When this is possible, the nurse can learn how tolerant of pain the child is, as well as how the child expresses pain. This rating can be incorporated into a flow sheet so that a record is available of how effective the various pain relief measures are that the nurse uses. In this way the child becomes part of the pain management process.

McCaffery lists several guidelines for pain relief. The nurse is advised to:[19]

1. Use a variety of pain relief measures
2. Use the pain relief measures *before* the pain becomes severe
3. Include what the child or parent believes will be effective
4. Consider the patient's ability to be active or passive in the application of pain relief measures
5. Determine the potency of the pain relief measure on the basis of the patient behavior indicating the severity of the pain
6. Encourage the patient to try the pain relief measure at least one or two times more if it is ineffective the first time it is used

7. Be open-minded about what may relieve pain
8. Keep trying
9. Do no harm

Table 21-1 describes specific nursing measures for relieving pain.

Reactions to chronic illness

The child

Children with chronic illnesses, regardless of their seriousness or the child's developmental stage, exhibit specific and similar reactions during the period of diagnosis and initial attempts to stabilize the condition.[20] All children or adolescents with chronic illness suffer a *loss*. This may be of body parts, functional abilities, or health, but most of all disturbance of body image and loss of one's previous assessment of self. This loss is not easy to accept and almost all children find ways to deny its permanence. A child who was going to have an amputation said, "I will get it back." Another child with a permanent colostomy said confidently, "I won't always have to go to the bathroom this way."

A child also very deeply fears the loss of his role in the family. Each child contributes to the family in a unique way and jealously guards his place in the family structure. The need to defend his place in the family may cause the child to deny the illness, especially if he feels it will cause the family to reject him or to no longer need him.

The child can adjust to his loss or change in body image and role by first mourning the loss. Grief for what is past is a prerequisite to accepting one's new situation. The child who has successfully mourned his losses can then acquire a new image of himself and his place in the family and society.[21] Nursing interventions for the grieving chronically ill child are presented in Table 21-2.

Children also react to loss with anxiety, depression, and anger. Depression is frequent in chronically ill children, especially adolescents. (See Chaps. 16 and 40.) Feelings of helplessness and apathy may follow. The young child usually copes by using withdrawal and regression; the older child may become restless, bored, or completely submissive. (Nursing interventions are discussed in Table 21-3 and in Chap. 16.)

Table 21-1 Nonpharmacological pain relief measures available to the pediatric nurse

I. Nurse's relationship with the child and parents
1. Can be used to reduce anxiety with the child and parents.
2. Provides the basis for collaboration in planning pain relief. Nurse can learn from child and from parents what has helped control child's pain in the past.

II. Teach about pain
1. Have child touch and handle the actual equipment involved.
2. Have child meet physicians and nurses.
3. Have child play with dolls and other representations of the painful event.
4. Explain to child and parents when they will be separated and when they can be together during painful period.
5. Nurse should use hands to demonstrate location of pain and, by pressing and pulling the skin, the quality of pain.

III. Teach distraction strategies
1. Child's involvement in the distraction needs to increase as the pain intensity increases, but with fatigue or higher intensity of pain distraction needs to be less demanding. Younger child requires less complex distraction.
2. Distractions involving both rhythm and imagery tend to be most helpful; e.g., rhythmic, shallow breathing and making a sound with each exhalation can be coupled with image of steam locomotive ("choo-choo") taking child away from pain; train goes faster as pain increases. Nurse demonstrates method beforehand.

IV. Use cutaneous stimulation
1. Simple rhythmic rubbing. Use of pressure; electric vibrator; massage with hand lotion, powder, or menthol cream; application of heat or cold.
2. Stimulation is most effective if rhythmic or constant and moderate in intensity.

V. Use relaxation techniques
1. Teaching child to relax may decrease painful stimuli, e.g., release tension on abdominal incision, or may act as distraction.
2. Ask child to take deep breath and "go limp as rag doll" as he exhales slowly. Ask child then to yawn.
3. Older child may also need help into comfortable position (pillow under neck and knees), instruction in directing his attention away from pain, and testing relaxation of limbs so he will focus concentration on the task.

VI. Use desensitization and "fading in"
1. Desensitization: Threatening stimuli (dressing trays, needles, etc., employed in painful procedure) are introduced gradually, beginning with least frightening items, and presented in pleasurable surroundings. When child shows fear, nurse retreats to nonthreatening stimuli and begins again, hoping to develop child's tolerance of fear-provoking stimuli. Requires several repetitions.
2. Fading in: If child continues to respond with anxiety, the object is placed far away and gradually brought closer while the child is occupied with something pleasurable. If fear is again elicited, process is restarted with object farther away. Process needs to be repeated several times. Theoretically, child eventually will accept the object in his room and even be able to handle and discuss it.

Source: Adapted from Margo McCaffery, "Pain Relief for Child," *Pediatric Nursing* **3**(4):11–12 (1977).

Young children may feel angry that their parents have "allowed" the disease to happen to them. Older children resent their parents for transmitting a genetic disease to them. This anger may be repressed because the child depends on the parent as a caretaker and protector, or it may take the form of "acting out" feelings verbally or physically.

The parents

Parents' initial response to learning that their child has a chronic condition is one of *shock and disbelief*. This is true even when, as is often the case, parents are aware that something is seriously wrong with the child long before the fact is confirmed. A mother whose child was diagnosed as having cystic fibrosis said that she had known that something was wrong with the child since birth and didn't think she "would ever raise her." Even though she had consulted many physicians, she was still shocked when she learned the diagnosis and found it difficult to believe.

Shock increases anxiety levels and makes it difficult for the parent to comprehend information. Burton[22] quotes a father: "I can't recall what we were told on that occasion. An awful lot of what he said I lost."

Shock also causes distortion of information, such as "No one ever told me that." The mother usually has a better understanding of the information given about the condition than the father since he is often not present at the time the diagnosis is presented. Shock and disbelief are usually short-lived as the parents must make decisions about the child's care and treatment.

Denial is a defense mechanism used universally. It is effective in helping the parents cope with anxiety and pain. A mother, when told that her child had leukemia, called the hematology clinic and said, "You must have made a mistake!" At this time the parents may "doctor-shop" in hopes of learning of an error or misdiagnosis. This is a normal reaction but can interfere with the child's treatment.

Denial decreases anxiety by making the condition less fearsome while allowing the parents to gather their resources. Denial may be only an initial reaction or may continue throughout the course of the illness, but it usually decreases as the reality of the disease becomes increasingly difficult to ignore. It is usually not pathological and should not be destroyed by health professionals since it allows the parents the hope they need to face the future.

Guilt feelings also occur. As the relatives of a dying person search for a reason for death, so do the parents of the chronically ill child[23] accuse themselves and search for a cause. Feelings of guilt and personal responsibility are especially prevalent if the child's condition is genetic. Even though the parents usually do not know they are carriers of the defect before the birth of the child, they become aware of their own vulnerability and lack of power to prevent the disease. This increases their feelings of anxiety, anger, and guilt. A characteristic statement is: "If I had known I was a carrier, I wouldn't have had children." Guilt feelings may be observed frequently at the onset of the illness as overanxious, hovering behavior. They may persist throughout the illness. It is imperative that the nursing and medical staffs help the parents master their feelings of guilt; parents' acceptance of the child appears to center upon their mastery of self-accusation.[24]

Anger is a normal reaction and may be directed toward the nursing or medical staff, or even God. It may be expressed openly as in "Why would God let this happen to a child?" Anger and

Table 21-2 Nursing interventions to promote grieving in the chronically ill child

Nursing intervention	Rationale
1. Unconditionally accept the patient as he is.	1. Normality begins with loving or accepting the child as he is with his body shape and functions.
2. Present the loss as permanent if it is. Do not offer false hopes. Say, for example, "Your BM will always come out this opening."	2. Reality is a beginning point for grieving. False hope comes from adults' own feelings of guilt and helplessness.
3. Provide for continuity of care in hospital. Keep old care plans for a data base. Assign child to same unit, room, and favorite nurse. Keep environmental changes minimal.	3. Chronically ill children are vulnerable and tolerate change poorly. Consistent staff decreases anxiety, builds trust, and facilitates mourning.
4. Provide opportunities for patient to feel valued in hospital. Ask child to help younger patients or assign simple clerical jobs such as stapling papers. (See Chap. 16.)	4. The need to feel valued and contribute to family life can be transferred to the hospital staff. This increases self-esteem.
5. Provide for continuity of care at home. Begin discharge planning on admission. Plan detailed teaching plan. Provide for adequate instruction time, questions, and return demonstrations. Include child in planning. Include social worker, therapists, school nurse, and teacher in planning. Help family understand that major changes in family functioning are undesirable.	5. Chronic illness causes changes in all family members' roles. Maintaining family patterns of living and functioning increases the child's security and minimizes stress for other family members.

Source: Adapted from Richard A. Geist, "Onset of Chronic Illness in Children and Adolescents: Psychotherapeutic and Consultative Interventions," *American Journal of Orthopsychiatry* **49**(1):9–10 (January 1979).

Table 21-3 Nursing interventions to reduce depression or anger

Interventions	Rationale
1. Do not try to "cheer up" the patient or avoid discussing the loss.	**1.** Avoiding the child's behavior increases feelings of rejection and encourages repression of feelings. Acknowledgement relieves the child of burden of repression, builds trust, and frees psychological energy for building an appropriate new self-concept and patterns of coping.
2. Acknowledge child's anger: "You look really angry." Encourage safe expression of anger with appropriate toys and activities: Throwing bean bags, pillow fights, hammering, sawing. (See Chap. 16 for other suggestions.) Establish safety rules before play.	**2.** Movement is an important method of expressing anger and coping with anxiety.
3. Provide consistent structure of environment: "We understand your feelings but they will not affect our decisions. We are responsible for your care." Establish acceptable "acting out" behavior and consistent replies by staff. Assign same staff and hold team conferences. Support parents to avoid guilty behavior. Encourage them to make no excuses. Let the child know disease is unfair and often unexplainable. Help the child know the parents did nothing intentional to cause the disease.	**3.** Providing consistent structure promotes feelings of security. The parents' understanding helps the child understand and cope with his own feelings. Parental guilt undermines the child's (and other family members') family environment.
4. Encourage personal acceptance of anger. Anger may initially focus on a particular person: "I wish it had happened to my sister!" Accept initially with appropriate replies, such as "I know you wish it hadn't happened to you." Later help the child realize these feelings of unacceptance keep him dependent on other people.	**4.** Anger focused on another person is due to unresolved grief. Personal acceptance promotes independence and development of abilities for coping and achieving.

Source: Richard A. Geist, "Onset of Chronic Illness in Children and Adolescents: Psychotherapeutic and Consultative Interventions," *American Journal of Orthopsychiatry* **49**(1):12–13 (January 1979).

resentment may be directed at the spouse and toward the patient and may be repressed to assume the form of physical symptoms. Parents become angry at their own inability to produce a perfect child. As the parent's time and energy are increasingly invested in the child, they repress feelings of resentment and anger toward the child. This repressed anger may occasionally erupt in inappropriate outbursts of anger which further intensify guilt feelings. The increase in guilt and anger directly contributes to the formation of overprotection, discussed later in this section.

Depression and discouragement are commonly seen, especially in periods of exacerbations. Routines that must be followed every day become monotonous and trying. Parents become discouraged when they cannot prevent the dis-

ease from progressing. Sometimes it is even uncertain if they will prolong life.[25]

Overprotection or overcompensation occurs when the parent gives excessive attention to the child. This occurs because the parent overcompensates or overreacts to feeling responsible for the child's condition or to resenting or not wanting the child. The parent may also have a neurotic need to keep the child dependent or may genuinely love the child.[26] Overprotective parents accept responsibility for the child's disability and punish themselves for feelings of guilt and anger. They devote themselves to the child and often feel they are the only ones who can adequately provide care. Overprotective parents carefully regulate and restrict all aspects of the child's life and commonly are not aware of the child's real capabilities. The child is exposed to few outside stimuli, kept very dependent, and is not allowed to do things he or she is capable of mastering. As a result of the sensory restriction, the overprotected child is often developmentally delayed. Discipline tends to be minimal and inconsistent, and the child is overindulged.

The overprotected child who is not allowed to cope with stress will be less able to cope with stress in adulthood. This may cause him or her to seek protection as an adult and may result in loss of self-esteem and immature, dependent behavior. If parents are permissive, the child may be rebellious and refuse medication and treatment. Such a child is often spoiled and lacking in self-control and commonly resented by siblings.[27]

Solnit and Green[28] describe a *"vulnerable child syndrome"* in children whose parents expect them to die prematurely because of an acute, life-threatening illness. The child accepts the parents' assessment of his or her vulnerability and a disturbance in psychosocial development occurs. Symptoms include difficulty with separation and sleep problems. The child is "babied," overprotected, and overindulged and becomes overdependent, irritable, and disobedient. The parents are unable to set limits and some of the children become physically abusive, hitting, biting, or scratching the parent. The parents are overconcerned with the child's health. The child underachieves in school. Predisposing factors include prematurity, congenital anomaly, acquired handicap, or a life-threatening illness. Parental factors include unresolved grief reactions, ambivalent feelings toward the child, or the presence of a hereditary disease in the family.

Rejection of the ill child may also occur. Parents who reject the child criticize, nag, or excessively punish the child. They may fail to obtain needed care or fail to follow medical regimens. The rejected child, as well as the smothered or overprotected child, needs the support and advocacy of the nurse; so do the parents.

Grief is universally experienced by the parents of the chronically ill child. They grieve for the loss of their "ideal," fantasy child who will be beautiful, competent, master the things they dreamed of achieving and who will help them achieve a kind of immortality by producing grandchildren. But most frightening of all, many must face the possibility that their child's life span is limited. Parents must be helped to grieve for their imagined, dream child. They must complete the grief process before they can bond with the child.[28]

Feelings of sadness are experienced and expressed by crying. Inability to sleep or such somatic symptoms as headache and abdominal pain are common. Parents with seriously ill children experience some anticipatory grief, whereby the loss of the child is anticipated.

Olshansky[29] noted that some parents who have a defective child experience *chronic sorrow* throughout their lives. This experience may vary in intensity because of such factors as personality, religion, and social class. This normal reaction may be shown openly but more often is concealed or denied. It does not prevent the parent from enjoying the child or feeling satisfaction from the child's achievements.

Parents frequently try to overcome their feelings of helplessness and lack of control over the illness by the defense mechanism of *intellectualization*. They are determined to learn everything they can about the disease and its treatment. Some try to find a cure by raising money for research. Many become quite knowledgeable and can be threatening to the medical or nursing staff.

Accepting parents, who have adjusted successfully to a chronically ill child, are aware of normal growth and development, encourage the child to develop strengths, discipline consistently, and encourage independence, self-care, school attendance, and playing with peers. The child feels loved and accepted.[30] These parents interact with their own friends. Even while experiencing emotional highs and lows, they cope with the child and feel satisfaction at attaining short-term goals. They meet the child's needs and family members support each other.

Effects on the family

Chronic illness affects *all* aspects of family functioning. It causes a loss of equilibrium in the family and changes in roles, communication, and outside social relationships.

Roles become confused as the family tries to adjust to the illness.[31] Role changes or reversals often occur with the father and siblings taking on some of the traditional maternal roles. The father feels resentment, anger, and physical exhaustion but is reluctant to criticize his wife because of her devotion to the ill child.

Breakdown in communication is a significant problem among all family members. Even families which usually communicate easily may find it difficult to talk to the child or siblings about the condition. This occurs because the parents wish to protect the child, are uncertain of what to say, or prefer to deny the problem. Many parents do not discuss the illness with the child, spouse, or siblings. The parents may not want neighbors or friends to know about the illness for fear the child will be told the truth, receive misinformation, or be pitied. Some families view the illness as a threat to their social status.

The involved child is often unable to discuss her illness with her parents because she senses it is a "taboo" subject. She also perceives the parents' anxieties, but instead of receiving their help and support she must cope with her fears alone. Her fears are then magnified; her feelings of trust and security in her parents are decreased and her self-esteem is diminished.

Disruption in communication also occurs between the parents. The mother is usually the caretaker of the child with the father having less involvement. If the mother tries to continue all of her other chores, in addition to caring for the child, she may become physically exhausted with repressed feelings of anger toward the father and child. There may be a lack of consistent discipline and affection and of family activities. Children express disappointment in the loss of peer relationships because parents are "always at the hospital" or too busy to have friends visit.

Siblings frequently express jealousy toward the ill child, are envious of the parents' time devoted to caring for him, are jealous of the lenient and inconsistent discipline toward him, and resent the ill child's ability to dominate and manipulate the family for secondary gain. Children may have difficulty relinquishing their play time to care for the child. Some children feel tension in school because of their sibling's appearance or absences.[32]

Siblings can adapt positively to the chronically ill child. A sense of responsibility, independence, and appreciation of one's own attributes are developed. They gain a sense of compassion, understanding, and respect for the ill sibling. They take pride in contributing to the family's unity.[33] Grandparents, who occasionally reject the child, are too often excluded from family decisions and plans made about the ill child. When grandparents are included in information-giving sessions and major decisions about the child, they can be a major source of support for the child and family. They can rally support from the extended family during times of crisis. Honest, open communication increases family solidarity.

Outside relationships

The families of chronically ill children may become isolated from social contacts.[34] They tend to interact less with neighbors and restrict themselves to people who have children with the same defect. It is extremely difficult to obtain competent baby-sitters for the handicapped child, and those available charge higher prices, adding additional stresses on the family budget. A vacation is also difficult to arrange if the child needs to have special equipment or be near a medical center for specialized care. These problems further increase the family's social isolation.

Each family should be assessed and helped to locate financial assistance. Financial screening is frequently coordinated by the social worker. The cost of medications, special equipment, and surgery can be financially devastating for the average family. The best insurance covers only 80 to 85 percent of the total cost. In some locations Title V (Crippled Children's Program) money is available or the patient may be eligible for Title XIX (Medicaid) benefits.[35]

Nursing management

No family is ever prepared for the multitude of problems caused by the chronically ill child.[36] The family is in crisis: previous solutions no longer solve problems. The family members are reestablishing their roles and are seeking new answers to problems. The period of crisis is *optimal* for the nurse to intervene with the family as a family advocate and coordinator of care.

The psychological effects of chronic illness on the child and family can be more devastating than the physical condition. The overall objectives of nursing care are to promote optimal adjustment of all family members, to maintain family unity, and to ensure that the child's primary needs for love and consistent discipline are met. In order to achieve these goals, the nurse uses the nursing process to continually assess, intervene, and evaluate the family's strengths and weaknesses, coping behaviors, communication patterns, reaction to the disability, level of knowledge, quality of the parent-child relationships, and the child's developmental level and place in the family.[37]

Over half of chronically ill children do not receive ongoing pediatric care. The assignment of one primary nurse to work with the family adds stability to the family's care and builds nurse-family trust. When one nurse coordinates the care, arranges consultations, and answers questions, clear communication is promoted. Many medical centers use medical teams to care for the chronically ill child, enabling the family to draw upon each specialist's expertise. The nurse, as team member, frequently coordinates all aspects of the child's care.

The nurse should be honest, sensitive, compassionate, and understanding, and should support the parents rather than "label" or accuse them. A nurse is occasionally repulsed by a child's disability or the family's reaction. This nurse needs to examine his or her feelings, seek their source, and recognize them. The slightest body or facial movement indicating rejection or displeasure will be conveyed to the parents. Nurse-family trust builds when the family observes the nurse's acceptance of the child.

Supporting the family The nurse uses knowledge of interviewing techniques, critical assessment, and sensitivity to the family to support the parents during the phase of shock and disbelief. The nurse should ensure that parents are informed of the diagnosis in a private room; this enables them to ventilate feelings privately. This is not the time for extensive, detailed explanations. After being told, the parents should be left alone to gather strength. The nurse and doctor should then reenter and answer further questions. The conference should end on a hopeful note, stressing the child's strengths, positive behaviors, and potential for rehabilitation. It is important to emphasize the constantly changing nature of the child's condition, the fact that the diagnosis is only a beginning label, and the child's potential.

During shock and disbelief the nurse encourages the parents to ask questions and supplies answers in simple, everyday language. Parents repeatedly ask the same question and may appear to be testing the nurse. The nurse should avoid becoming annoyed or defensive at the questions but should realize the parents are able to hear only portions of the information. During this stage parents need excellent teaching about the child's care and constant reassurance of their ability to provide that care.

During the phase of denial the nurse should be patiently aware that the parents' denial allows them to gather strength to confront the condition. Avoid detailed explanations; these will be denied by the parents. Instead give simple explanations about the condition.[38] When parents are angry and frustrated, the nurse encourages expression of these feelings and does not criticize parents for revealing intense emotion. Anger is often directed at the nurse, who must then objectively realize the anger is directed at the nearest safe target; it is better for the anger to be directed at the nurse than the child. Increase the parents' sense of power and competency by using the interventions discussed in Chap. 16.[39]

The nurse encourages the parents to ventilate feelings of guilt. If their self-accusations are incorrect, give the parents factual information. Positively reinforce their ability to care for the child. Use the interventions in Chap. 16 to teach them to care for their child (Fig. 21-1). Parents should participate in their child's care whenever possible.[40]

Overprotecting parents need the nurse's help in ventilating suppressed anger and guilt. The nurse motivates the parents to recognize the child's real capabilities. Parents can be helped to scrutinize the child, noting the slightest achievement. The nurse teaches the parent normal growth and development and emphasizes the child's normal behavior and newly acquired achievements. The nurse then helps the parents anticipate new developmental milestones. The nurse first focuses upon parents' strengths and then progresses to examining their overprotective behavior. Nursing interventions for the abused or rejected child are discussed in Chap. 41.

Long-term support Teaching for parents should be related to the parents' greatest need, worded in simple, nontechnical language, and based on the parent's educational level and past knowledge. The assessment of past knowledge prevents duplication. The nurse provides family members

Figure 21-1 By teaching parents how to care for their handicapped child (A), the nurse can influence the successful integration of the child into the family (B).

A

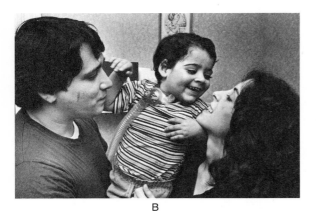

B

with information about physical condition, use of equipment, treatment regimens, prognosis, and time spans. (See teaching interventions in Chap. 16.)

The nurse also functions as an advocate to preserve child-family unity. At times the nurse may have to intervene to prevent the disability, treatment protocols, and health team members from disrupting the family unit.[41] To achieve unity the nurse coordinates treatments, promotes consistent discipline, plans and coordinates parent and patient teaching, and encourages mutually trusting relationships with health team members. Nurses must also advocate parent and patient rights by teaching them to be assertive by having them demand the right to review treatments, learn to speak up if angry at medical personnel, and seek clarification of unclear answers.[42] These assertive techniques will help parents develop trusting relationships with health team members. Assertion will aid parents to feel competent and powerful and to see themselves as partners with the medical and nursing staff in their child's care.

The nurse also guides the parents to anticipate sibling responses to the ill child. Role-playing verbal responses successfully prepares them for reacting to the children's feelings without punishment. The nurse should encourage parents to inform the siblings of the disability before it is heard from friends and to tell them about changes in the child's condition. Siblings, when receiving praise for help, are often glad to accept responsibility for helping to care for the ill child.

Support groups are tremendously beneficial for many parents. These groups, whether composed of friends, relatives, or parents of children with similar conditions, decrease parental feelings of isolation and loneliness. Group members with children having similar illnesses build trust and provide psychological support through discussing solutions to problems and learning positive coping mechanisms. The members may role-play responses to insensitive comments by people or rejection by family members. Accurate information and research results are shared.

The nurse, aided by data from home observations, helps family members communicate and divide caretaking responsibilities to relieve their physical exhaustion and sleep deprivation. For example, the nurse might suggest an alternative to both parents getting up several times each night; one parent could arise for two or three successive nights, allowing the spouse to obtain uninterrupted sleep. Nursing interventions are needed in these areas, for sleep deprivation and physical exhaustion decrease the family's ability to cope.

Parents of multiply handicapped children especially need the nurse's help in prioritizing child-caring problems. These parents are frequently overwhelmed by the child's numerous problems. The nurse can help the parent decide which concern should be treated first to provide the greatest relief.

Chronically ill children are mainstreamed into regular classrooms whenever possible. Special schools are available for educating deaf and blind children and those who have cerebral palsy and mental retardation. Vocational training should begin early and should include development of social skills. Children with cerebral palsy, orthopedic handicaps, or mental retardation especially need early vocational education.[43]

The following Nursing Care Plan is for a child with cystic fibrosis. Chapters 22 and 35 also include care plans for children with chronic disease.

Nursing Care Plan–Cystic Fibrosis *

Patient: Kathy Hanton   **Age:** 12 years old   **Date of Admission:** 1/10 10 A.M.

Assessment

Kathy Hanton, an underdeveloped 12-year-old Caucasian female with long-standing cystic fibrosis (CF), was brought to the CF clinic by her parents at the insistence of her pediatrician. Her mother stated that 3 weeks earlier Kathy had developed a fever and productive cough and had lost her appetite. The physician diagnosed bronchitis and started antibiotic therapy. The condition worsened to a chronic low-grade fever, persistent productive cough, and shortness of breath (SOB) after activity. Kathy lost 5 lb.

History

CF was first diagnosed after meconium ileus, which required surgery 24 h after normal labor and delivery. Kathy is an only child; her parents, fearing a genetic cause for CF, decided against having more children, although there is no family history of CF. Mr. and Mrs. Hanton followed prescribed CF therapy (daily mist tent, aerosol treatment, bronchial drainage twice a day) for 5 years and then discontinued it. Kathy appeared normal; therapy "didn't seem to make any difference." They also stopped visiting the CF clinic for follow-up care.

The father is a lawyer and the mother is a high school teacher. Kathy's CF is a major stress in their marriage. They had not told her she had CF, hoping to protect her from "the stigma of such an awful disease." Her mother would have told her years ago except for the opposition of the father. Both parents say they feel extremely guilty over "giving Kathy this terminal disease." The mother spoke of her concern that Kathy's father would never accept the diagnosis of CF and participate in daily therapy. They also disagree about child rearing and were inconsistent in their approach to Kathy. Mrs. Hanton expressed concern about her daughter's general growth and development, stating Kathy was the smallest girl in her class and frequently was teased about her size.

After history taking and physical exam, the physician recommended that Kathy be hospitalized for acute pulmonary infection and that CF therapy be resumed. Her parents agreed and then told Kathy the diagnosis of CF.

Physical exam

General inspection revealed a thin, anxious, and lethargic girl in moderate respiratory distress.

Vital signs temp.—37.8°C (100°F), pulse—120, respiration—34 and labored

Weight 30.0 kg (5th percentile for age)

Height 146 cm

Color Pale, slight circumoral cyanosis noted with coughing episode, nail beds pink

Chest Mild intercostal retractions with use of accessory muscles with respiration. Shortness of breath noted with activity. Respirations are shallow in depth. Chest expansion is limited on right side. Slight barrel chest configuration noted. Auscultation—crackles noted on both inspiration and expiration in right middle lobe and right lower lobe, expiration is decreased in all lobes, and expiratory wheeze noted in entire right lung

Cough Frequent, loose cough productive of moderate amounts of thick, green sputum. No hemoptysis noted

Extremities Thin with poor muscle mass. No edema noted. 1+ clubbing present

I & O Significant decrease in intake for past 3 weeks with diet consisting mainly of fluids, soup, and bland foods. Usual intake is above average for age; diet consists of three main meals with frequent between-meal snacks

Output Approximately six loose, oily, foul-smelling stools per day

Physician's orders

The attending physician ordered Kathy admitted to the hospital with the diagnosis of cystic fibrosis. The following regimen was ordered:

1. Mist tent at night
2. Aerosol treatment q6h followed by percussion and postural drainage (P & PD) to all lobes; aerosol solution consisting of 3 ml Mucomyst, 6 gtt Isuprel, 20 ml sterile water
3. Diet—high calorie, high protein with frequent between-meal snacks
4. VS—q3h

5. Medications—IV D$_5$W with ⅓ NS at 50 ml/h; IV antibiotics—100 mg tobramycin q6h, 3 g ticarcillin q6h, vitamins A and E every day, vitamin K every week, Pancrease, 2 caps with every meal, 1 cap with snack
6. Daily weights, I & O, calorie counts
7. Chest x-ray, sputum culture, heme work-up, pulmonary function test every week

Patient behavior

During Kathy's hospitalization intense education was begun regarding the disease process and treatment of CF for Kathy and her parents. Kathy had difficulty accepting her disease and need for therapy. She avoided learning about the disease, refused to listen to doctors and nurses when they attempted to teach her about CF, refused medications, and was a major behavior problem during chest physical therapy treatments. (She would kick, scream, and bite the therapist.)

Kathy also displayed socialization problems. She talked incessantly and constantly ran through the ward bumping into people, knocking equipment over, and disrupting other patients' care. Her roommates found her behavior intolerable and refused to continue sharing a room with her.

Finally, after 3 days of this behavior, a care conference was held during which a care plan was developed.

Nursing diagnosis	Goals	Nursing actions	Evaluation/revision
1. Impaired gas exchange secondary to pulmonary infection, increased mucus production, and bronchial obstruction	☐ Effective gas exchange ☐ Decrease in pulmonary infection ☐ Decreased mucus production ☐ Decreased bronchial obstruction evidenced by: **a.** Normal temperature **b.** Normal respiratory rate and pattern **c.** Decreased cough **d.** Decreased sputum production **e.** Increased activity level **f.** Resolution of SOB with activity **g.** Increased appetite **h.** Breath sounds clear on auscultation	☐ Obtain sputum culture, send to lab, and repeat every week ☐ VS q3h, observe quality of respirations ☐ Administer medications as ordered ☐ Pulmonary function test every Friday ☐ Mist tent at night ☐ Aerosol therapy q6h (8-2-8-2) ☐ Percussion and postural drainage to all lobes after aerosol therapy ☐ Patient to cough following each position of P & PD ☐ Teach patient appropriate breathing exercises; supervise breathing exercises tid ☐ Consult to physical therapy to begin an exercise program	☐ 1/10: T = 38.4C (101°F), RR = 34, using accessory muscles with respiration, moderate intercostal retractions. Crackles heard in RML & RLL, wheeze on expiration in RML. Frequent loose productive cough; sputum thick green; lethargic ☐ 1/11: Uncooperative with chest physical therapy, coughs effectively, taught breathing exercises. ☐ 1/12: T = 37.9°C (100°F), RR = 30, continues to use accessory muscles, slight intercostal retractions. Remains SOB with activity. Evaluated by Physical Therapy and begun on exercise program. Cough unchanged ☐ 1/14: Remains uncooperative with chest physical therapy. Does breathing exercises well, enjoys Physical Therapy (PT) ☐ 1/18: T = 37.4°C (99°F), RR = 22, no respiratory distress noted. No SOB with activity. Cough less frequent, productive of small–moderate amounts of yellow-green sputum, which is less thick. Crackles heard in RML, occasional expiratory wheeze in RML, other lobes clear. Pulmonary functions improved 8%,

Nursing diagnosis	Nursing goals	Nursing actions	Evaluation/revision
			more cooperative with chest physical therapy □ 1/24: T = 37°C (98°F), RR = 18, no respiratory distress noted. Activity level normal and well tolerated, occasional loose cough, productive of scant amounts of thin yellow-white sputum. Pulmonary functions improved 10%. Cooperative with exercise program and breathing exercises. Usually cooperative with P & PD
2. Delayed growth and development due to inadequate caloric intake and malabsorption	□ Maintain adequate caloric intake for weight gain □ Achieve proper digestion and absorption of nutrients	□ Consult to dietitian for patient-parent education regarding high-calorie, high-protein diet □ High-calorie, high-protein diet; offer between meal snacks □ Pancreatic digestive enzymes with each meal and snacks □ Nutritional supplements if needed for adequate caloric intake □ Daily calorie counts □ Daily weights □ Record I & O □ Monitor stool output; note amounts, consistency and characteristics of stool. Notify doctor if inappropriate so digestive enzyme supplements can be adjusted □ Effectively schedule mealtime and chest physical therapy □ Insure adequate intake of salt □ Administer water-soluble vitamins as ordered	□ 1/10: Appetite poor, picks at food. Refused breakfast and lunch. Emesis two times with coughing episode. Stool output: 6 loose, bulky, greasy stools. Dr. notified and Pancrease increased to three capsules with each meal □ 1/12: Daily caloric intake remains poor, weight down 1 lb. Appetite unchanged. Emesis x1 with coughing episode. Stool output: 4 soft, bulky, nongreasy stools. Dietitian in to talk with mother and Kathy □ 1/14: Daily caloric intake remains inadequate. Weight down 2 lb. No longer vomiting. Begun on Ensure plus malts (nutritional supplement) for caloric intake; offer midmorning, midafternoon, and before bed □ 1/16: Daily caloric intake improving, appetite improved. Taking malts well. Stool output: 2 formed, semigreasy stools □ 1/18: Caloric intake appropriate. Appetite much improved. □ 1/20: Appetite good, caloric intake excellent, weight up 0.5 kg □ 1/24: Caloric intake remains appropriate for weight gain. Weight up an additional 0.5 kg. Stool output appropriate (×2 nongreasy, formed)
3. Poor patient and parent comprehension of CF disease process and rationale	□ Parents and patient will understand the disease process of CF and related	□ Teach parents and patient pathophysiology of CF and complications of dis-	□ 1/11: Teaching begun with parents on disease process of CF and related

Nursing diagnosis	Nursing goals	Nursing actions	Evaluation/revision
for prescribed therapy associated with inability to accept diagnosis of CF and chronicity	complications ☐ Parents and patient will understand rationale for prescribed therapy ☐ Parents will be able to perform prescribed home therapy adequately	ease process ☐ Teach parents and patient rationale for prescribed therapy and need for consistent, ongoing home care ☐ Teach parents: **a.** How to perform chest physical therapy **b.** Care and operation of home equipment **c.** Administration of medications **d.** Proper diet ☐ Teach patient to assist in own care: **a.** Diet selection **b.** Use of pancreatic digestive enzymes **c.** How to cooperate with cares ☐ Reinforce teaching as needed	complications. See teaching flow sheet for documentation of all teaching done. ☐ 1/11: Teaching attempted with Kathy. She avoids hearing about CF. ☐ 1/13: Continued parent teaching, covered rationale for therapy. Comprehension appears good. ☐ 1/14: Arranged with RT to begin parent instruction on chest physical therapy. ☐ 1/14: Spent time with Kathy allowing her to vent her fears about CF. She states, "What I don't know won't hurt me!" Used approach that Kathy must learn how to keep herself healthy and well. Contracted with her to select topic for teaching each day. ☐ 1/15: Taught Kathy her medications today (her selection). She is to be responsible for taking her own pancreatic digestive enzymes with meals and snacks. ☐ 1/16: Parents taught care and operation of home equipment. Reviewed previous teaching done regarding disease process, complications and rationale for therapy. Comprehension is excellent. ☐ 1/17: Kathy taught about CF and its effect on her body (her selection). Initially she was somewhat hesitant to listen; eventually she was very interested and asking questions. ☐ 1/19: Parents able to demonstrate chest physical therapy and care and operation of home equipment. Also able to explain rationale for prescribed care (including medications and proper diet).
4. Inappropriate behavior of patient and parents secondary to inability to cope with diagnosis of CF	☐ Parents and patient will eventually accept diagnosis of CF and optimally adjust to life-style changes. ☐ Patient will cooperate with prescribed therapy. ☐ Patient will demonstrate age-appropriate behavior.	☐ Consult to child psychologist for individual and family counseling ☐ Involve patient in CF child support group ☐ Arrange for parent contact with other parents of CF children	☐ 1/11: Consult sent to child psychologist. Appointment scheduled with family for 10:00 A.M. ☐ 1/11: Call made to Mrs. Karey (CF parent). She will meet with parents tomorrow afternoon.

Nursing diagnosis	Nursing goals	Nursing actions	Evaluation/revision
	☐ Parents will resolve guilt feelings regarding CF.	☐ Encourage parents to become involved in parent support group at local CF foundation chapter ☐ Encourage patient and parents to verbalize feelings regarding CF ☐ Follow through with developed behavior modification chart and reward system, which will reinforce appropriate patient behavior (chart is in patient's room) ☐ Encourage parent participation in above plan and encourage consistency from parents ☐ Praise patient when behavior is appropriate and she is cooperative with care. Utilize reward system ☐ Be consistent and firm with patient at all times ☐ Allow patient some control by involving her in care (see nursing diagnosis no. 3 and action no. 4) and in decision making when appropriate	☐ 1/12: Discussed behavior modification plan with parents. They are agreeable to this and will cooperate and work on consistency ☐ 1/12: Parents met with Mrs. Karey. Discussed life with CF, common parental feelings and how to work them through. She will accompany parents to next CF parent support group. Parents beginning to verbalize their feelings regarding CF ☐ 1/14: Kathy interested in behavior modification plan. Earned three reward points for taking medications well and cooperating with morning chest physical therapy ☐ 1/16: Kathy continues to show interest in behavior modification plan. Earning daily reward points for cooperating with care and demonstrating appropriate behavior ☐ 1/17: Parents and Kathy have separately met with child psychologist on two different occasions. Child psychologist feels family is beginning to work through denial of CF. Will continue with counseling 1/18: Kathy's behavior more age-appropriate. Continues to earn reward points. Taking meds. well and handling responsibility of diet selection and pancreatic digestive enzymes 1/20: Kathy attended CF child support group. Verbalized anger at parents for giving her CF and fear of rejection from peers ☐ 1/23: Kathy remains motivated to cooperate with care and act appropriately through behavior modification plan. Has earned enough reward points for an evening pass—to go out with parents for pizza ☐ 1/25: Family continues to receive counseling. Feel they are adjusting to CF. Will continue counseling sessions following discharge

Nursing diagnosis	Nursing goals	Nursing actions	Evaluation/revision
5. Ineffective delivery of prescribed home therapy associated with denial of CF	□ Parents will follow through in providing prescribed home therapy to patient □ Patient will be cooperative for parents when providing prescribed home therapy	□ Assess parents ability to coordinate prescribed home therapy with life-style. □ Assist parents in problem-solving life style changes that may be needed to provide home therapy □ Assess parents ability to adequately perform: **a.** Chest physical therapy **b.** Administration of medications **c.** Care and operation of home equipment □ Encourage both parents to share the responsibility of providing home therapy. □ Encourage parents to communicate to each other any difficulties they encounter in providing home therapy. □ Refer family to public health nursing for: family support, to reinforce teaching done during hospitalization, to assess parents ability to perform and follow through with home care, and to evaluate status of home equipment □ Contact school nurse to describe home therapy program and to coordinate patient's care with school activities □ Before Kathy's discharge, primary nurse and primary clinic nurse attend conference on 1/25 with parents, physician, child psychologist, public health nurse, and school nurse. Decided: Kathy will continue weekly counseling with psychologist; public health nurse will provide support and reinforce teaching during home visits. PH nurse and school nurse will report family's progress to primary clinic nurse, who will coordinate outpatient health care	□ 1/17: Parents have agreed to share home therapy in following manner: Father will perform morning cares (his work allows more flexibility) and mother will perform evening care □ 1/19: Parents feel patient's daily care can be incorporated into their present life-style. Expressed concern about vacations; given community resources to utilize in providing home care in their absence □ 1/20: Parents able to adequately perform chest physical therapy following RT instruction and supervision. Are scheduled to perform total patient care for 2 days prior to discharge □ 1/22: Discussed parents' use of behavior modification plan used in hospital at home to encourage patient's cooperation with care. They are agreeable to this □ 1/23: Referral sent to public health nurse. She or he will contact family at discharge. Public health nurse to communicate with CF clinic primary nurse □ 1/23: Contacted school nurse and communicated patient's home therapy program. She will coordinate patient's therapy with school activities □ 1/25: Parents have adequately performed total patient care for past 2 days and feel comfortable in doing so. Patient cooperative for parents with care

* By Mary Jo McCracken, B.S.N., Pediatric Pulmonary Nurse Specialist.

References

1. Constance U. Battle, "Disruptions in the Socialization of a Young, Severely Handicapped Child," in Robert P. Marinelli and Arthur E. Dell Orto (eds.), *The Psychological and Social Aspects of Physical Disability*, Springer, New York, 1977, p. 51.
2. I. B. Pless and K. J. Roghmann, "Chronic Illness and Its Consequences: Observations Based on Three Epidemiological Surveys," *Journal of Pediatrics* **79**: 351–359 (1971).
3. Ake Mattson, "Long-Term Physical Illness in Childhood: A Challenge to Psychosocial Adaptation," *Pediatrics* **50**: 801–809 (November 1972).
4. Battle, op. cit., p. 52.
5. Cheryl Foster, "Chronic Illness and Handicapping Conditions: Coping Patterns of the Child and the Family," in P. Brandt, P. Chinn, et al. (eds.), *Current Practices in Pediatric Practice*, vol. 2, Mosby, St. Louis, 1978, p. 63.
6. J. Vipperman and P. Rager, "Childhood Coping: How Nurses Can Help," *Pediatric Nursing* **6**(2):11–18 (March–April 1980).
7. Paul D. Steinhauer, et al., "Psychological Aspects of Chronic Illness," *Pediatric Clinics of North America* **21**(4):830–831 (November 1974).
8. Battle, op. cit., p. 53.
9. Ibid., p. 61.
10. Frances P. Connor, "Education for the Handicapped Child," in John A. Downey and Niels L. Low, *The Child with Disabling Illness: Principles of Rehabilitation*, Saunders, Philadelphia, 1974, p. 580.
11. William A. Schonfeld, "The Body and the Body Image in Adolescents," in Gerald Caplan and Lebovici (eds.), *Adolescence: Psychosocial Perspectives*, Basic Books, New York, 1969, p. 44.
12. Patricia S. Yaros and Jeanne Howe, "Responses to Illness and Disability," in Jeanne Howe, *Nursing Care of Adolescents*, McGraw-Hill, New York, 1980, p. 94.
13. Ibid., p. 103.
14. Florence G. Blake, "Immobilized Youth: A Rationale for Supportive Nursing Intervention," *American Journal of Nursing* **69**(11):2366 (November 1969).
15. Mavis McGuire, et al., "Hospitalized Children in Confinement," *Pediatric Nursing* **4**(6):31 (November–December 1976).
16. Lynn Czarniecki, "Developmental Nursing Care: Infant Stimulation for High Risk Children," *Pediatric Nursing* **4**(5):33–38 (September–October 1978).
17. Nancy V. Schultz, "How Children Perceive Pain," *Nursing Outlook* **19**(10):672–673 (October 1971).
18. D. R. Haslam, "Age and the Perception of Pain," *Psychonomic Science* **15**:18(1969).
19. Margo McCaffery, *Nursing Management of the Patient with Pain*, 2d ed., Lippincott, Philadelphia, 1979, pp. 35–42.
20. Richard A. Geist, "Onset of Chronic Illness in Children and Adolescents: Psychotherapeutic and Consultative Interventions," *American Journal of Orthopsychiatry* **49**(1):4 (January 1979).
21. Ibid., p. 8.
22. Lindy Burton, *The Family Life of Sick Children: A Study of Families Coping with Chronic Childhood Disease*, Routledge and Legau, Boston, 1975, p. 35.
23. Pauline Cohen, "The Impact of the Handicapped Child on the Family," *Social Casework* **43**(3):137–142 (March 1962).
24. Beverly Lawson, "Chronic Illness in the School-aged Child: Effects on the Total Family," *American Journal of Maternal-Child Nursing* **2**:49–56 (January-February 1977).
25. Alan Tropauer et al., "Psychological Aspects of the Care of Children with Cystic Fibrosis," *American Journal of Diseases of Children* **119**:428 (May 1970).
26. Foster, op. cit., p. 58.
27. E. L. Cava, et al., *A Pediatrician's Guide to Child Behavior Problems*, Masson, New York, 1979, pp. 80–81.
28. M. Solnit and A. Green, "Reactions to the Threatened Loss of a Child: A Vulnerable Child Syndrome: Pediatric Management of the Dying Child, Part III" in J. Schwartz and L. Schwartz, *Vulnerable Infants: A Psychosocial Dilemma*, McGraw-Hill, New York, 1977, pp. 183–189.
29. Simon Olshansky, "Chronic Sorrow: Parental Responses to a Mentally Defective Child," *Mental Retardation* **4**:21–23 (August 1966).
30. Lawson, loc. cit.
31. E. James Anthony, "The Impact of Mental and Physical Illness on Family Life," *American Journal of Psychiatry* **127**(2):60 (August 1970).
32. J. Penny Iles, "Children with Cancer: Healthy Siblings' Perceptions during the Illness Experience," *Cancer Nursing*, October 1979, pp. 374–375.
33. Ibid., p. 375.
34. Anthony, op. cit., p. 61.
35. Robert S. Stone, "Administration of Hospitals for the Long Term Sick Child," in J. Downey and Niels Low, *The Child with a Disabling Illness: Principles of Rehabilitation*, Saunders, Philadelphia, 1974, p. 566.
36. Lawson, op cit., p. 49.
37. Lawson, op. cit., p. 51.
38. Ruth K. Young, "Chronic Sorrow: Parents' Response to the Birth of a Child with a Defect," *American Journal of Maternal-Child Nursing* **2**(1):38–42 (January–February, 1977).
39. Ibid., p. 40.
40. Ibid., p. 41.
41. Lucille F. Whaley and Donna Wong, *Nursing Care of Infants and Children*, Mosby, St. Louis, 1979, p. 791.
42. Ibid., pp. 799–800.
43. Usdane, William M., "Vocational Planning for the Handicapped Child," in Downey, J., and Niels Low, *The Child with a Disabling Illness: Principles of Rehabilitation*, Saunders, Philadelphia, 1974, p. 571.

Chapter 22 **The terminally ill child**

Marlene Singer Garvis, D. Gay Moldow, and **Ida M. Martinson**

Upon completion of this chapter, the student will be able to:

1. Describe two characteristics of the child's concept of death at each developmental level.

2. Identify one coping response of a terminally ill child in each age group.

3. Identify two characteristics of the terminally ill child's awareness of dying.

4. Compare responses of the parents to (a) diagnosis, (b) remission, and (c) the terminal phase.

5. Discuss the effects a child's terminal illness may have upon the parents' husband-wife relationship.

6. Identify at least two responses of the siblings of a terminally ill child.

7. List at least three factors that influence a child's adjustment to the loss of a sibling.

8. Identify at least two features of the mourning process.

9. Describe at least two feelings that may surface in the nurse caring for the terminally ill child.

10. Describe three resources that provide the nurse support and skill in caring for the terminally ill child.

11. List four examples that describe comfort care.

12. List at least two reasons why parents should be involved in the planning and providing of care to the terminally ill child.

13. List four areas of assessment when dealing with the family of a terminally ill child.

14. List four symptoms of impending death.

15. Describe the fear-pain-anxiety cycle and state how the nurse should intervene.

16. Describe the roles of the parents, nurse, and physician in home care for the dying child.

The use of the word *terminal* is often confusing. It is sometimes synonymous with fatal illness, but there are differences. While a child who is terminal usually has a fatal illness, a child with a fatal illness is not always terminal. For the purposes of this chapter the terminally ill child is defined as a child who has an illness from which he will soon die. There are many phases to living with a fatal illness; for example, diagnosis, remission, relapse, and even cure. The terminal phase brings the reality of death; hopes for cure or long remissions are no longer maintained. This phase can be quite short or may take weeks or even months.

Today, most childhood deaths result from accidents; however, cancer is the predominant illness that kills children between the ages of 3 and 14 years.[1] The focus of this chapter will be on the child with cancer, but the principles and concepts discussed apply to all children with terminal illnesses.

Children's experiences with death

Scientific and medical advances have significantly reduced infant mortality as well as extended the average life span. With the use of modern equipment and advanced technology, many diseases that were once devastating killers are now controlled or eradicated. At present, palliative treatment is used to prolong survival while awaiting a new therapy or cure. So, death occurs less often in early life and is increasingly an experience of the aged.

523

Death usually takes place in a hospital that is still likely to forbid the presence of young children. In their efforts to protect, parents compound their children's limited opportunity to understand death. Most children do not have a chance to see a person get sick, gradually grow worse, and die. Therefore, when death does occur, it is usually a new experience for the child. In his mind the person disappears into nowhere. Parents confuse children by providing misleading answers to their questions, such as "Grandpa is permanently asleep," or answers which are difficult to grasp, such as "Grandpa has gone to heaven."[2] In speaking of those who have died, people usually try to avoid the word *death* and say the person has "departed" or "passed away."

The child's concept of death

Age, education, and experiences with death among family members, friends, and relatives influence the child's ideas about death. A child's culture and religious beliefs also affect his responses to death. For most children, death seems very far away and in the remote future. The child's reaction to his own dying depends on his level of understanding and emotional maturity, how the disease process affects his self-concept, and the manner in which those around the child react. The child's awareness of the meaning of personal death changes according to the stages of childhood development.

The child under 3 years

During the first 2 years children have no understanding of death.[3] Young children live in the present and have little understanding of time. Personal dying has meaning to children under 3 only as it affects the people around them. A very young dying child may feel sad and upset because family members are sad and upset, but the child is not really mourning because he does not realize the significance of death. Young children do not worry that their existence may come to an end. But the child reacts to the anguish and sadness of the parents and may become depressed.[4]

When a child under 3 is hospitalized, the staff must understand that the parents can help the child cope with unfamiliar people, painful experiences, and unpredictable situations. They can support the child during treatments and assist the child in cooperating during necessary procedures. The decreased anxiety which often results from parent participation is beneficial to both the parents and the child.

The preschooler

During the preschool years, the growing child comes to understand the meaning of "myself" and "I," and while he is appreciating that he is a "me," he is sensing that one can become "not me." Over the preschool period the child gradually develops the concept of nonexistence. It has been observed that "while the very young preschooler could readily crush an ant or destroy a flower, this same child a few years later may become very protective of living creatures"[5]—an indication that the child understands the significance of life and "not life."

The preschooler believes that his existence is not limited by time. He understands that death is a departure; he believes it is gradual and temporary, but it is not a regular and final process. The child understands that one's condition can change periodically. Somewhat in the same way as one sleeps and wakes, so one "is made dead" and can return to ordinary life. The child believes that after death breathing, eating, and living are still possible, although perhaps in a style more restricted than when alive. For example, the dead person's eyes are closed to keep dirt out, and the dead do not move because the coffin restricts their mobility. He often concludes that anyone who goes away is dead.[6-8]

The older preschooler is prone to misinterpret superficial signals as being intrinsically involved with death. For example, he believes that if someone died in a hospital, then one must stay away from hospitals. As the child becomes increasingly aware that death is something that is both important and disruptive, he seeks to isolate the phenomena which cause or mean death.

When the preschool child is threatened by a fatal illness, nightmares may increase. Games may become more violent and he may act out accidents, disasters, or even funeral rituals complete with coffins. In his play, figures die but come back to life. This type of play permits the child to reemphasize that his newly achieved independence will not come to an end. The dying preschooler may ask: What will I look like when I die? Will I be able to breathe and have anyone to talk with? Will my death be painful? Have I been bad? Maybe my parents do not want me—is that why I am dying?[9]

The dying preschool child seeks comfort, reassurance, and support from parents. They are the child's main protectors. The young child fears separation, pain, and bodily harm, but not death. Time has no meaning to the child except as it pertains to his needs. For example, his mother's absence during lunch may seem an eternity, while time seems to fly when the child is absorbed in a play activity. For the child of this age, the emotional pain of parental separation may be far greater than any physical pain he has to endure. He often thinks that the painful experiences and his misery are a direct result of his misdeeds or bad thoughts. The child needs reassurances that good and bad private thoughts do not make things happen, that no one wants him to be sick and in pain, and that his parents do not want to be separated from him.

The child's anxieties may be evidenced by the child's regressing and becoming more dependent on parents. Or the child may maintain independence and yet deal with private feelings by withdrawing into a daydream world of fantasy, wish fulfillment, and happy endings. While regression and withdrawal do occur, they are less than desirable. Reassurance and support from staff and parents can encourage the child to express his concerns and maintain his achieved independence.

The preschool child should be approached on the basis of day-to-day reality. Questions should be answered when the child asks them. When the end stage occurs, the child should be assured that he will not die alone but will be supported by his parents. The child's anxieties and concerns need to be heard.

The school-age child

It has been found that children who are between 5 and 9 tend to personify death.[10] That is, they commonly think of "Death" as a person, either living or dead and with either good or bad intentions, who causes people to die. At the same time, school age children view death as removed from their lives. The child may say, "Only those die whom the deathman catches and carries off. Whoever can get away does not die."[11]

Piaget[12] observed that up to 6 or 7 years of age, children equate life with general activity. That is, anything active is viewed as being "alive." At ages 7 or 8 the child begins to discriminate between things which are alive and those which are not. At first, he believes all things which move, such as bicycles, are alive. Later, he attributes life only to things which move spontaneously and he realizes that bicycles are not alive. Finally, he learns that only humans, animals, and plants are alive.

The 6-year-old may worry about his own death and that of his parents, but unless he has had experiences with death, he usually relates death to old age. The 7-year-old realizes that he will die sometime. He is interested in the ceremonies which surround death, that is, the coffin, funeral, burial, and cemetery. The 8-year-old explores the cause of death and what happens after death.[13]

The older school-age child, 10 to 12 years, understands that death is the cessation of bodily life. For example, he may explain that "It means the passing of the body,"[14] or that death is something that no one can escape. "Everyone has to die once, but the soul lives on."[15] Evidence suggests that by age 10 most children formulate a close approximation of what is labeled as the adult view of life and death. This gives the preadolescent a framework within which the idea of death can be placed: Death is one general principle among many other general principles. He sees the world as a more comprehensible and predictable place.

As he grows, the grade-school child understands more and more that he may live and grow or he may die and disappear. He begins to fantasize an alternative to death—Heaven, Paradise, or even Hell. Even if this present existence is changed in some way, possibly by death, he believes that there will still continue to be a "me." Even hell is considered better than not existing at all. Heaven, of course, is by far the best solution.

The dying school-age child can understand the significance of a diagnosis and prognosis. Some children deduce their diagnosis on their own before they are even admitted or referred to a medical center. The child may feel his illness is a punishment for something he said or did, since he still believes that every act has a punishment or reward. The child has great difficulty with his feelings and tends to rely on authorities such as God, doctors, nurses, parents, or teachers for final protection. He knows he will die but also believes he will still be secure and protected. The school-age child mourns the loss of life. He worries about how his existence will end, and time begins to have meaning. Because he regards the prognosis more as a certainty than a statement of possibility, the child is usually eager to talk about and explore the meaning of death.

The school-age child needs his parents for support and security and for explanations of what is happening. It is important to help the child maintain independence and control whenever possible. Separation from the family should be kept to a minimum because it makes the child feel lonely, angry, and frustrated as well as depressed. When death is near and inevitable, the child's questions should be answered truthfully. The school-age child has the emotional ability to face the prospect of death and to reach out to parents, family, and friends for comfort and understanding. Support by those persons he trusts helps the child through this final experience.

The adolescent

Adolescents think of death as both fearsome and fascinating. Studies indicate that they do not want to die without having the opportunity of life's fulfillments. Some turn to religion as an insurance against the risk of death. The majority repress and deny their anxiety.[16]

The adolescent lives in an intense present. "Now" is so real to him that both past and future seem pallid by comparison. Everything that is important and valuable lies either in the immediate life situation or in the rather close future. Off in the distance stands death, the natural enemy to the developing self.

During adolescence, being accepted by others of one's own age is a high priority. Physical condition (strength, appearance, and ability to perform) has enormous influence on both peer acceptance and self-esteem. The terminally ill adolescent may express more concern over the physical changes in his body, such as weight gain or hair loss, than over the course of the disease process itself.

The emotional growth and increasing independence of adolescence bring feelings of guilt. The terminally ill teenager may believe death is a punishment for his assertive or "grown up" behavior. He may feel fearful and at the same time be unable to seek comfort from parents, God, or society.

Friends may withdraw, emotionally if not altogether, when they are faced with the impending death of a peer. The resulting isolation emphasizes the adolescent's basic vulnerability and makes him extremely uncomfortable. Illness also forces the peer-oriented adolescent to become increasingly dependent on his parents. The adolescent treasures his independence and struggles to maintain it against the total passivity of death. In his efforts to feel strong and powerful, he may well overtax his strength. While he longs for understanding, his fear of losing his independence may produce behavior which forces people away. The dying adolescent's responses to his fate include anger and bitterness.

Health team members should understand that emotional outbursts may well be a sign of the adolescent's anger at dying. The adolescent may need physical activity outlets as well as visible evidence of love and support. Signs of attention from those he cares for, such as visits, flowers, and letters, while difficult for the adolescent to accept, help him understand he is not really alone. These tokens make his loneliness more bearable and at times his bitterness less acute. Providing ways to support the adolescent's self-confidence, independence, and sense of control will help him accept the comfort and support of staff and parents as he faces death. A terminally ill adolescent should be given information about his diagnosis, prognosis, and the purpose and nature of treatments and procedures. The questions he asks will usually indicate how much information he can tolerate. The adolescent should be encouraged to talk and ask questions about his illness. He should be assured his dying is not a punishment. Like younger children, the adolescent should be told that he is loved and accepted and that he will not die alone.

Awareness of dying

One of the tasks of the staff and parents of a terminally ill child is communicating with the child about his illness and about death. While developmental level is an important factor in approaching the child, the adult's understanding, ability, and willingness to communicate also determine how and when the child is approached. Parents and staff may wish to protect a child, stating "She really doesn't know how ill she is—why should I upset her?" This assessment is hardly accurate, however. The terminally ill child does appear to be aware of being seriously ill, whether or not his parents or the health team staff have actually discussed this with him.

Early studies focused on anxiety as a sign of awareness of dying. In one study of leukemic children, it was observed that children tended to handle anxiety in one of three ways: younger children expressed the anxiety symbolically and physiologically; older boys tended to act out; older girls tended to become depressed. Death anxiety was most often present in older children.[17] In another study it was found that the primary source of anxiety in dying children differed by age group. For children age 10 years and older, fear of death and distress over the death of other children in the hospital were the most upsetting factors. Children age 5 to 10 years found traumatic procedures, such as venipunctures, the most distressing. Those up to 5 years found separation from their mother the greatest cause of distress.[18] A third study of children with a fatal illness reported that anxiety varied with prognosis. A study of four groups of children 6 to 10 years of age found that the poor prognosis group showed more anxiety and more threat to body integrity than did the comparison groups. Children in the poor prognosis group included loneliness, separation, and death content in their stories even when they had not talked about death with hospital staff or even if their parents believed their child did not know the prognosis.

Death anxiety, while present, was not expressed overtly.[19]

Recent evidence suggests that the speed and completeness with which children develop awareness about their terminal illness may be unrelated to age and intellectual ability. It has been reported that 3- to 9-year-old children with cancer acquire awareness about their illness in similar stages (see Table 22-1). Progress from one stage to another was dependent on (1) acquisition of additional factual information and (2) personal disease-related experiences. Changes in self-concept were also observed as the children developed awareness about their illness (see Table 22-1). Awareness occurred whether or not the children had been told about their disease and prognosis.[20]

Adults should be honest and supportive in their approach to the dying child. This helps establish a basis of trust and promote the child's coping with future events. The child is then able to ask as many or as few questions as he can emotionally handle. Evasive answers are not likely to shield the child from the reality of his illness since there are so many other cues that something serious is happening. In the end the child will be more comfortable and secure. While the child may usually rely on his own resources, "... he attempts also to enlist the support of others (including peers, parents, staff ...). The child is not always asking nor always talking about dying, even when he knows the prognosis. Much of his time is spent in becoming aware, putting together, and probing for more infor-

Table 22-1 A child's growing awareness of dying

Stages of awareness
  I. The disease is a serious illness
 II. Names of drugs and side effects
III. Purposes of the treatments and procedures
IV. The disease is a series of remissions and relapses
 V. The disease is a series of remissions and relapses which ultimately ends in death

Changing self-concept
1. I am seriously ill
2. I am seriously ill and will get better
3. I am always ill and will get better
4. I am always ill and will never get better
5. I am dying

From Myra Bluebond-Langner, *The Private Worlds of Dying Children*, Princeton, Princeton, N.J., 1978.

mation. A child who is terminally ill may only express himself in symbolic, not easily understood ways. One only has to listen to him, however, to realize that the child does know the truth of his illness. . . ."[21]

The family and the dying child

Impact on the parents

Parents usually experience the need to care for and protect their children. Having a child who has a terminal illness threatens the fulfillment of this need and may even be perceived by parents as an attack on their integrity and well-being.

Diagnosis The crisis of the diagnosis is the event which may have the greatest impact on the family.[22] According to Gyulay, "Diagnosis marks the juncture of two radically different life styles: the one before diagnosis, which was normal, and the one after, in which the future is unknown and at the mercy of the child's illness."[23]

With the diagnosis parents usually become depressed and may feel worthless. Some parents blame themselves for the child's condition and critically review their attitudes and behavior toward him. Most parents in our society have been reared to believe that conformity and good behavior will be rewarded; when their child is diagnosed as having a terminal illness, parents may feel singled out and punished.

Nurses and other health team members can help parents by being open and honest in their communication. Also, an important factor in parents' ability to trust health care professionals is their perception of a willingness on the part of these individuals to listen and to be open. Such interaction can help relieve anxiety and guilt, enable parents to participate in the care of their children, and give parents "confidence in their ability to master subsequent developments."[24] It is equally important that staff members support the decisions parents make and maintain a hopeful outlook without giving unwarranted reassurances or promising too much.

While they may not always voice them, parents do have some general concerns that must be anticipated:[25]

1. Of what long-term significance is the fact that the diagnosis was not made earlier?
2. Does previous illness or lack thereof make any differences in the success of the child's treatment?
3. Will my child be able to go to school or continue normal activity?
4. What do I tell my children, friends, and distant relatives?
5. What should I tell the child?
6. How long will the child be in the hospital?
7. Will my child be in much pain? How and when will he die?
8. What are my child's chances for remission? When might remission begin? How long will it last?

The initial hospitalization involves induction therapy and repeated procedures for the child. Parents may be interviewed by a variety of professionals, such as the social worker, psychologist, pediatric specialists, and many nurses. They may become frustrated by the intrusion in their lives of all these people. They may experience such distressing symptoms as depression, nervousness, sleep difficulties, and loss of appetite.[26] Continuity of nursing care helps the parents gain support and perspective at this time. Discharge from the hospital often comes before remission. While parents are relieved to go home, they have several questions: Who will help us? Who will answer our questions? Who will relieve us when we are exhausted?

Remission Remission is a time when life becomes more normal again and the family begins to build a new life. During this period of "normalcy" parents may deny the illness or vacillate between accepting the diagnosis and hoping that a mistake was made.[27] There are also strong fears about the return of the disease. Parents often hope that by suppressing their thoughts of the disease, it, too, can be suppressed. Even while things outwardly begin to return to normal, parents may become preoccupied with possible future developments. Any change in medical or nursing procedure or routine causes alarm. The periodic trips to the hospital or clinic can accentuate fears and anxiety. Staff members can provide support by assuring parents that other families experience the same concerns.[28]

Between clinic visits life is relatively normal; there is hope that the remission will continue.

Parents report that the most difficult aspect of the child's illness is wondering how long the remission will last, if there will be another treatment protocol, and when this will all be over.

Relapse Relapse brings back the reality of the diagnosis. "They were right." It sweeps away the dream of long-term remission and the hope for a cure. The anxieties and disruption of the diagnosis period reappear, including separation from the child's other parent, well siblings, and home. During relapse parents observe many emotional and physical changes in the child—anorexia, nausea, weight loss, bleeding, and fatigue. Some parents may still hope for additional medication and treatment and the corresponding extension in life expectancy. This was well stated by one parent who said, "Where there's life, there's hope, so I'm looking forward."[29] If the child again improves, family living can return to a semblance of normality. But living is likely to be without long-term plans and rather day-to-day. Taking things a day at a time tends to minimize resentments and frustrations for parents in adapting to the course of their child's illness.[30]

Terminal stage The terminal phase brings parents face to face with the reality of impending death. While a few parents continue to deny or bargain, most give up hopes for cure, new therapy, and long remissions. Parents have many fears at this time, which usually include:

1. Fear of prolonging the inevitable and the pain
2. Fear of losing control or not being able to cope
3. Fear of being physically or emotionally isolated
4. Fear of having other people take over
5. Fear that death will occur while they are away or while they are alone with the child
6. Fear of not being able to love again

Parents, of course, also have many fears as they anticipate what the actual death will be like: Will he bleed? Will he just stop breathing? Will the pain be terrible? Will he be alert (parents' wishes about this matter vary)? How much warning will I have?[31]

Knowing that death is near for a child with cancer may be a relief from the long period of stress created by the disease. But it may instead precipitate further stress and abnormal grief reactions. Parents vary widely in this regard, but most seek to make the most of their child's final days of life. Even children who are close to death can have a "good day" with their families.

The actual death comes as a shock to parents, no matter what the length of preparation. Most parents want to be with their child at the time of death, although they may dread what it will be like and how they will react. Parents should be told "Your child is dying." No euphemisms should be applied, such as "critical" or "very bad." If parents wish, they should be allowed to hold their child.

When the child has died, parents, along with other close family members, should have some private time to say goodbye to him. Parents should be encouraged to see their child before he is taken to the funeral home. Seeing the child dead is painful but helps parents accept the fact that death has occurred; this acceptance is essential to the mourning process. After the death the parents must plan the burial ceremony. The religious and ceremonial aspects of death are, for many people, important means of confirming the reality of the loss and providing family members support in their mourning.

Family relationships during the illness

When parents begin to appreciate the significance of their child's progressing illness, their relationship with him can change in many ways. Initially they may handle the child with greater care, extend greater patience, worry more about falls and bruises. As reality sets in, their expectations and hopes have to be altered. Whereas before diagnosis the child was "the embodiment of a promise," after the illness is discovered that promise is "either gone or at least reduced in value."[32]

While it is important that parents be aware of the child's actual physical limitations, it is equally important that they stimulate the child to achieve at a realistic level. As difficult as it may seem, parents should maintain their discipline practices, if they are reasonable ones. This provides the ill child with assurance that he is still normal in some respects; it also shows the well brothers and sisters that there are consequences for misbehavior for the ill sibling.

A father faces tremendous stress when he is

faced with the reality that his child has a terminal illness. In a study of parents of children with leukemia, it was observed that fathers found many ways of absenting themselves from painful involvement with their families. This was their way of coping, a way of avoiding the pain of ongoing involvement with the dying child. Such behavior can indicate a father's need for additional support.[33] A father's participation in the care of his dying child can be helpful to his wife as well as the child. A mother usually copes by becoming increasingly involved in the care of the child. She may give up employment and outside activities as well as isolate herself from friends and family in the effort to provide care and support to the ill child.

These coping behaviors place significant burdens on the husband-wife relationship. Financial concerns may limit social activities and involve increased time working to meet expenses. This combination of factors may reduce the amount of attention the husband and wife can focus on their relationship. This may lead both partners to feel an increasing sense of isolation and loss of support. An additional burden is placed on the marital relationship each time the child is hospitalized. While the mother may spend many hours at the bedside of the child, the father may visit only infrequently. The mother may wish to protect the father from the intensity of guilt, anger, and sadness she feels about their child's illness. At the same time her husband may believe it necessary to protect his wife from his own quite similar feelings. In such a situation, each excludes and isolates the other.

One of the ways that this gap in communication can be overcome is for husband and wife to become aware of what is happening, to learn to focus on the common aspects of their situation, and to develop some practical ways to support each other in time of stress. Researchers have shown that family strength rather than weakness is a result of coping with serious illness. Many parents have not only mastered the practicalities of their situation but consequently appeared to grow together as people.

Resources to assist parents include discussion groups of parents of terminally ill children. Such groups provide information about the illness as well as promote sharing of feelings among parents. Group sessions can help parents find ways for the family to cope with the child's illness. By hearing other parents discuss their experience with the death of a child, parents can begin to feel that they can survive this devastating experience and that they will be able to go through the grief process reasonably well.

Four advantages to parent groups have been identified. These include:[34]

1. Open communication among parents regarding their children's and their own personal problems relating to their special situation
2. Learning that one is not alone by informal sharing and mutual caring
3. Ability to focus on individual situations
4. Informational materials provided by the group which help parents face the course of their children's illness.

Impact on other family members

While parents bear the greatest stress with the terminal illness of a child, there are other family members who need special attention in such a situation: siblings and grandparents.

Siblings react to the illness and death according to their age and ability to comprehend. Their relationship to the ill child and their own place and adjustment within the family both play a part. Also important are the honesty and appropriateness with which the parents communicate with them about the dying child and the nature of the problem, that is, "how they are included, as a part of the family, in the family's adaptation to terminal illness."[35]

With the demands on the parents' energy, it is understandable that the needs of well siblings assume a lower priority. Brothers and sisters may grieve and fear that they also will fall ill and die.[36] It is important that parents be open and honest, provide age-appropriate and anxiety-reducing explanations, and listen to their children's questions. Even when parents try to protect their children from sorrow by attempting to be cheerful and by giving evasive answers, the children will know something is wrong. Young children, who believe in magic, may fear that they caused the death and must be reassured otherwise. Communication about the disease between parents and well siblings is essential to minimize jealousy and promote cooperation. Siblings frequently feel isolated by the uniqueness of their experience. Visits by siblings to the ill child in the hospital will help eliminate fears and build up positive relationships. Siblings can help care for an ill child at home. They will be able to learn about the ill child's needs, gain acceptance of the illness, and participate in the family's concerns and activities.

When death is near, the siblings should be informed. The parents may decide to allow the siblings to be present when it occurs. If not, parents should tell them that the child received the best care and did not suffer too much. The siblings should be encouraged to participate in the funeral and cemetery services.

Sibling responses to death can range from no apparent response to depression, nightmares, aggression, and bodily complaint.[37] Children may express a variety of feelings, including responsibility for the sibling's death, fears that they will die, resentment that the parents spent so much time with the ill child, anger at the parents for allowing the child to die, and preoccupations with fantasies about death.[38]

Parents should provide opportunities for siblings to discuss the illness and death. Otherwise their fears and anxieties will lie hidden below the surface and continue to distress them. They may need to be reassured that the death was not their fault, the illness was not contagious, that normally children grow up to be adults, and that parents have many years to live. As parents are able to accept and express their grief and provide for the emotional needs of their surviving children, the children in turn will be able to accept their own feelings.

The terminal illness of a child has a significant impact on grandparents. They grieve for the child, the parents, and also themselves. Initially, grandparents may be angry and hostile with the parents—"Why didn't you take the child to the doctor sooner?"—or with themselves—"We should have realized the child was sick." They may be less accepting of the diagnosis than the parents and thus complicate the parents' struggle to accept and cope with the reality of the illness. While grandparents may wish to be included in the parents' grief and to help with the care of the child, some parents are reluctant to put the burden of their fears and feelings on the grandparents, who may not be physically well. Like other family members, grandparents need

to have effective means of gathering information and expressing their feelings in order to cope with their impending loss. Grandparents may find help in "grandparent groups" which provide information and support. When they can participate in the care of the dying child or the well siblings, the grandparents feel needed and have increased self-esteem.

Mourning after the death

Mourning for a dead child is an intense and lengthy experience for the family. Shock and numbness are usually the first responses, regardless of preparation for the death. Family members may find it difficult to make judgments or function effectively. This phase of mourning is replaced by anger and guilt, restlessness and reality-testing, depression, and awareness of the reality of the situation. Finally, after months family members may begin to experience a sense of relief and renewed energy. According to Glen Richardson, the process of post-death mourning may last 12 to 18 months.[39] Mourning may reoccur at times of special significance for the family: anniversary dates of the death, birthdays of the dead child, and religious holidays. An important goal for the family is to rejoin the life of the community. Religious faith, support groups, and contact with the staff who cared for the dead child may be important resources which help family members cope. The death of the child is an irrevocable fact, but life should continue to be enjoyed. As Harriet Schiff said, "As long as I live I will be sorry Robby is dead. That is a fact . . . I carry always. There are times . . . when I miss him still. But there are still good times. We share joys as a family that he did not live to share and I am sorry. But we still have joys. That is as it should be."[40]

The impact of terminal illness on the nurse

Caring for a child who is dying can be a positive, rewarding component of the nurse's role. However, nurses, like physicians, often tend to view terminal illness and death as failure because the usual goals of disease prevention and health promotion cannot be achieved.

Work with dying children elicits many taxing emotional responses. Nurses, like family members and others who are close to the child, experience grief—denial, anger, guilt, and depression. The frustration over the prognosis and the wish that the child would not die are confounded by awareness that, at the same time, one wishes death to come quickly so that all involved may be relieved of their suffering. When the terminal state is the result of an accident, the staff may feel considerable anger at parents or others who seem at fault for not having protected the child adequately. If the patient is an adolescent whose behavior has resulted in the accident, nurses may feel angry toward the patient. This blamesetting can cause resentment that can decrease the quality of care.[41] Whether the terminal condition is caused by trauma or by an illness such as cancer, staff may wish to alleviate their own suffering by withdrawing from the child and the family.

There are several approaches nurses can take to deal with their own feelings and ensure effective care for both patient and family. First, it is essential to recognize that denial, anger, guilt, frustration, and depression are normal for nurses as they are for family members and patients. Nurses can learn to recognize and accept their own reactions and to deal with them in ways that promote satisfaction and effectiveness in providing for the dying child and helping the family and friends.

A supportive work setting is a major resource for enabling nurses to cope with the stresses of caring for the terminally ill. Institutional mechanisms should be established to give nurses and other health team members a forum in which to share and confront their reactions to being involved in relationships that must be interrupted by the child's death. Staff members need to discuss the positive and negative aspects of the child and the child's care, and they need to acknowledge and receive acceptance of their responses to the emotional and physical demands placed on personnel caring for the child. When such a support system is not available, there is real danger that the nurse may attempt to cope by withdrawing from patient contact and involvement with parents. The problems tend to accumulate from one dying patient to the next, and a nurse can, in addition to being ineffective as a care-giver, become more and more angry, depressed, and cynical as a result of unresolved frustration and unresolved grief.[42]

Some ways a support system can be established in the practice setting have been suggested.[43]

1. During the report session, discuss the patients who are dying, the reactions of the staff, and the care plans. Discussing specifics will also aid others to implement effective means of care.
2. During staff meetings identify those staff members who have, or will have, the greatest amount of involvement, thus alerting the remaining staff to those who may be most in need of reinforcement.
3. During interactions with other staff members, give both verbal and nonverbal reinforcement whenever interpersonal or physical care has been done well.
4. Set aside some time that could be used for sharing knowledge, ideas, and plans and for evaluating goal achievement. In this way the staff may come to feel a real sense of accomplishment.
5. Define and evaluate the purposes of care measures, in order to measure each experience against the stated goal.
6. Take time to give a word of encouragement and to let someone cry with you or to discuss a patient. This will influence the quality of care as well as the well-being of the staff.
7. Encourage each staff member to find one other person with whom to share his or her experiences; this will be an enrichment and a support to both staff and patient.

The nursing process itself provides the means by which nurses can avoid much of the frustration and distress they might otherwise encounter in caring for dying children. When a child becomes terminal, the overall goal of nursing care is death with dignity and optimal functioning of the surviving family members. Death with dignity means that physical and psychological suffering and deterioration will be minimized—that comfort will be maximized. The nursing process breaks a complex situation into discrete, manageable subparts. For example, planning includes anticipation of needs in order to prevent unnecessary pain, skin breakdown, and complications. When these kinds of realistic goals are established, the success of nursing care is not linked to such impossible objectives as cure and survival, and the evaluation phase of the nursing process allows the nurse to feel successful—even when the child dies—because the best possible physical and emotional care has been provided.

Nursing management of the terminally ill child

Philosophy of terminal care

The decision to stop or continue cure-oriented treatment when children are at the end stage of disease is often difficult to make. Frequently the parent, child, doctor, and nurse will have differing opinions. Many parents are reluctant to discuss stopping treatment with their physician. They wonder if further treatment will help or if they will jeopardize their relationship with the physician, and thus their child's care, by making this request.

Once a good relationship with the parents has been established, the nurse can be alert for direct comments or subtle clues which indicate that the parents are considering discontinuing treatment.

The nurse also needs to listen for clues from children. This should be done with an especially attuned ear as children often talk in symbolic language.[44]

Most children do not like hospitalization and find their cancer treatment uncomfortable. As previously discussed, it has been shown that children know their diagnoses, understand the meaning of their illness, and even know when they are dying.[45] If the nurse establishes a trusting relationship with the child and listens carefully, the child will tell the nurse when he no longer wants to be in the hospital and when he has reached the point of no longer desiring treatment. The nurse should allow children to discuss their thoughts and relay this information to the parents and physician.

The nurse can facilitate physician-family communication by sharing information with the physician about the family's preparedness for discussing the discontinuance of treatment. If the family appears uncomfortable or reluctant to discuss their feelings with the physician, the nurse may need to provide support and encourage them to speak freely and honestly with the physician.

The nurse may also have an opinion about discontinuing treatment and should feel free to discuss these feelings with other team members. It is important to be aware of personal feelings and not to impose them on the family. Instead, help them to review all the alternatives so that they can decide what is the best choice for their child.

If, after consultation with the medical staff, the family decides to continue cancer treatment, the child's medical and nursing care should continue as before. The nurse should utilize every opportunity to promote healing and prevent further physical deterioration. Survival should be the goal with a high priority on preventive nursing care, health maintenance, and treatment of nursing care problems.

If cure-oriented treatment is discontinued, the child's comfort is the primary goal. Once treatment is stopped, children can survive several hours or days to a year or more, depending upon the type of cancer. Comfort care should be provided when a child has only several days or weeks of life remaining. If it is thought that the child will live longer, nursing care for the chronically ill child should be instituted.

Comfort care includes any measures that the family feels will make the child comfortable. The child is therefore provided with whatever he wishes during his final days. Many children, when they are ill and dying, refuse nutritious foods and fluids. Comfort care includes giving children whatever they want to eat, whenever they desire it, regardless of nutritional value. Another important aspect of this care is effective pain control. Whatever the source of the pain, the child should be adequately medicated so that he can be held by his parents. Months of valuable physical and emotional support for the child and parents can be lost if they are not able to touch and hold each other. It is important that the child be allowed to spend his last days free of pain. In many instances, methods of health maintenance such as antibiotics and blood replacements are discontinued unless the family desires these for the child's comfort.

Hospital care of the dying child

When treatment is discontinued, the family needs to decide where the child will spend his final days. There are many reasons why a family may choose to have their child die in the hospital. In some instances, the family may feel that the physical care is too difficult for them to provide, or that the family social situation is not conducive to the child's dying at home. Parents of an infant may not feel that being "at home" is important to the child. If the family chooses death in the hospital, health professionals should support their decision. The hospital nurses can greatly influence the quality of the life of the child and the family during the final days of life.

Assessment Once treatment has been discontinued, the nurse should complete a nursing assessment of the child's physical and emotional status, keeping the principle of comfort care in mind. The assessment should be completed as quickly as possible because hospitalized children who are not receiving medical therapy usually die within a short period of time. The assessment should be as thorough for a dying child as for any other child. The nurse needs to plan for the child's complete comfort. The physical assessment should include a review of all major systems, with an especially close look at sources of discomfort—pain from the disease, skin breakdown, contractures, constipation, or bleeding. Information from parents regarding how they have solved problems and provided comfort at home can prove invaluable and should be elicited during the assessment phase. An emotional assessment of the child is of equal importance at this stressful time. It should include an appraisal of the child's knowledge of the illness and of his impending demise. The child's current emotional status and ability to cope with this knowledge should also be assessed. The nurse should meet with and observe the child, in addition to discussing the child's emotional status with the parents.

The nurse usually has frequent contact with other family members, parents, siblings, and grandparents during the dying phase and provides them with emotional support and assistance. The nurse should assess the current emotional status and coping abilities of these other family members. A final important area for assessment is the family's desire for involvement in the dying process.

Table 22-2 outlines the assessment of a terminally ill child and significant others. Information derived from this assessment can be used by the nurse to:

1. Identify and evaluate current health problems in the child and family
2. Develop an appropriate nursing care plan for the dying child

3. Plan strategies to assist the other family members through this difficult time
4. Plan for the family's involvement in the comfort care

Principles of planning care An individualized nursing care plan that addresses all pertinent physical and emotional health care needs is as important for the dying child as it is for the chronically ill child or the child who will completely recover from a brief illness. The death of a child is a highly stressful event for the child, family, and hospital staff. Thorough, highly competent nursing care should be provided so that the child will be as comfortable as possible, both physically and mentally. When the nurse provides good care, the family will not have the additional worry or concern that their child is not receiving the best possible care.

When writing a nursing care plan, the nurse should first ascertain the degree of life-supportive measures the physician and family have planned. The nurse should ask what supportive measures are to be used, such as transfusions or oxygen, in order to develop a plan that includes sufficient time for child and parent teaching and emotional preparation.

The anticipated life expectancy should also be used as a guideline for writing the nursing care plan. For a child who may die in a few days, care should consist primarily of providing comfort. If the child wishes to remain in bed or curled up on a parent's lap eating popsicles and potato chips, the nurse should accept the child's choice. The nursing care plan for this child would not include the health preventive and health maintenance aspects of the plan shown in the nursing care plan at the end of this chapter. This nursing care plan was written with the child's death expected 2 or more weeks in the future. Skin care and attention to muscle tone, which includes range of motion (ROM) exercises, frequent turning, and getting out of bed several times a day, were included to increase the child's comfort and prevent pain, contractures, and skin breakdown that could occur over a longer period of time.

The care plan for each child needs to include information about the interventions that the parent has found to be successful prior to this time. For instance, a child might be able to

Table 22-2 Assessment for care of a dying child

I. Patient's physical condition
 A. Prior to decision to discontinue treatment
 B. Present—length and duration of symptoms
  1. Pain
   a. Amount and severity of pain
   b. Location
   c. Current pain medications
   d. Other comfort measures utilized (e.g., massage, distraction)
   e. Limitation of child's activities as a result of pain
   f. Limitation of parent-child contact due to pain
  2. Nutrition and hydration patterns
   a. Child's food and fluid routine—how often, how much
   b. Favorite foods and liquids or foods tolerated
   c. Food and fluid dislikes
   d. Recent changes
   e. Nausea and vomiting
   f. Family's mode of coping with feeding at the present time
   g. Current weight, weight change
  3. Sleep patterns
   a. Recent changes
   b. Type of sleep: sound, restless, changes during hospitalization
   c. Support and comfort: blanket, bottle, toys, night light, bedtime routine
  4. Elimination patterns
   a. Toilet trained (when applicable)
   b. Urination
     Frequency (how many diapers used, if applicable)
     Color and odor
     Foley or condom catheter
     Pain on urination
     Hematuria
     Recent changes, describe
   c. Defecation
     Frequency
     Color and consistency
     Melena
     Pain on defecation
     Constipation—frequency, how managed
     Diarrhea—frequency, how managed
     Recent changes, describe
  5. Activity
   a. Walking, crawling, sitting
   b. Balance
   c. Amount of activity
   d. Limited by pain?
  6. Skin and mouth
   a. Turgor, color, temperature
   b. Area of breakdown or potential breakdown
     Favorite position, place to sit, place to sleep
     Current preventive skin care
   c. Current skin care, if breakdown exists
   d. Tumor
     Size
     Closed or draining
     Current care
     Painful?
   e. Mouth
     Hydrated, dry
     Blisters
     Bleeding

Table 22-2 Assessment for care of a dying child—(*Continued*)

     7. Respiratory
       a. Color of skin
       b. Shortness of breath, rate and quality of respirations
     8. Special problems
       a. Speech, aphasia
       b. Seizures
       c. Vision
       d. Paralysis
       e. Retardation
       f. Prostheses
II. Emotional assessment
  A. Knowledge and understanding of child's current health status and prognosis by child, parents, siblings, extended family members
  B. Emotional status of child—from history and observation
    1. Previous
    2. Present
      a. Psychological behaviors, feelings exhibited, how often

Angry	Anxious
Fearful	Crying
Depressed	Accepting
Calm	Flat or no affect

      b. Reaction to impending death—acceptance, denial, ambivalence
      c. Talks about illness and death, with family, hospital staff
      d. Talks with family only
      e. Accepts emotional support from family, hospital staff, others
      f. Cooperates with hospital staff, parents
      g. Prefers one parent
      h. Discipline problems
  C. Emotional status of parents—from history and observation
    1. Previous
    2. Present
      a. Psychological feelings exhibited, how often

Angry	Anxious
Fearful	Accepting
Depressed	Flat or no affect
Calm	Cries

      b. Reaction to impending death—acceptance, denial, ambivalence
      c. Talk about illness and death with child, family, hospital staff, others
      d. Accept emotional support from child, other family members, hospital staff, others
      e. Cooperate with hospital staff
  D. Emotional status of each sibling—from history and observation
    1. Previous
    2. Present
      a. Psychological feelings exhibited

Angry	Accepting
Fearful	Flat or no affect
Depressed	Cries
Calm	Curiosity
Anxious	

      b. Reaction to impending death—acceptance, denial, ambivalence
      c. Talk about illness and death with child, parents, other siblings, hospital staff, others
      d. Relationship to dying sibling—close in age, play often, get along well
      e. Accepts emotional support from child, other family members, hospital staff, others
      f. Emotional problems relevant to disease and impending death of sibling
III. Family involvement in dying (includes child, parents, siblings, grandparents)
  A. How much involvement does family want?
  B. Family wants to provide physical care?
  C. Family knows how to provide physical care?
  D. Family, including dying child, knows signs and symptoms of impending death?
  E. Family wants to be present at time of death, stay during night?
  F. How often do siblings want to visit; do parents want siblings present at time of death?

prevent constipation by eating Metamucil on cereal or taking milk of magnesia, or both, thereby avoiding suppositories and enemas.

Setting goals and planning care It is very important that the nurse involve the family in the development and implementation of the child's care plan. The family, including both child and parents, should participate in discussions to set goals and outline plans to meet those goals. Families differ in the extent to which they wish to be involved in their children's care, but there are three strong reasons why every child's parents (and perhaps other members of the family) should be included in planning and providing care: (1) Separation of parents and child, which is stressful,[46-49] is diminished; (2) children experience less discomfort when their parents take part in planning and giving care; and (3) child and parent involvement in care helps them regain some feeling of being in control.

From the time of diagnosis of a life-threatening disease and throughout the entire illness, parents feel out of control of the destiny of their child. This feeling is very difficult to withstand; it often gives rise to other distressing reactions, such as frustration, despair, depression, and anger. The family has also probably felt that much of their life-style was beyond their control during the illness, as they have had to adjust many of their activities to provide care for the ill child. For example, a mother may have stopped working in order to care for the child. A father may be forced to change his job, or a mother may need to work in order to cover the high cost of medical treatment. A recent study showed that during an illness one-fourth of the family's monthly income is spent on out-of-pocket non-reimbursable expenses. These expenses include food, lodging, gasoline, clothing of different sizes, wigs, and many other needs.[50]

These are only a few examples of the many changes and adjustments a family may have to make during the illness. When the child is at the end stage of life, the nurse has the opportunity to help the parents and the child reestablish control. The nurse can begin to do this by including them in goal setting and the formulation of the nursing care plan.

Nursing care goals must be realistic. Explain that decreased healing occurs during the dying phase of a terminal illness so that the child and parents will not become unduly distressed when a decubitus does not heal or a sore continues to drain. Stress the child's comfort as the most important goal. Goals should be written in terms of patient condition or behavior "outcome." For example, "Child able to move about in bed and be held by parents without pain."

The nurse should discuss the care plan with parents and also with the child if his or her age and emotional status permits. Select a quiet place where there are minimal interruptions for this meeting. Share the plan that is developed, encourage questions, and request comments from the child and parents. Clarify specific nursing care measures that have been incorporated into the plan. This is very important because the child and family may be unfamiliar with treatment measures and equipment which may be used to promote the child's comfort and well-being. Ask the parents when they will be available and what care they would like to provide. This should be noted on the child's care plan. Beds should be available for the parents so they can stay with the child through the night if they desire. The nurse should make it clear that he or she is available to assist the parents with the child's care whenever they wish.

Implementing the nursing care plan *Teaching* It is important that the nurse evaluate the family's understanding of the child's care. The nurse may need to instruct family members, including the parents, child, and siblings, in the correct way to perform care. Often, the nurse can offer suggestions which may improve the effectiveness of care provided by the family. It is important to realize that many parents feel inferior to hospital staff in their ability to perform medically oriented tasks. In addition, they may also be afraid of medical equipment and supplies. The nurse needs to anticipate these feelings and discuss them openly with the family. The nurse can support the family's desire to provide care by:

1. Providing teaching and having the parents give return demonstrations to demonstrate their competency
2. Praising the parents when they have learned a skill
3. Encouraging their involvement, pointing out that it is the parent who knows the child's needs and desires better than anyone else

Information regarding the process of dying is essential for the parents and child. Certainly, children from about 10 years old on need to know what to expect and even children as young as 5 or 6 may ask questions about their death. Regardless of age, all children should have their questions about death answered openly and honestly. The family should therefore receive information regarding the changes that occur as death approaches and the child's concurrent needs. See Table 22-3.

Another helpful area of information for the parents is an estimation of how long the child might live. Although no one can predict exactly when a child will die, an estimation helps the family to regain some control and provides them with a time framework within which to make plans. If one or both parents, or siblings, want to remain in the hospital with the child, they need to arrange for the care of their other children, make arrangements regarding work, and organize their time so that they can get adequate rest and sleep during this stressful,

exhausting time. The nurse can assist the family by asking the physician to give an expected time of death.

Physical care of the dying child Children who are dying of cancer often have numerous physical and mental symptoms caused by the disease process. Many of these symptoms (e.g., constipation, nausea and vomiting, temperature imbalance, sore mouth) can be managed using standard nursing care (see Chap. 35). The following are additional suggestions for nursing care of these routine problems as well as suggestions for specific problems related to cancer and dying. These measures may also be useful in providing care to children dying from other diseases.

PAIN One of the areas of greatest concern for parents and children is pain. Pain is not new to dying children and their families. These children often experience pain associated with diagnostic or treatment procedures or the disease itself. The pain may become chronic. Many children with cancer also experience a sudden onset of

Table 22-3 Signs and symptoms of approaching death and nursing interventions

Signs and symptoms	Nursing interventions
External temperature decreases, beginning at distal extremities and progressing toward upper body; child will probably not feel cold; skin color may be pale, grey, bluish	Offer to cover child with lightweight, loose-fitting bedding
Internal temperature may increase	Use lightweight blanket or sheet; fresh circulating air in room
Loss of sensation and movement, beginning in lower extremities and progressing toward upper body	Use loose clothing and bedding; child may prefer no clothing; gentle change of positioning
Decrease in muscle tone with resultant inability to swallow and cough, urinary and fecal incontinence, mouth breathing	Atropine sulfate may be used to decrease oropharyngeal secretions; suctioning may be used; place absorbent padding under child if incontinent; frequent mouth care
Difficulty breathing, shortness of breath or "air hunger"; respirations may increase, then become shallow and irregular; Cheyne-Stokes respirations may occur	Place child on side, head elevated and firmly supported; may administer oxygen
Senses decrease; although vision and speech may cease, hearing may continue until death; although tactile sensation decreases, touch may become annoying	Encourage family to continue communicating with child by speech until death; if child is comfortable, family and nurse should continue holding, caressing, touching child until death; if child is uncomfortable, it may be appropriate to stop bed baths and bed and clothing changes
Child may indicate pain by restlessness and verbal utterances even when comatose; if in deep coma, probably won't feel pain	Be alert for signs of pain and treat with pain medication
Eyes may become sunken or bulging	If child comatose, place moist bandage over bulging eyes to prevent corneal drying and subsequent corneal ulceration
Loss or faintness of pedal and radial pulses; apical pulse may become more rapid, then slower, irregular, and difficult to auscultate	

Table 22-4 24-h "round-the-clock" medication schedule*

Medication	Dose	Route	Time
Dolophine (methadone hydrochloride)	0.7 mg/kg per day in 4–6 divided doses	PO	Every 6–8 h: 7-3-11-7, etc.
Benadryl (diphenhydramine hydrochloride)	5 mg/kg per day in 4 divided doses	PO	Every 4 h: 7-11-3-7, etc.
Vistaril (hydroxyzine pamoate)	2–5 mg/kg per hour in divided doses every 6 h and/or HS	PO	HS: 7p

* Doses given in this table are minimum safe doses. Amount of pain medication given will vary greatly with the degree of pain and drug tolerance and will need to be individually titrated to control pain and keep symptoms of the drug at an acceptable level.

severe pain in their final days of life. These past and current experiences and the anticipation of future pain can increase anxiety and fear in both the child and family. Many terminal care facilities find that pain can be controlled effectively during the dying phase. These agencies place pain control as a top priority in providing comfort care.[51–54]

The most successful pain control, to date, is 24-h "round-the-clock" coverage (see Table 22-4). This includes a hypnotic and a mood changer in addition to a narcotic. The round-the-clock coverage is used to prevent the fear-pain-anxiety cycle.[55,56] This cycle can occur if the child takes a pain medication that does not take effect for one-half to three-quarters of an hour. After the medication takes effect, the child may worry when the pain will begin again, or about the period between pain onset and the time the next dose will provide relief. The fear and anxiety created by concern about the *next* pain often increases the *current* pain. When the child experiences this repetitive cycle, an ordinary dose of an analgesic is often inadequate for pain control. Unfortunately, this cycle often occurs, leading to more pain and increased dosages of medication.

It is essential that nurses get to know the children well in order to evaluate and assess complaints of pain. All health professionals and parents are aware that children can and do use pain to manipulate those around them and to gain attention. Dying children often have real physical pain, which is aggravated by the knowledge that they are dying. Nurses must be very sensitive toward dying children in pain. The nurse must be ready to administer round-the-clock total pain coverage which will provide these children with physical and emotional com-

fort so that they can be active and alert and enjoy the final days with those they love.

Many different medications have been used successfully with children dying from cancer. Narcotics are usually necessary for moderate to severe pain in the final days. Tylenol (acetaminophen) with codeine, Demerol (meperidine hydrochloride), Dilaudid (hydromorphone), Dolophine (methadone hydrochloride), and morphine sulfate are examples of effective narcotics. All of these drugs may be taken orally, the route preferred by children. Methadone hydrochloride has recently received increased usage because it can be taken orally and is effective for 6 to 8 h. Specific dosage ranges for use of these drugs in providing pain control to dying children have not yet been firmly established. Depending upon the duration of the use of the drug and the child's physical and emotional reaction to pain, a dose much higher than previously used might be needed to achieve complete relief.

In order to assist the physician in planning pain management, the nurse needs to closely observe the child's response to medications. The parents can be very helpful in assessing pain relief, because they know the child well. The nurse may need to alert the physician that the child's pain is not sufficiently controlled and that the child is still caught in the fear-pain-anxiety cycle. The child may need a very large "loading" dose of a medication to break the cycle. Medications that are sometimes given in conjunction with round-the-clock pain medications to facilitate sleep include Vistaril (hydroxyzine pamoate), Benedryl (diphenhydramine hydrochloride), chloral hydrate, and phenobarbital. Tranquilizers such as doxepin hydrochloride and diazepam are also used.

The side effects of pain medications can be

adequately controlled; they are a secondary consideration in care of the dying child. Some parents and children express concern over the sedative effect of high narcotic doses. In many instances, this sedation decreases after extended use of the drugs. The nurse should assist the family in discussing these concerns with the physician.

Additional measures that may be used to control mild pain, or when emotional anxiety appears to potentiate more intense pain, include:

1. Changes in temperature, such as room temperature, bedding, or clothing; dying children often prefer little or no bedding or clothing
2. Diversion with games, reading books, visits from siblings or friends
3. A change of environment, such as a wheelchair trip outdoors or to the hospital cafeteria
4. Partial or total body massage, as touching conveys closeness, caring, and love
5. Muscle relaxation techniques, such as those used for childbirth preparation
6. Changes in equipment such as a water bed, alternating-pressure mattress, gel flotation pad, or foam mattress

Some innovative methods of pain control which are being investigated and tested, such as hypnosis,[57, 58] acupuncture, and electrical stimulators, may prove effective for dying children. Surgical procedures, such as chordotomy, may also be used to control pain.

BLEEDING Children with cancers that affect the bone marrow, such as leukemia and lymphoma, or children who have had chemotherapy are susceptible to bleeding. Although major hemorrhage is often feared by parents and children, a more common problem is slight but persistent bleeding from the nose, mouth, or rectum.

Measures that can be utilized to stop the bleeding include:

1. Application of an ice pack over the bleeding area
2. Reasonable pressure applied by hand to the bleeding area
3. The use of packing such as Gelfoam or gauze for epistaxis
4. The application of topical thrombin to the bleeding site
5. The application of salt pork to bleeding gums

Measures to control bleeding may not be effective during advanced disease. The nurse should share this information with the family.

Additional comfort measures for the child who is bleeding include:

1. Providing a good supply of tissues, towels, or chux to absorb the blood.
2. Quickly removing soiled tissues and linen from the child's environment.
3. Keeping the clothing and bedding clean to decrease the child's anxiety about the amount of blood lost.
4. Using a large basin rather than an emesis basin, if the child is vomiting blood, is more efficient and makes it easier to keep the child clean.

Transfusions of blood products may be used if the family so desires. See Chaps. 27 and 35 for further discussion of nursing management of the child receiving transfusions of blood products.

RESPIRATORY NEEDS Respiratory pattern changes can occur as a result of tumor metastasis, infection, and fluid retention. Many families are afraid that their child will die while choking or fighting for breath. Respiratory difficulty can therefore create great anxiety in the parents and child. The nurse needs to remain calm and reassuring and institute comfort measures that are designed to alleviate respiratory difficulty. Aids which improve respiration include:

1. Placing the child in an upright position
2. Increasing the moisture in the room air by using a humidifier
3. Suctioning
4. Using oxygen

Suctioning should be used judiciously because it often causes discomfort and anxiety that can further interfere with respiration. When oxygen is used, children and families feel comforted because something is being done for the child. Children sometimes prefer nasal prongs to a face mask. Children who fear the face mask should be told that they can put it in their lap and hold it up to their face when they want to use it.

SEIZURES Children with brain tumors or tumors that metastasize to the brain, such as neuroblastoma or leukemia, may develop seizures at any point during their illness. They often exhibit seizures when they are close to death; these seizures may be almost constant. Many parents and children have expressed a desire for the child to be alert during the final days. Anticonvulsant medications may produce drowsiness, especially when they are used in conjunction with analgesics or tranquilizers. The nurse should alert the physician to the family's concern so that a medication regimen that produces the least amount of sedation can be provided. Sometimes families are willing to have the child experience numerous mild seizures in order to maintain the child's mental alertness.

Seizures are frightening to most people. If there is a possibility the child will develop seizures, the nurse should discuss this with the child and parents. The nurse should also teach them what to expect and what to do in the event of a seizure.

INADEQUATE NUTRITION AND/OR HYDRATION When children are in the dying phase of an illness, good nutrition is not likely to prolong life. The child should therefore be allowed to eat what he wants, when he wants to eat it. Mothers and fathers should be encouraged and aided by the hospital staff in the preparation of the child's favorite foods.

During the last days of life, the dying child usually greatly decreases or stops eating and may drink only sips of fluid. Children often find IV fluids painful and confining. Although it is traditional to use intravenous fluids for hydration of children dying in the hospital, the child or parent may request that they be discontinued. It is important to honor their request. Conversely, the family may request IV fluids to increase the child's comfort.

MOUTH SORES When children decrease their oral intake, the mouth may become dry and sore; cracks and blisters of the lips can also occur. A frequent problem for children with leukemia is superficial hematomas on the lips. These lesions are painful and may ooze blood.

The nurse should first try to treat these problems with standard measures such as petroleum jelly, mouthwashes, and lemon glycerine swabs. Additional measures to treat unrelieved pain include the use of topical agents such as viscous Xylocaine, Cetacaine, or a mixture of viscous Xylocaine and hydrogen peroxide. Elixir of Benadryl (diphenhydramine hydrochloride) and mild narcotics may be used systemically.

CONSTIPATION Constipation is a common problem which may be caused by a combination of factors, such as inactivity, poor nutrition, and certain chemotherapeutic and analgesic medications. The nurse should be alert for the possible development of constipation and should institute treatment immediately. Diet changes and laxatives are often successful.

Enemas and digital removal of stool are usually avoided in children who are highly susceptible to bleeding and infection, but may be used if the child is experiencing pain caused by constipation or impaction. These procedures should be performed carefully and gently.

SKIN CARE Dying children are highly susceptible to skin breakdown because of their poor nutritional status, decreased physical activity, neurological problems, and the effects of chemotherapy on tissue repair. Preventive measures such as frequent turning, repositioning, skin massage, and the use of mechanical appliances such as an alternating pressure mattress or heel protectors should be continued throughout the child's life. However, many children during the final days before death assume a specific posture of comfort and refuse to be moved. The dying child should be allowed to remain in this position, if it provides comfort, and skin breakdown problems should be treated if they occur. It is important that the nurse teach the family that healing will probably not occur because of the advanced disease process and that comfort is the most important consideration.

EYE CARE Tumors of the brain and cancers that metastasize to the brain can cause eye problems, such as crossed eyes, difficulty with vision, blindness, and protrusion of the eye from the socket. The latter is caused by a tumor behind the eye, which presses the eye forward. Because of pressure on the lacrimal gland(s), the eye(s) may not be adequately moistened. Artificial tears or normal saline should be applied to the eye as often as necessary. If the child cannot see or does not mind eye patches, the eye(s) may be closed and saline patches applied.

ACTIVITY Children should be encouraged to remain active for as long as possible. Activity will help maintain emotional health and prevent the physical complications of skin breakdown, constipation, and muscle weakness or tightening. The hospital should have a liberal pass policy that enables the child to leave the premises for brief periods. It would be ideal if the hospital could permit a nurse to accompany the child on brief visits at home if the family feels that a nurse would be helpful to them. Dying children often want to go home "one more time," sometimes to say goodbye.

EMOTIONAL CARE The emotional needs of dying children continue until the moment of death. Although children vary as greatly as adults in their acceptance of dying and their use of coping strategies, the nurse can anticipate some common basic emotional needs.

All dying children need to know that they are loved and cherished and will be sorely missed after they die. A nurse who has a special, loving relationship with a child should feel free to express feelings of love for this child and sadness at the impending loss of the child. Dying children need to share in honest communication. Nurses can help families provide for these needs by establishing honest communication at the time of diagnosis and maintaining open communication throughout the dying period. The question "Am I dying?" may be very difficult for the nurse or parent to answer. Children deserve an honest answer and will know when the hospital staff and family are being deceptive. Honest and open communication creates a relationship of trust. Dying children need to know that they will be able to die in comfort, free of pain, and surrounded by the people and things they love. Liberal ward policies that allow families to sleep in, visiting by siblings and pets, and toys from home will enhance the child's emotional comfort in the final days.

Dying children need to know that they will be supported by those they love through the moment of death. Children of all ages fear abandonment throughout their illness and especially at death. They may have already experienced changes in their relationships with their friends and relatives, who often decrease closeness in their relationships because they find it too difficult to be in frequent contact with the child and family. If the child has already experienced these losses, he may fear that others will abandon him, too. The hospital staff should assist the family to remain close to the child. Touching conveys closeness and warmth without words. Parents of dying children should be permitted and encouraged to lie in the child's bed, holding and comforting the child. The parent can easily reposition himself if a treatment is necessary.

Other people in the hospital who are important to the child should also be encouraged to visit. Other patients on the ward who may themselves be dying can be especially helpful to the dying child and also to the parents. In addition, if these children are encouraged and allowed to visit other dying children, they will learn that they too will not be abandoned when they die.

Dying children are often placed in private rooms. However, private rooms are not always necessary. The child may want to be near friends and the parents may benefit from the support of the other parents in the room. When the parents of dying children request remaining in a "nonprivate" room, the nurse should speak with the parents of the other children and assess the feelings of those parents and their children. The nurse can then make a decision based upon the needs of everyone in the room.

COMFORTABLE ENVIRONMENT Although the hospital can never be as comfortable as the child's home, many steps can be taken to make the environment as comfortable as possible. Throughout the illness, painful procedures and treatments should be performed in a treatment room away from the child's room. There should be a telephone in the child's room to help the child maintain contact with family and friends. The child should wear his or her own clothes and be encouraged to continue with normal activities as long as possible.

The child and family will need to have adequate privacy to rest and relax, to share special feelings, and just to be alone as a family unit. The hospital environment is very noisy, highly stimulating, and demanding. It is emotionally exhausting for the child and family alike. Privacy helps limit stress from the environment at this very difficult time. The nurse should discuss this with the family; together they can set time periods during which no treatments or procedures are performed. If the child is in a private room, a sign can be placed on the door limiting entrance to only those persons who first check with the nurse. The nurse should also ask the parents if they would prefer to be alone with their child at the time of death, or immediately thereafter, and communicate the parents' wishes to the ward staff.

CONTROL The child suffers from the sense of loss

of control of his or her destiny, as do the parents. Active participation in care and decision making will help the child to gain some control over the situation. Throughout the illness and at death, the nurse can find many opportunities for the child to participate in care and to make choices. Two especially important decisions that the child should participate in are the cessation of treatment and the choice of place of death. The dying child may also be permitted to choose the intravenous site, clothes to wear, foods to eat, whether to stay up all night, and when to get out of bed. If the child makes requests that seem unreasonable, the nurse should listen carefully. If the nurse evaluates these requests as signs of the child's effort to regain "control," the requests should be granted, if possible.

INFORMATION Information is very important during the dying process. The child can better cope with death when the fear of the unknown is decreased. The nurse should begin by eliciting the child's preconceived ideas about the act of dying and correcting misconceptions. The nurse can then ask what questions the child has about dying. Small children usually ask if their parents will be with them when they die. The nurse might therefore want the parents present at these discussions so they can reassure the child. Older children, starting at about 8 or 9, may want to know if they will suffocate, have pain, or be conscious or unconscious at death. The nurse should answer these questions honestly, while also giving reassurance that everything will be done to keep the child comfortable. The child should be told that someone will always be with him, and this promise must be kept.

NEEDS OF PARENTS AND SIBLINGS Parents, siblings, and other members of the dying child's family can benefit from the nurse's assistance with their emotional needs during the death of a child.

Just as the child needs emotional support, so does the family. The nurse should get to know the family well in order to provide support according to their individual needs. The nurse's consistent interest and willingness to be involved in the family's sorrow can be very supportive. Often the best help the nurse can offer is a willingness to listen, regardless of when or how long. Sharing in the parents' anticipatory grieving and acknowledging that the nurse, too, loves and will miss the child are helpful. The parents can also derive support when the nurse is available to answer questions honestly and to provide teaching.

Many parents are reluctant to leave their child's side or to sleep. They want to spend every remaining minute with their child and be present when he dies. The emotional and physical strain parents experience are exhausting; the nurse should encourage them to rest. Offer to help find someone (perhaps a relative or neighbor) to sit with the child while the parents sleep, assuring them that you will awaken them if any changes occur.

Many parents worry about their other children and feel that they are neglected at times during the illness. Siblings should be involved as much as possible in the family's and dying child's activities.

A nursing care plan for a terminally ill, hospitalized child with cancer is presented at the end of the chapter.

Intervention after death occurs Many bereaved persons have remarked about their feelings during the period immediately after their loved one dies in the hospital. They often complain that they were not allowed enough time to be with their loved one after the death. Acceptance of death begins when the bereaved person sees the reality of the dead body. Parents who are allowed to remain with their dead child, to hold, to touch, to cry over, and to say goodbye can begin to accept the reality of the death. When children die at home, it is not unusual for parents and siblings to sit with the dead child for 1 h or more. This experience should also be available when the child dies in the hospital. The family should be allowed to call in other family members who wish to see the child a last time. The nurse should be supportive of the family's desires. They may want the nurse to sit with them, or they may ask to be left alone. The hospital should provide something to eat and drink before the family leaves.

The nurse who has established a good relationship with the family should attend the funeral, if at all possible. A follow-up visit to the home several weeks after the death or, minimally, a phone call to inquire about the family should be made. Some hospitals now have bereavement follow-up programs where the nurse calls or visits the family once a month for a year and on special days, such as the child's birthday and death anniversary. Some programs also include home visits by the nurse. The nurse can be helpful to the family during their grief by listening, answering questions, being willing to talk about the child (often others will not be able to), and making referrals if the family needs additional physical or emotional support.

Home care for the dying child

Care that facilitates the child's dying near loved ones in the familiar home surrounding is becoming increasingly available in the United States. Once the family and hospital staff have decided that treatment is to be discontinued, the family should have the option of choosing where the child will die. Many children request to return home. Frequently, the parents also want the child to be at home so they can reunite their family. At this critical time, the other siblings also need their parents' presence. Brothers and sisters are usually fearful and upset about what is happening to their ill sibling. They need support and reassurance from their parents. The parents may also wish to recreate some normalcy in their lives. Home care enables the family to reestablish considerable control over their lives, as the parents once again assume their role as primary caretakers of the child and managers of their household.

Despite these important needs, parents may be afraid to take their child home to die. They may fear that they are incapable of learning treatments and technical procedures, that they will give inadequate care, or that they won't be able to handle the actual death. They may fear the pressure of neighbors, relatives, and sometimes even health professionals, who may say that a dying child at home is too much of a strain on the parents and may emotionally damage the siblings.

The hospital nurse can counsel the family that is considering home care for their dying child. Dying at home is a reasonable alternative to dying in the hospital. The nurse should address the fears the family is likely to have regarding home care, but the positive aspects should also be identified. The nurse needs also to explain the philosophy of quality home care and services available so the family can make a well-informed decision.

Philosophy of home care   The home care team for the dying child usually consists of four persons, the parents, the nurse, and the physician. In order to enable the family to regain control over their lives, a quality home care program must be structured so that the parents are the primary care-givers for the child. The professional must recognize the parents' need to be in control and facilitate this in every possible manner.

The home care nurse functions primarily as a consultant to the family. The nurse assesses the child, discusses a care plan with the parents, teaches the family, provides emotional support, assesses medication effectiveness, and identifies equipment and supply needs. The nurse is a liaison between the family and the physician, other health care professionals, and health agencies. In addition, the nurse provides physical care if the family desires, and medication, equipment, and supplies when necessary. Quality home care ensures that the nurse is available to the family by telephone 24 h a day 7 days a week and that the nurse visits whenever and for whatever reason the family deems necessary. If the child is readmitted to the hospital, either temporarily or to die, the nurse continues to visit the family if they desire. The home care nurse does everything possible to assist the family.

Because of the discontinuation of active treatment, the home care physician generally functions as a consultant to the family. The physician is readily available to answer questions, make recommendations for care, or see the child if the parents or nurse feel they need the physician's opinion on the child's current status. The physician also assures the family that readmission to the hospital is always an option.

Parents who take their child home to die often fluctuate from great confidence to ambivalence about their decision and their abilities. Quality home care programs organized as previously described give parents a great deal of physical and emotional support. Whether the parents succeed in keeping the child home until death or decide to readmit the child, time spent at home can be of great emotional benefit to the child and the whole family.

Assessment for home care *Hospital nurse assessment*   Once the family has decided to return home, the hospital nurse should anticipate the physical and emotional care needs the child will have at home in order to identify the teaching needs of the family. Once the decision is made to discontinue treatment, the family usually wants to leave the hospital immediately in order to spend as much time at home as possible with the child. Time for teaching during hospitalization may be very limited; teaching should be started early. Parent participation in the care of the child during the entire illness facilitates parent teaching in preparation for going home.

The hospital nurse, either in conjunction with a home care coordinator or independently, should initiate a home care referral and, if possible, should have the home care nurse visit the child in the hospital. This enables the home care nurse to meet the family, observe teaching, and consult with the hospital staff. They can discuss the family's needs and develop a home care plan that is consistent with the care given in the hospital.

Home care nurse assessment The home care nurse should telephone the family on the day they take the child home and visit either that day or the next day. Because there are many differences between the home and the hospital setting, the nurse should complete a total family assessment. An assessment of the family's teaching needs should be made at the initial meeting. The nurse then develops nursing diagnoses and establishes long- and short-term care goals for home care.

Planning home nursing care The process of developing a care plan differs when the parents are the primary care-givers and the nurse is the consultant. The home care nurse needs to inform the parents of the discharge recommendations sent by the hospital staff and of the nurse's recommendations for care based upon the assessment. The parents, child, and nurse discuss these recommendations and the care that the family desires for the child. A nursing care plan is then developed by the family and nurse together. There should be a clear understanding of who is to provide the care. If the family desires, the nurse can be included as a physical-care provider. Fathers are often excluded from care

during hospitalization, and even at home, because they work outside the home. The nurse should encourage the father to assume specific care duties during his off-work hours if he desires. This will enable him to spend time with the child and provide support for the mother. If the family desires, the care plan can be written and left in the home. Parents also usually want to maintain flow sheets which record the child's status and care given. The nurse's willingness to assist in any way and 24-h availability should be stated during this initial meeting with the family and at subsequent meetings. Knowing that the nurse is there to assist them whenever needed, regardless of the time or the apparent importance of the request, is very important and very reassuring to the family.

The concept of comfort care should be discussed at the initial meeting. The nurse may need to explain the wide range of comfort care measures so that the family will know what is available at home. Comfort care at home can include medical measures such as intravenous fluids, oxygen, hypnosis, hyperalimentation, and medications. Analgesics, psychotropics, anticonvulsants, steroids, antipruritics, antidiarrheals, and antipyretics may be used.

The goals the family and nurse set depend upon the child's life expectancy. If the child is expected to live for several months, disease-preventive and health-maintenance goals are appropriate. If the child's life expectancy is several days or a week, the child's comfort should be the only concern.

Implementing home care *Teaching* If the child's life expectancy is very short, the home care nurse should provide essential family teaching about physical care at the initial meeting.

The nurse should also begin, as soon as possible, to discuss what the dying process is like and to inquire about funeral arrangements. In many counties the county coroner must investigate deaths which occur outside a hospital or other institution where death is common. The home care nurse can help the family avoid the necessity of a police investigation in the home, which might involve the removal of the body to the county coroner for examination. The nurse can call the medical examiner's or coroner's office and alert them that the child is expected to die and that the home care physician will sign the death certificate. The nurse should also notify the funeral home of these arrangements. The nurse needs to discuss this with the family and obtain their permission to contact the coroner's office. If the life expectancy is longer, e.g., several months, the nurse should discuss these topics when appropriate.

Home visits Once the home care tasks have been assumed by the various members of the family, the nurse can determine how often visits are needed. How often the nurse visits depends upon the condition of the child (Fig. 22-1). If the child is in the final days of life, visits may be every day and more often if the family desires. A child with a brain tumor who will live for 6 months might need only weekly visits after the initial assessment, planning, and teaching visits.

Physical care The provision of comfort care for physical needs in the home is very similar to providing these measures in the hospital. With the few following exceptions, hospital care of the dying child can be applied to the physical care in the home.

Figure 22-1 Jeremy, age 8, at home with his home care nurse. (*From the film "Time to Come Home," produced by Ida M. Martinson and Kenneth D. Greer*).

Hospital equipment such as suction machines and alternating pressure mattresses may be difficult to obtain. Exploration of the community and surrounding communities might reveal equipment that can be borrowed for a brief time.

Blood products have not to date been given in the home. The child may, however, go to an outpatient clinic or hospital emergency room in order to receive transfusions.

Emotional care of the child The child's greatest emotional need, to be surrounded by and cared for by the ones he loves, can be fulfilled when he is cared for at home. The home care nurse is often not very involved with the younger child, who usually prefers to be cared for by the parents. Older children and teenagers often strive to maintain their independence from parents throughout the dying period at home. They are therefore usually more willing than young children to accept nurse involvement and assistance with their emotional needs.

The child dying at home has the same emotional concerns as the child in the hospital. The child may be fearful, depressed, or angry. (See the previous section "Emotional Care," under "Implementing the Nursing Care Plan.")

The fear of abandonment does not disappear because the child is at home, although the possibility of abandonment is lessened when the family is together at home. The child still needs to be reassured that his family will always be close at hand. The nurse can offer to stay with the child while the parents rest or sleep or get away from the house for a while if they desire.

Privacy is sometimes a problem for the child and the family if there are numerous friends and relatives who wish to visit. The nurse can assist with this by suggesting that a sign be posted on the front door to limit visit times.

Emotional needs of parents and siblings Parents need the emotional support provided by the nurse's consistent interest and concern about the family and their needs. Many parents also need reassurance throughout the home care period that they made the correct decision in taking their child home to die and that they are providing the best possible care. These parents are highly susceptible to feelings of guilt and

(*Continued on page 549*)

Nursing Care Plan – Terminal Illness

Patient: Patty Gary   **Age:** 8 years   **Date of Admission:** 4/21, 2:30 P.M.

Assessment

Patty Gary is 8 years old. Her family consists of her mother, stepfather, and brothers, aged 4 and 6 years. Patty was first admitted to the hospital 1½ years ago with symptoms of ataxia and petit mal seizures. A neuroblastoma with metastases to the brain and spine was diagnosed. During her first admission, a ventriculoperitoneal (VP) shunt was inserted to relieve intracranial pressure and the maximum dose of radiation was given to the brain. Ten courses of chemotherapy were completed during the subsequent year.

Fourteen months after diagnosis, Patty demonstrated vomiting, irritability, and weakness in both lower extremities; she reported severe headaches. Repeat CT scan revealed recurring metastases. The physicians decided that cure-oriented therapy would no longer help Patty. This was discussed with Patty and her parents. The family decided Patty should return home and that treatment should consist of supportive care to relieve her symptoms. At the time of discharge, Patty had no bowel or bladder control, weakness in both lower extremities, a poor appetite, and she was very irritable.

A referral to the local community health nursing agency was made in anticipation of Patty's return home. The agency began visits immediately and provided 24-h coverage 7 days a week. Patty's family cared for her with the assistance of the community health nurses for 4 months. Although Patty became progressively worse, her family wanted to keep her at home as long as possible. Her illness advanced rapidly, resulting in total paralysis from the waist down and periods of unconsciousness lasting 1 or 2 days.

Patty's mother found it increasingly difficult to care for Patty at home and also care for other members of the family. The family's severe financial difficulties forced Mr. Gary to obtain a second job. Thus, he was not often able to assist his wife in caring for Patty or the other children. Signs of physical and emotional exhaustion were evident in Mrs. Gary. Last week, the community health nurse expressed her concerns about Mrs. Gary's ability to continue Patty's care at home. A long discussion followed, and Mrs. Gary tearfully admitted that she wanted Patty to spend her last days in the hospital. Patty was readmitted the following day.

Nursing diagnosis	Nursing goals	Nursing actions	Evaluation/revision
1. Pain due to disease process	☐ Patty will indicate relief from pain and headache	☐ Administer analgesic, as ordered, PRN ☐ See nursing actions for impaired mobility, below	☐ Obtains relief from analgesic administered q6h ☐ *Continue plan*
2. Impaired mobility due to lower extremity paralysis	☐ Skin will remain intact ☐ Lower extremity muscles will remain firm and toned ☐ Joints of lower extremities will retain range of motion	☐ Turn q1–2h when in bed ☐ Use alternating pressure mattress ☐ Out of bed (OOB) in reclining wheelchair with flotation pad at least tid ☐ Range of motion exercises to all joints in both lower extremities, qid	☐ Skin is smooth and intact ☐ Muscles remain firm ☐ Full flexion of lower extremities is possible with passive exercise. ☐ *Continue plan*
3. Urinary incontinence due to paralysis	☐ Bladder sufficiently drained ☐ Urine clear ☐ Body temperature within normal limits	☐ Foley catheter (No. 10) to straight drainage ☐ Irrigate catheter with Renacidin, 50–100 ml, PRN, if clogged	☐ Catheter draining properly ☐ No bladder distention ☐ Urinary output averages within 200 ml of fluid intake

Nursing diagnosis	Nursing goals	Nursing actions	Evaluation/revision
		☐ Change catheter once a week	☐ Urine clear and pale straw color; nonodoriferous ☐ *Continue plan*
4. Bowel incontinence due to paralysis	☐ Soft, formed bowel movement q2–3d	☐ Dioctyl sodium sulfosuccinate, 70 mg, PO, qd ☐ Bisacodyl rectal suppository, every 3d day, if no BM ☐ Pediatric (67.5 ml) sodium biphosphate/sodium phosphate enema and digital removal, PRN	☐ No BM for 3 days, suppositories ineffective; enema yielded good amount of moderately hard stool ☐ *Continue plan*
5. Nutritional deficit due to poor appetite and disease process	☐ Daily caloric intake between 1800–2400 kcal	☐ Offer small amounts of food frequently (Patty likes chocolate milk shakes, lemon soda, pickles, and spaghetti); do not force food ☐ Administer nutrients via nasogastric feeding tube when unconscious	☐ Eats only a few bites of food at a time ☐ Average oral intake, 1000 kcal/day ☐ *Continue plan*
6. Fluid deficit due to poor appetite and disease process	☐ Daily fluid intake between 1500–1800 ml ☐ Moist mucous membranes ☐ Good skin turgor	☐ Offer small sips of fluid frequently ☐ Administer supplemental IV fluids as ordered, PRN ☐ Administer mouth care with glycerin swabs and mouthwash at least qid ☐ Petrolatum to lips, PRN	☐ Average oral fluid intake, 750 ml/day; requires supplemental IV fluids ☐ *Continue plan*
7. Periodic loss of consciousness due to disease process	☐ Clear respiratory passage to permit adequate ventilation; corneas will remain moist ☐ Freedom from injury	☐ Monitor vital signs ☐ Check gag and swallow reflexes qh ☐ Check corneal reflex q4h ☐ Instill lubricating agent in both eyes, PRN ☐ Keep both padded side rails up, unless responsible adult is at bedside ☐ Provide supportive physical care as specified elsewhere in plan	☐ Has not lapsed from consciousness since admission
8. Anticipatory grief of parents due to Patty's impending death	☐ Parents will be able to verbalize their questions, concerns, and feelings with the nursing staff	☐ Allow parents to provide as much of Patty's care as they are able ☐ Provide a private place and time for parents to discuss their feelings about admitting Patty to the hospital and about death ☐ Encourage parents to leave the hospital and spend time with their sons ☐ Allow siblings to visit for periods of 5–10 min if parents so desire	☐ Parents able to express grief and feelings to staff ☐ Parents participate in Patty's care each day

Nursing diagnosis	Nursing goals	Nursing actions	Evaluation/revision
		☐ Explain signs of death when parents are ready for this information	
9. Financial stress due to medical expenses	☐ Family will receive any financial assistance for which they are eligible	☐ Referral to hospital social worker	☐ Parents met with social worker; applications for financial assistance filed

remorse and need to be reassured repeatedly that they have made the correct decision for their family.

Home care can be exhausting. The nurse should help the family members plan for daily rest, sleep, and exercise.

As in the hospital, the siblings should be involved as much as possible, either providing direct care or helping by entertaining the dying child (Fig. 22-2).

Siblings also need open and honest communication. They are astute and will be aware of the changes in their sibling and of the impending death. A trusting relationship with their family and the nurse is very important at this time.

Intervention after death occurs The family's need for emotional support continues through the many months which follow the child's death. The home care nurse should attend the funeral and other burial activities and visit the family during the first week after death. The nurse should telephone the family during the month and make a home visit 1 month after the child's death. If the family-nurse relationship is good, the nurse should continue visiting once a month for a year, or at least 6 and 12 months after the child's death. Depression, guilt, anger, relief, low energy, and social isolation are but a few of the feelings and problems the family may encounter in the months following the death of their child. The nurse can assist the family by helping them to cope with these feelings and problems, or by referring them to other appropriate persons, such as a parent-support group or professional counselor.

Figure 22-2 Jeremy, age 8, and his brothers at home. (*From the film "Time to Come Home," produced by Ida M. Martinson and Kenneth D. Greer.*)

References

1. Ida M. Martinson and Gordon D. Armstrong, *Cancer Facts and Figures*, American Cancer Society, New York, 1978, p. 20.
2. ———, "Death, Dying and Terminal Care: Dying at Home," in J. Kellerman (ed.), *Psychological Aspects of Childhood Cancer* (in publication), p. 2.
3. Robert Kastenbaum, "The Child's Understanding of Death: How Does It Develop?" in E. A. Grollman (ed.), *Explaining Death to Children*, Beacon Press, Boston, 1967, p. 94.
4. William M. Easson, *The Dying Child*, Charles C Thomas, Springfield, Ill., 1970, p. 24.
5. Ibid., p. 31.
6. Carol S. Green-Epner, "The Dying Child," in R. E. Caughill (ed.), *The Dying Patient: A Supportive Approach*, Little, Brown, Boston, 1976, p. 131.
7. E. Mansell Pattison, *The Experience of Dying*, Prentice-Hall, Englewood Cliffs, N.J., 1977, pp. 20–22.
8. Maria Nagy, "The Child's Theories Concerning Death," *J. General Psychology* 73:3 (1978).

9. Easson, op. cit., pp. 32–33.

10. Nagy, op. cit., p. 32.

11. Kastenbaum, op. cit., p. 103.

12. Jean Piaget, *The Child's Conception of the World*, Routledge, London, 1929.

13. Jo-Eileen Gyulay, *The Dying Child*, McGraw-Hill, New York, 1978, p. 20.

14. Sharon L. Hostler, "The Development of the Child's Concept of Death," in Olle Jane Sahler (ed.), *The Child and Death*, Mosby, St. Louis, 1978, p. 20.

15. Kastenbaum, op. cit., p. 103.

16. Rose Zeligs (ed.), *Children's Experience with Death*, Charles C Thomas, Springfield, Ill., 1974, p. 26.

17. J. R. Morrissey, "Death Anxiety in Children with a Fatal Illness," in H. J. Parad (ed.), *Crisis Intervention*, Family Service Association of America, New York, 1965, pp. 324–338.

18. J. M. Natterson and A. G. Knudson, "Observations Concerning Fear of Death in Fatally Ill Children and Their Mothers," *Psychosomatic Medicine* 22:456–465 (1960).

19. E. H. Waechter, "Children's Awareness of Fatal Illness," *American Journal of Nursing* 71:1168–1172 (1971).

20. Myra Bluebond-Langner, *The Private Worlds of Dying Children*, Princeton, Princeton, N.J., 1978, pp. 166–197.

21. ———, "I Know, Do You? A Study of Awareness, Communication and Coping in Terminally Ill Children," in B. Schoenberg et al. (eds.), *Anticipatory Grief*, Columbia, New York, 1974, p. 180.

22. Susan F. Woolsey, Doris S. Thornton, and Stanford B. Friedman, "Sudden Death," in Olle Jane Sahler (ed.), *The Child and Death*, p. 101, Mosby, op. cit., St. Louis, 1978, p. 101.

23. Gyulay, op. cit., p. 83

24. Stanford B. Friedman, "Epilogue to the Loss of a Child," in Olle Jane Sahler, op. cit., p. 279.

25. Ida M. Martinson, *Home Care for the Dying Child*, Appleton Century Crofts, New York, 1976, p. 201.

26. Lindy Burton, *The Family Life of Sick Children*, Routledge, London, 1975, p. 48.

27. Gyulay, op. cit., p. 91.

28. Ibid., p. 93.

29. Burton, op. cit., p. 225.

30. Ibid., p. 229.

31. Martinson, *Home Care for the Dying Child*, p. 235.

32. Ibid., p. 139.

33. C. M. Binger et al., "Childhood Leukemia: Emotional Impact on Patient and Family," *New England Journal of Medicine* 280:414–418 (1969).

34. Martinson, *Home Care for the Dying Child*, p. 153.

35. Bernard Schoenberg, et al. (eds.), *Loss and Grief: Psychological Management in Medical Practice*, Columbia, New York, 1970, p. 96.

36. Burton, op. cit., p. 203.

37. Stephen W. Munson, "Family Structure and the Family's General Adaptation to Loss: Helping Families Deal with the Death of a Child," in Olle Jane Sahler (ed.), op. cit., p. 40.

38. Ibid., p. 40.

39. Glen Davidson, M.D., *Mourning—Living with Dying*, presentation at the University of Minneapolis, May 3, 1979.

40. Harriet Sarnoff Schiff, *The Bereaved Parent*, Crown, New York, 1977, p. 146.

41. John E. Schowalter, "The Reactions of Caregivers Dealing with Fatally Ill Children and Their Families," in Olle Jane Sahler (ed.), op. cit.

42. Carol A. Reese, "Support Systems: A Necessity for Professionals in Health Care," in Ida A. Martinson (ed.), *Home Care for the Dying Child*, p. 89.

43. Ibid., pp. 92–93.

44. Elizabeth Kubler-Ross, "The Languages of Dying," *Journal of Clinical Psychology*, Summer 1974, pp. 22–24.

45. Myra Bluebond-Langner, op. cit.

46. Barbara M. Korsch, "Issues in Humanizing Care for Children," *American Journal of Public Health* 68:831–832 (1978).

47. Patricia B. Jackson, "Child Care in the Hospital—A Parent/Staff Partnership," *MCN The American Journal of Maternal-Child Nursing*, March-April 1978, pp. 104–107.

48. Annette H. Ayer, "Is Partnership with Parents Really Possible?" *MCN The American Journal of Maternal-Child Nursing*, March-April 1978, pp. 107–110.

49. Carol B. Hardgrove and Rosime Kermoian, "Parent-Inclusive Pediatric Units," *American Journal of Public Health* 68:847–850 (1978).

50. Shirley Lansky et al., "Childhood Cancer," *Cancer*, vol. 43, January 1979, p. 403.

51. Richard Lamerton, "Drugs for the Dying," *St. Bartholomew's Hospital Journal*, November 1974.

52. ———, "Opiate Delusions," *World Medicine*, January 1978, pp. 44–45.

53. Sylvia A. Lack, "New Haven (1974)—Characteristics of a Hospice Program of Care," *Death Education* 2:41–52 (Spring-Summer 1978).

54. William M. Lamers, Jr., "Marin County (1976)—Development of Hospice of Marin," *Death Education* 2:53–62 (Spring-Summer 1978).

55. Richard Lamerton, "Opiate Delusions," *World Medicine*, January 1978, p. 44.

56. D. Gay Moldow and Ida M. Martinson, *Home Care for Dying Children: A Manual for Parents*, School of Nursing, University of Minnesota, Minneapolis, Minn., 1979.

57. Karen Olness and G. Gail Gardner, "Some Guidelines for the Uses of Hypnotherapy in Pediatrics," *Pediatrics* 62(2):228–233 (August 1978).

58. Wallace La Baw, et al., "The Use of Self-Hypnosis by Children with Cancer," *The American Journal of Clinical Hypnosis* 17(4):233–238 (April 1975).

59. Preparation of this manuscript was supported, in part, by grants from The St. Paul Foundation and DHEW, National Cancer Institute, Grant CA 19490.

Part Three Alterations in child health

Chapter 23 **Nutrition**

Lyn Steele Ultsch

Upon completion of this chapter, the student will be able to:

1. Describe two psychosocial influences of dietary intake.

2. Contrast the three forms of vegetarianism.

3. Identify the basic four food group guidelines for children.

4. Identify the four categories of information used in making nutritional assessments.

5. Describe one government-funded public nutrition program.

6. Identify the deficiency disease associated with selected nutrients.

7. Identify vitamins which are toxic if taken in excess.

8. Evaluate a weight loss diet using at least four of the seven criteria given in the text.

9. Identify foods associated most often with selected forms of food-borne illnesses.

10. Identify appropriate dietary restrictions for children with alterations of major organs.

11. Describe correct procedure for the administration of enteral nutritional supplements.

12. List two major classes of nutrients used in total parenteral nutrition solutions.

13. Identify appropriate nursing interventions for psychological problems associated with hyperalimentation.

Nutrition is a health science dealing with the consumption of food and its usage by the body. Through the processes of ingestion, digestion, absorption, and metabolism the body is supplied with the nutrients—carbohydrates, proteins, fats, minerals, vitamins, and water—necessary for growth and maintenance. Growth, increase in body size, requires basic building materials supplied from outside the body. Even during periods when growth is not acutely apparent, the body's cells are continuously replacing themselves, and so daily replacement of nutrients is necessary. Daily nutritional needs are influenced by an individual's age, sex, activity level, and environment. (The needs of specific age groups are found in Chaps. 10–15.)

Each individual is born with a specific genetic potential. During growth the child strives to fulfill this potential. This can only be accomplished if the child is provided with a healthy environment, including adequate nutrition. A child may have the potential of becoming a 7-ft basketball player but if adequate amounts of protein are not eaten, this height will not be attained. When nutritional inadequacies occur early in life, "catch-up" growth will occur once intake improves.

Factors that influence dietary intake

Cultural influences

What foods are eaten, how they are eaten, and when they are eaten are parts of an individual's behavior dictated by culture. In the United States a child learns that milk helps promote growth, especially that of bones and teeth, and yet many other cultures regard milk as animal waste and do not include it in their diets.[1] In the United States the main meal is eaten in the evening, while in Europe many consume their large meal at midday. Neither of these cultural approaches is necessarily incorrect.

Children begin to learn eating habits from birth. By the time they reach school their cultural and familial patterns are routine. At this time children come in contact with other children and begin to acquire new eating habits.

Many religions have dietary laws which influence the food intake of members. These laws often reflect some aspect of punishment or atonement for wrongdoing. Such is the Jewish observance of Yom Kippur, during which a 1-day fast is required. Longer periods of atonement or preparation are observed by many Christians, such as Lent. During such periods children are often asked to "give up" a favorite treat, such as candy or desserts, rather than abstain from eating.

Social and psychological influences

According to Maslow, human beings have a hierarchy of basic needs. The first three are the vital physiological needs for food, shelter, and clothing. For some people, such as those in poverty areas around the world, the primary reason for eating is to satisfy hunger. When food is plentiful and this basic need is easily met, eating satisfies other needs. A summary of these needs may be seen in Table 23-1. The further an individual moves from the basic physiological need level, the less he eats purely out of hunger. When a person is on the low level of the scale, any edible substance is consumed. In contrast, an individual who has reached the level of self-esteem may only satisfy his hunger with first-quality cuts of beef—what he perceives as status foods.

For children, the food offered at home will reflect the psychological-social meanings of food for the parents. Other abstract concepts also influence a child's intake. All too often food is used as a reward or punishment. In the United States especially, sweets (candy, cookies, cakes, etc.) are used to reward "good" behavior. Frequent use of such food items may lead to such nutritional problems as dental caries or obesity. Conversely, "bad" behavior may be punished by the withholding of particular foods or of entire meals. These practices may deprive the child of needed nutrients and if done frequently may lead to nutritional problems.

As the child advances in age, peer pressure plays an increasingly large role in food intake. Although sound eating habits may have been

Table 23-1 Correlation between Maslow's hierarchy of needs and individual food habits

Hierarchy of human needs	Hierarchy of food habits
Basic physiological needs	Foods satisfy feeling of hunger and thirst. Little regard is given to content of the food.
Safety needs	Food is used for maintenance of health and growth. Selection of foods is made to avoid harmful ingredients and to get necessary nutrients.
Need to be loved or to belong	Food is a social reinforcement. Food likes, dislikes, and usage are influenced by significant others in social realm. Use of food fads.
Need for self-esteem, recognition	Food selection is influenced by perceptions of status foods.
Need for self-actualization	Food growth and preparation is done by self. Experimenting is done to create new preparation, serving techniques, and recipes.

established earlier in their lives, adolescents often succumb to the influence of others and select fast food instead of following their previous training. For many teenage females the pressure to be thin and the concomitant use of various fad weight-loss diets or the elimination of meals can be a problem. Neither practice is advisable, especially during this critical growth period. These influences of peers relate to the third step in Maslow's hierarchy—the need for love and belonging.

Physical influences

Food selection may be limited by physical disability. Most often these limitations relate to the texture of the food. Soft or even pureed foods are easier to manage when the ability to chew is decreased because of some dental problem.

Larger problems with meals are encountered when a congenital anomaly or birth defect exists. If the child is unable to feed himself, he is totally dependent on another individual for his food intake. Time must be taken to ensure that the child receives a sufficient quantity of nutritious food. Educable mentally retarded individuals can be taught many aspects of food selection and basic food preparation techniques. Physical handicaps may require the involvement of an occupational therapist to help adapt conventional eating utensils (Fig. 23-1). A child who cannot grasp a spoon may be taught how to eat using a spoon attached to a band which is

Figure 23-1 Eating utensils for handicapped children. (*From "Feeding the child with a handicap,"* DHEW Pub. No. (HSM) 73-5609)

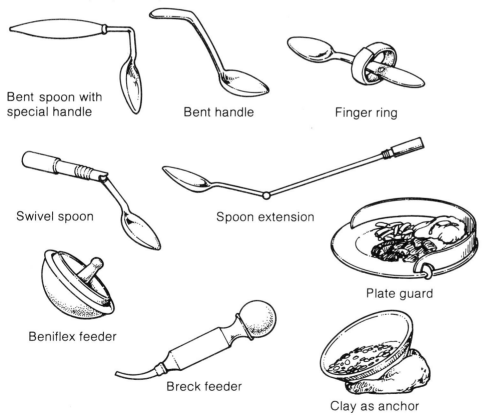

Bent spoon with special handle

Bent handle

Finger ring

Swivel spoon

Spoon extension

Plate guard

Beniflex feeder

Breck feeder

Clay as anchor

secured around the hand. Special nipples are available for use with infants who have a cleft palate or lip.

Current trends in food consumption

Health, natural, and organic foods *Health, natural,* and *organic* are adjectives currently used with the connotation that food so described is somehow better than other foods. *Natural* is used to refer to foods which have had minimal processing and contain no artificial colorings, flavorings, or preservatives. Some foods which have never contained any artificial items are now labeled *natural* in an effort to increase their marketability. This word may also be used to describe one ingredient in a food product that still may contain some preservatives or other artificial ingredients. Closer regulation of the use of the term *natural* is needed. This is difficult to do since a concrete definition of the word in the food industry is not available.

Natural has also been used to describe vitamin and mineral preparations. This leads the consumer to believe that the nutrients were taken from a substance which exists in nature rather than from a laboratory. To the human body a vitamin is a vitamin and a mineral is a mineral. If the nutrient is the chemical compound needed by the body, it will be used despite the nutrient's origin. Under chemical analysis the origin, nature or lab, cannot be determined. Natural vitamins and minerals do not have any greater effect on the human body than synthesized supplements.

Organic is used to describe foods grown without the aid of commercial fertilizers or pesticides. Many so-called organic foods, however, have been found to contain pesticide residues.[2] This occurs because pesticides can remain in the soil for several years and can be carried by the wind.

Another group of foods are those labeled *health foods.* Such items as honey, kelp, sea salt, and stone-ground flour are given the connotation that they possess some healthful property. This alleged healthfulness is generally attributed to minimal processing of these foods. The health qualities have not been proven and are questionable at best. For example, honey carries the connotation of being a healthful sweetener since it undergoes little or no processing. In comparing honey to table sugar, a processed sweetener,

neither sweetener contains any significant quantities of vitamin or minerals. Honey and sugar contain approximately equal amounts of empty calories. Both sweeteners also cause dental caries, elevated blood sugar levels, and obesity when taken in excess. Similar arguments can be made for many other so-called health foods.

It is important to keep in mind that the foods labeled *organic, natural,* or *health* often carry a premium price. Similar items may be found on supermarket shelves at lower costs if the shopper takes the time to read food labels carefully. Tighter control of this aspect of the food industry will assure the consumer that the food is what its name claims it is.

Fast foods On the opposite end of the scale from health, natural, and organic foods are fast foods, which also have grown in popularity. Many people believe that the foods offered at fast-food establishments are junk food. On the contrary, fast foods do provide some needed nutrients. Recent studies show that many fast-food entrees contain substantial amounts of protein and fair amounts of the B-complex vitamins.[3] Burgers are the major items at fast-food franchises. When compared to items in the basic four food groups (see Appendix C), these sandwiches contain half of the daily servings a child needs from the grain (one bun equals two slices) and meat (approximately 2 oz.) groups.[4] Fast foods are somewhat high in calories because of their high fat and starch content,[5] but these calories are not empty. For a teen whose energy needs are relatively high, fast foods offer the needed calories while supplying other needed nutrients.

Vegetarianism Another current trend is vegetarianism. Three forms of vegetarianism exist. The *vegan* is a vegetarian who eats foods only from plant sources, such as vegetables, fruits, grains, and legumes. A *lactovegetarian* uses milk and milk products in addition to plant foods. *Lactovovegetarians* use dairy items, eggs, and plant foods. The latter two forms of vegetarian diet generally contain adequate amounts of complete protein (proteins that contain all eight essential amino acids). These types of vegetarianism are easier to follow since a wider range of foods may be eaten. The strict vegetarian (vegan) must be careful to use foods whose amino acids complement one another.

For children, lactovegetarian or lactovovegetarian diets can supply most of the nutrients needed for growth. One problem with a heavy reliance on milk, however, is the possible development of iron-deficiency anemia. With such diets a good source of ascorbic acid should be included at each meal to aid with the absorption of iron from plant foods.[6] Children who follow vegan diets are at risk for low intakes of amino acids, vitamins D and B_{12}, riboflavin, and iron. Adequate amino acids can be obtained if foods are included at each meal which in combination supply all of the essential amino acids. Meat analogs made from plants contain the same needed protein. Fortified soybean milk will supply the needed vitamins along with protein. The use of this soy milk is strongly urged for vegan children.[7]

Nutritional assessment

Nutritional assessment is the evaluation of an individual's nutritional status. It involves the use of dietary, physical, anthropometric, and biochemical data. The first three of these give information which may indicate some nutritional problem. Biochemical data are then used to confirm the existence of such problems.

Dietary information

Purpose Information concerning an individual's dietary intake is important to determine the food and nutrient components of the diet. Such information can be obtained by the nurse while taking a nursing history. The amount of information needed will depend on whether or not there is a current health problem and the type and severity of such problems.

Methods of data collection A diet history provides data concerning general eating habits. This should be part of each child's health record (see Appendix C for a nutrition history form). As the child grows and changes in eating habits occur (e.g., addition of solid food), this record should be updated. Periodic well-child checkups provide the nurse with an opportunity to obtain this information. Items to be included are: amounts of foods eaten from the various food groups, frequency of meals and snacks, recent changes in food intake (such as special diets), the use of nutritional supplements, food likes and dislikes, and food allergies. In some instances information concerning the availability of food storage and preparation facilities may be needed. This type of information may be available from the child or parent, but it can also be obtained by a public health or visiting nurse through simple observation of the home.

Most diet histories are obtained by interviewing. Care should be taken so that interviewer bias is not present. Such things as tone of voice and word accentuation may convey interviewer prejudice or anticipated responses. In such instances the interviewee will respond with what is perceived to be the desired response rather than actual fact. Assumptions concerning meal habits should not be conveyed in the interview either. It is best for the nurse to ask, "What is the first item you normally eat or drink each day?" and proceed to ask questions about the rest of the day in a like manner. This avoids interviewer interference associated with the question "What do you eat for breakfast?" which assumes the child eats breakfast. When working with small children, the interviewer will find that plastic food models may be useful for obtaining estimates of portion sizes. Measuring utensils are generally more useful with older children and adolescents than with young children. Other information regarding food likes or dislikes and general food usage can be obtained by asking the parent or child to complete a questionnaire (Fig. 23-2). This should then be reviewed by the nurse so that any necessary clarifications can be made.

In some instances specific food intake during the previous 24 h (or some other specific time period) is important (e.g., in the case of allergic reactions or food poisoning). This differs from a diet history in that the 24- or 48-h diet recall must contain *all* food items consumed within the specified period and not a general picture of normal dietary habits. In some instances amounts of food and location of preparation and consumption are important. If the child was away from the parent during part of specified time period, it will be necessary to interview both parent and child to obtain an accurate 24- or 48-h diet recall.

Figure 23-2 Food preference form.

	Frequency				
Food	**Never**	**Seldom**	**Once a Month**	**Once a Week**	**Daily**
Milk					
Cheese					
Ice Cream					
Pudding, Custard					
Peanut Butter					
Eggs					
Liver					
Beef, Lamb, Pork					
Chicken, Turkey					
Fish					
Dried Beans (Lentils, Navy, Pinto, Kidney)					
Spinach					
Carrots					
Orange, Grapefruit					
Salad					
Squash					
Broccoli					
Cauliflower					
Corn					
Peas					
Green Beans					
Fresh Fruit					
Fruit Cocktail					
Applesauce					
White Bread					
Noodles					
Rice					
Cold Cereal (specify)					
Hot Cereal					
Whole Wheat or Rye Bread					
Potatoes					
Candy					
Soda					
Kool-Aid					
Chewing Gum (specify)					
Cake					
Popcorn					
Pizza					

When exact calorie or nutrient consumption levels are important, a food diary should be used. Such would be the case when working with an anorexic or obese child. With this form all foods (liquid and solid) consumed are recorded, as well as an exact specification of portion sizes. Generally such a record is completed by the dietitian. Food composition tables are used to determine the nutrient content of the food consumed. Most individuals, especially children, need help in estimating total portion sizes and amounts eaten. When working with some children, it may also be necessary to remind them to record their meals and all snacks. Occasionally monitoring of meals is necessary to verify that the food was actually consumed and not thrown in the trash or flushed in the toilet. If a food diary is done on an outpatient basis, clear and precise instructions should be given by the dietitian or nurse, with reinforcement as needed.

Once dietary data have been collected they are evaluated using the basic four food groups or recommended dietary allowances (RDAs). The basic four divides food into four broad categories (see Appendix C). Each food item within the group supplies similar nutrients. Such extras as fats and sugars are in a separate group known as *extras*. Any food record can be evaluated using this method. The foods consumed are placed into the appropriate group and an evaluation is made to determine if the recommended number of servings were consumed (Table 23-2). To evaluate a diet using the recommended dietary allowances, the food consumed is located in food composition tables (such as those in *Agriculture Handbook no. 8* or manufacturer's prod-

uct content charts) and all necessary nutrient levels are recorded. Then all components are totalled and matched against the child or adolescent's RDAs (see Appendix C).

Occasional or slight variations from the basic four food groups or RDAs will not be harmful. When a consistent variation is noted, therapeutic and educative measures are indicated. The degree of therapeutic measures will depend on what is found from other areas of data collection. Educative measures should be initiated by the nurse or other members of the health team to encourage proper food and nutrient intakes.

Physical status information

Physical assessment findings may be indicative of some nutrition problems. Relationships between certain physical observations and nutrition are listed in Table 23-3. For example, the nurse may note that a child is pale and has pale conjunctivae and brittle, ridged nails. Upon further investigation it is noted that the hemoglobin and hematocrit are significantly below normal. The physical observations of the nurse suggest iron deficiency, which is confirmed by biochemical data.

Table 23-2 Evaluation of a teen's diet using basic four food groups (*For a 24-h recall*)

Food	Amount	Food group
Breakfast:		
None		
Lunch:		
Hamburger on	3 oz	Meat
a roll	1	Bread
French fries	½ cup	Fruit and vegetable—fat
ketchup		
Cola drink	12 oz	Extra
Apple	1 medium	Fruit and vegetable
Snack:		
Ice cream cone	½ cup	Milk (at ⅓ of a full serving)
Chewing gum		Extra
Supper:		
Chicken thigh	2 oz	Meat
Mashed potatoes	½ cup	Fruit and vegetables
Green peas	¼ cup	Fruit and vegetable—½ serving
Lemonade	12 oz	Extra
Yellow cake	1 slice	Extra
Snack:		
Cola drink	16 oz	Extra
Potato chips	¼ bag—2 oz	Extra
Chocolate bar	3 oz	Extra

Table 23-3 Physical signs and causes of malnutrition

Body area	Signs associated with malnutrition	Nutrition-related causes
Hair	Lack of natural shine; dull, dry, sparse, straight; color changes (flag sign); easily plucked	Protein-calorie deficiency; often multiple coexistent nutrient deficiencies
Face	Dark skin over cheeks and under eyes (malar and infraorbital pigmentation), scaling of skin around nostrils (nasolabial seborrhea)	Inadequate caloric intake; lack of B-complex vitamins, particularly niacin, riboflavin, pyridoxine
	Edematous (moon face)	Protein deficiency
	Color loss (pallor)	Iron deficiency, general undernutrition
Eyes	Pale conjunctivae	Iron deficiency
	Bitôt's spots, conjunctival and corneal xerosis, soft cornea (keratomalacia)	Vitamin A deficiency
	Redness and fissuring of eyelid corners (angular palpebritis)	Niacin, riboflavin, pyridoxine deficiency
Lips	Redness and swelling of mouth or lips (cheilosis), angular fissure and scars	Niacin or riboflavin deficiency
Tongue	Red, raw and fissured, swollen (glossitis)	Folic acid, niacin, B$_{12}$, pyridoxine deficiency
	Magenta color	Riboflavin deficiency
	Pale, atrophic	Iron deficiency
	Filiform papillary atrophy	Niacin, folic acid, B$_{12}$, iron deficiency
	Fungiform papillary hypertrophy	General undernutrition
Teeth	Carious or missing	Excess sugar (and poor dental hygiene)
	Mottled enamel (fluorosis)	Excess fluoride
Gums	Spongy, bleeding; may be receding	Ascorbic acid deficiency
Glands	Thyroid enlargement (goiter)	Iodine deficiency
	Parotid enlargement	General undernutrition, particularly insufficient protein
Skin	Follicular hyperkeratosis, dryness (xerosis) with flaking	Vitamin A deficiency; insufficient unsaturated and essential fatty acids
	Hyperpigmentation	B$_{12}$ folic acid, niacin deficiency
	Petechiae	Ascorbic acid deficiency
	Pellagrous dermatitis	Niacin or tryptophan deficiency
	Scrotal and vulval dermatosis	Riboflavin deficiency
Nails	Spoon nails (koilonychia); brittle or ridged	Iron deficiency
Muscular and skeletal systems	Muscle wasting	Protein-calorie deficiency
	Frontal and parietal bosselation; epiphyseal swelling; soft, thin infant skull bones (craniotabes), persistently open anterior fontanel; knock-knees or bow-legs	Vitamin D deficiency
	Beading of ribs (rachitic rosary)	Vitamin D and calcium deficiency
Internal systems: gastrointestinal, nervous	Hepatomegaly	
	Mental confusion and irritability	Chronic malnutrition
	Sensory loss, motor weakness, loss of position sense, loss of vibration, loss of ankle and knee jerks, calf tenderness	Thiamine, niacin deficiency Thiamine deficiency
Cardiac	Cardiac enlargement, tachycardia	Thiamine deficiency

Source: Rosanne B. Howard and Nancie H. Herbold, *Nutrition in Clinical Care*, McGraw-Hill, New York, 1978. Used by permission of the publisher.

Anthropometric information

Anthropometric data are body measurements such as height, weight, specific body circumferences, and skin fold or subcutaneous fat measurements. When taken periodically, these measurements indicate growth.[8] Each child should have at least a height and weight record (see Appendix B). A child who falls above the 97th percentile or below the 3d percentile should be further evaluated.[9,10]

For infants under 24 months of age, head circumference measurements are part of the growth record. Increased head circumference may indicate such problems as hydrocephalus, which does not relate to nutrition. Abnormally small head circumference may be an indication of nutrient deprivation.[11] When malnutrition occurs during a period of rapid brain cell growth, children have a reduced brain size due to a reduction in the number of brain cells.[12] When an altered head circumference can be linked to altered nutritional intake, steps should be taken to change the nutrient intake and prevent any further alterations in growth.

Malnutrition, either from deprivation or excess, can also be discovered by taking the midarm circumference in relation to the head circumference. This ratio reflects lean body mass and skeletal body reserves.[13] Table 23-4 gives the ratio values and their relationships to nutrition. The midarm circumference should be taken at the midpoint between the acromial process of the scapula and the tip of the elbow.

Another anthropometric measure which indicates obesity is the triceps skinfold thickness. The midpoint of the upper arm is located and marked. The skin and subcutaneous fat are gently pulled from the muscle 1 in above the midpoint and this thickness is measured in millimeters using a Lange caliper (see Figure 23-3). For greatest accuracy, three measurements should be taken and averaged. The triceps skinfold measure can be used with children 2 years and older.[14]

Biochemical information

Biochemical information can be obtained from analysis of blood or urine. This form of data is used to confirm suspected alterations in nutrition. Deviations from the normal ranges for nutrient or waste levels in blood and urine are sometimes indicative of a nutritional problem. Some of the common blood tests include hemoglobin and hematocrit, serum albumin, glucose, and total iron binding capacity. Serum vitamin levels can also be measured. Care should be used when including lab results in nutritional assessments. These tests measure nutrient levels in the blood and do not indicate storage levels of these nutrients. Hemoglobin, for example, does not decrease below normal until stores of iron are depleted. A normal value therefore does

Table 23-4 Midarm and head circumference ratio (*3–48 months*)

Ratio	Relation to nutrition
<0.25	Severe undernutrition
0.25–0.28	Moderate undernutrition
0.28–0.31	Mild undernutrition
0.31–0.35	Normal
>0.35	Obese

not indicate if the stores are full or near empty. Further tests of storage iron levels give a more accurate picture of the body's nutritional status but are not done on a routine basis.

Urine analysis also provides some information relating to nutrition. When protein, sugar, or ketones appear in the urine, further study should be done to determine the cause and necessary adjustments in the diet should be made. If the child or adolescent is following a weight reduction program, the excretion of ketones will reflect a decrease in body fat and may indicate whether the reduction program is being followed or not.

Additional information

Besides the four major categories of data mentioned, some other information is useful to complete the nutritional picture. All allergies, especially food allergies, should be recorded. Any medications, especially vitamin and mineral supplements, should be recorded indicating name and dosage. Since more and more nutrient-drug interactions are being discovered, this information is becoming more important.

Prevention of nutrition alterations

The prevention of nutrition alterations in children has three main focuses—prenatal care of the mother, early detection of problems, and nutrition education.

Prenatal care of the mother

The diet of the mother from her birth until conception is just as important as the diet she follows during her pregnancy. Sound dietary habits during childhood and adolescence provide the nutrients needed for her growth and health and prepare her for a successful pregnancy. A pregnancy superimposed on the growth requirements of the adolescent mother increases nutritional needs tremendously because the

Figure 23-3 Taking skinfold measurements. (*A*) Location of the midpoint of the upper arm. (*B*) Application of the Lange calipers for measurement of triceps skinfold. (*C*) Representation of the tissues of the arm (bone, fat, and skin) and measurement of skinfold thickness. (*From Rosanne Howard and Nancie Herbold, Nutrition in Clinical Care, McGraw-Hill, New York, 1978. Used by permission of the publisher.*)

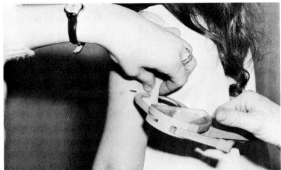

B

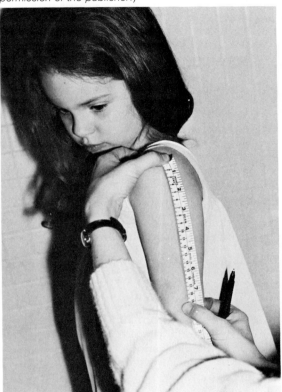

A

BONE
MUSCLE
FAT
SKIN

C

young girl does not have nutrient stores for herself and for the baby. Once the growth rate of a girl begins to decrease, these stores can begin to build. The same situation exists for a woman who has rapid successive pregnancies. Nutritionally her body has not recovered from the earlier pregnancy. Spacing pregnancies approximately 1 year apart permits full nutritional recovery. A woman who is in good health and has followed a well-balanced diet is nutritionally ready for a pregnancy. This preparation plus a good diet during pregnancy will provide the child with the best possible start in life and help to prevent later problems.

Early detection of problems

The sooner a nutritional problem is detected and treated, the fewer serious problems will develop. Good assessment skills are invaluable in early detection. Slight changes in a child's activity level or appearance may indicate a dietary problem. A diet history may pinpoint a problem with the diet. Corrective steps can then be taken to prevent the development of a serious nutritional problem. One example would be the nurse who observes that the child seems "chunkier." This observation is confirmed by the amount of weight gain over the past year. While talking to the child, the nurse learns that the child now has limited daily activity and eats a large amount of empty calorie snack foods. The child can be taught about nutritious snack foods and the importance of a well-balanced diet and daily exercise. With early detection the overweight child can be helped before becoming an obese child.

Nutrition education

Both prevention and correction of nutritional problems depend on good nutrition education. Through this process the child and parent are provided with sound information regarding food selection and preparation and the important part these play in health. The nurse can play a significant role in this process, as will be explained later. Nutrition education may be family-oriented or client-centered.

Family teaching deals with such topics as meal planning, budgeting, and food purchasing and preparation. Family members can be given information concerning a well-balanced diet using the basic four food groups. Appendix C, which lists the basic four food groups and minimal portion sizes needed by various age groups, can be used when planning food purchases. When shopping, the parents need to be aware of the cost of nutrients from each food group. Pertinent information is available from local health departments, extension services, and consumer buying guides.

For teaching a pediatric client, the information presented should be narrowed to that which applies directly to the child. From preschool age on, children can be taught their daily food needs using the basic four food groups. Teaching aids appropriate for various age groups are available from the American Dairy Council, the U.S. Department of Agriculture, local health departments, and many hospital dietitians. Children can also be taught basic food preparation skills. Such things as making sandwiches, cleaning fruits and vegetables, and stirring and mixing can be done by a child as young as 3 years. By doing these simple tasks a child takes more interest in food and is more likely to eat these items. Another area for education is meal habits. The importance of eating three meals can be stressed. Once the child reaches adolescence, more detailed information can be given. Often this will be done through science, health, home economics, and family life courses given in the schools.

Public nutrition programs

From the start of life, a child can receive needed nutrition from the Women, Infant and Children (WIC) Supplementation program. Through WIC low-income pregnant or lactating mothers and children up to 5 years of age receive selected food supplements. Vouchers are given monthly for such items as milk, cheese, eggs, certain fortified cereals, fruit juices, certain protein substitutes, and iron-enriched baby formula. The emphasis of the program is to provide such nutrients as calcium, iron, protein, and vitamins during the early rapid growth period. Eligibility for these supplements depends on family size and yearly income. The programs are administered through the local health department under the direction of a dietitian or nutritionist. When the nurse is dealing with low-income young mothers and children, encouragement for participation in this program should be given.

A complete family can receive aid through the Food Stamp Program. Again family size and income determine eligibility. Food stamps can be used in place of money to purchase any edible food except certain specialty import items (e.g., caviar). No restrictions as to quality or selection of food are made. This program is generally administered through local welfare offices. WIC and the Food Stamp Program are provided so that people can obtain necessary food to aid in the prevention of health problems.

Specific meal programs for children also exist. It has long been established that breakfast is the most important meal of the day. Children who eat breakfast generally are more alert and perform better during the day. These ideas supported the establishment of a breakfast program under the Child Nutrition Act of 1966. Through this program a school-age child is able to purchase a well-balanced breakfast at full or reduced rate prior to the start of the school day. Milk, fruit or juice, and entree are generally provided. This program is especially good for children who leave home very early because of the distance they travel by bus to school or those children who would normally skip breakfast. For many reasons the breakfast is not available in all school districts.

The School Lunch Program is available on a much wider scale. A "Type A" lunch provides a minimum of 2 oz of meat or a protein alternative, a half pint of milk, one slice of enriched bread or an enriched alternative (e.g., macaroni), and two servings of fruit, or vegetables, or both. For children or adolescents who can not afford to pay the full price, the lunch is given at a reduced price or is free depending on family economic eligibility. All lunches, like breakfasts, are subsidized by the federal government. The "Type A" lunch is intended to provide the child or adolescent with a balanced meal containing nutrients essential for growth.

Role of the nurse in nutritional care

The nurse is only one source of nutritional information and care. In a hospital setting the nurse generally assumes a primary role in the patient's nutritional care. As a member of the health team, the nurse generally has the most contact with the client. Seldom is the dietitian or physician with a child during meals—the nurse is. The nurse also spends more time communicating with the child and therefore may serve as the pivotal person in the child's nutritional care.

Initial assessments made by the nurse based on dietary history, physical observations, and other data will influence the selection of the child's diet. Continual assessments and observation of food intake are important to determine if the nutritional care is adequate. Therefore it is important that documentation of all meals (amounts of food and tolerance for foods) and snacks be made daily. When abnormalities in intake are noted, a consultation with the dietitian is needed. Oftentimes alternate food selections are available within the prescribed diet limitations. This will avoid the problems associated with constant diet order changes. If a change is indicated, the dietitian may make appropriate suggestions of other diets available, which can then be ordered by the physician. Other problems, such as disabilities, which may influence food intake should also be noted. The nurse may then arrange for special equipment needed by the child at meals.

Nurses can implement a child's nutritional care in several ways. If the child is permitted to select from a menu, the nurse can help. Instruction about well-balanced meals or dietary restrictions can be given at this time. This information can also be reviewed using the child's meal tray. Another important thing the nurse can do is provide a conducive atmosphere for eating. The nurse should:

1. See that proper mouth care has been given. This helps to remove bad tastes from the mouth.
2. Be sure the child is comfortable and in a full Fowler's position if permitted. It's much easier to eat when sitting up.
3. Have the child in a pleasant area. A sunny dayroom, play area, or group dining area encourages eating.
4. Be sure the child can manage the food. When necessary, cut meat, butter bread, and open beverage containers.
5. Periodically check to see that the child is eating. When necessary because of age or injury, feed the child.

Also, the nurse should check to see that needed dietary instructions have been given. Once the dietitian has completed instructions, the nurse may reinforce the information.

Daily nursing assessments serve as evaluation tools for the child's nutritional care. The nurse will note changes in the child's physical condition, which will indicate if the nutritional care has been successful or not. If the care must be changed, this should be done with the other members of the health care team.

In the community the nurse serves as a primary source of basic nutritional information. It is therefore important that each nurse study normal nutrition in addition to therapeutic nutrition. Many parents or children may ask the nurse questions regarding food sources of nutrients, use of "health" foods, fad diets, dietary supplements, and other topics. Many educational pamphlets, booklets, and other items are available for use by health professionals.

In school the nurse should serve as a member of the health teaching team. The nurse may teach or arrange for the school district's nutritionist or a dietitian to be a guest teacher. When doing school health examinations, the nurse should note any problems which may indicate a nutritional problem. Necessary referrals should then be carried out. In schools where a particular nutritional problem is widespread, the nurse may develop and implement special programs, such as group work with obese children within the school.

The nurse who works in a physician's office or well-child clinic can do more individual basic nutrition education. (Therapeutic nutrition education is the responsibility of a dietitian reinforced by the nurse.) Topics may include appropriate food intake for age, food sources of specific nutrients, meal planning, food preparation, and label reading. Since the parent is often primarily concerned with other health matters (immunizations, etc.), printed material about nutrition should be available. This way the parent can review the information at home. Teaching about diet should be emphasized when the nurse suspects some problem in relation to the child's nutritional health. Unless a child is in the hospital, a dietitian or nutritionist may never be seen. Therefore it is important that the nurse teach the parent or child, or both, the importance of good nutrition throughout life.

Malnutrition

The word *malnutrition* usually brings to mind an extremely thin, undernourished child. Few individuals think of a chubby cheeked, roly-poly 1-year-old as being malnourished. However, by definition both of these children are malnourished. Malnutrition is a discrepancy between the nutrient supply and the nutrient demand of cells,[15] whether caused by a lack or excess of nutrients.

The existence of malnutrition may be attributed to many things. Inadequate food supplies and poverty account for most malnutrition. Ignorance about and indifference toward the role of nutrition in health are other causes. Malnutrition can also arise as an effect of illness or medical treatment (e.g., chemotherapy).

Undernourishment

Infancy, including the neonatal period Infancy is the most critical and rapid postnatal growth period. The rate of growth requires adequate calories, protein, and other nutrients. Malnutrition may be seen at birth in the form of intrauterine growth retardation (IUGR). The infant is generally of a low birth weight—less than 2500 g—but gestational age is 37 weeks or more. The cause of IUGR is lack of necessary nutrients due to placental insufficiency, inadequate prenatal care (including diet), or other factors. These infants may have some type of congenital anomaly due to a growth insult, primarily during the first trimester.[16] Small brain size is often noted, which may be reversed if corrective measures are initiated during a period of hyperplasia.[17] Other problems such as hypoglycemia or hyperglycemia, acid-base imbalance, and food intolerances may also develop, presumably because of the immaturity of the various systems in the body.

Intrauterine growth retardation can often be prevented. The goal is for the fetus to receive adequate nutrients for growth. The pregnant woman's diet should be well-balanced, supplying all nutrients, especially protein and calories. Since cigarette smoking decreases birth weight,[18] women should be encouraged to stop smoking before or immediately after becoming pregnant.

The goal in the management of an infant with intrauterine growth retardation is to provide the necessary calories and nutrients for the child to attain full growth potential. Parenteral feedings of glucose water are given to help prevent hypoglycemia[19] and for adequate hydration.[20,21] The length of time for parenteral feedings depends on the infant's ability to consume and tolerate oral feedings. If the infant does not have a well-developed sucking or gag reflex, nasogastric feedings are given. A pacifier can be used to encourage the infant to suck. Once a good sucking reflex is established, oral feedings of formula or breast milk are given. The type of feeding depends on gastrointestinal and kidney function. Formulas with more than 20 cal/oz will provide the extra calories and protein needed by these infants. These formulas do contain less water and should not be used if renal output is inadequate. Soybean-based formulas (Isomil) are available for the infant who cannot tolerate lactose. In addition to formula, vitamin supplements and iron are necessary because of the rapid rate of growth.

Small, frequent feedings are initially used because of decreased stomach capacity. During feedings the infant should be wrapped to maintain body temperature. Frequent pauses for burping are needed. Accurate records of all oral feedings should be kept. When at all possible, the nurse should encourage the parent to participate in the child's feedings. This will aid in bonding and is especially important when the infant is in the hospital for a prolonged period of time.

Another nutritional problem seen during infancy is improper formula preparation. Formula can be overdiluted so that it supplies too few nutrients, or it can be underdiluted so that it supplies insufficient water. In the first case a decrease or cessation of growth will occur. This can be corrected by supplying adequate calories and nutrients for growth. If the formula is too concentrated, problems such as dehydration, hyperglycemia, acidosis, and other metabolic abnormalities develop.[22] These problems must be corrected before oral feedings can be reinitiated. Once the improper formula preparation is discovered, an important function for the nurse is the education of the parents. Directions for preparation of concentrated liquid and powder formulas are printed on the can. The nurse should review these directions with the parents. Measuring cups help when demonstrating correct water-measuring and formula-mixing techniques. It is important that the nurse ask the parent to repeat and possibly even demonstrate the correct procedure for formula preparation. If the parent is unable to read the directions on the can, then alternate directions should be obtained. This may mean that the directions be translated into the parents' language or into pictures. The nurse can obtain help with these tasks from other individuals in the hospital or the community health department.

Feeding practices are another area of infant nutrition problems. Ideally an infant should be held close to the body to be fed. Under no circumstances should an infant be left with a propped-up bottle. This unwise practice increases the possibility of aspiration of formula. The nurse should explain to the parent the proper way to feed the child and the importance of following this method. Before teeth begin to erupt, the parent should be educated about oral hygiene. This may help to prevent development of bottle mouth syndrome. The parents should not permit children to take a bottle of milk or juice to bed with them after the teeth erupt, because the sugar from the liquid remains in the mouth and leads to tooth decay or bottle-mouth syndrome. This should also be the policy of the nursing staff in the hospital.

When an infant is unable to consume formula or food, dehydration must be prevented. Clear fluids such as gelatin, ginger ale, broth, or apple juice may be given. These fluids, which provide water and some energy, should be offered frequently and in small quantities. Once the child begins to recover, solids may be added to the diet. Care should be taken to avoid strong flavors and spices.

Childhood and adolescence Once the child becomes mobile, many factors influence food consumption. One form of eating that may begin is *pica*, the consumption of nonfood items. All children at one time have eaten dirt. This is pica and is generally harmless. Problems arise when the consumption of such items as laundry starch or clay depresses a child's appetite and replaces food in the diet. The nurse should inquire about this form of eating. If it is discovered, it should be discouraged. It may mean substituting a food item with a consistency similar to the nonfood item. One example would be a dry milk powder with the gritty feeling of laundry starch. Pica can also take the form of eating peeling paint. If the paint is lead-based, lead poisoning will develop. This should be treated immediately (see Chap. 37). Iron-rich foods should be given to help correct the anemia that accompanies pica.

All children at one time or another experience periods of anorexia or food jags. For the most part these are inconsequential and the child soon returns to a more normal eating pattern. A low-dosage multiple vitamin supplement will provide needed nutrients during these periods. If anorexia persists, a cause should be investigated and treatment begun.

A sound nutritional background before puberty is especially important. The adolescent falls victim to many fad diets that generally are deficient in one or more nutrients, and when followed for long periods of time, may cause various health problems. For example, anemia commonly follows fad weight-loss diets. Few of these diets come close to supplying the 18 mg of iron needed daily by an adolescent female. Information regarding food sources of iron should be provided. Adolescent males seldom have nutritional deficits because of the large volume of food they consume. Often what they lack in quality is made up in quantity.

Overnourishment

Overnourishing a child can begin in infancy and may continue throughout life. Such practices as giving solids early and bottle-feeding rather than breast-feeding may lead to excessive calorie intake. Infant obesity is characterized by a weight at or above the 90th percentile for age and height and a body composition of excessive fat vs. muscle or bone. Upon physical observation the infant or child appears "fat." Anthropometric measures such as skinfold thickness or midarm circumference also indicate obesity (see Fig. 23-3).[23] When the nurse interviews the child or parent, eating habits reflecting excessive quantities of foods are generally found. When excessive weight gain is observed during the first few months of life, the mother should be encouraged to give the infant an occasional supplemental bottle of sterile water. This will provide oral stimulation and fluid without increasing caloric intake. Solid foods should be withheld until 4 to 6 months of age. At this time the infant is physiologically ready to take solids. The tongue begins to move laterally back in the mouth rather than thrusting forward. This aids in swallowing.[24] The mother who is bottle-feeding should be encouraged to watch for clues that the infant is finished eating even if the bottle is not empty. The "finish the last drop" approach may lead to excessive formula consumption. Infants will stop sucking and push the nipple out of the mouth when they are full. If the parent responds to such clues, the baby is less likely to consume excess food and gain excessive weight.

Obesity This is a "condition in which there is an accumulation of body fat in excessive proportion to total body mass."[25] The child generally is not just plump and does not just have a little leftover baby fat, but is 10 to 20 percent above weight norms for age and sex. A diagnosis of obesity is based on many forms of physical data. Physical observations may reveal rolls and flabby skin areas and ill-fitting clothes. Height-weight tables are used to plot the child's measurements with established norms. Children who are in the 90th percentile for height and weight may just be growing earlier than other children their age. However, if the child is in the 95th percentile for weight and only the 60th percentile for height, chances are the child is obese. The limitation in using height-weight tables is that body composition is not taken into account. The child may be very muscular or have a large bone structure which accounts for much of the weight. The use of skinfold measurements will help to determine if the mass is attributed to fat or muscle. Table 23-5 gives standards for skinfold measurements. Body density studies may also be done but the costs prohibit routine use.

Table 23-5 Triceps skinfold percentiles (*triceps skinfold measurements based on data obtained using Lange skinfold calipers on white subjects included in the Ten-State Nutrition Survey, 1968–1970*)

Age, yr	Percentiles, mm									
	Males					**Females**				
	5th	15th	50th	85th	95th	5th	15th	50th	85th	95th
Birth–	4	5	8	12	15	4	5	8	12	13
0.5–	5	7	9	13	15	6	7	9	12	15
1.5–	5	7	10	13	14	6	7	10	13	15
2.5–	6	7	9	12	14	6	7	10	12	14
3.5–	5	6	9	12	14	5	7	10	12	14
4.5–	5	6	8	12	16	6	7	10	13	16
5.5–	5	6	8	11	15	6	7	10	12	15
6.5–	4	6	8	11	14	6	7	10	13	17
7.5–	5	6	8	12	17	6	7	10	15	19
8.5–	5	6	9	14	19	6	7	11	17	24
9.5–	5	6	10	16	22	6	8	12	19	24
10.5–	6	7	10	17	25	7	8	12	20	29
11.5–	5	7	11	19	26	6	9	13	20	25
12.5–	5	6	10	18	25	7	9	14	23	30
13.5–	5	6	10	17	22	8	10	15	22	28
14.5–	4	6	9	19	26	8	11	16	24	27
15.5–	4	5	9	20	27	8	10	15	23	31
16.5–	4	5	8	14	20	9	12	16	26	31
17.5–24.4–	4	5	10	18	25	9	12	17	25	

Source: A. R. Frisancho, "Triceps Skinfold and Upper Arm Muscle Size Norms for Assessment of Nutritional Status. *American Journal of Clinical Nutrition* **27**:1052–1058 (1974). Table courtesy of Ross Laboratories, Columbus, Ohio.

The cause of most obesity is consumption of calories in excess of calories expended. This is influenced by many factors. Heredity is one factor which is believed to attribute to obesity. Children who have two obese parents have an 80 percent chance of being obese. If one parent is obese, the chance decreases to 40 percent.[26] This may be because of parental influences concerning eating habits, but the inheritance of body somatotypes (ectomorph, endomorph and mesomorph) must also be considered. Very few cases of obesity are due to endocrine imbalances (e.g., underactive thyroid), but this possibility should be ruled out. Another theory concerning cause of obesity is the adipose cell theory. This theory postulates that overfeeding early in life causes an increase in the number of fat cells which does not decrease later in life.[27] Therefore obese children would have a greater potential to be obese adults.

Environmental and social factors can also trigger obesity. Oftentimes feelings of depression, loneliness, or anxiety may stimulate food intake. Excess calories are consumed and weight increases. Then when the child is left behind by peers or ridiculed, the feelings which led to overeating resurface and cause more overeating. A vicious cycle begins.

To aid the obese child, the root of the problem must be identified. A good diet history will often reveal poor eating habits and little physical activity. Once the basic problems have been identified, a care plan can be formulated. (Planning should involve all members of the health team, the child, and the parents.)

The main mode of treatment is a low-calorie diet. A diet of 1000 to 1200 cals will afford a slow weight loss of $1\frac{1}{2}$ to 2 lb per week. Lower calorie levels can be used with caution for a limited time period. Too severe a restriction will produce excess ketone bodies. Although ketones indicate fat weight loss and curb the appetite, the danger of ketosis and serious harm prohibit the use of this type of diet for more than a couple of weeks. (These diets may be used in a hospital, where the child can be closely monitored, for longer time periods.)

Although the diet is low in calories, it should still contain needed nutrients. This can be achieved by using a diet which includes foods from all of the basic food groups. Weight-reduction diets which use food exchange lists offer a simplified way to plan daily menus which include a variety of foods. These diets are planned by the dietitian using information obtained from the diet history. In order to make the child feel less threatened, some aspect of former eating habits may be retained, such as an afterschool snack included as part of the daily meal pattern. This is a compromise by the health team which may encourage the child to make some compromise in return.

When taking the diet history, one often finds that obese children and adolescents have used various fad diets. Temporary success may have been achieved. To evaluate these and other weight reduction diets, seven basic questions should be answered.[28]

1. Is the diet deficient in calories?
2. Can adequate nutrients be consumed? (This can be done if foods from all four of the basic food groups are included daily.)
3. Does the diet have satiety value? (This prevents hunger shortly after eating, which may lead to cheating.)
4. Can the diet be easily adapted to family meals, school lunches, or eating at restaurants?
5. Is the cost reasonable? Can seasonal food buys and staples be used? (Meat and protein diets are very expensive.)
6. Can the diet be followed for a long period of time (months) without becoming boring?
7. Does the diet teach a new set of eating habits or goals?

The last question is most important if long-term weight loss is to be achieved. This is one reason why fad diets often have limited success. Once the child or adolescent loses weight, a return to old eating habits is made. Eventually this means a return of the weight also.

Besides the diet, the obese client will need weight-loss goals and help to establish new habits for attaining the goals. The weight loss goals and habit changes must be planned with the patient. It is easier for a pediatric client to see success when the large total weight loss (75 lbs) is broken down into smaller more manageable interim goals (15 lbs). Habit changes that help many people include:[29]

1. Eating while sitting in a specific chair at a table, preferably away from the television and other distractions

2. Taking time to taste food by counting number of chews or placing the fork down after each mouthful
3. Not leaving serving dishes on the table during meals
4. Not keeping junk food within sight or reach
5. Using smaller plates, which will give the illusion of having a large meal

Periodic evaluation is essential. This can be done individually or in a group. By forming a group, the nurse can work with a number of clients and the children or adolescents can help each other. This is especially good as a support mechanism.

Once a goal has been reached, some form of reward must be given. The exclusion of sweets, fast foods, and other treats may be very difficult. Therefore these foods may be used as a reward. These so-called binge items are permitted only as a reward. This also teaches the individual that these items can be part of a diet occasionally. Other rewards may include toys for children or clothes for adolescents. Some very special reward should be planned for the time when the total weight loss is achieved.

Special low- or no-calorie treats can easily be prepared and used as snacks. Gelatin cubes can be made using fruit-flavored, low-calorie beverages. Celery and carrot sticks or cucumber slices can be kept ready to eat in the refrigerator. Diet sodas or unsweetened soft drinks made with a sugar substitute make refreshing frozen treats. These provide the child with some items which may resemble popular treats so the child does not feel so oppressed.

It is important that parents and other family members be involved in the weight loss program. First the parent needs to know what the diet involves as far as food purchasing and preparation are concerned. If the child is able to select meals from the food prepared for the other family members, then greater compliance can be achieved.

Psychological counseling may be needed for some obese children and their families. Clues which may indicate this need are "depression, altered body image, problematic peer relationships and poor school performance."[30] These are often just symptoms of larger family problems which need to be resolved. Bowers et al. found such family characteristics as enmeshment, overprotectiveness, rigidity, and lack of conflict resolution.[31] When the nurse recognizes these traits, therapy should be considered. Unless these forms of family dysfunctioning are corrected, long-term weight loss can not be achieved. A nursing care plan for an obese child is given at the end of the chapter.

Excessive protein intake Protein, like other nutrients, can be consumed above daily nutritional needs. It is generally accepted that people in the United States consume excess protein. The majority of people can handle the metabolism of this protein and excretion of its nitrogenous waste products. Only if serious liver or kidney impairment is present does the body have problems with excessive protein intake. These disorders are not widespread in the pediatric population. However, excess protein does add extra calories to the diet. Protein is also the most expensive nutrient, and so an excess of its consumption increases the family's food costs.

Excessive carbohydrate intake Carbohydrates are being singled out as the root of many problems. Their role, if any, in hyperactivity is still under investigation. Excessive intake of carbohydrates is clearly the major cause of obesity and dental caries.

When calories are not used for energy, they are converted into fat and stored in the body. The use of sugars, natural or processed, greatly increases the caloric intake without significantly increasing the volume of food. This is one reason sugar has been omitted from most commercial baby food. The sugar only added unnecessary calories, which increased fat cell development.

Carbohydrate is the main culprit in causing dental caries, but not the only one. The bacteria in dental plaque break down the carbohydrates in the mouth to form organic acids. These acids cause teeth to demineralize and decay results. The longer a carbohydrate remains in contact with the teeth, the greater is the chance of decay. Sticky foods such as caramel or dried fruits are more hazardous to the teeth than carbonated beverages.

Proper nutrition and dental hygiene are also important in preventing caries. The nurse should educate parents and children about the importance of consuming adequate amounts of calcium, phosphorus, vitamin D, and fluorine for strong tooth formation (mineralization is completed at approximately 16 years of age).[32] Dental care is discussed in Chap. 6.

Excessive fat intake High fat intake has also been associated not only with obesity but also with cardiovascular disease. Saturated fats and cholesterol have been identified as the harmful fatty substances for the heart and arteries. By decreasing the use of dairy products, eggs, red and high-fat meats, the fat-cholesterol level of the diet can be decreased. When polyunsaturated vegetable (not coconut) oils are substituted for hydrogenated oil or animal fats, the polyunsaturated-fat-to-saturated-fat ratio of the diet is increased. Although recently the effectiveness of these measures has been questioned, their use is suggested when a family history of heart disease or diabetes mellitus exists.[33] Such measures are not recommended for children under 1 year of age.

Excessive salt intake The role of salt in causing hypertension is well-documented. By avoiding excessive amounts of salt, hypertension may be prevented. The best way to accomplish this is to discourage the addition of salt to food at the table. Out of habit, many individuals, including children, salt their food before tasting it. Other things to do would be to cook with lemon juice and use spices and herbs to season foods.

Alterations in vitamin and mineral intake

Vitamins and minerals are nutrients with specific functions needed by the body in small amounts. Although they interact with each other, they cannot substitute for each other. When inadequate amounts are consumed, deficiency signs and symptoms develop (see Table 23-3).

Vitamin A (retinol) This is a fat-soluble vitamin which aids in vision, growth, epithelial tissue health, and tooth development. Inadequate intake can lead to night blindness due to interferences with the chemistry of the retina. The cornea becomes dry and eventually Bitôt's spots form. If this is unchecked, severe visual damage and eventual blindness will result. Scaliness (keratinization) will also occur throughout all epithelial tissue, such as the skin, oral cavity, and respiratory tract. When the epithelial cells become dry, hair is lost and the body is more open to invasion by infectious organisms. In children vitamin A deficiency can also cause growth retardation.

Since vitamin A is fat-soluble, it is stored in the body. Consequently the development of a deficiency is generally slow. A diet which contains organ meats, whole milk, eggs, and butter will supply preformed vitamin A. Provitamin A (a precursor) is found in deep-green leafy or yellow vegetables (squash, spinach, pumpkin, carrots) and is readily used by the body. These items should be consumed every other day. If a deficiency does develop, administration of vitamin A will correct the problem—unless irreversible damage has been done.

Since vitamin A is stored in the body, it can be toxic if taken in large doses over a period of time. Nausea, dizziness, flaking of the skin, and headache are symptoms of toxicity. The nurse should educate parents and children in correct administration and dosage of vitamin supplements. Some vitamin A is good, but too much can be harmful.

Vitamin D Vitamin D is another fat-soluble vitamin. It aids in calcium absorption from the intestinal tract, bone mineralization, and regulation of serum calcium levels. In children the deficiency of vitamin D is known as *rickets*. The mineralization of long bones is inadequate, resulting in bow-legs and knock-knees. The wrists and ankles thicken. The ribs, skull, and other bones also exhibit changes. Since teeth contain calcium, they generally are poorly calcified and erupt late in children with rickets. Treatment consists of daily administration of vitamin D supplements until the bone ends have calcified.

Rickets can be prevented with an adequate daily intake of vitamin D. The most important sources of this vitamin are fish liver oil and fortified milk. Milk is fortified with 400 IU of vitamin D per quart. Exposure to sunlight is also a good source of the vitamin. This causes ultraviolet light to change 7-dehydrocholesterol into cholecalciferol, a form of vitamin D. Since few young children drink 1 quart of milk each day, it is important that the nurse encourage the parents to expose the children to sunlight. Playing outdoors or walking when the weather is nice is generally sufficient. Since breast milk is a poor source of vitamin D, nursing infants should be given a supplement of this vitamin. Care should be taken to prevent excess supplementation. This vitamin is stored, so toxic levels can accumulate and cause hypercalcemia.

Vitamin E (tocopherol) Vitamin E has received much publicity in recent years. It has been associated with sexual functioning, heart disease, and aging. Its exact functioning in the human body is unknown. It does function as an antioxidant, helping to stabilize unsaturated fats, vitamin A, and certain enzymes and cell components. Deficiencies have not been recorded except in premature infants. Infants are born with low levels of vitamin E, which generally increase within 1 month. However, hemolytic anemia has been noted in premature infants and in infants who receive iron supplements or fortified formulas and whose serum levels of tocopherol are low. Children who are unable to absorb fats, such as those who have cystic fibrosis, may also exhibit deficiency symptoms. Supplementation with vitamin E corrects this problem.

Vitamin E is widespread in the diet. Fats and oils, especially unsaturated fats, are the major food sources. Liver, eggs, and green leafy vegetables are minor sources of this vitamin.

Vitamin K Vitamin K is one nutrient that is essential but does not need to be consumed regularly. The main source is bacterial synthesis in the intestinal tract. This vitamin may also be obtained from spinach, kale, alfalfa, cabbage, cauliflower, and other leafy vegetables. A deficiency of vitamin K manifests itself as a disorder of the blood-clotting mechanism. Vitamin K aids in the formation of prothrombin, which is necessary for blood clotting. Deficiency is rare under normal conditions. Use of anticoagulants (coumarin) and salicylates is antagonistic to the action of Vitamin K. Newborns have a very low storage level of Vitamin K. This does not increase rapidly since the gut flora is absent at birth and takes time to be established. Newborns are given 1 mg of vitamin K intramuscularly at birth. Another pediatric population at risk is adolescents on prolonged antibiotic therapy (tetracycline) for acne. Such drugs diminish the bacterial flora, therefore decreasing the vitamin K supply to the body. Supplements need not be taken especially since an excess is toxic. The nurse should encourage patients on antibiotic therapy to consume cultured milk products such as buttermilk or yogurt to maintain the gastrointestinal flora and prevent possible problems.

Thiamine Thiamine is a water-soluble, B-complex vitamin needed by the body for carbohydrate metabolism. Its deficiency disease is known as *beriberi*. This affects the gastrointestinal tract, causing anorexia, indigestion, and vomiting; the nervous system, causing apathy, fatigue, and eventual damage of the myelin sheaths; and the cardiovascular system, causing cardiac muscle fatigue and peripheral dilation leading to edema (wet beriberi). Breast-fed infants whose mothers have a poor thiamine status are at risk of developing infantile beriberi. Symptoms such as insomnia, pallor, oliguria, and those previously mentioned develop, and death can occur in 24 to 48 h.[34] Treatment with thiamine injections will correct the deficiency disease. Infantile beriberi can be prevented if the lactating mother consumes adequate amounts of thiamine. Foods high in thiamine include pork, beef liver, whole or enriched grains, and legumes. These foods should be consumed daily by all children and adolescents to prevent the adult form of beriberi.

Daily needs for thiamine depend on the caloric level of the diet and range from 0.3 mg for infants to 1.4 mg for adolescent males. Recently the use of megadoses (10 times daily needs) of thiamine have been suggested for nervousness and stress. Although these dosages have not been proven to be beneficial, they should not be harmful since thiamine is water-soluble and excesses are excreted rather than stored.

Riboflavin Riboflavin is another B-complex vitamin. It functions as a coenzyme in protein and energy metabolism. A deficiency is most likely to occur during stress, such as that which comes from rapid growth, severe burns, surgery, or trauma, or when there is impaired absorption and utilization. Clinical symptoms include cheilosis (lesions of the lips), seborrheic dermatitis, glossitis, and eye irritations. Riboflavin deficiency often occurs along with other B-vitamin deficiencies. Treatment includes supplements of the vitamin and a diet rich in riboflavin. The main dietary sources of riboflavin are milk, organ meats, and some green, leafy vegetables. Enriched cereals contain small amounts of riboflavin but do contribute significantly to the total daily intake. No toxic side effects are associated with megadoses of this vitamin, but its excretion may cause urine to turn bright yellow.

Niacin Niacin, another B-complex vitamin, functions as a coenzyme in tissue oxidation. Pellagra, a disease due to a deficiency of niacin, is characterized by the 3 D's—dermatitis, dementia, and diarrhea. Death occurs if pellagra is untreated. Treatment is similar to that of the other B-vitamin deficiencies. Supplements of nicotinamide (a form of niacin) are given. Often other B vitamins are also given since their respective deficiencies may also be evident. A diet containing meat, enriched grains, and peanuts should be encouraged. Since tryptophan can be converted to niacin in the body, foods (meat, fish, and poultry) containing this amino acid should also be encouraged.

Niacin, unlike thiamine and riboflavin, does have toxic effects. When large doses of nicotinic acid (a form of niacin) are taken, vasodilation may occur. The person will become flushed and feel a tingling sensation. Liver toxicity, diabetes, and peptic ulcers are other possible complications associated with long-term megadoses of niacin.[35]

Pyridoxine Pyridoxine, Vitamin B_6, is needed for protein metabolism. It is also necessary for formation of the heme molecule and conversion of tryptophan into niacin. Deficiency of pyridoxine is rare. Symptoms of this deficiency are irritability and convulsive seizures. Children with absorptive disorders such as celiac disease or children receiving isonicotinic acid hydrozide (INH) are at risk of developing pyridoxine deficiency. Oral supplements are used in the treatment of celiac disease. Dosage is determined on an individual basis. Normal daily needs range from 0.3 mg for infants to 2 mg for adolescent males. These levels are easily obtained from a diet which includes meat, wheat, corn, and liver. No known toxic effects result from megadoses of pyridoxine.

Folate Folic acid is a water-soluble vitamin associated with blood cell production. Megaloblastic anemia is the disease associated with a deficiency of this vitamin. Other signs and symptoms of folate deficiency include diarrhea, glossitis, and growth retardation. Serum folate levels below 3 mg/ml indicate a deficiency.[36] Megaloblastic anemia may be seen in infants whose diets are low in ascorbic acid (ascorbic acid aids in the conversion of folic acid to the coenzyme form); children receiving anticonvulsant drugs (DPH, primidone, or barbiturates); or who suffer from malabsorption. In infant megaloblastic anemia 5 mg of folic acid daily will reverse the condition in a few days.[37] Children receiving anticonvulsant medications should take 1 to 5 mg of folate daily.[38] Large doses of folic acid can mask signs of vitamin B_{12} deficiency. For this reason over-the-counter preparations can not contain more than 0.1 mg of folic acid.[39] When larger doses of folic acid are prescribed, vitamin B_{12} is often given also to prevent this problem. Food sources of folic acid include liver, green leafy vegetables, asparagus, meat, and whole grains.

Vitamin B_{12} Vitamin B_{12}, cobalamin, is needed for blood cell production. Unlike other water-soluble vitamins, B_{12} is stored in the liver. Healthy individuals have approximately a 3- to 5-year store of this vitamin, except for growing children. Deficiency signs and symptoms include pernicious anemia and neurological disturbances. Children who regularly consume meat, milk, eggs, and other foods from animal sources usually get adequate amounts of B_{12}. (This vitamin is not found in plant foods.) Malabsorption disorders may lead to a deficiency. Vitamin B_{12} (the extrinsic factor) must combine with intrinsic factor in the stomach for absorption to occur. Parenteral doses of B_{12} are indicated in malabsorption. The child or parent can be taught how to give these injections.

One area for concern is the child following vegan (strict vegetarian) diets. Without animal foods, the diet lacks vitamin B_{12}. A diet which includes eggs and dairy products is therefore recommended for vegetarian children and adolescents. (This also assures adequate amounts of complete protein needed for growth.) Oral supplements of B_{12}, or B_{12}-fortified soybean milk can be used as a source of the vitamin also. Excessive intakes of vitamin B_{12} have not been proven harmful and are generally excreted in urine.

Ascorbic acid (vitamin C) Ascorbic acid, vitamin C, is a water-soluble vitamin. The exact biochemical action of this vitamin is unknown, but vitamin C plays a role in collagen formation. This most likely accounts for its high concentration in active tissue during growth and healing. Apparently ascorbic acid is also involved in protein (phenylalanine and tyrosine) metabolism. In premature infants false positive tests for phenylketonuria may occur as a result of low vitamin C levels. In recent years some researchers have advocated megadoses of vitamin C to cure or prevent the common cold. Studies have both supported and refuted this practice. Further study of the vitamin's exact biochemical function is needed to determine its potential as a pharmacological substance.

The ascorbic acid deficiency disease is *scurvy*. The vascular network appears to be very sensitive to decreased vitamin C stores. Perifollicular hemorrhage and bruising are noted with scurvy. Other signs and symptoms include weakness, swollen and bleeding gums, and loose teeth. In infants, scurvy alters bone formation, causing the "frog leg" position. Anorexia and tenderness in limbs and lips are also seen in infants.[40] Most infants receiving commercial formula have an adequate vitamin C intake. Breast-fed infants also generally have an adequate intake unless the mother's intake is very poor. Cow's milk is a poor source of vitamin C because pasteurization destroys the small amount of ascorbic acid in this food. Therefore infants receiving cow's milk or a home-prepared modified cow's milk formula should receive a vitamin C supplement. Liquid drops are generally used. Once fruit juices such as orange and grapefruit have been introduced, the child can meet daily vitamin C needs through food. Other foods which supply vitamin C are broccoli, strawberries, and cantaloupe. Raw cabbage, tomatoes, green pepper, and potatoes are fair sources of this vitamin. Clients and their parents should be instructed by the nurse not to leave these foods exposed to air (especially after cutting) or to cook them for long periods of time. Such preparation methods destroy the vitamin C in the food.

Although vitamin C is water-soluble, some toxic reactions have been observed from megadose intakes (5000 to 15,000 mg daily). Kidney stones, false positive urine glucose test, and elevated vitamin C requirements in newborns whose mothers took high doses during pregnancy[41] are among the possibilities.

Minerals Iron is a mineral needed by the body in relatively small amounts daily. Iron is stored in the liver, bone marrow, and spleen. In red blood cells, iron acts to transport oxygen to all body cells for respiration and metabolism. Iron deficiency is observed as anemia and may result from various causes. Nutritional anemia is due to an inadequate intake of iron; hemorrhagic anemia results from excessive blood loss; and malabsorption of iron and increased iron requirements also result in iron-deficiency anemia. The anemic individual experiences weakness and fatigue and appears pale. Hemoglobin and hematocrit levels are used to confirm a diagnosis of anemia. When a diagnosis of iron-deficiency anemia is made, supplements of ferrous gluconate or ferrous sulfate are prescribed. Care should be taken to avoid excessive iron intake since this may lead to hemosiderosis. Foods such as organ meats, egg yolk, red meats, green leafy vegetables, fortified cereals, and legumes should also be encouraged. (Chapter 27 discusses anemia in detail.)

In the pediatric population several groups are at risk to develop iron-deficiency anemia. Infants are born with a 3- to 6-month supply of iron. At approximately 4 months of age iron supplementation should be started to prevent anemia. Generally at this age cereals are introduced. Since infant cereals are fortified with iron, they can be used as the source of iron supplement. If the introduction of cereals is delayed, iron-fortified formula or iron drops can be used. Supplementation must be done since cow's milk is a poor source of iron. If during the first year a child continues to take more than 1 quart (32 oz) of formula or milk a day, the chances of anemia increase. This excessive quantity of milk generally satiates the child and prevents the addition of iron-containing foods to the diet. A good diet history will identify such an occurrence. The nurse should instruct the parent to introduce solid foods, especially those rich in iron; to have the older infant use a cup (especially at meals); and to discontinue extra between-meal bottles (water, juice, or finger foods can be substituted).[42] By assisting the parent with weaning, infant nutritional anemia may be prevented.

During childhood, anemia may result from lead poisoning due to pica. Part of the nursing care should include instruction about iron-containing foods.

This same education is needed by females once menarche is reached. At this point daily iron needs nearly double to 18 mg daily. This amount is very hard to consume without overeating. For this reason a small dosage (30 to 60 mg) of iron supplement may be recommended.

When oral iron administration is prescribed, certain procedures should be followed. For maximum iron absorption, the supplement should be taken on an empty stomach with orange juice (iron is absorbed in an acid medium). This method may cause gastrointestinal irritation. If the iron is taken approximately 10 to 15 min before meals, less irritation may occur. When iron is taken after meals, the absorption is decreased and larger doses may be needed to correct the problem. Small, frequent doses will also help to prevent gastric problems. The iron should be started slowly and gradually increased to full dosages. Iron therapy should be continued for 6 to 12 months to ensure that iron stores are replenished.

Calcium is essential for skeletal and dental development. Calcium deficiency causes rickets, previously discussed under vitamin D. Milk and milk products are the main sources of calcium. Other foods, such as green leafy vegetables, egg yolk, legumes, shellfish, and nuts, supply some calcium. For children who refuse milk, such foods as puddings, ice cream, soups made with milk, yogurt, and cheese can be substituted. Dry milk solids can be added to sauces, ground meat dishes, and casseroles to increase milk consumption. Some mothers have even blended powdered milk into peanut butter. If the child is unable to consume milk because of allergies or lactose intolerance, other calcium foods and calcium supplements should be given. Soybean-based milks used for lactose intolerance will supply adequate calcium.

Zinc, which is receiving increasing recognition, functions in digestion, cellular respiration, and glucose oxidation. Hypogonadism and dwarfism have been associated with zinc deficiency in some populations. Alterations in taste acuity and impaired wound healing are also related to zinc deficiency. Oral supplements of zinc are administered to correct deficiency states.

Fluoride is important for children. This mineral helps to prevent dental caries and possibly strengthens bone structure. For most people fluoridated drinking water is the major source of this nutrient. In areas where the drinking water is not fluoridated or where well water is used, children should be given fluoride tablets or multiple vitamins with fluoride. Excessive fluoride can cause teeth to become gray and pitted (mottled). For this reason the nurse should be sure that parents know how to accurately administer any fluoride supplements.

Nutrition in altered states of health
Alterations in gastrointestinal function
The gastrointestinal tract is the major organ system for food digestion and nutrient absorption. Alterations in gastrointestinal organs will affect both how nutrients enter the body and what nutrients are available to the body cells. Only the nutritional aspects will be discussed here; many of these disorders are included in Chap. 28, "Gastrointestinal Function."

Oral alterations Cleft lip or palate results when the maxillary and premaxillary processes fail to fuse embryologically. Feeding is disrupted to varying degrees depending on the extent of the defect. The child should be held upright during feedings to prevent formula from entering the nasal passage. The nipple of a Beniflex feeder or the tip of a Breck feeder (a bulb syringe with a soft tip) (see Fig. 23-1) is placed on the infant's tongue. The infant is encouraged to suck by moving the jaw or stroking the cheek. Once the infant begins to suck, gentle pressure is applied to the bulb of the syringe to aid the flow of the formula. It is important that the parent or nurse be patient since the infant often resists this form of feeding. Frequent stops to soothe the child are important. Large amounts of air are swallowed by these infants, which necessitates frequent bubbling or burping. After each feeding, be sure to give water to cleanse the mouth.

Breast-feeding can be successfully done with an infant with a cleft lip. The mother should manually extend the nipple and place it in the child's mouth. The milk is released through the pressure of the baby's jaw, gums, and tongue on the areola even if the cleft is severe enough to make sucking ineffective. The attitude of the mother is very important. Extra support from the nurse and family members should be given. The local chapter of La Leche League can provide additional guidance and printed materials for these mothers.

Corrective surgery for cleft lip is often begun at approximately 6 to 8 weeks of age. The correction of a cleft palate generally does not begin until at least 12 months of age. Before this time the child should be weaned to a cup and spoon at meals. Postoperative feeding is described in Chap. 28.

Gastric alterations During the first few months of life some infants experience excessive vomiting due to pyloric stenosis. The condition is generally treated surgically. Nutritionally, pyloric stenosis causes excessive nutrient losses. The major problem is loss of fluid and electrolytes. If the disorder is allowed to continue, weight loss will occur. After surgery oral feedings may be resumed beginning with glucose water. Once this is tolerated, formula feedings are reintroduced to the infant. The amount and strength are slowly increased until full feedings are reached. This takes approximately 48 h.

Similar nutritional management is used during gastroenteritis. Clear fluids (broth, tea, gelatin, clear juices) are initially given. The diet is then slowly increased to full fluids, which include most juices, strained soups, custards, puddings, and ice cream. Soft solid foods are added next. This type of diet progression eliminates gastric irritation due to excessive spices or fiber. Like pyloric stenosis, gastroenteritis causes excessive loss of nutrients and the subsequent problems.

Intestinal alterations Many intestinal and other disorders have diarrhea as one of their symptoms. Diarrhea causes rapid passage of nutrients from the body. This decreases digestion time and the availability of nutrients for absorption. Initially, food is withheld and intravenous fluid and electrolytes are administered to correct imbalances. Once oral feedings are permitted, the diet progression is similar to that for gastroenteritis. The addition of banana flakes, apple, or pectin agar will help to decrease diarrhea. Infants may be given diluted formula, which is slowly increased to full strength. A lactose-free formula may be used initially to prevent any problems due to temporary decreased lactose tolerance. When fat absorption is impaired, medium chain triglyceride (MCT) oil may be given. This is more readily absorbed and will aid in absorption of fat-soluble vitamins.

Lactose intolerance Lactose intolerance is a disorder in which the enzyme lactase is lacking. Without lactase the person is unable to digest lactose to form galactose and glucose. Lactose then ferments, causing severe cramping and intestinal distention and diarrhea. Failure to thrive and muscle wasting in children will result due to decreased nutrient absorption. A lactose tolerance test (LTT) may be used to confirm a possible diagnosis of lactose intolerance. An oral test load of lactose (2 g per kilogram of body weight) is given. Periodic blood samples are taken. A lactose level of 20 mg or less confirms the diagnosis. Treatment is the elimination of lactose from the diet.

Lactose, also known as *milk sugar*, is present in milk. Therefore all milk and milk products are eliminated from the diet. For infants this generally means the use of soybean-based formulas such as Isomil or ProSobee. The parents (and child, when old enough,) should be instructed to read all food labels carefully. Table 23-6 lists some foods which contain lactose.

Other disaccharides (galactose, sucrose) may also not be tolerated. These intolerances occur less frequently than lactose intolerance. In these instances treatment is to eliminate the particular disaccharide from the diet.

Gluten-induced enteropathy (celiac disease) Gluten-induced enteropathy may affect individ-

Table 23-6 Food sources of lactose

Milk: fluid, evaporated, condensed, dry, flavored	Candies, chocolate, caramels, toffee
Commerical baked products	Luncheon meats
Instant cereals	Monosodium glutamate
Ice cream, ice milk, sherbet	Spice blends
Custard, pudding	Breaded meats, vegetables
Cream: sour, sweet	
Butter, margarine	
Creamed meats, vegetables, soup	

uals at any age, but in children it often appears between 1 and 5 years of age.[43] The exact cause of the disease is unknown. When the child consumes food containing gluten, diarrhea and steatorrhea appear. Weight loss, muscle wasting, increased appetite, and nutrient deficiencies also occur.

Treatment of celiac disease is to remove gluten from the diet. Gluten is a protein found in wheat, rye, oats, and barley. Consequently, all foods which contain these grains must be eliminated. Generally these grains are found in bakery products, cereals, pastas, and some soups (barley). The parent and child should be instructed to read all ingredient labels to be sure the problematic grains are not present. Corn and rice are the two grains which can be used. These grains produce a baked product which differs in taste and texture from the harmful grains, but the product is quite palatable. Recipes for these grains are available from community health departments, hospital dietitians, and allergy associations. Wheat starch (all protein has been removed) is also available and its manufacturers have recipes for its use. Some health or specialty food stores carry baked products made with rice and corn flours.

Ulcerative colitis Excess nutrient losses also result from the diarrhea caused by ulcerative colitis, an inflammatory disorder of the large intestine. Ulcerative colitis is characterized by periods of exacerbation and remission. To provide adequate calories and nutrients and to promote healing and growth during exacerbations, hyperalimentation should be used. When food is reintroduced, it should be done slowly as with the malabsorptive disorders previously mentioned. When such secondary problems as anemia accompany ulcerative colitis, nutritional supplements of iron and vitamins may be given. It is important for the nurse to work closely with these afflicted children to identify food intolerances. Each child responds differently to foods so diet must be individualized.

Hyperalimentation Generally if the gastrointestinal tract is functioning, it should be used to nourish an individual. With ulcerative colitis and other disorders this mode of nourishment is not possible and hyperalimentation, or total parenteral nutrition (TPN), must be used. This form of parenteral alimentation supplies the needed protein, carbohydrates, vitamins and minerals (with a few exceptions), and water in usable form directly into the circulatory system. This form of nourishment can provide up to 6000 cal daily. It would be difficult for any individual, especially a child, to orally consume this number of calories in 1 day. This will supply energy for a child's growth while recovery occurs. Therefore TPN is the nourishment of choice when a large number of calories are needed or when the gastrointestinal tract cannot be used.

Hyperalimentation solutions are hypertonic. They require rapid dilution inside the body to prevent fluid and electrolyte complications. Therefore they are generally administered through the superior vena cava. If a 10% dextrose solution is used, then administration can be done through a peripheral vein. When the superior vena cava is used, a silicon-rubber catheter is surgically inserted. With infants a cutdown is used to insert the catheter through the jugular vein (Fig. 23-4). Either a percutaneous or cutdown subclavian approach[44] is used with children. In both cases catheter placement is checked by x-ray. The line is secured with sutures.

The TPN solution is administered using an infusion pump. This permits a continuous slow rate of flow without blood backup. The rate of infusion is generally 135 to 150 ml/kg per 24 h.[45] If the flow should fall behind schedule, do not try to catch up. Once the alteration is discovered, the solution infusion time should be recalibrated. The risk of thrombosis increases if the flow rate is too fast.

Children receiving hyperalimentation should be watched closely to prevent dislodgement of the catheter and kinks in the line. A mesh stocking cap can be placed over an infant's head. This will help to keep the line secure while the baby moves its head. Hand restraints may be needed also. If used, they should permit some hand movement but not enough so that the child can reach the IV line. Toddlers and older children should also be monitored so that they do not step on the line or place objects on the tubing that could cause the line to kink or break. If the tubing is gently coiled near the entry site and under the dressing, less pressure will be exerted on the catheter as the child moves about.

The major complication is infection, primarily with *Candida*. Since the solution is high in nutrients, it is an excellent medium for bacterial growth. To prevent contamination, hyperalimentation solutions should be mixed by qualified personnel under a laminate flow hood. The solution should not be mixed more than 24 h prior to use and should be kept under refrigeration. Once a bottle is used, it should not hang for more than 24 h.

The nurse must check the child daily to see that no redness or swelling occurs near the catheter site. Blood cultures for septicemia should be done when infection is suspected.

Prevention of infection also depends on proper line care. All IV tubing and filters should be changed every 24 h. This can be timed with the change of solution bottles or dressing changes. Dressing changes are done using sterile technique. The catheter exit site should be cleansed with an iodine or other solution. An antibiotic ointment is applied. A sterile gauze dressing is then applied. Since children often squirm or move around, it may be helpful for a second person to be present. This individual may divert the child's attention while solution, tubing, or dressing changes are done.

Psychological and developmental complications can occur. Since oral intake is eliminated, infants receiving TPN lack needed sucking. The use of pacifiers may stimulate this important reflex and prepare the child for eventual resumption of oral feedings. When permitted, hard sour candies or chewing gum can be given to older children. Older children are deprived of the social interaction associated with meals. Some other activity may be planned for these children during mealtimes.

When food is reintroduced, it should be done slowly. The gastrointestinal tract is unaccustomed to food after prolonged rest. Food is better tolerated if small, frequent meals are given. This also eliminates the chance of overwhelming the child with excess food. Many children who receive TPN for long periods of time do not have much appetite. The sight of large meals may therefore discourage the child. The child should be encouraged to eat what is tolerable. The child also needs reassurance that physical hunger and appetite will increase as the IV solution is slowly decreased.

The family is included in the care of the child receiving hyperalimentation. The procedure is thoroughly explained so parents can feel at ease

Figure 23-4 Catheter placement for an infant receiving hyperalimentation. (*From Rita Colley, Jeanne M. Wilson, and Mary Pat Wilhem, Intravenous nutrition—Nursing considerations, Issues in Comprehensive Pediatric Nursing,* **1**(5):50, 1977.)

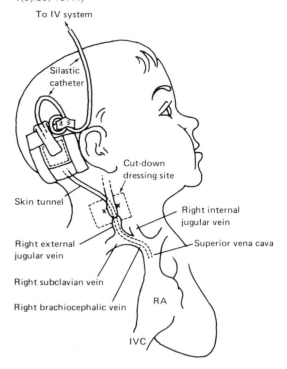

working with their child. Hygenic or mouth care can easily be given without disturbing the IV set-up. It is important that the child receive this care and attention from the family often. Generally, the child receiving TPN in the hospital is there for a long period of time. This may fragment the family unit if total family involvement is not encouraged by the nurse.

Home hyperalimentation has been developed to try to avoid some of the family and social problems which arise from prolonged hospital stays. The time required (approximately 10 to 14 h) to administer the solution can be scheduled so that the child may still participate in school or other activities. Another benefit is that the daily hospital costs are eliminated. A recent study demonstrated that adolescents with Crohn's disease can be managed at home using TPN.[46] Although few of those adolescents who responded to TPN remained in remission, the majority of the teens did show improved nutri-

Table 23-7 Central alimentation (total parenteral nutrition) solutions (per 1000 ml*)

0–40 kg		Over 40 kg	
Dextrose	20%	Dextrose	20%
Amino acids	3.5%	Amino acids	3.5%
NaCl	38 meq	NaCl	60 meq
KPO₄	10 mN	KPO₄	10 mN
Ca gluc	15 meq	Ca gluc	15 meq
MgSO₄	10 meq	MgSO₄	16 meq
KCl	12 meq	KCl	26 meq

* Supplies 0.94 kcal/ml.

Table courtesy of Dr. Robert J. Shulman, Section of Nutrition and GI, Texas Children's Hospital, Houston, Texas.

tional status and significant increases in height and weight.

When home TPN is used, the nurse should do extra patient and family education. The proper technique for tube changes, solution storage, and administration must be taught to all family members who will be working with the hyperalimentated child. Needed reinforcement can be given by a visiting nurse or on subsequent visits to the doctor, clinic, or hospital.

When speaking of total parenteral nutrition, it is important to recognize that the word *total* is misleading. The TPN solution supplies protein, carbohydrate, water, and some vitamins and minerals (see Table 23-7). Fats and certain vitamins and minerals are not included as part of the standard mixture. (These will be discussed later.) Protein is generally supplied in the form of crystalline amino acids or as a protein hydrolysate. To supply adequate calories, hypertonic dextrose solutions are used. Initially 10% dextrose and water is used. If this is tolerated, then the dextrose may be increased to 20% and then 25% solutions. This will provide adequate calories to permit protein anabolism.

The vitamin and mineral content (see Table 23-7) of a child's TPN solution is higher per unit of body weight than the level for adult TPN. This is due to the increased need for growth. Vitamins A and D, the B-complex vitamins, and folic acid are generally added. Since the levels of vitamins A and D are very high, hypervitaminosis can occur with prolonged administration of TPN. Vitamins E, K, and B₁₂ are not standard in some TPN solutions. Vitamins K and B₁₂ can be given

by injection if blood tests (prothrombin time and blood counts) indicate a need for these nutrients. (Vitamin E will be discussed later.)

Electrolytes constitute most of the minerals found in hyperalimentation solution. The blood levels of the electrolytes are checked daily so that frequent changes can be made to prevent electrolyte imbalances. Iron is not in the TPN solution. When needed, it is given intramuscularly.

Fat and vitamin E are not found in the primary hyperalimentation solution. An IV solution of a soybean-oil emulsion in glycerol and water with purified egg phosphatides—Intralipid—can be used to supply these nutrients. It will also supply a more concentrated form of calories—550 cals per 500 ml—than the hypertonic dextrose solution used. This will help to decrease fluid intake if needed. Intralipid is also used as a source of the essential fatty acid linoleic acid. Without linoleic acid eczema, sparse hair, and other signs of deficiency will develop. The pediatric population is especially at risk here.[47] Linoleic acid can also be supplied through oral ingestion of safflower, sunflower, or corn oil.

For the nurse several things are important when administering fat emulsions.[48] First, be sure to check that the emulsion is stable: It has a milky appearance and does not need shaking. It is best to keep the emulsions refrigerated until half an hour before use.[49] Secondly, no other liquids or medications can be added to the Intralipid solution. The Intralipid is generally given through a peripheral vein using a Y connector. Other fluids may be administered simultaneously since their mixture with the fat is limited before entering the blood system. Once the Intralipid solution is started, monitor vital signs frequently and check for other signs of adverse reaction (low-grade fever, headache, nausea, swelling at infusion site, etc.).

Alterations in metabolism

Ketosis This disorder, caused by alteration in fat metabolism, is characterized by an accumulation of ketone bodies and their excretion in urine. When carbohydrates are able to enter the cells, fatty acid output decreases and ketone production ceases. Ketosis often occurs in juvenile diabetes and will be discussed further in Chap. 29.

Phenylketonuria (PKU) This is an alteration in the metabolism of the amino acid phenylalanine due to the absence of phenylalanine hydroxylase. Without treatment, mental retardation and eventual death occur. Testing for this disorder is done during the first few weeks of life so that treatment may start early. Treatment for phenylketonuria is to decrease the phenylalanine content of the diet. This amino acid cannot be completely eliminated since it is an essential amino acid for growth. The length of treatment varies and often lasts until the child is at least school-age.

The major source of protein for a child with PKU is a special formula, such as Lofenalac. This is measured and mixed with water in a way similar to the preparation of powdered infant formula or dry milk. Small quantities of milk are added during infancy to provide the minimal amounts of phenylalanine and tyrosine needed for growth. Solids are given at the same time and sequence as for normal infants. Low-protein foods such as fruits, vegetables, and starches are permitted. Milk, meat, eggs, and other high-protein foods must be avoided because of their excessive phenylalanine content. Special baked products can be prepared using wheat starch. Food is selected using food groups which supply approximately 15 mg of phenylalanine per serving (1 equivalent). Equivalents are grouped into exchange lists, which are arranged into a daily meal pattern. This permits small amounts of phenylalanine to be evenly distributed throughout the day. The individual diet prescriptions are based on the child's growth needs and body size. Food selections should be as varied as possible to provide needed vitamins and minerals. Periodic dietary evaluations may be done to determine if a vitamin and mineral supplement is needed. Extra calories are provided from "free" foods (those containing no phenylalanine) such as sugar, hard candies, and specially prepared foods.

The success of the treatment for PKU depends on the thorough education of the family and others in the child's environment. It is important that the parents feel confident about preparing the infant's formula. Parents should realize that once the child achieves mobility, the child will begin to eat anything within reach. This increases the likelihood of obtaining excessive phenylalanine. Relatives, neighbors, and others who may give the child foods should be informed about the diet and taught what foods they can give to the child.

Health education should include the need for oral hygiene. Since many of the child's calories are provided from sugars, the need for proper dental care and regular dental checkups should be emphasized.

Further information on low-protein products is available from the manufacturers of low-phenylalanine foods. Dietitians and nutritionists can often provide recipes, pamphlets, and other materials to aid families in providing proper nutritional care for children with phenylkentonuria. With proper care and adherence to the restricted phenylalanine diet, these children can lead long, happy, and productive lives.

Galactosemia This is a metabolic disorder in which galactose (a monosaccharide) is not converted into glucose because of a deficiency of the enzyme needed for the conversion. Signs of the disorder include gastrointestinal disturbances, failure to grow, and jaundice. Mental retardation is evident during the second half of the first year if the child is left untreated. A diagnosis of galactosemia is made by testing urine for galactose or by a galactose tolerance test.

Since galactose is a component of lactose, milk sugar, products with this sugar are eliminated from the diet. Infant formulas which are soybean-based (Isomil), casein hydrolysate–based (Nutramigen), or meat-based must be used. When solids are introduced, foods which contain lactose, dry milk solids, whey and whey solids, and casein should be avoided. Since these items are often added to many foods, all food labels should be read carefully. The nurse should take care to see that the parents understand that galactose is part of lactose, since it is lactose which is added to many foods and is identified as such on food labels. Special recipes used for milk-free diets (see the section on lactose intolerance) are available.

Maple syrup urine disease (MSUD) This is a disturbance in the metabolism of the amino acids isoleucine, leucine, and valine. An infant with this disorder will exhibit poor appetite, severe vomiting and diarrhea, muscle hypertonicity, uncontrolled eye movement, lethargy, and convulsions. If the baby is untreated, death will occur. The disease gets its name from the characteristic maple syrup odor of the child's perspiration, earwax, and urine.

Treatment of MSUD requires the restriction of the three offending amino acids—isoleucine, leucine, and valine. Exchange lists of foods are used in daily meal planning. This type of restricted diet is complicated and needs to be planned and taught by a dietitian. The nurse should work with the dietitian to reinforce dietary instructions; the nurse may also act as an intermediate for communication between other health professionals and family.

Thyroid disease Iodine from the diet is needed to produce thyroxine. Iodized table salt is the most reliable source of this mineral for most people. The nurse can inform parents of the need for this nutrient and advise the use of iodized salt.

Thyroid disease influences the body's use of energy. Therefore an increase or decrease of calories may be needed to maintain proper body weight in children with thyroid dysfunctions.

Stress The body's need for nutrients changes during periods of physical stress, such as fever, burns, infection, and malignancies. These conditions require an increase in calories because of an increased metabolic rate. Protein requirement is also increased in the latter three conditions to promote healing and prevent physical deterioration. Three meals and three snacks daily generally provide the needed calories and protein without excessive quantities at one time. Such items as milk shakes, eggnogs, and sandwiches can provide the needed calories and protein. If necessary, special concentrated products such as Meritine, Vivonex, Ensure, and others can be used. Total parenteral nutrition may be necessary if the gastrointestinal tract is unable to handle food.

When special enteral feedings are given, it is important that proper administration techniques be followed. Such supplements as Meritine and Ensure (lactose-free) can be given the same as a milk drink. Small amounts should initially be given to check for any signs of intolerance. These products come in several flavors to facilitate acceptance by the child.

Elemental or low-residue supplements such as Vivonex or Precision may need to be given more carefully. These products often have a disagreeable taste. If these liquids are flavored and given ice cold, the taste may be more palatable. A second glass of water to wash the supplement down may also be helpful. When giving elemental products, such as Vivonex, which are hypertonic, encourage the child to sip them slowly. Allow 1 h or more to drink one full serving. This will aid absorption and decrease the chances of osmotic diarrhea. When given properly, enteral supplements can supply the needed calories, protein, and other nutrients to aid healing and prevent nutritional deterioration.

Alterations of major organs

Nutritional health is also jeopardized when an organ needed for metabolism is not functioning properly. Most of these alterations are discussed in detail in other chapters.

Hepatic disease The liver is involved in both the digestion of food (bile production for fat emulsification) and metabolism of nutrients. Generally, hepatic disorders involve restriction of the fat content of the diet. Carbohydrates are generally increased because of their protein-sparing affect. High-quality protein is encouraged in order to promote the healing process for acute hepatic illnesses. Such diets often include high-calorie–high-protein snacks. These snacks are an integral part of the child's treatment and should be planned by the dietitian with the child and the assistance of health team members.

Renal disease Although the kidneys are not involved in digestion or metabolism, their functioning is important to the child's nutritional status. When renal disease develops, alteration of the diet for protein, sodium, potassium, phosphorus, and fluid will decrease the work load of the kidneys. Calculation and instruction of such a restrictive diet should be left to the dietitian. The nurse, however, plays a role through reinforcement of the prescribed diet. The nurse can also help the child or parent manage fluid restrictions.

Pancreatic disease Like the liver, the pancreas is involved in the digestion and metabolism of food and nutrients. Children with cystic fibrosis have altered digestion of food due to changes in pancreatic enzyme secretions. Generally oral enzymes are given to correct this, but a low-fat diet is still followed. This may eliminate many childhood treats such as ice cream, but fruit ices and popsicles can be substituted. Special low-fat recipes for baked products are also available from local Heart Association chapters.

Juvenile diabetes mellitus (JDM) requires restriction of dietary carbohydrates. Concentrated forms of carbohydrates such as sugar, honey, and molasses are eliminated. A diet balanced in carbohydrate (45 to 55 percent of calories), protein (15 to 20 percent), and fat (30 to 35 percent) is prescribed. The total calorie level is generally based on the age of the child:

1000 kcal + (100 kcal × years in age)

For example, a 9-year-old child with JDM would require

1000 kcal + (100 kcal × 9) = 1900 kcal

The calories and carbohydrates are divided into three meals and two to three snacks daily. The exact distribution depends on type and amount of insulin, daily activities, and meal habits. Exchange lists provide the child with a variety of foods to use in daily meal planning.

At first, meal planning for a diabetic may seem difficult, but with practice it becomes much easier. If the child is in the hospital, the nurse may review the exchange lists with the child or parent once diet instructions have been given by the dietitian. The nurse has an excellent advantage to review and correlate all aspects of diabetes care. Parents should also be encouraged to obtain materials from local Diabetes Association chapters. A wide selection of cookbooks is available at reasonable cost. Many fast food chains and food producers provide information about how their foods work into the exchange lists. These can generally be obtained free or at minimal cost by writing to the company.

Food-borne illnesses

Illnesses due to food contamination result from three sources: parasites, bacteria, and viruses. These illnesses may be carried by other animals or human beings and are often transmitted via the fecal-oral route. With proper handling and preparation of foods, many of these illnesses can be prevented.

Parasites Trichina (*Trichinella spiralis*) and tapeworm (*Taenia saginata*) are two parasitic food contaminants. Trichinosis is generally associated with pork. It is spread when a hog eats garbage containing the trichina larvae, which then become embedded in the animal's muscles. Cooking the garbage before it is fed to hogs will prevent the spread of the parasites to the animals. When pork is prepared for human consumption, it should be thoroughly cooked (whitish grey with no evidence of pink remaining). This will kill the parasites and prevent their spread to a human host.

Tapeworms are spread in similar fashion to trichinae—through garbage. They can also spread through cattle grazing in polluted pastures. When humans eat raw or red meat (beef or pork) which contains the tapeworms, the organism matures and continues its life cycle in the intestinal tract. Again, thorough cooking will prevent the spread of this organism to humans.

Bacteria Several forms of bacteria may be responsible for food-borne illnesses. The exact type of illness—infection or poisoning—depends on the organism involved. (See Table 23-8.) With *food infection*, food which contains harmful bacteria is eaten. The bacteria then multiply in the host, causing symptoms specific for each organism. These food infections generally develop slowly in 12 to 24 h after the food is consumed. *Food poisonings* are caused by toxins produced by bacteria in food. Since the amount of toxin needed to produce illness is present before the food is eaten, symptoms develop rapidly in 1 to 6 h.

Viruses Some viral diseases can be spread through food, the most common of these being type A viral hepatitis. Generally this is spread by an infected food handler who does not properly wash his hands or carelessly prepares food. Hepatitis can also be spread by eating shellfish from contaminated water.

The nurse's role in food-borne illnesses is many-faceted. When a child is suspected of having a food infection or poisoning, the nurse will need to get a detailed 24-h food recall from the child, parent, or other persons. If any food was consumed in a public establishment or at a gathering, this should also be noted and the proper authorities must be notified and other

Table 23-8 Food-borne illnesses

Microorganism	Name of illness	Onset of symptoms	Symptoms	Duration	Foods susceptible
Salmonella	Salmonellosis	12 h	Cramps, fever, nausea, vomiting, diarrhea (sick people, infants, and elderly are more susceptible because of decreased resistance)	2–6 days	Poultry Eggs and egg products Milk Pork
Clostridium perfringens	Perfringens poisoning	10–20 h	Cramps, diarrhea, nausea	24 h	Meat
Staphylococcus aureus	Staphylococcus poisoning	2–8 h	Vomiting, diarrhea	1–2 days	Custards Sauces Gravies Soups Salads (chicken, tuna)
Clostridium botulinum	Botulism	12–36 h	Double vision, paralysis of respiratory muscles; can be fatal	3–8 days	Canned low-acid food Creamed soups Canned meat, mushrooms, etc.
Trichinella spiralis	Trichinosis	24–72 h	Nausea, vomiting, diarrhea, muscle pain, chest pain	Can be as long as 1 year	Pork and pork products

Source: Rosanne B. Howard and Nancie H. Herbold, *Nutrition in Clinical Care*, McGraw-Hill, New York, 1978. Used with permission of the publisher.

individuals involved located. Special attention should be paid to the foods associated most frequently with contamination (Table 23-8). If need be, the use of leading questions is appropriate in these instances.

Once the diagnosis is made, treatment will be established according to the type of illness. Since many of the food-borne illnesses affect the gastrointestinal tract, treatment often includes the use of a clear fluid diet and slowly reintroducing other foods as tolerated. Other treatments are used depending on the other systems of the body which are affected.

The nurse also has a responsibility to aid in the prevention of food-borne illnesses. The nurse should thoroughly wash hands to prevent the transmission of organisms between patients when helping patients with meals. Especially with pediatric hospital patients, the nurse should watch that the sharing of eating utensils is avoided.

Nursing Care Plan–Obesity

Patient: Susan K.   **Age:** 10 years   **Date First Seen:** 3/1, 10:00 A.M.

Assessment

Susan K., a 10-year-old female, was brought by her parents to the pediatrician's office for a routine physical exam because she is overweight. Susan lives with her mother and father, a 14-year-old brother, and an 8-year-old sister in a nearby middle-class neighborhood. The other children are of normal weight for their ages. The mother and father appear 10 to 20 lb overweight.

Mrs. K. explained that Susan is a straight-A student in school and does not participate in any after-school activities. She spends her free time reading, watching TV, and drawing, which she enjoys very much. Susan is driven to and from school by her mother.

Susan stated that she does not like physical education classes at school. She shrugged her shoulders when asked if she thought she needed to lose weight.

General appearance Eyes downcast, slumped posture; clothing ill-fitting due to excess weight
Vital signs Temp: 37°C.; Resp: 22; Pulse: 82; BP: 104/58
Weight 56.8 kg (125 lbs)—99th percentile
Height 139 cm (54½ in.)—50th percentile
Triceps skinfold 20 mm—85th percentile
Skin Clear complexion

Chest Clear on auscultation
Abdomen Negative
Laboratory tests Within normal range

24-hour diet recall

Breakfast None (normal habit)
11:30 School lunch: Spaghetti, 2 slices of bread with butter, tossed salad with French dressing, canned peach half, 1 pint whole milk
Extras from classmates: one half peanut butter and jelly sandwich, 1 slice chocolate cake with chocolate icing (4 × 4 × $\frac{3}{4}$″)
3:15 Large bowl of vanilla ice cream with chocolate sauce
5:30 Dinner with family: 2 helpings ($\frac{3}{4}$ cup each) mashed potatoes with gravy and butter, 1½ slices roast beef, $\frac{3}{4}$ cup candied carrots, 12 oz chocolate milk
7:00 3 cookies
8:00 3 cups buttered popcorn and 16 oz of soda (nondiet)

Susan said she usually snacks more often than on the day in question, mainly when she is reading or watching TV.

Nursing diagnosis	Nursing goals	Nursing actions	Evaluation/revision
1. Obesity secondary to excessive caloric intake	☐ Weight loss of 0.025–0.5 kg/week ☐ Total weight loss of 16 kg in 35 weeks	☐ Instruct Susan and parents on 1200-cal exchange list diet ☐ Have Susan and mother make out a daily menu plan for each week ☐ Plan reward with Susan for every 2 kg weight loss and for total 16-kg weight loss ☐ Check weight at clinic every Thursday	☐ 3/7: Susan finding it hard not to snack between meals. Reviewed list of free foods for snacks ☐ 3/15: Susan and parents able to plan weekly menu selection ☐ Mother reports finding new ways to season foods without increasing calories ☐ 3/15: Susan has decided she would like a new art supply item (< $5.00) for each 2 kg lost. Parents agree. Susan will get new fall clothes as final reward ☐ 3/21: Weight loss of 1.2 kg in 3 weeks ☐ *Continue plan and offer encouragement*

Nursing diagnosis	Nursing goals	Nursing actions	Evaluation/revision
2. Obesity associated with inadequate physical activity	☐ Increase energy output as evidenced by: **a.** Walking to and from school **b.** Regular physical activity at least every other day	☐ Plan exercise schedule with Susan ☐ Determine an acceptable physical activity for Susan	☐ 3/7: Susan has walked to and from school for 4 of last 5 days ☐ Susan began swimming lessons at YWCA 3 times a week
3. Inappropriate family health habits associated with lack of information and motivation	☐ Improve daily dietary and health practices as evidenced by: **a.** Eating 3 meals per day **b.** Reduction in high caloric foods **c.** Increase in level of physical activity	☐ Reinforce family's positive health practices, such as: **a.** Eating evening meals together **b** Including variety of foods from basic 4 food groups **c.** Eating breakfast together ☐ Encourage family to remove distractions during meals (TV, etc.). ☐ Suggest family participate in one physical activity together each weekend	☐ 3/7: Mother has fixed Susan daily breakfast of juice, boiled egg, and unbuttered toast ☐ 3/15: Family eating breakfast together on weekends ☐ 3/7: No TV viewed during meals ☐ 3/15: Family is swimming or riding bicycles to park one to two times per weekend

References

1. Sue Rodwell Williams, *Nutrition and Diet Therapy*, Mosby, St. Louis, 1977, p. 266.
2. "It's Natural! It's Organic! Or Is It?," *Consumer Reports* 45:410–415 (July 1980).
3. "Fast Food Chains," *Consumer Reports* 44:508–513 (September 1979).
4. Ibid.
5. Ibid.
6. "Position Paper on the Vegetarian Approach to Eating," *Journal of the American Dietetic Association* 77:61–69 (July 1980).
7. Ibid.
8. G. Christakis (ed.), "Nutritional Assessment of the Infant and Child," *American Journal of Public Health* 63:38–52 (November 1973).
9. Rosanne B. Howard and Nancie H. Herbold, *Nutrition in Clinical Care*, McGraw-Hill, New York, 1978, p. 214.
10. Kathryn H. Dansky, "Assessing Children's Nutrition," *American Journal of Nursing* 77:1610–1611 (October 1977).
11. Myron Winick and P. Rosso, "Head Circumference and Cellular Growth of the Brain in Normal and Marasmic Children," *Journal of Pediatrics* 74:774–778 (May 1969).
12. Myron Winick, "Cellular Changes During Early Malnutrition," *Ross Currents in Maternal and Child Health*, June, 1971.
13. J. M. Bengoa, *Nutrition, National Development and Planning*, M.I.T., Cambridge, Mass., 1972, p. 110.
14. Christakis, loc. cit.
15. Rosalinda T. Lagua, Virginia S. Claudio, and Victoria F. Thiele, *Nutrition and Diet Therapy Reference Dictionary*, Mosby, St. Louis, 1974, p. 146.
16. Robert H. Asher, "Clinical and Therapeutic Aspects of Fetal Malnutrition," *Pediatric Clinics of North America*, February 1970, pp. 169–183.
17. Myron Winick, "Cellular Growth in Intrauterine Malnutrition," *Pediatric Clinics of North America*, February 1970, pp. 69–78.
18. Carol Philipps and Nancy E. Johnson, "The Impact of Quality of Diet and Other Factors on Birth Weight of Infants," *American Journal of Clinical Nutrition*, February 1977, pp. 215–225.
19. Robert H. Usher, "Clinical and Therapeutic Aspects of Fetal Malnutrition," *Pediatric Clinics of North America*, February 1970, pp. 169–183.
20. Ibid.
21. Samuel J. Fomon, *Infant Nutrition*, Saunders, Philadelphia, 1974, p. 500.
22. Cyril A. Abrams, Louise L. Phillips, et al., Hazards of Overconcentrated Milk Formula, *Journal of the American Medical Association*, June 16, 1975, pp. 1136–1140.
23. Marie V. Krause and L. Kathleen Mahon, *Food, Nutrition and Diet Therapy*, Saunders, Philadelphia, 1979, p. 237.
24. Peggy Pipes, "When Should Semisolid Foods Be Fed to Infants?," *Journal of Nutrition Education*, April–June 1977, pp. 57–59.
25. Howard and Herbold, op. cit., p. 444.
26. Williams, op. cit., p. 504.

27. Howard and Herbold, op. cit., p. 447.

28. Helen A. Guthrie, *Introductory Nutrition*, Mosby, St. Louis, 4th ed., 1979, p. 927.

29. Deborah Dorsa Carman, "Infant and Childhood Obesity, Guidelines for Prevention and Treatment," *Pediatric Nursing*, November–December 1976, pp. 33–38.

30. Joan E. Bowers, Bonita Faulkner, and Susanne Michel, "Obesity in Children: An Ecological Approach," *The Journal of Continuing Education in Nursing:* 10(4):40–49 (1979).

31. Ibid.

32. Dominick P. DePaola and Michael C. Alfano, "Diet and Oral Health," *Nutrition Today*, May-June 1977, pp. 6–11, 29–32.

33. Committee on Nutrition, American Academy of Pediatrics, "Childhood Diet and Coronary Heart Disease," *Pediatrics*, February 1972, pp. 305–307.

34. Howard A. Schneider, Carl E. Anderson, and David B. Coursin, *Nutritional Support of Medical Practice*, Harper & Row, New York, 1977, p. 105.

35. Howard and Herbold, op. cit., p. 103.

36. Ibid., p. 106.

37. Schneider et al., op. cit., p. 112.

38. Ibid., p. 299.

39. Howard and Herbold, op. cit., p. 107.

40. Ibid., p. 95.

41. Robert S. Goodhart and Maurice E. Shils, *Modern Nutrition in Health and Disease*, Lea and Febiger, Philadelphia, 1980, p. 271.

42. Lea Whitby Heimann, "Weaning to Prevent Nutritional Anemia," *Pediatric Nursing*, May-June 1977, pp. 8–12.

43. Howard and Herbold, op. cit., p. 359.

44. Rita Colley and Jeanne M. Wilson, "Meeting Patients' Nutritional Needs with Hyperalimentation—Providing Hyperalimentation for Infants and Children," *Nursing 79*, July 1979, pp. 50–53.

45. Gladys M. Scipien, Martha Barnard, Marilyn Chard, Jeanne Howe, and Patricia Phillips, *Comprehensive Pediatric Nursing*, McGraw-Hill, New York, 1979, p. 755.

46. Cory T. Strobel, William J. Byrne, and Marvin E. Ament, "Home Parenteral Nutrition in Children with Crohn's Disease: An Effective Management Alternative," *Gastroenterology:* 77(2):272–279 (1979).

47. J. T. Goodgame, S. F. Lowry, and M. F. Brennan, "Essential Fatty Acid Deficiency in Total Parenteral Nutrition: Time, Course of Development and Suggestions for Therapy," *Surgery*, August 1978, pp. 271–277.

48. Nancy Tillotson Jacobson, "How to Administer Those Tricky Lipid Emulsions," *R.N.*, June 1979, pp. 63–64.

49. Ibid.

Chapter 24 **Fluid and electrolyte balance**

Patricia Maguire Meservey

Upon completion of this chapter, the student will be able to:

1. List five reasons why fluid balance is more critical in children than in adults.

2. List the major solutes of the extracellular, intracellular, and interstitial fluid compartments.

3. Compare the percentage of total water weight for the neonate, infant, toddler, preschooler, school-age child, adolescent, and adult.

4. Compare the size and major electrolytes found in the intracellular, extracellular, and interstitial fluid compartments.

5. List the fluid requirements, sources, and normal expenditures in children.

6. Identify the function, location, regulation, and dietary sources of sodium, potassium, calcium, magnesium, and chloride.

7. Compare the normal range of pH and that found in acidosis and alkalosis.

8. State examples of osmosis, diffusion, filtration, active transport, and pinocytosis.

9. Describe the function of the following buffer systems: carbonic-bicarbonate buffer, phosphate buffer, and protein buffer.

10. Describe the role of the respiratory system in the regulation of fluid and carbonic acid.

11. Describe the role of the kidneys in extracellular and acid-base regulation.

12. Describe the gastrointestinal regulation of fluids and nutrients.

13. Describe the integumentary regulation of hydration and temperature.

14. List the important fluid and electrolyte information to be elicited from a parent/child interview.

15. Compare the changes in isotonic, hypotonic, and hypertonic fluid deficit and excess.

16. Contrast the pathophysiology, symptoms, and treatment for hyponatremia, hypernatremia, hypocalcemia, hypercalcemia, hypomagnesemia, and hypermagnesemia.

17. Contrast respiratory and metabolic acidosis and alkalosis.

18. Identify changes in vital signs, hydration, intake and output, and general clinical status that are significant when assessing a child for fluid and electrolyte imbalances.

19. Describe the role of the nurse when caring for a child with dehydration caused by isotonic fluid deficit.

20. Plan care for a child with gastroenteritis causing fluid and electrolyte alterations.

Fluid and electrolyte balance is more critical in children than in adults. The younger the child, the more vulnerable he or she is to even slight alterations in fluid and electrolyte balance. The child with an impending imbalance needs meticulous nursing assessment, quick action, and frequent reevaluation of hydration status.

Physiological conditions that increase the vulnerability of children to fluid and electrolyte imbalances can be summarized as follows:

1. The metabolic rate of the infant and young child is two times as great as the adult's, with correspondingly greater production of heat and nitrogenous wastes. Physiological stress, such as fever or body heat loss, raises it still further.

2. The younger child experiences a greater turnover of body water than the adult. For example, infants excrete and must replace one-half of their extracellular fluid every 24 h; adults exchange one-sixth. This rapid turnover makes children more vulnerable to fluid shifts and imbalances.

3. Water comprises a higher percentage of body weight in the young child than in the adult. With the rapid turnover of body fluid, the infant's water reserve is less than that of the adult.

4. Certain normal physiological responses are inefficient because of the immaturity of body structures.

Until about age 2, for example, the kidneys are less able to concentrate urine than is normal, a condition which is thought to be due to their smaller capillary beds and the shorter loop of Henle of the nephrons.[1] They are also less able to maintain hydrogen ion concentration. Thus metabolic acidosis is more likely for a short time after birth; especially in the premature infant.[2] Furthermore, the nervous system of a child under age 2 is incompletely myelinated. Because the myelin sheath ensures rapid transmission of impulses along nerve pathways, an incompletely myelinated pathway may account for the unreliable response of renin and aldosterone mechanisms in maintaining homeostasis.[3]

5. The child has a greater body surface area per unit of weight than the adult and therefore undergoes greater loss of fluids, electrolytes, and body heat with exhaled air and through evaporation and radiation from the skin. For the same reason, children are more sensitive to changes in external temperature.

Water as a body constituent

Distribution of body fluid

Body water is divided into two main compartments, intracellular and extracellular. *Intracellular* refers to the contents of all body cells, including blood cells. *Extracellular* fluid consists of all other body water. It is subdivided into *intravascular fluid* (that is, plasma), *interstitital fluid* (fluid bathing the tissue cells), and *transcellular fluid*.[4] The last category includes fluid located in the eyes (ocular), joints (synovial), cerebrospinal system (cerebrospinal fluid), around the heart (pericardial), in the abdominal

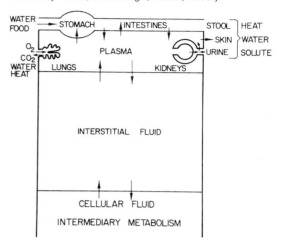

Figure 24-1 Body fluids approximate an open system in a steady state. (*Modified from Chart 1 in J. L. Gamble, Chemical Anatomy. Physiology and Pathology of Extracellular Fluid: A Lecture Syllabus, 6th ed. Harvard University Press, Cambridge, Mass., 1958.*)

cavity (peritoneal), and sometimes in the gastrointestinal and urinary tracts (see Fig. 24-1).

Although by weight an adult is approximately 60 percent water and 40 percent solid, the weight of a newborn child is 70 to 80 percent water and 20 to 30 percent solid (Table 24-1). Taking water alone, the newborn has 43 percent of the total in the intracellular compartment and 57 percent in the extracellular compartment. The figures for the adult are 75 percent intracellular and 25 percent extracellular. With so much body water in the extracellular compartment, the newborn is especially susceptible to fluid loss.

By adolescence, the distribution of body water

Table 24-1 Distribution of body water

Age	Total percent of body weight	Intracellular fluid	Extracellular fluid
Neonate	78%	34%	44%
Infant	70%	40%	30%
Toddler	64%	38%	26%
Preschool	62%	41%	21%
School age	62%	42%	20%
Adolescent	60%	45%	15%
Adult	60%	45%	15%

Source: Adapted from B. Friis-Hansen, "Body Water Compartments in Children: Changes during Growth and Related Changes in Body Composition," *Pediatrics* **28**:169 (1961).

is like that of adulthood. A sex difference in amount of weight that consists of water appears at this time. Girls have more adipose (fatty) tissue than boys, so that they have about 5 percent less water weight than boys, as adipose tissue holds less water than lean muscle (see Fig. 24-2).

Functions of water

Water is an essential substance for the body. It is the transport medium for the blood cells and substances that travel through circulatory vessels. It carries the enzymes, nutrients, and hormones through the interstitial compartment to tissue cells and waste products from these cells to the blood vessels. Within the cells, water provides the environment for the chemical reactions that fuel the body and maintain homeostasis.

Body temperature regulation depends, in part, on body water. By means of diaphoresis (sweating), water is released to the skin surface. As it evaporates, body heat is lost and the skin surface is cooled. Furthermore, blood carries heat from internal organs to blood vessels near the surface, where some of it leaves the body by radiation. Body heat carried by the blood also leaves with air expelled during expiration.

Daily water turnover

The normal healthy child maintains a balance between intake and output. The body receives its nutrients and normal fluids through the diet, and by metabolism, in the oxidation of food and body tissue. Fluid needs vary with age and will be discussed under requirements. Water intake is regulated by thirst, which is under the control of the hypothalamus. The feeling of thirst develops if the tonicity (level of electrolytes) of the extracellular fluids rises or if dehydration is present.[5]

Food provides fluid in two ways. The water content of food ranges from about 50 to 95 percent, fruits and vegetables having a much higher water content than meats. Food also provides fluid through the process of metabolism or oxidation. Fats, carbohydrates, and proteins produce different end products of metabolism as well as varying amounts of water. Complete oxidation of 100 g of fat yields 100 ml of water; 100 g of carbohydrates yield 60 ml of water; and 100 g of protein produce 45 ml of water.[6] The end products of fats and carbohydrates are carbon dioxide and water, while protein produces urea. Thus a child on a high-protein diet needs a higher fluid intake to dilute the nitrogenous wastes (urea) for excretion in urine. Oxidation of body tissues (metabolism) also produces some water, but the exact amount is difficult to determine.

Fluid output occurs through four routes: kidneys, lungs, skin, and stool. The kidneys are the largest excreters of water. Their product, urine, can be divided into *obligate* (the amount needed to excrete waste products) and *facultative* (variations occurring with diet and temperature). In general at most ages, approximately 50 ml of urine are excreted for every 100 calories metabolized.[7] However, because of the infant's much higher energy metabolism and immature kidneys, an increased urine output is required. The newborn's minimal urine output is 50 ml/kg, compared with the adult's minimal urine output of 20 ml/kg.[8]

Insensible losses account for the next largest category of fluid loss. This includes a total loss through the lungs and skin of 45 ml per 100 cal. Lungs utilize 15 ml fluid per 100 cal metabolized

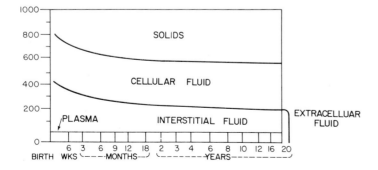

Figure 24-2 Approximate distribution of body fluids per kilogram. Body weight at various ages. (*Modified from N. B. Talbot, R. H. Richie, J. E. Crawford, and E. S. Tagrin, Metabolic Homeostasis: A Syllabus for Those Concerned with the Care of Patients, Harvard University Press, Cambridge, Mass., 1959, p. 3.*)

Table 24-2 Fluid expenditures and requirements

| Age/weight | Caloric expenditures | Fluid losses | | | | | Fluid requirements |
		Urine	Skin	Lungs	Stool	Total	
Newborn: 3 kg	300 cal	150 ml	90 ml	45 ml	15 ml	300 ml	300 ml
Infant: 6 kg	600 cal	300 ml	180 ml	90 ml	30 ml	600 ml	600 ml
Toddler: 15 kg	1250 cal	625 ml	375 ml	187.5 ml	62.5 ml	1250 ml	1250 ml
Preschool: 20 kg	1500 cal	750 ml	450 ml;	225 ml	75 ml	1500 ml	1500 ml
School-age: 30 kg	1700 cal	850 ml	510 ml	255 ml	85 ml	1700 ml	1700 ml
Adolescent: 60 kg	2300 cal	1150 ml	690 ml	345 ml	115 ml	2300 ml	2300 ml

and release this in exhaled air at the rate of 0.5 ml/kg/h.

The normal skin expenditure is 30 ml per 100 cal and does not include diaphoresis. Sweating can increase fluid loss significantly. It usually begins after the environmental temperature reaches 30°C (86°F).[9] Fluid loss increases by 30 ml per 100 cal for each 1°C rise in the environmental temperature. Children are much more susceptible to increased insensible fluid loss during increases in temperature of the body and external environment.

The fourth fluid loss occurs through the stool. Roughly 5 ml/kg per day (5 ml per 100 cal) metabolized are excreted in the feces of children compared to the adult output of 2.5 ml/kg per day.[10]

Fluid requirements

To determine fluid expenditure and requirements, several factors must be considered: metabolic rate, body weight, and skin surface area. It has already been stated that the child's metabolic rate is twice that of an adult per unit of body weight. Furthermore, the body surface area of an infant is three times that of an adult per unit of weight, supplying the means for a greater loss of heat and fluid.

There is a wide discrepancy in fluid needs between the infant and the adult, although both require 100 ml per 100 cal metabolized. To determine the number of calories metabolized, body weight in kilograms (kg) is used. For the first 10 kilograms of body weight, 100 cal/kg per 24 h are metabolized. For the second 10 kilograms (or kilograms 11 to 20), 50 cal/kg per 24 h are metabolized. Beyond 20 kg, the body utilizes 20 cal/kg per 24 h.[11]

For example: A 3-kg infant (approximately 6 lb, 6 oz) metabolizes 100 cal/kg, or 300 cal per 24 h. This is then easily converted into a fluid requirement by using the formula 100 cal = 100 ml. The 3-kg infant metabolizes 300 cal per day and therefore requires 300 ml of fluid per day.

Another example: A 30-kg, 9-year-old child utilizes 100 cal for the first 10 kg, 50 cal for the next 10 kg, and 20 cal for the last 10 kg. The totals are as follows:

$$0{-}10 = 10 \text{ kg at } 100 \text{ cal/kg} = 1000 \text{ cal}$$
$$11{-}20 = 10 \text{ kg at } 50 \text{ cal/kg} = 500 \text{ cal}$$
$$21{-}30 = 10 \text{ kg at } 20 \text{ cal/kg} = \underline{200 \text{ cal}}$$
$$\text{Total} \quad 1700 \text{ cal/24 h}$$

The 9-year-old child would burn about 1700 cal in 24 h and therefore requires 1700 ml of fluid during this period (see Table 24-2).

This formula is for maintenance fluids and does not consider abnormal losses. Losses from vomiting, fever, diarrhea, sweating, and increased exercise must be computed separately. Fever will increase caloric expenditure by 12 percent for every 1°C rise in body temperature. Likewise, hypothermia will decrease caloric expenditure by 12 percent for every 1°C drop in body temperature.[12] Enormous amounts of fluid (greater than 50 ml per kg every 24 h) may be lost through the gastrointestinal tract because of diarrhea, vomiting, fistulas, colostomy, or other causes.[13] Gastrointestinal losses represent the most common clinical cause of significant dehydration. A complete evaluation of fluid losses must precede administration of fluids to a child.

Electrolytes

Functions

Electrolytes are electrically charged chemical elements or compounds called *ions* that are found dissolved in all body fluids (Fig. 24-3). The positively charged ions are called *cations;* the negatively charged ions are called *anions.*

Electrolytes have many functions in maintaining the body's homeostasis. Two major ones are (1) to stabilize fluid distribution through osmotic pressure and (2) to maintain the acid-base balance. Each electrolyte will be discussed separately in this section. Abnormal electrolyte concentrations will be discussed in the section "Electrolyte Alterations."

Sodium Sodium (Na$^+$) is the major cation of the extracellular fluid, including interstitial and intravascular fluid (Fig. 24-3). Sodium is measured by serum level, and the normal range is 135 to 145 mEq per liter.

The major function of sodium is to maintain the osmotic pressure of the extracellular fluid and thus regulate the extracellular fluid volume. Sodium level is regulated by the kidneys. Sodium is reabsorbed by the kidneys and influences fluid reabsorption. When the concentration of sodium falls, aldosterone, a hormone secreted by the adrenal cortex, promotes sodium reabsorption. As the kidneys retain sodium, they also retain water. A deficit in body fluid volume causes a decrease in the glomerular filtration rate and enhances sodium retention. The body retains sodium so efficiently that a person may remain on a low-sodium diet for a long time without experiencing sodium depletion.

In contrast, when the sodium concentration in extracellular fluids rises, antidiuretic hormone (ADH) release causes the kidneys to retain water. This retained fluid dilutes the sodium to more normal concentrations. Sodium is excreted in the urine, feces, and sweat when the level exceeds normal.

Sodium is one of the ions responsible for the cell's membrane potential, which is essential for nervous system function and muscle contraction. Finally, sodium participates in maintaining the acid-base balance as a component of the buffer sodium bicarbonate. Commercially prepared foods contain high levels of sodium. Pickles, catsup, canned soups, cold cuts, ham, and bacon have very high sodium levels. Favorite children's foods such as potato chips, french fries, and cheese also have high sodium levels. Americans also use large amounts of table salt. A recommended intake of sodium is 2.5 mEq per 100 cal metabolized.

Potassium (K$^+$) Potassium is the major cation of the intracellular fluid. Values of intracellular potassium are difficult to obtain and are therefore approximately measured by the serum level. The normal serum potassium is 3.5 to 5.0 mEq per liter.

Figure 24-3 Differences in composition of intracellular and extracellular fluids. (*Modified from Chart 2 in J. L. Gamble, Chemical Anatomy, Physiology and Pathology of Extracellular Fluid: A Lecture Syllabus, 6th ed., Harvard University Press, Cambridge, Mass., 1958.*)

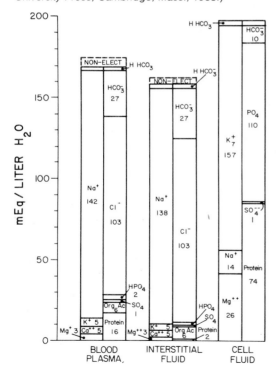

Potassium helps to maintain the normal fluid and electrolyte distribution of the intracellular compartment. As a component of a buffer pair, potassium also guards the acid-base equilibrium of intracellular fluids. The potassium ion, like sodium, establishes the membrane potential, essential for nerve and muscle action. Abnormal potassium levels are immediately reflected in disturbed functioning of nerve or muscle.

In the kidney, potassium is completely filtered out of the blood at the glomerulus and entirely reabsorbed in the proximal convoluted tubules. However, in the distal convoluted tubules, potassium is often excreted in exchange for sodium. Absorption is fairly complete in the upper gastrointestinal tract, but in the lower part of the tract potassium may be exchanged for sodium.

Daily dietary intake of potassium is required. The recommended rate is 2.5 mEq per 100 cal metabolized. Bananas, oranges, potatoes, carrots, celery, and peaches are excellent sources of potassium.

Calcium (Ca^{++}) Calcium is the primary electrolyte found in the teeth and bones. These locations account for 99 percent of the body's calcium. The remaining 1 percent is in the plasma and the cells. The plasma calcium is measured when a calcium value is given. The normal value is 9.0 to 11.5 mg per 100 ml.

It is difficult to identify a major function of calcium because all its functions are vital to the normal physiology of the body. The majority of the calcium in the body is used, along with phosphorus, to make the teeth and bones strong. Calcium is a component of cell cement, which determines the thickness, strength, and permeability of cell membranes. Furthermore, calcium is essential for contraction of muscle. Calcium abnormalities cause cardiac irregularities and skeletal muscle problems, such as leg cramps.

Other functions include the body's absorbing and using vitamin B$_{12}$, activating enzymes for chemical reactions, and converting prothrombin to thrombin in the clotting mechanism.

Calcium absorption and excretion are regulated by several means. Vitamin D promotes calcium absorption from the intestines while increasing renal excretion of phosphate. Parathormone, a parathyroid hormone, regulates the plasma phosphorus and calcium levels. Parathormone enhances calcium absorption from the intestine and kidneys to raise the serum calcium level. It also increases osteoclastic (bone-destroying) activity, which releases calcium into the bloodstream to raise the serum concentration. This results in the release of calcium from the bones and occurs in rickets (soft, porous bones). Calcitonin, a thyroid hormone, facilitates calcium excretion by the kidneys as the serum calcium level increases.

Sources of dietary calcium are milk, cheese, dried beans, kale, and brazil nuts. The recommended daily allowance is 1 g. Children refusing milk can be given cheese, ice cream, yogurt, puddings, and custards. Instant milk can also be camouflaged in baked goods.

Magnesium (Mg^{++}) The last major cation of the body is magnesium. Magnesium is found in the bone cells (50 percent), specialized cells of the heart, liver, and skeletal muscles (49 percent), and the extracellular fluid (1 percent). The normal serum magnesium is 1.67 mEq per liter.

The functions of magnesium are similar to those of calcium. Magnesium has been used successfully to treat cardiac arrhythmias and to reduce hyperactive muscle response in toxemia of pregnancy. This leads to the belief that magnesium has a role in nerve impulse transmission and muscle function. Magnesium is also used as a supplement to antihypertensive agents.

Recently, it has been found that magnesium activates enzymatic reactions related to vitamin B functions and the body's use of potassium, calcium, and protein. Like calcium, it inhibits muscle contraction.

Magnesium, like calcium, is regulated by the parathyroid gland. Magnesium and calcium compete for absorption, and as the absorption rate of one increases, the rate of the other decreases. Magnesium is also regulated by the renal system. As the magnesium level of the blood drops, the renal excretion of magnesium slows.

Magnesium's recommended daily allowance is 150 to 250 mg. Nuts, fish, whole grain, and legumes are excellent sources of magnesium and should be included daily in the child's diet.

Chloride (Cl$^-$) The principal anion of the extracellular fluid is chloride. Chloride's functions, regulation, and dietary sources are similar to those of sodium. Chloride also combines with hydrogen to form hydrochloric acid, a component of the gastric juice. The normal chloride level is 95 to 106 mEq per liter.

Other anions The other major anions include phosphate (PO_4^{3-}) and bicarbonate (HCO_3^-). Bicarbonate has the principal function of acid-base regulation and will be discussed in that section. Phosphate is a component of a buffer but has additional functions.

As calcium phosphate it is an important component of bones and teeth. More than 75 percent of phosphorus is employed in the skeletal system and the remainder is found in serum and the cells. In the latter, phosphorus takes part in many metabolic functions. The compound adenosine triphosphate (ATP) is important in the transfer of chemical energy. Phosphorus is also found in DNA and RNA.

Phosphorus is regulated along with calcium and requires vitamin B for absorption. It is absorbed at a much greater rate than calcium. In renal failure, there is an increase in phosphorus retention and calcium excretion. Dietary sources are beef, pork, dried beans, and peas.

Acid-base balance

Hydrogen ion concentration

Because the child is vulnerable to fluid and electrolyte imbalances, acid-base abnormalities are also more likely to occur. By one definition, an *acid* is a substance that, when added to a solution, produces hydrogen ions (H^+). Body cells cannot live in an environment with too little or too great a concentration of H^+; therefore the acidity (H^+ concentration) of body fluids is of great importance.

The pH scale expresses H^+ concentration in simplified form. For example, 0.0000001 g per liter of H^+ (which can also be expressed as 10^{-7} g per liter) is stated as pH 7.

A *basic*, or alkaline, substance, on the other hand, can be defined as one that produces hydroxyl (OH^-) ions when added to a solution. The pH scale tells not only the concentration of H^+ but also the proportion of H^+ to OH^-. At the midpoint, 7.0, the two ions are in equal concentration. The result is a neutral solution such as water.

An acidic solution, therefore, is one with a high concentration of H^+, a low concentration of OH^-, and a pH *lower* than 7.0. The more acidic the solution, the more hydrogen ions are available to be given to other chemical elements of the solution. For this reason, acids are also defined as *proton* (hydrogen ion) *donors*. A strong acid is one that releases large amounts of H^+; that is, all or most of its molecules dissociate into ions. Hydrochloric acid (HCl) is an example of a strong acid.

The opposite is true of basic solutions. These have low concentrations of H^+ and high concentrations of OH^-. The pH is greater than 7.0. The less H^+ in a solution, the more it can receive. For this reason, bases are defined as *proton acceptors*. For example, when H^+ is added to a basic solution, some hydrogen ions combine with the base. The two kinds of ions neutralize each other, producing a solution with a neutral pH (6 to 8). Therefore, by combining with H^+, the base succeeds in reducing the amount of H^+ at liberty in the solution.

The pH of extracellular fluid is normally held between 7.35 and 7.45. Extremes of 7.0 to 7.7 can be tolerated, but only for short periods. The body has evolved three systems to hold pH within this range: buffers, ventilation through the lungs, and excretion through the kidneys. Buffers tend to make their corrections within seconds, the lungs within minutes, and the kidneys within hours to days.

Buffers

Buffers of the body are compounds that, by releasing or absorbing H^+, enable body fluids to correct changes in pH when acidic or alkaline substances are added, as happens every day in the course of metabolism. Most buffers of the body consist of a pair of compounds and hence are called *buffer systems*. The three main ones are (1) bicarbonate, (2) phosphate, and (3) protein buffer systems.

The bicarbonate buffer system is the primary one and is found in all body fluids. It consists of bicarbonate (HCO_3^-) and carbonic acid (H_2CO_3) and operates as summarized in this equation:

$$H_2CO_3 \rightleftharpoons H^+ + HCO_3^-$$
Carbonic acid   Bicarbonate

When H^+ is added to a solution containing this buffer system, some of it immediately combines with bicarbonate molecules to form carbonic acid. As carbonic acid is a weak acid, it only partly ionizes (hence the shorter arrow pointing to the right). As a result, the increase in H$^+$ in the solution is much reduced. It could be said that the carbonic acid serves to tie up much of the added H$^+$ and hold the solution close to its original pH. The opposite would follow a decrease of H$^+$ below normal levels. The reactions would shift to the right, with breakup of carbonic acid and an increase in H$^+$ and bicarbonate (see Fig. 24-4).

For the buffer system to work, the buffer compounds have to be available in the right amounts. About 1 carbonic acid molecule is needed for every 20 bicarbonates. Maintaining this proportion is the job of the kidneys.

The phosphate buffer system works in a similar manner. The components are acid phosphate (H$_2$PO$_4$$^-$) and alkaline phosphate (HPO$_4$$^{2-}$). This buffer system is found in large quantities in the cells, including tubule cells of the kidneys. It is important in maintaining cellular acid-base balance.

The phosphate buffer system acts as follows:

$$H_2PO_4^- \rightleftharpoons H^+ + HPO_4^{2-}$$

The last buffer system to be described is the protein buffer system. It is found in the intravascular fluid in the form of plasma proteins. Proteins are amino acids with peptide bonds. Some proteins have extra acid radicals ($^-$COOH) and others have extra basic radicals ($^-$NH$_2$). Proteins therefore can donate or accept hydrogen ions as needed to maintain the normal pH of intravascular fluids.

Alterations in acid-base balance

Metabolic acidosis

Metabolic acidosis is a decrease in plasma pH below 7.35 resulting from an accumulation of acids or a primary bicarbonate deficit. It is an important concern in newborn and young children because their buffer systems may still be immature. Furthermore, the young child's high metabolic rate increases the formation of acids and the potential for acidosis. Metabolic acidosis appears in children most often with diabetes, diarrhea, salicylate intoxication, and a loss of bicarbonate due to renal disease and starvation. The normal newborn may be acidotic at birth, but this acidosis is resolved by the second day of life.

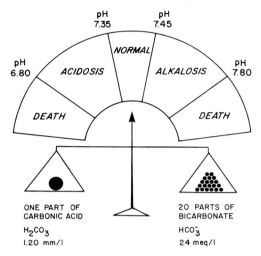

Figure 24-4 The bicarbonate buffer system. The body maintains a ratio of 1 part carbonic acid to 20 parts bicarbonate. Alkaline deficit or acid excess will bring a shift to the left. Alkaline excess or acid deficit will bring a shift to the right. (*Adapted from Fluid and Electrolytes: Some Practical Guides to Clinical Use, Abbott Laboratories, May 1969. From Rosanne B. Howard and Nancie H. Herbold, Nutrition in Clinical Care, McGraw-Hill, New York, 1978. Used by permission of the publisher.*)

Babies fed with cow's milk also have a greater tendency for metabolic acidosis because of the high phosphate and sulfate content of cow's milk. Any gastrointestinal losses (diarrhea or vomiting) from below the pyloric sphincter cause acidosis because the excreted fluid contains large amounts of bicarbonate (see Table 24-3).

Treatment of metabolic acidosis focuses on treating the underlying pathophysiology (an increase in the proportion of carbonic acid to bicarbonate). Sodium bicarbonate or sodium lactate provides relief by supplying additional buffers. This is only temporary but does allow extra time to diagnose and treat the cause of the acidosis.

Close observation of clinical symptoms and laboratory test results provide information signifying a change in the child's condition. The child's alertness and level of consciousness as well as an increased respiratory rate, are key factors in determining the severity of the acidosis. Life cannot be maintained if the pH stays below 7.0. The nurse must be alert to prevent drastic changes in pH from going unnoticed.

Respiratory acidosis

Respiratory acidosis (CO_2 excess) in infants and children may be caused by cystic fibrosis, asthma, croup, respiratory distress syndrome, muscular dystrophy, or aspiration of a foreign body. These diseases generally reduce pulmonary ventilation, causing retention of carbon dioxide (elevated P_{CO_2}) and an increase in the serum carbonic acid level. Respiratory acidosis occurs quickly and can be quickly resolved (see Table 24-3).

Treatment consists simply of aiding ventilation to the extent necessary. Oxygen, artificial ventilation, chest physical therapy, and suctioning are all possible methods of intervening to increase the effectiveness of respiration.

Nursing care of respiratory acidosis requires continuous monitoring, positioning in semi-Fowler's position, frequent turning, and encouraging coughing and deep breathing. Meticulous assessment of respiratory function and blood gasses and prompt interventions can prevent respiratory acidosis in many children. Early detection can decrease both the severity of the acidosis and the extent of medical treatment necessary to correct the problem.

Metabolic alkalosis

Metabolic alkalosis (primary bicarbonate excess) occurs when a metabolic malfunction brings about an increased amount of a base or a decreased amount of an acid. Four of the most common causes are (1) administration or ingestion of excess sodium bicarbonate, (2) loss of chloride as hydrochloric acid in vomiting or gastric suction, (3) excessive excretion of acid in urine, and (4) decreased serum potassium, which forces hydrogen ion to move from the serum into the cells. (See Table 24-3.)

Treatment is again to identify and eliminate the cause of the alkalosis and to prevent further acid and electrolyte loss. Potassium and chloride supplements may be necessary, and Diamox will promote bicarbonate excretion. Ammonium chloride given intravenously will temporarily relieve the alkalosis until the cause can be treated.

Safety of the confused, irritable child who

Table 24-3 Acidosis and alkalosis

Causes	Symptoms	Laboratory tests
Metabolic acidosis		
Excess acid, bicarbonate deficit, decreased plasma CO_2	Nausea and vomiting, diarrhea, headache, chest and abdominal pain, stupor or coma, hyperpnea, Kussmaul breathing, disorientation, muscle twitching, weakness	Increased: potassium Decreased: P_{CO_2}, sodium, chloride, bicarbonate (20–24 mEq per liter), urine pH (under 6), plasma pH (under 7.35), CO_2 combining power
Metabolic alkalosis		
Acid deficit, bicarbonate excess, increased plasma CO_2	Nausea and vomiting, diarrhea, irritability and confusion, tetany, depressed respirations, cardiac arrhythmia (low T wave merging into the P wave)	Increased: urine pH (above 7), serum pH (above 7.45), bicarbonate (above 27 mEq per liter) Decreased: potassium and possibly chloride
Respiratory acidosis		
Excess acid, increased plasma CO_2	Weakness and listlessness, diaphoresis, disorientation, depressed respirations, rapid, irregular pulse	Increased: P_{CO_2} (above 38 mmHg, arterial) potassium Plasma bicarbonate (normal or increased) Decreased: Serum and urine pH
Respiratory alkalosis		
Acid deficit, plasma CO_2 deficit, carbonic acid deficit	Headache, vertigo, carpopedal spasms, tetany, palpitations, circumoral paresthesias, chest discomfort	Increased: pH (above 7.45), P_{CO_2} Normal P_{O_2} and bicarbonate Decreased: P_{CO_2}

experiences convulsions, nausea, vomiting, or diarrhea is a primary concern. Observation for signs and symptoms of alkalosis, such as respiratory depression, that may require immediate attention is also a key nursing concern.

Respiratory alkalosis

Respiratory alkalosis (primary carbonic acid deficit) can occur in children as a result of hyperventilation or hysteria, meningeal irritation, or salicylate ingestion. The increased respirations cause an excessive release of carbon dioxide, resulting in a carbonic acid deficit (see Table 24-3).

Nursing care is the primary treatment in most cases of respiratory alkalosis. Reassurance and encouragement to slow respirations are the key to resolving the crisis. Sedation may be necessary while the underlying cause is identified.

Hyperventilation or hysteria is usually treated by rebreathing exhaled air from a bag. This elevates carbon dioxide levels and is effective in treating respiratory alkalosis.

Principles of fluid, solute, and acid-base regulation

Solutes in body water

Along with the electrolytes found in body fluids, there are other substances which have a role in the maintenance of fluid balance. Nonelectrolytes, such as urea, glucose, creatinine, and plasma proteins dissolved in body water, exert forces that affect water movement. These forces cause the constant movement of water (body fluids) back and forth across semipermeable membranes of the body compartments.

Fluid regulation and movement

Osmosis is the movement of water through a semipermeable barrier in response to a concentration gradient of solute, that is, a difference in solute concentration from one side of the barrier to the other. The water moves from the side where the solutes are in low concentration to the side of higher concentration. In doing so, the water equalizes the concentration of solute on the two sides of the barrier (see Fig. 24-5).

Any solution is said to exert osmotic pressure if it contains osmotically active particles. Proteins exert strong osmotic pressure. Osmotic pressure

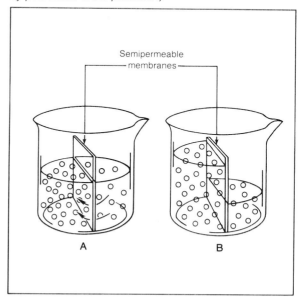

Figure 24-5 Osmosis. In (*A*) a concentration gradient exists between the two sides of the semipermeable membrane, causing the movement of water to the more concentrated side (*B*). (*From Dorothy Jones, Claire Ford Dunbar, and Mary Marmoll Jirovec (eds.), Medical-Surgical Nursing: A Conceptual Approach, McGraw-Hill, New York, 1978. Used by permission of the publisher.*)

due to proteins is called *colloid osmotic pressure* or *oncotic pressure*.

The osmotic pressure of a solution can be stated as *osmolarity*. Osmolarity is a way of measuring the concentration of osmotically active particles in a solution. It is also possible to classify solutions by tonicity. An *isotonic* solution has the same solute concentration as one used for reference—plasma, for example. Adding an isotonic solution to plasma does not change the osmotic balance between the plasma and the cells carried in it. A *hypertonic* solution is one with a greater solute concentration. Adding a hypertonic solution to plasma would cause blood cells to shrink as fluid crossed the cell membrane and entered the plasma. The opposite effect would follow the addition of a *hypotonic* solution. Cells would swell as water from the plasma entered, seeking to equalize the solute concentration.

Diffusion is the movement of solute through a solution down its concentration gradient, that is, from a higher to a lower concentration. Diffusion is the result of the natural random movement of particles, which leads them to spread evenly through a solution. Even a membrane, so long as it is permeable to the solutes, will not interrupt diffusion (see Fig. 24-6).

Certain substances, such as proteins, that are unable to cross cell membranes by means of diffusion, active transport, or filtration are taken in by another method, termed *pinocytosis*. In this method, a portion of the cell membrane folds inward, carrying with it any substance adherent to the membrane. This membrane segment with its contents enclosed breaks loose, forming a vesicle floating within the cell interior. Enzymes of the cell cytoplasm may then rupture the vesicle and digest its contents, making them available for cell metabolism.

Movement down a concentration gradient is characteristic of *passive transport*. Water and

Figure 24-6 Diffusion. As molecules randomly move, they bounce off each other, and the unequal concentration in (*A*) becomes progressively more equal (*B*) until they are equalized (*C*). (*From Dorothy Jones, Claire Ford Dunbar, and Mary Marmoll Jirovec (eds.), Medical-Surgical Nursing: A Conceptual Approach, McGraw-Hill, New York, 1978. Used by permission of the publisher.*)

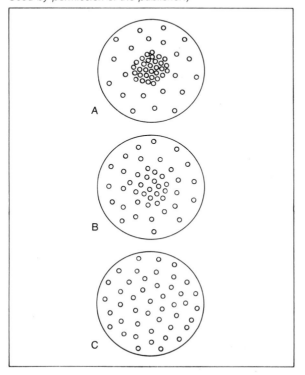

many metabolites that enter and leave the cells move by passive transport. Yet many substances are capable of moving up a concentration gradient (low to high concentration), and this kind of movement, termed *active transport*, requires assistance and energy expenditure to be carried out. The active transport mechanism of a given substance is known as a *pump*. For example, the membrane of the nerve cells maintains sodium in high concentration outside but in low concentration inside the cell, despite the tendency of sodium to enter by diffusion. The sodium pump of the membrane is so efficient that in the resting nerve cell, there is approximately 14 times the concentration of sodium outside as inside the cell.

Filtration is the transfer of water *and* solutes down a concentration gradient. The force behind filtration is hydrostatic pressure. In the vascular system, this pressure is created by the outward thrust of blood against the walls that confine it. The driving force is the pumping action of the heart.

Capillary fluid and solute dynamics Four factors determine the movement of fluids across capillary membranes: capillary hydrostatic pressure, interstitial hydrostatic pressure, capillary colloid osmotic pressure, and interstitial colloid osmotic pressure (Fig. 24-7).

Capillary hydrostatic pressure (CHP) is difficult to determine; measuring it directly would require invasion of the capillary. However, CHP is estimated to be the equivalent of 25 mmHg at the arterial end and 10 mmHg at the venous end of the capillary. The fluid within tissue also exerts pressure, *interstitial hydrostatic pressure*, but this is thought to be slightly below atmospheric pressure, so that its effect is to allow fluid to leave the capillary. Thus it reinforces the effect of CHP.

The proteins in the blood exert an osmotic pressure called *capillary colloid osmotic pressure* (CCOP). This pressure tends to draw water into the capillary and hence opposes the effects of the preceding two factors. The CCOP is estimated to be equal to 28 mmHg. Finally, *interstitial colloid osmotic pressure* (ICOP) must be considered. It is the result of the small amount of protein able to leak through the vascular membrane into interstitial fluid. The ICOP is estimated to equal about 5 mmHg.

Figure 24-7 Pressure dynamics in a capillary bed. Capillary hydrostatic pressure (CHP), interstitial hydrostatic pressure (IHP), and interstitial colloid osmotic pressure (ICOP) move fluid out of the capillaries, whereas capillary colloid osmotic pressure (CCOP) moves fluid into the capillaries. (*From Dorothy Jones, Claire Ford Dunbar, and Mary Marmoll Jirovec (eds.), Medical-Surgical Nursing: A Conceptual Approach, McGraw-Hill, New York, 1978. Used by permission of the publisher.*)

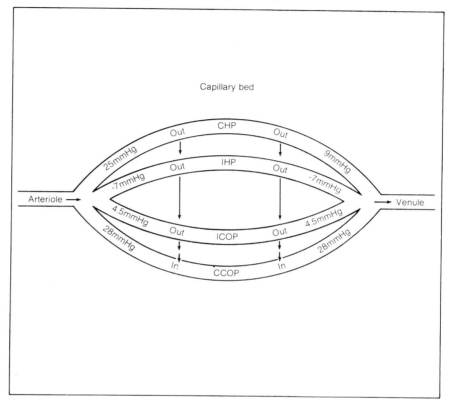

It is the net effect of these four factors that is of interest. The forces favoring outflow of fluid from the capillary are almost equal to those drawing fluid inward. The net outward pressure at the arterial end is equal to about 8.3 mmHg; this is called the *filtration pressure.* The reabsorption pressure is estimated to be equal to 6.7 mmHg. The small net difference of 1.6 mmHg favoring outward movement is actually still less when the mean pressure across an entire capillary bed is calculated. The effect of these forces is that while fluid leaves the capillary at the arterial end, almost all of it reenters at the venous end. The small amounts left in interstitial spaces enter the lymphatic system and are eventually returned to the vascular system. This balanced process is known as the *Starling equilibrium.*

Regulation of fluid and electrolytes by the kidneys The kidneys have both an excretory and a regulatory function. They participate in the adjustment of the composition of extracellular body fluids by determining both the volume of fluid and the amounts and kinds of electrolytes to be excreted or retained.

The functional unit of the kidney is the *nephron.* It is estimated that approximately 1 million nephrons are found in each kidney. Two types of nephrons, *cortical* and *juxtamedullary*, differing in tubular structure, are found in the kidneys. The cortical nephrons with short tubule loops are found in the renal cortex and are the most common type. Juxtamedullary nephrons have long loops of Henle that extend into the renal medulla and comprise only about 15 percent of the nephrons. Both types of nephrons have a vascular component (the glomerulus, peritubular capillaries, and vasa recti) and a tubular component (Bowman's capsule with the tubular system—the proximal tubule, loop of Henle, distal tubule, and collecting duct). Kidney function depends upon the interrelationship of these two components. See Fig. 24-8 for a diagram of a nephron.

Blood is supplied to the kidney by the renal artery. This artery subdivides into progressively smaller branches until it enters Bowman's capsule as the *afferent arteriole*, which then forms a bundle of capillaries called the *glomerulus*. Surrounding the glomerulus is *Bowman's capsule*, a double-walled, cuplike structure in which filtration takes place. As the glomerular capillaries leave Bowman's capsule, they recombine to form the *efferent arteriole*. This divides into the peritubular capillaries to form an intertwining network around the tubules. The *vasa recta* are the blood vessels around the loops of Henle. This vascular network reunites into a venous system by which the blood leaves the kidneys.

Glomerular *filtrate*, the product of filtration in Bowman's capsule, is similar to blood plasma but with little of the protein and none of the red blood cells. Hydrostatic pressure of the blood is the force behind filtration into the capsule. Whereas about one-fourth of the total cardiac output enters the kidneys every minute, only about one-fifth of the plasma undergoes filtration (passes into Bowman's capsule). The amount of glomerular filtrate produced each minute by all the nephrons of the kidneys is called the *glomerular filtration rate* (GFR).

As the filtrate passes through the tubules, the process of reabsorption back into the blood takes place. About 99 percent of the water in filtrate is reabsorbed, along with varying amounts of other substances. Reabsorption takes place chiefly by osmosis and diffusion, but the tubules are also the site of active transport of some substances.

While tubular reabsorption moves substances out of the tubules for return to the blood, another mechanism, *secretion*, moves substances from the peritubular capillaries into the lumen of the tubules. Secretion is the chief way in which levels of potassium and hydrogen ions are regulated. Potassium is almost entirely reabsorbed in the proximal tubules and the loop of Henle. It is actively secreted in exchange for sodium in the distal and collecting tubules.

When substances are actively transported into or out of the tubules, a carrier is required. Sodium

Figure 24-8 Schematic view of the nephron, with its functional units identified. (*From Rosanne B. Howard and Nancie H. Herbold, Nutrition in Clinical Care, McGraw-Hill, New York, 1978. Used by permission of the publisher.*)

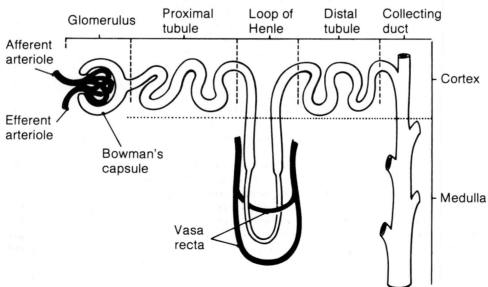

is involved in one of the most important active transport systems in the kidney. As sodium is reabsorbed, it carries chloride (Cl^-) with it, and the osmotic pressure exerted by these particles draws water out of the tubules. The proximal tubule accounts for 85 percent of the sodium reabsorbed. Aldosterone, secreted by the adrenal cortex in response to a series of stimuli beginning with the kidney's production of renin, causes sodium reabsorption to increase. This takes place in the ascending limb of the loop of Henle, the distal tubule, and the collecting duct (tubule).

The small amount of protein that manages to achieve filtration in the glomerulus is recaptured by pinocytosis.

Water regulation and sodium balance depend on the GFR and the tubular reabsorption rate. This is called *glomerulotubule balance*. Imbalances may occur from changes in (1) renal blood flow, (2) hydrostatic pressure in Bowman's capsule, (3) oncotic pressure due to such factors as dehydration, and (4) diseases that decrease the total area of the glomerular filter.

In a normal renal response, tubular reabsorption increases as the quantity of glomerular filtrate becomes greater. However, if the filtrate includes a high volume of solutes that fail to be reabsorbed, a proportional amount of water will remain in the filtrate because of its hypertonicity.

For example, the filtrate is hypertonic in diabetic hyperglycemic episodes. Protein and lipid metabolic end products, as well as glucose molecules, are present in the filtrate in high concentrations. When these products are not reabsorbed, the increased solute concentration draws fluid into the filtrate. The solutes and water are then excreted from the body. If unchecked, the person becomes dehydrated. Another example of the effect of hypertonic filtrate is the high-protein, low-carbohydrate diet some people adopt for quick weight reduction. The level of serum protein rises, causing an increase in colloid osmotic pressure. Fluid is drawn into the intravascular compartment as a result. An increase in the amount of protein in the glomerular filtrate follows. A proportional amount of water joins the filtrate. The outcome is rapid fluid and weight loss and partial dehydration, soon to be corrected by normal body mechanisms when the diet is abandoned.

On the other hand, if the colloid osmotic pressure in the peritubular capillaries is high, a large volume of water will be reabsorbed. Once

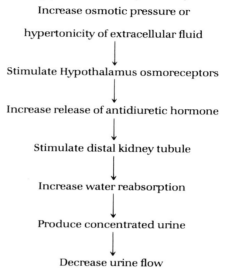

Figure 24-9 Antidiuretic hormone and water reabsorption. Interactions between the release of antidiuretic hormone by the hypothalamus and water reabsorption by the kidneys, serving to stabilize the osmotic pressure of the body fluids. (*From Roseanne B. Howard and Nancie H. Herbold, Nutrition in Clinical Care, McGraw-Hill, New York, 1978. Used by permission of the publisher.*)

Increase osmotic pressure or

hypertonicity of extracellular fluid

↓

Stimulate Hypothalamus osmoreceptors

↓

Increase release of antidiuretic hormone

↓

Stimulate distal kidney tubule

↓

Increase water reabsorption

↓

Produce concentrated urine

↓

Decrease urine flow

again, it can be clearly seen that water movement follows particle concentration.

Just as sodium loss is controlled by aldosterone, a mechanism exists to influence water reabsorption. When the osmolarity of the blood and the concentration of the filtrate rise, special "osmoreceptors" in the hypothalamus are stimulated to release ADH. ADH controls the amount of water reabsorbed from the ascending loop of Henle and the distal tubule. With an increase in reabsorption, the osmolarity of blood returns to normal and ADH secretion is inhibited (Fig. 24-9).

Changes in renal flow also influence the GFR, reabsorption, and secretion rates. The GFR is primarily controlled by the alteration of glomerular capillary pressures. A fall in arterial blood pressure decreases the GFR by lowering the glomerular capillary pressure. Conversely, an increase in arterial blood pressure increases the glomerular capillary pressure and the GFR.

In the former situation, reduced arterial pres-

Figure 24-10 Correction of low glomerular filtration pressure by means of the renin–angiotensin system.

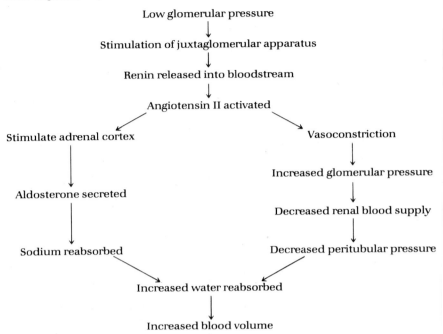

sure, correction is achieved by dilation of the afferent arteriole and constriction of the efferent arteriole, raising pressure in the glomerulus. In the latter situation, raised arterial pressure, the correction is provided by constriction of the afferent arteriole and dilation of the efferent arteriole. These corrective mechanisms are capable of maintaining a constant renal blood flow if aortic pressure does not drop below 80 mmHg or rise above 250 mmHg.[14]

Renal autoregulation of blood flow is not well understood. Just outside the glomerulus, in the nearby afferent arteriole wall, there are special *juxtaglomerular cells* that are capable of producing renin. It is postulated that renin is released from them in response to a high level of sodium chloride in the tubule filtrate and also in response to decreased renal blood flow and GFR. However release of renin is stimulated, its effects are certain (Fig. 24-10). Once in the blood, the renin stimulates formation of angiotensin II. This substance has two effects. The first is stimulation of aldosterone secretion by the adrenal cortex. Aldosterone induces the kidneys to retain

larger amounts of sodium and water, which increases blood volume and thus pressure throughout the circulatory system, including the renal artery. The second effect of angiotensin is vasoconstriction, by which means blood pressure is directly raised.

Acid-base regulation The kidneys will respond to either an increase or a decrease in the bicarbonate concentration of the plasma. They help regulate the acid-base balance of the body through excretion of hydrogen ions.

The proximal, distal, and collecting tubules are all able to excrete hydrogen by the following process. Carbon dioxide is joined with water within the tubule cell to form carbonic acid. The hydrogen ion thus set free is actively transported into the lumen of the tubule. Bicarbonate, meanwhile, is reabsorbed into the extracellular fluid. Sodium, exchanged for hydrogen in the filtrate, joins with bicarbonate in the extracellular fluid. As the pH decreases, the hydrogen ion secretion rate increases (to correct acidosis). As the pH increases, the hydrogen ion secretion decreases (to correct alkalosis). Through this mechanism, the renal system can restore the serum pH in 3 days.

Regulation by the gastrointestinal tract The most effective method of taking in water, electrolytes, and nutrients is by the gastrointestinal tract. The gastrointestinal tract efficiently utilizes nutrients because of its slow absorption rate and ability to tolerate large quantities of nutrients. Water is absorbed by both the small and large intestines. The absorption is accomplished by diffusion and osmosis over the intestinal membrane. As ions and nutrients are absorbed, causing hypertonicity of the extracellular fluid, a corresponding amount of water also crosses the membrane by osmosis.

Most ions, sodium, calcium, potassium, and phosphate, are actively absorbed by the small intestine. Chloride is absorbed in larger quantities in the large intestine in exchange for bicarbonate ions. The chloride, in combination with sodium, increases the osmotic gradient and creates a greater absorption of water. The excreted bicarbonate helps to neutralize the acid end products of bacterial action in the colon.

Regulation by the lungs The insensible water loss from the lungs averages 15 ml per 100 cal metabolized. Hyperventilation and low humidity can increase this loss. High environmental humidity or appliances such as vaporizers will decrease the water loss.

The lungs participate in the acid-base balance when carbonic acid is converted to carbon dioxide and water. Carbon dioxide is then released in the act of breathing. This response to acid buildup is quick (1 to 3 min) but may be only partially effective. Conversely, depressed respiratory function (hypoventilation), by reducing the discharge of carbon dioxide, will permit accumulation of carbonic acid.

Regulation by the skin Water loss and temperature regulation by the integument were discussed earlier in this chapter.

Electrolyte alterations

When there is an alteration in electrolyte balance it is common to find several conditions existing at the same time, for example, hypocalcemia, hypokalemia, and hypomagnesemia. Clear-cut individual electrolyte problems are most often seen with hyperkalemia and hypercalcemia.

Hyponatremia

Hyponatremia (serum sodium deficit) is uncommon because of the body's excellent ability to conserve sodium. When it does occur, however, hyponatremia is likely to be caused by decreased salt intake, gastroenteritis, renal salt-losing states, a potent diuretic, fluid overload, burns, wounds, inappropriate ADH secretion resulting from meningitis, head trauma, medication, parenteral infusion of an electrolyte-free solution, repeated water enemas, or freshwater drowning.

Hyponatremia is divided into degrees of mild (120 to 130 mEq per liter), moderate (114 to 120 mEq per liter), and severe (below 114 mEq per liter).[15] The signs and symptoms of hyponatremia are indices of the severity of the deficit. The neurological symptoms result from swelling of the brain cells with water as a fluid shift from extracellular to intracellular occurs.

Mild hyponatremia	Severe hyponatremia
Anorexia	Headache
Nausea and vomiting	Lethargy
Apprehension	Confusion
Anxiety	Convulsions
Weakness	Vasomotor collapse
Sense of impending doom	(decreased blood pressure)
	Fingerprinting of the sternum

Laboratory values in hyponatermia will show a serum sodium level lower than the serum chloride level (Table 24-4). The urine sodium will usually be decreased, the amount depending on the underlying cause. The specific gravity of the urine will decrease and the volume will increase because of a lack of sodium to be reabsorbed.

Nursing management The nursing care of the child with hyponatremia focuses on safety and close observation. The confused, anxious child requires frequent reassurance. Seizure precautions should be initiated in anticipation of possible convulsions.

Fluid intake will be restricted; initially a decrease in the urine output does not follow. The intake-output balance must be closely monitored

Table 24-4 Electrolyte concentration of body secretions and excretions, mEq per liter

Body fluid	Na+	K+	Cl-	HCO₃
Saliva	9	25	10	12–18
Gastric juices	60	10	85	10
Bile	142	4	98	40
Small bowel suction	105	4	98	30
Ileum suction	130	4	102	—
Ileostomy, recent	124	18	108	—
Cecostomy	78	20	50	—
Stool: normal	2	4	1	—
Diarrheal	12	18	8	—
Urine, per 24 h	80–180	40–80	110–250	—
Perspiration	82	10	84	—
Plasma	135–145	3.5–5.5	98–106	22–26

to correct hyponatremia without causing a fluid volume deficit.

Hypernatremia

Hypernatremia, or sodium excess, occurs in one of four ways. There may be (1) decreased water intake; (2) excessive water output; (3) decreased sodium output; or (4) increased sodium intake. The underlying causes of these imbalances are most commonly fever, diabetes insipidus, increased intracranial pressure, watery diarrhea, high-protein feedings, or saltwater drowning. Accidental use of salt instead of sugar in formula preparation has also resulted in hypernatremia, causing infant death.

The neurological symptoms result from the dehydration of brain cells that follows an intracellular to extracellular fluid shift. Symptoms of hypernatremia include dry, sticky mucous membranes, flushed skin, immense thirst, lethargy, dullness, irritability when disturbed, tremors and convulsions, nuchal rigidity, muscle rigidity, increased extracellular fluid volume, edema, and oliguria or anuria. Laboratory values include elevated serum sodium chloride levels and elevated specific gravity.

Nursing management Treatment for hypernatremia is focused on diluting the sodium concentration without diluting other electrolytes. A solution less concentrated than plasma is ad-

ministered to provide more fluid intake without additional sodium.

Safety of the child is again a major nursing concern. Padded side rails, frequent observation, and other seizure precautions should be implemented.

Anuria is a serious complication and may result in renal failure. Accurate monitoring of the hourly intake and output is mandatory to detect changes in the child's status.

Hypokalemia

Hypokalemia, or loss of potassium, occurs rapidly and frequently in sick children. Potassium must be ingested daily to maintain a normal level. Diarrhea may cause a child to lose one-fourth of total body potassium in 1 day. Any child who has taken nothing by mouth for 24 h should be assessed carefully and routinely for hypokalemia.

Diuretics are the main cause of hypokalemia. Other causes may include wound drainage, a decreased dietary intake, diarrhea, vomiting, gastric suctioning, adrenocorticosteroids, or massive trauma (burns). Metabolic alkalosis will cause a temporary serum hypokalemia as potassium goes into the cell when sodium and hydrogen leave the cell; it will rectify itself when the alkalosis is corrected. Hypokalemia causes impaired nerve conduction in cardiac, skeletal, and smooth muscle. Cardiac arrhythmias may occur. Other symptoms include apathy, malaise, neuromuscular weakness (especially in the legs), flaccid paralysis of muscles, diminished reflexes, muscle cramps, nausea, anorexia, paralytic ileus, and abdominal distention, hypotension, weak shallow respirations, weak or irregular pulse, low, flat T wave and depressed S-T segment, atrial flutter and fibrillation, prolonged QRS interval, and heart block.

Nursing management of hypokalemia Treatment of hypokalemia is aimed at replacing the lost potassium. It takes 5 to 7 days to replace a serious potassium loss. Potassium-rich foods and oral or parenteral supplements effectively restore the potassium level. These oral supplements are bad tasting and should be given in juice. Chilling also is helpful for the taste. The normal replacement dose is calculated at 2 mEq/kg per 24 h.

If intravenous potassium chloride is needed, care must be taken that infusion is not done too rapidly, less than 20 mEq per h, as potassium ion irritates vein walls and can cause cardiac arrest. If intravenous potassium is administered on a continuous basis ECG monitoring is imperative. Finally, IV potassium should never be given until renal functioning is assured as administration during renal failure will cause hyperkalemia.

The nurse must be aware of potassium's action in the body when treating hypokalemia. Cardiac and muscular irregularities and metabolic alkalosis may be life-threatening and require early detection. A frequent check should be made of the apical pulse, with irregularities noted, as well as the respiratory rate, which should be counted for 1 full minute. Be alert for signs of hyperkalemia as well as hypokalemia during potassium replacement.

Hyperkalemia

Hyperkalemia, or excess serum potassium, may result from renal failure, hemolysis, excessive or too rapid infusion of potassium supplements, and severe burns. Metabolic acidosis may temporarily cause a rise in the serum potassium, but this is usually reduced as the acidosis is corrected.

Excess potassium depresses cardiac, skeletal, and smooth muscle contraction and nerve conduction. Symptoms include muscle cramping, weak and flaccid muscles, irritability, possible paralysis, diarrhea, nausea, and cardiac arrythmias (elevated and peaked T waves, decreased or absent P waves, fusion beats, widened QRS interval, intraventricular conduction disturbances, arteriovenous dissociation, ventricular fibrillation, and cardiac arrest).

Nursing management Hyperkalemia may require immediate treatment if the potassium level exceeds 7 mEq per liter. Calcium gluconate can be administered parenterally to decrease cardiac irritability. Sodium bicarbonate given parenterally causes an alkalosis which forces potassium into the cells. Likewise, glucose and insulin administration will draw both potassium and glucose into the cells. Kayexelate, which exchanges sodium for potassium ions, may be given orally or rectally. Diuretics also increase potassium excretion. If these treatments do not bring immediate relief, dialysis may be necessary.

Good nursing care of a child with hyperkalemia is critical. All potassium supplements should be stopped immediately and potassium-rich foods eliminated from the diet. Close observation for signs and symptoms of hyperkalemia, metabolic acidosis, and possible cardiac arrest is mandatory. These must be precisely charted and promptly reported to the physician. Safety precautions to protect the child from the environment, such as decreased stimuli and side rails, are necessary. If cardiac monitoring is taking place, extra care should be taken to explain its use to the child and the family.

Hypocalcemia

Hypocalcemia, or calcium deficit, occurs when the serum calcium level falls below 4.5 mEq per liter. It results from prolonged inadequate dietary intake. Inadequate vitamin D intake and decreased absorption by altered metabolism, diarrhea, or copious wound exudate may cause hypocalcemia. Exchange transfusions with citrated blood, hypoparathyroidism, and increased excretion due to renal failure may cause hypocalcemia. Mothers with diabetes mellitus or hyperparathyroidism may deliver a newborn with transient hypoparathyroidism. Because the parathyroid gland controls the calcium level, this results in a temporary low serum calcium level. With inadequate calcium, the body's nerves become increasingly excitable and fire spontaneously. This causes contraction of muscles and paresthesias. Symptoms include numbness and tingling of the ends of fingers and the circumoral region, muscle cramps, carpopedal spasm, tetany and convulsions, laryngeal spasm, negative Sulkowitch's test (no precipitate formed in urine), rickets (osteomalacia in adults), memory lapse, irritability, seizures, hallucinations, and cardiac arrythmia (prolonged Q-T interval).

Nursing management Treatment of hypocalcemia is by parenteral administration of calcium gluconate or a high daily dietary intake. The course of treatment will depend on the severity of the deficit. Newborns may experience "tetany of the newborn" caused by milk formula with a high phosphorus/calcium ratio. Cow's milk has a higher ratio than human breast milk. The ratio can be altered with calcium supplements.

Nursing care focuses upon early detection of tingling in the fingers or muscle spasm and on the prevention of convulsions. When the nurse observes low-calcium diets in children, early recognition and health teaching can prevent these symptoms. The nurse can teach parents the importance of adequate daily calcium intake. Together, the parents and the nurse can discuss methods of camouflaging milk in other foods. If the child refuses or has an allergy to milk, it may need to be given in another form. Infiltration of intravenous calcium causes tissue sloughing; intravenous administration requires very close monitoring.

Hypercalcemia

Hypercalcemia, or excessive calcium, is present when the serum calcium level exceeds 5.2 mEq per liter. It is caused by vitamin D metabolism deficit or excessive administration during pregnancy or childhood, excessive milk ingestion, parathyroid, or bone tumors. Metabolic acidosis and idiopathic (cause unknown) hypercalcemia can also occur.

Calcium enhances the movement of sodium into the cell, causing depolarization. Excess calcium inhibits proper functioning of the sodium pump and sedates nerve transmission. Symptoms include depression, apathy, lethargy, weakness, diminished or absent tendon reflexes, anorexia, nausea and vomiting, peptic ulcers, constipation, abdominal pain and distention, deep bone pain, renal stones, x-ray signs (thinning of bone), and cardiac arrhythmia (shortened Q-T interval). A Sulkowitch test shows a dense precipitate.

In acute crises of hypercalcemia nausea and vomiting, dehydration, stupor, delirium, hallucinations, and coma occur. This is an emergency situation with possible cardiac arrest.

Nursing management Medical treatment of hypercalcemia is difficult and inefficient. Inorganic phosphate or sulfate solutions are used to increase the excretion of calcium. Treatment focuses on identifying the underlying cause and treating it.

Comfort measures for the hypercalcemic child are most important. Deep bone pain, abdominal pain, and nausea and vomiting make the child uncomfortable. Rest, quiet, diversional activities, medication, and the parent's presence help to relieve discomfort.

Along with the comfort measures, the nurse must be alert to signs and symptoms of hypercalcemic crisis. The treatment time is unpredictable; close observation continues until it is certain that the danger has passed.

Hypomagnesemia

Hypomagnesemia (serum magnesium level reduced below 1.5 mEq per liter) is rare. It may occur in the newborn as a result of a familial condition, hypoparathyroidism, renal damage, or chronic diarrhea. It usually occurs with other electrolyte abnormalities. A high dietary intake of calcium will decrease the absorption of magnesium. Kwashiorkor, severe protein/calorie malnutrition, inadequate dietary intake, or malabsorption syndromes may also cause hypomagnesemia.

Since magnesium stabilizes nerve impulse transmission, inadequate magnesium causes increased nerve irritability. Symptoms include weakness, hyperactive reflexes, neuromuscular irritability, painful parasthesias, tremors and convulsions, confusion and hallucinations, hypertension, and tachycardia.

Nursing management Magnesium supplements are given orally or parenterally. Nursing care centers upon providing early identification of the deficit, reassuring and reorienting the child during confusion, and preventing convulsions. Nutritional teaching of parents may also be necessary when the cause is poor dietary intake.

Hypermagnesemia

Hypermagnesemia (serum magnesium level elevated above 3.0 mEq per liter) is even more rare than hypomagnesemia. Renal disease, decreasing magnesium excretion, uncontrolled diabetic acidosis, or excessive administration to the child may cause this electrolyte abnormality. When a pregnant woman has received magnesium sulfate or taken magnesium-containing antacids or magnesium salt cathartics excessively, the residuals may be found in the newborn. Since magnesium stabilizes nerve impulse transmission, excess magnesium diminishes nerve transmission. Symptoms include flaccid, weak muscles, diminished deep tendon reflexes, lethargy and drowsiness, hypotension (decreased cardiac output), tachycardia, coma, respiratory failure, and cardiac arrhythmia (prolonged P-R and QRS intervals, tall T wave, arteriovenous block, and premature ventricular contraction).

Nursing management If the blood level is greater than 7.0 mEq per liter, decreased intake and dialysis comprise the usual treatment. Close observation for cardiac and respiratory failure is necessary, as they both may lead to cardiac arrest. Lethargy may progress to coma; therefore neurological and vital signs and behavior assessment should be monitored frequently.

Alterations in fluid volume

Fluid deficit (dehydration)

Disturbances in fluid volume, either excesses or deficits, are one of the most common and potentially life-threatening problems in nursing of children. When the child first becomes dehydrated, fluid is drawn from both the extracellular and intracellular compartments. Because of the extracellular fluid loss, the remaining extracellular fluid has an increased osmolarity. It draws more fluid from the intracellular compartment into the extracellular space. Intracellular losses then intensify, and the child's fluid and electrolyte imbalances may become life-threatening.

There are three types of fluid deficits: (1) isotonic, (2) hypotonic, and (3) hypertonic. These are identified by serum sodium values. The severity of the fluid loss is determined by the child's weight loss. A loss of 2 percent is mild, 5 percent is moderate, and 8 percent is severe.

Isotonic fluid deficit Isotonic fluid deficit, or isotonic dehydration, refers to the loss of both fluid and electrolytes with the same osmolarity as the blood. Serum sodium remains at a normal value of 130 to 150 mEq per liter. Since there is no osmotic gradient present to cause intracellular to extracellular fluid shifts, the fluid and electrolyte losses are primarily from the extracellular compartments. This loss eventually decreases the circulating blood volume. Symptoms of dehydration follow, and the child is in danger from hypovolemic shock. Isotonic fluid deficit is commonly caused by vomiting, gastric suction, hemorrhage, diarrhea, or repeated enemas.

Indications of isotonic fluid deficit include postural hypotension and giddiness on sitting up, irritability and lethargy, dry skin and mucous membranes, poor skin turgor, cold skin, pale,

gray, or mottled skin color, oliguria to anuria, normal or low blood pressure, rapid pulse, elevated or low temperature, rapid respirations, weight loss, decreased tearing and sunken, "mushy," or soft eyeballs, depressed fontanel and prominent suture lines (if patent). Laboratory values show elevated hematocrit, hemoglobin and blood urea nitrogen (BUN); normal sodium (130 to 150 mEq per liter), and high specific gravity.

Medical treatment includes identification of the underlying cause of the fluid deficit and rapid replacement of the lost fluid and electrolytes. This volume deficit is replaced over a 24-h period, with one-half given in the first 8 h and the remaining half over 16 h.

The nursing responsibilities are to monitor closely the intake and output of the child and to note continued losses. Signs and symptoms of fluid volume deficit should be recorded and improvement or regression during each shift and each day reported to the physician.

Renal failure, secondary to hypovolemia, is a major complication. Hourly intake and output and daily weights should be measured. Frequent monitoring of vital signs and laboratory tests will provide further information on the child's ability to compensate for the fluid loss.

Hypertonic fluid deficit Hypertonic fluid deficit (hypertonic dehydration) occurs when the child loses more water than sodium, as in profuse watery diarrhea. It may occur when the child receives abnormally large amounts of replacement sodium. Serum sodium values are greater than 150 mEq per liter.

The extracellular fluid receives the increased number of electrolytes. This causes the extracellular fluid's osmolarity to be higher than that of the intracellular fluid. Fluid is thus drawn from the intracellular compartment into the extracellular compartment in an attempt to equalize the concentrations. Because fluid shifts to the extracellular compartment, the urine output, pulse, and blood pressure may initially remain stable, masking the severity of the fluid loss.

Symptoms of hypertonic fluid deficit include extreme thirst, lethargy or irritability, gray, cold, or flushed skin, diminished or normal skin turgor, dry mucous membranes, no tearing, sunken and mushy eyeballs, sunken fontanels and suture lines, increased pulse, and increased respirations.

Hypotonic fluid deficit Hypotonic fluid deficit (hypotonic dehydration) occurs when the child loses more electrolytes than water or receives more water than electrolytes. Serum sodium values are less than 130 mEq per liter. This uncommon deficit occurs when a child with fluid loss, commonly from diarrhea, is given water or tea replacements with no (or minimal) amounts of electrolytes. Excessive water intake through intravenous infusion of water or freshwater drowning also cause this type of fluid shift.

In hypotonic dehydration, the extracellular fluid is less concentrated than the intracellular fluid. Water is thus drawn into the cell, swelling it, in an attempt to equalize the concentrations. Movement of water from the extracellular compartment into the cell reduces extracellular volume. This fluid shift frequently causes hypovolemic shock.

Symptoms of hypotonic fluid loss include confusion and lethargy, headache, coma, convulsions, anorexia, nausea and vomiting, abdominal cramps, diarrhea, gray, cold, clammy skin, very poor skin turgor, slightly moist mucous membranes, no tearing, sunken and mushy eyeballs, sunken fontanels and suture lines, low temperature, decreased blood pressure, rapid pulse, and rapid respirations.

Fluid volume excess

There are several terms used to denote fluid volume excess: *edema, circulatory overload, water intoxication,* and *isotonic extracellular fluid excess.* In all types of fluid volume excess, there is an increase in the extracellular, interstitial, and/or intracellular fluid compartments. This increase can be localized (for example, surrounding a bee sting or a bump on the head) or generalized (spread throughout the body, as in nephrosis or starvation).

In fluid volume excess, the child gains or retains excessively large amounts of isotonic fluids. The excessive fluids first expand the extracellular, then the interstitial, and even the intracellular fluid compartments. Fluid accumulation in the interstitial or intracellular compartments causes edema. Increase of extracellular fluid leads to circulatory overload.

Several factors cause an increased fluid gain in the child:[16]

1. Any disease reducing the excretion of fluid and electrolytes causes edema. Examples are renal disease, congestive heart failure, increased aldosterone secretion, and high doses of corticosteroids, which decrease excretion by enhancing sodium and thus fluid retention.
2. Conditions which increase venous pressure are cardiac defects, causing pulmonary edema, and hepatic diseases, causing increased portal hypertension.
3. Increased capillary permeability occurs in response to inflammation or trauma. A bump on the head or an allergic reaction causes histamine to be released. Histamine increases cell wall permeability, allowing fluid from the capillary to rush into surrounding interstitial tissue.
4. Decreased lymphatic circulation creates edema. This condition is rare in children but may result from injury to lymphatic tissue (lymph obstruction following surgery) or parasitic invasion.

Symptoms of isotonic fluid overload include shortness of breath, restlessness, puffy eyelids, distended neck veins, weight gain (2 percent gain is considered mild, 5 percent is moderate, and 8 percent is severe), peripheral edema, pulmonary congestion, and moist rales. Laboratory values are low hematocrit, hemoglobin, and specific gravity, elevated potassium and BUN.

Extracellular fluid compartment shifts

Intravascular to interstitial fluid shift

Intravascular to interstitial fluid shift occurs when the forces drawing the fluid out of the capillary are greater than the forces retaining the fluid in the intravascular system. A common term for this state is *hypovolemia.* For example, the cause may be a burn, arterial occlusion, malnutrition, or trauma. Symptoms include tachycardia and weak pulse, pallor, hypotension, cool extremities, disorientation and possible coma, and hemoconcentration, with elevated hematocrit and electrolytes.

The treatment of hypovolemia is aimed at replacing the fluid lost. This requires an increase in the osmotic pressure of the intravascular fluid to enable it to draw the fluid back into the blood vessel. Plasma or plasma expanders (dextran), administered parenterally, increases the plasma colloidal osmotic pressure, causing the fluid to shift into the intravascular space.

The role of the nurse is to monitor the shift of fluid from the interstitial to the intravascular compartment. Vital signs, pulse, and blood pressure will reverse from tachycardia and hypotension to normal readings. If the shift occurs too rapidly or in too great a volume, the result may be hypertension and bradycardia. Renal failure is a possible complication before corrective therapy can begin. Disorientation from a decreased cerebral perfusion necessitates the use of safety measures. Close observation or restraints may be required.

Interstitial to intravascular fluid shift

Interstitial to intravascular fluid shift, or hypervolemia, occurs during the recovery phase of intravascular to interstitial fluid shift. It may also be a compensatory mechanism for hemorrhage. Symptoms include pallor, weakness, bounding pulse, engorged veins, pulmonary congestion, cardiac failure, and hemodilution, with decreased hemotocrit and electrolytes.

The cause should be identified as soon as possible. While diagnosis is beginning, a diuretic or a phlebotomy may be necessary. These procedures will temporarily reduce the increased fluid.

Nursing care is similar to that of the child with intravascular to interstitial fluid shift. Close observation of vital signs, blood pressure, and pulse should be carried out. Cardiac monitoring to note arrhythmias may be required.

Pulmonary congestion will lead to air hunger and anxiety. Oxygen, high Fowler's position, and chest physical therapy will help to increase the available oxygen for the child and decrease the risk of pulmonary infection.

Bed rest, with diversional activities, will decrease the body's demand for oxygen and assist the child in coping with the illness. The nurse should encourage the parents to participate in the child's care to relieve both the parents' and child's anxiety.

Role of the nurse in management of alterations of fluid and electrolyte balance

When assessing a child's fluid and electrolyte status, the nurse must be alert to the slightest change in physical and mental behaviors. The child's fluid balance is precarious and can change rapidly to a life-threatening situation.

Assessment

History The nurse should first review what is already known about the child. Can the disease process, liquid feeding, or medication result in a fluid or electrolyte loss or gain? For example, pyloric stenosis causes vomiting of hydrochloric acid, diuretics may cause potassium depletion, and liquid feedings are very high in sodium. If the answer is yes, ask yourself what imbalance would be expected to occur. Review the signs and symptoms of that imbalance and then proceed with the assessment.

Obtain information about the normal and current intake and output of the child. If the child has had diarrhea or vomiting, ask about the frequency, duration, character, and volume of the lost fluid. Ask if the diarrhea or vomiting is related to any changes in the child's diet. When does the diarrhea or vomiting occur, what brings it on, and what relieves it?

Review all the body systems with the parents and/or other caretakers to obtain as much information as possible to formulate a diagnosis. Past colds, fevers, immunizations, or trauma may be significant in assessment.

Behavior Is the child's general behavior normal for the age group? Ask parents about the child's behavior, for they will more accurately observe changes in their child. Particularly observe the child's body movements, tremors, alertness, coordination, and state of consciousness. For example, a change in the state of consciousness may be a critical sign indicating the need for emergency treatment. Purposeless movements, lethargy, irritability upon arousal, and inappropriate responses to familiar people are signs of a seriously ill child. Many electrolyte imbalances may cause the child to lapse relatively quickly into unconsciousness or stupor, signaling death.

Intake and output Oral intake must be precisely assessed and recorded. The child's food and fluid intake varies widely with age and developmental stage. It is therefore critical for the nurse to know the expected fluid and food intake at different ages. The nurse then compares the child's present intake to the expected intake, intake at home, and recent intake variations in the hospital.

All ingested fluid and food intake should be recorded on the chart. Parents and children should be taught how to measure and record intake. Small medicine cups easily measure fluid in milliliters.

The child's output, including stool, vomitus, urine, and wound drainage, must be precisely and accurately recorded. Parents and children can be taught the importance and techniques of measuring fluid output. The 24-h urine bags help to collect urine output in an infant. When strict output assessment is indicated, sheets and clothing soaked with spilled urine and/or insensible losses can be weighed dry and wet using a gram scale (1 g = 1 ml). The subtracted difference equals the output. This method works well in calculating diarrheal stool fluid losses in a diapered infant. Expected urine outputs are[17] 6 months = 12 ml/h, 1 year = 22 ml/h, 5 years = 28 ml/h, 12 years = 33 to 35 ml/h.

The nurse's notes and reports to physicians should reflect an ongoing evaluation of the child's output. Changes in the amount, color, consistency, or character of stool, urine, or vomitus are important. The number of voidings or stools should be compared to that of a previous time period and communicated to the physician when significant. The content of vomitus gives clues to acid–base imbalance. Vomiting of undigested or partially digested food is accompanied by hydrochloric acid excretions and turns the child toward metabolic alkalosis. In contrast, a change in the vomitus to a bile color indicates that the child is now losing basic fluids containing sodium, potassium, and bicarbonate.[18] Metabolic acidosis will follow. Furthermore, regurgitation of small amounts indicates an upper gastrointestinal tract obstruction, while projectile vomiting points to a disorder of the lower gut (except in pyloric stenosis).

Weight loss The child's weight is a very sensitive indicator of fluid loss or gain. Compare the child's present weight to the average weight for the age and to the child's past weight. This provides a baseline for fluid and electrolyte replacement and for assessment of fluid gains or losses. The child should be weighed at the same time each day, *before* eating, and on the same scale to ensure accuracy. Record the time, the child's clothing worn (preferably none), and the scale used. A difference as slight as 2 percent may have a major influence on a child's assessed fluid and electrolyte status and indications for replacement. Marked intake–output imbalances should be reported to the physician.

The *degree* of weight loss or gain provides additional information about the hydration status. Weight loss or gain indicates the severity of the imbalance: mild, 2 to 4 percent, moderate, 5 to 9 percent, severe, over 10 percent.[19]

Skin: color and turgor The color of the child's skin is important in assessing hydration. Mild fluid loss will change the normal color to a pasty, pale color. Moderate to severe dehydration will change the pale color to a grayish, mottled hue. The mottled appearance of a child is a serious sign of severe fluid volume deficit and indicates decreased peripheral circulation.

Skin or tissue *turgor* refers to the *tone* (elasticity) of the skin. It is evaluated by pinching up a section of tissue and then observing as it falls back into place. Assess the skin turgor on the abdomen near the umbilicus in a young child or the inner thigh in an older child. The well-hydrated child's skin returns quickly to a normal state when released. The child's skin with a fluid volume deficit remains in a raised (pinched) position for several seconds after release (see Fig. 24-11). Normal skin turgor begins to be lost after a 5 percent fluid volume loss. The skin loses its elasticity as the fluid is reduced in the extracellular and cellular compartments. This fluid loss accounts for the skin's looseness.

Sodium deficit in addition to fluid loss causes a shift of fluid from extracellular to intracellular, and the tissues have a characteristic fingerprinting. Hypernatremia will cause the tissue to take on a thick consistency. Malnutrition may also decrease skin turgor, caused by inadequate protein needed to firm the cell.

Edema of the tissues occurs in fluid overload and hypernatremia. It results from a fluid shift from the intravascular to the interstitial fluid compartment. Edema should be assessed in the face, hands, and feet. *Pitting edema* refers to the "fingerprint" indentation that remains in the edematous tissue after pressing with fingers. The deeper the indentation, the greater the edema.

The child's mucous membranes provide clues to possible fluid volume deficit. By fingering the line joining the lips with the mucous membranes to check for dryness, the nurse further assesses potential dehydration. Remember that mouth breathing also causes dry mucous membranes. A smaller than normal tongue and decreased salivation further support a nursing diagnosis of possible fluid volume deficit.

Figure 24-11 Technique for determining skin turgor. A fold of skin over the sternum is lifted with the thumb and index finger and then released. In a young child, the abdomen near the umbilicus is used. In an older child, the inner thigh may also be used. (*From Dorothy Jones, Claire Ford Dunbar, and Mary Marmoll Jirovec (eds.),* Medical-Surgical Nursing: A Conceptual Approach, *McGraw-Hill, New York, 1978. Used by permission of the publisher.*)

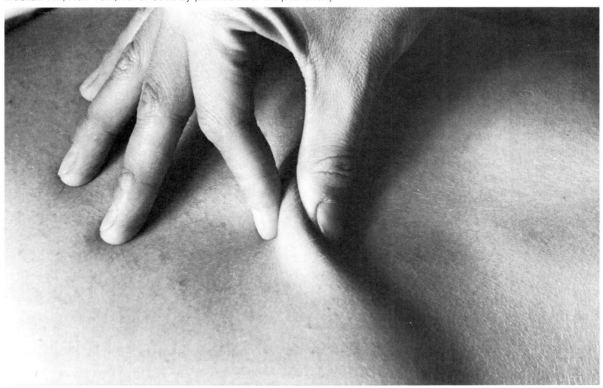

Tearing, fontanels, suture lines The absence of tearing also indicates fluid volume deficit and occurs in moderate dehydration. Moderate to severe dehydration will cause a decrease in the extracellular fluid around the eyes and in the intraocular pressure, causing the eyes to appear sunken. The eyeballs may also feel mushy, similar to a ripe banana, instead of showing their normal tension.

In the infant, the fontanels and skull suture lines provide additional information. The suture lines will become prominent and the fontanels depressed if a fluid deficit exists.

Alterations in vital signs *Temperature* The child with fluid and electrolyte imbalances may have an elevated or subnormal temperature. Fluid shifts in dehydration may initially cause an elevated temperature. However, the child's disease and immature temperature-regulating center in the hypothalamus may also cause the febrile state. Fever increases fluid expenditures by 12 percent for every 1°C rise in temperature.

Fluid volume deficit may cause a low temperature because of a decrease in energy production. Severe fluid volume loss causes cool skin, which is especially noticeable in the extremities. The peripheral vessels have poor perfusion in the young child, which is further decreased as blood is shunted to the vital organs.

Respirations The rate, depth, regularity, and character of the child's respirations must be assessed; they provide clues to the child's fluid and electrolyte status. Hyperpnea increases the insensible water loss from the lungs. Kussmaul breathing attempts to reduce metabolic acidosis by blowing off excess carbon dioxide and hydrogen during the prolonged respiratory phase. Shallow, irregular respirations in the older child indicate alkalosis.[20] As the rate increases, the depth generally decreases. Irregularities become more apparent and may indicate an improvement or worsening of the child's condition. Respirations should be counted for a full minute and abnormalities in rate, depth, and rhythm noted.

Pulse rate The pulse rate increases as the fluid volume and blood pressure decrease. The increased pulse rate is a compensatory mechanism whereby the heart pumps faster to provide adequate nutrients within a smaller amount of fluid to the cells. Irregularities in the heart rhythm may result from electrolyte imbalances such as hypokalemia. The pulse should be taken apically for a full minute to detect abnormalities.

Blood pressure Blood pressure is not the most reliable indicator of fluid volume deficit in children.

Laboratory tests

Laboratory test results provide additional information about the child's status (Table 24-5). They also validate or refute the nursing diagnosis. The hematocrit, blood electrolytes, BUN, and CO_2 are frequently drawn every 4 to 8 h to assess the degree of fluid volume deficit. An elevated hematocrit, BUN, hemoglobin, and specific gravity reflect the hemoconcentration of fluid volume deficit. When the above values are lowered below normal, hemodilution of fluid volume excess is is indicated. The serum sodium level indicates the child's type of dehydration. In hypertonic fluid deficit, the sodium level is often elevated; in hypotonic deficit, it is low; and in isotonic deficit, it is often normal. Potassium levels must also be assessed. Electrolyte imbalances also frequently result in electrocardiogram changes.

The specific gravity of urine provides information on the child's hydration status. A child with a fluid deficit will have a decreased urine volume and an increased urine concentration. This is reflected in a high specific gravity, above

Table 24-5 Laboratory test values and clinical implications

Test	Normal value	Some causes of excess	Some causes of deficit
Sodium	135–145 mEq per liter	High protein formula, diabetes insipidus, hydrocephalus, hypertonic dehydration	Gastroenteritis, hypotonic dehydration, inappropriate ADH secretion, fluid overload
Potassium	3.5–5.5 mEq per liter	Renal failure, exchange transfusion, crushing injury	Diarrhea, vomiting, diuretics, adrenocorticoid steroids
Calcium	9.0–10.6 mg/dl; infants 11–13 mg/dl	Idiopathic hypercalcemia, vitamin D metabolism defects, multiple fractures, bone tumors	Renal failure, inadequate dietary intake, diarrhea, hypothyroidism
Magnesium	1.67 mEq per liter	Renal disease, newborn of mother treated with magnesium sulfate	Hypoparathyroidism, familial, high-calcium dietary intake, malnutrition
Chloride	93–103 mEq per liter		Vomiting, diarrhea, diuretics
Protein	6.0–8.5 g per 100 m		Malnutrition, starvation
Glucose	80–120 mg per 100 ml	Diabetes mellitus, acute injury, brain lesions	Hyperinsulinism, liver disease, malnutrition
BUN (blood urea nitrogen)	5–25 mg per 100 ml	Renal disease, increased protein catabolism	
pH	7.35–7.45	Metabolic or respiratory alkalosis	Metabolic or respiratory acidosis
O_2 saturation	95% arterial 70–75% venous		High altitude, polycythemia
P_{O_2}	80–100 mmHg arterial 35–40 mmHg venous	Hyperventilation, high O_2 atmosphere	Hypoventilation
Total CO_2	25–32 mEq per liter	Hypoventilation, respiratory acidosis	Hyperventilation, respiratory alkalosis
P_{CO_2}	35–45 mmHg arterial 41–51 mmHg venous	Hypoventilation, respiratory acidosis	Hyperventilation, respiratory alkalosis

Table 24-5 Laboratory test values and clinical implications (*Continued*)

Test	Normal value	Some causes of excess	Some causes of deficit
Bicarbonate (HCO$_3^-$)	22–26 mEq per liter	Metabolic alkalosis	Metabolic acidosis
Hematocrit	Newborn 42–66%	Hemoconcentration, isotonic dehydration	Physiological anemia, blood loss, fluid overload
	Child 33–42%		
	Adolescent 34–40%		
	Adult male 42–52%		
	Adult female 37–47%		
Urine			
Electrolytes	Varies with diet		
Sulkowitch test	Positive	Heavy positive—hypercalcemia	Hypocalcemia
Protein	Negative	Renal disease, anabolic state, glomerular nephritis	
Glucose	Negative	Diabetes mellitus	
Ketones	Negative	High-protein diet, diabetes mellitus	
Creatinine clearance (24 h)	15–25 mg/kg per 24 h	Renal failure, decreased glomerular filtration rate	
Urea clearance (24 h)	6–17 g per 24 h	Renal failure, decreased glomerular filtration rate	
pH	4.6–8.0	Alkalosis	Acidosis
Specific gravity	1.010–1.030	Fluid volume excess, high fluid intake, diabetes insipidus	Fluid volume deficit
Osmolarity	500–800 mOsm per liter	Fluid volume excess, high fluid intake, diabetes insipidus	Fluid volume deficit
Volume	Varies with age	Fluid volume excess	Fluid volume deficit

Sources: Norma M. Metheny and W. D. Snively, *Nurse's Handbook of Fluid Balance*, Lippincott, Philadelphia, 1979; and Sarko M. Tilkian, Mary Boudreau Conover, and Ara G. Tilkian, *Clinical Implications of Laboratory Tests*, Mosby, St. Louis, 1979.

1.030. Excessive fluid overload will cause dilute urine and a low specific gravity, below 1.020.

Diarrhea*

Diarrhea is a good example of a disturbance that produces dehydration with severe fluid and electrolyte imbalances. It can be classified as acute or chronic. Acute diarrhea is a self-limiting disorder related to infection (viral, bacterial); ingestion of a toxic substance (arsenic, lead, iron); administration of antibiotics (ampicillin); overfeeding, changes in diet (new foods, excessive carbohydrates, unripe fruit); emotional stress, fatigue, and other infections (otitis media, urinary tract infections). Diarrhea that persists for 2 weeks or longer is termed *chronic*. Chronic diarrhea is often associated with malabsorption disorders (cystic fibrosis, celiac disease); nutritional deficiencies (kwashiorkor, marasmus); allergy (milk); inflammatory disorders (ulcerative colitis); and anatomic defects (intermittent or incomplete small bowel obstructions).

* The discussion of diarrhea is by Andrea Piens.

Diarrhea is a disorder in which the intestinal contents are propelled along so rapidly that there is inadequate time for absorption of digested foods, water, and electrolytes. Typically, there is an increase in the frequency and fluid content of the child's stools when compared to normal patterns. The stools contain undigested fat, carbohydrates, and to a lesser extent protein; are green, watery mucous-streaked, possibly blood-tinged; and are expelled with force. Water losses in the stool may be increased to 250 to 500 ml per 24 h. This is 10 to 15 times the normal rate. Electrolytes, specifically sodium, chloride, bicarbonate, and potassium, are also lost in amounts 10 times greater than normal. Altered fluid and electrolyte balance is the primary pathophysiological consequence of diarrhea. The child presents with symptoms of dehydration and metabolic acidosis.

The severity of diarrhea is determined by the percent of dehydration present and *not* the number of stools passed in 24 h. The classifications of diarrhea are: mild (less than 5 percent dehydration), moderate (5 to 10 percent dehydration), and severe (10 to 15 percent dehydration). Death occurs at 20 percent dehydration. Table 24-6 lists the physical changes caused by fluid and electrolyte losses that differentiate the severity of diarrhea. Diarrhea is the second leading cause of death among children under 2 years of age worldwide.

Mild diarrhea may be managed by the parent in the home. The child's intake is limited to clear fluids for 12 to 24 h to diminish intestinal motility and reduce the frequency and volume of stools. No solid foods and no milk or milk products are given. The parent should be instructed to provide 15 to 30 ml of clear fluid every 30 to 60 min and to observe the frequency and volume of stools relative to intake. If the diarrhea decreases, one may increase the intake to 60 to 90 ml every 2 to 3 h. Suggested clear fluids may include: water, weak tea, diluted grape or apple juice, diluted liquid Jello, Kool-Aid, Gatorade, and "flat" carbonated beverages (7-Up, ginger ale, Coca-Cola) (Table 24-7). To "flatten" carbonated drinks, open them and let them stand for several hours. After the first 24-h period, crackers, dry toast, cooked cereals (rice), raw ripe bananas, or unsugared applesauce may be added to the diet of clear fluids. The third day, the child may resume a regular diet. Milk and milk products should be reintroduced gradually, beginning with skim milk, adding half-strength milk, and progressing to full-strength milk over 2 to 3 days. If milk is reintroduced too rapidly, a secondary lactose deficiency may precipitate diarrhea from the lactose in the milk. The parent should be taught to observe for symptoms of progressive dehydration and told to notify the physician. These symptoms include dry mucous membranes, loss of skin elasticity, altered appearance (sunken eyes and fontanels, cool and pale extremities), diminished urination, and changes in behavior (increasing lethargy, seizure activity). Signs of dehydration are discussed in the assessment of fluid and electrolytes in infants and children in this chapter. Table 17-14 also lists signs of dehydration.

Hospitalization is necesary to reverse the symptoms of fluid and electrolyte imbalance in moderate and severe diarrhea. Medical treatment focuses on prescribing intravenous fluids to meet the child's normal fluid requirements and to replace fluids lost through diarrhea. In addition to maintenance of fluid requirements, an estimated 50 ml per kilogram of body weight are needed to replace fluid loss in mild (5 percent) diarrhea, 100 ml per kilogram of body weight for moderate (10 percent) diarrhea, and 125 ml per kilogram of body weight for severe diarrhea (10 to 15 percent). This additional fluid is administered over 8 to 16 h. The intravenous solution contains glucose for calories and normal saline. Potassium is added only after adequate kidney function is documented. If kidney function is impaired, the body retains potassium and excessive amounts may precipitate heart block.

Nursing management Since the child takes no oral fluids for 24 h or longer, it is important to provide frequent oral care, cleansing the mouth

Table 24-6 Physical changes from fluid and electrolyte losses due to diarrhea

	Severity of diarrhea		
	Mild	**Moderate**	**Severe**
Weight loss	Under 5%	5–10%	10–15%
Temperature	Normal	38.5–39°C	39.5–40°C
Number of stools	Loose stools, normal number	2–10	2–20
Signs of dehydration	Thirsty, tears absent, irritable	All symptoms of mild diarrhea, dry mucous membranes, poor skin turgor, sunken fontanels and eyes, tachycardia, lethargy, gray color	All symptoms of mild and moderate diarrhea, weak pulse, oliguria to anuria, increased urine specific gravity; skin changes: gray to mottled color, cool to touch; comatose or seizures. Death occurs at 20% dehydration

Table 24-7 Composition of oral fluids

Fluid	Na⁺	K⁺ (mEq/L)	Cl⁻	Solute (mOsm/L)	Calories (kcal/L)
Water 0	0	0	0	0	0
Sugar water (56%)*	0	0	0	0	200
Lytren	25	25	30	135	280
Pedialyte	30	20	30	115	280
Coca-Cola	0.5	13	0	27	435
Pepsi Cola	7	1	0	15	480
Ginger ale	3	1	1	10	380
Seven-Up	7.5	0.5	0	15	420
Orange juice	2	48	2	100	410
Gatorade	0.23	2.5	—	50	167
Boiled skimmed milk†	27	43	31	350	410
One-half boiled skimmed milk‡	13	21	15	175	205

Note: This table presents the electrolyte, solute, and caloric content of commonly used fluids given to infants who are unable to take their usual food intake. Reprinted with permission from W. Weil, *Fluid and Electrolyte Metabolism in Infants and Children*, Grune & Stratton, New York, 1977. p. 111.

* Prepared at home by using three tablespoons per quart of water.
† Assuming no evaporation. In practice, boiling creates an evaporative loss, producing higher values than those shown.
‡ This term refers to equal amounts of water and skimmed milk.

with lemon glycerine swabs and applying petroleum jelly to dry, cracked lips. Infants need to suck for comfort, so provide a pacifier. Sucking on a pacifier may produce excessive swallowing of air, leading to further abdominal cramping. It is necessary to bubble (burp) the infant frequently or to insert a cotton ball in the pacifier (if a regular nipple is used) to decrease this condition.

As the diarrhea decreases, the physician will prescribe clear liquids in small amounts given at specified intervals. A commercially prepared electrolyte solution may be used. Diet resumption follows the plan described in treatment of mild diarrhea.

The nurse observes, records, and assesses the status of the child's hydration on an ongoing basis. Specific nursing interventions include:

1. Observing skin turgor, moistness of mucous membranes, neurological function
2. Measuring weight daily or more frequently
3. Monitoring the color, odor, consistency, amount, pH, presence of pus, blood, and sugar (reducing substances) in the stool
4. Accurately measuring urine output by weighing diapers or by applying a collecting device for urine if unable to measure the urine because it is continually mixed with stool in the diaper
5. Maintaining prescribed intravenous rate, observing the intravenous site for patency, and restraining the child to prevent dislodgement
6. Monitoring vital signs. Take axillary rather than rectal temperature. Insertion of a rectal thermometer may stimulate intestinal motility, causing additional stools.
7. Providing perianal skin care to prevent or treat diaper rash. Care of the diaper area is described in Chap. 17.

Children who are hospitalized with diarrhea are placed on enteric isolation to prevent spread to others. This isolation, coupled with restraints imposed to maintain intravenous patency, decreases the child's ability to cope with this experience. To comfort the child, encourage the parents to be present whenever possible. Touching the child and providing security items, such as a favorite blanket or a stuffed animal from home, are important.

Nursing Care Plan–Fluid Imbalance*

Patient: Karen White   **Age:** 9 months   **Date of admission:** 3/18

Karen White, a 9-month-old infant, was admitted to the pediatric nursery at 9 A.M. with a tentative diagnosis of viral gastroenteritis and 5 percent dehydration. The following information was given by her mother during the admission interview.

Karen began vomiting and passing frequent watery stools, approximately 10 per day, 2 days ago. Karen's 3-year-old brother and 5-year-old sister have also been vomiting and passing diarrhea stools over the last 3 days. Mrs. White called her doctor and followed his instructions to limit Karen's oral intake to clear fluids, but the vomiting and diarrhea have continued. Over the past 24 h, Karen has been sleeping more and, when awake, is very irritable. Karen's temperature, taken axillary, has ranged from 37.8 to 38.3°C (100 to 101°F).

Her mother seems exhausted and very concerned. She commented, "I am so tired, what with all three children sick. The other two children seem to be getting better. They, at least, have stopped vomiting and are keeping down sips of soda. But I'm really worried about Karen. She's not even keeping soda down and is still having diarrhea. She hasn't had a wet diaper since 8 last evening."

Physical assessment

The following observations were made by the nurse:

Weight 8.1 kg (prior to illness at last well-child checkup 2 weeks ago, weight was 8.5 kg, or 19 lb)

Behavior Lethargic at present. Dozes to sleep when left alone, passively accepts all procedures, very irritable when aroused. Weak, whining cry. Hesitates in going to mother, then clings to mother.

Hydration Skin turgor decreased; slight delay in return to normal. Mucous membranes dry along cheek and gum line.

Eyes No tearing evident; eyeballs sunken and soft.

Fontanel Appears slightly depressed.

Intake Sips water only in last 24 h; vomited all intake within 10 min after each sip.

Output Last wet diaper at 8 P.M. yesterday, 13 h ago. Mother states that urine was bright yellow.

Abdomen Tense when palpated; hyperactive bowel sounds.

Extremities Pale color, cool to touch.

Vital signs Stable at 104/64, 108, 28; T 38°C.

Physician's orders

1. Private room, enteric isolation.
2. Strict record of intake and output.
3. Check urine specific gravity with each voiding.
4. Lab work: Hematocrit, BUN, Na, Cl, K, bicarbonate, stool specimens for ova and parasites, occult blood, sugar, pH.
5. NPO.
6. IV of D5/0.2 NaCl to run at 63 ml/h per 16 h. After child voids, add 20 mEq KCl per liter to D5/0.2 NaCl; then run at 38 ml/h (810 ml per 24 h is maintenance fluid, 405 ml per 24 h is replacement fluid).
7. Vital signs q4h.
8. Daily weights.
9. Record and describe all stools and emesis, including color, consistency, amount, and presence of pH, sugar, or blood.

Nursing diagnosis	Nursing goals	Nursing actions	Evaluation/revision
1. Potential dehydration and change in electrolyte status related to vomiting and diarrhea	☐ Karen will maintain normal fluid and electrolyte balance and will not be dehydrated	☐ Maintain IV fluids as ordered at D5/0.2 NaCl to run at 63 ml/h for 16 h; then reduce rate to 38 ml/h. Add 20 mEq KCl to each 1000 ml fluid	☐ 3/19: IV maintained at desired rate, 63 ml/h; then reduced to 38 ml/h. No signs of infiltration

Nursing diagnosis	Nursing goals	Nursing actions	Evaluation/revision
		☐ Monitor IV rate closely ☐ Check IV site frequently for infiltration: edema, redness, pain ☐ Restrain arm on IV board and pin board to sheet ☐ Check arm's circulation often ☐ Assess adequate voiding before adding KCl to IV ☐ Assess electrolytes	☐ 3/19–20: IV restrained. No signs of infiltration: no redness, pain, or edema at insertion site ☐ 3/19: Karen voided approximately 30 ml clear, dark yellow urine before KCl was added to IV
		☐ Observe for signs of dehydration: reduced BP, increased P, poor skin turgor, depressed fontanel, lack of tears or urine, high urine specific gravity ☐ Observe for possible signs of circulatory overload due to rapid infusion: high BP, weight gain, bulging fontanel, distended neck veins, copious urine ☐ Observe for signs of fluid balance: equal I&O, moist mucous membranes ☐ Maintain strict I&O. Use medicine cup to measure oral intake; apply 24-h urine-collecting bag (prevents mixing of urine with stool) ☐ Check and record specific gravity and pH of urine at each voiding	☐ 3/19–20: Signs of dehydration lessening. Fontanel is no longer depressed; voiding increased to 120 ml in 8 h; tears have appeared. Skin turgor remains flaccid, though more elastic. K level increased to 4.1 mEq per liter ☐ 3/19–20: Karen on strict I&O; approximately 20 ml urine lost with leaking urine bag; new one reapplied ☐ 3/19: Specific gravity done for each voided urine; decreased from 1.032 to 1.026
		☐ Observe and record amount, color, consistency, presence of blood, sugar, and pH of stool	☐ 3/19: Stool has remained negative for blood and sugar. Stools averge one per shift, firmer and yellower. Axillary temp. 38°C, P 106, R 26, BP 100/56, stable. Weight 8.2 kg
		☐ Measure, observe, and record color, consistency, and amount of vomitus ☐ Take axillary temperature (rectal temperature stimulates defecation) and vital signs q4h. Report significant changes to doctor ☐ Observe for abdominal cramping. Keep child NPO; label bed or door ☐ Provide pacifier for emotional satisfaction ☐ Give mouth care when NPO ☐ Instruct mother in reasons for Karen being NPO	☐ 3/19: No emesis ☐ 3/19: Mother stated "I'm so glad to know the reasons for the IV. I thought she was dying."

Nursing diagnosis	Nursing goals	Nursing actions	Evaluation/revision
		and for strictly measuring output ☐ Keep in private room on enteric isolation ☐ Use four-step teaching method to teach family members correct isolation technique ☐ Apply diaper tightly to prevent spread of feces ☐ Teach child importance of washing hands after use of potty	☐ 3/19: On mother's return, demonstrated isolation technique. Has forgotten technique once; took purse into room and laid it on the bed ☐ 2/19: Karen screams, clenches fists, and refuses to wash her hands ☐ *Continue plan*
2. Increased perianal skin irritation related to interaction of bacteria and digestive juices on skin	☐ Decrease Karen's perianal skin irritation	☐ Use absorbable cloth diapers (more ventilation) ☐ Assess if disposable diapers are causing rash ☐ Change diapers immediately after each voiding or stool ☐ Cleanse perianal area after each stool. Wash with warm water and antibacterial soap, and pat dry ☐ Apply Desitin, A&D ointment, or petroleum jelly after each stool	☐ 3/19: Cloth diapers changed quickly after wetting. Desitin applied after washing with soap and water. Buttocks still red with macular rash, but skin is no longer broken
		☐ As diarrhea becomes less frequent place Karen prone and expose buttocks to air; apply lights 18 in away from buttocks for 20 min qid ☐ Assess mother's knowledge of diaper rash care; praise her and instruct as needed	☐ 3/19: Lights applied 18 in from child. Mother visited and applied them 8 in from buttocks; reinstructed ☐ 3/20: Mother knew all aspects of diaper care but uses Desitin ointment sparingly ☐ *Continue plan*
3a. Potential for nutritional impairment and delayed recovery related to severe vomiting and diarrhea	☐ Prevent potential nutritional impairment and delayed recovery	☐ Assess parents' knowledge of diarrheal diet progression, using hospital's guidelines	☐ 3/19: Mother knew diet but admitted giving child "her favorites, orange juice and fried eggs"
3b. Inadequate parental knowledge of diarrheal diet progression	☐ Increase parents' knowledge of diarrheal diet progression	☐ Teach parents about diet; stress that purpose of NPO is to decrease GI tract motility and thus vomiting and diarrhea. Maintain NPO as ordered ☐ Begin giving sips of electrolyte solution (e.g., pedialyte) slowly at 5–10/ml per 15 min and progress as tolerated or ordered ☐ Observe child's response to oral fluids: Assess sucking strength, amount, color, character, and frequency of vomiting or stools	☐ 3/19: Karen eagerly gulped pedialyte; no emesis or hypermotility of bowel sounds. Stools remain firmer, yellow

Nursing diagnosis	Nursing goals	Nursing actions	Evaluation/revision
		☐ Schedule venipunctures to avoid meal times ☐ Reintroduce foods as ordered: Jello water, cola or other carbonated drinks, unsweetened applesauce, apple juice (controversial) ☐ Progress to liquid diet: skim milk, fresh bananas, rice cereal, white bread, added grease and sugar ☐ Adapt foods to family's food preferences; consult food buyer and cook	☐ 3/21: Karen retained cola, Jello water, and applesauce. No emesis or increase in stooling or bowel sounds ☐ 3/21: Mother stated that she had to use up orange juice, as she lacked money to buy food on diarrheal diet. Social worker contacted for financial screening ☐ *Continue plan*
4. Despair stage of separation related to mother's infrequent visiting	☐ Return to protest stage of separation anxiety	☐ Encourage mother to visit and room-in whenever possible ☐ Contact social worker to arrange child care at home; explore other probable sources of baby-sitters (church, neighbors) ☐ Instruct mother in reasons for child's behavior ☐ Have mother bring pictures from home and tape on bed ☐ Provide appropriate toys ☐ Bring object which child associates with her (purse, keys) ☐ Encourage child to express emotions; "Cry, Karen. I know you miss your mommy" ☐ Discuss mother's activities while at home (to strenghten bond with home) ☐ Schedule consistent nurses	☐ 3/20: Mother visited for 4 h. Karen went to her immediately ☐ 3/20: Social worker able to obtain financial aid for food, child care, and carfare. Karen's favorite neighbor will visit each morning ☐ 3/20: Karen had cried for 45 min after mother left. Nurse found mother's purse (had been lost); Karen clutched it to her chest and fell asleep within 3 min ☐ 3/20: Karen's favorite topics are: Mommy cooking, her dog, Sunny, and dolls ☐ *Continue plan*
5. Increased maternal anxiety related to IV, shaved head	☐ Reduce maternal anxiety	☐ Use four-step teaching method to assess mother's highest-priority need ☐ Instruct mother in reasons for IV therapy, shaved head, restraints, enteric isolation, collection of stool specimens if needed from family members, cause, prognosis, and "trouble signs" ☐ Provide liaison nurse's name for mother to call with questions	☐ 3/20: Mother's greatest concern was lack of money for special diets, carfare. She receives no child support, and family subsists on $800 per month ☐ 3/20: Mother not able to listen to teaching until financial worries are lessened ☐ *Continue plan*

* Written by Nancy L. Ramsey and Andrea Piens.

References

1. Margaret L. Dickens, *Fluid and Electrolyte Balance*, Davis, Philadelphia, 1974, p. 7.
2. Joyce L. Kee and Ann P. Gregory, "The ABC's (and mEq's) of Fluid Balance," *Nursing 74*, 4:28–36 (1974).
3. Peggy L. Chinn, *Child Health Maintenance*, Mosby, St. Louis, 1979, p. 143.
4. Robert A. Hoekelman at al. (eds.), *Principles of Pediatrics, Health Care of the Young*, McGraw-Hill, New York, 1978, p. 248.
5. Rosanne Howard and Nancie Herbold, *Nutrition in Clinical Care*, McGraw-Hill, New York, 1978, p. 129.
6. W. E. Lassiter and C. W. Gottschalk, *Volume and Composition of the Body Fluids*, in V. B. Mountcastle, *Medical Physiology*, 13th ed., Mosby, St. Louis, 1974.
7. Robert W. Winters (ed.), *The Body Fluids in Pediatrics*, Little, Brown, Boston, 1973, p. 123.
8. Rudolph Abraham (ed.), *Pediatrics*, 16th ed., Appleton-Century-Crofts, New York, 1977, p. 198.
9. Winters, op. cit., p. 120.
10. W. Weil, *Fluid and Electrolyte Metabolism in Infants and Children*, Grune & Stratton, New York, 1977, p. 49.
11. Winters, op. cit., p. 118.
12. W. E. Nelson, et al., *Textbook of Pediatrics*, 11th ed., Saunders, Philadelphia, 1979, p. 285.
13. Winters, op. cit., p. 131.
14. Dorothy A. Jones, Claire Ford Dunbar, and Mary Marmoll Jirovec (eds.), *Medical/Surgical Nursing: A Conceptual Approach*, McGraw-Hill, New York, 1978, p. 432.
15. Norma Metheny and W. D. Snively, *Nurses' Handbook of Fluid Balance*, 3d ed., Lippincott, Philadelphia, 1979, p. 376.
16. Lucille Whaley and Donna Wong, *Nursing Care of Infants and Children*, Mosby, St. Louis, 1979, pp. 1082–1083.
17. Kee and Gregory, op. cit., 31.
18. Joyce L. Kee, "Abdominal Surgery, Fluid and Electrolyte Complications," in *Monitoring Fluid and Electrolytes Precisely*, Nursing 78 Books, Horsham, Pa., Intermed, 1978.
19. Ibid., p. 30.
20. Ibid., p. 31.

Chapter 25 **Oxygen-carbon dioxide exchange**

Arlene V. Baia, Mary Jo McCracken, and **Marjorie J. Smith**

Upon completion of this chapter, the student will be able to:

1. Describe the embryological development of the respiratory system.

2. Describe the structure and functions of the upper and lower airway.

3. Describe the accessory structures of the respiratory system.

4. Contrast external and internal respiration.

5. List eight important nursing observations for a child experiencing alterations in respiratory function.

6. Explain the importance of measuring blood gases and pH in respiratory care.

7. Discuss the purpose of four methods used to improve respiratory function.

8. Describe nursing responsibilities in suctioning an artificial airway.

9. List four characteristics that make children more vulnerable than adults to upper respiratory infections.

10. Describe the nursing management of a child with an upper respiratory infection.

11. List four signs of respiratory failure in children.

12. Contrast nursing care priorities for a child with epiglottitis and one with croup.

13. Describe the nursing management of a child with a lower respiratory infection.

14. Contrast primary tuberculosis with reactivation tuberculosis.

15. Compare three methods used in diagnosing and screening for tuberculosis.

16. Compare the treatment program for tuberculosis in children who are exposed with the program for those who are infected or have active tuberculosis.

17. Describe the physiological changes produced by cystic fibrosis on the respiratory, gastrointestinal, and reproductive systems.

18. List six components of the therapeutic regimen used by children with cystic fibrosis.

19. Describe the psychosocial impact of cystic fibrosis on the child and his or her family.

Embryology of the respiratory system

The embryological development of the human respiratory system repeats in stages the respiratory systems of fish, amphibians, reptiles, and lower animals.[1] New structures were added while old ones were changed and kept as part of the respiratory system as the switch was made from a water- to an air-breathing environment. Respirations still occur in the predominantly wet environment of the lungs.

Oral and nasal cavities

During the fourth week of development, the beginnings of the nose, *olfactory pits*, appear on either side of the head end of the embryo as widely separated thickenings of depressed ectoderm (Fig. 9-7). These pits are surrounded by horseshoe-shaped elevations that gradually merge during the sixth week to form the nose and upper lip. Failure of these medionasal processes to merge results in a cleft lip.

Also located on the ventral portion of the head is the *stomodeum*, or mouth, which opens into the primitive pharynx and foregut. Around 6 weeks the thin membrane separating the stomodeum and nasal cavity disintegrates, creating a large *oronasal cavity*.

At about 7 to 8 weeks, a vertical plate grows down from the roof of the nasal cavity and forms the nasal septum. A horizontal plate grows toward the midline during the tenth to twelfth

619

week, forming the secondary palate. A cleft palate results when the horizontal plate fails to fuse.

Larynx and trachea

The rest of the respiratory system arises from the *laryngotracheal groove* that appears in the floor of the pharynx at about 26 days. As the groove deepens and grows caudally a tubular outpouching of endodermal cells is formed. The cranial part of the resulting tube becomes the *larynx*. The caudal part becomes the *trachea*. Mesodermal tissue surrounding the trachea develops into cartilage and muscle.

Also during the sixth week, the slit opening in the laryngotracheal groove, forerunner of the vocal cords, becomes bordered on each side by arytenoid swellings and anteriorly by the epiglottis. As the arytenoid cartilages grow toward the tongue, the glottis (opening of the larynx)

becomes T-shaped. The lumen of the larynx is then closed until the tenth week, when the vocal cords begin to develop.

Because the soft palate fits snugly around the larynx in the newborn, the infant can breathe and swallow liquid at the same time for at least 6 months. As the child grows, the opening of the larynx into the pharynx becomes lower. Beginning then, the pharynx serves as a common passageway for both food and air, and the danger of aspiration of food and fluids becomes real.

Bronchi and lungs

At about 6 weeks the caudal end of the trachea enlarges and bifurcates to form the *lung buds*, or beginnings of the bronchi and lungs. As the trachea elongates, the lung buds penetrate more deeply into the body.

Lung development can be divided into three phases:

1. The glandular phase, 4 to 17 weeks
2. The canicular phase, 17 to 24 weeks
3. The terminal sac phase, 24 weeks to term[2]

Glandular phase During the glandular phase, the right and left bronchi appear. Because the right bronchus is larger and comes off the trachea at less of an angle than does the left bronchus, it is more likely to be the site where foreign bodies lodge.

As the bronchi grow downward, secondary and tertiary bronchi develop to serve the three lobes of the right lung and two lobes of the left. At the end of the seventeenth week, the bronchial tree is formed (Fig. 25-1).

Canicular phase From 17 to 24 weeks, 17 orders of branching are completed and respiratory bronchioles appear. Each bronchiole forms three to six alevolar ducts that end in terminal sacs, or immature alveoli. Type I alveolar cells, which are necessary for gas diffusion, mucus-secreting cells, and ciliated cells are present.

By the twenty-fourth week, Type II alveolar cells begin to appear. These cells are essential for surfactant production. Surfactant lowers surface tension in the fluid layer lining the alveoli and prevents them from collapsing during expiration once respirations begin. Alveolar elastic tissue and capillaries proliferate and surround the terminal sacs.

Figure 25-1 Embryonic development of the respiratory system. (*From L. L. Langley et al.*, Dynamic Anatomy and Physiology, *McGraw-Hill, New York, 1980.*)

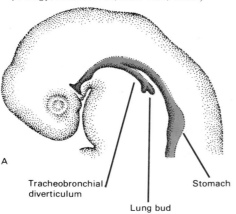

A

Tracheobronchial diverticulum

Stomach

Lung bud

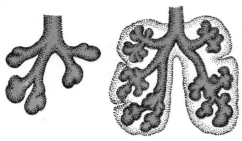

B Secondary bronchi   C Tertiary bronchi

Terminal sac phase During the terminal sac or alveolar period, the lungs are transformed from a glandular structure to a highly vascular alveolar structure.[3] By 28 weeks the fetus is capable of respiration because the alveolar-capillary membrane is thin enough and surfactant is being produced. Immature alveoli continue to increase in number until age 3 years. From 3 to 8 years, immature alveoli continue to increase not only in number but also in size. From age 8 on, the individual alveoli increase in diameter to fill the enlarging thorax. The surface area of the alveolar-capillary membrane is 32 square meters at age 8. Eventually the adult-sized surface area of the alveolar-capillary membrane—between 70 and 80 square meters—is achieved.[4]

Structure and function of the respiratory system

The respiratory system is made up of a series of conducting passages and the functional respiratory apparatus where oxygen and carbon dioxide exchange occurs. The *upper airway* is composed of the nose, nasopharynx, oropharynx, oral cavity, laryngopharynx, and larynx (the transition to the lower airway). The *lower airway* is composed of the tracheobronchial tree (trachea, bronchi, and bronchioles) and lung parenchyma (respiratory bronchioles, alveolar ducts, and alveolar sacs) (Fig. 25-2).

The upper airway

Nose Air enters the nose, where it is warmed, filtered, and 75 to 80 percent humidified as it passes through the choanae to the nasopharynx. The respiratory mucosa of the nose is supplied with cilia and mucus-secreting glands and has a rich supply of blood vessels. The nose also functions as a resonance chamber for speech and contains olfactory receptors. Upper airway humidification is lower in air inhaled through the mouth.

Pharynx The *pharynx* is common to both the respiratory and digestive systems. Its primary function is in swallowing. It is composed of three parts:

1. The *nasopharynx*, or portion lying above the soft palate

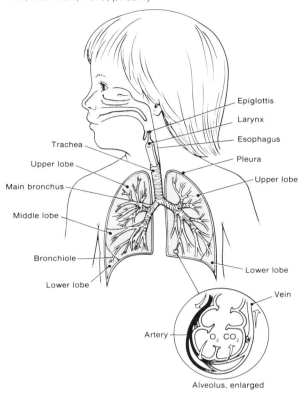

Figure 25-2 Structure of the respiratory system. (*From G. Scipien et al.*, Comprehensive Pediatric Nursing, *McGraw-Hill, New York, 1979, p. 594.*)

2. The *oropharynx*, or portion between the soft palate and the base of the tongue
3. The *laryngopharynx*, or portion below the base of the tongue to the opening of the esophagus

The pharyngeal tonsils (adenoids) are located on the upper posterior wall of the nasopharynx. When these tonsils become enlarged, they can block either the internal nares or the eustachian tubes. The eustachian tubes are channels connecting the nasopharynx to the middle ear. The eustachian tubes regulate air pressure in the middle ear and drain fluid from it.

The oropharynx receives air from the mouth and nasopharynx and food from the mouth. It contains the *faucial tonsils* or "tonsils."

The laryngopharynx contains the epiglottis or leaflike lid which lies over the glottis, protecting it during swallowing.

Larynx The *larynx* connects the upper and lower respiratory systems. It lies higher in the neck of the child than it does in the adult. Its shape is established by the thyroid, arytenoid, and cricoid cartilages, epiglottis, muscles, and ligaments. In the infant and small child, the cricoid cartilage is the narrowest part of the airway. Within the larynx lie the true and false vocal folds. The larynx not only conducts air to the lower airways but also protects them from foreign objects and aids in coughing and speech.

The lower airway

The lower respiratory system is divided into two sections: (1) the *tracheobronchial tree* and (2) the lung *parenchyma*.

The tracheobronchial tree The function of the tracheobronchial tree is to conduct, humidify, and heat inspired air. Gas exchange occurs in the lung parenchyma. At birth the bifurcation of the trachea is at the level of the third thoracic vertebra and by 12 years it is at the sixth thoracic vertebra. Its diameter is about 6 mm at birth, increasing to 12 mm at age 6 and to 18 mm by adulthood. Because of the small diameter in the young child, infection or inflammation takes on greater significance.

The trachea is a muscular tube in which 16 to 20 C-shaped cartilages are embedded. The area where it branches into two main stem bronchi is called the *carina*. The trachea lies in front of the esophagus.

The right main stem bronchus divides into three secondary bronchi (lobar branches) serving the three lobes of the right lung. The left bronchus divides into two secondary bronchi. Secondary bronchi further divide into segmental bronchi and smaller subsegmental bronchi. As the bronchi divide, their diameters become smaller and smaller. They are composed of (1) an epithelial lining of ciliated, mucus-secreting glands, (2) a loose fibrous tissue layer containing blood vessels, lymphatic vessels, and elastic fibers, and (3) an outer layer of cartilage. The many goblet cells in the tracheobronchial tree secrete a mucous blanket designed to trap dust and foreign particles. The cilia continually move this mucous blanket from the respiratory bronchioles toward the larynx, at a rate of 2 cm per minute, creating a self-cleansing mechanism in the normal lung. The cartilage ensures a relatively rigid open tube for air passage.

The bronchi further branch into bronchioles and terminal bronchioles. Bronchioles have diameters of less than 1 mm and lack cartilage. Terminal bronchioles have a diameter of less than 0.5 mm. Both mucus and surfactant are found in these terminal bronchioles, although mucous glands and cilia are absent.

The lung parenchyma Distal to the terminal bronchioles are the *respiratory bronchioles*—the first segment of the lung in which respiration takes place. Next come the thin-walled, fibroelastic alveolar ducts, which then lead to the *alveolar sacs*. The alveolar sacs exist in clusters of 15 to 20 and have common walls between them. The thin alveolar epithelium, which lines all the lung parenchyma, allows for diffusion of oxygen and carbon dioxide. Thirty-five percent of alveolar gas exchange occurs in the ducts, while sixty-five percent occurs in the sacs. The alveolar epithelium is lined with fluid containing Type III alveolar cells, or *macrophages*, which are an important part of the body's defense mechanism.

Accessory structures of the respiratory system

The thorax The thorax functions to house and protect the structures of the cardiopulmonary system. Each lung is enclosed in a double-walled serous membrane called the *pleura*. The inner *visceral* layer covers the lung surface. It folds back on itself at the *hilum* (where the bronchi enter the lungs) and becomes the parietal layer, which is attached to the chest wall. The pleural cavity, a serous, fluid-filled "potential" space, acts to decrease friction between the two layers of pleura. The pleura adheres to the chest wall, pulling the lung out with it on inspiration.

The two lungs are separated by the *mediastinum*, which lies in the midline and contains the heart, great vessels, trachea, esophagus, and thymus gland. The *thoracic cage* is composed of the sternum, ribs, and thoracic vertebrae. The thorax has a cylindrical configuration at birth but gradually changes with growth until the anterior-posterior diameter is less than the transverse diameter.

Muscles of respiration Three major groups of muscles function in respiration: the diaphragm, the intercostal muscles, and the accessory muscles. Contraction of the *diaphragm* vertically enlarges the thoracic cavity on inspiration. In the early years, ventilation is much more dependent on the diaphragm than it is later in life.

The *external intercostal muscles* contract on inspiration to increase the anterior-posterior chest diameter. The *internal intercostals* help in forceful expirations by pulling the rib cage down and in.

Accessory muscles of respiration, the scalene, sternocleidomastoid, trapezius, and pectoralis muscles, help stabilize the chest wall. They are not used with quiet inspirations but when greater than normal inspiratory effort is needed.

Neurochemical control of respirations

Because respirations are dependent upon the action of muscles, respirations must be controlled within the central nervous system.

Central chemoreceptors The respiratory center in the medulla transmits signals to muscles of inspiration. When inspiratory neurons fire, inspiration occurs. When they are inhibited, expiration occurs by elastic recoil. The central chemoreceptor cells stimulate inspiration when there is an increase in hydrogen ion (drop in pH) in cerebrospinal fluid, signaling an increase in arterial P_{CO_2}. First, the depth of respirations increases, then the rate. However, if hypoxia and hypercapnia (increased P_{CO_2}) exist for a long time, the respiratory center is depressed.

Peripheral chemoreceptors Chemoreceptors in the aortic arch and carotid bodies are very sensitive to a drop in oxygen supply. They stimulate the respiratory center when there is decreased blood flow, decreased hemoglobin amount or saturation, or increased P_{CO_2}. Stimulation of these receptors causes increased minute ventilation and cardiac output.

Physiology of respiration

The term *respiration* actually encompasses all the processes that are essential for cellular metabolism, not just ventilation. A continuous supply of oxygen and continuous removal of carbon dioxide are vital.

External respiration occurs in the lungs when gas is exchanged between the external environment and the blood. Through *diffusion*, oxygen and carbon dioxide pass across the alveolar epithelium to and from the pulmonary capillar-

ies. Gases are then transported by the blood and body fluids to and from the body cells. Gas exchange that occurs at the cellular level, involving systemic capillaries, is known as *internal respiration*. Thus, there are two different capillary beds where gas exchange takes place: pulmonary and systemic.

Mechanics of ventilation

The process of gas movement in and out of the pulmonary system is *ventilation*. Inspiration causes the thorax to enlarge and the diaphragm to descend. The pleural layers, held together by pleural fluid, expand the lungs as the thorax volume increases. The pressure inside the lungs decreases, becoming less than atmospheric, and air flows inward until the pressures inside and outside equalize. With the end of inspiration, the muscles relax and the elastic forces of the lungs and chest predominate, causing the capacity of the thorax to decrease. The pressure inside the lungs increases above atmospheric and gas flows outward.

The term *compliance* is used to describe the elastic forces of the lungs and thorax that must be overcome to expand the lungs. When a lung is highly compliant, little force is needed to expand it. When a lung has low compliance, the elastic forces are such that it can be expanded only with great difficulty.

The flow of gas in and out of the lungs is measured by resistance. Any increase in secretions or the narrowing of airways increases resistance. Normally the upper airway accounts for 45 percent of total airway resistance.

Pulmonary gas exchange

Gas exchange between the pulmonary capillaries and the atmosphere should equal that of the systemic capillaries. To ensure adequate perfusion across the alveolar epithelium, alveolar inflation (ventilation) and capillary blood flow (perfusion) should match. This means that ideally all alveoli are inflated with air and are surrounded by blood-filled pulmonary capillaries.

This is not the case, however. Air in the upper airways cannot participate in gas exchange and is part of the *anatomic deadspace*. It usually equals 1 ml per pound of body weight. *Alveolar deadspace* is the portion of ventilation that contacts alveolar epithelium where there is no blood flow. Together these two deadspaces make up the *physiological deadspace*.

Physiological shunt describes the part of cardiac output that does not exchange with alveolar gas. Blood passes by an unfilled alveolus or is shunted around a filled alveolus. Atelectasis leads to intrapulmonary capillary shunting and produces a *venous admixture*, the return of unoxygenated blood to the left heart. This condition occurs in pulmonary edema, obstructive pulmonary disease, and with retained secretions.

Assessment of respiratory status

In nursing the patient with pulmonary problems, the nurse often carries the responsibility for making life-and-death decisions. Therefore the nurse must develop the skills necessary to make a clinical evaluation of the patient's respiratory status. Although this text is not designed to teach complex physical assessment skills, basic information to assess the respiratory system must be included. The primary techniques used by the nurse include history taking, observation, palpation, and auscultation.

History

If the nurse is seeing the child for the first time, he or she will want to collect a history of the present illness in addition to the other components of a nursing history (Chap. 6). Either before or during the assessment of the child's respiratory status, the nurse will want to obtain the following information.

1. Has there been a change in the child's eating habits?
2. Has the child been worried, fatigued, or irritable?
3. Has the child had a fever?
4. Has the child experienced anorexia, nausea, vomiting, diarrhea, or abdominal pain?
5. Does the child appear frightened or restless?
6. What have the parents done for or given to the child because of this illness?
7. Has the child experienced similar problems before?
8. Has the child been exposed to others who were ill?

Specific information about respiratory status can be obtained by asking the following:

9. Has the child complained of difficulty in breathing? When?

10. Is a cough present? How frequently? When does it occur? What causes it, and how does it sound? Is the cough productive? If so, describe the color and consistency of sputum.
11. Has the child's activity level changed?
12. Are there any abnormal sounds during breathing? If so, describe.
13. Does the child complain of or appear to have pain?

Observation

It is extremely important to look closely at the child. Observe the size for age, posture, skin color, state of alertness, speech or cry, and degree of respiratory effort. Dyspnea is a subjective complaint of difficulty in breathing as reported by the patient. Very young children will not be able to complain. Therefore the observer must note "respiratory distress" or "shortness of breath." The nurse must look at the child's position and listen for signs of distress. Because an upper respiratory infection often signals the onset of a communicable disease, the child's skin must be checked for redness or rashes.

An orderly observation of general appearance includes the face, neck, chest, and abdomen in relation to ventilation. In observing the general shape and size of the chest, the nurse should note:

1. A funnel chest, characterized by sternal depression
2. A pigeon chest, characterized by a protruding sternum
3. A barrel chest, where the ribs form concentric circles

The nurse also looks for flaring of the nostrils on inspiration, use of accessory muscles in the neck and abdomen, and retraction of the intercostals. The position of the trachea should be noted; it will be deflected toward the unaffected side in a pneumothorax. The nurse should also look for bilateral chest expansion or paradoxical (see-saw) movement of the rib cage. (Fig. 19-1 describes the Silverman Index for Evaluation of Infant Respiratory Status.)

When observing color, look for pallor of the lips, mucous membranes, skin, and nail beds. Cyanosis is a very *late* sign of hypoxia. If present, it usually indicates cardiopulmonary disease due to hypoventilation or right-to-left shunting of blood. The fingers and toes should be examined for clubbing. Clubbing is characterized by hypertrophy of soft tissues at the nail base. The skin over the nail bed becomes stretched and shiny and the terminal phalanges enlarge, becoming puffy and blunt (Fig. 26-3). Usually the thumb and index finger are affected first. Clubbing is characteristic of chronic lung disease.

The rate, depth, quality, and pattern of respiration provide important assessment data (Table 25-1). In infants it is helpful to count the rise and fall of the central abdomen just below the xiphoid process. Look for head bobbing and listen for grunting or stridor. The respiratory rate should be monitored often in the newborn. Two hours after birth, a resting rate of more than 45 in the full-term and 60 in the preterm should be considered abnormal and reported.[5] Abnormal breathing is often the outstanding feature of cardiac problems in infants with congenital heart disease.[6]

The transition from abdominal respirations in the infant to costal respirations is gradual and is completed by 7 years. Average respiratory rates for children are given in Table 17-20. Ordinarily there are approximately four pulse beats to every respiration. As body temperature increases, so does the respiratory rate.

In addition to a careful assessment of respirations, the nurse should describe the child's cough. Usually an infant's or young child's cough is nonproductive. The cough, a basic defense mechanism, attempts to maintain adequate pulmonary hygiene when there is a problem with the mucous blanket. Coughing is the major defense against retained secretions.[7]

An expiratory paroxysmal cough followed by an inspiratory "whoop" is characteristic of pertussis. A loose, productive cough is seen in bronchitis, cystic fibrosis, and when a postnasal drip combines with an upper respiratory infec-

Table 25-1 Classification of respiratory patterns

Type	Rate	Rhythm	Depth	Respiratory cycle
Eupnea (normal)	Infant 30–60; child 15–25	Smooth, even	Variable	Active inspiration, passive expiration
Tachypnea	Increased	Regular or irregular	Within normal range or decreased	Active inspiration, passive expiration
Bradypnea	Decreased	Regular or irregular	Normal to increased	Active inspiration, passive expiration
Apnea	Variable	Irregular	Variable	Inspiration active; temporary cessation in the resting expiratory phase
Hyperpnea	Normal or increased	Regular	Increased	Inspiration active, usually prolonged and deep; expiration passive
Hypopnea	Normal or increased	Regular	Shallow	Shallow, active inspiration, passive expiration
Apneusis	Decreased	Regular or irregular	Variable	Inspiration active; cessation during inspiration; expiration passive
Cheyne-Stokes	Variable	Regular increases and decreases in rate	Sequential changes from increased to decreased	Inspiration active, expiration passive, with recurring periods of apnea of 10–15 s
Kussmaul	Variable	Regular or irregular	Increased	Inspiration active, expiration passive
Biot's	Variable	Irregular	Shallow	Shallow breathing followed by apnea

tion. A sharp, brassy, nonproductive, barking cough is heard with laryngeal diphtheria, a foreign body, croup, and tuberculosis. The cough heard with pneumonia is tight and nonproductive. A dry, irritating, persistent cough is characteristic of measles and laryngitis.

Palpation

In *palpation* the nurse places his or her hands over the sides of the chest wall to feel the degree of movement with each inspiration. Sometimes vibrations can be felt that are due to secretions or fluid. The symmetry of chest expansion is best felt by palpation.

Palpation of the chest wall will also pinpoint areas of tenderness. Feeling the trachea will help determine its presence in the midsternal line. Sometimes the grating sensation of a pleural friction rub or the coarse, crackling sensation of crepitation can be felt.

Auscultation

Auscultation is used to interpret the quality and quantity of breath sounds as air flows through the tracheobronchial tree and to detect the presence of fluid, mucus, or obstruction of air passages. Because the chest wall of the child is thin, breath sounds are louder and harsher than they are in the adult.

It is wise for the nurse to listen often to chest sounds in a variety of patients. When a condition is described by a physician, the nurse should listen and learn. Only by doing this will the nurse be able to distinguish the variety of sounds possible and become familiar with the normal ones. The nurse should listen to a complete breath cycle, systematically comparing each position with the same one on the opposite side of the thorax. Auscultation of breath sounds is important in evaluating the effectiveness of suctioning or chest physiotherapy. Auscultation in the infant and small child is very difficult.

Normal breath sounds *Vesicular breath sounds* are those of normal inspiration. They are heard all over the chest except over the manubrium and interscapular areas, and are characterized by a louder, longer, higher-pitched inspiration with a shorter, softer, lower-pitched expiration.

Bronchial breath sounds are those heard as air rushes through the large airways. They are normal only over the trachea. Elsewhere they indi-

cate consolidation. They are characterized by a shorter inspiratory phase and a longer expiratory phase and sound like air blowing through a tube.

Bronchovesicular sounds are a combination of vesicular and bronchial sounds commonly heard at the manubrium of the sternum and upper intrascapular areas. Inspiration and expiration are equal in quality, pitch, intensity, and duration.

Abnormal breath sounds *Adventitious sounds* are abnormal sounds. *Rales* are the most common and indicate the presence of fluid in the small airways and alveoli. They are heard on inspiration. Fine rales sound like the noise made when a lock of hair is rubbed between the thumb and forefinger in front of the ear. Medium rales originate in the bronchioles and sound like the fizz of a carbonated drink. Coarse rales are loud and bubbly. They originate in the trachea or bronchi. Rales are seldom cleared by coughing.

Rhonchi are loud, gurgling noises transmitted from secretions in the pharynx. They are usually more prominent during expiration. Since rhonchi suggest accumulated or retained secretions (or both), efforts should be made to mobilize the secretions and an evaluation made as to whether they disappear or change.

Wheezes sound more musical than do rales or rhonchi. The sound is produced by high-velocity airflow through a restricted air passage. Wheezes often accompany asthma or bronchoconstriction. Audible wheezes may be heard with aspiration of foreign bodies.

Other sounds helpful in assessing respiratory status include snoring, stridor, and grunting. "*Snoring*" while awake is associated with enlarged tonsils or other tissue obstruction of the upper airway. *Stridor* is produced by the flow of air through an obstructed upper airway. It can be loud or soft, high- or low-pitched, musical or harsh, depending on the type and extent of obstruction. Inspiratory stridor usually means obstruction at or above the larynx. Expiratory stridor usually indicates obstruction below the larynx. *Grunting* on expiration is a typical sign of severe respiratory distress in the infant (see Chap. 19).

Measurement of blood gases and pH

The most important basis for respiratory care today is the measurement of arterial blood gases

Table 25-2 Normal arterial blood gas values

	Normal	
pH	7.35–7.45	Acidity or alkalinity of blood in terms of hydrogen ion concentration
Pa_{CO_2}	35–45 mmHg	Partial pressure of CO_2 in arterial blood
Pa_{O_2}	80–100 mmHg 40–60 mmHg in newborn	Partial pressure of O_2 arterial blood
Sa_{O_2}	95–100%	Saturation of O_2—plotted on oxyhemoglobin dissociation curve—affected by pH, P_{CO_2}, temperature.
HCO_3-	22–26 mEq per liter	Bicarbonate ion, the basis of the buffer system
H_2CO_3	1.05–1.35 mEq per liter	Carbonic acid, formed by CO_2 + H_2O; is 3% of P_{CO_2} (ratio of hydrogen ion to carbonic acid is usually 20:1)

and pH (Table 25-2). These values provide information about acid-base balance, alveolar ventilation, and oxygenation. They can be used to determine the cause and degree of respiratory disturbance, to select treatment, and to evaluate patient progress. The more severely ill the child is, the more important the blood gas measurements become.

The measurement of the partial pressure of carbon dioxide in the arterial blood (Pa_{CO_2}) is a direct reflection of the adequacy of alveolar ventilation.[8] The normal Pa_{CO_2} range is 35 to 45 mmHg. When the Pa_{CO_2} rises *(hypercapnia)*, respiratory acidosis results. When it falls *(hypocapnia)*, respiratory alkalosis is present.

The measurement of dissolved oxygen gas tension in arterial blood (Pa_{O_2}) is closely related to the amount of oxygen carried by hemoglobin, that is, the saturation (Sa_{O_2}). The normal Pa_{O_2} is 80 to 100 mmHg; the normal Sa_{O_2} is 95 to 100 percent. Together these measurements indicate the oxygen content of arterial blood.

The Sa_{O_2} is reflected in the oxygen-hemoglobin dissociation curve. When the curve shifts to the right, as can occur with hyperthermia, chronic hypoxemia, hypercapnia, and acidosis, hemoglobin has less affinity for oxygen and more can be released to the tissues. When the curve shifts to the left, as in hypothermia, hypocapnia, and alkalosis, less oxygen is released.

The arterial pH measurement, the amount of free hydrogen ion concentration in arterial blood, reflects the acid-base balance in the body. The normal arterial pH is 7.35 to 7.4. Lower than 7.35 is acidotic; higher than 7.4 is alkalotic. Values less than 7 or more than 7.8 are incompatible with life. The three mechanisms for maintaining the acid-base balance are (1) the buffers in the bloodstream (hemoglobin, protein, and bicarbonate); (2) kidney regulation of bicarbonate (HCO_3^-); and (3) ventilatory regulation of carbon dioxide.

A decrease in arterial pH will stimulate an increase in the depth and rate of respiration. The Pa_{CO_2} than falls and the pH rises. An increase in pH suppresses alveolar ventilation, thereby increasing the Pa_{CO_2} and lowering the pH. Thus the pH and Pa_{CO_2} provide a physiological reflection of the ventilatory and acid-base status.

Pulmonary function testing

A spirometer is occasionally used in older children (more than 4 years) to measure the volume of air inhaled by and exhaled from the lungs. The total amount of air the lungs can hold at rest is the *total lung capacity*. It is dependent on the age, size, sex, and health of the individual. The amount of air inhaled and exhaled with each breath is called the *tidal volume* (Fig. 25-3). Other parts of the total lung capacity include:

1. *Inspiratory reserve volume*—the extra air that can be inhaled after a normal inspiration
2. *Expiratory reserve volume*—the extra air that can be exhaled after a normal expiration
3. *Vital capacity*—the sum total of tidal, inspiratory reserve, and expiratory reserve volumes.

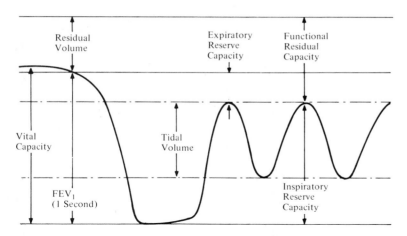

Figure 25-3 Pulmonary function studies graphically recorded on a spirometric printout. (*From L. Shortridge et al., Introductory Skills for Nursing Practice, New York, McGraw-Hill, 1980, p. 234.*)

Before spirometry is done, children will need an opportunity to familiarize themselves with the equipment and practice breathing through the mouthpiece with the nose pinched closed. (Normal values for height and sex will be available from the tester.)

Diagnostic procedures

Chest x-rays are used by the physician to diagnose such clinical conditions as atelectasis, pneumonia, pneumothorax, and mediastinal shift. Contrast media or dyes are also used to demonstrate defects or lesions or to observe motion.

Biopsies and aspiration of sputum and cells via bronchoscopy are used to obtain secretions for culture and sensitivity, for analysis, and for direct visualization of the upper and lower airways. Previously discussed principles should be incorporated into the preparation of the child (and the family) for the procedure.

Methods of improving respiratory function

Respiratory care of the child (or adult) is multidisciplinary. The nurse will share the responsibility for caring for the child with the pediatrician, anesthesiologist, respiratory therapist, and even the physical therapist. Although these other health professionals may have primary responsibility for certain treatment modalities, the nurse becomes involved in all treatment aspects through day-to-day care and in patient and family teaching.

Oxygen therapy

Oxygen therapy is used to treat hypoxemia and increase alveolar oxygen tension as well as to decrease the work of breathing and the work of the heart.[9] Oxygen makes up 21 percent of room air. The amount of oxygen delivered to the patient, Fi_{O_2}, can be increased by giving supplemental oxygen through high-flow (PEEP, CPAP) or low-flow (cannulas, hoods, masks) systems (Fig. 25-4). These methods are described in Chaps. 17 and 19.

Whenever oxygen therapy is used, the nurse must observe the child's response—color, vital signs, and respiratory effort. The oxygen content is analyzed and blood gases are obtained to monitor the child's response. Oxygen toxicity is possible when oxygen is given too long and at too high a concentration. Lung toxicity and retrolental fibroplasia can result (see Chap. 19 for a discussion of these two problems). Patients with chronic lung disease, in whom chronic hypoxia triggers the respiratory centers, can rapidly lose consciousness due to hypoventilation if given too much oxygen.

Humidity, aerosol, and IPPB therapy

Normally air is 100 percent humidified when it reaches the alveoli, maintaining the hydration of the mucous blanket. If disease interrupts the water balance, water must be added or water loss prevented. If the tracheobronchial tree becomes dehydrated, the following conditions occur:

1. Ciliary activity is impaired

2. Mucus movement is impaired
3. Inflammation results
4. Secretions are retained
5. Infection, atelectasis, and pneumonia can result

Therefore, whenever an artificial airway is necessary or oxygen therapy is needed, the gas delivered must be warmed and humidified.

Humidifiers function to restore dry oxygen to room air conditions. Aerosol machines, ultrasonic or jet nebulizers, break down a liquid (usually water) and suspend it in a gas. The gas and liquid are then deposited in the tracheobronchial tree to aid in bronchial hygiene or to deliver medication.

Intermittent positive-pressure breathing (IPPB) therapy is used to increase airway pressure, mechanically dilate the tracheobronchial tree, decrease the work of breathing, and increase the tidal volume. It is used to deliver medication, but, more importantly, it is used to stimulate the patient to cough and mobilize retained secretions. IPPB is difficult to use in the small child because it is frightening. Clear instructions, patience, and understanding are needed to teach an older child how to use IPPB.

Drug therapy

Medications are used frequently in the treatment of respiratory disease to control infection as well as to improve pulmonary function. Although medications given by inhalation may have a topical effect, they are rapidly absorbed systemically because of the thin alveolar membrane and generous capillary blood flow. Table 25-3 outlines the various types of pulmonary agents used in the treatment of respiratory disease. In addition, aspirin and acetaminophen may be used to decrease fever and control discomfort.

Chest physical therapy

Chest physical therapy is used to prevent pulmonary complications in some children, for example, children who have had surgical procedures, and to improve function in acute and chronic respiratory disease. It includes postural drainage, chest percussion, chest vibration, coughing, and exercise. Chest physical therapy may be combined with aerosol or IPPB therapy, especially when acute illness is superimposed on a chronic illness like cystic fibrosis or bronchiectasis. Percussion and vibration mobilize and

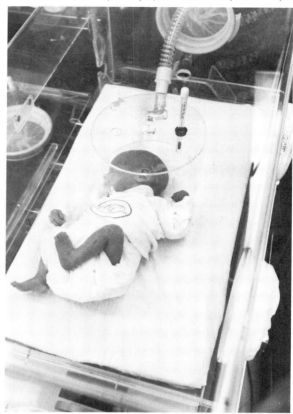

Figure 25-4 An infant receiving oxygen via an oxygen hood. (*Photo courtesy of Olympic Medical Corp. Seattle.*)

loosen secretions, which are then moved by gravity as the various postural drainage positions are assumed. These positions and techniques are explained in more detail in Chap. 17 (Fig. 17-29).

In order to help the child breathe properly, the nurse must understand normal respiration. With normal respiration, the abdomen rises as the diaphragm descends, the ribs flare, and there is a slight rise in the upper chest. During expiration, the diaphragm moves up and the abdomen falls.

Nurses must be able to tell a patient how to breathe more effectively as well as how to cough. Incentive spirometers, balloons, laughing, and crying may all aid in improving ventilation. To help the child cough properly, have the child take several breaths, then take one large one, hold it, and forcefully contract the abdominal muscles and expel the air by opening the glottis. Incisions will need splinting with hands or pillows. Sometimes nasopharyngeal or oropharyngeal suctioning will induce a cough.

Additional nursing measures that improve respiratory status include comfortable positioning in the semi-Fowler's or Fowler's position with the upper body and legs adequately supported. Because dehydration produces thick, tenacious mucus, every effort should be made to hydrate the child adequately by oral or intravenous fluids.

Table 25-3 Drugs used in respiratory disease

Type	Function
Noninhalation pulmonary agents	
I. Bronchospasmolytics	
A. Active bronchodilators	Promote relaxation of muscle fibers
1. Catecholamines (ephedrine)	Sympathomimetic agents; usually given in suboptimal doses combined with theophylline
2. Methylxanthines, (theophylline, aminophylline)	
3. Corticosteroids	Relieves bronchospasm
B. Preventive	
1. Cromolyn sodium	Prophylactic in allergic asthma, inhibits histamine release
II. Decongestants	Relieve swelling of mucosa and increase capillary blood flow in nasal and pulmonary tree
A. Alpha-adrenergic drugs	Constrict arterioles, thereby decreasing blood flow
1. Phenylephrine (Neosynephrine)	Most useful as a nasal decongestant
B. Allergic decongestants	Increase and thicken glandular secretions
1. Antihistamines (Benedryl, Chlor-trimeton)	Decrease histaminelike irritation to tissues and decrease cause of increased blood flow.
III. Mucokinetic agents (expectorants)	Improve removal of sputum
A. Water	Thins mucus and decreases viscosity
B. Vagal stimulants	Stimulate gastric mucosa, cause vagal activation of bronchial glands producing secretions
C. Direct bronchial gland stimulants (supersaturated potassium iodide)	Increase secretions
IV. Anti-inflammatory agents	
A. Corticosteroids	Decrease acute and chronic inflammation
V. Antiallergic agents (allergy shots)	Reduce sensitivity to allergen (cause)
VI. Antimicrobials	Given when pulmonary infection present
VII. Antitussives	Cough suppressants
A. Codeine	
B. Dextromethorphan	
Inhalation pulmonary agents	Topical application of drugs to the pulmonary tree through aerosol treatment
I. Bronchodilators	
A. Catecholamines	
1. Isoproterenol (Isuprel)	Beta adrenergic bronchodilator that causes vasodilation of pulmonary mucosal vessels. Side effects: tachycardia, palpitation, flushing
2. Isoetharine (Bronkosol)	Sympathomimetic
3. Metaproterenol (Alupent)	
4. Terbutaline (Bricanyl)	Potent, long-acting

Table 25-3 Drugs used in respiratory disease (*Continued*)

Type	Function
II. Decongestants	
A. Racemic epinephrine (Micronefrin, Vaponefrin)	Topical vasoconstrictor Aerosol decongestant, Mild systemic bronchodilator
B. Phenylephrine	
III. Mucokinetic agents	
A. Hypoviscosity agents	Decrease viscosity of mucus
1. Water	
2. Weak electrolyte solutions (sodium bicarbonate)	
B. Mucolytic agents	Liquefies purulent sputum by digesting DNA
1. Pancreatic agents (Dornavac)	Used only in cystic fibrosis: reduces tenacity of secretions; expectorant.
2. N-acetylcysteine (Mucomyst)	Decrease mucus viscosity and help mobilize secretions

Artificial airways

When respiratory failure occurs or there is obstruction of the upper respiratory tract, an artificial airway may be life-saving. Endotracheal tubes (Fig. 25-5) or tracheostomy tubes (Fig. 25-6) are designed to:[10]

1. *Relieve airway obstruction* due to soft-tissue obstruction or laryngeal obstruction
2. *Protect the airway* when the normal protective reflexes (gag, swallowing, cough) are absent due to anesthesia, drugs, or disease
3. *Facilitate suctioning*, especially of tracheal secretions
4. *Support ventilation* when it is needed for any length of time beyond extremely short periods

In children, nasal endotracheal intubation is preferred over tracheostomy when the airway problem is expected to be of short duration—1 to 2 weeks or less. For longer periods, tracheostomies are preferred. Cuffed tubes are seldom used in children. Table 25-4 compares endotracheal intubation to tracheostomy.

An alternative to intubation for providing a temporary airway is *cricothyroid puncture*. This procedure is done in an emergency room to ventilate the child whose breathing is obstructed due to epiglottitis or another cause. It allows air exchange until a more extensive procedure can be performed in the operating suite under better conditions.

Between the *thyroid cartilage*, the first prominence felt on the anterior aspect of the neck, and the *cricoid cartilage*, the second prominence, lies the cricothyroid space, which is covered by a membrane. A large-bore, 10-gauge needle with a stylet is inserted through the avascular cricothyroid membrane while the child's neck is hyperextended. After removal of the stylet, an adaptor is fitted to the needle and a positive-pressure breathing apparatus is connected to it.

Psychologically the insertion of an artificial airway is frightening, painful, and traumatic to the child and the family. Communication by

Figure 25-5 Endotracheal tube suitable for a small child. (*Photo by M. Smith.*)

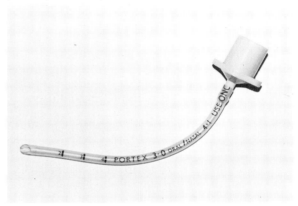

Figure 25-6 Tracheostomy tubes. (*A*) Metal tracheostomy tube. From left to right: (1) outer cannula; (2) inner cannula; (3) obturator. (*B*) Silastic tracheostomy tubes. From left to right: (1) tube with ties, obturator in place; (2) wing-tipped tube. (*Photo by M. Smith*)

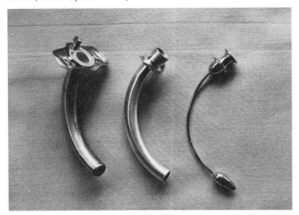

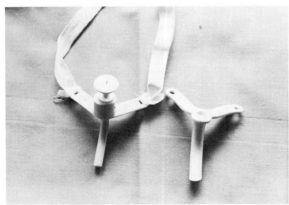

speech or crying is no longer possible while the tube remains in place. If a child writes, he or she should have a "magic slate" nearby. A call light or bell must be accessible, if the child can use it, to call for help. Above all, the child should never be left alone, at least during the initial crisis.

If a tracheostomy was done, the child needs to be observed closely for hemorrhage. The tube must be kept securely in place and removal prevented. When ties are changed, new ones may be secured in place before the old ones are removed. Wider Velcro straps may also be used. Elbow restraints may need to be applied to the very small child. Emergency equipment (a Trous-

seau dilator, extra tracheostomy tube) must be kept at the bedside in case the tube comes out.

Whenever the upper airway is bypassed, its normal function of humidifying and warming inspired air is lost. Children with artificial airways will either be placed in a mist tent or connected to a special "collar" or "T tube" that delivers humidified and warmed air. When air is properly humidified and the patient is properly hydrated, crusting of secretions is unlikely.

If mechanical ventilation is necessary, the child will usually be unable to handle secretions, making suctioning necessary. The patient is suctioned only when necessary, because the process is painful and frightening. Catecholamines are released, causing an increase in heart rate that can lead to arrhythmias. Hypoxia, tracheal irritation, hypotension, and lung collapse are other potential complications of suctioning. Constant reassurance and correct techniques are essential in making the procedure as nontraumatic for the child as possible. If it is necessary to suction the left bronchus, the infant's head is turned to the right and the chest tilted to the left. To suction the right bronchus, the patient's position is reversed. Table 25-5 describes a basic suctioning procedure in detail.

When it is necessary to suction the oropharyngeal area, a similar procedure is used. The patient is hyperventilated both before and after with oxygen to prevent hypoxia. The measurement used to approximate the depth to which the catheter should be inserted is the distance from the tragus of the ear (the cartilage projection in front of the external meatus of the ear) to the external nares. The basic suctioning procedure is the same as described in Table 25-5 (see also Table 17-17).

Although bacterial contamination of the lower airway is inevitable when the upper airway is bypassed, infection must be minimized by using careful aseptic technique during suctioning and tracheostomy site care. The site should be cleaned with an iodine-base scrub soap, rinsed with sterile normal saline, and covered with a sterile dressing.

All humidifying equipment should be changed often in the hospital. Endotracheal or tracheostomy tubes are changed according to hospital routine. Usually children under 5 years will not have the inner cannula in place in a tracheostomy tube. If an inner cannula is present, it may

Table 25-4 Comparison of nasotracheal intubation and tracheostomy in children*

Nasotracheal intubation	Tracheostomy
Advantages	**Advantages**
1. Simple procedure	1. Lower incidence of acquired subglottic stenosis
2. Can be done quickly	2. Larger tube, making obstruction less likely
3. No surgery: less infection, no scar or bleeding, less frightening	3. Less discomfort: less sedation needed
4. Lower mortality and morbidity in most institutions	4. Care relatively simple
5. Shorter hospital stay	
6. Simple extubation in most cases	
7. Simpler reintubation after accidental extubation	
Disadvantages	**Disadvantages**
1. Greater risk of acquired subglottic stenosis	1. More difficult procedure
2. Nasal excoriations	2. Usually takes longer than intubation
3. More postextubation stridor	3. Surgery: increased chance of infection, bleeding, scar; more frightening
4. Accidental extubation easier	4. Higher morbidity and mortality
5. Smaller tube: obstruction more likely	5. Longer hospital stay
6. More discomfort: sedation or restraint more necessary	6. Removal of tracheostomy more difficult: granulation tissue, edema, dependence
7. Intensive care needed	7. Accidental extubation more dangerous
	8. Needs intensive care initially

* Adapted from Aubrey Maze and Edward Bloch, "Stridor in Pediatric Patients," *Anesthesiology* **50**:132–145 (1979).

be removed, soaked in sterile normal saline, cleaned, rinsed, dried, replaced, and locked in place.

Complications of intubation

Whenever a foreign body is placed inside the trachea, there is risk of infection and tissue change. After the endotracheal tube is removed, the child will experience a sore throat and hoarse voice for a short period of time. Laryngospasm is more common in infants and children than in adults after extubation. It usually lasts 30 s or so and can be relieved by administration of high oxygen concentrations under positive pressure.

Edema of the glottis is caused by trauma during intubation, maintenance care, or an allergic response. One of the first signs of glottic edema is *inspiratory stridor*. The swelling progresses for about 24 h after removal of the tube. The sooner it appears, the more serious it is. Usually reassurance, careful observation, and aerosol treatment are helpful. Racemic epinephrine may be ordered for administration by IPPB or a hand-held nebulizer. Steroids may also be given by inhalation or intravenously. Usually this treatment will avoid the necessity of reintubation. Subglottic edema is even more serious and often requires the reestablishment of an artificial air-

way. Other complications that can develop from intubation include vocal cord granulomas, vocal cord paralysis, laryngotracheal webb (occurs 4 to 5 days or weeks after extubation and should be suctioned out), or tracheal stenosis due to scarring.

Tracheal stenosis appears 1 week to 2 years after endotracheal intubation in 2 to 5 percent of people. It is more frequent in those who had cuffed tubes and mechanical ventilation. It is also related to the length of time the tube was in place, the size of the tube, cuff pressure, infection, tube movement, and circulatory instability.[11] Tracheal stenosis may lead to permanent tracheostomy.

Home care of the tracheostomy

As more and more children with congenital and acquired defects of the trachea and related structures survive with long-term tracheostomies, nurses must be prepared to teach families how to manage their care at home. Aradine has listed parents' initial concerns about home care as follows:[12]

1. Obtaining needed equipment and keeping it in working order
2. Hearing the child at night

3. Fearing complications, such as infection, and not being able to manage the demanding care

Once the child is home, parents find that providing care is extremely demanding, forcing them to change their life-style. The family becomes isolated and confined because of the difficulty in transporting the child, the constant care needed, and often the great difficulty in finding someone else to care for the child so that they can be relieved. Parents also worry about the child's development in relation to language and learning at school.

Parents can be helped to cope with home care of a child with a tracheostomy when the nurse:

1. Includes the family in setting goals for the teaching-learning process
2. Carefully assesses the child's and family's perceptions, needs, readiness, and resources
3. Includes parents in the child's care from the very beginning
4. Encourages the siblings to be involved at a level appropriate for their development
5. Encourages self-responsibility in the child and family members
6. Provides consistency in teaching and continuity in teachers and care-givers
7. Includes another care-giver (grandparent or baby-sitter) and the community health nurse in the demonstration of home care techniques

Table 25-5 Two-nurse procedure for suctioning an endotracheal or tracheostomy tube*

First Nurse

1. Obtains needed equipment
   a. Disposable suction kit: one sterile glove, aspirating catheter (ratio of catheter size to lumen should be 1:3 or 1:2), container for sterile water.
   b. Sterile normal saline (if needed as a lavage to loosen secretions)
   c. Sterile gauze 4 by 4s (no filler)
   d. Sterile deionized water (to rinse catheter and lubricate tip)
   e. Ventilating bag connected to 100% (sometimes lower % for children) oxygen supply with flow meter
2. Opens sterile suction kit
   a. Adds sterile deionized water to container
   b. Puts on sterile glove (dominant hand)
   c. Using gloved hand, picks up sterile catheter and connects it to suction tubing, held by ungloved hand
3. Tests suction by occluding side hole and placing tip in sterile, deionized water

Second nurse

4. Stabilizes endotracheal or tracheostomy tube and disconnects it from ventilating machine or T-tube that delivers humidified air
5. *Carefully hyperventilates* patient four to five times with hand-operated ventilator bag that is connected to 100% oxygen at 10-liter flow rate. Manual ventilations should coincide with patient's respirations
6. Sterile normal saline may be ordered (0.5–2 ml) as a lavage to loosen secretions *before* hyperventilating

First nurse

7. Introduces catheter gently, *without suction,* beyond the end of the tube until slight resistance is felt; pulls back slightly
8. Intermittently *suctions* (60–100 mmHg) while withdrawing catheter. Catheter may be rotated if it has only one opening. Suctioning should take no longer than 10 s. Nurse may estimate time tube should be occluded by holding breath
9. Rinses catheter in sterile deionized water and wipes clean with the sterile 4 by 4s if necessary after each suctioning

Second nurse

10. Repeats step 5. This reinflates alveoli that were collapsed by suctioning

First nurse

11. Suctioning is repeated as necessary *after* second nurse has repeated step 5. Hyperventilation must be done before suctioning, between suctions, and at end of procedure before child is reconnected to ventilator or humidifier
12. Suctioning of oropharynx is done last if necessary. Glove is turned inside out over used catheter, and both are discarded
13. Auscultates child's chest, listening for retained secretions and noting respiratory status. Records procedure, child's response, and amount, consistency, and characteristics of secretions

*This procedure helps maintain patency of the airway and prevents stasis of secretions. It must take place in sterile conditions. Adapted from nursing procedures of St. Mary's Hospital, Rochester, Minn.

Congenital alterations in oxygen-carbon dioxide exchange

Choanal atresia

Choanal atresia is a congenital obstruction of one or both posterior nares at the entrance to the nasopharynx. The obstruction is usually membranous but may be due to bony growth.

If the obstruction is bilateral, the baby must breathe through the mouth. Because mouth breathing is difficult for the newborn, signs of respiratory distress are likely. The nasal obstruction also prevents the nasal discharge from draining posteriorly. Therefore, unilateral or bilateral rhinorrhea is a significant sign of this anomaly.

The diagnosis is suspected when a soft rubber catheter passed up the nose meets resistance. Contrast x-ray studies are usually done to confirm the diagnosis. An oral airway may be used initially to aid mouth breathing. The atresia plate is then pierced or removed by surgery.

Nursing management The infant must be closely observed for signs of respiratory distress. Feeding is done slowly with several rest periods. Usually the infant becomes adept at mouth breathing by 3 weeks.

Congenital laryngeal stridor

Congenital laryngeal stridor, also known as *laryngomalacia*, is the most common (70 percent) congenital problem of the larynx. The larynx is unusually flaccid, causing collapse of the supraglottic structures. There is high-pitched "crowing" on inspiration as the baby draws air through the narrow opening in the larynx. Crying, feeding, and a supine position usually make the stridor worse. This condition will normally improve as the larynx grows, and usually disappears by 1 year.

Nursing management The infant should be placed in a prone position for sleep and rest, allowing the soft supraglottic structures to fall away from the airway.

The noisy respirations can be very frightening to the baby's parents. They will need continued support and reassurance as they learn to feed and care for their baby. Feeding should be done slowly. Special handling, positioning, and nipples may be necessary. In extreme cases, a tracheostomy or intubation may be necessary.

Other congenital conditions causing stridor

Other congenital conditions that commonly are signaled by stridor include:

1. *Pierre Robin syndrome.* The infant has micrognathia, an oversized, posteriorly displaced tongue, and in half the cases a cleft palate. A prone position and an oral airway may be necessary. The child is managed conservatively while mandibular growth is awaited.
2. *Congenital subglottic stenosis.* Respiratory infection often causes distress and an inability to handle secretions. Mild stenosis is usually outgrown, but severe stenosis may require tracheostomy.
3. *Congenital laryngeal webs.* These make up a small percent of laryngeal anomalies and may be found above, at, or below the glottis.

Alterations in oxygen-carbon dioxide exchange due to infection

Infants and children are more susceptible than adults to infections of the respiratory tract because of their immunological immaturity and because they are in frequent contact with other immunologically incompetent children. The more contacts a child has, the more likely he or she is to experience a respiratory infection.

Anatomic factors also prevent children from handling respiratory infections as well as adults do. Children have decreased alveolar surfaces for gas exchange and narrower peripheral airways that are easily obstructed. In addition, accessory muscles of respiration are less well developed. These factors, together with a less rigid thorax, make it more difficult for the child to cough. Children also have a higher metabolic rate and oxygen consumption, making respiratory function even more critical.

Upper respiratory infections

Upper respiratory infections (URI) are often classified into three clinical entities: (1) nasopharyngitis, or the common cold; (2) pharyngitis, or pharyngotonsillitis; and (3) upper respiratory infection, or "flu." URIs are the most common acute infections in children and are caused by viruses, bacteria, fungi, or *Mycoplasma pneumoniae*. Age, allergies, chronic disease, number of exposures, environmental setting, and season all affect the incidence and severity of the host's response to the infection. In the winter, 50 percent of the population experiences a URI of some kind.

The common cold Children 1 to 5 years old are the most susceptible to colds, experiencing 10 to 12 per year. School-age children may have up to 6 colds a year. Younger children are also more apt to develop such complications as otitis media, bronchitis, and pneumonia. This is because viral invasion of the nasopharynx damages the epithelium and makes it more vulnerable to a superimposed bacterial infection.

The symptoms of a cold result from inflammation due to *viral* invasion of the epithelium. Hyperemia and edema cause *rhinorrhea*, the clear, profuse, watery nasal discharge that characterizes the beginning of a cold. Nasal obstruction, sneezing, mild sore throat and cough, and low-grade fever often accompany the rhinorrhea. The younger the child is, the higher the fever. After 2 to 3 days, the nasal secretions become yellow and thickened.

The typical cold lasts 4 to 7 days after an incubation period of 1 to 4 days. Fifteen to thirty percent of colds are due to the rhinovirus, with peak incidence in the spring and fall. Other viruses associated with a cold are respiratory syncytial, parainfluenza, and adenovirus.

Pharyngitis Infection and inflammation of the pharynx, tonsils, and cervical lymph nodes are characteristics of pharyngitis. The child is mildly to moderately ill with a sore throat, swollen glands, headache, malaise, anorexia, and a fever. Sixty percent of pharyngitis cases occur between 2 and 8 years. Viruses account for about 60 percent of cases. Group A beta hemolytic *Streptococcus* (GABHS) is responsible for the rest. GABHS peaks between 6 to 8 and 12 to 14 years.

Viral pharyngitis typically has a more gradual onset than does bacterial pharyngitis. Its symptoms more closely resemble those of a viral upper respiratory infection.

Bacterial pharyngitis ("strep" throat) often presents more suddenly with a temperature increase up to 40°C (104°F), headache, severe sore throat, abdominal pain, and localized, tender cervical nodes. A white exudate is typically seen on the reddened, enlarged tonsils.

Untreated children with pharyngitis due to GABHS can develop (1) acute rheumatic fever, (2) acute glomerulonephritis, or (3) abscesses, pneumonia, or osteomyelitis. Therefore, throat cultures are routinely done on all patients with pharyngitis who seek medical care. Those with a history of rheumatic fever or other chronic illness may be treated immediately with benzathine penicillin intramuscularly, oral penicillin, or erythromycin. Treatment for those with positive cultures is begun once the results of the culture are obtained. A 48-h delay in starting treatment does not increase the incidence of rheumatic fever or glomerulonephritis and is beneficial in that it gives the patient time to develop an antibody response. Oral antibiotics must be taken for 10 days to be effective. Since drug compliance decreases rapidly after treatment is begun, many physicians (and parents) prefer one injection of penicillin. Pharyngitis may also be the presenting symptom in diphtheria or gonococcal infection of the throat or retropharyngeal abscess.

Upper respiratory infection This third category of upper airway infection is more commonly known as "flu" or "grippe." The child becomes moderately ill without focal symptoms. There is muscle soreness, malaise, elevated temperature [37.8 to 41°C (100 to 106°F)], headache, a dry cough, and sometimes mild nausea and diarrhea. The bronchial epithelium is affected, and pneumonia is an infrequent complication.

Nursing management Most of the children with an upper respiratory infection will be treated at home. Therefore, the nurse becomes involved with educating and guiding parents in effective care.

Symptomatic care includes rest, control of fever, hydration, nutrition, and local comfort measures. The child should rest at home, separated from other children. Stories, quiet games, television, and naps as needed help the child relax.

Ingestion of fluids must be encouraged, especially those high in vitamin C or electrolytes (Gatorade). Often the child has favorites such as 7-Up, Sprite, apple juice, or Kool-aid. Jello, pudding, or ice cream are often pleasing. When anorexia or nausea is present, clear fluids may be all that are tolerated. When diarrhea exists, dehydration may be likely. The parents should be taught to observe for signs of dehydration (Chap. 17) and monitor the child's voiding pattern.

When the child has a fever, aspirin or acetaminophen can be given in age-appropriate doses every 4 to 6 h. Tepid sponge baths help to reduce high fever.

Measures to increase humidity are also very helpful in URIs. Steamers (hot and cold), vaporizers, or hot showers can be used. The child must be protected from burns when steam is used. (Cold steamers are difficult to keep clean and may become a breeding ground for certain organisms.)

A warm saline gargle (2 tsp salt per liter of water) is often soothing for the child who is old enough to manage the technique. If the cough is persistent, increasing hydration and lozenges, lollipops, or hard candy may help. Cough suppressants are seldom used—and then only at night.

Nose drops usually are avoided because of rebound engorgement of the nasal mucosa if they are used for several days. For the very young infant, saline nose drops before feeding and sleep may liquefy mucus, facilitating its removal. It is wise to clear the infant's nasal passages with a rubber bulb syringe before feeding. Petrolatum or a mild protective cream may be applied to the nostrils and upper lip to prevent excoriation from nasal secretions.

It is important for parents and children to understand that upper respiratory infections are very contagious. The severity of the infection, the amount of virus shed, and the length of contact all contribute to the possibility of spreading the infection. Careful hand washing, protected coughing or sneezing, use of paper cups and individual towels in the bathroom or kitchen, and a dishwasher all serve to reduce the spread of disease.

As stated earlier, antibiotics, although ineffective for viral infections, are very important in treating streptococcal pharyngitis. Emphasis in patient teaching should be on the difference between viral and bacterial infection. Parents should be instructed to seek professional attention for their child when (1) symptoms persist beyond 7 days; (2) symptoms localize in the ears, throat, or neck; (3) there is localization of URI symptoms in the lower chest with purulent or bloody sputum; (4) gastrointestinal (GI) symptoms or fever are prolonged.[13]

Tonsillectomy—adenoidectomy   Repeated bouts of pharyngitis and upper respiratory infections may lead to chronic tonsillitis and airway interference. At one time, removal of the tonsillar tissue was routine in almost all children. Most physicians currently believe that this surgery is undesirable as a routine because of the great surgical risk and is also detrimental because valuable protective lymphoid tissue is removed. Currently tonsillectomy and adenoidectomy or both are reserved for use in children who have severe chronic upper airway obstruction leading to alveolar hypoventilation, difficulty in swallowing, discomfort in breathing, distortion of speech, or recurrent ear infections leading to hearing loss.

Usually this surgery is performed around 4 to 6 years of age. Preoperative teaching is extremely important to reduce the trauma of hospitalization. Bleeding and clotting times are checked preoperatively because hemorrhage is the most common surgical complication. Preoperative care is similar to that for other surgical procedures. Postoperative care is summarized in Table 25-6.

Lower respiratory infections

Because the larynx can be considered the transition area between the upper and lower airways, infections that compromise its function are considered with those of the lower airway. Infections of the larynx are somewhat more likely to extend to the trachea and bronchi than are upper respiratory infections.

The nurse is reminded that at all times, in caring for children with any kind of respiratory disease, he or she must be on the alert for the following signs of respiratory failure and report them immediately:

1. Decreased or absent inspiratory breath sounds
2. Severe inspiratory retractions and use of accessory muscles
3. Depressed level of consciousness and diminished response to pain
4. Poor skeletal muscle tone
5. Cyanosis in 40 percent ambient oxygen
6. A Pa_{CO_2} equal to or more than 75 mmHg or a Pa_{O_2} of less than 100 mmHg in 100 percent oxygen.[14]

Epiglottitis   Epiglottitis is a life-threatening disease that can occur at any age. Without treatment, it can progress rapidly to death by closing off the airway.

Table 25-6 Summary of postoperative care for the child with tonsillectomy/adenoidectomy

1. Child is placed on abdomen or side to facilitate drainage from mouth until fully alert
2. Constant observation for signs of hemorrhage such as:
   a. Frequent swallowing—count number/min
   b. Tachycardia (> 120/min)
   c. Pallor
   d. Vomiting of bright red blood
3. Suction equipment should be available for airway obstruction. Suctioning must be done extremely cautiously to avoid trauma to surgical site
4. Comfort measures to ease sore throat include:
   Ice collar
   Analgesics
   Mild sedation
5. Once the child is fully awake and alert, give clear fluids—cool water, apple juice, Jello—then sherbet, soup, ice cream, pudding. Soft, nonirritating foods are continued for several days
6. Alert parents to signs of complications after discharge:
   a. Hemorrhage 5–10 days postoperatively due to tissue sloughing during healing
   b. Persistent cough or earache

Pathophysiology This acute bacterial infection is usually due to *Haemophilus influenzae*. Its onset is rapid, less than a day, with sore throat, high fever, muffled voice, and quickly developing signs of respiratory obstruction—inspiratory stridor, retractions, restlessness, inability to swallow, and respiratory distress. The child assumes an upright position, leaning forward with the mouth open, drooling, and a protruding tongue. The child appears pale, shocky, and frightened.[15] Table 25-7 compares epiglottitis and croup.

Medical management *The child must never be left alone.* Total airway obstruction may occur suddenly. Initially, humidified oxygen is given by mask. If respiratory distress is not too severe, an x-ray will be taken of the lateral neck to look for a swollen epiglottis. Once the diagnosis is made, swift intervention is essential. No one should even look in the child's throat (tissue manipulation can cause airway spasm) unless conditions are right for doing an emergency intubation. If the airway closes suddenly, a cricoid puncture may be necessary until a physician skilled in nasotracheal intubation is available.

The child will be cared for in an intensive nursing care unit. Intravenous fluids and antibiotics, usually chloramphenicol or ampicillin, are given. Direct humidification of the airway and mobilization of secretions are essential. Usually the endotracheal tube can be removed in about 48 h when the swelling has decreased and the temperature and white blood count are essentially normal. Complications of epiglottitis include pneumonia, tonsillitis, cervical lymphadenitis, and otitis media.

Nursing management Since epiglottitis is an emergency, the nurse must make an immediate assessment of the respiratory status and notify the physician. The parents and child will be extremely frightened. A calm, knowledgeable nurse is essential. The nurse's initial responsibilities include assisting the physician with airway placement, oxygen, humidity, intravenous fluids and antibiotics, measurement of arterial blood gases, and cultures. Once these emergency measures are instituted, the child will need rest and reassurance, endotracheal tube care, careful observation and frequent assessment of respiratory status, management of secretions, and care directed toward meeting his or her basic human needs.

Acute laryngotracheobronchitis (croup) The word *croup* is related to the old Scottish word *roup,* which meant "to cry out in a hoarse voice." Croup is usually caused by parainfluenza or influenza A viruses. Children between 6 months and 3 years are most commonly affected, with the peak incidence in the second year of life. Croup is a much more common cause of stridor in children than is epiglottitis. Some children have repeated episodes of croup known as *acute spasmodic laryngitis.*

Table 25-7 Epiglottitis compared with croup

	Epiglottitis	Croup
Peak age	3–7 years, but seen at any age	6 months–3 years
Causative agent	*Haemophilus influenzae*	Virus, especially para-influenza
Onset	Rapid, acute (<24 h)	1–3 days; gradual with URI
Appearance	Toxic, pale, shocky, drooling, dysphagic, sits forward with mouth open; respiratory distress with retractions	Less toxic, no drooling
Signs and symptoms	Usually no cough Fever higher than 39°C (> 102°F)	Croupy cough Fever less than 39°C (<102°F)
	Inspiratory stridor Sore throat	Inspiratory stridor

Pathophysiology The vocal cords, subglottic tissue, trachea, bronchi, and bronchioles are all involved in the inflammatory exudative process. Edema of the subglottic area, however, causes the characteristic inspiratory stridor and makes the greatest contribution to obstruction of the airway.

Typically the child at first has what appears to be a mild upper respiratory infection. The disease progresses to a characteristic barking or brassy cough and hoarse voice. Often the child goes to sleep in fairly good condition and awakens later with inspiratory stridor.

Because air is sucked in through the narrowed subglottic area, the negative pressure on inspiration tends to narrow further the already compromised airway (like sucking on a plugged straw). Respiratory effort is increased. The child appears distressed, frightened, and anxious. Suprasternal, supraclavicular, and substernal retractions are common. The respiratory rate increases to 50 or more per min. Coarse rales may be heard on auscultation.

As the obstruction increases, so does hypoxemia. Cyanosis may develop when the Pa_{O_2} falls below 60 mmHg. Decreased perfusion and decreased ventilation can combine to produce respiratory failure in severe cases, making artificial ventilation necessary.

Medical management When arterial blood gases indicate hypoxemia, the child is given humidified oxygen to raise the Pa_{O_2}. Humidification is usually given by ultrasonic nebulizer to thin secretions (Fig. 25-7). Fluids are administered parenterally to improve hydration. Antibiotics are not useful in treating this viral infection unless a bacterial infection is superimposed upon it.

If the child is particularly fatigued and is experiencing respiratory distress, racemic epinephrine by IPPB may aid in decreasing stridor and retractions. Mechanical ventilation becomes necessary when (1) Pa_{CO_2} rises progressively (> 45 mmHg), (2) oxygen therapy does not improve hypoxemia, and (3) the child has copious secretions that cannot be mobilized by coughing.

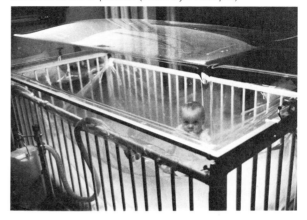

Figure 25-7 14-month-old child with group. Note ultrasonic nebulizer at left of picture. (*Photo by P. Sheps.*)

Nursing management Although most children with croup can be managed at home with increased humidity, fluids, antipyretics, and measures to decrease anxiety, some need hospitalization. The child and the parents will be frightened and anxious, and need calm reassurance.

Assessment of the child's respiratory status must be made frequently by monitoring color, cyanosis, arterial blood gases, respiratory pattern and difficulty, and vital signs. Often the mist or croup tent prevents soothing of the child by the parents, thus adding to the discomfort. The child also needs to be kept dry and prevented from being chilled in the moist environment.

An increase in heart rate and a decrease in respiratory rate and stridor may signal respiratory failure. If assisted ventilation is necessary, measures described earlier become part of the child's nursing care plan. A nursing care plan for a child with laryngotracheobronchitis is presented at the end of this chapter.

Some very young children will continue to have periodic bouts of croup that always occur at night. The child does not have a fever but may have been exposed to excessive cold or may have a history of allergies. Parents learn to cope with stridor and respiratory distress by providing cool or warm humidity at night. Parents need to know that for quick relief they can sit with their child near the shower, where forceful, hot water is producing steam. This procedure may prevent a trip to the emergency room.

Bronchitis *Bronchitis* refers to a condition in which the child has a chronic nonproductive cough. It is unusual for bronchitis to occur alone in children. Usually it follows croup, pneumonia, or an upper respiratory infection. Increasing humidity at night, lozenges and cough drops, postural drainage, and expectorants may be helpful.

Bronchiectasis Whenever a child develops a chronic cough that produces sputum, *bronchiectasis* may be present. It can follow repeated cases of pneumonia, measles, cystic fibrosis, or aspiration of a foreign body.

In bronchiectasis, saccular deformities of the bronchi and bronchioles develop. Secretions accumulate within them. Sputum is grayish-white. Usually the diagnosis is made by bronchoscopy. A positive throat culture should be treated with an appropriate antibiotic. Mist and postural drainage are helpful. If the disease continues to progress, surgery to remove the diseased area of the lung may be indicated.

Bronchiolitis *Bronchiolitis* is an infection of the lower respiratory tract caused by the respiratory syncytial virus (RSV). It is seen most commonly during the winter in infants under 1 to 2 years, especially aged 2 to 6 months.

Pathophysiology Initially the infant may appear to have an upper respiratory infection with a watery nasal discharge. The infection of the bronchiolar mucosa soon causes inflammation, edema, and production of mucosal exudates that lead to obstruction of the small and medium airways.

Air passes into the air sacs but becomes trapped, eventually causing overinflation. This condition leads to obstructive emphysema and patchy areas of atelectasis. Because of the increase in airway resistance, the infant has prolonged and difficult expirations.

The heart rate increases. Respiratory rates may go as high as 80 per minute. Wheezing and rhonchi are heard on auscultation. The baby may have a troublesome, distressing cough. The chest takes on a barrel shape, and retractions are common. The infant appears anxious and restless. Bronchiolitis will often get worse before it gets better, lasting 7 to 14 days.

Nursing management Basic supportive care is essential for these infants. Usually humidified oxygen is necessary to increase the PaO$_2$. Elevating the head of the bed 30° or placing the baby in a padded seat makes the work of breathing easier. Aerosol therapy may also be used occasionally. Sedation is avoided for fear of depressing respiration.

During the acute phase, intravenous fluids are necessary to maintain hydration. Arterial blood gases and pH are measured and the respiratory status is monitored frequently. See Chap. 5 for a nursing care plan for a child with bronchiolitis.

Because RSV epidemics can occur in hospitals, especially among chronically ill children, it is imperative to isolate these infants from others and to use strict hand-washing techniques. Any respiratory equipment used must be thoroughly cleaned before being used with another child.

Ninety-eight percent of infants with bronchiolitis will recover. Those who die may have underlying heart disease or another chronic problem. It is not unusual for some infants to have repeated chest problems with attacks of wheezing after recovery. A few go on to develop asthma.

Pneumonia When a child develops pneumonia, he or she has symptoms of respiratory tract involvement as well as those of a general infection. Pneumonia is more common in infants and young children but can occur at any age. It is caused by bacteria, viruses, *Mycoplasma pneumoniae*, or aspiration of foreign material.

Pathophysiology Pneumonia is a generalized inflammation and infection of the lung parenchyma. It may be disseminated throughout the lungs (bronchopneumonia) or confined to a specific area (lobar or lobular). An elevation in white blood cells, characteristic infiltration on x-rays, and culture of organisms from the trachea or blood all help in the diagnostic process.

In *pneumococcal* pneumonia, the alveoli become edematous and filled with inflammatory cells. Then, during the stage of *red hepatization*, serum and red blood cells enter the alveoli, thereby interfering with gas exchange. The stage of *gray hepatization* follows when leukocytes and fibrin fill the alveoli. Resolution occurs when the inflammatory reaction is over.

Viral pneumonia is seen in children of all ages. It has a gradual onset, often after an upper respiratory infection. The child develops a dry, hacking, nonproductive cough, has a slight increase in respiratory rate, and appears mildly ill. Abdominal distension is often present due to air swallowing and paralytic ileus. The child's temperature ranges from 37.8 to 40°C (100 to 104°F). On auscultation, inspiratory crepitant rales and expiratory rhonchi may be heard. X-rays reveal infiltration. Treatment of viral pneumonia is symptomatic.

Bacterial pneumonia, in contrast to viral pneumonia, usually has a sudden onset. The child appears very ill with a high fever, respiratory distress, and sometimes chest pain. The child may be restless and apprehensive. Circumoral cyanosis, retractions, tachypnea, and tachycardia indicate the seriousness of the illness.

Most bacterial pneumonias are caused by the pneumococci, but *Staphylococcus*, *Streptococcus* group A, and *Haemophilus influenzae* are also culprits. See Table 25-8 for a comparison of the last three.

Ten to twenty percent of hospital admissions for pneumonia involve the *M. pneumoniae* organism that causes atypical primary pneumonia. Usually school-age children are affected. Signs and symptoms include fever, chills, malaise, myalgia, anorexia, sore throat, and a dry, hacking cough that later becomes mucopurulent.

Medical management Children usually recover from viral pneumonias with supportive care at home. Bacterial pneumonias were a serious threat to a child's life before antibiotic therapy was developed. Pneumococcal pneumonia responds well to penicillin G. Erythromycin and cephalothin are also effective. For *M. pneumoniae*, erythromycin or tetracycline (in children over 7 years) is effective.

Antibiotics, fluids, antipyretics, and rest are the principal elements of care for children with pneumonia. For very young children, hospitalization may be more appropriate because of oxygen therapy, IVs, and variability in illness.

Because pneumonia is treated thoroughly and early, the complications of pneumothorax and empyema (accumulation of pus) do not occur as often as they once did. Nevertheless, a thoracentesis may be necessary to remove fluid or pus in the pleural cavity due to the infectious process. If purulent fluid is obtained, continuous closed-chest drainage is begun (see Chap. 26 for care of the patient with chest suction).

Signs of *pneumothorax*, the accumulation of air between the parietal and visceral layers of the pleura, include chest pain, difficulty in breathing, and cyanosis. Breath sounds are absent over the affected lung. With large amounts of air or fluid, there can be *mediastinal shift*—displacement of the heart, trachea, esophagus, vena cava, and aorta to the unaffected side. Arterial blood gases reveal a decreased Pa_{O_2}. Pulmonary function studies indicate a decrease in forced expiratory volume, vital capacity, and compliance. A thoracentesis must be done, a chest tube inserted, and a connection made to a closed-chest drainage system to allow reexpansion of the lung.

Nursing management As in other respiratory conditions, nursing care is directed toward support of vital functions and basic needs. With difficulty in breathing, oxygen therapy and cool

Table 25-8 Bacterial pneumonias*

Organism	Age	Signs and symptoms	Laboratory reports	Treatment
Staphylococcus	Under 1 year	History of furunculosis, recent hospitalization, or maternal breast abscess. Respiratory infection, upper or lower, for several days to 1 week followed by abrupt change—fever, cough, respiratory distress, tachypnea, grunting respirations, sternal and subcostal retractions, cyanosis, anxiety. Lethargic if undisturbed, irritable if roused. Pyopneumothorax, pneumatoceles, and empyema as clinical course progresses	WBC: normal range in young infant, 20,000/mm³ with predominant polymorphonuclear leukocytes in older infants. Tracheal aspiration and/or pleural tap culture positive. X-ray: patchy infiltration or dense (bronchopneumonia or lobar)	Symptomatic and supportive. Oxygen. Semi-Fowler's position. Parenteral fluids during acute phase. Methicillin or penicillin G for 3 weeks IV or IM. Thoracentesis. Closed chest drainage with extensive involvement for 5–7 days. Hospitalized 6–10 weeks
Streptococcus group A	3–5 years	Mild prodromal symptoms followed by sudden onset of high fever, chills, respiratory distress. Clinical course similar to staphylococcal. Complications: empyema and bacterial foci in bones and joints	WBC elevated with polymorphonuclear leukocytes predominating. ASO titer elevated. Positive culture. X-ray: disseminated infiltration	Symptomatic and supportive. Penicillin G. Thoracentesis. Closed drainage
Haemophilus influenzae	Infants and young children	Mild or severe. Insidious onset. Clinical course subacute and prolonged, of several weeks' duration. Signs and symptoms similar to pneumococcal. Signs and symptoms in young infants associated with bacteremia and emphysema. Complications: bacteremia, pericarditis, cellulitis, empyema, meningitis, pyarthrosis	Bacteremia. Positive cultures. Moderate leukocytosis with lymphopenia. X-ray: lobar consolidation	Symptomatic and supportive. Ampicillin

642

* From G. Scipien et al., *Comprehensive Pediatric Nursing*, McGraw-Hill, New York, 1979. Used with permission.

mist are essential. Lying on the affected side may reduce discomfort from pleural rubbing by splinting the chest.

Antipyretics are used as necessary. The respiratory status is monitored frequently. Usually young children are kept NPO until their respiratory status is improved. It is extremely important to regulate fluids carefully, monitor intake and output, and measure specific gravity.

Reassurance and reduction of anxiety also help to improve oxygenation. Often the child will fear being alone while awake. The strange environment becomes less frightening when a parent remains with the child.

Tuberculosis *Primary tuberculosis* refers to the initial infection with *Mycobacterium tuberculosis* (Mtb). After the primary infection occurs in the lung, any one of the following things can happen.

1. The infection can heal. This happens in more than 90 percent of those infected. Hypersensitivity to the tuberculin organism then occurs, causing a positive tuberculin skin test. A fraction of 1 percent of children entering school, but more than 50 percent of persons over 60 years, show evidence of infection, a positive tuberculin skin test.
2. The primary infection can develop into active disease. Active disease is usually discovered through a positive skin test or because of a history of exposure to a person with tuberculosis.
3. The primary infection heals but months or years later becomes reactivated. Factors that predispose to reactivation tuberculosis include menarche, poor nutrition, debilitating disease, diabetes, pregnancy, cancer, and steroid or immunosuppressive therapy.[16] About 30,000 people in the United States develop active or reactivation tuberculosis each year.[17]

Pathophysiology The tubercle bacillus is carried on an airborne droplet nucleus produced when an infected person coughs, sneezes, sings, talks, or laughs. Because these droplets are so small, they can be kept airborne by normal room air currents. These droplet nuclei then enter the body through the respiratory tract in almost all cases. Rarely, the Mtb enters through the GI tract or through a break in the skin or mucous membrane.

Persons with tuberculosis also shed larger particles containing bacilli that either fall to the floor or, if inhaled, are trapped in the mucous blanket of the upper airway and expectorated or swallowed. The tubercle bacillus is readily killed by heat, drying, or ultraviolet light. Therefore, infection is not normally transmitted by fomites.

Before milk pasteurization, cows infected with *M. bovis* were a significant source of tuberculosis in milk-drinking children. In developed countries, dairy herds are now carefully monitored and controlled for infection.

When tubercle bacilli reach the lungs in a susceptible host, they lodge in a respiratory bronchiole or alveolus. During the incubation period of 3 to 5 weeks, the bacilli multiply. They spread through the lymph channels to the lymph nodes and into the circulation. Systemic reticuloendothelial tissues usually destroy the disseminated organisms. The alveolar macrophages are the body's first line of defense and may be able to decrease the concentration of the Mtb in the alveoli.

Locally there is an inflammatory reaction resembling pneumonia. Edema, fluid, and white blood cells surround the bacilli. Within 2 to 10 weeks the T lymphocyte system is activated, producing cellular immunity.

Once the infected person acquires active immunity, further multiplication of the organism is limited unless primary pulmonary tuberculosis develops after the incubation period. Children, especially those under 2, are at higher risk for development of active disease. In most people, however, the lesion is walled off and healed by calcification. The individual then has a positive skin test and may have a positive x-ray showing a calcified, healed lesion and regional lymph node involvement—the *primary complex* or *Ghon complex*.

Within weeks or years after the initial infection, reactivation tuberculosis can develop in up to 10 percent of the infected people as dormant bacilli begin to replicate. Since the tubercle bacilli are aerobic organisms, they can live in the apices of the lungs, lying dormant until the body is stressed in one of the ways described earlier. During reactivation tuberculosis, there is necrosis of lung tissue and production of liquids containing large numbers of bacilli that are then easily spread throughout the lungs and the environment.

Diagnosis

TUBERCULIN SKIN TEST The single most valuable way to diagnose tuberculosis in children is through the skin test. When the antigen (culture extracts of tuberculin) is injected intradermally, an area of induration results in sensitized persons. The test is done using a tuberculin solution made from old tuberculin (OT) or from purified protein derivative stabilized with Tween 80 (PPD-T). The solution is injected under the skin in the volar or dorsal surface of the forearm via a needle (the Mantoux test), jet gun, or multiple puncture. The jet gun and multiple-puncture techniques are more likely to be used in screening rather than in diagnosis because they are not as reliable as the intracutaneous injection. Table 25-9 describes the interpretation of skin test reactions. A positive skin test in a child under 1 year indicates active disease and in a 1- to 3-year-old is highly suggestive of active disease. Currently one would expect a negative test to be *unreliable* in anyone who has a febrile illness, measles, or sarcoidosis; has just had a live virus vaccination or overwhelming miliary or pulmonary tuberculosis; or has received cortisone preparations or immunosuppressive drugs.

CHEST X-RAY X-rays are generally used only in tuberculin-positive children to look for the presence of a primary complex. The x-ray is often diagnostic in reactivation tuberculosis. Signs indicating disease include infiltration, fibrosis, calcification, cavity formation, and pleural thickening.

DEMONSTRATION OF THE TUBERCLE BACILLUS Diagnosis of tuberculosis is confirmed by culturing the Mtb organism from sputum or other body fluids. Since the culture grows slowly, as many as 8 weeks may be required before a culture is considered negative.

Children, because they are poor coughers, generally swallow their secretions, making sputum specimens difficult to get. Often gastric or bronchial washings are needed. It is important to get at least three specimens prior to beginning treatment. In older children, sputum may also be obtained by aerosol induction using hypertonic saline. Because mycobacterial disease can locate in any part of the body, urine, cerebrospinal fluid, pleural fluid, pus, or bone marrow biopsy specimens may be collected.

Once specimens are obtained, a smear is stained to look for acid-fast bacilli. If it is positive, the number of organisms present is significant. The smear is not diagnostic, however, because there are acid-fast bacilli other than Mtb. The culture allows precise identification of the organism and drug susceptibility testing.

Signs and symptoms Usually primary tuberculosis in children is discovered because the child has been in close contact with an affected adult. The clinical picture is variable. The child may be asymptomatic or may show any or all of the following: fatigue, anorexia, low-grade fever, irregular menses, night sweats (older children), and weight loss. Pulmonary signs and symptoms include an increasingly severe cough, upper respiratory infection, production of sputum, and a dull aching or tightness in the chest.

Extension of tuberculosis into other body systems causes a variety of symptoms. In *miliary tuberculosis* the organisms erode the blood ves-

Table 25-9 Interpretation of skin test reactions

	Positive reaction	Doubtful reaction	Negative reaction
Intracutaneous Mantoux test			
0.1 ml (5 TU) PPD tuberculin or jet injection tests (read 48–72 h after injection)	10 mm or more of induration	5–9 mm of induration	0–4 mm of induration
Multiple puncture test			
	Vesiculation	2 mm or more of induration	<2 mm of induration

* From "Diagnostic Standards and Classification of Tuberculosis and Other Mycobacterial Diseases," American Lung Association, New York, 1974, pp. 17–19.

Table 25-10 Categories of infection caused by *Mycobacterium tuberculosis**

Category	Exposure	Infection	Therapy
0	None; tuberculosis test negative	None	None
I	Tuberculosis exposure; tuberculosis test negative	No evidence	Primary prophylaxis for children under 6 years for 3 months after contact broken. Repeat tuberculosis test in 10–15 weeks
II	Positive Mantoux test	Tuberculosis infection *without* disease; negative chest x-ray; negative bacteriological studies	Treat all persons less than 35 years with primary prophylaxis for 12 months
III	Positive Mantoux test; positive x-ray	Tuberculosis infection *with* disease	Current tuberculosis is treated with two first-line drugs for 6 to 18 months or longer

* Adapted from American Thoracic Society, "Treatment of Mycobacterial Disease," *Am. Rev. Respir. Dis.* **115**(1), (1977).

sels in the lungs, giving them a "snowstorm" appearance on x-ray. Miliary tuberculosis is associated with osteomyelitis, arthritis, meningitis, and infection in the brain, kidneys, and GI tract. *Tuberculous meningitis* is characterized by headache, vomiting, and other signs of increasing intracranial pressure. These serious complications of tuberculosis are fatal in children if untreated. These children are very sick and require hospitalization and intensive treatment.

In *glandular tuberculosis* there is extension into regional lymph nodes, often the cervical nodes or tonsils. The nodes become tender and immobile and may drain externally.

Medical management and treatment All children under 6 years who are exposed to someone in their home with tuberculosis should receive primary prophylaxis with isoniazid (INH) for 3 months. A classification of patients for treatment is outlined in Table 25-10.

Infected children or adults (less than 35 years) are treated with INH for 12 months because the risk of developing tuberculosis later on exceeds that of 1 year's treatment with INH. INH prevents the progression of the infection to active disease by eliminating the Mtb organism from the body.

If active tuberculosis exists, the individual is treated with a *minimum of two first-line drugs* to which the organism is *sensitive.* First-line drugs (Table 25-11) are effective, less toxic, easy to administer, and usually less expensive than second-line drugs. Second-line drugs are more likely to be used with drug-resistant strains of Mtb. Patients receiving them must be watched much more closely for side effects. Occasionally three drugs will be used initially—especially in drug-resistant or systemic tuberculosis.

Chemotherapy reduces the number of infectious droplet nuclei very quickly. Within 2 weeks after treatment begins, patients are usually noninfectious. In addition, drug therapy reduces sputum production and cough. Since children are such poor coughers, they are unlikely to be very contagious unless they have advanced disease.

Oral medications are given on an empty stomach. Normally drugs are taken once a day, but some treatment regimens are successful with twice weekly dosages.

Because the single most important cause of unsuccessful treatment is failure to take medications regularly, a shortened period of daily doses or twice weekly doses may be helpful. For unreliable patients or families, the nurse may have to visit to administer the drug. Taking medications irregularly encourages the development of resistant organisms. Patient and family

Table 25-11 Treatment of mycobacterial disease in adults and children*

First-line drugs	Daily dosage	Most common side effects	Monitoring tests for side effects	Remarks
Isoniazid is the drug of choice in primary prophylaxis	5–10 mg/kg for child Up to 300 mg PO or IM Younger children need 20 mg/kg per day or 30 mg/kg per day with tuberculous meningitis. Can be combined with another first-line drug and given twice a week	Peripheral neuritis, hepatitis, hypersensitivity	SGOT/SGPT	Bacteriocidal. Pyridoxine (vitamin B₆) is given to prevent and/or treat peripheral neuritis. Monitor monthly for symptoms of hepatitis. Contraindicated in previous untoward reaction; patient taking diphenylhydantoin; daily use of alcohol; pregnancy
Ethambutol (used with isoniazid—most commonly for 18 months)	15–25 mg/kg PO	Optic neuritis, skin rash	Visual acuity and red-green color discrimination	Use with caution in younger children when eye testing is not feasible. Optic neuritis is reversible with discontinuance of drug—very rare at 15 mg/kg. Rash, GI upset, malaise. Do not give aminosalicylic acid within 8 h of drug
Rifampin (used with isoniazid)	10–20 mg/kg up to 600 mg PO	Hepatitis, febrile reaction, purpura (rare)	SGOT/SGPT	Bacteriocidal. Orange urine color. Negates effect of birth control pills
Streptomycin	15–20 mg/kg up to 1 g IM	Eighth-nerve damage, nephrotoxicity	Audiogram, vestibular function, BUN, creatinine	Use with caution in older patients or with renal disease

Second-Line Drugs (more toxic than first-line)

Drug	Dose	Toxicity	Tests for toxicity	Remarks
Viomycin (VM)	15–30 mg/kg up to 1 g IM	Auditory toxicity, nephrotoxicity	Audiogram, vestibular function, BUN, creatinine	Use with caution in older patients. Rarely used with renal disease
Capreomycin (CM)	15–30 mg/kg up to 1 g IM	VIIIth nerve damage, nephrotoxicity	Audiogram, vestibular function, BUN, creatinine	Use with caution in older patients. Rarely used with renal disease. Not for pediatric use
Kanamycin (KM)	15–30 mg/kg up to 1 g IM	Auditory toxicity, nephrotoxicity	Audiogram, vestibular function, BUN, creatinine	Use with caution in older patients. Rarely used with renal disease. Avoid ethacrynic acid, furosemide, mannitol, mercurial diuretics
Ethionamide (ETA)	15–30 mg/kg up to 1 g PO	GI disturbance, hepatotoxicity, depression	SGOT/SGPT	Divided dose may help GI side effects
Pyrazinamide (PZA)	15–30 mg/kg up to 2 g PO	Hyperuricemia (gout), hepatotoxicity	Uric acid, SGOT/SGPT	Combination with an aminoglycoside is bactericidal
Para-amino salicylic acid (PAS)	150 mg/kg up to 2 g PO	GI disturbance, hypersensitivity (fever, rash, etc.); sodium load, hepatotoxicity; may be used with isoniazid in very young children	SGOT/SGPT	GI side effects very frequent, making cooperation difficult
Cycloserine	10–20 mg/kg up to 1 g PO	Psychosis, personality changes, convulsions, rash	Psychological testing; drug blood levels if poor renal function	Very difficult drug to use; side effects may be blocked by pyridoxine, ataractic agents, or anticonvulsant drugs

* Adapted from American Thoracic Society, "Treatment of Mycobacterial Disease," *Am. Rev. Respir. Dis.* **115**(1), (1977).

education becomes extremely important in promoting compliance with the treatment and follow-up plan.

Prevention The best way to prevent tuberculosis is to identify people with the infection and then treat them. Those living in close proximity to the infected person should be tested and treated if appropriate. A circle of contacts is then tested; once all are negative, contact follow-up ceases.

The reduced incidence of tuberculosis and the current low risk for infection have made routine screening of the general population unjustifiable. As the incidence of tuberculosis decreases, however, the tuberculin test becomes more valuable as a screening test. In groups of people over 50, the chest x-ray is also used for screening because so many are positive skin testers.

Screening for tuberculosis is now recommended only where there is a high risk for developing tuberculosis in a group or where a sporadic case would represent a significant hazard. It is directed toward those who have not been identified as having the disease. Current guidelines suggest that screening be done when one or more of the following conditions exist:[18]

1. The group has a high rate of tuberculosis disease (example: Mexican immigrant workers).
2. The group has a high rate of tuberculosis infection and is at risk for developing the disease (persons over 50 years, Asian-American immigrants).
3. The people are in an environment where they are at high risk for becoming infected (health care or correctional institution workers).
4. The people, although at low risk for getting tuberculosis, have the potential of infecting young children or others with a suppressed immune response if they develop the disease (teachers in schools, day-care centers, or any resident facility for youth; personnel in acute or long-term health care facilities or correctional institutions).

As with any screening program, services for follow-up and treatment must be available to all involved.

Bacillus Calmette-Guérin (BCG) vaccination, which contains antigens, confers definite but only partial protection by preventing extension of the original infection to active disease. It is recommended for tuberculin-test negative children known to be exposed to adults with active or recently arrested disease.[19] It is also given to newborns of tuberculous mothers. BCG is used much more extensively in countries with a high incidence of tuberculosis than in the United States.

Nursing management Isolation of the child with tuberculosis is necessary only if he or she has a productive cough that cannot be made safe for others. The child should be taught to cover the mouth and nose with tissues when coughing. These tissues should be flushed down the toilet or placed in a paper bag and then burned. These protective measures should be used with any patient with a productive cough. The effectiveness of masks is questionable.

Ideally, room air is ventilated outside and not recirculated. Ultraviolet lights in the ceiling will kill bacilli in circulating droplets and are often used in sputum-collecting areas.

Unless the child is severely ill, hospitalization is rarely necessary. If the child has draining fistulas or cavitating tuberculosis, appropriate isolation techniques become necessary (Chap. 17).

Because motivation is such an important factor in continuing chemotherapy for the prescribed time, enthusiastic and encouraging nursing care is a key factor. It is imperative that parents and children understand and accept the importance of continuing treatment. Nurses must understand tuberculosis if they are to teach the family about its prevention and treatment ramifications.

The nurse must provide continuing support throughout the diagnostic and treatment program. It is helpful to the family if they can develop their own system of reminders to take the drug daily. Obstacles to clinic visits or to obtaining drug refills should be removed. The family should be monitored through home visits, clinic visits, and by telephone calls to follow up treatment and to observe for adverse drug effects. Families need to know what side effects to watch for and then must be interviewed monthly.

The need for adequate rest, a nutritious diet, and general health promotion measures should be stressed. Cigarette usage should be discouraged.

Any case of tuberculosis must be reported to the local health department by the physician. Although the private physician may manage the child's and family's treatment, the public health department is responsible for follow-up investigation of all contacts. In addition, the public health department is responsible for (1) education, (2) community screening programs, and (3) clinics for diagnosis, treatment, follow-up, and preventive treatment.

The community health nurse becomes involved with (1) contact investigation and follow-up and (2) case follow-up. Case follow-up includes teaching the patient and family about transmission and treatment of tuberculosis, helping with the chemotherapy program, and providing support and counseling.

Cystic fibrosis

Cystic fibrosis (CF) is characterized by widespread dysfunction of exocrine (mucous, salivary, and sweat-producing) glands. Chronic pulmonary disease, pancreatic enzyme deficiency, and abnormally high sweat electrolytes are manifestations of the disease. In the past, children with CF had little hope of living through adolescence. Today, with improved treatment and diagnostic tests, the mean age of survival is 19 years, with many persons living productive adult lives.

Incidence

CF is the most common lethal genetic disease of children, adolescents, and young adults; 1 out of every 15 to 20 people (males and females) carries the autosomal recessive gene for CF. The chance that two carriers will marry is 1:400.

Because of the carrier rate, CF occurs in 1 child out of every 1000 to 1600 live births. Although CF occurs mainly in Caucasians, there have also been cases in blacks, American Indians, and Orientals.

Parents of a CF child are both carriers of the gene for CF. With each pregnancy their chances of producing a child with CF are 25 percent, or one out of four. The risk for producing a carrier is 50 percent (two out of four) and the probability of producing an unaffected child is 25 percent (Table 25-12).

Pathophysiology

The widespread dysfunction of the exocrine glands causes them to secrete a thick, sticky mucus instead of normal thin mucus. This leads to systemic nutritional and metabolic alterations, progressive pulmonary disease, and elevated sweat sodium and chloride concentrations. The disease can be present in varying degrees, depending on the severity of organ involvement.

The child with CF is essentially normal at birth. Soon poor weight gain and malnutrition provide evidence of pancreatic involvement. Pulmonary changes develop gradually, and with appropriate treatment they are initially reversible. Early diagnosis is essential in preventing these complications.

The most reliable diagnostic test for CF is the sweat test. During the test, sweat glands of the arms and legs are stimulated by electrodes and pilocarpine. The sweat produced is collected

Table 25-12 Risk of producing a child with cystic fibrosis*

One parent	Other parent	Risk of CF in each pregnancy, ratio
With no CF history	With no CF history	1:1000–1:1600
With no CF history	With first cousin having CF	1:320
With no CF history	With aunt or uncle having CF	1:240
With no CF history	With sibling have CF	1:120
With no CF history	With CF child by previous marriage (carrier)	1:80
With no CF history	With parent having CF	1:80
With no CF history	With CF (each child will be a carrier, however)	1:40
With sibling having CF	With sibling having CF	1:9
With CF child	With CF child	1:4

* Adapted from Robert Hoekelman, Saul Blatman, Philip Brunell, Stanford Friedman, and Henry Seidel, *Principles of Pediatrics*, McGraw-Hill, New York, 1978.

and analyzed for chloride and sodium. Individuals with CF will have elevated levels (two to five times normal) at birth and all their lives.

In addition to a positive sweat test, the diagnosis of CF is established by objective evidence of pulmonary involvement, pancreatic involvement, or a positive family history. Signs and symptoms of CF include:

1. Failure to thrive (poor weight gain despite good intake)
2. A large amount of foul-smelling, fatty-appearing stool (malabsorption)
3. Rectal prolapse
4. Frequent cough, bronchitis, or pneumonia
5. A salty taste to the skin (a mother may notice this when she kisses her infant)

Because of these symptoms, CF is often confused with allergies, chronic respiratory infection, celiac disease, or failure to thrive.

Recent research by Breslow and others on cultured fibroblasts from CF patients and their parents and siblings showed a significant sodium-transport abnormality when compared to cells of normal subjects.[20] This test should be useful in identifying carriers of the CF gene in relatives of CF children.

The respiratory system Chronic changes in the upper respiratory system may cause chronic sinusitis and nasal polyps. Obstruction of the eustachian tubes can lead to chronic otitis media. Children with CF also tend to have an above-average incidence of allergies.

Chronic obstructive, infective pulmonary disease is the major cause of disability and death in children with CF. Progressive, irreversible pulmonary involvement is inevitable. It develops from the accumulation and retention of mucus in the airways. Mucus plugs lead to areas of overinflation and atelectasis in the lungs, impairing airflow.

Infection inevitably follows mucous obstruction. A vicious cycle results: infection → increased mucus production → inflammation→ further obstruction. Clearance of the airways is further inhibited.

Most infections are caused by *Staphylococcus aureus, H. influenzae,* or *Pseudomonas aeruginosa.* Infection with the mucoid strain of *Pseudomonas* is occurring more frequently in younger children and is almost impossible to eradicate with current antibiotic therapy.

Obstructive emphysema results from trapped air in the lung. Chronic, irreversible areas of bronchiectasis and abscesses result. Bronchiectasis is usually accompanied by bronchial artery hypertrophy and resulting hemoptysis. Overinflation with bleb formation, especially in the upper lobes of the lung, may lead to pneumothorax.

With the loss of gas exchange surface area, there is increased pulmonary insufficiency and respiratory failure. With severe pulmonary disease, pulmonary vascular resistance increases. The right side of the heart must work harder to pump blood through the lungs, leading to cardiac hypertrophy or failure (cor pulmonale). Signs of pulmonary involvement include (1) chronic productive cough; (2) enlargement of the thoracic cage (barrel chest); (3) increased respiratory rate; (4) use of accessory muscles of respiration; (5) clubbing of the ends of fingers and toes (Fig. 26-3); and (6) cyanosis.

Pancreas Mucous obstruction of the pancreatic ducts inhibits the flow of trypsin, lipase, and amylase (the digestive enzymes) to the duodenum. Malabsorption of food leads to poor weight gain and delays in growth and development. Stools are frequent, bulky, foul-smelling, and contain large amounts of fat (*steatorrhea*) and protein. The fat-soluble vitamins (A, D, E, and K) are poorly absorbed. Because of malabsorption, the child with CF often presents with a protruding belly, thin extremities, and poor muscle mass. With adequate treatment and improved nutrition, these signs resolve.

Pancreatic destruction caused by mucous obstruction and subsequent changes can lead to diabetes in the adolescent or young adult. CF children who develop diabetes are insulin dependent. The incidence of diabetes, however, is the same as in the rest of the population.

Liver Focal biliary cirrhosis of the liver can result from mucous obstruction of the bile ducts. A small percentage of patients with CF demonstrate abnormal liver function and clinical evidence of liver disease. Extensive liver involvement can result in portal hypertension, esophageal varices, GI hemorrhage, and ascites.

Intestine Meconium ileus is the earliest sign in 10 to 15 percent of babies with CF. Failure to pass the first stool is usually indicative of CF. Surgical correction is frequently required.

Mucus accumulation in the intestines can lead to bowel obstruction at any age. A mass is usually felt in the lower right quadrant of the abdomen. With appropriate medical treatment, surgical correction is rarely needed.

Abdominal pain is a common complaint of CF children. It is frequently caused by (1) undigested food due to failure to take pancreatic digestive enzymes; (2) intussusception of the small and large bowel; (3) partial obstruction by feces and mucus; (4) muscular soreness from coughing; (5) gallstones (10 percent of patients with CF over age 5 develop gallstones); and (6) subacute or chronic pancreatitis.

Rectal prolapse may result from poor control of steatorrhea. Once appropriate treatment is initiated and control of malabsorptive stools achieved, this problem is resolved. Surgical correction may be necessary in selected cases.

Reproductive system Generally males and females with CF have delayed development of secondary sex characteristics due to their chronic illness.

Ninety-nine percent of males are sterile. Mucous obstruction of the vas deferens prevents sperm from entering the semen. Sexual function is not impaired.

Females have decreased fertility as a result of thick cervical secretions. Menstrual irregularities and failure to ovulate due to poor nutritional status can further decrease fertility.

Sweat The rate of sweating is normal. The abnormally high concentration of sweat electrolytes usually poses no problem except in hot weather or during febrile episodes. Then excessive loss of electrolytes through increased sweating can lead to hyponatremia.

Treatment

Specific treatment for CF is not possible since the basic biochemical defect remains unknown. At the present time no cure exists, but medical advances, especially in the area of antibiotic therapy, have greatly increased the life expectancy for patients with CF. Since patients are ill from complications, treatment is aimed at con-

trol and prevention of these complications. Control of the pulmonary obstructive process, pulmonary infection, and pancreatic and nutritional deficiencies are the primary objectives of the treatment in CF.

Pulmonary therapy Since pulmonary complications account for the majority of disability and death in CF, successful treatment must focus on the maintenance of good pulmonary hygiene. Conventional pulmonary therapy includes the use of (1) mist tent, (2) aerosol inhalation, (3) postural drainage, (4) antibiotics, and (5) physical exercise. Controversy exists regarding these different aspects of therapy. Research is aimed at discovering more effective and less time-consuming methods of clearing the airways of obstructive mucus.

Mist tent The mist tent is designed to increase humidification of inspired air and to help thin mucus secretions by depositing water particles in the respiratory tract. Patients who use a mist tent sleep in it every night. To be effective, the mist cloud should be so dense that the child is barely visible. The usual mist tent solution is a combination of propylene glycol and distilled water. Because of the risk of mold and bacterial growth, the use of the tent is controversial. Proper care and cleaning of equipment is imperative if the mist tent is to be used safely and effectively. Many physicians feel that there is no clinical evidence of benefit from its use and are no longer prescribing it.

Aerosol inhalation Aerosol therapy is designed to thin and liquefy the thick bronchial secretions, thereby improving ventilation of the lungs and oxygenation of arterial blood. Medications used include bronchodilators, mucolytic agents, and antibiotics (see Table 25-3). Aerosol therapy is used both prophylactically and therapeutically on a daily basis prior to postural drainage. If needed, it may be used as frequently as every 4 h. Children 5 years and under receive aerosol therapy via a face mask. Usually children over 5 years are able to mouth-breathe totally and can receive the treatment via a mouthpiece. The ventilatory pattern should be slow, with moderately deep breathing and breath-holding at the end of inspiration to ensure deposition and retention of the aerosol. Presently, the use of daily aerosol therapy is also controversial. Some physicians prescribe it only during the acute phase of illness.

Postural drainage Postural drainage is an essential part of pulmonary therapy in CF. Its purpose is to (1) increase sputum expectoration and thereby reopen clogged airways and (2) improve ventilation by decreasing bronchial obstruction. This is accomplished through the use of physical maneuvers (percussion and vibration) and gravity, which stimulate the movement of the thick bronchial secretions toward the large airways. The patient is then able to cough up and expectorate the thick mucus. The frequency of postural drainage depends on the extent of pulmonary involvement. It is usually done one to two times daily. Postural drainage should be done at least 1 h after eating to avoid nausea and vomiting.

Older children with CF are usually able to perform certain portions of postural drainage on themselves. This should be encouraged to promote independence. Mechanical percussors and vibrators can be used when assistance with postural drainage is not available or to promote self-care. By adolescence children should be responsible for a good share of their care.

Antibiotics Antibiotics are used both prophylactically and therapeutically for treatment and control of pulmonary infection in CF. Many patients are routinely placed on prophylactic antibiotics (usually sulfa drugs) to decrease the incidence of pulmonary infection. All patients are placed on antibiotic therapy for treatment of specific organisms cultured out of their sputum. Sometimes antibiotics are given by aerosol to treat especially difficult pulmonary infections even though their usefulness remains questionable. The child's immunity to disease may be increased when antibiotics are not used prophylactically.

Physical exercise The value of physical exercise cannot be overemphasized. The patient with CF should be encouraged to be as physically active as possible. Exercise loosens mucus, helps remove it from the lungs, strengthens respiratory muscles, improves pulmonary function, and decreases pulmonary artery pressure. A form of aerobic exercise should be done on a daily basis.

Breathing exercises help establish normal patterns of breathing, strengthen respiratory muscles, and remove mucus from the lungs. The use of forced expiratory breathing has proven extremely beneficial in avoiding mucus retention and obstruction (see Table 25-13). This breathing technique should be done in conjunction with postural drainage and also practiced several times throughout the day.

A few words need to be said about coughing. The cough is the CF patient's best friend, for without coughing, mucus is not expectorated and remains in the lungs to obstruct airways and cause infection. The patient with CF needs to be encouraged to cough effectively throughout the day. School-age children often stifle their cough in school and in public. They need to learn that coughing is not a source of embarrassment but a natural mechanism working to keep them healthy and well.

Nutritional therapy Nutrition is of extreme importance in CF. A well-nourished child will cope better physically with pulmonary disease. A major objective for the child, therefore, is the achievement of an optimal nutritional state. A well-balanced diet with increased caloric intake is needed to offset malabsorptive losses due to pancreatic enzyme deficiencies. Dietary intake is balanced with pancreatic enzyme supplementation to achieve adequate absorption and digestion of food. Nutritional therapy for the patient with CF consists of (1) pancreatic digestive enzyme supplements, (2) vitamin supplements, and (3) a high-calorie, high-protein diet.

Pancreatic digestive enzyme supplementation The pancreatic digestive enzymes replace absent

Table 25-13 Forced expiratory breathing technique

Purpose: To force mucus out of the small airways

Instruct the child to:
1. Take in an average breath
2. Using *force*, breathe out *all* the air in the lungs
3. Squeeze the sides of the chest with the arms while breathing out
4. Then do relaxed diaphragmatic breathing (The child will need to cough to expectorate the mucus produced.)

This procedure should be used only one or two times per sitting, as it can be very tiring. It is used with postural drainage and three to four times during the day.

digestive enzymes so that food can be adequately digested and absorbed. The amount of supplementation taken depends upon the frequency, amount, and consistency of stool output. The patient is placed on a dosage that will control steatorrhea and limit stool frequency to one to two times per day. There are three different brands of pancreatic digestive enzymes available: (1) Viokase (the mildest form), (2) Cotazyme (available in packets, powder, and capsules), and (3) Pancrease (an enteric coated preparation which acts in the intestine). Pancreatic digestive enzymes must be taken with all meals and snacks. Bile salts may be added to promote digestion of fat. Signs and symptoms of inadequate pancreatic enzyme replacement are (1) abdominal cramping and distension, (2) poor weight gain despite good intake, (3) frequent, foul-smelling, fatty stools, and (4) rectal prolapse.

Pancreatic digestive enzymes are usually mixed in applesauce (a good vehicle that is not easily liquefied by the enzymes) before administration to infants and toddlers. It is important to apply petroleum jelly around the mouth before giving pancreatic enzymes to this age group to avoid skin breakdown. School-age children may not want to take their pancreatic enzymes while eating with friends.

Digestive enzymes should be increased to match increased intake. Currently, many CF children, especially adolescents, are not required to adhere to a rigid diet low in fats. Instead they are taught to take the needed amount of enzymes as necessary with their meals or snacks.

Sometimes schools do not want children to use medications without supervision. The child may be forced to take the enzymes or other medications at the office of the principal or nurse. Obviously this makes it difficult to take the enzyme at the recommended time in the middle of a meal. In addition, it isolates the child even further from his or her peers. A method should be worked out whereby children can manage their own medications at the most appropriate time and in the most convenient way.

Vitamin supplementation Vitamin supplements are used to correct vitamin deficiencies due to malabsorption. The usual vitamins supplemented are A, E, and K. Water-soluble preparations of vitamins A, D, and E are used. Some patients are also placed on vitamin C for control of *Pseudomonas* infections in the lung.

Diet Diet should be high-calorie, high-protein, and well balanced. Restriction of fat intake is sometimes required and depends on the degree of fat intolerance. Rigid fat restriction should be avoided. A 50 to 100 percent increase in calories and a protein intake of two to two and a half times above the normal requirement for age is recommended. Between-meal snacks are usually necessary to avoid excessive hunger and to satisfy above-normal intake requirements. Often nutritional supplements are needed for weight gain in patients with severe pancreatic dysfunction.

Infants are placed on predigested formulas such as Pregestimil or Probana. Some infants may need 28 cal per ounce of formula to ensure adequate weight gain. Breast-fed infants will need enzyme supplementation. Once solid foods are added, usually meat and fruit initially, the pancreatic digestive enzymes are needed. Cereals should be given in reduced amounts because they provide a less desirable source of calories than protein.

Overall, it is important to make foods attractive and mealtimes pleasant. The development of good dietary habits is essential for the well-being of the patient with CF.

Psychosocial aspects

Like any chronic illness, CF makes a significant psychosocial impact upon the patient and family. The stresses of daily therapy, life-style changes, the financial burden of the cost of medical care, and the constant threat of a limited lifespan can prove overwhelming.

The diagnosis of CF in a child produces feelings of shock, despair, and guilt in the parents. They must cope with the reality that their child has a serious, life-threatening, chronic disease. Parents feel guilty because the disease is genetic. Reassurance is needed that both parents carry the abnormal gene for CF and that mass screening for detecting carriers is not currently feasible.

Caring for the child with CF will make significant changes in the parents' life-style. Parents must share the burden of prescribed daily therapy. Feelings of anger and hostility may develop when one parent becomes the primary caregiver. A breakdown in communication can result, having a profound long-range effect on the marriage. The parents should be encouraged to be open and honest in talking with each other about CF and its effect on them and their life-style.

A consistent problem for the parents is the difficulty of obtaining relief from the daily cares and regimen CF imposes. Training babysitters, extended family members, or friends in chest physical therapy and utilizing community resources for assistance are beneficial in providing the opportunity for needed relief and time away from home.

Parent-support groups provide an opportunity to share experiences and exchange ideas in problem solving. Contact with another parent at the time of diagnosis also proves beneficial. Knowing that there are other parents who are successfully coping with CF in their lives and that their children are doing well proves supportive and facilitates acceptance.

CF imposes a great financial burden on the family. The cost of home equipment, medications, clinic appointments, and hospitalizations is astronomical. Being able to provide needed medical care for the child can be a continued stress for the parents. Often the family goes without other items to pay medical bills. This may cause feelings of guilt in the child with CF, who realizes the hardship placed on the family. Resources such as state government services for handicapped children are available for assistance with medical expenses for qualifying families.

Children with CF are prone to psychosocial problems. Daily chest physical therapy, medications, frequent clinic appointments, and hospitalizations make it apparent that they are different from other children. A chronic cough, clubbed fingers, a barrel chest, and small stature further reinforce the perception of being different. Concern with body image increases with age. Absence from school due to illness, frequent hospitalizations, and poor exercise tolerance can separate CF children from their peer group. A sense of isolation develops. As children attempt to gain some form of control in their lives, they may refuse chest physical therapy and medications. This becomes a real frustration for the parent, who is trapped between the need for providing prescribed therapy and the need for discipline and limit setting.

As the child reaches adolescence, the risk of psychosocial problems increases. Attempting to work through the normal tasks of adolescence while coping with the limitations imposed by CF can prove stressful and depressing. Delays in puberty coupled with an altered physical appearance contribute to a poor body image. The majority of adolescents with CF are dissatisfied with their bodies and find their obvious physical differences a source of great stress and embarrassment. While the normal adolescent is attempting to develop a positive self-image, the adolescent with CF finds this almost impossible to do. A poor self-image develops, leading to feelings of inadequacy and insecurity.

Gaining peer group acceptance is difficult for adolescents with CF because of body image problems, physical limitations, and frequent illness. CF appears to affect the way other adolescents react to them. Fearing rejection, the adolescent with CF develops few interpersonal relationships. The idea of dating and marriage produces anxiety, especially for boys, who experience feelings of sexual inadequacy due to sterility. Poor peer group acceptance and the dependency on others for assistance with daily chest physical therapy inhibit the development of independence, a major task of adolescence.

Awareness of the future and the prognosis of CF lead to anxiety and a preoccupation with death and dying. Making vocational decisions is difficult when adolescents question the ability ever to be physically and financially independent of their parents. The use of denial and avoidance in dealing with these issues leads to rebellion and poor compliance with treatment. Vocational counseling should be encouraged.

The young adult with CF faces the problems of achieving and maintaining independence of the family unit. Finding a suitable occupation that will provide financial security and not be physically detrimental is often difficult. For the married adult, the need for daily therapy and the financial burden of medical expenses, plus physical limitations and frequent illness, place great stress on the marriage. Family planning decisions are difficult. Many females with CF decide not to have children because of the physical risks involved and the fact that all the children will be carriers. Attempts at adoption are hindered because of the chronicity and prognosis of CF. Making a marriage succeed with a chronic illness is a difficult task. With CF, the threat of a serious illness and death from complications is always present.

Nursing management

An essential component of nursing management is providing for the physical, psychological, and social needs of the patient. However, before a nursing care plan can be established, the nurse must make an accurate assessment of the patient's needs. Data obtained from this assessment will provide guidelines for all areas of nursing management. Table 25-14 describes areas of assessment for the CF child and family.

Once the assessment is complete, the nurse is ready to incorporate the data into a care plan that will establish goals for the nursing staff, patient, and hospitalization. Since pulmonary hygiene is a major component of care in CF, the care plan should reflect this priority. Aggressive chest physiotherapy should be initiated, a sputum sample obtained and sent for culture and sensitivity, and appropriate antibiotic therapy begun. Oxygen therapy may be indicated. All equipment should be functioning properly and used safely. The patient's exercise tolerance should be evaluated and an exercise program begun. Continuous assessment of the respiratory status is essential.

Nutrition is another priority of care and weight gain a usual goal of therapy. The daily calorie intake should be counted and recorded. High-calorie, high-protein foods should be included in meals and between-meal snacks made readily available. Determining the daily calorie intake necessary for weight gain is important in setting realistic goals for the patient. Children must eventually be able to estimate their own caloric intake to know whether it is enough to ensure weight gain. Nutritional supplements may be indicated if weight gain is not achieved.

The nurse is responsible for coordinating all aspects of the patient's care effectively and efficiently. Scheduling of meals, chest physical therapy, medications, and exercise time can be a complicated task but is necessary for an optimal outcome.

Nurses must also communicate their nursing goals to the patient, family, and involved health team members. As discharge planning evolves, the nurse must often contact health professionals outside the hospital and clinic. Referrals to community health nurses may be vital to continuity of care.

Sometimes the stress of coping with this demanding illness causes a breakdown in communication or disruption among family members. Parents and siblings may have difficulty expressing their feelings about how CF affects their relationships and life-style. The nurse should facilitate the development of healthy communication between family members when it does not exist and reinforce it when it does.

Table 25-14 Nursing assessment of the CF patient

Respiratory status	Gastrointestinal status	Psychosocial status
General appearance	Height, weight	Family support system
Discomfort	Growth pattern	Financial status
AP diameter of chest	Usual intake	Understanding of CF
Vital signs	Number of calories	and treatment program
Temperature	Type of foods eaten	Compliance with
Pulse	Use of enzymes—type,	treatment program
BP	frequency	Other family stressors
Respirations	Stools	School adjustment
Rate	Quality	Peer relationships
Quality	Quantity	Community resources
Use of accessory	Odor	CF clinic follow-up
muscles	Abdominal pain,	
Retractions	discomfort	
Breath sounds	Supplements	
Color, cyanosis	(vitamins, etc.)	
Clubbing of digits		
Cough		
Usual pulmonary care		
Practiced at home		
Schedule		
Equipment—type, care		
Exercise program		
Medications		

Patient and family education When the diagnosis of CF is made, parents, and even the child or adolescent, are asked to absorb a great deal of information regarding the disease process, its treatment, and home care. The nurse, along with the physician and other health team members, is responsible for implementing a teaching program. Education is an ongoing process for the child and family since only so much information can be assimilated at one time. As the child grows older, pulmonary therapy techniques change, medications change, and the disease process may progress, creating new learning needs in the CF patient and family. Techniques of chest physical therapy require periodic evaluation whether they change or not. The Cystic Fibrosis Foundation* and state chapter affiliates provide educational materials and services to families and health professionals.

Principles of self-care should be taught as appropriate, often by age 10. CF, with its demanding home therapy, can foster dependency. The child should eventually assume responsibility for home equipment, medications, and chest physical therapy.

Parents need to understand that their child

* Cystic Fibrosis Foundation, 6000 Executive Boulevard, Suite 309, Rockville, MD, 20852.

will experience normal growth and development even though some steps may be delayed, such as puberty. Discipline, limit setting, and promotion of independence are important topics to explore.

Adolescents who are experiencing their illness with feelings of rejection and rebellion may be helped by support groups of others with CF. Group teaching situations may increase receptiveness and eventual compliance.

Health maintenance Usually CF children are followed up closely at regional CF centers. There the child is examined periodically and more thoroughly at least once a year. Children with CF may need hospitalization for periods of illness or for evaluation. Chest x-rays, pulmonary function studies, blood gases, sputum cultures, and various other tests are done to monitor status.

Very often the nurse acts as coordinator of the child's care. The nurse can facilitate referral to genetic and vocational counselors, social workers, respiratory therapists, nutritionists, and community health nurses. Providing comprehensive care to the child (or adult) with CF is a demanding, time-consuming job that no one person can accomplish alone.

See Chap. 21 for a nursing care plan for a child with CF.

Nursing Care Plan–Laryngotracheobronchitis*

Patient: Billy Dow   **Age:** 12 months, 7 days   **Date of Admission:** 1/13, at 2:30 A.M.

Assessment

The infant, Billy Dow, who is 12 months and 7 days old, was admitted to the pediatric unit on 1/13. Billy was brought first to the emergency room accompanied by his parents and 3-year-old brother, his only sibling. The mother stated that the infant "can't breathe." Billy Dow has not been hospitalized before. He had no history of allergies. The medical diagnosis is laryngotracheobronchitis.

General appearance

The child has circumoral cyanosis, pale color, substernal and intercostal retractions, nasal flaring, and prominent inspiratory stridor. Respiratory rate is 60 to 70 breaths per min, heart rate is regular at 140 beats per min. Rectal temperature is 38.8°C (101.8°F). He is very anxious, frightened, and has a hoarse, "seal-like" cough made worse by crying.

History

One week ago, Billy had an upper respiratory infection for which he was treated with aspirin 60 mg q4 to 6h for a temperature of 38.9°C (102°F) rectally. On 1/12 his mother noticed that her infant son seemed congested and hoarse when she put him to bed at 8 P.M. At midnight, the mother was awakened by the child's coughing and crying. Billy was standing in his crib, coughing, his hair wet from perspiration. As Mrs. Dow changed Billy's diapers, she noted that his chest seemed to "move in and out funny" with each breath. He made a high, shrill noise on inspiration. Rectal temperature was 38.3°C (101°F). Billy refused a bottle and would not settle down when his mother rocked him or walked with him. The pediatrician was called, and he told the parents to take Billy to the emergency room, where he would meet them.

In the emergency room the primary pediatrician took chest and lateral neck x-rays. These showed some subglottic narrowing below the vocal cords and edema of the vocal cords. Two trial doses of racemic epinephrine via IPPB were administered by a respiratory therapist, with no improvement in the chest retractions, color, or stridor. Billy was admitted to the pediatric unit at 2:30 A.M.

Physician's orders

The physician's orders for the first 24 h include:

1. Chest x-ray
2. Lateral neck x-ray
3. Throat culture
4. NPO
5. Cool mist tent
6. IV of D 5.2 NS or D4MRL to run at maintenance rate, which is:
   100 ml/kg for first 10 kg/24 h
   50 ml/kg for next 10 kg/24 h
   10 ml/kg over 20 kg/24 h
   KCl—2 meq/100 ml IV fluid added when child urinating
7. Vital signs: respirations and pulse qh
   Temp. q2h if fever present
   BP on admission and q4h
8. Rest—external stimuli kept to minimum
9. Aspirin 60 mg per rectum for rectal temp. > 39°C (102.5°F)
10. Emergency tracheostomy (intubation) equipment at bedside
11. Notify physician if: resp. > 60; HR > 160; T > 38.9°C (102°F) or color becomes ashen gray; increased restlessness; increased retractions

Nursing diagnosis	Nursing goals	Nursing actions	Evaluation/revision
1. Respiratory distress related to anxiousness and inability of air to pass glottis	☐ Effective oxygenation and breathing patterns as evidenced by: **a.** Pink mucous membranes, nail beds	☐ Administer cool mist with humidified oxygen as ordered according to blood gas determinations and assessment of respiratory rate, pattern, and color	☐ 1/13 Placed in cool mist tent with 40% oxygen. Pa_{O_2} 90%, Pa_{CO_2} 52%, pH 7.30. ☐ 1/14 Pa_{O_2} 96%, Pa_{CO_2} 43%, pH 7.36, Fi_{O_2} reduced to 21% in mist tent.

657

Nursing diagnosis	Nursing goals	Nursing actions	Evaluation/revision
	b. Decreased, rhythmic respiratory rate without retractions	☐ Observe for signs of increasing respiratory distress, degree and location of retractions, nasal flaring, inspiratory stridor, increase in restlessness. Record and report to physician if resp > 60, HR > 160, T > 38.3°C (101°F)	☐ 1/13 Four h after admission, resp. 54, retractions present but mild to moderate during rest. Bilateral breath sounds
	c. Absence of inspiratory stridor	☐ Provide a quiet environment; group nursing actions together to give longer periods of uninterrupted rest	☐ 1/13 Billy transferred to a private room per family's request. VS were checked q1h initially, with rectal T q2h. All nursing care limited to essentials. Parent states Billy is a stomach sleeper, so child positioned on stomach. Mist tent large enough to cover entire mattress
	☐ Oxygen transport to all tissues will be maintained at level needed for adequate perfusion	☐ Elevate head of bed 30°. Permit infant to assume position of comfort without compromising IV line	☐ 1/14 Oral mucosa pink when sleeping; circumoral cyanosis returns when agitated and crying
			☐ 1/16 Color remains pink when out of mist tent; nailbeds pink
		☐ Assess perfusion of extremities by assessing pedal pulses, capillary filling, warmth	☐ 1/14 Monitor perfusion q1h, keeping in mind that mist tent is cool. Billy was covered with bath blankets to keep extremities warm and to prevent vasoconstriction. Blankets were changed frequently. Pedal pulses equal to apical. Prompt capillary filling
2. Potential for fluid and electrolyte imbalance related to inability to take oral fluids and tachypnea	☐ Maintain fluids and electrolytes within normal limits for a 13-kg infant as evidenced by: **a.** Fluid intake of 40 ml/h **b.** Voiding quantities sufficient at least 4–5 times in 24 h **c.** Firm skin turgor, moist oral mucous membranes. **d.** Weight within 60 g of admission weight	☐ Maintain patency of IV line and administer fluids at rate ordered. Left hand secured to sheet and protected with medicine cup over insertion site ☐ Record intake and output. Weigh diapers. Check IV hourly. Maintain NPO first 24 h. Assess skin turgor. Weigh infant daily	☐ IV of D 5.2 NaCl with 2 meq of KCl/100 ml started to run at 50 ml/h. A no. 22 intracath was placed in the dorsum of Billy's left hand and secured to a padded arm board. Serum electrolytes: Na 137, Cl 96, K 3.9 ☐ 1/13 Elasticity of skin remains, no tenting ☐ 1/14 Urine output 10–15 ml/kg/24h, IV patent, site without edema or erythema. Weight 13 kg
3. Inability to mobilize and cough out secretions in lungs related to inflammation and infection	☐ Nonretention of secretions as evidenced by loose productive cough, adequate hydration, decreased resp. rate, no retractions or stridor	☐ Check fluid level in mist tent hourly and fill with distilled water when appropriate. Change equipment qod ☐ Explain to parent how much PO fluid Billy can have	☐ 1/13 Begun on clear liquids ☐ 1/14 Mist tent required filling q6h to maintain mist at desired concentration. Billy has loose productive

Nursing diagnosis	Nursing goals	Nursing actions	Evaluation/revision
		and schedule 120 ml during 7–3 shift, 90 ml during 3–11 shift, and 60 ml during 11–7 shift. Leave 1-oz paper measuring cups in room	cough now □ 1/15 Billy allowed to have broth, Jello water, 7-Up to drink, but total PO and IV fluid not to exceed 1200 ml per 24 h. Tolerating PO fluids well □ 1/15 Resp. rate 34–40 with mild retractions intercostally. Mild stridor on inspiration □ 1/16 IV discontinued and clear liquid diet maintained with PO intake of 600 ml on 7–3 and 450 ml on 3–11
4. Parental anxiety and feelings of inadequacy associated with Billy's hospitalization	□ The parents will be able to verbalize their feelings and support each other	□ Complete nursing admission information sheet in first 24 h; assign a primary nurse. Assess and identify: **a.** Parents' reactions to infant's illness	□ 1/13 Primary nurse: N. Horvath; associate nurse: G. Tolzman □ Mother states, "It was only a cold and he seemed OK when I put him to bed. What did I do wrong?" □ 9 A.M. Pediatrician told parents that child's condition is common at his age, gets worse at night, occurs in fall and winter; reinforced parents' positive actions: ability to assess need for medical intervention and notification of pediatrician
		b. Parents' relationship with each other **c.** Coping mechanisms used by parents **d.** Family support and reaction	□ 1/13 Parents appear close; touch and support each other verbally □ 1/13 Father asked maternal grandmother to take 3-year-old brother so he can stay with wife at hospital □ 1/13–16 Grandparents visit; minister and neighbors visit and assist mother by sitting with Billy so she can go home and rest for several hours and be with Billy's brother
	□ Involve parents in Billy's care	□ Encourage parents to change diapers but save so they can be weighed. Allow parents to take rectal temperature	□ 1/13 4:30 P.M. Mother and father less frightened and expressing need to assist in care. Nurse explains necessity of mist tent and how to tuck it under mattress. Mother or father changes Billy's diapers, takes rectal temperature if Billy becomes anxious when RN does it

Nursing diagnosis	Nursing goals	Nursing actions	Evaluation/revision
		□ Encourage mother to touch and talk to Billy. Assist with "making him better"	□ 1/15 Mother enjoys holding Billy and giving him bottle for short periods out of mist tent.
5. Irritability and restlessness of infant related to illness and strange environment	□ Billy will adjust to strange environment as evidenced by decreased anxiety, resting and napping 2–3 times per day	□ Ask parents to bring in familiar blanket or toy from home □ Place mobiles on crib that Billy can see and be stimulated by □ Encourage parents to visit and care for Billy as they can manage. Have cot available if parent wishes to stay overnight	□ 1/13 Father brought blanket from Billy's crib □ 1/13 7–3 nurses placed musical toy inside mist tent □ 1/13 Since grandparents are caring for 3-year-old sibling, mother able to stay with Billy all day

* By Nancy Horvath, BSN, St. Mary's Hospital, Rochester, Minn.

References

1. Edmund Crelin, *Development of the Lower Respiratory System*, Vol. 27, No. 4, *Clinical Symposia*, CIBA Pharmaceutical Co., Summit, N.J., 1975, p. 3.
2. Mary Tudor, *Child Development*, McGraw-Hill, New York, 1981, p. 244.
3. Crelin, op. cit., p. 19.
4. Ibid.
5. Arim Weinberg, Charles Christiansen, and Doreen Wise, "Respiratory Rate: Forgotten Clue in Early Detection of Congenital Heart Disease," *Pediatric Nursing* May:40 (1977).
6. Ibid.
7. Barry Shapiro, Ronald Harrison, and Caroll Trout, *Clinical Application of Respiratory Care*, Year Book Medical Publishers, Chicago, 1975, p. 150.
8. Ibid., p. 106.
9. Ibid., p. 127.
10. Ibid., pp. 231–233.
11. Ibid., pp. 277–281.
12. Carolyn E. Aradine, "Home Care for Young Children with Long-Term Tracheostomies," *The American Journal of Maternal-Child Nursing* 5:121–125 (1980).
13. Suzanne Champoux, "Upper Respiratory Tract Infection," *Nurse Practitioner* July–August:31–35 (1977).
14. Robert Hoekelman, Saul Blatman, Philip Brunell, Stanford Friedman, and Henry Seidel, *Principles of Pediatrics*, McGraw-Hill, New York, 1978, p. 1468.
15. Aubrey Maze, and Edward Bloch, "Stridor in Pediatric Patients," *Anesthesiology* 50:138 (1979).
16. Hoekelman, Blatman, Brunnell, Friedman, and Seidel, op. cit., p. 1207.
17. Lawrence Fahrer, "Tuberculosis in the United States Today," *American Lung Association Bulletin* 65(3):2 (1979).
18. American Thoracic Society, "Screening for Pulmonary Tuberculosis in Institutions," *American Review of Respiratory Disease* 115(5):1 (1977).
19. Hoekelman, Blatman, Brunell, Friedman, and Seidel, op. cit., p. 1208.
20. Jan Breslow, Joseph McPherson, and J. Epstein, "Distinguishing Homozygous and Heterozygous Cystic Fibrosis Fibroblasts from Normal Cells by Differences in Sodium Transport," *New England Journal of Medicine* 304:1–5 (1981).

Chapter 26 **Cardiovascular function**

Sandra Sonnessa Griffiths

Upon completion of this chapter, the student will be able to:

1. Describe the growth and development of the fetal heart during gestation.

2. Name the components of fetal circulation that differ from those of postnatal circulation.

3. Describe the changes in the heart and circulation that occur at or soon after birth.

4. List alterations in cardiovascular status that may be present if the child has congenital heart disease.

5. Identify the signs and symptoms of congestive heart failure.

6. Discuss the nursing care of a child with congestive heart failure.

7. Describe the hemodynamic components that differentiate acyanotic heart disease from cyanotic heart disease.

8. Suggest two reasons why either medical or surgical treatment may be appropriate for a child with congenital heart disease.

9. Describe selected examples of acyanotic heart defects and cyanotic heart defects.

10. State the nursing management involved in caring for a child after heart surgery.

11. Identify areas of health teaching to address with children, and their parents, who have atherosclerosis or hypertension.

12. Discuss the etiology and nursing management of acute rheumatic fever.

13. Identify the purpose of common drugs used for children with heart disease.

14. Discuss areas of teaching appropriate for the child and family when the child has congenital heart disease.

Ever since living organisms have evolved beyond the size of a few cells, a circulatory system that moves essential substances from the environment to each cell has been a necessity for all but the tiniest creatures. Similarly, as soon as cell division gets well under way in the human embryo, a primitive circulatory system is required, which is then transformed progressively in the developing embryo, ultimately acquiring its fully developed characteristics. The pumping structure of the developed circulatory system provides the force needed to circulate life-sustaining oxygen and nutrients. Any alterations in the normal heart structure affect the transportation of these vital materials.

A malformation in heart structure, or a *congenital heart defect*, occurs during early fetal development. The incidence of congenital heart defects is estimated at approximately 7 to 9 per 1000 live births. The exact etiology of congenital heart defects is often unknown, but theories center around a combination of genetic and environmental influences. It is known that the more genetic defects present in one child, the greater the chances of a coexisting heart defect. Approximately 50 percent of children with Down syndrome have atrial or ventricular septal defects. Prematurity has also been associated with a higher incidence of congenital heart disease in newborns.

Fetal heart development

From the time of fertilization until the third week of gestation, the developing embryo's nutritional needs are supplied by diffusion, since the embryo is merely a few cell layers thick. The heart and vascular system develop rapidly from the third to the eighth week of gestation. A primitive hollow, curved tube gradually develops into four highly specialized chambers of the heart. Simultaneously, the cell layers of the *pericardium* (the outer layer of the heart), the *myocardium* (muscle wall), and the *endocardium* (inner lining) develop. In the first 3 weeks, there is no separation of chambers. The blood flows freely into the right and left atria and to the right and left ventricles and leaves the heart in an undivided flow. By the end of the sixth week, the primitive tubular heart is differentiated into a parallel double-pump circulatory system and is a recognizable four-chambered structure similar to that present at birth.

Fetal circulation*

The fetal heart and vascular system develop in a way that will support the fetus in utero and permit rapid transition to extrauterine life at birth. *Arteries* are vessels that take blood away from the heart; *veins* bring blood back to the heart. In adult circulation, all arteries except the pulmonary artery carry blood enriched with oxygen in the lungs from the heart to the body tissues. The pulmonary artery transports oxygen-depleted blood from the heart to the lungs. The oxygenated blood then returns from the lungs via the pulmonary veins to the heart, where it is pumped out of the left ventricle to the systemic circulation. During gestation, the placenta is the site of carbon dioxide–oxygen gas exchange and nutrient absorption. The lungs do not develop sufficiently to support extrauterine life until 26 to 28 weeks of gestation.

The fetal circulatory system utilizes three blood-diverting mechanisms, called *shunts*, to direct oxygenated blood flow away from the liver and lungs. The three shunt systems are the

---

* The author gratefully acknowledges the assistance of Barbara Macpherson, B.S.N., and Sarah Sacksteder, B.S.N., of Fresno Valley Hospital in the preparation of this section and in the presentation of specific congenital heart defects.

ductus venosus, the *foramen ovale,* and the *ductus arteriosus* (Fig. 26-1). Closure of these shunts after birth is necessary if a normal extrauterine pattern of blood flow is to exist.

Oxygenated blood flows from the placenta through the umbilical vein to the liver. Here, some blood is directed into the hepatic circulation, while the rest is shunted directly through the ductus venosus to the inferior vena cava. The blood circulating through the liver returns to the inferior vena cava through the hepatic veins. Blood from the lower extremities and alimentary canal returns to the heart through the inferior vena cava. Blood entering the heart is a mixture of well-oxygenated blood received from the ductus venosus and blood with lower oxygen saturation received from the gastrointestinal system and lower extremities.

Upon entering the right atrium, most of the blood from the inferior vena cava is directed through the *foramen ovale* (an opening between the atria) into the left atrium, bypassing the right ventricle and the lungs. The foramen ovale allows blood to flow unidirectionally from the right atrium to the left atrium. Only small amounts of blood enter the left atrium from the pulmonary veins. Blood entering the left atrium flows into the left venticle and out through the ascending aorta.

Upper extremity and cerebral blood returns to the heart through the superior vena cava. This blood, low in oxygen content, and some blood from the inferior vena cava, flows from the right atrium into the right ventricle and then into the pulmonary artery. The ductus arteriosus directs most of this blood away from the immature lungs directly into the aorta. The pulmonary vascular resistance (the resistance to blood flow through the lungs) in the fetus is normally high partly because of the vasoconstriction caused by the hypoxia effect in the lungs of the fetus. A portion of right ventricular output still flows through the pulmonary circulation; this blood returns from the lungs to the left atrium through the pulmonary veins. Blood from the descending aorta is distributed to the alimentary tract and lower extremities and returns to the placenta through the umbilical arteries. The left ventricle does not meet high resistance when pumping blood into the systemic circulation because the placenta is a low-resistance system.

Before birth, the right atrium receives and

accommodates more blood volume than the other chambers of the heart. This causes the right side of the heart, especially the ventricle, to be slightly larger than the left. This normal right heart hypertrophy gradually diminishes after birth as the left ventricle begins to receive blood from the lungs. The left ventricle then enlarges to accommodate the increased blood volume and to overcome the increased systemic vascular resistance that occurs when the placenta is no longer part of the systemic circulation.

Circulatory changes at birth

At birth, the function of the three fetal circulation shunt structures—the ductus arteriosus, foramen ovale, and ductus venosus—changes drastically. The lungs assume the function of oxygen–carbon dioxide exchange. With initiation of respiration, the alveoli expand and blood flow through the lungs increases. Pulmonary vessel resistance decreases as the blood vessels dilate and vessel wall tension is lowered. The increased oxygen concentration is believed to be one of the primary stimuli for closure of the ductus arteriosus. Separation from the placenta causes increased resistance in the arterial system. Left atrial pressures exceed right atrial pressures and the foramen ovale, anatomically structured to permit flow only from right to left, closes. The heart now acts as a functioning unit rather than two parallel pumps. The ductus venosus eventually becomes a nonfunctional ligament.

Circulation in the heart after birth

The heart is a muscular pumping organ designed to circulate oxygen-depleted blood through the pulmonary system and oxygen-enriched blood through the body. The right atrium and ventricle and the left atrium and ventricle serve as two circulatory systems alternately contracting and relaxing in series. Venous blood returning from the systemic circulation enters the right atrium by way of the superior vena cava and inferior vena cava (Fig. 26-2). The oxygen-depleted, dark-red blood is propelled through the tricuspid valve into the right ventricle. The right ventricle pumps blood through the pulmonary artery to the lungs, where carbon dioxide–oxygen gas exchange takes place. Blood returning from the lungs is oxygen-enriched and bright red. It enters

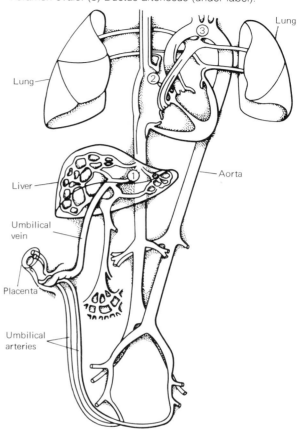

Figure 26-1* Fetal circulation. (1) Ductus venosus. (2) Foramen ovale. (3) Ductus arteriosus (under label).

the left atrium through the pulmonary veins and is propelled through the mitral valve into the left ventricle. Thus the *oxygen saturation* values (the amount of oxygen combined with hemoglobin) vary between the right and left heart chambers (Fig. 26-3).

The pressure within each chamber differs (Fig. 26-3) and has a characteristic waveform corresponding to a numerical value (Fig. 26-2). Because blood always flows from areas of higher pressure to areas of lower pressure, an increase in pressure in the chambers, lungs, or systemic circu-

* The author wishes to thank Kathleen A. Nyberg for the sketches on which the anatomical drawings in this chapter are based.

Figure 26-2 Adult circulation and normal pressure waves. (*After Netter, 1978.*)

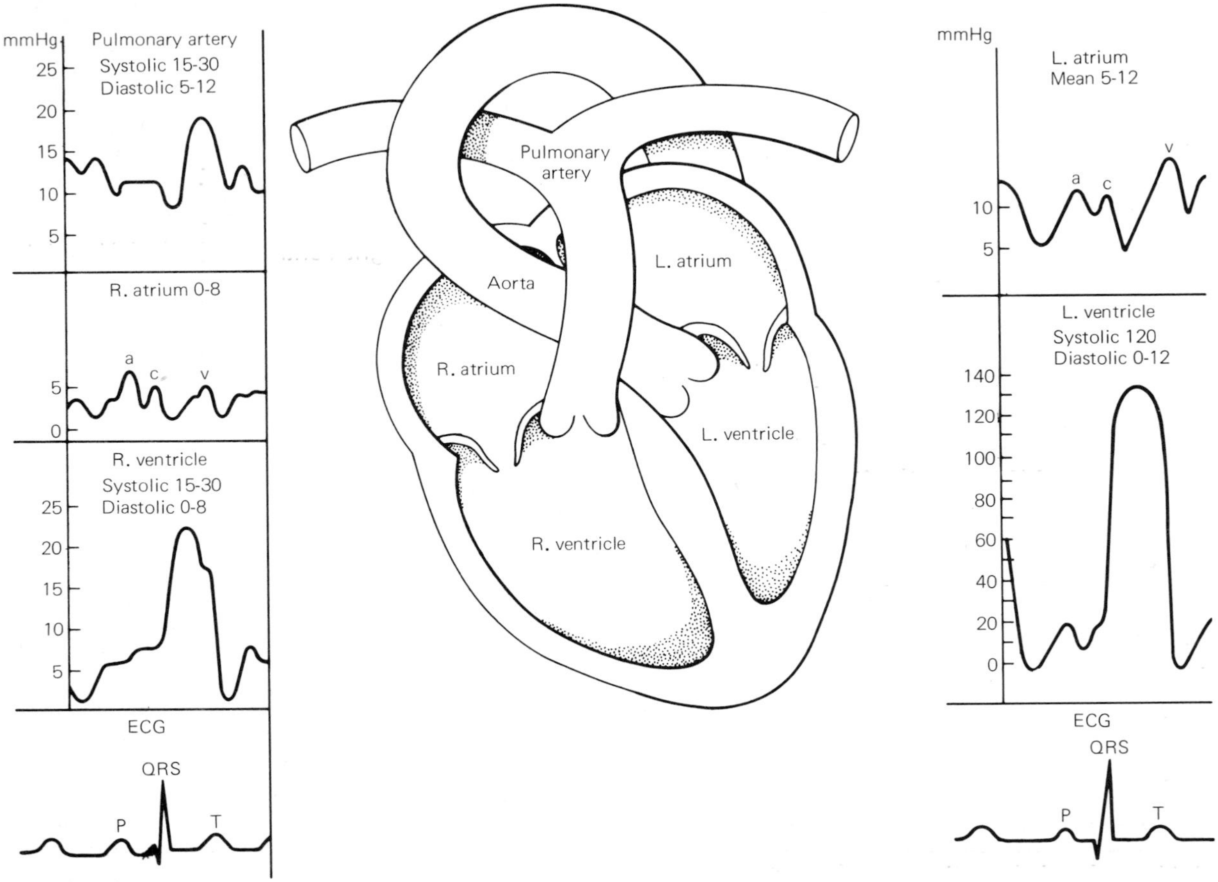

Assessment of cardiovascular function

Accurate cardiovascular assessment is vital to the child with a congenital heart malformation. The assessment includes a nursing history, a physical examination, and diagnostic studies performed by specialized cardiologists and technicians.

Nursing history

A thorough admission history is obtained to provide a data base of the child's health and social history and to help care-givers meet the child's individual needs (see Chap. 6). The pre-

lation causes the part of the heart pumping blood into that area to work harder. For example, when the right atrium contracts, its pressure is higher than that of the right ventricle during diastole (relaxation). The left ventricular musculature is much thicker than the right and provides the required contraction pressure to force the blood through the aorta and out into the higher-pressure systemic circulation to perfuse the body. The blood circulates through the systemic capillary system that connects the arteries with the veins. In the capillaries the oxygen and nutrients move out of the blood to the cells in exchange for carbon dioxide and other metabolic waste products.

Figure 26-3 Normal pressure and oxygen saturation of blood in heart chambers.

BLOOD PRESSURE

Right Atrium	Left Atrium
0-8 mmHg (mean)	5-12 mmHg (mean)
Right Ventricle	Left Ventricle
15-30/0-8 mmHg	100-120/0-12 mmHg*

A

BLOOD OXYGEN SATURATION

Right Atrium	Left Atrium
75%	96%
Right Ventricle	Left Ventricle
75%	96%

B

* lower in infants

senting problem, or chief complaint, parental history of heart disease and other pertinent illnesses, and patterns of daily living are areas which provide information about a child with suspected or confirmed heart disease (Table 26-1).

Even though a tentative medical diagnosis is made prior to admission, it is important to determine the parent's and child's own understanding of why hospitalization is necessary. Asking what brings them to the hospital (chief complaint) and exploring what they think is the problem with the child's heart facilitate assessment of understanding and of potential teaching needs.

Ask about past hospitalizations and illnesses, especially respiratory infections. Find out what medications the child has taken in the past and is presently taking, since the physician may want the child to receive these drugs while in the hospital. Record information regarding the dosage, frequency, side effects, and special precautions needed. Though parents are usually aware of the name of the drug, it is helpful to have them bring the prescription container to the hospital.

Inquire about family history related to heart disease, including cardiac defects, rheumatic fever, hypertension, atherosclerosis, sudden death, or myocardial infarctions. The presence of other disorders related to heart disease, such as genetic disorders, birth defects, and diabetes mellitus, should also be recorded in the family history.

If relevant, as in a child less than 2 years, investigate the maternal childbirth history, including illnesses, complications during pregnancy, use of medications, and exposure to x-ray therapy or rubella. Determine the type of labor and delivery, any complications, and initial newborn assessment. Low birth weight, prematurity, need for respiratory assistance or resuscitation, cyanosis, or heart murmur may indicate the presence of a congenital heart defect.

Assessment of the general health of the child, patterns of daily living, and appropriate developmental milestones give the nurse clues as to the severity of heart disease and the ability of the heart to function effectively. Ask objective questions. Ask the parents to clarify vague information by giving specific examples of the child's behavior.

Incorporate questions about activity tolerance into the parent's descriptions of usual patterns. Feeding difficulties, poor or weak sucking, and poor weight gain are common in infants with severe heart defects. They fatigue easily, become dyspneic, and may get cyanotic. Toddlers, preschool, and school-age children tire easily while playing and may become breathless. Identify the frequency of rest breaks by asking specific questions about usual age-related activities. For instance, ask how long the child plays outside, if the child can run for a moderate distance, climb to "reasonable" heights, or ride a bike. Any difficulties should be noted.

Explore the impact of heart disease on the child and family to assess how the family as a unit and the individual members are coping with the child's illness. The parents can describe the child's relationship to them, to siblings, and to friends. An older child or adolescent may find

Table 26-1 Outline of a history for a child with heart disease

---

1. Chief complaint or presenting problem

2. Past medical history

Hospitalizations
Medications
Frequency of respiratory infections

3. Family history

Hypertension
Atherosclerosis
Myocardial infarction
Rheumatic fever
Others: diabetes mellitus, genetic diseases, birth defects

4. Maternal history

Previous childbirth history
Illness or complications during pregnancy
Exposure to x-ray therapy or rubella during pregnancy

5. Newborn

Weight
Gestational age
Length of labor
Apgar score
Need for resuscitation
Cyanosis at birth (transient or persistent)
Breathlessness
Grunting or wheezing respirations
Feeding difficulties

6. Infant and toddler

Weight gain since birth
Diet and appetite
Feeding or sucking difficulties
Fatigue
Cyanosis
Developmental milestones:
    Holding head up (1–3 months)
    Sitting up without support (6–7 months)
    Crawling (8–10 months)
    Standing without support (12–14 months)
    Walking (by 18 months)
    Language development: sounds, words, sentences

Table 26-1 Outline of a history for a child with heart disease (*Continued*)

---

7. Preschool or school-age

Daily activities:
    Hours of sleep
    Rest breaks
    Meals
Play tolerance
    Running
    Climbing
    Riding bicycle
Fatigue
Breathlessness
History of rheumatic fever
Recent sore throat or upper respiratory infection:
    Joint pain
    Fever
    Loss of appetite
Days of school missed in last 6 months
Language development: sentences

---

it helpful to share feelings about having heart disease. If appropriate, once a therapeutic trusting relationship is established, explore how the parents felt when they learned about their child's heart problem. Some parents of children who are chronically ill may express feelings of guilt, grief, denial, and anxiety about the future. Collect data about other stress, financial or occupational, the family is experiencing.

Physical examination

Inspection A major part of the physical assessment of a child with congenital heart disease is inspection. A large portion of inspection can be done without touching the child.

First, assess the child's general features. Evaluate general temperament for signs of irritability, restlessness, or lethargy that may indicate *hypoxia* an inadequate supply of oxygen to body tissues. Assess growth by obtaining height and weight and plotting the values on a growth curve. Children with a congenital heart defect may be underweight for their age. Note the child's posture while standing or sitting. If possible, observe the child at play to note breathlessness, increasing cyanosis, or squatting to rest.

The nutritional status of the child should be evaluated since feeding difficulties and poor weight gain are common in children with severe heart defects. Observe the child's level of alertness, brightness of eyes, and brilliance of hair.

Redness of gums may indicate lack of vitamins. Note the number of teeth the child has and whether they are deciduous or permanent teeth. Observe the child's gait for unsteadiness.

Observe skin color when the child is at rest, agitated, or crying. The color may be difficult to assess if the child is anemic or jaundiced. In children with dark skin, subtle color changes are more difficult to assess. It is important to establish a baseline to aid in identifying cyanosis. The presence of *cyanosis*, a bluish discoloration of the skin, is indicative of oxygen-depleted blood circulating in the peripheral body tissues. The color of nail beds, lips and oral mucous membranes is the most reliable indicator of oxygen saturation in tissues. Cyanosis around the mouth, *circumoral* cyanosis, and around the eyes, *periorbital* cyanosis, may be observed in infants and young children and may or may not be related to heart disease. *Acrocyanosis*, blue-tinged hands and feet, is frequently observed in normal newborns and is not a reliable indicator of a heart problem. Besides cyanosis, note any pallor or diaphoresis (sweating). Flat, reddened, purplish pinpoint lesions called *petechiae* are also significant in children with suspected cardiovascular disease and may indicate blood-clotting disorders, circulatory stasis, or obstruction.

Inspect the nails of the fingers and toes for clubbing. *Clubbing*, a rounding of the tips of fingers and toes with a convex curved angle, indicates chronic tissue hypoxia that usually accompanies severe heart or pulmonary disease (Fig. 26-4).

Assess respiratory status after removing the child's clothing. It is vital to observe respirations since problems in the cardiac system can affect respirations. Note the pattern of breathing. Normal infants typically use their abdominal muscles in breathing. Count the rate and note the depth and regularity of the respirations. Compare the values to the appropriate range for the child's age. (See Table 17-20.) Observe for signs of respiratory distress: (1) *tachypnea*, increased respiratory rate for a given age; (2) *dyspnea*, difficulty breathing; (3) *retractions*, use of accessory muscles in the neck, clavicle area, sternum, and intercostal spaces; (4) *nasal flaring*; or (5) *audible breath sounds* such as inspiratory stridor or expiratory grunting.

Check for visibly bounding pulses in the neck and in the chest over the point of maximum

Figure 26-4 Clubbing. (*A*) Typical cyanosis and clubbing of the fingers in a young adult (left) compared to normal (right). (*B*) Close-up profile of clubbing (arrow). (*C*) Clubbing in a young child (*courtesy of Robert W. Feldt*). (*A and B, from Joseph Perloff, The Clinical Recognition of Congenital Heart Disease, 2d ed., Saunders, Philadelphia, 1978. Used with permission.*)

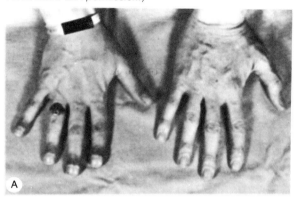
A

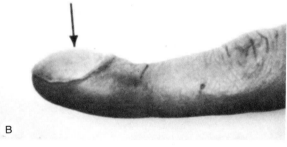
B

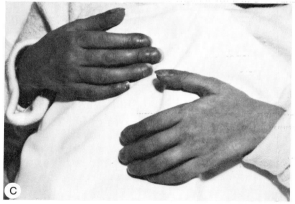
C

impulse (PMI). The PMI is located at the fifth intercostal space to the left of the sternal border (Fig. 26-5). Visible pulsations may indicate circulatory overload and heart failure.

Figure 26-5 Point of maximum impulse. (*From E. Hochstein and A. L. Rubin, Physical Diagnosis, McGraw-Hill, New York, 1964. Used by permission.*)

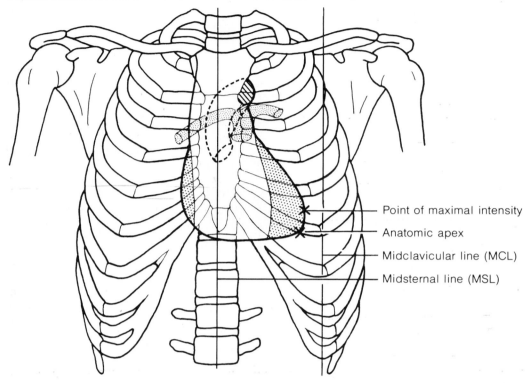

Point of maximal intensity

Anatomic apex

Midclavicular line (MCL)

Midsternal line (MSL)

Palpation The use of palpation is essential in assessing cardiovascular status. The skin should be evaluated for temperature (warm or cool), moisture (dry or clammy), and turgor. The presence of "tenting" (skin remains suspended) when the skin is pinched and pulled taut over the abdomen may indicate dehydration or electrolyte imbalance.

Body pulses should be evaluated for rate, rhythm, and volume. Palpate pulses in an orderly manner, beginning at the head and ending at the feet. Use a light touch and palpate pulses on both sides of the body simultaneously. The temporal and carotid artery pulses may be weaker than in adults. Check brachial and radial pulses in the upper extremities and the femoral, popliteal, and dorsalis pedis pulses in the lower extremities. The following may be used as a guideline:

4+ Bounding
3+ Strong
2+ Palpable but weak
1+ Barely palpable
0 Absent

Note and record any alterations in the rhythm or quality.

Observe *capillary refill* time by pinching the tip of a finger or toe. Count the time in seconds for the blanched or whitened area to resume its usual color. The color should return immediately if the heart is circulating blood effectively.

The child should be examined for evidence of edema. Fluid accumulation may occur in the interstitial tissues in heart failure, but evidence of overt peripheral edema is rarely seen in infants. In older children dependent edema may be observed in areas affected by gravity and position. Check the ankles and sacral area for edema. Note whether the edema is pitting or nonpitting. Press the edematous area. If the press mark remains, note the time in seconds it takes to lose the imprint. Pitting edema is frequently described on a 1+ to 4+ scale with 4+ as the longest time to lose the press mark.

Advanced physical assessment skills include palpation of the liver and percussion of the borders of the heart. These techniques are not within the scope of this text.

Auscultation The auscultation of blood pressure, breath sounds, and heart sounds is very important in cardiovascular assessment, but is often threatening to the young child. The child sometimes fears that some one listening to his heart can hear his private thoughts and wishes. The stethoscope and blood pressure apparatus are frightening and the child interprets these instruments as intrusive and harmful to the body. Allowing the child to handle the blood pressure cuff and stethoscope before and after using them may help to alleviate some fears of bodily harm.

Blood pressure should be taken when the child is quiet, if possible, since anxiety may increase the blood pressure. Using an appropriate cuff size (see Table 17-22), take the blood pressure in all four extremities. In young infants, the blood pressure of the arms and legs should be equal. Beyond 1 year of age, the blood pressure obtained in the leg is normally 10 to 40 mmHg higher than in the arms. Blood pressure in the legs lower than that in the arms may indicate coarctation of the aorta.

With infants and young children palpation of systolic blood pressure is much easier than auscultation. In premature infants and newborns, the technique of obtaining flush pressures may be used (see Chap. 17). When possible auscultate blood pressure to determine both systolic and diastolic components. After obtaining the pressure values, compare them to normal ranges for the age of the child (Table 17-21). The *pulse pressure,* or difference between the systolic and diastolic pressure, should be calculated. Though the normal pulse pressure spread is 20 to 50 mmHg, a greater pulse pressure may occur in hypertension, aortic regurgitation, or patent ductus arteriosus. A smaller pulse pressure may occur in tachycardia, severe aortic stenosis, pericardial effusion, or congestive heart failure. Abnormal blood pressure and pulse pressure findings should be noted and reported to the physician.

Auscultating breath sounds is important in the assessment of the cardiac and respiratory systems. Normally, breath sounds should be clear and equal bilaterally in all lobes of the lungs. Characteristically, breath sounds in the lower lobes are not as loud as in the upper lobes but they should still be heard. Any adventitious or abnormal sounds, such as rales, rhonchi, or wheezing, should be reported.

Normal heart sounds are condensed over the child's small chest area and are due to the combination of the closing of the valves, contraction of the heart, and vibrations of blood moving through the chambers. The first heart sound (S_1), *lub,* represents the closure of the mitral and tricuspid valves and is associated with the systolic portion of the cardiac cycle. It is heard over the entire precordium (area of anterior chest wall overlying the heart) with the child in any position.

The second heart sound (S_2), *dub,* signifies the closing of the aortic and pulmonary valves and is associated with the end of systole and start of diastole, or the filling phase of the cardiac cycle. It can be heard over the entire precordium and is affected by respiration. A normal physiological splitting of S_2 into two components may be heard on inspiration. In newborns and infants, it may be difficult to ascertain the difference between S_1 and S_2 since their heart rate is so rapid. Light palpation over the carotid, apical, or femoral pulse areas will help identify the first heart sound as the pulses are synchronous with S_1.

A third heart sound (S_3) may be heard in normal children. It reflects transmitted vibrations during ventricular filling. The presence of S_3 can be heard best in the fifth intercostal space with the child in a supine position. The presence of S_3 may also indicate right-sided heart failure or a systemic illness.

A fourth heart sound (S_4) is heard immediately before S_1 and, when audible, is heard best over the lower left sternal border. Though heard primarily in adults, S_4 represents an audible resistance to filling, as in aortic or pulmonary stenosis.

A nurse listening to the heart should first count the apical heart rate for 1 full minute when the child is resting or quiet. After this, identification of the audible heart sounds should be undertaken in a systematic manner—first, S_1; second, S_2; and then S_3. Abnormal heart sounds are often difficult to auscultate even by trained persons.

After counting the heart rate and comparing it to the normal range for the specific child, identify the rhythm and record whether it is regular or irregular. An increased heart rate, *tachycardia*, or decreased heart rate, *bradycardia*, should be reported.

Any noise heard between the heart sounds, which is not characteristic of a specific heart sound, is termed a *murmur*. The majority of murmurs heard in children are benign and do not represent heart disease. They are called *functional* or *innocent murmurs* and reflect the normal blood turbulence transmitted through the child's thin chest wall. Murmurs are also caused by changes within the structure of the heart. Murmurs are heard when some resistance in the circulatory system is present that creates turbulence in blood flow. In congenital heart anomalies, a narrowed or incompetent valve, an altered structure, or a backflow of blood may produce a murmur.

Murmurs are characterized by five factors.

1. *Intensity*, or loudness of a murmur, is often described on a scale ranging from grade I to VI. A grade I murmur is faint and each grade successively increases in intensity to the Grade VI murmur that can be heard without a stethoscope
2. *Frequency*, or pitch, of the murmur is related to the velocity of blood flow through or around the area of resistance. The greater the velocity of blood flow, the higher the pitch. Low-pitch murmurs are heard best using the diaphragm of the stethoscope while higher-pitch murmurs are heard best using the bell portion.
3. The *configuration* of the murmur can be demonstrated, if diagrammed, by a particular shape.
4. *Quality* of a murmur may be described as harsh, rasping, musical, whistling, rumbling, or blowing.
5. *Timing* in the cardiac cycle is one of the key diagnostic tools used to define the occurence of the murmur. Murmurs are either systolic, occuring between S_1 and S_2, diastolic, between S_2 and S_1, or continuous, occurring throughout the entire cardiac cycle.

Murmurs may radiate to other parts of the thorax. It is important to note if a murmur can be auscultated through the posterior chest wall or palpated over the apical area, sternum, or posterior thorax. Though detection of murmurs is difficult, the presence of even a loud murmur may not indicate a heart defect.

A *bruit* is a high-pitched murmur heard during systole over a specific part of the body other than the heart. Most bruits in children are not significant. Children with aortic or pulmonary stenosis, however, may have a systolic bruit heard over the carotid artery.

Diagnostic studies

Selected diagnostic studies may be done in conjunction with other components of cardiovascular assessment. The number and type of studies varies, depending on the clinical signs and symptoms present, the tentative diagnosis, and the plan of management of the particular problem.

Hematologic tests Hematologic studies measure specific blood components that may reflect cardiovascular function. The studies done and the normal ranges vary slightly from one institution to another (Table 26-2).

Serum electrolyte studies may be obtained as

Table 26-2 Hematologic values that may reflect cardiovascular function*

Factor	Normal range
Sodium	135–145 mEq/L
Potassium	3.5–5.0 mEq/L
Calcium	9–11 mg/100 ml
Chloride	98–106 mEq/L
White blood cells (WBC)	5,000–10,000/mm³
Red blood cells (RBC)	5,400,000/mm³—males
	4,600,000/mm³—females
Hemoglobin	19 ± 5—newborn
	14 ± 3—infant
	12 ± 2—child
	14 ± 2—adolescent
Hematocrit	40–52%—newborn
	35% ± 5%—infant
	35–37%—child
	38–40%—adolescent
Blood urea nitrogen (BUN)	10–20 mg/100 ml
Creatinine	0.7–1.5 mg/100 ml
Platelets	150,000–350,000/mm³
Prothrombin time (PT)	11–16 s
Partial thromboplastin time (PTT)	25–40 s
Cholesterol, total	120–230 mg/100 ml— 1–19 years
Triglycerides	25–150 mg/100 ml

* Values may vary slightly in different laboratories.

needed. Sodium, potassium, and calcium, important for intracellular and extracellular impulse conduction, have a significant effect on myocardial electrical conduction. Values within normal ranges are vital for efficient contractions of the muscular myocardium.

A complete blood count (CBC), including hemoglobin, hematocrit, and white blood cell count, helps to identify the quality as well as the quantity of the blood and plasma. An increased white blood cell value may indicate the presence of infection in the body. Children with cyanotic heart disease may have *polycythemia*, an increased number of red blood cells, due to elevated red blood cell production. This increase reflects the body's attempt to compensate for the oxygen-depleted blood flow to peripheral tissues.

Coagulation studies may be done if there is a history of abnormal bleeding or bruising, a family history of bleeding or bruising tendency, or as part of a screening procedure prior to invasive diagnostic studies or heart surgery. A platelet count, prothrombin time (PT), and partial thromboplastin time (PTT) evaluate the essential components of the blood-clotting mechanism. Blood urea nitrogen (BUN) and creatinine levels denote kidney function and may reflect the ability of the heart to perfuse the kidneys.

Blood gases may be done depending on the diagnosis and specific cardiovascular disorder (Table 26-3). Venous, capillary, or arterial blood may be used, but an arterial blood gas sample is preferred since it is the most accurate.

Type and crossmatch studies obtained prior to a surgical procedure on the heart include an analysis of various blood factors necessary to prepare whole blood, packed red blood cells, and plasma. Special permission is required to infuse blood and should be obtained prior to heart surgery.

Children with congenital heart disease are subjected to multiple venipunctures, arterial punctures, and capillary finger sticks. Due to their level of cognitive development, children may lack the ability to understand the reasons for the repeated intrusive procedures. Helpful and necessary medical procedures and treatments are painful and are viewed as harmful to the body. Until children are 8 or 9, they think their body is a hollow tube.[1] The child fears that any hole made in the skin surface will result in

Table 26-3 Normal arterial blood gas values*

Factor	Range
pH	7.35–7.45
P_{CO2}	35–45 mmHg
P_{O2}	80–100 mmHg
HCO_3^-	25–35 mmHg
Base excess (BE)	± 2 mEq
O_2 saturation	95–100%

* At normal body temperature.

blood loss. Adhesive strips used after various hematologic tests protect the "injured site" and help to maintain the child's image of an intact body surface. Children need support during these procedures and comfort and reassurance afterwards. Parents may choose not to be present during these procedures. A nurse must then provide the support the child requires.

Noninvasive studies Other diagnostic tests may involve noninvasive laboratory studies. One test or a combination of tests may be done depending on the type of defect involved and the mode of treatment.

Anterior-posterior and lateral chest x-ray films are not performed routinely on admission. For children with suspected cardiac disorders, chest x-rays are important in evaluating pulmonary status and the presence of cardiomegaly, an enlarged heart.

An *echocardiogram* is a relatively new, nontraumatic diagnostic tool that employs an ultrasound technique. The picture that results is a reproduction of the image of sound echoes of the various structures of the heart and great vessels. An echocardiogram can be useful to detect a cardiac defect.

Phonocardiography produces a graphic representation of the sounds of blood flow in the heart and great vessels. With the use of sound channels, an electrocardiography machine, and a pressure recording device, a phonocardiogram can display normal and abnormal heart sounds. Audible and occasionally inaudible vibrations are recorded and add more information regarding cardiac function.

An electrocardiogram (ECG) is a study of the electrical impulses created during cardiac contraction. The electrical activity of the heart is

Figure 26-6 Electrical impulse conduction pathway in the heart. [*From D. A. Jones and J. S. Martin, in D. A. Jones et al. (eds.), Medical-Surgical Nursing, McGraw-Hill, 1978. Used by permission.*]

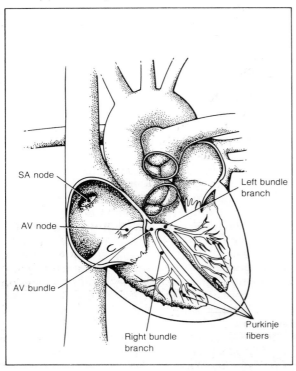

Figure 26-7 Normal electrocardiogram (ECG). Lead II pattern.

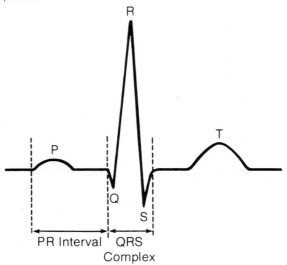

best measured by placing leads over the heart (chest leads) and the periphery (limb leads). The electrodes measure electrical activity that is generated during a cardiac cycle.

Normally, the electrical impulse originates in the *sinoatrial node* (SA node), located at the junction of the right atrium and superior vena cava (Fig. 26-6). From there, the impulse travels to the *atrioventricular node* (AV node), located at the base of the atrial septum. The impulse is delayed slightly at the AV node. The electrical impulse then travels along the ventricular septum via a collection of special myocardial fibers called the *bundle of His*. The traveling impulse eventually passes through the *Purkinje fibers* located in the right and left ventricles. Cardiac electrical impulses are transmitted through the remainder of the body via the intracellular fluid. The ECG is a reflection of the transmission of these impulses.

The waveforms usually recorded in an ECG represent the contraction and relaxation of the atria and ventricles (Fig. 26-7). The P wave represents *depolarization* (electrical discharge) of the atria and is usually associated with atrial contraction. The QRS complex depicts the depolarization of the ventricle or ventricular contraction. the P–R interval indicates the time of conduction of the electrical impulse from the atria to the ventricles. The T wave represents the *repolarization* or recovery period (electrical charging) of the ventricles. A more detailed discussion of the ECG is beyond the scope of this text.

A *vectorcardiogram* can be helpful in the diagnosis of certain heart defects. Vectorcardiography accurately depicts the relationship between electrical impulses and the degree of myocardium response. A vectorcardiogram is an alternate method to the ECG for displaying the electrical activity and is usually obtained at the same time the ECG is done.

Sympathetic and parasympathetic nerve fibers influence the conducting tissues of the heart. Stimulation of the *sympathetic* fibers accelerates the firing rate of the pacemaker (SA node) as well as abnormal pacemakers (ectopic foci) and speeds the rate of conduction, thereby increasing the heart rate. Stimulation of the *parasympathetic* nerve fibers produces an inhibitory effect (vagal influence), depressing the firing of the pacemaker and slowing conduction.

Normal sinus rhythm (NSR) represents a regular progression of the electrical impulse through the heart at a rate appropriate for a given child's age. *Arrhythmia* and *dysrhythmia* are synonymous terms used to describe cardiac rhythm irregularities. Arrhythmias can originate from any site within the heart since each cell in the myocardium has the potential to discharge an electrical impulse. Arrhythmias occurring along the conduction pathway are detected in the related area of the electrocardiographic tracing. A deviation in the P wave or P–R interval, for example, may suggest an abnormal contraction of the atria.

Although a wide variety of arrhythmias have been observed in children, they do not occur as frequently as in adults. A nurse should be alert for an irregular apical pulse signaling an arrhythmia. *Sinus arrhythmias*, commonly observed in healthy children, reflect a normal conduction pathway with an irregular rate that increases with inspiration and slows with expiration. *Sinus tachycardia* more specifically describes an increase in rate greater than a value appropriate for a child's age. The heart rate may be increased if the child is crying, anxious, or excited. The treatment for sinus tachycardia is symptomatic. Removing the cause will usually calm the child and the heart will resume its usual rate.

An important rate disturbance observed in children is *paroxysmal atrial tachycardia* (PAT). Its onset is heralded by a sudden increase in heart rate (greater than 250) with signs of tachypnea and dyspnea. The heart rate may revert to normal spontaneously or may require treatment. Prolonged episodes of PAT's diminish cardiac output and predispose the child to congestive heart failure.

Sinus bradycardia is a heart rate lower than normal. It should be reported to a physician immediately as treatment may be needed. It is important to remember that an adult's normal heart rate of 60 to 80 beats per minute would be considered bradycardic if auscultated in a newborn whose pulse ranges from 120 to 160 beats per minute

Many atrial and ventricular arrhythmias can be treated with medications that decrease the irritability of the foci by prolonging the *refractory period*, the time cells use to recover from an impulse discharge. Ventricular arrhythmias are more life-threatening than atrial arrhythmias since they more directly affect cardiac output. Ventricular fibrillation is life-threatening and denotes a cardiac arrest situation. The ventricles are quivering and cardiac output is nonexistent. Cardiopulmonary resuscitation must be initiated immediately. Defibrillation with electrical shock stimulation used in conjunction with emergency medications may help to restore normal sinus rhythm.

Invasive studies Invasive cardiac diagnostic procedures include cardiac catheterization and angiography. Both procedures carry additional risks to the child. Therefore, careful evaluation is required to ascertain that these tests are necessary.

Cardiac catheterization involves the passage of a thin, hollow radiopaque catheter into the cardiac chambers and great vessels. The route of entry depends on which side of the heart is to be visualized. To visualize the right side of the heart, the catheter is introduced via a cutdown into the antecubital fossa or percutaneously into a femoral vein. Left-sided cardiac catheterization carries more risks than right-sided catheterization because entry is made into the arterial system either by a brachial artery cutdown or percutaneous femoral artery entry. Major abnormalities can be visualized and functions of the heart valves can be evaluated. Oxygen saturation of the blood can be measured as the catheter is advanced through the cardiac chambers. The location, magnitude, and direction of blood flow can be determined in part by the measurement of oxygen saturation from various cardiac chambers. In addition, pressures in each chamber can be measured.

Preparation of the child and the family for cardiac catheterization is an important nursing responsibility. The procedure should be explained to the family and child (if appropriate for the child's age and level of understanding). Such visual aids as diagrams, photographs of the laboratory, a doll, and a miniature model of the lab equipment are effective teaching tools. A description of the sounds heard and the sensations felt is often helpful.

On admission to the hospital for the catheterization, vital signs, height, and weight are obtained. It is wise to make a comparison of the circulatory status of the right and left extremities before the cardiac catheterization to establish a baseline for post-catheterization evaluation. The child is usually not given anything to eat or drink after midnight or 2 A.M. prior to the catheterization. Sedation may be used to help the child relax. Occasionally, general anesthesia is employed during the procedure. The room is darkened and the large x-ray machine may be frightening. A familiar nurse should accompany the child to the catheterization lab to minimize anxiety and provide comfort.

After the catheterization, astute nursing management is of critical importance. Vital signs are taken every 15 to 30 min until stable and then frequently during the next 24 to 48 h. The pulse should be regular within limits appropriate for a given child. Report tachycardia or bradycardia to the physician. Observe the rate and depth of respirations and note signs of dyspnea or tachypnea. Do not measure blood pressure on the affected limb. Check the systolic and diastolic readings with precatheterization values and note any significant change, such as *hypotension.*

Temperatures should be recorded with vital signs. Though contamination during the sterile catheterization procedure is rare, the nurse should keep the puncture site clean and dry and observe the puncture site for signs of injection. Special consideration should be taken to prevent contamination from excreta, especially at a femoral catherization site in an infant or a young child.

In addition to vital sign checks, circulation is assessed frequently. A pressure dressing is placed over the puncture site to minimize the chance of bleeding and the formation of a hematoma. Record the type and amount of drainage on the dressing. If there is excessive oozing or bleeding, apply firm pressure directly on the dressing and notify the physician. Evaluate the circulation of the extremity used for the catheter entry. Adequate circulation is shown by pale-pink color of the nail beds and skin of the affected extremity (or precatheterization color in children with darker skin), warm temperature, equal and regular pulses, and rapid capillary refill. Signs of compromised blood flow such as cyanosis, coolness or mottling, numbness or tingling, and excessive bleeding from the puncture site should be reported to the physician immediately.

Intake and output should be monitored to evaluate circulatory status and renal function.

Decreased output or hematuria may result from the physiological response of the kidneys to the dye used for the catheterization x-ray studies.[2]

If no complications, such as hemorrhage, infection, arrhythmias, or allergic reactions, develop, the child will usually resume his diet as tolerated after the procedure. Activity may be limited after the catheterization but will return to normal after the puncture site has healed. If no other treatment is planned, the child may be discharged from the hospital in 2 or 3 days. Dismissal teaching should include information regarding care of the puncture site.

In *angiocardiography* a radiopaque medium is introduced by catheter into a selected part or parts of the cardiovascular system. A series of x-rays or moving pictures are taken as the contrast medium is introduced into the body and flows through the heart. An angiogram demonstrates anatomic detail of the heart structures and is usually done in conjunction with cardiac catheterization.

Congestive heart failure

Signs and symptoms of congestive heart failure at or soon after birth indicate that the heart of the newborn is unable to adapt to extrauterine life. *Heart failure*, or pump failure, reflects the inability of the myocardium to circulate sufficient oxygen and nutrients to meet the metabolic requirements of the body. *Congestive* refers to the symptoms related to fluid accumulation in various parts of the body.

Heart failure occurs when the heart is unable to keep up with its work load because of ineffective contractions, inability to fill properly, or hindrance in blood flow through the chambers of the heart. Congenital heart anomalies may cause heart failure either by a hindrance of blood flow through a narrowed valve or by increased work load on the heart. Increased work load occurs when blood is shunted from one chamber to another, leading to increased work for the affected chamber.

In order to supply enough blood to the body, the heart must maintain an adequate cardiac output. Cardiac output is the amount of blood ejected by the heart per minute. It is dependent upon the heart rate and *stroke volume*, the amount of blood ejected from the heart with each contraction. A congenital heart anomaly that blocks effective blood flow forces the heart to respond with *compensatory mechanisms* that maintain or improve circulation to the tissues and organs of the body.

Increased sympathetic nervous system activity is an early compensatory mechanism. As the heart fails, reserves of norepinephrine, a neurotransmitter substance, become depleted and circulating norepinephrine from the adrenal gland acts to constrict the blood vessels. This action returns more blood to the heart and augments the stroke volume. Another compensatory mechanism diverts blood from the stomach, intestines, and kidneys to the central nervous system and myocardium. The decreased blood volume through the kidneys leads to a decreased glomerular filtration rate. This stimulates the release of renin and aldosterone, causing sodium and water retention. Fluid and sodium retention aids cardiac output by increasing the volume of fluid returning to the heart. Hypertrophy and dilatation, a third compensatory mechanism, increase heart size to maximize pumping effectiveness. Tachycardia also helps the heart to compensate by increasing the rate to maintain an adequate cardiac output.

These mechanisms are unable to maintain the work load of the heart for long. *Cardiac decompensation* occurs and the child exhibits signs of congestive heart failure. Since the body tissues and organs are deprived of sufficient oxygen and nutrients for metabolic needs, *malaise* or lethargy may be present. *Tachycardia* and a gallop rhythm are usually observed. Decreased urinary output, *oliguria*, may occur if renal perfusion is impaired. *Weak peripheral pulses* are present and the extremities may be cool, mottled, and cyanotic because of peripheral vasoconstriction and diversion of blood to vital organs. On x-ray's, the heart is usually enlarged, signifying the compensatory mechanisms of hypertrophy and dilation in response to the increased stress and work load.

In adults, heart failure may be predominantly right-sided or left-sided before the whole heart becomes involved. In children, it is usually impossible to make a clear distinction between right- and left-sided heart failure.[3] It is helpful, however, to consider the specific signs manifested in left-sided or right-sided failure in order to understand the total process and effects on the body.

Failure which involves the left side of the heart is manifested by symptoms of altered respiratory function and respiratory distress. Tachypnea and dyspnea are the primary manifestations of left-sided heart failure. Wheezing, pulmonary rales, a hacking cough, and orthopnea (assuming an upright position to facilitate breathing) may also be present. A gallop rhythm is best heard with the bell of the stethoscope over the apex of the heart when the child is in a supine position. This signifies the decreased ability of the left ventricle to accommodate the increased blood volume. The presence of pink, frothy sputum and cyanosis would further indicate the severely impaired gas exchange due to fluid accumulation in the aveoli. It is important to note that infants and young children do not verbally communicate their breathing difficulty. The astute nurse must look for other signs of respiratory distress such as tachypnea, nasal flaring, retractions, wheezing, grunting, restlessness, or apprehension.

Right-sided heart failure is due to an increased volume of blood on the right side of the heart. The principle sign of right-sided failure is *hepatomegaly*, an enlarged liver, due to systemic congestion. Neck vein distention may be present in older children but is difficult to evaluate in newborns and infants because of their short necks. Peripheral edema is usually not present in young children though facial edema or ascites may be observed. Fluid retention in an infant may be subtly reflected in a weight gain of a few ounces. Anorexia and abdominal pain may be present.

Nursing management of a child in congestive heart failure is directed toward increasing the efficiency of the heart and lessening the work load of the stressed myocardium. These goals are accomplished through the use of specific medications, rest, positioning, close observation, and fluid and nutrition balance.

The chief method of improving the strength of cardiac contraction is through the administration of a digitalis preparation (Table 26-4). Though the types of preparations vary in their onset and dosage, each increases the force of contraction (inotropic action) and slows the heart rate (chronotropic action). These two effects enable the heart to empty more completely. In order to achieve a therapeutic blood level quickly, initial doses of the selected preparation are higher than usual (based on the child's weight). The administration of loading doses to achieve a therapeutic blood level is termed *digitalization*. After a therapeutic blood level is reached, lower maintenance doses are given twice a day. The administration of the correct dose is crucial. Two nurses should always double-check the order and dosage, comparing it to suggested dosage ranges for the child's weight. The elixir or liquid form of digitalis is useful for infants and young children. The nurse should

Table 26-4 Drugs used to improve myocardial efficiency in the treatment of congestive heart failure

Medication	Usual dosage	Pharmacological action	Side effects	Nursing implications
Digoxin (digitalization)	Premature infant: 0.035 mg/kg PO Newborn: 0.05 mg/kg PO <2 years: 0.05–0.07 mg/kg PO >2 years: 0.03–0.05 mg/kg PO IM or IV: 75–80% of PO dose; $\frac{1}{4}$–$\frac{1}{3}$ given in 2 divided doses in 24 h	Strengthens myocardial contraction by stimulation of the vagus nerve to decrease the heart rate; improves cardiac output; has some use in the treatment of arrhythmias	Gastrointestinal irritation "Digitalis toxicity," especially bradycardia or tachycardia	Check apical pulse for 1 full min Do *not* administer if pulse is less than 60 in adolescents and adults or 100 in infants. Check with physician Report low potassium level before digoxin administration Report signs of digoxin toxicity
Aminophylline	20 mg/kg per 24 h	Dilates pulmonary blood vessels to improve oxygen–carbon dioxide gas exchange Dilates coronary arteries Increases cardiac output	Gastrointestinal irritation Central nervous system stimulation, especially in children. Signs include: headache, restlessness, and irritability Hypotension with IV administration	Report signs of nausea and vomiting related to the drug Check signs of central nervous system stimulation Check blood pressure every 5 min during IV infusion and for 1 h following infusion
Lasix	1–3 mg/kg per 24 h PO IM or IV: 1–2 mg/kg per 24 h	Inhibits sodium reabsorption in the loop of Henle, promoting water excretion and thereby decreasing the circulating blood volume and reducing venous return as well as cardiac output	Hypokalemia	Monitor electrolyte levels, especially potassium Encourage intake of foods high in potassium: orange juice and bananas
Morphine sulfate	IM or IV: 0.1–0.2 mg/kg q4–6 h, usually PRN	Narcotic analgesic, relaxes smooth muscles and dilates pulmonary blood vessels Central nervous system depressant, relieving anxiety and restlessness	Depresses respirations and causes hypotension Causes constipation	Evaluate respiratory status and blood pressure frequently Use additional safety precautions

take an apical pulse for 1 full min before giving the medication. Though procedures vary slightly from one institution to another, the usual policy is to check with a physician before giving the drug if the pulse is lower than 100 in infants or below 60 in older children.

Oxygen therapy is employed to increase the amount of circulating oxygen in the blood and reduce the stress on the myocardium. In young infants, a hood may be used while a face mask will be used in older children. If oxygen is delivered with mist, as is frequently done, the nurse should observe that the amount of mist is not too great so as to increase the amount of fluid in lungs already filled with fluid. Aminophylline or a similar theophylline derivative (Table 26-4) may be used to dilate and relax the bronchioles and increase gas exchange.

Positioning is extremely important in the nursing management of a child with congestive heart failure. A semi-Fowler's (45° elevation) helps to decrease venous return of blood to the right atrium, prevents abdominal organs from placing pressure on the diaphragm, and allows fluid in the lungs to flow to the lower lobes. The surface area by which gas exchange takes place is increased. Car seats or infant seats are helpful in positioning infants in an upright position. The position should be changed every 2 h to prevent complications of immobility, such as pressure sores and pneumonia. Promote skin integrity by applying lotion and avoiding such drying agents as harsh soaps.

Provide periods of rest. Observe activity tolerance to prevent overexertion. Alternate periods of such activity as bathing with rest breaks. Feeding difficulties are common since infants with congestive failure are prone to dyspnea and fatigue. This can lead to frustration for the parents as well as the child. Use larger-holed nipples to minimize the energy needed for sucking. Formulas with increased calories per ounce may be helpful in providing optimal nutrition. Feed the infant in an upright position and allow him to pull away from the nipple to rest. Such quiet, age-appropriate activities as playing with musical toys and rocking for an infant and reading and listening to music for older children are helpful. Small amounts of morphine sulfate (Table 26-4) may be given to relieve anxiety and excessive restlessness.

Vital signs are taken frequently and respira-

Table 26-5 Guidelines for the care of a child on a monitor

1. Use grounded electrical equipment *only*.
2. Set high-low pulse parameters appropriate for the child's age.
3. Apply electrode pads to clean dry skin for a selected lead pattern. Lead II (RA,RL,LL) is a commonly used pattern.
4. Ensure a clear picture on the oscilloscope by:
   a. Checking electrode pads, wires, and cable for adequate electrical function
   b. Reapplying electrode pads every 1 to 2 days and when necessary
5. Explain basic monitor function and alarm sounds to the child and family.
6. Allow the child and family to express feelings about the monitor.

tions assessed for rate, regularity, and depth. The presence or absence of cyanosis and degree of edema should be accurately recorded. Although respirations and heart rate may be mechanically monitored (Table 26-5), the direct observation of the child must continue. The monitor is only an assessment aid.

Measure intake and output carefully. All intake (oral fluids, intravenous fluids) must be balanced or fairly equal with all output (urine, emesis, stools). A principle tool in assessing fluid balance is accurately weighing the child twice a day. Weigh the child at the same time each day, usually before breakfast, with the same amount of clothing on. Undress the infant and protect him from drafts. Disposable diapers are weighed before and after use and the dry weight is substracted from the wet to determine the quantity of urine (1 ml = 1g). It is wise to have another nurse double-check a child's weight when there is a significant change from the previous weight. A 24-h fluid balance is calculated at midnight or 6 A.M. Any significant discrepancies between the amount of fluid taken in and the amount of fluid excreted should be reported. Diuretics such as furosemide (Lasix), (Table 26-8) are administered to promote sodium and water excretion. Since potassium is excreted with the sodium, it is important to encourage intake of foods high in potassium.

Long-term follow-up care and parent education are important since many children with recurrent congestive heart failure will continue the therapeutic regime after discharge. Parents should be given written instructions regarding the medications the child will be taking at home. Teach the parents to follow guidelines in administering the digitalis preparation. Double-check the dose, take the apical pulse before giving the medication, and check it against designated high-low pulse parameters. Occasionally, a child may miss a dose of digoxin. Should more than one dose be skipped due to emesis, refusal, or other reason, the physician should be consulted. Parents should encourage children taking diuretics to eat foods high in potassium. Include in discharge teaching the importance of positioning, feeding suggestions, prevention of infections, and anticipatory guidance for future episodes of heart failure.

The prognosis of children with congestive heart failure depends on the cause and severity of the heart disease. Early diagnosis is a necessity. Accurate nursing assessment and appropriate intervention facilitate early recognition and prompt medical treatment.

A nursing care plan is presented at the end of the chapter for an infant with congestive heart

Figure 26-8 Patent ductus arteriosus.

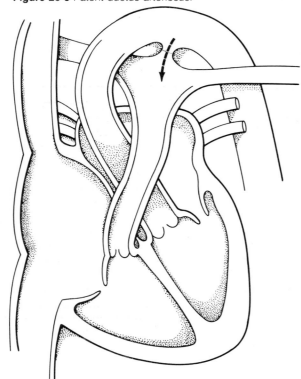

failure secondary to a congenital malformation, ventricular septal defect.

Congenital heart defects

There are many recognized types of congenital heart malformations. Nine common lesions represent 90 percent of all anomalies. Heart defects may be classified according to the presence or absence of cyanosis and the degree of pulmonary vascularity (blood flow to the lungs). The abnormality may be so minor that the individual is hardly affected. In other instances, it may be so major that other body systems must compensate in some way for the defective structure. The severity of the defect directly influences the symptoms exhibited and the overall prognosis. The signs and symptoms each child presents are merely a reflection of the hemodynamic alterations of each specific defect. Classification of congenital heart defects is difficult because of their variety and complexity. Traditionally, they are grouped into acyanotic and cyanotic categories, but it must be remembered that the types of lesions that usually cause cyanosis do not always do so; lesions that usually do not produce cyanosis will do so under special circumstances.

Acyanotic heart defects

Acyanotic heart defects are those that usually do not cause cyanosis. Acyanotic heart disease is more common than cyanotic heart disease. In acyanotic disease, either there is no shunting, or diversion of blood or else there is left-to-right shunting with blood diverted from the left side of the heart (oxygen-enriched) to the right side (oxygen-depleted); therefore, only bright red oxygen-enriched blood enters the systemic circulation. A left-to-right shunt causes increased amount of blood flow into the lungs and a tendency towards respiratory infections.

In patent ductus arteriosus, atrial septal defect, and ventricular septal defect, pulmonary vascularity is increased due to the larger volume of blood in the lungs. Normal pulmonary vascularity exists in coarctation of the aorta and aortic stenosis; these types of acyanotic lesions are not associated with shunting.

Patent ductus arteriosus During fetal life, the ductus arteriosus maintains communication between the pulmonary artery and the aorta. Failure of closure of the ductus after birth allows that communication to persist (Fig. 26-8). Patent ductus arteriosus (PDA) is one of the most common congenital heart defects. Specific populations known to be at increased risk include:

1. Premature infants
2. Infants with respiratory distress syndrome or neonatal hypoxia
3. Infants born at high altitudes
4. Infants whose mother had rubella the first trimester of pregnancy.

Blood flows from areas of higher to lower pressure. The direction of shunting through the ductus depends on the pressure difference between the aorta and the pulmonary artery. With the onset of respiration at birth, pulmonary vascular resistance begins to decrease. Separation of the placenta from the arterial system increases systemic vascular resistance, and aortic pressure rises. When aortic pressure exceeds pulmonary artery pressure, well-oxygenated blood is shunted from the aorta through the ductus to the pulmonary artery. The result of this increased flow is an increased volume load on the lungs, the left atrium, and the left ventricle. If the ductus is large, the right ventricle may have to generate higher pressures to eject its volume of blood into the pulmonary artery, as aortic pressures will be transmitted through the ductus to the pulmonary artery.

Presenting symptoms depend upon the size of the ductus, the pressure difference between the aorta and the pulmonary artery, and the volume of blood flow through the ductus. In severe cases, congestive heart failure occurs. With small shunts, the presenting symptoms may be minimal. The rapid runoff from the aorta through the patent ductus decreases peripheral vascular resistance. This lowers the diastolic pressure and increases the pulse pressure. Features found on physical examination include bounding peripheral pulses and a systolic or diastolic murmur heard best at the upper left sternal border and under the left clavicle. A history of fatigue, weak cry, breathlessness, feeding difficulties, and increased susceptibility to upper respiratory infections may be elicited. With large shunts, there is increased risk of congestive heart failure, pulmonary hypertension, and bacterial endocarditis.

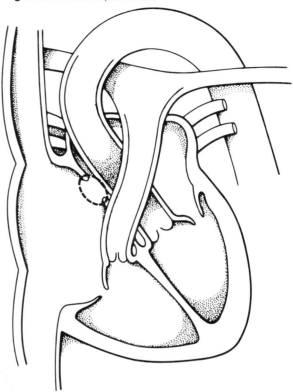

Figure 26-9 Atrial septal defect.

Correction of a PDA has traditionally been done by surgical ligation. Cardiopulmonary bypass is not required and the mortality rate is very low. Recently, investigation of indomethacin (Indocin) has begun. Indomethacin, a prostaglandin synthetase inhibitor, appears useful in producing closure of the PDA in premature infants.[4] Closure of the ductus restores normal circulation and children whose PDA has been closed can look forward to a normal life.

Atrial septal defects An atrial septal defect (ASD) is an abnormal opening in the atrial septum (Fig. 26-9). The two most common types are *ostium secundum* and *ostium primum*. An *ostium secundum* defect occurs in the midportion of the septum. An *ostium secundum* defect is more than just an anatomically open foramen ovale. The foramen ovale is normally held closed by left atrial pressure on a flap of septal tissue. An *ostium primum* defect is an abnormal opening low in the septum. It is nearly always associated with a cleft or abnormality in the mitral valve that may render the valve incompetent.

An ASD usually results in the shunting of blood from the left atrium to the right because pressure is higher in the left atrium. The flow through the ASD may range from small to very large amounts. With anything other than an extremely small defect, right and left atrial pressures tend to equalize. Once this occurs, the degree of shunting is dependent on the relative distensibility of the ventricles. The right ventricle, being thinner-walled and less muscular than the left, accepts an extra volume load more readily. In diastole, during ventricular filling, the presence of an ASD allows all four chambers of the heart to communicate. At this point, the blood in the left atrium will take the path of least resistance and flow through the right atrium into the right ventricle.[5]

Shunting of blood from left to right through an ASD causes an increase in the work load of the right ventricle and increased blood flow through the pulmonary circulation. This eventually leads to right ventricular hypertrophy and may result in congestive heart failure. Heart failure is unusual in the infant or child with ASD but more commonly develops in untreated adults.

Most infants and children with an ASD are relatively asymptomatic, especially if the defect is of the *ostium secundum* variety. Typically, the splitting of the second heart sound is wide and "fixed," and heard on expiration as well as inspiration. This is due to the increased stroke volume of the right ventricle, which delays closure of the pulmonary valve. The characteristic pulmonary ejection murmur heard during systole is often not present in the infant due to the existence of normal right ventricular hypertrophy. Growth may be somewhat retarded but generally tends to fall within normal limits. There may be less than the normal tolerance for exercise and the child may have frequent upper respiratory infections. If mitral regurgitation is associated with an *ostium primum* defect, there will be increased pressure in the left atrium and in the pulmonary vascular bed. These children are at greater risk for developing congestive heart failure.

In the presence of increased right atrial pressures due to alterations in heart structure or increased resistance to pulmonary blood flow, shunting will be from right to left. The same mechanism may cause right-to-left shunting through an anatomically patent foramen ovale. The child with right-to-left shunting is likely to manifest some degree of cyanosis. It should be noted that the newborn with an ASD may exhibit transient cyanosis. The right-to-left shunt in this situation is due to the high pulmonary resistance and the normal right ventricular hypertrophy found in the neonate.

Surgical correction of both types of atrial septal defects is relatively simple. By utilizing cardiopulmonary bypass, repair of the septum is accomplished either by oversewing the small defect or by closing larger openings with a pericardial or Dacron patch. In the *ostium primum* defect, the cleft in the mitral valve is also repaired. Complications after surgery are minimal but include, on occasion, air emboli and transient heart block if suturing was done near the bundle of His.

The ideal age for surgical closure is approximately 5 years. Children whose defects are repaired before they reach the age of 20 are often able to lead normal, active lives. Survival rates are high. Surgical risk is lowest during the first 10 years of life and increases only slightly for the next decade. After this, risk increases with age as do the number of postoperative complications.[6]

Ventricular septal defect Incomplete development of the ventricular septum during fetal life will establish communication between the right and left ventricles and result in an abnormal blood flow pattern (Fig. 26-10). If the defect is small or moderate in size, the amount of blood directed through the ventricular septal defect (VSD) will be limited by its size. When the defect is large, the relative resistance offered to flow out of the two chambers will determine the amount and direction of flow through the septal defect. The direction of flow is always determined by the difference in resistance to outflow from each ventricle. In the absence of other heart defects, the shunt is from the left ventricle to the right ventricle because pulmonary vascular resistance is lower than systemic vascular resistance.

A small- to moderate-sized VSD results in an increased volume in the right ventricle, pulmonary vasculature, left atrium, and left ventricle, whereas a large defect results in both an increased volume and pressure load. With large defects, the higher left ventricular pressures are transmitted to the right ventricle and pulmonary system. In response to this, pulmonary vascular resistance may rise as nature's method of reducing the extra blood flow through the lungs.

The symptoms of a VSD vary with its size. Children with small-to-moderate defects may be asymptomatic. Children with large defects present classic signs of heart failure after the first month of life. These include increased respiratory rate, difficulty feeding, irritability, excessive perspiration, tachycardia, mild cyanosis, repeated pulmonary infections, and slow growth.

Management of children with a VSD is influenced by the knowledge that many of the defects of small-to-moderate size will close spontaneously in the early months of life. Prophylactic antibiotic therapy prior to and following dental care or operative procedures is used to prevent bacterial endocarditis. Asymptomatic children whose defects do not close spontaneously or those with large shunts should have their VSD surgically corrected with a Dacron patch prior to starting school. If pulmonary hypertension is present, surgical repair before 2 years of age provides protection from irreversible damage to the small arteries of the lungs.

Symptomatic infants are treated with digoxin and diuretics. If this controls the symptoms, the operation is deferred until the infant is older and weighs 25 lb. For those infants who do not respond to medical management, either surgical closure of the VSD or a pulmonary artery banding to decrease flow through the pulmonary circulation may be indicated. Complete correction of the VSD is currently favored over banding since a large portion of children who have had banding require reconstruction of the pulmonary artery at some future time.[7] Postoperative complications primarily include congestive heart failure and arrhythmias due to injury of the interventricular septum. Most children with a repaired ventricular septal defect should reach adult life with a good prognosis and lead normal lives.[8]

Coarctation of the aorta Coarctation is a narrowing in the lumen of the aorta (Fig. 26-11). The constriction commonly occurs near the ductus arteriosus and is often described as "preductal" (before the ductus) or "postductal" (after the

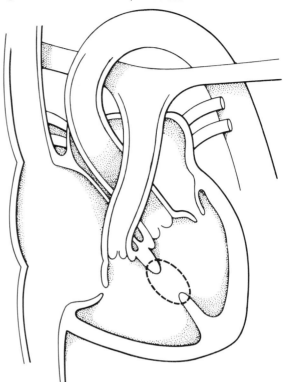

Figure 26-10 Ventricular septal defect.

ductus). The resulting obstruction of blood flow through the aorta presents two major hemodynamic problems. First, the left ventricle must generate higher than normal pressures to eject an adequate stroke volume. Second, there is a reduced systolic pressure distal to the coarctation. In many cases, the body compensates for the obstruction to blood flow by developing collateral vessels to carry blood around the obstruction.

Presenting symptoms vary according to the severity of the defect, its anatomic location, and the presence or absence of associated cardiac anomalies. The typical patient with coarctation is a male whose anomaly was discovered during a routine physical exam. When questioned, he may report episodes of sudden and unexplained epistaxis, frequent headaches, and leg fatigue. Examination frequently reveals full, bounding pulses in the upper extremities, weak or absent pulses in the lower extremities, and a systolic

Figure 26-11 Coarctation of the aorta.

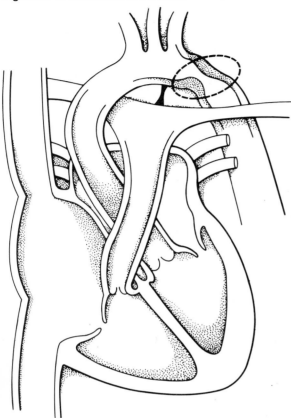

pressure that is higher in the arms than in the legs. Better development of head and shoulders than hips and legs is possible. A comparison of femoral and radial pulses will also show a delay in the femoral. Pulsation is often seen, and a thrill palpated, in the suprasternal notch.

The murmur of coarctation is systolic. It is heard posteriorly along the spine at the level of the obstruction. Both systolic and diastolic murmurs may be heard in other areas of the back and over the precordium. These are most often related to collateral circulation or to the coexistence of other cardiac anomalies.[9]

Congestive heart failure, poor weight gain, and feeding difficulties can occur early in the infant whose coarctation is severe. Other accompanying defects contribute to early congestive failure. The adult with uncorrected coarctation is at risk for congestive heart failure, a dissecting aortic aneurysm (blood-filled sac within the layers of the arterial wall), or aortic rupture. Bacterial endocarditis may also occur. Systemic hypertension may lead to cerebral hemorrhage. Infants who manifest early congestive heart failure are often managed medically and surgery is delayed until they are older. For those who do not respond to such treatment, surgical intervention provides the best chance for survival. Repair of coarctation involves removal of the narrowed segment of the aorta with either end-to-end anastomosis or insertion of an aortic graft. More recently, patch graft enlargement of the narrowed segment has been used, with either a cloth patch or the ligated and divided left subclavian artery as a patch. Ideally, the operation is delayed as long as possible to allow the aorta to grow. Repair is done sometime between 3 and 10 years before systemic hypertension becomes irreversible.

Prognosis is good for the asymptomatic child with simple coarctation. Surgical repair of the infant, the child with severe symptoms, or the adult increases the risk. High mortality rates accompany early repair in infants. Of those infants who survive, additional surgery may be needed later in childhood since stenosis can develop at the site of anastomosis. Without correction of the defect, few people will live past the age of 50.[10]

Pulmonary stenosis Pulmonary stenosis refers to any lesion obstructing flow from the right ventricle to the lungs. Obstruction to flow may occur above or below the pulmonary valve, but in the majority of patients with isolated pulmonary stenosis, the obstruction is stenosis of the pulmonary valve itself.[11]

Blood flow through the pulmonary vasculature may be normal or diminished as a result of pulmonary valve stenosis. To maintain pulmonary blood flow, the right ventricle must produce a high systolic pressure. The right ventricle hypertrophies, and the thickened ventricle offers more resistance to filling. Right ventricle diastolic pressure then rises with a corresponding rise in right atrial pressure. If the pulmonary stenosis is severe enough to start this chain of events, the high right atrial pressure may reopen the foramen ovale. A right-to-left shunt through the foramen ovale will then occur.

On examination, a thrill and murmur, which radiate upward and to the left, are heard loudest in the second or third left interspace near the sternal border. The second heart sound is notably split.[12] Children with mild stenosis are usually asymptomatic. Infants with severe pulmonary stenosis will have profound congestive heart failure. The symptoms most frequently seen in moderate-to-severe stenosis are dyspnea and fatigue. Major symptoms frequently do not occur until just prior to death.

The treatment depends on the severity of the stenosis. Pulmonary stenosis is not a static process. Children diagnosed as having this type of defect need to be followed closely. Surgery is necessary with a severe stenosis. Cardiopulmonary bypass is utilized and a valvulotomy is performed.

Infants who present with congestive heart failure with pulmonary stenosis have a less favorable prognosis than those without failure. Children with mild stenosis have a normal life expectancy without surgical repair. The long-term results of valvulotomy have been excellent. Without surgery, children with severe stenosis rarely live to their twenties.

Aortic stenosis Aortic stenosis has been identified in various forms. The largest percentage of children have valvular stenosis. The aortic valve may be bicuspid, unicuspid, or tricuspid.[13] In aortic stenosis, the left ventricle ejects its volume of blood through an orifice that is reduced in size. To accomplish this, the left ventricular systolic pressure rises, sometimes to as high as 250 mmHg. To generate these pressures, the left ventricle hypertrophies. The thickened ventricle offers more resistance to filling and so diastolic pressure also rises. This rise in diastolic pressure in the left ventricle is transmitted to the left atrium, pulmonary vein, lungs, pulmonary artery, and right ventricle. The hypertrophy of the left ventricle leads to increased oxygen demand. Coronary artery blood flow may not be adequate to meet that demand.

Males have a higher incidence of aortic stenosis than females. Most children with aortic stenosis develop normally and are asymptomatic. The presence of a murmur at the aortic area raises the suspicion of this congenital defect.

On examination, a thrill is present and the cardiac impulse is heaving. The first heart sound is normal. The second heart sound is altered due to prolonged left ventricular ejection. The second heart sound may become single; the split may become narrow or aortic closure may follow pulmonary closure. The murmur is systolic and is usually heard throughout the precordium.[14] A careful history may reveal symptoms of mild fatigue and dyspnea. Symptoms of angina or syncope, though they seldom occur, are important, as are signs of congestive failure in infants since they may indicate the presence of significant stenosis.

There is an increased incidence of sudden death in the presence of severe aortic stenosis.[15] Children with moderate stenosis may not be allowed to participate in competitive sports. Children with mild stenosis are not limited in activities. Follow-up management is required because the degree of stenosis may progress. Most children lead normal lives through childhood and adolescence. Signs and symptoms of the stenosis often do not become obvious until the fourth or fifth decade of life.

Surgery is indicated for those who have significant stenosis with symptoms or severe stenosis in the absence of symptoms. The repair requires cardiopulmonary bypass. A valvulotomy, considered a palliative procedure, may be performed. Although it relieves the stenosis the best way possible, usually some degree of stenosis remains. An additional operation for valve replacement may be required at a later date.

Cyanotic heart defects

As described earlier, cyanosis reflects the presence of reduced oxygen in the blood circulating through the tissues. A right-to-left shunt usually exists, allowing some of the systemic venous blood to bypass the lungs and re-enter the systemic arterial circulation. Pulmonary vascularity may be increased (as in most children with transposition of the great arteries or in truncus arteriosus) or decreased (as in tetralogy of Fallot and tricuspid atresia) depending on the presence or absence of an obstructed blood flow between the heart and the lungs.

Cyanosis is typically associated with (1) clubbing of fingers and toes (Fig. 26-4) due to lack of oxygen-enriched blood circulating in the periphery, (2) poor growth, (3) a tendency to develop cerebral abscesses, and (4) polycythemia. In polycythemia, the tissue hypoxia related to cyanosis stimulates bone marrow to increase red blood cell production for additional oxygen-carrying ability. Elevated hemoglobin and hematocrit result. Infants, however, are prone to develop iron-deficiency anemia that may disguise the elevated values. A low or normal hemoglobin in children with cyanotic heart disease may reflect an iron deficiency requiring an iron supplement.

Complete transposition of the great arteries

Complete transposition of the great arteries (TGA) involves reversal of the anatomic positions of the aorta and the pulmonary artery (Fig. 26-12). The aorta originates from the *right* ventricle and the pulmonary artery originates from the *left* ventricle. Therefore, venous blood entering the right atrium will go to the right ventricle and return to the systemic circulation via the aorta without having passed through the lungs to be oxygenated. Oxygenated blood entering the left atrium from the pulmonary circulation will travel to the left ventricle and return to the lungs without having supplied any oxygen to the body. Thus,

Figure 26-12 Complete transposition of the great arteries.

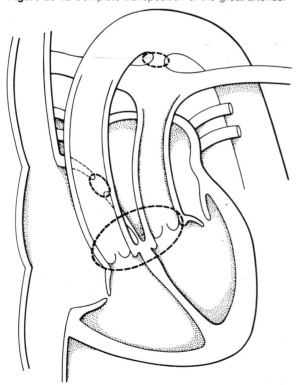

two entirely separate circulatory systems are established.

The separation of the systemic and pulmonary circulations will result in death shortly after birth unless there is a communication between them. This communication is usually present in the form of a ventricular septal defect, an interatrial opening, or a patent ductus arteriosus. These, either alone or in combination, allow for the mixing of oxygenated with unoxygenated blood. In this way, the body receives enough oxygen to allow survival. Shunting of blood must be balanced, with equal amounts going in either direction, or overload of one or the other system will occur.

The typical infant with complete transposition is a male of normal or high birth weight who is visibly cyanotic. Tachypnea is often present due to pulmonary venous congestion. Closure of the ductus arteriosus can lead to sudden deterioration in the condition of an infant who is dependent on that structure for a large portion of systemic oxygenation.

Auscultation may yield little information. It is possible that a variety of abnormal sounds may be heard, depending on the nature of the communication between the right and left heart. Conversely, there may be no murmurs.

If the child survives early infancy, growth and development are generally retarded. Clubbing of fingers and toes is seen. Polycythemia develops and, if severe or prolonged, puts the child at risk for thrombosis and congestive heart failure. Respiratory infections are common.

If the infant is in severe distress, a palliative procedure is often done in the first few days or weeks of life. The desired objective is to allow better mixing of the oxygenated blood circulating through the lungs with the oxygen-depleted blood circulating through the body. The method preferred, because of its relatively low mortality rate and simplicity, is that of *balloon atrial septostomy*. During cardiac catheterization, a catheter with a balloon tip is passed from the right to the left atrium via the foramen ovale. The tip is then inflated and pulled forcefully through the atrial septum, tearing it. This procedure is repeated until maximum effect is achieved. In many cases, arterial oxygen saturation is greatly improved. When atrial septostomy is not effective, an atrial septal defect may be created surgically.

The infant with complete transposition accompanied by a large ventricular septal defect is subject to high pulmonary blood flow. In order to control congestive heart failure and to prevent the development of increased pulmonary vascular resistance, a pulmonary artery banding may be done to decrease the amount of blood flow to the lungs.

Attempts to correct the transposition by reversing the positions of the aorta and the pulmonary artery have been associated with high mortality rates.[16] At present, the most common type of corrective operation is accomplished by redirecting the blood flow inside the atria so that the blood from the inferior and superior venae cavae flows to the left ventricle and then to the lungs. The blood from the pulmonary veins then flows to the right ventricle and to the body. Thus, venous blood will be oxygenated in the lungs and carried to the body in the correct functional sequence, even though the right ventricle still pumps to the aorta and the left ventricle to the pulmonary artery.

When transposition is associated with a VSD and pulmonary stenosis, the Rastelli operation gives both functional and anatomic correction. It involves tunneling blood inside the heart to connect the left ventricle to the aorta and using a conduit (tube) outside the heart to connect the right ventricle to the pulmonary artery.

Surgical repair of transposition has significantly improved the prognosis of the infant with this defect. Problems encountered following surgery include arrhythmias and pulmonary vascular and venous obstruction due to baffle occlusion.[17] The ability of the right ventricle to continue to perform left ventricular work over a long period of time is difficult to determine.

Truncus arteriosus Truncus arteriosus is an uncommon lesion consisting of a large ventricular septal defect and a single artery supplying the systemic and pulmonary circulations (Fig. 26-13). The truncus valve structure is frequently abnormal. Both ventricles eject their contents into the common artery, where oxygenated and oxygen-depleted blood mix. The oxygen saturation of this mixture is largely dependent upon the relative volume of pulmonary blood flow. If pulmonary vascular resistance is high or the pulmonary arteries are small, arterial oxygen levels will be low. When the pulmonary arteries

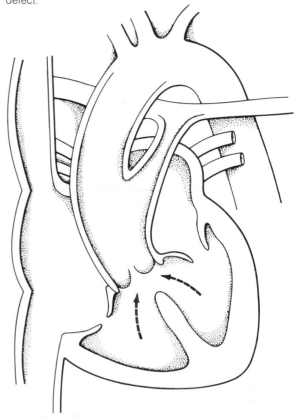

Figure 26-13 Truncus arteriosus with ventricular septal defect.

are of normal size and pulmonary resistance is low, saturation of the truncus blood is greatly improved and cyanosis is absent.

Infants with truncus arteriosus are characteristically ashen and cyanotic; the degree of cyanosis depends upon which variety of the defect they have. Other symptoms frequently seen are dyspnea and fatigue associated with congestive heart failure. Generally growth and development are retarded. A systolic murmur is usually present and the second heart sound is single.

Most infants who present with this defect are very sick. Initial medical treatment is aimed at control of congestive heart failure, but for many surgical intervention provides the only possibility for long-term survival. When a large pulmonary flow is present, the pulmonary arteries may be banded to prevent the development of high pulmonary vascular resistance. Complete correction closes the VSD, leaving the truncus to serve as the aorta, and re-establishes communication between the right ventricle and the pulmonary arteries by means of a conduit. Mortality is high if the patient is under the age of 2 years or if high pulmonary vascular resistance exists.[18]

Tetralogy of Fallot   Four abnormalities are classically present in tetralogy of Fallot. They include: (1) right ventricular outflow obstruction, (2) a large VSD, (3) overriding of the VSD by the aorta, and (4) right ventricular hypertrophy (Fig. 26-14). The obstruction to right ventricular outflow may be located in the infundibulum of the right ventricle (smooth area directly below the pulmonary valve), in the pulmonary valve, or in the pulmonary artery or its branches. Pressures in the left and right ventricle are equal because of the large VSD. Since right ventricular pressures cannot exceed left, blood flow through the pulmonary system is limited by the amount of resistance offered by the obstruction to pulmonary flow. The blood which is not ejected into the pulmonary circulation crosses the VSD and is ejected into the aorta.

The right-to-left shunt and limited pulmonary blood flow are responsible for the outstanding clinical features of the disease. Cyanosis, usually not present at birth, appears sometime during the first year of life and generally becomes progressively severe. Clubbing of the fingertips may be seen in older infants and children. The knee-chest position is frequently preferred by these children; squatting is characteristic following exercise or walking. They are frequently small for their age and their activities are limited. A systolic murmur and a single second heart sound will be heard on physical examination.[19]

Many of these children have hypoxic spells characterized by increased rate and depth of respirations accompanied by increasing cyanosis. This may progress to unconsciousness, seizures, and even death. These episodes may occur frequently, rarely, or never. Treatment of hypoxic spells includes placing the child in knee-chest position to increase systemic venous return to the heart. Morphine sulfate, propranolol (Inderal), sodium bicarbonate, and even general anesthesia have been utilized to interrupt the attack.[20] Polycythemia develops early in children with tetralogy to increase the oxygen-carrying ability of the blood. Over time, collateral circulation to the lungs may increase. Both the knee-chest position and polycythemia are mechanisms for relieving hypoxia.

Palliative shunt procedures are utilized to increase blood supply to the lungs until the child is older and is physically more able to undergo total correction (Table 26-6).

Complete correction includes relieving the obstruction of right ventricular outflow and closing the VSD. In some centers, complete correction is being done at earlier ages, thus avoiding the palliative shunt procedures. The immediate postoperative course following complete correction of tetralogy of Fallot may be difficult. Problems frequently encountered include hemorrhage, low cardiac output, and arrhythmias (especially heart block).

Tricuspid atresia   Tricuspid atresia is a defect accompanied by a number of anatomic varia-

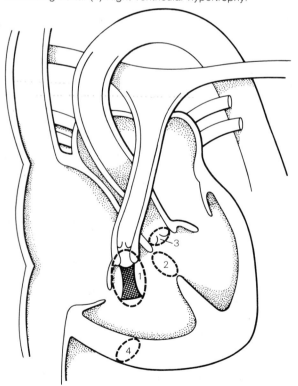

Figure 26-14 Tetralogy of Fallot. (1) Right ventricular outflow obstruction. (2) Ventricular septal defect. (3) Overriding aorta. (4) Right ventricular hypertrophy.

tions. The hallmark sign is absence of the tricuspid valve (Fig. 26-15). No direct communication from the right atrium to the right ventricle and pulmonary vasculature is present. Blood flows from the right atrium through the interatrial septum to the left atrium and into the left ventricle. Blood flow through the pulmonary vasculature usually occurs via a ventricular septal defect. In the absence of a VSD, pulmonary blood flow is dependent on the ductus arteriosus or bronchial artery collaterals. The right ventricle is small. The right atrium is usually enlarged, and congestive heart failure is common. Pulmonary edema is rare since pulmonary blood flow is usually diminished. As a result of the abnormal flow pattern, venous and arterial blood meet and mix in the left atrium. The left ventricle is enlarged and hypertrophied. Blood delivered to the general circulation is low in oxygen because of the venous and arterial mixing in the left atrium.

These children are sick from birth. They appear undernourished and are poorly developed. Cyanosis is obvious except in the presence of adequate pulmonary flow. Dyspnea, fatigue, anoxic spells, clubbing, and signs of venous congestion are present. The first and second heart sounds are usually single. The murmur is variable or, in some cases, absent.[21] The prognosis for these children is poor, and death frequently occurs in the first year of life.[22]

Previously, a palliative shunt operation was all that was available. Now, a more corrective type operation, the Fontan operation, is done for patients who do not have pulmonary hypertension. This operation involves connection of the right atrium to the small right ventricle or to the

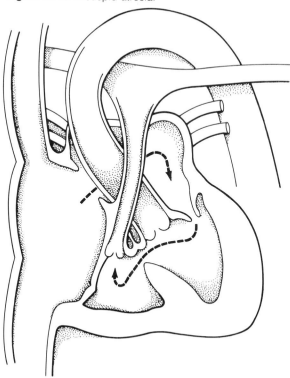

Figure 26-15 Tricuspid atresia.

pulmonary artery either directly or with a conduit. The blood then flows from right atrium to pulmonary artery without being pumped by a developed ventricle. Initial reports are encouraging, but long-term evaluation is not yet possible.[23]

Single ventricle* When no partition exists between the two ventricles or when both the mitral and tricuspid valves empty into one ventricle and the opposite one remains underdeveloped, a *univentricular* defect is present. The terms *double-inlet right ventricle* (DIRV) and *double-inlet left ventricle* (DILV) are synonymous with single ventricle.[24]

Signs and symptoms are similar to those of a child with a large VSD (poor growth, frequent upper respiratory infections, and congestive heart failure). Some right-to-left shunting may

Table 26-6 Palliative shunt procedures for children with tetralogy of Fallot

Methods of choice
1. Blalock-Taussig (BT) procedure: An anastomosis between the subclavian artery and the pulmonary artery is established.
2. Waterston procedure: A communication between the ascending aorta and right pulmonary artery is established.

Infrequently used

Potts' procedure: A communication between the descending thoracic aorta and the left pulmonary artery is established.

*The author wishes to thank Dr. Dwight McGoon, Rochester, Minnesota, for the information he provided in these sections.

occur because of the mixing of blood in the ventricle.[25]

Efforts to surgically create an artificial septum with a patch have not been encouraging. However, for persons with associated pulmonary stenosis, a modification of the operation described for tricuspid atresia has been successfully applied. A patch is sewn, closing the orifice from the right atrium to the right ventricle. Then, a drainage pathway is established directly from the right atrium to the pulmonary artery. Thus, right atrium blood flows directly into the lungs without passing through a ventricle and the one ventricle now pumps blood only to the aorta. After surgery, problems such as high right atrium pressure and other pulmonary difficulties such as pleural effusions complicate recovery.

Double-outlet right ventricle*
This defect is similar to tetralogy of Fallot in that the aorta orifice overrides the VSD. In double-outlet right ventricle (DORV), the aorta is so far displaced to the right that all or nearly all of the aorta originates from the right ventricle. If the pulmonary artery continues to originate from the right ventricle as it normally does, then both great arteries have right ventricular origin. Pulmonary stenosis may or may not be associated with DORV.

Signs and symptoms include frequent upper respiratory infections, S_3 heard at the apex of the heart, and a systolic thrill at the third and fourth intercostal space along the left sternal border.[26]

Repair is accomplished by closing the ventricular septal defect in such a way that the patch forms a tunnel which leads blood being ejected from the left ventricle through the ventricular septal defect and out the aorta.

Nursing care of the child undergoing heart surgery

When such medications as digoxin and diuretics are no longer effective in treating a child with congenital heart disease, surgical intervention may be necessary. Surgery may be emergency or elective. Usually elective surgery is done before the child enters school, around 3 to 5 years of age. When heart surgery is done, it may be

*The author wishes to thank Dr. Dwight McGoon, Rochester, Minnesota, for the information he provided in these sections.

palliative—a temporary, partial correction done at birth, or soon after, to shunt blood, thus improving oxygenation until the infant gets older. A balloon septostomy, done to create a small opening between the atria, is an example of a palliative procedure. A total correction of a defect is attempted when the risks and possible complications of the surgical procedure are less than those of not having the surgery. Generally, the younger the child, the more risks entailed in the surgery. This is especially true for newborns and infants.

Preoperative management
Assessment of a child having heart surgery is multifaceted. A cardiac catheterization may have been performed prior to surgery. Studies done before surgery include a chest x-ray and 12-lead ECG. A routine urinalysis is obtained.

Various blood studies are performed. Electrolyte and clotting studies are done as well as a complete blood count. Blood gases may be drawn if the child has a cyanotic heart defect. All the studies done provide a data base for comparison during and after surgery.

On admission, it is important to obtain accurate baseline vital signs, including apical pulse rate, blood pressure in all extremities, and an assessment of respiratory status. Record the presence, severity, and location of cyanosis. An accurate height and weight is necessary since amounts of future medications and intravenous fluids will be based on these measurements. Weigh the child without clothes. It is helpful to have another nurse double-check the weight if the infant or young child is agitated and moving around. Determine any allergies to food or medications and record these in the chart, the Kardex, and on the medication sheet. The child may be given a special allergy band (like an ID band) listing the drugs to which he is allergic. Loose teeth should be reported to prevent aspiration during intubation for surgery. Review immunization status and possible recent exposure to any communicable diseases.

Preoperative teaching
Include the child and family in preoperative teaching. Assess their level of understanding about the heart defect and the impending surgical treatment. Simple direct explanations using diagrams, drawings, miniature models, and dolls aid learning. Teaching may be

accomplished through short frequent sessions or condensed into one or two longer periods—depending on the child's age and condition.

Areas to cover in teaching include the anatomy of the heart and particular defect and preoperative, intraoperative, and postoperative procedures. Table 26-7 provides a checklist useful in teaching.

Preoperative activities prior to surgery are often frightening and overwhelming for the child. Visits by the cardiac surgeon, anesthesiologist, and, if possible, the primary ICU nurse who will care for the child after surgery help to clarify information that may be confusing or misunderstood. Explain that the child will not eat nor drink after midnight, emphasizing the importance of an empty stomach during the operation. Tell the older child about the morning preoperative medication and how it will make him feel. Even though parents are unable to go with the child to the operation, stress that they will be waiting for the child's return. Knowing loved ones are nearby waiting and taking a favorite toy along helps a child through this difficult experience (see Chap. 16).

When explaining the operative procedure, show the child as many items as possible that he will be exposed to in the coming days. Allowing the child to play with such equipment as surgical garments, anesthesia masks, and intravenous fluids and tubing facilitates the introduction of these new intrusive devices in a nonthreatening manner. Some hospitals allow visits to the operating room and intensive care

Table 26-7 Preparation of a child undergoing cardiac surgery—a checklist*

Equipment for teaching kit

Doll
Soap
Foley catheter
Intravenous equipment
Monitor leads
Cardboard model of a monitor with picture of EKG across screen
Oxygen mask
Balloons
Chest tube
Stethoscope
Syringes
Dressings or adhesive strips
"Safe" (nonthreatening) toy
Plain drawing paper and crayons or felt-tip pens

Table 26-7 Preparation of a child undergoing cardiac surgery—a checklist* (Continued)

Checklist for teaching sessions (adapted for individual child's needs)

☐ Review anatomy of heart and defect
☐ Understanding of surgical procedure
☐ Preoperative procedures explained
  1. Bath/shower with skin preparation
  2. Visits by:
      Cardiac surgeon, Dr. _____
      Anesthesiologist, Dr. _____
      ICU nurse, _____
  3. No food or drink in the morning
  4. Transportation to the OR
  5. Parents (where they will be)
☐ Operation
  1. Show equipment
      Mask, hat, gown
      Rubber face mask
  2. Visit to OR, if possible
  3. Anesthesia is a special sleep in which all body parts go to sleep. (Name a few parts.)
  4. No pain will be felt during operation
  5. Incision—type (location and size); illustrate on doll
☐ Postoperative appearance and feelings
  1. Feel sleepy
  2. Tube in mouth to breathing machine
  3. Tubes—demonstrate on doll
      a. Nasogastric
      b. Chest tube
      c. Foley catheter
      d. Pacemaker wires
      e. IV in leg or arm
      f. Arterial pressure line
      g. RA or LA line
  4. ECG monitoring shows TV picture of heart beats
  5. Suctioning, deep breathing, and coughing (blow balloons)
  6. Pain medication
  7. Oxygen mask—demonstrate on doll
☐ ICU routines
  1. Visiting hours
  2. Usual length of stay (for parents visiting and child)
  3. Special nurse with child
☐ Surgical unit transfer
☐ Response to teaching
  Child _____
  _____
  Parents _____
  _____

* Adapted from "Pre-Op Teaching Checklist for Use with Children Undergoing Cardiac Surgery," prepared by Nancy Horvath, B.S.N., Instructor, Nursing Service—Pediatrics and Pediatrics Intensive Care Units, St. Mary's Hospital, Rochester, Minn. Used by permission.

unit to further decrease anxiety in older children. A videotape of the sights and sounds on the way to the OR may be helpful.

It is comforting to the parents and child to stress the care, attention, and close observation the child will receive during and after the operation. Emphasize the presence of the anesthetist or anesthesiologist during the operation. Tell the child that he will be in a "special" kind of sleep and will feel no pain during the operation. It is helpful to reinforce that the anesthesiologist will help the child wake up as well as go to sleep.

The size of the "cut" or incision is nearly always exaggerated in children's minds. Asking them to show how big they think the incision will be or drawing a picture gives the nurse an idea of their fantasy level. Illustrating the location and size of the incision and sutures on a doll or diagram may aid in the explanation.

Further teaching regarding the postoperative experience greatly depends on the child's age. It is important to stress that a nurse will always be nearby, that the child will feel sleepy or drowsy, and that medicine will be available for pain. Showing a doll with the various equipment used after surgery to monitor body functions (IV lines, endotracheal tube, and Foley catheter)

Figure 26-16 Preoperative teaching. These sessions prepare the child for procedures done before and after surgery. Blow bottles and devices such as balloons and Tri-Flow equipment make deep breathing exercises fun.

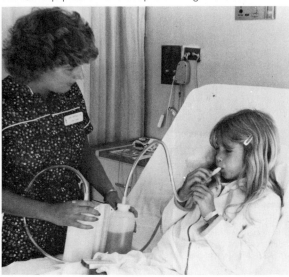

helps to prepare the child and family. Encourage the child to handle the equipment during and after the teaching sessions. Practice deep breathing and coughing exercises with the child (Fig. 26-16). Balloons are useful to simulate lung inflation (inspiration) and deflation (expiration). A small pillow is helpful in demonstrating splinting, as is applying pressure to support the thoracic cavity while coughing.

It is important to remember that children need to feel safe and secure. Fears of insecurity, impending danger, and bodily harm and mutilation due to their lack of cognitive understanding increase their anxiety level and diminish their ability to cope with the surgical experience. Remember that it is far worse to tell a child *too much* information in preoperative teaching than *too little*. Careful preparation and thoughtful preoperative teaching appropriate for the level of the child and family promotes cooperation and makes the surgical experience less frightening.

Preoperative activities In some agencies, a Phisohex or Betadine shower or bath may be taken daily for 1 to 3 days prior to surgery. The skin is shaved in the operating room after the child is asleep. The night before surgery, the child may have a light supper. The child is not allowed to eat or drink after midnight, and so it is good to allow the child a cool drink before bedtime. Remove all fluids and food from the bedside table and place a label at the foot of the bed to signify that the child is not allowed food or drink. Vital signs are taken the evening before and the morning of surgery. Any increase in temperature or sign of an upper respiratory infection should be reported to the physician. If there is any infection, surgery will usually be delayed until the child is better.

Preoperative sedation helps to relax the child and facilitate induction of anesthesia. Medications used include various narcotic analgesics such as meperidine HCl, pentazocine HCl, or morphine sulfate. Occasionally, a narcotic sedative such as secobarbitol or pentobarbitol may be administered. Atropine sulfate or scopolamine is frequently given in conjunction with a narcotic analgesic or sedative. Nurses must double-check the ordered dosage of the preoperative medication with the child's weight before administration and notify the anesthesiologist if there are any questions.

Sometimes parents are allowed to wait with their child before the surgery in a holding area outside the operating room. Encourage parents and other family members to wait in the designated area so they can hear immediately of the child's condition and speak with the surgeon after the operation.

Intraoperative period Depending on the type of defect being repaired, the procedure is accomplished through either open or closed heart surgery. *Closed heart surgery* is done for relatively simple corrections of defects outside the heart such as a PDA ligation. *Open heart surgery* involves cutting into the myocardium and carries more risks than closed heart surgery.

During the surgery, vital signs are monitored closely. As soon as the child is asleep, various intravenous lines are initiated. Frequently, an intraarterial line is started percutaneously or by a cutdown in the radial artery or femoral artery. Then a *thoracotomy* or *sternotomy* incision is made, depending on the type of defect and route of entry into the body needed to correct it.

Open heart surgery is accomplished in a bloodless field with the use of *extracorporeal* (outside the body) circulation. The right atrium is cannulated (a small tubular catheter is inserted). Blood then flows from the cannula through a cardiopulmonary bypass machine where it is oxygenated with a membrane or bubble-type oxygenator. The machine acts as an artificial set of lungs. The warmed, filtered, and oxygen-enriched blood is returned through a cannula in the aorta and circulated throughout the body.

Deep hypothermia may be used in young children. During deep hypothermia, the child's body surface may be partially cooled with dry ice packs while appendages and genitals are protected. Then, the blood vessels are cannulated and the cardiopulmonary bypass machine centrally cools the blood and thus the body temperature to 12 to 20°C (53 to 76°F). Around 20°C, cardiac arrest occurs and the surgeons correct the defect in a quiet, nonbeating heart. Though there is a time limit (60 to 90 min) in circulatory arrest, no brain damage occurs since metabolic processes are considerably slowed. After the correction, the body is warmed gradually by warming blood in the bypass machine. The heart usually begins beating on its own, but defibrillation may be needed if the rhythm is irregular.

Chest tubes are inserted during the suturing process as are additional intravenous lines. A central venous pressure (CVP) line, right and left atrial (RA, LA) lines, or a pulmonary artery (PA) line help to monitor cardiac function in the initial postoperative period.

Heart surgery is delicate and complicated and may take several hours. During the period of the child's surgery, the family should be informed of the child's progress at regular intervals.

Nursing management in the postoperative period

After surgery, the child is transferred directly to an intensive care unit or similar critical care setting for 1 to 3 days or more until vital signs and related systems of the body are stable and functioning well. The goal of nursing management is the restoration and maintenance of optimal cardiovascular, respiratory, renal, and neurological function. It is vital that the nurse be able to identify subtle changes in the body systems which may herald impending complications. The need for intelligent assessment of children after cardiac surgery is intensified because of their limited physiological reserves for compensating for physical insults like surgery. To detect subtle symptoms of compromised reserves, each system is continuously monitored through careful nursing observations and mechanical recording devices.

There is great trauma to the body and heart during cardiac surgery from manipulation and replacement of parts such as valves or patches and from cutting through delicate impulse conduction and muscle fibers. The anesthesia used during surgery also depresses the contractility of the myocardium and affects ventilation capacity.

General assessment Vital signs are taken every 15 min for 1 h, every 30 min for 2 h, then every hour for 24 to 48 h (Fig. 26-17). The apical pulse is auscultated for 1 full min. The nurse must report an irregular heart rate, muffled or distant heart sounds, and murmurs or gallops. A cuff blood pressure may be taken in an arm or leg and, if necessary, the sound may be amplified using an ultrasound device.

Temperature is monitored closely since young children, especially infants and newborns, have minimal stores of subcutaneous fat and immature thermal-regulating mechanisms. Initially, on

Figure 26-17 Immediate postoperative period. The child requires constant observation and support. Monitoring equipment facilitates assessment of cardiovascular status after surgery. (*Courtesy of Barbara Macpherson.*)

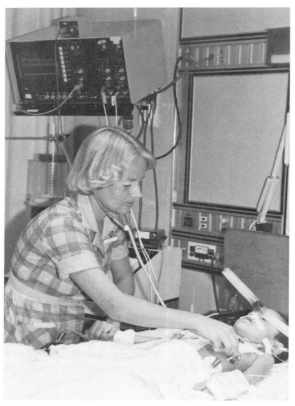

admission to the intensive care setting, the child is *hypothermic* (has a low temperature) due to the cold operating room and, in some cases, to the deep hypothermia used during repair of the defect. Warmed blankets or a heat lamp may be used to gradually increase the child's temperature to the normal range. *Hyperthermia* (increased temperature) is common in the first 24 to 48 h after surgery because of the trauma of the surgery and cardiopulmonary bypass. Though antibiotics are given prophylactically, if a child's temperature remains elevated for longer than 48 h after surgery, cultures and sensitivities (C & S) of urine, blood, wound, and sputum are obtained to identify infection.

Cardiovascular function The child's vital signs are recorded by a cardiac monitor with modules depicting the ECG (usually lead II pattern), respiratory rate, and circulatory pressures. A pressure-sensing device is used to record arterial and venous pressure waves with corresponding numerical values visualized on an oscilloscope. These lines must not become kinked since they are important in monitoring circulatory status within the chambers and great vessels of the heart. The mean arterial pressure (MAP), in addition to the systolic and diastolic values of the arterial pressure, is a valuable tool in assessing circulatory blood volume.

Assess the skin, primarily of the extremities, for color, temperature, moisture, and capillary refill. Palpate peripheral pulses on the right and left side simultaneously. If all tissues are receiving an adequate blood volume and cardiac output is good, the nurse will see: (1) warm hands and feet; (2) equal, palpable peripheral pulses in all extremities; (3) pink or pale lips, oral mucous membranes, and fingernail beds; and (4) rapid capillary refill. Cyanotic or mottled skin and membranes, cool extremities, delayed capillary refill, and weak, thready pulses indicate decreased ability of the heart to pump oxygenated blood through the body tissues. Notify a physician immediately if signs of compromised circulation are noted.

Measurement of circulatory blood volume and cardiovascular function is accomplished with a central venous pressure line (CVP). A CVP line is usually inserted into the right cephalic or basilic vein and is threaded into the right atrium, where the pressure is normally 0 to 5 mmHg. The placement of the CVP line is verified with a chest x-ray. The pressure reading is obtained with the child in a supine position. A low CVP value may indicate the need for fluid or blood replacement while a high reading may indicate fluid overload, deteriorating cardiac function, or cardiac tamponade (bleeding into the pericardial sac).

Measuring chest tube drainage is essential to monitoring circulatory volume. Placement of chest tubes at the conclusion of surgery ensures proper drainage of blood from around the heart and pleural cavity, decreases the pressure around the heart and pulmonary structures, enhances return of pulmonary function, and prevents infection in the pleural and mediastinal space. Underwater-seal chest drainage bottles were used in the past (Fig. 26-18). The one-bottle gravity system is an elementary water-sealed system. It is appropriate when the pleural cavity

Figure 26-18 Water-seal drainage systems. (*A*) The one-bottle gravity system. Note that tube A, from the patient's pleural cavity, is submerged in water. Some surgeons may elect to attach tube B to suction apparatus. (*B*) The two-bottle gravity system. If bottle X fills, the excess flows to bottle Y via tubes B and C. Fluid thus does not re-enter the pleural cavity. Bottle Y is called the "trap" bottle. Some surgeons may elect to attach tube D to suction apparatus. [*From Gladys Scipien (ed.) et al., Comprehensive Pediatric Nursing, 2d ed., McGraw-Hill, New York, 1979. Used by permission of the publisher.*]

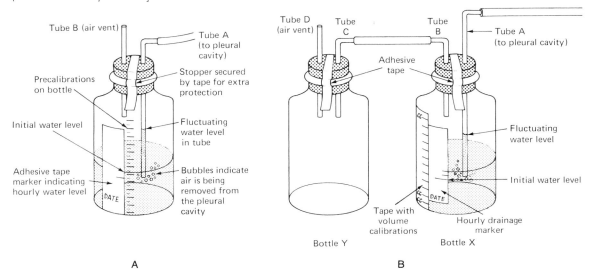

is used to drain air and only a small amount of fluid. When there is a need to drain large amounts of fluid, the two-bottle system is employed, the second bottle serving to hold any overflow from the first. Today such underwater-seal systems are employed only when pneumothorax is present or, in the older child, when drainage is expected to be minimal. Disposable chest tube drainage sets (Fig. 26-19) are capable of measuring drainage more accurately and are more popular than bottle systems.

Nurses must maintain patency of the chest tubes for proper drainage. There should be no kinks in the tubing and connections between the chest tube and the drainage container must be intact and secured with adhesive tape (Fig. 26-20). The tubing should lie without tension to give the child room to move freely. Chest tubes are stripped or "milked" from the child to the drainage container every 15 min on admission and thereafter every 30 min and when necessary. The type of drainage and quantity (in milliliters) is recorded hourly. Initially drainage will be sanguineous (bloody), then serous-sanguineous, and finally serous. Although drainage usually does not exceed 500 ml per 24 h, older children and those in surgery for transposition of the great arteries, tetralogy of Fallot, and truncus arteriosus experience increased sanguineous drainage. Any significant increase in amount or type of drainage should be reported.

Chest tube drainage is computed as output along with all other body drainage. Two Kelly clamps or hemostats for each chest tube and petroleum gauze are kept at the bedside in case a chest tube becomes disconnected or falls out. A hissing sound alerts a nurse to a lack of patency in the tubing. *Never* clamp a chest tube that becomes disconnected when the child is on a respirator, however, because the child will develop a spontaneous tension pneumothorax.

Respiratory function Respiratory function has a two-fold relationship to cardiac function. If arterial blood oxygenation is not maintained within required amounts, myocardial and tissue metabolism may be adversely affected leading to decreased cardiac output, poor perfusion, metabolic acidosis, and further cardiac depression. The muscular work of respiration also depends upon the oxygen supplied by an effectively pumping heart. Respiratory function is also affected by anesthesia, sedation, and incisional pain.

After heart surgery, mechanical ventilation assistance may be required. The child will have an oral or nasal endotracheal tube in place. The position of the tube is verified with a portable chest x-ray done routinely after the child is admitted to the unit. As the child wakes from the surgery, tell him that he will not be able to talk. It is comforting to the child to instruct him to shake his head yes or no in order to communicate and to understand that a nurse is

Figure 26-19 Disposable chest tube drainage system. Before use, the water-sealed chamber is filled to the 2-cm level to eliminate the possibility of air flow back into the pleural cavity. When suction pressure is desired, the suction control chamber is filled to provide the amount of negative pressure needed to facilitate drainage of the pleural cavity. When the collection chamber tubing is attached to the chest tube from the child, the drainage flows into the columns via the inlet tubing. The calibrated markings allow accurate measurement of drainage. If the drainage system fills to capacity, a new one may be attached to the chest tube(s). (*Photo courtesy of Deknatal, Inc., New York.*)

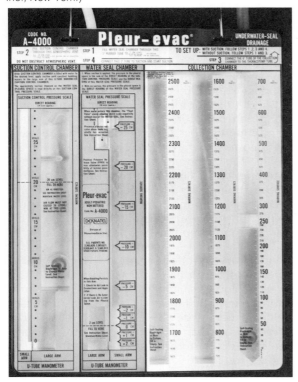

Figure 26-20 Chest tube care. Careful measures and precautions are vital in the nursing management of a child with chest tubes. The tube should be checked frequently for patency.

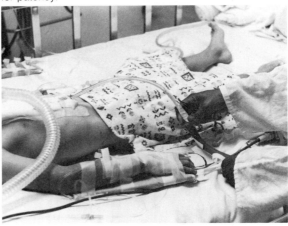

always nearby if he needs anything. To keep the endotracheal tube patent, the child is suctioned (Table 25-5) every 1 to 2 h or when needed. Always ventilate the child with 100% oxygen before, during, and after suctioning. Initially secretions may be blood-tinged due to the intubation process. If the child does not have an endotracheal tube, a face mask or oxygen hood will be used to deliver oxygen with mist.

General respiratory care for any child includes noting the respiratory rate, depth, and presence of retractions. Observe skin, lips, mucous membranes, and fingernail beds to assess oxygen saturation. Breath sounds are auscultated bilaterally and absent or diminished sounds should be reported. Blood gases are drawn on admission to the intensive care unit and thereafter, when necessary, or after any change in oxygen concentration, tidal volume, or ventilatory rate. Position is changed, usually from side to side, every 2 h to prevent stasis of secretions and respiratory infection. The head of the bed may be flat for the first 24 h after surgery and then elevated to promote maximum lung expansion. Good skin care is vital since children are not usually able to relieve pressures themselves until they wake sufficiently from the anesthesia.

Once the child is more awake, chest physiotherapy (see Chap. 17), coughing, and deep breathing exercise are initiated every 2 h. A splint pillow is helpful to decrease the tension on the incision site as the child coughs. Nasotracheal suctioning may be done, if necessary, to stimulate the child's cough reflex.

Renal function Renal status is monitored carefully after heart surgery. Intake and output are accurately reported. Urinary drainage systems are used to facilitate close monitoring of urine output. Indwelling catheters may be used. In neonates and infants, blood taken for lab studies is counted as output.

The level of hydration is frequently assessed (Table 17-14). Skin turgor, fontanels, lips, and mucous membranes are checked. Children are not overly hydrated after surgery to prevent fluid overload and myocardial stress. Intravenous fluids infuse at a rate appropriate for the child's body surface and usually contain a 10% concentration of dextrose (D_{10}) for infants and children up to age 12.

Blood is monitored for BUN and creatinine levels. Urine specimens are tested for pH, glucose, ketones, protein, blood, and specific gravity. It is important to remember that circulatory status directly affects renal perfusion. The quantity of urine reflects the circulating vascular status, whereas the quality of urine reflects the renal function.

Neurological function The central nervous system is monitored closely after surgery. Cerebral blood flow may be hindered by a blood clot, or *embolus*, from the surgical procedure. A sleeping child should be easy to arouse, alert, and oriented. Though children are frequently confused and frightened in the intensive care unit, normal confusion must be distinguished from disorientation. Ask simple questions and have the child say yes or no or nod his head. Wipe away the lubricating ointment placed in the eye during surgery. Then check the pupils for size, equality, position, reaction to light, and accommodation. Muscle strength is evaluated by observing facial symmetry, hand grasp, and extremity movements. The response to pain can be assessed easily since many procedures are occurring simultaneously. Withdrawal from the direction of painful stimuli is an expected and appropriate response. It is important to have an accurate preoperative assessment recorded to compare with postoperative findings.

Hematologic studies Blood studies are simultaneously monitored to enhance assessment of the body systems. Blood clotting studies are especially important since heparin is administered to the child before extracorporeal circulation to minimize the chance of emboli. Serum electrolytes, hemoglobin, and hematocrit are evaluated closely since a significant increase or decrease would directly affect cardiac function. Serum glucose levels may be increased since the bypass machine is primed with a parenteral glucose solution. Finger sticks can be done in infants to estimate serum glucose levels by placing a drop of blood on a test tape. A 50% dextrose IV is used for severe hypoglycemia.

Potassium levels are monitored closely and supplemented to prevent arrhythmias from developing. Sodium and calcium levels must also be measured. Usually a continuous infusion of calcium is given during the immediate postoperative period.

White blood cell count is evaluated for an increase due to infection. Based on the results of lab studies, vital signs, and chest tube drainage, blood is replaced using packed red blood cells, washed blood cells from the bypass machine, or plasma. As much as possible, a balance is maintained between blood lost and blood replaced.

Additional nursing care A nasogastric tube may be used to prevent aspiration and maintain decompression of the gastrointestinal tract while the child is not eating or drinking. After checking its placement, irrigate it with 10 to 15 ml of normal saline every 1 to 2 h to maintain patency. Record the amount, color, and consistency of the drainage hourly.

The child may be restrained during the immediate postoperative period. Use proper restraint techniques (Table 17-5) and maintain good skin care.

Parents should be allowed to visit the child as soon as possible (Fig. 26-21). Though visiting policies vary, the parents' limited time with the child should be uninterrupted if possible. Describe the child's appearance to the family beforehand. Explain that the child will look pale. Simple explanations such as "This tube helps your child to breathe" are adequate. A chair by the bedside is helpful so one member can sit, hold the child's hand, and talk to the child. The nurse should be aware that normally the parents

Figure 26-21 Postoperative parental visit. The nurse should describe the child's appearance to the parents in advance and provide support during visiting periods in the intensive care setting. The parents' presence is vital to the child during this difficult experience.

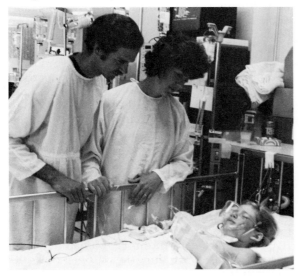

are overwhelmed by the amount of tubes and monitoring equipment. It is helpful to plan well-spaced visits at a time convenient for the family to prevent severe emotional stress.

As the child wakes from the anesthesia, he may be restless and uncomfortable. If there are no signs of hemorrhage (increased chest tube drainage, decreased blood pressure, or increased pulse) and neurologic and respiratory difficulties have been ruled out, then the child is probably in pain. Narcotic analgesics are used cautiously after surgery. Controversy exists about the degree of pain children perceive. Occasionally, morphine sulfate is administered intravenously in small doses to ease the child's discomfort; yet avoid masking signs of complications. Morphine's relaxation effect on smooth muscles may cause the blood pressure to decrease slightly.

Drug treatment after cardiac surgery may include prophylactic antibiotic therapy for 4 to 10 days, electrolyte replacements such as calcium and potassium to promote optimal myocardial efficiency, and digoxin when indicated. In cases of hemodynamic instability, vasopressors such as dopamine HCl and nitroprusside are used cautiously.

As soon as the child can maintain satisfactory ventilation, the endotracheal tube is removed. After the tube is removed, tell the child that his voice will be hoarse and he'll have a sore throat for a few days. Continue to monitor respiratory status for any signs of respiratory distress. Coughing, deep breathing, and ventilation exercises are continued. The nasogastric tube is removed when bowel sounds are heard, and the child can then begin taking sips of clear fluids according to the prescribed fluid regime. Chest tubes are discontinued when there is minimal serous drainage. A chest x-ray is taken after the removal of the chest tubes to check for pneumothorax.

Complications may arise during surgery or in the immediate postoperative period. (Table 26-8). The frequency and severity of the complications necessitate close observation and immediate attention. Respiratory problems are the most common complications following cardiac surgery.[27]

Cardiac arrest may occur following heart surgery and is usually a result of one or more complications. It may happen suddenly or may be preceded by subtle warning signs. Astute assessment of changes in skin color, vital signs,

Table 26-8 Postoperative cardiac surgical complications

Respiratory
Mucus accumulation
Pneumonia
Atelectasis
Pneumothorax
Pulmonary embolus

Cardiovascular
Arrhythmias
Cardiac tamponade
Hypovolemic shock
Heart failure
Embolus

Renal
Renal failure

Neurological
Embolus
Decreased cerebral blood flow

Infection
Mediastinitis
Wound infection

and blood gases with subsequent appropriate intervention may prevent cardiac arrest. An absence of pulse, respirations (if not receiving ventilatory assistance), and blood pressure denotes an arrest. Prompt action is necessary to increase the child's chance of survival (Table 17-18). A patent airway must be obtained and maintained throughout the resuscitation procedures. Cardiac compressions at a rate appropriate for the age of the child are initiated by external or internal massage to maintain circulation. Once the arrest team is present (or if an arrest protocol is in existence), emergency cardiac drugs are administered to correct acidosis and stimulate the myocardium. Specific amounts of medications given are based on the child's weight. Guidelines should be available on the emergency equipment. The outcome of the arrest depends on the reason for the arrest, status of the myocardium, and timing of resuscitation.

Convalescence

Once the child is transferred out of the intensive care area, the goals of nursing management focus on helping the child become stronger and preparing the child and family for discharge. Coughing and deep breathing exercises are continued as well as auscultation of breath sounds. Fluids may continue to be restricted and the child may be placed on a low-sodium diet. An ambulation schedule is followed and the child is encouraged to alternate activities with rest breaks to avoid overexertion. External sutures, if present, and temporary pacemakers are removed before the child is discharged. With minimal postoperative complications, children are discharged 7 to 10 days after surgery.

Dismissal teaching should be initiated once the child is transferred from the intensive care setting. Families will need teaching about medications, activity, wound healing, and follow-up care. Important information should be written down and given to the family prior to discharge.

Directions given to parents should include the action, frequency of administration, and side effects of the medications the child will be taking home. If the child is taking digoxin, instruct the parents to check the child's pulse and give guidelines for withholding the drug or reporting an abnormal pulse. Similar information is necessary if the child will be taking a diuretic. Stress the importance of eating foods high in potassium and provide parents with a list of appropriate foods.

Activity limitations depend primarily on the type of repair done, postoperative course, and age of the child. Children under 2 years usually gauge their own activity level and sleep when they are tired. School-age children tend to overexert. They may return to school in 4 to 5 weeks but should not participate in physical education or vigorous sports for 1 to 3 months afterwards. Some children who have had extensive surgical repairs may take as long as 6 months before they are able to tolerate demanding sports.

Instruct the parents to keep the incision site clean and dry and observe for signs of infection around the suture line. Steri-strips may be kept on but will fall off in a week or two. Children may complain of itchiness as the incision heals.

Make follow-up appointments before discharge. Usually, the child will visit the cardiac surgeon and the pediatric cardiologist. Parents must advise other physicians (child's dentist and pediatrician) of the history of heart disease. Prophylactic antibiotics such as penicillin, or erythromycin if the child is allergic to penicillin, should be given before and after dental surgery, genitourinary procedures, or surgery on the upper respiratory tract. This helps to prevent *subacute bacterial endocarditis* (SBE), an infectious process usually caused by *Streptococcus viridans* involving altered or malformed tissues of the heart. SBE can occur in children with congenital heart disease or as a complication of cardiac surgery.

After discharge, children may have nightmares or temporary behavior changes. The nightmares usually disappear when the child becomes reaccustomed to the safe, nonthreatening environment of the home. Behavior tendencies range from hostile or aggressive actions to passive dependent mannerisms that disappear when the child has an opportunity to release unresolved feelings regarding the surgical experience. Therapeutic play sessions before discharge may help a child to overcome threatening, insecure feelings (Fig. 26-22). Younger children tend to regress and often need parental assistance with tasks they had previously mastered. Encourage parents to allow the child to pass through these stages and provide as much support as possible. Allow the child to verbalize feelings about the experience. A follow-up visit to the surgical and

Figure 26-22 Therapeutic play. Planned play activities help children cope with threatening procedures and hospitalization.

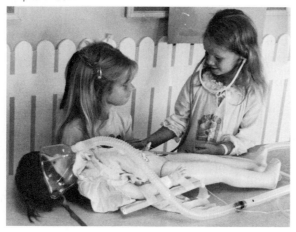

intensive care units after discharge also helps the child to deal with past experiences.

Siblings may be envious of the increased attention the child has received before, during, and after hospitalization. In some instances, younger siblings may feel that they caused the child's bad experience through "bad" wishes or thoughts. Encourage parents to deal with the siblings honestly and maintain firm, realistic discipline policies within a loving caring relationship.

Postperfusion syndrome is a long-term complication of heart surgery and extracorporeal circulation. The symptoms are vague and occur between the third and twelfth week after surgery when the child is usually home. The symptoms include fever, malaise, arthritis, skin rash, and splenomegaly (enlarged spleen). Treatment includes bed rest and salicylates.[28]

Acquired heart disease in children

Acute rheumatic fever

Acute rheumatic fever is the leading cause of postnatally acquired heart disease in children in the United States and Western Europe.[29] Incidence varies with geography, age, and economic status. There may be a familial predisposition to the development of rheumatic fever and rheumatic heart disease. Crowded conditions, poor housing, dampness, and poor nutrition—often found in families in low socioeconomic classes—are believed to predispose children to rheumatic fever.

Rheumatic fever is a systemic, inflammatory collagen disease. It usually develops 1 to 3 weeks after a group A, beta-hemolytic streptoccoccal, upper respiratory infection. There is a high prevalence following scarlet fever. Rheumatic fever primarily affects children over the age of 5 and young adults. There is a seasonal increase of rheumatic fever that correlates with the incidence of upper respiratory infections. Rheumatic fever peaks during spring on the east coast and during winter on the west coast.

Rheumatic fever seems to progress through four stages.[30] First there is the initial streptococcal infection that goes undiagnosed or untreated. The second stage is characterized by a latent period of 1 to 3 weeks when the fever and infection seem to disappear but the individual may not quite return to normal. This is followed by phase three, or the acute rheumatic episode, which may last 2 to 3 months. In the final phase, which exists for the rest of the child's life, all signs of rheumatic fever are gone, but varying degrees of residual heart disease may persist.

The initial streptococcal infection is characterized by a sudden onset of a sore throat, a temperature of 38.4 to 40°C (101 to 104°F), and cervical and mandibular adenitis. Headache, abdominal pain, and vomiting may also be present. Diagnosis is by culture and history of recent exposure. As many as 20 percent of streptococcal infections may be asymptomatic. Treatment consists of IM penicillin (1,200,000 units), oral penicillin (250,000 units four times daily for 10 days), or erythromycin (20 mg/lb per day for 10 days) when penicillin sensitivity exists.

Signs and symptoms of rheumatic fever involve target areas such as the joints, lungs, and heart. *Arthritis*, inflammation of the joints, is the most common complaint of children with rheumatic fever. Inflammation produces heat, redness, tenderness, swelling, pain, and limitation of joint movement. Such large joints as elbows, wrists, ankles, and knees may be involved and the discomfort mistaken for "growing pains." Characteristic nonpainful subcutaneous nodules may be found over the joints, vertebrae, and skull. In the acute state of rheumatic fever, the lungs may be the site of a pneumonia-type infection. *Carditis*, associated with congestive heart failure, is indicative of cardiac involvement. Cardiomegaly, demonstrated on x-ray, and pericarditis may be present with carditis. A friction rub, heard on auscultation, signifies pericarditis. As fluid accumulation increases in the pericardial sac from the inflammation, the rub diminishes.

Permanent or transient ECG changes in the P-R interval, T wave, and QRS complex may occur if carditis is present. Sydenham's chorea demonstrates involvement of the nervous system and is manifested by emotional instability, involuntary muscle movements that disappear during sleep, ataxia, and muscle weakness. Chorea does not usually appear at the same time carditis is present but 2 to 6 months after the initial infection.[31] Nonspecific skin manifestations include urticaria, petechiae, and an erythematous rash. Epistaxis and right lower quadrant abdominal pain may also be present.

Diagnosis of rheumatic fever is made by using the modified Jones criteria. Diagnosis is positive if any *two major* or *one major and two minor manifestations* are present. Major manifestations include carditis, polyarthritis, chorea, subcutaneous nodules, and erythema marginatum. Minor manifestations include fever, elevated erythrocyte sedimentation rate, a positive C-reactive protein, polyarthralgia, ECG changes, and previous history of rheumatic fever.

The prognosis depends on the severity and treatment of the rheumatic fever. Carditis occurs in approximately 50 percent of the cases and increases the severity of the illness. Rheumatic carditis causes temporary insult and may lead to permanent damage to any of the three layers of the heart. Endocardial involvement is usually restricted to the mitral, tricuspid, and aortic valves. Edema and inflammation of the valves occur in the acute phase and scarring may lead to valvular stenosis (constriction or narrowing of a valve lumen or orifice) or insufficiency (inability to perform a normal function, usually causing leakage). If acute inflammation progresses or recurs, scar formation and valvular damage may be permanent. Mitral insufficiency is the most common valvular lesion seen in the acute phase of rheumatic fever.

Immediate goals of nursing management are directed toward maintaining optimal cardiac functioning and promoting the child's comfort. During the acute phase, the child is hospitalized if carditis is present and intravenous antibiotics are given. Vital signs are taken frequently. The nurse should watch for signs and symptoms of congestive heart failure. A systolic murmur characteristic of mitral insufficiency or diastolic murmur due to aortic insufficiency may precede signs of heart failure. Since carditis may be fatal, it is imperative that the nurse report the presence of distended neck veins, pulmonary congestion, decreased urinary output, tachypnea, dyspnea, and tachycardia. Bed rest, which helps to promote myocardial efficiency but has not been proven to affect residual heart disease, may be especially difficult for a young child. Periods of rest, alternated with passive activities appropriate for a child's age, are helpful. Ambulation is gradually increased on the basis of the child's well-being and the severity of carditis.

Maintenance of fluid balance and assessment of hydration are important components of nursing management. Record daily intake and output and weight to evaluate myocardial function. Determine hydration by checking lips and mucous membranes, skin turgor, fontanels, and presence or absence of tears.

If chorea is present, additional safety precautions are instituted. Protect the child from the random involuntary movements of the extremities. Siderails must be padded and remain up at all times. Restraints may be needed and should be applied when appropriate. Remain with the child when he is in a cart or wheelchair.

Medications are used to eradicate the infection and promote comfort. Salicylates are used for their antipyretic quality, relief of joint pain, and treatment of mild carditis. Penicillin is the drug of choice. It is given orally, except when carditis is active. Then parenteral administration is used. Steroids help to decrease the effect of the inflammatory process in moderate-to-severe carditis. Diuretics and digitalis products are used for congestive heart failure.

Long-term care and follow-up are essential to prevent recurrence. Parents need information regarding the disease, the treatment, and medication. Maintenance of prolonged bed rest is often unrealistic and short periods of limited activity help to decrease the frustrations of the child. Home visits by a public health nurse, social worker, and school tutor can help to continue meeting the needs of the child and family following hospitalization.

Streptococcal prophylaxis should be continued until age 18, until at least 5 years after the last rheumatic fever attack with no residual heart disease, and indefinitely in those with rheumatic heart disease. Recurrences take place in more than 50 percent of those not following streptococcal prophylaxis.[32] The surest method of prevention is the administration of penicillin G intramuscularly every 28 days. 400,000 units potassium penicillin G orally every day can be used for the healthy, compliant child or adult.

Hypertension

Hypertension is an elevation of systolic or diastolic blood pressure, or both, exceeding the normal range for a child of a given age and sex. Prolonged hypertension is associated with permanent changes in the blood vessels of the eye, heart, kidneys, and cerebrum. These changes predispose an individual to optic nerve damage, atherosclerosis, renal disease, and stroke.

There are two types of hypertension. *Primary*, or *essential, hypertension* has no known cause. *Secondary hypertension* is due to a pathophysiological process such as renal disease (acute or chronic pyelonephritis), endocrine disorders (adrenal disease), and cardiovascular disease (coarctation of the aorta). Hypertension in young children is most often secondary to a known cause such as renal disease.

Although actual incidence is not known, estimates of primary hypertension in childhood range from 1 to 11 percent. Persons at risk for hypertension are the 15-to-30-year-old age group. Hypertension in adolescents is most likely to occur in families with other hypertensive members. Black people have a particularly high prevalence of hypertension.[33]

Because of increasing recognition of the detrimental effects of sustained hypertension, more activities are now directed toward early recognition of hypertension and medical intervention. Evidence suggests that adults who are at risk for developing primary hypertension can be identified in childhood. Thus, more attention is being placed on early detection of persons with a greater tendency to develop hypertension and on children with higher-than-normal blood pressure values. Though the exact cause of primary hypertension has not been firmly established, heredity, obesity, and excess salt intake may be important contributing factors.

Though blood pressure norms exist for definitions of systolic and diastolic hypertension in adults, there is still some question about specific ranges in children. Ranges may vary, (Table 17-21), but children who have persistent elevations in supine systolic and diastolic readings greater than the 80 or 90 percentiles for their age are considered to be borderline hypertensives.[34]

One of the reasons for lack of substantial data for hypertension in children is the difficulty in measurement. Current recommendations suggest that blood pressure be checked in any child over 3 years of age. Proper cuff size (Table 17-22) and a quiet, cooperative child are helpful in determining a proper pressure reading. Even then, it may be difficult to obtain a diastolic reading in infants and young children except through intraarterial pressure monitoring.

Symptoms of hypertension vary. Usually a child with increased blood pressure does not demonstrate any overt symptoms. With severe disease, children may experience blurred vision, severe frontal headaches, generalized or focal seizures, epistaxis, and on occasion severe back or abdominal pain. Signs of hypertension seen on physical examination include retinal hemorrhages or exudates, constriction of the retinal arteries, and papilledema (edema of the optic disc).

To aid in the diagnosis of hypertension, it is vital that the nurse obtain an accurate history in order to evaluate the family history for frequency of hypertension, myocardial infarctions, renal disorders, diabetes or other endocrine disease, and strokes (cerebral vascular accidents). Such special diagnostic tests as abdominal aortography may be done if a tumor or other mass in the kidneys or adrenal gland is suspected of causing the hypertension. An intravenous pyelogram (IVP) is frequently done to assess renal dysfunction. Through the injection of a contrast medium, aortography and IVP allow the examination of the vascular system and organs of the lower abdominal cavity. Various tests measuring urinary excretion of certain products are used to assess renal status. Hematologic studies include CBC, serum electrolytes, BUN, creatinine, and uric acid levels.

Medical management of the child or adolescent with definitive hypertension is varied. If secondary hypertension is diagnosed, the underlying cause is treated. If mild primary hypertension exists, follow-up care and monitoring are sufficient. Patient and family education includes diet modifications such as restriction of sodium, fat, and caloric intake, increased physical activity, medications, follow-up care, and promotion of compliance.

Avoidance of foods with high-sodium content has been established as an aid in decreasing blood pressure. Overweight children are counseled regarding diet, nutrition, and exercise. Family patterns and cultural practices regarding food are important considerations in diet teaching.

Adequate exercise without excessive fatigue is important to promote optimal circulatory function. When encouraging proper activities, include information about the postural effects on blood pressure of several of the drugs used in treating hypertension. In addition, female adolescents with hypertension who are sexually active should be counseled about appropriate methods of contraception and planning pregnancies. Oral contraceptives should be avoided since an increased blood pressure from using these medications has been described. For males, such antihypertensive drugs as methyldopa (Aldomet) and guanethidine (Ismelin) may cause impotence and inhibition of ejaculation.

At the present time, there is no single successful medication for treatment of hypertension. Diuretics and vasodilating and neural regulating agents are used in combination. Diuretics are used to diminish plasma and extracellular fluid volume by acting on the renal tubules at different sites to inhibit reabsorption of sodium. Thiazide diuretics such as chlorothiazide (Diuril) and hydrochlorothiazide (HydroDiuril) are frequently used. Chlorthalidone (Hygroton), another oral diuretic, is a useful agent because it has a longer duration of action than chlorothiazide. Given in a single daily dose, it is valuable with children who have a difficult time remembering multiple-dose schedules.[35] More potent diuretics that act on the loop of Henle are furosemide (Lasix) and ethacrynic acid (Edecrin). These diuretics are restricted for use when significant fluid retention is present and hypertension does not respond to thiazide therapy. Nursing management includes monitoring serum electrolytes and promoting of intake of foods high in potassium, such as orange juice and bananas.

Vasodilating agents directly affect smooth muscles by decreasing vascular tone and lowering peripheral resistance. Smooth-muscle vasodilators include such drugs as hydralazine HCl (Apresoline), minoxidil (Loniten) (currently in restricted use only for adults), and prazosin (Minipress).

Neural blocking agents act in various ways at the postganglionic nerve terminal to reduce the vasoconstricting responses elicited by stimulation of the sympathetic nervous system. Thus, the systemic blood pressure is lowered. Since the drugs decrease vasomotor tone, postural hypotension is a major side effect. Neural blocking agents include methyldopa (Aldomet), guanethidine (Ismelin), reserpine (Serpasil), propranolol (Inderal), and clonidine (Catapres).

Nurses have an important role in identifying children at risk for hypertension and in promoting maintenance of therapeutic regimes designed to lower blood pressure. Community health nurses may be the first to note an elevated blood pressure or detect the symptoms of hypertension in a client. Because hypertension is often asymptomatic, compliance is difficult for anyone, especially adolescents. Since some medications cause postural hypotension, adolescents may feel worse while taking the drugs. Every opportunity should be made to maintain communication with the child and family. Discussions should take place with the family unit about the therapeutic regimen, diet, medications, and their actions and side effects. Realistic goals should be set by the child and family. Small group meetings for older children and adolescents who have hypertension may improve compliance and provide an opportunity to share experiences and feelings with peers.

Follow-up care should continue with the same nurse in order to maintain communication between the nurse and the family and to help achieve a trusting relationship over a long period of time.

Atherosclerosis and lipid disorders

It is commonly accepted that coronary heart disease is the leading cause of death of adults in the United States. There is now evidence that one facet of coronary artery disease, *atherosclerosis*, begins in childhood and progressively worsens until symptoms appear in middle- and late-adult life. Atherosclerosis refers to the accumulation of fatty deposits in the intimal layer of arteries such as the aorta, femoral, carotid, and cerebral vessels. The lesions narrow the lumen of the blood vessel, thereby decreasing the blood flow and predisposing the artery to thrombosis. A weakening in the wall of the affected artery may result in an *anuerysm* (localized dilatation). The exact etiology of atherosclerosis is unknown. There is strong evidence that the progression and development of atherosclerosis is effected by heredity, hypertension, diet, hyperlipidemia, obesity, physical inactivity, and smoking.

An elevated plasma lipid concentration is considered to be a major risk factor in the development of atherosclerosis in children as well as adults. It has been suggested that fatty streaks develop in the aorta as early as fetal life.[36] These streaks progress into hardened plaques in childhood, adolescence, and young adulthood and constitute potential atherosclerotic lesions.

Hyperlipidemia is a borderline high or increased plasma concentration of cholesterol, triglycerides, or both (Table 26-2). Since the majority of children are asymptomatic and rarely obese, a positive family history of coronary artery disease (before 50 years), elevated cholesterol or triglyceride levels in a parent or grandparent, or the presence of xanthomas (fatty fibrous nodules on the knees, elbows, face, eyelids) provide clues of hyperlipidemia.

There are five basic types of hyperlipidemia. Each type is defined by increased cholesterol or triglycerides, or both, and the elevation of a specific type of lipoprotein. Blood studies identify the specific type of hyperlipidemia.

Primary familial hypercholesterolemia (type II-A hyperlipoproteinemia) is the most commonly recognized type of familial hyperlipidemia in children. Laboratory tests show an elevated low-density lipoprotein (LDL) value with increased cholesterol levels. Though the exact etiology is unknown, the possibility exists that hyperlipoproteinemia is inherited as an autosomal dominant trait.

Serum lipid and lipoprotein normative levels are not yet firmly established though guidelines for hyperlipidemia have been suggested.[37] Norms exist for values at the extremes. A fasting serum cholesterol level greater than 230 mg per 100 ml is indicative of the 95th percentile for American children.[38] Because of the need for early intervention, the higher the level of total cholesterol, the greater the effort that should be directed towards treatment if the family medical history is positive for atherosclerotic heart disease.[39] It is recommended that serum lipid levels be routinely monitored in hematologic studies on all school-age children.[40]

A modified dietary regimen is the main approach used to treat children with hyperlipidemia. Since it is not yet known whether one specific dietary factor is at fault in high lipid values, overall total caloric intake is reduced and modifications based on the lipid value are made in the intake of saturated fats, cholesterol, and sugar.

If dietary treatment alone does not decrease serum lipid levels sufficiently and there is a definite family history of atheroslcerotic heart disease, more stringent measures are instituted and lipid-lowering drugs are used. The effect of a specific drug on a lipid disorder is related to its mode of action. Certain drugs, such as cholestyramine (Questran, Cuemid), reduce the plasma cholesterol levels by preventing the reabsorption of bile acids while others, such as nicotinic acid (Clofibrate), alter lipoprotein production in the liver.[41]

Follow-up care is vital in promoting compliance. Clinic visits followed by home visits and telephone calls give the nurse an opportunity to evaluate the effectiveness and impact of a certain medical regime. The family's compliance is promoted by recording accurate weights, undertaking hematologic studies to recheck cholesterol and triglyceride levels, and positive reinforcement. When necessary, alterations and revisions in the regimen can be undertaken to help the child and family to reach the desired goal. Mutual contract-setting between the nurse and family promotes compliance.

Nursing Care Plan–Congestive Heart Failure*

Assessment

Manuel Oliverez, a 6-month-old male, was admitted to 3 East peds unit at 8:00 P.M. with a diagnosis of *congestive heart failure*. Manuel was diagnosed as having a ventricular septal defect (VSD) at 6 weeks of age and was placed on digoxin to stabilize him until corrective surgery could be performed.

1 week prior to admission Manuel had his routine 6-month checkup. At that time he weighed 6.1 kg, was eating well, and the pediatrician said, "Everything is fine." Three days prior to admission Mrs. Oliverez ran out of digoxin and didn't think she had to renew it until today, when she brought her other two children into the clinic for immunizations.

Social history

Mr. Oliverez worked at two jobs in order to support his family of five and relied on public transportation to get to and from work. Mrs. Oliverez didn't drive. Because she lived an hour's distance from the hospital, Mrs. Oliverez would not be able to visit Manuel every day.

Admission assessment

General Mother holding infant. Infant sleeping. Mucous membranes moderately cyanotic; skin color pale, slightly mottled. Anterior fontanel open 1.5 cm.

Temperature 37.4° C (99.4° F) rectally

Pulse Rate 142/min, regular rhythm. Radial and pedal pulses present but of fair quality.

Blood Pressure 98 by palpation

Respirations 58 per min; regular rhythm; shallow. Dyspnea with audible expiratory grunt. Moderate subcostal and substernal retractions with moderate nasal flaring. Equal bilateral breath sounds with scattered, coarse rhonchi

Extremities Edema, dorsum of both feet and hands. Warm and dry.

Abdomen Soft and nondistended.

Weight 6.4 kg.

Developmental assessment

Smiled 7 weeks
Held head up 6 weeks
Sits with support 5½ months
Sits without support not yet
Reaching for objects actively
Language development isolated vowel sounds

After the primary nurse finished the admission assessment, the physician came in, examined Manuel, and left the following orders:

V.S. (T.P.R. & B.P.) q2h
Elevate head of bed 45°
0₂ with hood and mist at 30%
NPO
Weigh bid
Accurate I & O
IV D5 in 0.2 NS at 25 ml/h
Stat arterial blood gases, serum electrolytes, CBC, BUN, and creatine
Furosemide (Lasix): 6 mg IM now; then 6 mg PO bid. starting in A.M.
Digoxin 0.04 mg IM now; then 0.04 mg PO bid. in A.M.
Electrocardiogram in A.M.

The primary nurse positioned Manuel in an infant seat in the tent. The IV was started by the physician with a No. 23 scalp vein on the dorsum of his left hand. A buretrol was hung between the 500-ml bag of D5 and 0.2 NS and the IV tubing and 35 ml of IV fluid was dropped from the bag into the buretrol. The physician left Manuel in the 0₂ for 20 min prior to obtaining the arterial blood gas. The other blood studies were also drawn at the same time.

Mrs. Oliverez stayed in the room during the admission procedures. She phoned her sister and asked her to take care of the two older children (4 and 6 years). Mrs. Oliverez left to go home at 10:30 P.M. Before she left, the primary nurse gave her the unit telephone number and encouraged her to call whenever she wished.

Nursing diagnosis	Nursing goals	Nursing actions	Evaluation/revision
1. Potential alteration in hemodynamic stability related to pump failure	☐ Stable hemodynamic status as shown by: **a.** Heart rate of 100–120/min	☐ Assess cardiovascular status q2h: **a.** Apical heart rate **b.** Peripheral pulses **c.** Color of oral mucosa **d.** Quality of pulses **e.** Depth and regularity of respirations **f.** Capillary refill of nail beds	☐ Pulse rate within proper range: > 160, tachycardia; < 100, bradycardia ☐ Pink, warm extremities
	b. Adequate renal perfusion, i.e., urinary output 1 ml/kg per hour	☐ Assess renal status: **a.** Weigh diapers and test specific gravity every void; record **b.** Check lab data, especially potassium; report abnormal values **c.** Administer furosemide (Lasix) as ordered **d.** Weigh bid **e.** Record abdominal girth **f.** Check for dependent edema	☐ Specific gravity; 1.005–1.015 within 24 h ☐ Voided 10–20 ml/h
2. Potential for fluid and electrolyte imbalance related to administration of furosemide and digoxin	☐ Edema will decrease ☐ Urine output will become adequate	☐ Record intake and output hourly ☐ Administer furosemide as ordered ☐ Keep NPO—offer pacifier	☐ Edema decreased in 6 h after admission; abdominal girth lessened; weight down 60 g; urine output adequate
3. Dyspnea and tachypnea with reduced cardiac output associated with pulmonary engorgement	☐ Respiratory rate will be 30–40/min. Chest clear upon auscultation. Respirations easy, without exertion	☐ Assess pulmonary status q2h; record dyspnea, tachypnea, breath sounds, grunting respirations, nasal flaring, lessen respiratory effort when crying, feeding, stooling	☐ Respiratory rate decreased to 30–40 in 6–12 h ☐ Respiratory effort has decreased ☐ Rhonchi and expiratory grunting diminished in first 12–24 h
	☐ Pink lips, mucous membranes, and nail beds	☐ Check capillary refill and color of skin, lips, mucous membranes q30min	☐ Skin color is pinker in 12–24 h
	☐ Raised cardiac output	☐ Maintain high Fowler's position in infant seat; change position q2h ☐ Check Fi_{O_2} q2h and record	☐ Capillary blood gases should reflect adequate oxygenation by morning ☐ Fi_{O_2} held at 30%
4. Fatigue and lethargy due to decreased cardiac output and pulmonary congestion	☐ Short periods of activity alternating with rest breaks	☐ Schedule only necessary activities: **a.** 8:00 A.M.: V.S., weight **b.** 10:00 A.M.: bath and V.S. **c.** 12:00: V.S.	☐ Diminished fatigue
	☐ Diminished fatigue as shown by infant's respirations, heart rate, and level of activity during procedures	☐ Maintain NPO until cardiac output increases and respiratory rate < 40	

Nursing diagnosis	Nursing goals	Nursing actions	Evaluation/revision
	☐ Feeding pattern modified to maximize caloric intake and minimize exertion	☐ Use preemie nipple with larger hole during feeding ☐ Feed infant q3h using SMA (low in sodium) ☐ Allow infant to rest with nipple in mouth during feeding ☐ Assess respirations during periods of activity	☐ Schedule modified to allow infant rest breaks ☐ Infant appears rested
5. Potential for separation anxiety due to parent's inability to be present during hospitalization	☐ Nursing care reflects continuity and incorporation of child's level of growth and development	☐ Assign primary nursing team to care for child ☐ Implement patterns of care and comfort similar to those at home ☐ Institute age-appropriate passive play activities: **a.** Have parents bring favorite toy or blanket from home **b.** Place brightly colored objects in crib; include musical objects and rattles (evaluate safety of toys) ☐ Use such comfort measures as rocking, cuddling	☐ Minimal trauma from separation and hospitalization
6. Parental anxiety and frustration due to physical condition of child and to hospitalization and long-term implications of illness	☐ Decreased parental anxiety and frustration level as shown by: **a.** Verbalization of questions and concerns **b.** Verbalization of future plans for medication and surgery **c.** Verbalization of family's coping mechanisms	☐ Schedule conference with parents, physician, social worker, and primary nurse at parents' convenience: **a.** Encourage communication **b.** Allow parents to verbalize their concerns **c.** Identify problem areas **d.** Provide explanations where needed **e.** Help family and health team solve problems regarding plans ☐ Permit mother to do care she feels comfortable doing: change diapers, hold Manuel while O_2 mask is in place, assist in bathing child	☐ Verbal and nonverbal communication shows decreased level of anxiety ☐ Mother seems relaxed while caring for Manuel
7. Potential readmission associated with family's insufficient knowledge of defect and need for continuous medication regimen for child	☐ Family demonstrates understanding of therapeutic regimen regarding: **a.** Cardiac defect **b.** Medication **c.** Activity **d.** Feeding schedule	☐ Explore parents' understanding about medical regimen **a.** Reinforce understanding and appropriate concerns **b.** Identify teaching needs **c.** Use appropriate AV aids	☐ Family states time, amount, and purpose of medications ☐ Family verbalizes age-appropriate activities and need for rest breaks; also, willingness to comply with medical regimen

Nursing diagnosis	Nursing goals	Nursing actions	Evaluation/revision
		such as diagrams of defect, written directions for digoxin: dose, time, side effects	☐ Family can describe signs and symptoms of recurring heart failure ☐ Evaluate by behavioral and verbal clues
	☐ Family verbalizes understanding and need for follow-up care	☐ Complete community health nursing referral form ☐ Make next cardiology appointment; meet family in clinic ☐ Telephone family after discharge of Manuel ☐ Write them how to complete Manuel's progress evaluation 1 month after discharge (enclose stamped, self-addressed envelope)	☐ Telephone conference with public health nurse, who later visited Manuel and Mrs. Oliverez prior to discharge and will follow Manuel at home

* The author gratefully acknowledges the assistance of Nancy Horvath, B.S.N, St. Mary's Hospital, Rochester, Minnesota, in the preparation of this nursing care plan.

References

1. S. Fraiberg, *The Magic Years*, Scribner, New York, 1959, p. 129.
2. A. Rudolf, "Complications Occurring in Infants and Children," in E. Braunwald and H. Swan (eds.), *Cooperative Study on Cardiac Catheterization*, The American Heart Association, New York, 1968, p. 64–65.
3. J. Keith, "Congestive Heart Failure," in J. Keith, R. Rowe, and P. Vald, *Heart Disease in Infancy and Childhood*, 3d ed., Macmillan, New York, 1978, p. 167.
4. R. Rowe, "Patent Ductus Arteriosus," in ibid., p. 443.
5. J. Perloff, *The Clinical Recognition of Congenital Heart Disease*, 2d ed., Saunders, Philadelphia, 1978, p. 280.
6. J. Keith, "Atrial Septal Defect: Ostium Secundum, Ostium Primum, and Atrioventricularis Communis (Common A-V Canal)," in op. cit., p. 398.
7. T. Graham, H. Bender, and M. Spach, "Defects of the Ventricular Septum," in A. J. Moss, F. H. Adams, and G. C. Emmanouilides, *Heart Disease in Infants, Children, and Adolescents*, 2d ed., Williams & Wilkins, Baltimore, 1977, p. 147.
8. Keith et al., op. cit., p. 398.
9. Perloff, op. cit., pp. 140–143.
10. A. S. Nadas and D. C. Fyler, *Pediatric Cardiology*, 3d ed., Saunders, Philadelphia, 1972, p. 460.
11. G. Emmanouilides, "Obstructive Lesions of the Right Ventricle and the Pulmonary Arterial Tree," in Moss et al., op. cit., p. 233.
12. Ibid., pp. 235–236.
13. P. Olley, K. Bloom, and R. Rowe, "Aortic Stenosis: Valvular, Subaortic, and Supravalvular," in Keith et al., op. cit., p. 698.
14. Ibid., pp. 700–701.
15. Ibid., p. 707.
16. B. Kidd, "Complete Transposition of the Great Arteries," in Keith et al., op. cit., p. 606.
17. M. Paul, "D-Transposition of the Great Arteries," in Moss et al., op. cit., p. 333.
18. D. Mair and D. Ritter, "Truncus Arteriosus," in Moss et al., op. cit., p. 428.
19. W. Gunderoth and I. Kwabori, "Tetrad of Fallot," in Moss et al., op. cit., p. 281.
20. Ibid., p. 287.
21. Perloff, op. cit., p. 628.
22. Ibid., p. 625.
23. A. Rosenthal, "Tricuspid Atresia," in Moss et al., op. cit., p. 298.
24. L. Elliott, P. Bream, and I. Gessner, "Single and Common Ventricle," in Moss et al., op. cit., p. 380.
25. Ibid., p. 284.
26. H. Neufield and P. Randall, "Double Outlet Right Ventricle," in Moss et al., op. cit., p. 359.
27. D. I. Begglin, "Complications after Open Heart Surgery," *Nursing Clinics of North America* 4:123–129 (March 1969).
28. W. Nelson, V. C. Vaughn, and R. J. McKay, *Textbook of Pediatrics*, 11th ed., Saunders, Philadelphia, 1979, p. 1327.
29. L. W. Wannamaker and E. L. Kaplan, "Acute Rheumatic Fever," in Moss et al., op. cit., pp. 515–532.
30. A. Diehl, "Clinical Aspects of Rheumatic Fever: An Update," *Comprehensive Pediatric Nursing*, 4:67–76, April 1980.

31. Wannamaker and Kaplan, op. cit.

32. Diehl, op. cit., p. 74.

33. J. Wood, "The Detection of Hypertension," in J. W. Hurst, R. B. Logue, R. C. Schlant, and N. R. Wenger (eds.), *The Heart: Arteries and Veins*, 4th ed., vol. 1 and 2, McGraw-Hill, New York, 1978, p. 1391.

34. National Heart, Lung and Blood Institute's Task Force on Blood Pressure Control in Children, "report of the Task Force on Blood Pressure Control in Children," *Pediatrics* 59(suppl.):799 (May 1977).

35. B. L. Mirkin and A. Sinaiko, "Clinical Pharmacology and Therapeutic Utilization of Antihypertensive Agents in Children," in M. I. New and L. Levine (eds.), *Juvenile Hypertension*, Raven, New York, 1977, p. 205.

36. H. Sinzinger, W. Feigl, C. Dadas, and J. H. Holzner, "Intimal Alterations of the Aorta and the Great Arteries of Newborn and Children," *Pathologica Microbiologica* **43**:129–133, 1975.

37. S. R. Srinivasan, R. R. Frerichs, and G. S. Berenson, "Serum Lipids and Lipoproteins in Children," in W. B. Strong (ed.), *Atherosclerosis: Its Pediatric Aspects*, Grune & Stratton, New York, 1978, pp. 102–103.

38. S. Blumenthal, M. J. Jesse, C. C. Hennekens, et al., "Risk Factors for Coronary Artery Disease in Children of Affected Families," *Journal of Pediatrics* **87**:1187–1192 (1975).

39. Srinivasan et al., op. cit., p. 103.

40. Srinivasan, et al., op. cit., p. 105.

41. G. Carter and R. Lauer, "Atherosclerosis," in Moss et al., op. cit., p. 715.

Chapter 27 **Hematologic function**

Joanette Pete James, Sylvia L. Lee, and Robert T. Miller

Upon completion of this chapter, the student will be able to:

1. List the components of blood and their functions.

2. Distinguish between normal and abnormal values of RBCs, WBCs, hemoglobin, and hematocrit for children from the newborn period through adolescence.

3. Identify the basic underlying pathology for the major anemias as they result from decreased production of cellular elements or increased destruction.

4. Describe three factors that may lead to iron deficiency anemia.

5. Compare sickle cell trait, sickle cell anemia, and sickle cell disease.

6. Describe the most severe form of thalassemia.

7. Describe the coagulation process.

8. Compare and contrast the two major types of hemophilia.

9. Outline the instruction for a home infusion program for a child with hemophilia.

10. Write a nursing care plan for a child with hemophilia or sickle cell anemia.

11. Describe the major signs and symptoms for thrombocytopenic purpura.

Embryology of blood

The formation of blood cells, *hemopoiesis,* begins as early as 15 to 16 days of embryonic development from undifferentiated stem cells called *hemocytoblasts.* The early cells, made by the yolk sac, bring nutrients and oxygen from the placenta to the embryo to promote growth and development of the fetus. By the second month of embryonic life, the liver, spleen, and lymph nodes begin to produce blood cells. Around the fourth month, the bone marrow becomes active in the production of blood cells. The ribs, sternum, and vertebrae produce a small amount of blood cells during intrauterine development, but shortly after birth all areas, except the red bone marrow, cease production of blood cells.

Blood composition and characteristics

Blood is composed of two portions, liquid (plasma) and formed cells (platelets and red and white blood cells). The cells normally constitute 38 to 52 percent of the total blood volume; the remainder is the straw-colored plasma, which is a complex mixture of 91 percent water and 9 percent solutes—proteins, electrolytes, hormones, and enzymes. The body contains approximately 90 ml of blood per kilogram of weight at birth. This decreases to approximately 75 ml of blood per kilogram of adult body weight or about 5 to 6 liters of blood.

Blood has a slightly salty taste, a pH of 7.35 to 7.40, and a specific gravity of 1.055 to 1.065.

Changes occur in blood volume and normal blood values as children get older. Table 27-1 describes average blood values for the newborn, infant, child, and adolescent/adult.

Morphology and function of blood

Erythrocytes (red blood cells)

Erythrocytes, or *red blood cells (RBCs)*, are biconcave, disc-shaped cells produced in the bone marrow and derived from the hemocytoblast. Fig. 27-1 shows the maturation process of blood cells. At each stage of RBC development, greater quantities of hemoglobin and more and more cells are formed. Finally, after the cytoplasm of the normoblast has become filled with hemoglobin to a concentration of approximately 34 percent, the nucleus is autolyzed and absorbed. About 1 percent of circulating RBCs are *reticulocytes*, immature erythrocytes; the rest are mature erythrocytes. The erythrocyte is very flexible, making it possible for the cell to bend and twist when squeezing through the narrowest of capillaries and then to regain its original shape when it enters larger vessels.

Erythrocyte production, or *erythropoiesis*, is

Table 27-1 Average range of normal blood values

Measure	Birth–1 mo Newborn	1 mo–2 yr Infant	2 yr–12 yr Child	Adolescent/adult		Comment
				Male	**Female**	
Hemoglobin (g/100 ml blood)	14–24	10–15	11–16	14–16	13–15.5	Chief means of transport for O_2 and CO_2 in blood
Hematocrit (ml packed cells/ 100 ml blood)	43–63	30–42	34–37	42–52	37–47	% of blood made up of RBCs; the relative volume of cells and plasma
Red blood cells (RBCs) millions per cubic millimeter	4.8–7.1	4.5–5.1	3.8–5.5	4.8–5.5	4.4–5	
Reticulocytes (% of total RBCs)	4–6 decreasing to 0.5–1.6 by 2 weeks	0.5–1.6	0.5–1.6	0.5–1.6	0.5–1.6	Immature RBCs. released from bone marrow within past 1–2 days
Erythrocyte indices						
MCH (mean corpuscular Hb), $\mu\mu g$	32–34	27–31	27–31	29–32	29–32	Amount of HGB in a cell $$MCH = \frac{Hgb \times 10}{RBC}$$
MCV (mean corpuscular volume), μm^3 per RBC	96–108	82–96	82–96	82–96	82–96	Volume of each RBC (size of cell) $$MCV = \frac{Hct \times 10}{RBC}$$
MCHC (mean corpuscular Hb concentration), percent	32–33	32–36	32–36	32–36	32–36	Av. Hgb content per deciliter packed cells $$MCHC = \frac{Hgb}{Hct} \times 100$$
White blood cells (WBC) (number per cubic millimeter)	9000–30,000	5000–17,000	5000–10,000	5000–11,000		

(Table continued next page)

Table 27-1 Average range of normal blood values *(Continued)*

Measure	Birth–1 mo Newborn	1 mo–2 yr Infant	2 yr–12 yr Child	Adolescent/adult		Comment
				Male	Female	
Differential count						
Neutrophils (%)	40–80	30–50	55–60	38–70	38–70	Important in phagocytosis
Basophils (%)	0–0.5	0–0.5	0–3	0–3	0–3	Release of heparin and histamine
Eosinophils (%)	5	2–3	2	1–5	1–5	Phagocytosis plus playing a role in allergies
Lymphocytes (%)	30–35	40–50	40–45	15–45	15–45	Key cells in immune responses
Monocytes (%)	5–10	5–10	1–8	1–8	1–8	Capable of becoming macrophages
Platelets (thrombocytes) (number per cubic millimeter)	140,000–300,000	200,000–473,000	150,000–450,000	200,000–400,000		Active in coagulation

stimulated by anything that decreases the amount of oxygen available to the bone marrow or body tissue. Hemorrhage, nutritional deficiencies, high altitude, physical activities, and endocrine disturbances may stimulate the kidneys to secrete *erythropoietin*, the hormone regulating erythropoiesis.

The normal life span of erythrocytes is about 120 days. Old, worn-out RBCs are destroyed by phagocytes in the spleen, liver, and red bone marrow (reticuloendothelial system). Normally the rate of destruction of RBCs equals the rate of production, so that the number of circulating cells remains remarkably constant.

Hemoglobin The *hemoglobin* (Hgb) molecule is formed during the manufacture of the RBCs in the bone marrow. It consists of an iron-containing pigment—*heme*—and a simple protein—*globin*. Heme is an organic ring compound—protoporphyrin—to which iron is bound. It is the heme portion that combines with oxygen and carbon dioxide for transport. Hemoglobin carries 98 percent of the oxygen transported by the blood; less than 2 percent is carried in simple solution in the plasma.

Globin is formed by two pairs of polypeptide chains. When the chemical makeup of the globin chain changes, different kinds of hemoglobin are formed. Fetal hemoglobin, Hgb F, is composed of two alpha and two gamma polypeptide chains. Most hemoglobin is replaced by adult hemoglobin, Hgb A, during the first 6 months after birth. Hgb A is made up of two alpha and two beta chains. Abnormalities of these hemoglobin chains produce disorders of hemoglobin, or *hemoglobinopathies*. Because hemoglobin is a protein, hemoglobin type is a genetically controlled characteristic.

At birth, between 40 and 70 percent of the infant's hemoglobin is fetal hemoglobin. Fetal hemoglobin serves the fetus well because it has the ability to absorb oxygen at the low oxygen tensions found in fetal circulation. Hemoglobin disorders often do not appear until fetal hemoglobin is considerably reduced.

Bilirubin When RBCs are destroyed, either by natural cell aging and cell death or by disease, hemoglobin is set free and broken down into globin and heme. Heme is further broken down into iron, which is reused by the marrow for manufacture of new RBCs and protoporphyrin. Protoporphyrin is degraded, initially into unconjugated (fat-soluble) bilirubin and eventually into conjugated (water-soluble) bilirubin that is then excreted in bile. The normal amount of circulating bilirubin in infancy is 0.2 to 1.4 mg per 100 ml of blood. When the level rises above 5 mg per 100 ml (hyperbilirubinemia), as happens when RBCs are being destroyed at a rapid rate because of some abnormality, bilirubin escapes from the circulatory system and causes yellow discoloration (jaundice) of the body tissues.

Leukocytes (white blood cells)

Leukocytes are classified on the basis of size, shape of nucleus, and staining qualities of cytoplasm. Granulocytes are the most numerous and include basophils, eosinophils, and neutrophils. The other major white blood cell (WBC) types are nongranulated lymphocytes and monocytes (Fig. 27-1).

Leukocytes are selectively attracted to areas where tissue has been invaded by microorganisms. Leukocytes are capable of engulfing (phagocytosis), neutralizing, and destroying bacteria and yeasts. They also digest inert foreign particles and inflammatory debris.

The total number and percentage of WBCs change with age (Table 27-1). Like the RBC count, the WBC count is highest at birth (approximately 12,000 per cubic millimeter) and decreases to an average of 7500 per cubic millimeter in adults.

Thrombocytes (platelets)

Platelets, the smallest cells in circulating blood, originate from megakaryocytes, the largest cells in the bone marrow (Fig. 27-1). They are irregular in shape and are capable of ameboid movement. They are minute oval, nonnucleated, granular bodies whose primary function is in clotting.

When a blood vessel is damaged, platelets adhere immediately to the site of damage. They assume bizarre, irregular forms and have numerous points protruding from their surfaces. An accumulation of platelets and fibrin at the site of an injured vessel is called a *clot*.

Platelets also provide defense against infections. They are the first cells to interact with bacteria, viruses, and other foreign particles in circulating blood. In addition, platelets assist in *fibrinolysis*, destruction of a clot. The normal concentration of platelets is lowest in the newborn (140 to 300,000 per cubic millimeter) and increases to 150,000 to 450,000 per cubic millimeter in adults (Table 27-1).

Plasma

Blood *plasma* is a straw-colored solution of water (91 percent) and chemical compounds (9 percent), mainly proteins. Plasma is the medium by

Figure 27-1 Diagrammatic summary of orderly development of blood cells from a stem cell or hemocytoblast.

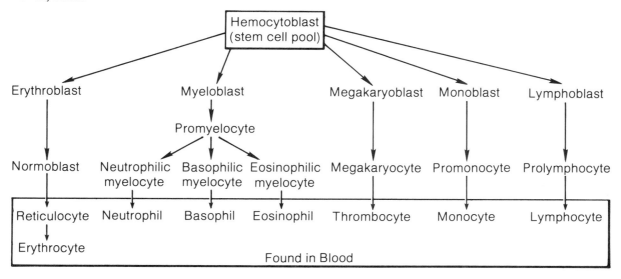

which the formed elements are transported in the blood vessels.

There are four major plasma proteins: albumin, globulin, fibrinogen, and prothrombin. Albumin, the most abundant, is important in maintaining the osmotic equilibrium of the blood. Since albumin cannot pass through the capillary wall, it remains in the bloodstream and exerts an osmotic pressure, attracting water from the tissue spaces back into the bloodstream. If dehydration or hemorrhage occurs, the plasma volume is reduced and shock may develop. In severe injuries, such as burns, albumin is able to escape from the capillaries, water cannot be retained, and blood volume drops. Infants are vulnerable to deficits in fluid volume because of their proportionately greater body fluid content and great extracellular fluid exchange.

Globulin is formed primarily in the liver. It combines with other proteins and transports them from one part of the body to another. The globulins also serve as antibodies (*immunoglobulins*) and provide immunity against some infections.

Fibrinogen and prothrombin are unstable proteins in the plasma that can split easily into smaller compounds, fibrin and thrombin. They are essential in clot formation.

The plasma proteins, low in early infancy, reach adult concentrations by 18 months. In health, the normal fluid volume of the plasma is maintained within relatively narrow limits.

The child who is suspected of abnormalities of the blood or hemostasis will undergo many blood tests. Repeated punctures are upsetting. The nurse must be ready to explain the tests, support the child, and help the child and parents cope with the procedures.

Alterations in erythrocytes

Anemia

Anemia, a sign of an underlying pathological process, is a reduced RBC volume or a hemoglobin (Hgb) concentration below the range of normal for the person's age. Children with anemia require a diagnostic search for the underlying cause.

A complete blood count (CBC) is the most valuable and most widely used laboratory test for the diagnosis and follow-up of anemia. A CBC includes all the cellular components of the blood (erythrocytes, leukocytes, and platelets). The RBC assessment includes both the number of erythrocytes and their shape (morphology). Morphology may also be determined by direct microscopic examination of a carefully prepared smear. Anemias may be classified according to the morphology of the erythrocyte size (microcytic, normocytic, or macrocytic) and the amount of hemoglobin pigment in the cells (normochromic or hypochromic) (Table 27-2).

The shape of the RBCs is important in making a diagnosis. In an anemic child, RBCs that are

Table 27-2 Erythrocyte morphology and related conditions

Terminology	Description of red blood cell	Condition in which found
Normocyte	Normal size and shape (biconcave disc)	Secondary anemia
Microcyte	Smaller than normal size	Secondary anemia, thalassemia
Macrocyte	Larger than normal size	Primary anemia due to folic acid and vitamin B_{12} deficiencies
Spherocyte	Slightly smaller than normal diameter. No central indentation or pallor	Hemoglobin C, thalassemia major
Normochromic	Normal pigmentation at edges of cell with normal central pallor	Acute blood loss; anemia due to extracorpuscular defects
Hypochromic	Pale-appearing cell with decreased color and accentuated central pallor	Any anemia
Anisocytosis	Variation in size of RBC	Any anemia
Poikilocytosis	Variation in shape of RBC	Any anemia

normocytic and normochromic point to the possibility of chronic infection, malignancy, endocrine hypofunction, marrow suppression, or blood loss. Macrocytic cells are caused by deficiencies of either folic acid or vitamin B_{12}. Erythrocytes that are microcytic and hypochromic are seen commonly in children with iron deficiencies but are also seen in children with thalassemia and lead toxicity. Other morphologic distinctions such as spherocytosis, fragmentation, or sickled cells signal a hemolytic process. The amount of reticulocytes indicates how much the bone marrow is responding to an anemic state by increased or decreased production of newly formed erythrocytes.

It is useful to classify further the anemias as resulting from either decreased production or increased destruction or loss of RBCs. To conceptualize them in this manner gives a better understanding of the underlying processes toward which the treatment is aimed.

Other laboratory tests used in the diagnosis and follow-up of anemias are bone marrow aspiration, bilirubin level and liver function tests, and Hgb electrophoresis. These and other tests are discussed later according to their use in specific disorders.

Signs and symptoms When the hemoglobin level drops to 7 or 8 g, signs or symptoms of physiological alterations begin to appear. Pallor of the skin and mucous membranes may become visible to the nurse. Anemias of about 8 to 11 g of Hgb are often detected on routine CBCs before surgery or during well-child examinations.

The body compensates for an anemic state by making adjustments to facilitate the transfer of oxygen. As the Hgb drops, cardiac output increases, heart rate increases, and the flow of blood is directed more to the vital tissues of the body. In addition, the affinity of Hgb for oxygen is reduced, allowing oxygen to be more freely taken up by the tissues. When the anemia is moderate to severe, the child may become weak or have shortness of breath upon exertion. After exertion, tachycardia may be marked. A baby may cry weakly and tire quickly after eating. Anorexia, irritability, and easy fatigability are noted by the parents of the anemic child.

Most anemias have an insidious onset and therefore give the body time to compensate for the loss of RBC mass. However, when there is rapid loss of blood from a major bleeding episode or a very rapid hemolysis (RBC destruction), the failure of the compensating mechanisms will eventually lead to congestive heart failure. Even anemia with a slow onset has the potential to cause cardiac failure when the level of Hgb falls below 4 to 5 g. Dyspnea, increasing weakness, edema, and weight gain may warn of impending cardiac failure. Children with chronic diseases or other intercurrent problems such as respiratory disorders may develop congestive failure when Hgb reaches 4 to 6 g.

The history obtained from the parents and the nurse's physical assessment of an anemic child can be diagnostically helpful. Certain physical signs or clues from the history point to different etiologies for the anemia. For instance, increased bruising or nosebleed alerts the clinician to look for a bleeding disorder resulting in blood loss anemia. A history of drug intake points to the possibility of toxic bone marrow suppression. Dark stools can mean blood loss into the intestinal tract, whereas a history of dark urine may mean that hemolysis is present with bilirubin being lost in the urine. Although various signs or symptoms are typical of certain disorders, many overlap and can complicate the diagnostic process. Laboratory confirmation is necessary to make a firm diagnosis.

Decreased production of RBCs

Physiological anemia Following birth, the normal infant's Hgb drops from a high of around 19 g to a low of 10 to 11 g in 6 to 8 weeks. Prematures or low-birth-weight babies may reach a low point of 7 to 9 g in 3 to 7 weeks since they have a smaller RBC mass at birth. The Hgb level declines because:

1. Rapid growth leads to an increase in blood volume and hemodilution.
2. RBCs survive only about 90 days during this period.
3. Erythropoietin drops, causing a decreased production of new RBCs in the bone marrow.

Treatment No therapy is indicated unless this "normal" anemia is aggravated by nutritional deficiencies, infection, or other intercurrent problems. The administration of iron will not prevent the normal decline of Hgb. When the Hgb level reaches its low point, erythropoietin is spontaneously secreted to stimulate bone marrow production. By 1 year of age, the normal Hgb will rise to about 12 g and will reach a mean of close to 13 g in the young teenager. Transfusions are used only in extreme cases and then only with small amounts of packed cells. If larger transfusions are used, they can delay the spontaneous return of normal bone marrow production.

Nursing management The infant's diet should contain sufficient essential nutrients to prevent deficiencies of iron, folic acid, and vitamin E. Iron stores are adequate in the full-term infant until 6 months of age, but prematures and low-birth-weight babies deplete storage iron earlier. Cow's milk and breast milk are low in iron, so supplemental iron is recommended after 4 months of age for full-term babies and earlier for prematures. Ferrous iron preparations or iron-fortified formulas are given until cereals and meats, which are high in iron content, can be introduced into the diet (usually at 6 months of age).

Iron-deficiency anemia Iron deficiency is the most common nutritional deficiency and occurs mainly during infancy or adolescence. Iron-deficiency anemia is more prevalent among low-income groups but is found at all economic levels.

When a deficiency of iron begins, the Hgb level initially remains constant while the body uses up stored iron to make RBCs. As the storage pool becomes depleted, the level of circulating serum iron falls. The RBCs then develop the characteristic hypochromic, microcytic morphology (also seen in lead toxicity and thalassemia), and the Hgb level begins to fall. The plasma ferritin level can be tested in order to measure the storage pool of iron in the body. Low ferritin concentrations can signal an early iron deficiency before the iron stores are depleted and before the Hgb levels begin to drop.

Iron-deficiency anemia is caused by four interrelated factors:

1. Deficient diet
2. Increased demand for growth
3. Blood loss
4. Poor absorption of dietary iron

A diet deficient in iron is the leading cause of the anemia and occurs commonly in a child who is fed mostly cow's milk without other foods for a source of iron. Adolescents may experience mild anemia especially if their diet is low in iron. Rapid growth during the first couple of years of life and during puberty increases the demand for iron. Third, blood loss for any reason reduces the amount of recycled hemoglobin iron available for erythrocyte production.

In addition to the varied disorders that cause bleeding in infancy, iron deficiency itself is associated with changes in the gut that promote blood loss. The mucosal lining is affected by the deficiency of iron, causing occult blood loss in the stool. Intestinal intolerance or hypersensitivity to whole cow's milk, especially when ingested in large amounts, may also cause loss of blood in the stools. Malabsorption syndromes or prolonged bouts of diarrhea prevent iron from being taken up by the body even though there is sufficient dietary intake.

Treatment Normally, the body absorbs about 10 percent of the dietary intake of iron. When a child is iron deficient, the absorption rises to around 20 percent. For this absorption to be of any consequence, a diet sufficient in iron must be provided.

The treatment of choice for the iron-deficient child is oral iron and diet counseling. Various forms of ferrous iron are effective in correcting the anemia. Although a prompt response can be noted on the CBC within the first week, treatment should be continued for about 3 months after the hemoglobin returns to normal in order to replenish the storage pool. The child's parents should be warned that oral iron causes the stools to become black or dark green. Oral iron is best absorbed in an empty stomach. Iron medication, like other medications, should be placed out of reach of young children to prevent overdose poisoning. Normally, reduced intake of cow's milk and the introduction of an adequate diet along with oral iron therapy is sufficient to correct the anemia.

Severe anemia with an Hgb of less than 4 g may require a packed RBC transfusion and follow-up treatment with oral iron. Intramuscular iron may be needed when parents fail to give the oral preparation or for a child who has intestinal malabsorption.

Nursing management When obtaining a history of the present illness, the nurse should note the presence of irritability, fatigue, weakness, and change in behavior. The usual diet should be described. Factors which may point to the cause of illness should be noted—history of drug intake, exposure to environmental hazards, pica, or episodes of bleeding. Racial origin, family history of anemia, jaundice, blood loss, and infection should be described.

Observations should include vital signs, color of stools or urine, bruising or petechiae, and response to normal activities. To determine pallor, both the conjunctiva and skin should be checked.

Anemic children need extended periods of rest and careful scheduling of nursing care to prevent undue fatigue. As the anemia is corrected, anorexia, irritability, and fatigue will lessen.

The severely anemic hospitalized child should be watched carefully for signs of congestive heart failure. Dyspnea, increasing weakness, edema, and weight gain are findings warning of impending cardiac failure. A *slow* transfusion of packed RBCs can correct the cardiac dysfunction. Blood loss in the stool should be monitored by guaiac testing, as even minor loss can worsen the anemia.

The nurse's role includes teaching. The parents should understand that the diet must contain sufficient amounts of iron-containing foods and that whole milk should be limited. Foods that are high in iron content include liver, dried fruits, beef, veal, carrots, beans, spinach, peas, sweet potatoes, peaches, and fortified cereals. *Pica*, or ingestion of nonfood substances, is associated with iron deficiency, and the parents should be warned that the child may be eating dirt or paint chips, which may lead to worm ingestion or lead poisoning. Pica should decrease when the anemia is treated. Furthermore, parents who have been unable to meet the dietary needs of their infant often need counseling for other well-child care such as immunizations, hygiene, and general approaches to infant care and well-being.

Prevention, of course, is the ideal way to handle this public health problem of iron-deficiency anemia. Counsel parents of newborns to provide an adequate diet and give supplemental iron as indicated for the age of the infant.

Aplastic anemia *Bone marrow aplasia* is moderate to severe depression in bone marrow production of RBCs, WBCs, or platelets. The term *hypoplasia* is used when there is at least some production by the marrow. Any or all of the cellular elements may be decreased to any degree. In *pancytopenia*, all three cellular components are decreased in the peripheral blood. Aplastic anemia may be congenital or acquired.

The commonest congenital aplastic anemia is *Fanconi syndrome*, a genetically transmitted anemia accompanied by microcephaly, limb deformities, heart and kidney anomalies, deafness, and short stature. The marrow aplasia is not evident until the age of 3 to 4 years, when bruising and nosebleeds appear. Confirmation of the diagnosis with a bone marrow aspirate and biopsy reveals marked hypocellularity of the marrow. Treatment includes combined corticosteroids and anabolic steroids (methyltestosterone).

Another congenital aplasia is *Blackfan-Diamond anemia*. This disorder is a pure RBC aplasia with normal numbers of circulating leukocytes and platelets. The bone marrow examination reveals markedly diminished to absent erythrocyte precursors. There is no known cause for this disorder and no commonly associated anomalies. The presenting signs and laboratory data are those of severe anemia in infancy, with normocytic, normochromic RBCs and a marked decrease in reticulocytes (new, young RBCs). Approximately 10 percent of children with this disorder will at some time during childhood or puberty begin spontaneously to produce their own RBCs and continue to do so. Corticosteroid treatment produces erythropoiesis in about 60 percent of children.

Acquired aplastic anemia can be caused by damage to the bone marrow from the effects of drugs, toxins, infections, or radiation. Cancer chemotherapeutic drugs known to cause marrow damage include antimetabolites and alkylating agents. Radiation also severely depresses bone marrow production. Other drugs associated with aplastic anemia include sulfonamides, quinicrine, phenylbutazone, mephenytoin, gold compounds and, more importantly, chloramphenicol (Chloromycetin). Acquired aplasia can follow infection with measles, hepatitis, and possibly other viruses. Insecticides, as well as benzene and related hydrocarbons found in glues and petroleum distillate solvents, also cause marrow damage. Aplasia may be the presenting sign of acute leukemia or systemic lupus erythematosus. No cause is found in 50 percent of the cases.

Treatment However vigorous the therapy, the prognosis for aplastic anemia is poor. With acquired aplastic anemia, death may be the result of a rapid progression of the disease when supportive therapy is unable to keep up. In the more chronic forms, such as Fanconi or Blackfan-Diamond anemia, the prognosis is somewhat better with the proper use of supportive transfusions and antibiotics. Life is often extended into the second and third decade. For the acquired forms of the anemia, removal of the offending agent is most important. Both forms require supportive therapy to replace the necessary components of the blood.

Spontaneous bleeding may occur when the platelet count falls below about 30,000 per cubic millimeter; many children, however, have only occasional bleeding with counts even below 5000 per cubic millimeter. Platelet transfusions are necessary during surgery or to stop severe bleeding. Transfusions with packed RBCs may be needed after a bleeding episode or to maintain the Hgb at an acceptable level—8 to 10 g.

Children with Blackfan-Diamond anemia, who depend upon monthly RBC transfusions, gradually accumulate iron in their body from the large amounts of iron in packed RBCs. This iron overload becomes an increasing problem, as none of the extra iron received in the transfusion is lost through hemorrhage. The iron overload is deposited in the heart, liver, and pancreas and causes failure of these organs after years of transfusions. Deferoxamine (Desferal) therapy attempts to chelate the excess iron from the body. Deferoxamine, however, cannot usually keep up with the large amounts of iron deposited in the system.

A very low WBC count predisposes the aplastic child to infection—the major cause of death. Because WBC transfusions are difficult and costly, they are not done routinely. When infection is suspected, antibiotics should be started promptly, and the child must be hospitalized or watched closely as an outpatient.

Corticosteroids and androgenic steroids are used individually or in combination to stimulate bone marrow production. If effective, it sometimes takes 2 to 4 months to see any benefit. Among the side effects of corticosteroids are increased appetite with ensuing cushionoid features, sodium retention, hypertension, and impairment of linear growth. The androgens cause masculinization of the child and a greater frequency of malignant hepatomas after prolonged therapy.

Bone marrow transplants have been of value in some children. Siblings who are HL-A compatible by tissue typing are candidates to provide the marrow for the transplant. Tissue typing should be done immediately after the diagnosis is made, because typing becomes more difficult after transfusion therapy has begun.

Nursing management The assessment of the child with aplastic anemia is related to the deficiencies in platelets, WBCs, and RBCs. The parents and the child should be taught what signs to watch for and under what conditions they should come to the hospital for care or guidance.

The child should be monitored closely for increasing signs of anemia or blood loss. Nasal packing is necessary for nosebleeds. Contact sports should be avoided. Acetaminophen should be used instead of aspirin, which affects the function of platelets. Suppression of menstruation (by hormone therapy) may be necessary if blood loss is excessive.

Depending on how well the child's body compensates for the depression in RBC production, transfusions will occasionally be necessary to bring the Hgb back up to an acceptable level.

The nurse must be extremely vigilant during a transfusion. The child should be kept comfortable and vital signs monitored closely. Signs of a transfusion reaction often occur within 10 min. Table 27-3 describes transfusion reactions and nursing responsibilities. When a transfusion reaction occurs, the blood should be stopped, the line kept open with intravenous fluid, and the physician notified.

The chance of overwhelming infection is a constant threat when the WBC count is very low. Parents should be instructed to seek medical care at the first sign of infection. With a serious infection, hospitalization and parenteral antibiotics are the safest way to manage the child. Avoidance of contact with ill children or adults and large crowds should be attempted.

Children and their families need help in dealing with the physical changes that are the com-

Table 27-3 Transfusion reactions

Type of reaction	Signs and symptoms	Nursing responsibilities
Febrile	Fever, chills, headache, nausea, vomiting	Check temperature q30 min. Observe closely. Physician may elect to discontinue transfusion or give acetaminophen before transfusion
Hemolytic	Fever, nausea, vomiting, abdominal and back pain, hematuria, oliguria, restlessness, flushing, tachypnea	Usually transfusion is discontinued and blood samples obtained. Monitor vital signs, intake and output. Encourage fluids. Diuretics may be ordered. Check urine for hemoglobin
Hypervolemic	Dyspnea, cough, cyanosis, pulmonary edema, pain, distended neck veins	Blood should always be administered evenly at the designated rate. Place child in upright position with legs dependent. Oxygen may help
Hypersensitivity	Pruritus, urticaria, fever, asthma, hypotension, nausea, vomiting	Have epinephrine, antihistamines, and resuscitative equipment available. Monitor vital signs. Physician may order diphenhydramine before transfusion to alleviate allergic response
Bacterial contamination	Fever, chills, shock, coma, convulsions	Monitor vital signs, temperature, and neurologic status. Emergency drugs need to be available—plasma expanders, corticosteroids, vasopressors. Sample of transfusion sent for culture and sensitivity
Citrate intoxication	Tingling in fingers, cramps, tetany, convulsions, respiratory arrest	Infuse blood slowly. Stop transfusion, maintaining patency of line, and call physician

mon side effects of steroids. High-dose prednisone leads to increased appetite and weight gain from both caloric intake and water retention. To prevent massive weight gain, parents can adjust the child's diet by providing low-calorie, high-nutrient foods. The masculinization caused by the androgens is also a troublesome problem. School-age girls are especially affected by increased hair growth, increased muscle mass, and masculine features. Support and explanations to peers and school personnel may be helpful.

Although the anemia is of great concern to the caretakers of the child and usually the most life-threatening condition, referral is necessary for the child with Fanconi syndrome to provide special education and follow-up for the accompanying problems.

Megaloblastic anemias Deficiencies of folic acid or vitamin B_{12} cause the two megaloblastic anemias most common in children. *Megaloblastic* refers to macrocytic RBCs as well as to enlarged forms of leukocytes, platelets, and their precursors in the bone marrow. The large cells are produced in response to impaired DNA synthesis brought about by a lack of sufficient folic acid or vitamin B_{12}. Leukopenia and thrombocytopenia often accompany these deficiencies.

Vitamin B_{12} deficiency is rare in children and can be due to dietary insufficiency or to juvenile pernicious anemia. In pernicious anemia a glycoprotein, the *intrinsic factor*, that is normally secreted by the gastric mucosa to aid in the absorption of B_{12}, is missing. The Shilling test, using radioactive B_{12}, tests for B_{12} absorption by the stomach.

Typical symptoms of anemia plus a painful, smooth tongue are characteristic of vitamin B_{12} deficiency. Involvement of the nervous system causes tingling and numbness of fingers and toes (paresthesias), ataxia, and impaired position sense. Treatment requires monthly injection of B_{12} for the child's lifetime.

Megaloblastic anemia is more often due to a deficiency of folic acid than of vitamin B_{12}. Impaired absorption, a diet deficient in folate, or an increased demand for folate are responsible for the developing anemia. Normal body stores of folate can sustain cell production for about 5 to 6 months after intake of folates stops. Therefore the peak incidence of folic acid deficiency in infancy occurs at 4 to 7 months, when prenatal supplies become depleted.

Folic acid is inefficiently absorbed in the child with chronic diarrhea, celiac disease, and surgical resection of portions of the small intestine. Folic acid antagonists such as methotrexate cause megaloblastic changes. Rarely, this complication accompanies anticonvulsant therapy with diphenylhydantoin or phenobarbital. Poor dietary intake also causes deficiency. Folic acid must be supplemented in the child who is drinking goat's milk.

Poor weight gain, irritability, diarrhea, and symptoms associated with low hemoglobin are manifestations of folic acid deficiency anemia. The neurologic effects of vitamin B_{12} deficiency are not seen in the folate-depleted child unless there is also a concomitant B_{12} depletion. Both forms of megaloblastic anemia, however, result in a smooth tongue that is sometimes painful and in gastrointestinal changes resulting in diarrhea.

Treatment Folic acid deficiency responds well to oral doses of folic acid (100 to 200 mg daily). Therapy should be continued for at least 3 to 4 weeks to restore the storage pool. Folic acid administration can also partially correct anemia caused by vitamin B_{12} deficiency but will not correct the associated neurologic symptoms.

Nursing management The child with pernicious anemia and vitamin B_{12} deficiency will have to begin a lifelong therapy program. In most cases, the neurologic symptoms disappear after the correction of the anemic state, but during the initial treatment the child will need to take safety precautions in order to compensate for neurologic impairment. Impaired balance makes such activities as bicycling dangerous.

In the patient with folate deficiency, after the folic acid stores of the body are replenished and the anemia is corrected to a normal Hgb level, no maintenance therapy is needed for the child who had a deficient diet. However, unless a proper diet is followed, the anemia can recur. Good sources of folic acid are human and cow's milk, fresh green vegetables, liver, kidney, beans, and nuts.

Increased destruction or loss of RBCs

Blood loss anemia Rapid blood loss may result from a variety of disorders or trauma and can quickly lead to shock. Disorders of coagulation such as hemophilia or a reduction in platelets can cause serious acute bleeding. Excessive bruising or a petechial rash suggests coagulation abnormalities. During the fetal and neonatal periods, blood loss may be acute or chronic. Rapid blood loss can occur through the cord, the placenta, or from obstetric trauma. Chronic bleeding can occur with feto-maternal or feto-fetal transfusion in utero. Chronic blood loss in childhood usually occurs through stools.

The erythrocytes in blood loss anemia are normocytic and normochromic. Three to five days after an acute bleed, the bone marrow will produce a higher percentage of new reticulocytes. In the patient with chronic bleeding, the reticulocyte count may be normal or increased depending upon how hard the bone marrow must work to keep up with the blood cells being lost. Blood loss anemia does not affect the WBCs or platelets; however, decreased platelets may be the cause of the blood loss.

Treatment Active bleeding must be stopped as quickly as possible by first aid measures. If there is a known coagulation factor deficiency or severely decreased platelets, transfusions of the missing factor may be life-saving.

Nursing management Transfusions with packed RBCs will be used to restore the oxygen-carrying capacity of the blood if the Hgb level falls dangerously low (e.g., 3 to 5 g). When the Hgb is very low, transfusion with packed RBCs should be done slowly to avoid volume overload, causing congestive heart failure or pulmonary edema. The lower the Hgb, the lower the number of milliliters per kilogram of weight per hour of the transfusion.

Hemolytic anemias *Hemolytic anemias* are characterized by premature destruction of erythrocytes caused by either a defect within the RBC (corpuscular) or damage from outside the cell (extracorpuscular).

With increased hemolysis, the bilirubin level becomes elevated. Many people with ongoing hemolytic disease have a yellowish tint in their sclerae that becomes more prominent as more rapid hemolysis occurs and decreases as hemolysis decreases.

The child with hemolytic disease is subject to episodes of rapid hemolysis that can lead to very severe anemia and shock. Signs of increased hemolysis include increasing jaundice, fatigue, weakness, and pallor. Hemoglobinuria may appear as a red pigment in the urine and is indicative of a rapid hemolytic process.

The diagnosis of hemolytic disease is based upon demonstration of shortened RBC survival (less than 120 days), evidence of increased erythrocyte catabolism (increased bilirubin), and an elevated reticulocyte count.

The causes of extracorpuscular hemolysis can be grouped in five categories:

1. Mechanical factors: conditions involving deposits of fibrin in vessels due to thrombocytopenia or prosthetic heart valves
2. Infections, such as infectious mononucleosis, hepatitis, malaria, and *Clostridium welchii* infections
3. Toxins from snake bites
4. Drugs such as quinine, phenylhydrazine, and substances such as lead
5. Isoimmune disorders such as hemolytic disease of the newborn and incompatible blood transfusions.

Corpuscular hemolytic anemias are usually inherited. Two major categories are those caused by enzyme deficiencies (pyruvate kinase deficiency, glucose-6-phosphate dehydrogenase deficiency) and those caused by membrane deficiencies (hereditary spherocytosis, hereditary elliptocytosis). Characteristics and treatment of diseases in these groups are reviewed in Table 27-4. Because these anemias have a genetic basis, their incidence is higher in some populations; for example, glucose-6-phosphate dehydrogenase deficiency is high among Sephardic Jews, among whom intermarriage is frequent. A final group of hemolytic anemias can be traced to

Table 27-4 Characteristics and treatment of hemolytic anemias due to corpuscular defects

Condition	Characteristics	Treatment
Enzyme deficiency		
Pyruvate kinase deficiency	Range in severity of symptoms from severe jaundice at birth requiring transfusions to a well-compensated hemolysis. Growth and development may be delayed	Some improvement after splenectomy, with less need for transfusions and better RBC production
Glucose-6-phosphate dehydrogenase deficiency (G6PD)	Increased incidence in blacks (10–15%), Sephardic Jews, Orientals, and those of Mediterranean descent. May have mild congenital anemia, but usually hemolysis is precipitated by the ingestion of certain drugs—antipyretics, analgesics, antimalarials, sulfonamides, nitrofurans—or infections	Supportive treatment with transfusions. Control infection. Remove or avoid drugs
Membrane deficiency		
Hereditary spherocytosis	Common in white population. Infant presents with anemia, splenomegaly, hyperbilirubinemia. Infection causes hemolytic crisis.	Supportive transfusions. Splenectomy—making child a greater risk for pneumococcal infection, so needs vaccine. Prophylactic folic acid
Hereditary elliptocytosis	90% have no symptoms, Otherwise, symptoms the same as in spherocytosis	Same as for spherocytosis

Table 27-5 Characteristics of hemoglobinopathies

Characteristic	Sickle cell trait	Sickle cell anemia	Hemoglobin SC disease	Sickle cell beta + thalassemia	Sickle cell beta O thalassemia
Hgb type	AS	SS	SC	S-beta + thal. (SA + thal.)	S-beta O thal. (S + thal.)
Usual Hgb range	Normal	6–9 g	10–15 g	10–12 g	7–10 g
Course of illness	No illness	Severe anemia plus complications	Mild anemia and complications less frequent	Mild anemia, infrequent complications	Anemia plus complications
Spleen	Normal size	Usually not palpable as in adult	Enlarged	Enlarged	Enlarged
Usual onset of crises	No crises	Early in life	Often adolescence and later	Often adolescence and later or none	Similar to SS
Amount of Hgb A present	More than 50%	No Hgb A	No Hgb A	Less than 40%	No Hgb A

defects in hemoglobin structure (e.g., sickle cell disorders) or production (e.g., thalassemias). The sickle cell disorders are found most often in blacks, the thalassemias (of the beta type) among people of or from Mediterranean countries. These hemoglobinopathies are summarized in Table 27-5.

Sickle cell hemoglobinopathies Sickle cell hemoglobinopathies are a group of inherited RBC disorders characterized by the presence of sickle Hgb (Hgb S). Hgb S results from a change in the composition of the beta globin chains. This abnormal hemoglobin replaces all or part of the normal adult Hgb (Hgb A). This defect causes the RBC to sickle, i.e., to change from a round, biconcave disc to a crescent shape when oxygen is released to the tissues in the course of normal functioning. Hgb S is the most common of the more than 250 Hgb mutations in humans.

Hgb S is present in the homozygous state, as sickle cell anemia, in 1 percent of American blacks. It is present in the heterozygous state, as sickle cell trait, in 8 percent. Hgb S is also found in Spanish-Americans, Indians, and those of Mediterranean descent.

The child who receives one gene for normal Hgb A and one gene for Hgb S from his or her parents inherits the sickle trait (Hgb AS). If the child receives a gene for Hgb S from each parent, he or she inherits sickle cell anemia (Hgb SS). A gene for Hgb S in combination with another gene for an abnormal Hgb also produces sickle cell disease. *Sickle cell disease* is the umbrella phrase for all hemoglobin types in which Hgb S is present.

Fig. 27-2 gives examples of mating between individuals with various types of Hgb. The reader is reminded that the risk of having an affected child is the *same* for each pregnancy—no matter what happened in previous pregnancies.

Sickle cell trait (Hgb AS) is the carrier state for sickle cell anemia (Hgb SS). The *trait* has been confused with the *anemia* and also with other Hgb types that sickle. Persons with Hgb AS are not anemic, and their RBC survival is normal. Only about 24 to 45 percent of their Hgb is Hgb S. Even though some of their cells do sickle, these individuals do not have the recurrent sickling crisis or frequent infections that are associated with sickle cell diseases. Rarely, they experience painless hematuria or splenic infarcts. It is very important for nurses to understand the difference between Hgb AS and Hgb SS in order to be able to explain the implications of each to parents and children and to the general public.

The common sickle cell hemoglobinopathies

known to have abnormal hematologic findings and clinical manifestations requiring frequent medical attention are (1) sickle cell anemia (Hgb SS), (2) sickle cell C disease (Hgb SC), (3) sickle cell thalassemia (Hgb S-Thal). These hemoglobinopathies are compared in Table 27-5 and will be discussed later in this chapter.

Hgb SS is the most common form of sickle cell disease and has the most severe clinical manifestations. Its problems are related to rapid destruction of RBCs, vasoocclusion, and infection.

RBCs that contain Hgb S cannot be distinguished in appearance from normal RBCs until they sickle (Fig. 27-3). The sickle cell is rigid; its membrane is not as flexibile as that of a normal RBC membrane. It becomes very fragile, with a life span of only 8 to 20 days. This results in chronic anemia. Under conditions of lowered oxygen tension, increased acidity, or increased viscosity, RBCs containing Hgb S will sickle, making it difficult for them to pass through the microcirculation (capillaries and sinusoids). Some remain in the irregular sickle shape and are called *irreversible sickled cells* (Fig. 27-4). The sickling process tends to increase the blood viscosity, which then leads to stasis and more sickling. With each sickle cycle, the membrane of the RBC is damaged. Sickle-shaped cells become wedged in the small blood vessels and block the flow of blood to parts of the body, producing ischemia and subsequent microinfarcts causing tissue death. Fig. 27-5 diagrams the effects of Hgb S on various body systems. Over a period of time, major organs are affected, leading to severe malfunctioning and organ failure in the following sites.

The *spleen* is one of the first organs to be affected. The gradual fibrosis and scarring will generally produce autosplenectomy by age 7 to 8 years. Because of the abnormally functioning spleen, these children have an increased susceptibility to infections.

The *liver* becomes enlarged, firm, and tender. Liver damage affects the adult more than the

Figure 27-2 Inheritance from parents of normal and sickling hemoglobin. The hemoglobin types of one parent are given in the left margin of each block and those of the other parent along the top. Each parent carries two alleles for hemoglobin. As combinations at conception are random, the risk of each possible outcome in the zygote can be calculated according to statistical laws. Key: A, normal adult hemoglobin; S, sickling hemoglobin; AA, normal; AS, sickle cell trait; SS, sickle cell disease.

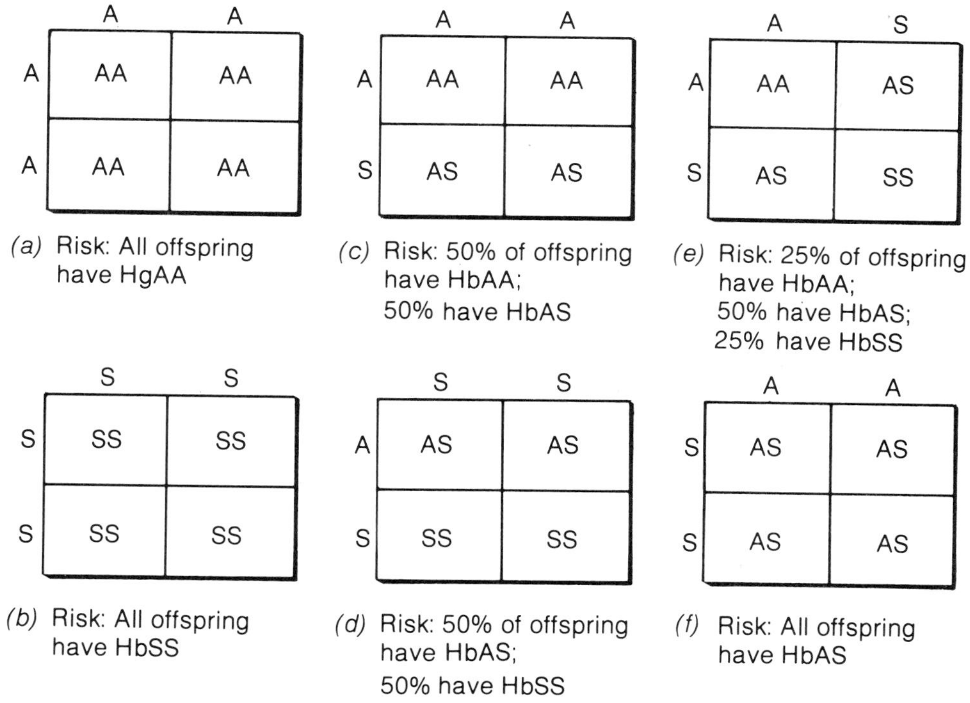
A A / A AA AA / A AA AA
(a) Risk: All offspring have HgAA
A A / A AA AA / S AS AS
(c) Risk: 50% of offspring have HbAA; 50% have HbAS
A S / A AA AS / S AS SS
(e) Risk: 25% of offspring have HbAA; 50% have HbAS; 25% have HbSS
S S / S SS SS / S SS SS
(b) Risk: All offspring have HbSS
S S / A AS AS / S SS SS
(d) Risk: 50% of offspring have HbAS; 50% have HbSS
A A / S AS AS / S AS AS
(f) Risk: All offspring have HbAS

Figure 27-3. Scanning electron micrograph of human sickled RBCs in the deoxygenated state accompanied by one normal biconcave cell (× 10,000). (*Courtesy of R. F. Baker, Department of Microbiology, University of Southern California Medical School.*)

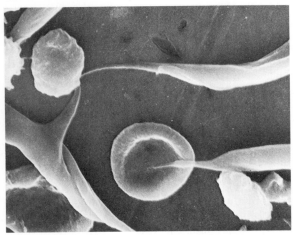

child. The rapid breakdown of RBCs produces an excessive amount of bilirubin, causing jaundice especially of the sclerae. Cholelithiasis may also contribute to jaundice.

A single episode of sickling in the *brain* can cause a cerebrovascular (CVA) accident or seizures or both. CVA is most common in children

Figure 27-4 Scanning electron micrograph of a mixture of sickled human RBCs and normal human RBCs. (*Courtesy of R. F. Baker, Department of Microbiology, University of Southern California Medical School.*)

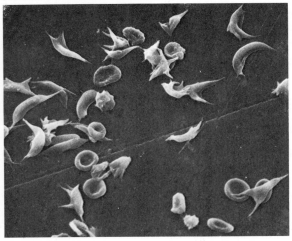

under 10 years. Usually there is no precipitating cause, although some are associated with hyperventilation.

The *heart* may become enlarged with a murmur related to the anemia that exists.

Any infection in the *lungs* causes edema and stasis, which precipitate sickling. Pneumonia is common, with treatment complicated by the impaired circulation. Pulmonary ventilation should be accomplished *without* hyperventilation. Therefore the incentive spirometer, IPPB, and blow bottles are all contraindicated.

In the *kidney*, sickling and microinfarcts can cause permanent damage manifested by hematuria and an inability to concentrate urine. Acute urinary tract infections can lead to pyelonephritis, particularly in older children and adults. Long-term sickling can destroy the glomeruli, leading to renal failure.

Bone infarcts involving the small bones of the hands and feet are common in infants and young children. The resulting swelling and pain are the "hand-foot syndrome" or sickle cell dactylitis. These bones usually heal without deformity. Older people experience aseptic necrosis of the femoral and humeral heads and deterioration of thoracic and lumbar vertebrae.

Because of the chronic hypoxia, bones become very susceptible to infection. *Salmonella* osteomyelitis is common and often requires years of continuous antibiotic treatment.

The *eye* manifestations in sickle cell disease develop gradually and are more common in Hgb SC and S-thal. Proliferative sickle retinopathy can lead to blindness. Photocoagulation has proven helpful.

The chronic, recurring problem of *leg ulcers* usually begins during the middle to late teens. These painful ulcers are subject to local and systemic infection. Una boots allow protection and mobility.

Priapism, a persistent, painful erection of the penis, may occur at any age but is associated with the onset of puberty. The longer the erection lasts, the more difficult it is to relieve. Hypotonic fluids and a warm bath may help. The erection should be relieved within two hours.[1] Aspiration of the corpora cavernosa may be necessary.

The RBC containing Hgb S may not function for more than 8 to 20 days, considerably less than the normal 120-day life span. This hemolysis and resulting chronic anemia stimulate eryth-

Figure 27-5 The pathophysiology of sickle cell disease related to the clinical expression of the illness.

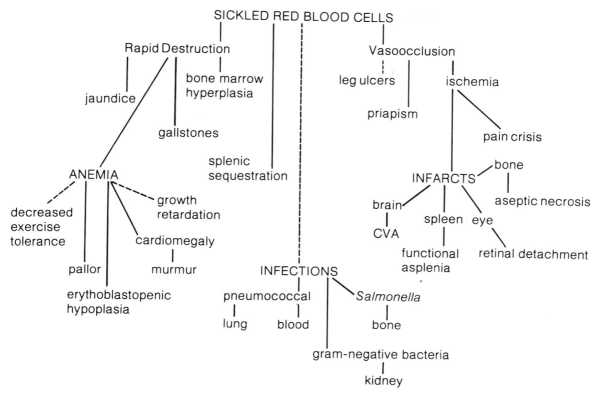

ropoiesis, causing hyperplasia of the bone marrow.

In addition to the effects of sickling on the various body organs, the child will have a variety of complaints such as fever, weakness, malaise, pain, anorexia, and vomiting. The disorder is not easily recognizable from the child's physical appearance, although the extremities may be disproportionately long.

Frequently physical activities are restricted because of the lack of stamina. Children need to be able to set their own limits and not be pushed beyond them.

The child experiences painful sickling episodes, called *crises*, that are often brought on by dehydration and infections. In early adolescence the child usually has fewer crises, but the frequency increases again in the later teens and early adult life. Despite reports suggesting little survival into adulthood, life expectancy is unpredictable at this time. Some people live into their fifth and sixth decades.

There are four events described as sickle crisis: (1) vaso-occlusive crisis or pain crisis; (2) aplastic crisis or reduction in RBC production; (3) splenic sequestration crisis; and (4) hyperhemolytic crisis or hyperhemolysis.

Vaso-occlusive crisis is the hallmark of the disease. The RBCs sickle and occlude the smaller blood vessels, producing pain due to lack of oxygen to the tissues. This may occur at any time after fetal Hgb diminishes sufficiently, usually at 3 to 6 months of age.

Painful episodes may be precipitated by dehydration, infection, stress, and exposure to extreme cold or heat. Pain may occur in the extremities, joints, back, or abdomen; older children and adults sometimes complain of pain everywhere. These episodes may last anywhere from 1 day to several days or weeks. They may follow a viral or bacterial infection and sometimes may be accompanied by local swelling and tenderness. Any fever should be evaluated as to the source and properly treated.

In *aplastic crisis* the rate of RBC production is severely or completely reduced. There are signs of increasing anemia, malaise, headache, and pallor. Aplastic crisis is thought to be precipitated by infections. When RBC production is severely reduced, the existing anemia becomes worse and requires transfusion support. Reticulocyte counts are used to determine the rate of RBC production, to diagnose, and to manage aplastic crisis. RBC production usually returns in a few days. Folic acid supplements are needed to aid in RBC production.

In *splenic sequestration crisis*, sickled RBCs get trapped, or sequestered, in the spleen, blocking blood flow. The spleen enlarges as more blood cells are trapped. Acute sequestration is often associated with septicemia. The infection and sudden worsening of the anemia are life-threatening. Transfusion is necessary as well as treatment for the infection. A splenectomy may be done after the child's first acute episode. Parents should be taught to check for signs of an enlarging spleen and increasing anemia and to seek immediate medical help if they occur.

In *hyperhemolytic crisis* RBCs are destroyed more rapidly than usual. It may occur in children while the spleen is still present, but in adults it probably either does not exist or is secondary to other complicating factors.[2] An increase in reticulocytes suggests hemolysis, but there is not necessarily a decrease in Hgb. Hyperhemolytic crisis is painless, generally requires no treatment, and would probably go unnoticed unless it occurs in conjunction with another complication.

TREATMENT Neither a cure nor an effective, safe treatment is available for sickle cell disease. Treatment is directed toward relieving the symptoms and complications. Correction of dehydration, acidosis, and hypoxia is essential. Vasoocclusive episodes must be recognized as forerunners of more severe complications. Analgesics and transfusions for severe anemia are needed. Infection must be treated promptly with antibiotics. Pneumococcal vaccine is recommended for children over 2 years of age.

Probably the single most important treatment for painful episodes is *water*—intravenously, orally, and by local application. Hydration through increased fluid intake increases plasma volume and blood flow, dislodging sickled cells from microcirculation.[3] Water is applied locally in the form of warm moist packs, tub baths or showers, or whirlpool baths or tanks.

Oxygen is often used during sickle cell crisis, especially with adults. It is seldom helpful in the child because it has no effect on sickling and does not decrease pain. Oxygen is helpful during episodes of dyspnea, severe pneumonia, and pulmonary infarcts.

Transfusions are used only when absolutely necessary because of risks of transfusion reaction, hepatitis, iron overload, and immune antibody production. Transfusions are most frequently indicated in the following conditions:

1. Any sudden drop in Hgb including splenic sequestration and bone marrow aplasia.
2. The need to increase the oxygen-carrying capacity, as in severe pneumonia, CVA, and complications of pregnancy.
3. Occasionally in preparation for surgery to reduce surgical and anesthesia risk.

Although several drugs have been used to treat Hgb SS, most offer no benefit and may be harmful. Iron is usually not necessary because the anemia causes increased absorption. When multiple transfusions are needed, they increase iron stores.

Multivitamins may be used, but a well-balanced diet is more important. Daily folic acid supplements are useful when the level is low due to increased RBC production.

Although extensive research is being done to find a drug that prevents sickling, it is hampered by the lack of a laboratory animal with sickle cells. The safety of any drug must be proven before experimentation is done on humans.

Ideally, surgery on the child with sickle cell disease is done only when absolutely necessary and when the child is in the best possible condition. Often transfusions will not be necessary unless the Hgb is well below 10 g. Certain precautions are required when emergency or elective surgery is necessary.

1. The surgeon and anesthesiologist must be aware of the child's sickle cell status.
2. Optimal oxygenation and hydration should be maintained at all times.
3. No tourniquets should be used during surgery.
4. No methods of hypoxia should be used in awakening the child.

5. Prophylactic antibiotics are necessary to prevent infections.

6. Prophylactic transfusions prior to surgery should be used only if absolutely necessary.

NURSING MANAGEMENT The pathophysiology of Hgb SS has been described in detail to provide a firm basis for nursing care. The nurse must determine the problems experienced by the child and provide nursing intervention accordingly.

During a sickle cell crisis, the child will need meticulous nursing care based on a comprehensive approach and a caring attitude. Since dehydration, infection, overfatigue, prolonged exposure to heat and cold, and emotional stress may all contribute to sickle cell crisis, their prevention is a major goal for the nurse and family.

Pain is a leading problem associated with the disease. Careful assessment, appropriate analgesia, and hydration are essential. Any swelling or painful area must be carefully described. Heat should not be applied to the abdomen unless appendicitis has been ruled out.

Oxygenation of tissues initially is achieved through bed rest with passive range-of-motion exercises and, later, progressive ambulation (Fig. 27-6). In addition, continuous moist heat, adequate hydration, pulmonary ventilation (by means of deep breathing and clearing of secretions), and prevention of infection contribute to oxygenation. Nursing care should be planned to allow adequate rest periods.

If blood transfusions are necessary, the nurse's responsibilities include observing for reactions and careful regulations of the transfusion rate to prevent hypervolemia.

Vital signs must be monitored closely to assess for impending shock, beginning infection, or problems with oxygenation. Gentle palpation of the spleen may be helpful when splenic crisis is anticipated.

Children under 10 years who develop an increased temperature of 39°C (102°F) or above should be hospitalized, cultured, and treated vigorously with antibiotics to protect against pneumococcal pneumonia—a disease that can cause death within a few hours if untreated. Temperature should always be checked before any antipyretic analgesic is given.

To promote hydration, the nurse should offer oral fluids frequently—every 30 to 60 min. If the

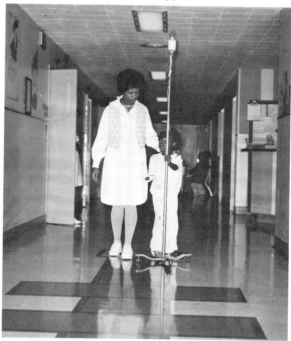

Figure 27-6 Child ambulating with the assistance of the nurse, receiving intravenous infusion, and pushing own intravenous pole for additional support.

daily goal is 2400 ml, then a plan must be implemented to insure approximately 200 ml every waking hour during the day. Intravenous fluids require careful regulation. (Review the nursing measures described in Chap. 17 regarding oral and intravenous fluids.)

Another nursing goal is the prevention of acidosis. Hydration and well-balanced meals are useful in preventing this problem. The child's electrolyte balance can also be monitored and changes reported to the physician. Daily weighing is helpful in checking for diuresis.

Because the kidneys do not concentrate urine well, fluids are easily lost. The child will need special protection in hot weather.

Due to the forcing of fluids, many young children have difficulty with toilet training. Increased frequency of urination is common, as is enuresis. The nurse can help parents understand the physiological basis for these problems and suggest coping measures such as:

1. Have the child void frequently during the day.
2. Get the child up to void once during the night.

3. Consider enuresis part of the disease and learn to live with it in that way.
4. Continue to force fluids.

The child needs play activities that are age and condition appropriate. Occupational therapy visits are useful. If the child is missing school, the school program must be implemented in the hospital or home.

Although puberty is often delayed in children with sickle cell disease, once it occurs they are usually fertile. The risk of producing offspring with the disease must be carefully explained. The nurse has an important role in these explanations and in providing birth control counseling. Neither oral contraceptives nor the intrauterine device is safe for the female with sickle cell disease. Barrier and chemical birth control methods, used carefully and competently, carry no risks of bleeding, infection, or emboli.

In pregnancy there are increased risks for the mother with sickle cell disease, and her baby. The pregnant patient needs careful follow-up, prompt, vigorous treatment of infection, and folic acid supplements. Some patients may be started on transfusion programs after a certain point in their pregnancy. Above all, the pregnant patient needs excellent care and the support of the health care team in the decision to have a child.

Table 27-6 Guidelines for teaching parents of children with sickle cell disease

1. Encourage intake of 2000–4000 ml per day. Give the child something to drink every 30–60 min. Restrict cola, coffee, and tea because of their diuretic qualities. Restrict cranberry juice because of acidosis.
2. Keep urine a light amber color through adequate fluid intake.
3. Any complicated illness with vomiting, diarrhea, pain, or elevated temperature of 39°C (102°F) or more should be treated in the hospital.
4. Provide and encourage the child to eat a well-balanced diet high in folic acid.
5. See that the child gets plenty of rest and sleep.
6. Avoid situations that may contribute to crisis—dehydration, infection, prolonged stress—emotional or physical, and fatigue, prolonged exposure to heat and cold.
7. Have the child wear a medical alert tag and keep people nearby informed of the illness.
8. Do not neglect regular health maintenance care—immunizations, eye examinations, dental care.
9. Avoid overprotectiveness and encourage the child to participate in age-appropriate activities as tolerated.

Parents especially need to understand that even with the best care there will be periods of crisis and setbacks from the disease. The greatest risk of death is in children under 5 years. Crisis incidence decreases thereafter. Nevertheless parents live constantly with the fear of losing their child.

Many parents feel guilty because of their genetic role in their child's disease. Methods of coping with those feelings vary. Helping them to explore their feelings and to learn to live with the situation positively are appropriate nursing responsibilities. Parents need to be encouraged to set reasonable limits for their children but to guard against overprotectiveness. Table 27-6 provides guidelines for teaching parents of a child with Hgb SS.

Education, testing, and counseling, in that order, are important when identifying those possessing the sickle gene. The federally funded sickle cell programs throughout the United States stress education first.

In the period immediately following 1972, when federal funds were first available for study and research in sickle cell disease, there were many mass screening programs. As a result of these programs, thousands of persons were tested before being properly counseled. People did not understand the difference between Hgb AS and Hgb SS. Inadequate information caused misunderstandings and many problems with employers and insurance companies. It is mandatory that people understand the difference between Hgb AS and Hgb SS and the implications of different test results before making the decision to be tested or to have their children tested.

Education is especially important to those of child-bearing age. General educational programs should also be directed toward other groups, such as employers, insurance companies, and school personnel in order to remove the stigma attached to having Hgb S.

Testing for Hgb S is a relatively easy procedure. The most accurate and definitive test is Hgb electrophoresis. It should be used *initially* and be followed by a sickling test, usually solubility testing, to distinguish Hgb S from other Hgbs that migrate in the same pattern. Hgb electrophoresis distinguishes between Hgb AS and sickle cell disease. Contrary to earlier thinking, Hgb S can be identified in the newborn by *microcolumn chromatography.*

Recently, procedures for identifying Hgbs prenatally have been used. Blood obtained by *fetoscopy* from the fetus, is examined by Hgb electrophoresis. Because this procedure is very technical and risky, it has been slow to emerge as the procedure of choice for prenatal hemoglobinopathy testing. A more acceptable procedure for Hgb testing is *amniocentesis*. Although amniocentesis is safer than fetoscopy, Hgb test results are not conclusive. Currently research is underway to refine this technique.

Counseling the person with sickle cell disease requires a special kind of expertise. Counselors should be aware that for some years there has been concern about the purposes and ethics of genetic counseling with regard to sickling. Parts of the black community have charged sickle cell programs with promoting genocide and believe that their real purpose has been to prevent blacks from reproducing.

The purpose and objectives of genetic counseling must be clearly defined to the clients. A counselor or a counseling program should have a philosophy known to the counselee. Basically, counseling is personal and private. Genetic counseling should consist of giving information, correcting misconceptions, and giving support. Genetic counseling should be nondirective and nonjudgmental. The goal should be to give information and support to individuals and couples enabling them to make decisions about marriage and/or reproduction that they can live with. This approach, based on adequate information, gives people respect and dignity and trusts in their ability to make decisions that are best for them.

SICKLE CELL C DISEASE *Sickle cell C disease (Hgb SC)* is the second most frequent sickle cell disease. It should not be confused with Hgb AS even though it has only one gene for sickle hemoglobin. A person afflicted with Hgb SC disease, a chronic disease, has *no* genes for normal adult Hgb. The clinical manifestations are often the same as in Hgb SS though less severe. Anemia and splenomegaly are present. Symptoms frequently do not begin until adolescence. The management and precautions taken to prevent or treat problems are the same for Hgb SC disease as for sickle cell disease.

SICKLE CELL THALASSEMIA The combined inheritance of Hgb S and thalassemia results in yet another sickle cell hemoglobinopathy. Thalassemias involve reduced production of a globin chain. In sickle cell thalassemia the beta chain may be affected in two ways, producing either a mild or a severe form of thalassemia.

In the mild form, beta chain production is only mildly suppressed, resulting in some normal Hgb A formation. This is known as *beta + thalassemia*. The condition resembles Hgb SC disease but is frequently confused with Hgb AS. Because more Hgb S than Hgb A is present, a sickle cell hemoglobinopathy results.

When Hgb S and severe thalassemia genes are inherited in the same offspring, the onset, course, and prognosis of the illness are similar to those in Hgb SS. This condition is called *sickle cell beta 0—no beta chain production—thalassemia*. The Hgb levels are approximately 9 to 11 g; the spleen, if present, may be enlarged.

Thalassemia *Thalassemia*, originally observed in persons of Mediterranean ancestry, is a term applied to a group of hereditary disorders of Hgb production that lead to the development of a chronic hypochromic, microcytic hemolytic anemia. The common characteristic of this group of anemias is a decreased *rate of synthesis* of one or more of the Hgb polypeptide chains. Subgroups are identified according to the polypeptide chain affected. For example, the major Hgb chains involved are alpha, beta, gamma, and delta. The two main categories presently identified are alpha thalassemia and beta thalassemia.

The clinical and laboratory features of these two categories are well defined. Beta thalassemia, although less common, is a more significant clinical problem. Most frequently, a person who has inherited one thalassemia gene and one normal gene is usually mildly affected and is said to have *thalassemia trait* or *thalassemia minor*. If a person has inherited two similar or identical thalassemia genes, the impairment of Hgb synthesis is severe and the person is said to have *thalassemia major*. There appears to be a genetic basis for the varying degrees of severity.

The alpha thalassemias show partial or total decrease in alpha chain production. The alpha globin chain is necessary for the formation of *all* Hgbs; thus any decrease in its production affects the formation of normal Hgb. The excess beta globin chains, which are then unable to participate in the formation of an Hgb molecule, precipitate inside the cell and damage the RBC membrane, shortening its survival. Normally, four genes are functioning to produce alpha chains, each gene being responsible for about 25 percent of alpha chain production. The activity of these four genes determines the degree of alpha thalassemia, which may range from one with three chains functioning that is undetectable to one with no alpha chain production that is incompatible with life.

Beta thalassemia is not usually detected at birth because of the presence of fetal Hgb. It appears later when Hgb A production takes over at 3 to 6 months of age. Beta thalassemia minor will show no incapacitating signs or symptoms. The children lead normal lives and are usually not diagnosed unless incidental to other studies. There may be mild anemia and splenomegaly. Hypochromia, anisocytosis, and poikilocytosis of RBCs occur.

Thalassemia major, not detectable at birth, results in a severe anemia during the first few months of life. It is transmitted to the offspring when both parents have thalassemia minor. It is also called *Cooley's anemia* or *Mediterranean anemia*. The homozygous state of the disease is a serious, life-threatening anemia. Growth retardation and failure to thrive are noticed in the first year of life. Hepatosplenomegaly is responsible for the large abdomen. The chronic severe anemia causes lifetime growth retardation, pallor, jaundice, patchy skin pigmentation, anoxic leg ulcers, anorexia, and retarded mental development. The mongol-like facies is the result of a combination of signs related to anemia—thickened cranial and prominent cheek bones, depressed nasal bridge, prominent overgrowth of the maxilla, and periorbital puffiness. The chronic hemolytic process and repeated transfusions cause hemosiderosis with arrhythmias, heart block, and early death. Excessive iron deposits are also found in the pancreas and liver.

TREATMENT Most of the thalassemia syndromes require no treatment because the anemia is either mild or incompatible with life. Beta thalassemia major, however, requires transfusions to maintain a functional hemoglobin level. Splenectomy may be of benefit if the spleen is sequestering RBCs.

Deferoxamine is administered once or twice daily intramuscularly, by slow intravenous infusion, or subcutaneously by slow (8 to 12 hours) infusion using a small portable infusion pump.

The last method has been proven to be more effective than a single intramuscular infusion.[4]

Undergoing research is a method that maintains the patient's hematocrit at normal levels by securing RBCs that will live longer in the body and not increase the blood volume. This would reduce cardiac work and the rate of iron accumulation.[5]

NURSING MANAGEMENT Generally, the nursing care with the thalassemia syndromes is supportive. There is no specific treatment, however, because transfusions are the mainstay of therapy. Most of the nursing measures, especially for physiological needs, are dictated by the complications encountered. Very important to the physical and emotional comfort of the child and family is the nurse's ability to give proper support during the care and treatment of a chronic and fatal illness.

The need for transfusions and their long-term effects should be explained well to parents. As many treatments as possible should be done on an outpatient basis. Home treatment, using chelating agents, should be a part of the child's care as soon as the child and parents are willing and comfortable with the procedure. When splenectomy is performed, parents should be aware of increased susceptibility to infections as well as the importance of compliance when prophylactic antibiotic therapy is instituted.

Improved methods of management are increasing survival potential. With this possibility in mind, the importance of health maintenance should not be overlooked. The major goals of health maintenance should focus on (1) education—including genetic information; (2) adaptation—daily activity with optimal exercise; (3) self-concept—encouraging a positive self-image and being alert to manifestations of a poor self-image; and (4) referrals—use of other agencies for parent and patient support services.

Increased production of RBCs (polycythemia)

Polycythemia, increased production of erythrocytes, is uncommon in children. The RBC count and Hgb levels may rise in response to decreased oxygen reaching the tissues of the body. Cyanotic heart disorders create a need for more oxygen-carrying capacity due to poor circulatory dynamics. The newborn may become polycythemic secondary to either maternal-fetal transfusion or excessive blood drained into the fetus from the placenta at birth. In people who live for an extended time in high mountains, polycythemia develops to help compensate for the decreased oxygen at that altitude.

An increase in the number of erythrocytes creates a higher viscosity in the blood. The high viscosity may cause headaches, lethargy, and pain in the extremities.

Polycythemia may require repeated phlebotomy to decrease the RBC count and the viscosity of the blood. In infants who have received maternal-fetal transfusion, the polycythemia will gradually resolve with growth and expanded vascular volume.

When the Hgb level rises above approximately 23 g, high blood viscosity can lead to respiratory distress, thrombosis, convulsions, or congestive heart failure from volume overload. Knowledge of normal Hgb concentrations for age will allow the nurse to be alerted to dangerously high levels.

Mechanism of coagulation

Coagulation, or clotting, of blood is a protective mechanism that guards against excessive loss of the body's life-sustaining fluid. At least 12 chemical substances known as *blood factors* are required for a clot to form (Table 27-7). These factors are present in the platelets and plasma or are produced during clotting reactions.

During the clotting process, blood loses its liquid quality and forms a jellylike mass at the injury site. Strands of fibrin appear, and together the mass and fibrin plug the hole in the vessel.

One type of clotting reaction starts when body cells as well as the vessel are damaged. The body cells release thromboplastin (Factor III), which initiates a series of reactions. This process continues (Fig. 27-7) until thrombin has been created from prothrombin and in turn causes activation of fibrinogen to fibrin. The reactions down to the creation of thrombin are known as the *extrinsic system* of clotting because the initiator, thromboplastin, is found outside (extrinsic to) the blood.

A clot created without the stimulus of thromboplastin is also possible. The process employs only blood factors and other normal blood substances, and hence is called the *intrinsic system*. In this situation a roughened surface, typically from a broken blood vessel, causes platelets to

Table 27-7 Coagulation factors

International name	Familiar name	Characteristics
Factor I	Fibrinogen	Produced in liver; average 3000 mµ/ml
Factor II	Prothrombin	Vitamin K necessary for production in liver
Factor III	Thromboplastin	Present in tissues and platelets
Factor IV	Calcium	Present in plasma and serum
Factor V	Proaccelerin, labile factor, Ac globulin	Used up in clotting
Factor VII	Stable factor, convertin, SPCA	Produced in liver; not used up in clotting
Factor VIII	Antihemophilic factor (AHF) Antihemophilis globulin (AHG)	Synthesized by vascular epithelium Used up in clotting
Factor IX	Plasma thromboplastin component (PTC) Christmas factor Antihemophilic factor B	Produced in liver; not used up in clotting
Factor X	Stuart-Prower factor	Produced in liver with vitamin K
Factor XI	Plasma thromboplastin antecedent (PTA)	Present in serum and plasma
Factor XII	Hageman factor Antihemophilic factor D	Unknown site of production
Factor XIII	Fibrin-stabilizing factor Laki-Lorand factor	High levels in plasma

adhere. Platelets release factors of their own, and once again a series of blood factors undergo rapid activation (Fig. 27-7). The intrinsic and extrinsic pathways end in a common pathway in which thrombin and finally fibrin are created.

The complex mechanism of coagulation is well understood today. A malfunction or absence of a clotting factor causes some degree of bleeding tendency. The factors most frequently involved are VIII and IX. A few such disorders are discussed in the next section.

Various coagulation tests are used to determine impairment in blood-clotting factors. Because individual laboratory values vary among laboratories, the norms for each setting need to be determined by the nurse. Five common tests of coagulation are described in Table 27-8.

Alterations in coagulation

Hemophilia A

Hemophilia A, classical hemophilia, occurs in 1 of every 10,000 American males. It is an X-linked recessive disorder characterized by a deficiency of plasma Factor VIII. The underlying defect is a congenital absence of the antihemophilic factor (AHF), which is vital in the formation of thromboplastin.

The disorder is transmitted by clinically unaffected female carriers to male offspring. Approximately 85 percent of all persons with hemophilia have the classical variety. Hemophilia is generally classified according to the deficiency of AHF: mild, moderate, or severe. Table 27-9 describes the severity of bleeding tendency according to the Factor VIII (AHF) plasma level. Normal level ranges from 60 to 200 percent. A female carrier with a Factor VIII of less than 30 percent may have excessive bleeding similar to that seen in hemophilic males with the same level of Factor VIII.

Classical signs of the disorder are a prolonged coagulation time (up to 2 h or more) and a tendency to bleed into joints, muscles, and body cavities. Bleeding is characteristically a prolonged oozing or trickling, occurring sponta-

Figure 27-7 Extrinsic and intrinsic systems of coagulation. (*From Sylvia A. Price and Lorraine M. Wilson,* Pathophysiology: Clinical Concepts of Disease Processes, *2d ed., McGraw-Hill, New York, 1982. Used by permission.*)

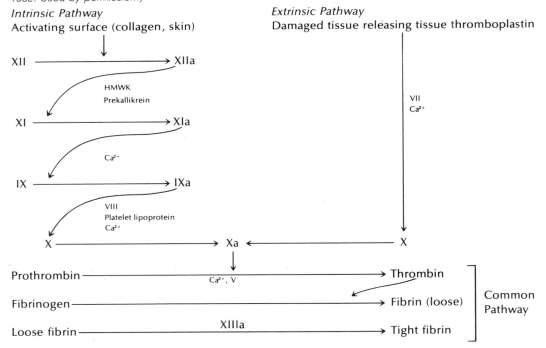

Table 27-8 Some coagulation test values

Test	Birth–1 mo Newborn	1 mo–2 yr Infant	2 yr–12 yr Child	Adolescent/adult Male Female	Characteristics
Bleeding time (min)	1–5	1–6	1–6	3–6	Usually normal if platelet count above 100,000 per cubic milliliter. Time required for a 2.5-mm-deep puncture wound to stop bleeding.
Coagulation time (min)	2	5–8	9–12	9–12	Time it takes venous blood to clot in vitro. Involves every factor in coagulation mechanism
Prothrombin time (PT) (sec)	12–20	12–14	12–15	10–13	Measures activity of prothrombin, fibrinogen, and Factors V, VII, X
Partial thromboplastin time (PTT) (sec)	90	90	90	90	Determines deficiencies of Factors V, VII, VIII, IX, X, XI, XII
Thrombin time (TT) (sec)	3–5	3–5	3–5	3–5	Time for plasma to clot in presence of added plasma. Measures level of fibrinogen

neously or after surgery or minor trauma. The diagnosis is usually made when prolonged bleeding occurs after circumcision or with severe bruising during the toddler period.

When the child reaches school age, he must cope with the most debilitating complications of the disorder, *hemarthrosis*, or bleeding into joints. Although any joint may be involved, the order of decreasing frequency of involvement is: knee, ankle, elbow, hip, and shoulder. The child is usually limited in play activities because of tenderness, pain, and restricted motion. If bleeding progresses the joint becomes swollen, hot, and immobile. The repeated presence of blood in joints causes degeneration of the synovial membrane with ankylosis, contractures, muscle weakness, and atrophy. If improperly treated, these changes can become permanent.

Because moisture is continually present in mucous membranes bleeding there is often persistent, with considerable blood loss. Following a dental extraction, slow oozing may occur up to 8 days. Bleeding can occur in any muscle but is seen most frequently in the calves, thighs, buttocks, and forearms. Retroperitoneal bleeding is fairly common; bleeding in the right iliopsoas region may mimic acute appendicitis.

Although it occurs infrequently, hemorrhage in the central nervous system is the major cause of death in hemophilia. Any trauma to the head or vertebral column should be treated immediately and the child carefully observed for 24 h in the hospital.

Diagnosis Contrary to common belief, a person with hemophilia does not bleed faster than normal; he simply bleeds longer. In patients with severe hemophilia, the coagulation time may range from 30 min to several hours. The partial thromboplastin time (PTT) is significantly prolonged. Factor VIII is virtually absent from the plasma. Capillary fragility, bleeding time, prothrombin time, fibrinogen content, and platelet values are all within normal limits. When these tests are within normal limits and the PTT test is prolonged, a Factor VIII assay should be performed, followed by a Factor IX assay if the Factor VIII is normal.

Treatment Special efforts should be made to ensure a safe environment for the infant and child. Cribs and playpens should be padded. As the child nears the toddler stage, large, hard toys and sharp pieces of furniture such as end tables

Table 27-9 Plasma level of Factor VIII related to severity of bleeding tendency

Plasma level of Factor VIII (AHF)	Degree of bleeding	Symptoms in child
Less than 1%	Severe	Severe, frequent hemorrhage into large joints
2–5%	Moderate	Occasional bleeding episodes related to trauma
6–30%	Mild	Bleeding with severe trauma or surgery
60–200%	Normal	No abnormal bleeding

should be removed to provide a safe area for exploration. As the child grows older, participation in noncontact sports such as swimming should be encouraged. Aspirin or aspirin-containing compounds should not be given since aspirin inhibits platelet function. Acetaminophen, pentazocaine, propoxythene, or plain codeine can be used to alleviate pain.

Superficial abrasions and cuts usually stop bleeding if firm pressure is applied for several minutes. The treatment of choice for larger lacerations or internal bleeding is administration of lyophilized concentrates of Factor VIII. The purpose is to raise the child's level of Factor VIII to a certain percentage and to maintain it at that level until hemostasis is obtained. The half-life of AHF in the body is about 12 h.

Concentrates, listed in Table 27.10, are prepared by pharmaceutical companies from pools of human venous plasma from as many as 1000 donors. Each unit of plasma utilized is nonreactive for hepatitis B surface antigen; unfortunately, this does not preclude the presence of the hepatitis virus. Because the hepatitis virus may

be present in the concentrate, the child should be carefully observed for signs and symptoms of hepatitis.

Plasma from freshly drawn blood that is immediately frozen and then slowly thawed forms a precipitate that is a source of AHF. This product, *cryoprecipitate*, is the treatment of choice for the child who is rarely treated. Because cryoprecipitate requires few donors, the probability of transmitting hepatitis with any one infusion is low. Carefully made cryoprecipitate contains about 100 units of Factor VIII per bag. Blood type-specific cryoprecipitate should be given when large amounts of Factor VIII are required, as in surgery.

Whether concentrate or cryoprecipitate is used, the child is given sufficient amounts to raise his AHF level by 30 to 100 percent depending on the severity of the problem. To determine the number of Factor VIII units needed to achieve a desired plasma Factor VIII level, estimate the child's plasma volume (40 ml plasma per kilogram of body weight) and multiply the plasma volume in milliliters by the desired increase in percent plasma Factor VIII. For example, a child who has less than 1 percent Factor VIII level and weighs 38 g has a plasma volume of 40 ml/kg × 38 kg, or 1500 ml. To raise his Factor VIII level to 50 percent, he will need 0.50 units/ml × 1500 ml, or 750 units of Factor VIII.

It is usually difficult to control a hemorrhage in the mouth, tongue, or gums because the formed clot readily breaks down in the presence of saliva. In addition to factor replacement which forms the clot, epsilon-aminocaproic acid (EACA or Amicar), a fibrinolytic enzyme, helps to preserve the clot until wound healing can occur. Parents should be instructed to give the epsilon-aminocaproic acid every 6 h, not four times during the day. This prevents the level from

Table 27-10 Commercial concentrates

Company	Name
Factor VIII	
Hyland	Hemofil
Courtland	AHG
Armour	Factorate
Alpha	Profilate
Cutter	Koate
Merieux	Actif-VIII
Factor IX	
Cutter	Konyne
Hyland	Proplex

dropping during the night and the hemorrhage from recurring. Because of the possibility of disseminated intravascular clotting, EACA is contraindicated in children with suspected renal bleeding or in those who are receiving Factor IX concentrate.

Inhibitors About 8 to 10 percent of the children with severe classical hemophilia have inhibitors, or Ig antibodies, to Factor VIII. The antibody destroys the infused factor, rendering it ineffective in a clot formation. There is no way to predict who will develop inhibitors. Most inhibitors appear in childhood but may develop at any age in those who have frequently received plasma products. In most children the inhibitor level increases if additional Factor VIII concentrate is administered; in a few, it remains low despite further exposure to Factor VIII.

The treatment of children with inhibitors is difficult. Most institutions prefer to avoid plasma products for mild or moderate hemorrhages and rely on conservative methods including ice, bed rest, and splinting.

Nursing management

Joints and muscles The initial symptoms of a joint or muscle hemorrhage are pain, stiffness, and discomfort. If the child is treated with a 30 percent dose of concentrate at this time, the hemorrhage will usually stop and there will be no need for joint aspiration or immobilization. Children with extensive hemorrhages in joints or muscles have swelling, increased warmth, and severe pain with motion; at this time a 50 percent dose will be required to stop the hemorrhage.

If the child has a painful effusion, aspiration may afford great relief of pain and rapid recovery of function. Padded posterior molded splints may be applied for 3 to 4 days or until the swelling subsides. The child should be encouraged to exercise the involved joints as soon as pain and swelling subside.

After any severe or prolonged hemorrhage, the nurse should evaluate the child for muscle atrophy or residual limitation of motion. Physical therapy should be instituted promptly and a prophylactic dose (30 to 50 percent) of concentrate given each day before the exercise. If corrections are not made promptly, the stress of the

abnormal distribution of weight during walking and the awkwardness of an abnormal alignment are likely to lead to further hemorrhage.

If a muscle or soft-tissue hemorrhage presses on a nerve and decreases sensory or motor function, the child should receive repeated doses of plasma products until the swelling subsides. The nurse carefully assesses, records, and reports any progressive signs of sensory or motor loss. A hemorrhage in the iliopsoas muscle causes pain in the groin that sometimes radiates into the scrotum or lower quadrant of the abdomen. The hip is held in a flexed position, and extension is painful. Bleeding into the hip joint causes pain on hip rotation, while an iliopsoas bleed does not. The nurse should explain to the child that bed rest for 1 to 2 weeks and daily or twice-daily doses of plasma products are usually needed to achieve resolution of iliopsoas hemorrhages. When the pain has stopped and hip flexion is less than 25°, gentle exercises may be instituted in the pool. Nurses should encourage children to progress slowly because iliopsoas hemorrhages recur easily. Encourage crutches until muscle strength returns.

Children with strong musculature have fewer hemorrhages than those with flabby muscles because strong muscles support joints. From early childhood, a planned exercise program should be a part of the child's daily routine.

Hematuria The nurse caring for the child with hematuria should encourage the child to drink 6 to 8 oz of fluids every 2 to 3 h. Children should be taught to observe the color of their urine and report any changes in color to their parents.

Emotional problems The diagnosis of hemophilia places stress upon the family unit, particularly the parents and the affected child, but also upon siblings and the extended family. From an early age, the child with hemophilia is expected to cope with untimely occurrences of painful hemorrhages resulting in immobilization, disruption of activities, hospitalizations, and joint deformities. At the same time, the child is expected to avoid dangerous endeavors, report hemorrhages promptly to his parents, balance his impulsive tendencies with his wishes for independence, and ignore the many disruptions in his educational plans. If the child is not helped to cope successfully with these encounters, then a broad range of crippling emotional problems are encountered. They include (1) low self-esteem and limited self-confidence, leading to excessive dependency and a failure to meet educational goals; (2) failure to accept the realities of hemophilia, leading to physical neglect; and (3) general prolonged immaturity and risk-taking behavior. Just as prompt factor replacement therapy and exercise can minimize joint deformity, crippling emotional problems can be prevented if they are recognized and treated in early childhood.

The most frequently observed problems in parents are (1) a tendency to overprotect the child or place undue restrictions upon his activity; (2) a feeling of being burdened by the constant responsibility to assess the child's daily health status and activity level; and (3) a lack of involvement in the child's care by the father.

Common problems encountered by other family members are (1) feelings of being unloved, resentful, or envious of the parents' attention given to the child with hemophilia; (2) fear of childbearing in carrier daughters or sisters; and (3) grandparents' experience of some of the stresses felt by parents.

Emotional problems in the child with hemophilia should be reduced if professional personnel and parents adopt attitudes and measures to help the child develop a positive attitude toward himself and his disorder. Early in the child's life, the following factors must be considered:

1. Emotional development is the same in all children. Frist, he is an individual; second, he has a disorder.
2. Interdependence requires the active participation of both parents.
3. Regardless of rigid supervision, the child will hemorrhage as a result of some daily activities.
4. The child should be allowed to discover appropriate activities at the preschool age.
5. The child should be allowed to participate in his own care.
6. The child should be included in decisions about his activities.
7. The child should be given the maximum amount of information about his disorder.

The nurse can be most helpful in solving emotional problems if he or she readily refers the child and his parents to the appropriate counseling service as soon as a problem is detected. (See the nursing care plan for a child with hemophilia A.)

Hemophilia B

Hemophilia B (Christmas disease, Factor IX deficiency, or PTC deficiency) is an X-linked disorder resulting from a deficiency of Factor IX coagulant activity. There are approximately seven cases of hemophilia A for every case of hemophilia B. Symptoms and management of hemophilia B are similar to those of classical hemophilia. It is important to distinguish between them in the laboratory because their treatment requires different replacement factors.

Home infusion program

In the past, children with hemophilia experienced many hospitalizations with periods of extended bed rest for blood transfusions or other treatments. The availability of commercial concentrates, however, has made the home infusion program possible. Participants in the program are taught to recognize early symptoms of bleeding. With prompt treatment, most bleeding episodes are controlled quickly (Table 27-11). Criteria for selection for the home infusion program:

1. An assessment of the family indicates readiness for the program.
2. The family has a desire to participate in the program.
3. The child must be 5 or 6 years old for parental participation. Younger children may be accepted if they will sit still for venipunctures.
4. Veins should be large enough for successful venipuncture.
5. The child must require infusion at least once per week.
6. Parents must demonstrate maturity and be able to read instructions.
7. The parents and child must have emotional stability to accept the responsibilities of the program.
8. The parents must not have a frost-free freezer if child is placed on cryoprecipitate on the home program.
9. The family must participate in follow-up.
10. The child must have a complete physical examination.

When a family has been selected for the home infusion program in an outpatient setting, the

Table 27-11 Guidelines for the home infusion instruction program for the child with hemophilia

I. Venipuncture
  A. Anatomy—circulatory system
   1. Use anatomic diagrams to help parents visualize appropriate veins. Allow for 7–10 instruction sessions.
  B. Actual practice of venipuncture
   1. Allay anxiety by allowing parent to attempt venipuncture in each session.
   2. Child may be given a small amount of concentrate during each instruction session.

II. Concentrate preparation
  A. Concentrate
   1. Prescribed by physician, dispensed by pharmacy or blood bank.
   2. Price varies greatly based on geographic location and type of center.
   3. Average 15–20¢ per unit factor VIII. Slightly higher for factor IX.
  B. Dosage calculation
   1. Based on weight.
   2. Multiply the child's weight in kilograms by plasma volume (see example in text).
   3. Note: It is difficult to determine exact factor VIII units. Concentrate dosages are approximate and are rounded to the nearest hundred.
  C. Equipment needed
   1. Concentrate (see Table 27-12), diluent, 23 g scalp vein needle, 30–50-ml syringe, antiseptic swab, tape, and bandage.
  D. Sterile techniques
   1. Stress throughout instruction sessions.
   2. Evaluate technique periodically.
  E. Storage of equipment
   1. Store equipment out of reach of children.
   2. Place concentrate in closed plastic container in refrigerator.
   3. Cryoprecipitate must not be stored in frost-free freezer. The temperature does not remain constant.
  F. Disposal of equipment
   1. Crush needles in side barrel of syringe.
   2. Place used equipment in double plastic bag or metal containers.
   3. Return to center for disposal.

III. Hemophilia—related information
  A. Definition
   1. Give parents a definition they can understand.
   2. Always include child in the teaching.
   3. Include genetic information.
  B. Safety
   1. Proper storage and use of equipment.
   2. Hand-washing techniques.
  C. Dietary habits
   1. Prevent obesity.
   2. Encourage proper nutrition.
   3. Eat foods with high iron content.
  D. Exercise program
   1. Swimming.
   2. Bicycling.
   3. Gradual, gentle exercise program to strengthen all muscles.
   4. Refer to physical exercise program.
  E. Disciplinary actions
   1. Use appropriate measures that do not cause bleeding episodes.
  F. School habits
   1. Encourage school attendance.
   2. When child is able to self-administer concentrate, get permission to keep one dose at school.
  G. Signs and symptoms of hemorrhages
   1. Discoloration, swelling, warmth, increasing immobility, and pain.
  H. Hepatitis
   1. Flulike symptoms, nausea, anorexia, malaise, fatigue, and moderate fever.
  I. Medications
   1. Instruct parents to read medication labels to make sure they do not contain aspirin.
   2. Use acetaminophen for pain relief.

(Continued next page)

Table 27-11 Guidelines for the home infusion instruction program for the child with hemophilia (*Continued*)

    J. Allergic responses
       1. Instruct parent to observe child during each infusion for allergic responses.
          a. Increased pulse and respirations.
          b. Tingling sensation in tongue and lips.
          c. Flushed.
          d. Itching, hives, or rash.
       2. (a)–(c) usually indicate that rate of infusion is too rapid.
       3. If hives or rash appear, stop infusion, record lot number, and report to physician.
    K. When to contact the center or physician
       1. After any head injury.
       2. Gastrointestinal bleed.
       3. Neck or throat bleed.
       4. Hemoptysis.
       5. Unimproved hemorrhage after three dosages of concentrate.

  IV. Follow-up evaluation
    A. Review venipuncture and preparation of concentrate
       1. Have parent demonstrate the process at least once a year.
       2. Inform parent of any new information.
    B. Evaluate records
       1. Evaluate records for correlation with instructions.
       2. Note frequency and areas of bleeds.
       3. Make appropriate referral for persistent problems.

  V. Termination from the program
    A. Poorly kept records
       1. Records must be accurate and complete.
       2. Concentrate and supplies must be accounted for.
    B. Complete annual physical examination
       1. Must have complete annual physical examination.
       2. Treatment regimen is altered if child develops an inhibitor.
    C. Misuse of the program
       1. Records or hemorrhage indicate a delay in treatment.
       2. Failure to report to center or physician certain hemorrhages.
       3. Drug abuse or use of supplies for other purposes.

nurse should individualize the plan of instructions to meet the family's needs. Several sessions should be devoted to information about hemophilia as well as the technical aspect of performing the venipuncture. Emphasis should be placed on sterile technique and signs and symptoms of bleeding and hepatitis, as well as when not to treat the child at home. Adequate recording and follow-up should be stressed. Before the course of instructions is complete, the parent or child must demonstrate several successful first attempts at venipuncture (Fig. 27-8). The nurse must emphasize the fact that the home infusion program is not a substitute for continuous supervised medical care.

Thrombocytopenic purpura

Thrombocytopenic purpura is a deficiency of platelets (less than 100,000 per cubic millimeter) that occurs most often in 3- to 7-year-olds. The etiology is unclear, but thrombocytopenic purpura may result from such causes as destruction of platelets, infection, drug sensitivity, or exposure to ionizing radiation.

Drugs which destroy the platelets in both mother and fetus or cause antibody formation against the fetal platelets are the thiazides, sulfonamides, and quinine. These drugs should be taken with extreme caution during pregnancy.

Characteristic symptoms of thrombocytopenia are spontaneous small hemorrhages (petechial lesions) into the skin or mucous membranes and bleeding from the nose, gastrointestinal, or urinary tract. The platelet count is always below 100,000 per cubic millimeter and may be as low as 10,000 per cubic millimeter.

Mothers who have thrombocytopenia may give birth to infants with the disorder. Maternal antibodies cross the placenta and destroy the infant's platelets by a mechanism similar to that of Rh isoimmune disease. Thrombocytopenia in newborns may also be caused by septicemia, congenital syphilis, or a congenital lack of megakaryocytes. In newborns the disorder is usually mild, and the platelet count rises within a short time after birth.

Acute thrombocytopenia, characterized by a sudden onset, most often affects children and young adults, especially females. It may follow a mild respiratory infection or rubella. Fever and prostration are present. Spontaneous disappearance of symptoms occurs in approximately 80 percent of children after a few weeks to a few months. Chronic thrombocytopenic purpura, which has a gradual onset, affects approximately 10 to 15 percent of the people with the disorder. It may start at any age but is seen infrequently in children. Clinical remissions and exacerbations occur, but the platelet count is always low. The size of the spleen is within normal limits. Children with thrombocytopenia have a tendency to bleed from many small capillaries rather than from large vessels.

The diagnosis is confirmed with a series of coagulation tests related to platelet function. Platelets cannot be seen in a peripheral blood smear. WBCs are not affected; anemia, if present, is secondary to blood loss. The bleeding time is prolonged, but partial thromboplastin time (PTT) and prothrombin time (PT) are normal. Clot retraction is poor since capillary fragility is greatly increased. Bone marrow is studied to rule out leukemia.

Treatment Corticosteroids are used to treat patients with moderately severe purpura of short duration, especially if the bleeding is from the gastrointestinal or genitourinary tract. The steroids produce a temporary increase in the platelet count and in some children will terminate the disorder within a few days. Transfusions of whole blood or platelets may be used when there has been substantial blood loss.

Splenectomy is usually the treatment of choice for patients with chronic cases of moderately severe purpura of more than 1 year's duration. It is also indicated in patients who do not respond to steroids or who have had two to three relapses with steroid therapy. The platelet count rises promptly following splenectomy and often doubles within the first 24 h. Maximum values are reached 1 to 2 weeks postoperatively.

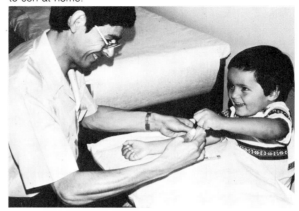

Figure 27-8 Father administering concentrate of Factor VIII to son at home.

A splenectomy is considered successful when the platelet count remains normal for at least 2 months. Splenectomy is curative in 70 to 90 percent of all patients.

Children with purpura should avoid trauma, contact sports, elective surgery, and tooth extraction. All unnecessary medications and exposure to potential toxins should be avoided. Children with mild purpura following viral infections do not require any treatment. They should be observed until petechiae disappear and the platelet count returns to normal.

Nursing management A primary concern in the nursing care of children with purpura is the concurrent bleeding tendency. Nursing assessment should begin with the prenatal history. A careful history of the mother's drug intake during pregnancy should be recorded. The nurse should observe the newborn's color and vital signs to detect the development of jaundice, ecchymoses, and petechial lesions. When the infant or child has an active period of bleeding, he or she should be observed closely for signs and symptoms of shock and possible internal and intracranial hemorrhage. If epistaxis (nosebleed) occurs, compression, packing, or hemostatic material may be utilized to control the bleeding.

The nurse must teach the child and parents to assess the child's limitations and help the child adjust to them. Contact sports should be discouraged. The nurse should assist the child and parents in making the school and community aware of the child's limitations. When blood

Nursing Care Plan–Hemophilia A

Patient: Rodney **Age:** 11 years **Date of Admission:** 4/10/81, at 10 A.M.

Assessment

Rodney, a 44.5 kg, 11-year-old boy, was admitted to the pediatric unit at 10 A.M. on 4/10/81 with a diagnosis of trauma-induced massive left retroperitoneal and calf hemorrhage secondary to hemophilia A.

General appearance

On arrival in the pediatric unit, Rodney complained of severe pain in the left calf, lower abdomen, and left groin area. He was pale and lethargic. His temperature was 38.9°C (102°F); pulse 120, irregular and weak; respirations 22/min. His skin was cold, clammy, and moist. Left calf measurement 38.5 cm. Lab tests: Hgb 6 g, WBC 20,000. AHF < 1%.

History

Rodney's mother explained that 2 days ago, he had been knocked down and kicked while playing soccer on the school's team. The next day he stayed in bed, "not feeling well." Late that afternoon, his mother noted that his left calf was swollen and that he was "curled up" in bed. She did not take him to the hospital because she thought "he would be all right." The next morning, Rodney was crying with pain and told his mother he had been kicked in the groin and calf area 2 days ago. She said she was angry because he should "know better" than to play soccer.

The nurse reported that Rodney's mother was visibly upset, stating that she did not know he was so sick. In the past she had waited, and he had always gotten better. She was also upset because she was "always the one" who had to bring Rodney to the hospital; his father was always "too busy."

Physician's orders

1. Transfuse 2 units of whole blood
2. AHF concentrate, 1000 units IV BID
3. Absolute bed rest
4. Ice packs to left calf and groin area
5. Clear liquids PO
6. Meperidine 50 mg IM q3–4h PRN for severe pain
7. Acetaminophen (300 mg) with codeine 30 mg PO, one tab q3h PRN mild pain
8. Acetaminophen 600 mg PO q4h until temp. is below 37.8°C (100°F)
9. Measure calf QD
10. Daily Hgb and Hct
11. D5$\frac{1}{2}$NS (5% dextrose in half-normal saline) IV 50 ml/h
12. Oxygen per nasal cannula 3 liters/min
13. Measure intake and output
14. Pre and post factor VIII assay qAM × 5 days
15. Vital signs q2h

Nursing diagnosis	Nursing goals	Nursing actions	Evaluation/revision
1. Severe pain secondary to bleeding in left calf and iliopsoas muscles	☐ Achieve comfort, as evidenced by: **a.** Decrease in frequency of IM Demerol **b.** Control of pain with Tylenol and codeine after 24–36 h **c.** No complaints of pain with movement	☐ Administer IM Demerol regularly q3–4h while pain is severe ☐ Observe and record effect of medication by having Rodney rate pain on scale of 1 to 10 ☐ Change ice pack to calf and groin areas q2h and PRN ☐ Support left leg with pillow	☐ 4/10 2 P.M.: Pain rated 4 2 h after Demerol IM ☐ Pain should decrease after 24–36 h ☐ Rodney expresses increased comfort from ice and pillow support *Continue plan*
2. Potential for continued bleeding due to antibody development to AHF	☐ Prevent further bleeding, as evidenced by: **a.** Decrease in size of calf **b.** Decrease in size of ab-	☐ Measure calf every 4 h ☐ Measure abdominal girth ☐ Administer concentrate q12h	☐ 4/10 2 P.M.: Calf and abdominal masses have not increased in size since first dose of concentrate

738

Nursing diagnosis	Nursing goals	Nursing actions	Evaluation/revision
	dominal mass **c.** Decrease in pain **d.** Increase in Hgb	☐ Check Hgb level and AHF level	☐ Assay should reflect calculated rise in AHF level *Continue plan*
3. Hypoxemia due to decreased Hgb	☐ Improved oxygenation of tissues, as evidenced by: **a.** Pink skin, nailbeds, and mucous membranes **b.** Respiratory rate 18–20, regular ☐ Hgb 11–14	☐ Administer whole blood as ordered; observe for transfusion reactions ☐ Observe and record skin color ☐ Administer O_2 at 3 liters per nasal cannula ☐ Place in semi-Fowler's position	☐ 4/10 6 P.M.: After completion of transfused whole blood skin, nailbeds, and mucous membranes pink ☐ Hgb 10 g *Continue plan*
4. Dehydration due to blood loss and elevated temperature	☐ Maintain adequate fluid and electrolyte balance, as evidenced by: **a.** Oral fluid intake of at least 50 ml/h **b.** IV fluids at 50 ml/h **c.** Urine output at least 30 ml/h **d.** Urine sp. gr. 1.006–1.015. **e.** Moist oral mucous membranes **f.** Good skin turgor.	☐ Encourage clear fluids PO q30–60min ☐ Maintain patent IV at 50 ml/h ☐ Record intake and output q2h × 24 ☐ Measure sp. gr. of each voiding ☐ Observe for abdominal pain after oral fluid intake	☐ 4/10 2 P.M.: Oral intake 400 ml, output 150 ml ☐ IV infusing well ☐ Urine sp. gr. 1.015 *Continue plan*
5. Alteration in thermal regulation due to bleeding in abdominal cavity	☐ Maintain temperature within normal range of 36°–37.5°C (97.5°–99.5°F)	☐ Monitor temperature q2h ☐ Encourage oral fluids PO q30–60 min ☐ Maintain IV at 50 ml/h ☐ Give Tylenol PO q4h for temp. above 38.8°C (101°F) ☐ Keep bed dry, room cool	☐ 4/10 2 P.M.: Temp. 38°C (100.4°F) Temp. will remain within normal range after reabsorption of blood from abdominal cavity *Contine plan*
6. Fatigue and lethargy due to pain, blood loss, and inadequate intake	☐ Decreased fatigue, as evidenced by: **a.** Relaxed state when resting **b.** Relaxed state while awake **c.** 12–14 h sleep per 24 h	☐ Schedule three 2-h nap periods within 16-h day ☐ Observe quality and quantity of sleep ☐ Administer analgesics ☐ Schedule nursing care to allow uninterrupted periods of rest ☐ Limit visitors during rest periods ☐ Monitor TV and radio use	☐ 4/10 4 P.M.: Rodney had two naps of 2 h each ☐ Resting more comfortably ☐ Facial expression more relaxed *Continue plan*
7. Potential left hip and knee contractures due to pain from bleeding	☐ Prevent permanent hip and knee contractures, as evidenced by: **a.** Full range of motion of hip and knees when pain and swelling subside **b.** Ambulation without pain	☐ Administer analgesics as necessary ☐ Give gentle range of motion to hip and knee during peak action of analgesics ☐ Elicit Rodney's cooperation in straightening his hip and knee as much as possible ☐ Maintain body in good alignment and change position every 2 h	☐ 4/11 2 P.M.: Improved extension of hip and knee; moves about on bed with greater ease *Continue plan*

Nursing diagnosis	Nursing goals	Nursing actions	Evaluation/revision
8. Delayed treatment due to Rodney's (and mother's) failure to recognize early signs of hemorrhaging	☐ Acceptance of illness and development of positive coping strategies, as evidenced by: **a.** Rodney sharing knowledge and feeling about hemophilia, injury, and participation in school activities **b.** Parents describing Rodney's health needs and problems **c.** Parents sharing feelings about hemophilia	☐ Encourage Rodney to share feelings about hemophilia and any limitations in activity he experiences ☐ Encourage parents to share feelings ☐ Plan teaching sessions for family, parents regarding hemophilia ☐ Evaluate father's participation in Rodney's care	☐ 4/11: Rodney verbally acknowledges need to have shared fact of injury with parents earlier ☐ Mother able to list early sign of bleeding ☐ Father not in to visit until 4/12 *Continue plan*

transfusions are indicated, the nurse should be supportive of both the parents and child because they will be anxious at that time.

In planning for the child's discharge from the hospital, the nurse should instruct the parents to identify signs of thrombocytopenia such as bleeding gums, petechiae, and ecchymoses. Parents should also be encouraged to continue medical supervision and to report any signs of bleeding to their physician immediately.

References

1. Darleen F. Powars, "Sickle Cell Disease Method of," in *Current Therapy*, ed. by Howard F. Conn. Saunders, Philadelphia, 1978.
2. David E. Comings, "Erythrocyte Disorders," in W. J. Williams et al., *Hematology*. McGraw-Hill, New York, 1972, p. 419.
3. Powars, op. cit.
4. Arthur W. Nienhuis et al., "Thalassemia Major: Molecular and Clinical Aspects," *Annals of Internal Medicine* 91:883-897 (1979).
5. Ibid.

Chapter 28 **Gastrointestinal function**

Catherine M. Kneut and Sandra A. Faux

After completion of this chapter, the student will be able to:

1. Describe the embryologic development of a patent gastrointestinal tract.

2. Identify the major functions of each organ in the gastrointestinal tract.

3. List nursing assessment components for the child with gastrointestinal tract alterations.

4. Compare the care of a colostomy and an ileostomy.

5. List the preoperative and postoperative nursing care for a child having gastrointestinal surgery.

6. Contrast the preoperative and postoperative nursing care given to the infant with cleft lip and the infant with cleft palate.

7. Identify the signs that indicate the presence of an esophageal anomaly.

8. Differentiate the preoperative care for the various types of tracheoesophageal anomalies.

9. Describe dehydration in the infant with pyloric stenosis.

10. Describe the anatomic defect present in omphalocele.

11. Compare the immediate newborn care with the postoperative care of an infant who has an omphalocele.

12. Describe the care of the infant with a diaphragmatic hernia.

13. Describe the nursing care for children with ulcers.

14. Compare ulcerative colitis and Crohn's disease.

15. Describe the possible courses of therapy for ulcerative colitis.

16. Identify the bowel anomalies related to defects in fetal development.

17. Differentiate between inguinal and umbilical hernia.

18. Describe the signs that might be seen in a child with appendicitis.

19. List the foods that must be eliminated from the diet of the child with celiac disease.

20. Compare the repair of high and low defect in imperforate anus.

21. List the functions of the liver.

22. Write an appropriate nursing care plan for the child with biliary atresia.

Embryology of the gastrointestinal tract

The digestive tube is formed from the part of the yolk sac contained within the embryo. The developing digestive system is divided into the foregut, midgut, and hindgut.

The *esophagus* begins as a short tube that develops from the foregut. It rapidly increases in length, and the lining proliferates so that the lumen is almost completely obstructed. Recanalization (hollowing out) occurs later.

The *stomach* begins as a dilation of the foregut during the fifth week of gestation.[1] The dorsal border grows to become the greater curvature of the stomach. The lesser curvature is formed from the anterior border.

The *duodenum* is formed from the end of the foregut and the first portion of the midgut. As with most of the esophagus, the cells lining the duodenum completely obstruct the lumen. Later, these cells degenerate and recanalization occurs. The *liver* and *pancreas* develop from buds on the duodenum.

The *jejunum, ileum, cecum, appendix, ascending colon,* and *proximal two-thirds of the transverse colon* develop from the midgut. The midgut elongates rapidly and forms a loop. The tip of the loop attaches to the vitelline (umbilical) duct. A small pouch appears at the caudal end of the loop and gradually evolves into the cecum and the appendix. The midgut returns to the abdominal cavity at about 10 weeks and rotates so that the cecum and appendix are positioned on the right side of the abdomen.

The *descending colon, pelvic colon, rectum,* and *upper half of the anal canal* evolve from the hindgut. This ends in a dilated blind pouch called the *entodermal cloaca.* A portion of the hindgut forms a structure called the *allantois,* which branches off and passes into the umbilical cord. The allantois and hindgut are separated by a wedge that forms gradually and penetrates the entodermal cloaca. This wedge, the *urorectal septum,* eventually divides the cloacal membrane into the urogenital membrane and the anal membrane. The anterior structure becomes the primitive bladder, and the posterior part forms the anorectal canal. The anal membrane breaks down when the protodeum (from the anus) invaginates, establishing a connection between the upper and lower anal canal.[2]

Physiology of the gastrointestinal tract

The transformation of edible substances to chemical energy utilized by the body involves the processes of ingestion, digestion, absorption, and elimination. *Ingestion* is the intake of food and is controlled by both physiological and psychological factors. *Mastication* (chewing) of food occurs in the mouth, and *deglutition* (swallowing) propels the bolus of food into the esophagus. This completes ingestion.

Digestion is the process that converts food into an absorbable form. This function begins in the mouth and is continued in the stomach and small intestine. Digestion is both mechanical and chemical. *Mechanical digestion* involves the changing of foodstuffs into minute particles and their movement through the gastrointestinal tract. *Chemical digestion* is the hydrolysis (breakdown) of proteins, carbohydrates, and fats into absorbable units.

In the *mouth,* ptyalin is secreted and initiates starch digestion. Peristaltic waves of the esophagus move the bolus of food to the stomach. The cardiac sphincter at the base of the esophagus prevents the reflux of stomach contents into the esophagus.

The *stomach* acts as a reservoir for food and mixes it with solution. This mass is called *chyme.* Hydrochloric acid and pepsin are secreted by the stomach and aid in the digestion of proteins. Mucus forms a protective covering over the gastric epithelial cells and buffers strong acids. The gastric mucosa cells secrete gastrin, which is absorbed into the circulation, increasing gastric motility and acid secretion. The intrinsic factor, responsible for vitamin B_{12} absorption, is also secreted by the stomach. Small amounts of chyme are slowly moved into the duodenum.

The *small intestine* is the final site of digestion. Table 28-1 lists the many secretions that act in the small intestine.

The *pancreas* releases into the small intestine proteolytic enzymes that convert protein molecules into smaller amino acids. Fat metabolism is carried out by pancreatic lipase. Pancreatic amylase breaks down polysaccharides. The beta cells of the pancreas secrete insulin, while the alpha cells secrete glucagon. Both are important factors in carbohydrate metabolism.

The liver secretes bile that is either stored in the gallbladder or released into the small intestine. Cholecystokinin is secreted by the small intestine in the presence of fat. This hormone is absorbed into the circulation and stimulates gallbladder contraction. When contraction occurs, bile is released from the gallbladder into the small intestine. Bile is responsible for the emulsification of fats.

The liver is responsible for glycogenesis (production of glycogen), glycogenolysis (freeing glucose from glycogen in the liver), and gluconeogenesis (formation of glucose from noncarbohydrate sources), which are essential components of carbohydrate metabolism. The liver also synthesizes serum proteins such as prothrombin, fibrinogen, and albumin, and plays a role in fat metabolism through the synthesis and release of bile.

Table 28-1 Digestive secretions acting in the small intestine

Secretion	Action
Maltase, sucrase, lactase	Convert disaccharides to monosaccharides
Amylase	Breaks down polysaccharides to disaccharides
Peptides	Breaks down proteins
Lipase	Changes neutral fats to fatty acids and glycerol
Enterokinase	Activates pancreatic trypsin
Enterogastrone	Released by stimulus of fat in the small intestines to decrease gastric activity
Bile	Emusifies fat

Absorption occurs mainly in the small intestine through diffusion, filtration, osmosis, and active transport. Limited absorption of glucose, water, and alcohol takes place in the stomach. The most absorptive area is the lower part of the duodenum and the first segment of the jejunum. Villi cover the mucosa of the small intestine, greatly increasing the surface area and therefore its absorptive abilities. The large intestine absorbs water and electrolytes.

The large intestine is mainly responsible for *elimination.* It secretes mucus that causes the waste material or feces to adhere as peristaltic waves move it through the large intestine. The waste products accumulate in the rectum, causing the descending colon to contract. The act of defecation is the release of fecal contents from the rectum. It occurs as a result of voluntary and reflex actions.

Assessment of common gastrointestinal tract alterations

Gastrointestinal signs and symptoms can be the result of either systemic diseases or gastrointestinal alterations. It is essential to obtain baseline data of the child's usual state of health before the significance of alterations can be established.

An accurate nursing history is beneficial to both health professionals and the child-family unit. The child's usual appetite, diet, meal schedule, food preferences, dislikes, and intolerances should be noted. Toileting habits, elimination patterns, and stool characteristics are also included in the nursing history.

Observation of the child's general appearance and nutritional state are important components of the assessment process. This can be beneficial in discriminating between an acute and a chronic illness. The child's weight and height are measured and recorded on growth charts. These parameters can then be compared to previous measurements of the child. The onset and duration of symptoms are discussed after baseline data have been obtained.

Physical assessment begins with examination of the oral cavity. The mouth is inspected for any condition that can interfere with sucking or chewing. In the older child, inspection of the gums for bleeding or ulcers is necessary. The condition of the teeth is important to note.

Table 28-2 Organs located in each of the four quadrants of the abdomen

Right upper quadrant	Left upper quadrant
Liver and gallbladder	Left lobe of liver
Pylorus	Spleen
Duodenum	Stomach
Head of pancreas	Body of pancreas
Right adrenal gland	Left adrenal gland
Portion of right kidney	Portion of left kidney
Hepatic flexure of colon	Splenic flexure of colon
Portions of ascending and transverse colon	Portions of transverse and descending colon

Right lower quadrant	Left lower quadrant
Lower pole of right kidney	Lower pole of left kidney
Cecum and appendix	Sigmoid colon
Portion of ascending colon	Portion of descending colon
Bladder	Bladder
Ovary and salpinx	Ovary and salpinx
Uterus (if enlarged)	Uterus (if enlarged)
Right spermatic cord	Left spermatic cord
Right ureter	Left ureter

Loops of small bowel are found in all four quadrants.

Dental caries can seriously hinder chewing and, consequently, nutrition.

The child or parents can be asked about swallowing problems (*dysphagia*). Difficulty with only solid foods probably indicates a mechanical obstruction such as a foreign body or a cyst. A neurologic problem is indicated when swallowing difficulties extend to include liquids. A distinction must be made between dysphagia and a sore throat.

The abdomen is divided into four quadrants for the purposes of physical assessment. An imaginary line is drawn from the middle of the sternum through the umbilicus to the symphysis pubis. A horizontal line intersects at the umbilicus. This separates the abdomen into right and left, upper and lower quadrants. Table 28-2 lists the organs underlying each quadrant.

The color of the abdomen is inspected and any distention noted. In children, distention must be differentiated from a normal "pot belly." The abdomen is also inspected for visible peristalsis and any masses. The abdominal girth is measured in children with suspected gastrointestinal alterations. Tissue turgor can be assessed by gently pinching a fold of skin and then quickly releasing it. Normally, the tissue immediately assumes its regular contour. If it remains creased, then dehydration is present.

The location of pain must be determined. Children have trouble verbalizing the source of pain. Hence, the nurse must observe the child's facial expression while gently palpating the abdomen to determine the locus of pain. Auscultation of the abdomen reveals the presence or absence of peristalsis. The gurgling sound heard is caused by air and fluid in the intestine. Gastrointestinal alterations can result in absent or diminished bowel sounds.

Sucking and feeding difficulties

Sucking and feeding difficulties in the neonatal period are sometimes due to congenital anomalies such as cleft lip, cleft palate, or tracheo-esophageal atresia or fistula. These defects require adaptive devices or alternate methods for feeding. They are discussed in detail later in this chapter. Infants with large, protruding tongues (as in Down syndrome) may also have difficulty sucking.

Foreign bodies

Children under the age of 5 years are the most likely group to swallow foreign bodies. Safety pins, buttons, coins, and any number of objects have been retrieved from the alimentary tracts of pediatric clients. Foreign bodies that lodge at the junction of the upper and middle third of the esophagus are removed by esophagoscopy with forceps extraction.

After esophagoscopy, humidity is provided by a mist tent or face mask depending on the child's age. Diet restrictions are unnecessary. Observation is required for a 24-h period, after which the child is discharged.

Objects that reach the stomach will generally move through the gastrointestinal tract without difficulty. It may take 3 weeks for some to be eliminated in the stool. Surgery is necessary if the object remains in the alimentary tract or obstructs the pylorus or ileocecal valve. Periodic x-rays are utilized to follow the progression of the foreign body.

Parents of children who swallow things frequently feel guilty and responsible for the child's predicament. The nurse must reassure the parents that no one is at fault.

Nausea and vomiting

Vomiting can indicate a host of problems both inside and outside the gastrointestinal tract. Nausea may or may not precede vomiting. Bile-stained vomitus usually indicates an obstruction below the ampulla of Vater, as in duodenal atresia or stenosis. Reflux of bile from the duodenum into the stomach can account for bile-stained vomitus without gastrointestinal obstruction in older children with persistent vomiting. Nausea and vomiting are symptoms of some underlying pathology. The definitive cause must be determined and treated.

It is a nursing responsibility to record the color, consistency, and amount of vomitus and any relationship between vomiting and other events such as meals or stressful situations. Vomiting in children can easily result in dehydration and fluid and electrolyte imbalance. Intravenous fluids with added electrolytes may be necessary to prevent or treat imbalances. Table 17-25 describes the care for a child with vomiting.

Diarrhea

Diarrhea is the passage of loose or liquid stools, usually with increased frequency. It may have an acute onset or become a chronic condition. The etiology of diarrhea may be bacterial, viral, food- or drug-related, the result of a disease process, or unknown. In some instances, fever is present, increasing water losses. The treatment and nursing management of diarrhea are discussed in Chap. 24.

Constipation

Constipation is the passage of hard, dry stools or stools of insufficient quantity. The feces eliminated vary from a large mass to small, hard pellets. An anal fissure may cause the stool to be blood-streaked.

Constipation in infancy is usually due to insufficient fluid intake or to the formula composition. Formulas with a high renal solute load draw water from the bowel contents to provide enough water for urine solute clearance.[3] Older children may withhold bowel movements for a variety of reasons, resulting in constipation. Emotional stress also contributes to constipation. Diets low in bulk or containing, excessive protein can also contribute to the problem.

Increasing the fluid intake or adding carbohydrates to the formula can remedy the infant's constipation. The addition of fiber and fluids to the older child's diet can be beneficial. Instruct parents to include in the child's diet fruits, vegetables, and whole-grain cereals moderately high in fiber. A stool softener or mild laxative may be employed on a temporary basis but should not be used for long-term management. If an anal fissure has resulted from dry, hard stools, the area must be kept clean and dry. Healing is usually spontaneous.

Gastrointestinal bleeding

Gastrointestinal bleeding is caused by various disorders. *Hematemesis*, vomiting of blood, usually indicates bleeding in the upper gastrointestinal tract. However, swallowed blood, as from epistaxis (nosebleed) or dental extractions, may also produce hematemesis. "Coffee-ground" emesis usually indicates bleeding in the esophagus, stomach, or duodenum.

Anal fissures or polyps are responsible for blood-streaked stools. Massive upper gastrointestinal bleeding may stimulate hyperperistalsis so that unaltered blood appears in the stool.[4] "Currant-jelly" stools are associated with intussusception. An infectious process produces acute bloody diarrhea, while chronic diarrhea with bleeding is more often associated with ulcerative colitis. Tarry stools (melena) result from upper gastrointestinal bleeding.

The darker the blood in the stool, the higher it originates in the alimentary tract. The underlying cause of the bleeding must be determined and treated.

The color, amount, and characteristics of bleeding are noted by the nurse. Labstix and guaiac testing of both stools and vomitus are done to determine the presence and amount of blood. A nasogastric tube may be inserted if hematemesis is continuous or of significant amounts. Transfusion of whole blood or packed red blood cells may be necessary if the child's hemoglobin is not stabilized. Frequent vital signs are essential to monitor the child's systemic response to blood loss.

Bleeding is very anxiety-provoking for both the child and parents. Even small amounts may appear great to them. It is a nursing responsibility to provide support, reassurance, and an explanation of treatments and nursing measures.

Gastrointestinal obstruction

Obstruction in the gastrointestinal system produces vomiting, abdominal pain, and distention. Bile-stained vomitus indicates that the obstruction is in the small intestine below the ampulla of Vater. Bile-stained vomiting occurs in obstructions such as duodenal atresia, duodenal stenosis, and meconium ileus.

Colonic obstruction causes vomiting of fecal material. Hyperperistalsis results from the bowel's attempt to move contents past the obstruction. Bowel movements are absent.

Signs and symptoms of obstruction also occur with paralytic or adynamic ileus. In this condition, nerve impulses that trigger peristalsis are absent or greatly decreased. Thus, bowel sounds are absent or diminished. Abdominal pain, distention, and vomiting are present. Foreign bodies may also cause obstruction. However, the clinical manifestations differ according to the size and location of the object.

Obstruction can progress to perforation and peritonitis. Fluid and electrolyte imbalances as well as dehydration are a result of vomiting, bowel edema, and accumulation of secretions within the intestine. The obstruction must be identified and corrected.

Gastrointestinal pain

Abdominal pain in children is a fairly common complaint. It is essential to inquire about the acuteness or chronicity of the pain. The location, duration, and characteristics of the pain must also be assessed. The child frequently is unable to provide this information, so parents' observations are very helpful. Associated problems such as fever, vomiting, and nausea are important. Any modification in the child's activity, particularly if self-imposed, is noted in the assessment.

Palpation of the abdomen aids in determining the pain locus. Most children tend to guard their abdomens, so it is important to have the child in a relaxed state. Generalized abdominal pain with rigidity may indicate peritonitis. *Rebound tenderness* (an increase in pain following the release of pressure applied to the abdomen) frequently occurs with appendicitis.

Pain is only a symptom. Efforts must be made to determine the etiology. In some children, the cause is never identified but is attributed to "school phobia" or other psychogenic factors.

Such labels should not be used without a thorough evaluation of the child.

Astute nursing observation of the pediatric client validates the information obtained from the parents. Any change in pain must be noted and reported to the physician. Heat should never be applied to the abdomen in the presence of undiagnosed pain. Perforation can result from such action. Cathartics and laxatives are also withheld for the same reason. Abdominal pain can have numerous causes. Specific nursing measures are discussed with each problem.

Types of stools

The newborn stool cycle is discussed in Chapter 10. Stools similar to adults' are seen by the time the child reaches 2 years of age.

Stools vary greatly in appearance. Small amounts of mucus in stools are of no significance. Large amounts occur in inflammatory bowel disease. Starvation stools are mucoid with a brownish tint.

Green stools result from the oxidation of bilirubin to biliverdin. Diarrhea stools are commonly green and watery. However, a green stool is not always abnormal. Swallowed blood, upper gastrointestinal tract bleeding, and iron cause the stools to turn black.

Protein stools are brownish yellow or greenblack and malodorous. These are found in children who either consume large amounts of protein or who are unable to digest it completely. Children with malabsorption syndromes, such as celiac disease or cystic fibrosis, have fatty stools. These are gray, greasy, and bulky with a foul odor.

Guaiac, Clinitest, and Labstix tests are routinely done on stools from children who have elimination or digestive alterations. Guaiac testing reveals the presence of blood, while Clinitest tablets monitor sugar content. Labstix measure protein in the stool and the pH.

Fluids and electrolytes

The stomach contains large amounts of hydrochloric acid. High concentrations of sodium are present in the gastric mucus. Fluid from the small intestine contains bicarbonate and sodium with lesser amounts of chloride and potassium. The large intestine absorbs water and electrolytes. Diarrhea, vomiting, gastric and intestinal suction, and other gastrointestinal alterations all contribute to electrolyte loss. Hypovolemic shock, electrolyte imbalances, and acid-base disturbance are potential complications of both alterations and treatments. The clinical manifestations and nursing management of these problems are discussed fully in Chap. 24.

Medical assessment and treatments

Diagnostic tests

Barium studies Alterations occur in all areas of the gastrointestinal tract. Many problems produce similar clinical manifestations. Diagnostic tests are used to determine the location and severity of the alteration.

Barium is a contrast material that outlines organ systems on x-ray examination. Barium is used for both upper and lower gastrointestinal x-ray studies. The child consumes barium prepared as either a liquid or a pudding. Fluoroscopy follows the progress of the contrast agent down the esophagus, into the stomach, and through the small intestine. Pictures are taken and examined in greater detail later. Barium is given by rectum to outline the lower gastrointestinal tract.

Food and fluids are withheld for 8 h prior to the barium swallow. Only clear liquids are allowed for 8 h previous to the barium enema. Mineral oil and cleansing enemas are given to empty the intestinal tract the night before the lower gastrointestinal study. After both procedures, all the barium must be eliminated to prevent impaction. Laxatives or enemas may be necessary to expel the barium. Check the stool for barium, which is white. A normal diet is resumed after the completion of the studies providing there are no contraindications.

Endoscopy *Endoscopy* is a broad term that refers to the visualization of an internal body cavity. It is possible to use a fiberoptic instrument (with an internal light source) to examine many parts of the gastrointestinal tract.

Esophagoscopy is utilized to (1) retrieve foreign bodies in the esophagus, (2) determine the presence and extent of stenosis, (3) determine the extent of esophageal varices, (4) assist in dilatation procedures, and (5) perform a biopsy. Esophagoscopy requires general anesthesia for pediatric clients. Nothing is given by mouth for 8 h prior to the procedure, and the child is pre-medicated. Normal activities and a regular diet are resumed after recovery from anesthesia.

Proctoscopy, sigmoidoscopy, and colonoscopy are used to diagnose intestinal conditions such as Hirschsprung's disease, ulcerative colitis, regional enteritis, and rectal polpys. The flexible fiberscopes (such as the colonoscope) allow the examiner to visualize the entire colon. Biopsies can also be performed at the time of examination.

Proctoscopy, sigmoidoscopy, and colonoscopy can be done without anesthesia or sedation. Bowel preparation (enemas, laxatives) are frequently deferred because they could cause mucosal changes that would distort the examination. The nurse is responsible for explaining the procedure to the child and enlisting his or her cooperation. The child is placed in either a knee-chest or left lateral position. The nurse should stay with the child to provide support and to help maintain the proper position. No restrictions are necessary after the procedure. The child should be observed for signs and symptoms of perforation and bleeding.

Biopsies *Rectal biopsy* is performed under anesthesia. After the specimen is obtained, the small surgical wound is closed with sutures. *Nothing* is inserted into the rectum for several days postoperatively.

A liver biopsy can be performed on the unit. Premedication with sedatives, narcotics, or tranquilizers promotes comfort. The child must be immobilized during the procedure. A small incision is made between the eighth and ninth ribs, and a Menghini needle is used to obtain the tissue specimen. Baseline vital signs are taken before the biopsy and frequently thereafter. Hemorrhage is a dangerous potential complication. Pressure is applied to the site for 10 min after the biopsy. The child remains on bedrest for 24 h and is positioned on the right side for splinting purposes.

Enemas

Enemas are not diagnostic tools but may be used prior to lower gastrointestinal studies or surgery to ensure adequate visualization of the bowel. They must be used judiciously to prevent electrolyte imbalances. Isotonic saline is used to prevent water intoxication and cerebral edema. Many commerical enema preparations are available for bowel preparation, and the specific directions for their use in children should be followed (see Table 17-3).

Colonic lavage, or irrigation, differs from enema administration. In this procedure, small amounts of solution are inserted and then aspirated back. It is most often used for children with Hirschsprung's disease and, occasionally, for those with encopresis.

The rubber catheter is lubricated and inserted into the rectum, using a gentle rotating motion, until resistance is felt (this is the initial point of aganglionic bowel, the underlying lesion in Hirschsprung's disease). Thirty milliliters of solution are instilled through the catheter, using a large syringe. This is then aspirated back. The process is repeated until the aspirate is free of fecal particles.

The entire length of the catheter is then inserted, using the same rotating motion. Force should not be used because of the danger of bowel perforation. The procedure is continued, with small amounts of solution instilled and aspirated back until the returns are clear. The catheter is withdrawn 1 in and the process repeated until the entire catheter is completely out.

Finally, the catheter is reinserted for its entire length to check for missed areas, and the lavage is repeated if necessary. All the solution instilled must be returned to prevent absorption into the circulatory system through the intestinal wall.[5]

Gastric intubation

Gastric intubation is the insertion of a nasogastric tube for the purpose of pre- and postoperative decompression, removal of gastric contents, obtaining specimens for diagnostic tests, or for feeding and medications. The catheters vary in size and have either single or double lumens (see Chap. 17). The older child is placed in an upright position for tube insertion. The child is encouraged to swallow as the catheter is inserted. Drinking water, if not contraindicated, may be helpful in this process.

Preoperatively, gastric intubation may be necessary to relieve distention and prevent vomiting. Manipulation of the bowel during surgery results in paralytic (adynamic) ileus. Decompression and drainage of gastric and intestinal secretions are necessary until peristalsis returns. The tube may be attached to suction to facilitate drainage.

The maximum suction force that can be used without causing mucosal damage is 25 mmHg.[6] Intermittent suction, set at "low," must be used with single-lumen (Levin) tubes. The "high" setting is used with Salem sumps, which have double lumens. The vent lumen of the Salem sump keeps the suction pressure below 25 mmHg. Because of the air vent, the Salem sump tubes may also be connected to continuous suction at 30 to 40 mmHg without adverse effects.[7] This vent must never be occluded or pressure will exceed the maximum and cause gastric mucosal injury.

It is a nursing responsibility to ensure patency of the nasogastric tube. Irrigations are performed with normal saline at specified intervals. The amount instilled is recorded as intake and the aspirate as output. The color and amount of the aspirate are noted, as well as any changes in its characteristics. Difficulty in irrigating or withdrawing solution, nausea, vomiting, distention, or discomfort must be reported to the physician. Nasogastric tubes are never clamped without a physician's order. When peristalsis returns, they are removed.

Gavage feedings are used for children whose physical conditions are such that oral feedings place an extreme burden on them (see Table 17-13). The formula is given slowly and at room temperature or slightly warmer. Feeding pumps or constant flow drips are other methods used for gavage feedings. The nurse must routinely check these to ensure that the correct volume is infusing.

Ostomies

An *ostomy* is a surgically created opening between an internal cavity and the body surface. After procedures such as ileostomies and colostomies, a *stoma* (opening) is present on the external surface

An *ileostomy* may be performed for ulcerative colitis or temporarily for meconium ileus. The terminal ileum opens onto the right side of the abdomen. The drainage from the ileostomy is liquid, continuous, and cannot be regulated.

There are several types of *colostomies*. The sigmoid colostomy is the most common. A transverse colostomy is performed for some types of imperforate anus and for Hirschsprung's disease. It is the most frequent temporary colostomy. The transverse colostomy is created either by the loop method or with surgically severed proximal

and distal stomas (double barrel). The stool is eliminated from the proximal stoma. The fecal discharge from the transverse colostomy is more formed than that from an ileostomy because the stool contains less water.

Children with either an ileostomy or a colostomy require meticulous nursing care. The peristomal area is vulnerable to skin breakdown (excoriation), particularly with an ileostomy. Digestive enzymes are present in the waste material and are harmful to skin integrity. The area must be protected from leakage and kept clean and dry.

The ostomy appliance (bag) must fit securely around the stoma to prevent spillage. Skin barriers such as zinc oxide or karaya powder can be used for infants. Stomahesive or karaya rings are better for older children.[8] Both of these protectors adhere directly to the peristomal area. The appliance is then fixed to either the Stomahesive or the ring. The appliance should be drainable so that it can be left in place for several days. Careful attention to skin care and appliance fixation minimizes the possibility of leakage and subsequent excoriation (skin breakdown). Odors from ostomies can be controlled with a variety of agents. Some experimentation may be necessary to find one that works optimally for the individual child.

It is a nursing responsibility to teach the parents ileostomy or colostomy care. Initially the parents may be frightened or overwhelmed by the surgery. They need support, guidance, and encouragement to participate in their child's care. Small tasks in the care of the ostomy are begun until, gradually, parents are able to assume total care. Teaching should take place over a period of time so that parents can perform return demonstrations in a nurse's presence. The child who is old enough can also be responsible for some aspects of ostomy care.

It is important to observe the type and amount of drainage. If the child has diarrhea, large amounts of sodium and water can be lost rapidly with an ileostomy. Dehydration can occur in a short period of time with either a colostomy or an ileostomy. Parents need to be provided with this information.

Body image and body integrity are important concerns for both child and parents. It is imperative that nurses recognize these issues and allow time for discussion. Peer relationships are major concerns of school-age children and adolescents, and anxieties can surface in regard to these relationships and the ostomy. The nurse needs to answer any questions the child has and to provide reassurance that social life need not be adversely affected.

A *cervical esophagostomy* is performed for esophageal atresia that ends in a proximal blind pouch. A stoma is created from the end of the pouch and opens onto the base of the neck, usually on the left side. A plastic or rubber catheter is inserted and remains in place for several days postoperatively. Nasal and oral secretions drain from the stoma.

Cervical esophagostomy does not cause skin breakdown because there are no proteolytic enzymes in saliva. A mild ointment will suffice to protect the skin from irritation due to constant wetness. The area needs to be wiped frequently with tissues and washed two to three times daily. A small dressing can be taped over the site and changed every 1 to 2 h, or an absorbent "bib" can be used.

To provide nutrition for the child with cervical esophagostomy, a *gastrostomy* is also performed.

The child with a gastrostomy and an esophagostomy may be given "sham" feedings.[9] Oral fluid is given and a towel or cup used to catch the fluid as it comes from the esophagostomy. Associated with the gastrostomy feeding, this method promotes essential learning of sucking, swallowing, and eating and avoids the difficulties of teaching the infant how to eat after the atresia is surgically corrected.

A *gastrostomy* (Fig. 28-1) is created by inserting a mushroom or Foley catheter through a small incision in the abdomen into the stomach. The anterior stomach wall is sutured to the anterior peritoneum to prevent seepage of gastric material into the peritoneal cavity. The gastrostomy tube is secured to the abdominal surface by a purse-string suture.

Tension on the gastrostomy tube should be avoided. It can widen the opening, causing leaking. The area is inspected for redness, excoriation, and leakage of gastric secretions. The skin can be protected by the use of a karaya paste, zinc oxide, or other products.

Feedings initially consist of clear liquids and

Figure 28-1 Child receiving a gastrostomy tube feeding. (*From L. Shortridge, and E. J. Lee*, Introductory Skills for Nursing Practice, *McGraw-Hill, New York, 1980. Used with permission of publisher.*)

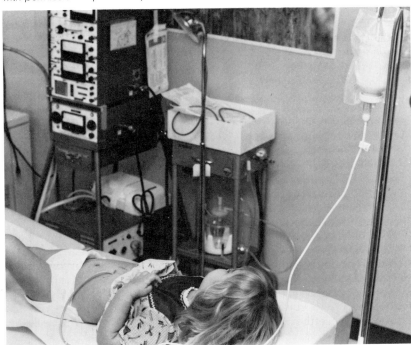

are advanced to full-strength formula according to the individual child's tolerance. Infants with long-term gastrostomy should have diets that progress as a normal infant's would. Cereal and strained baby foods can be mixed with the formulas at the normal developmental times. The gastrostomy tube is elevated and left unclamped to allow for the reflux of air and formula. The tube is clamped between feedings after the child demonstrates tolerance for the amount and type of formula used.

Dilatations

Esophageal dilatation is done to relieve strictures or prevent scar tissue formation such as may follow tracheoesophageal fistula repair or lye ingestion. Tucker or mercury dilators are the instruments used for esophageal dilatation. The procedure itself varies with the dilator used, but the principles are the same. Rubber tubes of various sizes are threaded into the esophagus. Dilatations are performed on a regular basis until the larger tubes pass easily. Anesthesia is usually required due to the child's difficulty in swallowing the dilators.

Anal dilatation is performed using Hager dilators. These are cone-shaped metal instruments of different sizes which are inserted into the anus. Dilatation may be required after pull-through surgery for Hirschsprung's disease or imperforate anus. The dilator is inserted and held in place for several minutes. It should be warmed and lubricated before insertion.

Principles of nursing care for the child with gastrointestinal surgery

Preoperative nursing management

Preoperatively, teaching is an essential component of nursing management for the child-family unit (see Chaps. 16 and 17).

The child is shown where the incision and dressing will be. If an ostomy procedure is to be done, the child must be told and prepared for the alteration.

Postoperative nursing management

When the child returns to the unit, he or she is positioned on the side to prevent aspiration and promote drainage of oral secretions. The child is encouraged to cough and deep-breathe frequently to prevent atelectasis. Infants and small children may require oral or nasotracheal suctioning of secretions. The patency of both the intravenous line and the nasogastric tube must be maintained. The dressing is inspected for drainage, and the color, odor, and amount are recorded.

It is important to observe for abdominal distention because this raises the diaphragm and exerts pressure on the abdominal cavity and the incision. Distention also compromises respiratory function, particularly in children under the age of 7 years, who are primarily abdominal breathers. Abdominal girth measurement once a shift, or more frequently, is a means of detecting distention.

Accurate intake and output are necessary, as well as urine specific gravity. Fluid and electrolyte balance can be precarious in children with gastrointestinal alterations, and it is essential to account for all gains and losses. The nurse must also be alert to any clinical manifestations of electrolyte imbalances.

Mouth care is given frequently for the child's comfort and to moisten the mouth and lips. Nothing is given by mouth until peristalsis resumes. This is indicated by the passage of flatus or stool and the presence of bowel sounds.

The incision should be inspected for signs of infection such as redness, warmth, and drainage. A culture should be taken of any wound exudate. Wound *dehiscence* is the separation of the edges of the incision. *Evisceration* is the protrusion of abdominal contents (usually bowel) through the separated incision. These two complications are not common in pediatric clients but may occur in debilitated children. The physician must be notified immediately. The wound edges are brought together and held in place with either a dressing or Steri-strips for dehiscence. If evisceration occurs, the abdominal contents are covered with a sterile towel which has been wet with normal saline. Vital signs should be monitored frequently, as shock is associated with evisceration.

Alterations of the mouth

Cleft lip

Cleft lip is a facial malformation involving a congenital fissure or fissures of the upper lip. Cleft lip with or without cleft palate occurs in about 1 in 1000 births, with about three-quarters

Figure 28-2 (*A*) a 3.6-kg newborn with cleft lip and a cleft palate that cannot be seen in this picture. (*B*) The same infant after repair of cleft lip at about 8 weeks of age (weight 4.5 kg). (*C*) The same child about 11 months old. Note the lower teeth. The upper teeth are in good position except for one that is missing. Cleft palate has not yet been repaired.

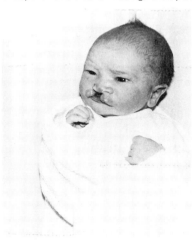

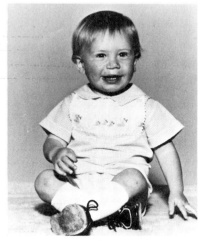

A   B   C

of the cases involving a unilateral (one-sided) cleft. Of the unilateral clefts, 70 percent are on the right side and 30 percent are on the left.[10] Cleft lip is twice as frequent in males as females and is more common in the relatives of affected persons. The defect is believed to be either an autosomal recessive or a conditioned dominant inheritance.[11]

Etiology The etiology of cleft lip is not conclusively known. Heredity is one possible factor, with approximately 15 to 20 percent of the children with clefts of the lip or palate having another family member with the condition. Recent research indicates that the etiology is a combination of genetic and environmental factors. Possible environmental factors include nutritional deficiencies, radiation, maternal infection, and a deficiency in the embryonic mesoderm.

Cleft lip is the failure of the facial processes to fuse between the fifth and eighth weeks of embryonic life. An alternative hypothesis is a rupture occurring after the fusion process is completed.[12]

The defect is visible and diagnosed immediately at birth (see Fig. 28-2A). Cleft lip varies in severity from an incomplete cleft lip, which can be simply a notch in the vermillion (red) border of the lip, to a complete separation of the lip

extending into the nostril and floor of the nose. The affected nostril is wider than normal, and there is a high incidence of poorly positioned, missing, or supernumerary (extra) teeth in the line of the cleft.[13]

In a bilateral cleft lip, the middle portion of the lip, the *prolabium*, is isolated in the midline and remains attached to the *premaxilla* and the *columella* (nasal septum). The nostrils are stretched and wide.

Medical management The treatment is surgical closure of the cleft. Some surgeons do this in the first week of life. However, most prefer to wait until 2 to 3 months of age, when the child has demonstrated a satisfactory weight gain and is completely free of oral, respiratory, and systemic infection.[14] The rule of 10 may be utilized; The infant should be 10 weeks of age, weigh 10 lb and have a hemoglobin of 10 (Fig. 28-2B, C).[15] The time delay also allows the development of normal maternal-infant bonding and permits the parents time to adjust to the defect and accept the child. Cleft lip may be accompanied by other congenital anomalies. The child needs thorough evaluation to detect the presence of any anomalies.

Surgical correction The surgical objective is to unite the cleft edges and produce a lip that is both functional and cosmetically attractive. The surgery, *cheilorrhaphy*, involves a Z-plasty technique which employs a staggered, Z-shaped suture line. Notching of the lip from retraction that usually occurs with healing and scar formation are reduced using this incision.[16] To protect the lip and to relieve tension on the suture line, the *Logan bar*, a wire bow, is attached to the infant's cheeks with tape (see Fig. 28-3) or a butterfly adhesive strip is placed over the suture line.

The defects that may remain after corrective surgery are a widened nostril and flattened tip of the nose on the side of the repair, a thinner area on the bottom of the upperlip, a lumpy or irregularly shaped vermillion lip margin, and a fine-line surgical scar.[17] The lip may need one or more revisions. Additional nasal corrective sur-

Figure 28-3 The infant has elbow restraints, and a Logan bow is in place to prevent tension on the suture line following cleft lip repair. (*From A. J. Ingalls and M. C. Salerno*, Maternal and Child Health Nursing, *4th ed., Mosby, St. Louis, 1979. Used with permission.*)

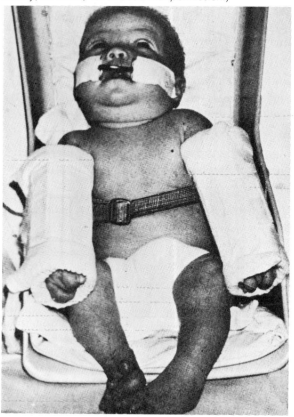

gery is often done in later childhood (about age 10) or early adolescence. The success of surgery depends on the severity of the cleft and the freedom from postoperative infection.

Preoperative nursing management Preoperatively, the role of the nurse focuses on providing adequate nutrition and preventing aspiration and infection. Because of the incomplete lip structure, the infant is unable to apply enough pressure to feed normally. Alternative feeding methods are implemented. Some infants can feed with a regular cross-cut or premature nipple when the hole has been slightly enlarged. A lamb's nipple can also be used. This nipple is very soft, long, and requires little sucking for milk to flow easily. Nipple feeding encourages the use of the infant's sucking muscles, which are needed for later speech development.[18] A third technique involves the use of a Breck feeder (an Asepto syringe with a rubber tubing tip attached) (see Fig. 23-1). The syringe's rubber tip should be directed to the side of the infant's mouth and the bulb squeezed with varying pressure to control formula flow. Medicine dropper or spoon feeding is tedious, time-consuming, and fatiguing for both infant and mother, but should be considered if other feeding methods are unsatisfactory. On occasion, gavage feeding may have to be employed.

The infant should be held in an upright position, fed slowly, and bubbled frequently. These infants swallow large amounts of air before and during feedings and are at increased risk for vomiting and aspiration. The nipple should be placed in the usual position in the mouth, not in the cleft. Due to the defect, feeding takes longer than for other babies. Some milk may come out through the nose. Warn the mother that because of incomplete suction, the feeding may be noisy but should be continued. When the feeding is completed, rinse the mouth with water. After feeding, position the child in an infant seat, on the abdomen, or on the side to prevent vomiting or aspiration.

A few days before surgery, the child should be taught the feeding techniques to be used after surgery. It is wise also to introduce the restraints so that the baby will become accustomed to restricted positioning and decreased mobility. The restraints used should immobilize the arms so that the infant cannot rub or disturb the suture line or turn over onto the abdomen. Jackets with pockets in the arms for tongue blades or arm restraints that do not allow bending of the elbows are needed.

Postoperative nursing management Postoperatively, the role of the nurse is to prevent trauma and infection of the suture line and maintain nutrition. The restraints should be sent with the infant to the operating room and applied in the recovery room. They also need to be pinned to the infant's clothing or diapers to prevent the infant from rubbing the mouth against the shoulder. The infant wears the restraints until the lip is completely healed. They should be removed one at a time at least every 4 h to allow range of motion and inspection of the skin condition. Discharge instructions should stress the correct use, precautions, and necessity for restraints (see Chap. 17).

Postoperative feeding will be by Asepto for about 3 weeks because a nipple would cause suture line pressure. The rubber Asepto tip should be directed toward the side of the mouth to avoid the suture line and prevent sucking motions. Feeding principles previously discussed should be utilized. After feeding, the mouth is rinsed with water to cleanse the oral cavity and prevent infection. Suture care of both the inner and outer lip is done to prevent crusting, infection, and subsequent scarring of the incision. Care consists of cleansing, not rubbing, the site gently with sterile swabs and a solution of water and hydrogen peroxide, then rinsing with sterile water or saline. Once the lip is cleansed, a thin layer of antibiotic ointment, such as bacitracin, may be applied to promote a supple suture line and prevent infection. The Logan bar or butterfly adhesive is not disturbed; any bleeding or separation of the suture line should be reported immediately to the surgeon. Crying stresses the suture line, increasing the chance of scarring. It is important to anticipate the infant's needs to prevent crying. Holding may be needed to keep the baby content.

Positioning of the infant postoperatively is very important. The infant may be positioned in an infant seat or on the back, but never on the abdomen. The side-lying position can be used, taking care to prevent the infant from rolling over and rubbing the face on the mattress.

Increased mucus production and laryngeal edema due to endotracheal intubation may cause airway problems. The nursing goal is to prevent aspiration and respiratory complications. The infant must be observed closely and constantly; humidifying the air may help reduce edema and make breathing easier. If suctioning is needed, it is done with care to avoid damaging the lip. A very soft catheter and low suction are employed. Avoiding the suture line is mandatory. If the infant develops acute respiratory distress, these precautions must be modified because preservation of life is primary. Positioning with the infant's head elevated, for example, in an infant seat, will make breathing easier. The side-lying position prevents aspiration.

The nurse's role as teacher and counselor is extremely important. After the initial diagnosis of the defect, the parents will have to be taught to care for the child. They will need to know why the child cannot suck efficiently and learn the appropriate feeding techniques. The parents should begin caring for and feeding the infant early, so that they will gain confidence before the infant's discharge. If mother and baby are at different hospitals, the mother visits the baby when she is physically able and has indicated her beginning acceptance of the defect. Initially, learning to feed the infant can be a frustrating and time-consuming experience. The parents will need constant support and praise from the nursing staff. The parents should be told of future surgeries, as well as the other problems that can occur, such as increased numbers of upper respiratory and ear infections. After surgery, discharge instructions need to include feeding techniques, restraints, positioning, and lip care.

When the parents are told of the defect initially, they will go through a grieving process for the loss of the normal, perfect child they had anticipated for 9 months and now do not have. With the resolution of this grieving process, the parents will begin to accept the child. The nurse can support the parents by listening to their concerns, encouraging them to care for the infant, praising their care-giving achievements, and encouraging them to make realistic plans. A positive aspect of this type of defect is that it can be surgically repaired.

A major component of the parental reaction to a cleft lip is its location. The face is the main means of communication in most cultures. Such a visible facial defect is one of the most difficult congenital defects to accept. The parents should be encouraged to cuddle, hold, and talk to the child, particularly emphasizing eye-to-eye contact. These interactions are needed in the development of normal parent-child relationships and for normal emotional and social development of the infant.

A Nursing Care Plan for a child who has undergone surgery for a cleft lip is presented at the end of this chapter.

Cleft palate

Etiology The isolated cleft palate is thought to be inherited as a simple dominant trait; it has an incidence of about 1 in 2500 live births.[19] Cleft palate is frequently associated with other congenital anomalies, especially those involving intellectual impairment. It is also found with many syndromes involving chromosomal abnormalities. The cleft palate results from the failure of the maxillary processes to fuse completely. The formation of the hard and soft palates takes place from the seventh to twelfth weeks of intrauterine life.[20] The lateral palatal processes of the maxilla grow upward and arch over the tongue. In the eighth week, the fusion of these processes begins anteriorly and extends posteriorly. This fusion is completed at the uvula at the twelfth week. Due to this directional developmental process of growth, from front to back, it is impossible to have a cleft of the hard palate without a cleft of the soft palate.

The extent of a unilateral cleft palate may range from an incomplete submucous cleft in the soft palate to separation through the entire soft and hard palates. With a bilateral complete cleft palate, the clefts extend through the hard and soft palates and the alveolus (dental ridge) on each side of the premaxilla. As a result, there is a direct connection between both nasal chambers and the oral cavity.[21] Feeding problems are similar to those of the infant with a cleft lip. The child cannot suck properly, and food is regurgitated through the nose.

Medical management Cleft palate, unlike cleft lip, may go undetected for a period of time. It can be detected in the newborn by exploring the palate with a finger. Some overt signs of cleft palate that might be noted by the nurse feeding the newborn include the inability of the infant

to suck properly, regurgitation of fluids through the nose, and difficulty in swallowing or breathing.

The primary objective of medical treatment is union of the cleft segments and achievement of intelligible and pleasant speech. Surgery can be done any time between the ages of 5 months to 5 years. However, the preferred timing is between 1 and 2 years of age, before faulty speech habits develop but after the palate has grown.[22] If the surgery is done too early, it will damage developing tooth buds. If surgery is to be delayed beyond 3 years, a palatal appliance may be used meanwhile to allow speech development to take place. If repair is not technically feasible or is medically contraindicated, a prosthodontic obturator (plastic device to cover the palate defect) may be used to create an artificial palate.

Preoperative nursing management Preoperatively, the goals are the same as those for the infant with a cleft lip: adequate nutrition and prevention of infections. Similar feeding principles and techniques are used with the infant, including the lamb's nipple, Asepto, or a duckbill nipple. Prior to surgery, the child needs to be fed by the technique to be employed postoperatively. The infant can become accustomed to the method, thus facilitating fluid intake in the postsurgical period. A cup or the side of a spoon can be used; an Asepto or nipple would disturb the surgical line. The mouth should be rinsed after feeding to prevent the collection of milk as a medium for bacterial growth.

Postoperative nursing management In the postoperative period, the nurse wants to prevent both trauma to the repair and infection. Respiratory problems can occur in the immediate postoperative period. Laryngeal edema due to intubation and learning to breathe through the smaller nasal passages may lead to respiratory difficulties; a croupette with mist will help alleviate these problems. Suctioning should not be done routinely, only as needed, because the catheter may injure the palate repair. Close observation of respiratory status and color is mandatory. Clots have been known to fall off the repair and block the airway.

Restraints are used to prevent the child from injuring the suture line by placing fingers or objects in the mouth. Positioning on the abdomen can be done; this will facilitate drainage of secretions and help prevent aspirations. An upright position in an infant seat is also useful.

Feeding should be done using the method selected preoperatively. A paper cup or the side of a plastic spoon is best. Metal utensils, straws, or any device that could harm the suture line must be avoided. The child will be fed only fluids for 3 to 4 weeks until healing is complete; a normal diet can then be resumed.

On discharge, the parents should be aware of the need to keep hands and toys away from the child's mouth. Sucking, laughing, and blowing all cause strain and should be avoided.[23] Feeding techniques and restraints also need to be discussed. Parents should be aware that further surgery may be needed to close any small residual fistulas of the palate, for scar revisions, and for correction of nasal deformities. The eustachian tube may also be partially blocked or abnormally positioned in the pharynx. Thus it may not drain properly, causing a high frequency of otitis media. Myringotomy (insertion of polyethylene drainage tubes into the eardrum) to treat chronic serous otitis media may need to be done.

The problems of the child with cleft palate are multiple and require the coordinated efforts of the entire health team. Recurrent ear infections can lead to permanent hearing loss. Dental decay and malpositioned teeth require extensive dental and orthodontic work. Speech defects remain even after closure of the palate, and speech therapy is required. Speech has a hypernasal quality for certain sounds—*p*, *b*, *d*, *t*, *s*, *h*, and *g*—due to the inadequacies remaining in the function of the palatal and pharyngeal muscles.[24]

Table 28-3 Frequency of the most commonly found types of esophageal atresia and tracheoesophageal fistula

Defect	Incidence
Type I	8%
Type II	1%
Type III	87%
Type IV	1%
Type V	4%
Type VI	No incidence listed Stenosis, not a true atresia

Source: Victor Vaughan et al., *Nelson Textbook of Pediatrics*, 11th ed., Saunders, Philadelphia, 1979. Used with permission.

The palate team is an interdisciplinary team of pediatric specialists who repair the defect and deal with dental, hearing, speech, social, and emotional problems. The child's physical problems can lead to social problems due to the speech impediment. Problems with self-image and peer relationships are common. The whole habilitative effort is team centered. Well-established cleft palate clinics have these wide-ranging facilities available for the child and family. The nurse plays an important role in coordinating care and dealing with the child on a long-term basis.

Alterations of the esophagus

Esophageal atresias and tracheoesophageal fistulas (TEF)

Embryology The esophagus develops from the primitive foregut. Between the third and sixth intrauterine weeks, it lengthens and separates from the trachea, which lies in front.[25] At one point in development, the esophagus is a solid tube that later hollows out.

Etiology The embryological failure of the esophagus to develop as a continuous, intact passageway[26] results in the defects of esophageal atresia and TE fistula. Six types of esophageal defects are shown in Fig. 28-4. Table 28-3 lists the frequency of the defects. Complete esophageal atresia occurs when the esophagus ends in two blind separate pouches with no connection between the mouth and stomach (Fig. 28-4, Type I). The most common, 87 percent, atresia and TE fistula, is Type III.[27] In this defect, the proximal (upper) esophagus ends in a blind pouch, while the lower esophageal segment has a fistula (opening) into the trachea or primary bronchus. The connection from the stomach to the trachea allows reflux of gastric contents into the lungs.[28] Passage of air from the lungs through the TE fistula progressively distends the stomach.

The etiology of the anomaly is unknown. The incidence is from 1 in 3000 to 1 in 4500 live births, and one-third of these infants are premature.[29] The anomaly occurs equally in both sexes, and there is often a history of maternal hydramnios (excessive amniotic fluid).[30] The normal fetus swallows amniotic fluid that is absorbed through the intestine. If the fetus cannot

Figure 28-4 Types of esophageal atresia. Type I, esophageal atresia with no fistula, blind pouches. Type II, lower esophageal atresia, fistula from upper pouch. Type III, esophageal atresia, blind upper pouch, fistula from lower pouch. Type IV, esophageal atresia with fistulas from both pouches. Type V, no esophageal atresia, connecting fistula. Type VI, esophageal stenosis. (*From Gladys M. Scipien, et al.,* Comprehensive Pediatric Nursing, *2d ed., McGraw-Hill., New York, 1979. Used with permission.*)

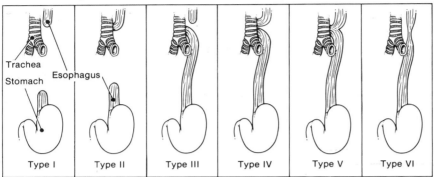

swallow or the gastrointestinal tract is blocked, maternal hydramnios results.

In approximately 30 percent of the infants with esophageal anomalies, other congenital defects are present.[31] The major associated defects are cardiac, anorectal, genitourinary, and vertebral.

Clinical manifestations Detection of this life-threatening defect immediately after birth is imperative. The usual symptoms are excessive oral and pharyngeal mucus, often flowing from the nostrils and bubbling from the mouth. Drooling, choking, and coughing are characteristic. Symptoms may not appear until the infant is fed for the first time; the baby may take a few swallows but immediately chokes and becomes cyanotic due to laryngospasm. Overflow of fluid from the blind esophageal pouch is aspirated into the trachea and bronchi.[32] Suctioning temporarily relieves the respiratory distress, but it will recur. Death may result from aspiration or aspiration pneumonia following feeding. (Since sterile water causes less irritation than glucose or milk, it is often used for a neonate's first feeding.)

Diagnosis Diagnosis is done by passing a radiopaque nasogastric catheter into the esophagus. Passing of a nasogastric tube and aspiration of stomach contents are done routinely in some delivery rooms to rule out TE fistula and atresia. Failure to aspirate gastric contents, obtaining

mucus and saliva instead, and a catheter that is visualized by x-ray coiled in the upper esophageal pouch are diagnostic of atresia. Radiopaque contrast material can be aspirated into the lungs and is not recommended unless absolutely necessary for diagnosis of TE fistula.

Medical management The medical management of the infant is directed toward treatment and prevention of pneumonia, which causes 75 percent of the deaths, and repair of the defect. Depending upon the type of defect, the surgery may be done in one stage or several. With a Type III defect, if the infant is a good surgical risk, the repair is done in one stage through a thoracotomy, with ligation of the fistula and an end-to-end anastomosis of the two segments of the esophagus. A gastrostomy may be done for decompression of the stomach and feeding. Occasionally the surgery is done in stages (repeated operations separated by a period of time to wait for growth). A premature or very sick infant with extensive pneumonia, other anomalies, or very short esophageal segments often has staging of the surgery. In this case, the fistula will be ligated and a gastrostomy done for gastric decompression and feeding. Primary fistula repair and esophageal anastomosis are done later.

Another type of surgery, a *colon transplant*, is done when the two esophageal segments are too short to allow primary anastomosis. The surgery is delayed until 6 to 24 months of age. To allow the child to survive until this surgery, the fistula, if present, is ligated and a gastrostomy done for feedings.

A *cervical esophagostomy* may be done to prevent aspiration by allowing drainage of the oral secretions. At the time of transplant or esophageal surgery, the cervical esophagostomy is closed and the gastrostomy removed. An earlier section in this chapter describes cervical esophagostomy and its care.

Complications following reconstruction of the esophagus include leakage at the anastomosis site, recurrence of the fistula, and stricture of the anastomosis due to the scar formation that accompanies healing. Many surgeons routinely do *esophageal dilatation* to eliminate strictures following surgery and repeat it as often as monthly after discharge and at growth periods. Stenosis (narrowing) of the esophagus can occur at any time after surgery. The parents should be aware of signs indicating this condition: dysphagia (difficulty in swallowing), increased coughing and choking, increased pharyngeal secretions, and decreased nutritional intake with weight loss. After surgery the swallowing mechanism is not entirely normal, and gastroesophageal reflux (backing up of gastric contents into the esophagus) with its attendant *peptic esophagitis* is common. The child experiences heartburn and bad breath, and vomiting may increase. The child is more susceptible to respiratory infections. A harsh, brassy cough may be present for as long as a year after surgery.

Preoperative nursing management The essential components of nursing care are removal of the secretions and promotion of adequate air exchange. Until surgery, oral secretions must be removed from the blind upper pouch to prevent overflow to the trachea. One method of accomplishing this is nasopharyngeal and oral suctioning as frequently as every 10 to 15 min. A second technique is placing an indwelling nasal catheter into the blind pouch and applying low, intermittent suction. The catheter is easily obstructed and needs to be changed daily. A third method involves the use of an *esophageal frame*. This is a canvas-covered frame which has an opening for the child's face and restraint straps. The infant is placed in the Trendelenburg position, face down, draining the secretions by gravity.[33] Obviously this method is useful only

with the Type I anomaly, in which there is no connection between the trachea and the stomach. If this method is used, nursing care includes frequently wiping and cleansing the face of mucus.

Other nursing care to promote air exchange includes the provision of humidified oxygen, usually by Isolette. Positioning is important. A head-down position can be used to facilitate mucus drainage if there is no fistula to the stomach. With the presence of fistulas, the supine position with the head elevated from 20° to 30° will decrease gastric reflux. If the child is turned from side to side, more time should be spent on the right side than on the left.

Intravenous fluids are needed to maintain fluid and electrolyte balance; hyperalimentation may be instituted if there is prolonged nutritional deprivation. Broad-spectrum antibiotics, such as penicillin and kanamycin, are used to combat respiratory infection. The infant is given nothing by mouth (NPO), and mouth care is essential. A pacifier should not be offered at this point. It will increase secretions in an infant unable to handle them adequately.

A gastrostomy is used to decompress the stomach and to prevent gastric aspiration. The gastrostomy tube drains by gravity; preoperatively, feedings and fluid irrigations are contraindicated. If the tube needs to be irrigated, air should be used.

When surgery is delayed, gastrostomy provides the method of nutrition. The gastrostomy tube is placed immediately after diagnosis. Feedings are initiated usually within 24 h if no TE fistula is present. The feeding techniques and care are similar to those for children with regular gavage tubes. Chap. 17 discusses gavage feeding.

Postoperative nursing management Many of the principles employed preoperatively also apply postoperatively. Once healing of the anastomosis has progressed sufficiently, oral feedings are begun. If a gastrostomy tube is present, it will be left open and positioned above the level of the stomach to promote gastric decompression and prevent gastroesophageal reflux, which could irritate the anastomosis and contribute to breakdown of the site. Suctioning, monitoring of intravenous fluids, positioning, and careful observations are essential.

Feedings may be started after the first week

postoperatively via the gastrostomy or after approximately 2 weeks orally. Oral feedings are started slowly and cautiously. The initial feeding is a few milliliters of glucose water. Feedings are given every 2 h by medicine dropper. The volume and type of fluid are advanced slowly until the infant is taking normal formula from a nipple every 2 to 3 h. This may take as long as 2 to 3 weeks to accomplish. The nurse has to be careful in feeding this infant and to use methods that minimize coughing, choking, and swallowing of excessive air. A slightly elevated position is best for feeding. The baby should be allowed to rest frequently during feedings and bubbled thoroughly. The care plan should include the feeding schedule and the reactions to feeding so that normal feeding behavior and experiences can be promoted. The feedings may be supplemented via gastrostomy until the infant's nutritional needs can be met by oral feedings. When the infant is taking adequate amounts and gaining weight, the gastrostomy tube is removed and the child is ready for discharge.

Parental discharge teaching includes effective feeding techniques, observations indicating increasing respiratory distress, the need to prevent swallowing of foreign objects, respiratory infections, and the possible need for further dilatations. If the child has esophageal atresia and has had palliative surgery, the parents need to know how to do gastrostomy feedings, suctioning, and esophagostomy care. They also need guidance concerning normal development and stimula-

tion, and to understand the need for later surgeries.

Alterations of the stomach and duodenum

Pyloric stenosis

Pyloric stenosis is an obstruction at the outlet of the stomach as a result of progressive hypertrophy of the circular muscle of the pyloric sphincter. It is the most common entity, after inguinal hernia, requiring surgery in the first few months of life. Pyloric stenosis is five times more common in males than in females.[34] The hereditary factor is speculative, but some reports have found a 15 percent familial incidence.[35] There is a preponderance of the condition in first-born males, and it is more likely to be found in full-term infants. Black and oriental infants are rarely affected.

Etiology The cause of the pyloric enlargement is unknown. There is some speculation that an acquired factor causing high levels of serum gastrin is present. It is not known whether this is a cause or a result of the condition. The circular muscle of the pylorus is thickened and elongated. The pyloric canal leading from the stomach to the duodenum becomes narrow and progressively obstructed. Diffuse hypertrophy and hyperplasia of the smooth muscle of the antrum of the stomach are present.[36] As peristalsis attempts to push food through the pylorus (Fig. 28-5), the stomach's musculature becomes

Figure 28-5 (*A*) Normal pylorus. (*B*) Pyloric stenosis. Notice the hypertrophied muscle mass and narrowed lumen. (*From M. Armstrong et al., eds.*, McGraw-Hill Handbook of Clinical Nursing, *McGraw-Hill, New York, 1979. Used with permission.*)

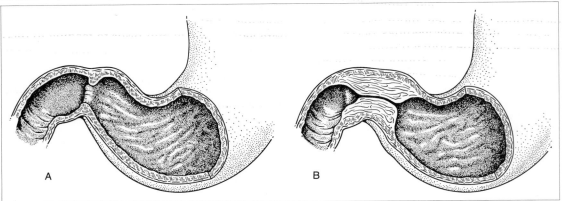

thickened. Pyloric obstruction leads to prolonged stasis of gastric secretions and may cause gastritis and bleeding.[37]

Clinical manifestations Vomiting is the cardinal symptom and usually begins between the third and fourth weeks after birth, but it may occur from the first week of life to as late as the fourth month. Initially, the history reveals that the infant does well after birth, with occasional vomiting or regurgitation, and may even have gained weight. During the second to fourth week, the infant begins vomiting more frequently and forcefully shortly after being fed. As the obstruction becomes more complete, the vomiting becomes more projectile, shooting out as far as 30 to 120 cm, and begins to occur after every feeding. The emesis is partially digested or undigested food without bile, although it may be brownish-tinged periodically secondary to the bleeding from gastritis.[38]

Hunger is ever-present, and the child refeeds eagerly. Progressive weight loss occurs. Varying degrees of dehydration may be present. The infant demonstrates the signs of dehydration; poor skin turgor, depressed fontanel, decreased urinary output, dry mucous membranes, and lethargy. With the inability to retain nutrients, severe nutritional depletion results, and the infant appears malnourished. The infant's stools and voidings decrease in number, quantity, and frequency depending upon the amount of food and fluid reaching the intestinal tract.[39]

Acute abdominal pain does not accompany pyloric stenosis, but the infant does seem uncomfortable. The upper abdomen is distended, and the enlarged pylorus is palpated as a hard, mobile, nontender, olive-shaped tumor in the right epigastrium.[40] It is felt more easily right after eating or vomiting. After feedings, peristaltic waves may be seen as the stomach works against the hypertrophied, closed sphincter. These waves move from left to right across the epigastrium.

Diagnosis Once the tumor is palpated, upper gastrointestinal barium x-rays are usually not needed. Clinical symptoms and the history confirm the diagnosis. In some cases, a barium x-ray will demonstrate delayed gastric emptying and the "string" sign, showing the threadlike,

elongated pyloric canal. X-rays may be used to rule out other possible diagnoses.[41]

Jaundice is found in a small number of infants with pyloric stenosis. It disappears soon after surgery and is thought to relate to poor nutrition and impaired liver enzyme function.[42]

Prolonged, frequent vomiting produces severe fluid and electrolyte disturbances that are revealed by lab tests. Loss of acid gastric juice containing chloride, sodium, and potassium causes hypochloremic metabolic alkalosis. With the alkalosis, bicarbonate and pH are elevated. The hematocrit and hemoglobin are increased secondary to the hemoconcentration of dehydration.

Medical management With only 1 percent mortality, the preferred method of treatment is *surgical*, the *Fredet-Ramstedt pyloromyotomy*. A right-upper-quadrant incision is made, and a longitudinal incision through the muscular fibers down to the submucosa of the pylorus is accomplished. This procedure is safe with a very high success rate, and reoperation is rarely necessary.

Nonsurgical treatment is seldom used, except in a baby who would be a poor surgical risk. With this treatment, there is a higher mortality and improvement is very slow, taking up to 8 months.[43] The long hospitalization can have deleterious effects on the emotional development of the infant. The conservative treatment basically consists of thickened (with cereal), frequent, small feedings.[44] The infant is fed in a semiupright position, burped frequently, and placed upright in an infant seat for an hour after feeding. If the infant vomits, he or she is immediately refed an amount equal to that vomited. Drug therapy includes sedation and cholinergic blocking agents such as methylscopolamine nitrate given 15 to 20 min prior to feeding to relax the sphincter. Intravenous fluids may be used to restore and maintain normal fluid and electrolyte balance. When gastric distention is present, a nasogastric tube used prior to feeding decreases the possibility of emesis with feeding.

Preoperative nursing management The surgical repair of pyloric stenosis is not an emergency. The nursing goal is to help restore the fluid and electrolyte balance so that the child will be a good surgical risk. The infant who is well hydrated and demonstrates no evidence of electrolyte imbalance will go to the operating room immediately. If severe fluid and electrolyte depletions are present, surgery will be delayed until the deficits are corrected, usually 24 to 48 h. Severe nutritional depletions of fat and protein may require a longer restorative period.

The infant is NPO, and a nasogastric tube is placed to prevent further vomiting and possible aspiration and to empty the stomach for surgery. Intravenous fluids with replacement of potassium and fluid deficits are maintained and are closely monitored for signs of water intoxication and circulatory overload. Vital signs and other indications of the infant's hydration are checked frequently. Intake and output, urinary specific gravity, daily weights, and skin turgor are evaluated. Restraints will be needed to prevent disruption of the intravenous and nasogastric tubes. Emesis and stools are noted for frequency and amount. Mouth care is very important since the child is dehydrated, NPO, and has a nasogastric tube in place. The infant needs to be protected from possible sources of infection because of particular susceptibility due to a poor nutritional status. Sensory stimulation should be provided, and a pacifier may meet some sucking needs.

The parents are usually apprehensive. The mother especially is often anxious and may even feel guilty, believing that in some way her skills as a mother and her feeding techniques have been a failure. It is important to help allay these very normal concerns and to prepare the parents for the various diagnostic procedures and the surgery.

Postoperative nursing management The nursing goal postoperatively is to return the infant to a normal feeding pattern and diet. A nasogastric tube is often left in place until feedings commence, to provide gastric decompression and prevent vomiting, which would strain the pylorus. The infant may have occasional postoperative vomiting. If vomiting persists for 3 to 5 days, it may indicate an incomplete division of the hypertrophied pyloric muscle, and reoperation is necessary.[45] Intravenous fluids are continued until the child is taking adequate amounts of formula. Vital signs, intake and output, and other preoperative nursing interventions are continued.

Feeding is initiated when the infant is alert, has bowel sounds, and the nasogastric tube is out, from 4 to 24 h after surgery, usually in the first 6 h. Small amounts of glucose water are started; then feedings progress slowly from half-strength to full-strength formula. An example of a feeding regimen would be 3 to 5 ml for the first feeding, repeated hourly. If no emesis occurs, the infant would progress a few milliliters more with each feeding until 2-h feedings have been achieved. Normal feeding amounts and timing should be accomplished within 2 days. If vomiting occurs at any time, the baby is kept NPO for 4 h and the regimen started again from the beginning.[46]

The infant is held in a sitting position, fed slowly with a medicine dropper, syringe, or nipple, burped frequently, and handled gently. Feeding techniques used preoperatively are continued. Turning the infant on the right side with the head elevated will aid emptying of the stomach. Intravenous fluids can be discontinued when daily weights indicate satisfactory oral intake.

With the breast-fed infant, two approaches can be taken. The mother can express her milk into a bottle and then feed it to the infant, or she may breast-feed the baby. For the first feeding, it is desirable to allow the baby only 1 min at each breast and then lengthen the time as the baby tolerates it.

The incision should be checked for inflammation and infection. Position the diapers low over the abdomen to prevent irritation to the incision and urinary contamination. Other postoperative complications are apnea, pneumonia, and hypoglycemia due to the preoperative glycogen depletion.

The parents should be included in the care and taught to feed the infant. A pacifier may be used to satisfy additional sucking needs, and sensory stimulation such as cuddling and holding is very important. The mother particularly may be apprehensive and hesitant after her prior feeding experiences but should be encouraged to participate in the child's feeding and care.

The infant will be ready for discharge by the third or fourth postoperative day. The parents need to learn feeding techniques, positioning, care of the incision, signs of incisional infection, and signs that might indicate pyloric or bowel obstruction.

Figure 28-6 Omphalocele before and after surgery. (*From Gladys M. Scipien et al.,* Comprehensive Pediatric Nursing, *2d ed., McGraw-Hill, New York, 1979. Used with permission.*)

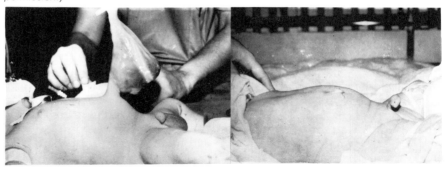

Omphalocele

Etiology Omphalocele is a rare anomaly in which a sac containing abdominal contents protrudes from the umbilical stump (see Fig. 28-6).[47] The defect may be small or very large, extending from the xiphoid to the umbilicus. The cause is unknown, but the condition seems to result from the failure of the intestines to return to the abdomen and the failure of the abdominal wall's lateral folds to fuse in the tenth week of fetal life.[48] Thus, the abdominal organs remain external without a skin covering. Omphalocele is associated with other gastrointestinal problems such as malrotation and small bowel atresia because the bowel normally rotates as it returns to the abdominal cavity. The sac can rupture easily with resulting peritonitis, sepsis, and death.[49]

Medical management The defect constitutes a medical emergency. Immediately after birth, the goals of care are to minimize heat and fluid loss, prevent trauma and rupture of the sac, and prevent infection. The treatment is surgery. With a small defect, complete closure of the muscular wall with the return of the bowel to the abdominal cavity is done.[50] A large defect may necessitate several stages of repair accomplished over days or weeks. A gastrostomy tube is placed for gastric decompression. The current procedure is to create a silo, which is a silicon-covered plastic sheet sutured around the edges of the abdominal opening. The silo is suspended perpendicular to the infant and attached to the top of the Isolette with a rubber band. The sac is wrapped in gauze soaked in a solution such as

Betadine, and parenteral antibiotics are started. Progressive shortening of the silo and consequent stretching of the sides of the abdominal opening by the physician may require two or three surgical procedures to complete the skin closure.

Preoperative nursing management Preoperatively, the nurse's major role is to provide care that prevents sac rupture and infection. Immediately after the birth, the infant is placed in a warmed, humidified Isolette. The exposed bowel is covered with sterile gauze soaked in warmed normal saline and covered with dry sterile towels to maintain the sterility of the inner dressings. *All* dressings are done with sterile technique. The intestine is not pushed into the abdominal cavity in any manner because respiratory distress, trauma, and shock may result. Prevention of tension on the area is mandatory. Extreme care should be taken in positioning, turning, and using restraints with the infant. Moving the infant for procedures such as x-rays may take two people.[51]

Intravenous fluid therapy is essential to promote perfusion of the major organs, to replace fluid lost through the bowel, and to prevent shock. The amount of fluid required varies with the size of the infant, the extent of the omphalocele, and the subsequent amount of bowel exposed. Shock is an ever-present problem, and the nurse must be constantly observant for the indications of fluid and protein losses. They occur continuously at varying rates until the abdomen is closed and healed. A volume expander, albumin, may be used to deal with this problem. A gastrostomy tube or nasogastric tube with low, intermittent suctioning keeps the stomach empty. Respiratory distress is often evident. The infant will need suctioning and humidified oxygen either by hood or through the Isolette. Cyanosis of the lower extremities is caused by the increased pressure on the descending aorta and its femoral branches. It is dangerous to try to move the bowel to correct this impaired circulation. Surgery should correct the problem.

Postoperative nursing management The major postoperative nursing goal is to promote healing and prevent trauma and infection. Respiratory assistance with oxygen provided by hood or ventilator may be required. Shock remains a major concern because of the possible fluid shift from the intestine to the silo and because of the surgical manipulation of the intestine. Close observation for the signs of shock—tachypnea, tachycardia, decreased urinary output and increased specific gravity, and hypotension—is mandatory. If the lower extremities remain mottled or dusky, the surgeon may shift the silo or increase its tension; the nurse does not do this. The infant may remain NPO up to several weeks and will be maintained on parenteral hyperalimentation.[52]

Positioning and movement of the infant are done with extreme caution to prevent trauma and tension to the wound. Sterile technique is used whenever the nurse is dealing with the wound, and parenteral antibiotics will be continued.

Complications after the repair include intermittent episodes of gastroenteritis, vomiting, abdominal distention, and malabsorption. Bowel obstruction and adhesions are not uncommon.

Maternal bonding will be delayed due to the prolonged hospitalization of the infant immediately after birth, the shocking appearance of the defect, and difficulty in handling the infant with the omphalocele. Parents should be encouraged to visit and care for the infant.

Diaphragmatic hernia

Diaphragmatic hernia is the protrusion of varying amounts of abdominal contents through a defect in the diaphragm into the chest cavity. This congenital defect is an acute emergency in the newborn and is associated with a 25 to 40 percent mortality.[53] It results from the failure of the *pleuroperitoneal canal* (opening between the chest and abdomen) to close completely during fetal development (Fig. 28-7).[54] Usually the herniation is on the left side; bilateral hernias are rare.

Small hernias produce few symptoms and may not be discovered until later in infancy when the child is seen for increased respiratory infections. Severe cases of herniation may include upward displacement of the stomach, small intestine, spleen, left lobe of the liver, left kidney, and even the large intestine. These organs enter the thorax,

Figure 28-7 Comparison of the pathological anatomies of diaphragmatic malformations. (*From Gladys M. Scipien et al.,* Comprehensive Pediatric Nursing, *2d ed., McGraw-Hill, New York, 1979. Used with permission.*)

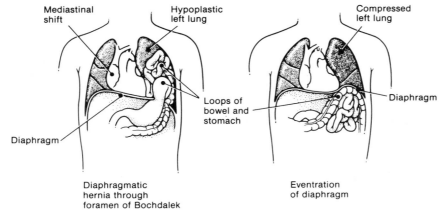

displacing the heart and lungs.[55] The left lung is usually *hypoplastic* (underdeveloped) and may be collapsed due to the pressure of the other organs.

Clinical manifestations Respiratory status is complicated by atelectasis, and the movement of the diaphragm is impaired as the herniated intestine and stomach fill with air and distend from the swallowing of air. Clinical signs include mild to severe respiratory distress usually within a few hours of birth. Chest sounds are dull to percussion, and breath sounds are decreased or absent on the left side; bowel sounds may be heard instead. The chest appears barrellike, especially on the left side. In contrast to the normal newborn's protruding abdomen, the abdomen will appear small and *scaphoid* (sunken) due to the absence of the abdominal contents. Heart sounds are shifted to the opposite side as the pressure in the left thorax increases.

Diagnosis Diagnosis is made by anterior-posterior chest x-ray, which differentiates this defect from other problems such as lung cysts and paralysis of the diaphragm due to phrenic nerve involvement. A definitive diagnostic sign is *dextrocardia* (shift of the heart to the right), with spasmodic attacks of cyanosis and difficulty in feeding, and gas-filled bowel loops are seen in the chest on x-ray. Signs of intestinal obstruction will also eventually present.

Medical management The treatment is immediate surgery. An abdominal approach is used with the presence of abdominal obstruction; otherwise, a thoracic approach suffices, with replacement of the abdominal organs and closure of the defect.[56] The prognosis depends upon the size of the defect, the degree of hypoplasia of the left lung, and the respiratory status of the right lung. Complications after surgery include spontaneous pneumothorax, circulatory problems, and pulmonary infection.

Preoperative nursing management Prior to surgery, the infant's respiratory status is stabilized and the respiratory and metabolic acidosis corrected. If oxygen is administered, it must be by endotracheal intubation to prevent further inflation of the intestine and stomach. Place the infant in the semi-Fowler's position to allow expansion of the thorax and prevent pressure on the lungs, diaphragm, and viscera. The baby is turned on the affected side to allow the unaffected lung to expand. Nasopharyngeal suctioning of secretions is needed to preserve airway patency. A nasogastric tube is essential for gastric decompression and will improve lung expansion. The child will be NPO and have intravenous fluids with prophylactic antibiotics.

Close observation of respiratory effort and status to facilitate respiratory functions is essential. The infant should also be kept from crying to prevent an increase in intrathoracic pressure and swallowed air.

Postoperative nursing management The infant's respiratory status continues to be of primary concern. Oxygen is continued, and often the infant is placed on a positive-pressure ventilator. Suctioning and chest physiotherapy will help to prevent atelectasis and other respiratory complications. Positioning is similar to the preoperative patterns. The thoracotomy tube is removed in 2 to 3 days when the left lung has expanded and air has been removed from the chest.

Intravenous fluids are continued, and a nasogastric tube remains in position.

Feedings are initiated slowly and cautiously. The infant often seems apathetic and fatigued, and gags and vomits easily. The feedings should be small and frequent, with a maximum amount set for any one feeding. The infant should be fed in a semiupright position and bubbled frequently. The infant is prone to abdominal obstruction. Vomiting, decreased number and frequency of stools, and abdominal distention should be noted and reported immediately. Before discharge, the parents should be taught appropriate feeding techniques with particular cautions about avoiding overfeeding, the signs of respiratory distress, indications of respiratory infection, and bowel obstruction.

Peptic ulcer
Etiology and pathology The incidence of *peptic (gastric and duodenal) ulcers* in children is not precisely known. Acute peptic ulcers are found most frequently in the first 3 years of life and during the 12 to 18 age span. Boys are affected more frequently than girls.[57] Under the age of 6, occurrence is related to an underlying

disease (leukemia, trauma, burns, sepsis, or bronchopneumonia) or a toxic substance and is referred to as a *stress ulcer*. Over 6 years of age, the ulcers are primary (not related to another condition). Distribution is equal between the stomach and duodenum.

Acute peptic ulcers, the result of erosion of the mucosal wall of the stomach, pylorus, or duodenum, are caused by two postulated mechanisms. One of these is the increased rate of gastric juice production. The other involves the interference with the normal protective mechanisms of the mucosal lining. As a result, there is a loss of normal mucosal barriers, and gastric acids digest the lining of the stomach and duodenum. Progressive edema, hemorrhage, and erosion of the mucosal lining occur.[58] Drugs implicated in the development of ulcers in childhood include the steroids and aspirin. Emotional stress is frequently a factor in older children.

In neonates, the ulcer formation is associated with birth hypoxia, a difficult labor and delivery, sepsis, dehydration, allergic disease, hypoglycemia, and tube feeding. Perforation and hemorrhage can occur very rapidly in the neonate. The baby needs to be observed for the signs of perforation—shock, rectal bleeding, distention, and absent bowel sounds. Emergency surgery may be necessary with ligation of the bleeding points.

Clinical manifestations The clinical symptoms may be few or include vomiting, poor eating, *hematemesis* (bloody emesis), melena, abdominal distension, crying after feeding, and anemia. Children up to the age of 10 may not consistently exhibit vomiting and abdominal pain before or after meals. They often have chronic anemia and a family history of peptic ulcers. The child over 10 follows the adult pattern of symptomatology. Complications of peptic ulcers are hemorrhage, perforation, pyloric obstruction, and intractable ulcers (those that do not respond to treatment).

Diagnosis Diagnostic assessment includes the history, with specific attention to the family history of ulcers and an explicit description of the presence and pattern of pain. Tests may include an upper gastrointestinal barium swallow, endoscopy (visualization of the gastric wall) that can be used as early as 1 month of age, and selective celiac and mesenteric arteriography

studies. Blood studies reveal anemia subsequent to chronic blood loss. Gastric acid measurements (to look for hypersecretion) may also be done. The stools are tested for occult blood. Studies are also done to rule out the possibility of other problems such as functional abdominal pain or gallbladder or pancreatic disease.

Treatment Treatment goals are to relieve pain, promote healing, and prevent recurrences and complications. Aspirin should be avoided; acetaminophen (Tylenol) is an acceptable substitute. Antacids are used to increase the pH of the gastric secretions. Anticholinergic agents are used to decrease gastric gland secretion. If the child is taking anticholinergic drugs, the child and parents need to be aware of side effects such as dry mouth, constipation, blurred vision, and urinary retention. These drugs are contraindicated with urinary retention or glaucoma.

Nursing management Management of peptic ulcer is primarily aimed at reducing acid production and protecting the mucosal tissues. Dietary control is advised. Meals should be frequent and small. Prolonged fasting and foods that cause the child discomfort should be avoided. A bland diet is ordered to avoid substances that increase gastric secretion and irritation. Substances to be avoided are tea, coffee, spices, fried foods, citrus, carbonated beverages, alcohol, and colas.

Milk and antacids are given hourly with the dosage adjusted to the age and size of the child. Many antacids contain magnesia, a cathartic, while others cause constipation. An alternating schedule of the two types may be appropriate. Liquid antacids are more effective than the tablets. As the child improves, the frequency of administration of antacids should decrease; when a child has been symptom-free for 3 months, some physicians discontinue them completely.

Nursing care involves close observation for bleeding and signs of shock. Vital signs are taken frequently; emesis and stools are examined for the presence of blood. "Coffee-grounds" or frank, bright red blood may be seen in the vomitus. Stools can be tarry; the presence of bright red blood in the stool indicates rectal rather than gastric bleeding. The amount, color, and site of any bleeding are recorded. Dyspnea and cyanosis indicate perforation. If active bleeding is occurring, the abdominal girth is measured hourly and blood replacement is done. During these acute episodes, the child is NPO and a nasogastric tube is inserted to decompress the stomach and to allow iced saline lavages to be done to provide local hemostasis.

Other therapy may include psychotherapy to help the child identify and deal with environmental stresses that have contributed to the ulcer formation.

Recurrent ulcers may lead to perforation of the ulcer and surgery. The surgery is a gastric resection, often removal of 70 to 80 percent of the stomach, or vagotomy with pyloroplasty. The aim is to reduce the amount of gastric acid. The child and family need support and teaching. Acute bleeding episodes are frightening, and the child and parents require ongoing information concerning tests, treatment, and possible surgery.

Upon discharge, the child and family should be knowledgeable about prescribed drugs and antacids, dietary restrictions, and general health maintenance measures. After a gastric resection, the possibility of dumping syndrome and its treatment should be discussed.

Alterations of the lower gastrointestinal tract

Intestinal atresias

Intestinal atresia is interruption in the continuity of the bowel, resulting in total obstruction. *Intestinal stenosis* is a narrowing or constriction of the bowel, causing incomplete obstruction. Single or multiple areas of atresia or stenosis involving varying lengths of bowel may exist.

Intestinal atresia or stenosis is due to failure of the embryological gut to recanalize. Duodenal obstruction usually occurs in the area where the common bile duct and the pancreatic duct enter. Atresia or stenosis below the duodenum is thought to be caused by ischemic injury to the bowel during intrauterine life.[59]

Clinical manifestations *Duodenal atresia* is the most frequently encountered form of intestinal atresia. This defect produces symptoms in the newborn within a very few hours after birth. Polyhydramnios is usually present before birth. Bile-stained vomiting occurs within the first 24

h of life. Abdominal distention is present intermittently, since the vomiting decompresses the bowel. The neonate fails to continue to pass meconium. Dehydration and weight loss occur rapidly. A flat plate x-ray of the abdomen reveals a "double-bubble" pattern due to the distended duodenum (Fig. 28-8). A significant number of children with Down syndrome have duodenal atresia. *Duodenal stenosis* has clinical manifestations similar to those of atresia. However, symptoms may appear later and may be less severe and more intermittent depending on the degree of stenosis. An upper gastrointestinal barium study may be required to establish a definitive diagnosis.

Jejunal and ileal atresia show more gradual onset of symptoms. Vomiting is less frequent, but larger amounts are lost. Abdominal distention is present and persistent. X-rays show dilated loops of bowel that relate to the length of intestine above the obstruction. A barium enema is performed to determine the presence or absence of large intestine atresia.

Medical management Surgery involves resection and anastomosis of the affected intestinal

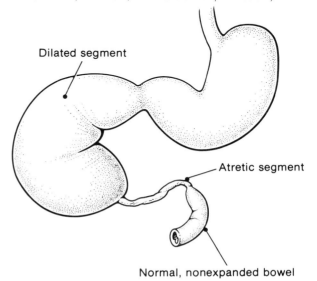

Figure 28-8 The "double-bubble" effect is seen in jejunal atresia due to the relationship of distended bowel to the atretic and normal nonexpanded bowel. (*From Gladys M. Scipien et al.,* Comprehensive Pediatric Nursing, *2d ed., McGraw-Hill, New York, 1979. Used with permission.*)

Dilated segment

Atretic segment

Normal, nonexpanded bowel

segment. One procedure performed for duodenal atresia, a duodenoduodenostomy, surgically joins the proximal and distal segments of the duodenum. Another corrective procedure, a duodenojejunostomy, involves a side-to-side anastomosis between the duodenum and the proximal jejunum. Surgical management of jejunal or ileal atresia includes resection and end-to-end anastomosis. The type of surgery performed depends on the segment of bowel affected. A gastrostomy is also done in conjunction with these procedures.

Some physicians place a transanastomotic catheter through the gastrostomy opening. This catheter extends below the surgical junction and allows for feeding earlier in the postoperative period. Others prefer to use total parenteral nutrition.

Nursing management Preoperatively, gastric decompression and fluid and electrolyte balance are of primary importance. The danger of aspiration is always present for a neonate who vomits persistently. The nurse must position the infant on the abdomen or side to avoid aspiration and observe for signs of this complication. Once the nasogastric tube is inserted, patency must be maintained. Observations for distention include measurement of the infant's abdominal girth. Intravenous fluids to correct imbalances and maintain hydration are initiated. Thermoregulation of neonates is essential, and some may require humidified oxygen if respiratory compromise is evident.

Postoperatively, gastric decompression and parenteral fluids are continued. Oral feedings begin when gastric drainage decreases, bowel sounds are present, and stools are passed. These feedings are initially small amounts of clear liquids. They are advanced slowly to full-strength formula according to the neonate's tolerance.

The nurse should be alert to vomiting, poor intake, diarrhea, and abdominal distention.[60] Special formulas may be necessary if any of these signs appear and persist. Once feedings begin, the nurse must observe stool characteristics and note changes related to feedings. Clinitest, Labstix, and guaiac testing of stools are done routinely.

A transanastomotic catheter requires careful handling to avoid displacement or inadvertent removal. The tube feeding is given slowly to prevent catheter slippage. Vomiting, unusual distention, milk seepage, or milk in the gastrostomy tube after feeding indicate catheter displacement.[61]

Total parenteral nutrition may be utilized for neonates with prematurity, malabsorption, or paralytic ileus, or at the discretion of the physician. Nursing management of the child receiving hyperalimentation is discussed fully in Chap. 23.

Meconium ileus

Meconium ileus, obstruction of the neonate's bowel caused by very thick, sticky meconium, is usually indicative of cystic fibrosis. While this complication occurs in only 15 percent of children who have cystic fibrosis,[62] almost 90 percent of infants with meconium ileus have cystic fibrosis. The meconium is thick and tarry, due to the deficiency of pancreatic enzymes and mucus from intestinal secretory glands. The meconium obstructs the distal ileum. Antenatal perforation can occur and, at birth, the infant then manifests meconium peritonitis.

Clinical manifestations Although the prognosis has improved, neonates with meconium ileus are critically ill. They appear toxic, vomit bile-stained material, and display uneven abdominal distention. Palpation reveals a firm, puttylike consistency to the intestinal contents. These newborns fail to pass meconium.

Diagnosis The diagnosis is difficult to confirm, as the findings mimic those of other intestinal obstructions. A family history of cystic fibrosis may be instrumental in the final determination. X-rays show air bubbles interspersed within the meconium, resulting in a "ground-glass" appearance.

Medical management Recently, Gastrografin enemas have been used to dislodge the impacted meconium. Extreme care must be utilized, as the solution is hypertonic and can promote fluid and electrolyte imbalances.[63] This technique cannot be utilized if bowel perforation is evident. Surgery is indicated if perforation has occurred or if the Gastrografin enemas fail to relieve the obstruction.

There are several surgical procedures that can be used. In some instances, an abdominal incision is made and the meconium is manually extracted, the remaining portion of the bowel is irrigated with warm normal saline, and the abdomen is surgically closed. Often a temporary ileostomy is necessary. A Mikulicz or "stovepipe" ileostomy allows for the irrigation of the intestine postoperatively to dislodge the meconium.

Postoperative nursing management Postoperatively, these neonates require close observation and expert nursing care. Respiratory complications can be prevented through the use of humidification and suctioning of secretions. Chest physiotherapy helps loosen thick pulmonary secretions. Hypothermia is prevented by placing the neonate in an incubator or on a warming table.

The ileostomy may require irrigation if impacted meconium is still evident. Various solutions are used for this purpose. It is important to observe the color and amount of return from the irrigations. The stoma and the peristomal area must be inspected for excoriation and breakdown. The skin must be kept clean and dry.

Feedings are initiated when peristalsis has resumed and the ileostomy is functioning adequately. Hyperalimentation may be used postoperatively until oral intake is sufficient.

Malrotation and volvulus

The cecum normally rotates into the lower right quadrant during the tenth week of gestation. At the same time, the mesentery of the ascending colon attaches to the posterior abdominal wall. Failure of the cecum to assume its normal anatomic position results in *malrotation*. The duodenum is pulled out of position, and partial obstruction occurs. The cecum is maintained in the abnormal position by duodenal bands. The mesentery remains unattached or is only loosely connected and allows the small intestine to twist around it. The twisted loop of intestine (*volvulus*) causes bowel strangulation and obstruction (Fig. 28-9).[64]

Malrotation and volvulus are found primarily in newborns. Only rarely are children over 6 months involved.

Clinical manifestations The clinical manifestations are bile-stained emesis, pain, and diminished or absent stools.[65] Symptoms are proportional to the degree of obstruction. Bowel strangulation may cause mucus and blood to ooze from the rectum. The infant may appear toxic or demonstrate signs of shock. The diagnosis is established by upper gastrointestinal series and barium enema.

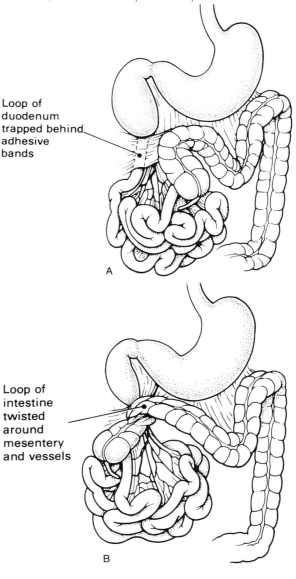

Figure 28-9 Malrotation and volvulus—causes of obstruction. (*A*) Loops of intestine trapped behind the mesentery of the descending colon. (*B*) A loop of intestine around the mesentery. (*From Gladys M. Scipien et al., Comprehensive Pediatric Nursing, 2d ed., McGraw-Hill, New York, 1979. Used with permission.*)

Loop of duodenum trapped behind adhesive bands

A

Loop of intestine twisted around mesentery and vessels

B

Medical management The surgical procedure involves correcting the volvulus, releasing the constricting bands across the duodenum, and freeing the cecum. If the bowel is gangrenous, the affected segment is resected.

Nursing management Both pre- and postoperatively, intravenous fluids and gastric decompression are utilized. Nursing management is essentially the same as previously discussed under postoperative care for children with intestinal surgery.

Meckel's diverticulum

This anomaly is due to the persistence of the embryological vitelline duct. It remains as a small outpouching on the terminal ileum (Fig. 28-10). The diverticulum can become infected, produce obstruction, and cause intussusception or perforation. It may also remain asymptomatic.

A previously healthy child may suddenly pass

Figure 28-10 This outpouching is an example of the type of abnormality present in Meckel's diverticulum. (*From Gladys M. Scipien, et al.,* Comprehensive Pediatric Nursing, *2d ed., McGraw-Hill, New York, 1979. Used with permission.*)

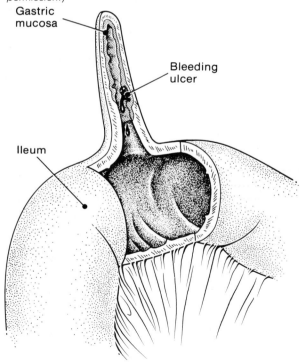

Gastric mucosa

Bleeding ulcer

Ileum

a bloody stool. Bleeding is of large volume and is initially dark, but rapidly becomes bright red with clots. There is no evidence of pain. An abdominal scan using sodium pertechnetate may aid in the diagnosis. However, a negative result does not rule out Meckel's diverticulum. Treatment is resection of the diverticulum and anastomosis.

Nursing management The child's massive bleeding can easily result in shock. Nursing responsibilities include frequent monitoring of vital signs along with blood pressure measurements. The child may have tachycardia and pallor due to blood loss. Transfusions may be necessary. Stool characteristics are also noted, particularly the amount of blood present.

Postoperatively, nursing care is similar to that for children with other intestinal procedures. Recovery is usually uneventful.

Intussusception

Intussusception is the telescoping of one portion of intestine in another, often causing intestinal obstruction (Fig. 28-11). The terminal ileum and ascending colon are the segments most commonly involved. This problem occurs most frequently in healthy, well-nourished male children at approximately 6 months of age, although it can be seen throughout childhood.[66] The child experiences extreme episodic abdominal pain, appears sweaty and pale, vomits reflexively, and tends to draw the legs up toward the abdomen. The pain episodes last 5 to 10 min, after which the child receives temporary relief.

The temporary relief is due to the initially incomplete bowel obstruction. As complete obstruction occurs, vomiting and "currant jelly" stools (blood and mucus) occur, along with abdominal distention. Between attacks of pain, an upper transverse tubular abdominal mass can be palpated.

In the first 1 to 2 days, a barium enema may correct the invagination. The pressure created by the flow of barium pushes out the telescoped bowel. This cannot be used if (1) evidence of complete mechanical small bowel obstruction is present or (2) peritonitis, sepsis, or shock have occurred. Surgery involves manual reduction of the telescoped bowel. Resection is done only if manual reduction fails or the intestine is severely damaged.

Nursing management After barium enema reduction, the child is observed for signs and symptoms of recurrence. Intravenous fluids are administered during this time. If clinical manifestations are absent, oral feedings are resumed within 24 h. The child is discharged shortly thereafter. If surgery is necessary, the usual postoperative care is given. Recovery is usually rapid and uncomplicated.

Ulcerative colitis

Ulcerative colitis, sometimes called *chronic inflammatory disease of the colon*, is characterized by remissions and exacerbations. It affects all age groups, but the peak incidence occurs between the ages of 10 and 28 years.[67] Ulcerative colitis is more severe in children and adolescents, and surgery may be needed earlier than for older age groups. The etiology is unknown, but there is a familial pattern. Males and females are equally affected. Emotional and psychogenic factors may play a role because children with ulcerative colitis tend to be overly dependent and insecure. One suggested cause of ulcerative colitis relates to bacterial invasion producing inflammation; another is that an autoimmune response takes place.[68]

Clinical manifestations The inflammatory process involves the colon mucosa, eventually extending to the submucosa. The rectum is first involved, and the disease progresses proximally. A *crypt* (glandular cavity in the intestines) abscess is the most typical lesion of ulcerative colitis. Ulceration occurs when these lesions become necrotic. The course of the disease is variable. Whaley and Wong describe two pattens of disease. The first is *acute remitting*. The disease produces episodic acute attacks, but between the attacks the child is relatively free of symptoms. There is usually a good response to medical treatment. With time, the disease either terminates or becomes chronic. The second pattern is *chronic continuous*. The disease tends to be milder, but chronic anemia and malnutrition are present. The response to medical treatment is usually poor, and complications are frequent.[69]

The most common clinical manifestations are diarrhea with tenesmus, rectal bleeding, and abdominal pain. *Tenesmus* is the continued feeling of a need to defecate. Pain is usually but not always located in the left lower quadrant.

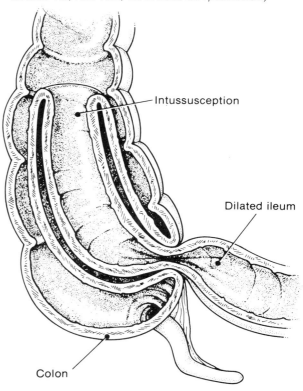

Figure 28-11 The presence of telescoped bowel produces the clinical symptoms in intussusception. (*From Gladys M. Scipien, et al.*, Comprehensive Pediatric Nursing, *2d ed.*, McGraw-Hill, New York, 1979. Used with permission.)

Intussusception

Dilated ileum

Colon

Stools may contain pus, mucus, and blood. Other signs and symptoms include weight loss, nausea, vomiting, fever, and weakness.

Diagnosis Diagnosis begins with a family history. An upper gastrointestinal series with small bowel follow-through is performed, as well as a barium enema. Ulcerations of the colon may be outlined by these studies. A rectal examination is done to rule out other diseases. Sigmoidoscopy and colonoscopy are also done to determine the extent of bowel involvement. A rectal biopsy for the presence of lesions and inflammation aids in the diagnosis.

Medical management The child with a *mild attack* of ulcerative colitis requires rest and dietary management. A low-residue, high-calorie, high-protein diet is necessary. Roughage is restricted during active disease. Sulfasalazine is one of the major therapeutic agents employed in the treatment of ulcerative colitis. It relieves diarrhea and associated symptoms and decreases the number of relapses. Sulfasalazine is introduced gradually due to its gastrointestinal side effects. Anticholinergics are used to relieve muscle spasm, and antidiarrheals may also be prescribed to decrease the frequency of stools. The nurse should be aware of the side effects of such medications and note the child's response to them.

Children with more *severe attacks* require intravenous fluid therapy to correct dehydration and electrolyte imbalance. Albumin, plasma, or blood transfusions may be necessary if severe anemia or hypoalbuminemia exists. Corticosteroids are administered parenterally to control the inflammatory process. Vitamins and iron are given as the child's symptoms subside and solid foods are tolerated. Sulfasalazine is added to the regimen after steroids are discontinued. Electrolyte imbalance can occur rapidly. Potassium and bicarbonate losses are high due to hyperperistalsis and decreased intestinal absorption. Metabolic acidosis can result from these losses.

The child with severe or prolonged symptoms is given nothing by mouth, and parenteral fluids are initiated. Nasogastric intubation and sedation are also required. *Hyperalimentation* is necessary when weight and protein losses are severe. Antibiotics may be added to the treatment protocol to control inflammation and prevent peritonitis.

Toxic megacolon is another indication for the use of antibiotics. This rare complication causes complete bowel obstruction and can produce perforation and peritonitis. Ampicillin, chloramphenicol, and clindamycin are usually employed, although other antibiotics may also be utilized. Arthritis is the most common systemic complication of ulcerative colitis (4 percent of children.)[71]

If conservative measures do not control the inflammatory process or if toxic megacolon, peritonitis, profuse hemorrhage, malignancy, or chronic growth failure occur, surgery is indicated.[72] A total proctocolectomy with ileostomy is done. Resection of only the diseased bowel segment does not stop the inflammatory process. Ileostomy and total colectomy are considered curative for ulcerative colitis.

Nursing management Nursing responsibilities include accurate intake and output measurements, administration of medications and recording of their effects, maintenance of fluid balance, and promotion of physical and emotional rest. It is essential that the nurse record the frequency and characteristics of stool. The child's environment should be as free of stress as possible. Odor control is also important to the child's sense of well-being. Skin care is important, as excoriation easily occurs. The anal area should be washed gently after each bowel movement and ointment applied.

Due to the child's debilitated condition, infection is always a potential hazard. Vital signs are monitored frequently to detect temperature elevation. Abdominal girth measurements are taken to determine distention. The nurse should also be alert for signs and symptoms of obstruction, which may indicate a worsening of the child's state.

Preoperative nursing management Preoperatively, every attempt is made to stabilize the child's condition. Electrolyte and blood values must be corrected to normal limits if the pediatric patient is to withstand the stress of major surgery. The bowel is prepared through the use of neomycin or another agent which affects bacterial flora.

Preparation also includes teaching the child and parents about the surgery and the ileostomy. The nurse must expect to deal with concerns and questions expressed by the child and family. Alterations in body image and in elimination are major issues that need to be explored. The nurse should reassure the child and parents that a normal life can be resumed with minimal, if any, restrictions. The stoma site that accommodates the clothing and activities of the child is selected preoperatively. The child should be shown and wear the appliance that will be used postoperatively.

Postoperative nursing management Fluid and electrolyte balance continues as a primary need postoperatively. Since the portion of bowel that is responsible for absorption of fluids has been removed, the ileostomy drainage is initially very liquid. Sodium losses from the ileostomy are great.[73] The nurse must note any signs of hyponatremia and be aware of the child's possibly low serum sodium level. The absorption of fat-soluble vitamins may also be impaired, and supplements may be necessary.

A nasogastric tube is used for decompression, and patency must be maintained. Drainage from this tube is noted and the amount recorded. This loss is included in the calculation of the child's fluid requirement. The nasogastric tube is removed when peristalsis resumes.

The nurse is responsible for ascertaining the condition of the stoma, the integrity of the peristomal area, and the type and amount of drainage. The ileostomy contents will never resemble formed stool but will gradually become thicker once the child begins to eat a more normal diet.

After peristalsis resumes, the child is allowed to drink clear liquids and, gradually, solids. The feedings are small to give the intestine a period of adjustment. The initial diet is high in protein and carbohydrates and low in residue. However, the child is allowed and even encouraged to consume a liberal diet after the postoperative period. Most children will avoid foods that cause discomfort or diarrhea. Ileostomy care must be taught to the child and parents (see the section on ostomy care). The nurse should take into account the child's concerns regarding body image and loss and expect periods of depression and rebellion as the child adapts to the ileostomy. Parents must also be prepared for their child's mood swings.

Ulcerative colitis is considered a premalignant disease. There is an increased risk of colon cancer in children whose disease began between 5 and 9 years of age and who had widespread colon involvement by the end of the second decade.[74] Those children who do not undergo surgery for ulcerative colitis should have biennial examinations, including sigmoidoscopy. These measures are essential for the early detection of malignant changes.

Crohn's disease

Crohn's disease is also known as *regional enteritis* and differs significantly from ulcerative colitis. Inflammatory changes occur beneath the intestinal mucosa, resulting in destruction and fibrosis of the muscle layer. Granuloma formation is common. There is no sex predilection in Crohn's disease. Abdominal pain and diarrhea are the predominating symptoms. Rectal bleeding is fairly common in children. Systemic signs such as arthritis, arthralgia, anemia, and growth failure may precede gastrointestinal manifestations by several years.

Unlike ulcerative colitis, which affects a continuous bowel segment, regional enteritis affects several parts of the intestine simultaneously. Therefore, the bowel has "cobblestone markings" that are seen on barium swallow. A sigmoidoscopy shows rectal-sparing as opposed to ulcerative colitis, which involves the rectosigmoid area. A rectal biopsy is also done as a component of the diagnostic process. Surgery is not indicated unless severe complications such as perforation, obstruction, or fistulas are present. Recurrences after surgery can be expected.

Nursing management The nursing management of children with Crohn's disease is similar to that for ulcerative colitis. The child may require hospitalization both for evaluation and for hydration. Total parenteral nutrition may be required for severe attacks. A diet high in protein and carbohydrate with limited fat is used to control the diarrhea. If malabsorption is present concurrently, an individualized diet for the child is necessary. Raw fruits and vegetables are eliminated, as well as high-residue foods.

Vitamins, iron, and folic acid are prescribed for deficiencies and anemia. Sulfasalazine is also used in the treatment of Crohn's disease. However, it may not be as effective as in the treatment of ulcerative colitis. Risk of bowel cancer is increased, but less than in ulcerative colitis.

Celiac disease

Celiac disease is second only to cystic fibrosis as a cause of malabsorption in children. The average age of onset is between 9 and 18 months.[75] It is characterized by an inability to digest and absorb gluten, a protein in wheat, oats, rye, and barley. Anorexia, irritability, chronic diarrhea, severe abdominal distention, muscle wasting, and failure to thrive are the clinical manifestations. Stools are bulky, foul-smelling, and contain large amounts of fat (steatorrhea) due to incomplete digestion and absorption. Abdominal pain and vomiting are present in some children.

Anemia is common due to iron, folate, or vitamin B_{12} malabsorption. Serum albumin and globulin studies reveal a protein-losing enteropathy. Hypokalemia is common, and hypocalcemia can lead to tetany in severe cases. Stool analysis shows a high fat composition.

Diagnosis A barium x-ray reveals dilatation of the small intestine lumen and segmentation due to hypersecretion of intestinal fluid. Biopsy of the small intestine shows mucosal changes in the jejunum that confirm the diagnosis of celiac disease.

Nursing management A gluten-free diet is the treatment for celiac disease. Parents must read labels carefully. "HVP," hydrolyzed vegetable products, containing grains are often food additives.[76] The mucosal changes are reversible if the diet is followed. Vitamins and iron are prescribed to correct deficiencies. The anorexic and irritable child is a nursing challenge. Patience and persistence are required for the child to accept a diet high in calories and protein. Small, frequent feedings are better tolerated than a few large ones. Lactose, found in milk products, may also be eliminated for 4 to 6 weeks to allow the mucosa to heal. Rice, soy, and corn flours can be substituted for grain products that contain gluten.

A dietitian should be consulted to help with meal planning. Parents must be taught dietary management to avoid products containing gluten (wheat, rye, barley and oats). They must comprehend the necessity of dietary controls, and the nurse must provide periodic reinforcement and support. The child will begin to gain weight and height once the diet is implemented. The child continues the gluten-free diet for life.[77]

Appendicitis *Appendicitis* is the inflammation of the vermiform appendix and is a common surgical problem of school-age children and adolescents. It is rare in infants. The appendix is located on the cecum and serves no discernible purpose. When the lumen becomes obstructed, the walls of the appendix become inflamed. Infection develops as a result of fecal stasis within the appendix. Perforation and peritonitis can result.

Due to the larger omentum in older children, peritonitis can remain localized to the right lower quadrant or lower abdomen. In young children, a generalized peritonitis results from perforation.[78]

The earliest sign of appendicitis is periumbil-ical pain. Vomiting may follow but is not characteristic. The pain shifts to the right lower quadrant after a few hours. The child has wincing tenderness in the right lower quadrant which progresses to guarding and then rebound tenderness. The temperature may have a low elevation if the appendix has not ruptured. The white blood cell count is usually elevated but does not exceed 20,000. Appendectomy is the surgical treatment.

Nursing management Postoperatively, the child receives intravenous fluids and is given nothing by mouth. A nasogastric tube may be used for gastric decompression. The child must be observed for signs and symptoms of abscess formation such as prolonged operative pain and irritability.

The operative site is examined for inflammation, pain, and drainage. The recovery period for uncomplicated appendectomy is generally short.

Peritonitis The child with a ruptured appendix and peritonitis is severely ill. He or she appears hot and dry, with a temperature elevation of 38.3 to 40°C (101° to 104°F). Vomiting is more frequent after perforation and contains small bowel contents. The right leg may be drawn up in an attempt to relieve the pain. The child may also have a small amount of diarrhea consisting of mucus or slime. Eventually bowel motility will decrease. Peritoneal inflammation leads to plasma loss within the abdominal cavity, and the child becomes dehydrated. An appendectomy is required immediately.

Nursing management Pre- and postoperatively, the child requires intravenous fluids and gastric decompression. A Penrose drain is inserted at the time of surgery to drain exudate. Antibiotics such as ampicillin, gentamicin, and clindamycin are given parenterally for 10 days postoperatively to prevent abscess formation. This treatment modality has significantly decreased the incidence of abdominal and pelvic abscesses.

The child is maintained in a semi- or high Fowler's position to facilitate drainage from the lower abdomen through the Penrose. The nurse must change the dressing as often as necessary. The characteristics of the exudate such as color, odor, and amount must be noted. The drain is advanced, by the physician, over a 1- to 2-week period and finally removed. Continued observation of the operative site is necessary to detect abscess re-formation.

Accurate measurement of intake and output are important nursing responsibilities. Albumin may be necessary to maintain intravascular fluid volume since plasma loss within the abdominal cavity is high. Patency of the nasogastric tube and the intravenous line must be preserved by the nurse. These measures are necessary for a longer period of time as compared to a simple appendectomy. The child is given nothing by mouth until the peritoneal inflammation subsides and stooling resumes.

The recovery period for the child with peritonitis is prolonged. The bed rest restriction limits interactions with other patients. The nurse should spend time with the child engaged in quiet activities. The child needs reassurance that the condition will improve and that normal activities can be resumed.

Hirschsprung's disease

This disease is characterized by constipation and megacolon. It is caused by the congenital absence of parasympathetic nerve ganglion cells. The aganglionic segment extends from the internal anal sphincter through varying lengths of rectum and colon (Fig. 28-12). The rectosigmoid area is the site most frequently affected. There is a 4:1 ratio of boys to girls. It is not uncommon for two or three siblings to have Hirschsprung's disease.

The diseased bowel segment lacks peristalsis and is unable to propel fecal material through the colon. The normal bowel proximal to it becomes greatly dilated (megacolon) in an attempt to move the accumulated fecal mass. Hyperperistalsis develops in the dilated bowel due to the functional obstruction of the affected segment.

In the neonate, manifestations range from complete intestinal obstruction to intermittent episodes of distention, feeding difficulties, and various degrees of constipation. Failure or delay in passing meconium, abdominal distention, and bile-stained vomitus are suspicious signs. Digital rectal examination results in immediate evacuation of meconium with or without the meconium plug.[79] Those infants with complete obstruction require immediate surgery. The diagnosis in newborns with intermittent problems may not

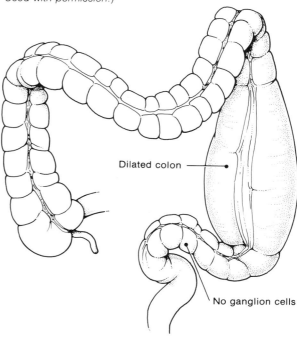

Figure 28-12 Notice the portion of the intestine without ganglia distal to the dilated colon typical of Hirschsprung's disease. (*From Gladys M. Scipien, et al.,* Comprehensive Pediatric Nursing, *2d ed., McGraw-Hill, New York, 1979. Used with permission.*)

Dilated colon

No ganglion cells

be made until intestinal obstruction or severe, persistent constipation occurs later in infancy.

The older child displays failure to thrive, a protuberant abdomen, chronic constipation, and megacolon. Anorexia and muscle wasting are related to poor intake and protein loss. Diarrhea may occur in both infants and older children as a result of liquid stool seeping around the fecal impaction. However, significant diarrhea may indicate the onset of enterocolitis. This complication can occur at any time and is the major cause of death in untreated infants.[80] Sudden abdominal distention, fever, dehydration, and shock are the manifestations of enterocolitis.

Diagnosis A barium enema aids in the diagnosis by outlining the dilated bowel segment. The usual bowel preparation before the enema is omitted, as it alters the radiologic picture. A rectal biopsy confirms the absence of ganglionic nerve cells. Abdominal x-rays show a distended colon that ends in an unexpanded rectum.

Medical management Medical management of Hirschsprung's disease involves the use of colonic irrigations and anal dilatations, discussed earlier in this chapter. These procedures are used with children in poor condition until a colostomy can be done. Definitive procedures in neonates are postponed until 4 to 6 months of age. A temporary colostomy is performed for elimination until definitive surgery can be undertaken.

The *Duhamel procedure* involves resecting the distended segment, and bringing normal bowel down to a surgically created retrorectal space. This segment is pulled through the posterior rectal wall and sutured side by side to the rectum. Crushing clamps are placed on the common wall, which sloughs in 5 to 8 days after surgery.[81] This anastomosis creates a new rectum with aganglionic rectum anteriorly and ganglionic colon posteriorly. The external sphincter remains intact.

The *Soave procedure* involves resection of the aganglionic bowel with separation of the mucosal layer of the rectum. This layer is then excised and a rectal cuff remains. The normal bowel is brought down through this conduit and is allowed to protrude. A spontaneous or autoanastomosis forms in 15 to 20 days. After this time, the protruding bowel is excised and the anastomosis is sutured. A rectal tube is in place from the time of surgery.

A *modified Soave procedure* involves the same principles, except that the normal bowel is sutured to the rectal cuff at the time of surgery and the protruding bowel is also excised.[83] The colostomy can be closed at the time of this surgery or a few months later.

Nursing management Preoperatively, bowel preparation is essential. Colonic irrigations are continued, with neomycin or kanamycin added to the solution. These drugs may also be given orally to suppress intestinal flora. A clear liquid diet is given for 24 to 48 h prior to surgery.

Postoperatively, intravenous fluids are required for several days. Gastric decompression is managed by insertion of a nasogastric tube. Perineal care is important for the child's comfort. Small amounts of bloody drainage or dark mucus are usually expelled from the anus. This area must be kept clean and dry. If a Soave procedure has been performed, the rectal tube must not be disturbed.

Stooling resumes approximately 4 days postoperatively and is usually liquid. The number and characteristics of the feces are observed and recorded. Large volumes of fluid and electrolytes can be lost, and it is important to have accurate measurements. Assessment of stool characteristics aids in establishing whether intestinal functioning is progressing toward normal or is compromised. Clinitest, Labstix, and guaiac tests are done routinely.

The child needs to be observed in the postoperative period for signs and symptoms of anastomosis breakdown or leakage. Sudden abdominal distention, fever, and irritability may signal the presence of this complication. Some children have intermittent periods of abdominal distention due to an inability to evacuate. Gentle insertion of a rectal tube will alleviate the problem. The diet initially consists of clear liquids and is gradually advanced to normal. If any foods contribute to diarrhea, they are avoided temporarily.

The success of surgery cannot be determined until the child reaches the toilet-training stage. Parents should receive support from the nurse during toilet training, as it may be very stressful for them. Long-range problems include staining, constipation, and delays in toilet training. The overwhelming majority of children experience satisfactory surgical results. However, perfect bowel function is not always attained.

Encopresis

Encopresis is a psychogenic dysfunction in which the child displays chronic constipation and persistent soiling. A functional megacolon develops as the result of stool retention. However, there are significant differences between the child with encopresis and one with Hirschsprung's disease. Table 28-4 compares encopresis and Hirschsprung's disease. There is disagreement over treatment modalities for this problem. However, the fecal impaction must be evacuated before any therapy can be instituted.

Family and/or child emotional disturbances are sometimes encountered in encopresis but are not necessarily its cause. Parents are involved in the training program once the initial bowel cleansing has been done. To prevent reimpaction, a regimen of cathartics and a high-fiber diet, along with specified toileting times, is instituted. Gradually, medications are eliminated from the program. Several months are required for the bowel training to be successful.

Nursing management Both parents and child require nursing support to deal with this difficult problem. The child should be praised for using the toilet appropriately. Incontinence is handled tactfully. Criticism or punishment for soiling is not effective. One approach is to have these children rinse out their clothes and clean themselves after soiling.

Consistent application of the regimen is essential for success. The nurse should reinforce this continuity with parents and praise both the child and family for their efforts.

Encopresis is further discussed in Chap. 40.

Imperforate anus

This disorder is the result of imperfect fusion of the entodermal cloaca with the proctodeum. (Refer to embryology of the gastrointestinal tract for further discussion.) Imperforate anus manifests itself in several different ways, but is commonly divided into high and low types designating whether or not the rectum passes through the puborectalis muscle (see Fig. 28-13 for the types and frequency of occurrence). Type III defects, high or low agenesis, are by far the most common. Fistulas to the vagina and rectum may coexist with imperforate anus.

Definitive diagnosis is accomplished by holding the infant with the head downward while an x-ray of the abdomen is taken. This position allows gas in the colon to rise and outline the blind rectal pouch and its distance from the anal opening.

The low anomalies may be treated surgically by removing the anal membrane, anoplasty, and anal dilatation. The high anomalies require more extensive surgery over many years. The degree of surgical difficulty is directly proportional to the space between the anus and the rectal pouch. A colostomy is performed in the neonate until definitive treatment can be undertaken. When the infant is 12 to 18 months of age, a pull-through procedure such as those discussed with Hirschsprung's disease can be performed. Studies which evaluate the innervation status of the pelvic muscles should be done prior to the pull-through procedure. Bowel continence is dependent on the levator ani muscle sling. If nerve impulses are weak or lacking, continence will

Table 28-4 Comparison of encopresis and Hirschsprung's disease

Encopresis		Hirschsprung's disease
Cause:	Psychogenic	Absence of colon ganglion cells
Onset:	Acquired at approximately 2 years of age	Neonatal period
Stools:	Large, formed	Small ribbons or liquid stools
	Incontinent Soiling	No soiling or incontinence
General state:	Healthy	Anorexic, muscle wasting, anemia, growth retardation

not be achieved and a permanent colostomy would be preferable.

Nursing management Frequently, the nurse discovers that the neonate has an imperforate anus when attempting to insert a rectal thermometer. Newborns may also develop signs of obstruction such as vomiting and distention. Postoperatively, the infant who has an anoplasty is positioned on the side to prevent tension on the suture line. The diaper is left off, and the area must be kept clean and dry. Ointments are not used, and nothing should be inserted into the rectum. Dilatation is initiated once healing has begun and is continued at home. Parents must be taught this procedure.

If a colostomy has been done, the infant will have a nasogastric tube and an intravenous line. These are continued until peristalsis resumes. Parents need to learn colostomy care prior to the infant's discharge. To allay their anxieties, they also should receive an explanation for the reasons that definitive surgery is postponed.

Nursing care of the child after the pull-through procedure is similar to that discussed previously for Hirschsprung's disease. Continence cannot be assessed until the child is older. A second procedure may be necessary to replace the colon in the puborectalis sling if bowel continence has not been completely achieved. Anal dilatations are necessary after the pull-through procedure and are continued at home. Parents need support during the toilet-training period, as they have many concerns in regard to the child's

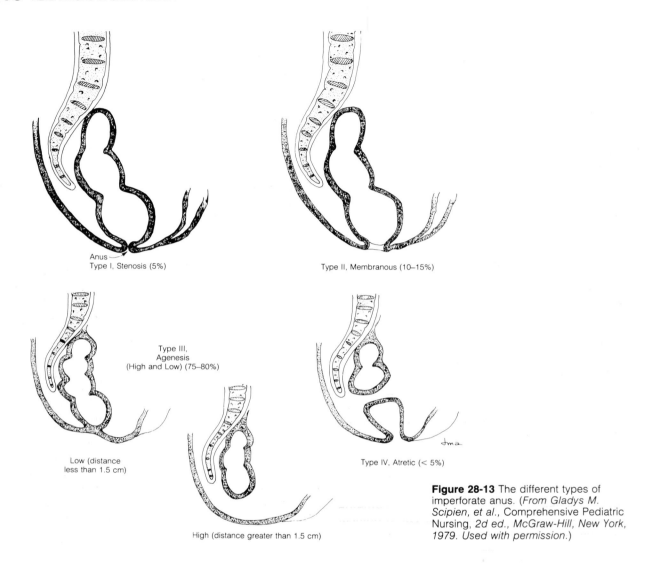

Anus
Type I, Stenosis (5%)

Type II, Membranous (10–15%)

Type III,
Agenesis
(High and Low) (75–80%)

Low (distance
less than 1.5 cm)

Type IV, Atretic (< 5%)

High (distance greater than 1.5 cm)

Figure 28-13 The different types of imperforate anus. (*From Gladys M. Scipien, et al.,* Comprehensive Pediatric Nursing, *2d ed., McGraw-Hill, New York, 1979. Used with permission.*)

ability to master this task.[83] These children and their parents should receive long-term follow-up by nursing personnel.

Hernias

Inguinal hernia *Inguinal hernia* is the prolapse of a portion of the intestine through the inguinal ring. The prolapse occurs as a result of a congenital weakness or an incomplete closure of the inguinal ring. During fetal development, about the eighth month, the testes descend with a portion of the peritoneum down the inguinal canal. This tract, called the *processus vaginalis,* closes and atrophies except for the peritoneum enclosing the testes in the scrotum. Incomplete closure can allow intestine or fluid to enter the scrotum. Ninety percent of the inguinal hernias occur in boys, usually under 5 years of age.[83] There is a high incidence in prematures, frequently associated with hydroceles and undescended testicles. Infrequently, inguinal hernias occur in females. The processus vaginalis in girls extends from the external inguinal ring to the labia minora.[84] Usually hernias produce few symptoms. When a child cries vigorously or strains, a bulging mass can be felt or the hernia becomes larger.

Medical management Hernias can become incarcerated or strangulated. An incarcerated or strangulated hernia becomes tightly bound in the inguinal ring. The blood supply to the bound intestine may be cut off, and bowel necrosis can occur. To prevent bowel damage, the hernia must be reduced (moved back out of the inguinal ring). The child is placed in the Trendelenburg position and ice is applied to the scrotum. Sedation may be necessary because pain can become intense. The hernia is usually manually reduced, but surgery will be done when the edema subsides.

When hernias are diagnosed at birth, surgery is usually done at 1 to 2 months or as soon thereafter as the infant's condition permits. Inguinal hernia repair is not a complicated surgery and in some settings is done on an outpatient basis.

Postoperative nursing management Postoperatively, the child is allowed to ambulate freely. The biggest nursing challenge is keeping the operative site clean and dry. Frequent diaper changes and careful attention to hygiene are necessary.

Umbilical hernia *Umbilical hernia* is the bulging of the intestine at the umbilicus. The umbilical ring that allowed the umbilical cord to penetrate the abdominal wall usually closes soon after birth. When an umbilical hernia is present, the umbilical ring remains as an opening of varying size. Strangulation is rare with umbilical hernias. Most of these begin to regress and gradually close as crawling and walking strengthen the abdominal muscles. The home remedies once commonly used are of no benefit. Assure parents that taping the umbilicus and using "belly binders" will not prevent or cure umbilical hernias. Surgery is indicated if the defect persists past the age of 5 years.

Postoperatively, the child will have a large pressure dressing over the abdomen. This is left in place for a week to 10 days. The hospital stay is 2 or 3 days.

Alterations of the liver
Normal liver function
The liver is essential for health and accomplishes multiple functions in the healthy child. Table 28-5 lists liver functions and some of the effects of impairment.

Liver dysfunction
Disease or obstruction of the liver can result in cell death, fibrosis, scarring, and decreased efficiency of function.

The liver is a very vascular organ, supplied with blood from two main sources: the portal vein and the hepatic arteries. Blood from the digestive tract normally passes through the portal veins to the portal circulation of the liver and then to the inferior vena cava and back to the heart. Obstruction of the portal blood flow whether due to disease inside (*intrahepatic*) or outside the liver (*extrahepatic*) leads to the development of increased portal pressure (*portal hypertension*).

The blood flowing through the portal veins is impeded by this pressure and forced to use an alternative route in its return to the vena cava. This results in the development of *collateral circulation*. The blood uses the collateral circulation provided by veins at the cardia of the stomach and lower esophagus, umbilicus, anus, and retroperitoneum.

As the pressure within the venous portal system increases due to obstruction or disease of the liver, it results in a large, tense liver, esophageal and gastric varices, hemorrhoids, distended umbilical veins, and ascites. The major danger is rupture of the varices and hemorrhage resulting in shock and death.

Diagnostic tests The laboratory tests used to diagnose liver disease will reflect the liver function impairment listed in Table 28-5. The tests usually done are:

Clotting function tests
Albumin levels
Bilirubin levels
Blood ammonia (NH_3) level and BUN
Blood glucose
Serum enzyme levels
A. SGOT (serum glutamic oxaloacetic transaminase) is an enzyme found in the liver and heart. Acute cell destruction will cause an increase after about

8 h with a peak in 24 to 36 h and decrease in 4 to 6 days.

B. SGPT (serum glutamic pyruvic transaminase) is an enzyme found only in the liver, but this laboratory test is not as sensitive an indicator as SGOT.

C. Serum alkaline phosphatase is an enzyme produced in the liver and bone and excreted in the bile. Its level in the blood is increased if the biliary pathways are obstructed.

Liver biopsy and liver and spleen scans are commonly done. A frequently done radioisotope test is the I 131 rose bengal test. With the rose bengal test, it is possible to measure the amount of dye that is excreted and to locate the biliary obstruction.

Medical management *Conservative management* of liver dysfunction includes promotion of nutrition, rest, protection from infection and trauma, and comfort measures. The diet will be limited in proteins and fats and high in carbohydrates. Additional fat-soluble vitamins, iron preparations, and intramuscular vitamin K will be needed. If the child is admitted to the hospital with bleeding, transfusions may be required.

Clinical symptoms seen in the child are jaundice, edema, ascites, portal hypertension, esophageal varices, dry, itching skin, splenomegaly, and color changes in the stool (clay-colored) and urine (dark). In children with portal hypertension, massive hemorrhage with symptoms of vomiting of blood and melena may be seen as early as 7 years old.[85] Control of bleeding from esophageal varices is essentially the same as for adults. The major method of control is gastric compression by the use of the Sengstaken-Blakemore tube.

Table 28-5 Summary of liver functions and the results of impaired function

Liver function	Results of impairment
Synthesis of fibrinogen, prothrombin, and clotting factors V, VII, IX, X	Clotting times and prothrombin and partial thromboplastin times are prolonged Bleeds and bruises easily Possibly hemorrhage Possible melena
Synthesis of albumin	Decreased albumin levels Edema and ascites result
Production of enzymes (SGOT, SGPT, LDH, alkaline phosphatase)	Elevated enzymes released from damaged liver cells
Metabolize and conjugate bilirubin	Increased bilirubin levels 　Indirect indicates damage to the cells 　Direct indicates a problem in the ducts Jaundice, itching
Deamination of amino acids to ammonia to urea	Increased levels of ammonia Confusion, toxic encephalopathy Hepatic coma
Drug metabolism and detoxification	Increased toxic levels of drugs Smaller dosages than normal are needed
Production of bile (pigments)	Stools white or clay-colored Reduced bile to intestines and impaired fat digestion
Storage of glycogen	Hypoglycemia
Metabolism of fats, proteins, and carbohydrates	Decreased metabolism and utilization of foods Reduced glycogen
Storage of vitamins and iron	Avitaminosis
Bile for absorption of fat-soluble vitamins (A, D, E, and K)	Anemia D—possible rickets K—not absorbed in intestines; influences clotting factors that require vitamin K for formation
Filtration, detoxification, excretion of corticosteroids (ADH and aldosterone)	Poor detoxification causes accumulation in the body Sodium retention and potassium loss

Surgery is usually done in children with severe hemorrhaging from esophageal varices. The surgical objective is to divert the blood through another pathway, around the liver, and thereby to relieve the pressure on the gastrointestinal tract. The *portocaval shunt* has the highest success rate and is done in children over 5 years old with intrahepatic obstruction. The portal vein is anastomosed to the inferior vena cava, thus bypassing the liver. The *splenorenal shunt* joins the splenic vein to the renal vein. It is used with extrahepatic obstruction. The splenic vein is too small to be used in children under 10 years old.

Biliary atresia

Etiology and diagnosis *Biliary atresia* is the failure of the biliary ducts to develop or may be related to an infection causing fibrotic changes in the liver.[86] Obstruction of the ducts, inside or outside the liver, is present, and as a result, bile builds up in the liver. It cannot be absorbed and causes jaundice, itching, and other symptoms of liver impairment

The primary symptom is persistent jaundice continuing in the newborn after 2 weeks of age. The direct bilirubin is elevated, and the stools are white or clay-colored and puttylike in consistency. The urine is dark. Laboratory studies reveal anemia, elevation of the serum alkaline phosphatase, and increased clotting times. Later (a few months to a year), fibrotic changes occur within the liver, leading to cirrhosis and the development of portal hypertension.[87] Enlarged spleen, esophageal varices, and ascites appear. As the child grows older, the skin color becomes more greenish gray or bronze, and itching becomes intense due to the buildup of bile salts. Growth is impaired, with malnutrition, especially hypoproteinemia, and wasting due to nutritional deficits. Hyperammonemia can result in hepatic coma and eventually death.[88]

The diagnosis is made using the rose bengal test, which is positive with biliary atresia. A liver biopsy and an exploratory laparotomy are done to evaluate the level of biliary obstruction.

Medical management Medical treatment is determined by the cause of the atresia. if the obstruction is in the extrahepatic systems, cholangiography and surgery may be used to remove it. If the problem is intrahepatic, palliative surgery such as portal-vena-caval shunts may be done. The ultimate treatment would be a liver transplant. This treatment, however, is still in the experimental stages. The prognosis for children with biliary atresia is very poor, and only about 5 percent survive early childhood.[89] The majority die during the second year of life.

Nursing management Nursing care is directed toward promoting nutrition and comfort for the infant. Intravenous fluids may be used until the infant has stabilized after the diagnostic workup. Feedings are then initiated. There is an increased risk of pulmonary infections, so frequent suctioning and turning are indicated. Vitamin K, needed for the synthesis of prothrombin, is given either parenterally or orally, and any signs of bleeding are noted. Gentle handling is necessasry to prevent trauma and bruising. Vitamin D, usually stored by the liver, is supplemented to prevent the development of rickets.

The skin is edematous, and the increase in bile salts causes intense pruritus, resulting in a fussy, irritable infant. Cholestyramine and antihistamines (Benedryl) may be used to decrease discomfort. Frequent cool or tepid baths, lotions, careful cutting of the fingernails, and mittens on the hands will prevent scratching and subsequent skin infections. The infant seems so uncomfortable that the mother may need additional encouragement to hold and cuddle the infant. The family is faced with frequent hospitalizations of the infant in future years with infections and bleeding difficulties. The parents need emotional support because this anomaly has essentially a terminal prognosis.

Nursing Care Plan—Cleft Lip Surgery

Patient: James Martin   **Age:** 3 months, 3 days   **Date of Admission:** 7/1 at 4:30 P.M.

Assessment

James Martin, age 3 months and 3 days, was admitted to the pediatric unit on 7/1. The reason for hospitalization was primary repair of unilateral cleft lip, which was performed 7/2. The infant has no history of hospitalization. He has no known allergies. His parents are married, and there are no siblings.

General appearance

Healthy, well-nourished, active infant. Weight 4.5 kg 84 g. Birth weight 3.15 kg 280 g. Height 57.5 cm. Alert and responsive to people.

Physical examination

Temp. 37.5°C (99.4°F) (R); P: 126, R: 30. BP not obtained

Health history

Diagnosed at birth to have unilateral left cleft lip and cleft palate. He is the first child of young (22-year-old) parents; there is a paternal family history of cleft lip. He has had two colds and one episode of otitis media. Both parents seem to be dealing well with the baby, holding, cuddling, playing with, and feeding the child. Immunizations have not been started.

Diet and elimination

Takes 112–208 ml of Enfamil with iron 4–5 times per day. Rice cereal added to the first feeding of the day. Lamb's nipple has been used, but has been fed with Asepto syringe for the last week. Takes about 30–35 min to eat. Both parents are comfortable in feeding the child. Voids 8–10 times per day and stools once per day—soft, brown, formed.

Sleep

Usually sleeps through the night, but may wake once during night. Mother gives him formula and he readily falls asleep.

Skin

Intact, pink, warm. Cleft of lip on left side—complete and extends into nostril. Buttocks—pinpoint maculopapular rash on inner thighs and buttocks.

Respiratory

Lungs clear to auscultation. Respirations regular, easy.

Neurologic

Normal reflexes for infant this age.

Growth and development

Smiles socially; beginning to roll over by self; babbles; sucks left fingers.

Family history

Father recently laid off from work. Blue Cross/Blue Shield in force temporarily. Live in apartment—baby has own room.

Laboratory data

Hbg 12 g; Hct 36%; WBC 4500. Urine clear and without WBC. Chest x-ray clear.

Postoperative orders

Surgery done 7/2. Postoperative orders include:

1. Mist tent for 24 h.
2. NPO until alert, then start clear liquids per Asepto; advance diet as tolerated.
3. IV fluids: D_5/0.2 NS to run at 15 ml/h. Discontinue when taking fluids well.
4. Arm restraints at all times.
5. Cleanse incision with hydrogen peroxide and normal saline and then apply bacitracin tid and prn.

Nursing diagnosis	Goals	Nursing actions	Evaluation/revision
1. Potential for respiratory complications due to anesthesia, cleft palate, and poor immune system of infancy	☐ Infant's lungs will remain clear to auscultation, with normal temperature, no cough, normal respiratory	☐ Note respiratory rate, color, and breath sounds every hour until stable, then q2h	☐ 7/2—11 P.M.: T increased to 38.3°C (101°F) Ice placed in croupette. Temp. 38.3 at 1 A.M. Lungs clear, respira-

Nursing diagnosis	Nursing goals	Nursing actions	Evaluation/revision
	rate, and clear chest x-ray	☐ Turn from side to side q2h ☐ Check mist tent for misting every 2 h; check linens for dampness ☐ Temperature, rectal, q4h ☐ Suction only if absolutely necessary	tory rate 32. No cough or excess secretions ☐ 7/3—12 noon: Respirations stable and no stridor or dyspnea. Temp. 37.8°C (100°F) at 11 A.M. Mist tent discontinued
2. Potential shock due to hemorrhage from surgery	☐ The infant's pulse and respiratory rate will remain within normal limits. The infant's hematocrit and hemoglobin will remain within normal preoperative limits	☐ Apical pulse and respiratory rate every hour until stable, then q2h ☐ Note any bleeding from wound ☐ Note color, skin temperature, and urinary output frequently	☐ 7/3: Pulse and respirations stable; VS now q4h. No visible bleeding. Color pink, and good urinary output. Hct 36
3. Potential for infection of wound	☐ The surgical site will remain intact and have normal wound healing without signs of infection or bleeding	☐ Arm restraints at all times. Remove q4h to check skin and circulation. Logan bar in place ☐ Place on side or back—*not* abdomen ☐ Cleanse lip with hydrogen peroxide and normal saline after feeding and apply bacitracin—sterile technique ☐ Check for signs of infection—temperature, erythema, purulent drainage ☐ Try to prevent crying and fussing	☐ 7/3: No signs of bleeding and incision intact. Incision being cleansed and appears clean and supple
4. Decreased hydration due to decreased fluids with surgery	☐ The infant will have adequate hydration, as indicated by good urinary output, good skin turgor, moist mucous membranes, normal pulse	☐ IV fluids—D_5/0.2 NS to run at 15 ml/h. Check rate hourly. Note signs of circulatory overload ☐ When alert, and bowel sounds present, start feeding with glucose water via Asepto. If retained, continue feedings and work up to normal formula, feeding q4h ☐ D/C IV when taking fluids well ☐ Check urinary output, skin turgor, mucous membranes	☐ 7/3: Taking clear liquids well; tolerated one feeding of half-strength Enfamil with iron. IV has been discontinued. Good urinary output, good skin turgor and moist mucous membranes
5. Disruption of skin integrity on buttocks due to diaper rash	☐ The infant's skin will be intact, pink, and healthy	☐ Cleanse buttocks well after every voiding. Check diapers frequently and change ☐ Air-dry buttocks 20 min, tid ☐ Apply A and D ointment at each diaper change	☐ 7/3: Diaper rash is decreasing

Nursing diagnosis	Nursing goals	Nursing actions	Evaluation/revision
6. Increased parental anxiety due to surgery and financial worries	☐ The parents will have decreased anxiety as seen by fewer questions, fewer verbal and nonverbal expressions of anxiety	☐ Explain surgery and keep them informed of all procedures and tests. Answers all questions as fully as possible ☐ Encourage visiting and caring for the child ☐ Explore any concerns they may have, i.e., finances	☐ 7/3: Parents remained concerned, but less than immediately after the surgery. They did express worry about finances; a social services referral has been initiated
7. Parental discharge teaching needed for care of child's lip repair and health maintenance	☐ The parents will demonstrate knowledge of health maintenance and discharge teaching	☐ Review immunizations—need and schedule ☐ Discuss growth and development—play, safety, normal milestones ☐ Discharge instructions regarding feeding, restraints, lip care, signs of infection, diaper rash	☐ 7/3: Plan to do this 2 days prior to discharge. Need to discuss future plans also—work with cleft lip/palate team and future surgeries for lip and palate
8. Promotion of normal growth and development	☐ The infant will exhibit normal growth and development, as seen by achieving the normal motor and social milestones	☐ Mobiles in crib. No toys which could injure mouth ☐ Sing, talk to, hold, and cuddle with feedings and when awake ☐ Encourage parents to visit frequently and care for and play with child ☐ Crib rails up at all times ☐ Discussion of normal growth and development with parents after assessing their level of knowledge and needs	☐ 7/3: Child seems happy and smiles in response to parents. Parents are visiting frequently

References

1. Jan Langman, *Medical Embryology*, 2d ed., Williams & Wilkins, Baltimore, 1969, p. 257.
2. Ibid.
3. Lyllis Ling and Sarah P. McCamman, "Dietary Treatment of Diarrhea and Constipation in Infants and Children," *Issues in Comprehensive Pediatric Nursing*, 3:24 (1978).
4. John G. Raffensperger, and Susan R. Luck, "Gastrointestinal Bleeding in Children," *Surgical Clinics of North America*, 56:413 (1976).
5. Katharine M. Jones, "Love and Lavage," *Nursing '78* 8:35 (1978).
6. Edwina A. McConnell, "Ensuring Safer Stomach Suctioning with the Salem Sump Tube," *Nursing '77* 7:54 (1977).
7. Ibid., 56.
8. Rosemary C. Watt, "Ostomies: Why, How and Where," *Nursing Clinics of North America* 11:396 (1976).
9. Lester W. Martin, Alice Gilmore, Judith Peckham, and Jean Baumer, "Nursing Care of Infants with Esophageal Anomalies," *American Journal of Nursing* 66:2462–2468 (1966).
10. Joyce Gryboski, *Gastrointestinal Problems in the Infant*, Saunders, Philadelphia, 1975, p. 23.
11. Ibid., p. 28.
12. Lucille F. Whaley, and Donna L. Wong, *Nursing Care of Infants and Children*, Mosby, St. Louis, 1979, p. 395.
13. Victor Vaughan et al., *Nelson Textbook of Pediatrics*, 11th ed., Saunders, Philadelphia, 1979, p. 1028.
14. Whaley and Wong, op. cit., p. 397.
15. Gladys M. Scipien et al., *Comprehensive Pediatric Nursing*, 2d ed., McGraw-Hill, New York, 1979, p. 768.
16. Ibid., p. 397.
17. Ibid., p. 398.
18. Ibid., p. 399.
19. Gryboski, op. cit., p. 34.
20. Whaley and Wong, op. cit., p. 395.
21. Vaughan et al., op. cit., p. 1028.
22. Whaley and Wong, op. cit., p. 398.

23. Scipien et al., op. cit., p. 770.
24. Vaughan et al., op. cit., p. 1029.
25. Whaley and Wong, op. cit., p. 401.
26. Ibid.
27. Vaughan et al., op. cit., p. 1040.
28. Gryboski, op. cit., p. 58.
29. Vaughan et al., op. cit., p. 1041.
30. Gryboski, op. cit., pp. 58–59.
31. Vaughan et al., op. cit., p. 1041.
32. Ibid.
33. Scipien et al., op. cit., p. 761.
34. Vaughan et al., op. cit., p. 1050.
35. Ibid.
36. Ibid.
37. Ibid., p. 1051.
38. R. Hoekelman et al., eds., *Principles of Pediatrics: Health Care of the Young*, McGraw-Hill, New York, 1978, p. 754.
39. Vaughan et al., op. cit., p. 1051.
40. Ibid.
41. Ibid.
42. Hoeckelman et al., op. cit., p. 755.
43. Vaughan et al., op. cit., p. 1052.
44. Ibid.
45. Ibid.
46. Ibid.
47. Ann Brueggemeyer, "Omphalocele: Coping with a Surgical Emergency," *Pediatric Nursing* 5:54–56 (1979).
48. Scipien et al., op. cit., p. 767.
49. Ibid., p. 765.
50. Brueggemeyer, op. cit., 54.
51. Scipien et al., op. cit. p. 767.
52. Brueggemeyer, op. cit., p. 55.
53. Gryboski, op. cit., p. 75.
54. Vaughan et al., op. cit., p. 1140.
55. Whaley and Wong, op. cit., p. 408.
56. Scipien et al., op. cit., p. 759.
57. Catherine Kneut, "Acute Stress Ulcers in Children," *Issues in Comprehensive Pediatric Nursing* 3:41–50 (1978).
58. Ibid., 42.
59. Richard S. Snell, *Clinical Embryology for Medical Students*, Little, Brown, Boston, 1975, p. 165.
60. Scipien et al., op. cit., p. 765.
61. Ibid.
62. Hoekelman et al., op. cit., p. 795.
63. Ibid., p. 796.
64. Scipien et al., op. cit., p. 777.
65. Ibid.
66. Hoekelman et al., op. cit., p. 847.
67. Ibid., p. 832.
68. Whaley and Wong, op. cit., p. 1281.
69. Ibid.
70. Vaughan et al., op. cit., p. 1096.
71. Hoekelman et al., op. cit., p. 833.
72. Vaughan et al., op. cit., p. 1101.
73. Barbara A. Given, and Sandra J. Simmons, *Gastroenterology in Clinical Nursing*, Mosby, St. Louis, 1979, p. 292.
74. Hoekelman et al., op. cit., p. 836.
75. Ibid., p. 813.
76. Vaughan et al., op. cit., p. 1085.
77. Vaughan et al., op. cit., p. 1085.
78. Scipien et al., op. cit., p. 787.
79. Vaughan et al., op. cit., p. 1057.
80. S. Kleinhaus et al., "Hirschsprung's Disease," a survey from the surgical section of the American of Pediatrics. Presented at the Section on Surgery, twenty-fifth and twenty-sixth annual meetings of the American Academy of Pediatrics, 1976 and 1977.
81. Snell, op. cit., p. 170.
82. Scipien et al., op. cit., p. 764.
83. Vaughan et al., op. cit., p. 1107.
84. Ibid.
85. Hoekelman et al., op. cit., p. 772.
86. Vaughan et al., op. cit., p. 1117.
87. Scipien et al., op. cit., p. 778.
88. Vaughan et al., op. cit., p. 1116.
89. Hoekelman et al., op. cit., p. 773.

Chapter 29 **Hormone regulation**

Patricia J. Salisbury

Upon completion of the chapter, the student will be able to:

1. Describe negative feedback as it applies to the endocrine system.

2. List the glands in the endocrine system.

3. Describe the pathophysiology of hypopituitarism.

4. List four actions to be taken to assure proper administration of Pitressin.

5. Discuss the nursing care involved with a water deprivation test.

6. Discuss the nursing care involved with a growth hormone stimulation test.

7. Discuss at least four areas of teaching to be covered with the family of a child with precocious puberty.

8. Identify at least five signs of hypothyroidism in infants.

9. Discuss the nursing care of the hypothyroid child when initially treated.

10. Discuss the nursing care of the hyperthyroid child when initially treated.

11. Discuss the nursing care of the child undergoing thyroidectomy.

12. Describe the functions of the hormones secreted by the cortex and medulla of the adrenal gland.

13. List at least five symptoms of hypoadrenocorticism.

14. Describe the pathophysiology of congenital adrenal hyperplasia.

15. List at least five physical symptoms of Cushing's syndrome.

16. Discuss the nursing care of the adrenalectomy patient.

17. Describe the pathophysiology of diabetes mellitus.

18. Describe the pathophysiology of ketoacidosis.

19. Compare and contrast short-, intermediate-, and long-acting insulins.

20. Discuss the nursing care of the patient in ketoacidosis.

21. Compare first-void and second-void urines.

22. List at least four principles of insulin injection.

23. Compare and contrast hypoglycemia and hyperglycemia.

The endocrine system is composed of a number of glands located throughout the body that are responsible for growth, maturation, reproduction, metabolic processes, and the reaction of the body to stress. The endocrine system controls these processes through the secretion of *hormones*, which are chemical substances released directly into the bloodstream.

Some endocrine glands—the thyroid, parathyroids, thymus, pancreas, adrenals, and gonads (ovaries and testes)—work under the coordination of the pituitary, for this reason known as the *master gland*. This system is kept in equilibrium through negative feedback control. The pituitary gland secretes several *tropic* hormones, each of which stimulates a specific endocrine gland (called the *target gland* for that hormone).

For example, the tropic substance thyroid-stimulating hormone (TSH) acts on the thyroid gland. Each target gland, in response to the pituitary hormone, releases its own hormones. In turn, elevated levels of the target gland hormone signal the pituitary to inhibit secretion of the tropic hormone. Likewise the pituitary detects low levels of the target gland hormone and then increases its tropic hormone secretion to cause increased secretion of the target gland hormone.

The *hypothalamus*, a portion of the brain located at the base of the skull, is also involved in hormonal secretion. For each pituitary hormone, a hypothalamic-releasing hormone (or factor) is secreted to regulate secretion of the pituitary hormones. Similarly, high levels of pituitary hormone inhibit the release of hypothalamic hormones, and low levels of target gland hormone increase secretion. For example, in the case of the thyroid gland, the pituitary secretes TSH, which causes the thyroid to release thyroxine (T_4) and triiodothyronine (T_3). Elevated levels of T_4 and T_3 inhibit the release of TSH. When circulating levels of T_4 and T_3 fall, the hypothalamus secretes thyrotropin-releasing factor (TRF), which stimulates the pituitary, and the cycle is begun again (see Fig. 29-1).

Thus, when a problem develops in the endocrine system, it can be based at the level of the hypothalamus, the pituitary gland, or the target endocrine organ. Disorders of the endocrine glands are mainly due to hyperfunction and hypofunction, *hyperfunction* denoting excessive secretion of the hormone and *hypofunction* denoting deficient secretion of the hormone.[1]

Pituitary gland

Anatomy and physiology

The pituitary gland, or *hypophysis*, is an organ about the size of a finger tip located at the base of the brain, surrounded by the bony cup in the skull known as the *sella turcica.* Its connection to the hypothalamus is the hypophyseal stalk. The pituitary is divided into three sections: the anterior pituitary, or *adenohypophysis;* the intermediate lobe, or *pars intermedia;* and the posterior pituitary, or *neurohypophysis.*

The anterior pituitary secretes six identifiable hormones: (1) adrenocorticotropic hormone (ACTH); (2) thyroid-stimulating hormone (TSH), or thyrotropin; (3) growth hormone (GH), or somatotropin; (4) follicle-stimulating hormone (FSH); (5) luteinizing hormone (LH); and (6) prolactin (PRL), or luteotropic hormone. Their principal functions are listed in Table 29-1.

Hypopituitarism

Hypopituitarism occurs when the secretion of one or more pituitary hormones is deficient. As mentioned previously, this can result from a problem in the pituitary or the hypothalamus, although it is often difficult to identify where the problem originates. When all pituitary hormones are deficient, the condition is called *panhypopituitarism.* Although this condition is uncommon in children, it may occur as the result of a congenital defect or the development of a craniopharyngioma. This nonmalignant cystic tumor

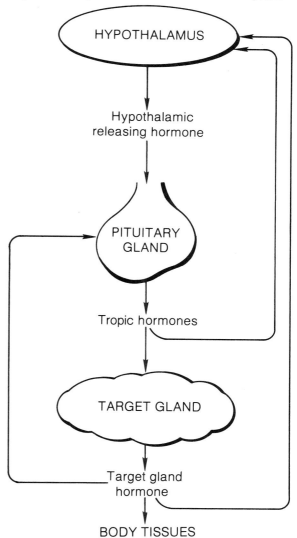

Figure 29-1 Negative feedback in the endocrine system.

of embryonic origin causes damage to the pituitary and hypothalamus by the accumulation of fluid in the tumor and the resulting pressure rather than through metastasis. These children usually present with headaches, vomiting, and visual disturbance, because of the proximity of the pituitary and hypothalamus to the optic nerves. The past growth records of many of these children show falling off on the growth grids as the children became increasingly deficient in GH. If the child has reached adolescence, he or

Table 29-1 Hormones of the pituitary gland

Hormone	Principal functions
Anterior pituitary hormones	
ACTH (adrenocorticotropic hormone)	Stimulation of cortisol production by adrenal cortex
TSH (thyroid-stimulating hormone)	Stimulation of thyroxine (T_4) and triiodothyronine (T_3) production by thyroid
GH (growth hormone)	Developmental enlargement of body tissues via cell hypertrophy and hyperplasia
FSH (follicle-stimulating hormone)	Stimulation of ovarian follicle growth in the female and spermatogenesis in the male
LH (leuteinizing hormone)	Stimulation of ovulation in the female and testosterone secretion in the male
PRL (prolactin)	Milk production in the lactating female
Intermediate lobe hormones	
MSH (melanocyte-stimulating hormone)	Involved in control of skin pigmentation
Posterior pituitary hormones	
ADH (antidiuretic hormone)	Functions in fluid and electrolyte balance by controlling reabsorption of water in the kidney
Oxytocin	Milk ejection in the lactating female; uterine contractions

she may be most concerned about the failure to progress to normal puberty.

Single deficiencies in anterior pituitary hormones are not uncommon. The most frequently seen problem is isolated GH deficiency. This appears to be an inherited condition, often occurring in more than one child in the family.[2] GH causes growth of the cartilaginous parts of the bone and increases protein synthesis and the mobilization of stored fat in muscle and adipose tissue. Children with GH deficiency are of normal size at birth but develop growth retardation within the first 2 years of life. Their growth curve, when plotted on normal growth grids (see Appendix B), appears to take a right turn somewhere before the age of 2. These children often have an infantile appearance, being chubby and round faced, and frequently show poor muscular development. If not diagnosed before their adolescent years, they will fail

to attain normal puberty even though they have normal pituitary sex hormones.

The diagnostic tests used to evaluate hypopituitarism are extensive, as each hormone must be evaluated. GH deficiency is evaluated by means of a stimulation test using exercise and a variety of substances such as arginine, insulin, estrogens, and L-dopa. Blood samples are obtained every 15 to 30 min over the course of several hours. All of these substances appear to stimulate the release of GH, and a rise in GH level is expected in the normal patient. Thyroid and adrenal function are both evaluated through simple blood tests not involving stimulation, although these may be combined with a GH stimulation test. TSH levels are measurable in the blood. It is difficult to measure levels of ACTH, and therefore adrenal function is evaluated by measuring cortisol levels. LH and FSH can be measured directly in the blood. Recent technological advances have resulted in the isolation of gonadotrophin-releasing hormone (GnRH) and thyrotrophin-releasing hormone (TRH). These substances are administered to individuals in an attempt to stimulate release of LH, FSH, and TSH, thereby differentiating pituitary and hypothalamic lesions. Frequently, bone age will be measured in order to evaluate a child's skeletal growth. X-ray pictures of the hands and wrists are taken, and the ossification of the child's bones is compared to standards for sex and age.

Diabetes insipidus

Diabetes insipidus (DI) is the most frequently occurring disorder associated with problems of the posterior pituitary. It results from an insufficiency in the production of antidiuretic hormone (ADH). ADH is produced in the hypothalamus and transported to the posterior pituitary, where it is released in response to an increased plasma osmolality and a decrease in extracellular fluid. ADH causes the renal tubules to reabsorb more fluid, resulting in retention of water in the body. True DI is a result of a deficiency of ADH, but a similar problem is caused by failure of the kidneys to respond to the action of ADH (nephrogenic DI) or compulsive water drinking (psychogenic DI).

DI may develop at any age. A central nervous system (CNS) tumor, often a craniopharyngioma, is a frequent cause in children, although a significant number of patients have idiopathic DI with no identifiable cause. DI may also be the result of congenital malformations of the CNS, histiocytosis X, or head trauma. Children with DI complain of polyuria and polydipsia. Infants often show a preference for water instead of milk. If the child has idiopathic DI, there will be no other symptoms. Headache, vomiting, and visual disturbance may indicate the presence of a CNS tumor, and there may be evidence of other pituitary deficiencies as well.

Since we are currently unable to measure vasopressin levels, DI is evaluated by the individual's response to a water deprivation test. The test is begun by giving the child nothing by mouth (NPO) for 8 h. Urinary specific gravity, urine volume, and body weight are then measured hourly. Serial determinations are obtained for sodium and urine and serum osmolality. Hematocrit and blood urea nitrogen (BUN) may also be obtained. In a child with ADH deficiency who is losing large amounts of free body water, it is expected that the urine specific gravity will remain below 1.005 and the urine osmolality will remain below 150 m0sm/kg, and there will be no significant reduction in urine volume. Serum osmolality and sodium are expected to rise. BUN and hematocrit are used to evaluate whether the patient received any water during the test.[3]

Diabetes insipidus is treated with the administration of synthetic vasopressin. However, all forms of the drug now available present difficulties in administration. The most commonly used form of this preparation is vasopressin tannate (Pitressin Tannate) in oil. In this preparation, tiny flecks of the vasopressin are suspended in peanut oil, which makes even distributin of the drug in the oil very difficult. The duration of effects from this preparation varies from individual to individual, and the administration schedule must be altered to meet the patient's response. Most individuals require injections every 36 to 48 h. Lypressin (Diapid), a synthetic antidiuretic nasal spray, is easy to administer and is preferred by some older patients. The duration of action varies from patient to patient, but most individuals have effects lasting 3 to 6 h. Frequent administration of the medication is a problem for some children, particularly at night. Absorption of the medication is also hindered by inflammation of the mucosa and therefore is less effective when the

child has any upper respiratory infection. DDAVP, desamino d-arginine vasopressin, a long-acting form of vasopressin nasal spray, is now available in the United States. This form requires administration approximately twice a day. However, because of the expense of this medication—several thousand dollars a year per child—it is prohibitive to most families.

Precocious puberty

Precocious puberty, or the development of secondary sex characteristics before the age of 8 or 9 years, is much more common in girls than in boys. Although CNS disorders, tumors, and adrenal disorders are causes for precocious puberty, the most common finding in girls is idiopathic precocious puberty. In these children there appears to be early release of GnRH from the hypothalamus, resulting in release of LH and FSH from the pituitary. These high levels of LH and FSH cause varying degrees of sexual precocity. The child may have precocious development of breast tissue (premature thelarche), most often occurring in girls between the ages of 6 months and 2 years of age, or precocious appearance of sexual hair (premature adrenarche), and usually occurring in older girls aged 5 to 8 years, or the child may progress to full puberty with menstruation.[4] With the onset of puberty, these children will have a corresponding growth spurt which makes them taller than their peers during childhood but ultimately leads to early closure of the epiphyses with a resulting short stature as an adult.

Although organic causes of precocious puberty in the female are rare, the possibility of organic disease or tumor must be investigated. Initial diagnostic tests include skull x-rays; bone age films; 24-h urinary 17-ketosteroids to evaluate adrenal function; T_4 to evaluate thyroid function; and serum LH and FSH. The most traumatic part of the evaluation is often the bimanual abdominal-rectal examination. For the young child, sedation or even anesthesia may be necessary to accomplish this examination.

A variety of drugs have been used to treat idiopathic precocious puberty with variable success. Provera (medroxyprogesterone acetate) is the most widely used drug. It appears to decrease gonadotrophin secretion, which results in halting the progression of puberty and cessation of menstruation; however, it does not alter the rapid growth rate of bone maturation.[5] Provera is used primarily with the menstruating young child when the problems of hygiene are not insignificant or when the anxiety level is very high in the patient and her family. Provera is administered as daily oral tablets or monthly intramuscular injection; the injections have been found to be more effective. See also Chap. 30.

Nursing management

The role of the nurse in caring for the child with pituitary problems can be extensive and may develop into a long-term relationship since these children need continuing health care supervision. Often the nurse is first involved with the patient and the family during the evaluation of the child's medical problem. This is usually an extremely stressful time for the family and the child, due to the physical discomfort from the many blood tests that are ordered and the time required to reach a diagnosis. Anxiety is increased when parents identify the problem as being "in the head" and envision craniotomy as the cure.

If craniotomy is the treatment of choice for pituitary tumor, the nurse is involved with the patient both before and after surgery. The child and the family need specific explanations as to what is to be done in surgery and what they can expect after surgery, as many fantasies are associated with surgery of the head. Because of the proximity of the optic nerves to the hypothalamic-pituitary region, blindness is always a danger in this type of surgery and the family needs to be aware of this potential complication.[6] The nurse should be available and encourage the family and the child to discuss their fears of blindness. If there is decreasing vision after surgery, the nurse can help the child make some initial adjustments to the situation. Two approaches are used for pituitary surgery: a frontal approach and a transsphenoidal approach. Postoperatively, the patient is observed for signs of cerebral edema or increased intercranial pressure. Vital signs and neurological status are assessed frequently, and the dressings are observed. Leakage of cerebrospinal fluid may occur around the incision site in the frontal approach and from the nose in the transsphenoidal approach. A muscle graft is used to close the opening made for the exposure of the pituitary in the transsphenoidal approach, and the patient is cautioned not to blow his or her nose in order to avoid moving the graft. The patient is checked for signs of infection, as meningitis is a serious complication of surgery. Diabetes insipidus is a frequent transient problem after surgery. The nurse needs to observe the hourly urine output. The physician should be notified when the hourly output is over 100 ml or the specific gravity is less than 1.010. Excessive fluid loss through the urine may result in dehydration. Postoperatively, the child may be required to undergo further testing to see if pituitary function has been altered by surgery.[7]

Children with hypopituitarism and their families need a great deal of education following the diagnosis. A variety of medications will be used to replace the hormones that are now deficient. These may include thyroid, vasopressin, cortisone, mineralocorticoids, and estrogens or androgens. The family needs to know which specific drugs the child is receiving, why their child is receiving those drugs, and the importance of daily administration of the medication. This is especially important if the child is receiving cortisone replacement, as these children are adrenally insufficient. Stresses such as minor illnesses, fever, and accidents raise the child's cortisone requirements, which must be met through larger doses of medication given by the family. The nurse is responsible for teaching, in collaboration with dietitians, occupational and physical therapists, in order to meet the diversified needs of the child with hypopituitarism.

The child being evaluated for GH deficiency has special problems. Many of these problems are psychological. The older child is very short in comparison to peers and as a result has usually taken a great deal of teasing. If his or her friends have entered puberty, then the teasing may center on sexual immaturity. Often these children are mistakenly believed to be much younger than their actual age, which can be most distressing to them. Younger children with severely impaired height have problems as well. They may be mistaken for infants even though their chronological age is 3 or 4 years and may be babied or overprotected by those around them, leading to delays in development. Parents may be torn between finding an answer for the child's short stature and wanting to keep a delightful child dependent even longer. The child may also be ridiculed by peers because of the obesity which results from a lack of GH. Initial evaluation will include a GH stimulation test. During this test, the nurse needs to supervise the child closely. A heparin lock intravenous needle is inserted to reduce the number of venipunctures needed for drawing blood during the test. The nurse must ensure that the needle is well anchored so that it does not become dislodged. This is particlarly important if exercise is used as part of the protocol for the GH stimulation test. Not only are repeat venipunctures painful, but they are often difficult to accomplish in children who are exceptionally small for their age. The most frequently used substance in GH stimulation tests is insulin. When insulin is injected intravenously, profound hypoglycemia is expected to occur. The nurse needs to be in attendance at all times when this test is being performed in order to pick up early signs of hypoglycemia so that the test may be terminated at this point.

Growth hormone deficiency is treated with GH derived from pituitary extracts of human autopsy material given as an intramuscular injection three times per week. The supply of GH is limited. The majority is available on a research basis, and candidates are screened extensively for admission to the program. Recently a small amount of GH has become available for purchase; however, the price is prohibitive for most families. This only adds to the stress that the family and the child are undergoing, and the nurse needs to be fully aware of this situation. If the child begins to receive GH, the family or the child is taught injection technique. Rotation of injection sites needs to be stressed, as treatment often takes several years. Although the child and family may be much relieved when GH injections have begun, they must be warned that the final height achieved may not be optimal. Some patients develop antibodies to exogenous GH. However, even if growth velocity is good, the National Pituitary Agency, which supplies experimental GH, currently provides pituitary extract only until the individual has reached a height of 5 ft to 5 ft 6 in.

The child who is being evaluated for DI has some problems similar to those experienced by the child being evaluated for GH deficiency. The water deprivation test is a long and difficult test for the child to endure. It is the nurse's major responsibility to assure that the child does not receive any type of fluid during the test period. Some children become so obsessed with obtaining fluids that they become devious in finding ways to get it. Children have been known to drink from toilets, vases of flowers, and urinals in an attempt to get fluid. It is often of benefit to have a plumber turn off the water supply to the sink in the patient's room during the time the test is being conducted. Some children require 24-h supervision during testing.

Accurate measurements of urinary output and specific gravity are essential during the test, as are accurate weights. If the test continues during a change of staff, it is essential that the nurse coming on duty weigh the child in exactly the same manner as had been done by the previous shift. If Pitressin is administered while the child is in the hospital, the nurse must observe for signs that the drug is diminishing in effectiveness, usually 36 to 48 h after administration. At this point, the child will begin to have increased urination, with a resulting increase in thirst. Before the child is discharged, the child and the family must be educated in the administration of vasopressin. If the child is placed on Pitressin, the family and/or the child must be taught injection technique. The nurse and the family must be aware of the difficulties in administering Pitressin. Holding the vial under warm water will aid in drawing up the thick oil. Uniform suspension of the flecks of vasopressin is essential. This is best accomplished by vigorous shaking and flicking of the vial for a full 5 min. If the full contents of the vial are not used at each injection, the remaining medication must be discarded, as there is no way to resuspend the preparation. Many children are allowed to decide when the next injection is due based on increasing symptoms rather than administering the drug at a set schedule. Likewise, children who are placed on Lypressin and DDAVP are taught to carry their medication with them so that they may use it when they have increasing urination.

Caring for the child and the family with precocious puberty can be a real challenge to the nurse. Many fears turn on sexual problems. Parents are often concerned that the child's psychosexual development will be advanced because of precocious puberty, although this is not the case. It is not uncommon to see little girls who are sexually mature playing with dolls during the course of their evaluation. Fathers frequently have many fears that the child will be sexually molested. All these problems need to be explored and dealt with openly with the parents. If the little girl has not begun to menstruate at the time of the evaluation, the family needs assistance in planning a discussion with her about impending menstruation in terms that she can understand. Unexplained bleeding can be frightening to the very young child. Hygiene also needs to be discussed with the family, as most individuals are not used to caring for a young child who has a vaginal discharge, adult sweat patterns, and normal oily adult skin. The problems of ultimate height also need to be discussed with the family. While the little girl is growing, she may be much taller than her peers, which only increases her visibility as a child who is different. However, as she grows older, her peers will soon catch up and pass her, and the problems of the adolescent with short stature will become apparent. If the child is placed on medication in order to stop menstruation, the family needs to understand the importance of maintaining the schedule for injections. Since the children started on medication are often very young, play therapy may be indicated in order to help them work through their frustrations and anger at having to get frequent injections for a condition they cannot understand.

Thyroid gland

Anatomy and physiology

The thyroid gland is an H-shaped organ located in the neck, anterior to the trachea. The gland is not normally visible in children, although the isthmus or cross bar may be palpable. An enlargement of the thyroid gland is termed a *goiter*.

The thyroid gland is concerned with control of metabolism. When foods containing iodine are ingested, the iodine passes into the circulation, where it is absorbed by the thyroid gland. This iodine then reacts with a protein called *thyroglobulin* produced by the thyroid, to form the two thyroid hormones thyroxine (T_4) and triiodothyronine (T_3). These thyroid hormones act on all body tissues to increase metabolic activity by causing the body to burn available carbohydrates very rapidly, increasing the utilization of fats and depleting fat stores. These actions have very visible effects on some body

systems. With the increased metabolic rate, all body tissues require increased quantities of nutrients. The cardiovascular system reacts by vasodilatation and increased cardiac output. T_4 also has a direct effect on the heart, increasing its metabolism as well as its rate and forcefulness of contraction. T_4 also greatly increases the reactivity of the nervous system, causing wakefulness with hypersecretion or sleepiness with hyposecretion of the hormone. Hypersecretion also causes a very fine but rapid tremor of the muscles. T_4 also increases the motility of the gastrointestinal tract and promotes a copious flow of digestive juices; therefore hypersecretion may cause diarrhea. On the other hand, lack of T_4 causes the opposite effects: sluggish motility and greatly diminished gastrointestinal secretion resulting in constipation. Excessive production of T_4 also causes a voracious appetite because of the rapid rate of metabolism. Inability to take in the needed nutrients can cause weight loss and vitamin deficiencies, particularly the B-complex vitamins.[8]

The thyroid gland, like other glands in the endocrine system, is kept in equilibrium through a negative feedback system. The hypothalamus secretes TRH, which acts on the anterior pituitary, causing it to secrete TSH. High levels of TSH inhibit the hypothalamus from producing more TRH. The TSH produced acts on the thyroid gland to produce T_4 and T_3. High levels of circulating T_4 and T_3 will then inhibit secretion of TSH by the anterior pituitary.

Hypothyroidism

Hypothyroidism in children can take two forms: (1) congenital hypothyroidism, or cretinism, and (2) acquired hypothyroidism. Thyroid deficiency in cretinism is present at birth, although the disease may not become obvious for several months, and occasionally is overlooked for years. *Acquired hypothyroidism* refers to thyroid deficiency beginning later in life, usually after the age of 2 years.

Congenital hypothyroidism results from malformation of the thyroid during embryonic development. The results may be a child with a total lack of thyroid tissue (*athyrotic cretinism*) or a child with a thyroid remnant which may be located anywhere along the embryonic migratory tract of the thyroid, for example, in the mediastinum or under the base of the tongue. Presently, the reasons for this malformation are not known. The incidence of congenital hypothyroidism is approximately 1 in 5000 to 10,000 live births.[9]

Lack of sufficient thyroid tissue to produce adequate amounts of T_4 and T_3 results in a variety of symptoms. The athyrotic child who has had a lack of thyroid hormone prenatally will often show symptoms at birth. Because of the effects of thyroxine on neuromuscular control, these children are lethargic and seldom cry and may actually be thought of as extremely good babies. Their reactions are slow, and they often have feeding problems. They often have a low-pitched, gruntlike cry. Constipation is a common problem. Other problems frequently seen include thick facial features, thick tongue, umbilical hernia, dry skin, falling hair, and frequent respiratory infections. The child with a thyroid remnant may exhibit few if any symptoms neonatally. As the child grows and the amount of thyroid hormone being produced by the thyroid remnant becomes increasingly inadequate, then symptoms slowly develop. In the older child, growth retardation may become more apparent, and strabismus is frequently seen.[10] Children with either congenital or acquired hypothyroidism are intellectually and developmentally delayed.

The diagnosis of hypothyroidism is made on the basis of several blood tests. T_4, T_3, and TSH are measured by radioimmunoassay (RIA). In the child with congenital hypothyroidism, T_3 and T_4 levels are low or nonexistent and TSH levels are elevated. In the past, serum protein-bound iodine (PBI) was used as a means of evaluating thyroid function. This test measures the amount of T_4 precursors in the blood; however, with the technological advances of RIA, this test is no longer done. Bone age x-ray films are frequently ordered to assess the level of growth retardation. Thyroid scans using radioactive iodine are frequently performed on children with congenital hypothyroidism to look for thyroid remnants. However, this test is usually delayed until the child is several years old. The child must be taken off the thyroid medication for a short period of time prior to the scanning, and therefore the scanning is delayed until major brain development has occurred. Cholesterol levels in older children may be markedly elevated due to the decreased utilization of fats.[11]

Treatment of congenital hypothyroidism consists of replacement of the deficient hormones with desiccated thyroid or a synthetic thyroid preparation such as sodium levothyroxine (Synthroid). Progress is evaluated by means of serial T_4, T_3, and TSH levels and x-rays for bone age. Periodic psychological and developmental assessments are beneficial. The infant is evaluated frequently because medication needs to be increased as the child grows in size. Recently, statewide screening of all newborn infants for congenital hypothyroidism has begun in some areas. It is hoped that with this type of screening, the asymptomatic hypothyroid child will be identified before serious complications result.

The prognosis for children with congenital hypothyrodism is always guarded. Once these children are placed on medication, their physical symptoms are reversed (Fig. 29-2); however, the damage done to the developing CNS is often permanent. The result may be a child who is severely retarded or one with apparently normal intelligence with developmental delays in one specific area. Speech problems are a common finding. There are children who, with thyroid replacement therapy, develop normally with no mental impairment; however, no guarantee can be made for any particular child.

Nursing management Once the child has been started on replacement medication, several weeks often elapse before symptoms disappear. The nurse dealing with the hypothyroid child must understand that the metabolism and general physical activity have been slowed down, and that it will take longer for the child to accomplish most tasks. The nurse must also be aware that the child may be mentally retarded as a result of hypothyroidism, and communication with the child must be aimed at the child's functional ability rather than his or her chronological age. Skin care is important. Avoiding soap and using skin lotions often help relieve some of the dryness that occurs. Feeding problems continue to be a difficulty. The nurse must remember that the child cannot be rushed, and a longer time period must be allotted for feeding. The hypothyroid infant may need to be suctioned during feeding in order to remove mucous secretions which may interfere with nursing. Constipation may continue. Offering the child increased amounts of fluid during the day will help to keep stools soft. In the older child, offering a variety of fresh fruits and vegetables

Figure 29-2 Hypothyroidism. (A) Ten-week-old baby showing typical thickened facial features and fragile hair, which is falling out. (B) The same child after 16 months of treatment. (From R. M. DeCoursey and J. L. Renfro, The Human Organism, 5th ed., McGraw-Hill, New York, 1980. Used by permission.)

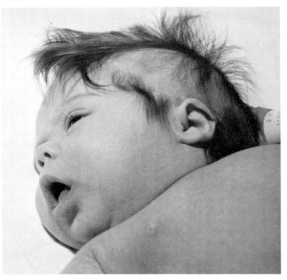

A

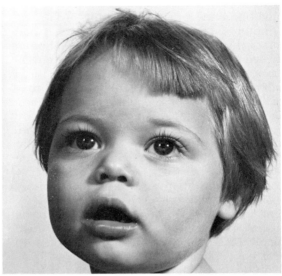

B

may help stimulate the gastrointestinal tract. In severe cases, enemas may be needed.

The family of the hypothyroid child will need a great deal of support from the nurse. The nurse must help the parents set realistic expectations for their child's development. The family can neither label the child mentally retarded nor expect that there will be no problems in the future. Many parents feel guilty, believing that they did something during the pregnancy which resulted in the hypothyroidism, and this needs to be discussed openly. The family needs a good understanding of the disease process, including the fact that the child will need to take medication for the rest of his or her life. Thyroid preparations come in tablet form only, so the family must be instructed how to crush tablets to give to small children. Medication must not be placed in the baby's bottle. Symptoms of hyperthyroidism must be explained to the family so that they can recognize any overtreatment in the child. It is not uncommon for symptoms such as a large tongue and strabismus to remain for many months after treatment has begun, and the family needs to be informed of this.

Hyperthyroidism

Hyperthyroidism, or *thyrotoxicosis*, in children is almost always secondary to Grave's disease (also called *Parry's disease, Basedow's disease*, or *exophthalmic goiter*). Grave's disease is a multisystem disorder composed of hyperthyroidism with thyroid enlargement and exophthalmos (protrusion of the eyeballs). In Grave's disease, the thyroid produces large quantities of T_3 and T_4 without apparent stimulation from the pituitary. These large amounts of T_3 and T_4 suppress TSH production and block the pituitary's ability to respond to TRH. The etiology of Grave's disease is unknown, although the incidence is five to six times more frequent in girls than it is in boys. It is not uncommon to find many other family members who have a history of other thyroid problems. Grave's disease occurs in approximately 4 out of 1000 patients in the general population.[12]

The course of Grave's disease is usually slow, although there may be an abrupt onset. When questioned at the time of diagnosis, families will often recall that there have been symptoms such as decreased school performance for the past year. The hyperthyroid period of Grave's disease lasts for several years, although the time varies from patient to patient. A significant number of patients will go on to develop hypothyroidism later in life; therefore, it is important that these patients have continuous follow-up.

Most children with Grave's disease present with complaints of nervousness, decreasing school performance, heat intolerance, excessive sweating, and increased appetite with or without weight loss. They show tachycardia, systolic hypertension with markedly widened pulse pressure, mild exophthalmos, lid retraction and stare, tremors of the outstretched hand, and smooth, moist, warm skin. Almost all patients have an obvious goiter.[13]

The diagnosis of Grave's disease is based on the history, physical examination, and laboratory findings. Levels of T_3, T_4, and TSH are measured. Ordinarily T_3 and T_4 are elevated and TSH is low; however, some hyperthyroid patients have an elevated T_3 and a normal T_4. This entity, T_3 thyrotoxicosis, is another form of hyperthyroidism. When the diagnosis of Grave's disease is questionable, a radioactive iodine uptake may be ordered. I 123 or I 131 is given to the patient by mouth. The radioactivity is then measured over the thyroid gland at various intervals, usually 4, 6, and 24 h. The results are read as a percentage of the tracer dose taken up by the thyroid.

There are three modes of treatment for Grave's disease, none of which are entirely satisfactory. The first and most commonly used form of treatment in children is the administration of oral medications. Propylthiouracil (PTU) and methimazole (Tapazole) block the production of thyroid hormones which produce the metabolic aspects of Grave's disease and allow the disease to subside spontaneously. Drug therapy can have significant complications, the most serious of which is granulocytopenia. Rashes, fever, urticaria, arthritis, and a severe lupuslike syndrome have also been noted. Therapy is continued 18 to 24 months and then discontinued. If signs of hyperthyroidism return, therapy may be reinstituted or often surgery is recommended. Subtotal thyroidectomy is the second mode of treatment in Grave's disease. Surgical treatment often involves significant complications. Vocal cord paralysis from cutting the recurrent laryngeal nerves, hypoparathyroidism from inadvertent removal or damage of the parathyroid glands, hemorrhage necessitating tracheostomy, and cosmetic disfigurement from keloid formation are all complications. Since the surgeon can only estimate how much thyroid to leave intact in an attempt to keep the patient euthyroid, the results are unpredictable. Most often the patient will become hypothyroid after surgery, requiring the daily administration of thyroid replacement. However, if too little thyroid is removed, the patient may still be hyperthyroid after surgery, requiring a second operation. Oral iodine (Lugol's solution or saturated solution of potassium iodide) is given for 10 to 14 days preoperatively to control the hyperthyroidism and to reduce the vascularity of the thyroid gland. The third form of treatment of Grave's disease is obliteration of the thyroid using radioactive iodine. This is a very popular form of treatment for adult patients; however, pediatricians generally limit its use to instances in which all other modes of therapy have failed or are contraindicated. Concerns center on exposure of the gonads of the young child to radioactivity with subsequent genetic damage, the development of thyroid cancer, and leukemia. It is common for children to become hypothyroid after treatment with radioactive iodine. This condition may develop in the first year after treatment or may not become evident for many years.[14]

Hashimoto's thyroiditis

Hashimoto's thyroiditis, or *chronic lymphocytic thyroiditis*, is the most frequently observed thyroid disorder in the United States. The disease is believed to have an autoimmune etiology. It appears that at some point the body begins to form antibodies against its own thyroid tissue. This causes an inflammatory response, leading to a moderately enlarged, firm, knobby goiter. This inflammatory response may have a varied effect on the functioning of the thyroid. The individual may be euthyroid, hypothyroid, or hyperthyroid (the last is sometimes called *Hashitoxicosis*).

The diagnosis is based upon the history, as there appears to be a familial tendency for Hashimoto's thyroiditis, physical findings of the typical goiter, and laboratory data. Circulating thyroid antibodies, antithyroglobulin, and antimicrosomal are measured, as well as T_3, T_4, and TSH to evaluate thyroid function. Treatment depends on thyroid function. Hypothyroidism, once present, is generally permanent and requires treatment with thyroid hormone. Hyperthyroidism is usually treated with oral medications, as in Grave's disease, although the length of treatment may be shorter. For the euthyroid patient, observation is all that is necessary; however, this is important, as the majority of patients will eventually become hypothyroid.[15]

Nursing management

It may be 10 to 14 days before patients with hyperthyroidism notice a change in symptoms once they have been started on oral medication, and 4 to 6 weeks before they become euthyroid.[16] Often these patients are extremely agitated, and any stress, either physical or emotional, will exaggerate the hyperactive symptoms. Environmental stimulation should be kept to a minimum. This is especially true at night, since there may be an increased need for sleep and rest due to constant fatigue from insomnia. Barbiturates may be ordered for sedation.

The effects of high levels of T_4 on the gastrointestinal tract may result in a need for high caloric intake and produce a ravenous appetite. Small, frequent feedings with high-quality foods may be needed to meet the caloric needs and the increased need for the B-complex vitamins. Diarrhea may also be a problem at this time. Limiting the intake of fluid at meals may be of some benefit. The nurse must observe for frequency, color, consistency, and character of stools. The goiter produced by hyperthyroidism may create a feeling of fullness in the throat. Because of this, the patient may find that some foods are easier to swallow than others. These preferences for certain food consistencies should be incorporated into the diet.

The patient with hyperthyroidism loses tolerance to heat. The room should be well ventilated and its temperature reduced if possible. Light-weight night clothing such as gowns and pajamas should be provided. These children may be more comfortable without any covers on the bed. During the day, quiet activities should be encouraged rather than vigorous exercises to decrease the amount of body heat produced. Frequent bathing and sponging may also offer relief for the patient who perspires heavily.

The patient and the family need to be taught a great deal about their medications before the patient is discharged. PTU is rapidly removed from the circulation and, therefore, is given every 8 h. A common schedule is administration at 8 A.M., 4 P.M., and 12 midnight. This will necessitate waking up the child to give a dose of medication. However, the parents need to understand the importance of the 8-h schedule rather than just giving the medication three times a day. PTU therapy has a possible side effect of agranulocytosis, and therefore, many children will have routine white blood cell and differential counts while they are on therapy. The family needs to report any signs of illness, particularly sore throat, skin eruptions, fever, headache, or general malaise. PTU has a very bitter taste which some children find objectionable. Placing the pill on the back of the tongue and offering copious fluids may be of some help. It is interesting to note, however, that a side effect of PTU therapy is a loss of taste, and it is not uncommon to see children chewing PTU tablets that would gag another person. Often a family will be asked to check sleeping pulses on their child once therapy has begun in order to assess how well the child is doing, and therefore, they need to be taught this technique. Medication therapy may be so effective that the child becomes hypothyroid, and so the family is warned to report any signs of possible hypothyroidism.

The patient who is to undergo thyroidectomy needs much information before surgery in order to alleviate fears and elicit cooperation. The patient will be placed on an iodine preparation prior to surgery. These preparations have a rather metallic taste which can be improved by being diluted in large quantities of water or fruit juice. Having the patient drink the preparation through a straw also helps alleviate the taste. Postoperatively, the patient is checked frequently for signs of hemorrhage, bleeding at the incision site, or change in vital signs. Since severe hemorrhage may compress the trachea and obstruct breathing, a tracheotomy tray is kept by the bedside. Signs of hypoparathyroidism such as tetany and numbness of the extremities must be reported immediately. Treatment may include increasing the amount of calcium in the diet or administering calcium lactate or calcium gluconate.

Thyroid storm is a condition which results from the rapid release of thyroid hormone into the circulation. It can be precipitated by physical and emotional stress, infections, surgery, and radioactive iodine therapy. It is occasionally seen when hyperthyroid children are removed from antithyroid medications. Thyroid storm can be a life-threatening situation. The patient progresses rapidly from fever and restlessness to delirium and shock. A nasogastric tube may be inserted to administer oral PTU. Intravenous fluids are started to combat shock. Medications include antipyretics, glucocorticoids, catecholamine-blocking agents, and vitamins.

Adrenal glands

Anatomy and physiology

The two adrenal glands are triangular-shaped organs directly above each kidney. Each adrenal gland is divided into two sections—the medulla or inner section and the cortex or outer section—whose functions are very different.

The medulla secretes two catecholamines, epinephrine and norephinephrine. When stress is placed on the body, either physical or psychological, the medulla responds with release of epinephrine and norephineprine, which have a profound effect on all parts of the body. This *fight-or-flight response* prepares the body to deal with the stress. The combined activities of epinephrine and norepinephrine result in stimulation of the CNS with increased alertness, increased cardiac output with increased force and rate of contraction, dilated coronary blood vessels, dilated blood vessels in skeletal muscle, elevated blood glucose, and an increase in free fatty acids (see Table 29-2). The adrenal cortex, or outer section, secretes three groups of hormones all derived from cholesterol. These include mineralocorticoids, glucocorticoids, and adrenal androgens. Because of their chemical structure, adrenal androgens are also known as *17-ketosteroids.*

A number of mineralocorticoids are produced in the adrenal cortex, although three are most common: aldosterone, corticosterone, and deoxycorticosterone, of which aldosterone makes up about 95 percent of the available mineralocorticoids. Their major function is to regulate electrolytes, particularly sodium, in the extracellular

Table 29-2 Adrenal hormones

Type	Major hormones	Action on body
Hormones of the cortex		
Mineralocorticoids	Aldosterone Corticosterone Deoxycorticosterone	Reabsorption of sodium by renal tubules Reabsorption of chloride→increased sodium chloride in extracellular fluid Increases water absorption Increases interstitial fluid and blood volume Increases cardiac output Increases arterial pressure
Glucocorticoids	Cortisol	Elevates blood glucose through gluconeogenesis Increases circulating amino acids Decreases rate of glucose utilization by the cell Mobilizes fatty acids from adipose tissue
Androgens	DHEA	Unknown in males Pubic and axillary hair growth in females Maintenance of normal libido in females
Hormones of the medulla		
Catecholamines	Epinephrine Norepinephrine	Increases alertness through CNS stimulation Increases cardiac output Increases force of contraction Increases heart rate Dilates coronary blood vessels Dilates blood vessels in muscles Elevates blood glucose Increases free fatty acids

fluids. This is accomplished through the action of aldosterone on the renal tubules, causing reabsorption of sodium into the blood. Increased absorption of sodium causes a corresponding reabsorption of chloride with a resulting increase of sodium chloride in the extracellular fluid. This elevation of salt in the extracellular fluid causes increased water absorption through osmosis and stimulation of osmoreceptors. Aldosterone's effect on electrolytes causes an elevated interstitial fluid volume and blood volume and increased cardiac output. Excess blood flow causes local vasoconstriction and increased peripheral resistance creating elevated arterial pressure.

The major glucocorticoid secreted is *cortisol*, also known as *hydrocortisone*. The major function of the glucocorticoids is to aid the body in resistance to physical stress. This is accomplished through effects on glucose, protein, and fat metabolism. As the name indicates, the glucocorticoids increase the glucose concentration in the blood through gluconeogenesis, the conversion of protein and fat into glucose. Protein metabolism is altered, allowing an increased quantity of amino acids to circulate. These amino acids are then available to provide energy or to repair tissue damage. This also causes a decrease in the rate of glucose utilization by the cells. Cortisol also affects mobilization of fatty acids from adipose tissue. This allows the body to utilize fat for fuel in times of starvation or other stresses.

The role of adrenal androgens in normal physiology is unknown. The major adrenal androgen is the 17-ketosteroid dehydroepiandrosterone (DHEA). Although two-thirds of the ketosteroids in the urine of males come from adrenal sources, these adrenal androgens have no significant masculinizing effect in normal amounts. In females they are believed to cause growth of pubic and axillary hair and to be important in maintaining normal libido.

The mineralocorticoids, glucocorticoids, and adrenal androgens are all kept under control through negative feedback. Corticotropin-releasing hormone (CRH) is secreted by the hypothalamus. This is carried through the circulation to the pituitary, causing ACTH release. ACTH is transported by peripheral circulation to the adrenal, where it causes steroid synthesis. Large doses of cortisol from the adrenal inhibit the release of CRH and ACTH, although this negative feedback can be overcome by stress. Large amounts of ACTH also feed back to inhibit CRH release. Aldosterone secretion is also regulated by angiotensin II, produced in the renin-angiotensin system, and stimulated by increases in potassium concentrations.

Hypoadrenocorticism

Lack of adrenal hormones can result from primary adrenal failure associated with the adrenal gland itself or from secondary adrenal failure related to insufficient ACTH secretion. Primary adrenal failure can be caused by a variety of conditions. Chronic adrenal insufficiency, termed *Addison's disease*, is an uncommon condition in children. In the past, tuberculosis of the adrenal was a frequent cause of Addison's disease; now, however, the majority of cases are attributed to idiopathic atrophy of the adrenal gland. In some cases, the disease may be the result of an autoimmune reaction, with the production of adrenal antibodies. This is frequently the case in children with multihormonal disorders. Congenital hypoplasia of the adrenals has also been reported as an inherited autosomal recessive trait.[17]

Infants with congenital hypoplasia of the adrenals and older children who present in adrenal crisis secondary to chronic adrenal insufficiency have nausea, vomiting, diarrhea, and dehydration. Hypoglycemia, hyponatremia, and hyperkalemia may be present as a result of the lack of mineralocorticoids and glucocorticoids. The child who is not in adrenal crisis may have weakness, anorexia, and weight loss. There may be hyperpigmentation of the skin due to excessive secretion of ACTH and melanocyte-stimulating hormone (MSH). Alopecia and monilial infections of the skin and mucous membranes are common.

Evaluation of children for chronic adrenal insufficiency is based on several diagnostic tests. These include cortisol determinations during the ACTH stimulation test. The patient is given synthetic ACTH (Cortrosyn) intramuscularly or intravenously, and cortisol levels are then drawn every 30 min for $1\frac{1}{2}$ to 4 h. In the normal individual, a rise in cortisol level is expected from the stimulation of the ACTH. This test will tell whether there is adrenal function or not, but it does not differentiate between primary and secondary adrenal insufficiency. Two tests can be used to evaluate whether there is normal pituitary function or secondary adrenal insufficiency. These include the metyrapone test and the insulin tolerance test. In the metyrapone test, the patient is given metyrapone either orally or intravenously and blood samples are obtained for 11-deoxycorticoids. Metyrapone inhibits an enzyme needed for the formation of cortisol in the adrenal gland. The resulting low cortisol level stimulates the pituitary to secrete higher levels of ACTH. However, since the chemical process leading to the formation of cortisol can not be completed, elevated levels of 11-deoxycortisol, the precursor of cortisol, result. In the patient with secondary adrenal insufficiency, there is no rise in the level of 11-deoxycortisol since the pituitary cannot be stimulated. Another test used to evaluate the same situation is the insulin tolerance test. This test, using insulin, is conducted in the same manner as the GH stimulation test. Since hypoglycemia is a potent stimulus to ACTH release, elevated cortisol levels following hypoglycemia are considered normal in this test (see "Hypopituitarism").[18]

Congenital adrenal hyperplasia

Another common cause of adrenal insufficiency in children is *congenital adrenal hyperplasia*, or *adrenogenital syndrome*. This inborn error of metabolism appears to be inherited as an autosomal recessive trait, and it is common to find more than one child in the family affected. The gene is found frequently in the normal population, with an incidence that may be as high as 1 in 35 individuals.[19]

In the formation of adrenal steroids from cholesterol, three pathways are used, leading to the formation of aldosterone, cortisol, and adrenal androgens. A variety of enzymes interact with precursor compounds ultimately to form these three substances. In congenital adrenal hyperplasia, one of the enzymes needed for aldosterone or cortisol production is missing, leading to overproduction of a precursor substance. This precursor then becomes part of the adrenal androgen pathway, leading to overproduction of androgens. Because insufficient amounts of aldosterone or cortisol are produced, the pituitary is stimulated through the negative feedback system to produce more ACTH. This ACTH stimulates the adrenal, causing adrenal hyperplasia and ultimately more precursor substance.

The most common type of congenital adrenal hyperplasia is 21-hydroxylase deficiency. The absence of this enzyme affects both the mineralocorticoid pathway and the glucocorticoid pathway, leading to the overproduction of progesterone, a precursor of aldosterone, and 17-alpha hydroxyprogesterone, a precursor of cortisol. These two substances are then rerouted into the third pathway, causing an overproduction of adrenal androgens and virilization. The enzyme defect is usually not complete, allowing the formation of small amounts of aldosterone. In approximately half of these children, the amount of aldosterone secreted is not sufficient to maintain the electrolyte balance and salt-losing crises occur, usually early in infancy.

The second most frequently seen type of congenital adrenal hyperplasia is 11-hydroxylase deficiency. In this condition, the enzyme interferes with both mineralocorticoid production and glucocorticoid production, leading to the formation of 11-deoxycorticosterone, a precursor of aldosterone, and 11-deoxycortisol, a precursor of cortisol. Because 11-deoxycorticosterone is a potent retainer of salt, these children do not have salt-losing crises but rather may have hypertension. These two substances feed back into the third pathway, and again there is overproduction of adrenal androgens. Several other types of congenital adrenal hyperplasia have been identified, although they are much less common.

The effect of the increased adrenal androgens is virilization. The time at which this change occurs varies from child to child. Virilization may occur in utero, resulting in a female with ambiguous genitalia. There is often clitoral enlargement and labial fusion, and in extreme cases the urethra may open at the tip of a malelike phallus. Male fetuses may be virilized, although the effects are not usually visible. After birth the male child will continue to be virilized and will progress to what appears to be puberty, that is, increased height, with epiphyseal maturation, development of pubic, axillary, and facial hair, acne, lowering of the voice, and increased growth of the penis. In spite of this, the testes do not grow and there is no spermatogenesis (Fig. 29-3). Female children also show signs of virilization with increased height and epiphyseal maturation, development of axillary and facial hair, and

Figure 29-3 A 3-year-old boy with congenital adrenal hyperplasia, showing marked virilization at the time of diagnosis. Height was 108.5 cm and bone age was 10 years.

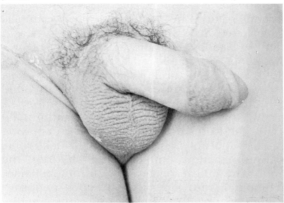

development of pubic hair with male escutcheon, enlarged clitoris, and hirsutism. If untreated, these children will be exceptionally tall during their early childhood years, but their epiphyses will close early and ultimately they will be very short.

Congenital adrenal hyperplasia may become evident at any point in childhood. An infant may be evaluated at the time of birth because of ambiguous genitalia and found to have congenital adrenal hyperplasia. Karyotyping may be done to identify the true sex of the child, although a female child who is severely virilized and phenotypically a male may nevertheless be reared as a boy.

The child may first be seen later in infancy or childhood when the marginally adequate adrenal function becomes inadequate due to a stressful situation. These children, who are salt losers, may have few if any signs of virilization at the time of their diagnosis. On the other hand, occasionally children are seen late in childhood, when both males and females may be fully virilized. It is interesting to note that frequently parents do not question the appearance of secondary sex characteristics in very young children.

Several laboratory tests are used in the diagnosis and evaluation of congenital adrenal hyperplasia. For example, urine collections may be obtained for 17-ketosteroids and pregnanetriol. Seventeen-ketosteriods are a general measure of

increased adrenal androgen production, and pregnanetriol is the urinary metabolite of the excessive precursors in 21-hydroxylase deficiency. A 24-h urine collection for 17-hydroxysteroids may also be made as a measure of total cortisol production. In some areas a blood test is now available to measure serum 17-alpha hydroxyprogesterone. This is the easiest and most definitive test for 21-hydroxylase deficiency. In the older child, a bone age test may be ordered to assess the degree of skeletal maturation.

If the child is admitted in an adrenal crisis, a medical emergency exists and treatment will be vigorous, including intravenous replacement of fluids and electrolytes with the addition of glucocorticoids and mineralocorticoids. Once the child has stabilized, the treatment consists of the administration of glucocorticoids or glucocorticoids and mineralocorticoids. Cortisone is used as the glucocorticoid replacement. This can be given as intramuscular injections every third day or orally in tablets or liquids (Cortef) given every 8 h. Several preparations are available for mineralocorticoid replacement. Desoxycorticosterone acetate (DOCA) may be given as intramuscular injections or placed under the skin in pellet form for slow absorption. DOCA pellets are slowly absorbed and need to be replaced several times a year. They are used primarily in infants who have difficulty retaining medications orally. Nine-alpha-fluorocortisol acetate (Florinef) is also used as a mineralocorticoid supplement. It is given once daily as an oral tablet. Salt is needed for the effective treatment with mineralocorticoids, and therefore, some children may be given prescriptions for sodium chloride tablets.[20]

Some children with congenital adrenal hyperplasia may undergo surgery to repair their physical defects. A female infant who is severely virilized may be assigned a male gender. These children will undergo subsequent surgery for removal of abdominal ovaries, repair of hypospadias, and implantation of testicular prostheses. Female infants who are less severely virilized will frequently need surgery to correct labial fusion. Enlargement of the clitoris is a concern to parents. If the child is young, surgery may be deferred in the hopes that as the child grows older, the labia will grow and surround the protruding clitoris. However, if the clitoris appears extremely hypertrophied, then surgery may be indicated. Recent surgical advances have allowed resection of the shaft of the clitoris, resulting in a functional organ. However, not all attempts have been successful, and clitoral amputation may be the end result. In the past, clitorectomy was the only treatment available.

Hyperadrenocorticism

Cushing's syndrome, a form of *hyperadrenocorticism*, although fairly frequent in adulthood, is a rare syndrome in infancy and childhood. Because of the negative feedback system, overproduction of the adrenal hormones can be the result of problems at the level of the pituitary or the adrenal itself. Increased ACTH production secondary to pituitary tumors results in bilateral adrenal hyperplasia. Adrenal tumors, either benign adenomas or highly malignant carcinomas, are also causes of Cushing's syndrome. Before 8 years of age, most cases of Cushing's syndrome are due to malignant adrenal tumors.[21]

The signs and symptoms of Cushing's syndrome are caused by overproduction of glucocorticoids (cortisol). The utilization of body proteins for the formation of glucose (gluconeogenesis) causes retardation of body growth and decrease in muscle mass with muscle weakness. Alterations in carbohydrate and fat metabolism may lead to obesity and abnormal glucose tolerance tests. These changes result in a patient who appears obese with thin arms and legs. The fat may be deposited in the facial area, producing "moon facies," or across the shoulders and cervical area, leading to "buffalo hump." The skin is often thin with prominent capillaries, bruising, and purple striae. There may be electrolyte imbalance with subsequent weakness. Some patients also have increased androgen secretion with resulting hirsutism and acne. Blood pressure may be elevated.

Diagnostic tests are used to differentiate between Cushing's syndrome and exogenous obesity. In Cushing's syndrome 17-hydroxysteroids, a measure of total cortisol production, and 17-ketosteroids, a measure of total androgen production, are both elevated. Blood cortisol levels are also elevated, and their diurnal variation is absent. A dexamethasone suppression test may be conducted. Dexamethasone, a potent glucocorticoid, is administered orally in order to turn off ACTH production, which then suppresses the production of cortisol. Blood cortisol levels and urinary 17-hydroxysteroids are evaluated. The test may be conducted for 24 h or over the course of several days. Various x-ray procedures may be performed in an attempt to visualize an adrenal or pituitary tumor.[22]

For the patient with adrenal tumor, surgery is the treatment of choice. Since tumors suppress the normal pituitary-adrenal axis, pre- and postoperative care includes hormonal replacement. Most patients with adrenal adenoma regain their own adrenal function within 6 months of surgery and are entirely normal thereafter. The prognosis for the patient with adrenal carcinoma, however, is poor. Radiation therapy and chemotherapy may be used in an attempt to elicit remission. The patient with a pituitary tumor may receive pituitary irradiation, although bilateral adrenalectomy is the most common form of treatment. In either case, the patient will remain adrenally insufficient.

Nursing management

The nurse has many opportunities to interact with the patient and family with adrenal problems. Often the first contact is when the child is hospitalized in adrenal crisis. This is a life-threatening situation, and administration of intravenous fluids at a uniform rate is critical. Careful monitoring of vital signs is essential, as these children are often dehydrated. Signs of increasing dehydration or overhydration as a result of too vigorous medical management need to be evaluated. Accurate collection of 24-h urine specimens is essential, particularly if a diagnosis has not yet been made.

During the evaluation phase of adrenal disorders, the nurse needs to work closely with the patient and family in order to accomplish the testing with the least trauma to the child. The 24-h urine tests need to be collected accurately, beginning and ending at the time specifically ordered. The nurse must ensure that no urine is inadvertently lost. If the child is an infant and not toilet trained, proper placement and good adherence of the collection bag are a must. Young children must also be restrained in order to be prevented from dislodging the collection apparatus. Signs should be posted at the bedside and in the bathroom to guard against inadvertent discarding of urine that needs to be saved. When medications are used in suppression tests, it is essential that they be given at precisely the times ordered to obtain the desired results.

Once a diagnosis has been made, surgery may be performed. In Cushing's syndrome, two approaches are used for surgery on the adrenal; an abdominal approach and a flank approach. Preoperatively, the patient needs to be informed about what to expect after surgery, including the possible insertion of a nasogastric tube to relieve abdominal distention and an indwelling catheter to measure urine output. Preparation in coughing, deep breathing, and the use of blow bottles is helpful. Postoperatively, breathing is often painful due to the close proximity of the incision to the diaphragm.[23]

Following adrenalectomy, the patient's vital signs are monitored carefully. Hypertension is a complication due to mineralocorticoid release secondary to manipulation of the adrenals. Urine output is observed closely as an indication of impending shock. Parenteral cortisol is given to replace the deficiency in mineralocorticoid production.

Children with congenital adrenal hyperplasia may require surgery for correction of genital abnormalities. The age of the child will influence the type of preoperative teaching that can be done, although it must be remembered that all children have a fear of genital surgery.[24] Adjustments in glucocorticoid and mineralocorticoid dosages are made preoperatively in order to deal with the stress of surgery. Postoperatively, the patient will most likely have in indwelling catheter in place. Vital signs are monitored frequently to assess steroid replacement. Infants need to be restrained in order to prevent damage to the surgical area or removal of the indwelling catheter. The operative site needs to be checked for trauma, infection, necrosis, or other signs that skin grafts might not be taking. Good perineal hygiene is essential to prevent contamination of the area with feces.

It is difficult for any parent to understand adrenal disease. The nurse may need to discuss the pathophysiology of the adrenal disease on many occasions. The physical changes that occur in adrenal diseases result in an altered body image for the child. The child needs help in dealing with those changes that will be permanent and needs assurance that certain body changes will disappear with therapy. For example, most children with Cushing's syndrome will have lost all external appearances of the disease within 1 year after surgery.[25] Parents of children with congenital adrenal hyperplasia have many of the same concerns as those of children with precocious puberty. Fears of sexual abuse need to be discussed openly. These families may also harbor guilt feelings when the child's ultimate height is compromised as a result of late detection of the disease. This guilt may be exaggerated by the child's poor body image related to height.

Daily medications remain the major form of treatment for adrenal insufficiency, and the nurse has an opportunity to do a great deal of teaching in this area. The family needs to know what type of medication the child is taking and the importance of following the prescribed schedule. Glucocorticoids need to be given every 8 h in order to suppress the release of ACTH. Administration three times a day will not accomplish this. Children with adrenal insufficiency frequently have increased salt needs secondary to poor aldosterone production. The family needs to understand the physiology of this process and allow the child to use the salt shaker freely, particularly in the summer when salt needs are increased due to sweating. Otherwise parents will often limit children's salt intake due to a fear of hypertension. Before discharge, the family will be given instructions for medication dosage schedules for sick day routines. For minor illnesses or fever, the dose is usually doubled, and for major illnesses or accidents the dose may be tripled. When the child is not able to take oral medication, intramuscular cortisol is given. The family and/or the child may be instructed in injection technique. When any type of illness occurs, prompt medical attention is important. The use of an identification (MEDIC-ALERT) necklace or bracelet is essential, as adrenal crisis is always a possibility.

Pancreas—islets of Langerhans

Anatomy and physiology

The pancreas is both an endocrine and an exocrine gland. The endocrine portion consists of the *islets of Langerhans*, clusters of secreting tissues scattered throughout the pancreas. The alpha cells secrete *glucagon*, a substance that raises the blood sugar, and the beta cells secrete *insulin*, a substance that lowers the blood sugar. In the normal individual, insulin is secreted in response to an elevation in the blood glucose level. This rise in insulin level causes a lowering of the blood sugar by facilitating the transport of glucose into the cells. This results in a nearly steady blood sugar level throughout the day. Without insulin, the body's cells are unable to utilize the glucose that is available to them. There are several exceptions, the most notable of which is the brain, which is able to utilize glucose directly from the circulation.

Insulin's major effect is on carbohydrate metabolism; however, it also affects fat and protein metabolism. Insulin also causes the transportation of fat into the fat cells, thus promoting fat storage. When insulin is not available, this transportation does not take place and fatty acids are released into the blood. Protein metabolism is affected when glucose cannot be utilized for energy. Large quantities of protein and fat are utilized for energy in place of carbohydrates, with the result that fewer amino acids are available for the building of new cellular tissue.

Diabetes mellitus

Diabetes mellitus is a deficiency in insulin production. This disease is a multisystem disorder with cardiovascular, renal, ophthalmic, and neurological complications. There appear to be two types of diabetes: juvenile-onset diabetes mellitus (JODM), usually diagnosed in childhood, and adult-onset diabetes mellitus (AODM), usually diagnosed in the middle-aged or elderly adult. Although these conditions have similar names, they are probably very different diseases.

Diabetes mellitus appears to be a multifactorial inherited disorder. That is, the individual inherits a predisposition for this disease, and then, given certain factors, unidentified at this time, certain predisposed individuals will go on to develop the disease. Several theories exist concerning these environmental factors. It is speculated that some individuals have developed viral infections which attack their susceptible pancreas. Mumps virus is one that has been implicated, since an increased number of individuals develop diabetes after mumps infection. Another theory is that diabetes results from an autoimmune process. It has been noted that individuals with diabetes mellitus have an increased frequency of other autoimmune endocrine disorders such as Hashimoto's thyroiditis and adrenal diseases.

In AODM the pancreas produces an insufficient amount of insulin for normal metabolism. Many of these individuals, if overweight, will have adequate insulin production if their weight is reduced, and this may be their only form of treatment. Others can be maintained on oral agents, pills, to stimulate the pancreas to produce more insulin. A small number of individuals will need to take insulin to supplement what their body is producing. In JODM, however, the pancreas stops producing insulin totally. In fact, in autopsies done on individuals with JODM, the beta cells have atrophied and disappeared. Thus, the only form of treatment that will be effective for individuals with JODM is the administration of insulin. Other differences such as the ability to develop ketosis, types of complications, and the age at which complications develop differentiate JODM and AODM. It should be noted that diabetes researchers are currently attempting to develop a new classification system for diabetes mellitus, and the designations JODM and AODM may change in the future.[26]

Although diabetes has been documented for thousands of years, we know relatively little about the disease. JODM occurs in about 1 in 600 school-age children. It affects males and females equally. JODM, unlike AODM, is uncommon in blacks. Diabetes may occur at any age, affecting children as young as 6 months, although it is most frequent in the school-age child. The two most frequent times of diagnosis are at 6 and 12 years of age.[27]

The onset of diabetes in children is rapid, with most having the symptoms for 2 weeks or less before diagnosis. Lack of insulin in the body causes decreased utilization of glucose by the cells, with the resulting elevation in blood sugar. When the kidneys are no longer able to reabsorb the glucose, sugar begins to spill over into the urine (the so-called renal threshold is surpassed). This large amount of glucose pulls water with it through osmotic pressure, causing dehydration and thirst. This alteration in glucose metabolism leads to a conversion to fat and protein metabolism. This utilization of body mass for energy results in weight loss and a corresponding increased appetite. The metabolic changes result in the classic findings of uncontrolled diabetes: polyuria, polydipsia, and polyphagia.

If the child is not diagnosed at this time, the signs and symptoms of ketoacidosis may develop. The body's dependence on fats and proteins for fuel leads to the formation of ketone bodies, a by-product of fat metabolism. The accumulation of the ketone bodies, acetoacetic acid, β-hydroxybutyric acid and acetone, causes a metabolic acidosis. As the level of ketones increases in the bloodstream, ketones begin to spill over into the urine. In an attempt to rid the body of the increasing quantities of carbon dioxide resulting from acidosis, the individual develops hyperpnea. Ketoacidosis also results in decreased peristalsis and stasis of fluid in the stomach, leading to nausea, vomiting, and abdominal distention. This loss of fluid combined with the osmotic diuresis leads to profound dehydration. At times the abdominal symptoms may be so severe that the child is thought to have appendicitis. If untreated, the child will become increasingly disoriented until coma develops. Renal shutdown may result, and ultimately death.

The findings of hyperglycemia, glucosuria, and ketosis are considered sufficient evidence to make the diagnosis of diabetes mellitus in a child. Glucosuria and hyperglycemia occur occasionally with stressful situations such as head injuries and hypothalamic lesions, and glucosuria alone is associated with alterations in the renal tubular handling of glucose; however, these situations are rare.

The child who is admitted with ketoacidosis may be moderately to critically ill. Blood is drawn for serum glucose, serum acetone, sodium, potassium, pH and CO_2 measurements. Serum lipids may also be checked. Glucose levels will be elevated, sometimes as high as 1000 mg/dl, although the glucose level does not indicate the severity of the child's condition. Serum acetone levels are a measure of the level of ketones in the blood. They are reported as positive at 1:2, 1:4, and so on, indicating that there is a positive reaction on an Acetest tablet when a dilution of one part of serum to two parts of water or one part of serum to four parts of water is used. Therefore, the higher the number the sicker the child, i.e., 1:16 is more serious than 1:4. Potassium, an intracellular ion, is driven out of the cells in the initial phases of ketoacidosis, which may result in a falsely high serum potassium level. However, this potassium is soon removed

from the system, leading to total body depletion of potassium. Blood lipids may be elevated due to the mobilization of fats for fuel, leading to falsely low electrolyte values. The pH and CO_2 give the best indication of the child's state of acidosis. Children who are critically ill have been known to have a pH as low as 6.8 and a CO_2 as low as 1.[28]

Once lab work has been obtained, parenteral fluids are begun to combat dehydration. Large amounts of fluids are administered rapidly, sometimes necessitating the use of two simultaneous intravenous lines. If there is any question of renal shutdown, an indwelling catheter may be inserted to monitor urinary output. Children are given nothing by mouth (NPO) due to the decreased peristalsis, and some children may have a nasogastric tube inserted to decrease abdominal distention.

Low-dose continuous insulin infusion is the treatment of choice for ketoacidosis. An initial bolus of insulin is given intravenously, and then the continuous infusion is begun. Sodium bicarbonate may be administered to the severely acidotic patient. A variety of intravenous solutions can be used to replace the electrolytes lost. Solutions containing glucose will be added to the intravenous as the blood sugar begins to fall. Most children respond rapidly to this regimen and are chemically normal, eating well and off intravenous maintenance within 24 to 48 h.

The nurse has a critical role in the management of the patient in ketoacidosis. Vital signs and urinary output are checked frequently. Urine is also checked for sugar and acetone at each voiding. The patient whose level of consciousness is decreased needs to be watched carefully for vomiting and possible aspiration. Accurate intake and output are essential. If continuous insulin infusion is being used, the nurse must keep in mind that insulin disintegrates rapidly once mixed in solution and, therefore, the insulin solution must be changed every 6 h. The rate at which this insulin is being administered must be kept steady, and a positive-pressure pump should be utilized. Too rapid an infusion of insulin may cause hypoglycemia, and too slow an infusion may delay the patient's response. A cardiac monitor may be used to evaluate the child's potassium level. A flattening or absence of the T wave may be the first indication of hypokalemia. Once the child has stabilized and the intravenous is to be discontinued, it is important to remember to give the first dose of subcutaneous insulin before discontinuing the intravenous. Intravenous insulin is utilized very rapidly and will be virtually gone when the intravenous is discontinued. If there is any delay between the time the intravenous is discontinued and the first dose of subcutaneous insulin is given, the child may slip back into hyperglycemia.

A variety of insulins are available for the treatment of diabetes. They are divided into groups of short-acting, intermediate-acting, and long-acting, according to their time of peak action and duration of action (see Table 29-3). Regular insulin is the only type that can be given intravenously; however, all insulin must be given by injection. Insulin is a protein and if taken orally would be digested by the individual's own digestive enzymes. Once a child has been taken off intravenous insulin, subcutaneous regular insulin is given three to four times a day. Once a dose has been established, the child is usually switched to short- and intermediate-acting insulins or an intermediate-acting insulin alone.

The majority of juvenile diabetics will experience a phenomenon known as the *honeymoon period* shortly after diagnosis. It appears that after an initial failing the pancreas gives one last surge of insulin before it totally depletes itself. After the child is stabilized on the initial dose of insulin, during the honeymoon period the insulin needs will fall and occasional children will need to be taken off insulin altogether. However, all will need to go back on insulin eventually. The honeymoon period usually begins several weeks after diagnosis and may last 1 to 6 months, although there have been cases in which the honeymoon period lasted as long as 2 years. The family needs to be aware of this phenomenon, as the child who remains on a large dose of insulin may experience hypoglycemic reactions. This can also be a stressful time for the child and the family who are having difficulty accepting the diagnosis. Often they will feel that the physician has made an error and that the disease is actually going away. Some physicians will keep the young child on a token dose of 1 unit of insulin a day, rather than remove the child from insulin completely because the psychological adjustment is so difficult.

The medical management of the child with

Table 29-3 Commonly used insulins

	Name	Peak	Duration of action
Short-acting	Regular	2 h	6 h
	Semilente	2–4 h	6–8 h
Intermediate-acting	NPH	8 h	24 h
	Lente	8 h	24 h
Long-acting	PZI	18 h	48 h
	Ultralente	18 h	48 h

JODM varies greatly from physician to physician. This is a philosophical issue. Some physicians feel that tight control, i.e., the maintenance of normal or near normal blood sugars, will prevent the vascular complications of diabetes in the future. Other physicians feel that research has not shown that tight control alters the course of the disease and that vascular problems are a result of the disease state, not a complication of poor control. Most pediatricians feel that the possible benefits of strict control do not justify the psychological and physical hazards associated with it. In general, management is aimed at the achievement of normal growth and development, psychological well-being, and minimal glucosuria. Evaluation of glucosuria may be based on testing of 24-h urine specimens. The calories spilled as glucose should be less than 5 percent of the total calories consumed in 24 h.

The course of the illness varies from child to child. Those children who are ketosis prone may have frequent hospitalizations or frequent absences from school due to ketoacidosis. However, many children are not ketosis prone and will have no hospitalizations other than at the time that they were diagnosed. Unlike AODM, the vascular problems in JODM develop after long-standing diabetes, usually 20 years or more. These microvascular complications include retinopathy and possible blindness, nephropathy with possible kidney failure, and neuropathy. Some patients develop complications in adolescence, although this is uncommon. Some patients never develop complications that are significant. It is impossible to predict the outcome for any particular child.

Nursing management

The long-term management of the child with diabetes mellitus requires participation by all members of the health care team. The nurse has a vital role on this team. After the initial diagnosis of diabetes is made, a great deal of information must be learned by the child and parents. It must be remembered that due to the shock, grief, and denial that families go through at the time of diagnosis, relatively little information may be retained at the beginning.

Several psychomotor skills must be learned by the family during the hospitalization. The first of these skills is urine testing. Most children are able to accomplish this task by 6 to 7 years of age. Two types of urine testing are done. One is testing on a first void specimen, i.e., the child goes to the bathroom and tests this specimen of urine. Results will be an average of the sugar and acetone values since the child has voided last, usually 2 h or more. A second type of test is a second void specimen, i.e., the child voids, then waits approximately 15 min, and voids again. The second specimen is then tested for sugar and acetone. This type of test reflects what is happening in the kidneys and, therefore, the circulation at the time of testing. Second void specimens should be routinely tested when the child is hospitalized or any time an insulin dose is being based solely on the results of urine testing. Most children test on first void specimens at home. Urine specimens are usually obtained before meals and at bedtime, although it is unrealistic to expect a child to test urine routinely while at school.

A variety of testing reagents are available for testing sugar and acetone. It is important to remember to utilize the proper color chart with each test, as they vary greatly. The American Diabetes Association has recommended that individuals with JODM test with tablet reagents rather than strip reagents, as tablets give a better quantitative reading. The 2-drop Clinitest tablets have the advantage of an upper limit of 5 percent. If families use Clinitest tablets, they need to be warned of the pass-through phenomenon, which occurs when the urine contains more sugar than the test tablet can accurately indicate; the color in the test tube then passes through the bright orange at the top of the color scale and changes to a darker color that may be misinterpreted as the lower end of the glucose scale. By watching the test tube constantly until the boiling reaction stops, one sees the full range of color that occurs and is not deceived by the pass-through phenomenon if it takes place. Strip preparations have the disadvantage of spoiling easily, particularly when the bottle caps are not screwed on tightly. It is now recommended that all tests be recorded in percentages rather than pluses (+ to + + + +). Currently each type of reagent is marked with percentages as well as pluses. There is no consistency between plus markings; for example 2+ using Testape indicates a 0.5 percent reading, while 2+ using 2-drop Clinitest tablets indicates a 2 percent reading. A log consisting of daily urine tests and insulin doses should be kept.

Currently more and more diabetic children (and their parents) are taught to monitor blood glucose levels at home using a method such as Chemstrip bG test strip. An Autolet is used to puncture a fingertip and a hanging drop of blood is transferred to the reagent area of the strip. After 60 s the blood is wiped off with a cotton ball. After another 60 s (total 120 s), the color on the strip is compared to colors on the vial label to determine the blood glucose level. The child and parents are taught how to adjust insulin, diet, and activity to maintain the blood glucose between 80 and 120 mg/dl. Because the Chemstrip retains the color, strips can be saved and shown to the physician later for follow-up. Since this method allows for blood glucose levels to be much more closely regulated, urine can be monitored with strip reagents—a method that is much more acceptable to the child than 2-drop Clinitest. Even more important, improved control of blood glucose levels appears to reduce or delay the onset of serious complications of JODM.

Insulin injection technique is taught to both the child and the family. Insulin is available in concentrations of 40, 80, and 100 units per milliliter. U 40 insulin is no longer being produced, although some pharmacies may still have a backlog in stock. U 80 insulin is expected to be phased out in the next several years. Although the concentrations are different, 1 unit of U 80 equals one 1 of U 40 or U 100. It is critically important that the type of syringe used (U 40, U 80, or U 100) be matched to the insulin concentration. Insulin is stable at normal temperatures, although it needs to be protected from extreme heat or freezing. The bottle or bottles in use should be kept at room temperature, as the insulin is then less irritating. Extra vials of insulin should be kept in the refrigerator. Injection technique is taught through demonstration and practice. A variety of sites are used throughout the body to foster site rotation in order to prevent atrophy or hypertrophy of the subcutaneous tissue, which interfere with insulin absorption. Sites commonly used are the posterior aspects of the arms, the deltoid regions, the upper outer quadrant of the buttocks, the abdomen, the thighs, and the calves. Often the best way of delineating the areas is to draw them on the child's body. This appears to be far more effective than using a teddy bear which has no anatomic landmarks. Children are able to master parts of the injection technique at a very early age, although there is some controversy as to how soon a child should be required to give his or her own injections (Fig. 29-4). Many people feel that the responsibility for giving injections should not be placed on a child until adolescence. However, before then, the child and family may share in the experience. Some children are able to draw up insulin into the syringe but are fearful of injecting themselves, while other children are able to inject themselves easily but have difficulty mastering the technique of drawing up insulin. Both situations allow the child to learn and share the experience with the family. Many children will learn to give their own injections at the time of initial hospitalization. Both parents need to give the child at least one injection before discharge so that they are capable should an emergency arise.

Diet is an integral part of therapy for the diabetic child. Diet prescriptions vary from a regular diet with the exception of no concentrated sweets to complicated diet plans based on divisions of calories into eighteenths of the total caloric intake. A common diet plan is based on American Diabetes Association exchange lists. All diet plans include snacks to cover peaks of insulin action and a bedtime snack to prevent nighttime hypoglycemia. Likewise, diets are planned to promote normal growth and development and allow for the frequently changing activities of the child. It is important that the family understand the need for yearly diet revisions to accommodate the changing caloric needs of the growing child.

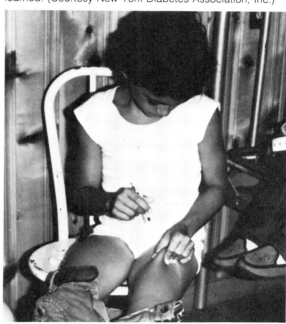

Figure 29-4 With supervision, a child can become capable of self-administering insulin in a short period. The New York Diabetes Association operates a summer camp for diabetic children where such skills and good dietary habits can be learned. (Courtesy New York Diabetes Association, Inc.)

Many factors affect the control of diabetes in the child. Stress most commonly raises the blood sugar, although in some children it may cause hypoglycemic reactions. Exercise allows the passage of glucose directly into the cell without the addition of insulin, thereby lowering the blood sugar. On days when an unusually high level of physical activity is anticipated, insulin should be injected into the abdomen or buttock; uneven absorption can result from the increased blood supply to vigorously contracting limb muscles, even though the insulin has of course been injected subcutaneously rather than intramuscularly. The production of GH and sex hormones in the growing child raises the need for insulin. Day-to-day management fluctuates with each child, and the family needs to be able to differentiate hyperglycemia and hypoglycemia (Table 29-4). Hypoglycemia is dangerous as well as embarrassing because repeated episodes may lead to brain damage. If the family is in doubt as to whether the child is hypoglycemic or hyperglycemic, they are taught to treat the episode as

Table 29-4 Comparison of hypoglycemia and hyperglycemia

		Hyperglycemia (acidosis)	Hypoglycemia (insulin reaction)
Clinical features			
Onset		Slow (days)	Sudden (minutes to hours)
Symptoms		Thirst	Nervousness, irritability
		Headache	Headache
		Nausea	Fatigue
		Vomiting	Personality change
		Abdominal pain	Weakness
		Dim vision (myopia)	Blurred vision (diplopia)
		Dyspnea	Paresthesias
			Lethargy, stupor, convulsions
			Tremor
			Pallor
			Shallow respirations
Signs		Flushing	Sweating
		Hyperventilation (Kussmaul), rapid, deep breathing, eventual respiratory failure	Variable pulse (early parasympathetic response, later sympathetic response)
		Dehydration (dry skin)	Positive Babinski reflex
		Rapid pulse	Normal eyes
		Soft eyeballs	
		Normal or absent reflexes	
		Acetone breath	
Chemical features			
Urine		Glucose, acetone	No glucose in second voided specimen
Blood glucose		↑ 240 mg/dl	↓ 60 mg/dl

hypoglycemia, since feeding the child a small amount of sugar will not make hyperglycemia appreciably worse, and hypoglycemia is far more dangerous than hyperglycemia. Families are given prescriptions for glucagon to be kept at home in case of hypoglycemia leading to unconsciousness. Glucagon works by mobilizing stored sugar from the liver, rapidly raising the blood sugar. However, when sugar stores are depleted the glucagon will have no effect, and the family needs to seek help rapidly. Before discharge, the family needs to know what to do if hyperglycemia or nausea and vomiting occurs. Over time, most families are able to learn to make minor adjustments in daily insulin doses to deal with elevated sugar and acetone levels.

Since the complications of long-standing diabetes do not occur in childhood, foot care and specialized skin care that are taught to adult diabetics are postponed for the child. Children with diabetes have no more foot problems, in-

fections, or difficulty healing than any other child. Therefore, the child needs to be taught normal good hygiene and normal first aid.

Some of the most difficult problems to deal with in a child with diabetes are the psychological effects of chronic illness. Many parents are overprotective and fear that something will happen to their child. Others make the child's life so rigid that a normal childhood no longer exists. Siblings may develop resentment for all the attention that the diabetic child receives. Adolescence can be a crisis period for the diabetic child and the family. Adolescents may use their diabetes as a way of acting out, resulting in poor control with frequent ketoacidosis and hospitalizations. In families where there are underlying family problems, diabetes tends to exacerbate these situations. The nurse needs to discuss these areas openly with the child and the family. It is far easier to prevent these problems than to deal with them in the future.

Nursing Care Plan–Diabetes Mellitus

Patient: Laurie Stewart **Age:** 14 years **Date of Admission:** 1/6 at 7:30 P.M.

Assessment

Laurie Stewart, a 14-year-old female, was admitted to the pediatric unit at 7:30 P.M. with a diagnosis of pharyngitis and diabetic ketoacidosis. The emergency room nurse who transported Laurie upstairs to the pediatric unit reported that Laurie was brought in by her mother at the advice of their doctor. Mrs. Stewart explained that the whole family had been sick with colds for the last week and that she herself had been confined to bed because of fever and cough for the last 3 days. Mrs. Stewart was unaware of Laurie's symptoms until late this afternoon, when Laurie "begged me to call the doctor."

Laurie explained that she felt well until 2 days ago, when she awoke with a sore throat. She felt progressively sicker during the day and had difficulty swallowing solid foods. This morning she took her normal dose of insulin, 17 units of Regular and 35 units of Lente. She was unable to eat any solid foods and had only small sips of Coca-Cola to drink, although she was very thirsty. By late this afternoon she was complaining of severe headache, abdominal pain, and difficulty breathing. Because Laurie had not tested her urine since becoming ill, her physician advised her to come to the hospital for further evaluation.

Admission assessment

Upon arrival on the pediatric unit, the evening nurse made the following observations:

General appearance Acutely ill-appearing, lethargic adolescent; answers questions but is somewhat disoriented.
Vital signs Weight 43 kg (down approximately 2 kg from normal weight),
temp. 38°C (100.4°F), pulse 88 per min, respirations 24 per min.
Skin Pale and dry; minimal tenting and poor turgor.
Mouth Mucous membranes dry, lips cracked and fissured, pharynx erythematous with white exudate on both tonsils.
Respirations Deep Kussmaul respirations, strong odor of acetone on breath (smells like mixed-fruit–flavor gum).
Abdomen Distended, no bowel sounds auscultated.

Urine Five percent sugar, large acetone.

Physician's orders

1. Blood sugar, serum acetone, pH, CO_2, electrolytes STAT
2. Blood sugar and serum acetone q2h × 4
3. Strep screen and Monospot
4. IV D 2.5 $\frac{1}{2}$ lactated Ringer's with 20 meq KCl to run at 200 ml/h
5. Four units Regular insulin IV push (done by physician)
6. IV 250 ml normal saline with 100 units Regular insulin to run at 4 units/h connect to IVAC pump
7. Complete bed rest
8. NPO except ice chips
9. Intake and output
10. Daily weight
11. Vital signs q2h
12. Urine sugar and acetone with 2-drop Clinitest tablets and Acetest tablets at each void
13. Cardiac monitor

The physician started the IV, drew the STAT blood work, and then gave the IV push insulin. While the evening nurse connected the cardiac monitor, she noted that Laurie moaned occasionally and complained of "stomachache." Mrs. Stewart stayed in the room during these procedures and then announced that she had to go home because she had left her 11-year-old son in charge of the other children. The nurse gave her the unit telephone number and encouraged Mrs. Stewart to call to find out how Laurie was doing.

Shortly after Mrs. Stewart left, the nurse from the diabetes clinic arrived and related the following history. Laurie had been diagnosed with diabetes 4 years ago. She is the oldest of seven children, and at the time of her diagnosis her mother stated that Laurie would have to take full responsibility for caring for her diabetes because she had too many other problems with the other children. Since her diagnosis, Laurie has not done particularly well with no family support. She has had a very difficult time following the clinic's recommendations. It is not uncommon for her to forget her insulin injections, and recently she stopped testing her urine.

Nursing diagnosis	Nursing goals	Nursing actions	Evaluation/revision
1. Alteration in glucose utilization secondary to infection	☐ Decreased hyperglycemia as evidenced by: **a.** Urinary glucose of 2 percent or less **b.** Negative urinary acetone **c.** Blood sugar 200 mg/dl or less **d.** Negative serum acetone	☐ Maintain IV insulin at 4 units/h ☐ Check urinary sugar and acetone at each void ☐ Blood sugar and serum acetone q2h ☐ When blood glucose falls to 200 mg/dl, observe for insulin reaction	☐ 1/6, 10:30 P.M.: IV infusing well, urine 5 percent sugar, negative acetone ☐ 1/7, 12:30 A.M.: Urine 2 percent sugar, negative acetone ☐ *Continue plan*
2. Fluid volume deficit and electrolyte imbalance secondary to osmotic diuresis	☐ Fluid and electrolyte balance as evidenced by: **a.** Firm skin turgor **b.** Moist mucous membranes **c.** Urinary volume approximately 1300 ml/24 h **d.** Normal T wave formation **e.** Return to normal weight **d.** Normal T wave formation	☐ Maintain IV 200 ml/h with 20 meq KCl ☐ Vaseline to lips q2h or PRN; ice chips PRN ☐ Record I and O q2h ☐ Monitor T wave q1h ☐ Daily weight ☐ Monitor T wave q1h	☐ 1/6, 8:30 P.M.: IV infusing well, normal T wave formation, increased comfort from ice chips and Vaseline ☐ 1/7, 12 noon: Weight up to 43.5 kg ☐ *Continue plan*
3. Abdominal pain and distention with decreased peristalsis secondary to ketoacidosis	☐ Decreased abdominal pain and distention and establishment of normal peristalsis	☐ Provide measures to resolve ketoacidosis as outlined in nursing diagnoses 1 and 2 ☐ Ice chips PRN ☐ Auscultate for bowel sounds q2h ☐ Position child on side ☐ Hospital gown without pants to bind at waist	☐ 1/6, 9:30 P.M.: IVs infusing well, taking ice chips without increased distention, no nausea or vomiting ☐ 1/7, 3:30 A.M.: Bowel sounds auscultated ☐ 1/7, 8 A.M.: Alert and hungry ☐ *Continue plan*
4. Dyspnea associated with metabolic acidosis	☐ Establishment of normal breathing patterns as evidenced by: **a.** Respiratory rate 14–18/min **b.** No acetone detectable on breath	☐ Provide measures to resolve ketoacidosis (nursing diagnoses 1 and 2) ☐ Elevate head of bed 45°	☐ 1/6, 10:30 P.M.: Breathing eased, appears more comfortable ☐ 1/7, 12:30 A.M.: No acetone detectable on breath ☐ *Continue plan*
5. Fatigue and disorientation secondary to diminished cell utilization of glucose	☐ Reorientation of time and place. Uninterrupted sleep between voidings	☐ Provide measures to resolve ketoacidosis (nursing diagnoses 1 and 2) ☐ While awake, give short reminders of time and place ☐ Evaluate physical signs without waking patient ☐ Offer ice chips when patient is awakened for voiding	☐ 1/7, 12:30 A.M.: Sleeping soundly ☐ 1/7, 8:30 A.M.: Awake and oriented ☐ *Continue plan*
6. Lack of compliance leading to insufficient insulin intake and hospitalization	☐ Test urine four times per day when confined to home because of illness	☐ Education program to cover: **a.** Relationship of insulin needs to urinary sugar and acetone **b.** Relationship of illness to insulin needs	☐ 1/7, 12:30 P.M.: Testing urine on own ☐ 1/7, 8 P.M.: Able to discuss relationship of illness, insulin, and glucosuria ☐ Continue plan

Nursing diagnosis	Nursing goals	Nursing actions	Evaluation/revision
		c. Psychomotor skills involved in urine testing ☐ Give urine testing equipment to patient to take home ☐ Review educational program with mother ☐ Encourage mother to become involved with diabetes care especially when patient is ill ☐ Introduce patient to other adolescents with diabetes on pediatric unit ☐ Suggest contacting Juvenile Diabetes Foundation children's group for support at home	

References

1. Jerome M. Hershman, *Endocrine Pathophysiology: A Patient Oriented Approach*, Lea and Febiger, Philadelphia, 1977, p. 1.
2. George E. Bacon et al.; *A Practical Approach to Pediatric Endocrinology*, Year Book, Chicago, 1975, p. 78.
3. Ibid., p. 216.
4. Ibid., p. 164.
5. Ibid.
6. Abraham M. Rudolph, ed., *Pediatrics*, Appleton-Century-Crofts, New York, 1977, p. 1817.
7. Mildred Fenske, "The Endocrine System," in Gladys M. Scipien et al., *Comprehensive Pediatric Nursing*, McGraw-Hill, New York, 1975, p. 766.
8. Arthur C. Guyton, *Textbook of Medical Physiology*, Saunders, Philadelphia, 1976, pp. 1009–1010.
9. A. H. Klein et al., "Improved prognosis in Congenital Hypothyroidism Treated Before Age Three Months," *Journal of Pediatrics* **81**:912 (1972).
10. Bacon, op. cit., p. 113.
11. Hershman, op. cit., pp. 46–47.
12. Ibid., p. 58.
13. Bacon, op. cit., p. 99.
14. Ibid., pp. 101–103.
15. Hershman, op. cit., pp. 64–66.
16. Bacon, op. cit., p. 102.
17. Rudolph, op. cit., p. 1636.
18. Hershman, op. cit., pp. 85–86.
19. Rudolph, op. cit., p. 1635.
20. Ibid., p. 1640.
21. Ibid., p. 1644.
22. Hershman, op. cit., pp. 96–97.
23. Fenske, op. cit., p. 776.
24. Madeline Petrillo and Sirgay Sanger, *Emotional Care of Hospitalized Children*, Lippincott, Philadelphia, 1972, p. 11.
25. Rudolph, op. cit., p. 1645.
26. Kelly M. West, "Standardization of Definition, Classification, and Reporting in Diabetes-related Epidemiologic Studies," *Diabetes Care* **2**:65–76 (1979).
27. Allan L. Drash, "Managing the Child with Diabetes Mellitus," *Postgraduate Medicine* **6**:86 (1978).
28. Rudolph, op. cit., p. 702

Chapter 30 Reproductive function and adolescent sexuality

Rosalyn Podratz and **Jacqueline Prokop Ficht**

Upon completion of this chapter, the student will be able to:

1. Describe the anatomy and physiology of the male and female reproductive tracts.

2. Describe alterations related to dysfunctional uterine bleeding.

3. Describe the causal relationships between embryologic development of the reproductive tract and alterations such as ambiguous genitalia, Kleinfelter syndrome, and monosomy X.

4. Identify several malformations of the male genital organs affecting normal urinary or reproductive function.

5. List reasons for the failure of adolescents to use birth control methods.

6. Compare the effectiveness of temporary methods of birth control for teenagers.

7. Identify teaching needed to orient the teenage girl for her first pelvic examination.

8. Describe the social, psychological, and health-related problems occurring with adolescent pregnancy.

9. Identify the predictors of success in young mothers.

Fertilization of the ovum by a sperm and continued embryologic development occur in an ordered and systematic way. Genetic sex is determined at the time of conception by the presence of the X or Y chromosome in the sperm fertilizing the ovum. When a sperm containing a chromosome complement of 23,X unites with an ovum containing a chromosome complement of 23,X, a normal female, 46,XX, will result. If a sperm with a chromosome complement of 23,Y unites with an ovum 23,X, a normal male, 46,XY, will result.

Embryonic origin of the reproductive tract

Although an infant's chromosomal sex is determined at conception, the reproductive system does not begin to develop until about the fourth week after fertilization.[1] Appropriate sexual development occurs if the subsequent steps of physical development proceed normally. These steps have a definite sequence: first, the differentiation of the bipotential gonad; second, the differentiation and development of the internal reproductive system; and third, the differentiation and development of external genitalia (Fig. 30-1).[2]

During the first 6 weeks of gestation, the embryonic sex glands, or *gonads*, are undifferentiated in the male and female. The gonad then is known as a *bipotential gonad* (able to form either testes or ovaries). It consists of a central medulla, which develops if the fetus is a male, and a cortex, which develops if the fetus is a female.

Figure 30-1 Differentiation of the bipotential gonad into testis or ovary. (A) The primordial germ cells have colonized the peripheral region of the indifferent gonad. (B, C) Male germ cells migrate into the central mass of gonadal tissue. The periphery becomes free of cells, forming a connective tissue layer. (D, E) Female germ cells are surrounded by migrating gonadal cells to form primary follicles. (*From S. Ohno, Sex Chromosomes and Sex-Linked Genes. Springer-Verlag, New York, 1967, p. 163. Used by permission.*)

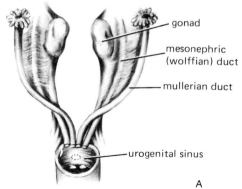

— gonad

— mesonephric (wolffian) duct

— mullerian duct

— urogenital sinus

A

INDIFFERENT STAGE

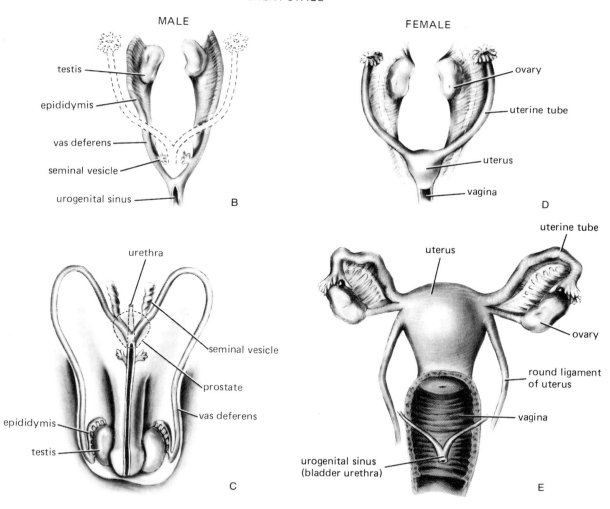

MALE

testis —
epididymis —
vas deferens —
seminal vesicle —
urogenital sinus —

B

FEMALE

ovary

uterine tube

uterus

vagina

D

urethra

seminal vesicle

prostate

vas deferens

epididymis —
testis —

C

uterine tube

uterus

ovary

round ligament of uterus

vagina

urogenital sinus (bladder urethra)

E

At about the seventh to eighth week of gestation, differentiation into the ovaries and testicles takes place. This process is poorly understood. Genes on sex chromosomes and probably also on autosomes are involved. The Y chromosome is required for diffentiation into testes.

In the fetus, external genitalia develop as female unless androgens from the testes are present. The presence of androgens and a non-steroid substance produced by the fetal testes induce growth of the Wolffian ducts into the epididymides, vasa deferentia, and seminal vesicles. At the same time, the growth of the müllerian duct is inhibited, and it later regresses.

Differentiation of the external genitalia is the final stage of reproductive system development (Fig. 30-2). The fetus is clearly recognizable as male or female by the third month. In the early embryonic stages of external genital development, the beginnings of the external genitalia are found in the genital tubercle, the urethral folds, and the two genital swellings or labioscrotal folds.

The external genitalia begin to develop sexual characteristics after 8 weeks of gestation. The genital tubercle elongates to form a central phallus. This extends to become either the penis or clitoris. The urethral folds develop, and the urethral groove becomes the opening of the urogenital sinus, forming the lower vagina and urethral opening or the perineal and penile urethra. The two urethral folds fuse to enclose the penile urethra. In the female, the unfused lips of the urethral folds become the labia minora. The genital swellings, or labioscrotal folds, fuse and become the scrotum or remain unfused to become the labia majora. If there is a failure of normal development, genitourinary tract anomalies often result. The exact reason for specific developmental genitourinary anomalies is unknown. These will be discussed under abnormal sexual development. Heredity, teratogenic agents, or infection during the first trimester of pregnancy may cause them (see Chap. 8).

Anatomy and physiology of the reproductive tract

The primary organs of reproduction are the *gonads:* the testes in the male and the ovaries in

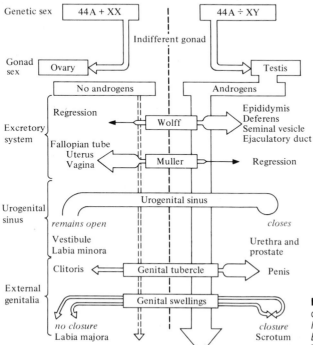

Figure 30-2 Developmental fate of the reproductive organs of the indifferent gonad and its hormonal regulation. (*From H. Tuchmann-Duplessis and P. Hagel, Illustrated Human Embryology, vol. 2: Organogenesis, Springer-Verlag, New York, 1974, p. 100. Used by permission.*)

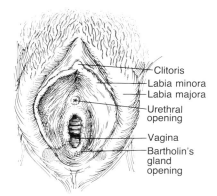

Clitoris
Labia minora
Labia majora
Urethral opening
Vagina
Bartholin's gland opening

Figure 30-3 External genitalia of the female. (*From Robert S. Hillman et al., Clinical Skills, McGraw-Hill, New York, 1981, p. 355. Used by permission.*)

the female. The *germ cells*, or sex cells, are the sperm in the male and the ova in the female. Collectively, they are known as *gametes*. Reproduction is possible only when all of the factors for fertilization are present. These factors include the internal and external organs of reproduction, the presence of appropriate hormones, and normal germ cell development.

Female reproductive anatomy
External female reproductive organs (Fig. 30-3)
The *perineum*, located between the vagina and rectum, is triangular in shape and composed chiefly of muscles, fascia, and fat. The *vulva* refers to the visible external genital organs. The *mons pubis* is the cushion of fat covered with hair which lies over the pubic bone. The *labia majora* are two skin folds from the mons pubis that pass downward and disappear in the posterior portion of the vulva in front of the anus. They are analogous to the scrotum in the male. At the base on either side are found the *Bartholin glands*. These glands are responsible for secretion of mucin that keeps the surface of the labia moist. The *labia minora* are folds of skin and mucous membrane found between the labia majora. At the upper margin, the labia minora unite above the clitoris to form the frenulum. The *clitoris*, analogous to the penis in the male, has erectile tissue, and sensory nerve endings, and is covered by the prepuce. The *hymen*, a fold of mucous membrane, partially covers the external opening of the vagina. The hymen is torn in most sexually active females. The *Skene's ducts* are located on each side of the urinary meatus. Both the Skene's ducts and Bartholin's glands can harbor infection.

Internal female reproductive organs (Fig. 30-4)
The *ovaries*, or female gonads, are the active source of female hormones, estrogen and progesterone. They are located one on either side of the uterus and consist of two layers, cortex and medulla. The *cortex*, or outer layer, contains the egg cells, or ova, and the *medulla*, or inner vascular layer, is the site of ova ripening. There are two *fallopian tubes*, each about 10 cm in length, that connect the ovaries to the uterus. These are narrower at the uterine end and have a funnel-shaped, fimbriated end over each ovary. Fingerlike folds of the inner muscle layer move by peristalsis, creating a current to transport the ovum through the tube toward the uterus.

The *uterus* is a muscular, pear-shaped organ located between the bladder and the rectum in the true pelvis. It has the ability to stretch to 500 times its normal capacity in full-term pregnancy and to return to near normal size. The *vagina*, or birth canal, is the connecting tube between the external genitalia and the uterus. The vagina is lined with mucous membrane that contains surface folds, or *rugae*. The vagina slopes down and back at an angle of 60 to 70° (see Fig. 30-4).

Male reproductive anatomy
Internal male reproductive organs (Fig. 30-5)
The internal male reproductive organs are the testes, canal systems, and accessory structures. There are two *testes* in the scrotal sac. They are compound glands divided into lobules. They contain the terminal portion of the *seminiferous tubules* (eventually forming the tube of the *epididymis*) and interstitial tissue (containing Leydig cells). The epithelial lining of the tubules consists

Figure 30-4 Midsagittal section through the female pelvis. (*From Charles E. Tobin and John J. Jacobs, eds., Shearer's Manual of Human Dissection, 6th ed., McGraw-Hill, New York, 1981, p. 188. Used by permission.*)

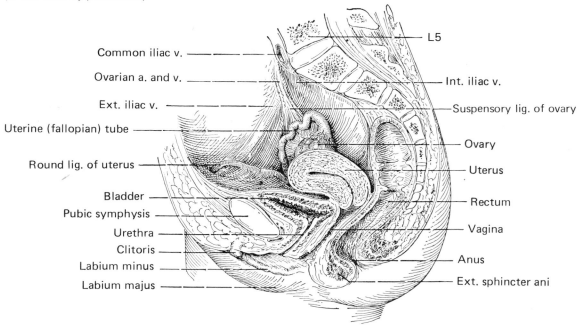

Figure 30-5 Sagittal section through the male pelvis. (*From Charles E. Tobin and John J. Jacobs, eds., Shearer's Manual of Human Dissection, 6th ed., McGraw-Hill, New York, 1981, p. 180. Used by permission.*)

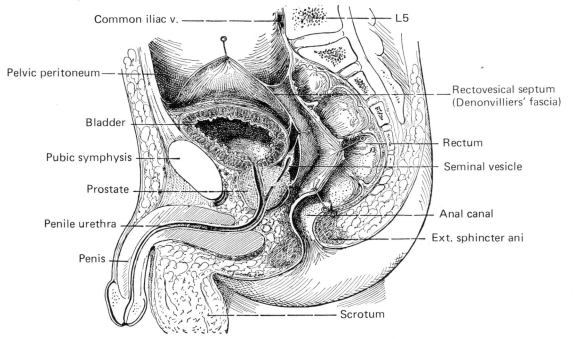

of supporting cells and *spermatogenic (sperm-producing) cells.* The Leydig cells function in the production of androgens, especially testosterone. Production of sperm begins at puberty, and the seminiferous tubules undergo a gradual involution with advancing age.

External male reproductive organs The external male reproductive organs are the *scrotum* and the *penis.* The scrotum contains the *testes* and is a continuation of the abdominal cavity. During fetal development, the testes develop in the peritoneal cavity. By about 36 weeks, the testes have descended into the scrotal sac and the canal connecting the sac with the abdominal cavity closes. The *penis* consists of *cavernous bodies* (erectile tissue) and the *urethra.* It is through the urethra that the seminal fluid is excreted. The cavernous bodies contain blood spaces that are empty when the penis is flaccid. When these spaces fill with blood, the penis becomes erect. The external urinary meatus is found in the *glans penis.* The glans is almost completely enclosed by a fold of skin called the *foreskin* or *prepuce.* This foreskin is removed when a circumcision is done.

Physiology of reproduction

Puberty

During adolescence, an individual's reproductive system matures and associated physical and behavioral changes take place. The physical changes that occur during adolescence are characterized by maturation of the reproductive organs, development of secondary sex characteristics, and a growth spurt affecting almost all the organs and tissues of the body. In boys, these changes occur from ages 12 to 20 and in girls from ages 10 to 18.

During childhood, a low level of follicle-stimulating hormone from the adrenal cortex is present in both sexes. The hypothalamus is responsible for releasing factors to the pituitary which stimulate release of gonadotropic hormones responsible for pubertal sexual maturation. At puberty, there is a growth spurt in the male's testes and the female's uterus and an activation of pituitary and gonadal hormones (estrogens and androgens). Chap. 15 describes the changes and endocrinology of puberty.

Male hormonal cycle

The pituitary gland secretes three *gonadotropic hormones* responsible for male sexual function, FSH, LH, and LTH. Androgens, principally testosterone, are secreted by the testes. FSH, *follicle-stimulating hormone*, stimulates and regulates spermatogenesis in conjunction with testosterone. LH, *luteinizing hormone*, stimulates the interstitial Leydig cells to produce testosterone. LTH, *luteotropic hormone (prolactin)*, does not play a significant known role in male sexual function.

Female hormonal cycle

The ovaries contain all the *primordial follicles* (immature ova) at birth. They continue growing slowly through childhood under the influence of low levels of FSH. At puberty, under stimulation of higher levels of ovarian hormones, the follicles develop into mature ova. There is a cyclic production of estrogen for about 2 years before menstruation begins.

Menstrual cycle The menstrual cycle is 28 to 35 days long in most women. The cycle begins with day 1 of the menses and progresses in well-defined steps. A single follicle (the *primordial follicle*) develops and matures in the ovary. It is stimulated by FSH and LH from the pituitary gland and estrogen from the ovaries. The primordial follicle matures in the ovary and becomes known as the *graafian follicle.* It secretes large amounts of estrogen. This process occurs during about the first 2 weeks of the menstrual cycle. At about 14 days before the onset of the next menses, the production of LH rises sharply *(LH surge)*, causing rupture of the graafian follicle and release of the egg *(ovulation).* The *corpus luteum* develops in the site of the former follicle and secretes large quantities of both progesterone and estrogen.

Endometrial cycle Many uterine cell changes occur during the *endometrial cycle.* These changes are the direct effect of estrogen and progesterone. *Estrogen* stimulates the growth of the uterine smooth muscle *(myometrium)* and the glandular epithelial lining *(endometrium).* The follicular, or proliferative, phase begins immediately after the menses are over and is under the control of estrogen. It is a period of rapid endometrial growth which ends at ovulation.

Figure 30-6 Summary of plasma hormone concentrations, ovarian events, and uterine changes during the menstrual cycle. (*From Arthur J. Vander, James H. Sherman, and Dorothy S. Luciano, Human Physiology, Mechanisms of Body Function, 3d ed., McGraw-Hill, New York, 1980, p. 497. Used by permission.*)

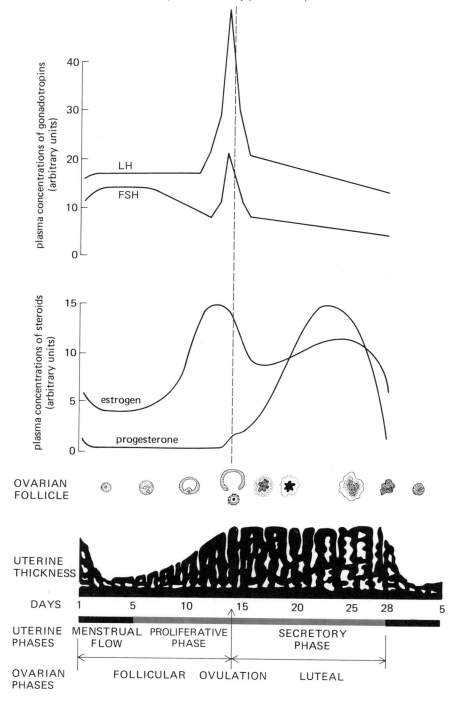

The *luteal* or *secretory phase* of the menstrual cycle begins after ovulation and ends with menstruation. In the luteal phase, progesterone acts on the endometrium to maintain and convert it to an actively secreting tissue. The glands become coiled and filled with glycogen; the blood vessels become spiral-shaped and more numerous; and the various enzymes collect in the glands and connective tissue in preparation for the implantation of a fertilized ovum.

If fertilization does not occur, the corpus luteum degenerates, and there is a characteristic decrease in blood estrogen and progesterone levels. This causes a constriction of the uterine blood vessels and a decreased supply of oxygen and nutrients to the endometrium. Disintegration and sloughing of the endometrium begin, and the menstrual cycle is initiated. Menses last 3 to 5 days, beginning a new cycle (Fig. 30-6).

Abnormalities of sexual development

Abnormality in any stage of embryologic sexual development can lead to a defect present in the infant at birth. These abnormalities can range from ambiguous genitalia, usually visible and seen at birth, to chromosomal defects, which may not be noticed until secondary sexual characteristics fail to develop at puberty.

Failure in any of the four stages shown in Fig. 30-1 can cause a defect. In addition, there may be excessive or inadequate amounts of hormones secreted or a failure of the male fetus to respond normally to androgens.

The following four mechanisms underlie most defects:

1. Abnormal sex determination based on faulty chromosomes
2. Failure of the bipotential gonad to differentiate
3. Incomplete development of the ductal system
4. Abnormal amounts of androgens or insensitivity of the male fetus to androgens[3,4]

Ambiguous genitalia

The first question normally asked by parents of a newborn is, "Is it a boy or a girl?". When the baby's sexual identity is *ambiguous*, not clearly male or female, this question becomes difficult to answer.

Ambiguous genitalia, sometimes also called *hermaphroditism*, result when a female fetus is masculinized or a male fetus is incompletely masculinized. All fetuses begin with a female sexual format, and this continues unless there is an interruption. Males born with incomplete male development result from the failure of fetal testes to develop and produce testosterone. This male fetus then continues to develop according to the female format.

True hermaphroditism is the presence of both ovarian and testicular tissue. This condition is very rare. The chromosome configuration usually appears as 46,XX but may be 46,XY. The choice of sex of rearing is determined by the external genitalia and gonads.

Masculinized females (female pseudohermaphrodites) have a chromosomal makeup of 46,XX and ovaries are present. External genitalia have varying degrees of labial fusion and enlargement of the clitoris. This can give the appearance of a penis and scrotum. These masculinizing symptoms are due to increased adrenal secretions of androgens. This may be caused by the mother's use of steroids and progestational agents but most often is the result of *congenital adrenal hyperplasia*. These androgens act on the external genitalia and the urogenital sinus, not the müllerian ducts. Therefore, the ovaries, tubes, and uterus are normal, while the external genitalia are affected (see Chap. 29). The female pseudohermaphrodite may be able to reproduce if treated with cortisone. Surgical correction is done in the first year and includes labial, clitoral, and vaginal reconstruction. Estrogen cream may also be used for mild labial fusion coupled with daily gentle, progressive manual separation for a few weeks.

Incompletely masculinized males (male pseudohermaphrodites) have a 46,XY chromosomal makeup. One or both testes may be undescended or atrophic (undeveloped). The penis may be fully formed, small, or hypospadiac, or a blind vaginal pouch may be present. Later pubertal development varies; with milder degrees of feminization, it is usually masculine. Treatment with testosterone may be used to stimulate growth of the penis in some males. Not all boys are responsive to testosterone treatment. Those who are unresponsive will be inadequate males. With reconstructive surgery and hormones, they can function as females sexually and should be raised as females.

Diagnostic tests for determining sex It may take up to 6 weeks to collect all the test results needed for sex determination. A careful search of the chromosomes, hormones, external appearance of the genitalia, and internal sexual makeup is needed to decide which direction, male or female, is best for this child. The appearance of the external genitalia is a major consideration when determining the sex.

The first step toward diagnosis is a *complete maternal history* and a *newborn physical examination.* Any signs of hypospadias, undescended testes, enlarged clitoris, labial fusion, or small penis should be investigated. Next, a *buccal smear* for nuclear chromatin (Barr body) is done. This usually gives enough data for an immediate assignment of gender. An X-chromatin-positive newborn is usually female. An X-chromatin-negative infant is a genetic male in 90 percent of the cases. Ideally, *total chromosome analysis* is also done. If further study is needed for an assessment of adrenal cortex imbalance, chemical tests to study urinary steroid excretion are done (17 ketosteroids). An exploratory laparotomy or, in some institutions, ultrasound may be used to look for gonads. Genitourinography, injection of dye used to visualize genitourinary structures, also will help determine which internal structures are present.

When a baby with ambiguous genitalia is born, the physician informs the parents of the infant's condition as honestly and sensitively as possible. Correct anatomic terminology should be used and defined. This allows the parents to talk more easily with friends and relatives about the condition. The baby's sex is assigned as soon as it is known, usually in the first weeks of life. Sex orientation and gender role are present in the $1\frac{1}{2}$- to $2\frac{1}{2}$-year-old child, and sex assignment should always be made before that time. This is an extremely embarrassing situation for parents, and they need much support.

After the gender has been ascertained, the condition should be fully explained to the parents. Pictures or sketches may be drawn to illustrate exactly what happened during embryonic growth. Emphasis should be placed on the fact that the child will not grow up with abnormal sexual desires and that sexual identity as a boy or girl is greatly dependent on how the child is reared.

As the child grows older, the need for psychological guidance may become greater. Children with ambiguous genitalia need explanations and understanding as they become aware of their differences. An honest approach to educating these children about their condition is important. The hermaphrodite child is all too aware that genitals are the focus of everyone's attention. If sterility is known, it is better that the child know about this early rather than discover it later.

Surgery Genital surgery is usually done at an early age. If surgery is delayed or done in stages, the child needs to be told about the prospective surgical and medical plans. The most frequent surgical procedures done are hypospadias repair, clitoridectomy, and vaginal and penile reconstruction.

Some adolescents request sex change surgical procedures after the development of secondary sex characteristics have encouraged this surgery. The change is made after intense psychological evaluation of both the parents and their child. For most of these children, the change is beneficial.

It is extremely important that each child be evaluated on an individual basis. No two cases or approaches will be the same, and they will depend upon the chromosomal findings, the developmental characteristics of the child, and the sexual organs present.

Delayed puberty

Puberty has been defined as the age at which males and females become capable of reproduction. Puberty begins earlier in the female than the male and is usually heralded by the development of secondary sex characteristics. Puberty depends upon the stimulation of the testes and the ovaries by the pituitary gonadotropic hormones. At puberty the male and female systems undergo full maturation.

Adolescents who do not experience pubertal changes, especially when they compare themselves with others of the same age, may become very impatient and upset. Although most adolescents will develop normally given time, during the waiting period they need to be treated with understanding. Any possible underlying disease process such as diabetes mellitus, malabsorption syndrome, anorexia nervosa, hypothyroidism, hyperthyroidism, and sometimes asthma could delay puberty and should be considered. An error involving sex chromosomes can also result in failure to develop secondary sex characteristics. A general physical examination and the same diagnostic studies discussed in sex determination with sexual ambiguity may need to be done.

Klinefelter syndrome The chromosome complement of these males is usually 47,XXY. *Klinefelter syndrome* is usually not apparent until puberty, when normal male secondary sexual characteristics fail to develop due to androgen deficiency. Instead, the boy begins to develop female characteristics, such as breast enlargement and fat deposits on the hips, and retains a high-pitched voice. These males have a small to normal-size penis, small testes, and an absence of sperm in their seminal fluid resulting in fertility problems. Mental impairment of varying degrees may also be present.

Diagnosis Diagnosis is seldom made before puberty, but a sex chromatin test will show an X-chromatin representing the inactivated X chromosome in 80 percent of the cases.

Treatment Treatment consists of administering testosterone by mouth, subcutaneous implantation (every 6 to 9 months), or stimulation of the testosterone-producing cells (Leydig cells) of the testes, utilizing gonadotropin, to improve the male appearance.

Monosomy X *Monosomy X*, or *Turner syndrome*, results in the failure of normal female sexual development due to the absence of an X chromosome. The ovaries are usually poorly developed or absent *(female gonadal dysgenesis)*. The sex chromosome complement of these females may be 45,X or 46 with an abnormal X. The symptoms in puberty relate to estrogen deficiency: primary amenorrhea, scanty menstruation, failure of sexual development, and a lack of growth (most of the females are less than 150 cm tall). Some girls have a characteristic webbing of the neck with the development of extra skin folds, lymphedema of the legs, thin hair, ptosis (drooping of the eyelids), shield chest (tapering of the anterior chest wall with widely spaced nipples and poor breast development), and mental retardation. Congenital anomalies, especially

cardiac, are found more frequently with this syndrome.

Diagnosis Diagnosis can be made by the absence of the X-chromatin body in cells from a buccal smear. Because many types of monosomy X are possible, however, a karyotype should be done. The excretion of estrogen in the urine is low, very similar to that of a postmenopausal woman.

Treatment Treatment of patients with monosomy X consists of estrogen replacement and psychological counseling. Initially, these patients receive continuous estrogen therapy until the secondary sex characteristics have developed. Then cyclical estrogen is given, consisting of 3 weeks on the therapy and 1 week off, during which simulated menstruation occurs. Synthetic androgens may also be given to stimulate growth. Surgical correction of the physical defect, the neck webbing, is also possible.

Nursing management The time of delayed puberty may be very stressful for both the child and the parents. The child may be subject to much social pressure and self-doubt. The nurse can instruct the child and parents that pubertal development will be slow even with the aid of medications. The child should have a follow-up examination every 6 months during this phase of maturation. Encourage age-appropriate behavior, rights, and responsibilities. Fears about sexuality must be discussed openly and honestly. The child with delayed puberty is usually fertile and able to reproduce, while the child with primary gonadal agenesis (absence of ovaries or testes) will be infertile and not able to reproduce. The male or female who has reached young adulthood should participate in discussion and understand the possibilities and limitations of the situation and treatment.

Alterations of male reproductive function

Hydrocele

A *hydrocele* can be defined as the presence of fluid anywhere within the course of the *process vaginalis* (the pathway through which the testes, preceded by a fold of tissue, descend from the peritoneal cavity to the scrotum). Small scrotal hydroceles are commonly present at birth and are often associated with inguinal hernias.

Noncommunicating hydroceles are those in which the process vaginalis has closed but fluid is trapped in the scrotum. These are usually stable, asymptomatic, not reducible, and have the capacity to transilluminate (showing the presence of fluid and testes). The peritoneal fluid trapped in the scrotum disappears slowly over a period of weeks or months. Most hydroceles resolve spontaneously in the first year of life, making surgical correction rarely necessary.

Communicating hydroceles are those in which the process vaginalis remains open and peritoneal fluid may be forced into the scrotum. The mother will usually notice a change in the size of the scrotum. It will be smaller in the morning, after the child has been asleep all night, and larger in the afternoon, after the child has been up most of the day. These hydroceles may be large enough to cause discomfort and allow herniation of the intestines. Surgical repair is required if they persist beyond the second year of life. Surgical repair is similar to inguinal hernia repair.

Nursing management Nursing management for an inguinal hernia repair is also appropriate for the surgical repair of a hydrocele. Postoperative patient care involves placing an ice bag to the scrotum to prevent swelling, instituting voiding measures to avoid retention, keeping the area clean, and maintaining planned rest periods.

Cryptorchism

Cryptorchism is the failure of one or both of the testes to descend into the scrotal sac. There are two types of undescended testes: ectopic and incompletely descended. Testes normally descend at 32 to 36 weeks of gestation. Failure of descent is linked to deficient quantities of fetal testosterone, an obstruction of the passageway to the scrotum, and prematurity. The testes are undescended in approximately 3 percent of full-term infants, 30 percent of premature infants at birth, and 0.3 to 0.4 percent of 1-year-old boys.[5] If by the end of the first year of life the testicle has not descended into the scrotal sac, it is unlikely to do so. Undescended testes usually occur as an isolated defect, but occasionally significant upper urinary tract abnormalities are found. About 13 percent of the boys with un-

palpable testes are found to have agenesis of the testes on surgery.[6]

For spermatogenesis to occur, it is important to place the testes within the scrotum before the onset of puberty. There is widespread controversy regarding the best time for repair. Many sources feel that repair should be done by 5 years of age. Others say that irreversible changes on biopsy have been demonstrated as early as 2 to 3 years of age.[7] Decreased fertility may result from the exposure of the testes to the higher internal body temperature. It has been noted that even with replacement in the scrotum, the sperm production in the testes may be lower.

Ectopic testes are testicles lodged in the perineum or in the pubopenile or femoral area during descent down the inguinal canal through the external inguinal ring. Ninety percent of ectopic testes are associated with inguinal hernias. Testes located somewhere along the normal path of descent that have never been in the scrotum are described as undescended, cryptorchid, or incompletely descended. Bilateral absence of palpable testes would require investigation for further signs of sexual-genetic malformations. There is also a higher incidence of testicular malignancy in undescended testes.

A short course of gonadotropin therapy is sometimes given for undescended testes before surgery is performed. Chorionic gonadotropin two to three times a week for about 3 weeks is used. This form of therapy is used to determine if the testes can be stimulated to descend into the scrotum on their own and mimics the onset of puberty when secretion of gonadotropin hormones by the anterior pituitary gland occurs. About 20 percent of cases respond to this therapy, eliminating the need for further surgery.

Orchiopexy

Surgical treatment of undescended testes is called *orchiopexy*. Surgery is recommended by the age of 5 years. Surgical exploration of the peritoneal cavity for the testes with relocation of the undescended testicles to the vas deferens and its blood supply is usually done.

Once the testes have been relocated in the scrotal canal, they will be secured with a suture tied to a rubber band that is taped to the child's thigh for tension and immobilization. An indwelling urinary catheter may also be put in place. Antibiotics given postoperatively help prevent infection. The suture and band are usually left in place for 5 to 7 days. The purpose of the tension of the suture is to retain the testes in the normal scrotal position. When healing is sufficient, the tension band and catheter are removed. The prognosis for fertility in these children is good if the testes can be placed in the scrotum before permanent damage has been done (Fig. 30-7).

Nursing management Families need a great deal of support, encouragement, and explanation to cope with this potentially emotional situation. If it is discovered that the child is infertile, parents may become confused and anxious and feel guilty for not having brought the child in earlier. The child, if he is old enough, also is aware that he is different from his peers and that his scrotum is not normal. Both the parents and the child should be encouraged to verbalize their concerns and feelings. The nurse requires much understanding to deal with parental anxiety during this trying time.

Testicular torsion

Testicular torsion occurs primarily in the newborn and adolescent age groups. In the neonate, it occurs because the testes have recently entered the scrotum and may be rotating freely. It is also caused by a contraction of the cremaster muscle or the absence of posterior attachments of the testes within the tunica vaginalis, thus permitting the testes to twist. Torsion, when it is complete, may result in blocking the blood supply and gangrene of the testes within 6 to 12 h. The presenting symptoms of children with torsion of the spermatic cord are sudden onset of scrotal pain, nausea, vomiting, swollen, tender, elevated testes, and scrotal edema. In the adolescent, the onset of pain is usually gradual, often occurring during sleep. The pain may become tolerable even though the testes are edematous. The torsion must be relieved within 4 to 6 h to prevent loss of function.

Treatment Treatment of testicular torsion is surgical and, if delayed more than 24 h, may result in loss of the affected testes. The scrotum is explored, the twisting of the spermatic cord is corrected, and an orchiopexy with fixation is performed. Recovery is usually uneventful (Fig. 30-8).

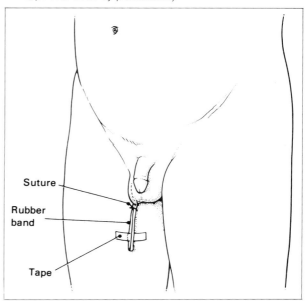

Figure 30-7 Traction apparatus used following orchiopexy. (*From Margaret E. Armstrong et al., eds., McGraw-Hill Handbook of Clinical Nursing, McGraw-Hill, New York, 1979, p. 448. Used by permission.*)

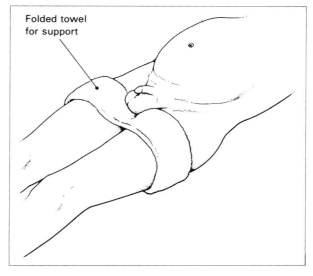

Figure 30-8 Bellvue bridge for scrotal support. (*From Margaret E. Armstrong et al., eds., McGraw-Hill Handbook of Clinical Nursing, McGraw-Hill, New York, 1979, p. 453. Used by permission.*)

Alterations of female reproductive function

Problems related to menstruation

The onset of menstruation is given more attention than any other sexual characteristic. Along with menstruation, secondary female sex characteristics serve as an index of sexual development. *Menarche* (onset of menstruation) requires normal function of the hypothalamus, pituitary, and ovaries. A mature uterus and a patent lower genital tract are also required. The average onset of menstruation is between 12 and 13 years of age. A delay much beyond 15 years, lack of development of secondary sex characteristics, and a short stature indicate the need for evaluation for possible abnormalities of sexual development. A complete workup should include a physical examination, pelvic examination, menstrual and sexual history, complete blood count, hormone levels, and pregnancy tests.

Amenorrhea *Imperforate hymen* is the first consideration in *amenorrhea* (absence of menstruation). In this situation, menstruation and ovulation occur but the blood cannot drain from the vagina because the *hymen*, a fold of mucous membrane, completely covers the external opening of the vagina. This collection of blood is called *cryptomenorrhea*. *Hematocolpos* is the term used when the vagina is distended with blood. The symptoms may include difficult urination, lower abdominal pain, and pain at the time of the menstrual cycle due to the pressure of increasing fluid in the vagina. On physical examination, the distended vagina appears as a lower abdominal and pelvic mass. Inspection of the perineal area shows a bluish, bulging hymen. Treatment for this condition includes incision and partial removal of the hymen. The retained blood is allowed to drain over a period of several days. Infection may be present because the retained blood is an excellent medium for bacterial growth.

In a broad sense, *primary amenorrhea* can be defined as the absence of menstrual periods. Causative factors of primary amenorrhea are congenital absence of the reproductive organs, disease affecting the genital organs before puberty, and endocrine disorders.

Congenital absence or *underdeveloped (infantile) reproductive organs* may involve absence of the uterus or a uterus that retains its infantile characteristics. With the absence of ovaries, secondary sex characteristics will fail to develop at puberty. Diseases that affect the genital organs before the onset of puberty may destroy their function, causing infertility. Infectious diseases such as mumps, anemia, poor dietary habits, anorexia nervosa, and venereal diseases (gonorrhea) may delay menarche and reduce fertility. The most common cause of primary amenorrhea is related to endocrine disorders. The effect of reproductive hormones (estrogen and androgen) on the child has already been discussed. The endocrine glands that may be involved are the pituitary, thyroid, ovaries, and adrenal glands (see Chap. 29).

Secondary amenorrhea can be defined as the absence of menstrual periods after the menstrual cycle has been initially established. Causative factors are multiple, with endocrine disorders being most common. Systemic disease and excessive dieting may also cause amenorrhea. Endocrine involvement usually includes the pituitary, thyroid, and ovaries.

Treatment for amenorrhea begins with finding and treating the primary cause, and this may be difficult. Counseling the adolescent about growth and body changes that are occurring is important. The absence of menstruation or any body changes different from those of the peer group will draw the adolescent's attention. She may become very sensitive and embarrassed. The adolescent tends to overemphasize her defects and underemphasize her assets. Her body is seen as a source of acceptance or rejection by others.

Dysfunctional uterine bleeding Abnormal uterine bleeding may be characterized as excessive, prolonged, or inadequate. From the ages of 10 to 20, there may be several causes of dysfunctional uterine bleeding: blood dyscrasias, inflammatory lesions, tumors, systemic disease or, most commonly, endocrine disorders.

Menorrhagia is an excessively long or heavy menstrual flow. There is usually failure of ovulation. Menorrhagia can occur at any time but usually takes place during the late childbearing years. If menorrhagia occurs before the age of 10 years, it is usually caused by an endocrine disorder or tumor of the pituitary, ovary, or adrenal glands. If the child fails to respond to the medical regimen of treatment, a D and C (dilatation and curettage) may be necessary. This is usually considered minor surgery but is done under a general anesthetic. In the procedure, the endometrial lining of the uterus is scraped and tissue specimens are sent to the laboratory for examination. During the preoperative period, problems of separation of the child and family are the paramount consideration (see Chap. 10). The family of a young girl needs much support during the extensive diagnostic testing to determine the underlying cause of menorrhagia. It is important to explain to the child what will be expected of her during any diagnostic tests done before the surgical procedure. Inform the child that after the procedure, she will get a light diet at the next scheduled meal, will have the first several voidings measured, may experience a small amount of vaginal bleeding, and have mild lower abdominal pain. Dismissal planning should include the observations listed in Table 30-1.

Oligomenorrhea (scanty menstrual bleeding) is another form of dysfunctional bleeding which involves irregularity of the menstrual periods. The interval between menstrual periods is abnormally long. Irregularity is common during the first few years of menstruation. Irregular periods after menses have been established usually indicate an imbalance between the endocrine glands that regulate the beginning and end of the endometrial cycle. The main endocrine gland of involvement is the ovary. Treatment involves hormone (estrogen and progesterone) therapy for about 6 months to regulate the cycle and then continued follow-up to be sure that normal ovulation has been established.

Dysmenorrhea *Dysmenorrhea* can be defined as painful menstruation. The term *dysmenorrhea* should be reserved for fairly incapacitating painful menstruation severe enough for the woman to seek self-medication or help from a physician. The amount of discomfort experienced during the secretory phase of the menstrual cycle is related significantly to the endometrial production of prostaglandins.[8] These are increased both at the end of the menstrual cycle and with the onset of menstruation. It has been shown likely that primary dysmenorrhea is due to myometrial contractions induced by prostaglandins originating in the endometrium.[9]

There are two major classifications of dysmenorrhea. The first, *primary dysmenorrhea* or painful menstruation, is unrelated to a pelvic abnormality. The second is *secondary dysmenorrhea* and can usually be related to specific organic pelvic pathology or an intrauterine device (IUD).

The common discomforts associated with dysmenorrhea include a sense of fullness in the pelvis, premenstrual tension, edema, enlargement and tenderness in the breasts, mild abdominal cramps, and backache.

The first step in dealing with dysmenorrhea is consulting with a physician to rule out the existence of pelvic pathology. This should include a complete gynecologic and pelvic examination. If no pathology is found, a second step might include a subjective assessment of the pain experienced through the use of a patient questionnaire or rating scale. These may be given to the patient to fill out before, during, and after the menstrual cycle and can be used to evaluate the experienced pain.

Table 30-1 Dismissal teaching following a dilatation and curettage

Vaginal bleeding	Hygiene	Pain	Infection	Contact doctor for
Light, pinkish vaginal bleeding may continue for 1 week after surgery Avoid heavy lifting, strenuous exercise for 1–2 weeks (may cause bleeding)	Cleanse perineum from front to back after elimination Change perineal pad three to four times daily No tampons	May experience mild abdominal cramps for 2–3 days following surgery	Signs of infection: **1.** Foul odor from vaginal discharge **2.** Elevated temperature **3.** Lower abdominal (uterine) pain	Signs of infection Severe pain or abdominal cramps Heavy, bright red flow or clots Elevated temperature

Symptomatic relief may be provided by utilizing the following general measures: routine genital hygiene, exercise, heat to the lower abdomen, vitamins, and teaching (including reassurance about the absence of serious pelvic disease and the likelihood that the pain will decrease after childbirth).

Further treatment may include the use of various drug regimens. Oral contraceptives which contain both estrogen and progesterone have been effective in treating dysmenorrhea because they inhibit ovulation. There is almost always complete relief of menstrual pain with this form of treatment. A new drug regimen under investigation is the use of prostaglandin inhibitors. The relationship between prostaglandin activity and dysmenorrhea has been mentioned. These new drugs decrease prostaglandin production through inhibition of the enzyme system which synthesizes the prostaglandin compounds.[10] By doing this, they inhibit the release of prostaglandin from the secretory endometrium, thus decreasing the pain of dysmenorrhea.

The specific drugs used for pain are nonsteroid, anti-inflammatory drugs such as salicylates (aspirin, phenacetin). Prostaglandin inhibitors, indomethacin, fenamoles (tolfenamic acid, mefenamic acid, e.g., Ponstel), naproxen sodium, and ibuprofen (Motrin) are also used for severe dysmenorrhea. The difficulty in using the prostaglandin inhibitors is the severity of the side effects of treatment. Side effects of prostaglandin inhibitors described in the literature include: headache, blurred vision, drug rash, severe gastrointestinal disturbances, and aplastic anemia. Motrin has been cited as the safest inhibitor with minimal side effects, but it is still under investigation for this purpose. The studies agree that when drug therapy is necessary, it should be started several (2 to 3) days prior to the onset of the menstrual flow and dysmenorrhea symptoms and continued until the flow and symptoms disappear.

Vulvovaginitis

Irritation and inflammation of the vulva and vagina are frequently seen in young girls. The vaginal tissue is thin, unestrogenized, and has a neutral pH, making it very susceptible to infections. The child may be reluctant to tell parents what is wrong and may resist medical examination, making diagnosis difficult. Signs of vulvovaginitis are a red and edematous perineal area, itching, foul-smelling or purulent vaginal discharge, and dysuria. Urinary tract infections often accompany vulvovaginitis, making it essential to obtain a clean catch urine specimen in addition to culturing vaginal discharge.

The common sources of vulvovaginitis are chemical irritations, trauma, and infections. Bubble bath, masturbation, placing foreign objects into the vagina, and injury from falls may all be causes of vulvovaginitis. Infections are often related to poor hygiene, especially wiping from the rectum toward the vagina and urethra. Pinworms, *Escherichia coli*, and other bacteria are common infection agents. Chap. 34 discusses the common sources, treatment, and nursing care for vaginitis.

Adolescent sexuality

How does the adolescent respond to developing sexuality and sexual activity? Girls may see intercourse as a means of obtaining affection, acceptance, or an identity. Their concept of sexual functioning is more related to love and is not so genitally based as that of boys. Boys often view intercourse with orgasm as an end in itself. They have fewer notions of romantic love and affection and more concerns about satisfying sexual needs. Neither girls nor boys have a completely developed capacity for intimacy and mature love and will complete that task in the next stage of development (see Chap. 15).

Sexual activity in teenagers

In 1976, Kantner and Zelnick found that 55 percent of young women were sexually active by age 19 and only 30 percent of sexually active teenagers consistently used birth control methods. The dispensing of birth control to minors is governed by state laws. These laws differ, but most allow dispensing of birth control methods, pregnancy diagnosis, early abortion, and treatment of sexually transmitted diseases without parental consent or knowledge. Though opposition still exists from some parental, church, and legislative groups, seeking health care and birth control when sexually active should be seen as a sign of a mature and responsible adolescent (Fig. 30-9).

Many teenagers are sexually active for long

periods of time without birth control methods. A number of factors contribute to this low use of contraception among adolescents.

1. An inability to accept the fact that one is sexually active and the feeling that using birth control methods means "planning" to be sexually active
2. Ignorance about body function, pregnancy, and types and availability of contraception
3. Fear of contraceptive side effects
4. Fear of medical exams and inability to pay for care
5. Embarrassment—many teenagers find it difficult to purchase tampons or sanitary pads, much less condoms or contraceptive foam
6. Adolescent magical thinking and denial ("It can't happen to me")
7. Poor impulse control, getting "carried away," resulting in intercourse
8. Belief that the use of contraception will inhibit spontaneity and thus pleasure
9. Lack of male commitment to the prevention of pregnancy and a lack of feeling of responsibility if pregnancy develops
10. A wish to become pregnant; the need to be loved and have someone (a baby) to love

Sex education programs that serve the adolescent should make the availability of contraceptive services offered widely known in the community. This is done through radio and TV ads, posters in schools and community centers, and organizing teen boards in adolescent care centers. With the increase in sexually active adolescents in recent years, programs to educate and provide adolescents with contraception have become a routine part of adolescent health care. One of the agencies well known for providing teenagers with health services is Planned Parenthood.

The most comprehensive program of sex education is offered by SEICUS, Sex Information and Education Council of the United States. SEICUS provides teaching materials and maintains that sex education programs should incorporate six areas: biological, social, health, personal adjustments and attitudes, interpersonal associations, and establishment of values. Contraception is only one facet of the program.

The adolescent's choice of contraceptive method should be safe, effective, and suited to the individual. The choice is usually based upon the adolescent's preference and the physician's or family planning practitioner's judgment. The

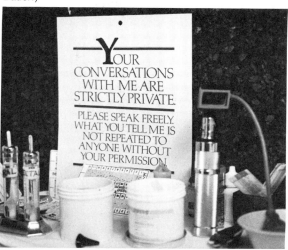

Figure 30-9 The teenager has the right to confidentiality and will feel more open to share health problems when assured that they will remain private. (*Photograph by Karel Bauer.*)

adolescent must be motivated to utilize whichever method is suited for her.

Choosing a birth control method

How does the nurse help a teenager choose a birth control method? First, it is important to remember that the best birth control method is the one the young person wants and will be comfortable using. Some questions the nurse might ask to aid in contraception counseling include:

1. What made you decide to begin using a birth control method?
2. What methods have you used in the past? Successfully? Unsuccessfully?
3. Have you discussed birth control with your partner?
4. Are your parents aware that you are sexually active? What is their reaction (or what would it be if they knew)?
5. What birth control methods do your friends use? What have their experiences been?
6. What would your reaction be if you became pregnant? Your boyfriend's, parents', friends' reactions?
7. How comfortable are you with your body? Do you masturbate? Do you use tampons?

8. How do you feel about having sex? Who usually initiates sex? Where do you most commonly have sex?

9. When did menstruation begin? How many days are there from the first day of menses to your next menses? Do you have cramping or a heavy flow? What is your vaginal discharge like between periods?

10. Do you or anyone in your family have any serious health problems—diabetes, cancer of the breast or uterus, hypertension, migraines, liver disease?

The answers to these questions, along with a full explanation of the risks and benefits of all methods, should be discussed with the teenager requesting contraception. This can be done individually or in groups of peers. It is important to provide an opportunity for the boyfriend or a significant other to participate in contraceptive counseling. Though teenage girls usually take responsibility for birth control, boys need education that emphasizes their sexual responsibility.

Birth control needs to be a personal choice suited for the individual. The teenager whose boyfriend is pressuring her to take the pill probably will not remember to take it. The young woman who is acutely uncomfortable touching herself will not do well with foam or a diaphragm. The young man who feels that condoms will cause him to enjoy sex less probably will not use them even if they are free. Teenagers who feel that the nurse is genuinely interested in helping them find the right birth control method will usually use birth control methods more effectively.

First pelvic examination

Although not a routine part of the physical examination for very young teenage girls, a pelvic examination is indicated for evaluation of menstrual irregularity, abdominal pain, vaginal discharge, and evaluation of possible pregnancy or venereal disease. Adolescent girls frequently have their first pelvic examination when receiving birth control for the first time. The use of tampons prior to the first pelvic examination is usually beneficial. It helps the teenager to be more familiar with her body and also relaxes the vaginal tissues.

Prior to their first pelvic examination all young women should have the opportunity to meet with a nurse educator who will familiarize them with the examination and equipment. This teaching should include:

1. Female anatomy and physiology. The use of charts, plastic models, and a hand mirror to visualize the perineum and cervix will acquaint the teenager with her body.
2. Feelings. Exploration of the teenager's feelings about her body and fears about the examination.
3. Equipment. The appropriate size speculum (usually a small Pederson) and Pap smear spatula and a swab should all be shown to the teenager, and she should have an opportunity to handle them prior to the examination.
4. Films. Teaching films showing a pelvic examination being performed are easily available and should be shown to the teenager to help allay her fears.
5. Support. A supportive person (if possible, the nurse who did the teaching) should remain with the teenager during the examination and prepare her for the sensations she will feel.

The teenager's reaction to her first pelvic examination is extremely important. The properly prepared teenager is usually able to undergo this examination without trauma. It should be stressed that if at any point she feels unable to continue with the examination, she should communicate this and her feelings will be respected. Often simply knowing that she will not be forced to undergo the examination gives the adolescent the control to tolerate some discomfort (Fig. 30-10).

The results of the examination should be shared with the teenager. If slides of vaginal secretions have been taken, she should be allowed to view them under the microscope. When properly prepared, the first pelvic examination can be a positive learning experience for most adolescent girls.

Effectiveness of contraceptive methods

Nurses doing contraceptive counseling must be aware of the effectiveness of each method. There are two types of effectiveness; theoretical and use effectiveness. Both are based on the number of pregnancies when a method is used by 100 women in one year.

Theoretical effectiveness is the effectiveness of a contraceptive method when used according to instructions and without errors. *Use effectiveness* includes the use of a method with and without errors. All of the errors involved in the use of birth control methods such as forgetting, losing, or using inappropriately are included in use effectiveness. When presenting information about birth control methods, the nurse must consistently provide either theoretical effectiveness or use effectiveness for all methods.

The ideal birth control method is 100 percent effective, has no side effects, is inexpensive and reversible (stopping the method allows healthy pregnancy), requires little motivation for use and can be used at a time remote from sexual intercourse. Obviously, this type of birth control does not yet exist. The types of birth control currently available are described in Table 30-2. Additional information not discussed in the table follows.

Oral contraceptives The birth control pill is the most effective method of contraception currently available, with a theoretical effectiveness approaching 100 percent. Since its development more than 20 years ago, the pill has been the most widely used birth control method. While oral contraceptives have risks, they are well suited to the sexually active adolescent at risk for pregnancy. The disadvantages of the pill include its unsuitability for young teenagers with irregular periods or those who are still growing. The estrogens can cause premature closure of the epiphyseal plate and stop growth.

Any young woman requesting birth control pills should have a complete physical exam, including blood pressure, pelvic and breast examinations, and a Pap smear. The laboratory workup should include a hematocrit or hemoglobin, urinalysis, culture for gonorrhea, and serological testing for syphilis. An assessment should be made of the patient's history, including family history, for contraindications to the pill. Table 30-3 lists the absolute and relative contraindications to birth control pills. All patients should be taught the warning signs and advised to contact their physician or clinic immediately if they occur. Table 30-4 lists the warning signs.

Birth control pill users should be interviewed at regular intervals to check for satisfaction, correct usage, side effects and blood pressure elevation. Routine visits are scheduled at 3-month intervals the first year and every 6 months

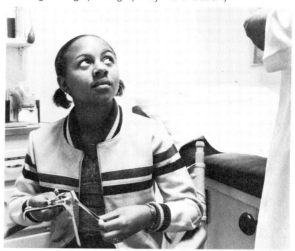

Figure 30-10 When the teenager has an opportunity to become familiar with equipment, the first pelvic exam is less frightening. (*Photograph by Karel Bauer.*)

thereafter. No patient should be given a prescription for more than a 12-month supply of pills. All patients on birth control pills should have an annual physical examination and be reevaluated.

IUD When the pill is contraindicated for teenage girls, the IUD is the second method of choice. With the advent of relatively small IUDs, this method can be used in even the *nulliparous* (never pregnant) teenager. There are a number of IUDs available. The most widely used at present in the teenager are the Copper 7 and the Lippes Loop. Young women requesting an IUD should have a thorough pelvic examination, gonorrhea culture, and an assessment of their history for contraindications. A second method of contraception, such as foam or condoms, should be used for 2 months after insertion. The length of time an IUD may be left in place varies for each type.

Barrier contraception

The diaphragm Barrier contraception includes those methods that prevent the sperm from reaching the egg. While the diaphragm is the most effective of these methods, it usually requires an extremely motivated young woman to be used successfully. The diaphragm requires a familiarity and comfort with one's body not

Table 30-2 Temporary methods of contraception

Method	Description of action	Instructions for use	Effectiveness* Theoretical	Effectiveness* Actual
Oral contraceptives ("the pill")	Tablets containing varying doses of estrogens and progestogens. Main action is suppression of ovulation. They also alter cervical mucus (making it hostile to sperm), and lead to an unfavorable endometrial environment.	1 pill daily for 21 days, at approximately the same time daily. Stop for 7 days. Menses will begin 1–4 days after pill has been stopped. Restart new pack of pills after 28-day cycle has been completed. Some pill packs contain 7 placebo or iron tablets, which can be taken instead of stopping for a week. Start on fifth day of menses; stop at end of pack. For early nausea, take at bedtime or with evening meal. For weight gain, reduce salt and caloric intake.	0.1	0.2
Mini-pill	A tablet form of contraception which contains only low doses of progestogens. Ovulation is probably not inhibited, but hostile cervical mucus and an unfavorable endometrial environment provide contraceptive effect.	1 pill daily, without stopping. Start on first day of menses; stop at end of pack.	1	3
IUD	A plastic or polyethylene device in various shapes and sizes. It is inserted into uterus and usually remains there until user wishes it removed. Action of IUD is unknown, but it is thought to cause a local inflammatory reaction inside uterus, which prevents fertilized ovum from implantation. Copper and progesterone have been added to some IUDs for an extra antifertility effect.	Approximately ½ in of IUD string will be in vagina. Insert finger to check for presence of string. (Can be checked by partner, also.) Notify care-provider if: no string is felt, string feels much longer than after insertion; plastic tip of IUD is felt protruding. Use another method of birth control until reexamined. Insert during menses; remove at any time during the cycle.	2	5
Diaphragm	A dome-shaped rubber cup on a circular metal spring. Used with spermicidal jelly or cream it fits over cervix and blocks entry of sperm into uterus. Must be fitted by a doctor or trained care-provider. Diaphragms come in sizes 55–105 mm in gradations of 5 mm, and are inserted and	Prior to insertion put spermicidal jelly in cup and on rim of diaphragm. In lying, standing, or squatting position, ease diaphragm into vagina. Hook rim under symphysis pubis. Check to see that cervix is covered. If intercourse is repeated, add an applicator of foam or jelly without removing	3	13

Early changes/minor side effects†	Other possible side effects	Contraindications	Advantages/disadvantages
Mild nausea; weight gain; breast tenderness; spotting, break-through bleeding; shorter, lighter menses; missed or "silent" periods; mood changes; chloasma	Depression Decreased libido Blood clots Heart attacks Hepatocellular tumors Prolonged amenorrhea after discontinuation	History or present evidence of thromboembolic phenomena Heart disease Hypertension Sickle cell anemia Severe depression Pregnancy Liver dysfunction or disease Impaired cerebrovascular function Known or suspected carcinoma of the breast or genital tracts Migraine headaches Epilepsy Lactation Ovarian dysfunction	*Advantages:* Nearest to 100% effective Regular menstrual cycle; period predictable Decreased menstrual flow Decreased dysmenorrhea and premenstrual tension Decreased iron-deficiency anemia Not related to intercourse *Disadvantages:* Increased susceptibility to VD, must take daily even if not having intercourse, must be started at specific time to be effective
Irregularity in amount and duration of menses, spotting between periods, missed periods	None currently known	None currently known	*Advantages:* No estrogen-related side effects Not related to intercourse *Disadvantages:* Irregular periods
Heavier and longer periods, cramps, spotting between periods	Spontaneous expulsion Perforation of uterus Embedding of IUD Pelvic inflammatory disease	Pelvic infections (acute, subacute, recurrent) Severe dysmenorrhea Acute cervicitis Uterine abnormalities Allergy to copper Wilson's disease Cervical stenosis Small uterine cavity Abnormal cervical cytology Anemia Congenital or rheumatic heart disease Pregnancy	*Advantages:* Little maintenance or attention needed after insertion Not related to intercourse *Disadvantages:* Higher rate of ectopic pregnancy Must be inserted and removed by care-provider (no self-involvement) Repeated pelvic infections can lead to decreased fertility
None	Allergy to rubber or spermicidal preparation	Damaged pelvic floor or relaxation which prohibits a proper fit Prolapsed uterus Severe cystocele, rectocele Severe retroversion or anteversion of the uterus	*Advantages:* Few side effects Effective for infrequent intercourse Holds back menstrual flow during intercourse Good for learning about female anatomy *Disadvantages:* Closely precedes sex act

(Continued)

Table 30-2 Temporary methods of contraception (*Continued*)

Method	Description of action	Instructions for use	Effectiveness*	
			Theoretical	Actual
	removed by wearer.	diaphragm. Do not remove diaphragm or douche for 6–8 h after last intercourse. Wash with warm water, dry, and powder with cornstarch. Check for holes or tears periodically.		
Foam, jelly, cream	Spermicidal preparations inserted into the vagina. They slow down and kill entering sperm. Can be used alone or in conjunction with other methods.	Insert an applicator full of foam, cream, or jelly into vagina within 30 min of intercourse. Insert an additional application each time before intercourse is repeated . Do not douche; foam or cream is absorbed into skin. If douching is desired, wait 6–8 h after last intercourse. Use with condom for increased effectiveness.	3	20
Condom (rubber prophylactic)	A thin rubber or skin sheath put over an erect penis. Creates a mechanical barrier which prevents sperm from getting into vagina.	Put condom on erect penis *prior* to penetration. If no tip on condom, allow ½ in slack in front to catch semen. Withdraw soon after ejaculation. Semen is more likely to leak out when penis is flaccid. Hold on to condom when withdrawing to prevent slipping off. If condom breaks during intercourse, insert an applicator of foam or jelly immediately. Use with foam for increased effectiveness.	3	15
Rhythm	A pattern of abstinence from intercourse around the time of ovulation, or greatest time of fertility. Records must be kept of menstrual cycles and calculations made for "safe days." New variations on this method include natural family planning and the Billings method, which add basal body temperature and evaluation of cervical mucus to the traditional rhythm system.	Keep record of menstrual cycles for 3–6 months. Subtract *18* from number of days in shortest cycle; subtract *11* from number of days in longest cycle. For example, cycles ranged from 28–30 days: 28 − 18 = 10 / 30 − 11 = 19 / Fertile or "unsafe" days are days 10–19 of cycle.	14	35–40

* Number of pregnancies per 100 woman-years of use. Data from S. Romney et al. (eds.), *Gynecology and Obstetrics: The Health Care of Women*, McGraw-Hill Book Company, New York, 1975, p. 552.

Source: Armstrong et al. (eds.): McGraw-Hill Handbook of Clinical Nursing, McGraw-Hill, New York, 1979. Used with permission.

Early changes/minor side effects†	Other possible side effects	Contraindications	Advantages/disadvantages
			May become dislodged during intercourse Can be messy
None	Allergy to spermicidal preparation	Allergy to spermicidal preparation	*Advantages*: Easily available No prescription needed Helps prevent VD *Disadvantages*: Can be messy
None	Allergy to rubber	Allergy to rubber	*Advantages*: Male method, allows for shared contraception Easily available No prescription Increased protection against sexually transmitted diseases *Disadvantages*: Requires interruption of coitus to put on May reduce sensitivity of glans
None	None	Irregular cycles	*Advantages*: Acceptable for those with rigorous or moral objections to artificial birth control methods Promotes learning about bodily systems *Disadvantages*: Irregular cycles make it difficult to follow successfully Abstinence may cause sexual frustration Problem if partner not cooperative

† Usually disappear within 2 to 3 months.

generally seen in adolescents. If a young woman is to use the diaphragm successfully, it is crucial to allow time for practice of insertion and removal after the diaphragm is fitted. The caregiver helps the patient locate the cervix by telling her where it is and telling her that it feels firm like the tip of the nose. The patient then feels the cervix both before and after it is covered by the diaphragm. She should also return in 1 to 2 weeks for a recheck of diaphragm placement.

The diaphragm requires refitting for the fol-

Table 30-3 Contraindications to estrogen-containing birth control pills

Absolute contraindications

Thromboembolic disorder (or history thereof)

Cerebrovascular accident (or history thereof)

Impaired liver function

Coronary artery disease (or history thereof)

Hepatic adenoma (or history thereof)

Malignancy of breast or reproductive system (or history thereof)

Pregnancy (known or suspected)

Strong relative contraindications

Migraine headaches

Hypertension

Less than 4 weeks postpartum

Prediabetes or diabetes (or strong history thereof)

Gallbladder disease

Acute phase of mononucleosis

Sickle cell disease

Undiagnosed abnormal vaginal bleeding

Relative contraindications

Frequent yeast vaginitis

Varicose veins

Asthma

Cardiac or renal disease

Chloasma

Uterine fibromyomata

Epilepsy

Depression

Menstrual irregularity or late menarche

Lactation

Adapted from Leonide Martin, *Health Care of Women*, Lippincott, Philadelphia, 1978, p. 76.

Table 30-4 Aches and pains which may be warnings of serious trouble

Signal	Possible problem
Headaches (severe)	Stroke or hypertension
Eye problems: blurred vision, flashing lights, or blindness	Stroke or hypertension
Chest pain (severe) or shortness of breath	Blood clot in lungs or myocardial infarction
Severe leg pain (calf or thigh)	Blood clot in legs
Severe abdominal pain	Gallbladder disease, liver disease, blood clot

lowing reasons: after each pregnancy, a 4.5-1 to 9-kg weight loss or gain; after pelvic surgery, if it causes discomfort; and after 1 year of use.

Spermicidal foams Spermicidal foam is a popular method of contraception because it can be obtained easily without a prescription. Foam is inserted deep into the vagina to block the cervical opening. It not only prevents sperm from entering the uterus but also immobilizes and kills them. It is important not to douche after using foam.

Contraceptive vaginal suppositories The product called Encare is relatively new on the U.S. contraceptive market. It is important to be sure that young women choosing to use contraceptive suppositories are not using feminine hygiene suppositories. Their effectiveness equals that of vaginal foams. They are convenient, easy to use, and available without a prescription. However, they may produce allergies or chemical irritation and may create a small amount of heat as they effervesce in the vagina, causing an unpleasant burning sensation. They should be inserted approximately 10 min prior to intercourse to allow time for melting, and douching should not be used after intercourse. One suppository should be used with each intercourse.

Condoms The condom is an excellent birth-control device for teenagers having sexual intercourse infrequently. It can also prevent sexually transmitted disease. A condom is made of rubber and processed collagenous tissue and is placed over the erect penis. It prevents semen from entering the vagina. Condoms are available at any drugstore without a prescription and are more effective when used with foam (Fig. 30-11).

Rhythm—natural contraception Natural methods of contraception, such as the rhythm-calendar method, basal body temperature, and evaluation of cervical secretion changes are not widely used in the adolescent population. Young women often have anovulatory cycles and irregular menses during their teenage years, and intercourse is often sporadic and unplanned. These methods require record keeping, temperature taking, and an intimate knowledge of the body. However, if young women are unable or unwilling to use other birth control methods, the nurse should work closely to instruct them about the use of natural contraception. The effectiveness of these methods varies greatly.

Calendar method The calendar method requires the use of a menstrual calendar. By keeping track of her menstrual period for the last 6 months, the teenager can calculate her fertile days and avoid intercourse.

Basal body temperature The basal body temperature, BBT, is the lowest temperature reached during waking hours. The temperature is taken every morning before getting out of bed, using a special basal thermometer with increments of 0.1°F instead of the usual 0.2°. It is possible to determine basal body temperature patterns after recording the temperature on a chart for 3 to 6 months. BBT drops about 0.2°F just before ovulation and then under the progesterone influence rises 0.6 to 0.8°F the day after ovulation. Unprotected intercourse is avoided until the temperature remains elevated for 3 consecutive days. It is important, when using a basal body thermometer, to be aware of the effect illness, irregular sleeping hours, and electric blankets have on BBT.

Cervical secretions For a young woman to use this method, she must be aware of the cervical secretion changes and the symptoms of ovulation. Adolescents, who already feel overwhelmed by the changes taking place in their bodies, find this method difficult. It is important to distinguish between the yellow, viscous mucus and the clear, sticky mucus, much like a raw egg white, present during ovulation. This colorless,

Figure 30-11 The teenager who considers many ordinary things embarrassing finds it very difficult to provide for contraception by purchasing condoms. (*Photograph by Karel Bauer.*)

watery mucus has the ability to stretch into a long thread of 6 cm or more. This property of stretching is known as *spinnbarkeit* and signals ovulation. Signs of ovulation may include abdominal pain on either side, *mittelschmerz*, a general feeling of heaviness, or slight vaginal bleeding. Unprotected intercourse should be avoided 4 days before ovulation, allowing 2 days for sperm life, and 3 days after ovulation, allowing 2 days for ovum life. It is sometimes possible to mistake semen, discharge due to vaginal infections, and vaginal lubrication for cervical mucus, thus confusing the interpretation of the cycle.

Abstinence Nurses doing contraceptive counseling with teenagers should include abstinence from intercourse as a birth control method. It has a theoretical effectiveness of 100 percent. Often teenagers do not see this as an option because they feel they must be sexually active to be part of the peer group. Young people who do not choose to become sexually active should be supported in their decision.

Coitus interruptus Coitus interruptus, "withdrawal," or "pulling out" is used by many teenagers. The male withdraws his penis from the vagina immediately prior to ejaculation. Sperm can be found in the lubricating fluid secreted by the penis *before* ejaculation, so the risk of pregnancy is high. It can also reduce sexual pleasure for both the male and female. This method is quite ineffective, resulting in a use effectiveness of 40 pregnancies per 100 woman-years of use.

Douching Douching with various fluids, even Coca-Cola, is seen by many adolescents as an effective birth control method. It provides no contraception and may even force sperm into the cervix more rapidly.

Lactation Breast-feeding prevents pregnancy by delaying ovulation and possibly menstruation after childbirth. It is most effective if the infant is totally breast-fed without supplemental formula but is less effective than every other method. It should not be advocated for a teenager, for whom an early second pregnancy may be more than she could handle.

Adolescent pregnancy

The girl who has an illegitimate child at the age of sixteen has 90% of her life's script written for her. She will probably drop out of school even if someone else in her family helps to take care of the baby. It will be difficult to find a steady job that pays enough to provide for herself and her child. She may feel impelled to marry someone she might not otherwise have chosen. Her life choices are few and most of them are bad. Had she been able to delay the first child, her prospects might have been quite different.[11]

Twenty percent of U.S. teenagers under the age of 15 have had intercourse. Of the 1 million girls who become pregnant each year, 30,000 are under the age of 15. Pregnancy in the older teens (15- to 17-year-old group) has increased 21.7 percent in the last decade. Statistics such as these help us understand the scope of the adolescent pregnancy problem. Adolescents are neither physically nor psychologically prepared for pregnancy and parenthood. Most teenage girls are not ready to assume the multiple roles of adolescence, pregnancy, motherhood, and sometimes marriage.

Complications of pregnancy

Morbidity and mortality for both mother and infant are higher in those under the age of 15. These teenagers have specific high-risk factors associated with physical immaturity. If conception occurs less than 1 year after menstruation, bone growth may be immature.[12] When a teenager becomes pregnant before her growth is complete, *cephalopelvic disproportion*, a baby too large to fit through the pelvis, may result, with the need for a cesarean section. The outcome of teenage pregnancy is closely related to adequate nutritional status. Anemia, prematurity, low birth weight, and preeclampsia are complications related to poor nutrition. Normal teenage caloric needs are very high; pregnancy increases the need for calories, protein, calcium, and iron. Consuming the additional nutrients needed may be difficult from a financial viewpoint or because of the teenager's poorly balanced diet. A food supplement program for needy pregnant women is the WIC, Woman-Infant Care, program. The pregnant teenager can receive additional protein, milk, cheese, eggs, orange juice, and fortified foods. Often the mother of the teenager needs instruction to help the teenager eat an adequate diet. Appropriate weight gain needs to be discussed to prevent dieting to maintain the thin body image so important in American culture. The pregnant teenager, like her adult counterpart, usually needs supplemental iron and folic acid but may be unwilling or unable to take them as prescribed. Unstable physiological and metabolic states also affect the outcome of her pregnancy.

Prenatal care

With good prenatal care, the physical risks of pregnancy to the adolescent can be substantially reduced. The overwhelming risk is the psychosocial effect pregnancy has on the young girl. Once the pregnancy is acknowledged, the teenager can begin receiving care. The problem of delayed prenatal care is often related to the gap between suspicion of pregnancy and diagnosis of pregnancy. The adolescent delays confirmation of pregnancy for many reasons: guilt, confusion, or fear. Pregnancy is usually an unwelcome interruption in school and association with peers, boyfriend, and family. Late prenatal care is correlated with increased maternal-fetal complications and allows little time for necessary health teaching.[13]

Pregnancy counseling

The pregnant adolescent usually knows little about conception and contraception. Denial of the fact that she is pregnant, even though she may have missed two or three menstrual periods, often accounts for her not seeking verification of pregnancy until the second trimester. Late recognition of pregnancy increases the complexity of choices for pregnancy outcome.

It is important for the pregnant teenager to understand that the outcome of pregnancy, whether it is abortion, continuing the pregnancy and keeping the baby, or placing it for adoption, is her decision. The nurse should encourage her to seek advice from her boyfriend and parents, if possible, but the final decision is hers. The teenager will need at least one responsible adult to whom she can turn for support—a parent, other relative, school nurse, or teacher. To come to a decision and resolve the crisis of pregnancy, the teenager must complete five tasks:[14]

1. Acknowledge the fact of the pregnancy
2. Formulate available alternatives
3. Choose between abortion and carrying the pregnancy to term
4. Commit herself to the decision
5. Carry it out.[15]

The adolescent needs counseling to help resolve these issues. There are no good alternatives; all involve some degree of pain and loss. Time is needed to make a decision, even though it may mean having a second-trimester abortion. The reality of each option should be fully discussed.

Abortion While statistically safer than delivery, abortion is not without risk, including infection and cervical trauma. A second-trimester abortion involves a greater risk than a first-trimester abortion. The adolescent who chooses to have an abortion will need to deal with her grief and sense of loss. Failure to do so will lead to increased depression and possibly repeated pregnancy.

Adolescents account for one-third of all legal abortions performed in the United States. As a result of the Supreme Court decisions (*Roe v. Wade* and *Doe v. Bolton*) in 1973, abortion in the first trimester is a matter between the woman and her physician. In 1976 the Supreme Court (*Planned Parenthood of Central Missouri v. Danforth* and *Bilotti v. Baird*) struck down parental consent as a requirement for abortion. A mature minor, who understands the risks and benefits of the procedure, may sign her own consent for abortion.

Keeping the baby Having and keeping the baby does not mean living "happily ever after," as so many teenagers expect. Often they are unwilling to hear from adults about the realities of parenthood and will continue to deny the impact it will have on their lives. Hearing from teenage mothers who have already delivered about the demands and rewards of parenthood is sometimes more palatable to them. Teenagers should make long-term plans about who will provide financial support and housing and raise and care for the child. Teenage marriages to "make the baby legal" are very fragile, have a high divorce rate, and should be approached cautiously.

Adoption The number of teenagers choosing to place their infant for adoption is steadily decreasing, as is the stigma of single parenthood. The teenager who chooses to place her child needs support both during and after her pregnancy. This decision is difficult, and the girl will need time during her pregnancy and after delivery to make this decision. If she is unsure about adoption, the baby can be placed in a foster home until her decision is firm. State laws vary, but some states also require written consent for adoption from the father, if he is named.

Forms of counseling The choice of group or individual counseling should be available. While group counseling can be valuable, peer pressure should not be used to force a teenager to make any decision. In some cases, the "misery loves company" theory can run rampant in a group. "I'm having my baby, you should be woman enough to have yours." All nurses working with teenagers must examine their own attitudes toward abortion and keeping or giving up the baby. While they are entitled to their own opinion, they should in no way attempt to impose their views on their teenage clients. The pregnant adolescent's decision may also conflict with the wishes of her family. Emphasis is placed on communication between the girl and her family until a satisfactory resolution is reached.

Contraception is an important issue to discuss while the teenager is still pregnant. *Denial* is often evident. Many young women emphatically state, "I'm never going to have sex again!" and then are seen for repeated abortions. They should be given information about all methods and their availability. Teenagers who choose to continue with a pregnancy should be involved in prepared childbirth and parenting classes. Groups for young and single parents should also be made available to them.

Adolescent parenthood

Parenthood is one of life's most difficult roles. For teenagers it is exceptionally difficult. Often they are poorly prepared to cope with the constant demands imposed on them by an infant. They lack knowledge about normal development and care. The financial strain, lack of sleep, and total dependence involved in caring for an infant often are too much for them to handle. Just as difficult as the infant is the toddler, who is beginning to rebel and needs constant surveillance. It is not surprising that child abuse is more frequently seen in the children of teenagers, who are little more than children themselves. The pregnant teenager must resolve the following issues:

1. *Loss of independence.* Until the time of her pregnancy, the teenager has looked ahead to increasing independence from her parents. Now, both she and her child may continue to be dependent on them for financial support. She also gives up a large share of her independence to her child, who will be totally dependent on her.

2. *Interruption of school/job training for the teenage mother.* Without an adequate education or vocational skills, she will be unable to support herself and her child. For many teenagers this means dependence on the welfare system, although it will not allow them to raise the child with the material benefits they would like to provide.

3. *Interruption of school/job training for the teenage father.* The adolescent father often lacks the strength to cope with pregnancy. His knowledge of conception may be minimal, and he may view the girl's pregnancy as a threat to his increasing need for independence. Financial resources needed to assist the girl by paying for an abortion or the costs of pregnancy and child rearing are often not available. The teenage father who drops out of school to support his child often finds that few jobs are available for unskilled workers, and those he finds pay very little. He may find himself in the ranks of the unemployed and on welfare as well.

While the picture of the adolescent father is generally presented negatively, some adolescent girls who remain unmarried do continue their relationship with the baby's father. Their dependence on the father is emotional and may be financial as well. Sometimes the couple express the feeling that they would like to have a baby together some time in the future, but not now. If given the opportunity, the father may want to support the girl in decision making and participate in the childbearing events.

4. *Stress of coping mechanisms.* Adolescence itself puts stress on coping mechanisms. A pregnancy may be more than the already stressed teenager can handle, and she may turn to drugs or alcohol. Many drugs have an adverse effect on the fetus, particularly in the first 3 months of pregnancy. Street drugs used by teenagers vary in composition, and the teenager herself may not be absolutely certain what she is taking. Counseling and support are essential to maintain intact coping mechanisms.

5. *Separation from the peer group.* The experiences and expectations of the peer group are usually similar. A pregnancy makes the teenager unlike the other members of the peer group. She now has little in common with her childless peers. While prior to her pregnancy the pain of adolescence has been made more tolerable by the peer group, it offers little support to the pregnant teenager. Pregnancy isolates the adolescent socially from her peer group.

6. *Exclusion from school.* While the pregnant teenager is no longer required to leave her school and attend a special school, many choose to do so. Schools for pregnant teenagers offer classes on prenatal and baby care as well as the regular school curriculum. Also, the pregnant teenager often feels more comfortable as one of many other pregnant teenagers rather than feeling on display in her regular school. Returning to school after birth of the baby may be prevented by the demands of the baby or the inability to cope with school after the drastic alteration of becoming a mother.

7. *Stressed relationship with the boyfriend.* Pregnancy is usually as overwhelming for the teenage father as for the teenage mother. Pregnancy rarely has a positive effect on even the most stable teenage relationship. It may, in fact, cause its termination, leaving the pregnant teenager feeling alone, unsupported and depressed.

8. Lack of a mothering role model. Good parenting is a learned behavior. If the teenager lacked good mothering herself, it is doubtful that she will be able to provide this for her child, resulting in a greater risk of neglect and abuse. The young mother needs her mother both as a support person and as a role model. The teenager often does not feel like a mother but instead like a sister and needs time to learn this role.

9. Unrealistic expectations. The teenager often views her infant as "someone to love me, be mine, always be there for me." The infant is unable to meet these needs but instead demands that his or her own needs be met, which also increases the risk of neglect and abuse. Teenagers rarely have a full understanding of what parenting actually entails. They often view a baby as little more than a doll who can be put aside when they tire of it.

10. Stressed relationships—marriage. Most teenage marriages are the result of pregnancy. The divorce rate of teenage marriage is astoundingly high, four times greater than that of adult marriages. Marriage requires maturity, a trait teenagers have not yet developed. Teenagers have not learned mature ways of dealing with the stresses involved in the give-and-take of marriage.

11. Family of the pregnant adolescent. Pregnancy usually results in great upheaval and emotional upset for families. If the family is already disorganized and troubled, the pregnancy compounds the situation. Goals and expectations of parents for the teenager must be changed. Many angry, hostile feelings toward the pregnancy become apparent. After the initial shock, the family responds in various ways. They may try to persuade the girl to terminate the pregnancy, marry the father of the child, or hide the pregnancy and place the child for adoption. Other responses may be to incorporate the girl and her baby into the existing family structure and support the girl through the family.

If all these problems exist, then, why do so many teenagers become pregnant each year? Teenagers often feel inadequate, unworthy, and not satisfied with their bodies or their family relationships. Their lives may be filled with conflict; often they are followers rather than leaders, defensive and unstable. It is common for such girls to believe that a baby would give their lives meaning, status, and love.[16]

Nursing management

How can the nurse help the teenager, her boyfriend, and their families deal with the crises of pregnancy? The pregnant adolescent needs comprehensive prenatal care with special emphasis on nutrition, a supportive environment, childbirth education, contraceptive counseling, and ongoing parenting classes. The teenage father should be included whenever possible. Although the changes brought about by pregnancy are more obvious in young girls, teenage fathers need support and education for parenthood as well.

While the focus has been on the problems of the pregnant adolescent, some time should be spent discussing how the nurse can expect a teenage mother to adapt to the mothering role. Mercer found in her study of young teenagers that girls 14 and under differ significantly from girls over 16 in their infant care-giving abilities.[17]

All girls under 16 need intensive follow-up and nurturing for themselves and their baby. If a supportive mother is not available for the young teenagers, a foster home with a surrogate mother should be sought.

The young teenager has difficulty giving priority to the baby's needs. She also needs much help in interpreting behavior and may feel, for example, that the baby who gets dirty on the floor and chews on everything in sight is intentionally misbehaving. Parenting education and maternal support are essential for adequate infant care.

The older teen (16 and over) is more capable of caring for a baby. There are some characteristics which Mercer says predict success with mothering in this age group. These include: past experience in caring for and positive feelings about infants, available support from the mate and mother, a mother who helps but recognizes the teenager's capabilities and independence, and family members such as siblings and grandparents who also give support. Emotionally, the older teenager is usually mature enough to be willing to put the infant's needs above her own. She understands and recognizes the infant's normal behavior. She knows that a baby that drools when teething is exhibiting normal, not naughty, behavior. She has a positive infant image and feels that she has produced a "good" baby, perhaps "better than average."[18]

Nurses working with pregnant teenagers will

find the experience challenging, rewarding, depressing, and even, at times, very surprising.

References

1. J. Langman, *Medical Embryology*, 3d ed., Williams & Wilkins, Baltimore, 1975, p. 175.
2. Lucille Whaley and Donna Wong, *Nursing Care of Infants and Children*, Mosby, St. Louis, 1979, p. 419.
3. Whaley and Wong, op. cit., p. 419.
4. R. L. Summit, "Differential Diagnosis of Genital Ambiguity in the Newborn," *Clinical Obstetrical Gynecology* 15:112–139 (1972).
5. Victor Vaughn et al., *Nelson Textbook of Pediatrics*, 11th ed, Saunders, Philadelphia, 1979, p. 1571.
6. Ibid, p. 1572.
7. Ibid.
8. Leon Speroff et al., *Clinical Gynecologic Endocrinology and Fertility*, 2d ed., Williams & Wilkins, Baltimore, 1978, p. 76.
9. Ibid.
10. Ibid.
11. A. A. Campbell, "The Role of Family Planning in the Reduction of Poverty," *Journal of Marriage and the Family* 30:236–245 (1968).
12. Suzanne Hall Johnson, *High-Risk Parenting: Nursing Assessment and Strategies for the Families at Risk*, Lippincott, Philadelphia, 1979, p. 199.
13. Ibid, p. 199.
14. M. B. Bracken and S. Kasi, "Delay in Seeking Induced Abortion: A review and Theoretical Analysis," *American Journal of Obstetrics and Gynecology* 121(8):1008–j1018 (1975).
15. Gladys M. Scipien et al., *Comprehensive Pediatric Nursing*, 2d ed., McGraw-Hill, New York, 1979, p. 826.
16. Johnson, op. cit., p. 197.
17. Ramona Mercer, *Nursing Care for Parents at Risk*, Charles B. Slack, Thorofare, N.J., p. 135.
18. Ibid, p. 144.

Chapter 31 **Renal function**

Lois L. Lux, Karen E. Roper, and **Geanne M. Friedland**

Upon completion of this chapter, the student will be able to:

1. Relate urinary system congenital anomalies to embryological development.

2. Explain the method and purposes of selected renal diagnostic tests.

3. Describe the methods for collecting serum or urine specimens for renal diagnostic tests.

4. Interpret the results of urine culture and sensitivity tests.

5. Describe three radiologic examinations used in urinary system disorder diagnosis.

6. Identify three measures employed after a closed renal biopsy to detect or minimize internal renal hemorrhage.

7. Differentiate the signs of lower and upper urinary tract infections.

8. List the common organisms responsible for urinary tract infection.

9. Formulate a plan of care for a child with a urinary tract infection.

10. Describe the anatomy and physiology present with vesicoureteral reflux.

11. Explain the treatment modalities for obstructions of the urinary tract.

12. Describe the physical appearance of a child with exstrophy and epispadias.

13. Prepare a preoperative teaching session for parents of an infant with hypospadias.

14. Describe the treatment modalities for children with neuropathic bladders.

15. Describe three symptoms of acute glomerulonephritis and the nursing measures for each.

16. Compare the drug therapies generally utilized for acute and chronic glomerulonephritis.

17. Describe four nursing care measures used for a child with severe active nephrotic syndrome.

18. Compare the advantages of peritoneal dialysis vs. hemodialysis for use in children.

19. Compare the advantages of an internal and external shunt for hemodialysis.

Embryology

Although the renal and reproductive systems are initimately related embryologically, they are discussed independently in this text to facilitate comprehension.

The kidney begins to function at approximately the eighth week of development after passing through three stages: (1) the pronephros (forekidney); (2) the mesonephros (mid kidney); and (3) the metanephros (hind kidney). The first stage is marked by the development of the pronephros, a primitive, transitory, nonfunctional unit that appears early in the fourth week. Later in the fourth week, it gives rise to the mesonephros, the second stage. The mesonephros may function as a temporary renal unit for a few weeks until the metanephros is formed. The mesonephros gradually disintegrates after the eighth week except for the mesonephric duct (which buds to form the ureters, renal pelvis, calyces, and collecting tubules) and a few tubules which later form part of the male reproductive system. The metanephros, or permanent kidney, begins to develop in the fifth week and is producing urine in the eighth week, signifying completion of the third stage of development.

The nephrons, the basic functioning unit of the kidneys, are derived from the metanephric mass of the mesoderm. The number of nephrons does not increase after birth except in premature infants. As a child matures, the increase in renal size results from growth in nephron size, not an increase in the number of nephrons.

Initially, the permanent kidneys are located in

the pelvis, but their ascent to an abdominal position begins by the seventh to ninth week of gestation. As they ascend, they rotate 90° and are supplied by successively higher arteries. At birth, one renal artery and one renal vein supply each kidney. Infrequently, the kidneys do not ascend, resulting in ectopic kidneys. Fusion may also occur during ascent, producing a horseshoe (u-shaped) kidney.

By the seventh week, the *cloaca* (common chamber to the hindgut and urogenital sinus) is divided by the urorectal septum into the rectum and the urogenital sinus (bladder, urethra, and lower vagina in the female). The mesonephric duct and the ureteric bud have separate open-ings into the urogenital sinus. In the male, the mesonephric duct eventually becomes the ejaculatory duct, whereas in the female, it simply degenerates. The ureteric bud, derived earlier from the mesonephric duct, becomes the ureter.

In the male, the urethra, except for the glandular portion of the penile urethra, develops from the urogenital sinus. The glandular portion of the urethra is formed by tubularization of a cord of cells that enter the glans by way of the tip. Various degrees of hypospadias occur if the urethra does not form correctly. In the female, the entire urethra is formed from the urogenital sinus (Fig. 31-1).

Anatomy and physiology

The urinary tract is composed of an upper tract (kidneys and ureters) and a lower tract (bladder and urethra). The kidneys are located in the retroperitoneal space, on the dorsal aspect of the abdominal cavity on either side of the vertebral column. Because of the location of the liver, the right kidney is usually lower than the left. They are not rigidly attached to the abdominal wall, but are supported by the renal fascia, renal arteries and veins, and perirenal fat. The kidneys of a newborn infant are proportionally about three times larger than those of an adult when general body mass is taken into consideration.

The kidneys participate in the regulation of fluids and electrolytes, body pH, and excretion of the end products of metabolism. Each kidney has approximately 1 million nephrons that serve as its functioning units. A nephron is composed of a glomerulus (a tuft of capillary loops) surrounded by Bowman's capsule and the renal tubule system (Fig. 31-2). The glomerulus is the center for filtration of water and solutes from the blood. The renal tubules are responsible for reabsorbing essential substances as well as for allowing waste products to remain in the filtrate and to be passed into the collecting tubules. The collecting tubules join to form central tubes called *the ducts of Bellini*. The contents of these tubes pass through the calyces into the renal pelvis. Urine is then transported into the bladder by way of the ureters. (For additional information on the role of the kidney in fluid and electrolyte management, refer to Chap. 24.)

The bladder is a hollow muscular organ that functions as a reservoir for urine. The internal

Figure 31-1 This drawing illustrates the three stages of development of the embryonic kidneys in the human fetus and the embryonic development of the collecting system. (*From Gladys Scipien et al., Comprehensive Pediatric Nursing, 2d ed., McGraw-Hill, New York, 1979. Used with permission of publisher.*)

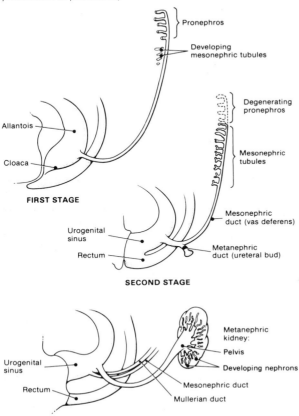

urethral orifice, located at the upper border of the symphysis in a neonate, gradually sinks until it is at the level of the lower border of the symphysis in the adult. For this reason, the bladder of a child is truly an abdominal rather than pelvic organ. It is therefore more accessible for suprapubic aspiration of urine or suprapubic surgery.

Assessment of the child with alteration of the urinary tract

Interview and history

The interview, history, and physical examination should be conducted in a manner conducive to health teaching. Participation appropriate for the child's age should be elicited during the assessment. Standard questionnaires designed to identify specific patterns of disease (such as urinary tract infection, enuresis) may be beneficial in establishing a data base and in planning for comprehensive care. They can also be important in providing continuity of care in a clinical setting.

A family history should be obtained, as should the physical and emotional history of the child. Any familial predisposition to renal disease, hypertension, urinary tract infections, and syndromes associated with urinary tract abnormalities is important to note. Specific questions to be asked include those that pertain to unexplained fever, flank or abdominal pain, changes in voiding habits (urgency, dysuria, enuresis, change in stream), and changes in the character of urine (color, odor). Medications the child is taking should be noted, paying particular attention to those that are potentially nephrotoxic or that may affect bladder function.

One must remember that some chronic renal conditions progress slowly and may not be associated with pain; in contrast, acute pyelonephritis causes a sudden onset of renal edema and will usually be accompanied by flank pain. Discomfort from the renal and ureteral areas may also be referred to the bladder, scrotum, and testicle in the male and to the bladder and vulva in the female.

Observation and physical examination

The general condition of the child is observed throughout the initial assessment. General malaise and failure to thrive may be associated with chronic urinary tract conditions. General skin

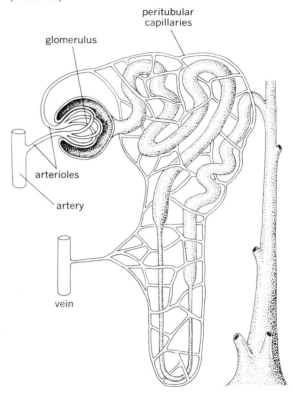

Figure 31-2 Basic structure of a nephron and the relationship between the blood supply and the renal tubular system. (*From Arthur Vander et al., Human Physiology, The Mechanisms of Body Function, 3d ed., McGraw-Hill, New York, 1980. Used with permission of the publisher.*)

condition and the presence or absence of periorbital, facial, or generalized edema should be noted. The physical examination should include palpation of the kidneys and bladder (if partially distended) and inspection of the genitalia. Accurate measurements of height and weight should be plotted on a standard growth grid. Blood pressure should be obtained, especially in children with reflux or renal disease. Follow-up physical examinations may not need to be as extensive, depending on the past history and the presenting symptoms.

Diagnostic tests

The nurse should discuss with the family the rationale for performing any diagnostic test, remembering to include an age-appropriate explanation for the child. If a urine specimen must be obtained, the method of collection should also be discussed and explained. Children (and parents) tend to be more cooperative when they understand the procedure as well as their participatory role.

Urine tests A voided sample usually is easily obtained, although catheterization of the bladder through the urethra, catheterization of a urinary stoma, or suprapubic aspiration may occasionally be necessary. A voided specimen may be obtained with a clean-catch, midstream collection or with a U-bag (refer to Chap. 17).

The procedure for catheterizing children is essentially the same as that for catheterizing adults. The use of a No. 5 or 8 French infant feeding tube is appropriate when catheterizing an infant or small child. The child should be told that the procedure will probably not be painful but will be uncomfortable. If a urine specimen is needed for culture and sensitivity testing in a child with a *urostomy* (nephrostomy, ileal conduit, or other urinary stoma), it will be necessary to obtain a catheterized specimen because of the high incidence of contamination associated with "bagged" or clean-catch specimens in these children. The procedure for stomal catheterization

is essentially the same as for sterile urethral catheterization.

Suprapubic aspiration is performed by a physician or pediatric nurse practitioner and should be attempted only in a child with a full bladder (i.e., not immediately following voiding). The bladder is situated just beneath the skin and can be easily palpated in an infant or small child. The skin should be prepared with Betadine solution. A needle of an appropriate size is used to puncture the bladder about 1 cm above the symphysis, and the specimen is aspirated via a syringe (Fig. 31-3).

Routine urinalysis When a routine urinalysis is ordered, instructions may include obtaining a fresh morning specimen. At this time, the urine will be more concentrated. Drinking large quantities of water to facilitate voiding is not advised because it may change the concentration.

Urine obtained for urinalysis should be kept at room temperature since refrigeration can cause precipitation of phosphates or urates, which could interfere with microscopic examination. It must not, however, be kept at room temperature for more than 1 to 2 h before examination. If it is allowed to stand at room temperature for a longer period of time, red cells may break up, casts may disintegrate, and bacteria may multiply, thereby affecting the accuracy of the test.

COLOR Urine is normally pale yellow or amber. A change in color may be due to food ingestion (dyes from beets or other vegetables), medications such as phenazopyridine (Pyridium) and Urised, red blood cells, or hemoglobin. It could also be very pale as a result of a low specific gravity or an osmotic diuresis (e.g., in diabetes mellitus).

ODOR An acetone odor is present with ketonuria and a strong ammonia-like or fecal odor may be present with bacterial growth.

SPECIFIC GRAVITY The normal range for children is approximately 1.000 to 1.030. Infants do not concentrate urine as well as older children and normally their urine specific gravity will not exceed 1.020. If fluids are restricted, the child's urine should become more concentrated and the specific gravity should reach the upper limits of normal. The specific gravity may be elevated if glucose, protein, or radiographic contrast material is present. Specific gravity can be measured

Figure 31-3 Suprapubic bladder aspiration is frequently the preferred method of obtaining a sterile urine specimen in infants. (*From Gladys Scipien et al., Comprehensive Pediatric Nursing, 2d ed., McGraw-Hill, New York, 1979. Used with permission of publisher.*)

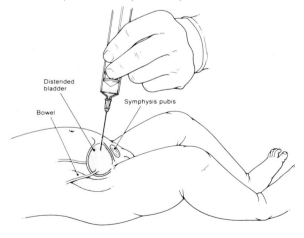

Distended bladder

Symphysis pubis

Bowel

easily on a nursing unit with a hydrometer or a refractometer; the latter requires only one drop of urine.

pH Normal kidneys participate in the control of total body pH by excreting urine in pH ranges of 4.5 to 7.5. Levels greater than 7.5 indicate that urea-splitting organisms are present (usually *Proteus*). These organisms make the urine very alkaline by relasing ammonia. Acid or alkaline food or medication may also affect the pH.

OTHER URINE ASSESSMENTS A dipstick screening test for protein, blood, ketone, and glucose is performed. Normally, these elements are not present in the urine. A microscopic examination is done to determine the presence or absence of red blood cells, white blood cells, epithelial cells, casts, crystals, bacteria, and yeasts.

One must consider the entire urinalysis when evaluating the results. For example, hematuria in the presence of bacteria and white blood cells would probably indicate a bladder infection. Hematuria with proteinuria and tubular casts would probably be the result of a glomerular disorder.

Urine culture and sensitivity Urine that has been collected for culture and sensitivity testing should be sent to the laboratory immediately as the number of bacteria doubles approximately every 30 min. An alternative to this practice is to use a dip-slide. This is a commercially prepared slide with culture media on both sides that can be dipped into the fresh specimen immediately and placed back in its plastic container. If dip-slides are not available, the urine may be placed in the refrigerator prior to transporation to the laboratory. A urinary tract infection may be diagnosed if: (1) more than 100,000 colonies of a single strain of bacteria are present in a voided specimen, (2) more than 10,000 colonies of a single strain of bacteria are found in a catheterized specimen, or (3) if any bacteria are detected in a suprapubic specimen. Antibiotic sensitivity testing should then be done so that appropriate antibiotic therapy can be initiated. A positive urine culture obtained on a specimen collected by U-bag is not reliable, since contamination from the skin or from possible reflux of the urine into the vagina of female patients may occur. Suprapubic aspiration or catheterization is indicated when positive results are obtained with U-bag specimens.

The importance of collecting a urine specimen correctly cannot be overemphasized. The risk of contamination is significant. A positive culture obtained from a single, clean voided specimen has a validity of only 80 percent. If two consecutive cultures are done correctly and they demonstrate the same organism and a high colony count, the validity rate increases to 95 percent.[1] A U-bag specimen has a very low validity and should be considered accurate only if it is negative. Positive cultures obtained by U-bags should be confirmed by suprapubic aspiration or by catheterization.

Timed urine collections When a 12-h or 24-h urine collection is required for an outpatient, written instructions are helpful. The child should be instructed to void before the test starts, discarding the urine. *All* of the urine that is voided from the time the test is initiated to the time it is completed should be saved. Timed collections begin and end with an empty bladder. The nurse should inform the family whether a preservative (formalin) or refrigeration is necessary.

CREATININE CLEARANCE This is a timed urine collection performed in conjunction with a serum creatinine test. (Refer to the section on blood tests.)

PROTEINURIA A patient with persistent proteinuria may undergo a timed test for total protein excretion. It is important to remember that transient proteinuria may occur with *orthostatic proteinuria* (caused by standing or exercising for long periods) or acute febrile illnesses or may follow a blood transfusion, exercise, or extensive burns. Therefore, it is not necessarily indicative of a severe renal disorder. Persistent, massive proteinuria generally accompanies glomerular disease and nephrosis. Mild proteinuria may be present or absent in many other renal conditions.

ADDIS COUNT A 12-h Addis count may be ordered to quantify the actual number of red blood cells, white blood cells, and tubular casts that have been passed within a specific period of time.

OSMOLALITY The ability to concentrate urine is decreased in such renal conditions as chronic renal failure and obstructive uropathy with hydronephrosis. In general, children over 2 months old should be able to concentrate urine to 900 mosmol per liter after a 12-h period of fluid restriction.

Renal function tests

Blood tests Renal function may be studied by blood tests and radiologic examinations. The most common blood studies are blood urea nitrogen (BUN), creatinine, creatinine clearance, and urea clearance.

Urea and creatinine are the major nitrogenous waste products normally cleared from the circulation by the kidney. Their concentration in the blood increases as kidney function decreases. These tests are considered only gross indicators of renal function since their values do not change until renal function is markedly impaired. The BUN and creatinine levels are elevated only after approximately 60 percent of kidney function is impaired.

Clearance tests report the milliliters of plasma that are completely cleared of a test substance each minute. Clearance values may relate primarily to glomerular function or to both glomerular and tubular function, depending upon the test substance being measured. The creatinine clearance test is generally considered more valuable than the urea clearance because creatinine clearance values are not affected by diet, fluid intake, or rate of urine flow. Normal values for the creatinine clearance test are approximately 100 ml/min. Normal urea clearance is approximately 70 ml/min.

Estimation of glomerular filtration rate is another important measure of kidney function. The glomerular filtration rate is measured by the clearance (removal from the bloodstream into the urine) of certain test substances. A normal glomerular filtration rate is 70 ml/min in children over 1 year of age.

Radiologic tests The most common radiologic test of renal function is the *intravenous pyelogram (IVP)*. This is a study of the upper urinary tract. An iodinized dye is given to the child through an intravenous line. The kidneys concentrate and excrete the iodine compound so that the kidneys, ureters, and bladder can be visualized on x-rays. Some patients are allergic to the dye compound, and so a small test dose is usually given prior to the examination. IV diphenhydramine (Benadryl) should be available for reactions. Patients are sometimes given a Fleets enema the evening before the examination so that bowel contents will not obscure the IVP

films. Fluids are usually restricted for some hours before the examination.

A *voiding cystourethrogram (VCUG)* may be performed to study the lower urinary tract. This examination consists of introducing contrast media into the bladder via catheter. The bladder is filled, and the child is asked to void. The child should be warned about this and told it is part of the test. Films of the bladder, bladder neck, and urethra are taken during voiding. This test is not done in the presence of an acute urinary tract infection, since filling the bladder via catheter may force infected urine up into the kidneys by reflux, causing upper tract infection. See Fig. 31-4*A* and *B*.

Renal arteriograms are performed for diagnosis of problems such as tumors, cysts, and aneurysms. An arteriogram provides detailed visualization of the large and small renal arteries. A cutdown is performed, and a catheter is passed via the femoral artery into the abdominal aorta. Contrast media can be injected into the aorta, thereby filling both renal arteries. The catheter can be directed into one of the renal arteries if only one kidney needs to be visualized.

Ultrasonography utilizes very high frequency sound waves transmitted through fluids and tissues. With this examination, the kidneys can be localized and measured. A mass can be identified as cystic, solid, or a mixture of both. The method is noninvasive and painless for the patient.

Radioisotope scanning is used to obtain detailed pictures of the pattern of blood flow and the excretory functioning of each kidney. A radioactive isotope is injected into the bloodstream. Films are taken as the kidneys concentrate and excrete the isotope. The test can define nonfunctional areas of the renal cortex and is of particular value in studying unilateral renal diseases and anomalies.

Cystoscopy *Cystoscopy* is a means of visualizing the lower urinary tract directly. In children, this procedure is usually performed under general anesthesia. The surgeon inserts the tubular cystoscope through the urethra into the bladder so that the bladder wall and ureteral openings are visualized. In additon to cystoscopy, the surgeon may perform *retrograde pyelography*. This involves visualizing the ureteral openings with the cystoscope and injecting contrast material into the openings through a catheter. The contrast material will ascend the ureters, and the appearance of the kidneys and ureters may then be filmed.

Renal biopsy At times, it may be necessary for the physician to examine a small piece (the diameter of a pencil lead) of kidney tissue to accurately diagnose a renal disorder and decide on appropriate treatment. A renal biopsy may also be done to determine the progression of a chronic kidney disease.

An "open" renal biopsy is a surgical procedure that exposes the kidney. It is done under general anesthesia. The preoperative and postoperative nursing care is similar to that of most pediatric surgical patients. A "closed" renal biopsy is

performed under local anesthesia, using a long needle to enter the kidney tissue. The procedure may be conducted using fluoroscopy or ultrasonography to assist in the placement of the needle. The child is premedicated to aid in relaxation and is positioned on the stomach. The biopsy should not be painful, although the child will feel the pressure of the needle.

To assure maximum cooperation, the child should be told ahead of time what to expect during and after the procedure. The most common complication of renal biopsy is internal renal hemorrhage. Postoperative care is designed to minimize hemorrhage and to detect it as early as possible. Strict bed rest is maintained for 24 h after a renal biopsy. The pressure dressing over the biopsy site should be checked frequently for bleeding. Vital signs, including blood pres-

Figure 31-4 (*A*) Radiographic study demonstrating a normal voiding cystourethrogram. (*B*) Voiding cystourethrogram showing gross reflux. (*Courtesy of J. W. Duckett, M.D., Director, Division of Urology, Children's Hospital of Philadelphia.*)

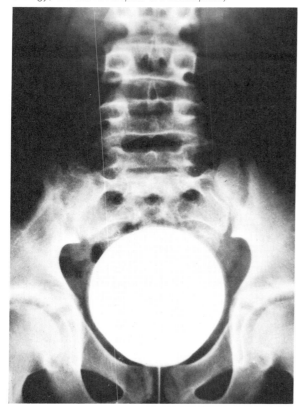
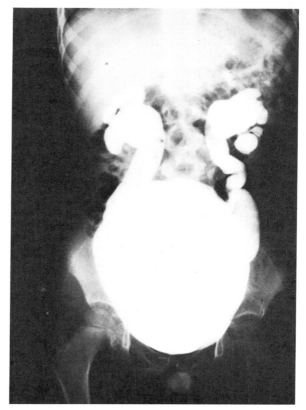

sure, should be taken every half-hour for 4 h and then every hour for 4 h. Fluids must be encouraged to maintain a good urine flow. Urine should be saved in separate containers with the date and time noted. Any profuse or persistent hematuria should be reported to the physician. Severe loin pain or abdominal pain should also be reported.

Structural and positional alterations of the urinary tract

Urinary tract infections

Urinary tract infections are very common in the pediatric age group. Girls, except as neonates, have a much higher incidence of urinary tract infections than boys, with a ratio of approximately 9 to 1.[2] At any given time, 1.2 percent of all school-age girls (through high school) have bacteriuria.[3] Many of them are asymptomatic. Five percent of all school-aged girls have had a urinary tract infection by the time they graduate.[4] Generally, bacterial invasions that cause urinary tract infections occur by a hematogenous (bloodborne) route in newborns (more commonly males) and a urethral route in older children (predominantly females).

Escherichia coli infections account for approximately 80 percent of all urinary tract infections. The next most common organisms are: *Klebsiella*, enterococci, *Proteus*, *Pseudomonas*, and *Enterobacter*. Antibiotic treatment is usually instituted after sensitivity tests are done, taking into consideration the child's age, renal function, past allergies, and urinary tract infection history (including response to treatment) as well as normal expected serum and urine concentrations of the antibiotic. Follow-up urinalyses are done at appropriate intervals to monitor the child's status.

Not all children with bacteria in their urine will develop an infection. Other factors are significant. The frequency of bladder emptying plays an important role. Overdistention will cause stagnant urine to remain in contact with bladder mucosa for prolonged periods. This may occur in a child who has a neuropathic bladder or in one with a functional disorder who holds large amounts of urine in the bladder before voiding. Obstruction, renal calculi, foreign bodies, and reflux may also interfere with the child's resistance. The characteristically short urethra

in the female may be one of the reasons for the increased incidence in girls. The body does, however, have natural defenses. For example, *Escherichia coli* does not colonize at pH levels of less than 5.5 or more than 7.5.[5] Some people advocate drinking alkaline juices (e.g., cranberry) that produce an acid ash to maintain or create an acid urine. If this is to be part of the treatment plan, the pH of the urine should be checked routinely because the amount of cranberry juice necessary to acidify the urine varies with the individual and, unfortunately, is usually large. This type of preventive care would probably be beneficial for a child (prone to infections) who drank large quantities of acidic juices (citrus). The family could then substitute cranberry juice for some of the citrus intake, thus reducing the chances for an alkaline urine. It is also thought that the bladder mucosa itself may have an intrinsic factor that repels colonization.

Symptoms of urinary tract infections depend upon the child's age and whether the upper or lower urinary tract is involved. An *infant* may present with anorexia, lethargy, irritability, abdominal pain, temperature change, or failure to thrive. Because of the wide range of symptoms in this age group, almost any unexplained illness could be a urinary infection and it is wise to obtain urine for culture. *Older children* with upper urinary tract infections may have the same symptoms as adults: elevated temperature, flank or back pain, and general malaise. Those with lower tract infections urinate frequently and urgently with a burning sensation and have urethral or lower abdominal pain after voiding or enuresis. Symptoms of lower urinary tract infections, in conjunction with a negative culture, may indicate a local urethral irritation. This may be secondary to taking a bubble bath, being infected with pinworms, or sexual activity.

Nursing management A child with a urinary tract infection may have less pain if he or she increases oral fluid intake. Many children with lower tract infections who complain of burning on urination are naturally reluctant to void. The nurse may suggest placing the child in a warm tub to stimulate voiding.

Children who are prone to urinary tract infections should be encouraged to empty their bladders frequently to prevent overdistension, and to avoid bubble baths. Girls should be taught to wipe from front to back after bowel movements to prevent fecal contamination of the urethra.

Vesicoureteral reflux

After a child has recuperated sufficiently (3 to 5 weeks) from the first urinary infection and a sterile urine is documented, a voiding cystoure-throgram and an intravenous pyelogram should be obtained to rule out urinary tract abnormal-ities. According to King, 45 percent of his female patients under 2 years of age and 20 percent of older girls who presented with a urinary tract infection demonstrated reflux.[6] Approximately 40 to 60 percent of all boys who have urinary tract infections will have a renal abnormality, most commonly reflux, demonstrated radi-ographically.[7] Because of this high degree of occurrence, radiography is a necessary diagnos-tic tool.

Vesicoureteral reflux occurs when urine backs up (refluxes) from the bladder into the ureters and possibly, into the kidneys. Reflux may vary in severity and may occur only at the time of voiding. After voiding, refluxed urine returns to the bladder, creating a good media for infection. In a normal system, the ureters enter the bladder at an oblique angle. The intravesical sections of the ureters, which are located in the submucosal tunnels, clamp off when the bladder contracts during voiding. In children who reflux, the ure-ter(s) tends to enter the bladder laterally. The configuration of the ureteral orifices, the position of the ureters in the bladder, and the length of the submucosal tunnels may be abnormal (Fig. 31-5). Diagnosis of reflux is confirmed by a voiding cystourethrogram, and its degree of severity is graded. If there is a small degree of reflux, the child may outgrow it and may be able to be managed conservatively. Medical treatment con-sists of low-dose antibiotic suppressive therapy and periodic urine cultures and radiographic examinations. The importance of continuous suppressive therapy must be emphasized to the parents because infections associated with reflux may cause permanent renal damage and arrested renal growth.

Ureteral reimplantation is performed when the child has a high degree of reflux, abnormal renal growth as evidenced on comparative x-ray films, breakthrough infections while on suppressive therapy, or all three. The operative procedure consists of reimplanting the ureter(s) obliquely into the bladder, simultaneously fashioning the submucosal tunnels. Postoperative care is gen-erally the same as with all abdominal surgeries. The child will have a catheter in the bladder for 4 to 5 days. The catheter will drain bloody urine because the bladder is a vascular organ. The catheter may cause bladder spasms, which may be treated with propantheline (Pro-Banthine) tablets or Banthine bromide and opium (B&O) suppositories. Ureteral *stents* (tubes) may be

Figure 31-5 Vesicoureteral reflux occurs if there is a malfunctioning ureterovesicular valve that permits urine to flow back into the ureter when the bladder becomes full. After voiding, when pressure within the bladder is lower, the refluxed urine reenters the bladder.

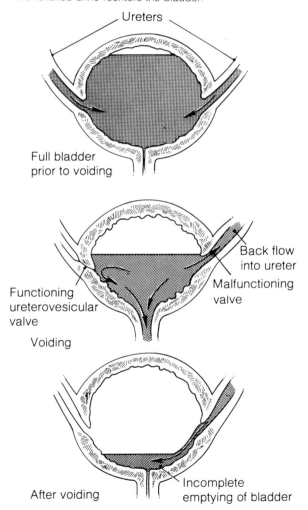

Ureters

Full bladder
prior to voiding

Functioning
ureterovesicular
valve

Back flow
into ureter

Malfunctioning
valve

Voiding

After voiding

Incomplete
emptying of bladder

used, depending on the preference of the surgeon. If the anastamosis has been difficult (due to the size of the ureters or the thickness of the bladder), stents will maintain patency by preventing edema from obstructing the flow of urine. It is important to measure all drainage from the catheter and stents separately so that it will be easy to detect obstruction of a tube. Kinking of these small stents does occur and the nurse should be alert to this.

Ureteral reimplantation has a very high degree of success in children with nonneuropathic bladders. The absence of reflux postoperatively should be verified by a voiding cystourethrogram. This is routinely obtained a few months after surgery. The child may continue to have bladder infections, but infected urine will not be refluxing up the ureters. For this reason, it is important to emphasize to the family that the primary reason for reimplantation is kidney preservation, not the prevention of future bladder infections.

Upper urinary tract obstruction

Obstruction of the urinary tract creates an increased pressure above the point of obstruction. The degree of dilatation in the ureters and kidneys depends on the severity and location of the obstruction. If the obstruction and backflow of urine raise the intrapelvic pressures to equal the glomerulus capillary pressure, filtration will cease. Early diagnosis and treatment of obstruction are essential to prevent permanent renal structure damage and dilatation of the upper urinary tract, which may result in hydronephrosis.

Obstruction of the ureteropelvic junction (UPJ)—hydronephrosis

The ureteropelvic junction is the most common site for obstruction in the kidneys and upper ureters. In most cases, it is considered to be a congenital defect caused by mechanical (narrowing or kinking of the ureter) or functional (no definitive etiology known) obstruction.

UPJ obstruction causing hydronephrosis is the most common renal mass that occurs in children under 1 year of age.[8] A palpable kidney mass and failure to thrive are the most common presenting symptoms in this age group. An older child will usually have vague gastrointestinal symptoms or recurrent attacks of colicky flank pain. Because of the vague symptoms, the correct diagnosis may not be made on initial examination.

Medical treatment may be instituted with a close follow-up examination that includes comparative radiologic examinations. In selected cases, surgical intervention in the form of pyeloplasty or, rarely, nephrectomy may be indicated. The choice of treatment depends on the severity of the obstruction and the resultant damage to the collecting system.

Occasionally, a temporary nephrostomy tube may be placed in the renal pelvis following a complicated pyeloplasty or preoperatively to decompress the system. One of the major advantages of the nephrostomy tube, its ease of reversibility, is also a disadvantage. If the tube should accidently be dislodged, the tract can close off in just 2 to 3 h, making replacement of the tube difficult. Nephrostomy tubes are usually sutured to the skin and taped in place to avoid this complication.

Lower urinary tract obstructions

Meatal stenosis The premise that meatal stenosis is the cause of most recurrent urinary tract infections and reflux is not accepted by many pediatric urologists. Meatal stenosis may, however, be the cause of abnormal voiding symptoms, and dilatation may occasionally be required.[9] In the male, the primary indications for a meatotomy are extreme narrowing of the urinary stream and prolonged voiding times. In both males and females, diagnosis is made by examining the urethra and observing the child while voiding.

Urethral strictures Basically, four types of strictures can be identified: "congenital," inflammatory, traumatic, and iatrogenic. *"Congenital" urethral strictures*, if they exist at all, are rare and occur mainly in boys. *Inflammatory strictures* are also rare in children and may be a sequela of gonorrhea. *Traumatic strictures* may occur following urethral trauma secondary to straddle or penetrating injuries. The use of instruments and catheters of inappropriate size may cause iatrogenic strictures at the meatus or at the penoscrotal junction.

Diagnosis of all but the traumatic strictures is difficult because symptoms vary. Strictures may become symptomatic because of a decrease in caliber or strength of the urinary stream or incomplete emptying of the bladder from outflow obstruction. A retrograde urethrogram may be necessary to establish a diagnosis. Depending on the severity of the stricture, urethral dilatation, urethrotomy, or urethroplasty may be performed.

Congenital posterior urethral valves Posterior urethral valves are membranous diaphragms found within the prostatic urethra that partially obstruct the flow of urine. The size of the opening in the valve determines the severity of the obstruction. Chronic bladder distention in utero may lead to a thickened bladder wall, ureterovesical junction obstruction, and, eventually, hydronephrosis. Reflux, if present, may cause further renal damage.

In newborn male infants, bilateral or unilateral smooth flank masses and a distended bladder would be suggestive of congenital posterior urethral valves. A dribbling stream is likely; however, significant valve obstruction has been observed in infants with a good stream. Many children with obstructive uropathy do not concentrate urine effectively. This becomes significant when the child has severe diarrhea or vomiting, as it can result in rapid dehydration.[10] If the diagnosis is not established in the newborn period, subsequent chronic urinary tract infections and failure to thrive may be diagnostic. In older boys, the symptoms may not be as definitive. The diagnosis should be confirmed by radiographic studies.

The treatment of choice is surgery that may be performed transurethrally or by perineal urethrostomy. Surgical treatment may have to be postponed in an infant until his general condition has stabilized. He may need fluids to correct dehydration and azotemia (elevated BUN), electrolytes to correct imbalances, and adequate urinary drainage to relieve hydronephrosis. Drainage may be provided by a temporary vesicostomy or placement of a nephrostomy tube.

Genital, bladder, and abdominal wall anomalies

External defects of the genitourinary tract are usually found during the physical examination at birth. Some may be mild, requiring little treatment. Severe defects, such as exstrophy of the bladder, require costly, time-consuming surgical repairs. Even minor defects may have a significant emotional impact on the parents because the genitourinary system is involved.

Patent urachus Patent urachus occurs when the epithelialized tube (urachus) that connects the bladder with the umbilicus prior to birth fails to close. When the urachus remains patent, urine leaks onto the abdomen and a persistently moist umbilicus may be noted. This anomaly may be seen alone or in conjunction with prune-belly syndrome or with obstruction of the urinary tract. If the urachus does not close during the newborn period, surgical intervention will be necessary.

Exstrophy of the bladder Bladder exstrophy results from failure of the anterior wall of the abdomen and bladder to fuse, leaving the bladder open and exposed on the abdomen (Fig. 31-6). Exstrophy occurs in approximately 1 in 30,000 births.[11] It is seen more often in males than in females. The anomaly rarely occurs more than once within the same family.

The most common form of the condition is

Figure 31-6 A newborn with exstrophy of the bladder. The pubic bones are widely separated. (*Courtesy of J. W. Duckett, M.D., Director, Division of Urology, Children's Hospital of Philadelphia.*)

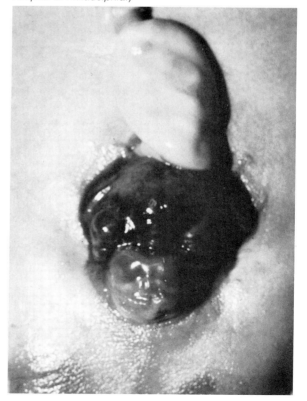

Figure 31-7 Surgical correction of bladder exstrophy in a male. Notice the splayed open penis with uncorrected subsymphysial epispadias. (*Courtesy of J. W. Duckett, M.D., Director, Division of Urology, Children's Hospital of Philadelphia.*)

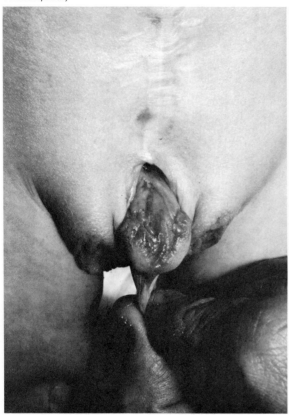

bladder exstrophy with complete epispadias. In this form, the bladder is turned out and the ureteral orifices are visible and are draining urine (Fig. 31-7). In the male, the urethra is splayed open with a dorsal groove and the testicles, although lying in the canal, are frequently undescended. In the female, there is an epispadiac urethra, a bifid clitoris, and widely separated anterior labia. The pubic bones are widely separated and the femoral heads are externally rotated. The child's gait will appear broad-based, but there is no associated permanent orthopedic disability. The separated pelvis often does not provide good suspensory support for the rectum and rectal prolapse may result. This tends to correct itself as the child grows older.

Many pediatric urologists operate on children with exstrophy within 48 h after birth. The rationale for this practice is that the pelvic structures move more freely during this period, allowing reconstruction without the aid of iliac osteotomies. This increased pliability is thought to be secondary to the same factors that allow the molding of the fetal skeleton during delivery.[12,13]

During this first surgical procedure, the bladder is either reconstructed or removed, according to its size and its potential for holding urine. The defect is thus partially corrected, leaving the child with an epispadiac urethra. Often a penis-lengthening procedure is necessary to achieve adequate sexual function in the male. This may be done at the time of the initial surgery or it may be postponed.

Future surgical procedures may include repair of the epispadias, bladder neck surgery for incontinence if the bladder is of adequate size, or a urinary diversion if it is not.

Some urologists prefer to delay the initial surgery until the child is older. If this occurs, the nurse will teach the parents how to protect the bladder mucosa and the surrounding skin from infection and irritation.

Nursing management Family support is especially difficult initially because the mother may still be hospitalized when the baby is transferred to a tertiary pediatric center. The father is then faced with the task of trying to spend time at both hospitals.

Often, the nurse serves as the liaison who coordinates care, education, and communication between the family and all of the involved disciplines. The nurse must foster positive feelings about the eventual outcome, while helping the family to realize the long-term medical supervision and multiple surgical procedures necessitated by this anomaly.

When the initial surgery is postponed, a fine-mesh petroleum gauze is placed over the bladder mucosa and a protective ointment is placed on the surrounding skin to prevent irritation. Frequent diaper changes and immediate cleansing after bowel movements are essential.

After the initial surgery, the baby is hospitalized for a few weeks, depending on the general condition. For 6 weeks postoperatively, the infant's legs may be flexed and wrapped in Kling or Ace bandages so that the femoral heads are internally rotated. The flexed knees keep additional pressure off the abdominal wall and the site of skin closure, facilitating healing. The wrapped legs maintain the hips in an internally rotated position and reduce tension on the sutures holding the pelvis together. Diapers must be applied in the same manner as a "wraparound skirt" in order to maintain correct alignment during this period. As an alternative to this method of immobilization, a cast or orthopedic traction may be used.

If a urinary diversion is required, either an *ileal conduit* or *ureterosigmoidostomy* is usually performed. The major advantage of a ureterosigmoidostomy is that there is no abdominal stoma. There are also disadvantages that make this type of diversion controversial. In this procedure, the ureters are taken out of the bladder wall and implanted into the sigmoid colon using an antireflux technique. The colon then becomes a reservoir for both stool and urine. Only children with normal kidneys, ureters, and good rectal tone (no history of rectal prolapse) are selected for this procedure. The parents should be made aware of the chronic care and long-term follow-up required. The parents and the child should receive continuous support as it will take time for the child to develop fecal and urinary continence and for the family to feel comfortable in their ability to assess all aspects of the child's care. Some patients develop full continence, whereas others are plagued with leakage.

Epispadias Epispadias is a rare congenital condition that is found more frequently in males than females in which a dorsal cleft of the urethra is present. In females, there is an associated bifid clitoris and the urethral cleft extends to and involves the bladder neck. In males, the cleft may involve only the glans (balanic), the glans and the penile shaft (penile), or the entire penis and the bladder neck (subsymphysial). If it involves the bladder neck, the patient is incontinent (Fig. 31-7).

The primary objectives for treatment are to: (1) reconstruct the urethra; (2) straighten the penis (or bring the bifid clitoris together); (3) produce a penis (or female genitalia) that is cosmetically acceptable and functional; (4) restore continence.[14] All of these goals are accomplished through surgical intervention. Achieving

bladder continence continues to be the major problem.[15–17]

Hypospadias Hypospadias, the congenital occurrence of an abnormally placed urethra on the ventral surface of the penis or the perineum has a high incidence (5 of 1000 male births).[18] There is no known single cause of this condition, although there is a familial tendency.

In hypospadias, the ventral foreskin is absent, a dimple or groove is often present at the tip of the penis, and the glans is usually spade-shaped. *Chordee*, a cobra-head-like bending of the penis, is often present and is corrected at the time of the hypospadias repair. Chordee may be noticeable only with erections (Fig. 31-8). Significant associated upper urinary tract anomalies are unusual. When the testes are undescended or nonpalpable, sexual determination may be difficult. Buccal smears and a karyotype may be necessary to determine gender.

Hypospadias in girls is uncommon and rarely causes problems. Occasionally, incontinence is present if the urethra is extremely short.

Surgery is usually performed after the child's penis is of sufficient size to facilitate the procedure (18 months to 2 years of age) and before the child starts school so that he will be able to void like his male peers. Depending on the severity of the defect and the preference of the urologist, the repair may be done in one or two stages. Neonates with hypospadias must not be circumcised. The foreskin is needed to repair the urethra.

Figure 31-8 Classification of hypospadias based on anatomic location of the urinary meatus. Associated chordee is best described in terms of its severity: mild, moderate, or severe. (*From P. Kalalis and C. King, Clinical Pediatric Urology, Saunders, Philadelphia, 1976. Used with permission of publisher.*)

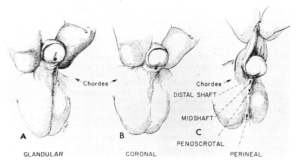

In the neonatal period, parents have to be reassured of the child's future normal sexual development. Often, they do not believe the penis will be normal after surgery and they may have difficulty verbalizing their fears.

A parent should be encouraged to stay in the

Table 31-1 Information for parents: home management for a child with hypospadias repair

We have designed this information sheet to help you with the care your son will require at home after his surgery.
1. Your son may play as he wishes except that he may not straddle a bicycle, rocking horse, or any other toy until your urologist says he can. This is to prevent him from damaging the operative area.
2. He will have a tube (catheter) in for approximately 10 days to 2 weeks after surgery. You will be furnished with a leg bag for daytime use and a larger drainage bag for overnight use. Most children do not like the feeling of the plastic bag against their leg. Before going home, please obtain a piece or two of stockinette from your nurse or the urology office on the third floor. This may be worn as a thigh-high sock so that the plastic will not bother him. If either of the bags develops urine crystals on the inside, you may rinse it with a solution of $\frac{1}{2}$ strength plain white vinegar and water.
3. As long as the tube (catheter) is in, your son may have bladder spasms. These cramping pains can be treated with B&O suppositories or Pro-Banthine tablets. Please follow the directions on the label. You may want to fill the prescription for B&O suppositories at the hospital pharmacy, because most outside pharmacies do not carry them.
4. You son should take tub baths twice a day for 20 to 30 minutes when he goes home. He may get completely wet, even the tube.
5. It is important to keep the tip of the penis from crusting over. You will be receiving a tube of Lacrilube to use to keep the opening at the end of the penis free of crusts. This is to be done while your son has a suprapubic tube in his bladder. Obviously, if he has a Foley catheter (tube) going into the opening of his penis (meatus), this will be done after the tube is removed.
6. Try to avoid constipation. Good oral fluid intake will help.

Please do not worry if:
1. There is bloody urine in the tubing or bag, especially when your son has bladder spasms.
2. There is mucus or sediment (whitish particles) in the urine.
3. Your son voids (passes water) in small amounts through his penis (if he has a suprapubic catheter in his bladder).
4. There is some swelling (edema) of his penis. Call us if it increases significantly.
5. The sutures on his penis start to come out. (They are dissolvable and will gradually fall out over the next several weeks.)
Please call us if there are any problems or questions.

hospital with the child. Children of this age do not tolerate parental separation well and are very much aware of their genitalia.

Preoperative instructions, including an explanation of dressings, catheter placement, and probable bladder spasms secondary to the presence of the catheter, are imperative. Propantheline (Pro-Banthine) tablets or Banthine and opium (B&O) suppositories may be prescribed to relieve these spasms. A "well-bandaged" penis and a Foley catheter or suprapubic tube that is adequately taped down will make it possible to leave the child's hands unrestrained. These children are usually out of bed the day following surgery and are in the playroom soon thereafter. They are not allowed to straddle toys or other objects, but because children usually limit themselves appropriately, they are otherwise unrestricted. Discharge teaching should be instituted early in the hospitalization, and written directions like those in table 31-1 should be provided.

Prune-belly syndrome A child with this rare congenital syndrome is identified by a wrinkled prunelike abdomen. This condition is actually composed of a triad of symptoms: abdominal muscle deficiency, cryptorchidism, and urinary tract anomalies. These anomalies usually consist of varying degrees of dysplastic kidneys, tortuous and redundant ureters, a large, thick-walled bladder, and an abnormal urethra (Fig. 31-9). Some children do not meet all three criteria and their condition is therefore known as *pseudo-prune-belly syndrome*. Only a few girls have been known to have pseudo-prune-belly syndrome, and, obviously, no girls have been diagnosed as having true prune-belly syndrome, as they have no testes.

The prognosis for these patients seems to depend on the degree of renal dyplasia rather than on the severity of the abdominal wall defect. They generally have a shortened life span.

Because of the large bladder and refluxing ureters (70 percent of the cases), stasis of urine leading to urinary tract infections is a primary problem. A cutaneous vesicostomy (see "Neuropathic Bladder") may be necessary to alleviate the situation. Because of the lack of abdominal musculature, these children have difficulty coughing and are prone to upper respiratory tract problems. Support of the abdomen when coughing is generally beneficial.

Neuropathic bladder

A neuropathic or neurogenic bladder is one that fails to function normally as a result of a neuromuscular defect. Children with neuropathic bladders may be divided into three groups. The first and most common group is composed of children with congenital sacral agenesis or myelomeningocele. The second group involves acquired lesions and includes children with traumatic injuries of the spinal cord, tumors of the spinal cord, sacrococcygeal teratomas, and surgical trauma associated with the repair of imperforate anus or extensive bladder dissections. The third group, children who have occult neuropathic bladders, is not well-defined. This discussion will be limited to neuropathic bladders in children with myelomeningocele.

Neuropathic bladders may be classified as either functional or neurological disorders. Further division into those that involve a failure to empty and those that involve a failure to store facilitates understanding of treatment modalities.

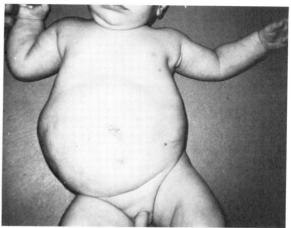

Figure 31-9 This male infant has the large distended abdomen of the prune-belly syndrome. A vesicostomy is present approximately midway between his umbilicus and his pubic symphysis. (*Courtesy of J. W. Duckett, M.D., Director, Division of Urology, Children's Hospital of Philadelphia.*)

Failure to empty An infant with a myelomeningocele should be initially evaluated with an intravenous pyelogram and a voiding cystourethrogram. If an infant fails to empty the bladder completely on voiding and does not demonstrate reflux, the parents may be taught to use Credé's method (manual bladder pressure) to express the residual urine from the child's bladder at specified intervals. This may be continued by the child in conjunction with a Valsalva maneuver (holding a deep breath while contracting abdominal muscles and straining) when the child is mature enough to be responsible and physically able to do it effectively.

If a child with this type of neuropathic bladder has reflux, the Credé method should not be used because the high pressure obtained during this mechanical decompression of the bladder will force urine up the ureters into the kidneys. Routine urine cultures and radiographic monitoring of renal growth and function are essential.

The objectives of treatment are to decompress the system in order to preserve renal function, to keep the child as free of infection as possible, and to promote the child's social acceptance. These goals may be achieved by temporary urinary diversion (usually a vesicostomy), clean intermittent catheterization, or a permanent di-

version such as an ileal or colon conduit. Permanent urinary diversion is rarely indicated.

In a newborn infant or young child, a *cutaneous vesicostomy* (an opening into the bladder) is probably the most desirable solution (Fig. 31-10). This technique is advocated because of its ease of reversibility as well as its ease of management for the family.[19] The dome of the bladder is brought to the skin surface, forming a 1- to 1.5-cm stoma that is situated between the umbilicus and the pubic symphysis. It allows urine to flow freely, decompressing the upper tracts. These children usually drain urine into diapers since urostomy appliances do not seem to adhere well in this area. Many ingenious parents have devised their own method for keeping their children dry. One child wears an elasticized band over a section of disposable diaper that covers the vesicostomy allowing her to wear panties rather than diapers. Another parent has found that taping an undershirt over the diaper helps to keep the diaper over the vesicostomy.

Clean intermittent self-catheterization (CIC) is initiated when these children reach an "age of concern," defined as the age when they become tired of being wet, be it at 5 years or 25 years. This clean, nonsterile method of emptying the bladder was introduced in this country in 1970.

Figure 31-10 Cutaneous vesicostomy (opening into the bladder) is shown in this illustration. The stoma is about 1 to 1.5 cm and is situated between the umbilicus and symphysis.

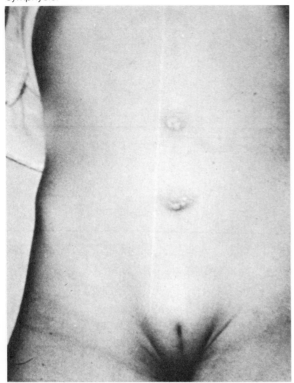

Patients who were on a regimen of self-catheterization demonstrated improvement, including continence and a decreased incidence of urinary tract infections.[20]

Teaching the child and family clean intermittent self-catheterization before the vesicostomy is closed and without emphasizing a projected date of competency takes the pressure off everyone. In this way, the family is not faced with a closed vesicostomy and the absolute necessity of learning clean intermittent self-catheterization before discharge from the hospital. The parents may be taught the procedure if the child is very young. Sometimes clean intermittent self-catheterization, rather than a vesicostomy, is undertaken in neonates, and responsibility is then transferred from parent to child at the age of concern.

It is important to evaluate the child's understanding and acceptance of the procedure and his or her mental or physical ability to perform the task. Parental attitude and willingness to comply plays an important role and must also be assessed. A knowledgeable, relaxed, and perceptive nurse-teacher is definitely an asset. Changes in body image and individual feelings regarding the genital area are a few of the major concerns that must be dealt with effectively.

A review of basic anatomy and physiology using diagrams and pictures will provide a sound basis for instruction. Boys, because they can see their meatus, are generally easier to teach than girls. Girls may be taught by learning to locate their urinary meatus by touch or by using a mirror. For specific information regarding types of catheters, lubricants, care of equipment, teaching methods, and follow-up, please refer to selected readings on clean intermittent self-catheterization.[21-22] It is essential to remember that the school nurse and the public health nurse are integral members of the health team and should be advised of treatment and consulted for assistance and follow-up when appropriate.

Failure to store Approximately one-third of the children with myelomeningocele and neuropathic bladders fail to store urine. These children are constantly wet and may require a permanent urinary diversion for social reasons alone if all other treatment modalities fail. This failure to store may be due to uninhibited bladder contractions or hypertonicity of the bladder itself. Medication such as propantheline (Pro-Banthine), imipramine (Tofranil), and oxybutynin chloride (Ditropan) is often given in an attempt to block uninhibited contractions and to decrease the hypertonicity of the bladder. The goal is to convert the problem with the child's bladder to one of "failure to empty," which can then be managed by Credé's method or clean intermittent self-catheterization.

An artificial sphincter was devised in 1973 and has been successful in selected children. This is an implantable Silastic prosthesis composed of a cuff which surrounds the bladder neck, a small reservoir for fluid used to inflate the cuff, and a bulb that moves the fluid from the cuff to the reservoir by releasing the pressure on the bladder neck and urethra each time the child voids. The bulb is located in the scrotum or in the labial folds and is activated by manual squeezing. The major problems associated with these devices have been infection and erosion.[23]

Ileal conduits

Candidates for ileal conduit diversion may include children with exstrophy of the bladder, unresolved urinary incontinence, or unremitting urinary tract infection with renal deterioration. When describing this surgery to the patient, it will be necessary to have diagrams or to draw pictures to illustrate the various steps. A small segment of ileum is excised, one end is sutured shut, and it is used to form the conduit. The remaining ileum is then rejoined, leaving a normally functioning intestinal tract. The ureters are disconnected from the bladder and inserted into one end of the conduit. The other end is then brought out onto the skin surface at a previously determined site, turned back, and fastened to the abdominal wall, creating a stoma. This ileal segment is not meant to function as a substitute bladder, rather it is a tube through which urine flows and should not store more than 5 to 10 ml of urine. Normal peristaltic movement of the ileal segment will assist urine flow (Fig. 31-11). The patient will have to wear an external appliance to collect urine. Obviously, these patients and their families will have to deal

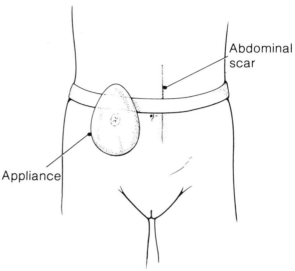

Figure 31-12 Position of the permanent drainage appliance after ileal conduit procedure. (*Adapted from Gladys Scipien et al., Comprehensive Pediatric Nursing, 2d ed., McGraw-Hill, New York; 1979. Used with permission of the publisher.*)

with feelings regarding an altered body image. A sound preoperative understanding of the surgery, the types of appliances available, skin care products, and general daily care will alleviate some of their fears (Fig. 31-12). Children will develop an understanding of the way an appliance functions and how it feels if they are encouraged to wear one that contains water for a day or two prior to surgery. This practice also aids in the selection of the stomal site.

The child will come back from the operating room with an appliance in place; this will be hooked up to a bedside drainage bag. Once the child is ambulatory, the use of the bedside drainage bag will be necessary only at night. Teaching is individualized and participation in care is encouraged as the child and family indicate their readiness.

Families should be made aware of the available community resources, such as public health nurses, visiting nurses, ostomy groups, and enterostomal therapists (E.T.). An E.T. is a nurse or technician who has received specialized training in ostomy management and who is certified by the International Association of Enterostomal Therapists. The United Ostomy Association, with

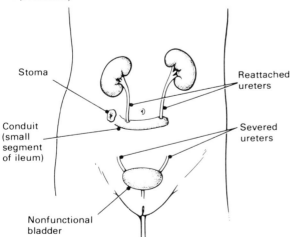

Figure 31-11 Anatomic drawing of an ileal conduit. (*From Gladys Scipien et al., Comprehensive Pediatric Nursing, 2d ed., McGraw-Hill, New York, 1979. Used with permission of the publisher.*)

headquarters in Los Angeles, California, publishes comprehensive educational material for children and adults. A list of publications and United Ostomy chapters in the area may be obtained by writing to them.

Emphasis should be placed on the positive aspects of diversion. The child will ultimately wear an appliance that will maintain continence and that will allow the resumption of a normal life-style, while providing protection from renal deterioration.

Structural and positional alterations of the kidney

Renal agenesis

Renal agenesis refers to the congenital absence of one or both kidneys. Unilateral agenesis is more common than bilateral absence and occurs more frequently in males. Renal agenesis is caused by degeneration of the ureteric bud in early fetal development.[24] Unilateral renal agenesis is usually associated with the absence of the ureter on the affected side. The opposite kidney is usually hypertrophied but otherwise normal. The single kidney may be in the pelvis.

Children with one missing kidney may be asymptomatic unless the one existing kidney is abnormal. On physical examination, the child with bilateral renal agenesis has no palpable renal masses, and intravenous pyelograms will show no renal visualization. Since bilateral agenesis is incompatible with life, these children die during the neonatal period.

Renal hypoplasia

Renal hypoplasia may involve one or both kidneys. In a true primary renal hypoplasia, the kidneys are much smaller than usual, but the anatomic structures present are normal. Normal kidneys have ten or more calyces, while a hypoplastic kidney contains five or less.

Most hypoplastic kidneys also function poorly. The severity of the kidney disease will depend on whether one or both kidneys are affected and on the amount of functional tissue present. Unilateral renal hypoplasia is usually asymptomatic and is not treated. If the disease is bilateral, varying degrees of renal insufficiency will be present. As the child grows older and greater demands are placed on the renal structures,

problems can develop. These children are treated for chronic renal failure, as discussed later in the chapter.[25]

Renal dysplasia

The diagnosis renal dysplasia describes a kidney that contains poorly functioning or nonfunctioning tissue. Renal structures are disorganized and some are abnormally developed.[26] Renal dysplasia may be bilateral, unilateral, or segmental within the kidney. The renal pelvis is usually absent, and the ureter on the affected side is almost always abnormal. The involved kidney is often hypoplastic and may contain cystic formations.

Children with dysplastic kidneys often have anomalies of other organ systems. Congenital obstruction of the lower urinary tract is frequently associated with renal dysplasia.[27] Unilateral renal dysplasia may be asymptomatic, or the child may have a mild degree of hypertension. Bilateral dysplasia generally leads to chronic renal failure.

Polycystic kidney disease

There are several types of polycystic kidney disease, each causing clinical symptoms at a different age. The prognosis depends on the severity of interference with kidney function.

The infantile form of the disease is bilateral and is genetically transmitted as an autosomal recessive. The kidneys are enlarged and filled with minute cysts. The anatomic structures of the kidney may be present but are distorted, and there is little functioning renal tissue. There are often associated cystic malformations of the liver. It is believed that the main cause of cystic disease in the kidney is abnormal embryological development of the collecting tubules.[28]

The large kidneys produce abdominal distension and the infant may exhibit respiratory distress as a result. Because there is little functioning kidney tissue, progressive renal failure develops. Urinary tract infections may complicate the course of the disease, and severe hypertension may be present early in the disease.

Treatment is directed toward the chronic renal failure. Death generally occurs early. Dialysis and eventual transplantation must be considered if the child is to survive. Genetic counseling should be offered to parents.

Hereditary renal disease

Inherited nephritis

Inherited nephritis, or familial nephritis, is transmitted as an autosomal dominant. The renal manifestations of the disease are similar to chronic glomerulonephritis. The most common type of inherited nephritis is known as *Alport's syndrome.*

Alport's syndrome is often initially diagnosed as acute glomerulonephritis until similar findings are discovered in other family members. It is more severe and progressive in males than in females. Remissions are common, and exacerbations may be associated with acute infections. The syndrome may include progressive nerve deafness, abnormality of the optic lens, and neurological dysfunction. Alport's syndrome is treated symptomatically and supportively with the therapy used for chronic glomerulonephritis. Steroids and cytotoxic drugs do not appear to alter the disease course. Genetic counseling should be made available for the family.

Acquired renal alterations

Acute nephritic syndrome

Acute nephritic syndrome is a clinical condition, a collection of signs and symptoms, that indicates a disease affecting the glomeruli of the kidney. There are several varieties of acute nephritic syndrome, the most important being acute glomerulonephritis itself. There are other variants of the syndrome, such as recurrent hematuria and proteinuria. Acute nephritic syndrome may be seen occasionally as part of a generalized disease affecting small blood vessels, such as Henoch-Schönlein purpura.[29] The treatment depends on the cause of the syndrome.

Acute glomerulonephritis

Broadly defined, acute glomerulonephritis may be considered an inflammation of the glomeruli. The cause is uncertain but is probably an antigen-antibody reaction stimulated by an infection somewhere else in the body. Any infection caused by group A beta hemolytic streptococcus may lead to acute glomerulonephritis. The infection is generally an upper respiratory tract infection but may also be scarlet fever, impetigo, or infected eczema.

Pathophysiology The actual glomerular injury is caused by the antigen-antibody complexes trapped in the glomerulus. Endothelial cellular swelling and proliferation obstruct the glomerular capillaries, decreasing the amount of glomerular filtrate. All the glomeruli in the kidney are involved, although the amount of proliferation varies among them. With the decreased glomerular filtration, the amount of sodium and water that is passed to the tubules for reabsorption is reduced and the end result is fluid retention with increased plasma volume and edema.

Symptoms Acute glomerulonephritis tends to occur in males between the ages of 3 and 7 years. The onset of symptoms generally occurs 1 to 3 weeks after the streptococcal infection. The symptoms vary from child to child and may be mild enough to be ignored or rapid and severe. There may be some or all of the following symptoms:

1. *Hematuria* is the usual presenting symptom. The urine will be grossly bloody, but not bright red. After a few days, the urine becomes a smoky brown color. This is caused by hemolysis and the release of hemoglobin, which is converted to brown hematin by the urine acidity.
2. *Edema* is also commonly seen in children with acute glomerulonephritis. Periorbital edema is most common, but the edema may become generalized. It usually does not proceed beyond a moderate degree.
3. *Mild hypertension* is also a common symptom. The diastolic pressure may rise as high as 100 to 120 mmHg.
   Hypertensive encephalopathy may then occur with headaches, vomiting, blurred vision, disorientation, convulsions, or all these symptoms.
4. *Oliguria or anuria* may occur in some cases. It is accompanied by a high urine specific gravity. The urine contains protein, red blood cells, white blood cells, and casts.
5. *A transient anemia* may develop because of the expanded plasma volume. As a result, these children are pale, tire easily, and have poor appetites.
6. *Abnormal laboratory values.* The blood urea nitrogen and creatinine may be mildly elevated. The erythrocyte sedimentation rate (ESR) (a nonspecific indication of acute inflammation) will usually be

elevated. Serologic tests for streptococcal infection (ASO titers) are often elevated.

7. *Severe circulatory congestion* may occur in the seriously ill child, because of the greatly expanded plasma volume. Cardiac enlargement and pulmonary vascular congestion may ensue.

Treatment There is no specific treatment for acute glomerulonephritis. Medical management is largely supportive and symptomatic, and most children can be cared for by their parents in the home.

Many children will limit their own activity so that strict bed rest is not usually necessary. Some ambulation and mild activity is generally acceptable to the child. If the child is hypertensive or at risk for cardiac failure, bed rest or hospitalization may be necessary. Most children will be able to resume their normal activities after 2 to 3 weeks.

During the acute phase of the disease, fluid intake should be limited to the amount of the previous 8-h output plus the calculated insensible water loss. Intake need not be limited when the child's output again reaches normal levels. Salt intake is usually not restricted unless the child is hypertensive or edematous. Potassium-free foods and fluids may be necessary if the child has a decreased urine output. Lowering dietary protein is usually not necessary unless blood urea nitrogen levels are grossly elevated. Dietary restrictions are usually moderated when diuresis ensues.

Drug therapy varies with the symptoms. Penicillin may be given if the child's infection was previously untreated. Penicillin, however, will not prevent acute glomerulonephritis from developing if the child has been exposed. It will not cure or reduce the severity of acute glomerulonephritis once it has developed. Antihypertensive drugs are given if the diastolic blood pressure is greater than 100 mmHg or if symptoms of encephalopathy develop. Reserpine is used initially for mild hypertension. Apresoline may be added to the regimen if needed. Digitalization and diuretics may be prescribed if the child develops severe circulatory congestion. If the child develops acute renal failure, dialysis may be necessary during the crisis phase.

Acute glomerulonephritis is a relatively brief disease. Improvement usually begins within 1 to 2 weeks. At that time, the grossly visible blood in the urine will disappear. The prognosis for acute glomerulonephritis is generally good although somewhat unpredictable. Reoccurrences are unusual, and death is very rare.

Nursing management The nursing management of a child with acute glomerulonephritis is based on an accurate assessment of the child and family (see Nursing Care Plan). Initial observations are important for establishing baseline data about the condition of the patient. Vital signs (including blood pressure) should be frequently checked. In those children showing signs of encephalopathy, blood pressures should be checked at least every 2 h. Any elevated reading should be reported to the physician along with the symptoms of encephalopathy the child is exhibiting. Symptoms include headache, vomiting, blurred vision, and convulsions.

In the acute phase, the child should be weighed daily and a careful record of intake and output kept. Urine must be carefully observed for amount and color. Testing for blood and protein is done as ordered. If the child is edematous, meticulous skin care should be part of the nursing care plan. Folds in the skin should be bathed and powdered frequently, and the child's position changed as needed.

The activity level allowed the child will depend on the acuteness of the illness. Quiet, ambulatory activities will enable the child to maintain relationships with peers. If bed rest must be maintained, it is helpful if the child can be positioned to see out a window or into the hallway. Games, puzzles, and books will help relieve the boredom of enforced bed rest.

Prevention of any further infection is an important part of the nursing care plan. The child should always be kept warm and dry, and away from anyone with an active infection. Family members may need cultures for strep. Those children who are returning to an infected environment may be placed on prophylactic penicillin for a few months. Discharge planning for the hospitalized child should include information from the nurse, physician, and dietitian. The social worker may also be involved if needed. The child can usually return home on a regular diet with no fluid restrictions and generally can return to school 2 weeks after discharge from the hospital, if no further hypertension or hematuria occurs. Competitive sports and other strenuous activities should be avoided until the urine is free of red blood cells.[30]

Chronic glomerulonephritis

Chronic glomerulonephritis is a term that can be used to describe any idiopathic, progressive form of renal disease. The clinical picture of protein-uria, hematuria, and hypertension indicates major involvement of the glomeruli.[31] There are several forms of chronic glomerulonephritis. The disease may be a late manifestation of nephrotic syndrome, result from hereditary nephritis, or occur as a complication of other diseases.

Pathophysiology Chronic glomerulonephritis reduces kidney size. Many of the renal tubules are atrophic or have totally disappeared. The tubules that remain are enlarged, although there is a reduction in the total number of glomeruli. The arterioles in the kidney are narrowed, thereby reducing the blood supply. This probably contributes to the increasing renal destruction.

Symptoms The progression of this disease is highly individualized. Symptoms vary from no obvious symptoms to those associated with severe renal failure and hypertension. Proteinuria is constant, although variable in amount. Creatinine and other urinary clearance tests and blood urea nitrogen indicate a gradual but progressive loss of function. The specific gravity is low and fixed, indicating the kidney's inability to concentrate urine. Hematuria is usually present, although it may only be seen microscopically. Anemia is present and progressive. The child is pale, tires easily, and has a poor appetite.

Periorbital edema is generally present. The edema may be limited to the eye region and to the ankles, or it may be severe and generalized. Hypertension is usual in chronic glomerulonephritis, and the child may suffer from episodes of encephalopathy and cardiac failure.

As the final stages of the disease are reached, the child may have muscular cramps, diarrhea and vomiting, headaches, anorexia, and convulsions. Overt uremia is not uncommon.

Treatment There is no known cure for chronic glomerulonephritis. The disease may be rapidly progressive or interrupted by intervals of freedom from symptoms. Each exacerbation may result in progressive functional deterioration of the kidney. With recent advances in dialysis and transplantation, there is some hope for these chronically ill children.

The treatment of chronic glomerulonephritis is symptomatic and supportive. Activity may be somewhat restricted by the child. During periods of exacerbation, the child may need to be kept in bed, depending on the amount of edema and degree of hypertension.

Adequate caloric intake is important in meeting the nutritional needs of the chronically ill child. A large body of research has accumulated suggesting that malnutrition, primarily calorie malnutrition, is a cause of growth failure in children with renal disease.[32] Salt is restricted only in the presence of edema or severe hypertension. Protein intake may be reduced if the blood urea nitrogen levels exceed 50 or 60. Supplemental vitamins and minerals are usually prescribed.

Varying drug therapies are ordered, depending on the child's symptoms. *Antihypertensives*, such as reserpine and Apresoline, are useful if the diastolic blood pressure rises over 100 mmHg. If the child develops heart failure, digitalization may be attempted. *Antibiotics* are utilized for infection. *Steroids and cytotoxic drugs* have been utilized in chronic glomerulonephritis, but the results to date have been unsatisfactory in most children.[33] All drugs primarily excreted by the kidneys should be given in reduced amounts, since an overdose due to poor renal function is possible. *Blood transfusion* for anemia may be given when the child's hemoglobin is low.

Peritoneal dialysis or hemodialysis is utilized for those children who may later be candidates for renal transplantation programs. Without dialysis, transplantation, or both, the life expectancy of children with chronic glomerulonephritis is generally 5 to 10 years after diagnosis.

Nursing management The nursing management of the child with chronic glomerulonephritis presents many problems (see Chap. 25). The problem of dealing with a chronic disease may be devastating to both the child and the family. It is difficult for the child to accept frequent bouts of illness while friends and siblings are actively pursuing their interests at home and at school. The stunting of growth may make the child and family embarrassed about the child's physical appearance. The nurse should play an active role in helping the family cope with chronic disease and the disruptions it causes. Parents must be helped so that the ill child is not treated as an invalid at the expense of other family members. Feelings of parental guilt often arise when siblings are neglected so that the ill child can receive most of the parents' attention. Parents must be taught about the disease and treatment so that they feel they have gained some control over the situation. Drug and dietary therapies must be carefully taught so that the treatment plan will be followed when the child is at home.

When the child with chronic glomerulonephritis is hospitalized with an acute exacerbation, the nursing management is similar to that for the child with acute glomerulonephritis. Frequent vital signs, emotional support, observation of symptoms, and monitoring drug therapy are all important. Discharge planning by the renal team should always occur.

Nephrotic syndrome (nephrosis)

The term *nephrotic syndrome* may be used to describe several clinical entities that have common symptoms and varied pathological manifestations, prognosis, and responses to therapeutic agents.[34] The cause of nephrotic syndrome is uncertain. Recurrences and exacerbations may sometimes be associated with acute respiratory infections.[35]

Pathophysiology Children with nephrotic syndrome have increased glomerular membrane permeability to large molecules, specifically proteins. The exact pathological lesion in the kidney varies with the type of nephrosis. In all types, large losses of protein from the blood into the urine occur. Albumin is lost in largest quantities, and the body is unable to replace it as fast as it is lost. The resulting low levels of blood protein decrease capillary osmotic pressure and result in a fluid leak from the capillaries. This causes a decrease in circulating blood volume, which stimulates the kidney to retain sodium and water. The end result of the process is edema.

Several forms of nephrotic syndrome are recognized. The three most common are minimal-change glomerular disease, focal glomerulosclerosis, and chronic proliferative glomerulonephritis. The differentiation is important since the various types differ in clinical course, response to drugs, and prognosis.[36]

Symptoms More males are affected than females. Each type of nephrosis is characterized early by edema, heavy proteinuria, hypoalbuminemia, and hypercholesterolemia.

The symptoms of minimal-change nephrotic syndrome usually appear between the ages of $1\frac{1}{2}$ and 4 years. Edema is the usual presenting symptom (Fig. 31-13 *A* and *B*). Initially it is found around the eyes and in the ankles and may then progress to the rest of the body. The patient may develop ascites that can cause respiratory distress. The genitalia, especially the scrotum, tend to become very swollen.

Proteinuria is probably the most important laboratory finding. The protein in the urine is mostly albumin. The urine specific gravity is elevated. Hyaline, granular, and cellular casts are also found in large numbers in the urine, and the urine appears foamy or frothy. Gross hematuria is not present.

The urinary output is decreased in relation to the amount of edema. Hypertension may occur, although the blood pressure is usually normal. Children with nephrotic syndrome exhibit pallor, poor appetite, lassitude, and irritability. Malnutrition may become severe since protein is lost in the urine and not replaced. The children are unusually susceptible to infection.

Treatment Nephrotic syndrome is a chronic disease. The course is one of recurrent accumulations of edema after partial or complete remissions. The duration and severity of nephrotic syndrome is variable.

Minimal-change glomerular disease is the most common form of nephrosis. More than 90 percent of children with this form of nephrosis will have remissions, and most have a good prognosis for eventual preservation of normal kidney function. The prognosis of children with *chronic proliferative glomerulonephritis* is not as good, because there is no known effective treatment. Children with *focal glomerulosclerosis* progress inexorably to renal failure.[37]

The treatment of nephrotic syndrome is aimed at prevention and control of acute infections, establishment of good nutrition, control of edema, and control of the progression of the renal lesion. During acute infections and when undergoing diuresis, the child may need to be in bed with only limited ambulation. Adequate rest is always important so that the child does not become fatigued. Generally, these children set their own activity limits.

Prevention of infection is important since edema fluid is an excellent culture medium. The edematous skin must be protected from injury since it is stretched thin and easily breaks down.

Since malnutrition is common in nephrotic children, dietary therapy is important. Sodium may be restricted to 1 to 2 g per day, or the child may simply be placed on a "no added salt" diet, depending on the degree of edema. Potassium is generally added to the diet. Water is usually restricted only during extreme edema. At those times, the child is generally allowed an intake equal to the previous day's output plus the calculated insensible water loss. There are varying opinions about the amount of protein that should be allowed. A high-protein diet is usually advocated since the child loses so much protein in the urine. Protein is necessary to help offset the growth failure and muscle wasting often seen in these children.

Drug therapy is usually effective with minimal-change glomerular disease. Corticosteroids are given with the goal of relieving edema. Diuresis usually occurs between day 8 and 14, after which the child's appetite and activity should improve. Prednisone is the steroid of choice because it has less tendency to cause sodium retention and potassium loss. The steroids may be given only every other day in an attempt to minimize side effects. Steroids are given for as short a time as possible because of their side effects, which include obesity, growth failure, hypertension, gastric ulcer, bone demineralization, and hypercoagulability. Nephrosis associated with focal glomerulosclerosis and chronic proliferative glomerulonephritis does not usually respond well to corticosteroids.[38]

Cyclophosphamide (Cytoxan) is an immunosuppressant given to children who are steroid-resistant. Initially it is given with prednisone, then alone if necessary. Immunosuppressants are used to attempt to prolong remissions. Serious side effects from Cytoxan include leukopenia, hair loss, cystitis, gastric ulceration, and sterility.

Diuretics are given to help control the edema. Thiazide diuretics are usually used. Spironolac-

tone may also be given to enhance the effectiveness of the thiazides. Intravenous albumin is given on occasion and helps reverse hypovolemia and replace plasma proteins.[39]

Paracentesis may be necessary to relieve fluid pressure in the abdomen and to ease the respiratory effort. Hypertension, if it occurs, is treated with antihypertensive drugs and bedrest. Infections are vigorously treated with antibiotics.

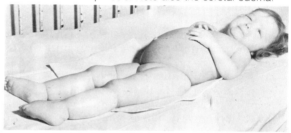

Figure 31-13 (*A*) Girl with active nephrosis. Note the severe generalized body edema and the periorbital edema that almost closes the eyes. (*B*) Boy with massive ascites associated with nephrosis. Note also the scrotal edema.

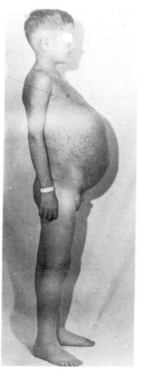
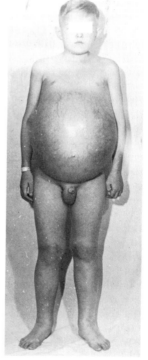

Nursing management Nursing care of a child with active nephrotic syndrome is complex and challenging. Meticulous skin care is necessary to prevent breakdown since the tissues have poor tone due to stretching by the interstitial fluid and since skin infections from abrasions can be very serious. Frequent position changes are necessary, although few positions may be truly comfortable. The head of the bed may need to be elevated to prevent respiratory embarrassment from ascites. Special localized care may be necessary for edematous areas such as the male genitalia. Frequent bathing, careful drying, and powdering should be utilized. Scrotal support may make the child more comfortable. Watch for hydrocele and rectal prolapse. Diarrhea may occur from intestinal malabsorption secondary to edema of the bowel wall. This may further compromise an already stressed area of the skin. The child should be kept as clean and dry as possible.

Vital signs (including blood pressure) should be checked frequently. Respiratory efforts should be observed since some respiratory distress is likely to develop. The child's temperature should be watched since nephrotic children are susceptible to infection. Edematous tissue is an excellent culture medium, and steroids often mask infection. The child should be kept away from crowds and infected persons. Daily weights and accurate intake and output help monitor the success of treatment.

The side effects and complications of the drugs should be understood by the nurse and carefully watched for. Tests will be performed to monitor the development of complications, such as leukopenia and diabetes.

Stimulate the child to eat as much of the prescribed diet as is possible. Since muscle wasting often occurs, a balanced program of rest and activities should be planned.

The child's mental status may be difficult for both the nurse and the family to deal with. The nurse can anticipate that the child will suffer some loss of self-esteem with the changes in body image and appearance. The parents and the child will need assistance in dealing with the restrictions of chronic illness.

Parental teaching is an important part of discharge planning. The parents need to know about the disease, diet, side effects of drugs, skin care, and urine testing in order to comply with the regimen of care at home.

Acute renal failure

Renal failure may be divided into two classifications—acute and chronic. Both types can have devastating implications for the child and family.

Acute renal failure, acute renal insufficiency, or acute uremia refer to a varied clinical picture of sudden and severely decreased kidney function that impairs homeostasis.

The symptoms and types of acute renal failure vary with the cause. Acute failure can be divided into three subclasses: (1) renal, (2) prerenal, and (3) postrenal. It is vitally important to ascertain the type of failure because prompt, appropriate treatment can prevent irreversible kidney damage and return renal function to within normal limits in relatively short periods of time. The total patient should be assessed since injuries or illnesses unrelated to the kidney can result in acute renal failure.

Renal failure This type of acute renal failure is relatively uncommon in children. Its causes are still uncertain, but are often external to the kidney, such as drugs, poisons, gastroenteritis, surgery, and, the most frequent, hemolytic-uremic syndrome.

Prerenal failure Prerenal failure results from decreased perfusion of blood to the kidneys. If blood flow and blood pressure are decreased below normal for a period of time, the body responds by trying to increase the blood volume to remedy the situation. This is accomplished by increasing reabsorption of sodium and decreasing the urine volume. The blood flow to the kidneys themselves is also decreased and they become progressively less efficient. If the decreased circulation is short-lived, no symptoms or problems other than decreased urine sodium with a subsequent drop in urine volume will occur. If the impaired circulation is prolonged and is accompanied by an increase in waste products to be excreted, acute renal failure and permanent kidney damage may result. This situation is called *prerenal* since the conditions causing it arise elsewhere in the body.

The most common cause of prerenal failure

in children is dehydration. This frequently is the aftermath of severe diarrhea, gastroenteritis, persistent vomiting, or, less commonly, bodily trauma, hemorrhaging, and burns. Prerenal failure can be easily reversed and urine flow restored by appropriate fluid replacement therapy and prompt treatment of the causative condition.

Postrenal failure

Postrenal failure is due to obstruction of urine from the kidney or the lower urinary tract. Obstructive causes for acute renal failure in children are relatively rare. Some cases are seen in the newborn and postoperatively. Sudden and complete obstruction of the outflow of urine from both kidneys will result in anuria and acute renal failure. It must be remembered that as long as one kidney continues to function and eliminate urine from the body, renal failure will not occur. Obstructions may occur anywhere in the system due to calculi, blood clots, sloughed tissue, or external pressure with compression of the ureters or urethra by tumors or retroperitoneal fibrosis. Complete recovery is possible with removal of the obstruction but is considered unlikely when total obstruction has lasted for more than 3 weeks.[40]

Clinical manifestations of acute renal failure

In most cases the child with acute renal failure is already very ill. A thorough history must be obtained to ascertain exposure to harmful drugs and chemicals as well as to evaluate symptoms of glomerulonephritis.

The most blatant symptom (probably the only true symptom) is oliguria. Although urine output may be only 40 to 60 ml in 24 h, anuria is relatively rare. Other symptoms, such as nausea, vomiting, and drowsiness, are usually due to the build-up of waste materials in the blood.

Laboratory values are usually abnormal and easily attributed to the lack of cleansing of the blood by the kidneys. *Azotemia* with rapid rises in serum creatinine and BUN is always seen. Metabolic acidosis occurs more slowly but can be life-threatening. *Hyponatremia* results from lack of urine output, and fluid requirements must be calculated frequently to prevent overhydration. *Hyperkalemia* is seen because of the normal release of potassium from the cells when the body is stressed. In renal failure the potassium cannot be excreted and blood levels increase. Many other blood values will change due to the failure itself and as a result of the treatment.

Treatment and nursing management Nurses play a major role in the prevention of acute renal failure. The nurse must be aware of potential situations that result in failure. By observing trends and communicating changes to the physician, acute failure can sometimes be prevented. For example, children undergoing treatment for burns or dehydration or receiving nephrotoxic drugs should be adequately hydrated and fluid output closely monitored.

The role of the physician in acute renal failure is supportive. Initially the blood and fluid deficits and the electrolyte imbalances must be corrected. Causative factors must be treated. Body fluid homeostasis must be maintained within limits that the body can handle until the failure is reversed or until more drastic measures, such as dialysis, are initiated.

Nursing care of children with acute renal failure involves close observation and monitoring as well as crisis intervention. These children are acutely and often critically ill and are very uncomfortable and irritable. Their families are understandably overwhelmed. The nurse needs to establish rapport with the family and help them cope with the illness, hospitalization, and possible guilt. Honesty and the sharing of factual data are vital. People can cope more effectively when they know what to expect. A team approach is usually quite helpful.

The child already in acute renal failure must have fluid intake and output monitored closely. Intravenous therapy rates must be maintained as ordered with no "catching up." These patients are often anorexic yet require a nutritious diet. The diet in acute renal failure is usually restricted in fluids, potassium, and protein. Urinary output may require catheters or collection bags. Nurses must be prepared to deal with this equipment and maintain accurate records.

Hyperkalemia can constitute a major emergency for the patient and may quickly result in cardiac arrhythmias and cardiac arrest. Laboratory values must be monitored and changes communicated to the physician quickly. Many children are placed on cardiac monitors. Nurses must observe for elevation of the T waves and widening of the QRS complex. Both oral and intravenous potassium are severely restricted in patients with hyperkalemia. Dialysis may be needed to relieve the symptoms and prevent permanent kidney damage.

Recovery from acute renal failure varies from complete recovery to permanent kidney damage requiring chronic dialysis or transplantation. The extent of recovery depends partially on the promptness of treatment, but more importantly on the causative agent.

Chronic renal failure

Chronic renal failure leading to end-stage renal disease and finally uremic syndrome may be defined as irreversible changes in the kidney that result in reduced function to the extent that the kidney no longer maintains normal body fluid homeostasis. The kidneys are able to maintain normal homeostasis until greater than 50 percent of the functioning renal tissue is destroyed. The signs of beginning chronic failure are more chemical than clinical and the patient's symptoms and degree of illness will vary.

Clinical manifestations The clinical manifestations of kidney failure may be predicted by considering the major kidney functions. The kidneys regulate both the volume and concentration of body fluids, play a role in acid-base balance, and maintain various solutes at optimal levels. They remove waste products of normal metabolism as well as toxic substances that may have been ingested. Their role in blood production revolves around production of *erythropoietin* (a substance stimulating RBC production). Another major function centers around blood pressure regulation. All of these vital functions suffer when the kidneys no longer function adequately. Although chronic renal failure is defined as irreversible damage to the kidney, a thorough history to attempt to find possible causative conditions is necessary. Sometimes treatment may increase renal function. When it is too late for improvement, the knowledge gained from the history may be helpful in preventing failure in siblings or in preventing further damage to the patient's kidneys.

As kidney failure progresses, the serum levels of creatinine, urea, and uric acid slowly but steadily increase. The kidneys attempt to compensate through hypertrophy of the functioning nephrons and by increased activity within the tubules. If the failure is treated, the kidneys can usually maintain some capacity to eliminate wastes unless they are overloaded.

Unless stressed, the kidneys can maintain a normal sodium-water balance even with minimally functioning nephrons. Changes occur within the nephron itself to increase filtration rates and decrease sodium reabsorption rates. It is only in the final stages of renal failure or when the body is unduly stressed that signs of edema and sodium retention are observed.

While hyperkalemia can be a major problem in acute renal failure, it usually occurs only in the latter stages of chronic failure. Potassium secretion by the tubules can be maintained as long as conditions remain within normal limits. If the potassium intake is increased, the kidney in failure may not be able to handle it. If salt intake is decreased, the normal exchange of sodium and potassium will be decreased, and this can lead to hyperkalemia.

In reality, the kidney will continue to excrete hydrogen ions to maintain acid-base balance but will be less efficient. Thus metabolic acidosis will result from a build-up of acids. A renal failure patient may have a pH of 7.2 to 7.3 and tolerate it well.

Central nervous system changes occur late in chronic renal failure. These may include a dulling of senses, muscle twitching, weakness and cramping, convulsions, lethargy, restlessness, and irritability. Some children experience a loss of vision. Others may hallucinate, usually because of hypertension and decreased cranial blood flow.

The anemia of chronic renal failure is normocytic and normochromic. The cause of this anemia is a complex interplay of a number of factors. Impaired production and a shortened life span of red blood cells and increased bleeding tendency with blood loss from the gastrointestinal tract are present. The negative effect on blood cell production is due to decreased erythropoietin production. Bleeding is related to platelet changes. The count is normal, but the platelets themselves lack adhesiveness.

One of the most distinctive and possibly most frustrating complications of chronic renal failure in children is their growth failure. It may be partially due to poor dietary intake. These children experience severe anorexia, refuse most foods, and thus have low caloric intake.

Another major factor in growth retardation is the change in calcium and phosphate metabolism due to the renal failure. Low serum calcium levels and high serum phosphate levels produce bone pain and deformities (rickets, renal osteodystrophy). The inability to excrete phosphates and metabolize vitamin D increases loss of calcium from the bone. With decreased serum calcium, parathyroid hormone is released, resulting in further demineralization of the bones. All of these changes result in severe bone disease and an obvious lack of growth.

With all these problems, what picture does this child present? The history states this usually active child now prefers to sit and watch television or sleep. There may be a history of growth slowing. The BUN and creatinine are elevated. The blood pressure may be elevated or could be normal and anemia may be present. The child eats poorly, is pale and listless, and apathetic about school or play. Adolescent girls may experience amenorrhea. Even minor illnesses such as colds or gastroenteritis can precipitate major changes in renal function. While these symptoms alone do not spell out renal failure, seen in combination, they usually are good indicators.

Because of health professionals' increasing knowledge and awareness of the symptoms of chronic renal failure, it is less common to see the end result of untreated failure; however, it can still occur. The clinical manifestations reflect continuation of the symptoms and changes of chronic renal failure already mentioned. These children have anorexia, vomiting, inflammation or sores of the mouth and lips, and many have bloody stools from intestinal ulceration. They complain of unrelieved itching and may accumulate urates on the skin, "uremic frost." The level of consciousness can decrease and progress to coma and death. Hypertension, congestive heart failure, and pulmonary edema are not uncommon findings.

Medical management and nursing care Medical management of chronic renal failure often provides only temporary relief of symptoms and more drastic treatment such as dialysis or transplantation is ultimately required.

The goals of medical management of chronic renal failure are few, but vital. These include promotion of renal function (whatever amount is possible), maintenance of body fluid homeostasis, treatment of symptoms, and maintenance of as normal and active a life as possible. Unfortunately, sometimes the treatment of one complication creates other complications, and so the medical regimen is one of constant change.

The team approach is vital in caring for these children. The team involves not only the physicians and nurses, but also the dietitians, pharmacists, play therapists, radiologist, social workers, psychologists, and psychiatrists. The parents are a vital part of the team and also need to be consulted.

The child in chronic renal failure must be allowed to resume normal activities at his or her own pace. This fosters growth and independence and ultimately ensures the cooperation of the child and parent (see Chap. 21).

In dealing with the chronically ill renal patient, a great deal of time, energy, and frustration is spent on diet. Adult renal failure patients have very restricted diets. In pediatrics, considerations other than just the kidney failure must be taken into account. Children need enough protein and calories to grow, yet not enough to cause needless overload to the kidneys. Sodium should not be drastically reduced unless edema or hypertension appears. Potassium can still be excreted, but should be monitored. Care should be taken to avoid overloading the patient with such high-potassium foods as orange juice and bananas. The diet is not a regular diet; some foods are avoided. Using salt makes what is left a little more palatable. The nurse must be patient, caring, and a good negotiator when helping the child eat. Sometimes it is wise to settle for a meal one-third eaten rather than argue and have the child not eat at all or become so agitated that emesis occurs. If you find a method that works, *write it in the care plan.*

While bone disease is not apparent at first it is inevitable. Hypocalcemia must be corrected to prevent further release of calcium from the bones. Vitamin D is given, but levels must be increased slowly to prevent toxicity. Parathyroidectomies are done in severe cases to control release of calcium from the bones. The most common and effective treatment is to bind the phosphates with aluminum hydroxide gels and give calcium. This eliminates the exchange of phosphates for calcium in the bones and tissue. Though phosphates are reduced in the diet, they cannot be completely eliminated because high phosphate foods, such as milk, are also, unfortunately, often high in calcium.

Care must be taken to avoid the CNS symptoms of aluminum toxicity. The gels will need to be discontinued or decreased if these occur. Nursing care includes watching for any bone changes, monitoring bone pain, observing for difficulty in walking, and administering the medications.

Children in chronic renal failure are always anemic. They appear pale and bruise easily. These children can function quite well on very low hemoglobins, less than 10 g/dl, and most centers will not transfuse them until hemoglobins reach 4 to 5 g/dl. Transfusing before this only creates the chance of transfusion reactions and a very temporary rise in blood values. Packed red blood cells are used for transfusion. Iron and folic acid supplements are given since the dietary intake is not a dependable source. The nurse's role is to monitor the blood values and assist the family to accept the appearance of their child. Many parents become quite perceptive and can tell when their child has reached the state of having critically low hemoglobin by behavior and color change (imperceptible to most medical staff!).

Cardiovascular involvement, with hypertension as a symptom, is the rule rather than the exception for renal failure patients. Treatment does not begin until the blood pressure is moderately high (higher than normal high values for age) since overtreatment can create as many problems as undertreatment.

Fluid and sodium restriction and diuretics are usually used in management of the hypertension. Antihypertensive drugs may be used to combat elevated blood pressure related to excessive activity of the renin-angiotensin system. Blood pressure needs to be monitored carefully for both hypertension and hypotension. Hypotension may be seen as a result of antihypertensive drugs. Intake and output are closely monitored. Sodium depletion should be avoided since it may increase the severity of the renal failure.

The nurse must know the patient and be able to recognize behavior changes, complaints, and changes in attitude that could mean increased blood pressure, pericarditis, or congestive failure. Early detection of these can mean more prompt treatment, shortened duration of treatment, and fewer residual effects.

Children with chronic renal failure tend to be more susceptible to infections, especially of the urinary and upper respiratory tracts. Treatment must be prompt and *specific*. For these patients, results of cultures and sensitivities must be obtained before treatment. Be aware that most of the drugs available are excreted by the kidney! Dosages must usually be reduced and blood values monitored as the drugs will remain in the bloodstream longer.

Hopefully, these children will spend most of their time at home. Follow-up in the community is necessary because many are treated in medical centers far from their homes. Public health nurses, local physicians, the school nurse, and the local hospitals are a good source of follow-up and should be sent a discharge summary. These children are pale, have abnormal blood values, are on medications, and have kidney failure. Both the parents and the child should be ready to explain the child's condition—pallor, abnormal blood values, and kidney failure—whenever medical attention is required.

The medical management of chronic renal failure is used alone for as long as the child's physical condition permits. Unfortunately it cannot maintain the child forever. Eventually these patients require peritoneal or hemodialysis and some receive renal transplants.

Hemolytic-uremic syndrome

Hemolytic-uremic syndrome is a combination of acute renal failure, severe hemolytic anemia, thrombocytopenia, and changes in the shape of red blood cells. It is a disease that occurs primarily in the first 3 or 4 years of life and is of unknown etiology.

The onset of hemolytic-uremic syndrome is similar to a respiratory tract infection in combination with gastrointestinal symptoms. The child is pale, restless, and prostrate. Severe oliguria or anuria develops rapidly, and the child may become stuporous and have convulsions. Pinpoint cutaneous hemorrhages may be present. The symptoms of severe acute renal failure are evident within a few days. The renal failure may be a result of clot formation in the small renal blood vessels.

Treatment There is no definitive treatment for hemolytic-uremic syndrome. Treatment is symptomatic and includes therapies for acute renal failure. Dialysis may become necessary. Transfusions of packed red blood cells and platelets may be given. Heparin may be ordered to limit coagulation within blood vessels. Many cases will resolve without permanent renal damage, although some children may progress to chronic renal failure.

Nursing management The nursing management is the same as that for acute renal failure. Close observation for bleeding is important. So much of the child's clotting factors may be used up that he begins to actively bleed.

Peritoneal dialysis

In peritoneal dialysis, the peritoneum acts as a semipermeable membrane allowing water and small-molecular-size solutes to pass back and forth, depending on their concentrations. The dialysis works on the basis of osmosis and diffusion. Hypertonic solutions are introduced into the peritoneal cavity, time is allowed for equilibration, and the hypertonic solution is then removed.

Peritoneal dialysis is used most widely with children to treat not only chronic renal failure, but also acute renal failure, poisonings, severe metabolic problems, congestive heart failure, and at times hepatic coma and Reye's syndrome.

Although acute catheters in pediatric sizes are available, many centers use a permanent Silastic catheter even for acute dialysis. From a nursing standpoint, the acute catheters are more difficult to stabilize, tend to occlude faster, and are more difficult to maintain. Permanent catheters may be inserted under local anesthesia on the patient unit or in the operating room. The family and child must be taught about what is to happen and what to expect afterwards. They may see dialysis as proof of worse disease or that the child is closer to death. They must be assured that this child is indeed very ill, but dialysis is another more involved treatment, but not a "last effort."

Once the catheter is in place, dialysis is begun. The returned fluid is initially bloody because of the catheter insertion, but slowly clears. The fluid of chronic dialysis patients is clear straw-colored, similar to urine, at the beginning of each dialysis and clear without color at the end of their dialysis session. Changes in color or odor, or pain or inflammation at the insertion or exit sites, can be signs of infection.

Children require 30 to 40 h of peritoneal dialysis a week either in the hospital or at home. Many children are dialyzed every other day during the night while they sleep to avoid interrupting their daily routine.

While a patient is being dialysed in the hospital setting, the nurse has the major responsibility for maintaining the dialysis and monitoring the child's progress. Tasks that are usually performed are BP monitoring, weighing at regular intervals, measuring the intake and output, and encouraging diet intake.

Nurses monitor for and initiate some interventions for complications arising from peritoneal dialysis. A common complication is obstruction to the fluid flow. Failure of the dialysis to flow in or out freely may be due to kinking, blockage, or displacement of the catheter. Repositioning or replacement of the tube and treatment of constipation may be needed. Additional fluid is not infused until the problem is corrected because distention, pain, and, in severe cases, rupture of the peritoneal membrane can occur. While abdominal pain often is present in the first month of dialysis, recurring pain after long periods without pain may indicate peritonitis. Shoulder pain is usually due to air in the abdomen and diaphragm irritation. This is treated with a mild analgesic.

Peritonitis may be caused by a bacterial or aseptic infection as well as by a systemic infection. The symptoms may include abdominal pain, cloudy fluid that does not clear, rebound tenderness, and, at times, fever. Cultures of the fluid will usually be positive. Treatment includes antibiotics in the dialysate and systemic antibiotics.

Other complications include dialysis that is too efficient in removal of fluids or causes an imbalance of potassium. Giving extra fluids, closely monitoring the weight loss and serum potassium levels, and adding potassium to the dialysate can prevent this.

Long-term or chronic complications are few and reflect the renal failure rather than the dialysis. Peritoneal dialysis is a safe method of maintaining a child who has chronic or acute renal failure, but it is less efficient than hemodialysis. While children can be maintained for lengthy periods on peritoneal dialysis and some patients refuse any further treatment, transplantation is usually the next step.

The emotional responses to dialysis differ; some children may shut the world out by sleeping the whole time (usually with their heads covered), by staring out the window, or by watching TV. The nurse must be aware of these behaviors and allow the child *some* time to be alone, but also make sure the child interacts with others. End-stage renal disease (chronic renal failure) patients tend to become depressed because of mental changes from the disease itself, the chronicity of their illness, feelings of abandonment, being "different," and isolation. Dialysis units can be busy and a quiet patient hiding under the covers can be easily ignored. Some units employ a buddy system; two patients of possibly opposite temperaments are paired. These children, especially adolescents, provide peer evaluation, support, and companionship.

Hemodialysis

Hemodialysis in children was not successful until approximately 10 years after its clinical use in adults. Much of this delay can be attributed to lack of trained personnel, technical difficulties in adapting adult equipment to pediatric use, and the variability of this age group. Hemodialysis tends to retard or at least does not encourage growth and physical maturation of children. Thus some physicians do not recommend it for long-term chronic use and suggest it should be considered only once transplantation is available.[41] However, more children are going on chronic hemodialysis programs since Medicare covers all chronic dialysis and transplantation expenses. There is a tendency to transplant earlier, which may eliminate some problems of long-term hemodialysis. Use of hemodialysis as an acute treatment in children is also limited because peritoneal dialysis is quicker, safer, and is sufficiently efficient in children.

Hemodialysis requires a direct blood access. This is accomplished in two ways; the external shunt and the internal fistula.

The external shunt (see Fig. 31-14A) consists of two cannulas—one to an artery and one to a vein. During dialysis the cannula to the artery is connected to the dialyzer and carries the patient's blood to the machine. The blood is returned to the patient via the cannula attached to the vein. The largest cannula that will fit into the vessel without harming it is used. In older children the radial artery and a vein in the forearm is used; in younger children, the brachial artery and cephalic vein are used; and in small children and infants, the femoral artery and saphenous vein are used.[42] These shunts are external to the skin and in areas that require some immobilization for safety. Children may respond negatively to this restriction. A shunt also requires dressings that may be hard to maintain and much teaching to prevent infection. The incidence of shunt infections and clotting problems tends to be higher with children, requiring more frequent revisions.

The internal fistula is a connection made between an artery and vein by a surgical procedure (see Fig. 31-14B). Since the vessels are quite small in children, grafts from the saphenous vein or bovine grafts are used to accomplish the anastomosis. After anastomosis, the vein will enlarge, become easily visible, and pulsate. During dialysis, two large-bore needles are inserted into the vein and attached to the dialyzer. Since the access is internal, the chance of infection between sessions is minimal. No dressings are required and movement is not greatly restricted. The major disadvantage is that it requires repeated venipuncture, which can be painful, frightening, and difficult as the skin and venous wall toughen. Many centers prefer this method because of its longer effectiveness.

While connected to the dialyzer, the child is monitored for BP, weight, intake and output, and clotting factors. Children on hemodialysis require dialysis usually two to three times a week for 4 to 6 h at a time. Dietary limitations are necessary and involve sodium, potassium, phosphorus, and fluid restrictions. Usually the child is allowed one less-limited meal during the dialysis. Medications are still required and must be even more carefully monitored since many can be removed during dialysis. Children generally respond well clinically to hemodialysis and receive temporary relief of symptoms.

Since home dialysis is costly and requires a great deal of teaching and because the pediatric patient is more difficult to clinically manage, hospital-based outpatient hemodialysis is more common in children. While families and patients are encouraged to assist in the care, the burden

Figure 31-14 External shunt for hemodialysis. During dialysis the cannula to the artery is connected to the dialyzer and carries the patient's blood to the machine. The blood is returned to the patient via the venous cannula. Between dialysis the cannulas are covered with a silastic tubing. (B) Internal fistula for hemodialysis. The internal arteriovenous fistula is made by connecting the radial artery and cephalic vein at the wrist. As blood shunts from the artery to the vein, the vein enlarges and can be used for easy venipuncture access.

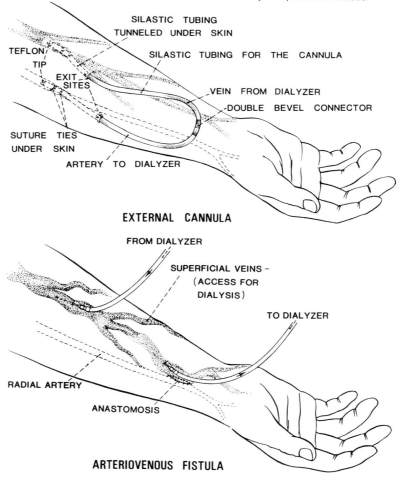

of initiation, maintenance, and discontinuation falls on the nurses and technicians.

The major complications to observe for include the disequilibrium syndrome and hepatitis. The disequilibrium syndrome occurs with a too rapid and efficient dialysis, causing a rapid shift of water, pH, and osmolarity between the CSF and blood. Cerebral edema results as evidenced by restlessness, confusion, nausea, and vomiting. Usually this is treated with IV saline. As with any treatment that involves the blood, hepatitis is always a possibility. The incidence is relatively small, but the precaution of routinely screening patients and staff should always be taken.

Renal transplant

Most chronic renal failure patients ultimately require kidney transplant. The criteria for accepting children into transplant programs are very liberal. Few children are permanently rejected. Age is not a real factor since successful transplants have been done on small children (under age 12 months is still debatable). Children with chronic conditions or with controlled malignancies have had successful transplants. Some children will have a reoccurence of their original disease in the transplanted kidney, but there is no predictable incidence with most diseases. The possibility of full renal function outweighs the chance of reoccurence. The child should be consulted and involved in the decision for transplantation if old enough.

The nursing assessment of the child and family must begin once transplanation as a treatment is accepted. The time before hospitalization for the transplant itself is filled with testing for *histocompatibility* (tissue compatibility), treatment of any medical problems, and teaching the family what is going to happen and what to expect afterwards. The prehospitalization time may be quite short or long. The waiting time depends on the type of transplant the child is going to receive, namely related donor or cadaver. Related donor (parent, sibling, or, best of all, identical twin) transplants are more successful and require a shorter waiting period. Cadaver transplants require being on a waiting list and being available when a suitable kidney is found.

Upon admission, the nursing care plan becomes more intense. The teaching continues, but with admission the child and family often become more tense, anxious, and excited. To combat the risk of overwhelming them, nurses often become coordinators of care and of visits by other team members.

The surgery itself varies little from adult transplantation. Younger, smaller children may have the new kidney placed in a different anatomic postion. Some children have nephrectomies either before or at the same time as the transplant; others retain their own kidneys.

Immunosuppression is begun preoperatively and continued postoperatively, sometimes for a year or more. At the present time immunosuppression is general and thus decreases the child's ability to fight infection. Research is being done to find ways to do specific immunosuppression. Teaching about these drugs must be specific and detailed. Many children and their families see transplant as a cure and expect all to be fine postoperatively. They must be helped to understand that this is the goal, but that medical care will still be very much required.

Rejection is still the major problem. It can occur immediately or even 6 months later. The child needs to be monitored for the usual postoperative problems (pneumonia, dehydration, etc.) as well as decreased urine output (once output is established), abdominal pain, changes in BP, changes in BUN and other blood values, and changes in consciousness, all of which could mean rejection. If rejection occurs, it means returning to dialysis to wait for another kidney.

Any complication can mean a major setback both physically and emotionally for the child and family. They need added support and teaching. They are frightened and need someone to care and to listen. The nurse is in an optimal position to help.

Nursing care continues long after transplantation and discharge. These children are followed both by the outpatient departments and the public health department. The team continues to evaluate and reevaluate the child and family for years afterwards.

Nursing Care Plan–Acute Glomerulonephritis

Patient: Martin Wilson   **Age:** 6 years old   **Date of Admission:** 1/6, 2:00 P.M.

Assessment

Martin Wilson, a 6-year-old male, was admitted to the pediatric unit with a tentative diagnosis of acute glomerulonephritis. The following information was given by his mother during the admission interview.

Mrs. Wilson had noticed that Martin's eyes were somewhat puffy 2 days prior to admission. The day before admission, Martin looked pale and didn't appear to have any energy. Mrs. Wilson called her doctor on the morning of admission when she noticed that Martin was going to the bathroom less frequently, his urine was red-colored, and his other symptoms had not improved. The physician immediately arranged for Martin to be admitted to the hospital. On the way to the hospital, Martin vomited twice.

When questioned, Mrs. Wilson recalled that Martin and his brother had sore throats about 3 weeks earlier. They had been treated with penicillin for 10 days and recovered without any problems. Mrs. Wilson appeared anxious about her son's illness. She repeatedly questioned the nurse about what was wrong with Martin and asked if his brother was also going to get sick. Mrs. Wilson stated that Martin had always been healthy and that the doctor said he was growing normally. There have been no previous hospitalizations. She decided to stay with Martin while he was in the hospital, since his brother could stay with his grandparents. Mr. Wilson, a plumber, can also help with child care and visit Martin in the evenings. She stated that she was upset with herself for not calling the doctor earlier.

The following observations were made by the nurse:

Vital signs Within normal limits (P 100, T 37°C, R 23) except blood pressure 138 mmHg systolic and 98 diastolic

Weight 21.9 kg (48.3 lb)—50th percentile

Height 117.5 cm (46.3 in)—50th percentile

Color pale

Edema Moderate amount of periorbital edema present

Urine Smoky brown

Behavior Lethargic, does not appear interested in his environment, vomited on the way to the hospital. When questioned, denies having a headache or blurred vision

Physician's orders

1. Bed rest with bathroom privileges
2. Strict record of intake and output
3. Complete blood count, BUN, creatinine
4. Urinalysis—save urine samples from each voiding to compare color; check urine specific gravity
5. Regular diet with no added salt
6. Vital signs q2h, including blood pressure
7. Notify physician for diastolic blood pressure greater than 100 mmHg
8. Chest x-ray
9. Weight bid

Nursing diagnosis	Nursing goals	Nursing actions	Evaluation/revision
1. Potential for alterations in neurological status related to hypertension	☐ Intact neurological status—no encephalopathy. Diastolic blood pressure of less than 90 mmHg	☐ Record vital signs including BP q2h ☐ Notify physician if diastolic BP is 100 mmHg ☐ Maintain bed rest with bathroom privileges ☐ Observe child for signs of encephalopathy—i.e., headache, vomiting, blurred vision, dizziness, seizures	☐ BP ranging from 130/90 to 136/94 ☐ No evidence of encephalopathy

Nursing diagnosis	Nursing goals	Nursing actions	Evaluation/revision
2. Potential for altered urine output, color, and consistency related to reduction in glomerular filtration	☐ Urine output 650–1000 ml/24 hr	☐ Maintain accurate intake and output records ☐ Obtain information from mother regarding child's normal voiding patterns ☐ Report urine output of less than 100 ml per shift to physician	☐ Urine output for this 24-h period is 400 ml
	☐ Urine color will be umber to light yellow	☐ Observe and record color of urine—save sample from each voiding to compare color (tape to bathroom wall)	☐ Urine continues to be smoky brown.
	☐ Urine specific gravity will be 1.000 to 1.030	☐ Check and record urine specific gravity with each voiding	☐ Specific gravity is 1.020
	☐ Urine protein will become negative.	☐ Record urine proteins by using Albustix to test each voiding	☐ Urine is showing 3 + proteins at present time
3. Potential for alterations of (periorbital) edema related to changes in plasma volume	☐ Periorbital edema will gradually disappear	☐ Record weights twice daily (at same time each day) ☐ Monitor and record degree of edema when taking vital signs	☐ Periorbital edema is resolving ☐ Weight loss of 0.5 kg ☐ Weight is slowly returning to normal
☐ Potential for altered body image (self-concept) related to periorbital edema	☐ Child will understand that changes in appearance are temporary and usually resolve within 5–10 days	☐ Allow child to ventilate feelings regarding puffy eyes ☐ Inform child that puffy eyes will disappear as he begins to feel better	
4. Potential for skin irritation and excoriation related to edema and immobility	☐ Skin will remain pink, smooth, and intact	☐ Observe and record skin condition every shift ☐ Reposition child q2h ☐ Bathe and powder skin fold areas bid and prn ☐ Cleanse eyelids with warm saline qid and prn	☐ Skin intact at present time. Continue to assess at every shift
5. Potential for impaired nutrition related to anorexia and change in diet	☐ Appetite will improve as symptoms subside	☐ Regular diet for age with no added salt ☐ Obtain information from mother and child regarding food likes and dislikes to aid in planning daily menus ☐ Provide afternoon and bedtime snacks	☐ Appetite is only fair and does enjoy snacks
6. Potential for circulatory overload related to increased plasma volume	☐ Improved renal function as evidenced by normal circulatory blood volume	☐ Observe for and record any signs of cardiac involvement, i.e., cardiomegaly, tachycardia, diaphoresis, dyspnea	☐ No evidence of cardiac involvement at present

Nursing diagnosis	Nursing goals	Nursing actions	Evaluation/revision
7. Potential for boredom related to continuing lethargy of disease and restrictions imposed on activity level	☐ Martin will gradually resume normal activity level: activities of daily living and participation in scheduled unit play activities alternated with rest periods	☐ Maintain bed rest with bathroom privileges ☐ Provide age-appropriate toys and games that maintain bed rest ☐ As symptoms subside, allow child to resume activities at own pace ☐ When activity increased, encourage interaction with peers	☐ From his bed, Martin plays Star Wars with his mother
8. Parental guilt and anxiety related to illness and hospitalization of child	☐ Mother will verbalize her feelings about Martin's illness	☐ Provide time and quiet area where mother can relax and talk with the nurse ☐ Allow mother to participate in Martin's care to the extent which she is able ☐ Teach mother about Martin's illness and its treatment so that she is able to accept what is occurring to him ☐ Teach signs of complications. ☐ Refer to appropriate agencies for follow-up after discharge	☐ Mother talked to nurse about her understanding of Martin's illness

References

1. Arnold H. Colodny, "Urinary Tract Infections, Pediatric Urology," *Urology Times*, March: 3 (1978).
2. C. R. Kleeman et al., "Pyelonephritis," *Medicine* 39:12 (February 1960).
3. C. M. Kunin et al., "Urinary Tract Infection in School Children: Epidemiologic, Clinical and Laboratory Study," *Medicine*, March 1964, p. 127.
4. Kunin et al., ibid., p. 122.
5. John R. Woodward, "Urinary Tract Infections," in P. O. Kelalis and L. W. King (eds.), *Clinical Pediatric Urology*, Saunders, Philadelphia, 1976, p. 185.
6. Woodward, ibid., p. 347.
7. Colodny, loc. cit.
8. John W. Duckett, in H. C. Filston (ed.), *Surgical Problems in Children: Recognition and Referral*, Mosby, St. Louis, in press.
9. Duckett, ibid.
10. Edmond Gonzales Jr., "Posterior Urethral Valves and Bladder Neck Obstruction," in R. Jeffs (eds.), *The Urologic Clinics of North America*, vol. 5, Saunders, Philadelphia, 1978, p. 64.
11. R. Sorrentino and P. Leonetti, "Terapia della estrofia vesicale," ESI, 1958, p. 1.
12. Tague C. Chishol and Felix A. McParland, "Exstrophy of the Urinary Bladder," in M. Ravitch (ed.), *Pediatric Surgery*, 3d ed., Yearbook, Chicago, 1979, p. 1239–1253.
13. Julian Ansell, "Vesical Exstrophy," in J. F. Glenn (ed.), *Urologic Surgery*, 2d ed., Harper & Row, Hagerstown, 1975, p. 316.
14. John W. Duckett, "Epispadias," in R. D. Jeffs (ed.), *Urologic Clinics of North America*, vol. 5, Saunders, Philadelphia, 1980, p. 428.
15. H. C. Bredon and E. C. Muecke, "Surgical Correction of Male Epispadias with Total Incontinence," *Journal of Urology*, May: 908 (1973).
16. O. S. Culp, "Treatment of Epispadias with and without Urinary Incontinence; Experience with 46 Patients," *Journal of Urology*, January: 125 (1973).
17. R. E. Gross and S. L. Cresson, "Treatment of Epispadias: A Report of 18 Cases," *Journal of Urology*, April 1952, p. 477.
18. A. Barry Belman, "Urethra," in P. P. Kelalis and L. W. King, (eds.), *Clinical Pediatric Urology*, Saunders, Philadelphia, 1976, p. 576.
19. John W. Duckett and D. M. Raezer, "Neuromuscular Dysfunction of the Lower Urinary Tract," in ibid., p. 416.

20. Jack Lapides et al., "Follow-up on Unsterile Intermittent Self-Catheterization," *The Journal of Urology*, February: 187 (1974).
21. Anne Altschuler et al., "Even Children Can Learn to do Clean Self-Catheterization," *American Journal of Nursing*, January: 98 (1977).
22. K. Devlin and D. Rheinheimer, "Clean Intermittent Catheterization in Children," *Pediatric Nursing*, July–August: 29 (1976).
23. Duckett and Raezer, op. cit., p. 413.
24. Jan Langman, *Medical Embryology*, 2d ed., Williams & Wilkins, Baltimore, 1969, p. 160.
25. J. R. Pascqual and P. L. Calcagno (eds.), *Nephrologic Problems of the Newborn*, Vol. 15, Basel, Switzerland, 1979, p. 58.
26. Ibid., p. 59.
27. Ibid.
28. Langman, op. cit., p. 159.
29. J. S. Cameron, A. Russell and D. Sale, *Nephrology for Nurses*, 2d ed., Medical Examination Publishing, Flushing, N. Y., 1976, p. 41.
30. John A. James, *Renal Disease in Childhood*, 3d ed., Mosby, St. Louis, 1976, p. 296.
31. Gladys Scipien, et al., *Comprehensive Pediatric Nursing*, (2d ed.) McGraw-Hill, New York, 1975, p. 740.
32. Donald Potter and Ira Greifer, "Statural Growth of Children with Renal Disease," *Kidney International* **14**:377 (1978).
33. James, op. cit., p. 245.
34. W. Nelson, V. Vaughan, R. J. McKay, and R. Behrman (eds.), *Nelson Textbook of Pediatrics*, 11th ed., Saunders, Philadelphia, 1979, p. 1517.
35. Ibid., p. 1496.
36. James, op. cit., p. 224.
37. Ibid.
38. Ibid.
39. Nelson et al., op. cit., p. 1498.
40. James, op. cit., p. 260.
41. Ibid., p. 261.
42. Ibid., p. 268.
43. Ibid., p. 370.

Chapter 32 **Integument**

Madeleine Lynch Martin

Upon completion of this chapter, the student will be able to:

1. Describe the local and systemic reactions to insect stings.
2. Identify the typical course of poison ivy dermatitis.
3. Describe the process of the development of acne.
4. Identify the methods of treatment used for acne.
5. Describe the physical, emotional, and social significance of a burn injury in the life of a child and the child's family.
6. Describe the initial physiological alterations which accompany burn injury.
7. Identify alterations in the body systems which develop as a response to thermal injury.
8. Describe the normal process of wound healing.

9. List the steps in initial first aid for the thermally injured child.
10. Discuss appropriate nursing intervention during the acute care management of the burned child.
11. Describe a thermal injury based on depth of tissue damage, amount of body surface involved, and type of injury.
12. List the steps and goals of burn care.
13. List four commercially available topical antimicrobial agents, including their advantages and disadvantages.
14. List the goals of physical and emotional rehabilitation of the burned child.

The integumentary system can be defined as the outside covering or shell of the body. This external surface of the body is formed by the skin and its associated structures. These are often called *skin appendages* and include: hair, nails, glands, and sensory skin receptors. The skin can be regarded as the single, largest organ of the body. It provides a supple, protective covering, serves as a barrier to loss of internal body fluids and electrolytes, and is a regulator of heat. The skin grows, changes, and renews and repairs itself efficiently. The appearance of the skin reflects the child's general state of health.

Embryonic origin

The epidermis is formed from the embryonic *ectoderm* (outer layer). By 7 weeks the epidermis is a single layer of cuboidal cells covering the embryo with primitive skin. It thickens to two layers by 11 weeks and continues to thicken to five layers, and closely resembles mature skin at birth. It is thin at birth, about 1 mm, and increases to about twice that thickness at maturity.

The dermis is derived from the *mesodermal* layer and forms the connective-tissue layer underlying the epidermis.

The skin appendages have a separate developmental timetable. Sebaceous glands are functional during fetal life and are responsible for the secretions that combine with dead epithelium to form vernix caseosa. From birth through infancy they gradually decrease in size and remain relatively inactive until puberty. *Eccrine* sweat glands appear at the fifth month but are not functional in fetal life. *Apocrine* sweat glands, associated with the hair follicles, are present at birth but will not mature until puberty. Nails appear at about 16 weeks and hair at about 20 weeks.[1]

Structure of the skin

Epidermis

The epidermis, the outer layer of the skin, is composed of five epidermal layers resting on a basment membrane (basal cells). These basal cells produce new epidermal cells, which constantly replace the older exterior cells by being pushed outward toward the skin surface. *Stratum corneum*, the most superficial skin layer, contains a layer of dead, flat, scalelike cells filled with keratin. These are shed continuously and rubbed off by contact with clothing, by washing, or by environmental exposure. The lower layer of the epidermis contains melanocytes, whose function is to form the melanin, or pigment, of the skin. It is the degree of activity of these cells, not the number of melanocytes, that gives the skin its characteristic light or dark color.[2]

Dermis

The dermal layer is directly under the epidermis. It is thicker; is composed of tough, elastic, connective tissue, and provides the structural and nutritional layer for the epidermis. It contains a network of blood vessels, nerves, and lymphatics that nourish the skin cells. The hair follicles and glands originate deep in the dermis. These glands invaginate into the dermal layers, incorporating epidermis as gland linings.

Subcutaneous layer

The subcutaneous layer, found under the dermis, is mainly composed of fat and loose connective tissue, with larger blood vessels, nerves, and lymph channels than the dermis. This layer provides fat and body fluid storage, acts as the body insulator from the elements, and provides for safety by cushioning the body.

Skin functions

The skin has four essential functions: protection of underlying parts, heat regulation, prevention of water and electrolyte loss, and reception of sensory stimuli.

Protection

The epidermis has keratinized (horny) cells that resist invasion of bacteria, chemicals, and parasites and protect the body from cold, heat, and injury. The sebum, oily secretions, of the sebaceous glands lubricate the skin, keeping it supple and decreasing fluid loss. The secretions of the glands provide a surface film of water, lipids, acids, and polypeptides that have a bacteriostatic effect.

The thickness of the epidermis varies in different parts of the body. The hands and feet are subjected to heavy use and have thick skin, about 5 to 6 mm. The thinnest skin is found in sensitive

Figure 32-1 Anatomy of skin and subcutaneous fat. (*Used with the permission of Shriners Burn Institute, Cincinnati, Ohio.*)

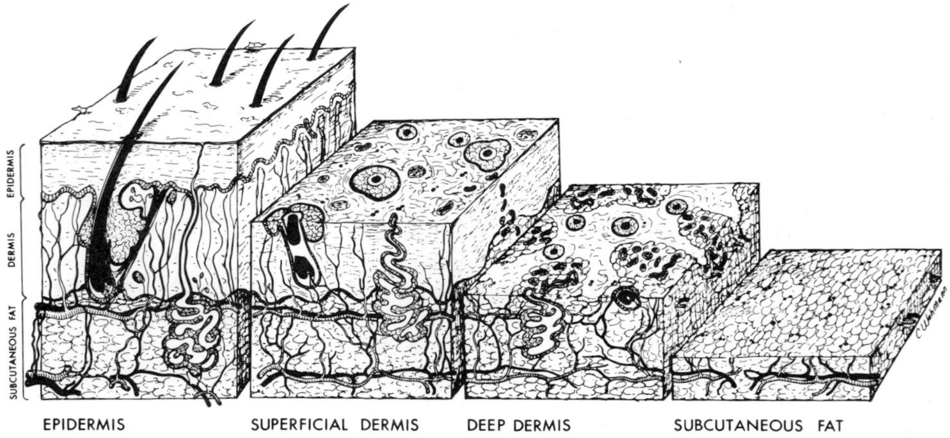

EPIDERMIS   SUPERFICIAL DERMIS   DEEP DERMIS   SUBCUTANEOUS FAT

areas of the body: eyelids, eardrums and on the penis, where it is about 1 to 2 mm thick. The epidermis and dermis are thin and loosely connected at birth. Thus in young children minimal friction can cause separation of the dermal and epidermal layer, resulting in blisters. The thin outer layer of skin in infants can easily be rubbed off, making them very susceptible to skin breakdown. The epidermal layer gradually thickens and becomes tougher with age.

At adolescence, sex-hormone secretion increases, causing skin changes. Estrogen in the female thickens the skin, making it soft and smooth, and increasing dermal fat and vascularity. Androgens in males cause the characteristic thickening and darkening of their skin.

Heat regulation

The skin helps to maintain the important function of temperature control of the body. This is accomplished by regulation of heat loss through sweating and cutaneous vascular changes. Sweating and vasodilation decrease the body temperature; vasoconstriction, shivering, and muscle activity raise the temperature. The eccrine glands are responsible for sweating in response to thermal stimuli. Children sweat much less than adults, and thus it is more difficult for them to regulate body temperature by sweating. Surface heat loss is also greater in children than in adults because children have a larger proportion of body surface area and less body fat with blood vessels closer to a thin skin surface.

Prevention of water and electrolyte loss

The intact skin is a relatively impermeable membrane that retards the exchange of liquids between the internal body and the outside environment. The intact skin effectively prevents excessive loss of essential body constituents. It does permit some water loss when water is evaporated on the skin surface to cool the body. The skin's effectiveness as a fluid barrier is clearly apparent when the profuse fluid and electrolyte loss following disruption of the skin by a burn is observed.

Skin as a sense organ

The skin is the major contributor to the touch sensation and can be described as a tactile organ. Touch, pressure, pain, cold, and heat are all sensations experienced through the skin. The skin conducts impulses to the brain, which are used to adjust the body to relieve uncomfortable sensations. Often these sensations are protective devices and permit the body to alter its position before damage to tissue occurs. Positive impulses are just as important as negative protective impulses: Pleasurable touch stimulates and motivates behavior from fetal life through adulthood.

Stinging-insect allergy*

The stings of bees, wasps, hornets, and yellow jackets pose a great danger to almost 1 million people in the United States. In the South, the sting of the fire ant can also be dangerous. At least 40 people die yearly in this country as the result of these stings. Children are especially vulnerable to stinging-insect allergies.

Types of reactions

The venom injected by the stinging insects has many components. If the child is allergic to stings, one or more of these components may trigger a reaction. The mildest form of reaction is called a *local reaction*. A very large swelling occurs but remains localized at the site of the sting. More dangerous reactions are called *systemic reactions.* At times only the skin is involved, producing superficial hives, or *urticaria*, and deep hives, or *angioedema*. In the most dangerous reactions, the sting may cause shock or suffocation. When the sting produces shock, it causes a reaction called *anaphylaxis*. The blood vessels throughout the body dilate and fluid leaks from the vessels into the tissues. The heart, with a diminished supply of venous blood returning, is unable to keep up blood pressure, which falls. Vital organs such as the brain are starved for the oxygen that the blood carries. The child begins to lose consciousness, and if the condition persists, vital organs of the body are severely damaged. The child dies if shock is not reversed.

Suffocation occurs if the air passages swell shut and prevent air from entering the lungs. This is called *laryngeal edema*. In a child, the air passages are smaller in size and the airway is blocked more quickly by swelling.

Treatment

The drug of choice is Adrenalin (epinephrine).

* By William E. Walsh, M.D.

The subcutaneous dose varies with age and size, between 0.1 and 0.5 ml, repeated in 20 min if necessary. Early treatment will usually reverse the systemic reaction. In those children who have shock and do not respond to epinephrine, rapid intravenous administration of saline or other solution will usually replace the depleted blood volume and allow the heart to resume efficient transport of the vital oxygen. Tracheostomy is often necessary in the patient with laryngeal edema to open the blocked airway.

The best treatment is prevention of the acute reactions. Children are instructed to avoid situations in which they may be stung. Shoes should be worn outside at all times to prevent stepping on a stinging insect. Perfumes and scented preparations attract insects and dark clothes attract them more than light colored clothes. An area where food is present, including at picnics and near garbage, attracts stinging insects. If a stinging insect is threatening, instruct children to leave the area. Undue excitement or slapping at the insect may cause it to sting.

Allergic children can be stung despite great efforts to avoid it. Kits containing epinephrine syringes with premeasured doses are available and should be carried at all times. The kit also contains an antihistamine and a tourniquet to use if the sting is on an extremity. A reaction can occur a few minutes after a sting. Injected adrenalin begins to work within minutes of administration. Antihistamine tablets take much longer to be dissolved and absorbed and must not be thought of as the first line of defense.

For the allergic person in danger of severe reaction, purified venom preparations are available for use in hyposensitization. Hyposensitization is described in Chap. 33. This is a complicated, long-term, and somewhat dangerous therapy. It does provide the protection against a severe reaction not provided by any other form of treatment.

Nursing management

Allergy to stinging insects is dangerous and can be fatal. A nurse must be ready to recognize the situation and treat it appropriately.

The danger of this allergy must be explained to the allergic person. Discuss means of avoiding the next sting. The nurse should be fully acquainted with the use of the insect sting kit, make sure the patient has one in his or her possession, and instruct the child and parents in its use. Use a kit for teaching purposes so the contents can become familiar. The syringe may be filled with water and the child and parents can practice administration on an orange. Many people are afraid of giving themselves a shot. To assist in overcoming this fear, encourage self-administration of an injection with 0.3 ml of sterile saline. The preferred injection site is the subcutaneous tissue in the anterior lateral area of the thigh.

The patient should be encouraged to seek consultation to find out if venom hyposensitization is appropriate.

Poison ivy dermatitis*

The skin eruption caused by touching the poison ivy plant is distinctly uncomfortable. Most people react by developing a rash that lasts for weeks.

Cause

Poison ivy is actually a type of sumac. Because it is a member of the *Rhus* genus of plants, the rash is called *Rhus dermatitis*. To recognize the plant, look for three leaves grouped close together. The outermost leaf has a long stem and the two leaves behind it have almost no stem. The plant will appear to have a shiny surface if the light strikes it at the proper angle. Red berries appear on it during the summer; they turn white and stay on the plant during the winter. The surface of the leaves and branches contains an *oleoresin* which is deposited on the skin when the plant is touched. Animal coats also pick up the oleoresin and can transfer it to people who touch the animal. The oleoresin produces the dermatitis.

Poison ivy dermatitis varies from mild to severe. The severe reaction is recognized by the intense itching and a certain sequence of events. After contact, the skin becomes extremely pruritic and the patient scratches the area, contaminating the fingers with the oleoresin. The fingers then transfer it to other parts of the body. It is important soon after contact to wash hands and affected areas thoroughly with soap and water.

Within 24 h the skin becomes swollen and blisters appear, which can grow large, break, and drain. During the first week, the blisters burst;

---

* By William E. Walsh, M.D.

the crusting, swelling, and pruritus lasts several weeks.

Characteristic locations are exposed areas such as the hands, face, and legs but can include any part of the body touched by the contaminated fingers. The rash is often found in linear streaks caused by the patient's scratching.

In severe cases, discomfort is marked, sleeping is difficult, and the patient will seek medical attention.

Treatment

In mild poison ivy dermatitis, a calamine-antihistamine topical preparation such as Caladryl will provide relief. Oral antihistamines such as diphenhydramine (Benadryl) may also relieve itching. With a severe eruption, systemic cortisone therapy is necessary for relief. Since the eruption is limited to a period of several weeks, there is no need for prolonged cortisone use. In the child, prednisone can be used at 1 mg per kilogram daily for 5 to 7 days, then the dose is rapidly reduced over the next 1 to 2 weeks. An alternate method is to continue the milligram per kilogram dose after 5 to 7 days but to use it only every other day at 8 o'clock in the morning for a total treatment of 2 to 3 weeks.

Controversy surrounds the various ways of reducing the patient's allergy to poison ivy. Desensitizing agents are available for oral and subcutaneous administration but studies do not show predictable protection. If used at all, they should be used only in those patients who are strikingly sensitive to the plant.

Nursing considerations

The nurse will often have first contact with the patient exhibiting poison ivy dermatitis. To identify the lesion and its cause, look for a history of exposure and for the characteristic rash. To prevent spread and secondary infections, impress parents and the child with the need to prevent touching and scratching the lesions. If done soon after initial contact, thorough washing with soap and water will remove much of the oleoresin and reduce the reaction substantially.

The nurse must educate the patient in the cause of dermatitis plus discuss the identification of the plants and the means to avoid it. If the patient lives in an area with poison ivy plants, special sprays are commercially available to kill them.

Acne vulgaris*

Acne vulgaris, commonly known as "pimples," is the most common skin disorder of patients in their early teens and twenties. It causes inflammation of conspicuous areas of the body: the face, the shoulders, the chest, and the back. When acne is active, the *comedones* (blackheads and whiteheads), papules, pustules, nodules, and cysts, are unsightly. After the acute process has subsided, the skin is often left scarred.

In most persons, acne begins in puberty and subsides at about 22 to 23 years of age. However, it can begin as early as 5 years of age and continue to be active into the forties.

As both males and females are affected by acne, the pattern of appearance in a family indicates acne is a dominant trait. Many factors point to androgenic hormone stimulation of the skin as a prime factor in its development. Acne seems to be aggravated by emotional stress, winter weather, some stimulant drugs, and the premenstrual period. Regardless of the cause, acne is a complex, chronic problem causing discomfort and mental distress to 80 to 90 percent of adolescents.

Pathogenesis

The pilosebaceous gland is found in large numbers on the face and in smaller, but significant, numbers on the back, chest, and shoulders. The gland is composed of a hair follicle and a large sebaceous (oil-producing) gland. At puberty, under the influence of the increased androgenic hormone secretions from the adrenal glands and gonads, the gland matures. Its size and secretions increase, and the cells lining the ducts grow more rapidly and are shed in greater numbers. The oily gland secretions are called *sebum* and are composed of keratin, lipids, and fatty acids and contain bacteria. The increased secretion of sebum, mixed with large numbers of gland-lining cells, should be extruded from the gland onto the skin.

In acne, the cells shed from the lining of the gland and block the opening to the skin surface. This plug prevents the gland from emptying its contents onto the skin. The melanin content of the plug gives it a dark color. If the pore is open to the air, the sebum also darkens through the oxidation process. Therefore, with the passage

* By William E. Walsh, M.D.

of time, the part of the plug at the skin surface develops a black pigmentation. This is called an *open comedo*, or blackhead. If the comedo maintains its opening to the skin surface, the contents of the gland can be slowly and continuously discharged without causing much damage. However, the pore containing the comedo often dilates and the blackhead becomes larger.

If the skin covers the pore, it is called a whitehead, or *closed comedo*. Beneath the plug, the gland continues to produce hair and sebum, causing progressive gland enlargement. This enlargement turns the gland into a distended sac which can be ruptured. The contents of the ruptured sac are irritating and cause inflammation around the gland.

Sebaceous glands that rupture and cause inflammation near the surface of the skin produce a pustule (pus-filled pimple). Ruptures deeper under the skin produce papules. These papules can become pus-filled and are prone to development of nodules, cysts, and scar formation.

Living in the pilosebaceous gland are bacteria called *Corynebacterium acnes.* The enzymes of the bacteria split the sebum into free fatty acids. These fatty acids are the most irritating part of sebum and significantly increase the inflammatory response around the ruptured gland.

Thus the acne process involves plugging of the pilosebaceous gland, glandular enlargement if the plugging is complete, followed by rupture and release of irritating glandular contents. These irritating substances, especially the free fatty acids released by *C. acnes* bacteria cause an inflammation as the body utilizes its defenses to remove the ruptured gland material. Secondary infection with staphylococci, from picking or squeezing the lesions, can complicate the problem.

Clinical manifestations

The comedo is the most characteristic lesion of acne. If the gland maintains its opening to the skin surface, the face has blackheads or open comedones. If the skin grows over the surface opening of the gland, a whitehead, or closed comedo, appears. With enlargement of the gland, a papule is formed. Enlargement and rupture causes swelling and the area becomes red and tender. Pustules and cysts are formed by this process. In more severe cases, scarring occurs with healing. The degree of scarring varies, depending on the person and the severity of the acne. These scars may be depressed pits in the skin or may become a nodule if the patient is susceptible to *keloid* (scar) formation.

Treatment

Diet Recent control studies show no evidence that diet has any influence on the course of acne. Some individuals believe that sweets and greasy foods make the process worse and that these foods should be avoided.

Topical treatment Various drying and *exfoliating* (peeling) agents provide the treatment of acne. This includes abrasive soaps, astringents, ultraviolet light, sulfur, resorcinol, and salicylic acid. Sulfur (1 to 5%) and resorcinol (1 to 10%) dry and peel existing comedones, papules, and pustules and allow them to empty, but fail to prevent closed comedones or whiteheads. The most potent topical agents currently in use are benzoyl peroxide and tretinoin.

Topical medications *Benzoyl peroxide* has been in use since 1934. Only recently have effective lotions and gel forms been developed. Benzoyl peroxide produces a fine *desquamation* (peeling) that helps to allow expression of the comedo. It also inhibits *C. acnes* and the formation of free fatty acids which this bacterium promotes.

Benzoyl peroxide can be irritating and drying and its use must be introduced gradually, especially in patients with sensitive skin. Depending on the individual, a thin film of benzoyl peroxide is rubbed into the skin gently, either daily or every second or third day. As the skin develops a tolerance for this treatment, the strength of the preparation and the frequency of application can be increased. This usually takes 2 to 3 weeks. If the skin becomes irritated or dry, the preparation can be discontinued for several days and lubricants used until the irritation subsides. Skin irritation from benzoyl peroxide will be reduced or avoided if the preparation is introduced and used cautiously.

Tretinoin (vitamin A acid) began to be used for topical treatment in 1969. Its use increases cell turnover within the pilosebaceous gland and decreases the "stickiness" of the cells that are shed into the sebum. It causes a thinning of the epidermis that promotes extrusion of the comedo and decreases comedo formation. It also assists the penetration of benzoyl peroxide and topical antibiotics into the pilosebaceous gland.

Tretinoin and benzoyl peroxide are both irritating. Treatment with tretinoin is begun cautiously in a schedule similar to that of benzoyl peroxide. Use a mild soap to wash the area, no more than two or three times a day. Wait at least 30 min after washing before applying tretinoin. Sun screens should be used if prolonged sun exposure is anticipated. The therapeutic affect of these medications is enhanced by using them in combination (one in the morning and one at night).

Salicyclic acid (5 to 10%) is less effective than tretinoin or benzoyl peroxide. It is sometimes used for teens with mild acne who have problems with tretinoin, or as an alternative to tretinoin in combination with benzoyl peroxide.

Topical antibiotics Topical tetracycline, erythromycin, and clindamycin can suppress the growth of *C. acnes.*

Systemic antibiotics In patients who have inflammation, pustules, or cysts, systemic antibiotics are helpful. They suppress the growth of *C. acnes,* causing a reduction in the irritating free fatty acids produced by the bacterial reaction. They are used less often at this time because of the effective topical treatment available.

Tetracycline is the most commonly used oral antibiotic because it is effective, inexpensive, and has few side effects. Therapy often begins with a dosage of 500 to 1000 mg per day, gradually decreasing to the lowest dose that gives a good response. This may be 250 mg every day or every other day. Usually a minimum of 3 to 4 weeks of treatment is necessary, with low-dose therapy continued for months. Complications include vaginal moniliasis, gastrointestinal irritation (nausea and vomiting), and allergy. It must be given on an empty stomach and not with milk, since it combines with calcium. Tetracycline is not used in patients younger than 12 years old nor in the first trimester of pregnancy because of the possibility of tooth discoloration in the child.

Erythromycin is often used for long-term acne treatment. When the patient does not respond sufficiently to tetracycline or erythromycin, clindamycin or minocycline can be used. *Clinda-*mycin can cause pseudomembranous ulcerative colitis and systemic use should not be long term. *Minocycline* causes a high incidence of headache and dizziness.

Nursing management

The person with acne vulgaris feels that each "zit" or acne lesion is an unsightly blemish and is self-conscious about them. This is especially true in the impressionable teenager, whose adult personality is being formed. This conspicuous and disfiguring process is traumatic to the personality and to self-esteem. The nurse must approach this teenager with kindness and understanding. A sympathetic approach will often gain the person's trust and the cooperation necessary to carry out a treatment program. The nurse's approach begins with gentle questioning about the patient's skin treatment. A treatment plan should be formulated. The plan begins with education concerning cause and treatment of acne. Topical therapy must be explained carefully and the patient followed while using it. When inflammation is prominent, systemic antibiotics are added to the program.

Sometimes removal of the comedones is advocated and instructions are given. Have the adolescent wash his or her face two to three times a day, wash the hair frequently, and keep it off the face to help reduce oiliness. Keeping hands away from the face is also important: "picking" and resting the face in the hands are to be avoided because they predispose to infection and scarring.

Instruction and encouragement are vital. The treatment can take weeks and some unpleasant side effects of the treatment will often arise, including erythema, redness, superficial peeling, and at times a temporary worsening of the acne process. A nurse who has established good rapport with the patient will be able to give emotional support that will encourage the long-term treatment necessary for control.

Burns

Management of the pediatric burn patient presents the nurse with a demanding and challenging opportunity to implement all aspects of nursing care. The stress involved in a burn injury cannot be overstated. Every major physiological organ system is potentially involved. Psychologically and socially the burn represents a major life event with dramatic effects. Furthermore, in a pediatric burn these physiological and psychosocial changes are interrelated with the progression of necessary developmental tasks. As a primary care giver on the burn care team, the nurse must have an understanding of the responses of the child to the injury. Such knowledge, combined with skill in accepted burn care techniques, serves as the basis for planning, implementing, and evaluating the care of the pediatric burn victim.

Scope of the problem

Approximately 2 million individuals are burned annually in the United States. It is estimated that 30 percent of these thermally injured are children. While some 6000 children still die annually as a result of burns, improved care techniques have greatly increased the child's chances of survival. Just 15 years ago, a child with 40 percent third-degree burn had only guarded chances for survival. Now, a child with this same burn injury has an 80 percent chance of recovery.

Certain types of thermal injury appear to be associated with selected age groups. Flame burns and house fires are frequent factors in infant burns. As the child begins to crawl, exploring the environment, he or she may chew exposed electrical cords, causing electrical injury to the mouth, lips, tongue, and teeth. Preadolescent and adolescent boys have a relatively high incidence of burns resulting from gasoline from either working with engines or throwing combustible liquids on an open fire. This age group also has frequent electrical injuries from high-voltage power sources. Girls in this same age group are more often burned while cooking or while tending such home heating sources as wood stoves and fireplaces. The majority of all childhood burns occur when children are unattended or in the care of babysitters.

Burns can be prevented. The importance of supervising children and leaving children in the care of a responsible person must be stressed to parents. Flameproof clothing greatly reduces the extent of injury from flame burns. Proper safety measures should be observed around combustible liquids and electrical appliances. Screens should be used with sources of open flames in the home. Fire exit drills should be practiced with children. Programs of fire and burn preven-

tion that include these facts and other safety measures should be developed for public education. In pediatric nursing the nurse must take every opportunity to educate families in the basics of prevention.[3]

Assessment of the injury

Care of the injury begins with an assessment and description of the burn. Burns are most efficiently described by: (1) type of injury, (2) amount of body surface involved, and (3) depth of tissue damage.

Types of injury

The type of injury is based on the source of tissue damage. The nurse should determine if the child has sustained an electrical burn, chemical burn, frostbite, scald, or direct-flame injury.

Electrical injuries result in extensive tissue destruction. Skin damage is seen at the point of entry of the electric current and the point of exit. Such surface burns are usually circumscribed, deep, charred, depressed wounds involving cutaneous and subcutaneous tissue. When the body acts as a conductor from the source of electricity to the ground, electricity passes through the body. As the electric current passes through the body it encounters resistance, and electrical energy is converted to heat energy, causing internal thermal tissue destruction. The current usually follows the path of least resistance, making blood vessels and nerve passages most susceptible to injury. However, damage to muscle and bones is frequently seen. Damage to major vessels may result in spontaneous hemorrhage during the post-injury period. The patient must be observed carefully for evidence of internal damage and ischemia which may not be immediately apparent. Amputation may be necessary if there is extensive muscle and bone involvement. In addition to thermal damage to skin and internal structures, the initial electrical contact may cause corresponding physiological disruption. The cardiopulmonary system is especially vulnerable and cardiac and respiratory arrest may result, demanding immediate resuscitation.

Although chemical burns are more frequently associated with adults and industrial accidents, chemical burn patients are also encountered by the pediatric nurse. Fireworks, flares, and improperly stored household chemicals may result in injury to the child. The chemical reaction of the agent on the skin results in tissue damage similar to that seen in other types of burns. Treatment focuses on removing the source of damage. Flushing with copious amounts of water or saline is indicated for most chemicals. Water is contraindicated in phosphorous injuries because it activates phosphorus. A 1% copper sulfate solution as a washing agent is recommended in such cases.[4]

Scalds, flame injury, and sunburn cause tissue damage as a result of excessive heat. The physiological response is similar for all these and will be discussed in detail later in this chapter. The most important factor in limiting tissue destruction is removing or extinguishing the source of heat as quickly as possible.

In some regions, cold injury or frostbite may also be encountered by the pediatric nurse. Such injury results from hypothermia rather than heat or hyperthermia. The results in terms of tissue destruction are similar to burns, however, and warrant inclusion in a discussion of care of the thermally injured child.

The most important factors causing tissue damage are wind, temperature, and humidity. Tissue damage results from direct freezing of tissue and extreme vasoconstriction causing local ischemia. First aid for frostbite is directed toward quick recognition and warming of the affected part. Warm, moist heat applied by immersion or wet packs is effective. The nurse must recognize that a patient with cold injury frequently experiences insensitivity to touch, pain, temperature, and other stimulation and cannot respond to the temperature of the warming agent. A moderate solution of 42°C (105°F) is recommended so as not to cause further tissue damage.[5]

Amount of body surface involved

The second factor used in describing a thermal injury is estimation of percentage of total body surface area (TBSA) involved. Generally, the greater the surface area damaged, the more serious the injury. The Lund and Browder technique, a convenient and useful tool in assessing a child's burn, allows for modifications based on the child's physical development and body proportions, but the nurse must be aware of normal growth and development as they relate to body

surface areas. For example, an infant who has a greater proportion of body surface in the head and trunk areas will present a very different burn profile than does a 10-year-old child with relatively more body surface distribution in the extremities (Figure 32-2).

Depth of tissue damage

In addition to estimating body surface and identifying the type of injury, the nurse also describes the depth of tissue destruction. Burns can be classified as first-, second-, or third-degree injuries (Table 32-1). *A first-degree burn* involves the covering layer of epidermis. It has characteristic redness, does not blister, has normal or increased pain sensation, and results from sources such as overexposure to the sun. Healing occurs spontaneously and rapidly.

Second-degree burns result in damage to all or most of the epidermis and some dermis. None of the underlying tissue structure is involved, however, and epithelization and spontaneous healing can occur. It has a moist, pink to cherry-red appearance, is painful, and frequently blisters. A second-degree injury can be converted to a third-degree injury if infection occurs that causes further tissue destruction (Table 32-2).

In contrast to first- and second-degree injuries, *third-degree burns* destroy the entire epidermis and dermis down to the underlying fat. In severe injury, fat, muscle, and bone may be damaged, but there is no pain sensation because the nerve endings are damaged. The appearance is cherry red to black or gray, and may be wet, or dry and leathery. Healing is not spontaneous and grafting is required for wound coverage. (Refer to Fig. 32-1.)

Pathophysiology

Immediate body response

The initial physiological alterations which accompany burn injury are commonly referred to as *burn shock*, and are associated with approximately the first 48 h after the burn. This phenomenon occurs in all age groups; however, the child presents a special risk during this period. Immature kidneys, unstable peripheral circulation, high metabolism, and the larger body surface in proportion to body weight are factors which increase the risk of the younger child;

Figure 32-2 Lund and Browder method of calculating burn size. (*Reproduced with permission from C. P. Artz and J. A. Moncrief, The Treatment of Burns, 2d ed., Saunders, Philadelphia, 1969*)

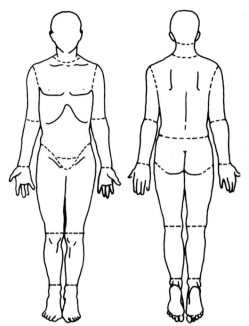

AREA	1 Yr.	1-4 Yrs.	5-9 Yrs.	10-14 Yrs.	15 Yrs.	Adult	2°	3°
Head	19	17	13	11	9	7		
Neck	2	2	2	2	2	2		
Ant. Trunk	13	13	13	13	13	13		
Post. Trunk	13	13	13	13	13	13		
R. Buttock	2½	2½	2½	2½	2½	2½		
L. Buttock	2½	2½	2½	2½	2½	2½		
Genitalia	1	1	1	1	1	1		
R.U. Arm	4	4	4	4	4	4		
L.U. Arm	4	4	4	4	4	4		
R.L. Arm	3	3	3	3	3	3		
L.L. Arm	3	3	3	3	3	3		
R. Hand	2½	2½	2½	2½	2½	2½		
L. Hand	2½	2½	2½	2½	2½	2½		
R. Thigh	5½	6½	8	8½	9	9½		
L. Thigh	5½	6½	8	8½	9	9½		
R. Leg	5	5	5½	6	6½	7		
L. Leg	5	5	5½	6	6½	7		
R. Foot	3½	3½	3½	3½	3½	3½		
L. Foot	3½	3½	3½	3½	3½	3½		
TOTAL								

children under 2 years old are especially vulnerable. Generally, the older the child, the better body systems can respond to the injury. In children there is usually a systemic response to burns which exceed 20 percent of total body surface area. Infants and very young children may suffer systemic responses to burns which cover 10 to 15 percent of their total body surface area.[6]

A major component of this burn shock response is the alteration of fluid balance. Approximately 50 to 70 percent of the body weight

is water, which is distributed in the intracellular and extracellular spaces. The *intracellular fluid*, contained within the cells, constitutes the majority of body fluid weight. *Extracellular fluid* is divided between interstitial fluid, which bathes the cells, and *intravascular fluid*, plasma. Thus the normal system is represented as having three compartments: the intracellular, interstitial, and intravascular. Through the process of diffusion and filtration, fluids within these compartments are constantly interchanging. Nutrients carried in the blood pass through the interstitial space

Table 32-1 Classification of burn depth

Traditional terminology	Anatomic terminology	Depth of involvement	Depth of anatomic involvement
1st degree	Epidermal	Partial thickness	Stratum corneum of the epidermis
2d degree	Intradermal Superficial Deep dermal	Partial thickness	Dermis to a variable extent
3d degree	Subdermal	Full thickness	Subcutaneous adipose tissue, fascia, muscles, and bones

Source: G. Scipien, et al., *Comprehensive Pediatric Nursing* 2d ed., McGraw-Hill, New York, 1979, p. 968. Used with permission of publisher.

Table 32-2 Characteristics of depth of injury

Depth of injury	Appearance	Pain sensitivity	Edema formation	Healing time	Scarring	Cause
1st degree	Pink to red	Painful	Very slight	3–5 days	None	Sunburn, flash, explosives
2d degree	Red to pale ivory and moist; may have vesicles and bullae	Extremely painful	Very edematous	21–28 days Variable		Flash, scalds, flame, brief contact with hot objects
3d degree	White, cherry red, or black; may contain bullae and thrombosed veins; dry and leathery	Painless to touch	Marked edema may require escharotomies	Requires grafting	Yes	Flame, high-intensity flash, electrical, chemical, hot object, scalds in infants and elderly

Source: by G. Scipien et al., *Comprehensive Pediatric Nursing* 2d ed., McGraw-Hill, New York, 1979, p. 968. Used with permission of publisher.

to the circulatory blood where they are filtered through the kidney.

Following thermal injury, there are disruptions in this distribution of body fluid. As a result of marked increase in capillary permeability, plasma leaks into the tissue, causing generalized edema or blistering. Red blood cells, which are larger, remain in the vessels. This loss of fluid in the vascular space results in decreased circulatory blood volume, which in turn causes a fall in blood pressure. The hematocrit rises because of hemoconcentration. Further, as plasma protein leaks into the tissue, there is a loss of the colloidal osmotic pressure difference between the capillaries and the tissue fluid, resulting in alterations in electrolyte balance. Potassium, contained primarily within cells, is lost into the interstitial space. Sodium passes into this space, contributing to edema and further fluid loss from the vascular system.

Resuscitation by fluid replacement must be monitored carefully to avoid either dehydration or overhydration.[7] As circulating blood decreases, renal vasoconstriction occurs, decreasing glomerular filtration rate. This will elevate blood urea nitrogen and creatinine levels. Permanent renal damage can be avoided by adequate fluid replacement, although the very young are more prone to permanent kidney damage. In addition, the child cannot excrete large volumes of non-electrolytic fluid and may suffer from fluid overload.

The most acute response is seen in the first 18 h. The response gradually decreases and by 48 to 72 h the capillaries generally heal. As permeability decreases fluid shift occurs as fluid from the tissues returns to the circulatory system. Throughout this period, urinary output should be monitored carefully and 10 to 30 ml hourly urine output should be maintained. Individual output is based on the child's age. Parenteral therapy may be decreased as the circulatory status improves and urinary output increases (Table 32-3).

Alterations of other body systems

Pulmonary Damage to the respiratory system associated with thermal injury has only recently been recognized as a major factor in morbidity of the burn patient. A burned child may exhibit respiratory involvement at the time of the injury, in connection with the acute burn shock response, or as a later complication during the post-injury course.

Direct respiratory damage at the time of injury is rare because the moist air in the respiratory

Table 32-3 Signs and symptoms of fluid deficit and overload

| | Extracellular fluid volume | | | |
| | Deficit | | Excess | |
	Moderate	**Severe**	**Moderate**	**Severe**
Cardiovascular	Orthostatic hypotension Tachycardia Collapsed veins Collapsing pulse	Cutaneous lividity (gray color) Hypotension Distant heart sounds Cold extremities Absent peripheral pulses	Elevated venous pressure Distention of peripheral veins Increased cardiac output Loud heart sounds Functional murmurs Bounding pulse High pulse pressure Increased pulmonary second sound Gallop	Pulmonary edema
Tissue signs	Soft, small tongue with longitudinal wrinkling Decreased skin turgor	Atonic muscles Sunken eyes	Subcutaneous pitting edema Basilar rales	Anasarca Moist rales Vomiting Diarrhea
Metabolism	Mild decrease in temperature (97–99°F)	Marked decrease in temperature (95–98°F)	None	None

tract dissipates the heat and has a cooling effect. However, indirect respiratory damage due to lack of oxygen in the burning environment may result in severe respiratory damage or death, even in cases where minimal or no cutaneous injury is present. Also, when victims are trapped in enclosed spaces such as automobiles or trailers, toxic fumes from burning materials can cause damage to their respiratory tract. Singed nares or facial hair, sooty tongue, blistering of the oral mucosa, or signs of products of combustion in the sputum should be observed by the nurse and are strong indicators of respiratory involvement. Since initial post-burn x-rays are frequently negative, repeated x-rays are indicated when a patient is suspected of having respiratory damage.

During the initial post-burn period, decreased circulating blood resulting in hypovolemic shock and shunting of unoxygenated blood can cause alterations in the child's respiratory status. Signs of early respiratory compromise include shallow, rigid breathing, disorientation, restlessness, and copious mucus secretions. Treatment should be aimed at increasing alveolar oxygen, increasing the ability of the lung to utilize available oxygen, and minimizing tissue oxygen requirements. Thus, humidified oxygen and gentle frequent suctioning are indicated. Careful precautions should be taken to avoid aspiration of oral intake or vomitus. If not monitored carefully, fluid therapy at this time can result in pulmonary edema. The importance of maintaining adequate fluid replacement while monitoring the acid-base balance and avoiding fluid overload must be stressed. If facial and neck edema are present or expected, early intubation should be considered. Such early intubation may avoid the necessity of emergency tracheotomy with accompanying risk of infection. Pain and thick, binding eschar (dead, burned tissue) may also inhibit adequate ventilation.

The patient should be made as comfortable as possible and reassured. There remains much controversy concerning the use of pain medications in children. Some institutions administer intravenous analgesics. Others believe that such analgesics alter cardiac and respiratory functioning and are contraindicated. The nurse should be familiar with the philosophy of her or his institution. It is imperative, however, that all such analgesics be administered intravenously rather than intramuscularly. During increased capillary permeability and edema, medications administered intramuscularly pool in the tissue. Upon fluid shift, such medications then enter the circulatory system and can result in severe overdose or death.

If the eschar, which is frequently leathery and binding, is a circumferential band around the chest wall, escharotomy should be considered. An escharotomy involves a surgical incision through the eschar only to release pressure. Because the incision goes only through the destroyed tissue, the patient experiences no pain and bleeding should be minimal.

Forced immobility and sepsis are two frequent causes of respiratory distress during the later post-burn course. To counter the immobility, turning, coughing, and deep breathing as well as active and passive exercises and early ambulation are done to improve ventilation. Infection control mandates the use of both topical and systemic antibiotics and aseptic technique including gloves, gown, mask, and sterile linens.

Renal A variety of renal changes are associated with burn injury. Such changes can be permanent or temporary. Initial decrease in glomerular filtration rate which results from hypovolemia and renal vasoconstriction have been discussed previously. Permanent renal damage can result in a patient with a history of past renal disease, or in the very young child if fluid replacement is not adequate. The most frequent causes of such renal damage are hypovolemia and the circulating byproducts of muscle necrosis and red blood cell destruction. While adequate fluid resuscitation is vital, osmolarity should be monitored. For example, increased urine output accompanied by increased specific gravity may indicate renal damage rather than inadequate fluid resuscitation. In such cases further fluid resuscitation will result only in fluid overload to the circulatory system with little assistance to the kidneys. Mannitol may be administered as an osmotic diuretic. Occasionally renal dialysis is necessary.[8]

Glycosuria may be seen during the first week post-burn. This condition is usually part of the overall physiological stress response to the trauma. Such glycosuria is usually accompanied by release of catecholamines and altered insulin response which allows the carbohydrate metabolism to shift from energy storage to utilization. Assessment of glucose metabolism through blood and urine testing in the patient is essential for proper burn management. Although glycosuria usually clears spontaneously, administration of insulin, fluid replacement, and dietary management must be considered in care planning.

Urinary tract infection is a potential complication following a serious burn. The child's defenses are weakened and frequently a urinary catheter is in place. Scrupulous care of the perineal area and removal of the catheter as soon as the circulatory status has stabilized are indicated.

Gastrointestinal Gastric dilatation and paralytic ileus usually occur early in the post-injury period, but the nurse should observe for signs of gastric distress throughout the recovery period. Stress ulcers, frequently referred to as *Curlings ulcers*, are also associated with burn trauma and are similar to acute stress ulcers seen in the general hospital population. The nurse must be alert for: (1) unexplained falling hematocrit, (2) distended abdomen, (3) occult blood in the stool (black stools), and (4) brown or red returns from the nasogastric tube.

For large burns in children it is often wise to insert a nasogastric tube attached to suction. Such a tube will prevent vomiting and aspiration, increase the child's comfort, and allow for easier, more accurate examination of the abdomen. It will also help prevent the common complications of gastric dilatation and paralytic ileus. An antacid regimen is usually initiated by mouth or nasogastric tube. Antacids are frequently prescribed every 2 h and alternated with milk or tube feedings so that something is given every hour. Knowledge that prophylaxis is the best treatment for Curlings ulcer will assist the nurse in realizing the importance of adhering to the time schedules for administering such medication. After adequate fluid resuscitation and return of bowel sounds, the NG tube is removed.

Integumentary healing

Following the initial shock response, capillaries begin to heal, edema is reabsorbed, and damaged tissue can be distinguished from living tissue. Epithelization begins and fibroblasts appear. At this point four main processes of wound healing begin: (1) separation of dead tissue (eschar), (2) regeneration of connective tissue and vasculature, (3) epithelization, and (4) contraction.[9]

Eschar separation occurs primarily by natural separation, surgical removal, or infection. Bacteria speed separation of eschar, but they also damage underlying tissue. After the eschar has separated, blood vessels redevelop in the wound. Fibroblasts, microphages, and collagens begin to form. New collagen tissue formation begins at the edge of the wound, slowly advancing for total coverage. In third degree injury, this process is slow. New tissue formed in the center of the wound is of poor quality and the wound requires surgical grafting.

Scar formation presents additional problems for the severely burned. As collagen advances it thickens and then shrinks, causing contractures. Although grafting eliminates contractures, good nursing care is also essential in contracture prevention. Splints applied properly to maintain the joints in positions of function are essential. Elastic pressure garments also help eliminate some of the thickening of the scar tissue. If contractures do develop, surgical release is frequently necessary. The nurse should remember that frequently a scar may not "mature" until 8 to 12 months after the injury. The patient is discharged with splints and pressure garments which must be reassessed and refitted during regular clinic visits.

Excessive scar formation (*hypertrophic scarring*) may also occur after a burn and presents special cosmetic problems for the burned child. Prevention of inflammation and full-thickness skin grafts may eliminate much hypertrophic scarring. However, in some cases surgery is again required. Hypertrophic scarring should not be confused with keloid formation. *Keloids* are large elevated masses of connective tissue which develop in certain individuals in spite of optimum medical and nursing care. While hypertrophic scars soften and decrease in time, keloids continue to grow unless treated with hormones or surgery.

Therapy

First Aid

The initial step in first aid for burns is to stop the burning process. This involves separating the person from the heat source by smothering flames and breaking the electric current. Then all smoldering clothing and such articles such as metal belt buckles or rings, which retain heat, should be removed. If clothing adheres to the skin, it should be dampened to extinguish any heat and left in place for removal at the hospital. With small surface burns the affected part is immersed in cool water. Specific first aid for chemical and electrical burns has been discussed previously. As a final step the victim should be wrapped in clean sheets for transport to a physician or hospital.

After these steps are taken, *minor burns* can be treated by washing the wound with a solution of mild soap and peroxide or, sterile saline, or both. The area may then be allowed to heal exposed or a sterile sheet of fine mesh gauze may be applied, held in place with a light bandage dressing. In selected cases, topical antibacterial ointment such as ampicillin is applied to the wound, but this is not routinely indicated. The parents of the burned child may wash and dress the wound at home on a daily basis, depending upon the area of the body involved and the amount of drainage. However, the dressing should be changed every 3 days by a professional, in order to observe healing or signs of infection.

A brief medical history including allergies, immunization record, last tetanus immunization, and relevant medical conditions is important for treatment. If tetanus immunization is not current (within 3 years), then prophylactic tetanus toxoid must be administered upon admission. Medical conditions such as diabetes, hypertension, and allergies will affect treatment plans and decisions concerning the necessity of hospitalization.

For more serious burns, more extensive measures should be taken. In the young child, second-degree burns over 15 percent, deep second- and third-degree injury, third-degree burns over 2 percent, or burns of the face, neck, hands, and feet usually require hospitalization. In addition, burn patients with fractures, respiratory involvement, electrical burns, and such preexisting conditions as renal disease or diabetes should be initially admitted.[10] See Table 32-4.

Acute care

Upon admission to the hospital, edema must be anticipated and preventive measures taken to ensure *adequate ventilation* with all major burns or burns of the face and neck. Endotracheal tubes, if inserted early, may prevent the need for subsequent tracheostomy. Suction equipment and humidified oxygen should be available.

Fluid resuscitation is a major consideration in the acute care phase of treatment. *Intravenous therapy* is directed toward maintaining the cardiocirculatory system. If possible a large vessel in an unburned area should be selected for the cutdown to avoid contamination and possible sepsis. Formulas for fluid resuscitation vary from institution to institution and the nurse should be familiar with the protocol in the hospital. Most formulas involve some calculation of percent of burn and body weight in kilograms. Colloids such as blood, plasma, and albumin are usually avoided during the first 24 h when vascular damage is greatest since colloids leak from the vascular space. Lactated Ringers is often the solution of choice. A formula of 3 ml of fluid per combined percentage of second- and third-degree burn multiplied by the child's weight in kilograms is a useful formula for calculating the total fluid needs for the first 24 h. (All burns over 40 percent are calculated at 40 percent, and no higher.) One half of this calculated amount is administered during the first 8 h after the burn. One-fourth of the total calculated fluid needs is then administered during the second and third 8-h periods. It is important that fluid replacement calculations be based on the time of injury, and not on the time of admission to the hospital. See Table 32-5.

During the second 24 h, fluid replacement includes addition of colloid solution or plasma. The total amount of solution needed during the second 24-h period is usually about one-half of the amount of solution calculated for the first 24-h period. This calculated amount is admin-

Table 32-4 Steps in acute care of a child with a large burn

1. Adequate airway
2. IV therapy—fluid resuscitation
3. Nasogastric tube inserted
4. Output monitored—catheter inserted
5. Pain control
6. Tetanus toxoid given if needed
7. Measures for infection control
8. Weight
9. Emotional support for child and family

Table 32-5 Fluid replacement formula*

Figuring fluid amount

3 ml × kg body weight × percent of combined 2d- and 3d-degree injury up to 40% = total 24-h fluid needs

Example:
3 ml × 30 kg × 40% = 3600 ml

Figuring rate of administration

½ First 8 h 1800 ml	¼ Second 8 h 900 ml	¼ Third 8 h 900 ml

* With permission of Shriners Burns Institute, Cincinnati, Ohio.

istered throughout the second 24-h period unless an alteration in urinary output indicates a need to increase or decrease fluid therapy. Sodium, potassium, and chlorides are also added. Subsequent fluid replacement depends upon the physiological response of the child and complications. Anemia may occur as a response to red blood cell breakdown. Blood specimens should be obtained to determine hematocrit, hemoglobin, and blood urea nitrogen (BUN) as well as type and cross matching for transfusions.

Also at the time of admission, a Foley catheter is inserted. Hourly vital signs and urinary output should be monitored to evaluate the adequacy of fluid replacement. Children's hourly output should be 5 to 10 ml under 1 year of age, 10 to 20 ml between 1 and 10 years old, and 15 to 30 ml from 10 to adulthood.[11] Urine specimens are obtained for pH, sugar, and acetone levels. A nasogastric tube inserted and attached to suction has been discussed as useful in avoiding gastric distress.

During the admission procedure the wound is washed with a solution of saline, peroxide, and mild detergent. For larger burns, when equipment is available, wound cleansing may be more effectively done in a whirlpool tank. A gentle washing technique should be used to remove loose skin and foreign materials. Following a complete cleansing and rinsing, a more accurate assessment of the extent of burn is possible, and if necessary alterations are made in fluid therapy. All solutions used for wound care should be warmed to body temperature. The importance of strict aseptic technique throughout the admission procedure must be stressed.

Infection

In a thermal injury, the skin, which is the body's first line of defense against infection, has been destroyed. During the overwhelming stress response, the immunological response of the body is taxed to the extreme, and infection is a major enemy of the burned child. Maintaining the overall physiological status of the child through optimum nursing and medical care assists the body in resisting infection. It is practically impossible to maintain a sterile burn wound. Common organisms which may colonize the burn wound are *Candida, Staphylococcus aureus, Streptococcus, Providencia stuartii,* and *Pseudomonas*. Although antibiotic therapy has made great advances in controlling burn wound infection during the past decade, resistant strains of organisms have developed. Therefore, prophylaxis through meticulous nursing care is still essential. Penicillin is often given on admission as a prophylactic against *Streptococcus* and *Staphylococcus* organisms, which are normal skin flora. Routine wound cultures done twice weekly for organism identification and antibiotic sensitivity are useful in determining the antimicrobial of choice. Many commercial antimicrobials are available and the nurse must be aware of the indication, dosages, and routes of administration of these agents.[12]

The patient and the patient's environment are also sources of infection, since normal skin bacteria may be present in hair follicles and on unburned skin. Other patients, personnel, and equipment are also possible reservoirs for contaminants to the burned wound. Good aseptic technique, prevention of cross-contamination, support of the patient's immune system, and constant monitoring for bacterial growth in wounds are essential for infection control. See Table 32-6.

Wound care

There are several generally accepted goals of wound care, including: (1) minimizing infection, (2) removing dead tissue, (3) preventing conversion of partial-thickness injury to full-thickness damage, (4) allowing for drainage from the wound, (5) preparing the wound for homografting and autografting, and (6) decreasing the severity of scars and contractures.

There are two major types of dressing procedures: exposed, or open, and closed. With the *open method*, after careful cleansing, the wound is left exposed to the air, but a dry, cool, clean environment is necessary. A crust forms over the wound that serves as a protective layer for underlying tissue and prevents bacterial growth. This method may be modified by the topical application of antimicrobial ointments or creams applied either directly on the wound or impregnated in fine mesh gauze.

When the *closed method* is used, again the wound must be carefully cleaned and rinsed prior to each dressing application. At least twice daily the wound is thoroughly cleaned of all exudate, creams, and ointments and the wound examined visually. After washing and rinsing and before applying the dressing, routine (twice a week) cultures should be obtained to determine a sensitivity profile for selection of topical antibiotics. Cleansing is done at the bedside with sterile basins of washing solution previously described or in a whirlpool tank. Manual debridement should be done at this time, and all loose eschar removed. A single layer of gauze, impregnated with the topical agent of choice, is applied to the wound. A useful hint for the application of topical agents is to use fine-mesh gauze for impregnating with ointments and coarse-mesh gauze for creams. The wound is then wrapped with coarse-gauze bandage in several layers to absorb drainage and protect the wound. When the impregnated gauze layer is applied, it should not be wrapped circumferentially around the extremity or trunk. If wrapped circumferentially, as edema forms or drainage saturates the gauze and dries, constriction may result with circulatory impairment. Rather, vertical strips should be placed next to each other, avoiding both overlapping of strips

Table 32-6 General factors associated with development of wound infections

Depressed cellular and humoral host resistance factors
Recurrent or remote infection
Malnutrition
Prolonged preoperative hospitalization
Obesity
Shock
Antibiotic therapy preceding operation
Certain chemotherapy such as cytotoxic drugs and steroids
Extremes of age
Certain diseases such as diabetes mellitus, advanced malignant disease, lupus erythematosus

and contact with unburned tissue. The gauze should be cut to match the approximate surface of the wound, because topical agents may cause irritation to healthy skin. Mesh may be used as a final layer to secure the dressing in place.

There are several commercially available topical agents. The agent chosen should not cause electrolyte imbalance, should present minimal discomfort to the patient, and should promote eschar separation as well as have antimicrobial effects. The following are representative of accepted agents in burn care.

Silvadene (silver sulfadiazine), a recognized silver substance in a water-soluble cream base, is an effective inhibitor of gram-negative, gram-positive, and *Candida albicans* organisms. Its mode of action is on the cell wall and membrane. Advantages include little delay in eschar separation, no pain or burning on application, and no known electrolyte imbalance. It is applied directly to the wound by "buttering" or may be impregnated in coarse mesh gauze (Fig. 32-3).

Sulfamylon (mafenide acetate) is also used as a topical antimicrobial. It is effective against gram-positive and gram-negative organisms, diffusing through the eschar for infection control. It is usually applied twice daily and thoroughly removed before reapplication. Because Sulfamylon is a carbonic anhydrase inhibitor, the renal buffering system may be inhibited. When used on patients with respiratory impairment, care should be taken to observe for acid-base imbalance. Patients may complain of stinging when the cream is initially applied. In addition some patients may develop a rash which should be noted and reported. The method of application is as discussed for Silvadene. Care should be taken with all topicals to avoid contact with healthy skin.

Betadine (povidone-iodine) has broad-spectrum germicidal action against common organisms. It is nonirritating, does not block air from the site of application, and easily washes off skin and natural fibers. It has the advantage of being available in an assortment of forms, such as ointments, solutions, sprays, foam, and swabs. The foam form is especially convenient for the nurse as it is water-soluble, adheres and conforms to the shape of the wound, and has little runoff while providing protection. Betadine is applied topically in a manner consistent with the form selected and a dressing may be applied.

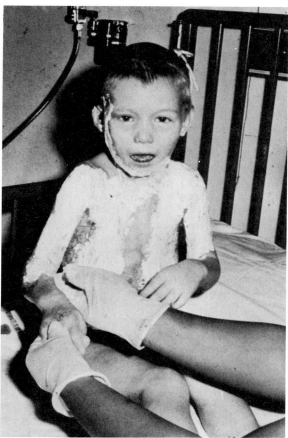

Figure 32-3 Application of silver sulfadiazine to the burned wound of a child with a 50 percent burn. (*Source: G. Scipien, et al., Comprehensive Pediatric Nursing, 2d ed., McGraw-Hill Book Co., New York, 1979, p. 971 Used with permission of publisher.*)

As with other topicals, the wound should be washed once or twice daily and fresh povidone-iodine applied.

Silver nitrate is a liquid which is applied to the burn wound as a continuous wet dressing, similar to saline soaks. The silver ion is considered bacteriocidal, but the solution can only penetrate 1 to 2 cm of burn eschar and is not effective on already deeply colonized wounds. Since the dressing must remain saturated, several layers of gauze dressing are saturated and held in place by stretch gauze wrap. While the patient is usually very comfortable with this solution, evaporative heat loss from the wet dressing is a problem. The child should be covered with a blanket to minimize heat loss and bed linens should be changed as they become wet. Children should be monitored carefully for loss of sodium and potassium ions and supplements given by mouth or intravenously, as tolerated. This type of dressing is especially tedious for the nurse. The child's bed must be kept dry while the dressings are kept saturated to avoid drying and concentration of the silver ion on the skin. In addition, the solution stains everything with which it comes in contact black. Walls, uniforms, and linens should be protected as special stain removers are required.

Gentamicin is a wide spectrum antibiotic and provides highly effective topical treatment in primary and secondary bacterial infections of the skin. Bacteria susceptible to the agent include sensitive strains of streptococci (including group A beta hemolytic), *Pseudomonas*, and *Klebsiella*. It is a bactericidal agent and has the same advantages as silver sulfadiazine. It may be buttered directly onto the wound or may be applied by application of impregnated fine-mesh gauze.

Surgical procedures (excision and grafting)

Removal of eschar is essential for ultimate wound closure, and the decision may be made to surgically remove (excise) the eschar rather than wait for natural sloughing. Such surgical excision may improve mortality risks, facilitate early rehabilitation, and decrease total hospitalization. Removal of eschar may be done by the nurse at the bedside or in the whirlpool tank, but only that tissue which can be removed with limited

Figure 32-4 Mesh dermatome reduces the size of the tissue needed for grafting by making slits to allow expansion of the graft. (*Used with permission of Shriners Burn Institute, Cincinnati, Ohio.*)

bleeding should be removed. Blunt, sterile scissors are used to clip away devitalized tissue. A gentle scrubbing motion is also effective in removing eschar. Aggressive scrubbing or probing with scissors and forceps is unnecessary and may damage the underlying wound bed, which is important for grafting.

Extensive removal of eschar is done in the operating room under anesthesia. Excision includes all deep dermal and full-thickness burned tissue down to the normal tissue layer. Because blood loss may be extensive during surgery, transfusions are often indicated on the day of surgery. The nurse should thus be aware of the risks, complications, and needs of the patient related to use of blood products.

If possible, the wound is closed with autografts at the same time that excision is performed. *Autografts* are skin grafts taken from an uninjured or healthy area on the patient. Such grafts may be of partial thickness (0.010 to 0.035 in) or full thickness (greater than 0.035 in). For most areas of coverage, partial-thickness grafts are used for greater area coverage, because when full-thickness grafts are taken, the donor site itself must be grafted for closure. Full-thickness grafts are indicated for selected reconstructive cases such as hands, where tissue strength is needed, or faces, for cosmetic purposes.[13] Partial-thickness grafts are expanded by passing the tissue through a mesh dermatone. Expansion in this manner allows for added coverage when limited good tissue is available for wound closure. It also decreases the size of the donor site needed. For expansion, the mesh dermatone makes small slits in the tissue. When expanded, these small slits become small diamond-shaped openings within the sheet of tissue, making it possible to expand the skin to two to three times its original width. These small openings can then epithelize from the margins of surrounding skin. These small openings also allow for adequate drainage of serum from the wound (Figs. 32-4, 32-5, and 32-6).

Care should be taken when changing dressings on grafted areas. An accepted procedure is for no dressing change to be undertaken until 3 days after grafting. The initial dressing change on the third day is then done by the physician to examine the area for graft take. As the nurse resumes dressing change procedures, he or she must be careful not to damage epithelizing tissue.

Strict aseptic technique is continued in order to prevent infection, which can destroy the graft and result in need for another grafting procedure.

Frequently the severely burned child has limited areas available for donor sites. In such cases, homografts or heterografts are used. *Homografts* are skin taken from a person other than the patient, usually cadaver skin available through tissue banks. *Heterografts* are taken from an animal, such as a pig or dog. Pig-skin dressings are frequently encountered by the nurse. They are applied in much the same way as dressings using topical antimicrobial agents. Heterografts and homografts decrease water and electrolyte loss from the burn wound and protect the area either until it is ready for autografting or until donor sites are available. They are changed every 2 to 3 days. When the underlying tissue is pink and vascularization has occurred, the wound bed is ready for autografting.

The donor site itself represents a second-degree injury and optimal nursing care is required. At the time of surgery, the donor site is covered with a single sheet of fine-mesh gauze. This remains in place and the wound is exposed to air and allowed to dry. As the wound heals,

Figure 32-5 A piece of skin after being put through the mesh dermatome. (*Used with permission of Shriners Burn Institute, Cincinnati, Ohio.*)

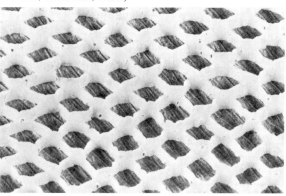

edges of the gauze will loosen and should be clipped away with scissors by the nurse. Prevention of infection and minimizing moisture and pressure on the donor site are important.

Nutritional support

Burn hypermetabolism continues to be a major concern in patient care. Evaporative water loss,

Figure 32-6 Hands showing the use of mesh autografts and progressive stages of healing. (*Used with permission of Shriners Burn Institute, Cincinnati, Ohio.*)

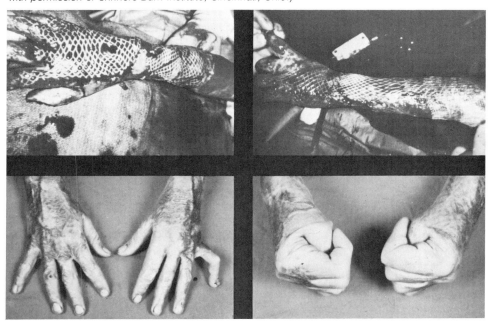

elevated temperature, and increased catecholamines may all contribute to the increased metabolic rate. The exact cause is still debated. Carbohydrates, as the main source of energy for muscle work and body heat production, are rapidly metabolized. Carbohydrate metabolism is shifted from energy storage to utilization. Body stores of fat and protein are depleted through catabolism. Post-burn dietary requirements may be two to four times that of the normal child and are essential for tissue repair and survival. A diet high in protein (150 to 200 g), calories (3000 to 5000), vitamins B and C, and iron is needed.

The nurse, dietitian, family, and patient must all be involved in meeting these requirements. The child's food likes and dislikes should be determined. Foods which taste good can be served attractively. Such in-between-meal feedings as milk shakes, ice cream, or electrolyte solutions such as Gatorade are all readily available. Nutritional supplements by feeding tube or by mouth are helpful as are supplements of vitamins and minerals. Commercially produced high-protein and high-calorie mixtures are available and may be served between meals. Such mixes tend to be hypertonic, pulling water into the gastrointestinal tract, so the nurse should observe for diarrhea. Supplemental vitamins, potassium, and calcium are frequently calculated into the nutritional regime. Total calorie intake and frequent weights are recorded. During the acute phase when edema is present, weight should be taken daily. During the healing period, the patient is weighed twice weekly to evaluate weight loss and adequacy of caloric intake. Treatments should be planned not to interfere with meal times. The nurse should make every effort to assist in conservation of the child's energy and body heat by avoiding unnecessary exposure of the burn wound, by properly applying the dressings, and by maintaining a comfortably warm environment.

Emotional Needs[14]

No matter how small the burn surface, the injury represents a change in body appearance which demands a process of adjustment. The nurse should not minimize the significance of the altered body image to the individual and should recognize the patient's attempt, over time, to deal with the alteration.

A pattern of response which can be anticipated after a burn injury has been described.[14,15] An understanding of this response helps the staff better meet the emotional needs of the child and family.

The initial response, or *impact*, is one of shock and disbelief. The child may be confused and frightened. Lack of oxygen, electrolyte imbalance, and strange surroundings all contribute to restlessness and disorientation. *Depersonalization* also occurs at this time. Often the patient perceives what is happening, but does not experience the event as happening to her or to him. The parents are also confused and frightened. They have no understanding of the severity of the illness or the expected treatment. They are overwhelmed by the many decisions which must be made. The nurse's intervention should be structured to decrease the family's anxiety. Procedures are explained to the family and child in a supportive, honest manner. Short, simple explanations are given in a calm tone. Honesty is essential as this is the beginning of the trust relationship which must develop between the staff, patient, and family.

As the shock begins to lessen, a second response, a period of *retreat* or withdrawal, may be observed. During this period a mechanism occurs whereby patient and family attempt to negate the seriousness of the situation and avoid it through repression and suppression. There is a sense of relief from this denial and it will persist until the individual is faced with reality. The nurse accepts this but does not reinforce it. Rather, the nurse presents reality in small amounts and in a supportive manner, maintaining a relationship with the child and family.

As the family begins to recognize the significance of the illness, a period of *acknowledgment* and mourning is observed. The child and family have experienced many losses and both anger and depression are common at this time. The child has lost independence, body image, and previous roles such as that of a sibling or a sixth-grader. The child must begin to assimilate the new role of patient. The nurse's acceptance of the patient will support the child's self-acceptance. Even if the burn is not fatal, the parents have lost the child as they knew him or her before the burn injury, and they may have had to give up some of the expectations they once had for the child's future. The family may experience feelings of guilt, anger, and depression, which may cause them to avoid the patient at a time when loving and caring are needed. Additional conflict may result as the staff carries out many of the functions previously performed by the family. The delegation of authority from parent to staff is often nonverbal and anxiety-provoking. The nurse should encourage the family to recognize and express their feelings. The nurse's support at this time can allow the family to maintain emotional contact with the child as the family moves toward future planning. The nurse should include the patient in the treatment plans and should be available to talk with the patient.

As these phases evolve, the family and child move toward the *reconstructive* phase. This is a time for new approaches to life. Doubts and fears of failure emerge as the patient tries new ways to manage the environment when confronted with his or her limitations. The nurse reinforces realistic goals through encouragement, acceptance, and collaborative planning.

The nurse should be aware that the burned child experiences a significant amount of both acute and chronic pain. The child's pain often has psychological implications. Chronic pain is associated with the loss of skin and exposed nerve endings. The most frequently encountered acute pain is during dressing changes and debridement. Fear, anxiety, and absence of parents often contribute to the pain response. Because pain is a subjective experience, the nurse should attempt to assess pain levels more objectively by eliciting the child's own report of pain, observing the child's behavior, and assessing preinjury behavior patterns. For care of the child in pain, see Chap. 21.

While little can be done to make such painful procedures as dressings, debridements, whirlpools, and physical therapy pleasant, there are steps the nurse can take to help the child. Explaining the procedure and its purpose may decrease anxiety. Skilled nursing care and removing the dressing as quickly and comfortably as possible are also important. Supporting the child in both the expression of feelings and allowing the child to participate in debridement and dressing removal give the child a feeling of some control over what is happening to him or her and a sense of importance.[16]

Play therapy is especially helpful in a pediatric burn unit. Play can be classified as therapeutic or diversional, and both are useful. Diversional play allows relaxation as children pass long weeks of hospitalization. Therapeutic play is more structured and serves several purposes: (1) expression of feelings such as aggression and fear; (2) clarification of distorted perceptions; (3) assessment of the child's emotional developmental level and degree of regression; (4) stimulation; and (5) preparation of the child for discharge.

To meet the emotional needs of the child and family, the nurse must be in touch with her or his own feelings. Caring for children with burns is emotionally difficult. Nurses frequently see their role as one of helping others, relieving distress, and returning the patient to society. Providing nursing care to burned children includes performing nursing care procedures which result in pain. The child may be discharged with scars and a future of further reconstructive surgery. In severe burns, death is an ever-present threat. The patient care team forms a mutual support group where feelings can be shared and accepted. Through such support and acceptance of their own feelings, the burn team can assist the family and child to reach optimal physical and emotional rehabilitation.

Good emotional care includes observing, assessing, interacting, and intervening. In some units a mental health team comprised of nurse, psychiatrist, physical therapist, and social worker may be formed. In other units, a mental health specialist is available for consultation. In all settings the nurse must remember that good emotional support is not the responsibility of one individual. It is the responsibility of all who come in contact with the child and family.

Rehabilitation

Rehabilitation begins early in the nursing process with the goal of returning the child to society with optimal physical, social, and emotional adjustment. If allowed to heal without proper positioning, exercises, and splinting, a third-degree burn can cause complete immobilization of a joint in a nonfunctional position which requires surgical release.[17]

Early mobilization is one of the best methods of preventing many complications. Active and passive exercises are used to strengthen the patient and maintain joint function. An excellent time to perform such exercises is during tubbing

Figure 32-7 Demonstrating the use of neck and elbow splints to prevent further contractures in a child with a 50 percent burn. (*Source: G. Scipien, et al., Comprehensive Pediatric Nursing, 2d ed., McGraw-Hill, 1979, New York, p. 977. Used with permission of publisher.*)

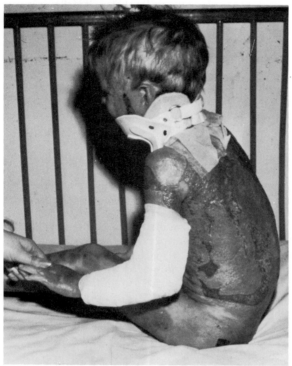

ing if it is allowed to be stuffed in a bag of toys or in the bedside table rather than worn by the child (Fig. 32-7).

Some of the frequently encountered problems which face the family at discharge are itching, appearance of the scar, unhealed wound tissue, and splints and braces. The scar may be rough and red; as the scar matures over time this usually decreases. Itching and flaking of the scar should be discussed with the parents. Scratching can damage the tissue and cause infection. Mild cream can be applied at home and massaged into the tissue. It will help eliminate itching and soften the scar.[18]

There may be small unhealed areas when the

Figure 32-8 Contractures resulting from inadequate follow-up care after a 50 percent burn. The photograph was taken 2 years after injury. (*Source: G. Scipien, et al., Comprehensive Pediatric Nursing, 2d ed., McGraw-Hill New York, 1979, p. 13 Used with permission of publisher.*)

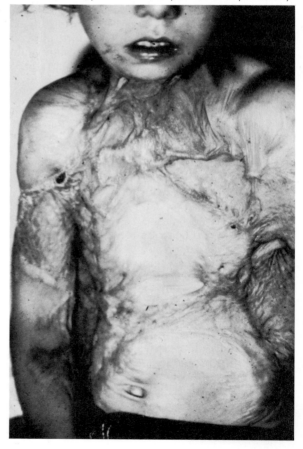

procedures. The soothing action and added buoyancy of the water help the patient exercise with less pain. Passive exercises are performed by the nurse, physical therapist, and parents during early hospitalization. As the wound is grafted and heals, the patient can assume more active exercise. Children are encouraged to exercise as they watch television. Such gross motor activities as ball throwing or gymnastic-type games also provide exercise and social stimulation. Formal exercise must be done at least twice a day.

Individually fitted splints and braces help maintain joint function. Some will be worn 24 h a day, removed only for washing, dressings, and exercise. Others are used when in bed or out of bed, depending on the purpose of the device. The nurse must see that these appliances are applied in the correct manner and at the times specified. A well-made splint accomplishes noth-

Figure 32-9 Molded hand splint demonstrated on therapist. (*Used with permission of Shriners Burn Institute, Cincinnati, Ohio.*)

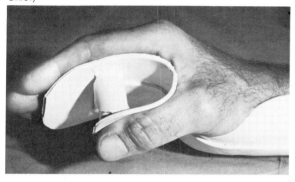

child is discharged, and a small dressing may be needed. Optimal cleansing and bathing should be stressed. A few days prior to discharge the person who will be responsible for the child's home care should come to the unit and begin performing these activities with the staff present for support and guidance. Parents are also instructed in the proper fit and application of splints and braces. They are encouraged to report any problems to the unit or physician.

Even with optimal care, some dysfunction or cosmetic problems cannot be prevented and surgery is necessary. This is especially true in children where scar tissue growth may not coincide with muscular skeletal development (Fig. 32-8). The scar is often allowed to mature 1 year before surgery is performed. The patient should understand at discharge the need for future surgical admissions. Most surgical contracture releases involve excision of the scar and inlay of a graft. Splints, molded appliances to maintain position, and special braces may be necessary for a short period following surgery to maintain the functional position obtained.[19] See Fig. 32-9.

As the child matures physical deformities will present unique problems at each phase of growth and development. Adjustment to school requires collaboration with the child, family, teacher, and school system. Adolescence brings preoccupation with physical attributes and social service agencies should be active to prevent psychological maladjustment. In addition, physical growth spurts and sexual development may necessitate surgery. If a child's chest wall has been extensively burned with resulting inelastic scar tissues, surgical release may be necessary for breast development.

The goal of rehabilitating the patient to assume his or her place as an optimally functioning member of society is the responsibility of all members of the burn team. Collaboration with the patient, family, community agencies, and family physician should be ongoing.[20,21]

References

1. James Crouch, and J. Robert McClentic, *Human Anatomy and Physiology*, 2d ed., Wiley, New York, 1976, p. 212.
2. Lucille Whaley and Donna Wong, *Nursing Care of Infants and Children*, Mosby, St. Louis, 1979, p. 258.
3. B. MacMillan, "Burns in Children," *Clinics in Plastic Surgery* 1(4):633–644 (October 1974).
4. Florence Greenhouse Jacoby, *Nursing Care of the Patient with Burns*, Mosby, St. Louis, 1972, p. 100.
5. Ibid., p. 89.
6. Ibid., p. 95.
7. Jacoby, *The Burn Patient: Management and Operating Room Support*, Ethicon, p. 6.
8. Wetald Rudowski et al., *Burn Therapy and Research*, Johns Hopkins, Baltimore, 1976.
9. Thomas Hunt, *Mechanisms of Repair and Spontaneous Healing*, Reprint, undocumented source.
10. Jacoby, *The Burn Patient: Management and Operating Room Support*, p. 5.
11. Rosanne Howard and Nancie Herbold, *Nutrition in Clinical Care*, McGraw-Hill, New York, 1978, p. 534.
12. Hiram Polk and Harlan N. Stine, *Hospital-Acquired Infections in Surgery*, University Park Press, Baltimore, 1977, pp. 39–50.
13. Ada K. Jacox, *Pain: A Source Book for Nurses and Other Health Professionals*, Little, Brown, Boston, 1977, pp. 391–403.
14. The author acknowledges the assistance of Connie Ragiel, M.S.N., in reviewing this portion of the manuscript.
15. Jacoby, *The Burn Patient: Management and Operating Room Support*, p. 24.
16. Jane M. Lee, "Emotional Reactions to Trauma," *Nursing Clinics of North America* 5(4): 577–587 (December 1970).
17. Jacoby, *Nursing Care of the Patient with Burns*, p. 74.
18. Jean Stoddard, "Rehabilitation of the Burn-Injured Patient," *Critical Care Quarterly* 1:30–33 (December 1978).
19. Jacoby, pp. 90–97.
20. Hunt, loc. cit.
21. Stoddard, op. cit., pp. 30–33.
22. The author acknowledges the assistance of Arlene Church Miller in the preparation of the Nursing Care Plan.

Nursing Care Plan–Burn

Patient: Joey M. **Age:** 2 years **Date of Admission:** 1/15 10:30 A.M.

Assessment

Joey M., 2 years old, was burned 3 days ago when his older sibling threw gasoline on burning trash. The flames quickly ignited the front of Joey's sweater. The child's parents immersed him in cool water immediately and summoned an ambulance.

Upon arrival at the emergency room (ER), Joey was crying with pain and he was obviously frightened. Both parents were distraught. Loud wheezing was audible (without the aid of a stethoscope) between Joey's sobs. Since Joey had burns around his head and neck, an endotracheal tube was immediately inserted to ensure a patent airway. An intravenous cut-down was performed in an unaffected lower-extremity and a Ringer's lactate infusion was initiated. Joey's weight was 28 lb (12.7 kg) on admission to the ER. Vital signs were stable and within normal limits.

The physicians determined that Joey's burns covered 35 percent of his body. He had second-degree burns on his face, ears, neck, upper anterior trunk, parts of both upper and lower arms, and both hands. He also suffered third-degree burns on both upper and lower arms and on a small portion of the anterior trunk (see burn evaluation chart). Fluid resuscitation and wound treatment were started in the ER. Before Joey was transferred to the pediatric unit, a central venous pressure line, a nasogastric tube, and a Foley catheter were inserted.

Joey responded well to therapy, and diuresis began 51 h postburn. His weight is now $29\frac{1}{2}$ lb (13.4 kg). Much of the facial and neck edema that resulted from his burns has subsided, but some periocular edema remains. He has full range of motion of his neck. Joey's endotracheal tube and Foley catheter were removed 24 h ago. His respirations are regular at 28 to 30 per min. Scattered bilateral wheezing is audible upon auscultation. His other vital signs are stable and within normal limits. Joey's bowel sounds returned 44 h postburn, and the nasogastric tube was removed 12 h later. Full range of motion of burned extremities can be elicited during dressing changes. Joey is generally cooperative, but he protests vigorously during dressing changes. Partial thickness skin grafts will be applied to areas that suffered third-degree burns. This surgery will be performed in approximately 4 days.

Joey lives with his parents, his $3\frac{1}{2}$-year-old brother, and his 5-year-old sister. Prior to his injury, Joey was in good health and demonstrated growth and development appropriate for his age. His immunizations are up to date, and he has no known drug sensitivities or allergies. He has not had any communicable diseases. There is no family history of heart disease or diabetes mellitus. At least one of Joey's parents has remained at his bedside since admission.

Burn Evaluation Chart

Area	% TBSA*	% Burned 2°	% Burned 3°
Head	17	5	0
Neck	2	1.5	0
Anterior trunk	13	6.5	4
Right upper arm	4	2	2
Left upper arm	4	2	2
Right lower arm	3	1.5	1.5
Left lower arm	3	1	2
Right hand	2.5	2	0
Left hand	2.5	2	0

* Represents percentage of total body surface area in a child between the ages of 1 and 4 years of age.

Nursing diagnosis	Nursing goals	Nursing actions	Evaluation/revision
1. Potential ineffective breathing pattern related to neck and facial edema and to restricted chest expansion	☐ Respiratory rate between 28 and 32 per min ☐ Clear breath sounds ☐ Symmetrical chest movements during respirations ☐ Skin and mucous mem-	☐ Monitor respiratory rate and rhythm q1h and record ☐ Auscultate lungs q1h; note abnormal sounds (rales, rhonchi, wheezing) ☐ Nasal and oropharyn-	☐ Respiratory rate stable; averages 28–30 per min ☐ Wheezing substantially diminished in last 24 h; faint bilateral scattered wheezing audible upon ausculta-

898

Nursing diagnosis	Nursing goals	Nursing actions	Evaluation/revision
	branes in unaffected areas will remain pink	geal suction, PRN; notify physician if Joey requires tracheal suctioning to remove secretions ☐ Observe for labored breathing, hoarseness, stridor, restlessness, paradoxical chest movement, cyanosis, sudden high fever ☐ Notify physician of abnormal breathing patterns ☐ Keep oropharyngeal airway, endotracheal tube and oxygen at bedside	tion only; Joey is able to cough effectively ☐ *Continue plan*
2. Impairment of skin integrity related to second and third degree thermal burns	☐ Burn wounds will heal (revascularization and reepithelialization)	☐ Wound care: **a.** Continuous wet AgNO$_3$ dressings to arms and anterior trunk; redress q8h (9 A.M., 5 P.M., and 1 A.M.) and re-wet q8h (1 P.M., 9 P.M. and 5 A.M.) **b.** Silver sulfadiazine and gauze dressing to face, neck and hands q8h (9A.M., 5 P.M. and 1 A.M.) ☐ Meticulous care of face, eyes, ears, and hands ☐ Handle wounds gently ☐ Avoid pressure by frequent turning and positioning ☐ Observe and record appearance of wounds at each dressing change ☐ Administer sedative or analgesic, as ordered, prior to dressing changes ☐ Carry out actions for "potential infection," specified in 4, below	☐ Even blood supply observed during dressing changes
	☐ Joey's ears will return to normal appearance	☐ Apply warm wet compresses to ears, as specified by physician ☐ Use sufficient layers of gauze to separate skin layers and facilitate drainage ☐ Examine ears q8h; observe pinna for edema, tenderness, pain, and redness ☐ Position Joey to prevent pressure on ears	☐ Ears are returning to normal appearance; some edema and redness remain ☐ *Continue plan*
3. Pain related to second-degree burns	☐ Joey will obtain sufficient relief from pain, enabling him to: **a.** Sleep at least 4 continuous h	☐ Observe frequently for signs of pain (irritability, crying, and "guarding" of affected areas)	☐ Acetaminophen elixir, 120 mg, appears effective; requires medication q5–6 h;

Nursing diagnosis	Nursing goals	Nursing actions	Evaluation/revision
	b. Perform active range of motion exercises **c.** Withstand dressing changes	☐ Administer analgesic, PRN, as ordered ☐ Coordinate administration of analgesic with dressing changes whenever possible; administer medication approximately 1 h prior to treatment	☐ Falls asleep within 45 min after receiving medication ☐ *Continue plan*
4. Potential infection related to thermal burns	☐ Burn wounds will remain free of infection	☐ Use strict aseptic technique; sterile gown, gloves, mask ☐ Employ reverse isolation ☐ Explain reason for precautions to parents ☐ Teach parents how to don and discard gown, gloves, and mask ☐ Wound care as specified ☐ Culture wound twice a week ☐ Prevent Joey from touching and picking at wounds and dressing ☐ Change soiled dressings immediately ☐ Administer antibiotic as prescribed by physician	☐ No exudate observed in wounds ☐ *Continue plan*
5. Potential fluid volume deficit related to burn sequelae	☐ Vital signs within normal limits as evidenced by: **a.** Rectal temp between 36.7 and 38.2°C (98° and 100.9°F) **b.** Pulse between 100 and 140 per min **c.** Respirations between 28 and 32/min **d.** BP between 88/54 and 98/60 **e.** CVP between 3 and 10 cm	☐ Monitor and record vital signs and CVP q2h and record	☐ Vital signs stable during previous 24h: *Temp.:* 37.2–38.2°C (99°–100.4°F) *Pulse:* 110–122/min *Resp.:* 28–30/min *BP:* 90/56–96/60 *CVP:* 4–6 cm
	☐ 24-h fluid intake (IV/PO) equivalent to amount specified by physician	☐ Maintain IV infusion at rate specified by physician and record amount infused q1h Sips of clear liquids after removal of NG tube; increase oral intake gradually, as tolerated	☐ Intake during previous 24 h: 2450 ml (IV, 1900 ml; PO, 550 ml)
	☐ Urinary function within normal limits as evidenced by: **a** Urinary output of at least 15 ml/h **b** Urine specific gravity (SG) between 1.002 and 1.028	☐ Notify physician if hourly oral fluid intake exceeds 40 ml for 3 h; regulate IV rate accordingly ☐ Measure and record intake and output q2h ☐ Use pediatric urine collection device to obtain *accurate* output	☐ Urinary output during previous 24 h: 1934 ml

Nursing diagnosis	Nursing goals	Nursing actions	Evaluation/revision
		□ Monitor and record SG q4h	□ SG during previous 8 h: 1.007 to 1.012
	□ Return to preburn weight of 28 lb. (12.7 kg) within 4 and 10 days postburn	□ Weigh q8h (*after* dressings have been removed)	□ Weight. 13.4 kg (29½ lb) (no change in last 24 h)
		□ Observe for signs of fluid volume overload (increased CVP, marked increase in urinary output, dyspnea, rales, irritability, seizures)	
		□ Observe for signs of fluid volume deficit (decreased urinary output, thirst, dry mucous membranes, urine SG above 1.030, tachycardia, poor skin turgor)	
		□ Notify physician of abnormal signs/symptoms, PRN	□ *Continue plan*
6. Potential alteration in thermoregulation related to burn sequelae	□ Rectal temp stable between 36.7 and 38.2°C (98° and 100.9°F)	□ Monitor rectal temp. q2h and record	□ Temperature stable during previous 24 h, ranging between 36.7 and 38.7° C (99° and 100.4°F)
		□ Observe for shivering, excessive diuresis	
		□ Warm AgNO$_3$ and saline prior to dressing changes and treatments	
		□ Avoid extremes in environmental temperatures, drafts, and damp clothing or linens	
		□ Maintain adequate calorie intake	
		□ Notify physician of temperature liability	□ *Continue plan*
7. Impaired mobility related to burn injury	□ Full range of joint motion in upper extremities and fingers	□ Encourage active motion of fingers and arms during waking hours	□ Joey demonstrates full range of motion in fingers while eating and at play; full range of wrist, elbow and shoulder elicited during dressing changes
		□ Encourage Joey to feed himself	
		□ Play games requiring use of arms and hands at least qid (Joey likes "Inky-Dinky Spider" and "Simon Says")	
		□ Passive range of motion exercises tid, during dressing changes (9 A.M., 5 P.M., 1 A.M.)	
		□ Splint hands in position of function when asleep. Bandage fingers carefully, preventing contact between skin surfaces. Tell Joey that the bandages are like "big mittens"	□ *Continue plan*

Nursing diagnosis	Nursing goals	Nursing actions	Evaluation/revision
8. Potential nutritional deficit related to burn sequelae	☐ Oral intake of at least 1980 Kcal per 24 h ☐ Protein intake of at least 73 g per 24 h ☐ Return to preburn weight within 4 to 10 days postburn, with maintenance of preburn weight thereafter (28 lb)	☐ Daily calorie count ☐ Daily weight and record ☐ Arrange meeting betwen Joey's mother and nutritionist to plan meals and snacks consisting of Joey's favorite foods ☐ Gradually increase diet once Joey has been able to tolerate clear liquids for 8 h ☐ Provide milk shakes, ice cream, and other high-caloric, high-protein supplements between meals and at bedtime ☐ Provide finger foods, such as hot dogs, small pieces of fruit, etc. ☐ Encourage but do not force Joey to eat ☐ Give small, frequent feedings ☐ Reward with praise when he does eat ☐ Plan care and activities to allow a rest period before and after meals ☐ Administer supplemental vitamins and iron as ordered by physician	☐ Joey's calorie intake for the last 24 h: 1650 Kcal ☐ Weight 13.4 kg (29½ lb) ☐ Joey has been taking liquids and soft foods for the last 16 h; will begin regular foods today ☐ Needs much encouragement; takes only small amounts at one time
	☐ Joey will maintain normal bowel sounds and gastrointestinal function	☐ Measure and record abdominal girth q4h ☐ Test all stools for guaiac ☐ Observe for vomiting "coffee-ground"–appearing vomitus, abdominal distention, and decreasing hematocrit and report to physician promptly ☐ Administer antacid as ordered by physician	☐ Bowel sounds returned 44 h postburn and remain audible upon auscultation ☐ Abdominal girth 55 cm; unchanged for last 48 h ☐ No BM since nasogastric tube removed ☐ *Continue plan*
9. Alteration in vision related to periocular edema	☐ Joey will return to preburn visual ability	☐ Identify self upon entering room until Joey's visual ability returns ☐ Give short, simple explanations of procedures just prior to carrying them out ☐ Irrigate eyes and instill ophthalmic ointment q4h, as prescribed ☐ Observe and record condition of periocular skin and extent of edema; note any exudate ☐ Tell Joey he will be able to see better when his eyes "open up"	☐ Eyelid edema subsiding; clear exudate easily removed by irrigation; no redness or purulent exudate ☐ Can open eyes about half-way ☐ *Continue plan*

Nursing diagnosis	Nursing goals	Nursing actions	Evaluation/revision
10. Potential separation anxiety related to injury and hospitalization	□ Joey will demonstrate behaviors expected of a toddler separated from his parents (crying, protest when parents leave, negativism)	□ Encourage rooming-in or frequent visiting by parents □ Encourage parents to participate in Joey's care when they feel ready to do so □ Minimize the number of staff caring for Joey (consistency) □ Keep all explanations simple and honest □ Provide physical contact, such as holding and rocking, as much as possible □ Allow Joey to demonstrate independence whenever appropriate (putting on slippers; selecting juice; selecting a toy for a play period, etc.) □ Expect some regressive behaviors (preference for a bottle, toilet "accidents," etc.) □ Suggest parents leave a small personal item with Joey for safe keeping until they return □ Suggest that siblings send drawings and little handmade projects to Joey □ Suggest a short visit by siblings	□ Continues to protest when parents leave and during treatments □ *Continue plan*
11. Guilt (parents and siblings) related to child's injury	□ Parents will be able to: **a.** Verbalize their feelings about Joey's injury and hospitalization **b.** Identify ways they can assist siblings to express their feelings about Joey's injury	□ Provide parents with time and privacy so they can verbalize their concerns □ Explain all treatments to parents □ Answer parents' questions honestly and patiently; refer them to physician when appropriate □ Suggest visits by grandparents or other adults who know Joey so parents can spend time with the other siblings □ Encourage parents to obtain enough sleep, to eat meals regularly, etc. □ Assure parents that nurses will be with Joey when they cannot be present □ Discuss methods of assisting siblings to express their feelings about Joey's injury **a.** Tell parents that it is nor-	□ Parents are able to discuss the accident and their feelings with nurse on one occasion; further verbalization should be ecouraged. □ Parents are willing to allow grandparents to relieve them for short periods □ Parents receptive to story telling and other methods suggested by nurse; parents verbalized intention to try suggestions

Nursing diagnosis	Nursing goals	Nursing actions	Evaluation/revision
		mal for the other siblings to feel guilty, not only because of the accident, but also because it is normal for children to "wish" that their siblings would "go away"	
		b. Suggest story telling; a parent starts a story about a child, *not* named Joey, who was accidentally hurt while playing with his brother and sister; the parent then encourages the siblings to continue the story and fill in the rest of "what happened." Explain that the parents can use a story to explain what is happening to Joey now, to assure the siblings that he will come home, how accidents can happen, etc.	
		c. Keep siblings informed about Joey's progress and his treatment (in simple terms)	
		d. Have Joey send some little items home to his siblings	
		☐ Before Joey is discharged, and when parents seem ready, introduce subject of accident prevention (do *not* blame parents); provide anticipatory teaching	☐ *Continue plan*

Chapter 33 **Immune system**

Linda Richelson

Upon completion of this chapter, the student will be able to:

1. Describe the specific function of each type of cell and tissue of the immune system.

2. Discuss the meaning of the term *antigen*.

3. Describe the body's response to antigen.

4. Distinguish between the two different types of immunity.

5. Write a plan for the early recognition and treatment of anaphylaxis.

6. Identify the pathophysiological changes commonly called asthma.

7. Distinguish between hypersensitivity and hyposensitization.

8. Describe the steps in the environmental and physical assessment of an allergic child.

Immunity and specific immunity

The immune system is the name given to the collection of cells, tissues, and organs that maintain body defenses against harmful substances. These defenses are both active and passive (see Chap. 34). Briefly, a passive defense is a physical barrier such as the skin or the hostile chemical environment of the stomach. The active defenses are the inflammatory reaction and the immune response. Related to the active defenses are the immune system's removal of worn-out "self" components (such as aged red blood cells) and its destruction of the abnormal cells that constantly arise by mutation.

Drugs, radiation, malnutrition, and illness are capable of disturbing the normal function of the immune system. An alteration can predispose the body to infection or malignant growths; it may also bring about immune system diseases.

One of the system's powerful active defenses is the *immune response*. This is a chain of reactions tailored to the unique characteristics of the harmful substance. It is therefore called a *specific defense*.

The term for a substance to which the immune system responds is *antigen*. Antigen is usually a protein but is more broadly defined as any substance capable of stimulating an immune response. It includes substances foreign to the body as well as constituents of the body that for some reason the immune system recognizes as foreign.

The steps in an immune response are: (1)

recognition of antigen, (2) production of antibody and cells prepared to attack that antigen, and (3) destruction of the antigen. Immunity against the antigen, sometimes life-long, is usually the outcome of such an immune response. Immunity is a quicker, stronger, more effective response to the same antigen if it is detected by the immune system again.

By virtue of its molecular weight and composition, each antigen is unique. One hypothesis for the mechanism underlying the immune response suggests that each antigen serves as a template (pattern) for the production of the antibody or cells capable of attacking it. This "lock and key" idea explains why each antibody fits only one antigen.

Cells, tissues, and organs of the immune system

The cellular elements serving the immune process are located throughout the body and are both fixed (attached) in tissues and floating in blood and lymph. The three most important cell types are:

1. Macrophages—cells highly specialized to ingest and destroy particulate matter by phagocytosis.
2. Lymphocytes—white blood cells that differentiate into T cells and B cells, which are the types active in immune responses. B cells produce antibody. T cells carry out direct attack on antigen.
3. Mediator cells—mast cells, basophils, and neutrophils. Platelets (cell fragments) are also included.

Table 33-1 Chemical mediators and their pharmacologic action

Mediator	Action
Histamine	Increased vascular permeability by dilation of small vessels
	Contraction of bronchiolar and other smooth muscle
	Increased gastric, nasal, and lacrimal secretions
SRS-A (slow reacting substance of anaphylaxis)	Sustained smooth muscle contraction
Serotonin	Increased vascular permeability
	Smooth-muscle contraction

Mediator cells release such chemicals as histamine, serotonin, slow-reacting substance of anaphylaxis (SRS-A), and vasoactive amines during inflammatory reactions and immune reactions (see Table 33-1).

The tissues of the immune system are:

1. Lymph—the fluid that flows through lymphatic vessels, nodules, and nodes and that carries foreign substances and T and B cells.
2. Lymph nodes—masses of lymphoid tissue surrounded by a capsule and placed in the path of lymphatic vessels so that lymph must circulate through them, where it is filtered and antigen is trapped for contact with lymphocytes.
3. Lymph nodules—tiny masses of lymphoid tissue without capsules. Nodules are scattered throughout the body, but dense collections are found near body surfaces in the submucosal tissues of the respiratory, genitourinary, and intestinal tracts. They function to trap invading particles.

Organs that serve the immune system include the following:

1. Bone marrow—produces cells destined to become T or B cells. Bone marrow is also believed to be where lymphocytes differentiate into B cells.
2. Thymus—place where lymphocytes become T cells.
3. Spleen—filtering organ of the blood, where foreign particles may be trapped for encounter with lymphocytes.

Sequence of immunologic events

An invader that penetrates the barriers of the skin, mucous membranes, and lymph nodules, or an internally arising "foreign" element, either will be eliminated by macrophages or will find itself in the lymph. Lymph flows through lymphatic vessels to lymph nodes. In the lymph nodes foreign matter (the antigen) is filtered from the lymph, trapped, held for contact with T or B lymphocytes, and phagocytized. T or B lymphocytes multiply in the lymph node after contact with the antigen. This causes the lymph node to enlarge from two to five times in size and become palpable when there is infection in the area of the node.

If the antigen escapes the lymph node, it is carried by the lymph through the thoracic duct and into the bloodstream. The blood can also be invaded directly through the capillaries and venules. The spleen, by filtering the blood, provides another arena for antigen-lymphocyte contact. Phagocytic elements in the spleen attempt to destroy the invader. The spleen is essential in the avoidance of overwhelming infection.

Two types of specific immunity

T and B lymphocytes each produce a different type of immunity. B lymphocytes, when stimulated by exposure to an antigen, differentiate into *plasma cells*, which produce antibody specific to the antigen. Other B lymphocytes that have encountered this antigen divide to produce a population of identical B cells primed to recognize this antigen in the future. These cells are responsible for immunologic *memory*; i.e., they "remember" the antigen when they encounter it again and begin rapidly to produce antibody.

The antibody produced by the transformation of the B lymphocyte floats freely in body fluids. For this reason, antibody can quickly reach antigen located almost anywhere in the body. Antibody is called *immunoglobin* (Ig) and there are five classes, each with a specific biological function. See Table 33-2 for a summary of the Ig classes.

Immunity produced by the B lymphocyte is called *immediate* because of the speed of the reaction. It is also known as *humoral* immunity (humor is from the Latin word for fluid) because the antibody floats freely in body fluids.

When an antigen triggers an immune response by a T lymphocyte, the T lymphocyte multiplies, producing a population of T cells identical to the T lymphocyte that first encountered the antigen but with antibody specific to the antigen attached to their cell surface. The movement of these "sensitized" lymphocytes through the body is slower than in B-cell immune reaction, and this type of immunity is called *delayed*. Because the whole T cell with antibody on its surface is involved in the reaction, it is also called *cellular* immunity.

Whether the T-lymphocyte or B-lymphocyte system is stimulated by an antigen depends on the characteristic of the specific antigen. See Table 33-3 for a summary of the two types of immunity and examples of types of antigens that stimulate them.

Table 33-2 Classes of immunoglobulins

IgG	Provides immunity to invaders with blood-borne dissemination; crosses the placenta to provide fetus and newborn with immunity to diphtheria, pertussis, tetanus, streptococcus, staphylococcus, measles, polio, herpes; used in passive immunization, in which preformed antibody is injected into host who is susceptible and has been exposed to a disease such as hepatitis. IgG = gamma globulin
IgM	First class of antibody to respond to infection, especially in extravascular spaces
IgA	Defends exposed body cavities; found in seromucous secretions of the lacrimal, salivary, and mammary glands and the gastrointestinal and respiratory tracts
IgE	Responsible for immediate hypersensitivity, including anaphylaxis. Responsible for allergic symptoms. Fixes to surface of mast cells. Induces release of vasoactive amines. Produced in greater quantity in allergic than nonallergic children
IgD	Functions unknown

How antibody works

Antibody works by neutralizing toxins with antitoxin, by making holes in cell membranes, or by making the surface of the antigen easier to phagocytize. Antibody works in conjunction with amplification systems that increase its destructive power. The complement system, discussed in Chap. 34, is the best-known amplification system.

In the T-cell system, antibody is attached to the surface of the lymphocyte. Known as a "sensitized lymphocyte," the entire cell becomes involved in the antigen-antibody reaction. The T-cell products released in the reaction are *lymphokines*, and they trigger inflammatory or tissue-damaging reactions.

Antigen-antibody reactions

When antigen is encountered by the immune system for the *first* time, it takes up to 2 weeks for the immunologic events of recognition, antibody production, and antigen destruction to be functioning optimally. This is called the *primary response*, and it is discussed in Chap. 34.

Table 33-3 Summary of the two types of immune response

Type	Characteristics	Gives immunity to:	Responsible for:
Humoral	Circulating antibody B cells Immediate reactions Persists months to years	Staphylococci Streptococci *Haemophilus influenzae* Pneumococci Rubeola, varicella, hepatitis (initial protection only)	Anaphylaxis Hay fever Asthma Hemolytic anemia Autoimmune disease
Cellular	Sensitized lymphocytes T cells Delayed reactions Persists for a lifetime	Acid-fast bacteria (TB) Rubeola Varicella Herpes Cytomegalovirus Fungi	Organ and tissue transplant reactions Contact dermatitis
Both humoral and cellullar	Formed in lymphoid tissue Antigen specific Stimulated by antigen Memory cells formed		

It is the *secondary, anamnestic,* or *memory* response, when a specific antigen is encountered for a second, third, or subsequent time, that can produce tissue-damaging reactions. Usually the secondary response is beneficial to the child and represents normal immune function. Vaccination works because of this secondary response. However, in some children dangerous malfunctions occur—tissue-damaging reactions, which can be divided into four major types.

Type I

Type I is the most immediate and acute reaction. Certain children have a genetic predisposition to produce large amounts of IgE that attaches itself to the surface of mast cells (in tissue) and basophils (in blood). When antigen combines with the antibody on the mast cell surface, the cell bursts and releases histamine, serotonin, and SRS-A. These pharmacologic agents are responsible for two major events: the contraction of smooth muscle, especially the bronchiolar muscles, and capillary dilation.

In its most severe form a Type I reaction causes *systemic anaphylaxis,* which can rapidly result in death if treatment is not initiated immediately. *Local anaphylaxis* occurs in allergic asthma (in the lungs), rhinitis (in the nose), hay fever (nose), and rash (skin). Allergens causing anaphylaxis can be ingested, inhaled, or injected. Drugs, insect bites, foods, and inhalants have all been

responsible for anaphylaxis. See Fig. 33-1 for diagrammatic representation of anaphylaxis. Table 33-4 presents its signs, symptoms, and treat-

Table 33-4 Nursing care in anaphylaxis

Whenever you give a drug:
1. Always check for history of allergy of any type
2. Always check for previous exposure to the agent being used

Watch 20–30 min for:
1. Generalized feeling of warmth
2. Itching palms, soles, throat
3. Hoarseness
4. Dysphagia
5. Tightness in chest and throat
6. Wheezing

If symptoms occur:
1. Report to physician
2. Administer:
   Antihistamine—Benadryl IV (blocks effects of histamine)
   Epinephrine—Adrenalin IV or IM (acts the opposite of histamine) to:
     a. Stimulate myocardium
     b. Increase cardiac output
     c. Increase blood pressure
     d. Relax smooth muscle of respiratory tract
   Aminophylline (bronchodilator)
3. Gather:
   Oral airway
   Endotracheal tube
   Tracheotomy set
   Tourniquets

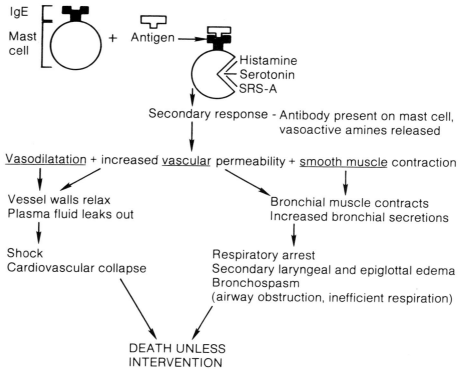

Figure 33-1 Diagrammatic representation of anaphylaxis.

ment. *Systemic anaphylaxis is a medical emergency, and the nurse must be able to recognize it and initiate treatment immediately.* All of the responses occuring in anaphylaxis are reversible by drug therapy if initiated immediately. This type of immune reaction represents hyperreactivity of the immune system and does not occur in all children.

Type II

IgG and IgM are responsible for a type II reaction. The antigen is on the surface of a body cell and the antibody is free-floating. When the antibody attaches to the cell-bound antigen, the cell breaks open and is destroyed. Autoimmune hemolytic anemia (a condition in which a child's own red cells are destroyed by antibody), transfusion reactions (each person possesses naturally occuring antibodies to blood group antigens different from his or her own), and organ transplant rejection reactions (the antigens on the surfaces of the transplanted tissue are immediately recognized as foreign and attacked) are examples

of type II antigen-antibody reactions. The type II reactions to blood transfusions and tissue transplants would be expected to occur in any immunologically competent child. Autoimmune hemolytic anemia is an immune disorder.

Type III

Type III reactions occur in body and tissue fluids. The antigen-antibody complexes deposit on small vessel walls, causing vasculitis, or in the dermis, epidermis, joints, choroid plexus of the skull, or glomeruli. Tissue damage is caused by proteolytic (protein-destroying) enzymes liberated during attempted phagocytosis of the complexes. Rheumatoid arthritis and glomerulonephritis are example of diseases that can be caused by this type of reaction.

Type IV

Type IV reactions are mediated by sensitized lymphocytes. Receptors on the surface of the sensitized lymphocyte recognize and combine with the antigen. This causes the sensitized lymphocyte to release products known as lymphokines, which trigger an inflammatory reaction that helps in destruction and elimination of antigen and can cause tissue damage. This reaction is responsible for: contact dermatitis, transplanted tissue rejection (delayed reaction), the prolonged reaction of insect bites, tuberculous lesions in the lung, skin lesions seen in measles and herpes simplex, and lesions seen in dermatomycosis, coccidioidomycosis, and histoplasmosis. This reaction is the one seen in a positive skin test for tuberculosis. If the person tested has had previous infection with TB, an area of induration and edema will develop at the injection site after several hours and persist to 48 h (see Table 33-3).

Alterations involving a deficiency or excess of immune system cells or tissues

Rarely occurring primary immunodeficiency diseases should be recognized by the nurse working with infants and children. Infantile sex-linked agammaglobulinemia (Bruton's disease) renders an infant unable to mount a humoral response (cannot produce free-floating antibody) and therefore subjects the infant to repeated bacterial infections. The cell-mediated responses are normal. Treatment is frequent injection of human gamma globulin. The gamma globulin is used up in antigen-antibody reactions and cannot be replenished by the child, and so it must be repeatedly injected.

Children with T-cell deficiency cannot mount an effective immune response to viral illness and can be overwhelmed by routine viral immunizations. These children also have weakened humoral system response. The cause of this problem is failure of the fetal thymus to develop and "process" the T cells. Grafting of neonatal thymus can restore immunocompetence, but the graft can later be rejected by the same T cells it "processed." The condition is known as thymic hypoplasia or Di George's syndrome.

When both T-cell and B-cell systems are deficient, Swiss type agammaglobulinemia is apparent within the first weeks of life. These children usually die by the age of 2 years from overwhelming infections. Bone marrow transplant has been attempted with minimal success.

These three *severe conditions* of immune deficiency are recognizable early in life by frequent infection, including sinopulmonary and gastrointestinal infections, by recurrent or continuous viral or fungal infections, and by failure to thrive.

Partial immunodeficiencies are more common. Premature infants may have a problem with transient hypogammaglobulinemia. Normally, there is a delay in the production of IgG (gamma globulin) by the infant for 15 to 30 weeks while the mother's IgG, transferred transplacentally, becomes used up. In the premature infant, the full amount of maternal antibody is not transferred and the baby's own immune response is delayed. These children are highly susceptible to infection but can be treated by human IgG injections (see Table 33-5).

Neoplastic changes can occur in the immune system of the child. Neoplasms termed *lymphomas* are cancers involving the immune system tissues while *leukemia* refers to the appearance of neoplastic lymphoid cells in large quantities in the blood. Thymic lymphoma of children and related acute lymphocytic leukemia are examples of immune system neoplasms characterized by excessive or deficient cell production, respectively.

Alterations producing tissue-damaging reactions

Much more commonly encountered in childhood are the immunologic disorders causing tissue-damaging reactions. This category of immunologic alterations includes allergy, antigen-antibody complex diseases, histocompatibility problems, and the development of autoantibodies.

Allergy (hypersensitivity)

The alteration in the immune system that is most commonly found in children is the tissue-damaging antigen-antibody reaction. This is caused by immunologic "memory," coupled with an excessive production of the immunoglobulin IgE. The antibody attaches itself to mediator cells that release histamine, serotonin, SRS-A, or all of them when they break open. When the antigen encounters its specific IgE antibody on a mediator cell, the chemical mediators are released and tissue damage occurs.

The terms *hypersensitivity*, *atopy*, and *allergy*

Table 33-5 Primary immunodeficiency disorders

Deficiency disorder	Cause, description, and treatment
Bruton's disease	Sex-linked hypogammaglobulinemia Defective B-cell function Recurrent invasive infections Recurrent sinopulmonary infections Malabsorption Protuberant abdomen Eczema Can be treated by IgG injections
Di George's syndrome	Deficiency in T-cell mechanism Absent or deficient thymus Tetany secondary to hypocalcemia Normal B-cell function Increased susceptibility to fungal and viral infections

Swiss type agammaglobulinemia	Both T cells and B cells are deficient
	Autosomal recessive transmission
	Apparent in first few weeks of life
	Die by age 2 from overwhelming viral or bacterial
	    infections, infant gastroenteritis, malabsorption,
	    Monilia, pulmonary infection, or failure to thrive

Ataxia-telangiectasia	Absence of IgA, deficiency of IgG Ataxia Oculocutaneous telangiectasia Recurrent sinopulmonary infections
Wiskott-Aldrich syndrome	Sex-linked recessive inheritance Bleeding secondary to thrombocytopenia Eczema Marked susceptibility to infection IgM deficiency—unusually prone to gram- negative infections Prone to lymphoreticular malignancies
Chédiak-Higashi syndrome	Autosomal recessive Decreased pigmentation in skin, hair, and eyes Skin and bowel infections If children survive, they develop malignancies
Transient hypogammaglobulinemia of infancy	Delay in initiation of infant's production of IgG for 15–30 weeks Highly susceptible to infections Treatment with IgG injections

are used interchangeably to indicate a situation in which a child is sensitized (has had previous experience with an antigen) and subsequent contact with the antigen causes tissue damage. When the antibody formed to an antigen is from the humoral (B-cell) system, the hypersensitivity reaction is *immediate*. In allergy, adverse physiological responses occur from antigen-antibody reactions induced by certain antigens (allergens) that do not normally cause reactions. Allergic or atopic children differ from normal children in their *overproduction* of IgE antibody. Everybody produces IgE to some antigens, but atopic children form IgE antibody in large amounts when exposed to such common environmental substances as house dust and pollen.

Atopic children have the following characteristics:

1. Hereditary or familial patterns of allergy
2. Production of IgE antibody on exposure to environmental substances
3. Hyperreactivity of airways
4. Hyperreactivity of skin

Conditions in children that may have an allergic origin are asthma, eczema, hay fever, gastrointestinal disorders, otitis, hyperactivity, and depression.

Any child suspected of having an allergic problem should receive a complete physical examination and diagnostic workup. A thorough medical history of the family and the child is essential. The child, family, and environment must be considered. Table 33-6 outlines the areas to be included in the history to help identify suspected allergies. Table 33-7 presents things to look for in the physical assessment of the child with suspected allergy. Table 33-8 summarizes diagnostic laboratory tests.

Table 33-6 History for suspected allergy

Environment	Attempt to relate child's symptoms and their absence (periods when symptom free) to:
Activity	Physical exercise, sleep, play (i.e., are symptoms increased or decreased during activity and sleep?)
Place	School, country, friends' homes, child's home: New or old Woolen rugs, furniture, blankets, feather pillows, stuffed toys, smokers, plants, family's hobbies (e.g., painting, furniture refinishing), household cleaning products, sprays, type of heating and cooling system, presence of pets, child's bedroom
Time of day	At night, morning, after meals, snacks
Season of year	Cold, humidity, wind, spring, summer, fall, winter, type of clothing, sweating
Animal contact	Schoolroom, at friends' houses, in home
Diet	Breast- or bottle-fed, length of time, introduction of foods, maternal food allergies and intolerances, other family food allergies, frequency of nausea, vomiting, diarrhea, rash, colic, stomach ache Complete diet history: everything in the mouth, including toothpaste, especially ingestion of cow's milk, milk products, eggs, wheat, cereals, chocolate, fish, nuts, (these foods are frequent allergic agents)
Medications	Use of any type of medication, length of time, reactions, time lapse since last used

Table 33-7 Physical assessment: indicators of possible allergic problem

Eyes*	"Allergic shiner"—discoloration, dark circles, and swelling under lower lid—from edema and venous stasis Spasm upper lid muscle—from edema and venous stasis Conjunctivitis; upper lid red, itchy, swollen; blepharitis; tearing
Ears	Hearing loss, pain, discharge, dizziness, bulging tympanic membrane, frequent otitis
Nose*	Transverse nasal crease from rubbing tip of nose upward to relieve itching Facial grimaces from wrinkling of nose to relieve itching, sinusitis Nasal congestion, discharge
Mouth*	Mouth ulcers, mouth breathing, high arched palate from mouth breathing, sore throat
Chest	Deformities—pectus excavatum, barrel chest, use of accessory muscles to breathe, wheezing, shortness of breath, frequent colds and pneumonia, cough
Skin	Presence of rash, evidence of scratching. Note color of rash (see Chap. 34 for rash assessment), observe back of knees, behind ears, antecubital fossae (front of elbows), crawling surfaces on babies, scalp, cheeks. Observe for patches of hair loss.
CNS	Headache, irritability, fatigue, depression.
GI tract	Frequent diarrhea, vomiting, stomach aches, flatulence, cramps.

* See also Fig. 33-4.

The three principles in the treatment of allergic children are: Remove the allergen, relieve the symptoms, and prevent future attacks. Table 33-9 discusses some methods of environment and food management that will be useful in instructing parents of allergic children. In lucky circumstances, removal of allergen will also prevent future attacks.

Once symptoms have occurred, they must be treated. In some cases allergic symptoms are short-lived and reverse themselves when the allergen is removed. When this is not the case, medication must be used.

The most frequently used drugs in allergy are *antihistamines*. These drugs work by competing for histamine receptors on the cells affected by histamine. The antihistamine has a high affinity for these receptor sites (it gets there rapidly and holds on tight), preventing the cell from responding to the histamine. The physiological effects of histamine (increased capillary permeability and smooth muscle contraction) cannot occur. The antihistamine drugs, because of the way they work, must be present before or early in an allergic reaction. These drugs cannot reverse allergic ractions once they have occurred. Antihistamine treatment is temporary and relieves only symptoms. It does not treat the cause of the allergy and every attempt should be made to identify the allergen and remove it.

If removal of an allergen is not possible, such as in ragweed or pollen allergies, *hyposensitization* or *desensitization* may be tried. The allergen must be identified and verified by *skin testing* (introducing minute quantities of the suspected allergen into the skin of the forearm or back in children and reading the reaction by recording its size, shape and character). Subcutaneous injections of dilute extracts of the identified allergen are given weekly or monthly and the dose is gradually increased.

Hyposensitization works by causing IgG antibody to be formed in response to injection of the allergen. IgG has a higher affinity for the allergen than IgE and therefore combines with it first. The allergen is destroyed by the IgG before

Table 33-8 Laboratory investigation of allergic disorders

Blood count	Eosinophilia—total eosinophil count is elevated in allergy
RAST	*Radioallergosorbent test*—used to estimate quantity of IgE antibody produced to cow's milk, egg, fish, nuts, pollens, house dust, mites, animal dander, molds, insect stings, penicillin. The test identifies the specific antibody the child is producing.
Serum immunoglobulins (antibody titers)	Specific antibody level can be measured.
Skin testing	Skin exposure to minute quantities of suspected allergens, followed by observation of skin for type of reaction. See text.
Challenge testing	Under carefully controlled conditions, the child is exposed to the suspect allergen and results of the exposure are observed. It is used to identify allergen.

Table 33-9 Management of the environment of allergic child

Removal of allergen

Remove house dusts, molds, animals (pets)
Remove dust-collecting items—venetian blinds, knickknacks, books, plants
Clean frequently, no fans, close doors and windows
Cover mattress and pillow with plastic casings (not plastic bags that may suffocate child), synthetic pillows, and blankets—*no wool, feathers, horse hair*
Use foam rubber furniture
Remove wool rugs
Avoid forced air heating and cooling
Close vents, cover with cheesecloth, clean frequently
Portable air filter and space heater can be rented (caution against fires and burns)
Avoid mold—damp basements, vaporizers, bathroom mold, (check behind wallpaper and headboard for mold growth)
Avoid wood piles, leaf piles, old unkept buildings

Restricted diet

Eliminate all suspect foods. Read *all* labels for products containing allergen*

Allergen	Form on label
Milk	Caseinate, sodium caseinate, casein, curds, whey, lactalbumin, lactoglobulin, lactose ("nondairy" products may contain these ingredients)
Egg	Albumin, ovoglobulin, livetin, ovomucin, ovomucoid, powered or dried egg, yolk, vitelin, ovovitellin—baking powder (sometimes has egg white in it)
Corn	Corn syrup, corn meal, corn flour, corn sugar coating on pills

* Consider everything the child ingests, including drugs, toothpaste, mouthwash, candy, soft drinks, chewing gum.

it comes in contact with IgE. Thus the problems of a type I hypersensitivity reaction are avoided. Hyposensitization can only work if the specific allergen can be positively identified. (*Note:* Because the children undergoing skin testing and hyposensitization are atopic, emergency precautions should always be taken. Epinephrine should be available during testing and hyposensitization injections in the event of an anaphylactic reaction.)

The family and especially the child with allergy should be well informed about the allergic problem. They should understand the cause and the treatment, especially if it may lead to local or systemic anaphylactic reaction. When allergy problems are severe or potentially fatal, the child should wear identification that tells the names of the known allergens. This is usually done in the form of a necklace or bracelet, but can be accomplished by a card with the important information pinned to the child's clothing. The Medic Alert Foundation, P.O. Box 1009, Turlock, Ca 95380, is a charitable, nonprofit organization which for a small fee will supply a Medic Alert bracelet or necklace. The emblem, which is recognized around the world, has the medical problem and a file number for the wearer engraved on its back. Medic Alert maintains a central file, accessible 24 h a day by telephone, with specific information about the wearer's problem. Children with severe allergies can benefit from this service.

Figure 33-2 Common precipitating factors in etiology of bronchial asthma. (*Copyright 1975 CIBA Pharmaceutical Company, Division of CIBA-Geigy Corporation. Reprinted with permission from Clinical Symposia. Illustrated by Frank H. Netter, M.D. All rights reserved.*)

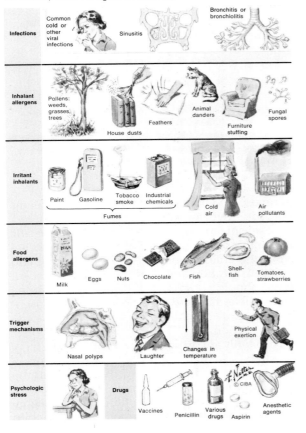

Major allergic diseases of childhood

Asthma The term *asthma* designates "episodic wheezy breathlessness" produced by a narrowing of the tiny airways (bronchioles) leading to the air sacs (alveoli) where gases are exchanged. The narrowing is due to *mucus* in the airway, *swelling* of the airway lining, *spasm* of the muscle in the wall of the airway, or all three combined.

There are two main types of asthma, *allergic* (also known as atopic and extrinsic) and *nonallergic* (intrinsic, infective, or idiopathic) asthma. Allergic asthma usually has its onset in childhood while nonallergic asthma usually begins after the age of 35. Children with allergic asthma have a positive family history of allergy, probably had infantile eczema, and have a heightened reactivity of the tracheobronchial tree to a variety of stimuli.

Clinical manifestations Asthma is recognized when whistling sounds are produced in the chest on *expiration* (wheezing). Air becomes trapped in the alveoli and the chest takes on an inflated appearance (barrel chest). The child's shoulders are pulled up and his sternal and abdominal muscles are used to help pull more air into the lungs. The child is short of breath and even minimal exertion may be difficult. He may not be able to speak more than a few words without taking a breath. In some children the production of frothy mucus is so great that the child seems to be drowning.

The child's respirations are rapid and shallow. With the stethoscope, noisy respirations producing little air movement are heard. At the end of expiration, the characteristic wheeze is noted as the last bit of air squeezes through the narrowed bronchioles.

An asthma attack, an acute onset of the above signs and symptoms, may be preceded by a rapid onset of sneezing, rhinitis, or paroxysmal coughing. Children with hyperactive airways may have attacks triggered by laughing, exercise, rapid change in humidity or temperature, or exposure to an allergen such as a cat or dog. The common cold and other illnesses of childhood can precipitate an asthmatic episode. See Figs. 33-2 and 33-3.

Management The approach to an asthmatic child should be calm and confident. Some acute attacks will reverse themselves, especially when the child and the precipitating allergen can be separated, but many will require treatment. Trips to the emergency room for epinephrine injections are not uncommon for asthmatic children. With treatment, most acute asthmatic attacks can be reversed within minutes.

Until emergency medical treatment is obtained or until prescribed medication begins to take effect, the child should have minimal exertion, be encouraged to breathe slowly, be reassured that the treatment will work, and be kept as occupied and distracted as possible. Rocking small children or rhythmically stroking the back of an older child to encourage relaxation may be helpful. Many children will be relieved of excessive mucus by spontaneously vomiting. Asthmatic children will not lie down during attacks. They are most comfortable sitting with their legs under them and leaning forward on their hands.

Emergency medical treatment The standard emergency treatment for a child with asthma is 1:1000 aqueous epinephrine, 0.01 mg/kg given subcutaneously. The effect is usually rapid. Within minutes high-pitched air movement sounds (rhonchi) become low-pitched (less airway resistance as epinephrine antagonizes effects of histamine and dilates airways). The breathing sounds may disappear completely as the airways fully dilate. After approximately 20 min, if the airways are not absolutely clear, the dose is repeated. Once the attack has been reversed, a dose of long-acting epinephrine (e.g., Sus-Phrine) may be given to make sure the attack does not return.

Epinephrine raises blood pressure and increases the heart rate dramatically. The child's pulse, respirations, and blood pressure are recorded, as quickly as possible, before epinephrine is administered so treatment is not delayed. Special care is taken with children who have hypertensive, hyperthyroid, and cardiac disorders.

The nurse must observe the child after injection for signs of respiratory distress. Sometimes dilating the airways causes the movement of mucus plugs that can precipitate further respiratory distress.

Children with an asthma attack that does not respond to epinephrine will be given intravenous aminophylline. This bronchodilator is *potent* and

Figure 33-3 General management principles for the asthmatic patient. (*Copyright 1975 CIBA Pharmaceutical Company, Division of CIBA-Geigy Corporation. Reprinted with permission from Clinical Symposia. Illustrated by Frank H. Netter, M.D. All rights reserved.*)

is *always given very slowly* over at least a 15-min interval. Side effects that indicate the dose is being given too fast or is too high are nausea and vomiting, nervousness, and diarrhea. Overdose can result in convulsions, coma, cardiac irregularities, and death. The nurse must respect the dangers inherent in administering drugs intravenously and pay special attention to the therapy.

Children who have asthma that is difficult to control may be given corticosteroids to decrease inflammation in the lungs and to potentiate the effects of the other asthma medications. These may be given intravenously initially and then orally. Because exogenous steroids can rapidly suppress the child's own adrenal function, steroid drugs that are to be discontinued must be tapered off rather than stopped abruptly. This allows the child's adrenals to begin to function normally as the drug is withdrawn.

Nursing management Along with careful attention to the administration of drugs to the asthmatic child, the nurse has a major role in the management of hydration, oxygenation, and maintenance of a clear airway. Hydration, to keep body fluid volumes up and to liquify secretions, may be done intravenously, orally, or both. Even oxygen, when ordered, must be humidified to avoid drying secretions. Maintaining a clear airway is difficult in the asthmatic child. While coughing is a frequent accompaniment to the onset of the attack, once the airways are narrowed, the forced expiration necessary for coughing is difficult or impossible. Coughing can further diminish airways by inducing bronchospasm. The removal of secretions must be aided by hydration, mucolytic expectorant drugs, deep slow breathing, chest percussion, frequent turning, and postural drainage (see Chaps. 17 and 25).

Excessive movement increases the child's need for oxygen. Shortness of breath produces anxiety and agitation in the child. It is essential in caring for the asthmatic child *not* to increase his or her anxiety and apprehension. The child should be talked to, not about. Short direct statements will aid understanding. When medication is to be administered, it should be given with minimal hesitation and maximum efficiency. The child can be told that the epinephrine injection is not painful but will burn or sting for a few seconds.

Most asthmatics require continuous, seasonal, or episodic treatment with bronchodilators, drugs that open up airways by action on bronchial muscles. A frequently used bronchodilator, theophylline (related to aminophylline), comes in liquid and chewable form for young children. Inhalant drugs can be used by children beginning at 5 years of age to provide rapid local relief without the systemic effects of oral preparations. Children younger than 5 years may have some difficulty with the technique involved in inhalation therapy.

As with other medications, children should be taught the proper name, dose, administration methods, and frequency of their medications, especially if therapy is continuous and the child is dependent on the drug. Children must be assured that their asthma medication is nearby, but they should be *supervised* in its administration, especially at night. Otherwise the child may wake up, require medication, take it, fall asleep, wake up later, and repeat the medication. Overdose can be fatal with many drugs used for asthma.

Chronic asthma can be controlled in from 50 to 80 percent of asthmatic children by cromolyn sodium (disodium cromoglycate, Intal). This drug, when inhaled, coats the mast cells in the lungs, preventing them from releasing histamine and SRS-A. It has no known serious side effects, but it must be taken from two to four times every day. It requires patience and practice on the parts of parent and child to properly inhale the powder. The medication prevents asthma attacks from occurring, but is not useful during an acute attack. Some children on cromolyn may also require bronchodilator drugs.

General principles to follow in assisting a family in the use of inhalant medications should include:

1. Be sure mouth is clear of food, gum, and all particulate matter before inhalation; rinsing the mouth with water is a good idea (this is to avoid aspiration of matter into the lungs).
2. Have airway extended; the chin should be pointing toward the ceiling to facilitate clear passage of medication into the bronchial tree.
3. Have the child practice exhaling forcibly to empty lungs of as much air as possible before inhaling medication.
4. Have child inhale as deeply as possible and hold the breath for several seconds. The medication should be dispensed at the moment inhalation begins if it is an aerosol. Cromolyn sodium is a powder and is sucked in when the child inhales.

Etiology of asthma Most allergists, pediatricians, and psychiatrists now accept a multiple etiology for asthma. They generally agree that heredity, allergy, infection, and psychology each play a role. Many early theories about asthma resulting from emotional maladjustments have not proven accurate. Children with chronic disorders of any type show a higher prevalence of adjustment problems than healthy children.[1] Emotional problems in the asthmatic child must be assessed to determine if they are primary or secondary to the asthma. Emotions alone may not be able to cause asthma, but it is suspected that in the asthmatic child emotional stress can precipitate an attack.

As in all allergies, the key to management is *prevention*. Identification of the allergen through skin testing or environmental manipulation is essential. Hyposensitization is the next step if the allergen is known and cannot be removed from the environment.

Eczema Like asthma, eczema is not a single disease but a state of hyperreactivity of the skin. It can be a tiny localized lesion or can cover the entire surface of the body. Children with eczema are atopic (have a hereditary allergic history). Eczema is itching, redness, weeping, and scaling of the skin. In infancy it is found on the face and crawling surfaces of the forearms and legs, and later, usually after 2 years, in the antecubital (front of the elbows) and popliteal fossae (behind the knees), face, and behind the ears. The cause is not known, but its development is influenced by immune, genetic, pharmacological, and environmental factors.

The pathophysiology of eczema is vasodilation with the release of histamine, lymphokines, serotonin, and other factors near the skin surface. The epidermis is invaded by inflammatory cells, causing edema. This activity in the cellular growth area of the skin results in abnormal skin formation. The lesions are not contagious, but are prone to secondary bacterial infection. Children with eczema are especially prone to develop herpes simplex and vaccinial infection. Vaccination for smallpox or contact with anyone recently vaccinated is absolutely contraindicated.

The management of this condition depends on an accurate diagnosis with care taken to identify characteristics of the particular child's eczema (things that seem to make it better and worse). The medical management is topical application of corticosteroids. These drugs are anti-inflammatory, suppress local immune function (immunosuppressive), and are vasoconstricting. These drugs should *not* be used in the presence of infection and should be used sparingly because they can be absorbed systemically. Antihistamines may be administered to reduce itching and promote sleep during an exacerbation of a child's eczema. See Table 33-10 for a summary of management of childhood eczema.

Table 33-10 Management of eczema in childhood

Hygiene	Avoid using soaps except baby soaps and shampoos (in some cases, use none at all). Keep fingernails short and clean.
Diet	Systematically eliminate suspect foods from diet. Encourage mother to breast-feed future babies.
Clothing	Use soft synthetic and cotton fabrics. Avoid wool or fabrics that cause excessive sweating (heat and humidity increase sweating which increases itching and irritation) and do not overdress.
Play	Encourage normal activity (swimming may be drying, but cream can be applied before). Low humidity and cool, sunny days are especially good for play.
Bathing	Avoid hot bath water. This is drying and increases itching. Use no bubble bath or fragrant oils. Nonirritating emulsifiers can be purchased to soften water.

Allergic rhinitis Allergic rhinitis can be seasonal (hay fever) or perennial (nonseasonal). The child with a positive family history of allergy becomes sensitized (first exposure and development of IgE antibody) by inhalation or ingestion early in life. These conditions are more common in young boys and are recognized by partial or complete nasal obstruction; sudden and recurrent episodes of sneezing and itching in nose and upper throat; watery nasal discharge, and watering, itchy, swollen eyes.

The pathophysiology is due to effects of histamine on the nasal mucosa, causing vasodilation and increased capillary permeability with leakage of fluid into the nasal passages, excessive mucus secretion, and swollen mucous membranes that close nasal passages. See Fig. 33-4.

The management of the child's environment has been discussed earlier (Table 33-9). Medication includes nose drops or nasal sprays that decrease nasal stuffiness by causing nasal vasoconstriction. These drugs should be used only as treatment, not for prevention. Overuse causes vasodilation (rebound phenomenon) requiring increasing doses to produce a therapeutic vasoconstriction. Antihistamines can prevent a full-blown attack and are sometimes effective in relieving itching and nasal obstruction. Reserve these medications for evening use because they

Figure 33-4 Facial characteristics of allergic rhinitis. 1. Allergic shiner, dark discoloration of the orbitopalpebral groove. 2. Transverse nasal crease due to constant rubbing of the nose upward (allergic salute). 3. Enlargement of the inferior turbinates. 4. Mouth breathing due to nasal obstruction (*After J. A. Kuzemo, Allergy in Children, Priory House, Priory Road, Standford, Linconshire, England, 1978. With permission.*)

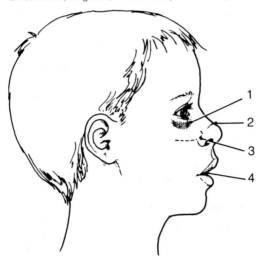

cause drowsiness. Hyposensitization may be useful when the allergen can be accurately identified.

Food allergy Symptoms of food allergy mimic symptoms of many other disorders. Food allergy can occur in anyone but is more likely in someone who has a positive family history of allergy or who has had an allergy to something else. Table 33-11 lists some of the symptoms attributable to food allergy. Many children suffering

Table 33-11 Symptoms sometimes attributable to food allergy

Headache	Tension
Abdominal pain	Learning problems
Earache	Hyperactivity
Otitis media	Drowsiness
Epigastric distress	Prostration
Emotional lability	Sweating
Rhinitis	Irritability
Enuresis	Depression
Muscle aches	Pallor
Fatigue	Nasal congestion
Poor dexterity	Circles under the eyes

from food allergy are referred to a psychiatrist because no pathology can be found after testing. Identifying food allergy is extremely difficult because of delayed symptoms, multiple ingredients in foods, and irregular exposure to the allergen. Immediate hypersensitivity reactions can also occur from foods.

Children can have allergy to the corn sugar coating or dyes on medications. Children with egg allergy can react adversely to immunization because vaccines are sometimes prepared in protein media including egg. Diabetics can react adversely to insulin prepared from pig pancreas (protamine insulin).

Food allergy should be considered in children with any of the symptoms listed in Table 33-11 when no other obvious reason for the symptoms can be determined. While difficult, prevention of attacks is somewhat easier in food allergy than in inhalation allergies because of the *elimination diet*. A registered dietitian should be consulted in the diagnostic process and in planning a long-term elimination diet that will provide the child with proper nutrition. The dietitian can assist with keeping an accurate diet history and can help provide recipes that will keep the child interested in food.

Histocompatibility (tissue compatibility)

The immune system recognizes components of the individual's body as "self" by recognizing histocompatibility (compatible tissue) antigens on the cell surface of all nucleated cells of the body. That is, there are certain configurations on a child's cells that enable the child's body to recognize "self" components and distinguish "self" from "nonself" or foreign. It is the "foreign" components against which the immune response is launched. This self-recognition system is known as *human leukocyte antigen system*, or HL-A. The HL-A system of every individual is genetically determined and unique. When tissue is transplanted, the HL-A system antigen on the cell surface of the donor tissue will be recognized as "foreign" by the recipient and the immune system will respond by destroying the tissue. When tissue transplants are planned, every effort is made to find a donor with HL-A configurations compatible with the recipient's. The highest probability of success with transplanted tissue occurs within families (mainly siblings) because genetic similarity exists.

The use of *immunosuppressive* therapy (therapy that prevents normal immune function) helps prevent graft rejection. The agents used are nonspecific and interfere either with the induction or the expression of the immune response.

Immunosuppression or immunologic depression is accomplished with steroids. It is also an unwanted effect of irradiation, cytotoxic chemicals, poor general health and nutrition, and some diseases.

Autoimmune diseases The body's system of recognizing components as "self" can break down. If this happens, the body forms antibodies against its own "self" components (autoantibodies) and the condition is an *autoimmune disease*. The lesions of autoimmune diseases are a result of inflammatory destruction of the target tissue, usually connective tissue of the skin, kidney glomeruli, joints, serous membranes, and blood vessels.

The pathophysiology of these diseases is tissue damage from an antigen-antibody reaction that results in inflammation, deposition of immune complexes (Ag-Ab) in small vessels of the involved area causing stasis, edema, and inflammation, or both inflammation and deposition. In *rheumatoid arthritis* enzyme products liberated at the site of inflammation destroy components of bone, cartilage, ligaments, and tendons, causing structural alterations in the joints.[2] Other autoimmune diseases that can occur in childhood include: systemic lupus erythematosus, polyarteritis, polymyositis, dermatomyositis, thrombocytopenic purpura, and Hashimoto's disease, which accounts for half of all childhood goiters.[3] The lesions of juvenile-onset insulin-dependent diabetes, occurring in the islets of Langerhans in the pancreas, have the pathological appearance of autoimmune disease. Glomerulonephritis is now recognized as a disease resulting from autoantibodies attacking the basement membrane of the glomeruli or by Ag-Ab complexes causing vasculitis when deposited in the glomerular capillaries. Each of these disorders is discussed in detail elsewhere in this book.

References

1. Ake Mattsson, "Psychologic Aspects of Childhood Asthma," *Pediatric Clinics of North America* 22(1): 77–88 (1975).
2. Max Samter (ed.), *Immunological Diseases, Volumes I and II*, 3d ed., Little, Brown, Boston, 1978, p. 1071.
3. Ibid., p. 1261.

Chapter 34 **Infectious processes**

Linda Richelson

Upon completion of this chapter, the student will be able to:

1. Describe the nurse's role in controlling infection and caring for children with communicable diseases.

2. List the specific and nonspecific defenses against infection.

3. Describe the types of immunity and how each is acquired.

4. Describe the cycle of infection transmission.

5. List the nursing measures for the clinical manifestations of communicable infections.

6. Describe the lesions of rashes.

7. Identify the properties of the following communicable diseases: bacterial, viral, rickettsial, parasitic, fungal.

8. Describe the common childhood diseases and their specific characteristics.

9. Compare the incidence of gonorrhea and syphilis with the incidence of other communicable diseases.

10. Describe the treatment, symptoms, and transmission of sexually transmitted diseases.

11. Explain the consequences of untreated sexually transmitted diseases in the male and female.

12. List the instructions for treatment of sexually transmitted diseases and maintenance of health in the adolescent.

The child's body must constantly defend itself against invasion by microorganisms to remain in a state of health. Infection is a major component of the spectrum of disease seen by the pediatric nurse. The nurse working with children can expect recognition, control, and prevention of infection to be a part of the care of every child.

Familiarity with the language used to describe the process of infection is basic to the nurse's understanding of the transmission of disease. The language describes the conditions of and relationships between the child (*host*), the organism (*agent*), and the *environment* that result in infection. Preventing the transmission of infection is a major function of the nurse. Understanding the process of infection helps the nurse to identify points at which intervention would interfere with the spread of disease.

Not every contact between an infectious agent and a host results in infection. For infection to occur there must be:

1. Adequate quantity of the infectious agent (*dose*)
2. Adequate strength of the agent (*virulence* or *pathogenicity*)
3. Adequate exposure time
4. A susceptible host
5. An agent entry into the host via the appropriate portal

Most organisms prefer a particular location in the body for growth, but the majority *enter* through the digestive and respiratory tracts.

When an agent successfully invades a host and multiplies, infection exists. If the infection provokes an *immune response* (the production of antibody) but no signs or symptoms of disease are evident, the infection is *inapparent* or *subclinical*. This is also known as the *carrier state:* The host is not sick, but is harboring the organism and can transmit it to others. The carrier state occurs in many infectious diseases during the *incubation period* (the time between the host's exposure to the organism and the appearance of symptoms). Disease exists when there are overt clinical manifestations of infection, such as pain, swelling, redness, rash, or fever.

The nurse's role in childhood infection

It is the responsibility of the nurse to prevent, recognize, and control infection. Educating the child and family in practices that promote and maintain health is the primary prevention role of the nurse. Good hygiene and immunization are the most effective infection-prevention measures. The ability to recognize infection or the potential for infection enables the nurse to limit the spread, initiate early treatment, and avoid complications of the infection. Special factors in the recognition of infection in children are discussed in the following section on the child's predisposition to infection. The basic mechanisms for controlling infection are:

1. Early recognition of infectious disease and the isolation of the host
2. Identification and follow-up of contacts
3. Hand-washing between patients
4. Screening for susceptible children who have been exposed to infectious disease before hospital admission,
   a. Do not admit, if elective.
   b. Isolate child.
   c. Determine susceptibility status of other patients.
   d. Provide protective isolation for other children who are highly susceptible. See Chap. 17 for information about isolation.

The nurse's role in caring for a child with an infection includes:

1. Observation for signs of infection, its spread, or impending complications
2. Assessing the child's and family's health practices to determine why the child acquired the infection
3. Assessing the health status of contacts

4. Providing optimal hydration and nutrition
5. Providing rest for the child, the infected body area, or both
6. Providing comfort measures for the clinical manifestations of the infection (itching, pain, dry skin, dry mouth, sensitive eyes, anxiety, etc
7. Providing control measures for fever, cough, nausea and vomiting, and diarrhea
8. Protecting the child from secondary infection
9. Educating the child and family about the infection, its treatment, prevention, and prevention of further infections

Childhood predisposition to infection

Understanding the nature of the child host will lead the nurse to an appreciation of the unique place of infection in childhood. Children have a high incidence of infection because of their physiological immaturity, high risk of exposure, and immunologic immaturity.

During early childhood the child is ill-equipped to resist infection. Air passageways are shorter and narrower, permitting rapid entry of an organism. The short, straight eustachian tube of the young child allows a throat infection to spread via the tube to the middle ear. Contamination of the urethra, also shorter in the young child, facilitates entry of microorganisms into the bladder. The use of diapers causes fecal contamination of the urethra and predisposes the skin to breakdown (diaper rash) and infection. The diaper area promotes the growth of organisms because it is rich in nutrients, moist and dark. If there is scratching in the diaper area, microorganisms from the hands are introduced. When the fingers become contaminated with fecal organisms, the organisms are spread to the nose, mouth, eyes, ears, and skin.

Sebaceous skin secretions are limited in childhood, causing the skin to be dry and easily injured. Skin injury permits entry of organisms. Excessive salivation, during teething and thumbsucking, breaks down the skin around the mouth, facilitating the entry of microorganisms. Contaminated fingers and foreign objects introduce microorganisms into the mouth and to the skin around the mouth. Foreign objects are inserted by some young children into the nose and ears, predisposing the child to infection.

Childhood is associated with a rapid rate of

growth. This great metabolic rate requires the child to have a high fluid, caloric, and nutrient intake to ensure good nutritional status. Poor nutritional status makes a child more susceptible to infection. The young child's dependence on milk products, a good medium for bacterial growth, also increases the likelihood of infection.

The young child's immune system is not completely developed, compromising the ability to react to infection. Immunity to many infectious agents develops only after exposure to them through illness or vaccination. The newborn and infant are largely unexposed to infectious agents. Increased social contact as the child grows older provides exposure to many different pathogenic organisms.

The anatomic and physiological immaturity of the child can easily be recognized when illness does occur. The cardiac sphincter of the stomach is more relaxed, predisposing the young child to vomiting. Marked elevation of temperature and convulsions indicate CNS immaturity. Fluid and electrolyte balance is easily upset by fever, diarrhea, or vomiting. The child becomes sick very rapidly, demonstrating how quickly children's defenses can be overcome. Children are generally less able to communicate the presence of pain, enabling an infection to progress unnoticed. For example, children with earaches may not complain until an eardrum has spontaneously ruptured. When pain is felt, the child may have difficulty in describing the pain or even in accurately locating the pain. To some extent this is due to the immature nervous system and the phenomenon of referred pain.

Social conditions of children also contribute to the frequency and spread of infection. Children often exchange clothing or toys and share food that may be contaminated, especially with saliva and nasal secretions. Children spend much of their day in close contact with other children, facilitating transmission of microorganisms. Siblings frequently share toilet articles (toothbrushes, combs, washcloths) and even bathe together. In colder months it is difficult to keep children properly clothed, setting the stage for upper respiratory infections, and in warmer months outdoor play without shoes leads to foot injury.

These are only some of the reasons why infection occurs so frequently in childhood and why the pediatric nurse can expect to be concerned about infection with every pediatric patient.

Defense against infection
Nonspecific defenses

The child has defenses that protect against invasion by microorganisms. Nonspecific defenses protect against invasion of any sort. The first line of defense is the epithelium that covers the exterior of the body and lines the internal surfaces. The intact epithelium provides a mechanical barrier to invasion. Other mechanical barriers result from the cleansing action of the flow of tears, urine, and saliva. The hairs in the nose filter and trap inhaled organisms and the mucus and cilia in the respiratory tract trap and propel organisms upward to be expelled by coughing, sneezing, or swallowing. The normal flora of the skin, mouth, and lower gastrointestinal tract provide a biological defense by competing with pathogens for nutrients, inhibiting their growth. The acidity of gastric secretions and of the skin also chemically inhibits the growth of pathogens. Lysozyme present in tears, nasal secretions, and saliva breaks down the bacterial cell wall, causing chemical destruction. All of these nonspecific defenses protect the child against the invasion of the body by microorganisms.

The child also possesses nonspecific defenses that protect against infection once invasion has occurred. These defenses are the white blood cells that ingest and destroy invading agents. This protection is known as *phagocytosis*. The most highly phagocytic cell is the *macrophage*. *Fixed macrophages* line the sinuses of the liver, spleen, bone marrow, and lymph nodes and are attached to the walls of the alveoli and lymph and blood channels. As microorganisms travel through these areas in the blood or lymph, they are removed by being engulfed by the macrophages. Macrophages in the liver remove invaders that have entered the portal circulation by traveling through the gastric mucosa. There are also *floating macrophages*, which circulate in the blood and travel to the site of infection. When microorganisms have penetrated into the tissue of the body, floating macrophages move to the site, proliferate, and "wall off" the infection from surrounding tissue, limiting its ability to spread.

Specific defenses

Immunity, the body's powerful adaptive response to invasion by microorganisms, must be developed specifically for each microorganism. Each microorganism or toxin has a unique chemical and physical composition that allows the cells of the immune system to identify it on first encounter and recognize it on subsequent encounters. The term for agents that stimulate a response by the immune system is *antigen* (Ag).

The immune response is the production of antibody (Ab), which works to destroy invading agents by creating conditions that enhance phagocytosis. Phagocytosis is facilitated when the antibody either covers the surface of the antigen or attacks the cell wall of an agent, causing the agent to rupture. This antigen-antibody complex then either clumps (agglutinates) or precipitates.

The antigen-antibody complex activates still another system of defense, *the complement system*. This is an amplification system; it increases the efficiency and effectiveness of antibody. The complement system consists of nine enzymes located in plasma and other body fluids that, when activated, attack invading organisms by either:

1. *Lysis*, digesting the cell membranes causing the cell to burst
2. *Opsonization*, coating the surface of the agent to make it more easily phagocytized
3. *Chemotaxis*, attracting phagocytic cells to the area
4. *Agglutination*, causing antigen to stick together, or
5. *Neutralization*, attacking the molecular structure of a virus

In addition, complement enzymes initiate a local inflammatory response preventing movement of the agent through the tissue. The inflammatory response is discussed later in the chapter.

Specific response to invaders, *immunity*, is an effective means of destroying invading agents and removing them from the body, and it is clearly essential to the survival of the child.

The immune response

The body does not respond immediately with the production of antibody on first exposure to an antigen. The invading agent, *antigen*, is transported to the lymphoid tissue, where most of it is destroyed by the white blood cell, the non-specific mechanisms of defense described earlier. If the antigen reaches the circulating blood, up to 90 percent may be removed on the first passage through the liver and spleen. This type of nonspecific immune destruction occurs for the first 4 to 7 days after the organism enters the host. On first exposure to an antigen, the antigen-specific immune response takes almost 2 weeks to become functional. This is why children usually show overt illness if they are exposed to an infectious disease they have not had before. Invasion has occurred by an agent unknown to the body and although the nonspecific defenses work to their capacity to destroy the invader, they are not so effective as the specific immune system.

When an agent is able to invade the body a second time, it is recognized by the immune system. This *secondary response*, much quicker than on the first encounter with the agent, is known as *anamnestic* or *memory response*. The immune response is altered as a result of the body's having experienced a particular antigen before. Larger quantities of antibody are produced much sooner than in the first exposure (*primary response*). The invading agent is destroyed before it can multiply enough to cause illness. See Fig. 34-1.

Development of antibody

Lymphocytes are responsible for immune responses. They must encounter the antigen and will then produce clones, i.e., identical cells all derived from a single cell. In a *humoral immune response*, the offspring cells produce antibody, which will circulate in body fluids and eliminate the antigen. A different kind of antigen will stimulate a *cellular immune response*. In this case, the clones will be specially prepared cells carrying antibody on their surface. These cells on contact with the antigen release lethal substances against it. The two types of immunity—cellular and humoral—are discussed in Chap. 33, and their distinct characteristics are summarized in Table 33-3. The types of antibody are described in Table 33-2.

Understanding immunoglobulins and their development gives the nurse a basis for understanding infection and immunization schedules in childhood. Children are especially prone to infection because their immune systems are not

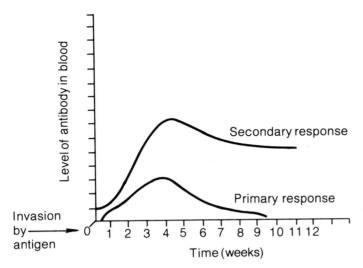

Figure 34-1 Primary and secondary immune response. Characteristics of the primary response are: (1) antibody production is delayed for several days; (2) it takes 2 to 3 weeks to increase antibody levels; and (3) after many weeks, antibody is largely used up and only low levels remain. Characteristics of the secondary response are: (1) shorter time from exposure to full antibody production; (2) higher levels attained; (3) antibody levels remain higher; and (4) second and subsequent exposure to antigen requires smaller doses of antigen to provoke full response.

entirely developed and they have not been exposed to many antigens. Therefore, little specific immunity has built up. Infants are born with some antibody protection, IgG that has crossed the placenta, but these antibodies are quickly used up or are broken down by the body. See Fig. 34-2 for a graphic presentation of the development of the four main immunoglobulin classes in the newborn and young child.

Immunization

The two principles underlying childhood immunization schedules are: to wait until antibody-forming mechanisms of the child are mature enough to respond and to avoid immunization when there is maternal antibody remaining in

the infant, which would neutralize the antigenic stimulus. The immunity the child receives from the mother through the placenta is called *passive immunity* because the baby's immune system was not involved in the production of the antibodies; they came preformed from the mother's system. Childhood immunization begins early so that the child's system can *actively* produce its own antibody. The child is immunized with antigenic material (bacteria, viruses, or their by-products) from major childhood infections (diphtheria, pertussis, tetanus, polio, measles, mumps, rubella). The antigen used in immunizations has had its pathogenicity (ability to produce disease) weakened or destroyed, but the immune system recognizes it as antigen. On first

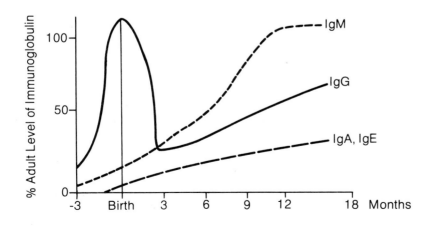

Figure 34-2 Immunoglobulin development in the young child. At birth the infant has more than 100 percent of the adult level of IgG, having received IgG from the mother across the placenta and also producing its own IgG for several months before birth. Maternal IgG has been used up or broken down by the child's body by about 4 months. (*Source: After J. R. Hobbs, in Ivan Roitt, Essential Immunology, Blackwell, London, 1971, p. 56.*)

immunization, low levels of antibody are produced. Second and third immunizations (*boosters*) produce a secondary response providing high levels of antibody that will persist for years to protect the child. The three main reasons for giving booster doses are:

1. To get a secondary, or memory, response from the immune system (Fig. 34-1)
2. Make sure that maternal antibody has not prevented the child's immune system from responding (Fig. 34-2)
3. To challenge the child's continuously developing immune system

The immune response in immunization is similar to the response that occurs during a *naturally acquired* infection, but the child does not get the disease. The development of immunity is an *active process* on the part of the child's immune system resulting in *acquired immunity* against a disease. Immunization is not a totally natural process because the natural phenomenon of acquiring the disease has been altered by reducing the ability of the organism to cause disease and by *purposely* introducing the organism into the host. Therefore, immunization produces *artificially acquired immunity.* The American Academy of Pediatrics in its *Report of the Committee on Infectious Diseases, 1977,* states that active immunization is the most effective tool in preventing infectious disease. See Table 6-5 for immunization schedules and Table 34-1 for a summary of the mechanisms of defense against infection.

Factors depressing defense

There are factors that interfere with the child's defenses against infection. Mechanical obstruction causing stasis of some drainage system of the body (e.g., bladder, sinuses, skin pores, or tear ducts) creates conditions favorable for infection. These, plus circulatory disturbances (ischemia or congestion and edema of an area or shock), interfere with the travel and function of white blood cells. Nutritional deficiencies, debilitating diseases, concurrent infections, and endocrine imbalance can adversely affect defenses. Steroid and radiation therapy depress the immune system and predispose the child to infection.

Table 34-1 Summary of the mechanisms of defense against infection

Type	Example
Nonspecific defenses	
Mechanical barriers	Mucus and cilia, skin, flow of tears and urine
Biological barriers	Competing organisms
Chemical barriers	Lysozyme and acidity
Nonspecific immunity	Interferon (see section on "Viral Infections")
Specific immunity	
Active	
Naturally acquired	Infection
Artificially acquired	Immunization
Passive	
Naturally acquired	Maternal IgG in baby
Artificially acquired	Preformed antibody injected, RhoGAM, gamma globulin

The process of infection

Once an agent has successfully invaded the tissues of the host, there are three main patterns of spread: to the lymphatics, though body spaces, and via the blood.

Organisms producing a local infection spread by the lymphatic vessels to the local lymph nodes. This spread can cause inflammation around the lymph vessels (*lymphangitis*) which, if superficial, appears as red streaks under the skin. Organisms reaching the lymph nodes cause swelling and tenderness of the node (*lymphadenitis*). If the organism is not stopped in the lymph node, it travels through the lymph vessels through the thoracic duct, to the blood.

The presence of bacteria or viruses in the blood is known as *bacteremia* or *viremia,* respectively. Bacteria in the blood are attacked by white blood cells. When the bacterial agent is engulfed but not destroyed, it can proliferate within the white blood cells. Eventually, the white blood cells rupture, releasing massive numbers of organisms into the blood, overwhelming the defenses of the host, and causing *septicemia.* Bacteremia is a laboratory finding confirming bacteria in the blood, while septicemia is a clinical diagnosis indicating a bacteremia with a serious clinical status.

Bacteria in the blood can be responsible for metastatic foci of infection. The direction and means of spread of an invading agent determine what the disease will become. A streptococcal sore throat can become acute otitis media or a brain abscess, depending on the direction and means of invasion of a particular strain of streptococcus.

Infection can also spread directly through tissue spaces like the peritoneal cavity, the pleural, subarachnoid, pericardial and joint spaces and through the tubes of the respiratory, genitourinary, and gastrointestinal tracts. Movement of the body or the infected part facilitates the spread of infection.

When the agent has entered the body but it is not yet detectable, the infection is *latent*. The agent is not being shed by the host and the host is not clinically ill. As the agent begins to multiply and reach numbers sufficient to produce signs and symptoms of disease, the *incubation period* ends and illness occurs. From some point after exposure but before the onset of illness, the agent can be transmitted. The period of communicability has begun. The infection is said to be *patent* when the agent is being shed by the host and can be transmitted. Figure 34-3 shows the relationships of these stages of the disease process to each other and to time.

The period of communicability continues until the end of the patent period, which varies greatly from disease to disease. The greatest spread of communicable disease occurs between the end of the latent period and the onset of the illness. The host is asymptomatic and hence unaware of the multiplication of the organism in his body,

and the numbers are sufficient to begin to be shed by the host. The host unknowingly spreads his disease.

Transmission of infection

Transmission is the movement of microorganisms from their *source* to the new host. The source is the person, place, or thing from which the infectious agent passes to the host by *direct contact* or *indirectly* through a vehicle or a vector. Table 34-2 lists the methods by which communicable diseases spread from one person to others.

In many infections of childhood, the portal of exit of the agent from the host is the source of transmission of the infection. It is important for the nurse to know the portals of exit of major childhood infections so he or she can interrupt the transmission and prevent spread of infection whenever possible.

The portals of exit for agents causing the major childhood illnesses are the respiratory and gastrointestinal tracts, skin, wounds, and blood. Table 34-3 lists the sources of agent for several illnesses. See Table 17-10 for isolation precautions to be taken in various infectious diseases.

Clinical manifestations of infection
Inflammation

The inflammatory response is a sequence of events aimed at limiting invasion of microorganisms. The tissue trauma caused by microorga-

Figure 34-3 General scheme of stages of infection.

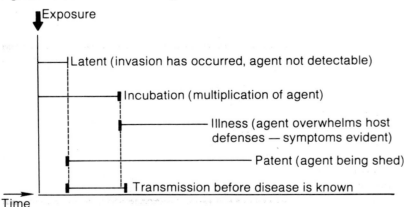

nisms metabolizing and multiplying stimulates damaged host cells to liberate histamine. Histamine increases local blood flow and the permeability of capillaries at the site. The increased blood flow brings white blood cells to the area and the increased permeability permits fluid and fibrinogen to leak into extravascular spaces. The area becomes "walled off" because both tissue spaces and lymph vessels become blocked, reducing movement and fluid flow and thereby limiting the spread of the agent. A cavity may form at the site of the infection and become filled with dead white blood cells and other necrotic material, or pus. Eventually, either the cavity breaks open at a body surface and releases the pus, or the pus is *autolyzed* (absorbed by surrounding tissue until gone).

The physiological purpose of inflammation is to destroy an agent, remove it and its products, limit its extension, and set into motion the mechanism for repair and replacement of damaged tissue.

The clinical signs of inflammation are redness, swelling, and heat. Symptoms include pain and impaired movement. Some children may have an inflammation and be unaware of it because of decreased sensitivity to pain. The nurse must observe for signs of inflammation in assessing the child.

Since inflammation can be caused by infection and infection can be spread by movement of the tissue fluids in the infected area, *rest of the area is essential in the treatment of infection.* Heat administered by compress, soaks, or lamps promotes healing by increasing circulation to the area. Cold is used to limit swelling. The application of either heat or cold may decrease pain associated with inflammation.

Pharmacological treatment of infection includes the use of analgesics, antipyretics, and organism-specific antibiotic therapy.

Fever

Fever is generally considered to be a sign of infection when it is above 37.8°C (100°F) orally or 38.3°C (101°F) rectally. Children have a daily variation in temperature with the lowest temperature in early morning and the highest elevation in the late afternoon or evening. Exercise can increase a child's temperature. Body temperature is an objective way to measure the presence of infection, the severity of disease, the

Table 34-2 Means of transmission

Contact spread

Direct:	Touching, physical contact between source and host
Indirect:	Host contacts a contaminated intermediate object
Droplet:	Agent expelled from source during talking, sneezing, coughing; most must be close by

Common vehicle

A *fomite* (contaminated inanimate object) which can deliver an agent to one or many hosts (through contaminated food, combs, towels)

Air-borne

Agent becomes suspended in air, droplets, or dust particles; travels in air movement, ventilation systems

Vector-borne

Agent is transported by an animal, such as infected household pets, mites, mosquitoes or a wild mammal (*vector*)

response to therapy, and the return to normal level of health.

The child's body regulates temperature by balancing heat production and loss. When fever occurs, there is both increased heat production and decreased heat loss. In infectious disease, fever can be caused by substances called *pyrogens*, which are secreted by toxic bacteria or degenerating tissue. Pyrogens work by causing the hypothalamic thermostat to be set at a higher level than normal. The body then works to raise the body temperature to the reset higher level by heat conservation and increased heat production.

Dehydration is another reason for fever during infection. When fever is due to dehydration or

Table 34-3 Portals of exit for major childhood illnesses

Feces	Mouth, nose, respiratory secretions
Salmonella infections	Pertussis
Polio	Pneumonia
Infectious hepatitis	Scarlet fever
	Meningitis
	Measles
	Mumps
	Polio
	Influenza
	Encephalitis

when pyrogenic substances cause the temperature setting to increase, it takes several hours for the body temperature to reach the new setting. Because the blood temperature is lower than the reset hypothalmus setting, the child feels cold or has chills. When the body temperature reaches the level of the new setting, the child feels neither cold nor warm. A child "feeling cold" may be in the process of temperature elevation and should be checked at frequent intervals. The nursing care of the child with fever is discussed in Chap. 17.

Rashes

Rashes are frequently seen in childhood infections. Skin eruptions or rashes are called *exanthema*. Rash on the mucous membrane is called *enanthema*. How rashes occur is not completely understood, but two pathological events take place. First, capillaries near the skin surface are damaged by toxins, infective agents, or antigen-antibody reactions. Skin cells are also damaged and the eruptions seen represent local inflammatory reactions.

The terminology used to characterize rashes is important in communicating findings (Tables 34-4 and 34-5). A *macule* is a flat, circumscribed area of inflammation and a *papule* is a raised area of inflammation. A *vesicle* is a raised, clearly circumscribed area of fluid in the skin and a *pustule* is a pus-filled vesicle. *Scabs* form at the site of pustules and vesicles. An *erythematous* rash is red.

In observing a child with a rash it is important to note the following:

1. Specific characteristics of the lesions such as size, shape, color, extent, raised, flat
2. The precise location on the body
3. How the rash progresses on the body, including where it is spreading and if the lesions are changing in character

Precision is essential in describing a child's rash. Is the rash red, salmon, pink, purple, brown? Does it have some characteristic that is predominant, like raised borders or unusual distribution? Does it itch? Does the child feel ill?

Table 34-4 Primary lesions of the skin

Types	Definition	Example	Diagram
Macule	A flat circumscribed area of color change in the skin without surface elevation Size: 1 mm to 2 cm	Freckles, vitiligo, purpura, petechia, flat moles, ecchymosis	
Papule	Circumscribed solid and elevated lesion Size: 1 mm to 1 cm	Ringworms, acne, psoriasis	
Nodule	Solid, elevated lesion extending deeper in the dermis Size: 1 to 2 cm	Erythema nodosum	
Tumor	Solid mass larger than a nodule Size: over 2 cm	Basal cell epithelioma	

Table 34-4 Primary lesions of the skin (*Continued*)

Types	Definition	Example	Diagram
Cyst	A papule or nodule containing fluid or viscous material Size: 1 mm or over	Sebaceous and epidermal cysts	
Wheal	A clustering of papular-type lesions creating an edematous plaque Size: 1 mm to several cm	Mosquito bites, urticaria	
Vesicle	A bulging, small, sharply defined lesion filled with serous fluid or blood Size: less than 1 cm	Herpes simplex, herpes zoster	
Bulla	Larger than a vesicle Size: over 1 cm	Pemphigus, second-degree burns	
Pustule	Vesicle or bulla filled with pus Size: 1 mm to 1 cm	Impetigo, acne vulgaris	

Source: M. Kinney et al. (eds.), *AACN's Clinical Reference for Critical-Care Nursing,* McGraw-Hill, New York, 1981, p. 265, 266. Used by permission

Table 34-5 Secondary lesions of the skin

Types	Definition	Example	Diagram
Crust	Dried serum, blood, pus, or sebum which forms on the surface of any vesicle or pustule lesion when it ruptures	Infectious dermatitis, eczema, impetigo	
Scale	Dried fragments of sloughed, dead epidermis	Exfoliative dermatitis, seborrheic dermatitis	

Source: M. Kinney et al. (eds.), *AACN's Clinical Reference for Critical-Care Nursing,* McGraw-Hill, New York, 1981, p. 266. Used by permission.

Ask the parent or child if they know what may have caused the rash and if they know anyone else with a similar rash. Establish the medication history of the child. Rashes from antibiotics or other medications can occur during or after drug administration. The child may not feel ill with a drug rash but will probably feel ill with measles or other rash due to infection. It is also important to note any other clinical signs or symptoms that have preceded or are occurring with the rash.

Nursing management of rashes is aimed at prevention of scarring and secondary infection from scratching. Soaks and baths in tepid to warm water can be soothing. Hot water increases itching. Some lotions are helpful, and systemic medications such as Benadryl can sometimes control itching. The child's nails should be kept short and clean. Mitts may be needed during sleep to prevent scratching. Sedation may be necessary. Dryness increases itching, and bathing excessively and the use of drying soaps should be avoided. Loose-fitting, soft cotton clothing may decrease friction irritation of the skin and prevent sweating. Clothing should be kept clean and changed frequently.

Once the reason for a child's rash has been established, the expected progression of the rash should be explained to the child and parents. They should be taught the importance of not scratching, rubbing, or breaking open any lesion because of the danger of secondary bacterial infection and scarring. The family of a child with a rash should be carefully interviewed to determine the immunization status of the family members to the childhood diseases that are currently preventable by immunization.

Agents of childhood infection

There are five major categories of microorganisms that cause infection in children. They are bacteria, viruses, parasites, rickettsia, and fungi.

Bacterial infections

Bacteria have several characteristics that enable them to cause disease. They are encapsulated, which inhibits phagocytosis. They have flagella (tails) that aid in motility, and their pili (hairlike structures) facilitate attachment to body tissues and other surfaces. They form spores when nutritional conditions are poor, permitting survival and making them highly resistant to physical and chemical attempts to destroy them.

Bacteria cause damage to the host by interfering with the body's attempt to "wall off" the invasion, interfering with phagocytosis, directly destroying body tissues, and causing reactions resulting in fever. Some bacteria produce toxins. *Exotoxins*, toxins released by the bacterial cell into the surrounding tissue and spaces, are antigenic; specific antibody known as *antitoxin* is formed.

Exotoxins inactivated by formaldehyde still retain their antigenicity. Inactivated toxins, *toxoids*, are used to stimulate an immune response. Diphtheria and tetanus toxoids are routinely used for this purpose. Preformed antitoxin is used when exposure has occurred or is suspected to have occurred. Tetanus antitoxin is given after puncture wounds.

The preferred methods of diagnosis in bacterial infections are *culture* and *smear* of infected tissue or fluid. Identification of the organism and its particular biological and biochemical activities is sought. Because drying destroys many bacteria, care must be taken to provide a sterile nutrient broth for the specimen. Prompt delivery to the laboratory is essential. When obtaining a specimen of blood, urine, spinal fluid, or other body fluid, extreme care must be taken to avoid contamination of the specimen. Skin-cleansing is crucial to obtaining an uncontaminated specimen. Special care must be taken in obtaining urine cultures. A contaminated specimen can result in an incorrect diagnosis, needlessly put the child through a course of anti-infective therapy, or lead to selection of the wrong medication.

Bacteria are remarkably able to adapt to environmental conditions. The clinical significance of this is apparent in increased tolerance of bacteria for antibacterial drugs. Strains of bacteria have become resistant to antibiotic drugs because of inadequate treatment of an infection with an antibiotic. When treatment is inadequate, either in dosage level or in length of time the drug is administered, the weaker organisms are destroyed while the stronger ones survive. The stronger organisms multiply, creating a more resistant strain.

Antibiotics, when used to treat an identified infection, should be administered for a full 10 to 14 days. When a culture is taken and an antibiotic started before the culture results are obtainable, it is appropriate to discontinue the drug if the organism is not one for which the antibiotic is specific.

Antibacterial agents include *antibiotics*, compounds produced by microrganisms and having the capability to inhibit or destroy other microorganisms, and *chemotherapeutic agents*, chemicals having the property of selecting the pathogen over the host cell for destruction. The drugs are either bacteriostatic or bactericidal. Bacteriostatic drugs inhibit growth and multiplication of micro-organisms. The host defenses then rid the body of the agent. Bactericidal drugs destroy bacteria directly. Antibacterial drugs that act against a specific agent are *narrow-spectrum* drugs. *Broad-spectrum* drugs interfere with the integrity, growth, and reproduction of a large group of bacteria.

Table 34-6 presents the major bacterial infections of childhood. Discussion of the body system affected and the nursing management appears in the appropriate chapter.

Viral infections

Viruses can complete their life cycle only within a living cell. Once a virus has invaded a cell,

Table 34-6 Common bacterial diseases of childhood

Agent	Source	Disease	Comments
Streptococcus pyogenes	Everywhere, skin, nasopharynx	Streptococcal pharyngitis	One of most common infections of children 5–15 years old Spread person-to-person Nasal droplets or saliva Crowding enhances spread Food or water-borne outbreaks explosive Not all infected will have symptoms; some have mild illness for few days Some temps. 38.3°C (101°F), sore throat, nausea and vomiting, abdominal pain, redness, edema, coryza, petechiae of mucosa Diagnosis by positive throat culture Antibiotics 10–14 days
		Scarlet fever Scarlatina (milder rash in children given penicillin)	Clinical syndrome same as above, but second day red rash, "blush," blanches on pressure, circumoral pallor, "strawberry" tongue. High fever: 39.5°C (103°F) Dick test for presence of antitoxin in host's blood

		Complications of streptococcus
		  Acute rheumatic fever
		  Acute glomerulo-nephritis
			Suspected cases of strep must be cultured and positives treated for 10–14 days to prevent complications
			Siblings and contacts of infected must be cultured

Streptococcus pneumoniae	Upper respiratory tract		Resistant to phagocytosis Produce toxins
		Pneumococcal pneumonia	Rapid growth to lungs; bronchopneumonia after aspiration; associated with anesthesia, seizures, coma
		Otitis media	More than one-half of otitis is strep Most children have first attack by age 6 Recurrent attacks lead to hearing loss and learning problems
		Mastoiditis, sinusitis, meningitis, endocarditis	

Table 34-6 Common bacterial diseases of childhood (*Continued*)

Agent	Source	Disease	Comments
Staphylococcus aureus	Skin, nose, gut, part of normal flora; nasal carriers common Improperly refrigerated cream- or egg-based food	Boils, wound infections, septicemia, endocarditis, osteomyelitis, impetigo, furuncles, styes, pneumonia, meningitis, food poisoning	Antibiotic-resistant strains exist in hospitals, where many children become infected. *Prevention:* 1. Wash hands after exposure and before working with susceptible persons. 2. Isolation of patients with staph. 3. Permit self-care when possible, especially new mother and baby. 4. Nurses are frequent carriers of resistant strains of staph in nose and skin. 5. Be alert to any skin infection, especially in people with IV, indwelling catheter, or shunts; skin infection can lead to septicemia and should be treated. 6. Antibiotic treatment must be continued 2–4 weeks.
		Impetigo (can be caused by *Streptococcus* as well as *Staphylococcus*) (See Fig. 34-4, p. 940)	Lesions begin as macule and progress to vesicle containing cloudy yellow fluid; rupture easily leaving red oozing lesion Usually on face or other exposed areas Most common: spring and summer in conditions of poor hygiene and nutrition Contagious—*itchy* Treatment: systemic and, less effectively, local antibiotics Avoid scratching and secondary infection Scabs may be removed to facilitate cleaning, treatment, and healing; saline soaks or compresses
Corynebacterium diphtheriae	Infected persons—initimate contact required for spread Droplets from nasopharynx; also, fomites, animals, milk; carriers exist	Diphtheria	May be symptomless or rapidly fatal; location of infection varies: anterior nasal, tonsillar, pharyngeal, laryngeal, bronchial Pseudomembrane forms, obstructing breathing Systemic effects on heart secondary to toxin High fatality rate Schick test for antitoxin Isolation, antibiotics, bed rest, 10–14 days in hospital Treatment includes DAT (diptheria antitoxin skin test first for sensitivity to horse serum) *Preventable* by active immunization in childhood Booster every 10 years Care to prevent infection secondary to pneumonia
Neisseria meningitidis	Nasopharynx; carriers exist; respiratory transmission	Meningococcal meningitis	Major worldwide health problem High fatality Petechial hemorrhagic lesions Circle area on skin and count lesions every hour to monitor progression
Pseudomonas aeruginosa	Soil water, vegetation	Infections of urinary tract, surgical wounds, Pneumonia Burns	Opportunistic pathogen (doesn't cause disease in healthy persons) Most frequent cause of death in patients with leukemia, cystic fibrosis, extensive burns Resistance to drugs common

Table 34-6 Common bacterial diseases of childhood (*Continued*)

Agent	Source	Disease	Comments
Salmonella	Infected feces; urine from humans; contaminating poultry, eggs, beef, pork, raw and powdered milk, pet turtles	*Intestinal:* gastroenteritis *Extraintestinal:* bacteremia, osteomyelitis, meningitis Typhoid fever	Sudden onset of abdominal pain, diarrhea, nausea and vomiting, dehydration, fever for several days Proper hand-washing and food handling can prevent it *Isolation required* Headache, malaise, diarrhea (occasionally constipation instead) and fever, abdominal pain and distention, rose spots on abdomen and chest. Danger of intestinal lesions perforating or hemorrhaging. All cases must be reported. Treatment by antimicrobials is useful
Shigella	Feces of infected human; contaminated food, water	Bacillary dysentery	Problem in young school-age children—contaminate hands touching toilet seat Excessive fluid loss from diarrhea and vomiting Acute onset of abdominal pain, cramping, diarrhea with mucus; feces may be blood-tinged Diagnosis should be confirmed and treatment instituted to eliminate reservoir of infection
Haemophilus influenzae	Nasopharynx of healthy or ill carriers	Otitis media, pneumonia Meningitis, bacteremia, cellulitis, epiglottitis, pericarditis	Symptoms may be vague. All children have some *Haemophilus* flu infection by age 3 Second leading cause of otitis media in children
Bordetella pertussis	Respiratory discharges from infected persons	Whooping cough	*Stage I. catarrhal:* Slow onset of common cold symptoms, cough becomes more severe, nocturnal, lasts 10–14 days *Stage II. paroxysmal (4–6 weeks):* Violent, sharp cough followed by inspiratory whoop—face and neck veins distended and face cyanotic during cough; vomiting of mucus *Stage III. Convalescent:* Gradual decrease in cough over 2 months Fatality rate high in children under 1 year old Most common late winter and early spring Immunization available, immunization must begin 6–8 weeks and series completed Immunity is not lifelong or complete
Clostridium tetani	Soil contaminated by feces of domestic animals and man	Tetanus	Organism is normal inhabitant of gut, but becomes dangerous when introduced into wound where anaerobic conditions exist (puncture wounds and under the crusts of burns) Tetanus neonatorum—unhealed umbilicus contaminated with feces Organism produces powerful neurotoxin

Table 34-6 Common bacterial diseases of childhood (*Continued*)

Agent	Source	Disease	Comments
			Hyperirritability of muscles, especially in face, neck and trunk; spasms of strong muscle groups produce lockjaw and opisthotonos (arched back), headache, fever, convulsions; difficulty with breathing, swallowing, and urinating due to muscle spasm
			Treatment includes tetanus antitoxin (test for horse serum sensitivity before giving), antibiotics; tranquilizers, sedatives, muscle relaxants; indwelling urinary catheter, IV fluids with electrolytes, tracheostomy, oxygen, suctioning
			Nursing care includes reducing all stimuli, especially, sound, light, and touch which may precipitate spasm; flatus-minimizing diet
			Immunization available
			Booster every 5–10 years and antitoxin at time of dirty wound

normal cell function ceases and the cell's machinery is used by the virus to reproduce itself. The host cell is fatally damaged when it either bursts open or slowly leaks new virus. The newly synthesized viruses move on to infect other host cells.

Viruses reach the human host by droplet, direct contact, and animal or arthropod vectors. The virus causes diseases predominantly by cell destruction. Viruses are responsible for the common cold, measles, mumps, chickenpox, polio, and many other diseases.

Viruses are generally prevented from invading the host by intact skin and mucous membranes. Once the host has been invaded, the inflammatory process resulting from cell injury can prevent the spread of the infection. Raising local temperature and increasing acidity from the chemicals released by damaged cells cause unfavorable conditions for viral growth. Viruses induce the host cells to produce *interferon*, a protein that inhibits viral multiplication, and *virus specific antibody.*

Viral diseases can be controlled through public health measures, including proper sanitation and hygiene, and some of them are preventable by immunization. Sanitary disposal of human feces, hand-washing by food handlers, and insect and rodent eradication programs have contributed to the control of many viral diseases. Immunization has worked well in reducing the number of cases of smallpox, polio, measles, mumps, and rubella. The common cold and some influenza viruses change their antigenic characteristics so frequently that vaccines are not useful.

Prevention of viral illnesses is very important because treatment measures are limited. Only symptomatic treatment can be given. Antibiotics are not useful. Antiviral therapy is difficult because the drug must destroy the virus and not the host's cell that it is inhabiting. Two specific therapeutic areas currently being developed are drugs that block viral movement into the cell and drugs that will stimulate the host's cells to produce interferon.

Viruses are difficult or impossible to grow in the laboratory so diagnosis of viral illness is based on the clinical presentation of the disease and on *antibody titers*, measurements of the host's blood levels of virus-specific antibody. An antibody titer is routinely done on women in their first trimester of pregnancy to determine whether they have levels of antibody against rubella sufficient to protect the fetus if the mother should be exposed to rubella during the pregnancy. Table 34-7 presents the major viral infections of childhood.

Table 34-7 Common viral infections of childhood

Disease/agent	Source	Communicability/immunization	Incubation	Clinical manifestations	Complications
Chickenpox (varicella-zoster virus) (See Fig. 34-5, p. 940)	Contact with discharge from skin, nose, or throat of infected person	1–2 days before to 6 days after rash appears (or until all lesions are crusted)/No immunization available for widespread use	14–21 days	Rash appears first on trunk, moves outward, rapid progression through macule, papule, vesicle, crusted vesicle, with all stages present simultaneously (noticeable in Fig. 34-5). Crusted vesicles itch. Prodrome may include malaise, fever, headache, anorexia, myalgia. Contagious until last lesion has crusted	Infection and scarring from scratching Encephalitis
Influenza (types A, B, C)	Contact with discharge from nose or throat of infected person; may be air-borne	Unknown; probably in early and febrile stages/Immunization available but of limited usefulness because of antigenic shift (virus frequently changes its antigenic characteristics); used in high-risk groups during epidemic years	24–72 hours	Chills, fever, myalgia, cough, headache	Pneumonia Bronchitis Bronchiolitis
Pneumonia (Coxsackie, echovirus, adenovirus, respiratory syncytial)	Contact with discharge from nose or throat of infected person	Communicability unknown	Few days to over week	Progression from mild upper respiratory infection to chills, malaise, headache, anorexia, cough that may be productive, fever 1–3 weeks (See Chap. 25.)	Rare
Diarrhea (summer diarrhea) echovirus	Contact via fecal-oral contamination	Unknown, probably around onset of symptoms; virus in feces up to 2 weeks	3–5 days	Vomiting and diarrhea (See Chaps. 24 and 28.)	Dehydration Electrolyte imbalance
Infectious hepatitis (A, B)	Contact, fecal-oral; blood or serum transfusions or skin punctures A, all ways B, never in feces	Few days before to 1 or more after onset of symptoms No immunization available Gammaglobulin given to contacts (preformed antibody to hepatitis virus)	15–50 days, A; 2–6 months, B	*Preicteric* (before jaundice): loss appetite, bad taste in mouth, chills, nausea, vomiting, diarrhea, fever; 24 h–3 weeks. *Icteric:* dark urine, clay-colored stools, jaundice; itching skin; 2 to 10 weeks. *Posticteric:* patient convalescent	Relapse Damaged liver

935

Table 34-7 Common viral infections of childhood (*Continued*)

Disease/agent	Source	Communicability/immunization	Incubation	Clinical manifestations	Complications
Measles (rubeola, red measles)	Contact with respiratory tract, secretions, blood, or urine of infected person or air-borne on droplet or dust	4 days before to 5 days after rash Immunization available; should be given at age 15 months; gamma globulin may be useful	10–12 days	Slow onset, symptoms of cold nasal discharge, tearing, sneezing, photophobia (sensitive to light), fever, to 40–40.6°C (104–105°F) for 3–4 days, then, Koplik's spots in mouth (pink macules with bluish spot in center) 2 days after Koplik's spots; dusty red rash, to maculopapular to coalesced, begins back of neck and forehead spreads to extremities; greatest on face and trunk; sickest day 2 or 3 of rash; skin desquamation as rash disappears; resolving day 6–8	Rare, usually secondary bacterial infections, otitis media, bronchopneumonia, encephalitis
Mumps	Contact with saliva of infected person	1 week before and after onset of parotitis; *inapparent infection is common* Immunization available; given at age 15 months	14–21 days	Sudden onset: headache, earache, anorexia, fever, uni- or bilateral parotid swelling, pain related to degree of swelling, swallowing difficult, acid food and drink increase pain	Rare in prepubertal ages Meningoencephalitis Postpubertal: orchitis, oophoritis Associated with sterility
Rubella (German measles, 3-day measles)	Droplet or contact with nasopharyngeal secretions, blood, feces, urine of infected person	7 days before to 5 days after rash Immunization available; given at age 15 months	14–21 days	Variable, may be headache, coryza, sore throat, malaise, mild conjunctivitis, fever, lymph node enlargement and tenderness; usually rash, pale pink, at hairline and spreads downward; symptoms and rash may appear together or rash may be delayed; rash gone 1–5 days	Rare Encephalitis Mild arthritis may last 3–28 days. Congenital rubella Teratogenic effect on fetus 1st 3 months of pregnancy. Infected infant may shed virus for 6 months Classical rubella syndrome Deafness Blindness (cataracts and congenital glaucoma) Cerebral defects (mental retardation microcephaly)

Disease	Method of transmission	Period of communicability	Incubation period	Symptoms	Complications
Roseola infantum	Uncertain	Uncertain		Sudden onset in children under 4; usually around 1 year. High fever for 3–5 days; after fever maculopapular rash appears, first on trunk later rest of body. Rash fades in 1–3 days; can be subclinical; often confused with rubella and allergies	Febrile seizures
Poliomyelitis (virus types 1, 2, 3) Infantile paralysis	Contact droplet, pharyngeal or intestinal excretions into mouth of host	Shortly before and during first week of illness. Immunization available; given in infancy	7–14 days	3 kinds of polio: prodrome same, headache, low fever, anorexia, nausea, vomiting, abrupt onset lasts 24–48 h. *Abortive poliomyelitis:* same as above, but intensified, with CNS involvement, stiff neck, pain on movement. *Paralytic poliomyelitis:* as above, but patient acutely ill; paralysis may be first sign; paralysis determines clinical signs; may be respiratory, extremities, bladder, circulatory, pharyngeal	Respiratory or circulatory failure, bacterial infections, emotional disturbances. Permanent paralysis
Rabies	Saliva of animals with disease, through bite or scratch. Dogs, cats, skunks, rodents, foxes, cattle, pigs, bats. Confine animal causing bite 14 days for observation.	In dogs and cats: 3–5 days before onset through disease. Antirabies vaccine available to exposed persons; hyperimmune serum of antirabies antibodies can prevent death in exposed person.	3–8 weeks	Occurs in 3 stages, affects CNS—damages pons, medulla, brainstem, thalamus. *Prodromal:* headache, malaise, fever, numbness and tingling at bite; lasts 2–4 days. *Excitation:* Increasing nervous irritability, apprehension, severe muscle spasm of muscles of swallowing and respiration. *Paralytic:* muscle spasms stop, stupor, coma, death	100% mortality unless antirabies vaccines is begun shortly after exposure. Treatment is a 14- to 20-day series of injections
Infectious mononucleosis Epstein-Barr virus (Diagnosed by Monospot test)	Humans, probably oral-pharyngeal spread	Unknown	Less than 2 weeks	Prodrome: 3–5 days malaise, fever, sore throat, enlarged tonsils with white membrane, fatigue, nausea. Day 5–20: prostration, enlarged lymph nodes and spleen, hepatitis, convalescence up to 3 months. Symptoms may reappear. Antibiotics do not affect progression of disease but may be used for secondary infections in throat. Relapse frequent. Bed rest, avoid trauma to spleen	Splenic rupture, extreme pharyngeal hyperplasia (avoid contact sports and trauma to spleen for at least 6 weeks)

Rickettsial diseases

Rickettsia are microorganisms that need the host cell to multiply. Their reservoir is some species of mammal. They are transferred to humans by lice, fleas, ticks and mites; therefore, the diseases they cause are known as *arthropod-borne diseases*. The arthropod either injects the agent when it bites the host or deposits the agent on the host's skin as it defecates during biting. The host scratches and inoculates the agent into broken or irritated skin.

Rickettsia establish themselves in the lining of small blood vessels in the host. The small vessels of the skin are most frequently involved, causing the characteristic rash associated with these diseases. The vascular lesions result from edema and obstruction and can also occur in the lungs, heart, liver, kidneys and central nervous system. Infection by *Rickettsia* stimulates the development of *Rickettsia* specific antibody and immunity is generally lifelong.

Diagnosis is made by clinical signs and symptoms, serologic tests, and isolation of the organism. Treatment is symptomatic. Removal of the arthropod vector is essential. Tetracyclines and chloramphenicol are frequently administered. See Table 34-8, "Major Rickettsial Infections of Childhood."

Parasitic diseases

Parasites depend on humans to complete some stage of their life cycle. They cause damage to humans by using nutrient materials the human body needs for their growth. Some parasites cause anemia by feeding on blood, and others cause local tissue inflammation and destruction by taking up space or by producing a toxin. Some parasites cause the host to have an allergic reaction. Many parasites have elaborate life cycles involving several hosts. Generally, parasites are either *endo-* (inside of) or *ecto-*(outside of) the body. The most common endoparasites of childhood are the helminths, or worms. The most common ectoparasites are lice. Table 34-9 discusses parasites and the diseases they cause.

Fungal Diseases

The study of fungal diseases affecting humans is known as *medical mycology*. The two major groups of fungi are yeasts and molds. The fungi

Table 34-8 Major rickettsial infections of childhood

Disease/agent	Vector/ transmission	Incubation	Clinical manifestations	Complications
Epidemic typhus (*Rickettsia prowazekii*)	Body lice Feces of lice scratched into skin	7–14 days	High fever, headache, generalized aches and pain, maculopapular rash by day 4–6, first on trunk near axillae, face spared, second week lesion petechial and purpuric	Otis media Parotitis Bronchopneumonia Gangrene of fingers, toes, nose, genitalia
Endemic typhus (*Rickettsia, mooseri typhi*)	Rat flea Feces of flea scratched into skin	8–12 days	Mild version of above rash; rarely hemorrhagic	Rare, same as above
Rocky Mountain spotted fever (*Rickettsia rickettsii*)	Tick Bite	3–12 days	Prodrome: headache, malaise, anorexia, then high fever, accentuation of prodrome Rash, bright red macules, begins at ankles, spreads to palms, soles, back, arms, thigh, and chest	Infrequent, if treated; severe or fatal in untreated cases, gangrene, deafness, encephalitis
Rickettsial pox (*Rickettsia akari*)	Mite Bite	7–14 days	Patient unaware lesion at bite; sudden-onset fever, chills malaise, headache; maculopapular red discrete rash	Rare

Table 34-9 Major parasitic infections of childhood

Disease/agent	Source/transmission	Incubation	Clinical manifestations	Control
Endoparasites; helminths				
Roundworm (*Ascaris*)*	Soil, with infected eggs from human feces Ingestion of eggs from soil-contaminated food, toys, hands, water, dust	8–10 weeks	*Larval stage:* Lung symptoms, asthma, wheezing, itching, malaise *Worm stage:* Abdominal pain, nausea, vomiting, malnutrition, dehydration, electrolyte imbalance *Complications:* Intestinal obstruction, peritonitis	Treatment with anthelmintics (pyrantel pamoate stains stools red)
Pinworm (*Enterobius vermicularis*)	Infected humans, contaminated hands, food, air (from shaking infected bedding or clothing)	2–6 weeks	Eggs stick to perianal skin; intense itching, may lead to loss of sleep, irritability, nausea, vomiting. Worms lay eggs at anus. Pressing cellophage tape on anus will pick up eggs or worms for inspection under microscope.	Improve personal hygiene; treat family members as well as patient. Treat as with roundworm
Hookworm (*Necator americanus; Ancylostoma duodenale*)	Soil contaminated with human feces. Larvae penetrate unbroken skin, usually of feet, enter blood, migrate to lungs, then are swallowed	6 weeks	Symptoms depend on number of worms; worms feed on host blood, cause anemia, pain, diarrhea, itching	Prevent spread. Treat as above
Ectoparasites				
Pediculosis (*Pediculus humanus capitis:* head lice; *P.h. corporis:* (body lice); *Phthirius pubis:* pubic lice, "crabs")	Infected persons or articles. Close contact with infested persons or articles	Days to weeks	Head lice is most common in children. Eggs attach to hair shaft (louse is on scalp); causes intense itching, excoriation. Secondary bacterial infection is common	Improve personal hygiene; shampoo and bathe with gamma benzene hexachloride (e.g., Kwell); cut hair
Scabies (*Sarcoptes scabiei:* "itch mite")	Infested persons. Close contact	4–6 weeks	Intense itching in area between fingers, toes; on wrists, abdomen, axillae, genitalia. Secondary bacterial infection common with pustules. Mite burrows under skin, leaving eggs and feces in black-red bumps	Treatment of skin with gamma benzene hexachloride (e.g., Kwell) Wash clothing, bedding, personal articles in hot, soapy water

* Adult roundworms lay eggs in intestines. Eggs pass to soil, incubating there in 2–3 weeks. When eggs in soil are swallowed, larvae penetrate intestines and move to lungs and back to gastrointestinal tract.

that cause disease are microscopic and are considered to be members of neither the plant nor the animal kingdom. Mycotic infections can be either superficial, involving skin and nails and known as *dermatophytoses*, or deep mycoses, producing systemic infection.

Fungi break down organic material, which produces carbon dioxide and alcohol. Economically, they are of value in the bread, cheese, alcoholic beverage, and drug industries. The most commonly recognized medically useful molds are *Penicillium notatum*, from which penicillin is purified and the *Streptomyces*, which produces streptomycin.

The superficial mycoses are acquired by direct personal contact. The dermatophytes cause disfigurement by digesting the keratin of the skin, hair, or nails. The disease is known as *ringworm* because of the sharply demarked red, ringlike border. The specific fungus can be identified by microscopic examination of skin scrapings. Local antifungal treatment is usually effective.

The deep fungal infections are transmitted by inhalation of air-borne or dust-borne spores. These fungi are weak antigens and they do not produce toxins. They cause damage by provoking a hypersensitivity reaction by the host against the agent's proteins. The most commonly oc-

Figure 34-5 Typical lesions of chickenpox (varicella). Notice the variety of lesions present. These present the typical rash which comes in "crops." Some macules and papules are present, but the predominant lesion is the vesicle. One lesion near the corner of the mouth shows a crust.

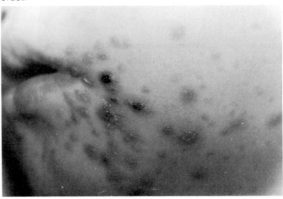

Figure 34-6 Ringworm of the scalp (tinea capitis) and of the body (tinea corporis). Tinea capitis of a child and tinea corporis on the arm of the mother. Though immune to tinea capitis, adults may get ringworm infection on the skin elsewhere. Note the partial alopecia (baldness) in the boy and the classical ringworm on the mother's arm. (*From R. Hoekelman et al., Principles of Pediatrics: Health Care of the Young, McGraw-Hill, New York, 1978, p. 1386.*)

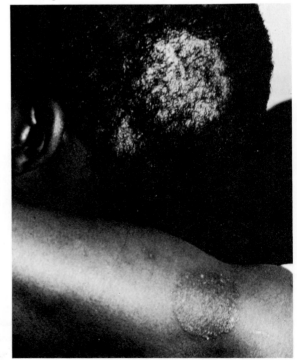

Figure 34-4 Classical impetigo. Superficial oozing and crusted ulcers. Note involvement of nares; the nose is the likely source of the infective organism (*From R. Hoekelman et al., eds., Principles of Pediatrics: Health Care of the Young, McGraw-Hill, New York, 1978, p. 1371.*)

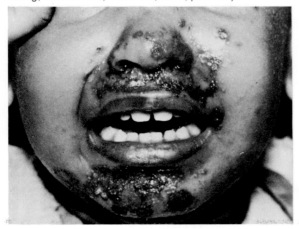

curring systemic mycosis in children is histo-plasmosis. The diseases caused by these agents are serious and can be fatal. They sometimes occur when host resistance is lowered or when normal flora is altered by prolonged antibiotic therapy. Deep fungal infections are difficult to treat and there are few specific antifungal agents. Amphotericin B is one sometimes used. See Table 34-10 for more discussion of specific fungal diseases.

Table 34-10 Major fungal infections of childhood

Disease	Source/Transmission	Clinical manifestations	Control
Tinea capitis (head ringworm) (See Fig. 34-6, p. 940)	Humans, animals Personal contact, combs, theater seats, clothing. Highly contagious	May begin with small itchy papules, hair loss, de-nuded scalp	Detect early, treat topically with lotions or systemically with griseofulvin, destroy or decontaminate head wear, and teach child not to use others head wear or combs
Tinea corporis (body ringworm)	Humans, animals Personal contact	Lesions circular, slightly raised and red at periphery, scaling, itchy, on smooth, nonhairy skin	Same
Tinea cruris (groin, jock itch)	Humans Direct contact skin, clothing, towel	Well-marginated, scaly, brownish, with tiny pustules, itchy	Keep area dry, clean; loose clothing; don't share towels; same as above
Tinea pedis (athlete's foot)	Public pools, showers, locker rooms Contact with skin, desquamated skin, colonies of fungi in damp areas	Vesicles between toes and on soles, skin becomes macerated and peels, fissures form	Prohibit infected persons from using public areas, treat; clean dry socks; avoid sweating feet. Treat as above and use antifungal powders or liquids topically
Candidiasis (moniliasis)	Human Newborns acquire during birth	Transient infection in mouth (thrush) or systemic involvement of lungs, liver, bone, kidneys, heart, vagina, brain; when defenses are depressed or during antibiotic therapy.	Hand-washing between patients. Further discussions under sexually transmitted diseases
Histoplasmosis	Soil with high organic content such as chicken houses, manured gardens Inhalation of air-borne spores	Onset 10–14 days after inhalation of spores; may be benign and asymptomatic or may have symptoms from lung lesion, fever, malaise, cough, chest pain, and weakness; lasts 4–6 weeks; very serious disease with high fatality rate. Occurs in children under 10 years when lung infection spreads throughout the body. Called acute disseminated, hepatosplenomegaly, fever, prostration; treatment, amphotericin B	Spray to reduce dust in chicken houses, barns, caves, starling roosts or wear masks

Sexually transmitted diseases*

The term *sexually transmitted diseases* (STD) has gradually replaced the more familiar term *VD*. Over the last several years, VD had become synonymous with two diseases—gonorrhea and syphilis. STD include a host of other diseases. See Table 34-11. All are diseases that may be spread simply by contact of skin to skin or mucous membrane to mucous membrane!

Gonorrhea (GC)

Gonorrhea ranks first among reported communicable diseases in the United States. Between 1966 and 1975 the number of cases of gonorrhea reported in the United States increased by 15 percent each year.[2] In 1977 there was a 2 percent decrease from 1976.[3] The age groups at greatest risk of acquiring the disease are young adults (20 to 24-year-olds), ranking first, and adolescents (15 to 19-year-olds), ranking second.[4] Adolescents in the process of formulating their identity are likely to risk contracting STD.

Gonorrhea ("clap," "dose," "drip," "GC") is caused by *Neisseria gonorrhoeae*, an anaerobic gram-negative diplococcus bacterium whose growth is enhanced in the presence of carbon dioxide. *N. gonorrhoeae* is sensitive to light, air, and temperature and can only penetrate mucous membranes such as those found in the cervix, urethra, mouth, throat, and anus and live in the submucosa. It is transmitted only by sexual contact, not by toilet seats or dirty towels.

Infection From a single sexual exposure with an infected person, boys have a 20 to 50 percent chance of contacting gonorrhea, while girls have more than a 50 percent chance.[5] Gonococcal infection in boys usually causes urethritis (pain on urination) and a thick creamy discharge (penile drip) within 2 to 14 days of infection. These symptoms cause most boys to seek treatment. After about 2 to 8 weeks, symptoms may spontaneously decrease. However, the disease is still present and can spread to the sexual partner or invade the posterior urethra, epididymis, and prostate gland. Five to ten percent of males infected may remain totally asymptomatic.[6] Sixty to eighty percent of females may have no symp-

*The section on sexually transmitted diseases was written by Nancy Schamber.

Table 34-11 Disease and infections that may be sexually transmitted

---

Chancroid
Condylomata acuminata (also called venereal warts)
Gonorrhea
Granuloma inguinale (also called donovanosis)
Herpes simplex type 1 (oral) and type 2 (genital) infections
Lymphogranuloma venereum
Syphilis
Urethritis due to *Chlamydia* or *Trichomonas vaginalis*
Vaginitis due to *Trichomonas vaginalis*, *Haemophilus vaginalis*, *Candida albicans*, and chlamydial organisms

---

toms or such mild discharge, dysuria, or pelvic tenderness that they do not seek medical care. Symptoms in girls seeking care usually include a yellow, irritating vaginal discharge, perineal soreness, and painful urination.

Diagnosis A definitive diagnosis in both sexes may be obtained by using a culture of Thayer-Martin medium (TMM, chocolate agar) or modified Thayer-Martin (MTM, Transgrow). A cotton swab is used to culture the cervix in a female or urethra, rectum, and mouth in either sex. The plate is then incubated in a carbon dioxide environment. The first ounce of freshly voided urine from the male will contain pus cells. This can be collected, centrifuged, and the sediment used for a culture. A diagnosis in males can also be done immediately by using a Gram stain, placing the urethral discharge on a glass slide and examining it. A Gram stain under the microscope is used to look for polymorphonuclear cells with gram-negative intracellular diplococci. A Gram stain is not reliable in females because the cervix has gram-negative bacteria as normal flora.

In 1976, a new type of gonococcus—*penicillinase-producing Neisseria gonorrhoeae* (PPNG), which is resistant to penicillin therapy and usually ampicillin—was recognized in the United States. Although cases of PPNG in the United States are few, testing every patient with gonorrhea for a cure is very important. If the repeat culture is positive and you suspect that the patient may have contracted PPNG, a test to detect the penicillinase enzyme can be done by the local health department. See Table 34-12 for treatment schedules.

Table 34-12 Recommended treatment for gonococcal infection*

Diagnosis	Therapy	Alternatives
Uncomplicated gonorrhea	*Procaine penicillin*, 4.8 million units IM at two sites with 1 g of probenecid PO	*Tetracycline*. Initial dose 1.5 g, then 0.5 g PO qid for 5–7 days *Ampicillin*, 3.5 g with 1 g of probenecid PO
Gonorrhea in pregnancy	Same as above	Penicillin allergy: *Erthromycin*, 1 g PO, followed by 0.5 g qid for 4 days *Cefazolin*, 2 g IM plus 1 g probenecid or *Spectinomycin*, 2 g IM
Treatment failures or penicillinase-producing strains	*Spectinomycin*, 2 g IM in single injection	
Pelvic inflammatory disease (outpatient)	*Tetracycline*, 0.5 g qid for 10 days	*Procaine penicillin*, 4.8 million units IM plus 1 g probenecid PO, followed by ampicillin, 0.5 g PO qid for 10 days
Pelvic inflammatory disease (hospitalized patient)	*Penicillin*, 20 million units IV per day until improvement then 15 g *ampicillin* PO qid for for 10 days	*Tetracycline*, 0.25 g IV qid until improvement then 0.5 g PO qid for 10 days
Disseminated gonococcal infection	*Penicillin*, 10 million units IV per day until improvement then 0.5 g *ampicillin* qid for a total of 7 days	*Ampicillin*, 3.5 g PO plus 1 g probenecid followed by 0.5 g *ampicillin* qid for 7 days *Tetracycline*, 0.5 grams PO qid for 7 days
Gonococcal ophthalmia (neonatal disease)	Penicillin 50,000 units per day in two doses IV for 7 days	
Gonococcal childhood disease	(Children who weigh 100 lb or more should receive adult regimen. Children who weigh less than 100 lb should be treated according to: "Gonorrhea: CDC Recommended Treatment Schedules, 1979, *Morbidity-Mortality Weekly Report* **28**(2):13–21.	

Modified from CDC recommendation, 1978.

Complications

Pelvic inflammatory disease (PID) There were 274,000 cases of PID in 1977;[7] 10 to 15 percent of female adolescents infected with gonorrhea develop PID. Symptoms classically begin after menses: fever, chills, and abdominal pain. GC grows well in blood, and because the cervix is slightly open during menses, the organism spreads into the uterus and up the fallopian tubes. Pertinent physical findings are exquisite bilateral lower abdominal pain and pain on gentle motion of the cervix (Chandelier sign) during vaginal exam. Lab tests result in positive gonorrhea culture, increased WBCs, and increased erythrocyte sedimentation rate. Hospitalization is required for severe infections. Gonococcal PID must be differentiated from ectopic pregnancy, appendicitis, endometritis, and torsion of *adnexa* (tubes and ovaries) which cause similar signs. *Fitz-Hugh-Curtis syndrome* (acute perihepatitis) with right upper quadrant abdominal pain and hepatic tenderness occurs in 30 percent of females with gonococcal PID.[8] Gonococcal PID can cause tubal-ovarian abscesses and tubal strictures. This is the largest cause of infertility in women and also predisposes them to ectopic pregnancy.

Disseminated gonococcal infection Gonococci can cause systemic disease by spreading via the bloodstream and lymphatics. Gonorrhea is the most common cause of acute arthritis in adolescents.[9] There were 5000 to 6100 cases of this in 1977.[10] The arthritis-dermatitis syndrome involves the wrists, knees, ankles, and small joints of the hands and feet. A typical rash with papular, petechial, and pustular skin lesions occurs primarily on the distal extremities. Sometimes the gonococcal organisms have been cultured from the skin lesions. Endocarditis and meningitis seen in response to a systemic infection occur, but are rare.

Ophthalmia neonatorum (conjunctivitis) This infection of the newborn's eyes is acquired during passage through the birth canal of infected mothers. Often bacteria are harbored in Bartholin's glands. The incubation period is 2 to 4 days. If symptoms of purulent conjunctival discharge and edema are not treated, blindness can result. Silver nitrate drops are inadequate treatment if the mother has gonorrhea at the time of the baby's birth. Even with silver nitrate treatment the infection persists in the deep tissues and organs—liver, heart, and brain. Systemic treatment is given to the newborn.

Preadolescent gonococcal infection In young girls symptoms of gonococcal infection are labial redness, swelling, and purulent discharge. Boys have the same symptoms as adults. In the first year of life, gonococcal vulvovaginitis is most frequently acquired nonsexually, especially when the infant shares the bed with an infected parent or poor hygiene is present. Beyond 1 year most pediatric infections result from sexual abuse (rape, sexual assault, or incest). Young children with suspected STDs should have cultures of the pharynx and rectum as well as the vagina and urethra.

Syphilis

Syphilis ("lues," "siff," "pox," "bad blood") is caused by *Treponema pallidum*, an aerobic spirochete which enters the body during sexual contact through mucous membranes or a cut in the skin. This fragile organism dies quickly outside the body and is easily killed by drying and common bacterial agents. Although syphilis ranks high among reported communicable diseases in the United States, the age group ranging from 0 to 19 has a very low disease incidence.

During the incubation period of 10 to 90 days (average is 21 days), the adolescent has no symptoms. The *primary stage*, in which a *chancre* (hard, painless ulcer) appears at the site of infection (usually the penis, cervix, vulva, mouth, or rectum), occurs about 21 days after contact. The chancre may not be noticed because there is no pain. If not treated, it will last 6 weeks or more and then disappear.

The secondary stage develops 2 to 6 months after the infection and lasts 2 to 6 weeks but may recur up to 2 years later. Symptoms of secondary syphilis are:

1. Skin eruptions: a copper-colored rash on the palms of the hands and soles of the feet; *mucous patches*, lesions in the mouth; *condylomata lata*, warts on the genital area. All these skin lesions are infectious.
2. Systemic symptoms: low-grade fever, headache, malaise, baldness (alopecia)
3. Adenopathy or swollen glands

These symptoms mimic other diseases and resolve slowly and spontaneously even without treatment.

The latent period (no overt symptoms) begins with resolution of the secondary symptoms and may persist for a few years or the remainder of the patient's life.

After 10 to 20 years, *tertiary syphilis* may be benign or may include the following: blindness, heart disease, paralysis, organic brain disease, or even death, depending on which body system the spirochetes affect. The lesions are generally divided into *gummas*, lesions affecting any body system but with a predilection for cardiovascular tissue, and *neurosyphilis*, called *general paresis* when it affects the nerve roots, or *tabes dorsalis* when it affects the dorsal roots of the spinal cord.

Congenital syphilis Syphilis may also be transmitted from an infected pregnant woman to her unborn infant (*congenital syphilis*). The spirochete may cross the placenta after the eighteenth week of pregnancy. A general rule is: "The longer the duration of the untreated infection before pregacy, the less likely it is that the fetus will be stillborn or infected."[11] Latent, or tertiary, syphilis is less likely to cause stillbirth and severe infection than primary or secondary syphilis. Adequate treatment of the mother before the eighteenth week of pregnancy prevents infection of the fetus. Because penicillin crosses the placenta, the treatment of the mother after the eighteenth week also cures the infected fetus. Treatment will not reverse damage done earlier. Early onset of newborn symptoms indicates more severe disease and a poor prognosis. Congenital syphilis is very rarely seen, probably because of early screening of pregnant women. See Table 34-13 for signs of congenital syphilis.

Diagnosis When a lesion or rash is present in primary, secondary, or congenital syphilis, the diagnosis may be made by visualizing the organism (*T. pallidum*) from the lesion under a darkfield microscope. The serologic tests, VDRL, FTA, and RPR, will be negative in the incubation period of syphilis, but positive in the primary, secondary, latent, and tertiary stages.

Treatment Primary, secondary, and latent syphilis infections of less than 1 year's duration are treated with 2.4 million units of long-acting benzathine penicillin intramuscularly in a single injection. If the adolescent is allergic to penicillin, treatment is 30 g total dosage of tetracycline or erythromycin. Syphilis of more than 1 year's duration is treated with 2.4 million units of benzathine penicillin intramuscularly weekly for 3 successive weeks. Cerebrospinal fluid examination is advisable in all patients with syphilis of greater than 1 year's duration to exclude neurosyphilis. All sexual partners are treated in the same way as the person with the active infection.

Adolescents treated for syphilis should be warned of the possibility of experiencing a Jarisch-Herxheimer reaction, which appears in 50 to 90 percent of people within a few hours of treatment and lasts for 24 to 48 h.[12] The reaction

Table 34-13 Signs of congenital syphilis

Early signs (newborn)

Skin lesions
Snuffles—profuse nasal discharge with resulting rhagades (facial scars or fissures)
Hepatosplenomegaly—enlarged liver and spleen
Abnormal cerebrospinal fluid (CSF) findings

Late signs (after 2 years of age)

Interstitial keratitis (blindness)
Hutchinson's teeth (widely spaced, notched central incisors)
Saddle nose (destruction of cartilage of nasal septum)

consists of headache, chills, fatigue, and transient fever. The cause is unknown but may be due to an allergic reaction or a release of endotoxins from the killed treponemas. The treatment is rest and aspirin.

Follow-up care includes repeat VDRLs at 3-month intervals the first year and treatment of suspected contacts.

Vaginitis

Vaginitis is an inflammation of the vagina. It is a common ailment that is not necessarily dangerous but can be very uncomfortable, painful, and anxiety-producing. Vaginitis is a special problem for adolescents who may keep silent and feel guilty because they connect vaginitis with "VD." Antibiotic therapy, long-term steroid therapy, mechanical irritation from foreign bodies or masturbation, chemical irritation (douching), diabetes, pregnancy, and sexual contact predispose individuals to vaginitis.

Normal vaginal discharge may be transparent or slightly milky in color, while a vaginal infection is characterized by an increase in amount of discharge that is usually bad-smelling, irritating, and purulent. The infection may spread from the vagina to include the vulva and cervix. *Monilia*, *Trichomonas*, *Chlamydia*, nonspecific vaginitis, and herpes simplex virus, type 1 and 2, will be discussed. Symptoms of most vaginal infections are similar: vulvovaginal itching, redness and soreness, burning on urination, and pain during intercourse. Variations in types of vaginal discharge help differentiate the disease.

Monilia *Monilia* (*Candida*, yeast) infection is caused by an overgrowth of a fungus, *Candida albicans*, which may be found in the normal vaginal flora. Yeast infections have a thick, white, (sometimes cottage cheesy) discharge. It is intensely itchy and the perineum appears inflamed and sore. Approximately one-third to one-half of all vaginal infections are caused by *Monilia*. Some predisposing factors for overgrowth of yeast in adolescents include: poorly controlled diabetes, antibiotic therapy, steroid treatment, poor health, poor hygiene, oral contraceptives, and pregnancy. *Monilia* can also be sexually transmitted.

Because *Monilia* needs a dark, warm, moist area for growth, males who are circumcised or have good hygiene usually do not develop symptoms. A local, red, itchy rash may develop on the penis after contact with the infected discharge. Treatment in the male consists of using a nystatin ointment on the rash and abstaining from sexual contact (or wearing condoms).

Treatment in females includes fungicidal or antibiotic vaginal cream or suppositories. Sitz baths, loose clothing, and cotton underwear may help. Decreasing free carbohydrates in the diet is also suggested. See Table 34-14 for a summary of vaginitis and its treatment.

Trichomoniasis Trichomoniasis is caused by the protozoan *Trichomonas vaginalis*. Human beings, insects, fish, fowl, and mammals are known to serve as a host to these flagellated parasites. They normally are carried in the intestinal tract. In the adolescent girl, *Trichomonas* accounts for up to 28 percent of genital infections and may be responsible for as much as 15 percent of urethritis in boys.[13] Trichomoniasis may be transmitted through sexual contact or by self-infection through contamination from the rectum. The discharge is usually very irritating, thin, foamy, and yellowish-green in color.

Males are usually asymptomatic (carriers) but can spread the infection to other sexual partners

Table 34-14 Symptoms, diagnosis, and treatment of vaginal infections

Vaginitis	Symptoms	Diagnosis	Treatment
Moniliasis (*Candida albicans*)	Itching, thick cheesy, white discharge; erythematous vulva and vagina; not malodorous; dyspareunia (pain on intercourse); dysuria	Use vaginal discharge material in potassium hydroxide on glass slide examined under microscope or Nickerson culture.	Nystatin (Mycostatin), 1–2 suppositories daily for 2–3 weeks inserted high in vagina Monistat cream, 1 applicator daily for 7–10 days
Trichomoniasis (*Trichomonas vaginalis*)	Malodorous, frothy, yellow-green discharge; itchy, erythematous vulvovagina and cervix; strawberry cervix; dyspareunia; dysuria	Use normal saline with vaginal discharge on glass slide examined under microscope (moving protozoa are seen).	Flagyl, 2 g orally in single dose Reinfection: Flagyl 250 mg PO tid for 10 days. Not used in pregnancy
Nonspecific (*Haemophilus vaginalis*) "clue cells"	Thinnish, gray-white discharge, malodorous; itchiness rare; dysuria; dyspareunia	Vaginal material and normal saline on glass slide examined under microscope, then cultured	Sulfa cream, 1 applicator bid for 10 days per vagina Ampicillin, 500 mg PO qid for 6–10 days Tetracycline, 250 mg qid for 7 days
Herpes genitalis (herpes simplex virus, types 1 and 2)	Initial infection 3–7 days after exposure, vesicles which rupture 1–2 days later, then painful, small round, shallow ulcers with red base that may last up to 2–4 weeks; dyspareunia and dysuria. Recurrent infection symptoms milder—last 7–10 days	Papanicolaou stain from scraping of ulcer. Viral culture. Antibody titer positive after 3 weeks of infection	*No cure.* Analgesics for pain, warm sitz bath; wet dressings of betadine

through the ejaculate. Therefore, both sexual partners should be treated with Flagyl. Avoid alcoholic beverages for 2 days after treatment with Flagyl since it has a minor Antabuse effect (alcohol causes nausea). Flagyl should not be used in pregnancy (Table 34-14).

Nonspecific vaginitis *Nonspecific vaginitis* (NSV) is a term applied to vulvovaginitis when gonococci, yeast, *Trichomonas, Chlamydia*, or an allergic reaction cannot be found. *Haemophilus vaginalis*, a bacterium, is responsible for more than 90 percent of vaginal NSV. Although adolescent boys are usually asymptomatic, *H. vaginalis* may be passed through sexual contact. Therefore, with recurrent infections, both partners should be treated to prevent reinfection. *Haemophilus* responds well to treatment with tetracycline (Table 34-14).

Herpes genitalis Teenagers may account for 25–50 percent of all patients with herpetic infections.[14] Herpes lesions, papules, blisters, and open sores around the perineal area, on the vagina or on the penis may be either type 1, oral herpes (10 percent of the time) or type 2, genital herpes. Type 1 is transmitted through oral-genital contact and type 2 through genital contact. There is no significant difference in the clinical manifestations of types 1 and 2. There is no cure for herpes; however, medications are used for the pain and to prevent infection of the lesions. Topical applications of antibiotics and steroids may be prescribed. Sexual intercourse will aggravate and spread herpes and should be avoided when active lesions are present.

After the sores have healed, the virus remains in the nerve cell, thus preventing the body's immune system from disposing of the virus. Since the herpes virus stays alive in the body, it can remain dormant or become active. Infections recur about 60 percent of the time. The adolescent is more likely to get herpes when the body is run down.

There is a more than 50 percent chance of severe herpetic infection occurring in the infant delivered through an area of active infection. If herpes lesions are noted within 4 weeks before delivery, a cesarean birth is preferred as long as membranes have not been ruptured for more than 4 hours. Recurrent infection may increase the likelihood of cervical cancer, so a pap smear every 6 months is suggested (Table 34-13).

Chlamydia *Chlamydia* is a bacterium which grows in the cells of the urethra or vagina and is spread by sexual contact. Not all physicians have the facilities to culture *Chlamydia*, and it is expensive. In those centers where cultures are done, incidence is higher then gonorrhea.

Symptoms vary in severity, but when present are like those seen in gonorrhea. Untreated, *Chlamydia* can produce PID exactly like gonorrhea but will not respond to penicillin. Tetracycline is required for treatment.

The newborn of a mother with *Chlamydia* can develop an eye infection called inclusion conjunctivitis which requires tetracycline for treatment. Inhaled vaginal secretions during birth can result in a fatal pneumonia from 2 weeks through 3 months after birth if not treated with tetracycline.

Venereal warts Venereal warts (condylomata acuminata), like skin warts, are caused by a virus. These warts can be spread by sexual contact and are usually found in the moist, warm, areas around the vagina or the rectum and on the penis. Usually they are treated if large and numerous. Do not confuse *condylomata acuminata* with *condylomata lata*, a very infectious manifestation of syphilis.

Condylomata acuminata are usually painted with a liquid, *podophyllin*, that is poisonous when taken orally and will damage normal skin. The skin around the wart may be protected with petroleum jelly. The warts often require multiple treatment, 2 to 3 times weekly, before they dry up and fall off. Podophyllin should be washed off after an hour or two or as soon as burning is felt. Large warts may be removed surgically or with cryosurgery.

Nursing management of STD

The nurse is in an important position to educate adolescents about STD. Many adolscents, especially girls, who suspect they have STD will go to a nurse rather than their parents. An assessment should be made concerning the adolescent's understanding of normal body functions and general hygiene. They need to understand the infection they are being treated for and the relationship of STD to gynecological problems.

Also assess their ability to carry out the prescribed treatment. Contacts will need to be identified, traced, and treated.

Laws for treatment of minors in the majority of states have enabled public and private health care agencies to check and treat adolescents for VD in complete confidence. Often adolescents will come for treatment sooner if they know their parents will not be notified.

To help the adolescent feel at ease, the nurse should be open, honest, able to listen, and nonjudgmental. Making reading material and visual aids available may be useful for those adolescents who find it difficult to verbalize their concerns. Ideally all adolescents should be required to take courses in family life and sex education that include factual information on STD.

The nurse may be asked to interview a child or family when a preadolescent infection is treated. Since a gonococcal or syphilitic infection may be connected with sexual abuse, the nurse must be an alert and objective listener. Assessing how an infection may have been contacted and whether the child or family need counseling is important. Role-playing with a doll sometimes brings out more information when trying to interview a child.

See Table 34-15 for some suggestions a nurse may convey to adolescents concerning maintaining good health. Additional instructions if an adolescent is being treated for a STD are listed in Table 34-16.

When seeking medical care, adolescents have the *right* to: *privacy, dignity, confidentiality, to understand, and to consent or refuse.* They also have *responsibilities* to: *be honest, understand, follow the treatment plan, report changes, and to keep appointments.* These rights and responsibilities are essential for optimum care.

Environmental considerations in childhood infection

A discussion of the process of infection and the nurse's role in prevention, recognition, and control of infection would not be complete without some attention to the role of *environment* in infection. Environmental factors influence either the agent, the host, or the host-agent relationship.

Environment is all that is external to the child and includes the agent and fellow children. The environment can be conceived of as including the inanimate, the animate, and the socioeconomic. The *inanimate* considerations in the transmission or acquisition of disease are geographic, climatic, and geologic. Cold weather keeps people indoors and in closer association, favoring the transmission of agents. Warm, humid weather promotes development and survival of many disease agents. The composition of the soil determines the quality of natural water

Table 34-15 Suggestions to the adolescent for maintaining reproductive tract health

1. Get enough sleep and exercise.
2. Eat a well-balanced diet.
3. Reduce sugar in your diet (sugar is a factor in some vaginitis).
4. Avoid douches (the vagina continuously cleanses itself).
5. Avoid harsh soaps, bubble baths, feminine hygiene sprays, or deodorized tampons (can produce irritations).
6. Wipe from front to back after a bowel movement.
7. Wear cotton underwear (allows more air circulation—less bacterial growth).
8. Begin yearly pelvic exams and Pap smears if sexually active.
9. Learn the symptoms of STD and seek medical help early.

Table 34-16 Instructions for the adolescent being treated for STD

1. The most important preventive factor is care in selecting a sexual partner. (Multiple partners produce higher risk of STD.)
2. Using condoms reduces the rate of STD. Foams and diaphragms may have some, but less, preventive effect. Pills and IUDs provide no protection.
3. Douching and washing with soap are of questionable value for preventing STD.
4. Sexual partners should be checked and treated, if necessary.
5. Use sitz baths for vaginal and perineal irritation.
6. Eliminate stimulants—caffeine, tea, colas (may be irritating to the inflamed area).
7. Take all medication as prescribed, even if symptoms disappear before the medication is completed.
8. If symptoms do not go away after all medication is completed, return for further examination and treatment.
9. The risks and complications of STD are so great that the teenager should understand them and provide protection through the use of condoms. (Both boys and girls should carry their own supply.)

purification and the types and quantity of food in an area. *Animate* considerations include types of agents in an area and its flora and fauna. Human nutrition depends on the quantity and quality of the food supply and on the adequacy of its distribution. The types of industry and occupations affect the conditions predisposing to exposure, injury, and infection. Agricultural areas, for example, have high potential for all three. The educational level of the population affects health knowledge and habits, and income level affects the ability to buy health care and a healthy life-style.

An important example of an environmental effect on infection for the nurse to understand is the high rate of infections acquired in hospitals. The environment of the hospital is unique and presents a high risk of infection for patients admitted. An estimated 5 percent of all patients admitted to hospitals in the United States develop an infection that was not present or incubating at the time of admission. The hospital environment contributes to infection by supporting a pool of organisms, a pool of susceptible hosts, and a variety of ways to transmit the agents to the host, including the hands of hospital employees.

References

1. William Bowie et al., "Roundtable: Venereology for Primary Physicians," *Patient Care*, Jan. 30, 1978.
2. Michael Rein, "New Approaches in the Management of Sexually Transmitted Disease," *Virginia Medicine*, 105(6):440 (June 1978).
3. *STD, FACT SHEET* Ed. 34 Basic Statistics on the Sexually Transmitted Disease Problem in the United States, U.S. Dept. of HEW, Center for Disease Control Division, Atlanta, Georgia 30333-"Summary of STD Problem: United States 1977," p. 2.
4. Ibid., p. 6.
5. Ibid., p. 6.
6. Donald Kaye, "Gonorrhea: An Old Malady Presents New Problems," *Modern Medicine* 48(15):40 (Sept. 15–30, 1978).
7. STD, op. cit., p. 2.
8. H. H. Handsfield, "Gonorrhea and Nongonococcal Urethritis, Recent Advances," *Medical Clinics of North America* 62(5): 925–943 (September 1978).
9. ————"Clinical Aspects of Gonococcal Infection," in R. B. Roberts (ed.), *The Gonococcus*, Wiley, New York, 1977, p. 57.
10. STD, op. cit., p. 2.
11. *Syphilis, A Synopsis*, U.S. Dept. of HEW, Ed. January 1968.
12. M. S. Stern and R. G. Mackenzie, "Venereal Disease in Adolescents," *Medical Clinics of North America*, 59(6):1395 (November 1975).
13. Ibid., p. 1395.
14. Stern and Mackenzie, op. cit., p. 1395.

Chapter 35 **Cellular proliferation**

Gladys M. Scipien

Upon completion of this chapter, the student will be able to:

1. Discuss the incidence, rates of survival, and mortality of cancer among children.
2. Discuss differences between malignant and nonmalignant neoplasms.
3. Cite at least three factors implicated in the etiology of childhood cancer.
4. Name and describe at least three types of malignant neoplasms affecting children.

5. Discuss the principles underlying the three treatment modalities for childhood cancer.
6. Discuss the impact cancer may have on the child, parents, and siblings.
7. Describe specific nursing responsibilities entailed in care of children with various forms of cancer.

Cancer in children and adolescents

Incidence

There is nothing more demanding, more challenging, or more emotionally draining than working with children who have cancer. These children and their families must cope with a disease process which, after accidents, is the leading cause of death in persons under 15 years of age. The incidence of childhood cancer is estimated at 10 per 100,000 children or approximately 6000 new cases each year. There has been a slight decline in its incidence since 1970. Although it occurs in all races, there are differences in frequency and survival rates among different races. See Table 35-1 for the incidence of common malignancies in children.

Survival

In the early 1950s, less than 20 percent of children with common forms of childhood cancer could be expected to live 2 years. Advancement in treatment modalities have resulted in dramatically improved survival rates. At present, about 80 percent of the children with Wilms' tumors survive. Approximately 60 percent of acute lymphocytic leukemic patients are expected to live beyond 5 years. Unfortunately, not all pediatric cancers are as responsive to treatment. The survival rates of patients with brain tumors or neuroblastomas have not improved substantially over the years. However, cancer in children is not always an acute or fatal disease. Rather, cancer nowadays should be viewed as a chronic illness which is controllable if not curable.

Table 35-1 Major forms of malignancies in children under 15 years of age

Form	Incidence (%)
Leukemia	30.7
Central nervous system tumors	18.6
Lymphoma	13.1
Sympathetic nervous system tumors	7.7
Soft-tissue sarcoma	6.5
Kidney tumors	6.1
Bone tumors	4.6
Eye tumors (retinoblastoma)	2.6
Other	10.1
	100.0

Adapted from: Kathy Hardin, "Solid Tumor in Children," *Issues in Comprehensive Pediatric Nursing* **4**(1):31 (1980).

Original source: Surveillance, Epidemiology, and End Results Program (SEER), National Cancer Institute, 1973–1976.

Mortality

Cancer continues to be the leading cause of pediatric deaths due to illness, but its mortality rate has decreased over the last 30 years. In 1950, there were 8 deaths per 100,000 children; by 1976, there were 5 per 100,000. The American Cancer Society estimates about 2800 pediatric deaths annually. Until the cause of cancer is known, slow progress will be made in lowering this statistic further.

Pathophysiology of malignant neoplasms

Types of neoplasms

Neoplasms, also known as tumors, are masses of cells that proliferate abnormally. This rapid cell growth may be benign or malignant. *Benign* neoplasms are generally not life-threatening but they sometimes exert pressure on adjacent structures. A benign brain tumor, for example, may apply pressure to vital centers in the cranium. *Malignant* neoplasms consist of cancer cells that have the ability to spread to adjacent and distant structures. Thus, malignant neoplasms are potentially life-threatening.

There are several types of malignant neoplasms. A *carcinoma* is a malignancy that consists of epithelial cells found in the skin, linings of lungs, and other body cavities. Carcinoma is predominantly seen in adults. *Adenocarcinoma* refers to a malignant, mixed mesodermal tumor, with glandular elements, which arises from the parenchyma of such glands as the breast, thyroid, or prostate. A neoplasm derived primarily from lymphocytic or histiocytic elements of lymphoid tissue is called a *lymphoma.* At the present time, lymphomas are further subdivided into two classifications: (1) Hodgkin's disease and (2) non-Hodgkin's lymphoma. A highly malignant tumor that consists of embryonic connective tissue arising in the mesoderm is called a *sarcoma.* It can involve bone, cartilage, muscle, blood vessels, and lymphoid tissue and takes its name from the predominant tissue of origin. For example, an osteosarcoma is a bone tumor, and a lymphosarcoma is a tumor of lymphoid tissue. A malignancy that occurs only in children is an *embryonic* tumor. It is a mixed mesodermal tumor arising from embryonic cells and manifested as a Wilms' tumor or a teratoma. *Leukemia* affects the hematopoietic tissue, causing a proliferation of leukocytes, their precursors, or both. This proliferative process can involve myeloid tissue (red bone marrow) responsible for manufacturing granular leukocytes (eosinophils, neutrophils, basophils). Leukemia can also affect red blood cells, platelets, and lymphatic tissue which produces nongranular leukocytes (lymphocytes, monocytes). The specific leukemic process is identified according to tissue primarily involved. Lymphoid tissue, for example, is affected in lymphocytic or lymphatic leukemia.

Etiologic factors

While cancer in adults can occur in the bowel, bladder, lungs, and skin with specific causes related to the length of exposure and a variety of carcinogenic and environmental agents, the cause of cancer in children is unknown. Most adult tumors arise in surface organs or glands while malignancies in children frequently occur in deep tissue, in bone marrow, blood, skeletal bone, neural crest tissue, muscle, or kidneys. The danger signs of cancer in adults are usually not evident in children.

The high incidence of malignancies in the first 4 years of life (41 percent of all types of childhood cancers)[1] points to the embryonic nature of some tumors. They may have been present at birth or in the postnatal period, but the tumor cells never matured. The rapid proliferation of these cells is similar to the growth of embryonic tissue.

Although the origin of cancer in children is unknown, there are several variables that seem to be implicated in some way. Perhaps when its etiology is eventually identified, researchers may find there are a number of interrelated causes.

Intrauterine exposure to carcinogens Between 1940 and 1970, diethylstilbestrol (DES) was often prescribed for pregnant women to prevent spontaneous abortions. It is now known that DES can result in vaginal adenocarcinoma and other abnormalities in female offspring 14 to 22 years later. Male offspring can demonstrate abnormalities that may predispose them to testicular malignancies. Since this drug demonstrates the ability to cross the placental barrier, it is assumed that other carcinogens can affect the embryo and fetus in utero. While many agents are suspected, the effect of physical and chemical substances is unclear at present.

Physical carcinogens Diagnostic radiation of pregnant women increases the incidence of leukemia and other malignancies in their children. Therapeutic doses of radiation to the necks of infants and toddlers who had thyroid enlargements several years ago has resulted in a higher-than-average incidence of cancer of the thyroid.

Genetic influence There is no established genetic cause of cancer in children, but some congenital defects are associated with malignancies. Examples are aniridia in Wilms' tumor and neurofibromatosis in connection with brain tumors. Leukemia has a higher incidence among children with certain chromosomal aberrations. Perhaps the best example of a heritable single-gene disorder is retinoblastoma, described later in this chapter. Some think that children with common malignancies may have inherited a predisposition through a single gene disorder. There is, however, no mechanism for identifying such children.[2]

Immune defects Some authorities believe that the body has a surveillance system that identifies and destroys neoplastic cells by immunologically reacting to them, before they are able to proliferate and develop into a detectable tumor. However, a malfunction of the surveillance mechanism could permit continued cellular division. Children with a number of immunodeficiencies are more prone to developing lymphoid malignancies. Individuals who are immunosup-

pressed for organ transplantations also have a higher than normal incidence of malignancies. Although not a direct cause of cancer in children, the immune system is implicated in some way.

Viruses Investigative work is being done to determine whether an oncologic virus is involved in the development of malignant neoplasms. A viruslike substance extracted from tumors of animals has produced leukemia, sarcoma, and other malignancies in mice. However, there is no conclusive basis for a virus-cancer etiology at this point. The Epstein-Barr virus has been identified in Burkitt's lymphoma, a non-Hodgkin type of lymphoma. For some reason, this disease occurs only in Africa and New Guinea. Some researchers think the interaction of viruses and certain chemicals may cause chromosomal damage which, in turn, results in malignancies. Although there is a great deal of speculation about viruses, their role in childhood cancer is unknown.

Characteristics of malignant tumors

Malignant neoplasms are composed of poorly differentiated cells with observable abnormalities of the nucleus and cytoplasm. The majority of tumors in children are malignant, and they possess characteristics that make some of them unique to the pediatric population.

Rapid growth. Normally, such cellular operations as replication, orderly growth, differentiation, maintenance of a repair system, and cessation of activities on maturation are controlled by some internal regulatory process. For example, when a wound occurs, healing epithelial cells divide at its margins and migrate across the wound in order to complete the repair. Once the wound heals, cellular division and motility cease. In malignant cells, signals which halt such activity are either ignored or ineffective in controlling proliferation. For example, in acute lymphocytic leukemia, the immature cells crowd out normal blood elements, inhibiting their production. It is the disregard for bodily need that typify malignant cells as they proliferate erratically.

Tissue invasion As these cells multiply, they invade and destroy normal tissue surrounding the tumor. Malignant tumors are not encapsulated, have irregular shapes and nondefined borders, and infiltrate along lines of least resistance, for example, into soft tissue. Cartilage, fascia, and ligaments are more resistant than softer tissues to this type of invasion. It is thought that malignant cells secrete toxins or enzymes that injure normal cells by breaking down the tissue matrix, thereby permitting an easy infiltration.

Two unique properties appear to enhance the ability of malignant cells to spread to adjacent or distant sites. Surface membranes of malignant cells reduce the ability of nearby normal cells to adhere to one another. This *decreased adhesiveness* allows the shedding of cells from the primary neoplasm and permits the development of foci in other sites. The second property is *loss of contact inhibition.* Contact inhibition is the normal cessation of cellular division and migration of cells when contact with other cells is established, as described in wound healing. When contact between malignant cells is made, chaotic proliferation continues. Normal and abnormal cells compete for essential nutrients and eventually the normal cells are destroyed. This localized, pathologically altered tissue is termed the *primary tumor.*

Metastasis After a local infiltration has occurred, malignant cells establish satellite foci of the same cell type as the primary lesion. This process is known as *metastasis.* (This feature distinguishes malignant tumors from benign neoplasms.) Malignant cells often spread through the *lymphatic* system. Cell "emboli" break away from the primary lesion and move to a lymph node, where a secondary site develops. As these cells multiply and involve the entire node, other malignant cells move on to the next group of nodes.

Another common route for metastasis in children is a *hematogenous spread,* which affects the circulatory system and such vascular organs as the lungs, liver, or bone. Infiltrating small veins or capillaries, free-floating neoplastic cells, held together by fibrin, penetrate the wall of a blood vessel, entering the surrounding tissue to establish a secondary site. A third type of metastasis seen in pediatrics occurs with abdominal neoplasms. The malignancy extends along tissue planes to adjacent organs. Cells may also be detached from the surface of a malignant neoplasm mechanically, by a surgeon doing a resection or biopsy, or during palpation of an abdominal mass. The transplantation of just a single malignant cell has the potential for establishing another site.

Treatment of malignant neoplasms in children and adolescents

Malignancies in childhood can be treated by chemotherapy, radiotherapy, or surgery. In some instances, one modality may be effective, while in other situations, two or possibly all three approaches may be utilized. Many factors determine treatment and they include: age, type of tumor, extent of disease at the time of diagnosis, and the unique tumor cell characteristics. It is not unusual for aggressive treatment to involve a combination of modalities. The sole purpose of therapy is to destroy or remove malignant cells which jeopardize a life.

Chemotherapy

General principles in therapy In the last 10 or 12 years, great strides have been made in treating malignancies systematically through the development of new agents and the combination of several drugs. As a result, both remissions and survival rates have increased significantly. The advantages to using drugs in combination include: (1) decrease in resistance to one drug; (2) lessening of the severe side effects of massive doses of a single agent; (3) breakdown of the tumor cell cycle at multiple sites.[3]

Malignant cells tend to proliferate at a steady rate, regardless of the body's need for that particular cell. However, it is important to remember that only a small percentage of the total tumor cells multiply at any given time. A tumor mass consists of four compartments with cells moving freely between them. The first compartment consists of temporarily differentiated cells, the bulk of the tumor. The second is a proliferating compartment, which is the target for chemotherapy and a source of metastasis. The third consists of a stationary differentiated compartment which often becomes differentiated cells of the host's tissue without further division. The fourth is the compartment of dying cells.[4] Cytotoxic agents are most effective when cells are proliferating.

Chemotherapeutic drugs are categorized according to their effectiveness in specific phases of a cell's generation time, and therefore it is necessary to know a cell's life cycle. See Table 35-2. Agents capable of destroying malignant cells only when they are in a specific phase of division are called *cell-cycle-specific* drugs. Some examples are vincristine, which inhibits mitosis, and methotrexate, which affects the synthesis of DNA. Others destroy proliferating cells without regard to their generational phases and they are considered to be *cell-cycle-nonspecific* agents. The antibiotic and alkylating agents are classified as such.

Most children and adolescents receive these cytotoxic drugs over varying periods of time. Initially, when treatment is most intense, large doses are administered in an effort to destroy as many proliferating cells as possible. Later, a maintenance dose is given at specific intervals. It is extremely difficult to predict the length of treatment, the duration of drug's effectiveness, or the individual patient's response to chemo-

therapy. That is one reason why treatment protocols are almost constantly changing.

Agents The drugs most often used in chemotherapy are divided into seven broad categories based on either their origins or their actions. These classifications are included in Table 35-3.

Since almost all these drugs are specific for neoplastic chemotherapy, it is necessary for the nurse to know the action of these medications, their side effects, and the nursing implications of each one of them. The most commonly used agents are found in Table 35-4. It does not include experimental drugs a child may receive.

Complications of therapy Selectivity is not a characteristic of these extremely potent cytotoxic drugs. As a result, normal cells are affected, especially those which have a high rate of proliferation. That is why gastrointestinal mucosa, hair follicles, and bone marrow respond as they do to these agents.

Toxic side effects demonstrated by the gastrointestinal tract include stomatitis, ulcerations, diarrhea, nausea and vomiting, while alopecia is characteristic of damage done to hair follicles. Patients are closely monitored for bone marrow depression (leukopenia, thrombocytopenia, agranulocytosis, anemia), which can present a life-threatening situation. White cells and platelets evidence toxic effects much more quickly than do red cells. Precipitous drops in either count may indicate the necessity for discontinuing a drug. This is why complete blood counts and bone marrow aspirations must be done frequently. Drugs can have a cumulative effect on the bone marrow with subsequent depression occurring weeks or months after treatment. Therefore, followup clinic or office visits are imperative.

Another potential complication is drug-induced immunosuppression which results in overwhelming infection. The extent of infection depends on many factors, such as the dose, route, schedule, duration, type, and number of agents being administered. It is almost impossible to predict the effect of these drugs on the immune response of human beings because they extend from no obvious ill effects to substantial inhibition.

The infection frequency increases when combinations of chemotherapeutic agents are being

Table 35-2 Cellular generation time

Phase	Activity	Dynamics
G_0	Resting or out-of-cycle phase	Cell remains in this stage until called to replenish cell population.
G_1	When signal is received, RNA and protein synthesis occurs.	Length of time in this phase varies and is dependent on and proportional to individual cells. Rapidly growing cells have a short G_1.
S	DNA synthesis occurs.	Chromosomes double and transcribe genetic material to RNA, including sequence for cellular function and renewal.
G_2	This is quiet phase in preparation for mitosis.	Here, protein synthesis provides material for mitotic spindle apparatus.
M (mitosis)	Cell passes through four phases (prophase, metaphase, anaphase, and telophase).	Results in two identical daughter cells, each with 46 chromosomes.

Table 35-3 Broad categories of antineoplastic drugs

Alkylating agents	Cell-cycle-nonspecific drugs which attach themselves to nucleic acid and interfere with mitosis	Cyclophosphamide, nitrogen mustard, the nitrosoureas (BCNU, CCNU)
Antimetabolites	These agents resemble cell metabolites so closely they are absorbed by a cell and inhibit certain biochemical reactions required for RNA synthesis and cellular growth.	Folic acid analog (methotrexate) Purine analog (6-mercaptopurine) Pyrimidine analog (cytosine)
Plant alkaloids	Natural products obtained from periwinkle plant which stop cell division in metaphase of mitosis, interfering with spindle formation and synthesis as well as processing for RNA.	Vincristine (Oncovin) and vinblatsine (Velban)
Antineoplastic agents Antibiotics	Cell-cycle-nonspecific drugs which are natural products of some soil fungi. They form stable complexes with DNA and inhibit DNA and sometimes subsequent RNA synthesis.	Actinomycin D, Adriamycin, daunorubicin, bleomycin
Hormones	Cortiocosteroids have a cytotoxic effect on protein receptors inside neoplastic cells.	Prednisone Dexamethasone
Enzymes	Extracellular supplies of the amino acid asparagine essential for survival of malignant cells are destroyed, killing the neoplastic cells.	L-Asparaginase
Miscellaneous	Synthetic substances whose cytotoxic properties are unknown Inorganic substances whose cytotoxic actions are unknown.	Procarbazine cis-platinum

administered. In addition, cyclophosphamide and Adriamycin appear to be most immunosuppressive. Fortunately, this tremendously increased susceptibility to infection is a reversible phenomenon.

Radiotherapy, an important treatment in some types of malignancies, is also immunosuppressive, primarily because a bone marrow field is almost always included in the site to be irradiated. Total body irradiation (TBI) in preparation for a bone marrow transplantation may result in a fulminating bacterial, viral, fungal, or protozoan infection which culminates in death.

Radiotherapy

Principles of treatment Radiotherapy is sometimes used in treating childhood neoplasms in combination with chemotherapy, surgery, or both. Its objective is to destroy malignant cells by an ionization process which damages the nucleus and eventually kills these cells, but it

can also be used to arrest the growth of a tumor or for palliative purposes.

The dosage is determined in "rads" (radiation absorbed dose), which refers to the quantity delivered to the site. It is divided into small doses and given over a period of weeks with rest between treatments, until the predetermined amount is received by a child. The time factor is important because malignant cells are unable to recover from the irradiation damage, while normal cells have an opportunity to do so.

Malignant cells demonstrate varying degrees of sensitivity to irradiation. Wilms' tumors and Ewing's sarcomas are most sensitive, rhabdomyosarcomas are moderately sensitive, and osteosarcomas are least sensitive.[5]

Normal body cells are selectively altered in this treatment. It is especially important to remember that in children growing tissue is involved. Radiotherapy can result in severe orthopedic deformities as the child grows.

Table 35-4 Common chemotherapeutic drugs

Drug	Route	Diseases in which drug is effective	Common side effects	Nursing implications peculiar to this drug
Alkylating agents				
Busulfan (Myleran)	PO	Chronic myelogenous leukemia	BMD; rare N/V; renal toxicity; hyperpigmentation of skin; interstitial pulmonary fibrosis with prolonged use; wasting syndrome	Check with patient frequently for anorexia or weight loss, which may indicate wasting syndrome.
Carmustine (BCNU)	IV	Brain tumors; lymphocytic lymphomas	Pain along vein and the flushed feeling during its administration; tissue necrosis if infiltrated; BMD 3–5 weeks after dose; N/V 6 h after dose; diarrhea; renal toxicity; mild hepatotoxicity	Drug darkens skin and hardens veins along sites used for injection. Warm soaks to hands/arms 3X/day helps. Giving drug IV drip can prevent burning during infusion.
Cytoxan (cyclophosphamide)	PO IM IV	Retinoblastomas; lymphocyctic and histiocytic lymphomas; neuroblastomas; ALL; AML; Rhabdomyosarcomas; ovarian tumors; Burkitt's; Hodgkin's; Ewing's; Wilms'; osteosarcoma	Hemorrhagic cystitis; stomatitis; liver dysfunction; BMD 1–14 days after dose; N/V 3–6 h after dose; facial flushing and hyperpigmentation of skin; sterility (amenorrhea and aspermia)	Good hydration is essential. Force fluids 1½–2X maintenance for 24 h prior to and 48 after dose. Have patient void qH for 24 h after receiving dose. The medication should be given in the morning to decrease time in the bladder.
Dacarbazine (DTIC)	IV	Hodgkin's disease	BMD 2–4 weeks after a dose; alopecia; pain along vein and a metallic taste during administration; N/V 1–2 h after administration; flulike syndrome with headache and malaise up to 10 days after dose; mild hepatotoxicity; renal toxicity	Give medication as on IV drip to prevent burning on infusion. The drug should be protected from the light by a covering bag during infusion. If the IV infiltrates, tissue necrosis will occur at the site.
Lomustine (CCNU)	PO	Brain tumors; Hodgkin's disease	N/V 2–6 h after dose; BMD 4–6 weeks after a dose; hepatotoxicity	Patient needs to be instructed to take medication on an empty stomach to decrease the likelihood of N/V.
Nitrogen mustard Mechlorethamine	IV IT	Histiocytic lymphoma Hodgkin's disease	N/V 1–6 h after a dose; alopecia; BMD 2–3 weeks after dose; hepatotoxicity; tinnitus and decreased hearing	Mix this drug cautiously; avoid contact with skin and eyes. If contact occurs, severe burns will result. If the IV infiltrates, tissue necrosis will occur at the site.
Plant alkaloids				
Vinblastine (Velban)	IV	Hodgkin's disease	Some N/V; diarrhea; BMD 4–11 days after a dose; neurotoxicity; alopecia; mental depression	If the IV infiltrates, there will be tissue necrosis at the site. Vinca drugs are metabolized primarily by liver; therefore, hepatotoxicity is possible.
Vincristine (Oncovin)	IV	Wilms'; retinoblastoma; Ewing's; AML; osteosarcoma; rhabdomyosarcoma; neuroblastoma;	Constipation; jaw pain; alopecia; stomatitis; neurotoxicity—ptosis; paralytic ileus; loss of deep	Patient needs to be checked frequently for signs of neurotoxicity. The drug may cause a decreased spermatogene-

Table 35-4 Common chemotherapeutic drugs (*Continued*)

Drug	Route	Diseases in which drug is effective	Common side effects	Nursing implications peculiar to this drug
		ALL; histiocytic and lymphocytic lymphomas; Hodgkin's; Burkitt's lymphoma	tendon reflexes; tingling or numbness of hands and feet	sis; therefore, the physician should tell an adolescent and his parents prior to beginning treatment.
Antimetabolites				
Cytosine arabinoside (Ara-C)	IV IM IT SC	Histiocytic and lymphocytic lymphomas; AML; ALL; Burkitt's lymphoma	N/V; BMD 7–14 days after a dose; diarrhea; stomatitis; esophagitis; hepatotoxicity; upper GI ulcerations	It is often administered as an SC injection on several consecutive days at home. Instruction critical, as is follow-up regarding administration of drug and care.
Hydroxyurea (Hydrea)	PO	AML; lymphocytic lymphoma	N/V; diarrhea; BMD with rapid leukopenia; stomatitis; GI ulcerations; rash, pruritis; renal toxicity.	Should be given cautiously to a patient with some renal dysfunction.
Methotrexate (MTX)	PO IV IM IT	Histiocytic and lymphocytic lymphoma; ALL; AML; Burkitt's lymphoma; osteosarcoma	Stomatitis; GI and mucosal ulcerations; N/V; diarrhea; BMD delayed; alopecia; renal toxicity; hepatic fibrosis.	The patient/family needs to be instructed to avoid vitamins or other drugs because this drug is a folic acid antagonist.
5-Azacytidine 5-Aza C	IV	AML	N/V; diarrhea; BMD	This drug should be infused slowly in order to decrease the severity of N/V.
6-Mercaptopurine (6-MP)	PO	ALL; AML	BMD 1–4 weeks after dose; renal toxicity; N/V; rarely-stomatitis and jaundice	The effect of 6-MP is potentiated when given with Allopurinol. Therefore, 6-MP dose should be decreased when both drugs are given together.
6-Thioguanine (6-TG)	PO	AML	N/V; diarrhea; BMD; hepatotoxicity; stomatitis; skin rash; photosensitivity; unsteady gait	Blood counts must be monitored because of the cumulative effect 6-TG has on bone marrow. These patients may need assistance when ambulating because of unsteady gait.
Antineoplastic antibiotics				
Adriamycin (doxorubicin)	IV	Retinoblastoma; osteosarcoma; ALL; AML; Hodgkin's; neuroblastoma; Ewing's sarcoma; Wilms' tumor, rhabdomyosarcoma	BMD; fever; stomatitis; N/V; alopecia; cardiomyopathy after cumulative doses above 550 mg/m^2	If the IV infiltrates, there will be tissue necrosis at the site. This drug colors urine red for approximately 24–48 h after a dose is administered, and the patient needs to be forewarned.
Bleomycin (Blenoxane)	IV IM SC	Hodgkin's disease	Anaphylaxis; allergic reaction may occur up to 3–5 h after dose; fever; hypotension; N/V; chills; stomatitis; darkened nail beds, palms, feet; macular rash of fingers and hands; anorexia; pulmonary fibrosis	First dose should be a *decreased* test dose. Observe patient for such pulmonary symptoms as dyspnea, coughing, or fever, which can occur immediately or gradually. Pulmonary fibrosis or pneumonitis more likely when radiation is concurrent or it has been completed.

Table 35-4 Common chemotherapeutic drugs (*Continued*)

Drug	Route	Diseases in which drug is effective	Common side effects	Nursing implications peculiar to this drug
Dactinomycin (actinomycin D)	IV	Rhabdomyosarcama; embryonic tumors; Ewing's sarcoma; Wilms' tumor; retinoblastoma	N/V 4–5 h after a dose; stomatitis; BMD 1–2 weeks after the last dose; alopecia; acne; diarrhea; hepatotoxicity	If the IV infiltrates, there may be tissue necrosis at the site. If radiotherapy has been or is being given, this drug potentiates its effect.
Daunorubicin (rubidomycin; daunomycin)	IV	ALL; AML; lymphocytic lymphoma	Same as Adriamycin	Same as Adriamycin
Enzymes				
L-Asparaginase Elspar	IV IM	Lymphocytic lymphoma; ALL	Anaphylaxis; chills; fever; hypotension; dyspnea; N/V; malaise; anorexia; hepatotoxicity; pancreatic toxicity with hyperglycemia; protein and coagulation abnormalities	When mixing the drug, swirl vial slowly; *do not shake!* The first dose should be a low test dose to determine sensitivity. Steroids, Adrenalin, and antihistamines should be drawn up and at bedside when this drug is administered.
Hormones				
Corticosteroids (prednisone, dexamethasone)	PO	Hodgkin's disease; ALL; AML; histiocytic and lymphocytic lymphomas	Increased appetite; weight gain; personality changes. Long-term: moon face; obesity; fluid retention; muscle weakness; osteoporosis; facial flushing; euphoria; hypertension; gastric irritation; immunosuppression	Explain effect of drug on appetite, weight, and personality changes. Antacid may be needed. Encourage the intake of foods rich in potassium—bananas and orange juice. Monitor blood pressure, urine (S, A), and stools (occult blood). Observe patient for potential infection.
Miscellaneous				
Procarbazine (Matulane)	PO	Hodgkin's disease; histiocytic lymphoma	N/V; BMD 2–5 weeks after dose; mild CNS toxicity; stomatitis; diarrhea; drowsiness; chills; fever; weakness; fatigue	This drug is a monamine oxidase inhibitor; therefore, foods such as ripe bananas, cheese, and alcohol, as well as such drugs as antidepressants and sympathomimetics, must be avoided. Otherwise, an "Antabuse" type of reaction may occur.
cis-Platinum	IV	Neuroblastoma; brain tumor; rhabdomyosarcoma.	N/V; renal toxicity; ototoxicity; BMD 3 weeks after dose	Since renal damage is possible during excretion, the patient should receive IV fluids prior to, during, and after the infusion of medication (at least 1½ maintenance). A strict I and O and vital signs q1h during infusion are essential. Tissue necrosis can occur if the IV infiltrates.

BMD = Bone marrow depression

N/V = Nausea and Vomiting

IT = Intrathecal

Adapted from : Ann S. Pryor, "Cancer Chemotherapy in Children," *Issues in Comprehensive Pediatric Nursing* **3**(5):50–55 (November 1978).

However, if radiation can destroy a neoplasm, then it may be necessary to take that risk.

Complications of treatment There are a number of local and systemic responses to radiation therapy. They vary according to the type being received, the dose, the length of treatment, and the age of the child. Most tissue responds to long-term treatment with local and systemic manifestations.

Local reactions usually consist of erythema, epithelial sloughing, desquamation, pigmentation, blistering, and alopecia. Some mild systemic reactions include anorexia, malaise, and fatigue. Later, nausea and vomiting may occur together with leukopenia, anemia, and an increased susceptibility to infection.

Surgery

Complete removal of a malignancy is the most effective treatment, but it is not always possible. In all too many children, diagnosis is made after the cancer has metastasized. At this point, the malignant cells cannot be completely removed. Chemotherapy, radiation, or both may precede an operation in order to decrease the size of the tumor and make surgical dissection possible.

In those instances where surgery is performed, the micrometastases which remain can be destroyed by antitumor drugs, radiotherapy, or both. Surgical intervention is palliative when there is regional or advanced tissue involvement. Specific surgical procedures which may be performed on children will be discussed later in this chapter.

Assessment of the impact of cancer

The child

Many factors influence a child's responses to cancer. A major one is stage of development. Younger children (toddlers, preschoolers) react very differently from school-age children or adolescents in spite of the fact that all of these children know they are not feeling well and want to know why.

Young children While toddlers and preschoolers do not comprehend a great deal, they realize their lives are changing and correctly perceive parental emotions. They can pick up cues from health professionals, too. Whispering in small groups, tearfulness, and showers of gifts are mystifying and convey that something is dreadfully wrong. The child's anxiety is related to mutilation, immobilization, and bodily changes. Principles described in Chap. 16 should be used to prepare the child for painful procedures and to promote coping.

Older children Older children are shocked and angry about their illness and the changes it imposes and demonstrate emotions similar to those of their parents. "Why me?" is a question they often ask. Some children believe they are being punished for wrong-doing. Adolescents may not wish to talk about what they are experiencing. Withdrawal and depression are common. Parents may not answer questions adolescents raise because they cannot bear the pain associated with sharing the information. The adolescent needs love, security, and support in addition to thorough explanations because he is old enough to understand. A family reluctant to respond to these queries compounds the dilemma for the adolescent because he has no recourse. When he is denied an opportunity to discuss his fears about his illness or its treatment, the adolescent supplies his own answers. Often, his ideas are more bizarre than the real truth. He loses control at the very time when he is striving for independence. Therefore, allowing him some control over decision making helps him immensely.

Older children have probably thought about career choices. They may need to alter their plans in view of the diagnosis. Extracurricular activities, especially contact sports like football, may not be possible, but alternatives, such as managing the team, may be acceptable. It is no wonder that adolescents demonstrate their anger so frequently. They seem to be losing so much.

Pain is one consequence of the disease that affects all children. It may be a direct result of the metastatic process or secondary to surgery or diagnostic tests, such as bone marrow aspiration. Children being treated for cancer live in constant fear of pain. Emotional outbursts and kicking and screaming can be expected if, for example, a decision is made to obtain a sample of marrow. The child must know that all efforts will be made to relieve his discomfort. Discussion of pain management can be found in Chaps. 21 and 22.

It is essential to develop a trusting relationship with the child and parents, but the honesty on which it must be based can be excruciating. Whether to tell a child the diagnosis or not is a difficult decision for parents. The problem is not a major issue when a child is unable to comprehend what is being said. However, children are extremely perceptive and it is difficult to deny the diagnosis when the individual involved is an older child or adolescent. Although the decision not to inform a child of the diagnosis may be an easy one initially, the reasons for follow-up blood examinations, bone marrow aspirations, or a relapse are hard to explain. Subsequent deceitful explanations often generate more hostility in the child.

The child's understanding of death is related to his cognitive development. A 4-year-old considers it a temporary state because he watches his favorite actor on television get shot, die, and appear again next week in another movie. A teenager understands that when death occurs, life ceases. His frustration and anger need resolution so that he can accept the inevitable. Children's understanding of death and their responses to fatal illness are discussed in Chap. 22.

Family

Parents are devastated by news that their child has a malignancy. They are shocked, angry, and cannot believe what is being said. During this initial period, nurses must often reiterate facts because parents may repeatedly ask the same questions, hoping to get "different" answers.

When the diagnosis is confirmed, there should be a frank, honest discussion with parents and other members of the family in order to provide them with as much information as they can absorb at that time. An overview of the course of the disease, treatment, and a prognosis are essential topics for the discussion even though the family may not be ready to hear what is being said. Unwarranted optimism or pessimism is inappropriate at this time and can be detrimental to the over-all management of the patient. Although the physician is responsible for informing the parents about the child's diagnosis and treatment, the nurse also has an important role at this time. Often the nurse participates in the physician's discussion with the parents. After the physician has explained the child's illness and treatment, it is important that the nurse confer frequently with the parents. They may have many unanswered questions and they may also need clarification of information the physician has given them. It is most important to maintain open lines of communication in spite of the time expended. How a family copes with this stressful situation often depends on the nurse's communication and support.

It is not unusual for parents to think the diagnosis is wrong and verbalize a desire to take the child to another doctor, another city, or another medical center for a second opinion. Although another consultation is the parents' right, it is important to point out the added financial burdens and home disruption that may result. Parents should not be deterred from seeking another opinion unless the diagnosticians are *absolutely* positive of the diagnosis and seeking another will only waste valuable time.

Consent to begin treatment is obtained after a complete discussion of protocols which are available for the primary cell type involved. Honest information about the side effects of radiotherapy or chemotherapeutic agents must be provided by the physician.

It is not unusual for parents to raise the issue of alternative methods of treating the malignancy. Media coverage of certain children who have been given "alternative" treatment is widespread. Laetrile, krebiozan and other drugs, dietary regimens, and a myriad of electrical gadgets do not cure cancer, despite the fact that medical quacks are eager to persuade people otherwise. Parents are vulnerable to the appeal of alternative treatment. They need reassurance regarding the legitimate research efforts being conducted by public (National Cancer Institute, Food and Drug Administration, U.S. Public Health Service) and private (medical centers, drug companies) sectors.

The family must cope with innumerable emotional and economic stresses almost immediately. Accepting the reality of the diagnosis takes time. Treatment is immediate, however, and it usually takes place in a specialized medical center. Therefore, a move to another city may be necessary. Without friends or relatives in the area, food and lodging become a substantial expense, especially when parents remain with their child. Parents are usually not compensated for their absence from work.

Other children in the family may have to stay with relatives while their sibling is hospitalized. This displacement is disruptive, especially for young children. While these problems are most substantial in the initial phase of illness, they may continue after the child's discharge. Follow-up visits for a physical examination, x-ray, blood and urine analysis, or bone marrow aspirations are repeated for an indefinite period. A relapse catapults the entire family into another stressful situation.

Financial burdens contribute to the family's woes. There may be no income as a result of absences from work. Health insurance plans seldom cover all medical costs. Cytotoxic drugs are expensive, and those used in maintenance may be needed for years. Bone marrow transplantation costs about $50,000. Transportation expenses for follow-up visits and special foods for a child who has stomatitis or gastrointestinal side effects must also be considered. An economic drain occurs rapidly in the presence of this catastrophic illness and can financially ruin a family for many years.

Support systems help families cope with what appear to be overwhelming circumstances. Parents who have a strong marriage and healthy perceptions of themselves in their roles as partners and parents are often drawn closer together by the illness. Families with strong religious beliefs can often sustain trying times. Extended families and grandparents can provide assistance, often in the form of financial support. Grandparents may assume responsibility for care of the siblings and they may also relieve parents during their hospital vigils.

A special bond unites parents of children who have cancer. A national group, "Candlelighters," consists of parents who have or who have had a child with this disease. They can assist in many ways, whether it be finding living accommodations in a distant city or helping the child's parents to resolve a particular problem. They are invaluable advisors because they *have experienced* similar situations.

Health-care providers can be an effective support system throughout the course of the illness. By establishing a relationship based on honesty and trust, healthcare providers help enhance a family's coping skills and decrease their stress.

Keeping parents informed of the child's progress and permitting them to exercise their parenting responsibilities by providing physical care to the child are important. Showing concern for and respecting parents' privacy while also being available to answer their questions serve to decrease their apprehension. It also demonstrates the extent of the nurse's caring about them and their child.

There are several issues which must be discussed before the child is discharged after initial treatment. Follow-up visits and compliance with drugs or treatments which continue after discharge are absolute imperatives. Children often determine their own activity levels, doing as much as they desire. One topic frequently raised by parents is discipline and what to do in a situation which demands a form of punishment. A child is more secure when parental expectations are very clear. Infringements of family rules should not be allowed and the child should be disciplined as before the illness was diagnosed. The child is often eager to return to school, primarily because of peer group interactions. Advising parents to meet with the school nurse (to inform her about medications the child is taking), teacher, and classmates before the child returns can help avoid severe consequences. They need to be told about body changes such as weight gain, alopecia, and a prosthesis, activities in which the child can participate, and his limitations. This anticipatory action may make it easier for the child to resume classroom activities.

Siblings When a child's malignancy is first diagnosed, he becomes the center of family life. His siblings who are well resent the new focus of attention. They become angry because established family routines are cast aside and because their parents spend most of their time at the hospital. In addition, very little, if any, information is being shared with them. The patient is showered with gifts, no longer responsible for performing chores and no longer punished for wrong-doings. This turn of events can be most frustrating for siblings who are not old enough to understand what is happening. Not only do healthy siblings resent parental preoccupation with their ill brother or sister, they also interpret it as a rejection of themselves. They may demonstrate a variety of problems at home and in the classroom setting, which extend from disruptive behavior to school refusal. Their creative imaginations may lead them to think they, too, have a fatal illnesses.

A healthy sibling's friends can create added pressures. Their making fun of the bodily changes evident in the ill brother or sister may increase the well child's anger or guilt. Often, the climate in the home prevents the sibling from turning to parents with these problems.

In some instances, a one-to-one confrontation between a patient and healthy sibling can precipitate a verbal encounter which allows the latter to share his feelings, clear the air, and promote greater understanding. It is important that parents take the time to offer thorough, comprehensible explanations to siblings. Once they are informed, siblings may assume greater responsibilities with regard to physical care or supervision of the ill child at play, thus adding strength and cohesiveness to the family by their cooperation.

The nurse

A nurse is committed to helping children return to optimum levels of health. This is reasonably easy to achieve when a child is admitted for a ruptured appendix. However, in oncology, the "unknown" factor is the nature of the child's response to therapy. Providing nursing care to these children is challenging, exciting, gratifying, and frustrating.

It is natural for a compassionate nurse occasionally to become discouraged, angry, and depressed at the extent of the child's disease or disappointed in the effectiveness or treatment. Coping strategies for nurses are described in Chap. 22.

Developing a strong relationship with the child and his family enables the nurse to make suggestions about the child's care. For example, if grandparents are available, the parents can be encouraged to spend a day at the park with other siblings or drive to a nearby town to watch their son play basketball. Parents need to get away, to talk, and put things into perspective.

The nurse can help family members learn about the disease, the child's care requirements, and the importance of returning for follow-up visits. The importance of preventing infection and the signs of infection must be stressed. In order to be an effective teacher, the nurse must first assess the learners' needs and determine their readiness to learn before using basic teaching-learning principles. Discharge teaching begins soon after admission, not the day before the patient leaves. The child's and family's learning can often be evaluated in future clinic or doctor's office visits. Changes in the treatment protocol can be reviewed with parents or child and instituted at home. Home care is discussed at length in Chap. 22.

Malignant neoplasms affecting children and adolescents

Leukemia

Leukemia is the most common type of cancer in children. It is a primary disorder of bone marrow, in which normal blood cells in the marrow are replaced by immature cells (blast cells) as a result of an uncontrollable proliferation of leukocytes. In the process of multiplying, the blast cells, which do not mature, accumulate in the marrow. This inhibits the production of other cells, such as erythrocytes or platelets.

While the cause of leukemia is unknown, several factors appear to have some relationship to its development. Exposure to ionizing radiation received a great deal of attention after a high incidence of leukemia resulted in survivors of atomic bomb blasts. The role of viruses in the etiology of leukemia has been demonstrated in mice. Similarities between animal and human leukemia are such that some investigators assume viruses are implicated. A genetic basis is suspected too because (1) the incidence of leukemia in siblings is four times the normal; (2) it has a high incidence in children with chromosomal abnormalities like trisomy 21; (3) it is present in children with genetically determined disorders like congenital agammaglobulinemia; and (4) if a child has a homozygous twin with leukemia, there is a 20 percent chance that he will also develop leukemia within a year.

Types of leukemia Leukemia is classified according to the specific predominating cell found in the peripheral blood smear and bone marrow aspiration. Two acute forms are most common in pediatrics: (1) acute lymphocytic, lymphatic, or lymphoblastic leukemia (ALL); and (2) acute myelocytic or myeloblastic leukemia (AML). About 80 percent of leukemic children have ALL, while the remainder have AML. ALL is usually diagnosed in Caucasian children over 1 year of age, especially between 2 and 5 years with males predominating over females. AML is usually seen in older children, without regard for sex or race.

Clinical manifestations The clinical manifestations are common to *all* forms of acute leukemia (ALL *and* AML), and a diagnosis is difficult to make because symptoms may appear in isolation or in various combinations. Their presence depends on the amount of bone marrow compromise as well as on the extent and location of extramedullary infiltration (disease in organs other than bone marrow). Petechiae and bruising are common parental observations. Complaints of bone pain and arthralgia, which are common, may be confused with other musculoskeletal disorders. Fever and pallor may be present. With an extensive marrow invasion, there is anemia, fatigue, dyspnea, and tachycardia. The central nervous system (CNS) can be infiltrated and those children are irritable, lethargic, vomit, and have headaches.

Diagnostic tests Since this disease involves the hemopoietic system, extensive blood tests are imperative. Hemoglobin, hematocrit, complete blood count, platelet count, and uric acid level are done. Although peripheral blood smears may contain many immature cells, a *bone marrow aspiration* is mandatory for a diagnosis and differentiation between ALL and AML. This technique enables the physician to obtain samples of bone marrow for microscopic cell examination. The posterior iliac crest is most often used as the aspiration site because it contains active bone marrow, is easy to locate, and permits easy restraint of the child. Other sites used for bone marrow aspiration in children are the femur and tibia. The latter site is most often used for children under 18 months of age. The nurse administers sedation prior to the procedure (if ordered) and positions the child. When the posterior iliac crest is the site, the child is placed in the prone position with a pillow or towel roll under his hips. The nurse also restrains the child as necessary and provides soothing words of support during the procedure. A bone marrow aspiration is extremely painful for individuals of all ages.

Chest x-rays, long bone surveys, an intravenous pyelogram, and a variety of other kidney and liver function tests serve to identify extramedullary sites and assess two systems that will play a vital role in the detoxification and excretion of cytotoxic agents. The high frequency of CNS involvement makes a lumbar puncture necessary in order to examine the cerebrospinal fluid.

Treatment At the time of diagnosis, there may be up to 1 trillion (10^{12}) leukemic cells in the body. In order to realize a clinical and a hematological remission, that cell count *must* drop to 1 billion (10^9) or less.[6] This goal is reached through the utilization of radiation and chemotherapy in the minimum amounts that are capable of obtaining maximum results. Drastic reduction in deaths from leukemia came about after combinations of agents were used, facilitating an increase in the number of remissions as well as prolonged periods of remission.

The treatment of a child with ALL is usually divided into three stages in an effort to arrest the malignant process. The first stage, known as *remission induction*, reduces the total number of leukemic cells in the body and allows the return of normal bone marrow production. It takes about 4 weeks for a remission to occur, and the drugs most frequently used are prednisone and vincristine, although there are medical centers that also incorporate daunorubicin and L-asparaginase. The second stage, also known as the *intensification* phase, can be prophylactic or a method of destroying leukemic cells located in the CNS. The CNS is often a sanctuary for malignant cells shielded from the chemotherapeutic agents because of the physiological blood-brain barrier. Specifically, the cranial vault is irradiated and methotrexate (MTX) is administered intrathecally. The last stage is called *continuation or remission maintenance*. When remission is successfully accomplished, the child takes MTX and 6-mercaptopurine (6-MP) to maintain this status. Children can remain in remission for an indefinite period of time. Medications are usually discontinued after 3 years of remission. Approximately 80 percent of children who sustain remission for 3 years continue to remain in remission and appear to be cured.

Relapse occurs when the drugs being used are no longer effective and abnormal cells reappear. The first relapse is especially significant because it is a very poor prognostic indicator. Every effort is made to prevent its occurrence. A relapse means that it is no longer possible to control the disease. Therefore, cytosine arabinoside and Adriamycin and possibly some investigative agents are often incorporated into the drug regimen in an effort to extend the effectiveness of the drugs available. After relapse, each remission becomes shorter and shorter until death occurs.

Treating the child with AML focuses solely on the use of drugs. There are a variety of inductive protocols, including prednisone, vincristine, daunorubicin, cyclophosphamide, cytosine arabinoside, 5-azacytidine, and 6-thioguanine. Unfortunately, AML has not been as responsive to treatment as ALL. The CNS prophylactic radiation does not seem to help these patients.

There are a couple of other treatment modalities which need a brief elaboration. One is bone marrow transplantation, and the second is the use of immunotherapy. One option available to terminal ALL patients and those with AML is bone marrow transplantation; however, one cannot approach this procedure simplistically. Donors are not readily accessible, the financial cost is high, massive doses of chemotherapy and total body irradiation are required, and transplantation is not yet available except in research settings. As a result of the radiation, these patients are susceptible to even the weakest strains of infections. They also may develop graft-versus-host disease. Transplantation appears more successful when patients are treated during the second remission rather than later. Research in this area is still quite limited.[7] Immunotherapy was a promising approach when it was found that BCG vaccine could stimulate immunity against leukemic associated antigens. It has not, however, generated or maintained remissions in many patients who have been studied. Some investigators do not believe immunotherapy should be a treatment for ALL.

Supportive measures A number of standard, supportive measures play an important role in care of the leukemic patient. Transfusions are essential in the presence of anemia and thrombocytopenia. To prevent volume overload, "packed" red cells are administered instead of whole blood. White cell and platelet transfusions are used frequently, especially in the presence of drug-induced depressed bone marrow. With-

out them, combating sepsis and hemorrhage is an overwhelming and, in some instances, impossible task.

Diminished humoral and cellular defense mechanisms, secondary to immunosuppression, make these patients most susceptible to infections. In fact, about 75 percent of leukemic deaths can be attributed to invading pathogens. Therefore, patients are isolated or placed in laminar flow units to combat this serious complication of leukopenia. Hemorrhage is the second most common cause of death because of the depressed marrow and thrombocytopenia.

Prognosis Survival rates have improved substantially, especially in ALL, but extramedullary infiltration is becoming more common. Sites such as the kidneys, ovaries, testes, and CNS may be invaded. Monitoring closely is imperative if disease control is to be achieved.

The over-all prognosis of ALL is favorable, but the eventual outcome depends on a number of variables, such as the child's age, the initial white count, and the presence or absence of extramedullary disease. Children between the ages of 2 and 10 years without extramedullary invasion and with white counts less than 100,000 have the best prognosis. On the one hand, about 90 to 95 percent of the children with ALL go into an initial remission, and 50 to 60 percent survive for at least 5 years, a statistic which seems to be improving annually. Until recently, the prognosis for children with AML was poor. For many years, the rate of initial remission was only 40 to 50 percent and remission seldom lasted longer than 6 months. Recent improvements in treatment protocols have, however, resulted in remission rates of about 70 percent which last approximately two years.[8] Ongoing research in the treatment of AML may provide a more promising prognosis in the future.

Response to therapy varies among children. It depends on the type of malignant cell present, the extent of involvement (local or disseminated), the age of the patient, treatment modalities available, and general physical health status, especially kidney and liver function.

Nursing management When a child suspected of having leukemia is hospitalized, his symptoms are usually minimal. The battery of tests essential for diagnosis are invasive and hurt. Explaining them, honestly and exactly, will help in developing a relationship which elicits the child's cooperation. Both the lumbar puncture and bone marrow aspiration are painful (the latter more so). They are important procedures which will be repeated in the future in order to assess response to chemotherapy or the extent of relapse. Being present when they are performed, reassuring the child, and the use of local anesthetics can decrease both anxiety and discomfort.

When chemotherapy begins, the side effects of cytotoxic agents cause many problems which can generate a number of complications. Corticosteriods, an exception, contribute to a euphoria and a marked increase in appetite. Drugs may also result in alterations in body image. Normal eating patterns are disrupted because of mechanical problems due to oral lesions and gingival bleeding. See Fig. 35-1A. A nurse is called upon to demonstrate creative ability in providing a high-protein, high-calorie diet to a child experiencing pain and an unpleasant taste. Supplemental high-calorie liquids can be used. The nutritionist should be consulted and parents may be asked to bring foods prepared at home. Children of different ethnic groups (Asian, Hispanic, Haitian) who may be unaccustomed to hospital-prepared meals improve their dietary intakes when food is brought in from home. Parents, frustrated and feeling helpless because

of the diagnosis, are pleased to help. Allowing children to select food they wish to eat may stimulate their interest.

Brushing teeth may be difficult with lesions present, and so a nurse needs to use good judgment in providing oral hygiene. A Water Pik cleanses teeth and provides gingival stimulation similar to chewing. Lemon and glycerine swabs or hydrogen peroxide mixed with saline or sterile water as a mouth wash are effective. In severely affected cases, water rinses may be the only alternative. The use of forks, spoons, and straws may be curtailed to prevent further injury.

Without exercise or foods high in bulk, these children have bowel problems. This is especially so when they are receiving vincristine, which exhibits a neurotoxic sign in constipation. Increasing fluid intake and giving stool softeners can prevent a potential problem.

Gastrointestinal side effects of some drugs may result in the development of rectal ulcers, which begin as small, tender, red lesions (see Fig. 35-1B). Assessing the anal area frequently and providing good skin care are effective in preventing necrosis. Leukemic children need to be turned and positioned frequently. A sheepskin or an alternating pressure mattress should be used if available. Rectal temperatures are *not* done and ointments, which tend to trap organisms (enhancing an infection) are never used. The child should be bathed after voiding or having a bowel

Figure 35-1 *A* Bleeding gums, common in AML. *B* A perianal lesion (*Pseudomonas* sepsis) in a child with leukemia. (*From G. M. Scipien et al., Comprehensive Pediatric Nursing, 2d ed., McGraw-Hill, New York, 1979, pp. 736–737.*)

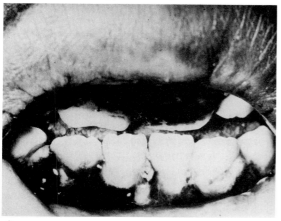

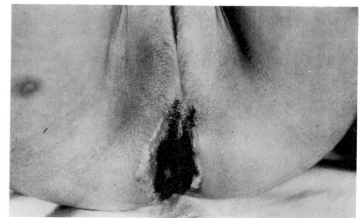

A   B

movement to decrease the likelihood of introducing contaminants.

Because infection is the leading cause of death, all efforts need to be directed toward lessening this possibility. Meticulous handwashing by the nurse with instructions to parents and child to do the same are essential. While venipunctures are necessary and can be a source of infection, injections are avoided, if possible, in an attempt to maintain skin integrity. A private room and protective isolation measures (see Chap. 17) or a laminar flow unit may be used to decrease the likelihood of infection. In the event that an infection does not respond to antibiotics, a white cell (granulocytes) transfusion can be done. Some patients may develop chills and an elevated temperature (more likely in repeated transfusions), which are monitored, recorded, and reported; however, this transfusion is not discontinued.

When a child is in the remission induction phase of treatment, blood transfusions are given to correct anemia. Transfusions are *not* administered prior to bone marrow aspirations or the confirmation of diagnosis, even in the presence of severe anemia. The administration of blood elements masks the true hematologic picture. Nursing responsibilities during a blood transfusion are directed toward observation of the patient and maintenance of a patent site. It may be necessary to immobilize the child (see Chap. 17). It is important to make him as comfortable as possible for the next few hours. The rate of blood flow is monitored closely to prevent circulatory overload. Since the risk of complications increases with successive transfusions, it is imperative that a nurse observe for signs of *transfusion reaction*. Most reactions occur in the first 10 minutes. They include chills, fever, restlessness, irritability, hematuria, or oliguria. When reaction is suspected, the transfusion *must be stopped* and a physician is called. If a double setup is used, saline can be infused in the interim, retaining patency. The remaining blood is sent back to the blood bank, where it is cultured and examined. A specimen of the patient's blood is drawn and sent for culture.

Hemorrhage is also a very serious problem in leukemic children. Their bodies must be examined often to determine the presence (and increase in) ecchymosis and petechiae as well as bleeding into soft tissue, which is a superb media

for infection. Platelet transfusions may be given during active bleeding episodes, such as uncontrollable epistaxis or in the presence of low platelet counts (20,000/mm^3). A temperature elevation can occur during a platelet transfusion. Simple measures often control minor local bleeding effectively. Ice or cold compresses and gentle pressure may be applied. A dry tea bag can be applied to control gingival bleeding. Salt pork, trimmed to size, acts as an astringent and provides pressure to control epistaxis. The removal of a salt pork pack (usually 12 to 24 h later) causes less disruption to the mucosa than does removal of a sterile gauze pack.

The child must cope with many bodily changes which accompany his illness and treatment. He should be free to select diversional activities, but the nurse needs to assist him in coping with the emotions he is experiencing. Play provides that opportunity. Pounding toys, story-telling, and role-playing are all effective avenues of expression (see Chap. 16).

Patient teaching is a high priority for the nurse. Both the child and his parents must anticipate radiation- or drug-induced alopecia and should be prepared to use a wig, baseball cap, or scarf. They also need to be reassured of regrowth in 3 to 4 months' time. Because the risk of infection is high, activities which bring the child in contact with crowds may need to be curtailed. This is especially true in the winter (stores, markets, movies). Explaining signs and symptoms of drug toxicity and the correct dose make parents more relaxed in relation to discharge. The biggest problem parents face is treating the patient as a normal child, a difficult task considering the unknown nature of this potentially life-threatening disorder. See the nursing care plan for a patient with acute lymphoblastic leukemia at the end of this chapter.

Brain tumors

The central nervous system (CNS) is the most common site of tumors in children. About 60 to 70 percent are located in the posterior fossa, while the remaining number are located in the anterior portion of the brain.

In general, tumors occur in both sexes, but there are exceptions. (These will be identified as specific tumors are discussed.) Brain tumors are diagnosed most frequently in the 5- to 8-year age group. Incidence decreases toward adolescence.

Although there are specific ages where the incidence "peaks," it is important to remember that *no* age is excepted.

Diagnosis of brain tumors It is extremely important to identify and treat brain tumors as early and as effectively as possible because a significant number are compatible with long-term survival. In addition, early recognition decreases the likelihood of residual neurological or visual disturbances which may be caused by the tumor.

Obtaining a careful history and attending to what a parent may consider inconsequential information, e.g., clumsiness, persistent inability to get the ball over home plate in Little League, or the evolution of a behavior problem in a formerly delightful, cooperative child, can all be of great importance in data collection.

Symptoms indicative of a CNS mass vary according to its anatomic site and size. Perhaps the most important nonlocalizing sign is increased intracranial pressure (ICP). This occurs because the lesion obstructs ventricles or displaces tissue by its growth. The latter is especially significant in children whose cranial sutures are closed. This symptom is not demonstrated in the infant or toddler (birth through 2) whose sutures are not closed and whose head expands to accommodate the growing lesion. This fact reiterates the importance of doing routine head measurements on young children.

A frequent complaint is a generalized, intermittent headache, which is worse on rising from a recumbent position (sleep or nap). Also, it is intensified by coughing, sneezing, or straining. Diagnosis may be delayed in the case of a young school-age child who complains of a headache which is misinterpreted as a classroom problem or a ploy to avoid school. Headaches are often accompanied by nausea and forceful vomiting as well as lethargy and irritability.

Eye problems are also evident in children with brain tumors, and they include diplopia, strabismus, nystagmus, squinting, or tilting the head in a peculiar manner to improve visual acuity. Children are incredible in their ability to compensate for these changes. As a result, they unknowingly complicate, and, in some instances, delay the diagnosis.

Once all the subjective data have been collected, the child undergoes a wide variety of neurological tests in order to locate, identify, and confirm the presence of a brain tumor. They include: lumbar puncture; cerebrospinal fluid analysis; anterior-posterior and lateral skull x-rays; EEG; CAT scan; brain scan; ventriculogram; arteriogram; pneumoencephalogram; and echoencephalogram. These tests are discussed in detail in Chap. 37.

Cerebellar astrocytoma This benign tumor, whose cells resemble astrocytes, has an insidious onset. It affects boys and girls equally, primarily those between the ages of 5 and 8 years. It has a very slow course and hence is capable of doing a significant amount of neurological damage before discovery.

Diagnosis and treatment Symptoms include increased intracranial pressure (ICP), tremors which indicate a focal disturbance, hypotonia, and diminished reflexes. Papilledema can result in nystagmus, optic atrophy, and blindness. A gait disturbance is present.

Treatment involves surgical removal of the lesion with a resulting cure in 80 to 90 percent of the patients. Although the abnormal gait and tremors persist postoperatively, they are not disabling.

Medulloblastoma This tumor is a highly malignant, rapidly growing lesion whose cells are similar to those in the primitive medullary tube. It tends to metastasize readily along the cerebrospinal fluid pathways, and it is this rapid invasion which makes excision so difficult. Its peak incidence is in 3- to 6-year-olds and this lesion is found twice as often in boys as in girls.

Diagnosis and treatment Initially, the clinical symptoms include early-morning headaches, anorexia, vomiting, and an unsteady gait. As the tumor grows, ataxia develops along with nystagmus, papilledema, and drowsiness.

Total excision of this tumor is almost impossible. The use of chemotherapy and radiation in combination can prolong life. Most children survive for about 12 months.

Brainstem glioma This malignant lesion, usually consisting of astrocytomas and, less frequently, glioblastomas, is particularly infiltrative because of its cellular makeup. Its location is capable of affecting vital control centers, such as those for respirations and heart beat, and so it is not amenable to surgery.

Diagnosis and treatment The presence of brainstem glioma is signified by a myriad of cranial nerve palsies (cranial nerves V through X involved), ataxia, indicating pyramidal tract involvement, and nystagmus. There is a positive Babinski's reflex and hyperreflexia, as well as a slow increase in ICP.

These tumors are inoperable because of their attachment to strategic centers. Palliative radiotherapy decreases the size of the tumor. Few children survive beyond a year.

Ependymoma

A slow-growing mass originating from the lining of the spinal cord canal and cerebral ventricles, this tumor most frequently involves the floor of the fourth ventricle. As it extends upward, it blocks the flow of cerebrospinal fluid, resulting in obstructive hydrocephaly. There is no specific age or sex predisposition to this neoplasm.

Diagnosis and treatment Symptoms include increased ICP, headache, nausea, vomiting, and unsteady gait. The presence of cranial nerve palsies and a positive Babinski's reflex can indicate brainstem infiltration. Young children with open cranial sutures may have head enlargement. An early sign is vomiting, but it is the episodes of *repeated* vomiting that are especially significant. Vomiting results from pressure on the emetic center, the site of the mass.

The location of this lesion makes the prognosis poor, in spite of its slow growth. The surgical treatment is removal of the bulk of the tumor. It cannot be removed completely because it is inseparable from the floor of the ventricle. A shunting procedure allows the cerebrospinal fluid to circulate. Survival of children with this problem can be as short as 12 months or as long as 10 years.

Craniopharyngioma

This tumor, located near the pituitary gland, arises from squamous epithelial cells which are remnants of the embryonic Rathke's pouch. Its growth characteristics resemble those of a benign neoplasm. It is associated with endocrine dysfunction, but it is also capable of producing a deformity of the sella turcica. A craniopharygioma can be diagnosed anytime in childhood or adolescence, showing no specific preference for boys or girls.

Diagnosis and treatment Its clinical manifestations include an increased ICP (early) and alterations in personality as well as memory. If it appears in adolescence, there is delayed sexual maturation. Visual problems develop slowly and are common. This is a result of the lesion's growth and subsequent pressure on the optic chiasma. Unfortunately, a child is usually unaware of his decreasing visual acuity.

Complete removal is not possible because of the tumor's adherence to such structures as the optic chiasma or an internal carotid artery. It is, however, possible to remove the bulk of this encapsulated mass. Although the tumor is radioresistant, future growth can be controlled with radiation. Repeated surgical procedures may be necessary to control tumor size since the cells remaining after the initial surgery continue to proliferate.

The survival rate is very high. Although hormonal replacement therapy is necessary, including antidiuretic hormone and corticosteroids, these children live relatively normal lives.

Nursing management

When children are admitted with suspected brain tumors, a nurse actively participates in observations and procedures which aid in confirming the presence and location of a neoplasm. The diagnostic tests (tomography) can be frightening. Children need explanations and the presence of a familiar person to allay their fears. A most distressing study is the pneumoencephalogram, which leaves the child with a headache. Even though the child must lie flat, headache is likely to persist for 24 h.

Parents are anxious about all aspects of diagnosis because the brain is involved. Many express feelings of guilt about ignoring the child's complaints and delaying the visit to a physician. Listening can relieve their anxiety and promote a therapeutic relationship which will be helpful in the months to come.

Most neoplasms of the brain are treated surgically, by radiotherapy, or both. In anticipating a craniotomy, the patient and family need to be prepared for the head shave, which is very upsetting to the child. They must expect a bulky dressing after the operation. Parents are also told that their child will have facial edema and will be comatose upon return to the unit. The day of surgery is extremely difficult for families, and they are grateful for any news a nurse can communicate from the operating room.

After recovering from anesthesia, the patient is transported to his room, where the nurse monitors vital signs closely until they are stable. Both pupillary responses are assessed frequently. Sluggish, unequal, or dilated pupils are promptly reported. The type of fluid infusing is checked, and the rate of flow is meticulously observed to prevent ICP. Placing the child on his unaffected side with the head of the bed elevated reduces edema and decreases ICP.

The head dressing is examined frequently for drainage. When present, the color, amount, and odor are recorded. The drainage area is circled with a pen or pencil and marked with the time, so that the rate of increase can be monitored. A felt-tip pen is *never* used because of its rapid absorptive qualities. Serosanguineous drainage is common, but if the amount increases substantially, it is necessary to reinforce the bandage with sterile dressings and notify the neurosurgeon. Infection is a prime concern because the incision provides a direct pathway to the brain. Sometimes a patient attempts to remove the dressing, and so it may be necessary to make mitts for his hands. If that intervention is ineffective, elbow restraints may be necessary (see Chap. 17). Under no circumstances should other types of restraints be used. If the child resists them, his ICP increases.

Facial and intracranial edema are normal consequences of surgery. Eyelids are edematous, but edema can extend to the neck. Since there is a potential for airway obstruction, both respirations and the extent of edema must be evaluated periodically. The child's blinking reflex is depressed, and so methylcellulose eye drops are used to prevent corneal damage.

The trauma of neurosurgery and the edema increase nervous tissue irritability. It can affect the respiratory control center necessitating mechanical ventilation. The temperature control center is easily irritated, too, resulting in fever. Since fever is a common postoperative response, hypothermia blankets are applied shortly after surgery. Because the elevated temperature is secondary to a CNS disturbance, it responds poorly to antipyretics. The nurse should remove bed covers and lower room temperature in addition to using hypothermia.

Positioning and giving skin care every 2 hours are essential because the child is unconscious. It is important to avoid jarring the bed. Turning is best done by two nurses, who can maintain the child's alignment. Although the child is unconscious, hearing is not impaired. It is, therefore, important to be mindful about conversations in the patient's presence.

Once the child wakes, alertness increases steadily. Levels of consciousness, general behavior, responses to stimuli, and assessments of cranial nerves (affecting gag, blink and swallowing reflexes) must be noted. Any deterioration to a lower level of consciousness warrants notifying a physician.

Once the swallowing reflex has been verified, clear oral fluids may be started. Diet is progressed gradually. Intravenous fluids are usually continued until the patient is eating and drinking well.

Some neurological residual damage may be evident when the child is allowed out of bed. This is probably due to edema or trauma. Gradually, there will be a steady improvement in strength and an increase in physical activity.

The head dressing remains until healing is complete. Later, hats, scarves, stocking-knit caps, or wigs are used until the hair grows back. Padded football helmets are used for young children who may fall.

The nurse needs to coordinate discharge planning. A referral to the local visiting nurses' association should identify teaching done in the hospital and patient-family needs. Parents need encouragement to visit the child's school and talk with the nurse, teacher, and classmates. The people at school should be told about the child's physical and behavioral changes and his activity limitations. It is best for the child to attend school part-time at first. After his fatigue level has been evaluated, a decision about increasing time in school can be made. Peer group contact is important in helping the child regain independence.

Malignant tumors of the eye

Rhabdomyosarcoma This common soft tissue sarcoma originates in the undifferentiated mesenchymal cells of muscle, lymphatic, vascular, or connective tissue. It is divided into four types:

(1) embryonic; (2) alveolar; (3) pleomorphic (very rare in children); and (4) a mixed type which can be a combination of the other three.

The embryonic rhabdomyosarcoma is seen most frequently in children, and although the primary sites can be the head, neck, abdomen, or genitourinary tract, the majority are confined to the head and neck. About 60 percent are orbital in origin.

Occurring equally in boys and girls, its peak is in children between the ages of 2 and 6 years. There are some patients less than 1 year old, which leads one to suspect some intrauterine factor as a causative agent.

Diagnosis and treatment Clinical symptoms depend on the site and rate of proliferation. When the orbit of an eye is affected, there is no optic atrophy and vision is not impaired. The first sign indicating a mass within the orbit is *proptosis*, a forward protrusion of the eye caused by the proliferating neoplasm. This neoplasm metastasizes early. Hence, at the time of diagnosis about two-thirds of the children have an extension of the disease to regional tissues or lymph nodes. A hematogenous dissemination to lungs, bone, or bone marrow is also possible.

The diagnostic tests include: complete blood count; chest x-ray; a metastatic survey; bone marrow aspiration; tomograms; and extensive opthalmologic examination. Diagnosis is confirmed only by a histologic analysis.

The combination of surgery, radiotherapy, and chemotherapy has resulted in a drastic improvement in survival. Prognosis is especially favorable when the tumor is confined to the orbit and can be completely excised. For children whose tumors are removed, a variety of agents can be used to suppress the growth of micrometastasis. They are vincristine, dactinomycin, doxorubicin, and cyclophosphamide. It is important to remember that prognosis is directly related to the extent of disease at the time of diagnosis. In the presence of disseminated disease, survival is highly doubtful.

Optic nerve glioma Gliomas make up the largest percentage of tumors which affect the optic nerve and about 95 percent are diagnosed in children. Their cellular composition consists of astrocytomas, which are benign and grow slowly.

There is strong association with neurofibromatosis, or von Recklinghausen's disease, and multiple *cafe au lait* spots are present on the bodies of about 25 percent of the children. There is no sexual predisposition. These tumors usually occur in the first 10 years of life.

Strabismus and nystagmus appear early, but it is possible for months to elapse before the correct diagnosis is made. When the glioma is confined to one orbit, exophthalmos and impaired vision can develop. If the lesion grows posteriorly, the optic chiasma and the other optic nerve are involved, resulting in bilateral eye problems. Should the foramen of Monro become obstructed, there is increased ICP. Optic nerve atrophy occurs because of constant compression exerted by the growing tumor.

Diagnosis and treatment Diagnostic tests are usually conducted by an ophthalmologist. If the optic chiasma is affected, a neurosurgeon is involved in diagnosis and subsequent treatment. The tests include measuring both visual fields and visual activity, skull x-rays, an intracranial pneumogram, and a funduscopic examination.

If the glioma is confined to a single orbit, a total resection may be feasible. This preserves the globe as a natural prosthesis. Reflex actions are controlled by the unaffected eye. Vision is lost because the optic nerve has been removed. If the bilateral optic nerve is involved or the chiasma infiltrated, one of two approaches is used. A significant portion of the tumor can be removed to restore flow of cerebrospinal fluid. The alternative is a ventricular shunt which circumvents the mass. Radiation may be utilized postoperatively to decrease the size of the tumor even further.

The prognosis varies greatly. It is very good when the glioma is confined to a single optic nerve; however, with greater infiltration the prognosis decreases substantally. It is very poor for those children who have increased ICP at the time of diagnosis.

Retinoblastoma The most common intraocular tumor in children is a congenital lesion consisting of embryonic retinal cells. Although it may be present at birth (1 per 15,000 to 20,000 births), it is usually detected in boys or girls during infancy or before 3 years of age.

Retinoblastoma can occur as a somatic mutation in the child's retina. In this case, it is usually unilateral and nontransmittable to offspring. Another cause can be a germinal mutation in one parent, free of the disease, who has transmitted it to his offspring. The majority of these children have bilateral involvement and will transmit it as an autosomal dominant gene to 15 percent of their children. Retinoblastoma can also be accompanied by a chromosomal aberration.

Retinoblastoma produces very few clinical signs or symptoms. The normal red reflex of the retina is missing. The pupil has a whitish appearance known as "cat's eye reflex." Strabismus is common. The eye may be red and painful, with or without glaucoma. Vision may be impaired or even lost, but this is difficult to assess because of the client's age.

Diagnosis and treatment Diagnosis is determined by ophthalmic examination under anesthesia and with x-rays and ultrasonography. Visualization of the tumor's calcified surface and seeding of the vitreous are characteristic, confirming findings.

Staging done by an ophthalmologist refers to the survival of the eye in reference to vision and *not* to the prognosis as it affects preservation of life. For clarification, group I tumors have either one small tumor or several very small tumors and a most favorable outcome. Those classified as group V are large tumors with vitreous seeding and a very poor prognosis.

When the tumor is unilateral and small, all attempts are made to preserve the child's vision. Radiation, cobalt implants, light coagulation with a laser beam, or cryotherapy may be used. If there is optic nerve involvement, an enucleation is done to decrease the likelihood of micrometastasis, and chemotherapy (vincristine, cyclophosphamide, Adriamycin) may be instituted.

If there is bilateral involvement, the eye affected most severely is removed. The remaining eye may be treated with radiation and light coagulation. Chemotherapy is generally used also. When bilateral involvement is severe, a bilateral enucleation may be performed. This treatment is traumatic for the child and family because the child will be blind after surgery. Enucleation does, however, spare the child the severe pain which inevitably accompanies tumor growth.

During an enucleation, the eyeball is replaced by a plastic implant. The child can be fitted with a plastic eyeball about 6 or 8 weeks after surgery.

Nursing management Malignant neoplasms which affect this sensory organ catapult a family into crisis because of: (1) a delay in diagnosis; (2) parental guilt about transmitting the gene; and (3) the loss of vision. It is important for a nurse to assist parents in coping with the guilt they are experiencing. Whenever possible, the nurse should emphasize positive aspects. For example, outcomes for retinoblastoma are more favorable than some other malignancies in children. If involvement is unilateral, vision in the unaffected eye remains. However, bilateral affliction compounds the difficulty of the situation.

It is especially difficult for the parents if they have been asked to give consent for an enucleation. Granting permission for surgery is an agonizing process for the parents. It is a difficult decision because denying permission decreases the child's life expectancy, while allowing surgery means that the child will lose his sight. It is crucial for a nurse to spend time with parents, allowing them to verbalize their fears about coping with their child's blindness, future resentment by the child regarding their decision, and possible disfigurement. If consent for an enucleation is given, the child must be prepared for the vision changes that result from surgery. If a bilateral enucleation is planned, it is important that the child be told he will not be able to see after the operation. When an eye prosthesis is planned, this should also be discussed with the child. These topics are difficult to discuss, but the child's and parents' fears and anxieties must be explored if resolution is to occur. The nursing care of children having eye surgery is discussed in Chap. 39.

Neuroblastoma

Neuroblastomas, the most common solid malignant tumors in children, arise from primitive sympathetic neuroblasts of neural crest origin. Primary sites can be the adrenal glands or areas anywhere along the sympathetic chain. Therefore, lesions may be found in the retroperitoneal area, the neck, abdomen, or chest. Unfortunately, metastasis occurs in about two-thirds of the children before a diagnosis is made.

This lesion is found slightly more often in

males than in females. While it is usually detected in the first 5 years of life, the majority are under 3 years of age.

Symptoms are related to the anatomic site involved. If a cervical gangloin is implicated, there is a painless mass in the neck. Should the chest be a primary site, dyspnea or a cough may be present. An abdominal mass can be detected by a parent or in a routine physical examination. A pelvic lesion usually causes a change in bowel habits, urinary frequency, or retention. Systemic signs are irritability, anorexia, fatigue, anemia, or a low-grade fever. Distant metastasis has occurred when the child has periorbital swelling, periorbital ecchymosis, and exophthalmos.

Diagnosis Diagnostic procedures include physical examination, complete blood count and platelet count, and x-rays of the chest, abdomen, and skeleton. An intravenous pyelogram (IVP) is done when an abdominal tumor is suspected. Urine collections for catecholamines and metabolic by-products, especially vanillylmandelic acid (VMA) are vital in confirming the presence of a neuroblastoma. Bone marrow aspiration is important in determining infiltration and, hence, staging. Diagnosis is confirmed by histologic examination at the time of excision or when a distant tumor is biopsied.

Staging Neuroblastomas are classified according to *stages*. These categories enable investigators to determine the effectiveness of treatment modalities and estimate prognoses in relation to tissue involvement.

Stage I Tumor confined to organ or structure of origin.
Stage II Tumor extends beyond organ or structure of origin, but it does not cross midline; regional lymph nodes on ipsilateral side may be involved.
Stage III Tumor extends beyond midline with bilateral regional lymph node involvement.
Stage IV Evidence of remote disease in soft tissue, parenchymatous organs, skeleton, and distant lymph node groups.
Stage IV-S Patients who would be classified as stage I or stage II except for remote disease confined to liver, spleen, or bone marrow. No evidence of metastasis on skeletal survey.

Treatment A complete excision is performed when the child has a localized neuroblastoma. This procedure generally results in a cure without further treatment. If the lesion cannot be totally removed, the residual regional disease is irradiated. Since the tissue is radiosensitive, favorable results can be achieved. The high incidence of metastasis necessitates the use of chemotherapeutic agents because surgery and radiation are no longer effective. The most effective drugs seem to be doxorubicin (Adriamycin) and cyclophosphamide while vincristine and dacarbazine (DTIC) are less useful.[9]

Prognosis The prognosis depends on the age and degree of dissemination at the time of diagnosis. About 50 percent of the children under 1 year survive regardless of the stage. The stage at the time of diagnosis is significant in children over 1 year of age. If the neuroblastoma can be excised, or if there is microscopic residual regional disease amenable to radiation, a cure is possible. Those children who are over 1 year of age, with either regional or distant metastasis, may achieve a clinical response to drug therapy; however, cure is very rare. Whether these patients have surgery alone, in combination with radiotherapy, or also receive chemotherapy, catecholamine and VMA urines need to be collected periodically to monitor their bodies' responses to treatment.

Nursing management The unpredictable nature of this malignancy, with its poor prognosis, contributes to the anxiety and apprehension of parents. They feel guilty because the child was not seen earlier and occasionally demonstrate it as hostility. A nurse needs to understand why they are experiencing these emotions in order to help them cope and hence function more effectively.

The large number of radiological studies and 24-h urine collections need to be explained in detail. Since parents will collect urine for examination months after discharge, involving them preoperatively can help in acquiring skill in doing so. Many of these children are not toilet-trained, which complicates the collection process.

Surgical sites may be abdominal, thoracic, or cervical. Dressing changes are done using sterile technique. Parents may be taught to do them. Intravenous therapy, monitoring vital signs, and turning and positioning are routine nursing actions. Infection is not a major risk.

Parents should be fully informed of the side

effects of radiotherapy, chemotherapy, or both, and the necessity for collecting urine specimens. The nurse must stress the importance of returning to the physician's office or clinic for follow-up after discharge. These parents face the probability of losing their child earlier than most, and supportive measures as described in Chap. 22 can be effective.

Wilms' tumor (nephroblastoma)

This malignancy is the most common abdominal tumor found in children. Derived from primitive renoblasts, it arises in the parenchyma of the kidney and grows by expanding into the renal cavity. Occurring equally in boys and girls, it is usually diagnosed before the age of 5 years, with the majority seen in 2-and 3-year-olds

Often, this nontender lesion is first discovered by parents or palpated by a physician doing a routine physical examination. Symptoms develop late and include anorexia and pain. Hematuria and hypertension are late findings. When metastasis to the lungs is present, children have such pulmonary problems as dyspnea or a cough.

Diagnosis and treatment Radiographic studies include chest x-ray, bone survey, inferior vena cavagram, and angiogram. Intravenous pyelogram (IVP) demonstrates a distorted caliceal system indicative of a mass. Renal function is assessed through blood urea nitrogen (BUN), creatinine, creatinine clearance, and uric acid determinations. A complete blood count and a battery of liver function tests are performed to detect infiltration by this neoplasm. In addition, a total protein, serum glutamic-oxaloacetic transaminase (SGOT), serum glutamic-pyruvic transaminase (SGPT), lactic dehydrogenase (LHD), and alkaline phosphatase are done.

Once the diagnosis is made, a histologic confirmation is essential. Therefore, surgery is scheduled 24 to 48 h later. Staging is done to precisely identify the extent of the tumor and facilitate the selection of an effective treatment protocol. Table 35-5 lists stages, modes of treatment, and prognoses. In the course of the transabdominal exploratory laparotomy, a nephrectomy is performed, the contralateral kidney and liver are examined, and lymph nodes are inspected (and biopsied), while other structures are all carefully scrutinized.

Subsequent treatment depends on the stage assigned. Radiotherapy and chemotherapy are both effective and combinations of approaches have resulted in the highest number of cures and best survival rates among the various malignancies seen in children.

Nursing management These children should have signs at the head of their cribs or beds reading "Do Not Palpate Abdomen." There is risk

Table 35-5 Stage, treatment, and prognosis of Wilms' tumor

Stage	Extent of involvement	Treatment	Prognosis
I	Tumor confined to renal capsule; completely resected	*Surgical:* Nephrectomy *Chemotherapy:* Vincristine, dactinomycin	About 90% cured
II	Tumor extended through renal capsule; completely resected	*Surgical:* Neprhectomy *Chemotherapy:* Vincristine, dactinomycin *Radiotherapy:* To renal bed	About 60% of these patients can be cured.
III	Tumor extended into or beyond renal bed	*Surgical:* Nephrectomy *Chemotherapy:* Vincristine, dactinomycin, and doxorubicin	About 60% of these patients can be cured.
IV	Hematogenous metastasis to lungs, liver, bone, or brain	*Radiotherapy:* Radiation to residual areas of tumor	About 50% can survive.
V	Bilateral renal involvement, either initially or later	*Surgical:* Removal of most affected kidney *Chemotherapy:* Vincristine, dactinomycin, and doxorubican *Radiation:* To remaining kidney	Disease-free, long-term control can be achieved in about 50% of the cases.

Primary source: James G. Hughes, *Synopsis of Pediatrics*, 5th ed., Mosby, 1980, p. 770.

of rupturing the renal capsule during palpation. This can cause malignant cells to break away from the primary mass. The nurse should tell parents of a child who will have a nephrectomy for Wilms' tumor that there will be a large incision, which is necessary because internal organ examination is essential during the laparotomy.

Postoperatively, the intake and output is monitored closely because parenteral fluid replacement is necessary. The patency of the nasogastric tube is maintained by normal saline irrigations every 2 h. Abdominal girth measurements are done every 2 hours to check for distention. The location at which abdominal girth measurements are taken should be marked. In this way, all nurses measure the same circumference and the results are valid. Dressings are checked for excessive drainage. Vital signs and rate of the intravenous flow are monitored and recorded.

These children recover rapidly from surgery and then begin radio- and chemotherapy shortly thereafter. Side effects and toxic symptoms that can be expected to result from therapy must be described to parents. The prognosis is more favorable than for other types of malignancies, thus allowing families to resume their prior lifestyles readily.

Bone tumors

Malignant tumors of the bone usually appear in the second decade of life. These children frequently appear well when they are seen initially for a traumatic injury such as a fracture, which is identified as pathological in nature. Osteogenic sarcoma and Ewing's sarcoma are the two most common malignancies which involve bone. The same bones are usually implicated in both disorders. Any bony structure may be involved, but the long bones of the skeleton are often affected.

Osteogenic sarcoma (osteosarcoma) Osteosarcoma arises from bone-forming osteoblasts, and as a result this neoplasm contains primitive cells that are forming the matrix of true bone. As the lesion grows within the medullary cavity, it eventually penetrates the periosteum and extends into soft tissue. There is destruction of preexisting bone. Any major long bone can be affected, especially the metaphysis of the lower end of the femur or upper end of the humerus.

Most clients are between 10 and 15 years of age at the time of diagnosis. This lesion affects both sexes equally at a young age, but almost twice as many males are afflicted during adolescence. The increased incidence may be due to the rapid growth spurt which occurs at this stage of development.

Osteosarcoma has been diagnosed in children following exposure to irradiation. Also, it is seen in some patients who have survived retinoblastoma.

While pathological fracture may be the first indication of a problem, some children also complain of pain. Initially, pain is intermittent. Later, it becomes intense and continuous. Local swelling and tenderness follow. An x-ray of the affected limb usually reveals: bone destruction; periosteal, new bone formation; a soft mass with some calcification. See Fig. 35-2. Metastasis to the lungs is common and rapid.

Diagnosis and treatment Extensive radiologic studies are necessary to evaluate the lesion, determine its extensiveness, and screen for metastasis. They include a bone scan, bone survey, chest x-ray and tomograms, urinalysis, complete blood count, and platelet count. Liver function tests including alkaline phosphatase, transaminase, and protein electrophoresis are also performed. Absolute confirmation requires histologic examination.

An amputation of the affected limb, with a sufficient margin of normal bone ensuring complete removal of the tumor, is the treatment of

Figure 35-2 This x-ray demonstrates the bone destruction, soft tissue mass, and new bone in a patient with osteosarcoma of the femur. (*From Seymour I. Schwartz et al., Principles of Surgery, 2d ed., McGraw-Hill, 1974, p. 1778.*)

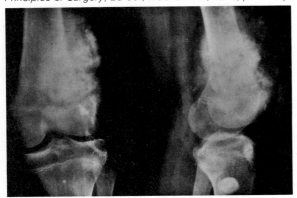

choice, *if* there is no evidence of metastasis. Chemotherapy is instituted postoperatively for about 1 year. The agents used frequently are: cyclophosphamide, doxorubicin, and a high dose of methotrexate with leucovorin rescue. With metastasis present, these neoplasms may be irradiated and chemotherapy started. Pain needs to be controlled.

Some medical centers are trying to avoid the need for amputating a limb, a drastic procedure for a child or an adolescent to experience. In those settings, chemotherapy is started, and after the neoplasm is resected, a reinforcing prosthesis is inserted into the affected bone. There are no longterm statistics regarding the success of this procedure at present.

The prognosis is difficult to determine. In cases where radical amputations can be done without evidence of metastasis, there is a good chance for survival. Unfortuantely, 75 to 95 percent die in about 5 years.[10]

Ewing's sarcoma This malignancy has an affinity for such long bones as the femur or tibia, but such flat bones as the ribs or scapula can also be primary sites. Arising from primitive bone marrow cells, myeloblasts, this neoplasm is capable of metastasis to the lungs and other bone. It appears primarily in the second decade of life, and for some unexplained reason, affects males twice as often as females.

The initial findings, localized pain in the affected bone, followed by tenderness, swelling, and heat are very similar to those seen in patients with osteosarcoma. An x-ray of the involved part demonstrates bone destruction and a soft tissue mass, with a characteristic "sunburst" sign of calcification.

Diagnosis and treatment Some of the initial studies are hemoglobin, hematocrit, white blood count, platelet count, SGOT, alkaline phosphatase, and uric acid in addition to urinalysis. A 24-hour urine for vanillylmandelic acid (VMA) or catecholamines is done to rule out neuroblastoma. Radiologic studies include chest x-ray, bone survey and scan, tomograms, and an x-ray of the involved area. The diagnosis is confirmed by biopsy.

Surgical intervention, either excision or amputation, has not improved the survival rate for this sarcoma, and therefore radiation and chemotherapy are used in an effort to extend life. Combinations of vincristine, dactinomycin, and cyclophosphamide have been especially effective. Some oncologists have also included doxorubicin in the protocols of patients with advanced disease.

The prognosis for these clients continues to be poor. In spite of aggressive treatment, about 95 percent die within the first few years.[11] These grave outcomes may be due to the presence of undetectable micrometastasis at the time of the patient's initial complaints.

Nursing management of children with bone tumors Amputating the limb of a child with osteosarcoma is a drastic, albeit almost imperative intervention for which he must be adequately prepared. School-age children and adolescents are able to convey their fears and anxieties about the operation. The alteration in body image initiates a grieving process, which is normal. The nurse should expect anger, depression, hostility or withdrawal. All of these are legitimate responses. The nurse must allow the patient an opportunity to vent his feelings. Issues related to the prothesis, peer group reactions to the amputation, or environmental handicaps can affect the success of rehabilitation.

Some orthopedic surgeons apply a temporary prosthesis after surgery. It can avoid serious complications such as contractures, stump edema, or phantom limb pain. However, the presence of this appliance prevents observation of the pressure dressing, which can be displaced, affecting both the incision and stump healing. An elastic bandage is used to decrease edema formation. For the first 24 h after surgery, the stump (with or without a prosthesis) is kept elevated to improve venous return and decrease the edema. If the child does not have a prosthesis, specific exercises are done to condition the stump for receiving one.

Early ambulation is essential. The physical therapist begins to work with the child early, teaching him to use his prosthesis or, if he does not have one, to crutch-walk.

The nurse assumes responsibility for coordinating these rehabilitative activities. The nurse's observations are important in assessing the child's readiness for crutch walking. A team conference is held to evaluate the child's overall (physical, emotional) progress and to identify activity levels. Discharge planning and consultation with appropriate nurses in the community begins soon after surgery. A community health nurse, knowledgeable in services available to a family, and a school nurse who can evaluate physical barriers which will confront the child on school re-entry are important resources.

Chemotherapy is used for those with either osteosarcoma or Ewing's sarcoma. Instructions given to the family are similar to those previously described. The discharge teaching emphasizes compliance (office or clinic visits, medications, activities) and a gradual resumption of activities which allow a child to work toward functioning at his maximum potential.

Rhabdomyosarcoma

As described previously, this malignancy arises anywhere, and its most frequent site is the orbit. However, since it arises from striated muscle, it can be found anywhere in the body. Although the head and neck regions are most common, it can also be retroperitoneal. Most children are between 2 and 6 years of age or less than 1 year old.

The symptoms a child demonstrates vary according to the structures involved. Middle ear involvement, often mistaken for chronic otitis media, include pain and drainage. Hence, a delay in diagnosis is not unusual because clincial manifestations can resemble a more common childhood problem. If these neoplasms are on the trunk or an extremity, they appear as painless, firm swellings attached to underlying tissues, which cannot be explained. An abdominal mass is most difficult to diagnose because it produces no symptoms until there is fairly extensive metastasis. This malignancy metastasizes (regional tissue, lymph node, or hematogenous dissemination to lungs, bone, and marrow) easily, often before it is recognized.

Diagnosis and treatment A complete blood count, bone marrow examination, skeletal survey, chest x-ray, tomograms, and appropriate radiologic studies of the region of origin are done. Confirming the lesion's presence and identifying its extensiveness is crucial. Definitive diagnosis is made on histologic tissue examination.

Removing the neoplasm entirely is the treatment of choice because it is highly malignant. This is not always possible, however, since the site is a crucial factor. Amputation of a lower limb is most successful, but complete removal cannot be accomplished if the primary site is the middle ear. In children who have nonresectable disease, irradiation and chemotherapy are effective treatment modalities. The cytotoxic agents frequently used in various combinations are vincristine, cyclophosphamide, dactinomycin, and doxorubicin.

The prognosis depends on the extent of disease at the time of diagnosis. If *total* excision is possible, in combination with chemotherapy, the majority of children are cured. As the extent of disease increases, the likelihood of a cure decreases, and long-term survival is questionable.

Nursing management Since this neoplasm is highly malignant, many children with rhabdomyosarcoma require postoperative care following radical surgery. The type of surgery performed depends on the tumor site. Since radiation and chemotherapy are used, patient teaching focuses on these approaches. Parents are intimately involved because these children are young and, hence, unable to understand.

The prognosis is not as favorable as in other neoplasms. It is important for the nurse to be supportive. These parents may need to deal with the prospect of caring for a terminally ill child.

Lymphomas

Hodgkin's disease This disease is characterized by a progressive, painless enlargement of lymph nodes, predictable extension to adjacent nodes, and subsequent extralymphatic metastasis. The cause of this lymphoma is unknown. There are four histologic types: (1) lymphocytic predominance; (2) nodular sclerosis; (3) mixed cellularity; and, (4) lymphocytic depletion. The first two classifications are the most favorable, while the last has the poorest prognosis.

Predominantly found in males, it is rare before 5 years of age. Increasing in frequency during the school-age period, the incidence rises sharply in adolescence and persists until about 30 years of age.

Initially, there is a firm, movable nontender mass. About half of these neoplasms are found in the cervical area, with others identified in the axillary, inguinal, mediastinal, or retroperitoneal regions. Tumor enlargement can cause serious complications such as tracheobronchial compression and subsequent airway obstruction when it is present in the mediastinum. Compression of the esophagus can effect swallowing. Systemic symptoms include fatigue, anorexia, an intermittent fever, nausea, pruritus, and weight loss. An enlarged spleen is present early, but there are no common hematological abnormalities if the disease process is localized. In advanced cases, there is leukopenia, polymorphonuclear leukocytosis, lymphopenia, and eosinophilia.

Diagnosis and treatment Clinical staging, confirmed by pathological examination, is imperative for treatment. See Table 35-6. The stages are classified further as A or B, indicating the presence or absence of a fever, night sweats, or an unexplained weight loss.

After obtaining a detailed history, a physical examination, complete blood count, urinalysis, and a battery of radiologic studies are done to determine the extent of involvement. They include a chest x-ray, skeletal survey, inferior vena cavagram, lymphangiogram, and, in the presence of hilar adenopathy, whole-lung tomograms. If risk of extensive involvement is present, an excretory urogram, liver function tests, and bone marrow aspiration are completed. The biopsy completes the workup.

Since a definitive diagnosis can only be made from a histological examination of tissue from an affected node, a staging laporatomy is performed. Tissue from lymph nodes, liver, and bone is obtained for biopsy. A splenectomy is also performed at that time. After the procedure is completed and tissue is examined, the patient's disease stage is determined. The presence of a unique type of cell called the Reed-Sternberg cell is essential for the diagnosis of Hodgkin's disease. The ultimate prognosis depends on the stage of disease at the time of diagnosis and the histologic type.

Table 35-6 Stage, treatment, and prognosis of Hodgkin's disease

Stage	Extent of involvement	Treatment	Prognosis
I	Limited to one anatomic region, or two contiguous anatomic regions on the same side of diaphragm	Irradiation to an extended field	With a favorable histologic picture, more than 90% achieve long-term disease-free control (more than 10 years).
II	Present in more than two regions or two noncontiguous regions on same side of diaphragm.	Irradiation to an extended field. Some centers may institute chemotherapy.	About 80% can achieve long-term control with a favorable histology.
III	Present on both sides of diaphragm but not extending beyond involvement of lymph nodes, spleen, or Waldeyer's ring	Irradiation therapy to an extended field and/or total modal (mastoid to groin); may be given chemotherapy: **a.** (1) Mustargen; Oncovin, prednisone, and procarbazine (MOPP); (2) Cyclophosphamide, Oncovin, prednisone, and procarbazine (COPP); or (3) a combination of the above agents, also including vincristine, bleomycin, and vinblastine	With a favorable histology about 50% can expect to be disease-free, long-term.
IV	Involvement extends to bone marrow, lung parenchyma, pleura, liver, bone, skin, GI tract or any tissue or organ in addition to lymph nodes, spleen, or Waldeyer's ring	**b.** With evidence of recurrence, BCNU, Adriamycin, or DTIC may be used effectively.	About 25% can survive for about 5 years.

Source: Phillip Lanzkowsky, "Diseases of the Blood and Childhood Malignancies" in Robert A. Hoekelman et al. (eds.), *Principles of Pediatrics*, McGraw-Hill, New York, 1978, p. 1049.

Overall, life expectancy has improved substantially. Irradiation and the combinations of cytotoxic drugs which are affective in combating this lymphoma have achieved long-term disease control even in those patients with more disseminated disease.

Non-Hodgkin lymphoma (NHL) or lymphosarcoma

This lymphoma is three to four times more common in children than Hodgkin's disease. Categorized according to the predominent cell involved, the Rapport classification subdivides NHL as follows: (1) undifferentiated, Burkitt's or non-Burkitt's; (2) lymphocytic, well or poorly differentiated; (3) mixed, histiocytic or lymphocytic; and (4) histiocytic. Each is also subdivided into a nodular or a diffuse type.[12] Burkitt's lymphoma is endemic in Africa and New Guinea, but its incidence is very rare in this country. The mixed as well as nodular types have a good prognosis, but they are very rare in children.

NHL can occur at any age in childhood or adolescence, but most cases are diagnosed between the ages of 9 and 11 years. It is more common in boys than in girls by a 3:1 ratio.

Although it can develop in the head and neck (adenoids, tonsils, sinuses) abdomen, or lymph nodes (cervical, axillary, inguinal), 60 percent arise from the posterior cervical triangle. Patients with a mediastinal lymphosarcoma have the most grave prognosis. Also, NHL has a tendency for greater extranodal involvement than patients with Hodgkin's disease.

Clinical manifestations depend on the site and the extent of involvement. Usually a painless enlargement, which has proliferated rapidly, is discovered. If the primary site is the retroperitoneal area, there may be signs of abdominal obstruction with pain and vomiting. The child may demonstrate weight loss, irritability, anorexia and fever.

Diagnosis and treatment Blood and marrow infiltration is common, which may make it difficult to distinguish this neoplasm from ALL. In many instances, diagnosis is made after dissemination to other sites has resulted in some obvious complaints.

Tests to confirm the diagnosis of lymphosarcoma are similar to those utilized in determining the presence of Hodgkin's disease. A complete blood count, lactic dehydrogenase, and serum uric acid levels as well as an intravenous pyelogram (IVP) are done. Bone marrow aspiration and lumbar puncture for analysis of spinal fluid are performed to assess the possibility of extranodal dissemination. Liver, spleen, brain, bone, and whole-body scans along with a lymphangiogram also can reveal other sites.

Although the staging process is similar to the one used in Hodgkins's disease, there are certain limitations which need to be identified. For example, when a mediastinal lymphosarcoma is present, a stage I classification carries with it a grave prognosis. In addition, a true stage III is almost nonexistent in children.

The treatment in NHL is not based on staging. While confirmation of the diagnosis is based on a tissue examination, there is great controversy as to whether a laporatomy should be performed or not. In any case, a biopsy *must* be performed. If complete excision is possible, then it should be done. Extensive surgical procedures are not indicated, however. They do not increase survival and can be responsible for "seeding," spreading malignant cells through the circulatory system to distant sites. This malignancy is sensitive to radiation and hence irradiation and chemotherapy are the two most effective treatment modalities.

The combination of cytotoxic drugs used most often is predisone, vincristine, cyclophosphamide, doxorubicin, and L-asparaginase. Methotrexate and 6-MP are effective in maintaining remissions.

Prognoses for stage I (excepting a mediastinal NHL) is a 75 percent survival rate, while those with regional disease in stage II have 40 to 50 percent survival. More extensive involvement has a poorer prognosis, with only 10 to 20 percent of these children surviving. Relapses for those assigned to stages beyond II occur within 6 months or so, at which time 40 to 60 percent experience a leukemic transformation.[13] At that time, the normal elements of blood are partially or completely replaced by immature cells and the patient's blood picture resembles that of a child with acute lymphoblastic leukemia.

Nursing management

The diagnostic procedures are frightening unless they are thoroughly explained to the adolescent. After a staging laparotomy, routine postoperative measures are instituted. Since these patients are treated with radiotherapy and chemotherapy, the emphasis for teaching is related to those treatments. Although treatment may be started in the hospital, it is primarily done on an outpatient basis.

Considering the age of most of these patients, school and peers are most significant. Resuming a normal life-style is crucial. Many times, activities can be scheduled around the chemotherapy. If nausea and vomiting routinely occur after drug administration, no activities should be scheduled for that day. Such counseling allows an adolescent to participate in his treatment and avoids embarrassing as well as frustrating situations he cannot control. Likewise, irradiation can result in delayed sexual maturation, an especially sensitive topic for the adolescent. While both parents and patient should be apprised of that fact, the nurse should make clear that development will eventually take place. The treatment does not affect sexual function.

In planning for discharge, the nurse needs to consider activity restrictions. The patient tires easily. Through the cooperation of the school nurse, a short nap is feasible. It may not be possible for the child to participate in physical education classes. This is a time when many adolescents turn to hobbies, such as playing an instrument, playing chess, or becoming involved in a debating team.

While follow-up visits are extremely important in the care of patients with malignancies, they are vital for patients with NHL. Leukemic conversion is possible. Teaching related to that complication should be delayed until its appearance emerges.

Activities should be limited or expanded, depending on how the adolescent feels. With the improved prognosis, planning for college should be encouraged.

Malignant tumors of the reproductive tract

Adenocarcinoma This neoplasm is found in children of women who took DES during pregnancy. The primary site is the vagina; however, if can be found in the cervix or ovaries. A majority of patients are adolescents or young adults (14 to 22 years old). The most common symptom is prolonged, persistent, irregular bleeding. It is often confused with the irregular bleeding which occurs with the onset of menarche. The tumor consists of tubules and glands lined with glycogen and "hobnail" cells. It is sometimes called *clear cell carcinoma.*

Diagnosis and treatment A vaginal mass is discovered upon examination. The necessary vaginal and rectal digital examinations are most anxiety-provoking for an adolescent. Diagnostic tests include a CBC, urinalysis, abdominal x-rays, and tomograms. Diagnosis is confirmed by histologic examination.

If the site is within the ovaries, a radical hysterectomy is done. Uterine involvement is treated with a radioisotope implantation, followed by a radical hysterectomy. While these tumors are relatively uncommon, the prognosis depends on early diagnosis and aggressive treatment.

Teratomas A *teratoma* is a true neoplasm, which is composed of bizzare, chaotically arranged tissue. It is histologically and embryologically foreign to the area in which it is found.[14]

Ovarian teratomas An *ovarian teratoma* is the most common tumor found in young females. It is also called a *dermoid cyst* or *benign cystic teratoma.* A variety of well-differentiated cells, such as squamous epithelium and sebaceous and sweat glands as well as hair, bone, and teeth, are found in this type of tumor. About 50 percent of these ovarian neoplasms are benign.[15] It is found in infancy, childhood, or adolescence.

Abdominal pain is a common symptom. In children, ovaries are considered abdominal (rather than pelvic) organs because the child's body is small (see Fig. 35-3). Hence, the neoplasm produces pain because of its pressure on other abdominal organs. Consequently, Wilms' tumor and neuroblastoma need to be ruled out. Nausea and vomiting, suggestive of appendicitis, are also present. A pelvic mass can be palpated.

Diagnostic tests include a CBC, urinalysis, pelvic and rectal examinations. X-rays of the abdomen and kidney-ureters-bladder (KUB) complete the radiologic assessment.

Treatment consists of removing the neoplasm surgically. To preserve ovarian tissue, an ovarian cystectomy is done. The prognosis is excellent. If a pathological examination reveals malignant changes, surgery is more radical, followed by

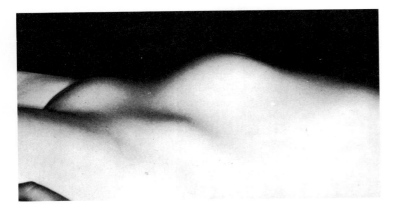

Figure 35-3 An ovarian mass in a 4-year-old, which emphasizes the need to remember that ovaries are abdominal organs in childhood. (*From Robert A. Hoekelman et al., Principles of Pediatrics, McGraw-Hill, 1978, p. 1331.*)

radiotherapy and possibly chemotherapy. Cure can be realized if there is no evidence of metastasis. With metastasis, the prognosis is doubtful.

Testicular teratomas. These tumors may be found at birth, infancy, or in early childhood. It is a benign neoplasm, detected by enlargement of the the testis. Testicular teratomas are often misdiagnosed as hydroceles.

Histologically, the tumor involves all three germ layers. It is not unusual to find cartilage, bone, adipose, and lymphoid tissue in a testicular teratoma. Tests in a diagnostic workup include a CBC, urinalysis, KUB x-rays, and a rectal examination. The teratoma is removed when an orchiectomy is performed. The prognosis is excellent.

Nursing management. Children suspected of having teratomas need support when certain procedures are done. Vaginal and rectal examinations are frightening to young children. A nurse's explanations and presence can be instrumental in obtaining the child's cooperation.

Since the majority of these neoplasms are benign, the anxiety and stress experienced by these families is substantially less. However, providing time for them to discuss the medical problem and seizing opportunities to teach are still important nursing functions.

Nursing Care Plan–Acute Lymphoblastic Leukemia

Patient: Joseph ("Skip") Jasinski   **Age:** 4 years   **Date of Admission:** 5/3 6:00 P.M.

Assessment

"Skip" Jasinski, 4 years old, was admitted because of a high white blood cell count and anemia. His father, John, 33 years old, is a drug company representative and his mother, Jean, a former teacher, is 32 years old. Skip has a 6-year-old sister, Mary, and a dog named Muffin. Skip is a handsome, friendly child who gets along well with others. His growth and development are normal for his age.

Skip was well until 3 weeks ago when his mother noted he was pale, more tired than usual, and had a poor appetite. The normal bruises on his lower extremities had increased in number, and there were black-and-blue marks on his thighs and arms, too. Skip complained of "hurting all over," which resulted in a visit to the pediatrician.

Upon admission, Skip was placed on reverse isolation because his blood tests identified anemia, low platelet count, high white cell count, and an elevated uric acid level. His physical examination revealed enlarged lymph nodes, hepatosplenomegaly, and many large ecchymotic areas over his body. When a bone marrow aspiration was done, the hematologist found an excessive number of blast cells and diagnosed the problem as acute lymphoblastic leukemia. Cerebrospinal fluid obtained from a lumbar puncture revealed no leukemic infiltration of the central nervous system. After sharing the results of the tests with Skip's parents and obtaining their consent, treatment was started. Mr. and Mrs. Jasinski were visibly upset after meeting with the hematologist. However, they remained calm and quiet while with Skip. Their sudden somber demeanor seemed to puzzle Skip.

The plan of treatment included prednisone, vincristine, and daunorubicin. Skip's head was to be irradiated prophylactically, and he was to receive methotrexate intrathecally.

Nursing diagnosis	Nursing goals	Nursing actions	Evaluation/revision
1. Potential blood volume deficit due to therapy-induced myelosuppression	☐ Skip will remain hemorrhage-free	☐ Monitor vital signs q4h and assess for signs of hemorrhage. ☐ Avoid IM injections ☐ Use firm, gentle pressure for at least 5 min to control bleeding at venipuncture and injection sites ☐ Post "Bleeding Precautions" sign at bedside	☐ Vital signs stable since admission; no signs of hemorrhage since admission
2. Alteration in blood constituents due to therapy-induced myelosuppression		☐ Avoid play activities which could result in accidental injury ☐ Inspect skin q8h for evidence of ecchymoses and petechiae. ☐ Handle Skip gently to prevent bleeding.	☐ 5/21: Out of isolation; needs supervision when with others ☐ No new ecchymoses or petechiae since admission
	☐ Skip will demonstrate: **a.** No increase in ecchymotic areas **b.** Intact gingival, oral, nasal, and rectal mucosa with no evidence of bleeding	☐ Check nasal, oropharyngeal and rectal mucosa q8h ☐ Control local bleeding PRN:	☐ 5/5: Gingival bleeding at 9:30 A.M.; tea bag effective

Nursing diagnosis	Nursing goals	Nursing actions	Evaluation/revision
		a. Dry tea bag compress to oral mucosa **b.** Ice or cold compress and gentle pressure for at least 10 min to area or nostril **c.** Salt pork topical application to nasal mucous membranes	☐ 5/6: Episode of epistaxis at 2 P.M.; salt pork effective ☐ No bleeding since 5/6
3. Alteration in body defense mechanisms due to therapy-induced myelosuppresion	☐ Skip will remain free of infection	☐ Private room; reverse isolation precautions, including gown and mask ☐ Careful, thorough handwashing by all who enter room ☐ Visitors limited to parents and necessary personnel ☐ Encourage parents' presence as much as possible ☐ Exclude anyone with evidence of infection	☐ 5/3: Reverse isolation instituted; procedures explained ☐ One parent remains with Skip at all times, assisting with care and providing diversions
	☐ Skip's temp. will remain below 38.3°C (100.8°F).	☐ Monitor temp. orally q4h, or q1h if temp. 38.2°C (100.8°F) ☐ Report temp. elevation to physician promptly ☐ Use alcohol and iodine prep prior to venipunctures and injections ☐ Assess for infection in target areas, such as venipuncture sites, skin, oral mucous membranes and perianal area ☐ (See related nursing actions listed with nursing diagnoses 4, 9, and 13)	☐ Skip's temp. ranges between 37.7–38°C (99.8°–100.4°F). ☐ No signs of infection noted since admission ☐ 5/21: Reverse isolation discontinued; retain private room and strict handwashing; continue other measures specified in plan.
4. Potential impairment of skin and mucous membrane integrity due to therapy-induced myelosuppression and mechanical pressure	☐ Skip will maintain an intact integument	☐ Meticulous skin and scalp cleanliness ☐ Avoid use of drying soaps ☐ Apply lotion and gentle massage to pressure areas q8h ☐ Check mouth and perianal area q8h	
	☐ Skip will experience minimal mucosal disruption due to oral lesions ☐ Skip will experience minimal mucosal disruption due to perianal lesions.	☐ Oral hygiene before and after eating and at bedtime: **a.** If no lesions, use soft toothbrush and gentle strokes **b.** If lesions present, use cotton swab with lemon and glycerine	☐ 5/13: Three lesions, approx. 0.3–0.4 cm, on lips; four lesions on oral mucous membranes (three on right, one on left), measuring approx. 0.4 cm ☐ 5/13: Tolerates lemon glycerine swab well. Skip eager to use Water Pik with warm solution

Nursing diagnosis	Nursing goals	Nursing actions	Evaluation/revision
		c. Use four parts sterile H_2O and one part H_2O_2 for mouthwash **d.** Use Water Pik, if possible; let Skip select temp. of solution ☐ Avoid introducing sharp instruments into mouth ☐ Use caution with drinking straws ☐ No rectal temps ☐ Wash perianal area with hexachlorophene and H_2O frequently and after every voiding and BM ☐ Change position frequently; avoid pressure on sacral area; use sheepskin or alternating-pressure mattress ☐ Expose lesions to air and heat lamp 20 min. 3–4 times a day (nap and sleep times are best)	☐ 5/16: Skip says his mouth feels better; lesions appear smaller and less inflamed ☐ 5/22: Lesions on mucosa almost healed; one lesion, approx. 0.1 cm, remains on left lower lip ☐ 5/14: Three small lesions, approx. 0.7 cm in diameter, in anal area ☐ 5/16: Lesions still approx. 0.7 cm ☐ 5/18: Lesions approx. 0.3 cm ☐ 5/20: Perianal lesions resolved; discontinue heat lamp; continue preventive measures
5. Fatigue due to anemia	☐ Skip will be able to tolerate activities of daily living (ADL) and moderate activity without fatigue	☐ Observe Skip's tolerance of ADL and other activity ☐ Discourage active play until hgb. and hct. improve ☐ Encourage foods high in protein and calories. (Skip likes ice cream, milk shakes, yogurt, tuna fish, and peanut butter.)	☐ 5/4: Playing with truck in room about 1 h, with fatigue (hgb. = 8.8, hct. = 28). Activity terminated and story-telling and drawing substituted
	☐ Skip will engage in at least two 1-h naps or rest periods per day ☐ Skip will obtain at least 8–10 h of sleep per 24 h	☐ Schedule 1-h nap for 11 A.M. to 12 noon and for 3:30 to 4:30 P.M. ☐ Plan meals and treatments around rest periods ☐ Maintain "quiet" even if Skip can't/won't sleep. (He likes puzzles, books, "cards," drawing, TV.)	☐ 5/7: Skip usually sleeps during rest periods and all night
	☐ Skip will experience little or no side effects from the administration of blood products	☐ Administer blood products cautiously: **a.** Double-check blood type, blood slips, and ID band with another nurse before hanging blood **b.** Use Y-type infusion set with NSS as alternate infusion, in case of reaction **c.** Take temp. before starting transfusion q1h during and at 1 and 2 h after transfusion **d.** Observe Skip closely for first 10–20 min of transfusion	☐ 5/5: Packed cells, 100 ml, administered between 5 and 8 P.M.; temp. = 37.7°C (99.8°F) to 38°C (100.4°F). No reaction observed

Nursing diagnosis	Nursing goals	Nursing actions	Evaluation/revision
		e. *Stop* transfusion if: chills, fever, urticaria, headache, low back pain, dyspnea, or wheezing occur **f.** Run transfusion no faster than 3 h.	
6. Potential nutritional deficit due to anorexia, nausea, vomiting, and oral lesions	☐ Skip will be able to ingest at least 1800 cal a day	☐ Fortify custards, puddings and milk shakes with powdered milk supplement ☐ Add polycose to all liquids ☐ Place small snack of a favorite food in front of Skip q2h ☐ Make foods visually appealing ("faces," shapes, colors) ☐ Encourage parents to assist Skip with meals ☐ Permit Skip to choose menu as much as possible ☐ Administer antiemetic 30–40 min a.c. when nausea/vomiting are present. ☐ Obtain order for local anesthetic for oral lesions if they interfere with po intake ☐ Try cool, bland foods when Skip's mouth is sore ☐ Provide meals in peer-group setting when isolation is discontinued	☐ 5/6: Poor intake due to nausea and vomiting ☐ 5/9: Snacks eaten erratically; Skip likes "white" (vanilla) the best ☐ 5/12–5/14: Nausea and vomiting; poor intake despite medication ☐ 5/17: Eating much improved; drank 1790 ml ☐ 5/13–5/16: Anesthetic not necessary; nausea and vomiting seem to interfere with eating ☐ 5/21: Began eating meals with peers; appetite improved
7. Potential alteration in renal function due to chemotherapy-induced hyperuricosuria	☐ Skip will have: **a.** Urinary output of approx. 85–100 ml/h **b.** Fluid intake of 1900–2100 ml per day **c.** Urine specific gravity between 1.004 and 1.015 **d.** Urine pH between 7.5 and 8.5	☐ Strict I and O ☐ Report urinary output which is 200 ml or more below intake for a 24-h period ☐ Offer fluids which promote alkalinization of urine, such as milk and citrus ☐ Administer IV fluids if oral intake is insufficient and during periods of nausea and vomiting ☐ Specific gravity q void; notify physician if <1.020 or >1.002 ☐ Check pH each void; notify physician if pH <7.4 or >8.6 ☐ Visually examine all urine in good light for sediment or particles ☐ Strain all urine ☐ Administer prophylactic allopurinol as ordered	☐ 5/4–5/10: Intake avg. 1970 ml per day; output avg. 1935 ml per day ☐ 5/11–5/17: Intake avg. 2057 ml per day; output avg. 1983 ml per day ☐ 5/18–5/24: Intake avg. 2036 ml per day; output avg. 1978 ml per day (see daily I and O sheets). IV fluids necessary on day of vincristine therapy and for about 2–3 days following therapy ☐ 5/4–5/24: SG: 1.007–1.011 ☐ 5/4–5/24: pH ranges between 7.6 and 8.1

Nursing diagnosis	Nursing goals	Nursing actions	Evaluation/revision
8. Alteration in metabolism due to steroid therapy	□ Skip will: **a.** Maintain balance between fluid intake and output **b.** Remain infection-free	□ Assess for side effects of prednisone (moon face, red cheeks, protuberant abdomen, fluid retention, supraclavicular fat pads) □ Weigh daily, before breakfast □ Strict I and O; observe for fluid intake in excess of output (See nursing action 2 for nursing diagnosis 7) □ Observe for signs and symptoms of infection; steroids can mask fever □ Take advantage of increase in appetite which can result from therapy	□ 5/4: Prednisone therapy initiated □ 5/9: Appetite not improved; moon face and red cheeks apparent. Skip does not appear concerned about these changes. □ 5/9–5/10: Fluid intake 197 ml above output □ 5/11–5/12: Intake and output approximately equal □ 5/14: Intake and output continue to balance □ 5/16: Protuberant abdomen evident; no signs of infection; and no change in appetite
9. Potential alteration in social behaviors due to steroid therapy and isolation	□ Skip will: **a.** Maintain a social interaction pattern similar to his previous pattern **b.** Be able to tolerate periods of 1–1½ h alone in room if parent or nurse cannot be present	□ Observe for mood swings and euphoria □ Provide company (parent or nurse) and diversional activities □ Set limits on behavior if necessary; involve parents in limit setting □ Visit with Skip in his room for 20 min q1–1½ h, during waking hours when parent not present □ Supervise type and amount of interaction with other children when reverse isolation discontinued (euphoria may cause him to overdo) □ Provide guidance to parents regarding activity with peers	□ 5/7: After period of nausea and vomiting passed, Skip became "happy," constantly chattering and calling out to all passing in corridor ("Hi ya!") and laughing deliberately at only slightly humorous incidents □ 5/12–5/16: Rapid change in behavior; weepy and quiet during period of nausea and vomiting □ 5/20: Can tolerate about 55 min alone, if given something to "finish" before parent or nurse returns, such as a drawing □ 5/21: Out of isolation; mother supervising activity
10. Potential alteration in elimination due to vincristine therapy	□ Skip will have normal, formed bowel movements at least qod	□ Record frequency and consistency of BMs. □ Administer stool softener. □ Maintain fluid intake.	□ 5/4–5/10: Normal BMs qod. □ 5/11–5/17: Normal BMs qod. □ 5/18–5/23: Normal BMs qod.
11. Potential alteration in perception and coordination due to therapy-induced neuropathy and, leukemic invasion of the CNS, or both	□ Skip will: **a.** Report normal sensation in extremities **b.** Demonstrate equal strength in extremities which is adequate to perform ADL **c.** Demonstrate normal gait **d.** Demonstrate normal joint mobility **e.** Maintain normal body alignment	□ Check extremities for weakness bid □ Ask Skip how his hands and feet "feel" to assess for tingling, numbness, or both □ Institute food board prn □ Assess gait and mobility qd □ Keep padded tongue blade, airway, and O_2 at bedside □ Observe for irritability, lethargy, or headache	□ 5/12: Foot drop noted; foot board instituted □ 5/16: Numbness and weakness in right hand □ 5/18: Weakness and numbness has subsided □ 5/18–5/23: No ataxia or abnormal gait observed; continue observations

Nursing diagnosis	Nursing goals	Nursing actions	Evaluation/revision
	f. Demonstrate orientation to time, place, person	☐ Report all symptoms suggesting neuropathy to physician ☐ Maintain fluid intake between 1900 ml and 2100 ml during chemotherapy ☐ Curtail activities prn	
12. Potential alteration in comfort due to pain	☐ Skip will be able to report: **a.** That he is comfortable and free of pain **b.** A minimal number of painful episodes	☐ Change position at least q2h ☐ Move body parts gently ☐ Avoid pressure on bony prominences or painful sites ☐ Assess for vincristine therapy-induced jaw pain ☐ Administer nonsalicylate analgesics prn ☐ Provide quiet, pleasing environment	☐ 5/4–5/11: Moving self about; pain-free ☐ 5/12–5/19: Remains pain-free ☐ 5/20–5/24: Remains pain-free; continue observations and plan
13. Parental lack of knowledge about ALL and its treatment	☐ Parents will be able to: **a.** Verbalize correct information regarding Skip's illness and his treatment	☐ Assess parents' understanding of information given by physician ☐ Correct misinformation and misunderstandings verbalized ☐ Provide explanations about Skip's illness and treatment ☐ Keep sessions short (30 to 45 min) ☐ Do not overload parents with too much information at one time; observe their responses ☐ Allow sufficient time for parents to ask questions; answer questions frankly; refer parents to physician for further information prn ☐ Content of teaching: **a.** Alteration in blood constituents; role of platelets in blood; rationale for curtailing potentially vigorous play **b.** Reason for protective isolation; importance of good handwashing and excluding persons with infections; encourage parents to visit as much as possible; suggest appropriate diversions; assure parents that isolation will be discontinued when Skip's WBC approaches normal **c.** Need for good skin care; skin lesions may	☐ 5/3: Handwashing, gown-and-mask technique return demonstration by parents satisfactory ☐ 5/4: Parents able to repeat information regarding: alterations in blood, potential for bleeding, anemia, and Skip's reactions to isolation during A.M. discussion ☐ 5/4: Parents able to repeat information discussed during P.M. discussion: Skip's need for increased fluids and effects of prednisone. Asking many questions about Skip's reaction to illness. Parents still upset, but seem to comprehend information ☐ 5/5: Preventive skin care and nutritional needs dis-

Nursing diagnosis	Nursing goals	Nursing actions	Evaluation/revision
		occur as a side effect of therapy despite preventive measures; measures to minimze discomfort and help resolve lesions will be used **d.** Skip's fatigue and the need for adequate rest **e.** Anorexia, nausea, and vomiting are frequent side effects of therapy; measures which may help Skip eat an adequate amount of nutrients; enlist parents' cooperation **f.** Necessity for high fluid intake and, possibly, IV fluids **g.** Side effects of prednisone therapy; euphoria may alter Skip's behavior and cause him to overdo; mood swings from "happy" days to "blue" days can occur **h.** Other side effects of therapy: constipation, neurological changes, alopecia, pain **i.** Potential stressful impact of illness, hospitalization, and treatment on Skip **j.** Prior to discharge, discuss Skip's limitations and abilities, i.e., avoiding crowds, head covering, fatigue, preschool attendance, discipline ☐ Repeat all explanations PRN, as parents' comprehension may be affected by their own stress	cussed with Skip's mother; able to accurately repeat information to Skip's father later in day; side effects of therapy discussed with both parents in P.M.; both appeared distressed and ventilated concerns. Parents concluded that side effects can be endured if the therapy can help Skip ☐ 5/6: Explanation of need for high-fluid intake during therapy repeated prior to starting IV infusion; mother verbalized understanding ☐ 5/7: Side effects of therapy and Skip's responses to illness and hospitalization discussed; parents verbalized understanding correctly
14. Potential alteration in body image due to therapy-induced alopecia	☐ Parents and Skip will be able to: **a.** Verbalize their understanding of reason for hair loss **b.** Verbally acknowledge that hair will grow back **c.** Formulate an explanation for children and adults who ask questions about Skip's appearance	☐ Prepare Skip and parents for hair loss ☐ Acknowledge that hair loss is upsetting to most people ☐ Careful daily scalp care ☐ Expose scalp to air as much as possible when in room or at home ☐ Suggest use of "doctor's" cap, baseball cap, or other head covering when Skip is with others, at school or play	☐ 5/15: Moderate amount of hair lost as Skip's mother was combing his hair; mother initially dismayed, but nurse reminded her that hair loss will be temporary. Skip aware of hair loss, but does not seem concerned ☐ 5/16: Skip's father brought him a baseball cap with the emblem of Skip's favorite team; Skip wants to sleep with it on

Nursing diagnosis	Nursing goals	Nursing actions	Evaluation/revision
		☐ Stress that hair will grow back in 3–6 months, but its color and texture may differ ☐ If repeated therapy with the same drugs is necessary, hair loss may be less severe ☐ Prepare Skip and parents for others' questions, which may be blunt and upsetting. Children, in particular, may say things that upset Skip or his sister.	☐ 5/19: Parents have decided that a short, truthful answer would be best, and then the subject should be changed ☐ 5/23: Skip told inquiring children in the hospital that his medicine made his hair fall out, adding . . . "It don't bother me, though, cause it's gonna grow back."
15. Emotional stress due to hospitalization and invasive procedures	☐ Skip will be able to: **a.** Tolerate necessary procedures **b.** Use acceptable means to discharge his anger, tension, and fear	☐ Explain each procedure to Skip just prior to and during procedure (explaining procedures too far in advance will increase his anxiety) ☐ Use words to describe the sensations Skip will experience during the procedure, such as "cold" skin cleaning medicine; a quick "sting" to get the "numbing medicine"; be honest; *don't* say it won't hurt if it will hurt ☐ Use simple, clear words in all explanations ☐ Ask Skip to tell "what comes next" in the procedure to distract him ☐ Tell Skip he can cry if it hurts, but he must remain still ☐ Tell Skip that the nurse or his parents will help him to hold still so the doctor can finish and the hurt will be over sooner ☐ Allow parents to be present, if they wish, and encourage them to comfort Skip after painful procedures and praise his bravery ☐ Do not allow parents, visitors, or health-providers to carry on conversations about Skip or any other matters within his hearing as he may misunderstand and fantasize unnecessarily	☐ 5/10: Explanations are on-going; both parents and Skip appear to have less fear and stress ☐ 5/6: Skip cried during venipuncture for IV infusion, but remained still; he is able to do the same during blood tests

Nursing diagnosis	Nursing goals	Nursing actions	Evaluation/revision
		☐ Tell Skip's parents that his need to express himself and release tension is normal and expected ☐ Suggest suitable means of play and expression to help channel Skip's feelings; activities might include: toy workbench and hammer, punching bag, water play, play with character dolls (doctor, nurse, family members), syringes, IV tubing, bandages. ☐ Use story-telling to elicit Skip's fears and fantasies. ☐ Caution parents that unacceptable behaviors should be limited, just as they would be ordinarily. Overindulgence should be avoided.	☐ 5/10: Through play, Skip "vigorously" performed a bone marrow aspiration on an astronaut doll. ☐ 5/18: Tolerated bone marrow aspiration better than previously. Skip often jumps right into a story and takes over, relating frightening episodes, such as bone marrow aspiration 5/21: Initially, maternal grandmother was very overindulgent. Parents better understand consequences of this now, and grandmother has refrained from excessive indulgence when she visits
	☐ Parents will be able to allow Skip to express his feelings in an acceptable manner and impose limits when necessary		
16. Parental stress due to the suddenness and seriousness of Skip's illness	☐ Parents will be able to: **a.** Verbalize their fears to the nurse **b.** Ask the nurse questions they may have about Skip's condition and his care **c.** Express their anger and tension in an acceptable manner **d.** Provide Skip with supportive physical and emotional care	☐ Initiate discussions with Skip's parents regarding his illness and their feelings; do *not* wait for parents to ask questions ☐ Provide a private place for discussions ☐ Acknowledge that it is upsetting for parents to find out that their child has leukemia as a way of helping them to verbalize their feelings and fears ☐ Assure them that there is *nothing* they could have done to prevent Skip's illness ☐ Remind parents that the physician has given them a hopeful prognosis for Skip ☐ Encourage parents to ask any questions they may have; tell them that *no* question is a silly question ☐ Provide parents with a private place to vent their feelings after they have assisted Skip during a traumatic procedure, such as a bone marrow aspiration ☐ Assure parents that the nurse is available to speak with Skip's sister and grandparents	☐ 5/3: Met with both parents after Skip's admission; both upset but able to understand basics of Skip's diagnosis; further discussion deferred because of parents' obvious anxiety and fatigue ☐ 5/4: Parents tearful during meeting and kept asking why this has happened to Skip. After initial release of feelings and tears, parents began asking questions about Skip's illness and treatment ☐ 5/5: Skip had first dose of vincristine while mother was present. After the procedure, mother confided to the nurse: "It hurt me, too." Both parents able to ask questions freely ☐ 5/6–5/16: Discussions held with parents every day or every other day; parents have good rapport with nurses ☐ 5/13: Met with maternal grandparents and answered their questions ☐ 5/18: Skip much improved after 3 days of nausea and vomiting; parents

Nursing diagnosis	Nursing goals	Nursing actions	Evaluation/revision
		☐ Expect that parents may not always be able to control their feelings; they may become hostile, angry, or critical of health-providers or the hospital. They may also become tearful or upset in front of Skip. Provide parents with a private place to express themselves if these episodes occur ☐ Initiate private conferences with parents at least every other day. Focus on positive aspects of Skip's progress, but allow parents to discuss distressing side effects that Skip is experiencing. These conferences are essential as the success of remission induction cannot be determined for several weeks ☐ Encourage parents to spend a quiet evening together on occasion. Assure them that the nurses will take care of Skip	went out to celebrate their ninth wedding anniversary (which was the day of Skip's admission) upon urging of nurse and Skip. Skip said, "I'll be okay with the nurse!" ☐ 5/20: Met with Skip's sister and parents; she's afraid Skip won't come home. Discussed Skip and explained that the doctors and nurses are helping Skip to get well enough to go home. After preparing her for changes in Skip's appearance, Mary visited with Skip for about 30 min. She told him that she's keeping his room neat for when he comes home and that all the neighborhood "kids" can't wait for him to come home. Visit with Skip seemed to benefit all family members

References

1. John L. Young, Jr. et al., *Cancer Incidence, Survival and Mortality for Children under 15 Years of Age*, American Cancer Society, New York, 1978, p. 2.
2. James G. Hughes, "Cancer in Childhood," *Synopsis of Pediatrics*, 5th ed., Mosby, St. Louis, 1980, p. 764.
3. Ann S. Pryor, "Cancer Chemotherapy in Children," *Issues in Comprehensive Pediatric Nursing* 3(5):46(1978).
4. Ibid., 47.
5. Kathi Hardin, "Solid Tumors in Children," *Issues in Comprehensive Pediatric Nursing* 4(1):36 (1980).
6. Patricia Ellis Greene and Laura Marie Bloomquist, "The Hemopoietic System," in Gladys M. Scipien et al. (eds.), *Comprehensive Pediatric Nursing*, 2d ed., McGraw-Hill, New York, 1979, p. 732.
7. W. A. Smithson, G. S. Gilchrist, and E. O. Burgert, "Childhood Acute Lymphocytic Leukemia," *CA—A Journal for Clinicians* 30(3):169 (1980).
8. Howard J. Weinstein et al., "Treatment of Acute Myelogenous Leukemia in Children and Adults," *New England Journal of Medicine*, 303(9):473–78 (1980).
9. Hughes, op. cit., p. 769.
10. Sherrilyn Passo, "The Musculoskeletal System," in Gladys M. Scipien et al. (eds.), *Comprehensive Pediatric Nursing*, 2d ed., McGraw-Hill, New York, 1979, p. 936.
11. Ibid., p. 937.
12. Joseph Simone, "Non-Hodgkin's Lymphoma," in Abraham Rudolph et al. (eds.), *Pediatrics*, 16th ed., Appleton-Century-Crofts, New York, 1977, p. 1193.
13. Philip Lanzkowsky, "Diseases of the Blood and Childhood Malignancies," in Robert A. Hoekelman et al. (eds.), *Principles of Pediatrics*, McGraw-Hill, New York, 1978, p. 1050.
14. Arthur Osol (ed.), *Blakiston's Gould Medical Dictionary*, 3d ed., McGraw-Hill, New York, 1972, p. 1537.
15. William A. Daniel, Jr. et al., "Diseases of the Reproductive System," in Robert A. Hoekelman et al. (eds.), *Principles of Pediatrics*, McGraw-Hill, New York, 1978, p. 1330.

Chapter 36 **Mobility**

Stephanie Wright

Upon completion of this chapter, the student will be able to:

1. Briefly describe the embryological development of the musculoskeletal system.

2. Identify on a human skeleton the skull, vertebral column, clavicle, humerus, radius, ulna, femur, tibia, fibula, and hip acetabulum.

3. Define and/or describe bone, cartilage, tendon, ligament, diaphysis, epiphysis, metaphysis, periosteum, joint, synovial membrane, and callus.

4. Demonstrate flexion, extension, abduction, adduction, internal rotation, external rotation, pronation, and supination.

5. List five areas to be assessed by the nurse before planning care for a child with an alteration in mobility.

6. Name the seven items to be assessed when checking the neurovascular status of an extremity.

7. Identify five effects of immobilization upon a child and family.

8. Describe the preparation of a child for cast application.

9. Describe the skin care of a child in a cast.

10. Describe how to keep a cast clean and dry.

11. Describe preparation of a child for cast removal.

12. List four basic rules for caring for a child in traction.

13. List two of the major causes of trauma to the musculoskeletal system in children.

14. Describe two ways of preventing injury to the musculoskeletal system.

15. Identify and describe five conditions that cause alteration in mobility in children.

Origin, structure, and function of the musculoskeletal system

Bones and cartilage make up the supportive and protective framework of the body. Bones also provide the surfaces to which are attached the muscles, tendons, and ligaments. Bones and muscles work intimately together to provide for support and motion of the human body.

Origins of muscles and bones

The musculoskeletal system begins to form in the third week of embryonic life. It arises from the mesodermal or middle germ layer which appears in the developing embryo about this time. The embryo, at this stage in development, has a primitive trunk support called the *noto-*chord. From the mesoderm, blocks of tissue appear called *somites*. The somites develop specialized cells which migrate toward the notochord and surround it. These cells develop into the backbone and ribs by about the sixth week of embryonic life. From the somites, specialized tissue also develops that is the precursor of muscles. These cells differentiate and develop into separate muscle groups, beginning about the fifth week of embryonic life, eventually forming the trunk muscles.

Meanwhile, arm and then leg buds have appeared in the embryo about the fourth week. Growth occurs very rapidly with fingers developing by the sixth week. The growth of the lower extremity lags about a week behind with toes appearing about the seventh week. Refinement of the limbs continues until, by the end of the third month, the shape and form of the hands and feet are completed. The bones and joints of the limbs develop from the mesodermal layer at that location, with the muscles developing around the bones. By the end of 8 weeks of development, a complete miniature skeleton has been formed, comprised either of cartilage or fibrous membrane. Muscle development continues so that by the beginning of the third month of intrauterine life the baby begins to move spontaneously.

The skeleton of cartilage provides a support system which can grow rapidly with the developing embryo. The cartilage begins to be replaced by bone during the eighth week. The bony skeleton is needed for a more substantial support as the baby grows. This process, called *ossification*, will continue throughout intrauterine life and childhood. By 16 weeks of intrauterine life enough of the baby's developing skeleton has been replaced by bone that the skeletal structure can be seen on an x-ray of the mother's abdomen. At birth, the central portions of most of the larger

bones have ossified, although the ends are still mainly cartilage. Figure 36-1 illustrates how ossification proceeds in a long bone.

The bones of the face and skull do not develop from cartilage. Bone is laid down directly over a fibrous membrane, and therefore these bones are referred to as *membranous bones*, rather than cartilaginous bones. Ossification of the skull also is only partially completed at birth. The skull is still composed of separate bones, separated by the sutures. The fontanels, or soft spots, are apparent at the corners of the adjoining membranous bones. Ossification will not be completed until later in childhood when the skull becomes one solid bony structure.

Anatomy and physiology of bone

The major bones of the body are illustrated in Fig. 36-2. There are generally considered to be four classes of bones: (1) long bones, (2) short bones, (3) flat bones, and (4) irregular bones. *Long bones* are found in the limbs and fingers and toes. They are easily identified by their long central shaft. *Short bones* are found in the wrist and ankle (carpals and tarsals). Short bones are generally cuboidal in shape. *Flat bones* are thin and may be somewhat curved (skull and ribs). *Irregular bones* would include all those not classified in the previous groups. The vertebrae are examples of irregular bones.

Figure 36-3 shows the major divisions of a typical long bone. The *diaphysis* is the central shaft. Ossification of long bones begins in this area and spreads outward. This area is often referred to as the *primary ossification center*. The ends of the long bones are the *epiphyses*. A separate secondary center of ossification begins here. Most of the secondary centers of ossification appear after birth. Between the diaphysis and epiphysis is a line of cartilage, the epiphyseal line or plate. It is from this area that all growth in length takes place. The epiphyseal line tends to become smaller as growth and ossification proceed. For this reason, x-rays of bones, particularly those of the hands, can be used to establish a "bone age" for the child. This is a helpful tool in diagnosing certain endocrine disorders that affect bone growth. The epiphyseal line will not disappear or close until all growth is completed. The area on the central shaft directly adjacent to the epiphyseal plate is the *metaphysis*.

Figure 36-1 Ossification of a long bone. Ossification begins in the central shaft, or diaphysis. Separate ossification centers develop in the epiphyses. (*From R. M. DeCoursey, The Human Organism, 3d ed., McGraw-Hill, New York, 1968. Used by permission of the publisher.*)

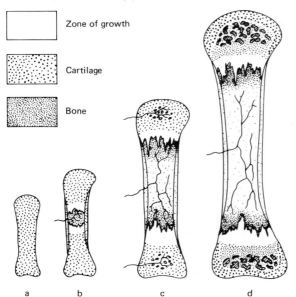

Zone of growth

Cartilage

Bone

a   b   c   d

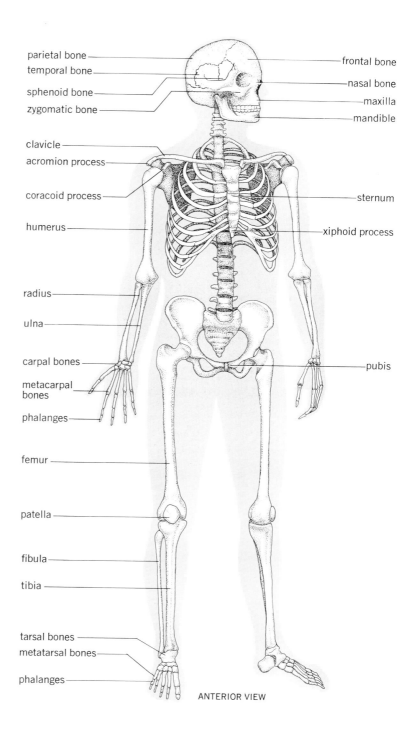

parietal bone

temporal bone

sphenoid bone

zygomatic bone

clavicle

acromion process

coracoid process

humerus

radius

ulna

carpal bones

metacarpal bones

phalanges

femur

patella

fibula

tibia

tarsal bones

metatarsal bones

phalanges

frontal bone

nasal bone

maxilla

mandible

sternum

xiphoid process

pubis

ANTERIOR VIEW

Figure 36-2 Major bones of the human body. (*From R. M. DeCoursey and J. L. Renfro, The Human Organism, 5th ed., McGraw-Hill Book, New York, 1980. Used by permission of the publisher.*)

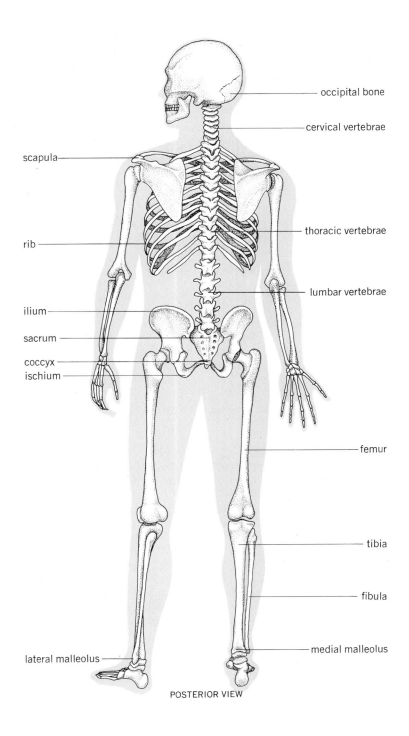

occipital bone

cervical vertebrae

scapula

thoracic vertebrae

rib

lumbar vertebrae

ilium

sacrum

coccyx

ischium

femur

tibia

fibula

medial malleolus

lateral malleolus

POSTERIOR VIEW

Bone is living tissue. It consists of approximately two-thirds inorganic material, mainly calcium phosphate, which provides for hardness. The remainder is organic material. The *osteocytes*, or bone cells, maintain the structure of the bone and are found scattered throughout the bone, separated by intercellular substance, which is composed of inorganic salts and collagen. The osteocytes produce and maintain the intercellular substance, continually exchanging the inorganic material within the bone. There are two types of bone tissue: compact bone, which is extremely dense, and spongy bone, which has a more open texture.

Bones are covered by a membrane, the *periosteum*. The blood supply for the osteocytes originates in the periosteum and reaches the cells through small pathways in the bone called *Haversian canals*. The periosteum is divided into a fibrous outer layer and an osteogenic inner layer. The osteocytes originate in this inner layer and form intercellular substance around themselves. As they do this, growth in bone diameter occurs.

Joints and body motion

The junction of two bones is a *joint*, or articulation. Joints may be nonmovable or movable. At a movable joint, the bone end is covered with a thin layer of cushioning articular cartilage. The joint is surrounded by a capsule of fibrous tissue which helps hold the bones together. Bones may also be directly joined by ligaments. The joint capsule is lined with the synovial membrane, which provides lubrication for the joint. Further stability is provided by overlying muscles and tendons. Joints may be further classified by the shape of their surfaces and the type of movement of which they are capable.

Muscles give motion to joints. Muscles are structures of specialized cells capable of shortening. Muscle attached to the skeletal system is under voluntary control. Most muscles have two or more attachments to the skeleton. Some attach directly to the periosteum while others are attached to the bone by tendons. The more fixed attachment is the muscle origin; the more movable is the insertion. When the muscle contracts or shortens, the two attachments come closer to each other, producing movement at a joint.

Nurses who work with children having alterations in mobility should be familiar with the

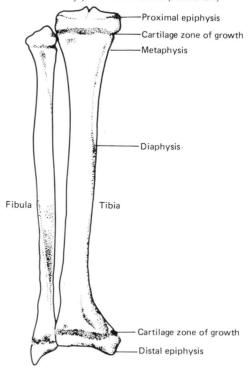

Figure 36-3 A typical long bone. (*From R. M. DeCoursey, The Human Organism, 3d ed., McGraw-Hill, New York, 1968. Used by permission of the publisher.*)

Proximal epiphysis
Cartilage zone of growth
Metaphysis
Diaphysis
Fibula
Tibia
Cartilage zone of growth
Distal epiphysis

following terms used to describe body movement (Fig. 36-4):

Flexion Movement that brings two bones closer together. Flexing of the arm brings the radius and ulna closer to the humerus.

Extension Movement that takes two bones farther away from each other. In standing, most of the body parts are in a state of extension.

Abduction The movement of a part away from the midline.

Adduction The movement of a part toward the midline.

Internal rotation The revolving of a part toward the midline.

External rotation The revolving of a part away from the midline.

Inversion Turning inward.

Eversion Turning outward

Supination Turning upward.

Pronation Turning downward.

Figure 36-4 Movements and terms describing them. (*From L. L. Langley, I. Telford, and J. Christensen, Dynamic Anatomy and Physiology, 5th ed., McGraw-Hill, New York, 1980. Used by permission of the publisher.*)

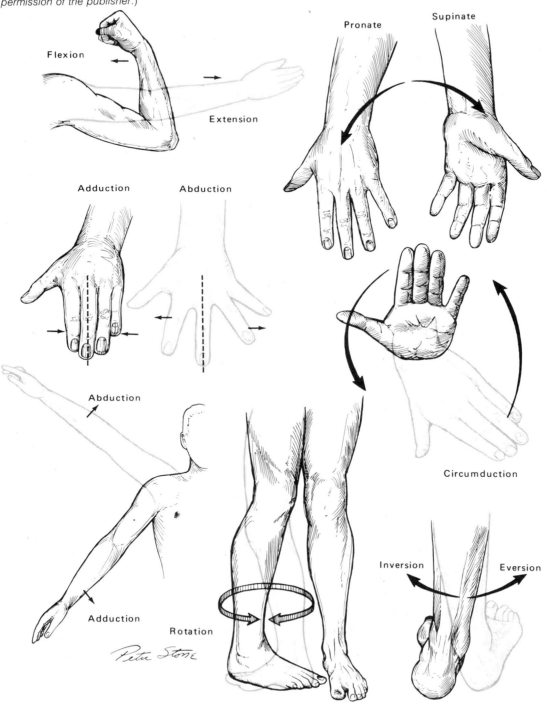

Assessment of children with alterations in mobility

Nursing assessment related to the musculoskeletal system is utilized in a variety of settings. The nurse caring for newborns and using a newborn assessment guide may be able to discern early alterations in mobility. Public health nurses and school nurses often utilize their assessment skills in these areas. Alterations in mobility are seen in any pediatric screening program or pediatrician's office as well as by nurses who deal primarily with children with musculoskeletal disorders. In the hospital orthopedic setting, nurses will encounter children who will fall primarily into two broad categories: those with long-term disabilities and victims of trauma. Assessment should be tailored to the special needs of these two quite different groups.

Nursing history

Assessment begins with the child's view or description of the problem, if possible, with supplemental information from the parents. With small children there will be no subjective data base from which to begin. The child's view of the nature of the difficulty is extremely important, not only in isolating and identifying the individual problems involved with physical care, but also in obtaining an initial impression of the impact of this particular episode upon the child's life and state of well-being. Many adolescents are encountered in an orthopedic setting. Some of these patients can supply a history with little parental assistance and should be given this opportunity. Respecting their independence creates a favorable climate for establishing a working relationship. Children with long-term physical disabilities are often extremely knowledgeable about their condition. Allowing them to supply as much information as possible fosters some autonomy in a situation where opportunities for developing competence may be limited.

The history should include all pertinent medical facts plus social, developmental, and emotional results of physical changes. What physical difficulties or limitations are currently present? What effect have these had upon the current lifestyle? A description of the child's pattern of daily life will usually elicit the changes evoked by the present difficulty. It will also provide a base for planning daily routines while hospitalized and

a goal for rehabilitation. In children hospitalized for trauma, try to obtain a clear account of the nature of the accident and what first-aid measures and means of transportation were utilized.

Has the child been using any special orthopedic equipment or devices, such as braces, splints, crutches, prostheses, or shoes? While some of these items may be fairly obvious, corrective shoes may not look unusual. Use of these devices may need to be a part of planning the child's care while hospitalized. It is also helpful to know how much assistance the child requires in applying or utilizing these devices.

A review of other body systems should include bowel and urinary habits and any difficulties pertaining to these areas. Functioning of the elimination systems will be influenced by immobilization. If a child has been previously immobilized, the parents or the child may be able to provide helpful prophylactic measures that are successful and will avoid problems of elimination for this particular child.

When assessing the area of family relationships in children with long-term problems, the nurse needs to attempt to ascertain the nature of the parent-child relationship. Do the interactions between the parent and child seem appropriate to the child's age and developmental level? Does the parent allow the child to express feelings and points of view during the interview? Is the manner and content of verbal exchanges significant? With victims of trauma, is the parent expressing many feelings of guilt? Is the child being rebuked for the accident?

In cases where hospitalization or immobilization at home will require a prolonged absence from school, it is important to explore this area more thoroughly. Has the child been attending a regular classroom and at what grade level? How are the child's grades? Have any plans been made to continue the child's education away from school? What subjects does the child enjoy? In what extracurricular activities is the child involved? Is distance to the home such that it is likely that peers will visit?

Areas of interest that can be used recreationally or therapeutically during immobilization should be explored. What are the child's hobbies? Does the child enjoy some sort of craft activity? What television programs are favorites? What kind of music does the child like?

A diet history should pay particular attention

to food preferences. During prolonged periods of immobilization, food takes on added significance as meals become one of the day's highlights.

Physical examination

Physical examination usually begins with body measurements. Where movement is painful or contraindicated, questioning the parents or child about usual height and weight may have to suffice. For children admitted with casts, weight can only be estimated. For scoliosis patients, height upon admission for treatment is of particular significance because correction of the curve will result in an increase in height.

Physical observation should include an initial look at the child's stance and posture. Note the symmetry of the body and limbs. If a limb is affected, does the child hold it in a particular fashion? Does it appear in normal alignment? Can the child walk and does the gait appear normal? A simple description of what one sees is sufficient in these areas. Relative measurements of extremities may be necessary if one limb appears smaller than another.

Assessment of the condition of the skin is important for two reasons. For a child having surgery, skin lesions can be a source of infection. If a cast will cover areas of skin, the skin should be intact before cast application.

The neurovascular status of all extremities should be assessed. This provides a valuable and necessary baseline for checking neurological function and circulatory status following surgery or cast application. Does the child have normal sensation everywhere? Does the child have normal range of motion? Both sensation and motion should be checked by demonstration, if possible. Asking, "Can you feel this?" will often evoke a positive response, even where the child does not have good sensation. Color and temperature of the extremities should be noted. Is there any edema present? A further check of circulatory status may be obtained by pressing on the skin or nail bed. The area blanches with pressure, but color should quickly return when pressure is released and the capillaries refill with blood. Any alterations from normal should be noted.

Is the child currently having pain? Where is it and under what circumstances does it occur? What provides relief? For victims of trauma, the nurse needs to know what pain medication might have been administered prior to assessment that will influence the findings.

In completing data collection, the nurse will wish to review the physical exam findings of the physician. In children with musculoskeletal problems, a physical therapist is a vital part of the care of many children. If an appraisal by the physical therapist has been completed, this should be included in the data base.

X-rays are the main diagnostic tool utilized with children with musculoskeletal problems. These are often repeated over long periods of time. Sometimes perspective on a child's long-term problem can be obtained by a review of x-ray findings.

Immobilization

Disorders of the musculoskeletal system often require immobilization of a body part during the treatment regimen. Healthy children are by nature active beings and immobilization of a child may not be easy to accomplish. It invariably has some ramifications. The degree of immobilization will influence the effects: The greater the extent of immobilization and the longer the time period that it is required, the more pronounced the side effects will be.

Physical effects

Body systems commonly affected by immobilization are: the urinary, digestive, cardiovascular, skin, and musculoskeletal systems. *In the musculoskeletal system*, immobilization is used to place a body part at rest and to place a body part in normal alignment for a sufficient period of time for healing to occur. While this is occurring, certain undesirable changes are taking place. Any muscle group that is not being used is subject to atrophy. This is usually quite apparent when a cast is removed. The casted extremity is smaller than the uncasted extremity because of disuse atrophy. Any joints encased in plaster will have lost some of their mobility. This means that strength and range of motion must gradually be restored to that extremity through exercise. Since the flexors of a joint are generally stronger than the extensors, any joint not held in position by plaster or traction will be subject to a flexion contracture. Areas particularly vulnerable to this are the hip, knee, and foot.

Loss of some of the mineral portion of the bone begins to occur with disuse of that body part. Although this change is more pronounced in older persons, it also occurs in children who have great degrees of immobilization for prolonged periods of time.

Every attempt should be made to minimize these effects upon body parts by movement and exercise of any body part whose immobilization is not necessary for treatment. Preferably this movement should be actively performed by the child. A physical therapist can work with the child to establish a daily exercise program. The nurse working with the child can establish a simple daily exercise program for most children. Observe the movement of the child. Young healthy children often exercise all their mobile extremities without prompting (Fig. 36-5). Take note of what areas need an exercise program. Follow the basic principles below.

1. Have the child perform active range of motion exercises whenever possible.
2. When a child cannot actively move a part or when the child is too young to follow instructions, put the joints through passive range of motion.
3. Have the child exercise the quadriceps muscle over the anterior portion of the thigh. Quadriceps setting is done by pressing the back of the knee down onto the bed. When done on a regular basis, this helps to prepare the muscles of the leg for ambulation.
4. Encourage the child to strengthen the upper extremities by the use of a trapeze attached to the bed.

Duration and frequency of exercise sessions will need to be based upon the child's general condition and strength. Two sessions a day is often a good starting point. To encourage the continuation of an exercise program, it is helpful to establish a regular routine and make the program enjoyable. Establish certain goals for the child. Make the exercises playlike whenever possible. Examples of this would include using a throwing game or having the child kick an object attached to the bed frame.

If possible, avoid having the hip or knee continuously flexed. This is often a comfortable position for the child, but the hip and knee need regular extension to avoid the development of flexion contractures. In children with traction applied to the lower extremity, a support for the foot should be provided to prevent footdrop.

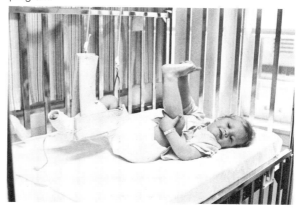

Figure 36-5 This 22-month-old in skeletal traction illustrates why young healthy children may not need an exercise program.

All the vital functions tend to slow with immobilization. Circulation may be sluggish. This, along with pressure on the skin, makes skin breakdown more likely. Change of position or massage of areas subject to pressure helps to reduce the likelihood of skin breakdown. Healthy, well-nourished children with a normal layer of subcutaneous fat will have fewer problems with skin breakdown.

Decreased motility of the gastrointestinal tract because of lack of activity may produce constipation. A record should be kept of the child's bowel function. A dietary regimen that includes fresh fruits and vegetables, other sources of fiber, and adequate amounts of liquid will often eliminate the necessity for stool softeners, enemas, and suppositories. Appetite may be diminished, but this problem is often related to the unfamiliarity of the food in the hospital and may be remedied temporarily by some familiar foods from home until the child has an opportunity to adapt. Smaller, more frequent feedings may be more attractive to a child when there is little physical activity to stimulate appetite. Allowing the child as much choice as possible in diet is always beneficial.

As kidney function slows, there may be a tendency for the kidneys to form stones. Increasing fluid intake will help to prevent this. Although the child needs normal calcium intake for bone healing, excessive amounts of milk should be avoided. High serum calcium levels encourage kidney stone formation.

Emotional effects

The emotional reaction of the child to immobilization will be influenced by the child's age, the amount of preparation provided for the experience, and the circumstances surrounding the event. Older children can obviously be better prepared when immobilization is anticipated. Discussion of what it will be like to be in a cast or traction should be instituted by the parents. The family can prepare favorite activities, books, and games to pass the hours. When immobilization is not forseen, as in the case of an accident, then the child must do all his adapting after the fact.

Some children, particularly young ones, will show an immediate reaction to being immobilized. It is common to see older children quietly accepting their imposed restraint the first few days and then to see some reaction occurring. Depression, withdrawal, and disobedient and aggressive behavior are all seen in children as a reaction to immobilization and hospitalization. Some sort of reaction should be considered usual and the normal result of immobilizing a healthy child. Physical capabilities are a part of each person's identity. Immobilization of a child limits these capabilities, alters the child's self-image, and may threaten the child's self-esteem. Also, many children use physical activity as a means of discharging feelings of anger and hostility. This normal and healthy way of handling emotional energy is denied them once they are immobilized. Although an uncooperative child is more difficult for the parents and staff to handle, this child needs freedom to express his or her feelings within certain bounds. These bounds need to be clearly defined for the child. Most children will show signs of making a good adaptation to their limitation of activity and their surroundings within a week.

If a child physically resists immobilization to the point where it interferes with treatment, then some sort of restraint may be required. Restraint is to be avoided, if at all possible, since this may be traumatic to the child. However, sometimes restraints relieve the child of the burden of maintaining a position by acting as a gentle reminder that certain movements are not allowed. Restraints should never be used in a punitive fashion. The child needs to understand that this is a necessary part of treatment to ensure that healing takes place.

Achievement of normal developmental goals for the child's age must be stimulated. Appropriate toys are an important part of this planning. See Chap. 17 for some of the basic needs of the hospitalized child.

Environmental stimulation might include decorating the room, bed, or traction apparatus with toys, posters, or cards. A child's bed should be positioned to provide as much of a view of surrounding activity as possible; a view out the window or down the hall will help to lessen the feeling of isolation. Whenever possible, the child should be moved out of his or her room. With casted patients this can be by means of a stretcher, wagon, cart, or someone's arms. Movement of a child may be time-consuming and hard work, but it is definitely worth the time and trouble. A trip to the playroom or another area for a meal may stimulate appetite. Just having the opportunity to observe activity in the hall provides diversion and stimulation. This also allows for more contact between children. Friendship may prove to be the most therapeutic measure of all in assisting the child in adjusting to illness and limitation of activity, and it may even make the illness a personal growth experience. Many of these friendships continue long after hospitalization and completion of treatment.

Care of a child in a cast

The types of casts commonly used in the treatment of children are illustrated in Fig. 36-6. A cast may be used as a gradual correction of a deformity, as an initial treatment to provide immobilization for a fracture, as a followup to traction, or as a means of immobilization following surgery to bones, joints, or muscles.

A plaster cast is made from a gauze bandage impregnated with plaster of paris. During application, the plaster bandage is wet and then applied over an underlying layer of padding or a piece of stockinette. Figure 36-7 shows a cast being applied to a foot. During the application of the cast, the chemical reaction taking place generates heat and the cast feels warm. Complete drying of the cast takes 24 h or longer. Fiberglass is a newer casting material which is being tested in some areas.

Preparation for casting Care of the child begins with preparation for casting, when the child is to be awake. In an emergency situation, there may be little time for preparation, but every child needs to have certain things explained:

1. Steps of cast application

2. Extent of pain or discomfort and what will be done to help
3. Warmth of the cast during application
4. What the cast will look like and what area it will cover

Figure 36-6 Casts commonly used in the treatment of children. (*From Nancy E. Hilt and William E. Schmitt, Jr., Pediatric Orthopedic Nursing, Mosby, St. Louis, 1975. Used by permission of the publisher and authors.*)

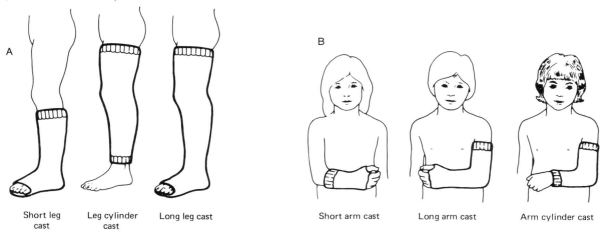

A

Short leg cast   Leg cylinder cast   Long leg cast

B

Short arm cast   Long arm cast   Arm cylinder cast

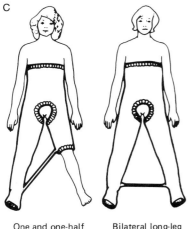

C

One and one-half hip spica cast   Bilateral long-leg hip spica cast

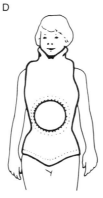

D

Risser localizer cast

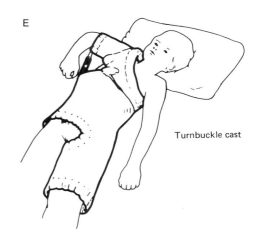

E

Turnbuckle cast

Figure 36-7 Short leg casts being applied.

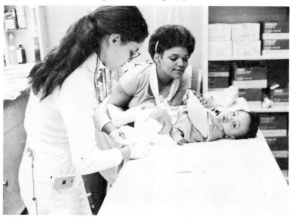

It is helpful to have the child see a drawing of the cast or to see a similar cast on another child. The child may apply a cast or see one applied to a doll. The apprehension of some older children may be allayed by talking with another child who has had a cast application. Books are excellent ways to help prepare children for casting or to help them express feelings about it afterward. Blue Cross provides member hospitals with a book entitled *Wearing a Cast*.[1] It covers many aspects of concern to children about casts and their use.

Physical preparation should include an assessment of skin areas to be covered by plaster. If stockinette is to be used under the cast, this will need to be applied.

Once the cast is applied, care must be taken that it is not dented or damaged until drying is completed. The cast should be supported and handled gently. When lifting the cast, avoid indenting the plaster with the fingers by lifting the cast with the palms of the hands. The cast should not be covered during the initial 20 to 24 h after application as this will slow the drying process. The child needs to be turned regularly to allow for all surfaces of the cast to dry.

Neurovascular status A plaster cast must be snug enough to provide the necessary immobilization without interfering with circulation. Every cast application carries with it the risk of circulatory impairment. Since impairment of circulation can result in irreparable damage and even permanent loss of function, the checking of neurovascular status is of extreme importance. If injury or a surgical procedure preceded cast application, then swelling may further compromise circulation.

Using as a baseline the initial assessment of neurovascular status prior to cast application, the nurse will begin assessing this area immediately following application and hourly for about 12 to 24 h. The length of time hourly checks are continued will be determined by the amount of swelling. Following the initial hourly checks, neurovascular status will be assessed every 4 h. Each check should include an assessment of: temperature, color, blanching, amount of edema, sensation, motion, and pain in the area distal to the cast application (Fig. 36-8). If there is impairment of circulation, there will be edema, coldness, pallor or cyanosis, and poor return of color upon blanching. If circulatory compromise continues, there will be pain, numbness, and loss of sensation and motion. When an arm or leg is casted, each finger and toe should be checked individually, since impair-

Figure 36-8 Nurse checking the neurovascular status of a casted extremity. When plaster covers most of the extremity, good lighting is essential. A flashlight may be necessary.

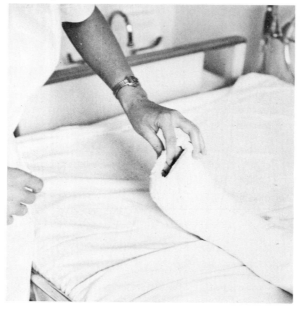

ment to some can occur without impairment to others.

When edema is present, elevating the casted extremity above the level of of the heart is often indicated to help reduce swelling. Coldness of the extremity may be partially due to the contact with the wet cast. It is not uncommon for one or two signs of slowing of circulation to appear. The nurse must then carefully check for any other signs that appear.

The physician should be aware of the child's neurovascular status and should be apprised of any changes. For example, if a child's extremity following casting is slightly edematous and cool, with a rapid color return on blanching and normal sensation and motion, then the nurse should observe carefully for any deterioration in blanching sign or sensation and motion. Pain may be more difficult to assess since some pain will normally accompany fracture or surgery. Extreme pain or pain poorly relieved by medication should be reported. Pain is usually confined to the operative or fracture area. Pain in other areas should be investigated. In small children, only the amount of pain can be assessed, and other signs of neurovascular status must be relied upon. If circulation is compromised, cutting or removal of the cast may be necessary to restore circulation. Some orthopedic units employ a separate chart for recording checks of neurovascular status (Fig. 36-9). Each check of neurovascular status should be

Figure 36-9 Neurovascular status checklist.

NEUROVASCULAR STATUS CHECKLIST

Procedure:							
Date:							
Time:							
SKIN TEMPERATURE							
Warm							
Cool							
Cold							
SKIN COLOR							
Normal							
Pale							
Dusky (bluish)							
Red							
CAPILLARY REFILL							
Normal							
Sluggish							
Faster							
EDEMA							
Not present							
Mild							
Moderate							
Severe							
SENSATION							
Touch							
Sharp (to pin)							
Dull (to pin)							
Tingling							
Numbness							
None							

Date:							
Time:							
MOTION							
Present							
Absent							
Foot							
Dorsiflex							
Plantarflex							
Fingers							
Flexion							
Extension							
Abduction							
PAIN							
None							
Mild							
Moderate							
Severe							
PULSES							
Pedal							
Tibialis							
Radial							

carefully noted on the child's chart. This facilitates the detection of any changes in the child's condition.

Skin care Care of the skin includes daily inspection of all visible skin at the edges of the cast and as far under the cast as possible with a flashlight for signs of redness or breakdown. This can occur as a result of pressure or abrasion from the cast edge. Following cast application, all plaster particles need to be removed from under the cast edges. Cast edges should be finished and smoothed to minimize skin abrasion. If the cast is lined with stockinette, this can be streched over the cast edge and secured with tape or plaster. The cast edges can also be finished with adhesive tape or moleskin. This is commonly referred to as a *petalling* since the tape or moleskin are cut into petal shapes and applied to the cast edges as illustrated in Figs. 36-10 and 36-11. Finishing of the cast edges in this manner should be delayed until the cast is dry.

Skin edges adjacent to the cast should be kept clean and dry. If the cast indents adjacent skin areas, some trimming of the cast following application may be necessary for comfort. Trimming is first checked with the physician to be certain that it will not affect the therapeutic value of the cast. A piece of padding may be placed under an edge that is uncomfortable for the child. The application of alcohol to the skin

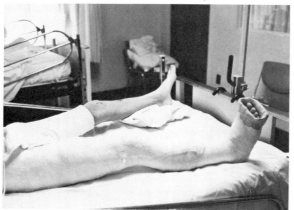

Figure 36-10 Petalled cast edges. The cast edges on the right foot are finished with moleskin, while the edges above the left knee are finished with adhesive tape.

around the cast edges may help toughen the skin and may also provide some relief from itching.

The cast may apply pressure to skin areas under the cast that are not visible. Pressure may be sufficient to produce skin breakdown. This is most likely to occur over bony prominences. The main indicator of pressure and skin breakdown is pain. It is continuous and intense at the location of pressure. An older child will be able to pinpoint the painful area. A younger child will be fussy and irritable beyond the time usually required for cast adjustment. Pain over a period of days followed by sudden relief may indicate that breakdown has progressed through the full skin thickness and sensation has been lost.[2] If skin breakdown occurs, an unpleasant odor may accompany it. Smelling the cast may provide a clue.

A pressure area or the suspicion of one may require removal of a cast or "windowing", i.e., removing a piece of the cast over the pressure area. This may be done to inspect the area and then determine what action needs to be taken. The removed piece may be reapplied with plaster.

Skin care includes frequent turning of all children who are not ambulatory. In larger children with large heavy casts, this may require several persons. Parts of the cast should not be used for lifting or turning since this may damage the cast.

Keeping the cast clean The casts must be kept clean and dry. If the lining of the cast becomes wet, it is extremely difficult to dry. Moisture allowed to penetrate the cast itself will soften the cast. A clean, relatively odorless cast will be more pleasant for the child and those who care for the child. The two main sources of soiling of the cast are eating and elimination. Protection of the cast when eating is fairly easy to accomplish by the use of bibs or a towel covering the cast. Protection of the cast from the products of elimination is more difficult when the cast approaches the perineal area.

In children who have bowel and bladder control, this problem consists of protection at the time of toileting. This is best accomplished by protecting the cast edges with plastic. With long leg casts, plastic placed over the tops of the casts and tucked inside will suffice. When a child

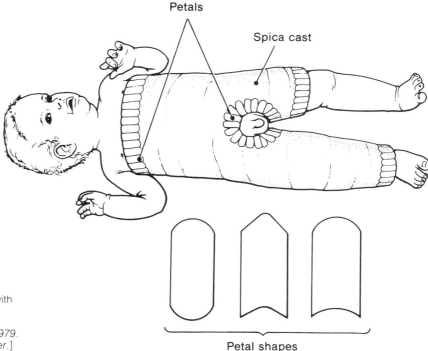

Petals

Spica cast

Petal shapes

Figure 36-11 Spica cast finished with petals. [*From Gladys Scipien et al. (eds.), Comprehensive Pediatric Nursing, McGraw-Hill, New York, 1979. Used by permission of the publisher.*]

wears a plaster jacket and must remain recumbent, care must be taken to prevent soiling to the posterior cast edge and to prevent urine from running up inside the cast. Boys will use a urinal and will have less problem with toileting. Some patients find a fracture pan more comfortable because of its lower height. A standard bedpan may be used satisfactorily if the upper torso is elevated slightly with pillows to prevent urine from running into the cast.

The following technique usually provides good results. Roll the child onto one side. Tuck a sturdy piece of plastic about 12 in wide into the back of the cast. Place a pillow or two behind the shoulders and upper portion of the cast for elevation, if necessary. Place the bedpan under the child's buttocks and roll the child back onto the pillows and bedpan. Tuck the lower edge of the plastic into the bedpan and tuck a similar piece of plastic under the front edge of that cast and into the bedpan between the child's legs. The plastic will help to funnel the products of elimination into the bedpan. Always check to see that the upper torso is not lower than the perineal area. After elimination is completed,

remove both pieces of plastic and place in the bedpan. Turn the child onto one side and remove the bedpan and pillows.

The technique for toileting a child in a spica cast is similar, but since the cast also covers the inner thigh area, the entire cast edge around the perineal area must be protected. This may take several pieces of plastic, all of which will be funneled into the bedpan. Encourage children to request the bedpan before elimination becomes urgent, since some time is required for proper preparation.

In children without bowel and bladder control, maintaining cast cleanliness becomes more difficult. In children with long leg casts usual diapering techniques can be utilized with frequent changes. Children in plaster jackets or spica casts will usually require a split Bradford frame for protection of the cast. Figure 36-12 shows a split Bradford frame. Use of the frame is indicated in any child who has poor bowel or bladder control. The frame is elevated on blocks on the bed and secured with the head slightly higher than the perineal area to prevent urine from entering the cast. The child is placed either

Figure 36-12 A split Bradford frame.

prone or supine on the frame with the perineal area over the opening (Fig. 36-13). The child is secured to the frame. A piece of linen placed around the frame and the child's casted torso and pinned with several safety pins usually works well. Plastic is tucked into the cast edges and funneled into a bedpan placed under the frame. All products of elimination drain into the bedpan while the cast remains clean and dry. The bedpan and plastic need to be changed frequently to control odor. The child's perineal area can easily be washed at this time. It is usually convenient to do this when turning the child on the frame and as often as needed between turning.

Disposable diapers can be cut down and used for short periods of time tucked into the perineal

Figure 36-13 A child in a hip spica cast on a split Bradford frame.

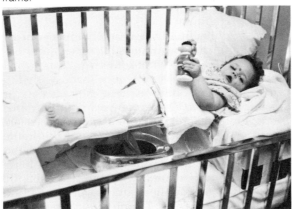

opening of the cast. This is convenient for transporting the child from one area to another. These must be changed very frequently to avoid wetting or soiling the cast.

Activity for casted children The child should be permitted as much activity and mobility as possible. Children who cannot ambulate should be provided with another means of transportation (Fig. 36-14). Children on a Bradford frame may have the frame placed on a wagon or cart.

When planning diversionary activities for a child in a cast, care must be taken that small children do not drop or place small objects down inside the cast. Children should be instructed not to place anything except the fingers inside the cast.

Removal of a cast The cast may be removed after healing is completed or for purposes of

Figure 36-14 A child with a hip spica cast in a cart.

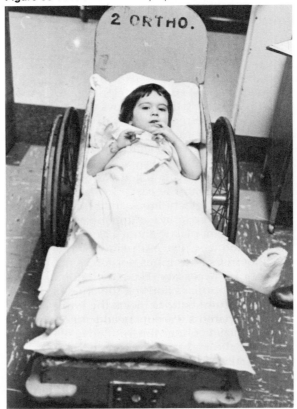

assessing the healing process, after which a new cast will be applied. Casts are usually removed with a vibrating cast cutter or cast saw, as shown in Fig. 36-15. A child should see the cast cutter and it should be explained that it will cut the cast, not him or her. The cast cutting is noisy and many children are frightened, even with adequate preparation. Distraction with toys may be helpful. The child may be fearful that the casted part may be painful without the support of the cast, once it is removed.

The child and parents need preparation for the appearance of the casted part. The skin area under the cast will be covered with dead skin cells that would normally have been sloughed but remain in place under the cast to form a yellow scale. Muscle areas will appear flabby. The casted extremity will usually appear smaller than the uncasted one.

The child may experience some discomfort as movement is resumed after the cast is removed. The previously casted area needs gentle handling with movement slowly instituted. An exercise program will be prescribed by either the physician or the physical therapist to restore normal function to the part. In many hospitals a trip to the physical therapy department is a routine part of cast removal.

Cleansing of the skin should be done gently. The best method of removing accumulated dead skin is soaking the area with mineral oil and then gently rubbing. Vigorous scrubbing will damage the skin beneath the scaly outer layer.

Home care of the child in a cast Instruction for the parents begins as soon as the cast is applied and they observe the care of the child. In hospitalized children, parents should be encouraged to assume as much responsibility for care as they are willing to assume. This instruction should include positioning, skin care, toileting, and checking circulation, for all of these will be continued after discharge. When a child has been cared for on a Bradford frame, this will often be continued at home. Many hospitals rent frames to parents. Parents need to know how to set the frame up as well as how to place and care for the child on the frame.

The parents must receive thorough instructions concerning the child's exercise program and what activities are permitted. The child needs to be a part of family activity at home and

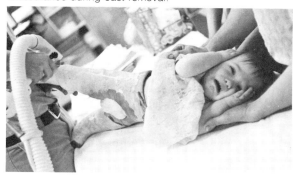

Figure 36-15 Removal of a hip spica cast. The noise of the cast cutter is very frightening. Children need much reassurance during cast removal.

not be confined to a bedroom, if at all possible. Small children can easily be carried from one room to another or up and down stairs. Older children may need to have their sleeping quarters relocated. A wagon or other wheeled vehicle may be adapted for use at home. Parents are often ingenious at finding ways to allow a child to be more mobile. A large skateboard-type vehicle may be constructed. This permits a child in a spica cast to move about on the abdomen, using the hands for self-propulsion.[3]

Oral instructions followed by complete written instructions are given. At the very least, the parent should receive written guidelines on conditions that should be reported to the physician. These would include any signs of circulatory impairment, skin breakdown, or weakening of the cast.

Care of a child in traction

Traction is the application of a pulling force to a part of the body. It is used to maintain proper alignment or to straighten a part of the body. *Manual traction* is the application of this force with the hands. This is commonly done when setting and casting a fracture. *Skin traction* applies the pulling force directly to the skin. It is generally used in situations that require light or intermittent traction. Skin traction may be applied to the skin with slings, halters, or bandages. Adhesive may be used to apply the traction more permanently to the skin.

Skeletal traction applies the force directly to bone through the use of a pin or wire placed through the bone. Insertion of the device is a surgical procedure and the child will be anesthetized.

The traction is mounted on a frame secured to the bed. A rope travels from the traction application device through a pulley and is attached to a weight. The weight and the arrangement of the pulleys determine the force and direction of the pull applied to the body.

Traction is initially applied by the physician. Some types of skin traction may be applied by the nurse at the direction of the physician.

Preparation for application of traction The child needs preparation for the application of traction. In emergency situations, this may be limited to describing briefly what is to occur and answering questions. When time permits, drawing the traction or seeing another child in traction will supplement this. Traction itself is not usually painful. When it is used to treat a fracture, traction helps to alleviate some of the fracture pain by overcoming the muscle spasm that accompanies it. Therefore, the child can usually be reassured that there will be less pain once the traction is applied. The child will continue to have some pain from the fracture. When traction is used for stretching or straightening, as in patients with scoliosis, there may be discomfort when it is applied or as weight is added to the traction. Children need reassurance that medication is available for relief of pain or discomfort when it does occur.

Basic rules
Once traction is applied, some basic principles need to be observed.

1. Traction pull should never be interrupted unless this is specifically ordered by the physician. Generally skin traction that is not adherent to the skin will be periodically removed and reapplied (Fig. 36-16). Skin traction that is adherent to the skin and skeletal traction are never interrupted.
2. Ropes should be free of knots and in the center of the pulley track so that they move freely through the pulleys. Weights should hang free. Frayed ropes should be replaced.
3. The child should be positioned to provide effective countertraction. The effectiveness of traction in many cases depends upon the countertraction, or pull away from the traction, applied by the child's body weight. Therefore, the child must be properly positioned to allow this countertraction to be applied. For example, the child in Bryant's traction must have the buttocks clear the bed so that the body weight applies countertraction. The child in split Russell's traction may have to be periodically moved to the head of the bed as sliding to the bottom of the bed interferes with the countertraction.

Neurovascular status The application of traction can interfere with circulation and neurological function. Some children in traction have fractures which may affect neurovascular status

Figure 36-16 A child in split Russell's traction. This skin traction is nonadherent and is periodically removed and reapplied by the nursing staff.

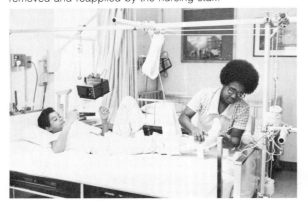
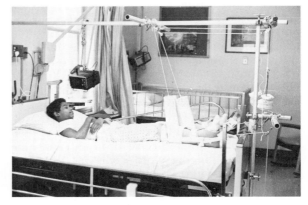

as well. Checking of neurovascular status should be carried out immediately following application of traction. The frequency of checking is determined by the type of traction and whether there was preceding trauma. Where trauma has occurred or where skeletal traction has been applied, hourly checks of neurovascular status for the first 24 h are indicated. This is followed by neurovascular checks every 4 h. When skin traction is applied, checks every 4 h will usually suffice. See Fig. 36-9.

Positioning and activity The position and alignment of the child will be determined by the type of traction. The amount of movement allowed will be determined by the physician. The child needs to have clear instructions concerning position and activity. Restraints should be used only when attempts at explaining and reminding have not been effective. A Bradford frame may be used for restraint purposes as well as for toileting purposes. Securing the child to the frame prevents excessive movement that may interfere with traction.

The child in traction has greater imposed immobility than the child in a cast. Some types of traction may allow for turning of the child, but in many cases, the child cannot be turned. The child in traction will be most likely to show the physical and emotional effects of immobilization.

All joints not directly involved in traction should be positioned to maintain function. This is particularly important for the feet to prevent foot-drop when traction is applied to a lower extremity. A foot board or foot support should be used. All joints not immobilized should be exercised and put through normal range of motion if this activity does not interfere with the immobilization of the affected part.

A trapeze is often attached to the bed frame when a child is placed in traction. This permits the child to move when toileting and gives the nurse some assistance when changing linen or providing skin care. It also allows an older child a means of movement when traction applied to a lower extremity gradually pulls him or her to the bottom of the bed. A trapeze also provides beneficial exercising and strengthening of arm and shoulder muscles. If the child will be using crutches at some time, this is particularly useful in preparing the arm muscles for crutch-walking.

General care Maintaining skin integrity in areas subjected to long-term pressure requires vigilance. Skin areas require stimulation of circulation three or four times a day. All areas subject to pressure should be rubbed and inspected; back, heels, and elbows are common problem areas. Sheepskin will reduce the irritation of linen on problem spots. Foam cushions may alleviate pressure on heels and elbows. A child who has little subcutaneous fat or who will be in traction for extended periods of time without turning may require an alternating-pressure mattress.

When skin traction is applied, the friction and pressure of the traction apparatus on the skin may cause irritation. Often this type of traction is removable for short periods of time for skin care.

Care of the area where a skeletal pin or wire penetrates the skin differs greatly from one institution to another and from one physician to another. Some physicians direct that no care be given to pin sites while others have an elaborate routine. Regardless of what procedure is used to care for the area, regular observation is important. Any redness or drainage must be reported to the physician since it may indicate infection. The position of the pin should be noted on a daily basis since slippage sometimes occurs.

Children in traction have large amounts of skin area exposed. It may be difficult to use bed clothing to properly cover the child without interfering with the traction. The child also has little muscle activity to generate body heat. Extra warmth may need to be provided. The room temperature should be adjusted to the child's comfort, not the family's or personnel's. A pair of warm socks or small pieces of linen for covering extremities may increase comfort.

Changing the bed linen or toileting may require some ingenuity and improvisation when a child is in traction. Sometimes it is more convenient to change the bed linen from the top to the bottom rather than from side to side. A fracture bedpan will require less lifting or movement of the child and may be more comfortable.

Psychological considerations Traction looks uncomfortable and the child and the parents need some time to adjust to the appearance of all the equipment. They need to understand the purpose of various parts of the traction device.

Parents need to know exactly how much movement is allowed. As the parents and child become accustomed to the traction, parents will usually become actively involved in the care of the child with some encouragement and instruction from the staff.

A child in a cast can be moved to provide some diversion, but this is often not possible for the child in traction. Particular attention should be paid to this child's immediate environment. Providing stimulation through cheerful decoration may also serve to camouflage some of the traction equipment.

Trauma

Trauma to the musculoskeletal system is a common occurrence. Children who are very active and athletic are more likely to find themselves in situations where trauma may occur. Motor vehicle accidents are a common cause of trauma to muscles and bones. Children are injured both as pedestrians and passengers. Other causes of musculoskeletal injury in children are falls, sports or athletic injuries, and lawn mowers.

While parents are becoming more conscious of automobile safety and the importance of proper restraint systems for children, more public education is needed for safety in sports. School-run athletic programs are usually fairly conscientious about safety, but children are frequently lacking in supervision in other sports areas. Skateboarding is a good example of an activity that results in many arm, leg, and head injuries.[4] Many children ride skateboards without proper safety equipment and in unsafe locations. Many parents are also not aware of the dangers from power lawnmowers. Young children are most frequently injured by falling into the path of a lawn mower or falling from a riding mower.[5] These children have extremely mutilating injuries, frequently with loss of a limb or a portion of it.

Nurses must take every opportunity in every setting to talk about safety to help parents prevent fractures and other injuries.

Sprains and dislocations

A sprain is trauma to one of the ligaments that stabilizes or unites a joint. In children sprains are most likely to occur as a result of sports activity.[6] Pain and swelling commonly occur.

Treatment usually consists of some degree of immobilization until swelling begins to subside and then gradual return to use of the joint. Elastic bandages are commonly used to provide support to the joint during the healing period. Ice may be used initially to reduce swelling and pain following injury. Warmth may be used once initial swelling has subsided to provide comfort, to increase circulation, and to promote healing.

Dislocations and subluxations as a result of trauma are not particularly common in children with the exception of the elbow. A dislocation of a joint occurs when the two bone surfaces that come together to form the joint are completely separated from one another. A subluxation occurs when the bones are displaced but not completely separated.

"Pulled elbow" is a subluxation of the elbow that occurs in small children as a result of a sudden pull on the extended arm. This might occur as a child suddenly pulls away from an adult holding his hand or when an adult lifts a child by the arm. Sometimes a click can be heard as the joint is displaced. The child experiences immediate pain and will refuse to use the arm, often holding it next to the body with the other arm. Once the subluxation is reduced, immediate relief of pain is experienced. Usually no other treatment is necessary. Parents should be cautioned to avoid pull on the arm to prevent recurrence of the injury.

Fractures

A fracture is a break in the continuity of the bone. Some common types of fractures are illustrated in Fig. 36-17. Generally the skeletal structures of children can withstand more force without fracture than can those of an adult. The larger amount of cartilage present in the child's skeleton means that bones are less brittle and more flexible. In small children this may result in a greenstick fracture. In this case, the bone is not completely broken but is bent on one side. Bones of children may bow considerably before fracture occurs.

Fractures in children tend to occur in the long bones and in the areas where bone growth is occurring—the epiphyseal plate. This area of the bone does not have the strength of the more solid structures around it and tends to be subject to injury. Damage to the epiphyseal plate is always a major concern when dealing with frac-

Figure 36-17 General classification of fractures. (*From J. Barry, Emergency Nursing, McGraw-Hill, New York, 1978.*)

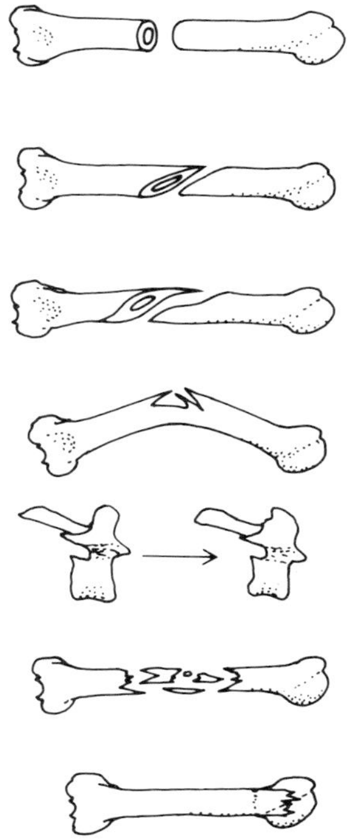

TYPE OF FRACTURE		DEFINITION
1. Transverse		1. Usually produced by angulating force; once the fragments are aligned and immobilized, stability is assured
2. Oblique		2. Fragments tend to slip by one another unless traction is maintained
3. Spiral		3. Produced by twisting or rotary force; reduction difficult to maintain
4. Greenstick		4. Caused by compression force in long axis of the bone; often seen in children under age of ten
5. Compression		5. Usually produced by severe violence applied to cancellous bone, such as the spine
6. Comminuted		6. Always more than two fragments
7. Impacted		7. Produced by severe violence, driving bone fragments firmly together

tures in children. If the trauma damages the bone producing cells in this area, longitudinal bone growth may stop completely in that limb or it may occur in an asymmetrical fashion.

As a child's bone grows following a fracture, it may remodel the fracture site. This means that if the alignment of the bones is not perfect following reduction, the bony deformity that is produced will often correct itself as growth occurs. The younger the child, the more correction takes place.

When a bone is broken, there is always some trauma to the soft tissues surrounding the fracture, causing swelling. This can be as a result of the force that caused the fracture or the fractured bone ends themselves may cause trauma to the soft tissues. Of particular concern is trauma to the major blood vessels or nerves that may occur as a result of fracture, particularly in the area of the elbow.

When a fracture occurs, the periosteum is torn and pulled away from the bone and bleeding occurs. This results in the formation of a hematoma around the fracture site. Osteoblasts are released from the broken ends of the bone into the area surrounding the fracture. The bone ends that have lost their blood supply become necrotic and degenerate. The hematoma around the bone ends changes to a fibrous connective tissue bridge and then into cartilage and bone through the action of the osteoblasts. This initial union of the bone ends is called *callus formation.* As callus is gradually changed into solid bone, remodeling and reshaping of the fracture area will occur.

During the period of healing, the bone must be immobilized to maintain correct position of the bone ends and to allow for solid healing of the bone before it is subjected to normal stress. Bone healing is more rapid in children. The younger the child, the more rapidly bone healing will take place. A femoral fracture in a newborn may heal in 2 to 3 weeks while in an adolescent this same degree of healing may take 8 to 10 weeks. This means that the period of immobilization required is generally shorter in children, especially young children.

Treatment of fractures Any child who is suspected of having a fracture will first be x-rayed. The child may be in considerable pain and need to be assured that gentleness will be used during this procedure. Once the fracture is diagnosed and if the bone ends are displaced, they will have to be replaced in alignment for proper healing to occur. This replacement is called *reduction* of the fracture. Reduction may be closed or open.

Closed reduction is accomplished through a combination of manual traction and force applied with the hands to push the bone ends into position. Closed reduction may require general anesthesia, or it may be done while the child is awake with the aid of analgesic and sedative medications. This helps to reduce the amount of pain the child experiences.

Open reduction involves direct exposure of the bones through a surgical procedure. It is always done under general anesthesia and some type of internal-fixation device is inserted to stabilize the fracture.

Once the fracture is reduced, it will be held in position by either a plaster cast or traction. For complete immobilization the cast will usually incorporate the joint above and the joint below the fracture site. Traction is more likely to be needed in fractures of bones where large muscles pull on the bone fragments. In these cases, a plaster cast may not hold the bones in the correct position. When traction is needed, it will be used until callus formation provides sufficient stability to the fracture that a cast may be applied.

Fractures that can be treated with a closed reduction and casting may not require admission to the hospital. Sometimes children are admitted for purposes of observing neurovascular status for a period of time, particularly if there is extensive swelling. Children whose fractures require closed reduction and traction will require several weeks of hospitalization.

Nursing care of children with fractures

If the fracture is untreated, the basic rule of first aid is to splint the fracture as it lies. The principle is to avoid movement at the fracture site since this may cause further injury to the limb. The child may arrive for treatment with the fracture splinted. Whether the fracture has been treated or not, assessments of neurovascular status should begin immediately and continue hourly for at least 24 h.

The child is usually in pain and will require regular pain medication for the first days following the injury. Children are often fearful of physical care from the nurse because any jarring or moving of the affected extremity causes considerable pain. When the child is in traction, caution should be taken to avoid bumping the bed or any part of the traction apparatus. All movement for physical care needs to be done with extreme gentleness to prevent increasing discomfort in the period immediately following the fracture. As callus formation begins and swelling subsides, pain will decrease and the child will be better able to tolerate movement for physical care.

In emergency situations children and parents need accurate explanations of procedures to be performed. These explanations may be brief because of the need for prompt medical attention. The child's pain may interfere with the child's perception of any information that is given. The parents are often visibly upset in situations where trauma has occurred. Their ability to process any information given to them under these circumstances may be limited. This means that detailed explanations of the nature of the injury and the treatment may be more meaningful after the initial crisis has passed. It is best not to assume that parents have received or understood information given in emergency situations.

Parents are often feeling responsible or guilty after a traumatic injury has occurred. Some parents will express these feelings while others will find these feelings so painful that they will avoid discussion and choose to concentrate on the physical problems. Some parents will attempt to blame or rebuke the child, especially if disobedience had anything to do with the injury. Staff usually have more difficulty accepting this type of reaction from parents. Indeed, the staff may feel angry with the parents for allowing the accident to occur. Parents need to express these feelings without judgment being placed upon them. In the period following injury, parents may be extremely solicitous or overprotective of the child in an attempt to relieve these guilt feelings.

The child's response to injury could include any of the usual responses to illness. Sudden unexpected injury carries with it a threat to physical well-being that may manifest itself in fearfulness or phobic reactions in the child following injury. This is a very understandable reaction. Usually these fears can be resolved by allowing the child to express these feelings without ridicule. Many children need to talk at length about the circumstances surrounding the accident. This helps to dissipate some of the anxiety surrounding the event.

Fracture of the clavicle The clavicle is one of the most frequently broken bones in children.[7] Fracture can occur at birth because of pressure on the shoulders at delivery. It commonly occurs as a result of falls from a bed or high chair onto an outstretched arm, elbow, or shoulder. While older children may complain of pain, in infants the only symptom may be lack of spontaneous movement on the affected side.

When fracture of the clavicle occurs at birth, healing and remodeling of the bone occur easily and rapidly. No treatment at all may be utilized, or the affected arm may be immobilized by using tape or by pinning the sleeve of the shirt to the shirt body. On older children a figure-eight bandage may be used to brace the shoulders back and prevent the bone ends from overlapping. This is usually worn for several weeks.

Leg fractures Fractures of the tibia and fibula can often be treated with reduction and casting. Fractures of the femur often require traction to maintain reduction. In children under 2 years of age, Bryant's traction is commonly used (Fig. 36-18). For older children, there are several types of traction used, depending upon the nature of the fracture. One type that is commonly used is called *90-90 traction*, which is illustrated in Fig. 36-19. The traction is applied to a pin placed in the distal fragment of the femur. Three or four weeks of traction are often required before casting can be done. Fractures of the femur require a $1\frac{1}{2}$ hip spica cast for immobilization following traction.

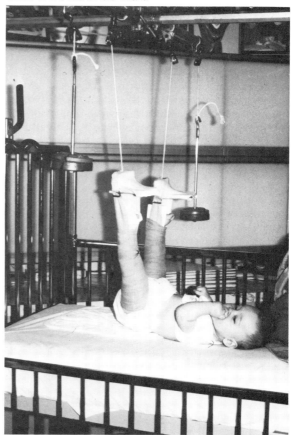

Figure 36-18 Bryant's traction for treatment of fractured femur in a 6-month-old infant.

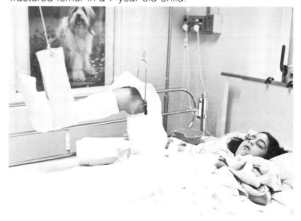

Figure 36-19 90-90 skeletal traction for treatment of a fractured femur in a 7-year-old child.

Arm fractures Falls are the common cause of arm fractures. Many can be treated with reduction and casting. Of particular concern are fractures near the elbow because there is considerable danger of damage or compression of the brachial artery. The *supracondylar fracture* of the humerus, a common fracture in children, is a fracture in which the distal humerus just above the elbow fractures. How this fracture is treated is determined by the amount of displacement of the bone fragments and the amount of swelling.[8] Some will be treated by closed reduction and casting. Others will require skeletal traction for a period of time following reduction (Fig. 36-20). Regardless of treatment, of primary importance is the assessment of neurovascular status because trauma to the brachial artery or ulnar or median nerve is not uncommon.

If undetected, trauma to the brachial artery can result in *Volkmann's contracture*, a disabling and permanent loss of function in the hand. It is produced by ischemia to the muscles of the forearm as a result of injury or spasm of the brachial artery. Within 24 h swelling and compression can produce permanent damage to the muscles and nerves. The child can be left with paralysis of the muscles of the wrist and fingers. Symptoms of disruption of circulation include: pain in the forearm, pallor of the hand, absence of the radial pulse, and inability to flex or extend the fingers or wrist. If ischemia occurs, cast removal or immediate surgery may be necessary to prevent permanent damage.

In cases of supracondylar fracture, the physician may establish a specific protocol for assessing neurovascular status. If not, the nurse should assess neurovascular status hourly. This assessment should include checking for radial pulse and checking the child's ability to flex and extend the wrist and all fingers. Any change warrants immediate attention from the physician.

Skull fractures Trauma to the head may include a skull fracture. Usually the skull fracture itself is not the main concern, but a blow that is forceful enough to fracture the skull may have injured the brain beneath. The fracture will heal without treatment unless a fragment of the skull is depressed or displaced. Surgery may be required to elevate the bone fragment.

Traumatic amputations

Loss of a body part in children is most likely to occur as a result of motor vehicle accident or lawn mower injury. Treatment is aimed at mak-

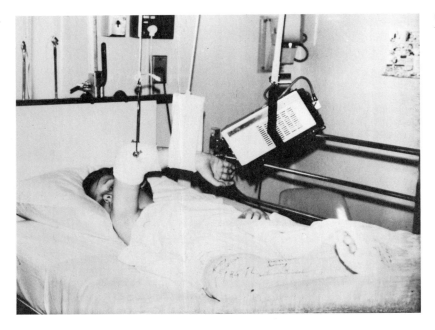

Figure 36-20 Overhead skeletal arm traction for treatment of a fractured humerus.

ing the limb as functional as possible with the use of prosthetic devices.

This type of injury has a devastating effect upon the family and they may be incapacitated with guilt. The grief reaction of the child at the loss of a body part varies with age. Younger children often make an amazing adaptation both physically and emotionally to this profound change in body function and body image. Older children have longer periods of mourning and adjustment. Parents and child require the maximal support possible to help the child make a healthy adjustment.

Care of the child with orthopedic surgery

Most orthopedic surgery in children is elective in nature. Common procedures include:

1. Various corrective procedures on bones themselves, such as surgical procedures for congenital dislocation of the hip
2. Muscle or tendon transplants to improve function of a part that has been damaged by trauma or other problem
3. Removal of bone tumors
4. Spinal fusion for scoliosis

Healing following surgical trauma usually requires some degree of immobilization. Most children with orthopedic surgical procedures will have casts applied immediately following the surgical procedure while they are still anesthetized.

Preoperative care

Preoperative diagnostic work consists mainly of x-rays and routine blood work. Preoperative nursing care concentrates heavily upon preparing the child and the family for the surgery and postoperative routine. The child who is to have surgery of the musculoskeletal system will require preparation similar to any other pediatric surgical patient. The child needs details on preoperative routines, an explanation of the surgery in appropriate language, an indication of the site of the incision, and details on the appearance and "feel" of the cast. As with all children, familiarity with the physical surroundings will reduce anxiety; visits to the surgical and recovery areas are helpful.

There is adequate time to prepare the surgical patient for casting. Some hospitals routinely use dolls with casts to demonstrate what the cast looks like. The child may see another child with a similar cast. In the absence of these, a simple drawing will be helpful.

The child and family need a thorough discussion of the degree of immobilization that will follow surgery. Parents may express concerns about their ability to care for the child if the child is to be discharged in a cast. They need answers to specific questions and reassurance that they will receive thorough instructions once the surgery has been performed.

Physical preparation includes shaving the incisional area. Care must be taken not to damage the skin in any way. Any skin lesion or break should be pointed out to the surgeon since this increases the chances of infection being transmitted to the bone. Usually, preoperative injections are not given near the operative area.

Whether or not the child will require preoperative teaching of coughing and deep breathing or using blow bottles will depend upon the extent of the surgery and the degree of immobilization. Children undergoing spinal fusion for scoliosis require careful attention in this area.

Both the parents and the child need preparation for postoperative pain. Orthopedic surgery is physically traumatic because the manipulation of bone requires much physical force, including sawing and chiseling. Orthopedic surgical procedures are accompanied by a considerable amount of pain. Besides pain in the immediate surgical area, children may complain of muscular aches and pains in other areas. Trauma to muscle may also produce muscle spasm following surgery. Morphine is the usual postoperative pain medication used with orthopedic procedures. Most children will require it regularly for 12 to 24 h after surgery, following which the child is progressed to some milder pain medication. A muscle relaxant may be required for the relief of muscle spasm as well.

Postoperative care

Postoperatively vital signs would be assessed at regular intervals, as they would after any surgical procedure. The length of the interval would be determined by the type of surgery. Assessment of vital signs will always include assessment of neurovascular status. The same procedure is used as when a cast is applied. Some swelling accompanies surgery and is to be expected. Postoperative elevation of an extremity is indicated to help prevent and reduce swelling (Fig. 36-21). Care should be taken when elevating an extremity that the cast is well supported since it will be wet when the child returns from surgery. Elevation on several pillows is often effective. Suspension of an extremity with slings and weights may also be used.

In most cases the incisional area and wound dressing are covered with plaster. Once blood saturates the dressing, it will be absorbed by the cast. Some staining of the cast with blood immediately over the incision is usual. If the staining is increasing, it is common to outline the stain with a ball point pen and mark the time on the cast. When the nurse or physician returns to recheck the child, they can see how much more staining has occurred in that period of time. The nurse should also describe the inten-

Figure 36-21 Elevation of an extremity following surgery to reduce swelling.

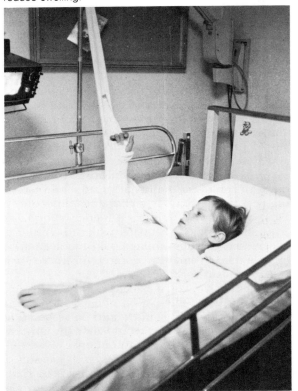

Figure 36-22 Staining of casts with blood following surgery.

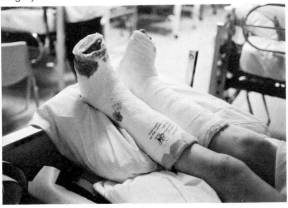

sity of the staining, just as one would with any surgical dressing. Figure 36-22 shows a cast stained with surgical drainage. This staining can be covered with more plaster before discharge to improve the appearance of the cast.

During the postoperative period, parents need to learn to care for the child in preparation for discharge. These instructions would be the same as any parents would receive when their child is being discharged with a cast. Parents of children with surgery also need to be aware of the signs of infection: temperature elevation, wound drainage staining the cast, or a foul odor emanating from the cast.

Children may return to the surgeon's office for cast removal. Children with more extensive procedures may be readmitted to the hospital for cast removal and physical therapy.

Congenital disorders

Clubfoot

In clubfoot (talipes equinovarus) the foot is adducted and there is inversion and equinus (plantar flexion) of the foot. A clubfoot is illustrated in Fig. 36-23A. The true clubfoot has an anatomic deformity of the muscles and bones that prevents it from being manipulated into a normal position. In contrast, some infants are born with a positional deformity of the foot simulating clubfoot, but with manipulation this foot can be placed in a corrected position. The most common method of treating clubfoot is serial casting. Starting shortly after birth, plaster casts are applied to gently and gradually correct the deformity. These are changed at weekly intervals until correction is obtained, usually within a few months. Once correction is obtained, the parents are instructed in exercises for the feet. Bivalved casts may be used to hold the foot in the corrected position during sleep. These are casts that have been applied, dried, and split into anterior and posterior halves. They may be reapplied periodically and held in place by wrapping with elastic bandages. Corrective shoes may also be used for maintaining correction. These may be used in conjunction with a Dennis-Browne bar. This is a metal bar fastened to the soles of the shoes which will help maintain the feet in the desired position.

Most infants will have good correction with treatment. A small percentage may require more extensive surgical treatment, such as a tendon transplant, to prevent recurrence of the problem.

Metatarsus adductus

In this condition, also called *metatarsus varus*, the forefoot is adducted in relation to the posterior portion of the foot (Fig. 36-23B). In some infants the condition can be passively corrected by holding the hindfoot and pressing the forefoot into a normal position. In these cases, corrections can be obtained through an exercise program as the parents regularly place the forefoot in the normal position. Straight last or reverse last shoes may be used to achieve or maintain correction. Normal shoes have a last that curves inward at the forefoot. A straight last shoe has no curve while a reverse last shoe curves outward at the forefoot. The shoes may be placed on a Dennis-Browne bar at night so that the child sleeps with the feet turned outward.

If the feet cannot be placed in the correct position passively, then a true bony deformity exists. This usually requires serial casting. Casts may then be followed by straight or reverse last shoes to maintain correction.

Congenital dislocation of the hip

Dislocation of the hip at birth is just one extreme of a problem usually referred to as *congenital hip dysplasia*. This condition consists of an instability of the hip joint where (1) the head of the femur may be easily dislocated, (2) the head of the femur may be subluxed or riding higher in the hip socket than usual, or (3) the head of

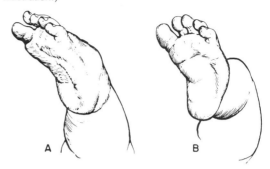

Figure 36-23 Congenital foot deformities. (*A*) Clubfoot. (*B*) metatarsus adductus. (*Courtesy of Craig Gosling, Indiana University School of Medicine, Department of Medical Illustration.*)

the femur may be dislocated or actually out of the hip socket (or acetabulum). All gradations of the problem require immediate treatment in order that the hip may develop normally.

The exact cause of congenital hip dysplasia is not known. There is some familial tendency and the condition is more prevalent in females. There may be some relationship between relaxation of the hip capsule (the ligaments that surround and stabilize the hip) and congenital hip dysplasia. Position of the baby in the mother's uterus and breech birth may contribute to the condition as well.

The hip joint at birth is still largely cartilage. It is necessary that the head of the femur be in the correct position in the hip socket so that the socket develops a normal shape and configuration as growth and ossification proceed. If the condition is left untreated, as the child begins to walk the hip will develop an abnormal configuration. Once this has occurred, treatment is much more difficult. For this reason, early diagnosis and treatment are extremely important.

Part of every newborn assessment is aimed at assessing the hips. Typical signs of congenital hip dysplasia are: unequal skin folds on the thigh or buttocks, unequal height of the knees when the infant is lying on a firm surface with the hips and knees flexed, limitation of abduction of the affected hip, or a click (Ortolani's sign) heard or felt as the hip is abducted. These three signs can be checked for easily and quickly by any nurse doing a newborn assessment. Figure 36-24 shows how this is done. Presence of any of the signs should be reported to the physician and usually

Figure 36-24 Checking for signs of hip dysplasia. The nurse checks: (A) abduction of the thighs (there is full abduction on the right and limited abduction on the left), (B) relative height of the knees (the right knee is higher than the left) and (C) symmetry of the skin folds in the gluteus and thighs (skin folds are asymmetrical). [*From Gladys Scipien et al. (eds.), Comprehensive Pediatric Nursing, McGraw-Hill, New York, 1979. Used by permission of the publisher.*]

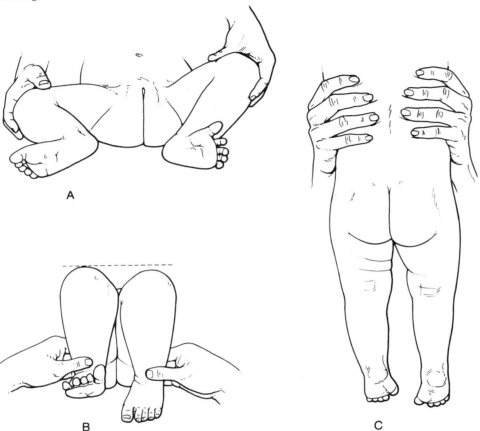

would indicate that x-rays of the hips be taken. If some degree of hip dysplasia is present, treatment in early infancy is relatively simple. The head of the femur is placed in the acetabulum and kept there. This is accomplished by keeping the legs in a position of abduction. How this is accomplished is dependent upon the severity of the problem. In very mild cases of dysplasia, triple diapering and pinning from front to back may be used to hold the legs in abduction. The Frejka splint, a pillow-like device worn over the diapers and secured over the infant's shoulders to keep the legs abducted, may be used. When the condition is more severe, the position of the

hip may be maintained by a cast. The length of treatment is determined by the progress of the hip on x-ray. Usually within several months the hip is developing normally.

Children with undiagnosed and untreated congenital dislocation of the hip develop an abnormal gait when they begin to walk, which may cause parents to seek medical attention. When the child bears weight on the affected hip, the pelvis drops on the opposite side. When dislocation is bilateral, this results in a waddling gait. The longer congenital hip dysplasia goes undetected, the more difficult the treatment. Walking tends to increase the upward displacement of the head of the femur. Older infants and children may require traction to bring the head of the femur down to the level of the acetabulum. Older children may require traction and surgical reduction to place the head of the femur in the acetabulum. These treatments are followed by immobilization in a spica cast. The success of treatment decreases as the child's age increases.

Torticollis

Contraction and fibrosis of the sternocleidomastoid muscle produce a condition known as *torticollis*, or *wryneck*. The shortening of the muscle results in the head being tilted toward the affected side and the chin being rotated to the opposite side. There may also be a fibrous mass within the affected muscle. The cause of this congenital condition is not known. Torticollis may be evident at birth or may not appear until several weeks after birth.

Treatment consists of gradual stretching of the contracted muscle with exercise. Parents are also encouraged to position the child so that he or she will turn the head toward the affected side when the child's attention is attracted to help stretch the muscle. If these exercises are started early and continued faithfully, most children will obtain good correction within a few months. A small number of cases may require surgical treatment.

Congenital amputation and phocomelia

Infants are born with all degrees and varieties of absence and deformity of the extremities. Various terms are used to describe these conditions. *Syndactylism* is the joining of two digits. *Polydactylism* is the presence of extra digits. *Amelia* is the absence of an extremity (sometimes called *congenital amputation*), and *phocomelia* is the attachment of a limb directly to the trunk with an intervening portion missing. Severity of limb deformities varies from the presence of a small extra digit to the complete absence of all four extremities.

All of these conditions arise in embryonic life when the limb buds are developing. Drugs administered in the first 3 months of pregnancy may induce these defects, as occurred in Europe with the use of the drug thalidomide.

Treatment is aimed at allowing the child to develop as much normal function of the involved extremity as possible. This may include surgical procedures. Extra digits may be surgically removed. Attachments, or webbing, between digits may be removed or reduced. A finger may be moved to serve as a thumb. In some cases amputation of a deformed limb is necessary to allow for the use of prosthetic devices that will allow the child more normal function.

Nursing management Initial nursing care is aimed at helping the parents deal with the grief response accompanying the diagnosis of a congenital problem. Although musculoskeletal problems are not usually life-threatening, they may have long-term effects upon the child's physical mobility and life-style. They are also quite visible to others. Parents often have questions about the long-term effects. Will the child be able to run and play normally or participate in athletics? How will it affect the child's appearance? These may seem like minor concerns to some, but they are major to the parents.

Parents need careful explanations of treatments, especially those to be continued at home. The nurse must take into consideration that the parents are just learning to care for a newborn. Caring for a newborn in a cast may seem overwhelming at first. If an exercise regimen is part of the treatment plan, parents should have the opportunity to demonstrate correct execution of the exercises several times, since the success of the treatment may depend upon this.

Developmental problems

Shoes for normal feet

Parents often have questions about shoes for their children. Shoes are basically protection for the feet from physical trauma and temperature extremes. Children with normal feet do not need shoes for support. Usually a baby needs shoes when beginning to stand or walk outdoors, where foot protection and warmth are needed. Infant shoes are made somewhat higher around the ankle so that the child will keep them on the foot. In infants the heel tends to be rounded and a shoe with a lower cut will easily slip off the foot. No ankle support is needed. When the heel is sufficiently developed so a regular oxford or sneaker will stay on the foot, these may be worn. Shoes do not need to be expensive but need to fit properly, allowing some room for growth.

Flat feet

When the medial arch of the foot is absent upon standing, this is commonly described as *flat foot*. This causes the foot to pronate or roll toward the medial or inward side. Infants almost always assume this position when they first stand or walk with the feet wide apart. There is very little medial arch apparent on an infant's foot. As the child gradually brings the feet closer together, the body weight is shifted towards the center of the foot. With growth and redistribution of body fat, the medial arch becomes more developed.

In older children, flat feet need treatment if they cause the child discomfort or limit his physical activity. Often the foot has a normal looking medial arch without weight bearing down on it, but the arch disappears when the child is bearing body weight. This may be caused by weakness or laxity of the foot ligaments. Children with flat feet may toe-in because it changes the weight distribution on the foot and alleviates foot strain.

The treatment is to supply support for the medial arch of the foot. A shoe with a heel will sometimes improve the weight distribution on the foot. A Thomas heel, which has a forward extension on the medial side, is sometimes used for flat feet.[9]

Toeing-in and toeing-out

There are many reasons for children walking with the toes pointing in or out. It can result from problems with the foot itself or problems elsewhere in the leg, including the hip. The position of the knees will indicate whether the problem is above or below the knees. If the knee is in the midline position while the foot turns, the problem is below the knee. If the knees deviate as well, then the problem is above the knees. Most causes of toeing-in and toeing-out correct themselves with growth and maturation.

Internal torsion, or twisting, of the tibia is a fairly common occurrence in infants. It causes a toeing-in gait but is self-correcting within the first few years of life. It usually requires no treatment. Torsion of the tibia or femur and the associated toeing-in or toeing-out gait may be associated with persistent postures assumed by the child: sleeping with the legs turned inward or sitting on the floor with the knees bent and the feet turned outward. Discouraging assump-

tion of these positions may help to correct the problem.

Bow-legs and knock-knees

Both of these occur normally in the process of growth and development of the lower extremities. Infants often appear bow-legged, but by the age of 3 may appear knock-kneed. The degree to which these occur is influenced by the hereditary pattern. By age 7 or 8, most children's legs are straight.

Pains in the musculoskeletal system

Pain in muscles and joints is a common occurrence in children. It may be due to excessive activity. Growth itself places some stress upon bone and muscle. Many children experience what are commonly called "growing pains." These typically occur during the night. The child awakens complaining of pain. There is no redness or swelling and pain does not seem to increase with joint motion. It is usually relieved by rubbing or by applying heat or cold. The pain is gone in the morning. Any pain that is regular and persistent or does not follow this pattern needs to be investigated by a physician.

Hereditary disorders

Muscular dystrophy

This hereditary disease occurs in several different forms. Two common forms of inheritance are recognized.

Pseudohypertrophic, or Duchenne's, muscular dystrophy is transmitted in a sex-linked recessive pattern. This means that the vast majority of victims are boys. The onset of the disease is usually early childhood, often before 5 years of age. There is a characteristic enlargement, or pseudohypertrophy, of certain muscle groups caused by infiltration of the muscle with fat. Initially, the child may experience difficulty with walking or playing. Progressive weakness in all skeletal muscles occurs until the child is confined to a wheelchair. Death usually occurs before adult life.

Another less severe form of the disease follows a dominant pattern of inheritance. Onset in this form occurs later in childhood. The first muscle groups affected are those of the upper torso and face, and weakness gradually spreads downward.

There is no effective treatment for this disorder.

Since these children tend to develop contractures, exercises may be prescribed to help prevent or delay this occurrence. Braces may be used for support.

Nursing Management During the diagnostic phase, the nurse's main concerns are preparing the child for diagnostic tests and assisting family members as they confront the possibility of a diagnosis of muscular dystrophy and its long-term ramifications.

Diagnostic tests include: drawing of blood for enzyme levels, which are typically elevated in muscular dystrophy; giving an electromyelogram; and performing a muscle biopsy. An electromyelogram involves the insertion of needles into the muscle mass to measure electrical activity; it is a painful test for the child. Muscle biopsy is a surgical procedure and requires preparation for anesthesia and surgery.

Parents need to understand the pattern of transmission of the disease and the possibility of bearing future children with the disorder. A referral to a genetic counselor is usually helpful.

Osteogenesis imperfecta

This condition is characterized by fragile bones which fracture easily. Also associated with it is the characteristic eye trait of having blue sclerae. Some persons with this condition also develop deafness later in life. Osteogenesis imperfecta is thought to be a dominant hereditary trait.

Two forms are recognized. In the congenital form, fractures occur in utero or at birth. In these cases the disease is usually severe and produces a great deal of deformity or death. In the late form of the disease, fractures may not appear until several years after birth. These cases are usually milder with fewer fractures, and the tendency to fracture disappears after puberty. Children with osteogenesis imperfecta have some degree of growth retardation, depending upon the severity of the disease.

Treatment of the disease aims at preventing deformity as a result of the frequent fractures. In children with severe osteogenesis imperfecta, the use of rods surgically placed within the long bones may prevent further fracture and deformity.

Nursing Management Caring for these children requires delicate and gentle handling to avoid breaking a bone. Usually the parents or the child alone can give excellent instructions in this regard with their knowledge of just how much stress the bones can tolerate.

During the period of diagnosis, parents need genetic counseling to recognize the risks to future offspring and the risk factors for their children when they arrive at childbearing age. In some areas parent support groups are available for parents of children with this condition.

Acquired alterations in mobility
Juvenile rheumatoid arthritis

Juvenile rheumatoid arthritis, or Still's disease, is a systemic disease of the connective tissues in which the primary manifestation is joint involvement. It shares many symptoms with other diseases of the connective tissues, such as lupus and rheumatic fever, and must be distinguished from them. The cause of the disease remains unknown, although it is felt by many to be a hyperimmune or hypersensitivity response of the body. The highest incidence occurs in children under 6 years of age.[10]

The onset of the disease may be very sudden with rash, fever, anemia, and enlargement of the lymph nodes, liver, and spleen. Joint pain may be present initially or the systemic symptoms may precede the joint pain. Other children will develop a more insidious onset of the disease with the gradual development of joint stiffness, swelling, and pain. Joint involvement varies from one to many joints. During acute phases, joints appear swollen and are warm to touch.

Involvement of the joint begins with edema, inflammation of the synovial membrane, and an increase in the amount of joint fluid. Inflammation and scarring may cause permanent damage to the joint. The pathological changes produce pain and limitation of movement. The child also tends to limit motion as a protective mechanism and holds the joint in a position of flexion, leading to flexion contractures. Most children experience considerable morning stiffness in involved joints. Other complications may include pericarditis and *iridocyclitis*, or inflammation of the iris and ciliary body of the eye.

The disease is often characterized by periods of recurrent exacerbation and remission of the disease. Usually the first episode is the most severe with the greatest systemic symptoms.

During remission the only symptom may be morning stiffness.

The general prognosis is good. Some children will recover completely within a few years. In the majority, the disease will be in permanent remission by adolescence. The amount of residual damage to joints will depend upon the severity and length of activity of the disease and the treatment.

Treatment is aimed at maintaining normal function and preventing deformity of the joints. Although the child may need bed rest during acute phases, this rest should not include prolonged immobility of the joints. A program of physical therapy is instituted. During periods of remission, the child and family may be taught exercises to maintain joint mobility. Aspirin is the most effective medication for these children, providing relief from pain and an anti-inflammatory action. Corticosteroid medications may be used in severe cases, but prolonged administration of these drugs may interfere with growth.

Nursing management The lack of any specific treatment or cure and the unpredictable course makes this a frustrating and frightening disease for the parents and child. The child is usually hospitalized only during acute episodes. The family needs continuous support and encouragement and sometimes they can obtain this help from their private physician or a public health nurse.

Since the child is on long-term aspirin therapy, the nurse must be familiar with the signs of aspirin toxicity and teach these to the parents. These signs include: ringing in the ears, a rash, bruising easily, or any unusual bleeding. Aspirin is very irritating to the stomach and will be better tolerated if administered with food. When aspirin therapy is instituted, the dosages will usually be checked by the drawing of blood samples for blood salicylate levels. Most parents think of aspirin as a benign medication to be taken intermittently for relief of pain. The importance of regular administration and maintenance of a therapeutic level of the medication in the child's bloodstream must be carefully explained to them.

During acute episodes, an exercise program will often be prescribed to be carried out by the nurse or physical therapist. Whenever possible, active motion of the joint by the child is best. Hot compresses to joints or warm baths may be used to help alleviate stiffness. Night splints may be used to hold joints in extension and help prevent flexion contractures. Since movement produces pain, the child is afraid of movement. Gentleness in handling and moving is indicated.

Osteomyelitis

Infection in the bone, or osteomyelitis, arises from one of three sources: contamination of a fracture, introduction of infection during a surgical procedure, or blood-borne infection secondary to infection elsewhere in the body. The causative organism is usually streptococcus or staphylococcus.

When the condition is blood-borne, it tends to localize in the bone metaphyses, but may then spread to other parts of the bone. The initial symptoms are: fever, pain, and decreased movement of the affected part. There may be swelling, redness, or heat depending upon the extent of the infection. The child may be seriously ill with septicemia.

The treatment is intravenous antibiotics for a period of several weeks, combined with immobilization of the extremity by the use of splints, bivalved casts, or skin traction. Many infections respond well to this treatment. If abcess formation occurs, surgical drainage of the infected area may be necessary. Treatment is aimed at preventing the spread of the infection to other areas of the bone, particularly the epiphyseal area, since the infection can damage the epiphyseal cartilage and interfere with normal growth. Inadequate treatment can lead to a chronic osteomyelitis, which may resist treatment.

Nursing Management The child will have several weeks of immobilization and intravenous antibiotic therapy. Protection and care of the intravenous injection site will ensure that the child receives antibiotics at regularly scheduled intervals (see Chap. 17).

If the infected area is open or has been surgically drained, careful precautions must be taken to avoid the spread of organisms to other patients or visitors.

Children with osteomyelitis are discharged on oral antibiotics, often to be continued for a period of months. The family must understand the importance of regular, long-term administration of antibiotics, even when symptoms are absent.

Synovitis of the hip

Synovitis is an acute inflammation of the hip that is self-limiting and of short duration. It may occur secondary to trauma. When there has been no trauma, there has often been an acute respiratory illness a week or two before the hip symptoms appeared. It usually occurs in males between 3 and 10 years of age.[11]

The child complains of pain, sometimes referred to the knee, and may limp. A fever is often present. The range of motion of the joint is limited, and there is usually a flexion contracture of the hip. The joint may be tender when palpated.

The hip is immobilized with traction, often split Russell's traction. This usually provides relief of pain and corrects the hip flexion contracture. Within a few days, full motion of the hip without pain has returned. Sometimes weight-bearing is limited for a short period after initial treatment with traction.

Legg-Perthes disease

Synovitis must be differentiated from Legg-Perthes disease, or aseptic necrosis of the head of the femur. Synovitis may precede the onset of Legg-Perthes, or it may begin with no previous hip problems. The onset is less acute than in synovitis. The child complains of knee pain, and there may be a limp for a period of weeks. There is limitation of motion and a hip flexion contracture. The prime incidence is again in males in the 3 to 10 year group.[12]

The disease generally progresses in three stages: (1) onset period with pain and limp lasting several weeks, (2) necrosis of the head of the femur, lasting a year or longer, and (3) regeneration of the head of the femur, which may take several years.

Initial treatment is bed rest and immobilization with traction. This relieves pain and restores motion to the hip. When initial symptoms have subsided, the child may be permitted to ambulate without bearing weight on the affected hip. A number of orthopedic appliances have been devised to allow this. Whatever method is used, it will be continued until the regenerative phase of the disease is well under way. Bearing weight prior to that time results in flattening of the head of the femur and permanent distortion of the hip joint.

Nursing management Since traction in Legg-Perthes makes the child more comfortable, it is usually well-accepted initially. As pain subsides, it will be more difficult for the child to understand why bed rest is necessary. It is extremely important that the parents understand the course of the disease since successful treatment is based upon a long period of the child's not bearing weight. It is the parents who must be diligent in enforcing strict compliance with the prescribed regimen. Parents need to discuss adaptation in the child's daily living pattern that will make adjustment to this change in mobility as easy as possible for all concerned.

Slipped femoral epiphysis

In a growing child the epiphyseal plate represents a weak area in the bone. Stress to this area can result in slippage across the epiphyseal line, displacing the epiphysis from its usual position. The most common place for this to occur is at the upper femoral epiphysis. Figure 36-25A shows a normal hip and Fig. 36-25B shows one in which a medial slip of the femoral head has occurred.

This condition occurs most commonly between 10 and 17 years of age in boys. Girls are less frequently affected.[13] It occurs more frequently in overweight children and in children who are thin and have recently had a period of rapid adolescent growth.

The onset of symptoms is insidious. The child complains of pain in the hip, knee, or thigh over a period of time and may have a limp. The leg tends to externally rotate and range of motion may be limited. The diagnosis is made by x-ray visualization of the slip.

Once the condition is diagnosed, weight-bearing is immediately stopped and the child is placed in traction. The most common treatment is surgical; a pin or screw is inserted through the epiphyseal line to secure the epiphysis and prevent further slippage. Care must be taken during treatment and surgery that no further trauma to the epiphyseal plate occurs and that the blood supply to the femoral head is not disturbed. Interference with the blood supply can result in necrosis of the head of the femur.

Postoperatively, the child will be placed in

Figure 36-25 (*A*) A normal hip. (*B*) A medial slip of the head of the femur. [*From Robert A. Hoekelman et al. (eds.), Principles of Pediatrics, McGraw-Hill, New York, 1978. Used by permission of the publisher.*]

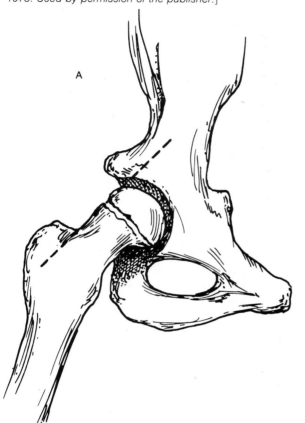

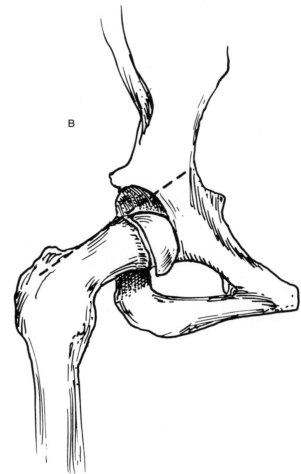

traction and progressed to partial weight-bearing with crutches for discharge. The child will be gradually progressed to full weight-bearing. The pin is removed after the epiphysis has closed, which may be as long as several years after surgery.

Nursing management If the child has been a very active, athletic adolescent, this condition is going to greatly change the child's life-style. The nurse needs to explore how the patient and the family are responding to this anticipated change. Some families and some adolescents place great emphasis on athletic achievements and may find this a difficult adjustment. The patient and family must understand the rationale for and the importance of instructions regarding activity.

If the adolescent is overweight, then a consultation with the dietitian and discussion of weight control is needed. Extra body weight places more stress on the epiphyseal plate.

During follow-up care, the other hip is observed for signs of slippage, since some children will develop the condition bilaterally.

Scoliosis

Scoliosis is a lateral curvature of the spine. In *functional scoliosis*, the spinal curvature can be voluntarily corrected by the patient. This type of curvature results from poor posture or compensation for some other problem, such as unequal leg length. Attention to the underlying problem will correct the spinal curvature. In *structural scoliosis*, the curve cannot be voluntarily corrected by the patient. The curve is typically S-shaped. Some of the curvature of the spine is an attempt by the body to compensate for the change in posture that is resulting from the scoliosis (Fig. 36-26).

Structural scoliosis can result from a large number of underlying diseases or conditions involving bones, muscles, or nerves that result in an imbalance of the forces usually placed on the spine. The majority of cases of scoliosis are idiopathic in nature; i.e. no known underlying cause can be identified. About 85 percent of cases of idiopathic scoliosis are girls.[14] There is sometimes a family history of scoliosis. The curve can begin to develop at any time, but idiopathic scoliosis most frequently appears in adolescence, because there is rapid growth during this period.

The curve may be detected by the parents. Improperly fitting clothes or a crooked hemline sometimes prompt the parents to have a closer look at the child's body. The curve may be detected during a routine physical exam at school or by the family physician. Early diagnosis of the curve before it becomes severe makes it more likely that nonoperative means of correction will be successful. Some schools have

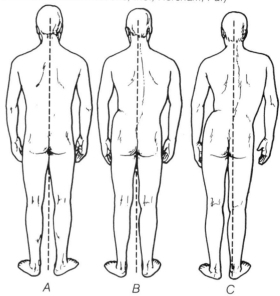

Figure 36-26 A normal spine is shown on the left. The middle figure demonstrates a compensated scoliosis; i.e., fairly normal posture has been maintained despite the curvature of the spine. The scoliosis on the right has progressed to the point where compensation for the curvature is no longer possible. (*Reprinted with permission from the May issue of Nursing 77. Copyright © 1977, Intermed Communications, Inc., Horsham, Pa.*)

A   B   C

Table 36-1 Examination of the back as done in routine scoliosis screening

Position of student	Observations by the examiner*
1. Standing erect, feet together, arms hanging straight down (Examiner seated, observing student's back)	**1.** Shoulder level unequal? **2.** Hip level unequal? **3.** Waistline uneven? **4.** Spine curved? **5.** One shoulder blade more prominent than other? **6.** Distances between arms and body unequal?
2. Bending forward at the waist, back parallel with floor, feet together, knees unbent, arms hanging freely, palms together (Examiner seated, observing front and rear of student)	**1.** Difference in level between two sides of the back? **2.** Hump on one side of the upper back? **3.** Compensating hump on other side of lower back?

* If findings are positive, there is a possibility of scoliosis. From G. Scipien et al. (eds.), *Comprehensive Pediatric Nursing*, 2d ed., McGraw-Hill, New York, 1978.
Source: Adapted from "Scoliosis Screening for Early Detection," Multi Video International Inc., Minneapolis, MN, 1975.

screening programs for detection of scoliosis. See Table 36-1.

Treatment is based upon the measurement of the lateral curves on x-rays. If the curve is mild, then the child will be followed with regular x-rays to observe for progression of the curve. Many cases will never progress to the point where treatment is required. The pattern of progression of the curve is unpredictable. Increase in the curvature often accompanies a growth spurt. Once growth is completed, no further increase in the curve will occur.

Nonoperative treatment is based upon use of the Milwaukee brace, illustrated in Fig. 36-27, in conjunction with an exercise program. The brace applies corrective force to the curve, achieving some correction and preventing an increase in the curvature. The brace may have to be worn until growth is completed. If the curve is severe when seen initially or continues to progress despite treatment with the Milwaukee brace, then surgical treatment is indicated.

Figure 36-27 Milwaukee brace. (*From Nancy E. Hilt and William E. Schmitt, Jr., Pediatric Orthopedic Nursing, Mosby, St. Louis, 1975. Used by permission of the publisher.*)

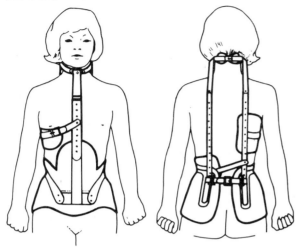

Surgical treatment involves straightening of the spine as much as possible through the use of casts or traction and then fusing the vertebrae in that position so that the curvature cannot recur or progress. During surgery, the vertebrae to be fused are curretted. Over this are laid small pieces of bone graft taken from the patient's iliac crest. The curve may be further stabilized by the insertion of a metal rod—the Harrington rod. Postoperatively, as the bone heals, it will fuse into a solid mass of bone.

There are several methods of straightening or decreasing the curve preoperatively. Commonly used is the application of a localizer cast, extending from the neck down over the hips (Fig. 36-28). This is applied over a piece of body stockinette with the patient on a special table. Pressure is applied to the curve to straighten it while the cast is applied. The plaster then holds the spine in the corrected position before, during, and after surgery. The cast may be applied a few days or a few weeks before the spinal fusion. Usually, the back of the cast is cut out for the surgery and replaced afterwards. Before discharge a new cast is applied.

In children with more severe curves that require more correction than can be obtained with a localizer cast, the straightening process will be more gradual. A turnbuckle cast may be used

(Fig. 36-6). The cast is applied and a turnbuckle apparatus allows the cast and spine to gradually be straightened over a period of weeks. When sufficient correction is obtained, a fusion is performed. Halofemoral or halopelvic traction may be used to straighten severe curves. Skeletal pins are inserted into the skull and attached to a metal halo encircling the head and into either the distal femurs or pelvis. These pins are attached to traction and the spine is gradually pulled into a straighter position. After surgery, the halo apparatus may be incorporated into a cast.

Following surgery, the patient may be on bed rest for several months at home. When a rod stabilizes the surgical area, ambulation may be permitted. After about 6 months, the patient is

Figure 36-28 Adolescent in a localizer cast following spinal fusion.

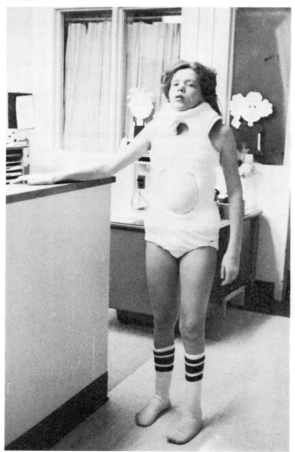

readmitted for evaluation and cast change. The cast is often reduced in size at this time and worn for another 6 months (Fig. 36-29). Once healing is completed and the cast removed, very strenuous or contact sports may be permanently prohibited.

Nursing management Adolescents with scoliosis face a frightening physical ordeal. Wearing a bulky, strange-looking brace for many years will not be easily accepted by the adolescent. Proper use of the Milwaukee brace requires that it be worn 23 h a day. Use of the brace does not guarantee that surgery will not be necessary. Caring for adolescents with scoliosis and spinal fusion requires incorporation of all the principles of nursing care involved with immobilization, casts or traction, and orthopedic surgery. They are challenging patients.

The scoliosis occurs at a time when the patient's body is changing from child to adult form, and there are already many concerns about body appearance. X-rays and examinations of the spine require that the adolescent disrobe extensively—something they often find extremely embarrassing. Every effort should be made to protect the patient's modesty when possible and to explain why these examinations are necessary. When a cast is applied, the nurse can be sure that the body stockinette is applied before the patient is taken to the cast room, so that he or she will not be unnecessarily exposed.

Preparation for casting should also include seeing the table that is used for cast application and explaining the sensations experienced. Patients may receive a tranquilizing medication prior to cast application. The stockinette is frequently pulled over the patient's head during the cast application. This helps to keep plaster dust out of the patient's nose and mouth. The patient needs reassurance that he or she can breathe through the stockinette.

If the cast is too tight, it may produce "cast syndrome"—vomiting from compression of the stomach. A hole cut in the cast over the abdominal area will often alleviate this.

Skeletal traction apparatuses look painful and frightening. Patients seem to experience little pain from the skeletal pins themselves but may experience pain or muscle spasm as weights are applied or increased to the traction.

Adolescents are always concerned about the

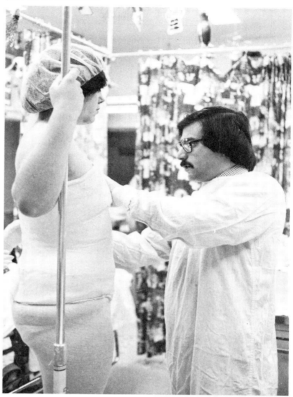

Figure 36-29 Body jacket being applied to an adolescent 6 months after spinal fusion for scoliosis. Localizer cast had just been removed.

effect of the treatment on their appearance. The correction of the curve will improve their general appearance, and this has a very positive effect on the acceptance of treatment. Patients may have specific questions about scarring from surgery or pin sites. They are always concerned about being accepted by their peers in a strange-looking cast. Adolescent girls may be concerned about the effect of a tight cast on breast development; breast development will not be affected.

These patients have extensive surgery with significant blood loss, often requiring transfusion. They need careful and frequent assessments of vital signs and neurological function. Spinal fusion always carries with it some risk of disruption of the blood supply to the spinal cord or spinal nerves, interfering with neurological function below that point. Postoperatively, the

(Continued on page 1031)

Nursing Care Plan–Surgery for Scoliosis Repair

Patient: Janet Myers **Age:** 16 years, 2 months **Date of Admission:** 4/27, 9:30 A.M.

Assesssment

Janet Myers, a 16-year-old girl, was accompanied by her mother and father on admission for spinal fusion to straighten her back. She appears to be a healthy and well-nourished adolescent. Her weight is appropriate for her height. She appeared neatly dressed in jeans and a sweater.

Janet has had no prior hospitalization. She has no allergies. Her health has been good; the only previous illnesses that required treatment were respiratory illnesses. She has a history of recurrent middle-ear infections, but the last episode was several years ago. Her regular physician has given her the usual childhood immunizations. He noted the beginning of scoliosis 2 years ago and referred her to an orthopedist, who has followed the case since then. She has been wearing a Milwaukee brace for almost 2 years, but during the past 6 months her scoliosis has worsened despite the brace and exercises. She is admitted for cast application and fusion with insertion of Harrington rods. She was not wearing the brace upon admission.

Physical assessment Height: 5'4", Weight: 110 lb, Temp.: 36.7°C (98.0°F), Pulse: 80, Respirations: 24/min, BP: 102/74

Diet and Elimination: Eats three meals a day plus a snack after school. Eats most foods. Describes her appetite as good. Likes pork chops and lasagna. Dislikes cauliflower. Liquid intake at home consists of milk, tea, fruit juice, and occasional soft drinks. Has had no problems with elimination.

Dental: Janet is wearing braces. Sees dentist and orthodontist on a regular basis.

Reproductive: Menarche occurred 6 months ago. Menstrual periods have been somewhat irregular. Last menstrual period was about 3 weeks ago. Experiences some cramps on first day of menstrual period. Some breast development is apparent, and patient wears a bra.

Skin: Appears intact and healthy. Face breaks out occasionally. Skin over back is clear.

Musculoskeletal: Limbs appear equal in size. Gait appears normal. Scoliosis is apparent. Left hip is higher than right. Shoulders appear of even height. Able to move all body parts normally. Plays volleyball at school. Scoliosis has not interfered with normal activity. Patient has had no pain. Has normal response to touch and prick in extremities. Lower extremities appear pink, warm, and evidence good capillary filling.

Daily patterns: Arises at 7:00 A.M., dresses, eats breakfast, and catches school bus at 7:40 A.M. Attends school from 8 A.M. until 2:30 P.M. Often visits with friends after school. Sometimes helps with dinner preparation. After dinner, does homework or watches TV. Usual bedtime is 10 P.M.

Hobbies and activities: Enjoys reading, painting, and listening to music. Art is her favorite subject at school.

Reaction to illness: Feels scoliosis is becoming noticeable. Has many questions about cast application. Concerned about cast appearance and what clothing she'll be able to wear over the cast. Expressed no explicit concerns about the surgery itself. Wonders how she will feed herself and care for herself in a cast. Parents had numerous specific questions about how surgery is performed and about pre-operative and postoperative routines. Hair was long, but patient recently had it cut at the suggestion of the surgeon to make care easier in the cast. She has had short hair before and did not seem to object to this.

Nursing diagnosis	Nursing goals	Nursing actions	Evaluation/revision
1. Confusion about course of treatment because of lack of information	☐ Patient will understand: **a.** Sequence of treatment and procedures **b.** Amount of discomfort associated with each	☐ Explain casting procedure thoroughly, including subjective sensations ☐ Take patient to see cast room	☐ 4/27: Patient evidences good understanding of treatment regimen. She is particularly concerned about the cast application.

Nursing diagnosis	Nursing goals	Nursing actions	Evaluation/revision
	c. Final appearance of cast d. Limitations of mobility e. Usual length of each treatment phase	☐ Have patient talk with Rita S., who has had the same surgery ☐ Explain bivalving of cast for surgery ☐ Explain reasons for bed rest ☐ Explore questions about surgery (areas not clear from surgeon's explanation) ☐ Explain postoperative routines and care, including pain medication.	She thinks it will feel "tight—like I can't breathe." Reassured that cast will be snug, but she will have no difficulty breathing ☐ 4/27: Taken to cast room. Patient asked many questions about equipment. Did not seem overly anxious about procedure
2. Potential skin breakdown due to cast application and immobilization	☐ Patient's skin will be intact, comfortable, and normal in color	☐ Examine cast edges for roughness and pressure on skin ☐ Finish or pad edges, if necessary ☐ Examine skin at cast edges daily ☐ Keep cast clean and dry by careful toileting	☐ 4/28: Cast is very tight over iliac crests. Explained that cast will be slightly looser when bivalved tomorrow ☐ 4/29: Chin red—extra padding placed under front neck edge ☐ 5/10: Recasted—cast tight under arm; trimmed
3. Potential atelectasis from restriction of chest by cast, anesthesia, and immobilization	☐ Patient's lungs will remain clear on auscultation	☐ Teach coughing and deep breathing preoperatively ☐ Cough and deep breathe at least q2h upon return from RR for 24–48 h; then q4h ☐ Turn patient q2h ☐ Encourage patient to move about in bed	☐ 4/30: Coughing and deep breathing q2h. Needs much encouragement to cough effectively. IPPB ordered by surgeon. Lungs clear ☐ 5/1: Lungs clear
4. Potential hemorrhage from surgical procedure	☐ Patient's blood pressure, temperature, and pulse will remain within normal limits ☐ There will be usual amounts of bloody drainage from the wound	☐ Check VS and drainage q1h for 12 h ☐ Check VS and drainage q2h for 12 h ☐ Check VS and drainage q4h thereafter ☐ Check drain following surgery.	☐ 4/30: VS stable. Small amounts of bright red bloody drainage on back of cast ☐ 5/1: VS stable. No increase in drainage on cast
5. Potential neurovascular impairment from cast or surgery	☐ Neurovascular status of lower extremities and bladder function will remain normal following surgery	☐ Check NVS with each check of vital signs following surgery ☐ Encourage patient to void following surgery. Measure urine in each voiding ☐ Check bladder for distention	☐ 4/30: Moves lower extremities without difficulty. Responds to pin prick and touch ☐ Voided 500 ml 2 h after return from recovery room. Continues to void in large amounts at regular intervals without difficulty
6. Discomfort from cast and surgery	☐ Patient will be comfortable	☐ After cast application, position patient comfortably ☐ Administer pain medication promptly when required	☐ 4/28: Patient had difficulty sleeping night after cast application. Sleeping medication ordered; she

Nursing diagnosis	Nursing goals	Nursing actions	Evaluation/revision
		☐ Change position frequently ☐ Plan care to allow for uninterrupted rest periods	slept for about 3 h. She couldn't seem to find comfortable position ☐ 4/30: She requested sleep medication and slept soundly ☐ 4/30–5/1: Requesting pain medication about every 3 h. Medicated with morphine. Appears to have good relief of pain ☐ 5/3: Patient requests percodan several times a day ☐ 5/5: Requires pain medication once or twice a day, more often at night ☐ 5/9: Requires only Darvon compound for pain
7. Physical dependency due to surgery and immobilization	☐ Patient will accept temporary dependency but will gradually regain independence	☐ Elicit patient's feelings on being confined to bed and being dependent ☐ As she feels able, instruct in how to assist in turning, bathing, eating, and toileting	☐ 4/28: Patient accepts care of parents and nurses but attempts to help when possible. Accepts this as a temporary necessity ☐ 4/30: Attempting to assist with turning shortly after return from recovery room ☐ 5/1: Mother feeding liquids ☐ 5/2: Patient attempting to feed self ☐ 5/5: Able to turn and feed herself. Assists with toileting and bathing
	☐ Patient will attain as much mobility as possible within confines of the treatment regimen	☐ Ambulate after initial casting ☐ Encourage movement of arms and legs when confined to bed ☐ Assist with walking when recasted	☐ 4/28: Following casting, seemed to rapidly become accustomed to cast; balance is good ☐ 4/30: Moves well in bed ☐ 5/5: Exercising arms and legs ☐ 5/10: Ambulating well in new cast
8. Potential boredom or lag in development due to immobilization	☐ Patient will find stimulating activities once physically able	☐ Explore interests and activities ☐ Plan visit from recreational therapist	☐ 4/27: Learning to knit; yarn brought to hospital. Reads a great deal. Will ask library volunteer to stop by ☐ 5/3: Watching TV ☐ 5/5: Tried knitting, but arms get too tired; reading
9. Inability to attend school for about a month because of surgery	☐ Patient will remain current in school work	☐ Discuss plans for school work at home	☐ 4/28: Parents have arranged for a home-bound teacher for 2 weeks postop at home
	☐ Patient will maintain contact with peers	☐ Encourage visits from peers	☐ 4/28: Distance too far for friends to visit while hospi-

Nursing diagnosis	Nursing goals	Nursing actions	Evaluation/revision
		☐ Encourage contact with other adolescent patients	talized, but mother is sure they will visit at home ☐ 4/28: Friendly with other girls in room
10. Concern about body image and appearance because of developmental stage and effects of scoliosis treatment	☐ Patient will be comfortable with her appearance	☐ Try to elicit specific concerns about appearance ☐ Emphasize the positive effect upon appearance the correction of the scoliosis will have ☐ Discuss clothing patient can wear over cast ☐ Encourage patient to take an interest in her appearance	☐ 4/28: Concerned about her classmates reaction to her when she returns to school. Seemed to feel better when she saw herself in mirror after casting. "It's not as bad as I thought." ☐ 5/5: Mother brought in some new larger tops to wear over cast. This seemed to have a positive effect on Janet's morale ☐ 5/8: Patient has good personal hygiene habits and takes an interest in her appearance
11. Parental anxiety due to concern over surgical complications and lack of information	☐ Parents will be comfortable with treatment regimen and their child's progress	☐ Encourage questions ☐ Answers all questions thoroughly	☐ 4/27: Parents express much anxiety about surgical risks. Have discussed all these with surgeon and realize the chances of complications are small. Fears are realistic
	☐ Parents will feel confident in their ability to care for their child	☐ Involve in care as soon as they are willing ☐ Discuss adaptations to be made at home for care ☐ Give parents printed discharge instructions day before discharge so they can read and discuss questions ☐ Arrange for parents to call following discharge, if needed	☐ 4/30: Parents assisting with care as soon as child returned from RR. Asking how to turn ☐ 5/6: Mother employed; will take 1 week of vacation following discharge. After that, an Aunt will stay with Janet during the day until she is able to resume normal routine ☐ 5/9: Parents seem confident things will go well at home. Will call, if needed. Read dicharge instructions; no questions

neurovascular status of both lower extremities will be regularly checked. The patient's ability to void is also of special importance in ensuring that neurological function of the bladder has not been impaired.

Prevention of atelectasis needs special attention for several reasons. If the patient has had a severe curve, this may have interfered with pulmonary function. The cast may inhibit chest expansion. The patient has had a long period of general anesthesia and will be on bed rest for at least 10 days. Intermittent positive-pressure treatments may be indicated for lung expansion in addition to using blow bottles or coughing and deep breathing.

Most patients will have a nasogastric tube in

place for a day or so following surgery. Surgical pain involves not only a large incision at the fusion site but also an incision over the iliac crest graft site.

If the patient is to be discharged on bed rest, parents will need to learn physical care and discuss arrangements at home. Ambulatory patients will need assistance with physical care as they recover from surgery and become adjusted to daily life in a cast.

There is often long-term contact with adolescents with scoliosis during several hospitalizations. This makes working with them an extremely enjoyable and rewarding experience for the nurse.

References

1. Arthur Greenwald and Barry Head: *Wearing a Cast*, Family Communications, Pittsburgh, 1977.
2. Nancy E. Hilt and William E. Schmitt, *Pediatric Orthopedic Nursing*, Mosby Company, St. Louis, 1975, p. 91.
3. Ibid., p. 117.
4. Robert Jacobs: "Skateboard Accidents," *Pediatrics* 59:939–942 (June 1977).
5. Paul Ross, Edward P. Schwentker, and Hugh Bryan, "Mutilating Lawn Mower Injuries in Children, *Journal of the American Medical Association* 236:480–481 (August 2, 1976).
6. Ted J. Hartman, *Fracture Management: A Practical Approach*, Lea and Febiger, Philadelphia, 1978, p. 42.
7. Mihran O. Tachdjian: *Pediatric Orthopedics*, Saunders, Philadelphia, 1972, p. 1545.
8. Ibid., p. 1581.
9. Albert Barnett Ferguson: *Orthopaedic Surgery in Infancy and Childhood*, Williams & Wilkins, Baltimore, 1975, p. 84.
10. Ibid., p. 591.
11. Ibid., p. 237.
12. Ibid., p. 242.
13. Ibid., p. 226.
14. Ibid., p. 319.
15. The author wishes to acknowledge the assistance of the patients, personnel, and administration of Children's Hospital of Pittsburgh in the preparation of this chapter.

Chapter 37 **Perception and coordination**

Susan Steiner Nash and **Marjorie J. Smith**

Upon completion of this chapter, the student will be able to:

1. Describe the protective mechanisms of the brain.

2. Identify five neurological functions and the methods used to evaluate them in a nursing assessment.

3. Describe the nurse's responsibility before, during, and after neurological diagnostic tests.

4. List six signs and symptoms of increasing intracranial pressure.

5. Contrast two types of partial seizures and two types of generalized seizures.

6. Describe the nursing management of a child with a myelomeningocele.

7. Contrast communicating and noncommunicating hydrocephalus.

8. Describe three types of cerebral palsy.

9. Contrast developmental dyslexia with hyperkinesis in terms of nursing management.

10. Describe the nursing management of the child with bacterial meningitis.

11. Describe the nursing management of an unconscious child.

12. Describe the differences between concussion and contusions.

13. Describe the signs of spinal shock.

14. Discuss the nursing management of a child with spinal cord injury.

15. Identify signs and symptoms of lead poisoning.

Embryology of the nervous system

The foundation of the nervous system is established with the appearance of the *primitive streak* late in the second week of gestation. The primitive streak, formed from the ectoderm, establishes the longitudinal axis of the embryo. Cranial thickening of the primitive streak leads to development of a column of cells known as the *notochord.* The ectoderm overlying the notochord in the midbody region thickens and is known as the *neural plate.*

As the neural plate thickens and widens, it develops a groove. Its sides pull inward and gradually fuse, forming the *neural tube.* As the neural tube closes, the cephalic part of the tube begins to enlarge and expands to form the embryonic brain. The remaining and longest part of the neural tube becomes the spinal cord. The *lumen* (cavity) of the neural tube forms the central canal of the spinal cord and the *ventricles* (hollow chambers) of the brain. Genetic miscoding or exposure of the embryo to teratogenic agents (drugs, infections, or radiation) during the third to fourth week may result in failure of the neural tube to close, leading to serious defects such as myelomeningocele or anencephaly.

During the fifth week of gestation, the brain begins to separate into three major parts: (1) the forebrain (cerebrum), (2) the midbrain, and (3) the hindbrain (cerebellum and brainstem). The hindbrain further develops to form the *pons* and *cerebellum* and later the *medulla oblongata.* Cavities develop within the three sections and later become the ventricular system. At the same time the vertebral arches develop from the mesoderm.

During the eighth to twelfth weeks, the cerebellar hemispheres become evident. The growth of the head slows down as the body begins to catch up. The ventricles and the choroid plexuses within them, the medulla, and the midbrain continue their development.

Anatomy and physiology of the nervous system

Central nervous system

The central nervous system (CNS) is composed of two major components—the brain and spinal cord (Fig. 37-1). The brain is made up of the cerebrum, the cerebellum, and the brainstem.

The *cerebrum*, or cerebral cortex, is divided by a longitudinal fissure into the right and left hemispheres. Each hemisphere is further divided (Fig. 37-2) into the frontal, parietal, temporal, and occipital lobes, and the insula (deep within brain).

The *cerebellum* lies between the cerebrum and brainstem. Acting on information coming into it through the spinal cord and brainstem, it is responsible for smooth and coordinated movements by refining signals from the cortex.

The *brainstem* lies between the cervical vertebrae and the cerebellum. It is made up of the medulla, pons, midbrain (mesencephalon), and diencephalon. The brainstem manages the basic life support systems of the body. Within the brainstem is the *reticular formation*. It has con-

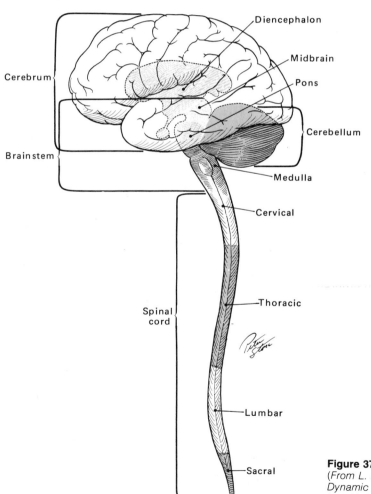

Figure 37-1 Lateral view of the central nervous system. *(From L. L. Langley, I. Telford, and J. Christensen, Dynamic Anatomy and Physiology, 5th ed., McGraw-Hill, New York, 1980. Used with permission.)*

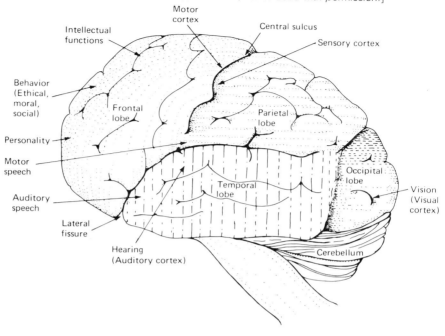

Figure 37-2 Lateral view of the cerebrum. [*From G. M. Scipien et al. (eds.), Comprehensive Pediatric Nursing, 2d ed., McGraw-Hill, New York, 1979. Used with permission.*]

nections to the rest of the brain and controls the overall degree of central nervous system activity. Its main function, performed by the *reticular activating system* (RAS), is control of wakefulness, sleep, and attention.[1]

The cylindrical spinal cord is an elongated mass of nerve tissue descending from the foramen magnum two-thirds of the distance down the spinal column. Central nervous system input and output moves to and from the cord along nerve fibers that travel bundled together as *spinal nerves.* Thirty-one pairs of spinal nerves emerge from the spinal cord. Each spinal nerve consists of a dorsal (sensory, afferent) and a ventral (motor, efferent) root. Each root is composed of many nerve fibers. The spinal nerve is formed just outside the spinal cord by the dorsal and ventral roots. Spinal nerves are named by the vertebral level at which they leave the spinal canal. Thus there are 8 pairs of cervical nerves, 12 of thoracic nerves, 5 of lumbar nerves, 5 of sacral nerves, and 1 pair of coccygeal nerves.

Peripheral nervous system

The nerves connecting the CNS with the "periphery" are for convenience described as belonging to a *peripheral nervous system* (PNS).

The periphery consists of everything outside the central nervous system, including sensory receptors, muscles, and glands. Within most of these nerves there are both afferent and efferent fibers. Some of these fibers connect the CNS to glands, the heart, and smooth muscle. Fibers with these functions are considered part of an *autonomic nervous system* (ANS). Even the ANS is further divided (Fig. 37-3). The nerve fibers that leave the spinal cord at the cervical, thoracic, and lumbar levels are *sympathetic* fibers. Those that leave the brainstem and the sacral level of the spinal cord are *parasympathetic* fibers. Although the ANS network is anatomically different from the rest of the PNS and the ANS nerve fibers give rise to different effects, the various systems (ANS, PNS, and CNS) work together, not in isolation. Table 37-1 summarizes the divisions and functions of the nervous system.

The neuron

The basic cell of the nervous system is the *neuron.* It is composed of a cell body and fibers. The fibers conducting impulses to the cell body are called *dendrites;* those carrying impulses away from the cell body are known as *axons.* Neurons are incapable of reproducing them-

Figure 37-3 The autonomic nervous system, schematic view. The nerves emerging from the brainstem and from sacral levels are parasympathetic. Nerves emerging from T1 to L2 are sympathetic. (*From L. L. Langley, I. Telford, and J. Christensen, Dynamic Anatomy and Physiology, 5th ed., McGraw-Hill, New York, 1980. Used with permission.*)

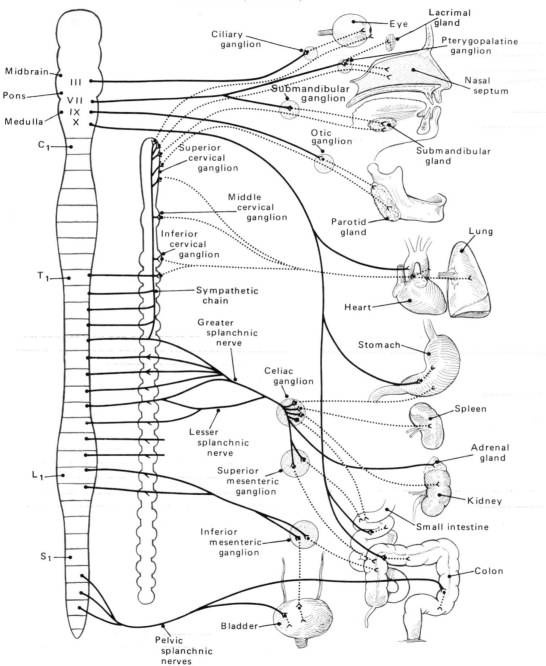

Table 37-1 Divisions of the nervous system

I. Central nervous system
  A. Brain
    1. Cerebrum
      a. Cerebral cortex—controls voluntary motor, and sensory function. Center for behavior, emotions, speech
      b. Cerebral nuclei or basal ganglia—help control muscle tone and tremor, inhibit movement
    2. Cerebellum—coordination of all muscular activity, muscle tone, position sense (proprioception), and reflexes
    3. Brainstem
      a. Diencephalon
        1. Thalamus—organizes sensory messages, emotions, and expression
        2. Hypothalamus—maintenance of homeostasis
      b. Midbrain—relay station for motor and sensory fibers
      c. Pons—relay station of motor and sensory fibers
      d. Medulla—contains vital centers (cardiac, respiratory, vasomotor)
  B. Spinal cord

II. Peripheral nervous system (includes cranial and spinal nerves)
  A. Afferent system—carries information from sensory receptors (*to* CNS)
  B. Efferent system—carries impulses to muscles (*away from* CNS)
    1. Somatic nervous system—supplies motor and sensory fibers to skin and skeletal muscles
    2. Autonomic nervous system—supplies smooth muscle, cardiac muscle, and glands in viscera. The fibers of these systems have opposing effects and work to maintain homeostasis.
      a. Sympathetic—emergency mobilization of energy
      b. Parasympathetic—stimulates visceral functions during relaxation.

selves and die if deprived of oxygen for as little as 4 or 5 min. If the cell body dies, loss of the neuron is permanent. However, if the damage is to an axon or dendrite, regeneration is possible for neurons outside the CNS. For example, in the case of a severed finger that is carefully sutured back together, regeneration of the axons is possible. This happens slowly—at the rate of 1 cm per month. However, nerve fibers within the CNS do not regenerate. Therefore, a severed portion of the spinal cord, for example, remains nonfunctional.

Neurons form circuits that integrate all functions of the nervous system. About 75 percent of neuron cell bodies are found in the cerebral cortex, the outermost layer of the cerebrum. However, there are other important clusters of cell bodies as well. In the CNS these are called *nuclei*. In the PNS they are termed *ganglia*.

Meninges

The brain and spinal cord are encased in three connective tissue membranes—the *meninges* (Fig. 37-4). The inner layer next to the brain, the *pia mater,* is a delicate membrane filled with a network of tiny blood vessels that nourish neural tissue. The *arachnoid* (spider) is a thin, transparent layer that forms a cobweblike structure between the pia mater and *dura mater*, the outermost layer. The dura mater has two extensions. The *falx cerebri* divides the right and left cerebral hemispheres and the *tentorium cerebri* separates the cerebral hemispheres from the cerebellum.[2]

Cerebrospinal fluid

Cerebrospinal fluid (CSF) is a cushion of colorless fluid that fills the ventricles and surrounds the brain and spinal cord. It protects the brain from jarring movements of the head. CSF contains

Figure 37-4 A section of the brain and skull showing the meninges and associated structures. [*From G. M. Scipien et al. (eds.), Comprehensive Pediatric Nursing, 2d ed., McGraw-Hill, New York, 1979. Used with permission.*]

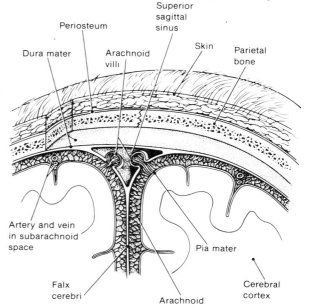

minute traces of white blood cells, protein, and glucose.

CSF is formed in clusters of blood vessels, the choroid plexus, of the ventricles. It flows from the lateral ventricles through the interventricular foramen (foramen of Monro) to the third ventricle through the cerebral aqueduct and into the fourth ventricle (Fig. 37-5). From there it passes through the medial aperture (foramen of Magendie) out to the subarachnoid space of the brain and spinal cord. Aided by circulatory, respiratory, and postural changes, it flows to the top of the outer surface of the brain. There it is absorbed into the vascular system through one-way valves in the arachnoid villi.

Blood-brain barrier

The blood-brain barrier is a protective mechanism that controls both the *kinds* of substances entering the extracellular spaces of the brain and the *rate* of entrance. It regulates the electrolyte and nutrient composition of the neurons and protects the neurons from undesirable substances (some drugs) in the bloodstream. Oxygen, carbon dioxide, water, and lipid soluble drugs enter the brain freely.

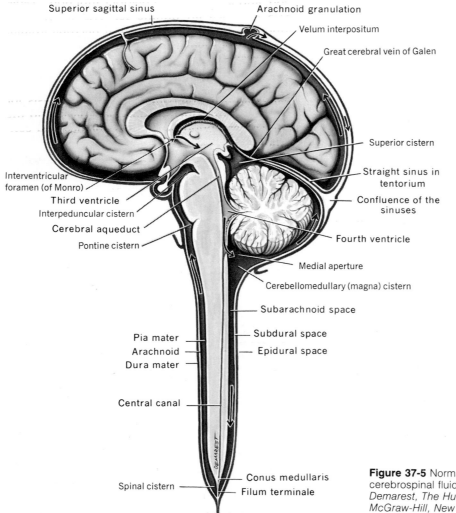

Figure 37-5 Normal circulation of the cerebrospinal fluid. (*From C. Noback and R. Demarest, The Human Nervous System, 3d ed., McGraw-Hill, New York, 1981. Used by permission.*)

Under normal conditions 15 percent of total cardiac output flows to the brain. The brain consumes more oxygen than any other single organ of the body. Much of that oxygen is used for oxidation of glucose, the brain's chief source of energy. Without adequate glucose, oxygen, and enzymes, the brain first ceases to function and then catabolizes itself, causing destruction of its substance.[3]

Diagnostic tests

Table 37-2 describes frequently used diagnostic tests and appropriate nursing interventions for alterations of the nervous system.

If the child is prepared for the sensations to be experienced during diagnostic testing, his anxiety will be reduced.[4] A tape recording of the sounds in the x-ray room may be helpful. If a lumbar puncture is needed, the nurse can describe the quiet of the room, the coolness of the antiseptic solution on the lower back, the sharp prick of the needle through which local anesthetic is injected, and the pressure the child will sense during needle insertion. All these will help the child prepare for the actual experience. However, preparation must be timed to avoid creating needless anxiety in the child.

After a procedure a child needs verbal praise and reassurance about his handling of pain. Further approval can be shown by awarding him a "trophy," which serves as a "badge of courage," gives recognition to the fear or pain he faced, and helps him assimilate the experience.

Nursing assessment of perception and coordination

An important part of newborn assessment is estimation of gestational age. (See Chap. 19.) As an infant matures, developmental progress should be monitored closely. By 4 months the Denver Developmental Screening Test (described in Chap. 6) can be used to assess developmental progress. As the child becomes older, the neurological exam more closely resembles that given to an adult because myelinization of the nerves and fiber tracts draws to completion.

The physician uses the medical neurological exam to diagnose a disease and locate its origin. Since the primary purpose of nursing is to assist people with the basic needs and activities of daily living, the nurse's purpose in assessing neurological dysfunction is to determine the effect any alteration may have on those activities and needs.[5] The nurse can use the physician's methods to detect life-threatening illness but will modify them to determine problems in self-care experienced by the patient.

The nurse's assessment of neurological function can be structured around the integrated functions of eating, communication, thinking, moving, and elimination. Lyons has described five functions to be evaluated by the nurse. They are: (1) consciousness, (2) mentation (includes language), (3) motor function, (4) sensory function, and (5) bowel and bladder function.[6] Table 37-3 provides an outline for evaluating these functions and the parts of the nervous system that control them.

Assessment of the child's neurological status begins with data collection and a thorough history. This can be done on admission or during daily care. An interview provides the basis for evaluating thinking, memory, language, and the child's perception of his own abilities and condition.

In order to make reliable and relevant nursing assessments, and to interpret the data gathered, the nurse must have a background knowledge in neuroanatomy and physiology. That knowledge must be combined with an understanding of normal growth and development. For example, incontinence in a 6-year-old may indicate pathology. In a 6-month-old incontinence is normal and only indicative of immaturity of the nervous system.

Assessment of consciousness

Disturbances of consciousness are caused by anything that interferes with the functioning of the cerebral cortex or reticular activating system. There are many classification systems for describing progressive changes in consciousness. One example is given below.

Level 1—conscious The child is alert and responsive to stimuli.
Level 2—lethargy, drowsiness There is clouding of consciousness. The child's senses are dulled and he may fall asleep even when the conditions are not conducive to sleeping. After arousal, the child will make appropriate verbal and motor responses to painful stimuli.

Table 37-2 Neurologic diagnostic tests

Name	Purpose	Procedure	Nursing care (before test)	Nursing care (after test)
Electroencephalogram	To examine brain waves and electrical activity to: Identify damaged or nonfunctioning areas Identify seizure disorders Follow progress of child after encephalitis, encephalopathy, or head injury	Multiple electrodes are placed on various areas of head with adhesive. Readings are taken sleeping, awake, and hyperventilating. May be done on outpatient basis	Explain purpose to parents and child. Explain placements of electrodes and that EEG is not painful. May shampoo hair to remove oils that would interfere with electrode readings Do not give coffee, tea, Coca-Cola, or alcohol on the day of the examination (contain stimulants or depressants). Do not give medications unless specifically ordered. Sleep-deprive 8–10 h prior to study if ordered.	Wash electrode paste from hair. Allow patient to rest. Provide means of resolving feelings, e.g., therapeutic play.
Skull series	To study bone configuration of skull to identify: Skull fractures Developmental disorders of bony growth, e.g., premature or postmature closing of fontanels Tumors or hemorrhage Presence of old fractures to rule out child battering	X-ray taken of head May be done on outpatient basis	Explain to parents and child x-ray equipment, which may be frightening; explain that there is no pain and describe procedure. Remove glasses, hearing aids, dentures, barrets, hairpins, etc., from mouth or head.	Allow child to express feelings created by this procedure.
Pneumoencephalogram	To demonstrate shape, size, symmetry, and position of ventricular system and subarachnoid spaces to identify: Space-filling abnormality of brain and meninges (except hydrocephalus) Tumors or masses	Air is injected into subarachnoid space from lumbar or cisternal site. X-rays of head General anesthetic given Hospitalization required	Explain to parents and child the procedure. NPO for 6–8 h prior to study, preoperative and postoperative occurrences.	Keep flat, at rest, and check neurological signs q½ h × 4, then q1–2 h, as appropriate. Observe and care for headache, vomiting, irritability, fever, meningeal irritation, intracranial pressure. Encourage fluids if not contraindicated to assist in repletion of CSF. Provide for means of resolving feelings when condition is satisfactory.

Procedure	Purpose	Method	Preparation	Nursing Care
Brain scan	To identify brain tumors, some vascular lesions, and masses	Iodinated human serum (^{131}I HSA) or [203]Hg Neohydrin is given IV 2 h prior to scan. X-rays taken of head. May be done on outpatient basis	Explain to parents and child the procedure, its purpose, that IV medication is given; describe x-ray equipment.	Allow child to express feelings, e.g., through therapeutic play.
Ventriculogram	To visualize ventricles of brain to identify: Hydrocephalus Masses, lesions	Air injected into ventricles. X-rays taken during and after. General anesthetic given. Hospitalization required	Explain to parents and child NPO 6–8 h prior to study, medication, preoperative and postoperative occurrences.	Keep flat, at rest, and check neurological signs q½ h × 4, then as appropriate. Severe headache likely for 12–48 h—provide comfort. Encourage fluids to replenish CSF. Observe for alteration in intracranial pressure. Provide for therapeutic play when condition is improved.
Myelogram	To visualize subarachnoid space of spinal cord to identify: Tumors, masses Interference in flow of CSF Fractures, dislocations, foreign bodies	Air or iodinized contrast medium injected into subarachnoid space via lumbar or cisternal puncture. X-rays taken. Iodinized medium is removed. Hospitalization preferred	Explain to parents and child procedure, purpose, NPO for 6–8 h prior to study, sedative PRN.	Keep flat, at rest. Observe for headache, alterations in intracranial pressure, temperature for 24–48 h. Comfort. Encourage taking fluids. Provide for therapeutic play to resolve feelings.
Angiogram	To identify: Vascular anomalies, lesions Hemorrhage Tumors, masses	Radiopaque substance is injected into carotid, brachial, vertebral, or femoral artery or vein or a dural sinus. General anesthetic given. Surgical exposure of vessel to be injected may be necessary. Hospitalization required. X-rays taken	Explain to parents and child NPO for 6–8 h prior to procedure, sedative, preoperative and postoperative procedures.	Observe for complications of: transient hemiplegia, seizures, petechiae, transient loss of vision, thrombus at injected site, hemorrhage or hematoma at injected site (emergency tracheostomy may be needed if jugular was used), alterations in intracranial pressure, and level of consciousness. Provide for complications if they occur. Comfort. Help to resolve feelings with therapeutic play.

Table 37-2 Neurologic diagnostic tests (*Continued*)

Name	Purpose	Procedure	Nursing care (before test)	Nursing care (after test)
Lumbar puncture	To identify: Intracranial pressure Culture, sensitivity, cell count, sugar, protein of CSF Hemorrhage in CNS To reduce intracranial pressure	Needle is inserted into lumbar area of subarachnoid space. Manometer attached to determine pressure Queckenstedt test performed CSF is collected in tubes which have to be numbered and labeled accurately. May be on outpatient or inpatient basis.	Explain to parents and child procedure, purpose, need for sedation, and that some pain is encountered. During procedure: Position child on side with knees flexed on abdomen and head flexed on chest to open lumbar space. Hold child firmly. Provide constant verbal support. Observe child for tolerance of procedure. Label and number tubes of CSF in order of their collection.	Keep flat, at rest. Observe and care for headache. Encourage taking fluids. Provide for therapeutic play.
Subdural tap	To identify: Subdural effusions Subdural or ventricular hemorrhage Bacteria in subdural or ventricular spaces To obtain fluid for laboratory analysis To relieve intracranial pressure To instill medication	Needle is inserted into subdural space or ventricle through open anterior fontanel or during craniotomy Hospitalization usually required	Explain to parents and child procedure and need to consent concerning shaving area on head. Shave the hair over open anterior fontanel. During procedure: Position child on back with head facing forward Hold head securely Observe child for tolerance of procedure. Label tubes in order they were collected. Tape tubes of fluid to the child's bedside unit and label tubes according to day and time of collection.	Keep flat, at rest. Observe for alterations of intracranial pressure and leakage of fluid from tap site.

Ventricular tap (procedure is the same as for a subdural tap)

Procedure	Purpose	Description of procedure	Nursing interventions	Post-procedure care
Computerized transaxial tomography (CAT scan)	To identify by a combination of computer and x-ray techniques slight differences in density of tissue of intracranial structures: vascular anomalies, lesions, hemorrhage, tumors, masses, ventricular size	Patient is placed in a supine position on a special couch that moves into the scanning unit. To facilitate the study, the area to be scanned is placed in a soft latex material, eliminating air between the head and the diaphragm of the machine and permitting the x-ray beams to penetrate more effectively. The patient must remain motionless during the procedure, which takes up to about an hour. In some instances the physician may choose to inject a contrast medium into a vein and repeat the scanning procedure to obtain additional information. The procedure may be done on an outpatient basis.	Explain to parents and child the procedure, its purpose, and that IV medication may be given. Describe the equipment. Keep the child NPO, if so ordered prior to the study. Explain the need for sedation, if the patient is an infant or young child.	Allow the child to express feelings created by this procedure. If contrast material was injected, observe for thrombi at injection site.
Intracranial pressure monitoring	To monitor increased intracranial pressure in cases of extremely high intracranial pressure	A burr hole is made behind the hair line of the forehead. After nicking the dura, a Richmond screw is placed 1 mm below the dura into the subarachnoid spaces. Screw is connected to tubing that is connected to a graph.	Explain to parents the need and procedure. Shave hair at hair line. During procedure: Position child on back with head facing forward. Hold head securely. Carefully monitor graph read out. Assess for leakage around site and connecting tubes	Keep flat, at rest. Observe for alterations of intracranial pressure and leakage of fluid from burr hole site.

Source: Adapted from G. M. Scipien et al. *Comprehensive Pediatric Nursing*, 2d ed. McGraw-Hill, New York, 1979. Used with permission.

Table 37-3 Neurological dysfunctions and nursing assessment methods*

Functional category	Origin in nervous system	Methods of evaluation
1. Consciousness	Reticular activating system	State of alertness (see later description of altered level of consciousness)
		Reaction to pain, noise, stimuli
		Vital signs
2. Mentation		
Thinking	Cerebral hemispheres	Oriented to time, person, place
Feeling		Recognition of family members
Memory		Recognition of simple objects, color
Perceptual disorders		Recent and past memory (What did you eat for supper last night?)
3. Language and speech		
Dysarthria (defects in articulation, enunciation, and speech rhythm)	Brainstem, cerebellum Cranial nerves VII, IX, X, XII**	What is the child's cry like?
		Child must be old enough to talk. Have the child repeat a phrase.
Dysphonia (abnormal sounds)		Look for a hoarse voice.
Aphasia (inability to use and understand written word)	Temporal and parietal lobes	Child must have learned to speak (2–3 years).
		Child must have learned to read (6–8 years).
		A child who has been in school 2 years should be able to send and receive written messages.
Agnosia (inability to recognize objects by means of touch, sight)	Parietal, temporal, occipital lobes	Have child close his eyes. Place a familiar object in his hand and ask him to identify it when his eyes are shut.
4. Motor function		
Expression	N. III	Look at symmetry of smile, frown, raising of eyebrows; blow out candle.
Eating, swallowing	N. V, IX, X, XII	Ability to chew, swallow, and presence of gag reflex
Eye movements	N. III, IV, VI	Extraocular movement (follow examiner's finger)
		Check pupil size, reaction to light, accommodation.
		Is double vision present?
		Do eyes move rhythmically side to side or up and down (nystagmus)?
Movement (posture, balance, gait)	Cerebellum, spinal cord	Posture of newborn is flexion.
		Have the child walk across room; walk by putting one foot directly in front of the other.
		Balance—stand with eyes closed and feet together
Muscle strength		Test hand grip, each side.
Muscle tone		Check flexion and extension of forearms, upper arms, legs, hips.
5. Sensory function		
Vision	N. II Occipital lobe	Check with Snellen eye chart.
Smell	N. I	Can child detect familiar odors (coffee, peppermint)?
Hearing	N. VII	Whisper or use ticking of watch.
Taste	N. VII, IX	Taste of sugar or salt on tongue.
Sensation: pain, temperature, touch, proprioception	Peripheral nerves plus brain N. V	Note paresthesias or abnormal sensations such as numbness, tingling, or burning.
		Check sensation on face, corneal reflex
6. Elimination		
Bowel	Spinal nerves S3–5	Check for incontinence, fecal impaction.
Bladder	Autonomic nerves	Urinary incontinence
	Spinal nerves T9–L2, S2–S4	Urinary incontinence due to flaccid or spastic bladder

* **Source:** Adapted from Marilyn Lyons, "Recognition of Neurological Dysfunction," *Nurse Practitioner*, September–October: 35–37 (1979).

** Names of cranial nerves:

I—Olfactory	VII—Facial
II—Optic	VIII—Acoustic
III—Oculomotor	IX—Glossopharyngeal
IV—Trochlear	X—Vagus
V—Trigeminal	IX—Spinal accessory
VI—Abducens	XII—Hypoglossal

Level 3—delirium In this state the child experiences disorientation, fear, irritability and sensory distortions. Agitation, loud talking or crying, and suspiciousness may be present. The child may be incontinent.

Level 4—stupor The child may be restless, but purposeful physical and mental activities are minimal. The child barely responds to verbal stimuli and reacts to strong stimuli by reflex withdrawal, grimacing, or unintelligible sounds. Spontaneous movements are common. The child may be incontinent.

Level 5—coma, semicoma In light coma, the child may respond semipurposefully to painful stimuli.

Reflex reactions may be present, but the plantar reflexes maintain an upward flare. The child is usually incontinent.

Deep coma This is a profound state of insensibility. The child does not respond to painful stimuli. The child's muscles are flaccid and he is incontinent.

A more precise scale, known as the *Glasgow coma scale*, has been developed to measure level of consciousness where impairment is suspected. This scale has been proved to be an accurate and reliable tool that allows standardization of observations (Table 37-4 and Fig. 37-6).[7] Because one-third of the scale is based on

Table 37-4 Glasgow coma scale

Category of response	Appropriate stimulus	Response	Score
Eyes open	Approach to the bedside	*Spontaneously*	4
	Verbal command	*To speech.* Eyes open to name or to command.	3
	Pain (pressure on the proximal nail bed)*	*To pain.* Does not open eyes to previous stimuli, but does to pain.	2
		None. Does not open eyes to any stimulus.	1
Best verbal response	Score best response patient makes with maximum arousal. Painful stimulus may be needed.	*Oriented.* Converses; knows who he or she is; where he or she is; year and month	5
		Confused. Converses but disoriented in one or more spheres	4
		Inappropriate words. Without sustained conversation; words disorganized or inappropriate (for example, cursing)	3
		Incomprehensible. Makes sounds (moaning, for example) but no recognizable words	2
		None. No sound even with painful stimuli	1
Best motor response	Verbal command (for example: "raise your arm; hold up two fingers.")	*Obeys command.*	6
	Pain (pressure on proximal nail bed)	*Localizes pain.* Does not obey, but "finds" offending stimulus and attempts to remove it.	5
		Flexion withdrawal.† Flexes arm in response to pain, without abnormal flexion posture.	4
		Abnormal flexion. Flexes arm at elbow and pronates, making a fist.	3
		Abnormal extension. Extends arm at elbow; usually adducts and internally rotates arm at shoulder	2
		None	1

* Produces least inter-rater variability.

† Added to the original scale by many centers.

Figure 37-6 Neurological assessment record employing the Glasgow coma scale (reduced from original size). An operational definition of coma is a score of 7 or less (no eye opening, no comprehensible verbal response, and no motor response to command). [*From M. Kinney et al. (eds.), AACN's Clinical Reference for Critical Care Nursing, McGraw-Hill, New York, 1980.*]

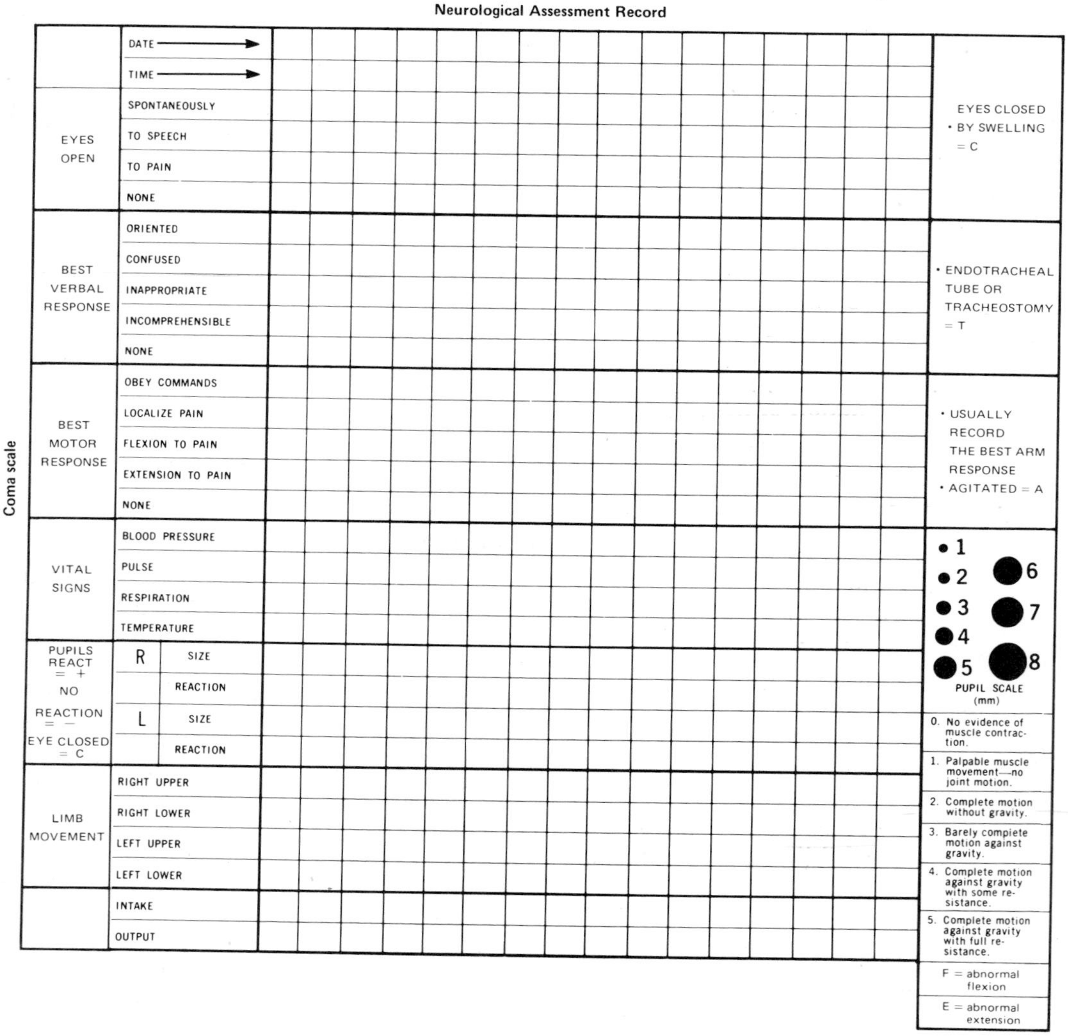

Neurological Assessment Record

verbal responses, however, its use is limited to children who can talk.

Whenever disturbances of consciousness are present in children, other, related disturbances are also present and must be monitored by the nurse.

Breathing patterns Children who are comatose may experience one of the abnormal respiratory patterns described below.[8]

1. *Cheyne-Stokes respirations*—rapid, deep breathing alternating with slow, shallow breathing or apnea
2. *Central neurogenic hyperventilation*—sustained, regular, rapid, deep breathing
3. *Apneustic breathing*—a prolonged inspiratory

phase alternating with expiratory pauses, causing irregular rhythm

Other breathing patterns are characterized by apnea, irregular rhythm and depth of breathing, hiccups, and yawning.

Eyes The pathways of the sympathetic system that control pupil size lie alongside those areas controlling consciousness. Observation of pupil size and reactivity closely relates to level of consciousness. The nurse must observe the equality, size, and reactivity to light of each pupil.

To assess the corneal light reflex, ask the child to look straight ahead. Bring a penlight in from the side of the face. Note the response of the pupil into which the light is shone (the direct response) and the response of the opposite pupil (the indirect response). Dilatation of the pupil is a result of sympathetic nerve activity; constriction is a parasympathetic response.

Assessment of mentation

An initial assessment of the child's mentation includes level of awareness, general behavior and appearance, and facial expression. Are they appropriate for the child's age and condition? To assess language and memory and thinking process the nurse must know what is normal behavior within each child's age range.

Assessment of motor response

Purposeful motor function is assessed by observing the child during eating, feeding, ambulating, or playing. Is the child's spontaneous behavior restless, agitated, or calm? Are strength, muscle mass, and coordination similar in each side of the body?

Specific changes in motor function help pinpoint the origin of any disease process. Localized lesions usually do not affect consciousness but may cause motor or sensory changes. A child in a coma will usually exhibit abnormal motor responses. Early reflexes that normally are gradually replaced by voluntary muscle activity are described in Chaps. 9 and 10. Persistence of the Babinski sign, or its reappearance after age 2, indicates an abnormal response.

Assessment of sensory function

The nursing history must carefully describe the sensory loss or abnormality in terms of location, duration, frequency, and aggravating or alleviating factors. With his or her eyes shut, the child can be asked questions like the following. "Tell me when you feel something by saying 'now.' "Do you feel something hot or cold? Do you feel something sharp or dull? Is your finger (toe) moving up or down?" Other methods of checking cranial nerve sensation are described in Table 37-3. Disturbances of sensation may be evident in terms of pain, numbness, tingling, or loss of touch, pressure or pain.

Assessment of elimination

Because a child's maturational level is so important in assessing neurological function, the significance of incontinence depends on age. Any change in bowel or bladder control should be carefully described. Nursing management must focus on preventing incontinence and keeping the child clean and dry. Distention should be avoided and impactions or infections prevented.

Nursing the neurological patient

Because the child experiences the world around him through his nervous system, any neurological dysfunction places him at risk. Nursing care must be planned and administered to protect the child when he is helpless and vulnerable. Nursing care must also provide the human interaction and environmental support that will enable the child to make the best possible adaptation to his illness.

Many times a child with an alteration in neurological function will need long-term care. The child then becomes particularly dependent on the willingness and ability of others because he is helpless.

The safety of the child is of paramount importance to the nurse. When a child loses sensation in a body part, he may forget to protect it. No warning system exists to remind him to move that part away from a dangerous object. If a child is in bed, he may not feel the small toy under his body. The nurse must check the bed, keep it smooth and clean, and schedule a routine inspection of all vulnerable areas.

Nursing care cannot be given haphazardly, without attention to planned outcomes and desired results. Scientific principles must be translated into intelligent nursing interventions that are consistently carried out to enhance the child's recovery and adjustment. In the following sections of this chapter the nursing management of each alteration is outlined to promote improved nursing care.

Increased intracranial pressure

Assessment

Diligent assessment of signs of increasing intracranial pressure (ICP) is essential when caring for the pediatric neurological patient (Table 37-5). Bleeding, growing tumors, and a buildup of cerebrospinal fluid all can raise intracranial pressure. If cerebral blood vessels are compressed, brain anoxia may follow. If the brainstem is compressed, the functioning of vital centers for heart rate, respiration, and consciousness may be disrupted.

In children less than 18 to 24 months of age, open suture lines accommodate increasing pressure by spreading apart. The head circumference increases and the fontanels become tense and bulge. The head and chest circumferences normally enlarge at approximately the same rate in a child's first 2 years and are almost the same (1 to 2 cm difference). If increased ICP is suspected, therefore, both head and chest are measured daily. If the head grows markedly faster, this is a confirming sign.

Increased ICP makes the infant irritable and lethargic. The infant's cry becomes high-pitched and weak. Early reflexes used to evaluate the neurological status of the neonate and infant are described in Chaps. 9 and 10.

After the cranium has become a rigid enclosure with closing of the fontanels by 18 to 24 months of age, one place where increased pressure in or against the cerebrum will seek release is at the tentorial incisure. The tentorium cerebri, an extension of the dura, acts as a floor for the occipital area of the cerebrum and a roof for the cerebellum. Its inner free border fits around the midbrain, and the area within this ring is the *tentorial incisure.* A rise in intracranial pressure may cause tentorial herniation, with brain tissue forced over the edge of the incisure and down against the midbrain (Fig. 37-7). Lesions below the tentorium cause pressure on the cerebellar tonsils and compress the medulla.

Signs of tentorial herniation include dilatation of the pupil on the same (ipsilateral) side as the lesion because of pressure on the oculomotor nerve. Dilatation of the pupil and sluggish reaction to light may precede, accompany, or be followed by a decrease in consciousness. The child becomes restless, cannot remember names or people, and is hard to arouse. As the brain is increasingly shifted and more pressure applied to the brainstem, Cheyne-Stokes respirations develop and a positive Babinski reflex is present. The respiratory pattern changes to hyperventilation, inspiration length increases, and finally an irregular pattern leads to cessation of respirations. Pupils become dilated. The nurse *must* become familiar with the signs of tentorial herniation because it can rapidly bring about permanent brain damage and even death.

The sole outlet of the cranium after closure of the fontanels is the foramen magnum, where the brainstem and spinal cord merge. With increased intracranial pressure there is a special hazard to

Table 37-5 Signs and symptoms of increased intracranial pressure

Early symptoms	Intermediate symptoms	Late symptoms
Irritability	Projectile vomiting	Decreased level of consciousness
Restlessness	Tense, bulging fontanel in child under 18	Decreased reflexes
Anorexia	months of age	Decreased rate of respirations or change in
Headache	Severe headache	pattern
Nausea	Sluggish, unequal response of pupils to light	Elevated temperature
	Papilledema (edema of optic disc)	Herniation of optic disk (creates blindness)
	Blurred vision	Dilated pupils
	Diplopia (double vision)	Sunset eyes
	Decrease in pulse and increase in systolic	Decerebrate rigidity
	blood pressure	Death
	Seizures	

Source: Adapted from G. M. Scipien et al., *Comprehensive Pediatric Nursing*, 2d ed., McGraw-Hill, New York, 1979. Used with permission.

a procedure such as lumbar puncture. A sudden release of pressure may cause the brainstem to be sucked down (herniate) through the foramen magnum, which would be lethal.

Rapidly increasing intracranial pressure is a medical emergency. Medical management includes fluid regulation, hypertonic drug therapy (Table 37-6), intracranial pressure monitoring, and surgical intervention.

Nursing management

Children experiencing increasing ICP may also experience nausea and weakened suck responses and so have difficulty in eating. Extra encouragement to eat may be necessary. Intake and output must be carefully measured and recorded. A quiet environment is needed. Loud television should be prohibited. Bumping of the bed should be avoided. Every effort should be made to prevent undue stimulation that might cause seizures. A padded tongue blade should be available at the bedside, and padded siderails used in case of seizures.

Regular neurological assessment includes evaluation of (1) level of consciousness, (2) pupillary response and eye movement, (3) motor and sensory function, and (4) vital signs and patterns of respiration. All are assessed at 15-min to 2-h intervals.

A patent airway must be maintained. Suctioning is used for this as needed. Chest physiotherapy (see Chap. 17) is done regularly, at least every 2 h. When artificial ventilation is necessary, blood gases must be routinely monitored. Hyperventilation may be used to reduce cerebral blood flow and give the brain room to expand.

The head of the bed is elevated 20 to 30° to reduce cerebral edema and discomfort. The neck is kept straight to improve venous return. Since straining at stool elevates cerebral pressure, it must be avoided.

Increased ICP can lead to loss of consciousness. If this happens, the principles of care are those for any unconscious child, regardless of cause. The child requires meticulous nursing care with careful attention to observing, recording, and evaluating neurological signs.

Unconscious children need careful skin care and bathing. Massage and turning, every 1 to 2 h, prevents skin breakdown. Often a urinary catheter is left in place to protect skin from incontinence and to allow accurate measure-

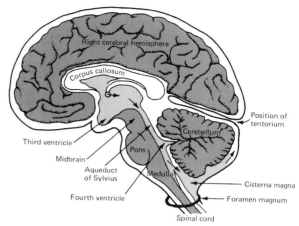

Figure 37-7 The brain and brainstem, sagittal section. [*From M. Kinney et al. (eds.), AACN's Clinical Reference for Critical Care Nursing, McGraw-Hill, New York, 1980. Used with permission.*]

ment of output. Range-of-motion excercises help maintain muscle tone and circulation.

Intravenous fluids (usually normal saline), tube feedings, or hyperalimentation are used to provide hydration and nutrition. Fluids are often restricted to prevent fluid overload in the brain.

Nurses must remember that the child's sense of hearing is often the last to be lost and the first to return. The nurse should speak to the child in a caring voice and encourage parents to do the same. The child can be stroked, held, and rocked.

Parents are extremely frightened and concerned when their child is unconscious. They feel guilt, fear, extreme anxiety, and even anger. They must be helped to express their feelings and given support. They are worried about their child's normalcy and future development. Remember that children often have amazing recoveries from trauma that causes unconsciousness. Help the parents not to give up hope too soon!

Headaches

Forty percent of children will have experienced a headache by the age of seven.[9] Causative factors include systemic illness or infection, neurological disease, tension, or migraine. Headache may also accompany increased ICP.

A detailed history of the headache pattern is necessary. The child should be asked to describe

Table 37-6 Commonly used hypertonic drugs

Drug	Indications and actions	Dosage	Nursing actions	Side effects
Mannitol	Used in emergency situations (not satisfactory for long-term use). Give as rapidly as possible—usually in 10–20 min.	Parental administration, 50–200 g qid, (20% solution) flow rate adjusted to urine output	Assess cardiovascular baseline. Maintain patent urinary catheter—careful assessment of urinary output, check Mannitol for crystalization. Twenty percent mannitol needs filter. Do not give directly with blood transfusion.	Congestive heart failure, rapid breathing, cough, hyponatremia, apprehension, twitching, convulsions
Urea (Urevert)	Used in emergency situations (not satisfactory for long-term use)	Parental administration, no more than 120 g per day, infuse slowly, 4 ml/h or 30% solution	Maintain IV site. Patent urinary catheter. Hazardous in patients with renal, hepatic, or cardiac failure	Skin necrosis at IV site, hypokalemia, weakness, irritability, elevated blood ammonia levels
Glycerol	Slow acting, useful in long-term treatment	Administration orally or through nasogastric tube, 0.5 g/kg q3–4 h	Mix with iced lemon juice or other juice to make it taste better	Hypernatremia, agitation, dry membranes, dehydration
Corticosteroids (Decadron and prednisone)	Useful in local and generalized cranial edema	Oral administration, or IV. 10–16 mg dexamethasone qd, 100–200 mg prednisone qd	Observe for signs of infection	Decreased immune response

its onset, character, location, severity, frequency, duration, and any aggravating or alleviating factors. Accompanying symptoms of dizziness, nausea, vomiting, or pallor should be described.

Diagnostic tests will be used to look for the cause. Headaches due to increased ICP may be aggravated by lying down, coughing, or sneezing. The underlying cause must be treated quickly in these children.

Migraine headaches occur in 5 percent of all children.[10] Although children can be affected from age 3 to 17 years, they usually experience migraine headaches around age 12. There is often a family history of migraine. The child may experience a visual disturbance, or *aura*, before the headache. Some headaches will cause changes in EEG patterns and even improve with anticonvulsant medications.[11]

Occasionally tension headaches will cause real disruption in the child's life. Support, reassurrance, and the use of methods designed to reduce stress have proved helpful. The child will need help in learning to cope with anxiety in a more acceptable manner.

Seizure disorders

Epilepsy, also called *convulsive disorder*, is a chronic condition of recurring seizures. A seizure is characterized by a temporary, uncontrolled alteration in behavior or consciousness, caused by abnormal electrical discharges in the brain. A seizure is a symptom indicating an underlying disorder, just as a fever indicates an infection. The area of electrical or chemical abnormality in the brain determines the nature of the seizure.

A single seizure may be due to high fever, metabolic alterations, toxins, hemorrhage, drug withdrawal, tumors, or anoxia. Recurrent seizures, or epilepsy, may be genetic, idiopathic (cause unknown), or secondary (organic) to trauma or conditions that cause a single seizure. In 70 percent of epilepsy cases, the cause is unknown.[12] Confirmation of the diagnosis of epilepsy is made by careful history of onset, characteristic behaviors during the seizure, and coincidental brain wave alterations indicated in the electroencephalogram (EEG).

The risk of developing epilepsy during a lifetime is between 1 and 3 percent for the general population. If one parent has epilepsy, the risk is 6 percent; if both parents are affected, the risk

is 10 to 12 percent.[13] Approximately one-third of convulsive disorders appear during the first 5 years of life, one-third during elementary school age, and one-third during adolescence and young adulthood.[14]

Newborn seizures

The neonate is quite susceptible to seizure activity because of nervous system immaturity. Metabolic alterations such as hypocalcemia, hypoglycemia, anoxia, uremia, infection, or excessive hydration can irritate the neonate's sensitive nervous system. Infants of diabetic mothers and drug addicts, and other high-risk infants are particularly prone to seizures.

Nursing observations include measurement of blood glucose and assessment of neurological status. It is essential to distinguish between seizure twitching and normal random movements or reflexes.

Febrile seizures

Because of a lowered seizure threshold, children between 6 months and 6 years (but especially under 3 years) are susceptible to seizures when their temperature rises above 38.8°C (101.8°F). Temperature thresholds vary with each child, but dehydration, allergies, and history of birth trauma seem to be contributing factors to febrile seizures.

Phenobarbital is used for prophylactic treatment of febrile seizures in children who:

1. Experience their first seizure before 18 months of age
2. Demonstrate associated neurological abnormalities
3. Experience complex seizure patterns lasting more than 15 min
4. Have family members with a positive history of seizures[15]

Dosage of phenobarbital is 3 to 5 mg per kg of body weight daily for 2 to 4 years. Since it takes 48 h for phenobarbital to reach therapeutic levels, giving phenobarbital at the first sign of a febrile illness is not as effective as constant medication. Diazepam (0.3 mg/kg) may be given intravenously for immediate control of the seizure.

Initially the nurse will gather a careful nursing history. If the seizure occurred outside the hospital (as it usually does), the parents will be asked to describe the events leading up to the seizure and the child's behavior during and after the seizure.

The key nursing responsibility is prevention of febrile seizures by carefully monitoring the child's temperature, administering acetaminophen or aspirin in appropriate dosages, and if, necessary, sponging with tepid water.

Parents should be taught to watch their child for signs of infection and dehydration such as listlessness, fussiness, poor urine output, nausea, and vomiting. The child should be given antipyretic medications every 4 h for a minimum of 24 h after onset of a fever [37.8°C (100°F)]. Parents should be reminded not to immerse their child in a tub of cold water as this can precipitate a seizure.

Epilepsy

Seizures have been classified according to their etiology, site of origin in the brain, or characteristics. The International Classification of Epileptic Seizures (idiopathic or organic chronic seizures) uses four major categories based on location of excess neuronal discharge in the brain as shown by the electroencephalogram.[16]

1. *Partial seizures*—seizures beginning locally
   a. Simple or elementary: motor, sensory, or autonomic, including Jacksonian (generally with impairment of consciousness)
   b. Complex: temporal lobe or psychomotor, repetitive, automatic, inappropriate behaviors (generally with impairment of consciousness)
   c. Partial seizures that become generalized
2. *Generalized seizures*—bilaterally symmetrical without local onset
   a. Absences (petit mal)—brief loss of consciousness with no change in muscle tone
   b. Bilateral myoclonic—sudden brief contractures of a muscle or group of muscles
   c. Infantile spasms—brief, symmetric muscle contractions, usually associated with cerebral abnormalities
   d. Clonic—jerking spasms alternating with relaxation
   e. Tonic—sustained contraction of all body muscles
   f. Atonic—lack of muscle tone
   g. Akinetic—sudden momentary loss of muscle tone and posture control
3. *Unilateral seizures*—usually in children
4. *Unclassified epileptic seizures*—due to incomplete data

Partial seizures *Partial seizures* begin locally and may or may not generalize. There are two primary forms: *Jacksonian* and *psychomotor*. *Jacksonian seizures* are focal motor seizures that generally do not involve loss of consciousness. The characteristic "Jacksonian march" begins with localized motions of the thumb, hand, or foot and progresses in clonic, marchlike movements to involve the same side of the body. It may end in a grand mal seizure. This seizure is associated with organic brain lesions and is uncommon in children. *Psychomotor* or temporal lobe seizures comprise about one-third of the chronic seizure disorders and may occur at any age. Psychomotor seizures involve the most complex patterns of behavior and high levels of cerebral motor and sensory function. Altered behavior includes chewing, changes in color perception, and arrest of activity with staring, picking at clothing, and wandering. Since some aspects of memory originate in the temporal lobe, the child may not remember the seizure. It may last several minutes or hours. The child should not be restrained. A soft, calm voice should be used to reorient the child to the environment.

Generalized seizures *Generalized seizures* have diffuse effects on cerebral functions. Characteristically the child does not experience an *aura*, a peculiar sensation or *warning* such as peculiar taste or smell or "butterflies" in the stomach.

Petit mal Petit mal seizures may go unrecognized because the only clue may be a teacher's complaint about the child's not paying attention in school. Petit mal epilepsy rarely occurs before 2 or after 14 years of age. This state of absence, or unawareness, can occur 50 to 200 times per day if untreated and is most often seen between the ages of 6 and 14. The child may demonstrate staring spells, rapid eye blinking, small twitching movements, or daydreaming lasting 3 to 30 s. Following the seizure the child resumes the interrupted activity as if nothing had happened.

Myoclonic infantile spasms Infantile spasms usually appear in the 3- to 8-month-old as brief jerks of the head or brief periods of opisthotonos. Initially these spasms last only a few seconds. Gradually the head bobbings increase in frequency and power and may progress to a generalized seizure. The spasms occur 20 to 300 times a day, usually during periods of awakening or falling asleep. Ninety percent of the children will develop moderate to severe mental retardation. Ten to fifteen percent will develop other forms of seizures.[17]

Grand mal The *grand mal* seizure is the most dramatic form of epilepsy. Most grand mal seizures last only a few minutes. The child experiences a sudden loss of consciousness and alternating tonic and clonic movements involving the entire body. Facial muscles begin jerking and the jaws clamp shut. There may be frothing of saliva, dyspnea, and bowel and bladder incontinence. Respirations are irregular, pharyngeal secretions are increased, and tachypnea and hypertension are also noted. Following the seizure the child enters a drowsy, calm period called the *postictal* state. During this period the child cannot be easily aroused or may awaken in about 5 min and be confused. Often the child sleeps several hours after the seizure.

Status epilepticus *Status epilepticus* is characterized by recurrent seizures, usually grand mal, with no interval or relatively short intervals between them. This condition constitutes a medical emergency since successive tonic and clonic seizures can lead to exhaustion, respiratory failure, and death. Vital functions must be supported, the seizures stopped, and the cause determined. Diazepam or phenytoin given intravenously is used to stop the seizures. Rectal administration of paraldehyde may also be helpful.[18]

Medical treatment of seizures Medical treatment is designed to determine the type and cause of the seizures the child has experienced. A complete medical examination includes a detailed history and neurological exam, electroencephalography, computerized axial tomography, and skull x-rays. Occasionally, biofeedback and surgery are used to treat selected cases of idiopathic epilepsy. The most valuable treatment for epilepsy, however, is anticonvulsant therapy.

Anticonvulsants raise the seizure threshhold or prevent spread of the abnormal electrical discharge through the brain. Drugs are chosen to fit the individual's epilepsy type, needs, and growth pattern and to produce the minimum number of side effects.[19] A comparison of the most common anticonvulsants, indications for use, usual dosage, therapeutic serum level, and side effects is found in Table 37-7. With proper use of drugs, 50 percent of people with epilepsy can have their seizures completely controlled and another 30 percent nearly controlled.

An anticonvulsant is absorbed through the gastrointestinal tract and metabolized in the liver. A steady state is achieved within the body when the amount of drug absorbed equals the amount excreted. Children usually metabolize drugs faster than adults do.

Each drug has a therapeutic blood level. Measurement of the amount of drug in the blood is useful to determine what dose is necessary to reach a therapeutic level, to evaluate patient compliance, and to assist in patient teaching.[20]

Drug therapy is begun using one medication at a time until the therapeutic blood level is reached. If control of seizures is achieved, the dose is increased until toxic side effects develop.[21] Then the dose is decreased until toxic effects disappear. If control is not achieved with one drug, another will be added. Children and parents need to understand that a therapeutic drug program can take months to establish. When drug therapy is individualized in this way, there are fewer side effects and improved drug compliance results.

Follow-up examinations include complete blood counts, liver studies, and serum blood levels. Drug therapy will need reevaluation during periods of rapid growth, during physical or emotional stress, or when the child is seizure-free for 2 to 3 years. If drugs are discontinued, they must be tapered off gradually because sudden withdrawal can cause an increase in the number and severity of seizures.

Seizure assessment The type of seizure is determined by the site of the abnormal electrical discharge in the brain. The onset and progression of the seizure may help the physician determine the area involved. It is the nurse's responsibility to carefully describe the child's behavior prior to, during, and following the seizure.[22] Questions to be answered include:

What happened immediately before the seizure?
Did the child experience an aura or cry out?
Was the child restless or calm?
What was the child doing?
What was the first sign of the seizure?

Table 37-7 Common anticonvulsants

Drug	Indications	Usual dosage	Therapeutic serum level	Side effects or adverse reactions
Carbamazepine (Tegretol)	Complex partial psychomotor temporal lobe Generalized: grand mal	10–20 mg/kg per day in children 200–400 mg per day in adults	4–8 μg/ml	Nystagmus, slurred speech, drowsiness, dizziness, blurred/double vision, lethargy, decreased white blood cells and platelets, liver toxicity
Clonazepam (Clonopin)	Generalized: absences, akinetic, myoclonic	0.1–0.2 mg/kg per day maintenance in children 20 mg per day maximum in adults	20–50 μg/ml	Lethargy, drowsiness, dizziness, nausea and vomiting, ataxia, behavior changes, hypersalivation
ACTH	Myoclonic infantile spasms	40–80 units per day IM × 28 days Gradually tapering doses × 28 days		Increased appetite, Cushingoid obesity, facial acne, muscle weakness, peripheral edema, increased blood pressure, increased irritability, increased susceptibility to infection
Phenytoin (diphenylhydantoin, Dilantin)	Generalized: grand mal	5–10 mg/kg per day in children 30–120 mg per day in adults	10–20 μg/ml	Ataxia, nystagmus, drowsiness, gum hyperplasia, rash, gastric distress, deformed teeth in children in predental ages, acne, increased hair growth. Dilantin suspension form may be difficult to measure in the small amounts necessary for infants. Careful parental teaching required
Phenobarbital (Mebaral or Luminal)	Generalized: grand mal, petit mal Parietal: all forms	5–10 mg/kg per day in children 30–120 mg per day in adults	10–25 μg/ml	Drowsiness, ataxia, nystagmus, rash, hyperactivity, megaloblastic anemia
Primidone (Mysoline)	Generalized: grand mal Parietal: psychomotor (temporal)	10–20 mg/kg per day in children 750 mg to 1.5 gm per day in adults	5–12 μg/ml	Drowsiness, nausea, ataxia, nystagmus, rash, anemia
Valproic acid (Depakene)	Partial simple and complex Absences Multiple seizures	15 mg/kg per day initially 30 mg/kg per day maximum	50–100 μg/ml	Anorexia, nausea and vomiting, diarrhea, drowsiness, temporary hair loss, hepatic toxicity, decreased platelets
Ethosuximide (Zarontin)	Generalized: absences, minor motor	205 mg 2 × day in children 500 mg 4 × day in adults	40–100 μg/ml	Nausea and vomiting, abdominal pain, headache, drowsiness, dizziness, hiccups, blood dyscrasia

The nurse should always document the child's behavior during the attack:

When did the seizure start? Was there jerking or twitching? Did it spread to other parts of the body?

What was the position of the child's body during the seizure? Did it change?

What was the child's breathing pattern and color?

Where there pupil changes? (If the seizure is of focal origin, the eyes may point away from the irritating focus.)

In an older child, was there incontinence of urine or feces?

How long did the seizure last?

The nurse should make note of the child's behavior following the seizure activity:

Was the child sleepy or groggy?

Was the child's speech clear? If not, describe changes.

Could the child move all extremities?

Were reflexes normal after the seizure?

Did the child complain of unusual feeling in any body part?

Was the child fearful, irritable, or confused?

Nursing management Providing a safe environment for the child who has a seizure disorder is one of the most important nursing goals. The nurse must consider the child's age and developmental needs as well as the type and frequency of seizure activity. A protective helmet may be appropriate for a child with frequent seizures so that he can ambulate and play freely. Crib and siderails should be padded and only soft, safe toys allowed in bed. The child, parents, and nurses work together to identify cues that indicate a seizure is imminent. A padded tongue blade should be available at the bedside or transported with the child when he leaves the room. It can be inserted only at the beginning of a seizure—*before* the jaws are clenched.

A seizure is dramatic and may be frightening to those around the child. When a generalized seizure occurs, certain precautions are essential for the safety of the child.

1. Keep calm. You cannot stop the seizure once it had begun. Do not try to wake the child. He is not in pain. Your goal is to maintain a safe environment and carefully observe the seizure pattern. Note the *time* of onset. *Do not leave the child.*

2. Prevent the child from falling. If he is standing, or in a chair, gently ease him to the floor. Loosen any constricting clothing around the neck.

3. If the teeth are *not* clenched, a padded tongue blade or corner of a towel can be placed between the teeth. *Do not force open* clenched jaws. The tongue may already be bitten and teeth broken. *Do not put your fingers in the mouth!*

4. Keep the child's head and body from striking hard or sharp objects. Crib and bedrails should be padded. A towel or blanket can be tucked under the child's head. Maintain the child's airway by hyperextending the neck and head. Do not physically restrain the child; movement restrictions contribute to muscle strain and may cause dislocation or fracture.

5. Once quieted, turn the child to a side position with the face pointed downward so that saliva or vomitus can drain out. This decreases the chance of aspiration. Carefully evaluate the need for pharyngeal suctioning.

6. Allow the child to rest—perferably in bed.

7. When the child awakens, be honest and tell the truth. "You had a seizure. I will stay with you awhile." Help the child become reoriented to the environment.

8. Document the pattern and length of the seizure and the child's response.

When the child is being regulated on a drug, the nurse is responsible for assessing the drug's effect. The nurse should look for idiosyncratic side effects that are not related to the amount of drug taken but rather to the body's response outside the central nervous system. Skin, gums, liver, and bone marrow may be involved.

Dose-related signs of toxicity usually affect the central nervous system. Signs of toxicity include drowsiness, ataxia (incoordination of voluntary muscle activity), diplopia, and mental dullness. To assess for drug toxicity in the child the following tests are helpful:[23]

1. Test the eyes for *nystagmus* (rhythmic oscillation of the eyeball) by asking the child to follow your finger as it is moved from one lateral extreme of the visual field to another. Nystagmus without double vision is usually present when a child takes anticonvulsants. Nystagmuus with diplopia suggests toxicity. Describe your observations.

2. Check coordination by asking the child to touch his finger to his nose and to walk by placing one

foot directly in front of the other. Difficulty with balance during walking or inability to maintain an upright position with eyes closed and feet together (Romberg's sign) may be evidence of ataxia and drug toxicity.

Because individuals differ in their ability to absorb, distribute, metabolize, and excrete drugs, seizure control is achieved with varying doses and types of anticonvulsants. Other medications may also affect the dose of the anticonvulsant and, in turn, may have their effectiveness altered by anticonvulsants. For example, the serum level of phenytoin can be decreased by phenobarbital, dexamethasone, digitoxin, and ethanol.[24] Oral contraceptive drug levels are lowered by such drugs as phenytoin, phenobarbital, primidone, and carbamazepine.[25] The nurse will need to be familiar with the child's other medications so that appropriate counseling and education can be made available.

Infants who are receiving daily ACTH for infantile spasms become cranky and irritable and very hungry. They may benefit from early introduction of solids and dilution of formula based on recommended dietary requirements. If acne develops, warm soapy washes with baby soap are helpful. Infant stimulation programs and physical therapy should be implemented when delayed motor development exists. Blood pressure must be checked weekly.[26]

Nurse's role with parents Like other chronic conditions, epilepsy requires major adjustments on the part of the child and family. When the diagnosis of epilepsy is made, parents may respond in many ways but at times will experience an overwhelming sense of grief. Denial, guilt, and anger are also common. Parents may have fears about their child's intellectual potential and social adjustment.

These reactions are not surprising when the historical view of epilepsy is considered. The person with epilepsy used to be considered possessed, insane, or mentally retarded. These misconceptions even crept into the legal system and resulted in laws concerning involuntary sterilization, adoption, and proscription of marriage or immigration. Since the American culture values independence, beauty, self-control, health, and physical perfection, it is no wonder the child with epilepsy may seem frightening and repulsive to others. When children experience rejection from their families or peers, their self-esteem decreases and they may be unable to adapt effectively to their illness.

Nurses must stress to parents that their main responsibility is to make sure that their child takes the proper amount of medication at the correct time. A written record of seizure activity and medication use is desirable. Drug compliance is essential for the control of epilepsy. Parents and children must be familiar with drug action and side effects.

Parents need help in understanding the nature of their child's seizure disorder and the medical treatment indicated. They need to be told the facts gently but firmly. They must be helped to develop realistic expectations for their child. Nurses who expect that parents care and can cope with this situation will usually elicit this behavior in parents. Nurses should emphasize the family's strengths and build on them. Parents can be shown how to emphasize their child's strengths and build on them.

Parents can help their child by providing a structured, supportive home environment where adequate rest and nutrition are possible. The child also will benefit from regular physical exercise. A child needs to be encouraged to develop as normally as possible and discouraged from using epilepsy as an excuse or "crutch" to avoid responsibility. When seizures are well controlled, a child should be able to participate in normal activities.

Parents can help their child by being honest and open in discussing epilepsy. The child should be helped to anticipate problems, and he should know what to do if a seizure occurs. If the epilepsy is not totally controlled, the people around him must know his seizure history, the medications he uses, and what to do during a seizure.

It is important for parents to divide their attention and concern among all their children. The pitfalls of giving special attention and dividing responsibilities unequally must be pointed out and avoided.

Encourage parents to get in touch with other parents of a child with *similar* seizure disorder. The older child will also benefit from contact with another child who is coping well with a similar problem. Local and state epilepsy organizations offer support groups, information, and classes on medical, psychosocial, and vocational aspects of living with epilepsy. Families may find group support very helpful.

Nurses who carefully examine their own attitudes and biases about epilepsy will be better able to relate to families in an open, accepting manner. How the nurse reacts to a child during a seizure reflects inner concern, caring, and acceptance.

Nurses may be called upon to educate children and teachers in school so that they will be better able to support and accept their classmate with epilepsy. Nurses may also act as patient advocates in the community and in employment settings. State and national epilepsy programs have information available on affirmative action, employment rights, social security benefits, driver's licenses, and worker compensation.

Congenital alterations of the central nervous system

Faulty closure of the neural tube or bony protection of the central nervous system leads to mild defects, such as spina bifida occulta, or to severe defects that are incompatible with life, as in anencephaly. Table 37-8 describes types of neural tube malformations. These defects make up a significant proportion of all congenital anomalies and affect 3 to 4 infants among every 1000 born.[27]

When a family has a child with a neural tube defect, the risk of recurrence increases in relation to the family history. With a negative history the risk of having another child with a neural tube defect is 1 in 20, or 5 percent. With a positive

family history the risk increases to 1 in 10, or 10 percent. An affected adult or a sibling of an affected person is also at greater risk for producing a child with a neural tube defect than the general population.[28]

Open neural tube defects (anencephaly, meningocele, and myelomeningocele) can now be diagnosed during the second trimester of pregnancy by amniocentesis and measurement of *alpha-fetoprotein* (AFP) level in amniotic fluid. Closed defects (spina bifida occulta) do not communicate with amniotic fluid and AFP does not rise. Because most children with neural tube defects are born to families with no previous history of the problem, efforts are underway to develop a screening program for pregnant women to measure their serum AFP level at 16 to 18 weeks' gestation. Two tests that show increased serum AFP suggest a defect and the need for amniocentesis and examination of the amniotic fluid.[29]

Cranial malformations

Encephalocele A defect associated with a cleft in the cranium—or *encephalocele*—can occur anywhere in the skull but is most common in the occipital area. In *occult cranium bifidum* only the bone is affected; there is no involvement of the CNS, thus giving the infant a good prognosis. When nervous tissue, meninges, and CSF are involved, as in *encephalomeningocele*, brain damage is inevitable and seizures, hydrocephalus, and mental retardation are frequent complications. Differential diagnosis is made by palpation, transillumination, and pneumoencephalography.

Table 37-8 Neural tube malformations*

Cranial bifidum or encephalocele	Defect in closure of bones of the skull
Occult cranium bifidum	Bony defect of skull only
Simple cranial meningocele	Meninges and cerebrospinal fluid protrude·through the skull defect.
Encephalomeningocele	Brain tissue, meninges, and CSF protrude through the defect.
Anencephaly	Absence of skull, brain, and other vital tissues
Spina bifida	Defect in closure of vertebral column
Spina bifida occulta	Bony defect of vertebrae only; no external sac
Meningocele	Meninges and CSF protrude through defect (normal spinal cord usually)
Myelomeningocele	Meninges, CSF, and abnormal spinal cord protrude through defect
Rachischisis	Incomplete closure of vertebrae, meninges, and spinal cord. Not repairable. Death usually results from infection.

* **Source:** Adapted from Sherrilyn Passo, "Malformations of the Neural Tube," in Diane McElroy and Gayle Davis (eds.), *Nursing Clinics of North America* **15**(1):6 (March 1980).

With severe defects the decision may be made not to repair the defect surgically. Whether or not surgery is done, the sac must be carefully protected. Pressure on an encephalocele can cause impaired consciousness, impaired respirations, and bulging fontanels.

Anencephaly Anencephaly is a severe neural tube defect immediately evident at birth. The protective cranial skull and cerebral hemispheres are absent. Most fetuses with anencephaly are aborted early in pregnancy or are stillborn. Some may live a short time if the brainstem functions. Reflex reactions of respirations, swallowing, and sucking may keep the child alive for a few days.

Nursing management Parents whose child has a severe cranial malformation must be supported in their grief and disappointment. Usually seeing the baby helps the parents come to terms with reality and prevents even worse imaginary visions. In anencephaly the parents have no hope. With a severe encephalocele, the parents will need accurate information and support in their decision making regarding surgical treatment.

When surgical repair is feasible, special care must be taken by the nurse to keep the sac clean and to prevent rupture.[30] Vital functions are monitored closely. Postoperatively the wound must be kept free of any contamination. Parents are encouraged to help with care. They will need nursing support to learn the best methods of feeding and bathing their child. Long-term management requires a team approach to the many physical, social, emotional, and financial problems associated with an encephalocele. Parents will need to know the signs of infection, hydrocephalus, and the risk of recurrence in future children.

Microcephaly With this defect the head size is significantly smaller than normal. The baby has a long, narrow, receding forehead, a small cranium, and a flat occiput. Brain weight may be less than 1000 g, or one-fourth normal size. Fontanels are either small or closed.

Careful assessment of microcephaly is necessary to rule out *craniostenosis* (premature closure of sutures). Craniostenosis is due to faulty bone growth, not to faulty brain growth as in microcephaly. Surgical treatment is done for cosmetic reasons, to relieve pressure, and to allow normal brain growth.

The impaired brain growth of microcephaly may be due to an autosomal recessive disorder, a chromosomal abnormality, or a teratogenic insult during pregnancy. The degree of neurological abnormality and mental retardation varies from mild to severe.

Nursing management The major objective of care is to promote the highest level of development possible for each child. Nursing care is directed toward helping parents adapt to this situation. A multidisciplinary approach is necessary with continued family support available as choices are made regarding the child's care and education. Genetic counseling may be helpful to the family if more children are desired.

Spinal malformations
Spina bifida occulta The incomplete fusion of the vertebrae may be signaled by an overlying dimple or tuft of hair. Neuromuscular disturbances of bladder and bowel control and paraparesis (partial paralysis) can occur in rare instances (Fig. 37-8A).

Meningocele The meningocele, varying in size from an acorn to an orange, contains meninges and CSF. It generally occurs in the lumbar area and is covered by abnormal skin or meninges. Because no nervous tissue is present, it allows the passage of light (transillumination) when a light is shone through it. Early surgical repair is done to prevent infection. Neurological complications are less severe than when nervous tissue protrudes into the sac, but hydrocephalus can develop (Fig. 37-8B).

Myelomeningocele This defect, also called *meningomyelocele*, is more severe than meningocele because it contains meninges, spinal fluid, *and* neural tissue. The sac may be as large as a grapefruit and is prone to leakage through the thin membrane or skin that covers it (Figs. 37-8C and 37-9). The spinal cord and nerve roots may stop at the sac, ending motor and sensory function below that point. Paralysis, sensory loss, and bowel and bladder dysfunction are common and are determined by the level of lesion.

A lesion at the thoracic level causes total lower extremity paralysis. If the lesion is at T12, pelvic flexion is possible. Thoracic lesions are rarer than lumbar or sacral defects. At L1 and L2 hip flexion is possible. Children with these defects will ordinarily be confined to a wheelchair. When L3 and L4 levels of paralysis are present, the child has potential knee movement and may become ambulatory with long or short leg braces and crutches. Lesions at L5 or below allow varying degrees of foot and ankle movement. Some of these children may be ambulatory without braces.[31]

Medical treatment In order to assess the extent of neurological damage the physician performs a complete neurological examination, paying careful attention to lower extremity motor func-

tion. X-rays of the skull, spine, hips, and chest are done. Cultures are done to determine the presence of infection. Developing hydrocephalus will be monitored by daily measurement of head circumference (and chest for comparison), palpation of fontanels, and computerized axial tomography.

Figure 37-8 Congenital malformations of the spine. (*A*) Spina bifida occulta, an incomplete fusion of the vertebral arches without an external sac. A dimple or tuft of hair may signal its presence. (*B*) Meningocele: The external sac contains meninges and CSF. (*C*) Myelomeningocele: The external sac contains meninges, CSF, and immature spinal cord tissue. [*From Beverly A. Bowens, "The Nervous System," in M. Armstrong et al. (eds.), McGraw-Hill Handbook of Clinical Nursing, McGraw-Hill, New York, 1979. Used with permission.*]

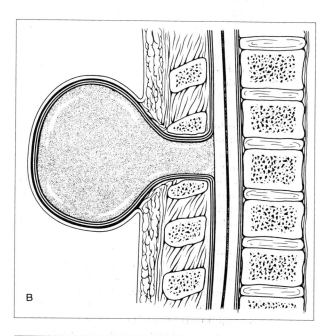

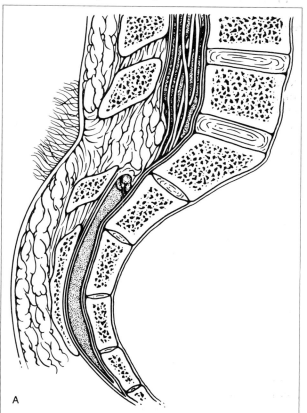

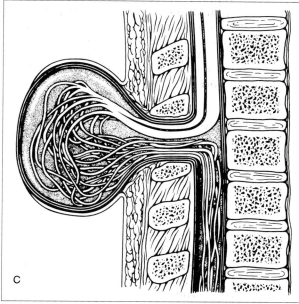

Figure 37-9 Myelomeningoceles. (A) With skin covering. (*Photo courtesy of D. Jack Mayfield, Department of Orthopaedic Surgery, University of Minnesota.*) (B) With thin, abnormal membrane covering. (*Photo courtesy of Dr. Edward R. Laws.*)

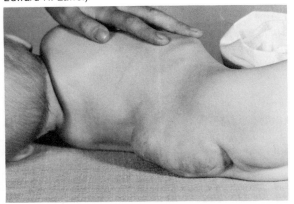

A

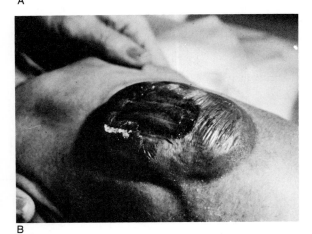

B

Surgical repair is done within the first 24 h, or as soon as feasible after birth, to reduce the risk of infection and further nerve damage. There continues to be controversy among physicians regarding the most appropriate treatment for children born with myelomeningocele. If the child has other severe defects as well as infection and hydrocephalus, some physicians recommend no intervention. Others advocate repair of every defect. Parents must be involved in the decision-making process and supported in their choice.

Once surgical repair is done, the goals of the health care team include: (1) maintenance of renal function, (2) control of bladder and bowel function, (3) promotion of independent locomotion, (4) independence in activities of daily living, and (5) achievement of social acceptance.[32] With vigorous early treatment and careful follow-up, a large percentage of myelomeningocele victims can meet these goals.

Nursing management Nursing care of the child with meningocele or meningomyelocele can be divided into the acute and chronic phases. The immediate problems relate to preoperative and postoperative care. Long-term care includes management of the associated complications (Table 37-9).

ACUTE CARE Nursing care is directed toward observation of neurological status, recognition of complications, and provision of basic needs during the preoperative and postoperative phase.

The nurse should observe the baby for spontaneous movement, usual position, and the response to body stimulation. Voiding and defecation patterns are monitored for amount and frequency. The presence or absence of the *anal reflex* (constriction of the sphincter upon stroking) is determined. When periodic spasms of the bladder cause incomplete emptying, the physician may order manual compression applied over the suprapubic area to promote complete emptying. This Credé procedure is discussed in Chap. 31.

Because hydrocephalus may be a secondary complication in at least 80 to 90 percent of children, the nurse must measure the head and chest daily. Fontanels are palpated often for fullness and bulging. Increasing lethargy or irritability and other signs of increasing intracranial pressure should be noted.

The nurse must watch for signs of infection. Meningitis is a common complication although early surgery and prophylactic antibiotic therapy have reduced its frequency. Restlessness, irritability, increased sensitivity to noise and light, excessive crying, and fever may indicate meningitis.

Care of the sac is extremely important. Correct positioning in a *prone* position is achieved through use of the Bradford frame or with small rolls and sandbags. Usually a low Trendelenberg position is favored to decrease pressure in the sac. The baby's head is turned to the side and the legs are abducted to counteract hip subluxation. Pressure on the sac must be avoided

Table 37-9 Complications of myelomeningocele

Hydrocephalus—occurs in 75–90% of children with lumbar
    myelomeningoceles
Impaired bladder and bowel control
Motor impairment: partial or complete paralysis
Sensory impairment: skin disturbances, decubitus ulcers
In utero joint deformities
    Flexion or extension contractures
    Talipes valgus or varus (club feet)
    Congenital hip dislocation
Kyphosis or scoliosis
Osteoporosis: leads to spontaneous fractures
Obesity
Hydrosyringomyelia (dilatation of the spinal cord central
    canal by CSF pressure with formation of fistulas within
    spinal cord tissue): scoliosis, spasticity, weakness and
    paralysis, personality changes

because rupture could cause a sudden loss of cerebrospinal fluid, leading to herniation of the brainstem and pressure on vital centers.

The sac is carefully observed for leakage or abrasions. Dressings, although seldom used, are applied with aseptic technique. A plastic wrap may be applied below the spinal defect to protect it from stool that can spurt out erratically (Fig. 37-10). Glycerine suppositories may be used to prevent constant stooling in the newborn.

Since early repair is the norm, feeding may not be begun until after surgery. However, if feeding is indicated, it will be difficult if the infant cannot be held or is irritable. If possible, the head should be elevated slightly and turned to the side. A soft nipple and chin support will help if the baby has difficulty sucking. Feeding should be a time of fondling and stimulation by touch. The baby can be stroked on the head, arms, and upper back. The normal cuddling situation should be imitated as closely as possible for the infant who must be fed lying on his or her abdomen. Intake is recorded accurately; daily weights may be ordered, depending on progress.

Following surgical closure of the sac, nursing care is similar to that described above. Special emphasis is given to observation for shock, development of increased ICP, hydrocephalus, wound leakage, infection, and adequacy of respiratory status and neurological function. Precautions are used to prevent contamination of the wound from feces or urine.

The infant may be placed on the abdomen or

Figure 37-10 Use of ordinary kitchen variety plastic wrap to protect a spinal defect from contamination. When the plastic wrap is folded back to expose the area it can be taped to thighs. [*From Beverly A. Bowens, "The Nervous System," in M. Armstrong, et al. (eds.), McGraw-Hill, Handbook of Clinical Nursing, McGraw-Hill, New York, 1979. Used with permission.*]

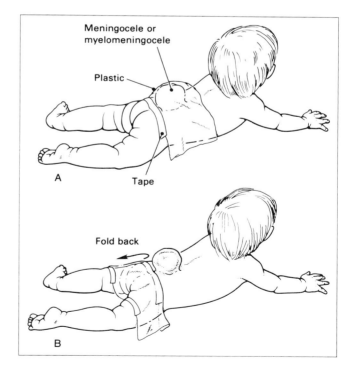

side. The head may be elevated if hydrocephalus is present. If leakage of CSF occurs, the head is lowered to reduce pressure on the wound.

The parents need a great deal of psychological support. Usually the baby has been rushed from the local hospital to the large medical center, leaving the new mother behind. Anxiety and fears are great. The mother may experience some guilt and wonder, "What did I do to make this happen?" Once the parents are assured the baby will survive surgery, they begin to realize how extensive their child's problems may be. Surgical intervention is the first step in a long series of future hospitalizations, surgeries, and crises.

Nurses are responsible for teaching parents about the defect, what surgery involves, and how to cope with the child's impairments. Table 37-10 outlines a teaching guideline that can be used postoperatively to prepare parents for discharge and long-term care of their child.

LONG-TERM CARE Long-term management includes a balanced diet and maintenance of an adequate fluid intake. With decreased mobility, the child is predisposed to constipation. Milk is recommended for the young child but may be restricted in the adolescent to decrease formation of renal calculi.

Since urinary reflux and infection can cause permanent renal damage, bladder dysfunction is the most threatening of the child's long-term problems. Continued monitoring of urologic status is essential. Prophylactic antibiotics and blad-

der training may be used. Chapter 31 provides a more complete discussion of bladder management in myelomeningocele. The neuropathic (neurogenic) bladder is one of the most difficult problems associated with myelomeningocele. Once a child enters school, bladder control becomes more important. Intermittent catheterization (see Chap. 31) has proven very successful for some children. Gradually the child is taught the procedure until he or she is totally independent. Indwelling catheters or external collecting devices may also be used.

Bowel training is established through chemical and mechanical stimulation. Prune juice at bedtime may be helpful to the older child. A suppository before a meal, warm fluid after the meal, and planned time on the potty chair or toilet are helpful. Sometimes a stool softener is necessary. A balanced diet high in bulk and fiber and adequate fluids help maintain the consistent stool necessary for regulation.

Long-term orthopedic management includes exercise, casting, traction, braces, and surgical correction of deformities. By 1 year the child should be equipped with appropriate braces and should be weight-bearing. Scoliosis is a common complication in adolescents with higher defects.

Providing for the emotional needs of the family is important. Each developmental hurdle that is not mastered by the child reactivates their grief. The grief process is a cyclic process that repeats itself. Families can be given anticipatory guidance and assurance that the feelings they experience are normal. By teaching the parents about the malformation and its implications and management, the nurse returns a sense of control to the child and family. Plans are made jointly with the parents and child.

The developmental changes of adolescence bring new or greater concerns to the child regarding body image, sexual identity, and peer acceptance. The child will need information about sexuality and his or her sexual potential. Females ordinarily are able to experience normal intercourse, pregnancy, and delivery. Hygienic problems may occur for both sexes because of immobility and incontinence, but these can be worked out.

The sexual potential of males will vary with the height of the lesion. Whether or not erection is possible, few males will be able to father a child.[33]

Table 37-10 Checklist for teaching and dismissal planning following repair of meningomyelocele

_____ Feeding
_____ Skin care
_____ Positioning
_____ Wound care
_____ Elimination
        Bladder drainage program
        Bowel
_____ Range-of-motion exercises
_____ Stimulation program
_____ Orthopedic problems
_____ Complications to watch for
        Hydrocephalus
           Fontanels
           Head circumference
        Infection
           Temperature
           Other signs

Hydrocephalus

Pathophysiology Hydrocephalus is an abnormal accumulation of cerebrospinal fluid (CSF) in the brain caused by excessive production, inadequate reabsorption, or obstruction of circulation of CSF through the ventricles.

Noncommunicating hydrocephalus (internal or obstructive) is due to blockage in the ventricular system that prevents CSF from flowing to the subarachnoid spaces of the brain where it is absorbed. Most cases of noncommunicating hydrocephalus are due to developmental malformations, neoplasms, infections, or trauma. *Arnold-Chiari* malformation, a *noncommunicating* obstruction of the fourth ventricle, results from the downward displacement of the lower brainstem and cerebellum into the cervical canal. It is associated with myelomeningocele and abnormal development of the cerebral hemispheres.

In *communicating* hydrocephalus, an excessive amount of cerebrospinal fluid moves freely through the ventricles but is not absorbed by the arachnoid villi. Nonabsorption, caused by fibrosis of the arachnoid villi, is often the result of hemorrhage or infection. Communicating hydrocephalus is the most common type.

The infant with hydrocephalus displays bulging fontanels, an enlarging head, prominent scalp veins, fixed downward gaze of the eyes with sclera visible above the irises (*sunset eyes*), and eventual thinning of the scalp (Fig. 37-11). In the older child whose sutures have closed, leaving no room for head expansion, signs and symptoms of increased intracranial pressure include headache, nausea, vomiting, papilledema, seizures, and decreasing levels of consciousness.

Diagnosis is possible in utero through the use of ultrasound. After birth transillumination, neurological evaluation, measurement of head circumference, and computerized axial tomography are used.

Medical treatment The treatment of hydrocephalus is almost always surgical. The obstruction to circulating CSF is reduced if possible. More often, a shunt is introduced into the ventricular system to reroute CSF and facilitate its absorption. A burr hole is drilled into the skull and the tip of a thin polyethylene catheter is inserted into the ventricle. The catheter is threaded behind the ear into the jugular vein

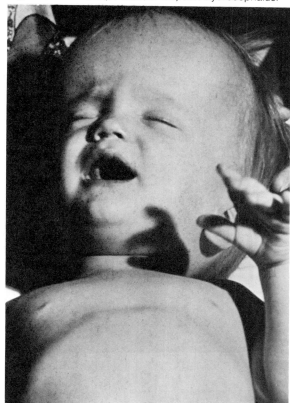

Figure 37-11 Infant (11 months old) with hydrocephalus.

and into the right atrium or peritoneal cavity (Fig. 37-12). A one-way valve in the catheter allows fluid to drain off when pressure increases. Some valves require "pumping" or pressing several times a day to keep the tube patent and draining. Several shunt revisions or replacements may be necessary during childhood because of:[34]

1. Dislodging of one end of the catheter
2. Infection
3. Clogging of the catheter
4. Failure of the pumping mechanism
5. Growth of the child (tubing becomes too short)

Untreated hydrocephalus has a 50 to 60 percent mortality rate. With treatment 80 percent of children will survive with one-half to one-third being intellectually and neurologically normal. Persistent infections and shunt revisions are emotionally, physically, and financially costly to both the child and the family.

Figure 37-12 Shunts used in hydrocephalus. (*A*) Ventriculoatrial shunt. The catheter is inserted into the anterior horn of the lateral ventricle, passed through a tunnel under the scalp, and connected to a catheter previously inserted into the atrium. [*From G. M. Scipien et al. (eds.), Comprehensive Pediatric Nursing, 2d ed., McGraw-Hill, New York, 1979. Used with permission.*] (*B*) Ventriculoperitoneal shunt. The ventricular catheter is threaded subcutaneously down the occipital-parietal area toward the anterior portion of the neck. There it is connected to the peritoneal catheter, which has been passed up the anterior abdomen and chest to the neck.

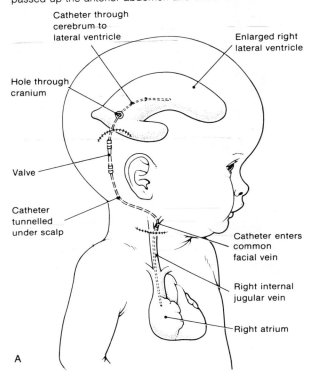

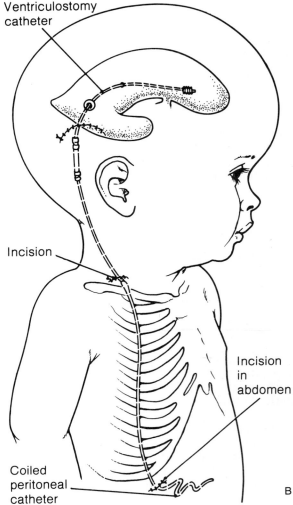

Nursing management The observations of the child before surgery are the same as those described for the child with increased intracranial pressure. Head circumference and fontanels are monitored closely in the infant. Eating may be difficult because the child is lethargic and irritable. If the head is large, it must be carefully supported and protected from developing pressure areas. Families will need support and education in regard to the purpose of surgery and expected care following surgery.

Postoperatively the child is positioned on the unoperative side and kept flat to avoid sudden reduction of intracranial pressure. The dressing is observed closely and neurological status monitored at least every 15 min. Total intake and output are measured. Because salt and fluid are lost through drainage of CSF, electrolyte replacement is done carefully. Signs of irritability, bulging fontanels, decreasing levels of consciousness, and increasing temperature are reported promptly. Prophylactic antibiotic therapy is routine.

Before discharge the parents must be taught how to recognize signs of increasing intracranial pressure, infection, or other signs indicating shunt malfunction. Usually children will need to avoid contact sports but can participate in most other activities. Sharing information helps allay parental anxiety and prevents overprotection of the child.

Infection, often due to *Staphylococcus epidermidis* or *aureus,* usually requires removal of the shunt and replacement. Shunt revisions are more common in children than in adults. The earlier a shunt is placed, the more likely it will need to be revised. Increased frequency of infection and revision create a poor long-term prognosis for the child.

Alterations in brain function

Cerebral palsy

Pathophysiology Cerebral palsy (CP) is a nonprogressive central motor deficit in which voluntary muscles are poorly controlled. It is a common crippling condition of childhood affecting at least 1 out of 1000 children.

Interference with oxygen supply before, during, or after birth increases the risk of developing CP. The severity of neuromuscular involvement is dependent upon the stage of fetal development and upon the duration of anoxia experienced. Maternal factors associated with increasing risk for CP in offspring are age (under 18), diabetes, rubella, and toxemia. CP is three times as common in the premature infant as in the full-term infant. Neonatal signs that are strongly predictive of increased risk of cerebral palsy are Apgar scores of 3 or less at 10 min and beyond, neonatal seizures, and abnormal neurological status in the newborn period.[35]

Detection In severe cases CP may be detected at birth. A feeble cry, general weakness, and difficulty eating alert the nurse to a CNS problem. Some babies may even be "too good." In contrast to these hypotonic infants, other children with CP are dramatically hyperextended with legs crossed in a scissor position. These infants are difficult to hold and cuddle. Other infants with CP may roll from a prone to a supine position very early.

Usually CP is diagnosed because the child is delayed in reaching developmental milestones and because of abnormal continuation of newborn reflexes (Moro, tonic neck, startle, or grasp). Twenty percent of infants with CP show persistence of the tonic neck reflex after 6 months. As the nervous system matures, deficits become more apparent. Delays in learning to roll over, sit, crawl, walk, and talk signal the parents and nurse that something is wrong. Exaggerated reflexes and asymmetry of limbs and muscles are warning signs. The sooner the diagnosis is made and treatment begun, the better it is for the child.

One-third of children with CP have some degree of mental retardation and one-half have seizures. Vision and hearing impairment frequently increase the child's difficulty with communication. Children with CP who can sit alone by 2 years will usually be able to walk. Those who are not sitting alone by age 4, however, seldom walk independently (Fig. 37-13).

Figure 37-13 Use of a four-point walker helps the child to learn balance and to walk. (*Photo courtesy of Dr. Daniel Halpern, Department of Physical Medicine and Rehabilitation, University of Minnesota.*)

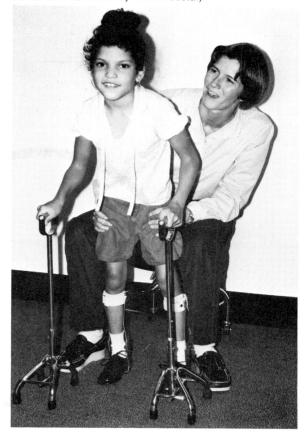

[handwritten annotations: Spastic movement / Exagerated / athetoid - dyskinetic ← Fingers / ataxic / walking]

Classification Cerebral palsy can be classified into three types: (1) spastic, (2) dyskinetic or athetoid, and (3) ataxic. Table 37-11 describes the incidence and main characteristics of the three types of CP.

Spastic CP is characterized by exaggerated reflexive movements of one or more limbs. Initially there may be hypotonicity in affected extremities with hypertonicity gradually appearing. Muscle groups become tight, shortened, and contracted. Reflexes are exaggerated. Difficulty in swallowing and drooling indicate head and neck muscle involvement. Communication difficulties because of muscle impairment may be misinterpreted as retardation in these children.

Athetoid or dyskinetic CP is characterized by involuntary slow, writhing (athetoid), random movements of all extremities, the head, and the face. Muscle hypertrophy can result from the constant motion. Usually muscle tone is decreased. The writhing, athetoid movements do not usually appear until 18 months, suggesting that a certain maturity of the CNS is necessary.

Ataxic CP is manifested by disturbances of balance, uncoordinated arms, hypoactive reflexes, and often a horizontal nystagmus. The infant exhibits little leg movement and when he begins crawling he may drag his legs. *[handwritten: Rolling eyes]*

Medical treatment Medical treatment is determined primarily by the extent of neuromuscular involvement. A comprehensive, interdisciplinary team approach provides the services needed to help the child achieve the highest possible level of neuromuscular functioning and independence. Goals and treatment are summarized in Table 37-12.

Nursing management The nurse is an integral member of the interdisciplinary team caring for the child with CP. Care plans designed by the team will be implemented by the nurse in the hospital, community, clinic, or school.

Frequently the child has some communication problem. It may take several minutes for the child to express himself. It is essential that nurses be patient, attentive, and interested. The nurse cannot assume a child with CP is retarded simply because difficulty in communication is present. Helpful aids designed to improve expressive or receptive communication include hearing aids, a spelling symbol or picture board, a typewriter, or sign language.

Children with CP may need assistance with nutrition (Fig. 37-14), elimination, activity, and other basic needs. Sometimes swallowing difficulties or tongue movements impair eating. Choking may be a problem. Constant movement increases nutritional requirements, while limited activity may decrease them.

Handling children with CP can prove difficult for everyone. The spastic child should be placed in a sitting position, held under the armpits, and then lifted while his arms are placed over the nurse's shoulders, his legs abducted, and knees flexed. The older child, and the child with athetosis, should be lifted from behind by placing the arms under the child's upper arms and

Table 37-11 Characteristics of cerebral palsy (CP)

Type	Frequency	Characteristics
Spastic	50–75% of all CP	Hypertonic muscle spasm varying from facial muscle to total body involvement. Poor control of posture, balance, and fine movement
Hemiparesis		One side of body affected with greater involvement of upper extremity
Quadriplegia		All four extremities involved to same degree
Diplegia		All four extremities affected but lower extremities involved to greater degree
Dyskinetic	25% of all CP	Slow, random writhing movements that disappear in sleep and are aggravated by stress
Ataxic	Less than 10% of all CP	Hypotonic state with intention tremor and muscle incoordination, especially of upper extremities. Loss of posture and balance

Table 37-12 Goals and treatment of cerebral palsy

Goal	Approach	Description
Maintain normal tone	Range of motion (active and passive)	Movement of joints to their fullest capacity
	Stretching exercise	Physical exercises designed to extend muscles to their fullest capacity
	Careful positioning	Braces, corsets, head halter, splints, appliances, and right-angle placement of all extremities
Increase voluntary control and inhibit involuntary random movement	Medications (used infrequently)	Maintenance levels of Valium may be administered
	Motor-point block	Injections of phenol with electrical stimulation
Prevent contractures	Range of motion	Movement of all joints to their fullest capacity
	Intermittent stretching	Daily short-term traction or casting of extremities to stretch muscles
Correct contractures	Surgical release	Prevent complete immobilization
Develop adequate communication skills	Visual exam and correction	
	Hearing exam and correction	Sometimes mental retardation is in reality an inability to hear
	Learn and practice movements of speech	Purposeful movements involving swallowing, lip movement, and chewing to improve speech patterns

grasping the inner aspects of the thighs. The nurse's chest supports the child's back and promotes a forward head position.[36]

When the child wears braces, meticulous skin care is essential. Skin needs to be checked every 4 h for redness, wrinkling, blistering, or cyanosis.

Brace cuffs are sufficiently tight when two fingers can be placed inside them.

Emphasis is placed on helping the child develop independence in locomotion and activities of daily living. If a child is hospitalized, the home treatment program must be adapted so progress

Figure 37-14 Special utensils for the handicapped. [*From Virginia F. Strange, "Dietary Assistance," in L. M. Shortridge and E. Lee (eds.), Introductory Skills for Nursing Practice, McGraw-Hill, New York, 1980.*]

is not lost. Parents are essential in helping the nurse develop an appropriate care plan.

Parents will need continued support and help as they are faced with the constant care and demands of raising a handicapped child. Discipline may be difficult. Siblings must be considered. Parents will need help in understanding their child's abilities and assets, how to parent the handicapped child, and how to keep the family system strong and supportive. Parents will need to understand the developmental and educational needs of their child as well as how to meet them. The parents and child bear the ultimate responsibility for the child's rehabilitation and for meeting the goals of optimum development, independence, and emotional adjustment.

Minimal brain dysfunction (attention deficit disorders)*

Minimal brain dysfunction (MBD) is a term associated with numerous behavioral learning disorders. These disorders can be divided into four main categories: (1) coordination, (2) attention, (3) language, and (4) perception. Most recently the term *attention deficit disorder* (ADD) has been used to replace MBD since the disturbance of attention seems to be at the core of the disorder.[37] A diagnosis of MBD is made if a child has a dysfunction in any one of the four categories, has normal intelligence, and does not have any sensory defects. MBD does not include learning disorders due to visual, hearing, or motor handicaps or to mental retardation. No single etiology of MBD has been identified. Possible causes that may overlap or act alone include neurochemical abnormalities, maturational lag, impaired development of cerebral dominance, central nervous system damage due to hypoxia, or inherited factors. Two major classifications of MBD (or attention deficit disorders) are *hyperkinesis* (hyperactivity) and *developmental dyslexia*.

Hyperkinesis Hyperkinesis, or attention deficit disorder with hyperactivity, is best described and diagnosed by its symptoms.[38,39] Characteristics can be classified into hyperactivity, inattention, and impulsivity. Table 37-13 describes the wide range of behaviors associated with hyperkinesis in the older child. Signs of hyperkinesis may also be evident in the newborn who reacts strongly to any stimuli, cries "all the time," and sleeps very little. As soon as he is mobile, he is "into everything." Precocious development of gross motor skills, even though the child is awkward, may be the result of increased activity. Language skills may be delayed. The general quality of the child's motor behavior tends to be haphazard and poorly organized. As the child gets older, he is difficult to be around because he is stubborn, bossy, and labile in mood. Family problems are not uncommon.

A common myth about hyperactivity is the belief that children outgrow the problem by adolescence. They do not. Instead they develop other problems such as poor achievement in school. Restlessness, inattention, and distractability persist. Low self-esteem, depression, and a sense of failure are not unusual.[40] Antisocial behavior causes difficulty in school and with juvenile authorities.

---

* This section on MBD is by Roberta Stroebel, B.S.N.

Table 37-13 Characteristics of hyperactive children*

Hyperactivity	Inattention	Impulsivity
Excess running or climbing	Often fails to finish things started	Often acts before thinking of consequences
Difficulty sitting still	Doesn't seem to listen	Excessive shifting from one activity to another
Fidgeting	Easily distracted	
Restlessness during sleep	Difficulty concentrating on schoolwork, play, or any activity requiring sustained attention	Difficulty organizing work
"Always on the go"		Needs a lot of supervision
		Finds it hard to take turns in games

* Children defined as hyperactive usually demonstrate two or three of the behaviors described in each column.
Source: Adapted from B. Shaywitz et al., "New Diagnostic Terminology for Minimal Brain Dysfunction," *Journal of Pediatrics* **95:**(1) 735 (November 1979).

Detection Early diagnosis allows careful management and counseling. A thorough evaluation of the child's physical and neurological status, behavioral patterns, social interactions, and learning skills is necessary for diagnosis. An accurate electroencephalogram is advisable to help rule out any neurological disease. Although food allergies (especially to milk products, food additives, and sugar) have been implicated as a causative factor, dietary treatment may not be as successful as drug therapy.

Drug management The drugs most commonly used in hyperactivity are central nervous system stimulants. Table 37-14 describes three commonly used drugs. These drugs promote attention to tasks and lessen tendency to impulsive behavior by increasing levels of norepinephrine. Dexedrine may cause decreased linear growth, but usually the child "catches up" when the drug is discontinued. Seventy-five percent of children respond favorably to drug therapy.[41]

Dietary management may include: no sugar (white, brown, raw), no honey, no boxed cereals, no milk or milk products, frequent small meals high in protein, and high-dose vitamin supplements.

Nursing management Within the hospital, the nurse provides for the safety and psychological needs of the child. A primary nurse and a consistent, predictable environment will increase the child's sense of control and decrease frustration. Short-term tasks and activities using large muscles are helpful.

Nutritional status should be observed closely. Height and weight graphs are kept. Children eat better if breakfast is served before the drug's action begins and if they are given several small, high-calorie meals during the day.

Parents should be helped to understand that the mild alterations in brain function will cause behavioral, motor, and learning problems. Suggestions for parents include:

1. Reduce distraction and stimuli in the child's environment.
2. Set reasonable limits and rules, and be firm in their enforcement.
3. Provide stable and predictable routines.
4. Learn and use behavioral modification techniques. Reward desirable behavior and promote the child's self-esteem.

Table 37-14 Central nervous system stimulants used in treatment of hyperkinesis (hyperactivity)

Drug	Average daily dose*	Side Effects
Dextroamphetamine sulfate (Dexedrine)	10–40 mg	Insomnia Anorexia Reduction of growth Headache Moodiness
Methylphenidate (Ritalin)	15–60 mg	Insomnia Anorexia
Pemoline (Cylert)	56.25–75 mg	Insomnia Anorexia Skin rash Depression

* Therapy is begun with the lowest dose possible. Therapeutic effect takes 2–3 weeks. A child on long-term drug therapy will usually benefit from a drug free trial periodically to assess necessity of continuing the medication.

5. Provide short lists of tasks to help the child remember what is expected.
6. Try to remain calm, noncritical, and nonirritable.
7. Remember the child will be "absent-minded" and accept it while being alert to problems it might cause in care of belongings, toys, etc.
8. Do not ask the child to make many decisions about unimportant items; instead involve him in major ones.

Parents need support in their role as limit-setters and help in developing parenting skills to manage their child. Parents need to understand the treatment program and the side effects of drug therapy. The nurse is the ideal professional for educating families and coordinating services between health and educational professionals.

Developmental dyslexia Developmental dyslexia is a specific language disability. It involves perception, integration, and expression of verbal and written tasks. Other names for this disability are specific language disability, specific learning disability, developmental reading disability, perceptual motor handicap, mirror reading, word blindness, and, incorrectly, attention deficit disorder and minimal brain dysfunction.

No single cause has been found for developmental dyslexia. Children with dyslexia have problems listening, thinking, speaking, reading, writing, spelling, or doing mathematics. Like hyperkinesis, the diagnosis is made by identification of signs and symptoms rather than cause. Table 37-15 describes the manifestations of developmental dyslexia.

The incidence of dyslexia in school-age children is estimated to be 5 to 15 percent. Boys are affected three to five times more frequently than girls. This gives support to the hypothesis that dyslexia is a genetic disability. According to Duane, the "frequency of specific reading retardation (developmental dyslexia) appears to equal or exceed the combined frequency of mental retardation, cerebral palsy, and epilepsy."[42] Obviously developmental dyslexia is an important public health problem.

A child with dyslexia may have a deficit in visual processing or auditory processing or both. Visual processing refers to the integration and expression of visual images in the brain after the eyes receive them. When a defect in visual memory occurs, the child has difficulty recognizing, reading, spelling, or recalling written words.

Auditory processing refers not to actual hearing but to what happens to the impulses in the brain. The child with less-than-average auditory memory may have difficulty in pronunciation, in remembering a series of directions, and in memorization of dates, word definitions, and multiplication tables. The child with dyslexia may have difficulty following oral instructions or com-

prehending written material even though he can read it.

Detection and treatment Dyslexic children are found in all ranges of intelligence and in all socioeconomic settings. Early detection is essential to prevent the child from being labeled as a slow learner, retarded, lazy, immature, or a daydreamer. As the child grows older, behavior may become disruptive or delinquent. In an unpublished study of Minnesota adolescents seen in juvenile courts, Dr. Dennis Hogenson, a psychologist, found one-third were reading 2 or more years below grade level despite average or above-average intelligence.

In addition to having a complete medical evaluation, the child should be evaluated by a language therapist who will pay particular attention to motor skills, left- and right-handedness, language development and error patterns, and school and social behavior. A planned remediation program is based on a multisensory approach. The child learns to "feel" letter shapes by tracing them and to be cued by the movement of lips and tongue when sounding and writing words. The student must "see it," "hear it," "feel it," "say it,"—all at the same time. Phonics are combined with rote memory of prefixes, suffixes, word roots, and spelling rules. In essence the logical structure of the English language must be learned. A classic example of spelling errors

Table 37-15 Manifestations of dyslexia

Signs	Observable behavior
Slow speech	Overactive
Difficult to understand	Demanding
Poor concentration	Disruptive
Reduced attention span	Impulsive
Poor coordination	Easily distracted
Difficulty with spoken or written word:	Disorganized
Recognizing	Excessive moodiness
Recalling	Anger
Reproducing	Frustration
Slow rate of word processing	Tenseness (nervousness)
Unusual difficulty with handwriting (dysgraphia)	
Direction disorientation (easily lost)	
Error patterns	
Reversals, misalignments of letters, numbers, symbols	
Distortions	
Omissions	
Substitutions	

made by a dyslexic child is shown in Fig. 37-15. To achieve full academic potential a dyslexic child must spend hours in drill, repetition, and reinforcement of correct responses. Progress will be determined by early intervention and appropriate treatment, innate intelligence, and individual motivation. Medication is not appropriate for a dyslexic child. Psychological symptoms that interfere with remediation or development may indicate the need for counseling. Academic failure can reduce the child's self-esteem and increase vulnerability to other stresses.

Nursing management The main responsibilities of the nurse in the area of developmental dyslexia are to recognize, teach, support, and refer. The reading and comprehension level of a child must be evaluated in order to teach him. A dyslexic child may have a short attention span. He will need to learn by a multisensory approach. The nurse must clarify written instructions. Are they understood? Can the child repeat them in his own words? Encourage the child to use a "hands on" approach whereby he acts things out. Several return demonstrations may be necessary when a procedure must be learned.

Pediatric and community nurses play an increasingly major role in referring a child for evaluation if a receptive, retentive, or expressive language problem is noted. The location of remedial centers can be learned from the Orton Society, 8415 Bellona Lane, Towson, MD 21204 or the Association for Children with Learning Disabilities (ACLD), 5225 Grace Street, Pittsburgh, PA 15236.

Figure 37-15 Handwriting sample from boy with developmental dyslexia. This sample was written by a 12-year, 4-month-old boy as his language therapist dictated from the quote below. This boy's IQ tested as 170 (Binet) and he was in seventh grade (grade 7, 2 months). Quote: "Truly the hour when he was compelled to develop a composition seemed the longest and grimmest of the whole week. He fretted, chewed his pencil, regretted that he had not applied himself earlier, and thought of other ways he would have preferred to spend the hour. In fact, he underwent every form of suffering except that which involves work. Finally, controlling his thoughts with an almost heroic effort, he ceased pitying himself and produced the weekly masterpiece." (*Courtesy of Marcia K. Henry.*)

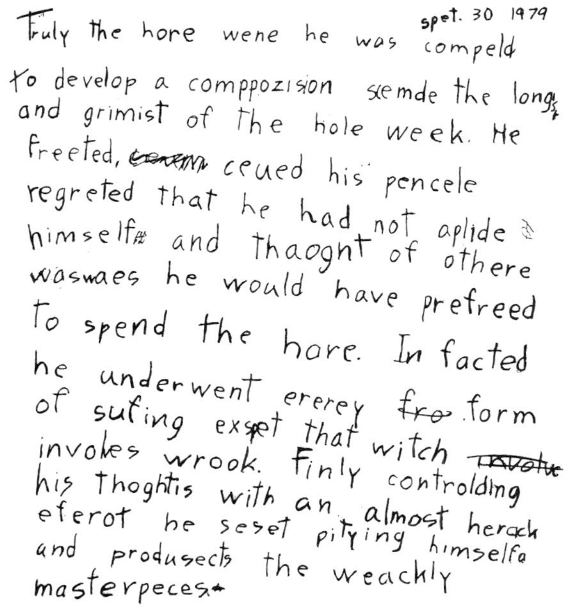

spet. 30 1979
Truly the hore wene he was compeld
to develop a comppozision semde the long
and grimist of the hole week. He
freeted, ceued his pencele
regreted that he had not aplide
himself and thaoght of othere
waswaes he would have prefreed
to spend the hore. In facted
he underwent ererey form
of sufing exspet that witch
involes wrook. Finly controlding
his thoghtis with an almost herack
eferot he seset pitying himselfa
and produsects the weachly
masterpeces

Alterations due to infection

Meningitis

Meningitis, or inflammation of the meninges, is a very serious disease and requires immediate treatment to prevent a rapid, fulminating course ending in death. With early recognition and treatment most children recover. Three different clinical entities of meningitis will be described: bacterial, viral, and neonatal meningitis.

Bacterial meningitis

Pathophysiology Meningitis can follow any infection of the head or face (otitis media, mastoiditis, sinus infection), gastrointestinal disturbance, or contamination of the meninges through penetrating head wounds or neural tube defects. Most cases in children over 2 years of age are caused by *Haemophilus influenzae,* type B; *Neisseria meningitidis,* types A, B, C, and Y (meningococcus); or *Diplococcus pneumoniae* (pneumococcus).

Symptoms of bacterial meningitis vary greatly according to age. Children over 2 years of age develop the classic signs of meningeal irritation: headache, neck stiffness (nuchal rigidity) and pain, and resistance of flexion of the neck and head. Neurological findings include:

1. *Brudzinski sign:* Brisk flexion of the knees occurs when the supine patient's neck is flexed.

2. *Kernig's sign:* Resistance to knee extension occurs when the supine patient's thigh is flexed at right angles to the trunk.

Opisthotonos occurs as the disease gets worse. Other classic symptoms of meningitis include fever, malaise, lethargy, chills, photophobia, vomiting, and seizures.

Infection in the brain causes hyperemia, brain edema, and formation of a purulent exudate. The flow of CSF may be obstructed by thick pus, fibrin, or even adhesions. Brain abscesses may develop. When the infection spreads to the cranial nerves, hearing, vision, and facial movement may be impaired.

Infants over 28 days often present with fever, vomiting, and irritability. As the disease progresses, seizures, a high-pitched cry, and a full, tense fontanel indicate increasing ICP.

Medical treatment Immediate hospitalization, lumbar puncture and analysis of CSF fluid, vigorous antibiotic therapy, and supportive care are necessary to ensure the best possible outcome for the child.

CSF typically shows an increase in white blood cells and protein and a decrease in glucose. The fluid is examined microscopically and a culture and sensitivity done. Table 37-16 contrasts normal cerebrospinal fluid analysis with that typical of meningitis and encephalitis.

The child is placed in respiratory isolation for at least 24 h. Intravenous antibiotic therapy is begun using large doses of broad-spectrum antibiotics until the exact pathogen is identified. Fever is reduced. Ventilation, reduction of increased ICP, control of seizures, and management of bacterial shock are all important elements of medical care. Subdural effusions are treated by repeated removal of small amounts of fluid from the subdural space.

Fluid deficits are corrected, but *overhydration* must be avoided to prevent additional cerebral edema. When *inappropriate antidiuretic hormone syndrome* occurs, as it does in 50 percent of patients with meningitis, water is retained, leading to greater cerebral edema. When this happens, as little fluid as possible is used to administer antibiotics and electrolytes (800 to 1,000 ml/m² per day).[43]

Viral meningitis Viral meningitis, or aseptic meningitis, is most often caused by enteroviruses or is the sequela of mumps, measles, or herpes. Onset may be abrupt or gradual with symptoms of headache, fever, malaise, nausea, vomiting, and other signs of meningeal irritation. The course is not as progressive as that in bacterial meningitis. Maculopapular rashes are associated with the echo viruses. Examination of CSF may reveal slight elevation in pressure and WBC, but the CSF is otherwise normal. Medical treatment is symptomatic. Nursing care is essentially supportive. Usually the child has an uncomplicated illness and a good recovery.

Neonatal meningitis Neonatal meningitis is a serious problem in neonates, accounting for 70 percent of all deaths from bacterial meningitis.[44] The mortality rate is high, varying from 40 to 80 percent. Pre-term infants are twice as susceptible as full-term infants. Gram-negative organisms such as *E. coli*, *Klebsiella*, *Pseudomonas*, *Salmonella*, and group B Streptococcus are the usual causative bacteria.

Diagnosis is difficult because infants do not show the classic signs of meningitis. They may have an elevated temperature or one that is

Table 37-16 Cerebrospinal fluid analysis

	Normal	Bacterial meningitis	Encephalitis
Pressure (mmH₂O)	40–200	Increased	Normal or moderately increased
Appearance	Clear	Cloudy	Clear
White cells (per mm³)	0–5	1000–4000	<500
Protein (mg/100 ml)	20–40	60–100 or more	Slightly increased
Glucose (mg/100 ml)	50–90	Decreased or absent	Normal
Culture	Negative	Positive in 80–90% of untreated children	

below normal. They may be lethargic or hyperactive. Typically they are septic, feed poorly, have loose stools, and experience respiratory distress. Seizures, hepatomegaly, and jaundice may be present.

Neonates with meningitis are critically ill and need intensive nursing care and multiple support systems. Many will experience neurological damage after recovery.

Nursing management Because meningitis affects so many children, it is frequently encountered by nurses. Nurses in community settings must recognize symptoms that suggest meningitis. Those nurses who care for the ill child must be highly skilled and knowledgeable to provide the needed nursing care.

Nursing care centers on the assessment of neurological status, support of the child during diagnostic procedures, provision of basic needs, and protection from injury. Observations of vital signs and blood pressure, sensory and motor function, and level of consciousness are made frequently.

The child with bacterial meningitis remains in respiratory isolation (Table 17-10) for at least 24 h. Parents must be taught the appropriate isolation procedures. They need opportunities to express their fears and to gain encouragement and support from those caring for their child. They may feel guilty because they did not seek care earlier. In some cases they may experience anger if a visit to the health professional for an upper respiratory infection did not result in the diagnosis of meningitis. They need help in understanding why the initial symptoms are often indistinguishable from other minor infections children often acquire.

When a lumbar puncture is done, the nurse must prepare the child and family for the procedure with a simple explanation of what will occur. The child is positioned on a bed or flat surface with his back next to the edge. The child lies on his side with his head flexed, knees drawn up on his abdomen, and back rounded (Fig. 17-11). This position widens the space between the lumbar vertebral spines, making puncture of the subarachnoid space easier. By holding the child with one arm behind the neck and one behind the thighs and locking hands in front of the child, the nurse can help the child maintain the

flexed position. Talking softly to the child throughout the procedure can be calming.

The lumbar puncture is a sterile procedure. After skin preparation, the physician injects a local anesthetic and then inserts the needle. After the stylet is removed, a few drops of CSF are allowed to drip out before the manometer is attached. Pressure is recorded at the point where CSF stops rising. Appropriate samples of CSF are taken in sterile containers. Closing pressure is measured and the needle withdrawn. An adhesive bandage is applied at the site.

The nurse must always be alert for respiratory complications when the child's head is flexed. If CSF pressure is very high, herniation of the brainstem through the foramen magnum is possible with sudden release of pressure upon puncture. The *Queckenstedt test* (manual compression of the internal jugular veins—normally causing rise in CSF pressure) is contraindicated when CSF pressure is elevated.

The child's room should be kept cool and quiet and all environmental stimuli reduced. Photophobia requires reduction of bright light. If the child has seizures or is unconscious, previously discussed nursing measures apply. Measures to reduce fever are used (Chap. 17).

Accurate measurement of intake and output is essential. If oral food or fluids are allowed, feedings may be very slow. A patent IV line will be needed for several days, making it essential to protect and preserve the infusion site. Observe for side effects of antibiotics used in therapy. Specific gravity of urine will be monitored along with careful balancing of intake and output. Daily weight may be ordered.

Grouping nursing care activities together allows the child periods of uninterrupted rest. Play and other diversionary activities are provided as recovery begins.

Encephalitis

Encephalitis is a complex inflammation of the central nervous system. It is often associated with mumps, rubeola, chickenpox, herpes, or mosquito-borne viruses (California, Eastern or Western equine, and St. Louis encephalitis). Encephalitis due to mumps or rubeola can be prevented by immunization. In more than one-half the cases of encephalitis the virus cannot be identified.

Onset may be slow or rapid. Characteristically there is headache, fever, and drowsiness with progressive decrease in consciousness. Nausea, vomiting, malaise, and signs of increased intracranial pressure point to cerebral involvement. CSF studies may show slight elevation in pressure and WBC (Table 37-16). Seizures are likely in the infant.

Medical and nursing care are primarily supportive. The acute stage is often a medical emergency and conscientious nursing care is essential. Careful monitoring of cerebral edema, fever, respiratory and neurological status, and fluid-electrolyte balance are important. Medications may be used to control increased intracranial pressure.

Prognosis is guarded. Death is not unusual. Recovery may be dramatic or may take several weeks. Mental retardation, seizures, or motor impairment may follow encephalitis. Family support, teaching, rehabilitation, and follow-up care depend upon the outcome of the illness.

Reye's syndrome

Pathophysiology In selected incidents a minor viral illness results in a severe encephalopathy called *Reye's syndrome*. This massive physiological crisis strikes with frightening swiftness and frequently fatal consequences.[45] Children 6 months through adolescence are affected.

Reye's syndrome is the result of an internal buildup of ammonia in the blood (more than 50 μg/ml) and a rapid form of liver damage due to

Table 37-17 Criteria for staging in Reye's syndrome*

Stage I	Drowsiness, lethargy, vomiting, temperature elevated; grade 1 EEG
Stage II	Disorientation, combativeness, hyperventilation, tachycardia, purposeful response to pain; grade 2 or 3 EEG
Stage III	Deepening coma, decorticate posturing in response to pain—dilated pupils. Respond to light; grade 3 or 4 EEG
Stage IV	Deepening coma, spontaneous decerebrate posture, dilated pupils, temperature elevated; grade 3 or 4 EEG
Stage V	Cessation of spontaneous respirations, temperature elevated; grade 5 or silent EEG

* **Source:** Adapted from R. Hoekelman, S. Blatman, P. Brunnell, S. Freidman, and H. Seidel, *Principles of Pediatrics*, McGraw-Hill, New York, 1978, p. 1855.

fatty tissue degeneration. Cerebral edema causes coma, hyperventilation, tachycardia, brain damage, or death. With vigorous medical intervention 60 to 80 percent of children recover.[46]

After an apparent recovery from influenza (often type B) or chickenpox (varicella), the child develops severe, persistent vomiting. Soon the child complains of fatigue, drowsiness, or general listlessness. A few hours to a few days after the vomiting develops, the first signs of encephalopathy appear. The child may become disoriented and combative, and may hallucinate and lose consciousness.

Diagnosis is based on history of viral illness, evidence of cerebral dysfunction (electroencephalographic changes), and a liver biopsy showing fatty degeneration. Laboratory tests reveal hypoglycemia, elevated ammonia, elevated SGOT and SGPT, and a prolonged prothrombin time—all reflecting a decrease in liver function. There is usually a combined respiratory alkalosis and metabolic acidosis.

Medical treatment Medical treatment varies from conservative approaches of supportive care to dramatic interventions of total exchange transfusions or total body washouts. Management is based on staging of the disease according to level of consciousness and EEG findings. Various clinical stages have been described and are used to determine the severity of the illness and aggressiveness of treatment (Table 37-17). The child who progresses rapidly through these stages, or who goes beyond stage 3, has a poorer prognosis than do others with less severe disease.

Medical treatment includes constant monitoring of (1) fluid and electrolytes (2) central venous pressure, (3) arterial blood gases, (4) liver function, (5) ventilation, and (6) intracranial pressure. Drug therapy may be used to sterilize the bowel to decrease ammonia formation and also to decrease cerebral edema. Exchange transfusions and total body washout are some of the methods used to remove toxins and ammonia and provide needed clotting factors.

Nursing management The child who is severely ill with Reye's syndrome requires intensive nursing care to support vital functions. Basic supportive care and accurate assessment of neurological status are essential. The child may have a nasogastric tube, endotracheal tube, urinary catheter, IV, and other equipment for monitoring pressures, gas exchange, and vital functions.

Providing emotional and psychological support for the family is a nursing priority. A sudden illness of such serious consequence is a terrifying experience for the family. Care must be taken in explaining the important function of each piece of equipment and in helping parents to support their child. They may be afraid to stay in the room much less to touch their child.

Although mortality is high, recovery can be very rapid and often occurs without any neurological damage. Usually the child experiences stress and anxiety when he awakens in a strange, frightening environment with no idea of what has happened. The child needs orientation to his surroundings and his illness. Above all he needs his parents with him during this difficult period.

Alterations due to trauma: physical or chemical

Head injuries

An injury to the head can cause a skull fracture or damage to the soft tissue of the brain, leading to bruising, edema, or hemorrhage. Children are especially prone to head injuries as a result of birth injury, falls, motor vehicle accidents, sports injuries, or physical abuse. One-half of all children who die from accidents have some kind of head injury. Children's resilient skulls, however, are more able to absorb and withstand a blow than can those of older individuals. Yet because their tissues are fragile and more easily damaged, long-term effects are more likely.

Pathophysiology The skull varies in thickness from 2 to 6 mm with the thinnest part found in the temporoparietal area. Fractures running through the grooves under the skull can cause tearing of blood vessels and severe hemorrhage. Most skull fractures are *linear* (no displacement of bone) and can be asymptomatic. *Depressed skull fractures* (broken pieces of bone pushed inward) are unusual in children under 3 years and usually follow a high velocity blow. A basal skull fracture with dural tears can allow seepage of CSF out of the nose (rhinorrhea) or ear (otorrhea).

Soft tissue injury to the brain is due to the forces of acceleration, deceleration, and deformation. These forces cause stress to brain tissue through movement of the brain within the cranium.

The term *coup* is used to describe the bruising of the brain at the site of trauma. Because the skull moves faster than the brain when hit, it also stops moving sooner. The slower moving brain rebounds off the skull and is injured on the opposite side—*contrecoup*.

Shearing stresses, due to this unequal movement of brain tissue, negative pressure, stretching and compression all act to cause shock, laceration with hemorrhage, increased cerebrospinal fluid, and cerebral edema. Regardless of the cause, the physical damage to the brain produces several clinical entities.

A *concussion* is the most frequent type of closed head injury in children. It is characterized by a transient and reversible neuronal dysfunction leading to a brief loss of consciousness. Memory loss for events before (retrograde amnesia) or after the event (anterograde amnesia) is common. Damage is diffuse with shearing of many axons in the brainstem and subcortical areas.[47] Signs and symptoms include headache, pallor, vomiting, apathy, and irritability.

Cerebral *contusions* or lacerations are more severe types of injuries with hemorrhagic lesions and tears in the brain tissue. They are deemed major head injuries and are considered a medical emergency. Contusions can cause focal neurological disturbances or more widespread damage when cerebral edema is present. Unconsciousness may last for a longer time than with concussion, and abnormal neurological signs are present. The posttraumatic period is characterized by more severe symptoms—mild fever, vomiting, headache, somnolence, confusion—lasting for a longer time than in a concussion.

When the brain injury is severe, hemorrhage may result. It is classified according to location as follows:

1. Extradural—between the dura and skull
2. Subdural—between the dura and arachnoid
3. Subarachnoid—bleeding into the subarachnoid space
4. Intracerebral—within the cerebral tissues themselves.

An *extradural hematoma* frequently follows a skull fracture that causes tearing of the middle meningeal artery (Fig. 37-16A). Brain compression occurs rapidly because of arterial bleeding with tentorial herniation likely. (See earlier section on increased intracranial pressure.) Treatment is removal of the clot. Mortality is 25 percent.

A *subdural hematoma* (Fig. 37-16B) occurs 10 times more frequently in children than do other hematomas.[48] It is usually bilateral and due to venous bleeding. A great deal of blood can accumulate in the young child's skull before signs of increased intracranial pressure occur (Table 37-5). Subacute and chronic subdural hematomas are frequently found in abused children (Fig. 37-16B). Subdural hematomas occur most frequently in children under 2 years.

An *acute subdural hematoma* is associated with meningeal tears, severe head injury, and cerebral edema. Mortality is over 50 percent. Symptoms of *subacute subdural hematoma* appear within 3 days to 3 weeks after the injury. Symptoms of a *chronic subdural hematoma* appear within 3 weeks to 6 months.[49] Subtle mood changes, irritability, drowsiness, seizures, and decreasing consciousness are signs of subdural hematomas. The very young child will have bulging fontanels and mild head enlargement.

Repeated subdural taps over a 10-day period are used to treat chronic subdural hematomas in infants. Excess blood is removed and accurately measured. Surgery is necessary if bleeding does not stop or in older children where the subdural space cannot be reached by subdural puncture. A shunt, similar to that used in hydrocephalus, is often put in place to treat communicating hydrocephalus, a frequent complication.

Diagnosis of head injuries is based on a complete neurological assessment, skull x-ray, CAT scan, echoencephalogram, or angiographic studies. Lumbar punctures are not done if any signs of increased ICP are present.

Medical treatment Treatment of head injury is based on the severity of the injury. With a mild concussion and loss of consciousness for less than 5 min, the child may be observed closely at home for 24 h. Indications for at-home observation include stable alertness, normal vital signs, normal neurological assessment, no more than three vomiting episodes, and reliable parent observers.

Parents may wonder about letting their child sleep. They need careful instructions about how to observe their child and what signs indicate danger. Parents should be instructed to check their child every hour in the following ways:

1. Wake up the sleeping child. Is it easy to wake him up? Is he alert and oriented to time, place and person?

Figure 37-16 Hematomas. (A) Epidural. (B) Subdural. [*From Beverly A. Bowens, "The Nervous System," in M. Armstrong et al. (eds.), McGraw-Hill Handbook of Clinical Nursing, McGraw-Hill, New York, 1979. Used with permission.*]

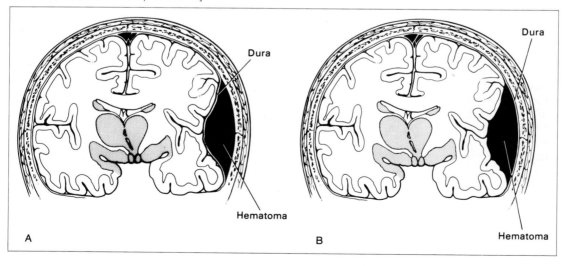

A   B

2. Check the pupils for size, equality, and reaction to light.
3. Check movement and strength of extremities. Are his hand grasps of equal strength?

Parents should be instructed to bring their child to the hospital if drowsiness is worse, the child does not respond, vomiting or headache increases, one-sided weakness develops, or pupils appear unequal in size or reaction to light.

More serious head injuries are characterized by longer periods of unconsciousness or a period of alertness followed by decreasing consciousness, seizures, or repeated vomiting. Treatment is based on assessment of neurological status and other injuries (Table 37-18). The child must be hospitalized.

Fluids are restricted to 75 percent of normal because of cerebral edema. Cerebral edema is also managed with corticosteroids (dexamethasone), hypertonic solutions (short-term usage), and hyperventilation via controlled ventilation. Hyperventilation, with the Pa_{CO_2} kept at 25 to 30 mmHg, will reduce cerebral blood flow. Less blood flow, and therefore volume and pressure, will give the swollen brain more room. Blood gases will be monitored closely if a respirator is used. Intracranial pressure monitoring may also be used.

Laboratory tests are done to monitor kidney function and sepsis. A urinary catheter is used to monitor output. Occasionally a cooling blanket is necessary if fever is difficult to control.

Clear drainage from the nose or ear should be checked with Dextrostix for the presence of glucose, which identifies the drainage as CSF. Antibiotics are used with any penetrating injuries to prevent infection.

Surgical treatment is used for depressed fractures and removal of hematomas. A Jackson-Pratt drain is often placed in the epidural space to drain off excess blood after surgery. It must be recharged periodically as it fills with blood. Since its suction decreases as it is filled, the bulb should be emptied frequently using sterile technique. The blood is measured accurately and may be replaced (by transfusion) with whole blood on a volume basis.

Nursing management The neurological examination forms the baseline for all future observations of the child and may be used in the

Table 37-18 Checklist for head injury assessment

Airway
Head
    Lacerations
    Depressed skull fracture
    Drainage from ears, nose, mouth
Neurological status
    Level of consciousness
    Vital signs
    Pupils, size, reaction, movement
    Motor and sensory function
    Breathing pattern
Bleeding
Broken bones
Bladder, bowel control

decision for surgical intervention. Level of consciousness remains the most sensitive indicator of neurological condition. Pupillary responses and vital signs must also be checked frequently.

It is imperative that nurses document their assessments clearly, accurately, and completely. Objective evidence is essential to document a trend or change in the patient's condition. Vital signs are often done every 15 min for 4 hours and then every hour. As the child improves frequency is decreased.

The child who is unconscious needs meticulous nursing care. Hypoventilation must be prevented and an airway maintained. The child is turned and suctioned as necessary. The head and neck should be kept in straight alignment, and the head of the bed elevated 30° to increase venous return from the head. With any fluid loss or drainage from a laceration, it is important to estimate the amount on the dressing. Dressings should be reinforced or changed before they become wet on the outside to prevent entrance of a pathogen into the wound. Catheter care, accurate intake and output, and daily weights are important. Passive range of motion and elastic stockings aid in venous return.

A child may be confused and combative. A screaming child is difficult to manage and may cause the nurse such unwelcome feelings as frustration and anger. The nurse must remember that bruising of the brain causes the irrational behavior. Restraining the child can lead to an increase in intracranial pressure and should be avoided.

It is helpful to talk soothingly to the child and

to touch and to stroke him. A calm, gentle touch and voice will be reassuring. The child's parents should be encouraged to keep contact with the child. The nurse should also remain with the child as much as possible.

If the child's condition changes, the nurse should make another neurological assessment and look for changes. Any localizing signs should be noted. A child may need to be checked every 3 to 4 min so that a detailed report can be given to the attending physician. Nursing care focuses on early recognition of complications.

Children recover from head injuries amazingly well, although long-term rehabilitation may be necessary after severe injuries. Posttraumatic amnesia, or loss of day-to-day memory, is related to the degree of brain damage and length of unconsciousness. Memory may be one of the last functions to return. For each day of decreased level of consciousness the child can be expected to experience 2 days of posttraumatic amnesia.[50]

Some children develop the *posttraumatic syndrome:* severe headache, dizziness, tinnitus, double vision, difficulty focusing, slight ataxia, personality changes, poor coordination, depression, or learning difficulties. Ordinarily children experience fewer problems than adults. By the end of a year, these symptoms usually disappear.

Table 37-19 Summary of activities of daily living possible according to level of cord injury

C1–3	Requires respirator because of complete respiratory paralysis. Quadriplegia—totally dependent
C4	Totally dependent. Needs externally powered devices for upper extremity function. Poor respiratory reserves
C5	Can perform self-grooming activities and feed self with assistive devices. Poor respiratory reserve. Can use electric wheelchair. Needs help to transfer, and with bowel and bladder care
C6	Performs self-grooming activities. Pushes wheelchair. Can drive using hand controls. May need help with bladder, bowel care
C7–8	Can transfer self. Manages self-care activities. Independent in wheelchair.
T1–10	Has full use of upper extremities. May have problem with balance
T10–12	Good trunk control. Can use braces, crutches
L3 or below	Floppy ankles. May get along without wheelchair by using short leg braces

Posttraumatic seizures develop more frequently in children than in adults—usually within 1 to 3 months. Prophylactic anticonvulsant therapy is sometimes begun during hospitalization and tapered off in a few years if no seizures occur.

Spinal cord injuries

Spinal cord trauma in childhood is most often the result of an accident or sports injury. Damage to the bone or cord and nerve roots can be caused by fracture, dislocation, interruption of vascular supply, compression, contusion, or laceration. Hyperextension, flexion, and rotation forces can all cause various degrees of damage. The sites most often affected in children include C1 to C2, C5 to C6, and T11 to L2.

Pathophysiology A cervical spinal injury can produce paralysis of all four extremities (quadriplegia) with involvement of respiratory muscles. Injury at C1 to C2 is usually incompatible with life. With a thoracic-level spinal cord injury the muscles of the lower extremities, bladder, and rectum are involved. Usually automatic urinary activity is possible. With a lumbar-level spinal cord injury, flaccid paralysis of lower extremities, bladder, and rectum results, with no automatic bladder activity. Table 37-19 describes the expected activities of daily living a child (or adult) can eventually manage according to the level of injury.

When injury occurs, edema, inflammation, and ischemia develop in the spinal cord at the site of the injury. The immediate signs of compression are loss of movement and sensation below the level of the injury, urinary retention, absence of reflexes, and pain at the injury site. *Spinal shock* occurs with the sudden disruption of central and autonomic pathways and leads to a *flaccid* paralysis, lack of reflexes, vasodilatation, and hypotension.

When spinal shock is present and reflexes absent, there will be (1) atrophy of both the paralyzed and noninvolved muscles, (2) atonic bladder with urinary retention, (3) respiratory difficulty with a higher lesion, (4) calcium loss, (5) great risk of pressure sores, and (6) inability to regulate body temperature (with higher lesions, also). Spinal shock lasts from 1 day to 6 weeks, when autonomic reflex activity returns. Usually the shorter the period of spinal shock, the greater the degree of recovery expected. With the return of some reflex activity, there may be muscle twitching, increased tone, and involuntary movement. This increase in activity may give false hope to the child and family for complete recovery.

The return of spinal reflexes can lead to contractures and *autonomic dysreflexia*. Autonomic dysreflexia constitutes an emergency. The increase in sympathetic activity causes systolic blood pressure to rise to over 200 mmHg. The patient experiences a severe headache, sweating, shivering, flushing of face and upper extremities, piloerection, and cardiac arrhythmias. Seizures and retinal or cerebral hemorrhages may be precipitated. Treatment consists of removing the stimulus and reducing blood pressure.

The usual causes of autonomic dysreflexia are an overdistended bladder, fecal impaction, or some other type of sensory overload such as leg spasms, decubitus ulcer, or overdistention of the stomach. Treatment is immediate removal of the cause. The bladder should be emptied gradually as sudden decompression can cause a quick drop in blood pressure. Careful, gentle manual removal of an impaction followed by a suppository is a reasonably safe approach for fecal impaction.

Initially the patient should be placed in a sitting position (if possible) and the physician notified. Ganglionic blocking agents may be necessary. The best treatment is prevention by immediate investigation of early signs of distress (gooseflesh, restlessness, perspiration) and prevention of triggering events. Both the patient and nurse must be alert for development of this complication.

In the final stages of cord injury, neurological signs stabilize. Young children with high thoracic and cervical lesions are prone to develop curvature of the spine because of unequal muscle tension and spasticity. Reflex activity in the child with a high injury reaches its maximum in about 2 years and then diminishes.

Medical treatment The initial care of a cord-injured child is very important. A coordinated team trained in stabilization and transfer techniques should move the child. Early management is supportive of vital functions. The last normal cord segment is used to classify the injury. A child with complete C7 function level has a functioning C7 root but no function below that level and should be able to bend and straighten the elbow (Table 37-20).

X-rays and a neurological exam are done. Oxygen, assisted respiration, maintenance of blood pressure, nasogastric suction, intravenous dexamethasone, and traction may be indicated. Surgery is done only if there is:

1. An increasing neurological deficit
2. Bone impinging on the cord or nerve root
3. An opening in the dura, or
4. Abdominal wounds communicating with the spinal cord

Nursing management Children with spinal cord injuries require excellent long-term nursing care. Although the care is similar to that required by the infant with a myelomeningocele, it differs considerably because of the child's age (usually adolescence) and suddeness of the injury.

When motor dysfunction is present, the nursing care goals are to maintain physiological functioning, to prevent complications of immobility, to help resolve issues of grief, dependency, and body image, and to promote adaptation.[51]

Initially vital functions must be maintained. Flexion of the neck must be avoided to prevent airway obstruction. Decreased vital capacity, oxygen distribution, and respiratory reserves all contribute to respiratory difficulty or arrest. Assisted ventilation and suctioning may be necessary. Some children will be helped with incentive spirometers. Chest physiotherapy may be done every 2 h. Assisted coughing is helpful with higher lesions. In assisted coughing, the child breathes in and out at least three times. Then the nurse pushes in and up on the diaphragm to help the child cough. This procedure may be necessary every 2 to 3 h with a new lesion.

Children with spinal cord injuries are at increased risk for pressure sores because they lack vasomotor control and sensation and have decreased peripheral circulation. Normal pressure from body weight can cause tissue ischemia in 30 min. It is imperative that these children be turned at least every 1 to 2 h; their skin must be kept clean and dry. Vigorous rubbing and soap should be avoided. Sheepskin elbow, heel, and sacrum protectors and gentle massage are helpful. Alternating pressure mattresses are used frequently. Donuts or rubber rings should never

Table 37-20 Spinal nerves and areas of innervation (sensory and motor)

Spinal nerve	Sensory (dermatome)	Motor innervation	Quick check of function after injury
C2	Occiput	C1–3: neck trapezius	
C3	Neck		
C4	Neck and upper shoulder	Diaphragm	
C5	Lateral aspect of shoulder	Deltoid, biceps (flexes elbow)	Lifts elbow to shoulder
C6	Radial arm, thumb, index finger	Extensor carpi radialis rotates arm externally	
C7	Middle finger, middle palm, and back of hand	Triceps, extends elbow, wrist and hand	
C8	Ulnar forearm, ring and little finger	Flexor digitorum	Grip
T1–2	Middle arm and axilla	T1: hand intrinsics	
T4	Nipple zone	T2–L1: intercostals	
T7	Lower costal margin	T1–T8: thoracic musculature	
T12–L1	Groin	T6–T8: abdominal musculature	
L3–4	Anterior knee, lower leg	L2–4: quadriceps (knee jerk)	Lifts leg or flexes hip
L5	Great toe, medium dorsum of foot	L5–S1: gastrocnemius	Extends knee
S1	Sole, Achilles tendon	S2–4: bowel and bladder	Pushes toe downward
S2	Posterior thigh	S1–2: ankle, foot	Ankle jerk
S3	Medial thigh		
S4–5	Genitals and saddle area		

be used. When patients are immobilized, their healing powers are diminished because cell breakdown is greater than cell production. If a decubitus ulcer develops, the child can lose up to 50 mg of protein a day. Maintaining intact skin requires much less nursing care time than does caring for decubitus ulcers!

The child should be properly positioned in bed as well as turned frequently. Once the acute phase is over, active and passive range-of-motion excercises are begun. If spasticity is present, the limb should be positioned in opposition to the position of contraction. Keeping the child in a prone position with the limbs straight for several short periods each day helps to prevent contractures. A great deal of care must be taken when moving anyone with a flaccid paralysis to protect limbs from strain or injury.

Nutritional needs are increased, requiring a diet high in vitamins, calories, and protein. Weight should be measured and monitored as soon as possible. Fluids should be maintained at 1500 to 2000 ml a day as soon as peristalsis returns. Inactivity and calcium loss from bones predispose the patient to renal calculi. Urine is checked for color, clarity, specific gravity, and amount.

Remobilization of the child begins after the acute phase to minimize osteoporosis. Gradually the patient is raised from a lying to sitting to an erect position. Vital signs must be checked closely and observations made for hypotension and syncope. Eventually wheelchairs, braces, and adaptive devices will be selected for the child to allow him to gain maximum mobility and independence.

Damage to the cord results in a neuropathic (neurogenic) bladder and bowel. Normally cerebral control provides an inhibitory influence over the micturition reflex when the bladder fills to keep it from emptying spontaneously. When upper motor neuron damage occurs, this control is gone and the bladder will empty automatically, but often incompletely, once reflex activity returns. If the conus medullaris or peripheral nerves to the bladder are damaged, the bladder has no innervation and will overdistend. Eventually this causes overflow incontinence. It is also possible to have mixed lesions producing varying degrees of the above.

Because bladder function may not always be predictable on the basis of the cord level injury, each child must be evaluated urologically. Reflex tests, blood tests, and kidney and bladder studies are performed to establish functional ability and to determine a baseline for future evaluation. Since renal failure from repeated infections is the most common cause of death in the postacute phase of spinal cord injury, bladder management is extremely important.

Bladder training is achieved through methods such as intermittent catheterization, Credé or other triggering mechanisms, pharmacological agents, and sometimes urinary diversion. (Bladder training is discussed in greater detail in Chap. 31.) Fluids are regulated and intake and output are measured carefully. The urine may be kept acidic with ascorbic acid (1 to 4 g daily) and cranberry juice to minimize the formation of stones.

Bowel training is based on a high-roughage diet, fluids, use of suppositories, stool softeners, activity, and manual stimulation. Usually regular bowel movements and good control can be established by following a regular routine.

Self-control in bowel and bladder functions is an important symbol of autonomy and self-control. "Accidents" can damage a child's self-esteem and increase his sense of isolation. Including the child in plans and goal setting increases his sense of participation and self-control.

The nurse must recognize that the child and family are totally unprepared for the effects of spinal cord injury. At first the situation may be too much for them to comprehend in all its ramifications. Shock, disbelief, and denial are common. During the acute phase the child may appear tense, jittery, and apathetic. Dependency needs are increased. Loss of control of body functions and abilities causes tremendous changes in body image and self-concept. Day by day the child and family are forced to face the impact the injury will have on future life.

After the initial acute phase subsides, anxiety, anger, and depression may become more evident. As the child is confronted with reality, issues of mobility and self-care arise. The child is faced with learning new skills when his self-image and self-esteem may be at a low ebb. The family is confronted with financial problems and long-term rehabilitation needs.

As in any grieving process, the emotional and physical changes that occur will cause the child to fluctuate among many emotional states. The nurse will need to be knowledgeable about the tentative nursing prognosis so preparation of the patient and family for the future can be accomplished. Appropriate communication shows concern and caring and emphasizes hopeful signs without giving false reassurance.

Gradually the child and family become ready for more information as recovery proceeds. The nurse must guard against overwhelming them with all that must be learned.

Slowly children and adolescents become curious about what their bodies can do. They decide that life is worth living after all and can then make amazing progress toward self-care.

Problems of self-concept can become particularly important in the adolescent. The adolescent normally is sorting out his identity, establishing his independence, and exploring his sexuality. Suddenly all is changed. Depression is normal as he grieves over this major loss.

Adolescents will have many concerns about sexuality. They will have many questions and concerns, which they may not be able to share. Information must be provided about what can be expected.

Usually sexual function in girls is unimpaired except that genital sensation and reflex vaginal lubrication are decreased. If menarche has occurred, menstruation will cease for about 6 months and then return. Usually a female can become pregnant and deliver vaginally.

Sexual function in the male is unpredictable and much more likely to be altered. Reflex erection is possible with a high lesion and intact sacral cord. With incomplete lesions, erection and ejaculation may be possible. With cauda equina lesions erection is not possible. Ordinarily males will be impotent. With the advent of intrapenile prosthetic devices a controlled erection may make intercourse possible for more males. The male with a penile implant, however, is sterile.

Openness in communication with adolescents will help allay their fears and encourage sharing of anxieties. Sexual counseling should include helping the adolescent learn to express initimacy and how to be a sexual human being within the limitations placed upon him. Nurses should examine their own attitudes toward sexuality and be familiar with all ways that individuals can find sexual gratification. When a child's sexual role is altered, testing will occur with those around him. The nurse may have to set limits on behavior. However, the nurse should keep communication lines open and understand the child's basic need to define his or her sexuality. The nursing care plan at the end of the chapter pertains to an adolescent male with a spinal cord injury.

Lead poisoning

Lead poisoning (plumbism) poses a serious health hazard to children under age 6, but especially to those between 1 and 3 years. Lead poisoning is usually due to the ingestion of nonfood substances (pica) and is an outgrowth of the toddler's tendency to mouth substances and objects in the environment.

Until the 1940s interior house paint contained lead. Young children often chewed on their painted cribs or window sills or ate paint chips. (A very small number of paint chips may contain up to 100 mg of lead.) In 1973 federal legislation was passed prohibiting the use of lead-base paint in homes. Unfortunately, many older homes and apartment buildings have underlying layers of lead-base paint and plaster. Often these dwellings are in deteriorating slum areas where children have limited environmental stimuli, poor diets, and families under social and economic stress.

Other sources of lead are improperly fired lead-glazed pottery; water from lead pipes; dirt; newspaper with colored print; and painted toys. Another common factor associated with lead poisoning today is atmospheric lead from automobile exhausts. On the average, children living near congested highways have higher lead concentrations in their blood than those living in rural areas. Older children who "sniff" gasoline can also be poisoned. Lead poisoning continues to be a serious problem today.

Pathophysiology The effect of lead on body systems is due to inhibition of certain enzymatic reactions that are essential to the transport of substances across cell membranes. Usually bone marrow is affected first. The production of heme is altered, leading to a hemolytic anemia, one of the initial signs of the disease. Although lead damages the cells of renal tubules and bone marrow, its effects on these tissues are reversible.

The effects of lead on the central nervous system are the most significant because they are probably irreversible. Symptoms range from mild neurological disability to acute encephalopathy

manifested by hypertension, increased intracranial pressure, cerebral edema, stupor, seizures, coma, and even death.

Symptoms of chronic lead poisoning may not appear for several months and depend upon the amount of lead ingested. Even when symptoms do occur, they may mimic viral infections or behavioral disturbances. Common symptoms are anorexia, abdominal pain, anemia, constipation, nausea, and vomiting. Behavioral changes include clumsiness, irritability, apathy, and lethargy. The young child may have difficulty with fine or gross motor skills that were mastered months before. Low-level lead poisoning may go undetected and manifest itself in under-achievement in school.

Detection Screening procedures for lead poisoning are based on measurement of the amount of lead or the erythrocyte protoporphyrin (EP) level in blood. In high-risk communities EP level is used for routine screening because it requires only a fingerstick.

Normal blood lead levels range from 15 to 40 $\mu g/100$ ml. When the blood level of lead is above 40 $\mu g/100$ ml further diagnostic study is indicated, and chelating (ability to bind with a metal) treatment becomes mandatory at levels over 50 to 60 $\mu g/100$ ml. EP levels above normal (40 to 75 $\mu g/100$ ml) may indicate anemia but are almost always caused by lead poisoning when they exceed 190 $\mu g/100$ ml. Usually several diagnostic tests are combined and clinical symptoms evaluated before a course of treatment is begun.

Other signs of lead poisoning include:

1. Increased density in long bones at the metaphysis
2. Lead in urine and hair
3. Blue lead line in gums
4. Increased protein and traces of lead in CSF

Medical treatment Acute lead poisoning (encephalopathy) or chronic lead poisoning with high lead levels requires immediate treatment with chelating agents. If ingestion of lead is recent and of large quantity, gastric lavage, magnesium sulfate, and milk will be used to remove lead, form insoluble salts in the intestines, and counteract the uptake of lead in the bones.

Lead is removed from the body by chelating agents that combine with lead in the blood and enhance its excretion in urine. Calcium disodium

Table 37-21 Antidotes for lead poisoning*

Antidote	Dose	Comments
Dimercaprol (BAL)	3–5 mg/kg q4h IM × 2 days then 2.5–3 mg/kg q6h IM × 2 days, then q12h × 7 days	Observe blood pressure, fever, myalgia, hypo- or hypertension, pulmonary edema. Also used for arsenic poisoning
Calcium disodium ethylenediamine-tetraacetate (Ca EDTA)	50–75 mg/kg per day IM or IV in 3 to 6 divided doses up to 5 days with encephalopathy or blood lead levels 100 mg/100 ml or more	Given till urine returns to nontoxic levels. Can cause renal tubular necroses, and so fluid must be given in adequate quantities
Penicillamine	100 mg/kg per day up to 1 g per day in divided doses up to 5 days	Do not give if allergic to penicillin. Monitor for proteinuria. Antidote for copper, lead, and mercury

* **Source:** Adapted from M. Wiener, G. Pepper, G. Kuhn-Weisman, and J. RImano, *Clinical Pharmacology and Therapeutics in Nursing*, McGraw-Hill, New York, 1979, p. 789.

edetate (Ca EDTA) and dimercaprol (BAL) are two chelating agents used as antidotes for lead or other heavy-metal poisoning. Penicillamine is an oral chelating agent used for children who do not tolerate Ca EDTA, or BAL. See Table 37-21.

Symptomatic treatment involves control of seizures, oxygen and respiratory support, close observation of neurological status and kidney function, and monitoring of calcium and phosphorous levels. Chelating agents, especially Ca EDTA, also remove calcium and can be toxic to the kidneys.

Nursing management Ideally nursing care focuses on the prevention of lead poisoning by identifying and helping screen children at risk. Prevention is especially important since the prognosis following lead poisoning is not very good. Mortality rate can be as high as 25 percent following acute encephalopathy. Even with treatment children with prolonged exposure to lead show residual effects such as mental retardation, seizure disorders, or behavioral disturbances.

For those children who are acutely ill the nurse must carry out the delegated medical regimen and administer chelating agents. When Ca EDTA and BAL are administered concurrently through the intramuscular route, a child can receive up to 12 injections per day or 60 in 5 days. Any child who receives that many injections will need careful preparation, an oppor-

tunity to "check off" each one on a chart, and play therapy to help work out his feelings about this invasive therapy.

Injections must be rotated carefully. If each site is divided into four corners and a center and if six muscles are used (right and left vastus lateralis, ventrogluteal, and gluteus maximus), then each specific location will be used only twice. A local anesthetic may be added to the medication and injected first so that pain is reduced.

Nursing care includes careful neurological assessment, measurement of intake and output, and support of basic needs. Seizure precautions are necessary because of cerebral edema. All aspects of nursing care described earlier for the unconscious child are appropriate for the child with acute encephalopathy.

Before the child leaves the hospital, the home environment must be evaluated and made lead-free if possible. All possible sources of lead must be removed and close supervision guaranteed to keep children away from sources that can't be eliminated.

The health department and medical social worker often must be involved along with other members of the health team. With increased awareness of symptoms, effective screening programs, and quick intervention, there should continue to be a decline in the incidence of lead poisoning in children.

Nursing Care Plan–Spinal Cord Damage*

Patient: Tim Jones   **Age:** 16 years   **Date of Admission:** July 6

Assessment

Date: September 4
Diagnosis: Fracture dislocation of C5–6
Sex: male
Religion: Catholic
Weight: 62 kg
Parents' marital status: Married
Siblings: 3 sisters—14, 13, and 12 years
Previous hospital experience: None
Reason for hospitalization: Quadriplegia
Allergies: None known

General appearance   Tim gives the appearance of a well-developed 16-year-old boy. He cannot move his lower extremities and lacks any sensation below the nipple line. He has gross movement of his upper extremities but lacks fine finger movement and has spotty areas of sensation in arms. His skin is in good condition with no pressure areas. His lungs are congested and upon auscultation scattered rales and rhonchi are heard throughout both lung fields. Vital signs: Temp.: 38.5°C (101.3°F); Resp.: 30; P: 92; BP: 100/60.

History of present illness   Tim is a 16-year-old white male who suffered a fracture dislocation of C5–6 when he dove into shallow water at a gravel pit. Shortly after admission, Tim underwent a cervical fusion and is now stabilized with a Philadelphia collar. Tim's motor and sensory levels are intact at C7. After spending 4 weeks on a neurology unit, Tim was transferred to a rehabilitation unit 1 week ago. As Tim's primary nurse, you assess that he is depressed and sometimes refuses his nursing care.

Although Tim's family lives 150 mi away, Tim's mother is with him from early morning until late at night and is available for anything he needs. Tim and his father were very close before the accident. His father now visits Tim on the weekends with the rest of the family.

Physician's orders

1. *Bladder retraining program*
   a. 1800-ml fluid program—400 ml at meals (8 A.M., 12 noon, 6 P.M.) 200 ml at 10 A.M., 2 P.M., 4 P.M.
   b. Tap bladder q3h (automatic or upper motor neuron bladder)
   c. Intermittent catheterization q6h (immediately after every other bladder tapping)
   d. Urine culture and sensitivity every week
   e. Sulfamethoxazole, trimethoprim (Septra) bid
2. *Bowel retraining program*
   a. Dulcolax suppository qod
   b. High-fiber diet
   c. Colace 100 mg bid
3. *Respiratory program*
   a. Chest physiotherapy and postural drainage q4h
   b. Deep breathing and supportive cough q1–2 h while awake
   c. Vital signs q6h
4. Skin maintenance program
   a. Turn q2h
   b. Sheepskin—full-length
   c. Up in wheelchair 1–2 hours tid as tolerated—with a cushion
5. *Nutrition*
   a. High-protein, high-fiber diet
   b. Weigh weekly

Nursing diagnosis	Nursing goals	Nursing actions	Evaluation/revision
1. Respiratory congestion secondary to decreased innervation of muscles utilized for breathing	☐ Tim will not show any signs of congestion in 1 week as evidenced by: **a.** Lungs clear upon auscultation **b.** Clear secretions brought up with supportive	☐ Auscultate lungs q4h before and after chest physiotherapy and postural drainage ☐ Chest physiotherapy and postural drainage q4h ☐ Encourage deep breath-	☐ 9/6: Patient's lungs were auscultated q4h—scattered rhonchi in bases of both lungs noted ☐ Deep breathing, supportive cough and chest physiotherapy often results in no

Nursing diagnosis	Nursing goals	Nursing actions	Evaluation/revision
	cough **c.** Respiratory rate within normal limits (less than 26)	ing and assist with supportive cough q1h while awake ☐ Observe for signs of respiratory distress, tachypnea, or restlessness	productive cough—when secretions are brought up they are clear ☐ Respiratory rate remains 20–24. Continue plan until lungs are clear of congestion then auscultate 1 × day
2. Inability to voluntarily empty bladder secondary to automatic neurogenic bladder.	☐ In 6 weeks patient will learn how to empty bladder by adhering to a bladder retraining program including: **a.** Suprapubic tapping of bladder q3h **b.** Fluid intake of 1800 ml, 400 ml at meals (8 A.M., 12 noon, 6 P.M), and 200 ml at 10 A.M., 2 P.M., and 4 P.M. **c.** Intermittent catheterization q6h until residuals are less than 75 ml consistently **d.** Perineal hygiene bid **e.** Septra—bid to aid in the prevention of urinary tract infections	☐ Instruct Tim in bladder retraining program ☐ Assist with tapping as needed—encourage Tim to tap his own bladder as able ☐ Make sure Tim has access to fluids at the specified times. Encourage Tim to keep track of own intake and output ☐ Reinforce importance of completely emptying the bladder with effective tapping technique to decrease residual urine volumes. Do intermittent catheterizations within 15 min after tapping is completed ☐ Explain importance of washing perineal area bid to help prevent UTIs ☐ Administer medication and describe how the medication helps keep the urine free from bacteria	☐ 9/16: Tim is beginning to tap himself—tires after 3 min and requires assistance. Urine volumes with tapping range from 75–150 ml. ☐ Patient is adhering to 1800-ml fluid program and keeping track of input and output himself ☐ Residual urine volumes running 150–250 ml ☐ Perineal hygiene performed by nurse in the morning and before sleep ☐ No urinary tract infections at present ☐ *Continue plan*
3. Inability to voluntarily evacuate bowels secondary to neurogenic bowel	☐ In 4 weeks Tim will be retrained to evacuate bowels at regularly scheduled intervals by adhering to a bowel retraining program including: **a.** Performing bowel care evacuation on a qod regular schedule **b.** Dulcolax suppository qod **c.** Eating at least 8 fiber-containing foods daily **d.** Maintaining 1800-ml fluid intake	☐ Instruct and explain bowel retraining program. Encourage optimal level of independence ☐ Determine with Tim his preference for time of day to complete bowel evacuation—preferably after a meal. Stress importance of establishing a *regular* schedule qod ☐ Explain purpose and action of Dulcolax suppository. Observe response to Dulcolax (length of time evacuation occurs after suppository) and nature of results ☐ Explain importance of bulk/fiber in diet. Give Tim a list of foods high in fiber ☐ Explain how fluid intake affects the bowels. Encourage patient to keep his fluid intake up to 1800 ml per day ☐ Give Colace 100 mg qid ☐ Observe for constipation, impaction	☐ 9/18: Patient has not been incontinent of bowel since beginning his bowel retraining program ☐ Currently receiving bowel care every other day after breakfast ☐ The bowel evacuation occurs 20–30 min after Dulcolax suppository ☐ When planning his daily menu, Tim chooses at least 8 fiber foods a day and eats them consistently ☐ Intake is consistently 1800 ml ☐ *Continue plan*

Nursing diagnosis	Nursing goals	Nursing actions	Evaluation/revision
4. Dependence on mother and nurse for activities of daily living (ADL) secondary to paralysis of extremities	☐ Tim will reach optimal level of independence in activities of daily living by discharge ☐ Tim will learn how to direct cares he is not able to perform physically ☐ Tim's mother (family) will continue to promote Tim's independence in ADL	☐ Follow up and encourage Tim to pursue the instructions received in his various therapies (occupational therapy, physical therapy) ☐ Assist Tim in utilizing assistive devices, orthotic (splinting) or prosthetic devices when performing ADLs ☐ Emphasize independence by instructing the individual to direct his daily living activities ☐ Encourage mother/family to support Tim's independence ☐ Teach mother/family rationale and skills needed to care for Tim at home	☐ 9/18: Tim is beginning to perform some activities of daily living with the help of assistive devices ☐ He is now starting to learn how to feed himself and brush his teeth ☐ Can wash his own face but cannot complete any more of his personal hygiene needs, including dressing ☐ Not able to direct his own cares at this point ☐ Mother learning how to manage some of Tim's care ☐ *Continue plan*
5. Potential for skin breakdown secondary to loss of sensation and impaired circulation	☐ Tim will understand importance of good skin care and will not develop any areas of skin breakdown during and after hospitalization as evidenced by: **a.** Absence of skin breakdown **b.** Ability to describe principles of preventing skin breakdown **c.** Ability to list signs of impending skin breakdown **d.** Taking responsibility for inspecting his skin (especially areas prone to injury) **e.** Taking appropriate precautions to prevent thermal injury	☐ Assess skin for redness, rashes, dryness at every turning. Turn and rub skin surfaces q2h when in bed. Sheepskin on bed. Use cushion in wheelchair ☐ Instruct and explain principles of good skin care ☐ Describe signs and symptoms of skin breakdown ☐ Provide a long-handled mirror so Tim can begin to inspect own skin ☐ Help Tim choose and value a high-protein diet ☐ Alert Tim to danger of hot or cold water, objects, etc., when loss of sensation is present	☐ 9/18: Skin intact ☐ Tim able to verbalize warning signs of skin breakdown ☐ Does not take responsibility for inspecting own skin or directing others to do it ☐ *Continue plan*
6. Potential joint contractures secondary to muscle spasm and weakness	☐ Tim will achieve optimum function as evidenced by: **a.** Absence of joint deformity **b.** Absence of contractures	☐ Maintain body alignment ☐ Inspect joints for impending contractures ☐ Apply splints as ordered ☐ Support/assist physical therapy program	☐ Hands, feet, limbs in good alignment ☐ Absence of joint stiffness ☐ *Continue plan*
7. Potential for altered male sexual response secondary to cervical injury	☐ Tim will display an optimum level of sexual health as evidenced by: **a.** Expresses feelings about change in sexual function **b.** Able to separate sexual function from sexuality	☐ Assess patient's concern about his sexuality ☐ Display attitude of acceptance and willingness to discuss sexual concerns ☐ Explore Tim's feelings about loss of masculinity ☐ Provide opportunity for Tim to acquire information about expected sexual function and fertility	☐ Tim remains hesitant in discussing his sexuality ☐ *Continue plan*

Nursing diagnosis	Nursing goals	Nursing actions	Evaluation/revision
8. Depression and grieving due to altered body image and prolonged hospitalization	☐ Tim's depression will lessen and he will learn to accept his disability within his lifetime through: **a.** Developing a trusting relationship with his primary nurse **b.** Verbalizing his feelings about his spinal cord injury and loss of function **c.** Exploring his future expectations and change in life-style with nurse, family, and friends	☐ Encourage Tim to look at his injury realistically and focus on his abilities rather than his disability ☐ Display acceptance of Tim's behavior ☐ Assist Tim in developing his independence and self-reliance ☐ Provide an environment conducive to nurse-patient interaction. Spend time with Tim ☐ Encourage Tim to share his feelings about his injury and life expectations ☐ Encourage Tim and his family and friends to discuss their feelings with each other ☐ Provide opportunity for involvement in group discussions with other patients	☐ Tim is beginning to look realistically at his injury ☐ He remains depressed and is not verbalizing much to anyone but primary nurse ☐ Has not discussed any future expectations at this time

Note: The nursing goals of this plan represent intermediate goals. Long-term goals would include restoration of sexual health, family adjustment, re-entry into the community, and achievement of an optimal level of independence in activities of daily living. It is possible that Tim will learn how to transfer, use a wheelchair, and even drive a car independently.

Tim's family will need support and education as they cope with changing roles, increasing financial burden, accommodation of living quarters to Tim and his wheelchair, and readjustment of their life-style to meet Tim's basic needs.

As Tim is prepared for discharge, weekly home visits should be encouraged. A public health nursing referral is helpful before discharge to promote dismissal planning. Tim's progress after discharge should be monitored to ensure that he is successfully reintegrated within his family, school, and community.

* Prepared by Kathy Orth, R.N., B.S. Former Head Nurse, Neuro-Rehabilitative Unit, St. Marys Hospital, Rochester, Minn. Currently Instructor, College of St. Teresa, Winona, Minn.

References

1. Rosanne Wille, George Jacobs, Robert Reibin, and John Hubbard, "Anatomy of the Brain and Skull," *Journal of Neuro-Surgical Nursing* 9(3):101 (September 1977).
2. Joyce Taylor and Sally Ballenger, *Neurological Dysfunctions and Nursing Interventions*, McGraw-Hill, New York, 1980, p. 51.
3. Ibid., P. 307.
4. Jean E. Johnson, Karin T. Kirckhoff, and M. Patricia Endress, "Altering Children's Distress Behavior during Orthopedic Cast Removal, *Nursing Research* 24:404–410 (November-December 1975).
5. Pamela Mitchell and Nancy Irvin, "Neurological Examination: Nursing Assessment for Nursing Purposes," *Journal of Neurosurgical Nursing* 9(1):23 (March 1977).
6. Marilyn Lyons, "Recognition of Neurological Dysfunction," *Nurse Practitioner*, September-October 1979, p. 34.
7. Cathy Jones, "Glasgow Coma Scale," *American Journal of Nursing* 79(9):1551–1553 (September 1979).
8. Taylor and Ballanger, op. cit., p. 142–143.
9. Robert A. Hoekelman, Saul Blatman, Philip A. Brunell, Stanford B. Friedman, Henry M. Seidel, *Principles of Pediatrics: Health Care of the Young*, McGraw-Hill, New York, 1978, p. 916.
10. Arnold Friedman, J. Gordon Millichip, and A. David Rothner, "When You Suspect Migraine in a Child," *Patient Care* September: 80 (1979).
11. Hoekelman et al., p. 953.
12. Barbara Lang Conway, *Pediatric Neurological Nursing*, Mosby, St. Louis, 1977, p. 235.
13. "Epilepsy: Medical Aspects," *Comprehensive Epilepsy Program*, University of Minnesota, 1978
14. Ibid.
15. Marvin A. Fishman, "Febrile Seizures: The Treatment Controversy," *The Journal of Pediatrics* 94:177–184 (February 1979).
16. H. Gastault, "Clinical and Electroencephalographical

Classification of Epileptic Seizures, *Epilepsia* 11:102–113 (1970).

17. Paula Russo and Kit Bakke, "Myoclonic Infantile Spasms," *Nurse Practitioner*, September October: 29 (1979).

18. Claire M. Chee, "Seizure Disorders," in Diane McElroy and Gayle Davis (eds.), *The Nursing Clinics of North America* 15(1):76 (March 1980).

19. Clyde R. Cooper, "Anticonvulsant Drugs and the Epileptic's Dilemma, *Nursing 76* 76:45–52 (January 1976).

20. Nancy Swift, "Helping Patients Live with Seizures," *Nursing 78* 8(6):25–31 (June 1978).

21. Margarethe Hawken, and Judith Ozuna: "Practical Aspects of Anticonvulsant Therapy," *American Journal of Nursing* 79(6):1065 (June 1979).

22. Loy Wiley, "The Stigma of Epilepsy," *Nursing 74* 74:37–45 (January 74).

23. Hawken and Ozuna, op. cit., p. 1062.

24. Ibid., p. 1067.

25. Ibid., p. 1066.

26. Russo and Bakke, op. cit., p. 28–29.

27. Hoekelman et al., op. cit., p. 922.

28. Sherrilyn Passo, "Malformations of the Neural Tube," in Diane McElroy and Gayle Davis (eds.), *The Nursing Clinics of North America* 15(1)8 (March 1980).

29. James Macri, James Haddow, and Robert Weiss, "Screening for Neural Tube Defects in the United States," *American Journal of Obstetrics and Gynecology* 133(2):119–125 (1979).

30. Passo, op. cit., p. 10.

31. Ibid. p. 13.

32. Barbara Lang Conway, (ed.), *Carini and Owens' Neurological and Neurosurgical Nursing*, Mosby, St. Louis, 1978, p. 235.

33. Passo, op. cit., p. 20.

34. Marie Louise Braney, "The Child with Hydrocephalus," *American Journal of Nursing* 73:831–838 (May 1973).

35. Gayle Tart Davis and Patty Maynard Hill, "Cerebral Palsy," in Diane McElroy and Gayle Davis (eds.), *The Nursing Clinics of North America* 15(1):47–48 (March 1980).

36. Ibid.

37. Dennis P. Cantwell, "Recognition, Evaluation and Management of the Hyperactive Child," *Pediatric Nursing*, September-October: 11 (1979).

38. Dennis R. Dubey and F. Kenneth Kaufman, "Home Management of Hyperkinetic Children," *Behavioral Pediatrics* 93:141–146 (July 1978).

39. Bob M. Van Osdol and Larry Carlson, "A Study of Developmental Hyperactivity," *Mental Retardation* 72:18–23 (June 1972).

40. Cantwell, op. cit., p. 13.

41. Ibid., p. 18.

42. D. D. Duane, "A Neurological Overview of Specific Language Disability for the Non-neurologist," *Bulletin Orton Society* 24:5–36 (1974).

43. Debra S. Gaddy, "Meningitis in the Pediatric Population," in Diane McElroy and Gayle Davis (eds.), *The Nursing Clinics of North America* 15(1):90 (March 1980).

44. Ibid., p. 92.

45. Kathryn R. Reeves, "Beware of Reye's Syndrome," *American Journal of Nursing* 74:1621–1622 (September 1974).

46. Richard J. Pickering and Rodrigo E. Urizar: "Abnormalities of the Complement System in Reye's Syndrome," *The Journal of Pediatrics* 94:218–222 (February 1979).

47. Taylor and Ballenger, op. cit., p. 401–402.

48. Connie Walleck, "Head Trauma in Children," in Diane McElroy and Gayle Davis (eds.), *The Nursing Clinics of North America* 15(1):120 (March 1980).

49. Ibid., p. 118–19.

50. Taylor and Ballenger, op. cit., p. 404.

51. Ibid., p. 235.

Chapter 38 **Developmental disabilities: Focus on mental retardation**

Linda L. Jarvis

On completion of this chapter, the student will be able to:

1. Define mental retardation in terms of scores on the Wechsler and Stanford-Binet tests of mental ability.

2. Give in your own words a definition of mental retardation.

3. State the term used for each degree of mental retardation.

4. Name four inherited abnormalities responsible for mental retardation.

5. Name four causes of acquired mental retardation in the prenatal, natal, and postnatal periods.

6. Describe the three stages of parental reaction to the diagnosis of mental retardation of their child.

7. Describe the assistance a nurse can give siblings of a mentally retarded child to ease their feelings about the child.

8. Identify six roles for the nurse of children with developmental disabilities.

9. Discuss what the nurse can do to prevent handicapping conditions when dealing with expectant mothers.

10. Name the three major stages of casefinding.

11. List three characteristics of the counseling role.

12. Discuss the scope of a nurse's role as advocate.

Introduction

Nurses working in health care settings frequently care for mentally retarded children. In order to provide effective care, it is important for nurses to have knowledge about mental retardation and to examine their own attitudes toward this condition. Primarily, nurses must remember that children who are mentally retarded are *children* first, with the same needs as all children (Fig. 38-1). The fact that they are mentally retarded certainly affects them and their future, but it is essential that their needs as children be met.

In the 1960s, President John F. Kennedy initiated the President's Committee on Mental Retardation. Since then, national interest, funds, and research have been directed toward the study, treatment, and understanding of mental retardation. To be mentally retarded in the United States often means relegation to second-class citizenship because educational, vocational, housing, and socialization options are severely restricted.

Nurses are involved in seeking ways to increase the intellectual and adaptive skill levels of mentally retarded children. Nurses assist families in developing effective ways of coping with the needs and demands of the mentally retarded family member. Educating health care peers and community members about the needs, abilities, and rights of the mentally retarded is another important role of the nurse. This chapter will explore the impact of a mentally retarded child on the family unit, the nurse's role in providing care to mentally retarded children and their

Figure 38-1 Mentally retarded children are first of all *children*, with the same needs as all children. (*Photo by Theresa Friedrich.*)

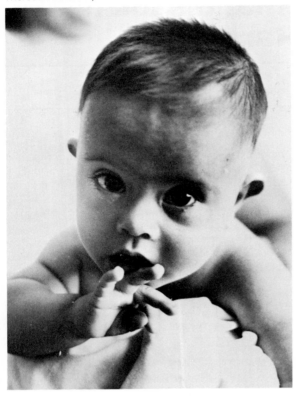

Table 38-1 Terms related to developmental disabilities

Mental retardation Significantly subaverage general intellectual functioning existing concurrently with deficits in adaptive behavior and manifested during the developmental period

General intellectual functioning The results obtained by assessment with one or more of the individually administered general intelligence tests developed for that purpose

Significantly subaverage IQ more than two standard deviations below the mean for the test

Adaptive behavior The effectiveness or degree with which an individual meets the standards of personal independence and social responsibility expected for the age and cultural group

Developmental period The period of time between birth and the 18th birthday

Source: Herbert J. Grossman (ed.), *Manual on Terminology and Classification in Mental Retardation*, American Association on Mental Deficiency, Washington, D.C., 1977, p. 11. Used by permission.

families, and the identification of helpful community resources.

Definitions of mental retardation

The American Association on Mental Deficiency (AAMD) provides a definition of mental retardation in its *Manual on Terminology and Classification in Mental Retardation*.[1] This broad definition has been designed to reflect current thinking in education, medicine, and psychology (see Table 38-1).

Measurements for both intellectual and adaptive skills reflect a child's level of functioning at the time of a given evaluation. These scores may later change due to the child's maturation and learning. A diagnosis of mental retardation is valid *only* when the child demonstrates deficits in intellectual *and* adaptive functioning.

Intelligence

A child who scores 67 or below on the Wechsler test is usually considered mentally retarded.[2] The Cattell scale and the Stanford-Binet test may be used successfully with infants and severely retarded children. Testing is sometimes not feasible if the child is uncooperative or severely retarded.[3] These tests must be administered and interpreted by individuals who are skilled in their use. A system for classifying mentally retarded children has been developed (see Table 38-2). It is important that caution be used before labeling a child mentally retarded.

Adaptive behavior

Measurement of adaptive behavior is more difficult than measurement of intelligence because it is hard to identify what the child usually does on a day-to-day basis. Adaptive behavior includes the child's general affect and social and motor skills. Caution must also be used in interpreting the results of adaptive tests. A child's adaptive behavior may change rapidly as a result of maturation, learning, and environmental modification. Thus, the child should be reevaluated frequently. The AAMD Adaptive Behavior Scale and the Vineland Social Maturity Scale are the most frequently used tests of adaptive behavior.[4] These tests identify adaptive behaviors which may range from "mild negative" to very poor.[5] Both tests were developed for use with institutionalized individuals, and they may not always

Table 38-2 Classification of mental retardation

Degree of mental retardation	Intelligence quotient obtained	
	Stanford-Binet test and Cattell scales (standard deviation = 16)	Wechsler scales (standard deviation = 15)
Mild ("educable")	67–52	69–55
Moderate ("trainable")	51–36	54–40
Severe ("dependent retarded")	35–20	39–25 (extrapolated)
Profound ("life support")	19 and below	24 and below

Source: Adapted from Herbert J. Grossman (ed.), *Manual on Terminology and Classification in Mental Retardation,* American Association on Mental Deficiency, Washington, D.C., 1977, p. 19.

be appropriate for testing noninstitutionalized children. Because of these disadvantages, adaptive tests are more useful *after* a diagnosis of mental retardation has been made.[6]

Developmental disabilities

Nurses should be aware of the definition of developmental disabilities in Public Law 95-602, signed into law by former President Jimmy Carter on November 6, 1978. It states:

> The term developmental disability means a severe, chronic disability which (a) is attributable to a mental or physical impairment or combination of mental and physical impairment (b) is manifested before the person attains age 22 years (c) is likely to continue indefinitely (d) results in substantial functional limitation in three or more of the following areas of major life activity—(1) self care (2) receptive and expressive language (3) hearing (4) mobility (5) self direction (6) capacity for independent living (7) economic self sufficiency and (e) reflects the person's need for a combination and sequence of special interdisciplinary or generic care, treatment or other services which are of a life long or extended duration and are individually planned and coordinated.[7]

This definition extends the focus of developmental disabilities further than previous definitions. It is not limited to a specific condition, such as cerebral palsy or mental retardation. The various components of the statement are critical to a clear understanding of the scope of the definition. Significantly, it means that physical, mental, or a combination of physical and mental impairments can occur prior to age 22 years which interfere with the complete development of the individual. Although several developmental disabilities are present and identified at birth, however, deficits which are later identified or which result from illness, accidents, poisoning, or deprivation can also be included within the scope of developmental disabilities. This is important because it allows the child and family to receive appropriate health and education services.

Because an age limit of 22 years is specified, children who become mentally retarded as a result of accident, trauma, or infectious disease during childhood and adolescence are included in the scope of services. This is particularly relevant, as the need for services for the mentally retarded probably will continue throughout their lifetime. Although the ability of states to provide educational programs is curtailed at ages 21 to 22, other state services can be utilized. These include vocational rehabilitation, human services, and various kinds of institutional care ranging from community residences and halfway houses to the traditional institutional settings for more protective care and supervision.

This definition also recognizes that areas such as self-help, the ability to live independently, and self-mobility skills directly influence the learning and independence potential of the individual and therefore should be a focus of intervention. The final point of the definition is the need for individualized multidisciplinary services and programming. Professional input for treatment programs comes from nurses, social workers, physicians, physical and occupational therapists, educators, vocational counselors, nutritionists, and psychologists. Since mentally retarded children are identified at different chronological and developmental ages, their needs may vary considerably. Thus, the composition of the interdisciplinary team may also vary. Individualization ensures that the needs of the specific child and his or her family are identified and addressed. The team approach also allows these professionals to pool their knowledge and skills in order to identify and address the child's numerous needs in a comprehensive manner.

Terminology and labeling

Terminology applied to the mentally retarded has changed over the years. This is due to increased knowledge about the complexity of various manifestations of mental retardation and sensitivity to the consequences of labeling for the child, family, and community. The term *developmental disability* or *disabilities* is now used for a large range of handicapping conditions affecting children, including mental retardation. It carries less social stigma than the terms *retardate, idiot, mentally deficient,* or others which have been used. Many parents find it far easier to say that their child is developmentally disabled than to say that he or she is mentally retarded. The term *mentally retarded* has been used over past decades to replace some of the older, less descriptive, and less accurate terms. It implies a degree of slowness in skill or ability, along with the hope that progress can be made in areas needing improvement. The term *mentally deficient* implies that something is missing and that replacement or improvement in deficit areas is not likely to occur. This loss of hope can severely curtail the effort by family members to provide for the special needs of their mentally retarded child. Many professionals in this field believe the term *developmentally disabled* has a positive influence on the family members. This allows families to focus on areas needing improvement rather than on the label of *mental retardation.*

Diagnostic labels are used by physicians primarily for identification and classification of the etiology and type of mental retardation. Once the diagnosis of mental retardation has been made, some labeling may occur if an intelligence quotient and adaptive rating are identified. Although labeling in itself is not negative, it can become detrimental to the progress of the child and family if the labels are regarded as concrete and unchanging. As a result of appropriate interventions and child maturation, intellectual and life skills often show remarkable progress. One's focus, therefore, should be on the *behavioral skills* which need to be developed rather than on the labels applied at a single, specific point in the child's life.

Labeling has long been a concern of parents and educators working with the mentally retarded. The general conclusion is that the label *mental retardation* has a negative impact which results in lowered expectations for the child. In 1974 an extensive review of the literature concerning this label was conducted. One conclusion was that research before 1970 did not support the negative effect of labeling.[8] The researchers found that individuals react to the label *mental retardation* on an individual basis and that the label is most important for the person functioning at the borderline level.[9] The impact of the label on children often depends on their ability to recognize the negative connotation of the label and their past history of success or failure in various endeavors. Mentally retarded children classified at the borderline level often know they are labeled *mentally retarded* and less capable in many areas than most of their peers. They are sensitive to the potential rejection by others because of both the label and their abilities. These children often have difficulty adjusting, particularly as they enter adolescence. They seek ways to look and behave like their nonretarded peers and actively resist placement in institutions or special classes.

Another study found that (1) labeling effects are less important when labels and other characteristics are combined for study, (2) the behavior exhibited by the children is often more biasing than are the labels, and (3) children interacting with mentally retarded peers are more likely to respond to behavior than to labels.[10] The importance of child behavior was cited by one expert, who observed that behavioral characteristics and academic achievement often identify a child as mentally retarded before special class placement or labeling occurs.[11] For peers of the mentally retarded, academic performance is more important than the label.[12]

The effect of labeling is questionable. It appears that both academic performance and behavioral characteristics often identify the child prior to the use of labeling. One authority states that "clinical labels may provide a way for children to understand retarded children's poor performances or appearance."[13] If this is true, the clinical label will help protect retarded children from the abuse that children labeled *retard* may receive. The label *mentally retarded* appears more objective in terms of the individual child's problems than the term *retard*, which implies negative concerns.[14] The effects of labeling are likely to continue as an area of concern for parents, educators, health professionals, mentally retarded and nonmentally retarded children, and the community at large.

Etiology

Vulnerable periods

The causes of mental retardation vary, and the condition can occur at any time during the child's developmental period. Handicapping conditions may appear singly or multiply. The three periods when mental retardation can occur are prenatal (conception to birth), perinatal (birth to 1 month of age), and postnatal (1 month to approximately 22 years of age). The causes of mental retardation are divided into two main categories—genetic and acquired conditions. Genetic conditions are those inherited from the parents through the gene pool. Acquired conditions are those one encounters as a result of toxic exposure, accident, infection, or deprivation. Table 38-3 lists common etiologies of mental retardation according to a developmental timetable.

Casefinding

Mental retardation conditions may not be readily identifiable at birth. Because of this, regular visits to health care providers are essential for obser-

Table 38-3 Causes of mental retardation

Prenatal		Natal (acquired)	Postnatal (acquired)
Genetic	Acquired		

I. Chromosal abnormalities
  A. Autosomal abnormalities
    1. Trisomy 21—Down syndrome
    2. Trisomy 18—Edward syndrome
    3. Trisomy 13—Patau syndrome
    4. Cri du chat—Cat-cry syndrome
  B. Sex chromosome abnormalities
    1. Klinefelter syndrome
    2. Turner syndrome
    3. XXX female
    4. XYY male
    5. Mosaic
II. Errors of metabolism
    1. Hurler syndrome
    2. Hunter syndrome
    3. Goitrous cretinism
III. Cranial abnormalities
  A. Anencephalus
  B. Microcephalus
  C. Hydrocephalus
	I. Intrauterine environmental factors
	  A. Viruses—rubella
	  B. Chemical—LSD (?), alcohol (?), thalidomide
	  C. Malnutrition
	  D. Radiation
	  E. Syphilis
	  F. Anoxia
	  G. Toxemia
	  H. Blood type incompatibility
		I. Birth
		  A. Birth trauma
		  B. Anoxia
		  C. Prematurity
		  D. Intracranial hemorrhage
		  E. Kernicterus
		  F. Infection
		  G. Hydrocephalus
			I. Exposure
			  A. Radiation
			  B. Toxic chemicals
			II. Physical trauma or injury
			  A. Head injury
			  B. Asphyxia
			III. Poisoning
			  A. Lead
			  B. Household cleaners
			  C. Drugs/medications
			  D. Insecticides
			  E. Toxic chemicals
			IV. Infections
			  A. Meningitis
			  B. Encephalitis
			  C. Viral or bacterial infections resulting in prolonged hyperpyrexia
			V. Brain tumors
			  A. Benign
			  B. Malignant
			VI. Social and cultural factors
			  A. Deprivation
			  B. Abuse
			  C. Malnutrition
			  D. Emotional impairment

Sources: Compiled from American Association on Mental Deficiency, Washington, D.C., 1977; Gladys Scipien et al. (eds.), *Comprehensive Pediatric Nursing*, McGraw-Hill, New York, 1979, p. 337; Lucille F. Whaley, *Understanding Inherited Disorders*, Mosby, St. Louis, 1974, pp. 806–89.

vation and recording of individual neurological and developmental progress. This is particularly important during the first year. It takes time for the infant's neurological system to develop. Hasty decisions should therefore be avoided until substantial data have been collected to support the definite presence of a developmental deficit.

Prevention

Prevention of mental retardation is a primary focus of health professionals. The causes of many kinds of mental retardation are known. Therefore, it is possible to identify high-risk groups and encourage consistent prenatal care. Offering child development education programs in junior and senior high schools, in social service agencies, and for adults in the childbearing period should be encouraged. These efforts may be useful in preventing many acquired conditions.

Amniocentesis is a medical procedure involving puncture of the amniotic sac (via the abdominal wall) for the purpose of obtaining a sample of amniotic fluid. Laboratory tests performed on the fluid sample can aid in prenatal diagnosis of some chromosomal disorders accompanied by mental retardation.

If the results of an amniocentesis indicate that the fetus is defective, the parents may decide to terminate the pregnancy. The ethical and moral implications of abortion are substantial, and they permeate all areas of society. The decision to terminate a pregnancy should be made only after the parents have been given enough information to make an informed decision. Regardless of their decision, it is important that the nurse offer the parents support during this time of stress. Once a genetic disorder is identified or suspected, it is important that the parents obtain genetic counseling. Genetic disorders and genetic counseling are discussed in Chap. 8.

The etiology of mental retardation is complex and may involve large numbers of factors. In many cases, the cause of mental retardation cannot be determined, but behavior and intellectual deficits indicate that it is present. Preventive efforts should be made where possible, and both lay and professional persons should be informed of actions that are effective. Current understanding of mental retardation etiology is incomplete, and more research and observation are necessary.

The mentally retarded child in the family and society

Attitudes of society

Ever so slowly, society is becoming more tolerant of mentally retarded individuals and their families. Parents were once told to institutionalize their child upon confirmation of a diagnosis of mental retardation. Now, parents often keep their mentally retarded child at home in order to provide love, nurturing, and educational opportunities. Mentally retarded children are no longer shut up in institutions away from the view of the uninvolved public. Mentally retarded children often stay in their birth homes, play at the playground, attend school, get sick and see the doctor, and learn academic and self-help skills. They also laugh, cry, feel, and give, just as children without this disability do.

As families acknowledge the presence of mentally retarded children and care for them at home, the rest of society can develop an understanding of the special needs, issues, and contributions of these children. Services for mentally retarded children and their families are available from a variety of public and private sources. These services will be described further later in this chapter.

Indifference is slowly giving way to understanding of mental retardation and the provision of services. Although there is still a long way to go before the mentally retarded child or adult will be accepted into the mainstream of society, progress is being made in that direction. People are learning that mental retardation is not contagious, that it can occur in any family regardless of status, and that it has many causes which are not fully understood. Most importantly, mental retarded children are first and foremost children, who have the same needs as their nonmentally retarded peers. Sensitivity opens the way for individualized, meaningful, and appropriate services for these children.

Parents' reaction

The reaction of parents to the birth of a mentally retarded child is one of shock, disbelief, anger, and guilt. Whether it is the first or a subsequent child, parents generally approach the birth of a new child with dreams and fantasies of the "perfect" child. Parents also give some thought to the possibility of having a disabled child. If the diagnosis of mental retardation is made at birth, the parents are immediately confronted with the loss of the fantasized perfect child. In many cases, however, a definitive diagnosis of mental retardation is not made until the child is several months old and has demonstrated developmental delays. In some cases, the diagnosis is not made until the child is ready to enter school. Even when parents suspect that their child is slow in development, their active coping mechanisms are not utilized until the diagnosis is made. As with other chronic, disabling, or fatal conditions, parents may "shop around" for other medical opinions before they are able to come to grips with the diagnosis of mental retardation.

Regardless of the time of the diagnosis, parents need support, information, and access to helping persons in order to work through their feelings successfully before they can begin to provide care and services to their child.

The reaction of parents to the diagnosis of mental retardation involves three stages of growth. Stage 1 is that of self-pity and subjective concern for oneself and the personal impact of the birth. Stage 2 is one of concern for the welfare and well-being of the child. Stage 3 is the time when the parents can examine and seek ways to serve other retarded children.[15]

This reaction to the diagnosis of mental retardation is often called *chronic sorrow*.[16-18] Some parents successfully reach stage 3, while others plateau at stage 1 or 2 or move among all three stages. Parents also say that the diagnosis both confirms their worst fears and suspicions and provides relief. Once the diagnosis is made, parents know that their observations are valid; something is wrong, but perhaps something can be done to assist their child. Parents repeatedly express a sense of guilt about their child's condition. They often say, "if only I did this" or "if I didn't do that," the mental retardation would not have occurred. The question "why me?" also surfaces when parents are faced with the diagnosis. Once the diagnosis of mental retardation is made, parents may be able successfully to incorporate their mentally retarded child into their home and family life. This mode of care is encouraged today. If this is not possible or feasible, a foster home or institutional placement may be necessary. Whatever their decision, the parents need support, encouragement, and guidance from professional team members.

Siblings' reaction

Siblings of the mentally retarded child require special consideration because their lives, too, will be affected. They may be required to take on extra household or child-care responsibilities. Siblings often need assistance in working through their own feelings about their brother or sister and may feel responsible for the condition. In addition, feelings of anger, fear, and resentment are common, and they should be discussed in an open, nonthreatening way. Their sibling's condition must be explained to them in terms appropriate for their development level. Brothers and sisters also need reassurance that they will still be loved even if their mentally retarded sibling requires increased amounts of parental time. Involvement in the care and special programs required by the retarded child can aid siblings in feeling a part of the family effort. It is also helpful if one or both parents can schedule their time so that all children in the family have the opportunity to have some "special" time with them without the presence of their mentally retarded sibling. This can provide all the family members with an opportunity to catch up on what each person is doing, to nurture and be nurtured, and to share some private time together. Keeping the family unit intact and functioning is an important nursing goal.

Family communication

The manner in which families communicate varies. Some find it easy to be open and honest and to share feelings, while others keep significant thoughts and feelings hidden, sharing only small parts of themselves. To aid families in communicating, the nurse should be aware of their past communication patterns. It is helpful to know how crises in the past have been resolved and which techniques were helpful. Honesty and openness should be encouraged. Because parents often express a sense of pain and shock when they learn of their child's mental retardation, they may need several opportunities to clarify with the health team the statements of the diagnosis and any specific information shared with them. It is not surprising to find that parents did not hear any of the explanations or treatment plans when they first learned of the diagnosis. Therefore, it is essential that this critical information be repeated until the parents are able to demonstrate their understanding. Access to the health team enables parents to clarify information if it is made clear that questions are expected and encouraged.

Some families find it very helpful to join groups of parents who also have mentally retarded children so that they can share in discussing their feelings, concerns, fears, and objectives. Such support often aids the parents in realizing that others are coping with similar issues and that they are not alone. Groups for siblings of the mentally retarded exist in some areas. They provide an opportunity for siblings to share their feelings, fears, and concerns and to realize that other peers are dealing with similar issues.

It is vital that intra- and extrafamily communication be open and maintained if progress is to occur. Communication may be difficult at this time if family members are not used to sharing their feelings and ideas. It is also important that health care providers be available for clarification of information about the child. They can also serve as a sounding board when necessary. The nurse often assists the family in establishing and maintaining communication channels for the family and interdisciplinary team.

Institutional placement

From the time of confirmed diagnosis, the potential for institutional placement exists. The decision to place the child depends on the attitude and abilities of the family, community resources, and severity of the mental retardation. In situations in which the child has been cared for at home, institutional placement may be necessary if the parents are no longer able to provide sufficient care. Siblings may be able to take their mentally retarded member into their own family, and for many this is a viable solution. However, what is to be done when the nuclear or extended family cannot provide needed care?

In general, the first choice for child placement is in the home, as mentioned earlier. With various community services, including early infant stimulation, self-help training, and educational opportunities through special classes or school, family integrity can often be maintained. When relief from home care is needed because of fatigue or illness, residential respite care services may be helpful. In such programs, the mentally retarded child can be cared for in an institution such as a school, or in a foster home or residence.

The time spent away from home varies with the needs of the family. It may range from a few days to 1 month. For many families, this kind of program provides sufficient relief from responsibilities to renew themselves and continue with the required care.

Foster home placement may be necessary on an extended or permanent basis. Residential programs, including schools for the mentally retarded, provide another option. Children are often placed in such settings temporarily or permanently if the family is no longer able to provide care or if additional care and supervision are needed. Sometimes effective education/training programs can be obtained through placement in a school. The decision to obtain institutional placement is not lightly made, and much ambivalence may be expressed by the parents regarding the wisdom of their decision. Some parents, after deciding on permanent placement, will reverse that decision, often based on the perceived or actual level of care provided in the institution, reevaluation of the family situation, and feelings of guilt. Regardless of the dynamics involved in the decision-making process, the parents should be encouraged to analyze the positive and negative aspects of the decision and to have available professional health team members for support and discussions.

The nurse's role with mentally retarded children

Nurses have played an increasingly significant role in developing awareness of and approaches to dealing with the mentally retarded child and his or her family in a healthful, supportive, and individualized manner. This section will explore in more detail some of the specifics of the nursing role with this client group. The exact role to be played depends in large measure on the nurse's educational and clinical preparation. Nurses who specialize in this field will need educational and clinical preparation beyond the baccalaureate level. Bean states that specialty preparation will be needed in such areas as pediatric neurology, orthopedics, cardiology, nutrition, assessment skills, anatomy and physiology, introductory genetics, child psychology, interpretation of growth and development, parameters and data, techniques of child management and parenting process, and counseling.[19]

What services can be provided by the nurse who does not have the above in-depth knowledge but is in contact from time to time with mentally retarded children and their families? There is much that can be done.

Nurses often come in contact with this special population in three main hospital settings—the maternity/gynecological unit, the pediatric unit, and the outpatient department. Each of these settings provides the nurse with many opportunities for interviewing, counseling, teaching, and referring on questions of real or potential mental retardation. Although the nurse may not be able to provide the services directly, the need for such action can be identified and appropriate referral(s) made. The depth of involvement will depend on the nurse's theoretical and clinical preparation, availability of support services in the medical facility and community, and extent of contact with the child.

Bean identifies six roles for the nurse: (1) casefinder, (2) teacher, (3) support source, (4) counselor, (5) coordinator of services, and (6) advocate.[20] In addition, Tudor specifies the importance of prevention and knowledge of community and state legislation when reviewing the scope of the nurse's role and responsibilities.[21] The following discussion will explore these specific activities.

The nurse in prevention and counseling

Prevention of handicapping conditions should be a primary goal of all nurses in all settings, particularly during the prenatal period. To this end, the encouragement of early, consistent, high-quality prenatal care is to be encouraged. Genetic counseling may be appropriate for couples hesitant about childbearing for such reasons as previous birth of a child with mental retardation, family history on one or both sides of mental retardation, or high risk of carrying a disease which could cause mental retardation.[22] To the above list of concerns, Tudor also adds multiple spontaneous abortions.[23] The purposes of genetic counseling are to advise parents on the risks of pregnancy, identify special risk situations, and reduce the number of affected children.[24] A very detailed family history is obtained which includes a pedigree chart. Analysis of findings and projected risk parameters are identified and shared with the involved couple.

Genetic counseling may be spontaneously sought by the couple or recommended to them by a health care professional. As a result of the genetic counseling, couples may make a decision to parent biologically or not. One must be aware that the information provided during the genetic counseling session may not be understood. Therefore follow-up contact with the couple should be initiated.[25]

When a couple has sought genetic counseling at pregnancy, the information obtained as well as that derived from an amniocentesis may result in a decision to terminate the pregnancy. The issues involved in such a decision are too broad for inclusion in this chapter. However, it should be remembered that pregnancy termination is an option for many people faced with the birth of a defective child. The nurse may be sought as a resource person as the couple struggle with this decision. The nurse's handling of such dilemmas is discussed in Chap. 18.

In addition to prenatal care and genetic counseling, adequate nutrition should be stressed. Cessation of smoking and alcohol consumption should be part of the pregnancy program to help ensure a strong, healthy baby of average birth weight. The ability of the nurse to give an appropriate rationale can increase desired health behavior compliance.

In the neonatal period especially and through infancy, attention should focus on adequate oxygenation and prevention of accidents and diseases. Childhood immunization should be started at 2 months of age and continued throughout the childhood years. High fever and infections should be carefully monitored and treated to prevent potential encephalitis or meningitis, which are sometimes the unfortunate result of some infections. Environmental safety at home, at school, and in the car should be stressed by the nurse.

The nurse as casefinder

Casefinding is a major focus for the nurse regardless of the work setting. Again, the primary site for such encounters would be newborn nurseries, pediatric units, and pediatric outpatient units. Tudor states that referrals for developmentally disabled children are often not made until 18 months or later because of two main reasons: (1) professionals often do not recognize or cannot define a developmental delay or abnormal physical or neurological finding, and (2) many are unaware of the existence or benefit of early intervention for infants and their parents.[26]

The first step to be taken in casefinding is the nursing assessment. A thorough history should be taken to determine attainment of developmental milestones, specific behavior patterns of the infant and child, and child-care and management techniques used by the parents. The date and duration of any high fever, illness, or trauma should be noted, as well as both routine and special medications received. All of this information should be carefully recorded and available for future reference. This history should be updated with each contact with the child and family. The style and format to be followed should be determined by the nursing team in each institutional setting, but the history needs to be clearly written and short enough to be used.

Following the history, there should be a physical examination. Nurses working in the newborn nursery are in a particularly critical setting to observe the infant for appropriate reflexes and neonatal behavior. Erickson describes in some detail the use of the Neonatal Behavioral Assessment Scale developed by T. Berry Brazelton. This scale measures six major categories of behavior: (1) habituation, (2) orientation, (3) motor maturity, (4) variation, (5) self-quieting activities, and (6) social behavior. It allows the nurse to observe the infant's adaptation to the environment.[27] As the infant grows, other development assessment tools may be used, as noted on the chart.

Because of the immaturity of the infant's nervous system and the difficulty in drawing conclusions from one observation or encounter, the results of tests, observations of the nurse, and statements from the parents must be carefully recorded. Behaviors or lack of behaviors may be normal at 3 months of age, borderline at 6 months, and abnormal at 9 or 12 months. Any suspicions or abnormalities should be referred to the physician or other members of the multidisciplinary team for further investigation, observation, and evaluation.

In addition to the physical and developmental investigation which must be conducted, a thorough assessment of the family structure and functioning as well as parenting activities needs to be completed. Parent-child interaction should be observed directly by the nurse, including such points as eye contact, touch, methods of child management, efforts to teach the child, verbal communication, and attempts to play with the child.[28] The nurse should also determine the level of self-help skills present, which include self-feeding, dressing, and toilet training. Reactions of siblings and husband-wife interactions should be observed, with the recommendation of intervention where necessary.

The nurse as care planner and care-giver

When the mentally retarded child is admitted to the hospital for illness, care needs to be planned on an individual basis, as for any other child. The initial history that is taken should carefully define the skills the child demonstrates at home, communication practices used, including any special terms used for him- or herself, dressing, feeding, and toileting. An outline of the daily routine should be obtained. Because of the need for clarity and repetition with this client population, it is important that the teaching technique used at home be continued in the hospital when possible.

Conversations should be carried on with the child in a normal tone of voice, using appropriate terminology for his or her comprehension. Regression can occur with any child who is hospitalized and can be expected with the mentally retarded child. Behavioral expectations can be readjusted to compensate for this change. Procedures need to be explained, as would be done with any other child. Play activities appropriate for the child's functional age and health condition should be planned individually and with other children when possible.

Frequent checks on the condition should be made, with specific questions asked about how the child feels, what he or she wants, where it hurts, etc. Parents need to be informed of hospital rules and regulations, and special accommodations should be made where possible. The child should be placed in the mainstream of hospital activity, not in an isolated care area, unless this is warranted for medical or safety reasons.

Mentally retarded children require extra attention, patience, and time when they are hospitalized. Nurses, by careful planning, can make the hospital stay for this client population and their parents a positive, supportive, and growing experience. The setting of nursing goals, the design and implementation of specific nursing interventions, and the reevaluation and revision of the nursing care plan are ongoing and should be available and shared with all involved persons.

The nurse as teacher

Teaching takes place in several areas. One is that of direct parent education, particularly during and after the specific diagnosis has been made. Parents should be provided with basic information about their child's condition, about the developmental prognosis if it is known, and about the various treatment approaches which might be used to treat and/or modify the disability. It is important that information to parents be repeated, that simple, nonmedical terminology be used, that parents be talked with and not to or down to, and that one or more resource persons be available at the health care site they use to clarify information and answer questions when they occur.

As the child grows, educational and training needs will change. It is important, particularly in the early years of childhood stimulation and training, that parental involvement be encouraged and reinforced. There should be no mystique about the site or equipment needed for adequate child stimulation. Parents should and can learn to work directly with infant stimulation programs, physical therapy programs, and self-help skills-learning programs as the primary teachers in the home. Mothers can be taught the techniques to be utilized, observed for appropriateness of techniques, and then reinforced as they proceed to implement the techniques. They should be taught to watch for cues for training readiness in such areas as feeding, dressing, and toilet training. Behavior modification techniques can be used by parents to teach their mentally retarded child may useful skills. Environmental modification can also aid the child in performing at a more independent level. Some modifications include feeding utensil adaptations such as padding the spoon or fork handle and using special suction cups or plates to keep them from sliding, cups with spillproof tops, food of a size and consistency which will allow for self-feeding, and clothes which are not buttoned or zipped but rather pulled over the head, have elastic waists and Velcro closures. Most of these and many other modifications are relatively simple to make and can significantly increase the independent functioning of the mentally retarded child.

Parents also need information about child management. Mentally retarded children need to have limits set for them, just as nonretarded children do. They need to know what is acceptable and what is nonacceptable behavior. Discipline should be encouraged. Where necessary, behavior modification techniques can be taught either to increase or to decrease specific behaviors. Mentally retarded children have enough special needs to cope with; they do not need to have disruptive or inattentive behavior further complicate their lives.

The nurse as giver of emotional support

The nurse can furnish needed support at many points as parents come to acknowledge and accept the mental retardation of their child. Parents need "to have their pain recognized, appreciated and validated," for they have experienced a loss, must grieve, and must reorganize their family unit to cope with the unanticipated needs of a mentally retarded child.[29] Providing a private area for expressing feelings is important in encouraging discussion of both the disappointments and joys involved in caring for their mentally retarded child. The nurse should keep in mind that parents may require frequent repetition of information before it is retained. The nurse often becomes the target of much of the parents' anger concerning their child. The ability to take this anger without backing away, retaliating, or becoming personally injured can often strengthen the bond between the nurse and family. It is not particularly pleasant, at times, to be in such situations, but the nurse is often the person who represents the professional at whom such anger can be safely vented. Quietly hearing parents out and being available for future contacts will deliver the message that anger and disappointment are acceptable.

The nurse in referrals and counseling

As the family deals with the many needs they face, referrals by the nurse to various agencies may be necessary. The nurse's availability by phone may provide the needed input or encouragement to deal with a major problem or a minor but irritating one. Nurses may be able to confirm the appropriateness of a decision and provide encouragement, or simply to "be there" when needed. The day-to-day efforts and time involved in caring for a mentally retarded child can be exhausting, and knowing there is a person available for discussion, encouragement, and reinforcement can be very helpful.

Counseling comes in many forms and again is dependent on the nurse's educational, clinical, and experiential preparation. Bean discusses three characteristics of the counseling role which must be present if such encounters are to be successful. The nurse must (1) present a professional appearance, (2) identify the parents' needs and help them to meet these needs before discussing the child, and (3) listen to the parents discuss their concerns about their child.[30] Work with parents to aid their mentally retarded child cannot adequately proceed if parents see the nurse as a threat or an awesome figure. Such perceptions are detrimental to the helping process and must be identified and corrected. If parents' energy is tied up in coping with their own needs, then the child's needs cannot be met. Again, by identifying these concerns and taking steps to meet them, the nurse can then make efforts to meet the needs of the child. Once steps 1 and 2 have been taken, the nurse is in a position to explore with parents their concerns about their child. These may run the gamut from confirming a disability to developing techniques to deal with a specific behavior issue. In all cases, the parents are ultimately responsible for the decisions they make. The nurse can be most helpful in supporting those decisions. It is important to keep in mind that values, ethics, and moral considerations held by a family unit may differ from those of the nurse. If the nurse cannot handle or therapeutically deal with the decisions made by a particular family, it would be most appropriate to refer the family to another, who could be more supportive.

The nurse as coordinator of services

Because the retarded child may have more than one problem and because of the multidisciplinary nature of the health team, the need for *coordination of services* is essential. The nurse is in an excellent position to provide this overseeing service. Appropriate referrals can be made through the health team and to outside agencies for specific services. The nurse can explain and clarify the roles of various providers to the parents and may be able to correct any misunderstanding which may occur between the parents and agencies or team members. Such efforts can be invaluable in maintaining families in

programs for the benefit of the child. Should parents develop concerns or difficulties with a specific agency, the nurse, because of his or her contact with and knowledge of the agency and its personnel and programs, may be able to resolve the problem, reevaluate the services, and/or make recommendations to the health team concerning its appropriateness for services.

The nurse and advocacy

Advocacy for the mentally retarded child and the family is a much needed nursing role. This involves speaking out for and supporting the establishment of special services for the mentally retarded at the local, state, and federal levels. Education of the community, both lay and professional, concerning the special needs, skills, and qualities of the mentally retarded is a necessary function. Misunderstandings, fears, and prejudices still exist which need the dedicated efforts of many to correct and put to final rest. Nurses committed to the field of mental retardation are in a position to do this. Evaluation of agencies can aid in continuing those which provide beneficial services and closing those which are without value. Supporting educational programs for nurses at the generic and continuing education levels can improve the contribution nursing makes to this field. As the pool of qualified nurses increases, the quality of the service should improve. Involvement in political lobbying efforts for the passage of pertinent legislation can have both long- and short-term impact on the mentally retarded and their families. Nurses can help by providing information, testimony, and assistance in the wording of legislation.

The final area of action, which often parallels that of advocacy, is *legislative action*. It is very important that the nurse be aware of state and federal legislation which will provide direct and indirect services to the mentally retarded. The nurse should be aware of state and federal senators and representatives and their position on mental retardation legislation. Where there is negative support, educational efforts via letters, phone calls, and personal visits may be in order. Where there is support, reinforcement of the legislator's stance is appropriate. When new legislation needs to be written or old legislation modfied, nurses can participate in such efforts. Sources of financial support for services from early childhood programs to vocational training need to be identified and utilized. Support for nursing education at the generic, graduate, and continuing education levels needs to be encouraged and reinforced. Education of the public to the need for appropriate legislation is an ongoing process and must constantly be lobbied due to the large number of competing causes.

Summary

The nursing roles in mental retardation are many and varied. The depth of commitment one may make to the field will depend in large measure on the educational, clinical, and personal preparation of the nurse. In mental retardation nursing, as in other specialties, nurses must come to grips with personal feelings about the condition, its various manifestations, and the nursing role. Their effectiveness will be greatly compromised until they know and understand their feelings about working with the handicapped.

In mental retardation nursing, the nurse works with the parents, who are in the best position to implement treatment programs, identify needs, and set goals and objectives. The mental retardation will not disappear, but its impact on the child's life can be modifed through consistent, diligent, goal-related actions. Nursing can aid the family in accepting the handicapping condition, modifying the family's life-style and expectations, and including their mentally retarded child in the family. It is time-consuming work filled with successes and failures, joys and disappointments, and the comforting knowledge that a service has been rendered to persons in real need.

Resources

The resources available to the family with a mentally retarded member will depend on such factors as geographical location, state of residence, and medical and other resources. Services may be provided through such agencies as the state crippled children's service, the United Cerebral Palsy Association, health departments, university affiliated centers, public and private schools, residential houses, halfway houses, and respite care centers. Headstart provides early childhood training for many developmentally disabled children. Infant stimulation programs are often offered at the state level to parents with a mentally retarded child.

In addition to the above, services may be provided through the National Associations for Retarded Citizens, the Easter Seal Society for Crippled Children and Adults, and the National Foundation—March of Dimes. These organizations can be contacted at the local, state, or federal level depending on access options. There are special camps, day-care programs, and recreation and social activities provided in many areas for this population.

As the mentally retarded individual ages, vocational training and placement are needed. These services are often provided through state departments of vocational training. Work training preparation and work placement may be provided in sheltered workshops and various industrial settings. The exact type of work can vary but must consist of repetitive-skill jobs and packaging activities.

Knowledge of various community resources is a time-consuming effort which requires persistence and frequent updating. Direct agency contact and visits, when possible, will aid in evaluation of agencies. The development of a resource file which includes at minimum the agency name, service provided, telephone numbers, contact person, and any fee charged can be most useful and worthwhile.

In summary, community resources vary in quality and quantity from location to location. Before using any given agency as a resource, it is imperative to evaluate it in terms of the service rendered. No service is usually better than poor service. Nursing plays a large role in identifying and evaluating community resources.

References

1. Herbert, J. Grossman (ed.), *Manual on Terminology and Classification in Mental Retardation*, American Association on Mental Deficiency, Washington, D.C., 1977, p. 11.
2. Ibid., p. 12.
3. Ibid., pp. 16–17.
4. Ibid., p. 20.
5. Ibid., p. 20.
6. Ibid., pp. 95–97.
7. The Rehabilitation Comprehensive Services Act and Developmental Disabilities Amendments of 1978, P.L. 95-602.
8. Donald L. MacMillan and Reginald L. Jones, "The Mentally Retarded Label: A Theoretical Analysis and Review of Research," *American Journal of Mental Deficiency* **79**(3):253 (1974).

9. Ibid.

10. Sheryl Freeman and Bob Algozzine, "Social Acceptability as a Function of Labels and Assigned Attributes," *American Journal of Mental Deficiency* 84(6):590 (1980).

11. Jay Gottlieb, "Attitudes toward Retarded Children: Effects of Labeling and Academic Performance," *American Journal of Mental Deficiency* 79(3):272 (1974).

12. Ibid.

13. Gary N. Siperstein, Milton Budoff, and John J. Bak, "Effects of Labels 'Mentally Retarded' and 'Retard' on the Social Acceptability of Mentally Retarded Children," *American Journal of Mental Deficiency* 84(6):597 (1980).

14. Ibid.

15. Dan Boyd, *The Three Stages*, National Association for Retarded Children, New York, 1969.

16. Susan E. Waisbren, "Parents' Reaction After the Birth of a Developmentally Disabled Child," *American Journal of Mental Deficiency* 84(4):345–351 (1980).

17. Albert J. Solnit and Mary H. Stark, "Mourning and the Birth of a Defective Child," reproduced by the U.S. Department of Health, Education and Welfare, Social and Rehabilitation Service, Children's Bureau, with permission from *Psychoanalytic Study of the Child* 16:523–537 (1961).

18. S. Olshansky, "Chronic Sorrow: A Response to Having a Mentally Defective Child," *Social Casework* 43:191–194 (1962).

19. Margaret Register Bean, "Nursing Roles in Developmental Disabilities," in Linda L. Jarvis (ed.), *Community Health Nursing: Keeping the Public Health*, Davis, Philadelphia, 1980, pp. 260–261.

20. Ibid., p. 261.

21. Mary Tudor, "Nursing Intervention with Developmentally Disabled Children," *The American Journal of Maternal Child Nursing* 3(1):28–30 (1978).

22. Lucille F. Whaley, "Genetic Counseling," in Judith Buckley Curry and Kathryn Kluss Peppe (eds.), *Mental Retardation Nursing: Approaches to Care*, Mosby, St. Louis, 1978, p. 89.

23. Tudor, op. cit., p. 26.

24. Whaley, op. cit., p. 99.

25. Ibid., p. 105.

26. Tudor, op. cit., pp. 27–28.

27. Marcene L. Erickson, *Assessment and Management of Developmental Changes in Children*, Mosby, St. Louis, 1976, pp. 49–50.

28. Bean, op. cit., p. 263.

29. Tudor, op. cit., p. 25.

30. Bean, op. cit., p. 274.

Chapter 39 **Special senses**

Carol J. Hill

Upon completion of this chapter, the student will be able to:

1. Describe the normal appearance of external eye structures.

2. Describe two methods for obtaining the cooperation of a toddler during an eye examination.

3. List five suggestions the nurse can make to parents for preventing eye trauma.

4. Recite the procedure for instilling eye medications.

5. Contrast congenital glaucoma and congenital cataracts.

6. List three symptoms of strabismus.

7. Describe preoperative preparation for a child undergoing eye surgery.

8. Construct a plan of care to meet the needs of a child in the postoperative period following eye surgery.

9. Describe the passage of a sound wave from the external ear to the brain.

10. Identify two methods for testing the hearing of a child.

11. List the steps involved in instilling ear drops.

12. Describe nursing measures to increase the comfort of a child with otitis media.

13. List five nursing interventions to increase the security of a sensory-impaired child who is hospitalized.

Alterations in the special senses of vision and hearing can occur prenatally and at any time throughout childhood although certain alterations are most apt to occur at specific times. Specific alterations will be considered in this chapter after a review of the development, anatomy, physiology, and assessment of the eye and ear.

Embryological development of the eye

From its first appearance in the fourth week of fetal life, the eye develops rapidly so that by the sixteenth week it appears to be a fairly typical human eye. The first portion to develop is called the *optic vesicle*, from which the retina later

develops. By the sixth week the nervous and pigment layers of the eye and the lens are being formed. The structures of the sclera, cornea, iris, ciliary body, choroid, and eyelids form between the sixth and twelfth week. Maternal disease, radiation, and drugs have the most disastrous effect on eye development during the period of 4 to 8 weeks. From sixteen weeks until birth further refinement of eye structures occurs. Initially the eyes are located on each side of the head; as the head and facial areas broaden, the eyes converge, which enables them to function together, resulting in binocular vision and depth perception.

Development of the eye is not complete at birth. The eyes of the newborn are sensitive to light; blinking and pupillary reflexes are present.

The newborn has peripheral vision and is able to follow objects to the midline. The macula matures over the first 4 months, making central vision possible. By the age of 2 vision is well-developed but it continues to mature until the child is approximately 6.

Anatomy of the eye

The eye is situated within the orbital cavity, which is made up of skull bones and provides some protection for the eyeball. The major struc-

tures of the eye and their functions are summarized on Table 39-1 and Fig. 39-1.

Physiology of the eye

To be visualized an object must go through several processes: refraction, accommodation, transformation of the visual images into nerve impulses, and transmission to the brain. When light rays are refracted they are bent so that the light from a large area can be focused on a small area. Light rays are bent successively by the

Table 39-1 Anatomy of the eye

Part	Function
Surrounding structures	
Extrinsic ocular muscles	Six muscles connecting eyeball to orbit to provide lateral, up-and-down movement
Eyelids, lashes	Protect eyeball from foreign objects, intense light, blunt force
Conjunctiva	Mucous membrane lining inner eyelid and outer eyeball
Lacrimal apparatus	Lacrimal gland and series of ducts; produces and drains away tears.
Eyeball	
Sclera	Outermost layer of eyeball; supports and protects eye
Cornea	Anterior 1/6 of eyeball; serves as principal refracting medium for light rays
Choroid	Vascular middle layer of eyeball; provides nourishment for retina
Ciliary body	Anterior extension of choroid consisting of ciliary processes, which secrete aqueous humor, and ciliary muscles, which regulate lens shape
Iris	Muscular, colored diaphragm which controls amount of light admitted to inner eyeball through the pupil
Lens	Biconvex, transparent structure which refracts light rays on retina by changing shape
Aqueous humor	Alkaline, watery fluid filling anterior and posterior chambers; nourishes lens and cornea
Vitreous body (humor)	Jelly-like substance making up 4/5 of eyeball; maintains eyeball shape
Retina	Provides conversion of light rays to nerve impulses
Optic nerve	Transmits nerve impulses from retina to visual area of occipital lobe in brain

Figure 39-1 Anatomy of the eye. (*From Gladys M. Scipien et al., Comprehensive Pediatric Nursing, 2d ed., McGraw-Hill, New York, 1979. Used by permission of the publisher.*)

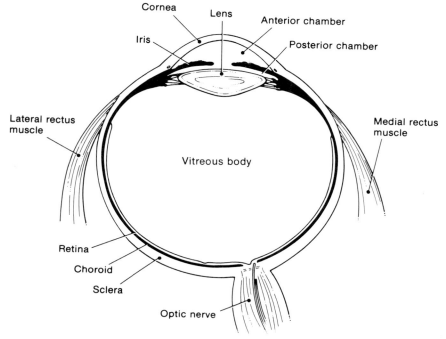

cornea, aqueous humor, lens, and vitreous body. Each refracting surface converges the light rays slightly more until the image of the object is formed on the retina.

In order for close objects to be projected on the retina, accommodation must take place. The lens provides this function by changing to a more convex shape. Pupillary constriction and the convergence of both eyes are also part of the accommodative process. When viewing distant objects, the lens resumes its usual biconvex shape.

The image formed on the retina is transformed into nervous impulses by the photosensitive cells of the retina, the rods and cones. Cones are sensitive to day vision and colors. They are most numerous at the center of the retina in the area known as the *macula*. Rods are sensitive to dim light. They are found outside the macula. The impulses generated by rod and cone cells pass along the optic nerve, out of the orbital cavity, and to the visual area within the occipital lobe, where the image is interpreted.

Assessment of the eye

Assessment of visual function includes a thorough history from the parent accompanying the child, inspection of the eyes for observable alterations as listed on Table 39-2, measurement of visual acuity, and assessment of extrinsic muscle balance. Evaluation of the internal structures of the eye is generally performed by a physician who has repeated experience in this area. Any deviation from normal will also be referred to an ophthalmologist for further evaluation and possible treatment.

The history obtained from the parents or caretaker should include both symptoms and functional alterations of the eyes. These areas are summarized on Table 39-3.

Nursing measures to facilitate assessment

The nurse can facilitate assessment of the eyes in several ways. Obtain the history first before handling the child. While obtaining the history, assess as much as possible indirectly, for ex-

Table 39-2 Examination of the eye by inspection

Part	Normal appearance	Abnormal appearance
Surrounding structures		
Orbit	Proportionate with other facial features Eyes aligned with each other	Edema Discoloration
Eyebrows		Thick, bushy, joined Scaliness, crusting
Eyelids, lashes	Lids open completely Lids open simultaneously	Drooping Discoloration Edema Excessive blinking or squinting Upward slant Sties Discharge Lice Masses Absent eyelashes Absent or excess tearing
Ocular muscles	Eyes move up, down lateral, obliquely Equal corneal light reflex	Crossing of eyes
Conjunctiva	Moist, smooth, non-reddened	Redness, pallor, jaundice
Eye proper		
Cornea	Clear, equal size	Scarring, ulcerations, opacities
Sclera	White color	Jaundiced, reddened
Iris	Same color both eyes Forms complete circle	Dull color
Pupil	Round, equal, react to light Constrict on accommodation	Nystagmus
Lens Globe	Red reflex present	Sunken Blank-looking Protruding

ample, symmetry of the eye position and how the child uses the eyes. Avoid sudden or hurried movement. The infant and young child feel most secure on the parent's lap. Use of a bottle or pacifier may keep the infant relatively quiet. To check the red reflex, have the parent hold the infant over the shoulder while the examiner approaches the child from behind. The *red reflex* is the reddish orange circular glow which nor-

mally fills the pupil when a light is shone into the eye. If necessary, the infant and young child can be restrained by placing the child on his back on the parent's lap with the head facing the examiner. The parent can hold the hands of the child and restrain the body at the same time with the child's legs placed around the parent's waist and restrained by the parent's elbows.[1]

To gain the cooperation of the older child, use

Table 39-3 Information about visual function gathered by interview

Symptomatic alterations

Presence of reddened eyes
Discharge from lids or eyes
Pain, discomfort, itching in or around eyes
Excessive tearing
Crossed eyes
Blurring of vision
Presence of spots before eyes
Swelling of eyelids
Rubbing eyes, squinting, frowning
Oversensitivity to light
Recurring sties

Functional alterations

Parent suspects child cannot see
Holding objects very close to eyes
Covering one eye while playing with toy or reading
Difficulty seeing chalkboard at school
Headaches after doing close work at school
Skipping over words when reading out loud
Stumbling over objects
Head tilt when looking at objects

positive suggestions such as "Look at the picture of the dog," rather than "Will you look straight ahead?" Allow the child time to become familiar with the penlight or ophthalmoscope. Ask questions of the child rather than talking over the child to the parent. The older child can be examined while seated on a chair or the examining table.

Assessment of visual acuity

Procedures used to assess visual acuity depend upon the age of the child. Table 39-4 lists assessment tools useful for various age groups. When checking the visual acuity of the preschooler with the E test, the child may respond better if the E is referred to as a table and the child is asked which way the legs point. Asking the parents to practice with the child the day before the test is also helpful. The Titmus Optical Tester is a machine in which the child sees letters or E's projected onto a screen. This machine helps to minimize distraction and memorization.

Extrinsic muscle balance testing

Testing the function of the ocular muscles can be accomplished by use of the Hirschberg test and the cover test. Both of these tests require fixation of the eyes on an object. This is more

easily achieved in a child if the fixation object is visually interesting, such as a small toy clipped to a paper clip.[2] When performing the Hirschberg test, the examiner shines a penlight into the child's eyes; the light should reflect on the same spot on both corneas.

The cover test is performed by covering one eye with a card or the examiner's hand while watching the uncovered eye for movement. Then the eye is uncovered and it is watched for movement. After the child rests for a few minutes, the test is repeated with the opposite eye. Any movement of the eyes indicates muscle imbalance. Another test for muscle function involves telling the child to follow the examiner's finger through the directions of gaze; small finger puppets may hold the child's attention.

Role of the nurse in teaching eye care

The teaching role of the nurse focuses on providing information to the parents and the child about maintaining healthy eyes, obtaining medical advice in case of injury or illness, and carrying out specific treatments, such as instillation of eye drops or ointments.

Maintaining healthy eyes

A child's eyes should be examined as a minimum at the following times: as a newborn, at age 3, before entering grade school, midway through elementary school, before entering high school, and at 2-year intervals thereafter.

Most eye injuries are preventable; most blindness is a result of trauma. Providing guidance to parents about prevention can be facilitated by using a developmental approach, that is, by determining which risks are greater at a certain

Table 39-4 Methods used to assess visual acuity

Infant and toddler

History: parent believes child can see
Ability to fixate on an object
Pupillary response to light

Preschooler

Snellen illiterate E chart, cards, or Titmus Optical Tester

School-age and older

Snellen letter chart
Color vision plates

developmental stage and providing suggestions on how those risks can be minimized or prevented. Table 39-5 presents a prevention guideline summary.

When to seek medical advice

The information listed on Table 39-3, in addition to the following symptoms, provides a useful guide to teach parents when to seek medical advice: presence of photophobia, enlargement of the eye, growths on the lid or surface of the eye, irregularities in pupil shape, and presence of white reflections from behind the pupil.

Parental eye treatment

Before the parents examine the child's eyes, their hands should be washed. Discourage use of over-the-counter drops for eye irritation because the drops may mask symptoms of disease and delay proper treatment; these drops are unnecessary

Table 39-5 Guidelines for prevention of eye injuries in children

Developmental stage	Risk	Preventive measures
Infancy	Pokes self or others with sharp objects	Dispose of broken toys Should not play with popsicle sticks, pencils, tinker toys, etc.
Toddler	Falls carrying objects	Should not run with pencils, lollipop sticks, etc.
	Drinks antifreeze	Keep antifreeze (all poisons) locked up in cabinet
	Throws sand or dirt	Supervise outdoor play
Preschooler	Waves sharp objects	Provide blunt-tipped scissors. Have child sit quietly at table when using scissors Teach child to walk holding point of scissors down
	Experiments with aerosol cans, perfumes	Place out of reach
School-age	Fireworks	Supervise rigidly if allowed at all
	Missiles such as BB guns, arrows	Supervised use only
	Football, hockey, baseball injuries	Playground supervision, explanation of risks
Adolescence	Same as for school-age, plus contact lenses	Proper cleaning, take out for sleeping, do not overwear
	Motorcycle accidents	Use of safety helmets
	Eye makeup—infection	Remove eye makeup with petroleum jelly or mineral oil at bedtime, do not share makeup with friends
All ages	Automobile accidents	Infant, toddler—dynamically tested car restraint Preschoolers and up—seat belts when over 40 lb or 4 years, shoulder harness when over 55 in
	Power lawn mowers—can throw objects such as rocks	Do not allow children to play nearby when lawn mower is in use
	Direct sunlight	Teach child not to look at sun

for normal eye hygiene. Caution parents to refrain from using an antibiotic prescribed for a child for a previous eye condition if symptoms recur. Drugs prescribed for another child with similar symptoms should not be used. Some of these medications lose their effectiveness after a period of time. Use of the wrong medication can be dangerous as well as delay essential medical treatment.

The nurse demonstrates to parents the proper procedure for instilling eye drops or ointments. Cleanliness of the parent's hands and the medication is important. The dropper or tip of the ointment tube should not touch the eye or any other surface. Several methods can be used to insert the medication. Rather than forcing the lids apart, the drops can be placed at the inner canthus; when the child opens his eyes, the drops will roll in. The child may need to be mummied or placed on the bed with the child's head stabilized between the parent's legs. If the child is a sound sleeper, arranging the schedule so that one dose is given at night may be successful. With the child in a supine position, gently pull down the lower lid and insert the drops in the lower conjunctiva (Fig. 39-2).

To instill eye ointments, place a thin ribbon along the inner margin of the lower lid without pressing the eyeballs or forcing the lids against the bony rims of the orbits. An ointment may be prescribed because a crying child tends to force drops out by squeezing his lids and dilutes drops with tears.[3]

Congenital alterations of the eye

Cataracts

Pathophysiology A *cataract* is a unilateral or bilateral opacity of part or all of the lens as a result of heredity or an environmental insult. The opacity of the lens makes it impervious to light. The most common environmental cause is maternal rubella during the first trimester of pregnancy. When an infant with cataracts is examined, the red reflex is absent or does not fill the pupil; a white glow may be seen behind the pupil when cataracts are far advanced.

Treatment Surgery can be performed as early as 6 months if vision is significantly impaired. In children the surgical procedure is an extracapsular procedure to prevent loss of the vitreous

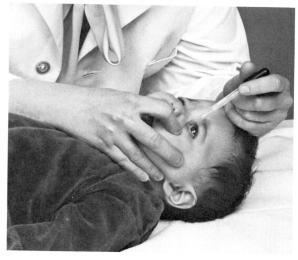

Figure 39-2 Instillation of eye drops.

fluid. The lens material, but not the lens capsule, is broken up, aspirated, and irrigated through an incision at the junction of the cornea and sclera. *Phacoemulsification*, a procedure in which the lens is broken up by high-frequency sound waves, may also be used. Extraction of cataracts caused by rubella may reactivate the rubella virus if removed before the child is 2 or 3, resulting in further eye damage.

Postoperatively, the operative eye is usually patched for 4 days. The child is ambulated the day after surgery. The total hospital stay is 4 to 5 days. Steroid and atropine sulfate drops are instilled two or three times each day for 6 weeks to prevent glaucoma, which can result from the adhesion of the iris to residual lens matter. Several weeks postoperatively, the child is fitted for glasses or contact lenses to replace the missing lens. Introduction of contact lenses in infancy has been successful; the lenses are modified as the eye changes with the child's growth. A 5-year-old child can be taught how to insert the lens.[4]

Prognosis varies, but in about 50 percent of the children with cataracts vision cannot be improved greater than 20/200.[5] Complications include glaucoma and retinal detachment, both of which may occur years after surgery has been performed. The coexistence of other eye anomalies, such as microphthalmia and poor retinal function, also affects the prognosis.

Glaucoma

Pathophysiology Congenital or infantile glaucoma is a result of inadequate drainage of the aqueous fluid from the anterior portion of the eye. Normally aqueous fluid leaves the eye through a trabecular meshwork located at the junction of the sclera, cornea, and iris. Obstruction of the flow of aqueous fluid in children is usually due to faulty development of the trabecular meshwork. The obstruction results in increased pressure within the eyeball, eventually leading to atrophy of the optic nerve. Most infantile glaucoma is apparent within the first 12 months of life. Early symptoms include extreme sensitivity to light and excessive tearing due to the irritation of the corneal epithelium. The photophobia may be so severe the infant keeps the eyes closed even when eating.[6] As the disease progresses, the cornea enlarges and becomes hazy; the eyeball itself enlarges if the child is under age 3. (See Fig. 39-3.)

Glaucoma may be hereditary or may result from congenital rubella, retrolental fibroplasia, retinoblastoma, or trauma. In many cases the cause is unknown. If the child is born with enlarged eyes, the vision may not be salvageable. If glaucoma occurs between 2 and 12 months and is treated before the eye enlarges, the prognosis is excellent 80 percent of the time.[7]

Treatment The treatment of congenital or infantile glaucoma is surgery. Preoperatively the child

Figure 39-3 Congenital glaucoma. Note enlargement of the cornea of the right eye. (*Courtesy of Dr. J. Olson, United Hospital, Grand Forks, N. Dak.*)

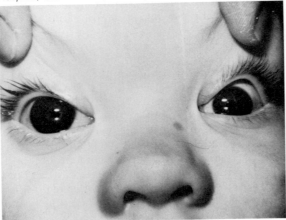

may be given pilocarpine hydrochloride eye drops to keep the pupil constricted and acetazolamide to lower the intraocular pressure and reduce corneal edema. The usual surgical procedure is a *goniotomy*, in which a fine knife is introduced through the cornea into the anterior chamber to incise the trabecular meshwork. The length of hospitalization may be 2 or 3 days. Complications of goniotomy are uncommon but include hemorrhage and infection. The child is examined under anesthesia 4 to 6 weeks postoperatively to measure intraocular pressure and examine the retina. Goniotomies may need to be performed several times to halt the disease.

Nursing management

When caring for infants with cataracts or glaucoma, the most important considerations for promoting the security of the child are consistency of routine and the presence of the parents. The age of the child precludes preparation for the experience. Obtain a thorough history from the parents at the time of admission, including sleeping and feeding routines and skills the child has mastered; record this information on the Kardex. Assure the parents that their presence throughout the child's hospital stay is welcome and helpful for their child.

Postoperatively, the nurse focuses on assessing the child's recovery from anesthesia, preventing injury to the newly operated eye, maintaining the child's fluid and electrolyte balance, and promoting the ability of the parents to comfort and care for their child. The child will have bandaged eyes. Elbow restraints can be applied to prevent pulling at the patch or rubbing the eyes. A child of this age usually needs to be distracted and comforted rather than told not to pull at the bandages. Preoperative preparation for the older toddler or preschooler is similar to that used for a child having strabismus repair. The child usually has a scratchy sensation in the operated eye rather than actual pain. While recovering from the anesthesia, the child is often restless. Crying will increase intraocular pressure; holding and gently rocking the child, especially by the parents, may decrease the crying. If possible, position the child who has glaucoma on his unoperated side to enhance serous drainage. Start oral fluids cautiously as soon as the child is awake; vomiting also increases intraocular pressure. Return to the child's room frequently in the early postoperative period to assess the child's condition and the parent's need for assistance, especially with a restless, crying child. Increasing restlessness may indicate intraocular hemorrhage.

The role of the nurse as a teacher includes preparation for discharge. Show the parents how to instill the prescribed eye drops following cataract surgery and if possible assist the parents to actually carry out this procedure while the child is still hospitalized. Stress the importance of continuing the drops until they are discontinued by the ophthalmologist.

Provide suggestions for prevention of injury to the operated eye. The surgeon may suggest use of a lightweight patch over the eye at night to prevent rubbing. Applying elbow restraints at home may help prevent rubbing when the child is not being held. Depending on institutional policy, the parents might be able to take home the tongue blade restraints used in the hospital. Or parents can make their own with rolled-up newspapers or magazines. Remind parents to remove restraints periodically to prevent skin irritation and to exercise the arms. Use quiet play rather than active play and avoid long periods of crying to prevent increased ocular pressure. The child may show increased sensitivity to light and will be more comfortable if direct light is avoided. If pain, increased swelling, or discharge in the eye occur, the parents should seek medical advice. They should also be given an appointment time with the child's physician.

Treatment of cataracts and glaucoma require ongoing long-term care. The nurse as communicator can help the family express their concerns for the child's visual deficit and the continuing care necessary to preserve remaining visual function. The nurse can also assist the parents in understanding the physician's explanations or in suggesting the physician talk with the parents again if a lack of understanding is apparent.

Acquired alterations in the eye

Retrolental fibroplasia

Pathophysiology *Retrolental fibroplasia* occurs as a response of the immature retina of a premature infant to high levels of oxygen. In the presence of high oxygen levels, the retinal vessels constrict; the resulting decreased oxygen levels

leads to dilatation of the vessels and new vascular growth extending into the vitreous body. Hemorrhages of these new delicate vessels result in retinal detachment. In the most severe cases, the retrolental space (space behind the lens) is filled with fibrous tissue, the eyes appear small and sunken, and the child is blind. If the process is not complete, the child has retinal scarring with reduced visual acuity. Retinal detachments can occur even into adolescence from the retinal scarring. Laser therapy is being used experimentally to control abnormally proliferating blood vessels.[8]

Nursing management In providing care to the premature infant, the nurse monitors arterial oxygen levels closely as long as an umbilical catheter is in place. An arterial oxygen level of 100 mmHg is generally considered the safe upper limit.[9] After the catheter has been discontinued, the oxygen levels in the isolette should remain below 40 percent. All newborns on oxygen therapy should have their eyes examined when oxygen is discontinued, before discharge, and between 3 and 6 months following discharge.[10] Infants who have any degree of retrolental fibroplasia should have their eye examinations every 3 to 6 months throughout the preschool years and yearly thereafter.[11] The nurse can help the parents understand the necessity of frequent eye examinations.

Parents of a premature infant are faced with acceptance of the premature birth and possible loss of the child. It may be difficult for them to accept that their child has defective vision or is blind as a result of treatment to save the child's life. The nurse can and should provide opportunities for them to ventilate their feelings.

Strabismus

Pathophysiology *Strabismus*, or crossing of the eyes, results from abnormal coordination of eye movements. (See Fig. 39-4.) It can be bilateral or unilateral. The eyes may turn in (*esotropia*), out (*exotropia*), up or down (vertical). It may be congenital, that is, present before 6 months, or acquired later in early childhood. The most common cause is an imbalance of the extraocular muscles, which control eye movement, but strabismus can also result from a difference in refractive ability of the two eyes. Aside from the cosmetic effect on the child, which may result

Figure 39-4 Bilateral strabismus—esotropia. (*Courtesy of Dr. M. Mariano, United Hospital, Grand Forks, N. Dak.*)

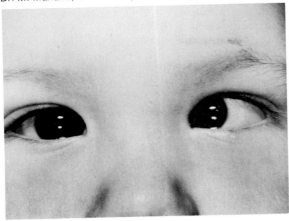

in teasing from peers as early as age 3, strabismus can result in suppression of vision in the deviating eye. This is known as *amblyopia*. When the eyes do not function together, the image seen by the child is not fused; this lack of fusion results in *diplopia*. To eliminate the confusing or double image, the brain suppresses the cells of the macula so visual stimuli are not registered; in time this leads to atrophy of the macula. This visual deficit tends to be more common in esotropia. The older the child, the longer treatment is necessary to reverse amblyopia. After the age of 6 treatment is generally not successful in restoring vision.

Symptoms indicating the presence of strabismus include, in addition to apparent deviation, complaints of double vision, difficulty reading, and unusual head positions, such as turning or tilting the head. Occasionally an infant is suspected of having strabismus, but in reality the appearance is due to the presence of epicanthal folds and the wide bridge of the nose. This *pseudostrabismus* is rechecked at 6-month intervals to be certain a true strabismus is not present.

Treatment Treatment of strabismus usually involves correction of amblyopia if present, surgery for muscle imbalance, and glasses to correct differences in refraction.

Amblyopia is treated by patching the normal eye in order to force use of the deviating eye. In the 1-year-old child correction may be obtained in less than 2 weeks while in the 6-year-old correction may take 6 months. The child is examined frequently to be certain the patched eye does not become amblyopic from disuse.

Surgery is performed after amblyopia has been corrected and involves resection or recession of one or more ocular muscles. Resection results in a shortened muscle, which strengthens it; recession weakens the muscle by lengthening it. Surgery may need to be performed more than once. The initial repair may be performed as early as 12 months for congenital strabismus and 18 months for infantile strabismus. The child is generally admitted the day before surgery and discharged the day following surgery. The operated eye is patched until the evening of the day of surgery.

The child is usually discharged with an antibiotic and steroid ointment. Some hospitals are now experimenting with performing strabismus surgery on an outpatient basis. Results have been satisfactory as long as the child is awake and drinking well before discharge.[12]

Nursing management In the outpatient clinic the nurse can teach the child and parents to correctly utilize patching for amblyopia. Parents need to know which eye is to be patched. They must understand that the patch is to remain on at all times. Elastoplast patches, which are available in most drug stores, can be applied with tincture of benzoin, which helps decrease skin irritation and increase adherence. The child often resists the patch because it is hot and uncomfortable, decreases the ability to see, and sets the child apart from peers.[13] The parents may need to apply mittens or elbow restraints to prevent an infant from pulling off the patch. The older child may have difficulty reading. Before being allowed to play alone outdoors, the child should be able to manage indoors without stumbling over objects.[14] Encourage parents to keep their child's appointments with the physician; progress of the amblyopic eye as well as the opposite eye needs to be monitored closely to prevent disuse amblyopia. When the vision in the amblyopic eye is close to normal, the child may be weaned from the patch. Because amblyopia can recur until about age 9, frequent examinations are still necessary after vision has been corrected and part-time patching may be continued.

Preoperative teaching In providing care to the child undergoing strabismus surgery, the same principles are utilized as for preparing any child for surgery. In addition the child can be told that the eye is going to be fixed and that when the child wakes up, the eye(s) will be covered. Assure the child that after the patches are removed, the child will be able to see. Blindfold the child the evening before surgery to have him experience not being able to see. Attach a call light to the bed and have the child practice using it when blindfolded.

Postoperative care When the child returns from surgery, suggest that the parents hold the child and assist them in doing so. Even when prepared, the child may panic when sight is not possible. Before touching the child or talking with the parents, the nurse's identity should be known to the child. It is helpful if the same nurse who prepared the child preoperatively cares for the child postoperatively so that the child hears a familiar voice.

Remain with the parents until they seem confident of their ability to comfort the child and return frequently to provide assistance as well as to check on the child's general condition. Although the possibility of increasing intraocular pressure is not a concern with this surgery, start oral fluids cautiously to keep the child more comfortable by preventing vomiting. A small amount of serous drainage from the operated eye is expected. Elbow restraints may be needed to prevent the child from pulling at the patch or rubbing the eyes. When the child is fully awake, usually distraction is enough to prevent eye rubbing. The child may enjoy putting a patch on a doll or stuffed animal; provide toys for quiet play. Before the eye patch is removed, prepare the parents for a swollen, reddened eye.

Before discharging the child, demonstrate to the parents how to insert the eye drops or eye ointment and explain the purpose of the medication. Alert them to symptoms of possible infection, such as increased drainage which becomes purulent or increased swelling. Explain the necessity for a return appointment with the surgeon and encourage them to call the physician at any time before that for questions. The operated eye may remain reddened and edematous for several days. The school age child may have to endure some teasing about the reddened eye and the loss of eyelashes. Any activity which may damage the eye such as contact sports, should be avoided.

Refractive errors
Pathophysiology There are three common types of refractive errors in children: *hyperopia* (farsightedness), *myopia* (nearsightedness) and *astigmatism*. (See Fig. 39-5.) Refractive errors are often familial and related to anatomical deviations in the eyeball. In hyperopia, the eyeball is shorter than normal so that the light rays converge behind the retina when viewing close objects, resulting in blurred vision. Many preschool children are slightly hyperopic and do not need corrective lenses. As the eyeball lengthens during growth, the problem may be outgrown. If there is a significant difference between the visual acuity of each eye, glasses will be needed to prevent development of amblyopia. A contact lens may be used in the hyperopic eye.

Myopia frequently develops after the age of 8. In this condition, the eyeball is too long so that light rays are focused in front of the retina. Myopia tends to increase in severity as the eyeball lengthens during childhood. These children do need corrective glasses and should be checked yearly. Unilateral myopia can result in amblyopia. A child who is nearsighted may complain of not being able to see the chalkboard or may be observed looking at distant objects with partially closed eyes.[15]

Astigmatism occurs because the cornea is curved irregularly so that some light rays are focused in front of the retina and others behind. As a result vision is blurred. Astigmatism is hard to detect before the child is 5 years old. Blurred vision results in complaints of headaches after close work. Glasses are necessary for correction.

Contact lenses Contact lenses may be used in place of glasses to correct refractive errors. The primary advantage of contact lenses is cosmetic; contact lenses frequently also provide more normal vision than glasses because the lenses are fitted right to the cornea and move with the eyes. There are no frames to block peripheral vision.

Most authorities suggest that contact lenses can be utilized successfully in children 12-years-old and older.[16] The child of this age, because of increased interest in improving appearance, is more likely to tolerate the initial discomfort

Figure 39-5 Hyperopia and myopia. (*A*) Hyperopia. At right, hyperopia is corrected with biconvex lens. (*B*) Myopia. At right, myopia is corrected with biconcave lens. (*From L. Langley et al., Dynamic Anatomy and Physiology, 4th ed., McGraw-Hill, New York, 1974. Used by permission of the publisher.*)

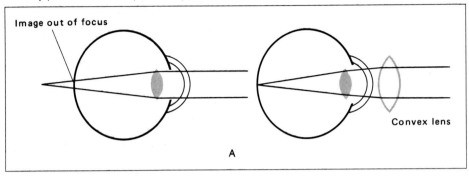

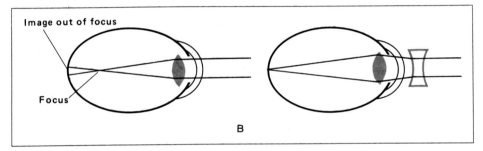

during the adjustment period. The child is also more dependable about caring for the lenses. As has already been mentioned, contact lenses are also used successfully in infants with cataracts.

Two types of contact lenses are readily available. The hard lens, which has been in use the longest, is made of a hard plastic material. This lens may provide better vision since it can correct for the irregularities of the corneal surface. Hard lenses are less expensive and resist wear-and-tear more easily than the soft lenses. The soft lens, which is made of a flexible plastic material, is easier to adjust to and the wearer is less likely to develop eye infections. However, soft lenses are more expensive, more difficult to clean, and have a shorter life span. Soft lenses also absorb eye medications and aerosols such as perfume and hair spray; these substances can damage the lens and the aerosols can continue to irritate the cornea when in contact with the lens.[17]

When a child is fitted for contact lenses, the nurse ensures that the child and parents understand how the lenses are to be worn and cared for. The nurse needs to know what instructions have been given to the child. The child should follow carefully the schedule established by the doctor during the initial adjustment period to wearing lenses. A special solution and procedure are necessary for cleaning the lenses. The child should be cautioned against using saliva to clean or reinsert a lens as this practice may lead to eye infection and may also result in the child swallowing the lens. Contact lenses should not be worn when sleeping as this decreases the amount of oxygen the cornea receives and may lead to corneal abrasions. Contact lenses should not be worn when swimming; they are easily lost underwater and the soft type may absorb the chlorine in the water. Lenses should be inserted before eye makeup is applied. The child's eyes should be examined every 6 months.

The most common complications of contact lens wear are corneal abrasions, which are terribly painful, and ocular infection, which can lead to loss of vision.[18] If the child follows the prescribed instructions carefully, both of these complications are rare. Symptoms indicating a need for evaluation include complaints of pain when wearing the lens or after removing it, inability to keep the eyes open, markedly increased light sensitivity, hazy vision, and extremely reddened eyes.[19]

Glasses Glasses should be shatterproof. Plastic frames are more desirable than metal ones because the metal bends out of shape too easily. Plastic lenses are of lighter weight but they may be unsuitable for children because they are so easily scratched. Athletic straps or headbands are useful in keeping glasses in place. The older child can be taught to clean the glasses with warm water and a soft cloth or paper towel. To prevent scratching, glasses should not be laid down on their lenses. To prevent breakage, they should be kept in a case when not being worn. Glasses should fit well to prevent irritation of the bridge of the nose and behind the ears; the child is more likely to wear the glasses if the skin is not irritated. Once the child realizes how much better vision is with glasses, the child is likely to keep them on. Persistence on the part of the parents may be necessary to keep glasses on the infant or toddler. Glasses require an initial period of adjustment; the child may complain of headaches for a few days. If headaches persist, the lenses should be rechecked by the prescribing physician to be certain the correction is accurate. The older child may need an opportunity to talk about feelings related to change in appearance and differences from peers.

Nursing management of children with refractive errors The functions of the nurse include encouraging frequent eye examinations in children, especially if visual difficulties have already been determined, providing follow-up referral of children detected in vision screening clinics, and providing information to the parents and child on the care and wearing of glasses or contact lenses.

Infectious processes

Ophthalmia neonatorum Any type of conjunctivitis in the newborn is referred to as *ophthalmia neonatorum*. The most common cause is a chemical reaction to the silver nitrate drops instilled after birth to prevent gonococcal conjunctivitis.

The newborn who develops a copious muco-purulent discharge from the eyes around the fifth day after birth usually has gonococcal conjunctivitis. If untreated, this infection can lead to corneal ulceration and ultimately blindness. The infant is isolated and treated with systemic and topical penicillin. Before instilling the topical penicillin, irrigate the involved eye with normal saline. Restrain the infant so that rubbing the eyes is not possible. If only one eye is involved, avoid contaminating the uninvolved eye. Open the involved eye frequently to release the pus. The pressure of the accumulating discharge can lead to corneal ulceration. Wearing protective glasses will prevent contamination of the nurse's eyes. Allow the mother to verbalize her feelings; she may express guilt because the infant has picked up an infection from her. With prompt penicillin treatment, loss of vision usually does not occur.

Inclusion conjunctivitis is caused by an organism similar to the one causing trachoma. It is also picked up during the birth process. Symptoms of mucopurulent discharge usually appear 5 to 10 days after birth. If untreated a chronic form may develop. This type of conjunctivitis is usually treated with oral and topical sulfonamides for 10 days.

Conjunctivitis in the older child Conjunctivitis in the older child may be due to drug reactions, allergies, disease of the cornea, or viral and bacterial infections. Most conjunctivitis is a result of infections. Symptoms include tearing, mucopurulent discharge, which may result in morning lid-sticking and a sandy feeling in the eyes. Conjunctivitis due to a bacterial infection, often staphylococcus or *Haemophilus influenzae*, produces more discharge. Instillation of antibiotic ointments or drops preceded by cleansing the eyes with sterile water are used to treat bacterial infections. Bacterial conjunctivitis is easily spread from one child to the next.

A viral conjunctivitis is usually accompanied by other symptoms of upper respiratory infection and is usually self-limiting. Many eye specialists recommend undertreating conjunctivitis, especially if the origin is viral. Use of steroid ointments can mask herpes virus or fungal infections and result in corneal ulcerations and scarring.

Nursing management The nurse in the teacher role can suggest that parents avoid over-the-counter remedies and seek medical advice for persistent conjunctivitis. The parents may need to be taught the instillation of eye drops or ointments; careful handwashing before and after should be emphasized. Towels and wash cloths should not be shared; swimming and bathing with siblings should be discontinued until the infection subsides.

Trachoma *Trachoma* is a chronic disease affecting both the conjunctiva and the cornea; it is caused by *Chlamydia trachomatis*, a virus like organism. Trachoma may be one of the leading causes of preventable blindness. Poor hygiene favors its spread. In the United States it is uncommon except in the Southwest. The infection is fairly mild in school-age children but is increasingly severe in adolescents and adults. Early symptoms include a mild amount of mucopurulent discharge and reddened eyes. As the disease progresses, the conjunctiva becomes scarred, resulting in malformed lids which may ulcerate the cornea. Inflammation of the cornea itself leads to vascularization and blindness. Treatment consists of oral sulfa drugs and topical tetracycline. Suggest to the parents or child that they irrigate the eyes before the medication is instilled. Edema can be reduced by the use of cold compresses and photophobia diminished by decreasing the amount of light in the room. Emphasize the need for careful follow-up. A newer method of treatment is the insertion of cellulose discs of antibiotics under the lids.[20]

Hordeolum A *hordeolum*, or *sty*, is a red, painful swelling due to infection of the sebaceous glands or hair follicles at the margin of the eyelids. Sties tend to occur in crops and can be spread from one hair follicle to the next by the fingers. The cause is usually staphylococcus. Sties are treated with topical antibiotics and warm, moist packs applied several times a day. Sties usually drain spontaneously; occasionally they will need to be drained surgically. Sties that recur call for further investigation. Extension of the infection to other parts of the eye is also possible.

Chalazions *Chalazions* are painless cysts which form in the connective tissue supporting the eyelid. They may disappear spontaneously within a month or may be surgically removed. They can become secondarily infected.

Trauma

Trauma to the eye includes foreign bodies, corneal abrasions, chemical burns, blow out fractures, lacerations, perforations, and hemorrhage of the globe. The causes of accidental injury have already been discussed. Children with eye injuries except for the simplest type of foreign body should be examined and treated by an ophthalmologist. Visual acuity should be determined whenever possible after an injury.

Nursing management Foreign bodies in the lower or upper lid can usually be removed with a cotton swab. Visible nonmetallic foreign bodies on the sclera or cornea can be irrigated off with normal saline or water.

Chemical burns can cause serious eye damage. Alkalis are most destructive because they penetrate rapidly through the cornea and deep into the eyeball. For a chemical burn, immediately flush the injured eye with large amounts of water for at least 10 min. In the emergency room, IV solution and tubing works well.[21]

Whenever the child is admitted to the hospital for an eye injury, the child will probably be placed on bed rest with one or both eyes patched. If the younger child is very apprehensive, only the injured eye may be patched. Place the child in a quiet room away from the activity of the nurse's station. Decrease the room lighting if one eye is not patched. Sensory deprivation and fear of loss of vision may concern the child most. The parent's presence is reassuring. The nurse can provide appropriate diversion and sensory stimulation by such means as reading to the child, providing a radio, and visiting with him.

The child may feel the accident is punishment for misbehavior. The accident may have occurred when the child was doing something he had been previously told not to do. Provide the child with the opportunity to express feelings either through play or talking. Assure the child the accident or treatment is not punishment. Parents may express guilt that they should have supervised the child's activity more closely.

Some eye injuries may require months before visual acuity, full or partial, is restored. If the child is of school age, the nurse can contact the hospital social services department to arrange for a tutor. Such complications as glaucoma, cataracts, and retinal detachment can occur years after the injury. Encourage parents to continue regular eye examinations after the eye has healed so that complications can be detected early.

Visual impairment/blindness

Visual impairment may be partial or total blindness. Legal blindness is the inability to see at 20 ft, even with corrective lenses, what a person with normal vision sees at 200 ft. Few persons are totally blind; most have some degree of light perception.

Congenital visual impairment

An infant may be diagnosed as blind in the hospital soon after birth or the parents may suspect that the child does not see. Whenever a child is diagnosed as being severely visually handicapped, parents will go through a grief process similar to the grieving that follows any loss. The nurse can support the parents in whatever phase of grieving they exhibit. Parents may ask for information about the cause, severity, and availability of treatment. They need assistance to accept the idea that their child is first of all a child and secondarily has impaired sight. They need information about available resources within or outside of the local community. Social services agencies should be able to provide referrals to state agencies and to community health agencies. In many states, teachers and counselors associated with a school for the blind can help the parents plan a home program to ensure full development of the child's potential. The community health nurse can work with the counselors and parents in implementing the program.

The infant blind from birth is at risk because most early learning takes place through visual cues. In addition, bonding of parents and infant occurs primarily through eye contact. The blind infant obviously cannot establish eye contact and the parents may feel rebuffed. The parents will need to learn different cues for interpreting pleasure or needs. The infant who is not stimulated will not develop mentally or emotionally but will withdraw. All of the tasks a sighted child learns by visual imitation, a blind child will need to be taught. Visually impaired children may crawl and walk later than sighted children be-

cause there is no visual incentive for them to move. Unless the child learns finger dexterity, he will be unable to read braille. When the child reaches school age, a decision will have to be made whether the child would gain the most from a residential school for the blind or the regular school system with special visual devices and teachers. The current trend is for visually impaired children to attend public schools whenever possible. With support from professionals and the family, the blind child can adapt well to a seeing world. Table 39-6 lists suggestions for promoting the child's development.

Rearing a congenitally blind child requires considerable emotional and physical investment on the part of the family. The needs of the other family members can become lost or secondary. An alert nurse can encourage the family to look at their own needs as well. (See Figs. 39-6 and 39-7.)

Acquired visual impairment

The child who has lost sight as a result of an illness or injury may assume that the loss is a result of misbehavior and needs to be given the opportunity to express those fears. The child may show regressive or openly hostile behavior. While hostility resulting in failure to cooperate with treatment or in aggressive behavior cannot be tolerated, the child does need the opportunity to express resentment at having lost his sight. Not until then can the child accept any assistance toward rehabilitation. Counseling may be necessary. The nurse can refer the family to social services for information about local rehabilitation services such as mobility training. The child's independence should be maintained as much as possible; this may be difficult for parents who may express their feelings of guilt and concern by trying to do everything possible for their child. If a sibling is responsible for the injury, that child may need assistance in working through feelings. Siblings may also feel that a similar accident could happen to them.

As soon as medically possible, the child should be ambulated. Help the child learn the placement of objects in the room and practice going from one object to the next. Make use of whatever residual vision, such as light perception, is present. Encourage the child to feed, bathe, and dress himself.

Table 39-6 Methods to promote the development of a blind child

Age	Intervention
Infancy	1. Tell child when you are picking him up 2. Hold, touch frequently 3. Carry from room to room in infant carrier on parent's back 4. String cradle gym across top of crib 5. Prop in sitting position to learn head control 6. Teach hand usage by playing patacake, splashing in water 7. Avoid leaving child in crib for long periods
Toddler	1. Use bowls with suction cups for feeding 2. Teach body parts 3. Describe what is happening while dressing child 4. Avoid playpen 5. Involve in household tasks 6. Teach to turn toward person child is talking to 7. Place objects on couch and place child up against couch to interest in walking
Preschooler	1. Provide play opportunities with sighted children 2. Sew tags on back of clothing to facilitate dressing 3. Explain where things come from such as water from faucet 4. Teach differences in textures—sandpaper, buttons, clay, etc
Schoolage—adolescence	1. Encourage skating, swimming 2. Teach use of typewriter and tape recorder, braille 3. Encourage activities with sighted friends 4. Assist with vocational testing, determining career choices

Figure 39-6 Visually impaired children from a residential school. (*Courtesy of North Dakota State School for the Blind, Grand Forks, N. Dak.*)

Admission of a blind child to the hospital

A blind child may be admitted to the hospital for an eye examination or for unrelated illness. When admitting the child, obtain a thorough history from the parents, including the length of time he has been blind, what self-help skills, such as feeding and dressing, the child performs at home, what limits are set at home, what kinds of activities are enjoyed, and whether or not the child has been hospitalized previously. Encourage the parents to remain with their child and participate in care; they can act as interpreters and security givers in a strange environment. Orient the child to the room and to the placement of objects, such as the bed or the bathroom. Walk the child around the unit several times. Explain the sounds the child may be hearing: the noise when a call light is pushed, the beep of a monitor or IV pump. If possible put the child in a room with another child of the same age.

Figure 39-7 Visually impaired child using a closed circuit television magnifier. (*Courtesy of North Dakota State School for the Blind, Grand Forks, N. Dak.*)

The blind child can become easily disoriented in a new environment and withdraw.

Before carrying out any procedure, explain it thoroughly and allow the child to handle the items if possible. Explain that siderails will be up when the child is in bed; keep the bed at its lowest height. Return objects in the room to the same place and guide the child's hands to them. Unless essential for safety, avoid hand restraints; the child needs hands to stay in touch with reality. Assist the child in remaining as independent as possible; for example, set up the meal tray but encourage self-feeding.

If the child leaves the unit for any reason, tape a note to the chart or pin a note on the gown. Use the information provided in the nursing history to assist the child in providing as much self-care as possible. Tell the child when entering or leaving the room. Provide play activities appropriate for age. Spend time with the child other than when procedures need to be carried out. Assess the interaction of the child and parents and the child's developmental level. Provide referral to community health nursing services or social service as appropriate.

Embryology of the ear

Development of the ear begins around 3 weeks of gestation. Each portion of the ear—external, middle, and inner—develops separately and follows its own timetable. The internal ear is the first portion to begin developing. By the eighth to tenth week the semi-circular canals are present; the cochlea is complete by 12 weeks. By the end of the eighth week an auditory tube is developing, which will become the middle ear. The tympanic membrane is not formed until 28 weeks.

The external ear is obvious by 8 weeks. By 11 weeks the ear approaches the typical adult appearance. Initially the external ear lies level with the lower jaw, but by the sixteenth week it rises to its higher position on the side of the head. At 20 weeks portions of the ear begin to ossify.

The ears of the newborn are functional at birth, but the infant is deaf until amniotic fluid drains from the ears and the pressure within the ear is equalized. This is usually accomplished within a few hours after birth. The newborn responds to noise by blinking or exhibiting the Moro reflex. By 9 months the infant localizes sounds, by 2 years the toddler responds to commands, and by 5 years hearing function is fully developed.[22]

Anatomy of the ear

The structure of the ear can be divided into three parts: external, middle, and inner ear. The anatomy and functions of the various parts are summarized in Table 39-7 and Fig. 39-8.

Physiology: Sound Conduction

The sound waves are caught and carried to the tympanic membrane by the auricle and external auditory meatus. Sound waves set the tympanic membrane in motion in harmony with the frequency of the sound waves. This vibration is passed on to the auditory ossicles within the middle ear. The third ossicle communicates with the oval window and sets it in motion. The vibration of the oval window creates waves within the fluid of the inner ear. These fluid waves are carried to the basilar membrane within the cochlea. The movement of the fibers of the basilar membrane stimulates the hair cells of the organ of Corti, which lies on top of the basilar membrane. The result is the stimulation of the axon fibers making up the auditory nerve. The impulses are then transmitted to the auditory area within the temporal lobe of the brain, where the sounds are interpreted.

Table 39-7 Anatomy of the ear

Part	Function
External ear	
Auricle	Thin cartilage structure which collects sound waves and channels them into external auditory canal
External auditory canal	S-shaped structure which brings sound waves to middle ear and helps protect and lubricate ear with cilia and cerumen
Middle ear	
Tympanic membrane	Thin, transparent membrane which vibrates when struck by sound waves
Auditory ossicles	Three small bones which move sound waves from tympanic membrane to fluid-filled inner ear across oval window
Eustachian tube	Small tube connecting middle ear to nasopharynx; made partially of cartilage; maintains equal air pressure between middle ear and external ear and prevents contents of nasopharynx from entering middle ear
Inner ear	
Oval window	Transmits sound waves from stapes into fluid of inner ear
Round window	Expands and contracts as fluid waves in inner ear change and serves as a relief valve
Vestibule	Central portion of inner ear
Semicircular canals	Maintain sensation of equilibrium and balance
Cochlea	Snail-shaped object in which sound waves are changed to nervous impulses by hair cells contained within it
Organ of Corti	Lies within the cochlea and contains the nerve cells which are sensitive to sound vibrations
Auditory nerve	Transmits nervous impulses to the auditory center within the upper part of the temporal area in the brain

When sound is transmitted by bone conduction through the skull, the waves are transmitted to the inner ear, bypassing the external and middle ear.

Assessment of the ear

Inspection

The assessment of the ear is performed primarily by careful inspection and palpation. Table 39-8 summarizes the major points that should be checked. The examination of the infant or small child can easily be carried out on the parent's lap. In order to examine the eardrum, the child will need to be restrained to prevent any movement which could injure the ear. The mother can hold the child against her body, tucking one arm behind her and holding the other arm while placing the child's legs between her knees. She can then hold the child's head against her body to stabilize the head. The child can also be examined on the examining table with the head turned to one side and the mother or nurse standing at the head of the table holding the child's arms up against the head to stabilize it. Evaluating the tympanic membrane requires repeated experience. The examiner will be looking for the color, mobility, presence of the light

Figure 39-8 Anatomy of the ear. (*From L. Langley et al., Dynamic Anatomy and Physiology, 4th ed., McGraw-Hill, New York, 1974. Used by permission of the publisher.*)

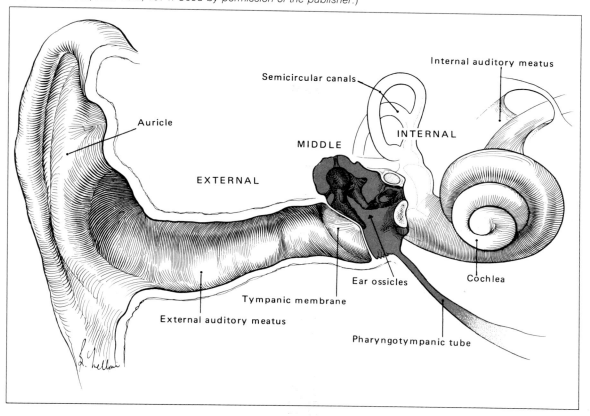

reflex, and evidence of perforation, retraction, or bulging of the tympanic membrane. Before using the otoscope, familiarize the child with it by showing him the instrument, allowing the child to "blow out the light," shining the light on the child's hand, or describing it as a flashlight.

Hearing tests

The child's hearing ability can be partially assessed by careful interviewing of the parent. Suggested questions follow the sequence of growth and development. These are summarized on Table 39-9.

Formalized testing of newborns has been carried out in some hospitals with a device called

Table 39-8 Assessment of the external ear

Auricles

Well-shaped, complete, absence of skin tags or fistulas
Lie flat against the head
Proportionate to rest of head
Pinna crosses line drawn from outer canthus of eye to occipital prominence
Flesh colored
Absence of tenderness behind ear

External ear canal

Appears patent
Absence of furuncles and foreign objects in canal
Absence of odor
Absence of dried or free-running discharge

Table 39-9 Assessment of hearing ability from interviewing

Infant
Responds to noise
Stops activity when someone enters room

Toddler—preschooler
Language development

School-age—adolescent
Described by teacher, parents as being inattentive
Complains of difficulty hearing in school
Excessive volume on radio or television
Complains of ear pain, dizziness, ear ringing

All ages
History of frequent ear infections
History of ear discharge

a *Crib-O-Gram*. This device consists of a transducer which is sensitive to motion, a strip chart recorder, timing system, and loudspeaker. The newborn lies on the transducer and a record is made of responses to sounds. The device can determine losses of 75 dB or greater, which would indicate moderate-to-profound hearing loss.[23]

A child from 2 months to 1 or 2 years can be tested by using various toys, such as a rubber squeeze toy with a whistle or a bell or rattle with known intensity and frequency. The child is distracted with a toy and the examiner then makes a noise and evaluates the child's response.[24]

For the toddler and early preschool-age child,

Figure 39-9 Testing the hearing of a 4-year-old child with an audiometer. (From *Pediatric Nursing*, vol. 2, no. 5, 1976. Reprinted with permission of the publisher.)

play conditioning techniques can be used. The child is taught to carry out a specific task when a sound is heard. The child will need to become familiar with the toys and the task first. Examples of tasks might include placing a ring on a peg or putting animals back into a toy barn. Each correct response is rewarded socially as well. The whisper test can also be used with the preschooler. Tuning fork tests are difficult to explain to young children.

The 4- to 5-year-old and school-age child can be tested with pure-tone audiometry. The audiometer provides a graphic chart of the child's hearing ability at various frequencies and intensities of sound. The record is made in terms of decibels (dB). Zero decibels is the intensity of sound heard 50 percent of the time by a person with normal hearing. Each ear is tested separately; the child is taught to respond to each sound heard by raising one hand. (See Fig. 39-9.)

Several specialized tests are also available for use on children who are too young or have behavioral problems which limit cooperation. In brainstem electric-response audiometry electrodes are placed on the child's head and an electroencephalogram recorded which detects changes when a sound stimulus is presented.[25] Electrocochleography is done under general anesthesia and a needle electrode is placed through the eardrum. Inroduction of a sound results in stimulation of the cochlea.[26]

Nursing management
Teaching general ear care The hearing ability of a child should be assessed at birth, every 6 months in the first 12 months, yearly until age 6, and then every 2 to 3 years.[27] This schedule does not imply formalized testing; an assessment of hearing ability will indicate the need for further testing.

Normally, ear hygiene consists only of washing the external ear and the edge of the ear canal with a soft washcloth. Cerumen (ear wax) serves a protective function and does not need to be removed under most circumstances. Remind parents not to use bobby pins, paper clips, or cotton-tipped applicators to remove wax. These instruments usually result in pushing the wax further into the ear canal against the tympanic membrane or in injuring the canal itself.

Symptoms of ear disease for which parents will need to seek medical advice include pain in the ear or behind it, especially if accompanied by fever, any discharge from the ear, any evidence or suspicion of decreased hearing ability, and complaints of dizziness or loss of balance.

If instillation of ear drops has been prescribed, demonstrate to the parents how the procedure is carried out. For an infant it is often easier for one parent to hold the child while the other parent instills the drops. The medication should be at room temperature to prevent dizziness. Have the child lie on the side. Straighten the ear canal by pulling down for an infant or young child and pulling up for an older child. Put in the required number of drops. After instillation, the child should remain on his side for a few minutes. He may complain that the drops tickle, but there should be no pain. (See Fig. 39-10).

Ear irrigations tend to be messy and time-consuming procedures which children dislike, but occasionally irrigations are necessary for removal of excessive ear wax. Either an ear syringe or Water Pik on low can be used. The Water Pik helps to break up the wax.[28] A mixture of warm water and hydrogen peroxide is often used. The solution is squirted forcefully into the ear canal and allowed to run out into a basin held below the ear. The procedure is repeated until the ear canal is free of enough wax for the tympanic membrane to be visualized.

Deafness

Pathophysiology

Hearing impairment varies from mild to profound. Losses are classified by decibels: Mild hearing loss ranges from 25 to 45 dB, and over 95 dB is a profound loss. (See Table 39-10.) If the child has a hearing loss before the age of 2 or 3 years, he cannot develop normal language skills. Hearing impairment can have a conductive or sensorineural basis. *Conductive loss* refers to any abnormality of the external or middle ear that prohibits a transmission of sound waves to the inner ear. Sensorineural loss may involve the cochlea, auditory nerve, brainstem, or central nervous system. Hearing impairment can also be a combination of conductive and sensorineural or mixed loss.

Deafness may result from heredity, prenatal rubella infection, prematurity, hyperbilirubinemia, mumps, measles, meningitis, and trauma.

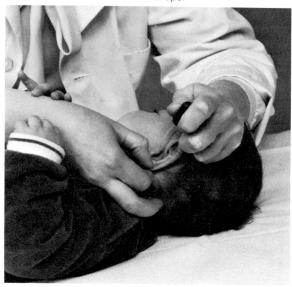

Figure 39-10 Instillation of ear drops.

Medications known to impair hearing include kanamycin, gentamicin, neomycin, and streptomycin. Incubator noise has been suggested as a positive factor in increased hearing loss in premature infants, but a more recent study failed to substantiate incubator noise as a cause of hearing loss while acknowledging it might play a role.[29]

Treatment

The child who has a congenital anomaly of the outer or middle ear is checked for inner ear function. If the inner ear is normal, the child is fitted with a bone conduction hearing aid. Reconstructive surgery is usually performed when the child is around 5.

Medical treatment is of no benefit to the child with a sensorineural loss. The child is fitted with hearing aids as early as 6 months if hearing loss is over 50 dB. Introduction of hearing aids is most successful in infants and helps prevent the language deprivation to which deaf infants are prone. Hearing aids which transmit the sound to both ears (binaural) are generally used. Body-type aids are usually used because the pinna of the infant and young child is not strong enough to support a behind-the-ear type. The older child may be unwilling to wear the body aid.

Table 39-10 Handicapping effects of hearing loss

Average hearing 500–2000 Hz (ANSI)	Description	Condition	Sounds heard without amplification	Degree of handicap (if not treated in first year of life)	Probable needs
0–15 dB	Normal range	Serous otitis, perforation, monomeric membrane, tympanosclerosis	All speech sounds	None	None
15–25 dB	Slight hearing loss	Serous otitis, perforation, monomeric membrane, sensorineural loss, tympanosclerosis	Vowel sounds heard clearly; may miss unvoiced consonant sounds	Mid auditory dysfunction in language learning	Consideration of need for hearing aid, lip reading, auditory training, speech therapy, preferential seating
25–40 dB	Mild hearing loss	Serous otitis, perforation, tympanosclerosis, monomeric membrane, sensorineural loss	Hears only some louder voiced speech sounds	Auditory learning dysfunction, mild language retardation, mild speech problems, inattention	Hearing aid, lip reading auditory training, speech therapy
40–65 dB	Moderate hearing loss	Chronic otitis, middle ear anomaly, sensorineural loss	Misses most speech sounds at normal conversational level	Speech problems, language retardation, learning dysfunction, inattention	All the above plus consideration of special classroom situation
65–95 dB	Severe hearing loss	Sensorineural or mixed loss due to sensorineural loss plus middle ear disease	Hears no speech sounds of normal conversation	Severe speech problems, language retardation, learning dysfunction, inattention	All the above plus probable assignment to special classes
95 dB or more	Profound hearing loss	Sensorineural or mixed loss	Hears no speech or other sounds	Severe speech problems, language retardation, learning dysfunction, inattention	All the above plus probable assignment to special classes

Source: Jerry L. Northern (ed.), *Hearing Disorders*, Little, Brown, Boston, 1976. Used by permission of the publisher.

Nursing management

When the diagnosis of hearing impairment is made, parents will need information regarding the cause and treatment as well as support. Parents who are successfully rearing a hearing-impaired child may provide the most support. The parents may express guilt, resentment, and anxiety over how to care for their child.

If the child is fitted for hearing aids, the parents will need to be taught how to insert the aids and maintain proper function. They will be taught to check the hearing aid daily for function, perform simple repairs, and replace the batteries. The ear mold must fit well to prevent ear irritation and squealing or whistling noises. Ear molds will be changed as the child grows.

Referral by the nurse to an agency that can provide a program of education and stimulation for the child and the audiological services necessary for evaluation of hearing impairment is essential. Hearing loss may be progressive especially in rubella syndrome children and hereditary diseases.[30] Unless the family lives near a major city, they may have to travel many miles to get the assistance they need.

It is essential for normal brain development that the child be able to use residual hearing as early as possible and be stimulated fully. Ideally, the infant is involved in a home program as soon as the diagnosis of hearing impairment is made. Parents are taught how to talk to the child and stimulate normal development. They also receive the support they need to express their feelings about the child and the stresses imposed on the family. After the age of 3 the child may be enrolled in a nursery school to learn further communication and socialization skills.[31] When the child reaches school age, parents will have to decide whether to use the public school system with special tutoring or a residential school for the deaf. There are several types of communication systems for the hearing impaired; which type is best remains controversial (Fig. 39-11). Some educators believe the child should not be taught any type of sign language until they can read lips well, which may be after the elementary school years; others believe in total communication, which includes lip reading, hand signs, finger spelling, and using residual hearing.

Hospital care of a deaf child

When a deaf child is admitted to the hospital, the nurse assesses

Figure 39-11 Teaching a deaf 2-year-old to speak. The race car set moves on the track when the child talks into the microphone. The set was made by the Telephone Pioneers Organization of Western Electric. (*Courtesy of Western Electric.*)

thoroughly the child's capabilities and needs just as was done for the blind child who is hospitalized. Hearing loss isolates the child from the external world. It is more difficult and takes longer for a hearing-impaired person to comprehend such abstract terms as pain. During the admission interview, ask how long the child has been deaf, whether deafness occurred before language ability was attained, what type of communication system the family has been using, and whether the child uses hearing aids.

During the admission procedure, teach the child how to call a nurse by having a nurse outside the door come into the room each time the child presses the call button. This activity may need to be repeated several times.

To maintain consistency, plan a time schedule for daily events and record it in the Kardex. The child will be more comfortable with the communication patterns that have been developed with the parents; encourage the parents to stay with the child and use the parents as much as possible in talking with the child or when explaining events or procedures. Assign one nurse to care for the child. To allow for scheduled days off, arrange for the primary nurse and the nurse caring for the child to work together for a day.

When entering the room, always touch the child before beginning to talk. Face the child at a distance of 3 to 4 ft. A female nurse can wear a contrasting lipstick so the child can read lips more easily. When it is necessary to perform a treatment behind the child, such as an enema, arrange for another person to stand in front of the child and explain the procedure as it is being carried out.

Use pictures or models of the actual objects to explain procedures or carry out preoperative teaching. If the child can read, use written communication as much as necessary.

Use every opportunity to orient the child to the new environment. Call attention to objects and events occurring in the area; allow the child to explore areas within the hospital with nursing personnel. Introduce the child to other children on the unit.

Words are easily misinterpreted by the hearing-impaired child; more cues are picked up by facial expression and body language. A frown or look of disgust or worry conveys more to the child than what the nurse says.

If the child uses hearing aids, be sure that the batteries are working and that the ear mold is clean and intact. If the child leaves the unit for any reason, the hearing aids should be in place.

For a child undergoing surgery, the experience is less threatening if the parents can accompany the child to the holding room and if surgery personnel leave their masks off until the child is asleep. The hearing aids should remain in place until the child is anesthetized; as soon as the child is brought to the recovery room, the hearing aids should be put back into place. To ensure that the hearing aids are not misplaced or damaged the circulating nurse can label and send them to the recovery room as soon as they are removed from the sleeping child. When the child returns to the unit, it is helpful to have the parents present.

The care provided by the nurse to the hospitalized deaf child will also be presented in the form of a case study—the Nursing Care Plan.

Acquired alterations

Acute otitis media

Pathophysiology *Acute otitis media* is an infection of the middle ear which occurs frequently in young children because of the anatomy of the eustachian tube. In infants the eustachian tube is wider, shorter, and placed more horizontally. The supine position of the infant also favors the introduction of bacteria from the pharynx through the eustachian tube into the middle ear. Older children often have enlarged lymphoid tissue which obstructs the eustachian tube; they also have more frequent upper respiratory infections, predisposing them to otitis media. The causative organisms include *Haemophilus influenzae*, streptococcus, and pneumococcus.

An infant may have vague symptoms, such as irritability and prolonged crying or fever or vomiting and diarrhea following a cold. The child may pull at the involved ear. For the older child, infection also follows a cold, and the child complains of ear pain in addition to having a fever. Pain is due to the distension of the tympanic membrane.[32] On examination, the tympanic membrane may appear red and bulging with the light reflex muddled. Mobility of the tympanic membrane may be decreased.

Treatment Treatment is usually carried out at home unless an infant becomes dehydrated. Oral ampicillin is usually prescribed for 10 days; decongestants or antihistamines may also be given, although their value has not been substantiated. The physician may reevaluate the child in several days. A *myringotomy*, which is a small incision in the tympanic membrane, may be performed to relieve the pressure and permit drainage from the middle ear. Two weeks after the infection, the ears should be examined again and the child checked for hearing loss.

Complications of acute otitis media include the development of a chronic form of otitis, mastoiditis, or meningitis. The child with chronic otitis media has recurring episodes of middle ear infection which can lead to mastoiditis or to hearing loss by immobilization of the ossicles and damage to the cochlea.

Nursing management Teaching parents how to care for a child with otitis media includes instructions on administration of ampicillin and comfort measures. Ampicillin is absorbed best when given 1 h before meals. The medication should be continued for the full 10 days. It is tempting to discontinue the medication after symptoms are relieved, especially if giving it involves a struggle. Occasionally administration of ampicillin results in the appearance of a maculopapular rash or diarrhea. The physician should be notified; in most instances the medication will be continued.

For relief of pain aspirin or acetaminophen can be given. Occasionally the child will require codeine. Suggest to the parents that they place the child with the head turned to the affected side and a heating pad on a low setting underneath the ear. When using heating pads with small children, constant supervison is necessary to prevent burns. If pain persists or increases, if the temperature rises, or if the child becomes lethargic and appears to have a stiff neck, the physician should be notified. Tell the parents the importance of returning to the physician for evaluation after the infection has subsided.

Serous otitis media

Pathophysiology Serous otitis media is the most common cause of school-age hearing loss and is usually the result of eustachian tube dysfunction or adenoidal hypertrophy. Allergy may also be involved. Chronic middle ear disease early in childhood may significantly delay the child developmentally, especially in the area of word and sentence usage.[33]

The most common symptoms of serous otitis media are a fluctuating hearing loss reported by the teacher or parents, mild intermittent pain, and a feeling of fullness in the ear. Blockage of the eustachian tube results in a negative middle ear pressure, which leads to increased mucoid secretion and increased permeability of the middle ear capillaries. On ear examination, the tympanic membrane will appear retracted, making the landmarks more visible, and dull or blue; a fluid level or air bubbles may be seen behind the drum. A tympanogram is a graph which represents the mobility of the tympanic membrane by measuring the air pressure on either side of the tympanic membrane; in serous otitis media, the tympanic membrane is immobile.

Treatment Medical treatment usually consists of antibiotics, antihistamines, and decongestants. The child is taught exercises such as blowing balloons to reopen the eustachian tube. If treatment is not successful within 4 weeks, a small Teflon tube which resembles a small dumbbell may be inserted into the tympanic membrane. The tube acts as a substitute eustachian

tube by providing aeration into the middle ear. The tube works itself out into the external ear canal within 6 months. It may need to be reinserted if the condition has not resolved by then. An adenoidectomy may be performed at the time the tube is inserted. A complication of tube insertion could be a permanent perforation of the tympanic membrane.

Nursing management Insertion of ventilating tubes into the tympanic membrane may be performed in the emergency outpatient department. The child is discharged several hours after the procedure when he is taking oral fluids and has voided. The child may be admitted to the pediatric unit if living some distance from the hospital or if an adenoidectomy is to be performed.

Ask the parents when the child is admitted if the child has decreased hearing, and if so, note it on the Kardex. Postoperatively, the child returns to the unit awake and alert. Slight serous or mucoid drainage may be noted in the operative ear; the discharge can be wiped away, but cotton balls should not be inserted into the ear.

The nurse's role in preparing the child and parents for discharge includes demonstrating the procedure for instilling ear drops and teaching the special precautions necessary as long as the tube is in place. Steroid ear drops may be prescribed to reduce inflammation. The medication should be discontinued if the child complains of pain. The parents will note hearing improvement when the drainage from the ear subsides.

Since the ventilating tube provides an open pathway into the middle ear, no water should be allowed in the ear. For bathing or shampooing, cotton balls coated with petroleum jelly can be inserted into the ears. Showering should be avoided until the tube is out. Swimming may be permitted if the child has well-fitting ear plugs. Diving is contraindicated; without an intact tympanic membrane, the change in pressure when diving may rupture the oval or round window, leading to permanent deafness. A new type of ventilating tube which is semipermeable and does not allow water into the middle ear is now being used in some hospitals.[34]

Parents should contact the doctor if hearing again decreases or if drainage increases. The child will be rechecked about 2 weeks after tube insertion and every 3 or 4 months until the tube is out. Frequent ear examinations after that will be continued to monitor reoccurrences.

Mastoiditis

Pathophysiology and treatment *Mastoiditis* occurs when the bony partitions between the mastoid air cells are destroyed and the area fills with purulent material. This complication is rare with the use of antibiotics. Symptoms include a dull ache behind the affected ear, low grade fever, increased irritability, and the appearance of a red, edematous area behind the ear. A mastoidectomy may need to be performed. The incision is usually made behind the pinna and is covered with padding and a head bandage. Drains may be inserted to prevent hematoma formation. The child may be dizzy and nauseated if the balance apparatus has been disturbed during surgery.

Nursing management postoperatively Increasing pain, swelling, and large amounts of serosanguineous drainage from the incision should be noted. Drooling from the mouth or drooping of the corner of the mouth on the operative side may indicate injury to the facial nerve. Begin oral fluids cautiously to prevent vomiting. Position the child on the unoperated side. Change the position of the child and ambulate slowly to decrease dizziness. The child will probably receive antibiotics which will be continued at home. Drains and packing may be removed the third or fourth postoperative day. When discharging the child, send home enough dressings so that the parents can keep the surgical area clean and dry and show the parents how to change the dressing as needed. No shampoos or showers should be taken until the surgical site is completely healed.

Otitis externa

Otitis externa is an inflammation of the external ear canal, often referred to as *swimmer's ear* because it is frequently due to contaminated water entering the ear. *Pseudomonas* is usually the causative organsm. The child complains of pain due to the edema of the skin in the external ear canal. When the tragus of the ear is moved, the child will feel pain. The child should be seen by a physician to differentiate between otitis externa and otitis media. Treatment usually consists of local heat and aspirin for pain relief plus antibiotic ear drops containing a combination of polymyxin B, neomycin, and bacitracin. Water should be kept out of the ears until the infection has subsided; swimming is usually contraindicated. This condition can become chronic although the chronic form is generally not seen in children.

Ear trauma

Trauma to the ear can result from foreign bodies, penetration of the ear canal or tympanic membrane with a sharp object, a blow to the head, or loud noise.

A foreign object may be an insect which as flown into the ear or small objects such as peas, beads, match sticks, or chewing gum. Small children frequently poke objects into their own or their friends' ears. The child may complain of pain and decreased hearing may be noted. The attempt to remove the object may result in more damage than the original object because the object may be pushed up against or through the tympanic membrane, dislocating the ossicles and pushing the stapes into the oval window. It is best to bring the child to the physician's office for removal of the object. Unless the object is a vegetable such as a pea or bean which will swell or the typanic membrane appears to be perforated, the object may be removed by irrigation. An insect will be killed first by instilling a few drops of alcohol. Suction or forceps may also be used to remove the objects. A small child may need a general anesthetic to prevent movement during removal.

Lacerations to the external auditory canal or the tympanic membrane are frequently the result of too vigorous ear cleaning. These lacerations usually heal spontaneously.

A blow to the head from a fall or a slap can rupture the tympanic membrane, round or oval window, or dislodge the cochlea, resulting in pain, partial deafness, and middle ear infection. Sudden loud noises can also damage the ear, as can the persistent use of amplified music. Children who have had an ear injury should have their hearing checked several weeks after the incident. Slapping the child across the side of the head is not an acceptable form of discipline. Parents may need counseling to learn more effective discipline techniques and to ventilate guilt feelings if slapping has resulted in hearing loss.

The deaf-blind child

Characteristics

Congenital rubella is the most common cause for a child to be both deaf and blind. Coexistence of other medical problems such as hydrocephaly, microcephaly, and cerebral palsy is common. It is difficult to determine whether these children are developmentally delayed because of injury to the brain or because the knowledge necessary for testing and stimulating development is lacking.

Everything a sighted, hearing child learns visually and through sound must be taught. Intersensory stimulation cannot be coordinated by the child; it is difficult for the child to learn what is external to himself. Characteristics of the deaf-blind child include hyperactivity, inability to distinguish between night and day, and addiction to light stimulation expressed by light gazing or moving fingers in front of the eyes. The child is more apt to resist any type of physical contact and has to learn to enjoy being held and touched.[35]

Effect on the family

Parents may react to their child by trying to meet every want or by ignoring the child and refusing to develop any type of communication system. It is difficult for the family to achieve a balanced integration of the child into their lives and there are as yet few professionals available to help them.[36] Even with professional assistance, rearing the child to take advantage of opportunities rather than withdrawing may require an investment few families can undertake without significant changes in their life-style and damage to their own physical and mental health.

Nursing management

Parents need professional intervention as soon as their child is identified as deaf-blind. Initiate a referral through the social services department and community health agencies as soon as possible. Provide opportunities for the parents to express their concerns.

When a deaf-blind child is hospitalized, it is usually because of an associated medical problem. Obtain a careful history from the parents or caretakers. The institutional caretakers will not be able to stay with the child, and although the parents may be requested to stay, they may legitimately need a break from the constant pressure of caring for the child. Determine what, if any, communication system the child is learning; use of finger spelling is common. For safety, a small child may need to be in a crib with a safety top. Take the child out of the crib frequently for holding, touching, or walking around the unit to prevent regression and withdrawal. Ask what kinds of play activities the child enjoys and continue them. Also, determine what skills the child has learned, such as feeding or dressing. If possible the same nurse should be assigned to provide for consistency; the nurse will be frustrated as well as challenged, however, and will need some relief. Assess the parents' acceptance of their child and assistance they are receiving, and if appropriate suggest other sources of help. Provide the parents the opportunities to verbalize frustrations and discouragement.

As a member of the community the nurse can encourage all parents to have children immunized for rubella and women considering pregnancy to have rubella titres checked. In some states rubella screening is part of the premarital blood work required to obtain a marriage license.

Nursing Care Plan–Hearing-Impaired Child

Assessment

Sara, age 8, was admitted to the hospital because of severe abdominal pain. After observation and laboratory study, the cause was diagnosed as acute appendicitis. Soon afterward the surgeon removed an inflamed appendix. Sara's mother was with her in the operating room until Sara was asleep. The girl's hearing aids were left in place until then and were replaced in the recovery room.

Sara wears binaural body-type hearing aids and has had moderate hearing loss since age 4, when she had meningitis. Hearing loss is in the range of 40 to 60 dB, where she misses most conversational speech. As her impairment occurred after development of language, her grasp of abstract terms is greater than would be true if the loss had preceded speech.

Sara is in the second grade, does well in school, but is about 1 year behind in academic skills. She receives special help from a resource teacher every school day. Sara is being trained to read lips and is in speech therapy. Her speech is understandable.

Sara's mother stays with her during hospital visiting hours. Her father visits when he can, and her grandmother manages the household, which includes a sister of 10 and a brother of 4. Sara's hospital roommate is a girl of 10 who is in traction because of a fractured femur.

Sara's birth history and development were normal. She has been well except for meningitis at 4, chickenpox at 6, and she contracts a few upper respiratory infections each year. This is her first hospital admission since the age of 4. Immunizations are up to date. Both her mother (age 34) and father (age 38) are well, as are her siblings. Her maternal grandmother has mature-onset diabetes, and her paternal grandfather died of lung cancer at 65.

Sara weighs 55 lb (25 kg) and is 50 in (127 cm) tall, both of which place her in the 50th percentile by age.

The patient's father manages a local men's clothing store. Her mother is not employed outside her home. Both parents hold college degrees. Sara shares a bedroom with her sister. Sara's family has accepted her hearing impairment. She has several playmates in the neighborhood and is a Brownie Scout. The family is active in their church.

Nursing diagnosis	Nursing goals	Nursing actions*	Evaluation/revision
1. Inability to hear normal conversation due to hearing loss	□ Sara will be able to communicate with hospital personnel	□ Tape over intercom button at nurses' station □ Note degree of hearing impairment on Kardex □ Teach Sara that nurse will come when call button is pushed by having a nurse standing outside the room and coming into the room immediately when the call light goes on; repeat until Sara understands □ Avoid approaching Sara from behind □ Touch Sara before talking to gain her attention □ Be certain light is on nurse's face; stand in front of Sara within 3 to 4 ft with face turned toward Sara; if female nurse, use dark or contrasting lipstick	□ Mother is staying with Sara and caring for hearing aids with Sara's assistance. Sara is able to cooperate with procedures.

Nursing diagnosis	Nursing goals	Nursing actions	Evaluation/revision
		☐ Use mother as communication source, but avoid directing all conversation to mother ☐ Print simple statements or words if necessary ☐ Make certain hearing aids are functioning, batteries are working, and ear molds are clean and intact. Ask mother how hearing aids are cared for at home	
2. Sara has potential feeling of insecurity and isolation due to hearing impairment and newness of environment	☐ Sara will feel secure in hospital environment as evidenced by: **a.** Calling for nurse when needed **b.** Initiating conversation with nursing personnel **c.** Asking questions about surroundings **d.** Maintaining interests she enjoyed at home **e.** Talking and playing with roommate	☐ Place in room close to nurse's station ☐ Encourage parents to stay with Sara; provide cot; also provide break time for parents ☐ Ask parents, if necessary, to interpret Sara's needs ☐ Assign same nurse to care for Sara each day; 2 days prior to assigned nurse's day off, introduce person who will be caring for Sara ☐ Follow the same time schedule each day as much as possible so Sara will know when routines occur and when a nurse will be with her. Give Sara a brief written plan for each day	☐ Sara uses call button to request nursing assistance. Sara smiles when the nurse is present, asks questions of nurse about hospital routines, and talks with nurse about home and school. She is observed carrying on animated conversations with parents and roommate
3. Decreased ability to understand environmental activities due to hearing impairment.	☐ Sara will understand what is happening to her as evidenced by: **a.** Being able to repeat accurately what she has been told **b.** Assisting nursing personnel when caring for her	☐ When entering room, explain what nurse will be doing; remember Sara is very aware of facial expression and body movement ☐ Explain to Sara what is happening when caring for roommate ☐ Make requests such as "Sit on this chair" rather than "Sit over there" ☐ Use pictures, actual equipment, and concrete words to explain routines and procedures. Avoid abstract terms such as *pain* ☐ When necessary to perform treatments or procedures behind Sara, have another person stand in front of Sara to explain what is happening	☐ Sara is able to explain procedures back to nurse and cooperates with nurse when care is being provided

Nursing diagnosis	Nursing goals	Nursing actions	Evaluation/revision
4. Sara has the potential to regress in developmental level due to stress of hospitalization	□ Sara will maintain her developmental level	□ Place in room with child Sara's age, introduce Sara to roommate, tell roommate Sara is unable to hear well □ Add to Kardex that room assignment should not be changed □ Call attention to surroundings and explain equipment in the room □ When Sara is ambulatory, show her around the unit and allow to explore under supervision; if possible, allow her to leave unit accompanied by mother or nurse □ Take Sara to the playroom, introduce her to the children playing there, staying with her until she seems secure and returning as necessary; suggest mother accompany her to the playroom at first □ Supply equipment for diversional activities, such as paper and crayons, clay, and books at second-grade level □ Arrange to play cards or table games with her or set up with roommate who is in traction □ Practice academic skills, such as printing or adding numbers	□ Sara appeared shy at interacting with roommate at first, but now enjoys card games with her. Roommate asks Sara about her hearing impairment, explains new occurrences, and enjoys her company. Sara has been reluctant to go to the playroom □ Revise plan by arranging specific times to take Sara to the playroom and arranging for other children Sara's age to be in the playroom at that time
5. Sara has potential postoperative complications due to anesthesia and abdominal surgery	□ Sara's physiological functions will return to preillness or prehospitalization state	□ See Chap. 28 for specific actions related to caring for child who has had abdominal surgery □ Demonstrate deep breathing and coughing in presence of mother □ Determine if she is in pain by pointing to incisional area and watching facial expressions rather than by asking about pain	□ Sara is taking a soft diet well. There is no abdominal distention. Sara had a bowel movement on the third postoperative day. The incision is healing, lungs are clear, and Sara is ambulating well. She dislikes injections; oral medication controls incisional discomfort.

* The author acknowledges the assistance of Keith Ellen Ragsdale in formulating the nursing actions.

References

1. Arthur H. Keeney, *Ocular Examination: Basis and Technique*, Mosby, St. Louis, 1976, p. 32.
2. Shiv K. Dube and Sophie H. Pierog, *Immediate Care of the Sick and Injured Child*, Mosby, St. Louis, 1978, p. 102.
3. Jules Baum, "The Eye," in Sidney S. Gellis and Benjamin M. Kagan (eds.), *Current Pediatric Therapy*, Saunders, Philadelphia, 1978, p. 510.
4. Everett A. Moody, "Amblyopia," in Robinson D. Harley (ed.), *Pediatric Ophthalmology*, Saunders, Philadelphia, 1975, p. 187.
5. R. Robb McDonald, "Disorders of the Lens," in ibid., p. 378.
6. Robinson D. Harley and Donelson R. Manely, "Glaucoma in Infants and Children," in ibid., p. 391.
7. Allan E. Kolker and John Hetherington, *Becker-Schaffer's Diagnosis and Therapy of the Glaucomas*, Mosby, St. Louis, 1976, p. 291.
8. Baum, op cit., p. 520.
9. Lee Shahinian and Natalie Malachowski, "Retrolental Fibroplasia: A New Analysis of Risk Factors Based on Recent Cases," *Archives of Ophthalmology* 96:70–74 (January 1978).
10. L. Stanley James and Jonathon T. Lanman, "History of Oxygen Therapy and Retrolental Fibroplasia," *Pediatrics* 57:591–642 (April 1976).
11. Frank W. Newell, *Ophthalmology*, 4th ed., Mosby, St. Louis, 1978, p. 329.
12. Stephen Weinstock and John Flynn, "Brief Hospital Admissions for Pediatric Strabismus Surgery," *American Journal of Ophthalmology* 80:525–529 (September 1975).
13. David Stager, "Amblyopia and the Pediatrician," *Pediatric Annals* 6:46–75 (February 1977).
14. Ben Esterman, *The Eye Book*, Great Ocean Publishers, Arlington, Va., 1977, p. 83.
15. Gunter K,. Noorden, "Chronic Vision Problems of School Age Children," *Journal of School Health* 66:334–337 (June 1976).
16. Oliver Dabezies, Joseph Dixon, and G. Peter Halberg, "When a Patient Asks about Contact Lenses," *Patient Care* 12:98–118 (March 15, 1978).
17. Walter Zinn and Herbert Solomon, *The Complete Guide to Eye Care, Eye Glasses and Contact Lenses*, Frederick Fell, New York, 1977, p. 102.
18. Dabezies et al., op. cit., p. 117.
19. Zinn and Solomon, op. cit., p. 108.
20. J. D. Trehane, "Trachoma," *Nursing Times* 72:523–525 (April 8, 1976).
21. Susan Shiery, "Insight into the Delicate Art of Eye Care," *Nursing 75* 5:50–53 (June 1975).
22. Colleen Caufield, "A Developmental Approach to Hearing Screening in Children," *Pediatric Nursing* 4:39–42 (March-April 1978).
23. George Mencher, "Screening the Newborn Infant for Hearing Loss: A Complete Identification Program," in Fred Bess (ed.), *Childhood Deafness*, Grune and Stratton, New York, 1977, p. 113.
24. Caufield, op. cit.
25. Derald E. Brachman and Weldon A. Selters, "Electric Response Audiometry: Clinical Applications," *Otolaryngologic Clinics of North America* 11:10–28 (February 1978).
26. Ralph Naunton and Stanley Zerlin, "The Evaluation of Peripheral Auditory Function in Infants and Children," *Otolaryngologic Clinics of North America* 10:51–58 (February 1977).
27. William K. Frankenburg, A. J. North, and A. Frederik, *Guide to Screening for the Early and Periodic Screening Diagnosis and Treatment Program*, American Academy of Pediatrics, Washington, D.C., 1974, p. 124.
28. George Larsen, "Removing Cerumen with a Water Pik," *American Journal of Nursing* 76:264–265 (February 1976).
29. F. J. Schulte and E. Stennert, "Hearing Defects in Preterm Infants," *Archives of Disease in Childhood* 53:269–70 (April 1978).
30. Sanford Gerber and David Mitchell, "Speech and Hearing Defects in Children," *Otolaryngologic Clinics of North America* 10:248–252 (February 1977).
31. Kathryn B. Horton, "Early Intervention Through Parent Training," *Otolaryngologic Clinics of North America* 8:143–157 (February 1975).
32. William M. Bruch, Otitis Media, *Pediatric Nursing* 5:9–12 (January-February 1979).
33. Peter Zinkus, Marvin Gottlieb, and Mark Shapiro, "Developmental and Psychoeducational Sequelae of Chronic Otitis Media," *American Journal of Diseases of Children* 132:1100–1104 (November 1978).
34. James Donaldson, "Surgical Management of Eustachian Tube Dysfunction and Its Importance in Middle Ear Effusion," *Pediatrics* 61:774–77 (May 1978).
35. Judith Bumbalo and Mary A. Seidel, "Identifying and Serving a Multiply Handicapped Population: Deaf-Blind Children and Their Families," *Nursing Clinics of North America* 10:341–352 (June 1975).
36. Corrine Klein, "Coping Patterns of Parents of Deaf-Blind Children," *American Annals of the Deaf* 122:310–312 (June 1977).

Chapter 40 **Behavioral problems**

Nada Light

Upon completion of this chapter, the student will be able to:

1. Compare children's and adults' responses to interviewing.
2. Compare typical behavior of healthy and disturbed children.
3. Describe the etiology and typical behavior associated with a reactive disorder.
4. Compare the child's behavioral symptoms of reactive depression with those of the adult.
5. Describe nursing management of a depressed child.
6. Summarize each of the four probable causes of pervasive childhood psychoses.
7. Compare the characteristic behavior, treatment, and nursing care of infantile autism and atypical childhood psychosis.
8. Contrast the etiology, symptoms, and nursing care of stuttering with those of elective mutism.
9. Describe the symptoms, treatment, and nursing care of encopresis and enuresis.
10. Describe the etiology and nursing management of childhood conduct disorders.
11. Compare the etiology, behavior, and nursing management of two anxiety disorders: separation anxiety (school refusal) and overanxious disorder.

Children with behavioral problems can appear in any pediatric nursing setting. The more severe disturbances are a mixture of neurological, perceptual, and behavioral problems. Symptoms are often observable from the beginning of a child's development. A definite organic (physiological) abnormality frequently underlies a severe disturbance. Other behavioral symptoms emerge from difficult parent-child relationships. Poverty, a poor marriage, and job loss can precipitate dysfunctional (maladaptive) patterns of child rearing. For example, the parent may demand behavior that is beyond the child's developmental level. The pediatric nurse must assess these behavioral problems and recommend specialized treatment for the child and family.

Psychological development is shaped by an individual's unique environment and by genetic endowment. Biological timetables determine the rate of certain behavioral capacities; maturation cannot be rushed. For example, an infant's capacity to remember images in the mind appears to begin near the end of the first year. Memory is an important tool in the child's psychological separation from parents and the process of individual development. (See Chap. 13 for further discussion.) Environmental forces, particularly parental and other socialization experiences, shape a child's personality through the processes of internalization and identification.

A child *internalizes* (learns and later uses) the behavior of other people. For example, the ways a father expresses tenderness or handles angry feelings are internalized by a child as "emotional methods" to be used in relating to others. *Identification* is a complicated process of internalizing social, physical, and sexual roles enacted mainly by parents. (See Chap. 13 for a discussion of identification.) Absence of a role model (parent) through death or divorce can compromise the identification process. Behavioral symptoms may develop, depending on the child's vulnerability at the time the parent is lost. Age is one critical factor. The loss of a father during a child's preschool years will have some impact on identification and the solidifying of self and role. The impact on a school-age child will vary with how effectively the remaining parent, extended family, and other adults contribute the adult companionship needed in many of the school-age child's activities.

Psychological assessment

Assessment of a child's developmental history and current functioning is essential when determining deviations from psychological health. There are three primary sources of information: (1) the developmental history (see Chap. 6 for guidelines); (2) interviews with the child, family, and significant others such as teachers, extended family members, police, or neighbors; and (3) diagnostic testing with psychometric and projective tests.

The child's reactions to interviewing are different from the adult's. The child is handicapped by:

1. Being less able to verbalize psychological distress. Younger children have more difficulty verbalizing internal conflicts.
2. Being less able to seek help independently.
3. Being cognitively immature and therefore lacking a fully developed ability to abstract and to think symbolically.
4. Being egocentric.

The preceding differences influence the interview process. If an interviewer questions a school-age child about school failure with "Why are you failing in your school work?" the child will find "why," a symbolic question, too difficult to answer. The nurse instead asks concrete questions such as "What is your favorite subject?" or "What happens at school to make you unhappy?" or uses the techniques discussed in

Table 40-1 Behaviors expressing psychological pain

1. Runs away
2. Destroys family, school, community property
3. Seeks the wrong kind of friend or group, enabling further acting out
4. Withdraws into a private fantasy world
5. Suicide
6. Homicide
7. Isolated incidents of bizarre behavior
8. Vague somatic symptoms: stomachaches, frequent upper respiratory illnesses, fatigue, or frequent visits to the school nurse

Chap. 16. There are numerous reasons for school failure. The length of the following list emphasizes the thoroughness required of the nurse. Incomplete assessment may lead to an incorrect nursing diagnosis. Causes might include (1) conflicts within the child; (2) family problems to which a child is reacting; (3) physical problems such as poor eyesight, hearing deficit, poor fine-motor coordination, or interference with writing; (4) learning disabilities; or (5) chronic illness. It is also true that children and adults express psychological pain differently (Table 40-1).

After the patterns and possible causes of the child's behavior are assessed, encourage parents to begin health screening. Always include a thorough physical examination, and begin exploring with the family and child possible internal psychological problems.

Usually, by the time a child's psychological problem attracts professional attention, a level of chaos has been reached that disturbs those in the child's immediate environment. Schools initiate the majority of psychological referrals. Disturbed children are often not identified before they start school for the following reasons:

1. Families tolerate unusual or peculiar habits in their children that are intolerable in a classroom.
2. A school experience may be the child's first contact with adults skilled in observing children.
3. Inability to pay attention or concentrate may not be noticed until the child goes to school, where these behaviors are required.

Some of the more frequent problems that emerge when a disturbed child enters school are listed in Table 40-2.

Helping a family recognize their child's psy-

Table 40-2 Problems identified at school

Problems with activity

Inability to concentrate
Inability to sit still in a chair or through an entire activity
Inability to follow directions
Impulsiveness: grabs others' materials, pushes, bites

Problems with personal habits

Strange tics, e.g., muscle twitches; head tilts or turning; strange shoulder, hand, or other body movements
Pulls hair out
Excessive nail biting, thumb or finger sucking
Incomplete toilet training
    Daytime urine accidents
    Fecal soiling

Problems with interpersonal relationships

No friends: excessive shyness or behaviors causing others to avoid contact with the child
Attention-seeking behaviors: calling out and other disruptive actions
Provocative fighting
Seeks only teachers as friends

chological difficulty requires a delicate balance between telling and facilitating. Child advocacy groups have tried to protect the rights of children. Even today, children basically remain possessions of their parents. Families rarely welcome outside authorities who investigate child abuse, neglect, or bizarre behavior. Parents may be unaware of or afraid to recognize their child's psychological difficulties. (See Chap. 21 for parental reactions to chronic illness.)

Reassuring and supporting parents will maximize cooperation and trust from the child. School-age children may be *fiercely loyal* to even the most chaotic families and disturbed parents. Once children feel their parents trust the nurse, most of them are willing to begin relating to the new adult. The pediatric nurse who can identify problems and begin a trusting parent-family-nurse relationship is in an optimal position to refer the family and child to more skilled psychological resources. The nurse can function as a *liaison* and ally for a family until treatment begins.

Healthy behavior

Psychological health is a dynamic state of adaptation; the child responds to crises and to both unexpected and expected events. By the time a

child enters the school years, a number of developmental steps have been taken to some degree: separation from parents, the autonomy struggle during toileting, and the preschooler's attainment of initiative and sexual identity. Situational crises have occurred and been mastered, in a healthy way, as in the following examples.

EXAMPLE: Five-year-old Kathy was excited about beginning kindergarten and had attended an orientation session. She had talked about her new school all summer to everyone. On the first day, Kathy refused to get dressed and wanted to stay home and play. Her mother was bewildered but patient as she helped the child get ready to go. At school, Kathy cried and clung to her mother. The teacher helped both to separate by holding and comforting Kathy. Later that morning, Kathy complained of a "tummyache" and said that she "needed her mommy." The school nurse was consulted and talked with Kathy about how hard it was to begin school.

With support, Kathy's anxiety disappeared in a few days and her original eagerness to attend school returned.

EXAMPLE: Eleven-year-old Bobby had been taking swimming lessons for several years. Suddenly, he announced that he hated swimming and refused lessons. When questioned about the class, teacher, and swimming mates, Bobby was very vague. He withdrew to his room and locked the door.

Bobby's father called the swimming teacher, but no clues emerged from their conversation. However, the teacher had noticed that Bobby was beginning to develop pubic hair and enlarged genitals. Bobby's father wondered if the other boys were also beginning to develop secondary sex characteristics, but the teacher said no.

Bobby's father approached his son cautiously but supportively. Father and son talked about body changes in boys and the coming event of seminal ejaculation. Bobby was relieved. He remained shy about undressing but rejoined his swimming group.

Disturbed behavior

Each culture identifies particular behavior that it deems unhealthy. Problem behaviors generally have two characteristics: (1) they *interfere* with the child's development and (2) they *continue* for a period of time. Any troublesome behavior continuing for 6 months should be investigated.

EXAMPLE: Johnny, age 11, has always been a quiet, studious boy but has failed to make any close friends for several years. He has remained withdrawn and isolated from group projects at school, rarely participates in games, and has no regular neighborhood playmates.

This child is reaching adolescence without the interpersonal skills needed to negotiate the final separation between parents and child. Peers and the accompanying activities provide this forum.

Table 40-3 Classification of symptoms caused by stress

Problems with bodily functions

Anorexia or overeating, bizarre dietary practices
Sleep disturbances: insomnia, night terrors, excessive sleeping
Elimination difficulties: enuresis, encopresis
Changes in speech: mutism, stuttering, unclear speech

Problems with motor and perceptual coordination

Very active, lethargic, or poorly coordinated

Problems with cognitive functions

Failure to learn
Difficulty with thinking and memory

Problems with emotional functions

Fears that interfere with daily life
Severe separation anxiety: cannot be separated from mother
Very anxious all the time: excessive worrying, anticipates the worst outcome in all new situations
Numerous physical complaints without clear physiological reasons: stomachaches, headaches, dizziness, colds, fatigue

Problems with social relationships

Unusual aggressiveness: rarely responds to limit setting; seems unable to control aggressive impulses
Antisocial behaviors: disregards other people and their property, shows little remorse or concern when reprimanded
Oppositional behaviors: always takes the opposite position even if this hurts the child
Isolates self from others
Depressed behaviors: initial aggressiveness or antisocial behavior; either high activity level different from usual pattern or more classical depressive symptoms of sadness, withdrawal, lethargy, anorexia, hopelessness, or discouragement; excessive clumsiness and poor motor coordination, which may be coupled wtih poor judgment; school work becomes difficult: concentration is poor, thinking is slowed and indecisive; comments about wanting to die, disappear, go away forever, or symbolic stories, e.g., "the sun that went to sleep in the clouds and never came up"; multiple "accidental" injuries: falling out of windows or off roofs, pill ingestion, and knife injuries

Table 40-4 Psychiatric problems in school-age children

I. Reactive disorders
  A. Reactive depression
II. Developmental deviations
  A. Pervasive developmental deviations
    1. Infantile autism
    2. Atypical childhood psychosis (formerly called *childhood schizophrenia*)
  B. Specific developmental deviations
    1. Specific language disorders: stuttering, elective mutism
    2. Problems with elimination: enuresis, encopresis
III. Conduct disorders
IV. Anxiety disorders

His school teacher, parents, school nurse, or pediatrician needs to investigate the reasons behind Johnny's withdrawal, which will interfere with his development.

The disturbed behavior of most school-age children can be categorized into the five groups listed in Table 40-3. Each of these groups must be considered in terms of *frequency of occurrence, severity, duration,* and *impact on the child's growth and development.*

The pediatric nurse needs a working knowledge of major psychiatric problems of this age group, listed in Table 40-4 and discussed below. Table 40-4 is based on the newest classification system developed by the American Psychiatric Association. Their broad developmental approach stresses observable signs and symptoms.

Reactive disorders

Reactive disorders are behavioral reactions to *specific,* emotionally traumatic events. Reactions can be *adaptive,* such as regression or withdrawal. The developmental milestones most recently mastered are temporarily lost as the child regresses; for example, bed-wetting and excessive fearfulness are common responses to traumatic events. Adults around a child often become alarmed at these reactions, but a healthy child usually uses these defense mechanisms temporarily. Reactive disorders occur most commonly in late preschool and early school-age children, who lack the capacity to express internal distress verbally.

Older children have a better command of language and, with support and encouragement by adults, can verbally express their reactions to a traumatic event. But some children may be overwhelmed by the event or too frightened to put their feelings into words. They may be surrounded by adults who are struggling to cope with the same trauma. Intervention by a psychotherapist is then necessary.

School-age children encounter a wide variety of social situations. Experiences can occur in which a child has no opportunity to express feelings. Secrecy is characteristic of school-age children. Frightening experiences may not be shared with parents.

Most reactive responses are precipitated by a traumatic separation from parents or a direct threat to the child's integrity of self, such as an accident, school pressure, or ridicule from peers. For example, in gym class during baseball season, a student broke his leg. A teammate later that week developed overwhelming malaise and mild fever, and had to stay home. A physical examination revealed nothing specific, and cultures were negative. The student dropped out of the school gym program for the rest of the year with the doctor's permission. This boy was unable to verbalize the overwhelming feelings he had about his classmate's accident. An astute school nurse connected the two events and arranged for the school psychologist to visit the family. Several family meetings and brief therapy with the student remedied the problem.

Nursing management

The nurse can use two guidelines in identifying behavioral problems: (1) Are these new problems interfering with development? (2) Have the problem behaviors continued for 6 months? If these two criteria are met, further assessment and intervention are needed. When assessing a child, the nurse should keep in mind the fact that a mild, unexpected incident may have a *profound*

Table 40-5 Masked symptoms of depression

I. Excessively aggressive behavior, unusual agitation and/or activity
II. Antisocial behavior, e.g., setting fires, injuring others or animals, destroying property
III. Radical changes in daily behavior patterns
    A. An outgoing child chooses "loner" activities
    B. A sports enthusiast becomes absorbed in television or repetitious empty projects
    C. School work slides and grades fall

effect on the child. The child may misinterpret what happened or blame himself for the event. The nurse can help a family trace through recent events that may have precipitated the child's current emotional distress. If the stress is not prolonged and emotional support is available, most children recover and develop new coping behaviors.

Reactive depression

Depression is a response to loss. The child must resolve the loss with the help of those close to him or her. The depression may deepen if the child's feelings are not relieved. A child needs opportunities to talk and to ask the same questions repeatedly. This may be painful to other family members who are also in mourning. Supportive counseling may best help the family to tolerate the child's continuous questions.

The school-age child has the capacity to become deeply despondent. A child can have feelings of extreme hopelessness and helplessness, and can even desire suicide. The younger suicidal school-age child may have an unclear understanding of the finality of death, but this does not influence the depth of the depression or the impulsive desire to end the hurt. While childhood depression is seen in this younger group, it occurs more commonly in the prepubertal years, ages 9 to 12, and is still more common in adolescence.

Depressive symptoms are initially masked by excessive aggressiveness and other antisocial behavior.[1] Underneath this aggressiveness, which is a defense, the child feels sad, discouraged, and hopeless. (See Table 40-5 for symptoms.) School work becomes difficult: Concentration is poor, thinking is slowed and indecisive, and excessive clumsiness may occur. Many childhood accidents and accidental deaths are masked suicide attempts. Adults have difficulty accepting the idea that a child's feelings of worthlessness could lead to suicide. When children are very angry, healthy ones feel free to express their wishes to banish or hurt their parents. A suicidal child turns these feelings inside toward the self rather than toward others or the outside world.

The injuries noted at the end of Table 40-3 should alert a pediatric staff to rule out attempted suicide. The pediatric nurse can assess possible indicators of suicide: In general, how cooperative is the child during physical care? Extreme passivity may indicate feelings of depression or hopelessness. Extremely agitated behavior, seen in wanting to escape, may reflect the desperation and impulsiveness of a child trying to find emotional relief through suicide.

Nurses can identify depression in hospitalized children (see Chap. 16). A mild depressive reaction usually occurs when the child is adjusting to the hospital. However, some children do not resolve these feelings and continue to be depressed after returning home. These children may show the following symptoms: anorexia, listlessness, loss of interest in surroundings (toys, children, adults), slowed speech or mutism, staring with blank despondency, failure to be comforted by physical tenderness, and overwhelming sadness expressed verbally or in drawings.

A severely depressed child requires hospitalization for safety while being treated. Antidepressants are used judiciously and require careful monitoring in a growing child. The environment must be kept safe: Medications and sharp objects must be removed from the room; bathroom doors should not lock and must be operable from the outside; and the child's room should be located near the nurse's station, away from elevators and exits.

Developmental deviations

Deviations from normal behavioral development can be divided into two major areas: pervasive and specific developmental deviations. These groups differ in two ways.

In *specific developmental deviations*, developmental milestones are delayed in timing and rate. The child's behavior and development are normal except for those specific delays. For example, John, 7 years old, is in the second grade, doing well, and is an active, coordinated child. However, he wets his bed several times a week. His enuresis is a specific developmental deviation. Bed-wetting is normal but only in children under 5 years of age.

In *pervasive developmental deviations*, the child's behavior is extremely abnormal and would not be normal at any age. For example, the object twirling, high-pitched shrieks, hand flapping, and rhythmic rocking of autistic children are very odd at any age. *Infantile autism*

and *atypical childhood psychoses* are the two subgroups of pervasive developmental deviations.[2] These severely disturbed children comprise a small percentage of disturbed children. There are 2 to 4 autistic children per 10,000,[3] and autism is more common in boys. Autistic children present a challenge to nurses when ill and hospitalized. Knowledge of their developmental struggle is essential in order to plan effective nursing care.

Pervasive developmental deviations

Infantile autism This condition generally occurs before 30 months of age. It is included here for comparison with atypical childhood psychoses and childhood schizophrenia. The behavior of autistic children at any age shows two characteristics: (1) isolation or withdrawal from human relationships and (2) an intense need to maintain sameness in the environment.

The autistic infant is a "good baby," lying quietly in the crib, self-absorbed, crying little, and demanding minimal nurturing. The parent may unknowingly reinforce the infant's withdrawn behavior by leaving it alone. The child then fails to attach (bond) to the parent. This lack of parent-child attachment is shown by the absence of separation anxiety, failure to mold to the parent's body when held, and failure to show anticipation of being picked up by the parent. The withdrawal from people influences other aspects of the child's development. Language and cognitive development lag. The autistic child repeatedly echoes words or phrases (echolalia), avoids eye contact, and is negativistic. To maintain sameness of the environment, the child adopts certain rituals, such as touching walls. He or she withdraws from outside stimuli into an inner world (see Fig. 40-1). Self-stimulatory behavior increases: body rocking, head banging, object twirling, staring at lights, and moving to music.

Special nursery school stimulation and habit training need to begin early. Educational training is the primary form of treatment for school-age autistic children. The family must be able to cope with sudden rage, fits of crying, strange fears, and other emotional outbursts. Autistic children lack the normal fears that promote safety, such as caution about cars and fire. Extra supervision must be provided. Family therapy may be needed to help parents and siblings cope

Figure 40-1 The autistic child is profoundly withdrawn from human relationships. (*Courtesy of Benhaven.*)

with the daily stress produced by having the child at home.

Nursing management Autistic children are usually quite healthy and require normal pediatric care. As they grow older, they are increasingly prone to seizures and require daily medication.[4] The question of placing such a child in an institution may arise. Parents may try coping with the youngster at home and with special schools but find that this does not work because the needs of the family outweigh those of one member. Locating an appropriate place for the child in the community may be impossible. It may be necessary to put the child in an institution far from home and visit infrequently. A nurse may be able to help with such decisions by serving as a sounding board and by providing referral to a social service agency for placement or home services.

Atypical childhood psychosis This condition was formerly called *childhood schizophrenia.* There is a severe impairment of emotional relationships. The child cannot make friends, clings to family members and caretakers, and lacks empathy with or regard for the feelings of others. Such tendencies are observable in infancy and the toddler years, but a diagnosis is usually confirmed between the ages of 3 and 12. The atypically psychotic child is initially less disturbed and shows fewer of the autistic child's peculiar behaviors (see Table 40-6).

Several of the following behaviors must be present before a diagnosis of atypical childhood psychosis is made:

1. *Acute, illogical anxiety* Unexplained panic attacks and hysterical reactions to everyday events (e.g., hearing a door bell ring or seeing a series of blue cars).
2. *Distorted emotional responses* Inappropriate fears, unexplained rages, extreme moodiness.
3. *Resistance to any change* The child requires special rituals and repetitive behavior to feel better: The same clothes are demanded each day, and furniture cannot be changed around or routines varied; repetitive touching of a particular object (for instance, an ashtray or the corners of a desk) reduces the child's anxiety when relating to another person.
4. *Hyper- or hypoactivity, strange body postures* (unusual arching of the back or extending of the neck), and *special hand and finger movements.*
5. *Strange vocal quality*—singsong or monotonous.
6. *Over- or undersensitivity to sensory and perceptual experiences* (touch, sound, vision).
7. *Self-mutilation* Biting or hitting oneself, head banging, or hair pulling.[5]

A disturbed child-parent relationship in the first years of the child's life appears to be a critical factor in atypical childhood psychosis, even though the condition may not appear until years later. Usually a particular traumatic event triggers the psychotic symptoms. A physical illness, separation from a parent, birth of a sibling, a family move, sexual molestation, or observation of violence may initiate the intense anxiety and result in personality fragmentation.

Parenting may have been highly ambivalent during the years before the outburst of psychotic behaviors. This ambivalence may have involved a pattern of rapidly alternating overgratification (pampering) and needless frustration coupled with a lack of nurturing and inadequate sensory stimulation. A developmental history may show that as a baby the child was fretful, sleepless, tense, and excessively demanding. The infant eventually gave up demanding that needs be met; feelings of helplessness and hopelessness increased, and gradually the infant withdrew into isolation. Parents may have misinterpreted this "good behavior" as calming down, not withdrawal.

Nursing management Early identification of these children is the most significant contribution a nurse can make. A parent may complain to a nurse about a child's peculiar and troublesome habits. For example, the child's need for rituals can be exasperating; the hysterical screaming for no reason is embarrassing in public places; strange fears may limit a family's outside activities; and unusual movements and self-mutilation can be frightening, especially when the child is out of control. The nurse may detect the parent's need to avoid the painful awareness that the child is different and even bizarre at times. The parent can be helped by critical, sensitive listening and can aid in identifying an area that can be managed through behavioral manipulation.

EXAMPLE: Three-year-old Ann arrived for a pre-nursery school physical. She was not toilet trained, ran around touching all corners of the room, and would suddenly burst into screams without tears and cling to her mother's leg. The nurse noticed that Ann's hairline on her forehead was irregular. Ann's mother described a bedtime ritual: Ann banged her head on the crib and rocked herself to sleep.

Ann needed immediate referral for a developmental and psychiatric examination. Ann's mother was reluctant to follow through because she feared her daughter would be labeled "crazy." She was also afraid of being blamed for Ann's peculiar behaviors. She had given up trying to toilet train Ann because the child was so unmanageable in other areas.

The nurse offered suggestions for behavior modification based on Ann's developmental needs. Toilet training, it was explained, proceeds much as it would for a normal child. However, each step is broken down into smaller behaviors for the child to master. The nurse pointed out that mastering toilet training would help Ann gain control over a natural function. This control would be transferred

Table 40-6 Comparison of autism and atypical childhood psychosis

	Autism	Atypical childhood psychosis
Onset	Before 30 months	After 30 months; onset follows period of normal development
Language	Gross language deficits: echoing words and sounds, speaking in metaphors, being mute, reversing pronouns, using immature grammatical structure; child demonstrates no abstract thinking	Language present but bizarre: sing-song, monotone, made-up words, rhyming (beyond the normal level of the preschool period)
Emotion	Lacks emotional responsiveness, does not mold to parents' bodies; self-involved	Emotional responses present but abnormal; rage and panic attacks; Child molds and clings to parents' bodies
Anxiety	Acute anxiety *not* present	Acute, illogical anxiety present
Genetic family history	Parents have high intelligence, emotional stability, low divorce rate; low rate of family mental illness	More average background; higher rate of mental illness in family
Orientation	Detached, self-absorbed	Disoriented and confused
Motor coordination	Refined gross and fine motor coordination; graceful	Poor balance and coordination

to other behavioral areas that eventually would be mastered.

Ann's mother found these suggestions helpful and began voicing some of her feelings about Ann's development.

If the nurse can establish a trusting relationship, it may support the family while they begin the painful experience of learning the limitations and strengths of their child.

Childhood schizophrenia *Childhood schizophrenia* is not a single disease entity but a label indicating a dramatic deviation from normal ego functioning. This classification is reserved for children exhibiting a majority of classically schizophrenic behaviors. These children lack the normal guides necessary for self-regulation, for achieving an identity, and for differentiating inner (their own) from outer (others') experiences. The onset of a schizophrenic episode can be gradual, depending on the family's awareness of their child's disturbed behavior. Current classification systems incorporate the younger disturbed child under the classification of atypical psychosis. Psychotic episodes may resemble more schizophrenic behaviors, especially in the preadolescent child with no previous psychotic episodes.

Childhood schizophrenia differs from adult schizophrenia in the following ways: Hallucinations are rare in childhood; bizarre motor behaviors—whirling, hand flapping, and sudden bursts of aggressive and self-mutilating behavior—are seen more frequently in children; and regression is less in children. The different subcategories of adult schizophrenia do not apply to children; this is because the child's personality trends are not well developed.

Nursing management Nurses need not deal with a classification enigma. The label is *not* the significant factor. Treatment approaches include a full range of therapies. The child will need special education. Depending on the child's level of functioning, this may be either a mainstream experience in a regular school or residential treatment. The trend today is toward intensive education and psychotherapy, and then the return of the child to the community if possible. Individual psychotherapy focuses on the child's anxiety and inner experiences. The educational setting provides the forum for learning how to handle bizarre feelings and thoughts when the child is with others. Behavioral modification is useful in controlling self-mutilating behaviors and eliminating the often strange body movements. Family therapy may be needed to help the whole family cope with the disturbed member and to identify any process within the family that may be fostering these peculiar behaviors.

The nature-nurture controversy regarding cause is avoided unless there is family pathology that directly contributes to the child's disturbance.

The pediatric nurse plays an important role in the health maintenance of disturbed children. These special children and their families need extra support during routine health care procedures. Ordinary experiences are frightening to severely disturbed children. Blood tests, throat cultures, rectal examinations, and even being weighed become insurmountable problems. Patience and desensitizing through planning with a parent will go a long way toward obtaining routine health care.

Etiology While the cause of these conditions remains unknown, the main hypotheses attribute them to (1) organic problems, (2) faulty parent-child relationships, (3) disturbed family interaction, and (4) multiple causation.

Organic problems Widespread neurological abnormalities are present in many of the children afflicted with pervasive developmental deviations. These neurological problems show up as seizures, abnormal electroencephalograms (EEGs), visual problems, extreme sensitivity to noise and touch, abnormal reflexes, and medical histories of infections, tumors, poisoning, and severe head injuries. Some researchers believe that the child's behavioral symptoms result from an impairment in the reticular formation of the brainstem.[6,7] Childhood schizophrenia has been defined as a maturation disorder of the central nervous system.[8] The mothers of large numbers of childhood schizophrenics had complications during prenatal and delivery periods. These included toxemia, vaginal bleeding, and severe maternal illnesses.[9] Other researchers have reported that autistic children have higher blood levels of serotonin than normal children.[10]

Parent-child relationship An early research project studied families composed of disturbed parents and a psychotic child. Three broad conclusions were drawn:

1. The mother-child relationship was disturbed in the first years of life and was characterized by unusually high ambivalence in the mother.
2. The father-child relationship was disturbed.
3. The infants had suffered severe gastrointestinal and respiratory problems in infancy. A recent traumatic event centering on separation from the parent had precipitated the child's acute psychotic symptoms.[11]

There is inadequate research evidence to support the earlier belief that parents cause psychological disturbances in their children. During the 1950s and 1960s, parents were frequently blamed for their child's autistic behavior. These parents were characterized as highly intellectual, oriented toward abstractions rather than toward people, and emotionally aloof from their children. The infant was thought to enter a non-nurturing, nonsupportive, nonloving world. However, some poorly functioning families produce healthy children, and some healthy families have disturbed children. Therefore many researchers now believe that environmental influences and both the parents' and child's vulnerabilities interact to cause the child's disturbed behavior.

Disturbed family interaction Some investigators believe that the psychotic child's withdrawal from a hostile world and overwhelming anxiety result largely from being the target of the family's conflicts. The family is the single most important social reinforcer in a child's life. Parental communication styles, values, disciplinary methods, and emotional expression have shaped the child from earliest infancy. The ways a child handles feelings of anger, disappointment, happiness, and sadness reflect the family's influence. The communication system in a family is the central concept of family interaction theory. Three dysfunctional family patterns appear to influence the development of behavioral problems in the children: marital schism, marital skew, and the double bind.

A married couple's mutual hatred and inability to solve interpersonal problems constitute a *marital schism*. Parents who continually argue, threaten to separate or divorce, and undercut each other's authority expose their children to dysfunctional emotional communication. A child's natural loyalty to one parent may be exploited and used to hurt the other. Parents in these families may disregard their children's emotional and developmental needs in favor of hurting the hated spouse.[12] A schism or split between the parents continually saps the emotional energy needed for effective communication within the family system.

A *marital skew* exists when one parent dominates a family by disturbed methods of communication and behavior. The conflict is less open in marital schism, but the feelings of hatred and resentment create anxiety in the children. Because problems are not discussed openly, a child may not understand what causes the anxiety he or she feels most of the time.[13]

Many children with pervasive developmental deviations experience contradictory, or *double bind*, messages from their parents. The double bind situation exists when the following criteria are met:

1. A message is communicated to the victim to do or not to do something under threat of punishment.
2. A second message is communicated to the victim which contradicts the first message. This contradictory message is given on another level, such as a frown or a serious message said with a smiling face.
3. The experience must be *repeated* many times between two people; one person is always the victim.
4. A third message binds the victim to the situation so that there is no escape.[14]

Double bind situations may severely harm the child's self-esteem because, since the messages are contradictory, the child is doomed to fail regardless of which message he or she attempts to obey. One escape from the double bind is to withdraw into a pathological world of fantasy.

Multiple causation The behavior of severely disturbed children may result from the interaction of inadequate nuturing, sensory deprivation, and organic causes. Sensorily deprived children, such as those who are blind or institutionalized, exhibit abnormal behaviors similar to those of autistic children. Autistic children are believed to experience reduced sensory input and impaired emotional responses because of neurological abnormalities.[15]

Recent research reveals that autistic children lack the ability to understand and use language. These children are unable to form relationships, learn normally, and integrate experiences. Without meaningful experiences, the child resorts to self-stimulatory behavior.[16] Intellectual inadequacy is common in psychotic children and may result from an organic dysfunction as well as from emotional and cultural deprivation.[17]

Nurturing and other aspects of the parent-child relationship are disturbed, as mentioned previously, so that the child receives suboptimal parenting. Mahler [18] and Bergman[19] observed that the "different" infant elicited irrational responses from the parents. The parents became more perplexed, discouraged, and exhausted after attempting to understand and respond to their child's needs while maintaining family integrity.

Inheritance also seems to contribute to childhood emotional disorders. Recent studies suggest that a genetic predisposition is involved in childhood schizophrenia. The incidence of this form of mental illness is higher among identical twins than among ordinary siblings, for example, even when the children are reared in separate environments.

Childhood psychoses have been conceptualized on a continuum. At one end may be an organic or genetic cause; at the opposite end are harmful environmental influences. The children midway on the continuum have disturbed behavior caused by both organic and environmental influences; they disprove the single-causation theories.[20] The multiple impact of these factors on a child may produce the more severe kinds of childhood psychoses.

Treatment A variety of treatments have been used with autistic children. *Psychodynamic* therapy establishes an environment designed to promote growth. The child is encouraged to learn that the world is not destructive, to experience and manage destructive impulses and feelings, and gradually to form relationships with adults.[21] *Behavior modification* techniques use the principles of reward and punishment to change the child's behavior. Behavior modifica-

tion reduces tantrums and self-destructive behavior, teaches basic speech and social responses, increases the attention span, and teaches letter and word recognition.[22] Pharmacologic therapy has been found useful but should be used judiciously with children. Blood levels and side effects should be closely observed, and medications should *never* be forced on children.

Specific developmental deviations

Stuttering *Stuttering* is a spasmodic action of the muscles involved with speech and difficulty in coordinating these muscles. The child articulates with difficulty and hesitates or repeats words or syllables. Three types of stutterers are classified by etiology: (1) children with defects due to anomalies, such as cleft palate; (2) children with defects in the central nervous system, such as cerebral palsy; and (3) children with functional disorders, including those with both a *physical potential* to become a stutterer and *tension-producing situations* in the environment that discourage an easy flow of language.

Stuttering in all three groups is more common in boys between the ages of 4 and 11 years, when expressive language is critical for the development of symbolic thought. Most children have had a parent or other relative with a history of stuttering.[23] Stuttering may be an isolated symptom or combined with other behavioral troubles. Careful assessment is important for the appropriate treatment. This section focuses on simple stuttering and the role of the parents and pediatric nurse.

Nursing management Parents and caretakers can be given two basic instructions to help their stuttering child. First, do not emphasize the expressive difficulty by calling attention to the stuttering, don't supply the word when the child is blocking, and don't tell the child to "start over and take it easy." Even offering praise is a type of negative labeling—"You aren't stuttering as much." Second, identify tension-producing situations in the child's life. Many families today are caught up in a hectic life-style that permits few relaxed moments. "Hurry up" may be frequently pressed upon a child, and the preschooler may find it impossible, under such pressure, to coordinate ideas and emerging speech patterns. Giving these children plenty of time, looking at them when they talk, and paying attention are important when they learn to talk.

Most young preschool children hesitate or repeat certain words or syllables, especially when excited or under stress. The family may fail to realize that this hesitancy or repetition is normal, and they may unknowingly make matters worse by offering corrections or otherwise calling attention to the "problem." Tension between parent and child then builds. A parent's disappointment and confusion over "why my child can't speak" lead to mounting irritation with each verbal exchange. The child cannot understand the parent's feelings. Simple guidelines for parents can be invaluable and may be sufficient intervention when language is emerging and stuttering is new (Table 40-7). Established stuttering in the late preschool period or afterward requires referral to a speech therapist.

Elective mutism A persistent refusal to speak is termed *elective mutism*. The child clearly understands what is being said. Elective mutism usually occurs before age 5 or when the child first enters school. Besides mutism, the child may also show excessive shyness or sensitivity over being teased, may cling to the mother, may refuse to go to school, and may wet the bed, soil himself, and engage in temper tantrums and other controlling or oppositional behavior, especially at home.

Early hospitalization and physical trauma involving the mouth are among the predisposing factors related to elective mutism. Other factors include excessive marital strife and the use of silence between parents to express hostility and to control each other's behavior. Foreign-speaking mothers who remain isolated at home may have children who simply refuse to speak the new language. Girls are affected more frequently than boys.[24]

Nursing management The nurse's role is to prevent and identify elective mutism. Adequate preparation and support of a family with a young hospitalized child can prevent this symptom choice. The nurse can identify vulnerable families, for example, the immigrant family isolated from the larger community. Most young children are constantly talking and making sounds. By being alert to the excessively quiet child or to the parents' comment that their child does not

Table 40-7 Guidelines for parents of preschoolers who are beginning to stutter

I. Ignore normal hesitation and repetitive sounds as speech emerges. Focus on intelligible sounds by reinforcing them through repetition and praise of clear words or sounds
II. Focus on what the child is trying to communicate *without* questioning and guessing; interruptions discourage speech in any young child
III. Slow your rate of speaking to the child's pace
IV. Simplify your language, speaking at the child's level
V. Set aside daily time to do a few verbal exercises with your child. Examples:
  A. Rhyming games, counting, naming all the blue objects in a room
  B. When reading a story, ask the child to "tell me about your favorite (animal, person, or object) in this story" or ask the child to describe something happening on a particular eye-catching page
  C. Play together for a short time and then ask the child to "tell me what is happening"

talk much or talks less than before, the nurse will help the child receive early treatment. An experienced clinician should differentially diagnose this disorder to rule out mental retardation, language disorders, childhood depression, anxiety disorders, and adjustment problems. The nurse should observe the child's mutism by asking, "Does the child use any syllables or gestures?" "Are there special people to whom the child directs some words or sounds?" Brief psychotherapy, often with the family as a unit, is usually effective.

Enuresis *Enuresis* is the *persistent, involuntary* voiding of urine either day or night after the age of 5 years at least once a month. Both nocturnal and daytime enuresis tend toward self-correction or spontaneous remission. *Primary enuresis* is enuresis, either during the day or at night, in a child never fully toilet trained. *Secondary enuresis* is incontinence that occurs at least once a month after urinary continence (toilet training) has been established for at least 1 year. The chance of developing secondary enuresis decreases with age. The birth of a sibling, divorce of parents, or hospitalization may precipitate secondary enuresis as a stress response in the younger child.[25]

Primary enuresis is due to delayed development of the neurological system. Boys are affected more often than girls, and there is a familial tendency. Every enuretic child should be evaluated for organic causes such as urinary tract infections, diabetes, or seizure disorders *before* psychological treatment is begun.

Enuresis affects families in a variety of ways. Parents who wish or demand that their child stop the inconvenient wetting are losing a maturational battle. Their child's neurological system needs further development. Some normal preschool children become absorbed in play, forget to heed the cues from their bladder, and void before reaching the toilet. Many children with psychiatric disorders of childhood have persistent enuresis. However, not all children with enuresis have emotional problems. If a thorough physical examination, including an emotional assessment, has linked no emotional difficulties to the enuresis, parents need the nurse's support to understand that their child will gradually outgrow the problem. Some parents unwisely continue using diapers to avoid inconvenience and extra laundry; this carries a clear message of "my child the baby." Most children are reaching for healthy, appropriate behaviors and may feel belittled or confused if diapered. The child's feeling of belittling is accentuated if there is a younger diapered child in the home. A particularly frustrating situation may exist when there is an older enuretic son and a younger daughter who is day- and night-trained. Careful consideration of the child's feelings is important for the development of self-esteem. Any accusations by parents, venting of anger while changing the sheets, or stating that the enuresis is voluntary or deliberate will only confuse and create unnecessary feelings of guilt in the child..

In the absence of identified psychiatric disorders, medication to control enuresis should be questioned by the parents. The nurse can act as patient and family advocate. Many medications prescribed to control enuresis during sleep have serious side effects, such as growth retardation and blood dyscrasias. A positive, patient "wait and see" attitude is most useful after any medical or surgical cause is ruled out. A few children do have "irritable bladders," and here medication can be useful.

Mechanical bells and electrical stimulus devices have been cited as successful behavior modification devices for treating bed-wetting.

The child is awakened by a bell or mild electrical impulse while wetting. It is imperative that these devices be used safely and in a positive manner if they are used at all. Behavior modification efforts cannot hasten neurological maturation, however. Techniques such as praising the child for having a dry bed are most useful when faulty training occurred initially and poor urination habits persist.

Encopresis *Encopresis* is the voluntary or involuntary passage of feces of near normal consistency in an inappropriate place. Most children are fully bowel- and bladder-trained by age 5. Children usually master first bowel and then bladder control. (See Chap. 12 for toilet training.) The former is easier to achieve because it is a more predictable physiological function. There are two groups of encopretics, primary and secondary. In *primary encopresis*, training was not completed by 5 years and soiling continues at least once per month.[26] Primary encopresis is associated with poor and inconsistent toilet training. However, most children achieve bowel control by 3 years with minimum help and maximum patience by the family.

Secondary encopresis occurs when a child who has achieved fecal continence begins withholding feces. This is usually associated with family problems, tensions, or life stresses. In most cases it is transient unless the family members focus upon it rather than alleviating the family's problem or tension.

Encopresis is more common in boys. Unlike enuresis, encopresis does not run in families. But bathroom habits may be unusual in many family members. Parents may excessively emphasize cleanliness related to bowel habits, or they may go to the other extreme and may have demanded no regular toileting of the child during the training period.

Soiling refers to the most common symptom of encopresis, defecating into underwear. Loose stools may seep around a bolus of impacted stool formed by withholding defecation. Some children also refuse to wipe themselves and so soil their underwear. While this may seem less serious, it is still considered a form of encopresis, and a closer look by the parents and nurse is warranted.

Many encopretic children defecate in unusual places, such as shoes or closet corners, to hide their bowel movements. Others develop severe constipation and overflow diarrhea. If soiling or inappropriate withholding of stool occurs beyond 3 years, a careful assessment of the child and the family system should begin (see Table 40-8). Prolonged withholding can produce distention of the large bowel and result in other medical complications.

Nursing management Pediatric nurses may help to cleanse an impaction using enemas and medication. This is obviously a very sensitive situation for the child because both the symptom, encopresis, and the treatment, enemas, occur in the same body part. Supportive talking and handling of the equipment, through doll play, are very useful for a child to "play out" feelings of body intrusion. A surprising amount of enema fluid may be absorbed by the child's bowel; careful monitoring of the quantity of fluid instilled and returned, and of vital signs, must be done and documented on the chart. Other useful play media are clay and paints (see Chap. 16). However, care must be exercised with these materials; encopretic children often have a strong aversion, despite their encopresis, to "messing" consciously. Offering a child a choice of several play activities is a more sensitive approach until the child's strengths and vulnerabilities are clearly understood.

Conduct disorders

Conduct disorders are characterized by repetitive and persistent patterns of antisocial behavior infringing on the rights of others. These behaviors are not mere pranks or occasional mischievous acts. These children fail to establish the normal bonds of friendship with peers and often use others exploitively. Their language is abusive. Persistent lying, truancy, vandalism, and early sexual activity are common. Frustration tolerance is low. For example, temper outbursts may occur when these children are simply asked to wait their turn. Aggression may be direct and violent or manipulative to meet the child's own self-centered needs.[27] Some children are relatively healthy but engage in acts that fall under the classification of conduct disorders. These children are often members of a group or gang and are influenced toward deviant behavior.

Table 40-8 Guide for assessing an encopretic child

I. When did bowel training begin and by whom?
II. Methods used: How long was each used, and why did several methods need to be used?
III. Child's response to (I) and (II): Was there self-initiated interest in bowel training?
IV. Presence of urinary incontinence
V. Presence of other behavioral disturbances or parent concerns:
   A. Temper tantrums
   B. Dietary patterns
   C. Child is too active by parent's standards
VI. Bowel habits and attitudes of other family members
   A. Demands of excessive cleanliness
   B. Unusual toilet habits of parents: regular use of laxatives, enemas, or other measures

Etiology

The psychosocial concept of conduct disorder and the legal concept of delinquency make it difficult to identify the incidence and causes of conduct disorders. The label of "delinquent" depends on the community's definition of morality and whether the deviant behavior falls within the scope of law enforcement. Each community has its own criteria and tolerance for acceptable behaviors.

Research points to the behavioral similarities between minimally brain-damaged children and children with conduct disorders. The hyperactivity, short attention span, impulsiveness, low frustration tolerance, irritability, inability to delay gratification, and unusual aggressiveness are problems in both groups (see also Chap. 37). Learning disabilities occur commonly in children with conduct disorders; dyslexia, a reading disability, is prominent.[28]

In attempting to explain the cause of conduct disorders, some investigators emphasize that the family is the most important socializing influence. The families of these children have a high incidence of severe marital problems, such as divorce, separation, and ongoing parental conflict.[29] Adult supervision and control over the child's behavior are the key factors missing in these families.

While studies have linked delinquency to low socioeconomic groups, the important factor actually appears to be deprivation: economic, social, and cultural. Socially deviant behavior among children is learned in small groups. If these friendships are the only ones available to a child, deviant behaviors are learned, and because they are not counterbalanced by more socially acceptable behaviors, they are incorporated into the child's general behavior. A child can be psychologically healthy and seemingly well adjusted and still act in a socially deviant way.

The emphasis on environmental influences in the development of conduct disorders is significant. However, the question of why some children in a disturbed family and a deprived social setting develop conduct disorders while others become well socialized remains unanswered.

Psychiatric explanations of conduct disorders view the central problem as defects in conscience development. Traumatic experiences and faulty identification contribute to a weakened character structure in the child's developing personality. The child develops the need to discharge impulses directly because his or her personality cannot delay or discharge them in an appropriate, more indirect way. Some children may act out their parents' impulsiveness as well as their own.

While causes of conduct disorders are not precisely known, it is clear that every child with a conduct disorder has difficulty with *self-control*. Punishments have not deterred the child; anxiety to avoid punishment was not sufficient to cause self-control. Constitutional differences are believed to contribute to some children's vulnerability to develop a conduct disorder if the environmental influences are sufficiently stressful.

Nursing management

Children with conduct disorders can wreak havoc on pediatric units with their aggressive destruction and disregard for other children's feelings and rights. Careful attention must be paid to safety, especially regarding drug paraphernalia, pranks, and leaving the hospital unit impulsively.

Developing a relationship with these children is difficult but not impossible. Endless testing of limits, rules, and the nurse's patience must be met by firm, authoritative discipline without punitive measures or angry feelings being inflicted on the child. More specifically, the pediatric nurse can:

1. Facilitate the child's experience with his or her body by helping the child through painful and uncomfortable hospitalization experiences, listening to the child's complaints, and offering concrete ways of handling the discomfort.
2. Teach the child about the body. This is a safe way to begin building trust between nurse and child (see Chap. 16).

The nurse must be aware that all people have their own biases about deviant behavior. Morality and values are subjective experiences. A child's conduct may make a nurse uncomfortable because it is in conflict with the nurse's and community's value systems. Socialization experiences for children with conduct disorders must occur without the nurse's showing harsh prejudice and expecting the child to fail.

Anxiety disorders

Anxiety disorders are characterized by *excessive anxiety*. The anxiety may be focused on specific concerns or may be a generalized response to most situations.

Separation anxiety

The child with *separation anxiety* experiences severe distress when separated from family and home. Abnormal separation anxiety occurs from the school-age period through adolescence and adulthood, *beyond* the periods when concern about separating from the parents is appropriate, under 3 years. School-age children with separation anxiety are preoccupied with horrible fantasies of harm that may occur to parents, usually the mother, or to themselves if separated. Preschool children have more vague concerns.

School refusal (previously called *school phobia*) becomes severe around 10 to 11 years but begins earlier for many children when forced separation occurs through mandatory schooling. These children are usually "model children" in the home and conscientious students, but they are fear-ridden about leaving home.[30]

Pediatric nurses and school nurses see these severely anxious children because somatic symptoms frequently develop. Extensive workups are often done for gastrointestinal problems, headaches, and influenza-like symptoms that plague the child and worry the parents. If school is missed too often, academic performance is compromised and lowered self-esteem further troubles the child. Care must be taken in talking with the families of severely anxious children. Interviewing must be conducted carefully because most of the mothers are highly ambivalent about separating from their anxious children. Coordination with the school-age child's teacher and school nurse may help a child feel safe despite eruptions of somatic symptoms. The nurse must be careful not to focus on the symptoms or accuse the child of malingering. *Anxiety is the root of the problem.* A pediatric-psychiatric liaison service is ideal for coordinating the physical findings and therapeutic approach for child and family. The pediatric nurse and school health nurse may be included in supporting the child and parent to tolerate the symptoms while trust is developed and anxiety is reduced. Helping a parent to feel separate and secure through psychiatric treatment may be the first step before a child can give up fears that the parent will be harmed if out of sight. The older school-age child has more specific fears and will need individual treatment. By the time a child reaches 10 to 11 years, internalized and fixed fears are more difficult to help with support alone.

EXAMPLE: Nine-year-old Rosie was referred by her school for excessive absenteeism. Rosie was from a close Hispanic family and had three older brothers. Rosie's mother worked in her daughter's school and could monitor Rosie and the teachers. Rosie knew her mother was nearby. They traveled to and from school together because the mother felt the city was dangerous. Their residing in an unsafe neighborhood only reinforced their mutual fear of separation.

Rosie was placed in a different class and finally in a Catholic school because both she and her mother did not like the public school teachers. Physical symptoms began to emerge in the second grade. Rosie became dizzy, had persistent headaches and stomach upsets, and "fainted in bed." Rosie had always missed many school days, but her absenteeism rapidly escalated to months.

Rosie's symptoms were treated by a pediatrician, but the etiology was uncertain. Finally, an EEG revealed a nonspecific abnormal wave pattern. This finding had no relationship to her physical symptoms, but her mother seized on the abnormality and again "doctor-shopped" until she found a physician who prescribed a low dosage of phenobarbital. At this point, a coordinated effort was made to help this family focus on the central issue of separation anxiety. Rosie was assigned to an individual psychotherapist. Her mother was seen individually after attempts to involve the whole family for at least one interview failed.

These interviews revealed that Rosie's mother had also stopped school at the second to third grade level for the same reason: a desire to be close to her mother.

Rosie was referred to a pediatric neurologist for examination and another EEG. While the results were explained endlessly to Rosie's mother, she was unwilling to give up her image of Rosie as "the sick child." A pediatric examination was arranged. All pediatric care was consolidated in hopes of discouraging Rosie's mother from seeking other advice.

Rosie was enrolled in home instruction even though this reinforced her desire to stay home. However, the problem was long-standing and symptoms had been present for 2 years. Rosie needed to continue learning basic skills and to complete the school year. Many therapy appointments were missed, a pattern similar to the school absenteeism. This was tolerated as long as more appointments were kept than broken.

A final treatment plan emerged after building trust with this approach for 6 months. Rosie was enrolled in the day treatment school program, a combination of school and psychotherapy. A school bus picked her up, alleviating her mother's anxiety about safety. Somatic symptoms occur occasionally, especially in the winter, but the plan remains in effect. Rosie shows gradual but definite progress.

Shyness disorder

Shyness disorder is often accepted by parents as a behavior peculiar to their child, unless the shyness begins to interfere with schoolwork or infringes on the parents' independence. For example, a teacher may observe a child's reluctance to participate in most activities or a parent may see the child always clinging when any babysitter arrives. Usually these children are warm and friendly within the family, but they are almost mute, may pale or blush excessively, stammer unintelligibly, and show excessive embarrassment outside the family setting. Participating in play, school, and other events is minimal, and clinging to parents is the child's usual response.

With support and encouragement, a child may gradually break out into the world. If the shyness increases and isolates the child further as adolescence approaches, the new pressures of adolescent development may be unusually stressful. Parents may share this concern with the nurse during a routine health checkup. The nurse can assess this area of the preadolescent's development by questioning his or her social adjustment. The nurse can observe how a school-age child contributes and answers questions during the examination.

Overanxious disorder

The overanxious disorder[31] is a generalized worrying and concern not focused on specific situations like those of school refusal or problems with relating to peers. These children worry about almost everything related to current and future events. Excessive anticipation, questions about the future, and overconcern about examinations and possible dangers plague them. Tasks are avoided through endless questions and stalling.

Characteristic somatic complaints—"lump in the throat," gastrointestinal problems, headaches, shortness of breath, feeling cold, and dizziness—appear when deadlines or dreaded events near. Nail biting, hair twirling, and other nervous habits are displayed by these highly verbal and often precocious children. Academic and social difficulties arise when school performance drops or the child misses trips, events, and games because of fearfulness. The physical symptoms and treatment for them can (unfortunately) confirm the "sick" role. When the anxiety disorder is recognized as the cause of the somatic complaints, a nurse can reassure the child that the physical problems will subside as self-confidence grows. Encouragement to explore new experiences, planning small steps toward new experiences, and talking about fears and failures can build a trusting nurse-child relationship.

References

1. Elva O. Poznanski, "Childhood Depression: A Psychodynamic Approach to the Etiology of Depression in Children," in Alfred P. French and Irving N. Berlin (eds.), *Depression in Children and Adolescents*, Human Sciences, New York, 1979, pp. 47–50.
2. Hector Jaso, "Disorders Usually First Evident in Infancy, Childhood, or Adolescence," in American Psychiatric Association, *Diagnostic and Statistical Manual of Mental Disorders*, 3d ed., American Psychiatric Association, New York, 1979, pp. 18–19.
3. Mary Coleman, *The Autistic Syndrome*, American Elsevier, New York, 1976, p. 2.
4. Lorna Wing, *Early Childhood Autism*, Pergamon Press, Elmsford, N.Y., 1966, p. 93.
5. *Ibid.*, pp. 18–19.
6. *Ibid.*, p. 35.
7. Lauretta Bender, "The Brain and Child Behavior," in *Archives of General Psychiatry* 4:531–538 (1961).
8. *Ibid.*
9. M. Pollack and M. G. Woerner, "Pre- and Peri-natal Complications and Childhood Schizophrenia: A Comparison of 5 Controlled Studies," *Journal of Child Psychology and Psychiatry* 7:235–242 (1966).
10. A. E. Yuweiler, E. Geller, and E. R. Ritvo, "Neurobiochemical Research," in E. R. Ritvo (ed.), *Autism: Diagnosis, Current Research and Management*, Spectrum, New York, 1976, pp. 85–106.
11. Beatta Rank, "Intensive Study and Treatment of Preschool Children Who Show Marked Personality Deviations or 'Atypical Development' and Their Parents," in G. Caplan (ed.), *Emotional Problems of Early Childhood*, Basic Books, New York, 1955, p. 493.
12. Theodore Lidz, S. Fleck, and A. R. Cornelison, *Schizophrenia and the Family*, International Universities Press, New York, 1965, p. 142.
13. *Ibid.*
14. *Ibid.*
15. Bernard G. Suran and V. R. Joseph, *Special Children: An Integrative Approach*, Scott, Foresman, Glenwood, Ill., 1979, p. 381.
16. *Ibid.*
17. Lorna Wing, op. cit., pp. 71–74.
18. M. S. Mahler and B. J. Goslinger, "On Symbiotic Child Psychoses," in *Psychoanalytic Study of the Child*, vol. 10, International Universities Press, New York, 1955, p. 201.
19. P. Bergman and S. Escalona, "Unusual Sensitivities in Very Young Children," in *Psychoanalytic Study of the Child*, vols. 3 and 4, International Universities Press, New York, 1948, pp. 333–352.
20. W. Goldfarb, *Childhood Schizophrenia*, Harvard University Press, Cambridge, Mass., 1961, pp. 21–23.
21. Suran and Joseph, op. cit., pp. 388–389.
22. *Ibid.*, p. 392.
23. Wendell Johnson et al. (eds.), *Speech Handicapped School Children*, Harper & Row, New York, 1967, pp. 262–263, 268–272.
24. Jaso, op. cit., p. 13.
25. Michael Cohen, "Enuresis," in Robert Hoekelman et al. (eds.), *Principles of Pediatrics: Health Care of the Young*, McGraw-Hill, New York, 1978, pp. 475–481.
26. R. G. Barr and M. E. Levine, "Encopresis," in Robert Hoekelman et al. (eds.), *Principles of Pediatrics: Health Care of the Young*, McGraw-Hill, New York, 1978, pp. 717–720.
27. Jaso, op. cit., pp. 10–11.
28. E. Critchley, "Reading Retardation, Dyslexia, and Delinquency," *British Journal of Psychiatry* 115:1537–1547 (1968).
29. R. E. Anderson, "Where's Dad? Parental Deprivation and Delinquency," in *Archives of General Psychiatry* 18:641–649 (1968).
30. Jaso, op. cit., pp. 11–12.
31. Ibid., pp. 12–13.

Chapter 41 **Child abuse and neglect**

Mona Clare Lotz Finnila

Upon completion of this chapter, the student will be able to:

1. Define child abuse, neglect, sexual abuse, emotional abuse, and institutional abuse.

2. Describe six hospital or community resources designed to assist abused children and their families.

3. Describe his or her emotional reaction to acutely injured or severely neglected infants and their parents.

4. State how this reaction may affect communication with the children and families.

5. Identify 10 common environmental problems which contribute to the abuse of children.

6. Detail 10 predictive signs prior to labor or after delivery of potential abuse of the infant by the parents.

7. Construct a support plan for a young family to prevent child abuse from occurring, utilizing a variety of community resources.

8. List 10 assessment findings about a child and family that indicate that abuse has occurred.

9. State five examples of patient goals and nursing actions to give adequate care to the abused child.

10. List five common diagnostic procedures and their rationale for use with the nonaccidentally injured (NAI) child.

11. Identify five common physical signs or symptoms of failure to thrive due to parental neglect.

Child abuse is a group of clinical health problems in children of all ages caused by inadequate or hostile adult caretakers or hazardous environments. The health problem may be acute (a duodenal rupture from a blow to the stomach) or chronic (verbal assault over many years, creating a poor self-concept). The clinical picture may be minor (welt marks on a child's back) or severe (a fractured skull which may cause death). The emotional, physical, social, and psychological health of the child may be impaired temporarily (a burn that will heal) or permanently (severe mental retardation from a head injury). Abuse occurs in children of all ages, from the fetal stage to late adolescence, and in *all socioeconomic classes*. Children of all races, religions, ethnic groups, and nations are abused.

The major categories of child abuse include fetal abuse, nonaccidental injury, neglect, sexual abuse, emotional abuse, and institutional abuse.

Child abuse is a tremendous problem in our world today. In the United States, 30 percent of the 2 million children in foster placement were abused or neglected in their natural home. It is estimated that 2 million children in the United States are moderately or severely abused each year: 1 million of these abuses are reported; 60,000 children have significant injuries; 2000 of these children die, and 6000 have permanent brain damage.[1,2] All children are mildly abused during their childhood from various environmental influences. Like the United States, many other nations are beginning to study child abuse problems.

As people have begun to look at how children are raised and to study the end results of various child care practices, parenting practices and children's environments are being modified to produce healthier, happier children. Although child abuse has been recognized as a problem for only 100 years, most progress has occurred in the last 20 years. Great strides have been made in helping families with nonaccidental injury and neglect. Work is underway in sexual abuse, while work in emotional, institutional, and environmental abuse has barely begun.

Nurses contribute to the identification and treatment of abused children. In addition, nurses help to prevent child abuse through careful assessment and treatment of parents, including preventive health education. As nurses continue cooperative work with persons in other disciplines for the long-term health benefits of fami-

lies, major contributions will be made to the health of children.

Historical perspectives

In ancient Greece and Rome, unwanted infants were left exposed in an open place. Mythology includes tales of heroes who began life in this manner. Infanticide (baby killing) may have been used as a form of birth control. Eskimos prior to 1900 encouraged the killing of female babies born before the birth of a male infant. This was on a tribal economic policy thought necessary for survival in their harsh environment. In certain African tribes, twin children were viewed as unlucky omens and killed. In many cultures, physically handicapped children were destroyed at birth. Children who were biracial were also in danger. In some countries even today, some infants are deliberately maimed so that they may become beggars and help support the family.

In the nineteenth century, during the era commonly called the Industrial Revolution, children were put to work in the fields and factories. Four- and five-year-old children worked in dungeon-like factories or mines 14 hours a day, 6 days a week. Farm children worked just as hard. The average life span for people of that era was 17 years. Malnutrition and epidemics of tuberculosis, cholera, typhoid, and typhus were rampant, especially among the poor and very young.[3] In 1916, a major law, the Child Labor Act, was passed preventing children younger than 9 from certain hazardous forms of labor. Not until 1938 were the present child labor policies enacted.[4] Children of migrant farm workers are still not adequately protected against excessive work, exposure to noxious chemicals, and poor housing and education. Some of the historical landmarks which signaled relief for children are listed in Table 41-1.

Table 41-1 Historical landmarks

1869	New York Foundling Hospital was established to care for unwanted babies (1060 infants were received the first year, 61% in critical condition)
1875	American Humane Society child protective services were established
1900–1920	Abused children were removed from their homes and their parents imprisoned
1920–present	Social workers began assisting families in the home setting. Foster care was used extensively
1960–1970	Kempe coined the term *battered child syndrome* and established some multidisciplinary approaches to treatment. Laws requiring that child abuse be reported were established in all states. Experimental programs were funded by the federal government
1974	The Child Abuse and Prevention Act was passed by the U.S. Congress. Eighty-five million dollars were earmarked for treatment of abused youngsters and their parents
1979	Multiple local parent and child treatment centers were operating throughout the country

Sources: C. H. Kempe, "Approaches to Preventive Child Abuse: The Health Visitor Concept," *American Journal of Diseases of Children* **130:**941 (1976). Vincent DeFrancis, "Progress and Problems in Protecting the Abused Child," *Speaking Out for Child Protection*, pamphlet of the American Humane Association, Englewood, Colorado, 1973, pp. 19–72.

Fetal and postpartal abuse

Fetal abuse is exposure of the child before birth to harmful influences from the maternal environment. These agents compromise the child's potential for a healthy life or even cause death. Inadequate maternal education, inadequate health care resources, and exposure to noxious drugs or infection are three major causes. These harmful prenatal influences are discussed in detail in Chaps. 8 and 9.

Clinical problems

What the health care team can do varies greatly according to the health problem. Heroin use by a pregnant woman, for example, can cause addiction in the unborn child, produce impaired neonatal adjustment, and sometimes bring about permanent neurological problems. Narcotic drug addiction must be reported to the law enforcement agency or public social service agency. An addict is likely to have poor emotional preparation for giving birth. It is not unusual that poor bonding behavior and even hostility toward the newborn follow. These problems are not reportable to the police. Children of drug abusers are often abused as infants. Regardless of particular factors such as these, the nurse can help parents safeguard their unborn infant by careful health care, education, and supervision. Parents who abuse drugs will need referral to specialized services such as Alcoholics Anonymous, stop-smoking clinics, and dietitians.

Prevention of child abuse

Adults in high-risk categories for child abuse can often be identified before, after, or during the birth of their child. The nurse, functioning as a parent health educator, can observe the parents' verbal and nonverbal behavior toward the baby even before it is born. An informal interview with the parents should follow. This assesses their emotional and physical preparation for childbirth and their responses to the child. Maintaining a nonjudgmental attitude toward the parents increases their cooperation and promotes the infant's safety. A partial list of warning signs for the nurse to observe is listed in Table 41-2.

When the nurse observes one or more of these warning signs, the behavior should be noted on the patient's record. Plans for further action can also be detailed. An example follows:

EXAMPLE: 3 P.M.: Mary fed John 1 oz, then returned him to his crib within 5 min of receiving him from the nursery and went to the visitor's room. She was found smoking and laughing loudly with a friend. When asked, "Why did you stop feeding John?" she replied, "He stinks and I needed a smoke." John was returned to the nursery, still clean and dry. He was alert and hungry (drank 1½ oz more).

Table 41-2 Predictive signs of potential child abuse

In the prenatal period

1. Mother living alone or with small children without supportive family and friends
2. Father uninterested in outcome of pregnancy
3. Mother living with a man unrelated to the infant
4. Mother overly concerned about the sex of the child
5. Mother hostile toward the biological father
6. Pregnancy was unplanned and comments suggest that the child is unwanted
7. Pregnancy was planned but woman wants baby in order to have "someone to love me"
8. Parents considered an abortion
9. Parents were children of abusing, neglectful parents
10. No telephone in home
11. Parents seem poorly educated, have learning and emotional problems, seem immature for their age, are underemployed, and have inadequate housing
12. Parents do not prepare "nest" for child—crib, clothing
13. Mother denies pregnancy, e.g., is late in seeking medical care, refuses to wear maternity clothes, and fails to gain weight

In the labor and delivery suite

1. Mother speaks angrily about the baby's "causing" her to be in pain
2. Parents don't touch, hold, or examine their baby, or they make disparaging remarks about the sex or appearance of the child
3. Mother is alone or father is remote or dutiful without affection

In the postpartum period

1. Mother does not enjoy or play with her baby
2. Mother avoids eye contact with her child
3. Mother feeds her child with minimal body contact
4. Mother is bothered by her child's crying and messiness
5. Child has congenital anomalies and requires a special-care nursery
6. Husband shows jealous behavior

Source: Jane D. Gray et al., "Prediction and Prevention of Child Abuse and Neglect," in M. L. Lauderdale et al. (eds.), *Child Abuse and Neglect: Issues on Innovation and Implementation*, vol. 1, Department of Health, Education, and Welfare, Washington, D.C., Pub. No. (OHDS) 78-30147, 1977, pp. 246–254.

Problem 1: Lack of interest in John resulting in inadequate feeding

Plan

1. Spend time with Mary tomorrow during a feeding period and some time with her alone.
2. Gather data: How does Mary handle John, how does she feed him, what are her current attitudes and plans for John? What personal life problems is she having? How has she prepared her home for John?

3. Gather data from other health care personnel who have given care to Mary.
4. Develop an intervention plan alone or with other nurses for Mary and John based on the above data.

Failure of the nurse to recognize or deal with parents' life problems and poor parent-infant bonding can result in abuse or even death of the child. In our present health care facilities, it is common for many health care personnel to ignore parent problems for the following kinds of reasons:

She's only here for 2 days. I can't change anything.
There are too many patients with too many problems.
Her problems are unsolvable.
It's the doctor's responsibility.

But nurses who do take the responsibility to communicate with patients effectively and help them establish an adequate support system to deal with their problems can facilitate a higher quality of life. Consider the contrast between these two examples:

EXAMPLE: A single teenager alone with a dog moved to a large city in the late stages of pregnancy. She secured a small, unfurnished apartment. She applied for welfare, but payments were delayed. She had no money to prepare the home for the baby. She did not know anyone in her apartment building. She delivered a son after normal labor and was hospitalized for 2 days.

On her discharge day, she returned home with the baby. The dog had not eaten for 3 days. She put the child on the floor and left to secure some dog food. On her return, she found that the dog had killed the baby.

EXAMPLE: Pregnant, 17-year-old Jennifer came to a prenatal clinic 1000 miles from her family's home. The physical examination indicated that she was in her sixth month of pregnancy. The clinic nurse interviewing her discovered that the girl had many problems, including infrequent illegal drug use, insufficient funds, poor education, poor nutrition, no close friends, no physical preparations for the baby, and a great deal of hostility. On the positive side, the girl revealed that she was dissatisfied with her previous life-style and wanted a better life for herself and the baby. She was willing to accept counseling from the nurse and other health care personnel. The clinic nurse worked closely with her for the next 3 months, introducing resources to Jennifer. The clinic nurse prepared the obstetrical unit to support Jennifer. A pediatric clinic contin-

ued to follow up Jennifer and her son, Jimmy, for the next 5 years.

Largely as a result of concerned health care personnel, Jennifer was able to utilize multiple resources to resolve her life problems. At 23 years of age, Jennifer had a stable marriage, two healthy, normal children, and a junior college education.

When the nurse develops an intervention program and cooperates with other health care personnel in the hospital and community, better family functioning and increased safety for children occur.

Nonaccidental injury

Nonaccidental injury (NAI) is physical injury to the child from hostile actions of an adult caretaker. For example, a parent dips a year-old boy in hot water to punish him for soiling his diapers. NAI may also occur from failure to protect a child when injury will result from inaction. For example, a toddler falls from an open and unscreened second-story window, or an infant drowns in a bathtub because a parent has left the baby to answer the phone.

Characteristics of nonaccidental injuries

Whenever a child is injured, NAI must be considered as a possible cause. There are some clues a nurse can assess. One is whether the injury makes sense in terms of the child's age. For example, an infant under 1 year of age rarely has a fractured femur from falling out of a crib or high chair. X-rays may reveal that the femur was fractured by a severe twisting movement which requires adult muscle strength. X-ray findings of old healed fractures along with a fresh injury suggest repeated abuse.

Another clue is whether the parent's explanation is compatible with the injury. The following case history is an example.

EXAMPLE: An 11-month-old girl is admitted with a fractured skull (cracked eggshell appearance on x-ray). The parents report that she fell off a couch while napping. A fractured skull is unlikely from a short fall. The x-ray finding of cracked eggshell usually results from being violently slammed against a wall. The injury does not match the parents' explanation.

When assessing an injury, problem solving is

helpful. Consider the child with bruises. Small bruises on a toddler's forehead, chin, and knees are normal consequences of learning to walk. Bruises on multiple surfaces (cheeks, back, trunk, and extremities) suggest that a toddler has been slapped (Fig. 41-1). If the bruises are in different stages of healing, multiple beatings may have occurred. Mongolian spots on the young child's lower back can resemble bruises but are normal findings. Do the bruises suggest the use of a weapon, such as a belt or electric cord? Using a weapon to hit a child is a reportable problem. Slapping sometimes leaves characteristic petechial marks (Fig. 41-2).

Reporting suspected abuse

It is not necessary for a nurse or other health care worker to know whether abuse has definitely occurred, who did it, or how the injury was suffered. A nurse who only suspects that child abuse has occurred is required by law to report the suspicion to the local police or protective child care service agency. The child has been injured under suspicious circumstances and needs protection until an investigation has taken place.

Figure 41-1 Thoroughly assess the undressed child for signs of injury. Note the welt marks on the child's body. (*Courtesy of Vincent J. Fontana, M.D. The New York Foundling Hospital.*)

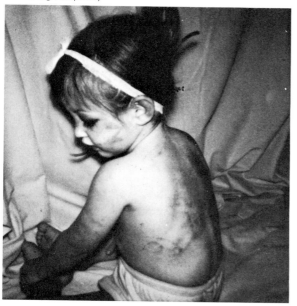

Figure 41-2 Hand slaps to the face of this 6-month-old child resulted in visible linear marks from the fingers and a subdural hematoma. (Cotton balls are routinely placed on the scalp after subdural taps for release of intracranial pressure.) (*Courtesy of Robert W. ten Bensel, M.D.*)

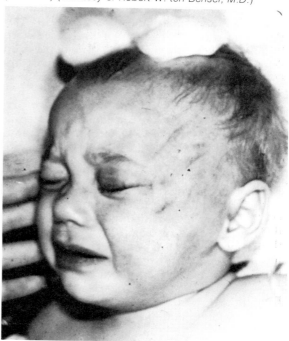

A nurse (as well as certain other professionals, including teachers and physicians) who fails to report suspected child abuse may be charged with a misdemeanor. Nurses have immunity from being sued when reporting suspected child abuse. In most emergency rooms, the physician will take the responsibility to contact the police or protective child care service worker. Every hospital and community health care agency needs a written policy on how the abused child will be admitted, assessed, treated, and returned to the general community, and who is reponsible for reporting the abuse to authorities. In many hospitals, this reponsibility is assigned to the medical or psychiatric social worker. In some states, a doctor can be charged with a felony for failing to report an obvious case of child abuse if that child is readmitted for another injury.

Some hospitals are developing child abuse teams that participate in identifying, reporting, assessing, treating, and follow-up of abused children and their families. Some team members have the very difficult task of informing the parents that child abuse is suspected and that the hospital staff, by law, must report the child's problem to the police. They also tell the parents that they wish to help the family through the process of assessment and treatment. The team members know that some of the parents' responses will be anger, denial, and depression. Sometimes a team member will support the family during the juvenile court or criminal court proceedings.

Absolute honesty with the parents regarding the court process and treatment recommendations is required. Empathic and nonjudgmental team members are a great comfort to the family members. The court respects the written reports of the team and most often follows their recommendations about treatment plans for the child and family. The child's primary nurse also joins the team to provide child and family data, observations, nursing diagnoses, nursing actions, and recommendations for discharge planning. All members of the team are responsible for accurately recording pertinent data in the patient's record.

Some child abuse teams utilize community resources for treatment and review the family's

Table 41-3 The path of abused and neglected children in the health care system

Entry

Relative, neighbor, or friend reports abuse
Brought in by school nurse
Child self-report
Parent report
"Accident story" in emergency room
Brought in by police or protective service worker
Private physician

Where decisions are made

Emergency room
Acute inpatient unit
Rehabilitation unit
Outpatient unit (usually a nonreportable mild abuse and neglect problem)

Exit

Home without court supervision
Home with court supervision (3 months to 18 years)
Shelter care facility until investigation is completed
Group home for mentally retarded or mentally ill children
Foster care, adoption, or other short-term or long-term relinquishment of child by parent
Death

progress only at specified periods. Other teams, in addition to making community referrals, participate in a therapy program for families during and after hospitalization. This participation may include supervising lay therapists (who work with families mainly at home) and conducting individual and group therapy sessions for children, siblings, and parents. Nurses often see great progress and experience a sense of satisfaction as families make tremendous gains in the quality of their child care. The threat of reinjury to a child is greatly reduced when a family participates actively in a treatment program designed by the multidisciplinary team.

How children enter and leave the health care system

Table 41-3 depicts the movement of an abused or neglected child through the health care system. The rehabilitation unit mentioned in the table refers to a special type of hospital unit. Children (and sometimes their parents) are housed in an informal, homelike setting. Children are dressed in street clothes and eat family style. Many health professionals, including nurses, psychologists, physicians, and physical and occupational therapists, work cooperatively for the benefit of the families.

Nurses' participation in the court process

The nurse's role in the investigation of abuse or neglect is rarely complicated, and court appearances are infrequently required. Usually the court wants accurate written data documenting the child's health problems, including injuries and illnesses. A sample of how data should be recorded on the chart follows:

EXAMPLE: A large, dark-purple bruise (approx. 6 cm in diameter and irregularly shaped) is on the upper right quadrant of Tommy's abdomen. Tommy's father said, "Tommy fell out of a tree, hitting a large rock on the ground." Tommy reported, when his father was out of the examining room, "My dad hit me."

Court processes vary in different cities. Usually the atmosphere in juvenile court is more casual than in civil or criminal court. A treatment plan is evolved, sometimes with the aid of the hospital child abuse team, that permits adequate supervision of the child and rehabilitation of the family. The child may be placed in a foster home or referred to an adoption agency. Foster placement can cause emotional disturbances in the child. Sometimes the child is placed with relatives or at home but under supervision. The child may stay under court supervision for months or until adulthood. Reevaluation is required approximately every 6 months to determine how these children are progressing.

Causative factors in nonaccidental injury

Families in all socioeconomic groups, religions, races, and cultural subgroups can become child abusers. People in the lower socioeconomic groups, who use impersonal health care facilities, are reported most often. Private physicians have been hesitant to report families in the past. This is gradually shifting as they become more familiar with the usual court process and the development of treatment centers for their clients.

Many researchers in different locations are attempting to delineate the multiple causes of child abuse.[5,6] There are some common findings. There is often parent pathology, with a history of abuse or neglect traced back three to four generations. The parent has learned violent methods of child discipline, such as beating with a belt or hitting with a board. Some abusive parents feel socially isolated or receive little if any support from spouse or family. Sometimes mental illness (rare) or mental retardation (more common) prevents the parent from nurturing a child well. The abusive parent has low self-esteem, unmet dependency needs, and inadequate knowledge of growth and development. Abusive parents characteristically expect the child to function as a little adult. The child is also expected to cater to the parents' needs and increase their self-esteem. In most instances, education and psychotherapy will assist these families to function well.

Often, the abused child is considered different from other children. The perception that the child is different may be based on a physical problem (e.g., crippling, retardation, or a heart defect). A negative emotional tie may occur if the child has been named after a disliked person or is a symbol of a former spouse.

When episodes of abuse are carefully studied, a precipitating stressor is often found. Although this stressor may seem minor to the nurse, it may be perceived as severe by the parent. For example, lack of sleep or the crying of an irritable infant may trigger an episode of abuse. One author has noted three common situations that cause abusive parents to erupt with anger. One is an infant's crying that the parent considers excessive. The parent is unable to stop the crying, becomes angry and impatient, and reacts violently toward the baby. It is very important that the nurse discuss infant crying with parents who have been identified as at risk to become abusive (Table 41-2). Normal crying patterns should be described (see Chap. 10), and the parents need to be taught to interpret why the baby is crying (pain, hunger, boredom, fear, etc.) and what to do about it. The parent needs to have a backup plan for times when the baby's crying becomes intolerable; for example, perhaps a neighbor can care for the infant while the mother takes a walk. Babies who cry excessively need evaluation to rule out organic disease as a cause of the irritability.

A second situation that provokes abusive episodes comes from toilet training too early or with poor understanding of what can and cannot be expected from the child. For example, if a $2\frac{1}{2}$-year-old child defecates in his pants or behind the couch, the parent may perceive the act as hostile and react violently. Or a parent may try to train a 1-year-old child and react with anger to the inevitable failure. Obviously, as a teacher, the nurse can learn parents' expectations and attitudes about toilet training and assist them to modify unrealistic expectations.

Third, a hyperactive school-age child may provoke child abuse. Excessive talking, movement, and reduced sleep needs produce stress for parents. Referring hyperactive children, or active children perceived by parents to be hyperactive, to a counselor can avoid child abuse.

Nursing management

When a child with suspected NAI is admitted to the hospital, immediate priorities are to assess, describe in writing, and treat injuries; to provide physical and psychological comfort; and to protect the child from further injury or removal by the parents. Long-range goals deal with changing the family's functioning to prevent further abuse.

Usually by the time the child reaches the inpatient unit from the emergency room, the police have been notified and custody of the child has been assigned to the hospital, pending a court hearing. The parents must be told about the custody and must be informed that they are not to take the child from the hospital.

Gentleness is important during the physical examination and any other handling of the child. Explanations and reassurance must be provided at the child's level of understanding. In addition to the usual apprehension all children experience when they come to the hospital, children who have been abused may have a generalized mistrust of adults. These children are watchful and fearful, not only of health care personnel but also of their parents. In spite of their apprehension, they passively submit to care-giving activities and protest or cry very little, because they have learned that complaining and resisting lead to punishment.

From the outset of nursing care, a major objective is to enable the child to establish a sense of security and trust. Consistent kindness and sustained interaction with the same staff members encourage the child's confidence in people and diminish anxiety. It is also critically important to remember that these children, like others (especially while young), have strong affectional and dependency ties to their parents; they are distressed by separation from the parents and need sustained contact with them and reassurance that the parents have not abandoned them.

The initial interview with the parents should deal with the child's present stage of development in order to provide the nurse with data on which to construct the care plan. (See Appendix D for a personal history form.) Parents need to be oriented to the hospital unit and its routines. They are told at this initial interview that the nurse will work closely with them and with the other members of the child abuse team to help the family change ineffective patterns and to increase the well-being of parents and child. Parents are generally upset at admission, and lengthy or sensitive aspects of the interview are deferred for another visit. It is important to convey the idea that the nurse wants to work with—not against—the parents, and that many families in similar situations have found ways to work out their problems. Parent visits to the hospital are encouraged (appointments with the nurse should be scheduled if parents do not routinely come in) so that intervention care can take place.

Nursing intervention with parents involves identifying and recording both the negative factors and the positive resources of the abusive family.

EXAMPLE: A 7-year-old girl is admitted to an inpatient unit because of welts and bruises on her back, upper thighs, and left cheek. A school nurse brought her to the emergency room. In gathering data for assessment, the nurse learned the following:

1. The stepfather, who admitted hitting the child, recently became unemployed.
2. The mother is a passive person, unable to stop the stepfather, and is 7 months pregnant.
3. The child displays hyperactive movements and sleeps only 4 h a day.
4. The child was a premature twin and, because of hospitalization (premature nursery), was not touched by her mother for 3 months after her birth.
5. The child is considered possessed (of devils) by her mother.
6. The child was jumping from a dresser onto a bed where her sister was sleeping at 3 A.M. when the incident occurred.
7. The stepfather is remorseful about the incident.
8. The parents are asking, "How can we help our child?"
9. The parents are willing to come in for appointments.

With these data, the nurse was able to collaborate with the hospital abuse team in an effective intervention approach. Guidelines for nursing care for children with NAI are presented in Table 41-7, following the discussion of child neglect.

Communication patterns When a nurse sees a severely abused child, an emotional response occurs. This reaction is based on the nurse's personal family history, child-rearing beliefs, and protective or rescue fantasies. The nurse's reaction affects the communication patterns with the child and other members of the family. In order to be an objective and effective nurse, it is vital to recognize this reaction, determine if it is blocking communication, and find a resource to help. The nursing staff often will gather for a conference to share and learn from each other. Since an effective intervention program depends on a firm trust relationship and bonding of the family to the hospital staff, clearly nonjudgmental behavior will enhance this. Greet the parents when they visit their child. Praise them for correct actions. Gather data on their knowledge

Table 41-4 Common diagnostic tests performed on children with suspected nonaccidental injury

Blood and urine tests	Radiologic examinations	Consultations
Bleeding tests to rule out underlying diseases which cause bleeding 　Platelet count 　Prothrombin time 　Ivy bleeding time 　Partial thromboplastin time Complete blood count Urinalysis Serum amylase for traumatic pancreatitis	Skeletal survey (particularly under 3 years of age) of all bones to identify fractures Serial x-rays to date healing, identify fracture not initially seen (chip fracture) X-rays of bones to rule out pathology which allows for abnormal fracturing Contrast studies of gastrointestinal tract (useful for children with forced ingestion of caustics or duodenal or jejunal injury from blunt trauma) CAT scans of brain/trunk when trauma is suspected, e.g., to identify subdural hematoma Radioactive scan for liver, spleen, or kidney trauma	Psychologist 　Psychometric testing 　Parent interview 　Interviews with child/sibling Psychiatrist 　Parent interview 　Child interviews Neurologist 　May order EEG Physical and occupational therapist to do developmental examination Pediatrician specializing in child abuse Photographer to document evidence of abuse

Source: James Apthorp, M.D. Children's Hospital, Los Angeles.

of growth and development and discipline problems.

Common diagnostic tests

Several diagnostic tests are commonly administered to NAI children with bruises, fractures, or suspected neurological damage. Table 41-4 is a brief guide to these tests.

Neglect

Neglect, another form of child abuse, occurs when the adult caretaker either deliberately or unintentionally fails to provide the supports necessary for developing a child's physical, intellectual, and emotional capacities. One form of neglect results in failure to thrive due to environmental deprivation. There are other forms of neglect, for example: failure to secure dental or medical care when needed for prevention or treatment of disease. In this section, failure to thrive due to environmental deprivation will be detailed. Children who are under the fifth percentile for height and weight and have no evidence of any organic disease are considered for this diagnosis (Fig. 41-3).[9] Head circumference is also frequently smaller than expected for the child's age. The growth retardation is generally accompanied by some other clinical manifesta-

tion. Characteristics of neglected children are listed in Table 41-5.

Most of the examples of clinical manifestations are reportable problems, except example 9, especially when a child shows more than one manifestation. When in doubt, consult protective service workers.

Rationale for intervention

There are many *organic* (nonenvironmental) causes for failure to thrive; neglect is not involved in them. When some organic problem, such as

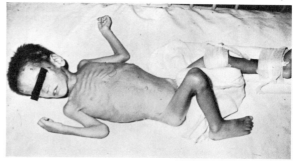

Figure 41-3 This 18-month-old infant was hospitalized for failure to thrive. No organic basis was found for the failure to gain weight. Physical examination findings included a dislocated knee. (*Courtesy of Robert W. ten Bensel, M.D.*)

Table 41-5 Clinical manifestations of neglect

1. Delayed development for age
2. Poor growth pattern
3. Poor or absent dental care
4. Chronic malnutrition, including eating excessive junk food and inadequate essential growth foods
5. Repressed personality
6. Evidence of poor supervision, e.g., repeated falls downstairs, repeated ingestions, child locked out of the house
7. Poor immunization pattern
8. Lack of medical attention for illnesses
9. Failure to protect children in motor vehicles
10. Inadequate stimulation for speech development
11. Skin problems, e.g., poor cleansing, seborrhea, impetigo and diaper rash
12. Small children left home alone
13. Unsanitary, unsafe or filthy home environment
14. Rumination
15. Marasmus
16. Chronic vomiting and/or diarrhea

intestinal malabsorption, is found in a youngster with growth failure, treatment must be initiated. When no organic problem can be found, environmental deprivation is usually the cause. If environmental deprivation occurs along with organic problems in the child, the treatment should be directed toward both problems.

Failure to thrive due to environmental deprivation can be a devastating life problem. Short-term and long-term problems of neglected children are listed in Table 41-6.

Parent characteristics

There are different kinds of parents who encourage the syndrome of failure to thrive due to environmental deprivation. Finnila et al.[7] identified five groups of parents as follows: inexperienced parents who are willing to learn, parents with low intellect, harried parents, neurotic and psychotic parents, and parents who are hostile

Table 41-6 Characteristic problems of neglected children

Short-term	Long-term
Malnutrition	Poor "catch-up growth"
Pneumonia	Mental retardation
Nonaccidental injury	Behavior problems
Disruption in brain development	Social problems
	Poor bonding with parents

toward the child. Nursing intervention varies widely according to the classification. Many parents respond quickly to a nurse's expressed acceptance and concern for themselves and their child. Neglectful parents were neglected as children and need to be bonded to the hospital staff before they can bond firmly to their child. Frequently, the parents are socially isolated and improve rapidly if a support system is created for the family.[8]

EXAMPLE: A 3-month-old boy was admitted to a medical facility because of poor weight gain, difficulty in feeding, seborrhea, severe diaper rash, and general irritability. The child was given a minimum of diagnostic tests (complete blood count, urinalysis, history, and physical examination). The 16-year-old mother, who lived alone, stated that the pregnancy, labor, and delivery had been normal (birth weight 3.15 kg, length 52.5 cm). Weight was now 3.37 kg and length 53.7 cm. The child was given well-child care (regular feeding or formula, baths, regular sleeping and cuddling periods). The mother visited her child infrequently and for short periods. She seemed to resent the baby's obvious return to health. The child gained 0.45 kg and grew 1.25 cm within a week. His skin problems and irritability disappeared.

He was transferred to a rehabilitation unit, and the nursing staff worked intensively with both the mother and child, using a variety of techniques, such as putting a radio in the child's room so that his mother would be more comfortable with her favorite music stations while feeding her baby and praising the mother when she exhibited positive mothering techniques. The nurse compared the child's handsomeness to the mother's beautiful features, giving the mother a sense of having produced a beautiful baby from her own beauty. Within 2 weeks the baby was discharged home to his mother. A support system was developed that included a lay home visitor and a special high school where the mother was enrolled while her baby was cared for in a school nursery. One year later, both mother and child were thriving.

General guidelines for nursing care of the neglected or NAI child

The guidelines in Table 41-7 are designed to define common patient problems, develop achievable patient goals, and suggest nursing interventions vital to achieving the patient's optimal health. Every child who enters the health care system is a different person and will require an individual care plan designed to meet his or her special needs.

Table 41-7 General guidelines for nursing care of children with neglect or nonaccidental injury

Patient problem and goal	Nursing actions
Growth delay: child will gain weight during hospitalization	Develop a baseline assessment and assessment of admission height and weight
	Interview parents regarding feeding patterns and types and amount of food taken at home
	Feed child a balanced diet appropriate for age
	Feed on demand unless child does not communicate hunger, then on schedule
	Weigh child daily
	Document food intake and response to feeding
	Hold infant for all feedings
	Provide eye contact and verbal communication during feeding
	Observe and record parent's feeding behavior with child
	Gently teach parent successful feeding behavior
	Reward successful feeding behavior when demonstrated by the parent
Developmental delay: child will show age-appropriate developmental milestones	Interview parents regarding developmental history (especially milestones)
	Assess and document current activity pattern, muscle strength, usual play interests and activities
	Provide verbal, tactile, and motor stimulation appropriate for age
	Vary toys, stimulation, and location regularly
Physical trauma: child will have maximum healing, recovery, and protection from bodily injury	Observe and document unusual physical findings
	Record the parent's explanation of the child's injuries
	Monitor all visitors in a discrete manner
	Observe and record parent-child communication
	Maintain a friendly, accepting attitude when dealing with parents
	Maintain a calm, gentle approach when giving care to child
	Identify and document family problems
	Teach normal well-child care, effective and safe discipline, and realistic expectations of behavior for age
	Guide parents in safety and accident prevention
Emotional deprivation and trauma: child will develop trust in and attachment to significant people	Assess and document parent-child interaction, child's affect, child's attachment behavior, and sibling interaction
	Assign consistent nursing personnel
	Secure social history, especially any problems promoting parental mistreatment, e.g., loss of job, drinking problem
	Provide substitute parenting and emotional stimulation
	Cuddle, hold, touch, and make eye contact for planned periods each day
	Respond immediately to crying
	Teach parent by example to comfort and play with child
Inadequate social situation: parents will have resources to utilize during crises	Introduce family to resources to use as lifelines in stress and crisis situations
	Assist family to utilize psychotherapies and self-help groups for more effective family function
	Assist families to identify physical environmental problems, e.g., housing, finances
	Assist parents to solve these environmental problems
Parenting inabilities and inadequacy	Assess and document parents' capabilities and inabilities by observation of parent behavior
	Accept the parents as worthy human beings capable of change
	Develop parents' trust: assign a staff person on each shift to act as a liaison
	Identify parent characteristics that prevent nurturing
	Reinforce parents' self-image
	Teach parents behaviors that strengthen their weak areas

Table 41-7 General guidelines for nursing care of children with neglect or nonaccidental injury (*Continued*)

Patient problem and goal	Nursing actions
Home care/long-term follow-up: parents will provide a safe, stimulating, and pleasant home environment for their children	Introduce parents to long-term treatment program while child is still in hospital Participate in the discharge planning for the child Inform the parents that child abuse is a long-term problem and needs long-term treatment Provide opportunities for parents and child regularly to discuss details of the treatment program Utilize the juvenile court social workers to promote compliance with the treatment plan Encourage parents to utilize foster care and adoption services if they decide not to participate in a treatment program and don't wish to keep their child Give them support if they make this decision

Sources: Mary Andrews, R.N., and Audrey H. Beatty, Director of Nursing, Children's Hospital, Los Angeles, "Standards of Care for Children with Failure to Thrive Syndrome," unpublished paper, 1977.

Audry Edberg, R.N., Clinical Coordinator of Rehabilitation Unit, Children's Hospital, Los Angeles, "Standards of Care for Children with Battered Child Syndrome," unpublished paper, 1977.

Sexual abuse

Sexual abuse is using a child for sexual gratification. It also includes allowing another person to use the child sexually, creating emotional and physical damage to the child.

Sexual abuse, thought by researchers to be more prevalent than NAI, is beginning to be widely identified. Innovative treatment programs are being established throughout the country. Sexually abused children are rarely hospitalized because they lack obvious external injuries. The following clinical manifestations should initiate measures to rule out or confirm sexual abuse.

1. A child becomes pregnant and the father of the baby is an adult.
2. Pornographic pictures involving a child have been taken.
3. A child seeks help for incest: a girl with an adult man, either the natural father or stepfather, or a boy with a stepfather (or, rarely, a boy with a natural mother or father). An uncle or other relative may be the abusing adult.
4. A child complains about adults getting overly friendly and "touchy" with him or her.
5. A child develops a vaginal discharge.
6. A child is raped or experiences oral or anal copulation and may have multiple bruises, lacerations, or bleeding.
7. A parent describes "deep kissing" with a child.

EXAMPLE: A 14-year-old girl runs away from home to an adult friend nearby. When questioned by the friend, she confesses in a guilt-ridden manner that she can no longer tolerate her father's "fooling around with her." After a police investigation and emergence of a treatment plan, the family (mother, father, and girl) gets individual and group therapy. The incest patterns stops, and a healthier family pattern develops.

EXAMPLE: A 4-year-old girl is seen in the emergency room exhibiting dirty skin and clothing, a discharge and hair in her underpants, and a frightened, watchful countenance. The mother brought her child to the emergency room to "fix" her boyfriend, with whom she was angry. The child was admitted to the hospital, where she improved immensely in physical and emotional health. After assessment, the family was felt to be "unworkable" and the child was placed in a foster home until she could be relinquished by the parents and adopted by a stable family.

Treatment of incest

A model treatment center has been established in Santa Clara County, California,[9] which has treated 300 families to date, with remarkable success. The father is usually in prison on a felony charge; the daughter is overwhelmed by guilt, fear, and anger and may exhibit self-abusive behavior; and the mother may be tormented by similar emotions. The siblings are confused and disturbed by the family crisis. The financial resources are spent, and the usual family support system is dissolved because of the revulsion and embarrassment of friends and relatives. In this program, all family members are immediately taken into a psychotherapy program. An important adjunct is assistance in locating community resources for housing, employment, financial aid, and legal assistance.

At first, only court-referred cases were involved in this treatment process. Now, self-referrals and those from voluntary agencies are accepted. With this treatment protocol, no reabuse has been reported, the children are returned sooner to their families, the self-abusive behavior of the girls is reduced, more marriages are saved (about 90 percent), and healthful father-daughter relationships are reestablished.

Nurses are beginning to take an active role in the referral or treatment of sexually abused children and their families.[10] Nurses are responsible for health interviewing, physical examination, counseling, education, collection of legal evidence for providing expert court testimony, and locating community resources for families. The nurse always stresses to the child that the sexual experience is not the child's fault.

For nurses interested in developing care plans for the sexually assaulted child, especially in the school and emergency room settings, Gorline and Ray's article (see References) will be helpful. The use of children's drawings to elicit a history and express feelings is especially innovative. See Chap. 20 for emergency care of rape victims.

Emotional Abuse

Emotional abuse is intellectual and psychological damage, inflicted either deliberately or by neglect, which is evidenced by observable damage to the child's ability to perform.[11] Common clinical manifestations of emotional abuse are listed in Table 41-8. Emotional abuse is included in most of the state child abuse laws but has been utilized very little to protect children. Over the next decade, as the process of emotional abuse is further studied, more children will be protected. Emotional abuse accompanies physical abuse and neglect.

Clinical manifestations

When discussing the child's signs and symptoms and the behavior of the parents, the terms *emotional disturbance* and *emotional abuse* become inseparable. Not all childhood emotional disturbances are linked to abuse, of course, as is clear in the example of a child's chronic grief reaction to a parent's death. Morever, mentally retarded parents or some other people may not understand that they are damaging their child by their child-rearing methods.

Health care personnel who can communicate with families in a friendly, nonjudgmental manner, expressing interest in both parent and child, will succeed in improving the emotional health of the child. Some families refuse to be treated. The family that is emotionally battering a child and refusing help or ignoring pleas from con-

Table 41-8 Sample parental behaviors that lead to emotional abuse of children

Parent behavior	Child behavior	
	If parent gives too little	If parent gives too much
Love	Poor growth	Overconfidence
	Poor self-steem	Overprotection
	Depression	Passivity
	Withdrawal	
Intellectual stimulation	Academic failure	Hyperactivity
	Development delay	"Stressed" student
Stability	Lack of trust	Inflexibility
Limits (moral and social)	Tantrums	Fearfulness
	Antisocial behavior	Lack of creativity

Source: Ira S. Lourie and Lorrain Stephana, "On Defining Emotional Abuse: Results of a NIMH/NCCAN Workshop," *Child Abuse and Neglect*, vol. 1, April 17–20, 1977, pp. 201–208. Chart designed by workshop members.

cerned friends, relatives, and health and educational personnel will necessitate legal intervention.

Nursing interventions with verbally assaultive parents

Verbal assault is one common form of emotional abuse. A large number of children are exposed to ridicule, shaming, threatened violence, and threatened withdrawal of love. The following statements are examples of assaultive language:

"My God, you're clumsy."
"I'm going to kill you!"
"What are you, deaf or something?"
"You're going to get hit 'til you're black and blue."
"I'm going to beat the shit out of you!"
"When you grow up, you're not going to amount to a hill of beans."
"Come here, stupid."
"Mommy won't love you anymore if you're bad."
"I don't want you, I don't love you, get lost!"

Sometimes only one child is selected for abuse in a family, and siblings join the parents in attacking that child. The end result of many years of this environment can be an adult with a very poor self-concept, little motivation for educational achievement or gainful employment, and some emotional disturbance.

EXAMPLE: Bob's mother, Barbara, was a lonely 25-year-old woman with a poor educational background (in relation to her family) when she met Joe at a roadside coffee stand. She conceived a child by him and subsequently married him, despite her family's concern about his suitability as a husband. Bob was a difficult child to feed and comfort from birth. Barbara's parents were ashamed of the inappropriate timing of the birth and offered limited support. The marriage broke up after 2 years, and Barbara quickly married again. She bore three children by her second husband. Verbal assault had begun when Bob was 1 year old and starting to walk. The siblings quickly learned to continue the parents's verbally abusive pattern when communicating with Bob, but they themselves were rarely verbally abused. Bob did poorly in school but was "pushed along" until he graduated from high school. At 21 years of age, he is living at home with his parents, is unemployed, has few friends, and aspires to become a writer of murder mysteries. He physically abuses his mother if she opposes him. She admits she is afraid of him. Both Bob's parents and Bob refuse to go for counseling.

When the nurse identifies a parent who is verbally abusive to a child, intervention is needed. Some suggestions for dealing with the parent (after a trust relationship is established) follow.

1. Encourage the parents to join Parents Anonymous, a parent self-help group which very effectively helps families who use verbal abuse. To do this, of course, parents must realize the consequences of this type of behavior and wish to change.
2. Give time and attention to the parents, using interviewing techniques and allowing them freedom to express their concerns, worries, and doubts.
3. Provide a lay volunteer, preferably a parent of similar age, to spend time with the family and to show them alternative responses to children, a different life-style, and an improved self-concept.
4. Teach or encourage parents to attend parent education classes where child care theories and practices are taught.
5. Encourage enrollment in a parent participation nursery school where the parents observe and practice under a skilled teacher.
6. Talk with a child protective service worker about the family, filing a formal report if requested.

Verbal abuse is usually considered a mild form of child abuse and is not usually prosecuted by the juvenile court. The long-range effects of this behavior can be crippling to a child and should be prevented or stopped if possible. The parent who verbally abuses a child is usually a needy person who will respond to an empathic, caring nurse.

Institutional abuse

Institutional abuse is abuse or neglect while a child is permanently or temporarily under the care of some group other than his or her family. Such care settings include hospitals, schools, shelters, detention centers, camps, and communes. The following are examples of institutional abuse.

1. A 5-year-old boy in a group home for emotionally disturbed boys has his arm fractured by an attendant.
2. A 10-year-old girl taken to a shelter facility suffers a detached retina from a fight with another child.
3. A 7-year-old, moderately retarded boy lies in a crib all day and night without stimulation and with minimal care.

4. A child in a religious commune is taken to a pit near a jungle and threatened with fake snakes and gruesome stories for being "bad."
5. A 9-year-old girl is belt-whipped in a public school for using foul language.
6. A child is placed in restraints to prevent night wandering in an institution for mentally retarded children.

Abuse and neglect should be reported to the supervisor. Suggestions of ways to improve patient care should be included in the written and oral reports. Reporting abuse creates a difficult position for a nurse, since harassment and loss of job may result. The American Nurses' Association may offer assistance to the nurse.

References

1. Ann W. Shyne and Anita G. Shroeder, "National Study of Social Services to Children and Their Families," National Center for Child Advocacy, U.S. Children's Bureau: Department of Health, Education, and Welfare, Washington, D.C., Pub. No. 78-30149, 1978.
2. Jane D. Gray, Christy A. Culter, Janet G. Dean, and C. Henry Kempe, "Prediction and Prevention of Child Abuse and Neglect," in M. L. Lauderdale et al. (eds.), *Child Abuse and Neglect: Issues on Innovation and Implementation*, vol. 1, Department of Health, Education, and Welfare, Washington, D.C., (CHDS), Pub. No. 78-30147, pp. 246–254, 1978.
3. S. C. Burchell (ed.), *Age of Progress*, Time-Life Books, New York, 1966, pp. 73–82.
4. *Encyclopedia Americana*, international ed., vol. 6, American Corporation, New York, 1964, pp. 461–464.
5. Garry B. McLain, "The Prevention and/or Treatment of Child Abuse in Head Start: An Eclectic, Ecologic Hypothesis," in M. L. Lauderdale et al. (eds.), *Child Abuse and Neglect: Issues on Innovation and Implementation*, vol. 2, Department of Health, Education, and Welfare, Washington, D.C., (CHDS), Pub. No.78-30147, pp. 19-32, 1978.
6. J. Kent, H. Weisberg, B. Lamar, and T. Marx, "Kent Data Child Abuse Cluster," unpublished paper, Children's Hospital, Los Angeles, 1977, pp. 1–10.
7. Mona C. Finnila, Robert Jacobs, and William Bucher, "Failure to Thrive Protocol," unpublished paper, Department of Psychiatry, Children's Hospital, Los Angeles, 1974, p. 3.
8. Ibid.
9. Henry Giaretta, "The Treatment of Father–Daughter Incest," *Children Today* 5:26, 34–35 (1976).
10. Lynne Lesak Gorline and Mary Moore Ray, "Examining and Caring for the Child Who Has Been Sexually Assaulted," *The American Journal of Maternal Child Nursing*, March-April: 110–114 (1979).
11. Henry L. Barnett and Arnold H. Einhorn, *Pediatrics*, 15th ed., Appleton-Century-Crofts, New York, 1972, pp. 575–577.

Chapter 42 **Substance abuse**

Christy Yapuncich

Upon completion of this chapter, the student will be able to:

1. Assess and analyze personal attitudes toward drug use by completing the self-assessment questionnaire.

2. Compare the following categories of drug usage: (a) nonuser, (b) experimental-occasional user, (c) recreational-regular user, (d) abuser, and (e) chemically dependent user.

3. Identify the four fundamentals of drug action and illustrate each with an example.

4. Identify and compare the major physiological action, side effects, and symptoms of overdosage and withdrawal for each of the following drug classifications: (a) narcotics, (b) depressants, (c) stimulants, (d) hallucinogens, (e) cannabis, and (f) inhalant-solvents.

5. Identify four major factors causing substance abuse during adolescence.

6. Compare nursing interventions for a patient with severe psychological side effects with interventions for a patient in withdrawal.

7. Identify the major components of a nursing assessment of a drug abuse patient.

8. List the six nursing intervention steps of a confrontation technique.

9. Compare and contrast the advantages and disadvantages of small discussion groups with the lecture style of teaching adolescents about drugs.

10. Identify the nurse's role in preventing drug abuse in the family, school, and community.

Since the late 1960s, the growing use of illicit mood-altering substances among children and adolescents has become a national health concern. Young teenagers today are using alcohol and other drugs in almost the same percentage as the adult population. Hospitals, schools, mental health centers, juvenile correctional institutions, youth centers, and other medical and social service agencies have been confused and unprepared to meet the complicated and acute health care needs of young people and families involved in substance abuse problems. Emergency rooms are now dealing routinely with a large variety of crises caused by ingestion of substances such as alcohol, tranquilizers, phencyclidine (PCP), and paint thinner. School teachers and school nurses must frequently respond to the needs of young students who pass out, overdose, or disrupt the classroom with occasionally violent behavior. In the last 5 to 8 years, urban and rural mental health centers across the United States have had to develop prevention, education, and treatment programs. These programs deliver services to less than 10 percent of the adolescents who urgently need them. In short, substance abuse is widespread among young people and constitutes a major health care challenge.

This chapter will examine the prevalence and patterns of adolescent drug usage, discuss theories of causation, describe the psychopharmacology of the substances used, misused, and abused, and describe the nursing management of the substance abuse patient.

Definitions

People can be grouped into five categories on the basis of their drug use.

1. *Nonuser-abstainer.* This person totally abstains from all mood-altering substances except perhaps tobacco and coffee. Mood-altering drugs may be used if prescribed by a physician, however. Obviously, nonusers are very rarely treated for any alcohol or other drug problems. They comprise 5 percent of the adult population.

2. *Experimenter-occasional user* This person infrequently uses alcohol or other drugs in moderation for social and recreational purposes. *Experimentation,* the first use of a particular drug, occurs frequently among children in junior high school. Use is not experimental when it exceeds one or two separate occasions. Experimental and occasional users account for 20 percent of the adult population. These adults are rarely treated for substance use problems; many more adolescents than adults in this category are treated for crisis and emergency situations related to their initial use of a drug.

3. *Recreational-regular user* People in this category have integrated regular drug use into their life-style to enhance the quality of social and recreational experiences. The frequency, quantity, and kinds of chemicals used vary. The person has individual standards and appropriate control for usage which reflect the surrounding culture. This type of user may experience an isolated, occasional problem requiring medical services. The recreational user comprises 45 to 50 percent of the adult population.

4. *Abuser* This person's substance use is characterized by (a) increasingly frequent ingestion, (b) ingestion of excessive amounts, (c) use in violation of social norms, and (d) physical or social problems related to drug use. This category includes 10 to 15 percent of the adult population.

   It is estimated that one in four teenagers today will have severe problems associated with abuse of alcohol or other drugs.[1,2] Physiological problems such as overdoses, "bad trips," abscesses, convulsions, coma, hyperactivity, malnutrition, cirrhosis, hepatitis, or bronchitis may be evidence of drug use. Psychological problems, truancy, behavioral and academic problems in school, family deterioration, and many legal problems are also common with drug abuse. The complex problems and pressures of adolescence precipitate and promote substance abuse.

5. *Chemically dependent user* Chemical dependency, formerly called *addiction,* is a primary, progressive, chronic, and ultimately fatal disease process.[3] Addicted persons constitute 10 percent of the adult population. Chemical dependency is a behavior disorder characterized by repeated ingestion of mood-altering chemicals that exceeds customary use within the community. It causes repeated physiological, psychological, social, and spiritual problems.[4] Chemical dependency is characterized by intense denial by the young person, his or her family, and friends. It is a treatable illness when diagnosed and treated within a holistic framework. Lack of awareness and delay in obtaining treatment are the largest deterrents to recovery. Communities deny adolescents' chemical dependency even more than that of adults. Community educational programs are still greatly needed to reduce substance abuse. Indications of chemical dependency are listed in Table 42-1.

The action of drugs

Pharmacology is the study of the effects drugs have on living organisms; *psychopharmacology* deals with the effects of psychoactive (mood-altering) drugs. The many varieties of psychoactive drugs are classified by their specific pharmacologic properties and by society's attitude toward them.[5] Four basic principles apply to all drugs:

1. *No drug is good or bad.* All drugs have the potential for good and bad effects. All drugs can be used constructively under appropriate circumstances, and all can be misused and abused. Tranquilizers, narcotics, barbiturates, and amphetamines are beneficial when used under medical supervision but can be very dangerous when self-administered for nonmedicinal purposes. Alcohol, volatile substances such as aerosol deodorants and hair sprays, and solvents such as glue and gasoline are useful products, but not for inhaling.

2. *Every drug has multiple effects.* All drugs act on different parts of the central nervous system to produce a wide range of effects. Depressants produce some excitatory effects, and stimulants ultimately produce depression. Hallucinogens cause complex emotional responses in addition to perceptual alterations.

3. *The effects of a drug depend on the dose.* Varying the dose changes both the magnitude and the

character of effects. The abuse potential of a drug increases in proportion to the dose. Certain dose levels constitute abuse, while others do not.

4. *The effect of a drug depends on the individual user and the circumstances under which it is taken.* Any

Table 42-1 Signs of chemical dependency

Physical status

Evidence of drug-related health problems (gastritis, hepatitis, etc.)
Changes in daily or hourly activity levels; alert and active at one time, tired and subdued the next
Neglected personal appearance
Frequent symptoms resembling influenza or coryza

Truancy

Chronic tardiness
Excessive absences (with or without pattern)
Leaving class early (with or without excuse)

Attitude

Low motivation and loss of interest
Hostile reaction when criticized
Frequent arguments
Extreme negativism
Stereotyped thinking
Denial of any problem
Low self-esteem
Remorseful, promises to change

Academic performance

Lower grades or lower achievement over a period of time

Contact with others

Avoids contact with family
Spends less time at home (time at home is spent alone in room or basement)
Schedules but does not arrive for appointments
Avoids talking about or minimizes drug use with adults but brags to peers

Chemical use

Frequent use and intoxication
Hides chemicals
Finds different ways to use drugs
Uses drugs in the morning, at school, or at work

Other behaviors

Involvement in arguments, fights, thefts, or other illegal activity
Noticeable change of friends over a period of time (new friends tend to use more known or suspected chemical subtances than old ones)
Obvious signs of being under the influence of a drug (smell of alcohol or other chemicals, inappropriate walking or movement, altered speech or inappropriate verbal responses)
Absenteeism, low job performance, or repeated job loss

psychoactive drug's effect is influenced by the user's environment, history, and makeup. Expectations of the drug's effect can significantly affect the user's perception of the experience. The following factors affect the drug's action in the body: body size, time of administration, route of administration, tolerance, dose, psychological state, physiological state, and rate of absorption.[6]

Classification of substances

Psychoactive drugs are classified according to eight factors:

1. The drug's actual or potential abuse factor
2. Scientific evidence of its pharmacologic effect
3. The exactness of current scientific knowledge regarding each substance
4. Its history and present pattern of abuse
5. The scope, duration, and significance of abuse
6. The risk to public health
7. Its physiological and psychological dependence liability
8. Whether the substance is an immediate precursor of an already classified substance[7]

Substances abused by children and adolescents are divided into six categories: (1) narcotics, (2) depressants, (3) stimulants, (4) hallucinogens, (5) cannabis, and (6) inhalant-solvents.

Narcotics

The term *narcotic* refers to opium and opium derivatives or synthetic substitutes. Narcotics include opium, morphine sulfate (morphine), dihydromorphinone hydrochloride (Dilaudid), codeine phosphate (codeine), meperidine hydrochloride (Demerol), methadone hydrochloride (methadone), oxycodone hydrochloride (Percodan), and pentazocine (Talwin). These drugs are the most effective pain-relieving agents known. They can be taken orally or by intramuscular injection.

As *"street drugs"* or drugs of abuse, narcotics can be snorted (inhaled), smoked, or injected either subcutaneously ("skin popping") or intravenously ("mainlining"). Narcotics have the highest potential for physiological and psychological addiction. Patients can become addicted in 1 week if drugs are taken daily in increasing dosages. Tolerance is developed rapidly. Withdrawal is acute and should be supervised by experienced medical personnel. The initial effects of these drugs are often unpleasant and may include nausea. Symptoms of narcotic intoxication (overdose) include pupillary contraction, drowsiness, slowed movements, apathy, euphoria, constipation, attention and memory impairment, and depressed vital signs. Excessive dosages may result in life-threatening emergencies: shock, coma, and death due to respiratory failure.

The withdrawal symptoms associated with narcotic addiction are watery eyes, runny nose, fatigue, loss of appetite, irritability, tremors, panic, chills, sweating, cramps, and nausea. Vital signs are elevated above normal limits. Complaints, pleas, and demands for the drug by the addict usually accompany the withdrawal syndrome. The withdrawal symptoms peak at 48 to 72 h after the last ingestion. Most of the symptoms disappear in 7 to 10 days. It may take weeks to restore fully physiological and psychological equilibrium. The withdrawal syndrome can be controlled by reducing the dose over a prolonged (1- to 3-week) period.[8]

Addicts often suffer a variety of other health problems caused by their excessive and unregulated use of narcotics. Malnutrition, infections, hepatitis, blood poisoning, and abscesses resulting from using dirty needles are seen frequently.

Depressants

These drugs depress the central nervous system by inhibiting the sending and receiving of messages by the nerve cells. Alcohol, tranquilizers, barbiturates, and hypnotic-sedatives are depressants. Examples include pentobarbital sodium (Nembutol), secobarbital sodium (Seconal), glutethimide (Doriden), diazepam (Valium), chlordiazepoxide hydrochloride (Librium), meprobamate (Miltown), and ethchlorvynol (Placidyl). They are prescribed for relief of acute anxiety, irritability, tension, and insomnia.

Alcohol Alcohol is the major social lubricant of our culture. The use of beer, wine, or liquor as an enhancer of a social occasion has been accepted and promoted for thousands of years. Alcohol is a drug, the only drug sanctioned by our society for social use. Its use varies widely from appropriate moderate usage to addiction, or *alcoholism*.

Alcohol is absorbed through the stomach and small intestine and then travels throughout the body. The rate of absorption is influenced by the amount of alcohol ingested, the speed of ingestion, the presence or absence of food in the stomach, and body weight. The effect of alcohol in the body is determined not only by the amount ingested but primarily by its concentration in the blood. This concentration can be measured and is called the *blood alcohol level* (BAL). The BAL is the number of grams of alcohol in each 100 ml of blood and is expressed as a percentage: 100 mg of alcohol in 100 ml of blood is reported as 0.1 percent. Behavioral impairment is noted when the BAL is at this level. A BAL of 0.2 to 0.25 percent is accompanied by extreme intoxication, and a BAL of 0.3 percent and over produces stupor or coma and, potentially, death (see Table 42-2).

Alcohol intoxication, or *inebriation*, is evidenced by slurred speech, incoordination, unsteady gait, mood lability (mood swings), uninhibited sexual and aggressive impulses, impaired judgment, and nausea. Alcohol intoxication sometimes produces *blackouts*, or amnesia, for events occurring while the individual was fully alert. Both psychological and physiological tolerance are produced by repeated frequent ingestion, potentially resulting in dependency.

The withdrawal syndrome begins shortly after the cessation of drinking, reaches its peak in 72 h, and disappears within 5 to 7 days. Withdrawal is characterized by tremors, nausea, vomiting, malaise, tachycardia, sweating, elevated blood pressure, anxiety, depression, insomnia, and grand mal seizures.

Chronic heavy usage of alcohol can produce other related disorders, such as Korsakoff syndrome, fetal alcohol syndrome, malnutrition, hepatitis, cirrhosis, gastritis, and heart disease.[9]

Other depressants The psychopharmacology of the other depressants (tranquilizers, barbiturates, and hypnotic-sedatives) is almost identical to that of alcohol. Depressant intoxication is characterized by slurred speech, incoordination, unsteady gait, mood lability, impaired judgment, and sedation. Tolerance develops rapidly, leading to a dangerously narrow margin of safety between an intoxicating and a lethal dose. When alcohol is used in combination with depressants, the effects are *synergistic*, that is, each drug increases the effectiveness of the other. Thus it may be dangerous and even become lethal to use alcohol in combination with other depressants.

The withdrawal from depressants is similar to alcohol withdrawal but is often far more acute. The cessation or reduction of high dosages of depressant should be treated as a serious med-

ical emergency. Detoxification and treatment must be carried out under medical supervision.

Stimulants

Stimulants excite, or stimulate, the sending and receiving of messages in the central nervous system. The two most prevalent stimulants are nicotine and caffeine. Because of their low potency levels and over-the-counter availability, they are not classified as controlled substances. More potent stimulants (cocaine, amphetamines, dexadrine, Preludin, Ritalin, etc.) are legally used for treatment of pain, narcolepsy, and hyperactivity (and, formerly, for short-term weight loss). Tolerance develops rapidly. These drugs are psychologically addicting but not physically addicting.

Many young people use stimulants to feel stronger, more mentally and physically fit, alert, and euphoric; some also use them for weight loss. Entertainers often use stimulants to give a "high" performance. Stimulant users are quickly reinforced for their behavior by our achievement-at-any-cost society. They enjoy the drug-induced exhilaration and euphoria and tend to repeat use frequently.

The symptoms and signs of stimulant intoxication are fine tremors, elation, feelings of grandeur, talkativeness, hyperactivity, resistance to fatigue, anxiety, mood swings, and physiological irritability (tachycardia, elevated pulse and blood pressure, nausea, anorexia, dilated pupils, and insomnia).[10]

Stimulants can be snorted, as is usual with "coke" (cocaine), ingested orally, or injected. Snorting may cause necrosis of the nasal septum. The heavier user generally develops a pattern of heavy use for a period of several days followed by a period of depression known as "crashing." Many times, the heavier stimulant user combines tranquilizers or other "downers" with use of "uppers." The side effects or complications associated with stimulant abuse are paranoia, tremors, malnutrition, depression, hostile behavior, and psychosis.

Hallucinogens

The hallucinogens dramatically distort one's perception of reality. They act on the central nervous system by interrupting the flow of messages sent from one site to another. These substances grow naturally or are manufactured. The medical

Table 42-2 Blood alcohol levels correlated with behavioral changes

Blood alcohol level	Drinks consumed	Behavioral effects
0.04%	1–2	Lowered alertness Release of inhibitions Relaxation Increased heart rate
0.06%	3–4	Impaired judgment Loss of coordination Apathy
0.10%	5–6	Impaired motor function Exaggerated emotions Clumsiness Impaired vision Impaired ability to drive a car
0.16%	6–8	Staggering Slurred speech Blurred vision Serious loss of judgment and coordination
0.20%	8–10	Sensory depression Mood swings Difficulty maintaining balance Double vision
0.30%	10–15	Uninhibited behavior Stupor and confusion Rowdy, unrestrained, or combative behavior Reality disorientation
0.40–0.50%	15–25	Loss of feeling Unconsciousness Shock
0.50%+	25+	Coma Death

Source: Adapted from Brent Q. Hafen, *Alcoholism: The Crutch that Cripples*, West Publishing, St. Paul, Minn., 1977. p. 41.

usage of such drugs has proven to be ineffective. Therefore, all synthetic hallucinogens are prepared in "home laboratories," and the exact content of these chemicals is never known. Peyote, mescaline, and psilocybin are found naturally as well as manufactured. Synthetic hallucinogens include LSD (lysergic acid diethylamide) or "acid," MDA and DOM (a combination of hallucinogen and a stimulant), and phencyclidine (PCP or "angel dust"). Hallucinogens can be ingested, injected, or smoked. They are not physically addicting, but they do produce psychological tolerance. The drug action is relatively long-term, with a "trip" lasting anywhere from 8 to 12 h.

The symptoms of hallucinogenic intoxication include perceptual distortions, *depersonalization* (a feeling of being outside the body), hallucinations, illusions, overattention to detail, anxiety, depression, fear of insanity, paranoia, and interference with judgment and functioning. Physical symptoms include sweating, pupillary dilation, increased pulse, and blood pressure fluctuations. The hallucinogenic experience is heavily influenced by the setting and by the user's expectations and personality. The hallucinations often focus on vivid color and forms, and voices are heard. A complication associated with this group of drugs is the phenomenon called *flashbacks*—fragmentary recurrences of the psychedelic effects long after hallucinogens are eliminated from the body.[11] Hallucinogens are highly unpredictable in their effects each time they are used.

Cannabis

Cannabis sativa, the hemp plant, grows wild throughout most of the tropic and temperate regions of the world. This plant contains delta-9-tetra-hydrocannabinal (THC), the psychoactive agent in the plant. Cannabis products, called *marijuana, hashish, Thai sticks,* and *hash oil*, are usually smoked in a hand-rolled cigarette called a *joint* or in a pipe, "bong," or water pipe. They are used alone or in combination with other substances. The effects are felt within minutes of inhaling, usually reach a peak in 10 to 30 min, and may linger for 2 h. Marijuana has been used throughout history for a variety of medical reasons, but not as extensively as opium. Its use had been strictly controlled by the Marijuana Tax Act of 1937; this act was declared unconsti-

tutional in 1969. Recent research indicates that marijuana may prove therapeutically effective (1) in the treatment of glaucoma by successfully reducing the fluid pressure in the eye; (2) in reducing the severe nausea caused by certain drugs used to treat cancer; and (3) in offering respiratory relief when taken during acute asthmatic attacks.

Marijuana is used as a "soft drug" by a large percentage of adolescents today. The marijuana "high" (being "stoned") is characterized psychologically by a dream state, mild euphoria, intensified perceptions, slowed sense of time, and apathy. Physiological effects are tachycardia, reddened, irritated conjunctivae, increased appetite, impaired motor coordination, and dry mouth. Most experts agree that infrequent usage of marijuana in low doses is relatively harmless. Chronic usage can produce impaired judgment and memory, chronic bronchial congestion, lack of motivation, and paranoid behavior.

The scientific debate continues on the long-term health effects caused by chronic, frequent use of marijuana. The most recent research classifies potential health problems into four major areas:

1. *The production of chromosome abnormalities* It has been proven clinically that moderate use of marijuana does not cause changes in the physical structure of the brain. However, research and clinical reports on chromosome changes disagree; some studies find abnormalities, others do not. Other drugs have a dose-related effect on chromosomes; marijuana probably does, too. It is very unwise for a pregnant woman to use marijuana or any nonessential drugs at any dose level because of possible effects on the fetus.

2. *The effects on testosterone levels in males* Significant clinical evidence finds that marijuana use reduces testosterone levels in males. Marijuana's effect on estrogen levels in the female is still unclear. Temporary impotence has been shown to occur. Chronic, heavy marijuana use clearly interferes with sexual development in pubescent males.

3. *The effects on the immune system of the body* Although there is controversy, marijuana use seemingly suppresses the immune system. Currently, marijuana users do not show a higher incidence of viral infections (other than low-grade bronchitis) or cancer. Significant long-term effects,

as with nicotine, will be more clearly known in the years to come.

4. *The effects on motivation and attitude* Marijuana affects the area of the brainstem that controls motivation. The introspective, passive, nonaggressive behaviors induced by heavy marijuana use will have a significant effect on those individuals and perhaps even on our culture.[12]

Inhalant-solvents

Inhalants are substances, usually household items, that produce a short-term high or "rush" when their toxic fumes are inhaled. Substances usually inhaled or "sniffed" by the user are nitrous oxide ("laughing gas"), ether, chloroform, amyl nitrate ("poppers"), and freon-containing aerosol cans. Solvents are usually household items extracted from petroleum. Examples of solvents are gasoline, cleaning fluids, glue, rubber cement, and products containing a variety of toxic chemicals such as benzene and toluene. Aerosol nonstick coatings for cooking utensils used to produce a most desired high for the inhalant-solvent abuser. The FDA has limited the use of freon in aerosol containers. This has effectively limited the availability of inhalant substances on the grocery market shelf.

Because inhalant solvents are immediately and widely available, grade school children and many adolescents have experimented with and regularly use these toxic substances. When inhaled, these substances produce a rush characterized by intense feelings of exhilaration, increased heart rate, hallucinations, loss of consciousness and, sometimes, death. Solvents cause freezing damage to the lungs, laryngeal spasms, and anoxia. Because *none* of these substances is meant to be inhaled, clinical research on the effects of inhalant-solvents is scanty. Chronic brain damage in users has been documented.[13]

The potential health problems of *any* user of these substances are immediate and grave. Detection of inhalation abuses is difficult. Any adult should be concerned about a peculiar chemical odor on a child, wet or damp handkerchiefs or tissues or plastic bags that smell similarly, or any inhalant substances among a child's belongings. Storekeepers should report any sudden increase in young people's purchases of these products to an appropriate health department. All children should be extensively educated on the *extreme* danger of using inhalant-solvents.

Prevalence and patterns of young people's substance use

The *Third Annual Special Report on Alcohol and Health* published in 1978 reported alcoholism and alcohol abuse problems in one out of every five teenagers.[14] Simultaneously, the National Institute on Drug Abuse reported other drug abuse problems in one out of every four teenagers.[15] The HEW* *Report to Congress on Alcohol and Health* reported:[16]

Ninety-three percent of students have used alcohol at some time during their lives. There are 3.3 million problem drinkers among adolescents between the ages of 14 to 17, which accounts for 19 percent of that age group.

Since 1965 there has been a steady increase in the proportion of students getting drunk. In 1966, 19 percent claimed to have been drunk at some time; in 1975, 45 percent claimed to have been drunk. Recent surveys indicate that this figure has risen to over 60 percent.

Eighty-seven percent of senior high school students reported usage of alcohol in the past 4 weeks.

Nineteen percent of teenagers today claim getting drunk in the last 4 weeks.

Sixty percent of people killed in drunk driving accidents are teenagers.

The frequent to heavy adolescent drug user will most likely combine alcohol with one or more substances from another drug category. The person who uses alcohol *and* other drugs is defined as a *multisubstance* user, as compared to a *polydrug* user (who uses only drugs other than alcohol) or the person who uses only alcohol. Extensive multisubstance usage is one of the major problematic characteristics of this age group, and the long-term results of this pattern of usage have not been studied.

A NIDA research study conducted from 1975 to 1977[17] noted the following:

Sixty-two percent of high school seniors report illicit drug use at some time in their lives. Twenty-five percent of that sample report marijuana usage only.

Marijuana is the second most widely used substance by this age group after alcohol, with 93 percent citing alcohol use and 56 percent reporting marijuana use at some time in their lives.

* Now the Education Department and the Department of Health and Human Services.

Thirty-six percent of high school seniors reported usage of illicit drugs other than marijuana. Stimulants are the most widely used, followed by tranquilizers-sedatives, hallucinogens, inhalant-solvents, and narcotics, respectively.

Just over 9 percent indicate *daily* marijuana use.

Regional differences in terms of illicit drug use among high school seniors are slight.

Overall illicit drug use is highest (54 percent) in the largest metropolitan areas.

An adolescent who does *not* use mood-altering substances is today in the minority, in contrast to 10 years ago, when adolescent drug use was growing but still a minor trend. Recent research clearly indicates that adolescent drug use can be expected to continue increasing. More young people are using more substances more frequently and are starting at a younger age. At the Adolescent Chemical Dependency Program of St. Mary's Hospital in Minneapolis, the average age of patients dropped from 17 years in 1972 to 16.6 years in 1976 and 15.2 years in 1979. The majority of the patients report that they began using alcohol or other drugs during junior high school; some started earlier.

Factors contributing to substance use

Adolescents use mood-altering substances for many of the same reasons as adults. They use alcohol and other drugs to enhance social situations, for relaxation, to alleviate anxiety, and to produce pleasurable states of euphoria. Use of mood-altering substances for these purposes is universal and has been noted in almost all past and present cultures. Some factors that contribute to the growing use of drugs by children and adolescents are:

1. *Curiosity* The illegal and forbidden nature of these drugs heightens curiosity and mystifies and attracts the novice user. Curiosity is a primary factor in experimentation.
2. *Peer-group influence* Peer influence is a primary factor in drug use among both adolescents and adults. Both age groups are under continual coercion to smoke, drink, and take a variety of pills to alleviate an extensive list of maladies. We live in a drug-oriented culture, and custom dictates and reinforces our substance use as a society. But peer influence has deeper implications for adolescents. An adolescent's self-image, behavior, and attitudes are greatly influenced by peers. The primary motivating factors for a teenager are not family, school, or church, but other teenagers. Adolescents today are under massive and extensive pressure to drink, smoke marijuana, and experiment with other drugs. The peer group approves, protects, reinforces, and sometimes even defines each other's drug-seeking and drug-using behavior. Substance use may admit and establish a teenager within a peer group.

3. *Lack of specific information* Adolescents are poorly informed about alcohol and other drugs. Unfortunately, community efforts to educate youth about substance abuse have only recently been developed on a wide scale. Past educational approaches have contributed to the lack of honest, factual information and have taught adolescents to trust only what they learn from their own experience and from peers. Encouraging results are being noted in schools that have integrated comprehensive educational programs in curricula throughout the junior and senior high school years. Educational programs stressing prevention are beginning to develop in kindergarten through sixth grades. Churches are increasingly sponsoring educational programs. More families are openly communicating with their children about alcohol, other drugs, and the role of substances in their lives. (This is important because blocked communication fosters substance abuse.) But denial and fear of the extent of usage among teenagers retard efforts to prepare young people more adequately to make appropriate decisions in this area of their lives

4. *Developmental limitations of adolescence* Adolescents generally are not prepared emotionally, mentally, physically, and socially to use alcohol and other drugs successfully and appropriately. The adolescent's egocentricity compounds the possible problems: The capacity to form mature judgments is not fully developed; values and goals are not formulated; risk-taking behavior is expected and reinforced during adolescence; and the need for immediate response and gratification is much higher.

5. *Escape* Many adolescents use mood-altering substances to escape boredom and psychological or physical pain resulting from family problems, school problems, or socioeconomic conditions. Children of families with a history of alcoholism, incest, physical abuse, or extremely moralistic expectations are more likely to abuse alcohol or other drugs.

6. *Imitation of adult behavior* Adolescents copy their

parents' use of alcohol and drugs to cope with the problems of life. The adolescent child of an alcoholic parent has less opportunity to observe more mature methods of coping with life's stresses.

Nursing management †

The use and abuse of chemicals by adolescents need to be of concern to *all* nurses. Nurses in the emergency room see trauma, overdose, inappropriate and withdrawn behavior, and potentially life-threatening situations related to drug use. Nurses on pediatric, medical, or surgical units may see adolescents with a drug problem who were originally admitted for medical or surgical treatment. Drug use may occur when friends bring drugs to add excitement to a dull hospital stay or when the patient leaves the unit and returns intoxicated. Family members may express concern over truancy or legal problems caused by drug use.

Nurses working with patients who abuse drugs need to examine closely their own beliefs, values, and attitudes regarding drug use and abuse. Drug abuse should not be condoned through silence or by aligning with the patient against people with opposing views. Not listening to the patient or labeling him or her guilty without adequate assessment does not help alleviate drug abuse. Therefore, a nonjudgmental approach is most effective in developing open communication and nurse-patient rapport. A negative, condescending attitude is conveyed by the nurse who views drug use as wrong; considers treatment for drug abuse a waste of time, effort, or money; or sees the drug abuser as an unmotivated individual who will never amount to anything. The patient readily perceives these judgmental attitudes that prevent rapport, block communication, and eventually lead to open hostility between nurse and patient. The nurse builds a trusting relationship by expressing genuine interest and caring concern in an honest, nonpatronizing, and straightforward manner.

John, 16 years old, left the party after drinking 10 beers in a few hours and drove his parents' car 1.6 km before crashing into a tree. His foot was pinned in the car, and he was brought to the emergency room by the police. Should the emergency room nurse merely assess the foot

† Compiled by Nancy L. Ramsey and Deane Hatteberg, R.N., B.S.N.

Table 42-3 Self-assessment: attitudes toward drugs

1. Do you see alcoholism as a self-inflicted disease?
2. How much alcohol do you keep at home?
3. Do you keep the alcohol flowing at a party or let it run out?
4. What does your medicine cabinet contain?
5. What things in your home contain alcohol? Look at labels of cooking and cleaning supplies.
6. What are your reactions to those who use alcohol or other drugs excessively?
7. What is written about alcohol or drug abuse in the media?
8. What is your reaction to the written material?
9. Does anyone in your family overuse alcohol or drugs?
10. Does this affect how you see others using chemicals? In what way?
11. Do you tend to avoid patients with a known history of alcohol or drug dependence? Why? Why not?
12. Do you obtain an alcohol or drug use history from patients? Why? Why not?

injury and ignore the odor of alcohol on John's breath? Too often the trauma is treated and the drug use is disregarded by medical personnel saying, "Boys will be boys ... at least he wasn't using drugs ... won't happen again." These excuses deny John's drug abuse problem and reflect a judgmental attitude toward drug use. If John is sent home to recover, has he been made aware of responsible drinking, living, and decision making? Suggestions for assessing your own beliefs and attitudes toward drug use are listed in Table 42-3.

Physical assessment

The presence of substance abuse must first be validated by physical assessment (see Table 42-4), history, and the results of laboratory tests.[18] The nurse's assessment of the adolescent's physical condition should focus upon (1) identification of the signs or symptoms of drug withdrawal or overdose, drug side effects, nervous system depression, and physical complications, and (2) identification of the extent and type of drug dependence (see Table 42-4). With knowledge of the drug's physiological action and resultant behaviors, the nurse will be prepared to assess the patient, anticipate future nursing problems, and put the patient's needs in order. Specific symptoms of withdrawal and overdose are discussed in an earlier section, "Classification of Substances."

Laboratory tests The nurse must validate physical symptoms of drug abuse with the results of laboratory tests. Thin layer chromatography (TLC) and gas-liquid chromatography (GLC) are laboratory tests used to analyze blood and urine for the presence of drugs. Heroin use is detected by fluorescing the urine at a specific wavelength. Conventional, complete blood counts and urinalyses will not identify specific drug use.[19]

Substance abuse occasionally results in life-threatening situations. Drug overdoses cause central nervous system depression. The following symptoms indicate an emergency and should receive highest-priority assessment and treatment: slurred speech, ataxic gait, slowed thinking, decreased attention span, inappropriate behavior, disorientation, pinpoint pupils, and impaired coordination. If a majority of the above symptoms are present, the nurse must observe carefully for behavioral changes indicating a progression to unconsciousness. Comatose patients have often mixed large amounts of alcohol

---

Table 42-4 A nursing assessment guide for a drug abuse patient

I. Physical assessment
  A. Assessment of body for trauma: injection sites, needle tracks, or scar tissue over veins (observe antecubital spaces, beneath tongue, in groin or penis, between fingers and toes, and along arms, hands, feet and legs)
  B. Assessment of skin: color, turgor, presence of sores, abscesses, or burns
  C. Assessment of central nervous system and eyes
    1. Neurological assessment
    2. Presence of red, irritated, or jaundiced eyes
  D. Assessment of secondary complications resulting from drug use: hepatitis, excessive nasal discharge, or pulmonary infections
  E. Assessment of nutritional and hygienic status
    1. Assess height and weight; compare to normal values
    2. Assess muscular development; note emaciation, flaking of skin, cracks in corners of mouth, or other symptoms of nutritional deficiency
    3. Assess mouth and teeth: decayed teeth, infection, or foul breath
    4. Assess clothing and personal cleanliness: dull or dirty hair, skin, or clothes; lice
  F. Assessment of hidden drugs in the following locations: clothes, hair, vagina, armpits, anus, or underclothing
  G. Physical assessment of drug use: assess for symptoms of withdrawal, overdosage, central nervous system depression, and side effects
  H. Past medical history

II. Drug history (focus on last 3 months)
  A. Nature of drugs: quantity and frequency of drugs used
    1. Do you use any prescription medications? In the recent past? What? How much? For what?
    2. What other drugs have you used? What drug did you first use? When? Do you use them now? What time? When was the last dose taken? How much? How often? Do you combine drugs? Are you allergic to any drugs?
    3. How much alcohol do you use? What kind? How often?
    4. Have you ever had a bad reaction to drugs?
    5. Have you ever had trouble stopping the use of any drugs?

II. Drug history (Cont.)
    6. Have you ever been hospitalized for drug use before? Where? When? What kind of therapy?
  B. Social assessment
    1. Have friends or family members talked with you about your drug use? Have they been concerned about your drug use?
    2. Have you had any legal problems? What? Were you using drugs at the time?
    3. Have you had difficulties with school? Missed school? Had failing grades? Were you using drugs at the time?
    4. Peer group: Do you like them? What do they value for their members? What do they require for continued membership?
  C. Patient's self-assessment
    1. Do you think you have a problem with drugs? Why or why not?
    2. Have you felt the need to cut down your use of drugs?

III. Mental-emotional assessment
  A. Reality orientation
    1. Assess if oriented to surroundings or hallucinating, confused, or not coherent
  B. Mental activity/levels of consciousness
    1. Assess if behavior is slowed or agitated
  C. Defense mechanisms
    1. Assess main defense mechanisms used, such as denying, minimizing, rationalizing (making excuses), or projecting blame or fault
  D. Attitude/behaviors
    1. Assess patterns of behavior, such as hostile-belligerent, depressed, or euphoric
  E. Assess psychological strengths

IV. Family assessment
  A. Assess family interactions
    1. Family configuration
    2. Perceived support from parents or family members
    3. Family's attitudes, beliefs, need for education
    4. Family chemical use
    5. Family–patient relationships

V. Any previous psychiatric history

with barbiturates. These two drugs have a synergistic action and potentiate each other's physiological action. This mixture results in a higher incidence of complications, risks, and accidental deaths than when one drug is used alone.

Nursing interventions must address the full range of the patient's health care needs. After the patient's condition is physiologically stable, it is often the nurse who deals with adolescents experiencing bad trips; the nursing interventions are listed in Table 42-5. Nursing interventions for the patient in drug withdrawal are listed in Table 42-6. Nurses should coordinate the drug-abusing patient's care among all health team members. The nurse can act as a liaison among team members by communicating the nursing assessment of the patient's status, clarifying the patient's needs and requests, coordinating treatments, and conducting team conferences to ensure a consistent approach by all team members. Clear communication among team members builds trust. It also decreases manipulation of team members by the adolescent, for drug abusers are often experts at manipulation. These young people require a holistic team approach because all facets of their lives are affected by substance abuse.

Psychological assessment

The nurse should conduct the psychological assessment after the physical assessment is completed and the patient's physiological condition is stabilized. The first step of the psychological assessment is to build a trusting relationship between the teenager and the nurse. Young drug abusers are often reluctant to share information. They have often been given incorrect information about drugs and have been lectured to in an

Table 42-5 Nursing interventions: A patient on a bad trip

General goal: To reduce the patient's terror and panic

Nursing interventions	Rationale
1. Provide a quiet, secure, nonstressful environment; small, separate room with adjustable lighting. Repeatedly tell the patient he or she is in a safe, secure environment and well cared for	1. A patient on a bad trip may misinterpret stimuli in the environment and may act out. The patient feels more frightened and less secure in a large room
2. Remove harmful objects from environment (syringes, medications, sharp objects). Provide safe environment (make certain that windows do not open from the inside and that bathrooms and room can be unlocked from the outside)	2. The patient may misinterpret the meaning of objects; may attack the nurse, objects, or self, or attempt to escape
3. Reassure patient that his or her experiences are drug-related and *temporary*	3. Self-control increases when the patient realizes the feelings are temporary. Panic and loss of control are caused by the overwhelming sensory input of the bad trip
4. *One* person should stay with the patient. Use a low-keyed, calm approach, a relaxed attitude, and a softly modulated voice; wear casual clothing	4. The patient's behavior is unpredictable; it may quickly change from calm to destructive. Authoritarian, critical attitudes and white uniforms increase the patient's anxiety level (panic) and terror. Consistent nurses increase the patient's trust and promote cooperation from the patient
5. Patients who are disoriented need *frequent* reorientation to reality: where they are and who you are. Encourage the patient to discuss his or her perceptions; clarify misconceptions. Do not support hallucinations. Do not touch the patient before saying what you intend to do. Use a gentle, soothing touch	5. Patients who are disoriented as to time and place are fearful and frequently paranoid (believing nurses will harm them). Amphetamine users are especially prone to misinterpret actions. The nurse's intent must be clear to the patient. This reduces the patient's anxiety level (panic) and reinforces reality
6. Don't threaten the patient or show hostility. Give short, clear directions with an attitude of expecting cooperation	6. All patients respond to a nurse's attitude of caring and understanding. A nurse's hostility blocks the development of trust, open communication, and cooperation. Hallucinogen users especially respond positively to an attitude of sincerity and care

Source: Adapted from Pamela Burkhalter, *Nursing Care of the Alcoholic and Drug Abuser*, McGraw-Hill, New York, 1975, pp. 213–215.

Table 42-6 Nursing interventions: A patient in withdrawal

Nursing intervention	Rationale
1. Monitor vital signs and neurological status	1. Alterations in vital signs and reflexes precede convulsions in adolescents withdrawing from barbiturates
2. Decrease sensory stimulation. Provide a serene, calm environment. Place the patient in a single, quiet room with adjustable lighting. Limit visitors	2. Adolescents with barbiturate withdrawal cannot tolerate excessive noise. Stimulation increases the patient's agitation and promotes seizures
3. Reorient the confused patient to reality and his or her location. Do not support hallucinations. Stay with the patient	3. Patients in withdrawal may become confused and disoriented and may hallucinate. Patients may feel panicky when left alone
4. Administer medication following a withdrawal schedule. Medication should be gradually reduced	4. The detoxification process usually takes 2–3 weeks
5. Monitor the patient's physical condition	5. Physical needs must be assessed and treated before long-term psychological treatment

Source: Adapted from Pamela Burkhalter, *Nursing Care of the Alcoholic and Drug Abuser*, McGraw-Hill, New York, 1975, pp. 209–213.

authoritarian manner by adults. Teenagers frequently avoid authority figures. Nurses and other medical personnel can encourage trust by wearing casual clothes and having a caring, calmly reassuring manner (Fig. 42-1).

The nurse should explain to the patient the rights of adolescents and the concept of confidentiality. This is an effective tool to build trust between the adolescent and the nurse. Reassure the patient that information will be shared *only* with other health team members, *not* with parents, outside institutions, or friends. When outside people or institutions must be informed or consulted, appropriate releases of information must be signed *first* by the adolesent. Adolescents have the same rights for treatment as adults. Fully inform the teenager of the serious reasons to consult parents or school personnel. Support and assist the young person in informing these people.

After informing the teenager of his or her rights and the confidentiality of information, begin the nursing assessment. Ask questions that will provide the information and keep defensiveness to a minimum. Explore the patient's use of prescription medications first and then progress to the more threatening issues of illegal drug use. Adolescents are often very guarded and unwilling to share information about their drug use pattern. Ask specific questions, such as "Have you ever used drugs?" or "Have you ever used pot?"

Each adolescent should be actively involved in the assessment, because motivation to change will occur only after the benefits of change after

a self-assessment are recognized. Because the adolescent frequently gives incorrect information, it is important to validate the history of drug use with family and friends. Peers, frequently also drug users, should be interviewed immediately because they often quickly disappear.

Psychological assessment is essential to determine the problems of the adolescent and the family and to clarify the need for long-term treatment. Drug abuse touches all areas of the family. The family of the drug abuser usually

Figure 42-1 A trusting relationship must be built between the teenager and the nurse. Nurses express honest, genuine concern, wear casual clothes, and encourage a relaxed atmosphere.

arrives in a state of crisis; their previous coping methods have been ineffective in solving the problems. Confusion about their child's behavior exists, and the entire family frequently uses denial to cope with the drug problem. As the adolescent progresses in the abuse pattern, family relationships and communication patterns change. The members adapt to altered behaviors, and a maladaptive system develops among family members. Family conflicts increase. The teenager frequently has had academic and behavioral problems in school.

Drug abuse is frequently a symptom of ongoing, maladaptive family patterns. Because all aspects of family life are altered by drug abuse, family therapy is often recommended for treatment. In this type of therapy, family members share their feelings, perceptions, and expectations of each other under the guidance of a therapist. Group members work together to express emotion-laden feelings, solve family conflicts, build trust, create new communication patterns, learn to communicate openly and honestly, and learn new methods of coping with stress.

The primary goal of psychological therapy with the adolescent is to increase motivation for self-help and to change behavior. Simply removing the drug does not cure the patient. The adolescent must be helped to recognize the reason for drug use.

The adolescent frequently grieves over the loss of drugs; he or she must confront and explore the meaning of this loss. Feelings of isolation, loneliness, frustration, insecurity, and anger resurface, no longer dulled by drug use. The coping skills of adolescents on drugs are at a minimum, and more mature coping methods must be learned. Drug abusers often skillfully manipulate others; new methods of communication must be learned. Self-esteem is low and has to be built up. A life-style of indiscriminate drug use to cope with any life problem or to obtain membership in a peer group must change. The temptation or desire to use drugs is high among adolescents. Teenage drug users are at a higher risk of

Table 42-7 Guidelines for confronting a person about drug use

Nursing interventions	Rationale
1. Ask to speak to the person alone	1. This respects the person's privacy and promotes open communication and trust
2. Describe the person's exact behavior, giving specific, descriptive (not labeling) statements. The person's behavior should be documented on the chart: "Ann, during the past two weeks, we have found pills hidden on your body four times—in your hair, underpants . . ." Do *not* say, "You are uncooperative and a bad girl"; this is labeling	2. Telling the patient your exact observations increases your credibility and reduces the person's opportunity to deny the statements and manipulate you
3. Tell the person how his or her behavior makes you *feel*. "Ann, I am frustrated and disappointed, and I wonder if you really want to get off drugs"	3. Communicating your feelings makes the person see things from your viewpoint; this enhances communiation and trust. Without the description of your feelings, the person's defenses and anxiety level will rise; the adolescent will be less able to hear you
4. Ask the person for a specific change in behavior. "Ann, I want you to stop hiding the pills now. Are you willing to do this?"	4. This does not force the person to agree but increases mutual understanding. Specific requests promote cooperation, emphasize self-control, and decrease dependency and insecurity
5. List the positive and negative consequences of the person's behavior. "Ann, when you cooperate and don't hide your pills, it tells us you are ready to get well," versus "Ann, if you continue to hide and take pills, we cannot keep you in our program. If we find pills one more time, you will be sent to another hospital"	5. The person knows exactly what is expected, and this increases motivation. It also increases the validity of evaluation
6. Use assertive body language: direct eye contact, erect body posture; speak clearly, distinctly, and do not whine; use hand gestures and facial expressions to emphasize important points	6. Assertive behavior, a learned skill, gives people clear, honest messages about your feelings and expectations of them

Source: Adapted from Sonya J. Herman, *Becoming Assertive, A Guide for Nurses*, Van Nostrand, New York, 1978, pp. 71–72, 92–94.

returning to drugs because their friends are often users. They feel pressured to use drugs to obtain and maintain membership in peer groups.

After a trusting nurse-patient relationship has been built, the nurse should confront the patient with his or her behavior, identifying destructive attitudes and behavior. Nurses should describe specific behaviors, facts, and observations on the chart and Kardex. This approach helps reduce the adolescent's denial. Even when a confrontation technique is used, the patient may respond with anger, denial, and defensiveness. (See Table 42-7 for a confrontation technique.) During counseling sessions the nurse repeatedly refers to specific, documented behaviors. Suspected drug abuse must be confronted; ignoring the problem is not a solution. During these sessions of group or individual therapy, adolescents must learn that they had a choice and chose to take drugs. In the future, they have the power to continue taking drugs or to choose a more mature and less self-destructive alternative (Fig. 42-2).

Education

Education is an indispensable part of nursing the drug abuser. The adolescent needs information about the drug, its physiological action, and its side effects. Small discussion groups are

Figure 42-2 Small groups are ideal for building trust and learning about drugs. These group members are learning that they chose to take drugs and have the power to choose more mature methods of solving problems.

Figure 42-3 Building the adolescent's self-esteem is the foundation for successful treatment. These teenagers are learning new, basic living skills in the occupational therapy department.

the ideal method of teaching this information to teenagers. Small group discussions build trust among group members faster than the lecture style of teaching. By sharing feelings, attitudes, and problems, members discover personal, relevant solutions to problems more easily than when solutions are presented in lectures. In working daily with the patient, the nurse should look for evidence of learning: Has a *change* in behavior taken place? If a patient repeats information verbatim but has no change in behavior, learning has not taken place.

Increasing the patient's self-esteem is the foundation of a successful treatment program (Fig. 42-3). The nurse and other health team members should design a plan to increase the adolescent's self-esteem. Remedial work in a school, assertiveness training, relaxation techniques, and activities planned to ensure success should be written in a detailed plan of care and instituted by the team. Teenagers often need help in setting achievable, short-term goals; praising their accomplishments increases their self-esteem and establishes expectations for success (Fig. 42-4). The nurse can also educate the adolescent by role modeling. When teenagers ask about the nurse's drug use and how he or she handles problems, the nurse can model more mature solutions to stress.

Figure 42-4 Praise by the nurse for this young man's woodworking project will increase his self-esteem. He is working out feelings of aggression and hostility in this type of aggressive (play) activity.

Long-term treatment

Drug-dependent adolescents often have difficulty making a long-term commitment to a treatment program. A recovered drug abuser has a more appealing approach to the patient. This ex-abuser often succeeds when health team members have failed. With his or her self-insight, the recovered abuser can act as a role model and motivator of adolescents.

The drug-using adolescent feels extremely vulnerable to peer pressure to restart drug use. A treatment and referral plan is therefore vitally important. Planning for the teenager's referral should begin soon after remission. To plan for a referral, the nurse must know the available community resources. When planning a referral, the nurse should consider the following questions: Is treatment necessary? Are resources available within the hospital to detoxify the patient? Does the family need long-term treatment and support? Community resources in many areas include Alcoholics Anonymous, Al-anon, Alateen, Narcotics Anonymous, outpatient family and/or individual counseling, court services (classes for people convicted of driving while drunk), social service departments, psychiatrists, detoxification units, inpatient treatment units, halfway houses, public health departments, schools, employee assistance programs, chemi-

cal dependency counselors, nurse counselors, and mental health centers. All of the above treatment programs can help the patient and family stop denying the problem and become involved in a treatment program.

Prevention

Prevention of drug abuse occurs on three levels: family, school, and community. The family provides the basis for the growing child's value formation, self-concept, self-control, and commitment to responsible living. Parents are role models for their children by showing them how to cope with life's problems through actions and attitudes that promote mature, constructive solutions. When parents use alcohol to the point of intoxication, supply large amounts of alcohol at parties, smoke marijuana, or use drugs when nervous or depressed, their teenage children learn and expect to solve problems by these same methods. Children and adolescents need to be given responsibility for their lives and to accept the consequences of their behavior. For example, if Joan never gets up by herself in the morning for school, and if her mother yells at her five times before she grudgingly arises and barely catches the school bus, is Joan learning responsible behavior?

Schools have a responsibility to educate the adolescent about drug problems, to present information on drugs, and to teach the consequences of drug use. Education ideally should begin in grammar school and continue through high school. Information taught should be based on facts, not on scare tactics, and moralizing by adults should be avoided. School nurses and counselors can form support groups for adolescents concerned about drug abuse in themselves, friends, or family members. Schools also have a responsibility to the parent. Communication and parenting classes can be offered at times accessible to working and nonworking adults. Assertiveness training and learning new methods to deal with anger, grief, or loss can be provided in these small groups. As the group members learn to trust each other, express themselves openly and honestly, and feel valued as group members, their self-esteem will grow. Mutual trust will enhance each member's decision to try out new methods of problem solving besides drug use.

Communities have a responsibility to evaluate their needs and to respond to those needs by enforcing laws and by providing hot lines, referral and evaluation agencies, treatment facilities, and recreational opportunities for adolescents. These facilities will prevent drug use. Schools, families, and communities must work together to solve this problem. America is a drug-oriented society, and drug use is here to stay.

References

1. National Institute on Alcohol Abuse and Alcoholism (NIAAA), *Report to Congress on Alcohol and Health*, Department of Health, Education, and Welfare, Washington, D.C., 1978, p. 3.
2. National Institute on Drug Abuse (NIDA), *Report to Congress on Drugs and Health*, Rockville, Md., 1979.
3. Vernon E. Johnson, *I'll Quit Tomorrow*, Harper & Row, New York, 1973, pp. 15–24.
4. Brent Q. Hafen, *Alcoholism: The Crutch that Cripples*, West Publishing, St. Paul, Minn., 1977, pp. 52–53.
5. Ray Oakley, *Drugs, Society, and Human Behavior*, C. V. Mosby, St. Louis, 1978, p. 57.
6. Ibid., pp. 59–61.
7. Horton Heath, "Drugs of Abuse," *Drug Enforcement* 6(2):5–7 (1979).
8. Edward M. Brecher and editors of *Consumer Reports: Licit and Illicit Drugs*, Little, Brown, Boston, 1972, pp. 8–87.
9. Ibid., pp. 249–253.
10. Brecher et al., op. cit., pp. 278–280.
11. Ibid., pp. 362–366.
12. Oakley, op. cit., pp. 268–272.
13. Brecher et al., op. cit., pp. 309–311.
14. NIAAA, *op. cit.*
15. NIDA, *op. cit.*
16. NIAAA, *op. cit.*
17. Lloyd Johnston, Jerald Bachman, and Patrick O'Malley, *Drug Use Among American High School Students, 1975–1977*, Department of Health, Education, and Welfare, Rockville, Md., 1977, pp. 1–11.
18. Dee Williams, "Substance Use and Abuse," in Jeanne Howe (ed.), *Nursing Care of Adolescents*, McGraw-Hill, New York, 1980, p. 190.
19. Ibid., p. 191.

Part Four **Appendix**

Appendix A Metric conversion tables

Table A-1 Celsius and Fahrenheit equivalents: Body temperature range

C°	F°	C°	F°	C°	F°	C°	F°	C°	F°
34.0	93.20	35.5	95.90	37.0	98.60	38.5	101.30	40.0	104.00
34.1	93.38	35.6	96.08	37.1	98.78	38.6	101.48	40.1	104.18
34.2	93.56	35.7	96.26	37.2	98.96	38.7	101.66	40.2	104.36
34.3	93.74	35.8	96.44	37.3	99.14	38.8	101.84	40.3	104.54
34.4	93.92	35.9	96.62	37.4	99.32	38.9	102.02	40.4	104.72
34.5	94.10	36.0	96.80	37.5	99.50	39.0	102.20	40.5	104.90
34.6	94.28	36.1	96.98	37.6	99.68	39.1	102.38	40.6	105.08
34.7	94.46	36.2	97.16	37.7	99.86	39.2	102.56	40.7	105.26
34.8	94.64	36.3	97.34	37.8	100.04	39.3	102.74	40.8	105.44
34.9	94.82	36.4	97.52	37.9	100.22	39.4	102.92	40.9	105.62
35.0	95.0	36.5	97.70	38.0	100.40	39.5	103.10	41.0	105.80
35.1	95.18	36.6	97.88	38.1	100.58	39.6	103.28		
35.2	95.36	36.7	98.06	38.2	100.76	39.7	103.46		
35.3	95.54	36.8	98.24	38.3	100.94	39.8	103.64		
35.4	95.72	36.9	98.42	38.4	101.12	39.9	103.82		

Table A-2 Fahrenheit and Celsius equivalents: Body temperature range

F°	C°	F°	C°	F°	C°	F°	C°	F°	C°
94.0	34.44	97.0	36.11	100.0	37.78	103.0	39.44	106.0	41.11
94.2	34.56	97.2	36.22	100.2	37.89	103.2	39.56	106.2	41.22
94.4	34.67	97.4	36.33	100.4	38.00	103.4	39.67	106.4	41.33
94.6	34.78	97.6	36.44	100.6	38.11	103.6	39.78	106.6	41.44
94.8	34.89	97.8	36.56	100.8	38.22	103.8	39.89	106.8	41.56
95.0	35.00	98.0	36.67	101.0	38.33	104.0	40.00	107.0	41.67
95.2	35.11	98.2	36.78	101.2	38.44	104.2	40.11	107.2	41.78
95.4	35.22	98.4	36.89	101.4	38.56	104.4	40.22	107.4	41.89
95.6	35.33	98.6	37.00	101.6	38.67	104.6	40.33	107.6	42.00
95.8	35.44	98.8	37.11	101.8	38.78	104.8	40.44	107.8	42.11
96.0	35.56	99.0	37.22	102.0	38.89	105.0	40.56	108.0	42.22
96.2	35.67	99.2	37.33	102.2	39.00	105.2	40.67		
96.4	35.78	99.4	37.44	102.4	39.11	105.4	40.78		
96.6	35.89	99.6	37.56	102.6	39.22	105.6	40.89		
96.8	36.00	99.8	37.67	102.8	39.33	105.8	41.00		

Table A-3 Length conversions

Meters	Centimeters	Yards	Feet	Inches
1	100	1.094	3.281	39.37
.01	1	.01094	.0328	.3937
.9144	91.44	1	3	36
.0348	30.48	1/3	1	12
.0254	2.54	1/36	1/12	1

Table A-4 Weight conversions (metric and avoirdupois)

Grams	Kilograms	Ounces	Pounds
1	.001	.0353	.0022
1000	1	35.3	2.2
28.35	.02835	1	1/16
454.5	.4545	16	1

Table A-5 Pound-to-kilogram conversion table*

Pounds	0	1	2	3	4	5	6	7	8	9
0	0.00	0.45	0.90	1.36	1.81	2.26	2.72	3.17	3.62	4.08
10	4.53	4.98	5.44	5.89	6.35	6.80	7.25	7.71	8.16	8.61
20	9.07	9.52	9.97	10.43	10.88	11.34	11.79	12.24	12.70	13.15
30	13.60	14.06	14.51	14.96	15.42	15.87	16.32	16.78	17.23	17.69
40	18.14	18.59	19.05	19.50	19.95	20.41	20.86	21.31	21.77	22.22
50	22.68	23.13	23.58	24.04	24.49	24.94	25.40	25.85	26.30	26.76
60	27.21	27.66	28.12	28.57	29.03	29.48	29.93	30.39	30.84	31.29
70	31.75	32.20	32.65	33.11	33.56	34.02	34.47	34.92	35.38	35.83
80	36.28	36.74	37.19	37.64	38.10	38.55	39.00	39.46	39.91	40.37
90	40.82	41.27	41.73	42.18	42.63	43.09	43.54	43.99	44.45	44.90
100	45.36	45.81	46.26	46.72	47.17	47.62	48.08	48.53	48.98	49.44
110	49.89	50.34	50.80	51.25	51.71	52.16	52.61	53.07	53.52	53.97
120	54.43	54.88	55.33	55.79	56.24	56.70	57.15	57.60	58.06	58.51
130	58.96	59.42	59.87	60.32	60.78	61.23	61.68	62.14	62.59	63.05
140	63.50	63.95	64.41	64.86	65.31	65.77	66.22	66.67	67.13	67.58
150	68.04	68.49	68.94	69.40	69.85	70.30	70.76	71.21	71.66	72.12
160	72.57	73.02	73.48	73.93	74.39	74.84	75.29	75.75	76.20	76.65
170	77.11	77.56	78.01	78.47	78.92	79.38	79.83	80.28	80.74	81.19
180	81.64	82.10	82.55	83.00	83.46	83.91	84.36	84.82	85.27	85.73
190	86.18	86.68	87.09	87.54	87.99	88.45	88.90	89.35	89.81	90.26
200	90.72	91.17	91.62	92.08	92.53	92.98	93.44	93.89	94.34	94.80

* Numbers in the farthest left column are 10-pound increments; numbers across the top row are 1-pound increments. The kilogram equivalent of weight in pounds is found at the intersection of the appropriate row and column. For example, to convert 54 pounds, read down the left column to 50 and then across that row to 4; 54 pounds = 24.49 kilograms.

Table A-6 Gram equivalents for pounds and ounces: Conversion table for weight of newborn*

Pounds	Ounces 0	1	2	3	4	5	6	7	8	9	10	11	12	13	14	15	Pounds
0	—	28	57	85	113	142	170	198	227	255	283	312	430	369	397	425	0
1	454	482	510	539	567	595	624	652	680	709	737	765	794	822	850	879	1
2	907	936	964	992	1021	1049	1077	1106	1134	1162	1191	1219	1247	1276	1304	1332	2
3	1361	1389	1417	1446	1474	1503	1531	1559	1588	1616	1644	1673	1701	1729	1758	1786	3
4	1814	1843	1871	1899	1928	1956	1984	2013	2041	2070	2098	2126	2155	2183	2211	2240	4
5	2268	2296	2325	2353	2381	2410	2438	2466	2495	2523	2551	2580	2608	2637	2665	2693	5
6	2722	2750	2778	2807	2835	2863	2892	2920	2948	2977	3005	3033	3062	3090	3118	3147	6
7	3175	3203	3232	3260	3289	3317	3345	3374	3402	3430	3459	3487	3515	3544	3572	3600	7
8	3629	3657	3685	3714	3742	3770	3799	3827	3856	3884	3912	3941	3969	3997	4026	4054	8
9	4082	4111	4139	4167	4196	4224	4252	4281	4309	4337	4366	4394	4423	4451	4479	4508	9
10	4536	4564	4593	4621	4649	4678	4706	4734	4763	4791	4819	4848	4876	4904	4933	4961	10
11	4990	5018	5046	5075	5103	5131	5160	5188	5216	5245	5273	5301	5330	5358	5386	5415	11
12	5443	5471	5500	5528	5557	5585	5613	5642	5670	5698	5727	5755	5783	5812	5840	5868	12
13	5897	5925	5953	5982	6010	6038	6067	6095	6123	6152	6180	6290	6237	6265	6294	6322	13
14	6350	6379	6407	6435	6464	6492	6520	6549	6577	6605	6634	6662	6690	6719	6747	6776	14

* 1 pound = 453.59 grams. 1 ounce = 28.35 grams. Grams can be converted to pounds and tenths of a pound by multiplying the number of grams by .0022.

Appendix B Growth charts

GIRLS: BIRTH TO 36 MONTHS
PHYSICAL GROWTH
NCHS PERCENTILES

NAME _____ RECORD # _____

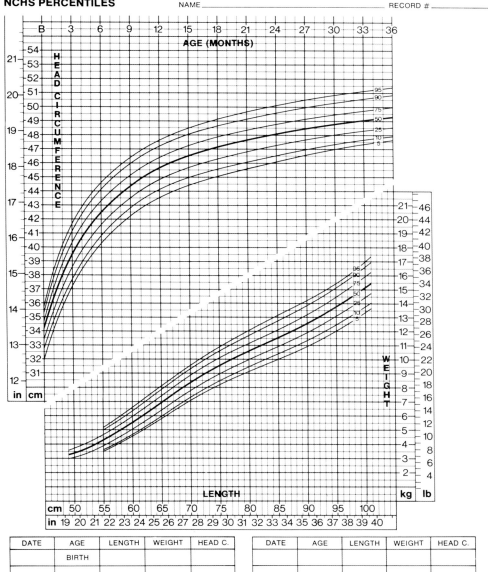

DATE	AGE	LENGTH	WEIGHT	HEAD C.
	BIRTH			

DATE	AGE	LENGTH	WEIGHT	HEAD C.

Figure B-1 Female infant growth chart: Head circumference–age and length-weight relationships from birth to 36 months. *(Adapted from the NCHS Growth Charts, 1976.)*

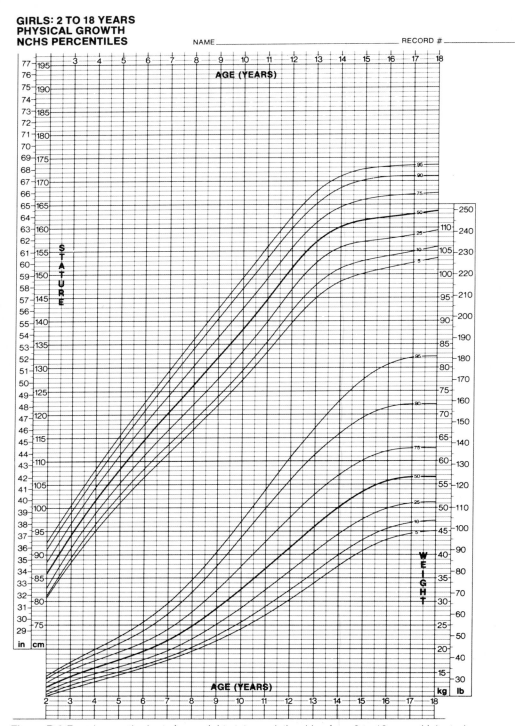

GIRLS: 2 TO 18 YEARS
PHYSICAL GROWTH
NCHS PERCENTILES

NAME_____ RECORD #_____

Figure B-2 Female growth chart: Age-weight-stature relationships from 2 to 18 years (*Adapted from the NCHS Growth Charts, 1976.*)

BOYS: BIRTH TO 36 MONTHS
PHYSICAL GROWTH
NCHS PERCENTILES

NAME _____ RECORD # _____

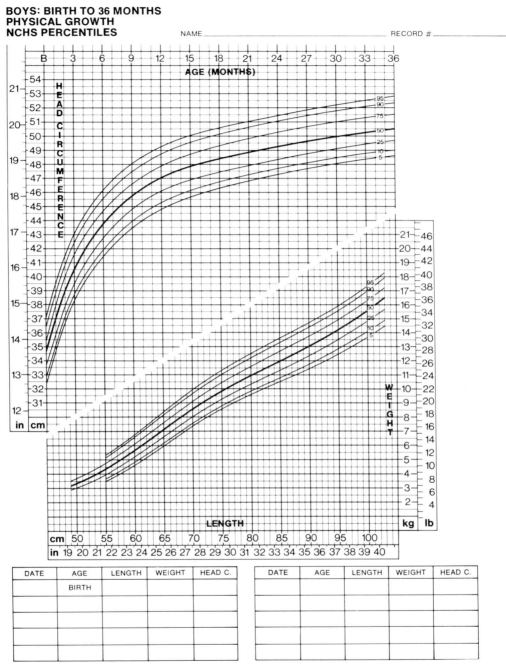

DATE	AGE	LENGTH	WEIGHT	HEAD C.
	BIRTH			

DATE	AGE	LENGTH	WEIGHT	HEAD C.

Figure B-3 Male infant growth chart: Head circumference–age and length-weight relationships from birth to 36 months. *(Adapted from the NCHS Growth Charts, 1976.)*

BOYS: BIRTH TO 36 MONTHS
PHYSICAL GROWTH
NCHS PERCENTILES   NAME_____   RECORD #_____

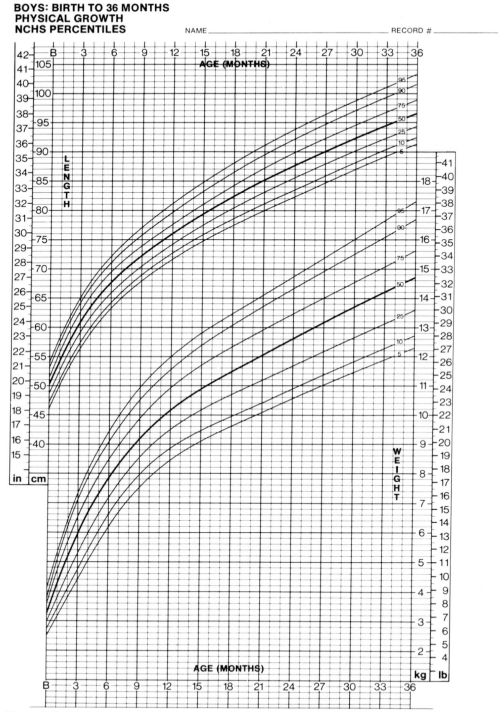

Figure B-4 Male infant growth chart: Length-age and weight-age relationships from birth to 36 months. *(Adapted from the NCHS Growth Charts, 1976.)*

**BOYS: 2 TO 18 YEARS
PHYSICAL GROWTH
NCHS PERCENTILES**

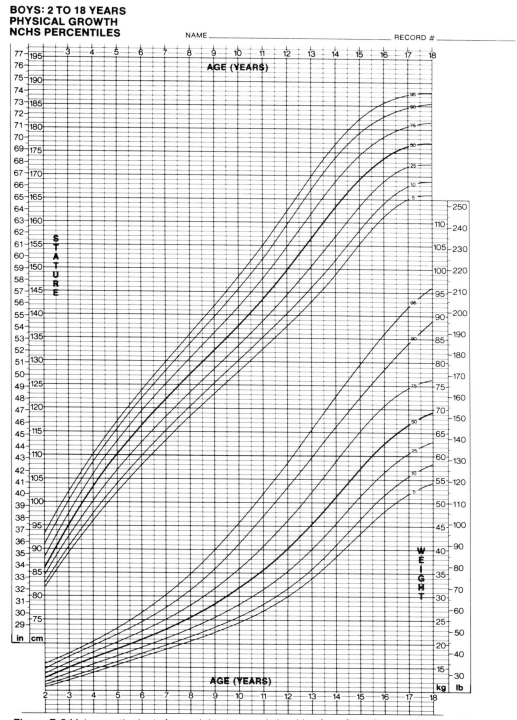

Figure B-5 Male growth chart: Age-weight-stature relationships from 2 to 18 years. (*Adapted from the NCHS Growth Charts, 1976.*)

Appendix C Nutrition

Table C-1 Nutrition history form

Name

Date

Age

Informant

Current weight _____ Height or length _____ Skin fold measurement _____

Birth weight _____ Length _____

Was the child breast-fed _____ or bottle-fed _____ ?
   Bottle-fed: Formula used
                 Frequency of feedings
                 Amount taken
                 Age of child when formula discontinued
   Breast-fed: Frequency of feedings
                 Length of time for feedings
                 Were supplemental bottles given? Give specifics.
                 Age of weaning and to what child was weaned

Was the infant given a vitamin and/or mineral supplement? Specify.

When did the child stop taking middle-of-the-night feeding?

At what age were solids introduced?
   Problems encountered.
   Length of time for a meal.

At what age did the child start eating table foods?
   Problems encountered.

At what age did the child feed itself?

At what age did the child begin to drink from cup?

List previous medical or nutritional problems.

Are there any current medical and/or nutritional problems? (Obtain all necessary data)

Current nutritional data

Do you use any vitamin or mineral supplements regularly? Specify.

Do you now or have you (child) ever followed a special diet? Explain.

What did you eat yesterday?

Time	Food	Amount

Table C-1 Nutrition history form (*Continued*)

Do you eat at similar times every day?

What was different about your meals yesterday compared to today or the day before?

Do you snack in the morning _____, afternoon _____, before supper _____. after supper _____, before bed _____?

What kinds of snack foods do you eat?

Do you ever skip meals?   Which ones and why?

Do you eat lunch at school?   If yes: Do you carry your lunch to school _____ or buy it at school _____

Do you help to prepare meals at home?   Which ones?

Name some of your favorite foods.

Name some of the foods you do not like.

Have you ever eaten nonfoods (clay, dirt, starch)?

Family nutritional data

In which room do you eat at home?

Do you eat meals with your family?

Is anyone in the family using a special diet? Specify.

Who purchases the food for the family?

Who prepares the food for the family?

Table C-2 Recommended daily dietary allowances (1980 revision)[a]

Age (years)	Weight (kg)	Weight (lb)	Height (cm)	Height (in)	Protein (g)	Fat-soluble vitamins Vitamin A (μg RE)[b]	Vitamin D (μg)[c]	Vitamin E (mg α-TE)[d]
Infants 0.0–0.5	6	13	60	24	kg × 2.2	420	10	3
0.5–1.0	9	20	71	28	kg × 2.0	400	10	4
Children 1–3	13	29	90	35	23	400	10	5
4–6	20	44	112	44	30	500	10	6
7–10	28	62	132	52	34	700	10	7
Males 11–14	45	99	157	62	45	1000	10	8
15–18	66	145	176	69	56	1000	10	10
Females 11–14	46	101	157	62	46	800	10	8
15–18	55	120	163	64	46	800	10	8
Pregnant					+30	+200[f] +	+5	+2
Lactation					+20	+400 +	+5	+3

Age (years)	Weight (kg)	Weight (lb)	Height (cm)	Height (in)	Water-soluble vitamins Vitamin C (mg)	Thiamin (mg)	Riboflavin (mg)	Niacin (mg NE)[e]	Vitamin B₆ (mg)	Folacin[f] (μg)	Vitamin B₁₂ (μg)
Infants 0.0–0.5	6	13	60	24	35	0.3	0.4	6	0.3	30	0.5[g]
0.5–1.0	9	20	71	28	35	0.5	0.6	8	0.6	45	1.5
Children 1–3	13	29	90	35	45	0.7	0.8	9	0.9	100	2.0
4–6	20	44	112	44	45	0.9	1.0	11	1.3	200	2.5
7–10	28	62	132	52	45	1.2	1.4	16	1.6	300	3.0
Males 11–14	45	99	157	62	50	1.4	1.6	18	1.8	400	3.0
15–18	66	145	176	69	60	1.4	1.7	18	2.0	400	3.0
Females 11–14	46	101	157	62	50	1.1	1.3	15	1.8	400	3.0
15–18	55	120	163	64	60	1.1	1.3	14	2.0	400	3.0
Pregnant					+20	+0.4	+0.3	+2	+0.6	+400	+1.0
Lactation					+40	+0.5	+0.5	+5	+0.5	+100	+1.0

Table C-2 Recommended daily dietary allowances (1980 revision)[a] (*Continued*)

	Age (years)	Weight (kg)	Weight (lb)	Height (cm)	Height (in)	Minerals Calcium (mg)	Phosphorus (mg)	Magnesium (mg)	Iron (mg)	Zinc (mg)	Iodine (μg)
Infants	0.0–0.5	6	13	60	24	360	240	50	10	3	40
	0.5–1.0	9	20	71	28	540	360	70	15	5	50
Children	1–3	13	29	90	35	800	800	150	15	10	70
	4–6	20	44	112	44	800	800	200	10	10	90
	7–10	28	62	132	52	800	800	250	10	10	120
Males	11–14	45	99	157	62	1200	1200	350	18	15	150
	15–18	66	145	176	69	1200	1200	400	18	15	150
Females	11–14	46	101	157	62	1200	1200	300	18	15	150
	15–18	55	120	163	64	1200	1200	300	18	15	150
Pregnant						+400	+400	+150	h	+5	+25
Lactation						+400	+400	+150	h	+10	+50

[a] The allowances are intended to provide for individual variations among most normal persons as they live in the United States under usual environmental stresses. Diets should be based on a variety of common foods in order to provide other nutrients for which human requirements have been less well defined.

[b] Retinol equivalents. 1 retinol equivalent = 1 μg retinol or 6 μg β carotene. See text for calculation of vitamin A activity of diets as retinol equivalents.

[c] As cholecalciferol. 10 μg cholecalciferol = 400 IU of vitamin D.

[d] α-tocopherol equivalents. 1 mg *d*-α tocopherol = 1α-TE.

[e] 1 NE (niacin equivalent) is equal to 1 mg of niacin or 60 mg of dietary tryptophan.

[f] The folacin allowances refer to dietary sources as determined by *Lactobacillus casei* assay after treatment with enzymes (conjugases) to make polyglutamyl forms of the vitamin available to the test organism.

[g] The recommended dietary allowances for vitamin B_{12} in infants is based on average concentration of the vitamin in human milk. The allowances after weaning are based on energy intake (as recommended by the American Academy of Pediatrics) and consideration of other factors, such as intestinal absorption.

[h] The increased requirements during pregnancy cannot be met by the iron content of habitual American diets nor by the existing iron stores of many women; therefore the use of 30 to 60 mg of supplemental iron is recommended. Iron needs during lactation are not substantially different from those of nonpregnant women, but continued supplementation of the mother for 2 to 3 months after parturition is advisable in order to replenish stores depleted by pregnancy.

Source: Food and Nutrition Board, National Academy of Sciences—National Research Council, Washington, D.C.

Table C-3 Estimated safe and adequate daily dietary intakes of selected vitamins and minerals[a]

	Age (years)	Trace elements[b]					
		Copper (mg)	Man-ganese (mg)	Fluoride (mg)	Chromium (mg)	Selenium (mg)	Molyb-denum (mg)
Infants	0–0.5	0.5–0.7	0.5–0.7	0.1–0.5	0.01–0.04	0.01–0.04	0.03–0.06
	0.5–1	0.7–1.0	0.7–1.0	0.2–1.0	0.02–0.06	0.02–0.06	0.04–0.08
Children	1–3	1.0–1.5	1.0–1.5	0.5–1.5	0.02–0.08	0.02–0.08	0.05–0.1
and	4–6	1.5–2.0	1.5–2.0	1.0–2.5	0.03–0.12	0.03–0.12	0.06–0.15
adolescents	7–10	2.0–2.5	2.0–3.0	1.5–2.5	0.05–0.2	0.05–0.2	0.10–0.3
	11 +	2.0–3.0	2.5–5.0	1.5–2.5	0.05–0.2	0.05–0.2	0.15–0.5

	Age (years)	Electrolytes		
		Sodium (mg)	Potassium (mg)	Chloride (mg)
Infants	0–0.5	115–350	350–925	275–700
	0.5–1	250–750	425–1275	400–1200
Children	1–3	325–975	550–1650	500–1500
and	4–6	450–1350	775–2325	700–2100
adolescents	7–10	600–1800	1000–3000	925–2775
	11 +	900–2700	1525–4575	1400–4200

	Age (years)	Vitamins		
		Vitamin K (μg)	Biotin (μg)	Panto-thenic acid (mg)
Infants	0–0.5	12	35	2
	0.5–1	10–20	50	3
Children	1–3	15–30	65	3
and	4–6	20–40	85	3–4
adolescents	7–10	30–60	120	4–5
	11 +	50–100	100–200	4–7

[a] Because there is less information on which to base allowances, these figures are not given in the main table of RDA and are provided here in the form of ranges of recommended intakes.

[b] Since the toxic levels for many trace elements may be only several times usual intakes, the upper levels for the trace elements given in this table should not be habitually exceeded.

Source: Food and Nutrition Board, National Academy of Sciences—National Research Council, Washington, D.C.

Table C-4 Mean heights and weights and recommended energy intake*

Age and sex group	Weight		Height		Energy			
					Needs		Range in kcal
	Kg	Lb	Cm	In	MJ	Kcal	
Infants							
0.0–0.5 yr	6	13	60	24	kg. × 0.48	kg. × 115	95–145
0.5–1.0yr	9	20	71	28	kg. × 0.44	kg. × 105	80–135
Children							
1–3 yr	13	29	90	35	5.5	1,300	900–1,800
4–6 yr	20	44	112	44	7.1	1,700	1,300–2,300
7–10 yr	28	62	132	52	10.1	2,400	1,650–3,300
Males							
11–14 yr	45	99	157	62	11.3	2,700	2,000–3,700
15–18 yr	66	145	176	69	11.8	2,800	2,100–3,900
Females							
11–14 yr	46	101	157	62	9.2	2,200	1,500–3,000
15–18 yr	55	120	163	64	8.8	2,100	1,200–3,000
pregnancy						+300	
lactation						+500	

* The data in this table have been assembled from the observed median heights and weights of children. Energy allowances for children through age eighteen are based on median energy intakes of children of these ages followed in longitudinal growth studies. Ranges are the 10th and 90th percentiles of energy intake, to indicate range of energy consumption among children of these ages.

Source: From Recommended Dietary Allowances, Revised 1980, Food and Nutrition Board, National Academy of Sciences—National Research Council, Washington, D.C.

Table C-5 Guide to good nutrition—basic four food groups

Food group	Recommended number of servings				
	Child	Teenager	Adult	Pregnant woman	Lactating woman
Milk 1 cup milk, yogurt, or **Calcium Equivalent:** 1½ slices (1½ oz) cheddar cheese* 1 cup pudding 1¾ cups ice cream 2 cups cottage cheese*	3	4	2	4	4
Meat 2 ounces cooked, lean meat, fish, poultry, or **Protein Equivalent:** 2 eggs 2 slices (2 oz) cheddar cheese* ½ cup cottage cheese* 1 cup dried beans, peas 4 tbsp peanut butter	2	2	2	3	2
Fruit-Vegetable ½ cup cooked or juice 1 cup raw Portion commonly served such as medium-size apple or banana	4	4	4	4	4
Grain Whole grain, fortified, enriched 1 slice bread 1 cup ready-to-eat cereal ½ cup cooked cereal, pasta, grits	4	4	4	4	4

* Count cheese as serving of milk or meat, not both simultaneously.
"Others" complement but do not replace foods from the Four Food Groups. Amounts should be determined by individual caloric needs.
Source: *Guide to Good Eating,* National Dairy Council, Rosemont, IL, 1978.

Appendix D Personal information forms

Table D-1 Sample personal information form: Infant to 6 years

---

Help Us to Know Your Child

Name _____ Nickname: _____ Age _____

Has your child been away from home before? _____

Why? _____ For how long? _____

Who cares for your child at home? _____

Has your child been told the reason for this hospitalization? _____

By whom? _____

Do you plan to stay with your child? _____

If not, when can you visit? _____

Is your child afraid of anything in particular?

What comforts your child best (bottle, toy, your arms, and so forth)?

Eating

Is/was your child breast-fed? _____

Is your child on a bottle? _____ When? _____

Does your child have any food allergies? _____

_____

Has feeding ever been a problem? _____

What food(s) does your child especially like? _____

Dislike? _____

Toilet training

Does your child stay dry during the day? _____ At night? _____

Is your child toilet trained for B.M.'s? _____

Does your child use a potty chair? _____ A toilet? _____

What word(s) does your child use for needing to go to the bathroom? _____

_____

Table D-1 Sample personal information form: Infant to 6 years (*Continued*)

Help Us to Know Your Child

Sleeping

Does your child sleep alone? _____ If not, with whom does your child share a bed or a room? _____

Would a doll or stuffed animal comfort your child at bedtime? _____

What? _____

Play

Does your child have a favorite toy? _____ Did you bring it along? _____ Is there a pet in your home? _____

What is it? _____ What are your child's favorite games, special interests, or hobbies? _____

Speech

Can your child speak well enough to make wants and needs understood with words? _____

What language is spoken in your home? _____

School

Does your child attend nursery school? _____

Head Start? _____ Day Care Center? _____

Is there anything else you would like us to know?

Source: Committee on Hospital Care, *Hospital Care of Children and Youth.* Copyright American Academy of Pediatrics, Evanston, Ill., 1978, p.00. Used by permission.

Table D-2 Sample personal information form: 6 to 12 years

Help Us to Know Your Child

Name: _____ Nickname: _____ Age: _____

Birthday: _____

How does your child take care of his own needs:

Dressing? _____ Eating? _____ School work? _____

Toileting? _____ Is your child on a special diet?_____

What? _____

Does your child know the reason for hospitalization? _____

Did your child tour the hospital before admission? _____

What interests your child most (toys, games, people, and so forth)?

Does your child prefer groups? _____ Is your child a loner? _____

Name of your child's school: _____

Grade: _____ Is your child in any special program? _____

Has your family moved recently? _____ Was the move within the same city? _____

Does your child have any particular fears? _____

Is there any thing special you would like us to watch for? _____

_____

We and your child want you to visit as much as possible. How can we help you with this?

Source: Committee on Hospital Care, *Hospital Care of Children and Youth.* Copyright American Academy of Pediatrics, Evanston, Ill, 1978, p.00. Used by permission.

Table D-3 Sample personal information form: Teenagers

Help Us to Know You: Tell Us about Yourself

Name: _____ Nickname: _____ Age: _____

Birthday (we would like to celebrate it with you if you are here): _____

Who lives in your household?

Names and ages of your brothers and sisters:

Have you ever been in the hospital before? _____

When? _____ Why? _____

Are you on a special diet at home? _____ What is it? _____

_____

Do you eat breakfast? _____

What are your special interests and hobbies? _____

_____

How can we provide for them here?

How can we help you keep in touch with your friends or school?

Is there anything else that might make your hospital stay easier?

Source: Committee on Hospital Care, *Hospital Care of Children and Youth,* Copyright American Academy of Pediatrics, Evanston, Ill., 1978, pp. 90–93. Used by permission.

National Poison Center Network ®

Poison Treatment Chart

Suggested general treatment for poisoning management

1. There should be no problem in small amounts.
   NO TREATMENT NECESSARY.
   Fluids may be given.

2. Induce vomiting. Give Syrup of Ipecac in the following dosages:

   UNDER ONE YEAR OF AGE:
   Two teaspoons followed by at least 2-3 glasses of fluid.

   ONE YEAR AND OVER:
   Give one tablespoon followed by at least 2-3 glasses of fluid.

   DO NOT INDUCE VOMITING
   IF THE PATIENT IS SEMICOMATOSE,
   COMATOSE, OR CONVULSING.

   Call Poison Center for additional information.

3. Dilute or neutralize with water or milk.
   DO NOT INDUCE VOMITING. Gastric lavage is indicated. Call Poison Center for specific instructions.

4. Treat symptomatically unless botulism is suspected. Call Poison Center for specific information regarding botulism.

5. Dilute or neutralize with water or milk.
   DO NOT INDUCE VOMITING. Gastric lavage should be avoided. This substance may cause burns of the mucous membranes. Consult E.N.T. specialist following emergency treatment. Call Poison Center for specific information.

6. Immediately wash skin thoroughly with running water. Call Poison Center for further treatment.

7. Immediately wash eyes with a gentle stream of running water. Continue for 15 minutes. Call Poison Center for further treatment.

8. Specific antagonist may be indicated.
   Call Poison Center.

9. Remove to fresh air. Support respirations. Call Poison Center for further treatment.

10. Call Poison Center for specific instructions.

11. Symptomatic and supportive treatment.
    DO NOT INDUCE VOMITING for ingestions.
    I.V. Naloxone Hydrochloride (Narcan) to be given as indicated for respiratory depression.
    Dosage:
    Adult—0.4 mg I.V.
    May be repeated at 2-3 min. intervals.

    Child—0.01 mg/kg I.V.
    May be repeated at 5-10 min. intervals.

Index